MANUAL OF CULTIVATED TREES AND SHRUBS

Hardy in North America

EXCLUSIVE OF THE SUBTROPICAL
AND WARMER TEMPERATE REGIONS

By

ALFRED REHDER

Second Edition

Revised and Enlarged

Biosystematics, Floristic & Phylogeny Series,
Volume 1
General Editor: Theodore R. Dudley, Ph.D.

Dioscorides Press
Portland, Oregon

© Alfred Rehder

Published by
Dioscorides Press
9999 S.W. Wilshire
Portland, Oregon 97225

ISBN 0-931146-00-3

Printed in Hong Kong

CONTENTS

Alfred Rehder on the occasion of his 70th birthday (1933). Photograph taken in front of the Administration Building of the Arnold Arboretum, Jamaica Plain, Massachusetts. (photo courtesy of the Arnold Arboretum)

FOREWORD TO THE COMMEMORATIVE REPRINT EDITION

Honoring: the 123rd birthday of Alfred Rehder

Commemorating: the 46th anniversary of the publication of the Second Edition of the *Manual of Cultivated Trees and Shrubs*

Treasuring and Celebrating: Alfred Rehder's still unsurpassed technical skills, highest levels of scholarship, generous sharing of knowledge and experience, mastery of communication, and unequivocably reliable judgement.

This Dioscorides Press Commemorative reprint edition of the *Manual of Cultivated Trees and Shrubs* is dedicated to the memory of a highly esteemed paragon whose scientific accomplishments, in consort with his irrefutable alliance with horticulture, reached the loftiest pinnacles of modern plant systematics.

The second edition of Alfred Rehder's *Manual of Cultivated Trees and Shrubs* (henceforth known as the "Manual") was last reprinted in 1960. Shortly after this ninth printing by the Macmillan Company the Manual was out-of-print and became an intensely sought collector's item. Rarely throughout the 1970s and 1980s has a copy been observed in bookstores or listed in book catalogues (although the 1927 first edition was indeed more commonly available). Yet, because of its impeccable accuracy and comprehensiveness, and its intrinsic timeliness and timelessness, the Manual has continued to be in high demand among professional, student, and amateur botanists and horticulturists. Anyone associated professionally, or even tangentially, with woody plants of either actual or potential landscape significance in temperate or subtemperate areas of North America or elsewhere must use the Manual for basic reference, bench-mark research and identification.

My own and only personal copy of the Manual was given to me as a wedding present in 1960. It would not be an exaggeration to state that it has been used several times a day since then. This copy is so dog-eared and falling apart that for several years I have been searching for an additional second copy, but to no avail.

I am certain that users of the Manual throughout the world could provide many reasons why it is so exceptionally popular. I feel that the two major reasons for its perpetual success are simple yet profound. An orderly compendium in the English language, like the Manual, intensely detailed, comprehensive and easily used had never before been compiled and has yet to be matched. There is simply nothing like it—not even remotely close. The Manual's wide-ranging impact is further due in large measure to Alfred Rehder's genius, personality and indefatigable productivity. He possessed an insatiable curiosity and outstanding originality, demanded of himself the very highest standards, and was dedicated to the systematics and biology of all woody plants. A measure of his greatness and prolificness might be the fact that in 66 years of publication, Alfred Rehder authored or co-authored over 1020 articles, book chapters and volumes!

The Manual was one of several crowning professional accomplishments in Alfred Rehder's career. It illustrates his commitment to the unending synthesis and elucidation of taxonomy and its inseparable affinity with nomenclature.

I could compile a great deal about Alfred Rehder's history, life, publications and accomplishments. However, I prefer to refer the reader to two excellent references: *Alfred Rehder, 1863–1949* by Clarence E. Kobuski (*Journal of the Arnold Arboretum 31(1):* 1–38, 1950) and *The Making of a Botanist* by Alfred's son, Gerhard Rehder (*Arnoldia 32(4):* 141–156, 1972). Since, unfortunately, I did not know Alfred Rehder personally, I feel that this commentary might be most effectively closed with remarks made to me a couple of years ago by Harald Rehder (Alfred's elder son): "He was indeed a wonderful and kindly person, who brought his children up to appreciate nature in all of its aspects. He was thoroughly happy in the pursuit of his chosen life's work. He told my mother shortly before his death that if he had his life to live over he would not change it in any way." Could there be a more poignant and fitting written memorial to Alfred Rehder?

The MANUAL:

Alfred Rehder's original Introduction and his Preface to the Second Edition, reprinted herein *verbatim,* explain in detail the philosophy, concept and format of the First (1927) and Second (1940) editions of the *Manual of Cultivated Trees and Shrubs.* I will not presume to try to improve on these. No attempt can be made at this time, in this reprint of the Manual, to correct typographic, indexing or other errors. Nor will I proceed to update the nomenclature in accord with the latest (1983) *International Code of Botanical Nomenclature* (E. Voss, *et al., Regnum Vegetabile* 111).

Additionally, since 1940 numerous woody plant taxa have been introduced to North America from all over the world. Also, since 1940 thousands of taxa new to science and taxonomic reappraisals have been described and proposed in many papers, monographs, revisions, and regional or political boundary floras. Yet, despite these new introductions, loss of taxa to cultivation, the numerous taxonomic re-appraisals and nomenclatural changes that have occurred over the past 46 years, the Manual remains practically indisputable and stands in center stage as the only printed resource of its kind in the world.

Alfred Rehder's 1927 and 1940 concepts and usage of "cultivated varieties", variety (var.) and form (f.) do not equate to the principles, concepts, definitions, rules and recommendations for the term "cultivar" as presented for the first time in the 1953 *International Code of Nomenclature for Cultivated Plants* (J. Gilmore *et al.* Royal Horticultural Society), and maintained (with amendments and additions) in the latest (1980, C. D. Brickell, *et al., Regnum Vegetabile 104*) edition of this International Code. Accordingly, numerous "f"s (or "forms") and "var."s (or "vars." of cultivated origin) correctly should ultimately be regarded as cultivars; i.e. *Taxus baccata* var. *variegata* is now correctly called *Taxus baccata* cv. Variegata or 'Variegata'.

Similarly, the designation of a hybrid species epithet, according to the latest *International Code of Botanical Nomenclature* (1983), must be preceeded by a × (multiplication sign); i.e. *Berberis × chenaulti* Chenault, rather than *B. chenaultii.*

I would strongly urge the users of this reprint edition of the Manual to make liberal and concurrent use of Alfred Rehder's *Bibliography of Cultivated Trees and Shrubs* (1949). This 825 page volume, published shortly before his death, was one of the largest, most meticulous and difficult works of his career. The *Bibliography* provides many solutions and answers to some of the seeming taxonomic and nomenclatural errors and anomalies in the Manual. The basis of this bibliography lies in a mammoth card file started by Alfred Rehder in 1915 and now probably containing at least 200,000 entries.

Dioscorides Press is deeply honored to present to the international botanical and horticultural communities this Commemorative Reprint Edition of Alfred Rehder's *Manual of Cultivated Trees and Shrubs* ("Second Edition Revised and Enlarged"). We would like to express our appreciation to the Rehder family, especially Dr. Harald Rehder, Gerhard Rehder and Sylvia Rehder (Mrs. Warren F. Witherell), for their most gracious support and advice, and for allowing this monumental work to once again be available.

Dr. T.R. Dudley
U.S. National Arboretum
1986

PREFACE TO THE SECOND EDITION

Since the publication of the first edition of this Manual thirteen years have elapsed and the edition has become exhausted, although the book was reissued several years ago. During this time many new species and varieties have been introduced into cultivation, new hybrids have appeared and changes in nomenclature have become necessary owing to a more intensive study of certain groups and to amendments to the International Rules of Botanical Nomenclature adopted by the International Botanical Congresses in 1930 and 1935.

Therefore the issue of a new revised and enlarged edition appears to be necessary and the author has been engaged for several years in bringing the book up to date. The number of species appearing in the keys and fully described has been considerably increased and now amounts to over 2550 instead of about 2350; the number of varieties and hybrids and of species only briefly described has grown accordingly.

In the systematic arrangement of the families, the system used by Engler and Prantl has for practical reasons been retained, with the exception that the Monocotyledons have been moved to the end of the system. They certainly do not form a connecting link between the Gymnosperms and the Dicotyledons and were not derived from the Gymnosperms, as their position between these two groups seemed to imply, but they originated from a dicotyledonous group, probably the Ranales, at an early period.

The zones of hardiness within the range of this Manual have been reduced from eight to seven, these being based on the average annual minimum temperatures. The old map showing the zones of hardiness was reproduced on too small a scale and has been replaced by a larger one showing the zones much more distinctly and clearly. The planting and testing of more recent introductions in more northern gardens has in many cases shown that these introductions possess a greater hardiness than was previously credited to them and the zones have accordingly been changed in many instances.

The use of the term variety intercalated between the specific name and that of a subdivision of the species has been abandoned to avoid making unintentional and unnecessary new combinations; instead the subdivisional name follows the specific name immediately and the category as proposed by the author who first published the subdivisional name under the binomial adopted in this book, is given after the name of the author, e.g., *Cephalotaxus drupacea fastigiata* (Carr.) Pilg., f. which indicates that Pilger when making this combination, published it as *C. drupacea* forma *fastigiata*. This does not mean that the author of this Manual considers the category given as correct in all cases, for many of the subdivisional names cited with the category "var." should really be classified as "forma" and similar discrepancies occur under other categories. Since a change in the category does not involve a change in the trinomial and therefore does not alter the name of the plant, it did not seem advisable to make numerous new combinations, perhaps more properly to be called "new status," considering the fact that the book is intended chiefly for horticultural usage, where as a rule, simple trinomials are used.

PREFACE TO THE SECOND EDITION

Also it seems more important to cite the author who first placed the variety or form under the correct binomial than a later author who only changed the rank. Since the scope and size of the Manual does not allow full citations of literature and synonymy, it is the intention of the author to follow its publication with a bibliographical supplement supplying for all the names mentioned in the Manual exact citations of their source and for trinomials the category considered to be botanically correct. This is particularly important for varieties and forms, since the source of their names is in many instances difficult to trace.

The list of authors' names cited in the book has been greatly increased, so as to include nearly every name cited as an authority of a botanical name, while in the first edition, mainly the abbreviations of the more frequently cited authors were given. For assistance in the search for biographical data appertaining to obscure and little known authorities, I am indebted to Dr. Leon Croizat, who obtained for me most of this information from the extensive collection of biographical data assembled by Dr. J. H. Barnhard of the New York Botanical Garden.

To many correspondents of the Arnold Arboretum too numerous to mention, I am indebted for additions and corrections of errors in the first edition. Acknowledgment is also due to my associates at the Arboretum for valuable assistance and suggestions. For help in the preparation of the account of the Bamboos, I am under obligation to Dr. F. A. McClure of Lingnan University and to Mr. B. A. Young of the United States Department of Agriculture.

ALFRED REHDER.

Arnold Arboretum, Harvard University,
Jamaica Plain, Massachusetts.
January, 1940.

INTRODUCTION

The purpose of this volume is to present a systematic and descriptive enumeration of the cultivated trees and shrubs hardy in North America, exclusive of the subtropical and warm-temperate regions, and to facilitate their identification by means of analytical keys. The plan and arrangement of the work is much the same as that of the manuals dealing with the spontaneous flora of the region indicated. Thus it may serve as a supplement and companion work to these, dealing with the cultivated ligneous flora which in an ever-increasing degree caters to our economic and esthetic wants; and furthermore tends greatly to modify the aspect of the original vegetation wherever man makes his home.

The term trees and shrubs is interpreted in a wide sense, so as to include not only woody vines, but also suffruticose plants, that is, plants of which only the lower part of the stems and branches persists and becomes woody, while the upper part dies back annually, or which have stems persisting for several years without becoming truly ligneous. The distinction between a suffruticose plant or subshrub and a perennial plant, however, is not always clear and definite, but in doubtful cases plants only slightly woody have been included, particularly if they belong to a genus or family otherwise not represented. It is the intention to treat in this book all hardy or supposedly hardy woody plants known to be at present in cultivation within an area whose southern limit is an isothermal line connecting points with the mean temperature of the coldest month near the freezing point; this corresponds approximately to a line running from Virginia through western North Carolina, northern Georgia and northern Alabama, central Arkansas, central New Mexico, central Arizona and then northward through northeastern California and Oregon along the western slope of the Cascade Mountains to northwestern Washington. In the East the area nearly coincides with that of the manuals of Gray and of Britton. Whether a plant is at present in cultivation or not is often impossible to say with certainty. Although we may have the record of its introduction into American or European gardens, it may not have persisted. As a rule woody plants known to have been successfully introduced have been included in this book. It has, however, been found necessary, in order not to exceed the limits of a single volume, to omit less known and rarely cultivated varieties and garden forms; likewise in some large genera as Salix, Crataegus, Rubus and Rosa species of neither economic nor horticultural importance, and not met with except in a few special collections, have not been mentioned. As these omitted species are almost exclusively those native to North America, their descriptions, in most cases, can readily be found in American manuals and floras; foreign species, even if but rarely cultivated, are usually mentioned, since information regarding these is not so easily obtainable.

The trees, shrubs and vines described in this book belong to 486 genera distributed among 113 families. The number of species, including a small number of horticulturally important hybrids, fully described and represented in the keys is about 2535 with about 2685 varieties. Besides these there are

INTRODUCTION

about 25 genera, 1400 species and 540 hybrids briefly described or mentioned and appended to the families, genera or species to which they are most closely related, or in the case of hybrids, to one of the parents. This cultivated ligneous flora is chiefly composed of plants introduced from the temperate and colder regions of the northern hemisphere. Only few species of the southern hemisphere and these mostly from the extreme southern part of South America and the higher altitudes of the Andes and from the high mountains of Australia and of New Zealand have proved to be hardy with us. A large percentage of this flora is native within our area and in the adjoining regions to the south. Perhaps an equal number came from eastern and central Asia, which has a very rich and varied ligneous flora. Less numerous are the contributions from Europe, western Asia and North Africa and, as stated above, from the southern hemisphere. In addition to the introduced species and varieties a large and ever-increasing number of hybrids and garden forms has originated under cultivation, and in many cases these hybrids have supplanted the original species in our gardens. Most of the foreign trees and shrubs, and even some native ones, have reached our gardens by the way of Europe, and it is only within the last 60 to 70 years that chiefly through the agency of the Arnold Arboretum and more recently through the U. S. Department of Agriculture, many plants have been introduced directly from their native countries, mostly from eastern Asia, to American gardens.[1] Lack of space in this work forbids the inclusion of details regarding the introduction of individual species, and only the year of the introduction into cultivation either in this country or in Europe, if known, is given. When the actual date of introduction could not be ascertained, the first record of the plant as being in cultivation is given, based either on mention in horticultural literature or on dated herbarium specimens.

The sequence of the families follows with few exceptions, the system used by Engler and Prantl in their "Natürliche Pflanzenfamilien" and in Engler's "Syllabus" which has been adopted with slight modifications in all, or nearly all modern American manuals. The chief deviation from this system consists in removing the Monocotyledons from their place between the Gymnosperms and Dicotyledons and placing them at the end of the system for reasons indicated in the Preface (p. vii). The descriptions have been made as concise as possible without omitting important matter, and in most cases characters used in the keys, and particularly in the shorter keys where the species can be referred to readily, are not repeated. Lack of space forbids the giving of full descriptions of all the species known to be in cultivation within the range of the manual, and less important and rarely cultivated ones are only briefly described in smaller type and appended to more fully described and related species. Also a selection had to be made from among the horticultural varieties and forms, very numerous in some groups, particularly in the Conifers, and only the more important and outstanding ones could find a place in the book. Similarly the hybrids, with the exception of a few horticulturally important and much cultivated ones, are not fully described, as these are usually very variable and should be recognized chiefly by their resemblances to the parent species; they are only briefly characterized and are appended to one of the parents with a reference from the other parent. In using the keys to the families and genera, it should be understood that the characters

---

[1] For dates of the introduction to North America of the more important species see: Rehder in Mitteil. Deutsch. Dendr. Gesell. 1932: 114–129, and in Nation. Hort. Mag. 15: 245–257 (1936).

INTRODUCTION

apply only to those genera of the families and those species of the genera which are described in this book, while the descriptions of families and genera include the characters of the entire group.

In regard to the botanical names, the International Rules of Botanical Nomenclature, as amended in 1935 by the VI. International Botanical Congress at Amsterdam, have been consistently followed. These Rules have now been accepted by nearly all botanists, in this country as well as abroad, and as far as botanical names are concerned are also generally followed in horticultural literature.

Authorities for the botanical names are cited, as is customary, mostly in abbreviated form. The explanation of the abbreviations with further data regarding the authorities will be found on pages 909 ff. The citation in parenthesis of the original author of a transferred specific or varietal name (epithet) is now obligatory and shows that the epithet did not originate with the author of the adopted combination, but was transferred from an older combination. Thus in *Malus baccata* (L.) Borkh. the parenthetical author indicates that the specific name was transferred by Borkhausen from *Pyrus baccata* of Linnaeus. As the author of a varietal name, the author who first placed the epithet under the accepted binomial is cited, his name being followed by the indication of the category or rank he assigned to the name, as subsp., var., f. (subspecies, varietas, forma), e.g., "*Rhododendron viscosum nitidum* (Pursh) Gray, var.," which indicates that Gray called the plant *Rh. viscosum* var. *nitidum*. If no indication of rank is given, it shows that the author published the name as a straight trinomial (ternary combination) without indication of rank. As this is the general usage in horticulture, it seems better to employ this form of citation rather than to use, as was done in the first edition, the designation "var." for every one of the several subdivisional categories and to create thereby what must be considered, according to the Rules of Nomenclature, as new combinations. In some cases the varietal designation for horticultural forms consists of two epithets, as in *Chamaecyparis pisifera plumosa aurea,* of which the second one has already been used under this species, namely in *Ch. pisifera aurea,* which is contrary to the Rules, since a subdivisional epithet can only be used under the same species. Instead of coining a new varietal name for such botanically unimportant forms, it seems preferable to treat them as garden names and indicate this by citing them in quotation marks, as *Ch. pisifera "plumosa aurea."*

The original orthography of the names has been preserved except in cases of an actual error or misprint. Thus names such as *Wisteria, Gleditsia, Penstemon, Gaultheria, Pyrus* are adopted as spelled by the original author. Also the genitive ending of personal names, whether single or double i, is given as originally published, although for practical reasons uniformity may be preferable; it seems an unnecessary burden on the memory to remember that one and the same name may sometimes end in a single and sometimes in a double i, as in *Viburnum Sargenti* Koehne and *Populus Sargentii* Dode, or in *Picea Engelmanni* (Parry) Engelm., and *Cirsium Engelmannii* Rydb. As this is a matter of secondary importance, no strong objection could or should be raised against either of the two ways of simplification,—to have these names all end in either a single or double i. In either case, certain exceptions should be made. If the choice should be to use the double i in all latinized surnames, as recommended by the International Rules, no change should be made in Christian names which have a recognized Latin form as Augustinus, Ferdinandus, Ernestus, Alfredus, and consequently they can have only a

INTRODUCTION

single i in the possessive case. On the other hand if the choice should be the use of a single i, as adopted by Standardized Plant Names, those surnames which end in i as Giraldi, Pampanini, Zuccarini should have a double i, since one i belongs to the original name and the other to the ending.

As an aid to the correct pronunciation, the botanical names are marked with accents, the grave (`) to indicate the long sound of the vowel, the acute (´) to indicate the short sound. The rules of Latin quantity have been followed as closely as possible in the accentuation of the words and in the latinized forms of proper names and other words unknown to classical Latin established custom has served as a guide. In the genitive ending of personal names, the penultimate vowel has usually been treated as long except in the English and German ending er, e.g., Pàlmeri, Éngleri, but Berlandièri, since in the French name Berlandier the last syllable is long and accented.

Only the more important synonyms are cited and chiefly those which occur frequently in horticultural and botanical literature.[1] English names are restricted to those which are in actual use and no attempt has been made to provide the less known and recently introduced plants with newly coined English names which would only have occupied valuable space to little purpose.[2] It has seemed desirable to cite illustrations; in general the references to illustrations are to the most easily accessible works, and only in cases where no other illustrations were available are rare and less readily accessible publications cited. Usually several illustrations are quoted which include colored plates and habit figures. These citations will also serve in most cases as a guide to further information and to citations of literature.[3]

Within the limits of one volume only very brief notes on the economic and ornamental properties of the trees and shrubs described could be given. Cultural directions had to be restricted to short hints in the case of such plants as could not be expected to thrive under ordinary conditions and to the indication of the approximate hardiness of each species, and in some instances of varieties. To this end the area has been divided into seven zones based on the annual minimum temperatures.[4] The average annual minimum of the temperatures of these zones are as follows:

Zone I: exceeding −50°; the treeless zone in extreme northern Canada. Zone II: −50° to −35°. Zone III: −35° to −20°. Zone IV: −20° to −10°. Zone V: −10° to −5°. Zone VI: −5° to +5°. Zone VII: +5° to +10°. These zones run nearly parallel to the southern boundary of the area as described above, but their boundaries are much modified by elevation, mountains, river valleys and other features, and often form considerable curves or loops; as a rule they tend to curve from the Atlantic coast southward, but beyond the 110° W. they turn rather abruptly northward and run for some distance almost parallel to the Pacific coast, extending here much farther to the north than on the Atlantic coast. A map showing these seven zones will be found opposite the title-page and with its help it can be easily ascertained to which zone a certain region belongs and which trees and shrubs described in this book may be expected to grow there. There

---

[1] It is the intention of the author to publish later a Bibliographical Supplement which is to contain the literature citations appertaining to the accepted names and of the important synonyms.

[2] For additional English names one may consult the new edition now in preparation of "STANDARDIZED PLANT NAMES" and for American plants the manuals covering our native flora.

[3] For additional illustration see INDEX LONDINENSIS TO ILLUSTRATIONS OF FLOWERING PLANTS, FERNS AND FERN ALLIES. Compiled by O. Stapf. 6 Vols. F. Oxford, 1929–31.

[4] See U. S. Dept. Agric., Atlas of American Agriculture, Phys. Base Land Relief, Climate, p. 9, map 7 (1936).

INTRODUCTION

are, however, many other factors besides winter temperature which influence the hardiness and growth of certain plants, such as soil, its physical as well as chemical composition, exposure, rainfall, humidity, air drainage and shelter from cold winds. As a rule, one may say that plants stand cold better in a drier situation than in a wet one and that deciduous trees and shrubs generally do well in more exposed situations and in a climate with higher summer temperature, while evergreen plants prefer a sheltered situation and respond to a more humid climate with less extreme summer and winter temperatures; for this reason many deciduous species grow best in the East, while evergreen plants and particularly broad-leaved evergreens thrive better on the northern Pacific coast. In the case of many rarer trees and shrubs hardy at the Arnold Arboretum, owing to lack of tests farther north and farther south, the limits of hardiness are not well known and had to be deduced from their behavior under approximately similar conditions in Europe. A few examples of well known trees and shrubs characteristic for each zone, as reaching there the northern limit of hardiness may be given here:

Zone   I. *Picea glauca, Populus tremuloides, Betula papyrifera.*
Zone II. *Quercus macrocarpa, Caragana arborescens, Acer Negundo, Viburnum Lantana.*
Zone III. *Berberis Thunbergii, Sorbus americana* and *S. aucuparia, Fraxinus americana.*
Zone IV. *Quercus coccinea, Cercidiphyllum japonicum, Robinia Pseudacacia.*
Zone   V. *Fagus sylvatica, Ilex opaca, Rhus chinensis, Koelreuteria paniculata.*
Zone VI. *Poncirus trifoliata, Paulownia tomentosa, Abelia grandiflora.*
Zone VII. *Albizzia Julibrissin, Firmiana simplex, Lagerstroemia indica.*

Under favorable conditions and with proper protection plants will survive in localities farther north than the zone to which they have been referred, but these exceptions should not change the indication of the proper zone. Such cases have been occasionally indicated by placing the zone in which the plant is not fully hardy in parenthesis, e.g., Zone (V) VI, which indicates that the plant is hardy in Zone V only precariously or under particularly favorable conditions, but is fully hardy in Zone VI.

As in most modern American floras the measurements are given in the metric system, which is understood the world over, and moreover, permits, particularly for smaller dimensions, a more exact and clearer designation than the various fractions into which an inch may be divided and which may not be indicated on the ruler at hand. Equivalents of the Metric and English systems of measurements and comparative scales of centimeters and inches are given on p. xix.

In most cases the keys will lead to the identification of the plant under consideration, but sometimes it may not be possible to arrive at a satisfactory conclusion, when either the material at hand is imperfect, or the plant represents some abnormal feature, or is very rare and only incidentally mentioned in the book or not at all. Doubtful identifications may be verified by comparing the plants with the illustrations cited or with correctly named specimens in a reliable herbarium, or if this does not lead to a definite result, by sending specimens for identification to a botanical institution.

The author hopes that the book, in spite of its imperfections, will serve the purpose for which it was written and will help to spread a more accurate knowledge of the wealth of trees and shrubs now at our command, and thus constitute a welcome contribution to the literature of botany and of horticulture.

ABBREVIATIONS OF REFERENCES TO ILLUSTRATIONS

An arrow after the volume number and the date indicates that the publication is continued. *Il.* refers to illustrations in the text, and *pl.* signifies plate, *col. pl.* colored plate. F, Q, and O refer to the size of the publications, as Folio, Quarto or Octavo.

Ad. ....Addisonia; Colored Illustrations and Popular Descriptions of Plants. Published by the New York Botanical Garden. Vol. 1→ O. New York, 1916→ Col. pl.
A.B. ......Arnold Arboretum. Bulletin of Popular Information. No. 1→ O. Jamaica Plain, Mass., 1911→ Il., pl.
A.C. ......Antoine, Franz. Die Cupressineen-Gattungen. F. Wien, 1857. 92 pl.
A.F. ......The American Florist. Vol. 1→ Q. Chicago, 1885→ Il. and few pl.
A.G. ......American Gardening. Vol. 1-25. Q. New York, 1880-1904. —Vol. 1-12, called "American Garden" (1880-91). Il.
A.I. ....Abrams, L. An Illustrated Flora of the Pacific States. Vol. 1. Q. Stanford University, Calif., 1923. Il.
A.R. ......Andrews, Henry. The Botanists' Repository. 10 vol. Q. London, 1797-1812. 664 col. pl.
B. ....The Botanist. Ed. by B. Maund. 5 vol. O. London, 1837-46. 250 col. pl.
B.B. ......Britton, N. L., & Addison Brown. An Illustrated Flora of the Northern United States, Canada, etc. 3 vol. Q. Ed. 2. New York, 1913. Il.
B.C. ......Bailey, L. H. Standard Cyclopedia of Horticulture. 6 vol. O. New York, 1914-17. Il. and pl., some col.
B.C.C. ....Bailey, L. H. The Cultivated Conifers in North America. O. New York, 1933. Il. and 48 pl.
B.D. ......Bulletin de la Société Dendrologique de France. Vol. 1906→ O. Paris, 1906→ Il. and pl.
B.E. ......Bailey, L. H. The Cultivated Evergreens. O. New York, 1923. Il. and pl.
B.F. ......Bulletin de la Société Botanique de France. Vol. 1→ O. Paris, 1854→ Il. and pl.
B.H. ......La Belgique Horticole. 20 vol. O. Gand, 1851-70. Col. pl.
B.J. ......Botanische Jahrbücher. Ed. by A. Engler. Vol. 1→ O. Berlin, 1881→ Il. and pl.
B.M. .....The Botanical Magazine. Ed. by Wm. Curtis and others. Vol. 1→ O. London, 1787→ Col. pl.
B.N. ......Beissner, L. Handbuch der Nadelholzkunde. Ed. 2. O. Berlin, 1909. Il.
B.N.F. ...Beissner, L. Handbuch der Nadelholzkunde. Ed. 3, rev. by J. Fitschen. O. Berlin, 1930. Il.
B.R. ......The Botanical Register. Ed. by S. Edward (Vol. 1-14) and J. Lindley (Vol. 15-33). O. London, 1815-47. Col. pl.
B.S. ......Bean, W. J. Trees and Shrubs Hardy in the British Isles. 3 vol. O. London, 1914-33. Il. and pl.
B.T. ......Britton, N. L. North American Trees. O. New York, 1908. Il.
C.B. ......Clinton-Baker, Henry. Illustrations of Conifers. Q. Hertford (Eng.), 1909. 171 pl.
C.Ba. ....Camus, E. G. Les Bambusées. Q (text). F (atlas). Paris, 1913. 100 pl.
C.C. ......Chun, W. Y. Chinese Economic Trees. O. [Shanghai], 1922. Il.
C.H. ......Chow, H. F. Familiar Trees of Hopei. O. Peking, 1934. 143 il.
C.L. ......Country Life [in America]. Vol. 1→ Q. New York, 1901→ Il.
C.Q. ......Camus, Aimée. Les Chênes; Monographie du Genre Quercus. Text. Vol. 1, 2→ O. 1936-39. Atlas. Vol. 1, 2→ F. Paris, 1934-36→ Pl. 1-236→
C.R. ......Clements, F. E. & E. S. Rocky Mountain Flowers. O. White Plains, New York, 1914. 47 pl., partly colored, each with several figures.
C.S. ......Camus, A. & E. G. Classification des Saules d'Europe. O. and F (atlas). 2 vol. Paris, 1904-5. 60 pl.
D.H. ......Dallimore, W. Holly, Yew and Box. O. London, 1908. Pl.
D.J. ......Dallimore, W., & A. B. Jackson. A Handbook of Conifers. O. Ed. 1 and 2. London, 1923 and 1931. Il. and pl.
D.L. ......Dippel, L. Handbuch der Laubholzkunde. 3 vol. O. Berlin, 1889-93. Il.
E.H. ......Elwes, H. J., & A. Henry. The Trees of Great Britain and Ireland. 7 vol. Q. Edinburgh, 1906-13. 419 pl. (5 col.)
Em. ......Emerson, G. B. A Report on the Trees and Shrubs Growing Naturally in the Forests of Massachusetts. Ed. 4. O. Boston, 1875. Pl. partly col.
E.N. ......Engler, A., & Karl Prantl. Die natürlichen Pflanzenfamilien nebst ihren Gattungen und wichtigeren Arten. Teil I-IV, each in several parts; suppl. 1-4. O. Leipzig, 1887-1915. Il. and pl.
E.N.R. ...Engler, A., & K. Prantl. Die Natürlichen Pflanzenfamilien. Ed. 2, rev. Vol. 1→ O. Leipzig, 1924→ Il.
E.P. ......Engler, A. Das Pflanzenreich; Regni Vegetabilis Conspectus. Part 1→ O. Leipzig, 1900→ Il.—Cited by the number of the family.
F. ....The Florist.—Continued as: Florist, Fruitist and Garden Miscellany. 14 vol. O. London, 1848-61. Il. and col. pl.

ABBREVIATIONS OF REFERENCES

F.C. ......Floral Cabinet and Magazine of Exotic Botany. Ed. by Knowles & Westcott. 3 vol. O. London, 1837–40. Col. pl.

F.D. ......Flora von Deutschland. Ed. by D. F. L. von Schlechtendal, Langethal und Schenk. Ed. 5 by Ernst Hallier. 30 vol. O. Gera-Untermhaus, 1880–87. 3470 col. pl.

F.E. ......The Florists' Exchange. Vol. 1→ F. New York, 1888→ Il. and few pl.

F.L. ......Forest Leaves. Published for the Pennsylvania Forestry Association. Vol. 1→ O. Philadelphia, 1886→ Il. and pl.

F.M. ......The Floral Magazine. 20 vol. O and Q. London, 1861–81. 1022 col. pl.

F.P. ......Florist and Pomologist. 22 vol. O. London, 1863–84. Il. and col. pl.

F.R. ......Flora and Sylva. Ed. by W. Robinson. 3 vol. Q. London, 1903–5. Il. and col. pl.

F.S. ......Flore des Serres et des Jardins de l'Europe. 23 vol. O. Gand, 1845–80. Il. and col. pl.

F.Sa. ......Forbes, James. Salicetum Woburnense. F. London, 1829. 140 col. pl.

F.W. ......The Floral World and Garden Guide. Ed. by Shirley Hibberd. 23 vol. O. London, 1858–80. Il. and col. pl.

G. ....Gardening Illustrated. Vol. 1–33. Q. London, 1880–1925. Il.

G.A. ......Gardeners' Chronicle of America. Vol. 19→ F. New York, 1915→ Il.

G.C. ......Gardeners' Chronicle. F. 1841–73.—F. London, 1841–1873.—New ser., vol. 1–26. London, 1874–86 (cited as II:1→)—Ser. III, vol. 1→ London, 1887→ (after vol. 26 cited by vol. only). Il. and pl., some col.

Gd.W. ...Goodale, G. L. Wild Flowers. O. Boston, 1882. Col. pl.

G.F. ......Garden and Forest. Ed. by C. S. Sargent. 10 vol. Q. New York, 1888–97. Il.

Gg. ......Gardening. Vol. 1→ Q. Chicago, 1892→ Il.

Gg.W. ...Gardening World Illustrated. Vol. 1–26. F and Q. London, 1884–1900. Il.

G.H. ......Guimpel, F., Willdenow and Hayne. Abbildungen der Deutschen Holzarten. 2 vol. Q. Berlin, 1815–20. 216 col. pl.

G.M. ......Gardeners' Magazine. Ed. by Shirley Hibberd and others. Vol. 1–59. O, Q, F. London, 1860–1916. Vol. 1–7 called "Gardeners' Weekly Magazine and Floricultural Cabinet." Il. and col. pl.

G.M.B. ...Gardeners' Magazine of Botany, Horticulture, Floriculture and Natural Sciences. Ed. by Thomas Moore and W. P. Ayres. 3 vol. O. London, 1850–51. Il. and col. pl.

Gn. ......The Garden. Founded by Wm. Robinson. Vol. 1–91. Q. London, 1871–1927. Il. and col. pl.

Gn.M. ....The Garden Magazine. Vol. 1–39. Q. New York, 1905–24.—Continued as: Garden Magazine and Home Builder. Vol. 40–47. F. Boston, etc., 1924–28.—Continued as American Home. Vol. 48→ Il.

Gn.W. ...Gardening World Illustrated. Vol. 1–26. F and Q. London, 1884–1909. Il. and pl.

G.O. ......Guimpel, W., Otto and Hayne. Abbildungen der fremden in Deutschland ausdauernden Holzarten. Q. Berlin, 1825 [1819–30]. 144 col. pl.

Gr.G. ....Gray, Asa. Genera of the Plants of the United States Illustrated. 2 vol. O. New York, 1849. 186 pl.

Gr.M. ....Gray, Asa. A Manual of the Botany of the Northern United States. Ed. 7; ed. by B. L. Robinson and M. L. Fernald. O. New York, 1908. Il.

Gs. ....Gartenschönheit. Ed. by K. Förster, C. Schneider and O. Kühl. Vol. 1→ F. Berlin-Westend, 1920→ Il. and col. pl.

Gt. ....Gartenflora. Ed. by Ed. Regel and others. Vol. 1–87. O. Erlangen, etc., 1852–1938. Il. and col. pl.

G.W. ......Gartenwelt. Ed. by Max Hesdörffer and others. Vol. 1–37. Q. Berlin, 1897–1933. (In 1934 united with Blumen- und Pflanzenbau.) Il. and some col. plates.

G.Z. ......Gartenzeitung; Monatschrift für Gärtner und Gartenfreunde. Ed. by L. Wittmack and W. Perring. 4 vol. O. Berlin, 1882–85. Il. and col. pl.

H.A. ......Hayne, F. G. Getreue Darstellung und Beschreibung der in der Arzneykunde gebräuchlichen Gewächse. 14 vol. Q. Berlin, 1805–46. Col. pl.

H.B. ......Horticulture. New ser.; vol. 1→ Q. Boston, 1923→ Il.—The volumes of the first series, 1904–23 (37 vol.) are cited by the year.

H.C. ......Hartig, Th. Vollständige Naturgeschichte der forstlichen Culturpflanzen Deutschlands. Q. Berlin, 1851. 118 col. pl.

H.D. ......Hornibrook, Murray. Dwarf and Slow-growing Conifers. O. London, 1923. Pl.

H.E. ......Hooker, W. J. Exotic Flora. 3 vol. O. Edinburgh, 1823–27. 232 col. pl.

H.F. ......L'Horticulteur Français. Ed. by F. Herincq. 21 vol. O. Paris, 1851–72. Il. and col. pl.

H.G. ......Hamburger Garten- und Blumenzeitung. 46 vol. O. Hamburg, 1845–90.—Vol. 1–7 have the title "Neue Allgemeine Deutsche Garten- und Blumenzeitung." Il. and col. pl.

H.H. ......Hough, R. B. Handbook of the Trees of the Northern States and Canada East of the Rocky Mountains. O. Lowville, N. Y., 1907. Il.

H.I. ......Hooker's Icones Plantarum. Vol. 1→ O. London, 1837→ Pl.

H.M. ......Hegi, Gustav. Illustrierte Flora von Mitteleuropa. Vol. 1–7. O. München, 1908–31. Il. and pl.

H.N. ......Hao, K. Sh. Caprifoliaceae in Liou, Flore Illustrée du Nord de la Chine. Fasc. 3. F. Peiping, 1934. Pl.

H.S. ......Hao, K. Sh. Synopsis of Chinese Salix. (Rep. Spec. Nov. Beih. 93.) O. Berlin, 1936. 44 pl.

H.U. ......L'Horticulteur Universel. Ed. by C. Lemaire. 8 vol. O. Paris, 1839–47. Col. pl.

H.W. ......Hempel, G., & K. Wilhelm. Die Bäume und Sträucher des Waldes. 3 parts in 2 vol. Q. Wien, 1889–99. Il. and col. pl.

ABBREVIATIONS OF REFERENCES

I.B. ......Icones of the Bamboos of Japan. [By H. Shirasawa.] F. [1912.] [In Japanese.]
15 col. pl.

I.G. ......Illustrierte Gartenzeitung. Ed. by A. Courtin & C. Müller (1857–79), by M. Lebl
(1880–95). Vol. 1–39. O. Stuttgart, 1857–95. Il. and col. pl.

I.H. ......L'Illustration Horticole. Ed. by C. Lemaire and others. 43 vol. Q and F. Gand,
1854–96. Il. and col. pl.

I.S. ....Hu, H. H., & W. Y. Chun. Icones Plantarum Sinicarum. Fasc. 1→ F. Shanghai,
1927→ Pl.

I.T. ......Icones Selectae Horti Thenensis. Ed. by L. van den Bossche. 6 vol. O. Bruxelles,
1899–1909. 240 pl.

J. ....Le Jardin. Ed. by H. Martinet. Q. Vol. 1–35. F. Argenteuil and Paris, 1887–
1921.—United with Revue Horticole in July, 1921. Il. and col. pl.

J.A. ......Journal of the Arnold Arboretum. Vol. 1→ O. Cambridge, etc., 1919→ Il. and pl.

J.C. ......Journal of the College of Science. Imp. University, Japan. Vol. 1→ Q. Tokyo,
1887→ Il. and pl.

J.F. ......Le Jardin Fleuriste. Ed. by C. Lemaire. 4 vol. O. Gand, 1851–54. Il. and col.
pl.

J.H. ......Journal of Horticulture. Vol. 26–63. Q. London, 1861–80.—Ser. III, vol. 1–71.
Sq. F. London, 1881–1915. Il.—Vol. 1–25 were issued under the title "Cottage
Gardener" and are not cited.

J.L. ......Journal of the Roy. Horticultural Society of London. 9 vol.—New ser. (II); vol.
1→ O. London, 1846→ Il. and pl.

J.P. ......Journal de la Société National d'Horticulture de France. 12 vol. (1855–66).—
Ser. II (1867–78).—Ser. III; 21 vol. (1879–99).—Ser. IV, Vol. 1→ (1900→). O.
Paris, 1855→ Il.

J.S. ....Jepson, W. L. The Silva of California. Q. Berkeley, 1910. Il. and pl.

K.B. ......Kew Bulletin of Miscellaneous Information. Vol. 1887→ O. London, 1887→ Pl.

K.D. ......Koehne, E. Deutsche Dendrologie. O. Stuttgart, 1893. Il.

K.S. ......Keeler, H. L. Our Northern Shrubs. O. New York, 1903. Pl.

K.V. ......Karsten, Georg, & Heinrich Schenck. Vegetationsbilder. Ser. 1→ Q. Jena, 1904→
Pl.

L.A. ......Loudon, J. C. Arboretum et Fruticetum Britannicum. 8 vol. O. London, 1838.
Il. and 418 pl.

L.B. ......Loddiges, C. and Sons. The Botanical Cabinet. 20 vol. O. London, 1818–33.
2000 col. pl.

L.D. ......Loiseleur-Deslongchamps, J. L. A. Herbier Général de l'Amateur. 8 vol. (1816–
27).—Ser. II; 6 vol. (1839–50). Q. Paris, 1816–50. 1036 col. pl.

L.G. ......Lounsberry, L. A Guide to the Wild Flowers. O. New York, 1900. Il. and col. pl.

L.H. ......Lowe, E. J., & W. Howard. Beautiful Leaved Plants. New ed. Q. London, 1865.
60 col. pl.

L.I. ....Lavallée, A. Arboretum Segrezianum; Icones Selectae Arborum et Fruticum. Q.
Paris, 1880–85. 36 pl., also 28 unpublished pl. without numbers or names.

L.S. ......Lounsberry, A. Southern Wild Flowers and Trees. O. New York, 1901. Il. and
col. pl.

M.A. .....Mouillefert, P. Traité des Arbres et Arbrisseaux. 2 parts and atlas. O. Paris,
1892–98. 195 pl., partly col.

M.Am. ...Millspaugh, C. F. American Medicinal Plants. 2 vol. Q. New York, 1887. 180
col. pl.

M.B. .....Mitford, A. B. Freeman. The Bamboo Garden. O. London, 1896. Pl.

M.B.G. ...The Magazine of Botany and Gardening, British and Foreign. Ed. by J. Rennie.
2 vol.—Ser. II; 3 vol. Q. London, 1836–37. Col. pl.

M.D. ......Mitteilungen der Deutschen Dendrologischen Gesellschaft. No. 1→ O. Berlin,
1893→ Il. and pl., few col.

M.G. ......Möller's Deutsche Gärtner-Zeitung. Vol. 1→ F. Erfurt, 1886→ Il.

M.I. ......Matsumura, J. Icones plantarum koishikavenses. Vol. 1–4. O. Tokyo, 1911–21. Pl.

M.K. ......Miyabe, K. & Y. Kudo. Icones of the Essential Forest Trees of Hokkaido. 3
vol. F. Sapporo, 1920–31. 86 col. pl.

M.M. ....Meehan's Monthly. Ed. by Th. Meehan. 12 vol. Q. Germantown, Pa., 1891–
1902. Il. and col. pl.

M.N. ......Meehan, Th. The Native Flowers and Ferns of the United States. 2 vol. Q.
Boston, 1878–9. 96 col. pl.

M.O. ......Mottet, S. Arbres et Arbustes d'Ornement de Pleine Terre. O. Paris, 1925. Il.
and pl.

M.S. ......Michaux, F. A. The North American Sylva. 3 vol. Q. Philadelphia, 1865. 156
col. pl.

N.D. ......Nouveau Duhamel; this is: Duhamel du Monceau, H. L. Traité des Arbres et
Arbustes. New ed. 7 vol. F. Paris, 1804–19. 487 col. pl.

N.F. ......New Flora and Silva. Ed. by E. H. M. Cox. Vol. 1→ O. London, 1928→ Pl.

N.H. ......National Horticultural Magazine. Vol. 1→ O. Washington, 1922→ Il.

N.I. ....Nicholson, G. The Illustrated Dictionary of Gardening. 4 vol. and suppl. Q.
London and New York, 1887–1900. Il.

N.K. ......Nakai, T. Flora Sylvatica Koreana. Vol. 1→ O. Tokyo, 1915→ Pl.

N.S. ......Nuttall, T. The North American Sylva. New ed. 3 vol. (vol. 4–6 of Michaux and
Nuttall's North American Sylva). Q. Philadelphia, 1865. 121 col. pl.

N.T. ......Nakai, T. Trees and Shrubs of Japan Proper. Vol. 1. Ed. 2, rev. O. Tokyo,
1927. Il.

N.V. ......Nederlandsche Dendrologische Vereeniging. Jaarboek. Vol. 1→ O. Waagenin-
gen, 1925→ Pl.

ABBREVIATIONS OF REFERENCES

P.B. ......Perrin, Mrs. I. S. British Flowering Plants. 3 vol. Q. London, 1914. 223 col. pl.
P.F. ......Paxton's Flower Garden. By J. Lindley and J. Paxton. 3 vol. Q. London, 1850-53. Il. and 72 col. pl.
P.G. ......Popular Gardening (and Fruit Growing). 6 vol. F. Buffalo, 1885–91. Il.
P.I. ......Pardé, L. Iconographie des Conifères. F. Paris, 1912–14. 30 col. pl.
P.M. ......Paxton's Magazine of Botany. 16 vol. O. London, 1834–49. Il. and col. pl.
R.B. ......Revue de l'Horticulture Belge et Etrangère. Vol. 1→ Q. Gand, 1875→ Il. and col. pl.
R.H. ......Revue Horticole. Vol. 1829→ O. Paris, 1829→ Il. and col. pl.
Rh. ......Rhodora; Journal of the New England Botanical Club. Vol. 1→ O. Boston, 1899→ Il. and pl.
R.I. ......Reichenbach, H. G. L. Icones Florae Germanicae et Helveticae. 25 vol. Q. Leipzig, 1834–1912. Col. pl.
R.Mo. ....Annual Report of the Missouri Botanical Garden. Vol. 1→ O. St. Louis, 1889→ Pl.
R.R. ......Redouté, P. J. Les Roses. Text by C. A. Thory. 3 vol. Ed. 3. 3 vol. O. Paris, 1835.—As neither pages nor plates are numbered, the plates are cited by the numbered groups "gr." followed by the number of the plate within the group according to sequence. The first folio edition (1817–24) is very rare and is not cited. 183 col. pl.
S.B. ......Sweet, R. The British Flower Garden. 3 vol. and ser. II, 4 vol. O. London, 1823–38. 300 col. pl.
S.C. ......Sweet, R. Cistineae. Q. London, 1825–30. 112 col. pl.
S.E. ......Sowerby, J. English Botany or Colored Figures of British Plants. Ed. 3. Ed. by J. T. B. Syme. 13 vol. O. London, 1863–1902. 1952 col. pl.
S.F. ......Sibthorp, J. Flora graeca. 10 vol. F. London, 1806–40. 966 col. pl.
S.H. ......Schneider, C. Illustriertes Handbuch der Laubholzkunde. 2 vol. and Index. O. Jena, 1906–12. Il.
S.I. ......Shirasawa, H. Iconographie des Essences Forestières du Japon. 2 vol. F. Paris, Tokyo, 1899–1909. 162 col. pl.
S.L. ......Silva Tarouca, E., and C. Schneider. Unsere Freiland-Laubgehölze. Ed. 3. Q. Wien and Leipzig, 1922. Il. and 16 col. pl. In a few cases ed. 2 is cited as "2:".
S.M. ......Sargent, C. S. Manual of the Trees of North America. Ed. 2. O. Boston and New York, 1922. Il.
S.M.E. ...Schwarz, O. Monographie der Eichen Europas und des Mittelmeergebietes. Vol. 1 (Text). Q. Vol. 2 (Atlas). Q. Dahlem bei Berlin, 1936→ Pl. 1–48→
S.N. ......Silva Tarouca, E., & C. Schneider. Unsere Freiland-Nadelhölzer. Ed. 2. Q. Wien & Leipzig, 1923. Il. and 12 pl. and 12 col. pl.
S.O. ......Schmidt, Franz. Oesterreichs Allgemeine Baumzucht. 4 vol. F. Wien, 1792–1822. 240 col. pl.
S.R. ......Species of Rhododendron. By the Rhododendron Society. O. Edinburgh, 1930. Il.
S.S. ......Sargent, C. S. The Silva of North America. 14 vol. Q. Boston, etc., 1891–1902. 740 pl.
S.St. ......Silva Tarouca, E., & C. Schneider. Unsere Freiland-Stauden. Ed. 4. O. Wien & Leipzig, 1922. Il. and 13 col. pl.
S.T. ......Sargent, C. S., ed. Trees and Shrubs. 2 vol. F. Boston, etc., 1905–13. 200 pl.
S.Z. ......Siebold, P. F., & J. G. Zuccarini. Flora Japonica. 2 vol. Q. Leyden, 1835–70. 151 col. pl.
T.M. ......Botanical Magazine. [Tokyo.] Vol. 1→ O. Tokyo, 1887→ Pl.
T.N. ......Torrey, J. A Flora of the State of New York. 2 vol. Q. New York, 1843. Col. pl.
U.S.Im. ..United States.—Bureau of Plant Industry; Bulletin of Foreign Plant Introduction. Nos. 1–100 (1908–14).—Plant immigrants. No. 101–219. Q. Washington, 1914–24. Pl.
U.S.Inv. ..United States.—Bureau of Plant Industry; Inventory of Seeds and Plants Imported. No. 1→ O. Washington, 1899→ Pl.
V.F. ......Vilmorin, M. L. de, & D. Bois. Fruticetum Vilmorinianum. O. Paris, 1904. Pl.
V.G. ......Vigué, Marie Th., & H. Gaussen. Révision du Genre Abies. O. Toulouse, 1928–29. (Bull. Soc. Hist. Nat. Toulouse. Vol. 58, fasc. 3.—Reprinted in: Trav. Lab. For. Toulouse. Tome II, art. 1.) Il.
W.A. ......Wilson, E. H. America's Greatest Garden; the Arnold Arboretum. O. Boston, 1925. 50 pl.
W.C. ......Wilson, E. H. The Conifers and Taxads of Japan. Q. Cambridge, 1916. 59 pl.
W.D. ......Watson, P. W. Dendrologia Britannica. 2 vol. O. London, 1825. 172 col. pl.
W.G. ......Wiener Illustrierte Garten-Zeitung. Vol. 1–30. O. Wien, 1876–1905. Vol. 1–3 issued under the title "Wiener Obst- und Garten-Zeitung." Il. and col. pl.
W.J. ......Wilson, E. H. The Cherries of Japan. O. Cambridge, 1916. 8 pl.
W.R. ......Willmott, Ellen. The Genus Rosa. 2 vol. F. London, 1910–14. Pl. and col. pl.

FURTHER ABBREVIATIONS USED IN CONNECTION WITH THE ABBREVIATIONS CITED ABOVE

(b) ....bark
(c) ....colored plate or illustration
f ....figure
(h) ....habit figure

(hc) ......habit figure colored
(l) ....leaf
t ....plate (Latin tabula)

xvii

VARIOUS ABBREVIATIONS AND EXPLANATION OF SIGNS

Afghan., Afghanistan
Afr., Africa
Ala., Alabama
Alb., Alberta
Am., America or American
Ark., Arkansas
Austr., Australia
auth., authors
B. C., British Columbia
br., brs., branch, branches
brt., brts., branchlet, branchlets
C., central
Calif., California
caps., capsule
Cauc., Caucasus
cm., centimeter, centimeters
Colo., Colorado
Conn., Connecticut
cult., cultivated, cultivation
Del., Delaware
diam., diameter
e., east or eastern
Eng., England
Eu., Europe
f., forma (in connection with a botanical name), or figure (in a citation of an illustration)
fl., flower
Fla., Florida
-fld., -flowered, as few-fld.
fls., flowers
fr., frs., fruit, fruits
Himal., Himalayas
Huds. B., Hudson Bay
Ill., Illinois
Ind., Indiana
intr., introduced into cultivation
isl., isls., island, islands or isles
Kamch., Kamchatka
Kans., Kansas
Ky., Kentucky
l., lusus, a slight variation ranking below forma (in connection with a botanical name)
L. I., Long Island, New York
Lab., Labrador
l. c., loco citato, at the place or in the work cited (in connection with the citation of an illustration)
lf., leaf
lft., lfts., leaflet, leaflets
-lvd., -leaved, as 3-lvd.
lvs., leaves
m., meter, meters
Mal., Malaysia, Malayan
Man., Manitoba
Manch., Manchuria
Mass., Massachusetts
Md., Maryland
Me., Maine
Mediterr., Mediterranean
Mich., Michigan
Minn., Minnesota
mm., millimeter, millimeters
mt., mts., mountain, mountains

n., north, northern
N. B., New Brunswick
N. C., North Carolina
N. D., North Dakota
n. e., northeast, northeastern
Neb., Nebraska
Nev., Nevada
Nfd., Newfoundland
N. J., New Jersey
N. H., New Hampshire
N. Mex., New Mexico
N. S., Nova Scotia
n. w., northwest, northwestern
N. Y., New York
nom. amb., nomen ambiguum; a name of varying application, an ambiguous name and one to be rejected in favor of the next oldest name
Okla., Oklahoma
Ont., Ontario
Ore., Oregon
Orig., origin, originated
Pa., Pennsylvania
Prol. proles, race; a subdivision of a species, ranking below subspecies
Que., Quebec, province of
R. I., Rhode Island
s., south, southern
Saghal., Saghalin
Sask., Saskatchewan
S. C., South Carolina
Scand., Scandinavia
S. D., South Dakota
s. e., southeast, southeastern
sensu, after the name of a plant, in the sense of a certain author, a misidentification, not the plant of the original author; also "of" used in the same sense
Sect., Section, a subdivision of a genus, ranking below the subgenus
spont., spontaneous, growing wild
subf., subform, a subdivision of a species, ranking below form (forma)
Subfam., subfamily, the primary subdivision of the family
Subgen., subgenus, the primary subdivision of the genus
subsp., subspecies, the primary division of the species
subvar., a subdivision of the species, ranking below variety
subtrop., subtropical
s. w., southwest, southwestern
t., plate (tabula), in citations of illustrations
temp., temperate
Tenn., Tennessee
tribe, tribe, a subdivision of the family, ranking below subfamily.
trop., tropical
Turkest., Turkestan
var., vars., variety (varietas), varieties
Vt., Vermont
w., west, western
W. Va., West Virginia
Wisc., Wisconsin

ABBREVIATIONS OF SIGNS

Wyo., Wyoming
? indicates doubt
§ section; see above under Sect.
× sign of a sexual hybrid, preceding the name of the hybrid, or connecting the names of the parents
+ sign of a graft-hybrid, preceding the name of the hybrid, or connecting the names of the parents

♀ pistillate flower or plant, also the seed-bearing parent of a hybrid
♂ staminate flower or plant, also the staminate parent of a hybrid
I–XII, Roman numerals (small capitals) after fl. (flowering time) and fr. (fruiting time) denote the months according to their sequence.

APPROXIMATE EQUIVALENTS OF THE METRIC AND ENGLISH SYSTEMS OF MEASUREMENTS

1 millimeter (mm.)	= 1/25 of an inch	5 centimeters	= 2 inches
2 millimeters	= 1/12 of an inch	10 centimeters (or 1	
1 centimeter (cm.)	= 2/5 of an inch	decimeter)	= 4 inches
2.5 centimeters	= 1 inch	30 centimeters	= 1 foot

1 meter (m.) = 3⅓ feet or 40 inches (less ¾ inch)

CENTIMETERS

INCHES

xix

SYNOPSIS
OF THE ORDERS AND FAMILIES CONTAINED
IN THIS BOOK

All the families treated in this book belong to the Division SPER-MATOPHYTA or SEED-PLANTS (*Phanerogamae, Phaenogamae, Embryophyta siphonogama*) differing from the other Divisions of the VEGETABLE COMMUNITY chiefly in the presence of true flowers containing stamens or pistils or both and in the reproduction by seeds containing an embryo.

Subdivision I. GYMNOSPERMAE. GYMNOSPERMS. Ovules naked, not inclosed in an ovary; fls. unisexual, rarely bisexual.
A. Lvs. fan-shaped, deciduous: fertilization by motile sperm-cells..Class I. GINKGOALES
Fam. 1. *Ginkgoaceae,* 1
AA. Lvs. scale-like or linear to oblong or elliptic, persistent, rarely deciduous: fertilization by passive sperm-cells.
B. Fls. without perianth...Class II. CONIFERALES
Fam. 2. *Taxaceae,* 1
C. Ovules solitary or few, developing into a drupe-like or berry-like seed.
Fam. 2. *Taxaceae,* 1
CC. Ovules borne on scales forming a cone which becomes woody, rarely berry-like at maturity and with 1 to many seeds; seeds often winged.
D. Each scale with 1 seed; fr. a large cone.................Fam. 3. *Araucariaceae,* 7
DD. Each scale with 2 or more seeds; fr. a cone or berry-like with 1 to many seeds; seeds often winged..Fam. 4. *Pinaceae,* 8
BB. Fls. with a 2-4 parted perianth...............................Class III. GNETALES
Fam. 5. *Ephedraceae,* 68

Subdivision II. ANGIOSPERMAE. ANGIOSPERMS. Ovules inclosed in an ovary: fls. usually with perianth, unisexual or bisexual.
Class I. DICOTYLEDONEAE. DICOTYLEDONS. Embryo normally with 2 opposite cotyledons: lvs. usually net-veined: parts of fls. mostly in whorls of 4 or 5: stem with clear distinction of bark, wood and pith; the wood forming annual layers.
Subclass I. CHORIPETALAE (*Apetalae* and *Polypetalae*). Petals wanting or free, or only some of the petals united at base.
A. Petals wanting (except in Fam. 21): lvs. simple (except in Fam. 15).
B. Sepals in one whorl or wanting: fls. unisexual, at least the staminate in catkins (except in some genera of Fam. 12).
C. Ovary superior or naked: fls. dioecious (sometimes monoecious in Fam. 8).
D. Fr. a many-seeded dehiscent caps.: fls. without perianth, dioecious.
Order I. SALICALES
Fam. 6. *Salicaceae,* 71
DD. Fr. a nut, drupe or berry, 1-, rarely 2-seeded.
E. Ovary with 2 ovules; staminate fls. with 4 sepals: lvs. opposite.
Order II. GARRYALES
Fam. 7. *Garryaceae,* 111
EE. Ovary with 1 ovule; staminate fls. without perianth: lvs. alternate.
F. Style with 2 stigmas: ovules orthotropous..............Order III. MYRICALES
Fam. 8. *Myricaceae,* 112
FF. Style not cleft, stigmatic at apex; ovule amphitropous.
Order IV. LEITNERIALES
Fam. 9. *Leitneriaceae,* 114
CC. Ovary inferior or partly so; staminate fls. with perianth; fls. monoecious.
D. Ovary with 1 basal orthotropous ovule: lvs. pinnate.........Order V. JUGLANDALES
Fam. 10. *Juglandaceae,* 115
DD. Ovary with 2 or 6 pendulous ovules, but fr. usually 1-seeded: lvs. simple.
Order VI. FAGALES
E. Fr. a nut or nutlet partly or wholly enclosed in a more or less leafy involucre, or nutlets disposed in a strobile or ament............Fam. 11. *Betulaceae,* 124
EE. Fr. a nut partly or wholly enclosed in a woody, often spiny involucre.
Fam. 12. *Fagaceae,* 146
BB. Perianth usually of 2 whorls; fls. usually not in catkins.
C. Fls. unisexual, rarely bisexual (sometimes so in Fam. 13 and 18).
D. Fr. not a caps.: ovary 1-celled.
E. Ovary superior ....Order VII. URTICALES

SYNOPSIS

SYNOPSIS

GG. Fls. perfect, rarely unisexual.
   H. Pistils 1 to many, often distinct, developing into achenes or follicles, or connate and forming a pome or drupe: fls. regular: stamens usually perigynous or epigynous..........................Fam. 39. *Rosaceae*, 322
   HH. Pistil 1, developing into a legume: fls. usually irregular (papilionaceous); stamens hypogynous...............Fam. 40. *Leguminosae*, 482
EE. Carpels united into a compound ovary; stamens hypogynous.
  F. Stamens as many as sepals or fewer, rarely more than twice as many as sepals.
   G. Stamens twice as many as sepals or as many and opposite the sepals (except in Fam. 58) or sometimes fewer.
    H. Ovules pendulous with ventral raphe, rarely ascending and with dorsal raphe ....Order XV. GERANIALES
     I. Fls. perfect or dioecious or polygamous: lvs. often compound.
      J. Fls. regular.
       K. Plants without secreting cells: fls. perfect: lvs. pinnate.
        Fam. 41. *Zygophyllaceae*, 522
       KK. Plants with secreting cells.
        L. Lvs. punctate, of aromatic or pungent odor when bruised.
         Fam. 42. *Rutaceae*, 523
        LL. Lvs. not punctate.
         M. Filaments distinct; fls. usually unisexual or polygamous.
          Fam. 43. *Simaroubaceae*, 530
         MM. Filaments usually wholly or partly united; fls. usually perfect ....Fam. 44. *Meliaceae*, 532
      JJ. Fls. irregular, papilionaceous...........Fam. 45. *Polygalaceae*, 533
     II. Fls. monoecious, often apetalous: fr. capsular, usually of 3 carpels, rarely indehiscent ....Fam. 46. *Euphorbiaceae*, 534
    HH. Ovules pendulous with dorsal raphe or erect with ventral raphe: disk usually conspicuous ....Order XVI. SAPINDALES
     I. Fls. apetalous or with 3 minute petals.
      J. Lvs. opposite: petals wanting: fr. capsular or fleshy.
       Fam. 47. *Buxaceae*, 536
      JJ. Lvs. linear, alternate; petals present: fr. drupaceous, berry-like.
       Fam. 48. *Empetraceae*, 538
     II. Fls. with petals, rarely apetalous.
      J. Lvs. simple, pinnately veined, or if compound, plants resiniferous.
       K. Each carpel with 1 pendulous ovule.
        L. Carpels distinct; fr. separating into 5–8 cocci; lvs. opposite, entire ....Fam. 49. *Coriariaceae*, 539
        LL. Carpels connate: fr. a drupe, berry or caps.: lvs. alternate.
         M. Plant resiniferous: lvs. often compound.
          Fam. 50. *Anacardiaceae*, 540
         MM. Plant not resiniferous: lvs. simple.
          N. Fr. a caps. or achene: fls. in racemes.
           Fam. 51. *Cyrillaceae*, 545
          NN. Fr. a drupe: fls. in cymes or solitary.
           Fam. 52. *Aquifoliaceae*, 546
       KK. Each carpel with 2 or more ovules: fr. a caps. or drupe.
        Fam. 53. *Celastraceae*, 553
      JJ. Lvs. palmately veined or compound (except in Fam. 58 and in a few species of Fam. 55).
       K. Lvs. opposite.
        L. Fls. regular.
         M. Fr. a bladdery caps.: lvs. pinnate.
          Fam. 54. *Staphyleaceae*, 563
         MM. Fr. a samara: lvs. simple or compound.
          Fam. 55. *Aceraceae*, 565
        LL. Fls. irregular: fr. a large leathery caps.
         Fam. 56. *Hippocastanaceae*, 586
       KK. Lvs. alternate.
        L. Stamens opposite the sepals, or more than sepals.
         Fam. 57. *Sapindaceae*, 591
        LL. Stamens opposite the petals: lvs. often simple.
         Fam. 58. *Sabiaceae*, 593
   GG. Stamens as many as sepals and alternating, opposite the petals: carpels 2–5, each with 1–2 ascending ovules...............Order XVII. RHAMNALES
    H. Fr. a caps. or drupe; petals involute: lvs. simple, penninerved.
     Fam. 59. *Rhamnaceae*, 595
    HH. Fr. a berry; petals valvate: lvs. palmately veined or compound.
     Fam. 60. *Vitaceae*, 608
  FF. Stamens usually numerous: disk inconspicuous or wanting.
   G. Sepals usually valvate: placenta usually central: pubescence stellate: tissue with mucilaginous cells.......................Order XVIII. MALVALES
    H. Stamens numerous.
     I. Anthers 2-celled; stamens fascicled or free...Fam. 61. *Tiliaceae*, 621
     II. Anthers 1-celled; filaments connate........Fam. 62. *Malvaceae*, 628
    HH. Fertile stamens as many as sepals, connate; anthers 2-celled; petals often wanting or reduced....................Fam. 63. *Sterculiaceae*, 629

SYNOPSIS

GG. Sepals usually imbricate: placentae usually parietal.

Order XIX. PARIETALES

  H. Styles usually free.

    I. Seeds usually with albumen.

      J. Fr. often berry-like: mostly climbing shrubs.

Fam. 64. Actinidiaceae, 630

      JJ. Fr. a caps., sometimes indehiscent: upright shrubs or trees.

        K. Sepals and petals 4: lvs. opposite.Fam. 65. Eucryphiaceae, 632

        KK. Sepals and petals usually 5: lvs. alternate.

Fam. 66. Theaceae, 633

    II. Seed without albumen.

      J. Lvs. usually opposite: styles present.....Fam. 67. Guttiferae, 636

      JJ. Lvs. alternate, small; style wanting or very short: seed with a tuft of hairs...........................Fam. 68. Tamaricaceae, 642

  HH. Styles united.

    I. Fls. perfect: fr. capsular.

      J. Stamens many ....Fam. 69. Cistaceae, 644

      JJ. Stamens 5 ....Fam. 70. Violaceae, 652

    II. Fls. often unisexual: fr. often berry-like.

      J. Sepals and petals usually 5...........Fam. 71. Flacourtiaceae, 652

      JJ. Sepals and petals 4; stamens 8.......Fam. 72. Stachyuraceae, 654

<small>*B.</small> Ovary usually inferior (except in Fam. 74, 75 and 76).

  C. Sepals and petals numerous: fleshy spiny plants.............Order XX. OPUNTIALES

Fam. 73. Cactaceae, 654

  CC. Sepals and petals usually 5: plants not fleshy.

    D. Ovules several or numerous in each cell (except in Fam. 75 and 76 with superior ovaries): infl. not umbelliform............................Order XXI. MYRTIFLORAE

      E. Ovary free, but enclosed in a tubular or campanulate calyx-tube.

        F. Ovary 1-celled, 1-ovuled; petals usually wanting.

          G. Ovule pendulous: lvs. not scaly.........Fam. 74. Thymelaeaceae, 658

          GG. Ovule upright: lvs. more or less scaly.........Fam. 75. Elaeagnaceae, 662

        FF. Ovary 2-6-celled; each cell with 2 to many ovules; petals present.

Fam. 76. Lythraceae, 666

      EE. Ovary adnate to the calyx-tube.

        F. Sepals and petals usually 5.

          G. Fr. with 9 carpels in 2 or 3 whorls, large, berry-like; petals 5-7.

Fam. 77. Punicaceae, 667

          GG. Fr. with the carpels in one whorl.

            H. Cells of ovary 1-ovuled: fr. drupaceous.

              1. Petals imbricate, small or wanting: ovary 1- or 6-10-celled.

Fam. 78. Nyssaceae, 667

              II. Petals valvate, 4-10, narrow: ovary 1-2-celled.

Fam. 79. Alangiaceae, 669

            HH. Cells of ovary 1-8-ovuled: fr. usually capsular or berry-like: aromatic plants ....Fam. 80. Myrtaceae, 670

        FF. Sepals and petals 4 or 2; calyx-tube cylindric......Fam. 81. Onagraceae, 670

    DD. Ovules 1 or rarely 2 in each cell, pendulous: fls. in umbels or corymbs.

Order XXII. UMBELLIFLORAE

      E. Fls. 5-merous; styles 2-5: fls. umbellate.

        F. Fr. a berry or drupe.................................Fam. 82. Araliaceae, 672

        FF. Fr. dry at maturity; splitting into 2 mericarps....Fam. 83. Umbelliferae, 680

      EE. Fls. 4-merous; style 1: fls. not umbellate: fr. a drupe..Fam. 84. Cornaceae, 681

Subclass II. SYMPETALAE Petals more or less united (free or nearly so in Fam. 85 and 86 and in some genera of Fam. 87, 94, 95 and 98).

A. Ovary superior (except in some genera of Fam. 87 and in Fam. 93).

  B. Stamens usually free or adnate only to the base of the corolla, twice as many as the lobes or alternate with the lobes, sometimes inserted at the sinuses of the corolla.

Order I. ERICALES

    C. Stamens free or nearly free.

      D. Petals free: fr. a caps.

        E. Ovary 3-celled: shrubs or trees......................Fam. 85. Clethraceae, 689

        EE. Ovary 4-5-celled; evergreen subshrubs.................Fam. 86. Pyrolaceae, 690

      DD. Petals united (distinct in a few genera): fr. a caps., berry or drupe.

Fam. 87. Ericaceae, 691

    CC. Stamens inserted at the sinuses of the corolla or connate into a tube.

Fam. 88. Diapensiaceae, 755

  BB. Stamens borne on the corolla.

    C. Stamens opposite the lobes and as many or more.

      D. Ovary 1-celled; stamens as many as lobes, usually 5.

        E. Ovary with 1 to many ovules, style 1: fr. a drupe or caps.

Order II. PRIMULALES
Fam. 89. Myrsinaceae, 756

        EE. Ovary with 1 ovule; styles 5: fr. an achene.........Order III. PLUMBAGINALES

Fam. 90. Plumbaginaceae, 757

    DD. Ovary 2-5-celled; corolla-lobes often 4.......................Order IV. EBENALES

      E. Ovary completely 2-5-celled; stamens usually as many as corolla-lobes.

Fam. 91. Sapotaceae, 757

xxiii

SYNOPSIS

Class II. MONOCOTYLEDONEAE. MONOCOTYLEDONS.

Embryo with one cotyledon: lvs. mostly parallel-veined: fls. usually 3- or 6-merous, not 5-merous: stem without annual layers, without clear distinction of bark, wood and pith.

ANALYTICAL KEY TO THE FAMILIES AND ABERRANT GENERA [1]

Ovules not enclosed in an ovary: fls. unisexual: resinous trees or shrubs (except *Ephedraceae*).

A. Seeds solitary or rarely 2, berry- or drupe-like: embryo with 2 cotyledons: lvs. alternate.
  B. Lvs. fan-shaped, deciduous: fr. yellow, drupe-like......................*Ginkgoaceae*, 1
  BB. Lvs. needle-shaped or linear, persistent......................................*Taxaceae*, 1
AA. Seeds several or many, forming a dry cone, rarely berry-like and with 1 or several seeds.
  B. Fr. a dry woody cone with often winged seeds between the scales or berry-like through union of the fleshy scales: fls. without perianth.
    c. Each scale with 1 ovule: cone large woody: lvs. alternate, ovate-lanceolate, 8–20 mm. broad at base ....*Araucariaceae*, 7
    cc. Each scale with 2 or more ovules: fr. a cone or berry-like: lvs. alternate, opposite or ternate, scale-like or needle-shaped or linear, rarely linear-lanceolate..*Pinaceae*, 8
  BB. Seeds nut-like, enclosed by the fleshy bracts, forming a small fleshy strobile: fls. with a 2–4-parted perianth: brs. virgate with scale-like lvs. in distant pairs or whorls: shrubs ....*Ephedraceae*, 68

Ovules enclosed in an ovary.

  I. Lvs. net-veined: parts of fl. mostly in whorls of 5, sometimes of 4, rarely of 3 or 2: stems with clear distinction of bark, wood and pith. (II. See on p. xxx.)

    1. *Fls. without corolla* (2, see p. xxvi).
A. Fls., at least the staminate ones, in catkins.
  B. Fls. of both sexes in catkins, without calyx; ovary superior or naked: lvs. simple, alternate.
    c. Fr. a many-seeded caps...*Salicaceae*, 71
    cc. Fr. 1-seeded.
      D. Style with 2 stigmas: lvs. often toothed.
        E. Each scale with a single pistillate fl.; catkins upright..........*Myricaceae*, 112
        EE. Each scale with 2 or 3 pistillate fls.; staminate catkins mostly pendulous.
          Betulaceae, 124
      DD. Style not cleft, stigmatic above: lvs. entire......................*Leitneriaceae*, 114
  BB. Fls., at least one sex, with calyx, usually only those of one sex in catkins.
    c. Ovary superior.
      Fr. fleshy, drupaceous. (See also *Rhus* sp. 13 and 14 on p. 545.)
      E. Pistillate fls. without perianth; those of both sexes in catkins: lvs. opposite.
        Garryaceae, 111
      EE. Pistillate fls. with perianth; only staminate fls. in catkins: lvs. alternate.
        Moraceae, 187
      DD. Fr. a caps.: styles and stamens 4...............................*Tetracentron*, 253
    cc. Ovary inferior.
      D. Lvs. pinnate ....*Juglandaceae*, 115
      DD. Lvs. simple.
        E. Fr. a nut..*Fagaceae*, 146
        EE. Fr. a caps.
          F. Fls. sessile, apetalous...*Sinowilsonia*, 317
          FF. Fls. pediceled, with minute petals...........................*Fortunearia*, 316
AA. Fls. not in catkins.
  B. Fls., at least staminate ones, without calyx or with indistinct calyx.
    c. Fls. in globular heads.
      D. Lvs. palmately lobed.
        E. Fr. a nutlet..*Platanaceae*, 320
        EE. Fr. a dehiscent 2-celled caps...................................*Liquidambar*, 312
      DD. Lvs. ovate, not lobed: fr. a drupe: head of many staminate and 1 pistillate fl.
        Davidia, 669
    cc. Fls. not in heads; carpels many.
      D. Lvs. alternate.
        E. Fr. drupaceous or of several 1-celled samaras...........*Trochodendraceae*, 244
        EE. Fr. a 2-celled samara...*Eucommiaceae*, 319
      DD. Lvs. opposite: fr. a dehiscent many-seeded pod.............*Cercidiphyllaceae*, 245
  BB. Fls. with calyx.
    c. Carpels distinct or nearly so, 2 or more.
      D. Sepals petaloid.
        E. Sepals valvate, usually 4...*Clematis*, 206

[1] The characters used in this key apply only to the genera and species treated in this book.

    EE. Sepals imbricate, 6 or more.
      F. Lvs. alternate.
        G. Lvs. compound: climbing shrubs.
          H. Carpels 3–12, many-seeded........................*Lardizabalaceae*, 220
          HH. Carpels numerous, 1-seeded.....................*Sargentodoxaceae*, 222
        GG. Lvs. simple ....*Magnoliaceae*, 246
      FF. Lvs. opposite: sepals many, spirally arranged...........*Calycanthaceae*, 255
  DD. Sepals not petaloid.
    E. Lvs. simple, palminerved: fr. a dehiscent dry pod...............*Firmiana*, 629
    EE. Lvs. compound: fr. a dehiscent pod or drupe.
      F. Lvs. not dotted: climbing shrubs........................*Lardizabalaceae*, 220
      FF. Lvs. with transparent dots: upright shrubs or trees............*Rutaceae*, 523
  CC. Carpels united into a 1–many-celled ovary.
    D. Ovary superior, free from the calyx.
      E. Lvs. alternate.
        F. Cells of ovary with 1 or 2 ovules.
          G. Fls., at least the pistillate, in globose heads or inclosed in a pyriform receptacle: fls. 4-merous.
            H. Trees or shrubs with milky juice: heads large, solitary..*Moraceae*, 187
            HH. Subshrubs without milky juice: heads small, in cymes.*Debregeasia*, 192
          GG. Fls. not in heads, nor inclosed in a receptacle.
            H. Anthers opening by pores: aromatic trees or shrubs.....*Lauraceae*, 257
            HH. Anthers opening by slits.
              I. Stamens as many and alternating with the sepals..*Rhamnaceae*, 595
              II. Stamens opposite the sepals or numerous.
                J. Styles or stigmas 2 or 3.
                  K. Fls. unisexual or polygamous (bisexual only in *Ulmus*).
                    L. Styles 2 or 1: lvs. usually serrate: fls. monoecious.
                      M. Styles usually 2: fr. a samara, nut or drupe: trees or large shrubs ....*Ulmaceae*, 174
                      MM. Style 1: fr. a nutlet: subshrub...........*Boehmeria*, 192
                  LL. Styles 3 or 2: fr. a caps. or drupe; shrubs or subshrubs with usually entire lvs.
                    M. Lvs. simple.
                      N. Fls. dioecious; stamens 5–18: lvs. entire.
                          Euphorbiaceae, 534
                      NN. Fls. monoecious; stamens 4–6.........*Buxaceae*, 536
                  MM. Lvs. pinnate: fls. dioecious, stamens 3–5....*Pistacia*, 540
                  KK. Fls. usually bisexual: low shrubs.
                    L. Stipules not sheathing: fr. an utricle, sometimes fleshy.
                        Chenopodiaceae, 200
                    LL. Stipules sheathing: fr. a dry achene......*Polygonaceae*, 196
                JJ. Style and stigma 1: calyx campanulate to tubular.
                  K. Stamens many: fr. a long-tailed achene.......*Cercocarpus*, 424
                  KK. Stamens as many or twice as many as calyx-lobes: fr. a berry.
                      Thymelaeaceae, 658
        FF. Cells of ovary with several ovules.
          G. Ovary several-celled ....*Sterculiaceae*, 629
          GG. Ovary 1-celled ....*Flacourtiaceae*, 652
      EE. Lvs. opposite.
        F. Fr. dehiscent, of 3 2-seeded carpels: lvs. entire...................*Buxus*, 537
        FF. Fr. not dehiscent.
          G. Fr. a drupe or berry....................................*Rhamnaceae*, 595
          GG. Fr. a samara.
           H. Samara 1-celled ....*Oleaceae*, 765
           HH. Samara 2-celled ....*Aceraceae*, 565
  DD. Ovary inferior or half-inferior or permanently inclosed in the calyx-tube.
    E. Fr. a dehiscent caps.
      F. Ovary 6-celled; calyx tubular, corolla-like: climbing shrubs.
                    Aristolochiaceae, 195
      FF. Ovary 2-celled; calyx of distinct sepals; upright shrubs.
                    Hamamelidaceae, 311
    EE. Fr. a drupe or rarely an achene; ovary 1-celled.
      F. Plant more or less covered with peltate or stellate scales...*Elaeagnaceae*, 662
      FF. Plant not scaly.
        G. Fls. in clusters on axillary peduncles; stamens 5–12: lvs. alternate: trees.
                   Nyssaceae, 667
        GG. Fls. axillary, subsessile or in spikes: lvs. often opposite: parasitic shrubs.
          H. Parasitic on brs. of trees: fr. a berry: lvs. opposite..*Loranthaceae*, 194
          HH. Parasitic on roots: fr. drupe or achene: lvs. alternate or opposite.
                    Santalaceae, 193

      2. *Fls. with a corolla.*
        a. *Petals free* (b, see p. xxviii).
A. Stamens numerous, at least more than 10.
  B. Ovary superior.
    c. Pistils several to many, distinct or united only at base.
      D. Stamens inserted on the disk or on the axis.

ANALYTICAL KEY

E. Sepals and petals imbricated, petals large.
    F. Fr. a pod or an achene.
        G. Carpels 1- or 2-ovuled...................................*Magnoliaceae*, 246
        GG. Carpels many-ovuled: fr. a dehiscent several-seeded pod.....*Paeonia*, 204
        FF. Fr. a 1-seeded drupe; petals usually 6, small...........*Menispermaceae*, 242
    EE. Sepals and petals valvate, in whorls of 3: carpels developing into many-seeded
        berries..*Annonaceae*, 257
  DD. Stamens inserted on the calyx.
    E. Lvs. alternate; sepals and petals unlike, in whorls of 5..........*Rosaceae*, 322
    EE. Lvs. opposite; sepals gradually changing into petals spirally arranged.
                                            Calycanthaceae, 255
cc. Pistil 1, consisting usually of 2 to many connate carpels.
  D. Lvs. opposite; fr. capsular.
    E. Lvs. punctate with pellucid dots: styles 3–5, usually distinct: ovary 1–5-celled.
                                            Guttiferae, 636
    EE. Lvs. not dotted.
        F. Styles 5–18; petals 4: lvs. evergreen, pinnate............*Eucryphiaceae*, 632
        FF. Style 1, with simple or 3-lobed stigma; petals 5 or 3............*Cistaceae*, 644
  DD. Lvs. alternate.
    E. Ovary 1-celled.
        F. Lvs. compound: fr. a legume...................................*Albizzia*, 484
        FF. Lvs. simple: fr. a berry or caps...........................*Flacourtiaceae*, 652
    EE. Ovary with 2 or more cells.
        F. Sepals imbricate.
            G. Style 1 or sometimes 5.
                H. Fls. 5-merous.
                    I. Fr. a 1–2-seeded drupe...............................*Sabiaceae*, 593
                    II. Fr. a caps.: fls. large...................................*Theaceae*, 633
                    III. Fr. a many-seeded berry: fls. dioecious, small.............*Eurya*, 636
                HH. Fls. 4-merous: fr. a many-seeded berry.............*Stachyuraceae*, 654
            GG. Styles more than 5: fr. a berry: twining shrubs.........*Actinidiaceae*, 630
        FF. Sepals valvate.
            G. Fr. a dehiscent many-seeded caps.: fls. showy............*Malvaceae*, 628
            GG. Fr. indehiscent: fls. rather small...........................*Tiliaceae*, 621
BB. Ovary inferior.
  C. Plants with thick fleshy stems and usually spiny, without foliage lvs.: fls. with many
    sepals and petals..*Cactaceae*, 654
  CC. Plants not fleshy.
    D. Lvs. with stipules..*Rosaceae*, 322
    DD. Lvs. without stipules.
        E. Sepals and petals connate and falling off as a lid: fr. a caps.: plants aromatic.
                                            Myrtaceae, 670
        EE. Sepals and petals not connate.
            F. Lvs. alternate: fr. drupe- or pome-like.
                G. Petals red: ovary 9-celled, many-seeded...................*Punicaceae*, 667
                GG. Petals white or yellow: ovary 1–3-celled: fr. a usually 1-seeded drupe.
                                        Symplocaceae, 760
        FF. Lvs. opposite: fr. a caps...................................*Saxifragaceae*, 263
AA. Stamens not more than twice as many as petals.
  B. Ovary superior.
    C. Carpels 2 or more, distinct or somewhat united.
      D. Stamens inserted on the calyx, perigynous.
        E. Lvs. without stipules..*Saxifragaceae*, 263
        EE. Lvs. with stipules...*Rosaceae*, 322
      DD. Stamens inserted on the axis, hypogynous.
        E. Lvs. simple.
            F. Lvs. alternate: fr. capsular: plant fleshy...................*Crassulaceae*, 263
            FF. Lvs. opposite or whorled: fr. fleshy.........................*Coriariaceae*, 539
        EE. Lvs. compound.
            F. Lvs. with pellucid dots.......................................*Rutaceae*, 523
            FF. Lvs. not dotted.
                G. Lfts. 3–7: low shrub....................................*Xanthorhiza*, 205
                GG. Lfts. 7–41: trees.....................................*Simaroubaceae*, 530
    CC. Carpels united, forming a 1–many-celled ovary.
      D. Ovary 1-celled.
        E. Ovules 2-many, parietal.
            F. Placenta 1: fls. usually irregular: fr. a pod..................*Leguminosae*, 482
            FF. Placentas 2 or more; stamens 5.
                G. Lvs., at least the lower ones, opposite.
                    H. Lvs. with pellucid dots...............................*Guttiferae*, 636
                    HH. Lvs. without pellucid dots.............................*Cistaceae*, 644
                GG. Lvs. alternate.
                    H. Lvs. small, scale-like: fr. a caps.; seeds bearded.....*Tamaricaceae*, 642
                    HH. Lvs. broad: seeds not bearded.
                      I. Stamens not connate...........................*Saxifragaceae*, 263
                      II. Stamens connate: lvs. entire, coriaceous.............*Violaceae*, 652

ANALYTICAL KEY

ANALYTICAL KEY

ANALYTICAL KEY

<small>BB.</small> Anthers united into a tube inclosing the style: fls. in a dense involucrate head.

    II. Lvs. parallel-veined: parts of fl. usually in whorls of 3: stems without clear distinction of bark, wood and pith.

<small>A.</small> Fls. without perianth or the perianth reduced to 1–3 minute scales: fr. a nutlet enclosed by scale-like bracts: stems hollow

<small>AA.</small> Fls. with perianth: fr. a caps. or berry, 3–many-seeded

DESCRIPTION OF TREES
AND SHRUBS

Subdivision I. **GYMNOSPERMAE** Lindl,

GYMNOSPERMS

Trees or shrubs with needle-shaped or scale-like, rarely fan-shaped or oblong to elliptic, mostly evergreen lvs. and unisexual fls.: ovules not enclosed in an ovary.

1. GINKGOACEAE Engl. GINKGO FAMILY

Resinous tree: lvs. deciduous, fan-shaped, parallel-veined: fls. dioecious, the staminate catkin-like, the anthers borne in stalked pairs on a slender axis; the fertile long-stalked with usually 2 ovules; fecundation by motile sperm-cells: fr. drupe-like, with a fleshy outer and a bony inner coat; embryo with 2 cotyledons. (Ginkgo, meaning silver fruit in Chinese.)—One monotypic genus.

GINKGO L. GINKGO. Characters of the family. One species.

G. bíloba L. Tree to 40 m., glabrous: lvs. alternate, partly in clusters of 3–5 on spurs, slender-stalked, fan-shaped, more or less incised or divided at the broad summit, 5–8 cm. across: fr. obovoid or ellipsoid, about 2.5 cm. long, yellowish, consisting of an ovoid angular nut surrounded by a pulpy ill-smelling and acrid outer coat; kernel sweet. Fl.v; fr.x. S.I.1:t.5(c). E.H.1:t.21–23(h). S.N.71(h). E.N.R.13:99. (*Salisburia adiantifolia* Sm.; MAIDENHAIR-TREE.) E. China, cult. in Japan. Intr. about 1730, about 1784 to Am. Zone IV. A rather sparsely branched picturesque tree, sometimes planted as a street tree; the nuts are edible.—**G. b. fastigiàta** Henry, var. Brs. ascending, forming a narrow-pyramidal or columnar head. Gn.M.31:383(h). —**G. b. péndula** Carr. Brs. pendulous. R.H.1907:272(h). M.G.16:164(h).— **G. b. laciniàta** Carr. Lvs. larger, deeply incised and divided. F.S.10:119. (*G. b.* var. *dissecta* Hochst.)—**G. b. variegàta** Carr. Lvs. yellowish-variegated. —**G. b. aùrea** (Nels.) Beiss., f. Lvs. bright yellow.

2. TAXACEAE Lindl. YEW FAMILY

Resinous trees or shrubs: lvs. persistent, alternate, rarely opposite, often 2-ranked, needle- or scale-like, rarely broad, entire, usually with a resin-duct: fls. dioecious, rarely monoecious, the staminate cone-like, with the anthers borne on peltate or apically thickened scales; ovules usually solitary, inverted or erect: fr. consisting of a seed with a bony shell, partly or wholly surrounded by a usually fleshy aril; embryo with 2 cotyledons.—Twelve genera with about

1

100 species in the temperate, subtropical and tropical regions of both hemispheres; sometimes divided into 3 families: TAXACEAE, CEPHALOTAXACEAE and PODOCARPACEAE.

A. Anthers 3–9-celled.   Tribe 1. TAXEAE Endl.
  B. Seed a small nut surrounded by a fleshy cup-like aril; lvs. with pale green to tawny-yellow broad bands beneath, without resin-ducts: brts. alternate..............1. *Taxus*
  BB. Seeds drupe-like; brts. opposite or subopposite.
    C. Fertile fl. of a single ovule; anthers 4-celled: lvs. sharply pointed with 2 glaucous or later fulvous lines beneath narrower than the green margin; brts. subopposite.
                                    2. *Torreya*
    CC. Fertile fl. of several 2-ovuled carpels, but only 1 or 2 seeds developed: lvs. with 2 glaucous lines beneath broader than the green margin; brts. opposite.
                     Tribe 2. CEPHALOTAXEAE Pilger
                                  3. *Cephalotaxus*
AA. Anthers 2-celled.   Tribe 3. PODOCARPEAE Endl.
  B. Seeds several, spiny-pointed, forming a small terminal head: lvs. with 2 glaucous bands beneath, 1–2.5 cm. long, midrib prominent on both sides.................4. *Saxegothaea*
  BB. Seeds solitary, drupe- or nut-like, on a usually fleshy stalk..............5. *Podocarpus*

1. TAXUS L. YEW. Trees or shrubs; bark reddish or reddish brown, scaly; brts. irregularly alternate; winter-buds with imbricate scales: lvs. spirally arranged, spreading in 2 ranks, linear, often falcate, with 2 broad yellowish or grayish green bands below, without resin-ducts: fls. axillary, dioecious, rarely monoecious, the staminate forming stalked heads of 6–14 stamens, each with 5–9 pollen-sacs; the female consisting of several imbricate scales, the uppermost bearing an ovule with a disk at base: seed ovoid, slightly angular, surrounded by a scarlet campanulate fleshy cup open at the apex; albumen uniform. (The ancient Latin name of the Yew.) About 8 species in the n. hemisphere, very closely related and often considered geographical varieties of one species.

A. Scales of winter-buds obtuse, not keeled.
  B. Lvs. gradually acuminate: bud-scales persistent at base of brts............1. *T. baccata*
  BB. Lvs. abruptly pointed: bud-scales deciduous...........................2. *T. chinensis*
AA. Scales of winter-buds acutish or acute, keeled: lvs. abruptly pointed.
  B. Lvs. 2–3 mm. broad, with prominent midrib above, on spreading brts. ascending, forming a V-shaped trough..3. *T. cuspidata*
  BB. Lvs. 1.5–2 mm. broad, with slightly elevated midrib, flatly 2-ranked.
    C. Low shrub: seed broader than high...................................4. *T. canadensis*
    CC. Small tree: seed ovoid...5. *T. brevifolia*

1. T. baccàta L. ENGLISH Y. Tree to 20 m., with broad roundish head, or shrubby; bark reddish, flaky; mature brts. greenish: lvs. abruptly narrowed into a very short greenish petiole, 1–2.5 cm. long, dark green and lustrous above, with 2 pale green bands below: seed broad-ellipsoid, slightly compressed and slightly 2-, rarely, 4-angled, about 6 mm. long, olive-brown. Fl.III–IV; fr.IX–X. H.W.1:t.11(c). K.V.131,134(h). Eu., N. Afr., W. Asia. Cult. since ancient times. Zone VI. A well known ornamental evergreen tree or shrub with numerous garden forms.

Color forms: **T. b. variegàta** West., var. Lvs. with white or whitish variegation. (*T. b.* var. *argentea* Loud.)—**T. b. aùrea** Carr. Lvs. yellow. (*T. b. elvastonensis aurea* Beiss.)—**T. b. elegantíssima** Beiss. Vigorous form of compact habit, or occasionally more open: young lvs. striped pale yellow, later whitish. (*T. b. aurea e.* Hort.)—**T. b. semperaùrea** Dallimore. Bushy with upright brs.: lvs. retaining their yellow color during the second year. (*T. b. erecta s.* Beiss.)—**T. b. lùtea** Endl., var. Fruit yellow. (*T. b. fructuluteo* Hort., f. *luteo-baccata* Pilger.)

Upright forms: **T. b. stricta** Laws. IRISH Y. Columnar form with crowded upright brs. and brts.: lvs. spirally spreading, not 2-ranked, obtusish, very dark green. H.B.5:195(h). Gt.85:187(h). D.H.198(h). (*T. b.* var. *fastigiata* Loud., *T. b. hibernica* Loud.) Intr. 1780. Variations are: **T. b. "fastigiàta** aurea" Standish, with golden yellow lvs.; and **T. b. "fastigiàta variegàta"** Carr., with the lvs. variegated yellowish white.—**T. b. erécta** Loud., var. A bushy upright form: lvs. narrower and shorter than those of *T. b. stricta,* sometimes 2-ranked. (*T. b. pyramidalis* Laws.)

Spreading forms: **T. b. Dovastónii** Laws. DOVASTON Y. A form with upright stem, horizontal wide-spreading brs. and pendulous brts.: lvs. very dark, usually falcate. G.C.27:147(h). Gn.9:341(h). (*T. b. D. pendula* Hort.) Cult. 1800.—**T. b. péndula** Jaeg., var. With slender pendulous brs. (*T. b. gracilis pendula* Beiss.)—**T. b.** expánsa Carr. A low bush with rounded top and elongated pendulous brs. in compact layers: lvs. light green, 1–2 cm. long. (*T. b. procumbens* Kent, not Loud.)—**T. b. repándens** Parsons. A low, almost prostrate form with long and wide-spreading brs. and dark bluish green, rather narrow and long lvs. partly falcate and curved upward. B.E.t.11(h). Zone IV.—**T. b. lineàris** Carr. Brs. spreading: lvs. long and narrow, bright yellowish green.—**T. b. adpréssa** Carr. Shrub or low tree with spreading brs.: lvs. oblong, 6–12 mm. long, obtuse and mucronulate: seed usually exceeding the cup. Gn. 35:37. S.N.285(h). (*T. b. f. tardiva* (Endl.) Pilger, *T. parvifolia* Wender., *T. brevifolia* Hort., not Nutt.) Orig. about 1828 or 1838 in England. —Variations are: **T. b. "adpréssa stricta"** Carr. with upright and ascending brs. forming a columnar bush; and **T. b. "adpréssa aùrea"** Henry, var., with ascending brs. and yellow lvs.

2. **T. chinénsis** (Pilger) Rehd. CHINESE Y. Tree to 15 m. or shrub, with fissured grayish or reddish bark; mature brts. yellowish green; bud-scales deciduous: lvs. distinctly 2-ranked, rather distant, horizontally spreading at nearly right angles from stem, usually falcate, 2–4 cm. long, very shortstalked, dark and lustrous green above and with slightly raised midrib, grayish green below: seed broad-ovoid, slightly 2-angled and slightly compressed; hilum orbicular, Fl.III–IV; fr.IX–X. C.C.43. I.S.2:t.53. S.N.35(h). (*T. baccata* var. *c.* Pilger, *T. cuspidata* var. *c.* Rehd. & Wils.) C. and W. China. Intr. 1908. Zone (V).

3. **T. cuspidàta** Sieb. & Zucc. JAPANESE Y. Tree to 16 m., with reddish brown park and spreading or upright-spreading brs.; mature brts. reddish brown; bud-scales generally ovate, the basal ones usually triangular-ovate: lvs. irregularly 2-ranked, 1.5–2.5 cm. long, abruptly contracted into a distinct yellowish stalk, dark and rather dull green above, with 2 tawny-yellow bands below about twice as broad as the green margin: seed ovoid, compressed, slightly 3–4-angled; hilum elliptic. Fl.III–IV; fr.X–XI. S.Z.2:t.62(c). S.I.1:t.15(c). M.K.t.1(c). W.C.t.5(h). Gn.M.30:214,215(h). (*T. baccata* var. *c.* Carr., *T. Sieboldii* Hort.) Japan, Korea, Manch. Intr. 1855. Zone IV. A very valuable evergreen on account of its hardiness and dense dark green foliage.—**T. c. nàna** Rehd., var. Low shrub, occasionally to 2 m. high or more, with wide-spreading brs. densely clothed with short brts., rather dense and compact while young; lvs. rather short, duller and more upright, not or slightly 2-ranked. B.E.t.10(h). Gn.M.30:214(h). (*T. b. brevifolia* Hort., var. *compacta* Bean.)—**T. c. Thayèrae** Wils. Wide-spreading low bush: lvs. rather light green, arranged in one plane; fruiting freely. H.B.8:424(h).—**T. c. densa** Rehd., var. Dwarf compact shrub with upright and ascending brts. forming a dense broad-conical or rounded bush, scarcely exceeding ½ m. H.D.165,t. (h).—**T. c. mínima** Slavin, f. Very dwarf, less than 30 cm. high; lvs. 4–12 mm. long, broad, shining dark green.—**T. c. auréscens** Rehd., f. Low compact form with the young lvs. yellow, changing later to green. (*T. tardiva aurea* Hort.)—**T. c. lùteo-baccàta** Miyabe & Tatewaki, var. Fr. yellow.

3

T. c. × *baccata* = **T. mèdia** Rehd. Intermediate between the parents. Older brts. olive-green, often reddish above; bud-scales obtuse, slightly keeled: lvs. similar to those of *T. cuspidata*, but more distinctly 2-ranked and often horizontally spreading. H.B.3:30(h). Orig. about 1900. Zone IV.—T. m. Hatfieldii Rehd., f. Compact conical bush with upright brs. and radially spreading lvs. Gn.M.33:25(h). H.B.3:21(h).—T. m. **Hicksii** Rehd., f. Columnar form with upright brs. and radially spreading lvs. B.C.C.t.5(h). (*T. cuspidata H.* Hort.) Similar to the Irish Y., but hardier.

T. c. × *canadensis* = **T. Hunnewellièna** Rehd. Resembling *T. cuspidata*, but of slenderer habit and with slenderer and narrower lvs. partly pointing forward, the green margin beneath more than ½ as broad as the stomatic band, lighter green and assuming mostly a reddish tint in winter. Orig. about 1900. Zone IV.

4. **T. canadénsis** Marsh. CANADA Y. Low shrub, often straggling, or with ascending brs. and occasionally 1–2 m. tall; mature brts. green, older reddish brown; bud-scales more or less lanceolate: lvs. abruptly narrowed into a fine point, 1.3–2 cm. long, very short-stalked, dark yellow-green above, with pale green bands below about as broad as the green margin, often indistinctly 2-ranked, assuming a reddish tint in winter. Fl.ɪv; fr.vɪɪ. B.B.1:67. Gn.M.2: 11(h). (*T. baccata* var. *c.* Gray, *T. baccata* var. *procumbens* Loud., *T. minor* Brit.—GROUND HEMLOCK.) Nfd. to Va., Iowa and Man. Intr. about 1800. Zone II. The hardiest of the Yews, but less handsome than the other species. —T. c. **stricta** Bailey, var. Form with stiff upright brs. Cult. 1933.

5. **T. brevifòlia** Nutt. WESTERN Y. Tree to 15, rarely to 25 m., usually with horizontally spreading brs. and slightly pendulous brts.; bark reddish brown; mature brts. yellowish green, older greenish or light brown; bud-scales usually cuspidate or mucronate: lvs. distinctly 2-ranked and horizontally spreading, 1–2 cm. long, abruptly and sharply pointed, contracted into a slender yellow petiole, with glaucescent bands below broader than the green margin: seed ovoid, 2–4-angled. Fl.vɪ; fr.vɪɪɪ–x. S.S.10:514. (*T. baccata* var. *b.* Koehne.) B. C. to Calif. and Mont. Intr. 1854. Zone VI.

2. **TÓRREYA** Arn. TORREYA. Trees with fissured bark and whorled brs.; brts. subopposite; winter-buds with few decussate deciduous scales: lvs. distinctly 2-ranked, linear, rigid, pungent, slightly rounded above and lustrous, with 2 rather narrow whitish or brownish bands beneath: fls. dioecious, occasionally monoecious, axillary; staminate fls. ellipsoid to oblong, about 8 mm. long, stalked, consisting of 6–8 whorls of 4 stamens each; female fls. sessile, in pairs of which only one fl. develops: seed ovoid, drupe-like, with a thin fleshy outer coat, ripening the second season; albumen ruminate. (After John Torrey, distinguished American botanist; 1796–1875.) Syn. *Tumion* Raf. Six species in N. Am. and E. Asia.

ᴀ. Two-year-old brs. yellowish green.
  ʙ. Lvs. about 3 cm. long, with scarcely impressed narrow bands beneath, of fetid odor
    when crushed..1. *T. taxifolia*
  ʙʙ. Lvs. about 2 cm. long, with impressed bands beneath, scarcely fetid.......2. *T. grandis*
ᴀᴀ. Two-year-old brs. reddish brown; lvs. of strong aromatic odor when crushed.
  ʙ. Lvs. 2–3 cm. long, linear-lanceolate;......................................3. *T. nucifera*
  ʙʙ. Lvs. 3.5–6 cm. long, linear..4. *T. californica*

1. **T. taxifòlia** Arn. FLORIDA T. Low tree, occasionally to 18 m.: lvs. linear, spiny-pointed, rounded at base, 2.5–3.5 cm. long, dark green and lustrous above; anthers truncate at apex: fr. obovoid, 2.5–3 cm. long, purple. Fl.ɪɪɪ; fr.vɪɪɪ. S.S.10:t.512. C.B.3:63. (STINKING CEDAR.) Fl. Intr. 1840. Zone VI? A tree with spreading slightly pendulous brs. forming a rather open pyramidal head.

2. **T. grándis** Fort. CHINESE T. Tree to 25 m.: lvs. linear, 1.2–2.3 cm. long, nearly rounded at base, abruptly spine-pointed, grooved above and dark

yellow-green; fr. oblong-ellipsoid, 2–3 cm. long; albumen slightly ruminate. (*T. nucifera* var. *g*. Pilger.) C.B.61. D.J.74. G.C.90:438(h). E. China. Intr. 1855. Zone VII?

Related species: **T. Fargèsii** Franch. Lvs. 1.5–2.5 cm. long, more gradually pointed, darker green above, with 2 more or 'ess distinct grooves along the midrib, bands below slightly narrower than the green margin; fr. globose-ellipsoid, 2–2.5 cm. long, deeply ruminate almost to the middle. C. and W. China. Intr. ?

3. T. nucífera (L.) Sieb. & Zucc. JAPANESE T. Tree to 25 m.; bark grayish brown, on old trees shallowly fissured and flaky; brs. wide-spreading: lvs. abruptly narrowed at base and nearly sessile, tapering into a spiny point, dark lustrous green and convex above, with 2 impressed bands below: anthers cristate-dentate at apex: fr. sessile, ellipsoid-oblong, about 2.5 cm. long, green, faintly tinged with purple; albumen slightly ruminate. Fl.v; fr.ix–x. S.Z.2:t. 129(c). S.I.1:t.15(c). M.D.25:16. W.C.t.3,4(h). Japan. Intr. before 1764. Zone V. Handsome tree with spreading brs. forming a pyramidal or ovoid head; seeds edible.

4. T. califórnica Torr. CALIFORNIA-NUTMEG. Tree to 20, occasionally to 35 m.; bark gray-brown, fissured into narrow ridges; brs. spreading, slightly pendulous: lvs. tapering to a slender spiny point, dark green above, with 2 narrow deeply impressed glaucous bands below; anthers truncate at apex: fr. ovoid to oblong-ovoid, 2.5–3.5 cm. long, light green, streaked with purple; albumen deeply ruminate. Fl.iii–v; fr.viii–ix. S.S.10:t.513. B.M.4780(c). S.N.294(h). (*T. Myristica* Hook.) Calif. Intr. 1851. Zone VII. Handsome tree with spreading slender brs. and drooping brts. forming a pyramidal head, round-topped in old age.

3. CEPHALOTÁXUS Sieb. & Zucc. PLUM-YEW. Trees or shrubs; brts. opposite; pith with a resin-duct in the centre; winter-buds with numerous imbricate persistent scales: lvs. dense, spirally arranged, but spreading in 2 planes, with 2 broad glaucous bands beneath and with a prominent midrib above: fls. dioecious, occasionally monoecious, axillary, the staminate in globose heads in the axils of lvs., the female in the axils of scales at base of the brts., consisting of several pairs of 2-ovuled carpels: seeds 1 or 2 on a stalk, ellipsoid, drupaceous, about 2.5 cm. long, greenish or purplish, ripening the second season. (Greek *kephale*, head, and *taxus;* referring to the shape of the staminate fls.) Five species in E. Asia.

A. Lvs. abruptly pointed, 2–5 cm. long, in semi-erect ranks....................1. *C. drupacea*
AA. Lvs. gradually tapering to a fine point, 5–8 cm. long, in nearly horizontally spreading ranks ....2. *C. Fortuni*

1. C. drupàcea Sieb. & Zucc. JAPANESE P. Small tree, to 10 m., with spreading brs.; bark gray, fissured into narrow detachable strips: lvs. linear, 2–4.5 cm. long, abruptly pointed, dark green above, with 2 grayish bands below, each with about 15 rows of stomata, 2-ranked, but semi-erect so as to form a V-shaped trough: heads of male fls. short-stalked, with the stalk 8 mm. long: fr. ovoid or obovoid, rarely globose (f. **sphaeràlis** Pilg.), 2.5–3 cm. long, 2 cm. across, green, on a stalk 6–12 mm. long. Fl.iii–v; fr.ix. B.M.8285(c). S.I.1: t.14(c). Japan. Intr. 1830. Zone (V.) In cult. usually a shrub of irregular habit with spreading brs., but at its best it is a small tree with wide-spreading brs. forming a broad round head.—**C.d. fastigiàta** (Carr.) Pilger, f. With upright or ascending brs., often columnar; lvs. spirally arranged, not 2-ranked. G.C.33:229. S.N.161(h). (*C. pedunculata* f. Carr., *Podocarpus koraiana* Sieb.) Cult. in Japan. Intr. 1830. Zone VI.—**C.d. nàna** (Nakai) Rehd., var. Shrub spreading by suckers, with upright or ascending stems, to 2 m. tall: fr. subglobose, 2 cm. long, edible. (*C. n.* Nakai.) N. and C. Japan. Intr. 1916. Zone (V.)—**C. d. pedunculàta** (S. & Z.) Miq., var. Lvs. to 5 cm. long: male fls. in stalked branched heads, with the stalk 1–2 cm. long. S.Z.2:t.132(c). G.C. 33:228. S.N.159(h). (*C. p.* Sieb. & Zucc., *C. Harringtonia* K. Koch.) Cult. in Japan. Intr. 1829.—**C. d. sinénsis** Rehd. & Wils., var. Shrub to 4 m.: lvs. linear-lanceolate, tapering to a sharp point. C. and W. China. Intr. 1907.

2. **C. Fórtuni** Hook. Chinese P. Tree to 10 m., usually with several stems; bark reddish brown, peeling off in large flakes leaving pale markings: lvs. spreading nearly horizontally, linear, 5–8 cm. long, glossy green above, with 2 pale bands below, each with about 20 rows of stomata: male fls. in short-stalked heads: fr. ovoid, purple, about 2.5 cm. long. Fl.v; fr.ix. B.M.4499(c). S.N.29(h). C. China. Intr. 1849. Zone VI. In cult. usually a spreading, rather sparingly branched shrub or a tree with slender spreading brs. pendulous at the ends and forming a broad ovoid head.

Related species: **C. Olíveri** Mast. Differs chiefly in its rather stiff spreading brs. and in its very close-set rigid and spiny-pointed lvs. truncate at base and about 2.5 cm. long. H.I.1933. G.C.33:226. W. China. Intr. 1900. Zone VI?

4. **SAXEGOTHAÈA** Lindl. Prince Albert Yew. Tree with whorled brs.: lvs. linear, indistinctly 2-ranked: fls. monoecious, the staminate in axillary cylindric spikes near the apex of the brts., the female with imbricate carpels, terminating short brts.: fr. subglobose, cone-like, consisting of fleshy connate carpels terminating in broad spine-like points. (After Prince Albert of Saxe-Coburg-Gotha, consort of Queen Victoria.)—One species in Chile.

S. conspícua Lindl. Tree to 14 m.: lvs. linear to linear-lanceolate, 1–2.5 cm. long, acute, abruptly narrowed at base into a short decurrent stalk: staminate fls. 6 mm. long: fr. 1–2 cm. across; seeds broad-ovoid, compressed, 2-edged, about 4 mm. long. B.M.8664(c). D.J.61(h). M.D.25:t.8. Chile. Intr. 1847. Zone VII? Densely branched with spreading brs. and pendulous brts.

5. **PODOCÁRPUS** Pers. Trees, rarely shrubs: lvs. alternate, sometimes opposite, linear to ovate, rarely scale-like: fls. dioecious, rarely monoecious, the staminate catkin-like, axillary, solitary or fascicled, rarely spicate, the female solitary, axillary, rarely at the end of short brts. or in spikes, consisting of 1 or 2 1-ovuled scales with several bracts at the base which usually become much thickened at maturity and form a fleshy receptacle bearing at the top the globular or ovoid, drupe- or nut-like seed. (Greek *pous, podos,* foot, and *karpos,* fruit; in reference to the fleshy fr.-stalks of many species.) About 60 species chiefly in the mts. of trop. and subtrop. regions.

A. Lvs. 5–10 cm. long, with a raised midrib above, usually acute: female fls. solitary.
  B. Lvs. abruptly pointed or obtusish, with a prominent midrib beneath.1. *P. macrophyllus*
  BB. Lvs. gradually tapering into a fine point; midrib beneath not prominent..2. *P. salignus*
AA. Lvs. 6–30 mm. long, obtusish or abruptly pointed; midrib not raised above.
  B. Lvs. 6–12 mm. long: fls. solitary...................................3. *P. alpinus*
  BB. Lvs. 8–30 mm. long: fls. in spikes...............................4. *P. andinus*

1. **P. macrophýllus** (Thunb.) Lamb. Tree to 20 m.; trunk with gray, shallowly fissured shreddy bark: lvs. linear-lanceolate, 7–10 cm. long, attenuate at the ends, dark green and glossy above, yellowish green or somewhat glaucescent beneath: staminate fls. fascicled, about 3 cm. long: fr. ovoid, about 1 cm. long, greenish or purplish, on a fleshy purple receptacle. Fl.v; fr.ix–x. S.Z.2:t.133(c). S.I.1:t.13(c). C.B.N.t.82. (*P. longifolius* Hort.) Japan. Intr. 1804. Zone VII. Tree with spreading short brs.—**P. m. Máki** Endl., var. Usually shrubby, with ascending brs.: lvs. crowded, 4–7 cm. long, obtusish.

6

S.Z.2:t.134(c). M.D.25:t.9. (*P. Makoyi* Bl., *P. chinensis* Endl., *P. japonica* Sieb.) China; cult. in Japan. Intr. 1840. Tenderer than the type. With some variegated forms.—**P. m. appréssus** (Maxim.) Matsum., var. Low bush with spreading brs.: lvs. scarcely exceeding 3.5 cm.; midrib above indistinct. (*P. a.* Maxim.) Cult. in Japan.

2. **P. salígnus** Lamb. Tree to 20 m., in cult. often shrubby; brts. green: lvs. linear-lanceolate, 5–10 cm. long, usually slightly falcate, tapering toward the apex, pointed, dark bluish green above, pale beneath: staminate fls. solitary, often crowded, 2.5 cm. long: fr. ovoid, 8 mm. long, solitary or in pairs on a stalk about 1 cm. long. Fl.iv; fr.xii–i. D.J.41. G.C.31:115(h). (*P. chilinus* Rich., *P. andina* Hort., not Poepp.) Chile. Intr. 1853. Zone VII?

3. **P. alpinus** R. Br. Dense shrub or low tree, to 5 m.: brts. slender, whorled: lvs. distinctly 2-ranked, linear-spatulate to linear-oblong, 6–12 mm. long, narrowed at base, obtuse at apex, sometimes mucronulate, dull green above, paler beneath: fls. dioecious; staminate fls. clustered, 4–8 mm. long: fr. ovoid, 5–6 mm. long, red. C.B.N.t.74. Fl.iii–iv. Tasmania, N. S. Wales. Cult. 1880. Zone VII?

4. **P. andìnus** Poepp. Tree to 5 or occasionally to 15 m.; brts. green: lvs. indistinctly 2-ranked, nearly sessile, linear, 1–3.5 cm. long, tapering at base, obtuse or abruptly pointed, dark green above, with 2 glaucous bands beneath: fls. in spikes, monoecious, staminate spike about 2.5 cm. long: fr. ovoid, yellowish white, 2 cm. long, usually only one developed in a spike. E.P. IV. 5:65. G.C.63:12(h),17. J.L.37:50,t(h). (*Prumnopitys elegans* Phil.) Chile. Intr. 1860. Zone VII? Small bushy tree with ascending and spreading much ramified brs. forming usually a dense round bush.

3. ARAUCARIACEAE Strasb. ARAUCARIA FAMILY.

Resinous trees with whorled brs.: lvs. persistent, broad or needle-shaped: fls. dioecious or rarely monoecious; staminate fls. cone-like, large, with numerous stamens; anthers many-celled; fertile fls. very numerous, spirally arranged, in a globose or ovoid terminal head becoming a large woody cone; scales without distinct bracts, with 1 seed each; seeds with or without wings; cotyledons 2, rarely 4.—Two genera with about 30 species in the southern hemisphere.

ARAUCÀRIA Juss. Evergreen tall trees with regularly whorled spreading brs.: lvs. alternate, decurrent, radially spreading, rarely more or less 2-ranked, closely set, awl-shaped to ovate-lanceolate, rigid: fls. usually dioecious; the male terminal and fascicled, large, cylindric; fr. a subglobose or ovoid cone falling apart at maturity, with wedge-shaped 2-edged scales and with large wingless seeds adnate to the scales; cotyledons 2, rarely 4. (Arauco, a province of s. Chile where the following species grows.) About 10 species in S. Am., Australasia and the Pacific Isls.

A. araucàna (Molina) K. Koch. MONKEY-PUZZLE. Tall tree to 30 m., with very stout spreading brs. in whorls of 5; brts. few, in opposite pairs, densely clothed with imbricate ovate-lanceolate, spiny pointed stiff lvs. slightly concave above, 2.5–5 cm. long, bright green on both sides, persisting for many years; male fls. 8–12 cm. long, cylindric: cone globose-ovoid, 14–20 .m. across; seeds oblong, slightly compressed, 2.5–3.5 cm. long; cotyledons 2, remaining below the soil. F.S.15:1577–80(c). G.C.III.21:288,t.(h); 24:154(h). E.H.1:t.17–20(h). (*A. imbricata* Pav.) Chile. Intr. 1795. Zone VII. Tree of striking appearance. The hardiest species of the genus.

7

4. **PINACEAE** Lindl. PINE FAMILY

Resinous trees, rarely shrubs; lvs. linear, rarely lanceolate, or scale-like, alternate or opposite, sometimes whorled, evergreen, rarely deciduous: fls. usually monoecious (dioecious in Juniperus), cone-like, rarely berry-like; staminate fls. consisting of numerous, rarely few scales bearing on the under side 2–6, rarely more, 2-, rarely 3–5-celled anthers; fertile fls. with few to numerous scales, each with 1 or 2, rarely more ovules on the upper side: fr. a more or less woody cone with usually winged seeds, or berry-like with fleshy coalescent scales enclosing the terete or angular seeds; embryo with 2–15 cotyledons.—Thirty-two genera distributed through both hemispheres chiefly in the temperate and subtropical regions. Sometimes divided into three families: PINACEAE, TAXODIACEAE and CUPRESSACEAE.

A. Lvs. and cone-scales spirally arranged, the former sometimes fascicled; ovules inverted; cotyledons 2–10.
  B. Cone-scales and bracts distinct; scales with 2 usually winged seeds; lvs. linear; winter-buds distinct with scarious scales.   Subfam. I. ABIETINEAE Endl.
    C. Lvs. solitary.
      D. Cone upright.
        E. Cone-scales deciduous from their axis; lvs. flattened, grooved above, usually with glaucous bands below, rarely 4-angled...........................1. *Abies*
        EE. Cone-scales persistent; lvs. flattened, keeled above, pale green below.
                                       2. *Keteleeria*
      DD. Cone reflexed or pendulous; scales persistent.
        E. Bracts exserted, conspicuous; brts. not roughened by lf.-bases; winter-buds elongated, pointed, not resinous.................................3. *Pseudotsuga*
        EE. Bracts not exserted; brts. roughened by persistent lf.-bases.
          F. Lvs. flattened and stomatiferous below or on both sides, narrowed into a short petiole, with 1 resin-duct below the fibrovascular bundle; cones 1.5–7.5 cm. long..4. *Tsuga*
          FF. Lvs. usually quadrangular or flattened and with stomatic bands above, sessile; resin-ducts lateral; cones 2–15 cm. long........................5. *Picea*
    CC. Lvs. in fascicles or clusters of 2 or more, solitary only on shoots.
      D. Lvs. many, clustered on short thick spurs; cone-scales flat at apex.
        E. Lvs. deciduous; cone ripening the first season.
          F. Bud-scales acuminate; staminate fls. clustered; cone-scales deciduous.
                                    6. *Pseudolarix*
          FF. Bud-scales obtuse; staminate fls. solitary; cone-scales persistent....7. *Larix*
        EE. Lvs. evergreen; cone ripening the 2d or 3d season, 5–12 cm. long......8. *Cedrus*
      DD. Lvs. in fascicles of 2–5, rarely to 8, sometimes reduced to 1, sheathed at base by scarious bud-scales; cone-scales usually much thickened at apex, persistent.
                                       9. *Pinus*
  BB. Cone-scales without distinct bracts, flat or peltate with 2–9 seeds.
                       Subfam. II. TAXODIINEAE Endl.
    C. Lvs. connate into pairs 8–15 cm. long, in whorls of 15–25 at the end of shoots; cone-scales thick and woody, with 6–9 seeds...............................10. *Sciadopitys*
    CC. Lvs. solitary, scattered.
      D. Cone-scales peltate: lvs. dimorphic or all scale-like and appressed.
        E. Brts. all persistent: staminate fls. solitary: cone-scales with 2–9 seeds.
          F. Lvs. dimorphic, on lateral shoots 2-ranked and linear: winter-buds scaly; cones with 15–20 scales...11. *Sequoia*
          FF. Lvs. ovate to lanceolate, appressed or slightly spreading; winter-buds naked: cones with 25–40 scales...................................12. *Sequoiadendron*
        EE. Lateral brts. deciduous: staminate fls. in panicles: cone-scales with 2 seeds.
                                      13. *Taxodium*
      DD. Cone-scales flattened, with 2–5 seeds: lvs. of one kind.
        E. Lvs. awl-shaped, curved; cone-scales with an upright toothed crest above the seeds ....14. *Cryptomeria*
        EE. Lvs. lanceolate, flat, glaucous below; cone-scales with narrow serrulate line above the seeds..15. *Cunninghamia*
AA. Lvs. and cone-scales opposite or whorled, the former small and usually scale-like; ovules erect; cotyledons 2, rarely 5–6.........................Subfamily III. CUPRESSINEAE Endl.
  B. Fr. a woody or leathery dehiscent cone.
    C. Lvs. ternate, linear; cone-scales ternate, valvate, only 1 whorl fertile....16. *Fitzroya*
    CC. Lvs. and cone-scales opposite; the former scale-like or sometimes needle-shaped.
      D. Cone-scales flattened, imbricate; cone ovoid or oblong-ovoid.
        E. Each cone-scale with 3–5 seeds; brts. much flattened, 5–6 mm. broad, with conspicuous glaucous patches beneath...........................17. *Thujopsis*
        EE. Each cone-scale with 2 seeds; brts. narrower, with or without whitish markings beneath.
          F. Pairs of cone-scales 6–8, the 2 upper pairs fertile..................18. *Thuja*

1. ÁBIES Mill. FIR.

Evergreen trees of pyramidal habit, with spreading whorled brs., bark usually smooth and thin on younger trees, often thick and furrowed on old trees; brts. smooth, or grooved in a few species; winter-buds usually resinous: lvs. often spreading in 2 ranks, linear or linear-lanceolate, contracted above the base and leaving a circular scar as they fall, usually flattened and grooved above, in most species with 2 white stomatiferous bands below, above without or rarely with stomata, with 2 or rarely 4 resin-ducts either internal (median) or marginal (external or subepidermal): male fls. pendent, oval to cylindric-oblong, with yellow or scarlet anthers: female fls. ovoid to oblong, consisting of numerous 2-ovuled imbricate scales: cone ovoid to oblong-cylindric with closely imbricated thin and leathery scales incurved at the apex, narrowed at base into a long stipe and subtended by narrow exserted or enclosed bracts; the scales falling at maturity from the persistent axis; seeds ovoid or oblong with large thin wing; cotyledons 4–10. (The ancient Latin name of the Silver Fir.) About 40 species in the temperate regions of the n. hemisphere ranging on the higher mts. s. to Guatemala, N. Afr. and the Himal.—The species of this genus are among the handsomest and stateliest Conifers; they succeed best in a cool and humid climate, but a few, particularly *A. concolor,* will stand a drier climate.

The description of the lvs. in the key and in the account of the following species refers to those of sterile lateral brs.; the lvs. of fertile brs. and of leading shoots are as a rule shorter and thicker, usually acute or acutish and often spiny-pointed and more or less upturned or ascending: in some species the resin-ducts of the lvs. of fruiting brs. are internal, while those of the lvs. of sterile brs. are marginal.

A. Lvs. green and lustrous above, stomatiferous only below (occasionally with one or few
    broken lines of stomata above in Nos. 1, 17, 23 and 24).
  B. Brts. deeply grooved, particularly on 2-year-old brts.: cones purple or violet (see also
      Nos. 8 and 12).
    c. Brts. glabrous: resin-ducts internal..............................14. *A. homolepis*
      cc. Brts. with brown pubescence in the grooves: resin-ducts marginal..15. *A. spectabilis*
  BB. Brts. not or slightly grooved.
    c. Lvs. with inconspicuous stomatic bands below (in nos. 10 and 12 sometimes more
        conspicuous).
      D. Lvs. acutish to spiny-pointed.
        E. Lvs. of upper ranks partly recurved; cones violet-purple: buds very resinous.
            11. *A. recurvata*
          EE. Lvs. spreading at nearly right angles, pectinate: cone green: buds thinly res-
              inous ....13. *A. holophylla*
      DD. Lvs. emarginate or bifid.
        E. Lvs. more or less pectinate: buds slightly or not resinous: cones green.
          F. Brts. glabrous: lvs. emarginate...........................10. *A. chensiensis*
            FF. Brts. slightly grooved, hairy in the grooves: lvs. sharply 2-pointed, rigid, on
                old plants obtusish...12. *A. firma*
          EE. Lvs. above directed forward, slender, often curved; bifid at apex: buds res-
              inous: cone purple...16. *A. Pindrow*
    cc. Lvs. with 2 white or glaucous bands beneath.
      D. Brts. more or less pubescent.
        E. Winter-buds resinous.
          F. Lvs. more or less pectinate.
            G. Lvs. 3–6 cm. long, distinctly pectinate; resin-ducts marginal; brts. soon
                glabrous ....27. *A. grandis*
              GG. Lvs. 1.5–2.5 cm. long, less distinctly pectinate; resin-ducts internal or
                  marginal.
                H. Brts. not grooved, ashy-gray, short-pubescent........24. *A. balsamea*
                  HH. Brts. slightly grooved, densely brown-pubescent; lvs. very white be-
                      neath ....8. *A. Faxoniana*

9

FF. Lvs. not pectinate.
  G. Lvs. spreading upward and outward, 1.5–2.5 cm. long.
    H. Buds thinly resinous: brts. soon glabrous, yellowish.
      ɪ. Lvs. 1–2 cm. long, margin flat, resin-ducts internal......4. *A. koreana*
      ɪɪ. Lvs. 1.5–2.5 cm. long, margin recurved, resin-ducts marginal.
                                        9. *A. Fabri*
    HH. Buds very resinous: brts. pubescent, brown or grayish.
      ɪ. Bark of 6-year-old and older brts. flaky: resin-ducts internal.
                                     6. *A. squamata*
      ɪɪ. Bark not flaky.
        J. Brts. brown, densely pubescent: resin-ducts marginal.
                                  3. *A. Veitchii*
        JJ. Brts. grayish: resin-ducts internal.
          ᴋ. Lvs. with 8–12 lines of stomata in each band....23. *A. Fraseri*
          ᴋᴋ. Lvs. with 4–8 lines of stomata in each band....24. *A. balsamea*
  GG. Lvs. at least the upper ones directed forward.
    H. Lvs. about 1.5 mm. broad, up to 3 cm. long; resin-ducts internal.
      ɪ. Brts. not grooved, minutely pubescent: lvs. with 4–5 lines of stomata
        in each band...1. *A. sibirica*
      ɪɪ. Brts. slightly grooved, hairy in the grooves: each band with 7–8 lines
        of stomata..2. *A. sachalinensis*
    HH. Lvs. at least 2 mm. broad; resin-ducts marginal or submarginal.
      ɪ. Pubescence of brts. rufous, dense: lvs. 1–2 cm. long....5. *A. Mariesii*
      ɪɪ. Pubescence of brts. pale, short: lvs. 2–3 cm. long....26. *A. amabilis*
EE. Winter-buds not resinous: resin-ducts marginal: cone green.
  F. Lvs. not pectinate.
    G. Lvs. spreading outward and upward: cone 16–20 cm. long, with hidden
      bracts ....20. *A. cilicica*
    GG. Lvs. directed forward: cone 12–15 cm. long, with exserted bracts.
                              21. *A. Nordmanniana*
  FF. Lvs. pectinate: bracts exserted....................................22. *A. alba*
DD. Brts. glabrous (see also Nos. 4 and 9): lvs. crowded, spreading, with marginal
  resin-ducts.
  E. Lvs. obtuse or emarginate: cone purple or violet.
    F. Winter-buds resinous: lvs. 1.5–3 cm. long, emarginate: resin-ducts internal
      on fruiting brs..7. *A. Fargesii*
    FF. Winter-buds not or slightly resinous: lvs. usually obtuse, rarely acutish,
      stout, 1.5–2 cm. long...17. *A. numidica*
  EE. Lvs. sharply pointed.
    F. Lvs. radially spreading, 2–3 cm. long......................19. *A. cephalonica*
    FF. Lvs. pectinate, to 5 cm. long: buds large, pointed, not resinous: cone bristly.
                              29. *A. venusta*
ᴀᴀ. Lvs. stomatiferous on both sides, grayish green or glaucous: buds resinous.
  B. Lvs. radially spreading, pointed, short and rigid: resin-ducts internal....18. *A. Pinsapo*
  BB. Lvs. not radially spreading.
    c. Lvs. flat: buds very resinous.
      D. Lvs. 2.5–4 cm long: resin-ducts internal: cone purple.............25. *A. lasiocarpa*
      DD. Lvs. 4–6 cm. long: resin-ducts marginal: cone green or purple......28. *A. concolor*
    cc. Lvs. often 4-sided, blunt or acute, those in the middle of brts. curving upward from
      an adpressed base; resin-ducts marginal: buds slightly resinous, with free acuminate
      scales at base: cone purple, large.
      D. Lvs. of sterile brs. flat or grooved above: bracts of cone exserted....30. *A. nobilis*
      DD. Lvs. 4-sided: bracts hidden or exserted.........................31. *A. magnifica*

1. A. sibìrica Ledeb. Sɪʙᴇʀɪᴀɴ F. Tree to 30 m.; bark smooth; buds globose; brts. gray, minutely pubescent: lvs. crowded above and directed forward, linear, slender, to 3 cm. long, rounded and entire or bifid at apex, shining bright green and grooved above, often with 2–3 short lines of stomata near apex, with narrow grayish bands beneath: cones cylindric, 5–8 cm. long, bluish before maturity; scales about 1.5 cm. high with denticulate margin; bracts hidden, about half as long as scales. Forbes, Pin. Wob. t.39(c). C.B.2:27. S.N.73(h). Act. Hort. Berg. 6:t.86(h). (*A. pichta* Forb., *A. Semenovii* Fedtch.) N. Russia to Kamch., s. to Turkestan and Manch. Intr. 1820. Zone II. Not satisfactory in the E. States; it demands a cool, moist climate and is apt to suffer from late frosts.

Closely related species: **A. nephrólepis** Maxim. Bark of trunk rough; brts. more pubescent: lvs. shorter: cones smaller; scales about 1 cm. high, with narrower bracts about ⅔ as long as scales. V.G.257 Act. For. Fenn. 24:t.18(h). (*A. sibirica* var. *n.* Trautv., *A. gracilis* Komar.) E. Siberia, N. China. Intr. 1908.—**A. n. chlorocárpa** Wils., f. Cone green or nearly so. Intr. 1918.

2. A. sachalinénsis Mast. Sᴀɢʜᴀʟɪɴ F. Tree to 40 m.; bark smooth, gray; buds small; brts. slightly grooved, pubescent in the grooves: lvs. similar to those of *A. sibirica*, but broader and to 4 cm. long, without stomata above and with 7–8 lines of stomata in each band below: cone blackish brown or blackish blue, cylindric, about 7 cm. long; scales with entire margin, densely pubescent on back; bracts exserted and reflexed. G.C.II.12:588. S.I.1:t.6(c). M.K.t.2(c). W.C.t.44,45(h). (*A. Veitchii* var. *s.* F. Schmidt.) N. Japan, Saghal., Kurile Isls. Intr. 1878. Zone II.—**A. s. nemorénsis** Mayr, var. Cones smaller, to 6 cm. long, with hidden bracts. M.K.t.4(c). (*A. Wilsonii* Miy. & Kudo.) Intr. 1914.—**A. s. Mayriàna** Miyabe & Kudo, var. Lvs. shorter, 1.5— 2.5 cm. long; bands beneath with 4–5 lines of stomata: cone-scales strongly auriculate. M.K.t.4(c). (*A. M.* Miyabe & Kudo.) N. Japan. Cult. 1929.

3. **A. Veìtchii** Lindl. Veitch F. Tree to 25 m.; bark smooth, grayish; buds purplish, very resinous; brts. brown, rather densely pubescent: lvs. crowded, directed forward and partly upward, nearly pectinate below, linear, 1–2.5 cm. long, truncate and notched at apex, lustrous dark green above, beneath with chalky white bands: cone cylindric, 4.5–6.5 cm. long, bluish purple while young; bracts slightly exserted and reflexed; seed with a broad wing scarcely as long as body. G.C.II.13:275. S.I.1:t.5(c). W.C.t.43(h). C. Japan. Intr. 1865. Zone III. Desirable species; thriving well in the E. States.—**A. V. olivàcea** Shiras., var. Cone green while young, grayish brown when ripe. Act. Hort. Berg. 6,4:t.1,f.9(c). Intr. 1914.—**A. V. nikkoénsis** Mayr, var. Cone smaller, with scarcely visible bracts.

4. **A. koreàna** Wils. Korean F. Tree to 18 m.; bark of older trees rough; brts. sparingly pubescent, yellowish, becoming glabrous and purplish; buds thinly resinous: lvs. crowded, 1–2 cm. long, usually broader toward the apex and rounded or emarginate, on young plants pointed, lustrous above, with whitish bands beneath: cone cylindric, 4–7 cm. long, about 2.5 cm. thick, violet-purple before maturity; scales about 2 cm. broad; bracts as long as scales, slightly exserted and recurved. G.C.69:77. V.G.214. S.N.149(h, as *A. holophylla*). Korea. Intr. 1908. Zone V.

5. **A. Marièsii** Mast. Maries F. Tree to 26 m.; bark smooth, pale gray, on old trees rough at base; buds small; brts. densely rusty-pubescent: lvs. crowded above, the middle ones directed forward and nearly appressed, the outer ones longer and spreading outward, linear, slightly broader above the middle, rounded or bifid at apex, 0.8–2 cm. long, shining green and grooved above, with white bands below: cone ovoid or oblong-ovoid, 4–9 cm. long, violet-purple while young; scales about 2.5 cm. wide; bracts hidden; seed-wing twice as long as body. G.C.II.12:788; III.69:103. S.I.1:t.4(c). W.C.t.40, 41(h). Japan. Intr. 1879. Zone V. This tree does not do well in the E. States, though it is hardy.

The closely related **A. Kawakàmii** (Hayata) Ito differs chiefly in the slightly longer and narrower lvs. with faint bands below, in the cylindric cone and black seeds and wings. C.B.N.t.15. V.G.211. (*A. Mariesii* var. *K.* Hayata.) Formosa. Cult. 1930. Zone VII?

6. **A. squamàta** Mast. Flaky F. Tree to 40 m.; bark purplish brown, exfoliating in thin flakes; buds subglobose, reddish brown, very resinous; brts. densely brownish pubescent: lvs. densely crowded and ascending, linear, 1.5– 2.5 cm. long, obtuse or acutish, bluish green and grooved above, with white bands below: cone oblong-ovoid, 5–6 cm. long, violet: scales about 1.5 cm. wide; bracts slightly exserted. G.C.39:299. V.G.351. W. China. Intr. 1910. Zone V? Remarkable for its flaky bark, beginning to show on brs. about 6 years old, the inner bark purplish red even on young brs.

7. **A. Fargèsii** Franch. Farges F. Tree to 35 m.; buds resinous; brts. glabrous, reddish brown or purplish, slightly grooved; lvs. pectinate below, crowded above, spreading at nearly right angles, the middle ones upright or sometimes reflexed, linear, sometimes falcate, emarginate or bifid at apex, 2–3 cm. long, dark green and grooved above, with white bands beneath: cones ovoid-oblong, 5–8 cm. long, purple or red-brown; scales 1.5–2 cm. wide; bracts slightly exserted and recurved. C. China. C.B.N.t.26. V.G.161. Gn.88:167 (h). S.N.142(h). Intr. 1901. Zone V. One of the most satisfactory and promising of the Chinese firs.

The closely related **A. sutchuenénsis** (Franch.) Rehd. & Wils. differs chiefly in its stouter and shorter ascending lvs. 1.5–2.5 cm. long, with distinct yellow petiole: cones 5–6 cm. long, with hidden bracts. (*A. Fargesii* var. *s.* Franch.) W. China. Intr. 1911.

8. **A. Faxoniàna** Rehd. & Wils. Faxon F. Tree to 40 m.; bark dark gray, furrowed: buds ovoid, purple, very resinous; brts. densely ferrugineous-pubescent, slightly grooved; lvs. crowded and irregularly spreading in 2 ranks, the upper shorter, linear, obtuse or emarginate, slightly revolute, 1.5–2.5 cm. long, shining dark green above, with white bands below; resin-ducts median or sub-marginal: cone ovoid-oblong, truncate at apex, 5–8 cm. long, violet-purple before maturity; scales 1.5–2 cm. wide; bracts somewhat exserted, upright or reflexed; seed-wings scarcely as long as body. C.B.N.t.5. V.G.165. (*A. Delavayi* var. *F.* A. B. Jacks.) W. China. Intr. 1911. Zone V?

Related species: **A. Geórgei** Orr. Tree to 25 m.; brts. densely reddish pubescent; lvs. nearly pectinate, 1.5–2 cm. long; resin-ducts marginal: cone ovoid, 9 cm. long; bracts distinctly exserted beyond its scale. C.B.N.t.10–12. W. China. Intr. 1923. Zone VI?

9. **A. Fabri** (Mast.) Craib. Tree to 40 m.; young brts. minutely pubescent, glabrescent, yellowish to brown; buds slightly resinous: lvs. crowded, 1.5–2.5 cm. long, rounded or subtruncate to slightly notched at apex, with acutish recurved margin, slightly pectinate below, the middle ones above smaller and nearly upright: cone oblong-cylindric, 6–8 cm. long, 3.5–4.5 across, bluish black; scales 2.2–2.4 cm. broad; bracts spatulate, with exserted and recurved appendage. B.M.9201, f.1–7,9(c). G.C.39:2.13 and C.B.N.,t.3,4 (as *A. Fargesii*). (*Keteleeria F.* Mast., *A. Delavayi* Mast., not Franch., *A. Faberi* Craib.) W. China. Intr. 1901. Zone VI.

Related species: **A. Forréstii** Craib. Tree to 20 m.; brts. dark reddish brown: lvs. to 4 cm. long, rounded or truncate, notched, very white beneath: cone to 9 cm. long, violet-purple; bracts short-exserted. B.M.9201,f.8(c). C.B.N.t.7,8. G.C.80:427(h). (*A. Delavayi* var. *F.* A. B. Jacks.) W. China. Intr. about 1910. Zone VII?—**A. Ernésti** Rehd. Tree to 60 m.; brts. yellowish, rarely slightly puberulous: lvs. crowded, 1.5–3 cm. long, acute or obtuse, rarely slightly emarginate, sometimes stomatiferous above near apex, with pale or glaucescent bands beneath: cone peduncled, gray-brown at maturity; scales half as long as bracts, hidden. V.G.97. (*A. Beissneriana* Rehd. & Wils., not Mottet.) W. China. Intr. 1904. Zone VII?—**A. Delavàyi** Franch. with the lvs. strongly revolute at the margin is not in cult.

10. **A. chensiénsis** Van Tiegh. Tree to 70 m.; buds ovoid, slightly resinous; brts. glabrous, yellowish gray, the older dark gray: lvs. horizontally spreading and more or less 2-ranked, linear, broader above the middle, 1.5–3.4 cm. long, usually rounded and emarginate at apex, rarely acutish, bifid and sharply pointed on young plants, shining dark green above, with grayish green or sometimes glaucescent bands beneath; resin-ducts marginal, on fruiting brs. internal: cones ovoid-oblong, 7–10 cm. long, green while young, finally cinnamon-brown; scales about 3 cm. broad, erose at margin and tomentose outside; bracts hidden. C.B.N.t.2,26. V.G.131. C. China. Intr. 1907. Zone V.

11. **A. recurvàta** Mast. Tree to 40 m., bark dark gray or reddish brown, rough; buds ovoid, very resinous; brts. glabrous, lustrous, pale yellowish gray; lvs. pectinate below and spreading, more or less recurved above, linear, 1.5–3.5 cm. long, acutish or sharply pointed, bright shining green or bluish green above, paler green beneath; resin-ducts marginal: cones oblong-ovoid, 5–10 cm. long, slightly resinous, violet-purple before maturity, finally grayish brown; scales 1.5 cm. broad; bracts hidden. B.J.48:642. C.B.N.t.21,22. W. China. Intr. 1910. Zone V.

12. **A. firma** Sieb. & Zucc. MOMI F. Tree to 50 m., with broad-pyramidal head; bark soon scaly, fissured on old trees: buds small, slightly resinous; brts. brownish gray, slightly grooved, short-pubescent in the grooves: lvs. pectinate, firm, to 3.5 cm. long, broadest about the middle, sharply bifid at apex in young plants, obtuse and emarginate on older plants, with 2 grayish bands beneath: resin-ducts sometimes 4, 2 marginal and 2 internal: cones cylindric, 10–12 cm. long, yellowish green before maturity; scales about 2.5 cm. wide; bracts exserted, not reflexed. S.Z.2:t.107(c). P.I.26(c,h). S.N. 145(h). W.C.t.35,36(h). (*A. momi* Sieb., *A. bifida* Sieb. & Zucc.) Japan. Intr. 1861. Zone (V), VI.

13. **A. holophýlla** Maxim. NEEDLE F. Tree to 30 m.; buds slightly resinous; brts. glabrous, slightly grooved, yellowish gray: lvs. pectinate below, spreading above at nearly right angles outward and upward, 2–4 cm. long, entire at apex, obtusish or acute, spiny-pointed in young plants, lustrous bright green above, with 2 pale or slightly whitish bands beneath; resin-ducts internal: cone cylindric, about 14 cm. long, light brown at maturity; scales 3–5 cm. wide, entire; bracts hidden. S.N.144(h, as *A. koreana*). V.G.199. C.B.N. t.13,14. Manch., Korea. Intr. 1905 to Am. Zone V. Handsome fir doing well at the Arnold Arboretum.

14. **A. homólepis** Sieb. & Zucc. NIKKO F. Tree to 30 m.; bark scaly; buds ovoid, resinous; brts. glabrous, grayish, deeply grooved, particularly on 2- and 3-year-old brs.: lvs. pectinate below, except a few small ones in the middle ranks, crowded above, spreading outward and upward and forming a V-shaped depression, the outer ones 2–3 cm. long, the middle ones shorter, rounded or pointed and slightly bifid at apex, lustrous dark green above, with broad white bands below: cones cylindric, slightly narrowed at base and apex, about 10 cm. long, purple before maturity: scales thin, 2 cm. wide, entire; bracts hidden. S.Z.2:t.108(c). S.I.1:t.3(c). B.E.t.25(h). W.C.t.37,38(h). (*A. brachyphylla* Maxim.) Japan. Intr. 1861. Zone IV. One of the most ornamental firs thriving well in the E. States.—**A. h. Tomòmi** (Bobbink & Atkins) Rehd., var. A more sparingly branched form with shorter lvs. (*A. t.* Bobbink & Atkins.)—**A. h. umbellàta** (Mayr) Wils., var. Cone green while young. S.I.2:t.2(c). (*A. u.* Mayr, *A. umbilicata* Mayr.)

15. **A. spectàbilis** (Don) Spach. HIMALAYAN F. Tree to 50 m., with wide spreading brs. forming a broad-pyramidal head; bark scaly, rough; buds large, globose, resinous; brts. reddish brown, deeply grooved, pubescent in the grooves: lvs. arranged as in no. 14, but larger, 2.5–6 cm. long, rounded and bifid at apex, lustrous dark green above, with broad white bands below: cones cylindric, 14–18 cm. long, violet-purple before maturity; scales 1.5–2 cm. broad; bracts hidden or slightly exserted. B.M.8098(c, as *A. Mariesii*). G.C. III.25:788. P.I.21(c,h). (*A. Webbiana* Lindl., *A. densa* Griff.) Himal., Sikkim and Bhotan. Intr. 1822. Zone VII.—**A. s. brevifòlia** (Henry) Rehd., var. Lvs. shorter, not exceeding 3 cm., with grayish bands below; brts. less grooved; bark smooth. (*A. Webbiana var. b.* Henry.) N.W. Himal. Zone VI or VII.

16. **A. Píndrow** Royle. PINDROW F. Tree to 60 m., with short brs. forming a narrow pyramid; bark smooth and gray on young trees, grayish brown on old trees; buds large, resinous; brts. smooth and glabrous, gray: lvs. nearly pectinate below, crowded above, those in the middle shorter and directed forward, narrowly linear, 3–6 cm. long, bifid and acute at apex (entire on young plants), lustrous dark green, with gray bands below: cone cylindric, 10–14 cm. long, deep purple while young; scales 3 cm. wide; bracts hidden. P.I.22(c,h). C.B.2:23. (*A. Webbiana* var. *p.* Brandis.) Himal. Intr. 1837. Zone VI.—**A. P. brevifòlia** Dallimore & Jackson, var. Brts. reddish brown; lvs. 2–3.5 cm. long, rigid, acute, paler green. C.B.N.t.9. V.G.185. (*A. Gamblei* Hick.) Himal. Cult. 1923. Zone VII.—**A. P. intermèdia** Henry, var. Intermediate between nos. 15 and 16, possibly a hybrid: lvs. up to 5.5 cm., convex below. Orig. unknown. Cult. about 1870.

17. **A. numídica** Carr. ALGERIAN F. Tree to 20 m.; bark gray, smooth, scaly and fissured on old trees; buds ovoid, large, not or slightly resinous; brts. glabrous and lustrous: lvs. pectinate below, much crowded above, spreading outward and upward, on stronger brts. backward, on weaker ones with a V-shaped depression in the middle, 1.5–2 cm. long, 2 mm. broad, often broadest above the middle, rounded at apex and bifid or entire, dark green above, often only faintly grooved and often stomatiferous near apex, with white bands beneath: cones cylindric, 12–18 cm. long; scales 3 cm. wide, entire; bracts hidden. F.S.17:t.1717(c). V.G.283. P.I.20(c,h). B.E.t.26(h). (*A. Pinsapo* var. *baborensis* Coss., *A. baborensis* Letourneux.) N. Afr. Intr. 1862. Zone VI or (V).—**A. n. glauca** Beiss. Lvs. shorter and broader, bluish, with more stomatic lines above. P.I.t.20,f.8,9,12,13(c).

Related species: **A. Párdei** Gaussen. Brts. pubescent; lvs. 1.5–2.8 cm. long, rounded or subacute at apex: cone 18–20 cm. long; bracts slightly exserted. V.G.287. Orig. unknown. Cult. 1912.

18. **A. Pinsàpo** Boiss. SPANISH F. Tree to 25 m.; bark smooth, fissured on old trees; buds ovoid, resinous; brts. glabrous, brownish: lvs. spreading radially at nearly right angles, thick, rigid, 1.5–2 cm. long, acute or obtusish, dark green, slightly convex and stomatiferous above, with pale bands beneath: cones cylindric, purplish brown, 10–12 cm. long; scales 2.5 cm. wide, entire; bracts small, hidden. P.I.19(c,h). G.C.III.3:140. E.H.4:t.212–3(h). Spain. Intr. 1837. Zone VI. A handsome fir of striking appearance thriving well in the E. States.—**A. P. argéntea** Beiss. With silvery white foliage.—**A. P. glaùca** Carr. With glaucous foliage.—**A. P. péndula** Beiss. With pendulous brs. S.N.147(h). M.D.1913:337(h).

A. P. × *cephalonica* = **A.** Vilmorinii Mast. J.L.26:107. Vilmorin, Hort. Vilm. t.12(h). Raised in 1868.—*A. P.* × *Nordmanniana* = **A.** insígnis Carr. B.H.128(h),129. Raised in 1872. Of this cross several forms are known: A. i. Beissneriana (Mottet) Rehd. (*A. B.* Mottet); A. i. Kentiana (Mottet) Rehd. (*A. K.* Mottet); A. i. Mastersiana (Mottet) Rehd. (*A. M.* Mottet); A. i. speciosa Bailly) Rehd. (*A. Nordmanniana s.* Bailly).

Closely related species: **A. marocàna** Trabut. Lvs. 1–1.5 cm. long, nearly flat above with 1 or 2 irregular lines of stomata, resin-ducts marginal: cone about 15 cm. long; bracts about ½ as long as scale. V.G.238,239. Morocco. Cult. ?

19. **A. cephalónica** Loud. GREEK F. Tree to 30 m.; bark grayish brown, smooth, fissured on old trees; buds ovoid, reddish, resinous; brts. lustrous, red-brown, glabrous: lvs. radially spreading and slightly directed forward, the middle ones above shorter, 1.5–2.8 cm. long, stiff, gradually narrowed into a sharp point, shining deep green above, with white bands beneath: cone cylindric, 12–16 cm. long and 4–5 cm. across, brownish; scales 3–3.5 cm. wide, undulate or entire; bracts exserted and reflexed. P.I.18(c,h). G.C.II.22:592.

D.J.92,t(h). (*A. panachaica* Heldr., *A. Reginae Amaliae* Heldr.) Greece. Intr. 1824. Zone V. Handsome tree distinct in its spreading, sharply pointed lvs.—**A. c. Apóllinis** (Link) Beiss. Brts. yellowish: lvs. more crowded above, only a few below spreading downward and forward, thicker and broader, slightly acute or sometimes obtusish.
     A. c. × *Pinsapo;* see under No. 18.
     Related species: **A. Borisii-règis** Mattf. Tall trees; brts. densely short-pubescent; buds resinous: lvs. to 3 cm. long, acute and subpungent, sometimes rounded or slightly emarginate: cones conical-cylindric, 15 cm. long; bracts exserted; scales 3–3.5 cm. wide. M.D.1925:t.1,f.7,t.4,5. Balkan Pen. Cult. 1883. Zone V.—**A. Bornmülleriàna** Mattf. Tall tree; brts. glabrous; buds resinous: lvs. to 3.5 cm. long, rounded or emarginate: cone 12 cm. long, cylindric; bracts exserted; scales 2.5–3 cm. wide. M.D.1925:t.2,f.9,t.6,7(h). Asia Minor. Intr.? **A. nebrodénsis** Mattei. Intermediate between Nos. 19 and 22.: brts. with short brown hairs: lvs. 1.2–2 cm. long, stiff, rounded or slightly emarginate at apex: cone about 8 cm. long. C.B.N.t.18,19. V.G.247. Sicily. Cult. 1930. Zone VII?

     20. **A. cilícica** (Ant. & Kotschy) Carr. Cilician F. Tree to 30 m.; bark ashy gray, smooth, scaly on old trees; buds small, not or slightly resinous, with few keeled scales free at the tips; brts. grayish brown, with scattered short hairs: lvs. above spreading upward and forward, on weaker brts. outward and upward, leaving a V-shaped depression, slender, 2–3 cm. long, rounded or acute and slightly bifid at apex, shining bright green above, with narrow whitish bands below: cones cylindric, 16–20 cm. long, reddish brown; scales 3.5–4 cm. wide, entire; bracts hidden. P.I.17(c,h). C.B.2:10. B.E.t. 27(h). Asia Minor, Syria. Intr. 1855. Zone V.

     21. **A. Nordmanniàna** (Steven) Spach. Nordmann F. Tree to 50 m.; bark grayish brown, slightly fissured on old trees; buds ovoid, acute, not resinous, with slightly keeled acute scales; brts. gray, loosely or densely short-hairy: lvs. pectinate below, above directed forward and densely covering the brts., 2–3.5 cm. long, rounded and bifid at apex, lustrous dark green above, with whitish bands beneath: cones cylindric, 12–15 cm. long, reddish brown; scales 3–4 cm. wide; bracts exserted and reflexed. B.M.6992(c). P.I.16(c,h). S.N.50,137(h). Cauc., Asia Minor. Intr. 1848. Zone IV. Handsome and desirable fir.—**A. N. aùrea** Beiss. Lvs. yellow.—**A. N. tortifòlia** Rehd., f. Lvs. of the middle ranks above falcate and twisted.
     A. N. × *pinsapo* = *A. insignis;* see under No. 18.

     22. **A. alba** Mill. Silver F. Tree to 50 m.; bark grayish, smooth, scaly on old trees; buds small, not resinous, with few obtuse scales; brts. gray, with short brown hairs: lvs. pectinate, those of the upper ranks shorter and pointing outward and upward, 1.5–3 cm. long, rounded and bifid at apex, lustrous dark green above, with white bands beneath: cones cylindric, 10–14 cm. long, green while young, finally reddish brown; scales 2.5–3 cm. wide, tomentose outside; bracts exserted and reflexed. H.W.1:87(h)–94,t.2(c). E.H.4:t.208–11 (h). (*A. pectinata* DC., *A. Picea* Lindl., not Mill.) Mts. of C. and S. Eu. Long cult. Zone IV. This species is not doing well in the E. States.—**A. a. compácta** (Parsons) Rehd., f. A dwarf compact bushy form with ascending crowded brs. and lustrous lvs. about 1.5 cm. long.—**A. a. péndula** (Carr.) Aschers. & Graebn., l. With pendulous brs. G.W.19:466(h). (*A. pectinata p.* Carr.)—**A. a. pyramidàlis** (Carr.) Voss, f. With ascending brs. forming a columnar head. (*A. pectinata p.* Carr., *A. alba* l. *fastigiata* Aschers. & Graebn.)—**A. a. columnàris** (Carr.) Rehd., f. With short spreading brs. of nearly equal length forming a columnar head. (*A. pectinata c.* Carr.)
     23. **A. Fràseri** (Pursh) Poir. Southern Balsam F. Tree to 25 m.; bark smooth, reddish and scaly on old trees: buds small, subglobose, very resi-

nous; brts. yellowish gray, densely covered with short reddish hairs: lvs. spreading upward and forward, pectinate below, 1.5–2.5 cm. long, rounded and bifid at apex, lustrous dark green above, with broad white bands beneath: cones oblong-ovoid or ovoid, 3.5–6 cm. long, purple before maturity; scales 2 cm. wide, usually auriculate; bracts exserted and reflexed. S.S.12:t.609. G.C.III.8:684. G.F.2:475(h). Alleghany Mts., W. Va. to N. C. and Tenn. Intr. 1811. Zone IV.—**A. F. prostràta** Rehd., f. Low, depressed shrub with horizontally spreading brs. Morton Arb. Bull. 4:56(h).

24. **A. balsámea** (L.) Mill. BALSAM F. Tree to 25 m.; bark grayish brown, scaly on old trees: buds reddish, very resinous: brts. ashy gray, short-pubescent: lvs. spreading upward, pectinate below, on weaker brts. pectinate, 1.5–2.5 cm. long, rounded and slightly bifid at apex, dark green above and often with a few stomatic lines near apex, with narrow whitish bands beneath: cones oblong, 5–7 cm. long, violet-purple before maturity; scales 1.5 cm. wide; bracts enclosed or sometimes exserted (f. **phanerólepis** Fern.). S.S.12:t.610. G.C.III.17:422. Act. Hort. Berg. 6:t.87(h). Lab. to W. Va., w. to Minn. and Iowa. Intr. 1698. Zone III. In the E. States not satisfactory outside of its natural habitat.—**A. b. hudsónia** (Jacques) Sarg., var. Dwarf depressed form with dark green shorter and broader lvs. (*A. b. hudsonica* Kent.) Intr. before 1810.—**A. b. nàna** (Nels.) Carr. Dense subglobose form with short dark green lvs. (*A. b. globosa* Beiss. & Jaeg.)—**A. b. macrocárpa** Kent, var. Lvs. longer and cones to 8.5 cm. long. Intr. from Wisc. about 1884. It forms a transition to the following species.

25. **A. lasiocárpa** (Hook.) Nutt. ROCKY MOUNTAIN F. Tree to 30 or occasionally to 50 m.; bark smooth ånd silvery gray, fissured on old trees; buds small, ovoid, resinous; brts. ashy gray, with short rufous pubescence: lvs. much crowded above and directed forward and upward, 2.5–4 cm. long, rounded or acutish at apex, rarely emarginate, pale bluish green, stomatiferous and slightly grooved above, with broad pale bands beneath: cones oblong-cylindric, 6–10 cm. long, truncate or depressed at apex; scales 2–2.5 cm. wide; bracts hidden. S.S.12:t.611. G.F.4:382(h). (*A. subalpina* Engelm.) Alaska to Ore., Utah, and n. N. Mex. Intr. 1863. It does not thrive in the E. States.— **A. l. compácta** (Beiss.) Rehd., f. A dwarf compact form. (*A. l.* var. *cònica* Hornibr., *A. subalpina c.* Beiss.) Orig. 1873.—**A. l. arizònica** (Merriam) Lemm., var. ARIZONA F. Bark creamy white, thick and corky: lvs. whiter beneath and emarginate at the apex, more distinctly pectinate. G.C.29:134. S.N.154(h). M.G.40:289(h). (*A. a.* Merriam.) N. Ariz. and n. N. Mex. Intr. 1901.

26. **A. amàbilis** (Dougl.) Forb. Tree to 80 m.; bark silvery white or pale, at the base of old trees thick and furrowed; buds globose, very resinous; brts. gray, densely pubescent: lvs. pectinate below, crowded above, the lower ranks spreading, the upper stouter and directed forward, linear, 2–3 cm. long, often broadest above the middle, truncate or bifid at the apex, shining dark green above and grooved, with broad white bands below: cones oblong, 8–14 cm. long, purple before maturity, puberulous; scales 2.5–2.8 cm. wide; bracts hidden. S.S.12,t.614. G.C.III.3:754. D.J.80,t(h). B. C. and Alb. to Ore. Intr. 1830. Zone V.

27. **A. grandis** Lindl. GIANT F. Tree to 100 m. tall and to 5 m. in girth; buds ovoid, resinous; brts. olive-green or olive-brown, minutely pubescent, soon nearly glabrous: lvs. pectinate, linear, 3–6 cm. long and 2–2.5 mm. wide, flexible, rounded and bifid at the apex, shining dark green and grooved above, with white bands below: cones cylindric, 5–10 cm. long, bright green; scales

2.5–3 cm. wide; bracts hidden. S.S.12:t.612. B.C.2:14. E.H.4:t.217–8(h). (*A. Gordoniana* Carr., *A. amabilis* Murr., not Forbes.) Vancouver Isl. to n. Calif., east to Mont. Intr. 1831. Zone VI.

28. **A. cóncolor** (Gord.) Engelm. Colorado F. Tree to 40 m.; bark smooth, gray, on old trees deeply fissured and scaly; buds globose, resinous; brts. yellowish green, minutely pubescent or nearly glabrous: lvs. irregularly arranged, mostly spreading outward and curving upward, some of the middle ranks above directed forward, linear, 4–6 cm. long, acute or rounded at apex, bluish green, slightly convex and stomatiferous above, convex below and with pale bands: cones cylindric, 7–12 cm. long, narrowed at the ends, greenish or purplish before maturity; scales about 2.5 cm. wide, bracts hidden. P.I.29 (c,h). S.S.12:t.613(partly). G.C.III.8:748. W.A.82,t(h). Colo. to s. Calif., n. Mex. and N. Mex. Intr. 1872. Zone IV. This species is one of the best firs for the E. States; the var. *Lowiana* is less satisfactory.—**A. c. violàcea** (Roezl) Beiss. Lvs. bluish white.—**A. c. Wattèzii** Beiss. Lvs. first pale yellowish, changing to silvery white.—**A. c. aùrea** Beiss. Young lvs. golden yellow.— **A. c. brevifòlia** Beiss. Lvs. short and thick, obtuse, twice as broad as in the type.—**A. c. globòsa** Niemetz. Of globose habit, with short brs.—**A. c. cònica** Slavin, f. Dwarf pyramidal form with lvs. 2–4 cm. long.—**A. c. péndula** Beiss. With strongly pendulous brs. forming a narrow columnar head. —**A. c. Lowiàna** (A. Murr.) Lemm., var. Tree to 80 m.; buds smaller; lvs. more pectinately arranged, 5–7 cm. long, rounded and bifid at the apex, shallowly grooved above. P.I.30(c,h). C.B.2:16. G.C.III.13:8. S.N.146(h). (*A. L.* A. Murr., *A. Parsonsiana* Barron, *A. lasiocarpa* Mast., not Nutt.) Ore. to Calif. Intr. 1851. Zone VI.

29. **A. venústa** (Dougl.) K. Koch. Tree to 50 m., the lower brs. pendulous; bark smooth, brown, fissured at the base of old trees; buds elongated, acute, 1.5–2.5 cm. long, not resinous; brts. greenish, glabrous: lvs. pectinate, linear to linear-lanceolate, 3–6 cm. long, rigid, spiny-pointed, shining green above, not grooved, with broad white bands below: cones ovoid, 7–10 cm. long, purplish brown, resinous, with the exserted bracts ending in rigid spines 2.5–5 cm. long, giving the cone a bristly appearance. S.S.12:t.615,616. E.H.4:t.224 (h). (*A. bracteata* Nutt.) Calif. Intr. 1853. Zone VII?

30. **A. nòbilis** Lindl. Noble F. Tree to 80 m., with a girth to 8 m.; bark on old trees reddish brown and deeply fissured; buds resinous above; brts. minutely rusty-pubescent: lvs. pectinate below, crowded above, the lower ranks spreading outward, those of the middle ranks much shorter, appressed to the brts. near the base, then curving upward, linear, 2.5–3.5 cm. long, 1.5 mm. wide, rounded and entire or slightly notched at the apex, bluish green, stomatiferous and grooved above, with narrow pale bands below: cone cylindric-oblong, slightly narrowed toward the apex, 14–25 cm. long, green before maturity, finally purplish brown; scales 3–3.5 cm. broad; bracts much exserted and reflexed. S.S.12:t.617. G.C.II.25;652. E.H.4,t.225(h). Wash. to n. Calif. Intr. 1830. Zone (V). This fir thrives well in the E. States.—**A. n. glauca** Beiss. With glaucous lvs.

31. **A. magnífica** A. Murr. Red F. Tree to 70 m. and to 10 m. in girth; buds and brts. like those of the preceding species: lvs. less crowded, longer, up to 4 cm. long, quadrangular in section, rounded and entire at apex, keeled and stomatiferous above, with 2 pale bands below: cones cylindric-oblong, 14–22 cm. long, pubescent, purplish violet before maturity; scales 3–3.5 cm. wide; bracts hidden. S.S.12:t.618.619. G.C.II.24;652. E.H.4:t.222–3(h). (*A. nobilis* var. *m.* Kellogg.) Ore. to Calif. Intr. 1851. Zone V. A handsome fir of

regular habit doing well in the E. States but less hardy than the preceding species.—**A. m. glauca** Beiss. With deep glaucous lvs.—**A. m. argéntea** Beiss. With bluish white lvs.—**A. m. shasténsis** Lemm., var. Bracts exserted and usually reflexed, covering nearly half the scales. S.S.12:t.620. G.C.II.24:652; III.41:114. (*A. s.* Lemm.) Ore. to Calif.

2. **KETELEÈRIA** Carr. Evergreen trees with spreading whorled brs., pyramidal while young, flat-topped in old age: buds ovoid or globose, not resinous: lvs. linear, rigid, flat or keeled and lustrous above, keeled and pale green below, on young trees usually spiny pointed, on old trees obtuse: male fls. clustered; female fls. composed of numerous 2-ovuled scales subtended by small bracts: cone upright, ovoid to cylindric-oblong, with broad, woody, persistent scales, ripening the first year; bracts half as long as scale; seeds 2, their wings as long or nearly as long as the scales; cotyledons 2, remaining below ground. (After J. B. Keteleer, a French nurseryman, born in Belgium; 1813–1903.) Two or 3 species in China and Formosa.—Trees of the aspect of firs, but with the lvs. keeled or flat, not grooved above and pale green below. Better suited for a drier climate than the firs.

A. Young brts. orange-red: lvs. spiny-pointed to obtusish: cone-scales suborbicular, slightly inflexed at apex..1. *K. Fortunei*
AA. Young brts. yellowish gray: lvs. on old plants obtuse or emarginate: cone-scales ovate, recurved at apex..2. *K. Davidiana*

1. **K. Fortùnei** (A. Murr.) Carr. Tall tree to 30 m.; bark corky; young brts. glabrous or with scattered hairs: lvs. linear, keeled on both sides, spiny pointed on young plants, obtusish on old trees, 2–3 cm. long: cone ovoid to ovoid-cylindric, 8–18 cm. long, purple while young. R.H.1904:130. I.S.t.12. G.C.II.21:348;III.90:327(h). G.W.3:125(h). (*Abies F.* A. Murr.) S. E. China. Intr. about 1845. Zone VII?

2. **K. Davidiàna** (Franch.) Beiss. Tree to 35 m.; bark dark gray, furrowed; young brts. short-pilose or glabrous: lvs. linear, keeled on both sides, on mature trees obtuse or emarginate, 2.5–5 cm. long: cone cylindric-oblong, 12–20 cm. long, greenish, while young. G.C.III.33:84. R.H.1904:131. S.N.30(h). (*Abies D.* Franch., *Abies sacra* David.) W. China. Intr. 1888 and 1901. Zone VII. Probably hardier than the preceding species.

    K. Evelyniana Mast. with smaller cones and oblong-ovate scales (G.C. 33:194) and *K. formosana* Hayata are probably varieties or synonyms of *K. Davidiana*.

3. **PSEUDOTSÙGA** Carr. Evergreen trees with irregularly whorled brs.; brts. nearly smooth, marked with oval scars after the lvs. have fallen: buds ovate, acute, glabrous, not resinous: lvs. spirally arranged, spreading into 2 onposite rows, linear, flattened, green and grooved above, with 2 stomatic bands below, and with 2 marginal resin-ducts and 1 vascular bundle: male fls. axillary, cylindric; female terminal on short brts. and consisting of numerous spirally arranged 2-ovuled scales: fr. a pendulous, ovoid to ovoid-oblong cone with rounded concave rigid scales subtended by exserted bracts 3-lobed at the apex with the middle lobe long and narrow; seeds 2 under each scale, winged; cotyledons 6–12. (Greek *pseudos*, false and *tsuga*; alluding to its relationship.) Five species in W. N. Am. and in E. Asia.

A. Lvs. entire at apex: 2-year-old brts. reddish brown, usually pubescent.....1. *P. taxifolia*
AA. Lvs. emarginate: brts. pale yellowish gray, glabrous........................2. *P. japonica*

1. **P. taxifòlia** (Poir.) Britt. Douglas-Fir. Tree to 100 m.; trunk to 12 m. in girth; bark smooth, on old trees thick and corky, deeply fissured into scaly ridges; brts. pubescent, rarely glabrous, pale orange at first, changing to

reddish brown and later to grayish brown: lvs. straight, rarely curved, 2–3 cm. long, obtuse to acute, dark or bluish green above, with grayish or whitish bands beneath; cone ovoid, 5–10 cm. long; scales slightly concave, about 2 cm. wide; bracts exserted, upright or sometimes reflexed, green while young, light brown at maturity. S.S.12:t.607. E.H.4:t.227–31(h). (*P. Douglasii* Carr., *P. mucronata* Sudw., *Abies mucronata* Raf., *A. Douglasii* Lindl., *Abietia Douglasii* Kent.) B. C. to Calif., Mont., Colo., w. Tex. and n. Mex. Intr. 1827. Very variable and recently split into about 10 species.—The typical form of the coast region has been distinguished as **P. t. víridis** (Schwer.) Aschers. & Graebn. (*P. Douglasii* subsp. *mucronata* Schwer.) It is a taller tree, with the young brs. spreading, larger green lvs., larger cones with upright and accumbent bracts. M.D.1909:79,t. Zone VI. Here belong the following three forms: **P. t. caesia** (Schwer.) Aschers. & Graebn. Lvs. bluish green.—**P. t. fastigiàta** (Knight) Sudw. A pyramidal form with upright brs. —**P. t. péndula** (Neumann) Sudw. Form with pendulous brs. M.D.1918:t.57 (h) ; 1921:t.24(h).—**P. t. glauca** (Mayr) Schneid., var., is the Rocky Mountain form. Tree of slower growth and more compact habit, with ascending young brs.: lvs. shorter and more or less bluish green: cone about 5 cm. long, with spreading or finally reflexed bracts. M.D.1909:79,t. M.G.20:124(h). S.N. 271(h). (*P.g.* Mayr, *P. Douglasii* var. *g.* Mayr, *P. Douglasii* subsp. *glaucescens* Schwer.) Zone IV. The Rocky Mountain form is doing well in the E. States and forms a handsome dense pyramidal tree, but is of slower growth than the tenderer typical form which on account of its more rapid growth and larger size is more valuable as a timber tree.—To this var. belong the following forms: **P. t. argéntea** (Koster) Sudw. Lvs. bluish white.—**P. t. "glauca péndula"** (Beiss.) Schneid., f. With pendulous brs. and bluish green lvs. (*P. Douglasii glauca pendula* Beiss.) M.D.40:t.75(h).—**P. t. compácta** (Carr.) Sudw. Compact conical form with short crowded lvs.—**P. t. globòsa** (Lutz) Aschers. & Graebn. Dwarf globose form, rather loosely branched.—**P. t. pùmila** (Beiss.) Schwer., f. Dwarf compact globose form.

2. **P. japónica** (Shiras.) Beiss. Tree to 30 m.; bark fissured, dull reddish brown, becoming grayish brown; brts. glabrous, pale yellowish gray, with a conspicuous dark brown line around the apex of the pulvini: lvs. directed more or less forward, linear, often slightly curved, emarginate, 1.5–2.5 cm. long, shining bright green above and grooved, with 2 whitish bands below: cone ovoid, 4–5 cm. long, dark violet while young; scales very concave, rigid, 2–3 cm. wide; bracts exserted and reflexed. S.I.2:t.7(c). C.B.1:59. G.C.76: 337. W.C.t.33,34(h). (*Tsuga j.* Shiras.) Japan. Intr. 1898. Zone VI.

Closely related species: **P. sinénsis** Dode from W. China differs chiefly in the pubescent brown brts., longer lvs., to 3 cm. long and more distinctly pectinately arranged, larger cones, about 6 cm. long, with puberulous scales and upright or reflexed bracts. I.S.t.10. Intr. about 1914.—*P. Wilsoniana* Hayata (*P. Forrestii* Craib) from Formosa and S.W. China is probably not hardy.

4. **TSÙGA** Carr. HEMLOCK. Evergreen trees with cinnamon-red furrowed bark and horizontal, often pendulous brs. irregularly ramified; brts. with prominent leaf-cushions; buds globose or ovoid, not resinous: lvs. spirally arranged, usually more or less 2-ranked, linear, usually flattened and grooved above and with 2 white stomatic bands below, rarely rounded above and stomatiferous on both sides, with one resin-canal below the vascular bundle: fls. solitary; male fls. globose, axillary, the female terminal on lateral shoots with imbricated 2-ovuled scales: fr. a usually small cone consisting of concave woody scales subtended by short, rarely exserted bracts and persisting

19

after the escape of the seeds; seeds 2 under each scale, small, winged; cotyledons 3–6. (*Tsuga* is the vernacular Japanese name.) About 10 species in temp. N. Am., Japan, China and Himal.

A. Lvs. flat, grooved above, with 2 white or pale bands below, pectinately arranged: cones small, 1.5–3 cm. long.
  B. Margin of lvs. entire.
    C. Brts. glabrous, grayish or yellowish brown: lvs. 8–25 mm. long, notched.
                                              1. *T. Sieboldii*
    CC. Brts. pubescent.
      D. Lvs. 8–14 mm. long, notched; brts. pubescent throughout, reddish brown.
                                            2. *T. diversifolia*
      DD. Lvs. 8–25 mm. long; brts. light yellowish brown or gray, pubescent chiefly in the grooves.
        E. Lvs. notched at the apex, with inconspicuous bands below: cone-scales suborbicular ....3. *T. chinensis*
        EE. Lvs. entire or obscurely notched at the apex, with conspicuous white bands: cone-scales oval-oblong ....4. *T. caroliniana*
  BB. Margin of lvs. serrulate: brts. pubescent.
    C. Lvs. beneath with well defined narrow bands and a distinct green margin: buds ovoid, pointed ....5. *T. canadensis*
    CC. Lvs. beneath with broad ill defined bands and indistinct green margin: buds globose.
                                          6. *T. heterophylla*
AA. Lvs. rounded or keeled above, rarely slightly grooved, stomatiferous on both sides: cones cylindric-oblong, 5–7 cm. long...7. *T. Mertensiana*

1. **T. Sieboldii** Carr. Tree to 30 m., with horizontally spreading brs. forming an oval head, in cult. usually small tree or shrub; buds ovoid, acutish, with glabrous ciliate scales: lvs. linear, 6–22 mm. long, to 3 mm. broad, emarginate at apex, glossy dark green above, with narrow white bands below: cone ovoid, 2–2.5 cm. long, stalked, with orbicular scales. S.Z.2:t.106(c). S.I.2:t.4(c). W.C.29,30(h). S.N.100,297(h). (*T. Araragi* (Sieb.) Koehne.) Japan. Intr. 1850. Zone (V).

2. **T. diversifòlia** (Maxim.) Mast. JAPANESE H. Tree, rarely to 30 m., with horizontal brs. forming a pyramidal head; buds obovoid, flattened, minutely pubescent and ciliate: lvs. crowded, linear-oblong, 5–15 mm. long, 2.4 mm. broad, emarginate at apex, very glossy and dark green above, with narrow white bands below: cones subsessile, ovoid, 2 cm. long; scales orbicular-ovate, lustrous, with slightly thickened bevelled margin. S.I.2:t.4(c). W.C.31, 32(h). S.N.298(h). (*T. Sieboldii nana* Carr.) Japan. Intr. 1861. Zone V. Graceful species doing well in the E. States.

3. **T. chinénsis** (Franch.) Pritz. CHINESE H. Tree to 50 m.; buds ovoid, obtuse, glabrous; brts. yellowish, later pale yellowish gray, hairy only in the grooves: lvs. linear, 1.5–2.5 cm. long, 2–3 mm. broad, emarginate, glossy dark green and slightly grooved above, with broad whitish bands beneath becoming inconspicuous: cones ovoid, 1.5–2.5 cm. long; scales suborbicular, lustrous yellowish brown, with slightly bevelled margin. B.M.9193(c). C.B.N.t.91. C.C.21. W. China. Intr. 1901. Zone (V). Handsome promising species.

Closely related species: **T. yunnanénsis** (Franch.) Mast. Differs chiefly in the more densely pubescent brts., shorter and narrower, obtuse, not emarginate lvs. 7–18 mm. long, deeply grooved above, always very white below, and in the dull cones with fewer scales slightly recurved at apex. G.C.39:236. C.B.N.t.93. W. China. Intr. 1908. Zone VI?

4. **T. caroliniàna** Engelm. CAROLINA H. Tree, occasionally to 25 m., with often pendulous brs. forming a compact pyramidal head; buds globose-ovoid, obtuse, pubescent; brs. orange-brown, slightly pubescent: lvs. linear, 8–18 mm. long, lustrous dark green above, with white bands beneath: cones shortstalked, ovoid-oblong, 2–3.5 cm. long; scales oblong-ovate, rounded, thin, puberulous outside. S.S.10:t.604. G.C.II.26:780. B.E.t.31(h). W.A.78,t(h). Mts. of S. W. Va. to Ga. Intr. 1881. Zone IV. Very desirable tree of more

compact habit than the common H.—**T. c. compácta** Hornibr., var. Slow-growing round-topped and denser form. H.D.186,t(h).

5. **T. canadénsis** (L.) Carr. COMMON H. Tree, occasionally to 30 m., with long and slender often pendulous brs. forming a broad pyramidal head; buds acute, slightly puberulous; brts. yellow-brown, pubescent: lvs. linear, 8–18 mm. long, rounded, rarely emarginate at apex, lustrous dark green and slightly grooved above, with narrow white bands beneath: cones short-stalked, ovoid, 1.5–2 cm. long, with roundish obovate scales. S.S.10:t.603. G.C.48: 350–1(h). E.H.2:t.70–1(h). (*T. americana* (Mill.) Farwell.) N. S. to Minn. and Ill., s. on the mts. to n. Ga. and n. Ala. Intr. about 1736. Zone IV. Handsome ornamental tree; also timber-tree of some importance and bark used for tanning.—**T. c. albo-spìca** Beiss. Tips of young shoots white.—**T. c. microphýlla** Sénécl. Lvs. 3–5 mm. long and 1 mm. broad. (*T. c. parvifolia* Beiss.) —**T. c. Jenkínsii** Bailey, var. Narrow-pyramidal graceful form with slender pendent brs. and small lvs. 1 cm. or less long. Cult. 1932.—**T. c. compácta** Sénécl. Dwarf conical form with short brs. and short lvs. B.E.t.32(h).—**T. c. grácilis** Carr. Slow growing form with spreading sparingly ramified brs. drooping at the ends: lvs. 6–8 mm. long.—**T. c. péndula** Beiss. Low form with pendulous brs. forming a dense hemispherical bush broader than high. M.G. 15:367–8,491(h). Gn.39:81(h). G.C.75:107(h). Jour. N. Y. Bot. Gard. 40: 156–164(h). (*T. c. Sargentiana* Kent, var. *Sargenti pendula* Bean.)

6. **T. heterophýlla** (Raf.) Sarg. WESTERN H. Tree to 70 m., with short usually pendulous brs. forming a narrow-pyramidal head; buds globose-ovoid, obtuse; brts. yellow-brown changing to dark red-brown, pubescent for 5 or 6 years and with long pale hairs while young: lvs. linear, 6–18 mm. long, rounded at apex, shining dark green and grooved above, with broad white bands beneath: cone sessile, 2–2.5 cm. long; scales obovate, longer than broad, puberulous outside. S.S.10:t.605. G.C.III.12:11. B.S.2:604,t(h). D.J.t.29(h). (*T Mertensiana* auth., not (Bong.) Carr., *T. Albertiana* (A. Murr.) Sénécl.) S. Alaska to Idaho and Calif. Intr. 1851. Zone VI. Handsome tree of rapid growth in humid soil, not doing well in the climate of the E. States.

Related species: **T. dumòsa** (D. Don) Eichl. Tree to 40 m.; buds globose, pubescent: lvs. 1.5–3 cm. long, tapering to an acute apex, silvery white below, with scarcely any green margin: cone-scales suborbicular, striate. G.C.II.26: 72, 500. E.H.2:t.72(h). (*T. Brunoniana* Carr.) Himal. Intr. 1838. Zone VII?

7. **T. Mertensiàna** (Bong.) Carr. MOUNTAIN H. Tree to 30 or occasionally to 50 m., with slender pendent brs. forming an open pyramidal head; buds ovoid, acute; brts. reddish brown, pubescent for 2 or 3 years: lvs. radially spreading, 5–25 mm. long, flattened, entire, bluntly pointed, usually bluish green: cones sessile, cylindric-oblong, 3–7.5 cm. long; scales suborbicular, thin, puberulous outside, usually bluish purple before maturity. S.S.10:t.606. G.C. III.21:150–1. G.F.10:6,7(h). E.H.2:t.67(h). (*T. Hookeriana* Carr., *T. Pattoniana* Sénécl., *Hesperopeuce Pattoniana* Lemm.) S. Alaska to n. Mont., Idaho and Calif. Intr. 1854. Zone (V).—**T. M. argéntea** (Beiss.) Sudw. Lvs. bluish white. S.N.302(h).—To avoid confusion one has to bear in mind that *T. heterophylla* was known for a long time as *T. Mertensiana* and is still not infrequently called so.

T. M. × *heterophylla* = **T. Jéffreyi** (Henry) Henry. Buds ovoid, acute: lvs. radially spreading and directed outward, green and grooved above, with stomata near apex, minutely serrulate. C.B.N.92. (*T. Pattoniana* var. *Jeffreyi* Henry.) Intr. 1851.

5. **PÍCEA** A. Dietr. SPRUCE. Evergreen pyramidal trees with scaly bark and whorled brs.; brts. with prominent leaf-cushions (pulvini) separated by

incised grooves and produced at the apex into a peg-like stalk bearing the leaf; buds ovoid or conical, with or without resin: lvs. spirally arranged, on the under side of the brts. usually pectinate, linear, usually 4-angled and stomatiferous on all 4 sides or compressed and stomatiferous only on the upper (ventral or inner) side which appears by twisting of the lvs. to be the lower one; with 2 marginal resin-ducts, rarely without: male fls. axillary, catkin-like, yellow or red, consisting of numerous spirally arranged anthers; female fls. terminal, green or purple, consisting of numerous 2-ovuled bracted scales: fr. an ovoid to oblong-cylindric pendulous or sometimes spreading to nearly upright cone, with persistent, suborbicular to rhombic-oblong scales subtended by small bracts; seeds 2 under each scale, small, compressed, winged. (The ancient Latin name, derived from *pix*, pitch.) About 40 species in the cooler and temperate regions of the n. hemisphere, from the arctic circle to the high mts. of the warm-temp. regions.

A. Lvs. quadrangular or slightly compressed, stomatiferous on all sides.
  B. Lvs. nearly equally stomatiferous on all 4 sides, in cross-section about as high as broad or higher than broad.
    C. Brts. glabrous (sometimes pubescent in No. 7 and in a var. of No. 15).
      D. Lvs. at least of the upper ranks more or less pointing forward.
        E. Winter-buds resinous; lvs. radially arranged.
          F. Brts. gray, pendulous; lvs. 2–4 cm. long......................1. *P. Smithiana*
          FF. Brts. yellowish to brown; lvs. 1–2 cm. long.....................6. *P. asperata*
        EE. Winter-buds not resinous.
          F. Lvs. radially arranged, 2–3.5 cm. long; brts. gray...........2. *P. Schrenkiana*
          FF. Lvs. more or less pectinate below and imbricate above, 1–2.5 cm. long.
            G. Winter-buds pointed, acute or acutish: lvs. acute: cones 4–15 cm. long.
              H. Brts. gray or whitish, with scarcely raised petioles.......3. *P. Wilsonii*
              HH. Brts. usually reddish or yellowish, with prominent petioles..7. *P. Abies*
            GG. Winter-buds obtuse: lvs. usually glaucous, obtusish or acutish: cones 3.5–5 cm. long...15. *P. glauca*
      DD. Lvs. more or less radially spreading at nearly right angles.
        E. Winter-buds very resinous: lvs. 8–15 mm. long..............4. *P. Maximowiczii*
        EE. Winter-buds not or slightly resinous: lvs. up to 2.5 cm. long.
          F. Bud-scales firmly appressed, dark brown; lvs. in cross-section higher than broad ....5. *P. polita*
          FF. Bud-scales revolute at apex, light yellow-brown: lvs. as high as broad: cone with loosely appressed scales....................................17. *P. pungens*
    CC. Brts. pubescent (leading shoot glabrous in No. 10).
      D. Terminal winter-buds without subulate scales at base.
        E. Brts. yellowish to grayish.
          F. Lvs. 1–1.8 cm. long, spreading: cone 6–12 cm. long, with obovate entire stiff scales ....6. *P. asperata*
          FF. Lvs. 1.5–2.5 cm. long, often glaucous, pointing forward, cone 3.5–7 cm. long, with rhombic erose flexible scales...........................16. *P. Engelmanni*
        EE. Brts. brown: lvs. dark green: cone-scales entire, stiff.
          F. Lvs. pointed, 8–20 mm. long, spreading.
            G. Leading shoot glabrous or nearly so: lvs. with more numerous stomata above than beneath......................................10. *P. Koyamai*
            GG. Leading shoot like other brts. pubescent: lvs. equally stomatiferous on all sides ....8. *P. obovata*
          FF. Lvs. obtuse, 6–12 mm. long, more or less appressed, dark green, very lustrous.
                                                                              9. *P. orientalis*
      DD. Terminal winter-bud with a ring of conspicuous subulate scales at base: lvs. often with more stomata above than beneath: cones 1.5–5 cm. long.
        E. Lvs. lustrous green: cones green when young, falling soon after maturity.
                                                                              13. *P. rubens*
        EE. Lvs. glaucous or dull bluish green: cones purple when young, persisting for several years ....14. *P. mariana*
  BB. Lvs. in cross-section broader than high, with at least twice as many stomatic lines above as below (see also Nos. 13, 14).
    C. Lvs. with about twice as many stomata above as below, slightly compressed: brts. at least partly glabrous.
      D. Leading shoot glabrous, the lateral brts. pubescent: lvs. 1–1.5 cm. long.
                                                                              10. *P. Koyamai*
      DD. Leading shoot pubescent, lateral brts. glabrous: lvs. 1–2 cm. long.....11. *P. bicolor*
    CC. Lvs. with only 1–2, rarely 3–4, often broken rows of stomata on each side beneath, with conspicuous stomatic bands above, compressed.
      D. Brts. reddish brown, pubescent: cone-scales orbicular, stiff..........12. *P. Glehnii*
      DD. Brts. yellow or grayish: cone-scales rhombic, thin, denticulate..18. *P. likiangensis*

AA. Lvs. flattened, with white bands above and without or occasionally with only a broken row of stomata beneath (see also *P. purpurea* under No. 19).
    B. Lvs. not radially spreading, more or less pectinate below: brts. short, not or slightly pendent.
        c. Brts. glabrous: cone-scales flexible, thin, erose-denticulate.
            D. Lvs. not pungent, though often pointed, 1–2 cm. long..............19. *P. jezoensis*
            DD. Lvs. pungent, 1.5–2.5 cm. long..20. *P. sitchensis*
        cc. Brts. pubescent or the leading shoots glabrous: cone-scales stiff, appressed before maturity.
            D. Brts. yellow to orange-brown,.the leading shoots usually glabrescent: winter-buds dark brown, without subulate scales at base: lvs. above usually without distinct green midrib ....21. *P. brachytyla*
            DD. Brts. brown, all pubescent: winter-buds with subulate scales at base: lvs. above with distinct green midrib..22. *P. Omorika*
    BB. Lvs. more or less radially spreading: brts. long and pendulous.
        c. Brts. pubescent: lvs. obtuse or obtusish............................23. *P. Breweriana*
        cc. Brts. glabrous: lvs. pungent...24. *P. spinulosa*

Sect. I. EUPICEA Willk. Lvs. quadrangular, stomatiferous on all 4 sides: cone-scales firm, closely appressed before maturity, usually entire and rounded at apex. (Sect. *Morinda* Mayr.)

1. **P. Smithiàna** Boiss. HIMALAYAN S. Tree to 50 m., with spreading brs. and pendulous glabrous gray and lustrous brts.; buds to 8 mm. long, ovoid, acute, dark-colored: lvs. radially spreading, slender, 2–4 cm. long, acute, straight or incurved, usually higher than broad, bright or dark green: cones cylindric, 12–18 cm. long, lustrous brown, green at first; scales broad-obovate, rounded and entire at apex. P.I.39(c,h). G.C.35:325;38:395. F.E.16:705(h). H.E.6:t.345(h). (*P. Morinda* Link, *P. Khutrow* Mast.) Himal. Intr. 1818. Zone VI.—Handsome tree of broad-pyramidal habit with pendulous brts.

2. **P. Schrenkiàna** Fisch. & Mey. Tree to 35 m. or more, with pendulous brts.: buds subglobose, the terminal one with acuminate, keeled pubescent scales at base: brts. glabrous, gray: lvs. nearly radially arranged, pointing forward, 2–3.5 cm. long, or on young plants often slightly shorter, finely pointed, straight or curved, dull green: cones cylindric-oblong, 7–10 cm. long; scales obovate, rounded and entire at apex. C.B.2:48. M.D.1910:227,229(h). (*P. obovata* var. *S.* Mast.) C. Asia. Intr. 1877. Zone V.

3. **P. Wilsónii** Mast. Pyramidal tree to 25 m., with short spreading brs.; buds ovoid, brown, lustrous, not resinous; brts. glabrous, pale or whitish gray, with scarcely raised lf.-stalks: lvs. slender, 1–2 cm. long, scarcely 1 mm. broad, acute or acuminate, dark green: cones cylindric-oblong, 4–6 cm. long, brown; scales suborbicular or broad-obovate, entire. G.C.33:133. C.B.N.t.66. Gn.88:167(h). (*P. Watsoniana* Mast.) C. and W. China. Intr. 1901. Zone V. Handsome spruce of dense habit with slender brs.

4. **P. Maximowíczii** Reg. Tree to 25 m., occasionally to 40 m., with horizontal brs. ascending at the ends: buds 3–4 mm. long, resinous, with firmly appressed scales; brts. glabrous, yellowish or reddish brown: lvs. spreading, rigid, 8–15 mm. long, acute, dark green: cones oblong, 3–6 cm. long, lustrous brown, green before maturity; scales rounded, entire. G.C.58:99,f.18–27. W.C.21,22(h). (*P. excelsa* var. *obovata japonica* Beiss., *P. Tschonoskii* Mayr.) Japan. Intr. 1865. Zone IV. In cult. usually a small bushy tree, without particular ornamental merit.

5. **P. polìta** (Sieb. & Zucc.) Carr. TIGERTAIL S. Tree to 30 or occasionally to 40 m., with slender brs. of moderate length; bark gray, rough; buds dark brown, acute, 6–10 mm. long, their scales long persistent as blackish sheath at base of brts.; brts. stout, pale yellow, glabrous: lvs. radially spreading, rigid, 1.5–2 cm. long, spiny pointed, often curved, lustrous dark green: cones oblong, 8–10 cm. long, brown, yellowish green before maturity; scales broad, rounded, irregularly denticulate. S.Z.2:t.111(c). S.I.2:t.2(c). G.C.III.21:251. W.C.t. 19,20(h). (*P. Torano* Koehne, *P. Thunbergii* Aschers. & Graebn.) Japan.

Intr. 1861. Zone V.—Very distinct tree with rigid spiny lvs. and conspicuous winter-buds.

6. **P. asperàta** Mast. Tree to 25 m.; bark grayish brown, peeling off in thin flakes: buds ovoid or conical, yellowish brown; brts. yellowish, pubescent or sometimes glabrous, with spreading petioles: lvs. 1–1.8 cm. long, acute, often curved: cones cylindric-oblong, 8–10 cm. long, fawn-gray, finally chestnut-brown; scales obovate, rounded and entire at apex. C.C.17. C.B.N.t.62. Gn.88:166(h). S.N.32,208(h). W. China. Intr. 1910. Zone V. The most vigorous of the Chinese spruces; similar in general appearance to the Norway S.—**P. a. notàbilis** Rehd. & Wils., var. Lvs. 1.2–2 cm. long: cones 9–12 cm. long, with rhombic-obovate scales narrowed toward the apex.—**P. a. ponderòsa** Rehd. & Wils., var. Bark thicker; brts. nearly glabrous: cones 12–15 cm. long.—**P. a. heterólepis** (Rehd. & Wils.) Cheng, var. Brts. reddish or yellowish brown: lvs. bluish green, often glaucescent: cone-scales rhombic-ovate, the lower ones deeply emarginate. (*P. h.* Rehd. & Wils.) W. China. Intr. 1910.

Closely related species: **P. aurantíaca** Mast. Brts. yellow, changing to orange, glabrous, often slightly bloomy: lvs. sharply pointed, pectinately arranged below: cone-scales slightly erose. W. China. Intr. 1908. Zone V.—**P. Meyeri** Rehd. & Wils. Brts. yellowish or light brown, pubescent, rarely nearly glabrous (a brt. may be densely pubescent one year and its continuation nearly glabrous the next year); lvs. obtusish, bluish green, often curved. N. China. Intr. 1910. Zone V.—**P. retrofléxa** Mast. Tree to 45 m.; bark gray, peeling off in thin flakes; brts. yellow, glabrous or nearly so: lvs. 1–2.5 cm. long, abruptly acuminate and pungent: cone-scales broadly rhombic to rounded. W. China. Intr. 1911. Zone V.

7. **P. Ábies** (L.) Karst. NORWAY S. Tree to 50 m., with spreading brs. and usually pendent brts.; bark reddish brown; buds reddish or light brown, without resin, scales often with spreading tips, the terminal bud with a few acuminate keeled pubescent scales at base: brts. usually brown, glabrous or minutely pubescent: lvs. 1–2, rarely to 2.5 cm. long, acute, dark green and usually lustrous: cones pendulous, cylindric, 10–15 cm. long, light brown, purple or green before maturity; scales thin, rhombic-ovate, with a truncate, erose-denticulate or emarginate apex. H.W.1:54–61,t.1(c). F.E.15:t.50(h). S.N.15(h). (*P. excelsa* Link, *P. rubra* A. Dietr., *Pinus Abies* L., *P. Picea* Du Roi.) N. and C. Eu. Long cult.; occasionally escaped in E. N. Am. Zone II. —Early intr. to Am. and much planted as an ornamental tree and also for shelters and wind-breaks. It is a rapidly growing pyramidal tree of graceful habit with dark green foliage, but like other spruces and firs it loses much of its beauty when growing older.—The typical form distinguished as **P. A. erythrocárpa** (Purkyne) Rehd., f., has the cones violet-purple before maturity and the lvs. usually spreading, while **P. A. chlorocárpa** (Purkyne) Th. Fries has the young cones green and the lvs. usually more or less appressed and obtusish and leafs later. Another spontaneous form is **P. A. nígra** (Loud.) Th. Fries (*P. excelsa* var. *n.* Willk.), a densely branched pyramidal tree with crowded falcate obtusish and dark green lvs.—A large number of garden forms is in cult.

Forms differing in color of lvs.: **P. A. argéntea** (Berg) Rehd., f. Lvs. variegated with white. (*P. exc. variegata* Beiss.)—**P. A. argénteo-spìca** (Beiss.) Rehd., f. Tips of young brts. white. S.N.221,223.—**P. A. finedonénsis** (Gord.) Nash, var. Lvs. pale yellow at first, changing to bronzy-brown and finally to green. (*P. exc. f.* Beiss.)

Columnar and narrow-pyramidal forms: **P. A. pyramidàta** (Carr.) Rehd., f. Brs. ascending at an acute angle, the lower ones long, decreasing toward the apex, forming a narrow slender pyramid. Gt.74:340(h). S.N.120(h). (*P. exc.* f. *pyramidalis* Voss.)—**P. A. cupréssina** (Thomas) Rehd., f. Tree with ascending densely ramified brs. forming a dense broad column. M.D.1909:t. 8(h).—**P. A. columnàris** (Jacques) Rehd., f. With very short horizontal or slightly pendulous much ramified brs. forming a narrow column. Conwentz, Beob. Waldb. Westpreuss. t.3(h). (*P. exc. c.* Carr.)

Pendulous or sparingly branched forms: **P. A. péndula** (Jacq. & Herincq) Nash, var. With pendulous brs. and brts. Gt.52:434(h).—**P. A. invérsa** (Beiss.) Nash, var. Similar to the preceding, with the brs. densely ramified and more closely appressed to the stem: lvs. thickish and lustrous. G.C.29: 363(h). F.E.22:765(h). S.N.211(h).—**P. A. viminàlis** (Alstroem) Th. Fries Brs. almost horizontal in remote whorls with very long and slender brts. often to 3 m. long. H.W.1:64(h). S.N.218(h).—**P. A. virgàta** (Jacques) Th. Fries. Sparingly branched, with much elongated straight or curved brs. destitute of brts., usually the upper ones ascending, the lower pendent. R.H.1854:102(h). M.G.9:31(h). (*P. exc.* var. *v.* Casp., *P. exc. Cranstoni* Carr.)—**P. A. monstròsa** (Loud.) Rehd., var. A form destitute of all brs., consisting of a single thick stem clothed with thick rigid lvs. Zeitschr. Forst. Jagdwes. 25:228(h). (*P. exc. m.* Schroet., *P. exc. monocaulis* Noerdl.)

Dwarf forms: **P. A. cònica** (Endl.) Th. Fries. Dense conical form with ascending brs. and light brown slender brts.: lvs. radially spreading, thin and pointed. (*P. exc. c.* Carr.)—**P. A. élegans** (Forbes) Rehd., f. Slender conical form similar to the preceding with very short crowded brts. densely clothed with short pointed laterally compressed lvs. (*P. exc. e.* Beiss.)—**P. A. Remóntii** (R. Smith) Rehd., f. Dense pyramidal or ovoid form with short crowded light yellow brts. and radially spreading fine light green lvs. F.E.16:491(h). M.G.21:556(h). (*P. exc. R.* Beiss.)—**P. A. pýgmaea** (Loud.) Rehd., f. Dense small pyramidal form with ascending brs. and bright green lvs. (*P. exc. p.* Carr.)—**P. A. Bárryi** (Beiss.) Nash, var. Conical form with thick brs. and rather distant short brts. S.N.47(h). (*P. exc. B.* Beiss.)—**P. A. Ellwangeriàna** (Beiss.) Rehd., f. Broad-pyramidal form with crowded slender brts. and small slender acute lvs.—**P. A. mucronàta** (Loud.) Rehd., f. Broad-pyramidal shrub, with ascending or sometimes spreading brs., stout reddish yellow brts. and rather distant dark green pungent lvs. 0.8–2 cm. long. (*P. exc. m.* Carr.) —**P. A. nàna** (Carr.) Schroet., l. Conical or subglobose form with short crowded ascending brs. and orange-yellow brts. partly swollen and irregular: lvs. stiff, appressed, about 1 cm. long and abruptly pointed. H.D.117,t.(h).— **P. A. parvifórmis** (Maxwell) Rehd., f. Broad-pyramidal form with slender regularly arranged brts. and crowded very short, acute, bright green lvs. (*P. exc. p.* Beiss.)—**P. A. microspérma** (Hornibr.) Rehd., var. Dense conical or subglobose form with crowded ascending brs. and gray-brown brts.: lvs. bright green, close-set and pointing forward, thick, slightly curved and bluntly pointed. B.E.t.34(h). H.D.116,t.(h).—**P. A. compácta** (Kirchn.) Nash, var. Subglobose dense form with slender brts. and acute lvs. F.E.16:t.65(h).— **P. A. Clanbrasiliàna** (Loud.) Th. Fries. Compact, subglobose, rather flat-topped bush, rarely exceeding 2 m. with very short crowded thin whitish brts.: lvs. nearly radiate and pointing forward or pectinate beneath, thin. 4–8 mm. long, slender-pointed, lustrous bright green. H.D.90,t.(h). (*P. exc. C.* Carr.)—**P. A. Gregoryàna** (Gord.) Nash, var. Dwarf subglobose or conical form, rarely exceeding 75 cm. in height, with short crowded spreading brs. and very crowded thin whitish to gray-brown brts. slightly pubescent in the grooves: lvs. radially arranged, 6–12 mm. long, gray-green. (*P. exc. G.*

Beiss.)—**P. A. Veìtchii** (Hornibr.) Rehd., var. Similar to the preceding, but less compact and more conical, with longer brts. inclined to droop: lvs. of lateral brts. thinner and flatter and pectinate beneath. H.D.98,t.(h). B.E.t. 34(h, as var. *Clanbrasiliana*).—**P. A. Parsónsii** (Hornibr.) Rehd., f. Similar to var. *Gregoryana*, but of looser more straggling habit, with spreading brs. and pendulous brts.: lvs. thinner and flatter, more distant, pectinate below on most brts. H.D.99,t.(h). (*P. exc. Gregoryana* f. *P.* Hornibr.)—**P. A. Mérkii** (Beiss.) Rehd., f. Dense low roundish form with rather fine yellowish white brts., and very thin, lustrous grass-green lvs. pectinate below. (*P. exc. M.* Ohlendorff.)—**P. A. pùmila** (R. Smith) Voss, f. Dwarf and dense, depressed-globose form with red-brown thick and stiff brts. and thin lvs. tapering to a blunt point, either dark green (*P. A.* f. *pumila nigra* Voss, *P. exc. p. n.* Beiss.), or bluish green (*P. A.* f. *pumila glauca* Voss, *P. exc. pumila glauca* Beiss.) S.N.43,219(h).—**P. A. Maxwéllii** (R. Smith) *Nash*, var. Low dense flat form, the brs. often with fascicled short brts.: lvs. bright green, radially arranged, rigid, finely pointed. H.D.103,t(h). (*P. exc. M.* Beiss.)—**P. A. procúmbens** (A. Murray) Rehd., f. Prostrate form with horizontal brs. and numerous short bright yellow brs. and pointed yellow-green thin lvs. (*P. exc. p.* Carr., var. *prostrata* Schneid.)—**P. A. tabulifórmis** (Carr.) Th. Fries. Prostrate form with slender horizontally spreading brs. and rather distant yellow-brown brts.: lvs. very thin, yellow-green, blunt.

8. **P. obovàta** Ledeb. Siberian S. Tree to 30 or occasionally to 50 m., similar to *P. Abies;* buds conical, not resinous, with closely appressed scales, the terminal buds with keeled, acuminate, ciliate scales at base; brts. brown, minutely pubescent: lvs. 1–1.8 cm. long, acute, slightly higher than broad in cross-section, deep green: cones cylindric-ovoid, 6–8 cm. long, brown, purple before maturity; scales obovate, with thin rounded and entire margin or slightly produced and sometimes emarginate. C.B.2:42 (*P. Abies* var. *o.* (Ledeb.) Voss). N. Eu. to Kamchatka and Manch. Intr. about 1852? Zone II. A smaller, more graceful tree than the Norway Spruce.—**P. o. fénnica** (Reg.) Henry, var. Lvs. dark green: cone-scales rounded, finely denticulate. (*P. exc.* var. *medióxima* Willk.) N. Eu.—**P. o. alpéstris** (Bruegger) Henry, var. Slow growing compact tree; brts. densely short-pubescent: lvs. obtuse or acutish, 1–1.5 cm. long, bluish or grayish green: cones 8–12 cm. long. Swiss Alps, at high altitudes. Resembles somewhat *P. glauca.*

9. **P. orientàlis** (L.) Link. Oriental S. Tree to 40 or occasionally to 60 m., with ascending or spreading brs. and slightly pendulous brts.; bark brown, scaly; buds acute, brown, not resinous, the terminal buds with a few keeled acuminate scales at base; brts. pale brown, short-pubescent: lv. stout, straight, 6–10 mm. long, obtuse, lustrous dark green, crowded and appressed to the brt.: cones cylindric-ovoid, 6–9 cm. long, brown, violet before maturity; scales obovate, rounded and entire. P.I.41(c,h). G.C.III.3:754. S.N.16(h). C.L. 11:311(h). Cauc., Asia Minor. Intr. 1837. Zone IV. Graceful compact tree with dark glossy foliage; of slow growth.—**P. o. aùreo-spicàta** Beiss. Young lvs. yellow, changing later to green.—**P. o. aùrea** Hesse. Lvs. bronzy-golden.— **P. o. nàna** Carr. Low broad-pyramidal form, with the lower brs. horizontal and wide-spreading.

10. **P. Koyamài** Shiras. Narrow-pyramidal tree to 20 m.; bark grayish brown, scaly; buds conical, brown, resinous; brts. reddish brown and slightly bloomy, the lateral ones glandular-pubescent, the primary nearly glabrous: lvs. slightly compressed, 8–12 mm. long, acute or obtuse, straight or curved, with 2 white bands above each with 5–8 rows of stomata, those below with

2–4 rows and inconspicuous: cones cylindric-oblong, 4–10 cm. long, pale brown, green before maturity; scales broad, rounded, denticulate, very firm. G.C.58:98. C.B.N.t.63. W.C.t.23(h). S.N.207(h). (*P. koraiensis* Nakai, *P moramomi* Hort.) Japan, Korea. Intr. 1914. Zone IV.

11. P. bícolor (Maxim.) Mayr. ALCOCK S. Broad-pyramidal tree to 25 m.; bark pale gray to gray-brown, fissured into thin flakes: buds ovoid or conical, brown, slightly resinous; brts. lustrous, yellow or reddish brown, the lateral shoots glabrous, the primary ones hairy: lvs. slightly compressed, 1–2 cm. long, acuminate, dark green, the stomatic bands above each with 5–6 rows, those below with 2 rows of stomata: cones cylindric-oblong, 6–12 cm. long, brownish, purple before maturity; scales obovate, rounded or somewhat narrowed at apex, slightly denticulate. S.I.1:19(c). G.C.II.13:212. S.N.14(h). W.C.t.19,20(h). (*P. Alcockiàna* Carr.) Japan. Intr. 1861. Zone IV.—**P. b. aciculàris** Shiras. & Koyama, var. Brts. finely pubescent: lvs. curved: cone-scales entire. G.C.58:98. Cult. 1923.—**P. b. refléxa** Shiras. & Koyama, var. Brts. pubescent: lvs. curved, 1–1.5 cm. long: cone-scales nearly entire, slightly attenuate and recurved at apex. G.C.58:98. Cult. 1923.

12. P. Glèhnii (Fr. Schmidt) Mast. SAGHALIN S. Tree to 40 m., with slender short brs.; bark red-brown, fissured into thin flakes; buds ovoid or conical, resinous, chestnut-brown, the terminal buds with subulate scales at base; brts. reddish brown, densely short-pubescent: lvs. slightly compressed, 6–12 mm. long, obtuse or on young plants pointed, deep green, with 2 bands of stomata above and 1 or 2 broken lines on each side below: cones cylindric-oblong, 5–8 cm. long, lustrous brown, violet, rarely green before maturity; scales suborbicular, rounded or slightly produced in the middle, entire or slightly erose. B.M.9020(c). K.M.t.5(c). W.C.25,26(h). Saghalin, Japan. Intr. before 1891. Zone III. Handsome narrow-pyramidal tree.

P. G. × *jezoensis hondoensis;* see under No. 19.

13. P. rubens Sarg. RED S. Tree to 30 m., with short and slender brs. forming a narrow-pyramidal head; bark red-brown, fissured; buds ovoid, acute, the terminal buds with pubescent subulate scales at base; brts. brown, pubescent: lvs. 1–1.5 cm. long, acute and mucronulate, lustrous dark or bright green, with about 6 stomatic lines above and 3 below: cone oblong, 3–4 cm. long, reddish brown, green or purplish green before maturity: scales obovate, rounded and entire or slightly denticulate at margin, rigid. S.S.12:t.597. B.M. 9446(c). P.I.44(c,h). Am. For. 22:705(h). (*P. rubra* (Dur.) Link, not A. Dietr., *P. australis* Small.) N. S. to the high peaks of N. C. Intr. before 1750. Zone II. A handsome tree of narrow-pyramidal habit, requiring a cool and moist climate.—**P. r. virgàta** (Rehd.) Fern. & Weatherby, f. Sparingly branched form with long brs. nearly destitute of brts. G.F.8:45(h).

14. P. mariàna (Mill.) B.S.P. BLACK S. Tree to 18 or occasionally to 30 m., with slender often pendulous brs. forming a narrow, often irregular head; bark, brts. and buds similar to *P. rubens*: lvs. 6–18 mm. long, obtusish, dull dark or bluish green, with the stomatic bands broader above than below: cones ovoid, 2–3.5 cm. long, dull grayish brown, dark purple before maturity; scales rigid, rounded and finely denticulate at the margin. S.S.12:t.596. P.I.43(c,h). Bot. Gaz. 55:452(h). (*P. nigra* (Ait.) Link, *P. brevifolia* Peck.) Lab. to Alaska, s. to Wisc. and Mich. and in the mts. to Va. Intr. 1700. Zone II. Usually a small tree of thin habit, but the following vars. are more ornamental.—**P. m. Doumétii** (Carr.) Schneid., var. Dense conical form with ascending crowded brs.—**P. m. Beissneri** Rehd., var. Similar to the preceding, but broader at the base and the lvs. of lighter bluish green. G.C.III.11:80(h).

B.H.263(h). (*P. nigra Mariana* Beiss., *P. m.* var. *Beissneriana* Rehd.)—**P. m. fastigiàta** (Carr.) Rehd., f. Columnar form with ascending brs. and short acute lvs. (*P. m. pumila* (Knight & Perry) Sudw.)—**P. m. ericoìdes** (Mast.) Rehd., f. Conical slow-growing form with very slender brts., the leading shoot glabrescent: lvs. very thin, blue-green and finely pointed. (*P. e.* Mast.) *P. m.* × *jezoensis;* see under No. 25.

15. **P. glaùca** (Moench) Voss. WHITE S. Tree to 30 m., with ascending brs. and usually pendent brts.; bark grayish, scaly; buds ovoid, obtuse, with glabrous loosely imbricated scales rounded and bifid at apex; brts. glabrous, grayish or pale brown: lvs. 8–18 mm. long, acute or acutish, slightly curved, more less bluish green, of strong disagreeable odor when bruised: cones cylindric-oblong, 3.5–5 cm. long, pale brown and glossy, green before maturity; scales suborbicular, with rounded and entire margin, thin and flexible; bracts spatulate, rounded at apex. S.S.12:t.598. P.I.42(c,h). F.E.29:81(h). S.N. 40(h). (*P. canadensis* (L.) B.S.P., not Link, *P. alba* Link.) Lab. to Alaska, s. to Mon⁀., Minn. and N. Y. Intr. 1700. Zone II. Dense pyramidal tree with light bluish green lvs.—**P. g. coerùlea** (Nels.) Rehd., f. Of dense habit and with glaucous lvs. (*P. alba c.* Carr.)—**P. g. aùrea** (Nels.) Rehd., f. With yellow lvs. (*l'. alba a.* Beiss.)—**P. g. nàna** (Jacques) Rehd., f. Dwarf dense form to 2 m. high, with ascending brs. and brts.: lvs. shorter, mostly radially spreading. (*P. alba nana* Carr.)—**P. g. parva** (Victorin) Fernald & Weatherby, f. Low depressed form with horizontally spreading brs.: lvs. crowded. G.W.38:206(h). (*P. g. f. tabuliformis* Slavin, *P. g. f. procumbens* F. Mey.)— **P. g. densàta** Bailey, var. BLACK HILLS SPRUCE. Slow growing compact tree: lvs. bright to bluish green. S. Dak. Cult. 1920.—**P. g. albertiàna** (S. Br.) Sarg., var. Tree to 50 m., of narrow pyramidal habit; buds with entire scales, slightly resinous; brts. with more prominent lf.-stalks; cones shorter, with stiffer scales; bracts shorter, narrowed at apex or acute. B.T.58. M.G.20: 117(h). S.N.206(h). (*P. a.* S. Br., *P. alba a.* Beiss., *Abies arctica* A. Murr.) Alaska and B. C. to Mont. Intr. 1904.—**P. g. cònica** Rehd., f. Dwarf form of the preceding var., of dense narrow-conical habit, with very thin, radially spreading lvs. G.C.75:107(h). B.C.C.t.27(h). N.H.17:217(h).

Sect. II. CASICTA Mayr. Lvs. quadrangular and with stomata above and below, or compressed and beneath without or with fewer lines of stomata than above: cone-scales loosely appressed before maturity, at maturity thin and flexible, usually rhombic, with erose and wavy margin.

16. **P. Engelmánni** (Parry) Engelm. ENGELMANN S. Tree to 50 m., with slender, spreading brs. in close whorls; bud brownish yellow, its scales usually revolute at apex; brts. pale brownish yellow, minutely glandular-pubescent: lvs. slender, 1.5–2.5 cm. long, acute, straight or slightly curved, usually bluish green, without resin-ducts, of disagreeable odor when bruised: cones cylindric-oblong, 3.5–7.5 cm. long, light brown, green and tinged with red before maturity; scales rhombic-oblong, narrowed and usually truncate at the erose apex. S.S.12:t.599. P.I.46(c,h). B.E.t.38(h). (*P. columbiana* Lemm.) B. C. and Alb. to Ore., Ariz. and N. Mex. Intr. 1862. Zone II. Desirable tree of dense pyramidal habit.—**P. E. glaùca** (R. Sm.) Beiss. Lvs. glaucous.—**P. E. argéntea** Beiss., var. Lvs. silvery gray. M.G.21:557(h).—**P. E. Féndleri** Henry, var. Brts. pendulous: lvs. slender, to 2.8 cm. long, with 2 bands of 4 rows of stomata above and half as many beneath.—**P. E. microphýlla** Fitschen, var. Dwarf globose form with shorter lvs.

17. **P. pungens** Engelm. COLORADO S. Tree to 30 or occasionally to 50 ın., with horizontal stout brs. in rather remote whorls; buds with brownish yellow

usually reflexed scales; brts. glabrous, bright yellowish brown: lvs. rigid, 2–3 cm. long, spiny pointed, incurved, bluish green, rarely dull green: cones cylindric-oblong, 6–10 cm. long, light brown; scales thin, flexible, rhombic-oblong, narrowed and erose at apex. S.S.12:t.600. B.E.283,t.38(h). Gng.7: 49(h). (*P. Parryana* Sarg., *Abies Menziesii* Engelm., not Lindl.) Colo. to N. Mex., Utah and Wyo. Intr. 1862. Zone II. Favorite tree for planting on lawns, particularly in its bluish and silvery white forms; for dry climates perhaps the best of all spruces.—**P. p. viridis** Reg., var. Lvs. green. (*P. commutata* Hort., not A. Murr.)—**P. p. glaùca** Reg., var. Lvs. bluish green. Gn.63:280(h). Gn.M.2:26(h).—**P. p. coerùlea** Beiss. Lvs. bluish white. G.W.1:357(h).— **P. p. argéntea** Rosenthal. Lvs. silvery white. Gt.53:493. M.G.16:178(h). (*P. p. Kosteri* Beiss., var. *Kosteriana* Hort.)—**P. p. Kosteriàna** Henry, var. With pendulous brs. and bluish lvs. (*P. p. glauca pendula* Beiss.)—**P. p. com-pácta** Rehd., f. Dwarf compact rather flat-topped form with the brs. in almost horizontal layers and with rigid dark green lvs. H.D.128,t(h). Gn.M.32:39(h). —**P. p. Hunnewelliàna** Hornibr., var. Dwarf form of dense pyramidal habit, with rather slender flexible lvs. 1.5–2 cm. long.

18. **P. likiangénsis** (Franch.) Pritz. Tree to 30 m. with horizontal brs.; bark gray, deeply furrowed; brts. pale yellow to brownish yellow or orange, more or less pubescent, rarely glabrous, with spreading yellow lf.-stalks about 1 mm. long; buds conic-ovoid, acute, resinous: lvs. compressed, 8–15 mm. long, acute or obtuse, with 2 white bands above, green beneath with bands of 1 or 2, rarely 3–4 broken rows of stomata; cones cylindric-oblong, 5–8 cm. long; scales rhombic-ovate to rhombic-oblong, thin, acutish or truncate at apex, erose and undulate at the margin. D.J.335. C.B.N.t.64. J.L.49:t.7(h). W. China. Cult. 1910. Zone (V).—**P. l. Balfouriàna** (Rehd. & Wils.) Cheng, var. Brts. densely villous: lvs. usually obtuse: cones violet-purple when young; scales narrowly rhombic-ovate. Gn.88:124(h). (*P. B.* Rehd. & Wils.) W. China. Intr. 1910.

Closely related species: **P. purpúrea** Mast. Tree to 30 m.; bark fissured into thin scaly flakes; brts. pale yellow-gray, densely pubescent: lvs. 5–10 mm. long, obtuse, much compressed, with 1–2 broken lines beneath or without: cones violet purple, 4–6 cm. long; scales rhombic-oblong. C.B.N.t.65. D.J.336. (*P. likiangensis* var. *p.* Dallim. & Jacks.) W. China. Intr. 1910. Zone (V).—**P. montígena** Mast. Tree to 30 m.; brts. pubescent: lvs. 8–15 mm. long, obtuse or acutish, beneath with inconspicuous bands of 2–3 rows of stomata each, bluish green: cones cinnamon-brown; scales rhombic-obovate, rounded at apex, slightly erose, not undulate. G.C.39:146 (excl. cones). W. China. Intr. 1908. Zone (V).

19. **P. jezoénsis** (Sieb. & Zucc.) Carr. YEDDO S. Tree to 50 m., with spreading slender brs.; bark gray, scaly, deeply fissured on old trees; buds conical, lustrous, resinous; brts. glabrous, lustrous, yellowish brown or green-ish yellow, with slightly swollen pulvini and recurved petioles: lvs. compressed, 1–2 cm. long, acute, slightly curved, slightly keeled on both sides, with white bands above, dark green and lustrous beneath: cones cylindric-oblong, 4–7.5 cm. long, light brown, green tinged with brown before maturity; scales rhombic-oblong, erose and denticulate. S.I.2:t.3(c). K.M.t.6(c). G.C.III.3:53. W.C.27:t.28,29(h). (*P. ajanensis* Fisch., *Abies Alcockiana* Veitch, partly.) Manch., Saghalin, N. Japan. Intr. 1878. Zone IV.—The typical form is not doing well in the E. States and suffers often from late frosts owing to early leafing; the var. is more satisfactory.—**P. j. hondoénsis** (Mayr) Rehd., var. Tree to 30 m.; brts. usually light reddish brown, with the pulvini much swollen: lvs. shorter, more obtuse, duller bluish green. B.M.6743(c). S.I.1: t.5(c). S.N.225,228(h). (*P. h.* Mayr, *P. ajanensis* var. *microsperma* Beiss., not Mast.) C. Japan. Intr. 1860. Zone V.

P. j. × *mariana* = **P. Mòseri** Mast. Brts. glabrous, olive-brown: lvs. quadrangular, slightly compressed, glaucous above, green beneath. Orig. before 1900.—*P. j.* × *glauca* = **P. Saaghyi** Gayer. Winter-buds resinous: lvs. triangular, glaucous above, green beneath, about 9 mm. long, pungent, spreading. Orig. about 1917.—*P. j. hondoensis* × *Glehnii* = **P. notha** Rehd. Brts. pilose, brown: lvs. with a few stomatic lines beneath: cone-scales broader, less undulate. Orig. 1894.

20. **P. sitchénsis** (Bong.) Carr. SITKA S. Tree to 40 or occasionally to 60 m., with slender horizontal brs. forming a broad-pyramidal tree while young; bark red-brown; buds conical, acutish, light brown, resinous; brts. glabrous, light brownish yellow: lvs. compressed, 1.5–2.5 cm. long, spiny-pointed, slightly keeled and silvery white above, rounded and lustrous bright green beneath: cones cylindric-oblong, 6–10 cm. long, pale yellowish or reddish brown: scales rhombic-oblong, rounded and erose at apex. S.S.12:t.602. G.C. II:25:728,729. S.N.229(h). (*Abies Menziesii* Lindl., ? *P. falcata* (Raf.) Suring.—TIDELAND S.) Alaska to Calif. Intr. 1831. Zone VI. Highly ornamental tree with handsome foliage, but it demands a cool humid climate and is not satisfactory in the E. States.—**P. s. speciòsa** Beiss. Of compact habit and slower growth with more ascending brs. and shorter more rigid lvs.

Sect. III. OMORICA Willk. Lvs. compressed, with glaucous bands above, green beneath: cone-scales closely appressed before maturity, firm, broad and usually entire or nearly so at apex.

21. **P. brachýtyla** (Franch.) Pritz. Tree to 25 m., with horizontal and ascending brs. and pendulous brts; bark grayish brown, darker, deeply fissured on old trees; buds ovoid, brown, not resinous, with obtuse firmly appressed scales; brts. yellow or orange-brown, glabrous or somewhat hairy, with short petioles: lvs. compressed, pectinately arranged below, 1–2.4 cm. long, about 1–1.5 mm. broad, obtusish or acute, white above, keeled and green beneath: cones cylindric-oblong, 6–12 cm. long, dull brown, greenish before maturity; scales broadly obovate, rounded and entire at apex. (*P. pachyclada* Patschke, *P. Sargentiana* Rehd. & Wils.) C. and W. China. Intr. 1901. Zone (V). A variable spruce of which several species were described based on unstable characters.—**P. b. rhombisquàmea** Stapf, f. Cone-scales narrowed toward the emarginate and erose apex. G.C.39:147 (fig. in upper right-hand corner). (*P. ascendens* Patschke.) W. China. Intr. 1910.—**P. b. complanàta** (Mast.) Cheng, var. Bark pale gray, separating into thin irregular plates: lvs. 1–2.5 cm. long, sharply pointed: cones brown or purple-brown before maturity; scales truncate or rounded at apex. G.C.39:147 (excl. cone in upper right corner). B.M.8969(c) and D.J.320, as *P. brachytyla*. (*P. c.* Mast.) W. China. Intr. 1903. Zone (V).

22. **P. Omórika** (Pančić) Purkyne. SERBIAN S. Tree to 30 m., with rather short spreading and ascending brs. forming a narrow-pyramidal head; buds dark brown, not resinous, the terminal bud with long subulate scales at base; brts. brown, pubescent: lvs. compressed, 8–18 mm. long, keeled on both sides, about 2 mm. wide, obtuse and mucronulate, with 2 broad white bands above, lustrous dark green beneath: cones ovoid-oblong, 3–6 cm. long, lustrous cinnamon-brown; scales suborbicular, finely denticulate. P.I.49(c,h). G.C. III.21:153. W.A.84,t.(h). E.H.1:t.28(h). (*Pinus O.* Pančić.) S. E. Eu. Intr. about 1880. Zone IV. Desirable spruce of slow growth, forming a dense narrow pyramidal tree; hardy and very satisfactory in the E. States.

23. **P. Breweriàna** S. Wats. Tree to 40 m., with spreading brs. and whip-like pendulous brts. often 2.5 m. long; buds conical, chestnut-brown; brts. reddish brown, pubescent, with long and spreading petioles: lvs. radially spreading, slightly compressed, 2–2.5 cm. long, obtuse, straight or slightly

curved, nearly flat and with white bands above, rounded and dark green below: cones cylindric-oblong, 6–12 cm. long, light orange-brown, purplish before maturity; scales obovate, entire. B.M.9543(c). S.S.12:601. G.F.3:66, 67;5:595. S.N.224(h). R.H.1922:49(h). S. Ore. and N. Calif. Intr. 1893. Zone (V). Remarkable for its whip-like brts., rare in cult.

24. **P. spinulòsa** (Griff.) Henry. Tree to 60 m., with long and slender pendulous brts.; buds ovoid, obtuse, scarcely resinous; brts. glabrous, yellow-ish gray: lvs. imperfectly radially spreading, slender, slightly compressed, 2–3.5 cm. long, acute, pungent, keeled on both sides, with 2 glaucous bands above, green below: cones cylindric-oblong, 6–10 cm. long; scales suborbicular, entire or slightly denticulate. B.M.8169(c). G.C.39:218. S.N.222(h). (*P. morindoides* Rehd.) Himal. Intr. about 1878. Zone VII? Handsome spruce of rather loose, broad-pyramidal habit.

6. **PSEUDÓLARIX** Gord. Golden Larch. Deciduous tree with horizontal whorled brs.: lvs. linear, spirally arranged and scattered on the long shoots, fascicled on the lateral spurs: fls. monoecious, terminal; staminate fls. catkin-like, slender-stalked and clustered on short spurs; female fls. solitary: cone ovoid, short-stalked, with ovate-lanceolate scales separating from the axis at maturity and with lanceolate bracts about half as long as scales; seeds 2 under each scale, with membranous wings nearly as long as the scale; cotyledons 5–6. (Greek *pseudos,* false, and *larix.*) Syn. *Laricopsis* Kent.—One species in China.

P. amàbilis (Nels.) Rehd. Tree to 40 m., with reddish brown bark, fissured into narrow scales: lvs. linear, 3–7 cm. long, 2.5–3.5 mm. broad, acuminate, soft, light green, bluish beneath: male fls. yellow, about 6 mm. long: cones ovoid, reddish brown, 6–7.5 cm. long and 4–5 cm. across; scales cordate at base, emarginate at apex, woody; seeds about 8 mm. long. B.M.8176(c). G.C.II.19:88. Gn.29:397(h). B.E.t.39(h). (*P. Kaempferi* Gord., *P. Fortunei* Mayr, *Larix a.* Nelson, *L. Kaempferi* Carr., *Abies Kaempferi* Lindl., in part.) E. China. Intr. 1854. Zone V. Tree of broad-pyramidal habit with light green feathery foliage turning bright yellow in fall; it dislikes limestone soil.

7. **LÁRIX** Mill. Larch. Deciduous trees with horizontal brs.; bark thick, scaly; buds small, subglobose, with imbricate scales, the inner ones accrescent: lvs. spirally arranged and remote on the long shoots, densely clustered on the lateral short spurs, linear, flattened, rarely nearly quad-rangular: fls. monoecious, solitary, terminal; male fls. globose to oblong, stalked or sessile, yellow, consisting of numerous short-stalked spirally ar-ranged anthers; female fls. subglobose, consisting of few or many 2-ovuled scales borne in the axils of larger usually scarlet bracts: cone subglobose to oblong; scales suborbicular to oblong, persistent on the axis, maturing the first year; seeds 2 under each scale, nearly triangular, with large membranous wing; cotyledons usually 6. (The ancient Latin name.) About 10 species in the cooler regions of the n. hemisphere, chiefly in the mts.; in Asia s. to the Himal.

A. Bracts conspicuous, exceeding the scales.
  B. Lvs. keeled on both sides...1. *L. Potaninii*
  BB. Lvs. rounded above, keeled only below...............................2. *L. occidentalis*
AA. Bracts shorter than scales, usually concealed: lvs. flat or rounded above.
  B. Cone-scales recurved at apex: lvs. with 2 conspicuous white bands below.
                                                        3. *L. leptolepis*
  BB. Cone-scales straight or incurved at apex: lvs. very narrow, without white bands.
    C. Cone-scales puberulous or tomentulose outside, 30–50.
      D. Cone-scales not incurved at apex, straight; bracts about half as long as scale.
                                                            4. *L. decidua*

DD. Cone-scales slightly incurved at apex, longitudinally convex; bracts ⅓ as long as scale ....5. *L. sibirica*
  CC. Cone-scales glabrous outside, lustrous, striate, 12–40.
    D. Brts. usually pubescent, reddish brown or yellowish: lvs. exceeding 3 cm.: cones 1.5–3 cm. long, with 20–40 scales....................................6. *L. Gmelini*
    DD. Brts. glabrous, brown, often glaucous: lvs. to 3 cm. long: cones about 1.5 cm. long, with 12–15 scales...7. *L. laricina*

1. L. **Potanìnii** Batal. CHINESE L. Tree to 30 m., with gray or grayish brown bark and rather short horizontal brs.; brts. pendulous, glabrous, lustrous, orange-brown or reddish brown, the buds of similar color but darker: lvs. compressed, slender, 1.5–3 cm. long, acute, grayish green, with stomatic bands on both sides each of 1 or 2 rows: cones ovoid-oblong, 3–4.5 cm. long, at maturity violet-purple changing to grayish brown; scales suborbicular, slightly incurved, entire; bracts long-acuminate, exserted, upright, purple. G.C.39:178. I.S.t.2 S.N.196(h). (*L. chinensis* Beiss., *L. thibetica* Franch.) W. China. Intr. 1904. Zone V.

Related species: L. **Masteriàna** Rehd. & Wils. Brts. pale yellowish brown, slightly pubescent when young: lvs. bright green, with 2 pale stomatic bands beneath: cone pale brown, with long acuminate purple bracts exserted and reflexed. W. China. Intr. 1908.—L. **Lyállii** Parl. Tree to 25 m., with remote long brs.; brts. stout, brown-tomentose: lvs. 4-angled, rigid, 2.5–3.5 cm. long: cones ovoid-oblong, 3.5–5 cm. long; scales pubescent, spreading at maturity and finally reflexed; bracts exserted, upright. S.S.12:t.595. S.N.(198(h). High mts. of B. C. and Alb. to Wash. and Mont. Intr. 1904, but not successful in cult.

2. L. **occidentàlis** Nutt. WESTERN L. Tree to 50 m., occasionally to 80 m., with short horizontal or sometimes elongated brs.; bark dark-colored, cinnamon-red on old trunks; buds dark, chestnut-brown; brts. pubescent when young, soon glabrous, orange-brown: lvs. triangular, 2.5–4 cm. long, rigid, sharply pointed, rounded above, keeled below, pale green: cones ovoid-oblong, 2.5–3.5 cm. long, with numerous suborbicular nearly entire scales tomentulose outside below the middle, spreading at maturity; bracts long-acuminate, exserted, upright. B.M.8253(c). S.S.12:t.594. M.D.1914:197,t(h). B. C. to Mont. and Ore. Intr. 1881. Zone V.

Related species: L. **Griffithii** Hook f. Tree to 20 m., with pendulous brs.; brts. dull reddish brown: lvs. flat above, obtuse: cones oblong, 7–10 cm. long; bracts lanceolate, reflexed. B.M.8181(c). G.C.41:130(h). Gn.82:445(h). (*L. Griffithiana* Carr.) Himal., S. W. China. Intr. 1848. Zone VII?

3. L. **leptólepis** (Sieb. & Zucc) Gord. JAPANESE L. Tree to 30 m., with short horizontal brs.; bark scaling off in narrow strips leaving red scars; brts. yellowish or reddish brown and usually bloomy, glabrous or slightly pubescent: lvs. flattened, 1.5–3.5 cm. long, rather broad, obtuse, light or bluish green, white bands below each with 5 rows of stomata: cones ovoid, 1.5–3.5 cm. long, with numerous truncate or slightly emarginate scales; bracts concealed. S.I. 1:t.2(c). W.C.t.15,16(h). (*L. Kaempferi* Sarg., not Carr., *L. japonica* Carr.) Japan. Intr. 1861. Zone IV. One of the handsomest and most rapidly growing larches.—The dwarf form of the high mts. of Japan (*L. K.* var. *minor* Sarg.) reverts under cult. to the normal form.

L. l. × *decidua* = L. **eurólepis** Henry. Differs from *L. leptolepis* chiefly in the less bloomy brts. yellow or grayish yellow the second year and the shorter and narrower lvs. with fewer rows of stomata. Proc. Irish Acad. 35B:t.11. C.B.N.51. Trans. Scott. Arb. Soc. 29:t.15(h). (*L. Henryana* Rehd., *L. hybrida* Farquhar, not Schroed.) Orig. about 1900. *L. l.* × *sibirica* = L. **marschlínsii** Coaz. Lvs. bluish green, to 3.5 cm. long: cones subglobose to ovoid; scales not recurved at apex. Orig. 1901.

4. L. **decídua** Mill. EUROPEAN L. Tree to 35 m., with a pyramidal, later often irregular head; bark dark grayish brown; brts. slender, glabrous, yellowish: lvs. flattened, 2–3 cm. long, keeled below, soft, bright green: female

fls. purple: cones ovoid, 2–3.5 cm. long, with 40–50 suborbicular scales, loosely appressed at maturity, the uppermost closing the apex; wings of seed extending to the upper margin of the scale. H.W.1:108–12,t(c). F.E.29:117(h). M.G.23:316,317(h). (*L. europaea* DC., *L. Larix* Karst.) N. and C. Eu. Long cult. Zone II.—**L. d. péndula** (Laws.) Henk. & Hochst. With pendulous brs. Gt.20:t.684,f.5(h). G.C.III.3:430,t(h). (*L. europaea* var. *pendulina* Reg., *L. europaea* var. *p.* Laws.)—**L. d. polònica** (Racib.) Ostenf. & Syrach, var. With smaller cones resembling those of *L. sibirica;* scales more rounded and less emarginate. Poland. Cult. 1910.

5. **L. sibírica** Ledeb. Siberian L. Tree to 40 m., with straight stem and rather short ascending brs.; brts. light yellowish gray; buds brown, at base very dark to nearly black: lvs. similar to those of the preceding species, 2.5–3.5 cm. long: female fls. usually green, sometimes whitish or brownish: cones ovoid, usually 3.5 cm. long, with about 30 scales truncate or rounded and entire at the margin, finely striate and tomentulose on the back, half-spreading at maturity; seed-wings not extending to the upper margin of the scale. Gt.20:t.684,f.1–2. G.W.18:390(h). S.N.46(h). (*L. decidua* var. *s.* Reg., var. *rossica* Henk. & Hochst.) N. E. Russia to Siberia. Intr. 1806. Zone II.

6. **L. Gmelíni** (Rupr.) Litvin. Dahurian L. Tree to 30 m., with rather long horizontal brs. fairly regular on young, but usually irregular on old trees and wide-spreading; brts. yellowish or reddish, usually pubescent; buds yellowish brown, darker or nearly black at base: lvs. flattened, about 3 cm. long, bright green: cones ovoid, 2–2.5 cm. long, with about 20 scales or more, thin, truncate or emarginate; bracts rounded at apex, with inconspicuous mucro. Gt.20:t.684,f.9,10. I.S.t.2. M.D.1914:191(h). (*L. dahurica* Turcz., *L. Cajanderi* Mayr.) E. Siberia. Intr. 1827. Zone II.—**L. G. japónica** (Reg.) Pilger, var. Young brts. bluish red, often gloomy, pubescent, sometimes pale. S.I.2: t.1(c). K.M.t.7(c). W.C.t.17,18(h). G.W.6:499(h). (*L. kurilensis* Mayr, *L. kamtchatica* Carr.) Saghalin, Kurile Isls. Intr. 1888. Zone II.—**L. G. Príncipis-Rupréchtii** (Mayr) Pilger, var. Cones larger, to 3.5 cm. long, with 30–40 scales truncate at apex; bracts at least the lower ones more than half as long as the scales. Mayr, Fremdl. Wald & Parkb. 309. B.D.1923: t.21(h). N. China, Korea. Intr. 1903. Zone IV.—**L. G. olgénsis** (Henry) Ostenf. & Syrach, var. Brts. strongly pilose: lvs. 1–2 cm. long; cones larger with broader scales. (*L. olgensis* Henry, *L. koreensis* Rafn.) E. Manch. Cult. 1920.

7. **L. larícina** (Duroi) K. Koch. American L. Tree to 20 m., with horizontal short brs. forming a narrow-pyramidal head; bark reddish brown; brts. glabrous, reddish yellow, usually bloomy, buds reddish brown: lvs. 2.5–3.5 cm. long, obtuse, light bluish green: cone globose-ovoid, 1.5–2 cm. long, with 12–15 suborbicular scales glabrous and striate outside, minutely crenulate and bevelled at the margin; bracts ¼ as long as scale. S.S.12:t.593. Em. 106,t(c). (*L. americana* Michx., *L. microcarpa* Desf., *L. alaskensis* W. F. Wight.—Tamarack, Hackmatack.) Alaska and Can. s. to Minn., Ill. and Pa. Intr. 1737. Zone I.

L. l. × *decidua* = **L. péndula** Salisb. It differs from *L. laricina* chiefly in its larger cones about 2.5 cm. long, with 20–30 scales pubescent below the middle: brts. usually pink, rarely glaucous. Lambert, Pinus t.36(c). G.C.58:178(h). (*L. americana* var. *p.* Loud.) Orig. before 1800. It has been confused with *L. laricina* and with *L. dahurica*.

8. **CÉDRUS** Trew. Cedar. Tall evergreen trees with spreading irregularly arranged brs.; bark dark gray, smooth on young, fissured and scaly

on old trees; buds minute, ovoid, with few scales: lvs. spirally arranged and scattered on the long shoots, densely fascicled on the spurs, acicular, usually triangular, rigid, pointed: fls. monoecious, terminal, solitary; staminate fls. cylindric, upright, about 5 cm. long; female fls. ovoid, purplish, 1–1.5 cm. long, consisting of numerous suborbicular, 2-ovuled scales subtended by small included bracts: cone upright, ovoid to ellipsoid-oblong, with numerous closely appressed very broad scales tomentose outside, maturing the second or third year: seeds irregularly triangular, with a membranous broad wing: cotyledons 9–10. (*Kedros* is the ancient Greek name of a resinous tree.)—Four closely related species sometimes considered races of one species.

A. Leading shoot stiff, upright or spreading; brts. usually not pendulous: cones truncate, often concave at apex.
  B. Brts. short-pubescent: lvs. usually less than 2.5 cm. long: cone 5–7 cm. long.
      1. *C. atlantica*
  BB. Brts. glabrous or slightly pubescent: lvs. usually 2.5–3 cm. long: cone 8–10 cm. long.
      2. *C. libani*
AA. Leading shoot and brts. pendulous, densely pubescent: lvs. to 5 cm. long: cones rounded at apex ....3. *C. Deodara*

1. **C. atlántica** Manetti. ATLAS C. Tree to 40 m., with upright leading shoot: lvs. bluish green: cone 5–7 cm. long, about 4 cm. across; scales 3.5 cm. wide, light brown. C.B.1:69. D.J.t.10(h). G.F.9:417(h). B.D.1925:69,t.(h). (*C. Libani* var. *a.* Hook. f.) N. Afr. Intr. before 1840. Zone VI.—**C. A. glaùca** Carr. Lvs. glaucous. G.C.76:227,t. Gg.8:275(h). Gs.1:198(h).—**C. A. argéntea** Murr., var. Lvs. nearly silvery-white; scarcely different from the preceding.—**C. A. péndula** Carr. Form with pendulous brs. and brts., sometimes nearly columnar in outline. G.C.66:287(h). M.D.1932:t.54(h).—**C. A. fastigiàta** Carr. Form of narrow-pyramidal or nearly columnar habit with ascending or upright brs. R.H.1890:32(h).

2. **C. libani** Loud. CEDAR OF LEBANON. Tree to 40 m., with upright or spreading leading shoot: lvs. dark or bright green: cones 8–10 cm. long, 4–6 cm. across, brown; scales about 5 cm. wide. B.C.1:71. B.E.294.t.40(h). G.F.2: 149;8:335(h). G.C.34:265;71:111,233(h). (*C. libanotica* Link, *C. libanitica* (Trew) Pilger, *C. Cedrus* Huth.) Asia Minor, Syria. Intr. 1638. Zone V.— Beautiful and stately tree of characteristic appearance; also of interest for its scriptural and historical associations.—**C. l. glaùca** Carr. Lvs. bluish white. (*C. Libani argentea* Gord.)—**C. l. nàna** Loud., var. Dwarf compact, usually broad-pyramidal form, with thinner lvs. 1–2 cm. long.—**C. l. péndula** Carr. Brs. pendulous: lvs. slender and rather long. (*C. Libani* var. *Sargenti pendula* Hornibro.)

Closely related species: **C. brevifòlia** (Hook. f.) Henry, differing chiefly in the much shorter glaucous lvs. usually 5–6 mm. long and the smaller cones, about 7 cm. long and 4 cm. wide and with a short umbo in the apical depression. B.N.328. C.B.N.t.42. R.H.1920:85(h). (*C. Libani* var. *b.* Hook. f.) Cyprus. Intr. 1881. Zone VII?

3. **C. Deodàra** (Roxb.) Loud. DEODAR C. Tree to 50 m.: lvs. dark bluish green, 2.5–5 cm. long, as high as broad: cones 7–10 cm. long, 5–6 cm. across, reddish brown; scales 5–6 cm. wide, less tomentose. C.B.1:70. B.E.t.41(h). G.C.III.25:139; 34:400(h). (*C. Libani* var. *D.* Hook. f.) Himal. Intr. 1831. Zone VII? Graceful tree of pyramidal outline.—**C. D. argéntea** Nelson. Lvs. bluish or silvery white.—**C. D. aùrea** Nelson. Lvs. yellow. G.W.11:87 (h).—**C. D. robústa** Carr. With stouter brs. and more rigid lvs. about 5 cm. long.

9. **PÌNUS** L. PINE. Evergreen trees with whorled spreading brs., rarely shrubby; bark furrowed or scaly; buds conspicuous, with numerous imbricated

scales: lvs. of 2 kinds, the primary lvs. spirally arranged and usually reduced to small scarious bracts bearing in their axils the acicular, semiterete or triangular secondary lvs. borne on an undeveloped brt. in clusters of from 2–5, rarely as many as 8 or reduced to 1, surrounded at base by sheaths of 8–12 bud-scales; only on young seedling plants and occasionally on shoots from the old wood the primary lvs. are subulate and green: fls. monoecious, the male fls. axillary, clustered at the base of the young shoot, catkin-like, yellow, orange or scarlet, composed of numerous spirally arranged 2-celled anthers; female fls. lateral or subterminal, consisting of numerous spirally arranged 2-ovuled scales, each subtended by a small bract: cone subglobose to cylindric, symmetrical or oblique, with woody scales closely appressed before maturity. The apex of the scales usually much thickened and the exposed part (apophysis) usually rhombic in outline, transversely keeled and in the middle usually with a prominent boss or umbo mostly terminated by a spine or prickle; in some species the apex of the scale is flat and bears the spineless umbo at the end; seeds usually with long articulate or adnate wing, rarely with short wing or wingless: cotyledons 4–15. (The ancient Latin name of the tree.) About 80 species distributed throughout the n. hemisphere from the arctic circle to Guatemala, to the W. Indies, N. Af. and the Malayan Archipelago.

The most important characters in the grouping of the species are the shape of the cone-scales and the structure of the lvs. which contain either one or 2 vascular bundles and usually 2 or more resin ducts which are either marginal (situated beneath the epidermis) or medial (enclosed by the tissue of the lf.) or internal (close to the fibrovascular bundle); in some species the lvs. have resin-ducts of 2 kinds. The fibrovascular bundles and the resin-ducts can easily be seen with a fairly strong lens in thin cross-sections made with a sharp razor from the middle of the lf. and placed on a glass plate. The shoot which develops in spring (spring-shoot) from the terminal winter-bud produces in most species only one internode with one whorl of brts. and is therefore called uninodal and bears the cones at the end of the shoot (subterminal), while in other species the spring-shoot produces 2 or more, often incomplete whorls of brts. (multinodal shoots) and bears the cones partly in the middle of the shoot (lateral); occasionally summer-shoots appear at the end of uninodal shoots and change it to an incompletely multinodal shoot.

Sheaths of lf.-clusters deciduous; base of bracts not decurrent; lvs. with 1 fibrovascular bundle.
  A. Lvs. 5 in 1 fascicle.
    B. Lvs. serrulate.
      C. Brts. pubescent or tomentose.
        D. Lvs. without conspicuous white lines on back, dark green.
          E. Brts. tomentose: cone indehiscent.
            F. Lvs. bright green: cones 9–14 cm. long, with often recurved apophyses.
                1. *P. koraiensis*
            FF. Lvs. dark green: cone 5–8 cm. long, with appressed apophyses..2. *P. Cembra*
          EE. Brts. pubescent: cone dehiscent.
            F. Bark of trunk smooth: cone 5–10 cm. long, with thickened convex scales: lvs. 2–8 cm. long...........7. *P. parviflora*
            FF. Bark of trunk fissured: cones 12–25 cm. long, with thin appressed scales: lvs. 4–10 cm. long...........10. *P. monticola*
        DD. Lvs. with conspicuous white lines on back: cone 25–50 cm. long..6. *P. Lambertiana*
      CC. Brts. glabrous or only slightly pubescent at first.
        D. Brts. bloomy: lvs. 12–20 cm. long....................9. *P. Griffithii*
        DD. Brts. not bloomy: lvs. 7–12 cm. long.
          E. Winter-buds cylindric, chestnut-brown: cone-scales much thickened; seed wingless ....5. *P. Armandi*
          EE. Winter-buds ovoid; cone-scales thin; seeds winged.
            F. Cone-scales convex, thickish: tree with ascending brs..........8. *P. Peuce*
            FF. Cone-scales thin, flat: trees with horizontal brs.
              G. Brts. pubescent at first: lvs. stiff: cones usually 12–25 cm. long.
                10. *P. monticola*
              GG. Brts. glabrous or slightly puberulous: lvs. slender: cones usually 5–12 cm. long ....11. *P. Strobus*
  BB. Lvs. entire: cones short-stalked.
      C. Sheaths deciduous the first year: lvs. with stomatic lines on back, rarely without, 3–7 cm. long.

35

    D. Cones indehiscent, 5–7 cm. long: brts. glabrous or puberulous: lvs. stout.
                                                      3. *P. albicaulis*
      DD. Cones dehiscent, 6–25 cm. long: brts. puberulous when young: lvs. slender, 1 mm.
          thick ....4. *P. flexilis*
    cc. Sheaths deciduous the 2d or 3d year: lvs. without stomatic lines on back, 2–4 cm.
      long.
        D. Brts. dark orange-brown, puberulous: cone-scales short-mucronate.
                                              14. *P. Balfouriana*
        DD. Brts. light orange, glabrous or nearly so: cone-scales aristate: lvs. resin-dotted.
                                              15. *P. aristata*

AA. Lvs. 1–4.
  B. Lvs. entire, 1–4, 2–5 cm. long.... ....12. *P. cembroides*
  BB. Lvs. serrulate, 3, 5–10 cm. long...13. *P. Bungeana*

Sheaths of lf.-clusters persistent; base of bracts decurrent: lvs. with 2 fibrovascular bundles, serrulate.

A. Lvs. usually 3, rarely 4 or 5 (partly 2 in a var. of No. 24 and in No. 38).
  B. Brts. bloomy: lvs. 12–30 cm. long: cones 15–35 cm. long.
    c. Lvs. bluish green.
      D. Lvs. stiff, 12–18 cm. long: seed-wing membranous, much longer than seed.
                                              25. *P. Jeffreyi*
      DD. Lvs. slender, 20–30 cm. long: seed with thick wing shorter than seed.
                                            39. *P. Sabiniana*
    cc. Lvs. dark green, stiff, 15–30 cm. long: seed-wing thick, longer than seed.
                                            40. *P. Coulteri*

  BB. Brts. not bloomy (sometimes slightly so in No. 27).
    c. Lvs. with internal resin-ducts, 20–45 cm. long: buds large, with white-fringed scales,
      not resinous ....26. *P. palustris*
    cc. Lvs. with medial or marginal resin-ducts: buds usually brown.
      D. Lvs. 15–30 cm. long: cones deciduous, prickly.
        E. Buds ovoid, acuminate, resinous: lvs. dark or yellow green, 2–5.24. *P. ponderosa*
        EE. Buds oblong-ovoid, not or slightly resinous: lvs. bluish green, 3....27. *P. Taeda*
      DD. Lvs. 7–18 cm. long: cone persistent.
        E. Lvs. dark green: tips of bud-scales slightly spreading: cone symmetrical.
                                             32. *P. rigida*
        EE. Lvs. bright or bluish green, slender: tips of bud-scales appressed: cone oblique.
          F. Bark on upper part of trunk and on brs. smooth: prickles of cone-scales stout.
                                      37. *P. attenuata*
          FF. Bark rough: lvs. sometimes 2: prickles of cone-scales minute....38. *P. radiata*
AA. Lvs. 2 (partly 3 in Nos. 23, 24, 28, 29, 33).
  B. Spring-shoots uninodal, with only 1 whorl of brts.
    c. Bark of 2-year-old brts. divided into sharply defined plates (the decurrent base of
      the bracts), each peeling off as a whole.
      D. Brts. grayish white: winter-buds not resinous...................20. *P. Heldreichii*
      DD. Brts. orange to brown or grayish yellow.
        E. Winter-buds brown.
          F. Young brts. not bloomy: winter-buds resinous.
            G. Lvs. with medial resin-ducts, not breaking when bent: conelet mucronate;
              cone falling off as a whole.
              H. Lvs. always 2: cone with obtuse umbo.......................21. *P. nigra*
              HH. Lvs. often 3: cones with prickly umbo............24. *P. ponderosa var.*
            GG. Lvs. with marginal resin-ducts on the flat surface, the others often medial,
             breaking when bent: conelet mutic; cone leaving a few basal scales on the
             stem ....16. *P. resinosa*
         FF. Young brts. bloomy: winter-buds not resinous: lvs. sometimes 3.
                                           23. *P. tabulaeformis*
        EE. Winter-buds grayish white, cylindric-oblong, with conspicuously fimbriate
          scales ....22. *P. Thunbergii*
    cc. Bark of 2- to 4-year-old brts. not conspicuously divided into plates, peeling off
      rather irregularly.
      D. Lvs. 2–8 cm. long: cone deciduous: winter-buds resinous.
        E. Lvs. bluish or grayish green: cone-scales with obtuse umbo: usually a tree.
                                        18. *P. sylvestris*
        EE. Lvs. bright green: cone with a more or less prickly umbo: usually a shrub.
                                        19. *P. Mugo*
      DD. Lvs. 7–25 cm. long: winter-buds not resinous.
        E. Young brts. bloomy: lvs. slender, bright green: cone deciduous..17. *P. densiflora*
        EE. Young brts. not bloomy: cones persistent.
          F. Lvs. with marginal resin-ducts, 6–18 cm. long: bark formation late.
                                        29. *P. halepensis*
         FF. Lvs. with medial or internal resin-ducts, 12–25 cm. long: bark formation
          early ....30. *P. Pinaster*
  BB. Spring-shoots multinodal, with more than one whorl of brts.
    c. Young brts. glaucous: resin-ducts medial.
      D. Winter-buds not, or little, resinous: lvs. 7–12 cm. long, sometimes 3: cones decidu-
      ous ....28. *P. echinata*
      DD. Winter-buds resinous: lvs. 4–8 cm. long: cones persistent........31. *P. virginiana*

cc. Young brts. not glaucous (sometimes slightly so in No. 30): cones persistent.
  D. Resin-ducts marginal: lvs. 7–15 cm. long: umbo obtuse...........29. *P. halepensis*
  DD. Resin-ducts medial.
    E. Lvs. 1–7 cm. long.
    F. Lvs. 1–3.5 cm. long: cone not prickly, curved................34. *P. Banksiana*
    FF. Lvs. 3–7 cm. long: cone prickly.
      G. Lvs. slightly twisted, with 2–5 resin ducts: cone symmetrical.
        33. *P. pungens*
      GG. Lvs. strongly twisted, with 1–2 resin-ducts: cone unsymmetrical.
        35. *P. contorta*
    EE. Lvs. 10–25 cm. long.
    F. Winter-buds not resinous: lvš. 12–25 cm. long: cone symmetrical.
      30. *P. Pinaster*
    FF. Winter-buds resinous: lvs. 10–15 cm. long: cones unsymmetrical.
      36. *P. muricata*

Subgen. I. HAPLOXYLON Koehne. SOFT PINES. Lvs. with one fibrovascular bundle, entire or serrulate, usually without stomata on back: bracts of lf.-fascicles not decurrent; sheaths deciduous: wood soft, with little resin.

Sect. I. CEMBRA. Umbo of cone-scales terminal; scales of young cone unarmed: lvs. in fascicles of 5.

Ser. 1. *Cembrae.* Cone indehiscent; seed wingless.

1. **P. koraiénsis** Sieb. & Zucc. KOREAN P. Pyramidal tree to 30 m.; bark scaly, gray-brown or gray; brts. with yellow-brown tomentum: buds oblong-ovoid, dark chestnut-brown: lvs. dark green, straight, 6–12 cm. long, serrulate; resin-ducts medial: cones short-stalked, 9–14 cm. long, conic-ovoid or conic-oblong, yellow-brown; scales with recurved obtuse apex. S.Z.2:t.116(c). S.I.1:t.2(c). F.E.18:333;25:35(h). W.C.t.6,7(h). (*P. mandshurica* Rupr.) Japan, Korea. Intr. 1861. Zone III. Hardy pine of slow growth and dense habit.

2. **P. Cembra** L. SWISS STONE P. Tree to 25 or occasionally to 40 m., with usually short brs. forming a narrow-pyramidal, in old age often broad round-topped head; brts. densely brown-tomentose; buds globose-ovoid, acuminate: lvs. straight, 5–12 cm. long, serrulate, dark green; resin-ducts medial: cones short-stalked, ovoid, 5–8 cm. long, light brown; scales often slightly reflexed at apex. H.W.1:174–7,t.8(c). B.S.2:176,t(h). E.H.5:t.275(h). Alps of C. Eu., N. E. Russia and N. Asia. Long cult. Zone IV. Handsome hardy Pine of slow growth and dense habit.—**P. C. columnàris** Beiss. Of columnar habit. M.G.32:34(h). G.W.2:209(h).—**P. C. sibìrica** Loud., var. Taller tree with shorter lvs. and larger cones. S.N.48, 51(h). (*P. s.* Mayr.) N. E. Russia to Siberia.

Closely related species: **P. pùmila** Reg. Shrub to 3 m., with prostrate stems: lvs. 4–7 cm. long, obscurely serrulate, with usually marginal resin-ducts: cones ovoid, 3–4.5 cm. long. S.I.2:t.1(c). K.M.t.9(c). G.C.46:193. W.C.t.8(h). N. E. Siberia, Japan. Intr. 1817. Zone III?

3. **P. albicaùlis** Engelm. WHITE-BARK P. Tree to 10, rarely to 20 m., with widespreading brs., sometimes shrubby; brts. puberulous or glabrous, brown or orange, tough and flexible: lvs. rigid, 4–7 cm. long, with stomata on back, entire: cone subsessile, ovoid or globose-ovoid, 5–7 cm. long, dull purple, finally brown; scales much thickened, often with stout-pointed umbo; seeds 8–12 mm. long. S.S.11:t.548. G.C.II.24:9. E.H.5:t.276(h). B. C. to Calif. and Wyo. Intr. 1852. Zone III.

Ser. 2. *Flexiles.* Cone dehiscent; seed wingless.

4. **P. fléxilis** James. LIMBER P. Tree to 15 or 25 m., narrow-pyramidal while young, broad and round-topped in old age; brts. puberulous at first, soon glabrous, tough and pliant; buds broad-ovoid, pointed: lvs. slender, 3–9 cm. long, with stomata on back, usually entire: cone short-stalked, ovoid to cylindric-ovoid, 7–15 cm. long, yellowish to light brown, lustrous; scales rounded at apex, with an obtuse dark umbo, the lower ones elongated and re-

flexed. B.M.8467(c). S.S.11:t.546,547. F.E.29:47(h). Alb. to Calif., w. to Mont. and w. Texas. Intr. 1861. Zone IV.

5. **P. Armándi** Franch. Tree to 20 m., with widespreading horizontal brs.; brts. glabrous; buds cylindric, chestnut-brown: lvs. slender, 8–15 cm. long, serrulate, bright green, without stomata on back: cones peduncled, conic-oblong, 10–20 cm. long, yellowish brown; scales much thickened, rounded at apex or tapering to an acute point, sometimes slightly recurved, umbo small, obtuse: seed ovoid, compressed, with a sharp edge all around. B.M.8347(c). G.C.33:34 (as *P. koraiensis*), 66. Gn. 85:181. R.H.1910:425(h). J.L.48:f.45 (h). (*P. scipioniformis* Mast., *P. Mastersiana* Hayata.) C. and W. China, Formosa, Korea. Intr. 1895. Zone V. Handsome pine of rather loose habit, with widespreading brs.

Ser. 3. *Strobi.* Cone dehiscent; seed with long adnate wing.

6. **P. Lambertiàna** Dougl. SUGAR P. Tree to 60 m., rarely taller, with spreading, somewhat pendulous brs. forming an open narrow pyramid; brts. brown, pubescent: buds oblong-obovate, apiculate: lvs. stout, 7–10 cm. long, sharply pointed, serrulate, with white lines on back: cones stalked, pendent, cylindric, 30–50 cm. long, light brown, lustrous; scales with rounded apex or tapering to a blunt slightly reflexed tip; seed about 1 cm. long, dark brown. S.S.11:t.542–3. E.H.5:t.272(h). M.G.20:126(h). Ore. to L. Calif. Intr. 1827. Zone (V).

The related **P. Ayacahuite** Ehrenb. is probably not hardy within our area. Tree to 40 m.; brts. glabrous or pubescent: lvs. 10–20 cm. long; cones 25–45 cm. long; scales elongated reflexed or revolute at apex. Shaw, Pines Mex. t.4. Mex. Intr. 1840.

7. **P. parviflòra** Sieb. & Zucc. JAPANESE WHITE P. Tree to 30 m., with slender brs., of dense pyramidal habit; bark of young trees smooth, of older trees fissured into thin flaky scales, red-brown beneath; brts. greenish brown, puberulous or glabrous; buds ovoid, scarcely resinous, the scales free at the tips: lvs. slender, 2–8 cm. long, serrulate, bluish green, conspicuously whitened on the ventral surface: cones ovoid to oblong-ovoid, 5–10 cm. long, nearly sessile; scales abruptly convex near the apex or irregularly warped, the umbo confluent with the thin margin; seed about 1 cm. long, with short broad wing. S.Z.2:t.115(c). K.M.t.8(c). A.G.14:212(h). W.C.t.9,10(h). (*P. pentaphylla* Mayr.) Japan. Intr. 1861. Zone V. As usually cult. it is grafted and forms a low tree with widespreading brs., the short usually twisted lvs forming brush-like tufts at the end of the brts. and the rather small ovoid cones usually profusely produced; the wild form has been distinguished as var. *pentaphylla* Henry.—**P. p. glauca** Beiss. has pale bluish green lvs.

8. **P. Peùce** Griseb. MACEDONIAN P. Tree to 20 m., with short ascending brs. forming a narrow dense pyramid; bark grayish brown, finally fissured into small plates; brts. greenish, glabrous; buds ovoid: lvs. straight, 7–10 cm. long, serrulate: cones short-stalked, sub-cylindric, 8–15 cm. long, tawny yellow; scales abruptly and prominently convex below the apex, with the umbo pressed against the scale beneath; seed small, with long wing. P.I.99(c,h). B.J.59:t.13(h). B.N.345(h). (*P. excelsa* var. *p.* Beiss.) Balkan Mts. Intr. 1863. Zone IV. Ornamental Pine of dense narrow-pyramidal habit and of slow growth.

9. **P. Griffíthii** McClelland. HIMALAYAN P. Tree to 50 cm., of broad and open pyramidal habit; bark grayish brown, fissured into small plates; brts. bloomy, glabrous; buds cylindric-obovate, acute, very resinous: lvs. slender, drooping, 10–18 cm. long, serrulate, grayish or bluish green: cones cylindric,

15–25 cm. long, tawny-yellow, on stalks 2–5 cm. long, the apophysis prominently convex, its umbo pressed against the scale beneath. P.I.69(c,h). F.E. 13:t.8(h). Gn.M.6:290(h). (*P. excelsa* Wall., not Lam., *P. nepalensis* De Chambray, not Forbes, *P. Wallichii* A. B. Jacks.) Himal., w. to Afghan. Intr. 1827. Zone (V). Handsome pine with widespreading brs. and drooping lvs.

    P. G. × *Ayacahuite* = **P. Holfordiàna** A. B. Jacks. Brts. usually hairy: cones broader; scales acute or acutish. C.B.N.t.68,69. Cult. 1906.—*P. G.* × *Strobus* = **P. Schwerìnii** Fitschen. Brts. bloomy, short-pilose: lvs. slender, pendulous, 8–13.5 cm. long: cones 8–15 cm. long, on stalk 2–2.5 cm. long; scales convex on back. Orig. about 1905.

    10. **P. montícola** Lamb. MOUNTAIN WHITE P. Tree to 30 or occasionally to 50 m., with slender brs. forming a narrow open pyramid; bark on old trees deeply divided into scaly plates, purplish; brts. yellowish or reddish brown, puberulous; buds ovoid, acute: lvs. stiff, 4–10 cm. long, serrulate, often slightly so, without or with few stomata on the back, bluish green: cones short-stalked, cylindric, tapering, sometimes curved, 10–25 cm. long, yellowish brown, their phyllotaxis 8/21; apophysis thin, apex sometimes slightly prolonged and reflexed. P.I.100(c,h). S.S.11:t.540–1. F.E.31:293(h). S.N.239(h). B. C. to Idaho and Calif. Intr. 1851. Zone V. Similar to the following species, but of narrower and denser habit.

    11. **P. Stróbus** L. WHITE P. Tree to 30 or occasionally 50 m., with a symmetrical pyramidal head, in old age usually broad and often very picturesque; bark thick, deeply fissured into broad scaly ridges, purplish; brts. greenish or light greenish brown, pubescent at first, soon glabrous; buds ovoid, acuminate, slightly resinous: lvs. slender, soft, 6–14 cm. long, serrulate, bluish green: cones narrow-cylindric, often curved, 8–20 cm. long, brown, their phyllotaxis 5/13; apophysis thin. H.W.1:183–5,t.9(c). S.S.11:t.538–9. Am. For. 19:613; 22:387; 26:223(h). Gn.M.33:352(h). (*Strobus S.* Small, *Leucopitys S.* Nieuwl.) Nfd. to Man., s. to Ga., Ill. and Iowa. Intr. about 1705. Zone III. Important timber tree and also very ornamental.—**P. S. glaùca** Beiss. Lvs. light bluish green.—**P. S. fastigiàta** Beiss. Form with ascending brs. forming a narrow-pyramidal head. Gn.M.31:384(h). (*P. S. pyramidalis* Hort.)—**P. S. nàna** Carr. Dwarf round or somewhat conical compact bush with short lvs.— **P. S. umbraculífera** Carr. Dwarf umbrella-shaped bush with short lvs. R.H. 1869:38. Gn.M.32:39(h). H.D.142,t(h). (*P. S. nana* Gord., not Carr.)—**P. S. prostràta** Beiss. Dwarf decumbent form with diffuse trailing brs.

    Sect. II. PARACEMBRA Koehne. Cone-scales with dorsal umbo; scales of conelet mucronate or aristate: lvs. with marginal resin-ducts.

    Ser. 4. *Cembroides*. Seed wingless: lvs. 1–4, rarely 5, entire.

    12. **P. cembroìdes** Zucc. NUT P. Small tree, usually not more than 7 m. tall, with stout spreading brs. forming a round-topped head; bark shallowly fissured into large red-brown scales; brts. dark orange, pubescent at first: lvs. usually 3 or 2, slender, much incurved, 2–5 cm. long, dark green, with stomata on all sides: cone subglobose, 2.5–5 cm. broad; apophysis pyramidal, strongly keeled, lustrous brown, with broad obtuse umbo; seed oblong-obovoid, 1–2 cm. long, dark brown, with very narrow wing. Shaw, Gen. Pinus, t.13, f.130–2. Am. For. 29:159(h). S. Ariz. to L. Calif. and Mex. Intr. 1830. Zone VII?— **P. c. monophýlla** (Torr. & Frém.) Voss, var. Tree to 15 m.: lvs. usually solitary, 2–3.5 cm. long, rigid, pungent, glaucous-green: cone broad-ovoid, 3.5–5 cm. long; umbo with minute incurved prickle. S.S.11:t.551. H.B.3:25 (h). S.N.264(h). (*P. m.* Torr. & Frém.) Calif. to Colo. and Ariz. Intr. 1848. Zone V.—**P. c. edùlis** (Engelm.) Voss, var. Tree to 15 m.: lvs. 2–3, rigid, 2–3.5 cm. long, dark green, without stomata on back: cone broad-ovoid;

umbo with minute incurved tip. S.S.11:t.552. F.E.29:205(h). S.N.263(h). (*P. e.* Engelm., *Caryopitys e.* Small.) S. Wyo. to Ariz., Tex. and n. Mex. Intr. 1848. Zone IV. In cult. like the preceding, a slow-growing round bush.— **P. c. Parryàna** (Engelm.) Voss, var. Lvs. 3–5, usually 4, rigid, 3–4 cm. long: cone subglobose; umbo with recurved prickle. S.S.11:t.549. M.G.18:97(h). (*P. P. Engelm.*) Calif. Intr. about 1885. Zone VII?

Ser. 5. Gerardianae. Seed with very short articulate wing: lvs. 3, serrulate.

13. **P. Bungeàna** Zucc. LACE-BARK P. Tree to 25 or 30 m., with long and slender brs.; bark exfoliating in large scales, leaving particolored areas, on old trees chalky-white; brts. grayish green, glabrous: lvs. rigid, 5–10 cm. long, with stomata on back, light green: cones subsessile, conic-ovoid, 5–7 cm. long, light yellowish brown; apophysis broad, keeled, the umbo forming a spine with broad base; seed broad-ovoid, with short wing. B.M.8240(c). P.I.89(c,h). Gn.89:165(b). B.D.1923:t.18(h). N. W. China. Intr. 1846. Zone IV. Slow-growing and bushy in cult. with rather sparse light green lvs.; remarkable for its exfoliating bark.

Ser. 6. Balfourianae. Seed with long articulate wing: lvs. 5, entire, without stomata on back and with marginal resin-ducts: sheath gradually deciduous.

14. **P. Balfouriàna** A. Murr. FOXTAIL P. Tree to 15, occasionally to 30 m., narrow-pyramidal while young, in old age with an irregular and open head; bark on young trees milk-white, on old trees deeply ridged, dark red-brown; brts. dark brown, puberulous at first: lvs. crowded, rigid, usually incurved, persistent for many years, 2–4 cm. long, dark green: cones short-stalked, pendulous, subcylindric, 7–12 cm. long, dark brown; apophysis tumid; umbo with short prickle. S.S.11:t.553. E.H.5:t.277(h). Calif. Intr. 1852. Zone (V).

15. **P. aristàta** Engelm. HICKORY P. Bushy tree, occasionally to 15 m., sometimes a prostrate shrub; brts. glabrous or puberulous at first, light orange: lvs. stout or slender, 2–4 cm. long, dark green, usually with conspicuous whitish exudations of resin: cones cylindric-ovoid, 4–9 cm. long; apophysis tumid, umbo with slender curved spine to 8 mm. long. S.S.11:t.554. G.C.III.20:719. M.D.1904:t.5(h). Gt.74:430(h). (*P. Balfouriana* var. *a.* Engelm.) Calif. to Colo. and Ariz. Intr. 1861. Zone V. In cult. usually a handsome low shrub with ascending brs. densely clothed with appressed lvs. sprinkled with white grains of resin.

Subgen. II. DIPLOXYLON Koehne. PITCH PINES. Lvs. with 2 fibrovascular bundles, and with dorsal and ventral stomata, serrulate; bracts of lf.-fascicles decurrent; sheaths persistent, rarely deciduous: cones with dorsal umbo: wood hard, with dark resinous bands and clearly defined annual rings.

Sect. III. PINASTER. Lvs. with persistent sheaths; seed-wings long and articulate: spring-shoots uninodal or multinodal.

Ser. 7. Lariciones. Lvs. 2–3; spring-shoots uninodal: cones dehiscent at maturity: ray-cells of wood with large pits.

16. **P. resinòsa** Ait. RED P. (NORWAY P.). Tree to 25, occasionally to 50 m., with stout spreading, sometimes pendulous brs. forming a broad pyramidal head; bark red-brown, shallowly fissured and scaly; buds ovoid, acuminate, light brown, resinous: lvs. 2, flexible, 12–17 cm. long: conelet mutic; cone subsessile, conic-ovoid, symmetrical, 4–6 cm. long, nut-brown, falling the 3d year, leaving a few basal scales on the br.; apophysis conspicuously keeled, with an obtuse small dark umbo. P.I.69(c,h). S.S.11:t.550–1. A.G.12:645(h). F.L.5: 152(h). N. S. to Man., s. to Pa., Mich. and Minn. Intr. 1756. Zone II.—**P. r. globòsa** Rehd., f. Dwarf and dense form of globose habit. H.D.138,t.(h). N.H.13:250(h).

17. **P. densiflòra** Sieb. & Zucc. JAPANESE RED P. Tree to 35 m., with hori-

zontal brs. forming an irregular, rather broad head; bark orange-red, thin, scaly; brts. orange-yellow, bloomy; buds oblong-ovoid, chestnut-brown: lvs. 2, slender, 8–12 cm. long, bright bluish green; conelets conspicuously mucronate; cones short-stalked, conic-ovoid to oblong, symmetrical, 3–5 cm. long, dull tawny-yellow; apophysis flattened, the small umbo with a short prickle or obtuse. S.Z.2:t.112(c). S.I.1:t.1(c). Gn.M.2:22(h). W.C.t.11(h). Japan. Intr. 1854. Zone IV.—**P. d. aùrea** Mayr, var. Lvs. yellow.—**P. d. òculus-dracònis** Mayr, var. Each lf. marked with 2 yellow zones. Mayr, Abiet. Jap. t.7,f.c.-d(c).—**P. d. péndula** Mayr, var. With pendulous or prostrate brs. N.H.13:137(h).—**P. d. globòsa** Mayr, var. Dwarf globose form with short lvs. N.H.13:251(h).—**P. d. umbraculífera** Mayr, var. JAPANESE UMBRELLA P. (TANYOSHO P.) Low form with spreading brs. forming an umbrella-like head, ultimately to 4 m. tall. H.D.134,t(h). Bull. N. Y. Bot. Gard. 14:22(h). (*P. d. tabulaeformis* Hort.)

The closely related **P. Massoniàna** Lamb. differs chiefly in the longer lvs., in the partly mutic, partly tuberculate or mucronulate conelet and the sublustrous nut-brown cone. Shaw, Gen. Pinus, t.20,f.176–8. I.S.t.6. S. China.—Confused with *P. densiflora* and *P. Thunbergii;* probably not in cult. and too tender.

18. **P. sylvéstris** L. Scots P. Tree to 25, or occasionally to 40 m., with spreading brs., pyramidal when young, round-topped and irregular when old: bark red or red-brown, rather thin and smooth on the upper part of the trunk, darker and fissured below; brts. dull grayish yellow; buds oblong-ovoid, brown, resinous: lvs. 2, rigid, usually twisted, 3–7 cm. long, bluish green: conelet reflexed, minutely mucronate; cone short-stalked, reflexed, conic-oblong, symmetrical or sometimes oblique, 3–6 cm. long, dull tawny-yellow; apophysis flat, sometimes pyramidal; umbo small, with a minute prickle or its remnant. H.W.1:121–6,t.4(c). F.E.29:157(h). E.H.3:t.160–9(h). Eu. to Siberia. Long cult. Zone II.—One of the most important timber trees of Eu.; naturalized in e. N. Am.—**P. s. argéntea** Stev., var. Lvs. light bluish green and of silvery hue.—**P. s. aùrea** Beiss. Young lvs. golden-yellow, changing to green in summer. F.E.13:t.14(h).—**P. s. fastigiàta** Carr. Of columnar habit with ascending brs. N.H.13:133(h). (*P. s. pyramidalis* Hort.)—**P. s. Wateréri** Beiss. Low dense pyramidal form with steel-blue lvs. N.H.13:257(h).—**P. s. péndula** Laws., var. With pendulous brs.—**P. s. nàna** Carr. Low dense and round bush with thick, very twisted lvs. about 2 cm. long. H.D.144,t(h). (*P. s. pygmaea* Beiss.)—**P. s. parvifòlia** Heer. Lvs. 1.5–2.5 cm. long.

The following are geographical varieties or races: **P. s. rigénsis** Loud., var. Bark very red; stem straight and tall. Silviculturally the most important race.—**P. s. scótica** Beiss. Bark redder: lvs. shorter, about 3.5 cm. long: cones shorter, about 3.5 cm. long.—**P. s. lappònica** Hartm., var. Of narrower pyramidal habit: lvs. broader and shorter, remaining alive for 4–7 years: cones more yellowish. Skogsvard. För. Tidskr.17:35, 37, 47(h). (*P. l.* Mayr.) N. Eu.— **P. s. engadinénsis** Heer. A slow growing pyramidal form with grayish green, thick and rigid lvs. 2.5–3.5 cm. long persisting for 7 or 8 years: cones oblique with partly convex apophyses. Tyrol.

19. **P. Mùgo** Turra. MOUNTAIN P. Usually low, often prostrate shrub, sometimes a pyramidal tree to 12 m.; brts. brownish: lvs. 2, crowded, stout, 3–8 cm. long, bright green: conelets mucronate; cones subsessile, ovoid or conic-ovoid, 2–7 cm. long, tawny-yellow or dark brown, lustrous; apophysis pyramidal or flattened, the umbo bordered by a dark ring and bearing the remnant of a mucro. H.W.1:140–3,t.5(c). (*P. montana* Mill.) Mts. of C. and S. Eu. Intr. 1779. Zone II.—As seen in a cross-section under the microscope

the cells of the epidermis of the lf. are much higher than broad with a dash-like space in the centre, while in *P. sylvestris* the cells are about as high as broad with a dot-like space in the centre.—This very variable species is usually divided into 4 vars. of which the first is the type. **P. M. Mùghus** (Scop.) Zenari, var. Cone symmetrical, conic-ovoid, with usually prickly umbo, not bloomy before maturity, yellowish brown, cinnamon-brown when ripe; apophysis sharply keeled, the prickly umbo in the middle: usually a prostrate shrub. M.D.1921:t.1. (*P. montana* var. *M.* Willk., *P. M.* Scop.) E. Alps to Balkan Pen.—Here belongs **P. M. Slavinii** Hornibr., f. Low spreading form with erect brts. G.C.81:146(h).—**P. M. pumílio** (Haenke) Zenari, var. Cone symmetrical, subglobose to ovoid, glaucous and usually violet purple before maturity, yellowish or dark brown when ripe; upper part of apophysis convex, lower part concave, the umbo below the middle, impressed: usually a prostrate shrub. M.D.1912:147–148(h);1921:t.1. (*P. montana* var. *p.* Willk., *P. mont.* var. *prostrata* Tubeuf, *P. p.* Haenke, *P. carpatica* Hort.) Alps to C. Eu. and to Balkan Pen. Here belongs **P. M. compacta** Slavin, f. Dense globose form: lvs. 2.5–3.5 cm. long, dark green. B.C.C.t.9(h). N.H.13:255(h). —**P. M. rotundàta** (Link) Hoopes. Cone oblique and asymmetrical, conic or ovoid, spreading or bent downward, with the lower and occasionally the middle scales of the outer side ending in a short and blunt, usually slightly reflexed apophysis: usually a tree to 10 m., with several stems. R.I.11:f.1128 (c). (*P. montana* var. *r.* Willk., *P. obliqua* Saut.) Mts. of C. Eu., Alps.— **P. M. rostràta** (Ant.) Hoopes. Cones asymmetrical and very oblique, conic-ovoid, 5–6 cm. long, directed downward; scales of the outer side strongly developed, the elongated pyramidal apophysis ending in a hook-like process directed toward the base of the cone: usually a tree with a single stem, sometimes to 25 m. Shaw, Gen. Pinus, t.21,f.186(cone),190(h). S.N.257(h). (*P. montana* var. *r.* Ant., var. *arborea* Tubeuf, *P. uncinata* Ramond.) Pyrenees to W. Alps.

P. m. × *sylvestris* = **P. rhaètica** Bruegg. Occasionally with the parents. (*P. digenea* Beck, *P. Celakovskiorum* Aschers. & Graebn.)

20. **P. Heldreìchii** Christ. Tree to 20 m., of pyramidal habit; bark gray, broken into angular plates; brts. brownish and usually bloomy when young, later grayish and somewhat rough: buds oblong-ovoid, not resinous, the scales brown with white tips or nearly grayish white: lvs. more or less incurved, 3–6 cm. long, stiff, pungent or obtusish, bright green, the vascular bundles separated by 1–2 rows (in *P. nigra* by several rows) of cells: cone ovoid, about 8 cm. long, similar to that of *P. nigra,* but yellowish or light brown, scarcely lustrous. K.V.18:t.39(h). Balkan Pen. Cult. 1891. Zone V.—**P. H. leucodérmis** (Ant.) Markgraf ex Fitschen, var. Tree of slower growth, with smoother more whitish bark; young brts. bloomy, grayish white and smooth when older: lower cone-scales with pyramidal apophysis and recurved umbo. H.W. 1:158–61. Gn. 89:184(h). E.H.2:t.119(h). M.D.43:t.27(h). (*P. l.* Ant.) Balkan Pen., s. Ital. Introd. 1865. Zone V.

21. **P. nígra** Arnold. AUSTRIAN P. Tree to 30, or occasionally to 50 m., with spreading brs. forming a pyramidal, in old age sometimes flat-topped, head; brts. usually light brown; buds ovoid or oblong-ovoid, light brown, resinous: lvs. stiff, 9–16 cm. long, dark green: conelets mucronate: cones sub-sessile, symmetrical, ovoid, 5–8 cm. long, yellowish brown, lustrous; apophysis strongly keeled; umbo usually with short prickle. C. and S. Eu., Asia Minor. Intr. 1759. Zone IV. A variable species with several geographical vars. of which the first is identical with the type.—**P. n. austríaca** (Hoess) Aschers.

& Graebn. Tall tree with dark gray bark and a broad ovoid head; brts. grayish or yellowish brown: lvs. rigid, 8–10 cm. long, dark green. H.W.1:151(h), t.6(c). F.E.18:t.84(h). B.E.t.42(h). (*P. Laricio* var. *a.* Loud., *P. a.* Hoess, *P. nigricans* Host.) Austria to Balkan Pen. Handsome Pine of vigorous growth.—**P. n. caramánica** (Loud.) Rehd., var. CRIMEAN P. Tree to 30 m., with long and stout ascending brs. forming a broad pyramidal head: lvs. dark green, lustrous: cones light brown, 8–10 cm. long, the upper and middle apophyses obtusely keeled. G.C.II.20:785;21:481. E.H.2:t.116–8(h). (*P. n. Pallasiana* Aschers. & Graebn., *P. Pallasiana* Lamb.) Asia Minor.—**P. n. Poiretiàna** (Ant.) Aschers. & Graebn. CORSICAN P. Tall tree to 50 m., with shorter ascending brs. forming a narrower head; bark gray; brts. reddish or light brown: lvs. lighter green, 10–14 cm. long, less crowded and usually curved; cone with the middle and upper apophyses obtusely keeled. R.H. 1897:355, 357(h). G.C.III.4:693,705. E.H.2:t.114(b). (*P. Laricio* Poir., *P. Laricio* var. *corsicana* Loud., var. *calabrica* Loud.) S. Eu.—**P. n. cebennénsis** (Gren. & Godr.) Rehd., var. Tree to 20 m.: brts. orange: lvs. slender, to 16 cm. long: cones 5–6 cm. long. B.E.318. (*P. n. tenuifolia* Aschers. & Graebn., *P. Salzmanni* Dun., *P. monspeliensis* Salzm. *P. pyrenaica* Carr., not Lapeyr.) Pyrenees and S. France.—Garden forms are: **P. n. péndula** (Carr.) Rehd., var., with pendulous brs.—**P. n. pyramidàlis** Slavin, f., a narrow pyramidal form with ascending curved brs. and bluish green lvs. to 12.5 cm. long. N.H. 13:132(h).—**P. n. Hornibrookiàna** Slavin, f. Low compact bush with stiff lustrous dark lvs. 5–6 cm. long. B. C. C.t.9(h). N.H.13:253(h).—**P. n. pýgmaea** (Gord.) Rehd., var. Dwarf globose form.—**P. n. prostràta** (Beiss.) Rehd., var. Prostrate form.

22. **P. Thunbérgii** Parl. JAPANESE BLACK P. Tree to 30 m., with spreading, often slightly pendulous brs. forming a broad-pyramidal, often irregular head; bark blackish gray, fissured into irregular plates; brts. orange-yellow; buds oblong, whitish, not resinous, with fimbriate scales free at the tips: lvs. stout, 6–11 cm. long, sharp-pointed, bright green, resin-ducts medial; conelet mucronulate; cones short-stalked, conic-ovoid, 4–6 cm. long, nut-brown; apophysis flattened, with small depressed, usually prickly umbo. S.Z.2:t.113 (c). S.I.1:t.1(c). W.C.t.13,14(h). (*P. Massoniana* Sieb. & Zucc., not Lamb.) Japan. Intr. 1855.—**P. T. òculus-dracònis** Mayr., var. Lvs. with 2 yellow zones.

23. **P. tabulaefórmis** Carr. CHINESE P. Tree to 25 m.: bark dark gray and fissured, on the limbs red; brts. pale orange or pale grayish yellow, slightly bloomy when young, often less conspicuously divided into plates; buds oblong, light brown, scarcely resinous: lvs. 2–3, mostly 2, stout, 10–15 cm. long, often glaucescent, resin-ducts marginal or marginal and medial: conelets mucronate; cones subsessile, ovoid, symmetrical or oblique, 4–9 cm. long, pale tawny yellow, changing to dark brown, persistent for several years; apophysis strongly keeled, with an obtuse or mucronate umbo. Shaw, Gen. Pinus, t.23,f.201–7. B.D.1923:t.20(h). S.N.34(h). (*P. sinensis* Mayr, not Lamb., *P. Henryi* Mast., *P. Wilsonii* Shaw, *P. leucosperma* Maxim., *P. funebris* Komar., *P. mongolica* Hort.) N. to W. China. Intr. 1862. Zone V.— **P. t. densàta** (Mast.) Rehd., var. Lvs. usually 2, rigid: cones ovoid, 5–6 cm. long, oblique, the posterior apophyses tumid and prominent. Shaw, Gen. Pinus, t.23,f.201. (*P. prominens* Mast.) W. China. Intr. 1909.

A closely related species is **P. yunnanénsis** Franch. Bark broken into large plates; lvs. slenderer, 10–18, rarely to 25 cm. long, usually in 3's: cone 6–9 cm. long, with flattened apophyses. (*P. sinensis* var. *y.* Shaw.) W. China. Intr. 1909. Zone VI.

Ser. 8. *Australes.* Cones dehiscent at maturity: spring-shoots uninodal or multinodal: ray-cells of wood with small pits.

24. **P. ponderòsa** Laws. WESTERN YELLOW P. Tree to 50 or occasionally to 75 m., with stout spreading or often pendent brs. forming a narrow-pyramidal head; bark usually cinnamon-red or dark brown to nearly black, fissured into ridges or on old trees into large plates; brts. orange-brown, fragrant when broken: buds oblong to ovoid, resinous: lvs. 2–5, usually 3, generally rigid, 12–26 cm. long, dark green: conelets mucronate; cones subsessile, often in clusters, ovoid-oblong or conic-ovoid, symmetrical, 8–15 cm. long, light reddish or yellowish brown, lustrous, usually leaving a few basal scales on the br. when falling; apophysis depressed-pyramidal or flattened, the umbo with a stout usually recurved prickle. S.S.11:t.560–1. G.C.III.8:557(h),569. S.N. 244, 246, 249(h). (*P. Benthamiana* Hartw.—BULL P.) B. C. to Mex., e. to S. D. and Tex. Intr. 1827. Zone V. One of the tallest pines and most important timber trees of the W. States.—**P. p. péndula** H. W. Sarg. A form with pendulous brs. G.C.II.10:37(h). G.F.1:391(h).—**P. p. scopulòrum** Engelm., var. Smaller in every part: bark nearly black, furrowed: lvs. sometimes 2, 12–16 cm. long: cones ovoid, smaller. S.S.11:t.564. C.B.N.t.70. S.N.246(h). (*P. s.* Lemm.) S. D. to Mex. and Tex. Zone IV.

25. **P. Jéffreyi** A. Murr. JEFFREY'S P. Tree to 40 or occasionally 60 m., with short spreading or often pendent brs. forming an open or sometimes narrow-pyramidal head; bark cinnamon-red, broken into large plates; brts. bloomy; buds oblong-ovoid, not resinous: lvs. usually 3, stout, 12–20 cm. long, pale bluish green: conelets mucronate; cones conic-ovoid, 14–26 cm. long, light brown; apophysis depressed; umbo with a slender recurved prickle. B.M.8257(c). S.S.11:t.562–3. Gn.89:329(h). G.F.5:185(h). S.N.250(h). (*P. ponderosa* var. *J.* Vasey.) Ore. to Calif. Intr. 1853. Zone V. Distinct ornamental pine remarkable for its long pale bluish lvs.

26. **P. palùstris** Mill. LONGLEAF P. Tree to 30 or 40 m., with ascending brs. forming an oblong open head; bark light orange-brown, separating into large thin scales; brts. orange-brown; buds oblong, whitish, fringed, not resinous: lvs. 3, crowded and forming tufts at the end of the brts., 20–45 cm. long, dark green: conelet short-mucronate: cones subsessile, cylindric, 15–20 cm. long, dull brown; apophysis keeled; umbo with a short reflexed prickle. S.S. 11:t.589–90. G.F.10:115(h). Am. For. 21:895(h). (*P. australis* Michx.— SOUTHERN P.) Va. to Fla. and Miss., along the coast. Intr. 1727. Zone VII. The most important timber tree of the S. E. States, also yielding excellent resin; brs. imported into n. cities for decoration.

27. **P. Taèda** L. LOBLOLLY P. Tree to 30 or occasionally to 55 m., with spreading brs., the upper ones ascending, forming a compact round-topped head; bark bright red-brown, fissured into scaly ridges; brts. yellowish brown, sometimes slightly bloomy; buds oblong, resinous: lvs. 3, slender but stiff, 12–25 cm. long, bright green; conelets spinulose; cones sessile, conic-ovoid, symmetrical, 6–10 cm. long, dull, pale reddish brown; apophysis distinctly keeled; umbo elongated into a stout triangular spine. S.S.11:t.577–8. F.L. 3:25,t(h). (OLD FIELD P., FRANKINCENSE P.) N. J. to Fla. and Tex. Intr. 1713. Zone VI.—Important timber tree.

28. **P. echinàta** Mill. SHORT-LEAF P. Tree to 40 m., with slender, often pendent brs. in regular whorls; bark light cinnamon-red, broken into large scaly plates, scaly on the brs.; brts. dark red-brown, bloomy at first: buds oblong-ovoid, brown: lvs. 2–3, slender, 7–12 cm. long, dark bluish green: conelet mucronate; cones short-stalked or subsessile, conic-ovoid, 4–6 cm. long,

dull brown; apophysis flattened or slightly thickened along the keel; umbo elevated, with a short prickle. P.I.71(c,h). S.S.11:t.587. Am. For. 22:513(h). (*P. mitis* Michx.—Spruce P.) N. Y. to Fla., w. to Ill. and Tex. Intr. 1726 Zone V. Handsome tree with broad ovoid head.

Ser. 9. *Insignes*. Cones tenaciously persistent, often serotinous (remaining closed after maturity for years); seed-wing articulate, long: ray-cells of wood with small pits.

29. **P. halepénsis** Mill. Aleppo P. Tree to 20 m., with short brs. forming an open round-topped head; bark gray, smooth for a long time, finally brown; brts. slender, yellowish brown or light greenish brown; buds small, cylindric, not resinous: lvs. 2, rarely 3, slender, 6–15 cm. long, light green; conelet obscurely mucronate near the apex; cones short-stalked, spreading or deflexed, conic-ovoid, symmetrical or nearly so, 8–12 cm. long, yellowish brown, lustrous, often serotinous; apophysis flattened or depressed-pyramidal, keeled; umbo obtuse. H.W.1:162–5,t.7(c). G.W.9:469,471(h). E.H.5:t.287–8(h). (*P. alepensis* Poir., *P. maritima* Mill. sensu Lamb., *P. pityusa* Stev.) Mediterr. Reg. Intr. 1683. Zone VII. Recommended for seaside planting; of little ornamental value.—**P. h. brùtia** (Ten.) Henry, var. Lvs. 10–16, rarely to 20 cm. long, more rigid, darker green: cone sessile, erect, usually in whorls of 2–6, 5–11 cm. long. H.W.1:172–3. G.C.III.4:268. R.H.1867:150–1. (*P. brutius* Ten., *P. pyrenaica* David, *P. eldarica* Medwed.) S. Eu., W. Asia.

P. h. × *Pinaster* = P. halepénsi-Pináster Saporta. Pyramidal tree; bark gray; lvs. 10–15 cm. long, slenderer than in no. 30, stiffer than in no. 29. Orig. in France before 1889.

30. **P. Pináster** Ait. Cluster P. Tree to 30 m., with spreading, sometimes pendent brs. forming a pyramidal head; bark deeply fissured into narrow scaly ridges, brown; brts. bright reddish brown; buds oblong, brown, not resinous: lvs. 2, stout and rigid, 10–20 cm. long, lustrous green: conelets minutely mucronate; cones short-stalked, clustered, conic-ovoid, symmetrical or nearly so, 9–18 cm. long, light brown, lustrous, sometimes serotinous; apophysis pyramidal, conspicuously keeled with prominent prickly umbo. H.W.1: 168–9. Gn.14:20;83:388(h). G.W.9:470(h). (*P. maritima* of Dur., not Mill.) Mediterr. Reg., near the coast. Intr. before 1660. Zone VII. Recommended for seaside planting.

31. **P. virginiàna** Mill. Scrub P. Bushy tree to 15 or sometimes to 30 m., with slender horizontal or pendent brs. in remote irregular whorls; bark shallowly fissured into scaly plates, smooth on the brs.; brts. bloomy; buds oblong, dark brown, very resinous, with appressed scales: lvs. 2, rigid, usually twisted, 4–8 cm. long: conelets with tapering sharp scales: cones conic-ovoid to oblong, symmetrical, 4–6 cm. long, reddish brown, lustrous, dehiscent at maturity; apophysis somewhat elongated along the keel; umbo prominent, ending into a slender prickle. S.S.11:t.581. (*P. inops* Ait.—Jersey P.) N. Y. to Ga., w. to Ohio and Ala. Intr. before 1739. Zone IV. Small tree with widespreading brs., valuable for planting on dry and barren soil.

32. **P. rígida** Mill. Pitch P. Tree to 25 m., with horizontal brs. forming an open irregular head; bark red-brown, deeply fissured into broad scaly ridges, on young stems thin and scaly; brts. light brown; buds ovoid or oblong-ovoid, chestnut-brown: lvs. 3, rigid, spreading, 7–14 cm. long, dark green: conelets with spiny scales; cones subsessile, often clustered, conic-ovoid, symmetrical, 3–7 cm. long, light brown, lustrous, dehiscent at maturity, rarely serotinous; apophysis somewhat elevated along the keel; umbo prominent, ending in a sharp slender prickle. Add.9:t.311(c). S.S.11:t.579. G.F.4:402(h).

E.H.5:t.286(h). N. B. to Ga., w. to Ont. and Ky. Intr. before 1759. Zone IV. Valuable for planting on dry and rocky soil. Old trees are often very picturesque.—**P. r. seròtina** (Michx.) Loud. POND P. Smaller tree, with shallowly fissured bark, lvs. to 20 cm. long and serotinous cones. S.S.11:t.580. (*P. s.* Michx.) N. J. to Fla. and Ala. Intr. 1713. Zone VII.

33. **P. pungens** Lamb. TABLE MOUNTAIN P. Tree to 10, occasionally to 20 m., with stout spreading brs. forming a broad open head; bark dark brown, thick, broken into scaly plates, on upper part of trunk and on brs. separating into thin scales; brts. light orange; buds oblong, obtuse, dark chestnut-brown: lvs. 2 or sometimes 3, rigid, twisted, 3–7 cm. long, dark green: male fls. red: scales of conelet prolonged into an acute triangle: cones conic-ovoid, symmetrical or nearly so, 5–9 cm. long, light brown, lustrous or sublustrous; apophysis much elongated along the keel; umbo conical, ending in a stout curved spine. P.I.73(c,h). S.S.11:t.584. (POVERTY P.) N. J. to Ga. and Tenn. Intr. 1804. Zone V.

34. **P. Banksiàna** Lamb. JACK P. Tree to 25 m., but usually lower, sometimes shrubby, with slender spreading brs. forming an open broad head; bark dark brown, slightly tinged with red, fissured into narrow ridges covered with thick scales; brts. purplish to yellowish brown; buds oblong-ovoid, light brown, very resinous: lvs. 2, rigid, twisted, spreading, 2–4 cm. long, acute or obtusish, bright or dark green: male fls. yellow: conelet minutely mucronate; cone erect, conic-ovoid, oblique and usually much curved, 3–5 cm. long, tawny-yellow, lustrous, serotinous; apophysis flat or convex; umbo small and unarmed. S.S.11:t.588. S.N.256(h). E.H.5:t.289(h). (*P. divaricata* Dum. Cours.) Huds. B. to n. N. Y. and Me., w. to Mackenzie River and Minn. Intr. before 1783. Zone II. For planting on dry and sandy soil.

35. **P. contórta** Loud. SHORE P. Tree to 10 m., with rather stout brs. forming a round-topped, usually dense head; bark deeply fissured into small scaly plates, dark red-brown, tinged with purple or orange; brts. light orange or orange-brown; buds ovoid, dark chestnut-brown, resinous: lvs. 2, rigid, twisted, 3–5 cm. long, acutish, dark green: conelet long-mucronate; cones sessile, conic-ovoid, very oblique, 2–5 cm. long, light yellowish brown, lustrous, serotinous; apophyses on the upper side of cone elevated; umbo dark, with a slender fragile prickle. S.S.11:t.567. G.C.II.19:45. D.J.384,t.(h, as *P. c. Murrayana*). (*P. Bolanderi* Parl., *P. inops* Bong., not Ait.) Alaska to Calif., the var. e. to Mont. and Colo. Intr. 1855. Zone VII?—**P. c. latifòlia** S. Wats., var. LODGE-POLE P. A slenderer pyramidal tree to 25 or occasionally to 50 m.: lvs. 3.5–8 cm. long, lighter green: cones less oblique. S.S.11:t.518. E.H.5:t.292(h). D.J.44,t(h). (*P. c.* var. *Murrayana* Engelm., *P. Murrayana* Balf., *P. Boursieri* Carr.) The most common coniferous tree of the n. Rocky Mts., often forming forests of great extent.

36. **P. muricàta** D. Don. BISHOP P. Tree to 15, occasionally to 30 m., with stout brs., pyramidal while young, finally usually round-topped; bark dark brown, tinged with red, broken into scaly plates on the lower, into thin loose scales on the upper part of the trunk; brts. orange-brown; buds ovoid, dark brown, resinous: lvs. 2, rigid, usually twisted, 10–15 cm. long, dark green: scales of conelet prolonged into a triangular spine; cones sessile, usually clustered, reflexed, conic-ovoid, oblique, 5–9 cm. long, chestnut-brown, lustrous, serotinous; apophyses of the upper side of cone much larger, conical, terminated by a stout spine. S.S.11:t.585–6. G.F.10:235(h). G.C.45:259(h),60–61. B.S.1:104,t(h). (PRICKLE-CONE P.) Calif. Intr. 1846. Zone VII? Handsome pine of regular pyramidal habit.

37. **P. attenuàta** Lemm. Knob-cone P. Tree to 10, occasionally to 30 m., with slender horizontal brs. ascending at the ends; bark at base of trunk dark brown, shallowly fissured into large loose scales, smooth and pale brown above; brts. dark orange-brown; buds oblong-ovoid, dark brown: lvs. 3, rarely 2, slender, 7–18 cm. long, pale yellowish or bluish green: scales of conelet prolonged into a triangular spine; cones short-stalked, usually clustered, oblique, comic-oblong, reflexed, 8–15 cm. long, tawny-yellow, lustrous, serotinous; apophyses on the upper side of cone prominent, conical, ending in a small incurved spine. S.S.11:t.575–6. G.C.II.24:784(h),785. For. & Irr. 8:246 (h). (*P. tuberculata* Gord., not Don, *P. californica* Hartw., not Lois.) Ore. to Calif. Intr. 1847. Zone VII?

38. **P. radiàta** Don. Monterey P. Tree to 30 m., with stout spreading brs. forming an irregular open head; bark of brs. and upper trunk rough, deeply furrowed below into broad scaly ridges, dark red-brown; brts. brown; buds ovoid, bright chestnut-brown: lvs. 2 or 3, slender, 10–15 cm. long, bright green; conelet mucronate; cones short-stalked or sessile, clustered, reflexed, conic-ovoid, oblique, 7–14 cm. long, nut-brown, lustrous, serotinous; apophyses of the upper side of cone prominent, rounded, with minute prickle. S.S.11:t. 573–4. G.C.III.9:341 (as *P. attenuata*). E.H.5:t.282–4(h). Gn.87:264(h). (*P. insignis* Dougl., *P. montereyensis* Hort.) S. Calif. Intr. 1833. Zone VII. Handsome pine with bright green lvs., of rapid growth when young.

Ser. 10. *Macrocarpae.* Wing-blades of seed thick; cone large: lvs. 3–5, long: ray-cells of wood with small pits.

39. **P. Sabiniàna** Dougl. Digger P. Tree to 15 or occasionally to 25 m., with short crooked brs. forming a round-topped head; bark dark brown, thick, deeply fissured into scaly ridges; brts. bloomy: lvs. 3, rather slender, 20–30 cm. long, pale bluish green: conelet large, the scales tapering to a sharp point; cones stalked, reflexed, ovoid, slightly oblique, 15–25 cm. long, red-brown, persistent; apophysis prominent, conical, sharply keeled, tapering into the umbo and ending in a sharp point; seed-wing very thick; not uniformly colored on the dorsal surface. S.S.11:t.569. G.C.III.4:43;5:45(h). E.H.5:t.280 (h). Calif. Intr. 1832. Zone VI. Very distinct pine of loose habit and with sparse and long pale lvs.

Related species is **P. Torreyàna** Carr. Soledad P. Tree to 15 or in cult. to 30 m.: lvs. 5, stiff, 20–30 cm. long. dark green: cone 10–15 cm. long; nut spotted. S.S.11:557–8. B.É.t.43(h). S.N.242(h). S. Calif. Intr. 1853. Zone VII?

40. **P. Coùlteri** Don. Tree to 25 m., with stout brs. forming an open pyramidal head; bark dark brown or nearly black, deeply fissured into rounded scaly ridges; brts. bloomy; buds oblong-ovoid, resinous: lvs. 3, very stout, 15–20 cm. long, dark bluish green: conelet very large, scales tapering to a long sharp point; cones reflexed, ovoid or oblong-ovoid, somewhat oblique, 25–35 cm. long, yellowish brown, persistent; apophysis elongated, pyramidal, with a large umbo forming a stout curved spine; seeds long-winged. S.S.11:t.571–2. G.C.III.4:765(h). E.H.5:t.279(h). (*P. macrocarpa* Lindl.) Calif. Intr. 1832. Zone VII? Tree of loose habit with sparse foliage.

10. **SCIADÓPITYS** Sieb. & Zucc. Umbrella-Pine. Evergreen tree with short and slender horizontally spreading brs. ascending at the ends; bark nearly smooth, separating in long thin shreds: lvs. of two kinds, small and scale-like, scattered on the shoots, crowded at the ends and bearing in their axils a whorl of 20–30 linear flat lvs. grooved on each side, more deeply beneath, and consisting each of two connate lvs. borne on undeveloped spurs

like the fascicled pine lvs.: male fls. in dense clusters at the end of the brts., consisting of spirally arranged 2-celled anthers; female solitary, terminal, consisting of numerous spirally arranged scales bearing 7–9 ovules and subtended by a small bract: fr. an ovate-oblong cone with thick woody broadly orbicular scales, ripening the second season; seeds ovoid, compressed, narrowly winged; cotyledons 2. (Greek *skias, skiados,* umbrella, and *pitys,* pine; alluding to the position of the lvs.) One species in Japan.

    S. verticillàta (Thunb.) Sieb. & Zucc. Tree to 40 m. with a trunk often 3 m. in girth and with a narrow-pyramidal head becoming thin in old age: lvs. linear, obtuse and emarginate, dark green and glossy above, with 2 white bands beneath, 8–12 cm. long: cone 8–12 cm. long; seeds 1.2 cm. long. S.Z.2; t.101,102(c). B.M 8050(c). F.E.21:t.115(h). W.C.t.46,47(h). C. Japan. Intr. 1861. Zone V. Handsome slow-growing tree of dense pyramidal habit.

    11. SEQUÒIA Endl. Tall evergreen tree; bark 15–25 cm. thick, furrowed into ridges with fibrous scales, reddish brown; winter-buds with acute imbricate scales: lvs. dimorphic, alternate, those of shoots scale-like, spirally arranged, appressed or slightly spreading, with stomatic bands on the ventral side, those of lateral shoots 2-ranked, petioled, linear to linear-lanceolate, with or without few broken rows of stomata above, with 2 white stomatic bands beneath: fls. monoecious, the staminate terminal and axillary, stipitate, with numerous spirally arranged stamens; pistillate terminal, with 15–20 scales, bearing 3–7 erect ovules in one row: cones pendulous, ovoid; scales obliquely shield-shaped, ridged, with a flattened, often deciduous mucro; seeds 2–5, near margin of scale, with 2 spongy wings slightly narrower than seed, ripening in one season; cotyledons 2. (After Sequoiah, inventor of the Cherokee alphabet; 1770–1843.) One species on the Pacific coast.

    S. sempérvirens (Lamb.) Endl. Redwood. Tree attaining 110 m., trunk up to 25 m. in girth: lvs. of leading shoots ovate-oblong, about 6 mm. long, with incurved callous tip, of lateral shoots linear to linear-oblong often falcate, 6–18 mm. long, dark or bluish green and slightly grooved above, with stomatic bands and a conspicuous midrib beneath: staminate fls. about 1.5 mm. long: cone ovoid, 2–2.5 cm. long, brown, ripening the first year; scales abruptly enlarged into a disk about 8 mm. long; seeds elliptic-oblong, 1.5 mm. long, light brown. S.S.10:t.535. B.S.2:510(h). B.E.t.23(h). S. Oreg. to Calif., near the coast. Intr. about 1843. Zone VII. The tallest of trees; demands a moist and cool climate; it suckers from the base and is occasionally seen in cult. as a bush of stool-shoots after the main trunk has died.—**S. s. adpréssa** Carr. Lvs. shorter, 6–8 mm. long, young tips creamy white. (*S. s. albo-spica* Hort.)—**S. s. glaùca** R. Sm. Lvs. glaucous.—**S. s. péndula** Rovelli. Brs. spreading and pendulous. S.N.276(h).

    12. SEQUOIADÉNDRON Buchholz. Tall evergreen tree with deeply furrowed spongy bark 25–50 cm. thick; winter-buds naked: lvs. spirally arranged, appressed or slightly spreading, scale-like, sharply pointed, with 2 stomatiferous bands above: staminate fls. sessile, terminal on short brts.; pistillate terminal, with 25–40 scales terminated by a long terete spine and bearing 3–12 or more erect ovules in 2 rows: cone ellipsoid, maturing the second year and remaining for many years on the tree, very woody; scales wedge-shaped, with 3–9 seeds in a single or double row; seeds with 2 thin wings broader than seed; cotyledons usually 4 (3–5). (*Sequoia* and Greek *dendron,* tree.) Syn.: *Wellingtonia* Lindl., not Meissn. One species in Calif.

S. gigantèum (Lindl.) Buchholz. BIG-TREE (GIANT SEQUOIA). Tree to 100 m. tall, occasionally 30 m. in girth above the enlarged and buttressed base, in old age free of brs. up to 50 m.: lvs. ovate to lanceolate, 3–6 mm. or on the main axis to 1.2 cm. long, convex below, concave above; staminate fls. 4–8 mm. long: cone 5–8 cm. long, 4–5.5 cm. in diam.; scales thickened into a disk to 2.5 cm. long and 0.6–1 cm. wide, pitted in the middle and when young with a slender spine; seeds oblong, 3–6 mm. long, light brown. S.S.10:536. P.I.112 (c,h). E.H.6:t.196(h). G.C.78:107(h). (*Wellingtonia gigantea* Lindl., *Sequoia gigantea* Dcne., not Endl., *S. Wellingtonia* Seem., *S. Washingtoniana* Sudw.) Calif., at 1450–2000 m. alt. Intr. 1853. Zone VI. The most massive of trees; in cult. when young, narrow-pyramidal, usually clothed to the ground with spreading brs.—**S. g. péndulum** (Carr.) Rehd., f. Brs. strongly deflexed and appressed to the stem so as to form a very narrow column. M.G.17:133 (h). R.H.1906:395(h). G.C.31:383(h);78:105(h).

13. **TAXÒDIUM** Rich. Deciduous or evergreen trees with light brown, furrowed and scaly bark and upright or spreading brs.; brts. of two kinds, those near the apex of the shoot persistent and with axillary buds, those on the lower part of the shoot without axillary buds and deciduous; winter-buds globose, scaly: lvs. alternate, subulate or flat and linear with two stomatic bands below, those of the deciduous brts. usually spreading in two ranks, those of the persistent brts. spreading radially: the staminate fls. ovoid, consisting of 6–8 stamens and forming terminal long and drooping panicles, the female ones scattered, near the ends of the brs. of the preceding year, sub-globose, consisting of 2-ovuled scales: fr. a short-stalked globose or ovoid cone ripening the first year and consisting of many thick, coriaceous peltate scales dilated from a slender stipe into an irregularly 4-sided, often mucronate, disk; each fertile scale with 2 unequally 3-angled seeds with 3 thick wings: cotyledons 4–9. (Greek; similar to Taxus.) Three species in e. N. Am. and Mex.

A. Lvs. linear, spreading, 2-ranked: brts. horizontal...........................1. *T. distichum*
AA. Lvs. subulate, appressed: brts. upright.......................................2. *T. ascendens*

1. **T. dístichum** (L.) Rich. BALD CYPRESS. Tree occasionally 50 m. tall. with a tapering trunk strongly buttressed at the base, pyramidal while young, in old age usually spreading with broad rounded head; young brts. green, becoming brown the first winter; the 2-ranked lvs. linear-lanceolate, apiculate, 1–1.5 cm. long, soft bright green, yellowish green or whitish below, turning dull orange brown before falling: panicle of staminate fls. 10–12 cm. long: cone globose or obovoid, about 2.5 cm. across; disk of scales rugose, usually without mucro. S.S.10:t.537. G.F.3:7(h). S.N.21&t.10(h). M.G.11:303(h). (*Cupressus disticha* L.) Del. to Fla., w. to s. Ill., Mo., Ar. and La.; in swamps and on banks of streams. Particularly in wet and occasionally inundated situations the roots produce woody cylindrical projections sometimes 2 m. high and 30 cm. in diam. known as "cypress-knees." Intr. 1640. Zone IV. A handsome ornamental tree with feathery light green foliage.– ·**T. d. pendens** Rehd., f. Brs. nodding at the tips and brts. drooping. H.B.3:446(h). N.H.12:50(h). (*T. d. nutans* Carr., not Ait., *T. d. pendulum* Horsey, not Carr.)

2. **T. ascéndens** Brongn. POND CYPRESS. Tree to 25 m.; trunk much enlarged at base; bark thick, furrowed: brs. spreading; brts. upright: lvs. appressed and incurved, subulate, 5–10 mm. long: fls. and frs. similar to those of *T. distichum.* B.M.5603(c). G.C.66:258,259. Jour. N. Y. Bot. Gard. 21:t. 246(h). (*T. imbricarium* Harper, *T. distichum* var. *imbricarium* Croom.)

Va. to Fla. and Ala.; in lakes, ponds and small rivers, usually over clay subsoil. Cult. 1789. Zone V. Less handsome than the preceding species, with a narrower and thinner head.—**T. a. nùtans** (Ait.) Rehd. With pendulous brts. B.N.468. (*T. a. pendulum* Schneid., *T. distichum* var. *n.* Sweet, *Glyptostrobus pendulus* Endl.) Cult. 1789.

A closely related genus from China is **Glyptóstrobus** Endl. which differs chiefly in its elongated, not peltate scales. The only species, **G. pénsilis** (Staunt.) K. Koch (*G. heterophylla* Endl., *G. sinensis* Loder), is not hardy within our area. Also the Mexican **Taxodium mucronàtum** Ten. (*T. distichum* var. *m.* Henry) with persistent lvs. is not hardy, but is occasionally planted in Calif.

14. **CRYPTOMÉRIA** D. Don. Cryptomeria. Evergreen tree with reddish brown bark peeling off in long shreds, pyramidal, with spreading brs.: buds minute: lvs. spirally arranged in 5 vertical ranks, decurrent, directed forward and curved inward, awl-shaped, laterally compressed: staminate fls. oblong, composed of numerous imbricate stamens, sessile, forming short spikes at the end of brts.; female fls. globular, solitary at the end of short brts.: fr. a brown, subglobose cone ripening the first year, but persistent after shedding the seeds; scales 20–30, woody, wedge-shaped, enlarged above into a disk with a recurved mucro in the middle and with 3–5 pointed rigid processes on the upper margin; seeds 2–5 to each scale, triangular-oblong and slightly compressed, narrowly winged; cotyledons 2–3. (Greek *kryptos*, hidden, and *meros*, part; meaning obscure.) One species in Japan.

C. **japónica** (L. f.) D. Don. Tree to 50 m. and to 6–10 m. in girth: lvs. linear-subulate, acutish, curved inwards, laterally compressed, keeled above and below, with stomata on both sides, 6–8 mm. long, bright green: staminate fls. about 6 mm. long: cone globose, 1.5–2.5 cm. across; seeds dark brown, 5–6 mm. long. S.Z.2:t.124(c). P.I.114(c,h). W.C.t.48(h). E.H.1:t.42(h). Japan, China. The typical form is **C. j. japónica** (L. f.) Henry, var. Pyramidal tree with stout dark green lvs: cone-scales with long-acuminate processes and long-pointed bracts, giving the cone a spiny appearance. Japan. Intr. 1861. Zone (V).—**C. j. sinénsis** Sieb. & Zucc., var. Tree of looser habit, with deflexed brs. and slender brts.: lvs. longer and slenderer: cone-scales about 20, with shorter mucro and shorter less pointed processes; seeds often only 2. H.I.7:668. (*C. Fortunei* Hooibrenk, *C. Kawaii* Hayata.) S. China. Intr. before 1840. Tenderer than the type.

The following are garden forms of the Japanese plant: **C. j. Lóbbii** Carr. Narrow-pyramidal tree with short and densely ramified brs.: lvs. rather short and lighter green. Intr. 1845. It differs scarcely from the type.—**C. j. compácta** Beiss. Compact conical form with bluish green short and stiff lvs.— **C. j. pungens** Carr. Compact form with stiff and spreading, sharply pointed dark green lvs.—**C. j. araucarioìdes** Henk. & Hochst. Brs. deflexed, with long and distant pendulous brts.: lvs. short, stout and stiff, incurved at apex, bright green. S.Z.2:t.124b,f.2,3—**C. j. dacrydioìdes** Carr. Brs. slender: lvs. 6–8 mm. long, close, stiff, brownish green, partly smaller and scale-like. Cult. 1867.— **C. j. spiràlis** Sieb. & Zucc., var. Slender shrub: lvs. strongly falcate and twisted spirally around the brts.—**C. j. nana** Carr. Dwarf and dense, spreading or procumbent form with short stiff lvs.—**C. j. élegans** (Henk. & Hochst.) Mast., var. Densely branched bushy tree; lvs. spreading and often recurved, soft and slender, flattened, grooved, 1–2.5 cm. long, glaucous green, changing in winter to a reddish bronze color. D.J.181g. B.E.t.24(h). Intr. 1861. Juvenile form, rather short-lived and rarely bearing cones.

15. CUNNINGHÁMIA R. Br. ex Richard. CHINA-FIR. Evergreen trees with spreading brs. pendulous at the ends: lvs. spirally arranged, decurrent, linear-lanceolate, serrulate, spreading in 2 ranks: staminate fls. cylindric-oblong, in terminal clusters: female fls. globose, 1–3 at the end of the brs.: cone subglobose with coriaceous, broad-ovate pointed and irregularly serrate scales, persisting after escape of the seeds: each scale with 3 narrow-winged seeds; cotyledons 2. (After J. Cunningham who discovered the following species in 1702.) Two species in E. Asia.

C. lanceolàta (Lamb.) Hook. Tree to 25 m.; bark brownish, scaling off in irregular plates and exposing the reddish inner bark: lvs. crowded, linear-lanceolate, with broad decurrent base, sharply pointed, 3–6 cm. long, lustrous above, with 2 broad white bands below: cone globose-ovoid, 2.5–5 cm. long. B.M.2743(c). S.Z.2:t.104,105(c). B.S.1:441,t.(h). (*C. sinensis* Richard.) S. and W. China. Intr. 1804. Zone VII. Handsome tree of broad-pyramidal habit; it sprouts from the roots and the stump if cut back.

The second species is **C. Koníshii** Hayata from Formosa with smaller and narrower lvs. and smaller cones. Intr. in 1918; tenderer.

16. FITZROỲA *Hook. f.* FITZROYA. Evergreen tree, irregularly branched; brts. angled: lvs. ternate, decurrent, their free part spreading: fls. dioecious, the staminate axillary, solitary, cylindric, consisting of 15–24 stamens in ternate whorls: cone small, globose, with 3 ternate whorls of valvate scales, the lower whorl small and sterile, the middle one sterile or fertile and the upper one fertile; each fertile scale with a prominent compressed umbo on back and with 2–6 seeds 2- or 3-winged; cotyledons 2. (After Capt. R. Fitzroy of the British Navy; died in 1855.) One species in Chile.

F. cupressoìdes (Molina) Johnston. Tree to 15 m., in cult. often shrubby; bark thick, reddish, deeply furrowed: lvs. ternate or occasionally opposite, spreading or somewhat imbricate, ovate-oblong to narrow-oblong, with incurved mucronate tip, about 3 mm. long, concave above and with 2 narrow stomatic lines, with 2 white bands beneath: cones globose, 8 mm. across. B.M. 4616(c). D.J.288,t.13(h). (*F. patagonica* Hook. f., *Pinus c.* Molina.) S. Chile. Intr. 1849. Zone VII.

17. THUJÓPSIS Sieb. & Zucc. Tree of pyramidal habit with spreading brs. and frond-like arranged brts. spreading in horizontal planes; brts. much flattened, broad: lvs. opposite, the lateral ones somewhat spreading, ovate-lanceolate and curved (hatchet-shaped), acutish, the facial ones ovate-oblong, obtuse: staminate fls. cylindric with 6–10 pairs of stamens; pistillate fls. with 4–5 ovules under each scale: cone subglobose; scales 6–8, woody, flat, imbricate, usually with a boss or mucro below the apex; the upper pair sterile, the fertile ones with 3–5 winged seeds; cotyledons 2. (Thuja and Greek *opsis*, likeness.) One species in Japan.

T. dolabràta (L. f.) Sieb. & Zucc. HIBA ARBOR-VITAE. Pyramidal tree to 15 m., with irregularly whorled or scattered horizontally spreading brs. nodding at the ends; brts. 5–6 mm. broad: lvs. glossy dark green above, with conspicuous white patches below, 4–6 mm. long: cone broad-ovoid, 1.2–1.5 cm. long; scales with a prominent often curved boss below the apex. (*T. d.* var. *australis* Henry, *Thuja d.* L. f.) S.Z.2:t.119,120(c). S.I.1:t.11(c). C. Japan. Intr. 1853, 1861 to Am. Zone VI. A handsome ornamental tree, of slow growth in cult.; not doing well in a dry climate.—**T. d. variegàta** Otto. Tips of brts. creamy-white.—**T. d. nàna** Endl., var. A dwarf and slow-growing form with slenderer brs. and smaller, lighter green lvs. (*T. d.* var. *laetevirens* Mast.,

T. *laetevirens* Lindl.)—**T. d. Hondai** Makino, var. Tree to 30 m.: brts. more closely set, partly overlapping: lvs. smaller: cones globose, 1.5–1.8 cm. across; the scales with a short mucro or only with a narrow ridge. M.K.t.10(c). W.C. t.50,51(h). (*T. H.* Henry.) N. Japan. Intr. 1915. This variety may prove hardier and more satisfactory in the Eastern States than the type.

18. **THÙJA** L. Arbor-vitae. Trees with scaly bark and short spreading or erect brs. forming a pyramidal head: brts. flattened, disposed in one plane: lvs. decussate, scale-like, the lateral lvs. nearly covering the facial ones: fls. monoecious, staminate ovoid, with 6–12 decussate stamens: cones ovoid-oblong or ovoid; scales 8–12, with a thickened ridge or a boss at the apex, the 2 or 3 middle pairs fertile; seeds 2 or 3 under each scale, thin and with broad wings or thick and wingless; cotyledons 2. (Ancient Greek name.) Six species in N. Am. and E. Asia. All the species except *T. setchuenensis* Franch. from W. China are in cult.

A. Brts. disposed in horizontal planes: cone-scales thin; seeds thin, winged.
         Subgen. I. EUTHUJA
  B. Lvs. of primary axes widely spaced, ending in a long point parallel to the axis.
    c. Primary axis flattened: lvs. conspicuously glandular, yellowish or bluish green below.
         1. *T. occidentalis*
    cc. Primary axis nearly terete: lvs. not or inconspicuously glandular, usually with whitish markings below..2. *T. plicata*
  BB. Lvs. of primary axes close, ending in a short spreading point; brts. with white markings below.
    c. Lvs. glandless, slightly or not concave below: brts. thickish, compressed, but scarcely flattened ....3. *T. Standishii*
    cc. Lvs. glandular, concave or grooved below and with conspicuous white markings: brts. much flattened...4. *T. koraiensis*
AA. Brts. in vertical planes, green on both sides: cone-scales thick; seeds ellipsoid, wingless.
  Subgen. II. BIOTA...5. *T. orientalis*

1. **T. occidentàlis** L. American Arbor-vitae. Tree to 20 m., with stout buttressed trunk and short spreading brs. forming a pyramidal head; bark reddish brown, fissured into narrow ridges covered with elongated scales: lvs. abruptly pointed, dark green above, those of the main axes conspicuously glandular, on the brts. sometimes inconspicuously so: male catkins globose, with 3 pairs of stamens: cone oblong, 8 mm. long, light brown; scales 8–10, usually 4 fertile, with a minute mucro at apex; seeds 3 mm. long. S.S.10:t.532. G.C.III.21:213. S.N.287(h). N. S. to Man., s. to N. C., Tenn., and Ill. Intr. about 1536. Zone II. Ornamental pyramidal tree of rather slow growth in cult., with numerous mostly shrubby horticultural forms.

Forms distinguished by color: **T. o. alba** Gord. Tips of young brts. white. (*T. o. albo-spicata* Beiss., *T. o.* "Queen Victoria" Hort.)—**T. o. variegàta** West., var. Brts. variegated with white. (*T. o. argentea* Carr., *T. o. albo-variegata* Beiss.)—**T. o. "Columbia"** Parsons. Columnar form: foliage with silvery variegation, more pronounced in winter. B.E.t.20(h).—**T. o. Vervaeneàna** Gord. Smaller and denser than the type; brts. slenderer, yellowish bronzy in winter. S.N.t.9(hc).—**T. o. aureo-variegàta** Henk. & Hochst. Lvs. variegated with golden yellow. (*T. o. aurea-maculata* Hort., *T. o. Wareana aurea* Hort.) —**T. o. lutéscens** Hesse. A form of *T. o. robusta* with yellow lvs. (*T. o.*' *Wareana lutescens* Hesse.)—**T. o. aùrea** Nels. Broad bushy form with deep yellow lvs.—**T. o. semperaùrea** Rehd., var. A vigorous form with golden-yellow lvs.—**T. o. lùtea** Kent, var. Pyramidal form with bright yellow lvs. (*T. o. elegantissima* Hort., *T. o.* "George Peabody golden.")

Pyramidal or fastigiate forms: **T. o. robústa** Carr. Pyramidal form, denser than the type; brts. stouter, bright green. R.H.1908:79(h). (*T. o. Wareana* Nels., *T. o. densa* Gord., *T. o. sibirica* Hoopes, *T. caucasica* and *T. tatarica* Hort.)—**T. o. Rivérsii** Beiss. Compact pyramidal form with yellowish green lvs.—**T. o. víridis** Beiss. Compact narrow-pyramidal form with lustrous dark green lvs. (*T. o. erecta viridis* Nichols.)—**T. o. Rosenthàlii** Beiss. Columnar form with lustrous dark green lvs.—**T. o. "Douglásii pyramidàlis"** Spaeth. Dense columnar form with crowded frond-like arranged brts., often cristate at end of brs.—**T. o. filicoìdes** Beiss. Narrow-pyramidal form with the short ultimate brts. pinnately arranged.—**T. o. theodonénsis** Beiss. Compact pyramidal form with thicker and broader brts. and dark green lvs. (*T. o. magnifica* Hort.)—**T. o. compácta** Carr. Pyramidal form of denser habit and slower growth than the type.—**T. o. Buchánani** Parsons. Graceful narrow-pyramidal form with slender brts. and rather remote and irregularly arranged thin brts., grayish green. B.E.t.20(h).—**T. o. fastigiàta** Jaeg., var. Columnar form with short brts. Gt.45:508(h). (*T. o. var. columnaris* Mast., *T. o. stricta* Hort., *T. o. pyramidalis* Hort.)—**T. o. Mastérsii** Rehd., f. Pyramidal tree, darker and denser than the type; brts. short, rigid, much flattened, disposed in vertical planes: lvs. distinctly glandular, brownish dark green above, bluish green beneath. G.C.III.21:258. (*T. plicata* Parl., not Lamb., *T. o. var. plicata* Mast., not Hoopes.)

Globose or dwarf forms: **T. o. globòsa** Gord. Compact globose form with bright green lvs. B.E.t.21(h). (*T. o. Spihlmannii* P. Smith, *T. o. globosa Speelmanni* Hort., *T. o. Froebeli* Hort., *T. o. compacta* Beiss., not Carr., *T. o. "Tom Thumb"* Hort.).—**T. o. Woodwárdii** Spaeth. Dense globose form with deep green lvs. B.E.t.21(h).—**T. o. Hóveyi** Hoopes, var. Dwarf globose-ovoid form with rather light green lvs.—**T. o. pùmila** Beiss. Dwarf dense form with dark green lvs. (*T. o. "Little gem"* Hort.)—**T. o. umbraculífera** Beiss. Dwarf dense form with umbrella-like top; brts. thin, dark green. S.N.288(h).

Pendulous or irregular forms: **T. o. péndula** Gord. Brs. bending downward and brts. tufted and pendulous.—**T. o. filifórmis** Beiss. Low bushy form with long and slender sparingly ramified brts., nodding at the tips, partly 4-angled and clothed with sharply pointed appressed lvs. B.C.C.t.38. M.G.16:357(h). (*T. o. var. Douglasii* Rehd.)—**T. o. Ohlendórfii** Beiss. Bushy form with two kinds of lvs., the upper brts. mostly similar to those of *T. o. filiformis,* the lower to those of *T. o. ericoides.* B.E.225. (*T. o. Spaethii* P. Smith.)—**T. o. cristàta** Carr. Irregular dwarf pyramidal form with crowded stout often recurved brts.

Juvenile forms: **T. o. ericoìdes** Hoopes, var. Dwarf broad-pyramidal or bushy form with slender brts. clothed with spreading linear soft lvs. dull green above, grayish green beneath and assuming a brownish tint in winter. R.H.1880:93,94. B.C.3336. (*Retinispora dubia* Carr., *R. ericoides* Hort., not Zucc.)—**T. o. Ellwangeriàna** Beiss. Low broad pyramid, with slender brts. clothed with two kinds of lvs., adult scale-like and juvenile linear and spreading lvs. R.H.1880:93. B.C.3336. A form with yellow lvs. is **T. o. "Ellwangeriana aùrea"** Beiss.

2. **T. plicàta** Lamb. GIANT A. Tall tree, to 60 m., with stout buttressed trunk and short horizontally spreading brs. pendulous at the ends and forming a narrow pyramidal head; bark cinnamon-red, fissured into scaly ridges; brts. slender, regularly and closely set: lvs. bright green and glossy above, with whitish marks below, those of the main axes ovate, acuminate and usually glandular, those of the lateral brts. acute and mucronate and not or scarcely glandular: cones oblong, 1.2 long; scales 10–12, usually 6 fertile; seeds often 3 to each scale, notched at apex. S.S.10t.533. G.C.III.21:215. S.N.292(h). (*T. gigantea* Nutt., *T. Menziesii* Dougl., *T. Lobbii* Hort.) Alaska to N. Calif. and Mont. Intr. 1853. Zone V. Ornamental tree of rapid growth with lustrous

bright green lvs.—**T. p. atróvirens** (Gord.) Sudw. Lvs. dark green. (*T*₁
Lobbii a. Hort.)—**T. p. fastigiàta** (Carr.) Mast., var. Columnar form. G.C.
41:200(h). (*T. gigantea* var. *pyramidalis* Bean.)—**T. p. péndula** (Beiss.)
Schneid., var. Brs. slender, pendulous.

3. **T. Standíshii** (Gord.) Carr. JAPANESE A. Tree to 18 m., with spreading
or somewhat ascending brs. forming a broad pyramid; bark reddish brown,
thin, separating into small scales leaving pale gray blotches; brts. rather thick,
compressed: lvs. bright green above, with triangular white marks below,
glandless, those of the lateral brts. ovate, obtuse: cones ovoid, 8–10 mm. long,
dark brown; scales 10–12, broad-ovate, the 2 middle pairs fertile; seeds 3
to each scale, with narrow wings, not notched at apex. S.I.1:t.11(c). G.C.
III.21:215. W.C.52,53(h). (*T. japonica* Maxim., *Thujopsis S.* Gord.) Japan.
Intr. 1860. Zone V. Handsome tree with broad head, quite different in habit
from the preceding species.

4. **T. koraiénsis** Nakai. KOREAN A. Low spreading shrub, usually with
decumbent brs., rarely a slender, narrow-pyramidal tree to 8 m. with spreading brs. ascending at the ends; bark thin, scaly, chocolate-brown; brts. much
flattened: lvs. of lateral brts. deltoid or rhombic, acutish or obtuse, bright
green above, glaucous beneath, glandular: cones elliptic-ovoid, about 8 mm.
long, light brown; scales 8, those of the 2 middle fertile pairs oval to narrow-
obovate; seeds emarginate at apex. C.B.N.t.90. Korea. Intr. 1918. Zone V.

5. **T. orientàlis** L. ORIENTAL A. Pyramidal or bushy tree, with spreading
and ascending brs. and with the trunk branching from near the base; bark
thin, reddish brown, separating into papery scales; brts. very slender: lvs.
bright green, nearly alike on both sides, those of the main axes glandular,
ending in a free, rather spreading point, those of the lateral brs. closely
appressed, glandular: cones ovoid, 1.5–2.5 cm. long, fleshy and bluish before
ripening; scales usually 6, thick, ovate, obtuse, produced below the apex into
a hooked boss; seeds 2 to each scale, ovoid, brown. S.Z.2:t.118(c). B.N.518.
S.N.65(h). (*Biota o.* Endl.) N. and W. China, Korea; much cult. in Japan.
Intr. before 1737. Zone V or VI. Ornamental tree; its garden forms more
often planted than the type.—**T. o. elegantíssima** (Gord.) Vos. Of compact
pyramidal habit, bright yellow in spring, greenish yellow later. S.N.t.11(hc).—
T. o. beverleyénsis Rehd., var. Pyramidal form with golden yellow lvs.—
T. o. conspícua Berckmans. Of compact fastigiate habit, golden yellow, suffused with green. Berckmans Cat. 1915–16:54(h).—**T. o. aùrea** Dauvesse.
Bushy subglobose form, golden yellow in spring, changing later to yellowish
green. (*Biota o. aurea nana* Sénécl.)—**T. o. semperauréscens** Nichols. Dwarf
subglobose form retaining its golden yellow color throughout the year.—**T. o.
Siebóldii** (Endl.) Laws., var. Low compact subglobose form with bright green
lvs. (*Biota o.* var. *S.* Endl., var. *japonica* Sieb., *B. o. compacta* Beiss.—**T. o.
strícta** Loud., var. Dense pyramidal form with ascending brs. and bright
green lvs. (*Biota o.* var. *pyramidalis* Endl., *T. pyramidalis* Ten., *T. tatarica*
Lodd.)—**T. o. flagellifórmis** Jacques. Pyramidal form with sparingly ramified thread-like pendulous brts. with distant and acuminate lvs. C.B.3:77.
S.N.291(h). (*T. o. var. pendula* Mast., *Biota o. filiformis* Henck. & Hochst.,
T. filiformis Lindl., *T. pendula* Lamb.)

Juvenile forms: **T. o. decussàta** (Beissn. & Hochst.) Mast., var. Dwarf
bushy form with spreading stiff linear-lanceolate and acute bluish green lvs.
(*Retinospora juniperoides* Carr.)—**T. o. meldénsis** (Beissn. & Hochst.) Mast.,
var. Of narrow-pyramidal, somewhat irregular habit: lvs. partly like those of
T. o. decussata, partly passing into the normal form.

Microbiòta decussàta Komar. from e. Manch. is probably only a variation of *Thuja orientalis* retaining the juvenile foliage up to the fruiting stage.

19. **LIBOCÉDRUS** Endl. Trees with scaly bark, spreading or erect brs. and compressed or rarely 4-angled brts. arranged in one plane: lvs. decussate, scale-like, decurrent at base, with or without gland: fls. monoecious, the two sexes on different brts., rarely dioecious; male fls. oblong, with 12–16 decussate stamens; female oblong; fertile scales with 2 ovules: cones oblong, with 4–6 woody, flat scales mucronulate at the apex, the lower pair short, reflexed and sterile; the middle pair oblong and fertile, the upper pair, if present, connate into an erect partition; seeds with one short and one long wing nearly equaling the scale; cotyledons 2. (Greek *libas,* drop, tear, and *cedrus,* referring to the resinous character of the trees.) Eight species in western N. and S. America, N. Zeal., N. Caledonia, N. Guinea, Formosa and S. W. China. Only the following species is hardy within our area, though possibly *L. chilensis* Endl. may survive in sheltered positions along the southern limit.

L. decúrrens Torr. INCENSE CEDAR. Tree to 45 m., with spreading short brs. forming a narrow-pyramidal head, irregular in old age; bark cinnamon-red, broken into irregular scaly ridges; brts. much flattened, bright green on both sides: lvs. oblong-ovate, acuminate, closely adnate to the brts., free at the apex, the lateral ones as long as and nearly covering the obscurely glandular facial ones, 3 mm. long on the lateral brts.: cones oblong, 2–2.5 cm. long, pendulous, light reddish brown; scales mucronate below the apex; the upper sterile pair connate; seeds oblong-lanceolate, 8–12 mm. long. S.S.10:534. B.S.2:25,t.(h). E.H.3,t.142(h). G.C.44:338(h). (*L. Craigana* Gord., *Heyderia d. K.* Koch, *Thuja gigantea* Carr., not Nutt.) Ore. to w. Nev. and L. Calif. Intr. 1853. Zone (V). Handsome tree of remarkably columnar habit with dark green foliage. A few garden forms as *L. d. compacta* Beiss., *L. d. glauca* Beiss. and *L. d. aureo-variegata* Beiss. are known.

20. **CUPRÉSSUS** L. CYPRESS. Trees, rarely shrubs, aromatic; brts. densely clothed with small appressed lvs., 4-angled or terete, rarely somewhat flattened: lvs. opposite, scale-like, minutely denticulate-ciliate, only on young plants or shoots subulate and spreading: fls. solitary, terminating short brts.: staminate fls. ovoid to oblong, yellow, the stamens with 2–6 pendulous globose anther-cells; female fls. subglobose: cone globose or nearly so, ripening the second season, consisting of 6–12 ligneous peltate scales, usually with a mucro at the flattened apex; each scale with numerous compressed and angled narrowly winged seeds; cotyledons 3–4. (The classical name of *C. sempervirens.*) About 12 species in the warmer temperate and subtropical regions; in America from Ore. to Mexico, in the Old World from the Medit. Reg. to China and Himal.—The majority of the species is tender, but the following which are the hardiest, will succeed at least in sheltered situations of the warmer parts of our area.

A. Lvs. obscurely glandular, dark or bright green: cone-scales 8–12.
  B. Brts. rather stout, 1–1.5 mm. thick: boss of cone-scales thick..........1. *C. macrocarpa*
  BB. Brts. slender, scarcely 1 mm. thick: boss of cone-scales thin..........2. *C. sempervirens*
AA. Lvs. with conspicuous, usually resinous gland on back: cone-scales 6–8.
  B. Lvs. dark or bright green, obtuse or acutish: cone-scales 6.................3. *C. Bakeri*
  BB. Lvs. bluish green, acute: cone scales 6–8....................................4. *C. arizonica*

1. **C. macrocárpa** Gord. MONTEREY C. Tree to 25 m., pyramidal when young, with a broad crown in old age: bark separating into broad scaly ridges: brts. terete or slightly 4-angled: lvs. uniform, rhombic, obtuse, dark green: staminate fls. ovoid, 4 mm. long: cone globose or broad-ellipsoid,

short-stalked, 2.5–3.5 cm. long; scales with a short ridge-like boss in the centre. S.S.10:t.525. G.C.III.22:53. G.F.7:245(h). Am. For. 29:270,271(h). (*C. Lambertiana* Gord.) Calif., s. of Monterey. Intr. 1838. Zone VII.—**C. m. fastigiàta** Carr. Brs. ascending forming a dense fastigiate head.—**C. m. lùtea** Webster. Narrow pyramidal form with yellow lvs. S.N.111(h). Gn.68: 237(h).—**C. m. Críppsii** R. Smith. A juvenile form with stiff brs. and spread ing subulate lvs.—**C. m. pygmàea** A. B. Jacks., f. Very dwarf and dense, to 10 cm. high, with dimorphous lvs. Cult. 1936.

C. m. × *Chamaecyparis nootkatensis* = *Cupressocyparis Leylandii;* see below.

2. **C. sempérvirens** L. ITALIAN C. Tree to 25 m. with erect or horizontal brs. and thin fissured bark; brts. terete or slightly 4-angled: lvs. uniform, rhombic, obtuse, dark green; staminate fls. oblong-cylindric, 4–5 mm. long: cone subglobose or ellipsoid, 2–3 cm. across; scales 8–14, contracted into a small point, sometimes flat or slightly impressed and mucronulate in the middle. H.W.1:196. C.B.2:73. S. Eu. and W. Asia. Planted since ancient times. Zone VII?—**C. s. strícta** Ait., var. COLUMNAR ITALIAN C. With erect or ascending brs. forming a columnar head. Gn.33:3(h). G.W.9:127(h). (*C. s.* var. *pyramidalis* Nym., *C. s. fastigiata* Hansen, *C. fastigiata* DC.)— **C. s. índica** Parl., var. Of columnar habit: cone globose, with 10 acutely mucronate scales.—**C. s. horizontàlis** (Mill.) Gord. With horizontally spreading brs. forming a broad-pyramidal head. (*C. h.* Mill.)

Closely related species: **C. Duclouxiàna** Hickel. Tree with spreading brs.; brts. usually slightly compressed: lvs. about 1 mm. long, obtusish, glaucescent: cones globose, 2–3 cm. across; scales usually 8, flat. Camus, Cyprès, 92. C.B.N. t.43. (*C. torulosa* Rehd. & Wils., not D. Don.) W. China. Intr. about 1900. Zone VII?

3. **C. Bàkeri** Jeps. MODOC C. Tree to 10 or sometimes 30 m.; bark thin, reddish, separating in thin plates: brts. slender, 4-angled: lvs. obtuse to acutish, keeled, with a conspicuous resin-gland, dark or bright green: cones subglobose, 1.5–2 cm. in diam., gray; scales 6, abruptly contracted into a short straight mucro, often an additional small pair at apex. Eliot, For. Tr. Pacific Coast, f.101–103. Ore. Intr. 1917. Zone (V). The hardiest of the true Cypresses.

Related species: **C. Macnabiàna** A. Murr. Shrub or tree to 10 m.; bark gray, slightly furrowed; brts. subterete: lvs. convex on back: cones 2–2.5 cm. long, with 6–8 scales, the upper ones with prominent incurved bosses. S.M.72. G.C. 56:411. S.S.10:t.528. B.C.2:915(h). S.N.178(h). Calif. Intr. 1854. Zone VII.

4. **C. arizònica bonìta** Lemm., var. Tree to 12, occasionally to 25 m.; bark red-brown, separating in large thin flakes or on older trees fissured and separating into long shreds: brts. rather stout: lvs. acute, thick, keeled, with conspicuous resinous gland, more or less glaucous: fr. subglobose to broadellipsoid, 2.5–3 cm. across; scales 6–8, flat or slightly depressed on back and abruptly contracted into a short mucro. I.T.3:t.145. G.C.57:315. M.D.13: t.4(h). (*C. glabra* Sudw.) C. and s. Ariz. Intr. 1882. Zone VII?—**C. a. compácta** Schneid., var. Low roundish bush. S.N.179(h).—**C. a. glauca** Woodall. Juvenile form of intensely silvery gray color.—The typical **C. arizonica** Greene differs from s. Ariz. differs chiefly in the usually glandless lvs. and in the smaller cones with larger, more prominent bosses.

20a. × **CUPRESSOCÝPARIS** M. L. Green. Hybrid between *Cupressus* and *Chamaecyparis;* only the following cross known.

C. Leylándii (A. B. Jacks.) M. L. Green (*C. macrocarpa* × *Ch. nootkatensis*). Similar in habit, brts. and lvs. to *Ch. nootkatensis:* cones to 2 cm. across, with about 5 seeds to each scale. K.B.1926:114,t(h). Orig. 1888

21. **CHAMAECÝPARIS** Spach. CYPRESS. Pyramidal trees; leading shoots nodding; brs. spreading; brts. mostly frond-like arranged, usually flattened: lvs. opposite, scale-like (only in the juvenile state subulate), ovate to rhombic, acuminate to obtuse, entire: staminate fls. ovoid to oblong, yellow, rarely red; stamens with 2–4 anther-cells: fr. globose, ripening the first season, with 6–12 peltate scales pointed or bossed in the middle; seeds 2, rarely up to 5, slightly compressed, with thin broad wings; cotyledons 2. (Greek *chamai*, on the ground, and *kyparissos*, cypress; in allusion to its affinity.) Syn. *Retinispora* Zucc., *Retinospora* Carr. Six species in N. Am. and in Japan and Formosa.

A. Lvs. green on both sides or somewhat paler below, the lateral not much larger than the facial ones.
  B. Brts. compressed, slender, not distinctly 2-ranked: lvs. glandular, bluish green: cone about 6 mm. across..1. *C. thyoides*
  BB. Brts. nearly 4-sided, stout: lvs. dark green, not glandular: cone nearly 1.2 cm. across.
                                                2. *C. nootkatensis*
AA. Lvs. with glaucous or whitish marks below: brts. arranged in horizontal planes.
  B. Lvs. closely appressed, obtuse to acute, the lateral much larger than the facial ones: cones 8–12 mm. across.
    c. Lvs. acute or acutish, glandular, the white markings below sometimes indistinct: staminate fls. red..3. *C. Lawsoniana*
    cc. Lvs. obtuse, not glandular, lustrous dark green, the white markings distinct.
                                                4. *C. obtusa*
  BB. Lvs. loosely appressed, acuminate, the lateral not much larger than the facial ones: cones 6–8 mm. across...5. *C. pisifera*

1. **C. thyoìdes** (L.) B.S.P. WHITE CEDAR. Tree to 25 m., with reddish brown bark fissured into flat connected ridges; brs. upright-spreading or horizontal, forming a narrow spire-like head; brts. slender, rather irregularly arranged; lvs. closely appressed or on vigorous brts. spreading at the apex, keeled, conspicuously glandular, dark bluish or light green: cones globose, finally bluish purple, bloomy; scales with acute, often reflexed bosses; seeds 1 or 2 on each scale, with wings as broad as the seed. S.S.10:t.529. B.N.529(h). M.G. 11:301(h). (*C. sphaeroidea* Spach, *Cupressus t.* L.) Me. to Fla., w. to Miss.; in cold swamps. Intr. 1727. Zone III. The least attractive, but hardiest species.—**C. t. glaùca** (Endl.) Sudw. Compact shrub with glaucous or nearly silvery white lvs. (*C. sphaeroidea* var. *kewensis* Hort.)—**C. t. variegàta** (Loud.) Sudw. Brts. variegated with yellow.—**C. t. ericoìdes** (Carr.) Sudw. Low compact pyramidal bush: lvs. linear, spreading, with 2 glaucous lines beneath, usually changing to reddish brown in winter. B.C.5:2922. B.N.532. (*Retinispora e.* Gord.)—**C. t. andelyénsis** Schneid., var. Of upright habit, with loosely appressed subulate lvs.; often part of the brts. like those of the type and others like those of the preceding form. B.C.5:2922. R.H.1880:36, 37(h). (*C. t. leptoclada* Sudw., *C. sphaeroidea a.* Carr., *Retinispora leptoclada* Gord., not Zucc.)

2. **C. nootkaténsis** (Lamb.) Spach. NOOTKA C. Tree to 40 m., with brownish gray irregularly fissured bark separating into large thin scales; brs. ascending or spreading, forming a narrow pyramid; brts. usually pendulous, terete or 4–angled, on the upper part of the tree arranged on vertical planes: lvs. closely appressed, or on vigorous shoots spreading, acute, keeled or rounded on back and usually not glandular: staminate fls. bright yellow: cones subglobose, about 1 cm. across, dark red-brown, bloomy; scales 4–6, with erect pointed bosses and often with resinous glands; seeds 2–4 on each scale, with broad wings. S.S.10:t.530. F.E.25:543(h). H.B.4:27(h). (*C. nutkatensis* Spach, *C. nutkaënsis* Lindl. & Gord., *C. nootkatensis* Sudw., *Cupressus n.* Lamb., *Thuyopsis borealis* Hort.—SITKA C., YELLOW CEDAR.) S. W. Alaska to Ore. Intr. 1853. Zone IV. Handsome narrow-pyramidal tree with dark

green lvs.—**C. n. glaùca** Beiss. Lvs. very glaucous (*Cupressus nutkatensis g.* Reg.)—**C. n. lùtea** Beiss. The young shoots light yellow changing finally to green. Gn.50:68(h). J.L.27:427(h).—**C. n. compácta** Beiss. Dwarf compact form. S.N.166(h).—**C. n. péndula** (Beiss.) Schneid., var. A form with spreading brs. and long pendulous brts. S.N.166(h). B.N.F.535(h).

C. n. × *Cupressus macrocarpa* = *Cupressocyparis Leylandii;* see p. 56.

3. **C. Lawsoniàna** (A. Murr. Parl. Lawson C. Tree to 60 m., in cult. usually a narrow-pyramidal tree furnished to the ground with brs.; bark reddish brown, divided into round scaly ridges: brts. flattened, frond-like arranged in horizontal planes: lvs. closely appressed, acute or acutish, glandular, bright green to glaucous, marked below with often indistinct white streaks: staminate fls. crimson: cone globose, 8 mm. across, reddish brown and bloomy; scales 8, with thin, acute, reflexed bosses; seeds 2–4 on each scale, broadly winged. S.S.10:t.531. F.E.23:309(h);33:559(h). P.I.t.32(c,h). B.S.1:444(h). (*C. Boursieri* Decne., *Cupressus L.* A. Murr.) S. W. Ore. to n. w. Calif. Intr. 1854. Zone (V). One of the most handsome Conifers, but not thriving well in a dry climate; it is very variable and about 80 garden forms are known in Eu.—**C. L. glaùca** (Jaeg.) Beiss. With steel-blue lvs. M.G.31:310(h). Here belongs "Triomphe de Boskoop."—**C. L. argéntea** (Gord.) Beiss. With nearly silvery white lvs.; here belongs "Silver Queen."—**C. L. lùtea** (R. Smith) Beiss. Of compact pyramidal habit; young growth bright yellow. S.N.t.5(hc).

Columnar forms: **C. L. erécta** (Gord.) Sudw. Columnar dense form with the brts. arranged in vertical planes, bright green. (*C. L. erecta viridis* Beiss., *Cupressus L. erecta viridis* Waterer.) G.C.58:272(h). S.N.168(h). A form of this with glaucous foliage is **C. L. "erécta glauca"** (R. Smith) Beiss.— **C. L. Állumi** (R. Smith) Beiss. Columnar form with bluish or steel-blue foliage. G.W.20:581(h).—**C. L. Fràseri** Beiss. Similar to the preceding, but less narrow in habit and with dark bluish foliage. M.G.33:250(h).—**C. L. Flétcheri** (Fletcher) Hornibr., var. Slow growing dense columnar form with ascending brs.: lvs. intermediate between the juvenile and adult form, glaucous. Gn.77:274(h). H.D.32,t(h).

Spreading and pendulous forms: **C. L. péndula** Beiss. With more or less spreading brs. and pendulous brts. F.E.27:187(h). A form of this with the brs. as well as the brts. pendulous is **C. L. "péndula vera"** Hesse.—**C. L. grácilis** Bailey, var. A graceful form with pendulous brts.: lvs. bright green with slightly spreading tips. (*C. L. gracilis pendula* Hort.)—**C. L. filifórmis** (Nichols.) Beiss. Brs. spreading or slightly pendulous, the terminal brts. much elongated and with few short lateral brts., pendulous. Gs.6:231.—**C. L. intertéxta** (R. Smith) Beiss. Pyramidal form with remote arching brs. and distant thickish brts., bluish green. B.N.550(h).

Dwarf forms: **C. L. nàna** (Dauvesse) Beiss. Dwarf globose or ovoid form with stiff short brts., dark green. B.N.553(h). A form of this with bluish green lvs. is **C. L. "nana glauca"** Beiss.—**C. L. "mínima glauca"** (R. Smith) Beiss. is a dwarf and compact conical form with dark steel-blue lvs. S.N. 132(h).

4. **C. obtùsa** (Sieb. & Zucc.) Endl. Hinoki C. Tree to 40 m., with broad-pyramidal head: bark reddish brown, rather smooth, peeling off in thin strips: brts. arranged in horizontal planes: lvs. closely appressed, obtuse, dark green above, with white marks below, the facial ones more acutish, often keeled, not glandular: cones globose, 8–10 mm. across, orange-brown; scales 8, rarely 10, depressed on back and with a small mucro: seeds 2–5 on each scale, narrowly winged. S.Z.2:t.121(c). S.I.1:t.10(c). W.C.t.54,55(h). (*Re-*

tinispora o. Sieb. & Zucc., *Cupressus* o. K. Koch.) Japan, and in a slightly differing var. in Formosa (var. **formosàna** Hayata). Intr. 1861. Zone III. An ornamental tree of rather slow growth; it does not do well in a dry climate and dislikes lime.

Forms differing in color: **C. o. albo-spica** Beiss. Young shoots at first creamy white, changing to pale green. (*C. o. albospicata* Beiss.)—**C. o. aùrea** (Gord.) Henk. & Hochst. With golden yellow lvs. S.N.t.6(hc). Gn.M.2: 27(h).—**C. o. Crippsi** (Cripps) Rehd., var. With pale yellow lvs.—**C. o. "grácilis aùrea"** (R. Smith) Nichols. A graceful form with slender slightly pendulous brts. golden yellow at first, changing to greenish yellow. (*C. o. aurea Youngii* Bobbink & Atkins.)—**C. o. "tetragòna aùrea"** (Barron) Nichols. A dwarf broad-pyramidal form, with crowded irregular brt. systems; brts. more or less 4-angled and partly golden-yellow. (*C. o. tetragona* Rehd.) H.D.43,t.(h). The green form, **C. o. tetragòna** (Gord.) Hornibr., var., is not now in cult.

Forms differing in habit: **C. o. breviràmea** (Maxim.) Reg., var. Tree of narrow-pyramidal habit, with short brs.; brts. rather thin, close, regularly arranged, the lateral ones overtopping the terminal one: cones slightly smaller, (*C. b.* Maxim.) Japan. Intr. 1919.—**C. o. magnífica** (R. Smith) Beiss. Vigorous form with stout brts. and lustrous bright green lvs.—**C. o. erécta** Beiss. Fastigiate form with ascending brs. and bright green lvs.—**C. o. grácilis** Rehd., var. Compact pyramidal form, dark green; brts. with slightly pendulous tips. —**C. o. filicoìdes** (R. Smith) Hartw. & Ruempl., var. Usually shrubby, of slow growth, with crowded and short brts. of nearly equal length on elongated brs., forming long and narrow frond-like brt.-systems; brts. keeled above. G.C.II.5:235. K.V.221 (*Retinospora f.* Veitch.)—**C. o. lycopodioìdes** (Gord.) Carr. Dwarf shrubby form, with irregularly ramified brs., the ultimate brts. crowded, not arranged in one plane, partly fasciated, not or scarcely compressed; lvs. appressed, elongated acute, spirally arranged or indistinctly 4-ranked, dark green. Gs.6:231.—**C. o. compácta** (Gord.) Hartw. & Ruempl., var. Dwarf broad-conical form with much crowded short brts. at the end of short brs. G.C.78:37(h). B.E.t.18(h, as var. *nana*).—**C. o. nàna** Carr. Low form of slow growth, with spreading brs. and short dark green brts. R.H. 1882:102. A form of this with the young growth golden yellow is **C. o. "nana aurea"** Carr.—**C. o. pýgmaea** (Gord.) Henk. & Hochst. Very dwarf form with horizontal almost creeping brs. and short close-set brts. R.H.1889: 376(h). Interesting form for rockeries.

Juvenile form: **C. o. ericoìdes** Boehmer. Dense broad-conical or subglobose bush with rather stout brts. and spreading linear obtuse lvs. 3–5 mm. long, thickish and bluish gray. G.C.33:f.107(h). H.D.42,t(h). (*Juniperus Sanderi* Hort., *Retinospora Sanderi* Sander, *Cupressus pisifera* var. *Sanderi* Dallim. & Jacks.)

5. **C. pisífera** (Sieb. & Zucc.) Endl. Sawara C. Tree to 50 m., with horizontally spreading brs. forming a narrow-pyramidal head; bark red-brown, rather smooth, peeling off in thin strips: brts. flattened, 2-ranked and arranged in horizontal planes: lvs. appressed, acuminate, ovate-lanceolate, with slightly spreading tips, obscurely glandular, dark green above, with whitish lines beneath: cones globose, 6 mm. across, dark brown; scales 10, sometimes 12, with a small mucro at the depressed centre; seeds 1–2, broadly winged. S.Z.2:t. 122(c). P.I.t.34(c,h). W.C.t.56,57(h). (*Retinispora p.* Sieb. & Zucc., *Cupressus p.* K. Koch.) Japan. Intr. 1861. Zone III. A narrow-pyramidal tree of fairly rapid growth and rather loose habit; it is apt to become soon thin and

to lose its lower brs.—**C. p. aùrea** (Gord.) Henk. & Hochst. Foliage golden-yellow. G.W.20:581(h).—**C. p. sulphùrea** (Kent) Schelle. Foliage light yellow.—**C. p. filífera** (Sénécl.) Hartw. & Ruempl., var. Pyramidal shrub of small tree with spreading and elongated pendulous thread-like brs. and with short and remote lateral brts.: lvs. subulate, distant, sharply pointed. (*Retinispora f.* Gord., *C. p. filifera pendula* Hort.) G.C.II.5:237. B.N.572,571(h). S.N.62(h). Forms of this variety are **C. p. "filifera aurea"** Beiss. with the young growth golden yellow and **C. p. "filifera aùreo-variegàta"** Voss, f., with the brts. variegated with yellow but less elongated.

Juvenile forms: **C. p. plumòsa** (Carr.) Otto, var. A transition between the type and var. *squarrosa*. Of dense conical habit: brs. ascending; ultimate brts. frond-like arranged, feathery: lvs. slightly spreading, subulate, 3–4 mm. long, bright green outside, whitened on the inner face. B.C.2:731. Gn.M.2:27(h). S.N.108(h). (*Retinispora p.* Veitch.) Intr. 1861. Color forms of this var. are: **C. p. "plumòsa argéntea"** (Sénécl.) Otto, var., with the tips of the brts. whitish; **C. p. "plumosa aurea"** (R. Smith) Otto, var., with the young growth golden yellow. B.E.215; **C. p. "plumosa flavéscens"** Beiss. with the tips of the young brts. yellowish.—**C. p. squarròsa** (Endl.) Beiss. & Hochst. Dense bush or small tree; brts. irregularly arranged, not frond-like, feathery: lvs. spreading, flat, linear, about 6 mm. long, rather soft, glaucous. B.E.215. B.C.2:731. M.G.24:44(h). Intr. 1843. A form with yellow foliage is **C. p. "squarròsa sulphùrea"** (Nichols.) Beiss.—**C. p. mínima** Hornibr. Low shrub of dense irregular habit with very crowded short brts.; lvs. 3–5 mm. long, partly recurved. (*C. p.* var. *squarrosa minima* Hornibr.)

22. **JUNÍPERUS** L. Juníper. Trees or shrubs with usually thin, shreddy, rarely scaly bark: lvs. opposite or ternate, acicular or scale-like, on young plants always acicular, on old plants either all acicular and ternate, or all scale-like or both: fls. dioecious or monoecious, axillary or terminal, the staminate yellow, consisting of numerous opposite or ternate stamens forming an ovoid or oblong catkin, the female of 3–8 pointed scales, some or all bearing 1 or 2 ovules; the scales become fleshy and unite into a berry-like indehiscent and usually succulent strobile subtended by scaly bracts, ripening the first, 2d or 3d year; seeds 1–12 usually ovoid, terete or angled, often grooved, brown, with a conspicuous hilum at base: cotyledons 2 or 4–6. (The ancient Latin name.) Including *Sabina* Spach. About 40 species widely distributed through the n. hemisphere from the arctic zone to the mts. of the tropics.

A. Lvs. all acicular, ternate, spreading, joined at base, with 2 white, often confluent bands above: winter-buds distinct: fls. axillary, dioecious: seeds usually 3.
  B. Fr. large, 2–2.5 cm. across; seeds connate into a 3-celled stone: lvs. decurrent, 3–4 mm. broad ....Sect. I. Caryocedrus Endl.
                                                                    1. *J. drupacea*
  BB. Fr. smaller; seeds not connate: lvs. 1.5–3 mm. broad, not decurrent.
                                                        Sect. II. Oxycedrus Endl.
    c. Lvs. with the white band above separated by a green midrib.
      D. White bands scarcely as broad as the green margin; lvs. spreading, sharply pointed: brts. spreading.
        E. Lvs. very rigid, 1.2–2 cm. long, tapering from the middle........2. *J. Oxycedrus*
        EE. Lvs. less rigid, 2-2.5 cm. long, tapering from the base..........3. *J. macrocarpa*
      DD. White bands broader than the green margin; lvs. directed forward: tree with pendulous brs. ....4. *J. formosana*
    cc. Lvs. with the white bands confluent.
      D. White band narrower than the green margin; lvs. sulcate above.
        E. Upright shrub or tree: fr. 6–8 mm. across...........................5. *J. rigida*
        EE. Procumbent shrub: fr. 8–12 mm. across............................6. *J. conferta*
      DD. White band broader than the green margin; lvs. concave above...7. *J. communis*

AA. Lvs. all or partly scale-like, less often all acicular, but not jointed at base, decurrent; without distinct winter-buds: fls. terminal, dioecious or monoecious: fr. with 1–6 seeds.
Sect. III. **SABINA** Endl.
  B. Lvs. always ternate and acicular.
    C. Brs. recurved and pendulous; tree: lvs. loosely appressed, channeled on the back near the base, without green midrib above: fr. 1-seeded.................8. *J. recurva*
    CC. Brs. prostrate or spreading; shrubs or tree: lvs. appressed or spreading, with a green midrib above, channeled from base to near apex.
      D. Brts. green and lvs. green below: procumbent shrub or tree: fr. 1-seeded.
9. *J. squamata*
      DD. Brts. glaucous on the edge of the pulvini: lvs. glaucous beneath spotted with white: procumbent shrub: fr. 2–3-seeded.........................10. *J. procumbens*
  BB. Lvs. at least on mature plants wholly or partly scale-like, usually opposite or opposite and ternate on the same plant.
    C. Lvs. minutely denticulate (under a strong lens).
      D. Acicular lvs. usually ternate.
        E. Fr. reddish brown or yellow, rather large, fibrous, dry.
          F. Scale-like lvs. obtuse or obtusish, opposite: seeds 3–6.
            G. Bark shreddy: fr. shining yellow...........................11. *J. phoenicea*
            GG. Bark scaly: fr. reddish brown, bloomy..................12. *J. pachyphloea*
          FF. Scale-like lvs. acute: seed 1...................................13. *J. utahensis*
        EE. Fr. blue or blue-black, usually bloomy, juicy.
          F. Brts. stout; scale-like lvs. usually ternate, conspicuously glandular: seeds 2–3 ....14. *J. occidentalis*
          FF. Brts. slender; scale-like lvs. opposite, rarely ternate, glandless or obscurely glandular: seed usually 1.
            G. Fr. globose or ellipsoid, bloomy, 3–6 mm. long..........15. *J. monosperma*
            GG. Fr. ovoid, broadest at base, not bloomy, 6–12 mm. long..16. *J. Wallichiana*
      DD. Acicular lvs. opposite; scale-like lvs. acute: fr. blue; seeds 2–4....17. *J. thurifera*
    CC. Lvs. entire: fr. blue-black, small, (brown or purplish brown and larger in Nos. 18 and 19).
      D. Acicular lvs. often ternate; scale-like lvs. obtuse: fr. brown, bloomy, seeds 2–3.
19. *J. chinensis*
      DD. Acicular lvs. opposite, ternate only on leading shoots: scale-like lvs. acute.
        E. Fr. dark purplish brown, bloomy, about 1 cm. across, with about 6 seeds: acicular lvs. rarely present; tree....................................18. *J. excelsa*
        EE. Fr. blue-black, 5–6 mm. across, with 1–4 seeds.
          F. Fr. erect or nodding; seeds 1–2; trees, rarely shrubby.
            G. Fr. ripening the first season: male fls. with 10–12 stamens..20. *J. virginiana*
            GG. Fr. ripening the second season: male fls. with 6 stamens..21. *J. scopulorum*
          FF. Fr. pendulous; seeds 1–4, usually 2: shrubs, often prostrate.
            G. Lvs. dark green, obtuse or acutish, of strong disagreeable odor when bruised ....22. *J. Sabina*
            GG. Lvs. bluish green or steel-blue, acute or cuspidate, of aromatic, less strong odor: prostrate shrub...................................23. *J. horizontalis*

1. **J. drupàcea** Labill. SYRIAN J. Tree to 20 m., of pyramidal habit, in cult. usually columnar; brts. triangular, with prominent ridges: lvs. linear-lanceolate, widest near base, sharply pointed, above with 2 white bands and a broad green midrib, 1.5–2 cm. long: fr. brown or bluish, bloomy, ripening the 2d season. G.C.III.19:519. B.C.3:14. S.N.114,205(h). M.D.1916:t.33(h); 1931:t.30(h). Greece, Asia Minor. Intr. 1853. Zone VII. Handsome ornamental tree of columnar habit; thrives well on limestone soil.

2. **J. Oxycédrus** L. PRICKLY J. Shrub or small tree to 10 m.: brts. angular, rather slender: lvs. linear, tapering from the middle to a spiny point, 12–18 mm. long and 1–1.5 mm. broad: fr. globose, 6–12 mm. across, reddish brown, without or with partial bloom. H.W.1:193. C.B.3:22. Medit. Reg. to Cauc. and Persia. Cult. 1740. Zone VII? In cult. usually a compact shrub.

3. **J. macrocárpa** Sibth. PLUM J. Bushy shrub or small tree to 4 m., of dense pyramidal habit: lvs. linear, tapering from the base, sharply pointed, 1.8–2.5 cm. long, 2 mm. broad: fr. globose, 1.2 cm. across, dark brown, glaucous. C.B.3:16. (*J. neaboriensis* Gord.) Medit. Reg. Intr. 1838. Zone VII.

4. **J. formosàna** Hayata. FORMOSAN J. Tree to 12 m., usually dividing into several stems, with spreading or ascending brs. and pendulous brts.: lvs. more or less directed forward, linear, spiny-pointed, 1.2–2.5 cm. long and 1.5–2 mm. wide, with two broad white bands above coalescent near apex, keeled below: fr. subglobose or broadly ovoid, 8 mm. across, reddish or orange brown.

Juniperus   PINACEAE   *Juniperus*

J.C.25,19:t.38. C.B.3:17. S.N.31(h). (*J. taxifolia* Parl., not Hook. & Arn., *J. oblonga pendula* Knight & Perry.) Formosa, China. Intr. probably 1844. Zone V. Handsome tree with pendulous brts.

5. **J. rígida** Sieb. & Zucc. NEEDLE J. Shrub or tree to 10 m., pyramidal or columnar, with ascending brs. and pendulous brts.: young brts. slender, triangular: lvs. spreading, linear-subulate, tapering from the middle into a spiny point, 1.2–2.5 cm. long, about 1 mm. wide, deeply sulcate above and with a narrow white band, prominently keeled below: fr. globose, 6–8 mm. across, brownish black, bloomy, finally slightly shining, ripening the second year. S.I.1:t.12(c). W.C.58(h). Japan, Korea, to N. China. Intr. 1861. Zone V. Graceful pyramidal tree or shrub with pendulous brts.

6. **J. conférta** Parl. Procumbent shrub: lvs. crowded, about 1.2 cm. long, bluish green, tapering to a spiny point, deeply sulcate above, keeled below: fr. globose 8–12 mm. across, black and bloomy. C.B.3:18. W.C.t.59(h). Gn. 88:142(h). (*J. litoralis* Maxim.) Saghal., Japan. Intr. 1915. Zone V.

7. **J. commùnis** L. COMMON J. Shrub or tree of pyramidal habit, to 12 m.; bark reddish brown, peeling off in papery shreds: lvs. linear-subulate to linear-lanceolate, tapering from the base to a spiny point, about 1.5 cm. long, concave above and with a broad white band sometimes divided at base by a green midrib, bluntly keeled below: fls. rarely monoecious: fr. globose or broadly ovoid, 5–6 mm. across, short-stalked, bluish or black, slightly bloomy, ripening the 2d or 3d year; seeds usually 3. H.W.1:t.10(c). S.S.1:t.516. E.H.6:t.348(h). N. Am., s. to Pa., Ill., N. M. and n. Calif.; Eu. to W. Himal. and N. E. Asia. Cult 1560. Zone II. A very variable species with some garden forms and several geographical varieties; the typical upright form (var. erécta Pursh) is common in Eu. and occasionally found in n. e. North Am.—
J. c. aùrea Nichols. Brts. drooping; young growth golden yellow, changing later to green. (*J. c. aureo-variegata* Beiss.)—**J. c. suècica** Ait., var. SWEDISH J. Columnar form with rather spreading, light bluish green lvs.; brts. with nodding tips. B.N.621(h). G.W.20:579(h). (*J. c.* var. *fastigiata* Parl., *J. s.* Mill.)—**J. c. hibérnica** Gord. IRISH J. Similar to the preceding, but lvs. shorter, less spreading, dark green; tips of brts. upright. B.N.623(h). (*J. c. stricta* Carr.)—**J. c. péndula** Carr. Shrub with spreading and recurving brs. and pendulous brts.—**J. c. oblóngo-péndula** Sudw. Broad-columnar shrub with pendulous brts. and thin and slender lvs. Am. For. 35:576(h). (*J. c.* var. *oblonga pendula* Loud.)—**J. c. compréssa** Carr. Slow growing dwarf fastigiate shrub with very short crowded brts. and thin lvs. 3–6 mm. long. H.D.70,t(h).

The following are geographical varieties: **J. c. depréssa** Pursh, var. PROSTRATE J. Low shrub, rarely exceeding 1.5 m., forming broad patches with numerous stems ascending from a procumbent base: lvs. somewhat shorter and broader. B.E.t.12(h). (*J. c.* var. *canadensis* Loud., *J. c. nana canadensis* Carr., *J. canadensis* Burgsd.) E. N. Am.—A variation with the young growth yellow is **J. c. aùreo-spìca** Rehd., var. (*J. nana canadensis aurea* Beiss., *J. canadensis aurea* Hort.)—**J. c. saxatilis** Pall., var. MOUNTAIN J. Spreading prostrate shrub, rarely over 60 cm. high: lvs. crowded, linear-oblong, 4–8 mm. long and 1–2 mm. broad, abruptly pointed, usually curved and very concave above: fr. globose, glaucous; seeds 1–3. E.B.8:t.1383(c). M.G.25:123(h). (*J. c.* var. *montana* Ait., *J. c.* var. *nana* Loud., var. *alpina* Gaud., *J. nana* Willd., *J. sibirica* Burgsd.) Arctic reg. and high mts. of Eu. and N. Am. Cult. 1789.—**J. c. Jáckii** Rehd., var. Prostrate shrub with flagelliform trailing brs. often to 1 m. long and nearly unbranched except a few clusters of short brts.:

lvs. linear-lanceolate, incurved. Ore., n. Calif. Intr. 1904.—J. c. nippónica Wils., var. Similar to var. *saxatilis,* but lvs. deeply sulcate above and keeled below. High mts. of Japan. Intr. 1915.

8. **J. recúrva** Buch.-Ham. Tree to 10 m., usually broad-pyramidal with spreading curved brs. and pendulous brts.: bark brown, peeling off in thin flakes: lvs. ternate, densely imbricated and loosely appressed, linear-lanceolate, 3–6 mm. long, sharply pointed, very concave above and whitish, dull green beneath and grooved below the middle: fls. monoecious: fr. ovoid, 8–10 mm. long, dark purple-brown, ripening the 2d year, 1-seeded. G.C.II.19:574. B.S.1:674,t(h). (*Sabina r.* Ant.) Himal.: Sikkim and Bhutan.; S. W. China. Intr. 1830. Zone VII?—A graceful tree with dull foliage.

Related species: **J. Coxii** A. B. Jacks. Large tree: lvs. about 1 cm. long, more acuminate, with 2 greenish white bands above, convex below: fr. ovoid, black, slightly bloomy. N.F.5:33. C.B.N.t.50. S. W. China, Burma. Intr. 1920. Zone VII?

9. **J. squamàta** Lamb. Shrub with long decumbent brs. and ascending brts.; young brts. green: lvs. ternate, crowded and loosely appressed or slightly spreading, linear, finely pointed, 3–4 mm. long, concave above and whitened, convex below and grooved from base to near apex, green: fr. ellipsoid, 6–8 mm. long, changing from reddish brown to purplish black, 1-seeded. C.B.3:29. S.N.192(h). (*J. recurva* var. *s.* Parl., *J. densa* Gord., *Sabina s.* Ant.) Himal., W. and C. China, Formosa. Intr. 1836 or before. Zone IV.— **J. s. prostràta** Hornibrook, var. Prostrate form with horizontally spreading brs. F.R.N.8:f.66(h). Intr. 1909.—J. s. Fargèsii Rehd. & Wils., var. Tree 5–20 m., with upright-spreading brs.: lvs. narrower and longer, usually 8 mm. long, acuminate, pale or bluish green: fr. ovoid, 5–6 mm. long. Not. Syst. Herb. Ross. 5:31. S.N.193(h). Gn.88:141(h). (*J. F. Komar., J. Lemeeana* Lévl. & Blin.) W. China. Intr. 1907. Zone V.—J. s. Wilsònii Rehd., var. Upright shrub to 2 m., with short crowded brts. recurved at the tips: lvs. shorter and broader, crowded, broad-lanceolate, about 4 mm. long. W. China. Intr. 1909. Zone V.—J. s. Meỳeri Rehd., var. Upright much branched shrub with ascending brs. and short straight brts.: lvs. narrow-lanceolate, straight, 6–8 mm. long, very glaucous on back. B.D.1923:t.20(h). H.B.1:76(h) China. Intr. 1914. Zone IV. Handsome with its dense habit and bluish white lvs.

10. **J. procúmbens** (Endl.) Sieb. & Zucc. Low spreading shrub, with ascending brts., to 75 cm. high; brts. glaucous: lvs. ternate, linear-lanceolate, 6–8 mm. long, spiny-pointed, concave above and glaucous with a green midrib, bluish below, with 2 white spots near the base from which 2 glaucous lines run down the edges of the pulvini: fr. subglobose, 8–9 mm. across, 2–3 seeded. S.Z.2:t.127,f.3. C.B.3:25. (*J. chinensis* var. *p.* Endl.) Cult. in Japan. Intr. 1843. Zone V. Handsome low shrub, often planted as a ground-cover.

11. **J. phoenícea** L. PHOENICIAN J. Shrub or tree to 6 m., with upright or ascending brs. forming a pyramidal head: lvs. usually scale-like, in 3's or opposite, rhombic-ovate, 1 mm. long, obtuse, rounded on the back, dark or bluish green: fls. usually monoecious: fr. variable, but usually globose, 8 mm. across, shining yellow or reddish brown, 3–6-seeded. B.S.1:673. C.B. 3:13. (*Sabina p.* Ant.) Mediter. Reg. Intr. 1683. Zone VII.

12. **J. pachyphloèa** Torr. ALLIGATOR J. Tree to 20 m., with a short trunk and stout spreading brs. forming a broad-pyramidal or round-topped head; bark dark brown, broken into small, closely appressed scales; brts. slender: lvs. usually scale-like, opposite, bluish green, rhombic-ovate, 1.5 mm. long, rounded or apiculate at the apex, obscurely keeled on the back and glandular;

acicular lvs. 3–6 mm. long, spiny-pointed, in 3's or in pairs, usually bluish green: fr. globose or broadly ellipsoid, 1.2 cm. long, tuberculate, reddish brown, bloomy, ripening the second year, usually 4-seeded. S.S.10:t.520. C.B. 3:23. M.D.1921:t.17(h). For. & Irr. 12:150(b). (*Sabina p.* Ant.) Ariz. and New Mex. to s. w. Tex. and Mex. Cult. 1873. Zone VII. One of the handsomest American Junipers, remarkable for its checkered bark; the acicular foliage of young plants is usually glaucous or nearly silvery white. Some named juvenile forms have been offered in Eu., e.g., **J. p. ericoìdes** Beiss., with glaucous lvs. R.H.1914:343.

13. **J. utahénsis** (Engelm.) Lemm. UTAH J. Bushy tree, rarely exceeding 6 m., with short trunk and erect or ascending brs. forming a roundish open head; bark shreddy; brts. slender: lvs. usually scale-like, opposite or occasionally in 3's, rhombic-ovate, acute or acutish, about 2 mm. long, rounded on the back and usually glandless: acicular lvs. usually in 3's: fr. subglobose or broadly ellipsoid, 6–10 mm. long, marked by the tips of the scales, reddish brown, bloomy, 1- or rarely 2-seeded. S.S.10:t.518. Contr. U. S. Nat. Herb. 25:t.13(h). (*J. californica* var. *u.* Engelm., *Sabina u.* Rydb.) Wyo. to Calif., Ariz. and New Mex. Intr. about 1900. Zone VII. Little known in cult. and of no particular ornamental value.—**J. u. megalocárpa** (Sudw.) Sarg., var. Tree to 18 m., with a single tall trunk; scale-like lvs. in 3's: fr. 1.2–1.5 cm. across. For. & Irr. 13:307(h). (*J. m.* Sudw.) Ariz., N. Mex. Intr. 1916.

Related species: **J. Pinchótii** Sudw. Shrubby tree to 6 m.; lvs. usually in 3's, acute, about 2.5 mm. long, conspicuously glandular-pitted: fr. subglobose, 6–9 mm. long, reddish brown, with 1–2 seeds. For. & Irr. 11:203(h),204. Texas. Intr.?

14. **J. occidentális** Hook. Tree to 15, rarely to 20 m., with short trunk and spreading brs. forming a low broad head, or a shrub with several stems; brts. stout, about 2 mm. thick: lvs. usually scale-like, in 3's, closely appressed, rhombic-ovate, acute or acuminate, about 3 mm. long, grayish green, glandular: fr. subglobose or ellipsoid, 6–8 mm. long, bluish black, bloomy, 2–3-seeded. S.S.10:t.521. C.B.3:21. S.N.191(h). (*Sabina o.* Rydb.) Wash. to s. Calif. Intr. 1840. Zone VII.

15. **J. monospérma** (Engelm.) Sarg. Tree, occasionally to 18 m., with short stout brs. forming an irregular head, or branching from the base and shrubby: brts. slender, about 1 mm. thick: lvs. mostly scale-like, opposite, rarely in 3's, acute or acuminate, often slightly spreading at the apex, 2 mm. long, rounded on the back and conspicuously glandular, grayish green; acicular lvs. in 3's, often 1 cm. long: fr. globose or ovoid, 3–6 mm. long, dark blue, bloomy, 1-seeded, rarely 2–3-seeded; seeds with 2 or 3 ridges, sometimes more or less exserted (f. *gymnocarpa* Rehd.) S.S.10:t.522. (*J. occidentalis* var. *m.* Engelm., *Sabina m.* Rydb.) Colo. to w. Tex., n. Mex. and Nev. Intr. about 1900. Zone VII. Of little ornamental value.

Related species: **J. mexicàna** Schlechtend. Usually shrubby tree, occasionally to 30 m.; brts. 4-angled: lvs. opposite, scale-like, ovate, acute, dark graygreen, usually without gland, keeled, on primary brs. in 3's, subulate, 3–4 mm. long: fr. globose-ovoid, 6–8 mm. long; seed 1, rarely 2, broad-ovoid, without ridges. S.S.10:t.523. S.M.87. (*J. tetragona* Schlechtend., *J. Ashei* Buchh.) S. Mo. and Okla. to c. Mex. Intr. about 1925. Zone VII.

16. **J. Wallichiàna** Hook. f. ex Brandis. Tree to 20 m. with spreading brs. or shrub; brts. slender: lvs. usually of 2 kinds; the scale-like lvs. opposite, closely appressed, narrowly ovate, acute, 1.5 mm. long, bright green, furrowed and glandular on the back; the acicular lvs. in 3's, whitened above, 4 mm. long: fls. dioecious: fr. erect, at the end of short curved brts., ovoid, 1 cm. long, dark, purplish brown, finally blue, 1-seeded. C.B.3:32. (*J. Pseudo-*

sabina Hook. f., not Fisch. & Mey.) Himal., S. W. China. Intr. 1849. Zone VII. Little known in cult.

Related species: **J. pseudosabìna** Fisch. & Mey. Low shrub with less acute lvs. and smaller recurved, often globose fr. Altai Mts., Turkest. Cult. 1900. Zone V.—**J. saltuària** Rehd. & Wils. Tree to 15 m.; lvs. acute or obtusish, obscurely glandular: fls. monoecious: fr. ovoid or subglobose, 5–6 mm. long, black. N. W. China. Intr. 1904. Zone VI or VII?—**J. glaucéscens** Florin. Small tree with spreading or pendent brs.: scale-like lvs. opposite, triangular-ovate to lanceolate, acute, conspicuously glandular, on shoots ternate, subulate: fr. pale blue, bloomy, ovoid to subglobose, 6–8 mm. long; seed obovoid with about 6 slight grooves on each side. N. W. China. Intr. 1926. Zone V?—**J. distans** Florin. Shrub to 2 m. with horizontal distant brs. and drooping brts.: lvs. ternate, on leading brs. triangular-lanceolate, to 6 mm. long, toward the apex and on lateral brts. scale-like, shorter, appressed, glandular; fr. red-brown, 8–12 mm. long; seed obovoid, obtuse or apiculate, acute at base, sulcate. N. W. China. Intr. 1926. Zone V?—**J. tibética** Komar. Tree to 30 m. with dense yellowish green head; lvs. opposite, deltoid, with a conspicuous oblong or linear dorsal gland: fr. dark brown, lustrous, 15 mm. diam.; seed at apex obtusely 4-angled, grooved and gibbous on the sides. E. Tibet, N. W. China. Intr. 1926. Zone V.

17. **J. thurífera** L. Tree to 12 m., narrow-pyramidal in cult.; brt.-systems pinnately divided and mostly in one plane: brts. slender: lvs. often of 2 kinds, always opposite, the scale-like ovate, free at the acuminate apex, 1.5 mm. long, with a glandular depression on the back; the acicular lvs. 3–4 mm. long, glaucous above with a green midrib: fls. dioecious: fr. subglobose, about 8 mm. across, dark blue, slightly bloomy; seeds 2–4. C.B.3:11,4. (*J. hispanica* Mill., *J. sabinoides* Endl., partly, *Sabina t.* Ant.) S. W. Eu., N. Afr. Intr. before 1750. Zone VII?

18. **J. excélsa** Bieb. Tree to 20 m., with upright or spreading brs., forming a narrow-pyramidal head: bark brown, peeling off in strips: brts. very slender: lvs. usually scale-like, opposite, rhombic-ovate, closely appressed, with incurved acute apex, glandular on back, on the leading shoots ternate; acicular lvs. opposite, 5–6 mm. long, with 2 glaucous bands above; fr. globose, about 8 mm. across, dark purplish brown, covered with bluish bloom, 4–6-seeded. Gt.46:t.26. C.B.2:75. S.N.78(h). (*Sabina e.* Ant.) S. W. Eu., Asia Minor, Cauc. Intr. 1836. Zone VII.—**J. e. stricta** Gord. Columnar form with juvenile glaucous foliage. (*J. e. Perkinsii* Gord., *J. e. venusta* Gord.)

A related species is **J. foetidissima** Willd. Tree; brts. thicker, distinctly 4-angled, of fetid odor when crushed: lvs. loosely appressed, acute to acuminate: fr. globose or ovoid, 6–12 mm. long. sometimes nearly black, bloomy; seeds 1–3. Antoine, Cupress.-Gatt.t.66–70. (*J. sabinoides* Griseb.) Greece, Asia Minor. Intr. 1910. Zone VII?

19. **J. chinénsis** L. Chinese J. Tree to 20 m., usually with ascending brs. forming a pyramidal head, or shrub, sometimes procumbent; brts. slender: lvs. often of 2 kinds, the scale-like narrowly rhombic, closely appressed, obtuse, 1.5 mm. long, the acicular ones usually ternate, spiny pointed, with 2 white bands above: fls. dioecious, the staminate yellow, with about 8 pairs of stamens, often on brs. with juvenile foliage: fr. subglobose, 6–8 mm. across, brown with a thick mealy bloom, ripening the second year; seeds 2–3. S.Z.2: t.126,127(c). S.I.1:t.12(c). B.N.603(h). (*J. sinensis* Hort., *Sabina c.* Ant.) China, Mong., Japan. Intr. before 1767. Zone IV. A variable species with many garden forms.—**J. c. variegàta** Gord. Compact shrub with the tips of the brts. creamy white: lvs. mostly scale-like. G.M.6:292. (*J. c. albo-variegata* Veitch.)—**J. c. aùrea** Young. Upright form with scale-like lvs., the young growth golden yellow. (*J. c. mascula aurea* Hort.)

Columnar or narrow-pyramidal forms: **J. c. mas** Gord. Dense columnar form with mostly acicular lvs. and usually with staminate fls. Handelsbl. Deutsch. Gartenb. 26:315(h). (*J. c. mascula* Carr., *J. c. neaboriensis* Beiss. *J. c. neoboracensis* Spaeth, *J. struthiacea* Knight.)—**J. c. pyramidàlis** (Carr.) Beiss. Very compact narrow-pyramidal form with upright brs. and crowded upright brts.: lvs. nearly always acicular and ternate, 4–10 mm. long, stiff and glaucous. (*J. japonica p.* Carr.)

Spreading and pendulous forms: **J. c. Pfitzeriàna** Spaeth. Broad-pyramidal form or often without leader, with wide-spreading brs. and nodding brts. and grayish green or glaucous scale-like lvs. B.N.606(h). B.E.t.13(h).—**J. c. péndula** Franch., var. With spreading brs. and pendulous brts.

Low or dwarf forms: **J. c. globòsa** Hornibr., var. Dwarf and dense subglobose form with short crowded thickish brts. clothed mostly with scale-like bright green lvs. (*J. virginalis g.* Hort.) A form, **J. c. aùreo-globòsa** Rehd., var., has the younger brts. variegated with golden yellow.—**J. c. plumòsa** Hornibr., var. Low plant with spreading and arching brs. and short nodding brts. clothed with mostly scale-like lvs., forming plumose sprays. (*J. c. procumbens* Beiss., in part.) A form with the young foliage golden yellow is **J. c. "plumòsa aùrea"** Hornibr., var. (*J. c. japonica aurea* Mast., *J. japonica aurea* Carr.)—**J. c. japónica** (Carr.) Lav. Low shrub with decumbent brs. and mostly with acicular lvs. (*J. c. nana* Hochst., *J. c. procumbens* Beiss. in part, var. *decumbens* Hornibr., *J. j.* Carr.) A form with the foliage variegated with white is **J. c. alba** Rehd., f. (*J. japonica a.* Standish, *J. c. procumbens albovariegata* Beiss.) A form variegated with yellow is **J. c. "japónica aùreovariegàta"** (Beiss.) Mast., var. (*J. j. aurea-variegata* R. Smith.)—**J. c. Sargénti** Henry, var. Prostrate shrub with creeping stems and ascending brts. forming dense mats; adult plants with the lvs. scale-like and bluish green, on young plants acicular and grass-green: fr. bluish, slightly bloomy. W.A. 98,t(h). B.E.t.14(h). (*J. c. procumbens* Takeda, *J. procumbens* Sarg., not Sieb.) Japan, Saghal., Kurile Isls. Intr. 1892. Handsome form valuable as a ground-cover.

The plant now in cult. as *J. sphaèrica* Lindl. does not differ from *J. chinensis.*

20. **J. virginiàna** L. RED CEDAR. Tree to 30 m., with upright or spreading brs. forming a narrow- or broad-pyramidal head; bark reddish brown, shredding in long strips; brts. very slender, less than 1 mm. thick; scale-like lvs. rhombic-ovate, acute or acuminate and free at apex, 1.5 mm. long, often with a small gland on back, acicular lvs. often present, 5–6 mm. long, spiny-pointed, concave and glaucous above, opposite, but on vigorous shoots and on young plants in 3's: staminate fls. with about 6 pairs of stamens: fr. subglobose or ovoid, 6 mm. long, bluish, bloomy, ripening the first season; seeds 1–2. S.S.10:t.524. G.F.8:65(h);10:145(h). (*Sabina v.* Ant.) Canada to Fla., east of the Rocky Mts. Intr. before 1664. Zone II.—A variable species divided into two geographical vars. and with many garden forms. The type is found in Va. and southward; usually a broad-pyramidal or ovoid tree with spreading often pendent brs.; mature lvs. appressed, broad-deltoid, obtuse or subacute: seeds deeply pitted.—**J. v. crebra** Fern., var., the northern form to which most garden forms belong is usually a narrow-pyramidal or columnar tree with ascending brs.: lvs. loosely appressed, narrow-ovate, acute: seeds slightly pitted. Rh.37:t.333.

Color forms: **J. v. albo-spica** Beiss. Tips of brts. white; here belongs 'Triomphe d'Angers" with the variegation more constant and more conspicuous.—**J. v. variegàta** Laws., var. Brts. variegated with white. (*J. v. albo-variegata* Beiss.)—**J. v. glauca** Carr. Pyramidal form with very glaucous lvs. S.N.189(h). B.E.t.15(h).—**J. v. elegantíssima** Hochst., var. Pyramidal tree with the tips of the brts. golden-yellow.—**J. v. "plumosa alba"** Beiss. Pyramidal form with mostly acicular lvs. and white tips. S,N.64(h). (*J. v.* var. *plumosa* Rehd., not Schneid.)

Columnar and narrow-pyramidal forms: **J. v. pyramidàlis** Carr. Dense columnar form. S.N.104(h). B.E.t.3(h).—**J. v. venústa** (Ellw. & Barry) Rehd., var. Columnar form with light or bluish green lvs. (*J. v.* Ellw. & Barry.)—**J. v. pyramidifórmis** D. Hill. Pyramidal form with the lvs. bright green in summer, soft-purple in autumn and winter.—**J. v. Schóttii** Gord. Narrow-pyramidal form with bright green scale-like lvs.—**J. v. Canaèrtii** Sénécl. A compact pyramidal form with dark green lvs. and bluish bloomy frs. usually profusely produced. (*J. v. Cannartii* Beiss.)

Spreading or pendulous forms: **J. v. péndula** Carr. With spreading brs. and slender pendulous brts.: lvs. scale-like. B.N.F.611(h).—**J. v. Chamberlaỳnii** Carr. With spreading and reflexed brs. and pendulous brts.: lvs. mostly acicular, grayish green.—**J. v. filífera** D. Hill. Broad-pyramidal form with slender much divided brts. and blue-gray lvs.

Low or dwarf forms: **J. v. globòsa** Beiss. Compact globose form with bright green scale-like lvs. S.N.64(h).—**J. v. tripartìta** Sénécl. Dwarf upright-spreading form of irregular dense habit with mostly acicular glaucous or bright green lvs.—**J. v. Kòsteri** Beiss. Low form with wide-spreading brs. and glaucous lvs. (*J. v. Kosteriana* Beiss.)—**J. v. réptans** Beiss. Low shrub with slender spreading brs. and pendent brts.: lvs. bright green. M.G.11: 296(h). (*J. v. horizontalis* Arb. Kew.)

The closely related **J.** silicícola (Small) Bailey from the s. states with slenderer brts. and smaller ovoid fr., and **J.** lucaỳana Britt. from the W. Indies, with slenderer brts. and smaller reniform fr., are too tender.

21. **J. scopulòrum** Sarg. WESTERN RED CEDAR. Tree to 12 m., with short trunk often dividing near base and with ascending brs. forming an irregular round-topped head; bark reddish brown, shreddy: brts. slender: lvs. rhombic-ovate, acute or acuminate, closely appressed, obscurely glandular, dark or yellowish green or glaucous: fr. subglobose, 6–8 mm. across, bright blue, bloomy, ripening the 2d season; seeds 1–2. S.S.14:t.739. C.B.3:28. G.F.10: 423(h). (*J. dealbata* Loud., not Dougl., *Sabina s.* Rydb.) Alb. to B. C., s. to w. Tex., n. Ariz. and Ore. Intr. 1836. Zone V.—**J. s. argéntea** D. Hill. Narrow-pyramidal form with very glaucous, almost silvery-white lvs.—**J. s. viridifòlia** D. Hill. Pyramidal form with bright green lvs.—**J. s. horizontàlis** D. Hill. Upright form with spreading brs. and very glaucous lvs.

22. **J. Sabìna** L. SAVIN. Shrub to 5 m., upright or more often low and spreading; brts. rather slender, of a strong disagreeable odor when bruised: scale-like lvs. rhombic-ovate, appressed, obtuse or acutish, 1 mm. long, glandular on back, dark green, acicular lvs. often present, slightly spreading, about 4 mm. long, concave and glaucous above with a prominent midrib: fls. monoecious or dioecious: frs. on scaly recurved brts., subglobose or ovoid, 5 mm. across, brownish blue, bloomy; seeds usually 2. C.B.3:26. B.N.586, 587(h). (*Sabina officinalis* Garcke.) Mts. of S. W. and C. Eu. to the Cauc. and Siberia. Cult. before 1580. Zone IV.—It does well on limestone soil.—**J. S. variegàta** (West.) Audib. Tips of the brts. creamy-white and lvs. scale-like.—**J. S. fastigiàta** Beiss. Columnar form with dark green, mostly scale-like lvs.—**J. S. cupressifòlia** Ait., var. Low spreading or ascending shrub, rarely erect, usually with scale-like, often bluish green lvs. (*J. S.* var. *humilis* Endl.)—**J. S. tamariscifòlia** Ait., var. Low spreading shrub with mostly

acicular, slightly spreading bright green lvs. on the primary brts. occasionally in 3's.—**J. S. lusitànica** (Mill.) Aschers. & Graebn. Upright shrub with scale-like acuminate lvs. S. Eu.

23. **J. horizontàlis** Moench. Creeping J. Procumbent shrub with long trailing brs. furnished with numerous short brts.: lvs. acute or cuspidate, glandular on back, bluish green or steel-blue, acicular lvs. usually present, 2–6 mm. long, mucronate, slightly spreading: fr. 6–8 mm. across, on recurved stalks, light blue, scarcely bloomy, 1–4-seeded. B.B.1:67. C.B.3:27. B.E.t. 16(h). (*J. prostrata* Pers., *J. virginiana* var. *prostrata* Torr., *J. Sabina* var. *prostrata* Loud., *J. Sabina* var. *procumbens* Pursh, *J. Sabina* Am. auth., not L.) N. S. to Alb., s. to N. J., Minn and Mont. Intr. 1836. Zone II.—Valued as ground-cover for sandy and rocky soil.—**J. h. variegàta** Slavin, f. Form with creamy white tips.—**J. h. Douglásii** Rehd., f. Waukegan J. Trailing form with bright steel-blue lvs. turning pale purple in autumn with glaucous bloom.—**J. h. alpìna** (Loud.) Rehd., f. Form with at first nearly upright stems becoming gradually procumbent, but with ascending or nearly upright brs., to 75 cm. high; lvs. mostly acicular, 3–4 mm. long, more or less glaucous, purplish in autumn.—**J. h. glomeràta** Rehd., f. Dwarf form, scarcely exceeding 20 cm., with very short brts. crowded into dense clusters, without long trailing brs.: lvs. all scale-like, minute, green.—**J. h. plumòsa** Rehd., f. Depressed shrub with flattened top and nearly horizontally spreading brs.: lvs. linear, upright-spreading, 2–6 mm. long, tinged purplish in autumn. (*J. depressa plumosa* Hort.)

5. EPHEDRACEAE Wettst. EPHEDRA FAMILY

Contains only the following genus.

ÉPHEDRA L. Upright, climbing or decumbent much-branched shrubs; brts. green, with distant opposite or whorled lvs. more or less connate at base and usually reduced to membranous sheaths: fls. dioecious, rarely monoecious, in axillary, rarely terminal infl., the staminate with a 2–4-lobed perianth and 2–8 stamens connate into a column with sessile or stipitate anthers, borne in the axils of bracts and forming a subglobose or oblong spike; female fls. 1–3, with 2-many bracts at base, each fl. consisting of a naked ovule enclosed by an urceolate integument (also called perianth) contracted at the apex into a more or less elongated tube, the tubillus, which has the appearance of a style: seed with leathery integument, globose-ovoid to cylindric, enclosed by the bracts which are either membranous and wing-like or form a berry-like syncarp. (Ancient Greek name, possibly of the horse-tail.) About 30 species in arid regions of S. Eu., N. Afr., W. and C. Asia, N. and S. Am.—Shrubs of very peculiar and distinct appearance with brs. resembling those of the horse-tail (Equisetum). Rarely cult.; they may be used as a ground-cover in arid regions and on dry slopes; of evergreen appearance on account of their numerous usually green brs. The red berry-like fr. is ornamental, but rarely produced in cult.—Monograph by Stapf, Arten Gatt. Ephedra (in Denkschr. Math.-Nat. Cl. Akad. Wiss. Wien, LVI. 1899), cited below as Stapf.

A. Lvs. ternate or occasionally 2: fr. dry, with winged bracts...................1. *E. trifurca*
AA. Lvs. opposite or occasionally 3–4: fr. fleshy, bracts not winged.
  B. Habit climbing or prostrate.
    C. Lvs., at least the upper ones, subulate, to 3 cm. long...................2. *E. foliata*
    CC. Lvs. reduced to scales or a membranous sheath.........................3. *E. fragilis*
  BB. Habit upright or sometimes prostrate at base.
    C. Brts. stout, 2–3 mm. thick..4. *E. intermedia*

cc. Brts. slender, 1-2 mm. thick.
　　d. Bracts of fr. not margined.
　　　e. Female spikes usually 2-fld., often terminal.
　　　　f. Staminate spikes with 4-8 pairs of fls...........................5. *E. distachya*
　　　　ff. Staminate spikes with 3-4 pairs of fls.......................6. *E. Gerardiana*
　　　ee. Female spikes 1-fld.
　　　　f. Inner bracts of female spikes ⅓ connate..........................7. *E. major*
　　　　ff. Inner bracts of female spikes ⅔ connate......................8. *E. equisetina*
　　dd. Bracts of fr. margined..9. *E. viridis*

1. **E. trifúrca** Torr. Upright much-branched shrub, 0.5-1.5 m. high, with rigid and spinescent, pale green or glaucescent, rather smooth brts.: lvs. scale-like, acuminate, 6-12 mm. long, ½-⅔ connate, conspicuous; becoming shreddy: male spikes short-stalked, with about 5 whorls of ovate bracts: female spikes nearly sessile, 1-fld. with 8-10 whorls of thin winged bracts: fr. 1-1.5 cm. long, with solitary smooth, 4-sided seed and large scarious bracts. A.I.1:78. Colo. to Calif. and Tex. Cult. 1897. Zone VII?

Related species: **E. Torreyàna** S. Wats. Shrub to 1 m.; brts. not spinescent, sometimes flexuose: lvs. 2-3 mm. long: staminate spikes with 6-7 whorls of fls.: female spikes short-stalked, 1-2-, rarely 3-fld., with 5-6 whorls of bracts: fr. about 1 cm. long. Stapf, t.1, f.7. Colo. to N. Mex. and Utah. Cult. 1912. Zone VII?—**E. Przewálskii** Stapf. Shrub to 1.5 m., with usually whorled yellowish green, rigid and scabrous brts.: lvs. ternate or opposite: male spikes sessile, with 4-6 whorls or pairs of fls.; female spikes 2-3-fld., with about 5 whorls of bracts, thickened on back and incurved at apex, with broad erose wing: fr. 5-6 mm. long. Stapf, t.1, f.4. C. Asia. Cult. 1912. Zone V?—**E. califórnica** S. Wats. Prostrate or ascendent shrub with rather thick yellowish green smooth brts.; male spikes with 4-5 whorls of fls.; female spikes short-stalked, 1-fld. with 4-6 whorls of narrow-margined entire bracts; fr. 8-9 mm. long, with subglobose or broad-ovoid black seeds. A.I.1:78. Stapf, t.1, f.8. Calif. Cult. 1899. Zone VII?

2. **E. foliàta** C. A. Mey. Shrub, climbing to 5 m., or prostrate; brts. flexuose, bright green or glaucescent, striate; internodes to 8 cm. long; buds minute: lvs. 2 or 3-4, subulate, to 3 cm. long, green, connate at base: male spikes clustered, rarely solitary, ovoid, obtusely 4-angled, with 4-12 pairs of fls.; female spikes in lax or dense cymes, 2- or rarely 3-fld., with usually 3 pairs of bracts, the outer ⅓, the inner ⅔ connate: fr. globose, 6 mm. long, red or whitish. Stapf, t.2, f.10. S.N.182(h). (*E. kokanica* Reg.) Persia, Turkestan, Arabia. Cult. 1895. Zone VII?

The closely related **E. altíssima** Desf. from N. Afr., climbing to 8 m., with the male spikes paniculate and with 2-6 pairs of fls., is probably too tender for our area. B.M.7670(c). G.C.III.7:792. Intr. 1823.

3. **E. frágilis** Desf. Upright shrub, rarely tree-like, or climbing, sometimes prostrate; brts. dark green, striate, fragile, straight or flexuose, to 4 mm. thick; lvs. 1-2 mm. long, ½-¾ connate: male spikes glomerulate, sessile or short-stalked, with 4-8 pairs of fls., anthers usually 6; female spikes usually solitary, short-stalked, 1-2-fld., with 2-3 pairs of bracts, the lower ⅓, the upper ¾ connate: fr. 8-9 mm. long, red; seed ovoid. Stapf, t.2,f.12. Mediterr. Reg. Cult. ?.—**E. f. campylópoda** (C. A. Mey.) Stapf, var. More or less climbing; brts. slenderer, 2-3 mm. thick, less fragile: female spikes 2-fld. C. A. Meyer, Ephedra, t.2. M.G.33:138(h). Cult. 1912. Zone VII.

4. **E. intermèdia** Schrenk & Mey. Densely branched upright shrub, or prostrate and ascending; brts. yellowish green or glaucous, striate, smooth or scabrous, internodes to 6 cm. long: lvs. 2, rarely 3-4, scale-like, scarious, ⅔ connate, 2-4, rarely to 6 mm. long: fls. sometimes monoecious; male spikes glomerulate, ovoid or obovoid, with 3-4 pairs of fls.; female spikes solitary, stalked, 2-3-fld., with 2-3 pairs of bracts ½-⅔ connate; tubillus twisted: fr. 6-7 mm. long, red; seeds slightly exserted. Stapf, t.2, f.15. C. Asia. Cult. 1902. Zone VI?

Related species: **E. pachýclada** Boiss. Upright shrub with rigid scabrous glaucous brts.: female spikes 1–2-fld., with about 3 pairs of bracts connate only at base or the inner ⅓: fr. 7–8 mm. long; seed much exserted. Stapf, t.2, f.14. C. Asia. Cult. 1899. Zone VII?

5. E. distáchya L. Low, usually procumbent shrub with rather rigid, dark green, finely striate upright brts.; internodes to 5 cm. long: lvs. scale-like, scarcely longer than 2 mm., ⅔ connate: female spikes 2, stalked, with 3–4 pairs of bracts, the outer to ⅓, the inner to ½ connate; tubillus straight: fr. globose, red, 6–7 mm. long; seed slightly exserted. R.I.11:t.539(c). S.N.181. (*E. vulgaris* Rich.) S. Eu., N. Asia. Cult. 1570. Zone V.—**E. d. monostáchya** (L.) Stapf, var. Very low; staminate spikes solitary. Intr. 1772.—**E. d. helvética** (C. A. Mey.) Hegi, var. Tubillus of the integument spirally twisted. Stapf, t.2, f.16. Cult. 1896.

Related species: **E. sínica** Stapf. Upright sparsely branched shrub, to 30 cm. high; upper internodes 2-edged: sheaths reddish brown at base; staminate spikes terminal, 4 mm. long, with 4–5 pairs of fls.; pistillate spikes 1–3 at end of brs., 2-fld.; upper bracts connate ⅔. I.S.t.56. N. China. Cult. 1937. Zone V.

6. E. Gerardiàna Wall. Usually very low; brts. slender, dark green, finely striate: lvs. scale-like, scarcely 2 mm. long, connate about ½: staminate spikes 1–2, sessile, globose-ovoid, with 3–4 pairs of fls.; female spikes solitary, sessile or stalked, with 3–4 pairs of bracts, ¼–⅓ connate; tubillus straight: fr. globose, 5–7 mm. long; seeds 1–2, exserted. Stapf, t.3, f.18. M.G.33:138(h). Himal., S. W. China. Cult. 1896. Zone V? The typical form scarcely exceeds 5 cm. in height.—**E. G. saxátilis** Stapf., var. Taller, ascending.—**E. G. sikkiménsis** Stapf, var. Upright robust shrub; brts. to 15 cm. long. Intr. about 1915. Zone VII?

7. E. màjor Host. Upright, rarely ascending shrub, to 2 m., densely branched; brts. dark green, finely striate; internodes to 2 cm. long, partly disarticulating in winter: lvs. scale-like, not exceeding 3 mm., scarious, ⅔ or more connate: male spikes 1–3, subglobose, with 2–4 pairs of fls.; female spikes 1–3, short-stalked, 1-fld., with 2, rarely 3 pairs of bracts connate about ⅓: fr. 5–7 mm. long, red. Stapf, t.3, f.20. S.N.131(h). (*E. nebrodensis* Tineo.) Mediterr. Reg. to Himal. Intr. 1750. Zone VI.—**E. m. procèra** (Fisch. & Mey.) Aschers. & Graebn. Brts. quite smooth: fr. more elongated. C. A. Meyer, Ephedra, t.4.

8. E. equisetìna Bge. Upright or ascending shrub to 2 m., with rigid brts. grayish green or glaucous, smooth or slightly scabrid: lvs. connate about ½, the free part triangular, about 2 mm. long: male spikes 1–3, sessile, with 2–4 pairs of fls.; female spikes subsessile, with 2–3 pairs of bracts, the lower connate ⅓, the upper ⅔: fr. subglobose, 6–7 mm. long; seed ovoid, scarcely exserted. Stapf, t.3, f.21. I.S.t.55. Turkestan to Mong. and N. China. Intr. 1909. Zone V.

9. E. víridis Cov. Upright shrub with rather crowded erect rigid brs.; brts. bright green, finely striate, somewhat scabrous: lvs. subulate, 4–7 mm. long, green, connate at base, the lower ones sometimes reduced to scarious sheaths: male spikes sessile, usually several, with 3–4 pairs of fls.; stamens 6–8; female spikes short-stalked, usually 2-fld., with 3–5 pairs of ovate acute bracts: fr. 7–8 mm. long, with usually 2 sharply angled, much exserted seeds; bracts slightly fleshy, reddish, nearly free. A.I.1:77. Calif. to Colo. and Ariz. Cult. 1906. Zone VII?

The closely related **E. nevadénsis** S. Wats. has spreading brs. and glaucous brts.: fr. with smaller and shorter seed and broader bracts. A.I.1:78. Nev. to Calif. Cult. 1894. Zone VII?—Another related species is **E. americàna** Humb. & Bonpl. Brts. with 3–9 internodes: lvs. usually more connate, sometimes subulate and to 1 cm. long: anthers sessile; female spikes 1–2-fld.: fr. 5–8 mm. long; seed brown, enclosed or slightly exserted. Stapf,t.3,f.25,26. Andes: Ecuador to Patagonia. Cult. 1896. Zone VII?—**E. a. andina** Stapf, var. Low shrub from the high Andes of Chile. Cult. 1896. Zone VII?

Subdivision II. ANGIOSPERMAE Brongn.
ANGIOSPERMS

Ovules borne in a closed ovary which at maturity becomes the fruit.

Class I. DICOTYLEDONEAE Juss. DICOTYLEDONS

Stems formed of bark, wood and pith; the wood increasing by annual layers below the bark: lvs. net-veined: parts of fls. mostly in 4's or 5's, rarely wanting: embryo with two opposite cotyledons.

Subclass I. ARCHICHLAMYDEAE Engl.

Flowers without or with a simple perianth not differentiated into calyx and corolla, or with calyx and corolla but the latter consisting of distinct petals, or petals wanting. (*Apetalae* Juss., *Polypetalae* Lindl., *Dialypetalae* Endl., *Choripetalae* Eichl.)

6. SALICACEAE Lindl. WILLOW FAMILY

Trees or shrubs with bitter bark and soft light wood: leaves alternate, undivided, stipulate: fls. dioecious, appearing before or sometimes with, rarely after the lvs., in catkins, each fl. in the axil of a bract, without perianth; stamens 2 to many; ovary 1-celled; stigma 2–4, often 2-lobed: fruit a dehiscent 2–4-valved capsule with 2–4 placentas bearing usually numerous seeds surrounded at base by long silky hairs; seed without albumen; cotyledons flattened.—Three genera with more than 200 species most abundant in the temperate regions of the northern hemisphere.

A. Scales of the catkins laciniate, very rarely entire: fls. surrounded by a cup-shaped disk; catkins pendulous: buds with several scales, terminal bud present, rarely lacking.
                                                                 1. *Populus*
AA. Scales of catkins entire; fls. without disk: buds with a single scale, terminal bud lacking.
  B. Styles 2, distinct, bifid; staminate catkins pendulous: stamens adnate to bract: fls. without gland ....2. *Chosenia*
  BB. Style 1 with 2 usually bifid stigmas, or stigmas sessile; staminate catkins upright; stamens free from the bract; fls. with 1 or more glands at base.................3. *Salix*

1. PÓPULUS L. POPLAR. Trees with furrowed pale bark and terete or angled brs. with terminal bud, rarely without; buds resinous: lvs. alternate, mostly ovate to ovate-lanceolate and long-stalked, entire or dentate, involute in bud: fls. in pendulous catkins before the lvs.; each fl. with an oblique cup-shaped disk at the base, in the axil of a laciniate, rarely incised to entire, bract; stamens 4 to many; style short; stigmas 2–4: fruit 2–4-valved, ripening before the lvs. are fully grown; seeds numerous, small, ovoid or obovoid, brown; cotyledons elliptic. (The classical Latin name of the poplar.)— About 30 species in N. Am., Eu., N. Afr. and in Asia, s. to the Himal.—Ornamental shade and street trees much planted on account of their rapid growth and the easy propagation of most species by cuttings.

A. Lvs. of long shoots white or grayish tomentose below; petioles terete: buds tomentose.
  B. Lvs. of long shoots lobed..1. *P. alba*
    BB. Lvs. not lobed.
      c. Lvs. to 15 cm. long..2. *P. tomentosa*
      cc. Lvs. to 10 cm long...3. *P. canescens*
AA. Lvs. glabrous or pubescent below, or thinly tomentose when unfolding; buds glabrous.
  B. Lvs. without translucent border.
    c. Petioles compressed; lvs. often suborbicular.
      D. Lvs. obtuse, acute or short-acuminate.
        E. Lvs. cuneate or rounded at the base, coarsely and irregularly dentate: brts.
          slightly tomentose..4. *P. grandidentata*
        EE. Lvs. rounded or subcordate at base, crenate-serrulate to sinuate-dentate.
          F. Glands at base of blade on short brts. usually wanting.
            G. Lvs. irregularly sinuate-dentate, often obtuse................5. *P. tremula*
            GG. Lvs. regularly crenate-serrulate, usually short-acuminate.6. *P. tremuloides*
          FF. Glands at base of blade usually well-developed: buds and young brts.
            slightly tomentose ....7. *P. Sieboldii*
      DD. Lvs. long-acuminate, glandular at base of blade..................8. *P. adenopoda*
    cc. Petioles terete.
      D. Lvs. light green beneath.
        E. Lvs. cordate at base, with white tomentum when young.
          F. Brts. pubescent when young.
            G. Lvs. floccose-tomentose when young, dark green above, to 15 cm. long.
              9. *P. heterophylla*
            GG. Lvs. pubescent beneath, bright green above with red midrib, to 30 cm.
              long ....10. *P. lasiocarpa*
          FF. Brts. glabrous: lvs. dull bluish green above..................11. *P. Wilsonii*
        EE. Lvs. rounded or broad-cuneate at base, lanceolate to ovate-lanceolate, glabrous.
          F. Petiole 1–4 cm. long; lvs. lanceolate to ovate-lanceolate...12. *P. angustifolia*
          FF. Petiole 3–7 cm. long; lvs. rhombic-lanceolate to rhombic-ovate.
            13. *P. acuminata*
      DD. Lvs. whitish beneath.
        E. Brts. brown.
          F. Brts. glabrous (puberulous in var. of No. 17).
            G. Lvs. broadest about or above the middle, 4–12 cm. long; petiole 0.5–2.5
              cm. long ....14. *P. Simonii*
            GG. Lvs. broadest below the middle.
              H. Brts. more or less angled: caps. 3–4-valved.
                15. *P. yunnanensis*
                I. Lvs. broad-cuneate at base; petiole 0.5–2.5 cm. long.
                II. Lvs. rounded or subcordate at base, 10–20 cm. long; petiole 2–4 cm.
                  long ....16. *P. szechuanica*
               HH. Brts. terete: capsule 2-valved; petiole 3–5 cm. long..17. *P. Tacamahaca*
          FF. Brts. pubescent, sometimes glabrous in No. 19.
            G. Lvs. cordate at base: caps. 2-valved......................18. *P. candicans*
            GG. Lvs. truncate to subcordate at base, rarely broad-cuneate.
              H. Brts. angled, light brown: petioles 3–6 cm. long; caps. pubescent, 3-
                valved ....19. *P. trichocarpa*
              HH. Brts. terete, dark brown; petiole 1.5–4 cm. long...........20. *P. tristis*
        EE. Brts. yellowish gray to orange-yellow.
          F. Brts. terete.
           G. Young brts. glabrous or puberulous, not viscid; petioles 1–4 cm. long.
            H. Lvs. glabrous, ovate or narrow-ovate, acuminate......21. *P. cathayana*
            HH. Lvs. pubescent on the veins beneath, elliptic, abruptly narrowed into
              a twisted apex....................................22. *P. Maximowiczii*
           GG. Young brts. glandular-viscid: petioles 0.5–2.5 cm. long......23. *P. koreana*
          FF. Brts. sharply angled, pubescent when young: lvs. sparingly pubescent be-
           neath, at least when young..................................24. *P. laurifolia*
  BB. Lvs. with a clearly defined translucent border.
    c. Petioles terete or nearly so; translucent border very narrow: brts. slightly angled.
      (Hybrids) ....25. *P. berolinensis*
    cc. Petioles compressed.
      D. Glands at base of blade absent (sometimes present in No. 27); blade not, or spar-
        ingly or minutely ciliate.
        E. Lvs. rhombic-ovate, cuneate at base: caps. 2-valved...............26. *P. nigra*
        EE. Lvs. truncate or broad-cuneate at base.
          F. Lvs. deltoid, irregularly and sparingly ciliate, sometimes with 1 or 2 glands
           at base (hybrids)...27. *P. canadensis*
          FF. Lvs. broadly triangular-ovate, minutely ciliate: caps. 3–4-valved.
           28. *P. Wislizenii*
      DD. Glands present at base of blade; lvs. truncate or subcordate, densely ciliate.
        E. Brts. terete, except very vigorous shoots: bracts of catkins laciniate.
          F. Buds pubescent, rarely glabrous: lvs. very broad at base and very coarsely
           dentate ....29. *P. Sargentii*
          FF. Buds glabrous: lvs. triangular-ovate.........................30. *P. deltoides*
        EE. Brts. sharply angled: lvs. ovate or nearly ovate-oblong, to 18 cm. long: bracts
          of catkins dentate...31. *P. angulata*

Sect. 1. LEUCE Duby. WHITE POPLARS, ASPENS. Bark smooth, rough only at the base of old trunks: buds tomentose or glabrous and glutinous: petioles compressed or nearly terete; lvs. tomentose at least on shoots, on short brts. less so or glabrous: bracts of catkins fringed; stigmas 2–4, narrow; stamens 5–20, anthers not apiculate: caps. oblong, usually 2-valved.

1. **P. alba** L. WHITE P. (ABELE). Tree to 30 m. or occasionally talier; bark whitish gray, smooth, rough at base of old trunks; young brts. and buds white-tomentose: lvs. on long shoots ovate, palmately 3–5-lobed, with triangular coarsely toothed lobes, acute, subcordate or rounded at base, 6–12 cm. long, dark green above, white-tomentose beneath, on short brts. smaller, ovate to elliptic-oblong, sinuate-dentate, usually gray-tomentose beneath; petioles tomentose: pistillate catkins about 5 cm. long, the staminate longer; scales dentate, fringed with long hairs; stigmas 4; stamens 6–10: R.I.11:t.614 (c). H.W.2:135(h),t.34(c). M.D.1914:277(h);1916:231(h). C. and S. Eu. to W. Siberia and C. Asia; naturalized in N. Am. Long cult. Zone III.—Large tree of irregular habit, chiefly planted for the contrasting white-felted under side of its lvs.—**P. a. nívea** Ait., var. Lvs. densely silvery-white-tomentose beneath, lobed. (*P. a. argentea, P. a. acerifolia* and *P. a. arembergica* Hort.) —**P. a. Richárdii** Henry, var. Lvs. yellow above.—**P. a. pyramidàlis** Bge., var. Columnar tree: lvs. of the short brts. orbicular, coarsely toothed, glabrescent and green beneath. G.C.II.18:556. R.H.1891:188(h). M.D.1916: t.28(h);1917:t.38(h). (*P. a. Bolleana* Lauche, *P. Bolleana* Lauche.) Intr. from Turkest. in 1872.—**P. a. globòsa** Spaeth. Shrub or small tree with dense oval head: lvs. slightly lobed, gray-tomentose beneath, pinkish when unfolding. Intr. 1886.—**P. a. péndula** Loud., var. With pendulous brs.

2. **P. tomentòsa** Carr. CHINESE WHITE P. Tree similar to *P. alba;* brts. gray-tomentose; buds slightly tomentose; lvs. of long shoots triangular-ovate, acuminate, subcordate or truncate at base, doubly dentate, to 15 cm. long on young trees, dark green above, gray-tomentose beneath, on old trees smaller, sinuately toothed and glabrescent beneath, on short brts. much smaller, ovate or triangular-ovate, sinuately toothed, glabrous beneath. R.H. 1903:355. S.H.1:f.7t-u. B.D.1923:t.16(h). (*P. alba* var. *t.* Wesm., *P. alba* var. *denudata* Maxim., *P. pekinensis* L. Henry.) N. China. Intr. 1867. Zone V.

3. **P. canéscens** (Ait.) Sm. GRAY P. Tall tree, similar to *P. alba,* but lvs. of long shoots deltoid-ovate, cordate, gray-tomentose beneath, with a few triangular teeth and irregularly glandular-serrate, ciliate, on short brts. suborbicular to ovate, obtuse, subcordate, not ciliate, with a narrow translucent border, light green beneath, glabrescent: staminate catkins 6–10 cm. long, pistillate 2–3 cm. long; stamens 8–15. R.I.11:t.615,616(c). H.W.2:137. E.H. 7:t.382(h). (*P. alba* var. *c.* Ait., *P. alba* Willd., not L., *P. hybrida* Reichenb., *P. Steiniana* Bornm.) Eu., W. Asia. Long cult. Zone IV.—Often considered a hybrid between *P. alba* and *P. tremula*.—**P. c. péndula** Dipp., f. With pendulous brs.

4. **P. grandidentàta** Michx. LARGE-TOOTHED ASPEN. Tree to 20 m., with rather narrow, round-topped head; brts. rather stout, gray-tomentose at first, becoming reddish or orange-brown; buds ovoid, gray-pubescent: lvs. of long shoots ovate, acuminate, truncate to broad-cuneate at base, coarsely sinuate-dentate with callous-mucronate teeth, 7–10 cm. long, dark green above, gray-tomentose beneath at first, soon glabrescent and glaucescent, those of short brts. elliptic, with sharper teeth; petiole glabrescent: catkins 3.5–6 cm. long; scales lobed and fringed with long hairs; disk and ovary pubescent; stigmas

4; stamens 6–12. S.S.9:t.488. N. S. to Ont. and Minn., s. to N. C., Tenn, Ill. and Iowa. Intr. 1772. Zone III.

Related species: **P. pseudo-grandidentàta** Dode. Brts. pendulous, tomentose at first: lvs. similar to those of *P. tremula*, but 7–10 cm. across, of thicker texture and with cartilaginous margin: stamens 5; disk glabrous. E.H.7:t.409, f.8. *(P. tremula p.* Aschers. & Graebn., *P. grandidentata pendula* Hort.) Origin unknown; probably a hybrid with *P. tremula*.

5. **P. trémula** L. EUROPEAN ASPEN. Tree to 30 m., usually much smaller, with round open head; suckering; brts. terete, glabrous; buds ovoid, acute, slightly viscid: lvs. thin, suborbicular or ovate, rounded or acute at apex, truncate or subcordate at base, sinuately crenate-dentate, 3–8 cm. long, tomentose when unfolding, quickly glabrous, glaucescent beneath: petioles compressed, glabrous, often as long as blade; lvs. of suckers ovate, to 15 cm. long, pubescent beneath: catkins 8–10 cm. long; scales deeply lobed and fringed; stamens 5–12; stigmas 2, 2-parted: fruiting catkins to 12 cm. long. R.I.11:t.618(c). H.W.2:131(h),t.33(c). Eu., N. Afr., W. Asia and Siberia. Long cult. Zone II.—**P. t. péndula** Loud., var. With pendulous brs. Gn.59: 337(h). G.W.7:447(h).—**P. t. villòsa** (Láng) Wesm., var. Lvs. and brts, silky-pubescent while young. R.I.11:t.617(c). (*P. v.* Lang, *P. canescens* Reichenb., not Sm.)—**P. t. Davidiàna** (Dode) Schneid., var. Lvs. with smaller and shallower serrations, often rounded and mucronate at apex. N.K.18:t.47,48. (*P. D.* Dode.) China, N. E. Asia. Intr. 1907. Zone II?

Of the closely related **P. rotundifòlia** Griff. from the Himal. only var. **Duclouxiàna** (Dode) Gombocz is in cult. It differs chiefly in the often cordate and short-acuminate lvs. and in the fruiting catkins being 15–16 cm. long. Dode, Monog. Pop. t.11,f.34a. (*P. D.* Dode.) W. China. Intr. 1908?

6. **P. tremuloìdes** Michx. QUAKING ASPEN. Tree to 30 m.; young brts. glabrous, reddish brown, slender; buds ovoid, pointed, slightly viscid: lvs. thin, ovate to orbicular, short-acuminate, truncate to broad-cuneate at base, finely glandular-serrate, 3–7 cm. long, glabrous and glaucescent beneath; lvs. of suckers ovate, large, glabrous: fr. like those of *P. tremula*, but smaller and catkins slenderer. S.S.9:t.487. For. & Irr. 10:424(b). (*P. graeca* Loud., not Ait., ? *P. atheniensis* Ludwig.—AMERICAN A.) Lab. to Alaska, s. to Pa., Mo., n. Mex. and L. Calif. Intr. about 1812. Zone I.—**P. t. péndula** Jaeg., var. With pendulous brs. (*P. t.* var. "Parasol de St. Julien").—**P. t. aùrea** (Tidestr.) Daniels is the Rocky Mtn. form: lvs. broader, often broadest near the middle, with a short slender point and more remotely and irregularly serrate, changing to bright or orange-yellow in autumn. For. & Irr. 12:151(b). Contrib. U. S. Nat. Herb. 25:t.15(h). (*P. a.* Tidestr., *P. cercidiphylla* Brit.) Intr. 1916.—**P. t. vancouveriàna** (Trel.) Sarg., var. Brts. pubescent or puberulous: lvs. coarsely crenate-serrate, tomentose when unfolding, becoming glabrous. S.M.122. (*P. v.* Trel.) B. C. to Ore. Intr. 1922. Zone V?

7. **P. Sieból dii** Miq. JAPANESE ASPEN. Tree to 20 m.; brts. rather stout, with whitish tomentum partly persisting during summer; buds tomentose: lvs. thickish, ovate, short-acuminate, rounded to cuneate at the glandular base, minutely toothed or glandular-serrulate, 4–8 cm. long, pubescent while young, later glabrescent or finally glabrous; petioles 1–4 cm. long, pubescent: fls. like those of the preceding species, but scales more villous. S.I.1:t.18(c). K.M.t.12(c). E.H.7:t.408,f.6. (*P. tremula* var. *villosa* Franch. & Sav., not Wesm., *P. rotundifolia* Simon-Louis, not Griff.) Japan. Cult. 1881. Zone V.

8. **P. adenópoda** Maxim. CHINESE ASPEN. Tree to 25 m. or more; brts. slender, pubescent when young, becoming grayish brown or brown; buds conical, acute, glabrous: lvs. of long shoots ovate, acuminate, truncate or

cordate and with 2 prominent glands at base, crenate-serrate with incurved gland-tipped teeth, 7–10 or occasionally to 15 cm. long, glabrous above or pubescent on the veins, pale green and grayish pubescent beneath at least when young, those of short brts. smaller, ovate to orbicular-ovate, 5–8 cm. long; petioles 1.5–3 or sometimes to 6 cm. long: staminate catkins 6–10 cm. long; scales deeply lobed and long-ciliate: fruiting catkins 12–16 cm. long; caps. short-stalked. Nuov. Giorn. Bot. Ital. n.s.17:247(l). B.D.1922:23,t(h). (*P. tremula* var. *a.* Burk., *P. Silvestrii* Pampan.) C. and W. China. Intr. 1907. Zone V.

Sect. 2. LEUCOIDES Spach. Bark of trunk rough, scaly: lvs. of long and short shoots scarcely different, cordate at base; petiole only at apex slightly compressed; buds conical, scarcely viscid, glabrous: fls. with deeply lobed disk; ovary pubescent; stamens 12–40; anthers oblong, apiculate; style elongated; caps. 2–3 valved.

9. **P. heterophýlla** L. SWAMP COTTONWOOD. Tree to 30 m., in cult. often shrubby; brts. stout, tomentose at first, dull brown or gray at maturity, rarely orange: lvs. broad-ovate, acute or obtuse, cordate or sometimes rounded at base, crenate-serrate, 10–18 cm. long, tomentose when unfolding, becoming glabrous or remaining floccose beneath, dark green above, paler and reticulate beneath, with yellow midrib; petioles 6–8 cm. long: staminate catkins 3–6 cm. long; stamens 12–20; scales filiform-lobed; pistillate few-fld., 3–5 cm. long; scales fimbriate; stigmas 2–3, thick: fr. slender-stalked. S.S.4:t.489. (DOWNY P., BLACK COTTONWOOD.) Conn. to Ga., w. to Ill., Mo. and La. Intr. 1656. Zone V. Rarely cult.

10. **P. lasiocárpa** Oliv. Round-headed tree, to 20 m.; brts. angled, tomentose when young; buds large, slightly viscid, the basal scales pubescent: lvs. ovate, acuminate, cordate, crenately glandular-serrate and revolute at margin, 15–30 cm. long, glabrous and bright green above, pubescent and light green beneath; petiole about half as long as blade, usually red like the midrib; catkins to 9 cm. long; scales glabrous, slightly laciniate; stamens 30–40; fruiting catkins 15–24 cm. long; caps. short-stalked, pubescent; disk glabrous, lobed. H.I.20:1943. B.M.8625(c). J.L.28:65;34:f.111(h). M.D. 1921:t.10(h). (*P. Fargesii* Franch.) C. and W. China. Intr. 1904. Zone V. Very striking and handsome on account of its large bright green lvs. with red midrib and petiole.

Related species: **P. violáscens** Dode. Lvs. elliptic-ovate to oblong-ovate, 10–15 cm. long, acute, subcordate, of smaller brts. ovate to lanceolate, glandular-serrate, glabrescent above, white-villous beneath chiefly on the veins; petiole 2–3 cm. long, glabrate, violet. B.D.1921:24(1). China. Cult. 1921. Zone V?

11. **P. Wilsònii** Schneid. Tree to 25 m., with pyramidal head; brts. terete, glabrous, purple when young, older grayish brown; buds slightly viscid, glabrous: lvs. broad-ovate to broadly ovate-oblong, obtuse, cordate to rounded at base, crenate-dentate, 8–18 cm. long, 7–15 cm. broad, glabrous and dull bluish green above, reddish and floccose-tomentose beneath when unfolding, soon nearly glabrous; petiole 6–11 cm. long: pistillate catkins about 7 cm. long, pubescent, in fr. to 15 cm. long; caps. nearly glabrous. B.D.1921:25(h). G.W.31:684(h). C. and W. China. Intr. 1907. Zone V. Similar to the preceding but lvs. smaller and of duller color.

Sect. 3. TACAMAHACA Spach. BALSAM POPLARS. Bark of trunk furrowed; buds large, very viscid, exhaling a strong balsamic odor: lvs. usually whitish below, with translucent margin, cuneate to subcordate at base. often different on shoots and short brts.; petiole terete or quadrangular, usually grooved above: stamens 18–60; anthers oblong to subglobose; stigmas 2–4, with short style or subsessile, broad; caps. 2–4-valved.

12. **P. angustifòlia** James. NARROW-LEAVED COTTONWOOD. Pyramidal tree to 20 m., with slender brs.; bark smooth, only on old trunks shallowly fissured; brts. glabrous, terete, orange at maturity; buds small, sharply pointed, glabrous: lvs. lanceolate or ovate-lanceolate, gradually acuminate, rounded or broad-cuneate at base, glandular-serrulate and revolute at margin, 5–10 cm. long or occasionally longer, light green beneath: catkins dense, glabrous; stamens 12–20; stigmas 2 on a short style; caps. 2-valved. S.S.9:t.492. M.D. 1912:119(h). (*P. fortissima* Nels. & Macbr., *P. balsamifera* var. *a.* S. Wats.) Assinib. to Nev., Ariz., and N. Mex. Intr. 1893. Zone II.

13. **P. acuminàta** Rydb. Round-topped tree to 15 m., with more or less upright brs.; brts. terete, glabrous, pale yellow-brown; buds acuminate, chestnut-brown: lvs. rhombic-lanceolate to rhombic-ovate, acuminate, broad-cuneate at base, crenate-serrate, 5–10 cm. long, lustrous and dark green above, light green beneath and glabrous; petioles slender, terete, 2–7 cm. long: catkins slender, glabrous, 2–7 cm. long; ovary broad-ovoid, with nearly sessile stigmas; caps. 3- or 2-valved. S.S.14:t.731. (*P. coloradensis* Dode.) Assinib. to Neb. and Colo. Intr. 1898. Zone II.

P. a. × *Sargentii;* see under No. 29.

14. **P. Simònii** Carr. Tree to 12 m. or more, of rather narrow habit; shoots angled; brts. slender, terete, glabrous, reddish brown; buds pointed upright: lvs. rhombic-ovate or rhombic-elliptic, 4–12 cm. long, 3–8 cm. broad, abruptly acuminate, broad-cuneate to narrowly rounded at base, crenate-serrulate, glabrous, bright green above, pale green or whitish beneath; petiole on brts. 1–2.5, on shoots 0.5–1.5 cm. long, reddish: staminate catkins 2–3 cm. long; stamens 8; pistillate catkins slender, 2.5–6 cm. long, in fr. to 15 cm. long: caps. small, 2(–3)-valved. S.H.1:f.6o-q. C.C.52. B.D.1923:t.16(h). (*P. Przewalskii* Maxim.) N. China. Intr. 1862. Zone II. Handsome poplar with slender brs. and rather small bright green lvs.—**P. S. fastigiàta** Schneid., f. Narrow-pyramidal tree with upright brs.; brts. slightly angled. U.S.Im.124:t. 202(h).—**P. S. péndula** Schneid., f. With pendulous brs.; brts. strongly angled.

15. **P. yunnanénsis** Dode. Tree; brts. angled, glabrous, brown at maturity; buds glabrous, viscid: lvs. of long shoots elliptic-ovate, acuminate, broad-cuneate at base, crenate-serrulate, 6–15 cm. long, bright green above, whitish beneath, glabrous; petiole 5–25 mm. long, often red like the midrib; lvs. of fruiting brs. ovate, subcordate at base, about 15 cm. long: fruiting catkins 10–15 cm. long; caps. nearly sessile, 3–4-valved. Dode, Monog. Pop. t.11,f.103a. B.D.1922:81(h). M.D.1938:t.15(h). S. W. China. Intr. before 1905. Zone V.

16. **P. szechuánica** Schneid. Tree to 40 m.; young brts. angled, glabrous, often purplish, older yellowish brown, nearly terete; buds purplish, glabrous, viscid; lvs. reddish when young, glabrous, bright green above, whitish beneath, those of shoots ovate-oblong, acute or short-acuminate, rounded or subcordate at base, or ovate-lanceolate and broad-cuneate, crenately glandular-dentate, 11–20 cm. long and 5–11 cm. broad; petioles 2–4 cm. long; those of fruiting brts. broad-ovate on petioles 3–7 cm. long: fruiting catkins to 16 cm. long, glabrous; caps. subsessile, 3–4-valved. G.C.61:46. B.D.1921:25(l). W. China. Intr. 1908. Zone V. Handsome tree with large lvs.

17. **P. Tacamaháca** Mill. BALSAM P. Tree to 30 m., with ascending brs.; brts. terete, glabrous; buds elongated, pointed, viscid: lvs. rather thick and firm, ovate to ovate-lanceolate, acute or short-acuminate, rounded or rarely broad-cuneate at base, crenate-serrate, minutely ciliate, 7–12 cm. long, glabrous, whitish beneath; petiole terete, slender, 3–5 cm. long: catkins 5–7 cm.

long; stamens 12–20; fruiting catkins 12–14 cm. long; caps. ovoid, stalked, 2-valved. S.S.9:t.490. E.H.7:t.387(h). (*P. balsamifera* Muenchh. & auth., not L.) Lab. to Alaska, s. to N. Y., Mich., Neb., Nev. and Ore. Intr. before 1689. Zone II.—**P. T. Michaùxii** (Dode) Farwell, var. Lvs. subcordate or rounded at base, sometimes slightly pubescent on the veins beneath. G.C.59: 230. (*P. M.* Dode.) N. E. N. Am. Intr. 1917.

P. t. × *deltoides* = P. Jáckii Sarg. Lvs. broad-ovate, long-acuminate, cordate at base, more coarsely serrate and with a narrow translucent border. G.C.III. 59:231. B.C.5:2763. (*P. Baileyana* Henry.) Ontario to Vt. and Mich. Intr. 1900.

18. **P. cándicans** Ait. BALM OF GILEAD. Tree to 30 m., with stout spreading brs.; brts. terete or slightly angled, pubescent; buds large, viscid: lvs. broadly ovate-deltoid, acuminate, cordate, rarely truncate at base, coarsely crenate-serrate, ciliate, usually 12–16 cm. long and about 10 cm. broad, dark green and slightly pubescent above, whitish and sparingly pubescent beneath, densely so on the veins; petioles terete, 3–6 cm. long, pubescent; fruiting catkins about 16 cm. long; caps. stalked, 2-valved. S.S.9:t.491 (excl. stam. fls.). M.A.t.19a(h). G.C.III.87:364(h). (*P. balsamifera* var. *c.* Gray, *P. ontariensis* Desf.—ONTARIO P.) Origin unknown. Cult. 1755. Zone IV. Often planted and escaped from cult. It has been confused with *P. tacamahaca* var. *Michauxii* and supposed to be native to N. Am.

P. c. × *berolinensis* Schreiner & Stout. Here belongs "Maine P."

19. **P. trichocárpa** Hook. WESTERN BALSAM P. (BLACK COTTONWOOD.) Tree to 60 m.; brts. slightly angled, pubescent or glabrous; buds elongated, glabrous: lvs. broad-ovate to rhombic-oblong, acute or short-acuminate, truncate, rounded or subcordate at base, finely crenate-serrate, 8–12 cm. long, or on vigorous shoots to 25 cm. long, thickish and firm, dark green and glabrous or puberulous above, whitish or rusty beneath and reticulate; petioles 3–6 cm. long: staminate catkins 3.5–6 cm. long; stamens 40–60; pistillate catkins slender, 6–8 cm. long; ovary tomentose: caps. 3-valved, pubescent. S.S.9: t.493. G.F.5:281(h). E.H.7:t.388(h). M.D.38:t.44(h). Alaska and B. C. to s. Calif. Intr. 1892. Zone IV.—**P. t. hastàta** Henry, var. Lvs. mostly oblong-ovate, acuminate, rounded at base, glabrous or nearly so; ovary less pubescent; caps. often nearly glabrous. Dode, Monog. Pop. t.12,f.105. N. Calif. and northward. Intr. 1892.

P. t. × *angulata* = P. generòsa Henry. Lvs. coarsely serrate, pale green beneath, with narrow translucent margin; petiole nearly terete. G.C.56:258(h), 259;71:321. Empire For. Jour. 4:182(h). Orig. 1912. Of very vigorous growth. —*P. t.* × *Maximowiczii* Schreiner & Stout. Here belongs "Androscoggin P."— *P. t.* × *nigra* Schreiner & Stout. Here belongs "Roxbury P."—*P. t.* × *nigra betulifolia* Schreiner & Stout. Here belongs "Andover P."

20. **P. trístis** Fisch. Small tree; brts. pubescent, terete, dark red-brown; buds pubescent, viscid, often subtended by persistent ovate stipules: lvs. narrow-ovate to oblong-ovate, about 10 cm. long and 5 cm. wide, acuminate, rounded or subcordate at base, crenate-serrate, ciliate, whitish and pubescent beneath; petiole 1.5–4 cm. long: fls. and frs. unknown. E.H.7:t.410,f.23. C. Asia. Intr. before 1831. Zone V.

21. **P. cathayàna** Rehd. Tree to 30 m. with upright brs.; brts. terete, olive-green while young, later orange-yellow to grayish yellow; buds elongated, viscid: lvs. of short brts. ovate or narrow-ovate, 6–10 cm. long, 3.5–7 cm. broad, acuminate, rounded at base, rarely subcordate, or smaller ones broad-cuneate, glandular-crenate-serrulate, glabrous, bright green above, whitish beneath, with 5–7 curved veins, slightly raised above, more strongly so and reticulate beneath; lvs. of shoots 10–20 cm. long, often subcordate;

petiole glabrous, 2–6, on shoots 1–3 cm. long: staminate catkins 5–6 cm. long; fruiting catkins 10–20 cm. long; caps. glabrous, rather distant, nearly sessile, ovoid, acute, 7–9 mm. long, 3–4-, rarely 2-valved. G.C.53:198. U.S.Im.124: t.200(h). B.D.1923:t.16,17(h). (*P. suaveolens* auth., not Fisch.) N. W. China to Manch. and Korea. Intr. about 1908? Zone V. Handsome tree with large lvs. on young plants.

A closely related species is **P. Purdómii** Rehd. Lvs. ovate to narrow-ovate, 10–13 cm. long, or on shoots oblong-ovate and to 25 cm. long, rounded to sub-cordate at base, pilose on the distinctly raised veins and veinlets beneath or sometimes glabrous, more coarsely glandular-serrate. U.S.Inv.42:t.5(h). N. W. China. Intr. 1914. Zone V. Handsome large-leaved poplar.—Another related species is **P. suavéolens** Fisch. Brts. terete: lvs. oval or elliptic to elliptic-oblong, rarely obovate-oblong, mostly broadest about the middle, 5–12 cm. long, 2–5.5 cm. broad, abruptly acuminate with very short often twisted acumen, veins above often slightly impressed, beneath near the base usually slightly pilose; petioles 0.5–3, rarely 4 cm. long, often slightly pilose: fruiting catkins about 10 cm. long, rather dense. Pallas, Fl. Ross. 1:14,excl.f.B. D.L.2:206. E. Siberia. Intr. 1834. Zone II. Rare in cult.—**P. s. pyramidàlis** Reg., var. Narrow-pyramidal tree with ascending brs.: lvs. oval or elliptic-ovate; petiole pilose, 1.5–2 cm. long. Cult. 1928.

22. **P. Maximowíczii** Henry. Tree to 30 m., with wide-spreading brs.; bark of old trunks gray and deeply fissured; brts. terete, densely pubescent, reddish at first, finally gray: lvs. nearly subcoriaceous, elliptic to elliptic-ovate, rarely suborbicular, abruptly short-acuminate or acute with twisted apex, subcordate, glandular-serrate and ciliate, 6–12 cm. long, dull dark green and wrinkled above, whitish beneath, pubescent on veins and veinlets on both sides; petioles 1–4 cm. long, puberulous; staminate catkins 5–10 cm. long; stamens 30–40; fruiting catkins 18–25 cm. long; caps. subsessile, 3–4-valved, glabrous. Fr.VII. K.M.t.11(c). N.K.18:198(h),t.50. G.C.53:198. N. E. Asia, Japan. Intr. before 1890. Handsome poplar of vigorous growth.

P. M. × nigra plantierensis Schreiner & Stout. Here belongs "Rochester P."—*P. M. × berolinensis* Schreiner & Stout. Here belong "Geneva P." and "Oxford P."—*P. M. × trichocarpa;* see No. 19.

23. **P. koreàna** Rehd. Tree to 25 m., brts. terete, viscid-glandular at first, later pale brown: lvs. of shoots elliptic or elliptic-ovate to ovate-oblong, short-acuminate, with rarely twisted apex, rounded or sometimes subcordate at base, 7–15 cm. long and to 8.5 cm. broad or occasionally larger, on short brts. elliptic-oblong or elliptic-lanceolate and 4–12 cm. long, cuneate or rounded at base, glandular-crenate-serrulate, dark green and wrinkled above, whitish beneath, glabrous, or those of short brts. sometimes minutely pilose on veins beneath and petioles; petioles 5–10 or on short brts. to 20 mm. long: staminate catkins 3–5 cm. long; stamens 10–30; fruiting catkins 10–14 cm. long; caps. sessile, 2–4-valved. N.K.18:198(h),t.49. F.R.N.1:17(h). Korea. Intr. 1918. Zone V. Handsome poplar, its large bright green lvs. with red midrib.

24. **P. laurifòlia** Ledeb. Tree to 15 m.; brts. slender, sharply angled, pubescent at least near apex, at maturity grayish yellow; buds elongated, upright, but not appressed: lvs. of shoots ovate-lanceolate to lanceolate, acuminate, rounded at base, finely glandular-serrate, 7–12 cm. long, bright green above, whitish beneath and sparingly pubescent, at least on the midrib; petioles short, pubescent; lvs. of short brts. elliptic to elliptic-ovate, short-acuminate, rounded at base; petioles rather long; catkins about 5 cm. long; scales large, pubescent; stamens 20–30 (or to 60?): caps. 2–3-valved, slightly pubescent. E.H.7:t.410,f.30. B.C.5:2764(l). B.D.1922:23,t(h). (*P. balsamifera* var. *viminalis* Loud.) Siberia. Intr. about 1830. Zone IV.—**P. l. Lind-**

leyàna (Carr.) Aschers. & Graebn. Lvs. narrower, rounded or broad-cuneate at base, with usually wavy margin, those of long shoots generally lanceolate, of short ones narrow-elliptic. B.C.5:2763. (*P. L.* Carr., *P. salicifolia* Hort., *P. crispa* Hort.) Orig. before 1867.

P. l. × tristis? = P. Woóbstii (Reg.) Dode. Similar to *P. laurifolia*, but brts. glabrous, slightly ribbed: lvs. lanceolate, widest about the middle. P.H.1:10(1). (*P. suaveolens* var. *Woobstii* Reg.) Orig. unknown.—*P. l.* × *nigra;* see No. 25.—*P. l.* × *balsamifera;* see under No. 25.

Sect. 4. AEGEIROS Duby. COTTONWOODS, BLACK POPLARS. Trees with furrowed bark; buds viscid: lvs. green and stomatiferous on both sides and with a well-defined translucent border, usually triangular-ovate and very broad at base or rhombic-ovate, long-acuminate and more or less coarsely crenate-serrate: stamens 15–30; anthers subglobose: caps. 2–4-valved.

25. × **P. berolinénsis** Dipp. (*P. laurifolia* × *nigra* var. *italica*.) Columnar tree with ascending brs.; brts. slightly angular, pubescent, yellowish gray the 2d year; buds greenish, viscid: lvs. ovate or rhombic-ovate, long-acuminate, rounded or cuneate at base and with or without basal glands, crenate-serrate, with a very narrow translucent non-ciliate border, 7–10 cm. long, about 5 cm. wide, slightly whitish or greenish beneath; petiole terete, with scattered pubescence; catkins glabrous, 4–7 cm. long; stamens about 15. E.H.7:t.410, f.29. Gn.80:124. (*P. certinensis* Dieck.) Orig. before 1870. Zone II. A very hardy poplar, perhaps the best for planting on the prairies of the Northwest. Here belong also "Strathglass P.", "Frye P." and "Rumford P." (*P. laurifolia* × *nigra*.)

P. b. × **candicans;** see under No. 18.—*P. b.* × *Maximowiczii:* see under No. 22.—Similar hybrids are: P. Rasumowskyàna Schneid. (?*P. laurifolia* × *nigra*). Brts. glabrous, angled: lvs. of long shoots orbicular-ovate, rounded or subcordate at base, to 14 cm. long, those of old trees smaller, elliptic. S.L.1:f.4q-s(1). Orig. before 1882.—P. Petrowskyàna Schneid. (?*P. laurifolia* × *deltoides*.) Brts. angled, like the petioles minutely pubescent: lvs. ovate, acuminate, rounded or cordate at base and usually with 1 or 2 glands, strongly crenate-serrate, to 16 cm. long, pale beneath. S.L.1:f.4t-v. Orig. before 1882.—Also *P. Nolestii* Hort. seems to belong here.

26. **P. nígra** L. BLACK P. Tree to 30 m., with wide-spreading stout brs. and usually short trunk; bark deeply furrowed, often with large burs; brts. terete, glabrous, orange, changing to ashy gray the 2d year; buds viscid, reddish, elongated and curving outward at apex: lvs. rhombic-ovate, long-acuminate, broad-cuneate, finely crenate-serrate, non-ciliate, 5–10 cm. long, 4–8 cm. wide, glabrous, light green beneath, on short brts. smaller and broader and often truncate or rounded at base; petioles slender: staminate catkins 4–6 cm. long, scales laciniate; stamens 20–30; fruiting catkins 10–15 cm. long: caps. 2-valved; pedicels slender, 3–5 mm. long. H.W.2:139(h),t.35(c). R.I.11:t.619 (c). M.A.t.85(h). Eu., W. Asia. Long cult. Zone II.—**P. n. itálica** Muenchh. LOMBARDY P. Brs. closely ascending, forming a narrow columnar head; lvs. usually more narrowly cuneate: usually staminate. B.C.5:2758(l). H.W.2: 140(h). Gn.M.31:293,317,319(h). (*P. n. pyramidalis* (Borkh.) Spach, *P. i.* Moench, *P. dilatata* Ait.) Orig. before 1750. Intr. to Am. 1784. The few pistillate trees known have less strictly upright brs. and a broader head. E.H. 7:t.383(h). Striking tree on account of its formal columnar habit; often planted as street tree.—**P. n. thevestìna** (Dode) Bean, var. Bark of older brs. grayish and of the trunk whitish, otherwise like var. *italica*. Dode, Monog. Pop. t.12,f.80. (*P. t.* Dode.) W. Asia, N. Afr. Cult. 1903.—**P. n. plantierénsis** (Simon-Louis) Schneid., var. Of fastigiate habit, with pubescent brts. and pubescent, usually reddish petioles. Probably cross between var. *italica* and var. *betulifolia*. (*P. n.* var. *elegans* Bailey.) Orig. before 1885.—**P. n. betuli-**

fòlia (Pursh) Torr., var. Young brts. and petioles pubescent: lvs. pubescent when young: rachis of catkins pubescent or sometimes glabrous. B.M.8298(c, except pist. catkins which belong to *P. Lloydii*). E.H.7:t.409,f.12. (*P. n.* var. *hudsonica* Schneid., var. *pubescens* Parl., *P. hudsonica* Michx., *P. b.* Pursh.) Eu. Intr. to Am. before 1800. Zone IV.

P. n. × *deltoides;* see No. 27.—*P. n.* × *angulata;* see under No. 31.—*P. n.* × *laurifolia;* see No. 25.—*P. n. plantierensis* × *Maximowiczii;* see under No. 22.— *P. n. betulifolia* × *trichocarpa;* see under No. 19.

27. × **P. canadénsis** Moench (*P. deltoides* × *nigra*). Tall tree with spreading or more or less ascending brs.; buds viscid; brts. nearly terete or slightly angled, glabrous, rarely pubescent: lvs. deltoid, acuminate, truncate and without or with 1 or 2 glands at base, crenate-serrate, the serration at base of lf. distant, short-ciliate, 7–10 cm. long, glabrous, green beneath; petiole reddish; staminate catkins about 7 cm. long, glabrous; stamens 15–25; (? *P. helvetica* Poederle.) Orig. probably first in France about 1750. The following forms which apparently originated independently in different places have been distinguished: **P. c. serótina** (Hartig) Rehd., var. Tree to 40 m., with wide-spreading and ascending brs.; brts. brownish yellow, grayish the second year: lvs. truncate at base; stamens 20–25. E.H.7:t.386(h),409,f.16. (*P. s.* Hartig.) Only the staminate plant known. The following 2 forms belong here: **P. c. erécta** (Selys-Longchamps) Rehd., f. Of fastigiate habit. B.H.14: 260(h). E.H.7:t.385(h). G.C.56:47(h). Cult. 1818.—**P. c. aùrea** (Dipp.) Rehd., f. Lvs. yellow. I.H.23:t.232(c). (*P. serotina* var. *a.* Henry.) Orig. 1871.—**P. c. regeneràta** (Schneid.) Rehd., var. Similar to *P. c. serotina*, but leafing 2 weeks earlier; catkins about 6 cm. long; stigmas usually 2. (*P. canadensis* Aschers., *P. r.* Henry.) Orig. about 1814. Also known as "Peuplier regeneré" and "Peuplier suisse rouge."—**P. c. Eugènei** (Simon-Louis) Schelle. Tree of narrow-pyramidal habit; brts. glabrous, slightly angled; buds small, viscid; lvs. unfolding early, reddish while young, long-acuminate, usually broad-cuneate, about 6 cm. wide, coarsely crenate-serrate, sparsely ciliate; staminate catkins 3.5–5 cm. long; stamens 15–20, with thread-like filaments. E.H.7:t.409,f.17. G.C.56:68,f.17. B.C.5:2761(h). Am. For.21:995(h). Here belongs probably *P. charkoviensis* Schroed. M.G.17:393(h). Often planted as a street tree under the name "Carolina Poplar."—**P. c. marilándica** (Poir.) Rehd., var. Similar to var. *serotina*, but with the brs. more distant and not regularly ascending; brts. terete; leafing earlier: lvs. rhombic-ovate, long-acuminate, cuneate, crenate-serrate, sparsely minutely ciliate while young, about 10 cm. long and 7.5 cm. broad; petioles greenish; pistillate catkins about 6 cm. long; stigmas 2–4. E.H.7:t.409,f.19. (*P. m.* Poir.) Cult. 1800.—To this group of hybrids belong *P. Henryana* Dode, G.C.56:46(h),68,f.18, and *P. Lloydii* Henry, G.C.56:67(h),68,f.21; the first differing chiefly in its pubescent buds and the second in its minutely pubescent brts. and petioles; this seems to indicate *P. nigra* var. *betulifolia* as one of the parents.—Also *P. Krauseana* Dode, *P. ramulosa* Dode and *P. pseudo-canadensis* Schneid. belong here.

28. **P. Wislizèni** (S. Wats.) Sarg. Tree to 30 m., with stout spreading brs.; bark fissured only on old trunks; brts. terete, glabrous, yellowish; buds puberulous, viscid: lvs. broadly deltoid-ovate, abruptly short-acuminate, truncate and usually abruptly cuneate and without glands at base, coarsely and irregularly crenate-serrate, 5–10 cm. long and as broad or broader, yellowish green, glabrous on both sides; petioles slender, 3–5 cm. long: catkins 5–10 cm. long; disk of pistillate fl. cup-shaped: caps. ovoid, about 10 mm. long, 3–4-valved, on slender pedicels about 1.5 cm. long. S.S.14:t.732. (*P. Fremontii*

var. *W*. S. Wats.) W. Tex., N. Mex. Intr. 1894. Zone VI? Often planted as street and shade tree in its native country like the following 4 related species.

Closely related species, all differing in the short-stalked caps., the pedicel not exceeding 6 mm., are the following: **P. Fremóntii** S. Wats. Tree to 30 m.; brts. stout; winter-buds glabrous: lvs. truncate or subcordate at base, more finely toothed. S.S.9:t.496. M.D.1922:t.11(h). Calif. to Ariz. Intr. 1904. Zone VII? —**P. arizònica** Sarg. Tree to 25 m.; brts. slender: lvs. deltoid, long-acuminate, truncate or broad-cuneate at base, coarsely serrate, 3.5–5 cm. long: caps. about 6 mm. long. S.M.131. M.D.1922:t.12(h). Calif. to Ariz. and n. Mex. Cult. 1916.—**P. texàna** Sarg. Tree to 20 m.; brts. stout: lvs. long-acuminate, truncate, coarsely serrate, 4–6 cm. long: disk of pistillate fl. minute; pedicel of fr. 2–3 mm. long. S.M.132. N. W. Tex. Cult. 1916.—**P. Macdougálii** Rose. Tree to 35 m.; brts. slender, puberulous at first: lvs. broad-ovate, short-acuminate, truncate to subcordate, usually rather finely crenate-serrate, 4–8 cm. long, pubescent beneath on the veins at first; petiole slightly compressed: disk minute; pedicel of fr. 3–5 mm. long. S.M.133. S. Calif. to Ariz. Cult. 1913. Zone VII?

29. **P. Sargéntii** Dode. GREAT PLAINS COTTONWOOD. Tree similar to *P. deltoides,* smaller; brts. lighter yellow; buds pubescent: lvs. often broader than long, 7–10 cm. wide, more coarsely serrate with fewer teeth, glabrous, yellow-green; pedicels shorter; fr. obtuse. S.T.2:t.183. S.M.135. Am. For. 26:414(h). (*P. deltoides occidentalis* Rydb.) Sask. and Alb. to Neb., N. Mex. and w. Tex. Intr. 1908. Zone II.

P. S. × *acuminata* = **P. Andrèwsii** Sarg. Differs chiefly in its oblong-ovate, finely crenate-serrate lvs., rounded or cuneate at base, 9–10 cm. long; petiole nearly terete; brts. light orange-brown. B.D.1921:25(l). Colo. Intr. 1913. Zone II.

30. **P. deltoìdes** Marsh. COTTONWOOD (NORTHERN C.) Tree to 30 m. with upright-spreading brs. forming a rather open broad head; brts. slightly angled or nearly terete, on vigorous shoots often strongly angled, glabrous; buds brownish, viscid: lvs. deltoid-ovate or broad-ovate, acuminate, subcordate to truncate and with 2 or 3 glands at base, coarsely crenate-dentate with curved teeth, entire at base and apex, densely ciliate, 7–12 cm. long and about as broad, bright green below, glabrous; catkins 7–10 cm. long; scales divided into filiform lobes; stamens 40–60; stigmas 3–4; fruiting catkins 15–20 cm. long; caps. short-stalked, 3–4 valved. S.S.9:t.495. S.M.137. B.C.5.2759,2760 (h). F.L.7:184,t.(h). (*P. balsamifera* var. *virginiana* Sarg., *P. monilifera* Ait., *P. deltoidea* var. *monilifera* Henry, *P. canadensis* Michx. *f.,* not Moench.) Que. to N. D., Kans., Tex., and Fla. Intr. before 1750. Zone II. The cottonwood is much planted on account of its rapid growth and luxuriant foliage; in Eu. also planted as a timber tree. The tree here considered the typical form and described above is the Northern Cottonwood, **P. d. virginiàna** (Castiglioni) Sudw.,while the two following varieties are southern: **P. d. missouriénsis** Henry, var. SOUTHERN COTTONWOOD. Brts. often more strongly angled: lvs. broad-ovate to ovate, 10–16 cm. long and usually longer than broad, more finely crenate-serrate; petioles usually with 3–4 glands at apex, glabrous, rarely pilose on the veins beneath when young. S.S.9:t.494,f.7. S.M.136. (*P. angulata* var. *m.* Henry, *P. angulata* Michx. f., not Ait., *P. deltoidea* var. *angulata* Sarg., *P. balsamifera* L., not Muenchh. and later auth.) Vt. to Ohio, Mo., Miss., and Fla. Intr. before 1800? Zone V.—**P. d. pilòsa** (Sarg.) Sudw. A form of the preceding with the petioles and lvs. pubescent when young and often remaining so on the veins beneath until fall. Ga. to La., Okla. and Kans.

P. d. × *Tacamahaca;* see under No. 17.

Related species: P. Pàlmeri Sarg. Tree to 20 m.; brts. slender, glabrous: lvs. ovate, 6–12 cm. long, acuminate, broad-cuneate to rounded at base, rather finely crenate-serrate, ciliate at first: fruiting catkins 12–15 cm. long; pedicels 6–8 mm. long. S.M. 138. Texas. Intr. 1918. Zone V.

31. **P. angulàta** Ait. Tall tree with stout spreading brs. forming an open head; brts. angled, glabrous, the shoots with projecting ribs; buds greenish, slightly viscid: lvs. ovate or broadly oblong-ovate, rather abruptly short-acuminate, truncate to cordate and with 2 or more glands at base, crenate-serrate and ciliate, to 18 cm. long and to 12 cm. wide, glabrous light green beneath; catkins 5–7 cm. long, glabrous; scales concave, crenate-dentate, not lacerate; stamens 30–40; pistillate fls. sessile; stigmas 3–4. S.L.1:f.1o-p,3q-r. E.H.7:t.384(h),409,f.15. G.C.56:68,f.15. Orig. before 1789. Zone V or VI. Differs from the other poplars of this group in the crenate-dentate scales but otherwis resembles *P. deltoides missouriensis.*—**P. a. cordàta** Simon-Louis is a staminate tree and said to be hardier than the type.

P. a. × *nigra plantierensis* = **P. robústa** Schneid. Vigorous tree with ascending brs.; brts. angled, minutely pubescent while young: lvs. cuneate to subcordate at base. E.H.7:t.409,f.20. G.C.56:66(h). M.D.1927:t.43,44,f.1(h). (*P. a. cordata robusta* Simon-Louis.) Orig. before 1900. Here belongs *P. Bachelieri* Solemacher.—*P. a.* × *trichocarpa:* see under No. 19.

To the sect. TURANGA Bge. characterized by polymorphous concolor lvs., brts. without terminal bud, pubescent not viscid winter-buds and laciniate deciduous disk, belongs **P. euphrática** Olivier. Tree with slender brs. or shrub: lvs. suborbicular or reniform to narrow-lanceolate or linear, coarsely dentate or entire, reticulate, grayish to bluish green, reticulate; petiole 0.5–4 cm. long: pistillate fls. slender-stalked; stigmas 3, on short styles: caps. oblong-ovate. Brandis, For. Fl. t. 63. Wesmael, Monog. Populus, t.10–13. Gn.89:597(h). (*P. diversifolia* Schrenk, *Turanga e.* Kimura.) N. Afr., W. to C. Asia. Cult. 1920. Zone VII?—Closely related species: P. pruinòsa Schrenk with usually reniform larger lvs. entire or toothed only near apex and glaucous and the disk cut nearly to the base. Wesmael, Monog. Populus, t.14. U.S.Im.67:476,t.(h). (*Turanga p.* Kimura, *Balsamiflua p.* Kimura.) C. Asia. Intr. 1911.

2. **CHOSÈNIA** Nakai. Deciduous tree; winter-buds with 1 scale: lvs. serrulate, short-petioled, estipulate: fls. in slender catkins, with the lvs.; staminate catkins pendulous, pistillate upright or ascending: fls. in the axils of entire bracts, without perianth or glands at the base; staminate fls. with 5 glabrous stamens shorter than bract, filaments glabrous, adnate to the base of the bract; pistillate fls. with a short-stipitate glabrous ovary; styles 2, distinct, each divided about ½ into 2 stigmas; ovary 1-celled, 4-ovuled: caps. 2-valved. (Chosen, the Japanese name of Korea.)—One species in N. E. Asia.

C. bracteòsa (Trautv.) Nakai. Tree to 30 m., with upright brs.; bark brownish gray; brts. glabrous, bloomy: lvs. oblong-lanceolate to lanceolate, 5–8.5 cm. long, 1.5–2.3 cm. broad, acuminate, cuneate at base, obscurely serrulate or nearly entire, glabrous, bloomy, with many pairs of veins; petiole 1–5, on shoots 5–7 mm. long: catkins with glabrous axis and broad-elliptic bracts pilose on back, the staminate short-stalked, 1–2.5 cm. long, with 3–5 leaf-like bracts at base, the pistillate 1–2 cm. long, on short leafy brts.; styles 0.5 mm. long, shorter than stigmas: caps. 3.5–4 mm. long. N.K.18:t.3–5, p. 60 (h). (*C. eucalyptoides* Nakai, *C. splendida* (Nakai) Nakai, *Salix eucalyptoides* Schneid.) N. E. Asia. Introd. 1906. Zone IV?

3. **SÁLIX** L. WILLOW. Deciduous shrubs or trees, rarely evergreen, with usually terete brs.; winter-buds with a single scale: lvs. alternate, rarely sub-opposite, petioled or sessile, mostly lanceolate, dentate or entire; stipules often developed, chiefly on vigorous brs.: fls. in usually upright catkins, before or after the lvs., sessile or on bracted or leafy peduncles or brts.; each fl. in the axil of a bract (scale), with 1 or 2 glands or rarely a small lobed disk at base; staminate fls. with 1–12, usually 2 stamens; filaments slender, free or sometimes connate, exceeding the scale; pistillate fl. of a single ovary, com-

posed of 2 carpels, sessile or stipitate (pedicelled), with 2, often bifid stigmas sessile or on a usually short style; ovules many, rarely few: caps. 2-valved, 1-celled. (The ancient Latin name.) About 300 species chiefly in the colder and temperate regions of the n. hemisphere, few in the s. hemisphere, none in Australia. Some arboreous species are important timber-trees; the tough flexible brs. of some are used in making baskets; the bark contains tannic acid and salicin. Many species are ornamental.

The difficulty of the classification and determination of the numerous often polymorphic species is increased by frequent hybrids and by the fact that the sexes are separated and that the fls. mostly appear before the lvs. are developed. Within the scope of this book it is impossible to give a complete enumeration of all the species and forms known to have been introduced into the gardens and collections and only the more important and more widely cultivated species and hybrids are found in the following enumeration.

GENERAL KEY TO THE SERIES AND SPECIES

Stamens 3–9; caps. glabrous; scales yellowish, deciduous: fls. with 2 glands.
   A. Lvs. linear-lanceolate or linear, green on both sides; petiole glandless. (Ser. 1. NIGRAE
      Loud.) ....1. *S. nigra*
   AA. Lvs. elliptic to lanceolate.
      B. Pistillate fls. with 2 glands: petioles glandular.
         C. Stigma thick; style short and thick: lvs. elliptic to lanceolate, not reticulate. (Ser.
            2. PENTANDRAE Dum.)
            D. Lvs. acute to acuminate; stipules oblong-ovate....................2. *S. pentandra*
            DD. Lvs. caudate-acuminate: stipules semicordate.........................3. *S. lucida*
         CC. Stigma narrow, bifid, about as long as the slender style: lvs. broad-ovate to elliptic,
            reticulate beneath. (Ser. 3. URBANIANAE Seemen.)..................4. *S. cardiophylla*
      BB. Pistillate fls. with 1 gland: lvs. lanceolate. (Ser. 4. TRIANDRAE Dum.)
         C. Petioles glandular: lvs. acuminate....................................5. *S. amygdalina*
         CC. Petioles glandless, slender: lvs. caudate-acuminate................6. *S. amygdaloides*
Stamens 2, rarely 1.
   A. Staminate fls. with 2 glands; scales yellowish or reddish, not dark at apex; catkins on
      leafy brts., with or after the lvs.
      B. Upright trees or shrubs.
         C. Filaments villous at base.
            D. Catkins 2–7 cm. long: lvs. not reticulate beneath: scales deciduous.
               E. Lvs. lanceolate to elliptic: catkins on short leafy brts. with the lvs. shorter than
                  the catkins.
                  F. Pistillate fls. with 2 glands: lvs. glabrous or soon glabrous. (Ser. 5. FRAGILES
                     W. D. Koch.)
                     G. Ovary glabrous.
                        H. Petiole 6–20 mm. long; pedicel as long or longer than gland.
                                                                              7. *S. fragilis*
                        HH. Petiole 2–8 mm. long: ovary sessile....................8. *S. Matsudana*
                     GG. Ovary thinly pubescent below the middle, short stalked: tree with pendu-
                        lous brs. ....9. *S. elegantissima*
                  FF. Pistillate fls. with 1 gland: lvs. more or less silky. (Ser. 6. ALBAE Borrer.)
                     G. Ovary pubescent; petiole 2–5 mm. long; lvs. silky beneath.
                                                                              10. *S. jessoensis*
                     GG. Ovaries glabrous.
                        H. Lvs. more or less silky; ovary sessile.......................11. *S. alba*
                        HH. Lvs. only slightly silky at first or glabrous: brs. pendulous.
                           I. Ovary sessile: lvs. linear-lanceolate, 8–15 mm. broad.12. *S. babylonica*
                           II. Ovary short-stalked; pedicel longer than gland: lvs. lanceolate, 15–
                              22 mm. broad..13. *S. blanda*
               EE. Lvs. linear to linear-lanceolate: catkins on elongated leafy brts.; lvs. about as
                  long as catkins. (Ser. 7. LONGIFOLIAE Anderss.)..................14. *S. longifolia*
            DD. Catkins 8–12 cm. long: lvs. reticulate beneath, 6–20 cm. long. (Ser. 8. PSILO-
               STIGMATAE Schneid.) ....15. *S. phanera*
         CC. Filaments glabrous: scales persistent.
            D. Lvs. serrulate, pubescent on the veins beneath; catkins 5–13 cm. long. (Ser. 9.
               ERIOSTACHYAE Schneid.) ....16. *S. moupinensis*
            DD. Lvs. entire, glaucous and glabrous beneath; catkins 10–30 cm. long. (Ser. 10.
               MAGNIFICAE Schneid.) ....17. *S. magnifica*
      BB. Low, often prostrate shrubs, not exceeding 1 m; lvs. never linear, not exceeding 8 cm.:
         catkins on leafy brts.: scales persistent.
         C. Ovary glabrous: scales yellowish; pistillate fls. with 1, rarely 2 glands; creeping
            shrubs; lvs. glabrous. (Ser. 11. HERBACEAE Borrer.)
            D. Lvs. suborbicular, obtuse or emarginate: catkins 4–10 fld.; stigma sessile.
                                                                              18. *S. herbacea*
            DD. Lvs. elliptic or obovate to oblong: catkins many-fld.; ovary with short style.

E. Stamens 2; scales yellow: lvs. green beneath, not reticulate........19. *S. retusa*
 EE. Stamen 1; scales rose-red at tip: lvs. pale beneath, reticulate....20. *S. uva-ursi*
CC. Ovary pubescent; pistillate fls. with 2 glands.
 D. Style wanting; scales yellowish; lvs. reticulate, silky at least when young. (Ser. 12. RETICULATAE E. Fries.)
  E. Petiole 8–20 mm. long: prostrate shrub with glabrous brts......21. *S. reticulata*
  EE. Petiole 4–8 mm. long: upright shrub, rarely to 50 cm. tall; brts. pubescent.
   22. *S. vestita*
 DD. Style distinct; pistillate fls. with 1 gland; scales dark above the middle: lvs. entire.
  E. Filaments glabrous: lvs. glabrous at maturity. (Ser. 13. OVALIFOLIAE Rydb.)
   23. *S. petrophila*
  EE. Filaments pilose: lvs. pubescent at least beneath. (Ser. 14. GLAUCAE E. Fries.)
   F. Lvs. 1–3 cm. long: catkins 1–2 cm. long.....................24. *S. brachycarpa*
   FF. Lvs. 3–8 cm. long: catkins to 4.5 cm. long......................25. *S. glauca*
AA. Staminate fls. with only 1 gland: catkins usually sessile or subsessile, before or with the lvs.; scales persistent, usually dark-colored at apex (pale in Nos. 27, 36, 39, 40).
 B. Stamens distinct, 2 (partly connate in No. 31).
  C. Style wanting or very short, shorter than stigma (about as long in Nos. 26 and 27).
   D. Ovary pubescent (glabrous in *S. silesiaca* under No. 28).
    E. Pedicel shorter or little longer than scale.
     F. Tall shrubs or small trees: lvs. usually rather large and broad; petiole usually 1–2.5 cm. long. (Ser. 15. CAPREAE Bluff & Fing.)
      G. Brts. glabrous, or pubescent only the first year.
       H. Lvs. smooth above, glaucous beneath, not reticulate, glabrous or pubescent: brts. soon glabrous.
        I. Lvs. acute; stipules small.............................26. *S. discolor*
        II. Lvs. acuminate; stipules usually conspicuous......27. *S. Wallichiana*
       HH. Lvs. rugose above, reticulate and pubescent beneath: brts. pubescent until autumn.
        I. Brts. stout; catkins large: lvs. 6–10 cm. long............28. *S. caprea*
        II. Brts. slender; catkins rather small: lvs. 3–8 cm. long....29. *S. aurita*
      GG. Brts. persistently tomentose until the 2d year.
       H. Stamens distinct: lvs. 5–9 cm. long, puberulous above.....30. *S. cinerea*
       HH. Stamens connate below: lvs. to 16 cm. long, glabrate above.
        31. *S. Medemii*
     FF. Low shrubs, rarely to 3 or 4 m. tall; petiole 2–10 mm. long; lvs. usually small. (Ser. 16. INCUBACEAE Dum.)
      G. Brts. glabrous or glabrate: lvs. glabrous to pubescent beneath.
       H. Pedicels 2–3 times as long as gland: lvs. 3–6 cm. long......32. *S. repens*
       HH. Pedicel 4–6 times as long as gland: lvs. 5–8 cm. long....33. *S. petiolaris*
      GG. Brts. pubescent: lvs. pubescent beneath.
       H. Lvs. silky-pubescent and lustrous beneath, serrulate......34. *S. sericea*
       HH. Lvs. grayish tomentose and dull beneath, crenate or subentire.
        35. *S. humilis*
    EE. Pedicel longer than scale: petiole 4–10 mm. long. Ser. 17. FULVAE Barrett.)
     36. *S. Bebbiana*
   DD. Ovary glabrous.
    E. Ovary stalked.
     F. Lvs. cuneate at base, entire: shrubs to 1 m. (Ser. 18. ROSEAE Anderss.)
      37. *S. pedicellaris*
     FF. Lvs. rounded or subcordate at base, glandular-serrulate: large shrub or small tree. (Ser. 19. BALSAMIFERAE Schneid.)........................38. *S. pyrifolia*
    EE. Ovary sessile or subsessile. (Ser. 20. LONGIFLORAE Schneid.)....39. *S. hypoleuca*
  CC. Style distinct, longer than stigma.
   D. Ovary distinctly stalked; style shorter than half the ovary.
    E. Ovary pubescent (but usually glabrous in No. 42).
     F. Scales light yellow-brown: pistillate catkins in fr. 6–10 cm. long, slender: lvs. entire, glaucous and glabrous or slightly silky beneath. (Ser. 21. HETEROCHROMAE Schneid.)....................................40. *S. heterochroma*
     FF. Scales dark brown at apex.
      G. Lvs. lanceolate, tomentose beneath. (Ser. 22. CANDIDAE Schneid.)
       41. *S. candida*
      GG. Lvs. glabrous or pubescent, green or pale beneath. (Ser. 23. PHYLICIFOLIAE Dum.)
       H. Lvs. glabrous or pubescent beneath
        I. Ovary usually glabrous: lvs. blackening in drying..42. *S. myrsinifolia*
        II. Ovary pubescent: lvs. not blackening.............43. *S. phylicifolia*
       HH. Lvs. with white silky tomentum beneath.............44. *S. subcoerulea*
    EE. Ovary glabrous. (Ser. 24. HASTATAE Borrer.)
     F. Lvs. silky-pubescent and serrulate, green beneath..........45. *S. adenophylla*
     FF. Lvs. glabrous or glabrescent, glaucous beneath.
      G. Brts. not bloomy.
       H. Lvs. lustrous above, glabrous from the first: caps. 9–11 mm. long.
        46. *S. glaucophylloides*
       HH. Lvs. dull above, pubescent at first: caps. shorter.
        I. Petioles 3–8 mm. long: lvs. acute.......................47. *S. hastata*

            II. Petioles 5–15 mm. long: lvs. acuminate.................48. *S. cordata*
        GG. Brts. bloomy, pedicels very short...........................49. *S. irrorata*
DD. Ovary sessile or subsessile (stalked in No. 52); style usually about half as long
     as ovary.
     E. Catkins on leafy peduncles: lvs. elliptic to lanceolate, 1–5 cm. long: ovary
        pubescent. (Ser. 25. MYRSINITES Borrer.).....................50. *S. myrsinites*
     EE. Catkin sessile or subsessile.
        F. Ovary glabrous.
          G. Lvs. pubescent or tomentose beneath, broad-elliptic to oblong-obovate.
            (Ser. 26. CHRYSANTHEAE W. Koch.)
            H. Ovary subsessile: lvs. 2.5–7 cm. long........................51. *S. lanata*
            HH. Ovary on a stalk 2–3 times as long as gland..........52. *S. Hookeriana*
          GG. Lvs. lanceolate, glabrous: brts. usually bloomy. (Ser. 27. DAPHNOIDES
            Dum.) ....53. *S. daphnoides*
        FF. Ovary pubescent (glabrous in No. 54): lvs. usually pubescent or tomentose
          beneath. (Ser. 28. VIMINALES Bluff & Fingerh.)
          G. Ovary glabrous or sparingly pubescent: lvs. lanceolate, silky or glabrescent
            beneath ....54. *S. Rehderiana*
          GG. Ovary densely pubescent.
            H. Lvs. 2.5–6 cm. long, elliptic-oblong to lanceolate........55. *S. lapponum*
            HH. Lvs. 10–25 cm. long, lanceolate to linear lanceolate, tomentose beneath.
                                          56. *S. viminalis*
BB. Stamens 2, more or less connate or only 1: catkins sessile or subsessile (stalked in No.
     57).
     C. Stamens 2, connate.
        D. Style wanting or short, not more than half as long as ovary.
          E. Lvs. white-tomentose beneath, linear: catkins stalked; stamens connate ½ or
            less: ovary glabrous. (Ser. 29. CANAE Kern.)...................57. *S. Elaeagnos*
          EE. Lvs. glabrous or silky beneath; stamens wholly connate: ovary pubescent.
            (Ser. 30. PURPUREAE E. Fries.)
            F. Fls. in spring before the lvs.
              G. Lvs. 5–15 cm. long: filaments wholly connate.
                H. Lvs. lanceolate to narrow-lanceolate, alternate: staminate catkins to 5,
                  pistillate to 8 cm. long in fr...........................58. *S. Miyabeana*
                HH. Lvs. often subopposite, usually oblong-obovate to oblanceolate: catkins
                  about 2 cm. long.......................................59. *S. purpurea*
             GG. Lvs. 1–4 cm. long: broad-oval to oblong: filaments only ½–4/5 connate.
                                        60. *S. caesia*
            FF. Fls. in autumn, sessile in the axils of lvs.: lvs. oblong to obovate, 6–15 mm.
              long ....61. *S. Bockii*
        DD. Style longer than the pubescent ovary: lvs. elliptic-oblong to oblong, 5–10 cm.
          long. (Ser. 31. GRACILISTYLAE Schneid.)..........................62. *S. gracilistyla*
     CC. Stamens 1 or 2 in fls. of the same catkin: ovary stalked, pubescent; style distinct:
        lvs. oblong-obovate to oblanceolate, 5–12 cm. long. (Ser. 32. SITCHENSES Bebb.)
                                       63. *S. sitchensis*

KEY BASED ON STAMINATE SPECIMENS [1]

[1] On account of the great variability of the species, the numerous hybrids and the often slight differences if not all the characters can be taken into consideration this and also the following keys allow in many cases only an approximate determination and cannot be considered final without further study of descriptions and specimens.

Stamens 3 or more: catkins on leafy or at least bracted stalks.
A. Stamens more than 3.
    B. Scales oval to oblong, villous on back, at least toward the base.
        C. Catkins slender, about 5 mm. thick; young lvs. usually slightly silky.
          D. Lvs. linear-lanceolate, green on both sides.............................1. *S. nigra*
          DD. Lvs. ovate-lanceolate to lanceolate, glaucous beneath..........6. *S. amygdaloides*
        CC. Catkins about 1 cm. thick: young lvs. glabrous.
          D. Stalk of catkins about 2 cm. long, its lvs. more than 1 cm. wide...2. *S. pentandra*
          DD. Stalk of catkins about 1 cm. long, its lvs. less than 1 cm. wide.........3. *S. lucida*
    BB. Scales glabrous, except ciliolate: young lvs. glabrous..................4. *S. cardiophylla*
AA. Stamens usually 3...5. *S. amygdalina*
Stamens 2 or rarely 1.
A. Staminate fls. with 2 glands: filaments distinct.
    B. Upright shrubs or trees.
        C. Catkins 6–18 cm. long.
          D. Bracts and rachis pubescent: catkins 6–12 cm. long: lvs. denticulate or serrulate.
            E. Lvs. silky-tomentose beneath.....................................15. *S. phanera*
            EE. Lvs. only sparingly pubescent on the veins beneath...........16. *S. moupinensis*
          DD. Bracts and rachis glabrous; catkins 12–18 cm. long: lvs. entire glabrous, glaucous
            beneath ....17. *S. magnifica*
        CC. Catkins 2–7 cm. long.
          D. Tall shrubs or trees.
            E. Lvs. lanceolate to elliptic-oblong: catkins with the lvs., longer than the some-
             times bract-like lvs. of the peduncles.
            F. Trees with upright brs. or spreading.

G. Young lvs. and brts. more or less silky.
    H. Scales broad-ovate ....10. *S. jessoensis*
    HH. Scales oblong-ovate to lanceolate............................11. *S. alba*
GG. Young lvs. and brts. glabrous or slightly silky.
    H. Catkins 2.5–6 cm. long; brts. brown or olive.
        I. Catkins 2.5–4.5 cm. long; brts. brittle at base...........7. *S. fragilis*
        II. Catkins 4–6 cm. long; brts. not brittle..............11. *S. alba calva*
    HH. Catkins 1–1.5 cm. long; scales oval; brts. yellowish...8. *S. Matsudana*
  FF. Trees with pendulous brts.
    G. Catkins 2–4 cm. long.
      H. Brts. brown or olive.
        I. Peduncles and young lvs. slightly silky..............12. *S. babylonica*
        II. Peduncles at base and young lvs. glabrous..............13. *S. blanda*
      HH. Brts. yellow ....11. *S. alba tristis*
    GG. Catkins 1–1.5 cm. long; brts. yellowish.........8. *S. Matsudana pendula*
  EE. Lvs. linear: catkins on elongated leafy brts......................14. *S. longifolia*
DD. Low shrubs not exceeding 1 m.: catkins after the lvs. on leafy brts.
  E. Lvs. linear or linear-lanceolate; stamens villous to the middle..14. *S. longifolia*
  EE. Lvs. broader: stamens pilose only at base.
    F. Brts. densely villous: catkins 1–2 cm. long.................24. *S. brachycarpa*
    FF. Brts. glabrous or glabrescent.
      G. Lvs. obtuse and rugose above: catkins slender; scales pale....22. *S. vestita*
      GG. Lvs. acute, not rugose: scales dark at apex...................25. *S. glauca*
BB. Prostrate or creeping shrubs.
  C. Lvs. 1.5–5 cm. long, rugose above, strongly reticulate beneath; petiole 8–20 mm. long.
                                      21. *S. reticulata*
  CC. Lvs. smaller, not rugose above; petiole short.
    D. Lvs. obovate to oblanceolate: catkins many-fld.
      E. Fls. with 2 stamens.
        F. Catkins about 1.5 cm. long; scales yellowish, slightly darker at apex.
                                    19. *S. retusa*
        FF. Catkins 2–3 cm. long; scales dark...........................23. *S. petrophila*
      EE. Fls. with 1 stamen..20. *S. uva-ursi*
    DD. Lvs. suborbicular: catkins 4–10-fld................................18. *S. herbacea*
AA. Staminate fls. with only one gland.
  B. Filaments distinct; stamens 2.
    C. Catkins with or after the lvs. on leafy or bracted brts.
      D. Brts. pubescent or villous.
        E. Catkins 1–2 cm. long; brts. finely pubescent..................42. *S. myrsinifolia*
        EE. Catkins larger: brts. villous.
          F. Catkins densely clothed with yellow villous hairs, 3–4 cm. long and 1.5 cm.
            thick ....51. *S. lanata*
          FF. Catkins white-woolly.
            G. Lvs. entire: catkins 4–5 cm. long, 1.5 cm. thick..........52. *S. Hookeriana*
            GG. Lvs. glandular-serrate: catkins 3–4 cm. long and 1 cm. thick.
                                   45. *S. adenophylla*
      DD. Brts. glabrous or nearly so.
        E. Scales yellowish or light yellow-brown.
          F. Scales nearly glabrous.
            G. Catkins 1–1.5 cm. long...................................37. *S. pedicellaris*
            GG. Catkins 3–6 cm. long.....................................39. *S. hypoleuca*
          FF. Scales pubescent: catkins 4–5 cm. long, densely silky......40. *S. heterochroma*
        EE. Scales dark at apex or sometimes only pinkish.
          F. Anthers red: catkins 1.5–2 cm. long, slender; scales dark brown.
                                    50. *S. myrsinites*
          FF. Anthers yellow or only slightly reddish at first.
            G. Lvs. rather densely glandular-denticulate.
              H. Catkins up to 5 cm. long; scales dark; basal lvs. short-petioled,
                cuneate ....46. *S. glaucophylloides*
              HH. Catkins up to 3 cm. long; scales rather light; basal lvs. slender-
                petioled, rounded at base..............................38. *S. pyrifolia*
            GG. Lvs. remotely denticulate or nearly entire.
              H. Lvs. glabrous or silky only on midrib beneath: catkins 2–3 cm. long.
                I. Lvs. usually rounded at base...........................47. *S. hastata*
                II. Lvs. cuneate at base.............................43. *S. phylicifolia*
              HH. Lvs. more or less pubescent when young, blackening in drying: catkins
                1–2 cm. long...42. *S. myrsinifolia*
    CC. Catkins before or with the lvs., sessile or subsessile; without or with only 1–3 small
      bracts at base.
      D. Brts. bloomy.
        E. Catkins 3–4 cm. long, with long silky hairs little shorter than stamens.
                                      53. *S. daphnoides*
        EE. Catkins 2–2.5 cm. long; stamens distinctly longer than hairs.
          F. Young lvs. glabrous...49. *S. irrorata*
          FF. Young lvs. silky beneath...................................44. *S. subcoerulea*
      DD. Brts. not bloomy.
        E. Brts. pubescent at least toward the apex.

    F. Hairs of bracts yellow or yellowish, nearly as long as stamens.
      G. Catkins 1.5 cm. thick, to 4.5 cm. long, hairs with golden sheen.51. *S. lanata*
      GG. Catkins about 1 cm. thick, to 3.5 cm. long, hairs yellowish.55. *S. lapponum*
    FF. Hairs shorter, whitish.
      G. Anthers red.
        H. Brts. short-pubescent; catkins 1–1.5 cm. long............35. *S. humilis*
        HH. Brts. woolly-floccose; catkins about 2.5 cm. long..........41. *S. candida*
      GG. Anthers yellow.
        H. Brts. persistently pubescent, rather stout: catkins 2 cm. or more long
          and more than 1 cm. thick................................30. *S. cinerea*
        HH. Brts. finely pubescent, becoming glabrous: catkins 2 cm. or less long
          and scarcely 1 cm. across.
          I. Brts. yellowish or gray-brown; catkins nearly 1 cm. across.
            56. *S. viminalis*
          II. Brts. red-brown: catkins about 7 mm. thick: brts. slender.
            J. Catkins 1.5–2 cm. long: upright shrub................34. *S. sericea*
            JJ. Catkins 1–1.5 cm. long: prostrate or ascending shrub.
              32. *S. repens*
EE. Brts. glabrous.
    F. Anthers red.
      G. Scales with yellowish hairs as long as stamens; anthers sometimes yellow;
        catkins at least 10 mm. thick..............................55. *S. lapponum*
      GG. Scales with whitish shorter hairs: catkins about 8 mm. thick.
          54. *S. Rehderiana*
    FF. Anthers yellow.
      G. Catkins 2–5 cm. long: brts. rather stout.
        H. Scales dark brown or nearly black above the middle.
          I. Catkins ovoid-oblong, 1.5 cm. thick....................28. *S. caprea*
          II. Catkins cylindric-oblong, usually less than 1.5 cm. thick.
            J. Catkins sessile, about 3 cm. long.
              K. Winter-buds finely pubescent................53. *S. daphnoides*
              KK. Winter-buds glabrous ....26. *S. discolor*
            JJ. Catkins short-stalked, with a few bracts at base.
              K. Catkins 3.5–5 cm. long...................46. *S. glaucophylloides*
              KK. Catkins 2.5–3 cm. long............................48. *S. cordata*
        HH. Scales paler, light red-brown to pinkish toward the apex.
          I. Filaments about 6 mm. long, glabrous............27. *S. Wallichiana*
          II. Filaments about 1 cm. long, villous at base..........36. *S. Bebbiana*
      GG. Catkins 8–15 mm. long: brts. slender; scales red-brown.......29. *S. aurita*
BB. Filaments connate or fls. with only 1 stamen.
  C. Stamens 2; filaments partly or wholly connate.
    D. Fls. before or with the lvs.
      E. Brts. tomentose: filaments connate ½...........................31. *S. Medemii*
      EE. Brts. glabrous (pubescent the first year in Nos. 57 and 62.)
        F. Anthers reddish when young.
          G. Catkins 1.5–2.5 cm. long; shrub with long slender brs.......59. *S. purpurea*
          GG. Catkins 1 cm. or less long: low shrub, less than 1 m. tall......60. *S. caesia*
        FF. Anthers yellow.
          G. Scales obtuse.
            H. Filaments connate ½ or less; catkins usually short-stalked, with the
              lvs. ....57. *S. Elaeagnos*
            HH. Filaments wholly connate; catkins sessile.............58. *S. Miyabeana*
          GG. Scales ovate-lanceolate, acuminate...........................62. *S. gracilistyla*
    DD. Fls. in late summer or autumn in the axils of lvs......................61. *S. Bockii*
  CC. Stamen 1 and 2 in fls. of the same catkin: brts. tomentose or glabrescent: catkins on
    short bracted stalks...63. *S. sitchensis*

KEY BASED ON PISTILLATE SPECIMENS

Ovary glabrous.
  A. Scales yellowish to yellow-brown, not dark at apex (reddish in No. 20); catkins usually on
    leafy stalks: brts. glabrous.
  . Upright shrubs or trees.
    C. Ovary stalked.
      D. Fls. with 2 glands.
        E. Style distinct: petioles glandular: lvs. glandular-serrulate, glabrous.
          F. Stigmas short, thick.
            G. Pedicels about twice as long as gland.....................2. *S. pentandra*
            GG. Pedicel 3–4 times as long as gland...............................3. *S. lucida*
          FF. Stigmas narrow, bifid......................................4. *S. cardiophylla*
        EE. Style wanting.
          F. Catkins slender, 2–5 cm. long.
            G. Tree with upright brs...7. *S. fragilis*
            GG. Tree with pendulous brs.: ovary slightly pubescent at base.
              9. *S. elegantissima*
          FF. Catkins short and dense, 1–2 cm. long; pedicels short........8. *S. Matsudana*

  DD. Fls. with 1 gland.
    E. Scales villous: lvs. serrulate or denticulate: caps. green.
      F. Catkins on rather short brts., longer than the basal lvs.: lvs. serrulate.
        G. Lvs. linear or linear-lanceolate.
          H. Lvs. green on both sides, glabrous............................1. *S. nigra*
          HH. Lvs. whitish-tomentose beneath........................57. *S. Elaeagnos*
        GG. Lvs. elliptic-oblong to lanceolate, more or less glaucous beneath and
        glabrous.
          H. Trees with upright or spreading brs.
            I. Pedicels 4 or 5 times as long as gland; petiole slender.
              6. *S. amygdaloides*
            II. Pedicel 2 or 3 times as long as gland: petiole short..5. *S. amygdalina*
          HH. Tree with pendulous brts.: pedicel short.................13. *S. blanda*
      FF. Catkins on elongated brts.: lvs. about as long as catkins, narrow, remotely
      denticulate ....14. *S. longifolia*
    EE. Scales nearly glabrous: lvs. entire, oblong to obovate, obtuse: caps. reddish
    green ....37. *S. pedicellaris*
  CC. Ovary sessile or subsessile (see also No. 8); fls. with 1 gland.
    D. Catkin 2–7 cm. long.
      E. Scales villous at least on margin.
        F. Lvs. pubescent: brts. upright or pendulous and yellow.
          G. Lvs. white-tomentose beneath, linear or nearly so........57. *S. Elaeagnos*
          GG. Lvs. silky beneath, lanceolate...................................11. *S. alba*
        FF. Lvs. glabrous or slightly silky when young.
          G. Brts. upright ....11. *S. alba calva*
          GG. Brts. pendulous ....12. *S. babylonica*
      EE. Scales glabrous: stigma sessile: lvs. elliptic to oblong...........39. *S. hypoleuca*
    DD. Catkins 8–30 cm. long, glabrous or sparingly pubescent.
      E. Lvs. serrulate; catkins sparingly pubescent...................16. *S. moupinensis*
      EE. Lvs. entire; catkins quite glabrous............................17. *S. magnifica*
BB. Low prostrate shrubs: lvs. small.
  C. Lvs. suborbicular, serrulate: catkins few-fld.; style distinct..........18. *S. herbacea*
  CC. Lvs. elliptic to oblanceolate, remotely and slightly toothed.
    D. Scales yellowish: lvs. green beneath...............................19. *S. retusa*
    DD. Scales rose-red at tip: lvs. glaucescent beneath.....................20. *S. uva-ursi*
AA. Scales dark at apex: upright shrubs or trees.
  B. Catkins on leafy or bracted stalks, with or after the lvs.
    C. Brts. pubescent or villous.
      D. Catkins densely clothed with yellow villous hairs; ovary sessile; style rather long.
        51. *S. lanata*
      DD. Catkins white-villous: ovary stalked.
        E. Lvs. entire: catkins about 1.5 cm. thick........................52. *S. Hookeriana*
        EE. Lvs. glandular-serrulate; catkins about 1 cm. thick.........45. *S. adenophylla*
    CC. Brts. glabrous or glabrate.
      D. Pedicels as long or longer than scale: catkin in fr. 4–7 cm. long.
        E. Veins of lvs. prominent beneath.................................38. *S. pyrifolia*
        EE. Veins of lvs. not raised beneath............................46. *S. glaucophylloides*
      DD. Pedicel shorter than scale.
        E. Style much longer than stigma: catkins very villous..............47. *S. hastata*
        EE. Style slightly longer than stigma: catkins moderately pubescent.
        42. *S. myrsinifolia*
  BB. Catkins sessile or subsessile, before or with the lvs.
    C. Brts. bloomy.
      D. Ovary short-pedicelled ....53. *S. daphnoides*
      DD. Ovary sessile ....49. *S. irrorata*
    CC. Brts. not bloomy.
      D. Ovary pedicelled ....48. *S. cordata*
      DD. Ovaries subsessile ....54. *S. Rehderiana*
Ovary pubescent.
A. Scales yellowish to yellow-brown, not dark at apex: catkins on leafy or bracted stalks.
  B. Catkins 1–5 cm. long; stigma sessile or subsessile.
    C. Brts. glabrous; catkins 3–5 cm. long.
      D. Catkins on rather short leafy stalks, its lvs. shorter than the catkins.
        10. *S. jessoensis*
      DD. Catkins on elongated leafy brts., its lvs. about as long as catkins.
        14. *S. longifolia*
    CC. Brts. pubescent: catkins 1–2 cm. long: low shrub.................24. *S. brachycarpa*
  BB. Catkins 6–30 cm. long; style distinct.
    C. Pedicel not exceeding the gland or wanting.
      D. Lvs. glabrescent ....16. *S. moupinensis*
      DD. Lvs. silky-villous beneath...15. *S. phanera*
    CC. Pedicel several times longer than gland..........................40. *S. heterochroma*
AA. Scales dark at apex.
  B. Catkins on leafy stalks or brts.
    C. Prostrate or creeping shrubs.
      D. Lvs. broad-elliptic to obovate; petiole 8–20 mm. long: fls. with 2 glands.
        21. *S. reticulata*

DD. Lvs. elliptic to oblanceolate; petiole 3–6 mm. long: fls. with 1 gland.

　　　　　　　　　　　　　　　　　　　　23. *S. petrophila*

cc. Upright shrubs.

　D. Style distinct; ovary stalked.

　　E. Lvs. glabrous or nearly so.

　　　F. Lvs. entire: pedicels 3–4 times as long as gland............43. *S. phylicifolia*

　　　FF. Lvs. usually serrate: ovary short-stalked....................50. *S. myrsinites*

　　EE. Lvs. pubescent beneath.

　　　F. Ovary short-stalked: lvs. entire, 3–8 cm. long...................25. *S. glauca*

　　　FF. Ovary long-stalked: lvs. entire or serrate, 5–16 cm. long.

　　　　　　　　　　　　　　　　　　　52. *S. Hookeriana tomentosa*

　DD. Style wanting; ovary sessile: lvs. pubescent.........................22. *S. vestita*

BB. Catkins sessile or subsessile, without or with 1–3 small bracts at base.

　c. Style wanting or shorter than stigma.

　　D. Brts. pubescent: pedicels distinct; stigma sessile or subsessile.

　　　E. Caps. attenuate at apex: winter-buds pubescent.

　　　　F. Catkins up to 9 cm. long: tall shrubs.

　　　　　G. Pubescence of brts. dark gray...............................30. *S. cinerea*

　　　　　GG. Pubescence of brts. light gray or whitish....................31. *S. Medemii*

　　　　FF. Catkins 1.5–3, rarely to 4 cm. long; stigma sessile or on a short style: low shrub ....35. *S. humilis*

　　　E. Caps. obtuse, about 4 mm. long; stigma sessile: winter-buds glabrate or minutely pubescent ....34. *S. sericea*

　　D. Brts. glabrous.

　　　E. Ovary stalked.

　　　　F. Style distinct, but short.

　　　　　G. Pedicels, at least the lower ones, longer than scale: catkins not bracted at base ....26. *S. discolor*

　　　　　GG. Pedicels shorter than scale: catkins usually with small bracts at base.

　　　　　　　　　　　　　　　　　　27. *S. Wallichiana*

　　　　FF. Style wanting.

　　　　　G. Pedicel about as long as scale.

　　　　　　H. Catkins 5–6 cm. long.....................................28. *S. caprea*

　　　　　　HH. Catkins up to 3 cm. long..................................29. *S. aurita*

　　　　　GG. Pedicel longer than scale...................................36. *S. Bebbiana*

　　　E. Ovary sessile or subsessile.

　　　　F. Fls. in early spring before the lvs.

　　　　　G. Style distinct ....54. *S. Rehderiana*

　　　　　GG. Style wanting.

　　　　　　H. Catkins about 1 cm. long: low shrub, not exceeding 1 m....60. *S. caesia*

　　　　　　HH. Catkins 2–4 cm. long: taller shrubs or trees.

　　　　　　　I. Catkins often subopposite; scales shorter than half the ovary, nearly black: shrub ....59. *S. purpurea*

　　　　　　　II. Catkins alternate; scales longer than half the ovary, brown: tree.

　　　　　　　　　　　　　　　　　58. *S. Miyabeana*

　　　　FF. Fls. in late summer; catkins in the axils of lvs.................61. *S. Bockii*

cc. Styles as long as stigma or longer.

　D. Ovary sessile or subsessile.

　　E. Style shorter than ovary; scales oblong, obtusish...............56. *S. viminalis*

　　EE. Style longer than ovary....................................62. *S. gracilistyla*

　D. Ovary stalked, on a stalk as long or longer than gland.

　　E. Brts pubescent.

　　　F. Tomentum of brts. floccose; scales long-villous; style red, longer than stigma ....41. *S. candida*

　　　FF. Tomentum of brts. villous; scales short-pubescent; style about as long as stigma ....63. *S. sitchensis*

　　E. Brts. glabrous.

　　　F. Brts. bloomy: catkins subsessile...........................44. *S. subcoerulea*

　　　FF. Brts. not bloomy: catkins on short bracted stalks.

　　　　G. Pedicel about twice as long as gland.....................42. *S. myrsinifolia*

　　　　GG. Pedicel 3–4 times as long as gland......................43. *S. phylicifolia*

KEY BASED ON VEGETATIVE CHARACTERS

Upright shrubs or trees.

A. Lvs. glabrous or only slightly pubescent beneath at maturity.

　B. Lvs. green on both sides.

　　c. Lvs. oblong-lanceolate to lanceolate.

　　　D. Petiole glandular: lvs. 4–12 cm. long, glandular-serrulate.

　　　　E. Lvs. acuminate ....2. *S. pentandra*

　　　　EE. Lvs. caudate ....3. *S. lucida*

　　　D. Petiole glandless.

　　　　E. Lvs. 6–12 cm. long, glandular-serrulate......................16. *S. moupinensis*

　　　　EE. Lvs. 1–5 cm. long, serrulate or sometimes entire (see also *S. myrtillifolia* under No. 38) ....50. *S. myrsinites*

　　c. Lvs. linear-lanceolate to linear; petiole glandless.

　　　D. Lvs. closely serrulate...1. *S. nigra*

      DD. Lvs. remotely denticulate..14. *S. longifolia*
  BB. Lvs. glaucous or glaucescent beneath (sometimes green in Nos. 5 and 7).
    C. Lvs. lanceolate to linear-lanceolate, at least 4 times longer than broad.
      D. Lvs. distinctly serrate or denticulate.
        E. Lvs. quite glabrous at maturity.
          F. Brts. bloomy.
            G. Lvs. obscurely serrulate or subentire; petiole about as long as bud or
                shorter, scarcely exceeding 1 cm............................49. *S. irrorata*
            GG. Lvs. usually serrulate; petiole always longer than bud, up to 2 cm. long.
                                                53. *S. daphnoides*
          FF. Brts. not bloomy.
            G. Brs. upright.
              H. Petiole glandular.
                I. Brts. brittle at base; petiole 6–25 mm. long..............7. *S. fragilis*
                II. Brts. not brittle at base; petiole 3–12 mm. long......5. *S. amygdalina*
              HH. Petiole glandless or sometimes obscurely glandular in No. 11.
                I. Lvs. caudate-acuminate; petiole slender, 1–1.5 cm. long.
                                         6. *S. amygdaloides*
                II. Lvs. acuminate or acute; petiole not longer than 1 cm.
                  J. Lvs. long-acuminate, closely serrulate, broadest below the middle.
                    K. Lvs. slightly silky at first, soon glabrous......8. *S. Matsudana*
                    KK. Lvs. more or less silky beneath.....................11. *S. alba*
                  JJ. Lvs. acute or acuminate, often broadest above the middle.
                    K. Stipules lanceolate, as long or longer than petiole; lvs. alter-
                        nate, sinuate-serrulate ....58. *S. Miyabeana*
                    KK. Stipules usually wanting or minute; lvs. often opposite and
                        often subentire ....59. *S. purpurea*
            GG. Brs. pendulous.
              H. Brts. yellow; lvs. usually slightly silky beneath........11. *S. alba tristis*
              HH. Brts. olive- to red-brown, sometimes yellowish: lvs. glabrous.
                I. Lvs. narrow-lanceolate, 8–15 mm. wide, finely serrulate.
                  J. Petiole to 8 mm. long; brts. brown.............12. *S. babylonica*
                  JJ. Petiole not exceeding 5 mm.: brts. olive or yellowish.
                                      8. *S. Matsudana pendula*
                II. Lvs. broader, usually 15–22 mm. wide.
                  J. Lateral veins diverging at an angle of more than 45°.
                                    9. *S. elegantissima*
                  JJ. Lateral veins diverging at an angle of 45° or less....13. *S. blanda*
  EE. Lvs. pubescent beneath, at least along the midrib.
      F. Pubescence of white silky hairs.
        G. Petiole glandular: tree...11. *S. alba*
        GG. Petiole glandless: shrub.....................................33. *S. petiolaris*
      FF. Pubescence of brown hairs: brts. usually purple.................34. *S. sericea*
    DD. Lvs. entire, 1.5–4 cm., silky beneath..............................32. *S. repens*
  CC. Lvs. ovate or elliptic to ovate- or elliptic-lanceolate, less than 4 times as long as
    broad.
    D. Lvs. entire or indistinctly toothed (see also No. 36).
      E. Lvs. 1–10 cm. long.
        F. Lvs. glabrous.
          G. Lvs. oblong, glaucous and finely reticulate beneath......37. *S. pedicellaris*
          GG. Lvs. elliptic to elliptic-oblong, not reticulate.
            H. Petiole 2–6 mm. long: lvs. glaucous beneath, 2–5 cm. long.
                                    39. *S. hypoleuca*
            HH. Petiole 1–3 mm. long; lvs. pale green beneath, 1.5–3 cm. long.
                                      60. *S. caesia*
        FF. Lvs. more or less pubescent.
          G. Brts. and petioles pubescent.
            H. Lvs. 3–8 cm. long, acute or acuminate, villous; petiole 2–8 mm. long.
                                    25. *S. glauca*
            HH. Lvs. 1–3 cm. long, obtusish to acute, silky beneath; petiole 1–3 mm.
              long ....32. *S. repens*
          GG. Brts. and petioles glabrous, at least at maturity; lvs. acuminate, 4–8 cm.
            long; petiole 5–15 mm. long..........................40. *S. heterochroma*
      EE. Lvs. 10–20 cm. long, elliptic or elliptic-obovate, rounded or subcordate at base.
                                      17. *S. magnifica*
    DD. Lvs. toothed.
      E. Lvs. quite glabrous at maturity.
        F. Lvs. reticulate beneath.
          G. Lvs. acute or acutish, 4–9 cm. long......................38. *S. pyrifolia*
          GG. Lvs. acuminate to acute, 6–18 cm. long.................4. *S. cardiophylla*
        FF. Lvs. not reticulate beneath.
          G. Lvs. distinctly acuminate, usually rounded at base.
            H. Lvs. caudate-acuminate ....5. *S. amygdaloides*
            HH. Lvs. acuminate.
               I. Midrib of lvs. puberulous above......................48. *S. cordata*
               II. Midrib of lvs. glabrous above; lvs. very glaucous beneath.
                              46. *S. glaucophylloides*

GG. Lvs. acute or abruptly short-acuminate, usually cuneate at base and often broadest above the middle.
   H. Lvs. always alternate.
      I. Lvs. usually 5–10 cm. long, generally oblong............26. *S. discolor*
      II. Lvs. usually 3–6 cm. long, generally elliptic.
         J. Petiole 1–4 mm. long; lvs. sometimes subcordate, usually stipulate.
                                    47. *S. hastata*
         JJ. Petiole 3–10 mm. long; lvs. never subcordate, without or with minute stipules....................................43. *S. phylicifolia*
   HH. Lvs. often subopposite................................59. *S. purpurea*
EE. Lvs. slightly pubescent.
   F. Lvs. more or less acuminate, generally oblong.
      G. Petiole 2–6 mm. long: brts. glabrous: lvs. oblong-lanceolate to lanceolate.
                                54. *S. Rehderiana*
      GG. Petiole 5–15 mm. long; young brts. pubescent: lvs. usually oblong.
        H. Lvs. cuneate at base, 4–8 cm. long.
           I. Pubescence of white and brown hairs: lvs. rarely subentire.
                                26. *S. discolor*
           II. Pubescence of white hairs: lvs. often subentire or entire.
                                36. *S. Bebbiana*
        HH. Lvs. often rounded or nearly so at base, larger.
           I. Lvs. to 20 cm. long, reticulate beneath...............15. *S. phanera*
           II. Lvs. to 12 cm. long, not reticulate..................27. *S. Wallichiana*
   FF. Lvs. acute or abruptly acuminate, elliptic to broad-oblong.
      G. Lvs. 6–12 cm. long.
        H. Winter-buds pubescent; petiole 3–8 mm. long: lvs. obovate-oblong to oblong ....62. *S. gracilistyla*
        HH. Winter-buds glabrous or nearly so; petiole 5–15 mm. long.
           I. Lvs. generally oblong............................27. *S. Wallichiana*
           II. Lvs. generally elliptic.................................28. *S. caprea*
      GG. Lvs. 3–6 cm. long.
        H. Lvs. reticulate beneath, not turning black in drying........29. *S. aurita*
        HH. Lvs. not or slightly reticulate, turning black in drying.
                               42. *S. myrsinifolia*
AA. Lvs. densely pubescent or tomentose beneath.
   B. Lvs. villous, with rather loosely appressed long hairs or floccose-tomentose.
      C. Lvs. broad-elliptic to oblong-lanceolate or oblanceolate.
        D. Lvs. crenate or serrate.
          E. Lvs. glandular-serrulate, green beneath, cordate: brts. densely pubescent.
                                45. *S. adenophylla*
          EE. Lvs. crenulate or crenate-serrate.
            F. Lvs. obtuse or acutish, crenulate, 2–6 cm. long..................22. *S. vestita*
            FF. Lvs. acute to acuminate, crenate-serrate, larger.
               G. Lvs. crenate-serrate, sometimes obscurely so, 5–8 cm. long...30. *S. cinerea*
               GG. Lvs. of shoots with rather prominent acuminulate teeth, up to 16 cm. long.
                                31. *S. Medemii*
        DD. Lvs. entire or indistinctly toothed.
          E. Lvs. subsessile, elliptic-oblong to oblanceolate................24. *S. brachycarpa*
          EE. Lvs. petioled.
            F. Stipules ovate, acute, about as long as petiole: lvs. broad-elliptic to elliptic.
                                51. *S. lanata*
            FF. Stipules small or wanting.
               G. Lvs. 5–16 cm. long; brts. densely tomentose..............52. *S. Hookeriana*
               GG. Lvs. 3–8 cm. long; brts. thinly villous, becoming glabrous.
                  H. Pubescence of lvs. loose, of long straight hairs............25. *S. glauca*
                  HH. Pubescence of lvs. dense, of matted hairs..............55. *S. lapponum*
   CC. Lvs. lanceolate or oblong-lanceolate to linear-lanceolate.
      D. Brts. floccose-tomentose ....41. *S. candida*
      DD. Brts. villous.
        E. Lvs. oblong-lanceolate to lanceolate, entire or subentire..........35. *S. humilis*
        EE. Lvs. narrow-lanceolate to linear, serrulate toward the apex....57. *S. Elaeagnos*
   BB. Lvs. closely and densely silky-pubescent beneath.
      C. Brts. pubescent.
        D. Lvs. more than 5 cm. long.
          E. Lvs. oblong-obovate to oblanceolate...........................63. *S. sitchensis*
          EE. Lvs. lanceolate to narrow-lanceolate...........................56. *S. viminalis*
        DD. Lvs. 6–30 mm. long.
          E. Lvs. with 5–8 pairs of lateral veins, usually entire.................32. *S. repens*
          EE. Lvs. with 10 or more closely set pairs of lateral veins, usually remotely denticulate ....61. *S. Bockii*
      CC. Brts. glabrous.
        D. Lvs. serrulate..10. *S. jessoensis*
        DD. Lvs. entire or indistinctly serrulate............................44. *S. subcoerulea*
Prostrate shrubs with often rooting stems.
   A. Petiole 8–25 mm. long: lvs. broad-elliptic to broad-obovate, entire........21. *S. reticulata*
  AA. Petiole 2–10 mm. long.
   B. Lvs. pubescent beneath, rugulose above, crenulate........................22. *S. vestita*

BB. Lvs. glabrous or glabrescent.
  C. Lvs. crenate-serrulate, suborbicular, green on both sides..............18. *S. herbacea*
  CC. Lvs. entire or only slightly toothed near apex.
    D. Lvs. reticulate beneath and pale or glaucous.
     E. Lvs. 1–2 cm. long; petiole 2–6 mm. long........................20. *S. uva-ursi*
     EE. Lvs. 2–3.5 cm. long; petiole 4–10 mm. long....................23. *S. petrophila*
    DD. Lvs. not reticulate, green on both sides.............................19. *S. retusa*

1. **S. nígra** Marsh. BLACK W. Tree to 12 m., with dark brown, rough and scaly bark and slender spreading brs.; brts. yellowish, slightly pubescent when young: lvs. linear-lanceolate to lanceolate, 6–12 cm. long, cuneate, acuminate, serrulate, pale green and sometimes pubescent on the veins beneath; petiole 3–6 mm. long; stipules semicordate, persistent: catkins on leafy brts.; staminate 3–5 cm. long, slender, pistillate 4–8 cm. long; stamens 3–7; ovary glabrous; pedicel much longer than gland; stigma subsessile. S.S.9:t.462. H.H.78, 79(b). N. B. to w. Ont., Fla. and Cal. Cult. 1809. Zone III. Graceful species. —S. n. falcàta Torr., var. Lvs. only 4–6 mm. wide, falcate, green on both sides. S.S.9:t.463. Mass to Ohio and Fla.
    S. n. × *alba* = **S. Hankensònii** Dode. Lvs. lanceolate, glaucous beneath; stamens 2–4; ovary sessile; style short. G.F.8:425. Orig. before 1890.

2. **S. pentándra** L. BAY W. Tree to 20 m.; bark gray, fissured; brts. lustrous, brownish green; young growth viscid; buds yellow: lvs. elliptic or ovate to elliptic-lanceolate, 4–12 cm. long, short-acuminate, rounded or subcordate at base, glandular-denticulate, lustrous dark green above, lighter beneath, midrib yellow, petiole 6–10 mm. long, glandular; stipules oblong-ovate, often small: catkins on leafy stalks, its lvs. serrulate; the staminate 3–5, the pistillate 3–6 cm. long; stamens 5–12, villous to the middle; ovary glabrous; pedicel slightly longer than glands; style short; stigma 2-lobed. R.I.11:t.612,f.1268(c). S.E8:t.1303(c). H.W.2,1:103. (*S. laurifolia Wesm.*) Eu. to Cauc.; escaped in the E. States. Long cult. Zone IV. One of the handsomest willows with lustrous dark green foliage and golden yellow catkins in spring.
    S. p. × *fragilis* = **S. Meyeriàna** Rostk. Lvs. generally oblong-elliptic, acuminate, broad-cuneate, often glaucescent beneath; stamens usually 4; pedicel 2–3 time as long as ventral gland. R.I.11:t.611(c). S.E.8:t.1304–5(c). Cambridge Brit. Fl.2:t.19. (*S. cuspidata* Schultz.) Eu. Cult. 1829.—*S. p.* × *alba* = S. Ehrhartiàna Sm. Lvs. oblong, slender-pointed, usually silky at first, green beneath: stamens usually 4. Andersson, Monog. t.3,f.27. C.S.t.39a-e. (*S. hexandra* auth., not Ehrh.) Eu. Cult. 1894.—? *S. p.* × *purpurea* = **S. heterándra** Dode. Lvs. lanceolate, remotely serrate, glaucous beneath: stamens 3–5, partly connate. B.F.55:653c. Cauc. Cult. 1910.
    Related species: **S. paraplèsia** Schneid. Tree to 7 m.: lvs. ovate to elliptic-obovate or elliptic-lanceolate, 4–10 cm. long, glaucous or pale green beneath. H.S.f.10. W. China. Intr. 1908. Zone V.—**S. seríssima** Fern. Lvs. elliptic-lanceolate to oblong-lanceolate, 4–8 cm. long, glaucous beneath; staminate catkins 1–1.5, pistillate 2–3.5 cm. long: fr. ripening in autumn. Gray Man. ed. 7:322. Que. to Alb., s. to N. J., w. N. Y. Cult. 1880. Zone III.

3. **S. lùcida** Muhlenb. SHINING W. Shrub or tree to 6 m., brts. yellowish brown, lustrous: lvs. ovate-lanceolate to lanceolate, 7–12 cm. long, long-acuminate, broad-cuneate to rounded at base, glandular-serrulate, green and lustrous on both sides, glabrous or pubescent on midrib; petiole 6–12 mm. long, glandular: stipules semicordate, very glandular, usually persistent: catkins on leafy brts.; the staminate 3–6, the pistillate 5–7 cm. long, dense; stamens usually 5, villous to the middle; stigmas subsessile. S.S.9:t.453. H.H. 80,81(b). Nfd. to N. W. Terr., s. to N. J., Ky. and Neb. Cult. 1830. Zone II? Handsome willow with lustrous lvs.
    Related species: **S. lasiándra** Benth. Tree to 20 m.; brts. pilose or tomentose at first: lvs. lanceolate to narrow-lanceolate, glaucous or glaucescent beneath and pubescent at first: stamens 5–9; scales glandular-dentate, those of pistillate catkins often entire. S.S.9:t.469,470. A.I.1:489. (*S. Lyallii* Heller,

S. lancifolia Anders.) B. C. and Alb. to Calif., Mont., Colo. and N. Mex. Cult. 1883. Zone VI?—**S. lóngipes** Shuttlew. Tree to 10 m., with spreading or slightly drooping brs.: lvs. lanceolate to oblong-lanceolate, 6–18 cm. long, sub-cordate to broad-cuneate at base, whitish and slightly pubescent beneath; petiole glandless; stipules foliaceous, acute: catkins 5–10 cm. long; stamens 3–7; caps. slender-stalked. S.S.9:t.465,466. (*S. occidentalis* Bosc ex Koch, not Walt.) Va. to Fla., Cuba.—**S. l. Wárdii** (Bebb) Schneid., var. Lvs. very glaucous beneath; stipules broad, obtuse; catkins slenderer, pedicel less than half as long as caps. S.S.9:t.464. H.H.76,77(b). (*S. Wardii* Bebb.) Md. to Mo., Miss. and Ala. Intr. 1895. Zone VI?

4. **S. cardiophýlla** Trautv. & Mey. Tree to 25 m.: lvs. elliptic to oblong-ovate, 6–15 cm. long, acuminate, usually rounded at base, glandular-serrate, glaucous and reticulate beneath, glabrous; petiole 1–3 cm. long, usually glandless; catkins slender, the staminate 4–8, the pistillate to 10 cm. long; stamens 5–9; ovary short-stalked, glabrous; style distinct, cleft at apex; stigmas slender, 2-parted. Tokyo Bot. Mag. 19(18):t.2. Middendorf, Reise Sib. 1.2,2:t.19, 20a-i. Saghal., Korea, Japan. Intr. 1919. Zone V.

5. **S. amygdálina** L. ALMOND-LEAVED W. Shrub or tree, sometimes to 10 m.; bark separating in flakes; brts. slightly pubescent at first, reddish brown or olive-brown: lvs. lanceolate or ovate-lanceolate, 5–10 cm. long, acuminate, cuneate or nearly rounded at base, serrulate, lustrous and dark green above, light or bluish green beneath, glabrous; petiole 3–12 mm. long, glandular; stipules usually semicordate, serrate: catkins on short leafy brts.; the staminate 3–8, the pistillate 3–7 cm. long; stamens 3, rarely 2, pilose at base: pistillate fls. with 1 gland; ovary long-conical, glabrous; pedicel 3–5 times as long as gland; stigmas subsessile, often emarginate. R.I.11:t.604(c). S.E.8: t.1313,1315(c). H.W.2:t.29,f.1–5(c). (*S. triandra* L., *S. Hoppeana* Willd.) Eu., W. to E. Asia. Long cult. Zone IV. Much cult. in Eu. for basketmaking.—**S. a. glaucophýlla** (Ser.) Seemen, var. Lvs. grayish or whitish beneath. (*S. a.* var. *discolor* Wimm. & Grab., *S. triandra* var. *amygdalina* Babingt., var. *nipponica* Franch. & Sav.)—**S. a. cóncolor** Wimm. & Grab., var. Lvs. light green beneath (*S. triandra* L.)—**S. a. angustifòlia** (Ser.) Seemen, prol. Lvs. narrow-lanceolate, green or grayish beneath.

    S. a. × *fragilis* = **S. speciòsa** Host. Brts. brown: lvs. oblong to lanceolate, dark green above, pale or bluish green beneath: stamens 2–3; pistillate fls. with usually 1 gland. Host,Sal.t.17(c). C.S.t.23a-c. (*S. alopecuroides* Tausch.) Eu. Cult. 1821.—*S. a.* × *viminalis* = **S. mollissima** Ehrh. Lvs. lanceolate, serrate or undulate-denticulate, thinly gray-tomentose beneath: ovary pubescent. I.T.4: t.140. (*S. multiformis* Doell.) Eu. Cult. 1809.—Here belong also **S. undulàta** Ehrh. (*S. lanceolata* Sm.) with less pubescent lvs. and usually glabrous ovary (S.L.8:t.1312), **S. hippophaifòlia** Thuill. with linear-lanceolate glabrate lvs. and villous ovary (R.I.11:t.599), and **S. Treviràni** Spreng. with linear-lanceolate glabrate, long-acuminate lvs. and usually glabrate ovary (C.S.t.24s).

    Related species: **S. Medwedéwii** Dode. Small glabrous shrub: lvs. linear-lanceolate, 6–10 cm. long and 5–6 mm. wide, remotely glandular-serrate, bluish white beneath; pistillate catkins dense. B.F.55:653g. Asia Minor. Cult. 1910.

6. **S. amygdaloìdes** Anders. PEACH-LEAVED W. Small tree, sometimes to 20 m., with ascending brs.; brts. red-brown or orange, lustrous, glabrous: lvs. lanceolate or ovate-lanceolate, 8–12 cm. long, cuspidate-acuminate, broad-cuneate to rounded at base, sharply serrulate, pale or glaucous beneath, pubescent when young, soon glabrous; petiole 6–15 mm. long, glandless; catkins on leafy brts., the staminate 3–5, the pistillate 4–10 cm. long, in fr. very loose; stamens 5–9, slightly pilose at base; pedicel nearly as long as caps. S.S.9:t.467. H.H.74,75(b). Que. to B. C., s. to N. Y., Tex. and Ore. Cult. 1895. Zone IV.

7. **S. frágilis** L. CRACK W. Tree to 30 m., with rough thick bark; brts.

glabrous, olive or brown, lustrous, growing at an angle of 60–90° to the br., brittle at base: lvs. oblong-lanceolate to narrow-lanceolate, 6–16 cm. long, long-acuminate, cuneate, glandular-serrate, lustrous, light green or bluish green beneath, usually slightly silky at first, soon glabrous; petiole 6–25 mm. long, glandular; stipules semicordate, serrate: catkins on leafy stalks, its lvs. entire; the staminate 2–4.5, the pistillate 3–6 cm. long; fls. of both sexes with 2 glands; filaments villous at base; ovary conic-ovoid; pedicel as long or longer than glands. R.I.11:t.609(c). H.W.2:t.28(c). H.H.82,83(b). Kew Bull. 1907:312, t.(h). Eu., W. Asia, sometimes escaped in the E. States. Long cult. Zone IV. **S. f. bullàta** Spaeth. A compact subglobose bush. M.D.1935:t.20(h). (*S. f.* var. *sphaerica* Hryniewecki & Kobenza.)—**S. f. decípiens** (Hoffm.) Koch, var. Brts. yellowish or reddish at first; winter-buds dark brown, often nearly black: lvs. lanceolate, pale green beneath. F.Sa.t.29(c). S.E.8:t.1307(c). Possibly a hybrid with *S. amygdalina.*

    S. f. × *alba* = **S. rúbens** Schrank. Intermediate between the parents and very variable: lvs. usually silky when young, becoming glabrous, usually glaucous beneath; pistillate fls. usually with 1 gland; pedicel short; style short. (*S. Russelliana* Willd.)—**S. r. víridis** (Fries) Schneid., var. lvs. pale green beneath, glabrescent. S.E.8:t.1306(c, as *S. fragilis*). (*S. v.* Fries.)—**S. r. palústris** (Host) Schneid., var. Lvs. silky-pubescent. Host, Sal.t.24–5(c). (*S. p.* Host, *S. Russelliana* Sm.)—*S. f.* × *pentandra;* see under No. 2.—*S. f.* × *babylonica;* see No. 13.—*S. f.* × *amygdalina;* see under No. 5.

8. **S. Matsudàna** Koidz. Tree to 13 m., with upright or spreading brs., yellowish or olive-green and glabrous when young: lvs. narrow-lanceolate, 5–8 cm. long, long-acuminate, rounded or rarely cuneate at base, sharply glandular-serrate, glaucescent or whitish beneath, slightly silky at first, soon glabrous; petiole 2–8 mm. long; stipules lanceolate, often wanting: catkins 1–1.5 cm. long; peduncle with entire lvs.; glands obtuse; ovary subsessile; style wanting or very short. C.C.51. B.D.1923:t.14(h). Transbaikalia, N. China, Manch., Korea. Intr. 1905. Zone IV.—**S. M. umbraculífera** Rehd., f. A form with a broad umbrella-shaped or semiglobose head. U.S.Intr.80:t(h). G.C.86: 307(h). B.D.1923:t.15(h). Intr. 1906.—**S. M. tortuòsa** Rehd., f. Brs. twisted and contorted. G.W.37:71. Gt.84:68. Cult. 1925.—**S. M. péndula** Schneid. f. Brs. pendulous. Intr. 1908.

9. **S. elegantíssima** K. Koch. THURLOW WEEPING W. Tree with long pendulous brs.; brts. brown, glabrous, lustrous: lvs. lanceolate, 8–15 cm. long, about 2 cm. broad, long-acuminate, sharply serrulate, bright green above, bluish green beneath, glabrous except midrib above; petiole 1–1.5 cm. long: stipules semicordate: pistillate catkins to 5 cm. long; the peduncle with entire lvs.; ovary short-stalked, thinly pubescent near base; style short; ventral gland emarginate or 2-parted, slightly longer than pedicel. M.G.13:88(h). Origin unknown, possibly *S. babylonica* × *fragilis*. Intr. about 1860. Zone IV. Ornamental tree with long pendulous brs.

10. **S. jessoénsis** Seemen. Tree to 25 m., with spreading brs.; bark light brownish gray, somewhat flaky; brts. light brown, grayish pubescent when young; winter-buds pubescent: lvs. lanceolate to narrow-lanceolate, 5–9 cm. long, acuminate, mucronate-serrulate, densely silky when young, later slightly silky above, densely so and glaucescent beneath; petiole 2–5 mm. long; stipules ovate-lanceolate, small, silky: catkins on short leafy stalks, the staminate 2–3 cm. long, rather loose; scales oblong-elliptic, slightly villous at base; filaments villous at base; pistillate catkins dense, to 4.5 cm. long; scales obtuse or emarginate; ovary pubescent; stigmas oblong, undivided. Seemen, Sal. Jap. t.3,f.f-1. M.K.t.14(c). Japan. Intr. 1897. Zone V.

Related species: **S. koreénsis** Anders. Tree to 20 m.; glabrous: lvs. lanceolate to narrow-lanceolate, 6–12 cm. long, sharply serrulate; petiole 5–10 mm. long, yellowish like the midrib; style distinct, rather long; ovary pubescent or glabrate; style emarginate. N.K.18:t.38. Korea. Intr. 1919. Zone V.—Other species which may belong here are: **S. lispóclados** Dode. Brts. reddish, glabrous: lvs. subsessile, ovate-lanceolate, about 6 cm. long, glandular-serrate, bluish white beneath, glabrous: staminate catkins 1–1.5 cm. long; stamens 2–3. B.F.55:653H. Asia Minor. Cult. 1910.—H. Tomínii Dode. Brts. dark brown, glabrous, young growth villous: lvs. lanceolate, 8–10 cm. long, nearly rounded at base, remotely serrulate, glabrate above, appressed-silky beneath and bluish white; petiole 5–8 mm. long: staminate catkins to 2 cm. long; stamens 2, connate at base. B.F.55:653A. Cauc. Cult. 1910.—S. óxica Dode. Brts. reddish brown, glabrous, young growth silky: lvs. lanceolate to 12 cm. or more long, cuneate, serrate, bluish gray and appressed-silky beneath; staminate catkins 4–6 cm. long; scales lanceolate; ovary glabrous, short-stalked. B.F.55:653B. Turkest. Cult. 1910.

11. **S. alba** L. WHITE W. Tree to 25 m., with spreading brs. pendent at ends; brts. silky when young, olive-brown, spreading at an acute angle (30–45°) from the br.: lvs. lanceolate, 4–10 cm. long, acuminate, cuneate, serrulate, glaucous and silky beneath; petiole 6–12 mm. long, with small glands; stipules lanceolate: catkins on leafy stalks, 4–6 cm. long; stamens villous at base; ovary subsessile, conic-ovoid, glabrous; style short. R.I.11:t.608(c). S.E.8:t.1309(c). H.W.2,1:100(h),t.27(c). S.H.1:35(h). Eu. and N. Afr. to C. Asia. Long cult. Zone II.—Planted as timber-tree, also var. *vitellina* as basket-willow and var. *tristis* for ornament.—**S. a. ovàlis** Wimm., f. Lvs. elliptic-oblong.—**S. a. calva** G. F. W. Mey. Brs. more upright; brts. dark brown: lvs. slightly silky at first, finally glabrous or nearly so; ovary slightly stalked. (Var. *coerulea* Koch, *S. coerulea* Sm.—CRICKET-BAT W.) S.E.8:t.1310(c). B.S.2:480,t(h). E.H.7:t.381(h).—**S. a. serícea** Gaud., var. Lvs. densely silky beneath and more or less so above. (*S. a.* var. *leucophylla* Hartig, var. *splendens* Anders., var. *argentea* Wimm., var. *regalis* Hort.)—**S. a. vitellìna** (L.) Stokes, var. Brts. yellow: lvs. narrow-lanceolate, long-acuminate, glaucous beneath and slightly silky; catkins longer; scales longer. F.Sa.t.137(c). S.E. 8:t.811(c). (*S. v.* L.)—**S. a. chermesìna** Hartig, var. Brts. bright red. (*S. vitellina britzensis* Spaeth.)—**S. a. trístis** Gaud., var. With bright yellow pendulous brs. M.G.13:88(h);32:322(h). Gn.86:603(h);89:143(h). (*S. a.* var. *vitellina pendula* Rehd., *S. chrysocoma* Dode.)

S. a. × *nigra;* see under No. 1.—*S. a.* × *pentandra;* see under No. 2.—*S. a.* × *fragilis;* see under No. 7.—*S. a.* × *babylonica;* see under No. 12.

12. **S. babylònica** L. WEEPING W. Tree to 10 m., with long pendulous brs.; brts. brown, glabrous, only young growth slightly silky: lvs. lanceolate to linear-lanceolate, 8–16 cm. long, long-acuminate, cuneate, serrulate, dark green above, grayish green beneath, with distinct venation, glabrous; petiole 3–5 mm. long; stipules rarely developed, ovate-lanceolate: catkins short-stalked, curved, the staminate to 4, the pistillate to 2 cm. long; scales villous only at base, nearly as long as ovary; ovary sessile or subsessile, glabrous; style very short; stigmas oblong, 2-lobed; gland about ⅓ as long as ovary. Brandis, For. Fl. t.59. Seemen, Sal. Jap. t.3a-e. Gn.M.31:318–20(h). B.S.1:64(h). (*S. pendula* Moench.) China. Intr. about 1730. Zone V or VI.—Handsome weeping tree, often planted; frequently confused with *S. elegantissima* and *S. blanda.*—**S. b. crispa** Loud., var. Lvs. folded and spirally curved. F.Sa.t.41(c). (*S. b. annularis* (Forbes) Aschers., f., *S. a.* Forbes, *S. Napoleonis* F. Schultz.)

S. b. × *alba* = **S. sepulcràlis** Simonk. Tree with spreading brs. and pendulous brts., similar to *S. babylonica*, but of more vigorous growth and less weeping; young growth silky: lvs. bluish or whitish beneath and silky-pubescent or sometimes glabrous: catkins pistillate or androgynous, thicker, their axis more pubescent; scales shorter, acute, long-ciliate. B.F.45:t.6. C.S.t.22e-i. Gn.55:

19(h). B.S.1:98,t(h). (*S. Salamonii* Carr., *S. babylonica Salamonii* Simon-Louis.) Orig. before 1864. Zone IV.—*S. b.* × *fragilis;* see No. 13.

13. S. blanda Anders. (*S. babylonica* × *fragilis.*) WISCONSIN WEEPING W. (NIOBE W.) Tree with widespreading head and long pendulous brs.; brts. dull green or brown, brittle at base: lvs. lanceolate to narrow-lanceolate, 8–15 cm. long, long-acuminate, cuneate, serrulate, dark green above, bluish green beneath, glabrous; petiole 5–12 mm. long; stipules ovate or oblong-ovate; catkins slender, 2–3 cm. long; stamens pubescent at base; ovary short-stalked; pedicel about twice as long as gland; style short; stigmas emarginate. Andersson, Monog. t.3,f.31. C.S.t.22d. M.G.13:89(h). (*S. babylonica* var. *dolorosa* Rowlee, *S. Petzoldii pendula* Hort., ? *S. pendulina* Wender.) Orig. before 1830? Zone IV.

14. S. longifòlia Muhlenb. SANDBAR W. Shrub 1–4 m. tall, forming thickets, sometimes a slender tree to 8 m., with rather smooth bark; brts. orange to purplish red, glabrous: lvs. linear-lanceolate, 6–10 cm. long, acuminate, cuneate, remotely denticulate, bright green, distinctly veined, silky beneath when young, later glabrous; petiole 3–5 mm. long; stipules minute or wanting: catkins on rather long leafy brts., the staminate dense, 2–4 cm. long, sometimes panicled, the pistillate to 5 cm. long in fr. and rather loose; ovary silky when young, short-stalked; scales ovate or obovate; stigmas subsessile, with short elliptic lobes; stamens pilose at base. S.S.9:t.474. H.H.84,85(b). (*S. fluviatilis* Sarg., in part, not Nutt.) Que. to Va. and La., w. to Man., Wyo., N. Mex. and n. Mex. Cult. 1873. Zone IV.

Related species: **S. exígua** Nutt. Shrub or small tree to 5 m.: lvs. subsessile, linear to linear-lanceolate, nearly entire, yellowish green, silky. B.T.195. A.I.1:493. B. C. to Calif., w. to Mont., Idaho, Colo. and N. Mex. Intr. 1921. Zone V?—**S. melanópsis** Nutt. Shrub·or small tree; lvs. elliptic-lanceolate to oblanceolate, 4–6 cm. long, serrulate, rarely nearly entire, glaucous beneath, silky when young, soon glabrous: petiole 1–5 mm. long; catkins 5–7 cm. long; scales linear-oblong; ovary glabrous. A.I.1:493. B. C. to Ore. and Mont. Intr. 1921. Zone V.—**S. argophýlla** Nutt. Shrub or small tree; lvs. subsessile, narrow-lanceolate, 4–8 cm. long, usually entire, silky-pubescent on both sides, silvery-white beneath: ovary densely pubescent. N.S.1:t.20(c). B.T.196. Wash. and Mont. to Calif. and Tex. Cult.?

15. S. phánera Schneid. Large shrub or tree to 12 m.; brts. tomentulose at first, soon glabrous: lvs. ovate-lanceolate or broadly elliptic-lanceolate, 6–20 cm. long, short-acuminate or acute, rounded at base, crenate-denticulate, sparingly puberulous or glabrate and impressed-reticulate above, tomentose beneath, finally glabrescent and reticulate beneath, midrib and the numerous parallel veins glabrate and yellowish; petiole 1–2 cm. long; stipules semicordate, glandular-serrate; staminate catkins 10–12 cm. long, slender; rachis villous; filaments villous at base; scales broad-ovate, rounded, yellow-brown, villous on both sides. H.S.f.33. W. China. Intr. 1911. Zone (V). Handsome willow with large lvs.

16. S. moupinénsis Franch. Shrub or tree to 6 m.; brts. glabrous, becoming orange to red-brown: lvs. narrow-elliptic to oblong, 6–12 cm. long, acute or short-acuminate, broad-cuneate or rounded at base, sharply glandular-serrulate, glabrous above, light green and reticulate beneath, silky on the veins or quite glabrous; petiole 1–1.5 cm. long, glabrous, glandless; stipules wanting: catkins on short leafy brts., the staminate 6–9, the pistillate to 14 cm. long, loose, with the fls. subverticillate; scales yellow-brown, glabrous or nearly so, persistent; rachis sparingly pubescent; ovary glabrous, short-stalked; style about ⅓ as long as ovary, with oblong bifid stigmas. W. China. Intr. 1911. Zone (V). Handsome willow with large bright green lvs.

Closely related species: **S. Fargèsii** Burk. Lvs. elliptic to elliptic-oblong, up to 18 cm. long, usually more densely pubescent beneath; petiole to 2.5 cm. long: staminate catkins to 12, pistillate to 16 cm. long; scales long-villous; style slender; caps. subsessile. B.J.29:t.3a-f. W. China. Intr. 1911. Zone (V).

17. **S. magnífica** Hemsl. Shrub or small tree to 6 m.; glabrous; young shoots and buds purple: lvs. elliptic or elliptic-obovate, 10–20 cm. long, abruptly acuminate, rounded or subcordate at base, entire or denticulate near apex, dull bluish green above, glaucous beneath; petiole 1–3.5 cm. long, purplish: catkins on leafy brts., glabrous, the staminate 10–18, the pistillate 18–30 cm. long in fr.: ovary subsessile; style distinct. J.L.39:f.148. Gt.75:29. W. China. Intr. 1903. Zone VI? Very distinct willow, remarkable for its large and broad lvs. and the very long catkins.

Related species: **S. pella** Schneid. Shrub: lvs. elliptic-oblong to elliptic, 4–13 cm. long, acute or obtusish, serrulate, silky-pubescent on the veins beneath; petiole 6–15 cm. long: fruiting catkins 4–9 cm. long; scales glabrous; rachis pubescent. W. China. Intr. 1911. Zone VII.

18. **S. herbàcea** L. DWARF W. Depressed shrub with partly underground creeping stems and slender angled brts. to 15 cm. long; young growth slightly pubescent, soon glabrous: lvs. suborbicular, 8–20 mm. long, rounded or emarginate at apex, rounded or cordate at base, crenulate-serrate, bright green and lustrous on both sides, reticulate-veined, glabrous; petiole 4–8 mm. long: catkins on 2-lvd. brts., 4–10-fld.; scales obovate, obtuse, yellowish, glabrous or nearly so; glands mostly incised or lobed; ovary short-stalked, glabrous; style short, with 2-parted stigmas. R.I.11:t.557,f.1182(c). S.E.8:t.1378 (c). High Mts. of Eu. and N. Asia; arctic N. Am. s. to N. H. Cult. 1789. Zone II.

S. h. × *formosa* = **S. simulátrix** B. White. Creeping shrub: lvs. suborbicular to ovate, to 1.5 cm. long: catkins many-fld., on leafy brts.; ovary pubescent. Gs.5:91(h). Switzerland. Cult. 1922.

A similar species is **S. polàris** Wahlenb. Lvs. smaller, entire: scales dark at apex; stamens sometimes slightly connate at base; pistillate fls. with 1 gland; ovary pubescent. S.H.1:f.19g,27d. S.L.67(h). M.G.25:141(h). Arctic Eu. and Asia. Cult. 1910. Zone I.

19. **S. retùsa** L. Prostrate shrub with rooting glabrous brs.: lvs. obovate to oblong, 8–35 mm. long, obtuse, rarely emarginate or acutish, cuneate, entire or with few small teeth, green on both sides, glabrous or slightly pubescent beneath; petiole 2–5 mm. long: catkins on leafy brts., the staminate to 18 mm. long, loose, the pistillate to 2 cm. long; scales oval to oblong, yellowish, glabrous or sparingly hairy; pedicel ¼ as long as the glabrous ovary; style about ⅓ as long as ovary, bifid; stigmas short, bifid. R.I.11:t.558,f.1186–7(c). H.W. 2,1:107a. Mts. of Eu. Intr. 1763. Zone I.

S. r. × *myrsinifolia* = **S. Cottéti** Kerner. Low, usually prostrate: lvs. elliptic to oblong, 2–4 cm. long, obtuse or acute, serrulate, pubescent when young; catkins short-cylindric; scales darker toward apex, pubescent. C.S.2:t.12e-g. G.W.9:542(h). Eu. Alps. Cult. 1905. Zone V.

Related species: **S. serpyllifòlia** Scop. Lvs. 4–8 mm. long: catkins about 5 mm. long; pedicel shorter than ventral gland. R.I.11:t.558,f.1185(c). (*S. retusa* var. *s.* Ser.) Alps and mts. of s. e. Eu. Cult. 1898.

20. **S. ùva-úrsi** Pursh. BEARBERRY W. Prostrate shrub with glabrous brs. to 30 cm. long: lvs. elliptic to obovate, 5–25 mm. long, acute or obtuse, cuneate, slightly toothed or entire, lustrous above, pale or glaucous beneath, strongly veined; petiole 2–4 mm. long; catkins on slender leafy brts., about 1 cm. long, the pistillate 2–4 cm. long in fr.; scales obovate, rose-red at apex, silky; usually 1 stamen, rarely 2; caps. conic-ovoid, glabrous, short-stalked; style short, but distinct. Fl. Dan. 17:t.3053(c). B.B.1:601. (*S. Cutleri* Tuckerm.) Lab. to Alaska, s. to alpine summits of N. Y. and N. H. Intr. 1880. Zone I.

21. **S. reticulàta** L. Low procumbent shrub; brts. angled, glabrous: lvs. broad-elliptic to broad-obovate, 1.5–5 cm. long, obtuse, sometimes emarginate, broad-cuneate to subcordate at base, entire, rugulose above, gray-green and usually silky beneath at first, soon glabrous, reticulate; petiole 8–20 mm. long; catkins slender, long-peduncled, on leafy brts., the staminate to 2, the pistillate to 3 cm. long; scales light brown, oval, villous; stamens villous below the middle; ovary sessile, tomentose; style very short. R.I.11:t.557,f.1184(c). S.E.8:t.1369(c). M.G.25:124(h). Gs.5:91(h). (*S. orbicularis* Anders., in part.) Eu., N. Asia, in N. Am. from Lab. to Alaska. Cult. 1789. Zone I. An attractive species for the rock-garden.

22. **S. vestìta** Pursh. Low shrub to 20 cm., usually prostrate; young brts. pubescent: lvs. obovate or elliptic, 2–5 cm. long, obtuse or emarginate, broad-cuneate to rounded at base, slightly crenate, silky above at first, soon dark green and glabrous, silky-tomentose beneath; petiole 4–8 mm. long: catkins on leafy brts., the staminate to 3.5 cm. long, the pistillate in fr. to 5 cm. long;. fls. similar to those of No. 21. A.I.1:507. B.B.1:603. Lab. and Que. to Man.— **S. v. erécta** Anders., var. Upright to 50 cm. tall: lvs. thinner, narrower, often acutish: caps. more obtuse. A.I.1:507. (*S. Fernaldii* Blankinsh.) B. C. to Calif. and Mont. Intr. 1892? Zone V.

Related species: **S. nivàlis** Hook. Cespitose creeping shrub: lvs. oval to oblong, about 1 cm. long, acute at ends, entire, glabrous, dark green above, glaucous beneath: catkins 1 cm. or less long, on leafy brts.; scales yellow, nearly glabrous; caps. pubescent, sessile. B. C. and Wash. to Mont. and Alberta.— **S. n. saximontàna** (Rydb.) Schneid., var. Brts. thick: lvs. 1.5–3.5 cm. long, 0.8–2 cm. broad; petiole to 1.8 cm. long: staminate catkins to 1.2, pistillate to 1.8 cm. long. Rocky Mts. Intr. 1921. Zone II?

23. **S. petróphila** Rydb. Creeping shrub to 10 cm. tall: lvs. obovate or elliptic to oblanceolate, 1–3 cm. long, obtuse or acutish, cuneate, entire, bright green above, slightly paler and strongly veined beneath, glabrous or sparingly silky at first; petioles 3–6 mm. long: catkins on leafy brts., 2–3 cm. long; scales obovate, blackish, sparingly silky-villous; caps. sessile, white-villous; style distinct, 0.5 mm. long, with elongated bifid stigmas. A.I.1:500. B. C. and Alb. to Calif., Wyo., Colo. and N. Mex. Intr. 1922. Zone V.

A closely related species is **S. árctica** Pall. Creeping shrub with thick brts.: lvs. obovate, 2.5–4, rarely to 7 cm. long, obtuse, broad-cuneate at base, sometimes sparingly denticulate, glaucous beneath; petiole 0.5–2 cm. long; catkins 2–4 cm. long. Proc. Wash. Acad. Sci. 3:t.40. Arctic N. Am., N. Eur., N. Asia. Cult. 1902. Zone I.

24. **S. brachycárpa** Nutt. Upright shrub to 1 m.; brts. densely villous: lvs. subsessile, elliptic-oblong to oblanceolate, 1–3 cm. long, entire, villous on both sides, more densely so beneath: catkins on leafy brts., 1–2 cm. long, dense; scales obovate, yellowish, villous; ovary subsessile, densely villous; style very short; caps. 4–5 mm. long. S.H.1:f.26e,27b-b. (*S. desertorum* Anders., not Richards.) B. C. and Wash. to Man., Colo. and Utah. Intr. about 1890. Zone V.

25. **S. glaùca** L. Shrub to 1 m.; young brts. silky or whitish tomentose, later brown or yellowish, lustrous: lvs. lanceolate to obovate, 3–8 cm. long, acute at ends or sometimes obtuse at apex, entire, silky above, later glabrate or glabrous, silky- or white-tomentose and grayish green or glaucous, rarely green beneath; petiole to 1.5 cm. long; stipules usually small or obsolete: catkins on leafy stalks, to 4.5 cm. long; scales oval to oblong, dark above the middle; filaments glabrous or villous at base; ovary short-stalked, silky or tomentose; ventral gland truncate or 2-parted, as long or longer than pedicel; style not more than ⅓ as long as ovary, with oblong, deeply emarginate stig-

mas. R.I.11:t.571,f.1214(c). H.W.2,1:122,f.206. Eu. Alps; N. As.; n. w. N. Am., from Alaska to B. C., Alb. and Mont. Cult. 1813. Zone II?—The Am. plant has been separated from the Eu. type as **S. g. acutifòlia** (Hook.) Schneid., var. (*S. Seemannii* Rydb.), differing chiefly in the usually well-developed stipules, the longer pedicels, sometimes twice as long as the gland and in the glabrescents filaments, and as **S. g. glabréscens** (Anders.) Schneid., var, similar, but less pubescent.

Related species: **S. pyrenàica** L. Lower: lvs. not more than 3 cm. long, scales usually pale; pistillate fls. with 1 gland. C.S.1:t.10b. Trautvetter, Sal. Frig. t.4. Gs.5:90(h). Pyrenees. Cult. 1875.—**S. argyrocárpa** Anders. Erect or ascending, to 0.5 m.: lvs. short-petioled, oblong to oblanceolate, 3–5 cm. long, silky-pubescent beneath, entire or crenulate and slightly revolute: catkins 1.5–2.5 cm. long; style elongated; pedicels about ½ as long as the silky caps. B.B.1:603 Anderson, Mon. Sal. t.6,f.60. Lab. and Que. to N. H. Intr. 1883. Zone II.

26. S. díscolor Muhlenb. Pussy W. Shrub or small tree to 7 m.; young brts. pubescent at first, soon glabrous: lvs. elliptic-oblong to oblong-oblanceolate, 4–10 cm. long, acute at ends, irregularly crenate-serrate or nearly entire, pubescent when young, glabrous or nearly so at maturity, glaucous beneath, rather thin; petiole 8–25 mm. long; stipules usually conspicuous, semi-cordate, deciduous: catkins before the lvs., subsessile, the staminate dense, to 3.5 cm. long, the pistillate to 7 cm. long in fr.; filaments glabrous; pedicel glabrous, ¼–⅓ as long as the pubescent rostrate ovary; style distinct, short, with narrow bifid stigmas. S.S.9:t.478. F.Sa.t.147(c). H.H.92,93(b). (*S. conifera* Wangh.) N. S. to Man., s. to Va. and Mo. Cult. 1809. Zone II.—**S. d. latifòlia** Anders., var. Brts. pubescent: lvs. pubescent beneath, often ferrugineous: catkins smaller. (*S. d.* var. *eriocephala* Anders.)

Closely related species: **S. Scouleriàna** Barratt. Large shrub or tree to 10 m.; lvs. elliptic to oblong-obovate, acute to short-acuminate, entire to slightly crenate-serrulate, white- or rusty-pubescent to glabrous and reticulate beneath; pedicels shorter, villous; stigma sessile. S.M.161. A.I.1:505. (*S. flavescens* Nutt.) Alaska to Mont., n. Calif., Ariz. and N. Mex. Intr. 1918 Zone V.

27. S. Wallichiàna Anders. Shrub or small tree; young brts. silky, soon glabrous; winter-buds glabrous: lvs. ovate-lanceolate to oblong-lanceolate, 5–10 cm. long, acuminate, cuneate to broad-cuneate, entire or sometimes serrulate, silky at first, later glabrous and smooth above, glaucous and nearly glabrous or sometimes pubescent beneath, with many lateral veins and indistinct veinlets; petiole 8–15 mm. long, glabrous; stipules small: catkins on short bracted stalks or subsessile, very villous, the staminate 2–3, the pistillate 2–5, in fr. to 10 cm. long; scales black-brown, obtuse; filaments glabrous; pedicels short, rarely ⅓ as long as the pubescent rostrate ovary; style short, with upright, oval to oblong and emarginate to bifid stigmas. Andersson, Mon. t.5,f.46. Brandis, For.Fl.t.61. Himal., China. Intr. 1911. Zone V.

Related species: **S. lívida** Wahlenb. Low shrub or sometimes small tree to 8 m.; brts. glabrous or nearly so, lustrous: lvs. obovate to oblong-lanceolate, up to 6 cm. long, acute, entire or crenate, glabrous or nearly so; petiole 2–5 mm. long; scales obtuse, yellow, usually dark at apex; pedicel about as long as ovary; style short. R.I.11:567(c). H.W.2,1:118. (*S. ? Starkeana* Willd., *S. depressa* E. Fries, not L.) Eu., N. Asia. Cult. 1872. Zone III?—**S. l. cineráscens** Wahlenb., var. Young brts. and lvs. pubescent. R.I.11:t.567,f.2008(c).

28. S. cáprea L. Goat W. Shrub or sometimes tree to 9 m.; young brts. gray-pubescent, later glabrous, brown and lustrous; winter-buds becoming glabrous: lvs. broad-elliptic to oblong, 6–10 cm. long, acute, rarely rounded at base, irregularly and slightly toothed or nearly entire, pubescent at first, finally glabrate, rugulose and dark green above, gray-pubescent beneath and reticulate; petiole 8–20 mm. long; stipules oblique-reniform, serrate: catkins subsessile, with 3–6 bracts at base, densely villous, the staminate oval, 2.5–3.5 cm. long, dense, the pistillate to 6, in fr. to 10 cm. long; scales lanceolate; filaments glabrous or slightly villous at base; pedicel ⅔ or as long as the gray-pubescent ovary; style wanting or very short; stigma oval, emarginate or bifid; gland short, ⅛ to ¼ as long as pedicel. R.I.11:t.577(c). H.W.2:t.32(c). S.E.8:t.1331–2(c). Eu. to N. E. Asia and n. Persia. Long cult. Zone IV. The rather large bright yellow catkins are conspicuous in early spring.—**S. c. varie-gàta** West., var. Lvs. variegated with white. ˙Cult. 1770.—**S. c. péndula** Th. Lang. KILMARNOCK W. With stiffly pendulous brs. Cult. 1853.

S. c. × *myrsinifolia* = **S. latifòlia** Forb. Lvs. broad-elliptic or obovate to oblong, silky-pubescent beneath, later glabrate, turning blackish in drying; catkins on short bracted stalks; ovary silky or nearly glabrous, on pedicel of about equal length. C.S.t.44,f.l-o. F.S.t.118(c). Eu. Cult. 1829.—*S. c.* × *phyli-cifolia* = **S. laùrina** Sm. Brts. pubescent at first: lvs. obovate to obovate-oblong, 4–8 cm. long, short-acuminate, lustrous above, glaucescent and glabrous beneath at maturity, pubescent at first; stigma thick, usually not bifid, about as long as style. R.I.11:t.564,f.2004(c). S.E.8:t.1333(c). (*S. bicolor* Sm., not Willd.) Cult. 1809.—*S. c.* × *daphnoides;* see under No. 53.—*S. c.* × *lapponum;* see under No. 55.—*S. c.* × *viminalis;* see under No. 56.—*S. c.* × *Elaeagnos;* see under No. 57.—*S. c.* × *purpurea;* see under No. 59.

Closely related species: **S. grandifòlia** Ser. Lvs. to 15 cm. long, at maturity glabrous or pubescent only at midrib and closely reticulate beneath; petiole to 1 cm. long: catkins with 1–3 bracts at base, smaller, less densely villous; pedicel as long or longer than ovary; style short. R.I.11:t.578(c). H.W.2,1:117A-E. (*S. appendiculata* Vill.?) Mts. of Eu. Cult. 1871.—*S. g.* × *purpurea;* see under No. 59.—**S. silesíaca** Willd. Lvs. lanceolate or ovate to obovate, to 14 cm. long, crenate-serrate, silky when young, later glabrate and pale green and closely reticulate beneath: pedicels as long as the usually glabrous ovary; style short. R.I.11:t.574(c). H.W.2,1:117F-H. Mts. of Eu. and Transcauc. Cult. 1876. Zone V.

29. **S. aurìta** L. Shrub to 2, rarely to 3 m.; brts. slender, tomentulose when young, later glabrous, usually dark brown; wood of 2–5-year-old brs. under the bark with short raised striations: lvs. obovate to oblanceolate, 3–8 cm. long, acute or obtusish, cuneate, obscurely serrate, dull green and rugose above and usually slightly pubescent, closely reticulate beneath and gray-tomentose at first, usually later glabrate; petiole 4–10 mm. long; stipules conspicuous, reniform, serrate: catkins sessile, staminate to 2.5, pistillate to 3 cm. long; scales brownish yellow, dark at apex; filaments villous at base; pedicels about as long as the pubescent ovary; stigmas oval, emarginate or bifid, subsessile. R.I.11:t.575(c). S.E.8:t.1330(c). H.W.2,1:116A-E. Eu., W. Asia. Long cult. Zone V.

S. a. × *cinerea* = **S. multinérvis** Doell. Brts. densely pubescent: lvs. obovate to oblong-obovate, acute, cuneate, gray-pubescent, later usually glabrate above; catkins small. C.S.1:t.30s-y. (*S. lutescens* Kern.) Eu. Cult. 1873.—*S. a.* × *repens* = **S. ambígua** Ehrh. Low shrub with often prostrate brs.; young brts. silky or silky-tomentose: lvs. elliptic or oblong to lanceolate, rather small, serrulate, silky-tomentose, later glabrescent above; stipules usually inconspicuous: catkins small; scales ovate, acute; pedicel about ⅓ as long as ovary. R.I. 11:t.592,f.1243b(c). S.E.8:t.1354(c). Eu. Cult. 1872.—*S. a.* × *phylicifolia* = **S. ludíficans** F. B. White. Brts. glabrous at maturity: lvs. elliptic to narrow-obovate, crenulate, glabrous at maturity and glaucous beneath; stipules usually persistent: catkins on bracted stalks. N. Eu. Cult. 1900.—*S. a.* × *viminalis;* see under No. 56.—*S. a.* × *Elaeagnos;* see under No. 57.—*S. a.* × *purpurea;* see under No. 59.—*S. a.* × *phylicifolia* × *purpurea;* see under No. 59.

30. **S. cinérea** L. GRAY W. Shrub to 5 m., sometimes tree-like, 1- and 2-year-old brts. and winter-buds tomentose; wood with striation as in No. 29: lvs. elliptic or obovate to obovate-lanceolate, 5–9 cm. long, acute, cuneate to rounded at base, crenate or remotely serrate, often obscurely so, tomentose at first, later glabrescent and dull green above, gray or bluish gray and densely

pubescent beneath; petiole to 1 cm. long: catkins subsessile, with 4–7 bracts at base, staminate to 5, pistillate to 8 cm. long in fr.; filaments villous at base; pedicel about ⅓ as long as the pubescent or tomentose, rarely glabrate ovary; style as long as the oval emarginate stigmas. R.I.11:t.576(c). S.E.8:t.1327–9 (c). H.W.2,1:116F-G. Gn.87:131. Eu. to Kamchatka and n. Persia. Long cult. Zone II.—**S. c. trícolor** Dipp., f. Lvs. variegated with yellow and white or white and red.

S. c. × ? = **S. renécia** Dode. Lvs. oblong to oblong-lanceolate, 8–10 cm. long, pubescent and glaucous beneath; pedicels slender; style longer than stigmas. B.F.55:653F. Eu. Cult. 1910.—*S. c.* × *phylicifolia* = **S. Wardiàna** F. B. White. Young brts. pubescent: lvs. oblong-obovate or narrow-elliptic to oblong, 4–8 cm. long, glaucescent and slightly pubescent and slightly reticulate at maturity beneath; style as long as the often bifid stigmas. C.S.1:t.31s-u. Eu. Cult. 1896.—*S. c.* × *aurita;* see under No. 29.—*S. c.* × *lapponum;* see under No. 54.—*S. c.* × *viminalis;* see under No. 56.—*S. c.* × *purpurea;* see under No. 59.

31. **S. Medémii** Boiss. Shrub to 4 m. with stout brs.; brts. tomentose: lvs. oblong, rarely oblong-obovate, 6–15 cm. long, acute, rounded to broad-cuneate at base, crenate-serrate or irregularly and rather coarsely dentate, pubescent at first, later glabrate above, sparingly pubescent and glaucous beneath; petiole to 2 cm. long; stipules semicordate: catkins sessile, thick, staminate to 3.5 cm. long; pistillate to 9 cm. long in fr.; filaments connate about ½, hairy at base; pedicel about ½ as long as the pubescent ovary; stigmas subsessile, bifid. S.H.1:f.15h,20e-f. G.C.77:129. Armenia, Persia. Cult. 1880. Zone V. Handsome willow, one of the earliest to bloom.

32. **S. rèpens** L. CREEPING W. Low shrub to 1 m., with prostrate stem and ascending brs.; young brts. pubescent, later glabrous, brown: lvs. elliptic to lanceolate, 1.5–3.5, rarely to 5 cm. long, acute and recurved at apex or obtuse, entire or nearly so and revolute, silky when young, usually glabrous above at maturity, with 6–8 pairs of veins; petiole 2–3 mm. long; stipules small, only present on vigorous shoots: catkins with or shortly before the lvs. on short bracted stalks, staminate 1–1.5, pistillate to 3.5 cm. long; scales obtuse, brown at apex; pedicel about ½ or sometimes as long as the narrow-conical caps.; style very short. R.I.11:t.589(c). S.E.8:t.1356–61(c). H.W.2,1:123. Eu. to W. and N. E. Asia. Long cult. Zone IV.—**S. r. nítida** (Ser.) Wender., var. Lvs. broad-elliptic to oblong, densely silky when young, later glabrescent above. (*S. r.* var. *arenaria* Anders., var. *argentea* (Smith) Wimm. & Grab., var. *sericea* Gaud.) R.I.11:t.589,f.1243(c). S.E.8:t.1362(c).—**S. r. rosmarinifòlia** (L.) Wimm. & Grab., var. Lvs. linear to oblong-lanceolate, acute and not recurved at apex, with 8–12 pairs of veins. R.I.11:t.591,f.1242(c). S.E.8:t.1363–4(c). (*S. rosmarinifolia* L., *S. r.* var. *angustifolia* Gren. & Godr.)

S. r. × *aurita;* see under No. 29.— *S. r.* × *S. daphnoides;* see under No. 53.—*S. r.* × *viminalis;* see under No. 56.—*S. r.* × *Elaeagnos;* see under No. 57.— *S. r.* × *purpurea;* see under No. 59.

33. **S. petiolàris** Sm. Low shrub; brts. slender, soon glabrous, purple: lvs. lanceolate or narrow-lanceolate, 4–8 cm. long, acuminate, cuneate, serrulate, slightly silky when young, soon glabrous, remaining green in drying; petiole 4–10 mm. long: catkins on short bracted stalks, with the lvs., staminate 1–2, pistillate to 4 cm. long in fr.; scales yellowish or pale brown; caps. pubescent, narrowed from an ovoid base; pedicel ⅓–½ as long as caps.; stigmas subsessile. E.B.16:t.1147(c). B.B.1:599. Gr.M.f.659. N. B. and Man., s. to Wis. and Tenn. Cult. 1802. Zone II. Valuable basket-willow.

34. **S. serícea** Marsh. SILKY W. Shrub to 4 m., with slender purplish brs. puberulous when young; lvs. lanceolate or narrow-lanceolate, 4–10 cm. long,

acuminate, cuneate to rounded at base, serrulate, silky when young, later dark green and glabrous above, minutely silky beneath; petiole 4–14 mm. long; stipules narrow, deciduous: catkins sessile, before the lvs., staminate about 2, pistillate to 4 cm. long in fr.; filaments pilose at base; pedicel about ⅛ as long as the ovoid-oblong, obtuse ovary; stigmas short, sessile. Gr.M.f.662. S.H.1: f.15g,21m-m′. (*S. grisea* Willd.) Me. to Mich. and Va. Cult. 1809. Zone III. Handsome willow.

     S. s. × *cordata;* see under No. 48.

     35. **S. húmilis** Marsh. PRAIRIE W. Shrub to 2.5 m.; brts. pubescent or tomentose: lvs. oblanceolate or oblong-lanceolate, 5–10 cm. long, acute at ends, or the lower ones obovate and obtusish, sparingly denticulate and slightly revolute, dull dark green and puberulous or glabrate above, glaucous and tomentose beneath; petiole 4–6 mm. long; stipules semi-ovate, usually persistent: catkins sessile, before the lvs., ellipsoid, 1.5–4 cm. long; anthers red; pedicels about ¼ or ⅓ as long as the beaked caps.; stigma sessile or on a short style. B.B.1:600. Gr.M.f.660. Nfd. to Minn. and N. C. Intr. 1876. Zone III?

     Closely related species: **S. tristis** Ait. Shrub to 0.5 m.: lvs. oblanceolate or linear-oblong, 2–5 cm. long; petiole 2–3 mm. long; stipules minute, deciduous; catkins small, subglobose to ovoid; pedicel longer than scale. B.B.1:600. Gr.M. f.661. (*S. humilis* var. *t.* Griggs.) Me. to Minn., s. to Fla. and Tenn. Intr. 1765. Zone II.

     36. **S. Bebbiàna** Sarg. BEAK W. Shrub or sometimes tree to 8 m.; brts. pubescent or puberulous: lvs. elliptic to oblong-lanceolate, 3–10 cm. long, acute or acuminate, rounded or narrowed at base, sparingly serrate or entire, dull green and puberulous above, reticulate and tomentose beneath, or glabrate on both sides when old, firm; petiole 4–12 mm. long; stipules semi-cordate, deciduous: catkins subsessile, bracted at base with the lvs., staminate to 3, pistillate to 6 cm. long; scales pale, rose-tipped, thinly villous; filaments villous at base, 1 cm. long; pedicels slender, about half as long as ovary, longer than scale; caps. long-beaked, stigma subsessile. S.S.9:t.477. B.B. 1:599. (*S. rostrata* Richards., not Thuill.) Nfd. to Alaska, s. to Pa., Ill., Utah and Calif. Intr. 1889. Zone II.—**S. B. perrostràta** (Rydb.) Schneid., var. Brts. glabrescent: lvs. glabrescent, smaller and often thinner. Neb. to Colo., N. Mex. and Utah. Intr. 1922.

     Closely related species: **S. Geyeriàna** Anders. Shrub to 3 m.; mature brts. often bloomy: lvs. linear-oblanceolate, 2–6 cm. long, densely silky when young, sometimes becoming glabrate: catkins on very short bracted stalks; pedicel ⅓ or ¼ as long as ovary; style short, but distinct. A.I.1:506. B. C. to Ore., Mont. and Colo. Intr. 1918. Zone V.

     37. **S. pedicellàris** Pursh. BOG W. Upright shrub to 1 m.; brts. glabrous, light brown: lvs. linear-oblong to elliptic-obovate, 1.5–7 cm. long, obtuse or acute, cuneate, entire and revolute, reticulate, glabrous, pale or glaucous beneath; petiole 2–4 mm. long: catkins on leafy stalks, staminate 1–2, pistillate to 3 cm. long; scales yellowish or brownish, obtuse, slightly villous; ovary conic-oblong, often reddish; pedicel slender, exceeding the scale; style short. T.N.t.120(c). B.B.1:602. (*S. myrtilloides* var. *p.* Anders., S. *myrtilloides* Tuckerm., not L.) Que. to B. C., s. to Pa., Iowa, Idaho and Wash. Intr. 1911. Zone III.

     Closely related species: **S. myrtilloìdes** L. Shrub to 0.5 m., with creeping subterranean stem: lvs. orbicular-elliptic to narrow-elliptic, acute, cuneate to subcordate: staminate catkins subsessile, 1–1.5 cm. long. R.I.11:t.593,f.1244(c). H.W.2,1:124,f.209. N. Eu. to N. E. Asia. Intr. 1772. Zone II?

     38. **S. pyrifòlia** Anders. BALSAM W. Much-branched shrub, rarely tree, to 7 m.; brts. glabrous, lustrous, red-brown or olive: lvs. elliptic-ovate to

ovate-lanceolate, 4–9 cm. long, acute or occasionally obtuse, subcordate or rounded at base, slightly crenulate-serrulate, dark green above, glaucous and reticulate beneath, thin, glabrous; petiole, slender, 6–15 mm. long: catkins with the lvs., bracted at base, staminate cylindric, about 2, pistillate 5–7 cm. long in fr., rather loose; ovary glabrous, rostrate; pedicel 6–8 times as long as gland; style very short; stigmas short, thick, 2-lobed. S.S.14:t.728. B.B. 1:596. (*S. balsamifera* Barratt.) Lab. to Man., s. to ,Me. and Minn. Intr. 1880. Zone II. Handsome willow, conspicuous in winter with its lustrous brs. and bright red buds.

39. **S. hypoleùca** Seemen. Shrub to 4 m.; brts. glabrous, yellow-brown: lvs. elliptic or elliptic-obovate to oblong, 2.5–5 cm. long, acute or acuminulate, cuneate to nearly rounded at base, entire or indistinctly denticulate, dark green above, glaucous beneath, glabrous; petiole 3–5 mm. long; catkins on short leafy stalks, slender, cylindric, 3–6 cm. long; axis slightly villous; scales pale, oval, obtuse, glabrous; stamens villous at base; ovary sessile, ovoid, glabrous; stigmas subsessile, elliptic, bifid. H.S.f.52. W. China. Intr. 1911. Zone V. Graceful willow with neat foliage.

Related species: **S. cathayàna** Diels. Shrub to 4 m.; young brts. pubescent: lvs. oblong or narrow-elliptic, obtuse or acutish, entire or minutely glandular-denticulate, glaucescent and slightly pubescent on midrib beneath or silky all over: scales ciliate; style short, but distinct. W. China. Intr. 1909. Zone V?— **S. macroblásta** Schneid. Shrub to 6 m.; brts. yellowish or yellowish brown, pubescent; winter-buds oblong, twice as long as petioles: lvs. narrow-lanceolate, 1.5–3 cm. long, acute, rounded or subcordate at base, glaucous beneath, glabrous; fruiting catkins 2.5–3 cm long; ovary glabrous, with very short style and short emarginate stigmas. H.S.f.49. W. China. Intr. 1911. Zone V?

40. **S. heterochròma** Schneid. Shrub or tree to 15 m.; brts. glabrous or slightly pubescent at first, later yellow- to purple-brown: lvs: elliptic-ovate or elliptic to oblong-lanceolate, 5–10 cm. long, acuminate, cuneate, entire, dark green above, glaucous beneath and silky at first, soon glabrous or sometimes remaining silky; petiole 5–15 mm. long; stipules minute or wanting: catkins on short bracted stalks, with or shortly before the lvs., staminate 3–5.5, pistillate in fr. 6–10 cm. long; scales oblong, very villous, light yellow-brown; caps. gray-pubescent, 5 mm. long; pedicel about 4 times as long as gland; style about ⅓ as long as caps., with narrow-oblong bifid stigmas. H.S. f.59. (*S. Henryi* Burk.) C. China. Intr. 1908. Zone V?

41. **S. cándida** Fluegge. HOARY W. Shrub to 2 m.; brts. white-woolly, older red: lvs. oblong-lanceolate to linear-lanceolate, 4–12 cm. long, acute at ends, slightly revolute and denticulate or entire, dull and pubescent or finally glabrate above, white-tomentose beneath; petiole 3–5 mm. long; stipules lanceolate, deciduous: catkins sessile, with the lvs., cylindric, densely villous, staminate about 2.5, pistillate 3–5 cm. long in fr.; anthers red; ovary conic-ovoid, pubescent; pedicels as long or longer than gland; stigmas short, spreading. Torrey, Fl. N. Y. t.117(c, as *S. incana*). F.Sa.t.91(c). Gr.M.f.665. Nfd. and Lab. to Athabasca, s. to N. J., Iowa and Mont. Cult. 1809. Zone I. Very distinct willow on account of its white-woolly tomentum.

42. **S. myrsinifòlia** Salisb. Shrub to 4 m., rarely tree-like, with spreading brs.; young brts. densely pubescent, tardily glabrescent, rarely glabrous: lvs. orbicular-ovate or elliptic to oblong-lanceolate, 2–10 cm. long, acute or acuminate, rounded or sometimes subcordate to cuneate at base, irregularly- or undulate-serrate, dark green and glabrous or nearly so above, glabrous or pubescent, rarely tomentose beneath and gray-green or bluish gray, turning black in drying; petiole 1–2 cm. long; stipules reniform or oblique-ovate: catkins shortly before or with the lvs., on short leafy stalks, staminate to 2.5

cm. long, oval to oblong, pistillate to 6 cm. long; scales dark-colored at apex, villous; filaments villous at base; pedicel ½–⅔ as long as the glabrous, rarely pubescent ovary, nearly twice as long as gland; style ¼–⅔ as long as ovary; stigmas oblong. R.I.11:t.573(c). S.E.8:t.1347,1351–4(c). H.W.2,1:119. (*S. nigricans* Sm., *S. Andersoniana* Sm., *S. phylicifolia* Willd., not L., ? *S. spadicea* Vill.) Eu. to W. Asia and W. Siberia. Long cult. Zone IV. An extremely variable species of which numerous varieties have been described, but neither of horticultural nor economic importance.

S. m. × *hastata* = S. **Mielichhòferi** Saut. Small shrub; young brts. silky-pubescent, rarely glabrous: lvs. elliptic to lanceolate, inequally and closely serrate, near base and petiole pubescent, later glabrous, dark lustrous green above, lighter beneath; petiole 5–10 mm. long: pedicel ½ as long as the glabrous ovary. C.S.2:t.42g-k. S.H.1:f.19q,20c-d. Eu. Cult. 1888.—*S. m.* × *retusa;* see under No. 19.—*S. m.* × *caprea;* see under No. 28.—*S. m.* × *phylicifolia;* see under No. 43.

43. S. phylicifòlia L. Upright shrub to 1, rarely 3 m.; brts. glabrous or pubescent when very young, later dark brown and lustrous: lvs. elliptic or obovate to lanceolate, 2–8 cm. long, acute or short-acuminate, rounded or cuneate at base, serrate or crenate-serrate, lustrous above, glaucous or gray-green beneath, glabrous or slightly pubescent at first, subcoriaceous, not blackening in drying; petiole 8–10 mm. long; stipules semi-cordate, rarely present: catkins on short bracted stalks, before or with the lvs., staminate to 2.5, pistillate to 6 cm. long in fr.; scales oblong to obovate, acutish, dark except at base; filaments glabrous; pedicel 3–4 times as long as gland; caps. pubescent, rarely glabrous, 7–10 mm. long. R.I.11:t.563,f.2002(c). S.E.8:t.1335–6, 1340,1345(c). F.Sa.t.38,44,46,47(c). (*S. bicolor* Ehrh., *S. Weigeliana* Willd.) Eu. to N. E. Asia. Cult. 1809. Zone III?

S. p. × *myrsinifolia* = S. **tetrápla** Walker. Lvs. more or less pubescent when young; blackening in drying; foliaceous stipules usually present: filaments villous at base; ovaries often only partially pubescent. S.E.8:t.1337,1341–4,1348-50(c). Eu. Cult. 1829.—*S. p.* × *aurita;* see under No. 29.—*S. p.* × *caprea;* see under No. 28.—*S. p.* × *aurita* × *purpurea;* see under No. 59.

Closely related species: **S. formòsa** Willd. Dense procumbent or upright shrub, to 0.5, rarely to 1 m.; brts. and lvs. glabrous or slightly pubescent at first, the latter 1–5 cm. long, serrate or entire; scales pale, darker at apex; pedicel much shorter than the narrow gland; anthers red or reddish at first. R.I.11:t. 561(c). S.E.8:t.1371–4(c). H.W.2,1:120. (*S. arbuscula* L., in part, *S. prunifolia* Sm.) Eu. to Cauc. and Siberia. Cult. ? Zone V.—*S. f.* × *herbacea* = *S. simulatrix;* see under No. 18.—**S. planifòlia** Pursh. Shrub to 3 m.; brts. purplish, sometimes bloomy: lvs. elliptic to lanceolate or oblong-obovate, 2–5 cm. long, entire or indistinctly denticulate, glaucous beneath, glabrous; catkins smaller; pedicels as long or slightly exceeding the gland; caps. 5–6 mm. long. B.B.1:600. Gr.M.668. (*S. chlorophylla* Anders., *S. phylicifolia* Tuckerm., not L.) Lab. to Alb., s. to N. H., Vt., Colo. and Calif. Cult. 1816. Zone I.

44. S. subcoerúlea Piper. Shrub to 2 m.; brts. glabrous or slightly pubescent at first, later purple and sometimes bloomy: lvs. lanceolate to oblanceolate, 3–6 cm. long, acute or short-acuminate, cuneate or rounded at base, entire or indistinctly crenulate, glabrous above, with lustrous, white silky tomentum beneath, with conspicuous yellow glabrescent midrib, of firm texture; petiole 2–7 mm. long; catkins subsessile, staminate 2–3.5, pistillate 2.5–5 cm. long in fr.; pedicels about half as long as gland; caps. 5 mm. long. A.I.1:502. (*S. pellita* Anders., in part.) Wash. to Wyo., Colo., N. Mex., Utah and Calif. Cult. 1890. Zone V. Handsome willow, conspicuous in winter on account of its often bloomy brs.

Closely related species: **S. pellìta** Anders. Brts. bloomy: lvs. lanceolate or oblanceolate to linear-lanceolate, 4–12 cm. long, white silky-villous beneath, later glabrescent; catkins longer; pedicel longer than gland. B.B.1:598. Gr.M.f.667.

Nfd. to Lake Winnipeg, s. to Me., Vt. and Mich. Intr. 1918. Handsome willow.
—**S. Drummondiàna** Barratt. Brts. tomentulose, not bloomy; lvs. obovate or obovate-oblong to elliptic-oblanceolate, 3–8 cm. long, obtuse or acute, velutinous-tomentose beneath; pedicel longer than gland. A.I.1:503. B. C., Alb. Intr. 1921.

45. **S. adenophýlla** Hook. FURRY W. Straggling shrub to 2.5 m.; brts. silky-villous: lvs. ovate to ovate-lanceolate, 3–6 cm. long, short-acuminate, cordate or rounded at base, glandular-serrulate, densely silky-villous on both sides, green beneath; petiole 3–6 mm. long, dilated at base, shorter than the cordate-ovate, persistent stipules: catkins on short leafy stalks, cylindric, staminate about 2, pistillate 4–10 cm. long in fr.; scales light brown, obtuse, scarcely darkened at apex; ovary glabrous, conic-ovoid; pedicel about as long as gland, shorter than scale; style longer than stigma. B.B.1:597. (*S. syrticola* Fern.) Lab. to Wisc., s. to Pa. and Ill. Cult. 1900. Zone II. Handsome and distinct willow.

46. **S. glaucophylloìdes** Fern. Shrub or shrubby tree to 5 m.; brts. glabrous: lvs. ovate or obovate to oblong-lanceolate, 5–12 cm. long, short-acuminate, rounded or cuneate at base, glandular-serrulate, dark green above, glaucous beneath, glabrous, subcoriaceous at maturity; petiole 3–10 mm. long; stipules large, persistent; catkins cylindric, on leafy stalks, very silky, staminate 3–5, pistillate, 4–7 cm. long in fr.; scales obtuse; pedicel about as long as scale; caps. rostrate, 9–11 mm. long, glabrous. B.B.1:596. Gr.M.f.652. (*S. glaucophylla* Robins. & Fern., not Schleich. et al.) N. B. to Que. and Me.—**S. g. glaucophýlla** (Bebb) Schneid., var. Lvs. firmer, thicker; pedicels longer, exceeding the scale; style longer. (*S. glaucophylla* Bebb, not Schleich. et al.) Ont. to Ohio, Ill. and Wisc. Intr. 1894. Zone III.

Closely related species: **S. montícola** Bebb. Shrub to 7 m.: lvs. elliptic to ovate or obovate, 3–5 cm. long; catkins subsessile, in fr. to 4.5 cm. long; caps. 5–7 mm. long. (*S. padophylla* Rydb.) Mont. to Colo., N. Mex. and Utah. Intr. 1898. Zone V.—**S. Barclàyi** Anders. Shrub; brts. villous: lvs. elliptic-oblong to oblong, usually cuneate, glandular-denticulate, villous above at first, glaucous and glabrous beneath: catkins on leafy stalks; scales mostly acute; caps. 5–8 mm. long, sometimes slightly silky. A.I.1:498. B. C. to Ore. and Mont. Intr. 1919. Zone V.

47. **S. hastàta** L. HALBERD-LEAVED W. Much-branched shrub to 1.5 m.; young brts. pubescent, soon glabrous, red-brown the 2d year: lvs. very variable, elliptic to ovate or obovate, 2–8 cm. long, rounded to cuneate, or on vigorous shoots cordate at base, irregularly serrulate, dull green above, glaucous and glabrous beneath or slightly pubescent when young, of firm texture; petiole 3–8 mm. long: stipules usually large, semicordate: catkins on leafy stalks, with the lvs., staminate to 3.5, pistillate to 5 cm. long; scales with long villous hairs; filaments glabrous; pedicel 2–4 times as long as gland; style as long or slightly longer than stigma. R.I.11:t.570(c). H.W.2,1:121. Mitt. Thuering. Bot. Ver. 29:10(h). Mts. of C. and S. Eu. to N. E. Asia and Kashmir. Intr. 1780. Zone V.

S. h. × *myrsinifolia;* see under No. 42.

Related species: **S. glàbra** Scop. Brts. and lvs. quite glabrous, the latter broad-elliptic or ovate to oblong, crenulate; scales long-c̄liate, otherwise glabrous; filaments villous near base. R.I.11:t.568(c). H.W.2,1:121. Alps and mts. of S. E. Eu. Cult. 1870. Zone V.—**S. japónica** Thunb. Lvs. elliptic-oblong, 5–12 cm. long, acuminate, cuneate, sharply serrate with glandular teeth, those of peduncle entire, silky-pubescent when young, soon glabrous: catkins with the lvs., thin and slender, to 10 cm. long; filaments villous at base; pedicel longer than gland. Seemen, Sal. Jap.t.7. S.H.1:f.20z,23b. Jap. Cult. 1874. Zone V?— **S. pyrolaefòlia** Ledeb. Shrub or small tree to 5 cm.; brts. pubescent when young: lvs. oblong-elliptic, 3–7 cm. long, or on vigorous shoots orbicular-elliptic, acute, serrate, bluish gray beneath, soon glabrous; petiole 1.5–2 cm. long;

stipules large, suborbicular: catkins before the lvs., short-stalked, to 5 cm. long; pedicel 2–3 times as long as gland. S.H.1:f.20z′,23n. Ledebour, Ic. Pl. Ross. t.476. N. E. Asia. Intr. about 1900. Zone III?

48. **S. cordàta** Muhlenb. Shrub to 4 m.; brts. glabrous or puberulous at first: lvs. oblong-lanceolate to lanceolate, 5–14 cm. long, acuminate, rounded to subcordate or often cuneate on flowering brts., sharply serrulate, dull green above, green or paler beneath, glabrous or slightly pubescent beneath; petiole 5–15 mm. long; stipules reniform or ovate, usually large: catkins on short bracted stalks before the lvs., rather slender, staminate 2–5, pistillate 2.5–6 cm. long in fr.; caps. 4–7 mm. long, its pedicel ¼–⅓ as long; style 0.5–0.8 mm. long. B.B.1:596. Gr.M.f.650. (*S. rigida* Muhlenb.) N. B. to B. C., s. to Va., Mo., Colo. and Calif. Intr. 1812. Zone III. Staminate catkins conspicuous.—**S. c. purpuráscens** (Dieck) Schneid., f. Lvs. purple when young. (*S. Nicholsonii* f. *p.* Dieck.) Orig. before 1889.

S. c. × sericea = **S. myricoìdes** Muhlenb. Brts. pubescent: lvs. lanceolate, cuneate, glaucous or glaucescent beneath and glabrate or more or less silky beneath; stipules small: caps. often silky when young. (*S. cordata* var. *m.* Carey.) Mass. to Wisc. and Kans. Cult. 1880.

A closely related species is **S. missouriénsis** Bebb. Large shrub or tree to 15 m.; brts. pubescent: lvs. lanceolate to ovate-oblong, rarely obovate, 8–15 cm. long, glaucous beneath: fruiting catkins 6–10 cm. long; caps. 8–10 mm. long. S.S.9:t.480. B.T.193. H.H.90,91(b). Ky. to Mo., Iowa and Neb. Intr. 1898. Zone V.—Another related species is **S. myrtillifòlia** Anders. Shrub to 0.5 m.: lvs. elliptic to oblanceolate, 1–5 cm. long, acutish to obtuse, crenate-serrate, green on both sides, glabrous; petiole 2–4 mm. long: catkins on short leafy stalks, 1–3 cm. long; style very short. (*S. pseudomyrsinites* Anders., in part.) Proc. Wash. Acad. Sci. 3:325. Alaska to Alb. Intr. 1922. Zone V.

49. **S. irroràta** Anders. Upright shrub to 3 m.; brts. glabrous, purple, rarely yellowish, bloomy: lvs. oblong to linear-lanceolate, 6–10 cm. long, acuminate, cuneate, bright green and lustrous above, glaucous beneath, remotely serrate or entire, glabrous, firm; petiole 3–10 mm. long, usually yellow: catkins subsessile, usually naked at base, short and dense, 1.5–2.5 cm. long; scales dark, densely white-villous; pedicel about 0.5 mm. long; style rather short; stigmas short and thick. Colo. to N. Mex., Ariz. Intr. 1898. Zone IV. Conspicuous in winter with its bloomy brs.

50. **S. myrsinìtes** L. Shrub to 0.4 m., with short densely leafy brs., pubescent when young, later glabrous, dark brown and lustrous: lvs. short-petioled, elliptic or obovate to lanceolate, 1–5 cm. long, acute at ends, rarely obtuse, serrate with usually glandular teeth, pubescent at first, later glabrous and lustrous green or both sides; stipules little developed: catkins on leafy stalks, dense, staminate to 4, pistillate to 5 cm. long; scales purple, darker at apex; anthers purple; ovary short-stalked, pubescent, later glabrescent; style ⅕–½ as long as ovary, purple, with narrow stigmas. R.I.11:t.559(c). S.E.8:t.1375–6(c). H.W.2,1:124. (*S. m.* var. *serrata* Neilr.) Mts. of Eu., N. Asia to Kamch. Cult. 1789. Zone IV.—**S. m. Jacquiniàna** (Willd.) Koch, var. Lvs. entire or sparingly serrulate. R.I.11:t.559(c). (*S. J.* Willd.)

51. **S. lanàta** L. Shrub to 1.5 m.; young brts. and winter-buds woolly: lvs. elliptic-orbicular to oblong-obovate, 2.5–7 cm. long, acute, broad-cuneate to subcordate at base, entire, sometimes undulate, silky-villous above when young, later glabrescent and dull green, glaucous and reticulate beneath and clothed with long silky hairs; petiole 5–15 mm. long; stipules often large, entire: catkins with the lvs., densely yellowish silky, staminate ovoid-oblong, subsessile, about 5 cm., pistillate 4–6, in fr. to 8 cm. long, short-stalked; scales dark brown; filaments glabrous; ovary glabrous, subsessile or the lower short-stalked; gland linear; style about ⅓ as long as the glabrous ovary, with nar-

row bifid stigmas. S.E.8:t.1367 (c, excl. stamens). S.H.1:f.21a-b,25l. C.S.2:t. 36a-e. N. Eu. and N. Asia. Cult. 1789. Zone III? Handsome willow on account of its long silky pubescence.

52. **S. Hookeriàna** Barratt. Shrub, sometimes with prostrate brs., or tree to 10 m.; young brts. densely tomentose: lvs. oblong to oblong-obovate, 5–16 cm. long, usually acute, entire or crenate-serrate, tomentose above when young, glaucous and pubescent or tomentose beneath; petiole 5–15 mm. long, pubescent; stipules wanting or small: catkins subsessile, with few bracts at base, 3–5, the pistillate in fr. to 8 or 12 cm. long; ovary glabrous, sometimes tomentose (var. **tomentòsa** Schneid.); pedicel 2–3 times as long as gland; stigmas short, spreading, emarginate. S.S.9:t.485. S.H.1:26g,27n-o. A.I.1:500. B.C. to Ore. Cult. 1891. Zone V.

Related species: **S. Pìperi** Bebb. Shrub to 6 m.; brts. slightly villous, soon glabrous: lvs. similar to those of the preceding species: filaments hairy at base; caps. slightly hairy at apex. A.I.1:499. Wash. to Ore. Intr. 1898. Zone V.

53. **S. daphnoìdes** Vill. Large shrub or tree to 10 m.; brts. slender, yellowish or brown, bloomy, sometimes slightly pubescent when young: lvs. oblong-lanceolate to narrow-lanceolate, 5–10 cm. long, acuminate, finely glandular-serrulate or nearly entire, pubescent when young, soon glabrous, dark lustrous green above, glaucous beneath, of firm texture; petiole 2–4 mm. long; stipules semicordate, large: catkins cylindric, about 3 cm. long, densely silky; scales oblong-obovate, dark brown; filaments glabrous; ovary conic-ovoid, glabrous, short-stalked; gland linear; style nearly half as long as ovary; stigmas linear-oblong, entire. R.I.11:t.602(c). F.Sa.t.26(c). H.W.2,1:110. Eu. to C. Asia and Himal. Cult. 1829. Zone IV. Conspicuous in winter with its bloomy brs.—**S. d. pomerànica** (Willd.) Koch, var. Usually shrubby: lvs. narrower: catkins slender. Eu.

S. d. × *caprea* = **S. Erdíngeri** Kern. Young brts. pubescent: lvs. obovate to oblong, acuminate, silky when young, later glabrous and lustrous above, gray-green and glabrate beneath; pedicel about ½ as long as the silky ovary; style about ¼ as long as ovary; stigma upright. C.S.2:t.46a-c. (*S. cremensis* A. & J. Kern., *S. Figerti* A. & G. Camus.) Eu. Cult. 1872.—*S. d.* × *repens* = **S. marítima** Hartig. Brts. and lvs. beneath silky at first; brts. purple: lvs. oblong or oblong-lanceolate, 2.5–5 cm. long, acute, rounded at base; petiole 2–5 mm. long: catkins 1.5–2 cm. long; ovary sparingly silky. Cult. 1873.—*S. d.* × *purpurea* = **S. calliántha** Kern. Brts. not bloomy: lvs. smaller than in No. 53, lanceolate, glaucous beneath and pubescent when young: catkins 2–3.5 cm. long; stamens connate at base, sparingly pubescent; ovaries nearly sessile; stigmas oval. Cult. 1872.—*S. d.* = *Elaeagnos;* see under No. 57.

Closely related species: **S. acutifòlia** Willd. Less tall; brs. slenderer, violet- or red-brown, bloomy: lvs. lanceolate to linear-lanceolate, 6–12 cm. long, long-acuminate, cuneate; stipules lanceolate: catkins slender, remote; style shorter; stigmas emarginate. R.I.11:t.603(c). S.E.8:t.1366(c). H.W.2:t.29, f.6–9(c). (*S. daphnoides* var. *a.* Doell.) Russia to E. Asia. Cult. 1809. Zone IV. Brs. used for coarse basket-work.

54. **S. Rehderiàna** Schneid. Shrub or tree to 9 m.; young brts. sparingly villous or glabrous, later red-brown: lvs. lanceolate, 5–12 cm. long, short-acuminate, rounded to broad-cuneate at base, irregularly glandular-crenulate, rarely nearly entire, grayish white and silky beneath or sometimes glabrescent and glaucous; petiole 2–8 mm. long, usually puberulous: catkins sessile or subsessile, with 2–3 bracts at base, 2–3 cm. long; scales oblong, obtuse, sparingly silky-villous; filaments glabrous or pilose at base; anthers purple at first; ovary glabrous or sparingly silky-villous, subsessile; style about ½ as long as ovary, with short emarginate stigmas. W. China. Intr. 1908. Zone V.

55. **S. lappònum** L. Dense much-branched shrub to 1.5 m.; brts. pubescent, later glabrous, dark brown and lustrous; winter-buds pubescent: lvs.

elliptic-oblong to obovate-oblong or lanceolate, 2.5–6 cm. long, acute or acuminate, rounded to cuneate at base, entire, soft-pubescent and dull green above, gray- or white-tomentose beneath; petiole to 1 cm. long; stipules wanting or minute: catkins subsessile with few small bracts, staminate about 2.5 cm. long, pistillate 2.5–5 cm. long; scales oblong, obtuse or acutish, silky-villous; filaments glabrous; anthers yellow or reddish; ovary densely pubescent, subsessile or the lower ones short-stalked; gland linear; style slender, longer than the narrow, usually divided stigmas. S.E.8:t.1368–9(c). F.Sa.t. 70,72,73(c). M.G.25:140(h). Mts. of Eu. to the Altai. Cult. 1789. Zone III?

S. l. × *caprea* = **S. Laestadiàna** Hartm. Young brts. hoary-pubescent: lvs. obovate-oblong to elliptic-lanceolate, acute at ends, silky-pubescent beneath: pedicel slightly longer than gland; style short, about as long as stigmas. C.S.2:t. 39m-p. Eu. Cult. 1873.

Closely related species: **S. helvética** Vill. Low shrub, to 0.6 m.: lvs. oblong to elliptic-lanceolate, entire, slightly pubescent or glabrous above, white-tomentose beneath: catkins on leafy stalks with the lvs. R.I.11:t.572,f.1216(c). H.W. 2,1:122. (*S. lapponum* var. *h.* Anders.) Alps. Cult. 1872. Zone V.

56. **S. viminàlis** L. COMMON OSIER. Upright shrub or tree to 5 or occasionally 10 m.; young brts. densely pubescent, later glabrescent; winter-buds pubescent: lvs. linear-lanceolate to lanceolate, 10–25 cm. long, broadest below the middle, acuminate, cuneate, nearly entire or obscurely crenate, undulate, dull green and glabrate above, grayish white and silky-tomentose beneath; petiole 4–12 mm. long; stipules small, lanceolate, deciduous: catkins subsessile, dense, staminate 2–4, pistillate about 2.5 and in fr. 3–6 cm. long; stamens long, glabrous; ovary conic-ovoid, pubescent; pedicel much shorter than the linear gland; style nearly as long as ovary, with narrow stigmas. R.I.11:t. 597(c). S.E.8:t.t.1322(c). H.W.2,1:112,t.31(c). Eu. to N. E. Asia and Himal.; naturalized in the E. States. Long cult. Zone III? One of the best basket willows.—**S. v. Gmelìni** (Pall.) Anders., var. Young brts. pubescent or glabrescent: lvs. equally narrowed at both ends, slightly pubescent above: catkins short-stalked; ovary always sessile; style shorter than the slender stigmas. (*S. splendens* Ledeb.) Russia, W. Siberia. Cult. 1905.

S. v. × *caprea* = **S. Smithiàna** Willd. Tall shrub to 6 m.; brts. later glabrescent: lvs. oblong-lanceolaᴛe or ovate-lanceolate, 6–12 cm. long, soon glabrate above, grayish and soft-pubescent beneath; stipules large: catkins about 2.5 cm. long; pedicel finally as long or longer than gland; style as long as stigmas. F.Sa.t.134(c). C.S.1:t.29a-f. (*S. mollissima* Sm., not Ehrh.) Cult. 1829.— *S. v.* × *aurita* = **S. fruticòsa** Doell. Shrub to 3 m.; brts. soon glabrous: lvs. lanceolate or oblong-lanceolate, 3–10 cm. long, crenate-serrate, slightly wrinkled above, reticulate and pubescent or glabrescent beneath; pedicels about as long as gland; style as long as stigmas. F.Sa.t.128(c). Eu. Cult. 1829.—*S. v.* × *cinerea* = **S. holosericea** Willd. Shrub to 4 m.: brts. persistently pubescent; wood under bark with short raised striations: lvs. oblong-ovate to lanceolate or oblanceolate, 5–12 cm. long, crenulate, dull green and pubescent above, light gray and silky-pubescent beneath; stipules ovate-lanceolate, subentire: catkins about 3 cm. long; pedicel finally as long as gland; style about as long as stigmas. S.E.8:t.1324(c). F.Sa.t.128(c). C.S.1:t.29m-r. Eu. Cult. 1829.—*S. v.* × *repens* = **S. Friesiàna** Anders. Lvs. lanceolate to narrow lanceolate, 2–7 cm. long, entire, sometimes revolute, densely silky when young, later glabrate above; catkins sessile or subsessile: style about as long as ovary; stigmas linear, bifid. F.Sa.t.87(c). Andersson, Mon. Sal.t.6,f.66. (*S. rosmarinifolia* L., in part?) Eu. Cult. 1829.—*S. v.* × *alba;* see under No. 5.—*S. v.* × *purpurea;* see under No. 58.

Closely related species or hybrids with species of the Caprea group, but differing from the 3 hybrids described above in the subsessile or sessile ovaries, are the following two: **S. stipulàris** Sm. Large shrub, similar to No. 56, but lvs. broader with foliaceous stipules longer than petioles; brts. densely woolly; lvs. narrow-lanceolate, 12–20 cm. long: catkins about 3 cm. long; stigmas linear, undivided, as long or longer than style. F.Sa.t.132(c). R.I.11:t.598(c). S.E.8:

1323(c). Eu. Cult. 1829.—**S. dasýclados** Wimm. Tall shrub or tree to 6 m.; brts. densely woolly: lvs. oblong-lanceolate or lanceolate to obovate-lanceolate, to 20 cm. long, acuminate, dull green above and slightly pubescent, soft-pubescent and glaucescent beneath; stipules large, ovate-lanceolate: catkins large, staminate to 4.5, pistillate to 5.5 cm. long; stigmas thick, undivided, about as long as style. F.Sa.t.131(c). S.E.8:t.1326(c). (*S. acuminata* Sm., not Mill., nor Pall.) Eu. Cult. 1829.—Another related species is **S. sachalinénsis** Fr. Schmidt. Tree to 10 m.; young brts. thinly pubescent, becoming glabrous: lvs. lanceolate, to 14 cm. long and 2.2 cm. broad, dark green above, glaucous and slightly pubescent or glabrescent beneath; stipules ovate-cordate, serrate: pedicel of ovary about as long as gland or slightly shorter. S.I.2:t.9(c). M.K.t.18(c). (*S. opaca* Seemen.) Saghal., Japan. Intr. 1905. Zone IV.

57. **S. Elaeágnos** Scop. Shrub or sometimes tree to 15 m., with slender brs. gray-pubescent when young: lvs. linear to narrow-lanceolate, 5–15 cm. long, acute at ends, revolute and finely serrate toward the apex, densely tomentose when young, later glabrous and dark green above, white-tomentose beneath; petiole 4–8 mm. long; stipules usually wanting: catkins on short bracted stalks, about 3 cm. long; scales oval, truncate or slightly emarginate, pale; filaments connate at base or ½; ovary glabrous, short-stalked; style about ⅓ as long as ovary; stigmas linear-oblong, cleft. R.I.11:t.596(c). H.W. 2,1:109. Gs.4:48. (*S. incana* Schrank.) Mts. of C. and S. Eu. and Asia Minor. Cult. Zone IV. Handsome with its grayish feathery foliage turning yellow in fall.

   S. E. × *caprea* = **S. Seringeàna** Gaud. Brts. tomentose: lvs. lanceolate or oblong-oblanceolate, revolute and irregularly serrulate, finally glabrous above, gray-tomentose beneath: catkins before the lvs.; stamens connate and villous at base; pedicel about ½ as long as ovary; style short. R.I.11:t.580(c). C.S. 1:t.28h-l. (*S. salviaefolia* Link, *S. Flueggeana* Willd., in part, *S. oleafolia* Vill., in part.) Eu. Cult. 1872.—*S. E.* × *aurita* = **S. pátula** Ser. Brts. gray-pubescent: lvs. oblong to lanceolate, acute at ends, at maturity slightly pubescent above, gray-tomentulose beneath; catkins cylindric, on bracted stalks; filaments connate and villous at base; pedicel about ½ as long as ovary; stigmas oblong, somewhat shorter than style. F.Sa.t.96(c). C.S.1:t.28n-p. (*S. pallida* Forb., *S. oleafolia* Vill., in part.) Eu. Cult. 1829.—*S. E.* × *repens* = **S. subalpìna** Forb. Lvs. lanceolate, entire or remotely serrulate, silky-tomentose beneath: catkins oblong to cylindric; stamens connate at base; style about ¼ as long as ovary. C.S.1:t.28q-t. Andersson, Monog. Sal. t.6,f.68. Alps. Cult. 1829.—**S. E.** × *daphnoides* = **S. Reùteri** Moritzi. Often tree-like; young brts. gray-pubescent, often bloomy when older: lvs. lanceolate or narrow-lanceolate, silky-tomentose beneath: stipules small, lanceolate; catkins subsessile; scales dark brown above the middle: filaments slightly connate at base. C.S.1:t.27r-x. Eu. Cult. 1870.

58. **S. Miyabeàna** Seemen. Shrub or small tree to 5 m.; brts. light brown, glabrous: lvs. lanceolate to narrow-lanceolate, 5–15 cm. long, acute at ends, crenate-serrate, glaucous beneath, glabrous; petiole 3–10 mm. long; stipules lanceolate, about as long as petiole: catkins before or with the lvs., cylindric, staminate 3–5.5 cm. long, sessile, pistillate 4–8 cm. long in fr. and rather lax, on short leafy-bracted stalks; scales oval, dark brown, villous; filaments wholly united; anthers yellow; ovary ovoid, sessile, tomentose; stigmas short, undivided, sessile. M.K.t.19(c). Seemen, Sal. Jap. t.12-e. Japan. Intr. 1897. Zone V. Handsome small tree.

   Related species: **S. Pierótii** Miq. Shrub: brts. glabrous, brown: lvs. lanceolate, 7–15 cm. long, broadest below the middle, serrulate, glaucous beneath, pubescent at first, soon glabrous: catkins smaller; style about ½ as long as ovary. Seemen, Sal. Jap. t.13e-f. S.H.1:f.23a,271-m. (*S. japonica* Dipp., not Thunb.) Amurl., Japan. Cult. 1893. Zone V?

59. **S. purpúrea** L. PURPLE OSIER. Shrub to 3 m., with slender tough brs., purplish at first, later gray or olive-gray, glabrous: lvs. oblanceolate, rarely oblong-obovate, often opposite, 5–10 cm. long, acute or acuminate, cuneate, serrulate toward the apex, dull green above, pale or glaucous beneath, glabrous

or slightly pubescent at first, turning black in drying; petiole 4–8 mm. long; stipules small or wanting: catkins subsessile, usually curved, before the lvs., slender, staminate 1.5–2.5, pistillate to 2 cm. long; scales obovate, obtuse, villous, dark above the middle; filaments wholly connate; anthers reddish; ovary ovoid, sessile or subsessile, tomentose; stigmas thick, usually entire, sessile or subsessile. R.I.11:t.582(c). S.E.S:t.1316,1319(c). H.W.2:t.30(c). Eu. and N. Afr. to C. Asia and Jap. Long cult. Zone IV. Graceful willow, often planted for ornament, also for finer basket-work.—**S. p. péndula** Dipp., f. Brts. very slender, pendulous. (*S. p. scharfenbergensis* Bolle, *S. nigra pendula* and *S. americana pendula* Hort.)—**S. p. grácilis** Gren. & Godr., var. A slender-branched, narrow-lvd. form. (*S. p. uralensis* Hort.)—**S. p. Lambertiàna** (Sm.) Koch, var. Brs. purplish, stouter: lvs. obovate, oblong. R.I.11: t.585(c). S.E.S:t.1318(c). (*S. L.* Sm.)—**S. p. serícea** (Ser.) Koch, var. Young brts. and lvs. beneath silky-tomentose at first, becoming glabrous.—**S. p. amplexicaùlis** (Bory & Chaub.) Boiss., var. Lvs. always opposite, subsessile, oblong to oblong-lanceolate, acutish, rounded to subcordate at base. S. E. Eu. and W. Asia.—**S. p. multinérvis** Matsum., var. Similar to the preceding var., but lvs. broader, narrow-elliptic to oblong, up to 2.5 cm. broad, usually obtuse. S.I.2:t.8,f.7(c). Seemen, Sal. Jap.t.11f-k. (*S. Savatieri* Camus.) Japan. Intr. ?

S. p. × *caprea* = **S. Wimmeriàna** Gren. & Godr. Young brts. sparingly gray-pubescent, later glabrous, lustrous: lvs. oblong to oblong-lanceolate or lanceolate, irregularly serrulate, thinly silky at first, becoming glabrous, dark green above, grayish or glaucescent beneath: catkins subsessile; filaments connate at base and slightly villous; pedicel about ½ as long as ovary; stigmas oblong, emarginate, subsessile. Host, Sal. t.60,61(c, as *S. discolor*). Eu. Cult. 1872.—*S. p.* × *grandifolia* = **S. austríaca** Host. Lvs. lanceolate or oblong-oblanceolate, serrulate, glabrous except when young; filaments partly connate, villous at base; anthers reddish at first; pedicel ½ as long as ovary; style very short. Host, Sal. t.64,65(c). (*S. neriifolia* Schleich., *S. Pontederana* Parl., not Willd.) Eu. Cult. 1870.—*S. p.* × *aurita* = **S. dichròa** Kern. Brts. glabrous or nearly so: lvs. oblong-obovate or oblanceolate, glaucescent and slightly pubescent beneath, acute or abruptly contracted into a short acumen; filaments connate below and pilose at base; stalk nearly ½ as long as ovary; stigmas nearly sessile. Cult. 1870.—*S. p.* × *aurita* × *phylicifolia* = **S. sesquitértia** F. B. White. Shrub to 2 m., with slender brs. pubescent when young: lvs. oblong-obovate, crenate-serrate, rugulose above, glaucous beneath, soon glabrous: catkins usually androgynous; filaments connate; ovaries short-stalked; style distinct. Eu. Cult. 1900. —*S. p.* × *cinerea* = **S. Pontederàna** Willd. Brts. becoming glabrous: lvs. obovate-lanceolate to lanceolate, at maturity glabrous or nearly so above, silky and glaucous beneath; filaments usually connate ½; anthers reddish at first; style short. R.I.11:t.587(c). F.Sa.t.43(c). (*S. sordida* Kern.) Eu. Cult. 1829. —*S. p.* × *repens* = **S. Doniàna** Sm. Young brts. thinly pubescent, soon glabrous: lvs. oblong to lanceolate, serrulate toward the apex, minutely silky when young, later glabrous above, glaucous and glabrescent beneath; catkins oblong; filaments more or less connate; anthers red; pedicel ¼ as long as ovary; stigmas subsessile, oval, emarginate. S.E.8:t.1365(c). F.Sa.85(c). (*S. parviflora* Host.) Eu. Cult. 1829.—*S. p.* × *viminalis* = **S. rúbra** Huds. Shrub to 3 m., with long brs. pubescent at first, later glabrous and yellow: lvs. lanceolate to oblanceolate, 6–14 cm. long, acuminate, glaucescent and glabrescent beneath or sometimes pubescent: catkins 2–3 cm. long; filaments more or less connate; anthers reddish at first; style distinct. R.I.11:t.586(c). S.E.8:t.1320(c). F.Sa.t.6(c). (*S. Helix* L.?) Eu. Long cult.; brs. used for basket-work.—*S. p.* × *pentandra;* see under No. 2.—*S. p.* × *daphnoides;* see under No. 53.

Related species: **S. Wilhelmsiàna** Bieb. Shrub; young brts. tomentose: lvs. linear, 1.5–4 cm. long, not more than 4 mm. broad, remotely denticulate or entire, tomentose on both sides when young: catkins on leafy stalks, thin; scales pale, villous only near apex; ovary pilose. Mem. Div. Sav. St. Petersb. 3:t.3. S.H.1:f.20x-y. (*S. angustifolia* Willd., not Wulf.) Cauc. to E. Asia. Cult. 1887. Zone V.—**S. microstáchya** Turcz. ex Trautv. Similar to the preceding: brts. glabrous: lvs. silky-pilose at first, becoming glabrous: ventral gland of male fl. ½ as long as scale; ovary glabrous. (*S. Wilhelmsiana* var. *m.* Herd.) W. Siber. to Mongol. Cult. 1933. Zone III.—**S. Gilgiàna** Seemen. Shrub to 3 m.; brts. slender, light yellow-brown, pubescent or glabrous: lvs. sometimes opposite, linear or linear-lanceolate, 3–6 cm. long, acute at ends, glaucescent beneath, gray-pubescent when young, later glabrous: catkins sessile, 1.5–3 cm. long; scales broad-oval, black-brown, thinly villous; anthers yellow; ovary short-stalked; stigmas oblong, bifid, about as long as style. Seemen, Sal. Jap. t.13a-d. Japan. Intr. 1897. Zone V.

60. **S. caèsia** Vill. Low shrub to 1 m.; brts. glabrous, brown, lustrous: lvs. crowded, broad-oval or obovate to oblong, 1–3.5 cm. long, acute or acuminulate, rarely obtuse, broad-cuneate to subcordate at base, grayish green above, pale or whitish beneath, glabrous; petiole 2–3 mm. long: catkins on short bracted stalks, with the lvs., about 1 cm. long; scales oval, yellowish, darker at apex, sparingly silky; filaments connate at base, rarely more, villous at base; anthers violet; ovary sessile, villous; stigmas subsessile, red. R.I.11:t.565(c). Alps. to C. Asia and Dahur. Cult. 1871. Zone V.

61. **S. Bóckii** Seemen. Shrub to 3 m.; young brts. densely gray-pubescent: lvs. oblong to obovate, 6–15 mm. long, obtuse or acute, entire or sparingly denticulate, revolute at margin, deep green and glabrous above, bluish white and silky beneath: catkins in autumn in the axils of lvs., sessile, staminate 1–2.5 cm. long, pistillate 3–3.5 cm. long; scales lanceolate, acute, pale: filaments wholly connate; ovary sessile, pubescent; stigmas subsessile, bifid. B.M.9079(c). Gn.87:609. W. China. Intr. 1908. Zone V. Distinct species with small deep green lvs., remarkable for its catkins appearing in late summer and autumn.

62. **S. gracilistỳla** Miq. Upright shrub, to 3 m.; young brts. gray-tomentose, glabrescent the 2d year: lvs. elliptic-oblong to oblong-obovate or oblong, 5–10 cm. long, acute at ends, serrulate, silky-pubescent when young, later glabrate above, grayish or bluish gray and pubescent beneath; petiole 4–8 mm. long, pubescent; stipules semicordate: catkins before the lvs., sessile, densely silky, staminate to 3.5, pistillate to 8 cm. long in fr.; scales lanceolate, acute, dark at apex; filaments connate, glabrous; anthers yellow; ovary subsessile, silky-pubescent; gland linear; style slender, longer than ovary. S.I. 2:t.7,f.1–9(c) B.M.9122(c). N.K.18:t.17. T.M.42:570(h). (*S. Thunbergiana* Bl.). Japan, Korea. Cult. 1900. Zone V. One of the earliest willows to bloom and conspicuous with its large catkins.

63. **S. sitchénsis** Bong. Tree to 10 m.; brts. tomentose, glabrescent the 2d year and brown or orange, sometimes bloomy: lvs. oblong-obovate to oblanceolate, 5–12 cm. long, acute or acuminate, sometimes obtuse, entire or glandular-denticulate, pubescent above at first, later dark lustrous green and glabrous, shining silky-tomentose beneath; petiole to 1 cm. long; stipules wanting or small: catkins on short bracted stalks before the lvs., cylindric, staminate 3–5, pistillate 5–7.5 cm. long; fls. partly with 1, partly with 2 stamens; filaments more or less connate; ovary short-stalked, pubescent; style short. S.S.9:t.486. Alaska to Ore. and Mont. Intr. 1918. Zone V?

7. GARRYACEAE Lindl. GARRYA FAMILY

Evergreen shrubs or rarely trees; usually more or less pubescent; brts. quadrangular at first: lvs. opposite, petioled, oval to lanceolate, entire, estipulate: fls. dioecious, in axillary or terminal catkin-like racemes, apetalous, 4-merous; staminate fls. with 4 valvate sepals; stamens 4, with introrse, elliptic to linear anthers on short filaments; pistillate fls. without sepals, but sometimes with 2 small adnate bracts which have been taken for sepals; ovary 1-celled, 2-ovuled, with 2 subulate styles; fr. a rather dry globose or ovoid berry, 1–2-seeded; seed ovoid to subglobose with copious albumen and a minute embryo.— Contains only the following genus with about 15 species in W. N. Am. from Ore. to C. Mex and 1 species in the W. Indies.

GARRYA Lindl. Characters of the family. (After Nicholas Garry, secretary of the Hudson Bay Company; about 1820.)

A. Lvs. pubescent below, at least while young: staminate infl. usually simple; pistillate infl. dense, with usually 3 fls. in the axils; bracts broadly connate at the base.
   B. Lvs. beneath with curly or woolly hairs...1. *G. elliptica*
   BB. Lvs. beneath with appressed silky hairs.
      c. Mature lvs. densely appressed-silky beneath.........................2. *G. flavescens*
      cc. Mature lvs. nearly glabrous beneath.................................3. *G. Fremontii*
AA. Lvs. glabrous: staminate infl. branched; pistillate infl. with remote solitary fls.; at least the lower bracts leaf-like, narrowed at base.................................4. *P. Wrightii*

1. **G. ellíptica** Lindl. Shrub to 2.5 m.; brts. densely pubescent while young; lvs. thick, leathery, elliptic to elliptic-oblong, acute or obtusish and mucronulate, usually rounded at base, revolute and usually undulate at the margin, 4–8 cm. long, densely woolly-tomentose beneath, glabrous above at maturity; staminate spikes to 20 cm. long; pistillate spikes dense, 5–9 cm. long; fr. globose, densely silky-tomentose. Fl.ɪ–ɪɪɪ; fr.vɪ–vɪɪɪ. B.R.1686(c). G.C.35:42.43;60:254. B.S.1:578. Gn.78:114(h). Ore. to Calif. Intr. 1826. Zone VII?

A hybrid of this species with *G. Fadyenii* Hook. from the W. Indies is **G. Thurétii** Carr. raised 1862 in France: lvs. narrower and longer, to 10 cm. long; pistillate spikes slenderer with usually one fl. in each axil. Zone VII?

2. **G. flavéscens** S. Wats. Shrub to 2.5 m.; brts. silky-pubescent at first: lvs. elliptic, acute and mucronulate, cuneate at base, quite entire, 3–7 cm. long, densely silky-pubescent below, sparingly so above while young; spikes short, the staminate not or little branched; the pistillate dense, 2.5–5 cm. long: fr. globose-ovoid, appressed silky-pubescent. Fl.ɪɪɪ; fr.vɪɪ–vɪɪɪ. (*G. Veitchii* var. *f.* Coult. & Evans.) Nev. and Utah to N. Mex. Intr. before 1904. Zone VII?

3. **G. Fremóntii** Torr. Shrub to 2 m.; brts. soon glabrous: lvs. elliptic to elliptic-obovate, acute or obtusish, mucronulate, cuneate at base, entire or slightly undulate, 4–6 cm. long, at first slightly appressed pubescent on both sides, finally quite glabrous above and slightly pubescent or glabrous beneath: staminate spikes 5–15 cm. long, simple; pistillate spikes 3–7 cm. long, dense; bracts short, triangular, acuminate; fls. usually solitary; ovaries pilose: fr. ovoid, stalked, slightly pubescent or nearly glabrous, dark purple. Fl.ɪv–v; fr.vɪɪɪ–ɪx. Wash. to Calif. Intr. 1842. Zone VII?

4. **G. Wrìghtii** Torr. Shrub to 2 m.; brts. at first sparingly appressed-pubescent, soon glabrous: lvs. elliptic or ovate to oblong, acute at the ends, entire or sometimes rough at the margin, 2.5–5 cm. long, slightly appressed-pubescent at first, soon quite glabrous: spikes slender, staminate more or less branched, 3–4 cm. long, pistillate 3–7 cm. long, with remote pairs of globose ovaries, the lower bracts leaf-like, but smaller and narrower, the upper lanceolate. Fl.vɪɪ–vɪɪɪ; fr.vɪɪɪ–xɪ. E.P.IV.56a:13. Ariz. and N. Mex. to W. Tex. Intr. 1901. Zone VI? Apparently the hardiest species.

8. MYRICACEAE Lindl. SWEET GALE FAMILY

Deciduous or evergreen shrubs or trees; buds small, scaly: lvs. alternate, entire to dentate or pinnatifid, resinous-dotted: fls. monoecious or dioecious, solitary in the axils of bracts, forming catkins; perianth wanting; stamens

2–16, with the filaments somewhat united below; anthers 2-celled; ovary 1-celled, with one erect ovule; style short, with 2 filiform stigmas: fr. a small, globose or ovoid drupe or nut usually coated with resinous grains or wax. Two genera with about 35 species widely distributed through both hemispheres chiefly in temp. and subtrop. regions.

A. Lvs. entire or toothed, deciduous or evergreen, estipulate......................1. *Myrica*
AA. Lvs. pinnatifid, deciduous, stipulate...2. *Comptonia*

1. MYRÌCA L.

Deciduous or evergreen shrubs: leaves alternate, short-petioled, entire or toothed, estipulate: fls. monoecious or dioecious; stamens 2–8, rarely to 16: fr. with or without a waxy covering or resinous-dotted, without or with 2–4 small adnate bracts not exceeding the fr. (*Myrike*, ancient Greek name of a shrub, probably the Tamarisk.) Syn. *Morella* Lour., *Cerothamnus* Tidestr.—About 50 species of the same distribution as the family.

A. Fr. more or less coated with wax, globular, bractless, on the growing wood: fls. with or after the lvs.
  B. Fr. grayish white, thickly covered with wax: fls. dioecious.
                                               Subgen. MORELLA (Lour.) Endl.
    C. Lvs. obovate to oblong-obovate, obtuse or acutish, 1.5–4 cm. broad.
      D. Lvs. deciduous, pubescent; fr. pubescent when young..........1. *M. pensylvanica*
      DD. Lvs. evergreen, glabrous or pubescent: fr. glabrous when young.2. *M. heterophýlla*
    CC. Lvs. oblanceolate or oblong-lanceolate, acute, evergreen, 1–1.5 cm. broad.
                                              3. *M. cerifera*
  BB. Fr. dark purple, thinly coated with wax: fls. monoecious: lvs. serrate, persistent.
                                              4. *M. californica*
AA. Fr. resinous-dotted, ovoid with 2 adnate, wing-like bracts, in cone-like axillary catkins at the end of last year's brts.................................Subgen. GALE (Adans.) Endl.
                                              5. *M. Gale*

1. **M. pensylvànica** Lois. BAYBERRY. Deciduous shrub to 3 m.; brts. gray pubescent and glandular: lvs. obovate to oblong-obovate or oblong, 4–10 cm. long, 1.5–4 cm. broad, obtuse or acutish, shallowly toothed toward the apex or entire, dull green and pubescent above, pubescent beneath, resinous-dotted: fr. 3.5–4.5 mm. thick. Fl.III–IV; fr.IX–IV. Em.255,t(c). G.F.7:477. F.E.23:825 (h). S.L.238(h). (*M. caroliniensis* auth., not Mill., *M. cerifera* var. *latifolia* Ait.) Nfld. to w. N. Y. and Md., chiefly along the sea-shore. Intr. 1727. Zone II. The aromatic lvs. fall late in autumn; conspicuous in winter with its grayish white fr. Valuable for planting on sterile dry soil.

2. **M. heterophýlla** Raf. EVERGREEN BAYBERRY. Evergreen shrub or small tree to 5 m.; brts. pubescent, blackish brown: lvs. coriaceous, obovate to oblong, occasionally lanceolate, 4–7 cm. long, 1.5–2.5 cm. broad, rounded or apiculate at apex, cuneate, entire or sharply toothed toward the apex, pubescent on both sides, finally glabrous and lustrous above: fr. about 3 mm. across. Fl.III; fr.X–IV. (*M. Curtissi* var. *media* Chev.). N. J. to Fla. and Ark., inner Coastal Plain. Cult. 1903. Zone VI.—**M. h. Curtíssi** (Chev.) Fern. Brts. glabrous, reddish brown: lvs. glabrous above, sparingly glandular beneath. (*M. C.* Chev.) Md. to Fla. and La. Intr. ?

3. **M. cerífera** L. WAX-MYRTLE. Shrub or small tree, occasionally to 12 m.; brts. reddish, glabrous or puberulous: lvs. evergreen, lanceolate to oblong-lanceolate, acute, entire or serrate toward the apex, 3–8 cm. long, 1–1.5 cm. broad, resin-dotted, dark green and glabrous above, glabrous or sometimes puberulous beneath: fr. 2.5–3 mm. thick. Fl.III–IV; fr.X–IV. S.S.9:t.459. G.F. 7:476. (*M. caroliniensis* Mill.) N. J. to Fla. and Tex. Intr. 1699. Zone VI.

4. **M. califórnica** Cham. CALIFORNIAN BAYBERRY. Shrub or slender tree, occasionally to 12 m.; brts. pubescent: lvs. coriaceous, lanceolate to oblong-lanceolate, acute, remotely serrate, 5–10 cm. long, resinous-dotted, lustrous above, glabrous or puberulous beneath and black-dotted: fr. globose or glo-

bose-ovoid, 4–6 mm. long, purple. Fl.v–vi; fr.ix–i. S.S.9:t.461. A.I.1:509. J.H.1852:283. Wash. to Calif. Intr. 1848. Zone VII. Handsome shrub with ornamental fr.

5. **M. Gàle** L. SWEET GALE. Shrub to 1.5 m., with upright virgate dark brown brs.: lvs. deciduous, oblanceolate, obtuse or acute, toothed toward the apex, 3–6 cm. long, dark green and glabrous above, usually pubscent beneath: staminate catkins with glabrous brown scales, 7–10 mm. long: fr. compressed, 3-pointed, in dense catkins 8–10 mm. long. Fl.iii–iv; fr.ix. Em.255,t(c). B.B.1:584. H.W.2:97. (*Gale palustris* Cheval.) N. Am., s. to Va., Mich. and Wash.; Eu. to N. E. Asia. Cult. 1750. Zone I.—**M. G. subglábra** (Cheval.) Fern., var. Lvs. glabrous or nearly so throughout. (*Gale palustris* var. *s.* Cheval.) N. Am., Eu. Cult. 1864.—**M. G. tomentòsa** C. DC., var. Brts. pubescent: lvs. pubescent on both sides, more densely below. (*M.t.* Aschers. & Graebn., *Gale japonica* Cheval.) E. Siberia, Japan. Intr. 1892.

2. **COMPTÒNIA** L'Hérit. Deciduous shrub, pubescent: lvs. alternate, petioled, pinnatifid; stipules semicordate: fls. usually monoecious; staminate fls. with 3–4, usually 4 stamens, in cylindric catkins; pistillate fls. with 8 linear-subulate, persistent bracts, at the base, in globose-ovoid aments: fr. a glabrous, ovoid, obtuse nutlet subtended by the elongated subulate bracts, in bur-like heads. (After Henry Compton, bishop of Oxford; 1632–1713.) One species.

C. peregrìna (L.) Coult. SWEET FERN. Shrub to 1.5 m.; brts. brown, covered with spreading hairs: lvs. linear-oblong, deeply pinnatifid with roundish-ovate, oblique, often mucronulate lobes, 5–12 cm. long and 1–1.5 cm. broad, pubescent, fragrant: staminate catkins about 1.5 cm. long, with acuminate brown ciliate bracts: fruiting aments 1.5–2.5 cm. in diam.; fr. about 5 mm. long, olive-brown, lustrous. Fl.iv–v; fr.viii. Em.255(c). N.D.2,t.11(c). S.L.2:273(h). Rh.40:t.415,f.7–10. (*C. asplenifolia* Ait., *Myrica a.* L., in part.) N. S. to N. C., Ind. and Mich. Intr. 1714. Zone II. Graceful aromatic shrub, doing well in peaty or sandy soil.—**C. p. asplenifòlia** (L.) Fern., var. Brts. minutely puberulous: lvs. smaller, sparingly puberulous or glabrous except the midrib: fruiting aments 8–15 mm. in diam. Rh.40:t.415,f.1–6. (*Myrica a.* L., in part.) Long Island to Va.

9. LEITNERIACEAE Drude. CORKWOOD FAMILY

Deciduous tree or shrub, with light soft wood and pale slightly fissured bark; buds scaly: lvs. alternate, petioled, entire, penninerved, estipulate: fls. dioecious, without perianth, in the axils of bracts, forming axillary catkins, appearing before the lvs.; staminate fls. with 8–12 stamens; anthers oblong, yellow; pistillate fls. consisting of a 1-celled, 1-ovuled ovary subtended by 3–4 gland-fringed scales; style slender, curved, caducous: fr. a drupe.—One monotypic N. American genus.

LEITNÈRIA Chapm. Character of the family. (After Dr. E. T. Leitner, a German naturalist, killed about 1840 during the Seminole war in Fla.)

L. floridàna Chapm. CORKWOOD. Shrub or tree, occasionally to 6 m. tall with open loose head, the trunk swollen at base; brts. tomentose at first, later glabrous and brown; buds tomentose: lvs. elliptic-lanceolate to lanceolate, acuminate, cuneate at base, 8–15 cm. long, firm, bright green and pubescent above at least on the veins, paler and reticulate and silky-pubescent below; petioles slender, 3–5 cm. long, tomentose: staminate catkins 2–4 cm. long, with acuminate silky-pubescent bracts, pistillate smaller and slenderer: fr. 1–4 on one ament, oblong, 1.5–2 cm. long, light olive brown. Fl.ɪɪɪ(v); fr.v(ɪx). S.S.7:t.330. H.I.11:t.1044. R.Mo.6:t.30–44. S. Mo. to Tex. and Fla. Intr. 1894. Zone V. Without particular ornamental qualities, but botanically interesting; it demands peaty humid soil and spreads by suckers.

10. JUGLANDACEAE Lindl. WALNUT FAMILY

Trees, rarely shrubs, aromatic; brts. terete; buds scaly or naked, usually several superposed: lvs. alternate, odd-pinnate, with short-stalked or sessile lfts., estipulate: fls. monoecious, with or after the lvs.; the staminate fls. in lateral, usually drooping catkins; stamens 3-many, with or without an irregulaɪly lobed perianth: filaments short; anthers oblong; pistillate fls. terminal, solitary or in racemes, in the axils of bracts and subtended by 2 bractlets; calyx 3–5-lobed; ovary inferior, 1- or incompletely 2–4-celled, with one erect ovule; styles 2, stigmatic only on the inner face; fr. a drupe or nut; seed 2–4-lobed, without endosperm; cotyledons usually corrugate and very oily.— Six genera with about 40 species distributed through the temp. regions of the n. hemisphere.

A. Fr. a winged nutlet.
  B. Frs. in the axils of persistent lanceolate bracts forming an upright cone-like catkin: pith of brs. solid...1. *Platycarya*
  BB. Frs. in pendulous racemes: pith lamellate.....................................2. *Pterocarya*
AA. Fr. an indehiscent or dehiscent large drupe, solitary or in pendulous racemes.
  B. Pith lamellate: husk indehiscent; nut sculptured or rugose...................3. *Juglans*
  B3. Pith solid: husk splitting; nut smooth, often angled.........................4. *Carya*

1. **PLATYCÁRYA** Sieb. & Zucc. Deciduous tree; pith solid: buds small, scaly, brown, nearly glabrous: staminate and pistillate aments upright; fls. without perianth; staminate catkins slender, short-peduncled, usually several below the terminal pistillate catkin; stamens 8–10 in the axils of lanceolate bracᵗs; pistillate catkin solitary, ovoid-oblong; bracts adnate to the ovary forming the wings of the fr.; style 5, short and thick; fr. a small compressed winged nutlet in the axils of stiff lanceolate bracts, forming a small strobile. (Greek *platys*, broad, and *karya*, nut; alluding to the compressed nutlet.)— One species in China.

P. **strobilàcea** Sieb. & Zucc. Shrub or tree to 12 m.; brts. hairy at first, soon glabrous, yellowish brown or chestnut-brown: lvs. 15–30 cm. long; lfts. 7–15, sessile, ovate- to oblong-lanceolate, slightly falcate, acuminate, doubly serrate, 4–10 cm. long, sparingly pubescent at first, finally nearly glabrous; staminate catkins 5–8 cm. long; fruiting catkins ovoid to oblong, 3–4 cm. long, brown; nutlets about 5 mm. long. Fl.vɪ; fr.ɪx. S.Z.2:t.149(c). S.I.1:t. 17(c). M.O.t.37. N.K.20:t.16. (*Fortunaea chinensis* Lindl., *Petrophiloides s.* Reid & Chandler.) China. Intr. 1845. Zone (V). Handsome shrubby tree with graceful foliage.—*P. sinensis* Mottet is probably only a form of this species.

2. **PTEROCÁRYA** Kunth. WING-NUT. Deciduous trees; pith lamellate; buds stalked, usually several, naked or with a few deciduous scales: lvs. alternate, pinnate, estipulate: fls. monoecious, in pendulous catkins, staminate axillary, on last year's brts., or at base of the new shoots; fls. with 1–4 sepals and two bractlets adnate to an elongated bract; stamens 6–18; pistillate fls. consisting of a 1-celled ovary enclosed in a connate perianth 4-pointed at apex, with 2 bractlets at base; style short, divided into 2 stigmas: fr. a rather

small winged nutlet 1-seeded, 4-celled at the base; cotyledons 4-lobed, raised above ground and becoming green. Fls. appearing in June; fruit ripening in September and October. (Greek *pteron*, wing, and *karya*, nut; referring to the winged nut.)—Eight species; 6 in China, 1 in Japan and 1 in W. Asia.

A. Buds naked, several, superposed. (Sect. I. EUPTEROCARYA Rehd. & Wils.)
  B. Fr. with 2 distinct wings.
    c. Wings of fr. suborbicular: rachis of lf. terete.
      D. Lfts. 11–25 ....1. *P. fraxinifolia*
      DD. Lfts. 5–9 ....2. *P. hupehensis*
    cc. Wings of fruit oblong: rachis more or less winged; lfts. 11–21.......3. *P. stenoptera*
  BB. Fr. winged all around: lfts. 7–9. (Sect. II. CYCLOPTERA Franch.)...........4. *P. Paliurus*
AA. Bud with 2–3 dark brown scales, falling during winter, accessory buds wanting: leaflets 11–21. (Sect. III. CHLAENOPTEROCARYA Rehd. & Wils.).......................5. *P. rhoifolia*

1. **P. fraxinifòlia** (Lam.) Spach. CAUCASIAN W. Tree to 30 m., often divided into several stems near base, with wide-spreading head; bark deeply furrowed; brts. minutely scurfy while young, soon glabrous: lvs. 20–45 cm. long; rachis terete, glabrous; lfts. 11–20, ovate-oblong to oblong-lanceolate, acuminate, sharply serrate, 8–12 cm. long, thin, glabrous except stellate hairs in the axils and along the midrib beneath: fr. with semiorbicular wings, 1.5–2 cm. broad, in racemes 20–45 cm. long. L.I.t.20,21. G.C.III.4:381. B.S.2:262, t(h). E.H.2:t.121–3(h). (*P. caucasica* C. A. Mey., *P. Spachiana* Lav., *P. laevigata* Hort., *P. sorbifolia* Dipp.) Cauc. to N. Persia. Intr. 1782. Zone (V). Tree with handsome dark green lvs. and long drooping racemes of light green frs. during summer. It prefers humid soil.—**P. f. dumòsa** (Lav.) Schneid., var. Shrubby; brts. yellowish brown: lfts. smaller, 5–7 cm. long. (*P. d.* Lav., *P. fraxinifolia* K. Koch, not Spach.)

  P. f. × *stenoptera* = **P. Rehderiàna** Schneid. Lf.-rachis more or less winged, at least on vigorous brs.; lfts. somewhat smaller and narrower: wings of fr. oval or oval-oblong, longer than broad. S.T.2:t.137. B.C.5:2854. R.H.1925:372. 373(h). Orig. 1880.—Apparently more vigorous and hardier than either of the parents; spreading by suckers.

2. **P. hupehénsis** Skan. Tree to 20 m., with pale gray smooth bark deeply fissured on old trunks; brts. minutely scurfy: lvs. 15–30 cm. long; rachis terete, glabrous: lfts. 5–9, oblong to oblong-lanceolate or oblong-obovate, acuminate, serrate or serrulate, 6–14 cm. long, stellate-pubescent in the axils beneath: fr. including the semi-orbicular wings 2.5–3 cm. across, in racemes to 45 cm. long. C. China. Intr. 1903. Zone VI.

3. **P. stenóptera** DC. Tree to 30 m.; young brts. and petioles pilose or nearly smooth: lvs. 20–40 cm. long; rachis winged, the wings sometimes serrate; lfts. 11–23, the terminal one often wanting, oval-oblong to narrow-oblong, acute or sometimes obtusish, serrulate, 4–10 cm. long, slightly pubescent on the midrib and veins beneath: fr. with oblong to oblong-lanceolate upright wings, with the nutlet 1.5–2 cm. long, in racemes 20–30 cm. long. C.C.65. L.I.t.19. R.H.1920:91(l). M.O.415(h). (*P. sinensis* Hort., *P. japonica* Hort.) China. Intr. about 1860. Zone VI.

4. **P. Paliùrus** Batal. Tree to 20 m.; young brts. and the terete leaf-rachis tomentulose or scurfy while young; lvs. 15–25 cm. long; lfts. 7–9, oblong-ovate to oblong-lanceolate, acuminate, very oblique at base, serrulate, 6–15 cm. long, firm, pubescent on the midrib and often on the veins beneath or nearly glabrous: fr. forming with the large wing a circular disk 3–7 cm. across, in racemes 15–25 cm. long. J.H.28:65. C.C.66. C. China. Intr. 1901. Zone VI?

5. **P. rhoifòlia** Sieb. & Zucc. Tree to 30 m.; brts. and the terete leaf-rachis finely pubescent while young or nearly glabrous; buds with 2–3 large brown glabrous scales, about 1.5 cm. long, deciduous during the winter or

early in spring; lvs. 20–40 cm. long; lfts. 11–21, ovate-oblong to ovate-lanceolate, acuminate, sharply and finely serrate, 6–12 cm. long, pubescent on the veins beneath or nearly glabrous: fr. with the broad rhombic wings which are broader than long, 2–2.5 cm. across, in racemes 20–30 cm. long. S.I.1:t.16(c). K.M.t.21(c). J.L.50:f.75(h). Japan. Intr. 1888. Zone V.

3. JÙGLANS L. WALNUT.

Deciduous trees, rarely shrubby; brs. with lamellate pith; trunk with scaly furrowed bark; buds with few scales, sessile, rarely short-stalked: lvs. alternate, odd-pinnate, large, aromatic, estipulate; lfts. opposite, serrate or entire: fls. monoecious; the staminate fls. on last year's brts. in lateral pendulous catkins, each consisting of a bract bearing 8–40 stamens, 2 bractlets and 1–4 calyx-lobes; pistillate fls. in few- to many-fld. terminal racemes, with 4 calyx-lobes and a 3-lobed involucre consisting of a bract and 2 bractlets; style divided into 2 plumose stigmas; fr. a large indehiscent drupe; nut thick-walled, incompletely 2–4-celled, indehiscent or finally separating into 2 valves; seed 2–4-lobed, remaining within the shell in germination. Fls. appearing with or shortly after the lvs.; fruit in autumn. (Ancient Latin name for *J. regia*, derived from *Jovis glans*, Jupiter's acorn.)—About 15 species in N. and S. America, in the Old World from S. E. Eu. to E. Asia.

A. Lfts. entire or nearly so, glabrous, usually 7–9: nut with thin partition, splitting.1. *J. regia*
AA. Lfts. serrate, 9–25: nut with thick bony partition, not splitting.
  B. Frs. glabrous or finely pubescent, solitary or few: leaf-scars without a prominent pubescent band on their upper edge: nut 4-celled at base.
    c. Width of lfts. 1–2.5 cm., rarely more: nut grooved or smooth.
      D. Lfts. 17–23, about 1 cm. broad: fr. 1.5–2 cm. thick..................2. *J. rupestris*
      DD. Lfts. 9–19, 2 cm. broad or more: fr. 2.5–5 cm. thick.
        E. Lfts. on the midrib beneath and rachis more or less pubescent, 9–13, rarely to 19: nut deeply grooved...3. *J. major*
        EE. Lfts. nearly glabrous at maturity, 15–19: nut obscurely or not grooved.
                                     4. *J. Hindsii*
    cc. Width of lfts. 2.5–5 cm.: nut prominently and irregularly ridged...........5. *J. nigra*
  BB. Frs. viscid-pubescent, racemose: leaf-scars with a prominent band of hairs on their upper edge: nut 2-celled at base.
    c. Nut strongly 6–8-ridged.
      D. Mature brts. red- or purplish-brown; lfts. with spreading teeth......6. *J. cinerea*
      DD. Mature brts. grayish or yellowish brown; lfts. with shallow teeth directed forward.
        E. Lfts. densely pubescent on the veins beneath: fr. 6–10 in pendulous racemes.
                                  7. *J. cathayensis*
        EE. Lfts. often glabrescent: fr. in short racemes.................8. *J. mandshurica*
    cc. Nut rugose or nearly smooth; frs. in long pendulous racemes........9. *J. Sieboldiana*

1. **J. règia** L. ENGLISH W. (PERSIAN W.) Broad-headed tree to 30 m., with silvery gray bark remaining smooth a long time; brts. glabrous: lfts. 5–9, rarely to 13, elliptic to obovate or oblong-ovate, acute or acuminate, entire, rarely and chiefly on young plants obscurely serrate, 6–12 cm. long, glabrous except small axillary tufts of hairs beneath: staminate catkins 5–10 cm. long; fr. subglobose, glabrous, green, 4–5 cm. across; nut usually ovoid, or ellipsoid, pointed, more or less wrinkled, usually thick-shelled. H.W.2:87–89,t.36(c). M.D.1911:197(h). E.H.2:t.74,75(h). S. E. Eu. to Himal. and China. Long cult. Zone (V).—Much planted as a fruit tree in the warmer parts of the country, particularly in Calif. Variable in size and shape of the nut and the thickness and sculpturing of the shell. Several geographical varieties have been distinguished: **J. r. turcománica** Popof, ssp. Lfts. oblong-ovate to ovate-lanceolate: nut with a hard thick or thin shell. Bull. Appl. Bot. 22:295,296,298. Turkest.—**J. r. kamaònia** DC., var. Lfts. ovate-lanceolate, pubescent on the veins beenath: nut with thin shell. B.D.1906:82,96. (*J. k.* Dode.) Himal.—**J. r. fallax** (Dode) Popof, ssp. Lfts. usually elliptic, up to 16 cm. long and 10 cm. broad: shell very thick, with protruding ridges inside. B.D.1906:83,96. Bull. Appl. Bot. 22:296,299. J.A.11:t.19(h). (*J. f.*

Dode.) C. Asia.—Here belongs *J. Duclouxiana* Dode. Lfts. elliptic-ovate, short-acuminate: nut thin-shelled. B.D.1906:82. Cult. in S. China, Himal. Cult. 1917.—The following are horticultural forms: **J. r. laciniàta** Jacques. Lfts. pinnately dissected. M.G.23:717(h). (*J. r. filicifolia* and *aspleniifolia* Hort., *J. heterophylla* Loud.)—**J. r. monophýlla** DC., var. Lvs. simple or 3-foliolate. S.H.1:f.44g.—**J. r. péndula** Pépin. Brs. pendulous.—**J. r. praepartùriens** Lem., var. A shrubby form producing rather small thin-shelled nuts at an early period, sometimes on plants 2 or 3 years old. (*J. r. fertilis* Kirchn., *J. r.* f. *fruticosa* Dipp.)

    J. r. × *mandshurica* = **J. sinénsis** (DC.) Dode. Lfts. oblong-ovate: sparingly denticulate: shell of nut with large lacunes. (*J. r.* var. *sinensis* DC.) B.D.1906:83,96. N. and E. China.—*J. r.* × *Hindsii;* see under No. 4.—*J. r.* × *nigra;* see under No. 5.—*J. r.* × *cinerea;* see under No. 6.—*J. r.* × *Sieboldiana;* see under No. 9.

    2. **J. rupéstris** Engelm. Shrub or small tree, rarely 10 m. tall; brts. pubescent when young: lfts. 15–23, lanceolate to narrow-lanceolate, acuminàte, finely serrate or nearly entire, 4–8 cm. long, soon glabrous or nearly so, or pubescent on the midrib beneath: stamens 20; ovary pubescent or tomentose: fr. globose, rarely ovoid, 1.5–2 cm. across, sometimes nearly glabrous at maturity; nut thick-shelled, with deep longitudinal grooves, about 1.5 cm. across. S.S.7:t.335. S.L.206(h). Texas, N. Mex. Cult. 1868. Zone V. Shrubby graceful species, the lvs. with numerous small and narrow lfts. Somewhat similar is *J. californica* under No. 4.

    3. **J. màjor** (Torr.) Heller. Tree to 20 m. with a rather narrow head; brts. pubescent while young: lfts. 9–13, rarely to 19, oblong-lanceolate to ovate, acuminate, cuneate or rounded at base, coarsely serrate, 7–10, the lowest pair 3–5 cm. long, soon glabrous or pubescent on the midrib beneath; stamens 30–40: fr. subglobose or ovoid and sometimes pointed, 2.5–3.5 cm. across, rufous-tomentulose; nut subglobose, slightly compressed, deeply grooved, thick-shelled, 2–3 cm. across. S.M.172. (*J. rupestris* var. *m.* Torr., *J. Torreyi* Dode.) N. Mex., Ariz. and Colo. Intr. 1894? Zone VII.

    4. **J. Híndsii** (Jeps.) Jeps. Round-headed tree to 15 or occasionally to 25 m.; brts. densely pubescent while young: petioles villous; lfts. 15–19, ovate-lanceolate to lanceolate, long-acuminate, usually rounded at base, coarsely serrate, 6–10 cm. long, pubescent on the midrib and veins beneath: stamens 30–40: fr. subglobose, 3–5 cm. across, soft-pubescent; nut nearly globose, 2.5–3.5 cm. across, thick-shelled, faintly grooved. (*J. californica* var. *H.* Jeps.) S.S.7:t.337,f.5–8. S.M.175. Gn.49:278(h). C. Calif. Cult. 1878. Zone VII? Much planted in Calif. as a street tree and used as stock for the English Walnut.—**J. H. quercinifólia** Babcock, mut. Lfts. usually 3, rarely 1, ovate to elliptic, obtuse or truncate, 1.5–5.5 cm. long. Univ. Calif. Pub. Agr. Sci. 2:t.20,f.1–2.

    J. H. × *regia* = "Paradox" of Burbank.—*J. H.* × *nigra* = "Royal" of Burbank. Am. Nut Jour. 11:61(h).

    Closely related species: **J. califórnica** S. Wats. Shrub or small tree: lfts. usually 11–15, oblong-lanceolate, acute, 2.5–6.5 cm. long, glabrous: fr. globose, 1–2 cm. across; nut not deeply grooved. S.S.7:t.337,f.1–4. S.M.174. A.I.1:509. S. Calif. Cult. 1889. Zone VII?—**J. c. quercìna** Babcock, mut. Lfts. 1–5, usually 3, broad-ovate to oblong. J.S.51–53. (*J. quercifolia* Pierce.) Orig. 1900.

    5. **J. nígra** L. BLACK W. Tall tree to 50 m. with round head; bark deeply furrowed, brown; brts. pubescent; upper margin of lf.-scar notched: lfts. 15–23, ovate-oblong to ovate-lanceolate, acuminate, rounded at base, irregularly serrate, 6–12 cm. long, at first minutely pubescent above, finally nearly glabrous and somewhat lustrous, pubescent and glandular beneath: staminate

catkins 5–12 cm. long; stamens 20–30; pistillate fls. 2–5: fr. globose or slightly pear-shaped, 3.5–5 cm. across, pubescent; nut ovoid and pointed or subglobose and sometimes broader than high, slightly compressed, strongly and irregularly ridged, 3–4 cm. across. S.S.7:t.333,334. Em.211(c). E.H.2,t.76–77 (h). G.C.30:303(h). Mass. to Fla. w. to Minn. and Tex. Cult. 1686. Zone IV. Tree with round head and dark green foliage; its timber highly valued.

J. n. × *regia* = J. **intermèdia** Carr. Similar to *J. regia*: lfts. usually 11, ovate to elliptic-ovate, remotely denticulate, dark green and glabrous except axillary tufts of hairs below: fr. smooth; nut deeply sculptured. The type of the hybrid is J. i. **pyrifòrmis** Carr. Young shoots glandular-pubescent: fr. obovoid. R.H.1863:30. Gn.50:478.—J. i. **Vilmoreàna** Carr. Brts. glabrous: fr. subglobose, apiculate. G.F.4:52(h),53. M.D.1911:197(h). B.C.3:1724(fr). (*J. Vilmoriniana* Vilm.)—Here belongs probably the so-called "James River Hybrid." F.L.2:133,134(h), which has large oblong-ovoid nuts about 5 cm. long very much like *J. regia gibbosa* Carr. (R.H.1861:428) in shape, but with numerous longitudinal irregular ridges separated by deep grooves.—*J. n.* × *Hindsii;* see under No. 4.

6. J. **cinérea** L. BUTTERNUT. Tree occasionally to 30 m., with gray deeply fissured bark; brts. pubescent, glandular while young; upper margin of lf.-scar straight or rounded: petiole and rachis glandular-pubescent; lfts. 11–19, oblong-lanceolate, acuminate, appressed-serrate, 6–12 cm. long, finely pubescent above, pubescent and glandular beneath: staminate catkins 5–8 cm. long; pistillate spikes 5–8-fld.: frs. 2–5, ovoid-oblong, 4–6.5 cm. long, viscid-pubescent; nut ovoid-oblong, with 4 prominent and 4 less prominent, sharp irregular ridges and many broken ridges between, thick-shelled. S.S.7:331,332. Em.207,t.(c). H.H.50,51(b). F.L.7:56,t.(h). N. B. to Ga., w. to Dak. and Ark. Cult. 1633. Zone III. Less handsome and less valuable than No. 5.

J. c. × *regia* = J. **quadrangulàta** (Carr.) Rehd. Similar to *J. regia*: lfts. usually 9, oval to oblong, obscurely and remotely serrate, slightly pubescent beneath: fr. sparingly produced, subglobose; nut ovoid-oblong, deeply sculptured; walls thinner than those of *J. cinerea*. G.F.7:435. R.H.1870:494. Gn.50: 578. (*J. intermedia quadrangulata* Carr., *J. intermedia alata* Carr., *J. alata* Schelle.) Orig. before 1870.—*J. c.* × *Sieboldiana;* see under No. 9.

7. J. **cathayénsis** Dode. CHINESE W. Tree to 25 m.; brts. glandular-pubescent: lvs. up to 1 m. long; lfts. 9–17, ovate- or obovate-oblong, acuminate, obliquely rounded or subcordate at base, serrulate, 8–15, or occasionally to 22 cm. long, dark green and sparingly pubescent above, more densely pubescent beneath, midrib and petiole glandular: staminate catkins 20–35 cm. long: frs. in racemes of 6–10, ovoid, pointed, 3–4.5 cm. long; nut ovoid, pointed, 6–8-angled with broken and spiny ridges. G.C.50:189;77:203. C. China. Intr. 1899. Zone V. Vigorous tree with large foliage; the nut is edible, but the walls thick and the kernel small.

8. J. **mandshurica** Maxim. MANCHURIAN W. Tree to 20 m., with broad round head; brts. glandular-pubescent: lfts. 9–17, ovate-oblong to oblong, acute, serrulate, 7–18 cm. long, sparingly pubescent above at first, finally glabrous or nearly so, pubescent below and usually densely glandular-pubescent on the midrib and rachis: staminate catkins about 10 cm. long; pistillate catkins 5–10-fld.: fr. subglobose or ovoid, pointed, 4.5–5.5 cm. long; nut ovoid, pointed, with 8 prominent, sharply edged ridges and irregular broken ridges between, 4–4.5 cm. long. N.K.20:t.17,18. G.C.30:302. Manch., Amurland. Intr. 1859. Zone V.

Related species: J. **stenocárpa** Maxim. referred often to *J. mandshurica,* but the plant in cultivation differs in its nearly glabrous brts., in the absence of the prominent hairy band above the leaf-scars, in the glabrescent lvs. and in the very large terminal lfts. which is up to 18 cm. long and to 10 cm. broad: nut cylindric-oblong. Mél. Biol. 8:632(fr). Manch. Cult. 1903. Zone V.

9. **J. Sieboldiàna** Maxim. Tree to 20 m., with broad round head, very similar in its brts. and lvs. to the preceding species, but quite different in its fls. and fr.: the staminate catkins 15–30 cm. long, the pistillate 12–20-fld.; fr. globose to ovoid, viscid-pubescent, nut subglobose or ovoid, pointed, with thick projecting sutures, rugose, thick-shelled, 2.5–3.5 cm. long. S.I.2:t.5(c). M.K.t.20(c). R.H.1878:414,415. (*J. ailanthifolia* Carr.) Japan. Intr. 1860. Zone IV.—**J. S. cordifórmis** (Maxim.) Mak., var. Nut heart-shaped or ovoid, much flattened, sharply 2-edged, with a shallow longitudinal groove in the middle of the flat sides, smooth, rather thin-shelled. S.I.1:t.17(c). G.C.30: 292,t. B.C.3:1724. (*J. c.* Maxim.) Japan. Intr. 1862 or 1863.—To this species belong the following names of Dode: *J. Allardiana, J. coarctata, J. Lavallei* (L.I.t.1,2), *J. subcordiformis;* the last named is scarcely different from the var. *cordiformis,* while the second and third are intermediate between this variety and the type (B.D.1909:33,38,39).

    J. S. × *regia* = **J. notha** Rehd. Lfts. 7–9, elliptic to elliptic-oblong, glabrous above, glabrescent beneath, sparingly and minutely denticulate: nut much like that of *J. Sieboldiana.* Orig. 1878.—**J. n. Batèsii** Rehd., var. (*J. S. cordiformis* × *regia.*) Nut slightly compressed, more acuminate and smoother.—*J. S.* × *cinerea* = **J. Bíxbyi** Rehd. Nut rough-shelled, but less deeply and less sharply ridged than in *J. cinerea.* Orig. about 1903.—**J. B. lancastriénsis** Rehd., var. (*J. S. cordiformis* × *cinerea.*) Nut slightly compressed and more acuminate.

4. CÁRYA Nutt. HICKORY. Deciduous trees; brs. with solid pith; buds scaly: lvs. alternate, odd-pinnate, estipulate; lfts. 3–17, opposite, serrate: fls. monoecious, with the lvs.; staminate fls. in axillary, usually ternate pendulous catkins, each fl. in the axil of a 3-lobed bract; stamens 3–10; pistillate fls. sessile, in terminal 2–10-fld. spikes, consisting of a 1-celled ovary enclosed by a 4-lobed involucre; stigmas 2, short: fr. globose to oblong, with a husk separating more or less completely into 4 valves; nut smooth or slightly rugose, often angled, 4-celled at base, 2-celled at apex; cotyledons remaining enclosed in the shell. (Greek *karya,* Walnut tree.) Syn. *Hicoria* Raf. About 20 species in E. N. Am., s. to Mex.; 1 in China and 1 in Tonkin.—Trees with handsome foliage, the head usually oblong or ovoid in outline; often planted as ornamental trees. Most species have edible nuts, some of commercial importance; see Rep. U. S. Dept. Agric. Div. Pomol. Nut-culture (1896) for illustrations of nuts. Several species are valued for their strong and tough wood.

A. Bud-scales 4–6, valvate: lfts. 5–17, usually lanceolate and often falcate: fr. with winged sutures; nut usually thin-shelled. (Sect. APOCARYA DC.)
  B. Nuts mostly elongated, nearly terete; husk thin, splitting to the base; kernel sweet; cotyledons entire or emarginate.
    c. Lfts. 11–17, tomentose and glandular when young: fr. 3.5–8 cm. long.....1. *C. Pecan*
    cc. Lfts. 5–11, scurfy-pubescent when young: fr. about 3.5 cm. long.
                                        2. *C. myristicaeformis*
  BB. Nuts usually as broad as long, compressed, irregularly angled and reticulate; kernel bitter; cotyledons deeply 2-lobed.
    c. Winter-buds dark reddish brown: lfts. 7–13: husk splitting to the base.
                                               3. *C. aquatica*
    c. Winter-buds bright yellow, glandular: leaflets 5–9: husk splitting somewhat below the middle ....4. *C. cordiformis*
AA. Bud-scales imbricate, more than 6: fr. not or slightly winged; nut usually thick-shelled: lfts. 3–9, not falcate; the uppermost larger and often obovate. (Sect. EUCARYA DC.)
  B. Buds small, 6–15 mm. long: nut slightly or not angled; husk usually thin.
    c. Petioles and lvs. beneath glabrous: lfts. 5–7: nut thin-shelled.
      D. Fr. obovoid, splitting only to the middle: kernel usually bitter........5. *C. glabra*
      DD. Fr. ovoid, splitting tardily to the base: kernel sweet...................6. *C. ovalis*
    cc. Petioles and lvs. beneath at least on the veins pubescent; lfts. usually 7.
                                             7. *C. pallida*
  BB. Buds large, terminal ones 1.5–5 cm. long: nut angled; kernel sweet.
    c. Brts. and petioles tomentose: bark close: husk not separating quite to the base.
                                            8. *C. tomentosa*

cc. Brts. and petioles glabrous or pubescent: bark shaggy: husk separating to the base.
  D. Lfts. 7–9: brts. pale orange..9. *C. laciniosa*
  DD. Lfts. usually 5: brts. light red-brown...............................10. *C. ovata*

1. **C. Pècan** (Marsh.) Engl. & Graebn. PECAN. Tree to 50 m.; bark deeply furrowed; buds pubescent, yellow; brts. pubescent while young: lfts. 11–17, short-stalked, oblong-lanceolate, serrate or doubly serrate, 10–18 cm. long, glandular and tomentose when young, becoming glabrous; petiole glabrous or pubescent: frs. in spikes of 3–10, oblong, 3.5–8 cm. long; nut ovoid or oblong, 2.5–5 cm. long, smooth, light brown marked with dark brown, 2-celled at base; kernel sweet. S.S.7:t.338,339. R.Mo.7:t.1(h),2(b). Am. For. 28:459 (h). (*Hicoria P.* Brit., *C. olivaeformis* Nutt., *C. illinoensis* K. Koch.) Iowa and Ind. to Ala., Tex. and Mex. Intr. about 1766. Zone (V).—Planted in the S. States as a fruit tree; many named vars. are in cult. (see B.C.5:2522–3).

C. P. × *cordiformis* = **C. Bròwnii** Sarg. Similar to *C. Pecan,* but differing chiefly in its 11 or rarely 9 lfts., in the ovoid fr. rounded at base and 3.5–4 cm. long and in the compressed nut. S.T.2:t.178. Intr. 1909.—There are also hybrids with *C. tomentosa* = **C. Schneckii** Sarg. and with *C. laciniosa* = **C. Nussbaùmeri** Sarg. (see R.Mo.7:t.20–23).

Closely related species: **C. texàna** (Le Conte) DC. Lfts. 7–11, broader and nearly sessile: nut smaller, red-brown, rough and obscurely 4-angled. S.S.14:t. 719. (*Hicoria t.* Le Conte.) E. Tex. Intr. 1900. Zone V.

2. **C. myristicaefórmis** (Michx. f.) Nutt. NUTMEG H. Tree to 30 m.; bark dark brown, broken into small appressed scales; buds with brown scurfy pubescence; brts. coated with yellow or brown scales, dark reddish brown the second year: lfts. 5–11, short-stalked or subsessile, ovate-lanceolate, the upper ones oblong-obovate, acuminate, pubescent or glabrous and silvery white beneath, 8–12 cm. long: fr. usually solitary, obovoid or ellipsoid, 4-winged to the base, 3–4 cm. long, husk splitting nearly to base; nut ovoid, reddish brown, marked with irregular bands and spots, thick-shelled, 4-celled below; kernel sweet. S.S.7:t.342,343. (*Hicoria m.* Brit., *H. Fernowiana* Sudw.) S. C. to Ark. and Mex. Intr. 1890. Zone VI. Tree with handsome foliage.

Related species: **C. cathayénsis** Sarg. Tree to 20 m.; young brts. covered with orange-yellow scales: lfts. 5–7, short-stalked, ovate to ovate-lanceolate, 10–14 cm. long, yellow-scurfy beneath and pilose on the midrib: fr. obovoid, 4-winged, nut ovoid, obscurely 4-angled, 2–2.5 cm. long; kernel sweet. C.C.63. Jour. Hered. 9:280(h). E. China. Intr. 1917.

3. **C. aquática** (Michx. f.) Nutt. BITTER PECAN. Small tree rarely to 30 m.; bark light brown, separating into long and thin, plate-like scales; buds dark reddish brown; brts. slightly glandular or loosely tomentose at first, finally dark red-brown: lfts. 7–13, lanceolate, long-acuminate, serrate, 8–12 cm. long, yellow-tomentose while young, glabrous at length: frs. often 3–4, ovoid or obovoid, compressed, 4-winged, 2.5–3.5 cm. long; nut broadly obovoid, much compressed, 4-angled, irregularly and longitudinally wrinkled, dull reddish brown; kernel bitter. S.S.7:t.344.345. R. Mo. 7:t.3(h),4(b). (*Hicoria a.* Brit.) Va. to Ill., s. to Fla. and Tex. Intr. about 1800. Zone VII?

4. **C. cordifórmis** (Wangh.) K. Koch. BITTERNUT. Tree to 30 m.; bark broken into thin scales, light brown; brts. rusty pubescent at first, finally glabrous, lustrous and reddish brown: lfts. 5–9, ovate-lanceolate to lanceolate, acuminate, serrate, 8–15 cm. long, light green and pubescent below, particularly along the midrib, nearly glabrous at length: fr. obovoid to subglobose, 4-winged above the middle, 2–3.5 cm. long; husk thin, splitting somewhat below the middle; nut subglobose to broadly ovoid, slightly compressed, abruptly contracted into a short point, nearly smooth, gray, thin-shelled; kernel bitter. S.S.7:340,341. E.H.3:t.170,171(h). F.L.5:81,t(h). (*Hicoria c.*

Brit., *H. minima* Brit., *C. amara* Nutt.) Que. to Minn., s. to Fla. and La. Intr.
about 1689. Zone IV. Tree with rather broad head and handsome foliage.
C. c. × *Pecan;* see under No. 1.

5. **C. glábra** (Mill.) Sweet. PIGNUT. Tree sometimes to 40 m.; bark dark
gray, fissured, close; buds with the outer glabrous scales deciduous, the inner
pubescent; brts. glabrous or nearly so, slender: lfts. 3–7, usually 5, oblong to
oblong-lanceolate, acuminate, sharply serrate, 8–15 cm. long, nearly glabrous;
petioles and rachis glabrous, green: fr. usually obovoid, slightly winged toward
the apex, about 2.5 cm. long and 2 cm. across, smooth; husk splitting usually
only to the middle; nut usually brownish, not angled; kernel usually astringent. S.T.2:t.179. S.M.192. E.H.3:t.172(h). B.C.2:677(h). R.Mo.7:t.7
(b). (*Hicoria g.* (Mill.) Brit., *C. porcina* (Michx. f.) Nutt.) Me. to Ont., s.
to Fla., Ala., and Miss. Intr. about 1750. Zone IV. Tall handsome tree.—
C. g. megacárpa (Sarg.) Sarg., var. Fr. 2.5–5 cm. long and about 3 cm. across,
obovoid, slightly flattened, with thick husk splitting earlier and a thick-shelled
nut. S.T.2:t.180. S.M.193. N. Y. to Mo. and Fla. Intr. 1912. Zone V.

6. **C. ovàlis** (Wangh.) Sarg. SWEET PIGNUT. Tree similar to the preceding; bark close and furrowed on young trees, often shaggy on old trunks; brts.
scurfy-pubescent at first, soon glabrous, stout: lfts. 5–7, oblong-ovate to
oblong-lanceolate or oblong-obovate, 8–15 cm. long, finely serrate, often
scurfy-pubescent while young, becoming glabrous; petioles often red: fr. subglobose to ellipsoid, 2–3 cm. long, densely scaly, slightly winged, splitting
tardily to near the base; nut slightly flattened, usually rounded at apex, sometimes slightly angular, brownish, rather thin-shelled; kernel sweet. S.M.194.
A.G.11:381,f.1,2,5,8,10. B.C.2:678(h). R.Mo.7:t.10(b). (*C. microcarpa* Nutt.,
partly, *Hicoria m.* Brit.—FALSE SHAGBARK.) Mass. to Wis., s. to Ga., Ala. and
Miss. Intr. probably before 1800. Zone IV.—Very variable in the shape of
its fr.: **C. o. obcordàta** Sarg., var. Fr. subglobose or broad-ellipsoid, to 3 cm.
diam.; nut angled, broader than high, often obcordate. S.S.7:t.354,f.5,6,7,9.
S.M.194.—**C. o. odoràta** (Sarg.) Sarg., var. Lfts. usually broader, glandular
beneath: fr. subglobose to ellipsoid, with distinctly winged sutures, splitting
freely to the base, to 2 cm. high; nut slightly higher than broad, very slightly
ridged, gray. S.S.7:t.354,f.8. S.M.195. R.Mo.7:t.8(b). Conn. to Pa. and Mo.
—**C. o. obovàlis** Sarg., var. Fr. obovoid, about 2.5 cm. high; nut much compressed, pointed or rounded at apex, rounded at base. S.M.196. Mass. to Va.
and Mo.—**C. o. boreàlis** (Ashe) Sarg., var. Bark scaly; brts. and lvs. pubescent at first: fr. ellipsoid, flattened, about 2 cm. high, very narrowly winged,
often incompletely splitting; husk rather thick; nut ellipsoid, ridged, whitish.
B.T.236. Mich. and Ont.—**C. o. hirsùta** (Ashe) Sarg., var. Bark scaly; petioles and lfts. beneath pubescent: fr. obovoid, narrowed at base, compressed.
(*Hicoria glabra h.* Ashe.) N. C. Intr. 1919.

7. **C. pállida** (Mill.) Engl. & Graebn. Tree with very rough pale bark;
brts. purple-brown; buds acute, with 5–9 scales: lfts. usually 7, sometimes 9,
oblong-lanceolate to lanceolate, 8–12 cm. long, finely serrate, bright green
above, beneath with silvery scales and scurfy-pubescent while young; petiole
and rachis pubescent with stellate hairs at least while young: middle lobe of
the staminate bract longer than lateral lobes: fr. subglobose to obovoid, 2–3
cm. long; husk rather thin, tardily splitting to the base; nut flattened, whitish, rather thin-shelled. G.F.10:305. S.M.190. Ala. and Tenn. Intr. 1898.
Zone V.

Related species: **C. Buckleyi** Durand. Tree 10–15, rarely to 20 m.; bark
dark, furrowed; young brts. rusty-pubescent: lfts. usually 7, lanceolate or ob-

lanceolate, 8–15 cm. long, pubescent on the veins beneath; petioles rusty-pubescent and villous when young: fr. subglobose, about 3.5 cm. long; husk splitting to the base; nut acute at apex, 4-angled above the middle, red-brown; kernel sweet. S.T.2:t.182. S.M.197. (*C. texana* Buckl., not Le Conte.) Tex. to Okl. and Ark. Intr. 1909. Zone V.—**C. B. arkansàna** (Sarg.) Sarg., var. Tree to 25 m.: fr. obovoid, rounded at apex, 3.5–4 cm. long, splitting to the middle or nearly to the base; nut rounded at ends, often slightly obovoid, slightly angled, pale brown. S.T.2:t.181. S.M.198. Ark. and Okl. Intr. 1910. Zone V.—**C. B. villòsa** (Ashe) Sarg., var. Tree to 15 m.: lfts. 5–7, oblong-elliptic to oblanceolate, more pubescent beneath: fr. broad-ellipsoid or obovoid, rounded at apex, 2–3 cm. long, tardily splitting to base by 1–2 sutures or indehiscent; nut broadovoid, pointed at apex, slightly angled, faintly tinged red. S.S.7:t.355. S.M.199. R.Mo.7:t.9(b). (*C. v.* Schneid., *C. glabra* var. *v.* Robins.) Mo. Intr. 1915.

8. **C. tomentòsa** (Lam.) Nutt. MOCKERNUT. Tree sometimes to 30 m.; bark rather close, ridged: brts. tomentose, sometimes nearly glabrous in autumn; terminal bud 1.5–2 cm. long: lfts. 7–9, oblong to oblong-lanceolate, acuminate, serrate, 8–18 cm. long, densely pubescent and glandular below, very fragrant when crushed; petiole and rachis hirsute or tomentose: fr. subglobose or pear-shaped, 3.5–5 cm. long; husk thick, splitting to the middle or nearly to the base; nut subglobose to ellipsoid, slightly flattened, angled, light brown, thick-shelled; kernel sweet. S.S.7:t.350. B.S.1:301,t.(h). R.Mo.7:t.11(b). (*C. alba* K. Koch, not Nutt.—BIG-BUD H.) Mass. to Ont. and Neb., s. to Fla. and Tex. Intr. 1766. Zone IV. Handsome tree.

C. a. × *Pecan* = *C. Schneckii;* see under No. 1.

9. **C. laciniòsa** (Michx. f.) Loud. BIG SHELLBARK-H. Tree to 40 m.; bark shaggy; brts. pubescent while young, later nearly glabrous and orange; terminal bud to 2.5 cm. long: lfts. 7, rarely 5 or 9, oblong-lanceolate, 10–20 cm. long, acuminate, serrate, pubescent beneath; petiole and rachis pubescent or glabrous, often persistent during winter: fr. ellipsoid to subglobose, 4–7 cm. long, 4-ribbed above the middle; nut ellipsoid or subglobose, compressed and obscurely 4-angled, pointed at ends, yellow or reddish, thick-shelled; kernel sweet. S.S.7:t.348,349. (*C. sulcata* Nutt.—BOTTOM SHELLBARK H., KINGNUT.) N. Y. to Iowa, s. to Tenn. and Okl. Intr. about 1800. Zone V.

C. l. × *Pecan;* see under No. 1.

10. **C. ovàta** (Mill.) K. Koch. SHAGBARK H. Tree, occasionally to 40 m.; bark light gray, shaggy; brts. scurfy-pubescent at first, usually soon glabrous and bright reddish brown; inner bud-scales becoming large and conspicuous when unfolding: lfts. 5, rarely 7, elliptic to oblong-lanceolate, 10–15 cm. long, acuminate, serrate and densely ciliate, pubescent and glandular below when young, finally glabrous: fr. subglobose, 3.5–6 cm. long, husk thick, splitting to base; nut ellipsoid to broad-obovoid, slightly flattened and angled, white, rather thin-shelled; kernel sweet. S.S.7:t.346,347. G.F.2:460(b). F.L.4:56,t (h). E.H.3:t.173(h). (*Hicoria o.* Brit., *C. alba* Nutt.—LITTLE SHELLBARK H.) Que. to Minn., s. to Fla. and Tex. Cult. 1629. Zone IV.—Next to the Pecan this species is the best as a fruit tree and several named varieties are in cult.; one of the best known is **C. o. Halèsii** Hort. with large, thin-shelled nuts.—**C. o. Nuttállii** Sarg., var. Fr. smaller; nut subglobose, usually obcordate, much compressed and angled, about 1.5 cm. across. N.S.1:t.13(c). (*C. microcarpa* Nutt.) Mass. to Pa. and Mo.—**C. o. fraxinifòlia** Sarg., var. Lfts. lanceolate or oblanceolate, the terminal one 12–15 cm. long and 4–5 cm. broad; fr. smaller, pointed. S.M.185. W. N. Y. Intr. 1911.

C. o. × *cordiformis* = **C. Làneyi** Sarg. Bark close, dark gray; terminal bud about 1 cm. long, the outer scales glabrous, deciduous, the inner lepidote, yellow: lfts. 5, lanceolate to oblanceolate: fr. ovoid, 3–5 cm. long; nut compressed, slightly obovoid, thin-shelled; kernel large, sweet. W. N. Y. Intr. 1913.—**C. L.**

chateaugayénsis Sarg., var. resembles more the Bitternut and has usually 7 lfts., a smaller fr. with a bitter kernel or sometimes sweet. Que. Intr. 1895.
Closely related species: **C. carolìnae-septentrionàlis** (Ashe) Engl. & Graebn. Lfts. 3–5, lanceolate, glabrous: fr. smaller; nut thin-shelled. S.S.14:t.720. N. C. to Ga. Intr. 1904. Zone V.

11. BETULACEAE Agardh. BIRCH FAMILY

Deciduous trees or shrubs: lvs. alternate, petioled, usually straight-veined, stipulate: fls. monoecious, rarely dioecious; staminate fls. in catkins, pistillate in clusters, spikes or catkins; stamens 2–10 to each bract, with or without calyx; ovary 2-celled, with 2 pendulous ovules in each cell; styles 2: fr. a 1-seeded nut; seed without albumen.—Six genera with more than 100 species in the temp. and colder regions of the n. hemisphere.—Monograph by Winkler in E.P.IV.101.

A. Nut small, compressed and often winged, without involucre, 2–3 in the axils of scales forming catkins; stamens 2–4, with 2–4-parted calyx......Subfam. 1. Betuleae (Döll) Aschers.
  B. Scales of fruiting catkins thin, 3-lobed, deciduous; stamens 2, bifid: buds sessile with 3 or more scales..1. *Betula*
  BB. Scales of fruiting catkins, 5-lobed, woody, persistent; stamens 4: buds usually stalked and with 2 valvate scales..2. *Alnus*
AA. Nut with a foliaceous involucre, forming clusters or spikes; stamens 3–10, without calyx: buds with several scales..........................Subfam. 2. Coryleae (Meissn.) Aschers.
  B. Frs. in pendulous slender spikes: buds elongated, acute; lvs. with 9 or more pairs of veins.
    c. Involucre of the fr. flat, 3-cleft or dentate, leafy; staminate catkins appearing in spring ....3. *Carpinus*
    cc. Involucre a bladder-like closed bag; staminate catkins formed in autumn..4. *Ostrya*
  BB. Frs. in clusters: buds ovoid, obtuse or acute: staminate catkins naked during winter: lvs. ovate or orbicular-ovate, with usually 5–8 pairs of veins.
    c. Anthers undivided, not hairy at apex: fls. with the lvs.: nut small, enclosed by the tubular involucre 3-fid at apex..5. *Ostryopsis*
    cc. Anthers divided, with tufts of hairs at apex: fls. before the leaves: nut large, wholly or partly enclosed by a leafy involucre irregularly laciniate at apex........6. *Corylus*

1. **BÈTULA** L. Birch. Deciduous shrubs or trees: buds with several imbricate scales: lvs. petioled, generally ovate, serrate or dentate to lobulate, with few or many veins: fls. monoecious; staminate catkins elongated, formed in autumn and remaining naked during winter, every bract with 3 fls., each fl. with a minute 4-parted calyx and 2 stamens divided at the apex; pistillate catkins oblong or cylindrical, each bract with 3 fls. without calyx: fr. a minute nut usually with membranous wings, at maturity dropping together with the 3-pointed bract from the slender rachis. (The ancient Latin name of the Birch.) About 40 species in the n. hemisphere, in N. Am. s. to Colo., Ala. and Calif., in Asia s. to the Himal.—Ornamental trees or shrubs, some valued as timber trees; they are essentially northern trees and mostly short-lived; most of them are well suited for planting on poor sandy or boggy soil.

A. Lvs. with 7 or more pairs of veins, usually more or less impressed above.
  B. Strobiles cylindric, pendulous, racemose or solitary and 3.5–11 cm. long; wing of the fruit much broader than the nutlet: lvs. 1–14 cm. long..........Ser. 1. Acuminatae Reg.
    c. Lvs. cordate at base: strobiles 2–4, racemose, 1.5–7 cm. long....1. *B. Maximowicziana*
    cc. Lvs. rounded or subcordate at the base: strobiles solitary; bracts without distinct lateral lobes..2. *B. luminifera*
  BB. Strobiles solitary, 2–5 cm. long, bracts with distinct lateral lobes: wings of fr. not or not much broader than nutlet...Ser. 2. Costatae Reg.
    c. Lvs. light green beneath: strobiles subglobose to cylindric.
      D. Strobiles cylindric or subcylindric, sometimes ellipsoid in No. 3.
        E. Wings of fr. ⅓–½ as broad as nutlet: lvs. triangular-ovate to ovate-oblong.
          F. Petioles 1–2 cm. long.
            G. Lvs. triangular-ovate, truncate or subcordate at base........3. *B. Ermani*
            GG. Lvs. ovate to ovate-oblong rounded, rarely broadly cuneate at base.
              H. Brts. glandular and villous: lvs. ovate, pubescent beneath..4. *B. utilis*
              HH. Brts. glabrous, sometimes slightly glandular: lvs. often ovate-oblong, glabrous beneath ....5. *B. albo-sinensis*

124

FF. Petioles 0.5–1 cm. long; leaves rounded or broad-cuneate at base, 4–8 cm. long ....**6.** *B. Schmidtii*
EE. Wings much narrower than nutlet: lvs. ovate to elliptic or obovate, 6–12 cm. long ....**7.** *B. Medwediewi*
DD. Strobiles subglobose to ellipsoid.
  E. Lvs. oblong-ovate, acuminate, 5–12 cm. long: petioles 0.5–2.5 cm. long: wings of fr. about ½ as broad or as broad as nutlet: bark of young brs. aromatic.
    F. Veins very prominent, 3–4 mm. distant; lvs. firm, long-acuminate, 5–8 cm. long ....**8.** *B. costata*
    FF. Veins less prominent, about 5 mm. distant; lvs. rather thin, 6–12 cm. long.
      G. Serration of lvs. coarse, usually 2 teeth between two veins: lvs. usually subcordate; petiole 1–2.5 cm. long...........................**9.** *B. grossa*
      GG. Serration fine, usually 3–4 teeth between two veins: petioles 0.5–1.5, rarely 2 cm. long.
        H. Bracts of strobiles glabrous: young brts. nearly glabrous: bark close, brown ....**10.** *B. lenta*
        HH. Bracts of strobiles pubescent: young brts. pubescent: bark yellowish, flaky ....**11.** *B. lutea*
  EE. Lvs. broad-ovate to elliptic, acute, rarely acuminate, 2–7 cm. long; petioles 3–12 mm. long: wings of frs. very narrow.
    F. Pairs of veins 7–10: petioles 6–12 mm. long.
      G. Lvs. broad-ovate, usually short-acuminate, 4–7 cm. long: strobiles 2.5–3 cm. long ....**12.** *B. globispica*
      GG. Lvs. ovate, acute, 2–5 cm., rarely to 6 cm. long: strobiles 1.5 cm. long. **14.** *B. chinensis*
    FF. Pairs of veins 10–20; lvs. acute, usually rufous-villous beneath on the veins; petioles 3–8 mm. long: shrub...................................**13.** *B. Potanini*
CC. Lvs. whitish beneath, rhombic-ovate, with 7–9 pairs of slightly impressed veins: strobiles cylindric-oblong ....**15.** *B. nigra*
AA. Lvs. with 3–7 pairs of veins (sometimes 8 in No. 24).
 B. Wings of fr. broader than the nutlet (½ as broad in No. 24): trees, rarely shrubs.
                                                        Ser. 3. ALBAE Reg.
  C. Bracts of strobiles with the lateral lobes spreading or recurved, usually longer than the middle lobe: brts. resinous-glandular and glabrous: bark white.
    D. Lvs. quite glabrous, rhombic-ovate, cuneate at base.
      E. Lvs. long-acuminate: bark chalky- or ashy-white, rather close.
                                      16. *B. populifolia*
      EE. Lvs. acuminate: bark creamy-white, flaky......................**17.** *B. pendula*
    DD. Lvs. slightly pubescent beneath and with axillary tufts of hairs at least while young, triangular-ovate or ovate, usually truncate at base.
      E. Lvs. bright green, usually truncate or subcordate...........**18.** *B. mandshurica*
      EE. Lvs. dull green above, usually rounded or truncate at base.
                                      19. *B. coerulea-grandis*
  CC. Bracts with the lateral lobes ascending, rarely spreading, shorter than the middle lobe: brts. pubescent, sometimes glabrous, not or slightly, rarely densely glandular.
    D. Bark flaky.
      E. Wings of fr. as broad as nutlet: bark white or sometimes brown.
        F. Lvs. usually truncate or subcordate at base, 5–10 cm. long: strobiles 3–5 cm. long ....**20.** *B. papyrifera*
        FF. Lvs. usually cuneate at base, 3–6 cm. long: strobiles 2.5–3 cm. long.
                                      21. *B. pubescens*
      EE. Wings ½ as broad as nutlet, rarely as broad: bark brown; brts. glandular and pubescent: strobiles 2–2.5 cm. long...................**22.** *B. davurica*
    DD. Bark close, brown: wings as broad as nutlet: lvs. 3–5 cm. long....**23.** *B. fontinalis*
BB. Wings of fr. much narrower than nutlet, rarely as broad: shrubs: lvs. small, 0.5–3, rarely to 5 cm. long, with 2–5 pairs of veins.......................Ser. 4. HUMILES Koch.
  C. Brts. pubescent with long hairs: lvs. 1–3 cm. long.
    D. Lvs. glabrous, acute: brts. glandular and pubescent.................**24.** *B. humilis*
    DD. Lvs. more or less pubescent at least when young.
      E. Brts. glandless, densely pubescent: lvs. obtuse...................**25.** *B. pumila*
      EE. Brts. sparingly glandular and pubescent: lvs. acute or acutish.
                                      26. *B. glandulifera*
  CC. Brts. glabrous or minutely puberulous: lvs. rounded at apex, glabrous.
    D. Brts. densely glandular: lvs. 8–25 mm. long....................**27.** *B. glandulosa*
    DD. Brts. glandless: lvs. 5–15 mm. across, suborbicular.....................**28.** *B. nana*

1. **B. Maximowicziàna** Reg. Tree to 30 m.; bark gray or orange-gray, peeling off in papery flakes; brts. dark reddish brown, glabrous: lvs. broad-ovate, acuminate, deeply cordate at base, 8–14 cm. long, doubly serrate, pubescent on young trees, nearly glabrous on old trees, with 10–12 pairs of veins; petiole 2.5–3.5 cm. long, glabrous or pubescent: strobiles 2–4 in a raceme, 1.5–7 cm. long, cylindric, nodding; bracts with ascending lateral lobes shorter than the middle lobe. B.M.8337(c). K.M.t.25(c). S.I.1:t.23(c). E.P.IV.61:90.

(*B. Maximowiczii* Reg., not Rupr., *B. candelae* Koidz.) Japan. Intr. 1888 Zone V. Very handsome vigorously growing tree with large lvs.

2. **B. lumínifera** Winkl. Tree to 20 m.; bark of old trunks dull yellowish gray, not exfoliating; brts. brown: lvs. ovate, acuminate, subcordate or rounded at base, 6–12 cm. long, sharply and unequally serrate with acuminate teeth, tomentulose or nearly glabrous beneath, with 10–13 pairs of veins; petiole 1–2.5 cm. long: strobiles solitary, 3.5–11 cm. long; bracts with the middle lobe much longer than the reduced lateral lobes. E.P.IV.61:92. Gn. 89:698(h). (*B. Wilsoniana* Schneid., *B. hupehensis* Schneid., *B. alnoides* var. *pyrifolia* Burk., partly.) C. and W. China. Intr. 1901. Zone VI? Ornamental tree with handsome large lvs.

Related species: **B. alnoìdes** Hamilt. Tree to 20 m.; bark brown; young brts. short-pubescent or nearly glabrous: lvs. ovate-oblong, 6–14 cm. long, rounded or cuneate at base, with appressed teeth, nearly glabrous: strobiles several, 3–9 cm. long. E.P.IV.61:90.f.22a-c. I.S.3:t.101. (*B. acuminata* Wall.) Himal., S. W. China. Intr. 1901. Zone VII?

3. **B. Ermáni** Cham. Tree to 20 m.; bark grayish or reddish to nearly white, exfoliating in thin sheets; brts. usually glandular; older brs. orange-colored: lvs. triangular-ovate, 5–10 cm. long, acuminate, truncate or subcordate at base, unequally coarsely serrate, glabrous and usually glandular beneath or pubescent on the veins, with 7–11 pairs of veins: petiole 5–35 mm. long: strobiles erect, oblong, 2–3 cm. long; bracts with linear-oblong lobes, the middle one longer than the ascending lateral ones; wing nearly half as broad as nutlet. S.I.1:t.21(c). E.P.IV.61:63,f.18D-F. K.M.t.26(c). N.K.2:t. 16. (*B. ulmifolia* Reg., not Sieb. & Zucc.) N. E. Asia, Japan. Cult. 1880. Zone V. Ornamental tree with handsome foliage, early leafing.—**B. E. subcordàta** (Reg.) Koidz., var. Brts. less glandular: lvs. more often subcordate, often with 10–14 pairs of veins. Later in leafing than the type. (*B. E.* var. *nipponica* Maxim.) N. E. Asia, Japan. Cult. 1903.

4. **B. ùtilis** D. Don. Tree to 20 m.; dark brown, peeling off in thin flakes; brts. villous and glandular: lvs. ovate to ovate-oblong, 5–8 cm. long, acuminate, rounded to broad-cuneate at base, unequally serrate, subcoriaceous, with 10–14 pairs of veins impressed above, pubescent beneath, otherwise glabrous or slightly hairy; strobiles penduncled, cylindric, about 3 cm. long; bracts pubescent, with oblong lobes, the middle lobe dilated above and usually longer than the ascending lateral ones; wings of fr. about half as broad as nutlet. E.H.4:t.269,f.7. Brandis, Ind. Trees, 622,f.191. G.C.100:316-7 (h). (*B. Bhojpathra* Wall.) Himal. Cult. 1880. Zone VII?—**B. u. Práttii** Burk., var. Bark orange-brown to pale gray: lvs. pubescent below, chiefly on the midrib: bracts of strobiles ciliate; lateral lobes spreading, spatulate. W. China. Intr. 1908. Zone V.

Closely related species: **B. Jacquemontiàna** Spach. Bark white; brts. short-pubescent, slightly glandular: lvs. ovate, 5–7 cm. long, rounded or slightly cuneate at base, doubly serrate, glandular beneath and hairy on the veins, with 7–9 pairs of veins: strobiles on long pubescent stalks; bracts with linear middle lobe. E.H.4:t.270,f.15. (*B. utilis* var. *J.* Henry.) W. Himal. Cult. 1880. Zone VII?

5. **B. albo-sinénsis** Burk. Tree to 30 m.; bark bright orange or orange-red, exfoliating; brts. glabrous, sometimes glandular: lvs. ovate to ovate-oblong, acuminate, rounded or sometimes truncate, rarely subcordate at base, doubly serrate and often slightly lobulate, 4–7 cm. long, dark yellow-green above, light green and glandular beneath, with 10–14 pairs of veins, like the midrib sparsely silky or nearly glabrous; petioles 5–15 mm. long, glabrous or sparingly silky; strobiles cylindric, pendulous, 3–4 cm. long; bracts ciliate, the

middle lobe linear-oblong, much longer than the broad ascending lateral lobes. I.S.3:t.103. (*B. utilis* var. *sinensis* Winkl.) C. and W. China. Intr. 1910. Zone V. Handsome tree; particularly the bark is beautiful.—**B. a. septentrionàlis** Schneid., var. Bark dull orange to orange-brown; brts. more glandular: lvs. oblong-ovate, 5–9 cm. long, more densely silky on the veins beneath and with axillary tufts of hairs. W. China. Intr. 1908.

6. **B. Schmídtii** Reg. Tree to 30 m., with dark gray or nearly black bark broken into thick small plates; brts. pubescent and glandular, finally glabrous, brown; lvs. ovate, acuminate, rounded or broad-cuneate at base, unequally serrate, 4–8 cm. long, light green and resin-dotted beneath, with 9–10 pairs of veins pilose like the midrib; petioles 5–10 mm. long, pilose: strobiles cylindric, upright, 2–3 cm. long; bracts with narrow ciliate lobes, the middle one much longer. S.I.1:t.23(c). N.K.2:t.19. N. E. Asia, Japan. Intr. 1896. Zone V. Handsome tree.

7. **B. Medwedièwi** Reg. Tall tree; brts. rather stout, smooth, pilose while young; buds large, glutinous; lvs. ovate to elliptic or obovate, short-acuminate, usually rounded or sometimes subcordate at base, unequally or nearly doubly serrate, 6–12 cm. long, dark green above and glabrous or sparingly appressed-pubescent, light green below, with 8–11 pairs of veins impressed above glabrous or pilose below: strobiles cylindric-oblong, 2.5–4 cm. long; bracts with linear-one lobes, the middle one nearly twice as long as the ascending lateral ones; wing of fr. about ¼ as broad as nutlet. Gt.36:383, f.95,1–4. S.L.105(h). Transcauc. Intr. 1897. Zone III. Distinct on account of its large and broad lvs.

8. **B. costàta** Trautv. Tree to 30 m.; bark grayish brown, exfoliating in papery flakes; brts. glabrous or finely villous when young, brown: lvs. ovate to oblong-ovate, 5–8 cm. long, long-acuminate, rounded or rarely subcordate at base, finely and doubly serrate with acuminate teeth, firm, sometimes sparingly pubescent above, glandular beneath, with 10–16 pairs of veins pilose beneath at least when young; petiole 8–15 mm. long: strobiles ellipsoid, about 2 cm. long, short-stalked: middle lobe of bracts about twice as long as the ovate or obovate somewhat spreading lateral ones. S.H.1:f.53o–o¹,54k–k¹. (*B. ulmifolia* var. *c.* Reg., *B. ulmifolia* Dipp. partly, not Sieb. & Zucc.) N. E. Asia. Cult. 1880. Zone V. Graceful tree with rather small and narrow lvs.

9. **B. gróssa** Sieb. & Zucc. Japanese Cherry B. Tree to 25 m.; bark dark gray or nearly black, smooth, fissured on old trees; brts. glabrous, with small scattered lenticels, usually yellow-brown at first, chestnut-brown later: lvs. ovate to oblong-ovate, 5–10 cm. long, acuminate, usually subcordate at base, rather coarsely doubly serrate, rather thin, glandular beneath, with 10–15 pairs of veins silky beneath; petiole 1–2.5 cm. long, silky: strobiles nearly sessile, ellipsoid, 1.8–2.5 cm. long; bracts ciliate; middle lobe narrow-oblong, longer than the ovate lateral ones; wings of the fr. often narrowed toward the base. S.I.1:t.22(c). T.M.8:t.6,f.16–19. (*B. carpinifolia* Sieb. & Zucc., *B. ulmifolia* Sieb. & Zucc.) Japan. Intr. 1896. Zone IV. Similar to *B. lenta*.

10. **B. lenta** L. Cherry B. Tree to 25 m.; bark dark reddish brown, close, fissured into thick plates on old trunks; young bark aromatic and of agreeable flavor; brts. slightly pilose when young, soon glabrous and red-brown: lvs. oblong-ovate, 6–12 cm. long, acuminate, usually cordate at base, sharply and doubly serrate, silky-pubescent below when young, with 9–12 pairs of veins; petiole 1.5–2.5 cm. long: strobiles nearly sessile, ovoid-oblong, 2–3.5 cm. long and less than 1.5 cm. thick; bracts about 4 mm. long, glabrous, with short lobes of nearly equal length; wings about as broad as nutlet. S.S.9:t.448. H.T.124,

125(b). Em. 232,t(c). (*B. carpinifolia* Ehrh.—Sweet or Blue B.) Me. to Ala., w. to Ohio. Intr. 1759. Zone III.—Handsome tree pyramidal while young, round-headed in age, attractive in spring with its long and slender pendulous catkins.—**B. l. laciniàta** Rehd., f. Lvs. deeply lobed. Me. spont. Not yet intr. *B. l.* × *pumila* = *B. Jackii;* see under No. 25.

11. **B. lùtea** Michx. Yellow B. Tree to 30 m.; bark yellowish or silvery gray, separating into thin flakes, reddish brown on old trunks; young bark aromatic and somewhat bitter; brts. pilose: lvs. ovate to oblong-ovate, 8–12 cm. long, with long pale hairs on the veins above and below, nearly glabrous at maturity, at the end of vigorous shoots often pubescent below, with 9–11 pairs of veins; petiole slender, 1.5–2.5 cm. long: strobiles short-stalked or subsessile, 2–3 cm. long and 1.5–2 cm. thick; bracts 5–8 mm. long, pubescent with narrow ascending lobes, the middle lobe longer; wing slightly narrower than the nutlet. S.S.9:t.449. Em.235,t(c). H.T.126,127(b). (*B. excelsa* Pursh, not Ait.—Gray B.) Nfd. to Man., s. to the high peaks of Ga. and Tenn. Cult. 1800. Zone III. Similar to the preceding, but not succeeding as well in warmer regions; a valuable timber tree.—**B. l. macrólepis** Fern., var. Bracts of strobiles 8–12 mm. long; fr. usually suborbicular. B.B.1:610,f.1500 and B.T.f.217, as *B. lutea.*—**B. l. alleghaniénsis** (Brit.) Ashe. Bracts similar to those of No. 10, but ciliate. (*B. a.* Brit.) Alleghany Mts. with the type.

B. l. × *glandulifera;* see under No. 26.

12. **B. globispìca** Shirai. Tree to 20 m.; bark nearly white, exfoliating; brts. yellowish gray or grayish brown with prominent lenticels: lvs. orbicular-ovate or broad-ovate, 4–7 cm. long, short-acuminate, usually broad-cuneate or nearly rounded at base, sharply and coarsely unequally serrate, with about 10 pairs of veins pilose beneath like the midrib; petiole 5–15 mm. long, pilose: strobiles globose-ovoid, 2.5–3.5 cm. long; bracts with linear ciliate lobes. S.I.1:t.21(c). E.P.IV.61:68,f.19D–F. C. Japan. Intr. 1896. Zone V.

13. **B. Potaníni** Batal. Shrub to 3 m., with often prostrate brs.; brts. densely villous: lvs. ovate or oblong-ovate, acute or acutish, rounded or broad-cuneate at base, unequally and sharply serrate, with acuminate teeth, 2–4 cm. long, glabrous above, rufous-pubescent chiefly on the nerves beneath, with 10–22 deeply impressed pairs of veins; petioles 2–4 mm. long, hairy: strobiles ellipsoid, 1.5–2 cm. long; bracts ciliate, with obtusish suberect lateral lobes about half as long as the middle lobe; nutlets with narrow wings. (*B. Wilsonii* Bean.) W. China. Intr. 1908. Zone VI? A very distinct shrubby birch easily recognized by its small acutish lvs. with numerous deeply impressed veins.

Related species:. **B. Delavàyi** Franch. Small tree or shrub: lvs. ovate or elliptic-ovate, 2–4 cm. long, acute or obtuse, sparingly silky above, silky on midrib and veins beneath, with 10–14 pairs of impressed veins: strobiles 1.5–2 cm. long; bracts long-ciliate, the lateral lobes acute, more spreading. E.P.IV. 61:f.19m. W. China. Intr. 1910. Zone V.—**B. Forréstii** (W. W. Sm.) Hand.-Mazz. Shrub to 5 m.: lvs. ovate or oblong-ovate, 3–6 cm. long; petiole 2–8 mm. long: strobiles 2–3 cm. long; bracts with the lateral lobes suberect, about ⅓ as long as middle lobe. (*B. Delavayi* var. *F.* W. W. Sm.) W. China. Intr. 1919. Zone V.

14. **B. chinénsis** Maxim. Shrub or small tree with grayish bark; brts. villous while young, later brown: lvs. ovate, acute, rounded at the base, unequally serrate with mucronulate teeth, 2–5, rarely 6 cm. long: pilose beneath along the midrib and base of veins, with 8–10 pairs of veins; petiole 4–8 mm. long: strobiles ellipsoid, 1.5–2 cm. long; bracts with lanceolate, acute ciliate lobes, the lateral ones 2–3 times shorter, sometimes reduced; nutlets

with very narrow wing. E.P.IV.61:f.68G–L. N.K.2,t.20. I.S.3:t.106. (*B. exalata* S. Moore.) N. E. Asia, N. China. Intr. 1906. Zone V.

Into this affinity seems to belong **B. Raddeàna** Trautv. Tree with densely villous and sparingly glandular brts.: lvs. ovate, rounded at base, 3–4.5 cm. long, pubescent along the veins beneath, with 6–7 pairs of not impressed veins; petioles 1–1.5 cm. long: strobiles ellipsoid; wings about as broad as nutlet. Gt.36:385,f.95,5–11. Trav. Acad. Sci. St. Petersb. 12:76,79. Cauc. Intr. ?

15. B. nígra L. RIVER B. Tree to 30 m.; bark reddish brown or silvery gray on younger brs., exfoliating in papery flakes; brts. pubescent: lvs. rhombic-ovate, acute, doubly serrate, 3–8 cm. long, dark green above, whitish below and pubescent when young, finally only on the nerves, with 7–9 slightly impressed pairs of veins; strobiles oblong-cylindric, 2.5–3.5 cm. long; bracts pubescent, with upright, linear-oblong, nearly equal lobes; wing ½ or nearly as broad as nutlet. S.S.9:t.452. G.F.2:593(h). Gn.55:161(h). H.T.122,123(b). (*B. rubra* Michx.—RED B.) Mass. to Fla., w. to Minn. and Kan. Cult. 1736. Zone IV. Graceful tree with an ovoid head and slender brts., remarkable for its torn and ragged bark; it likes moist sandy soil.

Related species: **B. corylifòlia** Reg. Tree to 20 m.; bark pale gray or nearly white; brts. glabrous or nearly so: lvs. elliptic to obovate, 4–6 cm. long, glaucescent below and silky on the nerves, with 10–14 impressed pairs of veins: strobiles subcylindric; bracts pubescent, with narrow upright lobes; nutlet with narrow wings. S.I.2:t.14(c). E.P.IV.61:60. C. Japan. Intr. ?

16. B. populifòlia Marsh. GRAY B. Small tree to 10 m. with usually ascending stem; bark chalky or ashy white, rather close; brts. densely glandular: lvs. triangular-ovate or deltoid, 6–8 cm. long, long-acuminate, truncate at base, coarsely and doubly serrate, glutinous when young, lustrous above; petiole 1.5–3 cm. long, slender: strobiles slender-stalked, cylindric, 1.5–3 cm. long; bracts spreading, puberulent. S.S.9:t.450. H.T.118,119(b). B.T.248(h). G.C.60:302(h). (*B. alba* var. *p.* Spach.—WHITE B.) N. S. and Ont. to Del. Intr. 1750. Zone IV. A small and graceful but short-lived tree; suited for dry and poor and also for boggy soil; useful as nurse for more valuable trees.— **B. p. laciniàta** Loud., var. Lvs. pinnately lobed.—**B. p. purpúrea** Ellw. & Barry. Lvs. purple when young, green at length.—**B. p. péndula** Loud., var. Brs. pendulous.

B. p. × *papyrifera* has been observed in Mass. G.F.8:356.

17. B. péndula Roth. EUROPEAN B. Tree to 20 m.; bark white, exfoliating; brs. usually pendulous, at least in older trees; brts. resinous-glandular: lvs. rhombic-ovate, 3–7 cm. long, acuminate, usually cuneate at base, sometimes truncate, doubly serrate, glutinous when young, glabrous; petiole slender, 2–3 cm. long: strobiles cylindric, 2–3 cm. long, slender-stalked; bracts puberulous or glabrous. H.W.2:20(h),t.15(c). E.P.IV.61:76. B.C.1:498(h). (*B. verrucosa* Ehrh., *B. alba* L. partly.) Eu., Asia Minor. Long cult. Zone II. A handsome but comparatively short-lived tree. Of its vars. var. *dalecarlica* is most often planted; it forms a very graceful tree.—**B. p. purpúrea** (André) Schneid., f. Lvs. purple. R.B.4:t.185(c). (*B. alba atropurpurea* Jaeg. & Beiss.) —**B. p. dalecárlica** (L.) Schneid, f. Lvs. deeply lobed, with irregularly serrate acuminate lobes. R.I.12:t.627,f.1289(c). (*B. laciniata* Wahlb.)—**B. p. trístis** (Beiss.) Schneid., f. Form with slender pendulous brs. forming a round regular head.—**B. p. grácilis** Rehd., var. Habit like that of the preceding form but with laciniate lvs. smaller and more finely dissected than in var. *dalecarlica.* Gt.85:148(h). (*B. alba laciniata gracilis pendula* Hort., *B. a. elegans laciniata* Hort.)—**B. p. Yoùngii** (Th. Moore) Schneid., f. Primary brs. spreading and recurving forming an irregular head; brts. very slender and pendulous.

F.1873:60(h). R.H.1869:136(h). Gn.84:93(h). (*B. p. f. elegans* Winkl., *B. alba pendula Youngii* Th. Moore.)—**B. p. fastigiàta** (Clemenceau) K. Koch. With straight upright brs. forming a columnar head: lvs. very dark green. G.C.41: 151(h). M.G.16:169(h). (*B. p.* var. *pyramidalis* Dipp.)—**B. p. viscòsa** (Bean) Rehd., f. Bushy small tree; young growth very viscid: lvs. crowded, 2–3.5 cm. long, coarsely doubly serrate or lobulate; petiole 1–1.5 cm. long. (*B. verrucosa* var. *dentata viscosa* Bean.)—Of the several geographical vars. the best known is **B. p. oycoviénsis** (Bess.) Schneid., f. Shrubby, with very glandular brts.: lvs. rhombic, much smaller. S.H.1:f.60s. (*B. o.* Bess.)

　　B. p. × *papyrifera* = **B. Koèhnei** Schneid. Somewhat doubtful. Cult. 1905.
—*B. p.* × *pubescens* = **B. auràta** Borkh. (*B. hybrida* Bechst.) Spont. in Eu.—
B. p. × *nana* = *B. fennica;* see under No. 28.

　　18. **B. mandshùrica** (Reg.) Nakai. Tree to 20 m.; bark white; brts. resinous-glandular: lvs. ovate or deltoid-ovate, 4–6 cm. long, acuminate, truncate to broad-cuneate at base, unequally serrate, paler and glabrous beneath or sometimes with axillary tufts of hairs, glandular-dotted: petioles 1–2.5 cm. long; strobiles cylindric, pendulous, puberulous; middle lobe of bracts triangular, shorter or about as long as the spreading broad lateral lobes; wings as broad or broader than nutlet. N.K.2:t.13. I.S.3:t.108. (*B. alba* ssp. *mandshurica* Reg. *B. japonica* var. *m.* Winkl.) Mandsh., Korea. Intr. ?—**B. m. kamtschática** (Reg.) Rehd., var. Lvs. thinner, broad-ovate to triangular-ovate, 5–7.5 cm. long, unequally serrate-dentate and slightly lobulate, with axillary tufts of hairs beneath, rarely slightly pilose on the veins. S.I.2:t.11 (c). Bull. Soc. Nat. Moscou,38,2:t.7,f.16–20. (*B. alba* var. *k.* Reg., *B. japonica* var. *k.* Winkl.) N. E. Asia, Jap. Cult. 1917. Zone II?—**B. m. szechuànica** (Schneid.) Rehd., var. Tree with wide-spreading brs.: lvs. ovate or rhombic-ovate, rounded to broad-cuneate at base, short-acuminate, unequally dentate-serrate, dull green above, densely glandular-dotted beneath and glabrous or slightly pilose. W. China. Intr. 1872 and 1908. Zone V. Remaining green until late in fall.—**B. m. japónica** (Miq.) Rehd., var. Lvs. broad-ovate to triangular-ovate, 4–7.5 cm. long, to 6 cm. broad, truncate or subcordate at base, puberulous or glabrous below, usually with axillary tufts of hairs. K.M.t.62q. (c). S.H.1:f.62q. Gn.89:719(h). (*B. japonica* Winkl., not Thunb., *B. pendula* var. *Tauschii* Rehd., *B. Tauschii* Koidz., *B. latifolia* Komar., not Tausch.) Japan, N. China. Intr. 1902. Zone IV.

　　19. **B. coerúlea-grándis** Blanchard. Tree to 10 m.; brts. glabrous; slightly resinous-glandular: lvs. ovate or triangular-ovate, acuminate, usually rounded or truncate at base, 6–8 cm. long, sharply and usually doubly serrate, bluish green above, yellowish green beneath and slightly hairy on the veins at first, soon glabrous or nearly so; petioles 1.5–2.5 cm. long; strobiles cylindric, pubescent, 2.5–3 cm. long and 8–10 mm. thick; lateral lobes of bracts spreading, as long or slightly longer than middle lobe. S.M.211a. (*B. coerulea* var. *Blanchardi* Sarg.) N. S. to Que., Vt. and N. H. Intr. 1905. Zone II?

　　B. c. × *populifolia* = **B. coerúlea** Blanchard. Lvs. usually broad-cuneate at base, slightly smaller: strobiles to 3.5 cm. long, slenderer. S.M.211. N. S. to Vt. Intr. 1905.

　　20. **B. fontinàlis** Sarg. Small shrubby tree, usually forming clumps, occasionally to 12 m.; bark close, reddish brown; brts. slender, densely resinous-glandular: lvs. broad-ovate, 2–4 cm. long, acute, usually rounded at base, sharply and often doubly serrate, bright green, glandular-dotted beneath, with 3–4 pairs of veins; petiole 5–15 mm. long: strobiles 2–3 cm. long, 5–10 mm. thick; bracts pubescent, the lateral lobes ascending, shorter than the narrow middle lobe, all acute. S.S.9:t.453. N.S.1:t.8(c). (*B. occidentalis*

Hook., in part, *B. rhombifolia* Nutt., not Tausch.) Alaska to Ore. and through
the Rocky Mts. to Colo. Intr. 1874. Zone IV. Graceful tree with slender
spreading and pendulous brs.—**B. f. Pìperi** (Brit.) Sarg., var. Small tree:
lvs. ovate or elliptic, 5–6 cm. long, usually broad-cuneate at base, pubescent
on the veins beneath when young: strobiles cylindric, 3–5 cm. long; lateral
lobes of bracts broad and spreading, auricled at base. S.M.219. B.T.255.
(*B. P.* Brit.) Wash., Mont. Intr. 1903. Zone V.

    21. **B. papyrífera** Marsh. CANOE B. Tree to 30 or occasionally 40 m.;
bark white, exfoliating; brts. pubescent when young and often slightly glandular: lvs. ovate to narrow-ovate, 4–10 cm. long, acuminate, cuneate or rounded
at base, coarsely and usually doubly serrate, glabrous above, pubescent on the
nerves beneath or nearly glabrous; petiole stout, 1.5–3 cm. long, pubescent:
strobiles cylindric, 3–5 cm. long, slender-stalked, usually pendulous; bracts
pubescent, with suberect or spreading lateral lobes slightly shorter than the
middle lobe. S.S.9:t.451. Em.238,t. H.T.121(b). W.A.26,t(h). M.G.29:145
(h). (*B. papyracea* Ait., *B. latifolia* Tausch.—PAPER B., WHITE B.) Lab. to
B. C. and Wash., s. to Pa. and Mich., Neb. and Mont. Intr. 1750. Zone II.
Handsome tree, often planted in the N. E. States; the vars. occasionally seen
in collections.—**B. p. cordifòlia** (Reg.) Fern., var. Small tree with usually
white bark, sometimes shrubby; brts. pubescent while young: lvs. broad-
ovate, subcordate at base, doubly serrate, pilose on the veins beneath. S.S.14:
t.724. (*B. c.* Reg.) Lab. to Minn. Intr. 1876.—**B. p. mínor** (Tuckerm.) Wats.
& Coult., var. Shrub or low bushy tree: lvs. elliptic-ovate or ovate, truncate
or broad-cuneate at base, 1.5–4 cm. long, glabrous beneath, glutinous: strobiles 1.5–3 cm. long, 5–10 mm. thick. Am. Jour. Sci. 14:t.5,f.9–12. Lab. to
N. H. and Minn. Intr. 1904.—**B. p. occidentàlis** (Hook.) Sarg., var. Large
tree to 40 m.; bark orange to dark brown, sometimes nearly white: lvs. ovate
or broad-ovate, acute or acuminate, rounded or truncate at base, doubly serrate, bright or dark green, rather thin: strobiles 3–4 cm. long; lateral lobes
of bracts spreading, much shorter than the middle lobe. S.S.14:t.725. A.I.1:
512. (Var. *Lyalliana* Henry, *B. Lyalliana* Koehne, *B. o.* Hook., in part.) B. C.
and Wash. to Mont. Intr. about 1885.—**B. p. kenáica** (Evans) Henry, var.
Bark usually white, tinged with orange and brown; brts. minutely pubescent
and slightly or not glandular: lvs. usually cuneate at base, about 5 cm. long:
strobiles shorter; bracts glabrous, ciliate. S.S.14:t.723. (*B. k.* Evans.) Coast
of Alaska. Intr. 1897.—**B. p. subcordàta** (Rydb.) Sarg., var. Small tree with
silvery gray purple-tinged bark; brts. glabrous or puberulent, rarely slightly
glandular: lvs. ovate or broad-ovate, acute, rounded to cordate at base, glabrous, rarely slightly pubescent near base beneath, unequally dentate-serrate;
bracts of strobiles pubescent and ciliate. Bull. Torr. Bot. Club, 36:436. (*B. s.*
Rydb.) B. C. and Alb. to Idaho and Mont. Intr. 1918.—**B. p. neoalaskàna**
(Sarg.) Raup, var. Bark reddish brown to dull white; brts. densely resinous-
glandular: lvs. triangular-ovate, usually truncate at base: strobiles 3–3.5 cm.
long; bracts glabrous or puberulent; the rhombic lateral lobes shorter than
the middle lobe. S.S.14:t.726. (*B. n.* Sarg., *B. alascana* Sarg., not Lesquereux.)
Sask. to Alaska. Intr. 1905.

    B. p. × *populifolia;* see under No. 16.—*B. p.* × *pendula;* see under No. 17.
—*B. p.* × *pumila;* see under No. 25.—*B. p.* × *glandulifera;* see under No. 26.

    22. **B. pubéscens** Ehrh. Tree to 20 m.; with usually ascending or spread-
ing brs.; bark white, exfoliating, dark and rough at base of old trunks; young
brts. densely pubescent, glandless: lvs. rhombic-ovate or ovate, 3–5 cm. long,
acute, truncate or cuneate at base, usually unequally doubly serrate, pubes-

cent beneath, at least while young, often with axillary tufts of hairs; petiole pubescent, often finally glabrous, 1–2.5 cm. long; strobiles cylindric, 2.5–3 cm. long; bracts puberulous, lateral lobes suberect to recurved, slightly shorter than the middle lobe; wing as broad or twice as broad as nutlet. R.I.12:t.625 (c). H.W.2:24,25(h). (*B. alba* L. in part, *B. odorata* Bechst.) N. and C. Eu. to Siberia. Cult. 1789. Zone II. A very variable species with many geographical vars. and forms which are scarcely cult. in this country, except perhaps **B. p. urticifòlia** (Loud.) Schelle. Lvs. coarsely doubly serrate or lobulate, dark green and slightly pubescent above, more densely beneath: wing much narrower than nutlet. S.H.1:f.64m-m⁴. (*B. u.* Reg., *B. alba* var. *u.* Loud.) Orig. unknown; said to have been found wild in Sweden. Cult. 1836.

B. p. × *pendula;* see under No. 17.—*B. p.* × *nana;* see under No. 28.

Related species: **B. turkestànica** Litvin. Tree with yellowish or whitish bark; brts. pubescent and resinous-glandular: lvs. ovate, cuneate to rounded at base, pubescent when young, later only beneath along the veins, without axillary tufts: strobiles about 2.5 cm. long; lateral lobes of bracts suberect, about ½ as long as central lobe. Trav. Acad. Sci. St. Petersb. 12:t.12,f.5. Turkest. Intr. ?—**B. microphýlla** Bge. Tree; bark yellowish; brts. pubescent and densely glandular: lvs. rhombic-ovate to rhombic-obovate, 2–5 cm. long, cuneate at base, acute, coarsely dentate, almost glabrous and glandular beneath: lateral lobes of bracts ascending, slightly shorter than middle lobe. Trav. Acad. Sci. St. Petersb. 12:t.12,f.12. C. Asia. Intr. ? Plants seen under this name in cult. belonged to *B. Middendorffii.*—Here may be also mentioned: **B. coriàcea** Gunnarsson. Tree or shrub; bark gray or grayish brown; brts. glabrous, often minutely verrucose: lvs. broad-elliptic or ovate, rounded at base, subglabrous, thickish, reticulate beneath: middle lobe of bracts scarcely longer than lateral loves. Gunnarsson, Monog. Scand. Betul. t.1,f.3;t.4,f.3. Scand.—**B. concínna** Gunnarsson. Tree or shrub; bark blackish brown: lvs. elliptic-ovate, acute, equally serrate, slightly reticulate beneath and pilose on the veins: middle lobe of bract distinctly longer than lateral lobes. Gunnarsson, t.1,f.2;t.4,f.2. Scand.

23. **B. davùrica** Pall. Tree to 20 m.; bark purplish brown, exfoliating in thin and small flakes; brts. glandular and pubescent: lvs. rhombic-ovate or narrow-ovate, 4–8 cm. long, acute or acuminate, cuneate, unequally dentate-serrate, gland-dotted beneath, with 6–8 pairs of veins pubescent on both sides, finally glabrescent above; petiole 5–15 mm. long, slightly pilose: strobiles 2–2.5 cm. long: bracts glabrous, lustrous, firm, middle lobe triangular, about as long as the lateral rounded and spreading lobes; wing of fr. about half as broad as nutlet. S.H.1:f.60p. N.K.2:t.14. I.S.3:T.107. Gn.89:719(h). (*B. Maximowiczii* Rupr., *B. Maackii* Rupr., *B. wutaica* Mayr.) N. E. Asia, Japan. Intr. 1883. Zone V or IV? Tree with wide-spreading brs. and peculiar bark similar to that of the Red Birch.

24. **B. húmilis** Schrank. Shrub to 3 m.; brts. resinous-glandular and hairy: lvs. ovate or elliptic, rarely obovate, 1.5–3 cm. long, acute or acutish, cuneate, rarely rounded at base and apex, irregularly dentate-serrate, glabrous and green on both sides, with 4–5 pairs of veins; petiole 1–4 mm. long: strobiles upright, oblong, 5–15 mm. long; bracts ciliate, middle lobe usually thinner and larger than the lateral lobes; wing about half as broad as nutlet. R.I.12:f.1279 (c). H.W.2:f.122a-d. S.H.1:f.55a-e. Eu., N. Asia to Altai Mts. Intr. 1818. Zone II. Small-leaved shrub, rarely cult.

Closely related species: **B. fruticòsa** Pall. Brts. often less glandular: lvs. 2–5 cm. long, more distinctly serrate with finer serrations, with 5–6 pairs of veins, slightly pubescent on the midrib beneath: wing ½–¾ as broad as nutlet. S.H.1:f.56d-e,57b-b¹. N.K.2:t.15. (*B. Gmelini* Bge.) N. E. Asia to Altai, N. China. Cult. 1876. Zone IV.—**B. Middendórffii** Trautv. & Mey. Brts. resinous-glandular and finely pubescent when young or quite glabrous and smooth: lvs. orbicular-ovate or broad-ovate, 2–4 cm. long, rounded or acutish at apex, usually rounded at base, coarsely serrate, pale yellow green beneath; strobiles 1.5–2 cm.

long; wing about as broad as nutlet. Middendorff, Reise, I.1:t.21. N. E. Asia. Cult. 1904. Zone III?

25. B. pùmila L. Low B. Shrub to 5 m.; brts. densely tomentose when young, not glandular: lvs. suborbicular to broad-elliptic or obovate, 1–3 cm. long, obtuse or acutish, rounded or broad-cuneate at base, coarsely crenate-dentate, usually densely pubescent beneath while young and grayish white and reticulate-veined, often becoming quite glabrous, with 4–6 pairs of veins: strobiles cylindric-oblong, upright, stalked, 1.5–2.5 cm. long; bracts pubescent, lateral lobes spreading, shorter than the middle lobe; wing about half as broad as nutlet. B.B.1:511. E.P.IV.61:f.20g-m. (*B. excelsa* Ait.) Nfd. to Assina., s. to N. J., Ohio and Minn. Intr. 1762. Zone II.

B. p. × *lenta* = **B. Jáckii** Schneid. Bark aromatic: lvs. ovate or elliptic-ovate, 3–5 cm. long, glabrate, with about 7 pairs of veins: strobiles about 1.2 cm. thick. G.F.8:243. Orig. 1888.—*B. p.* × *papyrifera* = **B. Borggreveàna** Zabel ex Winkl. Bark gray; brts. pubescent: lvs. ovate or rhombic-ovate, broad-cuneate or rounded at base, coarsely serrate, slightly pubescent and glandular-punctate beneath; petiole 1–1.5 cm. long: bracts similar to No. 25. S.H.1:f. 59r²-r³. (*B. excelsa* auth., not Ait.) Cult. 1872.

26. B. glandulífera (Reg.) Butler. Shrub to 2 m.; brts. slender, reddish brown, slightly resinous-glandular and pilose: lvs. obovate or elliptic to suborbicular, 2–5 cm. long, usually acute, cuneate, serrate or crenate-serrate, pubescent on the veins beneath when young, reticulate and resin-dotted: strobiles 1.5–2 cm. long, cylindric; lateral lobes of bracts ascending, shorter than the obtuse middle lobe. Bull. Torr. Bot. Club, 36:424,f.2. A.I.1:511. (*B. pumila* var. *g.* Reg.) Ont. and Mich. to B. C. Intr.?

B. g. × *lutea* = **B. Purpusii** Schneid. Lvs. usually oblong-ovate, 2.5–5 cm. long, pubescent beneath, with 7–9 pairs of veins: strobiles 1.5–2 cm. long; lateral lobes ascending, about ½ as long as middle lobe. S.H.1:f.58a-a¹. Cult. 1900.— *B. g.* × *papyrifera* = **B. Sandbérgi** Brit. Tree or shrub; bark gray or yellowish gray; brts. pubescent: lvs. rhombic-ovate, cuneate or broad-cuneate at base, slightly hairy beneath: strobiles 2–2.5 cm. long. B.T.256. Minn. Intr. 1914. Zone II?

Closely related species: **B. Hàllii** Howell. Brts. finely or velvety-pubescent and sparingly glandular: lvs. obovate, rounded at apex, cuneate, crenate-serrulate, bright green, glabrous and resin-dotted beneath: lobes of bracts obtuse, of about equal length, the lateral suberect. Bull. Torr. Bot. Club, 36:428,f.6. (*B. pumila* var. *fastigiata* Rehd.) Ore. to Alaska and Yukon. Intr. about 1898. Zone II.

27. B. glandulòsa Michx. Shrub to 2 m.; brts. resinous-glandular, glabrous: lvs. suborbicular to broad-elliptic or obovate, 8–25 mm. long, rounded at ends or broad-cuneate at base, crenate-dentate, pale and gland-dotted beneath, glabrous; petiole 3–8 mm. long: strobiles 1.5–2 cm. long; bracts with nearly equal lobes, the lateral suberect; nutlets with very narrow wings. B.B. 1:510. Nfd. to Alaska, s. to N. Y., Mich., Colo. and Calif. Intr. 1880. Zone II.

28. B. nàna L. Low spreading much-branched shrub, to 0.5 m.; brts. velutinous, later often nearly glabrous, not glandular: lvs. orbicular to broad-obovate, rounded or truncate at apex, 5–15 mm. long, crenate, glutinous when young and slightly pubescent beneath; petiole very short: strobiles nearly sessile, 7–10 mm. long; bracts with rather narrow nearly equal lobes, the lateral ascending; nutlets with very narrow wings. R.I.12:f.1278(c). E.P.IV. 61:f.20d-f. N. Asia, N. and C. Eu., Greenl., Alaska. Cult. 1789. Zone II.— **B. n. Michaùxii** (Spach) Reg., var. Lvs. cuneate-flabellate, deeply crenate: strobiles with oblong-lanceolate, entire bracts or the lower ones 3-lobed. B.B. 1:612. E.P.IV.61:f.20a-c. (*B. M.* Spach.) Lab., Nfd. Intr. ?

B. n. × *pubescens* = **B. intermedia** Thomas. Shrub to 3 m.: lvs. suborbicular to ovate, 8–25 mm. long. S.H.1:f.58e-e²,59o-p¹. (*B. alpestris* Fries.) Spont. in Eu. Cult. 1895.—*B. n.* × *pendula* = **B. fénnica** Doerfl. Similar to *B. intermedia*, but brts. glandular. S.H.1:f.58g-g⁴,591-n. Spont. in Eu. Cult. ?

2. **ALNUS** B. Ehrh. ALDER. Deciduous trees or shrubs; buds stalked and with 2 or 3 subsequent scales or sessile and with imbricate scales: lvs. usually serrate or dentate: staminate catkins elongated, each bract with 3 fls., each fl. with a 4-parted calyx and 4, rarely 1–3, undivided stamens; pistillate catkins short, each bract with 2 fls. without calyx; the bractlets adnate to the bract; fr. a minute compressed, usually narrowly winged nutlet, in pairs in the axils of woody, 5-lobed or truncate persistent scales forming an ellipsoid or ovoid strobile. The fls. appear before or with the lvs.; the fr. ripens in autumn. (The ancient Latin name of the alder.) About 30 species in the northern hemisphere, in America s. to Peru.—Ornamental trees or shrubs; some species valued as timber trees. Mostly moisture-loving and essentially plants of cool climates.

   A. Buds sessile, with 3–6 imbricate, rarely with 2 unequal scales: pistillate catkins terminal enclosed during the winter in the bud: fr. with broad membranous wing: fls. with the lvs. (Subgen. ALNASTER Endl.)
     B. Lvs. with 12–26 pairs of veins.
       c. Strobiles 1–2: lvs. with 12–18 pairs of veins: brts. grayish or yellowish brown.
                                 1. *A. firma*
       cc. Strobiles 2–5, pendulous: lvs. with 18–26 pairs of veins: brts. dark red-brown.
                               2. *A. pendula*
     BB. Lvs. with 5–10 pairs of veins, glutinous when young.
       c. Lvs. not lobed, finely serrulate.
         d. Lvs. broad-cuneate or rounded at base, usually pilose on the midrib..3. *A. viridis*
         dd. Lvs. rounded or subcordate at base...................................4. *A. crispa*
       cc. Lvs. distinctly lobulate, thin, glabrous...................................5. *A. sinuata*
   AA. Buds stipitate, with 2 or 3 subequal scales. (Subgen. ALNUS Endl.)
     B. Aments appearing in autumn at the end of the brts.
       c. Lvs. plicate in bud, usually lobulate, with straight veins: pistillate catkins several from each bud.
         d. Lvs. green beneath, glutinous while young.
            e. Lvs. serrulate, not or scarcely lobulate: strobiles partly sessile.....6. *A. rugosa*
           ee. Lvs. lobulate, dentate or denticulate.
              f. Strobiles all stalked: lvs. obtuse or acutish, coarsely and doubly dentate.
                               7. *A. glutinosa*
              ff. Upper strobile sessile: lvs. acute or acuminate, lobulate and doubly serrate.
                                 8. *A. tenuifolia*
         dd. Lvs. glaucous beneath or glaucescent.
            e. Lvs. crenate-serrate and lobulate, with revolute margin; petioles and veins orange-colored: brts. glabrous.......................................9. *A. rubra*
           ee. Lvs. not revolute on the margin sharply and doubly serrate.
              f. Lvs. strongly lobed, 8–14 cm. long, hirsute on the midrib beneath or glabrous.
                             10. *A. hirsuta*
              ff. Lvs. not strongly lobed except on shoots, usually smaller, tomentose or nearly glabrous beneath ....11. *A. incana*
       cc. Leaves not plicate in bud, irregularly and rather remotely serrate, not lobulate; veins arching: pistillate catkins solitary or 2–3 from each bud.
         d. Fls. opening in spring.
            e. Lvs. rounded to cordate at base.
              f. Lvs. suborbicular to ovate, cordate at base, appressed-crenate-serrate: brts. and lvs. glabrous...12. *A. cordata*
              ff. Lvs. ovate to oblong-ovate, coarsely and unequally serrate: brts. and lvs. pubescent ....13. *A. subcordata*
           ee. Lvs. cuneate, rarely nearly rounded at base, oblong-ovate to oblong-lanceolate.
                              14. *A. japonica*
         dd. Fls. opening in autumn: lvs. elliptic or obovate to oblong, cuneate at base.
                             15. *A. maritima*
     BB. Aments of both sexes solitary in the axils of lvs.; pistillate catkins long-stalked; staminate fls. naked. (Subgen. CREMASTOGYNE Winkl.)..............16. *A. cremastogyne*

1. **A. fírma** Sieb. & Zucc. Shrub or small tree to 3 m.; brts. glabrous; lvs. ovate-oblong, 5–12 cm. long, acuminate, usually rounded at base, sharply and irregularly serrate, pubescent on the veins beneath; strobiles about 2 cm. long, on stalks to 2.5 cm. long. S.I.2:t.12(c). (*A. Sieboldiana* Matsum.) Japan. Not yet intr. and probably tenderer than the var. Ornamental shrub or small tree with handsome foliage remaining green until late in autumn —**A. f. hirtélla** Franch. & Sav., var. Shrub or tree to 10 m.; brts. pubescent;

lvs. ovate-oblong to ovate-lanceolate. E.H.4:t.268,f.2. S.H.1:f.66n–n[1],67b–c[1]. G.C.75:255. (*A. yasha* Matsum., *A. firma* var. *yasha* Winkl.) Japan. Intr. 1892. Zone V.

2. **A. péndula** Matsum. Shrub or small tree to 8 m.; young brts. pubescent, soon glabrous: lvs. oblong-lanceolate, 5–12 cm. long, acuminate, irregularly and sharply serrate, pubescent on the veins beneath, finally nearly glabrous: strobiles 8–15 mm. long, slender-stalked, in nodding racemes 3–6 cm. long. S.I.2:t.12(c). M.K.T.31(c). S.H.1:f.66o,67d–d[2]. (*A. firma* var. *multinervis* Reg., *A. m.* (Reg.) Callier.) Japan. Intr. 1862. Zone V. Similar to the preceding species, but smaller and more graceful.

3. **A. víridis** DC. European Green A. Shrub to 2 m.; brts. pubescent when young, finally gray or red-brown: lvs. ovate or elliptic, sometimes roundish ovate, 2.5–6 cm. long, acute, usually broad-cuneate, pale green and glabrous beneath or pubescent on the veins, rarely on the whole under side: pistillate catkins on glabrous or puberulous stalks: strobiles about 1 cm. long, slender-stalked, racemose. H.W.2:t.14(c). L.B.12:1141(c). R.I.12:t.678(c). (*A. Alnobetula* Hartig, *A. ovata* Lodd.) Mts. of Eu. Intr. 1820. Zone III. Smaller in every part than the following species and not as handsome.

4. **A. críspa** (Ait.) Pursh. American Green A. Shrub to 3 m., sometimes decumbent; young brts. glabrous or sparingly pubescent: lvs. ovate or broad-elliptic, 3–8 cm. long, acute, usually rounded or slightly subcordate at base, finely and closely serrulate or biserrulate, glabrous beneath or slightly pubescent on the veins, glutinous while young: stalks of pistillate catkins pubescent; filaments longer than perianth; anther-cells connate their whole length: strobiles 3–6, racemose, 1–1.5 cm. long, on stalks 5–15 mm. long. B.B.1:612. (*A. Mitchelliana* M. A. Curt., *A. Alnobetula* var. *crispa* (Ait.) Winkl., *A. viridis* of Am. auth.) Lab. to N. C. in the mts. Intr. 1782. Zone II. Shrub with bright green lvs. exhaling an aromatic fragrance when young; prefers cool and moist situations.—**A. c. móllis** (Fern.) Fern., var. Young brts. and lvs. beneath pubescent; lvs. usually larger; strobiles to 2 cm. long. G.C.77:41. (*A. m.* Fern.) Nfd. to Lake Winnipeg, s. to Mass. Intr. 1897.

5. **A. sinuàta** (Reg.) Rydb. Shrub or small tree to 12 m.; brts. glandular and puberulous when young: lvs. ovate, 6–12 cm. long, acute, rounded to broad-cuneate at base, usually lobulate, sharply serrate, light green and glabrous beneath or villous along the midrib; anther-cells free at ends and spreading; filaments shorter than perianth: strobiles about 1.5 cm. long, 3–6 in sometimes leafy racemes, on slender peduncles to 2 cm. long. S.S.14:t.727. (*A. sitchensis* Sarg., *A. Alnobetula* var. *stenophylla* Winkl.) Alaska to n. Calif. Intr. 1903. Zone II. Shrub with rather large bright green lvs.; like the preceding species it prefers cool and moist situations.

Closely related species: **A. fruticòsa** Rupr. Lvs. ovate, sometimes broad-cuneate at base, glabrous beneath; filaments shorter than perianth. S.H.1:f. 66h. (*A. viridis* var. *sibirica* Reg.) N. E. Asia. Cult. 1888. Zone IV.—**A. Maximowíczii** Callier. Lvs. abruptly short-acuminate, truncate or cordate at base; anther-cells free at base and apex. M.K.t.30(c). S.H.1:f.66k. M.D.1918: t.9. (*A. viridis* var. *sibirica* Reg. in part.) Japan. Intr. 1914. Zone V.

6. **A. rugòsa** (Du Roi) Spreng. Smooth A. Shrub or small tree to 8 m.; brts. nearly glabrous or pubescent, rarely densely villous; stipules oval: lvs. elliptic to obovate, 5–10 cm. long, acute or obtuse, cuneate, rarely elliptic-ovate and rounded at base, finely and nearly regularly serrulate, green beneath and glabrous or pubescent on the veins, rarely pubescent all over: strobiles 4–10, the upper sessile, the lower short-stalked, ovoid, 1–1.5 cm. long; nutlet ovate. Add 7:t.237(c). Em.248,t(c). B.B.1:613. (*A. serrulata* Willd.) Me.

to Minn., s. to Fla. and Tex. Cult. 1769. Zone IV.—A tall rather coarse shrub adapted for planting along water-courses and banks of ponds.

A. r. × *incana* = **A. Aschersoniàna** Callier. Differs chiefly in the more pointed, rather coarsely serrate lvs. usually yellowish pubescent beneath and often slightly glaucous. S.H.1:f.72b-c. Occasionally among the parents, first observed in Eu.—*A. r.* × *glutinosa* = **A. silesíaca** Fiek. S.H.1:f.69r-r[1]. Observed in Eu.

7. **A. glutinòsa** (L.) Gaertn. BLACK A. Tree to 25 m.; young growth very glutinous; brts. usually glabrous; stipules ovate to lanceolate; lvs. oval or obovate to suborbicular, 4–10 cm. long, rounded or emarginate at apex, usually broad-cuneate, coarsely and doubly dentate, usually nearly glabrous except axillary tufts of hairs beneath, with 5–6 pairs of veins: strobiles 3–5, distinctly stalked. H.W.2:12(h),t.12(c). H.T.130. G.C.II.2:294,295(h). E.H. 4:t.252–3(h). (*A. vulgaris* Hill, *A. rotundifolia* Mill., *A. communis* Desf.) Eu. to Cauc. and Siberia, N. Afr.; occasionally escaped in N. E. Am. Long cult. Zone III. Tree with an ovoid or oblong head and very dark foliage remaining green until late in autumn; growing well in swampy soil. Besides No. 10 silviculturally the most important Alder.—**A. g. aùrea** Versch., var. Lvs. yellow. I.H.13:t.490(c). Cult. 1866.—**A. g. laciniàta** (Leske) Willd., var. Lvs. deeply and regularly lobed about halfway to the middle, with ovate to lanceolate, dentate or nearly entire lobes. Gt.37:585. E.H.4:t.268,f.7. S.H. f.69o–o[1]. Cult. 1750.—**A. g. imperiàlis** (Lem.) Kirchn., f. Similar to the preceding, but lvs. smaller, more deeply lobed, with linear nearly entire lobes. I.H.6:97,t. Gt.37:585. Orig. 1853.—**A. g. quercifòlia** Loud., var. Lvs. deeply lobed, with irregular ovate lobes. S.H.1:f.69m.—**A. g. sorbifòlia** Dipp., f. Similar to the preceding, but lvs. smaller with broader partly overlapping lobes. S.H.1f.69n.—**A. g. incìsa** Willd. Lvs. small, deeply lobed or pinnate, with broad rounded dentate lobes. E.H.4:t.268,f.10. S.H.1:f.69p–p′. (*A. g.* var. *oxyacanthifolia* Loud.) Cult. 1800.—**A. g. rubrinérvia** Dipp., f. Lvs. lustrous, dark green, with red veins and petioles; a very handsome form of vigorous growth and broad pyramidal habit. Intr. about 1870.—**A. g. pyramidàlis** Dipp., f. Habit narrow-pyramidal: lvs. dark green, rather short and broad. K.B.1929:t.12(h). (*A. g. pyramidalis Birkiana* Hort.) Cult. 1880.—Besides these forms the following geographical vars. are sometimes cult.: **A. g. denticulàta** (C. A. Mey.) Ledeb., var. Lvs. broad-elliptic, obtuse or short-acute, denticulate, not or slightly lobed except on vigorous shoots. M.D.1918:t.20. S.H.1:f.691. Cauc., W. Asia, Italy, N. Afr. Intr. 1759?—**A. g. barbàta** (C. A. Mey.) Ledeb., var. Lvs. ovate-oblong, denticulate, beneath like the petioles pubescent. (*A. b.* C. A. Mey.) Cauc. Cult. 1870.

A. g. × *incana* = **A. hýbrida** A. Br. Not uncommon in Eu. with the parents. R.I.12:f.1292(c). S.H.1:f.69s-s′. (*A. pubescens* Tausch, not Sartorelli, *A. ambigua* Beck, *A. spuria* Callier.)—*A. g.* × *rugosa;* see under No. 6—*A. g.* × *cordata;* see under No. 12.

8. **A. tenuifòlia** Nutt. Tree, occasionally to 10 m.; brts. slightly pubescent at first, finally light brown or often red; buds red; stipules ovate to lanceolate: lvs. ovate to ovate-oblong, 4–10 cm. long, rounded or less often subcordate or broad-cuneate at base, lobulate with obtuse lobes and usually obtusely toothed, usually yellowish green, glabrous or slightly pubescent and light green or sometimes glaucescent beneath; petiole 1.5–2.5 cm. long: stamens 4: strobiles 3–9, ovoid-oblong, 1–1.5 cm. long, on peduncles 3–8 mm. long. S.S.9: t.455. (*A. incana* var. *virescens* S. Wats., *A. occidentalis* Dipp.) B. C. to L. Calif., e. to Sask., Colo. and N. Mex. Cult. 1880. Zone V. Small shrubby tree with slender brs. forming an ovoid round-topped head. Its more n. form with

larger more sharply toothed lvs. slightly glaucescent beneath has been distinguished as var. **occidentális** (Dipp.) Callier (*A. o.* Dipp.) Intr. 1891.

Related species: **A. rhombifòlia** Nutt. Tree to 25 m.: lvs. ovate to elliptic, acute or obtuse, usually finely serrate, not lobulate, pubescent when young, later only below: stamens 2–3. S.S.9:t.456. Wash. to Idaho and S. Calif. Intr. about 1885. Zone V.—**A. oblongifòlia** Torr. Tree to 10 m.: lvs. oblong-ovate to ovate-lanceolate, 4–8 cm. long, usually acute, cuneate, sharply and usually doubly serrate, not lobulate or slightly so, glabrous or puberulous below: stamens 2–3; strobiles 1.5–2.5 cm. long. S.S.9:t.457 (as *A. acuminata*). N. Mex. and Ariz. to n. Mex. Intr. ? Zone VII?

9. **A. rúbra** Bong. Tree to 20 m.; bark light gray, nearly smooth; brts. tomentulose at first, soon glabrous, finally dark red; buds red, scurfy: lvs. ovate to oblong-ovate, 7–12 cm. long, acute, broad-cuneate or truncate at base, lobulate and crenate-serrate with slightly revolute margin, at maturity glabrous above, grayish green or glaucous beneath and glabrous or with short rusty pubescence, with 12–15 pairs of veins; petiole and nerves red or yellow: strobiles 6–8, ovoid to ovoid-oblong, 1.5–2.5 cm. long, on stout orange-colored stalks or sessile. N.S.1:t.9(c). S.S.9:t.454. (*A. oregana* Nutt.) Alaska to Calif., e. to Idaho. Cult. 1884. Zone IV.—**A. r. pinnatisécta** Starker, var. Lvs. deeply pinnately lobed, with 5–7 pairs of oblong-ovate to oblong lobes Jour. For. 37:416. Intr. 1939.

10. **A. hirsùta** (Spach) Rupr. Tree to 20 m.; brts. villous at first, later glabrous; buds pubescent: lvs. broad-ovate to elliptic-ovate, 8–14 cm. long, acute, rounded at base, coarsely doubly serrate and shallowly lobed, dark green above, glaucous and rufous-pubescent beneath; petiole 2–4 cm. long, pubescent: strobiles usually 3–4, ellipsoid to oblong-ovoid, 1.5–2 cm. long, short-stalked or sessile. S.I.2:t.3(c). M.K.t.29(c). G.F.10:473. S.L.82(h). (*A. tinctoria* Sarg., *A. incana* var. *h.* Spach.) N. E. Asia, N. Japan. Intr. about 1888. Zone IV. Handsome tree of broad-pyramidal habit and of vigorous growth while young.—**A. h. sibírica** (Spach) Schneid., var. Brts. glabrous or nearly so: lvs. hirsute only on the midrib and sparingly on the veins beneath. S.H.1:f.68h-h²,721;2:f.557i. (*A. incana* var. *s.* Spach, *A. s.* Fisch. ex Komar.)

Related species: **A. Matsúmurae** Callier. Lvs. smaller, broad-elliptic or obovate, emarginate, scarcely lobulate and nearly glabrous beneath. S.H.2:f. 557k. M.D.1918:t.15. (*A. incana* var. *emarginata* Matsum.) Japan. Intr. 1914. Zone V.

11. **A. incàna** (L.) Moench. Speckled A. Shrub or tree to 20 m.; brts. pubescent while young; bark smooth, light gray; stipules lanceolate: lvs. broad-elliptic to ovate, 4–10 cm. long, acute, usually rounded at base, doubly serrate and usually slightly lobulate, dull dark green above with impressed veins, glaucous or grayish green and pubescent or nearly glabrous beneath: strobiles 4–8, sessile or short-stalked, about 1.5 cm. long. H.W.2:16(h),t.13 (c). Eu., Cauc., N. Am. Long cult. Zone II. A very variable plant; the typical European form, distinguished as var. **vulgàris** Spach, is a shrub or tree to 20 m.: lvs. usually pubescent beneath, 4–8 cm. long; petiole more than ⅕ as long as blade. Eu., Cauc. Many forms of this var. are in cult.—**A. i. aùrea** Dipp., f. Lvs. yellowish, pubescent beneath; brts. reddish yellow.—**A. i. coccínea** Schelle, f. Lvs. yellowish, nearly glabrous beneath: brts. reddish yellow.—**A. i. acuminàta** Reg., var. Lvs. lobed about halfway to the middle, with lanceolate serrulate lobes. S.H.1:f.72p. (*A. i.* var. *pinnatifida* Spach, f. *incisa* Dipp., var. *laciniata* Loud.)—**A. i. pinnatifída** Wahlenb. Lvs. small, deeply lobed, with broad serrate lobes. Mem. Soc. Nat. Mosc. 13:t.21,f.5,6. M.D.1918:t.21,f.13.—**A. i. péndula** Callier, f. Brs. pendulous. Lustgard,4:143

(h).—**A. i. glauca** (Marsh.) Loud., var. Shrub, rarely small tree to 6 m.: lvs. usually glabrous and glaucous, 5–12 cm. long, sometimes pubescent beneath; petiole usually less than ⅕ of blade. Em.251,t. B.B.1:613. (*A. g.* Michx., *A. i.* subvar. *americana* Reg.) Nfd. to Sask., s. to Pa., Iowa and Neb.—**A. i. tomophýlla** Fern., f. Form with deeply and irregularly dissected lvs.; not yet intr.

A. i. × *rugosa;* see under No. 6.—*A. i.* × *glutinosa;* see under No. 7.—*A. i.* × *subcordata;* see under No. 13.—*A. i.* × *japonica;* see under No. 14.

12. **A. cordàta** Desf. Tree to 15 m.; young brts. viscid, glabrous, finally reddish brown: lvs. suborbicular or broad-ovate, 5–10 cm. long, abruptly acuminate, cordate at base, serrulate, light green beneath, pubescent on the veins only when young and with axillary tufts of hairs; petiole about ⅓ as long as lf.: strobiles 1–3, ovoid, 1.5–2.5 cm. long, stalked. B.M.8658(c). B.S.1:179. G.C.III.19:285. (*A. cordifolia* Ten., *A. tiliacea* and *pyrifolia* Hort.) Italy, Corsica. Intr. 1820. Zone V. Round-headed tree with handsome glossy lvs. resembling those of a pear-tree.

A. c. × *glutinosa* = **A. elliptica** Requien. Lvs. obtuse or emarginate, rounded or subcordate at base; strobiles 2–5, smaller. M.D.1918:t.19,f.6,7. S.H.1:f.66q[1]. (*A. cordata* var. *nervosa* Hort.)

13. **A. subcordàta** C. A. Mey. Tree to 15 m.; brts. usually pubescent, reddish brown; buds puberulous: lvs. ovate to oblong-ovate, 5–16 cm. long, short-acuminate, rounded or subcordate at base, serrate, usually pubescent on both sides while young, later glabrous above, light green and pubescent on the veins beneath; petiole ⅕–¼ as long as lf.: strobiles 1–4, oblong-ovoid, 1.5–2.5 cm. long, stalked. S.H.1:f.69a. (*A. cordifolia* var. *s.* Reg., *A. macrophylla* Hort.) Cauc., Persia. Cult. 1860. Zone VI. Tree with large broad lvs.

A. s. × *incana* = **A. Koèhnei** Callier. Brts. more densely pubescent: lvs. usually elliptic, acute; strobiles short-stalked or nearly sessile. S.H.1:f.69b-c. (*A. orientalis* var. *pubescens* Dipp.) Orig. unknown.—*A. s.* × *japonica* = **A.** Spaèthii Callier. Lvs. ovate-lanceolate, sharply serrate, violet-purple when unfolding. S.H.2:f.555n-o. Orig. before 1908.

Related species: **A. orientàlis** Dcne. Tree to 15 m.; brts. glabrous: lvs. rounded or broad-cuneate at base, glabrous. S.H.1:f.66r-r[1]. Syria. Cult. ?

14. **A. japónica** (Thunb.) Steud. JAPANESE A. Tree to 25 m.; brts. glabrous or slightly pubescent while young: lvs. narrow-elliptic to oblong-lanceolate, rarely ovate-oblong, 6–12 cm. long, acuminate, broad-cuneate, serrulate, glabrous or slightly pubescent when young, light green beneath; petiole 1.5–2.5 cm. long: strobiles 1–3, peduncled, about 1.5 cm. long. S.I.1:t.19(c). G.F. 6:345. (*A. maritima* var. *j.* Reg.) Japan, N. E. Asia. Intr. 1886. Zone V. Pyramidal tree with dense dark green foliage.—**A. j. argùta** (Reg.) Callier, var. Lvs. elliptic to elliptic-obovate, cuneate, irregularly or doubly serrate. M.K.t. 28(c). N. Jap. Intr. ?

A. j. × *incana* = **A. spectàbilis** Callier. Lvs. dull green above and sometimes slightly lobed. S.H.1:f.69h-h[1]. Orig. before 1908.—*A. j.* × *subcordata;* see under No. 13.

Related species: **A. trabeculòsa** Hand.-Mazz. Tree: lvs. elliptic to elliptic-oblong, acuminate, broad-cuneate to rounded at base, serrate, glabrous and green beneath, veins connected by conspicuous parallel veinlets: strobiles axillary, solitary, about 2 cm. long, short-stalked. I.S.1:t.16. (*A. Jackii* Hu.) S.E. China. Intr. 1926. Zone VI?

15. **A. marítima** (Marsh.) Nutt. SEA-SIDE A. Shrub or sometimes tree to 10 m.; brts. pubescent at first, finally dull orange or reddish brown; buds acute, scurfy-pubescent: lvs. oblong or obovate, acute or short-acuminate, rarely obtuse, cuneate at base, remotely serrulate, 6–10 cm. long, lustrous dark green above, light green and glabrous or nearly so beneath: strobiles 1–3, about 2 cm. long, short-stalked. Fl.ix. S.S.9:t.458. (*A. oblongata* Reg., not Ait. nor

Willd.) Del., Md. and Okl. Intr. 1878. Zone V. Attractive in autumn with its dark green foliage and the yellow pendulous catkins.

Related species flowering in autumn is **A. nítida** Endl. Tree to 30 m.: lvs. ovate to ovate-oblong, entire or remotely serrulate, 6–10 cm. long, glabrous; staminate catkins up to 15 cm. long: strobiles about 2.5 cm. long, stalked. B.M. 7654(c). Himal. Intr. 1882. Zone VI.

16. **A. cremastógyne** Burk. Tree to 40 m.; brts. pubescent while young, soon glabrous, finally reddish brown or dark purple: lvs. obovate to obovate-oblong or elliptic, abruptly acuminate, broad-cuneate at base, regularly and rather remotely serrate, 6–14 cm. long, dark green above, light green and usually floccose-pubescent beneath while young, soon glabrous, rarely pubescent on the veins: catkins of both sexes solitary in the axils of the young lvs.: strobiles 1.5–2 cm. long on slender stalks 2–6 cm. long, pendulous; nutlets with broad membranous wings. E.P.IV.61:128. C.C.75. K.B.1913:164,t(h). W. China. Intr. 1908. Zone VII?

Closely related species: **A. lanàta** Duthie. Lvs. rufous-pubescent beneath: stalks of the strobiles not exceeding 4.5 cm. W. China. Intr. 1908. Zone VII?

3. **CARPÌNUS** L. Hornbeam. Deciduous trees or sometimes shrubs; brts. slender; bark gray, smooth or scaly; buds acute with many imbricate scales: lvs. more or less 2-ranked, with 7–24 pairs of straight veins, serrate: staminate catkins pendulous, inclosed in the bud during winter; fls. without perianth, each bract with 3–13 stamens 2-forked at apex; pistillate catkins terminal, slender; each bract with 2 fls. subtended each by 2 bractlets; perianth adnate to the ovary, with 6–10 teeth at apex; style short, with 2 linear stigmas; fr. a ribbed nutlet subtended by a large bract. Flowers in spring with the lvs.; fr. ripening in autumn. (The ancient name of the Hornbeam.) About 26 species from Eu. to E. Asia, s. to the Himal., and in N. and C. Am.— Small or medium-sized trees with usually short trunk and deliquescent stem and with handsome foliage; the pendulous light green fruiting catkins are attractive in some species. The wood is very hard and tough.

A. Lvs. with 7–15 pairs of veins: bracts of staminate fls. broad-ovate, subsessile; bracts of fruiting catkins ovate to lanceolate, not imbricate, chartaceous: bark smooth. (Sect. Eucarpinus Sarg.)
  B. Lvs. 4–12 cm. long, usually acuminate: fruiting bracts lobed at base.
    c. Brts. glabrous or only slightly pubescent when young: fruiting bracts with a lobe on each side.
      D. Lvs. acuminate or acute: fruiting bracts 2–5 cm. long.
        E. Buds small, about 3 mm. long, hairy at first; fruiting bracts 5–7-nerved at base.
                                          1. *C. caroliniana*
        EE. Buds about 5 mm. long, glabrous; fruiting bracts 3–5-nerved......2. *C. Betulus*
      DD. Lvs. cuspidate: fruiting bracts about 1.5 cm. long.................3. *C. laxiflora*
    cc. Brts. densely pubescent: fruiting bracts lobed only on one side......4. *C. Tschonoskii*
  BB. Lvs. 2.5–5, rarely 6 cm. long, usually acute: fruiting bracts without distinct lobes or with a very small lobe at base.
    c. Lvs. serrate on both sides...5. *C. orientalis*
    cc. Bracts not or slightly serrate on the inner side....................6. *C. Turczaninovii*
AA. Lvs. with 15–24 pairs of veins deeply impressed above: bracts of staminate fls. ovate-lanceolate, stipitate: fruiting bracts ovate, serrate, imbricate, membranous: bark scaly. (Sect. Distegocarpus Sarg.)
  B. Lvs. ovate-lanceolate, 2.5–3.5 cm. broad, with 20–24 pairs of veins, usually rounded at base ....7. *C. japonica*
  BB. Lvs. ovate, 4–7 cm. broad, with 15–20 pairs of veins, cordate at base......8. *C. cordata*

1. **C. caroliniàna** Walt. American H. Small tree, rarely to 12 m.; trunk fluted: lvs. ovate-oblong, 6–12 cm. long, 2.5–6 cm. broad, acuminate, rounded or subcordate at base, sharply and doubly serrate, glabrous except pilose on the nerves beneath and with axillary tufts of hairs: fruiting catkins slender-stalked, 5–10 cm. long; bracts ovate to ovate-lanceolate, 2–3 cm. long, with short and broad lateral lobes, usually with 1–5 pointed teeth. S.S.9:t.447.

Em.t.199(c). (*C. americana* Michx.; Blue Beech.)—N. S. to Minn., s. to Fla. and Tex. Intr. 1812. Zone II. Handsome bushy tree with fluted trunk and slender often slightly pendulous brts.; lvs. turning scarlet and orange in autumn.—The tree described above is the northern form extending s. to N. C. and Ark. distinguished as var. **virginiàna** (Marsh.) Fern. The southern form extending n. to s. Ill. and Va. has ashy-gray bark, smaller and narrower lvs. with shorter teeth; bracts with few blunt teeth or entire. Rh.37:t.394.

2. **C. Bétulus** L. European H. Tree to 20 m.: lvs. similar to those of the preceding species, ovate to ovate-oblong, cordate or rounded at base, to 12 cm. long, of somewhat thicker texture, with the veins more impressed above: fruiting catkins 7–14 cm. long; bracts 3–5 cm. long with ovate-lanceolate middle lobe and ovate lateral lobes, entire or remotely toothed on the margin. H.W. 2:31,32(h),t.17(c). E.P.61:29. E.H.3:t.148–152(h). G.C.53:397(h). Eu. to Persia. Long cult. Zone V. Used sometimes for tall hedges.—**C. B. purpúrea** K. Koch, f. Lvs. purple when young, later green.—**C. B. incìsa** Ait., var. Lvs. rather narrow, deeply lobed, with often nearly entire lobes. S.H.1:f.76d-d. (*C. B. aspleniifolia* Hort., *C. B.* f. *heterophylla* Kirch.)—**C. B. quercifòlia** Desf. Lvs. smaller than of *C. B. incisa,* deeply lobed with broader serrate lobes. S.H.1:f.76e-e[1]—**C. B. fastigiàta** Jaeg., var. Of upright habit forming a narrow-pyramidal tree. (*C. B. pyramidalis* Moehl.)—**C. B. columnaris** Spaeth is similar but slenderer.—**C. B. péndula** Kirchn., f. With pendulous brs.—**C. B. Carpinízza** (Host) Neilr., var. Differs chiefly in the usually entire fruiting bracts and the smaller lvs. often cordate at base and with only 7–9 pairs of veins.

3. **C. laxiflòra** Bl. Tree to 15 m.: lvs. ovate or elliptic, abruptly long-acuminate, obliquely rounded or subcordate at base, doubly serrate, 4–7 cm long, glabrous beneath except in the axils of the veins: fruiting catkins loose, 5–7 cm. long; bracts slightly 3-lobed at base, with the middle lobe lanceolate, acute, serrate on one side; nutlets slightly resin-dotted. S.I.1:t.25(c). Japan. Intr. 1914. Zone V.—**C. l. macrostáchya** Oliv., var. Lvs. ovate-oblong, not lobulate; fruiting catkins 6–9 cm. long; bracts obtusish, less distinctly lobed at base. H.I.20:1989. (*C. Fargesii* Franch.) W. and C. China. Intr. 1900. Zone VI?

4. **C. Tschonóskii** Maxim. Tree to 15 m.; young brts. and petioles soft-pubescent: lvs. elliptic-ovate to ovate-oblong, acuminate, rounded at base, irregularly or doubly, rather finely serrate, with mucronulate teeth, 4–9 cm. long, pubescent on both sides when young, later only pilose on the nerves beneath, with 12–15 pairs of veins; fruiting catkins 5–7 cm. long, with pubescent stalk and rachis; bracts ovate to lanceolate, acute, serrate on one side, with a small lobe at base of the entire side; nutlet glabrous. S.I.2:t.11(c). I.S.3:t.117. N.K.2:t.9. (*C. yedoensis* Maxim., *C. Fauriei* Nakai.) Japan, N. E. Asia, N. China. Intr. 1894. Zone V. Graceful shrubby tree.

Closely related species: **C. Henryàna** Winkl. Lvs. ovate-lanceolate, simply and rather coarsely serrate, 4–7 cm. long; bracts ovate; nutlet puberulous. I.S. 3:t.124. B.J.50(Suppl.):507.f.7. (*C. Tschonoskii* var. *H.* Winkl.) C. and W. China. Intr. 1907. Zone VI?—**C. Fargesiàna** Winkl. Tree to 20 m.: lvs. ovate-to elliptic-oblong, short-acuminate, doubly serrate, 4–6.5 cm. long: bracts semi-ovate; nutlets pilose at apex and sparingly glandular, otherwise glabrous. E.P. IV.61:f.10G. I.S.3:t.118. (*C. yedoensis* Winkl., not Maxim.) China. Intr. 1920. Zone V.—**C. exímia** Nakai. Tree to 10 m.: lvs. ovate to ovate-oblong, doubly serrate, 8–10 cm. long, pubescent above and on the veins beneath, pairs of veins 14–16: bracts semi-ovate, about 2.5 cm. long; nutlet pilose at apex and sparingly glandular. N.K.2:t.8. Korea. Intr. 1921. Zone V?

5. **C. orientàlis** Mill. Shrub or small tree to 5 m.; young brts. and petioles

silky-pubescent: lvs. ovate or elliptic-ovate, acute, usually rounded at base, sharply and doubly serrate, 2.5–5 cm. long, lustrous and dark green above, glabrous beneath except pilose on the midrib, with 11–15 pairs of veins: fruiting catkins 3–6 cm. long, with ovate bracts serrate on both sides, pilose below; nutlet pilose at apex. R.I.12:t.634(c). H.W.2:34. S.H.1:140. (*C. duinensis* Scop.) S. E. Eu., Asia Minor. Intr. 1739. Zone V.

6. **C. Turczaninòvii** Hance. Small tree to 5 m.; brts. and petioles tomentulose; stipules linear, persistent during the winter: lvs. ovate to broad-ovate, acute, usually rounded at base, doubly serrate, 3–5 cm. long, pilose on the nerves beneath and bearded in the axils, with 10–12 pairs of veins: fruiting catkins 3–4 cm. long, slender-stalked; bracts semi-ovate, acute, or obtuse, incisely serrate on one side, on the other with 1–3 small teeth at apex and with a very small lobe at base; nutlet resin-dotted. E.P.IV.61:34,f.10a–c,11. N.K. 2:t.12. I.S.3:t.116. (*C. Paxii* Winkl., *C. stipulata* Winkl.) N. China, Korea. Intr. 1905. Zone V. Graceful shrubby tree with small foliage.—**C. T. ovalifòlia** Winkl., var. Lvs. ovate or nearly ovate-oblong, scarcely doubly serrate, 3–6 cm. long: bracts not lobulate at base. E.H.3:t.201,f.5. (*C. Turczaninowii* Franch., not Hance, *C. polyneura* Burk. in part, not Franch.) W. China. Intr. 1889. Zone V.

7. **C. japónica** Bl. Tree to 15 m.; young brts. pubescent: lvs. oblong-ovate to oblong-lanceolate, acuminate, rounded or subcordate at base, irregularly and sharply serrate, 5–10 cm. long, glabrous or nearly so except brownish pubescent beneath on the nerves while young, with 20–24 pairs of veins: fruiting catkins slender-stalked, ovoid-oblong, 5–6 cm. long; bracts ovate, dentate, appressed and overlapping, about 2 cm. long; nutlet covered by a small bractlet opposite to the bract. S.I.1:t.24(c). G.F.6:365. R.H.1895:427. G.C. 66:107. (*C. carpinoides* Mak., *Distegocarpus Carpinus* Sieb. & Zucc.) Japan Intr. 1879, 1892. Zone IV. Small tree with handsome lvs.

8. **C. cordàta** Bl. Tree to 15 m.; young brts. and petioles slightly hairy at first, soon glabrous; terminal winter-bud about 2 cm. long: lvs. ovate to oblong-ovate, acuminate, cordate at base, irregularly and doubly serrate, 7–12 cm. long, slightly pubescent on the veins beneath or glabrous, with 15–20 pairs of veins: fruiting catkins slender-stalked, 6–8 cm. long; bracts appressed, overlapping, dentate, inflexed at the base and covering the nutlet. S.I.1:t.24(c). K.M.t.22(c). G.F.8:295. N.K.2:t.6. Japan, N. E. Asia, N. and W. China. Intr. 1879. Zone V. Small tree with large handsome foliage.— **C. c. chinénsis** Franch., var. Brts. and petioles densely pubescent: lvs. smaller. S.H.2:f.558f. C. and W. China. Intr. 1901. Zone V.

4. **ÓSTRYA** Scop. Hop-Hornbeam. Deciduous trees; bark scaly, rough; buds pointed, with many imbricate scales: lvs. doubly serrate, generally ovate to oblong-ovate: staminate catkins slender, pendulous, naked during the winter: fls. without perianth, each bract with 3–14 stamens, the filaments bifid at apex; pistillate catkins upright, slender, with 2 fls. in the axil of each deciduous bract; calyx adnate to the ovary which is enclosed in a tubular involucre formed by the union of a bract and 2 bractlets and open at the apex; stigmas 2, linear: fr. a ribbed nutlet, enclosed by the bladder-like involucre with rigid hairs at base, these imbricated into a short, slender-stalked pendulous strobile. Flowers appearing in spring with the lvs.; frs. ripening in autumn. (The ancient Greek name of a tree with hard wood.) Seven species in N. and C. Am., and in Eu. and in W. and E. Asia.—Ornamental

141

small or medium sized round-headed trees with handsome foliage and attractive in autumn with their light green fruits.

A. Lvs. acuminate, 4–12 cm. long.
  B. Lvs. slightly pubescent or nearly glabrous, with 11–15 pairs of veins.
    C. Nutlet ovoid: petioles 5–10 mm. long, glandless; lvs. usually rounded at base.
                    1. *O. carpinifolia*
    CC. Nutlets spindle-shaped: petioles 3–6 mm. long, like the brts. often with stalked
       glands: lvs. usually subcordate..2. *O. virginiana*
  BB. Lvs. soft-pubescent beneath, with 9–12 pairs of veins: nutlet narrow-ovoid.
                                   3. *O. japonica*
AA. Lvs. acute or obtusish, 3–5 cm. long, with 5–8 pairs of veins..............4. *O. Knowltonii*

1. **O. carpinifòlia** Scop. EUROPEAN H. Tree to 20 m.; bark gray; young brts. pubescent: lvs. ovate to ovate-oblong, acuminate, usually rounded at base, sharply and doubly serrate, 4–10 cm. long, dark green and sparingly hairy above sparingly hairy chiefly on the nerves beneath, with 12–15 pairs of veins: fruiting clusters 3.5–5 cm. long; nutlet ovoid, 4–5 mm. long, with a tuft of hairs at apex. H.W.2:35,t.18(c). R.H.1895:188(h),189. G.C.III.8:274. E.H.3:t.153(h). (*O. italica* Winkl., *O. vulgaris* Willd.) S. Eu., Asia Minor. Intr. 1724. Zone V.

2. **O. virginiàna** (Mill.) K. Koch. AMERICAN H. Tree to 20 m., similar to the preceding species; bark brown: lvs. 6–12 cm. long, usually subcordate at base: nutlets spindle-shaped, 6–8 mm. long, glabrous at apex. S.S.9:t.545. Gn.24:230,231. (*O. virginica* Willd., *O. italica* subsp. *v.* Winkl.—IRONWOOD.) Cape Breton, Ont. and Minn. to Fla. and Tex. Intr. 1690. Zone IV.—**O. v. glandulòsa** (Spach) Sarg., var. Young brts., petioles and peduncles with stalked glands. (*O. virginica* var. *g.* Spach.) The northern form.

3. **O. japónica** Sarg. JAPANESE H. Tree to 25 m.; similar to *O. carpinifolia;* brts. densely pubescent: lvs. irregularly, but scarcely doubly serrate, soft-pubescent on both sides: nutlet oblong-ovoid, 5–6.5 mm. long, glabrous at apex. S.I.1:t.25(c). K.M.t.24(c). G.F.6:384. (*O. virginica* var. *j.* (Sarg.) Burk.) Japan, N. E. Asia, China. Intr. 1888. Zone V.

4. **O. Knowltònii** Cov. Tree to 10 m.; bark gray; lvs. ovate to elliptic, acute, sometimes obtusish, usually rounded at base, sharply serrate, 2.5–5 cm. long, soft-pubescent beneath, with 5–8 pairs of veins: fruiting catkins about 3 cm. long; nutlets oblong-ovoid, 6 mm. long, pilose at apex. S.S.9:t.446. G.F.7:115. N. Ariz. Intr. 1914. Zone V.

5. **OSTRYÓPSIS** Dcne. Deciduous shrubs; buds acute, with many imbricate scales: lvs. ovate, doubly serrate, plicate in bud: staminate fls. in pendulous, oblong-cylindric catkins, naked during winter; each bract with 4–6 stamens; fls. without perianth; filaments bifid at apex; anthers pilose at apex; pistillate fls. in very short spikes, each bract with 2 fls., fl. enclosed in a 3-fid involucre; calyx adnate to the ovary; ovary with one ovule in each cell; style bifid: fr. a small nutlet enclosed in a tubular involucre 3-fid at the apex; cotyledones above ground, green. Fls. appearing with the lvs. (Ostrya and Greek *opsis*, appearance.) Two species in China.

O. Davidiàna Dcne. Shrub to 3 m., suckering from the base; young brts. pubescent: lvs. broad-ovate, acuminate, cordate at base, doubly serrate and usually lobulate, 3–7 cm. long, with scattered hairs above, pubescent and gland-dotted beneath; petioles about 5 mm. long; frs. 6–12 in a long-stalked dense cluster; involucre about 1.2–1.8 cm. long, finally splitting open on one side; nutlet ovoid, beaked, about 8 mm. long. L.I.t.3. E.P.IV.61:19. N. and W. China. Intr. about 1865. Zone V. Small shrub similar to a small-leaved hazel, but may be distinguished by the sessile red glands on the under side of the leaf.

Related species: **O. nòbilis** Balf. & W. W. Sm. Differs chiefly in larger, 4–12 cm. long, scarcely lobulate lvs. brownish tomentose beneath. S. W. China. Intr. ?

6. CÓRYLUS L. HAZEL. Deciduous shrubs, rarely trees; buds obtuse, rarely acute, with many imbricate scales: lvs. generally ovate, usually doubly serrate and more or less pubescent, conduplicate in bud: staminate catkins cylindric, pendulous, naked during the winter; fls. without perianth, each bract with 4–8 stamens, filaments bifid, anthers pilose at apex; pistillate inflorescence head-like enclosed in a small scaly bud, with only the red styles protruding; ovaries with 1, rarely 2 ovules in each cell; style bifid to the base: fr. a subglobose or ovoid nut, with ligneous pericarp, included or surrounded by a large leafy variously toothed or dissected involucre, often tubular, in clusters at the end of the brts.; cotyledons thick, fleshy, remaining inclosed in the nut. Fls. appearing before the lvs. in early spring; frs. ripening in autumn. (The ancient Latin name.) About 15 species in N. Am., Eu., and temp. Asia.—Large shrubs or trees, some cult. for their edible nuts and some for ornament.

A. Involucre spiny: lvs. glabrous except pubescent on the veins beneath, teeth acuminate: winter-buds acute...Sect. ACANTHOCHLAMYS Spach.
          1. *C. tibetica*
AA. Involucre not spiny: lvs. usually pubescent, teeth scarcely acuminate: winter-buds obtuse.
          Sect. AVELLANA Spach.
  B. Involucre divided into linear recurved lobes; petiole about 2 cm. long.
    c. Involucre campanulate, deeply divided, glandular........................2. *C. Colurna*
    cc. Involucre tubular, contracted above the nut into a short tube with recurved lobes.
          3. *C. chinensis*
  BB. Involucre irregularly divided into lanceolate to ovate lobes: petiole usually about 1 cm. long.
    c. Involucre consisting of 2 distinct or partly connate bracts.
      D. Lobes of involucre dentate-serrate.
        E. Involucre not or only slightly longer than nut....................4. *C. Avellana*
        EE. Involucre about twice as long as nut, usually tightly inclosing it.
          5. *C. americana*
      DD. Lobes of involucre triangular-ovate, entire or sparingly dentate..6. *C. heterophylla*
    cc. Involucre tubular.
      D. Involucre pubescent, slightly contracted into a wide tube............7. *C. maxima*
      DD. Involucre setose, abruptly contracted above the nut.
        E. Petiole 1.5–2.5 cm. long: anthers reddish........................8. *C. Sieboldiana*
        EE. Petiole 6–12 mm. long: anthers yellow............................9. *C. cornuta*

1. C. tibética Batal. TIBETAN H. Shrubby tree to 8 m.; brts. glabrous, brown, with conspicuous lenticels: lvs. broad-ovate to obovate, subcordate or rounded at base, long-acuminate, unequally and sharply serrate, 5–12 cm. long, with silky hairs on the veins beneath; petioles 1.5–2.5 cm. long: bracts of staminate fls. acuminate, glabrous at apex: nuts 3–6 with spiny and glabrous involucres forming a bur about 4–5 cm. across; nut subglobose, compressed, 1–1.5 cm. long. V.F.206(h). R.H.1910:203,t(c). M.O.432. (*C. ferox* var. *t.* Franch.) C. and W. China. Intr. 1897. Zone VI. Remarkable for its fruit-clusters which resemble the burs of the chestnut.

    C. t. × *Avellana* = **C. spinéscens** Rehd. Similar in habit and lvs. to *C. tibetica*: involucre of fr. with a few spiny bristles on the face, its lobes and teeth ending in rigid spiny points. Orig. before 1911. Zone V.

    The closely related **C. férox** Wall. with narrower more oblong lvs. and pubescent spiny involucre from the Himal. is tenderer. E.P.IV.61:45. Intr. 1924.

2. C. Colúrna L. TURKISH H. Tree to 25 m.; bark light yellowish gray; brts. glandular-pubescent, older brs. furrowed, corky: lvs. broadly ovate to obovate, acuminate, cordate at base, doubly serrate or crenate-serrate and sometimes lobulate, 8–12 cm. long, nearly glabrous above, pubescent on the nerves beneath; petioles 1.5–2.5 cm. long, glandular-pubescent at first: staminate catkins 5–7 cm. long: frs. clustered; involucre deeply divided into linear recurved glandular lobes; nut 1.5–2 cm. across. B.M.9469(c). G.C.40:257(h). Gn.31:260,261. E.H.3:t.147(h). Gt.54:532;62:355(h). S. E. Eu., W. Asia. Intr. 1582. Zone IV. Tree of regular pyramidal habit.—**C. C. glandulífera** DC., var. Petioles, peduncles and involucre glandular-setose. R.I.12:t.638,f. 1303(c).

C. c. × *Avellana* = **C. colurnoìdes** Schneid. Shrubby tree with short-acuminate, more sharply serrate lvs.; involucre glandular-setose, divided to about the middle into narrow dentate lobes sometimes partly connate. Goeschke, Haseln. t.76. S.H.1:f.83r. (*C. intermedia* Lodd., not Fingerh.) Orig. before 1835.

Closely related species: **C. Jacquemóntii** Dcne. Lvs. distinctly obovate and sharply serrate; involucre not glandular-bristly. K.B.1913:163,t. (*C. colurna* var. *lacera* A.DC.) Himal. Cult. 1898.

3. **C. chinénsis** Franch. CHINESE H. Tree to 40 m.; bark furrowed, light colored; brts. brown, pilose and glandular: lvs. ovate to ovate-oblong, acuminate, very oblique and cordate at base, doubly serrate, not lobulate, 10–18 cm. long, glabrous above, pubescent on the nerves beneath; petiole 1–2.5 cm. long, sometimes longer, pubescent and glandular: frs. 4–6, clustered; involucre, striate, finely pubescent, much contracted above the nut into a short tube divided into linear lobes usually forked at apex; nut subglobose, about 1.5 cm. across. C.C.73. E.P.IV.61:f.14h,15. S.H.2:f.560c,561d. M.O.t.40. C. and W. China. Intr. 1895. Zone V. Tree with spreading brs. forming a broad-oval head.

C. c. × *Avellana* = **C. Vilmorìnii** Rehd. Similar to *C. chinensis* in habit: lvs. smaller and less cordate: involucre little constricted above the nut, occasionally split to the base on one side, divided above the apex of the nut into laciniate and, toothed nearly upright lobes; nut larger, with thinner shell. Orig. before 1911.

4. **C. Avellàna** L. EUROPEAN H. Shrub to 5 m.; brts. glandular-pubescent: lvs. suborbicular to broad-obovate, abruptly acuminate, cordate at base, doubly serrate and often slightly lobulate, 5–10 cm. long, slightly pubescent or nearly glabrous above, pubescent beneath, particularly on the nerves; petioles 8–15 mm. long; staminate catkins 3–6 cm. long: frs. 1–4; involucre shorter or rarely slightly longer than the nut, deeply and irregularly divided into narrow, often toothed lobes; nut globose to ovoid, 1.5–2 cm. long. H.W. 2:28 t.16(c). R.I.12,t.636(c). Eu. Long cult. Zone III? The larger fruited forms of this species are much cult. for the edible nuts.—**C. A. aùrea** Kirchn., f. Lvs. yellow; brts. yellowish. Goeschke, Haseln., t.8.—**C. A. fusco-rúbra** Dipp., f. Lvs. dull purple or brownish red. Goeschke, Haseln., t.4. (*C. A.* f. *atropurpurea* Winkl., *C. A.* var. *purpurea* Bean.)—**C. A. heterophýlla** Loud., var. Lvs. pinnately lobed with acute serrate lobes. Goeschke, Haseln., t.5. S.H.1:146,f.83d. (*C. A.* f. *laciniata* Kirchn., var. *pinnatifida* Hort.)—**C. A. péndula** Dipp., f. With pendulous brs. Goeschke, Haseln., t.7. G.W.2:13; 19:94(h).—**C. A. contórta** Bean, var. With twisted and curled brs. G.C.III. 16:380. Intr. before 1863.—**C. A. grándis** Ait., var. COBNUT. Nut large, usually subglobose. R.I.12:t.638,f.1302(c).—**C. A. póntica** (K. Koch) Winkl., var. Lvs. suborbicular, pubescent beneath; petioles short; involucre longer than the nut, with much divided spreading lobes; nut large, broad-ovoid. F.S.21,t.2223–4(c). Goeschke, Haseln., t.13,14,29. Jour. N. Y. Bot. Gard. 14: 13,t.3(h). (*C. p.* K. Koch.) Cauc.

C. A. × *tibetica;* see under No. 1.—*C. A.* × *Colurna;* see under No. 2.—*C. A.* × *chinensis;* see under No. 3.—*C. A.* × *maxima;* see under No. 7.

5. **C. americàna** Marsh. AMERICAN H. Shrub to 3 m.; young brts. and

petioles glandular-pubescent: lvs. broad-ovate or oval, short-acuminate, rounded or subcordate at base, irregularly and doubly serrate, 6–12 cm. long, sparingly pubescent above, soft-pubescent beneath; petioles 8–15 mm. long: staminate catkins 3.5–7 cm. long: frs. 2–6, rarely solitary; involucre about twice as long as nut, usually tightly enclosing it, deeply and irregularly lobed, downy and often glandular-bristly; nut subglobose, about 1.5 cm. across. B.B.1:607. Goeschke, Haseln., t.71,72. (*C. calyculata* Dipp.) N. E. to Sask. and s. to Fla. Intr. 1798. Zone IV.

6. **C. heterophýlla** Fisch. Shrub or small tree to 7 m.; brts. and petioles glandular-hairy: lvs. orbicular-ovate to obovate, abruptly acuminate from a usually nearly truncate apex, cordate or rounded at base, irregularly serrate and usually lobulate, particularly near the apex, 5–10 cm. long, glabrous above, pubescent on the nerves beneath; petiole 1–2 cm. long: frs. usually 1–3; involucre campanulate, longer than the nut, striate, glandular-setose near the base, with 6–9 triangular, entire or sparingly dentate lobes; nut subglobose, about 1.5 cm. across. S.I.1:t.20(c). N.K.2:t.1. E.P.IV.61:49,f.14b. N. E. Asia, Japan. Intr. 1882 or earlier? Zone V.—**C. h. sutchuenénsis** Franch., var. Lvs. less truncate at apex and usually glabrous or glabrescent beneath: lobes of the involucre often dentate and involucre sometimes shorter than nut. C. and W. China. Intr. 1909. Zone V.—**C. h. yunnanénsis** Franch., var. Lvs. densely soft-pubescent beneath; petioles 5–10 mm. long, like the young brts. densely pubescent and stipitate-glandular. S. W. China. Intr. about 1910.—The typical form is easily recognized by the broad truncate and abruptly acuminate apex of its lvs., a character usually not so pronounced in the varieties.

7. **C. máxima** Mill. FILBERT. Shrub or sometimes small tree to 10 m.; young brts. and petioles glandular-hairy: lvs. roundish-ovate to broad-obovate, abruptly acuminate, cordate at base, doubly serrate and usually lobulate, 7–14 cm. long; petioles 8–15 mm. long: staminate catkins 5–7 cm. long: frs. 1–3; involucre tubular, about twice as long as nut, downy and setose-glandular at base, at the apex irregularly lobed with serrate lobes; nut ovoid-oblong; kernel with thin red or white skin. H.W.2:30. E.P.IV.61:49,f.14a. R.I.12,t.637(c). (*C. tubulosa* Willd.) S. E. Eu., W. Asia. Long cult. Zone IV.—**C. m. purpúrea** (Loud.) Rehd., var. Lvs. dark purple. Goeschke, Haseln. t.57. F.E.21325(h). (*C. m.* var. *atropurpurea* Bean, *C. Avellana* var. *p.* Loud.)

Hybrids of this species and *C. Avellana* are occasionally planted for their fruits. The involucre is more deeply divided and often little longer than the nut, sometimes split nearly to the base on one side. Goeschke, Haseln. t.65–70.

8. **C. Sieboldiàna** Bl. JAPANESE H. Shrub to 5 m.; brts. hairy; lvs. elliptic or obovate to oblong, acuminate, usually rounded at base, doubly serrate and slightly lobulate, 5–10 cm. long, nearly glabrous above, pilose on the veins beneath, often with a red blotch in the middle when young; petiole 1.5–2 cm. long: nuts 1–3; involucre tubular, 1.5–4 cm. long, much constricted above the nut, divided at the apex into short entire lobes, densely covered with loosely accumbent bristles; nut conical. S.I.1:t.20(c). N.K.2:t.4. E.P. IV.61:f.16b. (*C. rostrata* var. *S.* (Bl.) Maxim.) Japan. Cult. 1904. Zone V. —**C. S. mandshùrica** (Maxim.) Schneid., var. MANCHURIAN H. Lvs. usually cordate at base, more distinctly lobulate, chiefly near apex, 7–12 cm. long, pubescent beneath chiefly on the veins; petiole to 2.5 cm. long: involucre slightly contracted above the nut, to 5 cm. long, with spreading bristles. B.M. 8623(c). N.K.2:t.3. E.P.IV.61:f.14e. (*C. m.* Maxim. & Rupr.) N. E. Asia to

N. China and N. Japan. Intr. 1882. Zone IV. The var. is a vigorous shrub; its large bristly frs. conspicuous in fall.

9. **C. cornùta** March. BEAKED H. Shrub to 3 m.; young brts. slightly hairy: lvs. ovate to obovate, rarely ovate-oblong, acuminate, subcordate at base, densely serrate and sometimes lobulate, 4–10 cm. long, glabrescent above, downy beneath on the nerves; petioles 6–15 mm. long: frs. 1–2; involucre tubular, much constricted above the nut, 2.5–4 cm. long, densely bristly; nut ovoid, 1–1.5 cm. long, thin-shelled. B.B.1:607. G.F.8:345. S.H. 1:f.83i-k,87a-c. (*C. rostrata* Ait.) Que. to Sask., s. to Mo. and Ga. Intr. 1745. Zone IV.

Closely related species: **C. califórnica** (A.DC.) Rose. CALIFORNIAN H. Similar to the preceding species: leaves more downy beneath, cordate at base: fr. with a short beak about as long or little longer than the nut. E.P.IV.61:f. 14d. A.I.1:510. (*C. rostrata* var. *c.* A.DC). Wash. to Cal. Intr. 1910. Zone V.

Fam. 12. **FAGACEAE** A. Br. BEECH FAMILY

Deciduous or evergreen trees, rarely shrubs; buds with imbricate scales: lvs. alternate, petioled, penninerved, entire, dentate to pinnately lobed, stipulate with usually deciduous stipules: fls. monoecious, usually axillary on the young shoots; perianth 4–7-lobed; staminate spikes slender, each bract with 1 fl.; stamens as many or twice as many as perianth-lobes, rarely more; filaments usually slender; pistillate fls. solitary or in 3's forming spikes or short clusters, sometimes at base of the staminate spikes; ovary inferior, 3- or rarely 6-celled at base, with 3 styles, each cell with 2 ovules; fr. a nut 1-seeded by abortion, solitary or 2–3, partly or wholly enclosed by an involucre or cupula; seed without albumen; cotyledons fleshy.—Six genera with over 600 species in the temp. and subtrop. regions of both hemispheres.

A. Staminate and pistillate fls. solitary or in stalked heads: involucre 2–4-lobed; nuts triangular: lvs. 2-ranked, entire or shallowly toothed: cotyledons above ground, green.
  B. Staminate and pistillate fls. solitary or 3: lvs. evergreen or deciduous, usually small: involucre with transverse entire or toothed scales.........................1. *Nothofagus*
    BB. Staminate fls. in many-fld. heads; pistillate fls. 2: lvs. deciduous, rather large: involucre with prickly, subulate or bract-like appendages, with 2 nuts....................2. *Fagus*
AA. Staminate fls. in slender spikes; pistillate fls. solitary or in spikes; involucre not or irregularly splitting: cotyledons remaining in the seed.
  B. Staminate fls. in upright spikes.
    C. Lvs. deciduous, dentate, 2-ranked: ovary 6-celled; 1–3 frs. in one symmetrical prickly involucre: terminal bud wanting...................................3. *Castanea*
    CC. Lvs. evergreen, entire or dentate: ovary 3-celled: terminal bud present.
      D. Involucre usually spiny, asymmetrical, usually wholly enclosing the 1–3 frs.: lvs. usually 2-ranked ....4. *Castanopsis*
      DD. Involucre of fr. not spiny, usually cup-shaped; nut always solitary; styles cylindric with the stigma at apex: lvs. not 2-ranked................5. *Lithocarpus*
  BB. Staminate fls. in pendulous catkins; styles flattened, with the stigma on the upper surface: lvs. entire to lobed, deciduous or evergreen............................6. *Quercus*

1. NOTHOFÁGUS Bl.

Deciduous or evergreen trees or shrubs: lvs. usually small, 1–5 cm. long, rarely larger, short-petioled, usually plicate in bud, entire or serrate: staminate fls. short-stalked, solitary or in 3-fld. cymes; stamens 8–40; calyx campanulate, 4–6-lobed: pistillate fls. 1–3, in a sessile or short-stalked involucre: nuts 3-angled, usually 3 in a 2–4-lobed involucre bearing outside transverse, entire, toothed or lobed lamellae, with or without gland-tipped appendages. (Fagus with prefix *nothos*, Greek for spurious; probably mistake for *notos* south, referring to the southern habitat.) About 17 species in antarctic S. America, Australia and N. Zeal.—Little known in cult. and probably hardy only near the southern limit of our area.

A. Lvs. evergreen, 1.5–3.5 cm. long.......................................1. *N. fusca*
AA. Lvs. deciduous.
  B. Lvs. 1–3 cm. long...2. *N. antarctica*
  BB. Lvs. 3.5–7 cm. long..3. *N. obliqua*

1. N. fúsca (Hook. f.) Oerst. Tree to 35 m.; brts. zigzag, puberulous: lvs. broad-ovate to suborbicular, acute or rounded at apex, cuneate to truncate at base, coarsely dentate, 1.5–3.5 cm. long, glabrous except ciliate on the margin, with usually 3–4 pairs of veins; petioles pubescent, 2–4 mm. long: involucre sessile, scarcely 1 cm. long, 4-lobed, with large toothed lamellae, with 3 nuts. Kirk, For. Fl. N. Zeal. t.90. Gn.88:845. (*Fagus f.* Hook. f.) N. Zeal. Intr. about 1880. Zone VII?

Related species: **N. betuloìdes** (Mirb.) Bl. Tree with viscid young shoots and ovate, serrulate, very close-set lvs. 1–2.5 cm. long. G.C.33:11. Chile. Intr. 1830.—**N. cliffortioìdes** (Hook. f.) Oerst. Tree with entire lvs. 6–15 mm. long. Cheeseman, Ill. N. Zeal. Fl. 2:t.183. N. Zeal. Intr. about 1880? Zone VII?— **N. Dombeÿi** Bl. Tree: lvs. ovate to ovate-lanceolate, 2–3.5 cm. long, finely toothed, lustrous above, black-dotted on both sides. Chile. Intr. 1916.

2. N. antárctica (Forst.) Oerst. Tree to 35 m.; brts. tomentulose: lvs. broad-ovate to oblong, obtuse, truncate or cordate at base, irregularly crenulate or serrulate and sometimes lobulate, 1.5–3 cm. long, glabrous except puberulous on the midrib beneath, with 3–4 pairs of veins; petioles puberulous, 2–5 mm. long: involucre 4-lobed, with entire lamellae; nuts 3. B.M.8314(c). B.S.2:98. (*Fagus a.* Forst.) Chile. Intr. 1830. Zone VII?

3. N. oblìqua (Mirb.) Bl. Tree to 35 m.; brts. glabrous; lvs. ovate to oblong-ovate, obtuse or acutish, rounded or broad-cuneate at base, serrate, lobulate below the middle, 3–7 cm. long, glabrous, with 8–11 pairs of veins; petioles about 6 mm. long; staminate fls. solitary, with 30–40 stamens: involucre 4-lobed, with 2 triangular and one flattened nut. J.L.37:53,f.25. Gn. 83:511;88:831. (*Fagus o.* Mirbel.) Chile. Intr. 1849. Zone VII?

Related species: **N. procèra** (Poepp. & Endl.) Oerst. Tree: lvs. oblong, rounded at both ends, doubly and finely serrate, 3–10 cm. long and 14–18 pairs of veins pubescent beneath. Chile. Intr. 1913. Zone VII?

2. FÁGUS L. BEECH. Deciduous trees; bark smooth; buds elongated, acute: lvs. 2-ranked, dentate or nearly entire, plicate in bud: staminate fls. many, in slender-peduncled heads; perianth 4–7-lobed, stamens 8–16; pistillate fls. usually 2, surrounded by numerous bracts united below into a 4-parted peduncled involucre; styles 3, slender, recurved: nuts ovoid, triangular, 1 or 2 in a woody 4-valved involucre covered outside with prickly or bract-like, rarely short and deltoid appendages. Fls. appear with the lvs.; frs. ripen in fall. (The ancient Latin name of the beech.) Ten species in the temp. regions of the n. hemisphere; in Am. s. to Mex.—Ornamental trees with handsome lvs.; the nuts are edible and contain oil. An important timber tree in Eu.

A. Stalk of involucre stout, 5–25 mm. long, pubescent: lvs. green beneath.
  B. Appendages of involucre all subulate.
    c. Lvs. with 9–14 pairs of veins, serrate..............................1. *F. grandifolia*
    cc. Lvs. with 5–9 pairs of veins, denticulate.........................2. *F. sylvatica*
  BB. Appendages at base of involucre bract-like, linear to spatulate.
    c. Lvs. broadest above the middle, nearly entire; stalk of fr. 2–2.5 cm. long.
                                              3. *F. orientalis*
    cc. Lvs. broadest below the middle; stalk of involucre 5–1.5 cm. long......4. *F. Sieboldii*
    BBB. Appendages deltoid, very short and closely appressed........................5. *F. lucida*
AA. Stalk of involucre slender, 2.5–7 cm. long, glabrous or nearly so: lvs. glaucescent beneath.
  B. Involucre about as long as nut.
    c. Lvs. pubescent beneath; petioles 1–2 cm. long: appendages of involucre all subulate.
                                           6. *F. longipetiolata*
    cc. Lvs. glabrous beneath; petioles 5–10 mm. long; appendages at base of involucre bract-like ....7. *F. Engleriana*
  BB. Involucre about half as long as nut, covered with short deltoid processes: lvs. glabrous beneath ....8. *F. japonica*

1. F. grandifólia Ehrh. AMERICAN B. Tree to 30, rarely to 40 m.; bark light gray; winter-buds lustrous brown: lvs. ovate-oblong, acuminate, usually

broad-cuneate at base, coarsely serrate, 6–12 cm. long, dark bluish green above
and light green and usually glabrous below at maturity, silky when unfolding;
petiole 3–8 mm. long: involucre with slender straight or recurved prickles,
about 2 cm. long; stalk 5–10 mm. long. S.S.9:t.444. Em.182,t(c). G.F.8:125(h).
A.G.12:711(h). (*F. ferruginea* Ait., *F. americana* Sweet, *F. atropunicea* Sudw.)
N. B. to Ont., s. to Fla. and Tex. Intr. about 1800. Zone III.—**F. g. pubéscens**
Fern. & Rehd., f. Lvs. more or less soft-pubescent beneath.—**F. g. caroliniàna** (Loud.) Fern. & Rehd., var. Lvs. darker green and of firmer texture,
ovate to obovate, less coarsely toothed: involucre rufous-tomentose, prickles
shorter and fewer. (*F. ferruginea* var. *c.* Loud.) E. Mass. and s. Ill. to Fla.
and Tex. Cult. 1836. Zone V.

2. **F. sylvática** L. EUROPEAN B. Tree to 30 m.; bark gray; winter-buds
slightly silky, dull: lvs. ovate or elliptic, acute, broad-cuneate or rounded at
base, remotely denticulate, 5–10 cm. long, lustrous dark green above, light
green beneath and usually glabrous at maturity, silky and ciliate while young;
petiole 5–10 mm. long: involucre about 2.5 cm. long, with usually upright
prickles; stalk 1–15 mm. long. H.W.2:42,t.20(c). F.E.33:615(h). M.G.17:
579–582(h). E.H.1:t.1–12(h). Centr. and S. Eu., e. to Crimea. Long cult.
Zone IV. Numerous forms differing in shape and color of the lvs. and in habit
are in cult., of which the following are those best known: **F. s. atropunícea**
West., var. PURPLE B. (COPPER B.) With purple lvs. A.G.18:837(h). F.E.13:
472(h) ;14:874(h). (*F. s.* var. *purpurea* Ait., *F. s. atropurpurea* Kirchn., *F. s.
sanguinea* Ktze.); here also belong var. *cuprea* Loud., var. *Riversii* Rehd.,
F. s. nigra Hort., *F. s. purpurea macrophylla* and *F. s. p. major* Hort., differing in the deeper or lighter color of the lvs. and in other slight characters.
Known since 1680.—**F. s. trícolor** (Simon-Louis) K. Koch, f. Lvs. nearly
white, spotted green, and with pink margin. R.B.12:145,t(c). (*F. s. atropurpurea tricolor* Pynaert.)—**F. s. roseo-marginàta** Henry, var. Lvs. purple with
an irregular light pink border. Ill. Monatsh. Gartenb. 7:t.10(c).—**F. s. Zlàtia**
Spaeth. Lvs. yellow when young, finally nearly green.—**F. s. lùteo-variegàta**
West., var. Lvs. variegated with yellow. (*F. s.* f. *aureo-variegata* Schneid.)
Intr. before 1770.—**F. s. álbo-variegàta** West., var. Lvs. variegated with
white. (*F. s.* var. *argenteo-variegata* Henry.) Intr. before 1770.—**F. s. laciniàta**
Vignet. FERNLEAF B. Lvs. narrowly elliptic to lanceolate, incisely serrate to
deeply lobed, sometimes linear and nearly entire. L.A.3:f.1875. S.H.1:155,f.
911. F.E.18:314(h). B.S.1:552,t(h). (*F. s. incisa* Hort., var. *heterophylla*
Loud.)—**F. s. asplenifòlia** Duchartre. Similar to the preceding, but lvs. very
narrow, often linear. S.H.1:f.91m. (*F. s.* f. *comptoniaefolia* Kirchn., *F. s.
salicifolia* Hort.)—**F. s. Rohánii** Koerber. With purple lvs. similar in shape
to *F. s. laciniata.* M.G.23:499. Intr. about 1894.—**F. s. quercifòlia** Schneid.,
f. Lvs. ovate-oblong, with short and broad obtusish lobes often undulate and
sometimes slightly toothed. (*F. s. quercoides* Kirchn., not Persoon; the latter
is a form with oak-like bark: M.G.24:509. M.D.1924:t.31.)—**F. s. cristàta**
Loud., var. Slow-growing form with small, clustered lvs. deeply toothed and
curled. L.A.3:f.1877.—**F. s. rotundifòlia** Cripps. With very small close-set
lvs. suborbicular and often subcordate at base, only 1.5–3 cm. long. Intr. 1872.
—**F. s. latifòlia** Kirchn., f. Lvs. very large and broad, nearly entire, up to 15
cm. long and to 10 cm. broad. (*F. s.* f. *macrophylla* Dipp., not DC.)—**F. s.
fastigiàta** K. Koch, f. Tree of fastigiate habit with glabrous glossy lvs.
Hesse, Cat. 1913–14,t(h). (*F. s. Dawyckii* Hesse, *F. s. pyramidalis* Hort., not
Kirchn.)—**F. s. péndula** Loud., var. With pendulous brs., the larger limbs
usually horizontally spreading. Gg.6:258(h). G.F.1:32(h). G.C.51:114(h).

B.S.1:552,t(h).—**F. s. purpúreo-péndula** Rehd., var. A pendulous form with purple lvs. (*F. s.* var. *purpurea pendula* Jaeg.)—**F. s. tortuòsa** Pepin. Dwarf spreading form with twisted and contorted brs. pendulous at the tips. R.H. 1864:130(h). M.D.1911:269(h);1912:111-3(h);1913:308-9(h). G.W.14:511(h). (*F. s. remillyensis* Simon-Louis, *F. s. suentelensis* Hort.) Similar forms partly intermediate between this and *pendula* are: *F. s. pagnyensis* Simon-Louis, var. *borneyensis* Henry, var. *miltonensis* Henry, f. *retroflexa* Dipp.

3. **F. orientàlis** Lipsky. ORIENTAL B. Tree to 40 m.; brts. pubescent: lvs. elliptic to obovate or obovate-oblong, acute or short-acuminate, broad-cuneate or rounded at base, with entire or slightly undulate margin, 6-12 cm. long, glabrous except silky pubescent on the nerves beneath, with 7-10 pairs of veins curving before reaching the margin; petioles pubescent, 5-15 mm. long: involucre about 2 cm. long, the lower prickles changed into spatulate bracts; stalk pubescent, 2-2.5 cm. long. S.H.1:f.88. (*F. sylvatica* var. *macrophylla* DC., *F. macrophylla* Koidz., *F. Winkleriana* Koidz.) Asia Minor, Cauc., N. Persia. Intr. 1904. Zone V.

4. **F. Siebóldii** Endl. SIEBOLD'S B. Tree to 30 m.; young brts. nearly glabrous: lvs. ovate to rhombic-ovate, short-acuminate, broad-cuneate or rounded and sometimes subcordate at base, shallowly crenate, 5-10 cm. long, with 7-10 pairs of veins, at maturity glabrous except slightly pubescent on the nerves beneath; petioles 3-10 mm. long, nearly glabrous, slender: involucre 1.5-2 cm. long, with long bristles, the lower ones changed into linear or spatulate bracts; stalk 5-15 mm. long, pubescent. M.K.t.32(c). S.I.1:t.35(c). (*F. sylvatica* var. *asiatica* DC.) Japan. Intr. 1892. Zone V.

5. **F. lùcida** Rehd. & Wils. Tree to 10 m.; bark gray: lvs. ovate to elliptic-ovate, 5-8 cm. long, acute or short-acuminate, rounded to broad-cuneate at base, lustrous green on both sides and glabrous except silky on the midrib above, slightly sinuate, the 8-12 pairs of veins ending into minute teeth in the sinuses; petiole about 1 cm. long: involucre about 8-10 mm. long, brown tomentose, covered with very short closely appressed deltoid mucronate scales; nuts slightly exserted; sfalk 5-10 mm. long, rather stout. I.S. 3:t.130. W. China. Intr. 1905. Zone V.

6. **F. longipetiolàta** Seemen. Tree to 25 m.; bark pale gray; brts. glabrous: lvs. ovate to ovate-oblong, acuminate, broad-cuneate at base, remotely serrate, 7-12 cm. long, finely and densely pubescent beneath and glaucescent, with 9-12 pairs of veins ending in the teeth; petioles slender, 1-2 cm. long, glabrous: involucre 2-2.5 cm. long, with slender, mostly recurved bristles; stalk 3-6 cm. long, glabrous except near the apex. H.I.20:1936. I.S.1:t.17. C.C.81. (*F. sinensis* Oliv.) C. and W. China. Intr. 1911. Zone V.

7. **F. Engleriàna** Seemen. Tree to 23 m., usually smaller, dividing at base into many stems; brts. glabrous: lvs. ovate to elliptic-ovate, rarely oblong-ovate, short-acuminate, broad-cuneate or sometimes rounded and subcordate at base, with sinuate margin, 4-8, rarely to 11 cm. long, glaucescent and glabrous beneath except long silky hairs along the nerves, with 10-14 pairs of veins curving before the margin; petioles slender, 5-10 mm. long, glabrous: involucre about 1.5 cm. long, covered with linear foliaceous bracts; stalk slender, 4-7 cm. long, glabrous. C.C.83. (*F. sylvatica* var. *chinensis* Franch.) C. China. Intr. 1911. Zone V.

8. **F. japónica** Maxim. JAPANESE B. Tree to 25 m., dividing at base into several stems; brts. glabrous: lvs. ovate or elliptic-ovate, short-acuminate, rounded or subcordate, rarely broad-cuneate at base, slightly sinuate-crenate or nearly entire, 5-8 cm. long, glaucescent and glabrous beneath except silky

hairs along the midrib, with 9–14 pairs of veins bending before the margin; petioles about 1 cm. long, glabrous: involucre 6–8 mm. long, with short deltoid processes; nut exserted; stalk slender, glabrous, about 3 cm. long. S.I.1: t.35(c). Japan. Intr. 1905. Zone V.

3. **CASTÁNEA** Mill. CHESTNUT. Deciduous trees, rarely shrubs; bark furrowed; buds with 3–4 scales; brts. without terminal bud: lvs. 2-ranked, serrate, with numerous parallel veins: staminate fls. in erect cylindrical catkins; calyx 6-parted; stamens 10–20; pistillate fls. on the lower part of the upper staminate catkins, rarely on separate catkins, usually 3 in a prickly symmetrical involucre; styles 7–9; ovary 6-celled; nuts large, brown, with a large pale scar at the base, 1–3, rarely 5 or 7 in a prickly involucre, splitting at maturity into 2–4 valves. (The ancient Latin name of the chestnut.) About 10 species in the temperate regions of the n. hemisphere. Monograph by A. Camus, Châtaigniers (1929), cited below as Camus.—Chiefly nos. 1, 3 and 4 are planted in many varieties as fruit trees for their large edible nuts which are an important article of food in some countries; also as ornamental trees for their large handsome foliage and for the attractive staminate flowers. The coarse-grained wood is very durable in the soil. The Chestnut trees like warm situations, well-drained soil and stand drought better than most trees.

A. Nuts usually 2 or 3 in one involucre, usually broader than high.
  B. Lvs. glabrous, cuneate at base, 12–24 cm. long: winter-buds glabrous or nearly so.
                                                                                      1. *C. dentata*
    BB. Lvs. pubescent beneath, at least while young: often rounded at base: winter-buds pubescent.
      c. Lvs. without lepidote glands beneath: brts. short-pubescent and with long spreading hairs at least on vigorous shoots.....................................2. *C. mollissima*
      cc. Lvs. more or less lepidote-glandular beneath, at least near the nerves: brts. tomentose or puberulous while young.
        D. Lvs. tomentose beneath, at least while young.
          E. Lvs. coarsely serrate, 12–22 cm. long: frs. at end of brts.: tree......3. *C. sativa*
          EE. Lvs. crenate-serrate, 8–16 cm. long: frs. often lateral: usually shrubby.
                                                                                      4. *C. crenata*
        DD. Lvs. pubescent beneath only on the veins, densely lepidote-glandular: usually shrubby ....5. *C. Seguinii*
AA. Nuts solitary, terete and usually higher than broad, only exceptionally 2.
  B. Lvs. tomentose beneath, usually elliptic-oblong...........................6. *C. pumila*
  BB. Lvs. glabrous, usually oblong-lanceolate, long-acuminate, slender-petioled..7. *C. Henryi*

1. **C. dentàta** Borkh. AMERICAN C. Tree to 30 m.; brts. glabrous or nearly so: lvs. oblong-lanceolate, acuminate, cuneate at base, coarsely serrate, 12–24 cm. long, glabrous except minute glands beneath when young: nut 1.5–2.5 cm. across, usually 2 or 3, rarely 5; involucre 5–6 cm. across. S.S.9:t.440-1. Em. 187,t(c). G.F.10:373(h). Am. For. 21:957;26:619;27:43(h). (*C. americana* Raf.) S. Me. to Mich., s. to Ala. and Miss. Cult. 1800. Zone IV.

C. d. × *pumila;* see under No. 6— *C. d.* × *crenata;* see under No. 4.—*C. d.* × *sativa;* see under No. 3.

2. **C. mollíssima** Bl. CHINESE C. Tree to 20 m.; sometimes shrubby; brts. short-pubescent and, at least on vigorous shoots, with long spreading hairs: lvs. elliptic-oblong to oblong-lanceolate, 8–15 cm. long, acuminate, rounded or truncate at base, coarsely serrate, whitish tomentose or green and soft-pubescent beneath, at least on the veins, without lepidote glands; petiole short-pubescent and pilose: nuts 2–3 cm. across, usually 2–3, the scar smaller than the base; spines of involucre pubescent. C.C.85. N.K.3:t.2–6. S.H.2: f.563c-d. Camus t.13,14,73,f.6–8. U. S. Inv. 36:t.2,3,(h). (*C. Bungeana* Bl., *C. Duclouxii* Dode, *C. hupehensis* Dode, *C. sativa* var. *m.* (Bl.) Pampan.) China, Korea. Intr. 1853 and 1903. Zone IV.

C. m. × *pumila* = **C. Burbánkii** A. Camus. Husk splitting into 4 or sometimes 2 valves; nuts 1–3. Camus,t.73,f.10–15. Orig. 1899.—*C. m.* × *alnifolia* = **C. Morrísii** A. Camus. Orig. before 1914.

3. **C. satìva** Mill. SPANISH C. Tree to 30 m.; trunk sometimes with a
girth of 10 m.: brts. soon glabrous: lvs. oblong-lanceolate, 12–22 cm. long,
acute or short-acuminate, broad-cuneate or rounded or sometimes subcordate
at base, coarsely serrate, pubescent or tomentose beneath while young and
with lepidote glands at least near the veins, glabrous or nearly so at maturity,
upright: nuts 2–3 cm. across, 1–3. H.W.2:37(h),t.19(c). E.H.4:t.232–6(h).
Gg.3:209(h). S.H.1:158(h). (*C. vesca* Gaertn., *C. vulgaris* Lam.) S. Eu., W.
Asia, N. Afr. Long cult. Zone V.—**C. s. aspleniifòlia** Loud., var. Part of the
lvs. linear with irregularly lobed or crenate margin, others nearly normal
but narrower and more deeply serrate. S.H.1:f.91r. G.C.74:309. (*C. s.* var.
heterophylla Henry.)—**C. s. prolífera** K. Koch, f. Lvs. narrower, at least
the upper ones with persistent tomentum beneath; fr. smaller.—**C. s. pyramidàlis** Mottet. Of narrow pyramidal habit. Cult. 1925.—**C. s. fastigiàta**
A. Camus, var. Of columnar habit.—**C. s. purpúrea** Bean, var. Lvs. purple.
There are also variegated forms.

C. s. × *dentata* = **C. Blaringhémii** A. Camus; here belongs probably "Paragon." Orig. before 1880.—*C. s.* × *pumila* = **C. pulchella** A. Camus. Fruits on
two year old sprouts: fr. smaller. Jour. Hered. 9:113–6(h,fr). Orig. about
1903.—*C. s.* × *crenata;* see under No. 4.

4. **C. crenàta** Sieb. & Zucc. JAPANESE C. Shrub or small tree to 10 m.,
occasionally taller; brts. finely pubescent, soon glabrous: lvs. elliptic to
oblong-lanceolate, acuminate, rounded or subcordate at base, crenate-serrate,
the teeth sometimes reduced to bristles, 8–16 cm. long, usually tomentose and
glandular-lepidote beneath, sometimes nearly glabrous, or pubescent only on
the nerves: spines of involucre nearly glabrous; nuts 2–3, rarely 5, 2–3 cm.
across, the scar covering the whole base. S.I.1:34(c). M.K.t.33(c). Camus
t.10–12,73,f.3. E.H.4:t.237. (*C. japonica* Bl., *C. sativa* var. *pubinervis* Mak.)
Japan. Intr. 1876. Zone V.

C. c. × *dentata* = **C. Endicóttii** A. Camus. Sometimes 7–8 nuts in one husk.
Jour. Hered. 13:305–13(h,fr.). Orig. 1908.—*C. c.* × *sativa* = **C. Coudércii** A.
Camus. Tree: lvs. larger: frs. larger, lateral. Camus t.21,22. Cult. 1919.—
C. c. × *pumila* = **C. Fleetii** A. Camus. Husks several together, usually with 3
nuts each. Camus t.20,f.11;t.73,f.1–2. Orig. before 1911.

5. **C. Seguìnii** Dode. Shrub or small tree to 10 m.; young brts. short-
pubescent: lvs. elliptic-oblong or oblong-obovate to lanceolate-oblong, acuminate, rounded or sometimes subcordate or broad-cuneate at base, coarsely
serrate, 6–14, rarely to 16 cm. long, green beneath and lepidote-glandular,
pilose only on the nerves or sometimes nearly glabrous, with 12–16 pairs of
veins; involucre 3–4 cm. across, with sparsely pilose spines; nuts usually 3,
rarely 5 or 7, 1–1.5 cm. across. U. S. Inv. 54:t.3(fr). B.D.1908:151,154(fr). S.H.
2:f.563e–f(fr). Camus t.13,f.4–5,t.15–17. (*C. Davidii* Dode.) E. and C. China.
Intr. 1853 and 1907. Zone VI?

6. **C. pùmila** Mill. CHINQUAPIN. Shrub or small tree; brts. tomentose:
lvs. elliptic-oblong or oblong-obovate, acute, rounded or broadly cuneate at
base, coarsely serrate or the teeth reduced to bristles, 7–12 cm. long, white-
tomentose beneath; involucre 2.5–3.5 cm. across; nut solitary, rarely 2, ovoid,
pointed, 1.5–2 cm. long and about 1 cm. across. S.S.9:t.442–3. Gn.88:821(h).
M.O.t.39(h). Pa. to Fla. and Tex. Intr. 1699. Zone V.

C. p. × *dentata* = **C. neglécta** Dode. Lvs. less pubescent: fr. larger. B.D.
1908:143,f.9. N. C. Cult. 1923.—*C. p.* × *sativa;* see under No. 3.

Closely related species: **C. ozarkénsis** Ashe. Tree to 20 m.: lvs. 12–20 cm.
long, coarsely toothed, white-tomentose, rarely glabrous beneath: fr. densely
spiny, about 3 cm. across; nut 1.5–1.7 cm. high. (*C. arkansana* Ashe.) Camus
t.74,f.3–6. Ark. to s. w. Mo. Intr. 1891. Zone VI.—**C. alnifòlia** Nutt. Low shrub
to 0.5 m., with creeping root-stock: lvs. oblong or oblong-obovate, usually obtuse,

5–15 cm. long, thinly tomentose or pubescent: involucre with fewer and shorter rigid spines. Bull. Torr. Bot. Club, 21:t.206. Camus t.19,f.6–8. (*C. nana* Muhlb.) Ga. to Fla. and La. Cult. 1906. Zone VI.—*C. a.* × *mollissima;* see under No. 2.

7. C. Hénryi (Skan) Rehd. & Wils. Tree to 25 or 30 m.; brts. glabrous: lvs. oblong-ovate to oblong-lanceolate or lanceolate, long-acuminate, truncate to cuneate at base, with bristle-like teeth, 8–16 cm. long, light green and glabrous and somewhat reticulate beneath, with 12–16 pairs of veins, chartaceous; petioles slender, 1–1.5 cm. long, glabrous: involucre about 2 cm. across with slightly pubescent spines; nut solitary, globose-ovoid, pointed, 1.5–2 cm. high. B.D.1908:156(fr). Camus t.20,f.1–5. S.H.2:f.563h-k,564e. (*C. Vilmoriniana* Dode, *C.Fargesii* Dode, *Castanopsis Henryi* Skan.) C. and W. China. Intr. 1900. Zone V.

4. CASTANÓPSIS Spach. Evergreen trees, sometimes shrubby; buds with numerous scales: lvs. 2-ranked or 5-ranked, entire or dentate, coriaceous, convolute in bud: staminate fls. in upright simple or branched spikes; calyx 5–6 parted; stamens usually 10 or 12; pistillate fls. usually in separate short spikes, sometimes at the base of the staminate spikes, 1–3 in one involucre; ovary 3-celled; styles 3, terminating in minute stigmas: fr. a nut ripening the second year, 1–3 in an ovoid or subglobose asymmetrical involucre, dehiscent or indehiscent, covered outside with spines or tubercles or interrupted transverse ridges. (Greek *kastana*, chestnuts, and *opsis*, resemblance: alluding to its resemblance to the chestnut-tree.) About 30 species in s. and e. Asia, one in Calif.—Ornamental evergreen tree adapted for cult. only in warmer regions.

C. chrysophýlla (Hook.) DC. Tree to 35 m., sometimes shrubby; bark deeply ridged; brts. scurfy: lvs. ovate-oblong to oblong-lanceolate, narrowed at ends, entire, 5–14 cm. long, dark green and lustrous above, coated beneath with golden-yellow scales: husk subglobose, dehiscent, densely clothed with rigid spines; nut usually solitary, globose-ovoid, about 1.5 cm. high. S.S.9: t.439. B.M.4953(c). G.C.36:145. Jepson, Silv. Cal. t.74(h). (*Castanea c.* Hook.) Ore. to Calif. and Nev. Intr. 1845. Zone VII.—**C. c. mínor** DC., var. Shrubby form with smaller 5–8 cm. long lvs., very golden yellow beneath, often slightly trough-shaped. Zone VII.

None of the Chinese species introduced have proved hardy within the range of this Manual.

5. LITHOCÁRPUS Bl. Evergreen trees: buds with few foliaceous scales: lvs. dentate or entire, coriaceous: staminate fls. in upright simple or branched spikes with rudimentary ovary; calyx 4–6-lobed; stamens usually 10–12, much longer than the calyx; pistillate fls. at the base of the staminate spikes or in separate catkins; ovary 3-celled; styles 3, cylindric, stigmatic only at apex: fr. a nut, partly, rarely nearly wholly enclosed by a cup-like involucre, its scales distinct and imbricate or connate into concentric rings. (Greek *lithos*, stone, and *carpos*, fruit, alluding to the hard shell of the nut of the type species, *L. javensis.*) Including *Pasania* (Miq.) Oerst., *Cyclobalanus* (Endl.) Oerst., *Synaedrys* Lindl. About 100 species in s. and e. Asia and in Malaysia, one in W. N. Am.—Ornamental evergreen trees adapted only for warmer temperate regions.

L. densiflòrus Rehd. TANBARK OAK. Evergreen tree to 25 or rarely 30 m.: brts. tomentose: lvs. oblong or oblong-obovate, acute, cuneate or rounded at base, dentate with callous teeth, 7–12 cm. long, rusty-tomentose beneath, becoming finally glabrate and bluish white; petioles stout, about 1.5 cm. long, tomentose; pistillate fls. at base of the staminate spikes: frs. 1–2 on a stout peduncle 1–2.5 cm. long; nut ovoid, 2–2.5 cm. long, embraced at base by the shallow cup covered with subulate spreading or reflexed scales. B.M.8695(c). S.S.9:t.438. G.F.5:523(h). J.S.t.7(h). (*Quercus d.* Hook. & Arn., *Pasania d.* Oerst.) S. Ore. to Calif. Intr. 1874. Zone VII?—**L. d. montànus** (Mayr) Rehd., var. Shrubby form with entire usually obtuse lvs. 3–5 cm. long. (*Quercus d.* var. *echinoides* Sarg.) S. Ore. to N. Calif. Intr. ? Zone VII?

None of the Chinese species introduced have proved hardy within the range of this Manual.

6. QUÉRCUS L. OAK.

Deciduous or evergreen trees, rarely shrubs; buds with many imbricate scales: lvs. short-petioled, penninerved, serrate, dentate, lobed or pinnatifid, rarely entire: staminate fls. in slender pendulous catkins; calyx 4–7-parted; stamens 4–12, usually 6; pistillate fls. solitary or in 2- to many-flowered spikes; ovary 3-, rarely 4–5-celled; styles short or elongated, dilated above and stigmatic on the inner face; fr. a nut (acorn) subglobose to oblong or cylindric, surrounded at base or sometimes nearly inclosed by a cup-like involucre covered outside with imbricate scales or scales connate into concentric rings. (The ancient Latin name of the Oak-tree.) Including *Cyclobalanopsis* Oerst., *Erythrobalanus* (Spach) Schwarz, *Macrobalanus* (Prantl) Schwarz (*Q.* §*Macrocarpaea* Oerst.) More than 200 species in the temp. regions of the n. hemisphere and in the tropics at high altitudes south to Colombia in America and to the Mal. Archipelago in Asia.—Much planted as ornamental trees on account of their handsome foliage assuming in most species brilliant autumnal tints. Many species are important timber trees and of some the acorns are edible.

I. Lvs. deciduous

A. Lvs. entire.
  B. Lvs. oblong or lanceolate to linear-oblong.
    C. Lvs. lanceolate to linear-oblong, 1–1.5 cm. broad.........................2. *Q. Phellos*
    CC. Lvs. oblong to oblong-lanceolate, 2–5 cm. broad.
      D. Under side of lvs. pubescent.......................................3. *Q. imbricaria*
      DD. Under side of lvs. glabrous..4. *Q. laurifolia*
  BB. Lvs. obovate to oblong-obovate, sometimes slightly 3-lobed at apex..........5. *Q. nigra*
AA. Lvs. toothed or lobed.
  B. Lobes or teeth bristle-pointed.
    C. Lvs. lobed: cup with imbricate scales except No. 22.
      D. Lvs. broadly obovate, 3–5-lobed at apex, more or less rusty-pubescent beneath.
                                 6. *Q. marilandica*
      DD. Lvs. elliptic to oblong, with 5–9, rarely only 3 lobes (if lvs. narrow, with few irregular lobes or partly entire, see hybrids under Nos. 2 and 3.)
        E. Lvs. whitish or grayish tomentose beneath, lobes entire or occasionally with few teeth.
          F. Lobes triangular.
            G. Lvs. with usually 5 lobes; cup with appressed scales..........7. *Q. ilicifolia*
            GG. Lvs. with 9–13 lobes; cup with spreading scales..........22. *Q. macrolepis*
          FF. Lobes narrow, often falcate.................................8. *Q. falcata*
        EE. Lvs. green beneath, glabrous or pubescent.
          F. Lvs. pubescent beneath at least when young; upper scales of cup loosely imbricated.
            G. Winter-buds tomentose; lvs. with axillary tufts of hairs beneath.
                                9. *Q. velutina*
            GG. Winter-buds puberulous; lvs. without axillary tufts........10. *Q. Kelloggii*
          FF. Lvs. glabrous beneath.
            G. Longest lobes of the lvs. 2–6 times as long as the narrow middle portion; lvs. lustrous.
              H. Lvs. with conspicuous axillary tufts of hairs beneath.
                I. Lvs. usually cuneate at base; acorn 8–13 mm. long; cup saucer-shaped ....14. *Q. palustris*
                II. Lvs. usually truncate at base; acorn 1.5–2.5 cm. high.
                  J. Winter-buds chestnut-brown: cup turbinate, 1.2–1.8 cm. wide.
                                11. *Q. ellipsoidalis*
                  JJ. Winter-buds light yellowish or grayish brown: cup hemispheric or saucer-shaped, 1–3 cm. wide.....................12. *Q. Shumardii*

HH. Lvs. with small axillary tufts; buds whitish pubescent above the middle; acorn inclosed about ½ by the cup..............13. *Q. coccinea*

GG. Longest lobes almost equaling the width of the broadish middle portion of the leaf; lvs. dull...15. *Q. borealis*

CC. Lvs. serrate: cup with spreading or recurved scales.

D. Lvs. white-tomentose beneath.....................................17. *Q. variabilis*

DD. Lvs. glabrous beneath or pubescent only on the veins.

E. Lvs. glabrous beneath except axillary tufts of hairs, with 10–16 pairs of veins.
18. *Q. acutissima*

EE. Lvs. pubescent on the veins beneath, with 9–12 pairs of veins......20. *Q. libani*

BB. Lobes or teeth not bristly pointed, but sometimes mucronate.

c. Axillary and terminal buds with long filiform persistent stipules; brts. pubescent or tomentose.

D. Lvs. with 8–14 pairs of small triangular mucronate teeth; cup with subulate spreading scales ....19. *Q. castaneaefolia*

DD. Lvs. with 4–10 pairs of lobes.

E. Lvs. elliptic to oblong, 5–10 cm. long, lobes often acutish: cup with spreading subulate scales ....23. *Q. Cerris*

EE. Lvs. obovate, 10–14 cm. long: cup with appressed scales....36. *Q. macranthera*

CC. Axillary buds without persistent stipules: cup with appressed scales except Nos. 21 and 59.

D. Lvs. serrate or sinuately dentate.

E. Lvs. with small mucronate teeth.

F. Lvs. with 15–20 pairs of veins, 10–15 cm. long...................34. *Q. pontica*

FF. Lvs. with less than 13 pairs of veins.

G. Lvs. short-stalked, usually broad at base.

H. Lvs. with 9–12 pairs of veins, acute at apex, auricled at base: cup with spreading scales ....21. *Q. trojana*

HH. Lvs. with 7–9 pairs of veins, usually obtuse at apex, broad-cuneate or rounded at base.......................................33. *Q. lusitanica*

GG. Lvs. slender-stalked, cuneate at base, usually glaucous beneath.
57. *Q. glandulifera*

EE. Lvs. with rather large rounded or sometimes acute and gland-tipped teeth. See also EEE.

F. Brts. glabrous or nearly so.

G. Lvs. glabrous beneath at maturity or pubescent only on the veins or along the midrib.

H. Petioles very short; lvs. auricled at base, hairy on the veins beneath.
58. *Q. mongolica*

HH. Petioles 1–2.5 cm. long; lvs. with brown floccose tomentum along the midrib ....35. *Q. canariensis*

GG. Lvs. tomentose, tomentulose or soft-pubescent beneath.

H. Lvs. obovate to obovate-oblong.

I. Lvs. with 4–8 pairs of veins.

J. Lvs. 6–12 cm. long, with 4–7 pairs of veins and usually acute teeth: shrub ....54. *Q. prinoides*

JJ. Leaves 10–20 cm. long, with 6–8 pairs of veins: fr.-stalk much exceeding the petiole.................................51. *Q. bicolor*

II. Lvs. with 10–17 pairs of veins: fr.-stalk short.

J. Petioles 1.5–3 cm. long; lvs. with 12–17 pairs of veins.

K. Lvs. dark green above, usually tomentose beneath: scales of cup free to the base.............................52. *Q. Prinus*

KK. Lvs. yellow green above, minutely downy beneath: scales of cup free only at tip.............................53. *Q. montana*

JJ. Petioles 1–2 cm. long; lvs. with 10–15 pairs of veins..56. *Q. aliena*

HH. Lvs. lanceolate, acuminate.........................55. *Q. Muhlenbergii*

FF. Brts. pubescent: lvs. obovate, 12–30 cm. long.................59. *Q. dentata*

EEE. Lvs. entire or sometimes slightly 3-lobed at apex..............45. *Q. Durandii*

DD. Lvs. deeply lobed or pinnatifid.

E. Brts. glabrous or nearly so.

F. Lvs. glabrous or slightly pubescent beneath.

G. Petioles less than 1 cm. long; lvs. usually auricled at base: fr. slender-stalked ....41. *Q. robur*

GG. Petioles 1–2.5 cm. long; lvs. usually cuneate at base.

H. Lvs. glaucous or glaucescent beneath, 10–16 cm. long, with 3–4 pairs of lobes: fr. stalked...42. *Q. alba*

HH. Lvs. green beneath, 6–12 cm. long.

I. Lvs. usually lobed less than halfway to the middle with 4–6 pairs of obtuse lobes: scales of cup not thickened..............40. *Q. petraea*

II. Lvs. usually pinnatifid more than halfway to the middle, with 3–5 pairs of acute or acutish lobes: scales of cup thickened.
46. *Q. novo-mexicana*

FF. Lvs. pubescent or tomentose beneath.

G. Lvs. green beneath, soft-pubescent, 6–12 cm. long........47. *Q. utahensis*

GG. Lvs. white-tomentose beneath, sometimes green and soft-pubescent.

H. Lvs. usually sinuate-dentate, with 6–8 pairs of lobes, sometimes pinnatifid, 10–15 cm. long: cup much shorter than acorn......51. *Q. bicolor*

    HH. Lvs. deeply pinnatifid, with 3–4 pairs of lobes, 15–20 cm. long: cup
        large, usually entirely inclosing the acorn..................49. *Q. lyrata*
  EE. Brts. pubescent or tomentose.
    F. Lvs. 15–30 cm. long.
      G. Lvs. pubescent and green beneath, sinuately lobed, short-stalked: cup with
        lanceolate spreading scales....................................59. *Q. dentata*
      GG. Lvs. white-tomentose beneath, lyrate, deeply lobed below the middle:
        upper scales of cup subulate, forming a fringe............50. *Q. macrocarpa*
    FF. Lvs. 5–15 cm. long: cup with small appressed scales.
      G. Lvs. glabrous above or only sparingly stellate-hairy.
        H. Lvs. auriculate at base, 10–18 cm. long, with usually dentate lobes.
                                   37. *Q. Frainetto*
        HH. Lvs. cuneate or rounded at base, rarely subcordate.
          I. Petioles more than 1 cm. long; lvs. 10–15 cm. long...44. *Q. Garryana*
          II. Petioles 1 cm. or less long.
            J. Lvs. soft-pubescent beneath, deeply pinnatifid, 8–12 cm. long.
                                    47. *Q. utahensis*
            JJ. Lvs. usually tomentose beneath, rarely divided more than halfway
              to the middle, 5–10 cm. long......................39. *Q. pubescens*
      GG. Lvs. pubescent above.
        H. Leaves usually 5-lobed, with broad sinuses and broad lobes, 10–14 cm.
        long ....48. *Q. stellata*
        HH. Lvs. 7–13-lobed.
          I. Lobes of lvs. broadly ovate to obovate, obtuse, 6–10 cm. long: fr.
          subsessile, acorn elongated, conical......................43. *Q. lobata*
          II. Lobes of lvs. ovate to ovate-lanceolate, acutish, 6–14 cm. long: fr.
          stalked; acorn subglobose or ovoid..................38. *Q. pyrenaica*

II. Lvs. evergreen

A. Lvs. pubescent below.
  B. Lvs. nearly sessile, subcordate or rounded at base, ovate or elliptic, tomentose beneath.
                                28. *Q. semecarpifolia*
  BB. Lvs. petioled, cuneate to rounded at base, rarely subcordate.
    C. Lvs. beneath with yellow or yellowish tomentum.
      D. Lvs. orbicular to obovate, 3.5–5 cm. long, with prominent veins..27. *Q. alnifolia*
      DD. Lvs. ovate or elliptic to ovate-oblong, 3–10 cm. long, finally glabrous and glaucous
        beneath ....31. *Q. chrysolepis*
    CC. Lvs. beneath with white or grayish tomentum.
      D. Lvs. entire or spinose-dentate, with 7–10 pairs of veins: bark scaly.
        E. Lvs. usually oblong, obtuse, cuneate at base, rarely acute and rounded at base.
                                32. *Q. virginiana*
        EE. Lvs. usually ovate to lanceolate, acute, usually rounded at base......30. *Q. Ilex*
      DD. Lvs. with mucronate teeth or lobes and with 5–7 pairs of veins.
        E. Lvs. toothed, evergreen: bark corky.................................25. *Q. Suber*
        EE. Lvs. lobed, half-evergreen: bark slightly corky.................26. *Q. hispanica*
AA. Lvs. glabrous beneath at maturity.
  B. Lvs. acute or obtuse, 2.5–5, rarely to 7 cm. long.
    C. Lvs. serrate, rounded at base....................................29. *Q. phillyraeoides*
    CC. Lvs. with spiny-tipped teeth, subcordate at base.
      D. Lvs. 2–10 cm. long: scales of cup appressed..........................16. *Q. agrifolia*
      DD. Lvs. 1.5–5 cm. long: scales of cup spreading..........................24. *Q. coccifera*
  BB. Lvs. acuminate, 7–10 cm. long..................................1. *Q. myrsinaefolia*

Subgen. I. CYCLOBALANOPSIS Prantl. Cupula with the scales connate
into concentric rings: styles short; aborted ovules near the apex of the fr.: lvs.
evergreen, entire or dentate. (*Cyclobalanopsis* Oerst.)

1. **Q. myrsinaefòlia** Bl. Evergreen tree to 18 m.: lvs. lanceolate to oblong-
lanceolate, 5–12 cm. long, 1.5–3 cm. broad, acuminate, cuneate at base, serrate,
glabrous, lustrous above, glaucescent beneath: frs. in short spikes; acorn
ovoid-oblong, 1.5–2 cm. long, inclosed about ⅓ by the glabrous cup. S.I.1:
t.29(c). N.K.3:t.25. C.Q.t.16,f.7–21. (*Q. Vibreyana* Franch. & Sav., *Q. bam-
busaefolia* Fort., not Hance.) Japan, E. China. Intr. 1854. Zone (VI). Confused with *Q. acuta, Q. glauca* and *Lithocarpus glaber (Q. thalassica).* This
seems to be the only species of this subgenus which survives in Zone VII.

Subgen. II. ERYTHROBALANUS Spach. Scales of cup not connate into
rings, appressed; style elongated, capitate; aborted ovules near apex of fr.;
walls of nut tomentose inside; fr. ripening the second year: lvs. deciduous or
evergreen, lobed or entire, lobes and apex bristle-pointed.

2. **Q. Phéllos** L. WILLOW O. Tree to 30 m.; brts. slender, reddish brown,
glabrous; lvs. linear-oblong to lanceolate, acute at ends, 5–10 cm. long, lus-

trous above, pubescent below while young, glabrate at length and light green; fr. nearly sessile; acorn hemispherical, about 1 cm. high, inclosed only at base by the saucer-shaped cup. S.S.8:t.435. M.S.1:t.14(c). H.H.158,159(b). Am. For. 27:461(h). J.L.45:207(h). N. Y. to Fla., w. to Mo. and Tex. Intr. 1723. Zone V. Tree with conical round topped head and willow-like lvs. turning pale yellow in fall.

    Q. P. × *borealis maxima* = **Q. heterophýlla** Michx. f. Brts. glabrous: lvs. oblong to elliptic, with 3–5 pairs of teeth, or entire, glabrous beneath except axillary tufts of hairs. M.S.1:t.18(c). S.S.8:t.486. N. J. to Tex. Cult. 1822.—
Q. P. × *falcata* = **Q. ludoviciàna** Sarg. Lvs. oblong, 10–15 cm. long, usually with 3–4 triangular-ovate teeth or lobes near apex or entire, green and pubescent to glabrate beneath. (*Q. subfalcata* Trel.) With the parents. Intr. ?—
Q. l. microcárpa (Sarg.) Rehd., var. Lvs. oblong-lanceolate, 7–9 cm. long, shallowly lobed. D.L.2:107. (*Q. Phellos microcarpa* Hort., *Q. subfalcata* var. *m.* Sarg.) Cult. 1880. Zone V.—*Q. P.* × *palustris* = **Q. Schochiàna** Dieck. Lvs. oblong to narrow-oblong, usually with 1–3 teeth or lobes on each side, rarely entire, 6–12 cm. long, green and nearly glabrous beneath. Cult. 1896.—*Q. P.* × *marilandica* = **Q. Rudkínii** Britt. With the parents. Intr. 1925.—*Q. P.* × *velutina* = **Q. inaequàlis** Palmer & Steyerm. With the parents. Intr. 1925.

    3. **Q. imbricària** Michx. Shingle O. Tree to 20, rarely to 30 m. tall; brts. slender, soon glabrous, light brown: lvs. oblong or oblong-lanceolate, acute or rounded at ends, 7–16 cm. long, with slightly thickened revolute margin, dark green and glabrous above, pale green or brownish and pubescent beneath; petioles 5–15 mm. long: fr. short-stalked; acorn hemispherical, 1–1.5 cm. high, inclosed ⅓ to ½ by the turbinate cup. S.S.8:t.432. M.S.1:t.15(c). H.H.162,163(b). M.M.6:91(h). Pa. to Ga., w. to Neb. and Ark. Intr. 1724. Zone V. Pyramidal while young, round-topped when old, with lustrous lvs. turning russet-red in fall.

    Q. i. × *velutina* = **Q. Leàna** Nutt. Brts. scurfy: lvs. sinuately toothed, rarely entire, rounded at base, 8–16 cm. long, scurfy beneath. N.S.1:t.bis(c). S.S. 8:t.434. With the parents. Intr. before 1850.—*Q. i.* × *palustris* = **Q. exàcta** Trel. Brts. glabrous: lvs. oblong-lanceolate, coarsely toothed or entire, soon glabrous, 10–15 cm. long: cup turbinate. With the parents. Cult. 1889.—
Q. i. × *borealis maxima* = **Q. runcinàta** Engelm. Lvs. slender-stalked, elliptic-oblong, 10–16 cm. long, with usually 3 lobes on each side, usually broad-cuneate to nearly rounded at base, glabrous and usually pale green beneath. With the parents. Intr. 1883.—*Q. i.* × *marilandica* = **Q. tridentàta** Engelm. With the parents. Intr. ?

    4. **Q. laurifòlia** Michx. Laurel O. Tree to 20, rarely to 30 m.: brts. slender, glabrous, dark brown: lvs. oblong or oblong-obovate, 5–14 cm. long, acute or rarely rounded at ends, entire or sometimes slightly lobed, lustrous and dark green above, light green beneath, puberulous at first, soon glabrous; petioles yellow, 5–8 mm. long: fr. short-stalked; acorn subglobose to ovoid, 1–1.5 cm. long, inclosed only at base by the saucer-shaped cup. S.S.8:t.429,430. M.S.1:t.15(c). H.H.160,161(b). F.E.16:396,t.62(h). Va. to Fla. and La. Intr. 1786. Zone VII? Dense round-topped tree with half-evergreen lustrous foliage.

    5. **Q. nígra** L. Water O. Tree to 25 m.: lvs. obovate, 3-lobed at apex, or sometimes entire, rarely pinnately lobed above the middle, 3–7 long, dull bluish green above, paler beneath, soon glabrous except axillary tufts of brown hairs; petioles 5–10 mm. long: frs. short-stalked; acorn globose-ovoid, 1–1.5 cm. long, inclosed ⅓ or ¼ by the saucer-shaped cup; scales acute, closely appressed. S.S.8:t.428. M.S.1:t.19(c). H.H.156,157(b). E.H.5:t.312(h). (*Q. aquatica* Walt., *Q. uliginosa* Wangh.) Del. to Fla., w. to Ky. and Tex. Intr. 1723. Zone VI. Tree with rather slender brs. forming a conical round-topped head. Often planted as an avenue tree.·

Related species: **Q. obtùsa** (Willd.) Ashe. Tree to 40 m.: lvs. rhombic to rhombic-oblong, rarely oblong-obovate or lanceolate, 6–10 cm. long, dark green and lustrous above: acorn about 1 cm. long; scales obtuse, loosely appressed. S.M.262. (*Q. rhombica* Sarg.) Va. to Fla. and La. Cult. 1927. Zone VII.

6. **Q. marilándica** Muenchh. BLACK-JACK. Tree to 10 or sometimes to 18 m. high: leaves broad-obovate, 10–20 cm. long, and often nearly as broad at apex, rounded at base, 3–5-lobed at apex, with broad, entire or sparingly toothed lobes, dark green and glabrous above, brownish tomentose beneath, finally nearly glabrous and yellowish green; petioles 1–2 cm. long: frs. short-stalked; acorn ovoid-oblong, 2 cm. high, often striate, inclosed ⅓ to ⅔ by the turbinate cup, its upper scales smaller and forming a thick rim round its inner surface, occasionally reflexed and covering the upper half of the inner surface. S.S.8:t.426,427. M.S.t.20(c). H.H.154,155(b). (*Q. nigra* Wangh., not L., *Q. ferruginea* Michx.) N. Y. to Fla., w. to Neb. and Tex. Intr. before 1739. Zone VI. Tree with stout spreading brs. forming a narrow, often irregular head, with large lustrous lvs. turning brown or yellow in fall.

Q. m. × *texana* = **Q.** Hastíngsii Sarg. Lvs. more deeply lobed, 6–8 cm. long, glabrous: fr. smaller. With the parents. Intr. about 1925. Zone VI.—*Q. m.* × *velutina* = **Q.** Búshii Sarg. With the parents. Cult. 1931. Zone V.—*Q. m.* × *Phellos;* see under No. 2.—*Q. m.* × *imbricaria;* see under No. 3.—*Q. m.* × *ilicifolia;* see under No. 7.

Related species: **Q. arkansana** Sarg. Lvs. broad-obovate, 5–8 cm. long, cuneate, slightly 3-lobed at apex, or on sterile branches elliptic to ovate, rounded at base and undulately lobed, stellate-pubescent beneath at first, later glabrous or nearly so: acorn broad-ovoid, 1.5 cm. across. S.T.2:t.152. Ark. Intr. 1909. Zone V.

7. **Q. ilicifòlia** Wangh. SCRUB O. Intricately branched spreading shrub, to 3 m., rarely small tree to 7 m.; brts. hoary-pubescent: lvs. obovate or rarely oblong, 5–12 cm. long, broad-cuneate at base, sinuately lobed with usually 2 pairs of broad triangular lobes entire or with few bristly teeth, dark green and glabrous above, whitish tomentulose beneath; petioles 2–3.5 cm. long: fr. short-stalked; acorns globose-ovoid, about 1 cm. high, inclosed about ½ by the saucer-shaped cup. S.S.8:t.424. M.S.1:t.21(c). (*Q. Banisteri* Michx., *Q. nana* Sarg.) Me. to Va., w. to Ohio and Ky. Intr. about 1800. Zone V. Densely branched spreading shrub with dull dark green foliage.

Q. i. × *coccinea* = **Q.** Robbínsii Trel. Lvs. 8–12 cm. long, with usually 3 pairs of lobes, slightly tomentose or often glabrescent at maturity beneath: acorns about 12 mm. long, inclosed about ½ by the cup. With the parents. Intr. 1913.—*Q. i.* × *velutina* = **Q.** Rèhderi Trel. Lvs. 8–10 cm. long, with 2–3 pairs of lobes, slightly tomentulose or glabrate at maturity beneath: cup with larger tomentulose scales. Rh.3:t.24. With the parents. Intr. about 1905.— *Q. i.* × *marilandica* = **Q.** Brittónii W. T. Davis. With the parents. Cult. 1888.

8. **Q. falcàta** Michx. SPANISH O. Tree to 25 or occasionally to 30 m.; brts. rusty-tomentose: lvs. elliptic-oblong or obovate, 8–20 cm. long, broad-cuneate or sometimes rounded at base, deeply sinuately lobed, with 3–7 acute lobes gradually narrowed from a broad base, often falcate, entire or repand-dentate, the terminal lobe elongated, dark green and glabrous above, tawny or grayish pubescent beneath, drooping; petioles 2.5–5 cm. long: fr. short-stalked; acorn subglobose, 1–1.5 cm. high, inclosed only at base or sometimes ⅓ by the saucer-shaped cup puberulous inside. S.S.8:t.420. M.S.1:t.23(c). G.F.8:104 (b). F.E.29:943(h). (*Q. rubra* L., not Du Roi, *Q. digitata* Sudw., *Q. triloba* Michx., *Q. cuneata* auth., not Wangh.) N. J. to Fla., w. to Mo. and Tex. Intr. before 1763. Zone VI. Tree with stout spreading brs. forming an open round-topped head, with dark green deeply cut drooping lvs.—**Q. f. pagodae-fòlia** Ell., var. SWAMP SPANISH O. Tree to 40 m.; brts. hoary-tomentose: lvs.

usually rounded at base, less deeply lobed, with 5–11 broader lobes, white-tomentose beneath. S.S.14:t.772. (*Q. p.* Ashe.) Va. to Fla., w. to s. Ill. and Ark. Intr. 1904. Zone VII?

    Q. f. × *Phellos;* see under No. 2.

    Related species: **Q. laevis** Walt. Tree to 20 m.: lvs. similar to those of *Q. falcata* but with petioles 1–2 cm. long, at maturity lustrous and glabrous below; cup turbinate; scales extending above the rim and down the inner surface. S.S. 8:t.417. (*Q. Catesbaei* Michx.) N. C. to Fla. and La. Intr. about 1834. Zone VII?

    9. **Q. velutìna** Lam. BLACK O. Tree to 30 or occasionally to 50 m.; bark dark brown, inner bark orange; brts. scurfy-tomentose, glabrescent the first winter; buds pubescent: lvs. ovate to oblong, 10–25 cm. long, cuneate to truncate at base, sinuately lobed halfway to the middle or beyond, with 7–9 broad, repand-dentate lobes, lustrous dark green above, brown-pubescent beneath at first, finally often glabrous except in the axils of the veins; petioles stout, 3–6 cm. long, yellow: fr. short-stalked, acorn ovoid, 1.5–2 cm. high, often striate, inclosed about ½ by the turbinate cup, with loosely imbricated pubescent scales, the free tips of the upper scales forming a short fringe-like border. S.S.8:t.414,415. M.S.1:t.24(c). H.H.148,149(b). Em.160,t(h). G.F. 5:55(h). B.T.289(h). (*Q. tinctoria* Bartr.) Me. to Fla., w. to Minn. and Tex. Intr. about 1800. Zone IV.—Large tree of rapid growth with rather slender brs. forming an open narrow head, and with lustrous lvs. turning dull red or orange-brown in fall. The bark is used for tanning.—**Q. v. missouriénsis** Sarg., var. Lvs. with permanent rusty pubescence beneath; cup-scales tomentose. W. Mo. to Ark. Intr. 1905. Zone V.

    Q. v. × *Phellos;* see under No. 2.—*Q. v.* × *imbricaria;* see under No. 3.— *Q. v.* × *ilicifolia;* see under No. 7.—*Q. v.* × *borealis maxima;* see under No. 15.

    10. **Q. Kellóggii** Newb. CALIFORNIAN BLACK O. Tree to 30 m.: bark dark brown or nearly black; brts. hoary-tomentose at first; buds puberulous or nearly glabrous: lvs. oblong, 8–15 cm. long, cuneate or truncate at base, sinuately 7- or rarely 5-lobed about halfway to the middle, with oblong repand-dentate lobes, pubescent at first, at maturity thick and firm, glabrous and lustrous above, glabrous or pubescent beneath or sometimes hoary-tomentose; petioles slender, 3–5 cm. long: fr. short-stalked; acorn ovoid-oblong, 2.5–3.5 cm. long, inclosed about ¼ or ⅔ by the deep cup-shaped cup with glabrous loosely imbricated scales. S.S.8:t.416. G.F.9:145(h). (*Q. californica* Coop.) Ore. to Calif. Intr. 1878. Zone VII? Tree with stout spreading brs. forming an open round-topped head.

    11. **Q. ellipsoidàlis** E. J. Hill. Tree to 25 m.; bark gray, close and smooth or shallowly fissured; brts. tomentose at first; buds slightly puberulous: lvs. elliptic, 8–12 cm. long, truncate to broad-cuneate at base, deeply sinuately 5–6-lobed, with oblong, coarsely repand-dentate lobes, soon glabrous except the sometimes very small axillary tufts beneath; petioles 3–5 cm. long: fr. short-stalked or nearly sessile; acorn ellipsoid to subglobose, 1.2–2 cm. long, inclosed ⅓ or nearly ½ by the turbinate cup with closely appressed pale brown-puberulent scales. S.S.14:t.771. H.H.144,145(b). S. Mich. to Man. and Ia. Intr. 1902. Zone IV. Similar to the Pin Oak in habit.

    12. **Q. Shumárdii** Buckl. Tree to 40 m.; bark gray or reddish brown, broken into small scaly plates; brts. glabrous; buds glabrous, rarely pubescent, grayish: lvs. obovate to elliptic-oblong, 8–18 cm. long, 5–9-lobed, on the lower brs. usually 7-lobed, with broad, rather short lobes, on the upper brs. 7–9-lobed and deeply divided by broad sinuses more than halfway to the middle, lobes toothed and often lobulate, dark green and lustrous above, lighter

green beneath, with conspicuous axillary tufts of hairs; petioles 4–6 cm. long: fr. short-stalked or subsessile; acorn ovoid to oblong-ovoid, 1.5–3 cm. long, inclosed only at base by the saucer-shaped cup sometimes to 3 cm. across and covered with appressed often tuberculate scales. S.M.243. (*Q. texana* var. *S.* Sarg.) Kans. and s. Mich. to N. C., Fla. and Tex. Intr. 1907. Zone V. Handsome tree with widespreading brs., resembling *Q. coccinea* in foliage and *Q. borealis maxima* in fr.—**Q. S. Schnéckii** (Brit.) Sarg., var. Fr. with deep cup-shaped cup, inclosing about ⅓ of the nut, with usually thin, rarely tuberculate scales. S.S.8:t.411 (excl.f.5–7). S.M.244. G.F.7:515. (*Q. S.* Brit., *Q. texana* var. *S.* Sarg., *Q. texana* Sarg., in part.) Ill. and Ohio to Tex. Intr. 1897.—**Q. S. acerifòlia** Palmer, var. Shrub or small tree: lvs. about as broad as long, 6–10 cm. long, often deeply 3-lobed in outline; acorns 6–12 mm. long, enclosed ⅕–⅓ by the shallow cup. Ark. Intr. 1924. Zone V.

Q. S. Schneckii × *palustris* = **Q. mutàbilis** Palmer & Steyerm. With the parents. Intr. 1923.

Closely related species: **Q. texàna** Buckl. Tree to 10 m.; buds pubescent; lvs. not dimorphous, smaller, 6–9 cm. long, usually 5-lobed, rarely with small axillary tufts of hairs beneath: acorn smaller; cup turbinate. S.M.245. G.F. 7:517. Texas. Probably not hardy.—*Q. t.* × *marilandica;* see under No. 6.— **Q. Nuttállii** Palmer. Tree to 25 m.: lvs. deeply 5–7-lobed with wide sinuses and rather narrow lobes: acorn oblong-ovoid or short-cylindric, enclosed ⅓–½ by the usually turbinate cup; scales looser, more pubescent. Miss. and s. e. Mo. to e. Texas. Intr. 1923. Zone V.

13. **Q. coccínea** Muenchh. Scarlet O. Tree to 25 m.; bark gray, the inner reddish; brts. soon glabrous becoming orange-red; buds dark reddish brown, pubescent above the middle: lvs. oblong or elliptic, 8–15 cm. long, truncate or rarely broadly cuneate at base, sinuately pinnatifid, with 7, rarely 9, oblong, sparingly repand-dentate lobes, bright green and glabrous beneath except small axillary tufts of rusty hairs; petioles slender, 3–6 m. long: fr. short-stalked; acorn ovoid, 1.3–2 cm. long, inclosed about ⅓–½ by the turbinate or hemispheric cup with rather large appressed and glabrate scales. S.S.8:t.412,413. M.S.1:t.25(c). Em.1:164,t.(c). H.H.146,147(b). Me. to Fla., w. to Minn. and Mo. Intr. 1691. Zone IV. Tree with gradually spreading brs. forming a round-topped, rather open head, and with handsome bright green lvs. turning brilliant scarlet in fall.

Q. c. × *borealis maxima* = **Q. Bénderi** Baenitz. Buds and lvs. intermediate: cup turbinate. Orig. in Eu. before 1900; also spont. with the parents.—*Q. c.* × *ilicifolia;* see under No. 7.

14. **Q. palústris** Muenchh. Pin O. Tree to 25 or occasionally to 40 m.; brts. soon glabrous, becoming dark red-brown or orange; buds chestnut-brown, glabrate: lvs. elliptic or elliptic-oblong, 8–12 cm. long, usually cuneate at base, sinuately pinnatifid, with 5–7 oblong to oblong-lanceolate repand-dentate lobes, bright green above, lighter green, lustrous and glabrous beneath except axillary tufts of hairs; petioles slender, 2–5 cm. long: fr. sessile or short-stalked; acorn nearly hemispheric, 1–1.5 cm. across, inclosed about ⅓ by the thin saucer-shaped cup; scales closely appressed, puberulous. S.S.8:t.422,423. M.S.1:t.27(c). R.H.1921:438,t(c). Em.167,t(h). B.T.284(h). Mass. to Del., w. to Wis. and Ark. Intr. before 1770. Zone IV. Tree with slender spreading brs., usually pendulous at the ends, forming a symmetrical pyramidal head while young, irregular and oblong in older trees. Of rapid growth while young and often used for avenues.

Q. p. × *borealis maxima* = **Q. Ríchteri** Baenitz. Lvs. deeply lobed with 4–5 pairs of lobes, cuneate at base: cup saucer-shaped. Orig. before 1900 in Eu.; also spont. with the parents.—*Q. p.* × *Phellos;* see under No. 2.—*Q. p.* × *imbricaria;* see under No. 3.—*Q. p.* × *Shumardii Schneckii;* see under No. 12.

Related species: **Q georgiàna** M. A. Curt. Shrub to 3 m. or small tree: lvs smaller, less deeply lobed, the lobes entire or with 1 or 2 small teeth: cup thick, cup-shaped. S.S.8:t.425. Ga. Intr. 1876. Zone V.

15. Q. boreàlis Michx. f. RED O. Tree to 20 or 25 m.; brts. soon glabrous, becoming dark red; buds glabrous except at apex: lvs. oblong, 12–22 cm. long, usually cuneate at the base, sinuately 7–11-lobed about halfway to the middle, lobes triangular-ovate or ovate-oblong, with a few irregular teeth, dull green above, grayish or whitish or sometimes pale yellow-green beneath and gla-brous except axillary tufts of brownish hairs; petioles 2–5 cm. long: fr. short-stalked; acorn ovoid, 2–2.5 cm. high; cup turbinate or hemispheric, inclosing the acorn about ⅓, 1.5–2 cm. across, with closely appressed puberulous scales. M.S.1:t.26(c). S.M.241. (*Q. ambigua* Michx., f., not H.B.K., *Q. rubra* var. *ambigua* Fern.) N. S. to Pa., w. to Minn. and Iowa. Intr. 1800. Zone IV. Beautiful Oak of rapid growth with stout spreading brs. forming a broad round-topped head and with large lvs. turning dark red in fall. Often planted as shade and avenue tree.—**Q. b. máxima** (Marsh.) Ashe. Tree to 25 or occa-sionally to 50 m.; fr. larger; acorn 2.5–3 cm. high; acorn inclosed only at base by the saucer-shaped cup 2.5–3 cm. broad. S.S.8:t.409,410. M.S.1:t.28(c). H.H.138,139(b). Em.168,t(h). E.H.5:t.314(h). (*Q. rubra* Du Roi, not L., *Q. m.* Ashe.) N. S. to Fla., w. to Minn. and Tex. Intr. 1724.

Q. b. m. × *velutina* = **Q. Pòrteri** Trel. With the parents. Intr. 1877.—*Q. b. m.* × *imbricaria;* see under No. 3.—*Q. b. m.* × *coccinea;* see under No. 13. —*Q. b. m.* × *palustris;* see under No. 14.

16. Q. agrifòlia Née. Evergreen tree to 30 m., often shrubby; brts. tomen-tose: lvs. broad-elliptic to elliptic-oblong, 3–7 cm. long, acute or rounded at apex, usually rounded at base, sinuately spiny-toothed, rarely entire, usually convex, dark green above, paler and rather lustrous beneath, glabrous and with axillary tufts of hairs or stellate-pubescent, subcoriaceous: fr. sessile; acorn conic-ovoid, usually elongated, 2–3.5 cm. long, inclosed ¼–⅓ by the turbinate cup silky-pubescent inside, puberulous outside. S.S.8:t.403. N.S. 1:t.2(c). B.C.5:f.3321,3322. J.S.t.71(h). Calif. Intr. 1849. Zone VII? A related species is **Q. Wislizèni** A. DC. Tree to 25 m.: lvs. coriaceous, oblong-lanceolate to elliptic, 2.5–4 cm. long, acute or rounded and mucronate at apex, entire or serrulate to sinuate-dentate, with spinescent teeth: fr. usually short-stalked; acorn enclosed usually about ½ by the thin turbinate cup. S.S. 8:t.406. Calif. and n. Mex. Intr. 1874. Zone VII?—*Q. W.* × *Cerris;* see under No. 23.

Subgen. III. **LEPIDOBALANUS** Endl. Cup with the scales not connate into rings, appressed or spreading: aborted ovules near base of fr.; walls of nut glabrous inside (except in No. 31); fr. ripening the first or second year.

Sect. 1. CERRIS Loud. Styles linear, acute, upright or recurved; scales of cup spreading or recurved; fr. biennial: lvs. deciduous, rarely half-evergreen.

17. Q. variàbilis Bl. Tree to 25 m.; bark yellowish gray, corky, deeply furrowed; brts. soon glabrous; buds acute: lvs. oblong to oblong-lanceolate, 8–15 cm. long, acuminate, usually broad-cuneate at base, crenately serrate with bristle-like teeth terminating the 9–16 pairs of parallel veins, dark green and glabrous above, white-tomentose beneath; petioles 5–25 mm. long: fr. nearly sessile; acorn subglobose or globose-ovoid, 1.5–2 cm. long, little longer than the cup; scales subulate, recurved. S.I.1:t.28(c). N.K.3:t.10. (*Q. chinensis* Bge., not Abel, *Q. Bungeana* Forb., *Q. serrata* Carruthers, not Thunb.) N. China, Korea, Japan. Intr. 1861. Zone V. Tree with distinct foliage resembling that of *Castanea crenata*.

18. Q. acutíssima Carruthers. Tree to 15 m.; brts. glabrous: lvs. obovate-oblong to oblong, acute, 8–18 cm. long, broad-cuneate or rounded at base, serrate with bristle-like teeth terminating the 12–16 parallel veins, lustrous and glabrous above, light green and glabrous beneath except axillary tufts of hairs, pubescent only when unfolding; petioles 1.5–2.5 cm. long: fr. sessile; cup with long, spreading and recurving scales, inclosing about ⅔ of the nut. S.I.1:t.26(c). N.K.3:t.9. (*Q. serrata* Sieb. & Zucc., not Thunb.) Japan, Korea, China, Himal. Intr. 1862. Zone VI? Tree with chestnut-like foliage.

Related species: **Q. Barònii** Skan. Half-evergreen shrub or small tree: lvs. short-stalked, ovate-oblong to lanceolate-oblong, 4–6 cm. long, with 5–7 pairs of small bristly teeth, glabrous or nearly so beneath except the tomentose midrib. W. China. B.J.29:291. Intr. 1915. Zone VII?

19. **Q. castaneaefòlia** C. A. Mey. Tree to 25 m.; brts. tomentulose at first, later glabrous; stipules persistent: lvs. elliptic-oblong to oblong-lanceolate, 7–16 cm. long, acute, cuneate or rounded at base, coarsely serrate with mucronate teeth, dark green above, grayish tomentulose or pubescent, rarely nearly glabrous beneath, with 6–12 pairs of veins; petioles 1.5–2.5 cm. long: fr. subsessile; acorn ovoid, 2–3 cm. long, inclosed ⅓ to ½ by the cup-shaped cup; scales recurved, the lower ones ovate. Kotschy, Eich. t.40(c). B.S.2:304,t(h). J.L.45:164(h). Cauc., Persia. Intr. about 1840. Zone VI? Tree with spreading brs. forming a broad round head and with chestnut-like lvs.—**Q. c. incàna** Batt., var. Tree of erect pyramidal habit with smaller comparatively broader lvs. 6–12 cm. long. E.H.5:t.323(h). (*Q. c.* var. *algeriensis* Bean, *Q. Afares* Pomel.) N. Afr. Intr. 1869. Zone VII?

20. **Q. líbani** Oliv. LEBANON O. Tree to 10 m.; brts. soon glabrous: lvs. oblong-lanceolate, 5–10 cm. long, acuminate, rounded at base, serrate with bristle-tipped triangular teeth terminating the 9–12 pairs of veins, glabrous and dark green above, light green beneath and sparingly pubescent on the nerves or finely short-pubescent all over; petioles 1–1.5 cm. long: frs. 1–2 on thick stalks about 1.5 cm. long; acorn broad-ovoid, about 2.5 cm. across, inclosed about ⅔ by the large cup with loosely appressed upright scales. B.S. 2:315. R.H.1872:155. S.L.287. Syria, Asia Min. Intr. 1855. Zone V? Handsome small tree.—*Q. l.* var. *angustifolia* Dipp. is scarcely distinct.

21. **Q. trojàna** Webb. Half-evergreen tree to 10 m. or shrubby; brts. scurfy: lvs. ovate-oblong to oblong, 3–7 cm. long, acute, usually rounded at base, sinuately toothed with mucronate teeth, terminating the 8–12 parallel veins, lustrous dark green above, light beneath, sparingly stellate-pubescent while young, finally nearly glabrous; petioles 2–4 mm. long: acorn ovoid, 2.5–3.5 cm. high, inclosed more than ½ by the large cup with the lower scales ovate and appressed, the middle ones recurved and the upper ones lanceolate and upright or inversed. H.W.2:83. S.H.1:f.170a. (*Q. macedonica* A. DC.) Maced., Albania. Intr. about 1890. Zone VI? Small tree or shrub with bright green rather small half-evergreen lvs.

22. **Q. macrólepis** Kotschy. Tree to 25 m.; brts. yellowish tomentose: lvs. elliptic to oblong, 5–10 cm. long, acute, usually subcordate at base, with 3–6 pairs of triangular, entire, bristle-tipped lobes, at first yellowish tomentose, finally glabrate above; petioles 1.5–3 cm. long: fr. sessile; acorn to 4.5 cm. long, inclosed ⅓ to ½ by the cup-shaped cup 3–4 cm. across; scales large and thickened, the upper ones narrower and reflexed. Kotschy, Eich. t.30(c, as *Q. graeca*). S.H.1:f.108m(l). C.Q.t.55,56. E.H.5:t.322(h). (*Q. Aegilops* Lam., not L.) S. Italy, Balk. Pen., W. Asia. Intr. 1731. Zone VII?

Related species: **Q. Ehrenbérgii** Kotschy. Lvs. usually distinctly lobed with acute lobes: acorn ovoid, about 3 cm. long, exceeding the subglobose cup about ½; scales upright or slightly inflexed, the lower ovate and mucronate. C.Q.t. 54,f.7–9. Asia Minor. Cult. 1880. Zone VII?

23. **Q. Cérris** L. Turkey O. Tree to 35 m.; bark dark, furrowed; brts. usually tomentose; buds ovoid, pubescent, surrounded by subulate persistent stipules; lvs. narrow-oblong to obovate-oblong, 6–12 cm. long, acute, rounded or subcordate at base, with 4–9 pairs of mucronate lobes entire or with 1–4 small teeth, dark green and somewhat rough above, light green beneath and stellate-pubescent at first, finally pubescent only on the nerves; petioles 1–2 cm. long: frs. subsessile, 1–4; acorn oblong-ovoid, 2.5–3 cm. high, inclosed about ½ by the cup-shaped cup covered with subulate recurved scales. H.W. 2:74–76,t.25(c). C.Q.t.62–66. F.E.14:1264,t.41(h). E.H.5:t.316–318(h). S. Eu., W. Asia. Intr. 1735. Zone VI. Ornamental tree with spreading and slender, rather short brs. forming a broad pyramidal head, and with dark green lvs. turning brown late in fall.—**Q. C. laciniàta** Loud., var. Lvs. pinnatifid, with acute, usually dentate lobes. C.Q.t.64,f.5,6. S.H.1:f.110c.—**Q. C. péndula** Loud., var. Brs. pendulous; lvs. pinnatifid.—**Q. C. austríaca** Loud., var. Lvs. shallowly lobed, with broad triangular obtusish and mucronate lobes. Kotschy, Eich. t.20(c). C.Q.t.65,f. S.H.1:f.110b,d.—**Q. C. Ambrozyàna** (Simonkai) Aschers. & Graebn., var. Stipules caducous; lvs. smaller, half-evergreen, glabrous above, with bristly teeth. Possibly hybrid. Orig. in Hungary before 1909.

Q. C. × *Wislizeni* = **Q. kewénsis** Osborn. Evergreen tree: lvs. oval to oblong, 5–8 cm. long, deeply lobed, glabrous and lustrous. G.C.90:475(h). Orig. 1914. Zone VII?—*Q. C.* × *Suber;* see No .26.

Sect. 2. Suber Reichb. Styles linear, acutish, upright or recurved; cup with recurved or loosely appressed scales: fr. ripening the first or second year: lvs. evergreen.

24. **Q. coccífera** L. Kermes O. Evergreen shrub or small tree: young brts. stellate-pubescent, finally glabrous: buds small, brown, nearly glabrous: lvs. rigid, broad-elliptic to ovate-oblong, 1.5–4 cm. long, spiny-pointed, rounded or subcordate at base, undulate and with 2–5 spiny teeth on each side, lustrous and glabrous on both sides; petioles 2–4 mm. long: fr. biennial, short-stalked; cup cup-shaped with short spreading spiny scales, inclosing more than ½ of the subglobose or ovoid acorn 1.5–3 cm. long. H.W.2:82,t. 25(c). R.I.12:t.643(c). B.S.2:306. S. Eu., W. Asia, N. Afr. Intr. 1683. Zone VII? Evergreen shrub with small lustrous lvs.; the host plant of the kermes insect.

Related species: **Q. callíprinos** Webb. Tree: lvs. usually oblong, mucronate-serrate, rarely spiny or subentire, to 5 cm. long: cup larger, with more elongated scales; acorn usually exserted ½ or less. C.Q.t.50,51,f.1–5. K.B.1919: 235;1920:257,t.(h). (*Q. palaestina* Kotschy.) W. Asia. Intr. 1855. Zone VII.

25. **Q. Sùber** L. Cork O. Evergreen tree to 20 m.; bark thick and corky, deeply furrowed; brts. yellow-tomentose: lvs. ovate to ovate-oblong, 3–7 cm. long, acute, rounded or subcordate at base, with 4–5 pairs of short teeth, rarely nearly entire, lustrous dark green above, grayish tomentose beneath, rarely glabrescent; petioles 8–15 mm.: fr. short-stalked, annual: acorn ovoid-oblong, 1.5–3 cm. long; cup cup-shaped, its upper scales elongated, upright or sometimes spreading. M.S.1:t.13(c). Kotschy, Eich. t.33(c). C.Q.t.40–47. H.W.2:80,81(h). E.H.5:t.328(h). Am. For. 19:525,527(h). S. Eu., N. Afr. Intr. 1699. Zone VII? Tree with broad round-topped head and short trunk; the thick corky bark is the source of the cork of commerce.—**Q. S. occidentàlis** (Gay) Arcang., var. Lvs. usually falling in spring; frs. biennial. C.Q.t.48,f.1–8. (*Q. o.* Gay.) S. W. Eu. Intr. about 1826. Zone VII?; said to be hardier than the type.

26. × **Q. hispánica** Lam. (*Q. Cerris* × *Suber.*) Half-evergreen tree to 30 m. or shrub; bark thick, slightly corky; brts. tomentose: lvs. subcoriaceous,

ovate-oblong to oblong, 4–10 cm. long, acute, usually rounded at base, with 4–7 pairs of short triangular, mucronate lobes, sparingly pubescent and dark green above, grayish tomentose beneath; petioles 5–10 mm. long: fr. subsessile, biennial; acorn ovoid-oblong; cup large, with stout recurved scales. Kotschy, Eich. t.35(c). H.W.2:82. C.Q.t.77,f.1–25. S.H.1:f.113c-h. Sparingly with the parents in S. France, Italy, Balkan Pen. Intr. 1830. Zone VII? The same cross has originated repeatedly in cult. and has given rise to several distinct variations: **Q. h. Lucombeàna** (Sweet) Rehd., var. Pyramidal tree 30 m., with corky bark: lvs. generally longer and narrower and usually more deeply toothed than in the type. S.H.1:f.119c. L.A.3:1852,1853(h). B.S.2:316,t(h). J.L.45:187(h). (*Q. L.* Sweet, *Q. Cerris* var. *L.* Loud., *Q. exoniensis* Lodd., *Q. pseudosuber* var. *aegylopifolia* DC.) Orig. about 1765 in England.—**Q. h. críspa** (Loud.) Rehd., var. Bark very corky; lvs. smaller, 5–8 cm. long, with wrinkled margin, densely white-tomentose beneath. L.A.3:f.1715,1717c, 1718(h). (*Q. Cerris* var. *c.* Loud., *Q. Lucombeana* var. *c.* Henry.)—**Q. h. heterophýlla** (Loud.) Rehd., var. Lvs. oblong, irregularly and deeply lobed, occasionally in the middle with a deep wide sinus on each side: scales of the turbinate cup mostly short. L.A.3:f.1719. (*Q. Lucombeana* var. *h.* Henry.) **Q. h. diversifòlia** (Nichols.) Rehd., var. Smaller tree with ascending brs. and very corky bark: lvs. about 5 cm. long and 2 cm. or less wide, usually in the middle with a deep wide sinus on each side, the lower portion with 1–4 lobes, the upper entire or toothed, white tomentose beneath, subcoriaceous: cup hemispheric, with short partly appressed scales. E.H.5:t.339,f.71. (*Q. Ilex* var. *d.* Nichols., *Q. Lucombeana* var. *d.* Henry.)—**Q. h. dentàta** (Wats.) Rehd., var. FULHAM O. Tree with slenderer brs.; bark less corky: lvs. smaller and broader than those of var. *Lucombeana*, about 8 cm. long and 3.5 cm. broad, rounded and occasionally auricled at base, white-tomentose beneath. W.D. 2:t.93(c). C.Q.t.77,f.26–29. E.H.5:t.319(h),335,f.21. (*Q. Cerris* var. *d.* Wats., *Q. Cerris* var. *fulhamensis* Loud., *Q. Lucombeana* var. *f.* Henry.)—**Q. h. latifòlia** (Henry) Rehd., var. Lvs. broader, elliptic, about 9 cm. long and 6 cm. broad, obtuse at apex, with broad shallow teeth, grayish tomentose beneath. (*Q. Lucombeana* var. *fulhamensis l.* Henry.)

27. **Q. alnifòlia** Poech. Evergreen shrub or small tree; brts. with yellowish gray pubescence: lvs. orbicular or broad-obovate to elliptic, 2.5–5 cm. long, with few small teeth and 5–8 pairs of prominent veins, the margins of older lvs. deflexed, lustrous dark green above, yellowish or grayish tomentose beneath; petioles pubescent, 5–10 mm. long: cup with lanceolate recurved pubescent scales, inclosing about ½ of the obovoid-oblong (club-shaped) pointed acorn 2.5–3.5 cm. long. Kotschy, Eich. t.6(c). C.Q.t.40,f.1–14. Gn.40:95. A.G.13:436. Cyprus. Intr. 1885. Zone VII?

28. **Q. semecarpifòlia** Sm. Evergreen tree to 30 m., sometimes shrubby; brts. fasciculate-pilose: lvs. coriaceous, ovate or elliptic-oblong, 3–8 cm. long, rounded at apex, subcordate or rounded at base, entire or sinuately spiny-toothed, glabrous and lustrous above, with a close brownish tomentum beneath, with 6–8 pairs of partly forking veins: frs. 1–3, usually short-stalked; acorn globose-ovoid, 1–2 cm. high, enclosed about ⅓ or ¼ by the thin cup-shaped cup; scales villous, loosely appressed, lanceolate, the upper linear, forming a fringe. Brandis, For. Fl. t.64. C.Q.t.36,f.1–16. C.C.102. Himal., S. W. China. (*Q. aquifolioides* Rehd. & Wils.) Himal., S. W. China. Intr. 1900. Zone VII?

Closely related species: **Q. monimotrícha** Hand.-Mazz. Shrub to 3 m.: lvs. elliptic-oblong to orbicular-ovate, 1–3.5 cm. long, sinuately spiny-toothed, with impressed veins and bullate above, densely fasciculate-pilose beneath, finally often glabrescent; acorns about 1 cm. high. (*Q. aquifolioides* var. *rufescens* Rehd. & Wils.) W. China, Upper Burma. Intr. 1908. Zone VII?—**Q. Gilliàna** Rehd. & Wils. Evergreen small tree to 7 m. or shrubby: lvs. subsessile, elliptic, rounded at the spiny-pointed apex, 2–5 cm. long, subcordate or rounded at base, glabrous at maturity: fr. sessile, annual; acorn ovoid, about 1.2 cm. long, inclosed nearly ½ by the cup. C.Q.t.38,f.7–11. W. China. Intr. 1910. Zone VII? —**Q. Engleriàna** Seemen. Evergreen tree to 10 m.: lvs. ovate, 6–12 cm. long, acuminate, rounded at base, with few spiny appressed teeth, glabrous at maturity; petioles about 1 cm. long: frs. short-stalked; acorn ovoid, 1 cm. long, cup with thin glabrescent scales. Icon. Pl. Koisikav. 1:t.56. C.Q.t.88,89. (*Q. sutchuenensis* Franch., *Q. obscura* Seem.) C. and W. China. Intr. 1900. Zone VII?

Sect. 3. **ILEX** Loud. Styles short, dilated toward the rounded apex: cup with appressed scales; fr. usually annual: lvs. evergreen, often entire, coriaceous.

29. **Q. phillyraeoìdes** Gray. Evergreen shrub or tree to 10 m.; brts. stellate-pubescent: lvs. broad-elliptic to obovate-oblong, 2.5–6 cm. long, obtuse or acute, rounded or subcordate at base, crenately serrate except at base, glabrous except on the midrib above and at its base below, with about 8 pairs of inconspicuous veins; petioles 2–5 mm. long: fr. subsessile, biennial; cup tomentose within and without; acorn ovoid, 1.3–2 cm. high. S.I.1:t.31(c). C.Q.t.39,f.1–6. (*Q. Ilex* var. *p.* Franch.) Japan, C. and E. China. Intr. about 1862. Zone VII?

30. **Q. Ìlex** L. HOLM O. Evergreen tree to 20 m.; bark gray, nearly smooth or finally scaly; brts. tomentose: lvs. ovate to lanceolate, 3–7 cm. long, acute, usually rounded at base, remotely serrate or entire, lustrous dark green and glabrescent above, yellowish or whitish tomentose beneath, rarely glabrescent; petioles 6–15 mm. long: frs. 1–3, usually stalked; acorn ovoid, 2–3.5 cm. high, inclosed about ½ by the cup-shaped or turbinate cup with thin appressed scales. H.W.2:78,79,t.25(c). Kotschy, Eich. t.38(c). E.H.5: t.324–326(h). Gn.65:320. M.G.1898:275(h). S. Eu. Intr. before 1580. Zone VII? Tree with broad round head and dense dark green foliage; one of the hardiest of the evergreen Oaks. The acorns of var. *rotundifolia* are edible.— **Q. I. angustifòlia** Lam., var. Lvs. narrow, lanceolate, entire or nearly so. S.H.1:f.118d.—**Q. I. Fórdii** (Loud.) Nichols. Of pyramidal habit; lvs. narrow-oblong, acute at both ends. R.H.1885:352,353.—**Q. I. rotundifòlia** (West.) Rehd., var. Lvs. suborbicular to ovate, rounded at base, entire or remotely serrate. (**Q. I.** var. *ballota* A. DC., *Q. r.* Lam.)—**Q. I. microphýlla** Aschers. & Graebn. Lvs. very small, to 1 cm. long, serrulate.—**Q. I. crispa** Loud., var. Lvs. small, orbicular, 1–1.5 cm. long, with decurved margin.—**Q. I. gramúntia** (L.) Loud., var. Lvs. suborbicular to broad-elliptic, often subcordate, with slender spiny teeth, 2.5–5 cm. long. (*Q. g.* L.)

Q. I. × *petraea* = Q. audleyénsis Henry. Tree with subcoriaceous deciduous lvs. entire or sinuately lobed. E.H.5:t.338,f.59,t.327(h). (*Q. Koehnei* Schneid., *Q. Pseudoturneri* Veitch.)—*Q. I.* × *robur;* see under No. 41.

31. **Q. chrysólepis** Liebm. CALIFORNIAN LIVE O. Evergreen tree to 20, rarely to 30 m.; brts. fulvous-tomentose: lvs. short-petioled, elliptic to oblong-ovate, 3–10 cm. long, acute, broad-cuneate to cordate at base, sinuately spiny-dentate or entire, with revolute thick margins, bright green and glabrous above, glaucous and fulvous-tomentose beneath, coriaceous; petioles 3–10 mm. long, yellow: fr. sessile or short-stalked, acorn ovoid to ovoid-oblong, 1.5–5 cm. long; cup cup-shaped or turbinate, broad-rimmed, with small hoary-pubescent scales often hidden by a thick fulvous tomentum. S.S.8:t. 398,399. G.F.5:127(h). S. Ore. to L. Calif. Intr. 1877. Zone VII? Tree with widespreading head and often pendulous brs.—**Q. c. vacciniifòlia** (Kellogg)

Engelm., var. Prostrate shrub with small narrow lvs., small acorns and shallow
thin cup with slightly pubescent scales. S.S.8:t.400. (*Q. v.* Kellogg.) Calif.,
high altitudes. Intr. about 1895; probably hardier than the type.

32. Q. virginiàna Mill. LIVE O. Evergreen tree to 20 m.; brts. tomentose:
lvs. elliptic to oblong, 4–12 cm. long, obtuse or rarely acute, usually entire,
rarely with a few spiny teeth above the middle, with revolute margin, lustrous
dark green above, whitish tomentulose beneath; petioles stout, 5–10 mm.
long: frs. 1–5, on peduncles 1–8 cm. long; acorn ovoid, about 2.5 cm. long,
inclosed about ¼ by the turbinate cup with thin appressed hoary-tomentose
scales. S.S.8:t.394,395. M.S.1:t.12(c). H.H.180,181(b). G.F.5:486(h);8:235
(h). Gg.8:1(h). (*Q. virens* Ait.) Va. to Fla., w. to Mex. Intr. 1739. Zone VII.
Tree with nearly horizontal limbs forming a widespreading head; often
planted as an avenue tree in the southeastern states; easily transplanted and
of rapid growth.

   Q. v. × *lyrata;* see under No. 49.
   To this group also belong the following species: **Q. reticulàta** H. B. K. Evergreen shrub or small tree to 12 m.; brts. tomentose: lvs. broad-elliptic or obovate, 4–12 cm. long, usually obtuse, rounded or cordate at base, remotely spiny-
dentate, fulvous-tomentose and reticulate beneath: frs. usually several on slender stalks; acorn 1–1.5 cm. long, inclosed about ¼ by the hoary-tomentose cup.
S.S.8:t.390. S. Ariz. and N. Mex., Mex. Cult. 1883. Zone VII?—**Q. obtusàta**
H. B. K. Large tree; brts. glabrous: lvs. obovate, 5–12 cm long, obtuse, cuneate
at base, irregularly and sinuately toothed, glabrous, glaucescent and reticulate
beneath, falling in spring: frs. stalked; acorn inclosed about ⅓ by the pubescent
cup. E.H.5:t.333,f.4(1). J.L.41:8,f.5(h). Mex. Cult. 1839. Zone VII?

   Sect. 4. GALLIFERA Spach. Like the preceding group, but lvs. thin, deciduous
or persistent only until spring, usually coarsely dentate or lobulate.

33. Q. lusitànica Lam. LUSITANIAN O. Deciduous shrub or tree to 20
m., with rough scaly bark; brts. pubescent: lvs. usually elliptic or obovate,
5–8 cm. long, obtuse or pointed, rounded at base, with 5–9 pairs of coarse
triangular teeth, grayish green above and scurfy pubescent at first, finally
nearly glabrous, grayish tomentulose beneath; petioles 5–10 mm. long: frs.
2–3, on stalks 6–25 mm. long; acorn about 2 cm. long; cup hemispheric or
turbinate, tomentose. H.I.6:562. Spain, Portugal. Cult. 1835. Zone VII?

   Closely related species: **Q. infectòria** Olivier. Half-evergreen tree: differing
chiefly in its glabrous or nearly glabrous lvs. and brts.; petioles slender, to 2.5
cm. long. Olivier, Voy. 1:t.14,15. C.Q.t.108–111. (*Q. lusitanica* ssp. *orientalis*
A. DC.) W. Asia, Cyprus. Intr. 1850. Zone VII?—**Q. fruticòsa** Brotero. Half-
evergreen shrub to 1, rarely to 4 m., sometimes partly prostrate: lvs. subsessile,
elliptic, 3–5.5 cm. long, rounded or subcordate at base, margin undulate, with
4–7 pairs of triangular mucronate teeth, tomentulose beneath; petioles 2–4 mm.
long. G.C.II.1:113. C.Q.t.114. S.H.1:f.108w. (*Q. humilis* Lam., not Mill.)
S. W. Eu., N. Afr. Intr. about 1829. Zone VII?—**Q. inérmis** Kotschy. Deciduous tree; brts. pubescent: lvs. elliptic-oblong, 3–8 cm. long, obtuse or acute,
usually broadly cuneate at base, with 5–9 pairs of shallow teeth, tomentulose
beneath or glabrescent; petioles 1–1.5 cm. long; acorn usually inclosed ½ by
the cup. S.H.1:191. C.Q.t.109. (*Q. Veneris* A. Kern.) Cyprus. Intr. 1862. Zone
VII?

   Sect. 5. ROBUR Reichenb. Styles short, dilated toward the apex and rounded:
scales of the cup appressed: lvs. deciduous, usually dark green, deeply lobed,
rarely dentate: frs. ripening the first year: bark of trunk dark, deeply furrowed.

34. Q. póntica K. Koch. Shrub or small tree; young brts. glabrous,
ribbed; terminal bud large, conspicuous: lvs. elliptic to obovate-oblong, 10–15
cm. long, acute, broad-cuneate at base, sharply and irregularly serrate, with
13–17 strong veins, bright green above with yellow midrib, glaucescent beneath and hairy on the veins; petioles 6–15 mm. long, yellow: fr. subsessile;
acorn ovoid, inclosed about ½ by the cup; scales ovate-lanceolate. Gt.40:510.

S.L.291. Armenia, Cauc. Intr. 1885. Zone V. Shrubby oak with distinct rather large lvs.

Q. p. × *robur* = **Q. Hickélii** A. Camus. Lvs. oblong-obovate, dentate or lobulate with acute or obtuse teeth, pairs of veins about 10. B.D.1933:13. C.Q. t.164,f.9. Orig. 1923.

35. **Q. canariénsis** Willd. Tree to 30 m. or more; brts. glabrous or nearly so: lvs. ovate-oblong to obovate, 5–12 cm. long, acute, subcordate at base, coarsely dentate, with 6–13 pairs of obtusish teeth and with 8–14 pairs of veins, lustrous above, at first floccose-tomentose beneath, soon glabrous; petioles 1–2 cm. long: frs. 1–3 on a peduncle 5–10 mm. long; acorn inclosed about ½ by the hemispheric cup. S.H.1:f.108i,109i. S.M.E.t.41,42. G.M.56:139. E.H.5:t. 323,332(h). (*Q. Mirbeckii* Durieu, *Q. lusitanica* var. *M.* Guerke.) Spain, N. Afr. Intr. 1844 or 1845. Zone VII?

36. **Q. macranthèra** Fisch. & Mey. Tree to 20 m.; brts. tomentose: lvs. obovate, 6–18 cm. long and to 11 cm. broad, rounded at apex, narrowed toward the base, with 8–10 ovate lobes on each side, the middle lobes the largest, dark green and nearly glabrous above, grayish tomentose beneath; petioles 1–1.5 cm. long, pubescent: frs. 1–4, sessile; acorn about 2 cm. long, inclosed about ½ by the cup; scales lanceolate, the lower ones very loose, S.H.1:f.108v. S.M.E.t.24. Mus. Cauc. 2,t.4(h). Cauc. and Armenia to n. Persia. Intr. before 1873. Zone V. Tree with rather large lvs.

37. **Q. Frainétto** Ten. Tree to 40 m.; brts. hairy at first, becoming glabrous; lvs. very short-petioled, obovate to oblong-obovate, 10–18 cm. long, narrowed toward the auriculate base, deeply lobed or pinnatifid more than halfway to the middle, with narrow sinuses and usually 7 mostly dentate lobes sometimes 3-lobed at their apex, dark green and glabrescent above, grayish green and pubescent beneath; petioles 2–5 mm. long: frs. 2–5, short-stalked; acorn ovoid-oblong, about 2.5 cm. high, inclosed ⅓ to ½ by the cup-shaped cup; scales rather large and loosely appressed. H.W.2:73(b,h),t.24(c). R.I. 12:t.646(c). C.Q.t.73,74,75,f.1–2. E.H.5:t.331(h). J.L.45:169(h). (*Q. conferta* Kit., *Q. Farnetto* Ten., *Q. hungarica* Hubeny, *Q. pannonica* Hort.) Balkan Pen., s. Italy. Cult. 1838. Zone V. Tree with gradually spreading brs. forming a round-topped open head, and with dark green lvs.

38. **Q. pyrenàica** Willd. Tree to 15, rarely to 20 m., suckering; brts. slender, yellowish tomentose; buds pubescent: lvs. obovate to obovate-oblong, 6–14 cm. long, rounded and auriculate at base, deeply pinnatifid halfway or more to the midrib, with usually 5–6 pairs of rather narrow and acute lobes with few coarse teeth or entire, pubescent above, becoming finally glabrate, yellowish tomentose beneath; petioles 5–20 mm. long: frs. 1–5, subsessile or on a stalk to 2 cm. long; acorn oblong-ovoid, inclosed ⅓ to ½ by the cup-shaped cup with rather loosely appressed tomentose scales. Kotschy, Eich. t.22(c). S.H.1:f.108k,f.109l–l″. S.M.E.t.31. E.H.5:t.330(h). (*Q. Tauzin* Pers., *Q. Toza* DC., *Q. crinita* Hort., not Lam., *Q. camata* Hort.) S. Eu. Intr. 1822. Zone VI? Tree with slender brs.—**Q. p. pèndula** (Dipp.) Schwarz, l. Form with pendulous brs.; lobes of lvs. rather narrow, often with 1 or few coarse broad teeth. (*Q. camata pendula* Hort.)

39. **Q. pubéscens** Willd. PUBESCENT O. Shrub or small tree to 15, rarely to 20 m.; brts. pubescent: lvs. obovate to oblong-obovate, 5–10 cm. long, broad-cuneate to subcordate at base, pinnately lobed with 4–8 pairs of usually shallow rounded lobes with undulate sinuses or pinnatifid sometimes halfway or more to the midrib and with acutish lobes, usually glabrous above, grayish green and pubescent or tomentose beneath; petioles 5–10 mm. long: frs. 1–4,

sessile or short-stalked; acorn ovoid, 1.5–2 cm. high, inclosed ⅓ to ½ by the tomentose cup with closely appressed scales. H.W.2:69,71(b,h),t.23(c). Kotschy, Eich. t.34(c). J.L.45:184(h). (*Q. lanuginosa* Thuill., not Lam., *Q. sessiliflora* var. *p.* Loud.) S. Eu., Cauc., W. Asia. Long cult. Zone V. Very variable in lf.-shape and pubescence.—**Q. p. pinnatífida** (Gmel.) Spenner, var. Lvs. 3–6 cm. long, deeply lobed with obtuse, often coarsely dentate lobes, tomentose beneath, silky on the veins. S.H.1:f.122a.—**Q. p. crispàta** (Stev.) Schwarz, f. Lvs. 2–3 cm. long, deeply lobed, with acute dentate and crisped lobes, tomentose beneath.

Related species: **Q. Virgiliàna** Ten. Brts. densely appressed-pubescent: lvs. 8–16 cm. long, cordate at base, rarely broad-cuneate, pinnately to sinuately lobed, lobes 5–7, 1–2.5 cm. broad, often with 1–3 broad teeth, pubescent beneath, finally often glabrescent and glaucous; petiole 5–25 mm. long, pubescent: frs. 2–4 on a pubescent stalk 3–8 cm. long; acorn 2–4 cm. long. S.M.E.:t.36. (*Q. robur* var. *Tenorei* DC., *Q. Dalechampii* Wenz., not Ten.) S. E. Eu. to Italy. Cult. 1890. Zone V.

40. **Q. petraèa** (Mattuschka) Lieblein. DURMAST O. Large tree, but usually smaller than *Q. robur;* brts. glabrous or slightly pubescent at first: lvs. obovate to obovate-oblong, 8–12 cm. long, cuneate to subcordate at base, with 5–9 pairs of rounded lobes, lustrous and bright green above, grayish green and glabrous beneath or slightly pubescent with branched hairs; petioles 1–2 cm. long, yellow like the midrib, glabrous: frs. nearly sessile or short-stalked; acorn ovoid to ovoid-oblong, enclosed about ⅓ by the hemispheric cup with closely appressed tomentose scales. H.W.2:66(h),67(b),t.22. M.S.1:t.2(c). E.H.2:t.92(h). (*Q. sessiliflora* Salisb., *Q. sessilis* Ehrh., *Q. robur* Mill., not L., *Q. robur* ssp. *sessiliflora* A. DC.) Eu., W. Asia. Long cult. Zone IV. Not as much planted as *Q. robur;* it keeps its lvs. longer and succeeds in drier situations.—Very variable: **Q. p. purpúrea** (Jaeg.) Schwarz, l. Young lvs. purple, changing to dark green with red veins. (*Q. sessiliflora* var. *rubicunda* Henry.) —**Q. p. mespilifòlia** (Wallr.) Schwarz, subf. Lvs. narrow, acute at ends, entire or nearly so. H.W.2:65. (*Q. sessiliflora Louettei* Kirchn., *Q. robur* var. *m.* Wallr.)—**Q. p. laciniàta** (Lam.) Schwarz, f. Lvs. incisely lobed with narrow irregular lobes pointing forward. Gt.61:495. M.D.1913:137. (*Q. sessiliflora* f. *insecata* Rehd.)—**Q. p. péndula** (Nichols.) Schwarz, l. Brs. pendulous.

Q. p. × *robur* = **Q. rosàcea** Bechst. Very variable; lvs. usually auricled at base. Jour. Bot. 48:t.502. M.D.1924:t.3. (*Q. hybrida* Bechst., not Brot., *Q. intermedia* Boenn.) With the parents in Eu. and cult.—*Q. p.* × *Ilex;* see under No. 30.

Related species: **Q. ibèrica** Bieb. Brts. glabrous: lvs. obovate-lanceolate, 8–16 cm. long, regularly sinuately lobed with 8–12 rounded lobes, subcordate or rounded at base, minutely puberulous beneath or finally glabrate; petiole 1.6–2.8 cm. long: fr. 1–3, subsessile or on a stalk to 1.5 cm. long. S.M.E.:t.4. W. Asia. Cult. 1890. Zone V.—**Q. polycárpa** Schur. Lvs. obovate to oblong-lanceolate, 7–12 cm. long, subcordate at base, puberulous beneath when young, finally glabrous, shallowly 5–8-lobed: fr. 1–6, subsessile or stalked; cup with much thickened gibbous scales. S.M.E.t.8. S. E. Eu., W. Asia. Cult. 1900. Zone V.—**Q. Dalechámpii** Ten. Brts. glabrous: lvs. oblong to obovate-lanceolate, 8–13 cm. long, deeply sinuately to pinnately lobed, with 5–7 ovate to oblong-lanceolate acutish lobes, truncate to subcordate at base, minutely puberulous at first, soon glabrate or glabrous: fr. 1–3, on a short stalk to 5 mm. long; cup with puberulous, much thickened gibbous scales. S.M.E.t.11. (*Q. aurea* Wierzb.) S. E. Eu. to Italy. Cult. 1900. Zone V.

41. **Q. ròbur** L. ENGLISH O. Tree to 25, occasionally to 50 m.; trunk thick, with dark deeply furrowed bark; brts. glabrous: lvs. obovate to obovate-oblong, 5–12 cm. long, subcordate or truncate at base, with 3–7 pairs of rounded lobes, glabrous, dark green above, pale bluish green beneath; petioles 4–8 mm. long: frs. 1–5 on a peduncle 3–8 cm. long; acorn ovoid to

ovoid-oblong, 1.5–2.5 cm. long, inclosed about ⅓ by the cup-shaped cup. H.W.
2:54(h), 55(b),t.21(c). M.S.1:t.2(c). Em.134,t(h). L.A.3:1742(h). E.H.2:
t.81–91,93–96(h). (*Q. pedunculata* Ehrh., *Q. robur* ssp. *p.* A. DC., *Q. femina*
Mill.) Eu., N. Afr., W. Asia. Long cult. Zone IV. Stately tree with short
thick trunk and wide-spreading stout limbs forming an open broad head;
the lvs. remaining green until late in fall.—Very variable species with more
than 40 garden forms of which the following are the best known: **Q. r.
variegàta** West., var. Lvs. variegated with white.—**Q. r. purpuráscens** (DC.)
A. DC. Lvs. purple when young, finally nearly green. Deutsch. Mag. Gart.
Blumenk. L875:23,t(c). (*Q. pedunculata* var. *p.* Loud., *Q. r. f. sanguinea*
Schneid.)—**Q. r. atropurpúrea** Hartw. & Rümpl., var. Lvs. dark purple or
violet-purple. F.S.17:t.1783–84(c). (*Q. r. nigra* Vanh., not var. *nigra* Lam.)
—**Q. r. Concórdia** (Kirchn.) Lem. Lvs. bright yellow, particularly when
young; habit upright. I.H.14:t.537(c). F.E.13:t.19(h). Orig. 1843.—**Q. r.
holophýlla** Rehd., f. Lvs. elliptic to oblong, 3–8 cm. long, obtuse, auricled at
base, entire; petiole about 1 cm. long. (*Q. ped.* var *longifolia* Bean, not
Kirchn.)—**Q. r. heterophýlla** (Loud.) K. Koch. Lvs. elongated, cuneate at
base, with few irregular obtusish lobes pointing forward, occasionally curved
and bullate, sometimes nearly entire. L.A.3:1733,1734. S.H.1:f.126a–b. (*Q. r.
f. laciniata* Schneid., *Q. Fenessei* Hort.)—**Q. r. aspleniifòlia** (Kirchn.) Hartw.
& Rümpl., var. Lvs. pinnatifid, cuneate at base, with triangular-lanceolate
or lanceolate lobes setosely acuminate, occasionally obovate and dentate or
linear and nearly entire. S.H.1:f.126f. (*Q. r. f. diversifolia* Schneid.)—**Q. r.
filicifòlia** (Lem.) Hartw. & Rümpl., var. Lvs. cuneate, irregularly and deeply
pinnatifid, with linear lobes directed forward, margins crisped. G.C.II.14:632.
S.H.1:126e.—**Q. r. pectinàta** (Kirchn.) K. Koch, f. Similar to the preceding
but lvs. regularly pinnatifid with somewhat broader lobes. Nederl. Fl. Pom.
t.42,f.3(c). S.H.1:f.126d.—**Q. r. péndula** (Loud.) A. DC., var. Brs. pendulous.
L.A.3:1733(h). J.L.45:203(h). (*Q. ped. Dauvessei* Hort.)—**Q. r. fastigiàta**
(Lam.) A. DC., var. Brs. upright, forming a columnar head, like that of the
Lombardy Poplar. G.C.41:149(h). J.L.45:203(h). Gt.65:86(h). (*Q. f.* Lam.,
Q. ped. var. *f.* Loud., *Q. pyramidalis* Gmel.) Several forms of similar habit but
with variations in the foliage are cult.

Q. r. × *Ilex?* = **Q. Túrneri** Willd. Half-evergreen tree to 15 m.; brts. stellate-pubescent: lvs. obovate and elliptic, 6–8 cm. long, acute or obtuse, rounded
and sometimes slightly auricled at base, remotely sinuately toothed with 5–6
broad, acute and mucronate teeth, dark green and finally glabrous above, glabrous except stellate-pubescent on the veins beneath; petiole 4–8 mm. long,
pubescent: frs. 3–7 on a slender tomentose peduncle; acorn ovoid, about 2 cm.
long; cup hemispheric, tomentose. Willdenow, Berl. Baumz. t.3,f.2. S.M.E.t.3.
J.L.45:217(h). Orig. in England before 1785.—**Q. T. pseudotúrneri** (Schneid.)
Henry, var. Lvs. longer and narrower, obovate-oblong to oblong, 7–10 cm. long
and 4–5 cm. broad, teeth usually longer and narrower, less pubescent beneath.
S.H.1:f.126g-h. G.C.II.14:714 (as *Q. glandulifera*). G.W.5:259(h). M.D.1933:
t.60(h). (*Q. pseudoturneri* Schneid., *Q. aizoon* Koehne, *Q. austriaca sempervirens* Hort.) This var. is better known in cult. than the type; it is a shrubby
tree with handsome dark green lvs. retained in milder climates until spring.
Zone VI.—*Q. r.* × *pontica;* see under No. 34.—*Q. r.* × *petraea;* see under
No. 40.—*Q. r.* × *montana;* see under No. 53.

Related species: **Q. Haas** Kotschy. Similar to *Q. robur*, but brts. finely
pubescent; lvs. larger, with broader lobes, yellowish tomentose beneath when
young, acorns to 5 cm. long. Kotschy, Eich, t.2(c). S.M.E.t.21. Asia Minor.
Cult. 1870. Zone V or VI.—**Q. Hartwissiàna** Stev. Lvs. obovate-oblong, 7–15 cm.
long, with 4–6 rounded or acutish and near apex with 3–4 small lobes, subcordate at base, thinly puberulous beneath: frs. 1–4, on slender stalks about
half as long as lf.; cup tomentose. S.M.E.t.15. Asia Minor to Cauc., E. Balkan
Pen. Cult. 1857. Zone V? The tree usually cult. under this name is a var. of

*Q. pubescens.—*Q. pedunculiflòra K. Koch. Brts. glabrous: lvs. obovate-oblong,
6–12 cm. long, cordate at base, deeply sinuately lobed, lobes 5–7, sometimes with
1–3 broad obtuse teeth, tomentulose beneath, later often glabrescent; petiole
3–10 mm. long: fr. 1–3 on a stalk about half as long as lf.; cup yellowish tomentose. S.M.E.t.20. (*Q. Haas* Wenzig, not Kotschy.) Asia Minor to Transcauc.,
Balkan Pen. Cult. 1870. Zone V.

Sect. 6. Prinus Loud. Styles short, broad at apex: lvs. deciduous, dentate
or lobed: cup with appressed scales, rarely the upper free and subulate: bark
usually thin, gray and scaly.

42. Q. alba L. White O. Tree to 30 m.; brts. soon glabrous, becoming
light reddish brown, often glaucous: lvs. obovate to oblong-obovate, 10–22
cm. long, narrowed at base, with 5–9 oblong and obtuse, usually entire lobes,
pubescent when unfolding, soon glabrous, bright green above, glaucescent
beneath; petioles 1.5–2.5 cm. long: frs. short- or long-stalked; acorn ovoid-
oblong, 2–2.5 cm. high, inclosed about ¼ by the cup-shaped cup with the
basal scales much thickened. M.S.1:t.1(c). S.S.8:t.356–358. S.M.301. G.F.3:
91;4:6,7;5:259(h). B.T.333(h). Me. to Fla., w. to Minn. and Tex. Intr. 1724.
Zone IV. One of the noblest trees of the n. states, with stout spreading brs.
forming a broad open head and bright green lvs. turning deep vinous-red or
violet-purple in fall.—Q. a. latíloba Sarg., var. Lvs. divided usually less than
halfway to the midrib into broad rounded lobes. S.M.302—Q. a. repánda
Michx., var. Lvs. with rather shallow sinuses and the frs. usually short-stalked.
—The typical form (var. *pinnatifida* Michx.) has the lvs. deeply pinnatifid,
with narrow often toothed lobes and usually slender-stalked frs.

Q. a. × *Durandii;* see under No. 45.—*Q. a.* × *stellata;* see under No. 48.—
Q. a. × *macrocarpa;* see under No. 50.—*Q. a.* × *bicolor;* see under No. 51.—
Q. a. × *montana;* see under No. 53.—*Q. a.* × *prinoides;* see under No. 54.—
Q. a. × *Muhlenbergii;* see under No. 55.

43. Q. lobàta Née. Valley O. Tree to 30 m.; brts. grayish, short-pubescent. glabrous the second year: lvs. obovate, 6–8 cm. long, cuneate to subcordate at base, with 7–11 ovate obtuse, sometimes dentate lobes, dark green
and stellate-pubescent above, grayish tomentulose beneath; petioles about
1 cm. long, pubescent: frs. nearly sessile: acorn narrowly conic-oblong, 3.5–5
cm. long, inclosed ¼ to ⅓ by the cup-shaped cup; upper scales with acuminate free tips, the lower ones much thickened. S.S.8:t.362. J.S.t.61,63–64(h),
62(b). G.F.3:611;10:55,202,205(h). (*Q. Hindsii* Benth.) Calif. Intr. 1874.
Zone VII. Tree with widespreading brs. forming a round or oblong head with
drooping brts.; scarcely planted outside of Calif.

44. Q. Garryàna Hook. Oregon O. Tree to 30 m., shrubby at high altitudes; brts. tomentose or pubescent, orange-colored, glabrous the second
year: lvs. oblong-obovate, 8–14 cm. long, cuneate or rounded at base, with
3–5 pairs of broad-ovate, obtuse, entire or toothed lobes and with rounded
sinuses reaching about halfway to the midrib, dark green and glabrous above,
bright green and pubescent or glabrate beneath: petioles pubescent, 1.5–2.5
cm. long: frs. sessile or short-stalked; acorn ovoid, 2.5–3 cm. long, inclosed
about ⅓ by the rather shallow cup pubescent or tomentose outside; scales
with thin pointed free tips, sometimes thickened. N.S.1:t.1(c). S.S.8:t.364,
365. G.F.7:495(h). F.E.32:919(h). B. C. to Calif. Intr. 1873. Zone VI. Tree
with spreading or ascending brs. forming a broad compact head.

Related species are: Q. undulàta Torr. Small tree to 10 m.; brts. tomentose:
lvs. persistent elliptic-oblong, 3–7 cm. long, coarsely sinuate-dentate or lobed,
the lobes often spinescent, bluish green, stellate-hairy above, pubescent below,
firm: acorn oblong-cylindric, 1–1.5 cm. long. Colo. to Nev., n. Mex. and w. Tex.
N.S.2:t.3(c). S.S.8:t.385. Intr. 1917. Zone V.—Q. Havárdi Rydb. Shrub to 1

m.; lvs. thickish, deciduous, similar to the preceding, lobes mucronate: acorn dark brown, 2–2.5 cm. long. Trel., Am. Oaks, t.160. C.Q.t.207,f.6–10. E. Tex. Cult. 1920. Zone V.

45. **Q. Durándii** Buckl. Tree to 25 m.: brts. soon glabrous or puberulous, light grayish brown: lvs. oblong to obovate-oblong, entire or slightly 3-lobed toward the obtuse or acutish apex, 4–10 cm. long, narrowed at base, green and lustrous above, paler and pubescent or whitish-tomentulose beneath; petiole 5–8 mm. long: fr. sessile or nearly so; acorn ovoid, about 1 cm. long, enclosed only at the very base by the saucer-shaped cup; scales thin, acute. S.M.289. (?*Q. sinuata* Walt.) Ga. to Ark. and e. Tex. Intr. 1924. Zone V.

Q. D. × *stellata* = **Q. Macnabiàna** Sudw. With the parents. Intr. about 1925. Zone V.

46. **Q. novo-mexicàna** Rydb. Tree to 10 m. or shrubby; brts. finely pubescent or glabrous, light brown: lvs. obovate to oblong-obovate, 6–10 cm. long, pinnatifid halfway to or nearly to the midrib, similar to those of the preceding species, usually somewhat smaller, glabrous above, puberulous or nearly glabrous below, with whitish, conspicuous veins: acorns 1–1.5 cm. high, obtuse, broad-ovoid to ellipsoid, inclosed ⅓ or ½ by the cup; scales ovate, slightly thickened and slightly pubescent. Bull. N. Y. Bot. Gard. 2:t.27. Mem. Nat. Acad. Sci. 20:t.164,165. (*Q. nitescens* Rydb.) Colo. to Utah and N. Mex. Intr. 1916. Zone VI?

Closely related species: **Q. Gunnisònii** Rydb. Lvs. mostly oblong, lobed halfway to the middle or less, rather dull above. Bull. N. Y. Bot. Gard. 2:t.26,f.3. Colo. to N. Mex. and Utah. Intr. 1916. Zone V.—**Q. Gambélii** Nutt. Lvs. lobed about halfway to the middle, less lustrous: acorns acute, inclosed about ½ by the cup. S.S.8:t.366–7. Colo. to Utah and N. Mex. Intr. 1894. Zone V.—**Q. leptophýlla** Rydb. Tree to 15 m.: lvs. broad-obovate, 10–15 cm. long, with 2–4 pairs of obtuse lobes, the sinuses halfway or less to the midrib, glabrous beneath except on the veins: acorn about 1.5 cm. high, inclosed about ½ by the cup; scales slightly thickened. B.T.340. S.M.299. Colo. Intr. 1911. Zone V.

47. **Q. utahénsis** Rydb. Tree to 15 m.; brts. densely yellowish pubescent, sometimes nearly glabrous in autumn, light brown: lvs. oblong to oblong-obovate, 6–12 cm. long, pinnatifid halfway to or nearly to the midrib, with 3–5 pairs of ovate or ovate-lanceolate, acutish or obtuse lobes usually entire or the middle ones with 1 or 2 teeth, the sinuses rather narrow, dark green and lustrous, sparingly stellate, at maturity glabrate or sometimes rough above, light green and soft-pubescent beneath and reticulate; petioles pubescent, 5–10 mm., rarely to 15 mm. long: frs. 1–2, subsessile; acorn ellipsoid or ellipsoid-oblong, 1.5–2 cm. high, inclosed about ⅓ by the cup-shaped cup 1.2–2 cm. wide with ovate pubescent much thickened scales. S.M.297. B.T.339. (*Q. submollis* Rydb.) Colo. to Utah, N. Mex. and w. Tex. Intr. 1916. Zone VI? Small tree with dark green foliage.

48. **Q. stellàta** Wangh. Post O. Tree to 20, rarely to 30 m.; bark reddish brown, deeply fissured and scaly: brts. tomentose: lvs. obovate, lyrate-pinnatifid, 10–20 cm. long, usually cuneate at base, rarely rounded, with 2–3 pairs of broad obtuse lobes, the middle pair much larger and mostly with a lobe on the lower margin, separated from the lower lobes by wide, from the upper by narrow sinuses, dark green and rough above, with grayish or brownish, rarely white tomentum beneath, finally glabrescent; petioles 1–2 cm. long: frs. sessile; acorns ovoid, 1.5–2.5 cm. high, obtuse, inclosed ⅓ or ½ by the cup-shaped or turbinate cup; scales thin, acute, loosely appressed, hoary-tomentose. M.S.1:t.5(c). S.S.8:t.368,369. H.H.166,167(b). (*Q. obtusiloba* Michx., *Q. minor* Sarg.) S. Mass. to Fla., w. to Neb. and Tex. Intr. 1819. Zone V. Tree with dense round head and large dark green lvs.

Q. s. × *alba* = **Q. Fernòwii** Trel. Lvs. narrower and more regularly lobed, mentulose beneath: fr. usually short-stalked. S.S.8:t.359. With the parents. atr. before 1898.—*Q. s.* × *macrocarpa* = **Q. guadalupénsis** Sarg. With the arents. Intr. 1916. Zone V.—*Q. s.* × *Durandii;* see under No. 45.

49. **Q. lyràta** Walt. OVERCUP O. Tree to 30 m.; brts. pubescent, glabresent during the first winter: lvs. obovate-oblong, 14–20 cm. long, cuneate at ase, deeply lyrate-pinnatifid, with 3–4 pairs of obtuse or acutish lobes, the 2 ower pairs much smaller and usually triangular and separated from the upper pairs by wide sinuses, the large middle pair usually with a small lobe on the lower margin, the terminal lobe usually 3-lobed, dark green and glabrous above at maturity, white-tomentose beneath or green and pubescent: petioles glabrous or pubescent, 1–2 cm. long: frs. sessile or stalked; acorn subglobose or ovoid, 1.2–2.5 cm. high, usually nearly entirely or rarely only ½ inclosed by the cup; lower scales much thickened, the upper thinner, acute and forming a ragged edge. M.S.1:t.6. S.S.8:t.374. H.H.170,171(b). Bull. Torr. Bot. Club 49:t.16,17(h). (SWAMP or SWAMP POST OAK.) N. J. to Fla., w. to Mo. and Tex. Intr. 1786. Zone V. Round-headed tree with short, often pendulous, brs. and large lvs.

Q. l. × *virginiana* = **Q. Cómptonae** Sarg. Lvs. oblanceolate, sinuately lobed, thickish with revolute margin: fr. slender-stalked, similar to No. 32. With the parents. Intr. 1920. Zone V.

50. **Q. macrocárpa** Michx. BURR O. Tree to 25 or occasionally to 55 m. tall; bark light brown, deeply furrowed and scaly; brts. stout, densely pubescent at first, later glabrescent, sometimes developing corky wings: lvs. obovate to oblong-obovate, 10–24 cm. long, cuneate or rarely rounded at base, lyrate-pinnatifid, the lower portion of the leaf usually with 2–3 pairs of lobes separated by wide and deep sinuses from the terminal lobe usually very large and with 5–7 pairs of ovate-obtuse lobes or smaller and 3-lobed, dark green and usually lustrous above, grayish or whitish tomentulose beneath: frs. sessile or short-stalked; acorn broadly ovoid or ellipsoid, 2–3.5 cm. high, inclosed ½ or less or more by the large cup, its upper scales ending into slender awns and forming a fringe-like border, the lower ones much thickened. M.S.1:t.3(c). S.S.8:t.371,372. H.H.168,169(b). G.F.2:500(b); 3:407(h). (MOSSY CUP OAK.) N. S. to Pa., w. to Man. and Tex. Intr. 1811. Zone II. Tree usually with tall trunk and spreading brs. forming a broad head; the often corky brs. conspicuous in winter.—**Q. m. olivaefórmis** (Michx. f.) Gray, var. Lvs. smaller, more deeply divided, often nearly to the midrib, the lobes almost all narrow: acorn smaller, ellipsoid-oblong, enclosed more than ½ by the turbinate cup higher than broad. M.S.1:t.2(c). S.S.8:373. M.G.16:67(h).

Q. m. × *alba* = **Q. Bebbiàna** Schneid. Lvs. with usually 5 pairs of less unequal lobes, pubescent beneath: cup scarcely fringed. S.S.8:t.560. With the parents. Intr. 1880.—*Q. m.* × *stellata;* see under No. 48.—*Q. m.* × *bicolor;* see under No. 51.—*Q. m.* × *Muhlenbergii;* see under No. 55.

51. **Q. bícolor** Willd. SWAMP WHITE O. Tree to 20, rarely to 30 m.; bark light grayish brown, scaly; brts. scurfy-pubescent at first: lvs. oblong-obovate to obovate, 10–16 cm. long, narrowed toward the base and acute or rounded, coarsely sinuate-dentate with 6–10 pairs of entire usually obtuse teeth, or sometimes lobed halfway to the midrib, dark green above, whitish tomentose or grayish green and velvety beneath; petioles 1–2 cm. long: frs. 1–2 on slender peduncles 3–8 cm. long; acorn ovoid-oblong, 2–3 cm. high, inclosed about ⅓ by the cup. M.S.1:t.7(c). S.S.8:t.380,381. H.H.172,173(b). G.F.4:246(h). E.H.5:t.329(h). (*Q. platanoides* Sudw.) Que. to Ga., w. to Mich. and Ark. Intr. 1800. Zone III. Tree with rather narrow round-topped open head;

easily recognized by the light scaly bark and the numerous brts. on the larger limbs; the lvs. turn yellow-brown or orange or red in fall.

Q. b. × *alba* = **Q. Jackiàna** Schneid. Lvs. with rather short lobes, thinly tomentulose or pubescent beneath: fr. usually stalked. With the parents. Intr. 1916.—*Q. b.* × *macrocarpa* = **Q. Schuèttei** Trel. Brs. sometimes with corky wings: lvs. intermediate: cup sometimes short-fringed. Proc. Am. Philos. Soc. 56:t.2,3. C.Q.t.226,f.6,7. With the parents. Intr. 1916.

52. **Q. Prìnus** L. BASKET O. Tree to 30 m.; bark light gray, scaly; brts. hairy at first: lvs. obovate to obovate-oblong, 10–16 cm. long, acute or acuminate, cuneate or rounded at base, coarsely and regularly toothed, with 10–14 pairs of obtusish, often mucronate teeth, bright green and lustrous above, grayish tomentulose beneath; petioles 1.5–3.5 cm. long: frs. short-stalked; acorn ovoid-oblong, 2.5–3.5 cm. high, inclosed ⅓ to nearly ½ by the cup; lower scales much thickened and the tips of the upper ones often forming a stiff fringe. M.S.1:t.8(c). S.S.8:t.382,383. H.H.174,175(b). (*Q. Michauxii* Nutt., *Q. Prinus palustris* Michx.) Del. to Fla., w. to Ind., Mo. and Tex. Intr. 1737. Zone V. Tree with round-topped, rather compact head, the lvs. turning rich crimson in fall. It prefers moist soil.

53. **Q. montàna** Willd. CHESTNUT O. Tree to 25 or 30 m.; bark dark brown, ridged; brts. pubescent at first or glabrous: lvs. oblong-obovate to lanceolate-oblong, 12–18 cm. long, acutish or acuminate, narrowed toward the acute or rounded base, coarsely crenate-dentate, with 10–15 obtuse teeth, lustrous and bright or yellowish green above, paler beneath and tomentulose when young, often nearly glabrous at maturity; petioles 1.5–3 cm. long, glabrous: frs. 1–2 on peduncles shorter than the petioles; acorn ovoid, 2.5–3.5 cm. high, inclosed ⅓–½ by the usually tuberculate cup. M.S.1:t.9(c). S.S.8: t.375,376. H.H.176,177(b). G.F.1:510(h). (*Q. Prinus* Engelm., not L., *Q. Prinus* var. *monticola* Michx.) Me. and Ont. to S. C. and Ala. Cult. 1688. Zone IV. Tree with broad irregular head and lustrous lvs. turning dull orange in fall. It grows well in rather dry rocky soil.

Q. m. × *robur* = **Q. Sargéntii** Rehd., a tree of vigorous growth, chiefly distinguished from *Q. montana* by the auriculate base of the lvs. and the fewer lobes. Gs.4:26(h). Orig. before 1830.—*Q. m.* × *alba* = **Q. Saùlii** Schneid. Lvs. with 6–8 nearly equal lobes on each side. S.S.8:t.361. Intr. about 1883.

54. **Q. prinoìdes** Willd. CHINQUAPIN O. Spreading shrub to 2 m., rarely slender tree to 5 m.; brts. soon glabrous: lvs. ovate-oblong to oblong, 6–12 cm. long, acute, cuneate at base, undulate-dentate, with 3–7 pairs of small acute or obtusish teeth, bright green and glabrous above, grayish tomentulose beneath; petioles 5–10 mm. long: frs. sessile; acorn ovoid, 1–1.5 cm. long, inclosed about ½ by the cup; scales tuberculate. M.S.1:t.11(c). S.S.8:t.378. Em.1:158,t. (*Q. Chinquapin* Pursh.) Me. to Ala., w. to Minn. and Tex. Intr. 1730. Zone V or IV?—**Q. p. ruféscens** Rehd., var. Brts. fulvous-pubescent: lvs. smaller, fulvous-villous along midrib beneath, lobes acutish: stamens smaller. (*Q. r.* Bickn.) Mass. to N. C. Intr. 1937.

Q. p. × *alba* = **Q. Faxónii** Trel. With the parents. Intr. ?

55. **Q. Muhlenbérgii** Engelm. YELLOW CHESTNUT O. Tree to 20 or occasionally to 50 m. tall; brts. hairy at first, soon glabrous: lvs. oblong to oblonglanceolate, 10–16 cm. long, acute or acuminate, usually rounded at base, coarsely toothed, with about 8–13 pairs of acute and mucronate, often incurved teeth, dark or yellowish green above, whitish tomentulose beneath; petioles 2–3.5 cm. long: fr. subsessile; acorns globose-ovoid to ovoid, 1.5–2 cm. long, inclosed about ½ by the thin cup; scales small, appressed. M.S.1:t.10.

S.S.8:t.377. H.H.178,179(b) (*Q. acuminata* Sarg., not Roxb., *Q. Castanea* Willd., not Née.) Vt. to Va., w. to Neb., N. Mex. and Tex. Intr. 1822. Zone V. *Q. M.* × *alba* = **Q. Deàmii** Trel. Lvs. rather deeply lobed, with 7–9 pairs of rather acutish lobes, tomentulose beneath: fr. short-stalked. With the parents. Intr. 1916.—*Q. m.* × *macrocarpa* = **Q. Hillii** Trel. With the parents. Intr. before 1930.

56. **Q. alièna** Bl. Tree to 20 m. tall or more; brts. glabrous: lvs. oblong-obovate, 10–20 cm. long, obtuse or acutish, cuneate at base, coarsely sinuate-dentate, with 10–15 pairs of usually obtuse teeth, dark yellowish green and glabrous above, whitish or grayish tomentulose beneath; petioles 1–2.5 cm. long, glabrous: frs. 1–3, short-stalked or subsessile; acorn ovoid to ovoid-oblong, 2–2.5 cm. long, inclosed about ⅓ by the grayish tomentulose cup; scales thin, acuminate. S.I.1:t.28(c). C.C.98. N.K.3:t.14. Japan, Korea to C. China.—**Q. a. acuteserràta** Maxim., var. Lvs. usually somewhat smaller and narrower and teeth acutish and usually incurved at the gland-tipped apex. Japan, C. China. Intr. 1905. Zone V. Similar in lf. to the Chestnut Oak.

Closely related species: **Q. Fabri** Hance. Tree to 25 m. tall; brts. pubescent and furrowed; lvs. with 6–10 pairs of short rounded lobes, grayish tomentulose and reticulate beneath: acorn cylindric-oblong, 2 cm. long. C.C.96. China. Intr. 1908. Zone VI?

57. **Q. glandulífera** Bl. Tree to 15 m. or occasionally taller; brts. silky-pubescent when young; lvs. oblong-obovate to ovate-lanceolate, 6–15 cm. long, acute, cuneate or rarely rounded at base, with 7–12 pairs of acute gland-tipped teeth, bright green and lustrous above, grayish beneath and appressed silky-pubescent; petioles 6–15 mm. long: frs. 1 or several on a short stalk; acorn ovoid, 1–1.5 cm. high, inclosed about ⅓ by the cup. S.I.1:t.26(c). N.K. 3:t.13. M.K.t.37(c). D.L.2:88. (*Q. serrata* Thunb., not auth., *Q. urticifolia* Bl.) Japan, Korea to W. China. Cult. 1877. Zone V. Small tree with lustrous bright green lvs. remaining green until late in fall.

58. **Q. mongòlica** Turcz. MONGOLIAN O. Tree to 30 m. tall; brts. glabrous: lvs. very short-stalked and crowded at the ends of the brts., obovate to obovate-oblong, 10–20 cm. long, obtuse, narrowed toward the auricled base, coarsely sinuate-dentate with 7–10 broad usually obtuse teeth, dark green above, paler beneath and pilose on the nerves or nearly glabrous; petioles 4–8 mm. long: frs. short-stalked or subsessile; acorn ovoid or ellipsoid, about 2 cm. long, inclosed about ⅓ by the thick cup; scales tuberculate, the uppermost thinner and acuminate forming a short fringe. M.K.t.35(c). D.H. 2:82. N.K.3:t.11. E. Siber., N. China, Korea, N. Japan. Intr. 1879. Zone IV. Tree of vigorous growth with large lvs.; easily recognized by its very short-stalked nearly glabrous lvs. clustered at the end of the brts.—**Q. m. grosseser-ràta** (Bl.) Rehd. & Wils., var. Lvs. somewhat smaller, usually acutish, with acute or acutish sometimes denticulate teeth: cup with closely appressed scales not fringed. S.I.1:t.27(c). M.K.t.36(c). S.M.E.t.2. (*Q. crispula* Bl., *Q. g.* Bl.) Japan, Saghal. Intr. 1893.

Closely related species: **Q. liaotungénsis** Koidz. Lvs. 5–9 cm. long, pinnately 5–7-lobed with obtuse lobes, glabrous, short-petioled: fr. short-stalked. Ic. Pl. Koisikav. 1:t.55. (*Q. mongolica* var. *l.* Nakai.) N. E. Asia. Intr. 1912. Zone V.

59. **Q. dentàta** Thunb. Tree to 25 m.; brts. stout, grayish pubescent: lvs. short-stalked, obovate, 10–20 or sometimes over 30 cm. long and up to 20 cm. wide, obtuse, narrowed toward the auriculate or rarely cuneate base, sinuate-dentate, with 4–9 pairs of broad rounded lobes, dark green above and at first short-pubescent, later glabrous, beneath grayish tomentose at first, later light

green and soft-pubescent; petioles 2–5 mm. long: frs. usually clustered and subsessile; acorn globose-ovoid, 1.5–2 cm. high, inclosed about ½ or more by the large cup covered with lanceolate spreading scales. S.I.1:t.27(c). M.K.t. 34(c). N.K.3:t.20. G.F.6:386(h). F.E.14:542,t.29(h). (*Q. obovata* Bge., *Q. Daimio* Hort.) Japan, Korea, N. and W. China. Intr. 1830. Zone V. Round-headed tree with very large lvs.—**Q. d. pinnatifida** (Franch. & Sav.) Matsum., var. Lvs. divided almost to the midrib into linear lobes with crisped margins. Cult. 1880.

13. ULMACEAE Mirb. ELM FAMILY

Trees, rarely shrubs with watery juice; buds with imbricate scales: lvs. 2-ranked, alternate, usually oblique at base, pinnately veined, serrate or rarely entire; stipules deciduous: fls. perfect or monoecious; perianth 4–5-, rarely 3- or 6–8-merous, usually more or less connate; stamens as many or rarely twice as many as perianth-lobes; filaments straight; ovary superior, 1-celled, with 1 suspended ovule; style 2-parted: fr. a samara, nutlet or drupe; seed usually without endosperm, with straight or curved embryo; cotyledons flat.—About 15 genera with more than 150 species, distributed through both hemispheres except the polar regions.

A. Lvs. with 7 or more pairs of parallel veins, the lowest pair not prominent: winter-buds somewhat spreading: perianth more or less connate.
  B. Fls. perfect, before the lvs. or in autumn; fr. winged: lvs. usually doubly serrate.
                                                              1. *Ulmus*
  BB. Fls. at least partly unisexual, the pistillate ones axillary on the young brts.; stamens 4–5: lvs. simply serrate.
    c. Fr. muricate, symmetrical; style centric...................................2. *Planera*
    cc. Fr. not muricate, oblique; style excentric.
      D. Fr. obliquely winged: brts. partly rigid and thorny, particularly on young plants.
                                      3. *Hemiptelea*
      DD. Fr. oblique, not winged: brts. always slender, never spiny..............4. *Zelkova*
AA. Lvs. 3-nerved at base; pairs of veins usually less than 6; winter-buds appressed: parts of perianth free: fls. unisexual.
  B. Fr. a small winged nutlet; anthers hairy at apex: veins of lvs. curving before the margin: brts. glabrous, chestnut-brown...................................5. *Pteroceltis*
  BB. Fr. a drupe: anthers glabrous: brts. usually grayish brown and pubescent.
    c. Veins curving before the margin: cotyledons broad..........................6. *Celtis*
    cc. Veins straight, ending in the teeth: cotyledons narrow...............7. *Aphananthe*

1. ULMUS L. ELM. Deciduous, rarely half-evergreen trees: buds conspicuous: lvs. short-petioled, usually oblique at base, usually doubly serrate: fls. perfect, appearing in spring before the lvs. or in autumn in the axils of the lvs., in fascicles or racemes; calyx campanulate, 4–9-lobed with an equal number of stamens: fr. a compressed nutlet surrounded by a broad rarely narrow membranous wing. Frs. ripening a few weeks after flowering. (The ancient Latin name of the tree.) About 18 species in the temp. regions of the n. hemisphere; in Am. s. to n. Mexico, but absent w. of the Rocky Mts., in Asia s. to the Himal.—Ornamental trees much planted as street or shade trees; of rapid growth and easily transplanted.

A. Fls. appearing in spring before the lvs.: calyx-lobes short.
  B. Fls. on slender pedicels, drooping: frs. ciliate.
    c. Fr. glabrous except the ciliate margin: lvs. ciliate: brs. not corky: fls. fascicled.
      D. Lvs. widest above the middle, densely pubescent beneath: buds elongated, pointed.
                                      1. *U. laevis*
      DD. Leaves widest about the middle, often nearly glabrous beneath: buds ovoid, obtusish or acute..2. *U. americana*
    cc. Fr. pubescent: brs. usually more or less corky: fls. racemose.
      D. Lvs. not ciliate, 5–10 cm. long: buds pubescent......................3. *U. Thomasi*
      DD. Leaves minutely ciliate, 3–6 cm. long: buds glabrous....................4. *U. alata*
  BB. Fls. short-pedicelled, not pendulous, in dense clusters.
    c. Buds covered with rusty hairs, obtuse: brts. scabrous: lvs. ciliate: fr. pubescent in the middle ....5. *U. fulva*

cc. Buds pale-pubescent or glabrous; brts. smooth, glabrous or pubescent: lvs. not
    ciliate; fr. glabrous.
    d. Lvs. doubly serrate, unequal at base, 5–20 cm. long.
        e. Young brts. pubescent: lvs. scabrous above.
            f. Fr. with the seed in the centre, about 2 cm. broad: petioles about 3 mm. long.
                g. Mature brts. reddish brown, hairy while young: lvs. rarely 3-lobed at
                    apex ....6. *U. glabra*
                gg. Mature brts. pale yellowish or grayish brown, glabrous or nearly so while
                    young: lvs. mostly 3-lobed at apex..........................7. *U. laciniata*
            ff. Fr. with the seed near the apex, 1.5 cm. broad or less; petioles 4–8 mm. long.
                g. Lvs. broad-elliptic or ovate, 5–7 cm. long: brts. not corky....8. *U. procera*
                gg. Lvs. obovate or elliptic, 7–10 cm. long: brts. often with corky wings.
                            9. *U. japonica*
        ee. Young brts. glabrous or with few scattered hairs: fr. with the seed above the
            middle.
            f. Lvs. 7–15 cm. long; petioles 6–8 mm. long...................10. *U. hollandica*
            ff. Lvs. 3.5–8 cm. long.
                g. Petioles 6–12 mm. long; lvs. smooth above, 5–8 cm. long..11. *U. carpinifolia*
                gg. Petioles about 5 mm. long; lvs. slightly scabrous above, 3.5–6 cm. long.
                            12. *U. Plotii*
    dd. Lvs. simply or nearly simply serrate, nearly equal at base, 2–5 cm. long.
                            13. *U. pumila*
aa. Fls. appearing in autumn in the axils of the lvs.; calyx divided beyond the middle.
    b. Lvs. simply serrate, small: fr. glabrous.................................14. *U. parvifolia*
    bb. Lvs. doubly serrate, 5–8 cm. long: fr. pubescent..........................15. *U. serotina*

Sect. 1. BLEPHAROCARPUS Dunn. Fls. before the lvs. on elongated unequal
pedicels, fascicled; calyx with 5–8 unequal short lobes: fr. ciliate.

1. **U. laèvis** Pall. EUROPEAN WHITE E. Tree to 30 m.; bark brownish
gray, smooth at first, later scaly and exfoliating, finally furrowed: brts. pubescent usually until the second year; buds elongated, acute: lvs. elliptic or
obovate, 6–12 cm. long, acuminate, very unequal at base, sharply and doubly
serrate, usually glabrous above, pubescent beneath; petioles 4–6 mm. long:
fls. on pedicels 6–20 mm. long; stamens 6–8, exserted; stigma white: fr. ovate,
1–1.5 cm. long, notched, the seed not reaching the nutlet, ciliate. H.W.
2:9(h),t.39(c). R.I.12,t.666(c). I.T.6:t.220. S.H.1:214(h). E.H.7,t.389,390(h).
(*U. pedunculata* Foug., *U. effusa* Willd., *U. racemosa* Borkh.—SPREADING E.)
C. Eu. to W. Asia. Long cult. Zone IV. Tall tree with spreading brs. forming
a broad open head; rarely cult.; very similar to the following species.

2. **U. americàna** L. WHITE E. Tree to 40 m.; bark light gray, scaly
and deeply fissured; brts. pubescent while young or sometimes nearly glabrous; buds ovoid, obtusish or acute: lvs. ovate-oblong, 7–15 cm. long, acuminate, unequal at base, doubly serrate, glabrous and rough above, pubescent
or nearly glabrous beneath; petioles 5–8 mm. long: fls. on pedicels 1–2 cm.
long; stamens 7–8, exserted; stigmas white: fr. elliptic, about 1 cm. long,
deeply notched at apex, the incision reaching the nutlet, ciliate. M.S.3:
269,t(c). S.S.7:t.311. H.H.182,183(b). G.F.3:443,467(h);6:175(h). F.E.15:
t.46(h). Dame & Brooks, Typ. Elms, 50tt.(h). (*U. alba* Raf.—AMERICAN
ELM, WATER ELM.) Nfd. to Fla., w. to foot of Rocky Mts. Intr. 1752. Zone
II. Tall tree with the limbs usually gradually spreading outward and forming a wide-spreading head with pendulous brts.; very variable in habit. A
favorite avenue tree in the N. E. States.—**U. a. columnàris** Rehd., f. Tree
with upright brs. forming a rather wide columnar head. A form with a narrower, more distinctly columnar head is **U. a. ascendens** Slavin, f. Other
columnar or narrow pyramidal forms are "Lake City Elm" and "Moline Elm,"
Nat. Nurseryman 40,6:10(h).—**U. a. péndula** Ait., var. Tree with long
pendulous brs.

Sect. 2. CHAETOPTELEA Schneid. Fls. before the lvs., on slender pedicels,
racemose: fr. pubescent and ciliate; seed near apex.

3. **U. Thomási** Sarg. ROCK E. Tree to 30 m.; brts. pubescent, usually
until the second year and developing later usually irregular corky wings; buds

large, acute, pubescent: lvs. elliptic to oblong-obovate, 5–10 cm. long, short-acuminate, unequal at base, doubly serrate, glabrous or somewhat rough above, pubescent beneath, without axillary tufts; petioles 2–6 mm. long: fls. in pendulous racemes to 5 cm. long; stamens 5–8, exserted; stigmas greenish white: fr. elliptic or obovate, 1.5–2 cm. long, with a small notch at apex, pubescent. S.S.7:t.312. H.H.184,185(b). (*U. racemosa* Thomas, not Borkh.— CORK E.) Que. to Tenn., w. to Neb. Intr. 1875. Zone II. Tree with short spreading brs. forming an oblong, round-topped head; of slow growth and rarely planted; the lvs. turn bright yellow before falling.

4. **U. alàta** Michx. WAHOO E. (WINGED E.) Tree to 15 m.; brts. nearly glabrous, developing usually 2 broad opposite corky wings; buds acute, glabrous: lvs. ovate-oblong to oblong-lanceolate, 3–6 cm. long, acute or acuminate, doubly serrate, glabrous above, pubescent beneath, with axillary tufts, subcoriaceous; petioles 1–3 mm. long: racemes short, few-fld.; stamens usually 5: fr. ovate-elliptic, about 8 mm. long, narrow-winged, with incurved beaks at apex, villous. M.S.3:275,t(c). S.S.7:t.313. H.H.186,187(b). Va. to Fla., w. to Ill. and Texas. Intr. 1820. Zone VI. Small tree with spreading brs. forming a round-topped oblong head, with small lvs. turning dull yellow before falling. Sometimes planted as a street tree in the s. States.

Sect. 3. MADOCARPUS Dum. Fls. before the lvs. on short pedicels, fascicled, calyx with 4–7 equal short lobes: fr. rarely ciliate: lvs. deciduous.

5. **U. fulva** Michx. SLIPPERY E. Tree to 20 m.; brts. pubescent and scabrous, red-brown or orange; buds large, fulvous-pubescent: lvs. obovate to oblong, 10–20 cm. long, long-acuminate, very unequal at base, doubly serrate, very rough above, densely pubescent beneath; petioles 4–8 mm. long: fls. short-stalked, in dense clusters; stamens 5–9; stigmas pinkish: fr. suborbicular to broadly elliptic, 1–2 cm. long, slightly notched, rufous-pubescent in the centre. M.S.3:278,t(c). S.S.7:t.314. H.H.188,189(b). Am. For. 19: 143,t.(h);22:278(b). (*U. rubra* Michx. f. *U. elliptica* Koehne, not Koch, *U. Heyderi* Spaeth.—RED E.) Que. to Fla., w. to Dak. and Texas. Cult. 1830. Zone III. Tree with spreading brs. forming usually a broad open head, with large lvs. turning dull yellow in fall.

Related species: **U. ellíptica** K. Koch. Tree with pubescent brts.; lvs. elliptic to elliptic-oblong, 8–14 cm. long, nearly smooth above, slightly pubescent beneath: fr. obovate, pubescent in the middle. Wolf & Palibin, Opr. Der. Kust. 626(l). Transcauc., Armenia. Intr. ?—U. macrocárpa Hance. Small tree or shrubby; brts. pubescent at first, often with 2 corky wings; lvs. broad-obovate or elliptic, 3–7 cm. long, usually abruptly short-acuminate, rough above, slightly pubescent beneath: fr. obovate, 2–2.5 cm. long, pubescent and ciliate. S.H.2: f.566h. C.H.136. N.K.19:t.5. China. Intr. 1908. Zone V.

6. **U. glabra** Huds. WYCH E. Tree to 40 m., without suckers; bark remaining smooth for many years (hence its name "glabra"); brts. pubescent while young, without corky wings; buds obtuse, pubescent: lvs. very short-petioled, oblong-obovate to elliptic or obovate, 8–16 cm. long, abruptly acuminate, very unequal at base, sharply and doubly serrate, scabrous above, pubescent beneath, rarely nearly glabrous; petioles 3–6 mm. long: fls. in dense clusters; stamens 5–6, slightly exserted; stigmas red: fr. obovate or broadly elliptic, 2–2.5 cm. long, with a small notch at apex, glabrous; seed in the middle. H.W.2:7,8(h),t.38(c). R.I.12:t.665(c, as *U. major*). E.H.7: t.394,400(h). G.C.39:152,suppl.(h). (*U. scabra* Mill., *U. montana* With., *U. campestris* L. in part.) N. and C. Eu., W. Asia. Long cult. Zone IV. There are many garden forms of which the following are most often cult.: **U. g purpúrea** (Dipp.) Rehd., f. Lvs. purple when young. (*U. scabra* var. *p.* Dipp.)

—**U. g. atropurpúrea** (Spaeth) Rehd., f. Lvs. dark purple. (*U. montana* var. *a.* Spaeth.) Orig. about 1883.—**U. g. lutéscens** (Dipp.) Rehd., f. Lvs. yellow. (*U. scabra* var. *l.* Dipp.)—**U. g. cornùta** (David) Rehd., f. Lvs. obovate, often broadly so and, at least on vigorous brts., with 3 or sometimes 5 acuminate lobes at the broad apex; brts. hirsute, red-brown in autumn. H.W.3: 7,f.231a. (*U. campestris c.* David, *U. scabra tricuspis* K. Koch, *U. triserrata* and *tridens* Hort., *U. mont.* var. *laciniata* Hort., not Maxim.) Orig. before 1845.—**U. g. crispa** (Willd.) Rehd., f. Lvs. narrow, incisely serrate, with twisted and incurved teeth: of slow growth. S.H.1:f.136y(1). (*U. mont.* var. *crispa* Loud., *U. asplenifolia* Hort., *U. urticaefolia* Audib.) Orig. before 1800. —**U. g. péndula** (Loud.) Rehd., f. Brs. horizontally spreading forming a low flat-topped head with long pendulous brts. G.C.50:221(h). Gn. 86:579(h). E.H.7:t.393(h). (*U. mont.* var. *p.* Loud., *U. mont.* var. *horizontalis* Kirchn.) Orig. about 1816.—**U. g. camperdòwnii** (Henry) Rehd., f. With pendulous brs. and brts. forming a globose head. G.C.50:221(h). (*U. mont.* var. *pendula Camperdowni* Henry, *U. mont. pendula* Kirchn., not Loud.) Cult. 1850.— **U. g. exoniénsis** (K. Koch) Rehd., f. With strictly upright brs. forming a narrow columnar head; lvs. smaller, broadly obovate, coarsely and deeply serrate, wrinkled above and often twisted. L.A.7:t.187a(h). (*U. mont.* var. *fastigiata* Loud., *U. scabra* v. *pyramidalis* Dipp., *U. exoniensis* K. Koch.) Orig. before 1826.—**U. g. nàna** (Dipp.) Rehd., f. Dwarf slow growing form with stunted brts. and small lvs., forming a rounded bush rarely more than 2 m. tall. Orig. before 1869.—**U. g. monstròsa** Schneid. Rehd., f. Compact shrub; brts. often fasciated; lvs. 5–8 cm. long, partly pitcher-shaped at base and on a slender stalk to 2.5 cm. long.—**U. g. nítida** (Fries) Rehd., f. Glabrous form with glabrous brts. and glabrous lvs. smooth above. (*U. mont.* var. *n.* Syme.) Spontaneous in Scand. and Eng. Intr. ?

U. g. × *pumila* = **U. arbúscula** Wolf. Shrubby tree with elliptic to ellipticoblong lvs. 2–7 cm. long (much longer on shoots), nearly equal at base, doubly serrate. Orig. 1902.—*U. g.* × *carpinifolia;* see No. 10. *U. hollandica*,

Related species: **U. Brandisiàna** Schneid. Brts. finely pubescent when young: lvs. elliptic to elliptic-lanceolate, 6–14 cm. long, long-acuminate, rough on both sides, slightly pubescent beneath at first; petioles 0.5–1 cm. long: frs. in very short racemes, broad-ovate, 12–18 mm. long. N. W. Himal., Afghan. Intr. 1919. Zone V.—**U. Bergmanniàna** Schneid. Tree to 23 m.; brts. glabrous: lvs. very short-petioled, obovate-oblong to elliptic, 7–12 cm. long, glabrous: fr. roundish-obovate, about 1.5 cm. long. S.H.2:f.565a-b,566a-b. C. China. Intr. 1900. Zone V?—**U. B. lasiophýlla** Schneid., var. Lvs. pubescent beneath. W. China. Intr. 1908. Zone V?

7. U. laciniàta (Trautv.) Mayr. Tree to 10 m., rarely taller; brts. glabrous or sparingly hairy when young, becoming pale yellowish brown or grayish brown in fall: lvs. obovate or obovate-oblong, 8–18 cm. long, at the broad apex usually with 3 or sometimes with 5 lobes, very unequal at base, doubly serrate, rough above, usually soft-pubescent beneath; petioles 2–5 mm. long: fls. in dense clusters: fr. elliptic, about 2 cm. long, glabrous; seed in the middle. S.I.2:t.15(c). M.K.t.39(c). N.K.19:t.2,3. (*U. mont.* var. *l.* Trautv., *U. major* var. *heterophylla* Maxim.) Manch., N. China, Japan. Cult. 1900. Zone V. Often confused with *U. glabra cornuta* which may be readily distinguished by the hairy brts. reddish brown at maturity and the presence of the 3-lobed lvs. chiefly on vigorous shoots.—**U. l. nikkoénsis** Rehd., var. Lvs. obovate, 6–11 cm. long, sparingly short-pubescent on the veins and veinlets beneath, purple when unfolding. C. Japan. Intr. 1905.

8. U. procèra Salisb. ENGLISH E. Tall tree to 40 or even 50 m.; suckering; bark deeply fissured; young brts. pubescent, sometimes developing **corky**

wings; buds ovoid, minutely pubescent: lvs. ovate or broad-elliptic, 5–8 cm. long, short-acuminate, very oblique at base, doubly serrate, with about 12 pairs of veins, dark green and scabrous above, soft-pubescent beneath and with axillary tufts; petioles 4–6 mm. long, pubescent: fls. short-stalked; stamens 3–5; stigmas white: fr. suborbicular, about 1.2 cm. across, with a small closed notch at apex; seed close to the notch. S.E.8:t.1285(c). Em.2:336(h). M.G.15:577(h). E.H.7:t.404,405(h),412,f.14. (*U. campestris* Mill., *U. surculosa* var. *latifolia* Stokes.) Eng., w. and s. Eu. Early intr. to Am. Zone V. Tall tree with straight nearly excurrent stem and spreading or ascending brs. forming an oval or oblong head. Much planted in England and also in this country, particularly in the N. E. States. The lvs. remain green several weeks longer than those of the American Elms.—**U. p. argénteo-variegàta** (West.) Rehd., f. Lvs. striped and spotted with white. (*U. camp.* var. *variegata* Dipp., *U. camp.* var. *a.* West.) Orig. before 1770.—**U. p. purpúrea** (Wesm.) Rehd., f. Lvs. tinged dark purple. (*U. camp.* var. *p.* Wesm.) Orig. before 1860.—**U. p. purpuráscens** (Schneid.) Rehd., f. Lvs. small, 2–3 cm. long, tinged purple. (*U. camp.* f. *p.* Schneid., *U. camp.* var. *myrtifolia purpurea* De Smet.) Orig. before 1877.—**U. p. Vanhoúttei** (Schelle) Rehd., f. Lvs. tinged with yellow. (*U. camp.* var. *V.* Henry, *U. camp.* "Louis van Houtte" Hort.) Orig. about 1886.—**U. p. Berárdi** (Simon-Louis) Rehd., var. Bushy tree with slender upright brs.: lvs. elliptic-oblong, 1.5–3 cm. long, with few large simple obtusish teeth, glabrous; petiole and brts. pubescent: fr. unknown. S.H.1:f.1361-m. (*U. camp.* var. *B.* Simon-Louis.) Orig. 1863. Similar to *Zelkova Verschaffeltii.*—**U. p. myrtifòlia** Rehd., f. Lvs. ovate or rhombic-ovate to oblong-ovate, 2–3(–5) cm. long, with nearly simple teeth, loosely pilose on both sides: fr. obovate, 12–15 mm. long. Cult. 1880.—**U. p. viminàlis** (Loud.) Rehd., var. Tree with ascending brs. and pendulous brts. slightly pubescent while young: lvs. obovate to narrow-elliptic, 2–6 cm. long, acuminate, incisely doubly serrate, scabrous above, slightly pubescent beneath: fr. unknown. G.C.51:326. S.H.1:f.215n-o. (*U. camp.* var. *v.* Loud., *U. antarctica* Kirchn., *U. stricta* Hort., not Lindl.) Orig. 1817.—**U. p. aùrea** (Morr.) Rehd., f. A form of the preceding var. with yellow lvs. I.H.14:t.513 (c). B.H.16:t.19(c). (*U. Rosseelsii* Hort., *U. camp. a.* Morr.) Orig. before 1866.—**U. p. marginàta** (Kirchn.) Rehd., f. A form of *U. p. viminalis* with the lvs. variegated creamy white near the margin. (*U. camp. viminalis m.* Kirchn., *U. camp.* var. *viminalis variegata* Nichols.) Orig. before 1860.—**U. p. austràlis** (Henry) Rehd., var. Lvs. thicker and firmer, prominently veined beneath, more cuspidate-acuminate. E.H.7:t.412,f.17. (*U. camp.* var. *a.* Henry.) S. Eu. Long cult.

9. **U. japónica** (Rehd.) Sarg. JAPANESE E. Tree to 30 m.; young brts. densely pubescent and tuberculate, pale yellowish brown, sometimes developing corky wings: lvs. obovate or elliptic, 8–12 cm. long, acuminate, doubly serrate, with 12–16 pairs of veins, scabrous and pubescent above, pubescent beneath, with small axillary tufts; petioles 4–5 mm. long, densely pubescent: fls. nearly sessile; stamens 4: fr. obovate-elliptic, about 2 cm. long, gradually narrowed at base; seed touching the open notch. S.I.2:t.101(c). C.H.139. N.K.19:t.8 G.F.6:327(h). (*U. campestris* var. *j.* Rehd., *U. Davidiana* var. *japonica* Nakai.) Japan, N. E. Asia. Intr. 1895. Zone V.

Related species: **U. Davidiàna** Planch. Brs. usually with 2 broad corky wings: lvs. short-petioled, broad-obovate or elliptic-ovate, 5–10 cm. long, slightly pubescent beneath: fr. elliptic, pubescent in the middle. C.H.141. N.K.19:t.9. N. China. Intr. ?.—**U. Wilsoniàna** Schneid. Tree to 25 m.; young brts. pubescent, becoming brown and often corky: lvs. elliptic or elliptic-obovate, 4–10 cm.

long, smooth above, finely pubescent or nearly glabrous beneath: fr. obovate, glabrous. S.H.2:f.565e,566c-d. C. China. Intr. 1910. Zone V.

10. × **U. hollándica** Mill. Under this name are united here a number of Elms which are apparently hybrids between *U. glabra* and *U. carpinifolia*, more or less intermediate between these two species. (*U. Dippeliana* Schneid.) As the type of this group may serve the following variety which probably is not different from Miller's *U. hollandica*. Zone IV.—**U. h. màjor** (Sm.) Rehd., var. Dutch E. Tree to 40 m. with short trunk and wide-spreading brs. and often pendulous brts.; suckering; bark deeply fissured; young brts. glabrous or with few hairs: lvs. elliptic-ovate or broad-elliptic, 8–12 cm. long, acuminate, very unequal at base, with 12–14 pairs of veins, lustrous dark green and nearly smooth above, sparingly and minutely pubescent and glandular beneath, with conspicuous axillary tufts; petioles 6–10 mm. long: fls. usually 4-merous: fr. elliptic-obovate, 2–2.5 cm. long; the seed touching the notch. R.I.12:t.662(c, as *U. montana*)? E.H.7:t.42,f.15. F.N.2:f.84(h). (*U. m.* Smith, *U. camp.* var. *m.* Planch., *U. scabra* var. *m.* Guerke.) Of unknown origin.— **U. h. végeta** (Loud.) Rehd., var. Huntingdon E. Tall tree with usually forked stem and rough bark; suckering; young brts. glabrous or sparingly hairy: lvs. elliptic, 8–12 cm. long, acuminate, very unequal at base, with 14–18 pairs of veins, smooth and glabrous above, glabrous below except small axillary tufts; petioles 6–8 mm. long: fr. elliptic-obovate with closed notch; seed above the middle. E.H.7:t.395(h),t.412,f.16. (*U. v.* Lindl., *U. glabra* var. *v.* Loud., *U. Huntingdoni* Hort.) Orig. about 1750.—**U. h. bélgica** (Burgsd.) Rehd., var. Belgian E. Tall tree with straight stem and broad crown; bark rough; young brts. more or less pubescent: lvs. elliptic-obovate, often narrowly so, 8–12 cm. long, acuminate, very oblique at base, with 14–18 pairs of veins, slightly scabrous above, soft-pubescent beneath, or only on the veins; petioles 4–6 mm. long: fr. elliptic, 2–2.5 cm. long, seed above the middle. E.H.7:t.412,f.18. (*U. b.* Burgsd., *U. latifolia* Poederle, *U. batavina* K. Koch, *U. camp.* var. *latifolia* Gillek.) Orig. in Belgium; much planted in continental Eu.—**U. h. Dumóntii** (Mottet) Rehd., var. Similar to the preceding, but with more ascending brs. forming a narrow head. (*U. belgica* var. *D.* Henry, *U. camp.* var. *D.* Mottet.)—**U. h. Klemmer** (Gillekens) Rehd., var. Tall tree with ascending brs. forming a narrow-pyramidal head; bark smooth; young brts. with short hairs: lvs. ovate, 5–10 cm. long, short-acuminate, oblique at base, with about 12 pairs of veins, glabrous but scabrous above, minutely pubescent beneath; petioles 5–10 mm. long: fr. with the seed close to the notch. (*U. camp.* var. K. Gillekens, *U. camp. Clemmeri* Hort., *U. Klemeri* Spaeth.) Orig. in Belgium where it is much planted.—**U. h. supérba** (Morr.) Rehd., var. Narrow-pyramidal tree; bark smooth; young brts. glabrous: lvs. ovate or elliptic-obovate. 8–12 cm. long, very oblique at base, with 15–18 pairs of veins, glabrous and smooth above, glabrous below except small axillary tufts; petioles 6–8 mm. long, sparingly pubescent: fls. 5-merous: fr. elliptic, 1.5–2 cm. long, with the seed near the middle. (*U. montana* var. *s.* Morr., *U. s.* Henry, *U. praestans* Schoch.) Orig. in Belgium.—**U. h. Dauvéssei** (Henry) Rehd., var. Broad-pyramidal tree; brts. hairy: lvs. to 12 cm. long, very unequal at base, soft-pubescent beneath; petiole about 5 mm. long: fr. with the seed near apex. (*U. mont.* var. *D.* Nichols., *U. D.* Henry.) Orig. before 1877.—**U. h. Pitteùrsii** (Kirchn.) Rehd., var. Vigorous growing tree with large broad-ovate lvs.; said to produce annual shoots to 3 m. long. B.H.2:133, 166. (*U. P.* Kirchn., "Orme Pitteurs" Morr.) Orig. in Belgium.—**U. h. péndula** (W. Mast.) Rehd., var. Tree with ascending brs. and pendulous brts.,

more or less pubescent when young; lvs. firm, elliptic, about 8 cm. long, long-acuminate, very unequal at base, glabrous and smooth above, sparingly pubescent beneath; petioles about 8 mm. long: stamens 3–5: fr. obovate, 2 cm. long, with open notch; seed above the centre. E.H.7:t.412,f.24. (*U. Smithii* Henry, *U. glabra* var. *p.* Loud.) Orig. in England before 1830.—The various hybrids are much planted in Europe, particularly on the continent as shade and street trees.

11. **U. carpinifòlia** Gleditsch. Smooth-leaved E. Tree to 30 m., suckering; bark gray, deeply fissured; brts. slender, glabrous or nearly so while young; buds minutely pubescent: lvs. elliptic to ovate or obovate, acuminate, very oblique at base, doubly serrate, with about 12 pairs of veins, lustrous bright green and smooth above, glabrous beneath except axillary tufts, glandular while young; petioles 6–12 mm. long, usually pubescent: fls. in dense clusters; stamens 4–5; stigmas usually white: fr. elliptic or obovate, cuneate at base, rounded at apex; seed close to the closed notch. H.W.2:3,t.37(c, as *U. campestris*). R.I.12:t.664(c) S.E.8:t.1286(c). E.H.7:t.399,401,402(h). (*U. foliacea* Gilib., *U. nitens* Moench, *U. glabra* Mill., not Huds., *U. campestris* var. *laevis* Spach, *U. surculosa* var. *glabra* Stokes.) Eu., N. Afr., W. Asia. Long cult. Zone IV. A tree with straight trunk and slender ascending brs. forming a pyramidal head, or spreading and forming a round-topped head; brts. often pendulous; foliage bright green. A very variable species with many garden forms: **U. c. variegàta** (Dum.-Cours.) Rehd., f. Lvs. marked usually densely with rather small white spots. (*U. camp. v.* Dum.-Cours.)— **U. c. péndula** (Henry) Rehd., f. With slender pendulous brts. (*U. nitens* var. *p.* Henry.)—**U. c. Webbiàna** Rehd., f. Narrow-pyramidal tree with ascending brs.: lvs. small, folded longitudinally. (*U. camp. W.* Lee.)—**U. c. Dampieri** (Wesm.) Rehd., var. Narrow-pyramidal tree: lvs. crowded on short brts., broad-ovate, deeply doubly toothed with crenately serrate teeth. N.V.12:133, t(h). (*U. nitens* var. *D.* Henry.)—**U. c. Wrèdei** (Juehlke) Rehd., f. Like the preceding, but lvs. yellowish. M.G.13:160(h). S.H.1:f.136p. (*U. camp. Dampieri W.* Juehlke. *U. W. aurea* Hort.) Orig. about 1877.—**U. c. cornubiénsis** (West.) Rehd., var. Cornish E. Narrow-pyramidal tree, with ascending brs.; young brts. often pubescent at the nodes: lvs. elliptic or broad-obovate, 5–7 cm. long, dark green and smooth above; petioles about 8 mm. long, pubescent: stigmas pink: fr. narrower than in the type. E.H.7:t.397(h), 412,f.20. (*U. stricta* Lindl., *U. camp.* var *stricta* Ait., *U. camp.* var. *c.* Loud., *U. glabra* f. *fastigiata* Dipp., *U. nitens* var. *stricta* Henry.) S. W. Eng. Long cult.—**U. c. sarniénsis** (Loud.) Rehd., f. Jersey E. A form of the preceding with more stiffly erect brs. and broader lvs. less conspicuously tufted beneath: stigmas white. G.C.41:150(h);87:165(h). E.H.7:t.398(h),412,f.21. B.S.1:86, i.(h). F.N.2:f.81(h). (*U. camp. Wheatleyi* Simon-Louis, *U. nitens* var. *W.* Henry, *U. sarniensis* Lodd., *U. campestris monumentalis* Hort., not Rinz.— Wheatley or Guernsey E.)—**U. c. umbraculífera** (Trautv.) Rehd., var. Tree with dense globose head; brts. slender, slightly hairy when young: lvs. elliptic or elliptic-ovate, 3–7 cm. long, often slightly rough above; petiole 4–8 mm. long. Gt.30:t.1034(h). M.G.15:579(h). M.D.1910:72,73(h). S.L.372(h). (*U. camp.* var. *u.* Trautv., *U. densa* Litvin.) Turkest. Cult. 1879.—**U. c. gracilis** (Spaeth) Rehd., f. A form of the preceding with slenderer brs. and smaller lvs. (*U. camp. umbraculifera g.* Spaeth.)—**U. c. Koopmánnii** (Spaeth) Rehd., f. Similar to *U. c. umbraculifera* but with an oval head; brs. often corky, brts. paler: lvs. grayish green beneath; petiole 3–5 mm. long. (*U. K.* Spaeth.) Intr. from Turkest. before 1880.—**U. c. suberòsa** (Moench) Rehd.,

var. Usually shrubby; the stiff brs. with corky wings: lvs. smaller, often slightly rough above. R.I.12:t.663(c) S.L.2:413(h). (*U. s.* Moench, not Ehrh., *U. camp.* var. *s.* (Moench) Wahlb.) C. Eu.—**U. c. propéndens** (Schneid.) Rehd., f. A form of the preceding with somewhat pendulous brs. and small lvs. 2–3 cm. long. M.G.16:166(h). (*U. suberosa pendula* Lav., *U. glabra* var. *suberosa* f. *pr.* Schneid.)—**U. c. itàlica** (Henry) Rehd., var. Lvs. more coriaceous than in the type, with 14–18 pairs of veins, quite glabrous except axillary tufts beneath. E.H.7:t.411,f.9. (*U. nitens* var. *i.* Henry.) Italy. Probably tenderer than the type.

    U. c. × *glabra;* see *U. hollandica,* No. 10.

    12. **U. Plotii** Druce. Tree to 30 m.; suckering; brts. sparingly and minutely pubescent, glabrous the second year: lvs. elliptic to obovate, 3.5–6 cm. long, acute or acuminate, only slightly unequal and often cordate at base, doubly serrate, with 8–10 pairs of veins, dull green above and slightly scabrous and puberulous, densely pubescent beneath at first, later glabrescent, with conspicuous axillary tufts: fls. very short-stalked; calyx with 4–6 pinkish lobes; stigmas pink: fr. narrowly obovate, 1–1.5 cm. long, with open notch. E.H.7: t.403(h),411,f.3. G.C.50:408(h),409;51:235. N.F.2:f.86(h). (*U. minor* Henry, not Mill., *U. sativa* Moss, not Mill., *U. surculosa* var. *angustifolia* Stokes.) Eu. Zone V.

    13. **U. pùmila** L. SIBERIAN E. Tree to 25 m. or shrub; bark rough; brts. slender, grayish or grayish brown, pubescent while young or nearly glabrous; stipules broad, often semicordate at base: lvs. elliptic to elliptic-lanceolate, 2–7 cm. long, acute or acuminate, usually nearly equal at base, nearly simply serrate, with the teeth entire or with only one minute tooth, dark green and smooth above, glabrous beneath or slightly pubescent when young, firm at maturity; petioles 2–4 mm. long: fls. very short-stalked; stamens 4–5; anthers violet: fr. suborbicular, 1–1.5 cm. long, with closed notch; seed slightly above the middle. C.C.109. N.K.19:20–22(h),t.6,7. Gn.65:133. S.H.1:f.137m–p, 139i–k. U.S.Im.125:t.204(h). (*U. campestris* var. *p.* Maxim.) E. Siber., N. China, Turkest. Cult. 1860. Zone IV. Recommended as a street tree for arid regions.—The typical form is a small-leaved shrub of E. Siberia and Mongolia; the plant of N. China, Manch. and Korea is a tree to 25 m. with round head (*U. manshurica* Nakai); this is the form generally cult.—**U. p. péndula** (Kirchn.) Rehd., var. Brs. slender, pendulous. U. S. Inv. 43;t.2(h).—**U. p. arbórea** Litv., var. Tree pyramidal while young, rather loosely branched: lvs. elliptic-ovate to ovate-lanceolate, 4–7 cm. long, teeth mostly with 1 or 2 small teeth, lustrous above, petiole 4–8 mm. long. (*U. turkestanica* Reg., *U. p.* var. *pinnato-ramosa* Henry.) Turkestan. Cult. 1894.—**U. p. Androssówi** (Litv.) Rehd., f. Tree with spreading brs. forming a dense broad head; older brs. corky. Sched. Herb. Fl. Ross. 8:t.2(h). (*U. A.* Litv.) Cult. 1934. Similar in habit to *U. carpinifolia umbraculifera.*

    U. p. × *glabra;* see under No. 6.

    Sec. 4. MICROPTELEA Spach. Fls. in autumn, fascicled; calyx deeply divided beyond the middle into 4–8 equal lobes: lvs. subpersistent or tardily deciduous.

    14. **U. parvifòlia** Jacq. CHINESE E. Small tree to 15 or 25 m.; bark smooth or rough; brts. pubescent; stipules linear-lanceolate, narrow at base: lvs. elliptic to ovate or obovate, 2–5 cm. long, acute or obtusish, unequally rounded at base, simply or nearly simply serrate, lustrous and smooth above, pubescent beneath while young, subcoriaceous at maturity; petioles 2–6 mm. long: fls. in August or Sept. in axillary clusters: fr. elliptic-ovate, about 1 cm. long, notched at apex; seed in the middle. S.I.1:t.37(c). M.O.

t.36,f.165(h). R.H.1909:399(h). Mo. Bot. Gard. Bull. 11:t.31(h). (*U. chinensis* Pers.) N. and C. China, Korea, Japan. Intr. 1794. Zone V. Tree with broad round head and small lvs. changing late in fall to red or purple or farther s. remaining green into the winter.—The species described as *U. Sieboldii* and *U. Shirasawana* Daveau (B.F.1914:24,25; S.I.1:t.37,f.1–9) and as *U. coreana* Nakai (N.K.19:t.11) differ little from *U. parvifolia;* all three are in cult.

Related species: **U. crassifòlia** Nutt. CEDAR E. Tree to 25 m.; brs. often with 2 opposite corky wings: lvs. ovate to ovate-oblong, 2.5–5 cm. long, acute or obtuse, often nearly simply serrate, subcoriaceous: fls. in short-stalked, 3–5-fld. fascicles: fr. small. S.S.7:t.315. Miss. to Ark. and Tex. Intr. 1876. Zone VII.

Sect. 5. TRICHOPTELEA Schneid. Fls. in autumn, in pendulous glabrous racemes: calyx 6-parted to the base: fr. pubescent and ciliate.

15. **U. seròtina** Sarg. RED E. Tree to 20 m.; brts. slender, glabrous or slightly puberulous at first, often developing irregular corky wings: lvs. oblong to oblong-obovate, 5–8 cm. long, acuminate, very oblique at base, doubly serrate, with about 20 pairs of veins, glabrous and lustrous above, pubescent on the veins beneath and somewhat reticulate; petioles about 6 mm. long; stipules narrowed from a broad clasping base, persistent nearly until the lvs. are fully grown: fls. in Sept., axillary in pendulous racemes about 3 cm. long: fr. elliptic, 1–1.5 cm. long, deeply notched, densely ciliate. S.S.14:718. Ky. to Ala., n. Ga. and Ill. Cult. 1903. Zone V. Tree with spreading or pendulous brs. forming a broad head.

2. **PLÁNERA** G. F. Gmel. WATER-ELM. Deciduous tree; winter buds subglobose, minute: lvs. pinnately veined, serrate: fls. polygamo-monoecious; calyx deeply 4–5-lobed; staminate fls. in clusters at base of the young brts.; stamens 4–5; perfect fls. 1–3 in the axils of the young lvs.: fr. a small muricate drupe; cotyledons thick, unequal. (After J. J. Planer, 1743–1789; professor of medicine at Erfurt, Germany.) One species in N. Am.

P. aquática (Walt.) Gmel. Tree to 12 m.; brts. puberulous: lvs. ovate to ovate-oblong, 3–6 cm. long, acute, unequal at base, unequally serrate, at maturity glabrous, scabrate above; petioles 3–6 mm. long: fr. ellipsoid, about 8 mm. long, with irregularly crested fleshy ribs. Fls. with the lvs.; fr.iv–v. M.S. 3:283,t.(c). S.S.7:t.316. R.H.1903:351(h). (*P. ulmifolia* Michx.) S. Ill. and Ky. to Fla. and Tex. Intr. 1816, but rare in cult. Zone VII? Small tree with spreading brs. forming a low broad head.

3. **HEMIPTÉLEA** Planch. Deciduous tree; brts. often rigid and spinescent; winter-buds globose-ovoid, minute: lvs. very short-stalked, penninerved, simply serrate: fls. polygamous, short-stalked, in 1–4-fld. clusters on the young brts. in the axils of bracts and lower lvs.; calyx 4–5-parted; stamens usually 4; fr. a small oblique nutlet with a crest-like wing on the upper half; cotyledons broad. (Greek, *hemi*, half, and *ptelea*, the ancient Greek name of the elm; referring to the shape of the wing.) One species in N. E. Asia.

H. Davídii (Hance) Planch. Shrubby tree; spines 1.5–10 cm. long, slender or stout, usually leafy, chiefly on young plants; brts. slightly pilose or densely hairy while young, becoming brown or grayish brown: lvs. elliptic to elliptic-oblong, 2–5 cm. long, acute, subcordate at the narrowed base, simply and coarsely serrate, with 8–12 pairs of veins, above at first with scattered hairs each leaving a dark circular depression, sparingly hairy on the veins beneath; petioles 1–3 mm. long: fr. obliquely conical, 2-edged, winged on the upper half, about 6 mm. long. Fl. with the lvs.; fr.viii–x. C.C.121. N.K.19:t.14. I.S. 1:t.21. R.H.1913:29. M.O.35. Gn.90:377(h). (*Planera D.* Hance, *Zelkova*

D. (Hance) Hemsl., *Z. Davidiana* Bean.) N. China, Manch., Korea. Cult. 1899. Zone V. Small much-branched tree, often shrubby. In N. China used as a hedge plant.

4. **ZÉLKOVA** Spach. Deciduous trees or shrubs; bark rather smooth, scaly; winter-buds ovoid, acutish, glabrous, with many imbricate dark brown broad scales: lvs. short-petioled, penninerved, simply serrate: fls. polygamous, short-stalked, appearing on the young brts., the staminate ones clustered in the axils of the lower lvs. and bracts, the pistillate fls. solitary or few in the axils of the upper lvs.; calyx 4–5-lobed; stamens 4–5; style eccentric; fr. a short-stalked drupe oblique and broader than high; cotyledons broad. Fls. in spring with the lvs.; fr. in autumn. (Zelkoua or Aselkwa, the Caucasian vernacular name of *Z. carpinifolia*.) Syn.: *Abelicea* Reichenb. Five species, including a doubtful one, in W. and E. Asia.

A. Lvs. acute, crenately serrate, with 6–8 pairs of veins......................1. *Z. carpinifolia*
AA. Lvs. acuminate, sharply serrate, with 8–14 pairs of veins......................2. *Z. serrata*

1. **Z. carpinifòlia** (Pall.) K. Koch. Tree to 25 m.; brts. slender, pubescent: lvs. elliptic to oblong, 2–5, rarely to 9 cm. long, acute, rounded or subcordate at base, coarsely crenate-serrate, with 6–8 pairs of veins, dark green and smooth or somewhat rough above, pubescent on the veins beneath; petioles 1–2 mm. long: fr. about 5 mm. across. E.N.III.1:65. Gn.24:371. E.H.4:t.249 (h). B.S.2:694,t(h). (*Z. crenata* Spach, *Z. ulmoides* Schneid., *Planera Richardii* Michx., *Abelicea ulmoides* Ktze.) Cauc. Intr. 1760. Zone VI. Tree similar to the following, but with an ovoid or oblong head.

2. **Z. serràta** (Thunb.) Mak. Tree to 30 m.; brts. usually glabrous: lvs. ovate to oblong-ovate, 3–6, or on shoots to 12 cm. long, acuminate or apiculate, rounded or subcordate at base, sharply serrate with acuminate teeth, with about 8–14 pairs of veins, somewhat rough above, glabrous or nearly so beneath; petioles 2–5 mm. long: fr. about 4 mm. across. S.I.1:t.36(c). G.F.6:325. N.K.19:t.12. S.L.391(h). H.B.3:483(h). E.H.4:t.250(h). (*Z. acuminata* Planch., *Z. hirta* Schneid., *Z. Keaki* Mayr, *Planera acuminata* Lindl., *P. japonica* Miq.) Japan. Intr. about 1860, 1862 to Am. Zone V. Tree with short trunk dividing into many upright and erect-spreading stems forming a broad round-topped head.

Closely related species: **Z. sínica** Schneid. Tree to 17 m.: lvs. ovate-oblong, 2–7 cm. long, obliquely rounded or broadly cuneate at base, crenate-serrate with acutish or slightly apiculate teeth, with usually 7–10 pairs of veins: fr. 5–6 mm. across. C. and E. China. Intr. 1908. Zone VI?—**Z. Schneideriàna** Hand.-Mazz. Lvs. elliptic-ovate to elliptic-oblong, 3–8 cm. long, crenate-serrate, pubescent beneath, veins 8–12. E. China. Intr. 1920. Zone VI.—A doubtful species is **Z. Verschafféltii** Nichols. Shrub or small tree: lvs. oval or ovate, 3–6 cm. long, with 6–9 pairs of coarse triangular teeth, rough above, pubescent beneath: fr. similar to that of *Z. carpinifolia*. S.H.1:f.141c. (*Z. japonica* var. *V.* Dipp., *Ulmus V.* Hort.) Cult. 1886. Possibly a native of the Cauc. and a form of *Z. carpinifolia*.

5. **PTEROCÉLTIS** Maxim. Deciduous tree: lvs. 3-nerved at base: fls. much like those of Celtis; anthers pilose at apex; fr. a small nutlet, surrounded by a broad wing, usually emarginate at apex; cotyledons broad. (Greek *pteron*, wing and *celtis;* referring to the winged fr. by which it differs from Celtis.) Only the following species known.

P. Tatarinòwii Maxim. Tree to 16 m.: bark pale gray, peeling off in long flakes; brts. glabrous, chestnut-brown, with few small lenticels: lvs. ovate to ovate-oblong. 3.5–8 cm. long, acuminate, broad-cuneate at base, irregularly and sharply serrate, glabrous: fr. slender-stalked, suborbicular, 1.5–2 cm. across, emarginate at apex. S.H.1:f.146. C.C.116. C.H.150. V.F.205. N. and

C. China. Intr. 1894. Zone V? Tree with short trunk and a broad wide-spreading head.

6. **CÉLTIS** L. HACKBERRY. Trees or rarely shrubs, deciduous, only the tropical and subtropical species often evergreen: bark usually gray, smooth, sometimes with corky warty excrescences; winter-buds small: lvs. 3-nerved at base, serrate or entire; petioles usually fairly long: fls. polygamo-monoecious, appearing on the young brts., the staminate ones in fascicles toward the base, the perfect fls. above, solitary in the axils of the lvs.: calyx 4–5-lobed; stamens 4–5: fr. a subglobose or ovoid drupe with a firm outer coat, usually scanty pulp and a bony stone with smooth or sculptured surface; embryo with broad folded cotyledons. Fls. with the lvs.; fr. ripening in autumn and often remaining long after leaf-fall. (The ancient Greek name of a tree with sweet fr.) About 70 species in the temp. regions of the n. hemisphere and in the tropics; the species cult. with us belong to the sect. Euceltis which contains more than 30 closely related species often difficult to distinguish.—The hackberries are planted as shade trees or for ornament, but do not present any particular ornamental features; a few have edible frs.

A. Lvs. entire or occasionally with few teeth (serrate in var. of No. 1): stone pitted.
  B. Lvs. ovate to oblong-lanceolate, long-acuminate, usually broad-cuneate at base, thin, glabrous: fr.-stalk longer than petiole..1. *C. laevigata*
  BB. Lvs. ovate to ovate-oblong, acute or short-acuminate, rounded or subcordate at base: fr.-stalk about as long as petiole.
    c. Lvs. strongly reticulate beneath: fr. orange..........................2. *C. reticulata*
    cc. Lvs. scarcely reticulate: fr. purple or tan-color..........................3. *C. pumila*
AA. Lvs. serrate (occasionally entire in No. 6).
  B. Lvs. acuminate.
    c. Lvs. glabrous or nearly so beneath (pubescent on the veins beneath and rough above in a var. of No. 4): fr. on stalks longer than the petioles.
      D. Lvs. green or yellowish beneath.
        E. Petioles slender, about 1 cm. long or longer; lvs. sharply serrate with acuminate teeth: stone pitted.
          F. Lvs. oblong-lanceolate, cuneate at base..........1. *C. laevigata* var. *Smallii*
          FF. Lvs. ovate to oblong-ovate, rounded or subcordate at base..4. *C. occidentalis*
        EE. Petioles stout, less than 1 cm. long; lvs. usually serrate only above the middle.
          F. Brts. glabrous; lvs. perfectly glabrous and lustrous green on both sides, crenate-serrate: fr. purplish black; stone smooth................5. *C. Bungeana*
          FF. Brts. pubescent: lvs. with appressed hairs and dark green above, lighter beneath, serrate, sometimes entire: fr. orange; stone pitted.....6. *C. Biondii*
      DD. Lvs. grayish or whitish beneath, sharply serrate except at base: fr. black; stone pitted ....7. *C. jessoensis*
    cc. Lvs. pubescent beneath at least on the veins.
      D. Lvs. densely pilose only on the veins, usually serrate only above the middle: frs. several, short-stalked small, orange...................................8. *C. labilis*
      DD. Lvs. soft-pubescent beneath: frs. long-stalked, large, over 1 cm. long.
        E. Brts. and lvs. beneath grayish pubescent; lvs. sharply serrate except at base: frs. black, on slender glabrescent stalks............................9. *C. australis*
        EE. Brts. and lvs. beneath yellow-tomentose; lvs. serrate only above the middle: frs. orange, on stout tomentose stalks...........................10. *C. Juliana*
  BB. Lvs. rounded or truncate at apex and abruptly cuspidate, coarsely serrate, 5.5–11.5 cm. broad ....11. *C. koraiensis*

1. **C. laevigàta** Willd. MISSISSIPPI H. Tree to 30 m.; bark light gray, usually covered with corky warts: brts. glabrous or pubescent at first: lvs. oblong-lanceolate, sometimes ovate, 5–10 cm. long, long-acuminate and usually falcate, broad-cuneate or rounded at base, entire or sometimes with a few teeth, dark green above, slightly paler beneath, glabrous, thin; petioles 6–10 mm. long: fr. 5–7 mm. across, orange-red or finally purple-black, on slender stalks 1–2 cm. long. S.S.7:t.318. G.F.3:41,f.9,11. M.M.7:225(h),227 (b). (*C. mississippiensis* DC., *C. integrifolia* Nutt.) S. Ind. and Ill. to Tex. and Fla. Cult. 1811. Zone V. Tree with spreading often pendulous brs. forming a broad round head.—**C. l. texàna** Sarg., var. Brts. often pubescent:

lvs. ovate to ovate-lanceolate, 3.5–7 cm. long, thicker, often pubescent on veins beneath. S.M.325. Kans. to Mo. and N. Mex. Intr. 1922.—**C. l. Smàllii** (Beadle) Sarg., var. Tree to 10 m.: lvs. sharply serrate. B.T.357. (*C. S. Beadle.*) N. C. and Tenn. to Ga. and Ala. Intr. 1909. Zone VI?

2. **C. reticulàta** Torr. Small tree to 15 m. or shrub; brts. pubescent: lvs. ovate, 3–7 cm. long, acute or acuminate, rounded or subcordate at base, entire or with few coarse teeth above the middle, scabrous above, conspicuously reticulate and glabrous or somewhat pubescent beneath, firm and thickish; petioles 5–10 mm. long: fr. 7–10 mm. across, orange-red, on stalks about 1 cm. long. G.F.3:41,f.12. S.M.323. (*C. mississippiensis* var. *r.* Sarg.) Colo. and Tex. to Wash. and S. Calif. Intr. 1890. Zone V? Small tree with rather rigid spreading brs. or spreading shrub; rarely cult.

Closely related species: **C. Douglàsii** Planch. Small tree: lvs. usually oblong-ovate, distinctly acuminate, sharply serrate to nearly entire: fr. on slender stalks usually twice as long as the petioles. S.M.321,f.292. A.I.1:523. (*C. rugulosa* Rydb.) Colo. to Wash. and Utah. Intr. 1898. Zone V.

3. **C. pùmila** Pursh. Shrub or small tree to 4 m.; brts. finely pubescent or at least puberulous while young: lvs. ovate to ovate-oblong, 3–8 cm. long, acute or short-acuminate, rounded or subcordate at base, smooth or slightly scabrous above, light green and nearly glabrous beneath, finely pubescent on both sides while young; petioles 5–10 mm. long: fr. dull orange to purplish, 6–8 mm. thick, on short stalks about as long as the petioles; stone subglobose, shallowly pitted. G.F.3:41,f.10. Bull. Torr. Bot. Club, 27,t.33. (*C. occidentalis* var. *p.* Gray.) N. J. to Fla., w. to Kansas, Colo. and Utah. Intr. 1876. Zone V. —**C. p. Deàmii** Sarg., var. Lvs. slightly pubescent on the veins beneath, rather thick: pedicels longer. Deam, Shrubs Ind. 149. Ind. Intr. 1919.—**C. p. georgiàna** (Small) Sarg., var. Shrub or tree to 10 m.: lvs rugose above, pilose along the veins beneath and on petioles; pedicels puberulous. S.M.326. B.T. 357. (*C. g.* Small.) N. J. to Fla., Ala. and Mo. Intr. 1906.

4. **C. occidentàlis** L. Tree occasionally to 40 m.; brts glabrous or puberulous: lvs. ovate to oblong-ovate, 5–12 cm. long, acute to acuminate, oblique and rounded or broad-cuneate at base, serrate except at base, bright green and usually smooth and lustrous above, paler below and glabrous or slightly hairy on the veins; petioles 1–1.5 cm. long: fr. 7–10 mm. thick, orange-red to dark purple, on slender stalks longer than the petioles; stone pitted. S.S. 7:t.317. G.F.3:40,43(h). B.T.354(h). E.H.4:t.251(h).—Que. to Man., s. to N. C., Ala. and Kans. Cult. 1636. Zone II. Tree with straight trunk and spreading rather rigid or sometimes pendulous brs. forming a round-topped head, and with bright green lvs. turning light yellow in fall; the var. *crassifolia* is of more vigorous growth and grows to a taller tree with darker lvs.— **C. o. canìna** (Raf.) Sarg., var. Lvs. narrower, oblong-ovate, 8–14 cm. long, long-acuminate, glabrous or rarely pilose on the veins beneath, usually light green; petiole to 1.8 cm. long. S.M.320. (*C. c.* Raf.) Que. to Ga. and Okl. Cult. 1898.—**C. o. crassifòlia** (Lam.) Gray., var. Tree with pubescent brts.: lvs. 9–15 cm. long, usually cordate at base, scabrous above, pubescent on the nerves beneath, of firmer texture. H.H.192,193(b). S.M.321,f.291. (*C. c.* Lam., *C. Audibertiana* Spach.) N. Y. to S. C., Tenn. and Kans. Intr. about 1825. Zone V.

5. **C. Bungeàna** Bl. Tree to 15 m.; bark light gray, smooth: brts. glabrous: lvs. ovate to ovate-oblong, 4–8 cm. long, acuminate, usually rounded at the oblique base, crenate-serrate usually only above the middle, lustrous bright green and glabrous on both sides; petioles 5–10 mm. long: fr. sub-

globose, 6–7 mm. thick, purplish black, on a slender stalk 1–1.5 cm. long; stone smooth. C.C.113. N.K.19:53,t.17. C.H.153. E.H.4:t.267,f.11. (*C. Davidiana* Carr.) C. and N. China, Manch. and Korea. Intr. 1868. Zone V. Tree with spreading brs. forming a broad round head, and with bright green lustrous lvs.

Related species: **C. Tournefórtii** Lam. Tree to 6 m. or shrub; glabrous: lvs. ovate, 3–7 cm. long, acute, rounded or subcordate at base, bluish or grayish green, sometimes slightly pubescent: fr. reddish yellow, about 8 mm. thick; its stalk about as long as the petiole. S.H.1:f.147m-p¹,148p1-p². (*C. orientalis* Mill., not L.) S. E. Eu., W. Asia. Intr. 1739. Zone V.—**C. glabràta** Stev. Differs chiefly from *C. T.* in the more acuminate and sharply serrate lvs. with cuneate base and in the slightly pitted stone. S.H.1:f.147l-l¹,148s. (*C. Tournefortii* var. *g.* Boiss.) W. Asia. Cult. 1870. Zone VI?

6. **C. Bióndii** Pampan. Tree to 14 m. or shrub; young brts. rufous-tomentulose: lvs. ovate to narrow-elliptic, 5–10 cm. long, acuminate, usually broad-cuneate at the oblique base, crenate-serrate above the middle, sometimes entire, pubescent at first, at maturity nearly glabrous, dark yellowish green above, paler and somewhat reticulate beneath; petioles 3–8 mm. long: fr. often 2 or 3, orange, about 6 mm. across, on stalks 1–1.5 cm. long; stone minutely pitted. C. China. Intr. 1894. Zone VI.—On young plants the lvs. are usually abruptly contracted at the apex into a long and slender entire point. T.M.28:266,f.2,b,g. **C. B.** var. **heterophylla** Schneid. (*C. Leveillei* Nakai.)

Related species: **C. sinénsis** Pers. Tree to 20 m.: leaves broad-ovate to ovate-oblong, broad-cuneate at base, crenate-serrate, dark green and nearly smooth above, reticulate and nearly glabrous below; petioles about 1 cm. long: frs. solitary, dark orange, on stalks about as long as the petioles; stone pitted and ribbed. Icon. Pl. Koisik. 1:t.2,f.2. S.H.1:f.147r-r²,148r. N.K.19:t.24. (*C. japonica* Planch.) E. China, Korea, Japan. Intr. about 1793. Zone VI?

7. **C. jessoénsis** Koidz. Tree to 23 m.; young brts. pubescent: lvs. ovate to ovate-oblong, 5–10 cm. long, long-acuminate, usually rounded at base, sharply serrate except at base, dark green above, whitish or grayish green beneath and sparingly pubescent on the nerves or glabrous; petioles 6–10 mm. long: fr. black, 8 mm. across, on stalks about 2 cm. long; stone pitted. N.K. 19:t.18. M.K.t.40(c). Korea, Japan. Intr. 1892. Zone V.

Related species: **C. cerasífera** Schneid. Tree to 10 m.: lvs. broad-ovate to ovate-lanceolate, short-acuminate, rounded or nearly subcordate at base, coarsely crenate-serrate; petioles 1–1.5 cm. long: fr. about 1 cm. thick, black, bloomy, on stalks 2–2.5 cm. long. C. China. Intr. 1907. Zone V.

8. **C. làbilis** Schneid. Tree to 18 m.; brts. yellowish-tomentose; the short fruiting brts. dropping off in autumn or winter: lvs. ovate-elliptic to elliptic-oblong, 5–10 cm. long, short-acuminate, unequally rounded at base, crenate-serrate above the middle, dark green and sparingly appressed-pubescent above, paler or brownish beneath and somewhat reticulate, short-pilose on the nerves; petioles 5–8 mm. long: frs. usually 2–3, subglobose, 7–8 mm. across, on stalks 6–8 mm. long; stone slightly pitted and ribbed. C.H.156. C. China. Intr. 1907. Zone VI? Easily distinguished by the dropping off of the short fruiting brts.

9. **C. austràlis** L. Tree to 25 m.; brts. pubescent: lvs. elliptic-ovate to oblong-lanceolate, 5–15 cm. long, long-acuminate, broad-cuneate or rounded at the oblique base, sharply serrate, scabrous and dark green above, soft-pubescent and grayish green beneath; petioles 5–15 mm. long: fr. dark purple, 1–1.2 cm. thick, sweet, on a stalk 1.5–2.5 cm. long; stone pitted. H.W.3:11(h), t.40(c). S. Eu., N. Afr., W. Asia. Intr. 1796. Zone VI? Tree with spreading brs. forming an ovoid round-topped head.

Closely related species: **C. caucásica** Willd. Lvs. rhombic-ovate to oblong-elliptic, 3–8 cm. long: fr. dark reddish brown, smaller, on a stalk about 1.5 cm. long. S.H.1:f.147e-e²,148t. Cauc., W. Asia. Intr. about 1885. Zone VI?

10. **C. Juliànae** Schneid. Tree to 25 m.; brts. densely yellowish tomentose and hirsute: lvs. broad-ovate to ovate-elliptic, 7–14 cm. long, acuminate, rounded or cuneate at the oblique base, crenate-dentate usually above the middle, slightly scabrous above, yellowish green and soft-pubescent beneath, firm and thick; petioles 1–1.3 cm. long; stamens usually 5: fr. orange, globose-ovoid, 1–1.3 cm. thick; stone nearly smooth. C. China. Intr. 1907. Zone V. Tree with straight trunk and stout spreading brs.; easily distinguished by its dense yellowish pubescence and large lvs.

11. **C. koraiénsis** Nakai. Tree to 12 m.; brts. glabrous or sometimes pubescent, brown: lvs. orbicular-ovate to broad-obovate or obovate, 8–15 cm. long and 5.5–11.5 cm. broad, rounded or subcordate at base, truncate or rounded and abruptly cuspidate at apex, coarsely serrate, the teeth near apex elongated, bright green above, glabrous or sometimes pubescent on the veins beneath; petioles 5–10 mm. long: fr. globose-ellipsoid, about 1 cm. long, dull orange; pedicels 1.5–2 cm. long. J.C.31:t.18. N.K.19:t.21. C.H.155. Korea, Manch., N. China. Intr. 1923. Zone V. Remarkable for the unusual shape of its large lvs. and the large fr.

7. **APHANÁNTHE** Planch. Deciduous or evergreen trees or shrubs: lvs. petiolate, serrate: fls. monoecious, unisexual, with the lvs., the staminate in axillary dense corymbs at base of the young brts., the pistillate fls. in the axils of the upper lvs., 5-, rarely 4-merous: fr. an ovoid or subglobose drupe; embryo involute with narrow cotyledons. (Greek *aphanes*, inconspicuous, and *anthe*, flower.) Three to 4 species in Australia and E. Asia.

A. áspera (Bl.) Planch. Deciduous tree to 20 m.: lvs. ovate to ovate-oblong, 5–9 cm. long, long-acuminate, 3-nerved and rounded at base, simply serrate, the veins straight, parallel, excurrent, scabrous from appressed hairs on both sides; petioles about 5 mm. long: fls. greenish: fr. globose, about 8 mm. thick, black, appressed-pubescent, short-stalked. S.I.1:t.37(c). N.K.19: t.15. S.H.1:f.154. (*Homoioceltis a.* Bl.) Japan, E. China, Korea. Intr. about 1880. Zone VII. Tree with a dense round head.

14. **MORACEAE** DC. MULBERRY FAMILY

Deciduous or evergreen trees or shrubs, or herbs, with milky juice: lvs. alternate, entire, serrate or lobed; stipules present, sometimes persistent: fls. monoecious or dioecious, small, regular, usually in spikes or heads or affixed to a variously shaped torus, or on the inside of a hollow receptacle; perianth of staminate fls. of 2–6, usually 4, free, or more or less united, parts; stamens as many as sepals and opposite, straight or inflexed and elastic; sepals of pistillate fls. 4, more or less united; stigmas 1 or 2; ovary superior or inferior, 1-celled, with one suspended, amphitropous ovule, rarely basal and orthotropous: fr. a small achene or drupe usually developed by the fleshy perianth, or on a fleshy gynophore, often assembled into an aggregate fr. (syncarp); embryo often curved; cotyledons thick, flat or folded, often very unequal.— About 55 genera and 1000 species, chiefly trop.

A. Fls. in spikes or heads: stipules free, not leaving a ring-like scar: lvs. folded or involute in bud.
  B. Lvs. serrate or dentate, undivided or lobed; brs. never spiny: staminate fls. in catkins; stamens inflexed.
    c. Syncarp ovoid to cylindric, fleshy, juicy: buds with 3–6 scales..............1. *Morus*

cc. Syncarp globose; the frs. at maturity exserted on fleshy gynophores: buds with 2-3
   scales: lvs. sometimes opposite...3. *Broussonetia*
BB. Lvs. with entire margin: brs. spiny: fls. of both sexes in heads or clusters: syncarp globose with a crustaceous rind.
   c. Lvs. undivided, 6–16 cm. long: fr. large: filaments inflexed................2. *Maclura*
   cc. Lvs. mostly 3-lobed, 3–7 cm. long: fr. about 2.5 cm. across: filaments straight.
                                                                          4. *Cudrania*
AA. Fls. in a hollow receptacle; filaments straight: lvs. entire or lobed, convolute in bud;
   stipules connate, enclosing the terminal bud, leaving a ring-like scar.............5. *Ficus*

1. **MÒRUS** L. MULBERRY. Deciduous unarmed trees or shrubs; bark
usually scaly; buds with 3–6 imbricate scales: lvs. undivided or lobed, serrate
or dentate, with 3–5 nerves at base; stipules lanceolate, deciduous: fls. monoecious or dioecious, both sexes in stalked axillary pendulous catkins; calyx
4-parted; the filaments inflexed in bud, later partly inclosed by the involute
sepals; stigmas 2: fr. an ovoid compressed achene, covered by the succulent
white to black calyx, aggregating into an ovoid to cylindric syncarp resembling
a blackberry; seed albuminous; cotyledons oblong, equal. Fls. with the lvs.;
frs. in late summer. (The ancient Latin name of the plant.) About 12 species
in the temperate and subtropical regions of the n. hemisphere.—Small trees
or shrubs grown for their edible frs. or for their lvs. which constitute the
chief food of the silkworm, or planted for ornament.

A. Lvs. glabrescent or only slightly pubescent below.
   B. Stigmas sessile or subsessile: lvs. smooth above, with axillary tufts of hairs beneath:
      usually tree-like ....1. *M. alba*
   BB. Stigmas borne on a distinct style: lvs. slightly rough above, without axillary tufts
      beneath: usually shrubby..2. *M. australis*
AA. Lvs. pubescent beneath, scabrous above, usually large and undivided.
   B. Lvs. deeply cordate, short-acuminate, pubescent beneath, chiefly along the veins.
                                                                          3. *M. nigra*
   BB. Lvs. truncate or slightly cordate at base, soft-pubescent beneath.
      c. Fruiting catkins narrow-cylindric: lvs. coarsely serrate with broad short teeth.
                                                                          4. *M. cathayana*
      cc. Fruiting catkins ovoid to oblong: lvs. rather closely and sharply serrate..5. *M. rubra*

1. **M. alba** L. WHITE M. Tree to 15 m.: brts. slightly pubescent at first
or glabrous: lvs. ovate to broad-ovate, 6–18 cm. long, acute or short-acuminate, rounded or cordate at base, coarsely toothed with often obtusish teeth,
often variously lobed, light green and usually smooth above, pubescent on
the nerves beneath or nearly glabrous; petioles 1–2.5 cm. long: pistillate
spikes 5–10 mm. long, the staminate about twice as long: syncarp 1–2.5 cm.
long, white, pinkish or purplish-violet, sweet, but insipid. Fl.v; fr.VII–VIII.
R.I.12:t.657(c). H.H.196,197(b). Koidzumi, Rev. Morus, t.10. G.C.75:37(h).
China, naturalized in other parts of Asia, in Am. and Eu. Zone IV–V. Small
tree with spreading brs. forming a round-topped head and with bright green
lvs.; the lvs. of this species are the chief food of the silkworm. Very variable,
with many forms and varieties of which the following are the most important: **M. a. macrophýlla** Loud., var. Lvs. large, 15–22 cm. long, undivided:
fr. red. (*M. Morettiana* Jacq.)—**M. a. skeletoniàna** Schneid., var. Lvs.
regularly and deeply divided into narrow long-pointed lobes. S.H.1:f.151b.
(*M. a. laciniata* Beiss., not K. Koch.)—**M. a. venòsa** Delile. Lvs. usually
rhombic-ovate, cuneate at base, acute or acuminate or sometimes rounded at
the apex, irregularly serrate, with strongly marked whitish veins. B.C.4:2070.
S.H.1:f.151c. (*M. a.* var. *nervosa* Loud., *M. urticaefolia* Hort.)—**M. a. pyramidàlis** Ser., var. Tree of narrow pyramidal habit; leaves usually lobed. U. S.
Im. 36:3,t.(h). (*M. a. fastigiata* Schelle.)—**M. a. péndula** Dipp., f. With long
and slender pendulous brs.; lvs. usually lobed. B.C.4:2070(h). M.G.17:27(h).
Gn.86:648(h).—**M. a. tatárica** (L.) Ser. Small tree with bushy head; lvs.
small, 4–8 cm. long, lobed or undivided; fr. small, about 1 cm. long, dark red,

sometimes white. B.C.4:2071. Supposed to be the hardiest form.—**M. a. multicaùlis** (Perrottet) Loud., var. Strong-growing shrub or bushy tree: lvs. large, 8–15 cm. long, undivided, dull and somewhat rough above, with obtusish teeth: fr. large, nearly black. Ann. Hort. Fromont, 1,t.3. Koidzumi, Rev. Morus, t.8,9. (*M. a.* var. *latifolia* Bur., *M. sinensis* Hort.)

2. **M. austràlis** Poir. Shrub or small tree to 8 m.; brts. glabrous: lvs. ovate, 6–15 cm. long, acute to long-acuminate, truncate or subcordate at base, sharply or sometimes crenately serrate, undivided or variously lobed, often deeply so, slightly scabrous above, minutely pubescent or nearly glabrous at maturity beneath; petioles slender, 1.5–4 cm. long, glabrous: fls. dioecious, staminate catkins 1.5–3 cm. long, the pistillate 5–10 mm. long; style nearly as long as the stigmas; syncarp 1–1.5 cm. long, dark red, juicy, sweet. Fl.iv–v; fr.vi–vii. S.1.2;t.6,f.1–11(c) Koidzumi, Rev. Morus, t,2,4. (*M. alba* var. *stylosa* Bur., *M. acidosa* Griff., *M. japonica* Bailey, not Sieb., *M. bombycis* Koidz.) China, Korea, Japan. Intr. 1907. Zone V. Broad shrub with spreading brs. or a small bushy tree; its lvs. not used as food for silkworm; the abundantly produced fruits are palatable.

Related species: **M. mongòlica** Schneid. Small tree or shrub: lvs. ovate to oblong-ovate, 8–16 cm. long, caudate-acuminate, cordate at base, coarsely serrate with cuspidate teeth, rarely lobed, smooth above, nearly glabrous: style distinct; fr. red or black. C.H.164. N.K.19:t.33,A. (*M. alba* var. *m.* Bur.) China, Korea. Intr. 1907. Zone V.—**M. m. diabólica** Koidz., var. Lvs. scabrid above, pubescent beneath, often deeply lobed. N.K.19:t.33B. Cult. 1923.

3. **M. nígra** L. BLACK M. Tree to 10 m.; brts. pubescent, becoming brown: lvs. broad-ovate, 6–12 or sometimes to 20 cm. long, acute or short-acuminate, deeply cordate at base, coarsely serrate, usually undivided, sometimes 2–3-lobed, dark green and scabrous above, lighter and pubescent beneath, chiefly along the veins; petioles 1.5–2.5 cm. long: fls. dioecious or sometimes monoecious, the staminate about 2.5 cm. long, the pistillate half as long; syncarp ovoid to oblong, 2–2.5 cm. long, dark red. Fl.v; fr.viii. R.I.12:t.658 (c). B.S.2:86,t(h). M.D.1812:203(h),204,205. G.W.18:434(h). W. Asia. Intr. 1548. Zone VI? Tree with short trunk and widespreading brs. forming a broad, rounded, often irregular and picturesque head, with dark green lvs.; sometimes grown for its fruit.

4. **M. cathayàna** Hemsl. Small tree to 8 m., or occasionally to 15 m., sometimes shrubby; bark gray, nearly smooth: brts. pubescent at first: lvs. ovate, 8–15 cm. long, short- or long-acuminate, truncate or rarely cordate at base, serrate with broad, often rounded teeth, sometimes 3-lobed, scabrous above, soft-pubescent beneath; petioles 1.5–3 cm. long, pubescent: staminate catkins 3–6 cm. long, pistillate about 2 cm. long: syncarp narrow-cylindric, 2–3 cm. long and about 7 mm. thick, white, red or black. Fl.v; fr.viii. C.H.166. C. and E. China. Intr. 1907. Zone V. Tree with widespreading brs. forming a flattened, round head: lvs. not used as silkworm food.

5. **M. rúbra** L. RED M. Tree to 20 m.; bark scaly, brown; brts. pubescent at first: lvs. broad-ovate to oblong-ovate, 7–12 or occasionally to 20 cm. long, abruptly long-acuminate, truncate or subcordate at base, rather closely and sharply serrate, scabrous or sometimes nearly smooth above, soft-pubescent beneath; petioles 2–3 cm. long, tomentose at first: staminate catkins 2–5 cm. long, pistillate 2–2.5 cm. long: syncarp 2–3 cm. long, finally dark purple, juicy. Fl.v; fr.vii–viii. M.S.3:232,t(c). S.S.7:t.320. H.H.198,199(h). G.F.7: 25(h). Mass. to Fla., w. to Mich., Neb., Kans. and Tex. Intr. 1629. Zone V. Tree with short trunk and stout spreading brs. forming a broad round-topped head, with dark green, rather large lvs. turning bright yellow in autumn.

Occasionally planted for its fruit used as food for hogs and poultry. A large-fruited form is grown as Lampasas Mulberry.—**M. r. tomentòsa** (Raf.) Bur., var. Lvs. whitish-tomentose beneath, glossy above. Tex.

Distinct on account of its small lvs. is **M. microphýlla** Buckl. Small tree to 7 m. or shrub: lvs. ovate, 3–7 cm. long, often 3-lobed, rounded to subcordate at base, serrate or crenate-serrate, rough above, pubescent or sometimes glabrous beneath; petiole 3–8 mm. long; staminate catkins 1–2 cm. long: fr. ovoid, 1–1.5 cm. long, edible. S.M.331. Tex. to Ariz. and s. to Mex. Intr. 1926. Zone VII?

2. **MACLÙRA** Nutt. Osage-Orange. Deciduous tree; brs. with axillary thorns; buds depressed-globose with few imbricate scales: lvs. slender-petioled, entire, involute in bud; stipules minute: fls. dioecious; calyx 4-lobed; staminate fls. pediceled in subglobose or sometimes elongated racemes on long peduncles axillary on spur-like brts.; stamens 4, the filaments inflexed in bud; pistillate fls. sessile in dense globose heads on short peduncles; ovary with a long filiform stigma: drupelets oblong, collected into a large globose syncarp covered by a mamillate rind; seed without albumen; cotyledons oblong, nearly equal. (After Wm. Maclure, an American geologist.) Syn.: *Toxylon* Raf. One species in N. Am.

M. pomífera (Raf.) Schneid. Tree to 20 m.; bark deeply furrowed, dark orange; brts. light green, soon glabrous, becoming light brown the first winter; spines 1–2.5 cm. long, stout: lvs. ovate to oblong-lanceolate, 5–12 cm. long, acuminate, broad-cuneate to subcordate at base, lustrous above, soon glabrous; petioles 3–5 cm. long: clusters of staminate flowers 2.5–3.5 cm. long; heads of pistillate fls. 2–2.5 cm. across: syncarp subglobose, 10–14 cm. across, orange; seeds nearly 1 cm. long. Fl.v–vi; fr.ix. N.S.1:t.37(c). S.S.7:t.322,323. H.H.202,203(b). G.C.III.16:693. (*M. aurantiaca* Nutt., *Toxylon pomiferum* Raf.) Ark. to Okla. and Tex. Intr. 1818. Zone V. Medium-sized spiny tree with an open, irregular, round-topped head and bright green lvs. turning clear yellow in fall; the orange-like large frs. are a conspicuous feature. Often used as a hedge plant in the Middle West.—**M. p. inérmis** (André) Schneid., var. Form with unarmed brs. R.H.1896:33.

M. p. × *Cudrania tricuspidata;* see under 4. *Cudrania.*

3. **BROUSSONÉTIA** Vent. Paper-Mulberry. Deciduous unarmed trees or shrubs; buds small, with 2–3 outer scales: lvs. petioled, serrate, undivided or lobed; stipules ovate-lanceolate, distinct, deciduous: fls. dioecious; the staminate in cylindric pendulous catkins, with 4-lobed calyx and 4 stamens inflexed in bud; pistillate fls. in globose heads; perianth tubular, including the stipitate ovary; stigma slender, filiform: syncarp a dense globose head consisting of the frs. with their persistent perianths and bracts; frs. exserted at maturity on fleshy gynophores; endocarp crustaceous; cotyledons oblong, equal. (After T. N. V. Broussonet, a French naturalist; 1761–1807.) Syn. *Papyrius* Lam. Two species in E. Asia.

A. Petioles 3–10 cm. long; lvs. pubescent..1. *B. papyrifera*
AA. Petioles 1–2 cm. long; lvs. glabrescent..2. *B. Kazinoki*

1. **B. papyrífera** (L.) Vent. Tree to 16 m.; bark smooth, gray; brts. stout, pubescent: lvs. occasionally opposite, ovate, 7–20 cm. long, acuminate, cordate at base, coarsely dentate, on young plants often deeply lobed, scabrous above, grayish and soft-pubescent beneath; petioles 3–10 cm. long: staminate catkins 6–8 cm. long: syncarps 2 cm. across, orange, the protruding frs. red. Fl.v; fr.ix. S.I.1:t.38(c). B.M.2358(c). H.H.200,201(b). M.D.1915: t.24;1918:t.26(h). (*Morus p.* L.) China, Japan; occasionally naturalized

from N. Y. to Fla. and Mo. Cult. 1750. Zone VI. Small tree with widespreading brs. forming a broad rounded head; often planted for ornament and sometimes as a street tree.—**B. p. laciniàta** Ser. Lvs. finely dissected into narrow segments often reduced to the nerves and only at the ends with small narrow lfts. R.H.1878:374(h),375. Gn.15:53. S.L.108(h). (Var. *dissecta* Hort., var. *Billiardii* Hemsl.)—**B. p. leucocárpa** Ser. Fr. white.—**B. p. variegàta** Ser. Lvs. variegated with white or yellow.

2. **B. Kazinòki** Sieb. & Zucc. Shrub to 5 m.; brts. slender, often sarmentose, soon glabrous, purplish: lvs. ovate to ovate-oblong, 5–20 cm. long, longacuminate, rounded or subcordate at base, serrate, sometimes 2–3-lobed, scabrous above, slightly pubescent beneath at first, later glabrous; petioles 1–2 cm. long: staminate catkins about 1.5 cm. long: syncarps about 1 cm. across, woolly. I.T.2:t.45. S.H.1:f.151i-k,155d-f. (*B. Sieboldü* Bl., *B. Kaempferi* Sieb. & Zucc.) Korea, Japan. Intr. about 1844. Zone VII.

4. **CUDRÀNIA** Tréc. Deciduous or evergreen trees or shrubs; brs. often thorny; stipules small, distinct; lvs. petioled, entire, sometimes 3-lobed: fls. dioecious in axillary globular heads; perianth of staminate fls. with 4 oblong segments and 2–3 bracts at base; stamens with 4 straight filaments; ovary of the pistillate fls. enclosed by the 4-parted perianth; stigma filiform: syncarp subglobose, fleshy: fr. with a crustaceous pericarp; seed with thin endosperm; cotyledons folded. (From its Malayan name Cudrang, Cudranus of Rumphius.) Syn.: *Vaniera* Lour. Five or 6 species from China to Austr. and New Caled.

C. tricuspidàta (Carr.) Bur. Shrub or small tree to 8, rarely to 18 m.; brts. glabrous, with slender thorns 5–30 mm. long: lvs. ovate to obovate; 3–8 cm. long, acuminate, rounded at base, sometimes 3-lobed at apex (or tricuspidate on young plants), glabrous, dark green above; petioles 8–15 mm. long: fl.-heads short-stalked, solitary or in pairs; syncarp subglobose, about 2.5 cm. across, with a firm rugose rind, red. R.H.1872:56;1905:363(h). H.I.18:1792. K.B.1888:291,t. (*Maclura t.* Carr., *Vaniera t.* Hu.) China, Korea, Japan. Intr. 1862. Zone VII? Bush or small tree with slender spiny brs.; the lvs. used in China for feeding the silkworm; the fr. is edible. Recommended as a hedge plant for the South.

C. t. × *Maclura pomifera* = **Macludrània hýbrida** André. Tree; brts. dark brown, with short straight spines: lvs. elliptic, up to 15 cm. long, acuminate, not lobed. R.H.1905:362. Orig. before 1905.

5. **FÌCUS** L. Fig-tree. Evergreen or rarely deciduous trees or shrubs; unarmed; stipules connate, enclosing the terminal bud, caducous and leaving a ring-like scar: lvs. alternate, rarely opposite, usually entire, rarely serrate or lobed. convolute in bud: fls. monoecious or rarely dioecious, borne inside of a hollow receptacle with a narrow orifice; the staminate fls. with a 2–6-parted perianth and 1 or 2, rarely 3–6 stamens; pistillate fls. usually with more segments; style eccentric, short or filiform; stigma peltate to filiform: syncarp subglobose, ellipsoid or pear-shaped, fleshy; fr. enclosed in the perianth; embryo curved, with equal or unequal cotyledons. (The ancient Latin name.) About 600 species in the trop. and subtrop. regions of both hemispheres.

F. Càrica L. Fig. Deciduous tree to 10 m.; brts. stout, glabrous: lvs. 3–5-lobed, rarely undivided, 10–20 cm. long and about as broad, usually cordate at base, palmately nerved, the lobes usually obovate and obtuse at the apex and irregularly dentate, scabrous above and below with stout, stiff hairs;

191

petioles 2–5 cm. long: receptacle axillary and solitary, pear-shaped, at maturity 5–8 cm. long, greenish or brownish violet. Fr.vii–x. G.O.t.108(c). B.C. 3.t.42(h). M.A.t.129,130(h). W. Asia. Cult. since early times. Zone (VI). Usually a spreading shrub with long, sometimes procumbent brs., rarely a small tree with short stem and widespreading brs. forming a broad flattened head. Grown for its edible fruit which is of great commercial importance; many pomological varieties are distinguished.

15. URTICACEAE Endl. NETTLE FAMILY

Herbs, shrubs or trees, with watery juice, sometimes with stinging hairs: lvs. alternate or opposite; stipules usually present: fls. monoecious or dioecious, rarely perfect, usually in axillary cymes, rarely solitary; perianth with 4–5 free or more or less connate segments; stamens as many and opposite the segments; filaments inflexed in bud, uncoiling elastically; ovary 1-celled, with one basal orthotropous ovule; style 1, stigma of various shape: fr. an achene or drupe; seed usually with copious endosperm: embryo straight; cotyledons fleshy, ovate or suborbicular.—More than 40 genera with about 500 species, chiefly trop.

A. Fr. dry: stigma linear: stipules free..1. *Boehmeria*
AA. Fr. fleshy: stigma capitate and penicillate: stipules connate, bifid..........2. *Debregeasia*

1. **BOEHMÈRIA** Jacq. Shrubs, small trees or herbs: lvs. alternate or opposite, 3-nerved at base, serrate; stipules usually free: fls. monoecious or dioecious, in small clusters collected into axillary, usually lax and pendulous spikes or panicles: perianth of staminate fls. 3–5-lobed or -parted; stamens 3–5: pistillate fls. with tubular perianth, 2–4-toothed, inclosing the ovary; stigma filiform: achene crustaceous, inclosed by the perianth; cotyledons ovate. (After G. R. Boehmer, professor at Wittenberg; 1723–1803.) About 50 species in the tropics, also in N. Am. and E. Asia.

B. **nívea** (L.) Gaudich. RAMIE. Suffruticose, to 2 m.; brts. and petioles densely pilose: lvs. opposite, broad-ovate, 8–15 cm. long, acuminate, broad-cuneate to truncate at base, coarsely crenate-serrate, scabrid above, white-tomentose beneath and pilose on the nerves; petioles 2–8 cm. long, unequal: fls. monoecious, in long, often pendent, panicles 5–15 cm. long. Fl.vi–viii; fr.ix–xi. Kew Jour. Bot. 3:t.8. (*Urtica n.* L.) China, Japan, S. Asia. Cult. 1850. Zone (VI). An important fibre plant cult. in La. and Fla.; sometimes planted as an ornamental perennial for its handsome lvs. snowy-white beneath.

2. **DEBREGEÀSIA** Gaudich. Shrubs or small trees: lvs. alternate, 3-nerved at base, serrate; stipules connate into a single bifid one: fls. monoecious or dioecious, in unisexual globose clusters arranged in axillary cymes: staminate fls. with usually 4-parted perianth and 4 short stamens; pistillate fls. with obovate or urceolate, 4-toothed perianth usually much contracted at the mouth; stigma capitate, penicillate: syncarp globose, consisting of fleshy drupelets; cotyledons short, broad. (After Prosper Justin de Brégeas (1807–), officer on La Bonite when Gaudichaud made his voyage around the world.) Five species in E. and S. Asia, Abyssinia.

D. **longifòlia** (Burm.) Wedd. Shrub or sometimes small tree to 6 m.; brts. pubescent: lvs. lanceolate to oblong-lanceolate, 6–16 cm. long, acuminate, serrulate, rugose and scabrous above, white-tomentose beneath; petioles 5–15 mm. long: fr. 5–6 mm. across, orange to red, 2 or more on a short dichotomous peduncle, Fl.v–vi; fr.vi–vii. R.H.1896:321. G.C.39:232,t. (*D. velutina* Gaudich.) China, Himal., Java. Cult. 1896. Zone VII? Spreading shrub attractive on account of the contrast of the dark green lustrous upper and the snowy-white lower surface of the lvs.

16. SANTALACEAE R. Br. SANDALWOOD FAMILY

Parasitic or half-parasitic (or independent?) herbs or shrubs, rarely small trees: lvs. alternate or opposite, undivided, sometimes scale-like; stipules wanting: fls. perfect or unisexual; perianth simple, usually tubular at base, at apex 4–5-, or 3- or 6-lobed; disk epigynous or perigynous; stamens as many as perianth-lobes; anthers 2-celled; ovary usually inferior, 1-celled; ovules 1–4, at the apex of a central placenta: fr. a 1-seeded nut or drupe; seed without testa, with copious endosperm; cotyledons narrow, semi-terete, often short.—Twenty-seven genera with about 250 species in trop. and temp. regions.

A. Lvs. opposite: staminate fls. in umbels; pistillate solitary.....................1. *Buckleya*
AA. Lvs. alternate: fls. in racemes or panicles.......................................2. *Pyrularia*

1. **BUCKLEŸA** Torr. Deciduous parasitic shrubs; buds acute with 3–5 pairs of outer scales; lvs. opposite, sessile or short-stalked, entire: fls. dioecious; staminate in small terminal and sometimes also axillary umbels; stamens 4, opposite the sepals and much shorter; pistillate fls. solitary, terminal on short brts., with 4 short deciduous sepals and immediately below but at the apex of the clavate calyx-tube with 4 linear-lanceolate persistent spreading bracts; style short, with 2–4-parted stigma; ovules 3–4: fr. an ellipsoid drupe. (After S. B. Buckley, an American botanist; 1809–1884.) Three species in Japan and China and one in N. Am.

B. **distichophýlla** Torr. Shrub to 4 m.: lvs. 2-ranked, sessile, ovate to ovate-lanceolate, 2–6 cm. long, acuminate, cuneate at base, nearly glabrous, ciliolate: fls. small, greenish: fr. ellipsoid, 1.2–1.5 cm. long, yellowish green or dull orange; the terminal bracts dropping at maturity. Fl.v; fr.ix. G.F. 3:237.—N. C. and Tenn., parasitic on the roots of *Tsuga*. Intr. 1842. Zone V. A graceful shrub with slender spreading brs. and bright green two-ranked narrow lvs. Cult. occasionally in botanical collections.

2. **PYRULÀRIA** Michx. OIL-NUT. Deciduous shrubs or small trees; buds with many imbricate green scales: lvs. alternate, entire: fls. subdioecious in terminal spikes or racemes, 4–5-merous; segments of perianth free above the disk, at base behind the short stamens with a tuft of hairs or a hairy scale: ovary inferior, with 2–3 ovules: stigma capitate: fr. a subglobose or obovoid drupe, rather large; seed subglobose; embryo terete, short. (Diminutive of Pyrus, in allusion to the shape of the fruit.) One species in N. Am., 2 in the Himal.

P. **pùbera** Michx. Shrub to 4 m.; the young parts puberulous; brts. stout: lvs. elliptic to obovate-oblong, 5–15 cm. long, acute or acuminate, cuneate at base, minutely punctulate; petioles 5–15 mm. long; staminate spikes many-fld., 2–6 cm. long, pistillate few-fld., short; fls. 5-merous: fr. pear-shaped or subglobose, about 2.5 cm. long, crowned by the ovate calyx-lobes, yellowish, containing an acrid oil as does the whole plant. Fl.v; fr.viii–ix. B.B.1: 641. Pa. to Ga. and Ala.; parasitic on the roots of *Calycanthus, Kalmia* and other shrubs. Cult. 1897. Zone VI? Straggling shrub with rather large lvs.; rarely cult. in botanical collections.

17. LORANTHACEAE Lindl. MISTLETOE FAMILY

Parasitic green shrubs or herbs, growing mostly on woody plants, rarely terrestrial; brs. usually brittle at base: lvs. opposite, sometimes reduced to scales, rarely alternate, entire, without stipules: fls. dioecious or monoecious, terminal or axillary; perianth of 2–6 parts, simple, rarely differentiated into calyx and corolla and fls. perfect; stamens as many as parts of perianth and opposite: ovary inferior, 1-celled, with 1 orthotropous ovule; stigma 1: fr. a berry; seed without testa, with copious endosperm; embryo terete or angled. —About 21 genera with 600 species in trop. and temp. regions.—Of no economic importance and not objects of horticulture, though many trop. species are highly beautiful. Occasionally cult. in botanical collections.

A. Lvs. flat.
  B. Lvs. deciduous, thin; brs. brown: parts of perianth 4–6...................1. *Loranthus*
  BB. Lvs. persistent, leathery: brs. green.
    c. Fls. in axillary spikes; anthers free, 2-celled, opening with a pore or slit.
                                           2. *Phoradendron*
    cc. Fls. 1–5 in terminal clusters; anthers adnate to the perianth-lobes, opening with
        many pores ....4. *Viscum*
AA. Lvs. scale-like; anthers 1-celled, free; fls. axillary......................3. *Arceuthobium*

1. **LORÁNTHUS** L. Parasitic trees or shrubs with usually brown terete br.: lvs. opposite, rarely alternate: fls. perfect or unisexual; parts of perianth 4–6, valvate, spreading, sometimes connate below; filaments at least partly free; style filiform: berry globose or ovoid. (Greek *loros*, strap, and *anthos*, flower; referring to the shape of the sepals.) About 200 species in the Old World, chiefly trop.

L. europaèus L. Deciduous glabrous shrub to 1 m.; brs. dark brown: lvs. opposite, petioled, ovate-oblong, 2–4 cm. long, obtuse: fls. small, yellowish green, in short racemes: fr. about 8 mm. across, yellow. Fl.IV–V; fr.X–XII. R.I.24:t.142. C. Eu., chiefly on Oaks and Chestnuts. Zone V.—Rarely cult. in European collections (see Jour. Bot. 11:90 for cult.).

2. **PHORADÉNDRON** Nutt. Parasitic shrubs wih terete, angled or flattened green brs.: lvs. opposite, leathery, rarely reduced to scales: fls. usually dioecious, extra-axillary and sunk in the joints of axillary or terminal spikes; calyx usually 3-lobed, rarely 2–5-lobed; anthers 2-celled, sessile, opening lengthwise; stigma sessile or subsessile, obtuse: fr. a sessile subglobose berry. (Greek *phor*, thief, and *dendron* tree; referring to the parasitic habit.) About 240 species in N. and S. Am.

P. flavéscens (Pursh) Nutt. AMERICAN MISTLETOE. Much-branched shrub to 1 m., with terete brs.: lvs. short-petioled, oblong or obovate, 2.5–5 cm. long, obtuse, cuneate at base and 3–5-nerved: spikes axillary, 1–3, 1.5–2.5 cm. long; berry globose, 4–5 mm. across, white. Fl.IV–V; fr.X(–IV). B.B.1:639. Trelease, Gen. Phoradendron, t.24,25. N. J. to Fla., w. to Ohio, Ind., Mo. and Tex. on various deciduous trees. Collected and sold for Christmas greens. Not known to have been cult.

3. **ARCEUTHÓBIUM** Bieb. Small fleshy plants parasitic on coniferous trees: lvs. opposite, scale-like: fls. dioecious in the axils of the scales; staminate fls. with 2–5-parted calyx; anthers sessile, 1-celled, opening by a circular slit; pistillate fls. with 2-parted calyx-limb; style short, with obtuse stigma: fr. an ovoid, flattened berry on a short recurved pedicel. (Greek *arkeuthos*, Juniper, and *bios*, life; the European species lives on Juniper.) Syn.: *Razoumowskya* Hoffm. About 10 species throughout the n. hemisphere.

A. pusíllum Peck. Plant 0.5–2 cm. high, olive-green to brown: brs. nearly terete when fresh; scale-like lvs. suborbicular, appressed: berry ovoid-oblong, about 2 mm. long. Fl.iv–v; fr.ix. B.B.1:638. Rhodora 2:t.12–14. (*Razoumowskya p.* Peck.) Me. to N. Y. and Pa.; on Picea and Larix. Zone IV. Cult. by grafting infested brs.

4. VISCUM L. Mistletoe. Parasitic shrubs with green brs.: lvs. opposite, leathery: fls. monoecious or dioecious, axillary or terminal, 3–4-merous; anthers adnate to the inside of the calyx-lobes and opening with many pores; pistillate fls. with capitate stigma sessile or on a short style: fr. a globose berry, often with several embryos in one seed. (The ancient Latin name.) About 15 species in Eu., Asia, Afr. and Australia.

V. album L. Shrub to 1 m.; brs. terete, regularly dichotomous: lvs. subsessile, obovate to oblong, 3–5 cm. long, obtuse: fls. dioecious, yellowish, terminal, sessile, the staminate in 3–5-fld. clusters, the pistillate 1–3: berries globose, about 8 mm. across, white, translucent, in the angles of the forking brts. Fl.iii–iv; fr.x(–iii). R.I.24:t.139(c). S.E.4:t.635(c). S.H.1:f.161,162l-o. Gn.89:107(h). Eu., N. Asia; on various dicotyledonous and coniferous trees, particularly on Malus, Populus and also Pinus. Zone IV. The true Mistletoe of which the fruiting brs. are imported as Christmas decoration. Often cult. in European botanical collections (for cult. see G.C.II.5:43;9:83. B.H. 21:206. R.H.1887:470).

18. **ARISTOLOCHIACEAE** Lindl. BIRTHWORT FAMILY

Herbs or shrubs, often twining: lvs. alternate, often palmately veined, without stipules: fls. perfect, regular or symmetrical; perianth simple, connate, 3-merous, often petaloid; stamens 6–36, free and inserted on the ovary or united with the stylar column; styles connate, with 3 or 6 spreading stigmas; ovary inferior, rarely superior, 4–6-celled, each cell with several or many horizontal or pendulous ovules: fr. a capsule; seeds with copious endosperm and small embryo. Five genera with about 210 species, mostly in trop. and subtrop. regions.

ARISTOLÓCHIA L. Birthwort. Herbs or deciduous or evergreen shrubs, often twining; buds small, usually several, superposed, with few outer scales: lvs. usually cordate, 5–7-nerved at base, entire, rarely lobed: fls. axillary, symmetrical; perianth usually with long curved tube, inflated at base, constricted at the mouth and enlarged abruptly into a spreading limb, or gradually widened; stamens usually 6, adnate to the thick fleshy style; ovary 6, rarely 4- or 5-celled; style 3- or 6-lobed at apex: fr. a caps. dehiscent into 6 valves; seeds many, flat. (Greek *aristos*, very good, and *lochia*, childbirth, referring to supposed medicinal virtues.) Syn.: *Hocquartia* Dumort. About 180 species in trop. and temp. regions of both hemispheres.

A. Fls. glabrous: lvs. reniform, 10–25 cm. long: limb of perianth brownish purple.
1. *A. durior*
AA. Fls. and lvs. more or less pubescent.
  B. Lvs. at least ¾ as broad as long, generally ovate, never lobed.
    c. Lvs. usually rounded at apex: limb of perianth yellowish............2. *A. tomentosa*
    cc. Lvs. pointed at apex: limb of perianth yellow, dotted with purple..3. *A. moupinensis*
  BB. Lvs. variable, partly narrower, ovate to ovate-lanceolate, often lobed at base.
    c. Pedicel with a leaf-like bract below the middle...................4. *A. heterophylla*
    cc. Pedicel with a small bract...............................5. *A. Kaempferi*

1. A. dùrior Hill. Dutchman's Pipe. Twining to 10 m.: brts. glabrous: lvs. reniform, 10–30 cm. long, pointed or obtuse, dark green and glabrous above, pale green beneath and pubescent at first, afterward glabrous; petiole 3–7 cm. long: fls. 1 or 2, axillary, on pedicels 3–5 cm. long, with a bract below the middle; perianth about 3 cm. long, its tube U-shaped, yellowish green and glabrous outside, constricted at the mouth and spreading into a 3-lobed smooth, brownish purple limb 1.5–2 cm. across; capsule 6–8 cm. long, 6-ribbed. Fl.v; fr.ix. B.M.534(c). G.F.5:509(h). Gn.28:585(h). (*A. macrophylla* Lam., *A. Sipho* L'Hérit.) Pa. to Ga., w. to Minn. and Kans. Intr. 1783. Zone IV. Vigorous climber with handsome large lvs.; an excellent vine for porches.

Closely related species: **A. manshuriénsis** Komar. Young brts. pubescent: lvs. pubescent beneath: perianth about 5 cm. long, yellowish, flushed purple; limb brown-purple, 3 cm. across. N.K.21:t.1. (*Hocquartia m.* Nakai.) Manch., Korea. Cult. 1909. Zone V.

2. **A. tomentòsa** Sims. Twining to 10 m.; brts. woolly: lvs. roundish ovate, 10–16 cm. long, usually rounded at apex, dull light green above and pubescent, more densely beneath; petioles 3–7 cm. long, woolly: fls. about 3.5 cm. long, the tube U-shaped, greenish yellow and pubescent outside, with a purple, nearly closed mouth and a reflexed yellow rugose 3-lobed limb about 2 cm. across: fr. about 5 cm. long, 6-ribbed. Fl.vi; fr.ix. B.M.t.1369(c). N. C. to Fla., w. to s. Ill. and Mo. Intr. 1799. Zone V. Vigorous vine similar to the preceding but with smaller lvs. of duller color.

Closely related species: **A. califórnica** Torr. Lvs. ovate to ovate-oblong, 5–10 cm. long, obtuse; petioles 1–2 cm. long: fls. little contracted at the mouth, slightly pubescent outside; limb 2-lipped, the upper lip of 2 obtuse lobes: fr. 4–5 cm. long, with 6 winged ribs. A.I.1:536. Calif. Intr. 1877. Zone VII?

3. **A. moupinénsis** Franch. Twining to 4 m.: brts. densely silky-pubescent, finally glabrous: lvs. broad-ovate, 7–12 cm. long, usually pointed at apex, slightly pubescent above, grayish pubescent beneath; petioles 2–5 cm. long: fls. about 3.5 cm. long; tube U-shaped, pubescent and greenish outside, with yellow mouth and a 3-lobed yellow limb dotted purple: fr. oblong, 7–8 cm. long, with 6 ridges. Fl.vi. B.M.t.8325(c). W. China. Intr. 1903. Zone VI?

4. **A. heterophýlla** Hemsl. Twining to 3 m.; brts. finely pubescent: lvs. ovate to ovate-oblong, or hastate-oblong, 4–10 cm. long, acute or acuminate, usually with a pair of rounded lobes at base, dull green above, pubescent beneath: fls. on nearly glabrous stalks 3–5 cm. long with a large leaf-life bract below the middle: perianth about 5 cm. long, U-shaped, yellow and pubescent outside, bright yellow inside the mouth, the limb lurid-purple, 3-lobed, the lower lobe rounded, flat, the 2 upper with recurved margins: fr. 5–7 cm. long, 6-ribbed. Fl.vi. W. China. Intr. 1904. Zone VI? Lvs. less handsome than in the preceding species, but fls. strikingly colored.

5. **A. Kaèmpferi** Willd. Tall climber; brts. pubescent; lvs. variable in shape, ovate to ovate-oblong, 8–15 cm. long, acute, often with a pair of rounded lobes at base, reticulate and silky-pubescent beneath; petioles 2–6 cm. long, pubescent: pedicel with a small bract; fls. with U-shaped tube, yellow outside, purple inside, with a 2-lipped limb, the upper lip emarginate. Fl.vi-vii. Kaempfer, Icon. Sel. t.49. Japan. Cult. 1854. Zone V.

19. **POLYGONACEAE** Lindl. BUCKWHEAT FAMILY

Herbs, shrubs or trees, sometimes twining: lvs. alternate, sometimes opposite or whorled, simple and usually entire; stipules usually united and forming a sheath (ocrea): fls. small, regular, unisexual or bisexual, solitary or collected into various inflorescences; perianth simple, of 2–6 parts, sometimes in 2 whorls, connate or distinct, persistent and sometimes accrescent; stamens usually 6–9, rarely less or more, usually opposite the sepals; ovary superior, consisting of 2–4 carpels, 1-celled, with 1 usually orthotropous ovule; styles 3, rarely 2 or 4: fr. a flat or angled achene, often inclosed by the accrescent calyx; seed with copious endosperm; embryo usually eccentric, curved or straight.—Thirty genera with about 700 species, mostly in the temp. regions of the n. hemisphere, few in the Tropics and in the s. hemisphere.

A. Petioles without ochrea: fls. in involucrate clusters forming corymbs or umbels; stamens 9: small under-shrubs ....1. *Eriogonum*
AA. Petioles with ochrea: fls. in the axils of bracts forming racemes or panicles; stamens usually 6–8.
  B. Upright shrubs: sepals 4 or 5, the 2 outer ones much smaller..............2. *Atraphaxis*
  BB. Twining or rarely prostrate shrubs: sepals or perianth-lobes nearly equal.
    C. Ocrea conspicuous, membranous: brs. without tendrils: fr. not inclosed by the tubular part of the perianth...3. *Polygonum*
    CC. Ocrea very short, not membranous: brs. often with tendrils: fr. inclosed by the thickened tubular part of the perianth, its stipe-like base with a broad wing.
                                                      4. *Brunnichia*

1. **ERIÓGONUM** Michx. Annual or perennial herbs or subshrubs: lvs. often whorled, usually woolly; ochrea wanting: fls. small, usually perfect, in involucrate clusters forming corymbs or umbels, white, pink or yellow; involucre 5–8-lobed; sepals 6, equal or the outer ones larger; stamens 9; styles 3, with capitate stigmas: achene 3-angled. (Name formed analogous to Polygonum, from Greek *erion*, wool, referring to the woolly tomentum of most species.) About 150 species in W. N. Am.—Essentially plants of arid regions requiring in cult. well drained soil and sunny position; well adapted for sunny rockeries. Most species are herbaceous and the few suffruticose species are of more southern distribution and probably not hardy North.

    E. Wrìghtii Torr. Subshrub to 60 cm., with slender brs. upright or procumbent: lvs. lanceolate or elliptic-lanceolate, 1–2 cm. long: fls. white or pink in terminal spike-like panicles 3–6 cm. long. Fl.vɪɪɪ–ɪx. S.L.197(h). N. Mex. to Calif. Cult. 1904. Zone VII?

2. **ATRAPHÁXIS** L. Deciduous shrubs with unarmed or spinescent brs., glabrous: lvs. short-petioled, usually small, with a conspicuous membranous orcrae: ns. small, perfect, white or pinkish, several in the axils of often scale-like lvs., forming terminal racemes; sepals 5 or sometimes 4, the 2 outer smaller and usually reflexed; stamens 8, sometimes 6, connate at base; ovary superior; styles 2–3, free or connate at base: achene 2-edged or 3-angled, inclosed by the enlarged inner sepals; embryo eccentric, slightly curved. (Ancient Greek name for Atriplex.) Syn.: *Tragopyrum* Bieb. About 18 species in C. and W. Asia, Greece and N. Afr.—Small shrubs of usually spreading habit with small lvs. and usually profusely produced white or pinkish fls. in terminal racemes remaining a long time nearly unchanged. Essentially desert plants requiring in cult. well drained soil and sunny position.

A. Sepals 4; stamens 6; fr. 2-edged: brs. rigid, often spinescent................1. *A. spinosa*
AA. Sepals 5; stamens 8; fr. 3-angled: brs. unarmed.
  B. Lvs. 1–3 cm. long.
    C. Lvs. lanceolate ....2. *A. frutescens*
    CC. Lvs. orbicular-ovate to broad-elliptic..................................3. *A. buxifolia*
  BB. Lvs. 2.5–8 cm. long, oblong-elliptic to oblong-lanceolate.............4. *A. Muschketowi*

    1. **A. spinòsa** L. Rigid shrub to 50 cm., with whitish, usually spinescent, brs.: lvs. ovate to elliptic, 5–10 mm. long, bluish green: fls. about 8 mm. across, white, tinged rose, in small clusters on short lateral brts.; sepals 4, the inner 2 roundish, accrescent, closely appressed to the 2-edged fr. Fl.vɪɪɪ. E.N.III. 1a:23,f.12a–e. S.H.1:255. W. Asia, S. Russia. Intr. 1732. Zone V.

    2. **A. frutéscens** (L.) K. Koch. Shrub to 80 cm., with slender whitish upright unarmed brs.: lvs. oblong to lanceolate or oblanceolate, 8–30 mm. long,

acute, wavy at the margin, grayish green: fls. whitish, in small clusters at the end of the brts., forming racemes 2–7 cm. long; inner sepals suborbicular, in fr. about 6 mm. across and pinkish. Fl.viii–ix. L.B.5:489(c). B.R.3:254(c). (*A. lanceolata* Meissn., *Polygonum f.* L.) S. Russia to W. and C. Asia. Intr. 1770. Zone III. Attractive small shrub with profusely produced fls. in late summer, changing from white to pinkish.

Related species: **A. Billardièri** Spach. Low, usually prostrate shrub with often spinescent brts: lvs. ovate to lanceolate, 3–5 mm. long, obtuse to acute, slightly wavy: fls. rosy-pink, in dense 5–8-fld. racemes. B.M.8820(c). G.C.76:43. S. E. Eu., W. Asia. Cult. 1903. Zone VI?

3. **A. buxifòlia** (Bieb.) Jaub. & Spach. Shrub to 60 cm., with rather short, sometimes slightly spinescent brs.: lvs. broad-obovate to broad-elliptic, 1–2.5 cm. long, acute or obtusish, with crisped and wavy margin: fls. pinkish-white, slender-stalked, forming short terminal racemes 2–4 cm. long; inner sepals orbicular, about 8 mm. across in fr. Fl.vii–viii. B.M.1065(c, as *Polygonum crispulum*). Transcauc. to Turkest. Intr. about 1800. Zone V.

4. **A. Muschketòwi** Krassn. Shrub to 2.5, of open straggling habit: young brts. pale yellowish brown, older brown with shreddy bark: lvs. elliptic-oblong to oblong-lanceolate, 3–8 cm. long, acute, with crisped margin, light green: fls. white, about 1 cm. across, slender-stalked, in terminal leafy racemes 2–5 cm. long; accrescent sepals about 8 mm. across in fr. Fl.v–vi. B.M.7435(c). B.S.1:225. G.C.78:406,t(c). (*A. latifolia* Koehne, *Tragopyrum lanceolatum* var. *latifolium* Reg.) Turkest. Intr. about 1880. Zone V. The most ornamental species on account of its larger fls. and bright green lvs.

The closely related genus **Callígonum** L. consisting of small-leaved or nearly leafless shrubs resembling Ephedra in habit and appearance, is apparently not now in cult. It differs chiefly in the not accrescent sepals, in the larger fr. which is either 4-winged, as in **C. aphýllum** Schneid. (*C. Pallasia* L'Hérit.), or densely covered with branched setae, as in **C. polygonoìdes** L. These species are native of W. and C. Asia and will be hardy within our area.

3. **POLÝGONUM** L. Knotweed. Herbs or shrubs often twining: lvs. alternate, petioled; ocrea conspicuous, membranous: fls. small, perfect, usually collected into large terminal spikes or panicles, rarely solitary; perianth 5-parted or 5-lobed, usually pinkish; the 3 outer parts often somewhat larger, accrescent and enclosing the fr. at maturity; stamens usually 8, rarely 5–7, adnate to a disk; styles 2–3, free or more or less connate; stigmas capitate: fr. compressed or 3-angled; embryo eccentric, more or less curved; cotyledons narrow, not folded. (Ancient Greek name, from *poly-*, many, and *gonu*, knee, referring to the numerous joints.) About 150 species throughout the earth, chiefly in temp. regions.

A. Prostrate subshrubs: fls. in terminal spikes..............................1. *P. vaccinifolium*
AA. Twining shrubs.
  B. Axes of infl. nearly glabrous; fls. pinkish..........................2. *P. baldschuanicum*
  BB. Axes of infl. minutely scabrous-pubescent; fls. white.....................3. *P. Auberti*

1. **P. vaccinifòlium** Wall. Prostrate subshrub with long trailing and rooting brs., glabrous: ocrea laciniate, about 1 cm. long, brown; lvs. broad-elliptic to elliptic, 1–2 cm. long, acute at ends, dark green above, glaucescent beneath; petioles 4–6 mm. long: fls. rose-red, in short-stalked slender spikes 5–7 cm. long, borne on short upright brts. Fl.viii–x. B.M.4622(c). Gn.45:159(h); 87:564(h). G.W.9:377(h). Himal. Intr. 1845. Zone VII? A handsome trailing plant, forming carpets with numerous upright rosy-red fl.-spikes; well adapted for rockeries, likes moist position.

Related species: **P. equisetifórme** Sibth. & Sm. Subshrub to 1 m., with ascending striped brs. with lanceolate revolute lvs. 1.5–3 cm. long near the base, leafless above, and with conspicuous lacerate sheaths, resembling stems of an Equisetum: fls. white, in axillary clusters forming terminal spikes, in autumn. S.F.4:t.364(c). Gn.83:517(h);87:604(h). Mediterr. Reg. Cult. 1912. Zone VII?

2. **P. baldschuànicum** Reg. Twining woody climber to 15 m.; brts. glabrous, green, older brs. gray: lvs. broad-ovate or ovate, 4–10 cm. long, acute or acuminate, cordate or hastate at base, glabrous, bright green; petioles 1–3.5 cm. long: fls. white, tinged with pink, 6–8 mm. across, in large terminal panicles at the end of the brs. and of lateral brts.; the 3 outer sepals winged on back, attenuated into a slender stipe; stamens pubescent at base; achene 3-angled, shining black. Fl.vii–ix; fr.ix–x. B.M.7544(c). Gt.37:t.1278(c). G.C.III.21:17;41:399(h). Gn.79:41(h). Gn.M.38:25(h). Bokhara. Intr. 1883. Zone IV. The large panicles of pinkish fls. often cover the upper part of the plant completely in late summer and fall.

3. **P. Aubérti** L. Henry. Similar to the preceding, but less woody: lvs. ovate to oblong-ovate, 4–9 cm. long, hastate at base, usually undulate at margin, bright green, reddish when young; petioles 3–5 cm. long: fls. about 5 mm. across, whitish or greenish white, sometimes slightly pinkish, in numerous slender lateral panicles along the upper part of the brs.; anthers white; the 3 outer sepals winged. Fl.vii–ix. R.H.1907:82,83. W. China. Intr. 1899. Zone IV. Vigorous climber with bright green dense foliage handsomer than that of the preceding species.

Related species: **P. multiflòrum** Thunb. Less woody: brs. hollow or nearly so: lvs. deeply cordate, 5–12 cm. long, long-acuminate; panicle smaller, slenderer, puberulous; fls. pink, 3 mm. across; stamens glabrous; outer sepals much enlarged in fr. S.H.1:f.169i-m. Japan. Intr. 1881. Less handsome and tenderer.

Closely related genera: **Pteroxýgonum** Dammer & Diels. Woody climber; differing chiefly in the not accrescent perianth, the 3-angled fr. being 3-winged at apex and 3-horned at base, with 2-winged pedicel. One species: **P. Giráldii** Dammer & Diels. Brts. sparingly pilose or glabrescent: lvs. long-petioled, cordate-triangular, acute to cuspidate, sparingly pilose on the veins: racemes stalked, pendulous; fls. short-pedicelled. C. China. Cult. 1935. Zone V.— **Polygonélla** Michx. Annual or perennial, often suffruticose plants; brts. conspicuously jointed, adnate at base to the internode: lvs. small, linear or narrow: pedicels solitary, in slender panicled racemes; the 2 outer sepals spreading or reflexed; stamens 8; styles 3: embryo straight or nearly so. About 6 species in N. Am.—**P. americàna** (Fisch. & Mey.) Small. Subshrub to 0.5 m., glabrous: lvs. linear, 5–20 mm. long: fls. about 4 mm. broad, white or rose, in racemes 2–5 cm. long and forming terminal panicles to 20 cm. long. Gr.M.363. (*P. ericoides* Gray.) S. Mo. to Tex. and Ga. Intr. ?

4. **BRUNNÍCHIA** Banks. Climbing shrubs; the brts. partly ending in tendrils: lvs. petioled, entire; ocrea very short, not membranous: fls. perfect, small, in large terminal panicled racemes; sepals 5; stamens 7–10, usually 8; styles 3; stigmas 2-cleft at apex; ovule pendulous: fr. obtusely 3-angled, enclosed in the tubular enlarged perianth, below with a long stipe-like winged base; seed deeply 6-grooved, the embryo in one of the angles. (After M. T. Brunnich, a Scandinavian naturalist of the 18th century.) One species in N. Am. and one in W. Afr.

B. cirrhòsa Banks. Climbing to 8 m.; stems grooved: lvs. ovate to ovate-lanceolate, 5–15 cm. long, acute or acuminate, truncate or subcordate at base, slightly pubescent or nearly glabrous beneath; petioles about 1 cm. long: racemes 3–15 cm. long, forming large terminal panicles; fls. greenish white, 6–7 mm. across; achene oblong-ovoid, lustrous brown, about 6 mm. long, inclosed in the tubular perianth, with the stipe-like broad-winged base 2.5–3 cm. long. Fl.vii–viii; fr.ix–x. E.N.III.1a:35,f.18a-d. B.B.1:677. S. C. to Fla.,

w. to Okl. and Tex. Intr 1787. Zone VII? Vine with handsome dark green lvs.
Related genus: **Muehlenbeckia** Meissn. Usually climbing or sometimes prostrate shrubs or subshrubs: lvs. usually small, with small, loosely sheathing stipules: fls. polygamous or dioecious, small, in axillary fascicles or in spikes, rarely solitary; perianth 5-parted; stamens usually 8; styles 3, short; stigmas usually fimbriate: fr. 3-angled, inclosed in the usually succulent perianth. About 15 species in Austral., Polynes., and S. Am.—**M. compléxa** (A. Cunn.) Meissn. Prostrate or climbing subshrub, glabrous, with thin wiry stems minutely warty when young: lvs. orbicular to elliptic, 4–20 mm. long, slender-petioled: fls. 2–3 mm. long, in axillary or terminal short spikes, sometimes panicled: fr. waxy-white, 5–8 mm. across; nutlet black, shining. B.M.8449(c). N. Zeal. Intr. 1842. Zone (V).—**M. axillàris** (Hook f.) Walp. Young brts. minutely puberulous: lvs. elliptic or ovate to suborbicular, 2–8 mm. long: fls. axillary, solitary or 2, or the staminate in short terminal spikes. Cheeseman, Ill. N. Zeal. Fl.2:t.165. (*M. nana* Hort.) N. Zeal. Cult. 1902. Zone V.

20. CHENOPODIACEAE Dumort. GOOSEFOOT FAMILY

Herbs or shrubs, rarely small trees: lvs. usually alternate, entire or irregularly toothed, often fleshy, sometimes reduced to scales; stipules wanting: fls. small, usually greenish, bisexual or unisexual, regular; perianth simple, of 1–5 parts; stamens as many as perianth parts or fewer; ovary superior, 1-celled; ovule 1, amphitropous; styles or stigmas 2, rarely 3 or 4: fr. dry, rarely fleshy, inclosed by the variously shaped perianth; embryo coiled; cotyledons usually long and narrow. About 74 genera with 550 species distributed all over the world.—None of the woody members of this family are of horticultural importance, but as they are almost all plants of alkaline or saline soil, they are useful for seashore planting. The species mentioned below are occasionally found in botanical collections.

A. Lvs. alternate, rarely opposite.
  B. Lvs. lanceolate to obovate or ovate: fls. unisexual.
    C. Lvs. scurfy or mealy, often glabrescent, without hairs: fruiting bracts usually toothed ....1. *Atriplex*
    CC. Lvs. stellate-pubescent.
      D. Lvs. pubescent while young; fruiting bracts entire, glabrous............2. *Grayia*
      DD. Lvs. persistently stellate-tomentose: fruiting bracts with 2 horns and densely pilose ....3. *Eurotia*
  BB. Lvs. linear or terete.
    C. Brs. slender: lvs. 4–10 mm. long: fls. bisexual.
      D. Plant pubescent: fr. inclosed in a 4-toothed hairy calyx..........4. *Camphorosma*
      DD. Plant glabrous: fr. inclosed in a 5-lobed calyx............................6. *Suaeda*
    CC. Brs. rigid, spinescent: lvs. 1.5–3 cm. long: fls. unisexual: fr. winged....5. *Sarcobatus*
AA. Lvs. opposite, reduced to scales: fr. winged..................................7. *Haloxylon*

1. **ÁTRIPLEX** L. ORACH. Herbs or shrubs: lvs. alternate, rarely opposite, scurfy, mealy or glabrous: fls. unisexual, sometimes mixed with perfect ones, in clusters usually forming terminal spikes or panicles; staminate fls. with 3–5-parted calyx, the pistillate with 2 large bracts and without calyx; stigmas usually 2: seed vertical with annular embryo, enclosed in the enlarged distinct or connate bracts. (Ancient Latin name of the plant.) About 120 species throughout the earth.

A. canéscens James. Shrub to 1.5 m. with whitish ascending or spreading brs.: lvs. subsessile, linear-lanceolate to oblanceolate or narrow-oblong, 2–5 cm. long, obtuse or acute, entire, grayish green: fls. usually dioecious, the staminate in simple or panicled spikes, the pistillate axillary or spicate: fruiting bracts united nearly to the apex, on each side with 2 longitudinal wings, undulate or dentate, 12–15 mm. broad. Fl.VIII. B.B.2:19. Clements, Rocky Mt. Fl.t.10,f.1,2. Bull. U. S. Dept. Agr. Bot. 27,t.6,f.1. (*A. occidentalis* D. Dietr.) S. Dak. and Ore. to Tex. and L. Calif. Cult. 1870. Zone V. One of

the hardiest of the woody species in cult. and rather conspicuous by the grayish white or grayish green color of its foliage.
Related species: **A. Nuttállii** S. Wats. Suffruticose, with erect or decumbent stems: lvs. oblong or obovate to oblanceolate, 2–4 cm. long, obtuse, grayish green: fruiting bracts united to above the middle, 3–4 mm. long, indurate, irregularly dentate. B.B.2:19. Man. and Sask. to Neb. and Utah. Cult. 1880. Zone II?—**A. confertifòlia** (Torr.) S. Wats. Shrub to 1 m.: lvs. ovate to suborbicular, 1–2.5 cm. long, short-petioled: fls. dioecious in small axillary clusters; fruiting bracts united at base, entire, 6–12 mm. long. Jepson, Fl. Calif. f.83. Contr. U. S. Nat. Herb. 25:t.7a(h). N. Dak. and Ore. to Calif. Cult. 1894. Zone V?—**A. Hálimus** L. Shrub to 2 m., with upright stout brs.: lvs. rhombic-ovate to ovate-oblong, 1.5–6 cm. long, acutish, silvery gray, petioled: fls. in large terminal panicles, greenish: fruiting bracts connate at base, entire. Fl.ix. R.I. 24:t.270(c). S. Eu. Intr. 1640. Zone VII?—**A. portulacoìdes** L. Straggling shrub to 0.5 m.: lvs. opposite, obovate to oblong, about 1 cm. long, grayish: fls. greenish, in slender panicled spikes: fruiting bracts 3-lobed, tubercled. R.I.24: t.271(c). S.E.8:t.1208(c). Seashores of Engl. and Denm. to Mediterr. Cult. 1800. Zone VII?

2. **GRAỲIA** Hook. & Arn. Deciduous shrubs, stellate-pubescent: lvs. alternate, entire: fls. usually dioecious; staminate fls. with 3–5-parted membranous calyx, in axillary clusters; pistillate fls. without calyx, inclosed by 2 connate bracts; stigmas 2: fr. nearly orbicular, inclosed by a winged involucre; seed erect; embryo annular. (After Asa Gray, noted American botanist; 1810–1888.) Syn.: *Eremosemium* Greene. Two species in N. Am.
G. spinòsa (Hook.) Moq. Erect much-branched shrub, to 1 m.; brts. short, often spinescent: lvs. narrow-oblong to oblanceolate, 0.5–4 cm. long, obtuse, pubescent while young, later glabrescent: staminate fls. in dense short spikes; pistillate fls. in dense spikes 2–7 cm. long: fruiting bracts suborbicular, 5–15 mm. long, glabrous, often tinged red. Fl.iv–v; fr.vii–viii. H.I.t.271. Jepson. Fl. Calif. f.86. (*G. polygaloides* Hook. & Arn., *Eremosemium spinosum* Greene.) Wyo. and Wash. to Colo. and Calif. Cult. 1897. Zone V?

3. **EURÓTIA** Adans. Low shrubs or subshrubs with stellate pubescence: lvs. alternate, entire, narrow: fls. dioecious, or sometimes monoecious; the staminate fls. in clusters forming spikes; calyx 4-parted; stamens 4; pistillate fls. axillary, solitary or clustered, with 2 bracts connate below and without calyx; stigmas 2: fr. inclosed by the connate bracts forming a long-pilose, 2-horned coat; seed vertical; embryo nearly annular. (Greek *euros*, mould; referring to the pubescence.) About 4 species in N. Am. and in S. Eu. to C. Asia.
E. lanàta (Pursh) Moq. Subshrub to 1 m., with upright brs., like the lvs. with dense stellate pubescence mixed with simple hairs: lvs. short-petioled or subsessile, linear to lanceolate, 1.5–5 cm. long, obtuse, with revolute margins: fls. usually incompletely dioecious: fruiting bracts about 6 mm. long. Fl.v–vii; fr.viii. B.B.2:20,f.1703. Jepson, Fl. Calif. f.87. Contr. U. S. Herb. 25:t.7b (h). Sask. and Wash. to Kans. and Calif. Cult. 1895. Zone V? The long-pilose frs. give to the brs. of the fruiting plant a feathery appearance and make it attractive; also the gray foliage is distinctive.
The related **E. ceratoìdes** (L.) C. A. Mey. differs chiefly in the broader, less densely pubescent lvs. greenish above, and with scarcely revolute margin. Mediterr. Reg. to C. Asia. R.I.24;t.273(c). S.H.1:264. S.L.175(h). Intr. 1780. Zone VI?

4. **CAMPHORÓSMA** L. Herbs or shrubs, often aromatic: lvs. alternate, terete or semi-terete: fls. perfect or pistillate, axillary and forming spikes; calyx campanulate, 4-toothed; stamens 4; style with 2, rarely 3 stigmas: fr.

included in the campanulate calyx; seed upright; embryo horse-shoe-shaped. (*Camphora,* camphor, and Greek *osme,* odor.) About 7 species from the Mediterr. Reg. to C. Asia.

C. monspelíaca L. Subshrub to 0.5 m., with procumbent or ascending woolly brs.; aromatic: lvs. alternate, with clusters of smaller ones in the axils, 4–8 mm. long, subulate, pilose: fls. in dense ovoid to oblong spikes; calyx 2–2.5 mm. long, pilose; styles red: seed black. R.I.24:t.274(c). S. Eu. and N. Afr. to C. Asia. Cult. 1880. Zone VII? Of heath-like appearance, adapted for seaside planting.

Related genus: **Kochia** Roth. Herbs or subshrubs, silky-pubescent: lvs. alternate: fls. perfect or pistillate, axillary, forming terminal spikes; calyx 5-lobed; stigmas 2–3: fruiting calyx depressed, with incurved lobes, winged on back: seed horizontal; embryo annular. About 30 species all over the earth. Possibly in cult. is K. **prostràta** (L.) Schrad. Subshrub to 0.6 m.: lvs. linear to filiform, 5–20 mm. long: fls. 3–5, axillary, forming leafy, panicled spikes: fruiting calyx 4–4.5 mm. across, each lobe with an oval to oblong striate horizontal wing on back. R.I.24:t.276(c). S.H.1:f.174. Mediterr. Reg. to C. Asia. Zone VI.

5. SARCÓBATUS Nees. Shrubs with spinescent brs. grayish or yellowish white: lvs. alternate or opposite, linear, fleshy: fls. monoecious or dioecious, without bracts; staminate fls. in cylindric catkins, each fl. consisting of a peltate scale, with 1–3 stamens underneath, without perianth; pistillate fls. sessile, axillary, 1 or 2; perianth turbinate, compressed, confluent with the ovary: fruiting calyx with a broad horizontal wing about the middle; seed erect; embryo spirally coiled, without endosperm. (Greek *sarcos,* flesh, and *batos,* a spiny shrub.) Two species in W. N. Amer.

S. vermiculàtus Torr. Much-branched rigid shrub to 3 m., glabrous or pubescent: lvs. 1–3 cm. long, the lower ones opposite and shorter and broader: staminate catkins 7–30 mm. long: fr. minutely stellate-pubescent, its body 4–5 mm. long, with the wing above 1 cm. across. Fl.vi–vii. B.B.2:f.1709. E.N.III.1a:78. S.L.336(h). Alb. and N. Dak. to Calif. and N. Mex. Cult. 1895. Zone V.

6. SUAÈDA Forsk. Herbs or shrubs, upright or procumbent; lvs. alternate, terete, fleshy, glabrous: fls. sessile, in axillary 3-fld. cymes or solitary, with 2 minute bracts, perfect, mixed with unisexual ones; perianth subglobose or urceolate, 5-lobed; stigmas 2–5: fr. enclosed in the spongy or fleshy perianth, its lobes subequal or the 2 or 3 outer ones tubercular on the back, rarely all winged; embryo spirally coiled; endosperm wanting or scanty. (From the Arabian name of *S. baccata* "Suidah.") Syn. *Dondia* Adans. About 40 species, essentially saline plants found on the seacoast of all continents and in inland regions with saline soil.

S. fruticòsa Forsk. Upright much-branched shrub to 1 m., glabrous, with whitish brs.: lvs. closely set, semi-terete, 5–15 mm. long, obtuse, grayish green: fls. solitary, rarely 3, greenish, small, the upper forming terminal leafy spikes; perianth subglobose, its lobes obtuse or acute, rounded on back; stigmas 3: fr. ellipsoid; seed ovoid, 1.6–1.8 mm. long, lustrous black. Fl.viii–ix. R.I.24:t.289,f.1–6(c). S.E.8:t.1178(c). (*Dondia f.* Druce.) Alb. to S. Calif. and n. Mex., also W. and S. Eu., Asia, Afr. Cult. 1789. Zone V? Low shrub of heath-like aspect, for planting in saline or sandy soil.

Related genus: **Sálsola** L. Herbs usually annual, rarely shrubs: lvs. usually alternate, sessile or clasping, usually pubescent: fls. perfect, small, with 2 large bracts, axillary, solitary or clustered, the upper ones forming spikes; perianth 5-, rarely 4–6-parted, with oblong or lanceolate segments, in fruit usually horizontally keeled or winged, connate or free at base, usually inflexed at apex.

About 40 species distributed nearly over the earth.—**S. laricina** Pall. Subshrub to 0.5 m., pubescent or glabrescent: lvs. subulate, 5–10 mm. long, obtuse: fls. solitary, in slender spikes; anthers with punctiform appendix: segments of fruiting calyx ovate-oblong, each below the middle with a reniform wing. Pallas, Ill. Pl. t.13. S. E. Russia to Siber. Cult. 1878. Zone IV?

7. HALÓXYLON Bge. Shrubs or small trees with articulate brs.: lvs. reduced to small scales: fls. perfect, axillary, with 2 broad bracts; sepals 5, free; stamens 2–5, inserted on a lobed disk; stigmas 2–5: fr. globose or cylindrical, surrounded by the accrescent sepals, all or some with a horizontal wing on back; seed horizontal; embryo spirally coiled. (Greek, *hal*, salt, and *xylon*, wood; referring to the saline habitat.) About 10 species from the Mediterr. Reg. to C. Asia.

H. Ammodéndron (C. A. Mey.) Bge. Saxoul. Shrub or tree to 6 m., with thick gnarled trunk; brts. light green, slender: scales short-triangular, obtusish, connate, puberulous inside: fruiting calyx with large suborbicular wings. Fl.v; fr.ix. E.N.III.1a:84,f.40a-g,t(h). Ledebour, Icon. t.47. Ural to Persia and Turkest. Intr. 1900. Zone V?

Closely related genus: **Anábasis** L. Herbs or small shrubs: brs. articulate, with opposite, terete, often scale-like lvs.: fls. with small, sometimes subulate, bracts; stamens 5; fruiting calyx with horizontal wings, rarely without; seed vertical. About 18 species from the Mediterr. Reg. to C. Asia.—**A. aphýlla** L. Shrub to 0.5 m., with upright green brs.: lvs. scale-like, connate, pubescent inside: fls. axillary, forming terminal spikes: fruiting calyx with 3 wings. Pallas, Ill. Pl. t.8(as *A. tatarica*). S. E. Russia to the Altai and Songaria. Cult. 1878. Zone V?

The genus **Salicórnia** L. has also articulate brs. and scale-like opposite lvs., but it is succulent and scarcely woody. Herbs or subshrubs: fls. sunk in the fleshy joints; perianth 3–4-toothed, stamens 1 or 2: embryo conduplicate. About 10 species chiefly on the seashore throughout the earth.—**S. perénnis** Mill. has prostrate, suffruticose rooting stems. B.B.2:22. S.E.8:t.1183(c). (*S. ambigua* Michx., *S. radicans* Sm.) N. H. to Miss., W. Eu., Algeria. Cult. ? Zone IV.— **S. fruticòsa** L. has erect stems to 0.6 m. R.I.24:t.287(c). La., Bahamas, Old World. Intr. about 1800. Zone VII?

21. CARYOPHYLLACEAE Reichenb. PINK FAMILY

Herbs, rarely suffruticose; brs. usually swollen at the nodes: lvs. opposite, often connate at base, entire, with or without stipules: fls. regular and usually perfect, mostly in cymes; sepals 4–5, free or united; petals 4–5, sometimes wanting; stamens usually twice as many as sepals or fewer, hypogynous or perigynous; styles 2–5, sometimes united; ovary superior, 1-celled: ovules 1 to many, attached to the base or on a free central placenta: fr. a dehiscent caps., or a 1-seeded utricle, rarely a berry; seeds albuminous, with coiled or curved, rarely straight embryo.—About 75 genera and 1200 species in both hemispheres, most abundant in temp. and colder regions; none of the suffruticose species are of particular ornamental or economic importance.

SILÈNE L. Catchfly, Campion. Annual or perennial herbs, sometimes suffruticose or shrubby: lvs. opposite, without stipules: fls. solitary or in cymes, white, pink or red; calyx 5-toothed or 5-cleft, ovoid to cylindric, 10 to many-nerved; petals 5, with a narrow claw and usually with a scale at base of blade; stamens 10; styles 3–5; caps. dehiscent, with 6–10 teeth at apex; seeds many. (Name probably derived from *Silenos*, companion of Bacchus in Greek mythology.) More than 400 species throughout the n. hemisphere.

S. chloraefòlia Sm. Woody at base, to 50 cm. tall, with upright or ascending brs., viscid above, otherwise glabrous and glaucescent like the lvs.: lower lvs. elliptic-spatulate, with the slender petiole 2–3 cm. long, upper sessile, suborbicular and acuminulate, 1–2 cm. across: fls. white or pinkish, slender-stalked in loose panicled cymes; calyx 10-nerved, glabrous, pale, 2.5–3 cm. long; petals bifid to middle of blade: caps. oblong, about 1½ as long as stipe. Fl.VII–VIII. B.M.807(c). B.R.1989(c). W. Asia. Intr. 1796. Zone VII.

Related species: S. fruticòsa L. Woody at base: lvs. oblong-spatulate to oblanceolate, 2.5–6 cm. long, ciliate, grayish green: fls. pink, in panicles, with long-ciliate bracts; calyx glandular-pubescent; petals bifid at apex; caps. about as long as its stipe. S.F.5:t.428(c). S. Eu. Cult. 1877. Zone VII?—**S. Tánakae** Maxim. Suffruticose, upright, to 60 cm.: lvs. elliptic to lanceolate-spatulate, 2.5–6 cm. long, puberulous; calyx about 2 cm. long, puberulous; petals purple, emarginate, with ciliolate claws; caps. about as long as stipe. S. Japan. Intr. 1884. Zone VII?

Other genera with suffruticose species probably hardy within our area are: **Paronýchia** Juss. Herbs or subshrubs: lvs. linear, small, with scarious stipules: fls. small, often clustered, with minute petals or without: fr. a 1-seeded, inde-hiscent utricle. **P. Jamèsii** Torr. & Gr. is a subshrub to 30 cm. tall, from Wyo. and Neb. to Tex.—**Acanthophýllum** C. A. Mey. Subshrubs with linear, rigid and pungent lvs., without stipules: fls. sessile, usually in clusters with 5-nerved calyx and pungent calyx-teeth; petals without crown-scales; stigmas 2; caps. circumscissile, few-seeded. About 15 species in W. and C. Asia.—**A. pungens** (Bge.) Boiss. Low compact subshrub: lvs. subulate, spiny, 2–3 cm. long: fls. with 2 spiny lanceolate bracts, in terminal short-stalked heads: petals pink, with elliptic-oblong limb more than ½ as long as the puberulous calyx. Ledeb. Ic. Fl. Ross. t.4. (*A. spinosum* C. A. Mey., not *Dianthus spinosus* Desf.) C. Asia. Cult. 1934. Zone V?

22. RANUNCULACEAE Juss. BUTTERCUP FAMILY

Herbs or woody plants: lvs. alternate or opposite, often dissected: fls. perfect, rarely unisexual, regular or irregular; sepals 2–15, usually 5; petals 2–15 or wanting; stamens numerous, rarely few; carpels 1–many, usually separate; fr. an achene or follicle, rarely berry-like; seeds with endosperm and a minute embryo.—Forty-eight genera with nearly 1300 species, chiefly in the temp. regions in the n. hemisphere.

A. Lvs. alternate; sepals imbricate, 5–10: fr. a follicle.
  B. Fls. large, solitary or few, with 5 or more petals; stamens many.............1. *Paeonia*
  BB. Fls. small, in compound racemes; petals wanting; stamens 5–10.........2. *Zanthorhiza*
AA. Lvs. opposite; sepals valvate, usually 4: fr. an achene.......................3. *Clematis*

1. PAEÒNIA L. PEONY.

Herbs or deciduous shrubby plants: buds large, with few outer scales: lvs. large, alternate, pinnately dissected: fls. terminal, usually solitary, sometimes several, red, white or yellow; sepals 5, persistent; petals large, 5–10; stamens numerous; carpels 2–5, developing into dehiscent follicles, each with several large seeds. (Ancient Latin name.) About 35 species in Eu., Asia, and one in W. N. Am.

A. Lfts. not decurrent, the lower ones stalked: fls. white to red, 10–30 cm. across: carpels
  pubescent ....1. *P. suffruticosa*
AA. Lfts. decurrent: carpels glabrous.
  B. Fls. dark crimson, 5–6 cm. across..2. *P. Delavayi*
  BB. Fls. yellow, 5–10 cm. across...3. *P. lutea*

1. P. suffruticòsa Andr. TREE P.

Shrub to 2 m., with stout brs.: lvs. without the petiole 10–25 cm. long, bipinnate; lfts. broad-ovate to ovate-oblong, stalked or sessile, 3–5-lobed, rarely entire, glaucescent beneath and glabrous or sparingly pubescent; petioles 5–10 cm. long: fls. solitary, 10–30 cm. across, white, rose or red: carpels densely pubescent, partly or nearly wholly enclosed by the disk. Fl.V–VI; fr.IX. Gn.52:325(h). M.G.11:201(h). S.L.245(h). (*P. arborea* Donn, *P. moutan* Sims.) N. W. China, long cult. in China and Japan. Intr. 1789. Zone V. The Tree Peony with its numerous garden forms is one of the most gorgeous of all ornamental shrubs; they are of slow growth and prefer rich loamy soil.—**P. s. spontànea** Rehd., var. Stoloniferous: lfts. pubescent on the veins beneath, at least toward the base when young, broad-ovate to ovate: fls. 10–12 cm. across, white to pink, with 5–10 petals. N. China. Intr. 1910.—The following are the first garden forms intr.; their lfts. are narrower, usually oblong-ovate and quite glabrous.—**P. s. papaveràcea** (Andr.) Bailey, var. Fls. nearly single, large, white, the petals thin and with a blotch of purple near base. A.R.7:463(c). B.M.2175(c). Gn. 52:325,t(c). Intr. 1806. (*P. moutan p.* Andr.)—**P. s. ròsea** (Andr.) Bailey, var. Fls. more or less double, sometimes nearly single, rose-colored. A.R.6: 373(c). L.B.11:1035(c). (*P. moutan r. plena* and *r. semiplena* Andr.) Intr. 1794.—**P. s. Bánksii** (Andr.) Bailey, var. Fls. more or less double; petals pale pink to nearly white at the margin, purplish toward the middle and base. A.R.7.448(c). B.M.1154(c). (*P. moutan B.* Andr.) Intr. 1789.—A cult. form which is probably nearest to the wild form is **P. s. Annéslei** (Sabine) Rehd., f., with almost single purple-pink fls. 10–12 cm. across. Trans. Hort. Soc. 6: 482,t(c). (*P. moutan A.* Sabine.) Orig. before 1826.

2. **P. Delavàyi** Franch. Subshrub to 1 m., stoloniferous, glabrous: lvs. bipinnatifid, the blade 15–25 cm. long, the segments ovate-lanceolate to lance-olate, 5–10 cm. long, decurrent at base, entire or with a few teeth, glaucous beneath; petioles 10–15 cm. long: fls. usually several, cup-shaped, 5–6 cm. across; petals 5–9, suborbicular to broad-elliptic, of firm texture; carpels included only at base by the disk, glabrous: follicles 2–2.5 cm. long. Fl.vi; fr.ix. G.C.68:93,97,98(fl,h). W. China. Intr. about 1908?—**P. D. angustíloba** Rehd. & Wils., var. Lvs. more finely divided, with narrow-lanceolate or linear-lanceolate segments 5–10 mm. broad: petals broad-elliptic. G.C.53:403. W. China. Intr. 1908. Zone V. The var. is a low shrub with much divided attractive lvs., but the fls. are not showy.

3. **P. lùtea** Franch. Subshrub to 1 m., glabrous: lvs. very similar to those of the preceding species: fls. usually solitary, 5–10 cm. across, golden-yellow; outer sepals leaf-like, the inner ones orbicular and yellowish green; petals 6–8, elliptic to obovate, concave, the outer ones irregularly crenate; anthers yellow; carpels 3, glabrous, inclosed only at base by the disk. Fl.vi; fr.ix. B.M.7788(c). R.H.1906:14,t(c). Gn.76:416. (*P. Delavayi* var. *l.* Fin. & Gagnep.) China. Intr. 1886. Zone VI? Particularly valuable on account of the yellow color of its fls.—**P. l. supérba** Lemoine. Lvs. bronzy red while young: fls. 8–12 cm. across, with 9–11 petals; filaments dark red. R.H.1906: 14,t(c). G.C.44:50,t(c). Intr. 1886.

P. l. × *suffruticosa* = P. Lemoinei Rehd. In habit and lvs. similar to *P. suf-fruticosa;* the form first raised is "L'Esperance" with single flowers, about 20 cm. across; petals 8–10, soft yellow, tinged red and buff particularly toward the base; filaments red, anthers yellow. "La Lorraine" is similar, but double. G.C. 57:56,t(c).

2. **XANTHORHÌZA** Marsh. YELLOW-ROOT. Deciduous low shrub; bark and root yellow and bitter; buds with few outer scales: lvs. alternate, clus-tered, long-stalked, pinnate or bipinnate: fls. polygamous, brownish purple, in terminal pendulous compound racemes; sepals 5; 5 small 2-lobed nectaries, sometimes called petals; stamens 5–10; carpels 10, 2-ovuled, developing into 1-seeded follicles. (Greek *xanthos,* yellow, and *rhiza,* root.) Syn.: *Zanthor-hiza* L'Hérit. One species in N. Am.

X. simplicíssima Marsh. Stems sparingly branched, to 0.6 m.: lfts. usually 5, ovate to ovate-oblong, 3–7 cm. long, incisely toothed, sometimes ternate;

racemes 5–10 cm. long; fls. 4 mm. across; sepals ovate, acute. Fl.iv–v. B.M. 1736(c). G.O.t.129(c). S.L.389(h). (*Z. apiifolia* L'Hérit.) N. Y. to Ky. and Fla. Intr. 1776. Zone IV. Suited for borders of shrubberies.

3. **CLÈMATIS** L. VIRGIN'S BOWER. Perennial herbaceous, or suffruticose or woody plants, often climbing; winter-buds with several pairs of outer scales: lvs. opposite, usually compound,[1] often ending in tendrils, rarely simple: fls. solitary or in panicles or cymes, perfect, rarely dioecious, apetalous; sepals usually 4, rarely 5–8, valvate in bud, rarely imbricate, petaloid; petaloid staminodes sometimes present; stamens numerous; carpels many, developing into 1-seeded achenes with a persistent, usually long and plumose style. (Greek name of a slender vine.) Including *Viorna* Reichenb., *Viticella* Dill. and *Atragene* L. About 230 species, widely distributed through the temp. regions chiefly of the n. hemisphere.

A. Sepals more or less upright forming a tubular, urceolate or campanulate fl.; stamens appressed, usually pubescent; fls. usually blue, violet, purple or red, rarely yellowish or whitish.
  B. Fls. without petaloid staminodes.
    C. Lfts. or lvs. entire, sometimes lobed; fls. solitary; stamens, including the connective, densely pubescent.
      D. Lvs. simple, sessile..1. *C. integrifolia*
      DD. Lvs. pinnate, or partly simple and often lobed.
        E. Style of fr. glabrous or silky.
          F. Lfts. not reticulate, the terminal one usually present.............2. *C. crispa*
          FF. Lfts. reticulate beneath, the terminal one usually replaced by a tendril.
                                    3. *C. Pitcheri*
        EE. Style of fr. plumose.
          F. Pedicels much longer than the sepals.
            G. Sepals pubescent outside.
              H. Lfts. reticulate, subcoriaceous...........................4. *C. reticulata*
              HH. Lfts. indistinctly veined, membranous...................5. *C. Viorna*
            GG. Sepals glabrous outside.
              H. Fls. purplish ....6. *C. divaricata*
              HH. Fls. scarlet ....7. *C. texensis*
          FF. Pedicels shorter than sepals; fls. axillary............................8. *C. fusca*
    CC. Lfts. or lvs. serrate or toothed: stamens pubescent or glabrous.
      D. Lvs. compound: fls. on the young growth.
        E. Lvs. ternate: fls. in axillary clusters: upright or sarmentose subshrubs.
          F. Fls. campanulate, purple to pale rose, 1 or few, axillary; filaments with long hairs ....9. *C. ranunculoides*
          FF. Fls. tubular, blue to bluish white, in axillary clusters; filaments sparingly pubescent with short hairs or glabrous....................10. *C. heracleifolia*
        EE. Lvs. pinnate or bipinnate: stamens pubescent.
          F. Fls. in axillary long-stalked panicles, yellowish.
            G. Sepals pubescent inside: lvs. glabrous......................11. *C. connata*
            GG. Sepals glabrous inside: lvs. silky beneath...............12. *C. Rehderiana*
          FF. Fls. 1–3 in the axils.
            G. Sepals glabrous outside, tinged violet-purple: lfts. serrate..13. *C. lasiandra*
            GG. Sepals slightly pubescent outside, whitish: lfts. small, deeply lobed or dissected ....14. *C. aethusifolia*
      DD. Lvs. simple: fls. axillary on last year's brs.: stamens glabrous......15. *C. cirrhosa*
  BB. Fls. with petaloid staminodes, solitary; stamens densely pubescent.
    C. Lvs. ternate ....16. *C. verticillaris*
    CC. Lvs. biternate ....17. *C. alpina*
AA. Sepals spreading (somewhat campanulate in Nos. 40–43); stamens divergent.
  B. Stamens glabrous (or only with few hairs below the anther or near base; hairy in No. 31).
    C. Fls. solitary or in fascicles from axillary buds on last year's brs.
      D. Lfts. or lvs. entire or occasionally lobed: fls. solitary, blue, violet, red or white.
        E. Style glabrous; sepals obovate, usually 4.
          F. Fls. 2–5 cm. across; filaments shorter than anthers: lvs. bipinnate.
                                    18. *C. Viticella*
          FF. Fls. 8–14 cm. across: lvs. pinnate............................19. *C. Jackmani*
        EE. Style pubescent; sepals 6 or more, elliptic or ovate, large; filaments as long or longer than anthers.
          F. Pedicels longer than sepals: lvs. glabrous or slightly pubescent beneath.
            G. Style of fr. silky; fl.-stalk with 2 bracts.....................20. *C. florida*
            GG. Style of fr. plumose; fl.-stalk without bracts.................21. *C. patens*

[1] The term flammuliform has been used in this genus for pinnate lvs. with all or part of the lfts. 3-foliolate, and biflammuliform, if the lvs. are bipinnate.

FF. Pedicels shorter than sepals: lvs. woolly beneath, simple or ternate.
22. *C. lanuginosa*
DD. Lfts. serrate: fls. white or rarely pink, fascicled, from the axils of last year's brs. (sometimes on the young growth in No. 24).
  E. Lvs. ternate.
    F. Lvs. glabrous or sparingly pubescent........................23. *C. montana*
    FF. Lvs. silky beneath: fls. sometimes on the young growth....24. *C. chrysocoma*
  EE. Lvs. pinnate; lfts. about 1.5 cm. long.........................25. *C. gracilifolia*
CC. Fls. in axillary or terminal panicles, rarely reduced to 3-fld. cymes, sometimes solitary in No. 33, on the young growth except in No. 26; sepals white, rarely pinkish (bluish in No. 31).
  D. Lfts. entire or nearly so or occasionally 3-lobed.
    E. Lvs. 3-foliolate; lfts. always entire.
      F. Fls. from scaly buds on last year's brs.: lfts. ovate, coriaceous.
26. *C. Armandi*
      FF. Fls. from the young growth: lfts. lanceolate, subcoriaceous.27. *C. Finetiana*
    EE. Lvs. pinnate or bipinnate.
      F. Lfts. 7–11, 8–20 mm. long, silvery white beneath: upright shrub.
28. *C. Delavayi*
      FF. Lfts. 3–7, larger, green beneath.
        G. Fls. white: woody climbers.
          H. Lvs. usually pinnate; lfts. 3–10 cm. long: achenes narrowed at base.
29. *C. paniculata*
          HH. Lvs. usually bipinnate; lfts. 1.5–4 cm. long: achenes rounded at base.
30. *C. Flammula*
        GG. Fls. bluish: upright or sarmentose subshrub..............31. *C. aromatica*
  DD. Lfts. or lvs. serrate or dentate, only occasionally nearly entire.
    E. Lvs. simple, serrate to pinnatifid: habit upright................32. *C. songarica*
    EE. Lvs. compound: habit climbing (except in No. 38).
      F. Lvs. ternate or biternate.
        G. Fls. perfect: lfts. ovate to ovate-lanceolate, sparingly incised-dentate.
34. *C. apiifolia*
        GG. Fls. dioecious: lfts. usually ovate, coarsely dentate.......35. *C. virginiana*
      FF. Lvs. pinnate or bipinnate.
        G. Fls. white: high climbing shrubs.
          H. Fls. 1–3, axillary: lvs. bipinnate..........................33. *C. Fargesii*
          HH. Fls. in panicels or cymes: lvs. pinnate.
            I. Sepals pubescent inside: lfts. glabrous or nearly so.
              J. Fls. dioecious: lfts. firm, usually 1–2.5 cm. broad.
36. *C. ligusticifolia*
              JJ. Fls. perfect: lfts. thin, usually 3–4.5 cm. broad......37. *C.Vitalba*
            II. Sepals glabrous inside: lfts. pubescent beneath.........39. *C. grata*
        GG. Fls. bluish white: plant subshrubby, to 2 m. tall..........38. *C. Jouiniana*
BB. Stamens with pubescent filaments; fls. yellow or yellowish: lvs. glabrous.
  C. Lfts. usually entire or lobed, bluish or grayish green: fls. 2–4 cm. across, usually several.
    D. Sepals pubescent inside: lfts. often oblong or lanceolate..........40. *C. orientalis*
    DD. Sepals glabrous inside: lfts. usually ovate or oval.....................41. *C. glauca*
  CC. Lfts. serrate: fls. 5–8 cm. across, usually solitary, long-stalked.
    D. Lvs. pinnate or bipinnate; lfts. dentate with spreading teeth......42. *C. tangutica*
    DD. Lvs. biternate; lfts. serrate with the teeth pointing forward....43. *C. serratifolia*

Sect. I. VIORNA Reichenb. Sepals more or less upright, with narrow margin or broad only above the middle; stamens upright, usually pubescent.

Ser. 1. CRISPAE Prantl. Lvs. or lfts. entire: fls. solitary, sometimes 2 or 3; stamens pubescent including the connective.

1. **C. integrifòlia** L. Herbaceous or subshrubby, upright, to 1 m.: lvs. sessile, ovate to oblong-ovate, 6–10 cm. long, acute, entire, slightly pubescent beneath or nearly glabrous, green on both sides, thin: fls. terminal, solitary, slender-stalked, 3–4 cm. long, violet or blue to white; sepals above the middle with broad margin and spreading, glabrous outside: frs. with plumose style. Fl.vi–vii. B.M.65(c). R.I.4:t.60,f.4663(c). Fl.vi–viii. S. E. Eu. to W. Asia and Altai. Cult. 1573. Zone V.

C. i. × *Viorna;* see No. 6.—*C. i.* × *Jackmani;* see under No. 19.—*C. i.* × *Viticella;* see under No. 18.—*C. i.* × *Fammula;* see No. 31.

Related species: **C. ochroleùca** Ait. Slightly woody at base, about 0.5 m. high: lvs. ovate to oblong-ovate, obtuse, reticulate, glabrous or pubescent beneath: fls. 2–2.5 cm. long, yellowish white, sometimes flushed purple; sepals thick, silky outside, without broad margin: style of frs. with yellowish brown hairs. L.B.7:661(c). T.N.1:t.1(c). (*Viorna o.* Small, *C. ovata* Pursh.) Fl.v–vi; fr. vii–xi. N. Y. to Ga. Cult. 1767. Zone V.—**C. albícoma** Wherry. Stems branched;

brts. with small lvs.: fls. about 2.5 cm. long, purple outside: achenes oblique; style with whitish hairs. Va. to W. Va. Cult. 1928? Zone V.

2. **C. crispa** L. Shrubby climber, to 3 m. high: lfts. 3–7, ovate to ovate-lanceolate, 4–8 cm. long, sometimes lobed or ternate, thin, glabrous: fls. solitary, long-stalked, nodding, bell-shaped, 2–4 cm. long, fragrant, bluish purple; sepals tubulose below, above the middle with a broad wavy margin and spreading, glabrous or nearly so outside: achenes with silky, not plumose styles. Fl.vi–ix. B.M.1160,1816,1860,1892(c). I.H.t.2:t.78(c, as *C. campaniflora*). Gn.34:147,t(c). (*Viorna c.* Small, *C. cylindrica* Sims, *C. Simsii* Sweet.) Va. to Fla. and Tex. Intr. 1726. Zone V. A slender vine with large and handsome fragrant fls.

C. c. × *texensis;* see under No. 7.

3. **C. Pitcheri** Torr. & Gr. High climbing vine; brts. pubescent: lfts. 3–6 or 7, usually ovate, 3–7 cm. long, entire or deeply 2–3-lobed, occasionally ternate, acute or obtusish and mucronulate, reticulate and somewhat pubescent beneath, the terminal one often changed into a tendril: fls. solitary, long-stalked, urn-shaped, 2–2.5 cm. long, purplish; sepals with recurved and margined tip, pubescent outside: achenes with glabrous or silky styles. Fl.vi–ix. B.M.1816(c, as *C. cordata*). Lavallée, Clemat. t.15. (*C. Simsii* of auth., not Sweet, *Viorna S.* Small.) S. Ind. to Neb. and Tex. Intr. before 1810. Zone V. Not showy and like the preceding lacking the feathery frs., an ornamental feature of most species.—**C. P. Sargénti** (Lav.) Rehd., var. Fls. smaller and paler: lfts. rarely lobed. Lavallée, Clemat. t.18. (*C. S.* Lav.)

C. P. × *texensis;* see under No. 7.

4. **C. reticulàta** Walt. Woody vine to 3 m. high or more: lfts. 3–7, broad-ovate or elliptic to ovate-lanceolate, 3–7 cm. long, obtuse or acute, strongly reticulate and glabrous or pubescent beneath, subcoriaceous: fls. nodding, urn-shaped, about 2 cm. long; sepals with recurved tips, dull yellowish and grayish pubescent outside, pale violet inside: achenes with long plumose styles. Fl.vii. B.M.6574(c). Lavallée, Clemat. t.16. (*Viorna r.* Small.) S. C. to Tex. and Fla. Intr. before 1884. Zone VI?

Related species: **C. versícolor** Small. Lfts. 4–6, oblong or ovate-oblong, entire, glabrous, reticulate, glaucous beneath: fls. glabrous outside, purple. B.B.2:124. Mo. to Ark. Intr. ? Zone V.

5. **C. Viórna** L. Slender woody vine to 3 m.: lfts. 5–7, ovate to ovate-oblong, 3–8 cm. long, obtuse or acute, cuneate to subcordate at base, entire or lobed and sometimes 3-foliolate, glabrous or nearly so, deep green: fls. nodding, urn-shaped, 2.5–3 cm. long, dull reddish purple; sepals thick, pubescent outside, with recurved tips: achenes with brownish plumose styles. Fl. v–viii. Lavallée, Clemat. t.17. Gn.54:240. (*Viorna V.* Small.) Pa. and Ohio to Ga. and Ala. Intr. 1730. Zone V.

Related species: **C. Addisónii** Brit. Glabrous and glaucous subshrub to 1 m.: lower lvs. simple, ovate or orbicular-ovate, 5–10 cm. long, obtuse, 2–4-lobed, upper mostly pinnate, tendril-bearing: fls. urn-shaped, purplish 1.5–2 cm. long, glabrous: plumose styles yellow. B.B.2:123. (*Viorna A.* Small.) Va. to N. C. and Tenn. Cult. 1902. Zone V.

6. × **C. divaricàta** Jacq. (?*C. integrifolia* × *Viorna.*) Upright bushy sub-shrubby plant: lvs. pinnate, or simple and deeply and irregularly lobed; lfts. 3–7, sessile and often decurrent, acute or obtusish, glabrous or nearly so beneath: fls. nodding, rather short-stalked, campanulate, about 2.5 cm. long, purplish; sepals spreading and margined above the middle, pubescent or glabrous outside: styles plumose. Fl.vi–vii. Jacquin, Eclog. Pl. Rar. t.13(c). G.W.14:562(h),563. (*C. integrifolia pinnata* Hort.) Orig. before 1805. Zone V

Related species: **C. troutbeckiàna** Spingarn. Lower lvs. elliptic to ovate, 7–10 cm. long, obtuse or retuse at apex, glaucescent beneath, upper lvs. pinnate: bracts of middle peduncle slender-stalked, of lateral subsessile; sepals lavender or pale pinkish purple outside, at the tip and inside pale green. N.H.13:89. Orig. unknown, probably hybrid. Cult. 1932. Zone V.

7. **C. texénsis** Buckl. Suffruticose vine to 2 m.: lfts. 4–8, the terminal one usually replaced by a tendril, broad-ovate, 3–8 cm. long, usually obtuse, subcordate at base, sometimes lobed, glaucous, subcoriaceous: fls. solitary, slender-stalked, urn-shaped, much narrowed at the mouth, 2–3 cm. long, carmine or scarlet; sepals thick, glabrous outside, with slightly spreading tips: achenes with long plumose styles. Fl.vii–ix. B.M.6594(c). Ad.21:675(c). Gt.32:86,t.(c). Gn.19:284,t.(c). R.H.1888:348,t.(c). (*C. coccinea* Engelm., *Viorna c.* Small.) Tex. Intr. before 1878. Zone IV. Handsome vine with bright scarlet fls.—**C. t. màjor** (Bean) Rehd., var. Fls. to 3.5 cm. long. (*C. coccinea* var. *m.* Bean.)

C. t. × *Jackmani* = **C. pseudococcínea** Schneid.; here belongs "Countess of Onslow" (G.C.III.16:9. Gn.52:304.t.fl(c);57:376[h]), "Duchess of York" (Gn.52:304,t.f.2[c]) and "Duchess of Albany" (Gn.52:304,t.f.3[c]).—There are also hybrids with *C. crispa* (see Gn.49:189. M.G.13:500) and with *C. Pitcheri* =**C. Morélii** Rehd. (see R.H.1893:376,t[c]).

8. **C. fúsca** Turcz. Suffruticose vine to 4 m.: young brts. pubescent: lfts. 5–7, the terminal one often wanting, ovate to ovate-oblong, 3–6 cm. long, acute, rounded or subcordate at base, glabrous or pubescent beneath: fls. nodding on villous pedicels shorter or as long as the sepals, urn-shaped, 2–2.5 cm. long; sepals thick, with recurved tips, densely brownish pubescent outside, violet inside: achenes with fulvous plumose styles. Fl.vi–viii. Lavallée, Clemat. t.20. N. E. Asia. Intr. about 1860. Zone IV. Interesting and hardy, but not particularly showy.—**C. f. violàcea** Maxim., var. Fls. slightly pubescent and violet outside. Gt.13:t.455(c). Manch. Intr. about 1860.

Into this group probably belongs **C. Práttii** Hemsl. Woody vine to 3 m., glabrous: lfts. 3, ovate-oblong, 2–3.5 cm. long, entire, glaucous beneath: fls. solitary, axillary, slender-stalked, tubular, 2 cm. long, bright yellow; styles plumose. W. China. Intr. 1908. Zone VI? Very distinct and graceful vine.

Ser. 2. **TUBULOSAE** Decne. Upright herbs often woody at base: lvs. ternate; lfts. serrate: fls. tubular, in axillary fascicles or in spikes, white to blue; filaments pilose, sometimes glabrous or nearly so.

9. **C. ranunculoìdes** Franch. Upright herb or sarmentose subshrub to 2 m.; stem pubescent or glabrous: lvs. 3-foliolate or 3-parted or partly pinnate; lfts. ovate or broad-ovate to elliptic-oblong, short-stalked or subsessile, 2–7 cm. long, 1–3 cm. broad, acute or acuminate, coarsely or incisely serrate, sometimes nearly entire, sparingly hairy to nearly glabrous: fls. purple to pale rose, axillary, solitary or several, nodding, on pubescent short or slender pedicels; sepals elliptic-oblong, 10–15 mm. long, recurved, with 3 prominent ribs or narrow wings and tomentulose on back; filaments silky-plumose, 1 cm. long; anthers 2–3 mm. long; achenes short-pubescent. Fls.ix–xi. B.M.9329(c). N.F.2:f.42(h). W. China. Intr. 1906. Zone VII? Very distinct, valuable for its late purple fls.

10. **C. heracleifòlia** DC. Upright plant, woody at base, to 1 m.: lfts. 3, broad-ovate, 6–15 cm. long, truncate or broad-cuneate at base, coarsely dentate and often slightly lobed, with mucronate teeth, slightly pubescent: fls. polygamous, in axillary clusters, tubular, 2–2.5 cm. long, blue and pubescent outside; sepals reflexed at apex; filament about as long as anther: achenes with plumose style. Fl.viii–ix. B.M.4269(c),6801(c). F.S.3:t.195(c). (*C. tubulosa* Turcz.) E. China. Intr. 1837. Zone IV. A rather coarse plant with stout stems and clustered blue fls. in size and shape similar to hyacinths; var.

Davidiana is the more showy.—**C. h. Davidiàna** (Decne.) Hemsl., var.
Slenderer and taller: lfts. usually cuneate: fls. dioecious, indigo-blue, fragrant;
the sepals tubular only at base, spreading above, not curling back. R.H.1867:
90(c). Gn.49:99;68:273. (*C. D.* Decne.) N. China. Intr. 1868.—**C. h. ichangénsis** Rehd. & Wils., var. Lfts. usually rounded at base, sparingly pubescent
above, more densely beneath: fls. densely silky outside; sepals curled back at
apex, deep blue inside: achenes densely villous. C. and N. China. Intr. 1908.
　　C. h. × *Vitalba;* see No. 38.
　　The closely related **C. stans** Sieb. & Zucc. with whitish or bluish white flowers
from Japan is scarcely woody. B.M.6810(c).

　　Ser. 3. CONNATAE Koehne. Shrubby climbers: lvs. pinnate or bipinnate;
lfts. serrate: fls. in axillary panicles, rarely 1–3, campanulate, usually whitish or
yellowish; sepals not or only at the tips recurved; filaments pubescent.

　　11. C. connàta DC. Climber to 8 m.; brts. glabrous or nearly so: lvs.
pinnate; lfts. 3–7, ovate to ovate-oblong, 5–12 cm. long, long-acuminate, cordate at base, coarsely, but rather regularly toothed with rounded mucronulate
teeth, not or slightly lobed on one side, rarely 3-lobed, glabrous or slightly
pubescent; petioles enlarged at base and surrounding the stem: fls. in slender-
stalked panicles 8–12 cm. long and with large leafy bracts, nodding, campanulate, 2–2.5 cm. long; pale yellow; sepals pubescent on both sides, recurved at
apex; filaments and connective pubescent: achenes with long plumose styles.
Fl.viii–x. Himal., S. W. China. Cult. 1887. Zone VI?
　　Closely related species: **C. trullífera** Finet & Gagnep. Lfts. 7–9, ovate, 4–10
cm. long, cordate or rounded at base, coarsely and incisely serrate, often 3-lobed,
glabrous or nearly so; petioles much enlarged at base and united, forming a flat
or cup-like expansion 1–2.5 cm. wide, bloomy: fls. in rather short-peduncled
panicles with small subulate bracts; filaments and connective densely pubescent.
W. China. Intr. 1903. Zone VI?

　　12. C. Rehderiàna Craib. Climber to 8 m.; brts. pubescent: lvs. pinnate;
lfts. 7–9, broad-ovate, 4–8 cm. long, acuminate, usually cordate at base,
coarsely or incisely toothed, usually 3-lobed, sparingly appressed-pubescent
above, more or less silky beneath and conspicuously veined: fls. nodding,
fragrant, campanulate, about 1.5 cm. long, pale yellow or yellowish white,
in many-fld. short panicles on upright stalks 8–12 cm. long; bracts at base of
the panicle ovate to lanceolate, 1–2 cm. long, often 3-lobed; sepals narrow-
oblong, downy outside, glabrous within; filaments pubescent: achenes with
plumose styles. Fl.viii–x. G.C.48:310;89:289,t(h). Gn.82:363;96:336. J.L.
64:f.37. R.H.1905:438 (as *C. Buchananiana vitifolia*). (*C. nutans* var. *thyr-
soidea* Rehd. & Wils., *C. nutans* Bean, not Royle.) W. China. Intr. 1898.
Zone VI? Vigorous climber with rather large lvs. and fragrant late fls.
　　Closely related species: **C. Veitchiàna** Craib. Differing chiefly in the
bipinnate more finely divided lvs.; pinnae 7–9, mostly 3-foliolate or 3-lobed;
lfts. ovate to ovate-lanceolate, less pubescent. W. China. Intr. 1904. Zone VI.
—**C. Buchananiàna** DC. Lfts. usually 5, rarely 3 or 7, coarsely toothed, rarely
slightly 3-lobed: fls. 2–3 cm. long; sepals ribbed and tomentose outside, pubescent inside. Himal. Intr. ?

　　13. C. lasiándra Maxim. Climber to 4 m.; young growth viscid: lvs.
bipinnate; pinnae 3–7, mostly 3-foliolate or 3-lobed, only the upper ones
often simple; lfts. ovate to ovate-lanceolate, 3–8 cm. long, long-acuminate,
sharply serrate, glabrous or sparingly pubescent, bright green; petioles enlarged at base and connate: fls. axillary, 1–3, on slender stalks 3–7 cm. long,
campanulate, 1.5–2 cm. long, whitish and more or less suffused with dull
violet; sepals with recurved tips, glabrous or nearly so outside; stamens about
as long as sepals, densely pubescent: achenes with plumose styles. Fl.viii–x.

C. and W. China. Intr. 1900. Zone V. Graceful vine with late rather dull colored and small fls.

Related species: **C. acutángula** Hook f. & Thoms. Large woody climber; stems sharply angled: lvs. bipinnate; pinnae 5–7, the lower ones 3-foliolate: lfts. ovate to ovate-lanceolate, 3–7 cm. long, coarsely toothed and often 3-lobed: fls. in axillary, short-stalked cymes on slender pedicels; sepals slightly pubescent outside and each with 3 longitudinal membranous wings on back. Fl.ix–x. Himal., W. China. Intr. about 1906. Zone VII?

14. **C. aethusifòlia** Turcz. Slender woody climber to 2 m.: lvs. pinnate or bipinnate; pinnae 5–9, the lower ones usually pinnate; lfts. small, 5–15 mm. long, deeply dissected into obovate-oblong or linear-oblong, acute or obtusish lobes, bright green, glabrous: fls. 1–3 on axillary slender stalks with a leaf-like bract above the middle, campanulate, about 1.5 cm. long, pale yellow; sepals narrow-oblong, not or little reflexed at apex, minutely pubescent outside: achenes with long plumose styles. Fl.viii–ix. S.H.1:f.186b[1](l). N. China,. Manch. Intr. 1910. Zone V. Much-branched vine with graceful foliage, flowering profusely in fall.—**C. a. latisécta** Maxim., var. Lvs. usually simple pinnate; lfts. to 3.5 cm. long, often 3-fid or deeply lobed and toothed with broad, ovate or obovate lobes. B.M.6542(c). Gt.10:t.342. R.H.1869:10. Gn.45:241. Manch. Intr. 1855. Zone IV.

Ser. 4. CIRRHOSAE Prantl. Woody climbers: lvs. simple or ternate, serrate: fls. from axillary buds on last year's brs., nodding, campanulate, with an involucre below the sepals; stamens glabrous.

15. **C. cirrhòsa** L. Climbing to 3 m., glabrous: lvs. persistent, simple, ovate to ovate-oblong, 2–4 cm. long, obtuse or acute, rounded or subcordate at base, coarsely crenate-serrate, sometimes 3-lobed: fls. 1–2, axillary, broadly campanulate, 3–5 cm. across, yellowish white; sepals broad-elliptic, 2–2.5 cm. long, downy outside; pedicels 1.5–3 cm. long, below the fl. with 2 bracts connate into a cup-shaped involucre: achenes with long plumose styles. Fl.iv–v. B.M.1070(c). L.B.19:t.1806(c). R.H.1924:186,t(c). S. Eu., Asia Minor. Intr. 1596. Zone VII. Desirable on account of its early fls.

Sect. II. ATRAGENE (L.) DC. Lvs. ternate to biternate: fls. from axillary buds of last year's brs., solitary, nodding, campanulate, with petaloid staminodes; stamens pubescent.

16. **C. verticillàris** DC. Trailing or climbing to 3 m.: lvs. 3-foliolate; lfts. slender-stalked, ovate to oblong-ovate, 3–8 cm. long, acuminate, rounded or subcordate at base, entire or coarsely toothed, slightly pubescent on the veins beneath: fls. purple or bluish purple, on slender stalks 2–7 cm. long; sepals 4, thin, oblong-lanceolate, 3–4 cm. long, slightly downy outside, strongly veined: staminodes and stamens about half as long as sepals: achenes with long plumose styles. Fl.v–vi. B.M.887(c). B.B.2:126. (*Atragene americana* Sims.) Hudson Bay to B. C., s. to Va. and Utah. Intr. 1797. Zone II? With showy fls. in spring; rare in cult.

Related species: **C. koreàna** Komar. Prostrate; lfts. 3, acuminate, 4–8 cm. long, coarsely dentate, the lateral ones ovate, truncate to subcordate at base, sometimes 3-lobed to 3-parted, the terminal one 3-lobed to 3-parted, sparingly pilose on veins beneath and sometimes on the face: fls. dull violet; sepals elliptic to elliptic-lanceolate, 2.5–3.5 cm. long; staminodes spatulate, ½ to ⅔ as long as sepals. Act. Hort. Petrop. 22:t.6. Korea. Cult. 1920. Zone V.—**C. k. lùtea** Rehd., f. Fls. yellow. Gs.9:285.—**C. chiisanénsis** Nakai. Similar to the preceding: lfts. nearly glabrous: sepals with 3 longitudinal winged keels on back, yellowish. M.I.2:t.107. Korea. Intr. 1917. Zone V.—**C. c. carunculòsa** (Gagnep.) Rehd., var. Lfts. hairy above, glabrous beneath: fls. yellow, sometimes flushed red; sepals outside at base with small bract-like appendages forming a kind of involucre. R.H.1915:534. M.O.19. (*C. alpina* var. *c.* Gagnep.) Korea. Intr. 1908. Zone V?

17. **C. alpìna** (L.) Mill. Woody climber to 2 m.: lvs. biternate or occasionally simply ternate: lfts. short-stalked or nearly sessile, ovate to ovate-lanceolate, 2–5 cm. long, acute, coarsely serrate, slightly pubescent beneath: fls. on slender stalks 4–12 cm. long, campanulate, violet-blue; sepals narrow-oblong, 3–4 cm. long, minutely downy outside, staminodes spatulate, about half as long as sepals: achenes with plumose styles. Fl.iv–v. B.M.530(c). R.I.4:t.60, f.4662(c). H.W.3:16. G.W.10:82(h). (*Atragenè a.* L.) C. and S. Eu. to N. E. Asia. Intr. 1792. Zone V. With early showy fls.—**C. a. sibírica** (L.) Ktze., var. Fls. yellowish white. B.M.1951(c). L.B.14:1358(c). R.H.1855:321,t.(c). (*C. a. alba* Hort., *Atragene s.* L.) Siberia. Intr. 1753. Zone V.

Closely related species: **C. pseudoalpina** (Ktze.) A. Nels. Lfts. usually more or less lobed and incisely toothed with few large teeth or lobes, glabrous beneath: staminodes narrower and fewer usually with a rudimentary anther at apex. S.H.1:f.186c(1). (*Atragene p.* Rydb., *C. alpina* var. *occidentalis* Gray.) Colo. to N. Mex. and Utah. Intr. 1916. Zone VI.—**C. macropétala** Ledeb. Lfts. incisely toothed and often lobed: fls. violet, 4–5 cm. long; staminodes narrowlanceolate, acuminate, nearly as long as the sepals, longer than stamens. G.C. 77:254. B.M.9142(c). A.B.1937:45. Gn.86:106(fl);88:223(h). N. China, Siber. Intr. 1910. Zone V. Has the largest fls. of any species of this section.

Sect. III. VITICELLA Link. Shrubby climbers: lvs. simple to bipinnate with entire or somewhat lobed lfts.: fls. 1–3, axillary or terminal, large; sepals spreading, 4–8, with broad margin folded in in bud; stamens glabrous or with a few hairs below the anthers.

18. **C. Viticélla** L. Slender woody climber to 4 m.: lvs. usually bipinnate, sometimes pinnate; pinnae 5–7, the lower ones usually 3-foliolate; lfts. ovate to ovate-lanceolate, 1.5–5 cm. long, usually obtuse, rounded at base, sometimes elliptic and acute at ends, entire to 3-lobed, glabrous or nearly so: fls. 1–3, slender-stalked, 3–5 cm. across, purple, rosy-purple or violet; sepals 4, spreading, obovate; filaments as long or shorter than anthers, usually with a few hairs below the anther: achenes large, nearly glabrous except at apex; style short, glabrous. Fl.vi–viii. B.M.565(c), R.I.4:t.65(c). H.W.3:15. Lavallée, Clemat. t.7. S. Eu. to W. Asia. Cult. 1597. Zone IV. Graceful woody climber flowering profusely in summer.—**C. V. albiflòra** Ktze., f. Fls. white (*C. V. alba* Hort., not Carr.)—**C. V. purpúrea** Loud., var. Fls. reddish purple. (*C. V.* var. *rubra* Bean.)—**C. V. kermesìna** Lem. Fls. bright wine-red.—**C. V. coerùlea** Loud., var. Fls. blue-violet.—**C. V. multiplex** G. Don., var. Fls. double, violet-blue. (*C. V. fl. pleno* Hort., var. *pulchella* Jaeg.)—**C. V. nàna** Carr. Dwarf form about 1 m. high, bushy.

Several hybrids of this species are known of which *C. V.* × *lanuginosa* = *C. Jackmani* (see No. 19) is the most important. Other hybrids are the following: *C. V.* × *integrifolia* = **C. eriostèmon** Decne. Sarmentose subshrub, to 3 m.; upper lvs. often simple, lower ones pinnate, the lowest pair of pinnae usually short-stalked; lfts. similar to those of *C. Viticella*: fls. slender-stalked, broadcampanulate, 4–6 cm. across, blue; filaments pubescent except at base: achenes slightly downy; style plumose below the middle, glabrous above. R.H.1852:341, t(c);1856:341(c, as *C. divaricata*). M.O.23. Lavallée, Clemat.t.10,12. (*C. Hendersonii* Hort., *C. Chandleri* Hort., *C. Bergeronii* Hort., *C. intermedia* Hort.) Origin. about 1830.—*C. V.* × *florida* = **C. venòsa** (Carr.) Schneid. Climbing shrub, similar to *C. Viticella*: lvs. bipinnate; lfts. ovate, acute, sparingly hairy beneath: fls. large, with 4–6 purple obovate sepals; styles glabrous. F.S.13:t. 1364(c). R.H.1860:183(c). (*C. Viticella v.* Carr., *C. florida* var. *v.* Lav.) Orig. before 1860.—*C. V.* × *patens* = **C. Guáscoi** Lem. Woody climber; young brts. pubescent: lfts. usually 5, nearly glabrous: fls. solitary, about 8 cm. across, violet-purple, with 4–6 obovate sepals, strongly 3-nerved, tomentose outside; style pubescent. I.H.4:t.117(c). B.H.7:226,t(c). Lavallée, Clemat. t.7bis. (*C. francofurtensis* Lav.) Orig. before 1857.—*C. V.* × *Flammula*; see under No. 30.

Closely related species: **C. campaniflòra** Brot. Woody climber to 6 m.; lvs. bipinnate; pinnae 5–9: lfts. ovate to ovate-lanceolate, 2–6 cm. long, acute, entire or sometimes lobed: fls. nodding on pubescent stalks 3–7 cm. long, broad-campanulate, 1.5–2.5 cm. across, white, tinged with violet; filaments broad, shorter than anthers, with a few hairs below the anthers: achenes with short appressed-pubescent style. Fl.vii–viii. L.B.10:987(c). Gn.31:187,t.(c). Lavallée, Clemat. t.8. Portugal. Intr. 1810. Zone VI.

19. × **C. Jackmáni** Th. Moore (*C. lanuginosa* × *Viticella*). Woody climber to 3 m.: lvs. pinnate, the upper ones often simple; lfts. ovate, rather large, usually slightly pubescent beneath: fls. usually 3, slender-stalked, 10–14 cm. across, usually violet-purple; sepals usually 4, sometimes 6, obovate; filaments often shorter than anthers, sometimes pubescent below the anther; styles glabrous or sometimes plumose up to the middle. Fl.vii–x. I.H.11:t. 414(c). F.S.16:t.1629(c). R.H.1868:390(c). Gn.71:507(h). (*C. splendida* Simon-Louis.) Orig. about 1860. Zone V or VI. One of the most important groups of large-flowered Clematis of which numerous forms are in cult., one of the best known being "Mme. André" R.H.1893:180,t.c.

C. J. × *integrifolia* = **C. Durándi** Ktze. Suffruticose climber to 3 m.: lvs. simple, ovate, 8–12 cm. long, acute, broadly cuneate to subcordate at base, nearly glabrous; petioles 2–5 cm. long: fls. slender-stalked, 8–12 cm. across, dark violet-blue; sepals spreading and recurving, usually 4, rarely more, obovate, with wavy margin; stamens yellow: achenes with plumose styles. Fl.vi–ix. Gn. 49:98,t(c). G.W.17:108,t.f.2(c). (*C. integrifolia D.* Hort., *C. integrifolia semperflorens* Hort.) Orig. before 1874.

20. **C. flòrida** Thunb. Deciduous or half-evergreen woody climber, to 4 m.: lvs. usually biternate, sometimes ternate; lfts. ovate to ovate-lanceolate, 2–5 cm. long, acute, entire or sometimes with 1 or 2 lobes or with a few teeth, dark green above, slightly pubescent or nearly glabrous beneath: fls. axillary, solitary, on slender pubescent stalks 6–12 cm. long, with 2 entire or lobed leafy bracts near the middle, 5–8 cm. across; sepals spreading, 4–6, ovate, acute, creamy-white with a green band on back; stamens purple, glabrous; styles silky or glabrous above. Fl.vi–vii. B.M.834(c). R.H.1856:41,t(c). Lavallée, Clemat., t.5. G.C.32:51. (*C. japonica* Makino, not Thunb.) C. China; cult. in Japan. Intr. 1776. Zone VI?—**C. f. Siebóldii** D. Don, var. Stamens partly changed into purple staminodes. B.R.24:25(c). Gn.22:142,t. (c):87:340(h). R.N.1915:552,t(c). (*C. f.* var. *bicolor* Lindl., *C. S.* Paxt.) Intr. 1837.—**C. f. plèna** D. Don, var. Fls. double, the stamens being changed into greenish white sepals shorter than the outer whorl of sepals. Intr. before 1798.

C. f. × *Viticella;* see under No. 18.

21. **C. pàtens** Morr. Deciduous woody climber to 4 m.: lfts. 3–5, ovate to ovate-lanceolate, 4–10 cm. long, acute or acuminate, usually rounded at base, entire, slightly pubescent beneath: fls. solitary and terminal on axillary brts. with one pair of long-stalked ternate lvs., 10–15 cm. across, white to violet or violet-blue; sepals 6–8, elliptic to oblong-elliptic, narrowed into a claw at base, not or slightly overlapping; style appressed-pubescent near apex, plumose below. Fl.v–vi. B.R.23:1955(c). P.M.4:t.193(c). Lavallée, Clemat. t.2. (*C. coerulea* Lindl.) China, cult. in Japan. Intr. 1836. Zone VI? This and the preceding species represent groups of the large-flowered Clematis valuable for their early flowering habit, while *C. lanuginosa* and *C. Jackmani* bloom in summer and fall.—**C. p. grandiflòra** (Hook.) Rehd., var. Fls. larger than in the type. B.M.3983(c). (*C. coerulea* var. *g.* Hook.)—**C. p. Standíshii** (Th. Moore) Rehd., var. Lfts. 3, small: fls. 12–14 cm. across; sepals light lilac-blue, of metallic lustre. (*C. florida* var. *S.* Th. Moore.) By some considered *C. florida* × *patens*.—**C. p. Fortùnei** (Th. Moore) Rehd., var. Fls. 8–12 cm. across, on a stout stalk with a whorl of simple or ternate long-stalked lvs. below the fl.: sepals very numerous, rather narrow, creamy white becoming pink; style appressed-pubescent above the middle, plumose below. F.S.

213

15:t.1553(c). G.C.1863:676. (*C. F.* Th. Moore, *C. florida* var. *F.* (Th. Moore) Davis.) Intr. about 1860.

C. p. × *Viticella;* see under No. 18.—*C. p.* × *lanuginosa;* see under No. 22.

22. C. lanuginòsa Lindl. Woody climber, not more than 2 m. tall: lvs. ternate or simple, ovate to ovate-lanceolate, 6–12 cm. long, acuminate, rounded or subcordate at base, entire, glabrous above, pubescent beneath, of firm texture: fls. terminal, 1–3 on woolly bractless stout stalks usually shorter than the sepals, white to pale lilac, 10–20 cm. across; sepals 6–8, ovate or elliptic, overlapping, woolly outside; styles long-plumose. Fl.vii–ix. F.S.8: t.811(c). I.H.1:t.14(c). G.C.29:23. Lavallée, Clemat. t.1. China. Intr. about 1850. Zone VI.

From this species most of our large-flowered summer-blooming Clematis have been derived and one of the most important groups of hybrids is that classed under *C. l.* × *Viticella* = *C. Jackmani;* see No. 19.—Another important group is *C. l.* × *patens* = **C. Lawsoniàna** Moore & Jackman. The typical form is said to be a cross of *C. patens Fortunei* and *C. lanuginosa.* Lvs. usually ternate: fls. large, on long stalks; sepals 6–8, usually elliptic and overlapping, rosy-purple and dark-veined in the typical form; style plumose. Here belong also **C. L. Symesiàna** (Anderson-Henry) Rehd., var.; **C. L. Hénryi** (Anderson-Henry) Rehd., var. G.M.43:318. B.C.2:795; **C. L. Gablénzii** (Courtin) Rehd., var. (*C. patens G.* Courtin.) G.Z.14:80,t(c), and many other garden forms. This group of hybrids resembles in many respects *C. Jackmani* which, however, may be distinguished by the usually 4 or sometimes 6, obovate or rhombic sepals, by the styles being glabrous above the middle, and by the fls. appearing usually in 3's.

Sect. IV. **FLAMMULA** DC. Upright herbs to climbing shrubs: lvs. simple to bipinnate: fls. white, pink or yellow sepals valvate, usually with narrow margin; stamens spreading, glabrous or pubescent at base, without nectaries.

Ser 1. MONTANAE Schneid. Woody climbers: lvs. ternate or pinnate, with serrate lfts: fls. rather large, white, sometimes pink, from axillary scaly buds of last year's branches; sepals with broad margin, folded in in bud; stamens glabrous.

23. C. montàna DC. Woody climber to 8 m.: lfts. 3, short-stalked, ovate to ovate-oblong, 3–10 cm. long, acute, incisely toothed, occasionally entire, glabrous or nearly so: fls. 1–5, fascicled, on slender stalks 5–10 cm. long, white, usually 2.5–5 cm. across; sepals elliptic-oblong, slightly pubescent outside; stamens yellow: achenes glabrous, with plumose styles. Fl.v. R.H. 1856:161,t.(c);1899:529(h). G.C.III,20:589(h). Gn.60:79(h);75:371(h);86: 111(h). (*C. anemoniflora* D. Don.) Himal., C. and W. China. Intr. 1831. Zone VI. One of the most beautiful of the early Clematises, particularly *C. m. rubens.*—**C. m. grandiflòra** Hook., var. Fls. 5–8 cm. across. B.M.4061(c). M.G.17:423(h).—**C. m. rubens** Ktze., f. Lvs. purplish, particularly when unfolding; fls. rosy-red to pinkish, 5–6 cm. across. R.H.1909:35.t(c). Gn.77:84 (h);87:339,632(h). B.S.1:364(h). Intr. 1900.—**C. m. lilácina** Lemoine. Fls. bluish lilac. G.34:345.—**C. m. Wilsònii** Sprague, var. Lfts. ovate, usually rounded at base, puberulous on the veins beneath: fls. 6–8 cm. across, white; sepals obovate-oblong, pubescent outside. Fl.vi–vii. B.M.8365(c). Gn.82: 287. M.G.27:26(h).

C. m. × *chrysocoma* = **C. vedrariénsis** Vilm. Similar to *C. montana*: fls. 5–6 cm. across, mauve-pink or rose-colored; sepals broad-elliptic. G.C.55:393(h); 61:94. (*C. verrieriensis* Gard. Chron.) Orig. before 1912.—**C. v. rósea** (Vilm.) Rehd., var. Fls light rose-colored, 8–10 cm. across. R.H.1922:214,t(c). (*C. Spooneri* var. *rosea* Vilm.) Orig. 1917.

24. C. chrysócoma Franch. Upright and shrubby or climbing to 6 m.; young brts., peduncles and leaves on both sides with dense yellow appressed pubescence: lfts. 3, short-stalked, ovate to elliptic or obovate, 2–5 cm. long, acute or obtuse, rounded or broad-cuneate at base, 3-lobed or coarsely toothed: fls. fascicled, 1–5 from axillary scaly buds, sometimes 3–5 on a peduncle 4–12 cm. long, or terminal and axillary on the young growth, white, tinged pink, 4–5 cm. across; sepals elliptic, densely silky outside, glabrous inside: achenes pubescent with plumose styles. Fl.vi–ix. B.M.8395(c). M.O.21. W. China. Intr. about 1890. Zone VII. The typical form is often shrubby and continues to bloom from the new growth through August and September, while the variety which has larger fls. only blooms from the old wood.—**C. c. sericea** (Franch.) Schneid., var. Fls. 1 or 2 from axillary buds, not on the young growth, 7–9 cm. across, white; sepals broad-obovate. Fl.vi–vii. M.O. 27. (*C. montana* var. *s.* Franch., *C. Spooneri* Rehd. & Wils.) W. China. Intr. 1909. Zone VII?

C. c. × *montana;* see under No. 23.

25. C. gracilifòlia Rehd. & Wils. Woody climber to 4 m.: lvs. pinnate; lfts. short-stalked or subsessile, 5–7, ovate to oblong-ovate, 1–2 cm. long, acute, rounded to cuneate at base, with few coarse teeth or 3-lobed, sparingly pubescent: fls. 1–4, fascicled, from axillary buds, on slender pubescent stalks 3–5 cm. long, white, 3–4 cm. across; sepals obovate to oblong-obovate, slightly pubescent outside: achenes glabrous with long-plumose styles. Fl.vi. W. China. Intr. 1910. Zone VI. Similar to *C. montana* but slenderer and with smaller more finely divided lvs.

Ser. 2. RECTAE Prantl. Upright herbaceous plants or woody climbers: lvs. simple to bipinnate; lfts. entire or serrate: fls. white, rarely pink, on the young growth in terminal and axillary panicles, rarely in axillary 3-fld. cymes occasionally reduced to 1 fl. or axillary on last year's brs.; sepals with narrow margin, rarely broad above the middle: anthers usually several times longer than broad and longer than the filaments.

26. C. Armándi Franch. Evergreen woody climber, to 5 m.: lfts. 3, on twisted stalks 1–3 cm. long, oblong-ovate to lanceolate, 8–12 cm. long, acuminate, rounded or subcordate at base and 3-nerved, entire, quite glabrous, lustrous above, coriaceous: fls. in leafy or leafless panicles from axillary scaly buds, white, 2.5–3.5 cm. across; sepals 4–5, oblong to oblong-obovate: achenes sparingly hairy with long plumose styles. Fl.v. Nouv. Arch. Mus. Paris II.8: t.2. R.H.1913:65. C. and S. China. Cult. 1907. Zone VII. Evergreen climber with showy white fls. in spring.—**C. A. Biondiàna** (Pavol.) Rehd., var. Infl. sessile; fls. 3.5–6.5 cm. across, with 5–6(–7) sepals. B.M.8587(c). G.C.38:30. Gn.87:631. N.H.17:22. (*C. B.* Pavol.) Intr. 1900.

C. A. × *Finetiana* = **C. Jeuneiàna** Symons-Jeune. Similar to *C. Armandi*, but infl. larger and looser. G.C.69:135.

Related species: **C. fasciculiflòra** Franch. Evergreen climber to 6 m.; lfts. 3, ovate to ovate-oblong, 4–12 cm. long: fls. in dense axillary fascicles on short woolly stalks 1–2 cm. long, creamy-white, densely woolly outside; anthers much shorter than filaments: achenes glabrous. S. W. China. Cult. 1910. Zone VII?

27. C. Finetiàna Lévl. & Vant. Subevergreen climber, to 4 m.: glabrous: lfts. 3, on twisted stalks, oblong-ovate to lanceolate, 5–10 cm. long, acuminate, subcordate or rounded at base, 3-nerved, entire, thinly coriaceous: infl. an axillary 3-fld. cyme or a few-fld. raceme with small lanceolate bracts; pedicels 2–4 cm. long: fls. about 3 cm. across; sepals lanceolate, nearly glabrous, white, greenish outside; outer filaments as long or longer than the linear anthers: achenes pilose; style plumose, fulvous. Fl.vi. B.M.8655(c). (*C. Pavoliniana* Pamp.) E. to W. China. Intr. 1908. Zone VII.

C. F. × *Armandi;* see under No. 26.

The following more or less closely related species have been intr., but are probably all tender: **C. Meyeniàna** Walp. Lfts. 3, ovate to ovate-oblong, 5–12 cm. long, usually cordate at base, glabrous: fls. 2–2.5 cm. across, in many-fld.

panicles with small subulate bracts: achenes hairy. B.R.599(c). B.M.7897(c). Japan, S. E. China, Indochina. Cult. 1821.—**C. quinquefoliolàta** Hutchins. Young brts., infl. and lvs. sparingly pubescent: lvs. pinnate, with 5 lanceolate lfts.: cymes 3–9-fld., leafy; filaments several times longer than anthers. V.F.3. (*C. Meyeniana* var. *heterophylla* Gagnep.) C. China. Intr. 1899.—**C. chinénsis** Osbeck. Lvs. pinnate; lfts. usually 5, ovate to oblong-lanceolate, 2–6 cm. long, rounded at base, slightly pubescent when young: fls. 1.5–2 cm. across, in many-fld. axillary leafless panicles; filaments partly longer than anthers. Retzius, Observ. 2:t.2. C. China to Indochina. Intr. 1900.—**C. uncinàta** Champ. Lvs. bipinnate or sometimes pinnate; pinnae usually 5, the lower ones 3-foliolate: lfts. ovate to ovate-lanceolate, 4–10 cm. long, glabrous, glaucescent beneath: fls. about 2.5 cm. across, white, fragrant, in many-fld. leafless panicles: achenes oblong-lanceolate, glabrous. H.I.1533. (*C. leiocarpa* Oliv.) C. China. Intr. 1901.—A form with emarginate lfts. and leafy infl. is **C. u. retùsa** Sprague, f. B.M. 8633(c). Cult. 1915.

28. **C. Delavàyi** Franch. Upright shrub to 1.5 m.: lvs. pinnate, 3–10 cm. long; lfts. 7–11, subsessile, ovate to oblong-ovate, 8–20 mm. long, acute, rounded at base, dark green above, densely silky and silvery-white beneath: fls. white, 2–3 cm. across, in terminal 3- to several-fld. cymes, on slender silky pedicels 2–5 cm. long; sepals 4–6, obovate-oblong, rounded at apex, with broad margin, densely silky outside; filaments longer than anthers: achenes pubescent; styles plumose. Fl.vii–viii. M.O.22. W. China. Intr. 1908. Zone VI? Distinct species, resembling more a white-flowered Potentilla than a Clematis.

29. **C. paniculàta** Thunb. Vigorous woody climber to 10 m.: lvs. ternate or pinnate; lfts. 3–5, ovate, 3–10 cm. long, acute, subcordate or rounded at base, entire or sometimes lobed, glabrous: fls. about 3 cm. across, white, fragrant, in many-fld. axillary and terminal panicles; sepals oblong, nearly glabrous outside; filaments longer than the linear-oblong anthers: achenes margined, thinly appressed-pubescent; styles plumose. Fl.ix–x. G.F.3:621; 5:91(h);9:75,185(h). R.H.1902:86. Gn.57:155. M.G.1898:487–9(h). (*C. recta* var. *p.* Ktze., *C. Flammula robusta* Carr.) Japan. Intr. 1864? Zone V. Desirable fast growing climber with white fragrant fls. profusely produced in fall.—**C. p. dioscoreaefòlia** (Lévl. & Vant.) Rehd., var. Lfts. generally ovate and cordate, usually rounded and mucronate at apex, in the floral region often emarginate, of thickish texture; sepals broader, obovate-oblong to oblong. (*C. d.* Lévl. & Vant.) Korea. Intr. 1911.

Closely related herbaceous species: **C. recta** L. Upright to 1 m.: lfts. 5–7, ovate to lanceolate, rounded or cuneate at base: fls. 2–3 cm. across, in terminal panicles. R.I.4:t.61(c). Middle and S. Eur., N. Asia. Cult. 1597. Zone III?—**C. r. plena** Lemoine. Fls. double. R.H.1860:512.—**C. r. mandshùrica** (Rupr.) Maxim., var. Usually decumbent, to 1.5 m.; lfts. usually larger, often subcordate at base, reticulate: fls. 3–4 cm. across, in axillary and terminal panicles; sepals usually 6. R.H.1909:423(h). N. E. Asia. Cult. 1889.—**C. angustifòlia** Jacq. Upright to 1 m.: lvs. pinnate to bipinnate; lfts. oblong to narrow-lanceolate, attenuate at base, often deeply divided into narrow lobes, strongly veined: panicle terminal; sepals 6, oval to oblong. R.I.4:t.62(c). L.B.t.918(c). N. Asia. Intr. 1787. Zone III?

30. **C. Flámmula** L. Woody climber to 5 m.: lvs. usually bipinnate, sometimes pinnate; pinnae usually 5, the lower ones usually 3-foliolate or 2–3-lobed; lfts. broad-ovate to narrow-lanceolate, 1.5–4 cm. long, acute or sometimes obtuse, usually rounded or cuneate at base, often lobed, but otherwise entire, bright green, glabrous: fls. white, fragrant, 2–3 cm. across, in large many-fld. panicles; stamens white; anthers shorter than filaments: achenes minutely appressed-pubescent; styles plumose. Fl.viii–x. R.I.4:t.63(c). H W.3:14. Gn.58:319(h);76:23(h). (*C. Pallasii* J. F. Gmelin.) Mediterr. Reg. to Persia. Cult. 1590. Zone VI. With profuse fragrant white flowers in fall.—

C. F. rotundifòlia DC., var. Lfts. broader, obtuse. R.I.4:6.62,f.4666(c). (*C. fragrans* Ten.) Mediterr. Reg. Zone VII?

C. f. × *Viticella* = **C. violàcea** DC. Climbing shrub to 4 m.: lvs. bipinnate or pinnate; lfts. entire: fls. about 3 cm. across, pale violet, in terminal panicles; sepals often 6; style pubescent. Ann. Soc. Bot. Gand. 1:t.45(c). Orig. before 1840. Zone VI or V?—**C. v.** rubro-marginàta (Cripps) Rehd., var. Sepals 4, white, with reddish violet margin. (*C. Flammula rubro-marginata* Cripps, *C. r.* Jouin.) Orig. before 1883.—*C. F.* × *integrifolia;* see No. 31.

31. × **C. aromática** Lenné & Koch (*C. Flammula* × *integrifolia*). Upright or sarmentose subshrub to 2 m.: lvs. pinnate; lfts. 3–7, short-stalked, ovate to elliptic, 3–6 cm. long, acute, rounded to broad-cuneate at base, entire, glabrous: fls. 3–4 cm. across, bluish violet, fragrant, on slender stalks about 5 cm. long, in loose terminal cymes; sepals oblong, spreading and reflexed; stamens with a few hairs below the anthers: achenes pubescent; styles plumose. Fl.vii–ix. (*C. coerulea odorata* Hort., *C. davurica* K. Koch, not Patrin.) Lavallée, Clemat. t.9. R.H.1877:15. Orig. before 1850. Zone V.

32. **C. songàrica** Bge. Upright shrub to 1.5 m., in cult. often sarmentose and suffruticose: lvs. simple, lanceolate to linear-lanceolate, 3–8 cm. long, acute, attenuate at base, serrate with spreading teeth or occasionally pinnatifid near base, sometimes entire, glaucous or grayish green, glabrous; petioles 8–20 mm. long: fls. yellowish white, 2–2.5 cm. across, on slender pedicels 2–4 cm. long, in terminal cymes; anthers very narrow, longer than the filaments: achenes pubescent; styles plumose, glabrous toward the apex. Fl. viii–ix. S.H.1:f.183x–x³,186d. (*C. Gebleriana* Bong.) Siber. to Turkest. Intr. before 1880. Zone V. Distinct species, but not very ornamental and rarely cult. The var. **integrifòlia** Ledeb. with entire lvs. is not in cult.

Closely related species: **C. fruticòsa** Turcz. Upright shrub: lvs. narrowly oblong to lanceolate, 2–5 cm. long, entire or incisely dentate (var. *lobata* Maxim.), green: fls. 1 or 3 on axillary short brts., light yellow, 2.5–5 cm. across; pedicels short or to 5 cm. long; sepals glabrous or pubescent outside: filaments glabrous, linear, longer than the anthers. N. China, Mong. Intr. ? Zone IV?

33. **C. Fargèsii** Franch. Woody climber to 6 m.: lvs. bipinnate; pinnae 5–7, the lower ones 3-foliolate; lfts. ovate, 2–5 cm. long, acute, usually rounded or truncate at base, irregularly incisely serrate and lobed, sparingly silky-pubescent: fls. 3.5–5 cm. across, pure white, in 3-fld. cymes or solitary, on slender pedicels with the peduncle 7–18 cm. long; sepals usually 6, obovate, rounded and mucronate at apex, outside tinged yellowish and slightly pubescent; anthers shorter than filaments: achenes glabrous; styles plumose. Fl. vi–ix. Gn.89:659(h). W. China. Intr. 1911. Zone V. Handsome vine with large pure white flowers.—**C. F. Soùliei** Finet & Gagnep., var. Lfts. usually narrower, sometimes broad-cuneate at base, nearly glabrous: fls. 5–7 cm. across, often solitary. B.M.8702(c). W. China. Intr. 1911.

34. **C. apiifòlia** DC. Woody climber to 3 m.: lvs. ternate, or occasionally biternate; lfts. ovate to ovate-lanceolate, 4–7 cm. long, acuminate, rounded or broad-cuneate at base, coarsely toothed and often lobed, pubescent on the veins beneath or nearly glabrous: fls. dull white, 1.5–2 cm. across, in axillary panicles with the peduncle 5–12 cm. long; anthers oblong: achenes pubescent, 5–8 in small fruiting heads with the rather short plumose styles about 3 cm. across. Fl.ix–x. S.H.1:f.183z–z⁴,186e. Japan. Intr. about 1863. Zone V. Not as showy as some allied species; valuable for its late fls.—**C. a. obtusidentàta** Rehd. & Wils., var. Lfts. broader and larger, coarsely toothed, with large rounded teeth, pubescent beneath: infl. larger. C. China. Intr. 1907.

Closely related species: **C. Pieròtii** Miq. Lvs. mostly biternate; lfts. ovate to ovate-lanceolate: infl. usually cymose, few- to many-fld.; achenes glabrous except the ciliate margin. G.F.5:139 (as *C. brevicaudata*). Japan. Cult. 1890. Zone V.

Ser. 3. VITALBAE Prantl. Similar to the preceding group: woody climbers: lvs. always compound: fls. perfect or dioecious, small, white; anthers elliptic-oblong, not more than twice as long as broad, several times longer than the filaments.

35. **C. virginiàna** L. Climbing to 6 m.: lvs. ternate, rarely pinnate with 5 lfts.; lfts. ovate, 5–9 cm. long, acuminate, rounded or subcordate at base, coarsely toothed, nearly glabrous: fls. dioecious, dull white, 2–3 cm. across, in axillary leafy panicles; sepals obovate-oblong to spatulate, pubescent outside; anthers elliptic: achenes pubescent, in large fruiting heads with the plumose heads about 5 cm. across. Fl.VIII–IX. B.B.2:122. Gd.W.t.12(c). N. S. to Man., s. to Ga. and Kans. Intr. 1720. Zone IV.—**C. v. missouriénsis** (Rydb.) Palmer & Steyerm., var. Lfts. usually 5, ovate or broad-ovate, 5–9 cm. long, appressed-pubescent beneath. Neb. to Mo. Intr. ?

36. **C. ligusticifòlia** Nutt. Climbing to 6 m.: lvs. pinnate; lfts. 5–7, ovate to lanceolate, 3–7 cm. long, acuminate, truncate to cuneate at base, coarsely toothed and often 3-lobed, sparingly strigose or glabrous, yellowish or bright green, of thickish texture: fls. dioecious, white, about 2 cm. across, in terminal and axillary cymes: achenes densely pubescent, with plumose styles, in large heads. Fl.VIII–IX. B.B.2:122. Jour. Intern. Gard. Club, 3:229(h). B. C. and N. D. to N. Mex. and Calif. Cult. 1880. Zone V.

37. **C. Vitálba** L. TRAVELERS' JOY. Climbing to 10 m.: lvs. pinnate; lfts. usually 5, the lowest pair occasionally 3-foliolate, ovate to ovate-lanceolate, 3–10 cm. long, acute or acuminate, rounded or subcordate at base, coarsely toothed or sometimes entire, occasionally 3-lobed, slightly pubescent or nearly glabrous, thin: petiolules 1–3 cm long: fls. about 2 cm. across, white, faintly fragrant, in axillary and terminal panicles; sepals densely pubescent outside: achenes pubescent, with long plumose styles, in large heads. Fl.VII–IX. R.I.4:t.64,f.4667(c). H.W.3:13. M.G.1898:319(h). Eu., N. Afr., Cauc. Long cult. Zone IV. Strong growing vine, profusely blooming in summer.

Related species: **C. Gouriàna** Roxb. Lfts. 5–7, ovate to ovate-oblong, 3–8 cm. long, long-acuminate, usually subcordate at base, often entire, glabrous or pubescent, chartaceous; petiolules 5–10 mm. long: fls. 1.5–2 cm. across. Wight, Icon. t.933–4. (*C. Vitalba* var. *G.* Ktze.) Himal., China. Intr. 1901. Zone VI? —**C. G. Finétii** Rehd. & Wils., var. Lvs. glabrous: achenes glabrous. C. & W. China. Intr. 1907.—**C. brevicaudàta** DC. Lvs. bipinnate; pinnae 5–7, the lower 3-foliolate, occasionally only 3-lobed: lfts. ovate to ovate-oblong, 3–7 cm. long, coarsely toothed or sometimes entire, glabrous or pubescent: fls. 1.5–2 cm. across, nearly glabrous outside, on long and slender pedicels in axillary loose cymes; sepals elliptic: achenes in small heads with the rather short plumose styles about 3 cm. across. Manch. to W. China. Has been confused with *C. apiifolia* and *C. Pierotii;* doubtful if in cult.

38. × **C. Jouiniàna** Schneid. (*C. heracleifolia* × *Vitalba*). Subshrubby climber, to 3 or 4 m.: lvs. ternate or pinnate; lfts. 3–5, ovate, 5–10 cm. long, acuminate, rounded or truncate at base, coarsely toothed, slightly pubescent: fls. white at first, finally suffused with lilac, 2.5–3 cm. across, in terminal and axillary cymes forming a large terminal panicle; sepals spreading, linear-oblong, pubescent outside; anthers shorter than the filaments. Fls. VIII–X. B.S.1:362. S.H.1:280,f.185l–l[4]. Gn.66:365;71:506(h, as *C. grata*). Orig. before 1900. Zone IV. Vigorous climber blooming profusely in fall.

39. **C. gràta** Wall. Vigorous climber: young brts. pubescent: lvs. pinnate; lfts. usually 5, the lowest pair sometimes 3-foliolate, broad-ovate, 3–6 cm. long, acute or acuminate, truncate or subcordate at base, coarsely and in-

cisely toothed, pubescent on both sides or glabrous above: fls. white, about
2 cm. across, on pedicels 1–2 cm. long, in terminal and axillary rather dense,
pubescent panicles or cymes; sepals oblong, densely pubescent outside, glabrous inside; buds obovoid, obtuse; filaments longer than anthers: achenes
pubescent, with long plumose styles. Fl.ix–x. Wallich, Pl. As. Rar. 1,t.98(c).
(*C. Vitalba* var. *g.* Ktze.) Himal. Intr. ? Vigorous climber similar to *C.
Vitalba.*—**C. g. lobulàta** Rehd. & Wils., var. Lfts. with coarser and fewer
teeth, often 3-lobed or 3-fid, densely pubescent on both sides. C. and W.
China. Intr. 1907. Zone VI?—**C. g. argentilùcida** (Lévl. & Vant.) Rehd., var.
Lfts. occasionally only 3, larger, 5–9 cm. long, with few large teeth, glabrescent
above. (*C. g.* var. *grandidentata* Rehd. & Wils.) C. and W. China. Intr. 1907.

Ser. 4. ORIENTALES Prantl. Woody climbers: lvs. biternate or pinnate to
bipinnate: fls. yellow, solitary or few; filaments pubescent, longer than the
linear-oblong anthers; achenes pubescent, with long plumose styles.

40. **C. orientàlis** L. Slender woody climber to 6 m.: lvs. pinnate or bipinnate, the lower pinnae usually 3-foliolate, sometimes 5-foliolate, or 3-fid;
lfts. ovate to oblong-ovate or lanceolate, 1.5–5 cm. long, lobed or coarsely
toothed, glabrous or minutely pubescent: fls. yellow, 3–5 cm. across, solitary
or few on slender stalks 4–10 cm. long; sepals elliptic to oblong-elliptic,
pointed, spreading and finally somewhat reflexed, pubescent inside and usually
outside: achenes pubescent with long plumose styles. Fl.viii–ix. B.M.4495
(c). Lavallée, Clemat. t.21. R.H.1855:321,t(c);1899:530. Gn.45:240,t(c);52:
501(h). (*C. crux-flava* Cock., *C. graveolens* Lindl.) Persia to Himal.; escaped
in N. Mex. Intr. 1731. Zone VI? Slender climber with glaucescent finely
divided lvs. and profuse yellow fls. in fall.

41. **C. glaùca** Willd. Slender woody climber, glabrous: lvs. pinnate to
bipinnate; lfts. elliptic to lanceolate, 1.5–5 cm. long, 2–3-lobed, otherwise
entire, very glaucous: fls. yellow, 3.5–5 cm. across, solitary or few on slender
pedicels 3–8 cm. long; sepals elliptic to elliptic-oblong, pointed, glabrous on
both sides, open-campanulate at first, finally spreading, not recurving: achenes
pubescent, with long plumose styles. Fl.viii–ix. Willdenow, Berl. Baumz.
t.4,f.1. R.H.1890:561. (*C. orientalis* var. *g.* Maxim.) W. China to Siber. Cult.
1752. Zone V. Similar to *C. orientalis,* but hardier.—**C. g. akebioìdes**
(Maxim.) Rehd. & Wils., var. Lfts. ovate to ovate-lanceolate, 2–3-lobed and
irregularly crenately toothed: fls. bronzy-yellow. W. China. Intr. 1904.—**C. g.
phaeántha** Rehd., f. A form of the preceding var. with the fls. dull violet
outside. Cult. 1918.—**C. g. angustifòlia** Ledeb., var. Lfts. narrow-oblong to
linear-oblong, or 2–3-lobed with narrow lobes. (*C. intricata* Bge.) Siber., N.
China. Intr. 1905.

42. **C. tangùtica** (Maxim.) Korsh. Woody climber to 3 m.; young brts.
usually slightly villous: lvs. pinnate or bipinnate; lfts. oblong-lanceolate to
lanceolate, 3–8 cm. long, serrate with spreading teeth, sometimes deeply 2–3-
lobed, glabrous, bright green: fls. large, bright yellow, usually solitary on
slightly pubescent stalks 8–15 cm. long; sepals ovate-lanceolate, 3–5 cm. long,
long-acuminate, glabrous on both sides, open-campanulate at first, finally
spreading: fruiting head with the plumose styles about 6 cm. across. Fl.vi,
and usually again in fall. B.M.7710(c). R.H.1902:528,t(c). G.W.14:651(h).
(*C. orientalis* var. *t.* Maxim., *C. eriopoda* Koehne, not Maxim.) Mong. to N.
W. China. Cult. 1890. Zone V. The handsomest of the yellow-fld. climatises;
also the large heads of feathery frs. are attractive.—**C. t. obtusiúscula** Rehd.
& Wils., var. Lfts. smaller: sepals elliptic to elliptic-ovate, obtusish to short-
acuminate, 2.5–3 cm. long. J.L.47:193. N. W. China. Intr. 1910.

43. C. serratifòlia Rehd. Woody climber to 3 m.: lvs. biternate; lfts. ovate-lanceolate to lanceolate, 3–6 cm. long, acuminate, serrate with the teeth pointing forward, and sometimes 2–3-lobed, glabrous, bright green: fls. 1–3, yellow, large, on slender stalks 4–6 cm. long; sepals ovate-lanceolate to oblong, 2–2.5 cm. long, acuminate, glabrous outside, slightly villous inside; filaments purple, much longer than the oblong anthers; head of frs. about 6 cm. across. Fl.viii–ix. Korea. Cult. 1909. Zone V. Similar to *C. tangutica*, with smaller fls., blooming later and more profusely.

23. LARDIZABALACEAE Lindl. LARDIZABALA FAMILY

Woody plants, mostly twining: lvs. alternate, compound, estipulate: fls. polygamous or unisexual, regular, in racemes, rarely solitary: sepals 6, rarely 3, petaloid; petals wanting, but nectaries often present; stamens 6; carpels 3–9, superior, free, with numerous ovules arranged in longitudinal rows; carpels baccate in fr., dehiscent or indehiscent; seed with copious endosperm and a small straight embryo.—Seven genera with about 20 species in E. Asia, Himal. and Chile.

A. Lvs. pinnate: upright shrub...1. *Decaisnea*
AA. Lvs. digitate: twining shrubs.
  B. Lfts. 3–9, subequal and all distinctly stalked.
    C. Lvs. evergreen; lfts. acute or acuminate: sepals 6......................2. *Holboellia*
    CC. Lvs. deciduous; lfts. emarginate: sepals 3...................................3. *Akebia*
  BB. Lfts. 3, the terminal one generally obovate, cuneate at base, the lateral ones of different
    shape and subsessile or short-stalked; carpels 3, many-seeded.........4. *Sinofranchetia*

1. DECAÌSNEA Hook. & Thoms. Upright shrub with stout sparingly branched stems: winter-buds large, ovoid, with 2 outer glabrous scales: lvs. odd-pinnate; lfts. opposite, entire: fls. polygamous, in elongated racemes forming panicles terminal on lateral brts.; pedicels slender; sepals 6, lanceolate, long-acuminate, petaloid; nectaries wanting; stamens 6, in the staminate fls. with long filaments connate into a column, short and nearly distinct in the pistillate fl.; pistils 3, free, developing into oblong fleshy follicles dehiscent along the ventral suture and with numerous seeds in 2 rows imbedded in a white pulp. (After Joseph Decaisne, French botanist; 1809–1882.) Two species in the Himal. and W. China.

D. Fargèsii Franch. Shrub to 5 m., glabrous: lvs. 50–80 cm. long; lfts. 12–25, short-petioled, ovate to ovate-oblong, 6–14 cm. long, acuminate, broad-cuneate or rounded at base, glaucous beneath: panicle drooping, 25–50 cm. long; pedicles about 1 cm. long; fls. pendulous, campanulate, greenish, 2.5–3 cm. long: fruiting carpels cylindric, curved, 5–10 cm. long and about 2 cm. thick, blue, bloomy; seeds ovoid, flattened, about 1 cm. long, black. Fl.vi; fr.x. B.M.7848(c). R.H.1900:270,271,273. G.C.73:161. G.W.17:533(h),534 (fr). W. China. Intr. 1893. Zone (V). Shrub with stout stems and large pinnate lvs.; fls. inconspicuous, but the large blue fruits are attractive; they are insipid, but eaten in China.

2. HOLBOÈLLIA Wall. Evergreen twining shrubs, glabrous: lvs. long-petioled, digitate; lfts. 3–9, entire, stalked: fls. monoecious, in few-fld. axillary racemes; sepals 6, petaloid, obtusish, fleshy; nectaries 6, small; staminate fls. with 6 free stamens and a rudimentary ovary; pistillate fls. with small stami-nodes and 3 carpels developing into indehiscent fleshy pods with numerous black seeds in several rows. (After F. L. Holboell, once superintendent of the Botanic Garden at Copenhagen.) Five species in China and Himal.

H. grandiflòra Réaubourg. Climbing to 6 m.: lfts. 3–7, oblong to oblanceolate, 6–14 cm. long, acuminate, usually cuneate at base, dark green above, glaucous and reticulate beneath; petiolules 1–4 cm. long: fls. campanulate, 2–3 cm. long, white, fragrant; pedicels 2.5–3 cm. long; staminate fls. with oblong-obovate, obtuse outer sepals, in the pistillate fls. broad-elliptic and acutish, the inner sepals narrower: fr. purple, 8–12 cm. long, edible. Fl.v.—W. China. Intr. 1908. Zone VII? Valued chiefly for its fragrant white fls., the largest in the genus.

Related species: **H. Fargèsii** Réaubourg. Lfts. 5–9, oblong-lanceolate to oblanceolate, 5–12 cm. long, glaucous below, with inconspicuous veins: fls. 1.5–2 cm. long, the pistillate greenish white. H.I.29:2848. (*Stauntonia longipes* Hemsl.) C. China. Intr. 1907. Zone VII?—**H. coriàcea** Diels. Lfts. 3, ovate or elliptic to oblong, 5–8 cm. long; pale green below with the veinlets invisible: fls. about 1 cm. long, on slender pedicels, the staminate white, the pistillate purple. G.C.71:270(h);77:391(h). C. China. Intr. 1907. Zone VII?

Of the closely related genus **Stauntònia** DC. which differs chiefly in the connate stamens and the thinner, acuminate sepals, only **S. hexaphýlla** Decne. is in cult. Lfts. 3–7, oval to oblong-ovate, short-acuminate, rounded at base, 4–9 cm. long, reticulate and whitish beneath, coriaceous: fls. 1.5–2 cm. long, white, tinged with violet. S.Z.1:t.76(c). G.C.II.5:597. N.K.21:t.2. Japan, Korea. Intr. 1876. Zone VII?

3. **AKÈBIA** Decne. Deciduous or half-evergreen twining shrubs, glabrous: buds with many imbricate glabrous scales: lvs. long-petioled, digitate; lfts. 3–5, stalked, emarginate at apex: fls. monoecious, in axillary racemes, the pistillate at the base, the staminate ones smaller, at the end of the raceme; sepals 3; stamens 6, with subsessile anthers; carpels 3–12, developing into ovoid-oblong fleshy pods opening along the ventral suture, with numerous black seed in several rows. (Akebi, its Japanese name.) Two species in eastern Asia.

A. Lfts. 5, entire...1. *A. quinata*
AA. Lfts. 3, sinuately toothed or entire...2. *A. trifoliata*

1. **A. quinàta** (Houtt.) Decne. Climbing to 10 m. or more, glabrous: lfts. 5, obovate or elliptic to oblong-obovate, 3–6 cm. long, emarginate, rounded or broad-cuneate at base, glaucous beneath: fls. slender-stalked, fragrant, the pistillate purplish brown, 2.5–3 cm. across, with broad-elliptic sepals, the staminate rosy purple, much smaller, on pedicels 5 mm. long: fr. 6–8 cm. long, purple-violet, bloomy. Fl.v; fr.ix–x. B.M.4864(c). G.F.4:137(fr.) N.K.21: t.3. Gn.51:151. H.B.1:157(h). C. China to Japan and Korea. Intr. 1845. Graceful vine with fragrant dark colored fls. in spring; the showy fruits are but rarely produced in cult.

A. quinata × *trifoliata* = **A. pentaphýlla** (Mak.) Mak. Lfts. 3–5. With the parents in Japan; orig. also in Am. in 1932.

2. **A. trifoliàta** (Thunb.) Koidz. Climbing to 6 m. or more: lfts. 3, broad-ovate to ovate, 3–7 cm. long, emarginate, usually rounded or truncate at base, undulate or sinuately dentate, sometimes entire, glaucescent or greenish beneath: pistillate fls. maroon-red, 2–2.5 cm. across, the staminate smaller, numerous, pale purple, on pedicels 1–3 mm. long: fr. 6–8 cm. long, pale purple, edible. Fl.v. B.M.7485(c). S.Z.1:t.78(c). A.G.1891:140. G.W.13:438. (*A. lobata* Decne.) C. China to Japan. Intr. before 1890. Zone V. Similar to the preceding species, but less handsome.—**A. t. austràlis** (Diels) Rehd., var. Lfts. ovate to ovate-oblong, entire or nearly so, subcoriaceous: pistillate fls. to 3 cm. across. C. and W. China. Intr. 1907. Probably tenderer.

4. **SINOFRANCHÉTIA** Hemsl. Deciduous twining shrub: terminal buds large, with about 9 imbricate mucronate glabrous outer scales: lvs. long-

stalked, 3-foliolate; the lateral lfts. short-stalked, oblique: fls. unisexual, probably dioecious, short-pediceled, in long, bractless racemes; sepals 6, obovate; nectaries 6; stamens (or staminodes in the pistillate fl.) free, 6; carpels 3, developing into ellipsoid many-seeded berries; seeds ovoid, compressed. (After Adrien Franchet, French botanist, who described many new Chinese plants; 1834–1900.) Monotypic.

S. chinénsis (Franch.) Hemsl. Climbing to 10 m., glabrous: lfts. 3, large, short-acuminate, dark green above, glaucescent beneath with yellowish veins and darker veinlets, subchartaceous, the terminal one rhombic-obovate to broad-obovate, cuneate at base, on a stalk 2–3 cm. long; the lateral ones obliquely ovate, 7–11 cm. long, very oblique at base and nearly rounded, short-stalked: racemes with the peduncle 10–30 cm. long: fls. 5–6 mm. across, whitish, on pedicels 2–3 mm. long: about 2 cm. long, lavender-purple; seeds 5–6 mm. long, black. Fl.v; fr.ix–x. H.I.29:2842. (*Holboellia c.* Diels.) C. and W. China. Intr. 1907. Zone VII? With large lvs. resembling those of Phaseolus in size and shape.

24. SARGENTODOXACEAE Stapf. SARGENTODOXA FAMILY

Deciduous twining shrub; buds with several imbricate scales: lvs. alternate, long-petioled, 3-foliolate: fls. dioecious, campanulate, in pendulous racemes on slender petioles with 2 minute bractlets; sepals 6, petaloid; nectaries 6, minute, suborbicular; staminate fls. with 6 stamens and few to many aborted carpels in the centre; filaments short, anthers oblong; pistillate fls. with very numerous spirally arranged 1-ovuled subulate-lanceolate free carpels on a globose or oblong torus and with 6 staminodes: fr. consisting of an ovoid torus with numerous stipitate subglobose berry-like carpels, each with a globose-ovoid seed truncate at base, with copious endosperm and a small straight embryo.—One monotypic genus in China.

SARGENTODÓXA Rehd. & Wils. Characters of the family. (After C. S. Sargent, director of the Arnold Arboretum; 1841–1927; Greek *doxe*, glory.)

S. cuneàta (Oliv.) Rehd. & Wils. Climbing to 7 m. or more: lfts. 3, unequal, short-acuminate, light green below, the terminal one rhombic-ovate, cuneate at base, 7–12 cm. long, on a stalk 5–10 mm. long, the lateral ones slightly larger, subsessile, semi-ovate, very oblique at base and palmately 2–3-veined: staminate fls. 1–1.2 cm. long, greenish yellow, fragrant, in pendulous racemes 10–15 cm. long; pedicels about 1.5 cm. long: mature carpels about 8 mm. long, dark blue and bloomy, on a fleshy stipe to 12 mm. long; seed 5 mm. long. Fl.v; fr.ix–x. B.M.9111,9112(c). (*Holboellia c.* Oliv., partly.) E. and C. China. Intr. 1907. Zone VII? With large lvs. resembling those of Phaseolus; valued for its fragrant yellowish fls.

25. BERBERIDACEAE Torr. & Gray. BARBERRY FAMILY

Herbs or woody plants: lvs. alternate, simple or compound; petioles dilated at base or stipulate: fls. perfect, solitary, or in cymes, racemes or panicles: sepals and petals imbricated, usually in whorls of 3, rarely 2 or 4; stamens free, as many as petals and opposite to them; filaments short; anthers opening with 2 valves, rarely by a longitudinal slit: ovary superior, consisting of one carpel, with few to many ovules, rarely only one, on the ventral suture or at base; style short or wanting; stigma usually peltate: fr. a berry or pod;

seeds anatropous, with endosperm; embryo usually small, straight.—Ten genera with more than 200 species distributed through the n. hemisphere, only Berberis extending in S. Amer. to the Straits of Magellan.

A. Lvs. compound, evergreen; unarmed shrubs.
  B. Lvs. tripinnately compound; lfts. entire: fls. white.........................1. *Nandina*
  BB. Lvs. simply pinnate; lfts. usually toothed: fls. yellow.......................2. *Mahonia*
AA. Lvs. simple or occasionally 3-foliolate: deciduous or evergreen: spiny shrubs, rarely unarmed.
  B. Lvs. usually simple with occasional 3-foliolate lvs. mixed in: unarmed half-evergreen
    shrub ....3. *Mahoberberis*
  BB. Lvs. always simple, deciduous or evergreen: usually spiny shrub.............4. *Berberis*

1. NANDÌNA Thunb.

Evergreen shrub: lvs. usually thrice pinnate; rachis articulate; lfts. entire: fls. in large terminal panicles; sepals in numerous whorls of 3, gradually passing into the white petals; nectaries 3 or 6; anthers opening with longitudinal slit: fr. a 2-seeded globular berry. (Its Japanese name.) Monotypic.

N. doméstica Thunb. Upright shrub with unbranched stems, glabrous: lvs. 30–50 cm. long; lfts. subsessile, elliptic-lanceolate, 3–10 mm. long, acuminate, cuneate at base, coriaceous: fls. about 6 mm. across, white, in upright panicles 20–35 cm. long: fr. globular, 8 mm. across, bright red or purplish, rarely white. Fl.vi–vii. B.M.1109(c). Gn.23:329;58:13. R.H.1923:340,t(c). G.M.51:665. C. China to Japan. Intr. 1804. Zone VII? Evergreen shrub with graceful foliage tinged red when unfolding, changing to purple in autumn; chiefly valued for its large panicles of bright red fr.

2. MAHÒNIA Nutt.

Evergreen unarmed shrubs, rarely small trees: terminal buds with numerous persistent pointed scales: lvs. alternate, oddpinnate, rarely 3-foliolate; lfts. usually spinose-dentate, the lateral sessile; stipules minute, subulate: fls. yellow in usually many-fld. racemes or panicles springing from the axils of the bud-scales; sepals 9; petals 6: ovary usually with few ovules: fr. dark blue and bloomy, rarely red or whitish. (After Bernard M'Mahon, a prominent American horticulturist; 1775–1816.) Syn.: *Odostemon* Raf. About 50 species in N. and C. Am. and in E. and S. Asia.— Most species are susceptible to the Black Stem Rust (Wheat Rust) of cereals, but Nos. 1, 2 and 5 are immune or highly resistant.

A. Lfts. leathery, 3–13.
  B. Petioles 2–5 cm. long; lfts. 3–9, spinulose-dentate.
    c. Lvs. dull green above; plant rarely exceeding 0.25 m., stoloniferous.....1. *M. repens*
    cc. Lvs. lustrous dark green above; plant 1–2 m. high..................2. *M. Aquifolium*
  BB. Petioles 5–15 mm. long; lfts. 7–13, sinuately spiny-toothed...............3. *M. pinnata*
AA. Lfts. rigidly coriaceous, sinuately spiny-toothed.
  B. Lfts. 3–7, 1–2.5 cm. long: racemes few-fld..............................4. *M. Fremontii*
  BB. Lfts. 9–19, large.
    c. Stem scarcely 0.25 m. high; petioles 4–12 cm. long......................5. *M. nervosa*
    cc. Stems tall: petiole short...6. *M. Bealii*

1. M. rèpens (Lindl.) G. Don. Stoloniferous shrub, to 0.25 m. high: lfts. 3–7, broad-ovate to ovate, 3–6 cm. long, spinulose-dentate, dull bluish green above, with distinct papillae below, leathery; petioles 2–3 cm. long: racemes 3–7 cm. long, clustered at end of the brs.: fr. black, bloomy, 6–7 mm. thick. Fl.v; fr.ix. B.R.1176(c). L.B.19:1847(c). (*Berberis r.* Lindl., *B. Aquifolium* Brit.; *Odostemon Aquifolium* Rydb., *B. nana* Greene.) B. C. to N. Mex. and Calif. Intr. 1822. Zone V. Low suckering shrub, less handsome than *M. Aquifolium*; the lvs. not changing to red in fall.—**M. r. rotundifòlia** (May) Jouin, var. Shrub to 1 m.: lfts. usually 5–7, broad-ovate, finely and sparingly serrate or nearly entire. R.H.1907:163. Gs.4:222. (*Berberis rotundifolia Herveyi* Hort.)—**M. r. subcordàta** Rehd., f. Lfts. 5–7, crowded and overlapping, broad-ovate, subcordate at base, with few mucronate spreading teeth.—**M. r. macrocárpa** Jouin, var. Upright, to 1 m.: lfts. 5–7, spiny-dentate, slightly lustrous: fr. larger. This is possibly a hybrid of this species and the following.

2. **M. Aquifòlium** (Pursh) Nutt. Shrub to 1, rarely 2 m. tall: lfts. 5–9, ovate to oblong-ovate, 3.5–8 cm. long, rounded or truncate at base, sinuately spiny-dentate, lustrous dark green above, rarely dull, without distinct papillae below, stiff and leathery; petioles slender, 2–5 cm. long: racemes fascicled, erect, 5–8 cm. long, at end of the brs.: fr. bluish black, bloomy, about 8 mm. across. Fl.ɪv–v; fr.ɪx. B.R.1425(c). L.B.18:1718(c). S.B.II.1:t94(c). Gn.86: 260(h). (*Berberis A.* Pursh, *B. nutkana* Kearney.) B. C. to Ore. Intr. 1823. Zone V. With dark green lvs. becoming purplish in fall, and bright yellow fls. in spring; prefers a partly shaded position.—**M. A. juglandifòlia** Jouin, var. Lfts. usually 7, often subcordate, smaller and of thicker texture; rachis usually red.

M. A. × *Fortunei* = M. heterophýlla (Zab.) Schneid. Lfts. 5–7, lanceolate, 4–8 cm. long, spiny-toothed, lustrous above. (*Berberis h.* Zabel, not Juss., *B. toluacensis* Hort.) Origin unknown.—*M. A.* × *pinnata;* see under No. 3.—*M. A.* × *Berberis vulgaris* = *Mahoberberis Neuberti;* see p. 225.

Related species: **M. grácilis** (Hartw.) Fedde. Shrub to 1.5 m.; lfts. 5–11, ovate to ovate-lanceolate, 3.5–6 cm. long, entire or obscurely crenulate-denticulate, lustrous above: fr. with distinct style. S.H.1:f.201,k,l. Mex. Cult. 1900? Zone VII?

3. **M. pinnàta** (Lag.) Fedde. Upright shrub to 4 m.: lfts. 7–13, ovate to ovate-lanceolate, sinuately spiny-toothed, slightly lustrous above, without distinct papillae and green beneath; petioles very short: fls. pale yellow, in fascicled racemes 6–8 cm. long, axillary along the stem: fr. globose-ovoid, purplish black. B.M.2396(c). B.R.702(c). R.H.1907:162. (*Berberis p.* Lag., *B. Aquifolium* var. *fascicularis* Bean, *M. fascicularis* DC.) Calif. and N. Mex. to Mex. Intr. 1819. Zone VII. Taller than *M. Aquifolium* and with similar foliage, but duller.

M. p. × *Aquifolium* = M. Wàgneri (Jouin) Rehd. Upright shrub to 2.5 m.: lfts. 7–11, usually ovate-oblong, with 4–7 teeth on each side, dark green and slightly lustrous above; petioles 5–30 mm. long: fls. and fr. like *M. pinnata*. M.D.1910:89(h). (*M. pinnata* var. *W.* Jouin.) Orig. before 1863. Zone VI? Similar in habit to *M. pinnata*, but hardier.

4. **M. Fremóntii** (Torr.) Fedde. Shrub to 4 m.: lfts. 3–7, ovate-oblong to lanceolate, 1.5–4 cm. long, with few large spiny teeth on each side, dull bluish green, rigidly coriaceous; petiole very short: fls. pale yellow, on slender pedicels to 2 cm. long in the axils of minute lanceolate bracts in few-fld. racemes: fr. subglobose, 8–15 mm. across, bluish black. Fl.v–vɪ; fr.vɪɪɪ. G.F.1: 497. B.C.4:1971. (*Berberis F.* Torr.) W. Tex. to Colo. and Calif. Cult. 1895. Zone VI. Upright shrub with pale bluish green small foliage and comparatively large bluish black fruit.

Closely related species: **M. haematocárpa** (Woot.) Fedde, chiefly distinguished by its red fruit about 8 mm. across. M.G.32:89(h). (*Berberis h.* Woot.) N. Mex., Colo. Intr. 1916. Zone VII? Handsome in fr. which like that of the following species is used for jams.—**M. Swaseÿi** (Buckl.) Fedde. Shrub to 1.5 m.: lfts. 5–11, elliptic to oblong-lanceolate, thinner, reticulate: infl. with broadovate bracts about 5 mm. long: fr. about 1 cm. across, red. Jour. Hered. 12:427. (*Berberis S.* Buckl.) Tex. Intr. 1917. Zone VII?—**M. trifoliolàta** (Moric.) Fedde. Shrub to 2.5 m.: lfts. 3, rigid; petiole 5–50 mm. long: fr. red. B.R.31: 10(c). F.S.1:t.56(c). (*Berberis t.* Moric.) N. Mex. and Tex. to Mex. Intr. 1839. Zone VII.

5. **M. nervòsa** (Pursh) Nutt. Shrub to 0.5 m. tall, usually lower; the stem with conspicuous persistent lanceolate bud-scales 2–3 cm. long: lvs. with the stalk 18–40 cm. long; lfts. 11–19, obliquely ovate to ovate-lanceolate, 4–8 cm.

long, with 3–5 nerves at base, sinuately spiny-dentate, lustrous above, pale beneath, rigidly coriaceous; petioles 5–12 cm. long: fls. bright yellow in erect racemes 10–20 cm. long: fr. ovoid, dark blue, bloomy, about 8 mm. across. Fl.v–vi; fr.vii–viii. B.M.3949(c). B.R.1426(c). L.B.18:1701(c). (*Berberis n.* Pursh.) B. C. to Calif. Intr. 1822. Zone V. With large lustrous lvs.

6. **M. Beàlei** (Fort.) Carr. Shrub to 4 m., with stout upright stems: lvs. 30–40 cm. long; lfts. 9–15, roundish ovate to ovate-oblong, 5–12 cm. long, with 2–5 large spiny teeth on each side, the lateral ones very oblique at base, the lowest pair much smaller and close to the base of the petiole, the terminal lft. stalked, truncate or subcordate at base, larger, dull dark bluish green above, glaucescent beneath, rigidly coriaceous; petioles 1–2 cm. long: fls. lemon-yellow, fragrant, in fascicled upright stout racemes 8–15 cm. long, fls. crowded, on pedicels about 5 mm. long, with small bracts at base: fr. bluish black. B.M.4846,4852(c). F.S.6:t.79. Gn.87:574(h);88:107(h);89:171. M.O.60(h). (*M. japonica* var. *B.* Fedde, *Berberis B.* Fort.) China. Intr. 1845. Zone (V). With large lvs. and large clusters of pale yellow fragrant fls. In cult. usually as *M.* or *Berberis japonica.*

Related species: **M. japónica** (Thunb.) DC. Similar to *M. Bealei;* lfts. usually ovate-oblong, 4–10 cm. long, with 1–3 teeth on the upper and 5–6 teeth on the lower side, mostly pointing forward, yellowish green beneath, less rigid: racemes 10–20 cm. long, rather lax, the fls. nodding, on slender pedicels 6–7 mm: or sometimes to 1 cm. long, with conspicuous ovate bracts: fr. dark purple, bloomy. Thunberg, Icon. Pl. Jap. 4.t.2. Gn.89:171. Cult. in Japan, rare in western gardens.—**M. Fortùnei** (Lindl.) Fedde. Shrub to 1.2 m.: lfts. 7–13, lanceolate to linear-lanceolate, cuneate, with 5–15 teeth on each side, 6–12 cm. long; petiole 2–5 cm. long, green beneath. S.H.1:201,f.u-v. China. Intr. 1846. Zone VII.—*M. F.* × *Aquifolium;* see under No. 2.—Probably not hardy within our area is **M. napaulénsis** DC. With up to 25 ovate to ovate-lanceolate lfts. lustrous above. P.F.3:t.79(c). (*B. nepalensis* Spreng.) Himal., India. Cult. 1850.

3. × **MAHOBÉRBERIS** Schneid. Unarmed half-evergreen shrub; a hybrid between *Mahonia Aquifolium* and *Berberis vulgaris,* the only one known so far between these two genera. Resembles Mahonia in the unarmed brs., in the solitary, not fascicled lvs. on the shoots and the occurrence of 3-foliolate or pinnate lvs.; the influence of Berberis is shown in the usually simple lvs., thinner and serrulate on the older brs., while those of the shoots are more coriaceous and sinuately spiny: fls. and frs. not known.

M. Neubérti (Baumann) Schneid. Shrub to 2 m.: lvs. usually simple, obovate-oblong or oblong, 3–7 cm. long, cuneate at base, serrulate or those of the shoots sinuately spiny, or compound with 3–5 lfts. (*Berberis N.* Baumann, *M. N.* var. *ilicifolia* Schneid.) Orig. before 1854.—**M. N. latifòlia** Schneid., var. Lvs. of the shoots broader, truncate or broad-cuneate at base. (*B. latifolia, B. ilicifolia* Hort., not Forst.)—Subevergreen shrub of little ornamental value.

4. **BÉRBERIS** L. Barberry. Evergreen or deciduous spiny shrubs, rarely small trees; the inner bark and wood yellow: lvs. alternate, simple, those of the shoots changed into usually 3-parted spines, the normal lvs. appearing in fascicles on short axillary spurs: fls. yellow in elongated or umbel-like, rarely compound racemes, or solitary or fascicled; sepals 6, with 2 or 3 bractlets below; petals 6, often smaller than the sepals and usually with 2 nectariferous glands at base; stamens 6, irritable, the anthers opening with 2 valves; ovary with 1 to many ovules; stigma sessile or on a short style: fr. a 1- to several-seeded red to black berry. (Name derived from the Arabic

name of the fr.) About 175 species, particularly well developed in E. and C.
Asia and in S. Am., few in N. Am., Eu. and N. Afr.—Almost all species are
desirable ornamental shrubs with handsome foliage, evergreen in some species
and in many deciduous ones assuming bright tints in fall, with conspicuous,
mostly bright yellow fls. in spring, and variously colored, often scarlet frs. in
fall and often persisting during the winter. Unfortunately most species are
alternate hosts of the pernicious wheat rust or black stem rust (*Puccinia
graminis*) of cereals, and their propagation and distribution is prohibited in
the northern central and some adjoining states, except the following which
are immune or highly resistant: Nos. 1, 3, 5, 6, 6 x 10, 12, 13, 13 x 35, 14, 17,
20, 35, 43, 46, and *B. candidula, sanguinea, aemulans, Edgeworthiana, Beaniana*
and *B. Potaninii*.

I. Lvs. evergreen or half-evergreen

A. Lvs. entire.
  B. Lvs. elliptic to obovate: fls. solitary.....................................1. *B. buxifolia*
  BB. Lvs. narrow-oblong to linear.
    c. Fls. 1–2: lvs. linear..2. *B. empetrifolia*
    cc. Fls. 2–6 in peduncled umbels: lvs. narrow-oblong..................3. *B. stenophylla*
AA. Lvs. dentate (sometimes entire in Nos. 4, 26, and 28).
  B. Brts. pubescent, puberulous or verruculose.
    c. Lvs. green beneath; brts. pubescent or puberulous.
      D. Lvs. evergreen, 1–3 cm. long, obovate: fls. in racemes.............5. *B. Darwinii*
      DD. Lvs. half-evergreen, 2.5–8 cm. long: fls. in panicles.................26. *B. Chitria*
    cc. Lvs. glacous or glaucescent beneath.
      D. Fls. in racemes or panicles: lvs. 2.5–8 cm. long: brts. puberulous..28. *B. Lycium*
      DD. Fls. 1–2: lvs. 1–2.5 cm. long: brts. verruculose...................6. *B. verruculosa*
  BB. Brts. glabrous: fls. in fascicles or solitary.
    c. Lvs. thinly coriaceous.
      D. Lvs. glaucous beneath.
        E. Brts. angled: lvs. half-evergreen.
          F. Lvs. obovate to broad-elliptic with several teeth on each side.
              16. *B. concinna*
          FF. Lvs. usually obovate-oblong with 1–2 teeth on each side or entire.
              4. *B. heterophylla*
        EE. Brts. terete: lvs. evergreen.
          F. Lvs. elliptic to elliptic-oblong, spiny-toothed: fls. yellow.....7. *B. pruinosa*
          FF. Lvs. lanceolate, with 1–2 small aristate teeth on each side: fls. whitish,
            tinged red ....8. *B. triacanthophora*
      DD. Lvs. green beneath, lanceolate to narrow-lanceolate.
        E. Young brts. reddish: fr. bloomy; pedicels 2–3.5 cm. long..........9. *B. Veitchii*
        EE. Young brts. yellowish: lvs. rarely more than 1 cm. broad.
          F. Fr. ovoid, bloomy, with sessile stigma: pedicels 1–2 cm. long.
              10. *B. Gagnepainii*
          FF. Fr. subglobose, jet-black, with distinct style: pedicels 0.5–1 cm. long.
              11. *B. atrocarpa*
    cc. Lvs. strongly coriaceous, rigid, narrow-elliptic to oblong-lanceolate.
      D. Lvs. green beneath.
        E. Brts. terete, reddish when young: lvs. slightly reticulate beneath.
              12. *B. Sargentiana*
        EE. Brts. slightly angled, yellowish brown when young: lvs. with the veinlets in-
          visible ....13. *B. Julianae*
      DD. Lvs. glaucous or white beneath (except in var. of No. 14).........14. *B. Hookeri*

II. Lvs. deciduous

A. Fls. solitary or fascicled or sometimes in few-fld. umbels (in very short dense panicles
  in No. 22).
  B. Lvs. all entire, small.
    c. Young brts. glabrous: lvs. not reticulate: fls. slender-stalked.....35. *B. Thunbergii*
    cc. Young brts. puberulous: lvs. reticulate: fls. in very short-stalked dense clusters.
              22. *B. Wilsonae*
  BB. Lvs. dentate or only partly entire.
    c. Fls. solitary on short pedicels not exceeding 5 mm.
      D. Lvs. green and reticulate beneath, finely toothed...................16. *B. sibirica*
      DD. Lvs. glaucous beneath, often entire: brts. usually bloomy.....15. *B. dictyophylla*
    cc. Fls. on slender pedicels or in umbels.
      D. Lvs. with rather remote teeth, often entire.
        E. Brts. terete or nearly so, red-brown and lustrous the second year: fr. bluish
          black and bloomy.
          F. Lvs. obovate to obovate-oblong, 1–1.5 cm. broad, bright green, usually
            toothed ....36. *B. virescens*

    FF. Lvs. broad-elliptic to obovate, 1.5-2.5 cm. broad, grayish green, usually
        entire ....32. *B. heteropoda*
  EE. Brts. grooved or angled, dull brown or gray.
    F. Fls. 1-2.
      G. Brts. puberulous: lvs. entire or with 1 or 2 teeth on each side.
                                        21. *B. angulosa*
      GG. Brts. glabrous: lvs. spiny-dentate..........................17. *B. concinna*
    FF. Fls. several, occasionally 1 or 2.
      G. Fls. 2-8, on a peduncle, rarely 1; pedicels 1-2.5 cm. long.
        H. Fr. with distinct style: fls. usually 2-5: lvs. usually serrate.
                                     18. *B. diaphana*
        HH. Fr. with sessile or subsessile stigma: fls. 3-8: lvs. usually entire.
                                     19. *B. yunnanensis*
      GG. Fls. in dense clusters: lvs. entire or 3-toothed at apex, 0.6-2 cm. long.
                                    22. *B. Wilsonae*
  DD. Lvs. closely setose-serrulate.
    E. Brts. grooved, dull grayish: lvs. obovate: fls. usually 2....20. *B. circumserrata*
    EE. Brts. angled, red-brown: lvs. oblong-obovate: fls. in 3-6-fld. umbels.
                                    41. *B. Sieboldii*

AA. Fls. in panicles. (**AAA** follows)
  B. Brts. angled: lvs. not exceeding 3.5 cm.
    c. Infl. 1-4 cm. long, upright...23. *B. aggregata*
    cc. Infl. 5-12 cm. long, pendulous.....................................24. *B. polyantha*
  BB. Brts. terete; lvs. 3-8 cm. long: infl. 5-12 cm. long.
    D. Brts. glabrous: lvs. deciduous.
      E. Fr. red: lvs. acute, serrate...........................27. *B. Francisci-Ferdinandi*
      EE. Fr. purple-black, bloomy: lvs. obtuse, often entire..............33. *B. oblonga*
    DD. Brts. puberulous: lvs. half-evergreen, often entire.
      E. Lvs. green beneath: infl. paniculate; peduncle 2-4 cm. long.....26. *B. Chitria*
      EE. Lvs. glaucescent beneath: infl. racemose or paniculate; peduncle usually short.
                                    28. *B. Lycium*

AAA. Fls. in simple racemes. (See also species under No. 27.)
  B. Lvs. glabrous.
    c. Brts. glabrous.
      D. Lvs. entire, all or most of the flowering brs.: brts. brown or purplish the second
        year.
        E. Brts. grooved or angled: fr. bright red.
          F. Lvs. obovate to obovate-oblong, glaucescent beneath.
            G. Racemes umbel-like; 3-10-fld.: lvs. always entire..35. *B. Thunbergii* var.
            GG. Racemes usually many-fld.; pedicels 1-2 cm. long: lvs. often serrate.
                                  34. *B. Silva-Taroucana*
         FF. Lvs. oblanceolate or oblong: racemes many-fld.
          G. Bracts at least ½ as long as the short pedicels: lvs. entire.
            H. Pedicels 1-2 mm., in fr. sometimes to 4 mm. long: racemes dense; fls.
              3-4 mm. across...31. *B. Vernae*
            HH. Pedicels 3-5 mm. long, in fr. sometimes 1 cm. long: racemes not
              dense; fls. about 6 mm. across..........................37. *B. Poireti*
          GG. Bracts much shorter than the slender pedicels: lvs. sometimes dentate.
                                    38. *B. chinensis*
        EE. Brts. terete or slightly angled.
          F. Racemes short, 5-7-fld.; ovules 4-6, long-stipitate: fr. bluish black.
                                    32. *B. heteropoda*
         FF. Racemes dense, many-fld.; ovules 2-3, subsessile
          G. Fr. dark red, bloomy: lvs. with stomata above........30. *B. turcomanica*
          GG. Fr. pale red: lvs. without stomata above..............29. *B. nummularia*
    DD. Lvs. serrate or dentate.
      E. Brts. brown, red or purple the second year.
        F. Lvs. remotely dentate or serrulate, occasionally entire; veinlets usually
        indistinct beneath.
         G. Fr. bright red.
           H. Pedicels 4-10 mm. long.
            I. Lvs. glaucescent beneath, often obtuse.
             J. Brts. slightly verruculose: pedicels as long or longer than the
              short-ovoid fr. ....39. *B. canadensis*
             JJ. Brts. smooth: pedicels usually shorter than the oblong-ovoid fr.
                                  44. *B. Henryana*
           II. Lvs. light green beneath, acute, elliptic-oblong to oblanceolate.
             J. Brts. nearly terete: fr. globose-ovoid, about 6 mm. long; pedi-
              cels 5 mm. long...40. *B. Fendleri*
             JJ. Brts. grooved: fr. oblong-ovoid, 1 cm. long; pedicels about 1 cm.
              long ....38. *B. chinensis*
           HH. Pedicels 1-2 cm. long: lvs. broad-obovate to elliptic, glaucescent
            beneath ....34. *B. Silva-Taroucana*
         GG. Fr. dark purple, bloomy, oblong-ovoid: racemes few-fld.: brts. terete.
                                    36. *B. virescens*
        FF. Lvs. densely serrulate, never entire, reticulate beneath.
         G. Lvs. serrulate, obovate to obovate-oblong: racemes usually many-fld.

H. Brts. grooved: lvs. rounded at apex, grayish green beneath: fr. sub-
   globose ....43. *B. koreana*
HH. Brts. terete or nearly so: lvs. acute or obtuse, light green beneath: fr.
   oblong-ovoid.
   I. Lvs. all short-stalked: racemes short, nodding.42. *B. Bretschneideri*
   II. Lvs. of fertile brs. mostly on slender stalks 2–4 cm. long: racemes
      upright, 5–7 cm. long.............................45. *B. dasystachya*
   GG. Lvs. densely ciliate, narrow-elliptic to oblong or oblong-obovate: racemes
      3–6-fld., umbellate ....41. *B. Sieboldii*
EE. Brts. gray or grayish yellow the second year: fr. oblong-ovoid.
   F. Brts. nearly terete, grayish yellow: fr. purplish blue; style distinct.
                                                                   25. *B. aristata*
   FF. Brts. grooved, gray: fr. scarlet or purple; stigma sessile.
      G. Lvs. reticulate beneath, densely ciliate-serrate; petals slightly emarginate.
                                                                   49. *B. amurensis*
      GG. Lvs. setulose-dentate, not reticulate: petals entire at apex.50. *B. vulgaris*
CC. Brts. puberulous: lvs. usually oblanceolate, often entire: fls. slender-stalked, in
   racemes: fr. bluish black...28. *B. Lycium*
BB. Lvs. pubescent, acute: racemes slender; pedicels very short.
   C. Brts. and rachis of infl. pubescent.
      D. Lvs. slightly pubescent above, 2.5–5 cm. long: brts. brown........46. *B. Gilgiana*
      DD. Lvs. densely pubescent above, 4–8 cm. long: brts. gray............47. *B. mitifolia*
   CC. Brts. and rachis glabrous: lvs. glabrous above, 4–8 cm. long.........48. *B. Giraldii*

Ser. 1. BUXIFOLIAE Schneid. Lvs. evergreen, small: fls. solitary or 2–5 fascicled; ovules 2–12; stigma sessile.

1. **B. buxifòlia** Poir. Evergreen upright shrub to 3 m.; brts. brown,
usually puberulous, grooved; spines 3-fid or simple, usually not longer than
1.5 cm.: lvs. obovate to elliptic, 1–2.5 cm. long, spiny-pointed, cuneate at base,
entire: fls. 1–2, orange-yellow, on slender pedicels 2–2.5 cm. long: fr. subglobose, dark purple. B.M.6505(c). L.B.20:1941(c). G.W.7:414. (*B. dulcis*
Sweet.) Chile, Strait of Magellan to Valdivia. Intr. 1826. Zone (V). Compact shrub, one of the hardiest of the evergreen barberries.—**B. b. nàna**
Mouillef., var. Dwarf compact form.—**B. b. pygmaèa** (Koehne) Usteri.
Dwarf tufted form with slender unarmed brts., and partly juvenile, stalked
and serrate lvs.—**B. b. spinosíssima** Reiche, var. Spines to 3 cm. long, usually
longer than the lvs.

2. **B. empetrifòlia** Lam. Evergreen shrub to 0.5 m.; brts. slender, often
prostrate, slightly angled, glabrous, often bloomy: spines 3-fid or simple, 5–15
mm. long: lvs. linear, 5–20 mm. long, spiny pointed, entire and strongly
revolute at the margin, bright green; fls. 1–2, golden-yellow, 8 mm. across,
on slender pedicels 5–15 mm. long: fr. nearly black. B.R.26:27(c). S.B.4:350
(c). Chile to Strait of Magellan. Intr. 1827. Zone VI? Suited for the
rockery.

B. e. × *Darwinii;* see No. 3.
Related species: **B. linearifòlia** Phil. To 3 m. high; brts. angular: lvs. linear-
oblong to narrow-elliptic, 2–4 (–6) cm. long, dark green above, glaucescent
below, slightly recurved at margin: fls. 3–7, orange to crimson, 1.5 cm. across:
fr. ellipsoid, dark blue-black. B.M.9526(c). Chile. Intr. 1927. Zone VII.—
B. l. × *Darwinii;* see under No. 5.

3. × **B. stenophýlla** Lindl. (*B. Darwinii* × *empetrifolia*.) Evergreen
shrub to 3 m.: brts. slender, terete, puberulous; spines usually 3-fid, 3–7 mm.
long: lvs. narrow-lanceolate, 1.5–2.5 cm. long, spiny-pointed, with revolute
margin, dark green above, whitish beneath: fls. golden yellow, 1 cm. across,
in small fascicles or short 2–6-fld. racemes; pedicels 5–10 mm. long: fr. subglobose, 6–7 mm. across, black, bloomy. F.M.4:252(c). G.C.III.7:619. R.H.
1906:417;1913:535,t(c). Gn.86:259,408(h) ;87:92(h). Orig. before 1864. Zone
(V). Many forms reverting more or less to one or the other parent have
been raised from seed.

Ser. 2. ACTINACANTHAE Schneid. Lvs. evergreen or half-evergreen, usually
toothed: fls. solitary or fascicled or in umbel-like racemes; ovules 2–6; style
short or wanting.

4. B. heterophýlla Juss. Half-evergreen shrub to 1.5 m.; brts. yellowish brown, glabrous, grooved; spines 3–7-fid, 1–2 cm. long: lvs. narrowly obovate and entire, or obovate with 3–5 large spiny teeth, 1–3 cm. long: fls. solitary; pedicel about .8 mm. long; sepals and petals incurved: fr. black, bloomy. H.E.1,t.14(c). Chile to Strait of Magellan. Cult. 1823. Zone VII? Very spiny straggling shrub.

Related species: **B. actinacántha** Mart. Half-evergreen; brts. pubescent; spines 3-parted or sometimes leaf-like: lvs. broad-obovate to oblong, 1–3 cm. long, sparingly spiny: fls. 3–6, fascicled. B.R.31:55(c). Chile. Intr. before 1845. Zone VII.—**B. hakeoìdes** (Hook. f.) Schneid. Evergreen shrub to 4 m.; spines small or leafy: lvs. suborbicular, 1.5–3 cm. long, rounded or subcordate at base, spiny-toothed: fls. in dense subglobose clusters: fr. bluish black. B.M.6770 (c). G.C.29:295. B.S.1:241. (*B. congestiflora* var. *h.* Hook. f.) Chile. Intr. 1861. Zone VII?

Ser. 3. ILICIFOLIAE Schneid. Lvs. evergreen, usually toothed: fls. racemose; ovules 3–5; style distinct.

5. B. Darwìnii Hook. Evergreen upright shrub to 3.5 m.; brts. subterete, red-brown, short-pilose; spines slender, 3–7-parted, 3–7 mm. long: lvs. obovate to obovate-oblong, 1–3 cm. long, cuneate at base, remotely spiny-toothed and usually 3-spined at apex, lustrous and dark green above, light green beneath: fls. golden-yellow, tinged with red, in pendulous racemes 4–10 cm. long: fr. ovoid, about 8 mm. long, dark purple, with long style. B.M.4590(c). F.S.7: t.663(c). R.H.1913:525,t.,f.1(c). Gn.86:260(h). Chile. Intr. 1849. Zone VII? With lustrous dark green lvs. and golden-yellow fls. in spring.

B. D. × *linearifolia* = **B. lologénsis** Sandwith. Lvs. rhombic-elliptic or rhombic-obovate with few unequal teeth to linear and entire: fls. in racemes or umbels; pedicels 5–15 mm. long. Argentine. Cult. 1933.—*B. D.* × *empetrifolia;* see No. 3.

Related species: **B. ilicifòlia** Forst. Evergreen straggling shrub with grooved glabrous or puberulous brts.: lvs. obovate, 2–5 cm. long, with a few spiny teeth toward the apex: fls. orange-yellow, in dense short racemes. B.M.4308(c). S. Chile. Intr. about 1843. Zone VII?

Ser. 4. WALLICHIANAE Schneid. Lvs. evergreen, elliptic to narrow-lanceolate: fls. solitary or fascicled, 2–25; ovules 1–8; style very short or wanting: fr. purple-violet or black.

6. B. verruculòsa Hemsl. & Wils. Evergreen shrub to 1.5 m. high; brts. terete, densely verruculose; spines slender, 3-parted, 1–2 cm. long: lvs. elliptic or ovate to ovate-lanceolate, 1.5–2.5 cm. long, remotely spiny-toothed with revolute margin, lustrous dark green above, glaucous beneath: fls. 1–2, 1.5 cm. across, golden-yellow; pedicel 5–10 mm. long: fr. ellipsoid, about 8 mm. long, violet-black, bloomy; stigma sessile. B.M.8454(c). M.G.32:34(h). S.L. 27(h). W. China. Intr. 1904. Zone (V). Dense shrub with glossy dark green lvs. and large yellow fls.

B. v. × *Gagnepainii* = **B. Chenaùltii** Chenault. Brts. slightly verruculose: lvs. narrow-oblong, 2–3.5 cm. long, spiny-toothed, glaucous beneath. Cult. 1928.

Related species: **B. candídula** Schneid. Dwarf shrub; brts. glabrous: lvs. elliptic, 1.5–3 cm. long, with few spiny teeth, white beneath; fls. solitary, pedicel 1–1.5 cm. long. V.F.15. Gs.13:26,f.3. (*B. Wallichiana* var. *pallida* Bois.) C. China. Intr. 1894. Zone V.—*B. c.* × *Gagnepainii* = **B. hybrido-Gagnepainii** Suringar. Lvs. about 4 cm. long, spiny-toothed, glaucous beneath. Gs.13:26,f.7. Cult. 1929.

7. B. pruinòsa Franch. Evergreen shrub to 3 m.; brts. terete, yellowish or brownish yellow; spines stout, 3-parted, 1–3 cm. long: lvs. strongly coriaceous, obovate or elliptic to elliptic-oblong, 2.5–5 cm. long, spiny-toothed, lustrous dark green above, white beneath: fls. 8–25; pedicels about 1 cm. long, fascicled or on a short peduncle: fr. oblong-ovoid, 6–7 mm. long, bluish black,

bloomy. N.H.9:39. S. W. China. Intr. 1894. Zone VII? Handsome evergreen shrub of vigorous growth.

B. p. × *diaphana?* = B. Vilmorìnii Schneid., which differs chiefly in the
grooved brts., in the thinner and smaller lvs. with smaller and more numerous
teeth and in the few-fld. infl. Orig. before 1905.

8. **B. triacanthóphora** Fedde. Shrub to 1.5 m., with spreading slender
brs.; brts. reddish, becoming red-brown the 2d year; spines slender 1–2.5 cm.
long: lvs. lanceolate to narrow-lanceolate, 2–5 cm. long, 4–8 mm. wide, with
1–5 small setose teeth on each side, bright above, glaucous or glaucescent
beneath: fls. 2–5, fascicled, subglobose, 7–8 mm. across, whitish, tinged red;
pedicels slender, 1.2–3 cm. long: fr. ellipsoid, 7–8 mm. long, blue-black, slightly
bloomy. Fl.v. C. China. Intr. 1907. Zone V. One of the hardiest of the
evergreen barberries.

9. **B. Veìtchii** Schneid. Evergreen shrub; brts. subterete, reddish when
young, yellowish gray the second year; spines stout, 3-parted, 2–5 cm. long:
lvs. lanceolate, 6–12 cm. long, sinuately spiny-toothed, dark green above,
lighter beneath, with indistinct veinlets, thinly coriaceous: fls. 1 cm. across,
in 4–8-fld. fascicles; pedicels 2–3.5 cm. long; ovules 2–4: fr. oblong, 1–1.2 cm.
long, black, bloomy. Veitch, Novelties, 1907:13. Gs.13:26,f.1. (*B. acuminata*
Veitch, not Franch.) C. China. Intr. 1900. Zone VI?

B. V. × *vulgaris?* = B. Vanfleètii Schneid. Brts. slightly terete: lvs. elliptic,
acute, spinose-serrate, with 8–12 teeth on each side, chartaceous: fls. in umbel-
like racemes: fr. dark cherry-red, slightly pruinose. Orig. before 1915.

10. **B. Gagnepaìnii** Schneid. Evergreen shrub to 2 m.; brts. terete, slightly
verruculose, yellowish gray; spines slender, 3-parted, 1–2 cm. long: lvs.
narrow-lanceolate, 3–10 cm. long, sinuately spiny-serrate, with revolute margin, light green beneath and indistinctly veined, thinly coriaceous: fls. in
fascicles of 3–10, 1 cm. across, bright yellow; pedicels 1–2 cm. long: fr. ovoid,
8–10 mm. long, bluish black, bloomy, with nearly sessile stigma. B.M.8185(c).
G.C.46:226. M.G.32:1(h). Gn.89:585(h). (*B. acuminata* Stapf, not Franch.)
W. China. Intr. 1904. Zone (V).

B. G. × *verruculosa;* see under No. 6.—*B. G.* × *candidula;* see under No. 6.
Closely related species: **B. sanguínea** Franch. Brts. smooth, grooved; lvs.
narrower, often nearly linear, with revolute margin and fewer teeth (6–15
pairs): pedicels and outside of fls. red. V.F.16. W. China. Intr. 1898. Zone
VII?—**B. replicàta** W. W. Sm. Brts. terete, yellowish; lvs. 2–3.5 cm. long, about
8 mm. wide, with 1–6 pairs of teeth, strongly revolute: fr. black. B.M.9076(c).
J.L.49:t.13(h). S. W. China. Intr. 1917.—**B. taliénsis** Schneid. Brts. grooved,
yellowish: lvs. oblong-lanceolate, 2–3.5 cm. long, 10–12 mm. wide. W. China.
Intr. ?1921. Zone VII?

11. **B. atrocárpa** Schneid. Evergreen shrub to 2 m.; brts. yellowish,
grooved; spines 1–4 cm. long: lvs. lanceolate or oblanceolate to oblong-
lanceolate, 2.5–7 cm. long, unequally spiny-serrate with spreading teeth, yellowish green beneath with indistinct veins, coriaceous: fls. 6–12, fascicled,
8–12 mm. across; pedicels 5–10 mm. long: fr. short-ovoid, 5 mm. long, jet-
black, not bloomy at maturity, with a short, but distinct style. B.M.8857(c).
(*B. levis* Bean, not Franch.) W. China. Intr. 1909. Zone VII?

Related species: **B. lèvis** Franch. Lvs. with fewer aristate subequal teeth
pointing forward: fr. bloomy. W. China. Intr. ?—**B. sublèvis** W. W. Sm. Brts.
angled: lvs. subcoriaceous, linear- to narrow-lanceolate, spinose-serrulate, veins
visible beneath: fr. red? G.C.101:437. (*B. Wallichiana* var. *microcarpa* Hook.
f. & Thoms.) S.W. China, E. Himal. Cult. 1935.

12. **B. Sargentiàna** Schneid. Evergreen shrub to 2 m.; brts. terete, reddish
while young, yellowish gray or grayish brown the 2nd year; spines rigid, 3-
parted, 1–3 cm. long: lvs. elliptic-oblong or oblong to oblong-lanceolate, 4–10

cm. long, rather closely spiny-serrate, dark green above, light green and
slightly reticulate beneath, firmly coriaceous: fls. fascicled, yellow, about 1
cm. across; pedicels 1–2 cm. long; ovary 2–3-ovuled: fr. ovoid, 6–7 mm. long,
bluish black, slightly bloomy; stigma sessile. C. China. Intr. 1907. Zone VI?
  Related species: **B. Soulieana** Schneid. Brts. gray, subterete: lvs. narrow-
lanceolate, usually spiny-serrate, 4–10 cm. long, 8–15 mm. broad, pale and indistinctly or scarcely veined beneath: fr. ovoid, bloomy, with short style; pedicels
1–1.5 cm. long. (*B. stenophylla* Hance, not Lindl., ? *B. sanguinea* Lemoine, not
Franch.) C. China. Intr. 1897. Zone VI?—**B. insígnis** Hook. f. & Thoms.
Brts. subterete, red-brown: lvs. oblong-lanceolate, 5–12 cm. long, acuminate,
spiny-serrate, green beneath, with elevated secondary veins: pedicels 5–10 mm.
long; ovules usually 4: fr. ovoid-oblong, black. Sikkim-Himal. Cult. ?—**B. i.
tongloénsis** Schneid., var. Brts. yellowish gray. Intr. about 1850? Zone VII?
—**B. dumícola** Schneid. Lvs. elliptic-lanceolate to elliptic-oblong, 4–10 cm. long,
densely and unequally serrulate: fls. small, reddish outside: fr. 1–2-seeded, with
short style. W. China. Intr. 1921. Zone VII?

13. B. Juliànae Schneid. Evergreen shrub to 2 m.; brts. slightly angled,
yellowish when young, light yellowish gray or yellowish brown the 2nd year;
spines rigid, 3-parted, 1–3 cm. long: lvs. narrow-elliptic to lanceolate or oblanceolate, 3–6 cm. long, spiny-serrate, dark green above, much paler and indistinctly veined beneath, rigidly coriaceous: fls. fascicled; pedicels 1–2 cm.
long; ovules 1–2: fr. ovoid-oblong, about 8 mm. long, bluish black, bloomy,
with a short, but distinct style. M.G.32:35(h). S.L.103(h). C. China. Intr.
1900. Zone (V). Of upright habit; one of the hardiest evergreen barberries.
  B. J. × *Thunbergii* = **B. mentorénsis** L. M. Ames. Brts. strongly grooved:
lvs. subcoriaceous, elliptic-ovate, 2–4.5 cm. long, sparingly spinulose toothed,
pale beneath: fls. 1–2: fr. ellipsoidal, dull dark red. H.B.13:48(h). Orig. 1924.
Zone V.
  Closely related species: **B. Bergmánniae** Schneid. Lvs. smaller, 3.5–6 cm.
long, sinuately serrate with 3–8 strong teeth on each side, pale and lustrous
beneath: fr. very bloomy, on reddish pedicels about 1 cm. long. W. China. Intr.
1908. Zone VII?

14. B. Hoòkeri Lem. Shrub to 2 m.; brts. slightly grooved, grayish brown:
lvs. elliptic to oblong-lanceolate, 2.5–7 cm. long, acuminate, sinuately spiny-
serrate, white beneath, secondary veins elevated: fls. 3–6, clustered, greenish
yellow, about 1.8 cm. across; pedicels 1–2 cm. long; ovules usually 3, stipitate:
fr. oblong, 1 cm. long, black-purple; stigma sessile. B.M.4656,9153(c). N.F.
1:f.18(h). (*B. Wallichiana* Hook., not DC.) Himal. Cult. 1859. Zone VII.—
B. H. víridis Schneid., var. Lvs. green beneath.
  Related species: **B. hypokèrina** Airy-Shaw. Shrub to 75 cm.: lvs. oblong-
elliptic, to 15 cm. long, sinuately spiny-serrate, silvery white beneath: fls. 6–10;
ovules about 4: fr. blue-violet; stigma subsessile. Burma. Cult. 1930. Zone
VII?—**B. Cóxii** Schneid. Brts. subterete: lvs. elliptic-oblong, to 7 cm. long,
closely serrate, lustrous above, white beneath: ovules 4–5: fr. bluish black,
slightly bloomy. Burma. Cult. 1928.—**B. calliántha** Mulligan. Shrub to 1 m.:
lvs. elliptic to elliptic-oblong, 2–6 cm. long, impressed-reticulate above: fls. 1–3,
2.5 cm. across; pedicels 2–4 cm. long; ovules 7–9: fr. ovoid to oblong-ovoid, 1–1.3
cm. long. G.C.97:390,391. N.F.10:f.85. S.E. Tibet. Intr. 1925. Zone VII?

  Ser. 5. ANGULOSAE Schneid. Lvs. usually deciduous, often papillose beneath: fls. usually 1–3, rarely 5; ovules 2–8; style wanting or very short: fr. red
or pink.

15. B. dictyophýlla Franch. Deciduous shrub to 2 m.; brts. slightly angular, usually reddish and very glaucous while young, red-brown the second
year; spines 3-parted, 5–15 mm. long: lvs. obovate to obovate-oblong, 1–2.5
cm. long, usually entire and rounded at the apex, sometimes spiny-toothed,
bright green and reticulate above, chalky-white beneath: fls. solitary, pale
yellow, 1.5 cm. across, short-stalked: fr. ovoid, 1 cm. long, red, with short, but
distinct style. Franchet, Pl. Delav. t.11. (*B. d. f. albicaulis* Hesse.) W. China.

Cult. 1890. Zone (V).—**B. d. epruinòsa** Schneid., var. Brts. more strongly angled, not bloomy: lvs. glaucescent or nearly green beneath. Intr. 1910.— **B. d. approximàta** (Sprague) Rehd., var. Lvs. 0.6–1.5 cm. long, mostly spiny-toothed: fls. smaller. B.M.7833(c). B.S.1:239(as *B. dictyophylla*). (*B. a.* Sprague.) Intr. about 1892.

16. **B. sibírica** Pall. Deciduous shrub, to 0.5 m.; brts. angled, gray or grayish brown the second year; spines 3–5-, or sometimes 7–11-parted, slender, 3–8 mm. long: lvs. obovate to obovate-oblong, 1–2.5 cm. long, sinuately spiny-toothed with spreading teeth, green and reticulate beneath: fls. 1–2, 1 cm. across, on short pedicels, nodding: fr. ovoid, 7 mm. long, red. B.R.6:487(c). G.O.t.64(c). S.H.1:309,f.194t–u. Siberia. Intr. before 1781. Zone IV?—Low densely branched shrub with small bright green lvs.

B. s. × *vulgaris;* see under No. 50.

17. **B. concínna** *Hook.* f. Deciduous or half-evergreen shrub, to 1 m.; brts. grooved, pale brown the second year; spines 3-parted, 1–2 cm. long: lvs. obovate, 1–3.5 cm. long, remotely spiny-dentate, bright green above, white and reticulate beneath: fls. 1–2, 1–1.5 cm. across; pedicels 2–3 cm. long: fr. oblong, 1.5–2 cm. long, red. B.M.4744(c). Sikkim-Himal. Intr. about 1850. Zone VI? Desirable shrub with handsome lvs., white beneath, and large bright yellow fls.

18. **B. diáphana** Maxim. Deciduous shrub to 1 or 2 m.; brts. rather stout, grooved, yellowish or yellowish gray; spines 8–30 mm. long: lvs. obovate to oblong-obovate, 2–3.5 cm. long, obtusish, spinose-serrulate or sometimes entire, glaucous and reticulate beneath: fls. bright yellow, 1.5 cm. across, solitary or 2–5 on a common peduncle; pedicels 1.5–2 cm. long; ovules 6–12: fr. ovoid-oblong, often attenuated at apex, with short style, 1–1.5 cm. long, bright or pale red, slightly bloomy. B.M.8224(c, as *B. yunnanensis*). S.T.2:t.109. M.G.32:90(h,fr.). W. China. Intr. 1894. Zone V. Lvs. turning scarlet in fall.

B. d. × *pruinosa;* see under No. 7.

Related species: **B. aémulans** Schneid. which differs chiefly in the reddish or purplish brts.: fr. 1.5–1.8 cm. long; pedicels 2–3 cm. long, 1–3, without or very short peduncle. W. China. Intr. 1908. Zone V.—**B. Tíschleri** Schneid. Brts. reddish or purple: lvs. rarely entire: infl. a 4–10-fld. raceme; ovules 3–5: fr. about 1 cm. long, with distinct style. W. China. Intr. 1910. Zone VI?

19. **B. yunnanénsis** Franch. Shrub to 2 m.; brts. reddish or yellowish, grooved; spines to 2.5 cm. long: lvs. obovate to obovate-oblong, 2–3.5 cm. long, obtuse or acutish, usually entire, on shoots often sparingly spinulose-serrate, slightly reticulate and green beneath: fls. 3–8, pale yellow, 1.5 cm. across, in short racemes or nearly umbellate, peduncled or sessile; pedicels 1–2.5 cm. long: fr. ovoid, 1.5 cm. long, bright red, with sessile or subsessile stigma. S.H.1:f.198h–n;2:f.573c. W. China. Cult. 1904. Zone VI.

Related species: **B. Faxoniàna** Schneid. Brts. slightly angled, often reddish: lvs. obovate-oblong, 1.5–3 cm. long, with 4–10 spreading teeth on each side: infl. 2–6-fld.: fr. ellipsoid, purple, with a very short style. Origin unknown, probably intr. from W. China before 1900. Zone V.—**B. consímilis** Schneid. Brts. grooved, yellowish brown, gray when older: lvs. obovate-oblong, 1.5–2 cm. long, spinulose-dentate: infl. 3–8-fld.; ovules usually 4: fr. ellipsoid, purple; stigma sessile. Origin unknown, cult. since 1904.—**B. tsarongénsis** Stapf. Brts. red to brown: lvs. obovate or elliptic to oblanceolate, 1.5–3.5 cm. long, entire or spinose-dentate with 1–4 teeth on each side: fls. 7–8 mm. across, in 3–8-fld. fascicles or umbel-like racemes; pedicels 5–15 mm. long: fr. oblong-ellipsoid, 1 cm. long, dark red. B.M.9332(c). W. China. Intr. 1917. Zone VI?

20. **B. circumserràta** Schneid. Upright shrub to 1 m.; brts. grooved, yellowish or slightly reddish; spines 1–5-parted, to 2.5 cm. long: lvs. obovate to obovate-oblong, 1.5–3.5 cm. long, rounded at apex, cuneate at base, densely

spinulose-serrate, those of the shoots sometimes nearly entire, reticulate and whitish beneath: infl. 1–3-fld.; peduncle to 2.5 cm. long; fls. yellow, 1 cm. across; ovules usually 4: fr. ellipsoid-oblong, 1.3–1.5 cm. long including the distinct style, yellowish red. N. W. China. Intr. 1911. Zone V. Similar to *B. diaphana,* but lvs. densely serrulate.

21. **B. angulòsa** Wall. Upright shrub to 1.5 m.: brts. grooved, puberulous; spines 1–5-parted, to 1.5 cm. long: lvs. obovate to oblong-obovate, 1.5–3.5 cm. long, with 1–3 spiny teeth on each side or entire, slightly revolute, whitish beneath: fls. solitary, globose, 1.5 cm. across, orange-yellow, on stalks 1–2.5 cm. long, or in short 2–4-fld. racemes: fr. ellipsoid, 1.5 cm. long, red. B.M. 7071(c). Himal. Intr. about 1850. Zone VI?

Related species: **B. suberécta** Ahrendt. Brts. glabrous: lvs. elliptic-obovate to elliptic-oblong, 1.2–3 cm. long, remotely setose-dentate: infl. 5–6-fld.; pedicels 6–10 mm. long: fr. oblong-ovoid, 1 cm. long, deep rosy-red; stigma subsessile. (*B. Giraldi* hort., not Hesse.) Orig. unknown. Cult. 1939.

Ser. 6. POLYANTHAE Schneid. Lvs. deciduous or half-evergreen: infl. paniculate, sometimes reduced to a short and dense raceme: fr. red; ovules 2–5; style distinct.

22. **B. Wilsònae** Hemsl. & Wils. Deciduous or half-evergreen shrub: brts. with very short internodes, angled, puberulous at first, yellowish or brownish red, brown or grayish brown the second year; spines 3-parted, slender, 1–2 cm. long: lvs. oblanceolate, 6–20 mm. long, obtuse or sometimes acutish and mucronulate, dull pale green above, glaucescent beneath, reticulate on both sides: fls. about 7 mm. across, golden yellow, in 3–many-fld. dense fascicles, or in short dense panicles not exceeding 1.5 cm.; pedicels 2–4 mm. long: fr. subglobose, 5–6 mm. long, salmon- or coral-red, often paler on one side, with short distinct style. B.M.8414(c). Gs.1:180,t(c),185. G.C.42:372. Gn.89:537. R.H.1920:9(h). W. China. Intr. 1903. Zone (V). Low, densely branched, very spiny shrub, sometimes prostrate, with small lvs. assuming brilliant autumnal tints and with profuse light red berries.—**B. W. Stapfiàna** Schneid., var. Brts. glabrous: lvs. oblanceolate to obovate-oblong, mucronulate: infl. 4–7-fld.: fr. ellipsoid. B.M.8701(c). (*B. Stapfiana* Schneid.) W. China. Cult. 1894. Zone VII?—**B. W. subcaulialàta** Schneid., var. Brts. glabrous, strongly angled: lvs. obovate to oblong-obovate, occasionally with 1 or few teeth near the apex, whitish beneath: infl. 6–8-fld. R.H.1920:29(h). G.C.79:24. Gn.85:501. (*B. s.* Schneid., *B. Coryi* Veitch.) W. China. Intr. 1894. Zone VII?— Probably "Tom Thumb," a dwarf dense form, is a form of this species. Gn. 87:555(h).

B. W. × *? aggregata* = **B. rubrostílla** Chittenden. Lvs. obovate-spatulate, 1–2 cm. long, entire and partly spiny-toothed; fr. ovoid, scarlet, about 1.5 cm. long, in pendulous few-fld. panicles or racemes, to 2 cm. long. G.C.60:236. Gn. 80:563;85:580. J.L.42:f.65. Orig. before 1916.—Here belong probably: "Comet" with ovoid coral-red frs. in dense, profusely produced clusters. G.C.75:59. Gn. 87:578.—"Autumn Beauty" with coral-red frs. in short panicles. G.C.74:209.— "Lady Beatrice Stanley" with subglobose coral-red frs. in short, dense, pendulous panicles. G.C.72:283. Gn.86:569.—Other named forms see Gn.85:566,567, 581.

Related species: **B. parvifòlia** Sprague. Low dense shrub: lvs. obovate-oblong to obovate, 5–15 mm. long, remotely spiny-dentate or sometimes entire, glaucescent: fls. 6 mm. across, in dense 2–10-fld. racemes shorter than lvs., pedicels 2–5 mm. long; fr. broad-ellipsoid, 6 mm. long, red, bloomy. W. China. Cult. 1896. Zone V.—**B. àrido-cálida** Ahrendt. Lvs. broad-elliptic to obovate, sparsely spiny-serrulate, often entire on shoots: pedicels 1–2 mm. long: fr. elliptic-oblong. N. W. China. Intr. 1916. Zone V?

23. **B. aggregàta** Schneid. Shrub to 3 m.; brts. strongly angled, puberulous, grayish brown the second year; spines 3-parted, slender, 1–2 cm. long:

lvs. obovate to obovate-oblong, 1–2.5 cm. long, spinulose-serrate or sometimes sparingly spiny-toothed, rarely entire, reticulate and glaucescent beneath: fls. pale yellow, about 6 mm. across, in sessile dense panicles 1–4 cm. long; pedicels 1–3 mm. long: fr. globose-ovoid, 5–6 mm. long, red, bloomy, with distinct style. Gn.88:645. S.L.101. M.G.32:82(fr.),83(h). (*B. Geraldii* Veitch.) W. China. Intr. 1908. Zone V. Densely branched shrub, handsome in fr.—**B. a. Práttii** (Schneid.) Schneid. Lvs. to 3.5 cm. long, usually obovate, often entire: panicles 3–6 cm. long, subsessile, or to 10 cm. long and peduncled. B.M.8549(c). S.L.102(h). (*B. P.* Schneid., *B. brevipaniculata* Bean, not Schneid.) W. China. Intr. 1904. Zone V.—**B. a. recurvàta** Schneid., var. Lvs. usually oblong-obovate, often entire: panicles, including the 1.5–3.5 cm. long stalk, 4.5–10 cm. long, cylindric, its lower brts. very short, 2–4-fld.; pedicels recurved in fr.: fr. subglobose, about 5 mm. long, scarlet. W. China. Intr. 1908. Zone V.

B. a. ? × *Wilsonae;* see under No. 22.

Related species: **B. Edgeworthiàna** Schneid. Lvs. elliptic to elliptic-lanceolate, 1.5–3 cm. long, acute, spiny-serrate, green beneath and coarsely reticulate: infl. 1.5–3 cm. long: fr. oblong, 8–10 mm. long, red; stigma subsessile. N. W. Himal. Intr. 1920. Zone VI?

24. **B. polyántha** Hemsl. Upright shrub to 4 m.; brts. angled, glabrous or slightly puberulous, grayish brown or dull brown the second year; spines solitary or 3-parted, 1–2 cm. long: lvs. obovate or broad-obovate, 1.5–3 cm. long, rounded at apex, spiny-dentate, rarely entire, dull green above, glaucescent or glaucous below, finely reticulate on both sides, fls. deep yellow, about 1 cm. across, in pendulous much-branched panicles 5–12 cm. long; pedicels 1–5 mm. long: fr. oblong-ovoid, 7–8 mm. long, 3–4 mm. thick, salmon red, narrowed into a distinct style. Gn.84:583;85:581. G.C.62:183;72:263. Gs.13: 193. W. China. Intr. 1904. Zone VI? Distinct with its large panicles of deep yellow fls.

Ser. 7. Tinctoriae Schneid. Lvs. deciduous or half-evergreen, usually obovate-oblong or obovate-lanceolate: fls. in umbel-like or simple racemes or in panicles; ovules 1–4, style usually distinct.

25. **B. aristàta** DC. Deciduous shrub to 3 m.; brts. nearly terete, gray or yellowish brown the second year: spines simple or 3-parted, to 3 cm. long: lvs. obovate-elliptic or obovate to obovate-oblong, 2.5–6 cm. long, acute or obtuse, spiny-dentate or sometimes entire, light green or whitish beneath and slightly reticulate, chartaceous at maturity: fls. bright yellow, often reddish outside, in 10–25-fld. racemes 5–10 cm. long: fr. oblong, about 1 cm. long, red or finally purple, bloomy, with short style; pedicels shorter or as long as the fruit. Bentley & Trimen, Med. Pl. 1:t.16(c). B.S.1:235. N. W. Himal. Intr. about 1820. Zone V.—**B. a. coriària** (Royle) Schneid., var. Young brts. grooved. B.R.27:46(c). (*B. c.* Royle, *B. aristata* var. *floribunda* Bean, partly.) N. W. Himal. Intr. 1835.

B. a. × *vulgaris* = **B. macracántha** Schrad. Tall shrub to 4 m.; brts. grooved or nearly terete, usually yellowish gray the second year; spines to 3 cm. long; lvs. usually obovate, remotely spinulose-serrate; racemes long, 10–20-fld.; fr. ellipsoid, purple; style short or wanting; the lower pedicels longer than frs. (? *B. alksuthiensis* Usteri.) Orig. about 1830.

Related species: **B. kewénsis** Schneid. Brts. angled, red-brown: lvs. narrow-elliptic to elliptic-obovate, 2.5–5 cm. long, spiny-serrate, glaucescent and distinctly veined beneath: infl. 4–8 cm. long; fls. 10 mm. across: fr. oblong-ovoid, 1 cm. long, dark violet, bloomy, with short style. Orig. unknown, possibly hybrid. Cult. 1889. Zone (V).

26. **B. Chítria** Lindl. Deciduous or half-evergreen shrub, to 3 m. or occasionally to 6 m.; young brts. terete or slightly grooved, puberulous, yellowish

gray to reddish brown the second year; spines; usually simple, to 3 cm. long: lvs. obovate or elliptic to obovate-lanceolate, 2.5–8 cm. long, acute or acutish, entire or with 1–5 teeth on each side, bright green beneath, slightly reticulate on both sides: infl. paniculate, pendulous, many-fld., peduncled; pedicels 5–10 mm. long; fls. pale yellow, about 1 cm. across; ovules 4–5, stipitate: fr. elliptic-oblong, 1.2 cm. long, dark red or purple, bloomy, with distinct style. B.R.9:729(c). B.M.2549(c). (*B. aristata* Sims, not DC.) Himal. Intr. 1820. Zone VII?

B. ? c. × *?* = **B. Spaèthii** Schneid. Brts. subterete, glabrous: lvs. elliptic to ovate-oblong or obovate, spinulose-serrate, light green or grayish beneath: infl. paniculate or racemose: fr. purple, bloomy, with very short style. Origin unknown; cult. 1902.

27. B. Francísci-Ferdinándi Schneid. Shrub to 3 m.; brts. nearly terete or slightly angled, purplish when young, red-brown the second year; spines usually simple, to 2.5 cm. long: lvs. ovate to ovate-lanceolate, 2–7 cm. long, spiny-dentate, rarely nearly entire, green beneath and somewhat lustrous, slightly reticulate; petioles 5–15 mm. long: fls. about 8 mm. across, in pendulous peduncled panicles 5–12 cm. long; pedicels to 1 cm. long; ovules 2, subsessile; fr. ellipsoid, 1.2 cm. long, scarlet, with very short style. B.M.9281(c). W. China. Intr. 1900. Zone V. Conspicuous with its drooping panicles of scarlet frs.

Related species: **B. Beaniàna** Schneid. Brts. slightly angled, reddish while young, gray when older; spines 3-parted, to 2 cm. long; lvs. elliptic-lanceolate, acute, 2–4 cm. long, spiny-dentate, whitish beneath: fls. 6 mm. across, in 10–20-fld. panicles to 4 cm. long; ovules 3–4, subsessile: fr. about 1 cm. long, purple, bloomy; stigma sessile. B.M.8781(c). G.C.72:351. Gn.83:591. (*B. Veitchii* Hort. Veitch.) W. China. Intr. 1904. Zone VI?

Related species with racemose infl.: **B. Jamesiàna** Forr. & W. W. Sm. Lvs. obovate to oblong-obovate, 1–3 cm., on shoots to 10 cm. long, entire or spinulose-serrulate, finely reticulate: fls. 6 mm. across, in pendulous racemes 2–10 cm. long, sometimes branched at base: fr. globose, coral-red. B.M.9298(c). G.C.78:168. W. China. Intr. 1913. Zone VII?—**B. leptóclada** Diels. Brts. purple, bloomy: lvs. obovate to oblong-obovate, 1–2 cm. long, obtuse and mucronate, entire or with few spiny teeth, reticulate: racemes few-fld., slender-peduncled; pedicels to 1 cm. long: fr. with short style. W. China. Cult. 1928. Zone VII.— **B. pallens** Franch. Brts. purple-brown, grooved: lvs. oblanceolate, 1.5–3 cm. long, obtuse and mucronate, entire or with few teeth, glaucescent beneath, reticulate: fls. 1 cm. across, in sessile, 5–12-fld. racemes, 2–5 cm. long; pedicels 5–20 mm. long: fr. oblong-ovoid, 1 cm. long, bluish purple, bloomy, with distinct style. W. China. Intr. 1929. Zone VI?

Ser. 8. ASIATICAE Schneid. Lvs. evergreen or half-evergreen, pale green or whitish and papillose beneath: fls. in racemes, panicles or fascicles; ovules 3–5, sessile; style short.

28. B. Lýcium Royle. Half-evergreen shrub to 3 m.; brts. terete, puberulous, yellowish gray, gray the second year; spines 3-parted, to 2 cm. long: lvs. oblanceolate to obovate-lanceolate, 2–5 cm. long, acute or obtuse and mucronulate, entire or with few teeth, light green above, glaucescent and papillose beneath: fls. bright yellow, in 10–20-fld. racemes, usually elongated, sometimes paniculate, to 10 cm. long, rarely short and umbel-like; pedicels to 2 cm. long: fr. ellipsoid, 8–12 mm. long, purple, bloomy, with distinct style. B.M.7075(c). (*B. ruscifolia* Lav., not Lam., *B. elegans* Hort.) Himal.: Kashmir to Nepal. Intr. about 1850. Zone VII.

Related species: **B. lycioìdes** Stapf. Brts. glabrous: lvs. oblanceolate, entire or slightly toothed, glaucescent, but not papillose beneath: infl. usually paniculate; fls. 1 cm. across; pedicels 5–10 mm. long; fr. ellipsoid-oblong, 1–1.2 cm. long, black-purple, with blue-white bloom. B.M.9102(c) Himal. Cult. 1925. Zone VII?

Ser. 9. INTEGERRIMAE Schneid. Lvs. deciduous, petioled, lanceolate to broad-obovate, entire or serrate, usually grayish green and reticulate on both sides: racemes elongated, dense, spike-like; ovules 2–4, subsessile or short-stipitate: fr. red; stigma sessile.

29. **B. nummulària** Bge. Shrub to 3 m. tall; brts. terete, purple and bloomy when young, purplish brown the second year; spines usually simple, 1–3 cm. long: lvs. oblong-obovate to oblanceolate, 2–4 cm. long, obtuse or acutish, gradually narrowed into a petiole 5–15 mm. long, entire or rarely with a few teeth, glaucescent and reticulate on both sides, subchartaceous; fls. yellow, 5–6 mm. across, in dense many-fld. racemes 3–5 cm. long; ovules 2–3; pedicels 3–6 mm. long in fr.: fr. globose-ovoid, 5–6 mm. long, red or pale red. Turkest., N. Persia. Intr. before 1878. Zone V. Spreading shrub with pale bluish green lvs.—The form described above is var. **pyrocárpa** (Reg.) Schneid.; the typical form differs in its broad-obovate lvs. S.H.1:f.198p-q.

Closely related species: **B. iliénsis** Popov. Lvs. oblong-lanceolate to lanceolate-spatulate; pedicels 5–7 mm. long, 4–6 times longer than bracts. C. Asia. Intr. 1936. Zone V.

30. **B. turcománica** Karelin. Shrub to 3 m.; brts. nearly terete or slightly grooved, usually purple and bloomy while young, purplish brown the second year; spines simple or 3-parted, 1–2.5 cm. long: lvs. very unequal, petioled, obovate-oblong, 2.5–4 cm. long, obtuse, narrowed at base into a petiole 1–2.5 cm. long, entire or sparingly spinulose-serrate, glaucescent on both sides and reticulate: fls. bright yellow, about 8 mm. across, in 12–25-fld., usually rather dense racemes 4–7 cm. long; ovules 3–4, subsessile; pedicels to 1 cm. long: fr. ellipsoid, to 9 mm. long, dark red, bloomy. S.H.1:f.198r-v'. Turkest. and N. Persia to Armenia. Cult. 1880. Zone V. Similar to the preceding species.— **B. t. integerrima** (Bge.) Schneid., var. (*B. i.* Bge.) has the lvs. papillose beneath, while the typical form and the following var. have no papillae.—**B. t. densiflòra** Schneid. Racemes denser; pedicels to 6 mm. long. Nouv. Mem. Soc. Nat. Mosc. 12:t.3,f.2. (*B. d.* Boiss. & Buhse, *B. integerrima* var. *serratifolia* Boiss.) N. Persia. Intr. before 1906. Zone V.

31. **B. Vérnae** Schneid. Shrub to 2 m.; brts. grooved, purplish; spines usually simple and short, sometimes to 3 cm. long: lvs. very unequal, spatulate to oblanceolate, 1–2.5 cm. long, rarely to 4 cm. long, obtuse, rarely acute, nearly always entire, green and slightly reticulate on both sides: fls. yellow, 3–4 mm. across, in dense racemes with the short peduncle 1.5–4 cm. long; pedicels 1–3 mm. long; ovules 2, sessile: fr. globose, about 5 mm. across, pale red. B.M.9089(c). M.G.32:82. (*B. Caroli* var. *hoanghensis* Schneid.) N. W. China. Intr. 1910. Zone V. Graceful spreading shrub with dense racemes of small fls.

Ser. 10. HETEROPODAE Schneid. Lvs. deciduous, petioled, usually entire: fls. in fascicles or in umbel-like or elongated racemes, sometimes compound at base: ovules 2–6, stipitate: fr. bluish black.

32. **B. heterópoda** Schrenk. Shrub to 2 m.; brts. terete, brown, lustrous, grayish brown the second year; spines simple or 3-parted, to 2.5 cm. long, sometimes wanting: lvs. broad-ovate to obovate or elliptic, 2–5 cm. long, obtuse, abruptly contracted at base into a petiole to 2 cm. long, entire or finely serrate, grayish green above, glaucous beneath, slightly reticulate on both sides: fls. orange-yellow, fragrant, 1.2 cm. across, in short, 3–8-fld. umbel-or fascicle-like racemes; pedicels to 1.5 cm. long; ovules 4–6, long-stipitate: fr. subglobose or ovoid, about 1 cm. long, black, bloomy; stigma sessile; seeds usually 3. G.F.8:455. B.C.1:591. Turkest. Intr. 1876. Zone V. Spreading shrub with bluish green lvs. and fragrant fls.

B. h. × ? *vulgaris* = **B. notàbilis** Schneid. Tall upright shrub; brts. slightly grooved, grayish brown while young: lvs. obovate to obovate-oblong, nearly always serrate: racemes elongated, 14–20-fld.: fls. smaller: fr. elliptic-ovoid, dark red, bloomy. Orig. 1895.

33. B. oblónga (Reg.) Schneid. Shrub to 2 m. or more; brts. terete or slightly grooved, chestnut-brown, lustrous, little changing the second year; spines simple or 3-parted, 5–15 mm. long: lvs. very unequal, obovate-oblong to elliptic, 2–5.5 cm. long, obtuse, abruptly contracted at base, entire or remotely serrulate, grayish green above, glaucescent beneath, slightly reticulate on both sides; fls. yellow, about 1 cm. across, in 10–20- or occasionally to 50–fld. panicles; pedicels 6–10 mm. long; ovules 2–3, short-stipitate: fr. ellipsoid, about 1 cm. long, purplish black, bloomy, with a very short style; seed usually 1. (*B. heteropoda* var. *o.* Reg.) Turkest. Intr. about 1874. Zone V. Similar to the preceding species, but with larger infl.

Ser. 11. TSCHONOSKYANAE Schneid. Similar to the preceding group, but fr. red and ovules 2, subsessile.

34. B. Silva-Taroucàna Schneid. Shrub to 3 m.; brts. grooved, reddish brown, older grayish; spines usually simple, small or wanting: lvs. obovate-oblong to oblong-lanceolate, 1.5–5.5 cm. long, obtuse, usually contracted at base into a petiole to 2 cm. long, entire or remotely serrate, green above, pale and pruinose beneath, slightly reticulate on both sides: fls. yellow, about 8 mm. across, in 8–12-fld. racemes 3–7 cm. long; pedicels 1–2 cm. long: fr. globose-ovoid, to 1 cm. long, scarlet; stigma sessile. W. China. Intr. 1908. Zone V.

Closely related species: **B. Mouillacàna** Schneid. which differs chiefly in the lvs. being lustrous green beneath and in the purplish brown brts.: pedicels 5–13 mm. long. W. China. Intr. 1908. Zone V.

Ser. 12. SINENSES Schneid. Brts. more or less purplish or red-brown the second year: lvs. deciduous, lanceolate to obovate, usually entire or remotely toothed: fls. in racemes, sometimes short, fascicle-like, rarely solitary; ovules 1–2; fr. usually red; stigma sessile.

35. B. Thunbérgii DC. Much-branched shrub to 2.5 m.; brts. strongly grooved, yellowish or purplish red, purple-brown the second year; spines usually simple, 5–18 mm. long: lvs. very unequal, obovate to spatulate-oblong, 1–3 cm. long, obtuse, rarely acute, narrowed at base into a petiole 2–10 mm. long, quite entire, bright green above, glaucescent beneath: fls. yellow, reddish outside, 8–10 mm. across, solitary or 2–4 and fascicled or umbellate and peduncled; pedicels 6–10 mm. long: fr. ellipsoid, about 1 cm. long, bright red. B.M.6646(c). G.F.2:53. A.F.8:526(h). (*B. sinensis* K. Koch, not Desf., *B. japonica* Hort.) Japan. Intr. about 1864. Zone V. Dense shrub much used for hedges; lvs. turning scarlet in fall, the bright red frs. remaining nearly unchanged during the winter.—**B. T. argénteo-marginàta** Schneid., f. Lvs. variegated with white. G.C.49:10 (as "Silver Beauty").—**B. T. atropurpúrea** Chenault. Lvs. deep purple.—**B. T. mìnor** Rehd., var. Low dense form, scarcely exceeding 0.5 m.; lvs. 1 cm. or less long. M.G.32:90(h). S.L.99(h). (*B. T.* var. *Dawsonii* Bean.) Orig. before 1900.—**B. T. erécta** Rehd., f. TRUEHEDGE B. Brs. strictly upright forming a dense column. H.B. 13:48(h).—**B. T. plurifìòra** Koehne, f. Infl. subumbellate, 4–10-fld.—**B. T. Maximowíczii** (Reg.) Reg., var. Lvs. narrower, usually acute, green beneath.

B. T. × *vulgaris* = **B. ottawénsis** Schneid. It differs chiefly in the 5–many-fld. umbellate or sometimes racemose infl., in the often serrate lvs. and in the yellowish brown, rarely purplish brts.; from *B. vulgaris* it may be distinguished by the color of the brts., by the obovate often entire lvs. usually not exceeding 3 cm., and by the shorter, usually subumbellate infl. (*B. auricoma* Lemoine.)

Cult. 1889.—**B. o. purpúrea** Schneid., var. Lvs. purple or purplish.—*B. T.* ×
Julianae; see under No. 13.

36. **B. viréscens** Hook. Shrub to 3 m. with slender upright brs.; brts.
terete, lustrous red-brown the second year; spines simple or 3-parted, slender,
1–2 cm. long: lvs. obovate to obovate-oblong, 1.5–3 cm. long, rounded or
mucronate at apex, remotely toothed or entire, bright green above, glaucous
beneath: fls. pale yellow, in few-fld. peduncled, usually umbel-like racemes;
pedicles slender, about 1 cm. long: fr. oblong, about 1 cm. long, purple,
bloomy. B.M.7116(c). Sikkim-Himal. Intr. about 1850. Zone V.—**B. v.
macrocárpa** Bean, var. Fr. larger, nearly black.
Related species: **B. oritrépha** Schneid. Brts. brighter red; spines stouter
and longer: lvs. more reticulate, partly setose-serrate, glaucescent beneath:
umbel-like racemes 3–6-fld., often subsessile. N. China. Intr. 1911. Zone V.

37. **B. Poiréti** Schneid. Shrub to 2 m.: brts. slender, grooved, purplish
brown; spines small, usually simple, about 5 mm. long; lvs. oblanceolate
to narrow-oblanceolate or lanceolate-spatulate, 1.5–4 cm. long, acute and
mucronulate, cuneate at base, entire, bright green above, light or grayish
green beneath, slightly reticulate: fls. bright yellow, reddish outside, about
6 mm. across, in peduncled, 8–15-fld. racemes: pedicels in fr. about 5 mm.
long; bracts 2.5–3.5 mm. long: fr. ovoid-oblong, about 1 cm. long, bright red.
B.S.1:248. (*B. sinensis* DC., partly, not Desf., *B. sinensis* var. *angustifolia*
Reg.) N. China, Amurl. Intr. about 1860. Zone IV. Shrub with spreading
brs. and dense racemes of bright yellow fls.
B. ? P. × *canadensis* = B. durobrivénsis Schneid., with reddish brown brts.,
small spines, serrulate lvs. obovate-oblong to oblanceolate and the racemes often
with longer stalked fls. at the base. Orig. before 1906.
Related species differing in having the bracts much shorter than the pedicels:
B. Boschànii Schneid. Spines to 1.8 cm. long: lvs. obovate, 1–2 cm. long: fr.
ellipsoid, about 5 mm. long, coral-red. W. China. Intr. 1908. Zone VI?—**B.
thibética** Schneid. Brts. slightly angled; spines to 2.5 cm. long: lvs. obovate-
oblong, 1–2.5 cm. long, entire or with few teeth: fr. ellipsoid, about 1 cm. long,
red, with short style. W. China. Intr. 1903. Zone VI?—**B. Lecómtei** Schneid.
Lvs. oblong-obovate, to oblanceolate or lanceolate, obtusish, entire: fls. in short
racemes, sometimes subumbellate: fr. ellipsoid, crimson. W. China. Cult. 1927.
Zone VI?—**B. lepidifòlia** Ahrendt. Lvs. linear-oblanceolate, 1.5–4.5 cm. long:
infl. subumbellate; pedicels 5–10 mm. long: fr. ovoid, blue-black, slightly bloomy,
5–6 mm. long; style very short, but distinct. W. China. Intr. 1923? Zone VII?

38. **B. chinénsis** Poir. Shrub to 3 m.; brts. grooved, purple- or red-brown;
spines simple or 3-parted, 5–18 mm. long: lvs. oblanceolate to obovate-
lanceolate, 1.5–4 cm. long, acute or obtusish, entire or with few teeth, bright
green above, pale green or slightly glaucescent beneath, slightly reticulate on
both sides: fls. 6–8 mm. across, in peduncled, 10–12-fld. racemes to 7 cm.
long; pedicels in fr. 7–15 mm. long, much longer than the bracts: fr. ellipsoid
to elliptic-oblong, about 1 cm. long, dark red and often bloomy. B.M 6573(c).
G.O.t.63(c, as *B. canadensis*). (*B. sinensis* Desf., *B. spathulata* Schrad., *B.
sanguinolenta* Schrad., *B. Guimpeli* K. Koch & Bouché, *B. serotina* Lge.)
Caucas. Cult. 1808. Zone V. Similar to the preceding, but with somewhat
broader leaves.
B. ? c. × *vulgaris* = B. laxiflòra Schrad. Brts. grayish brown the first, grayish the second year: lvs. obovate-oblong, 2–5 cm. long, remotely serrulate or
sometimes entire: racemes 4–9 cm. long, usually nearly sessile. Orig. before
1838.—**B. l. oblanceolàta** Schneid., var. Lvs. oblanceolate, rather densely serrulate. Orig. unknown; before 1880.—**B. l. Langeàna** Schneid., var. Brts. purplish brown, grayish brown the second year: lvs. obovate-oblong, 2–6 cm. long,
remotely dentate. (*B. Guimpeli* Hort., not Koch.) Orig. unknown.—*B. ? c.* ×
amurensis = B. Meehànii Schneid. Brts. angled, grayish brown or brownish,
grayish the second year; spines usually simple, to 2 cm. long: lvs. obovate to

elliptic, 2.5-4 cm. long, densely serrulate, reticulate beneath: racemes 4-9 cm. long: fr. ellipsoid, red, slightly pruinose. Orig. unknown (distributed by Meehan as *B. concinna*).
    Related species: **B. crataégina** DC. Young brts. nearly terete, brown, grayish the second year; spines usually simple: lvs. oblong-ovate to oblanceolate, 1-4 cm. long, entire or with few teeth: racemes 6-20-fld.: fr. ellipsoid, purpleblack. S.H.1:f.197r-t. Asia Minor. Intr. 1835, but doubtful if now in cult. Zone V.—**B. crètica** L. Much-branched shrub, sometimes procumbent; brts. nearly terete, purplish; spines usually 3-parted, 5-20 mm. long: lvs. oblanceolate to obovate-oblong, 8-15 mm. long, obtuse or acutish, entire, slightly reticulate: fls. in 2-7-fld. fascicles or short racemes: fr. purple-black, with short style. S.F.9:t.342(c). S.H.1:f.194d-f. Greece. Intr. 1703. Zone VII?

   39. **B. canadénsis** Mill. Upright shrub to 2 m.; brts. brown to dull purple, slightly angled, grayish the second year; spines usually 3-parted, to 1.2 cm. long: lvs. obovate to obovate-oblong, 2-5 cm. long, usually obtuse, remotely spinulose, grayish white beneath, with indistinct veins, firm at maturity: fls. bright yellow, in 5-15-fld. racemes 2-4.5 cm. long; pedicels 5-10 mm. long: fr. ellipsoid to short-ellipsoid, 7-9 mm. long, scarlet. Gr.G.1:t.31. G.W.1: 101,t(c). B.B.2:127. (*B. pisifera* Raf., *B. caroliniana* Loud., *B. angulizans* Massias.) Va. to Ga. and Mo. Cult. 1730. Zone V.—Lvs. turn scarlet in fall and the bright red frs. remain a long time unchanged. Often confused with *B. vulgaris*.
   B. ? c. × *vulgaris* = **B. declinàta** Schrad. Brts. yellowish or brownish, tinged violet, brownish gray the second year: lvs. obovate-oblong to ellipticobovate, remotely serrate or subentire, grayish beneath: racemes often umbellike, usually peduncled, 3-5 cm. long; pedicels partly whorled, 5-7 mm., the lower to 1 cm. long: fr. elliptic-oblong, about 1 cm. long, blood-red. Orig. before 1830.—Var. oxyphýlla Schneid. differs chiefly in the acute, densely serrulate lvs. Origin unknown, possibly a hybrid of *B. canadensis* and *B. amurensis.*—*B. ? c.* × *Fendleri* = **B. Rehderiàna** Schneid. Brts. slender, red-brown, slightly angled; spines 3-5-parted: lvs. obovate to oblong-obovate, 2-3 cm. long, spinydentate: racemes peduncled, 8-15-fld.: fr. subglobose, 5-6 mm. across, bright red, lustrous, persisting nearly unchanged through the winter. Orig. about 1880. Zone V.—*B. c.* × *Poireti* = *B. durobrivensis;* see under No. 37.

   40. **B. Féndleri** Gray. Shrub to 1.5 m.; brts. slender, red-brown, lustrous, nearly terete; spines 3-5-parted, to 1.2 cm. long: lvs. obovate-lanceolate to obovate-oblong, 2-3.5 cm. long, acute, entire or remotely spinulose, lustrous above, green and reticulate beneath: fls. bright yellow, tinged red outside, in short 6-10-fld. slender-peduncled racemes; pedicels 4-6 mm. long: fr. shortellipsoid, 5-6 mm. long, bright red, lustrous. Clements, Rocky Mtn. Fl. t.4,f.3. S.H.1:f.197h-l. Colo. to N. Mex. Cult. 1880. Zone (V). Attractive in fall with its bright red lustrous fr. and its lvs. changing to scarlet.
   B. ? F. × *canadensis;* see under No. 39.

   41. **B. Sieboldii** Miq. Shrub to 1.5 m.; brts. angled, two-edged toward the end, slender, red-brown the second year; spines slender, 3-parted, to 1.2 cm. long: lvs. elliptic to oblong, 3-8 cm. long, obtuse or acutish, densely ciliate, green beneath: fls. pale yellow, in 3-6-fld. peduncled, umbel-like racemes: fr. subglobose, 5-6 mm. long, bright red, lustrous. S.T.1:t.14. S.L.100(h). Japan. Intr. 1892. Zone V. Distinct species with the lvs. at first purplish and marked with green veins, changing to vinous red in fall; the frs. remain nearly unchanged until spring.

   42. **B. Bretschneìderi** Rehd. Spreading shrub, to 4 m.; brts. nearly terete or slightly grooved, reddish brown the second year; spines simple or 3-parted, 5-15 mm. long: lvs. obovate-elliptic to obovate-oblong, 3-8 cm. long, usually obtuse, attenuate at base, densely setose-serrate, light green or slightly glaucescent beneath and reticulate: racemes peduncled, 2.5-4 cm., rarely to 5 cm. long, 10-15-fld.; pedicels 6-10 mm. long: fr. ellipsoid, 1-1.2 cm. long,

purple, slightly bloomy. S.T.2:t.110. Japan. Intr. 1892. Zone V. Similar to *B. vulgaris* but with red-brown, nearly terete brts.

43. **B. koreàna** Palib. Shrub to 2 m.; brts. grooved, reddish and bloomy, dark brown the second year; spines usually simple, 5–10 mm. long: lvs. obovate or elliptic, 2.5–7 cm. long, rounded at apex, cuneate at base, rather densely spinulose-serrulate, paler and reticulate beneath, subchartaceous at maturity: racemes rather short and dense, without the slender peduncle 2–3.5 cm. long; pedicels 4–6 mm. long: fr. subglobose, about 6 mm. long, bright red. J.C.26,1:t.5. N.K.21:t.7. Gn.88:645. M.G.32:92(h),93. Korea. Intr. 1905. Zone V. The lvs. change to deep red in fall; the frs. retain their bright color a long time.

44. **B. Henryàna** Schneid. Shrub to 2 or 3 m.; brts. slightly angled, yellow or dark brown the second year; spines simple or 3-parted, to 3 cm. long: lvs. petioled, elliptic to broad-obovate-oblong, 2–5 cm. long, usually obtuse, entire or with few teeth to spinulose-dentate, grayish green and bloomy beneath, slightly reticulate; petioles, 3–12 mm. long: racemes peduncled, 2.5–6 cm. long, 10–20-fld.; pedicels 6–9 mm. long; fls. 9–10 mm. across: fr. ellipsoid, 9 mm. long, blood-red, slightly bloomy. C. China. Intr. 1907. Zone V. Shrub with slender brs., similar to *B. vulgaris*.

Closely related species: **B. Dielsiàna** Fedde; it differs chiefly in the narrower, acute lvs., greener beneath, in the longer raceme sometimes compound at base, and in the more brightly colored frs. W. China. Intr. 1910. Zone V.

Ser. 13. DASYSTACHYAE Schneid. Lvs. usually long-petioled and rounded at base, broad, serrulate: racemes erect, dense; ovules 1–2: fr. red; stigma sessile.

45. **B. dasystáchya** Maxim. Upright shrub to 4 m.; brts. reddish or light brown, terete or slightly angular, red-brown the second year; spines usually simple, 5–15 mm. long, rarely to 3 cm.: lvs. long-petioled, suborbicular or broad-ovate to broad-elliptic, 3–5 cm. long, obtuse, usually rounded at base, ciliate-serrate, glaucescent beneath; petiole 1–3 cm. long: racemes upright, slender, with the peduncle 5–6 cm. long; pedicels about 5 mm. long; peduncle 1–1.5 cm. long; fls. about 6 mm. across: fr. ellipsoid, 6–7 mm. long, coral-red. Maximowicz, Fl. Tangut. t.7,f.1–7. G.C.79:325. S.H.2:f.573f,574l. C. and N. W. China. Intr. 1893. Zone V. Distinct on account of its broad, long-petioled lvs. similar to those of *B. heteropoda,* but bright green.

Closely related species: **B. kansuénsis** Schneid. Brts. bright red, slender: lvs. more remotely and less setosely serrate, those at base of infl. broad, often suborbicular, subsessile, usually entire: fls. about 8 mm. across: pedicels 3–10 mm. long. N. W. China. Intr. 1910. Zone V?

Ser. 14. BRACHYPODAE Schneid. Lvs. and usually the infl. pubescent: racemes dense, spike-like.

46. **B. Gilgiàna** Fedde. Shrub to 2 m.; brts. grooved, slightly pubescent, yellow or purplish brown, red-brown the second year; spines usually 3-parted, 5–25 mm. long: lvs. elliptic or elliptic-obovate to oblong, 2.5–4.5 cm. long, acute, attenuate at base, remotely serrate, dull green and slightly pubescent or glabrous above, grayish green and pubescent beneath: fls. about 6 mm. across, bright yellow, in dense racemes 2.5–3.5 cm. long, on slender puberulous peduncles 1.5–2 cm. long; pedicels 1–3 mm. long; bracts shorter: fr. oblong-obovoid, 8–10 mm. long, deep blood-red, slightly bloomy. (*B. pubescens* Pampan.) N. C. China. Intr. 1910. Zone V.

47. **B. mitifòlia** Stapf. Shrub to 2 m.; young brts. finely grooved, minutely pubescent, grayish; spines simple or 3-fid, 1–2.5 cm. long: lvs. obovate or elliptic-obovate to oblong, 3–6 cm. long, acute or obtuse, minutely spinulose-serrulate or entire, bright green and sparsely puberulous above, pubescent

beneath chiefly on the veins: fls. 8–10 mm. across, in dense pubescent racemes 3–6 cm. long, sometimes branched near base; peduncle 1–2 cm. long; pedicels 2–4 mm. long, as long as the red subulate bracts; outer whorl of sepals oblong-lanceolate, puberulous, red; fr. oblong-ellipsoid, 10–12 mm. long, crimson. B.M.9236(c). Gn.87:555. M.G.32:90. G.C.74:251. (*B. brachypoda* Schneid., not Maxim.) C. China. Intr. 1907. Zone V. Distinct with its spike-like racemes and pubescent lvs.

Related species: **B. brachýpoda** Maxim. Young brts. angled: lvs. obovate, 3–6 cm. long, obtuse or acutish, strongly spinulose-dentate, chartaceous, often rugose above and pubescent when young, strongly reticulate beneath and pilose chiefly on the veins: infl. 2–4 cm. long; pedicels 1 mm. long: fr. ovoid, 5–6 mm. long, scarlet. Maxim. Fl. Tangut. t.7. N. W. China. Intr. 1926. Zone V.

48. **B. Giráldii** Hesse. Shrub to 2 m.; brts. slightly angled, glabrous, yellowish brown or dark brown; spines usually simple, sometimes to 2.5 cm. long: lvs. rhombic-ovate or oblong-ovate, 4–10 cm. long, acute, serrulate, dark green above and nearly glabrous, pubescent and bright green and reticulate beneath, reddish when unfolding: racemes spike-like, pendulous, to 10 cm. long including the peduncle, glabrous; pedicels 2–3 mm. long; fls. pale yellow, 9 mm. across: fr. ellipsoid, purple. M.D.1913:267. N. C. China. Intr. about 1900. Zone V. Similar to the preceding species, but lvs. and racemes larger.

Ser. 15. **VULGARES** Schneid. Brts. yellowish gray or gray, grooved: lvs. deciduous, serrate or dentate: racemes usually long and many-fld., pendulous; ovules 2–3; stigma sessile: fr. red or purple, usually bloomy.

49. **B. amurénsis** Rupr. Shrub to 3.5 m.; brts. grooved, yellowish gray, gray the second year; spines usually 3-parted, 1–2 cm. long: lvs. elliptic to obovate-oblong, 3–8 cm. long, obtuse or acute, densely and irregularly setose-serrulate, reticulate and bright green, rarely glaucescent beneath: racemes to 10 cm. long, 10–25-fld., pendulous; pedicels 5–10 mm. long; fr. ellipsoid, about 1 cm. long, bright red, often bloomy. N.K.21:t.5. S.H.1:f.200k-m. (*B. vulgaris* var. *a.* Reg.) N. E. Asia. Intr. before 1860. Zone II. Lvs. brighter green than those of *B. vulgaris* and habit more upright.—**B. a. japónica** (Reg.) Rehd., var. Lvs. broader, often rounded at apex, more densely serrulate and distinctly reticulate beneath: raceme shorter, 6–12-fld., slightly nodding. G.F.3:249. (*B. Regeliana* Koehne.) Japan. Intr. before 1875.

Related species: **B. dictyoneùra** Schneid. Young brts. reddish, older gray: lvs. elliptic- to oblong-obovate, 1.5–3 cm. long, spiny-serrulate, strongly and densely reticulate, grayish beneath: infl. short, 4–7-fld.: pedicels 2–4 mm., in fr. 6–10 mm. long; fr. ovoid or obovoid. N. W. China. Intr. 1911. Zone V.

50. **B. vulgàris** L. Shrub to 2.5 or occasionally taller; brts. strongly grooved, yellowish or sometimes yellowish red while young, gray the second year; spines usually 3-parted, 1–2 cm. long: lvs. elliptic-obovate to obovate-oblong, 2–4 cm. long, obtuse, rarely acutish, attenuated into a petiole to 1 cm. long, greenish and slightly reticulate beneath: racemes short-stalked, 4–6 cm. long; pedicels 5–12 mm. long; fr. ellipsoid or elliptic-oblong, 8–12 mm. long, bright red or purple. E.B.1:t.51(c). R.I.3:f.4486(c). H.W.3:17, f.243. Eu., frequently naturalized in N. Am. Long cult. Zone III.—**B. v. marginàta** Reg., var. Lvs. margined with white. (*B. v. argenteo-marginata* Usteri.)—**B. v. aureo-marginàta** Reg., f. Lvs. margined yellow.—**B. v. atro-purpúrea** Reg., f. Lvs. deeply purple (*B. v.* var. *purpurea* Bertin, not DC.) Gt.9:t.278,f.1(c).—**B. v. lùtea** DC., f. Fr. bright yellow.—Var. **B. v. alba** West., var. Fr. white or yellowish white. N.D.3:t.52(c). (*B. v. leucocarpa* Ktze.)—**B. v. enúclea** West., var. Fr. without seeds. (*B. v.* var. *asperma*

Willd., *B. v. apyrena* Schrad.)—**B. v. dúlcis** Loud., var. Fr. sweet or but slightly acid. (*B. v.* var. *edulis* Jaeg.)

　　B. v. × *sibirica* = **B. emarginàta** Willd. Densely branched shrub to 1 m. or taller; brts. angled, yellowish or purplish, yellow-gray the second year; spines sometimes 5–7-parted: lvs. obovate-oblong to obovate-lanceolate, 1.5–4 cm. long, acute or obtuse, setosely serrulate, grayish beneath: racemes dense, 1–3.5 cm. long, 5–16-fld.; pedicels 5–8 mm. long; fls. 8–10 mm. across; petals emarginate; fr. ellipsoid, about 1 cm. long, deep red, slightly bloomy, sometimes with very short style. G.O.t.68(c). (*B. vulgaris* var. *e.* Gord.) Orig. unknown, about 1800. —**B. e. britzénsis** Schneid., var. Young brts. brownish: lvs. more densely serrulate: racemes to 4 cm. long. Orig. unknown.—Probably also a hybrid with *B. sibirica*, but much nearer the latter species is **B. provinciàlis** Schrad. Brts. grooved, yellowish brown, grayish brown the second year; lvs. obovate-oblong to narrow-oblong, 1.2–2.5 cm. long, finely setose-serrulate, green and reticulate beneath: racemes 1–3 cm. long, sometimes subumbellate, 6–12-fld.; pedicels 3–6 mm. long: fls. 6–8 mm. across: fr. 8–9 mm. long with sessile stigma. (*B. vulgaris* var. *p.* Audib.) Orig. before 1830.—**B. p. serràta** Schneid., var. Low shrub; lvs. lanceolate or oblanceolate, 1–2 cm. long, acute, setose-serrulate with 6–10 teeth on each side, grayish green beneath and reticulate: fr. red, about 7 mm. long. (*B. s.* Koehne, *B. microphylla* var. *s.* Hort.)—*B. v.* × *Veitchii;* see under No. 9. —*B. v.* × *aristata;* see under No. 25.—*B. v.* × *heteropoda;* see under No. 32.— *B. v.* × *Thunbergii;* see under No. 35.—*B. v.* × *chinensis;* see under No. 38.— *B. v.* × *canadensis;* see under No. 39.—*B. v.* × *Mahonia Aquifolium* = *Mahoberberis Neuberti;* see p. 225.

　　Closely related species: **B. aetnénsis** Presl. Dwarf shrub, to 0.5 m.; spines stout, to 3 cm. long: lvs. 1.5–3 cm. long, sometimes nearly entire: racemes 5–15-fld. (*B. vulgaris* var. *a.* Reg.) Moris, Fl. Sard. t.5. S. Eu. Cult. 1894. Zone VII?

26. MENISPERMACEAE DC. MOONSEED FAMILY

　　Woody or suffruticose plants, mostly twining: lvs. alternate, usually palmately veined and often lobed: fls. dioecious, small, regular, usually in axillary racemes or fascicles, often panicled; sepals usually 6 in 2 whorls; petals 6, usually smaller than sepals, sometimes wanting; stamens usually 6, or more, free or connate; anthers 2- or 4-celled; carpels usually 3, each with 1 half-inverted ovule, developing into sessile or stipitate, much curved drupes with a usually sculptured bony or chartaceous endocarp; embryo usually curved; cotyledons flat or semiterete.—About 200 species in 63 genera, chiefly in the Tropics, in N. Am. n. to Man., none in Eu.

A. Lvs. not peltate, entire or lobed; stamens 6–12.
　　B. Lvs. deeply cordate at base and deeply 5–7-lobed; sepals 9; petals 0: drupes 2.5 cm.
　　　　long ....1. *Calycocarpum*
　　BB. Lvs. rounded or subcordate at base, entire or shallowly 3–7-lobed; sepals and petals 6:
　　　　drupes 1 cm. or less long.
　　　　C. Lvs. ovate to ovate-oblong, entire and obtuse or 3-lobed; fr. in clusters or spikes.
　　　　　　　　　　　　　　　　　　　　　　　　　　　　　　　　　　　　2. *Cocculus*
　　　　CC. Lvs. broad-ovate, entire and acuminate or 5–7-lobed: stamens 9–12: fr. in pendulous
　　　　　　panicles to 15 cm. long..3. *Sinomenium*
AA. Lvs. peltate, sometimes slightly so, shallowly palmately 3–7-lobed: stamens 12–24; sepals
　　4–10; petals 6–9...4. *Menispermum*

　　1. **CALYCOCÁRPUM** Nutt. Twining deciduous shrub; lvs. long-petioled, palmately lobed: fls. greenish, in large panicles; sepals 9; petals wanting; stamens 12; anthers 2-celled; pistillate fls. with 6 staminodes; carpels 3, with a short thick style: drupe ellipsoid or subglobose; stone deeply hollowed out on one side and erosely toothed on the margin of the cavity, convex and smooth on the other. (Greek *calyx,* cup, and *carpos,* fruit, referring to the cup-like stone.) One species.

　　C. Lyòni Nutt. High climbing; glabrous or slightly pubescent: lvs. broad-ovate or orbicular in outline, 10–20 cm. long, broad-cordate at base, deeply palmately 3–7-lobed, with ovate to oblong, acute or acuminate, repand or

entire lobes, bright green beneath: fls. in peduncled loose panicles 10–20 cm.
long: drupe about 2.5 cm. long, black. Fl.v–vi; fr.viii. E.P.IV.94:129. Gr.G.
1:t.30. B.B.2:130. Ill. to Kans., s. to Fla. and Tex. Intr. 1879 or before.
Zone VI? Strong growing vine with large leaves.

2. **CÓCCULUS** DC. Twining or erect shrubs, deciduous or evergreen:
lvs. entire or lobed: fls. in panicles or racemes; sepals and petals 6; stamens
6–9; anthers 4-celled; staminodes 6 or 0; carpels 3–6; style cylindric, with
lateral stigma: drupes obovoid or subglobose; stone compressed, transversely
ribbed. (Diminutive of Greek *kokkos,* berry.) Syn.: *Cebatha* Forsk. Eleven
species in E. and S. Asia., Afr., Hawaii Isls., and N. Am.

A. Fr. red: petioles 1.5–4 cm. long: lvs. glabrous above: petals emarginate or entire at apex.
1. *C. carolinus*
AA. Fr. bluish black: petioles 1–2 cm long; lvs. pubescent on both sides: petals bifid at the
apex ....2. *C. trilobus*

1. **C. carolìnus** (L.) DC. CAROLINA MOONSEED. Twining to 4 m.; brts.
pubescent: lvs. orbicular- to triangular-ovate, 5–9 cm. long, obtuse and
mucronulate at apex, rounded to subcordate at base, entire or shallowly 3–5-
lobed, pubescent and glaucescent beneath: fls. in short or sometimes spike-
like panicles to 10 cm. long: fr. red, 6–8 mm. long. Fl.vi–viii. Gr.G.1:t.28.
S.H.1:327. (*Cebatha carolina* Brit.) Va. and Ill. to Fla. and Tex. Intr. 1732.
Zone V.

2. **C. trílobus** (Thunb.) DC. Twining to 4 m.; brts pubescent: lvs.
usually ovate, sometimes ovate-oblong, 4–9 cm. long, obtuse and mucronate
or acutish, rounded to cordate at base, entire or 3-lobed with the middle lobe
usually elongated, pubescent on both sides: fls. in axillary cymes, sometimes
forming an elongated terminal spike· frs. subglobose, 7 mm. across, black,
bloomy, forming usually dense peduncled clusters. Fl.vi–viii; fr.x. B.M.8489
(c). I.T.6:t.231. B.S.1:376. S.H.1:f.205k-n. (*C. Thunbergii* DC.) Japan,
China, Philipp. Isls. Intr. before 1870. Zone V. Much-branched twining
shrub keeping its lvs. green until late in fall.

3. **SINOMÈNIUM** Diels. Deciduous twining shrub: lvs. long-petioled
and palmately lobed or entire: fls. inconspicuous, in large panicles; sepals 6;
petals 6; stamens 9–12; anthers 4-celled; pistillate fls. with 9 staminodes;
carpels 3; style recurved with lobulate stigma: drupe excentric; stone curved
with a tubercled dorsal rib and numerous transverse ribs. (*Sina,* China, and
Greek *men,* moon; meaning Chinese moonseed.) One species.

S. **acùtum** (Thunb.) Rehd. & Wils. Twining to 6 m.; brts. glabrous,
striped: lvs. ovate, 6–15 cm. long, acuminate, rounded or cordate at base,
entire or 3–7-lobed, usually with rather narrow elongated lobes, glabrous and
dark green above, glaucescent and slightly pubescent beneath or nearly glabrous: fls. in panicles 10–20 cm. long: drupe compressed, 6–7 mm. across,
bluish black. Fl.vi; fr.x. G.C.52:411. (*Menispermum a.* Thunb., *Cocculus
diversifolius* Miq., *C. heterophyllus* Hemsl. & Wils., *S. diversifolium* Diels.)
Japan, C. China. Intr. 1901. Zone VI? Vigorous climber with large handsome foliage.—**S. a. cinéreum** (Diels) Rehd. & Wils., var. Lvs. pubescent
above and densely grayish pubescent beneath. Intr. 1907.

4. **MENISPÉRMUM** L. MOONSEED. Twining suffruticose plants: lvs.
long-petioled, peltate, 3–7-lobed: fls. small, in peduncled racemes or panicles,
sepals 4–10; petals 6–9, suborbicular, shorter than the sepals, stamens 12–18,
rarely 24; anthers 4-celled; pistillate fls. with 6–12 staminodes; carpels 2–4,

243

with broad subsessile stigma: drupes 2–3; stone compressed, reniform or crescent-shaped, crested on back; endosperm copious; cotyledons semiterete, remaining enclosed in the seed. (Greek *men,* moon, and *sperma,* seed.) Two species in N. Am. and E. Asia.

A. Young growth pubescent: petiole attached just inside the margin.........1. *M. canadense*
AA. Young growth glabrous: lvs. distinctly peltate..............................2. *M. dauricum*

1. **M. canadénse** L. Common M. Climbing to 4 m.; brts. finely pubescent when young; lvs. slender-petioled, orbicular-ovate, 10–20 cm. long, acute or obtuse, rounded or truncate at base, entire or shallowly angulate-lobed, slightly pubescent beneath or nearly glabrous at maturity; petioles 5–15 cm. long: panicles loose, without the slender peduncle 2–6 cm. long; sepals 6–10: drupe subglobose, about 8 mm. across, bluish black. Fl.v–vi; fr.x–xi. B.M. 1910(c). E.P.IV.94:256. F.E.28:261(h). G.W.1:63(h). Que. and Man. to Ga. and Ark. Cult. 1646. Zone IV. Attractive in fall with its bluish black fr. resembling small grapes.

2. **M. daùricum** DC. Twining to 4 m.; brts. glabrous: lvs. orbicular-ovate, 6–12 cm. long, acute or acuminate, angulate-lobed, rarely entire, quite glabrous, glaucous beneath; petioles 3–12 cm. long: fls. in slender-stalked, short, often umbel-like panicles; sepals in the terminal fls. usually 6, in the lateral, 4; drupes about 1 cm. across, black, in dense clusters. Fl.vi; fr.x(–v). G.F.5:233. B.C.4:2034. E. Asia. Intr. 1883. Zone IV. Similar to the preceding, but lvs. and fruiting clusters smaller; spreading by suckers.

27. **TROCHODENDRACEAE** Prantl. TROCHODENDRON FAMILY

Trees or shrubs; buds large, acute, with many imbricate scales: lvs. alternate, long-petioled, penninerved, serrate: fls. perfect, without perianth, in fascicles or racemes; stamens numerous; carpels 5–many, free or immersed in the fleshy torus; stigmas linear; ovules 1 to many on the introrse ventral suture: fr. a samara or a dehiscent follicle; seed with copious endosperm and small embryo.—Two genera with 4 species in E. Asia.

A. Lvs. deciduous: fls. in small clusters before the leaves: fr. a samara............1. *Euptelea*
AA. Lvs. evergreen: fls. in terminal racemes: fr. consisting of dehiscent follicles.
                                                                              2. *Trochodendron*

1. **EUPTÉLEA** Sieb. & Zucc. Deciduous shrubs or small trees; buds with dark brown lustrous scales: lvs. dentate: fls. before the lvs., slender-stalked, in fascicles from axillary buds; stamens numerous with linear-oblong red anthers; carpels many, stipitate, oblique, with decurrent stigma, developing after the stamens have dropped; ovules 1 or few; carpels developing into stipitate obliquely winged samaras, 1–4-seeded. Fr.ix–x. (Greek *eu,* well, handsome and *ptelea,* elm; referring to the shape of the fruit.) Three species in E. Asia and Himal.

A. Lvs. coarsely and unequally dentate.......................................1. *E. polyandra*
AA. Lvs. fairly regularly sinuate-dentate.....................................2. *E. Franchetii*

1. **E. polyándra** Sieb. & Zucc. Shrub or tree to 15 m.; brts. reddish brown: lvs. roundish-ovate, 6–12 cm. long, cuspidate, broad-cuneate or nearly rounded at base, light green beneath, with a few scattered hairs on the veins; petioles 2–5 cm. long: carpels usually 1-seeded, incl. the slender stipe-like base 1.2–1.5 cm. long. S.Z.t.72(c). S.I.1:t.41(c). B.C.2:1174. Gng.16:162. Japan. Cult. 1877. Zone V. Slender tree with handsome foliage reddish when unfolding, changing to red and yellow in autumn.

2. E. Franchétii Van Tiegh. Tree to 15 m.; brts. dark grayish brown: lvs. roundish-ovate to ovate, 5–12 cm. long, cuspidate, broad-cuneate at base, grayish green and sparingly pubescent beneath; petioles 2–5 cm. long: samaras 1–3-seeded. H.I.28:2787. I.S.1:t.22. C.C.130. (*E. Davidiana* Hemsl., not Baill.) C. China. Intr. 1896. Zone V. Similar to the preceding.
Closely related species: **E. pleiospérma** Hook. f. & Thoms. Lvs. glaucescent and papillose beneath, of firmer texture; samaras with stipe to 2 cm. long. C.C. 131. (*E. Davidiana* Baill.) E. Himal., W. China. Cult. 1922. Zone VII.

2. TROCHODÉNDRON Sieb. & Zucc. Evergreen tree; terminal bud large, pointed, with imbricate scales: lvs. alternate and clustered, long-petioled, crenate: fls. perfect, without perianth, in terminal, upright racemes; stamens numerous, spreading, with long filaments; carpels 5–10, in a whorl, inserted on a fleshy torus; stigmas short, linear, spreading; ovules many: fr. consisting of 5–10 follicles, partly immersed in the torus and dehiscent at the free apex; seeds linear, several in each follicle. (Greek, *trochos*, wheel, and *dendron*, tree; referring to the aspect of the spreading stamens.) One species in E. Asia.

T. aralioìdes Sieb. & Zucc. Tree to 20 m., with spreading brs., glabrous: lvs. rhombic-obovate to elliptic-lanceolate, 8–15 cm. long, obtusely acuminate, cuneate at base, crenate-serrate, dark lustrous green above, paler beneath, coriaceous; petioles 3–7 cm. long: fls. about 1.5 cm. across, bright green, on slender pedicels 1.5–3 cm. long, forming racemes 6–8 cm. long: fr. brown, 1.5–2 cm. across. Fl.vi; fr.x. B.M.7375(c). S.I.1:t.42(c). G.C.III.15:725. M.O.t.3. J.H.27:867(h). Japan, Korea. Cult. 1894. Zone VII. Usually a spreading shrub in cult.

28. CERCIDIPHYLLACEAE Van Tiegh. KATSURA-TREE FAMILY

Deciduous tree developing short spurs bearing the flowers and a solitary lf.; buds with 2 outer scales: lvs. opposite or suboppposite on the shoots, solitary on the spurs, petioled, palmately veined, crenate-serrate: fls. dioecious, developing from axillary buds or spurs before the lvs., with small bracts and without perianth (what is called fl. here is by some botanists considered to represent an infl.); staminate fls. nearly sessile with slender filaments and linear red anthers; pistillate fls. pedicelled, consisting of 3–5 carpels with long purple styles, their sutures extrorse, developing into dehiscent many-seeded pods; seeds small, winged, with copious endosperm and small embryo. One monotypic genus in E. Asia.

CERCIDIPHÝLLUM Sieb. & Zucc. KATSURA-TREE. Characters of the family. (*Cercis* and Greek *phyllon*, leaf; referring to the shape of the lvs.)
C. japónicum Sieb. & Zucc. Tree to 10, occasionally to 30 m., usually divided from the base into several stems, glabrous: lvs. suborbicular or broad-ovate, 5–10 cm. long, obtusish, cordate or subcordate at base, crenate-serrate, dark bluish green above, glaucescent beneath; petiole 2–3 cm. long: pods 1.5–2 cm. long. Fr.x. S.I.1:t.41(c). M.K.t.42,43(c). G.F.7:106,107(h). Gn. 88:373,374(h). S.L.120(h). Japan. Intr. 1865. Zone IV. Ornamental tree of rather dense pyramidal habit, with slender, ascending, later spreading brs. and handsome foliage, purplish when unfolding, changing to bright yellow and partly scarlet in fall.—**C. j. sinénse** Rehd. & Wils., var. Tree to 40 m., usually with a single trunk: lvs. somewhat hairy on the veins beneath; petiole

about 2 cm. long: pods gradually narrowed at apex, 1–1.5 cm. long. C.C.135.
C. and W. China. Intr. 1907. Zone (V).

29. MAGNOLIACEAE Jaume St. Hil. MAGNOLIA FAMILY

Trees or shrubs; lvs. deciduous or evergreen, entire or lobed; stipules
present or wanting: fls. regular, usually perfect, hypogynous; sepals 3, often
not differing from the petals, rarely 4; petals 6 or more, rarely wanting;
stamens numerous, spirally arranged, rarely 4; carpels usually spirally arranged, rarely in a whorl; ovary 1-celled, with 1 to several ovules; seeds
anatropous; carpels developing into follicles, samaras or berries. Incl. *Win-
teraceae* and *Schisandraceae*.—Ten genera with about 80 species in the temp.
and subtrop. regions of Am. and Asia.

  A. Stipules present, large, enclosing the succeeding young lf.: fls. perfect: trees or shrubs.
                                               Subfam. MAGNOLIOIDEAE (DC.) Harms.
    B. Lvs. entire, acute or acuminate: ripe carpel a dehiscent follicle.............1. *Magnolia*
    BB. Lvs. lobed, truncate at apex: ripe carpel a samara.....................2. *Liriodendron*
  AA. Stipules wanting.
    B. Fr. capsular, dehiscent: fls. perfect: trees or upright shrubs.
      C. Lvs. penninerved, evergreen: fls. with many petals.
                                       Subfam. ILLICIOIDEAE (DC.) Harms,
                                            3. *Illicium*
      CC. Lvs. palmately 5–7-nerved, deciduous; fls. apetalous, 4-merous.
                                  Subfam. TETRACENTROIDEAE Harms.
                                         4. *Tetracentron*
    BB. Fr. of berrylike carpels: fls. unisexual: twining shrubs.
                                  Subfam. SCHIZANDROIDEAE (Gray) Harms.
      C. Carpels after anthesis spicate...5. *Schisandra*
      CC. Carpels after anthesis capitate...6. *Kadsura*

1. MAGNÒLIA L. Deciduous or evergreen trees or shrubs: buds with
a single scale, the terminal much larger than the lateral ones: lvs. petioled,
entire, large; stipules adnate to the petiole and inclosing the young successive
lf., their scar encircling the stem: fls. terminal, large, solitary, the bud enclosed in a stipular spathe; sepals 3, often petaloid; petals 6–15; stamens
numerous; carpels numerous, adnate to a usually elongate torus developing
into a cone-like fruit consisting of dehiscent 1–2-seeded carpels; seeds suspended at maturity for some time by long thin threads. (After Pierre
Magnol, director of the Botanic Garden at Montpellier; 1638–1715.) Syn.:
Kobus Nieuwl. About 35 species in N. and C. Am. and in E. Asia and Himal.

  A. Fls. after or with the lvs.: fr. subglobose to oblong, cone-like, usually symmetrical.
    B. Lvs. deciduous or half-evergreen.
      C. Fls. greenish or yellow: lvs. 18–25 cm. long, scattered.
        D. Brts. glabrous or nearly so: fls. greenish, 6–8 cm. high............1. *M. acuminata*
        DD. Brts. densely pubescent: fls. canary yellow, 4–5 cm. high............2. *M. cordata*
      CC. Fls. white, large.
        D. Lvs. cordate at base.
          E. Leaf-buds and brts. tomentose: lvs. scattered, 50–75 cm. long.
                                     3. *M. macrophylla*
         EE. Leaf-buds and brts. glabrous: lvs. crowded at end of the brts.
           F. Lvs. acute: tips of mature carpels nearly straight.............4. *M. Fraseri*
           FF. Lvs. obtusely pointed: tips of mature carpels incurved.....5. *M. pyramidata*
        DD. Lvs. cuneate at base, rarely rounded or subcordate.
          E. Lvs. 12–60 cm. long, crowded at end of the brts.: buds and brts. glabrous.
           F. Fr. 6–10 cm. long; carpels whitish during anthesis: lvs. gradually narrowed
              at base ....6. *M. tripetala*
           FF. Fr. 12–16 cm. long: carpels purple: lvs. usually abruptly contracted at base.
                                7. *M. obovata*
        EE. Lvs. 7–16 cm. long, scattered.
          F. Lvs. obovate or broadly elliptic, often rounded at base, 4–11 cm. broad;
            sepals pink.
           G. Young brts., petioles and peduncles pubescent: fls. 8–10 cm. across,
            slender-stalked ....8. *M. Sieboldii*
           GG. Young brts., petioles and peduncles glabrous or nearly so: fls. 12–15 cm.
            across, on stout peduncles...................................9. *M. Watsoni*

FF. Lvs. elliptic or ovate-oblong to oblong-lanceolate: fls. pure white.
  G. Lvs. acute or acuminate, deciduous: pedicel 1.5–3 cm. long..10. *M. Wilsonii*
  GG. Lvs. obtusish or obtusely short-acuminate, glaucous and nearly glabrous
    beneath, sometimes half-evergreen; pedicel 1–1.5 cm. long.
                                      11. *M. virginiana*
BB. Lvs. evergreen, ferrugineous-pubescent beneath: fls. 15–20 cm. across.
                                      12. *M. grandiflora*
AA. Fls. appearing before the lvs.: fr. cylindric, usually curved, unsymmetrical.
  B. Sepals 3, much smaller and narrower than petals, greenish (except in No. 16); petals 6.
    C. Fls. white.
      D. Lvs. oblong-lanceolate or narrowly elliptic; broadest below the middle: leaf-buds
        glabrous ....13. *M. salicifolia*
      DD. Lvs. obovate to obovate-oblong, broadest above the middle: leaf-buds slightly
        pubescent ....14. *M. Kobus*
    CC. Fls. purple, rarely nearly white.
      D. Sepals small, lanceolate, greenish; petals purple...................15. *M. liliflora*
      DD. Sepals usually half as long as petals and more or less petaloid; fls. sometimes
        nearly white ....16. *M. Soulangeana*
  BB. Sepals and petals alike.
    C. Sepals and petals obovate to oblong-obovate, 9–12, rarely more, 2 cm. or more broad.
      D. Lvs. abruptly acuminate: sepals and petals 9......................17. *M. denudata*
      DD. Lvs. usually rounded and often emarginate at apex: sepals and petals 12 or more.
                                18. *M. Sargentiana*
    CC. Sepals and petals narrow- or linear-oblong, 12–18, up to 1.5 cm. broad: lvs. 4–10 cm.
      long ....19. *M. stellata*

Subgen. MAGNOLIASTRUM DC. Fls. after the lvs.: buds with one bud-scale:
fr. globose-ovoid to oblong, symmetrical; carpels crowded, beaked.

1. **M. acumináta** L. CUCUMBER-TREE. Pyramidal tree to 30 m.; bark dark
brown, furrowed; brts. glabrous or slightly pubescent, red-brown, lustrous;
buds pubescent; lvs. elliptic or ovate to oblong-ovate, or sometimes oblong-
obovate, 10–24 cm. long, short-acuminate, rounded or acute at base, soft-
pubescent and light green beneath; petioles 2.5–3.5 cm. long: fls. campanulate, 6–8 cm. high; petals obovate-oblong, greenish yellow, bloomy; sepals
lanceolate, much smaller, soon reflexed: fr. ovoid to oblong, 5–8 cm. long,
red. Fl.v; fr.VIII–IX B.M.2427(c). L.B.418(c). S.S.1:t.4,5. F.E.20:64,t.102(h).
E.H.6,t.358(h). N. Y. to Ga., w. to Ill. and Ark. Intr. 1736. Zone IV. Pyramidal tree with rather short brs. upright at first, later spreading, and with
inconspicuous fls., but attractive red fr. in late summer.

2. **M. cordàta** Michx. Shrub or round-headed tree to 10 m.; bark dark
brown, scaly: brts. densely pubescent: lvs. oblong-obovate to elliptic, 8–15
cm. long, 6–11 cm. broad, short-acuminate or obtuse, broad-cuneate to
rounded, rarely subcordate, at base, pubescent and pale beneath; petiole 1–2
cm. long: fls. on short pedicels, campanulate, 4–5 cm. high; sepals ovate,
soon reflexed; petals obovate-oblong to oblong, yellow: fr. oblong-ovoid,
2.5–3.5 cm. long, dark red. B.R.325(c). L.B.474(c). S.S.1:t.6. S.M.345. (*M.
acuminata* var. *c.* Sarg.) Ga. Intr. 1801. Zone V. Fls. more conspicuous than
in the preceding species.

3. **M. macrophýlla** Michx. LARGE-LEAVED CUCUMBER-TREE. Tree to 18
m.; brts. tomentose at first; buds tomentose; lvs. oblong-obovate, 30–80 cm.
long, obtuse, subcordate-auriculate at base, glaucescent and finely pubescent
beneath; petiole 4–10: fls. cup-shaped, 25–30 cm. across, fragrant, creamy-
white; petals 6, oblong-obovate, 12–20 cm. long, reflexed above the middle,
purplish at base, thick; sepals somewhat shorter than petals: fr. globose-
ovoid, pubescent, 6–8 cm. long, rose-colored. Fl.v–VI. B.M.2981(c). S.S.1:t.
7,8. G.C.28:324. Gn.33:539. G.F.8:165(h). F.E.14:23(h). Ky. to Fla., w.
to Ark. and La. Intr. 1800. Zone (V). Round-headed tree with stout spreading brs., with large lvs. and large fls.

Closely related species: **M. Ashei** Weatherby. Shrub or tree to 8 m.: lvs.
subappressed-pubescent beneath on midrib: fls. smaller; petals 10–14.5 cm. long,
usually acute or acutish: fr. ovoid-cylindric, 5–11 cm. long. Jour. N. Y. Bot.
Gard. 34:151. Fla. Cult. 1933. Zone VI.

4. **M. Fràseri** Walt. Tree to 15 m.; brts. and buds glabrous: lvs. spatulate-obovate, 20–50 cm. long, acute, cordate-auriculate at base, glaucescent beneath, glabrous; petioles 4–7 cm. long: fls. 20–25 cm. across, creamy white, fragrant; petals 6–9, 8–12 cm. long, oblong-obovate, contracted below the middle; sepals 3, caducous, shorter than petals: fr. ovoid-oblong to oblong, 8–12 cm. long, rose-red. Fl.vi. B.M.1206(c). S.S.1:t.11,12. H.H.210,211(b). Gn.44:935. F.E.33:1071(h). (*M. auriculata* Lam.) Va. to Ga. and Ala. Intr. 1787. Zone V. Tree with wide-spreading brs. forming an open head, with large bright green lvs., large white fls. and attractive rose-colored fr.

5. **M. pyramidàta** Bartr. Tree to 10 m., glabrous; closely related to the preceding species: lvs. obovate, 14–22 cm. long, obtusely short-acuminate, auriculate at base, glaucescent beneath; petioles 2–4 cm. long: fls. 8–12 cm. across; petals gradually narrowed to the base; sepals much shorter: fr. oblong, 5–7 cm. long. Fl.vi. B.R.t.407(c). L.B.11:1092(c). S.T.1:t.51. Ga. to Fla. and Ala. Cult. 1825. Zone VI? Pyramidal tree with ascending brs.

6. **M. tripétala** L. UMBRELLA MAGNOLIA. Tree to 12 m.; brts. and buds glabrous: lvs. oblong-obovate, 25–60 cm. long, acute or short-acuminate, usually cuneate at base, pale and pubescent beneath, at least while young; petioles 1.5–3 cm. long: fls. 18–25 cm. across, white, of heavy odor; petals 6–9, oblong-obovate, 8–12 cm. long; sepals shorter, finally reflexed, light green; filaments purple: fr. ovoid-oblong, 7–10 cm. long, rose-colored. Fls.v–vi. L.D. 3:198(c). S.S.1:t.9,10. H.H.208,209(b). Gn.33:539. C.L.5:494. (*M. umbrella* Lam.) Pa. to Ala., w. to Ark. and Miss. Intr. 1752. Zone IV. Tree with widespreading brs. forming an open head, with large lvs. and large fls.; easily grown and often used as stock for species of this subgenus.

M. t. × *virginiana* = M. Thompsoniàna (Loud.) Sarg. Buds glabrous: lvs. elliptic to oblong, 12–22 cm. long, acute, glaucescent and pubescent beneath: fls. 12–15 cm. across, fragrant sepals shorter than petals. Fl.vi–vii. B.M.2164(c). G.F.1:269. Gn.24:511. (*M. glauca* var. *T.* Loud., *M. glauca* var. *major* Smith.) Orig. 1808. Zone VI.

7. **M. obovàta** Thunb. (not Willd. and later authors). Tree to 30 m.; brts. purplish, glabrous, like the buds: lvs. obovate, 20–40 cm. long, usually abruptly contracted at base, obtusely pointed, glaucescent and pubescent beneath at least while young; petioles 2.5–4 cm. long: fls. cup-shaped, 14–16 cm. across, white, fragrant; petals 6–9, obovate, leathery; sepals similar, but shorter, sometimes pink outside; filaments and pistils bright crimson; anthers 1.6–1.8 cm. long: fr. cylindric-oblong, 14–20 cm. long, scarlet. Fl.v–vi. B.M. 8077(c). M.D.1904:1,t(c). M.K.t.44(c). G.F.1:305. (*M. hypoleuca* Sieb. & Zucc.) Japan. Intr. 1865. Zone V. Similar to *M. tripetala,* but of more pyramidal habit and with showier fls.

Closely related species: M. officinàlis Rehd. & Wils. Brts. yellowish or grayish yellow; anthers 1–1.2 cm. long; fr. 10–12 cm. long. C. China. Intr. 1900. Zone VI?

8. **M. Siebóldii** K. Koch. Small tree to 10 m.; young brts. and buds appressed-pubescent: lvs. broad-elliptic or obovate to obovate-oblong, 6–15 cm. long, obtusely pointed, glaucescent beneath and pubescent at first, with 6–10 pairs of veins; petioles 1–2 cm. long, silky-pubescent while young, like the midrib beneath: fls. cup-shaped, 7–10 cm. across, white, fragrant, on a slender pubescent stalk 3–6 cm. long; petals usually 6, obovate; sepals somewhat shorter, reflexed, pink; carpels few, crimson like the filaments: fr. ovoid, 3–4 cm. long. Fl.vi–vii. B.M.7411(c). N.K.20:t.23. G.C.58:276(fr.);101:379, t(c). M.G.1913:484(h). (*M. Oyama* Kort, *M. parviflora* Sieb. & Zucc., not Bl.) Japan, Korea. Intr. about 1865. Zone (V) VI. A handsome species with showy fls.

9. × **M. Wátsoni** Hook. f. (*M. obovata* × *Sieboldii*). Similar to the preceding: brts. glabrous or nearly so: lvs. obovate to oblong-obovate, 10–18 cm. long, finely pubescent beneath, with 10–15 pairs of veins; petiole about 2.5 cm. long: fls. 10–14 cm. across, on stout pedicels usually 2–3 cm. long, glabrous or nearly so; carpels many: fr. larger. B.M.7157(c). Gt.48:t.1459(c). Gn.24:508(c, as *M. parviflora*). G.C.III.17:517. Orig. in Japan. Cult. 1889. Zone (V). Fls. large, fragrant with crimson center and pink sepals.

10. **M. Wilsònii** (Fin. & Gagnep.) Rehd. Shrub or small tree to 8 m.; brts. and buds pubescent: lvs. ovate-oblong to oblong-lanceolate, 6–12 cm. long, acute or acuminate, rounded or sometimes subcordate at base, glabrous above, silky-tomentose beneath; petioles pubescent, 1.5–4 cm. long: fls. cup-shaped, 10–12 cm. across, white, fragrant, on pedicels 1.5–2 cm. long; sepals and petals 9, obovate, of equal size, thin; filaments crimson; carpels green: fr. oblong-cylindric, about 6 cm. long. Fl.vi. B.M.9004(c). R.H.1923:338. (*M. parviflora* var. *W.* Finet & Gagnep.) W. China. Intr. 1908. Zone (V) VI. Distinct and handsome.—**M. W. taliénsis** (W. W. Sm.) Rehd., f. Lvs. glaucescent and glabrescent beneath except the rufous-pilose midrib. (*M. Nicholsoniana* Rehd. & Wils., *M. t.* W. W. Sm.) Intr. 1908.

M. W. × *sinensis* has been raised about 1927. N.F.10:f.33.
Closely related species: **M. globòsa** Hook. & Thoms. Lvs. ovate or broad-elliptic to elliptic-oblong, to 25 cm. long, obtuse to acute, rufous-pubescent beneath on the midrib and when young elsewhere; petiole rufous-pubescent: pedicels 3–6.5 cm. long, rufous-pubescent; carpels green. B.M.9467(c). N.F.10: f.92. (*M. tsarongensis* W. W. Sm. & Forrest.) E. Himal. to W. China. Intr. 1919. Zone VII.—**M. sinénsis** (Rehd. & Wils.) Stapf. Brts. and petioles pubescent: lvs. obovate to elliptic or oblong-obovate, 10–20 cm. long and 6–16 cm. broad, rounded or short-pointed at apex, grayish or whitish villous beneath: fls. 12–15 cm. across; pedicels 2.5–6 cm. long, loosely villous or nearly glabrous; carpels crimson. G.C.89:408. N.F.5:f.3(h). (*M. globosa* var. *sinensis* Rehd. & Wils., *M. Nicholsoniana* Hort., not Rehd. & Wils.) W. China. Intr. 1908. Zone VII?

11. **M. virginiàna** L. Sweet Bay. Deciduous shrub, or half-evergreen tree to 20 m. in the South; brts. slender, glabrous; buds pubescent: lvs. elliptic to oblong-lanceolate, 7–12 cm. long, acute or obtuse, broad-cuneate at base, rarely rounded, glaucous beneath and silky pubescent at first; petioles slender, 1–2 cm. long, glabrous: fls. subglobose, 5–7 cm. across, white, fragrant; petals 9–12, obovate, sepals shorter and thinner, spreading: fr. ellipsoid, 4–5 cm. long, dark red. Fl.vi–vii. Em.603,t(c). L.B.215(c). S.S.1:t.3. G.F.10: 403. (*M. glauca* L.: Sweet or Swamp Bay, Beaver-tree.) Mass. to Fla. and to Tex., near the coast. Intr. 1688. Zone V. Handsome shrub with lustrous lvs. persisting south until spring and with white fragrant fls.—**M. v. austràlis** Sarg., var. Young brts. and petioles densely silky-pubescent; pedicels tomentose. N. C. to Fla. and Tex.

M. v. × *grandiflora* Freeman. Lvs. evergreen: fls. 12–15 cm. across. N.H. 16:161. Orig. 1930.

12. **M. grandiflòra** L. Bull Bay. Evergreen pyramidal tree to 30 m.; brts. and buds rusty-pubescent: lvs. obovate-oblong or elliptic, 12–20 cm. long, obtusely short-acuminate or obtusish, cuneate at base, lustrous above, ferrugineous-pubescent beneath, firmly coriaceous; petioles stout, about 2 cm. long: fls. cup-shaped, 15–20 cm. across, white, fragrant, on a stout, tomentose pedicel; petals usually 6, rarely 9–12, obovate, thick; sepals 3, petaloid; filaments purple: fr. ovoid, 7–10 cm. long, rusty-tomentose. Fl.v–viii. S.S. 1:t.1,2. Gn.33:538. F.E.17:788,781(h). J.L.46:315(h). (*M. foetida* Sarg.) N. C. to Fla. and Tex. Cult. 1734. Zone VII. A magnificent evergreen tree, much planted in the warmer regions of this country and of Europe, with large

lustrous lvs. and very large fragrant white fls.—**M. g. lanceolàta** Ait., var. Lvs. oblong-elliptic to oblong-lanceolate, less rusty beneath: of narrow pyramidal habit. B.M.1952(c). L.B.814(c). (*M. g.* var. *exoniensis* Loud.) There are many other named varieties and forms of which **M. g. gallissoniénsis** *K. Koch* is said to be the hardiest.

Related species: **M. Delavaÿi** Franch. Tree to 10 m.; young brts. finely pubescent: lvs. ovate to ovate-oblong, 20–30 cm. long, dull green above, puberulous and glaucescent beneath; petioles 3–8 cm. long: fls. 15–20 cm. across, white, petals usually 7; sepals 3, reflexed: fr. about 12 cm. long. B.M.8282(c). Millais, Magnol. 32,t(h). I.S.2:t.66. S. W. China. Intr. 1900. Zone VII?

Subgen. II. GWÌLLIMIA Rottler. Fls. before the lvs.: buds with 2 bud-scales: fr. cylindric, unsymmetrical, usually curved and twisted; carpels distant, with semiorbicular valves, not or rarely beaked.

13. **M. salicifòlia** (Sieb. & Zucc.) Maxim. Slender tree to 10 m.; brts. and leaf-buds glabrous, slightly glaucous; fl.-buds densely pubescent: lvs. ellipticovate to oblong-lanceolate, 7–12 cm. long, acuminate, broad-cuneate at base, with about 12 pairs of veins, light green above, glaucescent and sparingly appressed-pubescent beneath; petiole slender, about 1–2 cm. long: fls. on short glabrous stalks, about 12 cm. across, white or purple at base outside, fragrant; petals 6, narrowly oblong-obovate, 5–6 cm. long; sepals lanceolate, about half as long as petals, greenish white: fr. cylindric, 4–7 cm. long. Fl.ɪᴠ–ᴠ. B.M.8483(c). S.I.1:t.40(c). G.F.6:67. G.C.51:223. Japan. Intr. 1892. Zone V.—**M. s. fasciàta** Millais, var. Brs. upright forming a densely branched broadly columnar shrub. Millais, Magnol. 213,t(h).

M. s. × *stellata* = M. Proctoriàna Rehd. Lf.-buds short-pubescent: lvs. broadest at or above the middle, green beneath: petals 6–12. Orig. 1928.

Closely related species: **M. Bióndii** Pampan. Lvs. green beneath; petiole 5–15 mm. long; pedicel silky-pubescent: fr. 8–13 cm. long; seed deeply concave on the ventral side. R.H.1924:41(h). (*M. aulacosperma* Rehd. & Wils.) C. China. Intr. 1908. Zone VI?

14. **M. Kòbus** DC. Tree to 10 m., usually shrubby in cult.; brts. glabrous; leaf-buds slightly, fl.-buds densely pubescent: lvs. broad-obovate to obovate, 6–10 cm. long, abruptly pointed, tapering to the cuneate base, light green beneath and pubescent on the veins, finally glabrous or nearly so; petioles 1–1.5 cm. long: fls. about 10 cm. across, white; petals 6–9, oblong-ovate, with a faint purple line at base outside; sepals narrow, about 1.5 cm. long, caducous: fr. cylindric, 10–12 cm. long. Fl.ɪᴠ–ᴠ. B.M.8428(c). S.I.1:t.39(c). G.C.37:264. S.T.2:t.126. (*M. Thurberi* Hort., *M. kobushi* Mayr.) Japan: Hondo. Intr. 1865. Zone V.—**M. K. boreàlis** Sarg., var. Pyramidal tree to 25 m.: lvs. larger, 6–15 cm. long: fls. about 12 cm. across, pure creamy white. M.K.t.45(c). N.K.20:t.24. G.F.6:66. B.C.4:1968. Japan: Hokkaido, N. Hondo. Intr. 1892. Zone IV. The hardiest of the Asiatic Magnolias, but not blooming freely while young.

M. K. × *stellata;* see under No. 19.

15. **M. liliflòra** Desrouss. Shrub to 3 m.; brts. glabrous, except near the tips; buds pubescent: lvs. obovate or elliptic-ovate, acute or short-acuminate, tapering at base, 10–18 cm. long, dark green and sparingly pubescent above, light green beneath and finely pubescent on the nerves: fls. large, campanulate, purple outside and usually white inside, on very short and stout pedicels; petals 6, oblong-obovate, obtuse, 8–10 cm. long; sepals lanceolate, about ⅓ as long, greenish, caducous: fr. oblong. Fl.ᴠ–ᴠɪ. B.M.390(c). N.K.20:t.25. Gn.46:49. (*M. purpurea* Curt., *M. obovata* Willd. and later authors, not Thunb., *M. discolor* Vent., *M. denudata* Schneid., not Desrouss.) China, much cult. in Japan. Intr. 1790. Zone (V). Shrub with very showy purple

fls. appearing in succession and partly with the lvs.; var. *nigra* seems to be hardier than the type.—**M. l. grácilis** (Salisb.) Rehd., var. Small shrub with slender brs. and narrower leaves and smaller dark purple fls. Salisbury, Parad. Lond. t.87(c). (*M. gracilis* Salisb.) Intr. 1804 from Japan.—**M. l. nígra** (Nichols.) Rehd., var. Fls. larger, about 12 cm. long, dark purple outside and light purple inside. Gn.25:276,t(c). (*M. Soulangeana* var. *n.* Nichols.) Intr. 1861 from Japan. Zone (V).

16. × **M. Soulangeàna** Soul. (*M. denudata* × *liliflora.*) Large shrub or small tree: lvs. obovate, more or less pubescent beneath: fls. campanulate, more or less purplish, rarely white, scentless or fragrant; sepals usually petaloid, half as long or sometimes nearly as long as petals. Fl.v. B.R.14:t.1164 (c). S.B.1:t.260(c). B.S.2:74,t(h). Gn.76:135(h);80:243(h). (*M. conspicua* var. *S.* Lindl.) Orig. 1820. Zone V. The forms of this hybrid are much more planted than either of the parents; they belong to the most gorgeous of the early flowering shrubs.—Among the numerous forms one of the most distinct is **M. S. Lénnei** (Topf) Rehd., var. Lvs. broad-obovate, pubescent on the nerves beneath: fls. rosy-purple outside, white inside; petals obovate, fleshy; sepals petaloid, narrower and paler and about half as long as the petals. F.S. 16:t.1693–94(c). R.B.1:145,t(c). (*M. Lennei* Topf.)—**M. S. rubra** (Nichols.) Rehd., f. Similar, but of lighter, more rose-red color. F.R.1:16,t(c). (*M. rustica rubra* Nichols.)—Forms with white or nearly white fls. are var. *spectabilis* (Millais, Magnol, 228,t.) and *alba* (*M. S. alba superba*). G.3:449.— White fls. tinged purple outside toward the base have *M. S. Alexandrina* (R.B.26:t.217(c). R.H.1912:317), *M. S. Brozzonii* (G.34:429,431; N.F.4:f.19), *speciosa, Candolleana* and others.

17. **M. denudàta** Desrouss. Tree with spreading brs., to 15 m.; young brts. and buds pubescent: lvs. obovate to obovate-oblong, 10–15 cm. long, short-acuminate, tapering at base, sparingly pubescent above, light green beneath and minutely pubescent chiefly on the nerves and slightly reticulate: fls. large, finally open campanulate, 12–15 cm. across, white, fragrant; petals and sepals alike, 9, oblong-obovate, concave, fleshy: fr. cylindric, 8–12 cm. long, brownish. Fl.iv–v. B.M.1621(c). L.B.12:t.1187(c). Gn.34:276,t(c);47: 402(h);51:474(h). C.L.3:173. M.G.20:253. (*M. conspicua* Salisb., *M. Yulan* Desf., *M. precia* Loisel.) C. China. Intr. 1789. Zone V.—**M. d. purpuráscens** (Maxim.) Rehd. & Wils., var. (excl. the Chinese plant). Fls. rose-red outside, pink inside; carpels and filaments rose-red. Ito, Shokubuts. 1:t.8(c). Japan. Intr. ? Zone V?

M. d. × *Campbellii* = **M. Veìtchii** Bean. Lvs. obovate, 15–30 cm. long, downy on the veins beneath; petiole 2–2.5 cm. long, pubescent: fls. pink, with 9 petals, about 15 cm. long. Orig. 1907. Zone VII?—*M. Campbellii* Hook. f. & Thoms. is not hardy within our area.

Closely related species: **M. Spréngeri** Pampan. Pyramidal tree to 20 m.: lvs. obovate, 12–17 cm. long, short-acuminate at the rounded apex, cuneate; fls. saucer-shaped, about 20 cm. across; sepals and petals 12, rose-carmine outside, white and flushed or streaked pink inside, much narrowed at base, outer obovate, inner narrower. B.M.9116(c). (*M. S. diva* Stapf, *M. denudata* var. *purpurascens* of Rehd. & Wils., in part.) C. China. Intr. 1901. Zone VII. Fls. very showy, resembling those of the tender Himalayan *M. Campbellii* Hook. f. & Thoms.—**M. S. elongàta** (Rehd. & Wils.) Stapf, var. Lvs. oblong-obovate: fls. white; sepals and petals narrower, oblong-obovate. G.C.97:249,t. C. China. Intr. 1901.

18. **M. Sargentiàna** Rehd. & Wils. Tree to 25 m.; brts. glabrous; buds oblong-ovoid, villous or glabrescent: lvs. subcoriaceous, obovate, 10–20 cm. long, 6–10 cm. broad, rounded or acutish, sometimes emarginate at the apex, cuneate or broad-cuneate, dark green, reticulate and somewhat shiny above,

pale green, reticulate and grayish villous beneath, with 8–12 pairs of veins; petioles 2–4.5 cm. long: fls. open-campanulate, rosy-pink outside, paler inside; sepals and petals 12, the outer about 7.5, the inner to 12 cm. long and 6 cm. broad: fr. cylindric, 10–14 cm. long, usually twisted. N.F.4:f.4,5(h). W. China. Intr. 1908. Zone VII. The showy fls. are similar to those of *M. denudata,* but pink.

Related species: **M. Dawsoniàna** Rehd. & Wils. Tree to 12 m.: lvs. obovate or elliptic-obovate, 8–14 cm. long, obtuse or apiculate, more leathery and more reticulate, glabrous: fls. unknown. W. China. Intr. 1908. Zone VII.

19. **M. stellàta** (Sieb. & Zucc.) Maxim. Shrub or small tree: young brts. and buds densely pubescent: lvs. obovate or narrow-elliptic to oblong-obovate, 4–10 cm. long, obtusely pointed or obtusish, gradually tapering at base, glabrous and dark green above, light green and reticulate beneath and glabrous or appressed-pubescent on the nerves; petioles 3–10 mm. long: fls. short-stalked, about 8 cm. across, white, fragrant; petals and sepals alike, 12–18, narrow-oblong, spreading and finally reflexed: fr. about 5 cm. long, twisted and with only a few fertile carpels. Fl.iii–iv; fr.ix–x. B.M.6370(c). R.H.1878:270,t(c). B.S.1:83,t(h). G.C.39:260(h),261. Gn.78:117;79:150(h). F.E.15:t.53(h). (*M. Halliana* Hort., *Buergeria s.* Sieb. & Zucc.) Japan. Intr. 1862. Zone V. Wide-spreading shrub with a profusion of early white fragrant fls.; flowering when quite small. It should have a sheltered position, as the delicate flowers are susceptible to the effects of high wind, rain and frost.— **M. s. ròsea** Veitch. Petals suffused outside with pink. R.B.30:85,t(h). J.H. 27:865(h).

M. s. × *Kobus* = **M. Loèbneri** Kache. Lvs. larger, more obovate: fls. larger, with about 12 petals. Orig. before 1910.—*M. s.* × *salicifolia;* see under No. 13.

2. **LIRIODÉNDRON** L. Tulip-tree. Deciduous trees; buds covered by the 2 coherent stipules which are also conspicuous on the growing shoot and envelop each successive leaf: lvs. long-petioled, with a broad truncate apex and usually 1 or 2 broad lobes on each side: fls. terminal, solitary, campanulate; sepals 3, spreading; petals 6, upright; stamens numerous, with extrorse linear anthers and slender filaments; carpels numerous, densely imbricated on a spindle-shaped column developing into a cone-like brown fr.; each carpel consisting of a 1–2-seeded nutlet with a long narrow wing, finally separating from the spindle; seed albuminous with a minute embryo. (Greek *lirion,* lily, and *dendron,* tree.) Two species in N. Am. and China.

A. Filaments about 1 cm. long; petals 4–5 cm. long: mature carpels acute at the apex.
1. *L. Tulipifera*
AA. Filaments about 5 mm. long; petals 3–4 cm. long: mature carpels obtuse or obtusish at the apex ....2. *L. chinense*

1. **L. Tulipífera** L. Tree to 50 m., rarely to 60 m.; glabrous: brts. brown: lvs. saddle-shaped, 7–12 cm. long and about as broad, the broad truncate apex with a short-acuminate lobe on each side and usually 1 or 2, rarely 3 or 4, acute or short-acuminate lobes on each side near the rounded or truncate base, pale green beneath; petioles slender, 5–10 cm. long: fls. tulip-shaped, 4–5 cm. long; sepals ovate-lanceolate, greenish white, spreading, deciduous; petals oblong-obovate, greenish white with a broad orange band near base; stamens slightly shorter than the petals: fr. 6–8 cm. long; carpels 2.5–3.5 cm. long. Fl.v–vi; fr.x. B.M.275(c). S.S.1:t.13. Em.2:605,t. B.S.2:35. E.H.1:t.24–27(h). G.C.55:255(h). Mass. to Wisc., s. to Fla. and Miss. Cult. 1663. Zone IV. Beautiful tree of pyramidal habit with large lvs. of unusual shape turning clear yellow in autumn, and with large fls. conspicuous on account of their size and shape though not brightly colored; in its

native forest it is a tall tree with a columnar trunk destitute of brs. for a considerable height.—**L. T. aureo-marginàtum** Schwerin. Lvs. edged yellow. F.S.19:t.2025(c);20,t.2181(c).—**L. T. obtusílobum** Michx., var. With one rounded lobe on each side at base.—**L. T. integrifòlium** Kirchn., f. Lvs. rounded at base, without lobes. S.H.1:f.218g(l).—**L. T. fastigiatum** Jaeg., var. Tree with upright brs. forming a narrow-pyramidal head. (*L. T. pyramidale* Lav.)

2. **L. chinénse** (Hemsl.) Sarg. Tree to 16 m., similar to the preceding; brts. gray: lvs. usually more deeply lobed, often halfway or more to the middle, with usually one pair of acuminate lobes near base, glaucescent and papillose beneath: fls. cup-shaped, green without, yellow within; petals 3–4 cm. long; filaments 5 mm. long: fr. 7–9 cm. long, with obtuse or obtusish carpels. S.T.1:t.52. H.I.28:2785. G.C.34:370;44:429(h). Jour. Hered. 9:274 (h). C. China. Intr. 1901. Zone VII?

3. **ILLÍCIUM** L. ANISE-TREE. Evergreen aromatic small trees or shrubs, glabrous: winter-buds with several outer scales: lvs. alternate, coriaceous, entire, minutely punctate, exstipulate: fls. perfect, axillary, solitary; sepals 3–6, petaloid; petals numerous, the inner ones narrower, in 3 to several series; stamens many in several series, on short thick filaments; carpels 6–18, in one whorl; style recurved: fr. star-shaped, a whorl of crustaceous 1-seeded follicles finally dehiscent; testa of seed smooth, lustrous. (Latin *illicium*, allurement, referring to the aromatic odor of the plant.) About 10 species in E. and S. Asia and Malaysia and 2 in U. S.

I. **floridànum** Ellis. Shrub to 3 m.: lvs. elliptic to elliptic-lanceolate, 6–15 cm. long, acuminate, cuneate, dark green above, pale beneath, obscurely veined; petiole 1–2 cm. long: fls. purple, nodding, 3–5 cm. across; pedicel 1.5–5 cm. long; sepals ovate or oblong, obtuse, membranous; petals 20–30, narrow-lanceolate to linear, 1.5–2 cm. long: fr. 2.5–3 cm. long broad. B.M. 439(c). N.D.3:t.47(c). Gn.36:151. Fla. to La. Intr. 1771. Zone VII.

4. **TETRACÉNTRON** Oliv. Deciduous tree; buds slender, pointed, upright-spreading with 2 outer sheathing scales: lvs. slender-petioled, palmately 5–7-nerved, crenulate-serrate, estipulate: fls. small, perfect, sessile, in slender pendulous racemes, apetalous; sepals 4, ovate, imbricate; stamens 4, opposite to the sepals, exserted; carpels 4, connate along the ventral suture; styles 4; ovules pendulous, several in each cell: fr. a 4-celled, deeply lobed dehiscent capsule; seeds linear-oblong. (Greek *tetra*, four, and *kentron*, spur; referring to the 4 spur-like appendages of the fr.) One species.

T. **sinénse** Oliv. Tree to 30 m., with smooth, rufous or gray bark: lvs. ovate to elliptic-ovate, 7–12 cm. long, acuminate, subcordate or rounded at base, closely serrulate with obtuse teeth: racemes 8–16 cm. long, short-stalked; fls. yellowish, minute; stamens 1.5 mm. long: fr. brown, about 4 mm. long. Fl.vi–vii. H.I.19:t.1892. C.C.133. I.S.1:t.23. C. and W. China. Intr. 1901. Zone (V) VI. Similar to *Cercidiphyllum* but easily distinguished by the alternate lvs.

5. **SCHISÁNDRA** Michx. Deciduous or evergreen twining shrubs, more or less aromatic; buds with several imbricate scales: lvs. slender-petioled, entire or denticulate, estipulate: fls. in few-fld. axillary clusters, slender-stalked, dioecious; sepals and petals 7–12, not differentiated; stamens 5–15, more or less connate; carpels numerous, densely imbricate in flower, developing into berries disposed on an elongated receptacle and forming a drooping

spike. (Greek *schizein,* to cleave, and *aner, andros,* man; referring to the cleft anthers of the type species.) Syn. *Schizandra* DC. About 12 species in E. and S. Asia and one in N. Am.

A. Pedicels 1.5–7 cm. long; stamens connate only at base: lvs. generally obovate, cuneate at base.
  B. Lvs. glaucous beneath...1. *S. Henryi*
  BB. Lvs. green beneath.
    C. Lvs. thickish: stamens with the free part of the filament as long as the anthers.
2. *S. grandiflora*
    CC. Lvs. thin, membranous: stamens with short filaments.
      D. Fr. black; seeds tuberculate: petioles often as long as the limb...........3. *S. nigra*
      DD. Fr. red; seed smooth: petioles about half as long as the limb.
        E. Stamens many ....4. *S. sphenanthera*
        EE. Stamens 5 ....5. *S. chinensis*
AA. Pedicels 5–10 mm. long; stamens connate into a globose head: lvs. ovate-lanceolate;
    petiole 5–15 mm. long...6. *S. propinqua*

1. **S. Hénryi** Clarke. Glabrous; brts. angled or winged, brown: lvs. broad-elliptic or ovate, 6–10 cm. long, short-acuminate, broad-cuneate or rounded at base, remotely denticulate, lustrous above, glaucous beneath, leathery; petioles 2–4 cm. long: fls. 1.5 cm. across, white, on slender stalks 4–7 cm. long: fr. red, 5–7 cm. long. G.C.38:162. (*S. hypoglauca* Léveillé.) W. China. Intr. 1900. Zone VII?

Related species: **S. glaucéscens** Diels. Differs in its subterete brts., thinner obovate lvs. gradually narrowed toward the base, shorter petioles and the orange-red fls. C. China. Intr. 1907. Zone VII?—**S. pubéscens** Hemsl. & Wils. Young subterete brts., petioles and under side of lvs. densely puberulous. C. China. Intr. 1907. Zone VII?

2. **S. grandiflòra** (Wall.) Hook. & Thoms. Glabrous; stems subterete, brown: lvs. obovate or sometimes ovate to oblong-obovate, 6–10 cm. long, acuminate, cuneate at base, light green beneath, leathery: fls. 2.5–3 cm. across, pinkish; petals suborbicular; pedicels 2–3 cm. long: fr. scarlet, 12–20 cm. long. Fl.v–vi. Wallich, Tent. Fl. Nep. t.14(c). Ann. Bot. Gard. Calcutta, 3:t.69a. Temp. Himal. Not yet intr.—**S. g. cathayénsis** Schneid., var. Lvs. usually smaller, more distinctly denticulate, sometimes glaucescent beneath and scarcely reticulate: fls. about 2 cm. across, fleshy-pink to blood-red. (*S. grandiflora* Fin. & Gagnep., not Hook. & Thoms.) W. China. Intr. 1907. Zone VII?—**S. g. rubriflòra** (Rehd. & Wils.) Schneid., var. Lvs. distinctly denticulate: fls. dark red, about 3 cm. across; pedicels 2–3 cm. long: fr. 8–12 cm. long. R.H.1925:450. M.O.t.4. G.C.78:271. (*S. r.* Rehd. & Wils.) Intr. 1908. Zone VII?

3. **S. nígra** Maxim. Glabrous; brts. terete, brown or grayish brown: lvs. broad-ovate to elliptic or obovate, 5–7 cm. long, short-acuminate, cuneate or sometimes rounded at base, light green beneath, membranous; petioles 2–4 cm. long: fls. about 1.5 cm. across, white; pedicels 2–3 cm. long: fr. black, 2–5 cm. long; seeds tuberculate. Fl.v–vi. N.K.20:t.19. Japan, Korea. Intr. 1892. Zone V.

4. **S. sphenanthèra** Rehd. & Wils. Glabrous; brts. red-brown, terete: lvs. elliptic or obovate to obovate-oblong or ovate-lanceolate, 5–10 cm. long, acuminate, cuneate at base, denticulate, light green beneath and glabrous, rarely pubescent on the veins; petioles 1–3 cm. long: fls. orange, about 1.5 cm. across; pedicels 2–4 cm. long; stamens 10–15, anthers emarginate or truncate at apex: fr. 6–8 cm. long, red. Fl.v–vi. B.M.8921(c). M.O.t.4. C. and W. China. Intr. 1907. Zone V?—**S. s. lancifòlia** Rehd. & Wils., var. Brts. angled: lvs. lanceolate, long-acuminate. W. China. Intr. 1908.

5. **S. chinénsis** (Turcz.) Baill. Climbing to 8 m.; brts. brown, slightly angled: lvs. broad-elliptic to broad-obovate to obovate, 5–10 cm. long, acute

or short-acuminate, cuneate at base, denticulate, lustrous above, light green and sometimes glaucescent beneath and usually slightly pubescent on the veins while young; petioles 1.5–3 cm. long: fls. 1.5 cm. across, creamy white or pinkish, fragrant; petals ovate-oblong; stamens 5, emarginate at apex: fr. scarlet, 3–10 cm. long. Fl.v–vi; fr.viii–ix. Gt.11:t.382. F.S.15:t.1594(c). N.K.20:t.20. G.C.50:2. M.G.14:568(fr.). (*Maximowiczia sinensis* Rupr.) N. E. Asia, Japan. Intr. 1858. Zone V. Vine with dense bright green foliage, attractive in autumn with its racemes of scarlet berries, but only produced if a male plant is near.

6. **S. propínqua** (Bl.) Hook. f. & Thoms. Brts. angled: lvs. ovate or elliptic to oblong-lanceolate, 7–12 cm. long, short-acuminate, broad-cuneate or nearly rounded at base, remotely denticulate or serrulate, rarely entire, pale green or glaucescent beneath, leathery; petiole 1–1.5 cm. long, rarely 2 cm.: fls. orange, about 1.5 cm. across; petals oblong; pedicels 5–10 mm. long, bracteolate: fr. scarlet, about 15 cm. long. B.M.4614(c). (*Sphaerostema propinquum* Bl.) Himal., Malay Arch. Cult. 1828. Zone VII?—**S. p. sinénsis** Oliv., var. Lvs. oblong- or ovate-lanceolate to lanceolate, 6–10 cm. long, long-acuminate, rounded or broad-cuneate at base: fls. smaller, yellowish. Fl. vii–ix. C. and W. China. Intr. 1907. Zone VII?

The N. American **S. coccínea** Michx. occurring from S. C. to Tex. is apparently not hardy within our area.

6. **KADSÙRA** Juss. Evergreen twining shrubs; buds with several imbricate scales: lvs. slender-stalked, dentate to entire, estipulate: fls. unisexual, axillary, usually solitary, slender-stalked; sepals and petals 9–15, gradually changing from the small and green sepals to the larger white or pinkish petals; stamens numerous, distinct or coalescent into a globular head; carpels numerous, 2–3-ovuled, developing into berries forming a globose head. (The Japanese name of the plant.) About 10 species in trop. and subtrop. S. and E. Asia.

K. japónica (L.) Dun. Climbing to 4 m., glabrous; lvs. elliptic to oblong-lanceolate, 5–10 cm. long, acuminate, cuneate at base, remotely dentate or denticulate, dark green above, lighter beneath; petioles 1–2 cm. long: fls. cup-shaped, about 2 cm. across, yellowish white, on slender stalks 1–5 cm. long: fr.-cluster scarlet, 2–3 cm. across. Fl.vi–ix. S.Z.1:t.17(c). N.K.20:t.21. Japan, Korea. Intr. 1846. Zone VII. Handsome in fall with its large scarlet fruiting heads.

30. **CALYCANTHACEAE** Lindl. CALYCANTHUS FAMILY

Deciduous or evergreen shrubs, with aromatic bark; buds scaly or naked: lvs. opposite, short-petioled, entire, penninerved, estipulate: fls. perfect, solitary, short-stalked, perigynous; parts of perianth numerous, spirally arranged, not differentiated into sepals and petals; stamens 5–30; anthers extrorse, innate; filaments short; carpels numerous, inserted inside of a hollow receptacle with the styles protruding, 1–2-ovuled, developing into one-seeded achenes inclosed by the urn-shaped receptacle, capsule-like at maturity, obovoid or ellipsoid; seeds without endosperm; cotyledons spirally rolled, broadly reniform, much broader than long, auriculate at base.—Two genera with 5 or C species in N. Am. and E. Asia.

A. Stamens 10–30; fls. brownish red; buds hidden or free.....................1. *Calycanthus*
AA. Stamens 5 or 6; fls. yellowish white: buds free...........................2. *Chimonanthus*

1. **CALYCÁNTHUS** L. Deciduous shrubs; buds hidden by the base of the petioles or free; fls. terminal on short lateral brts.; stamens 10–30; brown

or yellowish brown: fr. contracted at the mouth or campanulate. (Greek *kalyx*, calyx, and *anthos*, flower.) Syn.: *Butneria* Duh. Three or 4 species in N. Am.

A. Buds hidden: anthers oblong: fr. contracted at the mouth.
  B. Lvs. densely pubescent beneath...1. *C. floridus*
  BB. Lvs. glabrous or slightly pubescent beneath.................................2. *C. fertilis*
AA. Buds free; anthers linear: fr. campanulate...............................3. *C. occidentalis*

1. C. flòridus L. CAROLINA ALLSPICE. Shrub to 3 m.: lvs. ovate or elliptic to narrow-elliptic, 5–12 cm. long, acute or acuminate, rarely obtuse, cuneate or rounded at base, grayish green and densely pubescent beneath; petiole about 5 mm. long: fls. dark reddish brown, about 5 cm. across, fragrant: fr. obovoid, 6–7 cm. long, usually much contracted at the mouth. Fl.VI–VII. B.M.503(c). Gn.21:184;33:392. S.L.112(h). Va. to Fla. Intr. 1726. Zone IV. Chiefly grown for its sweet-scented fls.; all parts and particularly the wood when dry exhale a camphor-like fragrance.—**C. f. ovàtus** Ait., var. Lvs. ovate to ovate-oblong, rounded or subcordate at base. L.I.t.24.

Closely related species: **C. Mòhrii** Small. Lvs. broad-elliptic or elliptic-ovate, broad-cuneate to subcordate at base: fls. purple, 5–6 cm. across: receptacle little contracted at the mouth. Tenn. to Ga. and Ala. Intr. 1906. Zone V.

2. C. fértilis Walt. Shrub to 3 m.; glabrous or slightly pubescent: lvs. elliptic or ovate to elliptic-oblong, 6–15 cm. long, acuminate or acute, cuneate or rounded at base, glaucous beneath: fls. greenish purple to reddish brown, 3.5–5 cm. across: fr. obovoid, 5–7 cm. long, contracted at the mouth. Fl. VI–VII. B.R.5:404(c). L.D.3:172(c). (*C. glaucus* Willd.) Pa. to Ga. and Ala. Intr. 1806. Zone V. Similar to the preceding, but not quite as hardy and not as fragrant.—**C. f. férax** Rehd., var. Lvs. usually elliptic-oblong, green beneath. B.R.6:481(c). (*C. laevigatus* Willd.)—**C. f. nànus** (Lois.) Schelle, f. Low shrub: lvs. elliptic-ovate to ovate-oblong, 4–8 cm. long, green beneath. N.D.1:t.48(c). (*C. nanus* Lois.)

3. C. occidentàlis Hook. & Arn. Shrub to 3 m.: lvs. ovate to oblong-lanceolate, 8–20 cm. long, acute or acuminate, rounded or subcordate at base, scabrous above, green and glabrous or slightly pubescent beneath; petioles about 5 mm. long: fls. brownish purple, changing to a tawny color at the tips of the sepals, 5–7 cm. across, fragrant; anthers linear: fr. ovoid-campanulate, not contracted at the mouth, 4–5 cm. long. Fl.VI–VII. B.M.4808(c). F.S.11:t. 1113(c). Gn.33:392. (*C. macrophyllus* Hort.) Calif. Intr. 1831. Zone VI.— Of more straggling growth than the preceding species and with larger lvs. and fls., but blooming less profusely and less hardy.

2. CHIMONÁNTHUS Lindl. Deciduous or evergreen shrubs; buds with many imbricate scales: lvs. glabrous: fls. appearing long before the lvs., on very short scaly stalks from axillary buds on brs. of the previous year; sepals numerous, imbricate, yellow; stamens 5 or 6, short: fr. constricted at the mouth. (Greek *cheimon*, winter, and *anthos*, flower, referring to its flowering during the winter.) Syn.: *Meratia* Lois. Two species in China.

C. praècox (L.) Link. Shrub to 3 m.: lvs. elliptic-ovate to ovate-lanceolate, 7–15 cm. long, acuminate, rounded or cuneate at base; petioles about 5 mm. long: fls. about 2.5 cm. broad, very fragrant, the outer sepals yellow, the inner striped purplish brown; fr. ellipsoid, about 4 cm. long. Fl.XII–III. B.M.466(c). L.D.3:t.173(c). G.C.III.11:213. Gn.87:36(fl,h). M.O.t.2(h). (*C. fragrans* Lindl., *Calycanthus praecox* L., *Meratia p.* Rehd. & Wils.) China. Intr. 1766. Zone VII. Desirable shrub on account of its fragrant fls. produced in mild seasons during the winter.—**C. p. grandiflòrus** (Lindl.)

Mak., var. Lvs. usually larger, occasionally to 20 cm. long; fls. about 3–3.5 cm. across, purer yellow, not as fragrant. R.H.1924:11,t(c). B.R.6:451(c). (*C. fragrans* var. *g.* Lindl.)

31. ANNONACEAE Rich. CUSTARD-APPLE FAMILY

Deciduous or evergreen trees or shrubs: lvs. alternate, simple, entire, penninerved, exstipulate: fls. perfect, rarely unisexual, hypogynous, rarely perigynous: perianth usually of 9 parts in 3 whorls; stamens usually numerous, spirally arranged; carpels usually numerous, distinct, rarely connate, 1- to many-ovuled, usually berry-like at maturity; seeds with copious ruminate endosperm and a small embryo.—More than 70 genera with more than 600 species, chiefly in the trop. regions of Asia, Afr., Am., Austral.—Only one species of the N. American genus Asimina is hardly within our area.

ASÍMINA Adans. Deciduous or evergreen-shrubs, rarely trees; buds rather small, with 2–3 outer scales, brown-tomentose: lvs. usually large: fls. axillary, solitary or few, nodding, on short stalks: sepals 3, caducous, smaller than the petals; petals 6, the inner ones smaller and usually upright; filaments short; carpels 3–15, many-ovuled, with recurved styles: fr. of one or few oval to oblong berries with large compressed seeds in 1 or 2 ranks. (Assiminier, a French-Indian name.) Eight species in N. Am.

A. tríloba (L.) Dun. PAWPAW. Small tree to 12 m.: brts. fulvous-pubescent while young, later glabrous and brown: lvs. obovate-oblong, 15–30 cm. long, short-acuminate, usually gradually narrowed into a petiole 5–10 mm. long: fls. 4–5 cm. across, lurid purple, on short fulvous-pubescent stalks about 1 cm. long; sepals ovate, acute, greenish pubescent outside; outer petals broad-ovate, rounded and later reflexed at apex; the inner upright, much smaller, pointed: carpels in fr. ellipsoid to oblong, 5–7 cm. long, greenish yellow at first, finally brown; seeds 2–2.5 cm. long. Fl.IV–V; fr.IX–X. B.M.5854(c). S.S.1:t.15,16. G.F.8:495. G.C.74:293,295(h). R.H.1911:134,135. (*Annona t.* L., *Uvaria t.* Torr. & Gr.) N. Y. to Fla., w. to Neb. and Tex. Intr. 1736. Zone V. Small tree with large drooping lvs. and fls. of lurid purple color; the frs. are edible. It prefers rich and humid soil. Interesting as the only hardy member of the large tropical family of Annonaceae.

32. LAURACEAE Lindl. LAUREL FAMILY

Deciduous or mostly evergreen trees or shrubs, all parts containing an aromatic oil: lvs. usually alternate, simple, entire or lobed, usually with pellucid dots, exstipulate: fls. perfect or unisexual, regular, usually small; perianth usually of 6 parts, in 2 similar whorls; stamens in 3–4 whorls of 3 each, often partly staminodial; anthers opening by valves; ovary usually superior, 1-celled, 1-ovuled; ovule pendulous, anatropous; style 1; stigma 2–3-lobed: fr. a drupe or a berry, with the pedicel often thickened below the fruit; seed without endosperm; embryo straight, with large fleshy cotyledons. —About 45 genera with 1000 species chiefly in trop. and subtrop. regions.

1. PÉRSEA Mill. Evergreen trees: buds naked: lvs. entire, penninerved, revolute in bud: fls. in small panicles or cymes; calyx 6-parted, persistent; stamens 12, the 3 of the inner whorl sterile and gland-like; the first 2 whorls with introrse, the third whorl with extrorse anthers; anthers 4-celled; ovary sessile, with slender style: fr. a berry with the persistent calyx-lobes at base. (An ancient name of an oriental tree.) Syn.: *Tamala* Raf. About 50 species in trop. and subtrop. Am. and 1 in the Canary Isls.

P. Borbònia (L.) Spreng. RED BAY. Tree to 12 m.; bark furrowed; brts. soon glabrous: lvs. oblong to lance-oblong, 5–10 cm. long, obtusely pointed, cuneate at base, glaucescent beneath, glabrous; petioles 5–10 mm. long: fls. in peduncled several-fld. cymes, the peduncle about as long as the petiole: fr. subglobose, about 1.2 cm. long, dark blue or nearly black. N.D.2:t.33(c). S.S.7:t.301. H.H.220,221(b). (*P. caroliniensis* Nees, *Notaphoebe borbonica* Pax: BULL BAY.) S. Del. to Fla., in swamps. Intr. 1739. Zone VII. Attractive in fall with its bluish black frs. on red stalks.

2. UMBELLULÀRIA Nutt. Evergreen aromatic tree; buds naked: lvs. entire, penninerved, involute in bud: fls. perfect, on short pedicels in many-fld. stalked umbels enclosed before anthesis by an involucre of 5–6 imbricate scales; calyx 6-parted, deciduous; stamens of the third whorl with 2 conspicuous glands at base, those of the fourth whorl reduced to minute staminodes; style shorter than calyx-lobes. (From Latin *umbellula,* an umbelet; in reference to the inflorescence.) One species.

U. califórnica (Hook. & Arn.) Nutt. CALIFORNIAN LAUREL. Tree to 25 m., with scaly bark: lvs. short-petioled, ovate-oblong to lanceolate, 5–12 cm. long, obtusely acuminate, broad-cuneate at base, dark green and lustrous above, glaucous or glaucescent and reticulate beneath, glabrous at maturity: fls. yellowish green, in umbels about 1.5 cm. across; peduncle 1–2.5 cm. long: fr. ovoid, 2–2.5 cm. long, yellow green, sometimes purplish. Fl.I–v; fr.IX–x. B.M. 5320(c). S.S.7:t.306. J.S.t.10(h). (*Oreodaphne c.* Nees.) Calif. to Ore. Intr. 1829. Zone VII. Handsome tree with a dense head of lustrous foliage. —**U. c. péndula** Rehd., f. Tree with spreading brs. forming a broad head with pendulous brts. J.S.t.76(h).

3. SÁSSAFRAS Nees. Deciduous trees; buds with few imbricate outer scales: lvs. entire or 1–3-lobed at apex, 3-nerved at base, involute in bud: fls. dioecious, unisexual or apparently perfect, in several-fld. racemes before the lvs.; calyx 6-parted; staminate fls. with 9 stamens in 3 whorls, those of the inner whorl with a pair of stalked glands at base, with or without staminodes and with or without pistil; anthers 4-celled, opening with 4 valves or 2-celled; pistillate with an ovoid ovary, slender style and 6 rudimentary stamens or with 9 stamens and 3 staminodes: fr. an ovoid drupe supported by a club-shaped fleshy pedicel. (Spanish *salsafras* = Saxifraga, referring to its supposed medical properties.) Three species in N. Am., China and Formosa.

S. álbidum (Nutt.) Nees. SASSAFRAS. Tree to 20 or occasionally 38 m., with deeply furrowed bark; brts. and buds glabrous and glaucous: lvs. ovate to elliptic, 8–12 cm. long, entire or 1–3-lobed at apex, acutish or obtuse, cuneate at base, bright green above, glabrous and glaucous beneath; petioles 1.5–3 cm. long: fls. yellow, 7 mm. across, in racemes 3–5 cm. long; staminate fls. without staminodes and without rudimentary pistil: fr. ovoid, 1 cm. long, bluish black, bloomy, its fleshy stalk bright red. Fl.IV–v; fr.IX. Em.360,t.(c). S.S.7:t.304,305. G.C.76:96,97(h). B.S.2:501,t.(h). (*S. officinale* var. *albidum*

Blake). Mass. to S. C. and Tenn. Cult. 1630. Zone IV. Handsome pyramidal tree with bright green lvs. of distinct and peculiar shape turning orange
and scarlet in fall and with attractive dark blue red-stemmed fr.—**S. a. molle**
(Raf.) Fern., var. Buds and young brts. pubescent: lvs. glaucescent and
silky pubescent beneath at least while young. (*S. officinale* Nees & Eberm.,
S. variifolium Ktze.) Me. to Ont. and Mich., s. to Fla. and Tex. Cult. 1930.
    Related species: **S. Tzumu** Hemsl. Brts. and lvs. pubescent while young or
glabrous; lvs. more pointed, sometimes to 20 cm. long; petioles to 6 cm. long:
racemes with the peduncle 4–8 cm. long: fls. apparently perfect, with 9 fertile
stamens and 3 staminodes. C.C.150. H.I.29:2833. Jour. Hered. 9:275(h).
(*Pseudosassafras* T. Lecomte.) C. China. Intr. 1900. Zone VII?

4. LINDERA Thunb. Deciduous or evergreen aromatic trees and shrubs;
buds with few to several imbricate scales: lvs. entire or 3-lobed, penninerved
or 3-nerved at base, convolute in bud: fls. dioecious or polygamous in axillary
clusters, with an involucre of 4 deciduous scales; sepals 6, rarely more; staminate fls. with 9 stamens; anthers 2-valved; pistillate fls. with a globose ovary
and 9–15 staminodes: fr. a subglobose drupe. (After Joh. Linder, Swedish
physician; 1676–1723.) Syn.: *Benzoin* Fabric.; including *Daphnidium* Nees
and *Aperula* Bl. About 60 species in temp. and subtrop. E. and S. Asia; 2 in
N. Am.

A. Lvs. penninerved, always entire.
  B. Lvs. deciduous.
    C. Fls. before the lvs. on very short pedicels: pedicel of fr. 1 cm. long or less.
      D. Petiole 5–15 mm. long: fr. scarlet; buds with 2–3 outer pale scales...1. *L. Benzoin*
      DD. Petiole 1.5–2.5 cm. long, slender: fr. yellowish or brownish: buds with several lus-
          trous brown scales...2. *L. praecox*
    CC. Fls. with the lvs.: pedicels about 5 mm. long: fr. subglobose, black..4. *L. umbellata*
  BB. Lvs. persistent, 10–20 cm. long: fr. black, 1.5 cm. long................3. *L. megaphylla*
AA. Lvs. 3-nerved at base, entire or 3-lobed; fr. subglobose, black............5. *L. obtusiloba*

1. L. Bénzoin (L.) Bl. SPICE-BUSH. Shrub to 5 m.; glabrous or nearly so;
buds with 2–3 outer scales: lvs. oblong-obovate, 7–12 cm. long, acute or short-
acuminate, cuneate at base, light green above, pale beneath: fls. greenish
yellow, in dense subsessile clusters 5 mm. across: fr. elliptic-oblong, about 1
cm. long, scarlet. Fl.III–IV; fr.IX. M.Am.2:t.145(c). Em.365,t. B.B.2:135.
(*L. aestivalis* Nees, *Benzoin aestivale* Nees, *B. odoriferum* Nees.) Me. to
Ont. and Kans., s. to Fla. and Tex. Intr. 1683. Zone IV. Lvs. changing to
clear yellow in fall, when the brs. are studded with scarlet frs.; also attractive
in early spring with its yellow fls.—**L. B. xanthocárpa** (G. S. Torrey) Rehd.,
f. Fr. yellow. Mass.—**L. B. pubéscens** (Palmer & Steyerm.) Rehd., var.
Brts., petioles and lvs. beneath pubescent, at least on the veins, margin ciliate.
S. C. to Miss. and s. Mo. Intr. ?

2. L. praècox (Sieb. & Zucc.) Bl. Shrub or small tree to 8 m.; glabrous;
buds with lustrous brown scales; brts. brown with conspicuous white lenticels
while young: lvs. ovate or elliptic, 4–9 cm. long, acuminate, cuneate at base,
glaucescent beneath: fls. greenish yellow in subsessile or short-stalked umbels
about 1.5 cm. across: fr. subglobose, 1.5–2 cm. across, yellow or reddish
brown, on thickened pedicels about 1 cm. long; peduncle 3–5 mm. long.
Fl.IV; fr.IX. S.I.2:t.19(c). (*Benzoin p.* Sieb. & Zucc.) Japan. Intr. 1891.
Zone VI. Similar to the preceding; lvs. changing to yellow in fall.

3. L. megaphýlla Hemsl. Evergreen shrub or tree to 20 m.; brts. glabrous, dark purple-brown, with few pale penticels; terminal buds with many
imbricate velutinous scales: lvs. lance-oblong to oblanceolate, 10–20 cm. long,
acuminate, cuneate at base, lustrous dark green above, glaucous and glabrous
or slightly pubescent beneath; petioles 1–2 cm. long: fls. yellow, in many-fld.
dense short-stalked silky umbels about 2.5 cm. across: fr. globose-ovoid,

1.5 cm. long, black, on stout pedicels about 1 cm. long. Fl.III–IV; fr.x. C.C. 162. (*Benzoin grandifolium* Rehd.) C. and W. China. Intr. 1900. Zone VII? Evergreen shrub with large lustrous lvs.

4. **L. umbellàta** Thunb. Shrub to 3 m.; buds with 2–3 more or less silky outer scales; brts. yellowish or purplish, smooth, without lenticels: lvs. elliptic-obovate or elliptic to obovate-oblong, 6–12 cm. long, acutish or short-acuminate, cuneate at base, glaucescent beneath and usually slightly pubescent at least on the midrib; petioles 1–1.8 cm. long: fls. yellow, with the lvs. in short-peduncled silky-pubescent umbels 2–2.5 cm. across; pedicels 6–10 mm. long: fr. subglobose, about 8 mm. long, black, on slender pedicels 1.5–2 cm. long. S.I.2:t.18(c). (*Benzoin umbellatum* Ktze., *L. membranacea* Maxim.) Japan, C. and W. China. Intr. 1892. Zone VI?—**L. u. hypoglaùca** (Maxim.) Mak., f. Lvs. glabrous beneath except the silky midrib and with a distinct glaucous bloom. (*L. hypoglauca* Maxim.) Japan. Cult. 1880. Zone VI?

5. **L. obtusíloba** Bl. Shrub or thin tree, to 10 m.; buds glabrous, with 3–4 outer scales; brts. yellowish gray, rarely purplish, glabrous, with scattered lenticels: lvs. broad-ovate, 6–12 cm. long, acute or obtusish, cordate to broad-cuneate at the 3-nerved base, entire or 3-lobed at apex with the lateral lobes short and obtuse, grayish green and silky pubescent on the veins beneath; petioles 1–2 cm. long, silky-pubescent: fls. yellow, in subsessile silky-pubescent umbels 1–1.5 cm. across; pedicels 3–4 mm. long: fr. globose, 7–8 mm. across, black, on pubescent pedicels about 1 cm. long. Fl.IV; fr.IX. S.I.1:t.44(c). G.F.6:295. S.L.215(h). (*Benzoin obtusilobum* Ktze.) Japan, Korea, China. Intr. 1880. Zone VI. Tall spreading shrub with handsome lobed lvs.

Closely related species: **L. tríloba** (Sieb. & Zucc.) Bl. Shrub to 6 m.: lvs. usually broad-cuneate at base or rounded, deeply 3-lobed with nearly equal acuminate lobes; fr. subglobose, 1.2 cm. across, greenish yellow, on glabrous pedicels. S.I.2:t.19(c). (*Benzoin trilobum* Sieb. & Zucc.) Japan. Intr. 1915. Zone VI?—**L. cercidifòlia** Hemsl. Shrub to 8 m.: lvs. suborbicular to ovate, 3.5–10 cm. long, short-acuminate, rounded at base, usually entire, rarely with 3 short acute lobes at apex, glabrous or nearly so beneath: fr. globose-ovoid, 6–7 mm. long, dark red. (*Benzoin cercidifolium* Rehd.) China. Intr. 1907. Zone VI?

33. CRUCÍFERAE Juss. MUSTARD FAMILY

Herbs, rarely subshrubs or shrubs: lvs. usually alternate, entire to pinnatifid: fls. perfect, usually in terminal racemes, regular, rarely symmetrical; sepals 4; petals 4, rarely wanting; stamens 6, 4 longer and 2 shorter, rarely fewer or more; ovary superior, consisting of 2 carpels, 2-celled, rarely 1-celled, with 2 parietal placentae at the edges of the septum: fr. a dehiscent pod (silique or silicle), rarely indehiscent: seed with endosperm; embryo variously curved or folded.—More than 200 genera and 1600 species, chiefly in the temp. and colder regions of both hemispheres; few in the tropics. The family contains few shrubby plants; the genera enumerated below are only suffruticose with the exception of *Pseudocytisus* which is a shrub.

A. Plants without hairs or pilose with simple hairs.
  B. Plants suffruticose, usually glabrous, unarmed: pod compressed contrary to the septum.
    C. Petals unequal; fls. white or pinkish..1. *Iberis*
    CC. Petals equal, rosy-purple...2. *Aethionema*
  BB. Plant shrubby, pilose, spiny or unarmed: fls. yellow: pod scarcely compressed, 1–2-seeded ....3. *Pseudocytisus*
AA. Plant stellate-pubescent: fls. yellow: pod flattened in the plane of the septum..4. *Alyssum*

1. **IBÈRIS** L. CANDYTUFT. Herbs or subshrubs: lvs. glabrous or ciliate, entire to pinnatifid: fls. in usually umbel-like racemes; the outer 2 petals

much longer than the inner ones; stamens without appendages: pod much compressed, roundish or broad-elliptic, usually winged, often notched at apex; seed 1 in each locule. (Ancient Greek name for a kind of cress.) About 30 species in S. Eu., W. Asia and N. Afr.—The following species are all evergreen perennials with woody usually procumbent stems (erect in *L. semperflorens*) and ascending brts. and with thickish fleshy lvs.

A. Flowering brs. branching above; outer fls. pink, inner white: lvs. obovate-oblong, dentate near apex ....1. *I. gibraltarica*
AA. Flowering brs. simple: fls. white, rarely pinkish: lvs. usually entire.
  B. Lvs. linear to oblong or oblanceolate, rarely more than 5 mm. broad: pod winged; seeds wingless.
    C. Racemese umbel-like in fl.: lvs. ciliate and stems finely pubescent.
      D. Lvs. obtuse, oblong-linear, the lower obovate-oblong: fls. often pinkish.
                                                  2. *I. Tenoreana*
      DD. Lvs. acute, usually linear: fls. white...............................3. *I. saxatilis*
    CC. Racemes elongated; stems and the narrow-oblong obtuse lvs. glabrous.
                                                  4. *I. sempervirens*
  BB. Lvs. obovate-oblong, to 1 cm. broad, entire: pod wingless; seed winged.
                                                  5. *I. semperflorens*

1. I. gibraltàrica L. To 40 cm. high: lvs. obovate to spatulate-oblong, 2–5 cm. long, obtuse, dentate near apex, sometimes entire, slightly ciliate toward the base: infl. to 4 cm. across, umbel-like; the outer fls. lilac-pink: usually lateral infl. in the axils of the upper lvs.: fr. deeply notched at apex. Fl.iv–vi. B.M.124(c). R.H.1870:330,t(c). B.C.3:1635. G.C.46:158(h). Spain, Morocco. Intr. 1732. Zone VII?

2. I. Tenoreàna DC. To 20 cm. tall: brts. finely hairy: lower lvs. obovate, upper narrow-oblong, 2–4 cm. long, obtuse, entire or dentate, ciliate: infl. umbel-like, 4–5 cm. across, the outer fls. often pinkish: fr. 6–8 mm. long, deeply notched. Fl.v. B.M.2783(c). L.B.18:1721(c). Italy. Intr. 1822. Zone VII?—**I. T. petraèa** (Jord.) Nichols. Fls. tinged red in the centre. B.C.3: 1636(h). (*I. p.* Jord.) S. Eu.

    Closely related species: **I. Pruítii** Tineo. Differs chiefly in the glabrous often subdentate lvs. and white fls. Fiori & Paol. Ic. Fl. Ital. 173. Sicily. By some authors *I. Tenoreana* is referred to this species as *I. Pruitii* var. *hirtula* Ten.

3. I. saxátilis L. About 10 cm. tall; brts. and usually the infl. finely hairy: lvs. linear, 1–2 cm. long, acute, mucronate, ciliate: infl. umbel-like, 2–24 cm. across; fls. white: fr. about 7 mm. long, notched at apex. Fl.v. R.I.2: f.4200(c). S. Eu. Intr. 1739. Zone V?

    Related species: **I. corifòlia** (Sims) Sweet. Lvs. linear-spatulate, obtuse, glabrous. B.M.1642(c). J.H.58:453;III.11:177. (? *I. correaefolia* Nichols.) S. Eu. Cult. 1814. Zone VI?

4. I. sempérvirens L. To 30 cm. tall; glabrous: lvs. linear-oblong, 1.5–3 cm. long, obtuse, entire: infl. 2–3 cm. across, elongating and finally racemose: fr. orbicular-elliptic, 6–7 mm. long, slightly or deeply emarginate. Fl.v. R.I. 2:f.4198,4199(c). S. Eu., W. Asia. Intr. 1731. Zone V.—**I. s. Garrexiàna** (All.) Nichols. Lvs. linear-oblong, acutish, not mucronate: fls. rather small, umbellate, finally racemose. R.I.2:t.7(c). Gn.62:393(h). (*I. G.* All.) S. Eu. Cult. 1868.

5. I. semperflòrens L. Upright shrub to 60 cm., glabrous: lvs. obovate-oblong, with the petiole 3–6 cm. long, rounded at apex, gradually narrowed at base, entire: fls. white or sometimes pinkish, fragrant: infl. about 3 cm. across, becoming racemose: fr. broader than long, 8–10 mm. across, slightly emarginate, wingless; seeds winged. Fl.x–iii. R.I.2:4201. S. Italy, Sicily. Intr. 1679. Zone VII?

2. AETHIONÈMA R. Br. Herbs or subshrubs, sometimes spinescent: lvs. alternate, entire: fls. pinkish-purple or red, rarely whitish or pale yellow, in terminal racemes; sepals saccate at base; the longer stamens with usually dilated and often toothed filaments: pods compressed, winged, 2-celled, with 1 or several seeds in each cell, rarely 1-seeded and indehiscent. (Greek *aethein,* to scorch and *nema,* filament.) About 50 species chiefly mediterranean.

A. grandiflòrum Boiss. & Hohenack. Subshrub with slender simple brs. procumbent at base, to 40 cm. long, glabrous: lvs. linear-oblong to obovate-oblong, 2–4 cm. long, obtuse, bluish green: fls. in elongated racemes, to 7 cm. long and 2.5 cm. across, rose-colored, petals 4 times as long as sepals; filaments dilated at base, not toothed: pods suborbicular with the wings much broader than the locules, deeply notched at apex; stigma subsessile: locules 1-seeded. Fl.v–vⅢ. Gn.9:t.108(c). S.H.1:f.231a-h. Persia. Intr. 1879. Zone VI? Handsome subshrub well adapted for rockeries.

Related species: **A. pulchéllum** Boiss. & Huet. Stems branched: fls. smaller; petals about 2½ times as long as the sepals, obovate; pods with erose-dentate wings. Gn.25:320,t(c). G.C.105:147(h). (*A. coridifolium* Hort., not DC.) Asia Minor. Cult. 1887. Zone V?—**A. diástrophis** Bge. Fls. small: pods small with plicate deeply dentate curved wings; style slightly shorter than sinus. Bibl. Bot. No.58:t.1. Asia Minor. Intr. 1841.—**A. coridifòlium** DC. It differs chiefly in its shorter crowded linear to linear-oblong lvs. often acutish, in the shorter and denser racemes with smaller fls., and in the obovate-oblong narrowly winged pods. B.M.5952(c). Gt.33:t.1150(c). (*Iberis jucunda* Schott & Kotschy.) Asia Minor. Intr. 1871.—**A. membranàceum** DC. Upright, to 15 cm.: lvs. linear-oblong, upright: racemes subcapitate: fls. 6 mm. long; longer filaments toothed at apex: pods with very broad entire wings, style short. S.B.t.69(c). Persia. Intr. 1828.—**A. grácile** L. Ascending, to 20 cm.: fls. purplish, in dense racemes; longer filaments toothed at apex: pod obcordate with erose-dentate wings; style as long as sinus; locules 2–3-ovuled. R.I.2:t.11(c). Greece to Carniolia. Intr. 1820.—**A. iberídeum** Boiss. Cespitose, with scabrid brs., crowded narrow lvs. and white fls. in short and dense racemes: pods small, with curved wings; locules 2-ovuled. S.St.4,89(h). (*A. schistosum* Boiss. & Kotschy.) Greece, Asia Minor. Intr. about 1880.

3. PSEUDOCÝTISUS Ktze. Small shrubs, spiny or unarmed: lvs. alternate, entire, usually hirsute: fls. yellow, in racemes; longer filaments connate below: pod ovoid, slightly compressed, with convex valves; locules 1–2-seeded: seeds globose. (Greek *pseudos,* false, and *kytisos.*) Three species in Spain and Algeria.

P. spinòsus (Boiss.) Rehd. Upright spiny shrub to 30 cm.: lvs. linear, 1–2 cm. long, fleshy, like the stem furnished with scattered bristly hairs sometimes nearly wanting: fls. few, about 1.5 cm. across; petals yellow, with brown veins; sepals erect, 6 mm. long: pod ovoid, 6 mm. long, beaked. Fl.vɪ. S.H. 1:358. (*Vella spinosa* Boiss.) Cult. 1890. Zone VII?

P. integrifòlius (Salisb.) Rehd. is probably still tenderer: unarmed shrub to 60 cm. or more: lvs. obovate, 1.5–2 cm. long, bristly: fls. larger, in elongated many-fld. racemes. B.R.293. (*Vella Pseudocytisus* L., *V. integrifolia* Salisb.) Spain. Intr. 1759.

4. ALÝSSUM L. Herbs or subshrubs with stellate hairs: lvs. alternate, often forming rosettes, entire or toothed: fls. white or yellow, in terminal usually umbel-like racemes: longer stamens winged and toothed at apex: pods subglobose or ovoid, more or less compressed; valves convex, scarcely veined; each locule with 1 or 2 wingless seeds, rarely more. (Ancient Greek name.) About 100 species in Eu., the Mediterr. Region and Cauc.

A. saxátile L. GOLDEN-TUFT. Woody at base, to 30 cm., densely hoary-tomentulose: lvs. obovate-oblong to oblanceolate, obtuse or acutish, sometimes indistinctly toothed, the basal ones tufted, petioled, 6–10 cm. long with the petiole, the upper ones smaller, serrate: flowering stems much branched above, bearing numerous subumbellate heads about 1.5 cm. across of golden-yellow fls.; petals emarginate: pods suborbicular, compressed, 6–7 mm. long, glabrous. Fl.v. B.M.159(c). R.I.2:f.4280(c). B.C.1:269. C. and S. Eu. Intr. 1710. Zone IV. Low tufted plant covered with golden-yellow fls. in May.—**A. s. variegàtum** Nichols. Lvs. margined white. N.I.1:60.

Related species: **A. gemonénse** L. Differs chiefly in its broader and shorter lvs., in the incised petals and in the smaller slightly compressed pods about 4 mm. long. R.I.2:f.4281(c). S. Eu. Intr. 1710. Zone V.—**A. argénteum** Vitm. Subshrub to 40 cm., without tufted lvs. at base: lvs. obovate-elliptic to oblanceolate, 6–20 mm. long, acutish, green and pilose above, white-tomentose beneath: fls. golden-yellow, in small heads forming large termina. corymbs: pod suborbicular, 3–4 mm. long, much flattened, stellate-pubescent. Fl.vi–vii. R.I.2:f.4277,4378(c). B.C.1:269. S. Eu., Asia Minor. Cult. 1830. Zone V.—**A. spinòsum** L. Dense spiny shrub to 30 cm.: lvs. oblong-lanceolate, 1–5 cm. long, like the brts. and infl. silvery-scurfy: fls. white to pink, in short racemes: pod glabrous· Gn.88:182(h). J.L.64:f.38(h). S. W. Eu., N. Afr. Intr. 1683. Zone VII?

34. **CRASSULACEAE** DC. ORPINE FAMILY

Herbs or subshrubs, usually fleshy and mostly glabrous: lvs. usually alternate, entire or toothed: fls. mostly in terminal cymes, regular, usually perfect; sepals 5, rarely 3–30; petals as many; stamens as many or twice as many; carpels as many as petals, free, usually connate, usually each with a scale at base; styles subulate; ovules usually many, rarely few or 1: fr. consisting of dehiscent leathery or membranous follicles.—About 500 species in 14 genera, chiefly in the warmer regions, much developed in S. Afr. and S. Eu.

1. **SÉDUM** L. Herbs or subshrubs: fls. yellow, white, pink or blue, in terminal cymes, usually 5-merous; stamens 10, the epipetalous adnate to the base of the petals; follicles free, many-seeded, rarely 1-seeded, dehiscent on the ventral suture. (Ancient Latin name.) About 140 species in the temp. and colder regions of the n. hemisphere; in Am. s. to Peru.

S. populifòlium L. Upright subshrub to 30 cm. tall, glabrous; older brs. purple-brown: lvs. slender-petioled, ovate, 1.5–3 cm. long, acute, subcordate at base, coarsely and irregularly dentate: fls. whitish or pinkish, in terminal corymbose cymes, 3–8 cm. across; petals lanceolate, 5–6 mm. long; anthers purple. Fl.vii–viii. B.M.211(c). S.H.1:360. Gn.27:316;82:297(h). Siberia. Intr. 1780. Zone V.

35. **SAXIFRAGACEAE** Dum. SAXIFRAGE FAMILY

Herbs, shrubs or small trees: lvs. alternate or opposite, usually without stipules: fls. perfect, regular, hypogynous or perigynous; sepals 4–5, rarely more; petals as many, valvate or imbricate; stamens as many, or twice as many and the outer opposite to the petals; carpels 2–5, wholly or partly connate, rarely separate; styles or stigmas as many as carpels; ovules many: fr. a capsule or berry; seed small winged, with endosperm; embryo small with flat cotyledons. Including *Hydrangeaceae* Dum. and *Grossulariaceae* Dum.—About 75 genera with 100 species widely distributed in both hemispheres chiefly in temp. regions.

A. Lvs. opposite: fr. a capsule...........................Subfam. I. HYDRANGEOIDEAE Engl.
　B. Fls. all fertile with usually showy petals, in racemes or sometimes corymbose panicles.
　　C. Fls. 4–5-, rarely 6-merous.
　　　D. Stamens numerous.
　　　　E. Lvs. evergreen, penninerved: fls. 5–7-merous.....................1. *Carpenteria*
　　　　EE. Lvs. deciduous, usually dentate, 3–5-nerved at base: fls. 4-merous.
　　　　　　　　　　　　　　　　　　　　　　　　　　　　　　　2. *Philadelphus*

DD. Stamens twice as many as petals.
  E. Fls. 4-merous; ovary nearly superior: lvs. entire...................4. *Fendlera*
  EE. Fls. 5-6-merous: lvs. dentate.
    F. Ovary superior.
      G. Lvs. penninerved: fls. 5-merous.............................3. *Jamesia*
      GG. Lvs. 3-nerved: fls. 5-6-merous, small.......................6. *Whipplea*
    FF. Ovary inferior.
      G. Petals free, conspicuous: lvs. serrate. usually with stellate hairs.
                                                                      5. *Deutzia*
      GG. Petals cohering, falling off as a whole: lvs. entire, glabrous..10. *Pileostegia*
  CC. Fls. 7-10-merous; style 1: lvs. entire or nearly so.....................11. *Decumaria*
  BB. Fls. of two kinds, small fertile ones and sterile enlarged marginal ones, rarely the latter
      wanting: infl. corymbose, rarely paniculate; ovary inferior or semi-superior.
    C. Sterile fls. with connate sepals, sometimes wanting: stamens many: buds stalked.
                                                                      7. *Platycrater*
    CC. Sterile fls. with distinct sepals; stamens twice as many as sepals, rarely more: buds
        sessile.
      D. Styles 2-5, free: sterile fls. with 3-4 sepals...........................8. *Hydrangea*
      DD. Styles 4-5, connate: sterile fls. with 1 large sepal.................9. *Schizophragma*
AA. Lvs. alternate: stamens 4-5.
  B. Ovary superior: fls. in dense long racemes: fr. a caps......Subfam. II. ITEOIDEAE Engl.
                                                                      12. *Itea*
  BB. Ovary inferior.
    C. Fr. a caps.: lvs. usually coriaceous, serrate......Subfam. III. ESCALLONIOIDEAE Engl.
                                                                      13. *Escallonia*
    CC. Fr. a berry: lvs. usually palmately lobed: brs. often spiny.
                                              Subfam. IV. RIBESIOIDEAE Engl.
                                                                      14. *Ribes*

1. **CARPENTÈRIA** Torr. Evergreen shrub; brts. 4-angled: lvs. petioled, opposite, penninerved: fls. large, in few-fld. terminal cymes; sepals 5–7, valvate; petals as many, convolute, clawless; stamens numerous: ovary superior, 5–7-celled; style short, with 5–7-lobed stigma: caps. leathery, conical, 5–7-valved; seeds numerous. (After William M. Carpenter; 1811–1848.) One species.

C. califórnica Torr. Shrub to 2.5 m.: lvs. elliptic-oblong to oblong-lanceolate, 4–10 cm. long, narrowed at ends, entire or indistinctly denticulate, bright green and glabrous above, glaucous and sparingly pubescent beneath; petioles 5–10 mm. long: fls. in 3–7-fld. cymes, white, 5–7 cm. across, fragrant, sepals ovate-lanceolate; petals orbicular-obovate. Fl.VI–VIII. B.M.6911(c). G.C.40:6,7;44:112. Calif. Intr. 1880. Zone VII. Showy shrub when in bloom; demands sunny sheltered position and well-drained soil.

2. **PHILADÉLPHUS** L. MOCK-ORANGE. Deciduous shrubs; brs. with solid white pith and close or flaky bark; buds small, usually hidden by the base of the petiole, sometimes free, with imbricate scales: lvs. opposite, entire or dentate, 3–5-nerved at base: fls. white, rarely purple near base, often fragrant, terminal on lateral brts., usually racemose, but often solitary or in 2–3-fld. cymes, rarely paniculate; sepals and petals 4; stamens numerous, styles 4, more or less connate; ovary 4-celled, inferior or half-superior: fr. a 4-valved capsule with numerous minute seeds. (Ancient name of unknown application.) About 40 species in N. Am., S. Eu. and Cauc., and in E. Asia to the Himal.—Much planted on account of their showy mostly fragrant fls.; numerous hybrids make the distinction of the species difficult.

A. Fls. in racemes or panicles.
  B. Fls. in panicles, sometimes partly in racemes, but with the lower pedicels articulate.
    C. Calyx outside and lvs. glabrous.
      D. Lvs. subcordate at base...1. *P. cordifolius*
      DD. Lvs. broad-cuneate at base.......................................2. *P. californicus*
    CC. Calyx outside and lvs. pubescent.....................................3. *P. insignis*
  BB. Fls. in racemes.
    C. Calyx glabrous outside (pubescent in var. of 18).
      D. Brts. of the previous season yellowish or grayish brown, rarely gray or brown,
         with not or scarcely exfoliating bark.

E. Bark yellowish or brown.
  F. Lvs. acute or short-acuminate; racemes dense or only the lower pair remote.
    G. Lvs. glabrous or nearly so, entire or slightly denticulate......4. *P. Lewisii*
    GG. Lvs. pubescent on both sides, at least those of the shoots dentate.
                                                               5. *P. Gordonianus*
  FF. Lvs. long-acuminate: racemes loose; fls. 2–2.5 cm. across: bark brown,
      usually with longitudinal cracks............................15. *P. satsumanus*
  EE. Brts. light gray, with always close bark: lvs. large.........6. *P. pubescens* var.
  DD. Brts. of the previous season with brown exfoliating bark.
    E. Lvs. glabrous beneath or pubescent only near base or sparingly on the veins.
      F. Lvs. not bearded in the axils, sometimes sparingly pubescent beneath.
        G. Pedicels glabrous: lvs. rather small, petiole usually purplish: fls. yellowish
           white ....18. *P. pekinensis*
        GG. Pedicels pubescent: fls. pure white.
          H. Style glabrous.
            I. Lvs. 1.5–4 cm. long, entire or with 1–4 small teeth on each side.
                                                               31. *P. Lemoinei*
            II. Lvs. 4–8 (–12) cm. long, denticulae or dentate......19. *P. tenuifolius*
          HH. Style hairy at base.......................................20. *P. Schrenkii*
      FF. Lvs. bearded or pubescent near the axils at base, otherwise glabrous.
        G. Bark of brts. freely exfoliating: lvs. dentate.
          H. Style shorter than stamens: lvs. ovate or elliptic: fls. creamy-white,
             very fragrant ....21. *P. coronarius*
          HH. Style longer than stamens or nearly as long: fls. white, inodorous or
              slightly fragrant.
            I. Lvs. ovate or elliptic, short-acuminate: fls. 4–4.5 cm. broad.
                                                               22. *P. Zeyheri*
            II. Lvs. ovate-lanceolate to lanceolate, acuminate: fls. 3–3.5 cm. broad.
              J. Style nearly as long as stamens; petals elliptic, obtuse.
                                                               17. *P. nepalensis*
              JJ. Style longer than stamens; petals oblong, acutish.24. *P. Falconeri*
        GG. Bark slightly or scarcely exfoliating: lvs. denticulate or subentire.
                                                               4. *P. Lewisii*

  EE. Lvs. more or less pubescent all over beneath.
    F. Calyx green or greenish.
      G. Lvs. with rather small remote teeth, ovate to oblong-ovate: bark slightly
         or not exfoliating.
        H. Lower pedicels 0.5 cm. long: bark scarcely exfoliating: lvs. short-
           pubescent beneath ....15. *P. satsumanus* var.
        HH. Lower pedicels 0.5–1 cm. long: bark exfoliating: lvs. densely soft-
            pubescent beneath ....16. *P. tomentosus*
      GG. Lvs. of shoots coarsely toothed, broad-ovate, loosely hairy beneath: bark
          freely exfoliating ....23. *P. floribundus*
    FF. Calyx purple or purplish; petioles and veins beneath often violet-purplish.
      G. Young shoots glabrous: lvs. grayish tomentose beneath or nearly glabrous,
         3–10 cm. long..14. *P. Delavayi*
      GG. Young shoots pubescent: lvs. strigose-pubescent beneath, 2–5 cm. long.
                                                               13. *P. purpurascens*

CC. Calyx pubescent outside.
  D. Bark brown or yellowish brown, often exfoliating.
    E. Lvs. usually oblong-ovate, serrulate with the teeth pointing forward.
      F. Lvs. strigose-pubescent above; style hairy near base.......9. *P. Magdalenae*
      FF. Lvs. glabrous or glabrescent above.
        G. Lvs. pubescent beneath, at least on the veins.
          H. Style glabrous at base; lvs. densely pubescent or subtomentose beneath
                                                               10. *P. incanus*
          HH. Style usually pilose at base: lvs. strigose beneath at least on the veins.
                                                               11. *P. subcanus*
        GG. Lvs. glabrous or glabrescent beneath....................12. *P. sericanthus*
    EE. Leaves ovate or broad-ovate.
      F. Lvs. dentate or denticulate with spreading teeth, longer than 3 cm.
        G. Style shorter than stamens.
          H. Racemes 7–11-fld.: bark close, light yellowish or grayish brown.
                                                               8. *P. monstrosus*
          HH. Racemes 5–7-fld.: bark brown or grayish brown.
            I. Fls. single ....7. *P. verrucosus*
            II. Fls. usually double.................................34. *P. virginalis*
        GG. Style as long as stamens: fls. large, usually in 5-fld. racemes, sometimes
            cymose ....28. *P. magnificus*
      FF. Lvs. usually entire, shorter than 3 cm.: bark brown.......32. *P. polyanthus*
  DD. Bark close, light gray..6. *P. pubescens*
AA. Fls. solitary or 3, rarely 5, sometimes more and cymose.
  B. Buds enclosed in the base of the petiole.
    C. Lvs. large, usually over 3 cm., thin; style usually longer than stamens.
      D. Pedicels and calyx glabrous.
        E. Style with broad stigmas divided only at apex.
          F. Lvs. usually entire, ovate, glabrous..........................26. *P. inodorus*

FF. Lvs. dentate or denticulate, usually cuneate at base.
  G. Fls. 1–3.
    H. Lvs. usually oblong-ovate, dentate, usually glabrous.27. *P. grandiflorus*
    HH. Lvs. ovate-lanceolate to lanceolate, strigose beneath, denticulate.
                                                25. *P. laxus*
  GG. Fls. 5–9, rarely to 15: lvs. ovate, dentate................22. *P. Zeyheri* var.
  EE. Styles with narrow stigmas, divided nearly to base: fls. in 3-9-fld. cymes.
                                                33. *P. cymosus*
  DD. Pedicels and calyx pubescent.
    E. Styles as long or longer than stamens, with broad stigmas: fls. 1–3.
                                              29. *P. floridus*
    EE. Style shorter, with narrow stigmas; fls. 3 or more in cymes, usually double.
                                              34. *P. virginalis*
  CC. Lvs. small, 5–20 mm. long: fls. usually solitary; styles slightly shorter than stamens,
    usually wholly united..30. *P. microphyllus*
  BB. Buds exserted: styles united.
    C. Petals with purple blotch at base; stigmas free.............35. *P. purpureo-maculatus*
    CC..Petals pure white; stigmas partly united............................36. *P. hirsutus*

Ser. 1. GORDONIANI Koehne. Fls. in racemes or panicles; calyx glabrous, rarely pubescent; stigmas narrower than anthers; bark* of brts. brown, yellowish or gray, close, or slightly exfoliating.

1. **P. cordifòlius** Lange. Shrub to 2 m.; bark red-brown, slightly exfoliating: lvs. broad-ovate, 5–10 cm. long, acute or short-acuminate, rounded to subcordate at base, denticulate or entire, glabrous except in the axils below: fls. 2.5–4 cm. across, in 15–40-fld. glabrous panicles, leafy below; sepals lance-ovate; petals elliptic-oblong; style connate. Bot. Tidsskr. III.2:t.3(c). D.L. 3:344(as *P. Lewisii*). Calif. Intr. 1863. Zone VI. Shrub with large panicles of white fls.

2. **P. califórnicus** Benth. Shrub to 3 m.; bark pale brown to chestnut-brown, slightly exfoliating; buds slightly exserted: lvs. ovate to elliptic-ovate, rarely lance-ovate, 3–8 cm. long, acute, usually broad-cuneate at base, denticulate or entire, glabrous or sparingly hairy below; fls. fragrant, about 2.5 cm. across in 7–20-fld. panicles, occasionally in racemes, but the lower pedicels articulate; sepals ovate, short-acuminate; petals elliptic; styles connate. Fl.VI–VII. S.H.1:f.234a-a²,263a. (*P. Lewisii* var. *parvifolius* Torr.) Calif. Cult. 1858. Zone VI.

3. × **P. insígnis** Carr. (*P. pubescens* × *cordifolius* or *californicus*?) Tall shrub: bark light grayish brown, close or slightly exfoliating: lvs. ovate or broad-ovate, 3.5–7 cm. long, short-acuminate, broad-cuneate to slightly subcordate at base, entire or denticulate, glabrous above, grayish pubescent beneath: fls. about 3 cm. across, in 15–30-fld. leafy panicles; pedicels and calyx pubescent; petals obovate; styles connate. Fl.VI–VII. S.H.1:f.236g(1). (*P. Billiardii* Koehne, *P.* "Souvenir de Billiard" Carr.) Origin before 1870. Zone V. Shrub with large panicles of slightly fragrant fls.; one of the latest to bloom.

P. i. ? × *Lemoinei* = *P. polyanthus;* see No. 32.

4. **P. Lewísii** Pursh. Shrub to 2 m.; young brts. glabrous; bark red-brown or yellowish brown, with cross-cracks and tardily exfoliating: lvs. ovate to ovate-oblong, 3–7 cm. long, acute, usually cuneate at base, entire or denticulate, 3–5-ribbed, the strongest pair arising some distance from the base, usually villous in the axils of the veins below, otherwise glabrous, those of the shoots larger, denticulate and often rounded at base: fls. 2.5–3.5 cm. across, scentless, in 5–9 fld. dense racemes, only the lowest pair in the axils of lvs.; pedicels glabrous, the lower about 5 mm. long; sepals lance-ovate; petals elliptic to elliptic-oblong; styles divided only at apex or nearly to the middle. Fl.VI–VIII. S.H.1:f.236h,237a-b. Mont. to Wash. and Ore. Intr. 1823 or 1884? Zone IV.

* The description of the bark refers always to brts. of the previous season.

Closely related species: **P. confùsus** Piper. Chiefly distinguished by the yellowish or gray close bark and the ovate acute sepals. Wash. Cult. 1900. Zone V.

5. **P. Gordoniànus** Lindl. Shrub to 4 m.; young brts. slightly pubescent; bark yellowish or gray, not exfoliating: lvs. ovate or elliptic-ovate to elliptic-oblong, 4–8 cm. long, acuminate, cuneate at base, usually dentate, rarely nearly entire, coarsely dentate and rounded at base on shoots, usually strongly 5-ribbed, all ribs arising from the base, pubescent beneath: fls. 3–4.5 cm. across, slightly fragrant, in 7–9-, rarely 11-fld. dense racemes; pedicels pubescent; sepals ovate or lance-ovate, sometimes with a few hairs outside; petals elliptic to oblong; styles usually united ½ or ⅔. Fl.vi–vii. B.R.25:32 (c). D.L.3:342. N.I.3:f.107. M.O.224. (*P. Lewisii* auth., not Pursh.) B. C. to Idaho and N. Calif. Intr. about 1825. Zone IV. Shrub with spreading lateral brs. and profuse large fls., the var. smaller in every part.—**P. G. columbiànus** (Koehne) Rehd., var. Lvs. usually elliptic-ovate, 3–5 cm. long, 3–5-ribbed, the stronger ribs some distance from the base, those of the shoots ovate, with usually 2–4 coarse teeth on each side, the hairs of the upper surface often with pustulate bases. S.H.1:f.236k(l). (*P. c.* Koehne, *P. Gordonianus* var. *californicus* Dipp., in part?) B. C. and Idaho and N. Calif. Cult. 1890. Zone V.

P. G. ? × pubescens; see No. 8.—*P. G. × coronarius;* see No. 23.—*P. G. ? × grandiflorus;* see under No. 27.

6. **P. pubéscens** Lois. Shrub to 3 m.; bark light gray, close: lvs. ovate to elliptic, 4–10 cm. long, acuminate, rounded or broad-cuneate at base, sometimes subcordate on shoots, remotely dentate, rarely nearly entire, dark green and nearly glabrous above, densely grayish pubescent beneath: fls. 3–4 cm. across, scentless, in 5–9-fld. racemes, usually the 2 lower pairs in the axils of rather remote lvs.; pedicels and calyx pubescent; sepals ovate, acuminate; petals obovate or oval; style united about ⅔. Fl.vi–vii. L.D.4:t.268 (c). W.D.1:46(c). B.R.7:570(c) and Gn.40:289 as *P. grandiflorus*. (*P. latifolius* Schrad., *P. grandiflorus* var. *floribundus* Gray.) Tenn. to Ala. and Ark. Intr. 1800. Zone IV. Vigorous shrub with large dark green lvs.; the fls. partly hidden by the foliage.—**P. p. intéctus** (Beadle) A. H. Moore, var. Lvs. nearly glabrous beneath and calyx glabrous outside. (*P. i.* Beadle.) Intr. about 1880. Zone V.

P. p. × coronarius = P. nivàlis Jacques. Bark brown, usually exfoliating: lvs. ovate, usually rounded at base, less coarsely serrate and usually only sparingly pubescent beneath: fls. 3–4 cm. across, in 5–9-fld. racemes; pedicels 3–8 mm. long, rarely longer, like the calyx clothed with long villous hairs, rarely glabrescent; petals oval or obovate; style divided only at apex; stigmas longer than anthers, as broad. (*P. verrucosus* var. *n.* Rehd., *P. verrucosus* Hort., not Schrad.) Orig. before 1840.—**P. n. plènus** Rehd., f. Fls. double. (*P. verrucosus* var. *n.* f. *pl.* Rehd., *P. n. spectabilis pl.* Hort.)—*P. n. pl. × Lemoinei;* see No. 34. —*P. p. × ? laxus* = P. pendulifòlius Carr. Low shrub; bark chestnut-brown, tardily exfoliating: lvs. ovate or elliptic, pendent, pubescent beneath: fls. 2.5–3 cm. across, short-stalked, in 5–7-fld. racemes; styles as long as stamens, divided only at apex. Orig. before 1875.—*P. p. × californicus;* see No. 3.—*P. p. × Gordonianus;* see No. 8.—*P. p. × tomentosus;* see under No. 16.—*P. p. × grandiflorus;* see No. 28.—*P. p. × microphyllus;* see under No. 30.

7. **P. verrucòsus** Schrad. Shrub to 3 m.; bark brown or grayish brown, close or tardily exfoliating: lvs. ovate or elliptic-ovate, 4–7, on shoots 5–11 cm. long, acuminate, rounded or broad-cuneate at base, denticulate or dentate, glabrous above, pubescent beneath: fls. 2.5–3 cm. across, scentless or slightly fragrant, in 5–7-fld. racemes, the lowest or 2 lower pairs usually in the axils of lvs.; pedicels 3–5 mm. long, strigose-pubescent like the calyx; style usually divided ¼ or ⅓; stigmas narrower than anthers. Fl.vi. S.H.1:f.

235f-m,236l-m,237i-l. (*P. pubescens* Koehne, not Loisel.) Ill. Cult. 1828. Zone IV. The hybrid *P. nivalis* is very similar to this species.

P. v. ? × *laxus* = **P. congéstus** Rehd. Differs chiefly in its smaller and narrower lvs. and in the short and congested usually 5-fld. racemes: fls. 3–4 cm. broad; style shorter than stamens; stigmas as broad or nearly as broad and longer than anthers; calyx slightly pubescent chiefly toward the base. Origin unknown.

8. × **P. monstròsus** (Spaeth) Rehd. (*P.? Gordonianus* × *pubescens*). Tall shrub; young brts. nearly glabrous, light or sometimes yellowish brown; mature brts. light grayish brown, with cross-cracks, but not exfoliating: lvs. usually ovate, sometimes ovate-oblong, 3–8 cm. long, short-acuminate, usu-ally rounded or broad-cuneate at base, remotely denticulate, on shoots always ovate, with 4–8 pairs of rather shallow teeth, nearly glabrous above, densely grayish pubescent beneath: fls. 3–4 cm. across, scentless, in 5–13-, usually 7–9-fld. racemes, the lower pair usually remote; lower pedicels 3–5 mm. long, pubescent; calyx loosely pubescent; petals elliptic-oblong, rarely elliptic; style shorter than stamens, stigmas shorter and narrower than anthers. W.A. 104,t(h). (*P. Gordonianus m.* Spaeth). Orig. unknown; cult. 1897. Zone V.

Ser. 2. SERICANTHI Rehd. Bark of brts. brown with cross-cracks and usually more or less exfoliating: lvs. serrate-denticulate with the teeth pointing for-ward, never entire, more or less pubescent beneath, rarely glabrous: fls. sub-campanulate, in 5–11-fld. secund racemes; calyx usually pubescent, or glabrous and violet purple; style shorter than stamens; stigmas narrower than anthers.

9. **P. Magdalènae** Koehne. Shrub to 4 m.; young shoots pubescent at first, flowering brts. glabrous, older brts. brown or grayish brown, usually exfoliating: lvs. ovate to lance-ovate, 3–5, on shoots to 8 cm. long, long-acuminate, broad-cuneate or rounded at base, denticulate or dentate, pubes-cent above, densely strigose-pubescent beneath, chartaceous: fls. about 2.5 cm. across, scentless, in 7–11-fld. racemes; lower pedicels about 5 mm. long; calyx strigose-pubescent; sepals ovate; petals broad-elliptic; style connate to above the middle, pubescent at base. Fl.vi. V.F.129. S.L.256(h). W. China. Intr. 1894. Zone (V). Free-flowering shrub with spreading brs.; the secund racemes give this and the following species (Nos. 10–14) somewhat the aspect of a large-fld. Deutzia.

10. **P. incànus** Koehne. Shrub to 3, or occasionally 5 m.; young flowering brts. slightly, shoots densely pubescent; bark of older brts. brown, soon exfoliating in small flakes; lvs. ovate to oblong-ovate, 3–6, on shoots to 8 cm. long, acuminate, broad-cuneate or rounded at base, serrate, slightly pubes-cent or glabrescent above, densely grayish strigose-pubescent beneath: fls. 2.5–3 cm. across, scentless, in 5–7 fld. pubescent racemes; pedicels short; calyx densely grayish pubescent; petals broad-elliptic; style glabrous, rarely with a few hairs at base. Fl.vii. B.S.2:135. W. China. Intr. about 1895. Zone (V). Shrub with upright brs.; one of the last species to bloom.

11. **P. subcànus** Koehne. Shrub to 3 m.; young flowering brts. slightly pubescent, shoots pubescent; older brts. with light or dark brown exfoliating bark: lvs. usually oblong-ovate or ovate, 4–8, on shoots to 12 cm. long, acumi-nate, rounded or broad-cuneate at base, denticulate or serrulate, glabrous or nearly so above, strongly veined and strigose-pubescent chiefly on the veins and veinlets beneath: fls. 2.5–3 cm. across, in 5–9-fld. racemes; lower pedicels 5–10 mm. long, like the calyx densely pubescent; style usually pubescent at base. Fl.vi. C. and W. China. Intr. 1907 or before. Zone V. Closely related and similar to *P. incanus*, but less pubescent and blooming several weeks earlier.—**P. s. Wilsónii** (Koehne) Rehd., var. Larger in all parts, to 6 m.

tall; lvs. of flowering shoots 10–14 cm. long; racemes 9–15-fld. (*P. W.* Koehne.) Probably not in cult.

12. **P. sericánthus** Koehne. Shrub to 4 m.; young brts. glabrous, soon becoming red-brown; bark chestnut-brown, exfoliating: lvs. elliptic-ovate to lance-ovate, 3–6, on shoots to 10 cm. long, long-acuminate, broad-cuneate, rarely rounded at base, remotely serrulate, or serrate on shoots, with 3–10 pairs of teeth, dark green and sparingly strigose or glabrous above, lighter green below and glabrous or with few scattered hairs on the veins and bearded in the axils; veins beneath and petiole often red or violet: fls. 2.5–3 cm. across, scentless, in 5–11-fld. racemes; calyx and pedicels densely strigose-pubescent; lower pedicels 5–10 mm. long; petals broad-elliptic; style divided about ½, glabrous. Fl.vi. B.M.8941(c). S.H.1:f.236f,237m-o. C. and W. China. Intr. 1896. Zone V. Shrub with spreading brs. and numerous secund racemes. Possibly *P. parviflorus* Carr. is this species.—**P. s. Rehderiànus** Koehne, var. Lvs. larger, on the flowering brts. to 11 cm. long, sparingly pubescent on the veins beneath. W. China. Intr. 1908. Zone (V).

13. **P. purpuráscens** (Koehne) Rehd. Shrub to 4 m.; young flowering brts. glabrous, shoots sparingly strigose-pubescent; bark brown, exfoliating: lvs. elliptic-ovate or ovate to lance-ovate, 2–3, on shoots to 5 cm. long, acuminate, broad-cuneate or rounded at base, remotely serrulate or serrate, more or less appressed-pilose above, sparingly or sometimes densely strigose-pubescent beneath, rarely nearly glabrous: fls. about 2.5 cm. across, pure white, very fragrant, in 5–9-fld. racemes; lower pedicels 4–7 mm. long; calyx glabrous, violet-purple, rarely greenish; petals broad-elliptic; style connate to the stigmas. Fl.vi. B.M.8324(c, as *P. Delavayi*). (*P. brachybotrys* var. *p.* Koehne.) W. China. Intr. 1904. Zone V. Shrub with spreading and arching brs., and with small lvs. and an abundance of sweet-scented fls. whose white color is effectively set off by the purple calyx.

Closely related species: **P. venústus** Koehne. Bark grayish, not exfoliating: lvs. oblong-lanceolate, 3–4 cm. long, densely grayish pubescent beneath: racemes 3–5-fld. Tibet. Intr. about 1900. Zone V?

14. **P. Delavaỳi** L. Henry. Shrub to 5 m.: young brts. quite glabrous, purplish, bloomy; bark chestnut- or grayish brown, exfoliating, sometimes slightly so; lvs. ovate-oblong or lance-ovate, 3–6, or on shoots to 10 cm. long, acuminate, usually rounded at base, remotely serrulate or serrate, short-pubescent and dark green above, grayish tomentose beneath: fls. 3–4 cm. across, very fragrant, in 5–11-, sometimes 13-fld. racemes; lower pedicels 5–10 mm. long; calyx glabrous, violet-purple, often bloomy; petals oval, sometimes tinged slightly purplish outside; styles glabrous, connate ¾ or nearly to the stigmas. Fl.vi. R.H.1903:13. Yunnan. Intr. 1888. Zone (V). Vigorous upright shrub with large very fragrant fls.—**P. D. melanocàlyx** Lemoine is a form with dark purple calyx.—**P. D. calvéscens** Rehd., var. Lvs. pubescent beneath only on the veins, or nearly glabrous, sparingly strigose above. B.M.9022(c). (*P. Delavayi* Stapf, not L. Henry.) Intr. about 1915?

Ser. 3. CORONARII Koehne. Bark brown or grayish brown exfoliating (except in No. 15): lvs. dentate or denticulate, not entire: fls. early, in upright racemes; calyx glabrous, not purplish; stigmas narrow.

15. **P. satsumànus** Miq. Shrub to 2.5 cm.; bark brown or grayish brown, usually with longitudinal cracks, not or slightly exfoliating: lvs. ovate to ovate-lanceolate, 4–8 cm. long, rarely more, long-acuminate, broad-cuneate or rounded at base, remotely denticulate-serrulate, glabrous except bearded in the axils beneath and sometimes sparingly hairy on the midrib; petiole

5–10 mm. long: fls. about 2.5 cm. across, slightly fragrant, in 5–9-, usually 7-fld. rather loose racemes; lower pedicels about 5 mm. long, glabrous or pubescent; calyx glabrous or finely pubescent along the ribs ending in the sinuses; petals oval; style divided ¼ or ½. Fl.vi. Bot. Tidsskr. III.2:t.2(c). S.H.1:f.237f-h,238a. (*P. Satsumi* Koehne, not Lindl. & Paxt., *P. acuminatus* Lange.) Japan. Intr. before 1860. Zone V. Slender upright shrub with rather small slightly fragrant fls.—**P. s. nikoénsis** Rehd., var. Young brts. and lvs. beneath more or less pubescent, sparingly so above. Intr. 1892.

16. **P. tomentòsus** Wall. Shrub to 3 m.; young brts. sparingly hairy or nearly glabrous; bark brown, slightly or rather freely exfoliating: lvs. elliptic-ovate or ovate, 4–8 cm. long, long-acuminate, broad-cuneate or rounded at base, remotely denticulate or dentate, dark green and slightly pubescent or glabrous above, densely grayish soft-pubescent beneath: fls. fragrant, about 3 cm. across, in 5–7-fld. racemes; lower pedicels sparingly pubescent, 7–10 mm. long; calyx glabrous or with a few hairs; petals oval; style divided only at the apex. Fl.vi. Royle, Ill. Bot. Himal. 1:t.46(c). D.L.3:338. S.H.1:f.237 c-e, 238b. (*P. coronarius* var. *t.* Hook f. & Thoms., *P. nepalensis* Lodd.) Himal. Intr. 1822. Zone V. Similar to *P. coronarius*, but lvs. tomentose beneath.

P. t. × *pubescens* = **P. máximus** Rehd. Tall shrub; bark brown or grayish brown, close or slightly exfoliating: lvs. tomentose beneath: fls. with pubescent calyx. Orig. before 1885.

17. **P. nepalénsis** Koehne. Shrub to 2 m.; bark chestnut-brown, exfoliating: lvs. ovate-oblong to lance-ovate, 4–10 cm. long, long-acuminate, rounded or broad-cuneate at base, remotely denticulate-serrulate, glabrous, but conspicuously bearded in the axils of the veins beneath: fls. 3–3.5 cm. broad, scarcely fragrant, usually in 5-fld. racemes; pedicels glabrous, the lower 5–15 mm. long; calyx glabrous; sepals lance-ovate; style divided ⅓–¼, nearly as long as stamens. Fl.vi. S.H.1:f.238g(l). Himal. Cult. 1888. Zone V. Similar to *P. coronarius*, with larger pure white and scarcely fragrant fls.

18. **P. pekinénsis** Rupr. Shrub to 2 m.; young brts. quite glabrous, often purplish; bark chestnut-brown, rarely grayish brown, exfoliating: lvs. oblong-ovate, 2.5–5 cm., on shoots to 8 cm. long, long-acuminate, cuneate at base, remotely serrulate-denticulate, quite glabrous or slightly bearded in the axils beneath and grayish green, usually 3-nerved; petioles slender, 2–10 mm. long, like the nerves beneath purplish: fls. 2.5–3 cm. across, creamy white, slightly fragrant, in 5–7-, rarely 9-fld., dense and glabrous racemes; lower pedicels 2–5 mm. long; calyx pale yellowish green, sometimes tinged purplish; petals oval; style about as long as stamens, usually divided only at apex. Fl.vi. I.S.1:t.29. S.H.1:f.237p-r,238e-f. S.L.257(h). (*P. coronarius* var. *p.* Maxim., ?*P. rubricaulis* Carr.) N. China to Korea. Intr. 1883. Zone IV. Spreading shrub with small lvs. and small slightly fragrant creamy-white fls.; the following variety more upright.—**P. p. brachybótrys** (Koehne) Koehne, car. Bark more often grayish brown and less readily exfoliating; young brts. sparingly strigose; lvs. sparingly strigose usually on both sides, at least those on the shoot; petioles usually green: racemes usually 5-fld., short and dense. (*P. b.* Koehne.) Intr. 1892. Zone V.—**P. p. kansuénsis** Rehd., var. Lvs. sparingly pilose-setose above, beneath chiefly on the veins: fls. 5–7, fragrant; calyx strigose-villous. N. W. China. Intr. 1926. Zone IV.

19. **P. tenuifòlius** Rupr. & Maxim. Shrub to 2 m.; bark chestnut-brown or grayish brown, exfoliating; young flowering brts. sparingly pubescent, shoots glabrous or nearly so: lvs. ovate to oblong-lanceolate, 4–8, on shoots

to 12 cm. long, acuminate, rounded or broad-cuneate at base, remotely denticulate-serrulate or dentate on shoots, glabrous except sparingly hairy on the veins beneath, usually 5-nerved at base, thin, sometimes tinged violet when unfolding: fls. 2.5–3 cm. across, scarcely fragrant, in 5–7-fld. racemes; pedicels pubescent, the lower about 5 mm. long; calyx glabrous, sepals pale greenish white; style glabrous, divided about ½. Fl.vi. S.H.1:f.238m-n(l). (*P. coronarius* var. *t.* Maxim.) Manch. to Korea. Cult. 1890. Zone IV. Shrub with spreading slender brs. and rather large thin lvs.

Related species: P. Viksnei Zamelin. Upright shrub: pedicels pilose: fls. larger, fragrant. Act. Hort. Bot. Latv. 11–12:230(h). Manch. Cult. 1938. Zone IV?

20. **P. Schrénkii** Rupr. Very near the preceding species, but of more vigorous and upright habit; young brts. more or less hairy, flowering brts. often with minute black warts: young lvs. not violet, at maturity of firm texture: fls. 3–3.5 cm. across in 5–7-fld. racemes; rachis and pedicels more densely pubescent with spreading hairs; calyx often hairy along the nerves ending at the base of the calyx-lobes; style more or less pilose at base, rarely glabrous. Fl.vi. S.H.1:f.238c(l). N.K.15:t.12. (*P. coronarius* var. *mandshuricus* Maxim., *P. m.* Nakai.) Manch. to Korea. Intr. about 1874. Zone V or IV.—**P. S. Jáckii** Koehne, var. Lvs. sparingly hairy below: brts., rachis and pedicels more densely pubescent; calyx pubescent toward the base. N.K.15:t.13. (*P. lasiogynus* Nakai.) Korea, N. China. Intr. 1905. Zone V.

21. **P. coronàrius** L. Shrub to 3 m.; young brts. glabrous or slightly pilose; bark chestnut-brown, exfoliating: lvs. ovate to ovate-oblong, 4–8 cm. long, acuminate, broad-cuneate or rounded at base, remotely denticulate or dentate, glabrous except bearded in the axils of the veins beneath and sometimes hairy on the veins: fls. 2.5–3.5 cm. across, creamy-white, very fragrant, in 5–7 fld. racemes; pedicels glabrous or pubescent, the lower 5–10 mm. long; calyx glabrous, rarely sparingly pubescent; style usually divided about ½. Fl.vi. R.I.24:t.154(c). B.M.391(c). Gn.58:7(h). (*P. pallidus* Hayek.) S. Eu.: Italy to Cauc. Cult. 1560. Zone IV. Much planted for its fragrant fls.— **P. c. aùreus** Rehd., var. Lvs. bright yellow when young, later greenish yellow. Gn.15:476,t(c). (*P. c. fol. aureis* hort.) Orig. before 1878.—**P. c. variegàtus** West., var. Lvs. bordered creamy white. Orig. before 1770.—**P. c. dúplex** West., var. A semidouble or double form of dwarf habit; fls. often solitary. S.O.1:t.60(s, as *P. nanus*). (*P. c.* var. *fl. pleno* Loud.) Orig. before 1770.—**P. c. deutziaeflòrus** (Hartwig) Rehd., var. A double form with narrow acutish petals; racemes 3–5-fld.; pedicels glabrous. (*P. c.* var. *d. plenus* Hartwig.)—**P. c. primulaeflòrus** (Carr.) Nichols. A double form with broad petals. R.H.1870:305. Other double-fld. forms are *P. c. dianthiflorus, rosaeflorus, multiflorus plenus* (Gn. 15:476,t[c]).—**P. c. salicifòlius** (K. Koch) Jaeg., var. Lvs. lanceolate, 5–10 cm. long and 1.5–2 cm. broad, more or less curved. S.H.1:f.238l(l).—**P. c. pumilus** West., var. Dwarf dense shrub; brts. and lvs. on the veins beneath sparingly pubescent: lvs. smaller. (*P. nanus* Mill., *P. c.* var. *nanus* Schrad.)

P. c. × *pubescens*; see under No. 6.—*P. c.* × *inodorus* or *grandiflorus;* see No. 22.—*P. c.* × *Gordonianus;* see No. 23.—*P. c.* × *laxus;* see No. 24.—*P. c.* × *microphyllus;* see No. 31.

The closely related **P. caucásicus** Koehne with the lvs. pubescent beneath and the calyx slightly pubescent does not seem to be in cult.

22. × **P. Zeỳheri** Schrad. (*P. coronarius* × *inodorus* or *grandiflorus*). Spreading shrub to 2 m., glabrous; bark chestnut-brown, exfoliating: lvs. ovate or elliptic-ovate, 4–7, or on shoots to 10 cm. long, acuminate, remotely

denticulate, rarely nearly entire, on shoots remotely dentate, glabrous except
pubescent beneath along the veins near base or only bearded: fls. 3.5–5 cm.
across, cup-shaped, in 3–5-fld. racemes; pedicels about 5 mm. long; sepals
lance-ovate; petals broad-oval; style about as long as stamens, divided ⅓ or
sometimes nearly to the base; stigmas about as large as stamens. Fl.vi. Orig.
about 1820. Zone IV. Shrub with spreading and arching brs. bearing large
cup-shaped pure white and slightly fragrant fls.—See also *P. maculiflorus*
under No. 35.—**P. Z. Kochiànus** (Koehne) Rehd., var. Lvs. elliptic-ovate
to lance-ovate, sparingly pubescent on the veins or bearded beneath: fls. 3.5–4
cm. across; style longer than stamens, divided about ⅓. (*P. K.* Koehne.)—
P. Z. umbellàtus (Koehne) Rehd., var. Fls. 3–5 cm. across, in 7–15-fld.
cymes; stigmas as broad and often longer than anthers. (*P. u.* Koehne.)

23. × **P. floribúndus** Schrad. (*P. coronarius* × ? *Gordonianus*). Shrub
to 3 m.; bark chestnut-brown, exfoliating: lvs. ovate or elliptic-ovate, 3–7 cm.,
on shoots to 12 cm. long and often broad-ovate and very coarsely toothed,
acuminate, broad-cuneate or rounded at base, rather coarsely and irregularly
toothed, pubescent beneath: racemes 5–7-fld.; fls. 3.5–4 cm. across, slightly
fragrant; pedicels and calyx glabrous or sparingly hairy; the lower pedicels
1–2 cm. long; style divided about ½, as long or shorter than stamens. Fl.vi.
Orig. before 1828. Zone V.

24. × **P. Falcòneri** Sarg. (*P. coronarius* × ? *laxus*). Shrub to 2.5 m.;
nearly glabrous; bark chestnut-brown, exfoliating: lvs. ovate-lanceolate, to
oblong-lanceolate, 3–5, on shoots to 8 cm. long, long-acuminate, cuneate at
base, minutely denticulate or nearly entire, glabrous beneath except bearded
in the axils: fls. about 3 cm. across, fragrant, in 3–5-fld. racemes or occasionally in 7-fld. cymes; lower pedicels 1–1.5 cm. long, sometimes articulate and
occasionally branched; sepals lance-ovate; petals oblong, acutish; stamens
rather few, often sterile; style longer than stamens, deeply divided, with
narrow stigmas. Fl.vi. G.F.8:497. B.C.5:2581. Orig. before 1880. Zone IV.
Tall shrub of graceful habit with numerous rather small fragrant fls.

Ser. 4. SPECIOSI Koehne. Bark brown, exfoliating: lvs. over 3 cm. long:
fls. 1–3, rarely 5, usually large and cup-shaped; style longer than stamens, divided above; stigmas longer and broader than anthers.

25. **P. làxus** Schrad. Shrub to 1.5 m.; young brts. glabrous: lvs. elliptic-
ovate to oblong-lanceolate, 3–6 cm. long, on shoots to 8 cm., gradually acuminate, cuneate at base, remotely denticulate, sometimes nearly entire, usually
glabrous above, with scattered strigose hairs beneath, usually more or less
pendulous and curved, subchartaceous: fls. 1–3, scentless, 3–4 cm. across;
petals obovate to elliptic; lateral pedicels 5–10 mm. long, glabrous like the
calyx. Fl.vi. P.F.2:102 (as *P. satsumi*). (*P. grandiflorus* var. *l.* Torr. & Gray,
P. speciosus Schrad., *P. undulatus* Kirchn.) Ga. Cult. 1825. Zone IV.
Spreading shrub with arching brs., small pendulous lvs. and large fls.—**P. l.
strigòsus** (Beadle) Rehd., var. Lvs. densely strigose beneath and sometimes
sparingly so above. (*P. inodorus s.* Beadle.) S. C. Intr ?.

P. l. × *verrucosus;* see under No. 7.—*P. l.* × *pubescens;* see under No. 6.

26. **P. inodòrus** L. Shrub to 3 m.: lvs. ovate, 3–6 on shoots to 10 cm. long,
acute or acuminate, rounded at base, rarely broad-cuneate, entire or remotely
denticulate, glabrous and lustrous above, glabrous beneath except bearded
in the axils or sometimes sparingly strigose on the nerves, subchartaceous;
petiole 2–3 mm. long: fls. 1–3, cup-shaped, 4–5 cm. across; pedicels short;
calyx glabrous; sepals ovate, short-acuminate; petals orbicular-obovate.
Fl.vi. B.M.1478(c). N. C. to Ga. and Miss. Intr. 1738. Zone V. Shrub with

arching brs., lustrous dark green lvs. and large pure white cup-shaped fls. *P. i.* × *coronarius;* see No. 22.

27. **P. grandiflòrus** Willd. Shrub to 3 m.; lvs. elliptic-obovate to oblong-ovate, 4–7, on shoots to 12 cm. long, acuminate, cuneate or rounded at base, remotely denticulate or dentate, rather dull dark green above, glabrous or sparingly strigose beneath, rather thin; petiole 3–5 mm. long: fls. 4.5–5.5 cm. across; sepals lance-ovate; petals orbicular-obovate to oval. Fl.vi. S.B.II.1: 8(c). Gn.89:653(h). (*P. inodorus* var. *g.* Gray, *P. gloriosus* Beadle.) N. C. and Tenn. to Fla. and Ala. Intr. 1811. Zone IV. Similar to the preceding species, but lvs. larger and less lustrous and fls. slightly four-cornered in outline.

P. g. × *? Gordonianus* = **P. spléndens** Rehd. Similar to No. 28, but nearly glabrous: fls. usually 5; calyx glabrous; stigmas as broad as anthers, longer. H.B.1923:340(h). Gn.M.33:39(h). Orig. before 1900.—*P. g.* × *coronarius;* see No. 22.—*P. g.* × *pubescens;* see No. 28.—*P. g.* × *Lemoinei;* see No. 33.

28. × **P. magníficus** Koehne (*P. grandiflorus* × *pubescens*). Large spreading shrub: lvs. large, pubescent beneath: fls. about 5 cm. across, in 3–5-fld. racemes, sometimes in cymes; lower pedicels 5–15 mm. long; calyx pubescent; style as long as stamens; stigmas broader than anthers. ?B.R. 2003(c, as *P. grandiflorus*). Orig. unknown. Zone V.

29. **P. flòridus** Beadle. Shrub to 3 m.; similar to *P. grandiflorus*, but lvs. sparingly pubescent or glabrous above, rather densely pubescent beneath: fls. 1–3, about 5 cm. across; pedicels and calyx densely villous. Fl.vi. (*P. speciosus* Rydb., not Schrad.) N. C. and Ga. Intr. 1906. Zone V.—**P. f. Faxònii** Rehd., var. Resembling *P. laxus* in habit and shape of lvs.; lvs. and fls. smaller. Cult. 1917.

Ser. 5. MICROPHYLLI Koehne. Lvs. small, usually less than 2 cm. long: fls. 1–3; style wholly and stigmas usually partly connate.

30. **P. microphỳllus** Gray. Shrub to 1.5 m.; bark chestnut-brown, ex-foliating; young brts. appressed-pubescent at first, soon glabrous and lustrous red-brown: lvs. very short-petioled, elliptic-ovate to oblong-lanceolate, acute, broad-cuneate at base, entire, lustrous and glabrous or strigose above, glau-cescent and strigose beneath: fls. usually solitary, 2–2.5 cm. across, exqui-sitely fragrant; calyx glabrous or slightly strigose; pedicels 2–5 mm. long, strigose; style slightly shorter than stamens. Fl.vi–vii. Gn.40:288,t(c). G.C.51:225. G.W.19:561(h). Colo. to N. Mex. and Ariz. Intr. 1883. Zone V. Graceful upright shrub with small lvs. and numerous white fls. of pine-apple-like fragrance.

P.m. × *pubescens* = **P. látvicus** Zamelin. Act. Hort. Bot. Latv. 11–12:231. Cult. 1938.—*P. m.* × *coronarius;* see No. 31.

Closely related species: **P. argyrócalyx** Wooton. Lvs. elliptic to ovate-oblong, on shoots sometimes to 4 cm. long, densely silky-strigose beneath: fls. 3.5–4 cm. across; calyx white-tomentose. Fl.vii–viii. (*P. ellipticus* Rydb.) N. Mex. Intr. 1916. Zone V.—**P. serpyllifòlius** Gray. Straggling shrub to 1 m.; bark pale gray-brown, not exfoliating: lvs. obtuse or obtusish, hirsute-strigose above, densely strigose beneath: fls. solitary, nearly sessile; style much shorter than stamens, nearly wanting. N. Mex., w. Tex. Intr. 1917. Zone V.

31. × **P. Lemoinei** Lemoine (*P. microphyllus* × *coronarius*). Lvs. ovate to ovate-lanceolate, 1.5–4 cm. long, on shoots ovate, to 6 cm., acuminate, entire or with 1–4 small teeth on each side, glabrous above, sparingly strigose chiefly on the veins beneath: fls. 2.5–4 cm. across, very fragrant, in 3–7-fld. racemes; calyx glabrous; lower pedicels 2–5 mm. long; style shorter than stamens, connate to the apex or divided ½. G.F.2:617. Orig. 1884. Zone V. —The following horticultural forms belong here: "Avalanche" (G.C.III.21: 89. M.G.11:293,22:379).—"Boule d'argent," with double fls. (G.C.III.18:18;

23:f.123).—"Candelabre" (M.G.11:294).—"Erectus" (M.G.17:383).—"Manteau d'hermine," with double fls., sometimes in cymes.—"Mont Blanc" (Gs. 1:64.)—The forms of this hybrid are very handsome shrubs of different habit with rather small lvs. and very fragrant fls. produced in great profusion.—By crossing *P. Lemoinei* with other species and hybrids a bewildering variety of forms has been raised which may be classed under the following names:

32. × **P. polyanthus** Rehd. (*P. Lemoinei* × ? *insignis*). Bark brown, tardily exfoliating: lvs. ovate, 2–5 cm. long, usually entire, acuminate, on shoots sometimes with a few teeth, strigose-pubescent beneath: fls. about 3.5 cm. across, in cymose infl. or in racemes with articulate pedicels; calyx strigose-pubescent. (*P. Lemoinei multiflorus* Schelle.) Orig. before 1901.—Here belong "Gerbe de neige" (type), "Favorite" and "Pavillon blanc" (Gs.1:64. N.F.6:f.40).

33. × **P. cymòsus** Rehd. (*P. Lemoinei* × ? *grandiflorus* or closely related forms). Bark exfoliating: Lvs. 4–10 cm. long, remotely dentate or denticulate, pubescent beneath particularly near the base of the veins and along the veins or nearly glabrous: fls. 5–6 cm. across, double or single, in 3–9-fld. cymes or in racemes with the lower pedicels branched or articulate; calyx glabrous; sepals lance-ovate; style about as long as stamens, usually divided to the base. Orig. before 1903.—Here belong "Conquête" (G.W.17: 102), the type.—"Bannière," with semidouble fls. (N.F.6:f.41).—"Mer de glace" (G.W.17:102. Lemoine, Cat.176,t.).—"Norma," with single or double fls. (N.F.6:f.39).—"Nuée blanche."—"Rosace."—"Voie lactée" (Gn.82:267. J.H.28:f.117. G.M.55:554.)—Also "Perle blanche" may be referred here, but calyx pubescent.

34. × **P. virginàlis** Rehd. (*P. Lemoinei* × ? *nivalis plenus*). Bark brown exfoliating or gray-brown and little exfoliating; lvs. generally ovate, 4–6, on shoots to 8 cm. long, remotely dentate or denticulate, pubescent beneath: fls. double or semidouble, in 3–7-fld. racemes; calyx densely pubescent, rarely glabrescent; style shorter than stamens, divided ½. Orig. before 1910.—Here belong the following forms: "Virginal" (type) with exfoliating bark and semidouble fls. in 5–7-fld. racemes. G.C.64:3(h). Gn.82:267. R.H.1910:408, 409(h).—"Albâtre," with large semidouble fls. in usually 5-fld. racemes. N.F. 6:f.42.—"Argentine," with very double fls. usually in 3's; sepals usually 6.—"Glacier," with rather small double fls. in dense 5–7-fld. racemes. N.H.10:150. —Also "Bouquet blanc" may be referred here, though the calyx is scarcely pubescent. J.H.28:f.116. G.W.17:101.

35. × **P. purpúreo-maculàtus** Lemoine. (*P. Lemoinei* × *P. Coulteri*). Young brts. pubescent: lvs. ovate, 8–20 mm. long, acute, entire or with 1–2 teeth (or more in some vars.), strigose-pubescent on both sides; petioles 2 mm. long: fls. 1–3, about 3 cm. across, white, with a purple spot at the base of each petal; calyx sparingly pubescent; style connate, glabrous, shorter than the stamens; stigmas capitate, free. B.M.8193(c). Gn.82:267;87:396. Orig. before 1902. Zone VII?—Here belong: "Amalthée," "Etoile rose," "Fantaisie" (*P. phantasia* A. H. Moore), "Nuage rose," "Oeil de pourpre," "Romeo," "Sirène," "Surprise," "Sybille."

P. p. × *virginalis* = P. Burkwoòdii Burkwood & Skipwith. Fls. fragrant, 5–6 cm. across; petals rather narrow, with a lilac-pink blotch at base. Cult 1929.

Another plant with red spots at the base of the petals is P. maculiflòrus Koehne, but the spots are rather pale and the plant does not show the slightest influence of *P. Coulteri*, but resembles *P. coronarius,* though in the style which is longer than the stamens and in the broad stigmas it approaches *P. grandiflorus;* it may be a form of *P. Zeyheri.*

Ser. 6. GEMMATI Koehne. Buds free, not inclosed in the base of the petiole: fls. 1–3, or in racemes; styles and often the stigmas connate, pubescent or glabrous.

36. P. hirsùtus Nutt. Shrub to 2.5 m.: bark brown, exfoliating; young brts. pubescent: lvs. ovate to oblong-ovate, 3–8 cm. long, acuminate, cuneate or rounded at base, serrate, short-pubescent or nearly glabrous above, densely grayish pubescent beneath strongly 3-nerved: flowering brts. short, usually only with 1 pair of leaves; fls. usually 3, rarely 1, or 4–5, creamy white, scentless, 2–3 cm. across; pedicéls pubescent, the lower ones 5–20 mm. long; calyx pubescent; petals obovate; sepals triangular-ovate; style glabrous; stigmas oblong, partly united. Fl.v–vi. B.R.24:14(c). B.M.5334(c). S.L.254(h). (*P. Godohokeri* Kirchn.) N. C. and Tenn. to Ga. and Ala. Intr. 1820. Zone V. Straggling shrub with rather small scentless fls.; one of the least ornamental species, but the earliest to bloom.

The following two species of this series are in cult., but scarcely hardy within our area: **P. Coùlteri** S. Wats. Lvs. ovate to ovate-oblong, 2–4 cm. long, acute or acuminate, remotely denticulate, pubescent above, white-tomentose beneath: fls. solitary, about 3 cm. across, calyx white-tomentose, petals with a red spot at base; style hairy. G.F.1:233. (*P. mexicanus* var. *C.* Bean.) Mex. Intr. about 1840?—**P. mexicànus** Schlecht. Similar, but lvs. larger, sparingly strigose below; calyx short-villous; petals white, not spotted. B.R.28:38(c). G.C.34: 218. B.M.7600(c). Mex. Cult. 1842.

3. JAMÈSIA Torr. & Gr. Deciduous shrubs: brs. with exfoliating bark and solid pith; terminal bud with 2, lateral with 1 pair of outer scales, densely pubescent: lvs. opposite, short-petioled, serrate, penninerved: fls. perfect, in terminal cymes; sepals 5; petals 5, convolute, obovate-oblong, pubescent inside; stamens 10; ovary incompletely 3–5-celled, nearly superior; ovules numerous; styles 3–5, distinct, about as long as stamens, persistent: fr. a caps., half-inferior, 3–5-valved, little longer, or shorter than the upright sepals; seeds numerous. (After Dr. Edwin James, botanical explorer of the Rocky Mts.; 1797–1861.) Syn.: *Edwinia* Heller. One species in W. N. Am.

J. americàna Torr. & Gray. Shrub to 1 m., rarely to 2.5 m. tall; brts. pubescent while young: lvs. ovate to elliptic, 1.5–6 cm. long, acute, serrate, rugose and slightly pubescent above, grayish or whitish tomentose beneath; petioles 2–15 mm. long: fls. white, sometimes pinkish outside, slightly fragrant, about 1.5 cm. across, in many-fld. cymes, 2–4 cm. high; sepals ovate-lanceolate, acute, much shorter than the petals; stamens and styles somewhat shorter than petals; caps. about 4 mm. long. Fl.v–vi. B.M.6142(c). Gn.63: 105. Gt.53:231,232. L.I.t.6. (*Edwinia a.* Heller.) Wyo. to Utah and N. Mex. Intr. 1862. Zone IV. Attractive upright shrub, though not showy, with rather small dull green lvs. turning orange and scarlet in fall in sunny positions.— **J. a. ròsea** Purp., var. Fls. pink. Cult. 1905.

4. FÉNDLERA Engelm. & Gray. Deciduous rarely subevergreen shrubs: buds minute, with 1 or 2 pairs of outer pubescent scales; brts. striped, pale, bark of older branches fibrous: lvs. subsessile, opposite, entire, 1-3-ribbed, estipulate: fls. 1–3, on short lateral brts., pedicelled, perfect; sepals 4, valvate, longer than the calyx-tube; petals 4, clawed, with rhombic-ovate, erose-ciliate blades; stamens 8; filaments flattened at the top, with narrow upright appendages slightly exceeding the anthers; ovary half-superior, 4-celled, many-ovuled; styles 4, distinct: capsule 4-valved, longer than the persistent sepals; seeds 5–7 mm. long, oblong-triangular, narrowly winged. (After August Fendler, a German naturalist, botanical explorer of New Mexico; 1813–1883.) Three species from Colo. to Mex.

A. Lvs. green and strigose or nearly glabrous beneath..........................1. *F. rupicola*
AA. Lvs. grayish or whitish and strigose and tomentulose beneath...............2. *F. Wrightii*

1. **F. rupícola** Gray. Shrub to 2 m.; brts. minutely pubescent while young: lvs. elliptic to oblong or oblong-lanceolate, 1–3 cm. long, acute or obtusish, usually short-strigose and rough above, rarely nearly glabrous, sparingly or sometimes densely strigose beneath, chartaceous: fls. usually solitary, 3–3.5 cm. across, white or slightly tinged rose outside; sepals pubescent or nearly glabrous; stamens upright, about half as long as the spreading petals: caps. light brown, 1–1.5 cm. long. Fl.v–vi. Gray, Pl. Wright.t.5(excl. f. 2,6,7). Tex. and N. Mex.—**F. r. falcata** (Thornber) Rehd., var. Lvs. larger, 2–4 cm. long, narrow-elliptic to linear-lanceolate, usually nearly glabrous, often falcate: fls. often to 4 cm. across. (*F. f.* Thornber.) N. Mex. to Ariz. and Colo. Intr. 1916. Zone V?

2. **F. Wrìghtii** (Gray) Hell. Similar to the preceding: lvs. narrow-elliptic to lanceolate or narrow-oblong, 5–20 mm. long, scabrid above, grayish white and densely strigose and tomentulose beneath: fls. usually somewhat smaller; pedicels and calyx densely pubescent: caps. about 1 cm. long. Fl.v–vi. B.M. 7924(c). G.F.2:113 (as *F. rupicola*). G.C.36:410;73:177. G.W.19:562(h). (*F. rupicola* var. *W.* Gray.) N. Mex. and w. Tex. to n. Mex. Intr. 1879. Zone (V). Like the preceding a graceful shrub with slender often arching brs. bearing in late spring numerous white fls. resembling in shape a maltese cross.

5. **DEÙTZIA** Thunb. Deciduous or rarely evergreen shrubs; brts. hollow, with usually brown and exfoliating bark; buds with many imbricate scales, glabrous or nearly so: lvs. opposite, short-petioled, serrate, exstipulate: fls. in panicles or in cymes, rarely solitary, usually terminal on lateral brts., white, sometimes pink or purplish, epigynous; calyx-teeth 5, petals 5; stamens 10, rarely more, shorter than petals; filaments usually winged and toothed at apex, the 2 whorls often of different size and shape; styles 3–5, distinct: caps. 3–5-valved, with numerous minute seeds. (After Joh. van der Deutz, patron of Thunberg.) Including *Neodeutzia* Small. About 50 species in E. Asia and the Himal., 2 in Mex.

A. Petals valvate in bud.
 B. Fls. in panicels or racemes; calyx-lobes shorter than the tube.
  C. Filaments winged and toothed near apex (sometimes subulate in Nos. 2 and 3).
   D. Lvs. glabrous or nearly so beneath (sparingly stellate with 4–6-rayed hairs in Nos. 2 and 3).
    E. Infl. an elongated panicle or raceme; fls. white.....................1. *D. gracilis*
    EE. Infl. a broad loose panicle; fls. usually pinkish.
     F. Calyx-teeth lanceolate ....2. *D. rosea*
     FF. Calyx-teeth triangular-ovate ....3. *D. carnea*
   DD. Lvs. stellate-pubescent beneath with 10–15-rayed hairs.
    E. Calyx-teeth shorter than the tube; petals nearly upright.
     F. Panicle narrow: lvs. crenate-denticulate.......................4. *D. scabra*
     FF. Panicle broad and loose: lvs. sharply serrulate...........5. *D. Schneideriana*
    EE. Calyx-lobes about as long as tube..............................7. *D. magnifica*
  CC. Filaments, at least the longer ones subulate; panicle loose and broad: lvs. on the floral brts. subsessile; hairs with 4–5 rays........................6. *D. Sieboldiana*
 BB. Fls. in corymbs or cymes, sometimes solitary.
  C. Infl. many-fld. or several-fld.
   D. Calyx-teeth shorter than the tube, broad-ovate or triangular: fls. white, rather small ....8. *D. setchuenensis*
   DD. Calyx-teeth as long or longer than the tube, ovate-lanceolate or lanceolate.
    E. Fls. pink or purplish outside (see also Nos. 19 and 20).
     F. Anthers of the inner stamens borne on the inner side of the broad filaments.
      G. Lvs. green and sparingly stellate beneath, with 4–6-rayed hairs.
       9. *D. purpurascens*
      GG. Lvs. grayish or whitish beneath, densely stellate with 8–12-rayed hairs.
       12. *D. longifolia*
     FF. Anthers borne at the end of the filaments: lvs. slightly stellate and green beneath ....10. *D. elegantissima*

Deutzia SAXIFRAGACEAE *Deutzia*

EE. Fls. white.
 F. Inner filaments linear-oblong, exceeding the anthers: lvs. soft-pubescent
 beneath ....11. *D. glomeruliflora*
 FF. Inner filaments with 2 teeth near apex: lvs. with close stellate tomentum
 beneath.
  G. Infl. rather dense; the pedicels about 5 mm. long..........13. *D. discolor*
  GG. Infl. loose; the pedicels about 1 cm. long: lvs. usually with simple hairs
  along the midrib...14. *D. Vilmorinae*
 CC. Infl. 1-3-fld.; filaments with long recurved teeth; fls. large, white..15. *D. grandiflora*
AA. Petals imbricate in bud (or partly imbricate in Nos. 17-20).
 B. Lvs. soft-pubescent beneath with spreading hairs.
  C. Stamens subulate: lvs. densely soft-pubescent............................16. *D. mollis*
  CC. Stamens mostly abruptly contracted below the apex: lvs. with mixed pubescence
  beneath ....17. *D. Wilsonii*
 BB. Lvs. stellate-pubescent or glabrous beneath.
  C. Petals partly imbricate, partly valvate in bud: infl. paniculate: filaments dentate.
   D. Fls. white ....18. *D. Lemoinei*
   DD. Fls. pinkish outside.
    E. Fls. about 1.5 cm. across; calyx-teeth longer than tube........19. *D. maliflora*
    EE. Fls. about 2 cm. across; calyx-teeth ovate, as long as tube..20. *D. kalmiaeflora*
  CC. Petals all imbricate; infl. corymbose.
   D. Lvs. green beneath, sparingly stellate or glabrous.
    E. Calyx stellate-pubescent ....21. *D. parviflora*
    EE. Calyx glabrous ....22. *D. glabrata*
   DD. Lvs. glaucous and glabrous beneath: the inner filaments with the anther attached
   inside near the middle...23. *D. hypoglauca*

Sect. I. EUDEUTZIA Engl. Petals valvate in bud.
Ser. 1. LATISEPALAE Schneid. (*Scabrae* Rehd.) Infl. paniculate; calyx-teeth shorter than tube; petals more or less upright; filaments with teeth not exceeding the anthers or subulate; styles as long or slightly shorter than petals.

1. **D. grácilis** Sieb. & Zucc. Shrub to 2 m.; brts. with yellowish gray close bark: lvs. oblong-lanceolate, 3–6 cm. long, rarely to 8 cm., long-acuminate, broad-cuneate or rounded at base, unequally serrate, with scattered stellate hairs above, nearly glabrous and green beneath: fls. white, 1.5–2 cm. long, in upright panicles or racemes, 4–9 cm. long; calyx slightly scaly, with short triangular, greenish white lobes deciduous in fr.; petals elliptic to oblong; filaments with short spreading teeth. Fl.v–vi. S.Z.1:t.8(c). F.S.6:t.611(c).— Gn.39:200. Japan. Intr. about 1840. Zone IV. Graceful free-flowering shrub with slender often arching brs.; used for forcing.—**D. g. aùrea** Schelle, f. Lvs. yellow. There are also some variegated forms.

D. g. × *Sieboldiana* = **D. candelábrum** (Lemoine) Rehd. Brts. grayish brown: lvs. usually ovate-lanceolate, serrulate, scabrid above, thinly covered beneath with 3–5-rayed hairs; petioles of flowering brts. about 1 mm. long: fls. 1.5 cm. across, in many-fld. panicles 6–11 cm. long; filaments toothed. R.H. 1908:174. M.G.22:378(h). R.B.33:372(h). (*D. gracilis c.* Lemoine.) Orig. before 1907. Similar to *D. gracilis* in appearance, but panicles broader and denser.—**D. c. fastuòsa** (Lemoine) Rehd., var. (*D. gracilis f.* Lemoine) is scarcely different.—**D. c. erecta** (Lemoine) Rehd., var. (*D. gracilis e.* Lemoine) has shorter panicles and smaller fls.; the longer filaments usually gradually narrowed below the apex.—*D. g.* × *parviflora;* see No. 18.

2. × **D. ròsea** (Lemoine) Rehd. (*D. gracilis* × *purpurascens*). Brts. with brown, usually exfoliating bark: lvs. ovate-oblong to ovate-lanceolate, sharply serrulate, with scattered stellate hairs, those below with 4–6 rays; petioles 4–5 mm. long: fls. open-campanulate, about 2 cm. across, pinkish outside, in short panicles; calyx-teeth lanceolate, longer than the tube; filaments usually slightly toothed; styles usually longer than the stamens. F.E.30:423. Gn.M. 25:299. G.27:274. (*D. gracilis r.* Lemoine.) Orig. before 1898. Zone IV.— **D. r. campanulàta** (Lemoine) Rehd., var. Fls. white, about 2.5 cm. across; sepals lanceolate, purplish, petals broader; filaments strongly toothed. G.28: 485. Gn.M.25:229. (*D. gracilis c.* Lemoine.)—**D. r. venústa** (Lemoine) Rehd., var. Fls. white; filaments toothed; sepals deltoid, green. G.27:275. (*D. gracilis v.* Lemoine.)—**D. r. multiflòra** (Lemoine) Rehd., var. Fls. white;

filaments toothed; sepals lanceolate. (*D. gracilis m.* Lemoine.)—**D. r. carmínea** (Lemoine) Rehd., var. Fls. purplish outside; filaments strongly toothed; sepals deltoid, purplish. (*D. gracilis c.* Lemoine.)—**D. r. eximia** (Lemoine) Rehd., var. Fls. slightly pinkish outside; filaments short, strongly toothed; sepals deltoid, purplish. (*D. gracilis e.* Lemoine.)—**D. r. floribúnda** (Lemoine) Rehd., var. Fls. slightly pink outside, in rather dense upright panicles; stamens strongly toothed; sepals lanceolate. (*D. discolor f.* Lemoine.) J.P.1902:312(h).—**D. r. grandiflòra** (Lemoine) Rehd., var. Similar, but infl. less dense. Gn.M.25:229. (*D. discolor g.* Lemoine.)

    D. r. × *Vilmorinae;* see under No. 14.

    3. × **D. cárnea** (Lemoine) Rehd. (*D. rosea grandiflora* × *Sieboldiana*). Brts. brown: lvs. ovate to oblong-ovate, 3–5 cm. long, acuminate, usually rounded at base, sharply serrulate, with scattered stellate hairs on both sides; petioles 2–3 mm. long: fls. nearly 2 cm. across, pink outside, in loose upright panicles; sepals deltoid, purplish; stamens about as long as style, the filaments with short, sometimes obsolete teeth. (*D. discolor c.* Lemoine.) Orig. 1907.—**D. c. stellàta** (Lemoine) Rehd., var. (*D. discolor s.* Lemoine) differs chiefly in its narrower petals.—**D. c. densiflòra** (Lemoine) Rehd., var. (*D. discolor d.* Lemoine) has white fls. slightly pinkish in bud and **D. c. láctea** (Lemoine) Rehd., var. (*D. discolor l.* Lemoine) pure white fls.

    4. **D. scábra** Thunb. Shrub to 2.5 m.; brts. with red-brown, rarely grayish brown, tardily exfoliating bark, stellate-pubescent while young: lvs. ovate to oblong-lanceolate, 3–8 cm. long, acute or obtusely acuminate, usually rounded at base, crenate-denticulate, dull green, stellate-pubescent on both sides, beneath with 10–15-rayed hairs; petioles on flowering brts. about 2 mm. long: panicles upright, narrow, 6–12 cm. long, stellate-pubescent, often mixed with spreading hairs; fls. white or pinkish outside, 1.5–2 cm. long; calyx-teeth triangular, deciduous in fr.; petals oblong, nearly upright; filaments toothed below apex; the longer stamens nearly as long as petals; styles usually 3; caps. subglobose, about 5 mm. long. Fl.vɪ–vɪɪ. S.Z.1:t.6(c). B.M.3838(c). B.R.1718(c). I.S.5:t.220. Gn.37:315. (*D. crenata* Sieb. & Zucc., *D. dentata* Hort., *D. mitis* Hort.) Japan, China. Intr. 1822. Zone V. Handsome shrub with a profusion of white, often purplish tinted fls. late in June.—**D. s. angustifòlia** (Reg.) Voss, f. Lvs. oblong-ovate to ovate-lanceolate: infl. only with stellate hairs. (*D. crenata* var. *a.* Reg.)—**D. s. marmoràta** Rehd., var. Lvs. spotted with yellowish white. (*D. s. f. aureo-variegata* Schneid.)—**D. s. punctàta** Rehd., var. Lvs. sprinkled with white dots. (*D. s. f. albo-punctata* Schneid.)—**D. s. Wàtereri** (Lemoine) Rehd., var. Fls. white, tinted carmine outside. Add.8:t.264(c). G.C.39:340. (*D. s. f. punicea* Schneid., *D. crenata W.* Lemoine.)—**D. s. plèna** (Maxim.)Rehd., var. Fls. double, suffused with rosy purple outside. R.H.1867:70,t(c). F.S.17:t.1790;18:t.1850(c). (*D. crenata fl. pleno* Hort., *D. crenata* var. *p.* Maxim.) Here belongs "Pride of Rochester."—**D. s. candidíssima** (Froebel) Rehd., var. Fls. pure white, double. G.C.II.18:173. A.F.6:263. (*D. crenata c. plena* Froebel, *D. hybrida Wellsii* Hort.)

    D. s. × *Vilmorinae;* see No. 7.
    Closely related species: D. hypoleùca Maxim. Brs. slenderer: lvs. ellipticto oblong-lanceolate, long-acuminate, serrulate, white-tomentose beneath: panicles smaller; petals 1–1.2 cm. long, white. (*D. Maximowicziana* Mak.) Japan. Intr. 1915. Zone VI?

    5. **D. Schneideriàna** Rehd. Shrub to 2 m.; brts. with brown, tardily exfoliating bark: lvs. elliptic-ovate to elliptic-oblong, 3–7 cm. long, acuminate, usually rounded at base, sharply serrulate, whitish or grayish tomentose

beneath: fls. white in broad-pyramidal panicles; petals oblong; stamens slightly shorter, with strongly toothed filaments; styles usually 3: caps. about 6 mm. across. I.S.5:t.221. C. China. Similar to *D. scabra,* but with broader and looser panicles.—**D. S. laxiflòra** Rehd., var. Lvs. oblong-ovate to oblong-lanceolate, thinly stellate-pubescent and green beneath: panicles 4–8 cm. long and almost as broad at base, loose; petals 1.2–1.4 cm. long. Fl.vi–vii. Gn.M.27:21. C. China. Intr. 1907. Zone (V) VI.

Related species: **D. ningpoénsis** Rehd. Lvs. ovate-oblong, remotely denticulate, usually broad-cuneate; petiole 1–3 mm. long: panicle to 12 cm. long; petals oblong, 5–8 mm. long. I.S.5:t.222. E. China. Intr. 1937.—**D. Chunii** Hu. Lvs. oblong-lanceolate, remotely and minutely serrulate: panicle to 8 cm. long; petals ovate-oblong, 6 mm. long. I.S.2:t.71. E. China. Intr. 1935.

6. **D. Sieboldiàna** Maxim. Shrub to 2 m.; brts. with brown exfoliating bark: lvs. subsessile on flowering shoots, ovate to oblong-ovate, 3–6, on shoots to 8 cm. long, short-acuminate, rounded or subcordate at base, dentate-serrulate, rugose and scabrid above, green and stellate-pubescent beneath with 3–5-rayed hairs: panicles upright, broad-pyramidal and loose, 3–7 cm. long, stellate-pubescent and usually mixed with spreading hairs; fls. white, about 1.5 cm. across, with spreading elliptic-oblong petals; sepals triangular, acute, persistent; stamens slightly shorter than petals; the outer filaments without teeth, the inner often obscurely toothed; styles usually 3: fr. 3–4 mm. across. Fl.vi. S.Z.1:t.7(c). G.C.36:244. B.S.1:487. S.L.158(h). (*D. scabra* Sieb. & Zucc., not Thunb.) Japan. Cult. 1890. Zone V. Usually a low shrub with upright loose panicles.—**D. S. Dippeliàna** Schneid., var. Lvs. of flowering brts. broad-elliptic or broad-ovate: infl. only with stellate pubescence; all filaments without teeth. Japan. Intr. about 1875. Zone V.

D. S. × *rosea;* see No. 3.—*D. S.* × *purpurascens;* see No. 10.—*D. S.* × *Lemoinei;* see under No. 18.

7. × **D. magnífica** (Lemoine) Rehd. (*D. scabra* × *Vilmorinae*). Lvs. ovate-oblong, 4–6, on shoots to 8 cm. long, rounded at base, sharply serrulate, scabrid above, grayish green and rather densely stellate-pubescent beneath with 10–15-rayed hairs: fls. white, double, in short, rather dense panicles 4–6 cm. long; calyx-teeth ovate or deltoid, nearly as long as the tube; petals oblong, acutish; styles usually 4. Fl.vi. G.M.53:108. F.E.31:322. (*D. crenata m.* Lemoine.) Orig. before 1910. Zone (V). Similar to *D. scabra,* but the infl. shorter and broader and the filaments with larger ascending teeth.—**D. m. formòsa** (Lemoine) Rehd., var. (*D. crenata f.* Lemoine) has also double fls. while the following have single fls. and filaments with large ascending teeth.— **D. m. latiflòra** (Lemoine) Rehd., var. (*D. crenata l.* Lemoine.) Fls. nearly 4 cm. across, with spreading petals.—**D. m. supérba** (Lemoine) Rehd., var. (*D. crenata s.* Lemoine.) Fls. campanulate.—**D. m. ebúrnea** (Lemoine) Rehd., var. (*D. crenata e.* Lemoine.) Fls. campanulate, in rather loose panicles.—**D. m. erécta** (Lemoine) Rehd., var. (*D. crenata e.* Lemoine.) Fls. in dense panicles.

Ser. 2. CYMOSAE Rehd. Fls. in loose corymbose cymes; sepals broad-triangular; filaments with large teeth, those of the inner stamens elongated above the anther.

8. **D. setchuenénsis** Franch. Shrub to 2 m.; brts. with brown, tardily exfoliating bark: lvs. ovate-lanceolate to lanceolate, 2–4, on shoots to 8 cm. long, long-acuminate, usually rounded at base, scabrid above and sometimes with simple spreading hairs, grayish green beneath and densely stellate-pubescent with mostly 6-rayed hairs and mixed, particularly on the veins, with simple spreading hairs; petioles on the flowering brts. 2–4 mm. long:

fls. 1–1.2 cm. across, white, in few- to many-fld. loose corymbs; petals elliptic, spreading; stamens upright, scarcely half as long as petals, the outer filaments with broad ascending teeth, the inner lanceolate exceeding the anther; styles 3, shorter than stamens. Fl.vi–vii. G.C.76:165(h). (*D. corymbiflora erecta* Lemoine.) C. and W. China. Intr. about 1893. Zone VI. Of rather loose and straggling habit, less showy than most species.—**D. s. corymbiflòra** (Lemoine) Rehd., var. Lvs. broader and larger: fls. nearly 1.5 cm. across, in loose corymbs 5–10 cm. broad. B.M.8255(c). G.C.III.24:267(h). R.H.1897: 466(h),467. A.F.14:166(h). (*D. c.* Lemoine, *D. corymbosa* André, not R. Br.) Intr. with the type.

  D. s. × *parviflora;* see under No. 21.
  Related species: **D. Monbeigii** W. W. Sm. Lvs. ovate to ovate-lanceolate, 1.5–2 cm. long, obtusish or acutish, denticulate, densely white-tomentose beneath with 12–14-rayed hairs: fls. white, in 5–12-fld. corymbs; sepals triangular; petals about 1 cm. long; inner filaments with teeth shorter than the anther. G.C.100:92. J.L.59:409(h). W. China. Intr. 1921. Zone VI?

  Ser. 3. STENOSEPALAE Schneid. Fls. in corymbs; calyx-teeth elongated, as long or longer than the tube; filaments always toothed, the inner ones often elongated beyond the anther.

  9. **D. purpuráscens** Rehd. Shrub to 2 m.; brts. with brown exfoliating bark: lvs. oblong-ovate to oblong-lanceolate, 2–3.5, on shoots to 6 cm. long, acuminate, usually rounded at base, unequally serrulate, scabrid above, green and loosely stellate-pubescent beneath with 5–7-rayed hairs; petioles about 1–3 mm. long: fls. about 2 cm. across, purplish outside, in 4–10-fld. corymbs; sepals lanceolate, purplish, longer than tube; petals spreading, obovate or elliptic; stamens about ⅔ as long as petals; outer filaments with large teeth exceeding the anthers, the inner oblong, with the anther attached inside near the middle. Fl.v–vi. B.M.7708(c). G.C.III.2:45;26:45. G.F.7:287. R.H. 1895:64,t(c). (*D. discolor* var. *p.* Franch.) W. China. Intr. 1888. Zone VI? Spreading shrub with slender brs. and handsome star-shaped fls. more or less purple outside.

  D. p. × *gracilis;* see No. 2.—*D. p.* × *Lemoinei;* see No. 19.—*D. p.* × *parviflora;* see No. 20.

  10. × **D. elegantíssima** (Lemoine) Rehd. (*D. purpurascens* × *Sieboldiana*). Lvs. ovate to oblong-ovate, irregularly and sharply serrulate, sparingly stellate-pubescent beneath with 4–6-rayed hairs; petioles 1–2 mm. long: fls. nearly 2 cm. across, open, tinted rose inside and outside, in many-fld. loose corymbs; calyx-lobes lanceolate, purple, longer than tube; filaments with large ascending teeth. R.B.36:387. M.G.22:377,f.9. (*D. discolor e.* Lemoine.) Orig. before 1910. Similar to *D. purpurascens* but chiefly distinguished by its broader more abruptly acuminate lvs., shorter petioles, longer stamens with the inner filaments toothed at apex and by the more upright habit.—**D. e. fasciculàta** (Lemoine) Rehd., var. (*D. discolor f.* Lemoine) is very similar and **D. e. arcuàta** (Lemoine) Rehd., var. (*D. discolor a.* Lemoine) has white fls.

  11. **D. glomeruliflòra** Franch. Shrub to 2 m.; bark of brts. brown, quickly exfoliating: lvs. ovate-oblong to lanceolate, 2–4, on shoots to 7 cm. long, acuminate, cuneate or sometimes rounded at base, sharply serrulate, pubescent above, grayish white below and soft-pubescent with 5–6-rayed hairs mixed with simple hairs on the veins; petioles 1–2 mm. long: fls. white, about 2 cm. across, in usually dense corymbs 3–5 cm. across; calyx-teeth lanceolate, as long or longer than tube, purple; petals elliptic; stamens about half as long as petals; the outer filaments with large ascending teeth, the inner oblong or lanceolate with the anther attached inside; styles about 4. Fl.v–vi. I.S.5:t.224.

W. China. Intr. 1908. Zone (V). Easily distinguished from the related species by the soft pubescence of the under side of the lvs.

Related species: **D. Rehderiàna** Schneid. Brts. slender, densely stellate-pilose: lvs. ovate to ovate-lanceolate, .1.5–2.5 cm. long, acute, pale or grayish green below, densely covered with 5–10-rayed hairs; fls. white, in 3–5-fld. cymes; calyx-teeth triangular-lanceolate, about as long as tube: petals 6–7 mm. long: inner filaments with the anther attached inside, bifid at apex. (*D. dumicola* W. W. Sm.) W. China. Intr. 1913. Zone VI?

12. D. longifòlia Franch. Shrub to 2 m.; brts. with brown or grayish brown exfoliating bark: lvs. oblong-lanceolate to lanceolate, or sometimes narrow lanceolate, 5–8, on shoots to 12 cm. long, long-acuminate, usually cuneate at base, serrulate, scabrid above, grayish green or whitish beneath and densely covered with stellate, 8–12-rayed hairs, on the veins often with simple spreading hairs; petioles 2–3 mm., on shoots to 8 mm. long: fls. 2–2.5 cm. across, tinted light purple, in many-fld. rather dense corymbs; calyx-teeth lanceolate, longer than tube; petals elliptic-oblong; outer filaments with large ascending teeth, the inner usually lanceolate with the anther attached inside, sometimes similar to the outer ones; styles usually 4, sometimes 5. Fl.vi. B.M.8493(c). G.C.51:409. Gn.76:243;88:589(h). W. China. Intr. 1901. Zone VI. Shrub of vigorous habit with rather large lvs. and large purplish fls. in dense corymbs.—**D. l. Veìtchii** (Wils.) Rehd., var. With larger more brightly colored fls. in dense corymbs. R.H.1915:536,t(c). J.H. 40:f.53(h). (*D. V.* Wils.)—**D. l. élegans** Rehd., f. Fls. nearly 2 cm. across, rosy-purple outside, in rather loose corymbs along slender arching brs. Intr. 1908. Zone (V).—**D. l. Fárreri** Airy-Shaw, var. Fls. white; styles 4–5, distinct. B.M.9532(c). N. W. China. Intr. 1914. Zone V.

D. l. × *discolor* = D. hýbrida Lemoine. Here belongs "Mont-Rose" Lemoine. Also "Contraste" (G.C.89:485) and "Magicien" are hybrids of *D. longifolia*.

Related species: **D. àlbida** Batal. Shrub to 4 m.: lvs. ovate to oblong-ovate, 2–6 cm. long, obtusish to acute, denticulate, scabrid above, densely white-tomentose and reticulate beneath: fls. white, about 1 cm. across, in several-to many-fld. corymbs 3–5 cm. wide; pedicels shorter or partly longer than calyx: petals oval; filaments about half as long as petals, with large teeth exceeding the anthers. N. W. China. Intr. 1914. Zone V?

13. D. díscolor Hemsl. Upright shrub to 2 m.; bark of brts. red-brown or chestnut-brown, exfoliating: lvs. oblong-lanceolate, 3–7, on shoots to 10 cm. long, acuminate, cuneate at base, denticulate-serrulate, scabrid above, grayish green or whitish beneath and densely covered with 10–15-rayed hairs; petioles 2–3 cm. long: fls. about 2 cm. across, white, rarely slightly pinkish, in usually dense many-fld. corymbs; pedicels 3–6 mm. long; calyx-lobes lanceolate or triangular-lanceolate, about as long as tube; petals elliptic; stamens about half as long as petals, the large teeth of the filaments usually not reaching the base of the anthers, but on the inner filaments sometimes equaling the anthers, rarely the inner filaments prolonged beyond the insertion of the anthers; styles usually 3, longer than the stamens. Fl.vi. I.S.5: t.226. C. China. Intr. 1901. Zone (V) VI. Shrub with rather large lvs. and large white fls. in dense corymbs.—**D. d. màjor** Veitch, var. Fls. about 2.5 cm. across, slightly rose-tinted outside. B.S.1:482. G.30:307(h). R.B.32: 174(h).

D. d. × *mollis;* see No. 17.—*D. d.* × *longifolia;* see under No. 12.

Related species: **D. refléxa** Duthie. Lvs. with simple hairs beneath on the midrib and often on the veins: fls. smaller, the petals with reflexed margin and therefore appearing narrow. C. China. Intr. 1901. Zone (V).—**D. globòsa** Duthie. Lvs. smaller: fls. smaller, creamy white in smaller dense corymbs; filaments abruptly contracted below apex, without teeth. C. China. Intr. 1901. Zone (V).—**D. stamínea** R. Br. Lvs. ovate, 3–6 cm. long, long-acuminate, usually rounded at base, unequally serrate, densely covered with stellate hairs beneath: fls. about 1.5 cm. across, in corymbs 2–4 cm. across; filaments with large teeth. B.R.33:13(c). Himal. Intr. 1841. Zone VII.—**D. s. Brunoniàna** Hook. f. & Thoms., var. Lvs. less pubescent: fls. larger. B.R.26:5(c). (*D. corymbosa* Lindl., not R. Br., *D. canescens* Hort.)

14. **D. Vilmorìnae** Lemoine. Shrub to 2 m.; bark of brts. pale brown, tardily exfoliating: lvs. oblong-lanceolate, 3–6, on shoots to 9 cm. long, acuminate, broad-cuneate or rounded at base, serrulate, scabrid above, grayish green beneath, densely covered with 9–12-rayed hairs, and usually with simple spreading hairs along the nerves; petioles 3–5 mm. long: fls. white, 2–2.5 cm. across, in loose slender corymbs 5–7 cm. across; pedicels 1–1.5 cm. long; calyx-teeth lanceolate, slightly longer than tube; stamens slightly shorter than the petals, the filaments toothed usually much below apex; styles 3–4, almost as long as stamens. Fl.vi. F.V.126. I.S.5:t.225. R.H.1905:266,267. Gn. 81:224(h). M.O.221(h),222. C. and W. China. Intr. 1897. Zone (V). Graceful shrub with large white fls. in loose and large corymbs.

D. V. × *rosea grandiflora* = **D. excéllens** (Lemoine) Rehd. Lvs. ovate-oblong, 3–6, on shoots to 9 cm. long, acuminate, rounded or broad-cuneate at base, serrulate, scabrid above, grayish white beneath with many-rayed hairs and often with simple spreading hairs along the midrib; petioles 3–4 mm. long: fls. 2 cm. across, in loose corymbs 4–6 cm. across; pedicels 5–15 mm. long; calyx-teeth lanceolate, about as long as tube; filaments with large spreading teeth some distance below the apex. (*D. discolor e.* Lemoine.) Orig. before 1911.— *D. V.* × *scabra;* see No. 7.

Ser. 4. GRANDIFLORAE Rehd. Infl. 1–3-fld.; ovary partly superior; calyx-teeth narrow-lanceolate; filaments with long recurved teeth.

15. **D. grandiflòra** Bge. Shrub to 2 m.; bark of brts. usually grayish brown: lvs. ovate, 2–5 cm. long, acute or acuminate, rounded at base, closely and irregularly denticulate, scabrid above, white-tomentose beneath and reticulate; petioles 2–3 mm. long: fls. white, 2.5–3 cm. across, 1–3 on short lateral brts. usually only with one pair of lvs.; calyx-lobes linear-lanceolate, about twice as long as tube; petals elliptic-oblong, 1.2–2 cm. long; filaments with large spreading and recurved teeth; style 3, longer than the stamens. Fl.iv–v. I.S.5:t.228. N. China. Intr. 1910. Zone V. The earliest of all species to bloom and having the largest fls.

Another species with solitary flowers is **D. coreàna** Lév. which represents a distinct series COREANAE Rehd. characterized by solitary fls. originating from axillary leafless buds on the brts. of the previous year. Lvs. elliptic-oblong to lanceolate, 4–6 cm. long, with scattered, 4–6-rayed hairs on both sides. M.K.15: t.16. Korea. Intr. 1917. Zone V?

Sect. II. MESODEUTZIA Engl. Petals imbricate in bud: filaments subulate or toothed.

16. **D. móllis** Duthie. Shrub to 2 m.; brts. stellate-pubescent while young, older red-brown: lvs. elliptic or ovate to ovate-oblong, 4–8, on shoots to 12 cm. long, acute or short-acuminate, broad-cuneate to subcordate at base, closely serrulate, with scattered 3–4-rayed hairs above, grayish green and soft-pubescent beneath, the hairs with usually 4 horizontal rays and an upright central one; petioles 3–6 mm. long: fls. white, 1–1.2 cm. across, in rather dense corymbs 6–8 cm. across, with appressed and spreading hairs; calyx-teeth broad-ovate, shorter than tube; petals broad-obovate, rounded; filaments subulate; styles usually 3, shorter than the longer stamens. Fl.vi. B.M.8559 (c). I.S.5:t.230. B.S.1:484. C. China. Intr. 1901. Zone VI? Distinct but not showy, easily distinguished by the soft pubescence of its rather broad lvs.

17. × **D. Wilsònii** Duthie (*D.* ? *discolor* × *mollis*). Brts. with chestnut-brown exfoliating bark: lvs. elliptic to oblong-lanceolate, 6–9 cm., on shoots to 12 cm. long, acute or acuminate, broad-cuneate or rounded at base, irregu-

larly serrulate, scabrid and rugose above, grayish green beneath, densely
covered with 5-10-rayed stellate hairs mixed particularly on the veins with
numerous simple spreading hairs; petioles 3–5 mm. long: fls. white, about 2
cm. across, in rather loose broad corymbs; calyx-teeth ovate to ovate-oblong,
abruptly mucronulate, about as long as tube; petals broad-elliptic, partly
valvate in bud; filaments gradually or abruptly narrowed below apex, rarely
slightly dentate; styles 3–4, shorter than the longer stamens. Fl.vi. B.M.
8083(c). Gn.89:515(h). M.G.51:230(h). C. China. Intr. probably 1901.
Zone VI. Similar to *D. discolor,* but easily distinguished by the broader lvs.
hairy-pubescent below and the scarcely toothed filaments.

18. × **D. Lemoìnei** Lemoine (*D. parviflora* × *gracilis*). Shrub to 2.5 m.;
young brts. glabrous or nearly so, older with brown exfoliating bark; lvs.
elliptic-lanceolate to lanceolate, 3–6, on shoots to 10 cm. long, long-acuminate,
cuneate at base, sharply serrulate, green on both sides, with scattered 5–8-
rayed hairs beneath; petioles 3–5 mm. long: fls. 1.5–2 cm. across, in panicles
or pyramidal corymbs 3–8 cm. high; pedicels slender, glabrous; calyx-teeth
triangular, much shorter than tube; petals obovate, partly valvate in bud;
filaments toothed below the apex; styles 3, shorter than the longer stamens.
Fl.vi. G.F.9:285. Gt.46:383. G.C.III.18:389(h). A.F.11:437(h). Orig. in
1891. Zone IV. Handsome and free-flowering, one of the hardiest Deutzias.—
D. L. compácta Lemoine. Dwarfer and more compact: fls. smaller in numerous panicles. Gn.M.27:22.—Here belongs also "Boule de neige" with
larger fls. in dense corymbs. J.P.IV,3:309. Gng.8:306.

D. L. × *Sieboldiana* = **D. cándida** (Lemoine) Rehd. Bark of brts. brown,
scarcely exfoliating: lvs. ovate to ovate-oblong, 3.5–5 cm. long, acuminate,
rounded at base, serrulate, slightly scabrid above, green beneath, with scattered
5–7-rayed hairs; petioles 1–2 mm. long: fls. 1.8 cm. cross, slender-pedicelled, in
rather loose panicle-like corymbs 3–4 cm. across; calyx-teeth oblong-ovate, green,
almost as long as tube; petals elliptic, chiefly valvate: filaments with short
teeth or abruptly contracted, the longer ones often gradually narrowed. M.G.
22:376(h). (*D. discolor c.* Lemoine.) Orig. before 1907.

19. × **D. maliflòra** Rehd. (*D. Lemoinei* × *purpurascens*). Lvs. ovate-
oblong, 2.5–4 cm. long, acuminate, usually rounded at base, serrulate, green
beneath, with scattered 5–8-rayed hairs; petioles 1.5–3 mm. long: fls. about
2 cm. across, purplish outside, in corymbs 3–6 cm. across; calyx-teeth oblong,
acutish, purplish, longer than tube: filaments with large ascending teeth.—
Here belongs "Fleur de pommier" (Gn.M.25:228), the typical form of this
hybrid, and "Boule rose" which differs in its somewhat smaller lighter colored
fls., shorter calyx-teeth and in the less strongly toothed filaments; also
"Avalanche" which has large white fls., larger lvs. usually broad-cuneate at
base, and is nearer to *D. Lemoinei.* Fl.vi. Orig. about 1903.

20. × **D. kalmiaeflòra** Lemoine (*D. purpurascens* × *parviflora*). Young
brts. sparingly stellate-pubescent: lvs. ovate-oblong to ovate-lanceolate, 3–6
cm. long, acuminate, usually broad-cuneate at base, serrulate, light green
beneath, with scattered 6–8-rayed hairs; petioles 2–3 mm. long: fls. white,
carmine outside, cup-shaped, about 2 cm. across, in rather loose 5–12-fld.
corymbs; pedicels stellate-pubescent; calyx-teeth ovate, about as long as
tube; petals obovate, partly valvate in bud; filaments with large ascending
teeth, the inner often prolonged undivided above the anther. Fl.vi. Gn.W.
17:627. Gn.M.25:229. G.27:199. M.G.51:231. Orig. before 1904. Zone V.
Graceful shrub with rather large pinkish fls.

21. **D. parviflòra** Bge. Shrub to 2 m.; young brts. with scattered stellate
hairs; lvs. ovate or elliptic to ovate-lanceolate, 3–6, on shoots to 10 cm. long,
acuminate, usually cuneate at base, unequally serrulate with usually spread-

ing teeth, green on both sides and with scattered 5–6-rayed hairs above, beneath with 6–9-rayed hairs and with simple hairs along the midrib at least near base; petioles 3–5 mm. long: fls. white, about 1.2 cm. across, in many-fld. corymbs 4–7 cm. across; calyx-lobes broad-ovate, shorter than tube; petals roundish-obovate; filaments without teeth or the shorter indistinctly toothed; styles usually 3, shorter than the longer stamens. Fl.vɪ. (*D. p. musaei* Lemoine.) N. China. Intr. 1883. Zone IV. Free-flowering shrub, one of the hardiest species.—**D. p. amurénsis** Reg., var. Lvs. mostly ovate, above with 4–5-rayed hairs, paler beneath, without simple spreading hairs along the midrib and on the rather lax infl. N.K.15:t.20. I.S.5:t.232. Gt.43:65(h);46:382. G.F.1:361. G.C.III.14:153(h). (*D. a.* Airy-Shaw.) Korea, Manch. Intr. 1862.—**D. p. ovatifòlia** Rehd., var. Lvs. ovate, rounded at base, with 5–6-rayed hairs above, without simple hairs below. N. China. Intr. 1910.

    D. p. × *setchuenensis* = D. myriántha Lemoine. Lvs. oblong-ovate to oblong-lanceolate, 4–6, on shoots to 9 cm. long, long-acuminate, rounded or broad-cuneate at base, denticulate-serrulate, scabrid on both sides, the hairs beneath 5–6-rayed: fls. white, 2 cm. across, in loose corymbs, 5–8 cm. across; calyx-teeth triangular, short: filaments strongly toothed, the inner filaments often with the anther attached inside. G.C.52:45. A.F.31:100,101. M.G.22:376(h),377. Orig. before 1904. Zone VI.—*D. p.* × *gracilis;* see No. 18.—*D. p.* × *purpurascens;* see No. 20.

    Related species: **D. corymbòsa** R. Br. Brts. glabrous or nearly so: lvs. ovate to oblong-ovate, broad-cuneate or rounded at base, serrulate with usually incurved teeth, below with 8–12-rayed hairs: fls. about 1 cm. across; filaments all toothed. S.H.1:f.244g-i. (*D. parviflora* var. *c.* Franch.) Himal. Intr. 1830. Zone VII?—**D. compacta** Craib. Lvs. oblong-lanceolate, acuminate, serrulate, pale green beneath with 5–8-rayed hairs: fls. white, 6–9 mm. across, in many-fld. compact corymbs 3–5 cm. across; outer filaments with spreading teeth, inner truncate below apex; anthers reddish. B.M.8795(c). W. China. Intr. 1905. Zone VI?

    22. **D. glabràta** Komar. Shrub to 3 m.; young brts. glabrous, later with brown flaky bark: lvs. ovate-oblong or elliptic- ovate to ovate-lanceolate, 3–10 cm. long, acuminate, rounded or broad-cuneate at base, serrulate, bright green above, glabrous or with scattered 3–4-rayed hairs, pale green and quite glabrous beneath; petiole 2–6 mm. long: fls. white, 1–1.5 cm. across in loose many-fld. corymbs 4–8 cm. broad, glabrous; pedicels slender, 6–12 mm. long; calyx glabrous with short broad-ovate obtuse teeth; petals suborbicular; filaments subulate, the longer slightly shorter than petals; styles 3, about as long as stamens. I.S.5:t.231. N.K.15:t.19. Korea. Intr. 1918. Zone V. Vigorous upright shrub with rather large fls. in many-fld. corymbs.

    23. **D. hypoglaùca** Rehd. Shrub to 2 m.; young brts. glabrous, older with chestnut-brown exfoliating bark: lvs. ovate-oblong to oblong-lanceolate, 3–5, on shoots to 9 cm. long, acuminate, rounded or broad-cuneate at base, serrulate, sparingly stellate above, glabrous and glaucous beneath; petioles 1–2 mm. long; fls. pure white, 1.5–2 cm. across, in many-fld. convex corymbs 4–6 cm. across; calyx loosely stellate, teeth broad-triangular, obtuse, shorter than tube; petals roundish-obovate; outer filaments with large ascending teeth, the inner ones produced undivided beyond the anther. Fl.vɪ. B.M.9362 (c, as *D. rubens*). C. China. Intr. 1910. Zone V. Easily distinguished from all cult. species by the glaucous and glabrous under side of the lvs.

    Closely related species: **D. rubens** Rehd. Young brts. sparingly stellate: lvs. pale green beneath and loosely covered with 4–6-rayed hairs: fls. rosy-pink outside or tinged pink. I.S.5:t.233. W. China. Cult. ? Similar to *D. compacta* Craib (see under No. 21), but differing in the shape of the filaments.

    6. **WHÍPPLEA** Torr. Low deciduous shrub; buds small, with few outer scales: lvs. opposite, subsessile, 3-nerved, with few shallow teeth, exstipulate:

fls. small, in long-peduncled head-like compact cymes; sepals 5 or 6; petals 5 or 6; stamens 10–12, about as long as petals; ovary 3–5-celled, half-superior; cells 1-ovuled; styles 3–5, distinct; caps. subglobose, separating into 3–5 leathery, 1-seeded carpels. (After Lieut. A. W. Whipple, commander of the surveying expedition to the Pacific Ocean, 1853–54.) One species.

W. modésta Torr. Shrub with trailing or arching branches 20–50 cm. long and upright strigillose brts.: lvs. ovate or elliptic, 1–3.5 cm. long, acute or acutish, strigillose on both sides: fls. white, in dense cymes or racemes 1–2 cm. across; sepals ovate; petals rhombic, about 3 mm. long; caps. 2–2.5 cm. across. Fl.v. Rep. Exp. Surv. Pacif. Ocean, 4:t.7. S.H.1:f.241a-g. N. & middle Calif. Intr. before 1892. Zone VII? Low inconspicuous shrub.

7. PLATYCRÀTER Sieb. & Zucc. Deciduous shrub; buds with 2–3 pairs of acuminate outer scales: lvs. opposite, petioled, serrate, exstipulate: fls. white, in terminal loose cymes; the marginal fls. sterile with enlarged 3–4-lobed calyx; sepals 4, acute, petals 4, ovate; stamens numerous, with filiform filaments; styles 2, distinct; ovary inferior, 2-celled: fr. a turbinate caps. dehiscent at apex; seeds numerous, linear, winged at both ends. (Greek *platys*, broad, and *crater*, bowl; alluding to the broad calyx of the sterile flowers.) One species.

P. argùta Sieb. & Zucc. Prostrate shrub; brts. glabrous or nearly so, later grayish brown with exfoliating bark: lvs. oblong to lanceolate, 10–18 cm. long, long-acuminate, cuneate at base, coarsely serrate, with scattered hairs above and pilose on the veins beneath or nearly glabrous: fls. about 2 cm. across, slender-pedicelled, in 5–10-fld. cymes; sepals lanceolate, about half as long as petals, the marginal fls. with obtusely 3–4-lobed calyx. Fl.vii. S.Z.1:t.27(c). H.F.1870:206(c). H.S.1:f.245a-l. Japan. The form in cult. is **P. a. horténsis** Maxim., var., with smaller 3–5-fld. cymes usually lacking the sterile fls. Gt.15:t.516. Intr. 1864. Zone VII? It is of little decorative value; likes a shady and humid position.

8. HYDRÁNGEA L. HYDRANGEA. Deciduous upright, rarely climbing shrubs; brs. usually with ample white pith and exfoliating bark; buds with 2 or 3 pairs of outer scales: lvs. opposite, petioled, usually serrate, rarely lobed, exstipulate: fls. perfect, small, in terminal corymbs, rarely in panicles, often with sterile marginal fls.; calyx-lobes 4–5, short; petals 4–5, valvate, small; stamens 8–20, usually 10; ovary inferior or half-superior; styles 2–5, short: fr. a 2–5-celled caps. dehiscent at apex; seeds numerous, minute, winged or wingless. (Greek *hydor*, water, and *aggeion*, vessel; alluding to the shape of the caps.) About 35 species in N. and S. Amer., and in E. Asia south to Java.—Ornamental medium-sized shrubs with small white or sometimes blue or pink fls. in usually showy cormybs or panicles; the self-clinging *H. petiolaris* is valuable for covering walls and other objects. They prefer as a rule moist situations and rich soil.

A. Stems upright; stamens 10; petals free, expanding.
  B. Infl. paniculate.
    c. Lvs. lobed ....4. *H. quercifolia*
    cc. Lvs. not lobed, serrate...8. *H. paniculata*
  BB. Infl. corymbose, flat or hemispherical.
    c. Ovary partly superior, hence caps. ovoid, with the calyx-margin about or above the middle; styles usually 3–4.
      D. Fertile fls. blue or pink.
        E. Infl. sessile, with lvs. at the base: lvs. elliptic-lanceolate, pubescent on the veins beneath ....5. *H. Davidi*
        EE. Infl. peduncled, leafless or rarely with 1 or 2 leafy bracts.
          F. Lvs. obovate to broad-elliptic, glabrous or slightly puberulous beneath, fleshy ....6. *H. macrophylla*

ꜰꜰ. Lvs. ovate or elliptic to lanceolate, sparingly pubescent on both sides, rather
thin ....7. *H. serrata*
ᴅᴅ. Fertile fls. white.
  ᴇ. Lvs. villous or nearly glabrous beneath.
    ꜰ. Mature brts. with close brown or grayish brown bark......9. *H. xanthoneura*
    ꜰꜰ. Mature brts. with exfoliating brown bark...............10. *H. Bretschneideri*
    ᴇᴇ. Lvs. white-tomentose beneath................................11. *H. heteromalla*
  ᴄᴄ. Ovary inferior, hence caps. truncate, with the calyx-limb at apex.
    ᴅ. Corymb without involucre at base.
      ᴇ. Brts. glabrous or puberulous when young: seeds wingless.
        ꜰ. Lvs. glabrous below: corymbs without or very few marginal fls.
                                                              1. *H. arborescens*
        ꜰꜰ. Lvs. pubescent beneath.
          ɢ. Lvs. densely grayish pubescent beneath: corymbs usually with marginal
            fls. ....2. *H. cinerea*
          ɢɢ. Lvs. white-tomentose beneath, longer, acuminate: corymbs always with
            marginal fls. ....3. *H. radiata*
      ᴇᴇ. Brts. densely pubescent: seeds winged.
        ꜰ. Brts. densely covered with harsh spreading hairs: lvs. rounded at base.
                                                              14. *H. Sargentiana*
        ꜰꜰ. Brts. strigose.
          ɢ. Lvs. cordate or rounded at base...........................15. *H. longipes*
          ɢɢ. Lvs. cuneate at base.....................................13. *H. strigosa*
    ᴅᴅ. Corymbs enclosed before expanding by large bracts: upper pair of lvs. subsessile.
                                                              12. *H. involucrata*
ᴀᴀ. Stems climbing by aërial rootlets: lvs. broad-ovate, nearly glabrous: petals cohering at
apex ....16. *H. petiolaris*

Sect. I. Euhydrangea Maxim. Upright shrubs; petals free and spreading:
seeds winged at the ends or wingless.

Ser. 1. Americanae Maxim. Seeds wingless; capsule inferior, truncate at
apex; fertile fls. white; petals spreading or reflexed, persistent during anthesis.

1. H. arboréscens L. Upright straggling shrub, usually 1, occasionally to
3 m.; young brts. sparingly puberulous: lvs. ovate to elliptic, acute or acuminate, rounded or cordate at base, 6–20 cm. long, serrate, glabrous or sometimes
puberulous beneath: petioles 2–6 cm. long: corymbs 5–15 cm. broad, long-
stalked; sterile fls. few, 1.5–2 cm. across: capsule 2.5–3 mm. diam. and slightly
shorter, prominently 10-ribbed. Fl.ᴠɪ–ᴠɪɪ. W.D.t.42(c). B.B.2:231. G.W.15:
612(h). (*H. vulgaris* Michx., *H. a.* var. *cordata* Torr. & Gr.) N. Y. to Iowa,
s. to Fla. and La. Intr. 1736. Zone IV. Usually a round bush with conspicuous
creamy-white fl.-clusters in early summer.—H. a. grandiflora Rehd., f. Fls.
all sterile forming subglobose heads 10–18 cm. across; sepals ovate, acutish.
M.G.27:472. Gn.75:435. N.F.4:221(h). G.C.78:273(h). Found wild in Ohio
before 1900. A striking plant with large heads of white fls.—H. a. oblónga
Torr. & Gr., var. Lvs. rounded at base, elliptic-ovate to oblong-ovate. B.M.
437(c). (*H. a. laevigata* Hort.) Intr. before 1800.—H. a. stérilis Torr. &
Gr., var. A form of the preceding var. with all the fls. sterile; sepals broad-
oval, rounded or mucronate at apex. Gs.14:153(h). Found in Pa. before
1840, rare in cult.—H. a. austràlis Harbison, var. Lvs. cordate at base, more
coarsely serrate; petioles 1–4 cm. long. (*H. a. urticifolia* Hort.) W. Va.
Cult. 1888.

H. a. × *radiata* = H. canéscens Kirchn. Resembling the following species:
petiole shorter; lvs. smaller; the pubescence beneath usually thinner, the hairs
under the microscope nearly smooth (tuberculate in *H. cinerea*); sterile fls.
wanting or few. G.W.1931:534(h). (*H. arborescens* var. *c.* Nichols.) Orig.
before 1860.

2. H. cinérea Small. Spreading shrub, sometimes 2 m. tall; young brts.
puberulous: lvs. elliptic or broad-ovate to ovate-oblong, 6–15 cm. long, short-
acuminate, rounded or subcordate at base, serrate, bright green above, grayish
tomentose beneath; petioles 2–8 cm. long: corymbs 5–20 cm. across; sterile
fls. usually present, few. Fl.ᴠɪ–ᴠɪɪ. B.B.2:231. (*H. arborescens* var. *Deamii*
St. John.) N. C. and Tenn. to Ala. Intr. 1906. Zone V.—H. c. stérilis Rehd.,
f. A form with all the fls. sterile forming a head 8–15 cm. across; sepals broad-

ovate, obtuse. Gs. 4:27(h). (*H. arborescens* var. *Deamii* f. *acarpa* St. John.) Orig. before 1908. Similar to the sterile form of the preceding species.

3. **H. radiàta** Walt. Upright shrub, sometimes to 2.5 m.; young brts. puberulous: lvs. ovate to ovate-lanceolate, rather long-acuminate, subcordate or rounded at base, 6–12 cm. long, serrate, dark green and glabrous above, white-tomentose beneath and reticulately veined; petioles 1.5–6 cm. long: corymbs 5–12 cm. broad, often with numerous ray-flowers 2–3 cm. broad. Fl.vi–vii. W.D.1:43(c). F.E.32:11(h). (*H. nivea* Michx.) N. and S. Car. Intr. 1786. Zone IV.

H. r. × *arborescens;* see under No. 1.

4. **H. quercifòlia** Bartr. Shrub to 2 m. with upright and spreading brs.; young brts. reddish tomentose: lvs. ovate to suborbicular in outline, sinuately 3–7-lobed, usually truncate at base and decurrent into the petiole, 6–20 cm. long, lobes broad, serrate and often slightly lobed, whitish tomentose beneath: infl. paniculate, 10–30 cm. long with numerous white sterile fls. 2–3 cm. and finally 3–4 cm. across and turning purple, the sepals usually orbicular-obovate: caps. about 3 mm. high. Fl.vi. B.M.975(c). Add.5:t.175(c). G.C. II.22:369. Gn.M.32:260(h). Gs.2:305(h). Ga. and Fla. to Miss. Intr. 1803. Zone (V). Chiefly valued for the distinct shape and the size of its lvs.; also the large panicles are conspicuous.

Ser. 2. PETALANTHAE Maxim. Seeds wingless or with very short wing; caps. half or partly superior, ovoid: fertile fls. pink or blue; petals finally reflexed, usually persisting during anthesis: infl. corymbose.

5. **H. Davídi** Franch. Shrub to 2 m.; young brts. pubescent, older light brown: lvs. elliptic-lanceolate to oblong-lanceolate, long-acuminate, cuneate at base, 8–15 cm. long, dentate-serrate, yellowish green and nearly glabrous above, pubescent on the nerves beneath; petioles 1–2.5 cm. long; infl. a convex loose corymb 12–25 cm. across or sometimes paniculate, with 1 or 2 pairs of lvs. at base; fertile fls. bluish; petals lanceolate; styles 3–4; sterile fls. 2.5–4 cm. across, with orbicular-ovate entire sepals: caps. with the calyx-limb about the middle. Fl.vi–vii. I.S.3:t.132. W. China. Intr. 1908. Zone VII? Shrub with large loose corymbs of blue fertile fls. surrounded by white sterile fls.

Related species: **H. chinénsis** Maxim. Brts. glabrous: lvs. thickish, oblong or lance-oblong, 4–8 cm. long, acuminate, remotely denticulate or nearly entire, glabrous; petioles 4–10 mm. long; corymbs 6–10 cm. across with few or no sterile fls. S. E. China, Formosa. Cult. 1934. Zone VII?—**H. scandens** (L.) Ser. Brs. slender: lvs. elliptic to elliptic-lanceolate, 3–6 cm. long, acute or acutish, sparingly setose above: corymbs loose, 4–8 cm. across; sterile fls. white or whitish, 3–5 cm. across with usually 3 entire or slightly dentate sepals. S.Z.1:t.60(c). (*H. virens* Sieb. & Zucc.) Japan. Cult. 1904. Zone VII?

6. **H. macrophýlla** (Thunb.) DC. Shrub to 4 m.; brts. stout, glabrous: lvs. thickish, obovate to elliptic or broad-ovate, short-acuminate, broad-cuneate at base, 7–15 cm. long, coarsely serrate with triangular obtusish teeth, bright green and lustrous above, light green beneath, glabrous or slightly puberulous beneath and light green, petioles stout, 1–3 cm. long, leaving large scars, the opposite ones contiguous; corymbs peduncled, sparingly appressed-pubescent, in the sterile form globose and 15–20 cm. or more across; in the fertile form flattened; fls. blue or pink, rarely white; petals ovate-oblong soon deciduous; styles 3–4; sterile ray-fls. large, with entire or dentate sepals; caps. ⅓ or ¼ superior, ovoid, with the short styles 6–8 mm. long. Fl.vi–vii. (*H. opuloides* K. Koch, *H. hortensis* Sm., *H. Hortensia* DC., *Hortensia opuloides* Lam.) Japan. Zone (V), VI.—**H. m. Horténsia** (Maxim.) Rehd., f. Fls. all sterile, with broad-ovate, entire sepals; pink to

blue: lvs. usually elliptic. B.M.438(c). G.C.52:251;71:87(h). (*H. opuloides* var. *H.* Dipp., *H. japonica* var. *plena* Reg.) This is the type. Intr. from China in 1790.—**H. m. Otáksa** (Sieb. & Zucc.) Wils., f. Dwarfer, with smaller obovate lvs. and entire obovate sepals. S.Z.1:t.52(c). F.S.17:t.1732-3(c). R.H.1868:450,t(c). A.G.44:415(h). F.E.9:52,401(h). Intr. from Japan before 1861.—**H. m. Veìtchii** Wils., f. A form with deep rose-pink sterile fls. Gn. 50:122,t(c). G.W.7:582,t(c). (*H. Hortensia* var. *japonica rosea* Bean.) Intr. from Japan 1880.—**H. m. mandshùrica** (Dieck) Wils., f. Stems dark purple or nearly black: lvs. elliptic: fls. rose-colored, nearly all sterile. A.F.5:361. (*H. Hortensia* var. *nigra* Nichols., *H. m.* Koehne, *H. opuloides* var. *cyanoclada* Dipp.) Cult. 1870. Zone (V).— **H. m. normàlis** Wils., var. The wild type with a flat corymb of perfect fls. and with a few pink sterile ray-fls. 3–5 cm. across. C. Japan. Intr. 1917.—**H. m. ròsea** (Sieb. & Zucc.) Wils., f. Similar to the preceding but with toothed pink ray-fls. S.Z.1:t.53(c). (*H. japonica* Sieb.) Cult. 1841.—**H. m. Marièsii** (Bean) Wils., f. With rosy pink ray-fls., 5–8 cm. across, entire or sparingly toothed. Gn.54:390,t(c);87:341. G.C.III.23:f.122. Intr. 1879 from Japan.—**H. m. macrosépala** (Reg.) Wils., f. With white, toothed ray-fls. Gt.15:t.520(c).—**M. m. coerùlea** (Hook.) Wils., f. Perfect fls. deep blue and the ray-fls. blue or white. S.Z.1:t.55(c). B.M. 4253(c). (*H. Belzoni* Sieb. & Zucc., *H. japonica* var. *c.* Hook.) Cult. 1846. Zone VI. One of the hardier forms.—**H. m. maculàta** (Bl.) Wils., f. Lvs. edged white: infl. with fertile and sterile fls. F.S.7:t.696(c). (*H. hortensis variegata* Nichols.) Cult. 1850.

7. **H. serràta** (Thunb.) DC. Shrub to 1.5, rarely to 2.5 m., with rather slender brs. glabrous or pubescent àt first: lvs. elliptic or ovate to lanceolate, 5–10 cm. long, acuminate, cuneate, finely or coarsely serrate, sparsely appressed-pubescent on both sides, midrib with short curled hairs sometimes only above; petiole 1–2.5, rarely to 5 cm. long: fls. blue or white, in flat or slightly convex corymbs 4–8 cm. across, with few rather small, white, pink or bluish ray-fls.: caps. ovoid, 2–4 mm. long, with 3 short diverging styles. Fl. VII–VIII. S.Z.1:t.58(c). G.C.1870:1699. (*H. Thunbergii* Sieb., *H. opuloides* var. *s.* Rehd.) Japan, Korea. Cult. 1870. Zone VI or V?—**H. s. acuminàta** (Sieb. & Zucc.) Wils., f. Lvs. 9–18 cm. long, caudate-acuminate; ray-fls. usually blue. S.Z.1:t.56,57(c). R.H.1874:91,t(c). S.L.193(h). M.G.32:41(h). (*H. a.* Sieb. & Zucc.) Intr. about 1870.—**H. s. pubéscens** (Franch. & Sav.) Wils., f. Lvs. ovate or elliptic-ovate, caudate-acuminate, with appressed and spreading hairs on the veins beneath: ray-fls. pink or white. (*H. hortensis* var. *p.* Franch.`& Sav., *H. opuloides* var. *sinensis* Dipp.) Cult. 1888.—**H. s. rosálba** (Vanh.) Wils., f. Lvs. ovate to obovate, usually rounded at base, slightly pubescent beneath: ray-fls. white and pink, usually toothed. F.S.16: t.1649–50(c). R.H.1866:432,t(c). Gn.46:466,t(c). G.C.106:137. (*H. japonica r.* Vanh., *H. hortensis* var. *Lindleyana* Nichols., *H. opuloides* var. *r.* Rehd.) Cult. 1864.—**H. s. prolífera** (Reg.) Rehd., f. Lvs. ovate or elliptic-ovate, abruptly long-acuminate, pubescent on both sides: ray-fls. with numerous elliptic-ovate to oblong pointed sepals. S.Z.1:t.59(c). (*H. stellata* var. *p.* Reg., *H. st.* Sieb. & Zucc., *H. Hortensia* var. *st.* Maxim., *H. serrata* var. *stellata* Wils.) Cult. 1864.

Ser. 3. HETEROMALLAE Rehd. Seeds winged at the ends: fertile fls. white; petals caducous; styles usually 3: caps. half-superior.

8. **H. paniculàta** Sieb. Shrub or small tree to 10 m.; brìs. stout, pubescent: lvs. elliptic or ovate, acuminate, rounded or cuneate àt base, 5–12 cm. long, serrate, sparingly pubescent or nearly glabrous above, setose-

pubescent beneath, particularly on the veins: fls. in large panicles 15–25 cm. long; styles 2–3; sterile fls. with 4 entire, elliptic sepals, white, changing later to purplish: caps. with the calyx-limb about the middle. Fl.vɪɪ–ɪx. S.Z. 1,t.61(c). M.K.t.46(c). Gt.16,t.530(c). Gn.75:548(h);76:5(h). G.C.78:447, t(h). Japan, China. Intr. before 1864. Zone IV. The hardiest species; much planted in its sterile form.—**H. p. praècox** Rehd., var. Sepals of the sterile fls. narrow-elliptic: flowering about 6 weeks earlier than the type. G.F. 10:363. B.C.3:1621. Intr. 1892.—**H. p. grandiflòra** Sieb., var. Peegee H. Nearly all fls. sterile; panicle to 30 cm. long. F.S.16:t.1665–6(c). R.H.1873: 50,t(c). Gn.72:560(h). Gg.3:357(h);5:3(h). C.L.7:43(h). Intr. 1862.

9. **H. xanthoneùra** Diels. Shrub to 5 m.; brts. stout, pubescent, the 2d year with chestnut-brown close bark marked with conspicuous lenticels: lvs. elliptic to elliptic-oblong, abruptly acuminate, cuneate at base, 10–18 cm. long, serrate, bright green and nearly glabrous above and usually with yellowish veins, slightly pubescent on the veins beneath or nearly glabrous; petioles 1–3 cm. long, glabrous: corymbs rather loose, convex, 12–15 cm. across; sterile fls. 3–5 cm. broad, with oval obtuse sepals: capsule with the calyx-limb about the middle. Fl.vɪɪ. I.S.3:t.137. S.L.194(h). W. China. Intr. 1904. Zone V. Similar to the following, but with larger lvs. and more vigorous.—**H. x. Wilsónii** Rehd., var. Bark of 2-year-old brts. grayish or pale brown; lvs. usually oblong, lustrous above. M.G.1912:26(h). Intr. 1909.— **H. x. setchuenénsis** (Rehd.) Rehd., var. Two-year-old brts. light brown: lvs. to 20 cm. long, villous below. W. China. (*H. Bretschneideri* var. *s.* Rehd.) Intr. 1908.

Related species: **H. dumícola** W. W. Sm. Stout shrub to 5 m.: brts. and infl. densely and minutely scabrid: lvs. broad-ovate to ovate-lanceolate. 10–20 cm. long, acuminate, usually rounded at base, serrate-denticulate, pale and with long appressed white hairs beneath; petiole 2–4 cm. long: corymbs 25–30 cm. across. W. China. Cult. 1934. Zone VII.

10. **H. Bretschneìderi** Dipp. Shrub to 3 m.; brts. pubescent, two-year-old brts. with chestnut-brown bark peeling off in thin flakes: lvs. ovate or elliptic-ovate to oblong-ovate, acute or acuminate, cuneate at base, 7–12 cm. long, serrate, glabrous above, villous beneath; petioles 1–3 cm. long, not margined: corymbs 10–15 cm. across, slightly convex; sepals of sterile fls. broad-oval, obtuse, changing to purplish. Fl.vɪɪ. I.S.1:t.27. G.F.3:17;6:396(h). B.S.1: 624,t(h). (*H. vestita* var. *pubescens* Maxim., *H. pekinensis* Hort.) N. China. Intr. 1882. Zone IV. Shrub with spreading brs. forming a broad round bush very attractive when in bloom.—**H. B. glabréscens** Rehd., var. Lvs. smaller, usually elliptic and more coarsely serrate, sparingly pubescent beneath. (*H. serrata* Koehne, not DC.)

Closely related species: **H. hypoglaùca** Rehd. Lvs. glaucous beneath and silky-strigose on the veins. C. China. Intr. about 1901. Zone VI?

11. **H. heteromálla** Don. Shrub to 3 m.; young brts. densely pubescent, 2-year-old brts. with olive-brown close lenticellate bark: lvs. elliptic-ovate, acuminate, cuneate at base, 10–20 cm. long, densely setose-denticulate, nearly glabrous above, whitish tomentose beneath; petioles 2–6 cm. long, margined and deeply grooved, usually red: corymbs 12–20 cm. broad, pubescent, with bracts; sepals of sterile fls. elliptic or obovate: caps. with the calyx-limb above the middle. Fl.vɪ–vɪɪ. F.S.4:t.378–9(c). G.M.50:859. Himal. Intr. 1821. Zone VII? The dark green upper side of the lvs. forms a pleasing contrast with the red petioles and the whitish under side.

Ser. 4. Pɪptopetalae Maxim. (*Asperae* Rehd.) Seeds winged at the ends: ovary inferior; capsule truncate at apex; styles usually 2: fls. white, blue or pink.

12. **H. involucràta** Sieb. Shrub to 1.5 or 2 m.; young brts. densely strigose: lvs. elliptic-oblong or oblong, acuminate, cuneate at base, 10–20 cm. long, densely and sharply serrate, appressed-pubescent on both sides, denser beneath and more scabrid: corymbs enclosed before expanding by large suborbicular bracts; fertile fls. usually pinkish; sterile fls. whitish, 1.5–3 cm. across. Fl.vii–viii. S.Z.1:t.63(c). J.H.III.32:103. Japan. Cult. 1864. Zone VII.—**H. i. horténsis** Maxim., var. The fertile fls. double, often proliferous. S.Z.1:t.64(c). F.S.3:t.187(c). Cult. 1846.

13. **H. strigòsa** Rehd. Shrub to 2.5 m.; brts. densely strigose: lvs. oblong-ovate to elliptic-lanceolate or lanceolate, acuminate, cuneate or rounded at base, 7–18 cm. long, serrulate or serrate, sparingly strigose or nearly glabrous above, grayish beneath and densely strigose, particularly on the veins and veinlets; petioles 1–2.5 cm. long, strigose: corymbs 10–15 cm. across; sterile fls. white or purplish, 2–3.5 cm. across, with broad-ovate, entire or serrate sepals. Fl.viii. (*H. aspera* Hemsl., not Don.) C. China. Intr. 1907. Zone VII?—**H. s. macrophýlla** (Hemsl.) Rehd., var. Lvs. 20–30 cm. long; cymes to 20 cm. across, with the sterile fls. about 5 cm. broad. G.C.98:282(h).

Closely related species: **H. áspera** Don which differs chiefly in the fimbriate-denticulate lvs. grayish-white beneath and densely scabrid-villous: styles usually 3. Himal., W. China. Intr. ? Zone VII?—**H. villòsa** Rehd. Stems, petioles and cymes densely clothed with spreading villous hairs often ferruginous: lvs. fimbriate-denticulate, strigose above, grayish white and densely villous beneath. W. China. Intr. 1908. Zone VII? Possibly this species and *H. strigosa* are only vars. of *H. aspera.*—**H. v. strigòsior** (Diels) Rehd., var., has the petioles and brts. with few or sometimes without spreading hairs. Intr. Cult. 1905.

14. **H. Sargentiàna** Rehd. Upright shrub to 3 m., with stout brs.; brts. densely clothed with bristles and harsh hairs; young growth purplish: lvs. ovate to ovate-oblong, short-acuminate, rounded or subcordate at base, 15–25 cm. long, crenate-serrate, dull green and hairy above, densely rough-villous beneath; petioles 3–8 cm. long: corymbs nearly flat, dense, 12–16 cm. across; fertile fls. pale violet; sterile fls. white; styles 2–3. Fl.vii–viii. B.M. 8447(c). I.S.3:t.138. N.F.9:f.32(h). Gn.77:264(h). B.S.1:630. C. China. Intr. 1907. Zone VII? Striking plant with its large lvs., the dense purplish pubescence on the young growth and the large violet cymes with white marginal fls.

15. **H. lóngipes** Franch. Spreading shrub to 2, or occasionally 3 m., with rather slender lax brs.; brts. sparingly strigose: lvs. broad-ovate to ovate, rarely oblong-ovate, acuminate, rounded to cordate at base, 8–16 cm. long, sharply and unequally serrate or dentate, sparingly strigose above, strigose beneath on the veins and veinlets, sometimes glabrescent, rather thin; petioles 5–15 cm. long: corymbs 10–15 cm. across, pedicels densely strigose; sterile fls. about 3 cm. across, with orbicular-obovate, usually entire sepals. Fl.vi–vii. I.S.3:t.140. C. and W. China. Intr. 1901. Zone VI. Loosely branched shrub, remarkable for its long petioles.

Closely related species: **H. Rosthórnii** Diels. Larger and stouter shrub: lvs. 10–20 cm. long, unequally and densely fimbriate-dentate, grayish and densely strigose and reticulate beneath; petioles stouter, 3–10 cm. long: corymbs larger; sepals of sterile fls. toothed or entire. I.S.3:t.141. W. China. Intr. 1908. Zone VII?—**H. robústa** Hook f. & Thoms. Lvs. coarsely serrate, with brown hairs on the nerves beneath: fertile fls. blue; styles 2–3. B.M. 5038(c). (*H. cyanema* Nutt.) Himal. Cult. 1858. Zone VII?

Sect. II. CALYPTRANTHE Maxim. Shrubs climbing by aërial rootlets: petals cohering at apex and falling off as a whole: caps. truncate; seeds winged all around, compressed.

16. **H. petiolàris** Sieb. & Zucc. Climbing to 25 m.; older brs. with flaky brown bark: lvs. broad-ovate to ovate or oval, acute or acuminate, cordate

or rounded at base, 5–10 cm. long, serrate, nearly glabrous, dark green and lustrous above; petioles 2–8 cm. long: corymbs rather loose, 15–25 cm. across; stamens 15–20; styles usually 2; sterile fls. about 3 cm. across, with entire sepals. Fl.vi–vii. B.M.6788(c). N.K.15:t.22. S.Z.1:t.54(c),59,92(c). M.G.34: 57(h). Gn.88:144(h). B.S.1:628&t.(h). (*H. scandens* Maxim., not Ser., *H. volubilis* Hort.) Japan, China. Intr. 1865. Zone IV. Clinging firmly to walls and tree trunks, conspicuous in early summer with its large white fl.-clusters.

Closely related species: **H. anómala** Don. Lvs. ovate to elliptic-ovate or ovate-oblong, broad-cuneate, denticulate-serrate: corymbs smaller; stamens 10; sterile fls. wanting or few, about 2.5 cm. across. I.S.3:t.142. (*H. altissima* Wall.) W. China, Himal. Intr. 1839 from Himal., 1908 from W. China. Zone (V.)

9. **SCHIZOPHRÁGMA** Sieb. & Zucc. Deciduous shrubs climbing by aërial rootlets; bark of 2-year-old brts. close, splitting longitudinally on older brs.; buds with 2–4 pairs of chestnut-brown pubescent or ciliolate outer scales: lvs. opposite, long-petioled, dentate or entire, estipulate: fls. white, in loose terminal stalked corymbs with sterile marginal flowers consisting of a single large sepal; fertile fls. small, with 4–5 sepals and as many petals; stamens 10; style 1, short, with capitate 4–5-lobed stigma; fr. a 10-ribbed turbinate caps. opening between the ribs; seeds numerous, linear. (Greek *schizein*, to cleave, and *phragma*, wall; referring to the opening of the caps.) Three species in E. Asia.—Climbing shrubs very similar to *Hydrangea petiolaris*, but easily distinguished by the solitary sepal of the sterile fls. and in winter by the close longitudinally splitting bark and the winter-buds.

A. Lvs. coarsely dentate..1. *S. hydrangeoides*
AA. Lvs. entire or sparingly denticulate..2. *S. integrifolium*

1. **S. hydrangeoides** Sieb. & Zucc. Climbing to 10 m. or more: lvs. suborbicular or broad-ovate, short-acuminate, rounded or cordate at base, 5–10 cm. long, remotely coarsely dentate, nearly glabrous; petioles 3–7 cm. long, reddish: corymbs about 20 cm. broad; sepal of the marginal fls. oval to broadly ovate, 3–3.5 cm. long. Fl.vii. S.Z.1:t.26,100(c). B.M.8520(c). N.K. 15:t.24. Gn.34:281. R.H.1881:313,f.72. Japan. Cult. 1880. Zone V.

2. **S. integrifòlium** (Franch.) Oliv. Climbing to 4 m. or more: lvs. ovate or broad-ovate, acuminate, truncate or subcordate at base, 10–15 cm. long, entire or sparingly denticulate, usually pubescent on the veins beneath, of thickish texture: petioles 3–8 cm. long: corymbs to 25 cm. broad; sepals of sterile fls. ovate to ovate-oblong, 3.5–6 cm. long. Fl.vii. B.M.8991(c). I.S.1:t.30. H.I. 20:1934. J.L.28:f.21. M.O.215(h),217. (*S. hydrangeoides* var. *i.* Franch.) C. and W. China. Intr. 1901. Zone VII. Differs from the preceding in the larger sterile fls. and larger darker lvs.—**S. i. molle** Rehd., var. Petioles and lvs. beneath densely villous; sterile sepals 5–7 cm. long. W. China. Intr. 1908.

10. **PILEOSTÈGIA** Hook. f. & Thoms. Evergreen shrubs climbing by rootlets: lvs. opposite, entire or dentate: fls. whitish, small, fascicled along dichotomous brs. in terminal, broad, stalked corymbose panicles; sepals 4–5, small, imbricate; petals 4–5, caducous, cohering at the apex and falling off as a whole; stamens 8–10, with long filaments and subglobose anthers; ovary inferior, 4–6-celled; style short, clavate, with 4–6-lobed stigma: fr. a top-shaped caps. dehiscent irregularly along the ribs; seeds numerous, oblong, with a terminal extension of the seed-coat. (Greek *pileos*, hat, and *stege*, roof, tent; alluding to the shape of the stigma.) Three species in S. E. Asia.

P. viburnoìdes Hook. f. & Thoms. Climbing to 15 m., glabrous; young brts. brown, becoming gray: lvs. lanceolate to elliptic or obovate-oblong, 10–15 cm. long, 2.5–6 cm. broad, acuminate, cuneate, dark green and glossy above, lighter below, with 6–8 pairs of veins, midrib impressed above, prominent below; petiole 1–3 cm. long: panicle 7–10 cm. long and to 15 cm. broad; pedicels 1–3 mm. long; fls. in bud subglobose, about 4 mm. across; sepals triangular; petals ovate; filaments wavy, 4–5 mm. long; style about 1 mm. long: caps. turbinate 2–3 mm. long; seeds about 1 mm. long. B.M.9262(c). G.C.56:225;60:218. J.L.40:f.113. (*Schizophragma v.* Stapf.) S. China, Formosa, Liukiu Isls. Intr. 1908. Zone VII.

11. **DECUMÀRIA** L. Deciduous or half-evergreen shrubs climbing by aërial rootlets; bark of brs. exfoliating; buds small, pubescent, with indistinct scales: lvs. opposite, estipulate, petioled, entire or sparingly toothed: fls. perfect, white, small, in terminal corymbs; calyx-tube turbinate; sepals 7–10, minute; petals as many, valvate, oblong to narrow-oblong; stamens 20–30, with subulate filaments; ovary inferior, 5–10-celled; styles united, with capitate, 7–10-lobed stigma; caps. urceolate, ribbed, opening between the ribs; seeds numerous, minute, linear-clavate. (Latin *decumus = decimus*, ten; referring to the number of parts in the flower.) One species in N. Am. and one in China.

D. bárbara L. Climbing to 10 m.: lvs. ovate to elliptic, acute or abruptly short-acuminate, rarely obtuse, 5–10 cm. long and 2.5–5 cm. broad, glabrous and lustrous above, glabrous beneath or slightly pubescent on the nerves: corymbs round-topped, 5–10 cm. across: caps. urn-shaped, surrounded above the middle by the calyx-limb. Fl.v–vi. B.B.2:233. G.C.46:242,t. (*D. sarmentosa* Bosc.) Va. to Fla. and La. Intr. 1785. Zone (V), VI. Clinging firmly to walls and tree-trunks, preferring moist and half-shady positions.

Closely related species: **D. sinénsis** Oliv. Less high climbing: lvs. generally oblong and obtuse, 3–7 cm. long and 1–2.5 cm. broad; pedicels appressed-pubescent. H.I.18:1741. C. China. Intr. 1908. Zone VII?

12. **ÍTEA** L. Deciduous or evergreen shrubs or trees; brs. with lamellate pith; buds small, superposed, with 3–4 outer scales: lvs. alternate, serrulate to dentate, estipulate: fls. perfect, white, small, in terminal or axillary racemes or panicles; calyx-tube turbinate; sepals 5, persistent; petals as many, narrow, valvate; stamens 5, inserted under the edge of the disk; anthers oblong; ovary superior, 2-celled; styles united; ovules numerous; caps. elongated, 2-grooved, 2-valved; seeds flattened. (Greek name of the willow.) About 10 species in S. E. Asia and 1 in N. Am.

I. virgínica L. Upright shrub to 1 or sometimes to 3 m., with slender, virgate brs. pubescent while young: lvs. elliptic or obovate to oblong, acute or short-acuminate, usually cuneate at base, 4–10 cm. long, serrulate, glabrous above, often sparingly pubescent beneath; petioles 5–10 mm. long: fls. white, fragrant, in upright, dense pubescent racemes 5–15 cm. long; petals 4 mm. long; stamens as long as petals: caps. 6–8 mm. long, narrow, pubescent. Fl.vi–vii. B.M.2409(c). B.C.3:1707. S.L.203(h). N. J. and Pa. to Fla. and La. Intr. 1744. Zone V. Usually a low shrub with virgate brs.; the lvs. turn brilliant red in autumn.

Related species: **I. ilicifòlia** Oliv. Evergreen shrub to 3 m.: lvs. elliptic, obtuse, 6–11 cm. long, spiny-toothed: fls. greenish white, in dense drooping racemes 15–35 cm. long. H.I.16:1538. G.C.34:375;43:123;64:151(h). C. China. Intr. 1901. Zone VII?

13. **ESCALLÒNIA** Mutis. Evergreen, rarely deciduous trees or shrubs, usually glandular: lvs. alternate, usually serrate, estipulate: fls. white, pink

or red, in terminal racemes or panicles or axillary; calyx-tube turbinate to cylindric; sepals 5, short; petals usually narrow and with long claws; stamens 5, inserted under the margin of the disk; style 1, with capitate, 2- or 4–5-lobed stigma; ovary inferior, 2–3-celled; ovules numerous: fr. a 2–3-valved caps.. with small oblong often curved seeds. (After Escallon, a Spanish traveler.) Fifty or 60 species in S. Am., chiefly in the Andes.

E. virgàta (Ruiz & Pav.) Pers. Deciduous, much-branched shrub to 1 m.; brts. brown, glabrous: lvs. obovate to oblanceolate or lanceolate, acute, cuneate at base, 8–15 mm. long, finely serrate, usually entire below the middle: fls. white, about 1 cm. across, axillary, often forming short leafy racemes at the end of the brts.; calyx-lobes triangular; petals roundish-obovate scarcely clawed; stamens shorter than petals; style scarcely as long as sepals: caps. subglobose. Fl.vi–vii. G.C.II.10:108. J.L.37:52,t. Gn.83:518 (h);86:408(h),453. S.L.172(h). (*E. Philippiana* Mast., *E. v.* var. *Ph.* Engl.) Chile. Cult. 1866. Zone VI? Shrub with spreading brs.; the hardiest of all Escallonias.

E. v. × *punctata* DC. = **E. langleyénsis** Veitch. Evergreen shrub to 3 m., with arching brs.; brts. glandular: lvs. obovate to narrow-elliptic, 1–2.5 cm. long, serrate, glabrous, resinous beneath: fls. rosy-carmine, 1.2 cm. across. G.C.III. 22:15;24:11(h). Gn.74:351(h);79:315. B.S.1:528. B.C.2:1144. Orig. 1893. Zone VII?

Related species: **E. illinìta** Presl. Glabrous and resinous evergreen shrub to 10 m., with obovate or oval lvs. 2–6 cm. long and white fls. in terminal panicles to 10 cm. long. B.R.t.1900(c). Chile. Intr. 1831. Zone VII?

14. RÍBES L.

Deciduous or rarely evergreen, unarmed, or prickly shrubs; buds with several scarious or herbaceous scales: lvs. alternate, petioled, simple, usually palmately lobed, folded or rarely convolute in bud, estipulate: fls. perfect or dioecious, 5-merous, rarely 4-merous, in few or many-flowered racemes, rarely clustered or solitary; calyx-tube cylindric to rotate, like the sepals usually colored; petals usually smaller than the sepals, often minute, rarely wanting; stamens shorter or longer than the sepals; ovary inferior, 1-celled, many-ovuled; styles 2, more or less connate: fr. a juicy berry, usually many-seeded; seeds albuminous, with minute terete embryo. (Probably derived from *ribas*, the Arabian name for Rheum Ribes.) About 150 species in the colder and temp. regions of the n. hemisphere, in Am. in the Andes s. to Patagonia.—At least half of the species have been introduced to cult. Some are valued for their edible frs., particularly *R. sativum* and *R. Grossularia*, others are ornamental shrubs and planted for their handsome fls. or for their attractive frs. or lvs., while many are without particular merits and are found only in botanical collections. They are almost all early leafing shrubs flowering with or soon after the unfolding of the lvs. and ripening their fruit mostly in mid-summer, rarely later. Many species are carriers of the white-pine blister rust, particularly *R. nigrum* and most American Currants; they should not be planted where White Pine is growing.

A. Brs. unarmed or rarely with a pair of small prickles below the petiole: fls. usually in racemes; pedicels jointed.
  B. Fls. dioecious; racemes usually upright.
    C. Lvs. deciduous: fls. greenish to purple.
      D. Fls. in several- to many-fld. racemes.
        E. Brts. quite unarmed: lvs. generally suborbicular to ovate.
          F. Young growth viscid-glandular......................................2. *R. orientale*
        FF. Young growth glabrous or nearly so.
          G. Fls. greenish: lvs. with short obtuse lobes...................1. *R. alpinum*
          GG. Fls. red-brown or purple: lvs. acute or acuminate.
            H. Fls. rotate ....3. *R. tenue*
            HH. Fls. saucer-shaped ....4. *R. glaciale*

  EE. Brts. with slender paired prickles below the petiole: lvs. generally obovate, cuneate at base..5. *R. diacanthum*
 DD. Fls. solitary or in 2–8-fld. fascicles.
  E. Ovary glabrous ....7. *R. fasciculatum*
  EE. Ovary glandular-bristly ....9. *R. ambiguum*
CC. Lvs. persistent.
 D. Lvs. suborbicular, 3–5-lobed: fls. yellow..........................8. *R. Gayanum*
 DD. Lvs. ovate-oblong, crenate-serrate: fls. greenish..................6. *R. laurifolium*
BB. Fls. perfect, in usually pendulous or nodding racemes: lvs. deciduous.
 C. Color of fls. yellow; calyx-tube tubular: lvs. convolute in bud: glands crystalline.
  D. Calyx-tube less than twice as long as sepals; sepals spreading, connivent after flowering: young brts. glabrous or puberulous......................10. *R. aureum*
  DD. Calyx-tube at least twice as long as sepals, 2–2.5 mm. thick; sepals revolute or spreading, not connivent: young brts. and petioles pubescent, rarely glabrous.
                     11. *R. odoratum*
 CC. Color of fls. white, pink, red or greenish: lvs. plicate in bud.
  D. Calyx-tube tubular to campanulate.
   E. Ovary glandular: lvs. resin-dotted or viscid-glandular beneath.
    F. Leaves beneath and other parts of plant with viscid glands.
     G. Lvs. white-tomentose beneath: fls. usually red, in many-fld. racemes.
                   13. *R. sanguineum*
     GG. Lvs. not or slightly pubescent beneath.
      H. Lvs. 4–9 cm. broad.
       I. Calyx-tube cup-shaped: fls. greenish white in long-peduncled racemes ....12. *R. Wolfii*
       II. Calyx-tube cylindric or cylindric-campanulate.
        J. Sepals longer than tube; fls. red, rarely white, in many-fld. racemes ....14. *R. glutinosum*
        JJ. Sepals shorter than tube; fls. greenish or pinkish, in few- or several-fld. racemes ....15. *R. viscosissimum*
      HH. Lvs. 1–3.5 cm. broad; calyx-tube tubular; racemes few-fld.: fr. red.
       I. Bracts of racemes cuneate-obovate, toothed; fls. white, rarely pinkish ....16. *R. cereum*
       II. Bracts of racemes rhombic, usually acutish, entire or with a few teeth; fls. pink...17. *R. inebrians*
    FF. Lvs. resin-dotted beneath: fls. whitish or greenish.
     G. Calyx-tube tubular-campanulate; racemes many-fld...20. *R. americanum*
     GG. Calyx-tube broad campanulate; racemes few-fld...........21. *R. nigrum*
   EE. Ovary and fr. glabrous: lvs. not glandular or only with a few stalked glands beneath.
    F. Racemes dense; sepals ciliate; fls. purple, pink or reddish, broad-campanulate ....27. *R. petraeum*
    FF. Racemes loose; sepals glabrous; fls. pale, narrow-campanulate.
     G. Fls. sessile; racemes to 12 cm. long......................28. *R. moupinense*
     GG. Fls. stalked; racemes to 30 cm. long, very loose....29. *R. longeracemosum*
  DD. Calyx-tube rotate or saucer-shaped.
   E. Ovary and fr. glandular; racemes upright or ascending.
    F. Lvs. resin-dotted beneath: upright shrubs: fr. black.
     G. Bracts of racemes large, broadest in the middle; racemes 10–20 cm. long: fr. bloomy ....18. *R. bracteosum*
     GG. Bracts of racemes narrow, narrowed from the base; racemes 3–6 cm. long: fr. without bloom...........................19. *R. hudsonianum*
    FF. Lvs. not resin-dotted beneath, fetid: fr. red: prostrate shrub.
                   22. *R. glandulosum*
   EE. Ovary and fr. glabrous; racemes drooping or nodding.
    F. Stamens shorter than sepals, sepals spreading.
     G. Habit upright.
      H. Calyx-tube saucer-shaped, with plane disk; anther-cells contiguous: lvs. usually truncate at base.............................23. *R. rubrum*
      HH. Calyx-tube rotate, inside with a 5-angled elevated ring; anther-cells separated by a broad connective: lvs. cordate or subcordate.
                  24. *R. sativum*
     GG. Habit procumbent: anther-cells contiguous....................25. *R. triste*
    FF. Stamens as long as sepals; sepals recurved; racemes very dense and long.
                   26. *R. multiflorum*
AA. Brts. more or less prickly, rarely nearly unarmed: fls. 1–4 and pedicels not jointed (except in No. 30).
 B. Fls. in racemes; sepals broader than long; stems bristly................30. *R. lacustre*
 BB. Fls. 1–4; sepals longer than broad.
  C. Color of flowers white or greenish and often suffused with purple.
   D. Sepals white or sometimes greenish white.
    E. Stamens as long as sepals or longer.
     F. Filaments villous: brts. brown.
      G. Ovary glabrous; calyx-tube about as long as broad.........31. *R. niveum*
      GG. Ovary glandular or pubescent; calyx-tube twice as long as broad.
                  32. *R. curvatum*

    FF. Filaments glabrous; stamens nearly twice as long as the greenish white sepals: brts. yellowish or gray..........................33. *R. missouriense*
   EE. Stamens shorter than sepals; young brts. usually very bristly, grayish.
    F. Peduncle elongated; calyx-tube cyindric-campanulate.......34. *R. setosum*
    FF. Peduncle scarcely exceeding the bud-scales; calyx-tube campanulate.
                             35. *R. oxyacanthoides*
 DD. Sepals green or greenish, often tinged purplish.
  E. Style and calyx-tube inside pubescent.
   F. Fr. not prickly; stamens about as long as sepals (half as long in No. 40).
    G. Lvs. cuneate or rounded at base.
     H. Sepals about as long as tube; stamens as long or scarcely longer than sepals ....36. *R. hirtellum*
     HH. Sepals about twice as long as tube; stamens slightly longer than sepals.
                           37. *R. rotundifolium*
    GG. Lvs. subcordate or occasionally rounded at base; sepals recurved during anthesis.
     H. Ovary glabrous.
      I. Sepals longer than tube; stamens slightly longer than sepals.
                          38. *R. divaricatum*
      II. Sepals shorter than tube; stamens slightly shorter than sepals.
                          39. *R. inerme*
     HH. Ovary pubescent or glandular; stamens about half as long as sepals.
                          40. *R. Grossularia*
   FF. Fr. prickly, not glandular, rarely smooth; stamens less than half as long as sepals ....41. *R. cynosbati*
  EE. Style and calyx-tube inside glabrous.
   F. Fr. prickly: petals obtuse: brts. very bristly................42. *R. burejense*
   FF. Fr. not prickly, glandular-bristly or smooth.
    G. Petals elliptic, acute, connivent; fls. greenish or reddish....43. *R. alpestre*
    GG. Petals obovate, obtuse, upright; fls. white or pink......44. *R. leptanthum*
CC. Color of fls. orange, purple or bright red; style glabrous.
 D. Fls. 5-merous.
  E. Anthers oval; calyx-tube cylindric-campanulate.
   F. Fls. orange; sepals longer than stamens: fr. prickly........45. *R. pinetorum*
   FF. Fls. red or purple; sepals about as long as stamens: fr. densely glandular.
                         46. *R. Lobbii*
  EE. Anthers sagittate, lanceolate to lance-ovate.
   F. Calyx-tube cylindric; fls. not glandular: fr. prickly...........47. *R. Roezlii*
   FF. Calyx-tube campanulate: fr. glandular-bristly..............48. *R. Menziesii*
 DD. Fls. 4-merous, bright red; stamens 2-4 times as long as sepals....49. *R. speciosum*

Subgen I. **BERISIA** Spach. Fls. dioecious, usually in racemes; pedicels jointed: unarmed shrubs, rarely with small paired nodal prickles.

Sect. 1. **EUBERISIA** Jancz. Racemes upright; staminate fls. without ovary, anthers of pistillate fls. without pollen; petals minute; stamens much shorter than sepals: buds with scarious scales: brs. always unarmed.

1. R. alpìnum L. ALPINE CURRANT. Shrub to 2.5 m., nearly glabrous; buds acute: lvs. roundish or ovate, truncate or subcordate, 3–5 cm. across, 3-, rarely 5-lobed, with obtuse or acute dentate lobes: fls. greenish yellow, in upright racemes, the staminate 3–6 cm. long, with 20–30 fls.; the pistillate smaller; calyx-tube rotate; sepals ovate: fr. subglobose, scarlet, glabrous. R.I.23:t.135(c). L.B.15:1486(c). S.E.4:t.419(c). (*R. opulifolium* Hort.) Eu. Cult. 1588. Zone II. Early leafing shrub of dense habit with upright stems and spreading brs., usually broader than high, the pistillate form with attractive scarlet berries in summer and autumn. Well adapted for planting in shady places and as undergrowth.—**R. a. aùreum** Pynaert. Dwarf form with yellowish lvs. R.B.4:233,t(c). Cult. 1878.—**R. a. laciniàtum** Kirchn., f. Lvs. more deeply and incisely toothed. Cult. 1864.—**R. a. pùmilum** Lindl., var. A dwarf form with smaller lvs. (*R. a.* var. *humile* A. Br.) Cult. 1830.—The pistillate form is sometimes distinguished as var. *bacciferum* Wallr. and the staminate as var. *sterile* Wallr.

Related species: **R. tricúspis** Nakai. Lvs. subcordate, with acute or acuminate lobes: staminate racemes 1–2 cm. long with 8–12 often brownish fls.; sepals elliptic; pistillate with 2–6 fls.: fr. ellipsoid, small. N.K.15:t.5. Korea, Manch., Jap. Intr. before 1907. Zone V.—**R. distans** Jancz. Lvs. broad-cuneate or truncate at base, with acute lobes; staminate and pistillate racemes many-fld.: frs. globose, in 2–6 cm. long racemes. N.K.15:t.3. Manch. Cult. 1905. Zone IV?

—**R. Vilmorìnii** Jancz. Shrub to 2 m.; buds obtusish: lvs. 2–3 cm. across, 3–5-lobed: staminate racemes 5–20 mm. long; fls. greenish or brownish: fr. black, glabrous or glandular. Jancz., Monog. Gros. 462. W. China. Intr. 1902. Zone V.

2. **R. orientàle** Desf. Upright shrub to 2 m.; young growth with stalked viscid glands: lvs. roundish or reniform, truncate or cordate, about 4.5 cm. long and 5.5 cm. broad, 3–5-lobed with short rounded dentate lobes, bright green and lustrous above, pubescent on the veins beneath; petioles about 2 cm. long: racemes pubescent and glandular, the staminate 2–5 cm. long; fls. rotate, green, usually suffused with red; sepals ovate: fr. scarlet, pubescent and glandular. B.M.1583(c). (*R. resinosum* Pursh.) E. Eu. and W. Asia to Siber. and Himal. Intr. 1805. Zone V. Similar to *R. alpinum*, but easily distinguished by the viscid-glandular pubescence.—**R. o. heterótrichum** (C. A. Mey.) Jancz., var. Young shoots reddish: lvs. lustrous: fls. reddish: fr. not glandular. Ledeb., Icon. Fl. Ross. t.235. Siber. Cult. 1907.

3. **R. ténue** Jancz. Shrub similar to *R. alpinum*; glabrous; buds ovoid, obtusish: lvs. ovate, truncate, to 3.5 cm. long and to 3 cm. broad, 3–5-lobed, lobes acute, incisely toothed, the middle one longer; staminate racemes 3–5 cm. long, pistillate smaller: fls. rotate, brownish-red; sepals elliptic-ligulate: fr. short-stalked, red, globose. Jancz., Monog. Gros. 464. Himal., W. China. Intr. about 1900. Zone V. Flowering and leafing very early.

4. **R. glaciàle** Wall. Shrub to 5 m.; nearly glabrous; young brts. red or reddish; buds oblong, obtusish: lvs. roundish or ovate, cordate or truncate, to 6 cm. long, 3–5-lobed, the middle lobe longer, acute or short-acuminate, sparingly glandular-bristly; petioles 1–2 cm. long: staminate racemes 1.5–4.5 cm. long, 7–30-fld.; pistillate with 3–6 smaller fls.; fls. saucer-shaped or sub-turbinate, brownish purple; sepals ovate: fr. subsessile, globose or obovoid, scarlet, glabrous. Jancz., Monog. Gros. 468; suppl. 5:737. Himal., C. and W. China. Intr. from Nepal in 1823, from W. China about 1900. Zone V. Similar in habit to *R. alpinum*, chiefly distinguished by the longer acute middle lobe of the lvs. and the brownish cup-shaped fls.—**R. g. angustisé-palum** Jancz., var. Sepals ovate-lanceolate. C. China. Intr. 1907.

R. g. × *luridum* = R. Wallíchii Jancz. Lvs. similar to *R. luridum*, fls. to *R. glaciale*. Jancz., Monog. Gros. suppl. 4:619(fl). Orig. 1907.

Related species: **R. lùridum** Hook. f. & Thoms. Lvs. roundish, about 5 cm. long and 6 cm. broad, with short and broad sometimes obtusish lobes; petiole about 4 cm. long: staminate racemes 3–5 cm. long: fls. dark purple, turbinate: fr. black, glabrous. Leafing late; fr.x. Jancz., Monog. Gros. 469,470. Himal., W. China. Intr. about 1900. Zone V.—**R. Maximowíczii** Batal. Differing from the preceding species in the glandular-bristly fr.: lvs. usually ovate, 4–9 cm. long, slightly 3–5-lobed or nearly simple, coarsely dentate, pubescent on both sides: racemes pubescent, 3–5 cm. long; fls. red: fr. red, yellow or greenish. Jancz., Monog. Gros. 473(fl). W. China. Intr. ?—**R. M. floribúndum** Jesson, var. Racemes 10–15 cm. long; fr. with thinner and fewer bristles. B.M.8840(c). (*R. Jessoniae* Stapf.) W. China. Intr. 1903. Zone VI?

Sect. 2. DIACANTHA Jancz. Buds and fls. as in sect. 1: brts. with 2 small prickles at the nodes and often with smaller scattered prickles.

5. **R. diacánthum** Pall. Upright shrub to 2 m., glabrous: brts. with paired prickles at the nodes, often with scattered additional prickles, rarely nearly unarmed; buds small: lvs. ovate to obovate, cuneate or sometimes rounded, 2–3.5 cm. long, slightly 3-lobed, the lobes obtusish, sparingly dentate, lustrous, with obsolete veins: staminate racemes 2–3 cm. long, pistillate 1–2 cm. long; rachis glabrous, glandular; fls. greenish yellow, rotate; sepals ovate: fr. globose or globose-ovoid, scarlet, glabrous, small. S.O.2:t.97(c). N.K.15:t.2. S.H.1:f.258s-u,261f-i. (*R. saxatilis* Pall.) N. Asia, Tian-shan to n. Korea.

Intr. 1781. Zone II. Similar to *R. alpinum,* but with prickly brts. and of more upright habit and with lustrous lvs.

Related species: **R. pulchéllum** Turcz. Lvs. to 5 cm. long, more deeply 3-lobed, truncate or subcordate: staminate racemes to 6 cm. long; fls. saucer-shaped, reddish: fr. red, glabrous. Jancz., Monog. Gros. 453. N. China. Cult. 1905. Zone V.—**R. Giráldii** Jancz. Brts. pubescent while young, bristly, with larger nodal spines: lvs. truncate or subcordate, about 3.5 cm. broad, 3–5-lobed, pubescent and glandular: fls. cup-shaped, greenish brown: fr. glandular-bristly, red. N. China. Jancz., Monog. Gros. 455. Cult. 1905. Zone V.

Sect. 3. **DAVIDIA** Jancz. Fls. as in sect. 1: lvs. evergreen.

6. R. laurifòlium Jancz. Evergreen shrub to 1.5 m., glabrous, glandular at first: lvs. ovate to ovate-oblong, acute, rounded at base, 5–10 cm. long, crenate-dentate, coriaceous; petioles bristly, 5–15 mm. long: staminate racemes nodding, 3–6 cm. long; pistillate shorter, upright, 6–12-fld.; fls. greenish yellow, rotate; sepals oval; ovary tomentulose: fr. ellipsoid, puberulous, purplish black, 1.5 cm. long, in pendulous racemes. B.M.8543(c). G.C.55: 239;71:213(h). Gn.76:143;79:170,171. W. China. Intr. 1908. Zone VII?

Related species: **R. Hénryi** Franch. Brts. glandular-bristly: lvs. elliptic, to 10 cm. long, crenate; glandular beneath: fls. greenish, the staminate in racemes 2–4 cm. long: fr. obovoid-oblong, green, to 2 cm. long, stipitate-glandular. Jancz., Monog. Gros. suppl.5:738. C. China. Intr. 1908. Zone VII?

Sect. 4. **HEMIBOTRYA** Jancz. Fls. in 2–9-fld. umbels; staminate fls. with ovary containing sterile ovules; anthers of pistillate fls. with sterile pollen: buds with herbaceous scales; brs. always unarmed.

7. R. fasciculàtum Sieb. & Zucc. Shrub to 1.5 m. with upright or spreading brs.: lvs. roundish, truncate or cordate at base, 4–7 cm. wide, broader than long, 3–5-lobed with obtuse lobes, glabrous or slightly pubescent: fls. yellowish, cup-shaped, fragrant; staminate in 4–9-fld. umbels, pistillate only 2, sometimes 3–4: fr. subglobose, scarlet, crowned by the persistent calyx-tube, glabrous, insipid. Fl.ɪv–v; fr.ɪx–x. S.T.1:t.38. D.L.3:302. (*R. japonicum* Carr., *R. alpinum japonicum* Nichols.) Japan, Korea. Cult. 1884. Zone IV. Valued for the late persisting lvs. and the scarlet frs. remaining on the brs. the whole winter.—**R. f. chinénse** Maxim., var. Taller and more vigorous: lvs. larger, to 10 cm. across, pubescent beneath like the petioles and young brts., chartaceous, persistent into the winter. S.T.1:t.38,f.3,7–9. N.K.15:t.1. M.G. 14:571. (*R. Billiardii* Carr.) N. China to Korea and Japan. Cult. 1867.

Sect. 5. **PARILLA** Jancz. Fls. in racemes, otherwise like those of the preceding section: lvs. often persistent. S. Amer. species.

8. R. Gayànum (Spach) Steud. Evergreen shrub to 1.5 m.: young brts. and petioles villous: lvs. roundish, truncate to subcordate at base, 3–6 cm. long and slightly broader, with 3 or 5 short rounded toothed lobes, pubescent on both sides; petioles 1.5–2.5 cm. long, pubescent and glandular: fls. campanulate, pubescent, yellow, fragrant, in dense cylindric, erect racemes 3–6 cm. long borne on a stalk 2–4 cm. long: fr. globose, purple-black, hairy. B.M. 7611(c). S.L.311(h). (*R. villosum* C. Gay, not Nutt.) Chile. Cult. 1858. Zone VII? One of the hardiest of the S. Amer. species and chiefly grown for its fragrant fls.

Subgen. II. **RIBESIA** Berl. Fls. perfect, usually in racemes; pedicels jointed: unarmed shrubs; bud-scales herbaceous, but scarious in sect. 12.

Sect. 6. **MICROSPERMA** Jancz. Fls. 1 or 2, greenish; receptacle saucer-shaped; pedicels with 2 bractlets; ovary glandular-bristly; style undivided: seeds very small, more than 50.

9. R. ambíguum Maxim. Low shrub, often epiphytic: lvs. roundish, cordate, 2–5 cm. wide, 3–5-lobed, with short, often obtuse, dentate lobes, pubescent or nearly glabrous above, viscid-glandular beneath: fls. 1 or 2, greenish, on pedicels about 1 cm. long; sepals elliptic; filaments flattened, broad: fr. green, subglobose, about 1.2 cm. across, glandular-hispid. Jancz., Mon. Gros. 304. C. Japan, W. China. Intr. 1915. Zone V.

Sect. 7. SYMPHOCALYX Berl. (§ *Siphocalyx* Endl., *Chrysobotrya* Spach.) Fls. in racemes, yellow; receptacle tubular; ovary glabrous: fr. smooth, black or yellow: lvs. convolute in bud (plicate in all other sections): glands crystalline.

10. **R. aùreum** Pursh. GOLDEN CURRANT. Shrub to 2 m.; young brts. glabrous or puberulous: lvs. orbicular-reniform to obovate, cuneate to subcordate, 3–5 cm. wide, 3-lobed, the coarsely crenate-dentate lobes often with only 2 or 3 teeth, glabrous or sometimes puberulous beneath; petioles about as long as blade: fls. yellow, fragrant or slightly so, in 5–15-fld. racemes; bracts oblong to obovate; receptacle slender, 6–10 mm. long, 1.5 mm. thick, sepals more than half as long as the tube, spreading, upright and closed in the faded fl.; petals changing to red: fr. globose, black or purplish brown, 6–8 mm. across. B.R.1274(c). Card, Bush Fr.f.109. Jancz., Mon. Gros. suppl. 3:f.89. (*R. tenuiflorum* Lindl., *R. a.* var. *tenuiflorum* Torr., *Chrysobotrya aurea* Rydb.) Wash. to Assinib., Mont., N. Mex. and Calif. Intr. in ?1806. Zone II. Attractive shrub with golden yellow fragrant fls. appearing in spring with the lvs.—**R. a. chrysocóccum** Rydb. Fr. orange-yellow.

11. **R. odoràtum** Wendl. BUFFALO CURRANT. Shrub to 2 m.; young brts. pubescent: lvs. ovate to orbicular-reniform, cuneate or truncate, 3–8 cm. wide, deeply 3–5-lobed, with coarsely dentate lobes, glabrate or puberulous beneath: fls. yellow, fragrant, in 5–10-fld., usually nodding racemes; bracts ovate to oval, foliaceous; rachis pubescent; receptacle 12–15 mm. long and 2–2.5 mm. broad; sepals scarcely half as long as tube, revolute or recurved, not upright and closed in the faded fl.; petals reddish; fr. globose to ellipsoid, 8–10 mm. long, black. B.R.2:125(c). L.D.5:301(c). L.B.1533(c). Card, Bush Fr.f.108. B.C.5:2958. (*R. fragrans* Lodd., *R. longiflorum* Nutt., *R. palmatum* Thory, *Chrysobotrya revoluta* Spach, *C. odorata* Rydb.) East of Rocky Mts., S. D. to w. Tex., east to Minn. and Ark. Intr. 1812. Zone IV. Conspicuous in spring with its golden yellow fragrant fls.; with larger fls. and of more spreading habit than the preceding species. Large-fruited forms as the "Crandall" are sometimes grown for their fruit.—**R. o. xanthocárpum** Rehd., f. Fr. orange-yellow.—**R. o. intermèdium** (Spach) Berger, var. Racemes spreading; receptacle about 12 mm. long; sepals about 8 mm. long, spreading: fr. orange-brown. Jancz., Monog. Gros. suppl. 3:87. (*R. aureum i.* Jancz., *Chrysobotrya intermedia* Spach.)—**R. o. leióbotrys** (Koehne) Berger, var. Young brts. and rachis glabrous, glandular; sepals recurved, not revolute: fr. black. (*R. l.* Koehne, *R. aureum l.* Zabel.)

R. o. × *sanguineum;* see under No. 13.

Sect. 8. CALOBOTRYA Spach. Fls. in racemes, red, white or yellow, proterogynous; receptacle saucer-shaped to tubular: plant viscid-glandular: fr. often glandular, usually black and bloomy.

12. **R. Wólfii** Rothr. Shrub to 3.5 m.; young brts. finely puberulous or glabrous: lvs suborbicular, cordate, 4–9 cm. wide, 3–5-lobed with obtuse or acutish serrate-dentate lobes, pubescent on the veins beneath and glandular: racemes erect, dense, 2–3.5 cm. long, on a slender pubescent and glandular peduncle: ovary glandular, bristly; receptacle cup-shaped, puberulous; sepals ovate-oblong, 3–4 times the length of the receptacle, greenish white, spreading; petals white, much shorter than sepals; stamens half as long as sepals: fr. black, glandular-bristly, about 1 cm. across. B.M.8121(c). (*R. mogolloni-*

cum Greene.) Colo. to N. Mex., Ariz. and Utah. Intr. 1900. Zone V. An upright shrub of little ornamental merit.

13. **R. sanguíneum** Pursh. Shrub to 4 m.; young brts. pubescent and often sparingly glandular: lvs. reniform-orbicular, cordate to truncate, 5–10 cm. wide, 3–5-lobed, with obtuse irregularly dentate lobes, the middle one about as long as broad, dark green and puberulous above, whitish tomentose beneath; petioles pubescent and glandular: racemes ascending or pendulous, many-fld., pubescent and glandular; pedicels 8–10 mm. long; fls. red; sepals oblong, 5–7 mm. long, somewhat longer than the tubular receptacle; petals white or reddish, about half as long as sepals: fr. bluish black, bloomy, slightly glandular. Fl.v; fr.vɪɪɪ. B.M.3335(c). B.R.1349(c). B. C. to n. Calif. Cult. 1818. Zone (V). Ornamental free-flowering shrub; very attractive with its numerous racemes of red fls.; the young growth exhales an aromatic odor. —**R. s. Brocklebánkii** Bean, var. With yellow lvs.—**R. s. spléndens** Barbier. Fls. dark blood-red. R.H.1913:428,t(c). G.35:363. Orig. before 1900.—**R. s. atròrubens** Loud., var. Fls. dark blood-red, but smaller and in smaller racemes than in the preceding form. (*R. s. f. atrosanguineum* Kirchn.) Orig. before 1838.—**R. s. cárneum** Dipp., f. Fls. pink. (*R. c. grandiflorum* Carr.)— **R. s. albéscens** Rehd., f. Fls. whitish. (*R. s. albidum* hort., not Kirchn.) Gn. 58:208,t,f.2(c, as *R. album*.) G.M.53:125.—There are also double-fld. forms.

R. s. × *odoratum* = **R. Gordoniànum** Lem. Habit of *R. odoratum*: lvs. usually truncate, 3-lobed, glabrate: racemes about 20-fld., fls. yellow, tinged red outside, somewhat glandular, sterile. F.S.2:t.165(c). (*R. Beatonii* hort., *R. Loudonii* hort.) Orig. about 1837. Zone VI?—*R. s.* × *malvaceum* = **R. Bethmóntii** Jancz. Differs chiefly in the style being considerably longer and the sterile anthers shorter than the petals. Jancz., Mon. Gros. 490(fl). Orig. before 1904. —*R. s.* × *Grossularia* = **R. fontenayénse** Jancz. Unarmed: lvs. subchartaceous, subcordate, pubescent beneath; racemes horizontal, 3–6-fld.; fls. pubescent, vinous-red; receptacle cup-shaped; ovary pubescent-glandular: fr. rarely developed, purple-black, somewhat bloomy, glandular. Jancz., Mon. Gros. 492. (*R. sanguineum Fontenaysii* hort.) Orig. before 1877. Zone V?

Closely related species: **R. malváceum** Sm., which differs chiefly in the lvs. being bristly and rough above, in the usually rose-colored slenderer fls., with obtuse sepals shorter than the cylindric receptacle, in the densely white-pubescent ovary and the villous style, and in the viscid-pubescent fr. S.B.2:t.340. S.H.1:f.265m-n,266g-h. Calif. Intr. about 1832. Zone VII?—**R. nevadénse** Kellogg. Lvs. thin, sparingly pubescent or nearly glabrous and green beneath: racemes usually spreading; fls. rose-colored, smaller; pedicels 3–5 mm. long; sepals ovate to oblong, about 4 mm. long; receptacle campanulate, about 2 mm. long: fr. blue, glaucous, glandular. Jancz., Mon. Gros. 316,317. Proc. Calif. Acad. III. Bot. 2:t.23,f.4–5,t.24,f.6–7. (*R. sanguineum* var. *variegatum* S. Wats., *R. variegatum* A. Nels.) Ore. to Calif. and Nev. Cult. 1907. Zone VI?

14. **R. glutinòsum** Benth. Shrub to 4 m.: young brts., petioles and racemes pubescent and glandular-viscid: lvs. reniform-orbicular, cordate to truncate, 4–8 cm. broad, 3–5-lobed, with obtuse crenate-dentate lobes, at maturity glabrous above, green beneath, glandular, puberulous or nearly glabrous, rarely somewhat tomentose: racemes spreading or nodding; pedicels 8–10 mm. long; bracts reflexed; fls. red; sepals somewhat longer than the cylindric receptacle; style glabrous; ovary bristly-glandular, otherwise glabrous: fr. oblong, black, bloomy. Maund, Bot. Gard. t.597(c). Jancz., Mon. Gros. 318. S.H.1:f.265o,267a. (*R. sanguineum* var. *g*. Loud.) Calif. Intr. 1832. Zone VII?—**R. g. albidum** (Paxt.) Jancz., var. Fls. white, tinged pink. (*R. a.* Paxt.) P.M.10:t.55(c). Cult. 1840.

R. g. albidum × *nigrum* = **R. Carrièrei** Schneid. Intermediate between the parents without the odor of *R. nigrum*: fls. pink, glandular, in 10–15-fld. spreading racemes to 8 cm. long; receptacle campanulate: fr. black, not bloomy. Jancz., Mon. Gros. 489(fl). (*R. intermedium* Carr., not Tausch.) Orig. before 1867.

15. **R. viscosíssimum** Pursh. Shrub to 1 m.; young brts., petioles and infl. pubescent and viscid-glandular: lvs. reniform-orbicular, cordate, 5–8 cm. wide, usually 5-lobed, with short, rounded, crenate-dentate lobes, glandular-pubescent on both sides; petiole shorter than blade: fls. greenish white or pinkish, fragrant, in 3–8-fld. spreading or ascending racemes; receptacle cylindric-campanulate, 6–7 mm. long, about as long as sepals; ovary glandular: fr. black without bloom, glandular-bristly. Hooker, Fl. Bor. Am. t.76. Card, Bush Fr.f.103. S.H.1:f.265q,267b. B. C. and Mont. to Calif. and Colo. Intr. 1827. Zone V. The hardiest species of this section, but less handsome.

Sect. 9. CEROPHYLLUM Spach. Fls. small, white or pink, glandular, proterogynous, in 2–7-fld. racemes: receptacle cylindric, angled; ovary glandular or smooth: phyllotaxy of leaves ⅖ (⅗ in all other sections): plant glandular-viscid.

16. **R. cèreum** Dougl. Much-branched upright shrub to 1 m.; young growth glandular-pubescent: lvs. reniform, orbicular, cordate to broad-cuneate, 1–4 cm. wide, .3–5-lobed with obtuse crenulate lobes, glabrous or nearly so above, glandular-pubescent beneath; petioles almost as long as blade: fls. white or greenish, in few-fld. pendulous racemes; bracts cuneate-obovate, toothed at the truncate or rounded apex, glandular-pubescent and longer than the very short pedicels; receptacle cylindric, 6–8 mm. long; sepals ovate, about 2 mm. long, recurved; ovary glandular or smooth; style usually villous: fr. bright red, 6–7 mm. across. B.M.3008(c). Add.8:t.260(c). B.R.1263(c). B.C.5:2958. B. C. to Calif., east to Mont., Idaho and n. Ariz. Intr. 1827. Zone IV. Early leafing shrub with small light grayish green lvs. and attractive with its white or pink fls. and later with its bright red frs.—
R. c. farinòsum Jancz., var. Brts. violet: lvs. whitish puberulent: fls. pink.

17. **R. inébrians** Lindl. In habit and foliage scarcely different from the preceding species: fls. usually pink; bracts rhombic, usually acutish, entire or slightly toothed; ovary stipitate-glandular; style usually glabrous: fr. usually glandular, bright red. B.R.1471(c). B.B.2:238. (*R. Spaethianum* Koehne.) S. D. and Mont. to Calif. and N. Mex. Intr. 1827. Zone V. Similar to the preceding species.

Closely related species: **R. mescalèrium** Cov. Lvs. usually pubescent on both sides: fls. greenish white; bracts obovate, dentate at the obtuse apex; sepals oblong-ovate, about half as long as the receptacle; style glabrous: fr. sparingly glandular-pubescent, black. N. Mex. to w. Tex. Intr. 1916. Zone V?

Sect. 10. EUCOREOSMA Jancz. Racemes upright or pendulous: fls. proterandrous, greenish or brown, red or white; bracts usually linear; receptacle tubular or campanulate; ovary usually glandular: fr. black or brown: plant resinous-glandular.

18. **R. bracteòsum** Dougl. CALIFORNIAN BLACK CURRANT. Shrub to 3 m., with upright or ascending stems; young growth sparingly pubescent and glandular: lvs. thin, ovate, cordate, 5–20 cm. wide, deeply 5–7-lobed, with ovate to ovate-lanceolate, acute and sharply serrate lobes, resinous-glandular beneath; petioles about as long as blade or longer: fls. greenish or purplish in upright slender racemes to 20 cm. long; bracts spatulate, half as long as pedicels, the lower foliaceous; receptacle cup-shaped; sepals ovate-oblong, 3–4 mm. long: fr. globose, black with whitish bloom, resinous-glandular, edible. B.M.7419(c). Jancz., Mon. Gros. 339. Alaska to n. Calif. Cult. 1895. Zone VI? Remarkable for its large maple-like lvs. and the slender and very long upright racemes.

R. b. × *nigrum* = R. fuscéscens Jancz. which differs chiefly in the reddish-brown fls., in the smaller linear bracts of the shorter spreading or arching raceme and in the larger fr. Gt.55:162. Jancz. Mon. Gros. suppl.1:72. (*R. bracteosum* var. *f.* Jancz.) Orig. before 1905. Zone V.

Closely related species: **R. japónicum** Maxim. Brts. pubescent: lvs. 5-lobed to 17 cm. wide, glandular and pubescent beneath; racemes pubescent; fls. pubescent and glandular: fr. black, not glandular. Jancz., Mon. Gros. 340(fl). Japan. Intr. 1914? Zone V.

19. **R. hudsoniànum** Rich. Upright shrub: lvs. broader than long, cordate to subcordate, 3–10 cm. wide, 3–5-lobed, with ovate acute or obtusish, coarsely dentate lobes, pubescent and resinous-glandular beneath; petioles shorter than blade: fls. white, pubescent, in erect, loosely-fld. racemes 3–6 cm. long; pedicels short; bracts setaceous; sepals oval, spreading, longer than the cup-shaped receptacle: ovary resinous-glandular: fr. globose, black, 5–10 mm. thick. B.B.2:237. Hudson Bay to Alaska, s. to Minn. Cult. 1899. Zone II.

R. h. × *nigrum* = R. Saundersii Jancz. with pink fls. fading to whitish. Jancz., Mon. Gros. 488(fl). Orig. 1904.

Related species: **R. petiolàre** Dougl. Close to No. 19: lvs. glabrous or slightly pubescent, with sharply serrate lobes; petioles often longer than blade: racemes 5–10 cm. long. B. C. to Mont., s. to Ore. and Utah. Intr. 1827. Zone V.—**R. Dikúscha** Fisch. Upright shrub: lvs. 3–5-lobed, to 16 cm. broad, glabrous and glandular beneath; petioles shorter than blade; racemes loose, to 8 cm. long; fls. white, pubescent; bracts 1–1.5 mm. long; receptacle saucer-shaped: fr. bluish black, slightly bloomy. Jancz., Mon. Gros. 344(fl). E. Siber. Intr. before 1911. Zone IV.—**R. fràgrans** Pall. Lvs. shallowly 3–5-lobed, 2–6 cm. across, with short and broad obtuse to acute lobes, pubescent or glabrous beneath, rugose: racemes 4–7 cm, long; fls. white, about 1 cm. across; sepals oblong: fr. brownish. Jancz., Mon. Gros. 343(fl). E. Siberia, Manch. Intr. 1917. Zone IV.—**R. procúmbens** Pall. Procumbent shrub: lvs. subcoriaceous, reniform, to 8 cm. wide, 3–5-lobed, with short obtuse lobes, glabrous and glandular beneath: racemes upright, 1–4.5 cm. long; fls. glabrous, glandular, reddish or purplish; bracts wanting or minute: fr. brownish, glabrous. Jancz., Mon. Gros. 342. N.K.15:t.7. E. Siber. Cult. 1907. Zone IV.

20. **R. americànum** Mill. AMERICAN BLACK CURRANT. Upright shrub to 1.5 m., with rather slender spreading brs.; young brts. slightly pubescent and glandular: lvs. suborbicular, cordate to nearly truncate, 3–8 cm. wide, 3–5-lobed, with acute or sometimes obtuse dentate lobes, resinous-dotted beneath and pubescent at least on the veins; petioles pubescent, shorter than blade: racemes pendulous, many-fld., glabrous or pubescent; fls. yellowish white; bracts longer than pedicels; ovary glabrous; sepals obtuse, recurved, slightly longer than the cylindric-campanulate receptacle; petals and stamens ⅔ the length of the sepals: fr. black, smooth. S.O.2:t.92(c). G.O.t.1(c). B.B.2:238. (*R. floridum* L'Hérit., *R. missouriense* hort., not Nutt.) N. S. to Va., w. to Manit. and Colo. Intr. 1727. Zone II. The pendulous racemes of whitish fls. are rather conspicuous and the lvs. turn yellow and crimson in autumn.

21. **R. nígrum** L. EUROPEAN BLACK CURRANT. Shrub to 2 m. with rather stout brs.; young brts. glandular and puberulous or nearly glabrous: lvs. suborbicular, cordate, 5–10 cm. wide, 3–5-lobed, with broad-ovate, irregularly serrate acutish lobes, sparingly pubescent and resinous-dotted beneath; petioles pubescent: racemes pendulous, 4–10-fld., fls. dull white; bracts usually shorter than pedicels; ovary and receptacle pubescent and glandular; sepals oblong, recurved, longer than the broad-campanulate receptacle; petals almost half as long as sepals: fr. black, subglobose. S.E.4:t.523(c). R.I.23:t. 137(c). Card, Bush Fr. f.100. Eu. to C. Asia and Himal. Occasionally escaped in the Middle St. Cult. 1588. Zone IV. Cult. for its fr. which is used for jams, the varieties sometimes planted for ornament. All parts of the plant exhale a peculiar heavy odor when bruised.—**R. n. reticulàtum** Nichols. Lvs. densely mottled with yellow.—**R. n. heterophýllum** Pepin. Lvs. deeply divided, sometimes to the base, with irregularly and deeply incised lobes. (*R. n. laciniatum* Ktze., *R. n.* f. *aconitifolium* Kirchn.) Orig. before 1846.— **R. n. apiifòlium** Kirchn., f. Lvs. deeply divided usually to the base, the seg-

ments deeply and partly bipinnately lobed. (*R. n. dissectum* Nichols.) Orig. before 1864.—**R. n. xanthocárpum** Spaeth. Fr. yellow or whitish. Orig. before 1827.—**R. n. chlorocárpum** Spaeth. Fr. green. Gt.16:t.562,f.16(c). Orig. before 1838.

    R. n. × *Grossularia* = R. **Culverwellii** Macfarl. Fls. similar to those of *R. nigrum;* the glandless lvs. and infl. resembling those of the gooseberry: fr. dark red, hairy. G.C.III.12:271;44:120. J.L.28:169–73. (*R. Schneideri* Koehne.) Orig. about 1880.—*R. n.* × *glutinosum;* see under No. 14.—*R. n.* × *bracteosum;* see under No. 18.—*R. n.* × *hudsonianum;* see under No. 19.

    Closely related species: R. **ussuriénse** Jancz. Shrub with suckers: lvs. glabrous, resinous-dotted beneath, with the fragrance of camphor; petioles nearly glabrous: racemes 5–9-fld.; fls. pale; sepals spreading; receptacle campanulate; bracts at least half as long as pedicels: fr. black. N.K.15:t.6. Manch. to Korea. Cult. 1904. Zone V?

    Sect. 11. HERITIERA Jancz. Racemes upright; pedicels usually slender; fls. whitish or reddish, rotate or saucer-shaped, proterandrous; anthers recurved after anthesis; ovary glandular-bristly: fr. black or red: low or procumbent shrubs with crystalline glands.

    22. **R. glandulòsum** Weber. FETID CURRANT. Low shrub with prostrate or spreading and reclining stems and ascending brts.; young growth sparingly pubescent and sparingly glandular: lvs. thin, fetid, orbicular, cordate, 3–8 cm. wide, 5–7-lobed, with ovate, acute or acutish doubly serrate lobes, pubescent on the veins beneath; petioles about as long as blade: racemes ascending, 8–12-fld., glandular; pedicels much longer than the narrow bracts; fls. white or pinkish; ovary glandular-hispid; receptacle cup-shaped; sepals short, spreading, glabrous outside; petals much longer than broad: fr. red, glandular-bristly. S.O.2:t.95(c). B.B.2:237. Jancz., Mon. Gros. 308. Am. For. 22: 469,471. (*R. prostratum* L'Hérit., *R. rigens* Michx.) Nfdl. to B. C., s. to Mich. and Minn. and in the mts. to N. C. Cult. 1641. Zone II.

    Related species: R. **laxiflòrum** Pursh. Lvs. deeply 5-lobed, slightly pubescent beneath; sepals longer, pubescent outside, not glandular; petals as broad as long: fr. dark purple, bloomy, glandular. S.H.1:f.268b. Jancz., Mon. Gros. 307;suppl.5:728. Alaska to n. Calif. Intr. 1818. Zone IV.—R. **coloradénse** Cov. Young brts. puberulous; lvs. glabrous beneath or sparingly pubescent on the veins; sepals pubescent and glandular outside; petals nearly twice as broad as long: fr. black, not bloomy, sparingly glandular. Jancz., Mon. Gros. 310;suppl. 5:727. (*R. laxiflorum* var. *c.* Jancz.) Colo., N. Mex. Intr. 1905. Zone V?

    Sect. 12. RIBESIA Berl., emend. Jancz. Racemes pendulous or spreading, usually many-fld.; fls. rotate to turbinate, rarely campanulate, green, reddish or purple: fr. red or purple, rarely black: buds with scarious scales: upright, rarely prostrate shrubs with crystalline glands.

    23. **R. rúbrum** L. NORTHERN RED CURRANT. Shrub to 2 m.; young growth usually glabrous: lvs. suborbicular, truncate or rarely subcordate, to 12 cm. wide, 3–5-lobed, with serrate-dentate, acutish or obtusish lobes, usually nearly glabrous: racemes usually spreading; pedicels short; bracts very small: fls. greenish brown; receptacle nearly cup-shaped, without prominent ring or projections inside; anthers with contiguous cells: fr. usually red, the dried remnants of the fl. circular at base. S.E.4:t.522. Jancz., Mon. Gros. 287,288. (*R. sylvestre* Syme, not Mert. & Koch, *R. vulgare* Lam., *R. spicatum* Robs., *R. scandicum* Hedl.) C. and N. Eu., N. Asia. Long cult. Zone III. Rare in cult. outside of botanical collections and of the gardens of n. Eu., where forms with red, pinkish or whitish frs. are cult.—**R. r. pubéscens** Swartz, var. Young brts. slightly pubescent: lvs. pubescent beneath: fls. brownish or pinkish: fr. small. (*R. Schlechtendalii* Lange.) N. Eu.

    R. r. × *sativum* = R. **Houghtoniànum** Jancz. (Jancz., Mon. Gros. 479) to which several garden forms belong.—*R. r.* × *petraeum caucasicum* = R. **holoseríceum** Otto & Dietr. Lvs. pubescent beneath: fls. reddish or brownish: fr. blackish purple. Jancz., Mon. Gros. 483(fl).—**R. h. pállidum** (Otto & Dietr.)

Rehd., var., a hybrid with *R. petraeum bullatum* has the lvs. slightly pubescent beneath, pale fls. or tinged brownish and usually larger red fr. Jancz., Mon. Gros. 481,482. (*R. p.* Otto & Dietr.)—*R. h.* × *sativum;* see under No. 24.

Closely related species: **R. Warscewiczii** Jancz. Lvs. slightly pubescent beneath, chiefly on the veins, cordate at base: fls. pinkish; receptacle with a slightly elevated ring inside: fr. blackish purple, acid. Jancz., Mon. Gros. 285, 286. V.F.133. E. Siber. Intr. about 1860. Zone V.—*R. W.* × *sativum;* see under No. 24.

24. R. satìvum Syme. GARDEN CURRANT. Upright shrub to 1.5 m.; young growth pubescent and slightly glandular: lvs. suborbicular, cordate or subcordate, 3–7 cm. wide, 3–5-lobed, with short acutish serrate lobes, pubescent at least on the veins beneath: racemes drooping, many-fld., glabrous or nearly so; pedicels filiform, much longer than the bracts; receptacle saucer-shaped, green or slightly purple, inside with an elevated 5-angled ring; anthers with a broad connective separating the cells: fr. usually red, juicy, the dried remnants of the fl. 5-angled at base. S.E.4:t.520(c). B.B.2:237. Jancz., Mon. Gros. 277,278,280. (*R. sylvestre* Mert. & Koch, *R. hortense* Hedl., *R. domesticum* Jancz., *R. vulgare* Jancz., not Lam., *R. rubrum* auth., not L.) W. Eu. Cult. 1600. Zone IV. Cult in many varieties for its fr. which is eaten fresh or made into preserves.—**R. s. variegàtum** (West.) Rehd, f. Lvs. variegated or bordered irregularly with white or yellowish. S.O.2:t.93,f.(c). (*R. rubrum* var. *v.* West.)—**R. s. macrocárpum** Bailey, var. Of irregular habit on account of the lateral brts. being partly without buds: leaves large, deeply cordate, 3-lobed, with a large middle lobe: racemes without leaves at the base: fr. large, always red. (*R. vulgare* var. *m.* Jancz.) Jancz., Mon. Gros. 281,282. To this var. belong the large-fruited "Cherry Currants."

Hybrids of this species are **R. Gonduíni** Jancz. (*R. s.* × *petraeum.*) Jancz., Mon. Gros. 484,485.—**R. Koehneànum** Jancz. (*R. s.* × *multiflorum.*) Jancz., Mon. Gros. 486.—**R. futùrum** Jancz. (*R. s.* × *Warscewiczii.*)—**R. recens** Jancz., (*R. s.* × *holosericeum.*) Jancz., Mon. Gros. suppl.1:67.

25. R. triste Pall. SWAMP RED CURRANT. Shrub with creeping or ascending often rooting stems: young growth sparingly pubescent and sparingly glandular: lvs. thin, suborbicular, subcordate or cordate with a wide sinus, 5–10 cm. wide, 3–5-lobed, with acute or obtuse coarsely serrate lobes, glabrous above and light green with conspicuous veins, nearly glabrous beneath or pubescent to tomentose; petioles mostly shorter than blade: racemes drooping, 3–5 cm. long, glandular, otherwise nearly glabrous; fls. purplish or purple, rotate; sepals spreading, obtuse; anther-cells contiguous; fr. red, smooth, 6–8 mm. across. Jancz., Mon. Gros. 283. S.H.1:f.267g. (*R. albinervium* Michx.) Nfdl. to Alaska, s. to Mass., Mich. and Ore.; N. Asia. Intr. 1820. Zone II.—**R. t. alaskànum** Berger, var. Stems upright: lvs. cordate, with mostly obtuse lobes and rounded mucronulate teeth, glabrous: racemes 3–6 cm. long; fls. dark brown-red. N. Y. Agr. Exp. Sta. Tech. Bull 109:t.2. Alaska. Intr. 1914.

26. R. multiflòrum Kit. Upright shrub to 2 m., with stout brs.; young brts. pubescent; buds large: lvs. roundish, subcordate or truncate, to 10 cm. wide, 3–5-lobed, with acute or obtusish crenate-dentate lobes, densely grayish pubescent beneath, pubescent above while young; petioles pubescent, shorter than the blade: racemes pendulous, dense, to 12 cm. long, sometimes to 50-fld.; pedicels stout; fls. greenish yellow; receptacle saucer-shaped, inside with an elevated ring bearing 5 warts; sepals reflexed; stamens and style exserted, equaling the sepals: fr. dark red, glabrous. B.M.2368(c). R.I.23:t. 138a(c). L.I.t.31. Jancz., Mon. Gros. 274. E. Eu. Intr. about 1818. Zone V. Easily distinguished by the exserted stamens.

R. m. × *petraeum* = **R. urceolàtum** Tausch. Similar to *R. multflorum,* but fls. reddish and broad-campanulate; stamens slightly shorter than sepals. Jancz., Mon. Gros. 487:suppl.1:70. Cult. 1838.—*R. m.* × *sativum;* see under No. 24.

Closely related species: **R. manshùricum** Komar. Lvs. large, usually 3-lobed, with often acute or acuminate lobes, glabrous or pubescent beneath: racemes to 20 cm. long; receptacle inside with 5 warts not connected by an elevated ring. Jancz., Mon. Gros. 275;suppl.5:718. N.K.15:t.8. N. E. Asia. Cult. 1906.

27. **R. petraèum** Wulf. Upright shrub to 2 m.; young brts. usually glabrous: lvs. roundish, subcordate or truncate, 7–10 cm. wide, usually 3-lobed with acutish lobes, rugose and pubescent above while young, pubescent beneath at least on the veins; petioles pubescent, mostly shorter than blade: racemes rather dense, to 8 or 10 cm. long; pedicels short; fls. red or pink; receptacle broad-campanulate; sepals short, rounded, ciliate, spreading; petals nearly half as long as sepals, with a callosity below the base; stamens inserted below the petals, slightly longer than petals; ovary conical at apex, half-superior: fr. dark red, acid. R.I.23:t.138(c). S.O.2:t.94(c). Mts. of W. and C. Eu. Cult. 1794. Zone V.—**R. p. bullàtum** (Otto & Dietr.) Schneid., var., with the lvs. bullate above is the typical form. (*R. b.* Otto & Dietr.)— **R. p. carpáthicum** (Kit.) Schneid., var. Lvs. plane above, glabrescent: racemes looser and smaller. (*R. c.* Kit.) Carpath. Mts. Cult. 1838.—**R. p. Biebersteìnii** (Berl.) Schneid., var. Lvs. cordate, usually 5-lobed, with short obtuse lobes, not rugose, usually densely pubescent beneath: racemes long; fls. reddish: fr. dark purple. (*R. B.* Berl., *R. caucasicum* Bieb., not Adams, *R. petraeum* var. *caucasicum* Jancz.) Cauc. Cult. 1840.—**R. p. atropurpúreum** (C. A. Mey.) Schneid., var. Lvs. usually 3-lobed, with acutish lobes, to 12 cm. wide, glabrescent or pubescent beneath, not rugose: racemes short; fls. purple, the disk without callosities: fr. blackish purple. Jancz., Mon. Gros. suppl. 5:720. (*R. a.* C. A. Mey.) Siberia. Cult. 1878.—**R. p. altíssimum** (Turcz.) Jancz., var. Lvs. 3–5-lobed: racemes 5–7 cm. long; fls. small, paler red. Jancz., l.c.721. Siberia. Cult. 1910.—**R. p. tomentòsum** Maxim., var. Lvs. with elongated often subacuminate lobes, pubescent beneath: fls. pale: fr. pale red. Jancz., l.c.722. Manch. Cult. 1913.

R. p. × *rubrum;* see under No. 23.—*R. p.* × *sativum;* see under No. 24.— *R. p.* × *multiflorum;* see under No. 26.

Related species: **R. latifòlium** Jancz. Young brts. pubescent and stipitate-glandular: lvs. 3–5-lobed, to 18 cm. wide, cordate or subcordate, with often acute or acuminate lobes, pubescent or glabrous beneath: racemes 3–6 cm. long, loose; fls. greenish, often tinged red, subcampanulate, slightly pubescent; stamens inserted at the same height and about as long as petals; ovary inferior: fr. red. Jancz., l.c.723. (*R. petraeum* var. *tomentosum* Maxim., partly.) N. E. Asia. Cult. 1907.—**R. emodénse** Rehd. Young brts. glabrous, red while young: lvs. cordate, to 12 cm. wide, 3–5-lobed, with usually acute lobes, glandular, rarely pubescent beneath: racemes to 12 cm. long; fls. greenish, tinged purple, subcampanulate, pubescent or nearly glabrous; sepals broad-obovate, usually spreading; style as long as stamens: fr. red or black. Jacquemont, Voy. Inde.4:t.67. Jancz., Mon. Gros. 296. (*R. himalayense* and *R. himalense* Decne., not Royle.) Himal., C. China. Intr. 1908. Zone VI?—**R. e. urceolàtum** (Jancz.) Rehd., var. Fls. urceolate. Jancz., Mon. Gros. 297. W. China, Sikkim. Cult. 1900.—**R. e. verruculòsum** Rehd., var. Lvs. smaller, on the veins beneath and petiole with small wart-like excrescences: fr. red, edible. N. China. Intr. 1921.—**R. Meyeri** Maxim. Young brts. glabrous, reddish: lvs. cordate, to 9 cm. wide, usually 5-lobed, with acutish or obtuse lobes, glabrous: racemes reddish, 3–5 cm. long, loose, glabrous; fls. tubular-campanulate, nearly sessile, reddish; sepals upright; style longer than stamens: fr. black, lustrous. Jancz., Mon. Gros. 298;suppl.5: 725. C. Asia to N. W. China. Intr. about 1882. Zone III.

28. **R. moupinénse** Franch. Shrub to 5 m.; young brts. glabrous: lvs. cordate to truncate, usually 3-, sometimes 5-lobed, to 16 cm. wide, with acute or acuminate lobes, with gland-tipped hairs above and below, otherwise gla-

brous: racemes pendulous, short or to 12 cm. long; fls. sessile, turbinate-campanulate, red or greenish and tinged red; sepals upright, oval, glabrous; stamens half as long as sepals; style shorter than stamens: fr. black, lustrous. Jancz., Mon. Gros. 299. (*R. tripartitum* Batal.) W. China. Intr. 1908. Zone V. Vigorous shrub with large foliage.

29. **R. longeracemòsum** Franch. Shrub to 3 m.; brts. glabrous: lvs. cordate, to 14 cm. long and wide, 3–5-lobed, with acute or acuminate lobes, glabrous: racemes pendulous, to 30 cm. long, nearly glabrous, very slender, with remote, greenish or reddish fls. tubular-campanulate; pedicels 5–7 mm. long; bracts about half as long, ovate; sepals upright, ovate, much shorter than tube; stamens and style exserted: fr. black. Jancz., Mon. Gros. 301. W. China. Intr. 1908. Zone V. Vigorous shrub with large lvs.; remarkable for its very long and slender racemes.—**R. l. Wilsònii** Jancz., var. Young brts. red: racemes shorter; fls. salmon-red. C. China. Intr. 1907.

Subgen. III. **GROSSULARIOIDES** Jancz. (*Limnobotrys* Rydb.) Shrubs with spines and prickles: fls. perfect, in pendulous 6–20-fld. racemes; pedicels jointed beneath the ovary; bractlets minute or obsolete; fls. saucer-shaped: fr. black or red, glandular-bristly, disarticulating from the pedicel: buds with scarious scales.

Sect. 13. **GROSSULARIOIDES.** Characters of subgenus.

30. **R. lacùstre** (Pers.) Poir. Shrub to 1 m., with slender weak stems; brs. with slender usually clustered nodal spines and numerous scattered bristles: lvs. nearly orbicular, cordate, 3–6 cm. wide, with acutish incisely dentate lobes, glabrous or nearly so; petioles about as long as blade: racemes pendulous, 5–9 cm. long, 12–20-fld.; pedicels slender, about 5 mm. long; fls. greenish or purplish; receptacle crateriform; sepals spreading, short and broad; petals much broader than long: fr. purple-black, glandular-bristly. B.M.6492(c). L.B.9:884(c). Jancz., Mon. Gros. 353. (*R. grossularioides* Michx., *R. echinatum* Lindl., *Limnobotrys lacustris* Rydb.) Nfdl. to Alaska, s. to Pa., Mich., Minn., Colo. and n. Calif. Intr. 1812. Zone III? Graceful shrub with slender racemes of brownish red flowers.—**R. l. párvulum** Gray, var. Stems usually only slightly bristly: lvs. with obtusish lobes, the terminal one scarcely longer than the lateral ones. (*R. p.* Rydb.) Intr. 1918.

Closely related species: **R. hórridum** Rupr. Brts. yellowish, with more numerous spines and densely bristly: petioles and lvs. on both sides setose-bristly: racemes 6–7-fld. N.K.15:t.10. (*R. lacustre* var. *h.* Jancz.) N. E. Asia. Intr. 1918. Zone V.—**R. montígenum** McClatchie. Lvs. smaller, 1.5–4 cm. wide, pubescent and glandular: racemes 6–10-fld.; pedicels 2–5 mm. long: fr. red, glandular-bristly. Jancz., Mon. Gros. 355. (*R. lacustre* var. *molle* Gray, *R. lenturi* Cov. & Rose.) Wash. and Mont. to Calif., Ariz. and N. Mex. Cult. 1905. Zone V.

Subgen. IV. **GROSSULARIA** Rich. (*Grossularia* Mill.) GOOSEBERRY. Fls. perfect, in small, 1–4-fld. racemes; pedicels not jointed; receptacle turbinate to tubular, never rotate: fr. not disarticulating: buds with scarious scales: brs. with nodal spines, rarely nearly wanting, and often with bristles.

Sect. 14. **EUGROSSULARIA** Engl. Petals flat or somewhat concave; anthers obtuse, never glandular; style pubescent or glabrous: fls. greenish, whitish or purple, rarely red.

31. **R. níveum** Lindl. Shrub to 3 m., with upright or ascending brs.; brts. reddish brown with stout brown spines 1–2 cm. long, without bristles: lvs. thin, suborbicular, 2–3.5 cm. wide, 3–5-lobed, with short obtusish, few-toothed lobes, sparingly pubescent or glabrous: fls. 1–4, white, on slender peduncles; bracts ovate, much shorter than the filiform pedicels; ovary glabrous; receptacle campanulate; sepals narrowly lanceolate, 6–8 mm. long; filaments pubescent, longer than the sepals: fr. bluish-black, glabrous. B.M.8849(c). B.R.

1962(c). (*Grossularia nivea* Spach.) Idaho and Wash. to Nev. Intr. 1826. Zone V. Slender-branched shrub, attractive in bloom with its numerous small white flowers.

R. n. × ? *inerme* = R. robústum Jancz. Vigorous shrub with small spines: fls. white or pinkish; sepals broader and shorter and filaments shorter and less pubescent than in *R. niveum*. Jancz., Mon. Gros. 499. Orig. before 1890.—*R. n.* × *divaricatum* = R. succirúbrum Zabel. Lvs. similar to those of *R. niveum*: fls. pink or pinkish; stamens 1½ times as long as sepals: fr. black, slightly bloomy. Jancz., Mon. Gros. 500. Orig. in 1888.

32. R. curvàtum Small. Diffusely branched shrub to 1 m., with slender reddish brown brs.; spines slender, 4–6 mm. long: lvs. suborbicular, cuneate to subcordate, 1–3 cm. wide, 3–5-lobed with obtusish toothed lobes, sparingly pubescent; petioles slender, as long or shorter than blade: fls. 1–5, white, on slender peduncles; bracts often 3-lobed, ciliate; ovary glandular or pubescent; receptacle broad-campanulate; sepals linear-lanceolate, 6–7 mm. long, revolute; stamens as long as sepals; filaments villous: fr. greenish, glabrous. Jancz., Mon. Gros. 395. (*Grossularia curvata* Small, *G. campestris* Small.) Ga. to La. and Tex. Intr. before 1898. Zone V. Graceful shrub.

Closely related species: R. echinéllum (Cov.) Rehd. Brts. grayish; nodal spines 1–3, to 15 mm. long: lvs. 6–15 mm. long, finely pubescent; receptacle cylindric-campanulate, 4 mm. long; ovary densely glandular-bristly: fr. very spiny, 2–3 cm. across. Jour. Agric. Research, 28:t.1. (*Grossularia echinella* Cov.) Fla. Intr. 1925.

33. R. missouriénse Nutt. Shrub to 2 m., with grayish or whitish sometimes bristly brs.; spines 2 cm. long or less: lvs. suborbicular, broad-cuneate to subcordate, 2–6 cm. wide, 3–5-lobed, with coarsely dentate obtusish lobes, pubescent beneath: fls. greenish white, 2–3 on a slender peduncle; pedicels much longer than bracts; ovary glabrous; sepals linear, 2–3 times as long as the cylindric-campanulate pubescent receptacle, pubescent or glabrous; filaments glabrous, nearly twice as long as sepals, pubescent below: fr. glabrous, 8–15 mm. across, purplish, subacid. B.B.2:240. Card, Bush Fr. f.86 (as *R. gracile*). Jancz., Mon. Gros. 392 (as *R. rotundifolium*). (*R. gracile* Pursh, not Michx., *Grossularia missouriensis* Cov. & Brit.) Ill. to Minn., S. D., Kans., Mo. and Tenn. Cult. 1907. Zone IV. Similar to *R. niveum*, but fls. smaller and more greenish.

R. m. × *hirtellum;* see under No. 36.—*R. m.* × *Grossularia;* see under No. 40.

34. R. setòsum Lindl. Shrub to 1 m., with reddish brown, usually bristly brs.; spines subulate, to 2 cm. long: lvs. cordate to truncate, rarely cuneate, 1–4 cm. broad, 3–5-lobed, with dentate lobes, finely pubescent and somewhat glandular: fls. 1–3, white; bracts somewhat shorter than pedicels; ovary glabrous or slightly glandular; receptacle cylindric-campanulate, about twice as long as the recurved sepals; petals and stamens ½ or ⅔ as long as sepals: fr. red to black, glabrous or somewhat bristly. B.R.1237(c). B.B.2:240. Card, Bush Fr.f.91. (*Grossularia setosa* Cov. & Brit., *R. saximontanum* E. Nels.) Idaho to Assin., S. Dak. and Wyo. Intr. 1810. Zone II.

Closely related species: R. cognàtum Greene. Brts. white or buff-colored, usually bristly; receptacle greenish white, sparingly hirsute, ⅓ longer or nearly as long as the white or pink sepals: fr. smooth. Card, Bush Fr.f.90 (as *R. irriguum*). (*Grossularia cognata* Cov. & Brit.) Wash. and Ore. Intr. 1909. Zone V.

35. R. oxyacanthoìdes L. Low shrub, with slender often reclining brs. usually bristly, with stout spines 1 cm. or less long: lvs. cordate to broadcuneate, 2–4 cm. wide, deeply 5-lobed with dentate lobes, slightly pubescent or nearly glabrous, usually rugose at maturity: peduncles very short, scarcely exceeding the bud-scales, 1–2-fld.; pedicels short; fls. greenish white; sepals narrow-oblong, 2.5–4 mm. long, little longer than the receptacle; stamens and petals ⅔ as long as sepals: fr. red, smooth, about 1 cm. across. B.B.2:240. L.A.2:f.715. (*Grossularia o.* Cov. & Brit.) Hudson Bay to B. C., s. to Mich., N. Dak. and Mont. Intr. 1705. Zone II.

Closely related species: **R. irríguum** Dougl. Shrub to 3 m.; brs. often without bristles, usually gray: lvs. usually cordate, 3–7 cm. wide, 3–5-lobed, glabrous or nearly so above, pubescent and minutely glandular beneath: peduncles elongated, nodding, 1–3-fld.; sepals 5–8 mm. long, about twice as long as petals and stamens and nearly twice as long as the greenish receptacle. L.A.2:f.721. Jancz., Mon. Gros. f.110c. (*R. divaricatum* var. *i.* Gray, *R. leucoderme* Heller.) B. C. to Ore., Idaho and Mont. Intr. 1920. Zone IV.—**R. non-scriptum** (Berger) Standl. Small upright shrub; brts. usually without bristles: lvs. 5-lobed, deeply cordate, with crenate lobes, glandular beneath: peduncles shorter than petioles; sepals about as long or little longer than the receptacle; stamens as long as sepals. Colo.? Cult. 1900.

36. **R. hirtéllum** Michx. Shrub to 1 m., with slender, sometimes bristly brs., glabrous and gray when young, dark brown when older; spines wanting or small: lvs. ovate-orbicular or reniform-orbicular, usually broad-cuneate, 2–6 cm. broad, incisely 3–5-lobed, with acute dentate lobes, glabrous or sparingly pubescent; petioles slender, often with long hairs: fls. 1–3; bracts much shorter than pedicels; ovary glabrous, rarely pubescent or with stalked glands; receptacle greenish, narrow-campanulate, about as long as the green or purplish, spreading or upright sepals; stamens about as long as sepals; petals half as long: fr. purple or black, 8–10 mm. across, usually glabrous. B.M.6892(c, as *R. oxyacanthoides*). B.B.2:241. Card, Bush Fr. f.92 (as *R. oxyacanthoides*). B.C.3:f.1665–1667;5:2960. (*R. saxosum* Hook., *R. oxyacanthoides* of most auth., *R. gracile* Jancz., not Michx., *Grossularia hirtella* Cov. & Brit.) Nfdl. to Pa. and W. Va., S. Dak. and Man. Intr. 1812. Zone III. This is the most important edible native gooseberry, one of the best known improved forms being "Pale Red" which orig. about 1847.

Varieties as "Downing" (B.C.3:f.1668), "Houghton," "Smith" are referred to **R. rústicum** Jancz., apparently a hybrid with *R. Grossularia* and differing chiefly in its broader sepals and pubescent ovary. Jancz., Mon. Gros. 496. (*Grossularia downingiana* Berger.) Orig. about 1853 (Downing).—*R. h.* × *missouriense* = **R. arcuàtum** Jancz. Fls. whitish or slightly purple; sepals narrow-oblong, longer than the receptacle; stamens sometimes longer than the sepals: fr. red. Jancz., Mon. Gros. 498. Orig. before 1907.

37. **R. rotundifòlium** Michx. Shrub to 1 m., usually lower, with slender brown brs.; spines few and small: lvs. broad-cuneate to subcordate, 2–5 cm. wide, usually 3-lobed with coarsely dentate obtusish lobes, minutely pubescent or nearly glabrous; petioles usually shorter than blade: fls. 1–3, greenish purple; peduncles slender; pedicels much longer than bracts; sepals narrow, about twice as long as the campanulate receptacle; stamens somewhat longer than sepals: fr. purplish, smooth, 6–8 mm. across. G.O.t.3(c). L.B.11:1094 (c). B.B.2:241. Card, Bush Fr. f.88. (*R. triflorum* Willd., *Grossularia rotundifolia* Cov. & Brit.) Mass to N. Y. and N. C. Cult. 1809. Zone V. Often confused with the following species.

38. **R. divaricàtum** Dougl. Shrub to 3 m., with gray or brown, sometimes bristly brs.; spines usually stout, 1–2 cm. long, sometimes wanting: lvs. cordate to subtruncate, 2–6 cm. wide, usually 5-lobed, with coarsely crenate-dentate obtusish lobes, pubescent beneath along the veins or glabrous: fls. 2–4, greenish purple; peduncles slender, about as long as petioles; ovary glabrous; sepals oblong, slightly longer than the campanulate receptacle; petals white or purplish less than half as long as sepals; stamens somewhat longer than sepals: fr. black or dark purple, about 1 cm. across. B.R.1359(c).

Card, Bush Fr. f.87. Jancz., Mon. Gros. 390. (*Grossularia divaricata* Cov. & Brit.) B. C. to Calif. Intr. 1826. Zone V.—**R. d. pubiflòrum** Koehne, var. The more vigorous stems bristly: lvs. pubescent: flowers sparingly villous, smaller.

R. d. × *Grossularia* = **R. innominàtum** Jancz. Sepals broader; ovary glabrous or pubescent: fr. purple. Cult. 1906.—*R. d.* × *stenocarpum* = **R. gothoburgénse** Blom. Petals narrow-spatulate, slightly flushed reddish; style slightly pubescent: fr. subglobose to ellipsoid, purple. Orig. 1917.—*R. d.* × *niveum;* see under No. 31.—*R. d.* × *Lobbii;* see under No. 46.

39. R. inérme Rydb. Shrub to 2 m.: brs. with few small spines less than 1 cm. long, sometimes unarmed, rarely with few bristles: lvs. cordate to truncate, 1–6 cm. wide, 3–5-lobed with crenate-dentate, obtusish lobes, glabrous or sometimes pubescent and glandular: fls. 1–4, green or purplish; peduncles mostly shorter than petioles; bracts much shorter than pedicels; ovary glabrous; sepals oblong, reflexed during anthesis, slightly shorter than the narrow-campanulate receptacle; petals pink or white, about ⅓ as long as sepals; stamens shorter than sepals: fr. purplish red, smooth, about 8 mm. across, edible. Jancz., Mon. Gros. f.110 (except c). (*R. vallicola* Greene, *R. oxyacanthoides* Jancz., partly, *Grossularia inermis* Cov. & Brit.) Mont. to B. C. s. to N. Mex. and Calif. Cult. 1899. Zone V.

R. i. × *niveum;* see under No. 31.

40. R. Grossulària L. Shrub to 1 m.; brs. sometimes bristly, with stout spines about 1 cm. long and mostly 3-parted; lvs. cordate to broad-cuneate, 2–6 cm. wide, 3–5-lobed with crenulate-dentate obtusish lobes, glabrous or pubescent, of firm texture: fls. 1–2, greenish; ovary pubescent and often glandular-villous; sepals usually pubescent, about as long as the short-campanulate receptacle; stamens shorter than sepals: fr. globose to ovoid, pubescent and glandular-bristly or smooth, red, yellow or green. S.O.2:t.99(c). S.E.4:t.518(c). R.I.23:t.134(c). B.C.3:f.1663. (*R. reclinatum* L., *Grossularia reclinata* Mill.) Eu., N. Afr., Cauc. Cult. 1500. Zone IV. This species is the parent of the European gooseberries of which a large number of garden forms are in cult., varying greatly in size, color and pubescence of the fr.— **R. G. uva-críspa** (L.) Sm., var. Low shrub with pubescent brs. and lvs.; the tomentose ovary without or with few glands: fr. small, yellow, pubescent. (*R. G.* var. *pubescens* Koch, *R. uva-crispa* L.) S.O.2:t.100(c).

R. G. × *stenocarpum* = **R. vítreum** Jancz. Similar to *R. Grossularia uvacrispa;* ovary with only a few hairs near base: fr. greenish, transparent, tinged red, persisting until Oct. Jancz., Mon. Gros. Suppl. 4:613. Orig. before 1909. —*R. G.* × *cynosbati* = **R. ùtile** Jancz. Lvs. similar to those of *R. Grossularia:* fls. pale, slightly pubescent; sepals somewhat shorter than receptacle; style as long as stamens: fr. red, sometimes with a few spines. Jancz., Mon. Gros. 495. Orig. before 1896.—*R. G.* × *missouriense* = **R. Van-Fleetiànum** (Berger) Standl. Upright shrub with stout spines: lvs. 3-lobed, truncate to broad-cuneate, pubescent at first, later glabrous: ovary glabrous or pubescent; sepals much longer than receptacle; fr. ovoid, smooth, purple. Orig. before 1920.— *R. G.* × *sanguineum;* see under No. 13.—*R. G.* × *nigrum;* see under No. 21.— *R. G.* × *hirtellum;* see under No. 36.—*R. G.* × *divaricatum;* see under No. 38.

41. R. cynósbati L. Shrub to 1.5 m. high, usually lower; spines slender, 1 cm. or less long, simple or 3-parted, often wanting; bristles few or none: lvs. truncate to cordate, 3–5 cm. wide, deeply 3–5-lobed with crenately or incisely dentate lobes, usually somewhat pubescent; petioles shorter than blade, usually pubescent: fls. 1–3, green, glabrous; peduncles and pedicels slender; ovary setose; sepals broad, shorter than the broad-campanulate receptacle; stamens little longer than petals, shorter than sepals: fr. globose to ellipsoid, prickly, wine-colored, edible. S.O.2:t.98(c). B.B.2:239. Card,

Bush Fr. f.94. B.C.5:2961. (*R. gracile* Michx., *Grossularia c.* Mill.) N. B. to
Manit., s. to N. C., Ala. and Mo. Intr. 1759. Zone II.—**R. c. inérme** Rehd., f.
Fr. smooth, without prickles.—**R. c. glabràtum** Fern., var. Lvs. glabrous
or only sparingly pilose on the veins.
R. c. × *Grossularia;* see under No. 40.

42. **R. burejénse** Fr. Schmidt. Shrub to 1 m. or less; brs. usually very
bristly and with small nodal prickles: lvs. cordate to subcordate, 2–6 cm.
wide, deeply 3–5-lobed with dentate obtuse lobes, pubescent and glandular:
fls. 1–2, pale or reddish brown; peduncle 3–6 mm. long; sepals oblong, longer
than the broad-campanulate receptacle; petals rhombic, obtuse; stamens
longer than petals; style glabrous, divided only at apex: fr. about 1 cm. across,
green, prickly, edible. Jancz., Mon. Gros. 371. (*Grossularia burejensis* Berger.) N. E. Asia. Cult. 1903. Zone III.

Closely related species: **R. aciculàre** Sm. Nodal spines 5–7, small; lvs. glabrous, lustrous above, rarely pubescent and glandular; peduncles to 1 cm. long;
fls. pale or pinkish; stamens exceeding the obovate petals only by the anthers;
ovary smooth and glabrous, or sometimes glandular-bristly; style divided to the
middle: fr. red, green or yellow. Jancz., Mon. Gros. 373. Ledebour, Icon. Fl.
Ross. t.230. (*Grossularia acicularis* Spach.) Siber. Cult. 1903. Zone III?

43. **R. alpéstre** Decne. Upright shrub to 3 m.; brs. with stout spines to
2 cm. long and usually 3-parted, often bristly: lvs. cordate to truncate, 2–5
cm. wide, 3–5-lobed with incisely dentate obtusish lobes, slightly pubescent or
nearly glabrous: fls. 1–2, greenish or sometimes reddish, on short peduncles;
ovary glandular-bristly; sepals oblong, about as long as the campanulate
glandular receptacle; petals, white, upright, connivent, elliptic, acutish, half
as long as sepals; stamens exceeding the petals by the anthers; anthers with
a cup-shaped apical gland; style longer than stamens: fr. subglobose or ellipsoid, to 1.6 cm. long, purple, glandular-bristly. Jacquemont, Voy. Inde, 4:t.75.
Jancz., Mon. Gros. 376. (*Grossularia alpestris* Berger.) Himal., W. China.
Intr. 1902. Zone V.—**R. a. gigantèum** Jancz., var. Shrub to 5 m., with stout
spines to 3 cm. long: fls. glabrous: fr. smooth, green. W. China. Intr. 1908.
Zone V. Used in China as a hedge plant forming very dense tall hedges.

Related species: **R. grossularioìdes** Maxim. Shrub to 2 m.; brs. bristly,
glandular-bristly or glabrous: lvs. to 4 cm. broad, glabrous or slightly stipitate-
glandular: peduncle about 1.5 cm. long; style as long as stamens; anthers without apical gland: fr. glabrous, red. Jancz., Mon. Gros. 377. Japan. Intr. 1881.
Zone V?—**R. stenocàrpum** Maxim. Shrub to 2 m.: lvs. somewhat smaller;
anthers without apical gland: fr. oblong, 2–2.5 cm. long, greenish and tinged reddish. somewhat transparent, glabrous in the cult. form. Jancz., Mon. Gros. 375.
N. W. China. Cult. 1903. Zone V.—*R. s.* × *divaricatum;* see under No. 38.—
R. s. × *Grossularia;* see under No. 40.

44. **R. leptánthum** Gray. Slender shrub to 2 m.; brs. smooth or bristly,
with nodal spines about 1 cm. long: lvs. truncate to open-cordate, 0.5–2 cm.
wide, 3- or 5-cleft with crenate-dentate lobes, glabrous or pubescent and
somewhat glandular; petioles as long or shorter than blade: fls. greenish
white, 1–2 on a slender peduncle; pedicels short or wanting; ovary glabrous
or sometimes glandular-pubescent; sepals oblong, greenish white, about as
long as the nearly cylindric greenish receptacle; petals white or pinkish, about
half as long as the sepals and as long as the stamens; style glabrous, exserted,
bifid at the apex: fr. black, lustrous, smooth or glandular-hispid. Gt.53:409.
Jancz., Mon. Gros. 379. (*Grossularia leptantha* Cov. & Brit.) Colo. to N. Mex.
and Utah. Intr. 1893. Zone V. Graceful shrub.

Closely related species: **R. quercetòrum** Greene. Fls. 2–4, yellow; peduncles
pubescent: pedicels exceeding the bracts; petals slightly longer than the
stamens. Calif. and L. Calif. Cult. 1914. Zone VII?

45. R. pinetòrum Greene. Shrub to 2 m., with spreading and reclining brs., without bristles; spines 1 or 3, about 1 cm. long or less: lvs. thin, cordate, 2–3 cm. wide, usually 5-cleft with irregularly incised-dentate obtuse lobes, dull green and glabrous above, sparingly pubescent beneath, at least on the veins: fls. orange-red, 1 or rarely 2; peduncles puberulent, shorter than the petioles; ovary bristly; sepals linear-spatulate, pilose, nearly twice as long as the pilose cylindric-campanulate receptacle, ⅓ shorter than petals and stamens; style glabrous: fr. purple, 1–1.5 cm. long, prickly. Jancz., Mon. Gros. 370. (*Grossularia p.* Cov. & Brit.) Ariz., N. Mex. Intr. 1898. Zone V. Remarkable for the orange-red color of the fls.

Closely related species: **R. Watsoniànum** Koehne. Lvs. deeply 3–5-lobed, 3–5 cm. wide: fls. green; sepals fully twice as long as receptacle; petals white: fr. bristly. Jancz., Mon. Gros. f.97a. Wash. Cult. 1907. Zone VI?

Sect. 15. Robsonia Bert. Petals convolute, involute or convex; anthers sagittate or obtuse and glandular, rarely glandless; style always glabrous: fls. usually red or scarlet, 5- or 4-merous: fr. bristly or glandular, never glabrous.

46. R. Lóbbii Gray. Shrub to 2 m.; young brts. pubescent; spines 3, 1–2 cm. long: lvs. thin, cordate or subcordate, 2–3.5 cm. wide, 3–5-lobed with crenate-dentate obtuse lobes, slightly pubescent and glandular, often glabrous above: fls. 1–2, purple-red; peduncles glandular-pubescent; bracts ovate, as long as pedicels or shorter; sepals reflexed, about 1 cm. long, 2–3 times as long as the narrow-campanulate finely pubescent receptacle; petals whitish, half as long as sepals; stamens as long as sepals; anthers ellipsoid, glandular on back: fr. ellipsoid, purple, densely stipitate-glandular. B.M. 4931(c, as *R. subvestitum*). R.H.1908:30. G.C.II:19:11. Jancz., Mon. Gros. 359. (*Grossularia L.* Cov. & Brit.) B. C. to Calif. Intr. 1852. Zone VII?

R. L. × *divaricatum* = R. Knìghtii Rehd. Brts. puberulous: lvs. sparingly villous beneath, more densely on the veins: peduncle and pedicels glabrous or nearly so; receptacle campanulate, sepals about 6 mm. long: fr. sparingly glandular-setose. B. C. Cult. 1920. .

47. R. Roèzlii Reg. Shrub to 1.5 m.; young brts. pubescent, not bristly; spines slender, to 1.5 cm. long: lvs. rather thin, truncate to subcordate, 1.5–2.5 cm. wide, 3–5-lobed with incisely crenate-dentate lobes, finely pubescent on both sides or glabrous above: fls. 1–3, purple; ovary bristly and usually white-hairy; sepals lanceolate, longer than the pilose campanulate receptacle; petals involute, erose, white, about half as long as the sepals and as long as the filaments; anthers sagittate: fr. bristly, purple, 1–1.5 cm. across. Gt.28: t.982,f.1–3(c). R.H.1899:177. (*R. amictum* Greene, *Grossularia R.* Cov. & Brit.) M. and s. Calif. Cult. 1899. Zone VI? Fls. conspicuous on account of the contrast between the purple calyx-tube and the white petals.—**R. R. cruéntum** (Greene) Rehd., var. Lvs. and fls. glabrous. B.M.8105(c). R.H. 1908:32. S.L.312(h). (*R. c.* Greene, *R. amictum* var. *c.* Jancz.)

48. R. Menzièsii Pursh. Shrub to 2 m.; young brts. pubescent and densely bristly; spines 1–2 cm. long: lvs. firm in texture, cordate to subtruncate, 2.5–4 cm. wide, 3–5-lobed with crenate-dentate lobes, glabrous or slightly glandular above, velvety-pubescent and glandular beneath; petioles almost as long as blade: fls. 1–2, purple; peduncle slender, about as long as petiole; bracts shorter than the pedicels; ovary glandular-bristly; sepals oblong, about 3 times as long as the campanulate glandular-pubescent receptacle; petals whitish, erose, shorter than the filaments; stamens as long as sepals; anthers sagittate: fr. globose, bristly. G.C.45:242. R.H.1908:31. Jancz., Mon. Gros. 361,362. (*R. subvestitum* Hook. & Arn., *Grossularia M.* Cov. & Brit.) Ore. to m. Calif. Intr. 1830. Zone VII.

Related species: **R. califórnicum** Hook. & Arn. Brs. without bristles: lvs. glabrous or nearly so: fls. green or purplish; ovary bristly, only the shorter bristles sometimes glandular; petals obovate, nearly half as long as filaments: fr. prickly. Jancz., Mon. Gros. f.95. Card, Bush Fr.f.83. (*R. occidentale* Hook. & Arn.) Calif. Intr. ? Zone VII?

49. **R. speciòsum** Pursh. Evergreen shrub to 4 m.; brs. usually bristly; spines stout: lvs. coriaceous, orbicular to obovate, rounded to broad-cuneate, 1–4 cm. long, 3–5-lobed or crenate-dentate, glabrous or sparingly glandular-hairy: fls. bright red, 2–4 on slender pendulous peduncles, 4-merous; sepals upright, 6–10 mm. long, as long as the convolute petals and much longer than the broad-campanulate glandular-bristly receptacle; stamens 2–4 times as long as sepals; anthers oval: fr. glandular-bristly, red. B.M.3530(c). B.R. 1557(c). B.C.5:2968. G.C.34:71. Gn.34:230. M.G.32:65(h). (*Grossularia speciosa* Cov. & Brit.) Calif. Intr. 1828. Zone VII? One of the most showy gooseberries with its long pendulous bright red fls.

36. HAMAMELIDACEAE Lindl. WITCH-HAZEL FAMILY

Deciduous or evergreen shrubs or trees, often with stellate pubescence; buds scaly or naked; lvs. alternate, simple, stipulate, rarely estipulate: fls. usually rather small, in heads or racemes, unisexual or perfect, perigynous or epigynous; sepals 4–5, rarely 6 or 7; petals as many or wanting; stamens 4–5 or sometimes more; ovary 2-celled, with 1 or several pendulous ovules in each cell: fr. a woody 2-valved caps., with a separate inner layer of different texture; seeds often winged, albuminous, with straight embryo.— About 20 genera with 50 species chiefly in subtrop. and warm-temp. regions of both hemispheres.

A. Lvs. palmately veined, deciduous: ovary-cells with several ovules; fls. in heads: buds with 5–6 outer scales, rather large.
  B. Lvs. entire, broad-ovate: fls. in 2-fld. heads, with linear-lanceolate petals..1. *Disanthus*
  BB. Lvs. palmately lobed: fls. in many-fld. heads, apetalous................2. *Liquidambar*
AA. Lvs. penninerved: ovary-cells 1-ovuled.
  B. Petals wanting or minute.
    C. Lvs. deciduous, crenate-dentate.
      D. Fls. in heads or dense upright spikes; stamens usually more than 3; calyx-tube shorter than ovary.
       E. Stamens 5–7, pendulous, with linear-oblong anthers.................4. *Parrotia*
       EE. Stamens 10–24, with upright filaments; anthers oval.
        F. Filaments slender; infl. capitate, with large white bracts at the base.
                               5. *Parrotiopsis*
        FF. Filaments thickened toward the apex; infl. more or less elongated, without bracts ....6. *Fothergilla*
      DD. Fls. in long and slender racemes; stamens 5; calyx-tube urn-shaped, longer than ovary ....10. *Sinowilsonia*
    CC. Lvs. evergreen.
      D. Fls. in slender racemes; stamens 2–8; calyx-tube obsolete............3. *Distylium*
      DD. Fls. in heads or short racemes; stamens 8–10; pistillate fls. with urceolate calyx.
                                 9. *Sycopsis*
  BB. Petals conspicuous, longer than the sepals.
    C. Fls. in racemes, 5-merous.
      D. Petals broad: lvs. sinuate-dentate, with straight veins, each ending in a mucronate tooth ....7. *Corylopsis*
      DD. Petals subulate, minute; filaments very short: lvs. unequally denticulate, with much branched veins..8. *Fortunearia*
    CC. Fls. in clusters, 4-merous; petals linear: lvs. wavy-toothed..........11. *Hamamelis*

1. **DISÁNTHUS** Maxim. Deciduous shrub; glabrous except the pubescent calyx; buds ovoid, acute, with 5–6 outer scales: lvs. long-petioled, palmately 5–7-nerved, entire, with small caducous stipules: fls. perfect, in axillary, short-peduncled pairs, connate back to back; calyx 5-parted; petals 5, linear-lanceolate, spreading; stamens 5, shorter than sepals; ovary superior, with 2 short styles; caps. obovoid, 2-lobed at apex, with several black

glossy seeds in each cell. (Greek *dis*, twice, and *anthos*, flower, referring to the two-flowered heads.) One species in Japan.

D. cercidifòlius Maxim. Shrub to 5 m., with slender lenticellate brs.: lvs. orbicular-ovate, cordate to subcordate, obtuse or acutish, 5–12 cm. broad and usually less long, dull bluish green above, paler beneath, leathery at maturity: fls. dark purple, 1.5 cm. across; calyx pubescent, with short recurved lobes; caps. 1.5 cm. across; seeds about 5 mm. long, angular, very oblique at base. Fl.x; fr. the following Oct. B.M.8716(c). R.H.1910:363, t.(c). G.F.6:215. B.C.2:1021. M.D.1900:1,t(hc). S.L.164(h). Mts. of C. Japan. Intr. 1892. Zone VI or VII. A handsome shrub with cercis-like foliage turning in autumn to crimson-red suffused with orange.

2. LIQUIDÁMBAR L. Deciduous trees; buds ovoid, with 5 or 6 outer scales: lvs. slender-petioled, palmately 3–7-lobed, serrate, with small stipules: fls. apetalous, usually monoecious, in globose heads; staminate fls. without perianth, intermixed with small scales, in small heads forming a terminal raceme; pistillate fls. in slender-peduncled globose heads consisting of more or less cohering 2-beaked ovaries subtended by minute scales: fruiting head globose, spiny from the persisting styles, consisting of dehiscent capsules with 1 or 2 winged seeds. (Latin *liquidus*, fluid, and Arabic *ambar*, amber; referring to the fragrant resin exuding from the bark of *L. orientalis*.) Four species in N. and C. Am. and W. and E. Asia.

A. Lvs. 5–7 lobed: fr.-head with beaked caps. and short scales................1. *L. styraciflua*
AA. Lvs. usually 3-lobed: fr.-head with slender-beaked caps. surrounded by subulate bristles.
2. *L. formosana*

1. L. Styracíflua L. SWEET-GUM (BILSTED). Tree to 45 m.; bark deeply furrowed; brs. red-brown, often developing corky ridges or thick wings: lvs. cordate or subcordate, 10–18 cm. wide and about as long, 5–7-lobed with usually oblong-triangular acuminate, finely serrate lobes, dark green and lustrous above, paler beneath and glabrous except axillary tufts in the axils of the principal veins; petioles 6–12 cm. long: fr.-heads about 3 cm. across, consisting of lustrous brown capsules surrounded at base by short obtusish scales. Fl.v; fr.x, persisting during the winter. S.S.5:t.199. Am. For. 21:783 (h);22:641(b). F.E.18:90(h). Gn.24:166(h),167. Conn. and s. N. Y. to Fla., Ill., Mo. and Mex. Intr. 1681. Zone IV. Symmetrical tree with stout brs.; its maple-like lvs. turn deep crimson in fall; in winter the tree is conspicuous by its usually corky brs. and the pendulous frs.—**L. S. rotundíloba** Rehd., f. Lvs. with 3–5 short rounded lobes. J.A.12:71. Intr. 1930.—**L. S. péndula** Rehd., f. With deflexed pendulous brs. forming an almost columnar head. Intr. 1938.

Related species: **L. orientàlis** Mill. Tree to 20 m.; lvs. truncate, 4–5 cm. broad, usually with 5 ovate-oblong lobulate and obscurely toothed lobes, quite glabrous: fr.-heads about 2.5 cm. across, beaks of caps. slender. H.I.11:1019. F.R.3:87. (*L. imberbe* Ait.) W. Asia. Cult. 1750. Zone VI. Of slow growth.

2. L. formosàna Hance. Tree to 40 m.; young brts. pubescent or glabrous: lvs. cordate to truncate, 8–15 cm. wide, 3-lobed, with broad-ovate acuminate to slender-acuminate serrate lobes, glabrous or pubescent on the veins beneath or sometimes, particularly on young plants, pubescent on the whole under surface: fr.-heads about 3 cm. across, puberulous, of bristly appearance owing to the slender persisting styles and the subulate scales surrounding the capsules. H.I.11:t.1020. C.C.143. (*L. acerifolia* Maxim., *L. Maximowicziana* Miq.) W. to E. China and Formosa. Intr. 1884. Zone VII? Pyramidal tree, similar to the *L. styraciflua*, but the brs. without corky bark.

—**L. f. montícola** Rehd. & Wils., var. Lvs. always glabrous, usually truncate or rounded, cordate only in young seedling plants. Intr. 1907. Zone VI.

3. **DISTỲLIUM** Sieb. & Zucc. Evergreen trees or shrubs; buds ovoid, pubescent, with 2 outer scales: lvs. short-petioled, entire or dentate, penninerved, with deciduous stipules: fls. polygamous or dioecious, apetalous, subtended by small bracts, in axillary racemes; sepals 1–5 or wanting; stamens 2–8, almost spoon-shaped, with short filaments and flat anthers convex outside; pistillate fls. with a superior stellate-tomentose ovary and with several stamens or without; styles 2, slender, stigmatic on the inside: caps. with 1 seed in each cell. (Greek *dis*, two, and *stylos*, style; referring to the two conspicuous styles.) Six species in Japan, China and Himal.

D. racemòsum Sieb. & Zucc. Tree to 25 m., in cult. usually shrubby; brts. glabrous: lvs. elliptic to elliptic-oblong, sometimes obovate, acute or obtusish, narrowed at the base, 3–7 cm. long, glabrous: racemes stellate-pubescent, 1.5–4, in fr. to 8 cm. long; anthers red: caps. ellipsoid, 2-pointed, about 1 cm. long. Fl.III–IV; fr.VIII–X. S.Z.1:t.94(c). S.I.2:t.25(c). B.M.9501(c). S.L.164 (h). Japan. Cult. 1870. Zone VII?

4. **PARRÓTIA** C. A. Mey. Deciduous small tree with stellate pubescence; buds stalked, with 2 outer scales, brown-tomentulose: lvs. short-petioled, sinuate-dentate, with large lanceolate caducous stipules: fls. perfect, apetalous, in dense heads surrounded by large bracts; sepals 5–7, rather large, oval, inclosing the pubescent ovary about ½; stamens 5–7, opposite the sepals; anthers linear-oblong, opening with a slit, pendulous on slender filaments; styles slender, acute, with linear stigma: caps. ovoid, with the calyx-margin near the base; seeds oblong, shining, one in each cell. (After F. W. Parrot, a German naturalist and traveler, later professor of medicine in Dorpat; 1792–1841.) One species in Persia.

P. pérsica C. A. Mey. Small tree to 5 m. with smooth flaky bark; older brts. red-brown: lvs. oval to obovate-oblong, obtuse, rounded to subcordate at base, 6–10 cm. long, coarsely crenate-dentate above the middle, stellate-pubescent on both sides; petioles 2–6 mm. long: fls. before the lvs.; the heads with the brown-tomentose bracts about 1.5 cm. across: fr. broad-ovoid, about 1 cm. long, 2-lobed at the apex, with recurved beaks. Fl.III–IV. B.M.5744(c). Gs.3:237,t(c). S.L.246(h). M.O.t.21. Cult. 1840. Zone V. In cult. usually a shrubby tree with spreading brs.; lvs. similar to those of the Witch-Hazel, turning scarlet, orange and yellow in fall; the dull-colored fls. are insignificant.

5. **PARROTIÓPSIS** Schneid. Deciduous tree, with stellate pubescence; buds stalked, with 2 exposed scales, thinly tomentose: lvs. petioled, dentate with acute teeth; stipules oval: fls. perfect, apetalous, in many-fld. heads surrounded by large bracts; sepals 5–7, small; stamens about 15; anthers oval, yellow, opening with 2 valves, on upright slender filaments; styles slender, free, with linear stigmas: capsule ovoid, with spreading beaks, the calyx-margin below the middle. (Parrotia and Greek *opsis*, appearance; referring to its resemblance to that genus.) One species in the Himal.

P. Jacquemontiàna (Decne.) Rehd. Small tree to 7 m., with smooth gray bark; brts. yellowish gray, tomentulose at first: lvs. suborbicular, 5–8 cm. long, dentate with short acute or acutish teeth, light green beneath, sparingly stellate-pubescent above while young, more densely so on the veins beneath; petioles 6–12 mm. long, densely stellate-tomentose; fl.-heads with the spreading white bracts 3–5 cm. across; bracts dotted with purplish brown scurfy

tomentum on the back; stamens about 5 mm. long. Fl.v. B.M.7501(c). B.S.
2:123 (*P. involucrata* Schneid., *Parrotia* J. Decne.) Intr. 1879. Zone V. Similar to Parrotia, but lvs. resembling *Alnus glutinosa* in shape and serration,
changing to yellow in fall; fls. appearing with the lvs., conspicuous on
account of the large white bracts.

6. **FOTHERGÍLLA** L. Deciduous shrubs; buds with 2 exposed scales
densely stellate-pubescent, caducous: lvs. petioled, coarsely toothed, stipulate: fls. perfect, apetalous, in terminal heads or spikes, not subtended by
bracts; calyx 5–7-lobed; stamens about 24, the filaments white, thickened
toward the apex; anthers oval, yellow: caps. ovoid, with the calyx-margin
about the middle, tomentose and setose, with stout upright or spreading
beaks; seeds 1 in each cell, oblong and lustrous brown. (After John Fother-
gill, eminent English physician who introduced and cultivated many new
plants; 1712–1780.) Four species in s. e. N. Am.

A. Lvs. rarely exceeding 2–5 cm., stellate-pubescent above: low shrub..........1. *F. Gardeni*
AA. Lvs. 5–12 cm. long, glabrous or glabrescent above; upright shrubs.
  B. Lvs. glaucous beneath and more or less stellate-pubescent..................2. *F. major*
  BB. Lvs. green and sparingly pubescent beneath............................3. *F. monticola*

1. **F. Gárdeni** Murr. Low shrub to 1 m., with upright and spreading
slender brs.: lvs. obovate to oblong, rounded or broad-cuneate, 2–5 cm. long,
dentate above the middle, pale or glaucous and tomentose beneath; petioles
5–10 mm. long: fls. before the lvs.; spikes ovoid to oblong, 1.5–3 cm. long.
Fl.iv–v; fr.vii–viii. B.M.1341(c). L.B.16:1507(c). Gn.89:141(h). (*F. alnifolia* L., *F. carolina* Brit.) Va. to Ga. Intr. 1765. Zone V. Conspicuous in
early spring with its numerous spikes of white flowers.

2. **F. màjor** (Sims) Lodd. Upright shrub to 3 m.; brts. stout, stellate-
tomentulose: lvs. suborbicular to oval or obovate, cordate or truncate, 5–10
cm. long, coarsely crenate-dentate or sometimes denticulate above the middle,
dark green and glabrous above, glaucous and stellate-pubescent beneath at
least on the veins, leathery; petioles 5–10 mm. long, tomentose: fls. with the
lvs.; spikes 2.5–5 cm. long, with densely brown-tomentose bracts; stamens
8–14 mm. long: fr. including the upright beaks 1 cm. long, light brown inside
with red markings on the inner suture; seeds 7–8 mm. long. Fl.v; fr.ix.
B.M.1342(c). L.B.16:1520(c). M.G.17:395(h). B.S.1:561(h). Gn.78:229;79:
77(h);89:141(h). (*F. alnifolia* var. *m.* Sims.) Ga. Intr. 1780. Zone V. Ornamental shrub of pyramidal habit, conspicuous in spring with its numerous
spikes of white fls.; the lvs. turn orange-yellow in fall.

3. **F. montícola** Ashe. Shrub to 2 m., with spreading brs.; lvs. broad-oval
to obovate, usually cordate, remotely dentate, often from below the middle,
light green and sparingly pubescent beneath, often only on the veins; petioles
8–15 mm. long: spikes 3–6 cm. long: fr. with finally spreading beaks, darker
inside without red markings: otherwise much like the preceding species.
B.C.3:1271. Gn.89:141(h). N. C. to Ala. Intr. 1899. Zone V. Similar to the
preceding species, but of more spreading habit and with rather larger spikes.

7. **CORYLÓPSIS** Sieb. & Zucc. Deciduous shrubs with slender lenticellate brs., rarely small trees; buds with about 3 glabrous exposed scales, conspicuous: lvs. slender-petioled, strongly veined, dentate, stipulate: fls. perfect,
yellow, sessile or nearly so, in nodding racemes appearing before the lvs.,
with large bracts at the base; calyx-lobes short, petals clawed, 5; stamens 5,
alternating with short, entire or 2–3-parted staminodes; ovary half-superior,
rarely superior; styles distinct, slender: caps. broadly obovoid, truncate at

apex, with two spreading and recurved beaks, 4-valved, with 2 oblong, lustrous black seeds. (*Corylus,* and Greek *opsis,* likeness; alluding to the hazel-like foliage.) About 12 species in E. Asia and Himal.—All species are ornamental shrubs with handsome generally ovate leaves of moderate size and with yellow fragrant flowers appearing in nodding racemes in early spring before the lvs.

A. Young brts. and petioles pubescent: lvs. pubescent beneath, at least on the veins.
  B. Calyx and fr. glabrous...1. *C. Wilsonii*
  BB. Calyx and fr. pubescent.
    C. Lvs. obovate to oblong-obovate: racemes 10–18-fld.; its bracts loosely silky outside.
                                                  2. *C. sinensis*
    CC. Lvs. orbicular-ovate or orbicular-obovate: racemes 7–10-fld., its bracts glabrous
      outside ....3. *C. spicata*
AA. Young brts. glabrous or nearly so: lvs. usually glabrous.
  B. Calyx and floral bracts except the basal ones pubescent...............4. *C. Veitchiana*
  BB. Calyx and floral bracts on back glabrous.
    C. Racemes many-fld.
      D. Blade of petals broader than, or as broad as long, petals about 4 mm. long: lvs.
      generally obovate.
        E. Lvs. pubescent beneath, at least on the veins: nectaries deeply bifid.
                                         5. *C. Willmottiae*
        EE. Lvs. with scattered silky hairs when unfolding, soon quite glabrous: nectaries
          emarginate or truncate...6. *C. platypetala*
      DD. Blade of petals longer than broad, petals about 8 mm. long: lvs. generally ovate.
                                    7. *C. glabrescens*
    CC. Racemes 2–3-fld.; fls. about 1 cm. long...............................8. *C. pauciflora*

1. **C. Wilsónii** Hemsl. Shrub or small tree; young brts. stellate-pubescent: lvs. ovate to oblong-ovate or oblong-ovate or elliptic, acuminate, cordate or subcordate, 6–12 cm. long, sinuately dentate with bristle-like teeth, glaucous and sparingly pubescent beneath, more densely on the veins; petioles densely pubescent, 1–2.5 cm. long: racemes 5–7 cm. long; all bracts densely silky-pubescent on both sides, ovate or broad-ovate, acutish or obtuse; petals narrow-spatulate, about 6 mm. long, slightly longer than stamens; staminodes truncate or slightly emarginate: fr. 1–1.2 cm. across, contracted into a stout stipe 3–5 mm. long; seed 1 cm. long. C. China. Intr. 1900. Zone (V).

2. **C. sinénsis** Hemsl. Shrub to 5 m.; young brts. pubescent: lvs. obovate to oblong-obovate, short-acuminate, obliquely cordate or subcordate, 5–12 cm. long, sinuate-denticulate, grayish green and pubescent beneath, at least on the veins; petioles densely pubescent, 6–15 mm. long: fls. pale yellow, fragrant, in pendulous 10–18-fld. racemes 3–5 cm. long; petals orbicular-ovate, 7–8 mm. long, longer than style and stamens: fr. 7–8 mm. across, hairy. G.C.39:18. H.I.29:2820,f.17–20. C. and W. China. Intr. 1900. Zone (V).

3. **C. spicàta** Sieb. & Zucc. Shrub to 2 m.: young brts. pubescent: lvs. orbicular-ovate or orbicular-obovate, abruptly short-acuminate, obliquely cordate to rounded, 5–10 cm. long, sinuate-denticulate with bristle-like teeth, glaucous and pubescent beneath; petioles densely pubescent, 1–2.5 cm. long: racemes 7–10-fld., 2–4 cm. long; rachis pubescent; fls. bright yellow, fragrant; petals obovate, about as long as stamens; staminodes 2-parted: fr. pubescent, 7–8 mm. across. S.Z.1:t.19(c). B.M.5458(c). F.S.20: t.2135(c). S.I.2:t.26(c). G.C.III.25:210. Japan. Intr. 1863. Zone (V).

Related species: **C. Gríffíthii** Hemsl. Lvs. larger: racemes to 6 cm. long; bracts small, pubescent on both sides, the basal ones glabrous outside; stamens and style much shorter than petals. B.M.6779(c). Himal. Intr. 1879 Zone VII?

4. **C. Veitchiàna** Bean. Shrub to 2 m.; brts. glabrous: lvs. ovate or elliptic to oblong-obovate, short-acuminate, cordate or subcordate, 5–12 cm. long, sinuately dentate, sparingly silky and purplish beneath when young, glaucous and glabrous at maturity; petioles glabrous, 6–15 mm. long: fls. primrose-

yellow, fragrant, in many-fld. racemes 2.5–5 cm. long; basal bracts glabrous, the floral ones silky-pubescent outside; stamens as long or slightly longer than the oval or ovate petals; anthers red-brown; calyx hairy, with rounded lobes; staminodes 2-parted: fr. about 8 mm. across. B.M.8349(c). Gn.76:184. B.S.1:398. M.G.31:405(h). C. China. Intr. 1900. Zone (V).

5. **C. Willmóttiae** Rehd. & Wils. Shrub to 4 m.: brts. glabrous: lvs. oval or obovate, sometimes ovate, short-acuminate, subcordate to truncate, 3–8 cm. long, sinuate-dentate with mucronate teeth, pale green or glaucescent beneath, pubescent at least on the veins with long hairs or rarely villous, sometimes nearly glabrous at maturity; petioles 6–20 mm. long, glabrous or slightly pubescent; fls. soft-yellow, fragrant, in dense many-fld. racemes 5–7 cm. long; rachis villous; petals 3–4 mm. long, with short claw and suborbicular or reniform blade; stamens much shorter than petals, about as long as styles; staminodes 2-parted, shorter than sepals: caps. about 7 mm. across. B.M.8708(c). G.M.55:191. M.G.31:406(h). W. China. Intr. 1908. Zone VI.

6. **C. platypétala** Rehd. & Wils. Shrub to 3.5 m.; brts. glabrous, but stipitate-glandular: lvs. ovate or broad-ovate to elliptic, short-acuminate, cordate or subcordate, 5–10 cm. long, sinuate-dentate with bristle-like teeth, glaucescent beneath; petioles 1–2.5 cm. long, sparingly stipitate-glandular: fls. light yellow, fragrant, in many-fld. racemes with the stalk 3.5–5 cm. long; rachis slightly pubescent or nearly glabrous; petals about 3–4 mm. long, with short claw and reniform or suborbicular blade, staminodes truncate or emarginate, shorter than sepals; stamens shorter than petals, longer than styles: caps. 7–9 mm. long. C. China. Intr. 1907. Zone VI.—**C. p. levis** Rehd. & Wils., var. Young brts. and petioles without stipitate glands. W. China. G.C.95:276. Intr. 1908.

Related species: **C. yunnanénsis** Diels. Lvs. slightly pubescent beneath: floral bracts slightly silky on back; petals 6–7 mm. long, with obovate blade; stamens slightly shorter than petals; calyx-lobes ciliate, pubescent outside. S. W. China. Cult. 1910. Zone VII?

7. **C. glabréscens** Franch. & Sav. Shrub to 6 m.; young brts. glabrous: lvs. ovate, acuminate, cordate to subcordate, 3–8 cm. long, sinuate-dentate with bristle-like teeth, glaucescent beneath and sparingly silky on the veins or sometimes slightly pubescent while young, thin; petioles slender, 1.5–3 cm. long: fls. pale yellow, fragrant, in pendulous racemes 2–3.5 cm. long; rachis glabrous; petals 8 mm. long, with obovate blade, slightly longer than style and stamens; staminodes deeply bifid, about as long as sepals: caps. about 7 mm. across. (*C. Gotoana* Mak.) Japan. Intr. 1905. Zone V. The hardiest species.

8. **C. pauciflòra** Sieb. & Zucc. Spreading shrub to 2 m.: young brts. glabrous: lvs. ovate or broad-ovate, acute, obliquely cordate to subcordate, 3–7 cm. long, sinuate-dentate with bristle-like teeth, glaucescent beneath and sparingly pubescent on the veins; petioles 5–15 mm. long, glabrous: fls. primrose yellow, about 1 cm. long, 2 or 3 in short spikes; bracts glabrous outside, greenish yellow; petals oblong-obovate, longer than stamens. B.M.7736(c). S.Z.1:t.20(c). S.I.2:t.26(c). B.S.1:397. G.F.5:342(h). G.W.15:101(h). Japan. Intr. 1862 to Am. Zone VI.

8. **FORTUNEÀRIA** Rehd. & Wils. Deciduous shrub; buds naked, densely stellate-tomentulose: lvs. short-petioled, dentate, with small caducous stipules: fls. andro-monoecious, short-stalked, in terminal racemes appearing with the lvs.; racemes of bisexual fls. usually with 1–3 lvs. at base;

calyx turbinate, 5-lobed; petals 5, subulate, slightly shorter than calyx-lobes; stamens 5, with very short filaments; ovary partly superior; styles 2, filiform, revolute; staminate racemes short, catkin-like, developing in autumn, naked during winter, without lvs. at base; fls. with rudimentary pistil: fr. a 2-valved caps. with 2 glossy dark brown seeds; embryo with large cotyledons, revolute at the margin. (Dedicated to Robert Fortune, who traveled in China during 1843–62 and introduced many new plants; 1812–80.) One species in China.

    F. sinénsis Rehd. & Wils. Shrub to 7 m.; brts. and petioles densely stellate-tomentulose: lvs. obovate to obovate-oblong, short-acuminate, narrowed toward the rounded or truncate base, 7–15 cm. long, unequally sinuate-denticulate with small mucronulate teeth, glabrous above, pubescent on the veins beneath; petioles 3–8 mm. long: fls. about 4 mm. across, in stellate-pubescent racemes, those of perfect fls. 3–6 cm. long; pedicels 1–3 mm. long; style longer than the stamens, revolute: caps. 1–1.2 cm. across, brown, with pale lenticels; seeds about 1 cm. long. Fl.v; fr.x–xi. I.S.1:t.25. C. China. Intr. 1907. Zone (V). Shrub with rather large lvs. and inconspicuous fls.

    9. SYCÓPSIS Oliv. Evergreen trees or shrubs; buds naked, densely stellate-tomentulose: lvs. short-petioled, entire or sparingly denticulate, penninerved, with narrow caducous stipules: fls. monoecious, apetalous, small, terminal or axillary in heads or short racemes surrounded by pubescent bracts; staminate fls. with minute sepals, 8–10 stamens on slender filaments and with rudimentary ovary; pistillate fls. with urceolate, 5-lobed, stellate-pubescent calyx enclosing the superior ovary; styles distinct, slender, with decurrent linear stigmas: caps. with the irregularly splitting calyx at the base, 2-valved, with 2 brown lustrous seeds. (Greek *sykos,* fig, and *opsis,* likeness; referring to the resemblance of the shrubs to certain species of Ficus.) Six species in China, Himal. and in the Philippine Isls.

    S. sinénsis Oliv. Shrub or small tree to 7 m.: lvs. elliptic-ovate to elliptic-lanceolate, acuminate, broad-cuneate, 5–10 cm. long, remotely denticulate, above the middle or entire, lustrous and glabrous above, pale green and glabrous beneath or with scattered scale-like hairs; petioles 5–10 mm. long: fls. in rather small, short-peduncled heads, surrounded by brown-tomentose bracts; stamens 10, about 1.5 cm. long; anthers oblong, red; caps. ovoid, 3–5 together, with the short beak about 1 cm. long, covered with light brown tomentum mixed with setose hairs. Fl.ii–iii. H.I.20:1931;29:2834,f.1–3. B.S.2:562. G.C.72:91. C. and W. China. Intr. 1907. Zone VII.

    10. SINOWILSÒNIA Hemsl. Deciduous tree with stellate pubescence; buds naked, stalked, stellate-tomentulose: lvs. short-petioled, denticulate, penninerved; stipules caducous, lanceolate: fls. monoecious, apetalous, in pendulous racemes; staminate racemes catkin-like, from leafless buds; pedicels short; stamens 5, with short filaments adnate to the base of the linear-spatulate sepals disposed in an irregular whorl; ovary wanting; pistillate racemes terminal on short leafy brts.; fls. sessile; calyx-tube urceolate, pubescent, enclosing the ovary; sepals 5, spatulate, spreading; staminodes 5, with rudimentary anthers, opposite the sepals; styles free, exserted: caps. broad-ovoid, setose-strigose, enclosed partly by the calyx-tube; seeds elliptic-oblong, black. (After E. H. Wilson who traveled in China between 1900 and 1910 and introduced many new plants into cult.; 1876–1930.) One species in China.

    S. Hénryi Hemsl. Tree to 8 m.; brts. stellate-pubescent: lvs. broad-ovate to elliptic, acute or short-acuminate, subcordate to truncate, 10–15 cm. long, denticulate, with fascicled hairs on both sides while young, later glabrous or nearly so above, pubescent beneath chiefly on the veins; petiole about 1 cm. long, densely pubescent: staminate catkins 4–6 cm. long; pistillate racemes 1.5–3, in fr. to 15 cm. long; calyx-tube yellowish tomentulose, about 1.5 mm. long, little longer than ovary, later much elongated; sepals 2 mm. long: caps. about 1 cm. long, with short weak beak. Fl.v; fr.x. H.I.29:2817. C. and W. China. Intr. 1908. Zone V. Interesting shrub with large linden-like lvs., but fls. inconspicuous.

11. **HAMAMÈLIS** L. WITCH-HAZEL. Deciduous shrubs or small trees with stellate pubescence; buds naked, stalked: lvs. short-petioled, oblique at base, sinuate-dentate, with caducous, rather large stipules: fls. perfect, in short-peduncled, axillary few-fld. clusters; calyx 4-parted, with spreading ovate obtuse lobes, tomentose outside; petals 4, linear, crumpled in bud, yellow; stamens 4, with short filaments, alternating with scale-like staminodes; styles distinct, short: caps. 2-valved with the calyx-limb about or below the middle; seeds 2, lustrous black, oblong. (Ancient Greek name of a pear-shaped fr., probably the medlar.) Six species in N. Am. and E. Asia.— Ornamental shrubs interesting on account of the unusual time of flowering, from late autumn to early spring.

 A. Lvs. soon glabrous or glabrate, rarely pubescent below, subcordate to truncate.
  B. Fls. in autumn; lvs. bright green beneath..............................1. *H. virginiana*
  BB. Fls. during the winter or in early spring.
   C. Lvs. generally obovate with about 5 pairs of veins, often glaucescent beneath and
    sometimes tomentulose: petals 1–1.5 cm. long.........................2. *H. vernalis*
   CC. Lvs. generally broad-ovate, with about 7 pairs of veins: petals about 2 cm. long.
                          3. *H. japonica*
 AA. Lvs. densely soft-pubescent, cordate at base.................................4. *H. mollis*

1. **H. virginiàna** L. Shrub or small tree to 5 m.; lvs. obovate or elliptic, obtusely short-acuminate or obtusish, narrowed toward the base and sub-cordate, rarely broad-cuneate, 8–15 cm. long, coarsely crenate-dentate, nearly glabrous or pubescent on the veins beneath, with 5–7 pairs of veins; petioles 5–15 mm. long, pubescent: petals bright yellow, 1.5–2 cm. long; sepals dull brownish yellow inside: fr. broad-obovoid, 1.2–1.4 cm. long, with the calyx-limb slightly below the middle. Fl.ix–x; fr. the following autumn. Em.t.472 (c). B.M.6684(c). S.S.5:t.198. Gn.33:589;39:547;78:45. Can. to Ga., w. to Neb. and Ark. Intr. 1736. Zone IV. Spreading shrub with rather large lvs. turning bright yellow in fall, opening its fls. exhaling a heavy odor when the lvs. are falling.—**H. v. rubéscens** Rehd., f. Petals reddish; sepals yellowish or brownish green inside.

 Closely related species: **H. macrophýlla** Pursh. Lvs. smaller, with fewer, shallower and more rounded lobes, less unsymmetrical at base, more or less pubescent and roughened by persistent tubercles: sepals yellow inside; petals pale yellow. Fl.xii–ii. S.M.370. S. C. to Fla., Ark. and Tex. Intr. 1928. Zone VI.

2. **H. vernalis** Sarg. Upright shrub to 2 m. or rarely more, suckering; lvs. obovate to oblong-obovate, obtusely pointed, narrowed toward the broad-cuneate or truncate, rarely subcordate base, 6–12 cm. long, coarsely sinuate-dentate above the middle, green or glaucescent beneath, glabrous or nearly so, with 4–6 pairs of veins; petioles 5–12 mm. long, pubescent: fls. fragrant; petals 1–1.5 cm. long, light yellow, often reddish toward the base; sepals dark red inside: fr. like that of the preceding species. Fl.xii–iii; fr.ix–x. B.M.8573(c). Add.8:t.261(c). S.T.2:t.156. R.H.1913:131. F.E.88,2:23(h). Mo. to La. and Okl. Intr. 1908. Zone V. Fls. less showy than those of the following species, but fragrant. —**H. v. tomentélla** Rehd., f. Lvs. glaucescent

and more or less densely pubescent or tomentulose beneath: petals yellow or reddish.—**H. v. cárnea** Rehd., f. Petals red.

3. **H. japónica** Sieb. & Zucc. Shrub or small tree to 10 m., with spreading brs.: lvs. suborbicular to broad-ovate or elliptic, rarely obovate, acute or rounded at apex, rounded or subcordate, rarely broad-cuneate at base, 5–10 cm. long, light green and glabrous or slightly pubescent beneath, with usually 6–7 pairs of veins; petioles 5–15 mm. long, slightly pubescent: petals about 2 cm. long, bright yellow, sepals usually purple inside, with revolute lobes: caps. with the calyx-limb much below the middle. Fl.I–III; fr.IX–X. S.I.2:t.25(c). Gt.49:t.1481(c). G.F.4:257. B.C.3:1431. Gn.87:661. Japan. Intr. 1862. Zone V. Conspicuous in winter, the delicate petals withstand zero weather without injury; the lvs. turn bright orange-yellow late in fall.—**H. j. arbòrea** (Ottolander) Gumbleton, var. Of tree-like habit, more vigorous: lvs. somewhat larger and of firmer texture; calyx deep purple inside, stamens purple; petals golden-yellow. B.M.6659(c). R.H.1891:472,t.(c). G.C. II.1:187;III.9:247. Gn.39:546,t(c);87:660. Intr. 1862.—**H. j. Zuccariniàna** (Ottolander) Gumbleton, var. Tree-like, but brs. more upright; petals pale yellow and the calyx greenish yellow inside. Gn.17:251. R.B.28:62,t. Cult. 1882.—**H. j. flavo-purpuráscens** (Mak.) Rehd., var. Petals red or reddish, at least toward the base; sepals deep purple inside. (*H. obtusata* var. *f.* Mak., *H. incarnata* Mak.) Japan. Intr. 1919.

4. **H. móllis** Oliv. Shrub or small tree to 10 m.; young brts. densely tomentose: lvs. orbicular-obovate to obovate, short-acuminate, obliquely cordate to subcordate at base, 8–16 cm. long, sinuately denticulate, pubescent above, grayish tomentose beneath; petioles stout, 5–10 mm. long, densely pubescent; calyx ferrugineously tomentose outside, purplish red inside; petals golden yellow, reddish at the base, 1.5–2 cm. long: caps. enclosed ⅓ by the calyx. Fl.I–III; fr.x. B.M.7884(c). Add.7:t.229(c). G.C.52:488; 102:171,t(c). H.I.1742. Gn.90:3(h),94. C. China. Intr. 1879. Zone V. The handsomest of the Witch-Hazels; lvs. turning bright yellow late in fall.

37. **EUCOMMIACEAE** Van Tiegh. EUCOMMIA FAMILY

Deciduous trees: brs. with lamellate pith; buds ovoid, pointed, with about 6 exposed scales: lvs. alternate, petioled, serrate, estipulate: fls. dioecious, without perianth, in the axils of bracts at the base of the young brts., before or with the lvs.; staminate fls. pediceled, with 4–10 linear mucronate anthers on very short filaments; pistillate fls. short-pediceled consisting of a 1-celled ovary composed of 2 carpels with one locule aborted, bifid at apex with the lobes stigmatic on the inner side: fr. a stipitate, oblong, compressed and winged 1-seeded nutlet; seed albuminous with a straight embryo as long as the albumen; cotyledons narrow, flat.—Contains only the following monotypic genus.

EUCÓMMIA Oliv. Characters of the family. (Greek *eu*, well, and *kommi*, gum; referring to the fact that the plant contains rubber.)

E. ulmoìdes Oliv. Tree to 20 m.; brts. glabrous, light or yellowish brown, lenticellate: lvs. elliptic or ovate to oblong-ovate, acuminate, broad-cuneate or rounded, 7–8 cm. long, serrate, glabrous above and slightly rugose at maturity, pubescent beneath chiefly on the veins while young; petioles 1.5–2.5 cm. long, anthers about 1 cm. long, brownish red: fr. oblong, 3–4 cm. long. Fl.IV; fr.IX–X. H.I.1950,2361. K.B.1904:4,t. I.S.1:t.26. R.H.1909:226,227(h).

M.G.27:11,613(h) ;32:249(h). C. China. Intr. 1896. Zone V. Tree with ascending brs., resembling an elm-tree; interesting as the only rubber-producing tree hardy so far north, though the rubber is not present in sufficient quantity to make commercial exploitation pay.

38. PLATANACEAE Lindl. PLANE-TREE FAMILY

Deciduous trees with stellate pubescence; bark pale, exfoliating in broad thin plates; buds ovoid, acutish, with a single closed scale, at first hidden by the base of the petiole, the terminal one lacking: lvs. alternate, long-petioled, large, palmately veined and lobed; stipules usually sheathing with spreading margin; fls. monoecious, in dense globose heads; staminate and pistillate similar, but on separate peduncles; sepals 3–8, triangular, pubescent, petals as many, spatulate; staminate fls. with 3–8 stamens with very short filaments, connective enlarged at apex into a peltate scale; pistillate with 3–8 distinct carpels with elongated styles stigmatic on the inner side; ovary oblong, with 1 or 2 pendulous ovules: fr. a syncarp consisting of numerous narrowly obconical angled 1-seeded nutlets surrounded by long hairs; seed with scant albumen; embryo slender, with linear often unequal cotyledons.— One genus with 6–7 species in N. Am. s. to Mex. and from S. E. Eu. to India.

PLÁTANUS L. Plane-tree. Characters of the family. (Ancient Greek name, probably from *platys*, broad.)—The Plane-trees are ornamental trees with handsome large lvs., much planted as shade and street trees, particularly in cities, as they do not suffer much from dust and smoke and stand even severe pruning well.

A. Fr.-heads racemose 3 or more, bristly: lvs. usually deeply lobed............1. *P. orientalis*
AA. Fr.-heads 1 or 2, rarely 3 or more.
 B. Fr.-heads 2 or occasionally more: lvs. with the middle lobe about as long as broad.
 2. *P. acerifolia*
 BB. Fr.-heads usually solitary: lvs. with the lobes broader than long......3. *P. occidentalis*

1. **P. orientàlis** L. Oriental P. Tree to 30 m., with usually broad round head and comparatively short and thick trunks; bark exfoliating in large flakes, dull grayish or greenish white: lvs. broad-cuneate or truncate at base, 10–20 cm. wide, deeply 5–7-lobed, the sinuses reaching to or below the middle of the leaf, lobes longer than broad, coarsely toothed or entire, glabrous or nearly so at maturity; petioles 3–8 cm. long: fr.-heads 2–6, on long pendulous stalks, 2–2.5 cm. thick, bristly and with exserted hairs between the nutlets, their apex conical, with persistent style. Fl.v; fr.ix–x. S.O.3:t.128(c). Gn. 20:369. G.C.III.23:25,27(h). G.F.4:91(h). M.D.1915:3,t(h). H.E.3,t.174–176(h). (*P. vulgaris* Spach.—Sycamore.) S. E. Eu. and W. Asia. Zone VI. Tree with broad round head and short trunk often divided near the base into several stems, planted as a shade tree since ancient times in W. Asia and S. E. Eu.—**P. o. digitàta** (Gord.) Janko, var. Lvs. cuneate to truncate, deeply 5-lobed, with wide sinuses and narrow elongated coarsely dentate or lobulate lobes. Gn.20:371. G.C.76:250. (*P. digitata* Gord., *P. o. laciniata* Hort., *P. nepalensis* Hort.) Intr. about 1842.—**P. o. cuneàta** (Willd.) Loud., var. Smaller tree, sometimes shrubby: lvs. short-petioled, cuneate, or sometimes truncate, 3- or sometimes 5-lobed with ascending toothed lobes. G.C.29:363. Gn.20:371. (*P. c.* Willd.) This and the preceding var. are according to A. Henry possibly of hybrid origin.

Related species: **P. racemòsa** Nutt. Tree to 40 m.: lvs. deeply 3–5-lobed with narrow, entire or remotely dentate lobes, tomentose beneath: fr.-heads 2–7, sessile, bristly; achenes with conical or rounded apex. S.S.7:t.328. (*P. cali-*

fornica Benth.) S. Calif. and L. Calif. Cult. 1870. Zone VII?—**P. Wrìghtii** Wats. Tree to 25 m.: lvs. deeply 3–5-lobed, tomentose, finally often nearly glabrous beneath, with lanceolate, entire or remotely dentate lobes: fr.-heads 2–4, usually stalked, mostly smooth, the achenes truncate or rounded with a more or less deciduous style. S.S.7:t.329. Ariz. and N. Mex. to n. Mex. Cult. 1900. Zone VII?

2. **P. acerifòlia** (Ait.) Willd. LONDON P. (*P. occidentalis* ✕ *orientalis*.) Tree to 35 m., with tall upright stem and widespreading brs., the lower ones drooping; bark exfoliating in large flakes; young growth densely brownish tomentose; lvs. truncate to cordate, 12–25 cm. wide, 3–5-lobed, with triangular-ovate or broad-triangular not or sparingly toothed lobes, with acute or rounded sinuses extending to about ⅓ the length of the blade, glabrous or nearly so at maturity; petiole 3–10 cm. long: fr.-heads usually 2, rarely 1 or 3, about 2.5 cm. across, bristly; nutlet ovoid or rounded at apex and crowned by the persistent remnant of the style. G.C.66:48. E.H.3:t.204,f.1. Proc. Irish Acad. 35B:t.6. F.E.24:69(h). (*P. orientalis* var. *a*. Ait., *P. intermedia* Hort., *P. damascena* Dode, *P. densicoma* Dode, partly.) Origin unknown, probably before 1700. Zone V. Much planted as a street tree in Eu. and in this country: tall tree with straight trunk and broad round head. Like the other species it is conspicuous in winter on account of the large fruit-balls hanging from the brs. and of the light colored smooth bark mottled by darker blotches of old bark.—**P. a. Kelseyàna** (Jaennicke) Schneid., f. Lvs. variegated with yellow. (*P. a. aureo-variegata* Hort.)—**P. a. Sùttneri** (Jaennicke) Schneid., f. Lvs. blotched with creamy white. (*P. occidentalis argenteo-variegata* Hort.)—**P. a. pyramidàlis** (Janko) Schneid., f. Habit more upright, lower brs. not drooping: lvs. usually 3-lobed with slightly toothed lobes, often longer than broad, usually rounded at base. G.C.66:51.—**P. a. hispànica** (Muenchh.) Bean, var. Lvs. usually 5-lobed with toothed lobes, often to 30 cm. wide, truncate to subcordate. G.C.66:50.—To *P. acerifolia* also belong: *P. cantabrigiensis* Henry. Lvs. rather small, 5-lobed, truncate with cuneate centre: fr.-heads usually similar to those of *P. orientalis*. G.C.76:251.—*P. parviloba* Henry. Lvs. truncate to cuneate, with 3 triangular to oblong-triangular entire lobes and near base with 1–3 pairs of teeth or small lobes: fr.-heads 3–6.

3. **P. occidentàlis** L. BUTTONWOOD (BUTTONBALL, AMERICAN PLANE). Tree to 40 or occasionally to 50 m., with tall trunk and round or ovoid head; bark almost creamy white, exfoliating in rather small plates, dark brown and fissured at the base of older trunks: lvs. truncate or cordate, rarely cuneate, 10–22 cm. wide, often broader than long, 3- or sometimes 5-lobed with shallow sinuses and broad-triangular lobes, broader than long, coarsely toothed or rarely entire, floccose-tomentulose when young, at maturity pubescent only along the veins beneath: fr.-heads solitary, rarely 2, about 3 cm. across, rather smooth at maturity; nutlets with truncate or obtuse apex with a short style, without exserted hairs between the nutlets. Fl.v; fr.ɪx–x. S.S.7:t.326,327. Em.1:261,263,t. G.F.2:354,355(h);9:55(h). F.L.19:9,t(h). Am. For. 28:145 (h). Maine to Ont. and Minn., s. to Fla. and Tex. Intr. 1640. Zone IV. The most massive and perhaps the tallest deciduous tree of N. Am., often planted as shade and avenue tree, but not thriving well in Eu.—**P. o. glabràta** (Fern.) Sarg., var. Lvs. usually smaller and of firmer texture, mostly truncate at base, more deeply lobed, the sinuses extending to about ⅓ of the blade, the lobes long-acuminate and often entire, or coarsely and sparingly dentate. (*P. g.* Fern., *P. densicoma* Dode, partly.) Iowa to Tex. and n. Mex. Intr. ?

321

39. **ROSACEAE** Juss. ROSE FAMILY

Herbs, shrubs or trees, deciduous or evergreen, often thorny; buds usually with several exposed scales, sometimes with 2: lvs. alternate, rarely opposite; stipules usually conspicuous, rarely wanting: fls. perfect, rarely unisexual, usually regular, perigynous, the axis enlarged into a flat to urceolate or sometimes conical receptacle bearing the sepals, petals and stamens on its margin, inside usually lined with a glandular disk; sepals 4–5, imbricate; petals as many, imbricate, sometimes wanting; stamens 5–many; carpels 1–many, distinct or more or less united and often connate with the receptacle; carpels with 1–several upright or pendulous ovules; styles as many as carpels, sometimes connate: fr. a follicle, achene, drupe, hip or pome; seeds usually exalbuminous; cotyledons often fleshy with convex back, rarely folded or convolute.—About 100 genera with more than 2000 species widely distributed in all parts of the world, most abundant in the temperate regions.

Several families, as Spiraeaceae, Pomaceae (Malaceae) and Amygdalaceae (Drupaceae), chiefly distinguished by fruit characters, have been segregated, but they are all closely linked together by their floral characters and are perhaps best considered tribes or subfamilies of Rosaceae.

KEY TO THE SUB-FAMILIES

A. Fr. consisting of 1–5, rarely to 12 dehiscent follicles, indehiscent only in No. 12, or fr. a
   dehiscent caps.: stipules present or wanting...................................1. *Spiraeoideae*
AA. Fr. indehiscent: lvs. stipulate.
   B. Ovary inferior; the 2–5 carpels more or less connate and adnate to the cup-shaped receptacle: fr. a pome, sometimes berry-like................................II. *Pomoideae*
   BB. Ovary superior (apparently inferior in Rosa).
      c. Carpels usually many (if 1 or 2, not drupaceous); calyx persistent: lvs. often compound ....III. *Rosoideae*
      cc. Carpel usually 1, rarely 2 or 5, drupaceous; calyx usually deciduous: lvs. always simple ....IV. *Prunoideae*

I. Spiraeoideae

A. Fr. follicular, dehiscent; seeds not winged: fls. not exceeding 2 cm. in width.
   B. Lvs. simple, entire to lobed, or trifid in No. 8: pistils opposite to the petals or less than 5.
      c. Stipules present, caducous; lvs. lobed: staminal disk wanting; seeds shining.
         D. Follicles dehiscent along both sutures, often inflated, 1–5: fls. in umbel-like
            racemes ....1. *Physocarpus*
         DD. Follicles dehiscent only along the ventral suture, not inflated, 1–2: lvs. with
            acuminate lobes.
            E. Fls. in terminal elongated racemes or panicles; follicles usually 5-seeded.
                                                                2. *Neillia*
            EE. Fr. in small terminal corymbs, minute; style lateral; follicle 1, 1–2 seeded.
                                                        3. *Stephanandra*
      cc. Stipules wanting: carpels usually 5.
         D. Lvs. entire or lobed.
            E. Fls. in panicles, corymbs or umbel-like racemes.
               F. Carpels free: lvs. usually serrate or lobed (see also No. 12).
                  G. Petals orbicular to obovate; ovules 2–many.....................4. *Spiraea*
                  GG. Petals linear; ovules 2.......................................5. *Pentactina*
               FF. Carpels connate at base: fls. polygamo-dioecious, in panicled racemes: lvs.
                  entire ....6. *Sibiraea*
            EE. Fls. in racemes; carpels dehiscent on both sutures: lvs. entire: prostrate subshrub ....7. *Petrophytum*
         DD. Lvs. trifid with narrow segments: fls. in racemes: prostrate subshrub..8. *Luetkea*
   BB. Lvs. pinnate or bipinnate, stipulate: fls. in panicles, white; carpels connate at base.
      c. Lvs. pinnate; lfts. serrate..9. *Sorbaria*
      cc. Lvs. bipinnate; lfts. entire, very small............................10. *Chamaebatiaria*
AA. Fr. capsular, dehiscent or of 5 indehiscent achenes: lvs. simple; stipules wanting.
   B. Fls. about 4 cm. across, in racemes: fr. capsular........................11. *Exochorda*
   BB. Fls. small, in panicles: fr. of 5 achenes..................................12. *Holodiscus*

II. Pomoideae

A. Carpels bony at maturity; fr. with 1–5 nutlets.
   B. Lvs. entire or lobed.
      c. Lvs. entire or rarely serrulate: brs. unarmed.

   D. Fls. usually in several- to many-fld. corymbs, not more than 1 cm. across: fr.
      about 1 cm. across or less: pistils 2–5...............................13. *Cotoneaster*
   DD. Fls. solitary, 3–5 cm. across: fr. 3–5 cm. across, brown with foliaceous calyx-lobes:
      pistils 5 ....15. *Mespilus*
  CC. Lvs. crenate, dentate or lobed, rarely entire: brs. usually spiny.
      D. Lvs. persistent, crenate or entire: pistils 5, with 2 fertile ovules....14. *Pyracantha*
      DD. Lvs. deciduous, rarely subpersistent: pistils 1–5, with 1 sterile and 1 fertile ovule.
                                                                                    16. *Crataegus*
 BB. Lvs. pinnate; lfts. small, entire...17. *Osteomeles*
AA. Carpels with leathery or papery walls at maturity: fr. a 1–5-celled pome, each cell with
    1 or more seeds.
  B. Fls. in compound corymbs or panicles.
    C. Carpels partly free; styles 2–5, distinct or connate: fls. in corymbs or broad corym-
       bose panicles.
      D. Ovary in fr. free only at apex or ⅓ of its length; endocarp not dehiscent; styles
         2–5.
         E. Pedicels and infl. not verrucose: lvs. deciduous.
            F. Styles 2–5: lvs. pinnate or simple and often lobed, usually with excurrent
               veins: calyx-lobes sometimes deciduous.........................18. *Sorbus*
            FF. Styles 5, connate below: lvs. simple, with curving veins, glandular-denticu-
               late, glandular on midrib above: calyx-lobes persistent............19. *Aronia*
         EE. Pedicels and infl. verrucose, or smooth and lvs. persistent: lvs. simple, serrulate.
                                                                                    20. *Photinia*
      DD. Ovary in fr. (core) free to the middle and endocarp at full maturity dehiscent:
         lvs. persistent, entire or serrulate....................................21. *Stranvaesia*
    CC. Carpels wholly connate; styles 5, distinct: fls. in panicels: fr. pear-shaped, yellow,
       3–4 cm. long, with 1 or few large seeds: lvs. evergreen, with excurrent veins.
                                                                                    22. *Eriobotrya*
  BB. Fls. in umbels, racemes or solitary; sometimes paniculate in No. 23.
    C. Carpels 4–many-seeded.
      D. Styles connate at base: lvs. serrate or crenate, rarely entire.
         E. Ovules 4–10 in each cell; calyx tomentose outside; sepals persistent..27. *Docynia*
         EE. Ovules many in each cell; calyx glabrous outside; sepals deciduous.
                                                                                    28. *Chaenomeles*
      DD. Styles free; sepals persistent: lvs. entire............................29. *Cydonia*
    CC. Carpels 1–2-seeded.
      D. Ovary and fr. 2–5-celled; cells 2-ovuled.
         E. Lvs. evergreen: ovary 2-celled; fls. in upright racemes, sometimes panicled: fr.
            black; sepals deciduous..23. *Rhaphiolepis*
         EE. Lvs. deciduous: ovary 2–5-celled; fls. in umbel-like racemes.
            F. Styles connate at base: fr. usually apple-shaped, without or with few grit-
               cells ....26. *Malus*
            FF. Styles free: fr. usually pear-shaped, its flesh with numerous grit-cells.
                                                                                    30. *Pyrus*
      DD. Ovary and fr. incompletely 6–10-celled; cells 1-ovuled.
         E. Fls. usually in racemes; styles usually 5: lvs. serrate or crenate.
                                                                                    24. *Amelanchier*
         EE. Fls. in few-fld. umbels; styles 2–3: lvs. entire or denticulate, narrow.
                                                                                    25. *Peraphyllum*

III. ROSOIDEAE

A. Pistils borne on a flat or convex receptacle, usually many.
  B. Pistils 2–5: lvs. simple.
    C. Petals wanting; fls. in few-fld. corymbs.................................31. *Neviusia*
    CC. Petals present; fls. solitary.
      D. Lvs. alternate: fls. 5-merous, yellow..................................32. *Kerria*
      DD. Lvs. opposite: fls. 4-merous, white..................................33. *Rhodotypus*
  BB. Pistils many.
    C. Carpels becoming drupelets: brs. often prickly.........................34. *Rubus*
    CC. Carpels becoming dry achenes: brs. never prickly.
      D. Lvs. pinnate or lobed.
         E. Style deciduous: fls. yellow or white: lvs. pinnate.................35. *Potentilla*
         EE. Style persistent, plumose: fls. white: lvs. lobed.
            F. Calyx with bracts at base; pistils many: lvs. glandular..........36. *Fallugia*
            FF. Calyx without bracts; pistils few: lvs. glandless...............37. *Cowania*
      DD. Lvs. undivided, serrate, persistent: fls. 8–9-merous: prostrate subshrubs.
                                                                                    38. *Dryas*
AA. Pistils enclosed in a tubular or urn-shaped receptacle.
  B. Pistils 1–4.
    C. Receptacle tubular or campanulate, enclosing the achene loosely or partly; pistil
       usually 1.
      D. Fls. apetalous: lvs. simple, dentate or entire.......................39. *Cercocarpus*
      DD. Fls. with petals.
         E. Lvs. 3-fid at apex: fls. small, yellow..............................40. *Purshia*
         EE. Lvs. 3-pinnatifid: fls. white.....................................41. *Chamaebatia*
    CC. Receptacles urceolate, completely enclosing the 1–4 achenes: lvs. pinnate, small.

D. Receptacles with prickles, at least 1 under each sepal: fr. white (covered with spines in *Acaena*)..42. *Margyricarpus*
   DD. Receptacle without prickles: fr. red: fls. unisexual....................43. *Poterium*
BB. Pistils many: achenes enclosed in the fleshy receptacle: fls. usually large: lvs. pinnate, rarely simple: brs. usually prickly..44. *Rosa*

IV. PRUNOIDEAE

A. Carpels 1, rarely 2: lvs. usually serrate.
  B. Sepals 10; petals wanting or small...45. *Maddenia*
  BB. Sepals 5, petals present.
    c. Style terminal: pith of brs. solid..46. *Prunus*
    cc. Style lateral: pith of brs. lamellate..................................48. *Prinsepia*
AA. Carpels 5: lvs. entire...47. *Osmaronia*

Subfam. I. SPIRAEOIDEAE Focke. Unarmed shrubs, rarely trees or herbs: lvs. simple or compound, with or without stipules: fls. usually small, white to pink or purple, in usually large infl.; carpels usually 5, rarely more or less, free or connate, superior, developing into dehiscent follicles usually with several seeds, or rarely into achenes. (*Spiraeaceae* Maxim.)

1. PHYSOCÁRPUS Maxim. NINEBARK. Deciduous shrubs; bark peeling off in thin strips; buds rather small, with about 5 exposed brown scales: lvs. alternate, petioled, serrate and usually 3-lobed and 3-nerved at base: fls. perfect, in terminal umbel-like racemes; receptacle cup-shaped; sepals 5, valvate; petals spreading, suborbicular, little longer than sepals, white or rarely pinkish; stamens 20–40; pistils 1–5, united at base: follicles usually inflated, dehiscent along both sutures; seeds 2–5, yellowish, shining. (Greek *physa*, bladder, and *karpos*, fruit; referring to the inflated fruit.) Syn. *Opulaster* Raf. Thirteen species in N. Am. and one in N. E. Asia.—Ornamental shrubs of usually spreading habit with bright green foliage and with conspicuous though not very showy white fls. in dense umbels in June; in some species the inflated pods assume a bright red color in late summer.

A. Carpels 4–5, rarely 3.
  B. Pods glabrous ....1. *P. opulifolius*
  BB. Pods pubescent.
    c. Lobes of lvs. acute or acuminate......................................2. *P. amurensis*
    cc. Lobes of lvs. obtuse..3. *P. intermedius*
AA. Carpels usually 2, united half their length.
  B. Mature carpels turgid, styles spreading...............................4. *P. monogynus*
  BB. Mature carpels flattened; styles erect................................5. *P. malvaceus*

1. **P. opulifòlius** (L.) Maxim. Shrub to 3 m.; brts. glabrous or nearly so: lvs. roundish-ovate, 2–7 cm. long, usually 5-lobed, with crenate-dentate obtuse or acutish lobes, glabrous or nearly so beneath, those of the shoots to 10 cm. long, more deeply lobed and usually acute to acuminate: fls. white or pinkish, about 1 cm. across, in many-fld. corymbs 3–5 cm. broad; pedicels and calyx glabrous or sparingly pubescent; stamens purplish; pods glabrous, twice as long as sepals, acuminate. Fl.VI–VII; fr.IX–X. N.D.1:t.14(c). R.I.24: t.153(c). B.B.2:244. B.C.5:2610. (*Spiraea opulifolia* L., *Neillia o.* Brew. & Wats., *Opulaster o.* (L.) Ktze.) Que. to Va., Tenn. and Mich.; occasionally escaped from cult. Intr. 1687. Zone II.—**P. o. lùteus** (Kirchn.) Zabel, var. Lvs. bright yellow at first, changing to bronzy yellow. (*Spiraea o. lutea* Kirchn.) Orig. before 1864.—**P. o. nànus** (Kirchn.) Zabel, var. Dwarf form with smaller less deeply lobed and dark green lvs. (*Spiraea o. nana* Kirchn.) Orig. before 1864.

Closely related species: **P. capitàtus** (Pursh) Ktze. Brs. often sarmentose: lvs. 3–5-lobed, usually stellate-pubescent beneath; pedicels and calyx densely stellate-tomentose; fls. about 1.4 cm. across: pods glabrous at maturity. (*Spiraea capitata* Pursh, *S. o.* var. *mollis* Torr. & Gray.) B. C. to Idaho and n. Calif. Intr. 1827. Zone V.

2. **P. amurénsis** (Maxim.) Maxim. Shrub to 3 m.; brts. glabrous or slightly pubescent: lvs. ovate, subcordate to truncate, 5–10 cm. long, 3–5-lobed, with acute or acuminate doubly serrate lobes, slightly pubescent be-

neath: fls. 1.5 cm. across, in rather loose umbels; pedicels and calyx densely stellate-tomentose; stamens purple: pods usually 3–4, stellate-pubescent, about ⅓ longer than the calyx-lobes. Gt.14:t.489. N.K.4:t.15. (*Spiraea a.* Maxim., *Opulaster a.* (Maxim.) Ktze.) Manch., Korea. Intr. between 1854 and 1860. Zone IV. Similar to *P. opulifolius,* but lvs. and fls. larger.

3. **P. intermèdius** (Rydb.) Schneid. Shrub to 1.5 m.; brts. glabrous or nearly so: lvs. suborbicular to ovate, usually rounded to broad-cuneate, 2–6 cm. long, usually shallowly 3-lobed, with obtuse doubly crenate lobes, sparingly stellate or nearly glabrous beneath: fls. about 1.2 cm. across in rather dense umbels; pedicels and calyx stellate-pubescent or nearly glabrous: pods stellate-pubescent, inflated, nearly twice as long as sepals. B.B.2:244. (*P. Ramaleyi* A. Nels., *P. missouriensis* Daniels, *Opulaster i.* Rydb.) S. Ont. and w. N. Y. to Ill., Mo., Ark., Colo. and S. Dak. Intr. 1908. Zone IV.—**P. i. parvifòlius** Rehd., var. Dense form, with upright crowded brts.: lvs. ovate, acute, rounded to broad-cuneate at base, 1.5-2 cm. long, glabrous: fls. smaller; pedicels and calyx glabrous; bracts oblong, more or less persistent: pods usually 3, pubescent. Orig. before 1918.

Closely related species: **P. stellàtus** (Rydb.) Rehd. Brts. stellate-pubescent: lvs. stellate-pubescent beneath, often acute or acuminate on the shoots: umbels rather small and loose, pedicels and calyx densely stellate-pubescent: pods usually 4, abruptly acute. (*P. ferrugineus* Daniels, *O. alabamensis* Rydb.) S. C. to Ala. and Ga. Intr. 1906. Zone V.

4. **P. monógynus** (Torr.) Coult. Shrub to 1 m.; brts. glabrous or sparingly stellate: lvs. broad-ovate to reniform, rounded or subcordate, 1.5–3.5 cm. long, incisely 3–5-lobed, with rounded, incisely serrate lobes, glabrous or nearly so: fls. 1 cm. across, often pinkish, in rather few-fld. umbels; pedicels and calyx sparingly or rather densely stellate-pubescent; pods 2, rarely 3 or 1, united to about the middle, densely stellate-pubescent, with spreading beaks. G.F.2:5. B.C.5:2611. (*P. Torreyi* S. Wats., *Spiraea monogyna* Torr., *Neillia Torreyi* S. Wats.) S. Dak. and Wyo. to Tex. and N. Mex. Intr. 1879. Zone V. Neat shrub with small lvs. resembling those of *Ribes alpinum.*

Closely related species: **P. glabràtus** (Rydb.) Rehd. Differs chiefly in the glabrous or nearly glabrous pedicels and calyx, somewhat larger fls. and less deeply lobed lvs. with doubly crenate lobes. (*Opulaster g.* Rydb.) Colo. Cult. 1908. Zone V. A more showy shrub than the preceding.—**P. bracteatus** (Rydb.) Rehd. It differs chiefly in the many-fld. infl. with obovate or spatulate, often foliaceous and persistent bracts and in the larger lvs. 2–7 cm. long, broad-ovate, usually 3-lobed with doubly crenate lobes: fls. somewhat larger; pedicels and calyx densely stellate-tomentose. (*Opulaster b.* Rydb., *O. Ramaleyi* A. Nels., in part.) Colo. Cult. 1909. Zone V. Showier than *P. monogynus.*

5. **P. malvàceus** (Greene) Ktze. Shrub to 2 m.; brts. stellate-pubescent: lvs. orbicular to broad-ovate, cordate to truncate, 2–6 cm. long and about as broad, 3–5-lobed with broad rounded doubly crenate-dentate lobes, glabrous or stellate-pubescent above, stellate-pubescent beneath, rarely nearly glabrous: fls. white, about 1 cm. across, in rather few-fld. umbels with cuneate or spatulate caducous bracts; pedicels and calyx densely stellate-pubescent: pods usually 2, stellate-pubescent, flattened and somewhat keeled, dehiscent after falling, with erect beaks. B.M.7758(c, as *Neillia Torreyi*). (*P. pauciflorus* Piper, *Neillia malvacea* Greene.) B. C. to Mont., Wyo., Utah and Ore. Intr. 1896. Zone V.

2. **NEÌLLIA** D. Don. Deciduous shrubs, with slender brs.; buds ovoid, acutish, often superposed, with about 4 exposed scales: lvs. alternate, 2-ranked, doubly serrate and usually lobed, with conspicuous deciduous stipules: fls. perfect, in terminal racemes or panicles, with caducous bracts; calyx-tube

325

campanulate to tubular; sepals 5, erect, short, about as long as the suborbicular to oval petals; stamens 10–30, in 1–3 series; carpels 1–2, with slender terminal styles; ovules 5–10 in each carpel; pods enclosed by the persistent calyx-tube, dehiscent along the inner suture; seeds several, lustrous. (After Patrick Neill of Edinburgh, Scotch botanist; 1776–1851.) About 10 species in China and in the Himal.—Graceful shrubs with spreading, slender usually zigzag brs., bright green, generally ovate lvs. and white or pink fls. in terminal racemes.

A. Racemes forming terminal panicles: fls. whitish; calyx-tube campanulate.1. *N. thyrsiflora*
AA. Racemes solitary: fls. usually pink.
  B. Calyx-tube campanulate ....2. *N. affinis*
  BB. Calyx-tube cylindric, longer than the sepals.
    c. Pedicels short; lvs. pubescent...3. *N. thibetica*
    cc. Pedicels slender, about 5 mm. long; lvs. glabrous......................4. *N. sinensis*

1. **N. thyrsiflòra** D. Don. Upright shrub to 1 or rarely 2 m.; young brts. angular, glabrous: lvs. ovate to ovate-oblong, long-acuminate, cordate, 4–10 cm. long, doubly incised-serrate, 3-lobed, particularly on the shoots, pubescent on the veins beneath or nearly glabrous; petioles 5–10 mm. long: fls. white, short-stalked, in racemes 3–7 cm. long, forming terminal panicles; calyx-tube campanulate, with the lanceolate sepals about 8 mm. long, usually sparingly stipitate-glandular; ovary glabrous except a few hairs on the sutures. Fl.vⅢ–ⅸ. R.H.1888:416. L.I.,t.ined. Himal. Intr. about 1850. Zone (VI). Shrub with rather insignificant fls.; tender, but if killed to the ground the young shoots flower and fruit the same season .

2. **N. affìnis** Hemsl. Shrub to 2 m.; brts. angled, glabrous: lvs. ovate to ovate-oblong, long-acuminate, cordate or subcordate, 5–9 cm. long, lobulate and often with a pair of acuminate lobes at base, slightly pubescent on the veins beneath or nearly glabroùs; petioles 1–2.5 cm. long: fls. pink, in dense racemes 3–8 cm. long; pedicels 2–5 mm. long; calyx-tube campanulate, finely pubescent and usually sparingly stipitate-glandular, about as long as the lanceolate sepals; ovary villous. Fl.ⅴ–ⅵ. W. China. Intr. 1908. Zone V?

Related species: **N. Uékii** Nakai. Lvs. ovate, 4–8 cm. long, pubescent on the veins beneath; racemes 3–5 cm. long; fls. white, campanulate, about 6 mm. long; calyx-tube stipitate-glandular, otherwise glabrous, at maturity densely glandular-bristly. N.K.4:t.13. Korea. Intr. 1906. Zone V.

3. **N. thibética** Franch. Shrub to 2 m.; young brts. nearly terete, pubescent: lvs. ovate, subcordate, long-acuminate, 5–8 cm. long, doubly serrate and lobulate, sparingly pubescent above when young, pubescent beneath, densely so on the veins and veinlets; petioles 8–15 mm. long; stipules ovate, serrate, much shorter than petioles: fls. short-stalked, about 8 mm. long, in rather dense racemes 4–8 cm. long; calyx-tube cylindric, finely pubescent, twice as long as the sepals, at maturity glandular-bristly; ovary silky-pubescent. W. China. Intr. 1910. Zone V?

Closely related species: **N. longiracemòsa** Hemsl. Lvs. usually not lobulate, less densely pubescent beneath or glabrescent; stipules lanceolate, entire: racemes sometimes to 15 cm. long; sepals lanceolate; ovary hairy only at apex. W. China. Intr. 1909. Zone VI?—**N. ribesioìdes** Rehd. Lvs. 3–5 cm. long, incisely lobulate, pilose chiefly on the veins beneath; stipules oblong, entire, shorter than petioles: calyx-tube glabrous or puberulous; sepals triangular; ovary pilose only at apex. W. China. Cult. 1930. Zone VI?

4. **N. sinénsis** Oliv. Shrub to 2 m.; young brts. terete, glabrous: lvs. ovate to ovate-oblong, long-acuminate, rounded or truncate, 4–8 cm. long, incisely serrate and lobulate, sparingly hairy or nearly glabrous; petioles 5–15 mm. long, glabrous; stipules usually lanceolate, entire: fls. pinkish, 1–1.2 cm. long, nodding, in slender racemes 3–6 cm. long; pedicels 3–7 mm. long; calyx-tube

cylindric, glabrous, at maturity with glandular bristles; sepals triangular-ovate, long-acuminate, much shorter than the tube; ovary hairy at apex. Fl. v–vi; fr.viii–ix. H.I.16:1540. B.C.4:2116. B.S.2:95. M.O.175. C. China. Intr. 1901. Zone V. Graceful shrub with slender spreading brs. bearing numerous racemes of nodding pinkish fls.; lvs. bright green.

3. STEPHANÁNDRA Sieb. & Zucc. Deciduous shrubs, with slender brs.; buds superposed, small, with about 4 exposed scales: lvs. alternate, 2-ranked, serrate and usually lobed, stipulate: fls. perfect, white, small, slender-stalked, in terminal corymbs or panicles; calyx-tube cup-shaped; sepals 5; petals as many, of about equal length; stamens 10–20, short; carpel 1, with 2 pendulous ovules; follicles oblique, with lateral style, dehiscent only at base, with 1 or 2 globose-ovoid lustrous seeds. (Greek *stephanos*, crown, and *aner, andros,* man; referring to the persistent crown of stamens.) Four species in E. Asia.

A. Stamens 10: lvs. 2–4 cm. long, deeply lobed.....................................1. *S. incisa*
AA. Stamens 15–20; lvs. 3–8 cm. long, lobulate.....................................2. *S. Tanakae*

1. S. incìsa (Thunb.) Zabel. Shrub to 2.5 m., usually lower; brts. distinctly zigzag, nearly terete: lvs. ovate, long-acuminate, cordate to truncate, 2–4.5 cm., or on shoots to 6.5 cm. long, incisely lobed and serrate, the lower incisions halfway to the midrib, pubescent on the veins beneath; petioles 3–10 mm. long; stipules ovate-oblong to lanceolate, sparingly toothed; fls. 4–5 mm. across, greenish white, in loose terminal panicles 2–6 cm. long; bracts subulate, shorter than the slender pedicels. Fl.vi. Gt.37:537. Gn.88:55(h). B.C. 6:3237. N.K.4:t.14. M.O.t.14. (*S. flexuosa* Sieb. & Zucc., *Spiraea i.* Thunb.) Japan, Korea. Cult. 1872. Zone IV. Graceful shrub with widespreading slender brs. and finely divided bright green lvs. changing to reddish purple in fall; the small clusters of minute white fls. are rather insignificant.

2. S. Tánakae Franch. Shrub to 2 m.; brts. terete or angled: lvs. ovate, long-acuminate, subcordate, 3–8 cm. long, doubly serrate with acuminate teeth and lobulate, the lowest pair of lobes often rather large, spreading and long-acuminate, slightly pubescent on the veins beneath or nearly glabrous; petioles 5–15 mm. long; stipules ovate, serrate: fls. white, about 5 mm. across, in terminal panicles 5–10 cm. long; bracts oblong, often as long as pedicels, partly persistent. Fl.vi–vii. B.M.7593(c). Gt.45:t.1431(c). B.C.6:3237. S.L. 355(h). G.W.4:6. Japan. Intr. 1893. Zone V. More vigorous than the preceding species; lvs. coloring orange and scarlet or bright yellow in fall.

4. SPIRAÈA L. Spirea. Deciduous shrubs; buds small, with 2–8 exposed scales: lvs. alternate, simple, dentate or serrate, or sometimes lobed, rarely entire, usually short-petioled, estipulate, penninerved, rarely 3–5-nerved at base: fls. perfect, rarely polygamous, in umbel-like racemes, corymbs or panicles; receptacle cup-shaped or campanulate; sepals 5, usually short; petals 5, usually rounded and longer than the sepals; stamens 15–60, inserted between the disk and the sepals; pistils usually 5, distinct; follicles dehiscent along the inner suture, with several minute, oblong seeds. (Ancient Greek name of a plant used for garlands, derived from *speira*, wreath or band; probably first used for the present genus by Clusius.) More than 80 species in the temperate regions of the n. hemisphere, in Am. s. to Mex., in Asia to the Himal.—Most of the species have been introduced into cult.; many of them, including numerous hybrids originated in cult., are popular garden shrubs and much planted on account of their decorative fls.

KEY TO THE SECTIONS

A. Infl. a simple umbel or umbel-like raceme; fls. white................Sect. I. *Chamaedryon*
AA. Infl. compound; fls. white to rose-purple.
  B. Fls. in corymbs...Sect. II. *Calospira*
  BB. Fls. in panicles..Sect. III. *Spiraria*

Sect. I. Chamaedryon Ser.

A. Fls. in sessile umbels, without or with very few lvs. at base (in some hybrids the umbels on the lower part of the br. on short leafy stalks).
  B. Lvs. dentate or serrate: stamens about ⅓–½ as long as petals.
    C. Lvs. ovate to oblong-lanceolate.
      D. Umbels all sessile, 3–6-fld.: fls. often double........................1. *S. prunifolia*
      DD. Umbels on the lower part of the branch stalked.......................3. *S. arguta*
    CC. Lvs. linear-lanceolate, glabrous.......................................2. *S. Thunbergii*
  BB. Lvs. entire or crenate-dentate only near apex, often 3-nerved; stamens as long or nearly as long as petals...4. *S. hypericifolia*
AA. Fls. in umbel-like racemes on leafy brts. (sometimes the upper umbels nearly sessile).
  B. Lvs. entire or crenate or dentate near apex.
    C. Lvs. 3-nerved ....5. *S. crenata*
    CC. Lvs. penninerved.
      D. Lvs. glabrous or nearly so: infl. glabrous or slightly pubescent.
        E. Buds long-pointed, with 2 exposed membranous scales.
          F. Lvs. obovate to suborbicular, usually crenate at apex: buds shorter than petiole ....6. *S. nipponica*
          FF. Lvs. generally oblong, entire: buds longer than petioles........7. *S. gemmata*
        EE. Buds ovoid, small, with several exposed scales.
          F. Lvs. usually linear-lanceolate, acute, rarely oblong-obovate......9. *S. alpina*
          FF. Lvs. oval to obovate-oblong, obtuse............................10. *S. virgata*
      DD. Lvs. pubescent on both sides: infl. pubescent.
        E. Buds pointed, with 2 exposed scales, longer than petioles........8. *S. mollifolia*
        EE. Buds ovoid, obtuse, with imbricate scales, shorter than petioles.....11. *S. cana*
  BB. Lvs. serrate or dentate, sometimes slightly lobed (sometimes entire in No. 12).
    C. Stamens longer than petals; sepals reflexed in fr.; infl. racemose, the lower pedicels distant.
      D. Shoots terete, often pubescent: lvs. pubescent or nearly glabrous, often nearly entire ....12. *S. media*
      DD. Shoots angled, glabrous: lvs. glabrous or nearly so...........13. *S. chamaedryfolia*
    CC. Stamens shorter than or as long as petals; sepals erect, spreading in fr.; infl. umbel-like, the pedicels crowded.
      D. Lvs., infl. and follicles glabrous.
        E. Lvs. acute.
          F. Lvs. rhombic-lanceolate, penninerved......................14. *S. cantoniensis*
          FF. Lvs. rhombic-ovate, indistinctly 3-nerved.................15. *S. Vanhouttei*
        EE. Lvs. obtuse.
          F. Lvs. suborbicular, distinctly 3–5-nerved at base, usually 3-lobed. 16. *S. trilobata*
          FF. Lvs. rhombic-ovate to obovate, cuneate at base, penninerved or indistinctly 3-nerved ....17. *S. Blumei*
      DD. Lvs. pubescent beneath.
        E. Infl. and follicles glabrous.......................................18. *S. pubescens*
        EE. Infl. and follicles pubescent...................................19. *S. chinensis*

Sect. II. Calospira K. Koch

A. Corymbs on usually short lateral brts. appearing along the mostly arching brs. of the previous year.
  B. Fls. perfect, white.
    C. Winter-buds short, ovoid, with several exposed scales or with only 2 in No. 20.
      D. Stamens about as long as petals.
        E. Winter-buds with 2 exposed scales, pointed: brts. angled.......20. *S. canescens*
        EE. Winter-buds obtusish, with several exposed scales.
          F. Lvs. serrate at least toward the apex: infl. pubescent.
            G. Lvs. 1–2.5 cm. long.......................................21. *S. Sargentiana*
            GG. Lvs. 3–7 cm. long..22. *S. Henryi*
          FF. Lvs. entire or with few teeth. (See also *S. trichocarpa* under No. 6.)
            G. Lvs. pubescent above; infl. glabrous or sparingly pilose; follicles pilose. 23. *S. Wilsonii*
            GG. Lvs. glabrous above: infl. densely downy; follicles glabrous.24. *S. Veitchii*
      DD. Stamens 2–3 times as long as petals: lvs. doubly serrate............25. *S. Miyabei*
    CC. Winter-buds elongated, longer or about as long as petioles: lvs. doubly or incisely serrate.
      D. Lvs. glabrous, doubly serrate..................................26. *S. longigemmis*
      DD. Lvs. pubescent on the veins beneath, incisely serrate..............27. *S. Rosthornii*
  BB. Fls. dioecious, pink or white; sepals reflexed in fr.: lvs. sharply serrate.
    C. Lvs. glabrous above, pubescent only on the veins beneath, ovate to ovate-oblong. 28. *S. bella*

cc. Lvs. pubescent above, rarely nearly glabrous, more densely pubescent beneath, usually ovate-lanceolate ....29. *S. amoena*
AA. Corymbs terminal on upright shoots of the year.
 B. Stamens as long as petals; fls. white: procumbent shrub; lvs. 1–2.5 cm. long.
 　　　　　　　　　　　　　　　　　　　　　　　　　　　30. *S. decumbens*
 BB. Stamens longer than petals: upright shrubs.
 　c. Infl. very compound, flat, besides the terminal corymb, lateral ones blooming later appear beneath, only small brts. with a single corymb; infl. usually pubescent.
 　　D. Lvs. 4–10 cm. long, usually plane.
 　　　E. Brts. terete; fls. usually rose-colored.
 　　　　F. Ripe follicles diverging...31. *S. japonica*
 　　　　FF. Ripe follicles upright....................................32. *S. Margaritae*
 　　　EE. Brts. more or less angled, rather stiff, nearly glabrous: fls. white..33. *S. albiflora*
 　　DD. Lvs. 1–2 cm. long, bullate: plant rarely taller than 0.25 m...........34. *S. bullata*
 　cc. Infl. consisting of a single corymb, usually convex: follicles not diverging.
 　　D. Brts. striped: sepals reflexed in fr.
 　　　E. Lvs. generally oblong, acute: fls. pink or white..................35. *S. superba*
 　　　EE. Lvs. generally elliptic, obtuse, crenate-serrate: fls. white.......36. *S. betulifolia*
 　　DD. Brts. quite terete: sepals upright or spreading in fr.
 　　　E. Fls. white.
 　　　　F. Corymb puberulous ....37. *S. corymbosa*
 　　　　FF. Corymb glabrous ....38. *S. lucida*
 　　　EE. Fls. rose-colored ....39. *S. densiflora*

Sect. III. Spiraria Ser.

A. Infl. a broad panicle, about as broad as high, sometimes consisting of small panicles. (Hybrids between species of Sect. II and III = Sect. *Pachystachya* Zabel.)
 B. Panicles small, on lateral brts. at the end of last year's brs...........40. *S. fontenaysii*
 BB. Panicles large, terminal on upright brs.
 　c. Lvs. glabrous or nearly so...41. *S. pyramidata*
 　cc. Lvs. pubescent or tomentulose beneath............................42. *S. sanssouciana*
AA. Infl. an elongated panicle, much longer than broad. (Sect. *Spiraria* proper.)
 B. Lvs. glabrous or nearly so.
 　c. Lvs. sharply serrate, except at the very base, acute.
 　　D. Fls. light pink; infl. tomentulose, rather narrow, the lower brts. ascending and not exceeding their supporting lvs...................................43. *S. salicifolia*
 　　DD. Fls. white or slightly pinkish: infl. broad at base, the lower brts. spreading and exceeding their supporting lvs.
 　　　E. Infl. tomentulose: lvs. oblong to oblanceolate.....................44. *S. alba*
 　　　EE. Infl. glabrous: lvs. generally elliptic..............................45. *S. latifolia*
 　cc. Lvs. coarsely serrate above the middle, obtuse: fls. pink.............46. *S. Menziesii*
 BB. Lvs. pubescent or tomentose beneath: fls. pink.
 　c. Follicles glabrous.
 　　D. Lvs. acute at ends, pubescent or thinly tomentulose beneath.......47. *S. Billiardii*
 　　DD. Lvs. obtuse, tomentose beneath...................................48. *S. Douglasii*
 　cc. Follicles pubescent: lvs. usually light tawny beneath, usually oblong-ovate, acute.
 　　　　　　　　　　　　　　　　　　　　　　　　　　　49. *S. tomentosa*

Sect. I. Chamaedryon Ser. Shrubs with usually spreading and arching brs.: infl. a sessile fascicle or an umbel-like raceme on short leafy brts. axillary on the brs. of the previous season: fls. white.

1. **S. prunifòlia** Sieb. & Zucc. Shrub to 3 m., with slender pubescent or nearly glabrous angled brts.: lvs. elliptic to elliptic-oblong, acute at ends, 2–5 cm. long, denticulate, glabrous or finely pubescent beneath; petioles 2–3 mm. long: fls. pure white, about 8 mm. across, on slender pedicels in 3–6-fld. sessile umbels usually with a few leafy bracts at base; petals broad-obovate, longer than stamens: follicles spreading, glabrous. Fl.iv–v. J.C.22:t.12. N.K. 4:t.10. Korea, China, Formosa. Cult. 1864. Zone IV.—The form described above is **S. p. simpliciflòra** Nakai, f. The form commonly cult. is **S. p. plèna** Schneid., var., the type of the species. Young brts. pubescent: lvs. elliptic or ovate, lustrous above, pubescent beneath, of firmer texture; petioles to 5 mm. long: fls. double, about 1 cm. across. S.Z.1:t.70(c). F.S.2:t.153(c). A.G.18:425. F.E.9:503;31:602. Gn.53:185(h). (*S. p. fl. pleno* Bosse.) Intr. from Japan 1843.—*S. p. plena* is a handsome early-flowering shrub with dark green lustrous lvs. turning orange in fall; the single-fld. form is less showy.

2. **S. Thunbérgii** Sieb. Shrub to 1.5 m., with slender spreading brs.: brts. angled, pubescent while young: lvs. linear-lanceolate, acuminate, 2–4 cm. long, sharply serrate, glabrous, bright green: fls. pure white, about 8 mm.

across, slender-stalked, in 3–5-fld. sessile umbels; petals obovate, much longer than stamens: follicles diverging, with spreading terminal style. Fl.iv–v. S.Z.1:t.69(c). G.F.8:84,85(h). S.L.350(h). Japan, China. Intr. about 1863. Zone IV. Graceful early-flowering shrub, the brs. clothed with feathery bright green lvs. turning late in fall to orange and scarlet.

3. × **S. argùta** Zab. (*S. Thunbergii* × *S. multiflora*.) Similar in habit to the preceding, but taller and more vigorous: lvs. oblong-obovate to oblong-oblanceolate, acute, 2–4 cm. long, sharply and sometimes doubly serrate, finally glabrous: fls. pure white, 8 mm. across, in many-fld. umbels usually with small lvs. at base; pedicels glabrous; petals nearly twice as long as stamens. Fl.v. G.C.III.22:3;43:398. G.F.10:443. B.S.2:528. Gg.7:291(h). M.G.1900:16(h). Orig. before 1884. Zone IV. The most free-flowering and the most showy of the early spireas.

Closely related hybrid: **S. multiflòra** Zab. (*S. crenata* × *hypericifolia*). Lvs. obovate, 3–5-nerved at base, serrate above the middle, finely pubescent while young: lower umbels usually on short leafy stalks. Orig. before 1884.

4. **S. hypericifòlia** L. Shrub to 1.5 m., with upright and arching brs.: brts. subterete: lvs. nearly sessile, oblong-obovate to obovate-lanceolate, acute, rarely obtuse, 2–3.5 cm. long, with few small teeth near apex or entire, 3-nerved or penninerved, pubescent or nearly glabrous, grayish green: fls. white, about 6 mm. across; in 5–many-fld. sessile umbels; pedicels pubescent; petals suborbicular, slightly longer than stamens: follicles nearly glabrous, divergent. Fl.iv–v. Ledeb., Ic. Fl. Ross. t.438. S. E. Eu. to Siber. and C. Asia. Cult. 1640. Zone IV. One of the earliest Spireas to bloom.—**S. h. acùta** Ser., var. Lvs. oblanceolate: fls. yellowish white, 3–4 mm. across; petals obovate-spatulate, slightly shorter than stamens: follicles ciliate on the ventral suture. S.O.1,t.55(c, as *S. crenata*). G.O.t.9(c). (*S. acutifolia* Willd.) Cult. 1800.—**S. h. obovàta** (Waldst. & Kit.) Maxim., var. Lvs. obovate, rounded at the usually crenate apex, 3–5-nerved: fls. about 5 mm. across; petals about as long as stamens. S.O.t.56–57(c). G.O.t.11(c). (*S. obovata* Waldst. & Kit.) Cult. 1800.

S. h. × *media* = **S. micropétala** Zab. Lvs. obovate-oblong, entire or serrate at apex, 3-nerved or penninerved: umbels sessile and partly on leafy stalks; petals shorter than stamens. Orig. before 1878.—*S. h.* × *cana* = **S. cinérea** Zab. Lvs. oblong, usually entire: umbels usually sessile on the upper and on leafy stalks on the lower part of the brs.; petals longer than stamens. Orig. before 1884.—*S. h.* × *crenata;* see under No. 3.

Related species: **S. calcícola** W. W. Smith. Low shrub: brts. angled; buds scaly: lvs. obovate to elliptic, obtuse, 4–7 mm. long, entire, glabrous: fls. white, pink outside, in 6–8-fld. umbels; pedicels 2–5 mm. long. Yunnan. Intr. 1915. Zone V.

5. **S. crenàta** L. Shrub to 1 m., with slender brs., finely pubescent when young: lvs. obovate-oblong to oblanceolate, acutish or rounded at apex, cuneate, 2–3.5 cm. long, crenulate above the middle or entire, distinctly 3-nerved, puberulous when young, grayish green: fls. white, about 5 mm. across, in dense puberulous umbels on leafy stalks; petals orbicular-obovate, usually shorter than stamens: follicles finely pubescent, with erect styles; sepals upright. Fl.v. G.O.t.10(c). R.I.24:t.147(c). L.B.1252(c). (*S. crenifolia* C. A. Mey.) S. E. Eu. to Cauc. and Altai. Cult. 1800. Zone V.

S. c. × *media* = **S. pikoviénsis** Bess. Lvs. oblong, 2.5–5 cm. long, with a few teeth at apex or sometimes entire, penninerved to 3-nerved, nearly glabrous: infl. nearly glabrous; petals shorter than stamens: follicles with the upright style somewhat below the apex. (*S. Nicoudierti* Hort.) Found wild in Poland. Intr. 1807. *S. c.* × *cana* = **S. infléxa** K. Koch. Young brts. pubescent: lvs. usually 3-nerved, elliptic-obovate, acute or acutish, pubescent beneath, entire or with a few teeth at apex: infl. pubescent. (*S. conferta* Zab.) Orig. before 1850.—*S. c.* × *hypericifolia* = *S. multiflora;* see under No. 3.

6. **S. nippónica** Maxim. Shrub to 2.5 m., with upright and spreading brs.; brts. angled, glabrous; buds short, with 2 exposed scales: lvs. obovate to oval, broadly cuneate, 1.5–3 cm. long, crenate at the rounded apex, rarely entire, dark green above, bluish green beneath, chartaceous: fls. 8 mm. across in many-fld. umbel-like racemes, on leafy stalks, the lower pedicels often with a leafy bract and sometimes branched; petals orbicular, longer than the stamens: follicles upright, slightly hairy, with spreading style. Fl.vi. B.S. 2:529. (*S. bracteata* Zabel, not Raf.) Japan. Cult 1908. Zone IV. Shrub of rather stiff habit with dark green lvs. remaining green until late in fall and with pure white fls. in showy umbels.—**S. n. rotundifòlia** (Nichols.) Mak., var. Lvs. larger, broad-obovate or orbicular-obovate: fls. somewhat larger. B.M. 7429(c). G.F.7:305. G.C.37:149;43:399. J.L.33:f.43(h). Cult. 1882.—**S. n. tosaénsis** (Yatabe) Mak., var. Lvs. oblong-obovate to oblanceolate, 1–3 cm. long, entire or crenate at apex: fls. smaller, in dense umbels. Ad.19:613(c). (*S. t.* Yatabe.) Japan. Cult. 1935.

Related species: **S. trichocárpa** Nakai. Shrub to 2 m.: lvs. oblong to oblong-oblanceolate, 2.5–5 cm. long, acutish, entire or with a few teeth at apex: infl. pubescent, 2.5–5 cm. across, compound, its lower brs. with 2–7 fls. and often with a leafy bract: follicles pubescent. N.K.4:t.12. G.C.74:87(h). Korea. Intr. 1920. Zone V. Handsome shrub, similar to *S. nipponica*.

7. **S. gemmàta** Zab. Shrub to 3 m.; brts. slender, angled, red-brown, glabrous; buds elongated, pointed, with 2 exposed scales, longer than petiole: lvs. short-petioled, narrow-elliptic to oblong, acutish or obtuse, mucronulate, cuneate, 1–2.5 cm. long, entire, rarely with few teeth at apex, grayish green beneath: fls. white, 6–8 mm. across, in few- to many-fld. umbels, the upper ones sessile with lvs. at base, the lower on leafy stalks; the lower pedicels often with a bract in the middle; petals suborbicular, slightly longer than stamens: follicles diverging at the apex, usually hairy on the ventral suture; style terminal, upright or spreading; sepals spreading. Fl.v. S.H.1:f.289h, 290f-g. (*S. mongolica* Koehne, not Maxim.) N. W. China. Cult. 1886. Zone IV.

Related species: **S. arcuàta** Hook. f. Brts. sparingly pubescent, angled: lvs. elliptic to elliptic-oblong, 1–1.5 cm. long, entire, slightly pubescent: fls. about 6 mm. across, in pubescent umbels about 2 cm. broad, on short leafy brts.; stamens 18–25, slightly longer than petals; follicles glabrous. S.H.1:f.292i. Himal. Cult. 1908. Zone VII?—**S. Zabeliàna** Schneid. Similar to the preceding: lvs. larger, sometimes crenulate near apex, more pubescent: fls. 1 cm. across, in umbels to 4 cm. across; stamens 30–40, slightly shorter than petals; follicles pubescent. S.H.1:f.292k-m. N. W. Himal. Cult. 1921. Zone VI?

8. **S. mollifòlia** Rehd. Shrub to 2 m., with arching, strongly angled brs.; young brts. pubescent, purplish; buds elongated, pointed, with 2 exposed scales, longer than petiole: lvs. short-petioled, elliptic or obovate to oblong, acute at ends, 1–2 cm. long, entire or with a few teeth at apex, silky-pubescent on both sides: fls. white, about 8 mm. across, in rather dense pubescent umbels about 2.5 cm. across, on short leafy stalks: follicles upright, pubescent, with upright or spreading styles; sepals spreading. Fl.vi–vii. W. China. Intr. 1908. Zone V.

9. **S. alpìna** Pall. Shrub to 1.5 m., with upright or spreading brs.; brts. puberulous when young, angled, red-brown; buds small, ovoid, with imbricate scales: lvs. partly fascicled, short-petioled, oblong-obovate to oblanceolate, obtuse or obtusish, mucronulate, 1–2.5 cm. long, entire, glabrous: fls. yellowish white, about 5 mm. across, in small and dense glabrous umbels on short leafy stalks; petals suborbicular, slightly shorter than stamens: follicles diverging, with ascending styles; sepals half-spreading. Fl.v–vi. Pallas, Fl.

Ross. t.20. S.H.1:t.289i,290e-e[3]. N. E. Asia to W. China. Intr. 1886. Zone **V**. Much-branched small-leaved shrub of little ornamental merit.

10. **S. virgàta** Franch. Shrub to 2.5 m., with slender spreading brs.; brts. sparingly villous while young, angled, brown; buds ovoid, with imbricate scales: lvs. short-petioled, oval to obovate-oblong, obtuse, rarely acutish, 5-15 mm. long, entire, rarely denticulate at apex, glabrous above, paler beneath and sparingly pubescent and ciliolate or nearly glabrous: fls. white, about 6 mm. across, in dense hemispheric umbels sparingly pubescent or glabrous; petals suborbicular, about as long as stamens: follicles upright, glabrous, with spreading styles; sepals upright. Fl.v–vi. (*S. myrtilloides* Rehd.) W. China. Intr. 1908. Zone V? Graceful shrub.

11. **S. càna** Waldst. & Kit. Dense bushy shrub to 1 or rarely 2.5 m.; brts. slender, terete, pubescent; buds small, with imbricate scales: lvs. short-petioled, elliptic to oblong, acute at ends, mucronate, 1–2.5 cm. long, entire or rarely with a few teeth at apex, grayish pubescent on both sides, more densely beneath, very silky while young: fls. white, about 6 mm. broad, in dense pubescent umbels on leafy stalks; petals orbicular, about as long as stamens: follicles pubescent, with spreading styles; sepals reflexed. Fl.v. R.I.24:t.148(c). S. E. Eu. to Italy. Intr. 1825. Zone V.

S. c. × *chamaedryfolia* = S. Gieseleriàna Zabel. Lvs. ovate, sharply serrate, rarely nearly entire, pubescent: fls. rather large, in umbels on long leafy stalks, petals as long or slightly shorter than stamens: follicles pubescent on the ventral suture. Orig. before 1884.—*S. c.* × *hypericifolia;* see under No. 4.— *S. c.* × *crenata;* see under No. 5.

12. **S. mèdia** Schmidt. Upright shrub to 1.5 m.; brts. terete, glabrous or pubescent while young; buds small, pointed, with imbricate scales: lvs. ovate to oblong, acute, cuneate, 3–5.5 cm. long, incised-serrate above the middle or sometimes entire, pubescent or nearly glabrous; petioles 1–2 mm. long: fls. in many-fld. glabrous or nearly glabrous umbel-like racemes on usually rather long leafy stalks; petals orbicular, shorter than stamens; disk conspicuous, yellow: follicles pubescent, with spreading or reflexed styles somewhat below the apex; sepals reflexed. Fl.v. S.O.1:t.54(c). R.I.24:t.149(c). N.K.4:t.9. (*S. confusa* Koern.) S. E. Eu. to N. E. Asia. Intr. 1789. Zone IV. Similar to *S. chamaedryfolia*, but of more upright habit, easily distinguished by the terete brts.—**S. m. glabréscens** Simonkai, var. Nearly glabrous.—**S. m. mollis** (Koch & Bouché) Schneid., var. Lvs. villous on both sides: infl. pubescent. (*S. mollis* Koch & Bouché.) S. E. Eu. Cult. 1853.— **S. m. serícea** Reg., var. Lvs. more or less silky-pubescent, sometimes nearly glabrous. N. E. Asia.

S. m. × *chamaedryfolia* = S. oxýodon Zabel. Nearly glabrous; brts. slightly angled: lvs. serrate above the middle; follicles with terminal spreading style. Orig. before 1884.—*S. m.* × *hypericifolia;* see under No. 4.—*S. m.* × *crenata;* see under No. 5.—*S. m.* × *alba;* see under No. 40.

13. **S. chamaedryfòlia** L. Shrub to 1.5 m., with spreading and often arching brs.: brts. glabrous, angled, more or less zigzag; buds acuminate, with few scales: lvs. elliptic-ovate to oblong-lanceolate, acute to acuminate, usually cuneate, 4–6 cm. long, incised-serrate, nearly glabrous, bright green; petioles 5–10 mm. long: infl. several-fld., glabrous, on short-leafy brts., the upper ones sometimes sessile; fls. about 8 mm. across; petals orbicular, shorter than stamens: follicles slightly pubescent, somewhat diverging, with terminal, slightly spreading styles. Fl.v–vi. Ann. Sci. Nat. 1:t.26. (*S. flexuosa* Fisch.) N. E. Asia. Cult. 1789. Zone IV. Stoloniferous shrub with bright green lvs. and rather large fls.—**S. c. stenophýlla** Zab., var. Young brts. purplish; lvs. lanceolate.—**S. c. tránsiens** Zab., var. Lvs. ovate to narrow-ovate, incisely or

doubly serrate.—**S. c. ulmifòlia** (Scop.) Maxim., var. Taller and less spreading, with stouter brs.: lvs. ovate, usually rounded at base and doubly serrate: infl. many-fld., on longer stalks: follicles with upright styles. S.O.1:t.53(c). G.H.t.83(c). R.I.24:t.150(c). (*S. ulmifolia* Scop.) S. E. Eu. to N. E. Asia and Japan. Cult. 1790.

    S. c. × *trilobata* = **S. Schinabéckii** Zabel. Lvs. ovate to oblong-ovate, doubly serrate, the lower ones suborbicular, dark green above; fls. rather large; petals longer than stamens. Orig. before 1884.—*S. c.* × *cana;* see under No. 11. —*S. c.* × *media;* see under No. 12.—*S. c.* × *amoena;* see under No. 29.

    14. S. cantoniénsis Lour. Shrub to 1.5 m., glabrous, with slender arching subterete brs.; buds small, acute: lvs. rhombic-oblong to rhombic-lanceolate, cuneate, 3–5.5 cm. long, incised-serrate, dark green above, pale bluish green beneath; petiole 6–8 mm. long: fls. about 1 cm. across, in rather dense glabrous umbels; petals suborbicular to oval, longer than stamens: follicles parallel, with terminal spreading styles; sepals upright. Fl.vi. B.R.30:10(c). Gn. 34:304. A.G.18:356(h). G.C.II.19:569(h). (*S. Reevesiana* Lindl., *S. lanceolata* Poir.) China, Japan. Intr. 1824. Zone VI. With large pure white fls. and dark lvs. remaining green until late in fall.—**S. c. lanceàta** Zab., var. Lvs. lanceolate: fls. double. (*S. Reevesiana fl. pleno* Hort.) H. F. 1855:t.11 (c). F.S.11:t.1097(c). Cult. 1855.

    S. c. × *chinensis;* see under No. 19.

    15. × S. Vanhoúttei (Briot) Zab. (*S. cantoniensis* × *trilobata*). Shrub to 2 m., with arching brs., glabrous: lvs. rhombic-ovate to rhombic-obovate, acute, rounded or cuneate at base, 2–3.5 cm. long, incised-serrate with obtuse mucronate teeth and usually slightly 3–5-lobed, dark green above, pale bluish green beneath: fls. pure white, 8 mm. across, in many-fld. umbels; petals orbiculate, twice as long as the often partly sterile stamens: follicles slightly diverging; styles half-upright; sepals spreading. Fl.v–vi. Gn.53:251;71:334. G.F.2:317. F.E.14:389;31:600. Gng.5:210(h). S.L.351(h). (*S. aquilegiifolia* var. *V.* Briot.) Orig. before 1866. Zone IV. One of the handsomest of the spring-flowering spireas and much planted.

    16. S. trilobàta L. Shrub to 1.5 m., with slender spreading brs., glabrous; buds ovoid, obtusish: lvs. suborbicular, rounded or sometimes subcordate at base, 1.5–3 cm. long, incisely crenate-dentate, usually 3-lobed and palminerved, pale bluish green beneath; petiole 5–8 mm. long: fls. pure white, in many-fld. umbels; petals longer than stamens: follicles slightly diverging, obtuse, with ascending style; sepals upright. Fl.v–vi. L.B.1271(c). G.F.1: 452. F.E.30:45(h, as *S. crataegifolia.*) N. China to Siberia and Turkest. Intr. 1801. Zone IV. Similar to *S. Vanhouttei,* but smaller in every part.

    S. t. × *chamaedryfolia;* see under No. 13.—*S. t.* × *cantoniensis;* see No. 15.

    17. S. Blùmei Don. Shrub to 1.5 m., with spreading and arching brs., glabrous: lvs. ovate to rhombic-ovate, obtuse, 2–4 cm. long, incisely crenate-serrate and often indistinctly 3–5-lobed, pale bluish green beneath and rather prominently veined; petioles 6–8 mm. long: fls. white, polygamous, in many-fld. rather small umbels; petals roundish obovate, longer or as long as the stamens; follicles parallel, with reflexed or spreading styles. Fl.vi. B.H.8: 129,t(c). N.K.4:t.11(as *S. trilobata*). (*S. obtusa* Nakai.) Japan, Korea. Cult. 1858. Zone VI? Rare in cult.; often No. 16 is cult. under this name.

    18. S. pubéscens Turcz. Shrub to 2 m., with slender arching brs., pubescent while young; buds small, subglobose: lvs. rhombic-ovate to elliptic, acute, broad-cuneate, 3–4 cm. long, incisely serrate, sometimes slightly 3-lobed, pubescent above, grayish tomentose beneath; petioles 2–3 mm. long: fls. 6–8 mm. across, in glabrous many-fld. umbels; petals about as long as stamens: follicles ciliate on the ventral suture, otherwise glabrous, with the spreading styles slightly below the apex; sepals triangular-ovate, upright. Fl.v. G.F.1:331. N. China. Intr. 1883. Zone V.

19. **S. chinénsis** Maxim. Shrub to 1.5 m., with arching brs., yellowish tomentose when young: lvs. rhombic-ovate or obovate, acutish or rounded at apex, rounded or broad-cuneate at base, 3–5 cm. long, incisely serrate and sometimes 3-lobed, finely pubescent and dark green above, yellowish tomentose beneath; petioles 4–10 mm. long: fls. pure white, about 1 cm. across, in densely pubescent many-fld. umbels; sepals ovate-lanceolate, first spreading, later half upright: follicles pubescent with the spreading styles slightly below the apex. Fl.v. B.R.33:t.38(c). (*S. pubescens* Lindl., not Turcz.) E. China. Intr. 1843. Zone VI. Easily recognized by its yellowish tomentum.

S. c. × *cantoniensis* = S. blanda Zabel. Lvs. ovate to oblong, acute at ends, incised-serrate, glabrous above, grayish tomentose beneath: fls. pure white, in pubescent umbels: follicles pubescent, with the spreading styles slightly below the apex. (*S. Reevesiana nova* Hort.) Orig. before 1880. Zone VI.

Related species: S. dasyántha Bge. Lvs. rhombic-ovate, cuneate at base, incisely serrate or lobulate, white-tomentose beneath; infl. grayish tomentose; sepals triangular: follicles tomentulose on the ventral suture. N. China. Cult 1914. Zone V.—S. yunnanénsis Franch. Lvs. orbicular-ovate or oval to obovate, 1–2 cm. long, doubly dentate to lobulate or sometimes partly entire, rounded at apex, pubescent above, densely whitish or grayish tomentose below: umbels 1–2 cm. broad, densely pubescent; stamens about half as long as petals: follicles pubescent. (*S. sinobrahuica* W. W. Sm.) W. China. Cult. 1923. Zone VI?

Sect. II. CALOSPIRA K. Koch. Infl. a compound, flat or hemispheric corymb, broader than high: fls. often pink to purple, sometimes without glandular disk.

20. **S. canéscens** D. Don. Shrub to 2 or sometimes 4 m., with long arching brs.; brts. angled, pubescent; buds short-pointed, with 2 scales: lvs. very short-petioled, broad-oval to obovate, 1–2 cm. long, crenate-dentate above the middle, grayish green, pubescent or sometimes nearly glabrous beneath: fls. white, rather small, in dense hemispheric, pubescent corymbs 3–5 cm. across, on leafy brts. very numerous along the brs.; stamens about as long as or slightly longer than petals: follicles villous, with the styles slightly below the apex and ascending; sepals upright or spreading. Fl.vii. G.C.43:90. Gn. 61:380(h);62:414(h). (*S. cuneata, cuneifolia, flagellata, flagelliformis* and *rotundifolia* Hort., *S. vacciniifolia* Hort., not D. Don.) Himal. Intr. 1837. Zone VII? The arching brs. covered their whole length with clusters of white fls.—S. c. myrtifòlia Zab., var. Lvs. oblong, dentate near apex or entire, dark green above, glaucescent and slightly pubescent beneath. M.G.21:385.

S. c. × *amoena* = S. nívea Zab. Lvs. coarsely doubly serrate, 2–5 cm. long, pubescent: fls. white or pinkish white in looser corymbs to 10 cm. broad. (*S. expansa nivea* Billiard.) Orig. before 1867.—*S. c.* × *salicifolia;* see No. 40.— *S. c.* × *Douglasii;* see under No. 40.

Closely related species: S. uraténsis Franch. Brts. slightly angled: lvs. oblong-oblanceolate to oblong-obovate, 1–1.5 cm. long, entire, obtuse, glabrous, glaucescent beneath: corymbs glabrous, 1.5–3 cm. across, on leafy brts., leafless below the infl.; fls. 5–6 mm. across; stamens longer than petals: follicles pubescent at first, glabrous at maturity, with spreading styles. S. Mong., N. W. China. Intr. 1926. Zone V.—The two following related species resemble *S. bella* in habit; doubtful if now in cult.: S. vacciniifolia D. Don. Brts. terete: lvs. ovate, acute, crenate-dentate, rarely nearly entire, glaucous and nearly glabrous beneath: fls. white, in tomentose corymbs. B.R.26:17(c). P.F.2:98,f.183. (*S. laxiflora* Lindl.) Himal. Intr. 1835. Zone VII?—S. grácilis Maxim. Quite glabrous: brts. terete: lvs. slender-petioled, ovate, obtuse, entire or crenate toward the apex, glaucous beneath: fls. white, in lax corymbs. L.B.1403(c). (*S. vacciniifolia* Lodd., not D. Don.) Himal. Intr. 1824. Zone VII?

21. **S. Sargentiàna** Rehd. Shrub to 2 m., with slender spreading brs.; brts. terete, puberulous, at first, soon glabrous: buds ovoid, obtusish, with

several scales: lvs. short-petioled, elliptic-oblong to obovate-oblong, cuneate, 1–2.5 cm. long with few acute teeth at apex, puberulous above, villous beneath, chiefly on the veins: fls. creamy-white, about 6 mm. across, in dense villous corymbs 2.5–4 cm. across; petals about as long as stamens: follicles nearly glabrous, with spreading, nearly terminal style; sepals half-upright. Fl.vi. W. China. Intr. 1909. Zone (V). Similar to *S. canescens;* close to the following species, but smaller in every part.

22. **S. Hénryi** Hemsl. Shrub to 2.5 m., with spreading brs.; brts. terete, sparingly pubescent or nearly glabrous; buds ovoid: lvs. obovate to oblong or oblanceolate, acute or rounded, cuneate, 2–7 cm. long, usually coarsely dentate toward the apex, slightly hairy above, villous beneath, particularly on the veins; petiole 4–6 mm. long: fls. white, about 6 mm. across, in rather loose pilose corymbs about 5 cm. across; stamens shorter than petals: follicles hairy, slightly spreading. Fl.vi. B.M.8270(c). G.C.72:67. Gn.65:44. J.L.28:f.20. B.C.6:3211. C. and W. China. Intr. 1900. Zone (V).—**S. H. notàbilis** Farquhar. Corymbs larger.

23. **S. Wilsónii** Duthie. Shrub to 2.5 m., with arching brs.; brts. pubescent while young, dull purplish; buds ovoid, obtuse: lvs. very short-petioled, oval to obovate or oblong, obtuse or acutish, cuneate, 2–5.5 cm. long, dentate at apex or entire, dull green and pubescent above, grayish green and villous beneath, particularly on the veins: fls. pure white, about 6 mm. across, in dense glabrous corymbs, 3–5 cm. across; calyx glabrous; petals as long as stamens: follicles spreading, sparingly pilose on the ventral suture. Fl.vi. B.M.8399(c). G.35:851. C. and W. China. Intr. 1900. Zone V.

24. **S. Veìtchii** Hemsl. Shrub to 4 m., with long arching brs.; brts. puberulous while young, reddish, striped; buds ovoid, pointed: lvs. oval to oblong. rarely obovate, obtuse, broad-cuneate, 2–4 cm. long, entire, glabrous above, puberulous and glaucescent beneath; petiole about 2 mm. long: fls. 4–5 mm. across, white, in pubescent, rather dense corymbs 3–6 cm. across; calyx puberulous; stamens longer than petals: follicles glabrous, parallel. Fl.vi-vii. B.M.8383(c). J.L.35:f.98. Gn.89:567. S.L.352(h). C. and W. China. Intr. 1900. Zone V. Handsome shrub.

25. **S. Miyàbei** Koidz. Upright shrub to 1 m.; brts. slightly angled, puberulous while young; buds small, ovoid, with several scales: lvs. ovate to ovate-oblong, acute or acuminate, rounded to broad-cuneate at base, 3–6 cm. long, doubly incised-serrate, green and glabrous or nearly so beneath; petiole 2–5 mm. long: fls. white, about 8 mm. across, in pubescent corymbs 3–6 cm. across; stamens 2–3 times as long as the suborbicular petals: follicles tomentulose, diverging, with subterminal spreading style; sepals spreading. Fl.vi. N.K.4:t.5. (*S. silvestris* Nakai.) Japan. Similar to *S. chamaedryfolia ulmifolia,* but easily distinguished by the compound corymb.—**S. M. pilòsula** Rehd., var. Lvs. larger, to 8 cm. long, pubescent on the veins beneath: infl. sparingly pilose, to 8 cm. across. C. China. Intr. 1907. Zone V.—**S. M. glabràta** Rehd., var. Lvs. glabrous, larger: infl. glabrous, larger. C. China. Intr. 1907. Zone V.

26. **S. longigémmis** Maxim. Shrub to 1.5 m., with spreading slender brs., glabrous when young: buds long-pointed, longer than petioles, with 2 exposed scales: lvs. ovate-lanceolate to oblong-lanceolate, acuminate, cuneate, 3–6 cm. long, simply or doubly serrate, with gland-tipped teeth, bright green, glabrous: fls. white, about 6 mm. across, in rather loose pubescent corymbs 5–7 cm. across; stamens longer than petals; follicles nearly glabrous, with terminal spreading style; sepals spreading. Fl.vi. G.F.7:345. I.T.5:t.192.

B.C.6:3212. G.34:443. N. W. China. Intr. 1887. Zone IV? Graceful shrub with bright green foliage.

27. **S. Rosthórnii** Pritz. Shrub to 2 m., with spreading brs.; brts. sparingly hairy while young; buds elongated, pointed, with 2 exposed scales, often as long as petiole: lvs. ovate to ovate-oblong, acuminate, cuneate or rarely nearly rounded at base, 3–8 cm. long, incisely doubly serrate or lobulate, pubescent on the veins beneath and often loosely pubescent above; petioles 5–8 mm. long: fls. white, about 6 mm. across, in rather loose pilose corymbs 5–8 cm. across on elongated brts.; stamens longer than petals: follicles pubescent, diverging, with spreading styles. Fl.vi. W. China. Intr. 1908. Zone V. Graceful shrub with bright green foliage.

28. **S. bella** Sims. Shrub to 1 m. with slender spreading brs.; brts. nearly glabrous, slightly ridged: lvs. ovate or elliptic-ovate to oblong-ovate, 3–5 cm. long, rounded to broadly cuneate at base, acute, serrate from below the middle, pubescent on the veins beneath or glabrous; petioles 2–4 mm.: fls. dioecious, pink to white, about 5 mm. across, in pubescent corymbs 2–4 cm. broad; stamens shorter than petals in the pistillate, longer in the staminate fl.: follicles pubescent on the inner suture, with spreading styles; sepals reflexed. Fl.vi. B.M.2426(c). L.B.1268(c). (*S. expansa* Wall.) Himal. Cult. 1823. Zone VI?

29. **S. amoèna** Spae. Upright shrub to 2 m.; brts. terete, tomentulose like the infl.: lvs. ovate-oblong to ovate-lanceolate, rounded to cuneate at base, acute to acuminate, serrate usually only in the upper half, 6–10 cm. long, pubescent or sometimes glabrous above, soft-pubescent beneath: fls. dioecious, white or pinkish, in tomentulose corymbs 3–8 cm. broad on mostly long upright brts.; stamens as in no. 28: follicles pubescent. Fl.vii. Ann. Soc. Agr. Bot. Gand. 2:t.72(c). (*S. fastigiata* Wall., *S. expansa* K. Koch, not Wall.) N. W. Himal. Cult. 1843. Zone VI. Close to the preceding species.

S. a. × *? bella* = **S. pulchélla** Kunze. With large corymbs of pink fls. (*S. expansa rubra* Hort.)—*S. a.* × *chamaedryfolia ulmifolia* = **S. nudiflòra** Zab. Lvs. ovate, doubly serrate, nearly glabrous: fls. pinkish white, in compound or sometimes simple pubescent corymbs; longer stamens about twice as long as petals: follicles diverging; sepals reflexed. Orig. before 1890.—*S. a.* × *?* = **S. tristis** Zab. Similar to *S. amoena*, with small white or pink fls. in smaller corymbs; sepals upright in fr. Orig. before 1878.—*S. a.* × *canescens;* see under No. 20.—*S. a.* × *japonica;* see under No. 31.—*S. a.* × *albiflora;* see under No. 31.—*S. a.* × *alba;* see under No. 40.—*S. a.* × *Douglasii;* see under No. 42.

Related species: **S. micrántha** Hook. f. Lvs. ovate-lanceolate, 8–15 cm. long, acuminate, nearly rounded at base, serrate or doubly serrate, pubescent beneath: fls. pale pink, 4–5 mm. across, in loose leafy corymbs to 15 cm. across, densely fulvous-tomentose: follicles pubescent. E. Himal. Intr. 1924. Zone VII?

30. **S. decúmbens** W. Koch. Dwarf procumbent shrub with ascending brs., about 25 cm. high, glabrous; buds small, obtusish, with few scales: lvs. elliptic to elliptic-oblong, acute at ends, 1–3 cm. long, serrate or doubly serrate: fls. white, in small corymbs 3–5 cm. across, terminal on long leafy brts.; fls. imperfectly dioecious; petals about as long as stamens: follicles glabrous, parallel, with terminal upright style; sepals triangular, spreading or recurved. Fl.vi. R.I.24:t.151(c). G.C.II.11:752. M.G.27:186(h). G.M.57:746(h). (*S. lancifolia* var. *d.* Fiori, *S. procumbens* Hort.) S. Eu. Cult. 1830. Zone V. Prostrate shrub adapted for rockeries.

Closely related species: **S. lancifòlia** Hoffmanns. Grayish pubescent: lvs. narrower, serrate only toward the apex; sepals in fr. half-spreading. S.H.1:f. 291o,295d-d'. (*S. decumbens* var. *tomentosa* Poech, *S. Hacquetii* Fenzl & Koch.) N. E. Italy. Intr. 1885. Zone V.—*S. l.* × *decumbens* = **S. pumiliònum** Zabel. Slightly pubescent. S.L.352(h). Orig. before 1900.

31. **S. japónica** L. f. Upright shrub to 1.5 m.; brts. glabrous or puberulous when young, striped or nearly terete: buds ovoid, acute: lvs. ovate to ovate-oblong, acute, cuneate, 2–8 cm. long, doubly incised-serrate, pale or glauces-cent beneath and usually pubescent on the veins; petioles 1–3 mm. long: fls. pale to deep pink, sometimes white, 4–6 mm. across, in much-compound and rather loose, usually puberulous, corymbs; stamens much longer than petals; disk crenulate; follicles glabrous diverging with ascending styles. Fl.vi–vii. (*S. callosa* Thunb.) Japan. Cult. 1870. Zone V. Handsome shrub with upright brs. terminated by large very compound corymbs of usually pink fls.—**S. j. glabra** (Reg.) Koidz., var. Lvs. ovate, glabrous: fls. pink, in gla-brous corymbs. (*S. j.* var. *glabrata* Nichols., *S. glabrata* Lange.)—**S. j. ovali-fòlia** Franch., var. Lvs. elliptic, glabrous and glaucescent beneath: fls. white, in corymbs 7–12 cm. across. W. China. Intr. 1908.—**S. j. acumináta** Franch., var. Lvs. ovate-oblong to lanceolate, acuminate, green and pubescent be-neath at least on the veins: fls. pink, in corymbs 10–14 cm. across. C. and W. China. Intr. 1908.—**S. j. Fortùnei** (Planch.) Rehd., var. Taller; brts. quite terete, puberulous while young: lvs. oblong-lanceolate, acuminate, 5–10 cm. long, sharply and doubly serrate, with incurved callous-tipped teeth, rugose above, glaucous and glabrous beneath: corymbs much compound, puberu-lous; fls. pink; disk usually little developed, sometimes wanting. B.M.5164 (c). F.S.9:t.871(c). B.H.8:129,t.(c). (*S. Fortunei* Planch., *S. callosa* Lindl., not Thunb.) E. and C. China. Intr. about 1850. Zone V.—Forms of this var. are the two following: **S. j. atrosanguínea** Zab., var. Fls. crimson, in tomentose corymbs.—**S. j. rubérrima** Zab., var. Fls. deep pink, in puberulous corymbs.—**S. j. macrophýlla** Zab., var. Lvs. to 14 cm. long, bullate: corymbs small. (*S. Fortunei m.* Simon-Louis.) Orig. before 1866.

S. j. × *albiflora* = S. Bumálda Burvenich. Shrub to 0.75 m., with striped glabrous brts.: lvs. ovate-lanceolate, sharply and doubly serrate, glabrous: fls. white to deep pink; folicles diverging. R.B.17:12,t(c). S.L.353(h). (*S. pumila* Zab.) Orig. before 1890. A very handsome and variable hybrid, often difficult to distinguish from *S. japonica*, but usually of lower, more strictly upright habit and with slightly angled brts.—The best known forms are **S. B. Froèbeli** Rehd., var. A taller plant with broader, ovate-oblong lvs. and bright crimson fls. (*S. callosa F.* Hort.) F.E.31:604.—**S. B.** "Anthony Waterer." Compact shrub with rather narrow lvs. and bright crimson fls. Gn.45:49,t(c). G.C.III.14:365. —Here belongs *S. pruhoniciana* Zeman. (*S. B.* "Anthony Waterer" × *japonica ovalifolia*.)—*S. j.* × *amoena* = S. reviréscens Zab. Brts. slightly angled, pu-bescent while young: lvs. oblong-ovate, acuminate, 5–9 cm. long, incisely or doubly serrate, glaucescent beneath and densely yellowish pubescent on the veins: fls. rose-colored, in tomentulose corymbs; petals ¾ the length of the stamens: follicles small, parallel, pubescent. Fl.vi–vii and ix–x. Orig. before 1890.—*S. amoena* × *albiflora* = S. concínna Zab. Similar to the preceding: brts. pubescent: lvs. ovate-lanceolate, doubly and sharply serrate, pale green beneath and pubescent on the veins, midrib greenish, white near base: fls. pinkish white, in broad leafy corymbs. Orig. before 1890.—*S. j.* × *superba;* see No. 32.—*S. j.* × *corymbosa;* see under No. 32.—*S. j.* × *salicifolia;* see under No. 41.—*S. j.* × *Douglasii;* see No. 42.—*S. Bumalda* × *bullata;* see under No. 34.—*S. Bumalda* × *splendens;* see under No. 35.

32. × **S. Margarìtae** Zabel (*S. japonica* × *superba* [*albiflora* × *corym-bosa*]). Shrub to 1.5 m.; brts. nearly terete, finely pubescent while young, purple brown: lvs. short-petioled, elliptic-ovate to narrow-elliptic, short-acuminate, cuneate, 5–8 cm. long, coarsely and doubly serrate, pale green be-neath and slightly pubescent on the veins or nearly glabrous: fls. 7–8 mm. across, bright rosy-pink, in large leafy puberulous corymbs; calyx pubescent; stamens twice as long as petals: follicles parallel, glabrous, with upright styles; sepals spreading. Fl.vii. Orig. before 1890. Flowering freely in July and sparingly again in August and September.

Similar but less handsome is **S. Fóxii** Zabel (*S. corymbosa* × *japonica*). Brts. striped, nearly glabrous: lvs. elliptic, glabrous: fls. smaller, whitish or pinkish, in large puberulous corymbs: follicles parallel, with spreading styles. Orig. before 1870.

33. S. albiflòra (Miq.) Zab. Shrub to 0.5 m., with stiff upright brs.; brts. angled, glabrous: lvs. short-petioled, lanceolate, acuminate, cuneate, 6–7 cm. long, coarsely or sometimes doubly serrate, with callous-tipped teeth, glabrous and bluish green beneath: fls. white, in dense puberulous corymbs, the terminal one large with many smaller ones below; disk conspicuous: follicles glabrous, not or slightly diverging, with spreading styles; sepals reflexed. Fl.vii–viii. B.C.6:3212. (*S. leucantha* Lange, *S. japonica* var. *a.* Koidz., *S. jap. alba* Nichols.) Cult. in Japan. Intr. before 1868. Zone IV. Compact shrub with profusely produced white fls.

S. a. × *japonica;* see under No. 31.—*S. a.* × *amoena;* see under No. 31.— *S. a.* × *corymbosa;* see No. 35.—*S. a.* × *latifolia;* see under No. 41.—*S. a.* × *salicifolia;* see under No. 41.—*S. a.* × *Douglasii;* see under No. 42.

34. S. bullàta Maxim. Upright shrub to 0.4 m.; brts. villous while young, brown: lvs. short-petioled, roundish-ovate to ovate, acute, 1–3 cm. long, incisely serrate, nearly glabrous, thickish and bullate, grayish green beneath: fls. deep rosy-pink in small and dense corymbs forming usually a terminal corymb 4–8 cm. across; stamens reddish, slightly longer than petals; carpels sometimes 6–8, with usually aborted styles. Fl.vii–viii. Gt.35:t,1216(c). (*S. crispifolia* Hort.) Japan. Cult. 1880. Zone V.

S. b. × *Bumalda* = **S. Lemoìnei** Zab. Habit like *S. albiflora:* lvs. ovate, somewhat bullate: fls. rosy-pink. (*S. Bumalda ruberrima* Lemoine.) Orig. before 1892.

35. × S. supérba (Froebel) Zab. (*S. albiflora* × *corymbosa*). Low shrub with upright brs., nearly glabrous; brts. striped, dark brown: lvs. ellipticoblong to oblong, acute at ends, 4–7 cm. long, simply or doubly serrate: fls. light rose, or whitish pink, 7–8 mm. across, in a solitary terminal corymb; stamens about twice as long as the suborbicular petals; disk conspicuous: follicles nearly glabrous, parallel; sepals reflexed. Fl.vi–vii. (*S. callosa* var. *superba* Froebel.) Cult. 1873.

S. s. × *japonica;* see No. 32.—**S. assímilis** Zab. (*S. Bumalda* × *splendens.*) Similar to No. 35: low shrub: lvs. ovate or elliptic, 3–6 cm. long, rather finely doubly serrate, light green and puberulous beneath: fls. small rosy-pink in a puberulous corymb. Orig. before 1890.

36. S. betulifòlia Pall. Low much-branched shrub, sometimes to 1 m. high: brts. striped, red-brown, glabrous; buds ovoid, acutish: lvs. shortpetioled, broad-oval to elliptic, rounded, rarely acutish at apex, broadcuneate, rarely rounded at base, 2–4 cm. long, doubly or sometimes simply crenate-serrate, grayish green and reticulate beneath and glabrous or sometimes puberulous on the veins; petioles 1–3 mm. long: fls. white, in dense, glabrous corymbs 3–6 cm. across: follicles glabrous, parallel, with upright styles; sepals reflexed. Fl.vi. Pallas, Fl. Ross. 1:t.16(c). S.H.1:f.294n,295s-s'. N. E. Asia to C. Japan. Intr. 1812?, again in 1892. Zone IV?

Related species: **S. Fritschiàna** Schneid. Upright shrub to 1, rarely 2 m.; brts. sharply angled, glabrous, lustrous purple-brown: lvs. elliptic or ellipticovate to elliptic-oblong, 3–8 cm. long, acute to acuminate, usually cuneate, coarsely simply or doubly serrate, pubescent beneath or nearly glabrous; petiole 2–8 mm. long: infl. 3.5–8 cm. across, dense; fls. white or pink in bud: follicles lustrous, glabrous except pilose on the ventral suture. N.K.4:t.6. (*S. koreana* Nakai, *S. angulata* Schneid.) C. China to Korea. Intr. 1919. Zone V.

37. S. corymbòsa Raf. Low shrub, usually sparingly branched, rarely to 1 m.; brts. glabrous or puberulous, terete, purple-brown: lvs. suborbicular to elliptic, acute or obtuse, rounded or broad-cuneate at base, 3–8 cm. long, coarsely and often doubly serrate above the middle, pale bluish green beneath and glabrous or nearly so; petioles 3–8 mm. long: fls. white, rather small, in dense, somewhat convex puberulous corymbs 3–10 cm. broad: follicles upright, glabrous and lustrous; sepals upright. Fl.vi–vii. L.B.671(c). W.D. 67(c). G.O.t.82(c). B.B.2:246. (*S. crataegifolia* Lk.) N. Y. to Ga. and Ky. Intr. 1819. Zone V.

　S. c. × *japonica;* see under No. 32.—*S. c.* × *albiflora;* see No. 35.—*S. c.* × *latifolia;* see under No. 41.—*S. c.* × *Douglasii;* see under No. 42.—*S. c.* × *alba;* see under No. 44.

　Related species: **S. virginiàna** Brit. Slender shrub to 1.2 m.; brts. pubescent when young: lvs. oblong to oblanceolate, 3–5 cm. long, entire or with few teeth near apex, glabrous or finely pubescent on the veins: corymbs 3–5 cm. across, pubescent. B.B.2:246. Va. to N. C. and Tenn. Cult. 1907. Zone V?

38. **S. lùcida** Greene. Upright, sparsely branched shrub to 1 m., glabrous; brts. yellowish brown or brown, terete: lvs. broad-ovate to ovate-oblong, usually acute, sometimes rounded at apex, rounded or broad-cuneate at base, 2–6 cm. long, coarsely serrate or doubly incised-serrate, entire at the lower third or sometimes the lower half, shining above, pale beneath; petioles 3–6 mm. long: fls. white, in rather dense flat glabrous corymbs 3–10 cm. across. Fl.vi–vii. B. C. to Sask., S. Dak., Wyo. and Ore. Cult. 1885. Zone V.

　S. l. × *Menziesii;* see No. 41.

39. **S. densiflòra** Nutt. Low shrub to 0.6 m.; brts. glabrous, terete, dark red-brown: lvs. very short-petioled, oval or elliptic, rounded at ends, rarely acutish, 1.5–4 cm. long, crenate or serrate above the middle, paler beneath: fls. rose-colored, in rather dense glabrous corymbs 1.5–4 cm. across: follicles glabrous, parallel; sepals ovate, obtuse, erect or spreading. Fl.vi. B. C. to Mont., Wyo. and Ore. Intr. 1894. Zone V.

　Closely related species: **S. splèndens** K. Koch. Taller, to 1.2 m.; young brts. puberulous: lvs. oval to elliptic-oblong, sometimes acute, serrate, or doubly serrate, with acuminate teeth, entire toward the base: corymbs finely puberulous or nearly glabrous; sepals triangular, acute. (*S. arbuscula* Greene, *S. rosea* Koehne, not Raf., *S. betulifolia* var. *rosea* Gray.) Ore. to Calif. Cult. 1875. Zone VI? Possibly only a variety of the preceding species.

　S. s. × *Bumalda;* see under No. 35.—*S. s.* × *Douglasii;* see under No. 42.

　Sect. III. SPIRARIA Ser. Infl. a dense panicle, longer than broad; fls. white to rose.

40. × **S. fontenaỳsii** Lebas (*S. canescens* × *salicifolia*). Upright shrub to 2 m., with slender brs.; brts. angled, pubescent while young: lvs. short-petioled, oval to elliptic-oblong, obtuse at ends, 2–5 cm. long, crenate-serrate above the middle, pale bluish green and nearly glabrous beneath: fls. white in pubescent pyramidal panicles 3–8 cm. long; its lower brts. 1–3 cm. long, leafless, terminated by a short and small panicle; petals about as long as stamens: follicles nearly glabrous, spreading. Fl.vi–vii. (*S. fontenaysiensis* Dipp.) Orig. before 1866.—**S. f. alba** Zab., f. is the white-fld. typical form; **S. f. ròsea** Lebas has rose-colored fls.

　Hybrids of similar character are: **S. brachybótrys** Lange. (*S. canescens* × *Douglasii*). Brts. angled, pubescent while young: lvs. narrow-elliptic to oblong, 3–4 cm. long, with a few teeth at apex or serrate above the middle, gray-tomentose beneath: fls. pale rose, in rather dense, usually leafy, less tomentose panicles 3–10 cm. long, with short lateral brts. (*S. pruinosa* Zabel, *S. luxuriosa* Lav.) Orig. before 1867.—**S. microthýrsa** Zab. (*S. alba* × *media*). Glabrous; brts. terete: lvs. obovate to oblong or lanceolate, acute or obtuse, 4–6 cm. long, sharply serrate: fls. white, 6–7 mm. across, slender-pediceled, in rather small glabrous panicles to 4 cm. long or sometimes in few-fld. racemes; petals as long as stamens. Orig. before 1890.—**S. brumàlis** Lange. (*S. alba* × *? amoena*). Brts. puberulous: lvs. oblong-elliptic to oblong, acute at ends, 4–7 cm. long. sharply and often doubly serrate, glaucescent and nearly glabrous below: fls. white, slightly pinkish; infl. a broad terminal panicle with many smaller ones below on leafy brts. Orig. before 1882.

41. ✕ **S. pyramidàta** Greene (*S. lucida* ✕ *Menziesii*). Upright shrub to 1 m.; brts. glabrous, terete, red-brown: lvs. elliptic to oblong, obtuse or acutish, 3–8 cm. long, coarsely and sometimes doubly serrate above the middle, rarely below, glabrous or nearly so; petioles 2–5 mm. long: fls. white or pinkish in rather dense pyramidal, puberulous or sometimes glabrous panicles. Fl.vii. Occasionally with the parents from B. C. to Ore. and Idaho. Intr. 1911. Zone V.

Hybrids of similar character are: **S. conspícua** Zab. (*S. albiflora* ✕ *? latifolia*). Brts. slightly angled: lvs. elliptic-oblong, acute at ends, sharply serrate, nearly glabrous: fls. pinkish white, in broad-pyramidal puberulous panicles; stamens somewhat longer than petals. Orig. about 1875.—**S. syringaeflòra** Lemoine (*S. albiflora* ✕ *salicifolia*). Brts. slightly angled: lvs. oblong-lanceolate to lanceolate, acuminate, serrate above the middle, nearly glabrous beneath: fls. pink in pyramidal tomentulose panicles, usually with smaller panicles below; stamens twice as long as petals. Orig. before 1885.—**S. semperflòrens** Zab. (*S. japonica* ✕ *salicifolia*). Brts. terete: lvs. oblong-lanceolate, sharply and doubly serrate, glaucescent and nearly glabrous beneath: fls. rose-pink, rather large, in much-branched, broad-pyramidal puberulous panicles; stamens nearly twice as long as petals. (*S. kamaonensis* var. *spicata* Billiard.) Cult. 1870.—**S. notha** Zab. (*S. corymbosa* ✕ *latifolia*). Lvs. oval or ovate to elliptic, obtuse or acutish, broad-cuneate or rounded at base, 3–6 cm. long, coarsely or doubly serrate, glabrous or nearly so: fls. white or pinkish, in pyramidal glabrous panicles; stamens almost twice as long as petals. Orig. before 1890.

42. ✕ **S. sanssouciàna** K. Koch (*S. Douglasii* ✕ *japonica*). Shrub to 1.5 m.; brts. tomentulose while young, striped: lvs. oblong to oblong-lanceolate, usually obtusish, cuneate, 6–9 cm. long, coarsely and often doubly serrate, entire at the lower third or lower half, pale green and tomentulose beneath: fls. rose, in terminal tomentulose corymbs, composed of dense pyramidal obtuse panicles; stamens nearly twice as long as petals: follicles slender, glabrous, parallel, with spreading style; sepals recurved. Fl.vii–viii. B.M.5169(c). I.H.8:286,t(c). Gn.12:189. (*S. Nobleana* Hook., *S. japonica paniculata* Hort.) Orig. before 1857.

Hybrids of similar character are: **S. Watsoniàna** Zab. (*S. Douglasii* ✕ *splendens*). Lvs. elliptic-oblong to oblong, acute or obtusish, usually rounded at base, serrate usually only above the middle, grayish tomentulose beneath: fls. rose, in dense pyramidal tomentulose panicles: follicles small. (*S. Nobleana* Zab., not Hook., *S. subvillosa* Rydb.) Orig. in cult. before 1890, also found wild in Ore.—**S. pachystáchys** Zab. (*S. corymbosa* ✕ *Douglasii*). Similar to the preceding, but lvs. broader, elliptic to elliptic-oblong, rounded at base, very short-petioled: fls. light rose: follicles longer than the reflexed sepals. Orig. before 1878.—**S. intermèdia** Lemoine (*S. albiflora* ✕ *Douglasii*). Similar to *S. syringaeflora*, but the lvs. tomentulose beneath.—**S. rubra** Zab. (*S. amoena* ✕ *Douglasii*). Lvs. oblong-lanceolate, 7–9 cm. long, simply or doubly serrate toward the apex, grayish tomentulose beneath; petioles to 8 mm. long: fls. deep rose, in broad-pyramidal or ovoid tomentose panicles: follicles pubescent. (*S. ruberrima* Dipp., *S. expansa rubra* Hort.) Orig. before 1885.

43. **S. salicifòlia** L. Strictly upright shrub with slightly angled yellowish brown brts. puberulous when young: buds small, ovoid, scaly: lvs. short-petioled, oblong-lanceolate to lanceolate, acute at ends, 4–7 cm. long, sharply and closely, sometimes doubly serrate, glabrous and light green beneath: fls. rose, in slender pyramidal pubescent panicles with ascending brs.; calyx puberulous; stamens nearly twice as long as petals: follicles nearly parallel, ciliate on the inner suture, with recurved style; sepals ascending. Fl.vi–vii. S.O.1:t.50(c). R.I.24:t.152(c). S. E. Eu. to N. E. Asia, and Japan. Cult. 1586. Zone IV. Spreading by suckers; attractive in summer with its elon-

gated panicles of rose-colored fls.—**S. s. grandiflòra** Loud., var. With larger, light pink fls. L.B.1988(c). Intr. 1826.

S.s. × *alba* = **S. rosálba** Dipp. Lvs. generally lanceolate: fls. light rose, in panicles slender toward the apex, broad at base. Cult. 1892.—*S. s.* × *latifolia* = **S. rubella** Dipp. Similar to the preceding, but lvs. broader. Cult. 1892.— *S. s.* × *canescens;* see No. 40.—*S. s.* × *albiflora:* see under No. 41.—*S. s.* × *japonica;* see under No. 41.—*S. s.* × *Douglasii;* see No. 47.

44. S. alba Du Roi. Upright shrub to 2 m.; brts. puberulous while young, reddish brown, angled: lvs. short-petioled, oblong to narrow-oblanceolate, acute at ends, 3–6 cm. long, sharply serrate, puberulous on the veins beneath or nearly glabrous: fls. white, in leafy pyramidal tomentulose panicles, broad at base; stamens white, longer than the petals: follicles glabrous; sepals upright. Fl.vi–viii. W.D.133(c). B.B.2:245. (*S. salicifolia* var. *paniculata* Ait., *S. lanceolata* Borkh.) N. Y. to Mo., s. to Ga. and Miss. Intr. 1759. Zone IV.

S. a. × *corymbosa* = **S.** difformis Zab. Lvs. elliptic to lanceolate-oblong, serrate, glabrous or nearly so: fls. white, in a wide-spreading nearly glabrous panicle. Gn.84:348. Orig. about 1875.—*S. a.* × *media;* see under No. 40.— *S. a.* × *amoena;* see under No. 40.—*S. a.* × *salicifolia:* see under No. 43.—*S. a.* × *Douglasii;* see under No. 47.—*S. a.* × *tomentosa;* see under No. 49.

45. S. latifòlia (Ait.) Borkh. Shrub to 1.5 m.; brts. glabrous, bright or dark red-brown, angled; lvs. short-petioled, broad-elliptic or obovate to oblong, acute at ends, rarely obtuse at apex, 3–7 cm. long, coarsely and often doubly serrate, glabrous and slightly bluish beneath: fls. white or slightly pinkish, in glabrous broad-pyramidal panicles; stamens longer than petals; disk usually pinkish: follicles glabrous, with spreading style. Fl.vi–viii. W.D.66(c). Em. 485,t(c). G.C.43:417. (*S. salicifolia* var. *l.* Ait., *S. carpinifolia* Willd., *S. canadensis* Hort., *S. bethlehemensis* Hort., partly.) Nfd. and Can. to N. C. Cult. 1789. Zone II.

S. l. × *albiflora;* see under No. 41.—*S. l.* × *corymbosa;* see under No. 41.— *S. l.* × *salicifolia;* see under No. 43.—*S. l.* × *Douglasii;* see under No. 47.

46. S. Menzièsii Hook. Upright shrub to 1.5 m.; brts. puberulous when young, striped, brown, older ones dark purple: lvs. oblong-obovate to oblong, obtuse at ends, sometimes acute, 3–7 cm. long, coarsely and unequally serrate above the middle; pale green and glabrous or puberulous on the veins beneath; petioles 3–5 mm. long: fls. small, rose, in rather narrow and dense pubescent panicles 10–20 cm. long; stamens more than twice as long as petals: follicles glabrous, with spreading styles; sepals reflexed. Fl.vi–viii. (*S. Douglasii* var. *M.* (Hook.) Presl.) Alaska to Ore. Intr. 1838. Zone V. Handsome shrub with rose-colored flowers in summer.

S. M. × *lucida;* see No. 41.

47. × **S. Billiárdii** Herincq (*S. Douglasii* × *salicifolia*). Shrub to 2 m.; brts. pubescent, brown; lvs. short-petioled, oblong to oblong-lanceolate, acute at ends, 5–8 cm. long, sharply and often doubly serrate except at the lower third, usually grayish tomentulose beneath, at least when young: fls. bright rose, in tomentulose, usually rather narrow and dense panicles 10–20 cm. long; stamens nearly twice as long as petals: follicles glabrous, parallel, with spreading styles. Fl.vi–viii. H.F.1855:t.2(c). F.E.18:613(h). (*S. Menziesii* Zab., in part.) Orig. before 1854. Zone IV. Here belong probably *S. Lenneana, S. triumphans, S. eximia, S. Constantiae* Hort.

Similar hybrids: **S. fulvéscens** Dipp. (*S. alba* or *tomentosa* × *Douglasii*). Brts. yellowish tomentose: lvs. grayish or whitish tomentose beneath, sharply serrate above the middle, thinly tomentulose above, with fascicles of small lvs. in the axils of the upper lvs.: fls. bright rose in rather narrow panicles. (*S. Menziesii* f. *eriophylla* Zab.) Orig. before 1885.—**S. macrothýrsa** Dipp. (*S. Douglasii* × *latifolia*). Lvs. elliptic to obovate-elliptic, nearly glabrous above,

341

tomentulose and light green beneath: fls. bright pink, in dense panicles with almost horizontally spreading brs. (*S. Menziesii* var. *m.* Zab.) Cult. 1870.

48. **S. Douglásii** Hook. Shrub to 2.5 m.; brts. tomentose, reddish brown, striped: lvs. oblong to narrow-oblong, obtuse or acutish at ends, 3–10 cm. long, unequally serrate above the middle, white-tomentose beneath; petioles 2–4 mm. long: fls. deep rose, in rather narrow or sometimes broad tomentose panicles 10–20 cm. long; stamens twice as long as the obovate petals: follicles glabrous, lustrous, with upright-spreading style; sepals recurved. Fl.vii–viii. B.M.5151(c). F.S.2:t.66(c). R.H.1846:101,t(c). B. C. to Calif. Intr. 1827. Zone IV. Spreading by suckers, with large panicles of rosy pink fls.

S. D. × *canescens;* see under No. 40.—*S. D.* × *japonica;* see No. 42.—*S. D.* × *splendens;* see under No. 42.—*S. D.* × *corymbosa;* see under No. 42.—*S. D.* × *albiflora;* see under No. 42.—*S. D.* × *amoena;* see under No. 42.—*S. D.* × *salicifolia;* see No. 47.—*S. D.* × *alba* or *tomentosa;* see under No. 47.—*S. D.* × *latifolia;* see under No. 47.

49. **S. tomentòsa** L. HARDHACK. Upright shrub to 1.2 m.; brts. brownish tomentose, angled; lvs. ovate to ovate-oblong, acute, 3–7 cm. long, unequally and often doubly serrate, rugulose above, yellowish or grayish tomentose beneath; petioles 1–4 mm. long: fls. deep rose or rose-purple, in narrow and dense, brownish tomentose panicles 8–20 cm. long; stamens somewhat longer than the obovate petals: follicles pubescent, usually diverging; sepals reflexed. Fl.vii–ix. S.O.1:t.51(c). Em.485,t(c). B.B.2:245. G.M.5:344. N. Scotia to Ga., w. to Man. and Kans. Intr. 1736. Zone IV.—**S. t. alba** West., var. Fls. white. F.E.8833. Gng.5:149. (*S. t.* f. *albiflora* Macbr.) Cult. 1770.

S. t. × *Menziesii* = S. **pallidiflòra** Zab. Lvs. elliptic-oblong, abruptly acute, serrate only above the middle, light brownish tomentose beneath: fls. light pink: follicles sparingly pubescent, more densely on the ventral suture. Orig. before 1870.—*S. t.* × *Douglasii;* see under No. 47.—The spontaneous hybrid S. sub-canéscens Rydb. (*S. alba* × *tomentosa*) is probably not in cult.

5. **PENTACTÌNA** Nakai. Deciduous shrub; winter-buds with several outer pubescent scales: lvs. alternate, subsessile, dentate, estipulate: fls. perfect, small, in pendulous panicles; sepals 5; petals 5, linear, involute in bud; stamens 20; pistils 5, free, 2-ovuled: follicles glabrous, dehiscent on both sutures; seed spindle-shaped, brown. (Greek *penta-* five, *actine,* ray; referring to the 5 linear petals.) One species in Korea.

P. rupícola Nakai. Decumbent shrub, to 0.7 m.; brts. angled, glabrous; lvs. elliptic to oblanceolate, acute at ends, 2–3 cm. long, with few coarse teeth, glaucescent and sparingly pilose beneath: fls. in elongated panicles 6–8 cm. long; pedicels about 1 mm. long; sepals triangular, reflexed in fr.; petals linear, 5 mm. long; stamens short, white. Fl.vi; fr.ix. Nakai, Rep. Veg. Diamond Mts. t.1. Intr. 1918. Zone V. Suited for rockeries.

6. **SIBIRAÈA** Maxim. Deciduous shrubs; buds with 2–4 exposed scales, glabrous: lvs. alternate, subsessile, narrow, entire, estipulate, involute in bud: fls. polygamo-dioecious, small, short-pediceled, in terminal panicled racemes; calyx-tube campanulate; sepals short, erect; petals roundish-obovate, longer than sepals; stamens about 25, longer than petals in the stam. fls., half as long in the pist. fls.; pistils usually 5, connate at base: follicles oblong, upright, dehiscent along the whole ventral suture and on the dorsal one near apex; seeds usually 2, rather large, albuminous. (Name from Siberia, the habitat of the type species.) Two species in Siberia, W. China and S. E. Eu.

S. laevigàta (L.) Maxim. Shrub to 1.5 m., with stout upright terete and glabrous brs.: lvs. cuneate-oblong, obtuse or acutish, usually mucronulate, 4–10 cm. long, gradually narrowed at base, bluish green, glabrous; fls. white, in glabrous panicles 8–12 cm. long: follicles parallel, about 4 mm. long. Fl.v. G.O.t.89(c). S.O.2:t.49(c). S.B.2:537. S.H.1:f. 297e-f[1], 298i-p. (*Spiraea l.* L., *Sibiraea altaiensis* Schneid.) Siberia. Intr. 1774. Zone IV.—**S. l. angustàta** Rehd., var. Lvs. narrow-lanceolate or oblanceolate, rarely oblong, acute: infl. puberulous. W. China. Intr. 1908. Zone V.—**S. l. croàtica** (Degen) Schneid., var. Lvs. obtuse, sessile or subsessile: sepals acute, triangular. S. E. Eu. Cult. 1933.

Closely related species: **S. tomentòsa** Diels. Shrub to 0.6 m.: lvs. oblong-obovate to oblanceolate, acute and mucronate, densely silky tomentose beneath, glabrous above: fls. greenish yellow, in dense panicles about 5 cm. long. S. W. China. Intr. 1915.

7. PETROPHÝTUM Rydb. Low evergreen prostrate subshrub: lvs. crowded, generally spatulate, entire, estipulate: fls. small, white, short-pediceled, in terminal racemes, sometimes branched at base; sepals 5, valvate; petals 5, imbricate; stamens about 20; disk entire; pistils 3–5, hairy; style slender, longer than stamens: follicles leathery, dehiscent on both sutures; seeds few linear. (Greek *petros*, rock, and *phyton*, plant; alluding to the habitat of the plant.) Five species in W. N. Am.

P. caespitòsum (Nutt.) Rydb. Densely cespitose, forming flat patches on rocks: lvs. oblanceolate, obtuse and mucronulate, 6–15 mm. long, 1-ribbed, silky-pubescent: fls. small, white, in dense upright spikes 1.5–4 cm. long, on upright peduncles 2–8 cm. long; petals spatulate, obtuse, 1.5 mm. long; stamens exserted. Fl.vii–viii. Bot. Gaz. 15:t.14. S.H.1:f.297c-d[1]. S.L.37(h). N.F.11:f.97(h). (*Spiraea caespitosa* Nutt., *Eriogynia c.* S. Wats., *Luetkea c.* Ktze.) Mont., S. Dak. to Calif. and N. Mex. Cult. 1900. Zone V. Adapted for rockeries; likes limestone soil.

Related species: **P. cineráscens** (Piper) Rydb. Lvs. oblanceolate, 3-ribbed, 1–2.5 cm. long, gray, pilose: infl. short and dense. N.F.11:f.98(h). Wash. Cult. 1937. Zone VI?

8. LUÈTKEA Bong. Cespitose undershrub with stoloniferous creeping stems: lvs. alternate, usually twice trifid, estipulate: fls. small, short-pediceled, in upright racemes; sepals 5, acute, valvate; petals 5, oval, contorted in bud; stamens 20, shorter than petals; disk 10-lobed; pistils 5, as long as stamens: follicles dehiscent on both sutures; seeds several, linear-lanceolate. (After Fr. Luetke [Fedor Petrovich Litke], sea captain, in command of the fourth Russian voyage around the world [1826–29]; 1779–1882.) One species.

L. pectinàta (Pursh) Ktze. Glabrous undershrub with long trailing brs. forming dense carpets: lvs. twice or simply trifid, with linear 3-pointed lobes, with the margined slender petiole 1–2 cm. long, bright green: fls. white, 8 mm. across, in racemes 2–5 cm. long, terminating ascending leafy brts. Fl.vii–viii. (v–vi in cult.) Bot. Gaz. 15:t.14. Hooker, Fl. Bor. Am. t.88. (*Spiraea p.* Torr., *Eriogynia p.* Hook.) Alaska to Calif., high mtns. Cult. 1890. Zone V. Adapted for rockeries; similar to *Saxifraga decipiens*.

9. SORBÀRIA A. Br. Deciduous shrubs; brts. terete: buds ovoid, with several scales: lvs. alternate, large, pinnate, with serrate lfts., stipulate: fls. small, white, in large terminal panicles; calyx-tube cup-shaped; sepals 5, broad and short, reflexed; petals 5, oval to orbicular, imbricate; stamens 20–50, nearly as long or longer than petals; carpels 5, opposite to sepals, connate at base; follicles dehiscent on the ventral suture; seeds several. (From Sorbus; the lvs. resembling those of the Mountain-Ash.) Syn.: *Basi-*

lima Raf., *Schizonotus* Lindl. Seven species in E. Asia.—Rather large shrubs
with pinnate bright green lvs. and conspicuous panicles of white fls.

A. Lfts. doubly and sharply serrate, usually more than 1.5 cm. wide.
  B. Panicle with upright brs., rather dense: frs. upright.
    c. Stamens 40–50; lfts. with usually 20 pairs of veins....................1. *S. sorbifolia*
    cc. Stamens about 20: lfts. with 25 or more pairs of veins................2. *S. assurgens*
  BB. Panicle with spreading brs., loose: frs. on recurved pedicels.
    c. Lfts. with mostly simple hairs beneath when young; stamens as long as petals.
                                                                   3. *S. tomentosa*
    cc. Lfts. with stellate hairs beneath or glabrous; stamens longer than petals.
                                                                   4. *S. arborea*
AA. Lfts. simply or nearly simply serrate, less than 1.5 cm. wide, glabrous....5. *S. Aitchisonii*

1. **S. sorbifòlia** (L.) A. Br. Upright shrub, to 2 m., with stout stems;
brts. glabrous or puberulous: lfts. 13–23, lanceolate or ovate-lanceolate, long-
acuminate, 5–10 cm. long, doubly serrate, usually glabrous or nearly so beneath: fls. about 8 mm. across, in panicles 10–25 cm. long, more or less puberulous; stamens twice as long as petals; calyx glabrous: follicles glabrous,
with terminal recurved style. Fl.vi–vii. S.O.1:t.58(c). Gn.23:248. F.E.30:
777(h). (*Spiraea s.* L., *Sp. tobolskiana* Hort., *Basilima s.* Raf.) N. Asia from
Ural to Japan; sometimes escaped from cult. Cult. 1759. Zone II. One of the
first shrubs to burst into leaf in spring; freely spreading by suckers.—**S. s.
stellípila** Maxim., var. Lvs. beneath more or less stellate-pubescent: pedicels
and calyx puberulous: follicles pubescent. N.K.4:t.1. G.W.15:651(h). (*S. s.*
Schneid.) E. Asia. Cult. 1900.

Closely related species: **S. grandiflòra** (Sweet) Maxim. Shrub to 1 m.: lfts.
fewer, acute or acutish, obtusely doubly serrate, glabrous: fls. larger, in a
rather few-fld. corymbose infl.; stamens as long as petals. Gt.9:t.295(c).
(*Spiraea sorbifolia* var. *alpina* Pall., *Spiraea g.* Sweet.) E. Siber. Intr. 1852.
Zone II?

2. **S. assúrgens** Vilm. & Bois. Shrub to 3 m., with upright or ascending
stems: lfts. 13–17, oblong-lanceolate to narrow-lanceolate, long-acuminate,
often falcate, 5–8 cm. long, sharply doubly serrate, pubescent on the veins
beneath or nearly glabrous, with 25 or more pairs of veins: panicle 10–16 cm.
long, less dense than in the first species: calyx glabrous: stamens slightly
longer than petals: follicles with terminal slightly recurved or spreading
style, glabrous. Fl.vii. S.L.343(h). M.G.32:169(h). China? Intr. 1896. Zone
V. Similar in habit to No. 3.

3. **S. tomentòsa** (Lindl.) Rehd. Shrub to 6 m., with wide-spreading
brs.; brts. and petioles glabrous or nearly so: lfts. 15–21, lanceolate to narrow-
lanceolate, long-acuminate, 5–10 cm. long, doubly serrate, with simple hairs
on the veins beneath while young: fls. about 6 mm. across, in loose puberulous panicles with spreading brs., 20–30 cm. long and 15–20 cm. broad; stamens about as long as petals: follicles glabrous, 2.5 mm. long, with terminal
reflexed style, on recurved pedicels. Fl.vii–viii. F.S.2:t.108. B.R.31:33(c).
G.C.43:415(h). Gn.86:29(h);87:285(h). (*S. Lindleyana* Maxim., *Spiraea L.*
Wall.) Himal. Cult. 1840. Zone VII. Graceful shrub with large often nodding panicles.

4. **S. arbòrea** Schneid. Spreading shrub to 6 m.; brts. and petioles usually
slightly stellate-pubescent: lfts. 13–17, ovate-oblong to lanceolate, long-
acuminate, 4–10 cm. long, sharply doubly serrate, stellate-pubescent or nearly
glabrous beneath: fls. 6 mm. across, in large panicles similar to those of the
preceding species: stamens much longer than petals: follicles with the spreading style below the apex, on recurved pedicels. Fl.vii–viii. Gn.88:126. G.M.
61:603. G.35:697. C. and W. China. Intr. 1908. Zone V. Similar to the
preceding species, but much hardier.—**S. a. subtomentòsa** Rehd., var. Brts.
and petioles pubescent: lfts. elliptic-oblong, to oblong-lanceolate, densely

stellate-pubescent or tomentose beneath, with close-set veins. W. China.—
S. a. glabràta Rehd., var. Brts. and petioles glabrous, often purplish: lfts.
lanceolate to narrow-lanceolate, glabrous; stamens 2–3 times as long as
petals.

5. **S. Aitchisóni** Hemsl. Shrub to 3 m. with upright or ascending stems;
brs. glabrous, usually bright red when young: lfts. 15–21, lanceolate to linear-
lanceolate, acuminate, cuneate at base, 4–8 cm. long and about 1 cm. broad,
simply or slightly doubly serrate, quite glabrous: fls. about 1 cm. across, in
upright glabrous panicles 20–25 cm. long and 10–15 cm. wide, leafy at base:
follicles with recurved terminal style; stamens longer than petals. Fl.VII–VIII.
G.C.28:255;38:114;43:397. Gn.68:143;77:560. Gn.M.9:75(h). (*S. angustifolia* Zab., *Spiraea A.* Hemsl.) Afghan., Kashmir. Intr. 1895. Zone (V) VI.
Handsome shrub, the bright green graceful foliage contrasting well with the
bright red stems and petioles.

10. **CHAMAEBATIÀRIA** Maxim. Deciduous upright shrub, stellate-
pubescent and glandular: lvs. alternate, bipinnatisect, with numerous minute
segments; stipules lanceolate, entire: fls. white, in terminal panicles; calyx-
tube turbinate, with 5 erect sepals; petals 5, suborbicular, upright; stamens
about 60, inserted at the margin of the disk; carpels 5, pubescent, connate
at base, 6–8-ovuled: follicles dehiscent on the ventral suture and at the apex
on the dorsal one: seeds few, terete. (Name in allusion to the similarity of
the plant to Chamaebatia.) One species.

C. **Millefòlium** (Torr.) Maxim. Aromatic shrub to 1.5 m.: lvs. short-
petioled, ovate-oblong to oblong-lanceolate in outline, 2–7 cm. long, the primary segments linear, deeply pinnatisect with close-set obtuse segments 1–2
mm. long and occasionally toothed: fls. about 1.5 cm. across, short-pediceled,
in tomentose leafy panicles 8–15 cm. long; sepals lanceolate: follicles pubescent or nearly glabrous, about 5 mm. long, with upright style. Fl.VII–VIII.
B.M.7810(c). G.F.2:509. G.C.40:183. Gn.88:73. M.D.1905:t.11(h). M.G.23:
208(h). (*Spiraea M.* Torr., *Sorbaria M.* Focke.) Idaho and Nev. to Ariz. and
Calif. Cult. 1878. Zone V. Shrub with aromatic glandular pubescence;
retaining a few lvs. at the end of the brts. during the winter and leafing early
in spring; prefers sunny and well drained position.

11. **EXOCHÓRDA** Lindl. Deciduous shrubs; buds ovoid, pointed, glabrous, with imbricate scales: lvs. alternate, petioled, entire or serrate, estipulate or occasionally with small caducous stipules: fls. white, rather large,
in terminal racemes; calyx-tube broad-turbinate; sepals 5, very short and
broad; petals 5, broadly obovate, clawed, imbricate; stamens 15–30, inserted
at the margin of the large disk, with short filaments; carpels 5, connate: fr.
a 5-angled deeply furrowed caps. separating into 5 bony, 1–2-seeded carpels
dehiscent along both sutures; seeds winged. (Greek *exo*, external, and
chorde, chord; referring to the fibres on the external part of the placenta.)
Four species from C. Asia to Korea.—Handsome slender-branched shrubs
with large white fls. in terminal racemes; they belong to our most striking
and graceful spring-flowering shrubs.

A. Stamens 15–25, 3–5 in front of each petal; pedicels of the lower fls. to 5 mm. long; petals
abruptly narrowed into a short claw; petioles 5–15 mm. long..............1. *E. racemosa*
AA. Stamens 20–30; fls. short-pediceled or nearly sessile; petals gradually narrowed into the
claw.
  B. Lvs. of shoots without stipule-like appendages, oval to elliptic-oblong, broad-cuneate
  at base ....2. *E. Giraldii*
  BB. Lvs. of shoots at least partly with stipule-like appendages, oblong to obovate-oblong,
  gradually narrowed into the petiole.................................3. *E. Korolkowii*

1. **E. racemòsa** (Lindl.) Rehd. Slender spreading shrub to 3 or rarely 5 m., glabrous; lvs. elliptic to elliptic-oblong or oblong-obovate, acute and mucronate, cuneate, 3–6 cm. long, entire or on vigorous shoots serrate above the middle, whitish beneath: fls. white, 4 cm. across, in 6–10-fld. racemes; the lower pedicels to 5 mm. long, the upper shorter; petals suborbicular with a very short claw: fr. broad-turbinate or nearly subglobose, 8–10 mm. long. Fl.ɪv–v. B.M.4795(c). L.I.t.11,12. Gt.47:t.1455(c). G.C.III.7:613. Gn.62: 161(h). Gng.5:97(h). F.E.31:971(h). M.G.21:561(h). (*E. grandiflora* Hook.) E. China. Intr. 1849. Zone IV.—**E. r. prostràta** (Schwer.) Rehd., var. With prostrate brs. (*E. grandiflora* var. *p.* Schwer.)—**E. r. dentàta** (Chenault) Rehd., var. Young brts., lvs. on midrib beneath and rachis of infl. slightly pubescent: lvs. more often serrate. Cult. 1913.

    E. r. × *Korolkowii* = **E. macrántha** Schneid. Differs chiefly in its more upright habit and in the somewhat larger short-stalked fls. with about 20 stamens. R.H.1903:18(h),65. M.G.17:485(h). G.W.16:449. B.S.1:549. Orig. 1900.

2. **E. Giráldii** Hesse. Similar to the preceding: lvs. elliptic to ovate-oblong, acute, broad-cuneate, 4–6 cm. long, entire, rarely crenate-serrate above the middle; petioles 1.2–2.5 cm. long, often red: fls. subsessile or the lower ones short-stalked; petals obovate, gradually narrowed into the claw; calyx often reddish inside; stamens 20–30; caps. turbinate, 1–1.3 cm. long. Fl.v. B.S.1:548. M.D.1909:295. G.W.16:450. (*E. racemosa* var. *G.* Rehd.) N. W. China. Intr. about 1897. Zone IV. Handsomer than No. 1; particularly var. *Wilsonii* which is of more upright habit and more floriferous.— **E. G. Wilsònii** (Rehd.) Rehd., var. Lvs. elliptic to oblong, occasionally serrate; petioles 1–2 cm. long, green: fls. 5 cm. across; stamens 20–25: caps. to 1.5 cm. long. (*E. racemosa* var. *W.* Rehd.) C. China. Intr. 1907. Zone V.

    Related species: **E. serratifólia** S. Moore. Shrub to 2 m.: lvs. elliptic, 5–9 cm. long, 3–5 cm. broad, sharply serrate, usually entire below the middle, slightly pubescent beneath at least when young; petiole 1–2 cm. long: fls. about 4 cm. across; petals oblong-obovate, emarginate; stamens 25. N.K.4:t.2: Manch. and Korea. Intr. 1918. Zone IV?

3. **E. Korolkòwi** Lav. Upright slender-branched shrub to 4 m., glabrous: lvs. oblong to obovate-oblong, acute or rarely obtusish, mucronulate, 4–7 cm. long, entire or on stronger shoots often serrate above the middle, and at base with 1 or 2 small narrow lobes, gradually narrowed into a petiole 5–15 mm. long: fls. 3–4 cm. across, subsessile, in 5–8-fld. racemes; petals narrow-obovate; stamens 25: caps. about 1.5 cm. long, globose-ovoid, pointed. Fl.ɪv–v. G.W.16:451. G.31:505. (*E. Alberti* Regel, *E. grandiflora* var. *A.* Aschers. & Graebn.) Turkest. Intr. 1878. Zone V. Of more upright habit and less floriferous; one of the first shrubs to burst into leaf.

12. **HOLODÍSCUS** Maxim. Deciduous shrubs, more or less pubescent; buds small, ovoid, with several pubescent scales: lvs. alternate, petioled, incisely serrate or lobulate, estipulate: fls. very small, in terminal panicles or rarely racemes; calyx-tube cup-shaped; sepals 5, valvate in bud, upright in fr.; petals oval or elliptic, short-clawed, little longer than sepals; stamens 15–20, usually slightly longer than petals; disk entire; pistils 5, distinct, developing into short-stipitate, hairy 1-seeded achenes indehiscent and strongly convex on the lower suture; seeds broad-oblong. (Greek *holos*, entire, and *diskos*, disk, referring to the entire disk of the fl.) Syn.: *Schizonotus* Raf., not Lindl., *Sericotheca* Raf. About 14 closely related species have been distinguished ranging from B. C. to Idaho, Colo. and N. Mex. and s. through Mex. to Colombia.

H. díscolor (Pursh) Maxim. Shrub to 4 m., with spreading and arching brs.: lvs. broad-ovate to ovate, acute, truncate or sometimes broad-cuneate at base, 4–10 cm. long, doubly dentate and lobulate, with broad-ovate teeth, sparingly pubescent and finally glabrous or nearly so above, densely pubescent or whitish tomentose beneath; petioles 1–2 cm. long; fls. creamy white, about 4 mm. across, in ample drooping panicles 8–20 cm. long and 5–15 cm. wide; sepals ovate or ovate-oblong, obtusish; follicles semi-ovate, 1.5 mm. long, with a beak of the same length. Fl.vii. B.R.1635(c). G.F.4:617. B.S. 2:533. G.C.60:233;106:93(h). Gn.87:286(h). (*Spiraea d.* Pursh, *Sericotheca d.* Rydb.) B. C. to Calif., Idaho and Mont. Intr. 1827. Zone V. Handsome in bloom with its large panicles of creamy white fls. on slender arching brs.— **H. d. ariaefòlius** (Sm.) Aschers & Graebn. (*Spiraea a.* Sm.) is the commonly cult. form and has the lvs. grayish green and pubescent below, while the type has the lvs. whitish tomentose below.

Closely related species: **H. dumòsus** (Nutt.) Heller. Upright shrub to 5 m.: lvs. generally obovate, cuneate and decurrent at base, 2–5 cm. long, pubescent above, whitish tomentose below: panicle ovoid, narrow, 5–20 cm. long. Bull. Torr. Bot. Club, 25:338. (*H. australis* Heller, *H. discolor* var. *d.* Dipp., *Spiraea dumosa* Nutt.) Wyo. and Utah to N. Mex. and Mex. Intr. 1879. Zone V.— **H. Boursièri** (Carr.) Rehd. Shrub to 1 m.: lvs. flabellate or suborbicular, abruptly contracted into a short winged petiole, rounded at apex, 1–3 cm. long, grayish beneath: infl. 5–7 cm. long, simple or with few short brs. R.H.1859:519. (*Spiraea B.* Carr.) Calif., Nev. Intr. 1853, but apparently not now in cult.— **H. microphýllus** Rydb. Shrub to 1 m.: lvs. elliptic to obovate, 1–1.5 cm. long, cuneate, serrate, finely pubescent above, white silky-villous beneath: infl. 3–7 cm. long, with few spreading brs. Colo. to Wyo. and Utah. Intr. 1922. Zone V?

Subfam. II. Pomoideae Focke. Trees or shrubs: lvs. simple or pinnate, stipulate: fls. solitary or in umbels, racemes, panicles or corymbs; carpels 2–5, usually 2-ovuled, more or less united and adnate to the cup-shaped calyx-tube, forming an inferior ovary: fr. a fleshy pome. (*Pomaceae* Loisel., *Malaceae* Small.)

13. COTONEÁSTER B. Ehrh. Deciduous or evergreen shrubs or rarely small trees; buds small, with several imbricate scales: lvs. alternate, short-petioled, entire, with mostly subulate, caducous stipules: fls. white or pinkish, in few to many-fld. corymbs, sometimes solitary, terminal on short lateral brts.; calyx-tube usually turbinate; sepals 5, short; petals upright or spreading, imbricate in bud; stamens about 20; styles 2–5, distinct, carpels more or less connate except on the ventral side; carpels 2-ovuled: fr. a red or black small pome crowned by the persistent calyx-lobes, with 2–5 nutlets. (Latin *cotonea* (*cydonia*), quince, and *aster,* a suffix meaning "kind of"; the lvs. of some species resemble those of the quince.) About 50 species in the temp. regions of Eu., N. Afr. and Asia except Japan.—Ornamental shrubs much planted on account of their attractive frs. and some species also for their white spirea-like fls.

A. Petals upright, small, obovate, usually pinkish, solitary or in few-fld. or many-fld. and nodding corymbs: frs. red or black..........................Sect. I. Orthopetalum Koehne.
  B. Fr. red (or purplish black in No. 6).
    c. Lvs. glabrous or sparingly pubescent and green beneath, 5–30 mm. long: fls. 1–3, rarely 4: pubescence of brts. strigose.
      D. Habit prostrate.
        E. Stems appressed to the ground, irregularly branched: lvs. usually wavy at the margin ....1. *C. adpressa*
        EE. Stems horizontally spreading very regularly distichously branched: lvs. not wavy ....2. *C. horizontalis*
      DD. Habit upright.
        E. Lvs. dull green above, pubescent when young.
          F. Fls. usually solitary: calyx glabrous............................3. *C. disticha*
          FF. Lls. 2–4: calyx pubescent......................................4. *C. Simonsii*
        EE. Lvs. lustrous above.
          F. Fr. bright red: lvs. usually acute.............................5. *C. divaricata*

FF. Fr. purplish black: lvs. usually obtuse..........................6. *C. nitens*
CC. Lvs. tomentose or pubescent beneath (or nearly glabrous in Nos. 7, 14, 15): fls. 2–
many: pubescence of brts. appressed-villous (see also *C. rubens* under No. 3).
   D. Calyx glabrous or only slightly pubescent.
     E. Lvs. oval to oblong, often obtuse, 2–5 cm. long, smooth above.
       F. Lvs. glabrous or nearly so......................................7. *C. rosea*
       FF. Lvs. tomentose beneath..8. *C. integerrima*
     EE. Lvs. ovate to ovate-oblong, acute, 3.5–8 cm. long, rugose above...15. *C. bullata*
   DD. Calyx densely pubescent or tomentose: lvs. slightly pubescent above, dull green.
     E. Lvs. obtuse, rarely acutish.
       F. Lvs. whitish tomentose beneath: fr. with 3–5 nutlets........9. *C. tomentosa*
       FF. Lvs. yellowish tomentose beneath: fr. with 2 nutlets............10. *C. Zabeli*
     EE. Lvs. acute or acuminate, rarely acutish.
       F. Lvs. grayish or yellowish tomentose beneath.
         G. Fr. scarlet or orange: lvs. 1–3 cm. long.
           H. Fls. few: lvs. acute or acutish: fr. scarlet..............11. *C. Dielsiana*
           HH. Fls. in 6–15-fld. cymes: lvs. acute or acuminate: fr. orange-red.
                                        12. *C. Francheti*
         GG. Fr. dull brownish red: lvs. 2.5–4 cm. long....................13. *C. obscura*
       FF. Lvs. sparingly pubescent beneath, finally often glabrescent.
         G. Fr. ellipsoid, slightly pubescent, with usually 2 nutlets: calyx pubescent:
           lvs. pubescent above..14. *C. acuminata*
         GG. Fr. subglobose, with 4–5 nutlets: calyx slightly pubescent or glabrous:
           lvs. glabrous above, usually bullate..........................15. *C. bullata*
BB. Fr. black.
   C. Lvs. acute or acuminate.
     D. Lvs. pubescent above when young, dull green: calyx pubescent.
       E. Lvs. generally acuminate, 4–10 cm. long: fr. with 3–5 nutlets.
         F. Infl. many-fld.: lvs. rugose above, reticulate beneath......16. *C. moupinensis*
         FF. Infl. 3–7-fld.: lvs. neither rugose nor reticulate...............17. *C. foveolata*
       EE. Lvs. generally acute, 3–5 cm. long: fr. usually with 2 nutlets....18. *C. acutifolia*
     DD. Lvs. glabrous and lustrous above: calyx glabrous or slightly pubescent.
                                          19. *C. lucida*
   CC. Lvs. obtuse or acutish, whitish tomentose beneath: calyx glabrous.
                                      20. *C. melanocarpa*
AA. Petals spreading, suborbicular, white: fr. red (brown in *C. affinis* under No. 24, black in
C. Lindleyi under No. 23).............................Sect. 2. CHAENOPETALUM Koehne.
  B. Fls. in many-fld. corymbs: upright shrubs.
   C. Lvs. deciduous, green or grayish, not papillose beneath: anthers yellow.
     D. Lvs. suborbicular to elliptic, obtuse or acute, to 3.5 cm. long.
       E. Lvs. glabrous at maturity.....................................21. *C. multiflora*
       EE. Lvs. tomentose beneath.
         F. Lvs. ovate to elliptic, usually acute, grayish tomentulose beneath; calyx
           villous ....22. *C. hupehensis*
         FF. Lvs. suborbicular to elliptic, usually obtuse, white-tomentose beneath: calyx
           tomentose ....23. *C. racemiflora*
     DD. Lvs. narrow-elliptic to oblong-lanceolate, acute at ends, usually glabrous at ma-
      turity, to 10 cm. long..24. *C. frigida*
   CC. Lvs. evergreen or half-evergreen, subcoriaceous or coriaceous: anthers purple.
     D. Lvs. with persistent close white tomentum beneath, 1–3 cm. long (to 5 or 8 cm.
      long in related species)..25. *C. pannosa*
     DD. Lvs. with floccose or woolly tomentum beneath, finally usually more or less gla-
      brous and glaucous: 3–12 cm. long.
       E. Lvs. glabrous above, not or slightly papillose beneath, 1–2 cm. broad.
                                       26. *C. salicifolia*
       EE. Lvs. pubescent above while young, papillose beneath, 2–3 cm. broad.
                                      27. *C. Henryana*
  BB. Fls. 1–3: prostrate or trailing evergreen shrubs.
   C. Lvs. green or glaucescent, not papillose beneath, soon glabrous, 1–3 cm. long.
                                        28. *C. Dammeri*
   CC. Lvs. glaucous and papillose beneath (except in *C. buxifolia* under No. 29), less than
     1.5 cm. long.
     D. Lvs. suborbicular or broad-oval, 8–20 mm. long: fls. 1–3........29. *C. rotundifolia*
     DD. Lvs. obovate to cuneate-oblong, 5–10 mm. long: fls. usually solitary.
       E. Lvs. grayish pubescent beneath, obovate to cuneate-oblong..30. *C. microphylla*
       EE. Lvs. glabrous or nearly so beneath at maturity, obovate to oval..31. *C. congesta*

1. **C. adpréssa** Bois. Deciduous prostrate shrub, with irregularly branched creeping stems: lvs. broad-oval or obovate, acutish or obtuse, mucronulate, 5–15 mm. long, usually wavy at the margin, dull green above, ciliolate and sparingly pubescent beneath while young: petioles 1–2 mm. long: fls. 1–2, pinkish, subsessile; calyx slightly pubescent: fr. subglobose, 6–7 mm. long, bright red, usually with 2 nutlets. Fl.vi; fr.viii–ix. V.F.116. S.H.1:f.418k-m, 419e[1]. (*C. horizontalis* var. *a.* (Bois) Schneid.) W. China. Intr. 1896. Zone

IV. Brs. closely appressed to the ground and often rooting, with bright red fr. in late summer and fall; adapted for rockeries.—**C. a. praecox** (Vilm.) Bois & Berthault, var. More vigorous, to 0.5 m. tall: lvs. to 2.5 cm. long: fls. pink: fr. 8–12 mm. thick. R.H.1931:584,t.(c). Gt.81:15. G.W.33:584(h). Gs.16:37(h). (*C. p.* Vilm., *C.* "Nan-shan" Hort.) Cult. 1905.

2. **C. horizontàlis** Decne. Half-evergreen low shrub with horizontally spreading distichously branched stems: lvs. suborbicular to broad-elliptic, acute at ends and mucronate at the apex, 5–12 mm. long, dark green, glabrous and lustrous above, sparingly strigose-pubescent beneath; petioles 1–2 mm. long, strigose-pubescent: fls. 1–2, pinkish, subsessile; calyx slightly pubescent: fr. subglobose, about 5 mm across, bright red, with usually 3 nutlets. Fl.vi; fr.ix–x. R.H.1889:348,t(c). G.C.32:91. Gn.66:407(h);87:28. (*C. Davidiana* Hort.) W. China. Intr. about 1880. Zone IV. Distinct shrub with closely and regularly 2-ranked brts.; frs. smaller but more numerous than in the preceding species and ripen later; lvs. subpersistent, turning partly red and orange in late autumn.—**C. h. variegàta** Osborn. Lvs. variegated with white. R.H.1916:137(h).—**C. h. perpusílla** Schneid., var. More depressed: lvs. about 6 mm. long. W. China. Intr. 1908.—**C. h. Wílsonii** Wils., var. Similar to the preceding var. but more vigorous, lvs. somewhat larger. (*C. Wilsoni* Hort., not Nakai.)

3. **C. dísticha** Lange. Deciduous or half-evergreen shrub, to 2.5 m., with more or less distichously arranged brts.: lvs. suborbicular to broad-obovate or broad-oval, usually nearly rounded and abruptly mucronate at apex, broad-cuneate at base, 8–12 mm. long, dark green above, sparingly pubescent on both sides at least while young, but less so and lighter green beneath: fls. usually solitary, white, suffused with pink, short-pediceled; calyx glabrous; sepals broadly triangular: fr. broad-obovoid, 1 cm. long, scarlet. Fl.vi; fr.ix–x. B.M.8010(c). (*C. rotundifolia* Wall. ex Baker.) Himal., S. W. China. Intr. 1825. Zone V. In its mode of branching similar to the preceding species, but upright and with larger fr.

· Closely related species: **C. verruculòsa** Diels. Differs chiefly in the less pubescent densely verruculose brts. and in the more coriaceous glabrous lvs. often emarginate at apex. Yunnan. Intr. ?—**C. rubens** W. W. Sm. Irregularly branched; brts. whitish pubescent; lvs. suborbicular to broad-elliptic, to 1.5 cm. long, rounded at ends. mucronulate, yellowish tomentose beneath: fls. red; calyx slightly pubescent. W. China. Cult. 1927. Zone VI?—**C. apiculàta** Rehd. & Wils. Lvs. suborbicular to orbicular-ovate, apiculate, glabrous at maturity or only slightly ciliate, to 1.5 cm. long: fls. pink; sepals short-acuminate: fr. subglobose, subsessile. W. China. Intr. 1910. Zone IV.

4. **C. Simónsii** Bak. Deciduous or half-evergreen shrub to 3 or rarely 4 m., of upright habit: lvs. orbicular-obovate to broad-elliptic, acute or slightly acuminate, broad-cuneate, 1.5–3 cm. long, dark green above and pubescent while young, paler and pubescent beneath, chiefly on the veins; petioles pubescent, 2–3 mm. long: fls. white, in short, 2–4-fld. cymes; calyx appressed-pubescent; sepals triangular, acutish to acuminate: fr. short-ellipsoid or obovoid, 8 mm. long, scarlet. Fl.vi–vii; fr.x. Ref. Bot. 1:55(c). Gt.55:t.1551, f.5(c). Gn.87:42. (*C. Simmondsii* or *Symonsii* Hort.) Khasia. Cult. 1869. Zone V.

5. **C. divaricàta** Rehd. & Wils. Deciduous upright shrub to 2 m., with spreading brs.: lvs. elliptic or broad-elliptic, acute at ends or sometimes rounded at apex, 8–20 mm. long, lustrous dark green above, lighter and slightly pubescent or glabrous beneath: fls. pink, short-pediceled, in usually 3-fld. cymes; calyx slightly pubescent; sepals triangular, acute or acuminate: fr. ellipsoid, 8 mm. long, about 6 mm. thick, red; nutlets 1–3, usually 2. Fl.

vi; fr.ix. C. and W. China. Intr. 1907. Zone V. Handsome shrub with slender spreading brs. and bright red frs. profusely produced.

6. **C. nítens** Rehd. & Wils. Deciduous densely branched shrub, with slender spreading brs.: lvs. oval or sometimes ovate, rounded at ends or sometimes acutish, 8–20 mm. long, lustrous and dark green above, lighter and sparingly pubescent beneath while young, soon glabrous: fls. pink, in usually 3-fld. cymes; calyx slightly pubescent; sepals broad-triangular, obtusish: fr. globose-ellipsoid, 7 mm. long, purplish black; nutlets 1–2. Fl.vi; fr.viii–ix. W. China. Intr. 1910. Zone IV.

7. **C. ròsea** Edgew. Deciduous shrub with slender brs., to 2 m. tall or more; brts. pubescent at the tips, soon glabrous: lvs. elliptic or ovate to ovate-oblong, acutish or obtuse, mucronulate, rounded or broad-cuneate at base, 2–6 cm. long, bluish green above, grayish green beneath and slightly pubescent at first, soon glabrous: petioles 2–5 mm. long, glabrous: fls. pinkish in 3–9-fld. cymes; sepals broad-triangular to ovate, obtuse; petals slightly spreading: fr. globose-obovoid, 7 mm. long, red; nutlets 2. Fl.vi; fr.ix–x. S.H.1:f.423r–s,424n. Jour. N. Y. Bot. Gard. 37:135. N. W. Himal., Afghan. Intr. 1882. Zone V. In fr. similar to *C. racemiflora*, but glabrous.

8. **C. integérrima** Med. Upright bushy shrub to 2 m.; young brts. appressed-woolly, becoming glabrous and lustrous: lvs. suborbicular to broad-ovate or oval, obtuse or acute, usually mucronate, rounded at base, 2–5 cm. long; dark green and glabrous above, whitish or grayish tomentose beneath; petioles 2–4 mm. long, pubescent: fls. pinkish, in nodding glabrous 2–4-fld. cymes; sepals rounded: fr. subglobose, 6 mm. across, red; nutlets usually 2. Fl.v; fr.viii. H.W.3:73. R.I.25:t.96(c). G.H.t.71(c). (*C. Cotoneaster* Karst., *C. vulgaris* Lindl.) Eu., N. Asia to Altai. Intr. 1656. Zone V. A much branched round shrub with rather short and stiff brs. and ornamental red fr.

The closely related **C. uniflòra** Bge. with smaller lvs. glabrous at maturity and usually solitary short-stalked fls. from the Altai is possibly only a var. of the preceding species. Cult. 1907. Zone V or IV?—Another related species is **C. Silvéstrii** Pampan. Lvs. elliptic-ovate; calyx pubescent: fr. orange. C. China. Intr. 1907. Zone V?

9. **C. tomentòsa** (Ait.) Lindl. Shrub to 3 m.; young brts. tomentose: lvs broad-oval to elliptic or rarely oblong-ovate, obtuse or sometimes acutish, 3–6 cm. long, dull green above and pubescent while young, whitish or grayish tomentose beneath; petioles 3–6 mm. long: fls. pinkish, in nodding 3–12-fld. pubescent cymes: fr. subglobose, 7–8 mm. across, brick-red; nutlets 3–5. Fl.v–vi; fr.ix. G.O.t.105(c). R.I.25:t.97(c). H.W.3:73. W.D.55(c). S. E. Eu., W. Asia. Intr. 1759. Zone IV. Similar to *C. integerrima*, but larger in every part and more pubescent.

10. **C. Zàbeli** Schneid. Shrub to 2 m., with slender spreading brs.; young brts. densely pubescent: lvs. broad-oval to ovate, obtuse, rarely acutish, 1.5–3 cm. long, dull dark green and loosely pubescent above, grayish or yellowish tomentose below; petioles 1–3 mm. long: fls. pinkish, in 3–9-fld. pubescent nodding cymes; calyx villous, with obtuse lobes, soon glabrous: fr. globose-obovoid, 7–8 mm. long, bright red; nutlets usually 2. Fl.v; fr.ix–x. S.H.1:f. 420f–h,422i–k. C. China. Intr. 1907. Zone IV. Slender-branched shrub with bright red fruit.—**C. Z. miniàta** Rehd. & Wils., var. Fr. smaller, light orange-scarlet; lvs. turning yellow in autumn.

11. **C. Dielsiàna** Pritz. Shrub to 2 m., with slender spreading and arching brs.; young brts. densely pubescent: lvs. elliptic to ovate, acute or acutish, rarely obtuse, rounded or broad-cuneate at base, 1–2.5 cm. long, slightly pubescent and dark green above, yellowish or grayish tomentose beneath:

350

fls. pinkish, in short 3–7-fld. pubescent cymes; calyx pubescent; sepals triangular, mucronate: fr. subglobose, about 6 mm. across, scarlet; nutlets 3–5.
Fl.vi; fr.ix–x. Gs.1:185. S.L.142(h). (*C. applanata* Duthie.) C. and W.
China. Intr. 1900. Zone (V).—Graceful shrub with long arching or pendulous brs. densely studded with scarlet frs. in fall.—**C. D. màjor** Rehd., var.
Lvs. broader and larger.—**C. D. élegans** Rehd. & Wils., var. Lvs. subpersistent, smaller, finally nearly glabrous and somewhat shining above: fr. coral-
red. W. China. Intr. 1908.

12. **C. Franchéti** Bois. Half-evergreen upright shrub with spreading brs.;
young brts. densely pubescent: lvs. thickish, elliptic to ovate, acute or acuminate, broad-cuneate, 2–3 cm. long, pubescent above at first, finally glabrous
and somewhat lustrous, yellowish or grayish white-tomentose beneath; petioles 1–3 mm. long: fls. pinkish, small, in 5–11-fld. pubescent cymes, on lateral
brts. sometimes to 4 cm. long; calyx villous; sepals triangular, acuminate:
fr. ovoid, 6–7 mm. long, orange-red, sparingly pubescent or finally glabrous;
nutlets usually 3. Fl.vi; fr.ix–x. B.M.8571(c). R.H.1902:379;1907:256,t(c).
V.F.118. W. China. Intr. 1895. Zone VI? Shrub with small lvs. and profusely
produced orange-red frs.—**C. F. cineráscens** Rehd., var. More vigorous: lvs.
elliptic-ovate, to 4 cm. long, more loosely tomentose and grayish or greenish
beneath: infl. many-fld., on brts. to 5 cm. long. W. China. Intr. 1915. Zone
VII?

Related species: **C. amoèna** Wils. Differs chiefly in its bushy habit, with
short stiff brs., smaller lvs. and denser and smaller cymes with shorter pedicels,
and in the aristate sepals. G.C.51:2. Gs.14:25. S. W. China. Intr. 1904. Zone
VII?—**C. Wardii** W. W. Sm. Brts. white-tomentose: lvs. ovate, 2.5–3.5 cm. long,
acute or acutish, densely silvery white-tomentose beneath: infl. white-tomentose,
10–15-fld., on brts. to 4 cm. long; nutlets usually 2. S. E. Tibet. Cult. 1931.
Zone VII?—**C. newryénsis** Lemoine. Lvs. elliptic, 2–4 cm. long, acute or
abruptly mucronate, sometimes obtusish, villous and grayish green beneath: fls.
in dense corymbs; sepals broad-triangular, with very short or nearly without
mucro. (*C. Simonsii* var. *n.* Bean.) Origin unknown; possibly hybrid of Nos.
4 and 12. Cult. 1911. Zone VI?

13. **C. obscùra** Rehd. & Wils. Deciduous shrub to 3 m., with spreading
brs.; young brts. pubescent: lvs. elliptic-ovate or sometimes rhombic-ovate,
acuminate, rarely acute, broad-cuneate, 2.5–4, rarely 5 cm. long, dull green
above and slightly pubescent, at least while young, yellowish gray-tomentose
beneath; petioles 2–3 mm. long, pubescent: fls. pinkish, in short dense, 3–7-
fld. pubescent cymes, on very short lateral brts., sepals triangular, acuminulate; fr. broad-pyriform, dark red, 7–8 mm. long; nutlets usually 3. Fl.vi;
fr.ix–x. W. China. Intr. 1910. Zone V. Bushy shrub with numerous dark
red frs. in autumn.—**C. o. cornifòlia** Rehd. & Wils., var. Lvs. elliptic-ovate
to elliptic-oblong, 4–7 cm. long, less pubescent beneath, veins more deeply
impressed: fr. purple-black; nutlets 5. W. China. Intr. 1910.

Closely related species: **C. reticulàta** Rehd. & Wils. Lvs. subcoriaceous,
elliptic-ovate, 2.5–4 cm. long, wrinkled above, reticulate and yellowish tomentose
beneath: fr. subglobose, 3–6 in glabrous cymes, purplish black, 5–7 mm. across;
nutlets 5. W. China. Intr. 1910. Zone VI?—**C. glomerulàta** W. W. Sm. Lvs.
oblong-ovate, 3–5 cm. long, fulvous-tomentose beneath:·cymes dense, many-fld.:
fr. about 5 mm. long, crimson; nutlets usually 5. W. China. Intr. 1912?

14. **C. acuminàta** Lindl. Deciduous shrub to 4 m., of upright habit; young
brts. densely pubescent: lvs. elliptic-ovate to ovate-oblong, acuminate. or
acute, broad-cuneate, 3–6 cm. long, dull green above and pubescent while
young, paler green and more densely pubescent beneath, usually glabrescent
at maturity; petioles 2–5 mm. long, pubescent: fls. pinkish, in 2–5-fld. short,
pubescent cymes; calyx pubescent; sepals broad-triangular, acute or obtuse:

fr. ellipsoid, 8–10 mm. long, bright red, hairy near apex; nutlets 2. Fl.vi;
fr.ix–x. L.B.919(c). R.H.1899:348,t.f.5(c, as *C. nepalensis*). S.H.1:f.418r-t,
419i. Himal. Intr. 1820. Zone V. Ornamental in fall with its bright red
rather large fr.

Related species: **C. nitidifòlia** Marquand. Brts. densely pubescent: lvs. elliptic-
lanceolate, 4.5–6 cm. long, acuminate, glabrous and lustrous above, loosely pubescent beneath; infl. 3–9-fld., whitish tomentose; calyx-lobes deltoid, acute: fr.
5 mm. across, dark red. H.I.32:3145. W. China. Intr. 1924. Zone VI?

15. **C. bullàta** Bois. Deciduous spreading shrub to 2 m.; young brts.
pubescent: lvs. elliptic-ovate to ovate-oblong, acuminate, broad-cuneate,
rarely rounded at base, 3.5–8 cm. long, slightly pubescent or nearly glabrous
above and rugose or more or less bullate, paler or grayish green beneath and
reticulate, sparingly pubescent, more densely on the veins or sometimes nearly
glabrous; petioles 3–6 mm. long; fls. pinkish, 3–7; calyx glabrous; sepals very
short, rounded: fr. subglobose or obovoid, 6–8 mm. long, red; nutlets 4–5.
Fl.v–vi; fr.viii–ix. V.F.119. M.O.205. W. China. Intr. 1898. Zone V. With
large clusters of bright red frs. in fall.—**C. b. floribúnda** (Stapf) Rehd. &
Wils., f. Petioles shorter: cymes many-fld., 4–6 cm. across; calyx slightly
pubescent. B.M.8284(c). H.B.3:449. (*C. moupinensis* var. *f.* Stapf.)—**C. b.
macrophýlla** Rehd. & Wils., var. Similar to the preceding var., but lvs. 6–12
cm. long, often nearly glabrous: calyx nearly glabrous.

16. **C. moupinénsis** Franch. Shrub to 5 m., with spreading brs.: lvs.
elliptic- or rhombic-ovate to ovate-oblong, acuminate, broad-cuneate or
sometimes rounded at base, 4–10 cm. long, dull green, slightly pubescent,
rugose and usually bullate above, light green and pubescent beneath, at least
on the veins, reticulate; petioles 2–3 mm. long, pubescent: fls. pinkish, in
many-fld. corymbs; calyx slightly pubescent; sepals triangular, acutish: fr.
subglobose or obovoid, 6–8 mm. long, black; nutlets 4–5. S.H.1:f.421d-e,
423i-k. Fl.vi; fr.ix–x. W. China. Intr. about 1900. Zone VI? Similar to
C. bullata, but with black fr.

17. **C. foveolàta** Rehd. & Wils. Shrub to 3 m. with spreading brs.; brts.
densely pubescent, later gray or grayish yellow: lvs. elliptic or rhombic-ovate
to ovate-oblong, acute or acuminate, broadly cuneate or rounded at the base,
4–8 cm. long, slightly and loosely pubescent above while young, soon glabrous
and smooth, pubescent beneath, chiefly on the veins, finally often nearly
glabrous, veins prominent beneath and impressed above; petioles 2–3 mm.
long, pubescent or nearly glabrous: fls. pinkish in 3–6-fld. pubescent cymes:
calyx densely pubescent; sepals broad-triangular, acute: fr. subglobose, 6–8
mm. long, black; nutlets 3–4, furrowed and shallowly pitted on the back. Fl.
vi; fr.ix. C. China. Intr. 1907. Zone IV. Lvs. turning bright scarlet and
orange in autumn.

18. **C. acutifòlia** Turcz. Shrub to 4 m., with slender spreading brs.; brts.
pubescent, later red-brown: lvs. elliptic-ovate to oblong-ovate, acute, rarely
acuminate, broad-cuneate, 2–5 cm. long, dull green and slightly pubescent
above at first, lighter green beneath, sparingly pubescent, more densely on the
veins, finally often nearly glabrous; petioles 2–5 mm. long, pubescent: fls.
pinkish, in 2–5-fld. short pubescent cymes; calyx-tube pubescent, lobes triangular, acute: fr. ellipsoidal, about 1 cm. long, black, usually with 2 nutlets.
Fl.v–vi; fr.ix–x. S.H.1:f.421a-b,423d-f. (*C. pekinensis* Zab.) N. China.
Intr. 1883. Zone IV.—**C. a. villòsula** Rehd. & Wils., var. Lvs. more densely
villous beneath, somewhat larger; calyx-tube more densely villous: fr. thinly
pubescent. C. & W. China. Intr. 1900. Zone V.

Closely related species: **C. ambígua** Rehd. & Wils. which differs chiefly in its slightly pubescent or nearly glabrous calyx-tube and subglobose or obovoid fr. with 3–4 nutlets. W. China. Intr. about 1902. Zone V.—**C. tenúipes** Rehd. & Wils. Slender shrub to 2 m.: lvs. narrow-elliptic to ovate, 1.5–3.5 cm. long, densely villous beneath: cymes 2–4-fld., densely villous: fr. on slender, though short stalks; nutlets 2. W. China. Intr. 1910. Zone V.

19. **C. lùcida** Schlecht. Deciduous shrub to 3 m., of upright habit; young brts. pubescent: lvs. elliptic to ovate, acute, broad-cuneate, rarely rounded at base, 2–5 cm. long, glabrous and lustrous above, pubescent beneath, finally often nearly glabrous; petioles 2–5 mm. long, nearly glabrous: fls. pinkish, in 3–8-fld. slightly pubescent cymes; calyx-tube glabrous or slightly pubescent; fr. subglobose or obovoid, 8–10 mm. long, black, with 3–4 nutlets. Fl.v– vi; fr.ix. D.H.3:413. S.H.1:f.421c,423a-c. G.W.5:247. (*C. acutifolia* Lindl., not Turcz.) Altai Mts. Cult. 1840. Zone IV. Shrub with lustrous lvs. and rather large black frs.

20. **C. melanocárpa** Lodd. Shrub to 2 m., with spreading brs., brts. pubescent when young: lvs. broad-ovate to ovate-oblong, obtuse or acute, often mucronulate, sometimes emarginate, rounded at base, 2–4.5 cm. long, dull dark green above, slightly pubescent at first, whitish tomentose beneath; petioles 3–8 mm. long: fls. pinkish in 3–8-fld. nodding, glabrous or slightly pubescent corymbs; calyx glabrous: fr. subglobose, 6–7 mm. across, black; nutlets usually 2. Fl.v–vi; fr.viii. L.B.1531(c). R.I.25:t.98(c). (*C. nigra* Fries.) Eu. to C. and N. E. Asia. Cult. 1829. Zone IV.—**C. m. laxiflòra** (Lindl.) Schneid., var. Lvs. larger, to 6 cm. long; corymbs pendulous, 12– many-fld. B.R.1305(c). R.I.25:t.98,f.4–6(c). (*C. l.* Lindl., ? *C. polyanthema* Wolf.) C. Asia. Intr. 1826.—**C. m. commíxta** Schneid., var. Lvs. of shoots ovate, acute and mucrcnulate; infl. 8–15-fld. B.M.3519(c).

Closely related species: **C. ignàva** Wolf. Lvs. 2.5–5 cm. long, those of the shoots ovate, acute and mucronulate: infl. many-fld., pendulous, tomentose; calyx glabrous except at base; fr. dark purple. Yearb. For. Inst. Petersb. 15: 240,t. E. Turkest. Intr. about 1880? Zone V?

21. **C. multiflòra** Bge. Shrub to 2 m., with usually slender arching brs.; brts. pubescent at first, soon glabrous, purplish: lvs. broad-ovate to ovate, acute or obtuse, rounded or broad-cuneate at base, 2–5 cm. long, at first tomentose beneath, soon glabrous; petioles 3–10 mm. long: fls. white, 1–1.2 cm. across, in many-fld. usually loose glabrous corymbs; calyx glabrous: fr. sub- globose or obovoid, 8 mm. across, red; nutlets 1–2. Fl.v; fr.viii. R.H.1892: 327;1893:29. B.S.1:413,t(h). G.W.6:62(h). S.L.2:166(h). (*C. reflexa* Carr.) W. China. Intr. 1837. Zone V. Graceful shrub with arching brs., handsome in bloom and with ornamental fr.—**C. m. calocárpa** Rehd. & Wils., var. Lvs. larger and narrower: fr. larger, about 1 cm. across, very freely produced. W. China. Intr. 1900.—**C. m. granaténsis** (Boiss.) Wenz., var. Lvs. more pubescent: infl. laxer and more pubescent. Spain. Cult. 1854. Zone VI?

Related species: **C. submultiflòra** Popov. Mature lvs. puberulous beneath: infl. densely pubescent, half as long as lvs.: fr. bright red. Tian-shan, Pamir. Intr. 1935. Zone V.

22. **C. hupehénsis** Rehd. & Wils. Shrub to 2 m., with spreading and arching brs., pubescent at first, soon glabrous and purple: lvs. elliptic to ovate, obtuse or acute, mucronulate, usually rounded at base, 1.5–3.5 cm. long, glabrous above, thinly grayish tomentose beneath; petioles 2–5 mm. long, pubescent: fls. about 1 cm. across, in 6–12-fld. pubescent corymbs; calyx villous; anthers yellow: fr. subglobose, about 8 mm. across, bright red; nut- lets 2, closely cohering, the hypostyle covering only the apex. Fl.v; fr.viii–

IX. B.C.2:866. Gn.M.29:225(h). S.L.143(h). C. and W. China. Intr. 1907. Zone IV. One of the handsomest species in flower and fruit; the lvs. turning yellow in fall.

23. **C. racemiflòra** (Desf.) K. Koch. Shrub to 2.5 m. with slender spreading rarely upright brs.; brts. gray-tomentose while young: lvs. suborbicular to orbicular-obovate or oval, rarely ovate, usually obtuse and mucronate, sometimes emarginate, rarely elliptic and acute at ends, 1.5–3 cm. long, glabrous above, grayish or whitish tomentose beneath: fls. 8 mm. across, in 3–12-fld. short-stalked tomentulose cymes: fr. subglobose, about 8 mm. across, red; nutlets 2. Fl.v–vi; fr.ix–x. R.H.1867:31. S.H.1:f.424e-k,425d-f. (*C. nummularia* Fisch. & Mey., *C. Fontanesii* Spach.) S. Eu., N. Afr., W. Asia to Himal. and Turkest. Cult. 1829. Zone IV.—A very variable species, the typical form var. **Desfontaìni** (Reg.) Zab. (var. *typica* Schneid.) has generally elliptic acutish lvs., while var. **nummulària** Dipp.) (var. *Meyeri* Zab.) has broader usually obtuse lvs.—**C. r. soongòrica** (Reg. & Herd.) Schneid., var. Lvs. oval, usually obtuse and mucronate, less densely pubescent. Gn. M.33:38. W.A.114,t(h), (*C. nummularia* var. *s.* Reg. & Herd., *C. s.* Popov.) Song., W. China. Intr. 1910. Zone III.—**C. r. microcárpa** Rehd. & Wils., var. Similar to the preceding; lvs. smaller, 1–1.5 cm. long, fr. ellipsoidal, about 6 mm. long. W. China. Intr. 1910.—**C. r. Veìtchii** Rehd. & Wils., var. Lvs. generally elliptic, acute at ends, 2–3.5 cm. long; fls. 1.2–1.5 cm. across: fr. dark red, about 1 cm. across; nutlet usually 1. M.G.29:6. C. China. Intr. 1900.— **C. r. Royleana** Dipp., var. Low shrub: lvs. suborbicular or broad-obovate, rounded or emarginate at apex, 8–20 mm. long: infl. 3–6-fld. (*C. r.* var. *Kotschyi* Schneid., var. *orbicularis* Dipp., not Wenzig, *C. nevadensis* Hort., *C. Royleana* Hort.) Mediterr. Reg. ? Himal.

Related species: **C. hebephýlla** Diels. Lvs. subcoriaceous, suborbicular to broadly oval, 2.5–3.5 cm. long: anthers violet: fr. dark red, ovoid; nutlet usually 1. S. W. China. Intr. about 1910. Zone VII?—**C. Lindleyi** Steud. Brts. pubescent when young: lvs. broad-oval to broad-ovate, usually rounded at apex and mucronulate, sometimes emarginate, 2.5–6 cm. long, grayish tomentose beneath: infl. 5–12-fld.; calyx tomentose: fr. black. S.H.1:f.424a-b,425a. (*C. nummularia* Lindl., not Fisch. & Mey., *C. arborescens* Zabel, *C. compta* Hort.) Himal. Intr. 1924. Zone VI?

24. **C. frígida** Lindl. Tall shrub or small tree to 6 m.; brts. pubescent at first, soon glabrous: lvs. elliptic to elliptic-oblong or oblong-obovate, obtuse or sometimes acute, cuneate, 6–12 cm. long, dull green and glabrous above, paler beneath and tomentose while young, finally usually glabrous; petioles 3–8 mm. long, pubescent: fls. 8 mm. across, in dense tomentose corymbs 4–6 cm. across; sepals triangular, acute: fr. broad-ellipsoidal, about 5 mm. long, bright red; nutlets 2. Fl.vi; fr.viii–ix. B.R.1229(c). L.B.1512(c). Gn.87:28. G.C.72:365. M.A.t.6(c),37(h). Himal. Intr. 1824. Zone VII. Conspicuous in fall and early winter with its large clusters of bright red frs.—**C. f. aldenhaménsis** Gibbs, var. Lvs. oblong-lanceolate.—**C. f. Vicárii** Gibbs, var. Lvs. lanceolate. Gs.14:24.

C. f. × *pannosa* = **C. Críspii** Exell. Lvs. like those of *C. pannosa*, but 3–5 cm. long: frs. like *C. frigida*. Cult. 1928.—*C. f.* × *Henryana* = **C. Watereri** Exell. Intermediate between the parents: fruiting profusely. G.C.83:44,45. Cult. 1928.

Closely related species: **C. affìnis** Lindl. Tall shrub: lvs. elliptic to oblong-obovate, acute or sometimes obtuse, 3–8 cm. long, pubescent or tomentose beneath, finally glabrous: fr. subglobose, purple-brown or nearly black. L.B. 1522(c). S.H.1:f.426b-e,427a-f. Himal. Intr. 1828. Zone VII.—**C. a. bacillàris** (Lindl.) Schneid., var. Lvs. slightly pubescent at first, soon glabrous: young brts. and infl. slightly pubescent. G.C.56:412,t(c). (*C. bacillaris* Wall. ex Lindl.) Himal.—**C. Coòperi** Marquand. Tall shrub; young brts. tomentose:

lvs. elliptic-lanceolate, 5–7 cm. long, short-acuminate, cuneate, glabrous above, white tomentose beneath at first, soon glabrescent: infl. sparingly pubescent at first: fr. turbinate, 1 cm. long, dark purple. H.I.3146. Bhutan. Intr. 1914? Zone VII?—**C. c. microcárpa** Marquand, var. Brts. slender, arching: fr. subglobose, 6.5–7 mm. across, reddish purple. B.M.9478(c). Intr. 1914.

25. **C. pannòsa** Franch. Half-evergreen shrub to 2 m., with slender arching brs.; young brts. densely pubescent at first: lvs. elliptic, acute at ends, mucronate, 1–2.5 cm. long, dull green above and glabrous, white-tomentose beneath; petioles 2–7 mm. long: fls. 8 mm. across, in rather dense 6–20-fld. corymbs 1.5–4 cm. across, densely pubescent; sepals triangular, mucronate; anthers purple: fr. globose to ellipsoidal, 6 mm. long, dull red; nutlets 2. Fl.vɪ; fr.x–xɪ. B.M.8594(c). Gt.55:t.1551,f.2(c). R.H.1907:256,t(c). Gn.67: 118;80:66. N.F.3:f.3(h). S. W. China. Cult. 1888. Zone VII. Similar to *C. Francheti*, but lvs. glabrous above, petioles slenderer and fr. smaller with 2 nutlets.

C. p. × *frigida:* see under No. 24.
Related species: **C. Harroviàna** Wils. Lvs. elliptic to elliptic-oblong, 2.5–5 cm. long, leathery, densely villous beneath, finally glabrescent, with 5–10 not very prominent veins: infl. 3–4 cm. across. W. China. Intr. 1900.—**C. oligocárpa** Schneid. Lvs. oval or obovate to elliptic, acute or obtuse, 2.5–5 cm. long, dull and slightly pubescent above, with persistent tomentum beneath: fr. red, obovoid, 4–5 mm. long. W. China. Intr. 1915.—**C. turbinàta** Craib. Lvs. oblongovate to oblong-lanceolate, acute at ends, 3–4.5 cm. long, mucronulate: infl. white-tomentose: fr. turbinate, 4–5 mm. long, thinly silky, bright red. Fl.vɪɪ. B.M.8546(c). W. China. Intr. 1897.—**C. láctea** W. W. Sm. Brts. loosely whitetomentose: lvs. broad-elliptic, 3.5–8 cm. long, usually obtuse and mucronulate, rounded or broad-cuneate at base, dull green above, whitish tomentose beneath: infl. 4–6 cm. across, tomentose: fr. ovoid, 6 mm. long; nutlets 2. B.M.9454(c). N.F.3:f.1(h). W. China. Intr. 1930. Zone (V) VI.

26. **C. salicifòlia** Franch. Half-evergreen or evergreen shrub, to 5 m., with spreading brs.; young brts. floccose-tomentose: lvs. elliptic-oblong to ovate-lanceolate, acute or acuminate, cuneate, 3–8 cm. long, rugose and glabrous above, tomentose and glaucous beneath and with 5–12 pairs of prominent veins; petiole 2–5 mm. long, like the midrib often reddish: fls. small, in densely woolly corymbs 3–5 cm. across; anthers red: fr. subglobose, 5 mm. across, bright red, with 2–3 nutlets; hypostyle glabrous. Fl.vɪ; fr.x. B.M.8999(c). Gn.86:658. W. China. Intr. 1908. Zone VI? Graceful shrub with half-evergreen or in milder climates evergreen lvs. and attractive bright red fr. in late fall.—**C. s. floccòsa** Rehd. & Wils., var. Lvs. oblong to oblong-lanceolate, tomentose beneath while young, later partly glabrous, lustrous above, with 7–14 pairs of veins: fr. 6 mm. high, usually with 3 nutlets. G.C.71:114. Gs.14:25. Intr. 1908. Zone (V).—**C. s. rugòsa** (Pritz.) Rehd. & Wils., var. Lvs. elliptic-oblong, to 2.5 cm. broad, dull green above, beneath with dense woolly tomentum: fr. 6 mm. long; nutlets 3. B.M.8649(c). G.C. 56:412,t(c). Gn.87:42. (*C. r.* Pritz.) C. China. Intr. 1907.

Closely related species: **C. rhytidophýlla** Rehd. & Wils. Brts. and lvs. beneath densely whitish or yellowish tomentose: lvs. oblong-ovate to oblonglanceolate, 3–8 cm. long, strongly wrinkled above, reticulate beneath: corymbs dense, about 3 cm. across: fr. orange-red, pyriform, about 6 mm. long; nutlets 3 or 4. W. China. Intr. 1908. Zone VII?—**C. glabràta** Rehd. & Wils. Young brts. thinly pubescent, soon glabrous and red-brown: lvs. oblong-lanceolate, 4–8 cm. long, bright green and slightly rugose above, glaucous beneath and glabrous or slightly pubescent: corymbs dense, about 3 cm. across, slightly pubescent; styles 2. W. China. Intr. 1908. Zone VII?—**C. glaucophýlla** Franch. Lvs. elliptic to elliptic-oblong, 3–6 cm. long, glaucous beneath, glabrous or slightly pubescent at first: infl. slightly pubescent at first; calyx glabrous: fr. obovoid, 5 mm. long. Fl.vɪ. S.H.1:f.424m,427i. W. China. Cult. 1915. Zone VII?—**C. g. seròtina** (Hutchins.) Stapf, f. Infl. 3.5–7 cm. across; fls.vɪɪ–vɪɪɪ. B.M.8854, 9171(c). N.F.3:f.2. (*C. s.* Hutchins.) Intr. 1910.—**C. g. vestìta** W. W. Sm., var.

Lvs. densely fulvous-tomentose beneath when young: calyx densely white-tomentose. W. China. Cult. 1934.

27. C. Henryàna (Schneid.) Rehd. & Wils. Half-evergreen shrub, to 4 m., with arching pubescent brts.: lvs. oblong to oblong-lanceolate, acute at ends, 5–12 cm. long, sparingly pubescent above at first, grayish tomentose beneath, finally often glabrescent or pubescent only on the veins and otherwise nearly glabrous and glaucous, with 9–12 pairs of veins; petiole 5–15 mm. long, pubescent: fls. 1 cm. across, in rather loose pubescent corymbs 2.5–4 cm. across; anthers purple: fr. ovoid, 6 mm. long, dark crimson, with 2–3 nutlets; hypostyle pubescent. Fl.vɪ; fr.x. G.C.46:339. R.H.1919:264,t(c). M.G.29:15. (*C. rugosa* var. *H.* Schneid.) C. China. Intr. 1901. Zone VII? Lvs. larger than any other half-evergreen or evergreen species.

C. H. × *frigida;* see under No. 24.

28. C. Dámmeri Schneid. Evergreen shrub with trailing often rooting brs.; brts. slightly pubescent when young, soon glabrous: lvs. elliptic to elliptic-oblong, acutish or obtusish, mucronulate, rarely emarginate, cuneate, 1.5–3 cm. long, glabrous and lustrous dark green above, paler or glaucescent and slightly reticulate beneath, strigose pubescent at first, soon glabrous, petiole 2–3 mm. long: fls. usually solitary, 1 cm. across, short-stalked; calyx sparingly pubescent or nearly glabrous; anthers purple: fr. subglobose 6–7 mm. across, bright red; nutlets usually 5. Fl.v–vɪ; fr.x–xɪ. S.H.1:f.428a-b,429h-k. Gs.5:110. Gt.73:135(h). S.L.143(h). (*C. humifusa* Duthie.) C. China. Intr. 1900. Zone V? Very distinct on account of its prostrate habit with long trailing brs.—**C. D. radìcans** Schneid., var. Lvs. oval or elliptic to obovate, usually obtuse, often emarginate, more rugulose above, smaller: fls. 1–2, on pedicels 5–15 mm. long. Gn.88:35(h);87:27(h);89:226(h). W. China. Intr. 1904 or 1908.

29. C. rotundifòlia Lindl. Evergreen shrub to 4 m., with long arching brs.: lvs. broad-oval or broad-obovate, rounded or acute and mucronulate at apex, usually broad-cuneate, 8–20 mm. long, lustrous dark green above, glaucescent and sparingly strigose-hirsute below: fls. 1–3, 1–1.2 cm. across, short-stalked; calyx sparingly pubescent; anthers purple: fr. subglobose, 8 mm. across, red; nutlets 2. Fl.vɪ; fr.ɪx. Ref. Bot. 1:t.53(c). B.R.1187(c). (*C. prostrata* Bak., *C. microphylla* var. *uva-ursi* Lindl.) Himal. Intr. 1825. Zone VI? Forming dense masses of interlacing brs.—**C. r. lanàta** (Dipp.) Schneid., var. Lvs. elliptic to elliptic-oblong, tomentose beneath: fls. 3–8. Ref. Bot. 1:t.52(c). R.H.1889:348,t.f.4(c). Gn.55:186;87:28. (*C. buxifolia* Baker, not Wall., *C. Wheeleri* Hort., partly, ?*C. lanata* Jacques.)

Related species: **C. buxifòlia** Lindl. Low compact shrub; young brts. densely white-tomentose: lvs. elliptic to obovate, 6–15 mm. long, mucronate, dull green and hairy above when young, tomentose beneath, not papillose: cymes few-fld. Wight, Icon. 3:t.992. S.H.1:f.425k,l,429b. Nilghiri Hills. Intr. 1919. Zone VII? —**C. b. vellaèa** Franch., f. Prostrate shrub; brts. thinly pubescent, soon glabrate: lvs. 5–10 mm. long: fls. often solitary. W. China. Intr. about 1915, Zone VI?

30. C. microphýlla Lindl. Evergreen low shrub to 1 m. with spreading brs.: lvs. obovate to obovate-oblong, obtuse, rarely acutish or emarginate, cuneate, 5–8 mm. long, lustrous dark green above, glaucous and densely grayish pubescent beneath: fls. usually solitary, rarely 2–3, 1 cm. across; calyx pubescent; anthers purple: fr. globose, 6 mm. across, scarlet. Fl.v–vɪ; fr.ɪx–x. B.R.1114(c). R.H.1889:348,t,f.3(c). G.C.II.12:333;18:681. Gn.4:165. Jour. Intern. Gard. Club, 2:83(h). Himal. Intr. 1824. Zone (V). Forming dense masses with small lustrous lvs. studded in spring with white fls. fol-

lowed in fall by conspicuous scarlet fr.—**C. m. cochleàta** (Franch.) Rehd. &
Wils., var. Prostrate: lvs. obovate to nearly oval, rounded or emarginate at
apex, margin revolute, beneath with scattered long white hairs. W. China.
Intr. 1922.—**C. m. melanótricha** (Franch.) Hand.-Mazz., f. Lvs. obovate or
oval, glaucous and with scattered appressed, blackish hairs beneath. W.
China. Intr. 1915.—**C. m. thymifòlia** (Baker) Koehne, var. Lvs. narrowly
oblong-obovate; fls. 2–4, smaller: fr. 5 mm. across. Ref. Bot.1:t.50(c). R.H.
1889:348,t.f.2(c). G.C.II.12:333;18:681. (*C. thymaefolia* Baker.) Himal.
Intr. 1852.

Related species: **C. conspícua** Marquand. Spreading evergreen shrub to
2 m.: lvs. elliptic-oblong, 6–10 mm. long, on shoots to 2 cm. long, obtuse and
usually mucronulate, sparsely pilose above, densely so beneath: fr. subglobose
or obovoid, 9 mm. long, scarlet, profusely produced. B.M.9554(c). G.C.103:267.
W. China. Intr. 1925. Zone VII?—**C. c. decòra** Russell, var. Prostrate shrub
with ascending brs. (*C. d.* Hort.) Intr. 1925.

31. **C. congésta** Baker. Low compact shrub to 1 m.; brts. pubescent when
young, soon glabrous: lvs. obovate to oval, 6–12 mm. long, obtuse, cuneate,
dull green above, whitish beneath, sparingly pubescent at first, becoming
glabrous; petiole slender, nearly glabrous, 1–3 mm. long: fls. solitary, 6 mm.
across, pinkish white: fr. bright red, about 6 mm. across. Ref. Bot. 1:t.51(c).
(*C. microphylla* var. *glacialis* Hook., *C. pyrenaica* Hort.) Himal. Intr. 1868.
Zone VI.

14. **PYRACÁNTHA** Roem. Firethorn. Evergreen shrubs with usually
thorny brs.; buds small, pubescent: lvs. alternate, short-petioled, crenulate
or serrulate or entire, stipules minute, caducous: fls. white, in compound
corymbs; sepals short; petals suborbicular, spreading; stamens 20; anthers
yellow; carpels 5, free on the ventral side, on the dorsal one adnate about ½
to the calyx-tube: fr. a small pome with persistent calyx, red or orange;
nutlets 5. (Greek *pyr*, fire and *acanthos*, thorn; alluding to the spiny brs. and
bright red fr.) Six species from S. E. Eu. to Himal. and C. China.

A. Lvs. beneath and calyx glabrous, or lvs. slightly pubescent.
  B. Corymbs pubescent: lvs. elliptic to oblanceolate, acute...................1. *P. coccinea*
  BB. Corymbs glabrous except in var. of No. 2.
    C. Lvs. oblong to oblong-lanceolate, rarely oblong-obovate, usually acute, bristle-
      tipped serrate-crenate, 1–2 cm. broad...................2. *P. crenulata*
    CC. Lvs. generally obovate to obovate-oblong, obtuse, 1.5–2.5 cm. broad.
      D. Lvs. crenate-serrate, broadest above the middle, obtuse, green beneath.
                                    3. *P. crenato-serrata*
      DD. Lvs. usually entire, sometimes serrulate, widest at or near the middle, usually
        acutish, glaucescent beneath...................4. *P. atalantioides*
A. Lvs. beneath and calyx tomentose, entire or nearly so...................5. *P. angustifolia*

1. **P. coccínea** Roem. Shrub to 2 m., rarely to 6 m.; spines 1–1.5 cm. long;
young brts. grayish pubescent: lvs. narrow-elliptic to lanceolate or oblanceolate, rarely ovate-oblong, acute, rarely obtusish, cuneate, 2–4 cm. long,
closely crenulate-serrulate, slightly pubescent beneath at first or glabrous;
petioles 2–5 mm. long, pubescent: fls. 8 mm. across, in many-fld. corymbs
2.5–4 cm. broad: fr. subglobose, 5–6 mm. thick, bright red. Fl.v–vi; fr.ix–x.
S.O.2:t.90(c). R.I.25:t.99(c). B.S.2:268. M.D.1917:t.32(h). (*Cotoneaster
Pyracantha* Spach, *Crataegus P.* Borkh., *Mespilus P.* L.; Fiery Thorn, Ever-
lasting Thorn.) Italy to W. Asia. Naturalized Pa. and s. Intr. 1629. Zone
VI. Ornamental shrub doing particularly well trained against a wall; the var.
is more vigorous and hardier.—**P. c. Lalándii** Dipp. Of more vigorous
growth with slenderer and longer brs.: lvs. less deeply crenate: fr. bright
orange-red. R.H.1925:572,t,f.2(c). Gn.79:570;89:614 M.G.16:136(h). (*P. c.*
var. *latifolia* Zabel.) Orig. about 1874.

2. **P. crenulàta** (Roxb.) Roem. Shrub or small tree; young brts. and petioles rusty-pubescent: lvs. oblong to oblanceolate, rarely ovate-lanceolate, acute or obtusish and bristle-tipped at apex, cuneate, 2–5 cm. long, crenate-serrulate, lustrous bright green above, glabrous; petioles glabrous: fls. 8 mm. across, in rather loose corymbs 2–3 cm. broad; styles spreading from the base: fr. subglobose, 6–8 mm. across, orange-red. Fl.v–vi; fr.ix–x. B.R.30:52(c). G.C.57:101,t(c). R.H.1913:205,t(c). S.H.1:f.430c-d,413g-h. (*Crataegus c.* Roxb., *Cotoneaster c.* Wenz.) Himal. Intr. about 1844. Zone VII?—**P. c. Rogersiàna** A. B. Jacks., var. Lower: lvs. oblanceolate, 2–4.5 cm. long, unequally serrulate: fr. 7–8 mm. across, reddish orange. R.H.1925:572,t.f.3(c). G.C.60:309(l). Gn.85:567. (*P. R.* Chittenden, *P. R.* f. *aurantiaca* Bean.) S. W. China. Intr. 1911.—**P. c. flàva** Meunissier. A form of the preceding var. with yellow fr. R.H.1925:572,t.f.1(c). G.C.67:55.—**P. c. kansuénsis** Rehd., var. Lvs. narrow-oblong to oblanceolate, 1–2.5 cm. long: infl. pubescent: fr. about 5 mm. across. N. W. China. Intr. 1914.

3. **P. crenàto-serràta** (Hance) Rehd. Shrub to 3 m.; young brts. rusty-pubescent: lvs. elliptic or obovate to obovate-oblong, rounded or acute at apex, sometimes with a minute mucro, 2.5–6 cm. long, crenate, entire and gradually narrowed toward the base, dark green and lustrous above, light green beneath: fls. 1 cm. across; infl. 3–4 cm. across: fr. subglobose, 7 mm. across, coral-red. Fl.v–vii; fr.x–i. R.H.1913:204,t.B(c). B.M.9099,f.5–10(c). Gn.83:138;87:52. (*P. yunnanensis* Chittenden, *P. crenulata* var. *yunnanensis* Mott., *P. Gibbsii* Rehd., not A. B. Jacks.) C. and W. China. Cult. 1906. Zone VI? More vigorous and more freely fruiting than the preceding species.

P. c. × *Osteomeles subrotunda*; see *Pyracomeles*, p. 372.

4. **P. atalantioìdes** (Hance) Stapf. Shrub to 6 m.: lvs. elliptic to oblong-lanceolate, 3–7 cm. long, acutish or rarely rounded at apex, entire or serrulate to crenulate, glaucescent beneath and fulvous-pubescent when young; petioles 3–8 mm. long: corymbs many-fld., 3–4 cm. across, puberulous toward the base; pedicels glabrous; fls. 8–9 mm. across: fr. 6–7 mm. across, scarlet or bright crimson. Fl.v–vi; fr.x–iii. B.M.9099,f.1–4(c). G.C.60:309;63:47(h); 73:27. J.L.48:59. Gn.82:443. (*P. Gibbsii* A. B. Jacks., *P. discolor* Rehd., ?*P. Loureiri* Merr.) S. E. to W. China. Intr. 1907. Zone VI. Valued for its bright fr. remaining on the brs. through the winter.

5. **P. angustifòlia** (Franch.) Schneid. Shrub to 4 m., sometimes prostrate: lvs. narrow-oblong to oblanceolate-oblong, obtuse and mucronulate, sometimes emarginate, cuneate, 1.5–5 cm. long, entire or with few teeth near apex, pubescent above at first, finally glabrous and dark green, grayish tomentose beneath: fls. 8 mm. across, in rather dense corymbs 2–4 cm. across: fr. depressed-globose, 4–6 mm. across, short-stalked, bright orange to brick-red. Fl.v–vi; fr.x–iii. B.M.8345(c). Gn.67:24,105,t(c);87:110. G.C.36:441. (*Cotoneaster a.* Franch.) S. W. China. Intr. 1895. Zone VII. Retaining its bright-colored fr. until March.

15. **MÉSPILUS** L. MEDLAR. Deciduous tree, sometimes thorny; buds with imbricate scales, dark brown: lvs. alternate, short-petioled, serrulate or nearly entire, with deciduous stipules: fls. solitary, large, white, on short, not articulate stalks, terminal on short leafy brts.; sepals large; petals suborbicular or broad-obovate; stamens 30–40, with red anthers; styles 5 distinct, glabrous; carpels 5, completely connate, each with 2 fertile ovules: fr. a large pomaceous drupe, open at the top, with large leafy sepals; stones 5. (Ancient Latin name.) One species.

M. germànica L. Shrub or small tree, to 5 m. or more; brts. pubescent: lvs. oblong to oblong-lanceolate, short-acuminate, 6–12 cm. long, slightly pubescent and dull green above, more densely pubescent beneath: fls. 3–4 cm. across: fr. depressed-subglobose or pyriform, 2–3 cm. across. Fl.v; fr.x–xi. S.O.2:t.83(c). G.H.t.69(c). S.E.3:t.478(c). R.I.25:t.100(c). S. E. Eu. to Persia, doubtfully native in C. Eu. and Eng. Long cult. Zone V. Sometimes grown for its fr. which after incipient decay becomes soft and of agreeable acid taste.—**M. g. macrocárpa** (Duham.) K. Koch, with larger, much depressed fr. (*M. g. f. gigantèa* Kirchn.)—**M. g. abortìva** (Dum.-Cours.) K. Koch, var. A seedless form with small fr. (*M. g.* var. *apyrena* K. Koch.) There are also forms with variegated lvs.

M. g. × *Crataegus Oxyacantha* = *Crataegomespilus grandiflora;* see below.
—*M. g.* × *Crataegus monogyna* = *C. Gillotii;* see below.

× **CRATAEGOMÉSPILUS** Jouin. Deciduous trees or shrubs: graft-hybrids or sexual hybrids (*Cratae-mespilus* Camus) between *Crataegus* and *Mespilus:* similar to Mespilus but differing in the smaller fls., usually 1–3 at end of brts., with 14–28 stamens and in the smaller fr. with 2–3 sterile nutlets.

1. **C. grandiflòra** (Sm.) Bean (*Crataegus Oxyacantha* × *Mespilus germanica*). Shrub or tree: lvs. elliptic, acute at ends, 3–7 cm. long, unequally serrate or serrulate, or sometimes slightly lobed toward the apex, pubescent beneath: fls. 1–3, about 2.5 cm. across; calyx pubescent: fr. globose-ovoid 1–1.5 cm. across, pubescent. Fl.v–vi; fr.x. B.M.3442(c). R.I.25:t.107,f. 4–9(c). G.F.10:35. R.H.1869:80. (*Crataegus g.* K. Koch, *C. Smithii* Ser., *C. lobata* Bosc, *Mespilus g.* Sm., *Cratae-mespilus g.* Camus.) Orig. before 1800. Zone V.

A similar hybrid is **C. Gillótii** Beck (*Crataegus monogyna* × *M. germanica*), differing chiefly in its lobed, not serrate lvs. and smaller fls. with 2 styles. R.I.25:t.107,f.1–3(c). Orig. in France. Cult. 1890.

2. **C. Dárdari** Jouin (*Crataegus monogyna* + *M. germanica*). Lvs. and fr. similar to those of *Mespilus,* but brs. spiny: fls. 1.5 cm. across, in corymbs, pedicelled; stamens 15–20: fr. 1.5 cm. across, crowned by the upright calyx-lobes; stones 1–3. R.I.25:t.108(c). M.G.27:101. K.B.1911:268,t. R.H.1937: 446,t(c);1938:187.—**C. D. Asnierèsii** (Schneid.) Rehd., var. Resembling *Crataegus monogyna,* but pubescent: brs. slender: lvs. broad-obovate to ovate, serrulate and usually with 1 to 2 pairs of lobes: fls. in 3–12-fld. corymbs; stamens 20; styles 1–2: fr. subglobose, 1 cm. across. R.I.25:t.109(c). G.C. 50:183,185;77:3(h). Gn.75:310;86:189(h). K.B.1911:268,t(h). (C. "Jules d'Asnières" Jouin, *C. Asnieresii* Schneid.)—Both forms orig. on the same tree at Bronveaux near Metz, France. Sometimes brs. reverting to one of the parents are produced.

16. **CRATAÈGUS** L. Hawthorn. Deciduous, rarely half-evergreen shrubs or trees, usually spiny: lvs. alternate, serrate or lobed, stipulate: fls. white (red in some vars.), in corymbs, rarely solitary: sepals and petals 5; stamens 5–25; carpels 1–5, connate, but free at the apex and on the ventral side: fr. a pome-like drupe with 1–5 bony 1-seeded nutlets, their free part (hypostyle) differing in texture. (Ancient Greek name.) Temp. regions of the n. hemisphere; more than 1000 species have been described from N. Am., but much reduced by recent authors; about 90 in the Old World. Only some representative species of the different groups are described here; for other American species see Sargent, Man. Trees N. Am., ed. 2, 397–549, Small, Fl. S. E. St. 532–569, and Man. S. E. Flora, 637–644, Gray's Man. ed. 7,460–479, and

Britton & Brown, Ill. Fl. ed. 2, 2:294–321; also Palmer in J.A.6:5–128 for an enumeration of the American species.

A. Veins of the lvs. extending to the points of the lobes or teeth only: lvs. usually slightly or not lobed (except in Nos. 32–34): fr. not blue or black (except in Nos. 20 and 31).
  B. Nutlets without cavities on the inner surface: fr. usually mealy at maturity.
    C. Petioles elongated, usually slender.
      D. Petioles glandular at apex or sparingly glandular throughout.
        E. Petioles glandular only at apex; corymbs many-fld.: lvs. broad at base.
          F. Lvs. tomentose or pubescent beneath, at least on the veins.
            G. Stamens 20: lvs. leathery..1. *C. mollis*
            GG. Stamens 10; lvs. membranous..............................2. *C. submollis*
          FF. Lvs. glabrous beneath or nearly so.
            G. Fr. not bloomy.
              H. Stamens 20; anthers pink; infl. glabrous: lvs. truncate.
                            4. *C. coccinioides*
              HH. Stamens 5–10: lvs. broad-cuneate to truncate.
                I. Anthers pink or rose-colored; stamens usually 10.
                  J. Calyx-lobes usually glandular-serrate: nutlets usually 4.
                    K. Infl. densely villous...........................3. *Ellwangeriana*
                    KK. Infl. slightly villous or glabrous................5. *C. pedicellata*
                  JJ. Calyx-lobes entire or obscurely serrate; nutlets 2–3.6. *C. flabellata*
                II. Anthers yellow; stamens 5–10......................7. *C. chrysocarpa*
            GG. Fr. bloomy until nearly fully ripe....................8. *C. pruinosa*
        EE. Petioles sparingly glandular throughout; corymbs usually few-fld.: lvs. cuneate at base: stamens 10.
          F. Infl. glabrous or nearly so......................................9. *C. intricata*
          FF. Infl. pubescent.
             G. Corymbs many-fld. ....10. *C. Harbisonii*
            GG. Corymbs 2–5-fld. ....11. *C. triflora*
      DD. Petioles glandless or with few minute glands: lvs. usually 3-lobed toward the apex, lustrous above.
        E. Fr. bright red...12. *C. viridis*
        EE. Fr. dull dark red..13. *C. nitida*
    CC. Petioles usually short (except in No. 21): lvs. cuneate at base, not or very slightly lobed.
      D. Infl. many-fld.
        E. Fr. red.
          F. Stamens 10; corymbs glabrous............................14. *C. crus-galli*
          FF. Stamens 15–20.
             G. Lvs. lustrous above.
               H. Nutlets 1–3: lvs. 6–10 cm. long.
                I. Lvs. glabrous beneath.............................15. *C. persistens*
                II. Lvs. villous beneath................................16. *C. Lavallei*
               HH. Nutlets 3–5; lvs. 1–6 cm. long.
                I. Fr. 1–1.5 cm. across: anthers red: lvs. pubescent......17. *C. cuneata*
                II. Fr. 4–6 mm. across: anthers yellow: lvs. glabrous...25. *C. spathulata*
             GG. Lvs. dull above.
               H. Fr. juicy, edible: lvs. cuneate-oblong to elliptic-lanceolate, tomentose beneath ....18. *C. pubescens*
               HH. Fr. dry, mealy: lvs. obovate or oval....................19. *C. punctata*
        EE. Fr. bluish black...20. *C. brachyacantha*
      DD. Infl. 1–5-fld.: lvs. not exceeding 5 cm.
        E. Petioles glandless or with few glands.
          F. Fls. before the lvs., 2–5; sepals entire or minutely serrate; petioles 6–20 mm. long ....21. *C. aestivalis*
          FF. Fls. after the lvs., usually solitary: sepals foliaceous, glandular-serrate; petioles short ....22. *C. uniflora*
        EE. Petioles, margin of lf. and infl. densely glandular.................23. *C. aprica*
  B. Nutlets with furrows or irregular cavities on the inner surface (smooth in *C. dsunaarica* under No. 32): fr. usually lustrous and pulpy at maturity.
    C. Lvs. not or only slightly lobed.
      D. Fr. scarlet or orange; nutlets 2–3.
        E. Nutlets with shallow cavities: lvs. glabrous or nearly so: stamens 10–15.
                            27. *C. scabrida*
        EE. Nutlets with deep cavities: lvs. with impressed veins.
          F. Fr. ellipsoid or pear-shaped, upright: lvs. elliptic to oblong, pubescent below: stamens 20 ....28. *C. Calpodendron*
          FF. Fr. subglobose, nodding: lvs. broad-elliptic, pubescent only on the veins beneath.
             G. Stamens usually 20; anthers rose-colored................29. *C. succulenta*
             GG. Stamens usually 10; anthers yellow....................30. *C. macracantha*
      DD. Fr. black; nutlets 3–5: lvs. glabrous.............................31. *C. Douglasii*
    CC. Lvs. distinctly lobed and sharply serrate.
      D. Fr. black ....32. *C. chlorosarca*
      DD. Fr. red or yellow.

E. Lvs. cuneate, often pubescent; petioles stout: anthers pink or purple.
33. *C. sanguinea*
  EE. Lvs. truncate to broad-cuneate, glabrous; petioles slender: anthers pale yellow:
    fr. yellow or yellowish red.....................................34. *C. Wattiana*
AA. Veins of lvs. extending to the points of the lobes and to the sinuses, at least on the larger
leaves: fr. red or yellow (black in Nos. 35–36).
  B. Fr. 4–7 mm. across; sepals often deciduous.
    c. Lvs. triangular-ovate, 3–5-lobed, with broad-ovate lobes: fr. subglobose; calyx
      deciduous ....26. *C. Phaenopyrum*
    CC. Lvs. ovate, deeply 5–7-lobed: fr. ellipsoid...........................24. *C. Marshallii*
  BB. Fr. larger; sepals persistent.
    c. Fr. black; nutlets with cavities on the inner surface.
      D. Lvs. with about 5 pairs of lobes; anthers yellow: fr. lustrous, subglobose.
35. *C. nigra*
        DD. Lvs. with 2–3 pairs of lobes: anthers red: fr. dull, ellipsoid.......36. *C. pentagyna*
    CC. Fr. red or yellow.
      D. Nutlets 1–2, rarely 3, with cavities on the inner surface.
        E. Styles usually 2: lvs. 3–5-lobed with short and broad serrulate lobes.
37. *C. Oxyacantha*
        EE. Style usually 1: lvs. deeply 3–7-lobed, with usually entire or sparingly toothed
          lobes ....38. *C. monogyna*
      DD. Nutlets 2–5, without cavities.
        E. Brts. pubescent.
          F. Lvs. not glandular-serrate; lobes often entire.
            G. Lvs. lustrous above and glabrescent, finely pubescent below.
39. *C. Azarolus*
            GG. Lvs. dull and pubescent above, villous beneath: nutlets 4–5.
40. *C. orientalis*
          FF. Lvs. with glandular-serrate lobes, pubescent..............41. *C. tanacetifolia*
        EE. Brts. glabrous: lvs. deeply lobed, glabrous...................42. *C. pinnatifida*

Ser. 1. MOLLES Sarg.

1. C. mollis Scheele. Tree to 10 m., with short stout thorns: lvs. broad-
ovate, 6–10 cm. long, sharply and doubly serrate and with 4–5 pairs of short
and acute lobes, densely pubescent beneath at first, later chiefly on the veins:
infl. tomentulose; fls. 2.5 cm. across, with red disk: fr. usually pear-shaped,
1.2 cm. across, scarlet, pubescent, with sweet mealy flesh; nutlets 4–5. Fl.
IV–V; fr.VIII–IX. S.S.13:t.659. (*C. tiliaefolia* K. Koch, *C. acerifolia* Hort.,
C. coccinea var. *m.* Torr. & Gray.) S. Ont. to Va., w. to S. D. and Kans. Cult.
1683. Zone IV. This and the following species of this group are handsome
small trees with bright green foliage, large white flowers and brightly colored
rather large fr. in autumn.

    Closely related species: **C. arkansana** Sarg. with generally oblong-ovate lvs.
and frs. ripening in Oct. S.S.13:t.660. Ark. Intr. 1883.—A related species or
hybrid, probably *C. mollis* × *nigra*, is **C. peregrina** Sarg. Lvs. ovate, broad-
cuneate, with 4–6 pairs of narrow lobes, glabrous above, villous beenath: fr.
ovoid-globose, dark dull purple, pubescent at base and apex. S.T.2:t.191. Orig.
in Eu. before 1873.

2. C. submóllis Sarg. Tree to 8 m., with broad round head; spines thin,
usually straight, 5–7 cm. long: lvs. ovate, acute, broadly cuneate, 5–8 cm.
long, doubly serrate and with 3–4 pairs of acute short lobes, scabrous above,
soft-pubescent beneath at first, later puberulous on the veins: infl. tomentose:
fls. 2.5 cm. across: fr. pear-shaped or broad ellipsoid, 1.8 cm. long, bright
orange-red and lustrous, puberulous at base, with yellow mealy flesh; nutlets
usually 5. Fl.V; fr. early in Sept., soon falling. S.S.4:t.182(as *C. mollis*).
Em.494,t.(as *C. tomentosa*). G.F.5:221(h). Que. to Mass. and e. N. Y. Cult.
1830. Zone IV.

    Closely related species: **C. arnoldiàna** Sarg. Brs. zigzag; lvs. often truncate
at base, smooth and lustrous above; fr. subglobose, villous toward the ends;
nutlets 3–4. S.S.13:t.668. B.C.2:t.882. Mass. to Conn. and N. Y. Cult. 1900.

3. C. Ellwangeriàna Sarg. Tree, sometimes to 6 m. with ascending brs.
forming a broad symmetrical head: lvs. oval or ovate, acute, broad-cuneate
or rounded, 6–9 cm. long, coarsely and often doubly serrate, with many short

Ser. 9. TRIFLORAE Beadle.

11. **C. triflòra** Chapm. Large shrub or tree to 7 m.: lvs. ovate to elliptic, acute, rounded or broad-cuneate, 2–7 cm. long, serrate and with short acute lobes, pubescent: infl. usually 3-fld., pubescent: fls. 2.5–3 cm. across; sepals glandular-serrate, pubescent; stamens 20; anthers yellow: fr. globose, 1.2–1.5 cm. across, pubescent, red; nutlets 3–5. Fl.v–vi; fr.ix–x. Ga., Ala. Intr. 1912. Zone V.

Ser. 10. VIRIDES Beadle.

12. **C. víridis** L. Tree to 12 m., with spreading brs.; thorns slender: lvs. oblong-ovate to elliptic, acute or acuminate, cuneate, 2–6 cm. long, serrate, dark green and lustrous above, paler beneath, finally glabrous: infl. glabrous; pedicels slender; sepals lanceolate, entire: fr. globose, 4–6 mm. across, bright red; stones usually 5. Fl.v; fr.x(–iii). S.S.4:t.187. (*C. arborescens* Ell.) Md. and Va. to Ill., Iowa, Tex. and Fla. Cult. 1827. Zone IV.

13. **C. nítida** Sarg. Tree to 10 m. with spreading brs., unarmed or with straight thorns: lvs. elliptic to oblong-obovate, acuminate, cuneate, 2–8 cm. long, coarsely serrate and often slightly lobed, dark green and lustrous above, paler below, glabrous: infl. glabrous; sepals lanceolate, entire or sparingly glandular-serrate: fr. subglobose or short-ellipsoid, about 1 cm. long, dull red, with yellow mealy flesh; nutlets 2–5. Fl.v; fr.x(–iii). S.S.13:t.703. Gray Man. 465. Ill. to Mo. and Ark. Intr. 1883. Zone IV. Like the preceding a handsome round-headed tree with lustrous lvs. changing to orange and scarlet in fall and with red fr. persisting through the winter.

Ser. 11. CRUS-GALLI Loud.

14. **C. crus-gálli** L. COCKSPUR THORN. Large shrub or tree to 12 m., with wide-spreading rigid brs.; thorns slender, numerous: lvs. obovate to oblong-obovate, usually rounded at apex, cuneate, 2–8 cm. long, sharply serrate above the entire base, quite glabrous, subcoriaceous: infl. glabrous; fls. 1.5 cm. across; sepals entire or minutely glandular-serrate: fr. subglobose about 1 cm. across, red, with thin and dry flesh; nutlets usually 2. Fl.v–vi; fr. late in Oct. R.B.116(c). S.S.4:t.178. Em.492,t. G.F.7:295. G.C.28:244, suppl. Que to N. C. and Kans. Intr. 1656. Zone IV. Attractive in bloom and with decorative bright red fr. remaining during the winter; the lvs. changing to orange and scarlet in fall.—**C. c. salicifòlia** (Med.) Ait., var. Lvs. lanceolate to oblanceolate, thinner. (*C. c.* var. *linearis* Ser.)—**C. c. pyracanthifòlia** Ait., var. Lvs. elliptic to obovate, usually acute: fr. smaller, bright red. S.S.13:t. 637. W. N. Y. and Pa. to Fla. and Tenn.—**C. c. spléndens** Ait., var. Lvs. elliptic-oblanceolate, very shining.

C. c. × *pubescens;* see No. 16.—*C. c.* × *? macracantha;* see under No. 30. *C. c.* × *pentagyna;* see under No. 36.

Related species: C. **Fontanesiàna** (Spach) Steud. Lvs. thinner, elliptic to elliptic-lanceolate, or obovate-oblong: pedicels hairy; stamens 16–18, with yellow anthers: fr. ellipsoid or pyriform, 1.2 cm. long, brick-red. G.O.t.144. (*C. olivacea* Sarg.) Pa. Cult. 1830. Zone V.—C. **fecúnda** Sarg. Tree to 8 m.: lvs. thinner, ovate or elliptic to oblong-ovate, 5–8 cm. long, acute, rarely rounded at apex, coarsely doubly serrate, slightly pubescent on the veins beneath or nearly glabrous: infl. glabrous or slightly pubescent: fr. subglobose to short-ellipsoid, about 1.5 cm. long. W.A.62,t(h). Mo., Ill. Intr. 1883. Zone V.

15. × **C. persístens** Sarg. Low tree to 4 m. or more, with wide-spreading brs.; thorns stout, to 5 cm. long; young brts. glabrous: lvs. narrow-elliptic to oblong-obovate or oblong, acute or acuminate, cuneate, 5–7 cm. long, serrate from below the middle, dark green and lustrous above, paler beneath, gla-

brous, subcoriaceous: infl. slightly villous: calyx glabrous; fls. 2 cm. across; sepals glandular-serrate above the middle or entire; stamens 20, with whitish anthers: fr. ellipsoid or slightly pear-shaped, 1.5 cm. long, crimson, not lustrous; nutlets 2–3. Fl.v; fr.x. S.T.2:t.190. Orig. 1876? (Possibly hybrid of *C. crus-galli*.) Zone V. Similar to the Cockspur Thorn, but remaining green into the early winter and conspicuous with its persistent red fr.

16. × **C. Lavállei** Herincq (*? C. crus-galli* × *pubescens*). Small tree to 7 m., with spreading brs.; spines stout, to 5 cm. long; young brts. pubescent: lvs. elliptic to oblong-obovate, acute, cuneate, 5–10 cm. long, unequally serrate from below the middle, slightly pubescent above when young, finally glabrous and lustrous, pubescent beneath: infl. many-fld., villous: fls. 2 cm. across, with red disk; sepals linear, slightly serrulate; stamens 15–20, with yellow or red anthers: fr. ellipsoid, about 1.5 cm. long, brick-red or orange-red; nutlets 2–3. Fl.v; fr.x(–iii). R.H.1883:108,t(c);1924:59(h). L.I.t.7. G.C. III.4:737;21:118,119. M.A.t.31(h). (*C. Carrierei* Vauvel.) Orig. before 1880. Zone IV. Tree with the lvs. turning bronzy red late in fall and with conspicuous fls. and showy fr. remaining through the winter.

Ser. 12. Cuneatae Rehd.

17. **C. cuneàta** Sieb. Much-branched shrub to 1.5 m.; spines slender, 5–8 mm. long; young brts. pubescent: lvs. broad-obovate to obovate-oblong, gradually narrowed into a short petiole, 2–6 cm. long, incisely and irregularly serrate and often 3-lobed at apex, soon glabrous above, loosely villous beneath, at least on the veins; stipules semi-ovate, toothed: fls. 1.5 cm. across, in few-fld. pubescent corymbs; sepals entire or toothed; stamens 20; anthers red: fr. globose or pear-shaped with persistent large reflexed sepals and usually an adnate bract; nutlets 5. Fl.v–vi; fr.x. L.I.t.5. S.H.1:f.453s-v, 454a-c. (*C. alnifolia* Hort., not Sieb. & Zucc.) Japan, China. Cult. 1880. Zone (V). Small twiggy shrub, of no particular ornamental value.

Ser. 13. Mexicanae Loud.

18. **C. pubéscens** (H.B.K.) Steud. f. **stipulàcea** (Loud.) Stapf. Small tree to 10 m., unarmed or with straight spines to 4 cm. long; young brts. tomentose: lvs. elliptic-oblong or elliptic-obovate to oblanceolate, acute, cuneate, 4–8 cm. long, simply or nearly doubly serrate-crenate, sometimes lobed toward the apex, dark green above, pubescent at first, finally glabrous, slightly villous beneath, more densely on the veins; petiole 5–15 mm. long; stipules usually foliaceous, linear to lanceolate, infl. 6–12-fld., rather dense, villous: fls. 2 cm. across; sepals linear-lanceolate, entire or sparingly dentate near apex; stamens 15–20; anthers pink: fr. subglobose or pyriform, to 2.5 cm. thick, greenish yellow or orange; nutlets usually 2–3. Fl.iii; fr.x–xi. B.M.8589(c). B.R.t.1910(c). S.B.II.t.300(c). Gn.87:462. (*C. s.* Loud., *C. Loddigesiana* Desf., *C. hypolasia* K. Koch.) Mex. Intr. 1824. Zone VII? Tree with the lvs. turning orange and red late in fall and with edible fr.—The typical **C. pubescens** Steud. (*C. mexicana* DC., *Mespilus p.* H.B.K.) is probably not in cult.

C. p. × *crus-galli;* see No. 16.—*C. p.* × *?* = **C. grignonénsis** Mouillef. Lvs. with 2–4 pairs of acutish slightly crenate-serrate lobes: fr. subglobose, about 1.5 cm. thick, bright red. R.H.1936:16,t.(c). M.A.t.30(h). Orig. before 1870. Zone V.

Ser. 14. Punctatae Loud.

19. **C. punctàta** Jacq. Tree to 10 m., with horizontally spreading brs.; spines stout, short or wanting; young brts. pubescent at first: lvs. obovate,

5–10 cm. long, obtuse or acute, narrowed at base into a margined petiole to 1.5 cm. long, irregularly serrate, those of the shoots often slightly lobed above the middle, with impressed veins above, villous beneath: infl. villous, many-fld.; fls. 1.5–2 cm. across; sepals nearly entire; stamens 20: fr. subglobose or pyriform, 1.5–2 cm. long, dull red, dotted; nutlets 5. Fl.v–vi; fr. Oct., falling soon. S.S.4:t.184. W.D.57(c). A.F.28:805(h). W.A.60,t(h). Que. to Ont., Ill. and Ga. Intr. 1746. Zone IV.—**C. p. aurea** Ait., var. Fr. yellow. (*C. p.* var. *xanthocarpa* Lav., *C. crocata* Roem.) L.I.t.16.

C. p. × *tanacetifolia;* see under No. 41.
Related species: **C. collìna** Chapm. Lvs. 3–5 cm. long, nearly glabrous: fr. dark red, about 1 cm. across. S.S.13:t.654. Va. to Ala. and Kans. Cult. 1899. Zone V.

Ser. 15. BREVISPINAE Beadle (*Brachyacanthae* Sarg.)

20. **C. brachyacántha** Sarg. & Engelm. Tree to 15 m.; spines curved, 8–15 mm. long: lvs. obovate-oblong to elliptic, acute or sometimes obtuse, cuneate, 2–5 cm. long, crenulate-serrate, rarely slightly lobed, pubescent above when young, glabrous and lustrous at maturity: infl. many-fld., glabrous; fls. 8 mm. across, fading to orange; stamens 15–20: fr. subglobose, about 1 cm. across, blue and bloomy; nutlets 3–5. Fl.iv–v; fr.viii. S.S.4: t.177. Tex. to La. Intr. 1900. Zone VII?

Related species: **C. salìgna** Greene. Spines about 2 cm. long: fr. globose, 6 mm. across, red, finally blue-black, lustrous. S.S.13:t.636. Colo. Intr. 1902. Zone V?

Ser. 16. AESTIVALES Sarg.

21. **C. aestivàlis** (Walt.) Torr. & Gray. MAY HAW. Tree to 10 m. with a round compact head, unarmed or with stout spines 2–3.5 cm. long: lvs. elliptic to oblong-obovate, 2.5–3 cm. long, acute or rounded at apex, gradually narrowed into a petiole 6–20 mm. long, crenate-serrate or remotely dentate above the middle, on shoots sometimes 3-lobed, lustrous above, glabrous except axillary tufts of hairs beneath: fls. with the lvs., about 2 cm. across, in 2–3-fld. glabrous infl.: fr. ovoid, about 8 mm. across, bright red, fragrant, juicy; nutlets usually 3. Fl.iii–iv; fr.v–vi. S.S.4:t.192. N. C. to Fla. Intr. ? Zone VII?

Closely related species: **C. opaca** Hook. MAY HAW (APPLE HAW). Lvs. rusty-pubescent beneath, chiefly on the veins: fls. 2.5 cm. across in 3–5-fld. infl.: fr. subglobose, about 1.5 cm. across, ripening in May. S.M.436. Ala. to w. Tex. Probably not hardy. Fr. used for preserves and jellies.

Ser. 17. PARVIFOLIAE Loud. (*Uniflorae* Beadle)

22. **C. uniflòra** Moench. Dense low shrub, to 2.5 m., with numerous slender spines, rarely unarmed: lvs. short-petioled, obovate to oblong-obovate, obtuse, cuneate, 1.5–3.5 cm. long, coarsely or doubly crenate-serrate, pubescent on both sides, finally glabrous above: fls. 1–3, about 1.5 cm. across; calyx pubescent, with large serrate lobes: fr. globose or pyriform, about 1 cm. long, yellow or greenish yellow with conspicuous calyx; nutlets 3–5. Fl.v–vi; fr.x. W.D.65(c). S.S.4:t.191. (*C. parvifolia* Ait., *C. florida* Lodd., *C. tomentosa* L., in part, Eggl.) Va. to Fla. and e. Tex. Intr. 1704. Zone VI?

Closely related species: **C. trianthóphora** Sarg. differing chiefly in the usually 3-fld. infl. and obovoid orange-red fr.; scarcely different from the preceding. S.T.2:t.106. Mo. to Tex. Intr. 1906. Zone V.—**C. Brittònii** Eggl. differing in its elliptic or ovate acute lvs., in the 2–6-fld. corymbs and in the dull red fr. (*C. Vailiae* Beadle, not Brit.) Va. to Ga. and Ala. Intr. 1906. Zone V.

Ser. 18. FLAVAE Loud.

23. **C. áprica** Beadle. Shrub or small tree to 6 m., with spreading brs. and slender zigzag brts.; spines thin, straight, 2–3.5 cm. long: lvs. broad-

obovate or oval, acute or rounded, cuneate, 2–3.5 cm. long, serrate usually only above the middle, and often slightly lobed, with gland-tipped teeth, pubescent while young, finally glabrous, thickish: fls. 1.8 cm. across, in 3–6-fld. pubescent compact corymbs; sepals glandular-serrate; stamens 10; anthers yellow: fr. globose, 1.2 cm. across, dull orange red; nutlets 3–5. Fl.v; fr.x. S.S.13:t.698. Va. to Ga. and Tenn. Intr. 1876. Zone V. A very distinct and handsome species with small lvs.

Related species: **C. elliptica** Ait. Lvs. larger, 2–5 cm. long, crenately serrate and often slightly lobed: fls. few: fr. pyriform, green or reddish. B.R.1932, 1939. G.C.27:404. (*C. flava* var. *lobata* Lindl., *C. l.* Loud.) Orig. unknown; cult. 1789. Zone VI?—**C. flava** Ait. Differs chiefly in the less pubescent lvs., 20 stamens with purple anthers and in the ellipsoid orange-brown fr. S.S.13:t. 693. Ga., Fla. Cult. 1723.

Ser. 19. Apiifoliae Loud.

24. C. Marshállii Eggl. Shrub or small tree to 6 m.; brts. pubescent while young; spines 2–3 cm. long; lvs. broad-ovate to reniform, 2–4 cm. long, pinnately 5–7-cleft, serrate, glabrous or slightly pubescent when young; petioles slender, 1.5–2.5 cm. long: infl. 3–12-fld., villous; fls. 1.8 cm. across: fr. ellipsoid, 6–8 mm. high, scarlet; sepals reflexed, lanceolate, serrate, sometimes partly deciduous. Fl.iv–v; fr.x. S.S.4:t.188. (*C. apiifolia* Michx., not Med.) Va. to Fla., Ark. and Tex. Intr. 1812. Zone (V). With widespreading slender brs., abundant white fls. in spring and attractive fr. in fall.

Ser. 20. Microcarpae Loud.

25. C. spathulàta Michx. Shrub or small tree, to 8 m.: lvs. unarmed or with straight stout spines about 3 cm. long: lvs. rhombic-obovate to oblanceolate, acute or rounded and sometimes 3–5-lobed at apex, cuneate, 1–3.5 cm. long, crenate-serrate, glabrate at maturity: fls. about 1 cm. across in many-fld. glabrous corymbs: fr. subglobose, 4–6 mm. thick, with reflexed, deltoid, entire sepals, scarlet. Fl.v–vi; fr.x. B.R.1846(c). S.S.4:t.185. (*C. microcarpa* Lindl.) Va. to Fla., Okl. and Tex. Intr. 1806. Zone (V).

Ser. 21. Cordatae Beadle.

26. C. Phaenopỳrum (L. f.) Med. Washington Thorn. Tree to 10 m., glabrous; spines slender, to 7 cm. long; lvs. broad- or triangular-ovate, acute, truncate or subcordate, 3–7 cm. long, sharply serrate and 3–5-lobed, bright green and lustrous above, paler below; petioles slender, 1.5–3.5 cm. long: fls. 1.2 cm. across, in many-fld. corymbs; sepals entire, deltoid; stamens 20; anthers yellow: fr. depressed-globose, 8 mm. across, scarlet, lustrous; sepals deciduous, leaving a circular scar; nutlets 3–5. Fl.v–vi; fr.ix–x. B.R.1151(c). S.S.4:t.186. Gn.87:461. F.E.28:103(h). B.S.1:424(h). (*C. cordata* Ait., *C. acerifolia* Moench, *C. populifolia* Walt., ? *C. cordifolia* Mill.) Va. to Ala. and Mo. Intr. 1738. Zone IV. Tree with round head, beautiful in fall with its bright scarlet fr. in large clusters and the lvs. turning scarlet and orange.— **C. P. fastigiàta** Slavin, f. Small tree of columnar habit: fls. and frs. smaller. Cult. 1929.

Ser. 22. Anomalae Sarg.

27. C. scábrida Sarg. Shrub or small tree to 6 m.; brts. glabrous; spines 3–5 cm. long: lvs. elliptic to obovate, 5–7 cm. long, short-acuminate, broad-cuneate, with many short spreading sharply and irregularly glandular-dentate lobes, at first finely pubescent above, soon glabrous, thick at maturity, dark green; petioles 1–2.5 cm. long: fls. 1.8 cm. across, in many-fld. loose glabrous

corymbs; sepals linear-lanceolate, glandular-serrate; stamens 5–15; anthers
pink: fr. subglobose, scarlet, 1 cm. across; nutlets 2–4. Fl.v–vi; fr.ix. (*C.
Brainerdi* var. *s.* Eggl.) S. e. Can. to Pa. Intr. 1899. Zone IV.

Closely related species: **C. asperifòlia** Sarg. Shrub to 2 m.: lvs. with persistent hairs above: cymes sometimes slightly villous; fr. short-ellipsoid. (*C.
Brainerdi* var. *a.* Eggl.) S. e. Can. to N. Y. and N. H. Intr. 1902. Zone IV.

Ser. 23. MACRACANTHAE Loud. (*Tomentosae* Sarg.)

28. C. Calpodéndron Med. Shrub or small tree to 6 m., with spreading
brs., unarmed or with short spines; young brts. pubescent: lvs. elliptic to
obovate-oblong, acute, cuneate, 5–12 cm. long, serrate and often slightly
lobed, dull green and finally glabrous above, pubescent beneath: fls. 1.2 cm.
across in many-fld. pubescent corymbs 6–12 cm. across; sepals serrate; stamens
15–20; anthers pink: fr. ellipsoid or pear-shaped, about 1 cm. long, dull
yellow or yellowish red, pulpy; nutlets 2–3. Fl.vi; fr.x. B.R.1877(c). Ad.4:
t.154(c). S.S.4:t.183. G.F.2:425. Gn.22:145. (*C. tomentosa* auth., not L.,
C. pyrifolia Ait., *C. leucophloeos* Moench, *C. Chapmanii* Ashe.) Ont. to Ga.,
w. to Minn. and Kan. Intr. 1747. Zone IV.

Related species: **C. Wilsónii** Sarg. Shrub to 6 m.: lvs. ovate to obovate,
acute or obtuse, at maturity lustrous above, sparingly villous beneath: fr.
ellipsoid, about 1 cm. long, red. C. China. Intr. 1907. Zone V.

29. C. succulénta Lk. Tree to 5 m., with stout ascending brs.; spines
stout, 3–5 cm. long: lvs. broad-elliptic to obovate, acute or short-acuminate,
cuneate, 5–8 cm. long, coarsely and doubly serrate, lustrous above, pubescent
beneath on the veins, finally glabrous: fls. 1.8 cm. across, in many-fld. villous
corymbs; sepals glandular-serrate, stamens 15–20; anthers pink: fr. globose,
1.5 cm. across, bright red, pulpy. Fl.v; fr.ix–x. Lange, Rev. Crat. t.8B.
Ad.4:t.123(c). S.S.4:t.181(as *C. cocc.* var. *macracantha*). (*C. macracantha*
var. *s.* Rehd.) Que. and Ont. to Mass. and Ill. Cult. 1830. Zone III.

30. C. macracántha Lodd. Shrub or small tree to 5 m.; spines slender,
sometimes 10 to 12 cm. long: lvs. broad-elliptic to obovate, usually acute,
cuneate, 5–8 cm. long, doubly serrate, lustrous and dark green above, nearly
glabrous beneath; petioles about 1 cm. long: fl. 1.8 cm. across; infl. slightly
villous; stamens 10; anthers yellow; sepals glandular-serrate: fr. subglobose,
8 mm. across, dark cherry-red, lustrous, pulpy. Fl.v–vi; fr.ix–x. B.R.1912(c).
L.B.1012(c, as *C. glandulosa*). S.S.13:t.689. M.G.21:561(h). (*C. coccinea*
var. *m.* Dudley, *C. succulenta* var. *m.* Eggl.) W. N. Y. and Vt. to Pa. Intr.
about 1820. Zone IV. Shrub of dense habit with dark green shiny lvs. and
conspicuous lustrous red fr. in fall.

A related species or possibly hybrid with *C. crus-galli* is **C. prunifòlia**
(Poir.) Pers. Lvs. obovate or broad-obovate, pubescent on the veins beneath
when young: infl. pubescent; anthers pink: nutlets only slightly grooved on the
inner surface. B.R.1868(c). G.C.78:146,t. (*Mespilus p.* Poir., not Marsh.)
Orig. unknown; cult. 1797. Zone V.

Ser. 24. DOUGLASIANAE Eggl. (*Douglasii* Loud.)

31. C. Douglásii Lindl. Tree to 12 m. with slender, often pendulous brs.,
unarmed or with few short spines: brs. glabrous: lvs. broad-ovate to ovate-
oblong, acute or sometimes rounded, cuneate, 3–8 cm. long, serrate and
slightly lobed, pubescent on the veins at first, finally lustrous dark green
above, pubescent on the midrib, glabrous beneath; petiole about 1 cm. long:
fls. 1 cm. across, in glabrous corymbs; stamens 20; sepals triangular-ovate,
usually glandular-serrate above the middle: fr. short-ellipsoidal, 1.2 cm. long,
black and lustrous; stones 3–5. Fl.v; fr.viii–ix, soon falling. B.R.1810(c).
S.S.4:t.175. B. C. and N. Cal. to Mich. and Wyo. Intr. 1828. Zone IV.

Closely related species: **C. rivulàris** Nutt. Smaller tree, with ascending brs.: lvs. shorter-stalked, narrower, serrate; sepals shorter, entire. S.S.4:t.176. (*C. Douglasii* var. *r.* Sarg.) Idaho to Nev. and N. Mex. Intr. 1881. Zone V.

Ser. 25. SANGUINEAE Zabel

32. C. chlorosárca Maxim. Small tree of pyramidal habit; young brs. slightly pubescent, later purple-brown, lustrous: lvs. triangular-ovate to broad-ovate, acute or short-acuminate, broad-cuneate or rounded at base, 5–9 cm. long, with 3–5 pairs of short and broad, unequally serrate lobes, loosely pubescent on both sides, finally glabrous above and dark green; petioles slender, 8–20 mm. long: infl. 4–7 cm. across, nearly glabrous: fls. 1.2 cm. across, stamens 20; sepals serrulate; top of ovary pubescent; style inserted much below apex; fr. subglobose, about 1 cm. across, black; nutlets 5. Fl.v; fr.ɪx–x. S.H.Ɪ:f.437p–q,f.438n–o. Manch. Cult. 1880. Zone II.— **C. c. pubéscens** Wolf, var. Lvs. pubescent beneath. Cult. 1908.

Related species: **C. jozàna** Schneid. Brts. villous: lvs. with 5–7 pairs of lobes, pubescent beneath: infl. villous. M.K.t.51(c). Japan. Intr. 1888. Here belongs apparently *C. atrocarpa* Wolf. Yearb. For. Inst. Petersb. 15:250,t.— **C. dsungàrica** Zabel. Lvs. rhombic-ovate to broad-ovate, cuneate, 3–8 cm. long, more deeply lobed, lobes fewer, sparingly toothed, glabrous: infl. glabrous, loose; fls. 1.5 cm. across; style inserted slightly below apex; nutlet smooth on ventral surface. S.H.1:f.437k–m,438p–q. S.E. Siber., N. China. Cult. 1885. Zone V.

33. C. sanguínea Pall. Shrub or small tree to 7 m., with spreading brs., usually unarmed, or with short spines; brts. slightly hairy at first, soon glabrous: lvs. rhombic-ovate to broad-ovate, acute or short-acuminate, cuneate, 5–8 cm. long, with 2–3 pairs of short, sharply and sometimes doubly serrate lobes, slightly pubescent on both sides; petiole 8–15 mm. long: fls. 1.5 cm. across, in rather dense glabrous corymbs; stamens 20; anthers pink or purple; style inserted near apex: fr. globose, 1 cm. across, bright red. Fl.v; fr.vɪɪɪ–ɪx. W.D.60(c). S.H.1:f.437c–h,438d–f. (*Mespilus purpurea* Poir.) E. Siber. Intr. 1822. Zone III.—**C. s. chlorocárpa** (K. Koch) Schneid., var. Fr. yellow, smaller.

C. s. × *? nigra* = **C. Lambertiàna** Lge. Young brts. pubescent: lvs. pubescent beneath: infl. few-fld., pubescent: fr. blackish purple. Lange, Rev. Crat. 58. Orig. unknown. Cult. 1871.

Closely related species: **C. Maximowíczii** Schneid. Lvs. less deeply lobed, villous below: infl. densely villous; fr. villous when young. N.K.6:t.28. S.H.1: f.437a–b′, 438a–c. (*C. sanguinea* var. *villosa* Maxim.) N. E. Asia. Cult. 1904. Zone IV.—**C. dahùrica** Koehne. Lvs. rhombic-ovate, or elliptic-ovate, 2–5 cm. long, those of the flowering brts. often slightly or scarcely lobed; infl. glabrous: fr. subglobose, 7–8 mm. across, orange-red. S.H.1:f.437n–o,438g–i. S. E. Siber. Cult. 1895. Zone V. Graceful species, one of the earliest to burst into leaf.

34. C. Wattiàna Hemsl. & Lace. Small tree; brts. lustrous, red-brown, unarmed or with short spines: lvs. ovate, acute or short-acuminate, truncate or broad-cuneate, 5–9 cm. long, glabrous, with 3–5 pairs of usually ovate, acute or acuminate sharply and unequally serrate lobes, the teeth acuminate to aristate, the sinuses reaching rarely halfway to the middle; petioles 1–2 cm. long: infl. 5–8 cm. across; stamens 15–20; anthers whitish; top of ovary glabrous: fr. subglobose, 1–1.2 cm. across, orange- or reddish-yellow, pulpy. Fl.v; fr.vɪɪɪ–ɪx. R.H.1901:308,t(c). Jour. Linn. Soc. 28:t.40. (*C. Korolkowii* L. Henry.) Altai Mts. to Beluchistan. Cult. 1888. Zone V. With bright green lvs., large corymbs of white fls. and bright orange fr. in late summer.

Closely related species: **C. kansuénsis** Wils. Shrub or tree to 8 m.: lvs. broad-ovate, pinnately lobed, coarsely dentate or doubly dentate with triangular mucronate teeth, beneath with axillary tufts of hair; petioles 1–4 cm. long: infl. many-fld.; top of ovary villous: fr. 8–10 mm. across, red. N. China. Intr.

1926. Zone V.—**C. altáica** Lange. Lvs. usually smaller, with 2–4 pairs of lobes, the sinuses reaching usually more than halfway to the middle, and the lower ones often almost or quite to the midrib; petiole 1.5–3 cm. long: fr. 8–10 mm. across. Lange, Rev. Crat. t.5(excl.f.g). (*C. sanguinea* var. *incisa* and var. *xanthocarpa* Reg., *C. songarica* Reg.) Songaria to Turkest. Intr. 1876. Zone III.

Ser. 26. NIGRAE Loud. (*Pentagynae* Schneid.)

35. **C. nígra** Waldst. & Kit. Small tree to 7 m., with a round head of rather short brs.; brts. tomentose while young, unarmed or with short stout spines: lvs. ovate or triangular-ovate, acute, broad-cuneate or truncate, 4–9 cm. long, with 7–11 sharply and irregularly serrate lobes, the lower sinuses not more than halfway to the middle, pubescent on both sides, more densely beneath; petioles 1–2 cm. long: infl. dense, many-fld., villous; fls. 1.5 cm. across, white, fading to pink; anthers yellow; top of ovary glabrous: fr. subglobose, 1.2 cm. across, black, lustrous, pulpy. Fl.v; fr.vIII. R.I.25:t.102(c). L.B. 1021(c). L.I.t.30. (*C. carpathica* Lodd.) S. E. Eu. Cult. 1810. Zone IV.

C. n. × *mollis;* see under No. 1.—*C. n.* × *sanguinea;* see under No. 33.

36. **C. pentágyna** Waldst. & Kit. Shrub or small tree to 5 m.; young brts. pubescent; spines short: lvs. broadly rhombic-ovate or broad-ovate to obovate, truncate or broad-cuneate, 2–6 cm. long and usually nearly as broad, with 3–7 irregularly serrate lobes, on sterile shoots often elongated and with the lobes more than halfway to the middle, pubescent while young, finally nearly glabrous: fls. 1.2–1.5 cm. across, in pubescent corymbs 4–7 cm. broad; anthers pink; top of ovary pubescent: fr. ellipsoid, 1.2 cm. long, black-purple, dull; nutlets 4–5. Fl.v–vI; fr.ix. R.I.25:t.101(c). B.R.1874(c). R.H.1901: 310,t(c). (*C. melanocarpa* Bieb.) S. E. Eu., Cauc., Persia. Cult. 1836. Zone V.—**C. p.** Oliveriàna (Dum.-Cours.) Rehd. More pubescent, mature lvs. slightly pubescent above, more densely beneath: fr. smaller. B.R.1933(c). (*C. Oxyacantha* var. *O.* (Dum.-Cours.) Loud., *C. Oliveriana* DC.) W. Asia. Cult. 1810.

C. p. × *? crus-galli* = **C. hiemàlis** Lange. Lvs. densely serrate and often slightly lobed, pubescent on the veins beneath: infl. villous; stamens 15; anthers purple: fr. purple-black. Bot. Tidsskr. 13:t.2(c). Lange, Rev. Crat., t.9(c). Orig. before 1880.—*C. p.* × *?* = **C. Celsiàna** Bosc. Lvs. elliptic-ovate, cuneate, 4–8 cm. long, with 3–5 pairs of serrate lobes pointing forward: fr. ellipsoid, bright red; nutlets 2–3. Lange, Rev. Crat. t.3a. S.H.1:f.441q-r,442g-i. Orig. before 1830.

Ser. 27. OXYACANTHAE Loud.

37. **C. Oxyacántha** L. HAWTHORN (MAY of English literature). Shrub or small tree, to 5 m. with spreading brs.; spines stout, to 2.5 cm. long: lvs. broad-ovate or obovate, cuneate, 1.5–5 cm. long, with 3–5 broad serrulate, obtuse or acutish lobes, glabrous; petioles 6–15 mm. long: infl. glabrous, 5–12-fld., fls. 1.5 cm. across; stamens 20; anthers red; styles 2–3: fr. subglobose or broad-ellipsoid, 8–15 mm. long, scarlet, with 2 nutlets. Fl.v; fr.ix–x. B.R.1128(c). R.I.25:t.103(c). (*C. oxyacanthoides* Thuill.) Eu., N. Afr. Long cult. Zone IV.—**C. O. ròsea** Willd., var. Fls. rose. Orig. before 1770.— **C. O. punícea** Loud., var. Fls. dark red. L.C.1363(c). F.S.15:t.1509,f.1(c).— **C. O. Paùli** Rehd., var. Fls. double, bright scarlet. I.H.14:t.536(c). (*C. O. coccinea plena* Hort., *C. O.* f. *splendens* Schneid., *C. O.* "Paul's New Double Scarlet.") One of the most showy garden forms. Orig. 1858.—**C. O. plèna** West., var. Fls. double, white. F.S.15:t.1509,f.2(c). (*C. O.* var. *multiplex* Loud., *C. monogyna albo-plena* Rehd.) Orig. before 1770.—**C. O. aùrea** West., var. Fr. yellow. Orig. before 1770.

C. O. × *monogyna* = **C. mèdia** Bechst. R.I.25.t.105,f.2(c). Here may belong some of the garden forms.—*C. O.* × *?* = **C. sorbifòlia** Lange. Lvs. long-petioled, elliptic to ovate, with short obtuse crenate lobes, dark green and lustrous above, puberulous on the veins beneath, chartaceous: infl. several-fld.; stamens 12–18: fr. ellipsoid; nutlets 2–3. Lange, Rev. Crat. t.2(c). (*C. Oxyacantha* var. *s.* Dipp.) Orig. unknown. Cult. 1877. Zone V.—*C. O.* × *Mespilus germanica* = *Crataegomespilus grandiflora;* see p. 359.—*C. O.* × *Pyrus communis* = *Pyrocrataegus Willei;* see under No. 42.

38. C. monógyna Jacq. Shrub or tree to 10 m., similar to the preceding: lvs. more deeply 3–7-lobed, with narrower acute lobes usually only with a few teeth at apex; pedicels and calyx sometimes hairy; style 1, rarely 2: fr. ellipsoid, with 1 stone. Fl.v; fr.ix–x. R.I.25:t.104(c). R.H.1900:72. Gn.40: 500(h);52:266(h). (*C. Oxyacantha* var. *m.* (Jacq.) Loud.) Eu., N. Afr., W. Asia. Long cult. Zone IV.—**C. m.** pteridifòlia (Loud.) Rehd., var. Lvs. deeply lobed with broad closely incised-serrate lobes. F.S.20:t.2076(c). (*C. Oxyacantha filicifolia* Van Houtte.)—**C. m.** strícta (Loud.) Rehd., var. Of fastigiate habit with erect brs. (*C. Oxyacantha* var. *s.* Loud., var. *pyramidalis* Hort., var. *fastigiata* Hort., *C. m.* f. *fastigiata* Dipp.) M.G.21:390(h). M.A. t.36(h).—**C. m.** péndula (Loud.) Dipp., f. With pendulous brs. Gn.68:288(h). G.M.44:827. M.G.17:25,26(h). (*C. Oxyacantha* var. *p.* Loud.)—**C. m.** semperflòrens (André) Dipp., f. A low shrubby form flowering continuously or at intervals until August. R.H.1883:140. Gn.29:431;33:465. (*C. Oxyacantha Bruantii* Carr.)—**C. m.** biflora (West.) Rehd., f. GLASTONBURY THORN. Blooming in mild seasons in midwinter, producing a second crop of fls. in spring. Gn.84:40. (*C. m.* var. *praecox* Henry, not Dipp.) Cult. 1562.—**C. m.** Azarélla (Griseb.) Koehne, var. Young brts., lvs. and the loose infl. villous. (*C. A.* Griseb.) S. E. Eu. Intr. before 1880. Zone V.

C. m. × *Oxyacantha;* see under No. 37.— *C. m.* × *Mespilus germanica* = *Crataegomespilus Gillotii;* see p. 359.

Closely related species: **C. heterophýlla** Fluegge. Lvs. usually deeply 3-fid., the lower ones oblong, serrate only at apex, those of the shoots pinnatifid: infl. loose, glabrous; top of ovary glabrous: fr. larger, 1.5–1.8 cm. long. B.R.1161(c), 1847(c). ?W. Asia. Intr. about 1816. Zone V.—**C. ambígua** C. A. Mey. Lvs. deeply 4–7-lobed, slightly pubescent on both sides: infl. slightly hairy: fr. ellipsoid, usually with 2 nutlets. R.I.25:t.105,f.4–7(c). S. Russia. Intr. 1858. Zone V.—**C. microphýlla** K. Koch. Slender shrub: lvs. thin, 3–7-lobed, usually halfway to the middle or the lowest pair deeper, slightly pilose on the veins beneath or glabrous, lobes ovate, acute, serrate: infl. 2–5-fld., glabrous; pedicels slender, 1–2 cm. long; fls. 1 cm. across: fr. short-ovoid, 1 cm. across, red. S.H.1:f.445i-l, 447g-i. Cauc. to N. Persia. Cult. 1926. Zone V.

Ser. 28. AZAROLI Loud. (*Orientales* Zabel)

39. C. Azárolus L. Shrub or small tree to 10 m.; spiny or unarmed; young brts. tomentulose: lvs. rhombic-obovate or rhombic-ovate, cuneate, 3–7 cm. long, deeply 3–5-lobed, with narrow lobes nearly entire or incised at apex, pubescent on both sides, finally nearly glabrous above; petioles 1–2.5 cm. long: fls. 1.2 cm. across, in dense tomentose corymbs 5–7 cm. across; stamens 20; anthers purple: fr. subglobose, about 2 cm. across, orange-red or yellow, of apple-like flavor; nutlets 1–2. Fl.v; fr.ix. R.I.25:t.106(c). B.R. 1897(c). R.H.1856:441,t(c). M.A.t.35(h). (*C. Aronia* Ser., *C. maura* L. f.) S. Eu., N. Afr., W. Asia. Cult. 1700. Zone VI?—**C. A.** sináica (Boiss.) Lange, var. Lvs. glabrous: fr. usually reddish yellow. B.R.1855(c, as *C. maroccana*). Gn.22:146;28:634. (*C. s.* Boiss.) W. Asia. Intr. 1822. Zone VI?

Related species: **C. Físcheri** Schneid. Brts. glabrous or nearly so: lvs. deeply 5–7-lobed, the lowest pair often nearly to midrib; lobes incisely serrate with acuminate teeth, villous beneath on veins at least when young: infl. several-fld., loosely villous: fls. to 1.5 cm. across; styles 2: fr. short-ovoid, 1 cm. high, black or purple. S.H.1:f.450l-n,451y-z. C. Asia. Cult. 1926. Zone IV.

371

40. C. orientàlis Pall. Small tree to 7 m., with spreading brs. and pendent brts. tomentose while young: lvs. short-petioled, obovate or oblong-obovate, cuneate, 3–5 cm. long, pinnatifid with 5–9 narrow lobes incisely toothed at apex, pubescent above, tomentose beneath: fls. nearly 2 cm. across, in dense tomentose corymbs; sepals entire; fr. depressed-globose, 1.5–2 cm. across, brick- or orange-red, pubescent; nutlets 4–5. Fl.vi; fr.x. B.M.2314(c). B.R. 1885(c). G.C.72:310. Gn.28:632,t(c, as *C. tanacetifolia*). (*C. odoratissima* Lindl.) S. E. Eu., W. Asia. Intr. 1810. Zone V.—**C. o. sanguínea** Loud., var. Lvs. less pubescent, with broader lobes: fr. dark red, with 2–4 nutlets. B.R.1852(c). (*C. Tournefortii* Griseb., *C. orientalis* var. *T.* Schneid., *C. sanguinea* Schrad., not Pall.) S. E. Eu. Intr. 1910. Zone V.

Related species: **C. Heldreìchii** Boiss. Lvs. 1.5–3 cm. long, with rounded entire or nearly entire lobes: fr. red. S.H.1;f.448t-v′,451p-r. Greece. Cult. 1890. Zone V.

41. C. tanacetifòlia (Lam.) Pers. Shrub or small tree to 10 m., with upright brs.; unarmed or spiny: young brts. tomentose: lvs. short-stalked, obovate or rhombic-ovate, cuneate, 2–5 cm. long, pinnatifid, with 5–7 narrowly oblong glandular-serrate lobes, villous-pubescent on both sides; stipules large, curved, serrate: fls. 2–2.5 cm. across, in dense 5–8-fld. tomentose corymbs; sepals large, glandular-serrate: fr. yellow or reddish, 2–2.5 cm. across, with laciniate bracts at base; nutlets 5. Fl.v–vi; fr.ix. B.R.1884(c). Gt.43:15. J.L.41:f.10(h). G.C.71:285(h). W. Asia. Intr. 1789. Zone V.

C. t. × *? punctata* = **C. Dippelìàna** Lange. Lvs. lobed less than halfway to the middle, lobes acute, serrate, pubescent above, more densely beneath: corymbs dense; anthers red: fr. yellow, red or dull red. Lange, Rev. Crat. t.10(c). D.H.3: 452. (*C. Celsiana* Dippel, not Bosc, *C. tanacetifolia* var. *Leeana* Loud., *C. Leeana* Bean.) Orig. probably about 1830. Zone V.

Ser. 29. PINNATIFIDAE Zabel

42. C. pinnatífida Bge. Tree to 6 m.; brts. glabrous; spines wanting or short: lvs. broad- or triangular-ovate to rhombic-ovate, truncate or broad-cuneate, 5–10 cm. long, pinnately 5–9-lobed, the lower pair of lobes often divided nearly to the midrib, the lobes sharply and irregularly serrate, lustrous and dark green above, light green beneath, pubescent on the midrib′ and veins on both sides; petiole 2–6 cm. long; stipules large, serrate: fls 1.8 cm. across, in villous corymbs 5–8 cm. across; stamens 20; anthers pink: fr. subglobose or pyriform, 1.5 cm. across, red, punctulate; stones 3–4. Fl.v–vi; fr.ix. Gt.11:t.366. R.H.1901:308,t(c). N.K.6:t.26. N. E. Asia. Cult. 1860. Zone V. Tree with lustrous lvs. and showy fr., particularly large in var. *major* cult. in N. China for its edible fr.—**C. p. psilòsa** Schneid., var. Lvs. and infl. quite glabrous. N.K.6:t.26c.—**C. p. màjor** N. E. Br., var. Larger, more vigorous tree: lvs. larger, less deeply lobed, thicker: fr. about 2.5 cm. across, deep lustrous red. R.H.1901:308,t(c). G.C.II.26:620. N.K.6:t.27. U. S. Inv. 35:t.8(fr);40:t.2(h). (*C. Korolkowii* Schneid., not Henry, *C. Bretschneideri* Schneid., *C. tatarica* Hort.) N. China. Cult. 1880.

A supposed graft-hybrid between *Crataegus* and *Pyrus* is **Pyrocrataègus** Daniel of which only the following incompletely described form is known: **P. Willei** Daniel (*Crataegus Oxyacantha* × *Pyrus communis*). Lvs. similar to Pyrus; infl. corymbose: fr. pear-shaped, 1.5–3 cm. long. Norsk Havetid. 12:85, f.8. Orig. before 1896.

× **PYRACOMÈLES** Rehd. ex Guillaum (*Pyracantha* × *Osteomeles*). From the first differing chiefly in its unarmed brts. and pinnatisect lvs., from the latter in its pinnatisect lvs., the upper lfts. or lobes decurrent and usually crenate-serrulate at the apex.

P. Vilmorínii Rehd. ex Guillaum (*P. crenato-serrata* $\times$ *O. subrotunda*). Half-evergreen low shrub with slender brts.; brts. and lvs. grayish pubescent at first, soon glabrous: lvs. with the petiole 2.5–3.5 cm. long, pinnate below and pinnatisect toward the apex, lfts. or lobes 5–9, the upper decurrent, oval, obtuse or slightly mucronulate, usually crenate-serrulate at apex: fls. about 1 cm. across, in many-fld. glabrous or nearly glabrous corymbs: fr. 4 mm. across, coral-red, with 4–5 nutlets. G.C.103:125. Orig. 1922. Zone VII?

17. **OSTEOMÈLES** Lindl. Deciduous or evergreen shrubs; winter-buds small, with several narrow scales: lvs. pinnate, alternate; stipules linear to lanceolate; lfts. small, entire: fls. white, in terminal corymbs; calyx-teeth acute or acuminate; petals 5, ovate-oblong; stamens 15–20; styles 5, distinct; ovary 5-celled, each cell with 1 ovule: fr. a small pome with persistent calyx and 5 nutlets. (Greek *osteon*, bone, and *meles*, apple.) Three species in E. Asia and Polyn.

O. Schwerìnae Schneid. Deciduous or half-evergreen, slender-branched shrub, to 3 m.; brts., petioles and lvs. beneath grayish pubescent; lvs. 3–7 cm. long, with narrowly winged rachis; lfts. 15–31, elliptic to elliptic- or obovate-oblong, acute and mucronulate, 4–12 mm. long: fls. 1.5 cm. across, in loose terminal corymbs 3–6 cm. across; sepals lance-ovate, glabrous inside, pubescent outside; calyx-tube glabrescent; styles pubescent: fr. globose-ovoid or subglobose, 6–8 mm. long, bluish black, glabrous. Fl.v–vi; fr.ix. B.M.7354(c). G.C.50:533, both as *O. anthyllidifolia*. B.S.2:114. W. China. Intr. 1888. Zone VII? Graceful shrub with small pinnate lvs.—**O. S. microphýlla** Rehd. & Wils., var. Lfts. fewer, elliptic to obovate, 3–5 mm. long, glabrescent: infl. smaller and denser. Intr. 1908. Supposed to be hardier.

Related species: **O. subrotúnda** K. Koch. Brts. appressed-pubescent: lfts. 11–17, 4–8 mm. long, rounded and mucronate at apex, ciliate, thinly appressed-pubescent beneath; rachis appressed-pubescent: fls. 1 cm. across in loose corymbs 2–3.5 cm. across, thinly appressed-pubescent; styles glabrous. H.I.27:t. 2644. S. E. China. Cult. 1900. Zone VII?—*O. s.* $\times$ *Pyracantha crenato-serrata* = *Pyracomeles Vilmorinii*, see above.—O. anthyllidifolia Lindl. from Polynesia and Bonin Isls. is not hardy.

18. **SORBUS** L. Deciduous trees or shrubs; buds with imbricate scales, usually rather large; lvs. alternate, stipulate, simple and serrate, or odd-pinnate, folded or rarely convolute in bud: fls. white, rarely pink, in compound terminal corymbs; sepals and petals 5; stamens 15–20; carpels 2–5, 2-ovuled, either partly free and half-superior or wholly connate and inferior; styles free or connate at base: fr. a 2–5-loculed pome, usually rather small; the cells with cartilaginous walls, each with 1 or 2 seeds. (Ancient Latin name.) Including *Hahnia* Med. (*Aria* Host), *Cormus* Spach, *Torminaria* Roem. and *Micromeles* Dcne. More than 80 species distributed through the n. hemisphere, in N. Am. to N. C. and N. Mex., in Asia to the Himal.—The Sorbus are attractive in bloom with their large clusters of white fls. and most of them bear showy red fr. in fall.

Lvs. pinnate or at least partly so.
A. Lvs. all regularly pinnate.
  B. Fr. small, 4–10 mm. thick, red, rarely yellow or white.
    C. Lfts. 7–17, 1.5–10 cm. long.
      D. Fr. red or yellow.
        E. Stipules small, caducous.
          F. Winter-buds glabrous or slightly pubescent, viscid.
            G. Winter-buds glabrous or slightly whitish pubescent: lfts. serrate to near base, generally oblong-lanceolate.
              H. Lfts. acuminate, with acute or acuminate teeth, slightly pubescent beneath when young.....................................1. *S. americana*

HH. Lfts. long-acuminate, with aristate or mucronate teeth, quite glabrous
   beneath ....2. *S. commixta*
  GG. Winter-buds and infl. slightly rufous-pubescent.
    H. Lfts. short-acuminate or rounded at apex, generally oblong, dull above.
                                                              3. *S. decora*
    HH. Lfts. acuminate, generally oblong-lanceolate, lustrous above.
                                                           4. *S. sambucifolia*
   FF. Winter-buds densely white-villous.
     G. Lfts. acuminate, lustrous: brts. glabrous.................5. *S. tianshanica*
      GG. Lfts. acute, dull above: young brts. and lvs. pubescent.....6. *S. aucuparia*
     EE. Stipules large, persistent, at least below infl................7. *S. pohuashanensis*
   DD. Fr. white: lvs. glaucous and glabrous beneath; rachis usually purple.
                                                              8. *S. discolor*
  CC. Lfts. 19–29, 8–25 mm. long.
     D. Lfts. serrate usually only above the middle: infl. rufous-pubescent: fr. pale rosy-
        red ....9. *S. Vilmorini*
      DD. Lfts. serrate from near the base: infl. nearly glabrous: fr. whitish.
                                                              10. *S. Koehneana*
  BB. Fr. 1.5–3 cm. across, apple- or pear-shaped, yellowish, with red cheek and with grit-
     cells; styles 5...11. *S. domestica*
 AA. Lvs. pinnate only toward the base, the upper part lobed and serrate, occasionally only
    lobed. (See also Sorbaronia, p. 381.)....................................12. *S. hybrida*

Lvs. simple, lobed or serrate

 A. Fr. with persistent calyx.
   B. Lvs. glabrous beneath at length, broad-ovate, lobed: ovary inferior: fr. brown, with
      grit-cells...13. *S. torminalis*
   BB. Lvs. tomentose beneath or glabrescent and not lobed: ovary half-inferior: fr. usually
      red, without grit-cells.
      C. Lvs. lobed.
         D. Lvs. broad-ovate, usually rounded at base.........................14. *S. latifolia*
          DD. Lvs. ovate to ovate-oblong, broad-cuneate at base...............15. *S. intermedia*
      CC. Lvs. sharply and doubly serrate.
         D. Fls. white: lvs. white-tomentose beneath..........................16. *S. Aria*
          DD. Fls. pink, with upright petals: lvs. usually glabrous beneath.
                                                              17. *S. Chamaemespilus*
 AA. Fr. with deciduous calyx.
   B. Lvs. glabrous beneath or nearly so.
      C. Styles usually 2..18. *S. alnifolia*
      CC. Styles 5 ....19. *S. caloneura*
   BB. Lvs. white-tomentose beneath.
      C. Lvs. serrulate ....20. *S. Folgneri*
      CC. Lvs. lobulate ....21. *S. japonica*

Sect. I. SORBUS (L.) Pers. (Sect. *Aucuparia* K. Koch.) Lvs. pinnate:
carpels 2–4, rarely 5, more or less free above, partly superior: fr. red, yellow
or white, 5–15 mm. across.

1. S. americàna Marsh. AMERICAN MOUNTAIN-ASH. Small tree, to 10
m., sometimes shrubby: lfts. 11–17, lance-oblong to lanceolate, acuminate,
4–10 cm. long, sharply serrate, light green above, pale beneath and slightly
pubescent beneath when young, soon glabrous: infl. glabrous, dense, 7–14 cm.
across; fls. 5–6 mm. across: fr. globose, 4–6 mm. across, bright red, with connivent, very small calyx-lobes. Fl.v–vi; fr.x. S.S.4:t.171,172. F.E.23:209(h);
32:721(h). (*Pyrus a.* DC., *S. micrantha* Dum.-Cours.) Nfd. to Man., s. to
N. C. and Mich. Cult. 1811. Zone II. Particularly showy in fall with its
bright red fr.

   S. a. × *aucuparia* = S. spléndida Hedl. Winter-buds loosely pubescent and
viscid: fls. and fr. larger. Gs.5:181,t. Cult. 1850.—*S. a.* × *Aronia melanocarpa*
= *Sorbaronia sorbifolia;* see p. 382.—*S. a.* × *Aria;* see under No. 12.—*S. a.* ×
Aronia prunifolia = *Sorbaronia Jackii;* see p. 382.

   Related species: S. scopulina Greene. Shrub to 4 m.: lfts. 11–14, oblong-
lanceolate, 3–6 cm. long, acute to short-acuminate, dark green and lustrous
above, glabrous beneath: infl. sparingly pilose: fr. 7–8 mm. across. (*S. sambucifolia* auth., not Roem.. *S. angustifolia* Rydb., *Pyrus sitchensis* Piper in part.)
B. C. and Alb. to n. Calif. and S. Dak., s. to Ariz. and N. Mex. Intr. 1917. Zone
V.—*S. s.* × *Amelanchier florida* = *Amelasorbus Jackii*, see p. 382.—S. dumòsa
Greene. Shrub to 3 m.; winter-buds white-villous: lfts 9–11, oblong-lanceolate,
2–4 cm. long, dull dark green above: infl. less than 10 cm. broad, white-villous;
fr. to 8–10 mm. across. Ariz., N. Mex. Intr. ?

2. **S. commíxta** Hedl. Shrub or small tree to 8 m.; buds glabrous, viscid; stipules deciduous; lfts. 11–15, elliptic-lanceolate to lanceolate, long-acuminate, 2.5–8 cm. long, sharply and sometimes doubly serrate, with acuminate or aristate teeth, glaucescent beneath: infl. 8–12 cm. across, rather loose, glabrous; fls. 8 mm. across; styles usually 3: fr. globose 6–8 mm. across, bright red. Fl.vi; fr.x. S.I.2:t.31(c). M.K.t.48(c). N.K.6:t.3. (*S. aucuparia* var. *japonica* Maxim., *S. japonica* Koehne, not Sieb.) Korea, Saghal., Japan. Cult. 1880. Zone V. Small tree, similar to No. 1, but lvs. smaller and corymbs looser.

Closely related species: **S. reflexipétala** Koehne. Lfts. usually 15, to 5 cm. long: infl. nearly glabrous; petals reflexed; styles 3–4. Japan? Cult. 1890.— **S. serótina** Koehne. Lfts. usually 13, to 5 cm. long: infl. villous; petals reflexed: fr. smaller. Gs.1:183. Japan? Cult. 1900.

3. **S. decòra** (Sarg.) Schneid. Shrub or tree to 10 m.: lfts. 11–17, usually 15, elliptic to oblong, obtusish to abruptly short-acuminate, 3–7 cm. long, serrate with more or less spreading teeth, glabrous and dark green above, pale and usually pubescent beneath while young: infl. 5–10 cm. across, rather loose, slightly pubescent; fls. 8–10 mm. across; fr. globose-ovoid while young, with upright calyx-lobes, 7–10 mm. across, bright red. Fl.v; fr.x. N.S.2:t. 50(c). S.S.4:t.173,174. (*S. americana* var. *d.* Sarg., *S. scopulina* Britt., not Greene, *P. sitchensis* Rob. & Fern., not Piper.) Lab. to Minn., S. N. Y. and Vt. Cult. 1636. Zone II. Owing to its larger fr. this species is showier than *S. americana* and often planted.

S. d. × *Aronia prunifolia* = *Sorbaronia Arsenii;* see p. 382.

Related species: **S. cascadénsis** G. N. Jones. Shrub to 5 m; lfts. 9–11, ovate to oblong, acute, lustrous above, glabrous beneath: infl. 7–12 cm. across, sparingly pilose: fr. globose, 8–10 mm. across, scarlet. (*Pyrus sitchensis* Piper, not *S. s.* Roemer.) B. C. to n. Calif. Intr. ?

4. **S. sambucifòlia** (Cham. & Schlecht.) Roem. Shrub to 2.5 m.; young brts. slightly pubescent; buds slightly rufous-pubescent and viscid: lfts. 9–11, ovate-lanceolate to oblong-lanceolate, acuminate, very unequal at base, 3–7 cm. long, dark lustrous green above, lighter green beneath, soon quite glabrous: infl. 4–5 cm. across, sparingly rufous-pubescent; fls. 1–1.5 cm. across; calyx glabrous with ciliate lobes: fr. subglobose, 1–1.2 cm. across, with upright rather large sepals, red, slightly bloomy. Fl.vi; fr.ix. S.H.1:f.366a-b,367a-b. (*Pyrus s.* Cham. & Schlecht.) N. E. Asia, Japan. Cult. 1905. Zone II. Confused with *S. decora* and *S. sitchensis;* rare and apparently short-lived in cult.

Related species: **S. rufo-ferrugínea** (Schneid.) Schneid. Similar to No. 2, but winter-buds slightly rufous-villous: lfts. beneath, rachis and infl. rufous-villous when young; styles usually 5. (*S. commixta* var. *r.* Schneid.) Japan. Intr. 1915. Zone V.—**S. sitchénsis** Roem. Shrub to 4 ft.: lfts. 7–11, elliptic-oblong, obtuse or acutish, dull above, serrate to the middle or below: infl. 5–9 cm. across, rufous-pubescent to nearly glabrous; styles usually 3: fr. red, bloomy, about 8 mm. across. Hedl. Sorbus 40,f.4. Alaska and Yukon to Mont. and Idaho. Intr. 1918. Zone IV.—**S. occidentàlis** (S. Wats.) Greene. Shrub to 3 m.: lfts. 7–11, oval to oblong, 2–6 cm. long, obtuse, serrate only near apex, dull bluish green above: infl. 3–6 cm. broad, rufous-pubescent to nearly glabrous: fr. red, bloomy, 6–8 mm. across. Hedl. Sorbus 40,f.3. (*Pyrus o.* S. Wats., *S. sambucifolia* var. *Grayi* Wenz., ? *S. pumila* Raf.) B. C. to Ore. Cult. 1913. Zone V?

5. **S. tianshànica** Rupr. Shrub or small tree to 5 m.; buds pubescent; young brts. glabrous or nearly so, later red-brown and lustrous: lfts. 9–15, lanceolate, acuminate, 3–5 cm. long, serrate, entire near base, lustrous and dark green above, green beneath, glabrous: infl. glabrous, rather loose, 8–12 cm. across; fls. 1.8 cm. broad; stamens half as long as petals: fr. globose, 8 mm. across, bright red. Fl.vi. B.M.7755(c). Gt.40:8. (*Pyrus t.* Franch.) Turkest. Intr. 1895. Zone V. Handsome shrub with dark green lustrous lvs.

Related species: **S. Matsumuràna** (Mak.) Koehne. Small tree; buds glabrous: lfts. 9–13, oblong, 2.5–6 cm. long, acute, rarely rounded, serrate above the middle, pale beneath and pubescent only at base: styles 5: fr. 8–10 mm. across. S.H.1:f.366e-f,367c. Japan. Doubtful if in cult.—**S. Harrowiàna** (Balf. & W. W. Sm.) Rehd. Tree to 13 m., glabrous or nearly so; brts. 5–7 mm. thick: lfts. 5–9, narrow-oblong, 6–20 cm. long, obtuse, oblique at base, finely serrulate and slightly revolute at margin, glaucous beneath: infl. 15 cm. across, sparingly villous; styles usually 3: fr. ovoid, 6 mm. across. W. China. Intr. 1912. Zone VII? Distinct and handsome species.

6. **S. aucupària** L. ROWAN TREE (EUROPEAN MOUNTAIN-ASH.) Tree to 15, occasionally to 20 m.; young brts. pubescent, grayish brown when older; buds tomentose: lfts. 9–15, oblong to oblong-lanceolate, acute or obtusish, 2–5 cm. long, serrate, usually entire in the lower third, dull green above, glaucescent beneath and pubescent, at least when young: infl. 10–15 cm. across, villous or sometimes nearly glabrous; fls. 8–10 mm. across; stamens about as long as petals: fr. globose, about 8 mm. across, bright red. Fl.v; fr.VIII–IX. H.W.3: 78,79(h),t.54(c). R.I.25:t.114(c). (*Pyrus A.* Gaertn.) Eu. to W. Asia and Siber. Long cult. and naturalized in N. Am. Zone II. Handsome in fall with its showy bright red frs.—**S. a. Dírkeni** Schneid., f. Lvs. yellow (*S. a. Dirkeni aurea* Hort.)—**S. a. asplenifòlia** K. Koch. Lfts. incisely serrate, at base sometimes with 1 or 2 distinct small lobes, densely pubescent beneath. (*S. a. laciniata* Hort., not Hartm.)—**S. a. integérrima** Koehne, var. Lfts. entire or with few teeth at apex.—**S. a. xanthocárpa** Hartw. & Ruempl., var. With orange-yellow fr. (*S. a.* var. *Fifeana* Hartw.)—**S. a. fastigiàta** (Loud.) Hartw. & Ruempl., var. With upright brs. forming a tree of narrow-pyramidal habit. —**S. a. péndula** Kirchn., f. A form with long pendulous brs. M.D.1911:247 (h).—**S. a. edùlis** Dieck, var. Nearly glabrous; petioles purplish; lfts. 4–7 cm. long, serrate usually only above the middle: fr. larger, of slightly acid agreeable flavor and used for preserves. R.I.25:t.114,f.11(c). (*S. a.* var. *moravica* Zengerl., var. *dulcis* Kraetzl.) Intr. about 1886.—**S. a. róssica** Spaeth. Similar to the preceding, but lfts. larger and more serrate.—**S. a. Beíssneri** Rehd., f. A graceful form of var. *edulis* with pinnately lobed lfts. and the petioles and brts. bright red. G.W.3:267,t(c). (*S. a. dulcis laciniata* Beiss.)

S. a. × *americana;* see under No. 1.—*S. a.* × *discolor;* see under No. 8.— *S. a.* × *intermedia;* see No. 12.—*S. a.* × *Aria;* see under No. 12.—*S. a.* × *Aronia arbutifolia* = *Sorbaronia hybrida;* see p. 381.—*S. a.* × *Aronia melanocarpa* = *Sorbaronia fallax;* see p. 382.—*S.a.* × *Aronia prunifolia* = *Sorbaronia heterophylla;* see p. 382.

Closely related species: **S. amurénsis** Koehne. Lfts. acuminate, incisely serrate above the middle, slightly pubescent beneath when young: fr. 6–9 cm. across, orange-red. N.K.6:13(h),t.2. N. E. Asia. Intr. 1907. Zone IV.

7. **S. pohuashanénsis** (Hance) Hedl. Small tree; brts. villous; buds white-villous; stipules large, semi-ovate, toothed, persistent at least under the infl.: lfts. 11–15, elliptic-oblong to oblong-lanceolate, acute to acuminate, 2.5–6 cm. long, serrate usually from below the middle, glaucescent and pubescent beneath: infl. 10–12 cm. across, floccoso-tomentose: fr. subglobose, 6–8 mm. across. Fl.v; fr.x. N. China. Intr. 1883. Zone V or IV?

Related species: **S. Wilsoniàna** Schneid. Tree to 10 m.; brts. 5–7 mm. thick; buds silky at apex: lfts. 11–15, oblong to oblong-lanceolate, 6–8 cm. long, acute to acuminate, pubescent on midrib beneath: infl. 15–17 cm. across, slightly pubescent; styles 3–4: fr. orange-red. S.H.1:f.367k,368p. C. China. Doubtful if in cult.; confused with *S. hupehensis.*—**S. Esserteauiàna** Koehne. Shrub or tree to 8 m.; brts. 5–7 mm. thick; buds silky: lfts. 11–13, oblong to broad-lanceolate, 4–10 cm. long, sharply serrate, tomentose beneath, veins impressed above: fr. 4–6 mm. thick. B.M.9403(c). (*S. Conradinae* Koehne.) W. China. Intr. 1909. Zone VI?—**S. Sargentiàna** Koehne. Tree to 10 m.; buds slightly villous and viscid: lfts. 7–11, oblong-lanceolate, 8–13 cm. long, serrulate, tomentose beneath: infl. about 15 cm. across, densely villous: fr. scarlet, about 6 mm. across. W. China. Intr. 1908. Zone VI?—**S. S. warleyénsis** Marquand, var. Lfts. smaller; rachis dark purple: infl. larger and looser: fr. smaller. G.C.94:177. Cult. 1931.—**S. grácilis** (Sieb. & Zucc.) K. Koch. Shrub to 2 m.; brts. slender; buds finally glabrescent: lfts. 7–9, elliptic-oblong to oblong, 2–6 cm. long, the upper ones 4–8 cm. long, the lowest pair usually broad-oval, 1–1.5 cm. long, acute or obtusish, serrate above the middle, slightly pubescent or glabrescent beneath: infl. 2–4 cm. across, with large bracts; styles 2: fr. red. S.H.1:f.373a,374c. Japan. Cult. 1934. Zone VI?

8. **S. díscolor** (Maxim.) Hedl. Tree to 10 m.; buds slightly pubescent; young brts. glabrous or nearly so, like the petioles usually purplish; stipules leafy, digitately toothed, persistent; lfts. 11–15, oblong to lanceolate, acute or acuminate, 3–8 cm. long, sharply serrate except at base, glaucous beneath, glabrous: infl. loose, 10–14 cm. across, glabrous or nearly so; fls. about 1 cm. across; styles usually 3: fr. 6–7 mm. across, globose-ovoid, white or yellowish. Fl.v; fr.ix. Gt.55:t.1551,f.7(c). S.H.1:f.366l-m,367g. (*S. pekinensis* Koehne, *Pyrus d.* Maxim.) N. China. Intr. about 1883. Zone V. Remarkable for its white fr.

S. d. × *aucuparia* = **S. arnoldiàna** Rehd. Lfts. pubescent beneath when young: fr. pink. Orig. 1907.

Related species, but with deciduous stipules: **S. hupehénsis** Schneid. Buds glabrous: lfts. 13–17, elliptic to oblong, 2–3.5 cm. long, acute or obtusish, usually entire at the lower third: styles 4–5. (*Pirus mesogaea* Cardot.) C. and W. China.—**S. h. apérta** (Koehne) Schneid., var. Lfts. 9–11, 3–6 cm. long, usually acute. Intr. 1910. Zone V.—**S. h. obtùsa** Schneid., var. Lfts. 9–11, obtuse, 3–5 cm. long, serrate only near apex. W. China. Cult. 1912.—**S. Rehderiàna** Koehne. Shrub or small tree; brts. 5–8 mm. thick: lfts. 15–19, oblong-lanceolate or lanceolate, 2.5–5 cm. long, acuminate, serrulate, glabrous: infl. 2.5–6.5 cm. broad, sparingly rufous-villous; styles 5: fr. whitish to reddish, 6–7 mm. across. W. China.—**S. R. cúpreo-nítens** Hand.-Mazz., var. Rachis and midrib of lfts. beneath and infl. rufous-villous. Intr. 1932.—**S. Hélenae** Koehne. Tree to 7 m.; brts. 5–8 mm. thick; buds glabrous: lfts. 7–9, oblong, 5–10 cm. long, acute, crenate-serrate, slightly rufous-villous on veins beneath; rachis narrowly winged; infl. about 10 cm. across, slightly rufous-pubescent. W. China. —**S. H. rufídula** Koehne, f. Infl., rachis of lf. and veins beneath densely rufous-villous. Intr. 1932. Zone VI?

9. **S. Vilmorìni** Schneid. Shrub or small tree to 6 m., with spreading brs.; young brts. and buds slightly rusty-pubescent; stipules narrow, deciduous: lfts. 19–25, elliptic-oblong to oblong, acute, 1.5–2.5 cm. long, serrate from below the middle or sometimes only near apex, glabrous, grayish green beneath; rachis slightly winged and often slightly pubescent: infl. loose and slender-stalked, 5–10 cm. across; fls. 6 mm. across; styles 5: fr. globose, about 8 mm. across, pale rose-red. Fl.vi; fr.ix. B.M.8241(c). Gn.85:501;87:576. S.L.345(h). (*Pyrus V.* Aschers. & Graebn.) W. China. Intr. 1889. Zone V. With conspicuous white fls. in spring and rosy-red fr. in fall.

Related species: **S. microphýlla** Dcne. Shrub; brts. glabrous, later dark brown: lfts. about 25, oblong, 9–12 mm. long, obtusish, loosely villous and grayish beneath; infl. few-fld., loosely villous. S.H.1:f.374m-n. Sikkim. Cult. 1934.—**S. fílipes** Hand.-Mazz. Shrub to 4 m.; brts. glabrous or nearly so: lfts. 19–27, elliptic, 8–14 mm. long, with 3–4 teeth on each side: cymes 3–12-fld., glabrous, on slender peduncles 3–5 cm. long: fls. red: fr. red, 7 mm. across. W. China. Intr. 1932.—**S. rufopilòsa** Schneid. Tree to 5 m.: young brts., infl., lf.-rachis and lfts. beneath at least on midrib rufous-pubescent; lfts. 17–29, oblong, 1.5–2.5 cm. long, acute, serrate: infl. long-peduncled, 3–5 cm. across: fls. pink: fr. subglobose, 8–10 mm. across, red. S.H.1:f.374p-q,375o-p. W. China. Intr. 1932. Zone VI?

10. **S. Koehneàna** Schneid. Shrub to 3 m.; young brts. glabrous or nearly so; buds slightly fulvous-pubescent; stipules small, semi-ovate, with few teeth, partly persistent: lfts. 17–25, oblong to oblong-lanceolate, acute, 1.5–

3.5 cm. long, sharply serrate from near base, grayish green beneath, not papillose, slightly pubescent when young; rachis slightly winged: infl. 4–8 cm. across, slightly pubescent; fls. about 1 cm. across; anthers brown; styles 5; fr. subglobose, 6–7 mm. across, white. Fl.v–vi; fr.viii. S.H.1:f.374o(l). C. China. Intr. 1910. Zone V. Attractive in fall with its white fr. on red stalks.

Related species: **S. Práttii** Koehne. Lfts. 21–27, 1.5–2.5 cm. long, entire on lower third or half, glaucous beneath and papillose, usually villous, chiefly on midrib: fr. white. B.M.9460(c). W. China.—**S. P. tatsienénsis** (Koehne) Schneid., var. Lfts. smaller, 1–2 cm. long, often entire only at base. G.C.68: 153;72:226. Gn.87:556. Intr. about 1904. Zone V?—**S. P. subarachnoídea** (Koehne) Rehd., f. Lfts. with a rufous cobwebby tomentum beneath. B.S.3: 326(t). (*S. munda* f. *subarachnoidea* Koehne.) Intr. 1910.—**S. glomerulàta** Koehne. Buds glabrous: lfts. 23–29, 1.5–2.5 cm. long, serrulate above the middle or near apex, glaucous beneath and glabrous or nearly so: infl. glabrous, consisting of 12–20 small dense clusters; styles 5: fr. white. C. China. Cult. 1910. —**S. scalàris** Koehne. Shrub to 6 m.; stipules large, persistent: lfts. 23–29, oblong, 2–3 cm. long, serrate above the middle or nearly entire: infl. 12–14 cm. wide, rather dense, villous; styles 3–4: fr. 5–6 mm. across, bright red. W. China. Intr. about 1904. Zone V?—**S. pluripinnàta** (Schneid.) Koehne. Shrub: lfts. 21–25, oblong, 1.5–2.5 cm. long, grayish villous beneath: infl. about 9 cm. across: styles 4–5. S.H.1:f.374e'. (*S. foliolosa* var. *pl.* Schneid.) W. China. Cult. 1934. Zone VI?

Sect. II. CORMUS (Spach) Schneid. Lvs. pinnate: carpels 5, connate, inferior: fr. green or brown, 1.5–3 cm. long.

11. S. doméstica L. Tree to 20 m.: bark scaly, rough; buds viscid, lustrous, pubescent at apex; brts. soon glabrous: lfts. 11–21, narrow-oblong, acute, sometimes rounded, 3–8 cm. long, sharply serrate with acuminate teeth, entire near base, glabrous above, floccose-tomentose beneath, at least while young: infl. broad-pyramidal, 6–10 cm. across, tomentose; fls. 1.5 cm. across: fr. apple- (var. *pomifera* Hayne) or pear-shaped (var. *pyrifera* Hayne), yellowish green or brownish, tinged with red. Fl.v; fr.ix–x. R.I. 25:t.113(c). G.C.II.1:283;6:649. H.W.3:80,81(h). B.S.2:296,t(h). M.G.12: 376–8(h). (*Pyrus d.* Smith, *Cormus d.* Spach, *Pyrus Sorbus* Gaertn.) S. Eu., N. Afr., W. Asia. Long cult. Zone V. Sometimes grown for its fr., used in France and Germany in cider making.

SECT. I × III (AUCUPARIA × ARIA.)

12. × S. hýbrida L. (*S. Aucuparia × intermedia*). Tree to 12 m., with ascending brs.; young brts. and petioles floccose-tomentose: lvs. ovate to oblong-ovate or oblong, 7–12 cm. long, with 7–10 pairs of veins, below with 1–4 pairs of oblong decurrent lfts. acute or acutish and serrate toward the apex, the upper part lobed, tomentose beneath; petioles 1.5–3 cm. long: infl. 6–10 cm. across, tomentose; fls. 1 cm. across: fr. subglobose, 1.2 cm. thick, red. Fl.v; fr.ix–x. H.W.3:86. M.A.t.40(h). G.C.76:235. Gn.88:685. (*S. fennica* K. Koch, *Pyrus pinnatifida* Ehrh., *P. semipinnata* Bechst.) Scandinavia with the parents. Cult. 1779. Zone IV.—**S. h. Gíbbsii** (Osborn) Bean, var. With 1 or 2 pairs of distinct lfts.: fr. coral-red. G.C.77:234,t. (*Pyrus firma* Hort.) Cult. 1925.—**S. h. fastigiàta** Rehd., var. Form of fastigiate habit. G.C.41:185(h). (*P. pinnatifida* var. *fastigiata* Bean.)—**S. h. Meiníchii** (Lindb.) Rehd., var. A transition to *S. aucuparia* with 4–6 pairs of distinct lfts. S.H.1:f.370g. (*S. h. neuillensis* Cockerell.) Cult. 1907.

Closely related hybrid: **S. thuringíaca** (Ilse) Fritsch (*S. aucuparia × Aria*). Lvs. oblong-ovate, with 9–12 pairs of veins, with 1–3 pairs of distinct lfts., obtusish or rounded at apex with shorter and broader, less pointed teeth, the upper part lobed at base, very slightly so toward the apex. R.I.25:t.115(c). (*S. hybrida* var. *t.* Rehd., *S. decurrens* Hedl., *P. semipinnata* Roth partly, *S. quercifolia* Hedl.) This hybrid is less often cult. than the preceding.—An imperfectly known hybrid is **S. plantierénsis** Schneid., supposed to be *S. americana* × *Aria*.

Sect. III. ARIA Pers. (*Aria* Host, *Hahnia* Med., *Torminaria* Roem.) Lvs. simple, lobed or only serrate: fr. with persistent calyx-lobes.

13. **S. torminàlis** (L.) Crantz. SERVICE-TREE. Round-headed tree, to 25 m., with spreading brs.; buds glabrous, green; young brts. loosely tomentose: lvs. broad-ovate, slightly cordate to broad-cuneate at base, 5–10 cm. long, with 3–5 pairs of triangular-ovate lobes, the lower sinus reaching about half-way to the middle, bright green, thinly floccose-tomentose beneath when young, usually soon glabrous; petiole 2–5 cm. long: infl. 10–12 cm. across, rather loose, tomentose; fls. 1.2 cm. across; styles usually 2: fr. ellipsoid, about 1.5 cm. long, brown, dotted. Fl.v–vi; fr.ix–x. H.W.3:82(h),t.53(c). S.L.347(h). (*Pyrus t.* Ehrh., *Torminaria t.* Dipp.) Eu., Asia Minor, N. Afr. Long cult. Zone V. With light green lvs. turning bright red in fall.
S. t. × *Aria;* see No. 14.
A species with large brown fr. is **S. megalocárpa** Rehd. Shrub to 7 m.: lvs. elliptic-obovate to obovate-oblong, 12–24 cm. long, acuminate, crenate-serrate, glabrous: infl. 10–15 cm. across; styles 3–4, connate, glabrous: fr. ovoid, 1.5–3.5 cm. long, russet-brown. W. China. Intr. 1908. Zone VI?

14. ×**S. latifòlia** (Lam.) Pers. (*S. Aria* × *torminalis*). Tree to 16 m., similar to the preceding; buds olive-brown, glabrous: lvs. broad-ovate to ovate, usually rounded at base, 6–10 cm. long, pinnately lobed with short broad-triangular, sharply serrate lobes and with 5–8 pairs of veins, grayish or whitish tomentose beneath, rarely glabrescent: infl. 7–10 cm. across, tomentose; fls. 1.5 cm. across; styles 2–3: fr. globose to short-ellipsoid, 1.2 cm. long, orange or brownish red, dotted. Fl.v; fr.ix. Ad.7:t.225(c). H.W.3:85. N.D. 4,t.35(c). (*S. decipiens* Hedl., *Torminaria l.* Dipp.) Occasionally with the parents in C. Eu. Intr. before 1750. Zone IV.

15. **S. intermèdia** (Ehrh.) Pers. Shrub or tree to 10 m.: buds greenish or brownish, viscid, the scales with tomentulose margin; young brts. tomentose: lvs. elliptic to obovate-oblong, broad-cuneate, 6–10 cm. long, pinnately lobed, with short and broad irregularly serrate lobes and 6–9 pairs of veins, grayish white or grayish tomentose beneath; petioles 1.5–2 cm. long: infl. 8–10 cm. across, tomentose; fls. 1.2 cm. across; styles usually 2; fr. subglobose, about 1.2 cm. across, orange-red. Fl.v; fr.ix–x. S.E.3:485. S.H.1:f.377s-t(l). B.S.2:285,t(h). (*S. scandica* Fr., *Aria suecica* Koehne, *Pyrus i.* Ehrh.) N. Eu. Long cult. Zone V. Sometimes confused with *S. hybrida*, but its lvs. never have distinct lfts. and the sinuses do not reach farther than ⅓ toward the middle.—**S. i. mínima** (Ley) Bean, var. Slender shrub: lvs. oblong, shallowly lobed; fls. and frs. smaller. Jour. Bot. 35:t.372. England.—**S. i. arranénsis** (Hedl.) Rehd., var. Lvs. more deeply lobed, the lowest lobes more than halfway to midrib. Hedl. Sorbus. 60. Scotland.
Closely related species: **S. Mougeòtii** Soy.-Willem. & Godr. Tree to 20 m.: lvs. short-acuminate, with 8–12 pairs of veins, less deeply lobed, whitish tomentose beneath: fr. 8 mm. across, red, edible. H.W.3:83. S.H.1:f.377u-v(l). (*Pyrus M.* Aschers. & Graeb.) Mts. of C. Eu. Cult. 1880. Zone V.—*S. M.* × *Chamaemespilus;* see under No. 17.

16. **S. Aria** (L.) Crantz. WHITE BEAM-TREE. Tree with broad-pyramidal or ovoid head, to 15 m.: young brts. tomentose; buds greenish, viscid: lvs. elliptic to elliptic-oblong, acute or obtuse, usually cuneate, 5–12 cm. long, sharply and doubly serrate, glabrous except on the nerves and bright green above, white-tomentose beneath, with 8–12 pairs of veins, leathery; petioles 1–2 cm. long, tomentose: infl. 5–8 cm. across, tomentose; fls. 1.5 cm. across; styles 2, rarely 3, connate at base; fr. subglobose, 1.2 cm. thick, orange-red or

scarlet, with mealy flesh. Fl.v; fr.ix-x. H.W.3:t.52(c). G.M.44:291. (*Pyrus A.* Ehrh., *Aria nivea* Host.) Eu. Long cult. Zone V. Tree with handsome lvs. and attractive fr.—**S. A. aùrea** Hesse. Lvs. yellow. A form with deeper yellow lvs. is **S. A. chrysophýlla** Hesse; a form with yellowish lvs. is **S. A. lutéscens** Hartwig, var.—**S. A. edùlis** Wenzig, var. Lvs. elliptic-oblong to oblong, 7-14 cm. long: fr. ovoid, larger. S.H.1:f.377h-i(l).—**S. A. Decais-neàna** (Lav.) Rehd., var. Lvs. elliptic-ovate, 10-15 cm. long, irregularly and doubly serrate; petiole 2-2.5 cm. long: fls. 1.8 cm. acros; stamens longer than style: fr. larger, ovoid. B.M.8184(c). Gn.90:554. L.I.t.18. (*Aria D.* Lav., *S. Aria majestica* Zab., *Pyrus Aria* var. *majestica* Prain.) Cult. 1880.

S. A. × *aucuparia;* see under No. 12.—*S. A.* × *torminalis;* see No. 14.— *S. A.* × *Aronia arbutifolia* = *Sorbaronia alpina;* see p. 382.—*S. A.* × *Aronia melanocarpa* = *Sorbaronia Dippelii;* see p. 382.—*S. A.* × *Pyrus communis* = *Sorbopyrus auricularis;* see p. 382.

Closely related species: **S. umbellàta** (Desf.) Fritsch. Tree to 7 m.: lvs. orbicular to broad-elliptic, obtuse, cuneate, 3.5-6 cm. long, incisely lobed above the middle with short rounded coarsely toothed lobes and with 5-6 pairs of veins; petioles usually 1 cm. or less long: fr. depressed-globose. S.H.1:f.379a-d, 378f-g. (*S. flabellifolia* F. Schau., *S. meridionalis* Guss., *S. Aria* var. *flabelli-folia* Wenz.) S. E. Eu., W. Asia. Intr. before 1930. Zone V or VI?—**S. u. crètica** (Lindl.) Schneid., var. Lvs. broad-elliptic or elliptic, 5-9 cm. long, with 6-11 pairs of veins, scarcely lobulate. Gs.3:270. S.H.1:f.379e-i. (*S. graeca* (Spach) Hedl., *S. Aria* var. *graeca* K. Koch.) S. E. Eu. Cult. 1830.—**S. palléscens** Rehd. Lvs. elliptic, doubly denticulate-serrate, grayish-tomentose beneath: infl. small, sessile: fr. subglobose, pale, 8 mm. across. (*S. ochrocarpa* Rehd.) W. China. Intr. 1908. Zone V.—Also related to *S. Aria* are: **S. lanàta** (Don) K. Koch. Tree: lvs. elliptic, 10-16 cm. long, sharply and doubly serrate and slightly lobed, grayish villous-tomentose beneath, later often glabrescent; styles 2-3, woolly; sepals nearly glabrous outside; petals narrowed into a claw: fr. globose, 1.5-3 cm. across. S.H.1:f.383a-b,380o-p. M.D.47:146. (*Pyrus kumaonensis* Wall.) Cult. 1870. Zone VII?—**S. cuspidàta** (Spach) Hedl. Tree: lvs. elliptic to elliptic-oblong, acuminate, 7-16 cm. long, doubly serrate, densely white-tomentose beneath: infl. 8-10 cm. across; styles usually 5, distinct: fr. sub-globose, about 2 cm. across, reddish. B.M.8259(c). B.R.1655(c). G.C.II.1:17. (*Pyrus vestita* Wall., *Cormus lanata* Koehne, *S. nepalensis* Hort.) Himal. Intr. 1820. Zone VII. One of the handsomest species of the Aria group.

17. **S. Chamaeméspilus** (L.) Crantz. Shrub to 3 m.; young brts. loosely pubescent: buds glabrous, with ciliate scales: lvs. elliptic to oblong, acute, cuneate, 3-7 cm. long, serrate, glabrous beneath or slightly floccose-tomen-tose, with 6-9 pairs of veins; petioles 4-10 mm. long: infl. dense, about 3 cm. across, tomentose; petals pink, upright, gradually narrowed into the claw; styles 2: fr. ovoid, red. Fl.vi; fr.ix-x. H.W. 3:84. S.O.2:t.87(c). G.H. t.70. (*Pyrus C.* Ehrh., *Aria C.* Host.) C. & S. Eu. Intr. 1683. Zone V.—**S. Ch. sudètica** (Tausch) Wenz., var. Lvs. to 10 cm. long, grayish tomentose be-neath, (*S. s.* Nym., *Pyrus s.* Tausch, *S. chamaemespilus* var. *discolor* Neilr., not Hegetschw.) C. Eu. Cult. 1908. Possibly *S. Aria* × *Chamaemespilus.*

S. C. × *Mougeotii* = **S. Hostii** (Jacq.) Hedl. Shrub to 4 m.: lvs. elliptic to elliptic-obovate, sharply serrate, loosely tomentose beneath: fls. whitish pink, in corymbs to 6 cm. across: fr. globose-ovoid. S.O.4:t.193(c). S.H.1:f.381a-b. (*Aria Hostii* Jacq.) C. Eu. with the parents. Cult. 1820. Zone V.

Sect. IV. MICROMELES (Decne.) Rehd. Lvs. simple: fr. small, with deciduous calyx.

18. **S. alnifòlia** (Sieb. & Zucc.) K. Koch. Tree to 20 m.; brts. glabrous or slightly pubescent: lvs. ovate to elliptic-ovate, short-acuminate, rounded at base, 5-10 cm. long, unequally serrate, glabrous above, glabrous or slightly pubescent beneath, on vigorous shoots sometimes pubescent, with 6-10 pairs of veins: infl. loose, 6-10-fld., nearly glabrous; fls. 1 cm. across; styles usually 2: fr. subglobose, 8 mm. across, red and yellow. Fl.v; fr.ix-x. B.M.7773(c).

S.I.1:t.49(c). G.F.7:84. Gt.41:283,284. (*Micromeles a.* Koehne, *Pyrus Miyabei* Sarg.) C. China to Korea and Jap. Intr. 1892. Zone V. Tree with dense round head and bright green lvs. turning orange and scarlet in fall.

19. **S. caloneùra** (Stapf) Rehd. Shrub or tree to 6 m.; brts. glabrous: lvs. elliptic- to obovate-oblong, 7–12 cm. long, usually acute or sometimes obtusish, doubly crenate-serrate, pale beneath and sparingly hairy on the veins, at least at their base, with 10–12 pairs of veins impressed above; petiole about 1 cm. long: infl. dense, many-fld., loosely pubescent; fls. about 6 mm. across; styles 5: fr. pyriform, about 1 cm. high, brown, dotted. B.M. 8335(c). (*Micromeles c.* Stapf.) C. China. Intr. 1904. Zone V.

Related species: **S. meliosmifolia** Rehd. Tree to 10 m.: lvs. short-petioled, ovate to elliptic-oblong, 10–18 cm. long, doubly serrate, with 18–24 pairs of veins: infl. 5–10 cm. across: fr. subglobose, brownish red. W. China. Intr. 1910? Zone VI?—**S. Keissleri** (Schneid.) Rehd. Tree to 12 m.: lvs. elliptic-obovate, 5–8 cm. long, crenate-serrulate, with 8–10 pairs of veins: infl. tomentose; styles usually 3, connate below: fr. ovoid, red. (*S. Decaisneana* Rehd., not Zabel, *Micromeles K.* Schneid.) C. & W. China. Intr. 1900? Zone VI?

20. **S. Fólgneri** (Schneid.) Rehd. Tree with spreading and arching brs., to 8 m.; young brts. tomentose: lvs. ovate to elliptic-ovate, acute or short-acuminate, broad-cuneate or rounded at base, 5–8 cm. long, finely serrate or on shoots doubly serrate and often slightly lobed, dark green and glabrous above, white-tomentose beneath, with 8–9 pairs of veins; infl. many-fld., about 10 cm. across; styles 3: fr. ellipsoid, about 1.3 cm. long, red. Fl.v; fr.x. M.G.27:136(h). (*Micromeles F.* Schneid., *Pyrus F.* Bean.) C. China. Intr. 1901. Zone V. Graceful species.—**S. F. péndula** Rehd., f. Brts. pendulous.

Related species: **S. epidéndron** Hand.-Mazz. Shrub or tree to 15 m.: lvs. obovate to narrow-elliptic, 8–15 cm. long, acuminate, cuneate, serrulate, fulvous-tomentose beneath, with 10–12 pairs of veins; petiole 5–1.5 cm. long: infl. 5–10 cm. across, fulvous-pubescent. W. China. Cult. 1934. Zone VI?

21. **S. japónica** (Dcne.) Hedl. Tree to 20 m.; young brts. tomentose: lvs. ovate to oblong-ovate, short-acuminate, cuneate, 7–10 cm. long, doubly serrate and lobulate, pubescent above or sometimes glabrescent, grayish white or white-tomentose beneath, with 10–12 pairs of veins; petioles 1–2 cm. long: infl. tomentose, rather dense: fr. ellipsoid, 1.2 cm. long, scarlet, punctulate. Fl.v; fr.x. S.I.1:t.48(c). (*Micromeles j.* Koehne, *S. Koehnei* Zabel, *S. Aria* var. *kamaonensis* Maxim.) Japan, Korea. Intr. ? Zone V. Ornamental tree, particularly the var. with its lvs. white beneath changing to yellow in fall and with its bright orange fr.—**S. j. calocárpa** Rehd., var. Lvs. with purer white denser tomentum beneath, to 8 cm. broad: fr. orange, 1.5 cm. long, not punctulate. C. Japan. Intr. 1915. Zone V.

✕ **SORBARÒNIA** Schneid. Hybrids between *Sorbus* and *Aronia* and intermediate between the two genera. Deciduous shrubs with partly pinnate or simple, serrulate lvs., rather small and dense infl., 3–4 styles and red or nearly black fr.

1. ✕ **S. hýbrida** (Moench) Schneid. (*Sorbus aucuparia* ✕ *Aronia arbutifolia.*) Shrub or small tree, with slender, sometimes pendulous brs.; young brts. tomentose: lvs. ovate to oblong-ovate, obtuse, 3–8 cm. long, with 2–3 pairs of lobes or lfts. near base, crenate-serrate toward the apex, pubescent beneath: infl. about 3 cm. across, pubescent or nearly glabrous; fls. white or pinkish white: fr. subglobose or pear-shaped, 8–10 mm. long, dark purple. G.H.t.81(c). B.R.1196(c). (*Pyrus h.* Moench, *Aronia h.* Zab., *P. hetero-*

phylla Pott, *Sorbus spuria* Pers., *Sorbaronia heterophylla* Schneid.) Orig. before 1785. Zone V.

Similar hybrids: **S. fallax** Schneid. (*Sorbus aucuparia* × *A. melanocarpa*.) Similar, but nearly glabrous and fr. blackish. (*Sorbus heterophylla* Dipp., not Reichenb.) Cult. 1878.—**S. Jackii** Rehd. (*Sorbus americana* × *A. prunifolia*). Brts., infl. and lvs. beneath thinly villous; shoot-lvs. oblong-ovate to oblong-lanceolate, acute to acuminate, lvs. of fl. brts. acute to obtusish: fr. dark purple. N. Scotia. Intr. 1924.—**S. Arsènii** (Britt.) G. N. Jones (*Sorbus decora* × *A. prunifolia*). Lvs. abruptly acute or short-acuminate, slightly villous beneath: lateral lfts. obtuse: infl. small, nearly glabrous. Jour. N. Y. Bot. Gard. 27:228. Nfd. Cult. ?—**S. sorbifòlia** (Poir.) Schneid. (*S. americana* × *A. melanocarpa*). Similar to *S. fallax*, but lvs. more pointed and like the infl. glabrous: fr. nearly black. W.D.1:53(c). (*Sorbus s.* Hedl., *Sorbus Sargentii* Dipp.) Cult. 1893.

2. × **S. alpìna** (Willd.) Schneid. (*Sorbus Aria* × *A. arbutifolia*). Shrub similar to *S. Aria*, but lvs. smaller, glandular-serrulate, with fewer and less straight veins: infl. and fls. smaller; styles 3–4: fr. red or brownish red, 8 mm. across. S.H.1:f.385f-h(l). (*Pyrus a.* Willd., *Sorbus a.* Heynh., *Aronia densiflora* Spach, *A. Willdenowii* Zab.) Orig. before 1809. Zone V.

A similar hybrid is **S. Dippelii** (Zab.) Schneid. (*S. Aria* × *melanocarpa*). Similar, but lvs. and infl. finally glabrous: fr. blackish purple. (*Sorbus D.* Zab.) Cult. 1870.

× **SORBOPÝRUS** Schneid. Hybrids between *Pyrus* and *Sorbus* known so far only between *P. communis* and *S. Aria*. (*Bollwilleria* Zab., *Pyraria* Cheval.)

× **S. auriculàris** (Knoop) Schneid. (*Pyrus communis* × *Sorbus Aria*). Tree to 15 cm.; brts. and buds tomentose: lvs. broad-elliptic to elliptic, short-acuminate, usually rounded at base, 6–10 cm. long, irregularly and coarsely serrate or doubly serrate, pubescent beneath: fls. in 5–many-fld. corymbs; pedicels slender; calyx tomentose; styles 2–5: fr. pyriform, about 2.5 cm. across, greenish or reddish yellow. Fl.v; fr.x. B.R.1437(c). L.B.1009(c). B.S.2:278. S.L.344(h). (*Pyrus a.* Knoop, *P. Pollveria* L., *P. Bollwylleriana* DC., *Sorbus Bollwylleriana* Zab., *Bollwilleria a.* Zab.) Orig. before 1620. Zone V.—**S. a. bulbifórmis** (Tatar) Schneid., var. Nearer to Pyrus: fr. larger, to 4 cm. across. Wien. Obst-Gart.-Zeit. 1878:26. To this var. may belong *Pyraria malifolia* (Spach) Cheval. (*Bollwilleria m.* Zab., partly.) Dcne. Jard. Fruit. 1:t.32.

× **AMELASÓRBUS** Rehd. Hybrid between *Amelanchier* and *Sorbus;* from the former it differs chiefly in the partly incompletely pinnate lvs. and in the paniculate infl., from the latter in the partly simple, partly incompletely pinnate or lobed lvs., the paniculate infl., the oblong petals, the usually 5 styles and the incompletely 8- or 10-celled fr.; the false partitions extending about halfway to the middle.

× **A. Jáckii** Rehd. (*Amelanchier florida* × *Sorbus scopulina*.) Vigorous shrub: lvs. oval to elliptic, 3.5–6 cm. long, or on shoots to 10 cm. long and elliptic-oblong, rounded or acutish at apex, subcordate or rounded at base, coarsely dentate and partly pinnate or lobed below the middle, loosely pubescent at first, soon glabrous: infl. to 5 cm. long, with racemose brs.; petals oblong, 1 cm. long; styles 4–5: fr. subglobose, 6–8 mm. across, dark red, with blue bloom. Jour. N. Y. Bot. Gard. 27:228. Idaho, Ore. Intr. 1918. Zone V.

19. **ARÒNIA** Med. CHOKEBERRY. Deciduous shrubs; buds appressed, with about 3 outer scales: lvs. crenate-serrulate, with blackish glands on the midrib above, convolute in bud; stipules small, deciduous: fls. white or pinkish, in small corymbs; petals spreading; stamens numerous; anthers purple;

ovary 5-celled, woolly at the top; styles 5, connate at base; carpels connate, but partly free on their ventral suture: fr. a small pome without grit-cells, with persistent connivent calyx-lobes. (Derived from the generic name Aria.) Syn.: *Adenorhachis* Nieuwl. Three closely related species in N. Am.—Ornamental shrubs with handsome lvs. and attractive white fls. and decorative fr.

A. Lvs. beneath and infl. pubescent.
  B. Fr. red ....1. *A. arbutifolia*
  BB. Fr. purple-black or dark purple...2. *A. prunifolia*
AA. Lvs. and infl. glabrous or nearly so: fr. black............................3. *A. melanocarpa*

1. **A. arbutifòlia** (L.) Elliott. RED CHOKEBERRY. Shrub to 3 m.; brts. tomentose: lvs. elliptic to oblong or obovate, acute or abruptly acuminate, glabrous above except the midrib, grayish tomentose beneath: infl. tomentose, 3–4 cm. broad, rather dense, 9–20-fld.; fls. about 1 cm. across, white or reddish: calyx-lobes glandular: fr. subglobose or pear-shaped, 5–7 mm. across, bright or dull red. Fl.iv–v; fr.ix–x, long persistent. B.M.3668(c). G.F.3:417. G.W.5:245. (*Pyrus a.* (L.) L. f., *Sorbus a.* (L.) Heynh., *Mespilus a.* var. *erythrocarpa* Mich.) Mass. to Fla., w. to Minn., Ohio, Ark. and Tex. Intr. about 1700. Zone V. Ornamental shrub with bright red fr. persisting through the winter; the foliage turns red in autumn.—**A. a. macrophýlla** (Hook.) Rehd., f. Large shrub or tree to 6 m.: lvs. 5–9 cm. long. Ark. to La. and Tex. Intr. 1918. Zone (V).—**A. a. leiocalyx** Rehd., f. Calyx and pedicels glabrous or nearly so.—**A. a. macrocárpa** Zab., f. Fr. larger, 8–10 mm. across.—**A. a. pùmila** (Schmidt) Rehd., var. Dwarf shrub with smaller lvs. and darker red fr. S.O.2:t.89(c). (*Mespilus p.* Schmidt, *Pyrus depressa* Lindl.)

A. a. × *Sorbus aucuparia* = *Sorbaronia hybrida;* see p. 381.—*A. a.* × *Sorbus Aria* = *Sorbaronia alpina;* see p. 382.

2. **A. prunifòlia** (Marsh.) Rehd. PURPLE-FRUITED C. Shrub to 4 m., similar to the preceding; corymbs looser, calyx often less densely tomentose and calyx-lobes glandless or nearly so: fr. subglobose, 8–10 mm. across, purplish black, lustrous. Fl.iv–v; fr.viii–ix. Ad.3:t.81(c). B.R.1006(c). B.B.2:291. (*A. atropurpurea* Britt., *Sorbus arbutifolia* var. *atropurpurea* Schneid., *A. floribunda* Spach.) N. S. to Fla., w. to Ind. Cult. 1800? Zone IV. Intermediate between the preceding and the following, but not a hybrid.

3. **A. melanocárpa** (Michx.) Elliott. BLACK C. Usually low shrub, 0.5–1 m. tall; brts. nearly glabrous: lvs. elliptic or obovate to oblong-oblanceolate, abruptly acuminate or obtusish, 2–6 cm. long, bright green and glabrous or nearly so beneath: infl. glabrous or nearly so: fr. globose, 6–8 mm. across, lustrous black or black-purple. Fl.iv–v; fr.viii–ix. B.M.9052(c). B.B.2:291. D.H.3:385. (*A. nigra* Dipp., *Sorbus m.* Heynh., *Pyrus m.* Willd.) N. S. to Fla., w. to Mich. Intr. about 1700. Zone IV.—**A. m. subpubéscens** (Lindl.) Schneid., var. Lvs. pubescent beneath when young.—**A. m. elàta** Rehd., var. More vigorous shrub, to 3 m.: lvs. larger, generally oblong-obovate and acute: fls. and fr. larger.—**A. m. grandifòlia** (Lindl.) Schneid., var. Shrub to 3 m.: lvs. obovate to broad-obovate and abruptly acuminate, 4–8 cm. long and 2–6 cm. broad: infl. fls. and fr. larger. B.R.1154(c).—Particularly the two last vars. are handsome shrubs with lustrous dark green lvs., attractive white fls. in spring and shining black fr. in fall.

A. m. × *Sorbus americana* = *Sorbaronia sorbifolia;* see p. 382.—*A. m.* × *Sorbus aucuparis* = *Sorbaronia fallax;* see p. 382.—*A. m.* × *Sorbus Aria* = *Sorbaronia Dippelii;* see p. 382.

20. **PHOTÌNIA** Lindl. Deciduous or evergreen shrubs or trees; buds ovoid, with several outer scales: lvs. short-petioled, usually finely serrate, stipulate: fls. white, in corymbs or short panicles; petals 5, orbicular; sta-

mens about 20; styles 2, rarely 3–5, connate at least at base; ovary often nearly half-superior, in fr. free only at apex or ⅓ of its length: fr. a small, 1–4-seeded pome, red, rounded at top and with persistent connivent calyx-lobes. (Greek *photeinos*, shining, alluding to the lustrous lvs.) Including *Pourthiaea* Dcne. About 40 species, in S. and E. Asia.

A. Lvs. deciduous: fls. in corymbs or cymes, with conspicuously warty axes.
                                                              Sect. I. POURTHIAEA Schneid.
   B. Infl. compound, many-fld...1. *P. villosa*
   BB. Infl. subumbellate, 2–8-fld., glabrous....................................2. *P. parvifolia*
AA. Lvs. persistent: infl. corymbose-paniculate, not warty........Sect. II. EUPHOTINIA Focke.
                                                  3. *P. serrulata*

1. **P. villòsa** (Thunb.) DC. Shrub or small tree, to 5 m.; brts. slender, pubescent when young: lvs. short-stalked, obovate to oblong-obovate, 3–8 cm. long, acuminate, cuneate, finely and sharply serrate, dark green and glabrous above, villous beneath, with 5–7 pairs of veins, firm at maturity; petioles 1–5 mm. long: infl. 3–5 cm. across, villous; fls. 1.2 cm. across: fr. ellipsoid, 8 mm. long, bright red. Fl.vi; fr.x. S.I.1:t.49(c). M.K.t.50(c). G.F. 1:67. (*P. variabilis* Hemsl., *Pourthiaea v.* Dcne., *Sorbus v.* Zab.) Japan, Korea, China. Intr. about 1865. Zone IV. Ornamental shrubby tree, with bright red fr. persisting into the winter; the lvs. turn red in autumn.—**P. v. Maximowicziàna** (Lévl.) Rehd., f. Lvs. obovate, rounded and abruptly short-acuminate or truncate at apex, gradually cuneate, strongly veined with impressed veins above; petiole 1–2 mm. long. Korea. Cult. 1876.—**P. v. laèvis** (Thunb.) Dipp., var. Lvs. narrower and smaller, soon glabrous: infl. glabrous: fr. 1.2 cm. long. G.F.4:377. B.C.2596. (*P. l.* DC., *Pourthiaea arguta* Lav., not Dcne.) Cult. 1875.—**P. v. sínica** Rehd. & Wils., var. Shrub or tree to 10 m.: lvs. thinner, elliptic or elliptic-oblong, soon glabrous: infl. 5–8-, rarely to 15-fld., loosely villous. C. China. Intr. 1908.

Closely related species: **P. Beauverdiàna** Schneid. Lvs. obovate-oblong to oblong, 6–10 cm. long, glabrous, with 8–14 pairs of veins; petioles 5–10 mm. long: infl. 5 cm. across: fr. subglobose, 6 mm. across, scarlet. S.H.1:f.393p-q(l). C. and W. China. Intr. 1900? Zone VI?—**P. B. notàbilis** Rehd. & Wils., var. Lvs. elliptic-oblong, 7–12 cm. long: infl. 8–10 cm. across: fr. ellipsoid, 7–8 mm. long. Intr. 1908.

2. **P. parvifòlia** (Pritz.) Schneid. Slender shrub to 3 m.; brts. glabrous: lvs. elliptic to elliptic-ovate or rhombic-ovate, 3–6 cm. long, acuminate, broad-cuneate or rounded at base, sharply serrulate, glabrous, pale beneath: fls. 1–6, subumbellate, about 1.5 cm. across; pedicels 1–2.5 cm. long, glabrous: fr. ellipsoid, 8–10 mm. long, scarlet. Fl.v–vi; fr.x. S.H.1:f.392o,393g. (*P. subumbellata* Rehd. & Wils.) E. and C. China. Intr. 1908. Zone VI. Graceful shrub with scarlet fr.

Markedly different in its 5 styles and larger fr. is **P. amphidóxa** (Schneid.) Rehd. & Wils. Shrub to 3 m.; young brts. tomentose: lvs. elliptic to oblong or oblong-oblanceolate, acuminate, 5–9 cm. long, finally nearly glabrous: infl. 3–6-fld., tomentose; pedicels short; styles 5: fr. subglobose, 1–1.4 cm. across, scarlet. S.H.1:f.394k-l(fl). (*Stranvaesia a.* Schneid.) C. China. Intr. 1908. Zone VII?

3. **P. serrulàta** Lindl. Evergreen shrub or tree to 12 m., quite glabrous; buds ovoid, 4 mm. thick: lvs. oblong, acuminate, usually rounded at base, 10–18 cm. long, serrulate, dark green and lustrous above, yellowish green beneath, reddish when young; petioles 2–3 cm. long, pubescent: fls. 6–8 mm. across, in broad panicles 10–16 cm. across, with thick slightly angular brts.; petals glabrous: fr. globose, 5–6 mm. across, red. Fl.v–vii; fr.x. B.M.2105(c). L.B.248(c). G.W.15:247(h). China. Intr. 1804. Zone VII. Shrub with large lustrous lvs. and attractive white fls. followed late in fall by bright red fr.— **P. s. rotundifòlia** Bean, var. Lvs. shorter and broader.

Closely related species: **P. Davidsòniae** Rehd. & Wils. Buds about 1 mm. thick, acutish: young brts. appressed-pubescent: lvs. cuneate, 8–14 cm. long, pubescent on the veins beneath at first; petioles 1–1.5 cm. long: fls. 1 cm. across; infl. slightly pubescent: fr. 7–10 mm. long. C. China. Intr. 1900. Zone VII?— **P. glabra** (Thunb.) Maxim. Shrub to 3 m.: lvs. elliptic or obovate to oblong-obovate, cuneate, 5–8 cm. long; petiole about 1 cm. long: infl. 5–10 cm. across; petals bearded: fr. about 5 mm. across. S.I.1:t.47(c). (*Sorbus g.* Zab.) Japan. Cult. 1903? Zone VII?

21. **STRANVAÈSIA** Lindl. Evergreen trees or shrubs; buds small, with few acuminate scales: lvs. entire or serrate, with subulate stipules: fls. white, in terminal many-fld. corymbs; calyx turbinate, 5-toothed; petals 5, generally obovate, clawed; stamens about 20; styles 5, connate at least to the middle; ovary half-superior; cells 2-ovuled: fr. a small orange or scarlet pome; calyx-teeth persistent, connivent; upper part of ovary free to the middle or beyond, the whole ovary at full maturity easily separable from the fleshy receptacle and the valves splitting loculicidally. (After William Fox-Strangways, English botanist; 1795–1865.) Four or 5 species in China and the Himal.)

S. Davidiàna Dcne. Shrub to 8 m.; young brts. silky-villous, soon glabrous: lvs. oblong to oblong-lanceolate or oblanceolate, acuminate, cuneate, 6–11 cm. long, entire, green and glabrous on both sides except the sparingly pubescent midrib; petiole pubescent, 1–2 cm. long, often red: infl. loose, 5–8 cm. broad, villous: fls. 8 mm. across; anthers red: fr. subglobose, 7–8 mm. across, scarlet. Fl.vi; fr.x–xi. B.M.9008(c). M.O.t.19. G.C.71:199(h);84: 403. (*Photinia D.* Cardot.) W. China. Intr. 1917. Zone VII?—**S. D. undulàta** (Dcne.) Rehd. & Wils., var. Usually lower: lvs. elliptic-oblong to oblong-lanceolate, 3–8 cm. long, usually wavy at the margin: infl. 5–7 cm. across, sometimes nearly glabrous: fr. about 6 mm. across, coral-red to orange. B.M.8418(c). Gn.86:644. (*S. u.* Dcne.) W. and C. China. Intr. 1901. Zone (V).—**S. D. salicifòlia** (Hutchins.) Rehd., var. Lvs. narrow-lanceolate, with more numerous veins; stipules and bracts quickly deciduous: infl. densely pubescent: fr. red, about 8 mm. across. B.M.8862(c). Gn.87:no.2717;88:57 (h). (*S. s.* Hutchins.) W. China. Intr. 1907. Zone VII?

22. **ERIOBÓTRYA** Lindl. Evergreen trees or shrubs: lvs. short-petioled or nearly sessile, dentate, wtih straight veins ending in the teeth: fls. white, in terminal broad usually woolly panicles; calyx-lobes acute; petals 5, oval or suborbicular, clawed; stamens 20; styles 2–5, connate below; ovary inferior; cells 2-ovuled: fr. a pome with incurved persistent calyx-teeth, thin endocarp and one or few large seeds. (Greek, *erion,* wool, and *botrys,* cluster.) About 10 species in E. Asia.

E. japónica (Thunb.) Lindl. Loquat. Small tree to 6 m.; lvs. nearly sessile, obovate to elliptic-oblong, cuneate, 12–25 cm. long, remotely dentate, lustrous above, rusty-tomentose below: fls. fragrant, about 1 cm. across, nearly hidden in the rusty woolly pubescence of the panicle 10–16 cm. long: fr. pear-shaped, 3–4 cm. long, yellow; seeds 1–1.5 cm. long. Fl.ix–x; fr.iv–vi. S.Z.1: t.97(c). B.R.365(c). G.C.52:319. R.H.1913:107(fr). Gn.80:615(h). G.W.8: 314(h). C. China. Intr. 1784. Zone VII. With large lvs., fragrant fls. and edible fr. of agreeable acid flavor, for which the plant is cult. in E. Asia, S. Eu. and in the S. States.—**E. j. variegàta** Sander. Lvs. variegated with white. G.C.53:293.

23. **RAPHIÓLEPIS** Lindl. Evergreen shrubs: lvs. short-petioled, serrate or entire, with curving and anastomosing veins, leathery: fls. white or

pink, in terminal racemes or panicles; sepals triangular; petals 5, oblong to
obovate, obtuse; stamens 15–20; styles 2–3, connate at base; ovary inferior:
fr. subglobose, purple-black or bluish black, with deciduous calyx and with 1
or 2 large seeds. (Greek, *rhaphe,* needle, and *lepis,* scale; in reference to the
subulate bracts.) Three or four species in S. Japan and S. China.

    R. umbellàta (Thunb.) Mak. Shrub to 4 m.: lvs. elliptic to obovate,
rarely elliptic-oblong, obtuse or acute, cuneate, 3–8 cm. long, remotely dentate, dark green above, pale beneath and floccose-tomentose when young:
fls. white, 1.5–2 cm. across, fragrant, in dense upright tomentose panicles or
racemes: fr. about 1 cm. across, bluish black. Fl.v–vi; fr.ix(–iii). S.Z.1:t.
85(c). (*R. japonica* Sieb. & Zucc.) S. Japan. Intr. before 1859. Zone VII.)
Handsome evergreen shrub with fragrant white fls.—**R. u. ovàta** (Briot)
Schneid., f. Lvs. broad-obovate, rounded at apex, entire or sparingly toothed.
B.M. 5510(c). R.H.1870:348. G.W.4:129(h);14:323(h). (*R. japonica* var.
integerrima Hook. f., not Maxim.) Japan, Korea. Intr. before 1864.

    Doubtfully hardy is **R. índica** Lindl. Lvs. thinner and narrower, acute or
acuminate, more sharply serrate: fls. white or pinkish in loose glabrous or somewhat tomentose racemes with narrow lanceolate bracts; sepals lanceolate, acute
and usually red; petals narrow, acute. B.M.1726(c). B.R.1400,1468(c). S.
China. Intr. 1806.—*R. i.* × *umbellata* = **R. Delacoùrii** André. R.H.1900:698,
t(c).

    24. AMELÁNCHIER Med. Shadbush (Shadblow, Sarvis). Deciduous
shrubs or trees: buds conspicuous, pointed, with several scales: lvs. petioled,
serrate, with nearly straight veins; stipules small, deciduous: fls. white, in
terminal racemes, rarely solitary; calyx-tube campanulate, with 5 short
lobes; petals 5, obovate to lanceolate; stamens 10–20; styles 2–5, partly connate or distinct; ovary inferior, each cell with 2 ovules separated by a false
partition growing from the back of the cell; fr. a small berry-like pome, incompletely 4–10-celled, with one seed in each cell, crowned by the usually
reflexed calyx-lobes, bluish black or dark purple, usually juicy and sweet.
(Provençal name of *A. ovalis.*) About 25 species chiefly in N. Am. s. to
Mex., few in Eu. and in W. and E. Asia.—Ornamental trees or shrubs, handsome in bloom, particularly *A. laevis;* some as Nos. 3–7 and 10 have edible fr.
sometimes used for jellies and are occasionally cult. for their fr.

Styles free, 5, not exceeding the calyx-tube ....1. *A. ovalis*
Styles connate at least at base, longer than calyx-tube.
  A. Styles 5, often connate to the middle.
    B. Fls. in racemes: lvs. folded in bud; petioles slender.
      C. Lvs. rather coarsely serrate, 3–5 teeth per cm. on average lvs.; veins usually straight
        and close together; young unfolding lvs. soon flat: top of ovary woolly.
      D. Lvs. rounded or truncate at apex, usually serrate above the middle, glabrous or
        soon glabrous ....2. *A. florida*
      DD. Lvs. acute or acutish, densely woolly beneath when young.
        E. Shrub to 3 m.: lvs. serrate nearly to the base....................3. *A. sanguinea*
        EE. Shrub to 1.25 m.: lvs. serrate to below the middle.................4. *A. humilis*
      CC. Lvs. closely and finely serrate, about 6–12 teeth per cm.; young lvs. remaining folded
        for some time.
      D. Lvs. tomentose when young; pedicels usually rather short.
        E. Lvs. rounded or acutish at apex.
          F. Top of ovary woolly: lvs. generally elliptic.
            G. Sepals on fr. recurved: stoloniferous shrub to 1.25 m......5. *A. stolonifera*
            GG. Sepals on fr. slightly spreading: shrub to 4 m................6. *A. spicata*
          FF. Top of ovary glabrous or nearly so: lvs. generally oblong; sepals upright.
                                              7. *A. oblongifolia*
        EE. Lvs. short-acuminate or acute.
          F. Top of ovary woolly: lvs. glabrous above when young, rounded or subcordate
            at base ....8. *A. asiatica*
          FF. Top of ovary glabrous or nearly so: lvs. tomentose on both sides when
            young, usually cordate at base.............................9. *A. canadensis*
      DD. Lvs. glabrous from the beginning: pedicels slender, to 2.5 or in fr. to 5 cm. long.
                                           10. *A. laevis*

ВВ. Fls. 1–3: lvs. imbricate in bud, flat when unfolding, cuneate at base; petioles short.

                                                 11. *A. Bartramiana*

ᴀᴀ. Styles 2–3, usually connate only at base....................................**12.** *A. prunifolia*

1. A. ovàlis Med. SERVICE-BERRY. Upright or spreading shrub, 0.5–2.5 m., with rather stiff brs.; young brts. tomentose: lvs. oval to obovate, 2.5–5 cm. long, usually rounded at apex, subcordate at base, serrate from near the base, woolly beneath when young: racemes many-fld., tomentose; calyx glabrescent; petals linear-oblanceolate: fr. bluish black, bloomy. Fl.v; fr.vIII. B.M. 2430(c). H.W.3:87. G.C.II.9:793. M.G.1900:497(h). (*A. rotundifolia* Dum.-Cours., *A. vulgaris* Moench.) C. and S. Eu. Intr. 1596. Zone IV.

2. A. flòrida Lindl. Shrub with rather stout upright brs., sometimes small tree to 10 m.: lvs. broad-oval to oval, truncate or subcordate at base, 2–4 cm. long, coarsely and sharply toothed above the middle, rarely below, quite glabrous or slightly floccose-tomentose at first; racemes many-fld., upright, glabrous or slightly tomentose at first; sepals short; petals oblong to narrow-oblong, about 1 cm. long; summit of ovary woolly: fr. nearly black, bloomy. Fl.v; fr.vII. B.R.1589(c). S.S.4:t.196. G.F.185:5:515. G.M.52:143(h). (*A. alnifolia* var. *f.* Schneid., *A. alnifolia* auth., not Nutt., *A. oxyodon* Koehne.) Mich. to Ore. and Wash. Intr. 1826. Zone II.—**A. f. tomentòsa** Sealy, f. Lvs. glaucous and sparsely villous or glabrous beneath: infl. densely villous. B.M.9496(c). Cult. 1937.

    A. f. × *Sorbus scopulina* = *Amelasorbus Jackii;* see p. 382.

    Closely related species: **A. alnifòlia** Nutt. Usually low and shrubby; brts. pubescent: lvs. broad-oval to suborbicular, densely pubescent beneath, finally glabrate; racemes rather short and dense, silky-villous. Sask. to Colo. and Idaho. Intr. 1918. Zone V.—**A. Cusíckii** Fern. Lvs. elliptic to obovate-oblong, acutish to obtuse, 2–4 cm. long, serrate from near base or only above the middle: racemes 5–7-fld., glabrous; petals 1.5–2 cm. long; top of ovary glabrous: fr. scarlet, tardily turning black. S.H.1:f.410d. Wash. and Ore. to Mont. and Utah. Cult. 1934. Zone V?

3. A. sanguínea (Pursh) DC. Slender shrub with 1 or few stems, to 2.5 m.: lvs. orbicular-oval to oval-oblong, 3–6 cm. long, subacute, rounded or subcordate at base, serrate nearly to base: raceme usually loose and nodding: lower pedicels 7–10, in fr. to 25 mm. long; petals 1–1.4 cm. long; calyx-tube 3.5–6 mm. broad; top of ovary densely woolly; fr. rather large, nearly black, bloomy, sweet. Fl.v; fr.vIII. B.B.2:283. Rh.14:t.95. (*A. rotundifolia* Roem., *A. spicata* Robins. & Fern., not K. Koch.) Can. to N. Y., Neb. and Ind. Intr. 1824. Zone IV.

    Closely related species: **A. amàbilis** Wieg. Lvs elliptic-ovate, with veins more irregular, glabrescent: infl. loose; lower pedicels 2.5–4 cm. long; calyx-tube more shallow, 7–9 mm. broad; petals 1.6–2.2 cm. long. (*A. sanguinea* var. *grandiflora* Wieg., *A. grandiflora* Wieg., not Rehd.) N. Y. Intr. 1913.

4. A. hùmilis Wieg. Upright shrub, to 1.25 m., stoloniferous and forming patches: lvs. elliptic to elliptic-oblong, subcordate or rarely rounded at base, 2–5 cm. long, serrate to below the middle; racemes upright, rather dense, many-fld.; petals oblong-obovate, about 8 mm. long: fr. nearly black, bloomy, sweet. Fl.v; fr.vIII. Rh.14:t.95. Vt. to Alb., s. to N. Y. and Iowa. Intr. 1904. Zone IV.

5. A. stolonífera Wieg. Upright stoloniferous shrub to 1.25 m., forming patches: lvs. elliptic, rarely elliptic-oblong or suborbicular, rounded at base or rarely subcordate, 2–5 cm. long, finely serrate, usually quite or nearly entire at the lower third, densely white-tomentose beneath when young: racemes upright, short and densely tomentose or nearly glabrous; petals obovate-oblong, about 8 mm. long: fr. purplish black, bloomy, sweet. Fl.v; ε few days later than *A. laevis;* fr.VIII. Rh.14:t.95. (*A. spicata* Britt. & Br., not K. Koch.) Nfd. and Me. to Va. Intr. 1883. Zone IV.

6. × **A. spicàta** (Lam.) K. Koch (*A. oblongifolia* × *stolonifera?*). Bushy shrub with numerous stems, to 4 m.: lvs. elliptic to obovate, sometimes elliptic-oblong, rounded at base, 3–6 cm. long, serrate to the base, white tomentose beneath when young; racemes upright, dense, woolly; petals oblong-obovate, 8 mm. long: fr. bluish black, bloomy, with slightly spreading sepals; pedicels rather stout, 3–12 mm. long. G.O.t.79(c). M.G.15:496(h,fl). (*Crataegus s.* Lam., *A. ovalis* Borkh., not Med.) Orig. before 1800.

7. **A. oblongifòlia** Roem. Shrub with rather slender upright stems growing in rather dense clumps, to 6 m.: lvs. oblong to obovate-oblong, rounded or acute at apex, rounded or subcordate at base, 3–6 cm. long, finely serrulate nearly or quite to the base, white-tomentose beneath when young: racemes upright, short and dense, silky-tomentose; petals obovate-oblong to linear-oblanceolate, about 8 mm. long; top of ovary glabrous or sometimes slightly woolly: fr. nearly black, bloomy, sweet. Fl.v, with *A. laevis;* fr.VI. B.M. 7619(c). Em.2:503,t(c, lower fig.) S.S.4:t.195. G.C.III.21:333. S.L.84(h). M.G.15:497(h). (*A. canadensis* var. *o.* Torr. & Gr., *A. obovalis* Ashe, *A. Botryapium* Britt. & Brown in part.) Me. to S. C. Cult. 1641. Zone IV. This differs from all other species except Nos. 6 and 11 in the upright sepals of the fr.—**A. o. micropétala** Robins., var. Shrub to 1 m.: fls. inconspicuous, with linear petals 3–4 mm. long. (*A. m.* Ashe; possibly *A. o.* × *stolonifera*.) Mass. to Va. Intr. 1918.

Closely related species: **A. intermèdia** Spach. Usually low shrub: lvs. acute, often reddish when young, soon glabrous, those of shoots similar to lvs. of *A. laevis;* sepals irregularly spreading; pedicels slender, 8–20 mm. long. (*A. canadensis i.* Ashe.) Vt. to N. C. Cult. 1834. Zone V.

8. **A. asiática** (Sieb. & Zucc.) Endl. Shrub or tree to 12 m., with slender spreading brs.; lvs. ovate to elliptic-oblong, acute, rounded at base or subcordate, 4–8 cm. long, finely serrate to the base, densely white or yellowish tomentose beneath when young: racemes nodding, rather dense, woolly; top of ovary woolly: fr. bluish black. Fl.v; fr.IX. S.Z.1:t.42(c). S.I.1:t.47(c). (*A. canadensis* var. *a.* (Sieb. & Zucc.) Miq., *A. japonica* Hort.) Japan, Korea. Intr. 1865. Zone V.—**A. a. sínica** Schneid., var. Lvs. less tomentose, often finally glabrous, smaller, usually serrate only above the middle: infl. usually glabrous. I.S.1:31.. C.C.169. (*A. s.* Chun.) China. Intr. 1920.

9. **A. canadénsis** (L.) Med. Tree to 20 m., with ascending brs., sometimes shrubby: lvs. generally obovate, less often ovate, elliptic or oblong, acute to acuminate, usually cordate at base, 3–8 cm. long, sharply serrate nearly or quite to the base, when young densely tomentose beneath, less so above, tomentum usually partly persistent: racemes nodding, rather dense, silky-tomentose; petals linear to linear-oblong, 1–1.4 cm. long; top of ovary glabrous or slightly hairy: fr. maroon-purple. Fl.v, before the lvs.: fr.VI. B.R.1174(c). S.S.4:t.194. Rh.14:t.96. B.S.1:188&t(h). Me. to Ga. and La.; w. to Iowa, Mo. Intr. 1623. Zone IV. This is the only species with the young lvs. tomentose on both side.—**A. c. nùda** Palmer & Steyerm., f. Lvs. and petioles glabrous at maturity. Intr. ?

A. c. × *laevis* = **A. grandiflòra** Rehd. Tree or shrub: lvs. purplish when unfolding and floccose-tomentose, soon glabrous: racemes slightly villous; lower pedicels to 2.2 cm. long; petals obtuse; fls. rather large. Spontaneous with the parents. Cult. 1870. Very handsome, particularly the pink-fld. form.—**A. g. rubéscens** Rehd., f. Fls. purple-pink in bud, tinged pink when open. Cult. 1920.

Closely related species: **A. sèra** Ashe. Shrub to 4 m.: lvs. glabrous at maturity: racemes slender, glabrous or glabrescent; petals narrow, 2.5–3 mm. wide, acute; lower pedicels about 1.5 cm. long. Va. and Md. Intr. 1920. Zone V.

10. **A. laèvis** Wieg. Tree with spreading brs., to 12 m., sometimes shrubby: lvs. elliptic-ovate to ovate-oblong, short-acuminate, subcordate or rounded at base, rarely broad-cuneate, 3–7 cm. long, sharply serrate nearly to the base, quite glabrous and purplish when young: racemes slender, many-fld., nodding, glabrous or nearly so; pedicels to 3 cm. long, in fr. to 5 cm.; petals linear-oblong, 1–1.8 cm. long; top of ovary glabrous: fr. purple or nearly black, bloomy, sweet. Fl.v; fr.vi. Em.2:503,t.(c, upper fig.) H.T.242. M.G. 15:494,495(h). G.34:343(h). G.M.44:306(h). (*A. canadensis* Gray, not Med.) Nfd. to Ga. and Ala., w. to Mich. and Kans. Cult. 1870. Zone IV. One of the most graceful species in bloom, differing in the purplish young foliage and the drooping racemes.

11. **A. Bartramiàna** (Tausch) Roem. Shrub to 2.5 m.: lvs. elliptic to elliptic-oblong, acute or rounded at apex, cuneate, 3–5 cm. long, sharply serrate to below the middle or nearly to the base, glabrous when young: fls. 1–3, pedicels 1–2.5 cm. long, glabrous; petals obovate, about 8 mm. long; top of ovary woolly: fr. purplish black, bloomy. Fl.iv–v; fr.vii–viii. B.M.8499(c). G.F.1:247. B.C.1:273. (*A. oligocarpa* Roem.) Lab. to Mich. and Minn., s. to Pa. in the mts. Intr. about 1800. Zone II.

12. **A. prunifòlia** Greene. Much-branched shrub, to 4 m.; brts. pubescent: lvs. ovate to elliptic, rarely obovate, 1–2.5 cm. long, acute to obtuse, rather finely serrate, pubescent on both side, finally glabrate above, finely appressed-pubescent beneath; petiole 3–5 mm. long: racemes 3–6-fld., pubescent; pedicels 4–10 mm. long; ovary finely villous or sometimes nearly glabrous; sepals lanceolate, pubescent; petals oblong, 7–8 mm. long; stamens 10; styles usually 3, slightly pubescent at base; top of ovary villous. S.H.1:f.413a-ᴄ, 414a-f. (*A. rubescens* Greene.) Colo. to N. Mex. and Utah. Cult. 1900. Zone VI?

Related species: **A. Purpúsii** Koehne. Lvs. broadly oval or suborbicular, truncate or emarginate at apex, rather coarsely serrate: sepals pubescent inside; top of ovary glabrous. Colo. Intr. about 1900. Zone V?—**A. plurinérvis** Koehne. Lvs. oval, 1–1.5 cm. long, with few small teeth at the rounded apex, minutely puberulous, with 8–12 pairs of veins; stamens 10–15; ovary sparingly pubescent, top glabrous. Rocky Mts. Intr. about 1900. Zone V?

25. **PERAPHÝLLUM** Nutt. Deciduous shrub; buds small, acute, pubescent: lvs. partly fascicled, nearly sessile or short-stalked, entire or sparingly serrate, with minute caducous stipules; fls. white or tinged pink, in terminal 2–5-fld. umbel-like racemes; calyx-lobes lanceolate, entire; petals 5, obovate, spreading; stamens 20; styles 2–3, free, slightly longer than stamens: ovary wholly inferior, 2–3-celled, each cell with 2 ovules separated by a false partition: fr. a small pome 4–6-celled, each cell with one seed; calyx-lobes persistent. (Greek *pera*, excessively, and *phyllon*, leaf; alluding to the crowded leaves.) One species.

P. ramosíssimum Nutt. Upright shrub to 2 m.; young brts. tomentose: lvs. oblong to oblanceolate, narrowed at ends, 1.5–5 cm. long, silky-pubescent when young, later glabrous above; fls. 1.8 cm. across; disk rose-colored: fr. pendulous, globose, 8–10 mm. across, yellow with brownish or reddish cheek. Fl.v; fr.ix. B.M.7420(c). B.S.2:126. S.H.1:714. Ore. to Calif. and Colo. Intr. 1870. Zone V. Small shrub of little ornamental value.

26. **MÀLUS** Mill. **Apple.** Deciduous, rarely half-evergreen trees or shrubs, rarely with spinescent brs.; buds ovoid, with several imbricate scales: lvs. serrate or lobed, folded or convolute in bud, stipulate: fls. white to pink or carmine, in umbel-like racemes; petals usually suborbicular or obovate;

stamens 15–50, with usually yellow anthers; ovary inferior, 3–5-celled; styles 2–5, connate at base: fr. a pome without or with some grit-cells, with persistent or deciduous calyx. (Ancient Latin name.) About 25 species in the temperate regions of N. Am., Eu. and Asia; in N. Am. s. to Fla. and Tex., in Asia to the Himal.—Some species are important fruit-trees, others belong to our most valuable ornamental trees and shrubs with showy fls. in spring and attractive fr. in autumn.

Lvs. convolute in bud, always undivided..........................Sect. I. EUMALUS Zabel.
  A. Calyx persistent ....Ser. 1. PUMILAE Rehd.
    B. Calyx-lobes longer than tube, acuminate.
      c. Fr. depressed and usually ribbed at apex, with impressed calyx, short-stalked: lvs. crenate-serrate ....1. M. pumila
      cc. Fr. usually ovoid, attenuate at apex and without ribs, the raised calyx with tubular fleshy base, usually slender-stalked: lvs. sharply serrate.............2. M. prunifolia
    BB. Calyx-lobes shorter or as long as tube, acute: fr. slender-stalked: lvs. chartaceous, lustrous above.
      c. Lvs. broad-cuneate or nearly rounded at base; petiole 1.5–2.5 cm. long: fr. usually contracted into the pedicel..3. M. spectabilis
      cc. Lvs. gradually attenuate at base; petiole 2–3.5 cm. long: fr. impressed at base.
                                              4. M. micromalus
  AA. Calyx deciduous (partly so in some hybrids)........................Ser. 2. BACCATAE Rehd.
    B. Calyx-lobes longer than tube, narrow-lanceolate: fls. white; styles 5, rarely 4.
                                              5. M. baccata
    BB. Calyx-lobes shorter than tube or as long, triangular-ovate: fls. white or pink.
      c. Styles 3, rarely 4; calyx-lobes acute or acuminulate: fr. ellipsoid....6. M. hupehensis
      cc. Styles 4 or 5, calyx-lobes obtusish: fr. pyriform, small.................7. M. Halliana
Lvs. folded in bud, sharply serrate and at least those of the shoots more or less lobed (except in Nos. 8, 13 and 16).
  A. Calyx deciduous ....Sect. II. SORBOMALUS Zabel
    B. Styles villous at base.
      c. Calyx and pedicels glabrous or slightly pubescent.........Ser. 3. SIEBOLDIANAE Rehd.
        D. Lvs. never lobed, cuneate: fls. intense carmine in bud; styles usually 4, connate to the middle ....8. M. floribunda
        DD. Lvs. at least those at end of shoots lobed, usually rounded at base: fl.-buds white or pink; styles connate at base.
          E. Petals cuneate at base, often pink.
            F. Lvs. of flowering brts. entire or nearly so, only upper lvs. of shoots slightly lobed; sepals longer than tube...................................9. M. Zumi
            FF. Lvs. all serrate: lvs. of shoots lobed; sepals as long as tube..10. M. Sieboldii
          EE. Petals suborbicular, rounded at base: low shrub with spreading brs.
                                11. M. Sargenti
        DD. Calyx and pedicels tomentose: lvs. always lobed; styles 5.
                             Ser. 4. FLORENTINAE Rehd.
                                    12. M. florentina
    BB. Styles glabrous ....Ser. 5. KANSUENSES Rehd.
      c. Fr. without grit-cells, not dotted: styles 3–4.
        D. Lvs. undivided or partly 3-lobed.....................................13. M. fusca
        DD. Lvs. deeply lobed, sometimes undivided..........................14. M. toringoides
      cc. Fr. with grit-cells, dotted; styles 3: lvs. 3–5-lobed.................15. M. kansuensis
  AA. Calyx persistent; styles 5.
    B. Fr. with a cup-shaped cavity at apex and apex of core not free, 1–1.5 cm. across, dotted, with grit-cells: lvs. not or slightly lobed: styles glabrous or nearly so.
                                Ser. 6. YUNNANENSES Rehd.
      c. Lvs. glabrous or slightly pubescent beneath, not lobed.................16. M. Prattii
      cc. Lvs. tomentose beneath, often slightly lobed......................17. M. yunnanensis
    BB. Fr. with apex of core free and pointed; styles villous at base.
      c. Fr. without grit-cells, usually depressed, with impressed calyx; pedicels slender; fls. white, flushed pink.....................Sect. III. CHLOROMELES (Dcne.) Rehd.
        D. Lvs. ovate to elliptic, not or only slightly lobed on vigorous shoots: fr. about 5 cm. across ....18. M. platycarpa
        DD. Lvs. at least those of shoots lobed: fr. smaller.
          E. Calyx glabrous or sometimes villous: lvs. usually glabrous and rather thin.
            F. Lvs. acute or acuminate, serrate or doubly serrate.
              G. Lvs. glaucescent beneath, even those of flowering brts. slightly lobed, ovate to triangular-ovate: calyx thinly villous.................19. M. glaucescens
              GG. Lvs. green beneath; those of flowering brts. usually undivided, ovate to oblong-ovate.
                 H. Lvs. of flowering brts. ovate to oblong-ovate.........20. M. coronaria
                 HH. Lvs. of flowering brts. ovate-lanceolate to oblong-lanceolate.
                                   21. M. lancifolia
          FF. Lvs. of flowering brts. obtuse or acutish, crenate-serrate, cuneate at base, usually oblong. ....22. M. angustifolia

EE. Calyx tomentose: lvs. tomentose beneath, those of shoots thickish and strongly
veined ....23. *M. ioensis*
CC. Fr. with grit-cells, the calyx not impressed: fls. pure white; calyx tomentose.
D. Lvs. deeply lobed: fls. 6–8, slender-stalked: fr. 1.5 cm. across.
Sect. IV. ERIOLOBUS (DC.) Schneid.
24. *M. trilobata*
DD. Lvs. not or slightly lobed: fls. 2–5; styles villous below: fr. about 3 cm. across.
Sect. V. DOCYNIOPSIS Schneid.
25. *M. Tschonoskii*

1. **M. pùmila** Mill. COMMON A. Tree to 15 m., with short trunk and
round head; buds pubescent; young brts. tomentose: lvs. broad-elliptic to
elliptic or ovate, 4.5–10 cm. long and 3–5.5 cm. broad, usually broad-cuneate,
acute or acutish, crenate-serrate, pubescent on both sides at first, later glabrate above; petioles pubescent, rather stout, 1.5–3 cm. long: fls. white,
suffused with pink; pedicels 1–2.5 cm. long, like the calyx tomentose; styles
usually pubescent to the middle: fr. usually subglobose, 2 cm. across or larger,
impressed at apex and at base. H.W.2:76,f.295(b),t.51(c). R.I.25:t.112(c).
S.E.t.390(c). (*M. communis* DC., *M. Malus* Britt., *M. dasyphylla* Borkh.,
Pyrus Malus L., partly.) Eu., W. Asia. Cult. since ancient times. Zone III.
—This species is the parent of most of our cult. Apples, though some probably are the offspring of hybrids with *M. sylvestris*, *M. prunifolia* and also
M. baccata.—**M. p. apétala** (Muenchh.) Schneid., f. Fls. small, with deformed greenish petals, without stamens and with 10–15 styles: fr. open at
the top. B.C.5:2870,2871. R.H.1935:369. (*M. dasyphylla dioica* Zabel, *Pyrus
apetala* Muenchh., *P. dioica* Moench.) Cult. 1770.—**M. p. translùcens** (Hartwig) Schneid., f. Fls. double, pink in bud, changing to white. (*M. p.* var.
plena Bean.) Cult. 1811.—**M. p. péndula** (Zab.) Schneid., f. With pendulous
brs. ("Elise Rathke.")—**M. p. paradisíaca** Schneid., var. Shrubby form.
(*M. p. Med.*)—**M. p. Niedzwetzkyàna** (Dieck) Schneid., var. Young lvs.,
fls., fr. including the flesh, and bark and wood of the brs. red. B.M.7975(c).
R.H.1906:232,t(c). F.R.2:344,t(c). S.L.231(h). (*M. N.* Dieck, *Pyrus N.*
Hemsl.) S. W. Siber., Turkest. Intr. about 1891.

M. p. × *prunifolia* = **M. astracánica** Dum.-Cours. Differing chiefly in the
more sharply and coarsely serrate lvs. and in the longer-stalked usually bright
red and bloomy fr. (*Pyrus Malus* var. *a.* Loud., *P. a.* DC.) Orig. before 1800.—
M. p. × *spectabilis;* see under No. 3.—*M. p.* × *baccata;* see under No. 5.—*M. p.*
× *fusca;* see under No. 13.—*M. p.* × *coronaria;* see under No. 20.—*M. p.* ×
ioensis; see under No. 23.—*M. p. Niedzwetzkyana* × *atrosanguinea* = **M.** pur-
púrea (Barbier) Rehd. Young lvs. and brts. purple: lvs. smaller, lustrous, on
shoots occasionally slightly lobed; pedicels longer; petals oblong; styles often
4: fr. smaller, with sometimes deciduous calyx. G.C.62:221. (*M. floribunda p.*
Barbier.) Orig. before 1900.—**M. p. Eleỳi** (Bean) Rehd., var. Lvs. elliptic or
ovate, reddish when unfolding, pubescent beneath, with purple midrib: fls.
vinous-red, about 3 cm. across; petals ovate: fr. conic-ovoid, about 2.5 cm. long,
deep purple-red, on slender stalks about 3 cm. long. G.C.72:214;104:243,t(c).
Gn.88:81;91:760. B.S.3:321,t. (*M. E.* Hesse, *Pyrus E.* Bean.) Orig. before
1920.—**M. p. aldenhaménsis** (Gibbs) Rehd., var. Lvs. ovate to elliptic or ovate-
oblong, pubescent beneath on veins or nearly glabrous and reticulate-veined,
with purple midrib: fls. vinous-red, semidouble, 2.5–3 cm. across; calyx glabrous or slightly tomentose outside; sepals ovate to lance-ovate: fr. subglobose,
deep purple-red, with persistent calyx. R.H.1926:279,t.(c). (*Pyrus Malus a.*
Gibbs.) Cult. 1922.—**M. p. Lemoinei** (Lemoine) Rehd., f. Lvs. purple: fls.
dark crimson. G.C.83:349. (*M. floribunda L.* Lemoine.) Cult. 1922.—For other
hybrids of *M. p. Niedzwetzkyana* see *M. adstringens* under No. 5, *M. Scheideckeri* under No. 8, and *M. Soulardii* under No. 23.

Closely related species: **M. sylvéstris** Mill. differing chiefly in the nearly
glabrous or slightly pubescent lvs., the glabrous pedicels and glabrous or slightly
villous calyx; styles usually glabrous. R.I.25:t.111(c). S.E.3:t.389(c). (*M.
acerba* Mérat, *Pyrus Malus* var. *s.* L.) Eu. Rarely cult.

2. **M. prunifòlia** (Willd.) Borkh. Small tree; young brts. pubescent: lvs.
ovate or elliptic, 5–10 cm. long, acute or short-acuminate, rounded or cuneate

at base, sharply serrate, pubescent on the veins beneath, finally glabrous; petioles slender, 1.5–5 cm. long: fls. white, about 3 cm. across; pedicels 2–3.5 cm. long, like the calyx glabrous or sometimes villous: fr. subglobose or ovoid, about 2 cm. across, yellow or red, with a cavity at base, calyx not impressed, the sepals connate at base into a short tube. B.M.6158(c). (*Pyrus p.* Willd.) N. E. Asia. Intr. about 1750. Zone III. Cult. in E. Asia for its fr., particularly the var. As an ornamental tree chiefly valued for its bright red or yellow fr. produced in great abundance and persisting a long time on the tree.—**M. p. Rinki** (Koidz.) Rehd., var. Lvs. pubescent beneath: fls. pinkish; calyx villous; pedicels usually shorter. B.M.8265(c). N.K.6:t.14. B.S.2:291. B.C.5:2873. (*M. Ringo* Carr., *M. yezoensis* Koidz., *M. Matsumurana* Koidz., *M. asiatica* Nakai, *Pyrus p.* var. *R.* Bailey.) E. Asia. Intr. about 1850.—**M. p. fastigiàta** Rehd., f. A form of the preceding var. with ascending brs. forming a columnar head; pedicels 8–16 mm. long. Orig. 1908.—**M. p. péndula** (Bean) Rehd., f. Brs. pendulous. Zone IV.

M. p. ✕ *pumila;* see under No. 1.—*M. p.* ✕ *baccata;* see under No. 5.— *M. p.* ✕ *floribunda;* see under No. 8.—*M. p.* ✕ *Sieboldii;* see under No. 10.

3. **M. spectàbilis** (Ait.) Borkh. Tree to 8 m., of upright habit; young brts. sparingly pubescent, later red-brown: lvs. elliptic to elliptic-oblong, 5–8 cm. long, short-acuminate, cuneate, appressed-serrate, lustrous and glabrous above, pubescent beneath when young, finally nearly glabrous, subchartaceous; petioles 1–3 cm. long, pubescent: fls. deep rose-red in bud, fading to blush, 4–5 cm. across, semidouble or sometimes single; pedicels 2–3 cm. long, like the calyx glabrous or slightly villous; sepals triangular-ovate, shorter than tube: fr. subglobose, about 2 cm. across, yellowish, without cavity at base and stalk usually thickened at apex, sour. W.D.1:50(c). B.C.5:2873 (fr.). W.D.50(c, form with single fls.). B.M.267(c). L.B.1729(c). G.F.1:272. Gn.59:209(h). M.G.14:455(h). (*Pyrus s.* Ait.) Intr. before 1780 from China; not known wild. Zone IV.—**M. s. Rivérsii** (Booth) Nash. With larger and broader lvs. and larger double pink fls. F.P.1872:25,t.(c). Gn.84:387. (*Pyrus s. R.* Booth, *P. s. roseo-plena* T. Moore.)—**M. s. albi-plèna** Schelle, f. Fls. double, white.

M. s. ✕ *pumila* = **M. magdeburgénsis** Schoch. Lvs. broader, pubescent beneath; pedicels shorter, like the calyx tomentose: fls. semidouble: fr. subglobose, larger. M.G.20:254(h). (*M. herrenkrugensis* Hort., *? M. Kaido* Dipp.) Orig. before 1900.—*M. s.* ✕ *? baccata;* see No. 4.

4. ✕ **M. micromàlus** Mak. (*M. spectàbilis* ✕ *? baccata*). Small tree of upright habit; young brts. pubescent, soon glabrous: lvs. elliptic-oblong, acuminate, cuneate, 5–10 cm. long and 2–4 cm. broad, serrulate, pubescent beneath when young, finally glabrous, lustrous above, of firm texture; petioles slender, 2–3 cm. long: fls. pink, about 4 cm. across; calyx-tube villous, its lobes glabrescent, ovate to oblong-ovate, as long as tube, acute; pedicels slightly pubescent, 2–3 cm. long: fr. subglobose, 1–1.5 cm. across, red, with cavity at base; calyx persistent or deciduous. Ad.12:t.413(c). N.K.6:t.13. Gn.88:77(h). (*Pyrus m.* Bailey, *M. Kaido* Pardé, not Dipp.) Japan cult. Intr. about 1856. Zone IV. Of upright habit with showy pink fls.

5. **M. baccàta** (L.) Borkh. Siberian Crab. Tree to 14 m., with round head; young brts. glabrous, slender: lvs. elliptic or ovate to ovate-oblong, acuminate, cuneate or rounded at base, 3–8 cm. long, finely serrate, slightly pubescent beneath when young or glabrous; petioles 2–5 cm. long: fls. 3–3.5 cm. across, white; calyx glabrous, its lobes long-acuminate; pedicels slender, 1.5–4 cm. long; styles usually longer than stamens, slightly villous at base: fr.

subglobose, 8–10 mm. across, red or yellow; calyx deciduous. Gt.11,t.364(c). B.S.2:278,t(h). M.G.14:454(h). (*Pyrus baccata* L., *M. b.* var. *sibirica* (Maxim.) Schneid.) N. E. Asia to N. China. Intr. 1784. Zone II. Pyramidal when young, later with round head, with showy white fls. in spring and berry-like red or yellow fr. in fall.—**M. b. grácilis** Rehd., var. Small tree with pendent brs.; lvs. smaller, on longer stalks; fls. smaller. Intr. 1910.— **B. b. mandshùrica** (Maxim.) Schneid., var. Lvs. usually broad-elliptic, remotely serrulate, pubescent beneath when young; petioles pubescent: fls. fragrant; pedicels and calyx pubescent; styles scarcely as long as stamens: fr. larger to 1.2 cm. across, often broad-ellipsoid. B.M.6112(c). M.K.t.47(c). Gn.89:61(h, as *M. theifera*). (*M. cerasifera* Spach, *Pyrus cerasifera* Tausch, *Pyrus b.* var. *m.* Maxim.) C. Jap. to Amur Reg. and C. China. Intr. before 1825.—**M. b. Jáckii** Rehd., var. Similar to var. *mandshurica,* but glabrous: fr. red, about 1 cm. across. Korea. Intr. 1905.—**M. b. himaláica** (Maxim.) Schneid., var., with broad-elliptic coarsely serrate lvs. pubescent beneath on the veins. W. Himal., S. W. China. Intr. 1919?—**M. b. columnàris** Rehd., f. Columnar tree with large glabrous lvs. Cult. 1927.

Hybrids of *M. baccata* with *M. prunifolia* and *M. pumila* are cult. under the name "Siberian Crabs."—*M. b.* × *prunifolia* = **M. robústa** (Carr.) Rehd. Lvs. glabrescent or pubescent beneath: fls. slender-stalked, white or pinkish; calyx usually glabrous: fr. subglobose or ellipsoid, red or yellow, slender-stalked, up to 2 cm. across, usually partly with and partly without calyx. Beach, Apples N. Y. 2:264,t(c, as "Red Siberian"). (*M. cerasifera* Schneid., not Spach, *Pyrus cerasifera* Wenzig, not Tausch.) Intr. about 1815. Cult. in numerous forms.— **M. r. erécta** Rehd., f. Brs. ascending, forming a narrow nearly columnar head. Orig. 1905.—Another distinct form is **M. r. persicifòlia** Rehd., var. Lvs. oblong-lanceolate, peach-like. Intr. 1910 from N. China.—*M. b.* × *pumila* = **M. adstríngens** Zabel. Lvs. pubescent beneath: fls. usually pinkish with rather short villous stalk and villous calyx: fr. usually subglobose, up to 4 or 5 cm. across, rather short-stalked, red, yellow or green, calyx less often deciduous. Beach, Apples N. Y. 2:260,t(c, "Martha"),266,t(c, "Transcendent"),256,t(c, "Hyslop"). Gs.4:181,t(c). A great variety of forms is in cult, many of them probably the product of *M. robusta* × *pumila*. A handsome form with large purple-red fls. is "Hopa Crab" (*M. b.* × *pumila Niedzwetzkyana*). Orig. 1920. —*M. b.* × *Halliana;* see under No. 7.—*M. b.* × *floribunda;* see under No. 8.— *M. b.* × *Sieboldii;* see No. 9.

Related species: **M. sikkimensis** (Hook. f.) Koehne. Brts. and lvs. beneath tomentose: lvs. ovate to ovate-oblong, 5–7 cm. long, long-acuminate, sharply serrate: fls. pink outside; calyx pubescent: fr. obovoid, 1.5 cm. long, red, dotted. B.M.7430(c). B.S.2:294. (*Pyrus s.* Hook. f.) Himal. Intr. 1849. Zone (V).— **M. Rockii** Rehd. Young brts. villous: lvs. elliptic to elliptic-ovate, to 12 cm. long, mostly rounded at base, pubescent and reticulate beneath: pedicels and c lyx villous: fr. ovoid or subglobose, often attenuate at apex, 1–1.5 cm. long; calyx tardily dehiscent. W. China. Intr. 1923?

6. **M. hupehénsis** (Pamp.) Rehd. Tree to 8 m., with stiff, spreading brs.; young brts. pubescent, soon glabrous: lvs. ovate- to ovate-oblong, 5–10 cm. long, acuminate, sharply serrulate, pubescent on the veins beneath and finally glabrous, of firm texture; petioles 1–3 cm. long: fls. 3–7, white or pinkish, fragrant, 3.5–4 cm. across, on slender pedicels 3–4 cm. long, glabrous or slightly villous; sepals triangular-ovate, acute or acuminulate, purplish, glabrous; styles 3 or rarely 4: fr. globose, about 1 cm. across, usually greenish yellow with red cheek. C.C.174. I.S.1:t.32. Gn.89:221(h). (*Pyrus h.* Pamp., *M. theifera* Rehd., *Pyrus th.* Bailey.) China, Assam. Intr. 1900. Zone IV. Floriferous species of distinct habit.—**M. h. ròsea** (Rehd.) Rehd., f. Fls. pink.

7. **M. Halliàna** Koehne. Tree to 5 m., with rather loose open head; young brts. soon glabrous, purple: lvs. ovate or elliptic to oblong-ovate, 3.5–8 cm. long, acuminate, crenate-serrulate, quite glabrous except the midrib above, dark green and lustrous above and often purple-tinted; petioles 5–20 mm.

long: fls. 4–7, bright rose, 3–3.5 cm. across; pedicels slender, nodding, like the calyx purplish and glabrous; calyx-lobes ovate, obtusish; styles 4–5, the terminal fl. usually without pistil; petals usually more than 5: fr. obovoid, 6–8 mm. across, purplish, ripening very late. S.T.1:t.18. (*Pyrus H.* Voss.) Cult. in Japan and China. Intr. 1863. Zone V. Graceful species with bright rosy fls. on drooping purple pedicels and with the young foliage purplish.—
M. H. Parkmánii Rehd. Fls. semidouble. Ad.4:t.134(c). G.F.1:152. M.G. 14:457(h). Gn.89:313(h). (*Pyrus P.* Hort.)—**M. H. spontànea** (Mak.) Koidz., var. Lvs. smaller, elliptic or elliptic-obovate: fls. smaller, nearly white; pedicels shorter; styles usually 4. Asami, Crabappl. Jap. t.14,40d. (*M. s.* Mak.) Japan. Intr. 1919. Zone V.

M. H. × *Sieboldii* = **M. atrosanguínea** (Spaeth) Schneid. Spreading shrub with nearly glabrous serrate lvs. and rose-purple fls. similar to those of *M. floribunda,* but not fading to white and calyx-lobes shorter, acute. (*Pyrus floribunda* var. *a.* Bean, *P. a.* Spaeth.) Orig. before 1905.—*M. a.* × *pumila Niedzwetzkyana;* see under No. 1.—*M. H.* × *bacccta* = **M. Hartwígii** Koehne. Intermediate between the parents: fls. pink, changing to white; pedicels and calyx red. Cult. 1906.

8. **M. floribúnda** Sieb. Shrub or tree to 10 m., with wide-spreading brs.; young brts. pubescent, becoming glabrous: lvs. elliptic-ovate or ovate to oblong-ovate, acuminate, usually cuneate, 4–8 cm. long, sharply serrate, on shoots larger and incisely serrate, pubescent beneath or finally nearly glabrous; petioles 1.5–2.5 cm. long: fls. deep carmine in bud, changing to pale pink or finally nearly white, 2.5–3 cm. across; pedicels pubescent, purple, 2.5–3.5 cm. long; calyx pubescent, purple, its lobes acuminate, petals obovate-oblong; styles usually 4: fr. globose, 6–8 mm. across, red. F.S.15:t.1585(c). R.H.1866:311,t(c);1871:591,t(c). F.E.9:573(h). Gn.83:22(h);86:538(h) Gn. M.30:22(h). (*Pyrus f.* Kirchn., not Lindl., *P. pulcherrima* Aschers. & Graebn.) Japan? Intr. 1862. Zone IV. One of the handsomest crab-apples with the fls. changing from carmine to white; extremely floriferous.

M. f. × *baccata* = **M. arnoldiàna** (Rehd.) Sarg. Lvs. larger, ovate: fls. larger, of lighter color: fr. about 1 cm. across, yellow. M.G.24:27(h),28. Gn.M. 30:22(h). (*M. floribunda* var. *a.* Rehd., *Pyrus f.* var. *a.* Bailey.) Orig. before 1883. A very handsome and showy hybrid.—*M. f.* × *prunifolia* = **M. Scheidéckeri** (Spaeth) Zab. Small tree of upright habit; young brts. pubescent: lvs. ovate, 5–10 cm. long, sharply and coarsely serrate, pubescent beneath, at least on midrib: fls. pale pink, usually semidouble, 3–3.5 cm. across; pedicels and calyx pubescent: fr. yellow, 1.5 cm. across, with usually persistent calyx. Gt.53: t.1529(c). Gn.17:526,t(c);86:538(h). G.C.73:185. Gg.6:308(h). (*Pyrus S.* Spaeth, *P. pulcherrima* var. *S.* (Spaeth) Bailey.) Orig. before 1888.—*M. Scheideckeri* × *pumila Niedzwetzkyana* = **M. gloriòsa** Lemoine. Young lvs. bronzy-purple: fls. large, purplish rose. Orig. before 1931.

Related species or hybrid: **M. brévipes** (Rehd.) Rehd. Of lower and denser habit: lvs. smaller, more closely serrate with shorter spreading teeth: fls. nearly white, on glabrous pedicels about 1 cm. long; petals oval: fr. subglobose, about 1 cm. across, slightly ribbed, not pulpy at maturity, on stiff upright or spreading stalks. (*M. floribunda* var. *b.* Rehd.) Orig. unknown. Cult. 1883. Zone V.

9. × **M. Zumi** (Mats.) Rehd. (*M. baccata mandshurica* × *Sieboldii*). Tree of pyramidal habit; young brts. slightly pubescent: lvs. ovate to ovate-oblong or oblong, acuminate, 4–9 cm. long, those of flowering brts. entire or crenate-serrulate, of shoots serrate or occasionally slightly lobed, pubescent beneath when young, becoming glabrous: fls. pink in bud, becoming white, 2.5–3 cm. across; calyx slightly villous outside, its lobes acuminate; petals elliptic; styles 4–5: fr. about 1.2 cm. across, red. S.T.1:t.91. (*Pyrus Z.* Mats., *M. Sieboldii* var. *Z.* Asami.) Japan. Intr. 1892. Zone V. Similar to *M. Sieboldii* var. *arborescens,* but of more upright habit and lvs. scarcely lobed. —**M. Z. calocárpa** (Rehd.) Rehd., var. Habit spreading; only smaller lvs.

of flowering brts. entire, those of shoots more deeply lobed: fls. somewhat smaller; styles 3–4. (*M. Sieboldii* var. *c.* Rehd.) Japan. Intr. 1905.

10. **M. Siebóldii** (Reg.) Rehd. Torinco Crab. Shrub with spreading brs.; young brts. pubescent: lvs. ovate or elliptic, acuminate, 2.5–6 cm. long, sharply serrate, those of shoots broad-ovate, coarsely serrate and partly 3- or sometimes 5-lobed, pubescent on both sides, later glabrous or glabrescent above; petioles pubescent, 6–18 mm. long; fls. pink or deep rose in bud, finally nearly white, about 2 cm. across; pedicels 2–2.5 cm. long, like the calyx pubescent; petals obovate-oblong; styles 3–4: fr. globose, 6–8 mm. across, red or brownish yellow. R.H.1870:451,t(c);1881:296. M.G.14:456(h). N.K. 6:t.10. S.L.235(h). (*Pyrus Sieboldii* Reg., *M. Toringo* Nakai, *Pyrus Toringo* Sieb.) Japan (the cult. dwarf mountain form). Intr. 1856.—**M. S. arboréscens** Rehd. Tree to 10 m.: lvs. larger, less deeply lobed and less pubescent; fls. often nearly white. W.A.38,t(h). Japan, Korea (the wild form). Intr. 1892. Zone V. Graceful and handsome tree showy in bloom.

M. S. × *prunifolia* = **M. sublobàta** (Zab.) Rehd. Tree, usually pyramidal; young brts. tomentose; lvs. narrow-elliptic to elliptic-oblong, those of shoots broader, partly with 2 or only 1 short lobe, tomentose when young, pubescent beneath at maturity, 3.5–8 cm. long: fls. bluish; pedicels and calyx villous; styles 4–5, rarely 3: fr. subglobose, 1.5- 2 cm. across, yellow, usually with calyx, sometimes without. Gs.4:181.t(c). Orig. or intr. from Japan about 1892.— *M. S.* × *Halliana;* see under No. 7.

11. **M. Sargénti** Rehd. Low shrub to 2 m., with horizontally spreading brs., often spinescent; young brts. tomentose: lvs. ovate, acuminate, rounded or subcordate at base, acuminate, 5–8 cm. long, sharply serrate, villous when young, finally nearly glabrous, those of shoots usually broad-ovate, mostly 3-lobed; petioles 2–3 cm. long, pubescent: fls. pure white, 2.5 cm. across; pedicels 2–3 cm. long, like the calyx glabrous; petals oval, broad at base, overlapping; styles usually 4 (3–5): fr. subglobose, about 1 cm. across, dark red, slightly bloomy. B.M.8757(c). S.T.1:t.36. G.C.57:291;58:308;98:363, t.(h). Gn.M.30:22(h). S.L.235(h). (*M. Sieboldii* var. *S.* (Rehd.) Asami, *Pyrus S.* Bean.) Japan. Intr. 1892. Zone V. Low shrub of distinct habit, with abundant white fls. and attractive fr.; the lvs. turning orange and yellow in autumn.

12. **M. florentìna** (Zuccagni) Schneid. Small round-headed tree with upright brs.: young brts. villous: lvs. broad-ovate, usually truncate at base, 3–6 cm. long, all incisely lobed and serrate with several lobes on each side, tomentose beneath; petioles 1–2.5 cm. long, pubescent: fls. 6–8, white, 1.5–2 cm. across; pedicels 2–3 cm. long, villous; calyx tomentose; stamens 30; styles 5: fr. broad-ellipsoid, 1–1.2 cm. long, red. B.M.7423(c). G.C.59:7. (*Pyrus f.* Targ., *P. crataegifolia* Savi.) Italy. Cult. 1877. Zone V. Handsome small tree; the lvs. turning orange and scarlet.

13. **M. fúsca** (Raf.) Schneid. Shrub or small tree to 12 m.; young brts. pubescent: lvs. ovate to oblong-lanceolate, acute or acuminate, 3–10 cm. long, sharply serrate, often 3-lobed; pubescent on both sides, later glabrous above; petioles 2–3.5 cm. long, pubescent: fls. 6–12, white or pinkish, 2–2.5 cm. across; pedicels slender, like the calyx pubescent; styles 3–4: fr. ellipsoid, about 1.5 cm. long, red or yellow. B.M.8798(c). S.S.4:t.170. (*Pyrus f.* Raf., *P. rivularis* Dougl., *P. diversifolia* Bong.) Alaska to Calif. Intr. 1836. Zone V. Of little ornamental value.—**M. f. levipes** (Nutt.) Schneid., var. Pedicels and calyx glabrous or nearly so.

M. f. × *pumila* = **M. Dawsoniàna** Rehd. Lvs. elliptic to elliptic-oblong, 4–9 cm. long, not lobed: fls. slender-stalked, with 3–5 glabrous styles: fr. elliptic-oblong, 2.5–3 cm. long, yellow, with small calyx. S.T.2:t.111. G.C.74:377. Orig. 1881. Zone V.

14. M. toringoìdes (Rehd.) Hughes. Shrub or small tree to 8 m.; brts. slightly villous at first, soon glabrous: lvs. ovate to elliptic-oblong, 3–8 cm. long, with usually 2 pairs of crenate-serrate or appressed-serrate lobes, occasionally undivided and lanceolate- oblong to lanceolate, at maturity pubescent only on the veins beneath: fls. 2–2.5 cm. across, 3–6 in subsessile umbels; pedicels to 2 cm. long, slightly villous; calyx tomentulose, its lobes narrow-triangular; petals orbicular-obovate, hairy above; styles 4–5, rarely 3, glabrous: fr. globose-obovoid or obovoid-ellipsoid, 1–1.2 cm. long, yellow, usually with red cheek. B.M.8948(c). G.C.73:89. K.B.1920:207. W.A.102,t. (*M. transitoria* var. *t.* Rehd.) W. China. Intr. 1904. Zone V. In fr. one of the handsomest of the crab-apples.

Closely related species: **M. transitòria** (Batal.) Schneid. Smaller and slenderer; young brts. tomentulose: lvs. 2–3 cm. long, more deeply lobed, with narrower lobes and more pubescent: fls. 1.5–2 cm. across; sepals shorter; petals broad-oblong: fr. 6–8 mm. long. Gn.86:585. K.B.1920:207. (*Pyrus t.* Batal.) N. W. China. Intr. 1911. Zone V. Less handsome than the preceding species.

15. M. kansuénsis (Batal.) Schneid. Small tree to 8 m.; young brts. pubescent: lvs. ovate, truncate, rounded or broad-cuneate at base, 5–8 cm. long, 3- or sometimes 5-lobed, with triangular-ovate acute closely and partly doubly serrate lobes, pubescent beneath, at least on the veins; petioles 1.5–4 cm. long: fls. 4–10, white, 1.5 cm. across; pedicels 1.5–2.5 cm. long, like the calyx villous, sepals narrowly triangular-ovate, acuminate, as long as tube; styles 3, glabrous: fr. ellipsoid, about 1 cm. long, yellow or red. S.H.1:f. 403d-d', 404d-e. (*Pyrus k.* Batal.) N. W. China. Intr. 1904. Zone V.—**M. k. calva** Rehd., f. Lvs. beneath, calyx and pedicels glabrous, even when young.

Related species: **M. honanénsis** Rehd. Lvs. broad-ovate, rarely oblong-ovate, with 2–5 pairs of broad-ovate serrulate lobes, pubescent beneath: infl. glabrous; styles 3–4: fr. subglobose, about 8 mm. across, dotted. N. E. China. Intr. 1921. Zone V.

16. M. Práttii (Hemsl.) Schneid. Tree to 10 m.; young brts. pubescent at first, soon glabrous: lvs. ovate or elliptic to ovate-oblong, acuminate, usually rounded at base, 6–15 cm. long, and 3.5–7.5 cm. broad, finely and doubly serrate, with callous-pointed teeth and with 8–10 pairs of veins sparingly pubescent beneath; petioles 1.5–3 cm. long: fls. white, 2 cm. across, in many-fld. clusters; pedicels 1.5–3 cm. long, pubescent or glabrous like the calyx: petals suborbicular; styles 5, glabrous: fr. globose-ovoid or subglobose, 1–1.5 cm. across, red or yellow, punctate, on stout stalks; calyx persistent. (*Pyrus P.* Hemsl.) C. & W. China. Intr. 1909. Zone V.

17. M. yunnanensis (Franch.) Schneid. Tree to 10 m.; young brts. tomentose: lvs. ovate to oblong-ovate, rounded or subcordate at base, short-acuminate, 6–12 cm. long, sharply and doubly serrate, partly with 3–5 pairs of broad short lobes and partly or mostly without, tomentose beneath; petioles 2–3.5 cm. long, tomentose: infl. many-fld., 4–5 cm. across, rather dense; fls. white, 1.5 cm. across; pedicels 1–2 cm. long, like the calyx tomentose or villous; sepals triangular-ovate, acuminate, about as long as tube; petals suborbicular; styles 5, nearly glabrous: fr. subglobose, 1–1.5 cm. across, red, punctate; calyx reflexed. G.M.56:897. S.H.1:403e-g,404b-c. G.C.78:227. (*Pyrus y.* Franch.) W. China. Intr. 1908. Zone V. The lvs. turning orange and scarlet in fall.—**M. y. Veìtchii** (Veitch) Rehd., var. Lvs. cordate, ovate, all distinctly lobulate with short acuminate lobes, finally glabrescent beneath: fr. bright red, white-dotted. B.M.8629(c). (*Pyrus V.* Veitch, *P. yunnanensis* Bean, in part.) C. China. Intr. 1901.

18. **M. platycárpa** Rehd. Tree to 6 m. with spreading unarmed brs.; young brts. thinly tomentose, becoming glabrous: lvs. ovate to elliptic, rounded at base and at apex, but with short acute point, sharply and usually doubly serrate, those of shoots usually broad-ovate with several pairs of short triangular lobes and pubescent on veins beneath: fls. 3–4 cm. across; pedicels and calyx glabrous: fr. depressed-globose, deeply impressed at ends, about 5 cm. across. S.T.2:t.189. S.M.384. (*Pyrus p.* Bailey.) N. C. to Ga. Intr. 1912. Zone V. Fr. used for preserves.—**M. p. Hoopèsii** Rehd., var. Lvs. slightly or not lobed: calyx and pedicels pubescent. Intr. 1876.

19. **M. glaucescens** Rehd. Shrub or small tree, with sometimes spiny brs. forming a broad twiggy head; brts. glabrous or glabrescent: lvs. broad-ovate or triangular-ovate, acute or short-acuminate, truncate or subcordate, 5–8 cm. long, with short triangular lobes; those of shoots more deeply lobed, thinly tomentose when young, quite glabrous at maturity, dark green above, glaucous beneath; petioles slender, soon glabrous: fls. about 3.5–4 cm. across; pedicels glabrous; calyx thinly villous or sometimes glabrous; styles slightly shorter than stamens: fr. depressed-globose, 3–4 cm. across, yellow and waxy, fragrant. S.T.2:t.157. B.C.5:2876,2877. S.M.381. Ad.10:t.348(c). (*Pyrus g.* (Rehd.) Bailey.) N. Y. to N. C. and Ala. Cult. 1902. Zone V. Lvs. turning yellow and dark purple in autumn.

Related species: **M. glabràta** Rehd. with the lowest pair of veins springing directly from the cordate base, glabrous and purplish when young, green beneath, calyx glabrous and purplish; style longer than stamens. S.T.2:t.188. S.M.380. (*Pyrus g.* Bailey.) N. C. to Ala. Intr. 1912.

20. **M. coronària** (L.) Mill. Tree to 10 m.; brts. tomentose at first: lvs. ovate to ovate-oblong, acute, usually rounded at base, 5–10 cm. long, irregularly serrate and usually slightly lobed, those of shoots with short broad lobes, floccose-tomentose when young, finally glabrous, green beneath, or those at end of shoots pubescent on the veins, rather thin: fls. 3–4 cm. across; pedicels glabrous: fr. depressed-globose, about 3 cm. across, ribbed at apex, greenish. B.M.2009(c). B.R.651(c). S.S.4:t.167. Gn.29:395;34:206. S.L. 233(h). (*M. fragrans* Rehd., *Pyrus c.* L.) N. Y. to Ala., w. to Mo. Intr. 1724. Zone IV.—**M. c. elongàta** Rehd., var. Lvs. narrowly triangular-ovate or oblong-ovate, more deeply lobed and incisely serrate, sometimes cuneate. N. Y. to N. C. and Ala. Intr. 1912.—**M. c. dasycàlyx** Rehd., var. Lvs. paler beneath, those of shoots sometimes pubescent on the veins: calyx villous. Ont. to Ohio and Ind. Intr. 1920.—**M. c. Charlóttae** Rehd., f. A form of the preceding var. with semidouble large fls. Intr. about 1900.—**M. c. Nieuwlandiàna** Slavin, f. Similar to f. *Charlottae,* but fls. brighter; pedicels 3–5.5 cm. long: fr. 4–5 cm. across.

M. c. × *pumila* = **M. heterophýlla** Spach. Here belongs "Matthew's Crab" and some forms cult. as *M. Soulardii.* Differs from *M. Soulardii* chiefly in the broader less pubescent lvs. and slightly pubescent pedicels.

Related species: **M. bracteàta** Rehd. Lvs. less lobed, on flowering brts. elliptic-ovate to oblong, abruptly acute or obtusish, sparingly serrate or sometimes entire, on shoots slightly lobed, pubescent when young, soon glabrous, green or pale beneath. S.M.387. (*Pyrus b.* Bailey.) Mo. to Ga. and Ala. Intr. 1912. Zone V.

21. **M. lancifòlia** Rehd. Tree to 8 m., with spreading often spiny brs.; young brts. slightly pubescent or nearly glabrous: lvs. ovate-lanceolate to oblong-lanceolate, acute or acuminate, rounded or broad-cuneate, 4–8 cm. long, those of flowering brts. finely or sometimes coarsely serrate, those of shoots oblong-ovate, incisely serrate and slightly lobed, pubescent when young, glabrous at maturity and rather thin: fls. 3–3.5 cm. across; pedicels

and calyx glabrous: fr. subglobose, about 2.5 cm. across, green and waxy. S.T.2:t.158. S.M.385. B.C.5:2876. (*Pyrus l.* Bailey.) Pa. to Va. and Mo. Intr. 1912. Zone V.

22. **M. angustifòlia** (Ait.) Michx. Shrub or tree to 10 m., with slender brs.; brts. glabrous or slightly pubescent at first: lvs. ovate-oblong, oblong or lance-oblong, obtuse or acutish, usually broad-cuneate, 3–7 cm. long, coarsely crenate-serrate or sometimes nearly entire, rarely more sharply serrate, glabrous and light green beneath, usually turning brown in drying, those of shoots broader, coarsely serrate and often lobed, usually slightly tomentose below, subcoriaceous at maturity and under favorable conditions half-evergreen: fls. 2.5 cm. across; pedicels and calyx glabrous or sometimes slightly villous; style villous only at base: fr. subglobose or sometimes higher than broad, 1.5–2.5 cm. across. B.R.1207(c). L.D.3:154(c). S.S.4:t.169. (*M. coronaria* Brit., not Mill., *M. sempervirens* Desf., *Pyrus a.* Ait.) Va. to Fla. and Miss. Intr. 1750. Zone (V).—**M. a. péndula** Rehd., f. With slender pendulous brs.

23. **M. ioénsis** (Wood) Brit. Tree to 10 m.; brts. tomentose: lvs. ovate-oblong or elliptic-obovate, acute or short-acuminate, broad-cuneate or rounded, 5–10 cm. long, coarsely or incisely serrate or shallowly lobed, tomentose beneath, sometimes glabrescent at maturity except the veins, those of shoots more deeply lobed, at maturity of firm texture with strong veins; petioles stout, tomentose: fls. about 4 cm. across; pedicels stout, 2–3.5 cm. long, like the calyx tomentose: fr. subglobose or broad-ellipsoid, 2.5–3 cm. across sometimes angular, greenish, waxy. B.M.8488(c). S.S.4:t.168. (*Pyrus i.* Bailey, *M. coronaria* var. *i.* Schneid.) Minn. and Wisc. to Neb., Kans. and Mo. Intr. 1885. Zone II. The double-flowered form is often cult. as an ornamental tree and is very handsome in bloom.—**M. i. plèna** (Schneid.) Rehd., f. "BECHTEL'S CRAB." With double fls. G.C.III.25:397;65:229. B.A. 1931:31. R.H.1910:60,t.(c). (*Pyrus angustifolia fl. pleno* Hort., *P. angustifolia Bechtelii* Hort.) Orig. before 1840, intr. 1888.—**M. i. fimbriàta** Slavin, f. Lvs. narrower: fls. double, with fimbriate petals.—**M. i. Pàlmeri** Rehd., var. Shrub or small tree to 6 m.: lvs. smaller, oblong, usually obtuse or obtusish, thinly pubescent, those of flowering shoots usually crenate-serrate. Mo. Intr. 1910.—**M. i. texàna** Rehd., var. Similar to the preceding: lvs. smaller and much broader, not or only slightly lobed and densely villous. Texas. Intr. ?

M. i. × *pumila* = **M. Soulardii** (Bailey) Brit. Lvs. broad-ovate to ellipticovate, often obtuse at apex, irregularly crenate-serrate, occasionally slightly lobed, thickish and rugose, densely pubescent beneath: fls. on short and stout tomentose pedicels: fr. depressed-globose, often 5 cm. across or more, yellow and often with reddish cheek. Proc. Iowa Acad. Sci. 7:130,t. B.C.5:2871. B.A. 1934:50. (*Pyrus S.* Bailey.) Orig. before 1868. Occasionally wild from Minn. to Tex.—A form with red-purple fls. and red young lvs. is "Red Tip Crab" (*M. i.* × *pumila Niedzwetzkyana*).

24. **M. trilobàta** (Poir.) Schneid. Shrub or tree to 6 m., of upright habit; young brts. pubescent: lvs. deeply 3-lobed and serrulate, 5–8 cm. long, the middle lobe with one or two smaller lobes on each side, the lateral lobes usually with a basal lobe, pubescent beneath when young, later nearly glabrous and light green, lustrous and bright green above; petioles slender, 3–7 cm. long: fls. 6–8, white, 3.5 cm. across; pedicels about 2 cm. long, villous; calyx tomentose; sepals lanceolate, longer than tube: fr. ellipsoid, red. G.C. 72:341. B.M.9305(c). (*Pyrus t.* DC., *Eriolobus t.* Roem.) W. Asia. Cult. 1877. Zone V.

25. **M. Tschonóskii** (Maxim.) Schneid. Tree to 12 m.: brts. tomentose: lvs. elliptic-ovate to ovate-oblong, acuminate, rounded or subcordate at base, 7–12 cm. long, irregularly serrate or doubly serrate, sometimes slightly lobulate, tomentose when young, finally glabrous above, thinly tomentose beneath; petioles 2–3 cm. long: fls. white, 3 cm. across; pedicels 2–2.5 cm. long, tomentose like the calyx; sepals triangular-ovate, shorter than tube: fr. globose, 2–3 cm. across, yellowish green with purple cheek. B.M.8179(c). S.T.1:t.37. (*Pyrus T.* Maxim., *Eriolobus T.* Rehd.) Japan. Intr. 1892. Zone V. Tree of pyramidal habit; the lvs. turning orange and scarlet in fall.

27. **DOCÝNIA** Dcne. Evergreen or half-evergren trees: lvs. entire or serrate, sometimes slightly lobed, stipulate: fls. short-stalked, 2–5 in umbels, before or with the lvs.; calyx densely tomentose, with lanceolate lobes; stamens 30–50; styles 5, connate at base, villous; ovary 5-celled, each cell with 3–10 ovules: fr. subglobose to ovoid or pyriform, 2–3 cm. across; calyx persistent. (Anagram of Cydonia.) Five species in China, Himal. and Annam.

D. rufifòlia (Lévl.) Rehd. Half-evergreen or nearly deciduous tree: lvs. elliptic to oblong-lanceolate, acute or acuminate, rarely abruptly acuminate, broad-cuneate or nearly rounded at base, 5–8 cm. long, 2–4 cm. broad, serrate or serrulate toward the apex or entire, lustrous above, green and thinly pubescent or glabrescent at maturity beneath, chartaceous; petioles 5–20 mm. long: fls. about 2.5 cm. across, nearly sessile; stamens about 30; fr. subglobose or ellipsoid, 2–3 cm. across. S.L.165(h, as *D. Delavayi*). (*D. docynioides* (Schneid.) Rehd., *Malus docynioides* Schneid.) S. W. China. Intr. 1903. Zone VII.

The closely related **D. Delavàyi** (Franch.) Schneid. differs chiefly in its evergreen entire lvs. white-tomentose beneath. R.H.1918:133. (*Pyrus D.* Franch., *Eriolobus D.* Schneid., *Cydonia D.* Cardot.) S. W. China. Cult. 1890. Zone VII?

28. **CHAENOMÈLES** Lindl. Deciduous or half-evergreen shrubs or small trees, with sometimes spiny brs.; buds small, with about 2 outer scales: lvs. short petioled, serrate or crenate, stipulate, of firm texture: fls. solitary or fascicled, before or after the lvs., sometimes partly staminate; calyx lobes 5, entire or serrulate; petals 5, large; stamens 20 or more; styles 5, connate at base; ovary 5-celled, each cell with many ovules: fr. a large, many-seeded pome; seeds brown. (Greek *chainein,* to split and *meles,* apple; the fruit was supposed by Thunberg to split into 5 valves.) Including *Pseudocydonia* Schneid. Three species in E. Asia.

A. Fls. in leafless clusters, before or with the lvs.: calyx-lobes upright, entire; stipules large ....Sect. I. EUCHAENOMELES Schneid.
  B. Lvs. sharply serrate, acute: brts. smooth...............................1. *C. lagenaria*
  BB. Lvs. coarsely crenate-serrate, acutish or obtuse: brts. scabrous.........2. *C. japonica*
AA. Fls. solitary on leafy shoots; calyx-lobes serrulate, reflexed: stipules small.
                                    Sect. II. PSEUDOCYDONIA Schneid.
                                                3. *C. sinensis*

1. **C. lagenària** (Loisel.) Koidz. JAPAN QUINCE. Shrub to 2 m. with spreading spiny glabrous brs.: lvs. ovate to oblong, acute, 3–8 cm. long sharply serrate, lustrous above, glabrous: fls. 3.5–5 cm. across, scarlet-red in the type, varying to pink and white; style usually glabrous: fr. globose to ovoid, 3–7 cm. high, yellow or yellowish green, fragrant. Fl.III–IV; fr.x. L.B. 1594(c). G.O.t.70(c). G.C.34:434. R.H.1876:330,t.(fr). Gn.40:126,t.(c) ;71: 262(h). (*Pyrus japonica* Sims, not Thunb., *Cydonia Japonica* Pers., *Cydonia lagenaria* Loisel.) China, cult. in Japan. Intr. before 1800. Zone IV. Much

planted for its early conspicuous fls. and the dark green lustrous and long persisting lvs.; sometimes used for hedges.—Many garden forms with fls. varying from dark scarlet to pink and white and some with double or semi-double fls. are in cult.—**C. l. cathayénsis** (Hemsl.) Rehd., var. Shrub to 3 m.: lvs. elliptic-lanceolate to lanceolate, finely and sharply serrate, 3–11 cm. long and 1–3.5 cm. broad, pubescent on the midrib beneath when young: styles usually villous at base: fr. ovoid or conic-ovoid. H.I.2657–8. R.H. 1924:64(fr). (*C. c.* Schneid., *Cydonia c.* Hemsl.) C. China. Intr. before 1900. Zone VI.—**C. l. Wilsónii** Rehd., var. Shrub to 6 m.: lvs. fulvous-tomentose beneath: fls. salmon-pink: fr. ovoid, 10–15 cm. long. G.C.66:21, 22(h). J.L.41:f.122(h). W. China. Intr. 1910. Zone VI.

2. **C. japónica** (Thunb.) Lindl. Low shrub to 1 m.; brs. spiny, with short scabrous tomentum when young, verruculose the second year: lvs. broad-ovate to obovate, obtuse or acutish, 3–5 cm. long, coarsely crenate-serrate, glabrous: fls. brick-red, 2.5–3.5 cm. across: fr. subglobose, about 3 cm. across, yellow. Fl.iii–iv; fr.x. B.M.6780(c). G.C.34:435. R.H.1875:195,t(c). (*Pyrus j.* Thunb., *P. Maulei* Mast., *Cydonia Maulei* T. Moore, *C. Maulei* Schneid.) Japan. Cult. 1874. Zone IV.—**C. j. tricolor** (Parsons) Rehd., var. Lvs. variegated with pink and white.—**C. j. alpìna** Maxim., var. Dwarf shrub with procumbent stems and ascending brts.; lvs. orbicular-oval, 1–2.5 cm. long. R.H.1911:204,t.(c). (*C. Maulei* var. *a.* Schneid., *Cydonia Sargenti* Lemoine.)

C. j. × *lagenaria* = **C. supérba** (Frahm) Rehd. It differs from *C. japonica* in the larger, but comparatively narrower, more sharply serrate lvs., and in the larger fls. of deep blood-red color; from *C. lagenaria* in the pubescent brts. when young, slightly verruculose the second year in the smaller, generally obovate-oblong lvs., the smaller fascicled ones usually crenate-serrate, and in the lower habit with more upright brs. (*Cydonia Maulei s.* Frahm.)—**C. s. alba** (Froebel) Rehd., f., has white fls., **C. s. ròsea** (Froebel) Rehd., f. (*Cydonia Maulei grandiflora rosea* Froebel) has light rose-colored fls. and **C. s. perfécta** (Froebel) Rehd., f. (*Cydonia M. grandiflora perfecta* Froebel) has scarlet fl. with usually 6–8 petals and larger and broader lvs.

3. **C. sinénsis** (Thouin) Koehne. Shrub or small tree; trunk with flaky bark; brts. spineless, villous when young: lvs. elliptic-ovate or elliptic-oblong, acute at ends, 5–8 cm. long, sharply and finely serrate, villous beneath while young; stipules lanceolate, glandular-ciliate: fls. 2.5–3 cm. across, light pink: fr. oblong, 10–15 cm. long, dark yellow, woody. Fl.v; fr.x. B.M.7988(c). B.R. 905(c). R.H.1889:228,t.(c). U. S. Inv. 55:t.5(h). (*Cydonia s.* Thouin, *Pseudocydonia s.* Schneid.) China. Intr. about 1800. Zone (V). Lvs. turning scarlet in autumn.

29. **CYDÒNIA** Mill. Deciduous unarmed shrub or small tree; buds small, pubescent, with few scales: lvs. petioled, entire, stipulate: fls. white or light pink, terminal, solitary at the end of leafy shoots; sepals 5, entire, reflexéd; petals 5, obovate; stamens 20; styles 5, free, pubescent below; ovary inferior, 5-celled, each cell with numerous ovules: fr. a many-seeded pome. (Greek Cydon, now Caneà in Crete.) One species from Persia to Turkestan.

C. oblónga Mill. QUINCE. Shrub or tree to 8 m.; young brts. tomentose: lvs. ovate to oblong, acute, rounded or subcordate at base, 5–10 cm. long, dull green above, densely villous below; petioles 1–1.8 cm. long, tomentose; fls. 4–5 cm. across; pedicels and calyx tomentose; fr. pear-shaped, fragrant, yellow, villous. Fl.v; fr.x. G.H.t.81(c). N.D.4:t.36(c). F.D.25:t.2532(c). Gn.33:491. (*C. vulgaris* Pers., *Pyrus C.* L.) C. Asia. Cult. since ancient times. Zone IV. Grown chiefly for its fr. which is used for preserves; the lvs. turn yellow late in fall.—**C. o. marmoràta** (Dipp.) Schneid., f. Lvs. yellow and white variegated.—**C. o. pyrifórmis** (Kirchn.) Rehd., var. This is the typical form with pear-shaped fr.—**C. o. malifórmis** (Mill.) Schneid., var. Fr. apple-shaped.—**C. o. lusitànica** (Mill.) Schneid., var. Fr. pear-shaped and ribbed: lvs. large; a more vigorous form.—**C. o. pyramidàlis** (Dipp.) Schneid., var. Of pyramidal habit.

C. o. × *Pyrus communis* = *Pyronia Veitchii;* see below.—*C. o.* × *Malus* reported to have been obtained by I. V. Michurin.

× **PYRÒNIA** Veitch. Hybrids between *Cydonia* and *Pyrus*, known in several forms intermediate between the parents and representing sexual hybrids and graft-hybrids. Syn. *Pirocydonia* Hans Winkl.

P. Danièli (Winkl.) Rehd. (*Cydonia oblonga* + *Pyrus communis*, graft-hybrid.) Similar to Cydonia: lvs. ovate, 4–6 cm. long, rounded at base, irregularly serrate with setose teeth, less pubescent, involute in bud. Rev. Gén. Bot. 16:7,f.5,6. B.D.1925:63,t.f.4. Orig. 1902.—**P. D. Winkleri** (Daniel) Rehd., var. Lvs. elliptic-ovate, 1–4.5 cm. long, acuminate, broad-cuneate, more pubescent, conduplicate in bud. R.H.1914:28,29. B.D.1925:63,t,f.5. (*Pirocydonia Winkleri* Daniel.) Orig. 1913.

P. Veìtchii (Trabut) Guillaumin. (*C. oblonga* × *P. communis*.) Lvs. elliptic, 5–6 cm. long, acute at ends, entire, pubescent when young; petiole 1.5–2 cm. long: fls. 3 at end of brts., short-stalked, 5 cm. across; sepals glandular-dentate; stamens 20; anthers violet; ovules 6 in each cell: fr. ellipsoid, 7–8 cm. long. Jour. Hered. 7:417,418. (*P. V.* var. *John Seden* Guillaumin.) Orig. before 1913.—**P. V. luxemburgiàna** Guillaumin. Lvs. about 9 cm. long, acute or obtuse, rounded at base: fls. 3.5 cm. across; ovules 4–6 in each cell: fr. pear-shaped. B.D.1925:65,t. Orig. before 1913.

30. **PỲRUS** L. Pear. Deciduous, rarely half-evergreen trees or rarely shrubs, sometimes thorny; lvs. serrate or entire, rarely lobed, involute in bud, petiolate, stipulate; buds with imbricate scales: fls. with or before the lvs., in umbel-like racemes, white, rarely pinkish; sepals usually reflexed or spreading; petals clawed, suborbicular to broad-oblong; stamens 20–30; anthers usually red; styles 2–5, free, closely constricted at base by the disk; ovules 2 in each locule: fr. a usually pyriform pome; flesh with copious grit-cells; walls of locules cartilaginous; seeds black or nearly black. (Ancient Latin name of the pear tree; spelled *Pirus* in classical Latin.) About 20 species from Eu. to E. Asia, south to N. Afr., Persia and Himal.—Fruit- and ornamental trees with conspicuous white fls. with or just before the lvs. which usually turn red or scarlet in autumn.

Fr. with persistent calyx.
  A. Lvs. entire or crenate-serrulate, undivided.
    B. Lvs. usually oblong and obtusish, papillose beneath, entire or slightly crenulate toward
      the apex, glabrescent..1. *P. amygdaliformis*
    BB. Lvs. not papillose beneath.
      C. Lvs. entire, cuneate, usually pubescent beneath.
        D. Lvs. linear-lanceolate to lanceolate, lustrous above................2. *P. salicifolia*
        DD. Lvs. broader.
          E. Lvs. lanceolate to narrow-elliptic............................3. *P. elaeagrifolia*
          EE. Lvs. elliptic to obovate....................................4. *P. nivalis*
      CC. Lvs. crenate-serrulate all around, orbicular-ovate to oblong-ovate..5. *P. communis*
  AA. Lvs. at least partly pinnatifid..6. *P. Regelii*
  AAA. Lvs. setosely serrate, generally ovate, glabrous.........................7. *P. ussuriensis*
Fr. with deciduous or partly deciduous calyx, brown (yellow in No. 8).
  A. Lvs. dentate or sharply serrate.
    B. Lvs. sharply serrate or serrulate, often with appressed teeth; 6–12 cm. long.
      C. Fr. yellow: lvs. broad-cuneate at base; styles 5, rarely 4........8. *P. Bretschneideri*
      CC. Fr. brown: lvs. usually rounded or subcordate.
        D. Styles 5: lvs. setosely serrate or with appressed acuminate teeth...9. *P. pyrifolia*

DD. Styles 3–4; calyx occasionally partly persistent: lvs. serrulate with acute teeth.
                                                 10. *P. serrulata*
BB. Lvs. dentate-serrate with more or less spreading teeth: styles 2–4.
  c. Lvs. glabrous, 6–10 cm. long: styles 3–4, rarely 2: fr. subglobose or pyriform, 1.5–
    2.5 cm. long..11. *P. phaeocarpa*
  cc. Lvs. pubescent, 4–7.5 cm. long: styles 2 or 3: fr. subglobose, about 1 cm. diam.
                                        12. *P. betulaefolia*
AA. Lvs. crenate or crenulate-serrulate.
  B. Lvs. crenate-serrulate, orbicular-ovate to ovate, about 5 cm. long; styles 5.
                                        13. *P. longipes*
  BB. Lvs. crenate.
    c. Styles 3–5; stamens 25–30: lvs. ovate to oblong........................14. *P. Pashia*
    cc. Styles 2–3; stamens 20: lvs. orbicular-ovate to oblong-ovate......15. *P. Calleryana*

1. **P. amygdaliformis** Vill. Shrub or small tree to 6 m., with spreading
sometimes thorny brs.; young brts. slightly villous, soon glabrous, lustrous,
brown: lvs. oval to obovate or oblong, acutish or obtuse, cuneate or sometimes rounded at base, 2.5–7 cm. long, slightly crenate or entire, slightly
tomentose when young, soon glabrous and lustrous above, glabrescent and
glaucescent beneath, thickish; petioles slender, 1–3 cm. long: infl. 8–12-fld.,
grayish tomentose, rarely calyx glabrous outside; fls. 2–2.5 cm. across: fr.
subglobose, 2–3 cm. across, yellowish brown, on a stout stalk about as long
as fr. B.R.1484 (c, as *P. nivalis*). H.W.3:77. B.S.2:273. Dcne., Jard. Fruit.
1:t.13. (*P. parviflora* Desf., *P. Boveana* Dcne.) S. Eu., W. Asia. Intr. 1810.
Zone V.—**P. a. lobàta** (Dcne.) Koehne., var. Lvs. small, usually with few
round lobes. S.H.1:f.361h(l). (*P. collivaga* Velen., *P. a.* var. *heterophylla*
Dipp.)—**P. a. cuneifòlia** (Guss.) Bean, var. Lvs. smaller and narrower, attenuate at base. Gussone, Pl. Rar. t.39. (*P. c.* Guss., ? *P. pyrainus* Raf.)—**P. a.
oblongifòlia** (Spach) Bean, var. Lvs. oval to oblong, obtuse, rounded at
base: fr. larger. Dcne., Jard. Fruit. 1:t.14. S.H.1:f.361g. (*P. o.* Spach.)—
P. a. pérsica (Pers.) Bornm., var. Lvs. oblong, 3–7 cm. long, slightly crenulate: fr. slightly depressed-globose, 3 cm. diam., on a stalk 2 cm. long. Dcne..
Jard. Fruit. 1:t.15. S.L.321(h). (*P. p.* Pers., *P. sinaica* Dum.-Cours.) W.
Asia. Intr. before 1810.

P. a. × *nivalis* = P. Michaùxii Bosc. Lvs. ornate or elliptic-oblong, obtuse
or abruptly pointed, 3–7 cm. long, entire, villous-tomentose when young, later
glabrous and lustrous above, pubescent or glabrous beneath: infl. dense, tomentose: fr. globose or turbinate, greenish yellow. Decne., Jard. Fruit, 1:t.16. Cult.
before 1816.

2. **P. salicifòlia** Pall. Tree to 8 m., with slender more or less pendulous
brs.; brts. densely villous the first year: lvs. narrow-lanceolate, attenuate at
ends, 3–9 cm. long, 7–20 mm. wide, entire, white-tomentose when young,
later glabrous and lustrous above; petioles 3–15 mm. long: infl. tomentose,
dense, many-fld.; fls. 2 cm. across; pedicels about 1 cm. long: fr. pear-shaped,
2–3 cm. long, short-stalked. L.B.1120(c). B.R.514(c). G.O.125(c). Decne.,
Jard. Fruit. 1:t.12. S.L.284. S. E. Eu., W. Asia. Intr. 1780. Zone IV.

P. s. × *nivalis;* see under No. 4.

Related species: **P. glàbra** Boiss. Young brts. villous at first: lvs. narrow-
lanceolate, 4–10 cm. long, sometimes obscurely crenulate, glabrous from the
very first; petiole 8–35 mm. long; styles 3–4: fr. subglobose, small. Decne., Jard.
Fruit. 1:t.11. S.H.1:f.360a-a²,361a. Persia. Cult. ?

3. **P. elaeagrifòlia** Pall. Small tree, usually thorny; young brts. tomentose: lvs. lanceolate to obovate-lanceolate or narrow-elliptic, obtusish or
short-acuminate, cuneate, 4–7 cm. long, 1.2–2.5 cm. broad, entire, grayish or
whitish tomentose on both sides, often glabrescent above; petioles 1–4 cm.
long: infl. white-tomentose; fls. 2.5–3 cm. across; pedicels 1–2 cm. long: fr.
globose-turbinate or subglobose, 2–2.5 cm. across, green, short-stalked.
Decne., Jard. Fruit. 1:t.17. (*P. nivalis* var. *e.* Schneid.) Asia Minor. Intr.
1800. Zone IV.—**P. e. Kotschyàna** (Dcne.) Boiss., var. Usually thornless:

lvs. broader, 6–9 cm. long. Decne., Jard. Fruit. 1:t.18. G.C.98:405(h). (*P. nivalis* var. K. Schneid.) Asia Minor.

4. **P. nivàlis** Jacq. Snow P. Thornless tree, to 16 m.: young brts. tomentose: lvs. elliptic to obovate, acute, cuneate, 5–8 cm. long, 2–4 cm. broad, entire, white-tomentose when young, finally glabrous above; petioles 1–3 cm. long: infl. white-tomentose: fls. 2–3 cm. across: fr. subglobose, to 5 cm. across, yellowish green; stalk as long or longer than fr. G.H.t.77(c). H.C.t.79(c). Decne., Jard. Fruit. 1:t.21. S. Eu. Cult. 1800. Zone V.—**P. n. austríaca** (Kern.) Schneid., var. Lvs. elliptic, glabrescent. (*P. a.* Kern.)

P. n. × *salicifolia* = P. canéscens Spach. Lvs. lanceolate to narrow-elliptic, crenate-serrulate toward the apex, lustrous above at maturity: fr. pale green, short-stalked. Decne., Jard. Fruit. 1:t.19. Orig. before 1830.—*P. n.* × *communis* = P. salvifòlia DC. Lvs. elliptic to ovate, acute to acuminate, broad-cuneate or nearly rounded at base, usually crenulate, pubescent when young, finally glabrescent, long-petioled: infl. glabrescent: fr. pyriform, long-stalked. G.O.127(c). B.R.1482. S.H.1:f.361(1). Cult. before 1800.—*P. n.* × *amygdaliformis;* see under No. 1.

5. **P. commùnis** L. Common P. Broad-pyramidal tree to 15, rarely to 20 m.; sometimes spiny; young brts. glabrous or slightly pubescent: lvs. orbicular-ovate to elliptic, acute or short-acuminate, subcordate to broad-cuneate, 2–8 cm. long, crenate-serrulate, glabrous or villous when young; petioles slender, 1.5–5 cm. long: infl. villous or nearly glabrous; pedicels 1.5–3 cm. long; fls. about 3 cm. across: fr. turbinate or subglobose, on slender stalk to 5 cm. long. S.E.3:t.488. H.W.3:76(h);t.50(c). M.A.t.42(h). G.W. 16:368(h). Eu., W. Asia. Long cult. and often escaped and naturalized. Zone IV.—**P. c. Pyráster** L., var. Usually thorny: fls. 2–2.5 cm. across: fr. 1.5–2 cm. across. (*P. P.* Borkh., *P. c.* var. *achras* Wallr.)—**P. c. cordàta** (Desv.) Schneid., var. Lvs. suborbicular to ovate, subcordate, 2–3 cm. across: fls. smaller: fr. about 1.5 cm. across. Decne., Jard. Fruit. 1:t.3. Jour. Bot. 14:t. 180. (*P. c.* Desv., *P. com.* var. *Briggsii* Syme.)—**P. c. satìva** DC., var. Thornless tree: lvs. larger: fls. 2.5–3.5 cm. across: fr. large and juicy. Used as a collective name for the cult. varieties which, however, may be partly hybrids. —**P. c. sabauda** Dcne., var., is possibly a hybrid with *P. amygdaliformis*.

P. c. × *nivalis;* see under No. 4.—*P. c.* × *pyrifolia;* see under No. 9.—*P. c.* × *Crataegus Oxyacantha* = *Pyrocrataegus Willei;* see p. 372.—*P. c.* × *Sorbus Aria* = *Sorbopyrus auricularis;* see p. 382.—*P. c.* × *Cydonia oblonga* = *Pyronia Veitchii;* see p. 401.

Related species: **P. Balánsae** Dcne. Lvs. ovate to oblong-ovate, long-acuminate, rounded at base, 5–10 cm. long, entire or crenate, sharply serrulate on young plants: fr. turbinate, about 2.5 cm. across, long-stalked. Decne., Jard. Fruit. 1:t.6. S.H.1:f.361p(1). W. Asia. Intr. 1866. Zone V?—**P. syríaca** Boiss. Small tree, often thorny: lvs. oblong to oblong-lanceolate, 2–5, rarely to 10 cm. long, crenate-serrulate, glabrous or nearly so; petioles 2–5 cm. long: infl. tomentose: fr. pyriform, 3–3.5 cm. across. Decne., Jard. Fruit. 1:t.9. S.H.1:f.361o, 362e-f. M.D.1924:t.22(h). W. Asia, Cyprus. Intr. before 1874. Zone V?— **P. Korshínskyi** Litv. Tree; young brts. tomentose: lvs. oblong-lanceolate to ovate-oblong, acuminate, 5–8 cm. long, crenate-serrulate, villous-tomentose when young; petioles 1.5–3 cm. long: infl. villous; pedicels 2–3 cm. long; disk pubescent; style villous at base: fr. subglobose, 2 cm. across, on a stout stalk. S.H.1:f.359a-b. (*P. bucharica* Litv.) Turkest. Intr. 1890. Zone V.

6. **P. Regélii** Rehd. Shrub or tree to 10 m.; brts. glabrous or slightly pubescent at first, purple-brown the second year: lvs. very variable, ovate to ovate-oblong, rounded at base, partly undivided and crenate-serrulate, partly pinnatifid or lobed, 2–6 cm. long, with 5–7, usually narrow serrulate lobes, tomentose when young, soon glabrous; petioles 2–6 cm. long: infl. villous, few-fld.; fls. 2–2.5 cm. across; pedicels 1–1.5 cm. long: fr. pyriform or depressed-subglobose, 2–3 cm. across. B.S.2:284. G.C.III.7:115. S.H.1:f.

359e-f,361b. (*P. heterophylla* Reg. & Schmalh., not Pott, nor Steud.) Turkest. Intr. 1891. Zone V.

7. **P. ussuriénsis** Maxim. Tree; brts. glabrous or nearly so, yellow-gray to purple brown the 2d year, older brs. usually yellow-gray or yellowish brown: lvs. orbicular-ovate to ovate, acuminate, rounded or subcordate at base, 5–10 cm. long, setosely serrate, glabrous or nearly so; petiole 2–5 cm. long: infl. dense, hemispherical, glabrous, pedicels 1–2 cm. long; fls. 3–3.5 cm. across; petals obovate, gradually narrowed toward the base; styles pilose near base: fr. subglobose, short-stalked, greenish yellow, 3–4 cm. across. R.H. 1872:28.   B.C.5:2868.   N.K.6:t.19.   Gt.10:t.345.   U.S.Im.131:213,214(h). Gn.M.31:263(h). (*P. Simonii* Carr., *P. sinensis* Dcne., not Lindl., nor Poir.) N. E. Asia. Intr. 1855. Zone IV.—**P. u. ovoìdea** (Rehd.) Rehd., var. With spreading brs.; brts. brown: lvs. ovate to oblong-ovate: fr. ovoid to subglobose or ellipsoid; pedicels longer. N.K.6:t.17. B.C.5:2868. M.G.31:102. (*P. o.* Rehd., *P. Simonii* Hort., not Carr.) N. China, Korea. Intr. about 1865. Zone V.—**P. u. hondoénsis** (Kikuchi & Nakai) Rehd., var. Lvs. ovate to ovate-oblong, with finer more appressed and less aristate serration, at first like the young brts. often with ferrugineous floccose tomentum: pedicels longer. (*P. h.* Kikuchi & Nak.) C. Japan. Intr. 1917. Zone V?

Related species: P. Lindle`yi` Rehd. Lvs. serrate or denticulate, ovate, abruptly acuminate: fr. broad-ellipsoid, long-stalked, with persistent calyx. B.R.1248(c). M.G.31:111(l). (*P. sinensis* Lindl., not Poir.) China. Intr. 1820.

8. **P. Bretschneìderi** Rehd. Tree; brts. glabrous or nearly so, purple-brown the 2d year: lvs. ovate or elliptic-ovate, acuminate, broad-cuneate, rarely rounded, 5–11 cm. long, sharply serrate with acuminate setose teeth usually slightly appressed, floccose at first, soon glabrous; petioles 2.5–7 cm. long: infl. sparingly floccose at first, soon glabrous; pedicels 1.5–3 cm. long; fls. 2.5–3 cm. across: fr. globose-ovoid or subglobose, 2.5–3 cm. long, yellow; flesh soft and juicy; pedicels 3–4 cm. long. Hedrick, Pears N. Y. 74,t(c). M.G.31:103. N. China. Intr. 1882. Zone V.

9. **P. pyrifòlia** (Burm.) Nakai. SAND P. Tree; brts. glabrous or floccose while young, purplish brown or dark brown the 2d year: lvs. ovate-oblong, rarely ovate, long-acuminate, rounded or rarely subcordate at base, 7–12 cm. long, sharply setose-serrate with usually slightly appressed teeth, glabrous or slightly floccose while young; petioles 3–4.5 cm. long: infl. glabrous or floccose at first; fls. 3–3.5 cm. across, pedicels 3.5–5 cm. long; sepals long-acuminate, almost twice as long as tube; petals ovate; styles 5, rarely 4, glabrous: fr. subglobose, about 3 cm. across, brown with pale dots; flesh rather hard. N.K.6:t.23. B.C.5:2868. M.G.31:104. (*P. serotina* Rehd., *P. sinensis* auth., not Lindl. nor Poir., *P. montana* Nak.) C. and W. China. Intr. 1909. Zone V.—**P. p. Stapfiàna** (Rehd.) Rehd., f. With pyriform fr. B.M.8226(c). China. Cult. 1875.—**P. p. cúlta** (Mak.) Nakai, var. Lvs. larger and broader, to 15 cm. long: fr. larger, apple- or pear-shaped, brown or yellow. R.H.1879: 170,t(c);1880:110,t(c). (*P. montana* var. *Rehderi* Nak.) Cult. in China and Japan. Intr. before 1850 to Am. Here belong most of the forms known as Chinese or Japanese pears.

P. p. × *communis* = P. Lecontei Rehd. With serrulate or crenate-serrulate lvs. and yellow fr. with persistent calyx. Here belong Kieffer, LeConte, etc. B.C. 5:f.2809,2810. Hedrick, Pears N. Y. 180,187,tt(c). Orig. before 1850.

10. **P. serrulàta** Rehd. Tree; brts. woolly when young, soon glabrous, purple-brown the 2d year: lvs. ovate to ovate-oblong, abruptly or gradually acuminate, broad-cuneate or rounded at base, 5–11 cm. long, serrulate with

acute not setose teeth, floccose beneath at first, soon glabrous; petioles 3.5–7 cm. long: infl. slightly woolly; fls. 2.5 cm. across; pedicels 1.5–2 cm. long; sepals acute or acuminate, about as long as tube; styles 3–4, rarely 5: fr. subglobose, 1.5–1.8 cm. long, brown, with pale dots; calyx sometimes partly or wholly persistent. M.G.31:112. C. China. Intr. 1917. Zone V.

11. **P. phaeocárpa** Rehd. Tree; young brts. tomentose, glabrous and purple-brown the 2d year: lvs. elliptic-ovate to oblong-ovate, long-acuminate, usually broad-cuneate, 6–10 cm. long, dentate-serrate, with spreading teeth, loosely villous at first, soon quite glabrous; petioles 2–6 cm. long: infl. woolly, rarely nearly glabrous; pedicels 2–2.5 cm. long; fls. about 3 cm. broad; styles 3–4, rarely 2; fr. pyriform, 2–2.5 cm. long, brown with pale dots, soon becoming soft. B.C.5:f.3282. M.G.31:112. Monatschr. Ver. Gart. Preuss. 22:t.4(fr.). N. China. Intr. 1870. Zone V.—**P. p. globòsa** Rehd., f. Lvs. often ovate and rounded at base: fr. subglobose, 1.5–2 cm. across. Intr. 1882.

12. **P. betulaefòlia** Bge. Tree to 10 m.; young brts. tomentose until the 2d year: lvs. rhombic- to oblong-ovate, acuminate, broad-cuneate, 5–8 cm. long, sharply and rather coarsely serrate, finally bright green and lustrous above, tomentose beneath or finally glabrescent; petioles tomentose, 2–3 cm. long: infl. tomentose, 8–10-fld.; fls. 1.5–2 cm. across; pedicels 2–2.5 cm. long; styles 2–3: fr. subglobose, 1–1.5 cm. across, brown, dotted. G.F.7:225. Hedrick, Pears N. Y. 80,t(c). R.H.1879:318,319. Gng.6:309(h). N. China. Intr. about 1865. Zone IV. Brs. spreading and slightly pendulous.

13. **P. lóngipes** Coss. & Dur. Small tree with few thorns: lvs. ovate to orbicular-ovate, short-acuminate or obtusish, rounded at base, about 5 cm. long, crenate-serrulate, floccose beneath at first, soon glabrous; petioles slender, 1–3.5 cm. long: infl. floccose-tomentose, soon glabrous; fls. about 3 cm. across; pedicels slender: fr. globose, about 1.5 cm. across, brown, dotted, on slender stalks about 3 cm. long. Decne., Jard. Fruit. 1:t.4. S.H.1:f.365f. (*P. communis* var. *l*. Henry.) Algeria. Intr. before 1875. Zone VII.

Closely related species: **P. Boissieràna** Boiss. & Buhse. Lvs. ovate, rounded or subcordate, 2–3.5 cm. long; petioles usually longer than limb. S.H.1:f.363g, 364b. Persia. Intr. ?—Both species are probably closely related to *P. communis,* but differ in the deciduous calyx of the small fr.

14. **P. Páshia** D. Don. Tree to 12 m., mostly spiny; young brts. woolly, later glabrous: lvs. ovate to oblong-ovate or oblong, acuminate, usually rounded at base, 6–12 cm. long, crenate or crenate-serrulate, on young plants or suckers often lobed and sharply serrate, tomentose while young, finally glabrous or nearly so; petioles 1.5–4 cm. long: infl. tomentose; fls. 2–2.5 cm. across; pedicels short; calyx-lobes triangular, acute; stamens 25–30; styles 3–5: fr. subglobose, about 2 cm. across, brown; pedicels 2–3 cm. long. Decne., Jard. Fruit. 1:t.7. Collett, Fl. Siml. f.47. S.H.1:f.363h,364e-g. M.G.31:113. (*P. variolosa* Wall.) Himal., W. China. Intr. 1908. Zone V.—**P. P. kumaòni** Stapf, var. Lvs. and infl. glabrous or nearly so; calyx-lobes ovate, often obtuse. B.M.8256(c). B.S.2:290. Himal. Intr. 1825. Zone VI?

15. **P. Calleryàna** Dcne. Tree: brts. glabrous; winter-buds finely pubescent: lvs. broad-ovate to ovate, rarely elliptic-ovate, short-acuminate, rounded or broad-cuneate at base, 4–8 cm. long, crenate, usually quite glabrous; petioles 2–4 cm. long: infl. glabrous; fls. 2–2.5 cm. across; pedicels 1.5–3 cm. long; stamens 20; styles 2, rarely 3: fr. globular, about 1 cm. across, slender-stalked, brown, dotted. N.K.6:t.25. M.I.4:t.242. S.H.1:363p,364q-s. M.G.31:113. U.S.Im.160:t.243(h). China. Intr. 1908. Zone V.—**P. C. gracili-flòra** Rehd., f. Brts. tomentose toward the apex: fls. smaller; pedicels slenderer; anthers pink.—**P. C. tomentélla** Rehd., f. Brts. densely tomentose,

glabrous the 2d year: lvs. floccose at first, later glabrous except the midrib; those of shoots often serrulate: infl. villous.—This and the preceding form intr. with the type.—**P. C. dimorphophýlla** (Mak.) Koidz., var. Smaller lvs. 3–5 cm. long and mostly orbicular-ovate, rounded or subcordate at base, those at end of shoots ovate-lanceolate, on young plants deeply 3–5-lobed. Japan. Intr. 1918.—**P. C. Faurìei** (Schneid.) Rehd., var. Often shrubby and spiny; smaller in every part: lvs. 2.5–5 cm. long, often elliptic-ovate and broad-cuneate at base. N.K.6:t.24. (*P. F.* Schneid.) Korea. Intr. 1918. Zone V.

Subfam. III. ROSOIDEAE Focke. Herbaceous or woody plants usually shrubby, rarely trees: lvs. often compound, stipulate, sometimes evergreen: infl. variable: carpels distinct, usually numerous, forming a head on a torus, rarely solitary; style often lateral: fr. never dehiscent.

31. NEVIÙSIA Gray. Deciduous shrub: lvs. alternate, petioled, doubly serrate, stipulate: fls. perfect, apetalous, solitary or in cymes; calyx-tube flattish; sepals 5, petaloid, serrate, persistent, spreading; stamens numerous, longer than sepals; carpels 2–4, with slender styles shorter than stamens, becoming drupe-like achenes. (After its discoverer, Reuben Denton Nevius; 1827–1913.) One species in Alabama.

N. alabaménsis Gray. Upright shrub, 1–2 m. high: brts. terete: lvs. ovate to ovate-oblong, acute or acuminate, 3–7 cm. long, doubly serrate, those of shoots slightly lobed, nearly glabrous: fls. 3–8, rarely solitary, about 2.5 cm. across; pedicels 1.5–2 cm. long. B.M.6806(c). G.C.35:229;41:41. S.L.239(h). G.M.53:315. Fl.vi–vii. Intr. about 1860. Zone V. Cult. chiefly for its white feathery fls.

32. KÉRRIA DC. Deciduous shrub; buds small, with several scales: lvs. alternate, doubly serrate, stipulate: fls. yellow, solitary, perfect; sepals short, entire, calyx-tube flattish; petals 5; stamens numerous, half as long as petals; carpels 5–8, becoming dry achenes. (After William Kerr of Kew; d. 1814.) One species in China.

K. japónica (L.) DC. Shrub to 1.5 or 2 m.; brts. green, striped, glabrous: lvs. oblong-ovate, acuminate, 2–5 cm. long, doubly serrate, bright green and glabrous above, paler and slightly pubescent below; petioles 5–15 mm. long: fls. terminal on lateral brts., 3–4.5 cm. across; petals oval; stamens about half as long as petals; styles about as long as stamens: achenes brownish black. S.Z.1:t.98(c). B.R.1873(c). R.H.1869:293. F.E.9:593. A.G.18:425. (*Rubus japonicus* L.) C. & W. China; cult. in Japan. Intr. 1834. Zone IV. Planted for its bright green foliage and showy yellow fls. in spring; conspicuous in winter by its green brs.—**K. j. aureo-vittàta** Hartw. & Ruempl., var. Brts. striped green and yellow. (*K. j.* var. *vittato-ramosa* Zab., var. *ramulis variegatis aureis* Hort.) Intr. before 1864.—**K. j. pícta** Sieb., var. Lvs. edged white. I.H.9:336(c). F.M.5:296(c). (*K. j.* var. *variegata* T. Moore, var. *argenteo-variegata* Wyman.) Intr. 1844.—**K. j. aureo-variegáta** Rehd., var. Lvs. edged yellow. (*K. j.* var. *aurea variegata* Bean.)—**K. j. pleniflòra** Witte., var. Fls. double. B.M.1296(c). G.M.5:210. G.Z.9:48. Intr. 1805.

33. RHODÓTYPOS Sieb. & Zucc. Deciduous shrub; buds with several imbricate scales: lvs. opposite, short-petioled, doubly serrate, stipulate: fls. solitary, white; calyx-tube flattish; sepals 4, ovate, serrate, with 4 alternate small bracts at base; petals 4, suborbicular; stamens numerous; carpels usually 4, developing into black dry drupes surrounded by the large persistent calyx. (Greek *rhodon,* rose, and *typos,* type; alluding to the resemblance of the fl. to a single rose.) One species in E. Asia.

R. scándens (Thunb.) Mak. Upright spreading shrub to 2 m. or in Japan to 5 m.: lvs. ovate to ovate-oblong, acuminate, rounded at base, 4–8 cm. long, sharply and doubly serrate, dark green and glabrous above, lighter green and silky beneath when young; petioles 3–5 mm. long: fls. pure white, 3–5 cm. across; stamens half as long as petals, drupes obliquely short-ellipsoid, about 8 mm. long, shining black. Fl.v–vi; fr.x. B.M.5805(c). S.Z.1:t.99(c). Gt.15: t.505. Gn.43:138. B.C.5:2949. (*R. kerrioides* Sieb. & Zucc., *R. tetrapetala* Mak.) Japan and C. China. Intr. 1866. Zone IV. With showy white fls.; the black fr. conspicuous in winter.

34. RÚBUS L. Deciduous or evergreen shrubs or suffruticose or herbaceous plants, with erect to trailing mostly prickly and usually short-lived stems: lvs. alternate, simple, 3-foliolate or pinnately or pedately compound, stipulate: fls. perfect, rarely dioecious, white to pink, in racemes, panicles or corymbs, or solitary, terminal or rarely axillary; calyx 5-parted, rarely 3–7-parted, with persistent lobes; petals 5, sometimes wanting; stamens many; pistils many, sometimes few, on a convex torus; styles nearly terminal; mature carpels usually drupelets, sometimes dry. (Ancient Latin name.) Including *Bossekia* Neck., *Batidea* Greene, *Melanobatus* Greene, *Oreobatus* Rydb. and *Rubacer* Rydb. More than 400 species chiefly in the colder and temp. regions of the n. hemisphere, few in the tropics and the s. hemisphere. Latest monograph by Focke in Biblioth. Bot. parts 72 and 83 (1910–14).—Shrubby or suffruticose plants cult. for their foliage or handsome fls. or for their edible fr.; the fls. appear in spring or early summer and the frs. ripen in summer and early autumn.

The species of the subgenus Eubatus widely distributed in Europe and N. America are exceedingly polymorphous and hybridize readily which makes it almost impossible to define well marked species. In the following enumeration only the most important species are described; for other forms which may be found occasionally in special collections see Rydberg in N. Am. Fl. vol. XXII. 428–480 (1913) for American species and (including also cult. species and varieties) Bailey, Gent. Herb. 1:139–200;2:271–423,443–471;3:119–148,247–271; il. (1923–34); for European species see: Focke in Ascherson & Graebner, Syn. Mitteleur. Fl.VI.440–648 (1902), Sudre Rubi Europae with 215 pl. (1908–13) and Rogers, Handb. Brit. Rubi (1900).

KEY TO THE SUBGENERA

A. Stipules broad, often dissected, free: lvs. simple or compound.
  B. Stipules persistent: lvs. simple; stems unarmed......................I. DALIBARDASTRUM
  BB. Stipules caducous, often dissected: calyx-tube usually campanulate: stems usually prickly: lvs. simple or compound....................................II. MALACHOBATUS
AA. Stipules lanceolate to filiform, adnate to the petiole.
  B. Stems unarmed, upright, with flaky bark: lvs. simple, palmately lobed.
                III. ANOPLOBATUS
  BB. Stems prickly, rarely unarmed, usually biennial, upright, arching or trailing: lvs. usually compound.
    c. Fr. separating from the torus, therefore hollow: lvs. pinnate, ternate or rarely simple.
                IV. IDAEOBATUS
    cc. Fr. separating with the torus from the calyx, therefore not hollow; lvs. usually ternate or digitately compound..V. EUBATUS

KEY TO THE SPECIES
I. DALIBARDASTRUM

A. Lvs. ternate ....1. *R. nutans*
AA. Lvs. simple, cordate-ovate..2. *R. tricolor*

II. MALACHOBATUS

A. Lvs. ternate or quinate or partly simple and deeply lobed.
  B. Stipules and bracts entire or dentate..3. *R. Henryi*
  BB. Stipules and bracts fimbriate-pinnate..............................4. *R. Playfairianus*

AA. Lvs. simple.
  B. Fls. in terminal racemes.
    c. Infl. glandular ....5. *R. hupehensis*
    cc. Infl. glandless ....6. *R. malifolius*
  BB. Fls. in a compound infl.
    c. Lvs. not or slightly lobed.
      D. Lvs. suborbicular or broad-ovate, long-petioled.
        E. Lvs. reniform, rounded at apex: fls. in terminal clusters and below 1 or 2
          axillary fls. ....7. *R. irenaeus*
        EE. Lvs. broad-ovate, abruptly acuminate: fls. in a large terminal panicle.
                                   8. *R. chroosepalus*
      DD. Lvs. ovate to lanceolate.
        E. Infl. terminal, paniculate.
          F. Lvs. nearly glabrous, deeply cordate........................9. *R. ichangensis*
          FF. Lvs. pubescent or tomentose beneath.
            G. Petioles 2-5 cm. long; lvs. pilose on the veins beneath.10. *R. Lambertianus*
            GG. Petioles 1-2.5 cm. long: lvs. tomentose beneath, oblong-lanceolate.
                                     11. *R. Parkeri*
        EE. Infl. fasciculate, in the axils of old lvs........................12. *R. flagelliflorus*
    cc. Lvs. deeply lobed, mallow-like, with obtuse lobes................13. *R. setchuenensis*

III. ANOPLOBATUS

A. Lvs. large with acute lobes.
  B. Lobes broadly triangular: fls. in corymbs.
    c. Infl. many-fld.; fls. purple...14. *R. odoratus*
    cc. Infl. few-fld.; fls. white..15. *R. parviflorus*
  BB. Lobes ovate to oblong-ovate; calyx villous, glandless....................16. *R. trifidus*
AA. Lvs. 3-8 cm. across, with rounded incised lobes: fls. white, solitary.......17. *R. deliciosus*

IV. IDAEOBATUS

A. Lvs. simple.
  B. Fls. solitary; lvs. tomentose beneath (glabrous in var.): petals spreading.
                                     18. *R. corchorifolius*
  BB. Fls. several: lvs. glabrous beneath or pubescent only on the veins.
    c. Lvs. 5-lobed, green beneath: petals spreading....................19. *R. crataegifolius*
    cc. Lvs. of flowering brts. not lobed, glaucous beneath: fls. usually 3; petals and stamens
      upright ....20. *R. trianthus*
AA. Lvs. compound.
  B. Fls. solitary or few, rarely forming a loose, 2-8-fld. infl.
    c. Lvs. always ternate, nearly glabrous: fls. solitary..................21. *R. spectabilis*
    cc. Lvs. pinnate, with 3-11 lfts.
      D. Carpels more than 100 forming an ovoid fr.: fls. solitary or few: lfts. 5-7, lanceo-
        late, firm, pilose only on veins beneath.........................22. *R. illecebrosus*
      DD. Carpels 10-60, forming an hemispherical fr.
        E. Fls. solitary: lfts. 7-9.......................................23. *R. amabilis*
        EE. Fls. in 2-8-fld. loose infl.: lfts. 3-5; stems white-pruinose.
          F. Lfts. 3-5; stems glabrous, white-pruinose.
            G. Styles glabrous; fls. white..................................24. *R. biflorus*
            GG. Styles pubescent; fls. reddish, small......................25. *R. lasiostylus*
          FF. Lfts. 3; stems pubescent or glabrous...........................26. *R. stans*
  BB. Fls. in many-fld. usually dense infl.
    c. Terminal lft. elongated, pinnately lobed..........................27. *R. thibetanus*
    cc. Terminal lft. not elongated, serrate.
      D. Petals incumbent, adpressed to the stamens.
        E. Lvs. of flowering brts. 5-7-foliolate...........................28. *R. coreanus*
        EE. Lvs. of flowering brts. ternate or occasionally quinate.
          F. Plant not setose, nor stipitate-glandular.
            G. Terminal lft. lobed or incised, broad....................29. *R. parvifolius*
            GG. Terminal lft. coarsely serrate, long-acuminate..............30. *R. gracilis*
          FF. Plant densely glandular and setose.....................31. *R. phoenicolasius*
      DD. Petals erect or spreading.
        E. Infl. paniculate, elongated, only at base leafy.
          F. Lvs. 5-7-foliolate.
            G. Lfts. white-tomentose beneath; sepals tomentose.......32. *R. flosculosus*
            GG. Lfts. grayish tomentose beneath: sepals pubescent at apex: stems white-
              pruinose ....33. *R. Cockburnianus*
          FF. Lvs. of flowering brts. ternate, occasionally quinate.
            G. Lfts. white-tomentose beneath.........................34. *R. innominatus*
            GG. Lfts. green and villous beneath: infl. glandular..........35. *R. adenophorus*
        EE. Terminal infl. short, often augmented by lateral infls.
          F. Infl. loose and corymbose: stems pruinose: plant neither setose nor glandular.
            G. Prickles of infl. straight, scarcely flattened: lfts. dark green above.
                                   36. *R. occidentalis*
            GG. Prickles of infl. recurved, flattened: lfts. yellowish green above, often 5.
                                   37. *R. leucodermis*

FF. Infl. dense or with lateral brts.
    G. Lvs. often quinate: infl. consisting of terminal and axillary racemes: fr.
        tomentulose ....38. *R. idaeus*
    GG. Lvs. all ternate: infl. without or few lateral brts.: fr. glabrous.
                                      39. *R. mesogaeus*

V. EUBATUS

A. Fls. dioecious: lvs. ternate or pinnately quinate............................40. *R. ursinus*
AA. Fls. unisexual: lvs. ternate or digitately quinate.
  B. Stems erect or ascending and arching. BLACKBERRIES.
    C. Lfts. white-tomentose beneath.
      D. Stem green, with hooked prickles: fls. white.....................41. *R. Linkianus*
      DD. Stem pruinose, with nearly straight prickles: fls. pink or pinkish.42. *R. ulmifolius*
    CC. Lvs. green beneath, pubescent or nearly glabrous.
      D. Infl. densely glandular with long-stipitate glands; lvs. pubescent beneath.
                                  43. *R. allegheniensis*
      DD. Infl. not or slightly glandular; glands, if present, sessile or short-stipitate.
        E. Lfts. densely pubescent beneath (slightly so in *R. nessensis* under No. 44).
          F. Infl. racemose or paniculate.
            G. Stem with recurved prickles.
              H. Lfts. not dissected.....................................44. *R. fruticosus*
              HH. Lfts. dissected ....45. *R. laciniatus*
            GG. Stems with numerous long and straight prickles........46. *R. ostryifolius*
          FF. Infl. short, corymbose.......................................47. *R. frondosus*
        EE. Lvs. glabrous beneath or only sparingly pubescent on the veins: infl. racemose.
                                  48. *R. canadensis*
  BB. Stems prostrate, only the flowering brts. upright. DEWBERRIES.
    C. Stipules filiform: stem prickly or setose, not pruinose.
      D. Infl. with flattened prickles: lvs. persistent.......................49. *R. trivialis*
      DD. Infl. not prickly.
        E. Stem very bristly..50. *R. hispidus*
        EE. Stem prickly; the prickles confined to the angles of the stem..51. *R. flagellaris*
    CC. Stipules lanceolate: stems pruinose with sparse weak prickles..........52. *R. caesius*

Subgen. I. DALIBARDASTRUM Focke. Prostrate unarmed shrubs or subshrubs, bristly; lvs. simple or ternate; stipules broad, free; calyx setose.

1. R. nùtans Wall. Evergreen shrub; stems rooting, densely covered with purplish bristles; petioles bristly, 3–5 cm. long: lfts. short-stalked, rhombic or obovate, obtusish, sharply serrate and lobulate, the terminal one 3–6 cm. long, dark green and lustrous above, bristly on the veins beneath: fls. 1–3, white, about 3 cm. across, on slender bristly stalks 3–6 cm. long: fr. globose, dark purple, edible. B.M.5023(c). Himal. Cult. 1860. Zone VII?

2. R. trícolor Focke. Deciduous shrub; stems densely clothed with yellow-brown bristles; stipules laciniate: lvs. suborbicular to ovate, short-acuminate, cordate, 6–10 cm. long, irregularly and sharply toothed and sometimes lobulate, dark green above, white-tomentose beneath and bristly on the veins; petioles 2–3.5 cm. long, bristly: fls. white, 2–2.5 cm. across, in short terminal bristly racemes: fr. bright red, edible. Fl.VII–VIII: fr.IX. B.M.9534 (c). (*R. polytrichus* Franch., not Progel.) W. China. Intr. 1908. Zone VI?

Related species: **R. Treùtleri** Hook. f. Stems villous and bristly; stipules finely dissected: lvs. orbicular-ovate, pubescent on both sides, sometimes tomentose beneath, 5-lobed, middle lobe acuminate: fls. in terminal villous clusters; calyx setose, outer sepals laciniate. Himal., W. China. Cult. 1933. Zone VII?

To the subgen. CHAMAEMORUS belongs **R. Chamaemòrus** L. CLOUDBERRY. Herb with creeping root-stock and simple short stems: lvs. simple, long-petioled, reniform, 4–10 cm. across, with 3–5 short rounded crenate-serrate lobes; fls. solitary, 2.5–3 cm. across: fr. orange, edible. B.B.2:276. B.C.3022. Circumpolar, s. to Me. and N. H. Cult. 1789. Zone II.

Subgen. II. MALACHOBATUS Focke. Evergreen or deciduous, creeping or scandent, usually prickly shrubs, rarely herbaceous: lvs. usually simple, often lobed or digitate-compound; stipules free, broad, usually cleft into narrow lobes: infl. racemose or paniculate, rarely few-fld.; fls. small; sepals unequal, erect after anthesis: fr. separating from the torus.

3. R. Hénryi Hemsl. Evergreen scandent shrub to 6 m. long; stems tomentose-floccose when young, with few reflexed prickles: lvs. deeply 3-lobed, rarely 5-lobed, rounded at base, 10–15 cm. long, the lobes 2–2.5 cm.

wide, acuminate, remotely serrulate, white-tomentose beneath: fls. pink, nearly 2 cm. across, in terminal and axillary, glandular racemes; sepals caudate: fr. 1–1.5 cm. across, black, lustrous. Fl.vi; fr.viii. H.I.1705. Focke, Sp.Rub.44. M.G.30:7(h). C. and W. China. Intr. 1900. Zone VI?—**R. H. bambusàrum** (Focke) Rehd., var. Lvs. ternate; lfts. lanceolate or narrow lanceolate, very short-petiolate, 4–10 cm. long. G.C.42:251. S.L.328(h). (*R. b.* Focke.) C. China. Intr. 1900.

Related species: **R. Andersòni** Hook f. Upright; brts. like petioles minutely prickly; stipules ovate, entire: lfts. 3, rarely 5, elliptic, acuminate, 6–12 cm. long, silky beneath, with 25–35 close parallel veins: infl. terminal, paniculate; calyx setose. Himal. Cult. 1933. Zone VII?

4. **R. Playfairiànus** Focke. Half-evergreen sarmentose shrub, stems dark-colored, with small hooked prickles, floccose-tomentose when young: lfts. 3–5, stalked, oblong-lanceolate, acute, rounded at base, serrate, the terminal one 6–14 cm. long, dark green above, gray-tomentose beneath: fls. 1–1.5 cm. across, in small terminal and axillary racemes; calyx densely villous, not glandular: fr. black. Fl.v–vi; fr.vii–viii. G.C.51:165(h),166. (*R. Playfairii* Bean, not Hemsl.) C. and W. China. Intr. 1907. Zone VI?

5. **R. hupehénsis** Oliv. Deciduous or half-evergreen shrub; stems dark-colored, thinly floccose-tomentose when young, with few curved spines: lvs. oblong-lanceolate, acuminate, rounded at base, 7–11 cm. long, unequally serrulate, gray-tomentose beneath; petiole about 1 cm. long: fls. rather small in 3–7-fld. very glandular racemes; calyx gray-tomentose: fr. purple-black, austere. Fl.vi; fr.vii–viii. G.C.51:166. H.I.1816. (*R. Swinhoei* Bean, not Hance.) C. China. Intr. 1907. Zone VI?

6. **R. malifòlius** Focke. Deciduous prostrate or climbing shrub; stems with short recurved prickles: lvs. elliptic to oblong-elliptic, acuminate, rounded at base, 5–12 cm. long, remotely mucronulate-serrulate, glabrous above, puberulous on the veins beneath; petiole 5–15 mm. long: fls. about 2.5 cm. across, in terminal racemes 5–10 cm. long; calyx tomentose; petals suborbicular: fr. black, of unpleasant flavor. Fl.vi; fr.vii. H.I.1947 C. and W. China. Intr. 1904. Zone VI?

7. **R. irenaèus** Focke. Evergreen prostrate shrub; stems tomentose, with small prickles or unarmed: lvs. suborbicular, acuminulate or rarely rounded, broad-cordate or subcordate, 10–15 cm. across, mucronate-denticulate and usually slightly lobulate, dark green and glabrous above, whitish tomentose beneath; petioles 4–8 cm. long; stipules large, incisely dentate: fls. 1.5–2 cm. across, 1 or 2 in the axils or in several-fld. clusters; calyx tomentose: fr. red, large. Fl.vii. Focke, Sp. Rub. 115. C. and W. China. Intr. 1900. Zone VI?

8. **R. chroosépalus** Focke. Half-evergreen straggling shrub; stems with short curved prickles, puberulous when young: lvs. broad-ovate, abruptly acuminate, cordate, 7–12 cm. long, sharply and unequally serrate and often shallowly lobulate, glabrous above, white-tomentose beneath; petioles 3–6 cm. long, prickly, glabrous like the veins beneath: fls. apetalous, 1–1.5 cm. across, in large terminal panicles 12–20 cm. long; sepals tomentose outside, purple inside: fr. black, small. Fl.vii. H.I.1952. Focke, Sp. Rub. 51. G.C.51: 166. C. China. Intr. 1900. Zone VI? Lvs. resembling those of *Tilia tomentosa*.

9. **R. ichangénsis** Hemsl. & Ktze. Deciduous scandent or prostrate shrub; stems slender, with stipitate glands and scattered hooked prickles: lvs. ovate-lanceolate, acuminate, deeply cordate, 8–15 cm. long, remotely mucronate-serrulate and usually slightly lobulate toward the base, glabrous; petioles

2–3 cm. long, prickly like midrib beneath: fls. 6–8 mm. across, white, in slender panicles 15–25 cm. long or more; sepals erect: fr. red, small, of good flavor. Fl.vii; fr.x. Focke, Sp. Rub. 55. G.C.48:275(h). C. and W. China. Intr. 1900. Zone VI?

10. **R. Lambertiànus** Ser. Half-evergreen straggling shrub; stem angled, with scattered recurved prickles, tomentulose when young or nearly glabrous: lvs. ovate to oblong-ovate, acuminate, cordate, 7–12 cm. long, crenate-dentate and sinuate-lobulate or sometimes slightly 3-lobed, slightly pilose above, pilose beneath; petioles 2–4 cm. long: fls. white, 8 mm. across, in panicles 8–14 cm. long; calyx tomentulose or nearly glabrous, often glandular; petals scarcely exceeding the sepals: fr. red, small. Fl.viii–ix; fr.x–xi. G.C.48:276 (h);51:166. C. China. Intr. 1907. Zone VI?—**R. L. hakonénsis** (Franch. & Sav.) Focke, var. Lvs. nearly glabrous. (*R. L.* var. *glaber* Bean, *R. h.* Fr. & Sav.) Japan, C. China. Intr. 1907.

11. **R. Párkeri** Hance. Deciduous climbing shrub; stems grayish tomentose, with scattered curved prickles: lvs. oblong-ovate, acuminate, cordate, 10–16 cm. long, crenate-dentate and sinuate-lobate, hirsute above, grayish or brownish tomentose beneath; petioles 5–20 mm. long, pubescent and prickly: fls. white, about 8 mm. across, in large densely villous and glandular-setose panicles; calyx with reddish glandular hairs: fr. black with few drupelets. Fl.vi; fr.vii–viii. Focke, Sp. Rub. 66. G.C.51:166. C. China. Intr. 1907. Zone VI?

12. **R. flagelliflòrus** Focke. Evergreen climbing or creeping shrub; stems with very small recurved prickles, tomentulose when young: lvs. ovate to ovate-lanceolate, acute or acuminate, deeply cordate, 8–16 cm. long, crenate-serrulate, often obscurely lobulate, sparingly pilose above, yellowish tomentose beneath; petioles 3–6 cm. long, slightly bristly: fls. small, in short axillary fascicle-like racemes or clusters; sepals purple inside; petals white, quickly caducous: fr. black, edible. Fl.vi. Focke, Sp. Rub. 113. S.L.327(h). R.B.33:360,t(h). C. and W. China. Intr. 1901. Zone VII?

13. **R. setchuenénsis** Bur. & Fr. Deciduous straggling shrub; stems terete, velutinous, unarmed: lvs. suborbicular, 5- or obscurely 7-lobed, cordate, 7–16 cm. wide, lobes broad, obtuse, irregularly dentate, rugulose above, grayish tomentulose and somewhat reticulate beneath; petioles 5–7 cm. long: fls. 1–1.5 cm. across, in many-fld. panicles or partly in dense axillary clusters; calyx tomentose; sepals triangular, acute; petals purple: fr. black, of good flavor. Fl.vii–viii; fr.ix. (*R. omeiensis* Rolfe, *R. clemens* Focke, *R. pacatus* Focke.) W. China. Cult. 1898. Zone VI?

Subgen. III. ANOPLOBATUS Focke. Stems upright, rarely decumbent, with exfoliating bark, unarmed; stipules lanceolate, slightly adnate to petiole: lvs. simple, palmately lobed: fls. large, with spreading petals; styles club-shaped; torus flat.

14. **R. odoràtus** L. Deciduous upright shrub, to 3 m.; young shoots, petioles and peduncles villous and glandular: lvs. cordate, 5-lobed, 10–30 cm. broad, lobes broad-triangular, abruptly acuminate, irregularly dentate, green and pilose on both sides; petiole 2–8 cm. long, villous: fls. purple, fragrant, 3–5 cm. across, in short many-fld. panicles; sepals broad-ovate, abruptly caudate, acuminate, glandular outside; petals suborbicular: fr. red, flat, 1.5–2 cm. broad. Fl.vi–viii. B.M.323(c). N.D.6,t.24(c). Gn.34:230. B.B.2:276. F.E.22:557(h). (*Rubacer odoratum* Rydb.) N. S. to Mich., Tenn. and Ga. Intr. 1635. Zone III. Shrub with large lvs. and large purple fls.; likes shady position and humid soil.—**R. o. albus** Schneid., f. With whitish fls. and lighter-colored bark. (*R. o. albidus* Bailey.)

R. o. × parviflorus = R. Fràseri Rehd. Brts. and petioles less glandular-
hairy: lobes of lvs. acuminate: fls. pink fading to pale purple. G.C.73:50(h).
(*R. robustus* G. Fraser, not Presl.) Orig. 1918.—*R. o. × idaeus;* see under
No. 38.

15. **R. parviflorus** Nutt. Deciduous upright shrub, to 2 m.; young brts.,
petioles and infl. puberulous and more or less glandular: lvs. reniform, 3–5-
lobed, 6–20 cm. across, lobes triangular, short-acuminate or acute, dentate,
sparingly pilose on both sides; petioles 5–12 cm. long: fls. white, 3–6 cm.
across, in 3–10-fld. rather dense corymbs; sepals broad-ovate, abruptly caudate-acuminate, densely glandular outside; petals broad-oval or ovate: fr.
convex, red, 1.5–2 cm. across. Fl.v–vii. B.R.1368(c). B.M.3453(c). B.B.2:
276. Gn.81:31;84:339. (*R. nutkanus* Ser., *Rubacer parviflorum* Rydb.) W.
Ont. and Mich. to N. Mex. and n. Mex., w. to s. Alaska and Calif. Intr.
1827. Zone III. Similar to the preceding, but fls. white.—**R. p. Fraseriànus**
J. K. Henry, var. Petals incisely dentate: lvs. rather densely pilose beneath.
Gn.82:277. Torreya, 18:55. B. C. Intr. 1918.

16. **R. trifidus** Thunb. Half-evergreen upright shrub, to 2 m.; brts. glandular-pubescent at first, soon glabrous: lvs. suborbicular, cordate, deeply
5–7-lobed, 10–20 cm. across: lvs. oblong-lanceolate, coarsely double-serrate,
slightly hairy on the veins on both sides; petioles 3–6 cm. long: fls. rosy-
white, 2.5–3 cm. across, solitary in the axils and in a few-fld. terminal corymb;
calyx tomentose: fr. red, edible. Fl.iv–v. R.H.1908:298. S.L.326(h). (*R.
aceroides* Miq.) Japan. Intr. 1888. Zone V.

17. **R. deliciòsus** Torr. Deciduous shrub to 3 m., with spreading or arching brs.; young brts. puberulous: lvs. reniform to orbicular-ovate, truncate
or cordate at base, 3–7 cm. long, with 3 or sometimes 5 broad obtuse lobes,
or acute on shoots, irregularly dentate, glandular beneath and sparingly
pilose on the veins; petioles 2–3.5 cm. long, puberulous: fls. mostly solitary,
about 5 cm. across; sepals ovate, caudate-acuminate; petals oval: fr. hemispheric, dark purple, 1–1.5 cm. across. Fl.v. B.M.6062(c). Gt.24:t.837. R.H.
1882:356. B.S.2:457. Gn.80:286(h);86:37. J.L.35:362(h). (*Oreobatus d.*
Rydb.) Colo. Intr. 1870. Zone V. Graceful shrub with large white fls.—**R.
d. neomexicànus** Kearn., var. Lvs. with at least the terminal lobe acute,
pubescent on both sides, reticulate-veined beneath, usually larger; petioles
villous. S.H.1:t.307b(l). Card, Bush Fr. f.51. N. Mex., Ariz. and n. Mex.
Intr? Probably tenderer.

Subgen. IV. Idaeobatus Focke. Shrubs with deciduous upright or scandent
or procumbent stems usually prickly, setose or glandular, usually biennial: lvs.
usually ternate or pinnate, rarely digitate, sometimes simple; stipules linear,
adnate: fr. of many carpels at maturity separating from the torus. Raspberries.

18. **R. corchorifòlius** L. f. Upright shrub, suckering; stems prickly,
tomentulose when young: lvs. ovate-lanceolate, acuminate, cordate, 8–16 cm.
long, 3-nerved at base, with several short obtuse lobes near the base or without lobes, or 3-lobed on shoots with elongated middle lobe, irregularly serrulate, pubescent on veins above, gray-tomentose beneath; petioles 5–20 mm.
long: fls. white, about 3 cm. across, usually solitary or few on short lateral
prickly brts.; petals oblong, little longer than the ovate, mucronate sepals:
fr. bright, red, large, edible. Fl.iv; fr.vi. G.C.51:149. N.K.7:t,20. Japan,
China. Intr. 1907. Zone VI?—**R. c. Olíveri** (Miq.) Focke, var. Shoots glabrous: lvs. pubescent only on the veins beneath. (*R. O.* Miq.) China, Japan.
Intr. 1907.

Related species: **R. palmàtus** Thunb. Stems glabrous, prickly: lvs. palmately
3-5-lobed, 5-nerved at base, 3–8 cm. long, lobes unequally and coarsely dentate

and lobulate, nerves beneath puberulous and midrib prickly: fr. yellow, edible
B.M.7801(c). Focke, Sp. Rub. 133. Japan, China. Cult. 1899. Zone VII?

19. **R. crataegifòlius** Bge. Upright shrub to 3 m., suckering; stem
prickly, grooved, brownish red, pubescent when young, branching near apex:
lvs. palmately 3–5-lobed, cordate or truncate, 5–12 cm. long, those of flowering brts. smaller, 3-lobed, lobes ovate to ovate-lanceolate, acute, rarely acuminate or obtusish, unequally coarsely serrate, pubescent beneath on the
veins; petioles 2–5 cm. long, prickly: fls. white, about 2 cm. across, in few- or
several-fld. clusters; sepals ovate, acuminate, much recurved; petals elliptic:
fr. red. Fl.vi; fr.vii. Gt.17:t.591;27:t.924. N.K.7:t.21. S.H.f.307g,309r. Japan,
Korea, N. China. Intr. 1875. Zone V. Lvs. turning red and yellow in fall.

20. **R. triánthus** Focke. Shrub with upright arching stems; stems slender
glabrous, often bloomy, prickly: lvs. oblong-lanceolate, acuminate, subcordate or truncate, 5–8 cm. long, incisely serrate, those of shoots 3-lobed and
larger, the terminal lobe ovate-lanceolate, glabrous, pale or whitish beneath,
with 8–12 pairs of veins; petioles 1–4 cm. long, glabrous, prickly like the veins
beneath: fls. usually 3, white, 1 cm. across, on pedicels 1–2 cm. long; sepals
triangular, caudate-acuminate, glabrous outside, tomentose inside: fr. small,
red. Fl.v; fr.vii. Focke, Sp. Rub. 139. (*R. conduplicatus* Rolfe.) China.
Intr. 1907. Zone (V).

Closely related species: **R. Koehneànus** Focke. Stems upright, sparingly and
minutely prickly: lvs. ovate, 3- or rarely 5-lobed, 4–12 cm. long, the terminal
lobe usually ovate and acuminate; petioles often nearly as long as blade; fls.
nearly 2 cm. across: fr. orange, small. B.M.8246(c). Focke, Sp. Rub. 141. Gt.
53:555. (*R. incisus* Spaeth, not Thunb., *R. morifolius* Hort., not Sieb.) Japan.
Intr. 1890. Zone V?

21. **R. spectàbilis** Pursh. Stems upright, to 2 m., glabrous, with numerous
fine prickles below: lfts. 3, ovate, 10–15 cm. long, incisely serrate, nearly
glabrous, the terminal lft. the largest, rhombic-ovate, stalked, lateral lfts.
nearly sessile: fls. solitary, purplish-red, 2.5 cm. across, nodding, fragrant, on
short lateral brts.; calyx pubescent; sepals triangular-ovate, half as long as
petals: fr. orange, large, edible. Fl.iv–vi. B.R.1424(c). L.B.1602(c). Proc.
Iowa Acad. Sci.23,t.26. W. N. Am. Intr. 1827. Zone V.

22. **R. illecebròsus** Focke. Strawberry-Raspberry. Suffruticose or nearly
herbaceous; stems upright, to 1 m., angular, glabrous, prickly: lvs. pinnate;
lfts. 5–7, 3 at end of brts., oblong-lanceolate, acuminate, 4–8 cm. long, doubly
serrate, glabrous except pilose on veins beneath; petiole and rachis prickly:
fls. solitary or few, bracted, white, 4 cm. across; pedicels prickly, glabrous:
fr. scarlet, large. Fl.vii–x. G.C.III.20:82. Gn.64:412. Gt.47:27. G.W.4:233.
(*R. sorbifolius* Hort., not Maxim.) Japan. Cult. 1895. Zone (V). Particularly handsome with its large scarlet fr.

Closely related species: **R. rosaefòlius** Sm. Stems taller, pubescent: lfts.
5–11, pubescent below: fls. larger, sometimes double (var. *coronarius* Ser.
B.M.1783): fr. smaller. H.I.349. B.M.6970(c). Himal., S. Asia. Cult. 1816.
Zone VII.—A species similar in habit, though belonging to subgen. Cylactis is
R. xanthocárpus Bur. & Franch. Herbaceous: lateral lfts. several times smaller
than terminal lft. and obtusish: fls. smaller, 1–3: fr. yellow. W. China. Intr.
1885. Zone IV.

23. **R. amàbilis** Focke. Stems to 2 m., slightly prickly, unarmed above:
lvs. pinnate; petiole and rachis with subulate prickles; lfts. 7–9, ovate to
ovate-lanceolate, incisely double-serrate, pubescent on the veins and usually
prickly beneath, terminal lft. 2.5–6 cm. long, acuminate, lateral lfts. smaller,
usually acute: fls. solitary, white, 4–5 cm. across, nodding: pedicels silky-
pubescent and prickly; sepals broad-ovate, cuspidate; petals suborbicular,

overlapping: fr. large, red, edible. Fl.vi–vii; fr.viii. Focke, Sp. Rub. 164. W. China. Intr. 1908. Zone VI? With conspicuous white fls. and comparatively small lfts.

Closely related species: **R. pungens** Cambess. Lfts. 5–7, rarely 9, somewhat smaller: petiole and rachis with hooked prickles: fls. 1–3, smaller, sepals ovate to ovate-lanceolate, acuminate; petals obovate to oblong, 1–1.2 cm. long: fr. smaller. Jacquemont, Voy. Inde, 4:t.59. Himal., China, Japan. Intr. 1907. Zone VI?

24. **R. biflòrus** Buch.-Ham. Stems to 3 m., with straight prickles, glaucous-white like the upper brts.: lfts. 3–5, ovate or elliptic, acute or acuminate, 4–10 cm. long or the lateral ones smaller, incisely and irregularly serrate, white-tomentose beneath; petiole and rachis prickly: fls. 1–3, white, 2 cm. across: fr. yellow, roundish, 2 cm. across, edible. Fl.v–vi. B.M.4678(c). R.H. 1855,t.5(c). Gn.54:456. Himal. Intr. 1818. Zone VII? Striking plant with conspicuous white stems.—**R. b. quinqueflòrus** Focke, var. Taller and more vigorous: fls. usually 5, or sometimes to 8. G.C.66:212;73:23. Gn.76:624(h); 83:594;89:329(h). W. China. Intr. 1908. Zone VI?

25. **R. lasióstylus** Focke. Stems upright, to 2 m., with bristle-like prickles, glaucous-white: lfs. 3–5, the lateral acute, 5–10 cm. long, the terminal one much larger, acuminate, rounded or subcordate at base, often 3-lobed, unequally double-serrate, white-tomentose beneath: fls. 1–5, nodding, rather small; pedicels bristly; bracts large; petals reddish, shorter than the ovate-lanceolate cuspidate sepals: fr. subglobose, red, tomentulose. Fl.vi; fr.viii. B.M.7426(c). H.I.1951. G.C.51:167. Focke, Sp. Rub.168. G.28:631. S.L. 330(h). C. China. Intr. 1889. Zone (V). Conspicuous with its white stems; hardier than the preceding species.

26. **R. stans** Focke. Stems upright, to 1 m., with scattered slender prickles, like the brts. pilose and glandular: lfts. 3, on shoots sometimes 5, on fertile brts. sometimes 1, suborbicular to ovate or oval, 2–4 cm. long, rounded or acute at apex, broad-cuneate, the terminal one sometimes 3-lobed and rounded at base, doubly or unequally serrate, glandular-ciliate, pubescent on both sides and glandular, green beneath: fls. 1–3, 2–2.5 cm. across; calyx purplish, like the usually short pedicels villous and glandular; sepals lanceolate, longer than the obovate white or purplish petals: fr. orange, edible. Fl.vi; fr.viii–ix. Not. Bot. Gard. Edinb. 5:t.68. W. China. Intr. 1914. Zone VII?

Related species: **R. alexetèrius** Focke. Stems arching, to 2 m., glabrous, slightly bloomy, with curved prickles; lfts. elliptic to elliptic-oblong, 2.5–5 cm. long, acute to acuminate, coarsely doubly serrate, pubescent above, whitish-tomentose beneath: fls. 1–4; calyx aculeate: fr. yellow, large, edible. Focke, Sp. Rub. 265. W. China. Intr. 1914 or 1906. Zone VII?—**R. trullisàtus** Focke. Stems to 2.5, glabrous, with short prickles: lfts. ovate to ovate-lanceolate, acuminate, 4–6 cm. long, appressed crenate-serrulate, glabrous above, white-tomentose beneath: fls. usually 3: fr. subglobose, white-woolly. C. China. Intr. 1907. Zone VI?—**R. maciléntus** Cambess. Stems glabrous, with stout straight or slightly curved prickles: lvs. often simple; lfts. ovate to ovate-oblong, 1.5–5 cm. long, obtuse to acuminate, glabrous, midrib beneath and petiole prickly: fls. 1–3, white, on short brts., 1.5–2 cm. across; calyx slightly pubescent: fr. orange. Jacquemont, Voy. 4:t.60. Himal., W. China. Intr. 1908. Zone VII?

27. **R. thibetànus** Franch. Stems upright, with straight slender prickles: lfts. 7–13, incisely serrate, silky above, white or grayish-tomentose beneath, lateral lfts. elliptic to oblong, cuneate, 2–5 cm. long, terminal lft. longer, lanceolate, pinnatifid below; fls. 3–8 and sometimes some solitary ones in the axils below, 1–1.5 cm. across, purple; rachis and pedicels villous: fr. subglobose, black, bloomy. Fl.vi; fr.viii. Focke, Sp. Rub. 180. G.C.51:149. (*R.*

Veitchii Rolfe.) W. China. Intr. 1904. Zone VI? Distinct and attractive shrub.

28. **R. coreànus** Miq. Stems upright or arching, to 3 m. long, angled, with stout prickles, bloomy: lfts. 5–7, ovate or elliptic, acute, broad-cuneate or rounded at base, 3–7 cm. long, unequally and sharply serrate, pubescent on the veins beneath or white-tomentose; petiole and rachis prickly: fls. rather small, in corymbs 3–7 cm. across; petals pink, shorter than the ovate-lanceolate pubescent sepals: fr. small, red or black. Fl.v–vi; fr.vii–viii. N.K. 7:t.29. G.C.51:149. Korea, Japan, China. Cult. 1906. Zone V?

Related species: **R. níveus** Thunb. Stems to 2 m., terete, tomentulose when young or glabrous and bloomy, with hooked prickles: lfts. 5–7, usually elliptic or elliptic-ovate, 3–6 cm. long, acute or acuminate, broad-cuneate, the terminal usually ovate and rounded at base, usually simply and rather coarsely serrate, white-tomentose beneath: fls. small, rosy-purple, in terminal paniculate, many-fld. corymbs; pedicels and calyx white-tomentose: fr. dark red, becoming black. (*R. lasiocarpus* Sm.) India, W. China. Cult. 1934. Zone VII?—**R. inopértus** Focke. Lfts. 7–9, ovate to oblong-ovate, usually long-acuminate, glabrous or slightly pubescent: fls. in dense fascicles; calyx glabrous: fr. red. C. & W. China. Intr. 1908.—**R. Wilsònii** Duthie. Stems very prickly, the angles below the nodes nearly winged: lfts. 3–5, coarsely double-serrate, glabrous, terminal lft. broad-ovate, rounded or subcordate at base: fls. purple, in axillary fascicles and a dense terminal panicle; calyx purple-brown outside. C. China. Intr. 1901.

29. **R. parvifòlius** L. Stems rather low, arching, short-villous, prickly: lfts. 3, on shoots occasionally 5, usually broadly obovate or suborbicular, obtusish, rarely ovate and acute, lateral lfts. often elliptic, 2–5 cm. long, unequally dentate, terminal lft. often lobulate, strigose-pilose above, white-tomentose beneath: fls. rather small, in prickly and pubescent small corymbs or short racemes, partly axillary; calyx green outside; sepals spreading, later recurved; petals upright, pink or purplish: fr. roundish, red, edible. Fl.vi; fr.vii–viii. B.R.496(c). N.K.7:t.31. (*R. triphyllos* Thunb.) China, Japan. Intr. 1818. Zone V.

Related species: **R. telédapos** Focke. Lfts. usually ovate or oblong-ovate, acuminate, terminal lft. often nearly 3-lobed: infl. elongated: fr. dark red. W. China. Intr. 1908.

30. **R. grácilis** Roxb. Stems stout, erect, to 5 m. tall, sometimes sarmentose, densely velvety when young, with few minute prickles: lfts. 3–5, coarsely double-serrate, strigose-pilose above at first, later glabrescent, white-tomentose beneath, terminal lft. broad-ovate to oblong-ovate, acuminate, rounded or subcordate, 8–12 cm. long, lateral lfts. much smaller, obliquely ovate, nearly sessile: fls. white or pale pink, 1–1.5 cm. across, in few-fld. corymbs; petals obovate, shorter than the lanceolate sepals: fr. blue-black, small. Fl.vi–vii. (*R. niveus* Wall., not Thunb., *R. euleucus* Focke.) Himal., China. Intr. 1901 from China. Zone VII? The most robust of all Rubus.

31. **R. phoenicolàsius** Maxim. Stems upright, to 3 m. high, densely covered with reddish gland-tipped bristles and a few slender prickles: lfts. 3, rarely 5, broad-ovate, acuminate, 4–10 cm. long, coarsely and unequally mucronate-serrate, slightly pilose above, white-tomentose beneath: fls. in densely pilose and glandular short racemes and partly axillary; petals pink, shorter than the pilose sepals: fr. semiglobose, red, small, acid or insipid, with enlarged spreading bristly calyx Fl.vi–vii. B.M.6479(c). G.C.III.11:269; 28:137. Gt.52:564. N.K.7:t.28. Gng.3:263. Korea, Japan, N. China; occasionally escaped in E. U. S. Intr. 1876. Zone V. Handsome shrub conspicuous on account of the dense bristly pubescence of its stems.

R. p. × *idaeus* = **R. Páxii** Focke. Lfts. often 5, narrower, acute, less deeply serrate. Cult. 1906.

32. **R. flosculòsus** Focke. Stems usually arching, to 3 m. long, with few prickles, puberulous or glabrous, usually purplish brown, often bloomy: lfts. 5–7, usually ovate-oblong, acuminate, 3–5 cm. long, subequally serrate, terminal lft. often rhombic-lanceolate, to 7 cm. long and doubly serrate above the middle, white-tomentose beneath: fls. small, pink, 6–8 mm. across, in narrow panicles 5–10 cm. long; calyx tomentose; petals slightly longer than sepals: fr. small, dark red or black. Fl.vi; fr.viii. Focke, Sp. Rub. 193. C. China. Intr. 1907. Zone V–VI. With slender arching stems rooting at the tips in autumn.—**R. f. parvifòlius** Focke, f. Lfts. 1–2 cm. long.

33. **R. Cockburniànus** Hemsl. Stems upright, to 3 m. long, branching and curving above, white-glaucous, sparingly prickly: lfts. 7–9, oblong-lanceolate, unequally coarsely serrate, white-tomentose beneath, terminal lft. rhombic or ovate-lanceolate, often lobulate, acuminate; petiole and rachis prickly: fls. small, rose-purple, in terminal panicles 10–12 cm. long: fr. black. Fl.vi; fr.viii–ix. Focke, Sp. Rub. 194. G.C.51:147;65:248(h). Gn.76:624(h). J.L. 40:218(h). (*R. Giraldianus* Focke.) N. and C. China. Intr. 1907. Zone V. Conspicuous with its white stems.

34. **R. innominàtus** S. Moore. Stems upright, to 3 m., densely glandular-villous and prickly: lfts. 3–5, irregularly coarsely serrate, slightly pilose above, grayish white-tomentose beneath; lateral lfts. obliquely oblong-ovate, rounded at base, 5–10 cm. long, terminal lft. ovate, acuminate, subcordate, larger; petiole villous and prickly: fls. pink, about 1 cm. across, in glandular-villous racemes or panicles 10–35 cm. long: fr. orange-red, about 1.5 cm. wide, edible. Fl.vii–viii; fr.ix. G.C.38:290. R.B.33:360(h). S. E. and W. China. Intr. 1901. Zone VI? Remarkable for its large infl.; may be valuable for its fr.—**R. i. Kuntzeànus** (Hemsl.) Bailey, var. Stems and infl. glandless. S.L. 332(h). (*R. K.* Hemsl.) C. China. Cult. 1887.

35. **R. adenóphorus** Rolfe. Stems upright, to 3 m., stout, densely villous and stipitate-glandular like the petioles, with stout broad-based prickles: lfts. 3, often 5 on shoots, ovate, acuminate, rounded at base, 5–12 cm. long, the terminal lft. subcordate, doubly serrate, dull and pubescent above, more densely pubescent and grayish green beneath: fls. pink, small, in villous and stipitate-glandular panicles 10–12 cm. long: fr. black, edible. Fl.vii; fr.viii. Focke Sp. Rub. 197. (*R. sagatus* Focke.) C. China. Intr. 1907. Zone VI? Remarkable for its conspicuous glandular pubescence on stem and infl.

36. **R. occidentàlis** L. Stems to 3 m., very glaucous and often purplish, with short prickles: lfts. 3, sometimes 5 on shoots, ovate, abruptly acuminate, rounded or cordate at base, 5–8 cm. long, doubly serrate, white-tomentose beneath; petiole sparingly prickly: fls. white, 1–1.5 cm. across, in tomentose and prickly few-fld. corymbs; petals elliptic, shorter than the ovate-lanceolate sepals: fr. hemispherical, purple-black, bloomy. Fl.v–vi; fr.vii–viii. B.B.2: 277. B.C.5:f.3495,3496. Jour. Hered. 11:178. N. B. to Minn. and s. to Ga. and Colo. Cult. 1696. Zone III. Sometimes cult. in several vars. for its fr.— **R. o. pállidus** Bailey, var. Fr. amber-yellow. Gt.19:t.670(c).

R. o. × *idaeus* var. *strigosus* = R. negléctus Peck. Similar to the preceding, but petioles and infl. more or less glandular-hispid. B.B.2:277. B.C.5:f.3494. Occurs naturally; sometimes cult. with purple to yellow fr., e.g. "Royal," "Columbia Purple Raspberry" (Jour. Hered. 11:182).

37. **R. leucodérmis** Torr. & Gr. Stems upright, to 2 m., glaucous, armed with flattened recurved prickles: lfts. 3, on shoots often 5, coarsely double-serrate, white-tomentose beneath, terminal lft. broad-ovate, acute, often subcordate, 6–10 cm. long, lateral lfts. narrower, rounded at base; petiole and midrib beneath prickly: fls. white, in few-fld. tomentose and prickly corymbs;

petals shorter than the lanceolate sepals: fr. hemispheric, purple-black, bloomy, edible. Fl.v–vi. Card, Bush Fr. f.59. S.H.1:f.307n. M.G.16:429(h). (*R. occidentalis* var. *l.* Focke.) B. C. to Mont., Utah and C. Cal. Intr. 1829. Zone V. Horticultural varieties are grown for their fr.

38. **R. idaèus** L. Stems upright, to 2 m., finely tomentose when young and sometimes with a few prickles broad at base: lfts. 3, on shoots usually 5, coarsely double-serrate, finely pubescent or glabrescent above, white-tomentose beneath, terminal lft. broad-ovate, short-acuminate, often subcordate, 5–10 cm. long, lateral lfts. smaller, rounded at base; fls. white, small, in tomentose glandless and usually slightly prickly short racemes, usually with smaller axillary infl. beneath; petals shorter than the long-acuminate sepals: fr. red. Fl.v–vi; fr.vii–viii. S.E.3:t.442(c). F.D.25:t.2575(c). Circumpolar. Zone III. Very variable species, of which the following varieties are cult.— **R. i. vulgàtus** Arrhen., var. The typical form described above with the infl. without glands or bristles: fr. thimble-shaped. Eu., rare in N. Am. Much cult. in various horticultural forms and often escaped from cult.—**R. i. aculeatíssimus** Reg. & Tiling, var. Young stems glabrous and often glaucous, bristly and usually with strong prickles broad at base. Ill. Monatsh. Gartenb. 1894: t.(c). (*R. melanolasius* Focke, *R. i.* var. *m.* Focke.) B. C. to Mich., s. to Ore. and Colo., also in E. Asia. Intr. before 1894.—**R. i. strigòsus** (Michx.) Maxim., var. Young shoots glabrous and often glaucous, densely bristly and often glandular, with or without bristle-like prickles: infl. glandular and prickly: fr. hemispherical. B.B.2:277. Card, Bush Fr. f.58. (*R. s.* Michx.) Nfd. to B. C., s. to Va. and Wyo.; also in E. Asia. Some horticultural forms cult. for their fr.—**R. i. álbus** (Bailey) Fern., f. Form of the preceding var. with amber-white fr. (*R. strigosus* var. *a.* Bailey.)—**R. i. tónsus** Fern., f. A form with smooth not bristly shoots. Que. to Vt.—**R. i. canadénsis** Richards., var. Young shoots cinereous-tomentulose, with bristle-like prickles. (*R. subarcticus* Rydb., *R. carolinianus* Rydb.) Lab. to Alaska, s. to N. C. and Colo., also in E. Asia.

R. i. × *odoratus* = R. nòbilis Reg. Resembles in habit and fl. *R. odoratus*, but the lvs. are 3-foliolate, large, pubescent on both surfaces. Orig. about 1855. —*R. i.* × *phoenicolasius;* see under No. 31.—*R. i.* × *occidentalis;* see under No. 36.—*R. i.* × *? ursinus;* see under No. 40.—A hybrid with an unknown English Blackberry is shown in G.C.III.22:236. B.C.5:3021.

39. **R. mesogaèus** Focke. Stems long and slender, terete, densely tomentose, with small prickles: lfts. 3, unequally coarsely serrate, lobulate, pubescent above at first, finally glabrescent, grayish or whitish tomentose beneath, terminal lft. elliptic or rhombic-ovate, acuminate, rounded or subcordate, 5–8 or on shoots to 16 cm. long, lateral lfts. smaller, obliquely elliptic, very short-stalked; petioles 2–4 cm. long, prickly; stipules on shoots dissected: fls. white or pinkish, small, in rather loose or sometimes compact corymbs; petals obovate, 6–8 mm. long; sepals lanceolate: fr. small, globose, black. Fl.v–vi; fr.viii. Focke, Sp. Rub. 205. C. China. Intr. 1907. Zone VI.

Subgen. V. Eubatus Focke. Stems usually angled, rarely terete, prickly, usually biennial: lvs. ternate, or digitately 5-foliolate, rarely 7-foliolate (pinnate in No. 40); stipules adnate to petiole; petals always present; fr. falling off together with the torus, usually black or dark purple. Blackberries.

40. **R. ursìnus** Cham. & Schlecht. "Californian Dewberry." Evergreen; stems trailing, sometimes upright, pubescent when young, with straight prickles: lfts. 3 or sometimes 5, the upper ones simple; lfts. broad-ovate, acute, rounded at base, 3–6 cm. long, coarsely double-serrate, pubescent above, villous or white-tomentose beneath: fls. dioecious, white, in tomentose

Brainerd & Peitersen, t.10. B.C.ed.1,4;f.2208. (*R. Andrewsianus* Blanch., *R. argutus* auth., not Link.) N. S. to N. C., Kans. and Mich. Cult. 1822. Zone III.

Related species: **R. pergràtus** Blanch. Stems recurving, with smaller prickles: lfts. often oblong-ovate: infl. not prickly. Brainerd & Peitersen, Blackberr. N. Eng. t.11. (*R. amnicolus* Blanch.) N. Eng.—**R. laudàtus** Berger. Stems upright, moderately prickly: lfts. ovate to oblong-ovate: infl. not prickly, with large simple lvs., lower pedicels long and spreading. Bailey, Gent. Herb. 3:266. Mo., Kans. Here belongs "Bundy" and "Early Harvest."

47. **R. frondòsus** Bigel. Stems erect or recurved, glabrous, with rather stout straight or slightly recurved prickles: lfts. usually 5, thickish, sharply double-serrate, abruptly acuminate, sparingly hairy or nearly glabrous above, soft-pubescent beneath, terminal lft. suborbicular, cordate, 8–14 cm. long, its stalk 3–5 cm. long, lateral lfts. smaller, broad-elliptic, rounded or broadly cuneate at base, their stalk 1 cm. or less: flowering brts. villous: lfts. usually 3, elliptic or obovate, 3–7 cm. long: fls. white, in leafy villous and eglandular corymbs; petals broadly oval or suborbicular, about 1 cm. long, sepals broad-ovate, short-acuminate: fr. black, 1.5 cm. long, glabrous. Fl.vi; fr. vii–viii. B.B.2:279. Brainerd & Peitersen, Blackberr. N. Eng. t.12. Ont. to Va., Kans. and Iowa. Zone IV.—Several horticultural vars. belong here.

Related species: **R. flòridus** Tratt.; it differs chiefly in the flattened strongly curved prickles of the stem, in the narrower generally oblong-ovate lfts. of the shoots, glabrescent at maturity. Bailey, Evol. Nat. Fr. f.90,91. S.H.1:f.310g-g[1]. (*R. argutus* var. *f*. Bailey.) S. E. Va. to Mo., Tex. and Fla.

48. **R. canadénsis** L. Stems upright, recurving, to 4 m. long, grooved and round-angled, finely puberulous at first, purplish, with few weak prickles or without: lfts. on shoots usually 5, thin, glabrous or pubescent on the veins beneath, ovate, or obovate, abruptly long-acuminate, rounded or subcordate, sharply serrate, terminal lft. 7–15 cm. long, on a stalk 2–8 cm. long, outer lfts. nearly sessile; petiole 5–10 cm. long, glabrous, unarmed; lfts. on brts. usually 3, acute: fls. white, in villous or hairy leafy racemes 8–15 cm. long; sepals ovate, short-acuminate; petals obovate, 1–1.5 cm. long: fr. roundish, black, sour. Fl.vi; fr.vii. B.M.8264(c). B.B.2:279. Gn.84:338(h). (*R. Millspaughii* Britt.) Nfd. to N. C. and Mich. Cult. 1727. Zone II.

49. **R. triviàlis** Michx. Southern Dewberry. Half-evergreen; stems prostrate and trailing, hispid and with small slightly flattened prickles: lfts. 3–5, narrow-ovate to oblanceolate, acute, rounded at base, sharply serrate, 2–6 cm. long, glabrous, dark green and lustrous above; petiole and petiolules and often the midrib beneath with recurved prickles; lfts. of brts. smaller, more elliptic and obtuse: fls. usually solitary; peduncles 2–5 cm. long, tomentulose and prickly; petals obovate, 1–1.5 cm. long: fr. usually oblong, 1–1.5 cm. long, glabrous. Fl.iv–v; fr.vi. G.O.t.71(c). B.B.2:281. Card, Bush Fr. f.63. (*R. continentalis* Bailey.) Va. to Fla., Tex. and Okl. Cult. 1825. Zone VI? Sometimes cult. south for its fr.

50. **R. híspidus** L. Swamp Dewberry. Half-evergreen; stems prostrate, to 1.5 m. long, densely reflexed-bristly: lfts. 3, rarely 5, firm, coarsely and doubly serrate, glabrous, dark green above, middle lft. rhombic-ovate, acute or short-acuminate, broad-cuneate, 3–6 cm. long, short-stalked, lateral lfts. oblique, broad-ovate, nearly sessile; lfts. of brts. usually rounded at apex: fls. white, in tomentulose and bristly or unarmed few-fld. corymbs; petals obovate, 8 mm. long: fr. purple, with few glabrous druplets. Fl.vi–vii; fr. viii. B.B.2:281. B.C.5:3033. Brainerd & Peitersen, Blackberr. N. Eng. t.18. (*R. obovalis* Michx., *R. sempervirens* Bigel.—Running Blackberry.) N. S. to Ga., Mich. and Minn. Zone III. Sometimes used as a ground-cover.

Closely related species: **R. setòsus** Bigel. Stems at first erect, later reclining or decumbent: lfts. narrower, not evergreen: fls. smaller, in elongated glandular-hispid racemes: fr. red. Brainerd & Peitersen, Blackberr. N. Eng t.17. Mass. to Conn. and N. Y.

51. R. flagellàris Willd. NORTHERN DEWBERRY. Stems prostrate, to 2 m. long, glabrous, with scattered weak recurved prickles: lfts. on shoots 3–5, abruptly acuminate, rounded or broad-cuneate, 4–10 cm. long, coarsely double-serrate, sparingly hairy above, pubescent on veins beneath, terminal lft. broad-ovate or rhombic-ovate, on a stalk 1–2 cm. long; lateral lfts. ovate, subsessile: petiole 3–5 cm. long, like midrib beneath prickly; floral brts. sparingly villous, their lfts. obovate to oblanceolate, 3–5 cm. long, acute at ends: fls. solitary or rarely in 2–4-fld. cymes; pedicels sparingly villous; sepals ovate, acuminate, sparingly villous outside; petals elliptic-obovate, 1–1.5 cm. long: fr. hemispheric to thimble-shaped, 1–1.5 cm. long, black, glabrous. Fl. v–vi; fr.vii–viii. B.B.2:281. B.C.5:f.3501,3502. (*R. procumbens* Muhl., *R. trivialis* Pursh in part, not Michx., *R. canadensis* Torr. & Gr., not L., *R. villosus* Bailey, not Ait., nor Thunb.) Me. to Minn., Mo. and Va. Cult. 1809. Zone III. Some forms are cult. for their fr.—Here belongs "LUCRETIA DEWBERRY" (*R. fl.* var. *roribáccus* Bailey) with rather large fr. A.G.11:641,t. Bailey, Gent. Herb. 1:160.—**R. f. almus** Bailey, var. Spineless form. Bailey, Gent. Herb. 2:319.

Related species: **R. vèlox** Bailey. Robust plant with arching and prostrate angled stems armed with broad-based stout curved prickles: lfts. soft-pubescent beneath, the terminal one long-stalked: fls. solitary or in a forked cyme: fr. oblong, 2.5–3 cm. long. Bailey, Gent. Herb. 1:168,169. ? Tex. Several forms cult. for the fr.—**R. plicatifòlius** Blanch. Stems terete, with small prickles: lvs. of shoots nearly all 5-foliolate; lfts. large, with impressed veins, as if plaited: infl. cymose. (? *R. villosus* Ait., not Thunb.) N. E. States.

52. R. caèsius L. EUROPEAN DEWBERRY. Prostrate shrub; stems at first upright, soon procumbent and sometimes climbing, terete, glabrous or rarely slightly puberulous, pruinose, with scattered weak prickles: lfts. 3, rarely 5, coarsely and often incisely serrate, on both sides sparingly hairy, middle lft. rhombic-ovate or ovate, sometimes 3-lobed, subcordate, 3–7 cm. long, lateral lfts. nearly sessile, often 2-lobed; petioles pubescent, prickly; stipules dilated below the middle, lanceolate or linear-lanceolate above; fls. white, 3 cm. across, in few-fld. pubescent glandular and prickly corymbs; calyx pubescent often glandular; sepals ovate-lanceolate; petals broad-elliptic: fr. of few large drupelets, black, bloomy. Fl.vii–viii; fr.ix. S.E.3:t.456(c). F.D.t.2576(c). Sudre, Rub. Eur. t.207. Eu., in N. Asia to Altai Mts. Zone III.—**R. c. turkestànicus** Reg., var. Young stems slightly pruinose: terminal lft. often 3-fid: petals narrow-oblong: fr. oblong-cylindric, with numerous drupelets. Gt.41:107. Turkest. Cult. 1890.

Related species: **R. nemoròsus** Hayne. Stems slender, often to 8 m. long, pruinose, below rather thickly beset with small somewhat curved prickles: lfts. usually broad-ovate, irregularly serrate, bronzy in autumn, pubescent beneath: fls. small, corymbose; calyx grayish tomentose. F.D.25:t.2577(c). H.A.3:t.10 (c). Cauc., Eu. Cult. 1925. Zone V. Sometimes planted as ground cover.

35. POTENTÍLLA L. CINQUEFOIL. Herbs or small deciduous shrubs; buds with few scales: lvs. compound; stipules adnate to the petiole and sheathing: fls. in terminal cymes or solitary, white, yellow or red; sepals 5, with 5 alternate bracts at base; petals usually orbicular; stamens 10–30; pistils many, on a low conical receptacle, becoming small dry achenes; style deciduous. (Latin *potens,* powerful; referring to the medicinal properties of some species.) More than 300 species throughout the n. temperate and frigid zones; few of them woody.

A. Lfts. 3–7, entire: styles short, thickened upwards: much branched shrub....1. *P. fruticosa*
AA. Lfts. 5–9, serrate; styles slenderer, not thickened: sparingly branched, suffruticose.
2. *P. Salesoviana*

1. **P. fruticòsa** L. Low shrub, to 1.5 m., bark shreddy: lvs. pinnate; lfts. 3–7, usually 5, sessile, elliptic to linear-oblong, acute, 1–2.5 cm. long, with revolute margin, more or less silky: fls. usually bright yellow, 2–3 cm. across, solitary or few on slender stalks; sepals triangular-ovate, bracts usually linear. Fl.v–viii. N.K.7:t.35. S.E.3:t.436(c). B.B.2:262. (*Dasiphora f.* Raf.) N. hemisphere. Cult. 1700. Zone II.—Low rather dense shrub with conspicuous yellow or white fls. in early summer and sparingly until Sept. Very variable.—VARS. WITH BRIGHT YELLOW FLS.: **P. f. Fárreri** Besant, var. Spreading low shrub: lfts. oblanceolate to obovate-oblong, 6–10 mm. long, obtusish, dark green above, glaucescent and thinly silky, later glabrescent beneath: fls. about 2 cm. across. H.B.14:349. N. W. China. Intr. 1916.—**P. f. grandiflòra** Willd., var. Upright: lvs. larger, green, slightly pubescent: fls. 3–3.5 cm. across.—**P. f. micrándra** (Koehne) Schneid., var. Of lower spreading habit: lvs. rather broad: fls. rather small; stamens shorter than pistils. S.H.1:f. 313i-l. Intr. before 1890.—**P. f. tenuíloba** Ser., var. Lfts. narrow, often nearly linear, more pubescent. (*P. f.* var. *tenuifolia* Lehm.)—**P. f. pyrenáica** Willd., var. Dwarf alpine form of dense habit; lfts. small, lanceolate. (*P. prostrata* Lap.)—**P. f. parvifòlia** (Lehm.) Th. Wolf, var. Dwarf: lfts. usually 7, the 4 lower ones whorled, elliptic-oblong, 3–8 mm. long, glabrescent; fls. sometimes pale yellow. S.H.1:f.313n(1). (*P. p.* Lehm., *P. f.* var. *humilis* Spaeth.) C. Asia.—**P. f. pùmila** Hook. f., var. Dwarf: lfts. small, usually 5, densely silky-pubescent. (*P. lanuginosa* Hort. Vilm.) Intr. before 1910. C. Asia.— **P. f. rígida** (Lehm.) Th. Wolf, var. Low, upright: lfts. 3, elliptic-oblong, silky above, glabrous beneath: sepals subequal, the outer often 2-parted. Lehm., Rev. Potent. t.1. Himal. Intr. 1906.—**P. f. álbicans** Rehd. & Wils., var. Lfts. elliptic-oblong, pubescent and dull green above, white-tomentose beneath. W. China. Intr. 1909. Handsome form.—VARS. WITH PALE YELLOW OR CREAMY WHITE FLS.: **P. f. Friedrichsénii** (Spaeth) Rehd., var. Lfts. rather large, pubescent, glaucous beneath: fls. light yellow. (*P. F.* Spaeth.) Hybrid between the type and var. *dahurica*. Orig. 1895.—-**P. f. ochroleùca** (Spaeth) Bean, var. Lfts. nearly green beneath: fls. creamy white: seedling of the preceding var. (*P. Friedrichsenii* var. *o.* Spaeth.) Orig. before 1909.—**P. f. Purdómii** Rehd., var. Lfts. 7–10 mm. long, acute, glaucous and glabrous beneath except midrib: fls. pale yellow. N. China. Intr. 1911.—**P. f. Vilmorinìana** Komar., var. Lfts. pubescent above, white-tomentose beneath: fls. creamy white. R.H.1910:57. W. China. Intr. 1905.—VARS. WITH PURE WHITE FLS.: **P. f. Veitchii** (Wils.) Bean, var. Shrub to 1.5 m. Lfts. pubescent, glaucous beneath, 1–2 cm. long: calyx-bracts broader than the sepals. B.M.8637(c). B.S.2:222. G.C.83:79(h). J.L.40:222(h). (*P. V.* Wils., *P. davurica* var. *V.* Jesson.) C. and W. China. Intr. 1902. Very handsome.—**P. f. Beànii** Rehd., var. Lfts. pubescent: fls. with narrow calyx-bracts: seedling of var. *Friedrichsenii*. (*P. Friedrichsenii* var. *leucantha* Spaeth, **P. f.** var. *l.* Bean, not Mak.) Orig. before 1910.—**P. f. dahùrica** (Nestl.) Ser., var. Dwarf compact shrub, less than 0.5 m. high: lfts. about 1 cm. long, nearly glabrous, glaucous beneath; the lustrous brown stipules with a conspicuous tuft of hairs at apex: fls. usually solitary, 2–3 cm. across, with broad calyx-bracts. L.B.914(c). (*P. davurica* Nestl.) N. China, Siber. Intr. 1822.—**P. f. mandshùrica** Maxim., var. Low shrub: lfts. small, densely whitish silky-pubescent on both sides. G.C.76:233. M.G.34:233,234(h). (*P. davurica* var. *m.* Th. Wolf, *P. f.* var. *leucantha* Mak.) Manch. Cult. 1911.

Related species: **P. tridentàta** Ait. Stems slender, to 25 cm. high, woody at base: lfts. 3, oblanceolate, 1–5 cm. long, 3-toothed at apex, nearly glabrous, coriaceous: fls. white, several; receptacle and achenes hairy. B.B.2:262. Lab. to mts. of Tenn., w. to Man. Cult. 1789. Zone II.

2. **P. Salesoviàna** Steph. Suffruticose, 0.5–1 m. tall, little branched; stipules large, broadly scarious: lfts. 7–9, rarely 5, short-stalked, oblong, 2–3.5 cm. long, coarsely serrate, glabrous and dark green above, white-tomentose beneath: fls. white, rosy-tinted, 3 cm. across, in 3–7-fld. cymes; sepals lanceolate, as long as petals; bracts linear, half as long. Fl.vi–viii. B.M.7558(c). (*Comarum Salessowii* Bge.) Siberia. Intr. 1823. Zone III.

The closely related **P. palústris** Scop. with smaller purple fls. can hardly be considered suffruticose.

36. **FALLÙGIA** Endl. Deciduous shrub: lvs. alternate, partly fascicled, 3–7-lobed, petioled, stipulate: fls. terminal, perfect or polygamous, white; calyx-tube cupular; sepals 5, ovate, imbricate, with 5 alternate, narrow bracts at base; petals 5, suborbicular, spreading; stamens numerous; pistils many on a conical torus, pubescent; style slender; achenes with long persistent plumose style. (After Virgilio Fallugi or Falugi, an Italian botanical writer, end of XVIIth century.) One species in s.w. N. Am.

F. paradóxa Endl. Upright shrub to 1.5 m.; brts. slender, grayish white-tomentulose: lvs. cuneate, with 3–7 narrow-oblong lobes decurrent into the linear petiole, 8–15 mm. long, revolute, white-tomentulose beneath: fls. 1–3, 2.5–3.5 cm. across; achenes with feathery tails, 2.5–3.5 cm. long. Fl.vi–viii. B.M.6660(c). E.N.III.3:37. M.G.15:207(h,fl). S.L.177,178(h,fl). S. Nev. and Utah to n. Mex. Intr. 1877. Zone (V). Slender shrub with conspicuous white fls. and attractive heads of feathery fr.; demands sunny position and well drained soil.

37. **COWÀNIA** Don. Evergreen shrub: lvs. alternate and partly fascicled, lobed or dentate, petioled, stipulate: fls. terminal on short brts., often polygamous, white or purple; calyx-tube cup-shaped; sepals 5; petals 5, spreading; stamens numerous; pistils 1–12; achenes with persistent plumose style. (After James Cowan, English merchant who intr. many Peruvian and Mexican plants.) About 4 species in the S. W. States and Mex.

C. Stansburiàna Torr. Much-branched shrub to 2 m., with rather short stiff pubescent brs.: lvs. 3–5-lobed, with short oblong often cleft or toothed lobes, 6–15 mm. long, with revolute margin, dark green and glandular above, white-tomentulose beneath: fls. sulphur-yellow to white, about 2 cm. across; pedicels 2–8 mm. long, stipitate-glandular; calyx-tube turbinate; achenes usually 2, 4–5 cm. long. Fl.vii–ix. Trans. Linn. Soc. 14:t.22. E.N.III.3:37. (*C. mexicana* Gray, not D. Don.) Nev. and s. Colo. to s. Calif. and n. Mex. Cult. 1904. Zone (V). Aromatic shrub with conspicuous fragrant white fls. and feathery fr.; demands sunny position and well drained soil.

38. **DRÝAS** L. Mountain-Avens. Evergreen prostrate and suffruticose plants: lvs. alternate, dentate or entire; stipules adnate to petiole: fls. solitary, slender-pediceled, white or yellowish white; calyx-tube cup-shaped; sepals 8–10, persistent; petals 8–10, oval or obovate; stamens many; pistils many, on a flat torus: achenes with persistent plumose style. (Greek, wood-nymph.) Three species in the n. hemisphere on high mountains and in arctic regions.—Tufted creeping plants with showy white fls. from June to August and feathery fr.; suited for rockeries.

A. Lvs. usually subcordate at base: fls. white; stamens shorter or as long as sepals.
1. *D. octopetala*
AA. Lvs. usually cuneate at base: fls. yellowish; stamens longer than sepals.2. *D. Drummondii*

1. **D. octopétala** L. Lvs. elliptic to oblong, usually obtuse, deeply crenate, 1–2.5 cm. long, dark green and glabrous or slightly pubescent above, white-tomentose beneath; petioles 5–15 mm. long: fls. upright, 3–4 cm. across; pedicels 3–12 cm. long, pubscent; sepals linear to linear-lanceolate: achenes with style 2.5 cm. long. Fl.v–vii; fr.vii–x. B.B.2:273. Gt.9:t.286(c). S.E. 3:t.460(c). Gn.87:292. S.L.166(h). N. Am., Eu. and Asia, in Am. s. to Utah and Colo. Cult. 1750. Zone I.—**D. o. asiàtica** Nakai, var. Lvs. broad-elliptic to elliptic. N.K.7:t.17. E. Asia. Intr. ?—**D. o. integrifòlia** (Vahl) Hook. f., var. Lvs. oblong to oblong-lanceolate, entire or with one or two teeth at base, revolute: fls. slightly smaller. H.E.3:220(c). B.B.2:274. (*D. i.* Vahl.) N. Eu., Arct. Am. Intr. 1824.—*D. o. lanata* (Stein) Schneid., f., is scarcely different from the type.

    D. o. × *Drummondii* = **D. Suendermánnii** Sünderm. Fls. slightly nodding, yellow in bud, finally white. Gn.M.38:25(h). Orig. before 1920.

2. **D. Drummóndii** Hook. Similar to the preceding: lvs. usually oblong, crenate-dentate, to 3 cm.; petioles longer: fls. nodding, campanulate; pedicels often longer, floccose-pubescent; sepals ovate to ovate-lanceolate, glandular-pubescent: achenes with style to 4 cm. long. B.M.2972(c). B.B.2:274. (*D. octopetala* var. *D.* S. Wats.) Arct. Am. s. to Lab., Que. and Mont. Cult. 1830.

    D. tomentòsa Farr with obovate or elliptic lvs. tomentose on both sides, with tomentose not glandular sepals and yellow fls. from the Can. Rockies is probably not in cult.

39. **CERCOCÁRPUS** Kunth. MOUNTAIN-MAHOGANY. Evergreen or half-evergreen shrubs or small trees with hard and heavy wood; buds with several scales, pubescent: lvs. alternate, mostly fascicled, short-petioled, entire or dentate; stipules adnate to petiole, lanceolate, deciduous: fls. perfect, apetalous, small, greenish white or reddish, 1–10 in the axils of fascicled lvs.; calyx-tube cylindric, elongated, abruptly expanded into a cup-shaped 5-lobed deciduous limb, bearing 15–30 stamens with short filaments; ovary 1-celled, enclosed in the calyx-tube; style exserted: fr. a 1-seeded achene wholly or partly enclosed in the calyx-tube, with long plumose style. (Greek *kerkos*, tail, and *karpos*, fruit; referring to the long plumose style of the fr.) About 20 species or perhaps less in w. N. Am. from Ore. to s. Mex.—Grown occasionally in collections; attractive in autumn with their feathery tailed fr.; they demand well-drained soil and sunny position.

A. Lvs. dentate, usually obovate, chartaceous.
  B. Lvs. grayish or green beneath.
    c. Lvs. glabrous above at maturity and glabrescent beneath............1. *C. betuloides*
    cc. Lvs. pubescent above and tomentulose beneath......................2. *C. montanus*
  BB. Lvs. white-tomentose beneath..3. *C. argenteus*
AA. Lvs. entire, lanceolate, coriaceous, revolute................................4. *C. ledifolius*

1. **C. betuloìdes** Nutt. Shrub or tree to 10 m.; bark scaly; brts. glabrous or nearly so; lvs. obovate, 1.5–5 cm. long, crenate-serrate above the middle and rounded at apex, sparingly hairy when young, dark green above, paler beneath, with 5–6 pairs of veins: calyx-tube silky-strigose, 8–10 mm. long, sepals obtuse; style in fr. 6–7 cm. long. Fl.v; fr.ix. H.I.322. B.T.f.369. S.H.1:f.318f. W.G.4:554,555. (*C. betulifolius* Nutt., *C. parvifolius* var. *b.* Sarg.) C. and S. Calif. Intr. 1877? Zone VII?

2. **C. montànus** Raf. Shrub to 2 m.; bark persistent, fissured; brts. sparingly pilose when young: lvs. broad-obovate, 2–5 cm. long, rounded at apex, coarsely serrate with ovate teeth, pilose above, finely tomentulose and paler beneath, with 5–6 pairs of veins; petioles 3–6 mm. long: calyx-tube about 1 cm. long, pilose; sepals acute: style in fr. 6–8 cm. long. Fl.v–vi; fr.viii–ix.

B.B.2:274. S.L.122(h). N.V.12:67,70(h). (*C. parvifolius* Nutt.) Mont. and S. Dak. to Utah, N. Mex. and Kans. Cult. 1913. Zone V.

Closely related species: **C. Douglàsii** Rydb. Tree to 5 m.: lvs. oblong-obovate, dentate above the middle, with very short teeth, at maturity glabrate above, grayish tomentose beneath; petiole 5–10 mm. long: calyx-tube villous-tomentose. H.I.323. S.S.4:t.166. S.H.1:f.316a-e,318d-e(as *C. betulaefolius*). (*C. parvifolius* Nutt., in part.) S. Ore. to Calif. Intr. 1872. Zone VI?

3. **C. argénteus** Rydb. Shrub to 3 m.; young brts. white-villous: lvs. obovate to oblanceolate, 2–4 cm. long, crenate-dentate from the middle, with obtuse teeth, pilose above, white-tomentose beneath, with 4–5 pairs of veins; petioles 2–5 mm. long; calyx-tube silky: styles in fr. 6–7 cm. long. Fl.v; fr. VIII. Colo., N. Mex., and Tex. Intr. 1916. Zone VI?

4. **C. ledifolius** Nutt. Tree to 12 m., with furrowed bark; brts. pubescent at first: lvs. narrow-lanceolate to elliptic-lanceolate, 1–3 cm. long, lustrous and glabrate above at maturity, resinous and tomentulose beneath, with obscure veins; petioles 3–5 mm. long: calyx-tube white-villous; sepals acute, tomentose on both sides: style in fr. 5–7 cm. long. Fl.v–vi; fr.viii. H.I.324. S.S.4:t.165. N.S.2:t.51(c). Wash. and Mont. to Calif. and Ariz. Intr. about 1879.

40. **PÚRSHIA** DC. Deciduous shrub; buds small, scaly: lvs. alternate, partly fascicled, cuneate, 3-lobed; stipules small: fls. perfect, yellowish, solitary and subsessile at end of short brts.; calyx-tube tubular; sepals 5, elliptic to oblong; petals 5, spatulate; stamens about 25; pistil 1, rarely 2; style short, persistent: fr. a pubescent fusiform achene, exceeding the persistent calyx. (After F. T. Pursh or Pursch; 1774–1820; born in Germany; traveled in N. Am. and wrote Flora Americae septentrionalis.) Syn.: *Kunzia* Spreng. One species.

P. tridentàta DC. Spreading shrub to 3 m.; young brts. pubescent: lvs. obovate, gradually narrowed at base, 5–30 mm. long, 3-lobed at apex with obtuse lobes, revolute, slightly pubescent or glabrate above, whitish tomentulose beneath: fls. 8 mm. across; calyx villous and glandular: fr. about 1 cm. long, pubescent. Fl.v; fr.viii. B.R.1446(c). Hooker, Fl. Bor. Am. t.58. S.H. 1:f.315l-p,f.317a. S.L.283(h). Ore. and Calif. to Wyo. and N. Mex. Intr. 1826. Zone V. Distinct and interesting shrub.

Here may be mentioned **Coleógyne** Torr. of doubtful affinity, but usually placed near Purshia, though very distinct from it and all related genera on account of the opposite lvs. and brts. and the urceolate disk enclosing the carpel and most of the twisted style. **C. ramosíssima** Torr. is a small spinescent shrub: lvs. crowded, linear-clavate, 5–15 mm. long, with 4 grooves beneath: fls. solitary, apetalous, with 4 sepals and many stamens. Torrey, Pl. Fremont. t.4. S.H.1:f. 316p-v. S. Colo. to Ariz. and s. Calif. Intr. ? Zone VII?

41. **CHAMAEBÁTIA** Benth. Half-evergreen glandular-pubescent shrub: lvs. alternate, 3-pinnatifid, stipulate: fls. white, in terminal corymbs; calyx-tube broad-campanulate; sepals lanceolate; petals 5, obovate; stamens numerous; pistil 1, with short style and decurrent stigma: fr. a small obovoid achene, enclosed by the persistent calyx. (Greek *chamaibatos*, a kind of bramble; alluding to the bramble-like fls.) Two species in Calif. and L. Calif.

C. foliolòsa Benth. Shrub to 1 m.: lvs. nearly sessile, oval or ovate-oblong in outline, 3–7 cm. long, closely 3-pinnately dissected, ultimate segments 0.5–1 mm. long, villous and glandular: fls. 1.5–2 cm. across, in 4–8-fld. corymbs; pedicels 5–20 mm. long. Fl.vii. B.M.5171(c). E.N.III.3:f.18e-g. S.H.1:f.317 g-n. Gn.3:27. Calif. Cult. 1860. Zone VII? Shrub with finely divided aromatic lvs. and white fls.; suited for sunny rockeries.

Sect. 3. CANINAE

Lfts. more or less glandular beneath or often doubly serrate with gland-tipped teeth.
A. Prickles slender, straight or slightly curved: lfts. tomentose.
  B. Sepals upright, persistent: fr. large, about 2 cm. across: auricles incurved, falcate.
                13. *R. pomifera*
  BB. Sepals finally deciduous: fr. smaller: auricles short, divergent.........14. *R. tomentosa*
AA. Prickles hooked: lfts. glabrous or pubescent beneath.
  B. Lfts. suborbicular or broad-oval, usually obtuse, glandular on both sides: styles pubescent: sepals long-persistent..15. *R. Eglanteria*
  BB. Lfts. ovate or oval, acute or short-acuminate, eglandular above; styles glabrous or nearly so; sepals soon deciduous.......................................16. *R. micrantha*
Lfts. not glandular except sometimes on midrib; teeth usually simple.
A. Style exserted: sepals reflexed, deciduous.....................................17. *R. stylosa*
AA. Styles not or little exserted.
  B. Lfts. pubescent, at least beneath..................................18. *R. corymbifera*
  BB. Lfts. glabrous.
    c. Lfts. bright or dark green, lustrous above.............................19. *R. canina*
    cc. Lfts. bluish green, tinged with red, dull above, simply serrate, 7–9: brts. bloomy, with few prickles...20. *R. rubrifolia*

Sect. 4. CAROLINAE

A. Stipules more or less convolute, at least on the shoots; prickles hooked: lfts. serrulate.
                21. *R. palustris*
AA. Stipules flat: lfts. rather coarsely serrate.
  B. Lfts. 5–7: prickles slender, straight.....................................23. *R. carolina*
  BB. Lfts. 7–11.
    c. Infrastipular prickles usually curved: lfts. 7–9, usually elliptic......22. *R. virginiana*
    cc. Infrastipular prickles straight, slender: lfts. 7–11, elliptic-oblong to narrow-oblong.
      D. Brts. densely bristly: pedicels 1–3 cm. long.....................24. *R. nitida*
      DD. Brts. not bristly: pedicels 5–10 mm. long..........................25. *R. foliolosa*

Sect. 5. CINNAMOMEAE

Infrastipular prickles not present.
A. Brts. and prickles tomentose: lfts. thick, rugose above.....................26. *R. rugosa*
AA. Brts. and prickles glabrous.
  B. Brts. and stems bristly.
    c. Fls. solitary or few: lfts. 3–7, rarely 9.............................27. *R. acicularis*
    cc. Fls. corymbose: lfts. 7–11: low plants.
      D. Lfts. glabrous, acute...28. *R. arkansana*
      DD. Lfts. pubescent at least beneath, usually obtuse...................29. *R. suffulta*
  BB. Brts. and stems unarmed or the latter with weak bristles when young.
    c. Lfts. simply serrate, 5–7: fr. subglobose..............................30. *R. blanda*
    cc. Lfts. doubly serrate, 7–9: fr. usually oblong to ovoid...............31. *R. pendulina*
Infrastipular prickles present.
A. Stipules at least on shoots more or less convolute; prickles curved.....32. *R. cinnamomea*
AA. Stipules flat.
  B. Sepals persistent.
    c. Lfts. 3–7: brts. prickly, not bristly.
      D. Styles not exserted.
        E. Fls. usually several, less than 5 cm. across: lvs. usually simply serrate.
          F. Prickles straight or nearly so.
            G. Lfts. puberulous beneath, bright green; stipules broad...33. *R. pisocarpa*
            GG. Lfts. glabrous, bluish green; stipules narrow..............34. *R. Woodsii*
          FF. Prickles curved: lfts. villous beneath.......................35. *R. californica*
        EE. Fls. solitary, 5–6 cm. across: lfts. doubly glandular-serrate......36. *R. nutkana*
      DD. Styles exserted; infl. subumbellate: lfts. doubly serrate........37. *R. corymbulosa*
    cc. Lfts. 7–15 (5–9 in *R. persetosa* under No. 40, and *R. Forrestiana* under No. 46, and in No. 41).
      D. Fls. corymbose: lfts. 2–6 cm. long.
        E. Sepals entire.
          F. Styles exserted: lfts. acute, 3–6 cm. long.......................38. *R. Davidi*
          FF. Styles not exserted.
            G. Petals glabrous outside; inflorescence exceeded by the lvs.: lfts. simply serrate ....39. *R. caudata*
            GG. Petals slightly pubescent outside; inflorescence not exceeded by the lvs.: lfts. usually doubly serrate.................................40. *R. setipoda*
        EE. Sepals pinnate ....41. *R. Hemsleyana*
      DD. Fls. solitary, rarely several, on short lateral brts.; if corymbose, lfts. less than 2 cm. long.
        E. Style not exserted.
          F. Lfts. pubescent beneath, at least on the midrib (see also *R. Fedtschenkoana* under No. 45).
            G. Brts. with prickles and bristles, lfts. usually doubly serrate, 3–5 cm. long.
                42. *R. Sweginzowii*
            GG. Brts. only with prickles: lfts. usually simply serrate, 1–3 cm. long.
                43. *R. Moyesii*

    FF. Lfts. glabrous, 8–20 mm. long.
      G. Lfts. acutish, elliptic or ovate, 1.5–2.5 cm. long.................44. *R. bella*
      GG. Lfts. obtuse, orbicular to oblong, 6–20 mm. long.
        H. Lfts. serrate above the middle: pedicels short........45. *R. Webbiana*
        HH. Lfts. sharply serrate from below the middle: pedicels 1.5–3 cm. long.
                              46. *R. sertata*
    EE. Styles exserted, nearly as long as stamens: lfts. obtuse, 8–15 mm. long.
                             47. *R. multibracteata*
  BB. Sepals deciduous, falling off as a whole, together with their base: fls. solitary: lfts. 5–9, 8–25 mm. long.
    C. Stems without bristles: lfts. simply serrate.......................48. *R. Willmottiae*
    CC. Stems bristly and prickly.
      D. Prickles straight: lfts. glabrous, doubly serrate...............49. *R. gymnocarpa*
      DD. Prickles hooked: lfts. pubescent beneath, simply serrate.......50. *R. Beggeriana*

Sect. 6. SYNSTYLAE

Stipules pectinate; prickles usually infrastipular; styles glabrous.
                                     51. *R. multiflora*

Stipules entire or denticulate: prickles scattered.
  A. Habit upright, usually with arching brs.
    B. Lfts. 3–5 on flowering brts., pubescent at least on veins beneath.
      C. Fls. small, about 1 cm. across: lfts. linear-lanceolate...............52. *R. Watsoniana*
      CC. Fls. about 5 cm. across: lfts. usually ovate-oblong....................53. *R. setigera*
    BB. Lfts. 5–9 on flowering brts.
      C. Lfts. acute or acuminate, 3–10 cm. long; stems often sarmentose.
        D. Lfts. pubescent, at least beneath.
          E. Fr. ovoid, 1.5 cm. long; corymb umbel-like: lfts. usually 7–9, pubescent chiefly on the veins..54. *R. Helenae*
          EE. Fr. about 1 cm. long: corymb not umbel-like: lfts. 5–7, pubescent beneath all over.
            F. Lfts. usually 5, glabrous above, sharply and coarsely serrate: brts. glabrous: fr. subglobose ....55. *R. Rubus*
            FF. Lfts. usually 7, pubescent above: brts. often puberulous: fr. ovoid.
                              56. *R. Brunonii*
      DD. Lfts. glabrous or nearly so.
        E. Lfts. 5–7, green beneath.
          F. Styles pubescent: fl.-buds gradually acuminate..............57. *R. moschata*
          FF. Styles glabrous; fl.-buds abruptly acuminate.........58. *R. Maximowicziana*
        EE. Lfts. usually 5, glaucescent beneath.............................59. *R. Ernesti*
      CC. Lfts. obtuse or acutish, 1–2.5 cm. long, glaucescent: upright shrub..60. *R. Soulieana*
  AA. Habit trailing or prostrate.
    B. Lvs. evergreen or half-evergreen, lustrous on both sides: fls. usually several.
      C. Lfts. usually 9, obtuse, 8–20 mm. long; stipules dentate..........61. *R. Wichuraiana*
      CC. Lfts. usually 5, acuminate, 2–5 cm. long; stipules entire..........62. *R. sempervirens*
    BB. Lvs. deciduous, glaucescent beneath; lfts. usually 7: fls. often solitary..63. *R. arvensis*

Sect. 7. INDICAE

Stems with unform prickles: lvs. glabrous.
  A. Lvs. persistent or semipersistent.
    B. Fls. white, yellowish or light pink, very fragrant; sepals usually entire: fr. globose or depressed-globose; stipules without or with few marginal glands at the auricles.
                                    64. *R. odorata*
    BB. Fls. red or pink, rarely whitish, not or slightly fragrant; sepals usually pinnate: fr. ovoid or pyriform: stipules glandular-ciliate..........................65. *R. chinensis*
  AA. Lvs. deciduous: fls. many in a corymb...................................66. *R. Noisettiana*

Stems with prickles and bristles: lvs. slightly pubescent beneath: fls. solitary or few.
                                    67. *R. borboniana*

Sect. 8. BANKSIANAE

                                    68. *R. Banksiae*

Sect. 9. LAEVIGATAE

                                    69. *R. laevigata*

Sect. 10. BRACTEATAE

                                    70. *R. bracteata*

Subgen. III. PLATYRHODON

                                  71. *R. Roxburghii*

Subgen. IV. HESPERHODOS

                                  72. *R. stellata*

    Subgen. I. HULTHEMIA (Dumort.) Focke. Lvs. simple, estipulate: fls. solitary; receptacle urnshaped, constricted at the mouth by a disk, prickly. (*Hulthemia* Dumort., *Lowea* Lindl., Sect. *Simplicifoliae* Lindl.)
    1. **R. pérsica** Michx. Low shrub, to 0.5 m., with slender yellowish brown prickly brs: lvs. short-petioled, elliptic to oblong, acute at ends, 1.5–3 cm.

long, serrate, bluish green, finely pubescent: fls. solitary, yellow with purple
eye, about 2.5 cm. across: fr. globose, prickly. Fl.v–viii. B.M.7096(c). B.R.
1261(c). W.R.1(c). G.C.III.6:8,9,78. (*R. simplicifolia* Salisb., *R. berberi-
folia* Pall., *Lowea b.* Lindl.) Persia, Afghan. to Song. Intr. 1790. Zone VII?
A very distinct and remarkable species, but difficult to grow.

R. p. × *clinophylla* = R. Hardii Paxt. Lfts. 1–7, oblong-obovate, glabrous,
stipulate: fls. 5 cm. across, pale yellow, with orange eye: calyx-tube pubescent,
with few prickles. W.R.7,t(c). P.M.10:t.195(c). G.C.II.24:469. Gn.19:473.
Orig. before 1836.

Subgen. II. EUROSA Focke. Lvs. pinnate, stipulate: fls. usually corymbose,
sometimes solitary; receptacle urn-shaped, constricted at apex by a disk;
achenes basal and parietal: fr. smooth, glandular or setose.

Sect. 1. PIMPINELLIFOLIAE DC. Usually low shrubs; stems usually with
straight prickles and bristles: lfts. small, 7–9; stipules narrow, with divergent
and dilated auricles: fls. solitary, without bracts; sepals entire, erect and
persistent. Eu. and Asia. (Includ. Sect. *Luteae* Crép. and *Sericeae* Crép.)

2. R. spinosíssima L. BURNETT R. (SCOTCH R.) Low shrub, rarely exceeding 1 m., with spreading or recurving brs.; brts. usually densely prickly
and bristly: lfts. 5–11, usually 7–9, orbicular to oblong-ovate, 1–2 cm. long,
simply serrate, or doubly glandular-serrate, glabrous, sometimes glandular
beneath; stipules entire, rarely glandular-dentate: fls. solitary, but usually
very numerous on short brts. along the stems, pink, white or yellow, 2–5 cm.
across; pedicels usually glandular-hispid: fr. subglobose, black or dark
brown, 1–1.5 cm. across. Fl.v–vi; fr.ix. W.R.247,t(c). B.R.431(c). F.D.25:t.
2623(c). Gn.60:24;74:598;86:306. G.C.70:218. (*R. pimpinellifolia* L., *R.
illinoensis* Bak.) Eu., W. Asia; occasionally naturalized in N. Am. Cult.
before 1600. Zone IV.—A very variable species: R. s. pimpinellifòlia (L.)
Hook., var. Pedicels smooth.—R. s. altáica (Willd.) Rehd., var. More vigorous, less bristly: fls. large, white; pedicels glabrous. W.R.257,t(c). B.R.
888(c). Gn.53:t.170(c). Gng.5:307(h). W.A.104,t(h). (*R. a.* Willd., *R. grandiflora* Lindl.)—R. s. myriacántha (DC.) Koehne, var. Brts. very prickly:
lfts. doubly glandular-serrate, very small: fls. small, white, blushed. W.R.
261,t(c). R.R.1:gr.6,7.—R. s. inérmis (DC.) Rehd., var. Brts. almost unarmed: fls. pink. R.R.1:gr.6,6. (*R. s.* var. *mitissima* Koehne, *R. pimpinellifolia*
var. *i.* DC.)—R. s. Andrèwsii Willm., var. With double red fls. W.R.263,
t(c).—R. s. nàna Andrews. With double white fls. Andrews, Roses, 122(c).—
R. s. híspida (Sims) Koehne, var. Upright shrub to 2 m.: lfts. usually simply
serrate; pedicels smooth: fls. sulphur-yellow, 6–7 cm. across. B.M.1570(c).
W.R.259,t(c). Gn.56,t.398(c);62:17. J.L.27:508. (*R. h.* Sims, *R. lutescens*
Pursh.)—R. s. lutéola Andr. Similar to the preceding var.: lfts. 7: fls. pale
yellow, about 5 cm. across. W.R.255,t(c). G.28:281. (*R. ochroleuca* Swartz.)
—R. s. lùtea Bean, var. About 1 m. tall: lfts. broad-oval, to 2.5 cm. long,
pubescent beneath: fls. bright yellow. Orig. unknown, possibly a hybrid.

R. s. × *canina* = R. hibérnica Smith. Shrub to 3 m., with upright or arching stems, bristly and prickly: lfts.·5–9, bluish green, pubescent beneath: fls.
usually 3, pink, about 3 cm. across; sepals lobed: fr. globose, red. W.R.289,t(c).
Intr. 1802.—*R. s.* × *pendulina* = R. revérsa Waldst. & Kit. Shrub to 1.5 m.;
stems upright, with slender prickles and bristles: lfts. 5–9, 6–20 mm. long, dark
green: fls. solitary, red, 4–5 cm. across; pedicels glandular-bristly: fr. ovoid,
2 cm. long, pendulous, red. F.D.25:t.2624(c). (*R. rubella* Sm.) Eu. Cult.
1820.—Possibly of similar parentage is R. Màlyi Kern. Shrub to 2 m.: lfts. oval
or suborbicular, 1.5–3 cm. long, usually doubly serrate, glabrous: fls. usually
solitary, deep red, 3–4 cm. across: fr. oblong-ovoid. W.R.297,t(c). (*R. pendulina* var. *M.* Kern.) Dalmatia. Cult. 1902.—*R. s.* × ? *tomentosa* = R. involùta
Smith. Shrub to 3 m.; stems with prickles and bristles: lfts. 5–9, elliptic, simply
or doubly glandular-serrate, pubescent beneath: fls. pink or whitish, solitary:
fr. globose, red. W.R.281,t(c). Orig. in Scotland.—*R. s.* × *carolina* = R.

Kochiàna Koehne. Brts. densely bristly: lfts. 9–11, small: fls. 1–3, deep rose. (*R. oxyacantha* K. Koch, not Bieb.) Orig. before 1870.—*R. s.* × *foetida;* see under No. 6.

Related species: **R. koreàna** Komar. Dense shrub to 1 m.: brts. densely bristly, dark red: lfts. 7–11, elliptic or obovate-elliptic, 1–2 cm. long, obtusish, sharply glandular-serrate, glabrous or slightly pubescent beneath: fls. 2.5–3 cm. across, white, flushed pink; pedicels stipitate-glandular; fr. ovoid, 1–1.5 cm. long, orange-red. N.K.7:t.14. Act. Hort. Petrop. 22:t.11. Korea. Intr. 1917.

3. **R. Hugònis** Hemsl. Shrub to 2.5 m., with arching brs.; prickles straight, compressed, mixed on the shoots with bristles: lfts. 5–13, oval to obovate or elliptic, 8–20 mm. long, obtuse, sometimes acutish, finely serrate, glabrous or slightly villous on the veins when unfolding: fls. solitary on short brts., light yellow, 5 cm. across; pedicels 1.5–2 cm. long, like the receptacle glabrous: fr. depressed-globose, about 1.5 cm. across, dark scarlet to blackish red. Fl.v–vi; fr.vii–viii. B.M.8004(c). W.R.279,t(c). B.S.2:429. Gn.87:589. S.L. 324(h). Gn.M.31:373(h);38:37(h). C. China. Intr. 1899. Zone V. Free-flowering and early Rose, one of the best single yellows.

4. **R. xánthina** Lindl. Shrub to 3 m.; brts. brown with stout and straight prickles, shoots without bristles: lfts. 7–13, broad-oval or nearly suborbicular, rarely elliptic, 8–20 mm. long, obtuse, serrate, glabrous above, slightly villous beneath, at least when young: fls. solitary, yellow, double or semidouble, 4 cm. across. Fl.v–vi; fr.vii–viii. N.K.7:t.6. (*R. xanthinoides* Nakai.) Cult. in N. China, Korea. Intr. 1906. Zone V.—**R. x. spontànea** Rehd., f. Fls. single. The wild form. Franchet, Pl. David 1:t.15. N. China, Korea. Intr. 1906. Zone V.

Related species: **R. graciliflòra** Rehd. & Wils. Shrub to 4 m.; brs. with few prickles: lfts. 7–9, oval or elliptic, 1–2 cm. long, rounded or acutish at apex, doubly glandular-serrate, glabrous beneath or pubescent on midrib; stipules broad, glandular-ciliate: fls. pale pink, 3–4 cm. across; receptacle ovoid; sepals enlarged at apex and sometimes toothed: fr. red. W. China. Intr. 1932. Zone VI?—**R. Fárreri** Stapf. Stem densely bristly below: lfts. 7–9, ovate to elliptic, 5–18 mm. long, acutish, glabrous; stipules narrow, ending in a short tooth: fls. pale pink to white, 2–2.5 cm. across; pedicels 1.2–2.5 cm. long, glabrous; sepals scarcely leafy at tip: fr. ovoid-oblong, coral-red. N. W. China. Intr. 1915. Zone V.—**R. F. persetòsa** Stapf, f. Stems densely bristly throughout: fls. salmon-pink. B.M.8877(c). G.C.94:239.

5. **R. Prímula** Boulenger. Upright shrub to 2 m.; brts. slender with numerous stout wide-based straight prickles: lfts. 9–15, rarely 7, elliptic or elliptic-obovate to elliptic-oblong, 6–20 mm. long, acute or obtuse, minutely and doubly glandular-serrulate, glabrous, glandular beneath: fls. solitary, 3–4 cm. across, pale yellow or yellowish white; pedicels short, smooth: fr. globose or obovoid, red like its stalk, about 1 cm. long, with reflexed sepals. Fl.v–vi; fr.vii, soon dropping. N.F.8:f.83;11:f.95(h). (*R. xanthina* auth., not Lindl., *R. Ecae* Rehd., not Aitch.) Turkest. to N. China. Intr. 1910. Zone V. Valued for its early fls. and aromatic young foliage.

Closely related species: **R. Ecae** Aitch. Shrub to 1 m., densely prickly: lfts. 5–9, mostly obovate, 4–8 mm. long, rounded or truncate at apex: fls. 1.5–2 cm. across, yellow, short-stalked, often without lvs. at base. H.I.1329. B.M.7666(c). Afghan. Intr. 1880. Zone VI?

6. **R. foètida** Herrm. Austrian Brier. Shrub to 3 m.; stems slender, often sarmentose, brown, with straight prickles: lfts. 5–9, broad-oval or obovate, 1.5–4 cm. long, usually rounded at base, doubly glandular-serrate, dark green above, glandular and slightly pubescent beneath; stipules glandular-serrate: fls. solitary or sometimes several, deep yellow, 5–7 cm. across, of unpleasant odor; pedicels and receptacle smooth; sepals leafy at tip: fr. globose, red. Fl.vi. B.M.363(c). W.R.267,t(c). F.D.25:t.2622(c). Gn.53:22, t(c). (*R. lutea* Mill., *R. Eglanteria* Mill., not L.) W. Asia. Intr. before 1600.

Zone IV.—**R. f. bícolor** (Jacq.) Willm., var. AUSTRIAN COPPER BRIER. Fls. orange-scarlet or coppery-red inside. B.M.1077(c). W.R.269,t(c). Gn.53:23; 55:425. (*R. lutea* prol. *punicea* (Mill.) Aschers. & Graebn., *R. punicea* Mill., *R. b.* Jacq.) Intr. before 1590.—**R. f. persiàna** (Lem.) Rehd., var. PERSIAN YELLOW. With double fls. F.S.4:t.374(c). More floriferous than the double Sulphur Rose and fls. smaller, but more double. Intr. 1838.

   R. f. × *spinosissima* = R. Harisònii Rivers. HARISON'S YELLOW R. Lower, with shorter brs.: fls. paler and less double than Persian Yellow; pedicels and receptacle bristly: fr. nearly black. S.B.II.4:410(c). F.E.18:6. H.B.5:t.99(c). (*R. foetida* var. *H.* Rehd., *R. lutea* var. *Hoggii* Sweet, *R. Vorbergii* Graebn.) Orig. about 1830. Hardier than Persian Yellow.—*R. f.* × *Eglanteria* = R. Penzanceàna Rehd. LADY PENZANCE R. Low shub with arching brs. and hooked prickles: lfts. 7, fragrant: fls. pink with yellow eye. Orig. about 1890.

   7. **R. hemisphaèrica** Herrm. SULPHUR R. Shrub to 3 or 4 m.; stems slender, often sarmentose, with hooked prickles: lfts. 5–9, obovate, 1–3.5 cm. long, rounded at apex, cuneate, coarsely toothed, bluish green, glaucescent beneath and pubescent; rachis pubescent, sparingly glandular: fls. double, scentless, light yellow, 5 cm. across; pedicels glabrous or glandular-hispid; sepals with leafy toothed apex. Fl.vi. W.R.273,t(c). B.R.46(c). (*R. sulphurea* Ait., *R. glaucophylla* Ehrh.) W. Asia. Intr. before 1625. Zone VI? The wild form (*R. Rapinii* Boiss.) with single yellow flowers and globose fr. is not in cult.

   8. **R. omeiénsis** Rolfe. Shrub to 3 or 4 m.; stems upright, with flattened wide-based prickles, young shoots often bristly: lfts. 9–17, oblong or elliptic-oblong, 8–30 mm. long, acutish, cuneate, serrate, glabrous or puberulous on midrib beneath; petioles puberulous and prickly: fls. white, 2.5–3.5 cm. across; pedicels and receptacle smooth: fr. pear-shaped, 8–15 mm. long, bright red, on a thickened yellow stalk of about equal length. Fl.v–vi; fr.vii. B.M. 8471(c). I.S.2:t.81. B.C.5:2996. W. China. Intr. 1901. Zone VI. Distinct shrub with finely divided fernlike foliage; coloring of fr. unique; the stems of f. *pteracantha* conspicuous in winter.—**R. o. chrysocárpa** Rehd., f. Fr. yellow.—**R. o. pteracántha** (Franch.) Rehd. & Wils., f. Prickles much enlarged at base, decurrent and often confluent, forming wide wings, red and translucent when young. B.M.8218(c). Gn.69:300,t(c). G.C.38:260. J.L.27: 491. V.F.99(h). (*R. sericea* var. *p.* Fr.) Intr. 1890.

   Closely related species: R. serícea Lindl. Lfts. 7–11, oval or obovate, 1–2 cm. long, serrate only near apex, silky-pubescent beneath: fr. red, on a slender, not thickened stalk. B.M.5200(c). W.R.163,t(c). R.H.1897:444,445. Himal. Intr. 1822. Zone VII?

   Sect. 2. GALLICANAE DC. Upright usually low shrubs: stems usually with hooked prickles mixed with bristles; stipules narrow, adnate: lfts. 3–5, usually firm: fls. few, often with narrow bracts or solitary on a usually bractless pedicel; sepals often lobed, reflexed after flowering, deciduous; styles not exserted. Three or possibly one species in Eu. and W. Asia.

   9. **R. gállica** L. FRENCH R. Upright shrub, with creeping root-stock, rarely 1.5 m. tall; stems usually densely covered with prickles and bristles: lfts. 3–5, broad-elliptic or ovate, 2–6 cm. long, obtusish or abruptly acuminate, rounded or subcordate at base, doubly or sometimes simply glandular-serrate, dark green and rugose above, paler and pubescent beneath, firm, deflexed; petiole and rachis bristly and glandular-hispid; stipules glandular-ciliate: fls. solitary, pink or crimson, 4–7 cm. across, on rather long stout pedicels glandular-hispid and bristly; receptacle glandular-hispid; sepals glandular outside: fr. subglobose or turbinate, brick-red. Fl.vi. W.R.325,t(c). F.D.25:t.2634(c). B.M.1377(c). G.H.1:t.89(c). C. and S. Eu., W. Asia; occasionally naturalized in N. Am. Long cult. Zone V.—**R. g. pùmila** (Jacq.)

Reg., var. Dwarf form, with creeping root-stock: fls. red, single. R.R.2:gr.
16,12(c).—**R. g. officinális** Thory. APOTHECARY R. (DOUBLE FRENCH R.)
With double fls., otherwise like the typical form. W.R.359,t(c). (*R. g.* var.
plena Reg., *R. provincialis* Mill.)—**R. g. Ágatha** Thory. With rather small
double pink fls., the outer petals spreading, the inner ones concave. R.R.2:
gr.17,17–21.—**R. g. versícolor** L., var. Fls. semidouble; petals striped, white
and red. R.R.2:gr.16,12(c). (*R. g.* var. *rosa-mundi* West.) It has been confused with a similar form of *R. damascena*.

R. g. × *canina* = R. Waitziàna Tratt. With scattered, usually slightly curved
and unequal prickles: lfts. rather firm, usually simply serrate, nearly glabrous or
pubescent on the midrib beneath; pedicels stipitate-glandular; sepals glandular
on back: fls. large, usually deep rose-pink, 6–8 cm. across, often solitary. Eu.
Cult. 1874.—**R. W. macrántha** (Desportes) Rehd., var. Prickles nearly equal:
lfts. nearly glabrous beneath: fls. several; pedicels slightly glandular; fls.
flushed rose at first, becoming nearly white. Gn.52:465,t.f.1(c). R.H.1901:541,
t.f.2(c). W.R.2:403,t(c). Intr. about 1825.—*R. g.* × *tomentosa* = R. Marcyàna
Boullu. To 1 m. tall; stems prickly and bristly: lfts. 5–7, broad-oval, 2–5 cm.
long, pubescent on both sides: fls. pink to light purple, 6–7 cm. across, long-
stalked. W.R.335,t(c). (? *R. therebinthinacea* Bess.) Spont. in S. France.—
R. g. × *cinnamomea* = R. francofurtàna Muenchh. To 2 m.; stems with straight
or hooked prickles, flowering brts. nearly unarmed: lfts. 5–7, elliptic, serrate,
pubescent beneath; upper stipules much dilated: fls. 5–7 cm. across, single or
double, purple, slightly fragrant, receptacle at base and pedicels glandular-
hispid; sepals erect after flowering, entire or nearly so: fr. turbinate. Fl.VI.
F.D.25:t.2628(c). R.R.3:gr.23,1(c). (*R. turbinata* Ait.) Orig. before 1770.—
R. g. × *moschata;* see under No. 57.—*R. g.* × *arvensis;* see under No. 63.—
R. g. × *corymbifera;* see No. 12.

10. **R. centifòlia** L. CABBAGE R. Closely related to the preceding; taller,
to 2 m.; root-stock less creeping; prickles more unequal, partly stouter: lfts.
usually 5, pubescent on both sides or only beneath, often simple serrate,
larger and thinner; rachis not prickly: fls. usually pink, very double, nodding,
on long and slender, very glandular pedicels, fragrant; petals inflexed; sepals
persistent: fr. ellipsoid to subglobose. Fl.VI–VII. W.R.341,t(c). R.R.2:gr.14,
1–12. G.1:340. (*R. gallica* var. *c.* (L.) Reg.) E. Cauc. Zone V. Only the
double form in cult.; known to the ancients.—**R. c. muscòsa** (Mill.) Ser., var.
Moss R. Fls. rose, with pedicels and calyx glandular-mossy. B.M.69(c).
Gn.18:84(c). G.W.7:125.—**R. c. albo-muscòsa** Willm. Like the preceding,
but fls. white. B.R.102(c). W.R.349,t(c).—**R. c. cristàta** Prevost, var. Similar to var. *muscosa*, but the mossy excrescences confined to the edges of the
sepals. B.M.3475(c). W.R.351,t(c). G.W.7:125.—**R. c. pompònia** (DC.)
Lindl., var. POMPON R. Dwarf: lfts. elliptic, about 2.5 cm. long, glabrous
above: fls. bright red, double, 3–3.5 cm. across; pedicels densely setose. W.R.
353,t(c). (*R. pulchella* Willd., *R. dijonensis* Roess.)—**R. c. parvifòlia** (Ehrh.)
Rehd., var. BURGUNDIAN R. Similar to the preceding: lfts. 1–2 cm. long: fls.
about 2.5 cm. across; pedicels slightly setose. B.R.452(c). W.R.355,t(c). (*R.
p.* Ehrh., *R. burgundensis* West., *R. burgundiaca* Roess., *R. gallica* var. *p.*
(Ehrh.) Ser.)

Related species: **R. Richárdii** Rehd. Low shrub with unequal scattered
hooked prickles: lfts. 3–5, elliptic to ovate-oblong, rugose above, pubescent beneath: fls. few, pale rose, 5–7 cm. across; sepals large, pinnately lobed, leafy at
apex. W.R.337,t(c). (*R. sancta* Rich., not Andrews.) Abyss. Cult. 1902.
Zone VII?

11. **R. damascèna** Mill. DAMASK R. Shrub to 2 m.; stems usually with
numerous stout hooked prickles, sometimes mixed with glandular bristles:
lfts. usually 5, sometimes 7, ovate to ovate-oblong, 2–6 cm. long, simply
serrate, glabrous above, more or less pubescent beneath; petioles prickly;
stipules sometimes pectinate: fls. blush to red, double, in corymbs, on slender

433

glandular-hispid and prickly pedicels; sepals reflexed during anthesis, deciduous, glandular-hispid on back like receptacle: fr. obovoid, 2.5 cm. long, bristly, red. Fl.vi–vii. W.R.369,t(c). R.R.2:gr.16,6(c). (*R. belgica* Mill., *R. polyanthos* Roess., *R. gallica* var. *d.* Voss.) Intr. from Asia Minor in the 16th century. Zone IV.—**R. d. versícolor** West., var. York and Lancaster R. Fls. semi-double, white and striped and blotched pink, or some fls. white and some pink. Lawrance, Coll. Ros. t.10(c). (*R. d. variegata* Thory.)—**R. d. trigintapétala** Dieck, var. With semi-double red fls. Gt.38:129. G.C.III.7:45. Cult. in S. Eu. for the manufacture of attar.

R. d. × *chinensis;* see No. 67.

12. × **R. alba** L. (? *R. corymbifera* × *gallica*.) Upright shrub to 2 m.; stem with unequal hooked prickles, sometimes mixed with bristles: lfts. usually 5, broad-elliptic or ovate to oblong-ovate, 2–6 cm. long, simply serrate, pubescent beneath; upper stipules dilated: fls. more or less double, 6–8 cm. across, white or blush, fragrant, corymbose; pedicels glandular-hispid; receptacle usually smooth above; sepals glandular-bristly, deciduous: fr. oblong-ovoid, 2 cm. long, scarlet. Fl.vi. Andrews, Ros. t.10(c). Origin unknown. Intr. 1597. Zone IV.—**R. a. suavéolens** Dieck, var. Cult. in S. E. Eu. for attar of Roses.—**R. a. incarnàta** (Mill.) West., var. Fls. double, white, tinged with pink. W.R.413,t(c). (*R. incarnata* Mill., *R. alba* var. *rubicunda* Roess.)

The closely related *R. collina* Jacq. with rose-colored fls. and shorter sepals is probably of the same origin and referable to *R. alba*.

Sect. 3. CANINAE. Stems upright or arching, usually with numerous hooked or rarely straight prickles; upper stipules dilated: corymbs usually many-fld., with dilated bracts; outer sepals lobed, reflexed after anthesis and deciduous or erect and persistent.

13. **R. pomífera** Herrm. Densely branched shrub to 2 m., with almost straight slender spines: lfts. usually 5–7, on shoots sometimes 9, elliptic to elliptic-oblong, acute or obtuse, 3–5 cm. long, doubly glandular-serrate, grayish green and pubescent above, tomentose beneath and glandular, rarely glabrescent; auricles of stipules spreading or converging: fls. 1–3, pink, 3–5 cm. across; pedicels bristly and stipitate-glandular: fr. usually subglobose, to 2.5 cm. across, hispid, with persistent upright sepals. Fl.vi–vii. B.M. 7241(c). W.R.435,t(c). G.H.t.88(c). F.D.25:t.2632(c). (*R. villosa* L., in part.) Eu., W. Asia. Cult. 1771. Zone V.—**R. p. duplex** (West.) Rehd., f. With semidouble fls. W.R.436,t(c).

Cosely related species: **R. mollis** Smith. Low shrub; brts. purplish, bloomy: lfts. silky-tomentose beneath, less glandular, smaller: pedicels sparingly glandular: fr. smaller, not hispid, sometimes stipitate-glandular; sepals short, nearly entire. W.R.417,t(c). (*R. villosa* var. *mollissima* Rau.) Eu., W. Asia. Intr. 1818. Zone V.—**R. Sherárdi** Davies. Dense shrub to 2 m.; brs. often zigzag; spines often curved: lfts. broad-oval to elliptic, pubescent above, tomentose beneath, bluish green: fls. deep pink, usually several, exceeded by the basal lvs.; sepals appendaged: fr. ovoid or pyriform, 1.2–2 cm. across, with persistent sepals. (*R. omissa* Déségl.) N. and C. Eu. Cult. 1933. Zone IV.—**R. hawràna** Kmet. Flowering brts. usually unarmed: lfts. elliptic, glabrous above, pubescent beneath: fls. pink, 5 cm. across: fr. globose, densely bristly. W.R.431,t(c). Hungary. Cult. 1914.—Other related species: **R. orientàlis** Dup. Dwarf: prickles subulate; young brts. densely pubescent: lfts. 1–2 cm. long, simply serrate, pubescent on both sides: fls. solitary, pink, short-stalked; pedicels villous, glandular and bristly: fr. ellipsoid, sepals upright. S.H.1:f.321k-n,322g. S. E. Eu., W. Asia. Intr. ?—**R. Heckeliàna** Tratt. Very similar, but prickles stouter, hooked, and fls. smaller. S. Eu. Intr. ?—**R. elymaítica** Boiss. & Hausskn. Shrub to 1 m., with zigzag pruinose brs.; prickles stout, curved: lfts. usually 5, 5–15 mm. long, tomentose below: fls. pink, small; styles exserted, tomentose; pedicels and receptacle stipitate-glandular: fr. globose, about 1 cm. across; sepals reflexed. S.H.1:f.322g'(l). N. Persia. Intr. 1900. Zone VII᠙

14. **R. tomentòsa** Smith. Shrub to 2 m.; brts. often zigzag; young brts. often bloomy; prickles stout, curved or straight: lfts. 5–7, elliptic or ovate, acute or short-acuminate, 2–4 cm. long, doubly serrate, finely pubescent above, tomentose and glandular beneath; stipules with short triangular spreading auricles: fls. pale pink or nearly white, about 4 cm. across; pedicels often glandular-hispid; sepals lobed: fr. subglobose, 1–2 cm. across, stipitate-glandular; sepals usually deciduous before maturity. Fl.VI. W.R.421,t(c). S.E.3:t.467(c). F.D.25:t.2631(c). Gn.77:511. Eu. Cult. 1820; occasionally escaped in the e. states. Zone V.

R. t. × *gallica;* see under No. 9.—*R. t.* × *spinosissima;* see under No. 2.

15. **R. Eglantèria** L. SWEET-BRIER. (EGLANTINE.) Much branched shrub to 2 m.; prickles strong, hooked, sometimes mixed with bristles: lfts. 5–7, orbicular to oval, 1–3 cm. long, obtuse or acutish, dark green and glabrous above, pubescent beneath, glandular on both sides, fragrant: fls. 1–3, bright pink, 3–5 cm. across, on short glandular-hispid pedicels; receptacle glandular-hispid: fr. subglobose or ovoid, orange to scarlet, with more or less spreading, tardily deciduous sepals. S.E.3:468(c). D.F.25:t.2630(c). N.D.7:t.7(c). (*R. rubiginosa* L.) Eu.; often naturalized in N. Am. Zone IV. Planted for its aromatic foliage.—**R. E. duplex** West., var. With double fls. W.R.449,t(c).

R .e. × *foetida;* see under No. 6.

Closely related species: **R. inodòra** Fries. Dense shrub to 2 m.: lfts. elliptic to obovate-oblong, 1.5–3 cm. long, cuneate, pubescent beneath: fls. pinkish or white; pedicels short, usually eglandular. S.H.1:f.323h-i. W.R.469,t(c). (*R. elliptica* Tausch, *R. caryophyllacea* Bess.) Eu. Cult. 1875. Zone V.—**R. sícula** Tratt. Low shrub with slender, nearly straight, subequal prickles: lfts. 5–9, orbicular to elliptic, glabrous and glandular, 6–12 mm. long: fls. usually solitary, 2.5–3 cm. across: fr. small, globose. B.M.7761(c) and G.W.8:17(h), as *R. Seraphinii.* S. Eu., Afr. Intr. before 1894. Zone VII?—**R. glutinòsa** Sibth. & Sm. Dwarf; prickles unequal, partly scattered, straight, to 1 cm. long, and partly bristly, gland-tipped and very numerous: lfts. elliptic to obovate, 1–3 cm. long, densely glandular: fls. small, pink: fr. globose, small. S.F.5:t.482(c). W.R.467,t(c). (? *R. tuschetica* Boiss.) S. E. Eu., W. Asia. Intr. 1821.—**R. g. dalmàtica** (Kern.) Borb., var. Fr. ellipsoid, 2–2.8 cm. long. B.M.8826(c) (*R. d.* Kern.) Cult. 1882.

16. **R. micrántha** Sm. Much-branched shrub, to 2 m., with arching brs. armed with uniform curved prickles, without bristles: lfts. 5–7, broad-ovate, 1.5–3 cm. long, short-acuminate, doubly glandular-serrate, glabrous or pubescent above, pubescent and glandular beneath: fls. 1–4, pink to white, about 3 cm. across; styles glabrous, somewhat exserted; pedicels glandular-hispid: fr. ovoid or subglobose, with spreading or reflexed deciduous sepals. Fl.VI. W.R.461,t(c). S.E.3:t.469(c). D.F.25:t.2630,IIB(c). B.B.2:f.2316(as *R. rubiginosa*). Eu., Mediterr.; often escaped throughout N. Am. Zone V.

Related species: **R. hórrida** Fisch. Dwarf, with unequal prickles: lfts. broad-ovate to elliptic, 1–1.5 cm. long, glandular beneath and often above: fls. white, usually 3 cm. across; pedicels short; styles short. W.R.477,t(c). S.H.1:f.323 u-o,324e. (*R. ferox* Bieb., not Lawrance.) S. E. Eu., Cauc., Asia Minor. Intr. 1796.—**R. agréstis** Savi. Shrub to 3 m. with elongated brs.; prickles subequal: lfts. oblong to oblong-obovate, 1.5–5 cm. long, usually cuneate, pubescent or nearly glabrous: fls. whitish or pinkish; pedicels eglandular; style somewhat exserted. W.R.457,t(c). S.E.3:t.470(c). (*R. sepium* Thuill.) Eu., N. Afr. Cult. 1878.—**R. Serafinii** Viv. Low shrub with copious, unequal, partly hooked prickles: lfts. orbicular-ovate, 5–12 mm. long, glandular beneath, glabrous: fls. solitary, pink, on very short eglandular pedicels; sepals lobed, reflexed after anthesis, finally deciduous. W.R.475,t(c). (*R. Seraphinii* Viv.) Mediterr. Cult. 1914.

17. **R. stylòsa** Desv. Shrub to 3 m., with arching brs.; prickles stout, hooked: lfts. 5–7, elliptic to elliptic-oblong, 1.5–5 cm. long, acute, serrate, lustrous above, pubescent beneath, rarely glabrous, eglandular; rachis pubes-

cent, usually prickly: fls. 1–18, white or light pink, 3–5 cm. across; pedicels glandular; styles usually shorter than stamens: fr. ovoid, outer sepals with many lobes. W.R.47,t(c). S.E.3:t.475(c). S.H.1:f.323s-s², -324i-k. (*R. systyla* Bast.) Eu. Cult. 1838. Zone V.

18. **R. corymbífera** Borkh. Upright shrub to 3 m., with spreading or arching brs.; prickles stout, hooked: lfts. 5–7, closely set, orbicular-oval to elliptic, 2.5–4 cm. long, rounded or subcordate, usually simply serrate, pubescent on both sides or only below on the veins: fls. 1 to many, 4–5 cm. across; pedicels usually long, glabrous or glandular; sepals soon reflexed, deciduous: fr. ovoid or subglobose, 1.5–2 cm. long, orange-red, usually smooth. Fl.vi. W.R.397,t(c). S.E.3:t.491(c). Gs.3:134(h). (*R. dumetorum* Thuill.) Eu., W. Asia, Afr. Cult. 1838; rarely escaped. Zone V.
R. c. × *gallica;* see No. 12.
Closely related species: **R. coriifòlia** Fries. Lower: lfts. usually cuneate at base: fls. short-stalked; bracts large; sepals upright, long-persistent. W.R.391, t(c). S.E.3:t.472(c). Eu., W. Asia. Cult. 1878.—**R. c. Froebèlii** (Christ) Rehd., var. Of more vigorous habit: lfts. simply or doubly serrate, bluish green: fls. small, white. (*R. canina* var. *F.* Christ, *R. laxa* Froeb., not Retz.) Cult. 1890.

19. **R. canìna** L. Dog R. Shrub to 3 m., with often arching brs.; prickles stout, hooked: lfts. 5–7, oval or elliptic, 2–4 cm. long, doubly or simply serrate, glabrous or slightly pubescent beneath; upper stipules dilated: fls. 1–3, light pink or white, 4–5 cm. across; pedicels usually glabrous, 1–3 cm. long; receptacle ellipsoid, usually smooth; sepals usually lobed, later reflexed and finally deciduous: fr. scarlet, ellipsoid, 1.5–2 cm. long. Fl.vi. W.R.379,t(c). S.E.3:t.474(c). D.F.25:2629(c). N.D.7:t.11(c). B.B.2:f.2312. Eu.; occasionally naturalized in N. Am. Zone III. Much used as stock for grafting.—**R. c. éxilis** (Crép.) Keller, var. Low form: lfts. small, 6–10 mm. long: fls. pink, 2.5 cm. across. W.R.385,t(c). (*R. e.* Crép.)
R. c. × *gallica;* see under No. 9.—*R. c.* × *spinosissima;* see under No. 2.—*R. c.* × *rubrifolia;* see under No. 20.
Related species: **R. dumàlis** Bechst. Brts. often pruinose, very prickly: lfts. close-set, ovate to oblong-ovate, sharply and doubly serrate, bluish green, glaucous beneath: fls. rose-red; pedicels short; sepals lobed, upright, long-persistent. S.H.1:f.324p,325a. (*R. glauca* Vill., not Pourr., *R. Reuteri* God.) Eur., W. Asia. Cult. 1872.—**R. britzénsis** Koehne. Prickles slender: lfts. 7–11, elliptic, 2.5–3.5 cm. long, usually simply serrate: fls. 1–2, pale pink, changing to white, 3–4 cm. across: fr. brown, with upright sepals. M.D.1910:94. Gs.4:102. S.H. 2:f.593a-e. Kurdistan. Intr. 1901.—**R. montàna** Chaix. Prickles nearly straight: lfts. broad-ovate, cuneate, obtuse, often tinged bluish violet: fls. pink; pedicels with purplish black stalked glands and bristles: fr. large, oblong-ellipsoid, with persistent lobed sepals. S.H.1:f.325c-c¹,326b. S. Eu., N. Afr. Cult. 1872.—**R. marginàta** Wallr. Prickles straight or nearly straight, rather slender: lfts. 3–7, ovate to elliptic, doubly glandular-serrate, nearly glabrous, usually glandular beneath: fls. pink, 5–7 cm. across; pedicels long, glandular and bristly: fr. subglobose to ellipsoid, smooth; sepals deciduous. W.R.463,t(c). S.H.1:f. 321e-f,322f. (*R. Jundzillii* Bess.) Eu., W. Asia. Cult. 1870. Has some resemblance to *R. gallica.*

20. **R. rubrifòlia** Vill. Upright shrub to 2 m., with slender purplish bloomy brts.; prickles few, hooked or straight, rather small: lfts. 7–9, elliptic to ovate-lanceolate, 2–3.5 cm. long, simply serrate, bluish green and more or less tinged with purplish red, glabrous: fls. few, deep red, 3–3.5 cm. across; pedicels glabrous or with few bristles; sepals usually entire, longer than petals, deciduous; fr. subglobose, about 1.5 cm. across, bright red, smooth. Fl.vi–vii. W.R.399,t(c). B.R.430(c). G.W.7:139(h). F.D.25:2627(c). (*R. ferruginea* Déségl., not Vill., *R. glauca* Pourr.) Mts. of C. and S. Eu. Intr. 1814. Zone II.—Distinct with its purplish lvs. and purplish stems: fls. rather inconspicuous.

R. r. × canina = R. Pokornyàna Borbas. Stems with scattered prickles, purplish when young: lfts. usually 7, elliptic or oval, slightly doubly serrate, bluish green, tinged purple when young: fls. 1–3, deep red, 3.5–4 cm. across; sepals slender, with a few narrow appendages. Hungary. Cult. 1916.—*R. r. × rugosa;* see under No. 26.

Sect. 4. CAROLINAE Crép. Upright, mostly low shrubs; stems slender, with usually straight paired prickles and often with bristles; upper stipules usually narrow: corymbs usually few-fld.; sepals spreading after flowering, soon deciduous, the outer entire or with few erect lobes; pedicels and receptacle glandular-hispid, rarely smooth; achenes inserted only at the bottom of the usually depressed-globose receptacle.

21. **R. palústris** Marsh. Upright shrub to 2 m., with slender glabrous, sometimes reddish stems: lfts. 7, rarely 9, elliptic to narrow-oblong, acute at ends, 2–5 cm. long, finely serrate, usually pubescent beneath at least on the veins; stipules narrow, involute: fls. usually corymbose, pink, about 5 cm. across; bracts leafy; pedicels short, usually glandular-hispid: fr. about 8 mm. high. Fl.VI–VIII. W.R.211,t(c). Em.2:488,t(c). M.N.1:t.43(c). B.B.2:285. (*R. carolina* L. 1762 partly, not 1753, *R. pennsylvanica* Michx.) N. S., Minn., Miss. and Fla. Intr. 1726. Zone IV.

R. p. × virginiana = R. Marìae-Graèbnerae Aschers. Lfts. more shining, broader, more coarsely toothed. Fl.VI–IX. Gt.51:t.1504,t.4(c). Orig. about 1880. Also found wild with the parents.—*R. p. × rugosa;* see under No. 26.

22. **R. virginiàna** Mill. Shrub to 2 m., with few or no suckers; prickles often hooked, only young shoots bristly: lfts. 7–9, elliptic to obovate-elliptic, 2–6 cm. long, usually acute at ends, serrate with ascending teeth, dark green and lustrous above, glabrous or pubescent on veins beneath; upper stipules dilated: fls. usually few, sometimes solitary, 5–6 cm. across; pedicels and receptacle glandular-hispid: fr. 1–1.5 cm. across. Fl.VI–VII. W.R.197,t(c),199, t.,308,t(c). N.D.7:t.7,f.2(c). Gt.56:t.1564,f.2(c). Gn.55:428;71:493. B.B.2: 285. K.S.175. (*R. lucida* Ehrh., *R. humilis* var. *l.* (Ehrh.) Best, *R. blanda* var. *Willmottiana* Bak.) Nfd. to Va., Ala. and Mo. Intr. before 1807. Zone III. Handsome Rose with lustrous lvs. and bright pink fls.—**R. v. plèna** Rehd., var. Fls. double. Andrews, Ros. t.102(c). R.R.2:t,opp.p.7(c). (*R. rapa* Bosc.) Intr. before 1820.—**R. v. lamprophýlla** Rehd., var. Of very dense habit, usually lower than 1 m.: lvs. of shoots usually 9-foliolate; lfts. elliptic to obovate, acute or sometimes obtuse, cuneate, very lustrous above; petioles usually reddish. Me. to Conn. Intr. 1881.

R. v. × palustris = R. Mariae-Graebnerae; see under No. 21.

23. **R. carolìna** L. Shrub to 1 m., suckering; stems with slender straight prickles, usually very bristly when young; brts. sometimes unarmed: lfts. usually 5, rarely 7, elliptic to lance-elliptic, rarely oblanceolate, 1–3 cm. long, acute or obtuse, sharply serrate with ascending teeth, glabrous, not or slightly lustrous above, paler beneath, pubescent on veins or nearly glabrous; stipules narrow: fls. usually solitary, rose, about 5 cm. across; pedicels and receptacle glandular-hispid; outer sepals lobed: fr. about 8 mm. across. Fl. VI–VII. W.R.201,t(c). M.N.2:t.9(c, as *R. lucida*). B.B.2:f.2314. (*R. humilis* Marsh., *R. parviflora* Ehrh., *R. virginiana* var. *humilis* Schneid.) Me. to Wis., Kans., Tex. and Fla. Intr. 1826. Zone IV. Handsome Rose well suited for borders of shrubberies.—**R. c. grandiflòra** (Bak.) Rehd., var. Lfts. usually 7, obovate or oval; fls. about 6 cm. across. W.R.207,t(c). Lindl., Ros. Mon. t.3(c). (*R. obovata* Raf., *R. humilis* var. *g.* Bak., *R. virginiana* var. *g.* Bean.) Me. to Mich., Del. and Mo.—**R. c. glandulòsa** (Crép.) Rehd., var. Lfts. doubly glandular-serrate and rachis glandular-hispid or stipitate-glandular. Ont. and Mass. to Fla. and n. Mex. K.S.174(as *R. humilis*). (*R. serrulata* Raf., *R. parviflora* var. *g.* Crép.) Cult. 1902.—**R. c. villòsa** (Best) Rehd.,

var. Lfts. 5–7, pubescent beneath: fls. 1–4. House, Wild Fl. N. Y. t.102(c). (*R. humilis* var. *villosa* Best, *R. Lyonii* Pursh.) Mass. to Minn., s. to Ga. and Kans. Cult. 1887.—**R. c. alba** (Rehd.) Rehd., f. A form of the preceding with white fls. W.R.198,t.(c). A.F.12:1098. Gg.5:306. Intr. about 1870.

R. c. × *spinosissima;* see under No. 2.

24. R. nítida Willd. Shrub to 0.5 m.; stems densely bristly and with slender prickles 3–5 mm. long: lfts. 7–9, close-set, elliptic to oblong, 1–3 cm. long, finely serrate, lustrous above, slightly pubescent or glabrous beneath; stipules, particularly the upper ones, dilated: fls. solitary or few, rose, 4–5 cm. across; pedicels and receptacle glandular-hispid; sepals usually entire: fr. about 1 cm. across. Fl.vi–vii. W.R.215,t(c), 217,t. B.B.2:285. Nfd. to Conn. Cult. 1807. Zone III. Handsome dwarf Rose.

R. n. × *californica* = **R. Scharnkeàna** Graebn. Low shrub; stem with slender prickles, often bristly: lfts. 7–9, oblong, cuneate: fls. 1–5, rose-purple. Gt.51:t.1504,f,2(c). Orig. before 1900.

Related species: **R. rudiúscula** Greene. Stems to 1 m., densely bristly: lfts. 5–9, subcoriaceous, elliptic, acute at ends, densely pubescent and pale beneath: fls. few; pedicels usually glandular-hispid. Iowa and Mo. to Okla. Intr. 1917. Zone V.

25. R. foliolòsa Nutt. Low shrub to 0.5 m.; stem with short, straight, slightly reflexed prickles or nearly unarmed, rarely bristly; lfts. 7–9, rarely 11, narrow- to linear-oblong, 1–3 cm. long, acute, finely serrate, glabrous and lustrous above, glabrous or pubescent on the veins beneath; stipules usually narrow: fls. solitary or few, rose, sometimes white, about 4 cm. across; pedicels and receptacle sparingly glandular-hispid or the latter sometimes smooth: fr. subglobose, about 8 mm. across. Fl.vi–viii. B.M.8513(c). W.R.219,t(c). G.F.3:101. B.C.5:f.3445. Ark. and Okla. to Tex. Cult. 1880. Zone V.— **R. f. alba** Bridwell, var. Fls. white. Cult. 1919.

Sect. 5. Cinnamomeae DC. Upright shrubs; prickles usually straight, in infrastipular pairs or scattered; stems often bristly: lfts. 5–11: infl. usually many-fld. with dilated bracts; sepals usually entire, upright after flowering and persistent, rarely deciduous; receptacle usually smooth.

26. R. rugòsa Thunb. Upright shrub to 2 m.; stems stout, tomentose, densely bristly and prickly: lfts. 5–9, elliptic to elliptic-obovate, 2–5 cm. long, acute or obtusish, serrate, lustrous and dark green, rugose and glabrous above, glaucescent, reticulate and pubescent beneath, thick and firm; petioles tomentose and bristly: fls. solitary or few, 6–8 cm. across, purple to white; pedicels short, bristly; receptacle smooth: fr. depressed-globose, smooth, brick-red, 2–2.5 cm. across. Fl.vi(–viii). W.R.181,t(c). S.Z.1:t.28(c). B.R. 420(c). Gt.30:t.1049;42:537. Gn.52:384,t(c). G.C.II.14:372. C.L.A.2:76;7: 624. (*R. ferox* Ait., *R. Regeliana* André & Lind.) N. China, Korea, Japan; escaped in the N. E. States. Intr. about 1845. Zone II.—Forms of typical *R. rugosa* (*R. r.* var. *Thunbergiana* C. A. Mey.) are: **R. r. týpica** Reg., var. With purple fls.; the typical form. (*R. r. rubra* Hort.)—**R. r. ròsea** Rehd., var. With rose-colored fls.—**R. r. alba** W. Robins. With white fls. Gn.9:452.t (c). G.8:261. (*R.r.* var. *albiflora* Koidz.)—**R. r. albo-plèna** Rehd., var. With double white fls.—Geographical varieties are: **R. r. Chamissoniàna** C. A. Mey., var. Bristles almost absent from the brs.: lfts. narrower and smaller, less rugose. (*R. pubescens* Bak., not Roxb.)—A form with double purple fls. is **R. r. plèna** Reg., var. Gt.24:t.846. (*R. r.* f. *rubroplena* Rehd.)—**R. r. kamtchática** (Vent.) Reg., var. With slenderer, less densely armed brs., thinner and less rugose lfts. and smaller fls. and fr. B.M.3149(c). B.R.419(c). N.K.7:t.8. (*R. k.* Vent.) Intr. about 1770.—*R. rugosa* is one of the most ornamental and at the same time most vigorous and hardy of the wild Roses, much planted for its dark green lustrous foliage turning orange and scarlet in autumn, for its large fls. appearing during the whole summer and its large red fruits. Many hybrids have been raised.

    R. r. × *arvensis* = **R. Paùlii** Rehd. Procumbent shrub with large white fls. in corymbs. Gn.86:286(h). (*R. rugosa repens alba* Paul.) Orig. before 1903.—*R. r.* × *chinensis* = **R. calocárpa** Willm. With single rose-colored fls. and handsome, abundantly produced fr. W.R.189,t(c),199,t. R.H.1895:446,447. Gn.46:548;52:384. Orig. before 1891.—*R. r.* × *odorata* (or *dilecta*) = **R. Bruántii** Rehd. Here belongs "Mad. Georges Bruant" (B.C.5:2992) and "Blanc Double de Coubert." Orig. before 1887.—*R. r.* × *borboniana* = **R. arnoldiàna** Sarg. Large semidouble deep crimson fls. Orig. before 1914. The typical form is a cross between *R. r.* and "Général Jacqueminot." The same cross is represented by "Mrs. Anthony Waterer." Orig. before 1900.—*R. r.* × *palustris* = **R. Spaethiàna** Graebn. Fls. corymbose, large, purple. Gt.51:t.1504,f.3(c). Cult. 1902.—*R. r.* × *blanda* = **R. warleyénsis** Willm. Lfts. 5–7, small: fls. pink. W.R.185,t(c). Orig. before 1910.—*R. r.* × *carolina*. Procumbent shrub with purple fls. W.R.203,t(c). (*R. humilis* × *r.* Koehne.) Orig. before 1893.—*R. r.* × *Roxburghii* = **R. micrugòsa** Henkel. Upright, very prickly shrub: lfts. small, pubescent. Gt.59:t.1581(c). R.H.1905:144. (*R. Vilmorinii* Bean.)—*R. r.* × *multiflora;* see under No. 51.—*R. r.* × *Wichuraiana;* see under No. 61.—*R. r.* × *rubrifolia* = **R. rubròsa** Preston. Brts. less densely spiny and pubescent: lfts. leathery, glabrous and glaucescent beneath; rachis glabrous: fls. large pink. G.C.80:329(h). Cult. 1903; also raised in Ottawa 1920.

    27. **R. aciculàris** Lindl. Low shrub, to 1 m.; stems densely bristly with weak prickles; brts. sometimes unarmed: lfts. 3–7, broad-elliptic to oblong, 1.5–5 cm. long, usually acute at ends, simply serrate, dull and glabrous above, pubescent beneath; stipules usually broad: fls. solitary, deep rose, 4–5 cm. across, fragrant; pedicels glabrous, rarely slightly glandular-hispid: fr. usually pear-shaped with distinct neck, 1.5–2 cm. long. Fl.v–vi. W.R.147,149,235,t(c, as *R. Woodsii*). D.L.3:f.244. N.K.7:t.10. (*R. Sayi* Schwein.) Alaska to Wyo., Mich. and N. Y.; N. E. Asia. Intr. 1805. Zone IV.—**R. a. Engelmánnii** (S. Wats.) Crép., var. Flowering brts. usually bristly: lfts. doubly glandular-serrate, glabrous and glandular beneath: fr. ellipsoid or pear-shaped, smaller. G.F.2:377. B.C.5:2995. D.L.3:f.245. (*R. E.* S. Wats.) N. D. and Mont. to Colo. Intr. 1891.—**R. a. Bourgeauiàna** (Crép.) Crép., var. Lfts. broad-elliptic, usually obtuse, more or less doubly glandular-serrate, slightly pubescent and glandular beneath: fr. subglobose with very short neck. B.C. 5:2994. B.B.2:f.2309(as *R. acicularis*). (*R. B.* Crép.) Ont. to Colo., Mont. and Mackenzie.—**R. a. nipponénsis** (Crép.) Koehne, var. Lfts. 7–9, 1–3 cm. long, simply serrate, glabrous; petioles bristly: pedicels glandular-bristly: fr. ovoid, 1.5–2 cm. long. B.M.7646(c). W.R.151,t(c). (*R. n.* Crép.) E. Asia. Intr. 1894.

    28. **R. arkansàna** Porter. Shrub to 0.5 m.; stems very prickly and bristly: lfts. 9–11, elliptic, 2–6 cm. long, acute, coarsely and sharply serrate, glabrous and lustrous above, glabrous or sparingly pilose on the veins beneath; stipules dilated, glandular-dentate: fls. corymbose, pink, about 4 cm. across; pedicels glabrous: fr. subglobose, 1–1.5 cm. across. Fl.vi–vii. Wisc. and Minn. to Kans. and Colo. Cult. 1917. Zone IV.

    29. **R. suffúlta** Greene. Low shrub to 0.5 m.; stems densely prickly and bristly, usually green; lfts., 7–11, broadly elliptic to obovate-oblong, 1.5–4 cm. long, usually obtuse, cuneate, simply serrate, finely pubescent on both sides or finally glabrous above; stipules dilated, glandular-dentate; petiole and rachis finely pubescent: fls. corymbose, pink, about 3 cm. across; pedicels and receptacle glabrous; sepals sometimes lobed: fr. globose, about 1 cm. across. Fl.vi. B.B.2:284. (*R. pratincola* Greene, not H. Br., *R. heliophila* Greene.) Alb. and Man. to Ill. and w. Tex. Cult. 1880. Zone III.—**R. s. alba** Rehd., f. Fls. white. Intr. 1901.

30. R. blánda Ait. Shrub to 2 m. with slender stems, unarmed or with scattered bristles when young, brown: lfts. 5–7, rarely 9, elliptic to obovate oblong, 2–6 cm. long, usually acute, coarsely serrate, dull and glabrous above, paler and finely pubescent or glabrous beneath: stipules dilated: fls. solitary or few, pink, 5–6 cm. across; pedicels and receptacle smooth: fr. subglobose, about 1.2 cm. across, sometimes ellipsoid. Fl.v–vi. W.R.307,t(c). Miller & Whiting, Wild Fl. 152. B.B.2:283. (*R. Solandri* Tratt., *R. subblanda* Rydb.) Nfd. to Pa., Mo., N. D. and Man. Intr. 1773. Zone II?

R. b. × *chinensis* = R. Aschersoniàna Graebn. Stems with hooked prickles: fls. very numerous, small, bright light purple; styles usually exserted. Gt.51:t. 1504,f.1(c). Orig. about 1880.—*R. b.* × *rugosa;* see under No. 26.

31. R. pendulìna L. Stems slender, to 1 m., usually nearly unarmed, rarely bristly and prickly: lfts. 5–13, oblong-ovate or oblong-elliptic, 2–6 cm. long, obtuse, doubly glandular-serrate, usually pubescent, rarely pubescent on both sides, more densely so beneath; stipules dilated: fls. usually solitary or 2–5, about 4 cm. across, rose or purple; pedicels and receptacle smooth or glandular-bristly: fr. oblong, with neck, usually nodding, 2–2.5 cm. long, bright red. Fl.v–vi. B.R.424(c). W.R.2:293,t(c). F.D.25:t.2625(c). (*R. alpìna* L., *R. cinnamòmea* L. 1753, not 1759.) Mts. of S. and C. Eu. Cult. 1789. Zone V. Handsome Rose with conspicuous large fr.—**R. p. pyrenaìca** (Gouan) R. Keller, var. Dwarf with glaucous brts. and glandular-bristly pedicels and receptacle. B.M.6724(c). G.H.t.93(c). Gn.27:t.544. (*R. p.* Gouan.) Cult. 1815.—**R. p. oxýodon** (Boiss.) Rehd., var. Lfts. 5–9, usually glabrous, teeth acuminate, sometimes simple: fls. 2–7; receptacle smooth; pedicels glandular-bristly. (*R. o.* Boiss., *R. alpìna* var. *o.* Boulenger.) Cauc. Cult. 1896. Zone V.

R. p. × *chinensis* = R. Lheritieràna Thory. BOURSAULT R. Climbing to 4 m., sparingly prickly: lfts. 3–7, oblong-ovate, simply serrate, glabrous: fls. in corymbs, light or dark purple, double or semidouble: fr. subglobose, smooth. R.R.3:gr.26,3. W.R.301,t(c). (*R. reclinata* Thory, *R. Boursaultii* Hort.) Orig. before 1820.—*R. p.* × *spinosissima;* see under No. 2.

32. R. cinnamòmea L. CINNAMON R. Shrub to 2 m.; stems slender with short curved prickles, often unarmed: lfts. 5–7, rarely 3, elliptic to oblong, obtuse or short-acuminate, 1.5–4 cm. long, simply serrate, dull green and pubescent above, densely pubescent beneath: stipules dilated, more or less convolute: fls. solitary or few, purple, about 5 cm. across; pedicels 2–3 cm. long, like the receptacle smooth: fr. depressed-globose, 1.2–1.5 cm. thick, scarlet. Fl.v–vi. W.R.141,t(c). D.F.25:t.2626(c). A.G.13:343. (*R. spinosissima* L. partly.) Eu., N. and W. Asia, occasionally escaped in N. Am. Cult. 1596. Zone IV.—**R. c. plèna** West., var. With double fls. W.R.143,t(c). R.R.1:gr.9,1(c). B.C.5:2993. (*R. majalis* Herrm., *R. foecundissima* Muenchh.) Cult. before 1770. Sometimes escaped in the E. States.

R. c. × *gallica;* see under No. 9.

Closely related species: **R. davùrica** Pall. Prickles straight and slender: lfts., doubly serrate, glandular; stipules narrow: pedicels longer, glandular: fr. ovoid. N.K.7:t.9. S.H.1:f.327c,328b-b[1]. (*R. cinnamomea* var. *d.* C. A. Mey.) N. China, N. E. Asia. Intr. 1910. Zone V.—**R. laxa** Retz. Prickles hooked or straight: lfts. 7–9, glabrous or pubescent beneath: fls. several, white; pedicels glandular: fr. ovoid. S.H.1:f.325l-l[2]. Turkest., Song. Cult. about 1800.—**R. amblyòtis** C. A. Mey. Prickles slender, straight, pointing upward: lfts. rarely 9, elliptic-oblong or oblong-ovate, 3–5 cm. long, usually acute, sharply serrate, puberulous beneath at least on midrib: pedicels slender, to 2 cm. long, glabrous; fls. 5 cm. across, red; sepals caudate: fr. depressed-globose or pyriform. Kamchatka. Cult. 1917. Zone II?—**R. Marrétii** Lévl. Brts. dark purple; prickles slender, straight: lfts. usually 7, oblong, 2–4 cm. long, obtusish to acute, thinly pubescent beneath: fls. 1–3, pink; pedicels and calyx-tube smooth; sepals caudate, entire, stipitate-glandular on back: fr. subglobose. W.R.2:495,t. Saghalin. Cult. 1908. Zone II?

33. **R. pisocárpa** A. Gr. Shrub to 2 m.; stems slender, with weak slender usually ascending prickles 2–5 mm. long: lfts. 5–7, elliptic-oblong to oblong-obovate, 1–4 cm. long, acutish or obtuse, coarsely serrate, green and finely pubescent beneath, short-petioluled; upper stipules dilated, slightly glandular-dentate: fls. corymbose with leafy bracts, pink, about 3 cm. across; sepals glandular-hispid on back: fr. globose, sometimes with short neck, 8 mm. across. Fl.vi–viii. B.M.6857(c). W.R.227,t(c). B. C. to Calif. and Idaho. Intr. about 1882. Zone V.

34. **R. Woòdsii** Lindl. Shrub to 2 m.; stem with numerous straight or slightly curved prickles: lfts. 5–7, obovate to oblong-obovate, petioluled, 1–3 cm. long, simply serrate, glaucous and glabrous or nearly glabrous beneath; stipules entire or slightly toothed, like the petiole usually glandless, rather narrow: fls. 1–3, pink, rarely white, 3–4.5 cm. across; pedicels and receptacle glabrous: fr. globose, rarely ellipsoid and with distinct neck, 8–10 mm. thick. Fl.vi–viii. W.R.236,t(c). (*R. Maximiliani* Nees, *R. Sandbergii* Greene.) Sask. and B. C. to Kans. and Utah. Cult. 1880. Zone III.—**R. W. Féndleri** (Crép.) Rydb. Lower, with straight slender prickles; stipules and petioles glandular; lfts. usually doubly glandular-serrate. W.R.175,t.(c),177,t. B.B. 2:f.2311 (as *R. Woodsii*). (*R. F.* Crép.) B. C. and Minn. to Ariz. and Chihuahua. Cult. 1888.

Closely related species: **R. Macoùnii** Greene. Stems with straight prickles, bristly when young: lfts. obovate, pale or glaucous and finely puberulent beneath. B.R.926(c, as *R. Woodsii*). (*R. Woodsii* Lindl. 1826, not 1820.) B. C. to Sask., Ore., Neb. and W. Tex. Intr. before 1826.

35. **R. califórnica** Cham. & Schlecht. Shrub to 3 m., with stout flattened, recurved prickles 5–8 mm. long; young shoots sometimes bristly; flowering brts. usually prickly: lfts. 5–7, broad-elliptic to oblong-obovate, 1–3 cm. long, usually obtuse, usually simply serrate, not glandular, dull and appressed-pubescent above, villous beneath: fls. in leafy-bracted corymbs, pink, about 4 cm. across; sepals villous outside; pedicels glabrous or slightly villous: fr. globose, with a distinct neck, 1–1.5 cm. across. Fl.vi–viii. Armstrong, Field Book Wild Fl. 221,f. Ore. to L. Calif. Cult. 1878. Zone V.—**R. c. plèna** Rehd., f. With double or semidouble fls. W.R.223,t(c).—**R. c. nàna** Bean., var. Dwarf form.

R. c. × *nitida;* see under No. 24.

36. **R. nutkàna** Presl. Shrub to 1.5 m.; stems usually dark brown, upright, with rather large straight prickles; young stems sometimes bristly: lfts. 5–9, broad-elliptic or oblong-ovate, 1.5–5 cm. long, acute or obtuse, doubly glandular-serrate, dark green and glabrous above, somewhat glandular-puberulous beneath, rarely slightly pubescent on veins; upper stipules dilated, glandular-dentate, glabrous; fls. usually solitary, 5–6 cm. across, rose, rarely white; pedicels 2–3 cm. long, usually slightly glandular-hispid; receptacle glabrous: fr. globose, without neck, 1.5–1.8 cm. across. Fl.vi–vii. W.R.231,t(c). G.F. 1:449. B.C.5:2993. Alaska to Wyo. and Calif. Intr. about 1876. Zone V.— **R. n. híspida** Fern., var. Lfts. coarsely serrate; receptacle glandular-hispid. (*R. MacDougalii* Holz.) B. C. to Utah.

Related species: **R. Spaldíngii** Crép. Lfts. 5–7, oval, usually obtuse, with simple scarcely glandular teeth, puberulent beneath: pedicels glabrous. B. C. to Ore. and Utah. Cult. 1915. Zone V.—**R. oreóphila** Rydb. Stems usually with weak curved prickles: lfts. 5–7, oval or ovate, 2–3.5 cm. long, simply serrate, finely pubescent beneath; pedicels glabrous. Colo. Intr. 1898. Zone V.

37. R. corymbulòsa Rolfe. Shrub to 2 m.; stems upright or sarmentose: brs. with few slender straight paired prickles or unarmed: lfts. 3–5, ovate-oblong, 2–4 cm. long, acute, finely doubly serrate, dull green and slightly pubescent above at first, glaucescent and pubescent beneath; rachis puberulous and sparingly glandular; stipules narrow and glandular-ciliate: fls. red with white eye, 2–2.5 cm. across, in umbel-like many-fld. corymbs; pedicels slender, about 2 cm. long, like the receptacle glandular-bristly; styles pubescent, exserted; fr. subglobose or ovoid 1–1.3 cm. long, scarlet. Fl.vi–vii. B.M. 8566(c). G.C.79:23. W. China. Intr. 1908. Zone V. Handsome Rose with numerous small fls.

38. R. Davìdi Crép. Shrub to 3 m.; stems with straight stout scattered prickles 4–6 mm. long, much enlarged at base: lfts. 7–9, rarely 11, elliptic to ovate-oblong, 2–4, rarely 6 cm. long, simply serrate, glabrous above, glaucescent and puberulous beneath; rachis puberulous, sparingly prickly: fls. pink, 3.5–5 cm. across, corymbose; pedicels like the oblong receptacle glandular-bristly or sometimes only puberulous; styles exserted about 3 mm.: fr ovoid or oblong-ovoid, 1.5–2 cm. long, with long neck, scarlet. Fl.vi–vii. B.M.8679 (c). G.C.78:423. W. China. Intr. 1908. Zone V.—**R. D. elongàta** Rehd. & Wils., var. Lfts. 5–7 cm. long: fls. fewer: fr. 2–2.5 cm. long. Gs.16:1(c). Intr. 1908. Handsome in fr.

39. R. caudàta Bak. Shrub to 4 m.; stems with scattered straight stout prickles to 8 mm. long, broad at base: lfts. 7–9, elliptic-ovate or ovate to oblong-ovate, 2.5–5 cm. long, acute, simply serrate, glabrous and glaucescent beneath: rachis smooth or sparingly prickly and glandular-bristly; stipules rather broad, glandular-ciliate; fls. red, 3.5–5 cm. across, in few-fld. corymbs; pedicels and receptacle glandular-bristly, rarely nearly smooth; sepals entire, long-caudate, with leafy apex: fr. oblong-ovoid, with long neck, 2–2.5 cm. long, orange or coral-red; sepals upright. Fl.vi. W. China. Intr. about 1896. Zone V.

Related species: **R. banksiópsis** Bak. Prickles few or stems unarmed above: lfts. 7–9, oblong, usually pubescent beneath: fls. 2–3 cm. across; pedicels and receptacle glabrous. W.R.505(fr). W. China. Intr. 1907 or 1909.—R. macrophýlla Lindl. Large shrub, with few prickles or unarmed: lfts. 9–11, elliptic-ovate to elliptic-oblong, 2.5–6 cm. long, acute, pubescent beneath: fls. 1–3, red, about 5 cm. across; pedicels and receptacle glandular-setose or smooth: fr. oblong-ovoid, 2.5–3 cm. long. W.R.157,t(c).159,t. Himal. Intr. 1818. Zone VI.

40. R. setìpoda Hemsl. & Wils. Shrub to 3 m.; stem with infra-stipular, straight wide-based prickles to 8 mm. long: lfts. 7–9, elliptic or ovate, 3–6 cm. long, obtuse or acutish, usually doubly serrate, dark green and glabrous above, glaucous and usually glandular beneath and puberulous on the veins or sometimes glabrous; stipules broad, densely glandular-ciliate; rachis sparingly prickly and stipitate-glandular: fls. pale pink to rose-purple, about 5 cm. across, in loose corymbs; pedicels and receptacle copiously glandular-setose; sepals long-caudate, with foliaceous serrate tips; petals slightly pubescent outside: fr. oblong-ovoid, with narrow neck, about 2.5 cm. long, deep red. Fl.vi. J.L.27:486. (*R. macrophylla* var. *crasse-aculeata* Vilm.) C. China. Intr. 1895. Zone (V).—Conspicuous in June with its large pink fls. and in fall with its nodding clusters of red hips.

R. s. × *Moyesii;* see under No. 43.

Related species: **R. persetòsa** Rolfe. Stems densely bristly; lfts. 5–9, 2–5 cm. long, simply serrate, puberulous beneath: fls. deep pink, 2–3 cm. across, in large corymbs; pedicels and receptacle glabrous; sepals entire. J.L.27:487,488. (*R. Davidi* var. *p.* Boulenger.) W. China. Intr. 1895. Zone V.

41. R. Hemsleyàna Täckholm. Shrub to 2 m.; stem with few mostly infrastipular prickles: lfts. 7–9, rarely 5, oval or elliptic, 2–5 cm. long, acute or obtuse, slightly doubly glandular-serrate, glabrous beneath or pubescent on the veins; stipules broad, glandular-ciliate; rachis stipitate-glandular and with few small prickles: fls. 3–11, pink, 3–5 cm. across; pedicels 1–3 cm. long, densely glandular-setose; sepals caudate with broad serrate tip and lateral appendages: fr. ovoid-oblong, with long neck, about 2.5 cm. long. Fl.vi; fr.ix–xi. B.M.8569(c). C. China. Intr. 1904. Zone V?

42. R. Sweginzówii Koehne. Shrub to 5 m.; stems with large compressed prickles, sometimes mixed with smaller prickles: lfts. 7–11, elliptic to ovate-oblong, acute, 2–5 cm. long, doubly serrate, glabrous above, pubescent beneath, more densely on the veins; rachis prickly and glandular; stipules wide, glandular-ciliate: fls. 1–3, rose, about 4 cm. across; pedicels and receptacle glandular-hispid; sepals sparsely lobed and serrate at apex: fr. oblong, about 2.5 cm. long, bright red. Fl.vi. I.S.2:t.80. M.D.1910:96. G.C.72:135. Gn.87:588. N. W. China. Cult. 1910. Zone V.

Related species: **R. Muriélae** Rehd. & Wils. Shrub to 2.5 m.; stems with slender prickles and bristles: lfts. 9–15, elliptic to elliptic-oblong, 1–4 cm. long, acutish, pubescent on midrib beneath: fls. white, in 3–7-fld. corymbs; sepals entire: fr. ellipsoid, 1–2 cm. long. W. China. Intr. 1904. Zone (V).

43. R. Moyèsii Hemsl. & Wils. Shrub to 3 m.; stems with scattered and paired short straight prickles: lfts. 7–13, ovate or elliptic to oblong-ovate, 1–4 cm. long, acute, closely serrulate, glabrous except pubescent on midrib beneath; rachis puberulous, glandular and bristly; stipules wide, glandular-ciliate: fls. 1–2, deep blood-red, 4–6 cm. across; pedicels short, stipitate-glandular; receptacle stipitate-glandular or smooth; sepals ovate, long-caudate: fr. oblong-ovoid, narrowed into a neck, 5–6 cm. long, deep orange-red. Fl.vi. B.M.8338(c). W.R.229,t(c),230,t. J.L.27:489. B.S.2:435. G.C.70:219. Gn.72:313. V.F.95(h). (*R macrophylla* var. *rubrostaminea* Vilm.) W. China. Intr. 1894 and 1903. Zone (V). Handsome Rose, particularly the type with dark red fls.—**R. M. Fargèsii** Rolfe, var. Lfts. broad-oval to suborbicular, 1.2–2 cm. long, obtuse. G.C.65:19. Gn.86:543;87:590. Cult. 1900?—**R. M. rósea** Rehd. & Wils., f. Lfts. more coarsely serrate; fls. light pink. B.M.9248(c). (*R. holodonta* Stapf.) Intr. 1908.

R. M. × Willmottiae; see under No. 48.—Other hybrids of *R. Moyesii* are: **R. wintoniensis** Hillier (*R. M. × setipoda*) and **R. highdownensis** Hillier (*R. M. × ?*) Gs.18:166.

Related species: **R. saturàta** Bak. Stems unarmed or with few small prickles: lfts. usually 7, ovate to ovate-lanceolate, 2.5–6 cm. long, acute or short-acuminate, sharply serrate, pubescent on the veins beneath or nearly glabrous: fls. solitary, dark red, 5 cm. across; anthers purple; pedicels glabrous: fr. globose-ovoid, 1.5–2 cm. long, coral-red. C. China. Intr. 1907. Zone (V).

44. R. bélla Rehd. & Wils. Shrub to 3 m.; stems with slender straight prickles, bristly near base: lfts. 7–9, elliptic or ovate, 1–2.5 cm. long, acutish, rarely obtusish, simply serrate, glaucescent beneath, glabrous except stipitate-glandular on midrib; upper stipules broad, glandular-ciliate: fls. 1–3, bright rose, 4–5 cm. across; pedicels 5–10 mm. long, like the receptacle stipitate-glandular; sepals caudate, leafy and entire at apex: fr. ellipsoid; attenuate into the neck, 1.5–2 cm. long, scarlet. Fl.vi. I.S.2:t.79. N. China. Intr. 1910. Zone V.—**R. b. pállens** Rehd. & Wils., f. Fls. light rose-colored. Intr. 1910.

45. R. Webbiàna Royle. Slender shrub to 2 m.; brs. slender, often pruinose when young, with straight yellow prickles about 1 cm. long: lfts. 5–9, orbicular to obovate or broad-elliptic, 6–20 mm. long, rounded at apex, rarely acutish, serrate, entire toward the base, glabrous or sometimes slightly pubescent beneath; petiole prickly: fls. pale pink, 4–5 cm. across; pedicels short, glabrous or slightly glandular; sepals lanceolate, entire, glandular outside: fr. ovoid, 1.5–2 cm. long, bright red. Fl.vi. W.R.233,t(c). Himal. to Afghan. and Turkest. Intr. 1879. Zone (V).

Related species: **R. Fedtschenkoàna** Reg. Stems with prickles and bristles: lfts. 7–9, oblong, 2–3 cm. long, pubescent beneath: fls. 1–4, white; pedicels and receptacle hispid. B.M.7770(c). W.R.155,t(c). Turkest. Intr. 1876?

46. **R. sertàta** Rolfe. Slender shrub to 2 m.; brs. glaucous, with straight slender prickles: lfts. 7–11, oval to narrow-elliptic, 6–20 mm. long, obtuse or acutish, sharply serrate, glabrous, glaucescent beneath; stipules glandular-ciliate: fls. 1 or few, rose or rose-purple, 5–6 cm. across; pedicels 1.5–3 cm. long, glandular or glabrous; sepals caudate, entire: fr. ovoid, 1.5–2 cm. long, deep red. Fl.vi. B.M.8473(c). W.R.153,t(c). G.C.54:166. C. and W. China. Intr. 1904. Zone V. Handsome graceful Rose.

Related species: **R. Giráldii** Crép. Brts. with slender prickles: lfts. usually 7, suborbicular to ovate or elliptic, serrate, pubescent: fls. pink, 2.5 cm. across; pedicels short, like the receptacle glandular-setose: fr. ovoid, about 1 cm. long, scarlet. C. China. Intr. ?1897.—**R. G. venulòsa** Rehd. & Wils., var. Lfts. firmer, reticulate beneath, often glabrous or nearly glabrous above. Intr. 1907. Zone V?—**R. Práttii** Hemsl. Stems prickly and bristly or without bristles; lfts. 7–15, elliptic to oblong, 6–15 mm. long, obtusish, serrate, pubescent on the veins beneath; rachis puberulous: fls. 1 or several, 2 cm. across, pink, sepals ovate, abruptly acuminate; pedicels and receptacle glandular-bristly: fr. subglobose to ovoid, 6–10 mm. long; sepals finally deciduous. W. China. Intr. 1903 or 1908. Zone V.—**R. elegántula** Rolfe. Shrub to 2 m.; brts. usually densely bristly: lfts. 7–9, elliptic or elliptic-ovate, 1–2 cm. long, obtuse, usually simply serrate, glaucous: fls. deep pink, 2.5–3 cm. across; pedicels and the ovoid-oblong receptacle smooth. W. China. Cult. 1900. Zone V.—**R. Forrestiàna** Boulenger. Shrub to 2 m.; lfts. 5–7, rarely 9, oval to obovate, 1–2 cm. long, rounded at apex, glabrous or pubescent on midrib beneath, teeth simple or nearly so: fls. 1 or few, with large bracts at base, rose, 2–3.5 cm. across; styles exserted; pedicels 8–15 mm. long, stipitate-glandular. Bull. Jard. Bot. Bruxelles, 14:127. W. China. Cult. 1922. Zone VII?

47. **R. multibracteàta** Hemsl. & Wils. Shrub to 2 m.; brts. slender, glabrous, with slender straight paired prickles: lfts. 7–9, broad-oval to suborbicular, 6–15 mm. long, obtuse, doubly serrulate, glabrous or pubescent on midrib beneath; rachis glandular and often with few small prickles: fls. pink, 3 cm. across, paniculate or corymbose, with many crowded bracts; pedicels and receptacle glandular-bristly; sepals ovate, abruptly acuminate, entire; styles villous, exserted about 4 mm.: fr. ovoid, 1–1.5 cm. long, orange-red. Fl.vi. G.C.100:23. Gt.81:253. W. China. Intr. 1910. Zone VI.

48. **R. Willmóttiae** Hemsl. Densely branched shrub to 3 m.; stems with straight paired prickles, glaucous when young: lfts. 7–9, elliptic to obovate or nearly orbicular, 6–15 mm. long, usually rounded at apex, closely and often doubly serrate, glabrous: fls. usually solitary, rose-purple, about 3 cm. across; pedicels about 1 cm. long, glabrous; sepals lanceolate, caudate, smooth: fr. subglobose, about 1 cm. long, orange-red. Fl.vi. B.M.8186(c). Gn.87:588. S.L.323(h). W. China. Intr. 1904. Zone V?

R. W. × *Moyesii* = R. pruhoniciána Zeman. Dense shrub with bright pink fls. (*R. Hillieri* Hillier.) Orig. about 1920.

49. **R. gymnocàrpa** Nutt. Shrub to 3 m.; stems with paired very slender prickles and bristles: lfts. 5–9, broad-elliptic to elliptic-oblong, 1–3.5 cm. long, doubly glandular-serrate, glabrous; stipules glandular-ciliate and dentate: fls. usually solitary, rose, about 3 cm. across; pedicels glabrous or glandular-hispid: fr. ellipsoid or subglobose, 6–8 mm. across. Fl.vi–vii. W.R.221,t(c). B. C. to Calif. and Mont. Intr. 1893. Zone V.

Related species: **R. Albérti** Reg. Shrub to 1 m.; stems densely prickly and bristly: lfts. orbicular to obovate or ovate, 6–30 mm. long, often doubly serrate, appressed-pubescent beneath: fls. white, about 3 cm. across; pedicels glandular; receptacle smooth: fr. pear-shaped, 1.5–2 cm. long. Turkest. Intr. 1877. Zone V.

50. R. Beggeriàna Schrenk. Much-branched shrub to 2.5 m.; stems with hooked paired and scattered prickles: lfts. 5–9, oval or elliptic-obovate, 8–25 mm. long, simply serrate, pubescent beneath or glabrous, bluish or grayish green; fls. in several- or many-fld. corymbs, rarely solitary, white, rarely pink, 2–3 cm. across; pedicels and receptacle glandular or smooth; fr. subglobose, 6–8 mm. across, red, finally dark purple. Fl.vi;fr.viii–ix. W.R.171,t(c). I.T. 5:t.122. S.H.1:f.325i-k,¹326k-l. N. Persia to Altai and Song. Intr. 1881. Zone III.

Sect. 6. SYNSTYLAE DC. Stems climbing, trailing or sarmentose, rarely upright, with hooked prickles: fls. in corymbs, outer sepals pinnate, rarely entire, caducous; style connate into a slender exserted column.

51. R. multiflòra Thunb. Vigorous shrub with long reclining or climbing brs.: lfts. usually 9, obovate to oblong, 1.5–3 cm. long, acute or obtuse, serrate, pubescent: fls. in many-fld. pyramidal corymbs, 1.5–2 cm. across, usually white; sepals ovate, abruptly acuminate; styles glabrous: fr. small, globular. Fl.vi–vii. B.M.7119(c). G.F.3:405,4:535(h). Gt.67:185(h). Gg.5:120(h), 121. (*R. polyantha* Sieb. & Zucc., *R. intermedia* Carr., *R. Wichurae* Koch.) Japan, Korea. Intr. before 1868. Zone V.—**R. m. Thunbergiàna** Thory is the typical form described above, with small white fls. and pubescent pedicels. —**R. m. calva** Franch. & Sav., var. Lfts. pubescent beneath only on midrib: fls. small, white or pinkish; pedicels glabrous. (*R. c.* Boulenger.) Japan. N. and C. China.—**R. m. cathayénsis** Rehd. and Wils. Fls. pink, 2–4 cm. across, in few- to many-fld. rather flat corymbs; pedicels glabrous, sometimes glandular. Gn.89:35(h). (*R. calva* var. *c.* Boulenger, *R. c.* Bailey, *R. Gentiliana* Lévl. & Vant.) China. Intr. 1907.—**R. m. cárnea** Thory. A form of the preceding with double light pink fls. B.M.1059(c). B.R.425(c). (*R. m.* var. *plena* Reg., *R. florida* Poir.) Intr. 1804.—**R. m. platyphýlla** Thory. SEVEN SISTERS ROSE. Similar to the preceding, but lvs. larger and fls. deep pink. B.R.1372(c). Intr. 1817. Closely related to this form is the well known "Crimson Rambler." A.G.16:233.

R. m. × *rugosa* = R. Iwàra Sieb. with single, rather small white fls. W.R. 193,t(c). (*R. yedoensis* Mak.)—*R. m.* × *chinensis*. Here belong the Polyantha Roses (*R. polyantha* Hort., not Sieb. & Zucc. nor Roessig.) Upright low shrubs with numerous, rather small double fls. Gn.29:118,t. R.H.1884:501(h). Also "Baby Rambler" (*R. m.* × *chinensis minima*) belongs here.—*R. m.* × *moschata*. Here probably belongs the Rose known as *R. polyantha grandiflora*. W.R.34, t(c).—*R. m.* × *borboniana* "Général Jacqueminot." Here belongs the "Dawson Rose" (*R. Dawsoniana* Hort., not Ellw. & Barry which is typical *R. multiflora*.) G.F.6:316(h),317. G.W.7:125(h).—*R. multiflora* × *Wichuraiana;* see under No. 61.

52. R. Watsoniàna Crép. Shrub with sarmentose or recurving brs.: lfts. 3–5, linear-lanceolate, with entire wavy margin, 2.5–6 cm. long, pubescent beneath: fls. about 1 cm. across, white or pink in many-fld. pyramidal corymbs; style glabrous. Fl.vi. W.R.53,t.(c). G.F.3:477. R.B.14:183. (*R. multiflora* var. *W.* Matsum.) Cult. in Japan. Intr. 1870. Zone VI. Possibly a mutation of *R. multiflora;* peculiar rather than ornamental.

53. R. setígera Michx. PRAIRIE R. Shrub with glabrous climbing or recurving stems to 5 m. long: lfts. 3, rarely 5, ovate to oblong-ovate, 3–9 cm. long, short-acuminate, serrate, pubescent on the veins beneath: fls. about 5 cm. across, rose, fading to whitish, nearly scentless, in rather few-fld. corymbs; pedicels and receptacle glandular-hispid; styles glabrous: fr. glo-

bose, about 8 mm. across. Fl.vi–viii. W.R.71,t.(c). Mn.8:t.5(c). G.F.10:323.
Gng.1:325. C.L.A.4:339;7:473. S.L.320(h). Ont. to Neb., Tex. and Fla.
Intr. 1810. Zone IV.—**R. s. inérmis** Palm. & Steyerm., f. Stems unarmed or
with few weak spines: lvs. glabrous. Intr. 1923.—**R. s. serèna** Palm. &
Steyerm., var. Stems unarmed: lvs. pubescent beneath. Intr. 1924.—**R. s.
tomentòsa** Torr. & Gr., var. Lvs. tomentose beneath, dull above: fls. smaller,
more numerous. R.R.1:gr.5,3(c). L.A.2:f.516. (*R. rubifolia* Ait.) Intr. 1800.
—There are several double-fld. forms as "Baltimore Belle" (B.C.5:f.3439)
which are probably hybrids with *R. Noisettiana, R. gallica, R. multiflora* and
others.

Related species: **R. triphýlla** Roxb. Climbing; prickles few, small, recurved:
lfts. 3, rarely 5, ovate-lanceolate, acuminate, glabrous, glaucous beneath; stipules narrow, dentate: fls. corymbose, small, white, double, the inner petals
shorter and narrower than the outer ones; pedicels and calyx-tube glabrous.
R.H.1842:281,t(c). W.R.67:t(c). (*R. anemoneflora* Fort.) E. China. Intr.
1844. Zone VII.

54. **R. Hélenae** Rehd. & Wils. Sarmentose shrub to 5 m., with stout
hooked prickles: lfts. 7–9, rarely 5, oblong-ovate to ovate-lanceolate, 2.5–5
cm. long, short-acuminate, rounded or broad-cuneate at base, sharply serrate,
grayish green beneath and pubescent on the veins: fls. white, fragrant, 3 cm.
across, in many-fld. umbel-like corymbs 7–15 cm. across; pedicels slender,
·2–3 cm. long, stipitate-glandular like the receptacle; sepals lanceolate, sparingly pinnate; styles pubescent: fr. ovoid or oblong-ovoid, 1–1.5 cm. long,
scarlet. Fl.vi. I.S.2:t.77. J.L.47:195. Gn.89:35(h). Gs.6:108(h). (*R. floribunda* Bak., not Stev.) C. China. Intr. 1907. Zone (V).

55. **R. Rùbus** Lévl. & Vant. Sarmentose shrub to 6 m., with small hooked
prickles: lfts. usually 5, ovate-elliptic to obovate, 3–8 cm. long, abruptly
acuminate, sharply or coarsely serrate, pubescent beneath, rarely nearly glabrous: fls. white, fragrant, 2.5–3 cm. across, in dense corymbs; pedicels 1–2
cm. long, tomentose, glandular: fr. subglobose, 8 mm. across, scarlet. Fl.vi.
W.R.2:507,t. (*R. Ernesti* Bean.) C. and W. China. Intr. 1907. Zone VI?

Related species: **R. Mulligáni** Boulenger. Prickles strongly dilated at base:
lfts. 5–7, elliptic, to 6 cm. long, acute or acuminate, pubescent beneath on the
veins: fls. 4.5–5.5 cm. across; pedicels 2.5–3.5 cm. long; sepals 12–15 mm. long,
long-pinnate: fr. 10–13 mm. high. W. China. Intr. 1917–19. Zone VI?—**R.
glomeràta** Rehd. & Wils. Lfts. usually 5–7, oblong to oblong-obovate, 3–10 cm.
long, serrulate, rugose above, reticulate beneath and pubescent on the veins: fr.
orange-red. W. China. Intr. 1908. Zone VI?

56. **R. Brunònii** Lindl. HIMALAYAN MUSK-R. Tall shrub with arching or
sarmentose brs., glabrous or thinly villous while young; prickles hooked, short
and stout: lfts. 5–7, elliptic-oblong to oblong-lanceolate, 3–6 cm. long, acute
or acuminate, serrulate, slightly pubescent or glabrous above, soft-pubescent
beneath; petioles and rachis pubescent, usually with scattered prickles: fls.
white, 3–5 cm. across, fragrant, in many-fld. corymbs; sepals lanceolate, acu-
.much longer than the receptacle; pedicels slender, glandular-pubescent; styles pubescent: fr. ovoid, about 1 cm. long, glabrous. Fl.vi–vii. B.M.
4030(c). B.R.829(c). W.R.37,t(c). G.C.36:152,153. Gn.77:511;79:113(h),
519(h);86:363(h; as *R. moschata*). (*R. Brownii* Tratt.) Himal. Intr. 1822.
Zone VII? Usually cult. as *R. moschata*.

57. **R. moschàta** Herrm. MUSK-R. Shrub with arching or sarmentose
glabrous brs.; prickles straight or slightly curved; lfts. .5–7, elliptic-ovate to
oblong-ovate, 2.5–5 cm. long, acute or acuminate, serrulate, glabrous or nearly
so beneath, except pubescent on the midrib; petioles and rachis nearly
glabrous, usually prickly: fls. white, 3–5 cm. across, in usually 7-fld. corymbs,
of musky fragrance; pedicels slender, slightly pubescent and glandular; styles

pubescent: fr. ovoid, small. Fl.vi. W.R.33.t(c). (*R. ruscinonensis* Déségl.)
S. Eu., N. Afr., W. Asia. Long cult. Zone VII?—**R. m. plèna** West., var.
With double fls. R.R.1:99,t(c).—**R. m. nastaràna** Christ, var. More robust:
lfts. nearly glabrous beneath: fls. over 5 cm. across, tinged pinkish, more
numerous. W.R.39,t.(c). R.H.1880:314,315. (*R. Pissardi* Carr.) Persia.
Intr. 1879. Zone VI?

R. m. × *gallica* = **R. Dupóntii** Déségl. Stems prickly and bristly: lfts. fewer
and broader; fls. larger; styles shorter; pedicels glandular. B.R.861(c). W.R.
43,t(c). Gn.67:254;77:510. Orig. before 1817.—Here belongs also *R. Freundiana*
Graebn. Gt.57:471. G.25:311.

Related species: **R. longicúspis** Bertol. Sarmentose and climbing: lfts.
coriaceous, lustrous, ovate or elliptic to ovate-oblong, 5–10 cm. long, acuminate
or long-acuminate, usually rounded at base, reticulate beneath and usually quite
glabrous; stipules finely denticulate: fls. in many-fld. corymbs; petals silky outside; pedicels pubescent. Bertoloni, Misc. Bot. t.3. (*R. lucens* Rolfe.) Himal.,
W. China. Cult. 1915. Zone VII?—**R. Sinowílsoni** Hemsl. Similar to the preceding: lfts. glabrous or slightly pubescent beneath; stipules very narrow,
glandular-denticulate: fls. subumbellate or paniculate, in bud obtuse or abruptly
pointed; pedicels glabrous, not or slightly glandular. W. China. Intr. 1904.
Zone VI?—**R. cerasocárpa** Rolfe. Lfts. subcoriaceous, 5, sometimes 3, ovate
or elliptic-ovate, acute or acuminate, glabrous; stipules narrow, entire: fls. 2.5–3
cm. across, paniculate, pedicels and receptacle glabrous, glandular; bud abruptly
pointed: fr. globose, 1 cm. diam. B.M.8688(c). C. China. Cult. 1914. Zone VI?

58. R. Maximowicziàna Regel. Shrub with sarmentose or arching brs.;
young stems with scattered hooked prickles and bristles: lfts. 7–9, elliptic-
ovate to oblong, 3–6 cm. long, acute or acuminate, finely serrate, paler beneath, glabrous; stipules glandular-serrulate: fls. white, 3–3.5 cm. across,
in many-fld. corymbs with persistent bracts; sepals ovate, abruptly caudate-
acuminate; pedicels stipitate-glandular or glabrous; styles glabrous: fr.
subglobose or broad-ovoid, about 1 cm. across. Fl.vi–vii. N.K.7:t.1. (*R.
Fauriei* Lév.) Manch., Korea. Intr. ?—**R. M. Jáckii** (Rehd.) Rehd., var.
Stems without bristles. N.K.7:t.3. (*R. J.* Rehd., *R. Kelleri* Bak., not Dalla
Torre & Sarnth.) Korea. Intr. 1905. Zone V.

59. R. Hénryi Boulenger. Sarmentose shrub; brs. with hooked prickles,
often purplish; floral brts. unarmed: lfts. usually 5, elliptic to elliptic-ovate,
4.5–8 cm. long, acuminate, rounded or broad-cuneate at base, simply serrate,
glabrous and glaucescent beneath; stipules narrow, entire: fls. white, fragrant, 3–3.5 cm. across, in umbel-like corymbs; bud gradually acuminate;
pedicels 1.2–2 cm. long, pubescent and stipitate-glandular; receptacle pubescent; sepals pubescent and slightly glandular, with a few appendages; styles
pubescent: fr. globose, 8–10 mm. across, dark red. Fl.vi–vii. J.L.27:483. (*R.
Gentiliana* Rehd. & Wils., not Lévl. & Vant., *R. moschata* var. *densa* Vilm.)
C. and E. China. Intr. 1907. Zone VI.

Closely related species: **R. filipes** Rehd. & Wils. Lfts. usually 5–7, oblong-
ovate to lanceolate, 3.5–7 cm. long, acuminate, pale beneath and glabrous, but
glandular: pedicels glabrous and stipitate-glandular, 2–3.5 cm. long; fls. 2–2.5
cm. across: fr. globose, about 1 cm. across, scarlet. W. China. Intr. 1908. Zone
(V).—**R. crocacántha** Boulenger. Shrub to 2.5 m.; prickles orange-yellow:
lfts. 5–7, elliptic, to 5 cm. long, doubly serrate, glabrous or pubescent beneath:
fls. very numerous, 1–1.5 cm. across; pedicels 1–1.8 cm. long; styles glabrous.
W. China. Intr. 1917–19. Zone VI?—Another related species is **R. phoenícea**
Boiss. Lfts. usually 5, acute or obtuse; corymbs pyramidal, usually many-fld.;
styles glabrous. Asia Minor. Intr. about 1885. Zone VI?

60. R. Soulieàna Crép. Upright shrub to 4 m. with spreading brs.; prickles
stout, hooked: lfts. usually 7, elliptic or obovate to ovate-oblong, 1–3 cm.
long, acute or obtuse, serrulate, glabrous beneath: fls. white, 3–3.5 cm. across,
in many-fld. corymbs 10–15 cm. across: pedicels and receptacle glandular;

sepals ovate, acuminate: fr. ovoid, about 1 cm. long, orange-red. Fl.vi. B.M. 8158(c). W.R.57,t(c). Gn.89:35(h). W. China. Intr. 1896. Zone VI.

61. **R. Wichuraiàna** Crép. Memorial R. Half-evergreen, with long prostrate or trailing brs.; prickles strong, curved: lfts. 7–9, suborbicular to broadovate or obovate, 1–2.5 cm. long, usually obtuse, coarsely serrate, dark green and lustrous above, lighter green and lustrous beneath, glabrous; stipules dentate: fls. 4–5 cm. across, white, fragrant, in few- to many-fld. pyramidal corymbs; styles pubescent; pedicels slightly glandular-hispid: fr. ovoid, about 1 cm. long. Fl.vii–ix. B.M.7421(c). W.R.59,t(c). R.H.1898:105,t(c),106. G.F.4:569;6:337. G.C.II.22:99. M.G.13:580–5(h). (*R. Luciae* var. *W. Koidz., R. bracteata* Hort., not Wendl.) Japan, Korea, Formosa, E. China. Intr. 1891. Zone V. Adapted for covering banks and rocky slopes. Many hybrids have been raised.

R. W. × *rugosa* = R. Jacksònii Willm. Lfts. larger, rugose above; fls. bright crimson. R.W.63,t(c). Here belongs "Lady Duncan."—*R. W.* × *multiflora* "Crimson Rambler" = R. Barbieràna Rehd. Lfts. 5–7, larger: fls. single, carmine, 4–5 cm. across; petals whitish at the base. R.H.1901:20,t(c). (*R. Wichuraiana rubra* André.) Orig. before 1900.—There are also numerous hybrids of *R. W.* with Hybrid Teas and Hybrid Perpetuals (G.F.6:337. Mn.8:27,156)

Closely related species: R. Lùciae Franch. & Rochebr. Of more upright habit: lfts. usually 7, narrower and thinner: fls. smaller. E. China, Korea, Japan. Intr. ?

62. **R. sempérvirens** L. Evergreen or half-evergreen shrub with trailing or climbing stems: lfts. 5–7, ovate-lanceolate, 2–5 cm. long, acuminate, serrulate, lustrous above and beneath, glabrous: fls. 3–5 cm. across, in few-, rarely many-fld. corymbs, slightly fragrant; pedicels glandular-hispid; styles usually pubescent: fr. subglobose or ovoid, about 1 cm. long, orange-red. Fl.vi–vii. B.R.465(c). W.R.19,t(c). S. Eu., N. Afr. Zone VI?—**R. s. prostràta** (DC.) Desv. Lfts. elliptic, acute, smaller: styles glabrous; fr. ovoid. (*R. p. DC.)—* **S. s. scándens** (Mill.) Nichols. Lfts. elliptic to oblong, obtuse: fr. subglobose. (*R. s.* Mill.)—Some double-fld. forms like "Felicité perpetuelle" are probably hybrids with *R. chinensis*.

63. **R. arvénsis** Huds. Deciduous shrub with trailing stems: lfts. usually 7, ovate to elliptic-ovate, 1–3.5 cm. long, acute, serrate, dull above, glabrous or slightly pubescent beneath, rather thin: fls. 3–5 cm. across, scentless, in few-fld. corymbs or solitary; styles glabrous: fr. ovoid. Fl.vi–vii. B.M. 2054(c). W.R.11,t(c). S.E.3,t.476(c). F.D.25:t.2633(c). `Gn.60:233;77:510. (*R. repens* Scop., *R. silvestris* Herrm.) Eu. Cult. 1750. Zone V.—**R. a. Ayreshirea** Ser., var. Ayrshire R. More vigorous: lvs. green on both sides, remaining longer on the brs. B.M.2054(c). (*R. capreolata* Neill, *R. a.* var. *scandens* Sweet, *R. a.* var. *c.* Bean.)—The forms with double fls. often called Ayrshire Roses are probably hybrids with other Roses.

R. a. × *chinensis* = R. rùga Lindl. Trailing: fls. large, pink, double, fragrant, in several-fld. corymbs. B.R.1389(c). W.R.55,t(c). Orig. before 1830.—*R. a.* × *gallica* = R. Polliniàna Spreng. Upright or sarmentose: lfts. usually 5, of firmer texture, slightly pubescent beneath: fls. long-stalked, large, white te pink. W.R.333,t(c). Eu. Cult. 1820.—*R. a.* × *rugosa;* see under No. 26.

Sect. 7. Indicae Thory. Stems upright or procumbent, with sparse, hooked prickles: lfts. 3–5, rarely 7, glabrous; stipules and bracts narrow: infl. 1–many-fld.; sepals entire or sparingly lobed, reflexed after flowering: styles exserted, free. Two Chinese species.

64. **R. odoràta** Sweet. Tea R. Evergreen or half-evergreen, with long, sarmentose, often climbing brs.; prickles scattered, hooked: lfts. 5–7, elliptic or ovate to oblong-ovate, 2–7 cm. long, acute or acuminate, sharply serrate, lustrous above, glabrous: fls. solitary or 2–3, pink, on rather short, often glandular stalks, 5–8 cm. across. Fl.vi–ix. B.R.804(c). R.R.3:gr.25,19(c).

(*R. Thea* Savi, *R. chinensis* var. *fragrans* (Thory) Rehd., *R. indica fragrans* Thory, *R. indica* var. *odoratissima* Lindl.) China. First intr. in the double blush form in 1810. Zone VII.—**R. o. ochroleùca** (Lindl.) Rehd., f. With pale yellow double fls. R.R.3:gr.25,20(c). Andrews, Ros.2:t,77(c). Intr. 1824. —**R. o. pseudíndica** (Lindl.) Rehd., var. FORTUNE'S DOUBLE YELLOW. (Beauty of Glazenwood, Gold of Ophir.) Fls. salmon-yellow, outside tinged with red, double, 7–10 cm. across. B.M.4679(c). W.R.85,t(c). F.S.8:t.769(c). —**R. o. gigantèa** (Coll.) Rehd. & Wils., var. Very vigorous, climbing to 10 m.: fls. creamy white, single, 10–15 cm. across; pedicels and receptacle smooth. B.M.7972(c). W.R.34(c). G.C.III.6:13;37:136;51:314. Gn.67:179; 71:67. (*R. g.* Collett.) S.W. China, Burma. Intr. 1889. Zone VII.—**R. o. erubéscens** Rehd. & Wils., f. A form of the preceding var. with blush or pale pink fls., often smaller. W. China. Intr. ? This form or the preceding var. is probably the phylogenetic type of the Tea Rose.

R. o. gigantea × *Brunonii*. Here belongs "Madelaine," "Lemoine," "Montanosa," "Montecito" with paniculate fls.—*R. o.* × *borboniana* = R. dilécta Rehd. Here belong the hybrid Tea Roses which are hybrids between the Tea Rose and the Hybrid Perpetuals and of which "La France" may be considered a typical representative.—*R. o.* (or *dilecta*) × *rugosa;* see under No. 26.—*R. o.* × *laevigata;* see under No. 69.

65. **R. chinénsis** Jacq. CHINA R. Low upright shrub with stout more or less hooked prickles, sometimes nearly unarmed: lfts. 3–5, broad-ovate to ovate-oblong, 2.5–6 cm. long, acuminate, serrate, lustrous and dark green above, pale beneath, glabrous: fls. usually several, rarely solitary, on long, usually glandular stalks, rarely short-stalked, about 5 cm. across, crimson to pink or nearly white: fr. 1.5–2 cm. long. Fl.VI–IX. W.R.79,t(c). Jacquin, Obs. Bot. 3:t.55(c). (*R. indica* Lindl., not L., *R. sinica* L.—BENGAL R.) China. Cult. 1768. Zone VII?—**R. c. semperflòrens** (Curtis) Koehne., var. CRIMSON CHINA R. (CHINESE MONTHLY R.). Stems slender, prickly or nearly unarmed; lfts. rather thin, mostly stained with purple: fls. usually solitary on long slender pedicels, crimson or deep pink. B.M.284(c). W.R.89, t(c).—**R. c. mínima** (Sims.) Voss, var. FAIRY R. Dwarf shrub, rarely exceeding 25 cm., with small rose-red fls., about 3 cm. across, single or double. B.M.1762(c). B.R.538(c). R.R.3:gr.25,6,7(c). Gs.14:138. H.B.11:117. (*R. Lawranciana* Sweet, *R. Roulettii* Corr.) Hybrids of this var. with *R. multiflora* forms are the "Baby Ramblers."—**R. c. viridiflòra** (Lav.) Dipp., var. With monstrous green fls.; the petals transformed into small green lvs. F.S. 11:1136(c). Orig. about 1855.—**R. c. mutàbilis** (Corr.) Rehd., f. Fls. simple, first sulphur-yellow, changing to orange, red and finally crimson, 4.5–6 cm. across. R.H.1934:60,t(c). (*R. m.* Corr.) Cult. 1934.

R. c. × *arvensis;* see under No. 63.—*R. c.* × *moschata;* see No. 66.—*R. c.* × *rugosa;* see under No. 26.—*R. c.* × *blanda;* see under No. 30.—*R. c.* × *pendulina;* see under No. 31.—*R. c.* × *damascena;* see No. 67.

66. × **R. Noisettiàna** Thory (*R. chinensis* × *moschata.*) NOISETTE R. (CHAMPNEY R.) Shrub to 3 m. with upright or spreading stems; prickles reddish: lfts. 5–7, usually oblong-ovate to oblong-lanceolate, glabrous: fls. usually in many-fld. corymbs, white to pink or red, sometimes yellow; styles exserted, pubescent, loosely cohering. W.R.32(c). Gn.71:335. B.S.2:437. Orig. about 1816.—Here belongs the Manetti Rose (*R. Manetti* Crivelli, *R. chinensis* var. *M.* Dipp.), a vigorous shrub with semidouble or single fls. (B.C.5:2988), often used as stock for Tea and China Roses.

67. × **R. borboniàna** Desp. (*R. chinensis* × *damascena*). BOURBON R. Upright shrub with prickly and often glandular-hispid stems: lfts. usually 7, ovate to lance-ovate, acute, lustrous above, slightly pubescent beneath: fls.

solitary or few in a corymb, on glandular pedicels, double or semidouble, usually purple. W.R.339,t(c). (*R. borbonica* Morr.) Fl.vii–ix. Orig. before 1819. By crossing this hybrid with the different Roses of the Gallicae group, the Hybrid Bourbon Roses have originated and these crossed with *R. chinensis* and its vars. have produced the Hybrid Perpetuals or Remontant Roses. All these hybrids may be included in *R. borboniana* in an enlarged sense.

R. b. × *odorata;* see under No. 64.—*R. b.* × *rugosa;* see under No. 26.

Sect. 8. BANKSIANAE Lindl. Evergreen climbing shrubs with slender glabrous brs. armed with hooked prickles or unarmed: lfts. 3–7; stipules free, subulate, caducous: fls. in corymbs, white or yellow; sepals entire, reflexed after flowering, deciduous. Two species in China.

68. R. Bánksiae Ait. BANKS' R. Climbing to 6 m., with sparingly prickly or unarmed brs.: lfts. 3–5, rarely 7, elliptic-ovate to oblong-lanceolate, 2–6 cm. long, acute or obtusish, serrulate, glabrous except at base of midrib beneath; rachis pubescent: fls. white or yellow, 2.5 cm. across, slightly fragrant, on slender smooth stalks in many-fld. umbels: fr. small globose. Fl.vi–viii. Gn.83:107(h). China.—**R. B. normàlis** Reg., var. Fls. single, white. G.C. 31:539. J.L.27:501. Cult. 1877.—**R. B. albo-plèna** Rehd., var. Fls. double, white, fragrant. B.M.1954(c). Intr. 1807. The typical form.—**R. B. lùtea** Lindl., var. Fls. double, yellow, scentless. B.R.1105(c). (*R. B.* f. *luteo-plena* Rehd.) Intr. 1824.—**R. B. lutéscens** Voss., f. Fls. single, yellow. B.M.7171 (c). Intr. about 1870. Zone VII.

R. B. × *laevigata?* = **R. Fortuneàna** Lindl. Climbing shrub with sparingly prickly stems: lfts. 3–5, ovate-lanceolate, lustrous: fls. solitary, large, double, white; pedicels hispid. W.R.36,t(c). F.S.7:256(c). J.F.2:27. Intr. 1850. Zone VII?

Related species: **R. cymòsa** Tratt. Brts. slender, with hooked prickles: lfts. 3–7, elliptic to ovate-lanceolate, glabrous: fls. small, white, in many-fld. corymbs; styles exserted, pubescent: fr. small, globose. G.C.37:227. (*R. indica* L., in part, *R. microcarpa* Lindl., not Bess., nor Retz., *R. sorbiflora* Focke.) China. Intr. ? 1904. Zone VII?

Sect. 9. LAEVIGATAE Thory. Evergreen shrubs with scattered hooked prickles: lfts. usually 3; stipules free or adnate at base, caducous: fls. solitary, large, without bracts; sepals erect, entire, persistent; pedicels and receptacles densely bristly.

69. R. laevigàta Michx. CHEROKEE R. To 5 m. high: lfts. 3, rarely 5, elliptic-ovate to lance-ovate, 3–6 m. long, acute or acuminate, sharply and finely serrate, glabrous and lustrous, reticulate beneath: fls. white, rarely rose-colored, 6–8 cm. across, fragrant: fr. pyriform, bristly, 3.5–4 cm. long. Fl.v. B.M.2847(c). B.R.1922(c). W.R.117,t(c). G.C.III.6:497. Gn.68:206 (h);71:225(h). M.G.21:397. Gn.M.38:174(h). (*R. cherokeensis* Donn, *R. sinica* Murr., *R. ternata* Poir., *R. Camellia* Hort.) China; naturalized from Ga. to Fla. and Tex. Intr. before 1780 to Am. Zone VII.

R. l. × ? *odorata* = **R. anemonoìdes** Rehd. ("Anemone Rose"). With large single light pink fls. R.H.1901:548,t(c). W.R.41,t(c). M.G.11:345. Gn.62:413; 77:340;80:309. Orig. before 1896.—*R. l.* × *dilecta.* Here belongs "Silver Moon." —*R. l.* × *Banksiae;* see under No. 68.—*R. l.* × *bracteata;* see under No. 70.

Sect. 10. BRACTEATAE Thory. Evergreen shrubs with erect or sarmentose, tomentose or pubescent brs.; prickles in pairs; stipules slightly adnate and pectinate: infl. with large bracts; sepals entire, reflexed after flowering; receptacle tomentose. Two Asiatic species.

70. R. bracteàta Wendl. MACARTNEY R. Stems sarmentose or procumbent, tomentose, with stout hooked prickles: lfts. 5–9, elliptic to obovate, 1.5–5 cm. long, obtuse or acutish, crenate-serrulate, lustrous above, glabrous or pubescent on midrib beneath; rachis glabrous: fls. usually solitary, white, 5–7 cm. across, short-stalked, with large laciniated pubescent bracts at base: fr. globose, 3–3.5 cm. across, orange-red, woolly. Fl.viii. B.M.1377(c). B.B.

2:268. Gn.70:192. W.R.125,t(c). (*R. Macartnea* Dum.-Cours.) China; naturalized from Va. to Fla. and Tex. Intr. 1793. Zone VII.

R. b. × *laevigata.* Here belongs Marie Leonida (*R. alba odorata*) with creamy white double fls. W.R.1:127,t(c). Cult. 1832.

Closely related species: **R. clinophylla** Thory, with straight prickles and acute lfts. often pubescent beneath; rachis pubescent. B.R.739(c). R.R.3,gr. 24,2. (*R. involucrata* Roxb., *R. Lyellii* Lindl.) India. Intr. before 1817; probably not hardy.—*R. c.* × *persica;* see under No. 1.

Subgen. III. PLATYRHODON (Hurst) Rehd. Lvs. pinnate: stipules adnate, very narrow with subulate divergent auricles: fls. 1 or 2, with small caducous bracts: receptacle prickly, cup-shaped, achenes on a slightly elevated torus: stamens 150–175; sepals broad, erect, persistent, pinnate. (Sect. *Microphyllae* Crép., *Saintpierrea* Germ. de St. Pierre, *Platyrhodon* Dcne. ex Hurst).

71. R. Roxbúrghii Tratt. Spreading shrub to 2.5 m.; bark gray, peeling: lfts. elliptic to elliptic-oblong, 1–2 cm. long, acute, sharply serrate, glabrous beneath: fls. pale pink, 5–6 cm. across; pedicels and receptacle prickly: fr. depressed-globose, 3–4 cm. across, very prickly. (*R. microphylla* Roxb., not Desf.) China, Japan.—**R. R. plèna** Rehd., var. With double fls. Fl.vi. B.R. 919(c). B.M.3490(c). W.R.135,t(c). G.C.103:87. Gn.81:484,548. S.L.325(h). Intr. 1828. Zone VI? The type of the species.—**R. R. normàlis** Rehd. & Wils., f. The wild form with single fls. China. Intr. 1908.—**R. R. hírtula** (Reg.) Rehd. & Wils., var. Lfts. elliptic to ovate-oblong, 1–2.5 cm. long, pubescent beneath. B.M.6548(c). Japan. Intr. before 1880.

R. R. × *rugosa* = *R. micrugosa,* see under No. 26.

Subgen. IV. HESPERHODOS Cockerell. Lvs. pinnate; stipules adnate, with divergent dilated auricles: fls. solitary, without bracts; receptacle prickly, cup-shaped, without disk; achenes on a conical elongated torus; sepals pinnate, erect, persistent: fr. not fleshy. (Sect. *Minutifoliae* Crép., *Hesperhodos* Boulenger.)

72. R. stellàta Woot. Shrub to 0.6 m.; brs. with numerous slender yellowish white prickles and closely stellate-pubescent when young: lfts. 3, sometimes 5, broad-cuneate-obovate, 5–10 mm. long, incisely dentate, pubescent on both sides: fls. solitary, deep rose-purple, 3.5–5.5 cm. across: fr. broad-turbinate, 1–1.5 cm. across, dull reddish. Fl.vi–viii. W.R.305,t(c). J.L.27: 456. Bull. Torr. Bot. Club 25:t.335,f.1–5,9. (*Hesperhodos stellatus* Boulenger.) W. Tex. to Ariz. Intr. 1902. Zone (V).—**R. s. mirífica** (Greene) Cockerell, var. More vigorous, to 1.2 m. high; brs. without stellate pubescence: lfts. usually 5, sometimes nearly glabrous: fls. 3.5–6 cm. across. B.M.9070(c). Gs.20:179. (*R. m.* Greene.) N. Mex. Intr. 1916. Zone (V).

Related species: **R. minutifòlia** Engelm. Brts. pubescent, with slender brown prickles: lfts. 5–7, ovate to elliptic, 3–10 mm. long, pubescent: fls. pink or white, 2.5 cm. across. G.F.1:102. B.C.5:2996. J.L.27:456. L. Calif. Cult. 1910. Zone VII?

Subfam. IV. PRUNOIDEAE Focke. Trees or shrubs, sometimes spiny: lvs. simple, stipulate: fls. white to pink, solitary, umbellate or racemose; petals rarely wanting; stamens 10 to many; carpels usually 1, rarely 2–5, free, 2-ovuled, developing into a 1-, rarely 2-seeded drupe sometimes dehiscent; stone with usually bony endocarp. (*Drupaceae* DC., *Amygdalaceae* Reichenb.)

45. MADDÈNIA Hook. f. & Thoms. Deciduous trees or shrubs; winter-buds with many scales: lvs. alternate, serrate, stipulate: fls. appearing with the lvs., dioecious, apetalous, short-pedicelled, in racemes; sepals 10, very small; stamens 25–40; pistil with a long style and 2 ovules; in the staminate fl. sometimes 2 abortive pistils with sessile stigmas: fr. a 1-seeded drupe. (After Major E. Madden, plant collector in India; d.1856.) Five species in Himal., C. and W. China.

M. hypoleùca Koehne. Shrub or small tree to 6 m.; young brts. glabrous or sparingly pubescent: lvs. ovate-oblong to oblong, 4–6.5, on shoots to 16 cm. long, acuminate, rounded or subcordate at base, doubly serrate with acuminate teeth, glabrous, glaucous beneath, with 14–18 pairs of veins: racemes dense, 3–5 cm. long on leafy peduncles; calyx-tube 4 mm. long; sepals slightly shorter, unequal; stamens to 6 mm. long: drupe black, ellipsoid, about 8 mm. long. Fl.iv–v; fr.vi. C. and W. China. Intr. 1907. Zone (V).

46. PRÙNUS L. Deciduous or evergreen trees or shrubs; winter-buds with many imbricate scales: lvs. alternate, serrate, rarely entire, stipulate: fls. perfect, solitary or in fascicles or racemes; sepals 5; petals 5, usually white, sometimes pink or red; stamens numerous, perigynous; pistil 1, with elongated style, 2-ovuled: fr. a drupe, usually 1-seeded. (Ancient Latin name.) Nearly 200 species, mostly in the temperate zone, a few in the Andes of S. Am.—Many species are in cult. for their edible fr. and a few for their edible seeds; a large number are highly ornamental on account of their showy fls. appearing before or with the lvs.

Fr. sulcate, usually bloomy, sometimes pubescent: lvs. convolute or conduplicate.
  A. Axillary buds solitary; terminal bud wanting................Subgen. I. PRUNOPHORA
    B. Ovary and fr. glabrous; fls. pedicelled.
      c. Fls. 1–2, rarely 3; stone often sculptured: lvs. convolute..........Sect. 1. EUPRUNUS
      cc. Fls. 3 or more, rarely solitary; stone usually smooth: lvs. conduplicate, rarely convolute ....Sect. 2. PRUNOCERASUS
    BB. Ovary and fr. pubescent (glabrous in *P. brigantina*): fls. sessile (stalked in *P. dasycarpa*): lvs. convolute...Sect. 3. ARMENIACA
  AA. Axillary buds 3, the lateral ones fl.-buds; terminal bud present: fls. 1–2, sessile, rarely stalked: ovary and fr. pubescent, very rarely glabrous: lvs. conduplicate.
                                                                Subgen. II. AMYGDALUS

Fr. not sulcate, not bloomy; stone turgid, or subglobose; lvs. conduplicate: terminal bud present.
  A. Fls. solitary or few, sometimes in short, few-fld. racemes, usually with conspicuous bracts.
                                                                Subgen. III. CERASUS
    B. Buds 3 in each leaf-axil: pedicels usually short....................Sect. 1. MICROCERASUS
    BB. Buds solitary.
      c. Sepals upright or spreading: lvs. with sharp teeth............Sect. 2. PSEUDOCERASUS
      cc. Sepals reflexed.
        D. Petals emarginate: lvs. with sharp teeth.....................Sect. 3. LOBOPETALUM
        DD. Petals not emarginate.
          E. Involucre persistent; fls. in umbels: lvs. with short obtuse teeth.
                                                                Sect. 4. EUCERASUS
          EE. Involucre deciduous; fls. often racemose.
            F. Bracts small, deciduous; sepals shorter than tube, entire: lvs. with obtuse teeth ....Sect. 5. MAHALEB
            FF. Bracts leafy, persistent: lvs. with sharp teeth.
              G. Fls. 2–3 ....Sect. 6. PHYLLOCERASUS
              GG. Fls. 5–6, racemose ....Sect. 7. PHYLLOMAHALEB
  AA. Fls. in elongated racemes of 12 or more fls.; bracts small.
    B. Lvs. deciduous; peduncle usually leafy............................Subgen. IV. PADUS
    BB. Lvs. persistent: peduncle leafless......................Subgen. V. LAUROCERASUS

Subgen. I. PRUNOPHORA
Sect. 1. EUPRUNUS

Young brts. tomentose or pubescent; pedicels usually pubescent (glabrous in No. 1): fr. subglobose.
  A. Fls. usually solitary: fr. upright; stone more or less pitted.................1. *P. spinosa*
  AA. Fls. usually 2; stone nearly smooth: fr. pendulous............................2. *P. insititia*

Young brts. glabrous or glabrescent; pedicels glabrous, rarely pubescent.
  A. Fr. subglobose to oblong; lvs. spreading or drooping; veins diverging at an angle of about 45°.
    B. Lvs. pubescent beneath, to 10 cm. long: fr. generally ellipsoid, usually bluish black.
                                                                3. *P. domestica*
    BB. Lvs. glabrous beneath except along the midrib: fr. usually subglobose, yellow or red.
      c. Fls. usually solitary: lvs. 2–7 cm. long..............................4. *P. cerasifera*
      cc. Fls. usually 3: lvs. oblong-obovate, 6–10 cm. long.....................5. *P. salicina*
  AA. Fr. depressed-globose, very short-stalked: lvs. upright, narrow, with few veins diverging at a very acute angle...6. *P. Simonii*

452

2. PRUNOCERASUS

Lvs. round-ovate, obtuse or obtusish, incisely serrate, convolute in bud ..7. *P. subcordata*
Lvs. ovate to lanceolate, conduplicate in bud (convolute in No. 18, 19, slightly so in 9 and 17).
  A. Lvs. with acute or acuminate teeth, dull above, usually pubescent.
    B. Lvs. acute or gradually acuminate: brts. usually pubescent: calyx-lobes eglandular: fr. subglobose, usually dark purple, rarely yellow, 1–2 cm. across.
      c. Lvs. acute or obtusish, ovate to elliptic; petioles often glandular: low shrub.
                                       8. *P. maritima*
      cc. Lvs. acuminate, elliptic to elliptic-oblong; petioles eglandular: trees, sometimes shrubby.
        D. Calyx pubescent or puberulous outside; petals turning pink; petioles 7–12 mm. long ....9. *P. alleghaniensis*
        DD. Calyx glabrous or puberulous outside; petals white: petioles 5–9 mm. long.
                                    10. *P. umbellata*
    BB. Lvs. abruptly acuminate, usually obovate-oblong: fr. red or yellow, 2–3 cm. across: trees.
      c. Lvs. pubescent beneath and young brts. usually pubescent.
        D. Lvs. usually rounded or subcordate at base, thickish at maturity; petiole usually glandular at apex: not sprouting from the root....................11. *P. mexicana*
        DD. Lvs. usually cuneate, rather thin; petiole usually eglandular: sprouting from the root ....:2. *P. lanata*
      cc. Lvs. glabrous or nearly so and young brts. glabrous: sprouting from the root.
                                  13. *P. americana*
  AA. Lvs. with obtuse or obtusish teeth (sometimes acute in *P. orthosepala*, under No. 18); calyx-lobes usually glandular: fr. red or yellow.
    B. Lvs. elliptic or slightly obovate, 8–12 cm. long, coarsely or often doubly serrate, usually pubescent beneath: calyx and pedicel reddish; petals fading to pink: fr. 2.5–3 cm. across ....14. *P. nigra*
    BB. Lvs. ovate to lanceolate, rarely obovate-oblong, lustrous above, usually finely crenate-serrate, usually smaller: calyx and pedicels green; petals white.
      c. Lvs. 6–11 cm. long, pubescent along the midrib below: fr. 2–3 cm. across.
        D. Lvs. oblong-obovate or elliptic-oblong, obtusely serrate, rather thick.
                                  15. *P. hortulana*
        DD. Lvs. usually oblong-lonceolate, finely glandular-serrate, rather thin.
                                  16. *P. Munsoniana*
      cc. Lvs. 2–7 cm. long: fr. smaller.
        D. Young brts. glabrous: lvs. glabrous below, trough-shaped, lanceolate or lance-ovate.
          E. Calyx-lobes usually pubescent within: lvs. usually ovate-lanceolate and acuminate ....17. *P. Reverchonii*
          EE. Calyx-lobes glabrous within except at base or sparsely pubescent: lvs. usually elliptic-lanceolate, acute ....18. *P. angustifolia*
        DD. Young brts. pubescent: lvs. oval or ovate, pubescent below.........19. *P. gracilis*

Sect. 3. ARMENIACA

Fr. yellow or red: fls. short-stalked.
  A. Lvs. rather sharply and nearly doubly serrate, the teeth longer than broad.
    B. Ovary and fr. glabrous; pedicels glabrous, about as long as calyx-tube.20. *P. brigantina*
    BB. Ovary and fr. pubescent; pedicel shorter...........................21. *P. mandshurica*
  AA. Lvs. finely and simply serrate: fls. subsessile.
    B. Stone smooth: lvs. usually rounded at base.
      c. Lvs. ovate, long-acuminate: fr. about 2 cm. across...................22. *P. sibirica*
      cc. Lvs. round-ovate, short-acuminate: fr. about 3 cm. across..........23. *P. Armeniaca*
    BB. Stone pitted: lvs. usually broad-cuneate at base, often pubescent beneath; mature brts. green or greenish, slender..24. *P. Mume*
Fr. dark purple: fls. long-stalked...25. *P. dasycarpa*

Subgen. II. AMYGDALUS

Calyx-tube cup-shaped to campanulate, as long or little longer than lobes.
                                  Sect. 1. EUAMYGDALUS Schneid.
  A. Lvs. crenate or closely serrate: sepals erect-spreading: ovary tomentose except in var. of No. 27.
    B. Lvs. acuminate, 6–15 cm. long.
      c. Stone sulcate and usually pitted; petiole usually glandular.
        D. Sepals villous outside, at least on the margin.
          E. Fr. becoming dry and splitting at maturity: lvs. serrulate, broadest below the middle; petiole 1.5–2.5 cm. long............................26. *P. Amygdalus*
          EE. Fr. fleshy, not splitting: lvs. serrate, broadest above the middle; petiole 1–1.5 cm. long ....27. *P. Persica*
        DD. Sepals quite glabrous; petiole rarely glandular, 1–2 cm. long.....28. *P. Davidiana*
      cc. Stone smooth, ovate: lvs. lanceolate, villous beneath along the midrib...29. *P. mira*
    BB. Lvs. acute or obtusish, 1–3 cm. long: fr. dehiscent; stone rugose.......30. *P. tangutica*

AA. Lvs. deeply serrate or doubly serrate, broadly elliptic to obovate, 3–6 cm. long.
31. *P. triloba*
Calyx-tube tubular, much longer than sepals; lvs. usually elliptic-oblong, 3–7-cm. long.
Sect. 2. CHAMAEAMYGDALUS Focke.
32. *P. tenella*

Subgen. III. CERASUS
Sect. 1. MICROCERASUS

Fls. sessile or nearly so; calyx-tube tubular.
A. Lvs. pubescent, usually on both sides.
B. Fls. white: lvs. broad-elliptic to obovate, green and pubescent beneath.
33. *P. tomentosa*
BB. Fls. rose-colored: lvs. elliptic to oblong-lanceolate, white-tomentose beneath.
34. *P. incana*
AA. Lvs. glabrous, elliptic-oblong: fls. rose-colored......................35. *P. Jacquemontii*

Fls. and fr. distinctly pedicelled; calyx-tube cup-shaped; sepals serrulate.
A. Lvs. green beneath, finely serrate or serrulate from near the base; petiole 5–8 mm. long:
fr. red.
B. Lvs. ovate, rarely ovate-lanceolate, acuminate, broadest below the middle and rounded
or subcordate, sharply doubly serrate....................................36. *P. japonica*
BB. Lvs. obovate-oblong to lance-oblong, rarely elliptic, acute, finely serrulate or crenulate,
broad-cuneate.
C. Lvs. broadest about or below the middle; style glabrous or pilose at base.
37. *P. glandulosa*
CC. Lvs. broadest above the middle: style glabrous.......................38. *P. humilis*
AA. Lvs. glaucescent beneath, entire toward the base; petiole 8–18 mm. long: fr. purple-black.
B. Lvs. oblanceolate to obovate, ascending: fr. small, astringent...........39. *P. pumila*
BB. Lvs. elliptic to elliptic-lanceolate, spreading: fr. about 1.5 cm. across, sweet.
40. *P. Besseyi*

Sect. 2. PSEUDOCERASUS

Lvs. incisely and doubly serrate or lobulate: fls. white or pinkish, rather small.
A. Lvs. densely grayish pubescent beneath: fr. red: infl. with leafy bracts...41. *P. canescens*
AA. Lvs. glabrous or hairy only on veins beneath: infl. without leafy bracts.
B. Fr. purple-black: style glabrous; sepals entire or irregularly dentate, usually as long
as tube.
C. Petioles pubescent: pedicels usually short; fls. about 1 cm. across......42. *P. incisa*
CC. Petioles glabrous: pedicels 1.5–2.5 cm. long: fls. 2–2.5 cm. across....43. *P. nipponica*
BB. Fr. red, about 1 cm. across: style pilose at base; sepals glandular-serrulate, shorter
than tube ....44. *P. lobulata*
Lvs. simply or only slightly doubly serrate.
A. Fruiting pedicels conspicuously thickened: fls. pink or red.
B. Young shoots glabrous...46. *P. campanuiata*
BB. Young shoots rufous-tomentose...47. *P. rufa*
AA. Fruiting pedicels not thickened.
B. Fls. before the lvs. in sessile umbels.
C. Calyx-tube pubescent, narrowed at base: lvs. pubescent beneath at least on midrib,
with about 10 pairs of veins or more: involucre small, deciduous....45. *P. subhirtella*
CC. Calyx-tube glabrous: lvs. glabrous beneath at maturity or sometimes pubescent on
vigorous shoots: involucre persistent.
D. Lvs. 3–6 cm. broad, with more than 10 pairs of veins: calyx-tube abruptly con-
tracted at base: fr. red...50. *P. Conradinae*
DD. Lvs. 1.5–2.5 cm. broad with 8–10 pairs of veins: calyx-tube narrowed at base: fr.
black ....49. *P. concinna*
BB. Fls. with the lvs., often racemose.
C. Lvs. closely serrulate, lance-oblong or lanceolate: fls. white, rather small, 1–3 in
subsessile umbels: fr. red...48. *P. serrula*
CC. Lvs. rather coarsely serrate or doubly serrate: fls. large, usually in racemes: fr.
black or purple-black.
D. Lvs. and brts. glabrous or slightly pubescent.
E. Calyx-tube cylindric, usually pubescent: lvs. pubescent on the veins beneath.
51. *P. yedoensis*
EE. Calyx-tube campanulate, glabrous: lvs. glabrous, rarely sparingly pubescent
beneath.
F. Fls. in 2–4-fld. sessile umbels: lvs. with acuminate teeth.....52. *P. Sargentii*
FF. Fls. in 2–5-fld. bracted racemes: lvs. with aristate teeth....53. *P. serrulata*
DD. Lvs. beneath and brts. pubescent..................................54. *P. Sieboldii*

Sect. 3. LOBOPETALUM

Sepals shorter than calyx-tube...55. *P. cantabrigiensis*
Sepals longer than calyx-tube ....56. *P. Dielsiana*

Sect. 4. EUCERASUS

**Lvs. obtusely serrate, 4–15 cm. long; petiole 1.5–5 cm. long; sepals about as long as
calyx-tube.**
A. Lvs. pubescent beneath at least on veins, to 15 cm. long; inner bud-scales reflexed; infl.
without leafy bracts: fr. sweet..57. *P. avium*

ᴀᴀ. Lvs. glabrous, to 7 cm. long; inner bud-scales upright; infl. usually with a few leafy
    bracts at base: fr. sour...58. *P. Cerasus*
Lvs. crenate, 2–5 cm. long; petioles 8–15 mm. long; sepals about half as long as calyx-
tube ....59. *P. fruticosa*

Sect. 5. Mᴀʜᴀʟᴇʙ

Lvs. suborbicular or broad-ovate: fls. racemose ....60. *P. Mahaleb*
Lvs. narrower.
  ᴀ. Lvs. acute to acuminate, serrulate, rhombic-ovate to ovate-lanceolate, soon glabrous: fls.
    subumbellate ....61. *P. pennsylvanica*
  ᴀᴀ. Lvs. obtuse to acute, usually oblong, indistinctly crenulate..............62. *P. emarginata*

Sect. 6. Pʜʏʟʟᴏᴄᴇʀᴀsᴜs

Fls. few in a small short-stalked umbel....................................63. *P. pilosiuscula*

Sect. 7. Pʜʏʟʟᴏᴍᴀʜᴀʟᴇʙ

Fls. 5–6 in a raceme..64. *P. Maximowiczii*

Subgen. IV. PADUS

Peduncle leafy.
  ᴀ. Calyx persistent in fr.
    ʙ. Rachis of infl. and brts. glabrous......................................65. *P. serotina*
    ʙʙ. Rachis and young brts. pubescent.................................66. *P. alabamensis*
  ᴀᴀ. Calyx deciduous in fr.
    ʙ. Pedicels thickened in fr. and lenticellate..............................67. *P. sericea*
    ʙʙ. Pedicel not thickened and not lenticellate.
      ᴄ. Style shorter than stamens.
        ᴅ. Calyx-tube pubescent inside.
          ᴇ. Stone sculptured; petals 6–8 mm. long, twice as long as stamens..68. *P. Padus*
          ᴇᴇ. Stone smooth; petals 3–5 mm. long, about as long as stamens..69. *P. pubigera*
        ᴅᴅ. Calyx-tube glabrous inside; stone smooth or slightly rugose: petals as long or
          only ⅓ longer than stamens.
          ᴇ. Lvs. acute or short-acuminate.
            ꜰ. Lvs. 10–20 cm. long..70. *P. cornuta*
            ꜰꜰ. Lvs. shorter ....71. *P. virginiana*
          ᴇᴇ. Lvs. long-acuminate ....72. *P. Ssiori*
      ᴄᴄ. Style longer than stamens: lvs. long-acuminate.....................73. *P. Grayana*
Peduncle naked.
  ᴀ. Style about as long as stamens: lvs. gland-dotted beneath: calyx deciduous in fr.
                                   74. *P. Maackii*
  ᴀᴀ. Style shorter than stamens: lvs. not glandular beneath: calyx persistent in fr.
                                 75. *P. Buergeriana*

Subgen. V. LAUROCERASUS

Lvs. serrate, shorter than racemes ....76. *P. lusitanica*
Lvs. usually entire, longer than racemes.................................77. *P. Laurocerasus*

    Subgen I. PRUNOPHORA Focke. Fr. sulcate, glabrous and usually bloomy;
stone compressed, usually longer than broad and smooth or nearly so: fls. solitary
or in umbel-like cluster, before or rarely with the lvs.: stalk usually remaining
with the fr. (except in No. 6). Pʟᴜᴍ.
    Sect. 1. Eᴜᴘʀᴜɴᴜs Koehne. Fs. 1–2, rarely to 3, stalked, usually with the
lvs.; lvs. convolute in bud.
    1. P. spinòsa L. Bʟᴀᴄᴋᴛʜᴏʀɴ (Sʟᴏᴇ.) Much-branched spiny shrub, rarely
small tree to 4 m.; young brts. pubescent; buds small, globose-ovoid: lvs.
elliptic-ovate to oblong-obovate, 2–4 cm. long, obtuse, finely or crenately
serrate, pubescent while young, finally glabrous or sometimes pubescent: fls.
before the lvs., usually solitary, 1–1.5 cm. across; pedicels glabrous, rarely
pubescent: fr. globose, 1–1.5 cm. across, blue-black, bloomy, of astringent
taste; stone turgid. R.I.25:t.80(c). S.E.3:t.408(c). F.D.25:t.2554(c). H.W.
3:89. G.C.42:308. Eu., N. Afr., W. Asia. Long. cult. Zone IV.—**P. s. plèna**
West., var. With double white fls. Gn.59:76;61:363;88:107(h). G.M.44:165.
(*P. s. fl. pleno* Kirchn.)—**P. s. purpúrea** André. Less spiny: lvs. purplish,
larger: fls. pink. Orig. before 1903. ?Hybrid.
    ? *P. s.* × *insititia* = **P. frúticans** Weihe. Usually thornless; lvs. often acut-
ish, 4–5 cm. long: fls. larger: fr. 1.4–1.8 cm. across. R.I.25:t,81(c). Occasionally
found wild in Eu.
    Closely related species: **P. cúrdica** Fenzl & Fritsch. Lower, more spreading
and less spiny: lvs. elliptic, acute, to 9 cm. long, pubescent while young: fls. with

the lvs., about 2 cm. across, usually solitary: fr. bluish black; pedicel to 1.4 cm. long, upright. S.H.1:f.346e,347p-q. Armenia. Intr. before 1892.

2. **P. insitítia** L. BULLACE (DAMSON). Shrub or small tree to 6 m., sometimes slightly spiny: young brts. tomentose: lvs. elliptic to obovate, 4–8 cm. long, coarsely crenate-serrate, pubescent while young, at maturity usually glabrous and dull above; sparingly pubescent beneath, reticulate; petiole 1–2 cm. long: fls. white, 2–2.5 cm. across; pedicels pubescent; sepals glabrous or pubescent: fr. subglobose to ovoid, bluish black, sweet; stone little compressed; flesh clinging. R.I.25:t.82(c). S.E.3:t.409(c). D.F.25:2555(c). Hedrick, Plums N. Y. 34,t.(c). (*P. domestica* var. *i*. Fiori & Paol.) W. Asia, Eu. Cult. since prehistoric times. Zone IV.—**P. i. subsylvéstris** Boutigny. Spiny; sepals glabrous. The wild form.—**P. i. syríaca** (Borkh.) Koehne, var. MIRA-BELLE. Fr. subglobose, yellow. (*P. s.* Borkh.)—**P. i. itálica** (Borkh.) Aschers. & Graebn., prol. GREEN-GAGE (Reine Claude). Brts. thinly pubescent: fr. greenish often rather large. (*P. i.* Borkh., *P. Claudiana* Poir., *P. domestica* var. *i.* Schneid.)

P. i. × *spinosa;* see under No. 1.

3. **P. doméstica** L. GARDEN PLUM. Usually small tree to 10 or 12 m.: young brts. glabrous or slightly pubescent when young, becoming glabrous: lvs. elliptic or obovate, 5–10 cm. long, coarsely crenate-serrate, pubescent while young, at maturity glabrous and dull above, pubescent beneath and reticulate; petioles 1.5–2.5 cm. long: fls. greenish white, 1.5–2 cm. across; sepals pubescent inside: fr. usually ovoid to oblong, rarely subglobose, sweet; stone free, nearly smooth. R.I.25:t.83(c). S.E.3:t.410(c). D.F.25:t.2556(c). Hedrick, Plums N. Y. 12,t(c). (*P. communis* Huds., *P. oeconomica* Borkh.,. *P. damascena* Dierb., *P. pyramidalis* DC.) W. Asia, Eu. Long cult. in many forms for its fr. Zone IV.—**P. d. plantièrii** Carr. Fls. double, white. Gt.73: 59. (*P. plantierensis* Simon-Louis.)

4. **P. cerasífera** Ehrh. CHERRY PLUM. Slender-branched tree to 8 m., sometimes thorny; brts. glabrous: lvs. elliptic or ovate to obovate, 3–6 cm. long, finely obtuse-serrate, acute, broad-cuneate to rounded at base, light green, glabrous, except usually pubescent along the midrib beneath, with usually less than 6 pairs of veins: fls. usually solitary, 2–2.5 cm. across, white; stamens 25–30; pedicels glabrous, 5–15 mm. long: fr. subglobose, red, 2–3 cm. across, slightly bloomy. B.M.5934(c). R.I.25:t.84(c). Gn.33:252;87:109(h). (*P. domestica* var. *myrobalan* L., *P. myrobalana* Loisel. *P. Korolkowi* Vilm.) W. Asia, Caucas. Intr. about or before the 16th cent. Zone III.—**P. c. péndula** Bailey, var. With pendulous brs.—**P. c. élegans** Bean, var. Lvs. narrow, edged with white. R.H.1899:460. Orig. before 1899.—**P. c. atropur-púrea** Jaeg. Lvs. purple, larger: fls. pink; pedicel 1.5–2 cm. long: fr. dark wine-red. R.H.1881:190,t(c);1884:396,t(c). G.C.III.1:416;67:194(h). Gn. 32:224,t(c);55:315. S.L.278(h). (*P. Pissardi* Carr., *P. c.* var. *Pissardii* Bailey.) Intr. before 1881.—**P. c. Woodii** Spaeth. Lvs. dark purple, remaining so all summer. G.W.17:470,t(c). (*P. c. Spaethi* Wood ex Spaeth.)—**P. c. nígra** Bailey, f. Lvs. very dark purple.—**P. c. Purpùsii** Bailey, f. Lvs. dark red, variegated with yellow and bright rose.—**P. c. divaricàta** (Ledeb.) Bailey, var. Brs. slenderer: lvs. more often rounded at base: fls. smaller, with the lvs.: fr. yellow, not impressed at base, 1.6–2 cm. across. B.M.6519(c). (*P. d.* Ledeb.) The wild form. Intr. 1820.

P. c. atropurpurea × *Mume* = **P. blireiàna** André. Lvs. purple: differs from *P. c. atrop.* chiefly in its broader ovate acuminate lvs. rounded at base, semi-double pink fls. on pedicels 1–1.5 cm. long and pubescent ovary. R.H.1905:392,

t(c). Gn.78:240;85:109. J.L.40:f.37. M.D.1917:67,f.D. (*P. Pissardii b.*
Lemoine, *P. cerasifera* var. *b.* Bean.) Orig. 1895.—P. b. Mòseri (Moser)
Koehne, f. Lvs. less purple; petiole and midrib above glabrous (pubescent at
first in *P. b.*): fls. slightly smaller and paler. G.C.53:190. G.M.55:819. (*P.
Pissardii M. fl. pleno* Moser, *P. cerasifera purpurea M.* Spaeth.) Orig. 1894.—
Of similar origin is possibly *P. Boehmeri* Koehne. M.D.1917:67,f,C.—*P. c.* ×
Amygdalo-persica = **P. gigantèa** Koehne. Lvs. elliptic-oblong to elliptic-
lanceolate, 7-12 cm. long; petiole usually with 2 glands: fls. subsessile, sterile;
calyx-tube semiglobose; sepals roundish, slightly villous or subglabrous; petals
obovate, very concave, pale pink. R.H.1908:65. M.D.1917:67,f.B. Cult. 1877.—
P. c. × *Munsoniana* or *?angustifolia.* "Marianna." Lvs. narrow-elliptic to oblong-obovate, 3.5-7 cm. long, slightly pubescent along the midrib beneath: fr.
subglobose or globose-ovoid, 2.5-3 cm. across, red. R.H.1894:278,t(c). A.G.
1886:109. Hedrick, Plums N. Y. 274,t(c). Orig. about 1880.—*P. c.* × *salicina.*
"Motley Plum." With early dark red fr. U.S.Im.193:t.305(h),360(fr). Cult.
1910. Here belongs also "Purple-leaved Kelsey" (*P. c. atropurpurea* × *salicina*
"Kelsey"). Burbank, Cat.1893:16,f.—*P. c.* × *Armeniaca;* see No. 25.—*P. c.* ×
triloba; see under No. 31.—*P. c. atropurpurea* × *pumila;* see under No. 39.

Related species: **P. montícola** K. Koch. Close to No. 4: shrub to 4 m.: lvs.
glabrous, with more than 6 pairs of veins; petioles short: fls. usually 2; stamens
30 or more: fr. red. S.H.1:f.348a-c,349k. Asia Minor. Intr. 1854. Zone V.—
P. Cocomìlia Ten. Shrub or small tree with thorny brs.: lvs. elliptic to broad-
obovate, 3-5 cm. long, finely serrate: fls. usually 2, about 1 cm. across, white
or greenish white; pedicels short, about as long as calyx-tube: sepals erect-
spreading: fr. yellow, subglobose or ellipsoid, 3 cm. long. S.H.346m-n, 348l-n.
Tenore, Fl. Nap. t.144(c). Decaisne, Jard. Fruit. 8,t(c). Italy. Intr. 1824.
Zone VI?—**P. Pseudoarmenìaca** Heldr. & Sart. Close to the preceding: lvs. 1-3
cm. long, acute to acutish: fr. about 2 cm. long, purple-blue. S.H.1:f.346o(1).
Greece. Cult. 1934. Zone VI?—**P. ursina** Kotschy. Shrub to 3.5 m., sometimes
spinescent; brts. pubescent or glabrescent; lvs. oval or obovate, 2-5 cm. long,
acute to obtuse, crenate-serrulate, villous or glabrescent beneath: fls. 1.5-2 cm.
across; the short stalk and calyx villous: fr. about 2 cm. across. S.H.1:f.346s-t,
348o. Asia Minor, Syria. Cult. 1926. Zone VI?

5. **P. salícina** Lindl. Small tree to 10 m.; brts. glabrous, becoming lustrous red-brown: lvs. usually oblong-obovate or elliptic-obovate, 6-10 cm.
long, abruptly acuminate, cuneate, doubly obtuse-serrate, bright green and
lustrous above, light green and glabrous beneath except the bearded axils;
petioles 1-2 cm. long, with several glands: fls. usually 3, white, 1.5-2 cm.
across; pedicels 1-1.5 cm. long, glabrous; sepals oblong-ovate, glabrous,
slightly toothed: fr. globose-ovoid, with a deep depression at base, 5-7 cm.
across, yellow or light red, sometimes green, with deep suture and often
pointed at apex. N.K.5:t.26. R.H.1895:160,t(c). Gn.78:195. S.H.1:f.346c,
347d. (*P. triflora* Roxb., *P. ichangana* Schneid., *P. masu* hort., *P. botan* hort.)
China, cult. in Japan. Intr. 1870. Zone III.—**P. s. pùbipes** (Koehne) Bailey,
var. Pedicels densely pubescent, rarely glabrescent; calyx pubescent toward
base.

P. s. × *Armeniaca.* "Plumcot." Lvs. ovate, acuminate, broad-cuneate or
nearly rounded at base. J.L.1906:472,t.130. Orig. before 1906; also cult. in
China.—*P. s.* × *Persica.* "Hybrid Plum-Peach." Lvs. oblong, broad-cuneate at
b~se: fls. pink, stalked; style longer than stamens; ovary rudimentary, hairy.
G.C.41:256.257. J.L.1906:t.131. Orig. before 1906.—*P. s.* × *cerasifera;* see
under No. 4.—*P. s.* × *Simonii;* see under No. 6.—Also *P. s.* × *maritima, P. s.*
× *mexicana, P. s.* × *lanata, P. s.* × *americana, P. s.* × *Munsoniana, P. s.*
× *hortulana* and *P. s.* × *angustifolia* have been recorded.

Related species: **P. bokhariénsis** Schneid. Close to No. 5: lvs. oblong-elliptic
or oblong-obovate, acuminate, midrib beneath woolly, closely crenate-serrulate.
Kashmir? Cult. 1929. Zone VI?—**P. consociiflòra** Schneid. Small tree: lvs.
conduplicate in bud, oblanceolate to obovate, 3-7 cm. long, acuminate, narrowly
cuneate, finely glandular-serrate, glabrous except villous along midrib beneath;
petiole 4-7 mm. long: fls. 2-5, precocious, 1.2 cm. across: pedicels about 1 cm.
long. C. China. Intr. 1900. Zone VI?—**P. gymnodónta** Koehne. Lvs. 4-7.5 cm.
long, with glandless teeth, conduplicate in bud: fls. 1-2, coetaneous, 1.5 cm.
across; pedicels 1.5-3 mm. long. Manch. Intr. before 1910. Zone V.

6. **P. Simònii** Carr. Apricot Plum. Narrow-pyramidal tree with upright brs.; brts. glabrous: lvs. oblong-lanceolate to oblong-obovate, 7–10 cm. long, acuminate, finely and obtusely serrate, glabrous, dull green above, reticulate beneath; petiole short and stout, with 2–4 large glands: fls. 1–3, short-stalked, 2–2.5 cm. across: fr. much depressed, with a deep suture, 3–5 cm. wide, very short-stalked, maroon-red, with yellow flesh; stone small, suborbicular, rough, clinging. R.H.1872:110,t(c). Gn.70:225. N. China. Intr. 1863. Zone V. Sometimes cult. for its fr.

P. S. × *salicina* = P. sultàna Voss. Here belongs "Wickson." Hedrick, Plums N. Y. 376,t(c). M.G.14:544(h).

Sect. 2. Prunocerasus Koehne. Fls. in clusters of 2–5: lvs. usually conduplicate (convolute in Nos. 7, 18 and 19, slightly so in 9 and 17).

7. **P. subcordàta** Benth. Pacific Plum. Shrub or sometimes small tree to 8 m., with almost horizontal brs.; bark grayish brown; young brts. glabrous or pubescent, bright red: lvs. broad-ovate to suborbicular, 3–7 cm. long, obtuse or acutish, usually subcordate at base, sharply and often doubly serrate, pubescent below when young, at maturity glabrous or puberulous; petiole 1–2 cm. long, glandular: fls. 2–4, white fading to rose, about 1.5 cm. across, on pubescent or glabrous stalks 1 cm. or less long; calyx-lobes oblong, obtuse, pubescent on both sides: fr. red or sometimes yellow, bloomy, ellipsoid, 1.5–3 cm. long. S.S.4:t.154. Ore. to Calif. Intr. about 1850. Zone VI.— **P. s. Kellòggii** Lemm., var. Sisson Plum. Bark ashy gray: lvs. usually not cordate at base, nearly glabrous: fr. large.

8. **P. marítima** Marsh. Beach Plum. Straggling shrub to 2 m., the lower brs. often decumbent; young brts. pubescent: lvs. ovate or elliptic, rarely obovate, 4–6.5 cm. long, acute at ends, sharply serrate, dull green and glabrous above, paler and soft-pubescent beneath; petioles pubescent, rather stout, 4–6 mm. long, often glandular: fls. 2–3, white, 1.2–1.5 cm. across; pedicels 5–7 mm. long; calyx pubescent, lobes obtuse, oblong, entire or dentate at apex, pubescent within; petals oblong-ovate: fr. globose, about 1.5 cm. across, dull purple, bloomy, sometimes crimson; stone ovoid and turgid, truncate at base. B.M.8289(c). Gg.4:287. S.L.279(h). (*P. sphaerocarpa* Michx., *P. acuminata* Michx., *P. pubescens* Pursh.) Me. to Va., near the coast. Intr. 1818. Zone III. Rarely cult. for its fr.; sometimes for the early profuse white fls.—**P. m. flàva** G. S. Torrey, f. Fr. yellow.

P. m. × *americana* = P. Dunbàrii Rehd. Brts. glabrous at maturity: lvs. larger, acuminate, more sharply serrate, less pubescent; pedicels and calyx glabrescent: fr. purple, larger; stone more compressed. Orig. about 1900.

Related species: **P. Gravèsii** Small. Lvs. suborbicular, obtuse or apiculate: stone pointed at base. Conn. Intr. 19J2. Zone V.

9. **P. alleghaniénsis** Porter. Alleghany Plum. Straggling shrub or tree to 5 m., often forming thickets; young brts. pubescent or glabrous, soon reddish brown: lvs. narrow-elliptic to oblong-lanceolate, 6–9 cm. long, acuminate, cuneate, sharply and finely serrate, glabrous or sparingly pubescent above, pubescent beneath at least when young; petioles 7–12 mm. long, pubescent, rarely glandular: fls. 2–4, 1–1.2 cm. across; pedicels slender; calyx-tube pubescent, rarely glabrous; sepals oblong-ovate, sparingly hairy or glabrous within; petals round-obovate, turning pinkish: fr. subglobose, about 1 cm. across, dark purple and bloomy; stone turgid, slightly obovoid and obtusish at apex. S.S.4:t.153. F.G.3:429. B.C.5:2831. M.G.19:54(h). Conn. to Pa. Intr. 1889. Zone V.—**P. a. Davísii** W. F. Wight. Shrub: lvs. broader, less acuminate, pubescent beneath only at the midrib. Mich. Intr. 1912.

10. **P. umbellàta** Ell. Small tree to 6 m. with compact head and slender brs.; bark dark brown; brts. glabrous or slightly pubescent at first: lvs. ellip-

tic to lanceolate, 4–7 cm. long, acute, rounded at base or broad-cuneate, finely serrate with acute teeth, glabrous above, usually pubescent beneath along the midrib, rather firm at maturity; petioles 5–7 mm. long, pubescent: fls. 2–4, white, 1–1.8 cm. across; the slender pedicels and calyx glabrous; sepals ovate, obtuse, shorter than tube, slightly hairy without, pubescent within: fr. subglobose, 1–2 cm. across, red, yellow or dark purple, bloomy; stone oval or subglobose, obtuse, smooth or reticulate. S.S.4:155. S. C. to Fla. Intr.? Zone VII?—**P. u. injucúnda** (Small) Sarg., var. Lvs. elliptic to elliptic-oblong, acute or acuminate, broad-cuneate, pubescent beneath, slightly so above: stone usually pointed. N. C. and Ga. to Ala. and Miss. (*P. i. Small.*) Intr. 1900. Zone VI?—**P. u. tarda** (Sarg.) W. F. Wight. Bark light reddish brown: lvs. elliptic-oblong or sometimes obovate, acute or short-acuminate, cuneate, finely pubescent or glabrous above, tomentulose beneath; petioles tomentose. Fl.IV; fr.X–XI. S.M.560. Miss., Tex. to S. Ark. Intr. 1903.

11. **P. mexicàna** S. Wats. BIG-TREE PLUM. Tree to 12 m., not sprouting from the root; brts. pubescent or glabrous: lvs. obovate to oblong-obovate, 6–12 cm. long, abruptly acuminate, usually subcordate, sharply and often doubly serrate, short-pubescent above, at least when young, and rugose, pubescent and somewhat reticulate beneath, thickish at maturity; petioles glandular: fls. 2–4, white, 1.5–2 cm across, pedicels usually glabrous; calyx-lobes dentate at apex or sometimes entire, slightly glandular, pubescent within: fr. globose, sometimes ellipsoid, 2–3 cm. long, purplish red, bloomy; stone obovoid or subglobose, turgid. S.M.565. S.T.2:t.165. (*P. arkansana* Sarg., *P. australis* Munson.) S. W. Ky. and Tenn. to Okl. and Mex. Intr. 1910. Zone V. Used occasionally as stock.

P. m. × *salicina* and *P. m.* × *Reverchonii* have been recorded.

12. **P. lanàta** (Sudw.) Mack. & Bush. Small tree sprouting from the root and forming thickets; bark red-brown; brs. spreading, forming a broad round head; brts. glabrous or pubescent: lvs. obovate to oblong-obovate, 6–12 cm. long, acuminate, broad-cuneate, rarely rounded, sharply and often doubly serrate, pubescent beneath; petioles usually glandless: fls. 2–5, white, 2–3 cm. across, pedicels and calyx outside pubescent; lobes acuminate, entire: fr. usually subglobose, 2–3 cm. across, red or yellowish; stone flattened. Hedrick, Plums N. Y. 380,t(c). S.M.563. (*P. americana* var. *mollis* Torr. & Gr., in part, *P. americana* var. *l.* Sudw., *P. Palmeri* Sarg.) Ill., Iowa and Mo. to Tex. Intr. 1903. Zone V. Cult. occasionally for its fr.

13. **P. americàna** Marsh. Tree, much like the preceding; young brts. glabrous: lvs. obovate to oblong-obovate, 6–10 cm. long, acuminate, broad-cuneate, sharply and often doubly serrate, glabrous or slightly pubescent along the midrib beneath; petioles glandless: fls. 2–5, white, 2–3 cm. across; calyx outside and pedicels glabrous, lobes acuminate, entire: fr. usually subglobose, 2–3 cm. across, red, rarely yellowish; stone compressed. S.S.4: t.150. B.C.5:2827,2828. Hedrick, Plums N. Y. 56,t(c),382,t(c). S.L.278(h). Mass. to Man., s. to Ga., N. Mex. and Utah. Cult. 1768. Zone III.—Many pomological varieties are grown; sometimes planted for its fls.

P. a. × *maritima;* see under No. 8.—*P. a.* × *angustifolia;* see under No. 18. —*P. a.* × *salicina, P. a.* × *hortulana, P. a.* × *Munsoniana, P. a.* × *utahensis* and *P. a.* × *pumila* have been recorded.

14. **P. nígra** Ait. CANADA PLUM. Small tree to 6 m.; rarely 10 m. tall, with upright brs. forming a narrow head; bark red brown to gray brown; young brts. glabrous or pubescent: lvs. elliptic to obovate, 6–10 cm. long, acuminate, broad-cuneate to subcordate, coarsely and doubly obtuse-serrate,

glabrous above, pubescent or nearly glabrous beneath; petioles 1.5–2.5 cm long, biglandular: fls. 3–4, white fading to pink, 2–3 cm. across; calyx like the slender stalks reddish and glabrous, lobes acute, glandular-serrate, becoming reflexed; petals broad-ovate: fr. ellipsoid, 2–3 cm. long, red or yellowish red; stone compressed. S.S.4:t.149. B.M.1117(c). Em.2:511,t(c). S.L.279 (h). (*P. americana* var. *n.* Waugh, *P. borealis* Poir., *P. mollis* Torr.) N. B. to Assin., s. to N. Y., Ohio and Wisc. Intr. 1773. Zone II.

15. **P. hortulàna** Bailey. Tree to 10 m., not sprouting from the root; bark brown, thin, scaly; young brts. glabrous becoming dark red-brown: lvs. oblong-ovate to oblong-obovate, rarely oblong-lanceolate, 7–11 cm. long, glabrous and lustrous above, slightly pubescent beneath at least along the midrib and veins, rather thick at maturity; petioles slender, 1.5–2.5 cm. long, usually with 1 or more glands, pubescent above: fls. 2–4, white, 1.2–1.5 cm. across; pedicels sleǹder, like the calyx glabrous, lobes oblong-ovate, glandular-ciliate, as long or nearly as long as tube, acute or obtuse, sometimes slightly pubescent outside, pubescent inside, usually finally reflexed: fr. globose or short-ellipsoid, 1.8–3 cm. long, red or yellow, slightly or not bloomy; stone subglobose to ellipsoid, reticulate. S.M.568. B.C.5:2828. Hedrick, Plums N. Y. 384,t(c). (*P. hortulana* var. *Waylandii* Bailey.) Ky. and Tenn. to Iowa and Okl. Cult. 1890. Zone V. Often cult. for its fr.—**P. h. Mìneri** Bailey, var. Lvs. thicker and duller, more veiny beneath. Hedrick, Plums N. Y. 209,t(c),272,t(c).—**P. h. pubens** Sarg., var. Young brts. and lvs. beneath pubescent.

P. h. × *salicina, P. h.* × *americana* and *P. h.* × *Munsoniana* have been recorded.

16. **P. Munsoniàna** Wight & Hedr. WILD GOOSE PLUM. Tree to 8 m.; brts. glabrous, soon chestnut-brown: lvs. oblong-lanceolate to lanceolate, rarely obovate-oblong, 6–10 cm. long, acute or acuminate, rounded at base, finely glandular-serrate, bright green and lustrous above, paler beneath and rather sparingly pubescent along the midrib and veins, sometimes pubescent all over when young, rarely quite glabrous, rather thin at maturity; petioles 1.5–2 cm. long, usually biglandular, pubescent above: fls. 2–4, 1.2–1.5 cm. across; pedicels slender, glabrous; calyx-lobes ovate-oblong, as long as the glabrous tube, glandular-ciliate, glabrous or slightly pubescent outside, pubescent inside near base; petals obovate to oblong-obovate: fr. globose to short-ellipsoid, 1.5–2.5 cm. long, red, rarely yellow, slightly bloomy; stone oval, usually truncate at base. Fl.ɪv–v; fr.vɪɪ–vɪɪɪ. S.M.569. B.C.5:2830. Hedrick, Plums N. Y. 378,t(c). Ky. and Tenn. to Kans. and n. Tex.—Cult. occasionally for its fr. in many pomological vars. Zone V.

P. M. × *cerasifera;* see under No. 4.—*P. M.* × *salicina, P. M.* × *sultana, P. M.* × *americana, P. M.* × *hortulana, P. M.* × *angustifolia* and *P. M.* × *Persica* have been recorded.

17. **P. Reverchònii** Sarg. Hoɢ PLUM. Shrub to 2 m., forming dense thickets; bark gray; young brts. glabrous, chestnut-brown: lvs. lanceolate or lance-ovate, 5–7 cm long, acuminate, cuneate or rounded at base, crenately glandular-serrate, strongly trough-shaped, green and glabrous above, paler beneath and slightly pubescent, rarely densely so while young; petioles 7–12 mm. long, with 2–4 glands at apex, pubescent above: fls. 2–4, about 1 cm. broad; pedicels glabrous, 6–10 mm. long; calyx sparingly hairy outside, lobes oblong or oblong-ovate, glandular-ciliate, shorter than tube, pubescent within; erect or spreading; petals obovate or oblong-obovate: fr. globose or subglobose, 1.5–2 cm. across, usually yellow with crimson cheek, rarely red; stone oblong, pointed at ends, smooth or slightly reticulate. Fl.ɪɪɪ–ɪv; fr.

vii–viii. U. S. Dept. Agr. Bull. 179:t.3,f.2,t.10,f.13–22. (*P. pygma* Munson, not *P. pygmaea* Willd.) Okl., Tex. Intr. 1916. Zone V.

P. R. × *mexicana* has been recorded.

Closely related species: **P. rivulàris** Scheele. CREEK PLUM. Lvs. ovate to oblong-ovate, or slightly obovate, not strongly trough-shaped; petioles glandless or with 1 or 2 glands: sepals finally reflexed: fr. subglobose, 1.5 cm. diam., red, sligh 'y bloomy; stone subglobose or oval. U. S. Dept. Agr. Bull. 179:t.3,f.3; t.10,f.23.24. (*P. texana* Scheele, not Dietr.) Tex. Intr. 1917. Zone V.

18. **P. angustifòlia** Marsh. CHICKASAW PLUM. Twiggy shrub forming thickets, or small tree to 4 m.; brts. slender, zigzag, glabrous, reddish: lvs. lanceolate to oblong-lanceolate, strongly trough-shaped, 2–5 cm. long, acute or short-acuminate, broadly cuneate or rounded at base, finely glandular, serrate, glabrous and lustrous above, paler beneath and glabrous or pubescent along the midrib toward the base; petioles glandular or glandless: fls. 2–4, 8–9 mm. across; pedicels 3–6 mm. long, glabrous; calyx glabrous, the lobes ovate, shorter than tube, glandless, glabrous inside except near base: fr. subglobose, 1–2 cm. across, red or yellow, with thin skin; stone oval, obtuse at ends or acute at apex. Fls.iii–iv; fr.vii–viii. S.S.4:152. (*P. chicasa* Michx.) Md. and s. Del. to Fla., w. to Ark. and Tex. Intr. 1874? Zone V.—**P. a. Watsònii** (Sarg.) Waugh. SAND PLUM. Lvs. smaller, elliptic to elliptic-oblong, acute, less conspicuously serrulate: fls. smaller; fr. with thicker skin. G.F.7:135. B.C.5:2829. M.G.19:55(h). (*P. W.* Sarg.) Kans. to Tex. and N. Mex. Cult. 1879.—**P. a. vàrians** Wight & Hedr. Rather larger and more robust: lvs. larger; pedicels longer: stone usually more pointed at apex. Okla., Tex. Cult. for its fr.

P. a. *Watsonii* × *americana* = **P. orthosépala** Koehne. Spreading shrub to 2 m.; it differs from *P. angustifolia* chiefly in its oblong-lanceolate to obovate-lanceolate, slightly larger and broader and more sharply serrate lvs., the larger fls. and larger frs. about 2.5 cm. across. G.F.7:187. B.C.5:2830. Orig. in Kans. Intr. 1880. Zone V.—*P. a. Watsonii* × *Besseyi;* see under No. 40.—*P. a. varians* × *gracilis* = **P. Slavínii** E. J. Palm. Spinescent shrub to 2.5 m.: lvs. lanceolate to lance-ovate, 3.5–7 cm. long, paler and pubescent beneath: fls. 2–6; pedicels pubescent or nearly glabrous; calyx-lobes ovate-lanceolate, usually entire, slightly pubescent or glabrous outside. Okl. and Kans. Intr. 1916.— Also *P. a.* × *salicina* and *P. a. varians* × *Munsoniana* have been recorded.

19. **P. grácilis** Engelm. & Gr. OKLAHOMA PLUM. Straggling shrub to 1.5 m., forming thickets; young brts. pubescent, later reddish ·brown: lvs. elliptic to ovate, 2.5–5 cm. long, acute at ends, rarely obtuse, finely serrate with acute or obtuse teeth, finely and slightly pubescent above, reticulate and densely pubescent below; petioles pubescent, glandless: fls. 2–4, about 1 cm. broad; pedicels and calyx finely pubescent; calyx-lobes ovate, acute, entire or denticulate, pubescent on both sides: fr. subglobose, about 1.5 cm. thick, usually red, slightly bloomy; stone oval, obtusish at ends. S.H.1:f. 345i(l). (*P. normalis* Small.) W. Ark., Okl. and N. Tex. Intr. 1916. Zone V.

P. g. × *angustifolia varians;* see under No. 18.

Closely related species: **P. venulòsa** Sarg. Larger shrub: lvs. larger, ovate to oblong-ovate, often short-acuminate and rounded at base, strongly reticulate beneath: fls. smaller; pedicels glabrous or nearly so: fr. somewhat larger, dark red. U. S. Dept. Agr. Bull. 179:t.7,f.2;t.12,f.22–24. Tex. Intr. 1916.

Sect. 3. ARMENIACA (Lam.) Koch. Fls. usually sessile or short-stalked (long-stalked in No. 25), ovary and fr. pubescent (glabrous in No. 20): lvs convolute, round-ovate to ovate, simply or doubly serrate: stone smooth or pitted; thornless shrubs or trees, the fls. before the lvs., except in No. 20.

20. **P. brigántina** Vill. BRIANÇON APRICOT Shrub or small tree; young brts. glabrous: lvs. ovate, 4–7.5 cm. long, short-acuminate, often subcordate, sharply and doubly serrate, pubescent beneath, chiefly on the veins: fls. 2–5, with the lvs., white or pinkish, 1.5–2 cm. across, short-stalked: fr. yellow,

smooth, round. N.D.5:t.59(c). L.A.2:684. (*P. brigantiaca* Vill., *Armeniaca b.* Pers.) S. E. France. Long cult. Zone VI. The seeds yield a perfumed oil "l'huile de marmotte."

21. **P. mandshùrica** (Maxim.) Koehne. MANCHURIAN APRICOT. Small tree to 5 m., with spreading and slightly pendulous brs.: lvs. broad-elliptic to ovate, 5–12 cm. long, acuminate, rounded or broad-cuneate at base, sharply and doubly serràte, with narrow elongated teeth, green beneath and glabrous except axillary tufts of hairs; petioles 2–3 cm. long, puberulous: fls. solitary, pinkish, about 3 cm. across; pedicels 2–5 mm. long: fr. yellow, subglobose, 2.5 cm. across; stone small, with obtuse edges. N.K.5:t.25. S.H.:f.349e,350f. (*P. Armeniaca* var. *m.* Maxim.) Manch., Korea. Cult. 1900. Zone V.

22. **P. sibírica** L. SIBERIAN APRICOT. Upright tree or shrub to 5 m., lvs. ovate, 5–8 cm. long, long-acuminate, finely serrate, reddish when young: then bright green, glabrous except axillary tufts of hairs beneath; petioles 1–3 cm. long, reddish: fls. solitary, white or pink, 3 cm. across; pedicels and calyx nearly glabrous: fr. subsessile, yellow with reddish cheek, little fleshy and scarcely edible; stone smooth with sharp nearly winged edge. L.B. 1627(c). Gs.3:74. S.H.1:f.349c,350g-h[1]. (*P. Armeniaca* var. *s.* K. Koch, *Armeniaca* s. Pers.) E. Siber., Manch., N. China. Intr. about 1800. Zone IV.

23. **P. Armeníaca** L. APRICOT. Round-headed tree to 10 m.; bark reddish; brts. brownish: lvs. broad-ovate or orbicular-ovate, 5–10 cm. long, abruptly acuminate, subcordate or rounded, closely and obtusely serrate, glabrous or with axillary tufts of hairs beneath; petioles 2–3 cm. long: fls. solitary, white or pinkish, about 2.5 cm. across: fr. round, 3 cm. across or more, yellowish with red cheek, nearly glabrous; stone smooth with a thickened furrowed edge. N.D.5:t.49(c). R.I.25:t.85(c). F.D.25:t.2553(c). M.A. t.23(h). Gn.M.31:259(h). (*Armeniaca vulgaris* Lam.) W. Asia. Long cult. Zone V. Cult. for its fr. in many pomological varieties.—**P. A. variegàta** Schneid., f. With variegated lvs. Orig. before 1770.—**P. A. péndula** Jaeg., var. Brs. pendulous. Orig. before 1889.—**P. A. Ansu** Maxim. Lvs. broad-elliptic to broad-ovate, usually broad-cuneate or truncate at base: fls. usually 2, pink: fr. subglobose, red, tomentose; stone free, minutely reticulate and with a very sharp edge. (*P. a.* Komar.) Cult. in Japan and Korea. Cult. 1880.

P. A. × *salicina;* see under No. 5.—*P. A.* × *cerasifera* = *P. dasycarpa;* see No. 25.

24. **P. Mume** (Sieb.) Sieb. & Zucc. JAPANESE APRICOT. Round-headed tree to 10 m. or shrub; bark gray or greenish; brts. slender, green: lvs. broadovate to ovate, 4–10 cm. long, long-acuminate, usually broad-cuneate, finely and sharply serrate, pubescent on both sides or only on the veins beneath; petioles glandular: fls. 1–2, very short-stalked, light pink, fragrant; petals obovate: fr. globose, 2–3 cm. across, yellow or greenish, scarcely edible; stone pitted, the flesh adhering. R.H.1885:564,t(c). Gn.50:164,t(c). N.K.5:t.24. G.C.29:183. (*Armeniaca M.* Sieb.) Japan, China. Intr. 1844. Zone VI.— **P. M. alba** (Carr.) Rehd., f. Fls. white. R.H. 1885:564.—**P. M. Alphándii** Rehd., f. Fls. pink, double. (*P. M. fl. pleno* Bean.) R.H.1885:564,t(c).— **P. M. albo-plèna** Bailey, var. Fls. white, double.—**P. M. péndula** Sieb., var. With pendulous brs. U. S. Im. 23:t.325,326(h).—**P. M. tónsa** Rehd., var. Lvs. nearly glabrous, often broad-cuneate: fls. white. China.

P. M. × *cerasifera* = *P. blireana;* see under No. 4.

25. **P. dasycárpa** Ehrh. PURPLE APRICOT (BLACK A.) Small tree to 6 m.; young brts. glabrous, purplish: lvs. elliptic-ovate to ovate, 3–6 cm. long,

acuminate, finely and closely serrate, dull green above, pubescent beneath on the veins; petioles 1.5–2.5 cm. long, glandular or glandless: fls. white, 2 cm. across; pedicels slender, pubescent: fr. globose, 3 cm. across, dark purple, bloomy, minutely pubescent. B.R.1243(c). N.D.5:t.51,f.1(c). L.B.1250(c). Probably *P. Armeniaca* × *cerasifera*. Orig. before 1780. Zone V. Fls. early and showy, before the lvs.; fr. rarely produced.

Subgen. II. AMYGDALUS (L.) Focke. Fls. sessile or short-stalked, before the lvs.: fr. tomentose (glabrous in a var. of *P. Persica*), usually dehiscent; stone pitted or smooth: lvs. conduplicate in bud: buds 3 in each axil, the lateral ones fl.-buds; terminal bud present.

26. **P. Amýgdalus** Batsch. ALMOND. Tree to 8 m., with gray bark; brts. glabrous: lvs. ovate-lanceolate to narrow-lanceolate, broadest usually slightly below the middle, 7–12 cm. long, long-acuminate, broad-cuneate or nearly rounded at base, finely serrulate, glabrous; petioles to 2.5 cm. long, glandular: fls. 1–2, pink or nearly white, 3–5 cm. across, nearly sessile; calyx-lobes oblong, villous at the margin: fr. ellipsoidal, compressed, 3–6 cm. long, velvety, dry, splitting; stone smooth, pitted. N.D.4:t.29(c). D.F.25:t.2550 (c). G.O.t.141(c). R.I.25:t.87(c). Gn.50:312,t(c);54:122,t(c). (*Amygdalus communis* L., *P. communis* Arcang., not Huds.) W. Asia, ?N. Afr. Cult. since ancient times. Zone VI.—**P. A. variegàta** (Schneid.) Rehd., f. Lvs. variegated.—**P. A. albo-plèna** (Schneid.) Rehd., f. Fls. double, white.— **P. A. roseo-plèna** (Schneid.) Rehd., f. Fls. pink, double.—**P. A. purpúrea** (Schneid.) Rehd., f. Fls. rose-purple.—**P. A. péndula** (Schneid.) Bean, var. Brs. pendulous.—**P. A. amàra** (DC.) Focke, var. Fls. large, darker in centre: lvs. broadest about the middle: kernel bitter.—**P. A. dulcis** (DC.) Koehne, var. Lvs. somewhat glaucous, broadest toward the base: style exceeding the stamens: kernel sweet. (*P. A.* var. *sativa* Focke.)—**P. A. frágilis** (Borkh.) Focke, var. Stone with thin .ragile shell: kernel sweet.

P. A. × *Persica* = **P. An.ýgdalo-pérsica** (West.) Rehd. Lvs. similar to *P. Amygdalus*, but more sharply serrate: fls. large, pink: fr. more peach-like, but with rather dry flesh and finally dehiscent; stone with hard shell, pitted and furrowed. R.H.1908:64(fr.) Jour. Hered. 12:328(h),329. Gt.74:477. M.A.t. 20(h). (*P. persico-amygdala* Schneid., *P. persicoides* Aschers. & Graebn., *Amygdalus communis* var. *persicoides* Ser., ? *P. Pollardii* Hort.) Orig. before the 16th cent. Zone V.—*P. amygdalo-persica* × *cerasifera;* see under No. 4.

Related species: P. Fenzliàna Fritsch. Close to No. 26: lower, sometimes spinescent: lvs. narrowly oblong-ovate, broadest near base, 6–8 cm. long, grayish or bluish green: fls. whitish: fr. scarcely fleshy; stone shorter. S.H.1:f.333a, 334d-f. Cauc. Intr. before 1890. Zone VI.—P. scopària (Spach) Schneid. Upright shrub to 6 m. with virgate, sparingly leafy brts.: lvs. linear, remotely crenulate, 2–4 cm. long: fls. about 2.5 cm. across; petals suborbicular: fr. ovoid, about 2 cm. long, glabrescent. S.H.1:f.332e-h. (*Amygdalus s.* Spach.) Persia. Cult. 1934. Zone VII?—P. spartioìdes (Spach) Schneid. Similar to the preceding: to 1.5 m.: lvs. narrow-oblong, 1–1.5 cm. long: petals oblong; ovary pubescent: fr. glabrous or nearly so. S.H.1:332a-d. (*Amygdalus s.* Spach.) W. Asia. Cult. 1933. Zone VII?

27. **P. Pérsica** (L.) Batsch. PEACH. Tree to 8 m.; brts. glabrous; buds pubescent: lvs. elliptic-lanceolate or oblong-lanceolate, broadest about or slightly above the middle, 8–15 cm. long, long-acuminate, broad-cuneate, serrate or serrulate, glabrous; petioles glandular, 1–1.5 cm. long: fls. usually solitary, pink, 2.5–3.5 cm. across, very short-stalked; sepals pubescent outside: fr. subglobose, 5–7 cm. across, tomentose, fleshy; stone deeply pitted and furrowed, very hard. N.D.6:t.2,3(c). R.I.25:t.86(c). G.O.t.140(c). D.F. 25:t.2552(c). (*Amygdalus P. L., Persica vulgaris* Mill.) China. Cult. since ancient times. Zone IV.—**P. P. atropurpúrea** Schneid., f. Lvs. purple. F.S. 19:t.1986(c).—**P. P. alba** Schneid., f. Fls. white. B.R.1586(c).—**P. P. duplex**

(West.) Rehd., f. Fls. double, pink. R.H.1852:221,t(c). (*P. P. fl. pleno* and *fl. roseo-pleno* Hort.) Orig. before 1636.—**P. P. camelliaeflòra** (Vanh.) Dipp., f. Fls. semidouble, deep red. F.S.13:t.1299(c). I.H.5:t.165(c). B.H.8:164,t.(c). —**P. P. dianthiflòra** (Vanh.) Dipp., f. Fls. semidouble, pink. F.S.13:t.1300 (c).—**P. P. albo-plèna** Schneid., f. Fls. semidouble, white. F.S.10,t.969(c).— **P. P. rubro-plèna** Schneid., f. Fls. semidouble, red. F.S.10:t.969(c).—**P. P. magnífica** Schneid., f. Fls. double, bright red. G.C.104:331,t(c). Gn.56: 516,t(c).—**P. P. versícolor** (Vanh.) Voss, f. Fls. semidouble, white, red and striped on same plant. F.S.13:t.1319(c).—**P. P. pyramidàlis** Dippel, f. Of narrow pyramidal habit.—**P. P. péndula** Dipp., f. Brs. pendulous.—The numerous forms cult. for their fr. may be classed under the following varieties: **P. P. scleropérsica** (Reichb.) Voss, f. CLINGSTONE P. The flesh adhering to the stone.—**P. P. aganopérsica** (Reichb.) Voss, f. FREESTONE P. Stone separating from the flesh.—**P. P. Nectarìna** (Ait.) Maxim., var. NECTARINE. Lvs. usually more strongly serrate: fr. glabrous, smaller. (*Amygdalus Persica* var. *Nectarina* Ait., *Persica nucipersica* Borkh. *P. Persica* var. *laevis* Gray.) Of this var. there are two forms: **P. P. scleronucipérsica** (Schuebl. & Mart.) Rehd., f., stone adhering to the flesh and **P. P. aganonucipérsica** (Schuebl. & Mart.) Rehd., f., stone separating from the flesh.— **P. P. compréssa** (Loud.) Bean, var. FLAT P. Fr. much flattened from above, broader than high; stone small, irregular. R.H.1870:111,t(c). J.1:154. L.A.2:680. B.C.5:2493. (*Persica platycarpa* Dcne., *Persica vulg.* var. *compressa* Loud., *P. P.* var. *platycarpa* Bailey.) China. Cult. 1822.

P. P. × *salicina;* see under No. 5.—*P. P.* × *Munsoniana* has been recorded.
Closely related species: **P. kansuénsis** Rehd. Winter-buds glabrous: lvs. broadest below the middle, less closely serrate, villous along the midrib near base; style longer than stamens, about as long as petals; stone furrowed, but not pitted. G.C.101:119(h). (*Amygdalus k.* Skeels.) N. W. China. Intr. 1914.

28. **P. Davidiàna** (Carr.) Franch. Tree to 10 m., with upright slender brs.; young brts. glabrous: lvs. narrowly ovate-lanceolate, 6–12 cm. long, broadest near base, gradually long-acuminate, broad-cuneate, finely and sharply serrate, light green, glabrous; petioles glandular: fls. solitary, light pink, about 2.5 cm. across, on very short stalks; calyx-lobes oval, glabrous: fr. globose, 3 cm. across, yellowish; stone small, pitted, free. Fl.III–IV. R.H.1872:75. Gt.44:t.1412(c). G.F.10:503. G.C.III.11:529. (*Persica D.* Carr.) China. Intr. 1865. Zone III.—**P. D. alba** Bean, var. Fls. white. Gt.44:t.1412(c). Gn.50:165. (*P. D.* f. *albiflora* Schneid.)—**P. D. rubra** Bean, var. Fls. bright rosy red.—Ornamental tree, flowering very early.—**P. D. Potanínii** (Batal.) Rehd., var. Lvs. ovate-lanceolate, rounded at base, acute or acuminate, crenate, lustrous above, firm, 6–7.5 cm. long: fr. ellipsoid. U. S. Im. 106:858,t. (*P. Persica* var. *P.* Batal.) N. W. China. Intr. 1914. Zone V.

29. **P. mìra** Koehne. Tree to 10 m., with slender brs.; brts. glabrous, green: lvs. lanceolate, 5–10 cm. long, gradually long-acuminate, rounded at base, remotely crenate-serrulate, entire near apex, villous along the midrib beneath; petioles 8–15 mm. long, with 2–4 glands: fls. solitary or 2, white, 2–2.5 cm. across, very short-stalked; sepals oval, slightly villous on margin; petals roundish-obovate: fr. subglobose, about 3 cm. across, fleshy, densely tomentose; stone ovate, compressed, smooth. B.M.9548(c). W. China. Intr. 1910. Zone VI. Differs from all other species of this group in the smooth stone.

30. **P. tangùtica** Batal. Dense shrub to 4 m., with spreading spiny brs.; brts. glabrous, brown: lvs. usually fascicled, oblanceolate or oblong, 1–3 cm. long, acute or obtuse, mucronulate, cuneate, crenulate, dark green above,

pale green beneath with 5–8 pairs of veins: fls. sessile, solitary, 2.5 cm. across; sepals oval, glabrous, obscurely denticulate, about as long as tube; petals obovate; stamens about 30 in 2 series: fr. subsessile, about 2 cm. across, densely tomentose, with thin flesh, dehiscent; stone roundish, keeled on both sides, rugose. B.M.9239(c). G.C.77:200. (*P. dehiscens* Koehne.) W. China. Intr. 1910. Zone VI.

Related species: **P. mongòlica** Maxim. Close to No. 30: lvs. broad-elliptic, about 1 cm. long, with usually 4 pairs of veins: fr. smaller, slightly tomentulose; stone adhering to the flesh. Mongol. Intr. 1866. Zone III.—**P. buchàrica** (Korsh.) Fedtsch. Shrub to 2 m., scarcely spiny: lvs. elliptic to ovate or ovate-oblong, 2.5–4 cm. long, acute or obtusish, crenate-serrulate; petiole slender, to 1.5 cm. long: sepals with villous margin: fr. finally dehiscent; stone ovate to ovate-lanceolate, 2.5 to 3 cm. long, smooth or nearly so. (*Am. b.* Korsh.) Turkest. Cult. 1902. Zone VI?

Into this affinity belong: **P. argéntea** (Lam.) Rehd. Unarmed shrub to 3 m.; brts. whitish tomentose: lvs. elliptic or ovate, 2–3.5 cm. long, white-tomentose, obscurely serrulate, short-stalked: fls. rose, 2–2.5 cm. across: fr. ovoid, 1.5 cm. long, whitish-tomentose. L.B.1137(c). (*Amygdalus orientalis* Mill., *A. argentea* Lam., *P. orientalis* Koehne, not Walp.) W. Asia. Intr. 1756. Zone VII?—**P. fasciculàta** (Torr.) Gray. Shrub to 1 m., with spreading spinescent brs: brts. puberulous: lvs. fascicled, linear-spatulate, 1–2 cm. long, entire, finely pubescent: fls. 2–5, small, greenish white: fr. globose-ovoid, about 1.5 cm. long, villous. S.H.1:f.335f-h. Torrey, Pl. Frémont. t.5. (*Emplectocladus f.* Torr., *Amygdalus f.* Greene.) Calif. to Ariz. Intr. before 1881. Zone VII. —**P. pedunculàta** (Pall.) Maxim. Shrub to 2 m.: brts. tomentulose, dark brown: lvs. elliptic to oblong, irregularly dentate, 2.5–4 cm. long, pubescent at least beneath when young: fls. solitary, pinkish; pedicels as long or twice as long as calyx-tube: fr. ovoid, little over 1 cm. long, pubescent: stone smooth. S.H.1:f. 335a-c. R.H.1864:370. Nov. Act. Petrop. 7:t.8,9. (*Amygdalus p.* Pall., *A. Boïssieri* Carr.) Siberia. Intr. before 1860. Zone V.—**P. pilòsa** (Turcz.) Maxim. Close to the preceding: much-branched shrub to 1.5 m.; brts. pilose: lvs. obovate, 1–2 cm. long, glandular-serrate, pilose on both sides: fls. subsessile. Mongol. Cult. 1933. Zone V?—**P. spinosíssima** (Bge.) Franch. Rigid spiny shrub: lvs. elliptic-obovate to oblanceolate, 1–2 cm. long, glabrous: sepals villous at apex: petals oblong-obovate, 7 mm. long: fr. ovoid: stone smooth. S.H.1: 336p-r. (*Amygdalus s.* Bge.) Turk. to Persia and Transcasp. Intr. 1910. Zone VII?

31. **P. tríloba** Lindl. FLOWERING ALMOND. Shrub or small tree to 5 m.; young brts. glabrous or slightly pubescent: lvs. broad-elliptic to obovate, 3–6 cm. long, broad-cuneate at base, acuminate or sometimes 3-lobed at apex, coarsely and doubly serrate; slightly pubescent beneath; petiole about 5 mm. long: fls. 1–2, pinkish, 2–2.5 cm. broad; calyx-tube broad-campanulate, shorter than pedicel; sepals ovate, serrulate, glabrous or pilose outside; stamens about 30; ovary pubescent: fr. red, subglobose, 1–1.5 cm. across, hairy; stone with thick bony shell. (*P. ulmifolia* Franch., *Amygdalopsis Lindleyi* Carr., *Amygdalus t.* Ricker.) China.—**P. t. múltiplex** (Bge.) Rehd., f. Fls. double, pink; sepals usually 10. F.S.15:t.1532(c). R.H.1862:91,t(c);1883:367 (fr). I.H.S:t.308. B.S.2:256,t(h). Intr. 1855. Zone V. This is the original *P. triloba* and a favorite ornamental shrub.—**P. t. simplex** (Bge.) Rehd., f. Fls. single. B.M.8061(c). (*P. t. f. normalis* Rehd.) Intr. 1884.—**P. t. Petzóldii** (K. Koch) Bailey, var. Brts. glabrous: lvs. elliptic or ovate, broadest at the middle or below, never 3-lobed, glabrous beneath at maturity; pedicels as long as calyx-tube; sepals and petals about 10; calyx-tube, glabrous inside; petals rose. (*P. P. K. Koch, P. virgata* Hort.) Cult. n China. Cult. 1869.

P. t. × *cerasifera* = **P. arnoldiàna** Rehd. Differs chiefly in the white flowers appearing with the lvs., the longer pedicels, reflexed calyx-lobes pubescent inside, in the generally elliptic less coarsely serrate lvs. and larger more succulent and less hairy fr. Orig. 1902. Zone V.

Hort., *P. sinensis* Pers.) E. Asia. Cult. 1687. Zone VI. The double-flowered forms are very ornamental and often used for forcing.

38. **P. hùmilis** Bunge. Upright shrub to 1.5 m.; young brts. puberulous: lvs. obovate or elliptic, 2.5–5 cm. long, acute or short-acuminate, cuneate, serrulate, glabrous beneath; petioles 1–2 mm. long: fls. 1–2, with the lvs., white or slightly pinkish, 1.5 cm. across; pedicels 6–8 mm. long: fr. subglobose, 1.5 cm. across, bright red, acid. B.M.7335(c). M.D.1909:180,f.3. (*P. Bungei* Walp.) N. China. Intr. 1881. Zone V.

39. **P. pùmila** L. SAND CHERRY. Shrub to 2.5 m., with upright slender shoots, old stems often procumbent: young brts. glabrous, reddish: lvs. oblanceolate, 3–5 cm. long, acuminate or acute, cuneate, closely serrate, except toward the base, glabrous, dull green above, grayish white beneath; petioles 1–1.6 cm. long: fls. 2–4, about 1 cm. across, white; pedicels about 1 cm. long: fr. subglobose, about 1 cm. across, purple-black, lustrous, scarcely edible. G.O.t.119(c). L.B.1607(c). B.C.5:2833. M.G.19:57(h). W. N. Y. to Wisc. and Ill. Intr. 1756. Zone II.—**P. p. depréssa** (Pursh) Bean, var. Prostrate shrub: lvs. less acuminate, often obtusely spatulate, thinner, more glaucous beneath, teeth more crenate, veins less prominent; stipules less fimbriate: fr. globose-ellipsoid, edible. G.W.19:215(h). (*P. d.* Pursh.) N. B. to Ont. and Mass. Cult. 1864.—**P. p. susquehànae** (Willd.) Jaeg., var. Upright shrub to 1.3 m.: lvs. obovate or elliptic, strongly serrate. B.C.5:2833. (*P. p.* var. *cuneata* Bailey, *P. c.* Raf., *P. s.* Willd.) Me. to Pa., w. to Wisc. and Minn. Intr. 1805.

P. p. × *cerasifera atropurpurea* = P. cistena N. E. Hansen. PURPLELEAF SAND-CHERRY. Lvs. slightly pubescent along the midrib beneath near base, reddish like pedicels and calyx; petiole puberulous above; fls. 1–2, white: fr. blackish purple. M.D.1917:67,f.A. Orig. before 1910.—*P. p.* × *hortulana* and *P. p.* × *tomentosa* have been recorded.

40. **P. Bésseyi** Bailey. WESTERN SAND CHERRY. Similar to the preceding; stem usually prostrate: lvs. spreading, elliptic to elliptic-lanceolate, 2–6 cm. long, acute, appressed-serrate, glabrous; petioles 4–10 mm. long: fls. 2–4, white, 1.5 cm. across; pedicels about 8 mm. long: fr. subglobose, about 1.5 cm. across, purple-black, sweet. B.M.8156(c). B.C.5:2834. B.S.2:230. (*P. pumila* var. *B.* Waugh, *P. prunella* Daniels.) Man. to Wyo., s. to Kans. and Colo. Intr. 1892. Zone III. Cult. for its fr.

P. B. × *angustifolia* var. *Watsonii* = P. utahensis Dieck. Lvs. elliptic to elliptic-oblong or oblong-obovate, 3.5–6 cm. long, finely serrulate, lustrous above, reticulate beneath: fr. slightly bloomy, dark brownish red. S.H.1:f.345m-n. Orig. about 1865. Zone III.—*P. B.* × *tomentosa* has been recorded.

Sect. 2. PSEUDOCERASUS Koehne. Sepals upright or spreading: calyx-tube usually cylindric: fls. in fascicles or short few-fld. racemes.

41. **P. canéscens** Bois. Shrub with spreading brs., to 2 m.; brts. pubescent: lvs. ovate to ovate-lanceolate, 2.5–6 cm. long, abruptly acuminate, rounded at base, doubly serrate with abruptly acuminate teeth, pubescent above, densely grayish pubescent beneath; petioles 5–10 mm. long; stipules dentate, about ½ as long as petiole: infl. with leafy bracts; fls. 2–5, pinkish, about 1 cm. across; pedicels 5–10 mm. long; pilose like the calyx; sepals triangular, serrate, half as long as tube; petals caducous, oblong-obovate; style pilose at base: fr. subglobose, 1–1.2 cm. across, red. F.V.66(h),67. C. and W. China. Intr. 1898. Zone V. Distinct shrub, but of little ornamental value.

P. c. × *avium* = P. Schmittii Rehd. Small tree: lvs. elliptic-oblong, 5–8 cm. long, acuminate, glabrescent above, pubescent chiefly on the veins beneath; petiole 1–2.5 cm. long; pedicels 1–1.5 cm. long, with large involucre at base; calyx campanulate; petals broad-oval, 1 cm. long. Orig. 1923.

Related species: **P. dawyckénsis** Sealy. Young brts. pilose: lvs. elliptic, cuneate or broad-cuneate, doubly and obtusely dentate, loosely pubescent above, more densely beneath: peduncle short, in fr. to 2 cm. long; calyx-tube pubescent outside; style glabrous: fr. 1.2–1.5 cm. across, crimson. B.M.9519(c). (*?P. canescens* × *Dielsiana*). ?W. China. Intr. 1907.—**P. setulòsa** Batal. Shrub or small tree to 5 m.; bark flaky: lvs. ovate or elliptic-ovate, 1.5–4 cm. long, acuminate, doubly serrate, pilose beneath at least on the veins: fls. 2–3, pink, on a short peduncle, with leafy bracts: calyx villous outside; sepals entire. N. China. Cult. 1934. Zone V?

42. **P. incìsa** Thunb. Shrub or sometimes tree to 10 m.; brts. glabrous: lvs. purplish when unfolding, ovate to obovate, 3–5.5 cm. long, acuminate, incisely doubly serrate, pubescent above and beneath on the veins; petioles slender, 8–10 mm. long, pubescent, fls. 1–3, nodding, white to pale pink; pedicels short or sometimes elongated with leafy bracts at base; calyx vinous-red, usually glabrous; petals fugacious: fr. ovoid, 6–8 mm. long, purple-black. S.H.1:f.339g,340o. Wilson, Cherr. Jap. t.5(h). (*Cerasus i.* Lois.) Japan. Cult. 1910. Zone V. Early flowering shrub.—**P. i. serràta** Wils., f. Lvs. less distinctly biserrate or almost simply serrate, with long-aristate teeth. Intr. 1915.—**P. i. Yamadei** Mak., var. Young lvs., pedicels and calyx green; style greenish. Intr. about 1918.

Related species: **P. stipulàcea** Maxim. Lvs. oblong-lanceolate or obovate-lanceolate, 4–6.5 cm. long, glabrate except bearded in the axils beneath, with 7–10 pairs of veins; stipules about as long as petiole, coarsely serrate: fls. solitary, short-stalked; calyx glabrous; stone rugulose. N. W. China. Intr. 1873. Zone V?—**P. apétala** (Sieb. & Zucc.) Franch. & Sav. Shrub or small tree: brts. villous at first: lvs. oblong or obovate-oblong, 3–5 cm. long, long-acuminate, incisely doubly serrate, densely pubescent on both sides: fls. 1–2, with the lvs.; calyx-tube villous, purple; petals small, fugacious; pedicels pilose. S.I.2:t.28,f. 14–19. (*P. Ceraseidos* Maxim.) Japan. Intr. 1915. Zone V?—**P. latidentàta** Koehne. Tree to 6 m.; brts. strigose: lvs. ovate or elliptic-ovate, 2–5 cm. long, acuminate, deeply and sharply doubly serrate, minutely strigillose above, glabrous or slightly villous along the midrib beneath: fls. 1–3, white or pinkish, sometimes on a short peduncle with small bracts; pedicels and calyx glabrous; sepals sparsely denticulate: fr. red, about 1 cm. across. W. China. Intr. 1932. Zone VI?—**P. crataegifòlia** Hand.-Mazz. Prostrate and ascending shrub: brts. strigose: lvs. elliptic to oblong-elliptic, 2–8 cm. long, incisely doubly serrate or lobulate, glabrous except strigillose on the veins above: fls. 1–2, white or pink, 1.5–2 cm. across; pedicels and calyx glabrous; sepals broad ovate, glandular-denticulate. W. China. Intr. 1932. Zone VII?—**P. mùgus** Hand.-Mazz. Prostrate shrub, similar to the preceding: lvs. elliptic or obovate, 1.5–6 cm. long, acute, doubly serrate, sparingly strigillose above: sepals oblong-ovate, glandular-fimbriate: fr. dark red, about 9 mm. long. W. China. Intr. 1932. Zone VII?

43. **P. nippónica** Matsum. Bushy tree to 6 m.; brts. glabrous, chestnut-brown; lvs. ovate, 4–9 cm. long, long-acuminate, usually rounded at base, incisely doubly serrate, pubescent while young, chiefly on veins, finally nearly glabrous; petioles glabrous: fls. 1–3, white or pale pink, 2–2.5 cm. across; pedicels 1.5–2.5 cm. long, glabrous; calyx-tube campanulate or funnelform, glabrous; petals elliptic-oblong to roundish-obovate, rounded or emarginate: fr. globose, about 8 mm. across, black. S.I.2:t.28(c, as *P. incisa*). (*P. iwagiensis* Koehne, *P. nikkoensis* Koehne.) Japan. Intr. 1915. Zone V. Very ornamental in bloom.—**P. n. kurilénsis** (Miyabe) Wils. Petioles pubescent: fls. somewhat larger; pedicels and calyx-tube slightly pubescent. M.K.t. 54(c). (*P. k.* Miyabe.) Japan, Kurile Isls. Intr. 1905. Zone V.

44. **P. lobulàta** Koehne. Tree to 10 m., young brts. slightly pubescent: lvs. obovate to oblong-obovate or oblong-lanceolate, 3–8 cm. long, acuminate, cuneate to rounded at base, incisely doubly serrate with strongly acuminate teeth, nearly glabrous above, pilose on veins beneath: fls. white, 1–3; pedicels 1.5–2 cm. long, in fr. to 2.5 cm., glabrous; calyx-tube funnelform; sepals ovate-

oblong, shorter than tube, glandular-serrate, upright; petals obovate; style pilose toward base: fr. subglobose, about 1 cm. across, red; stone ovoid, ribbed, 8–10 mm. long. W. China. Intr. 1908. Zone V?

Closely related species: **P. glyptocárya** Koehne. Differs chiefly in its larger lvs. 6–11 cm. long, in its red-brown fr. with the stone roundish about 8 mm. long, reticulate-ribbed or ribbed. W. China. Intr. 1908. Possibly only var. of the preceding.—**P. pleuróptera** Koehne. Differs chiefly in its smaller lvs. 2–6 cm. long, in its black fr. with roundish foveolate stone about 7 mm. long; pedicels about 1 cm. long. W. China. Intr. 1908. Zone V.

45. **P. subhirtélla** Miq. Higan Cherry. Small, much-branched tree to 10 m.; young brts. pubescent: lvs. ovate to oblong-ovate, 3–7 cm. long, acuminate, sharply and often doubly serrate, pubescent on the veins beneath, with about 10 pairs of veins; petioles pubescent, about 6 mm. long: fls. 2–5, light pink, 1.8 mm. across; calyx-tube cylindric, pubescent; pedicels about 8 mm. long; petals emarginate: fr. about 8 mm. across, black. B.M.7508(c). M.D. 1917:42. M.G.15:320(h). S.L.273(h). Wilson, Cherr. Jap. t.1(h). (*P. Miqueliana* Maxim., in part.) Japan. Intr. 1894. Zone V. Handsome and free-flowering; much cult., particularly *P. s. pendula.*—**P. s. ascéndens** (Mak.) Wils., var. Large tree to 20 m., rather sparingly branched: lvs. usually elliptic-oblong, 6–10 cm. long. Wilson, Cherr. Jap. t.3(h). M.D.1917:42a^1-e^1. (*P. aequinoctialis* Miyoshi, *P. microlepis* and *P. Herincqiana* Koehne.) Japan. Cult. 1916.—**P. s. péndula** (Maxim.) Tanaka, var. Tree with slender pendulous brs.: lvs. similar to the preceding var., but broader; calyx-tube glabrescent. B.M.8034(c). L.I.35. Gn.50:454,t.(c). G.F.1:196;2:487. M.G. 15:319(h). S.L.274(h). (*P. p.* Maxim., *P. itasakura* Sieb., *P. Herincqiana* Schneid.) Japan. Intr. 1862.—"**Yae-shidare-higan.**" Pendulous form with double fls. N.H.18:65.—**P. s. autumnàlis** Mak., var. Shrub or bushy tree to 5 m.: fls. semidouble, appearing partly late in fall and partly in spring. Gn. 76:628;85:502;89:344(h). J.H.38:f.204(h). G.C.77:71(h). (*P. microlepis* var. *Smithii* Koehne, *P. microlepis* Bean, not Koehne, *P. Miqueliana* Hort., not Maxim.) Cult. in Japan. Intr. before 1909.

P. s. × *serrulata;* see No. 51.

46. **P. campanulàta** Maxim. Small tree to 8 m.; young brts. glabrous: lvs. ovate to elliptic-ovate or ovate-oblong, 4–10 cm. long, acuminate, closely and doubly or nearly simply serrate, with short teeth pointing forward, glabrous; pedicels slender, about 1 cm. long, glandular: fls. pendulous, deep rose, campanulate; calyx-tube deep rose, glabrous; pedicels 5–20 mm. long: fr. ovoid, 1.5 cm. long, red; stone smooth. Gn.56.t.1244(c, as *P. pendula*). B.M.9575(c). J.C.28,1:t.2,f.6–12;34,2:264. (*P. ceraseidos* var. *c.* Koidz.) S. Japan, Formosa. Cult. 1899. Zone VII? Beautiful Cherry, but probably not quite hardy.

Closely related species: **P. cerasoìdes** D. Don. Lvs. more coriaceous and more sharply toothed, rounded-oval: fr. apiculate. Wallich, Pl. As. Rar. 2:t.143. S.H.1:f.339a,340f. (*P. Puddum* Brandis.) Himal. Tender. Intr. ?

47. **P. rùfa** Hook. f. Tree to 7 m.; young brts. rufous-tomentose: lvs. elliptic-oblong to oblong-lanceolate, 5–10 cm. long, sharply serrate with gland-tipped teeth, pubescent on the veins beneath while young; petioles 1 cm. long: fls. 1 or few, pink; pedicels 1–2.5 cm. long; calyx-tube tubular-campanulate, glabrous; sepals triangular, serrate: fr. broad-ellipsoid. S.H.1: f.339n-n^1,340l.^{1} Himal. Intr. 1897. Zone VII.

Closely related species: **P. trichántha** Koehne. Infl. pubescent. Sikkim. Intr. 1897.

48. **P. sérrula** Franch. Tree to 10 m., with flaky brown bark; young brts. finely pubescent: lvs. lanceolate, 4–10 cm. long, long-acuminate, rounded at

base, slightly doubly or simply serrulate, pubescent along the midrib beneath and bearded in the axils, with 9–15 pairs of veins; petioles about 1 cm. long, with 3–4 glands: fls. 1–3, white; pedicels about 1 cm. long; calyx-tube glabrous, green; sepals ovate-triangular, glandular-denticulate; petals round-ovate, 8 mm. long, rounded or tricuspidate at apex: style finely pubescent below the middle: fr. oval, 1–1.3 cm. long, red; stone strongly reticulato-ribbed. (*P. s.* var. *tibetica* Koehne.) W. China. Intr. 1908. Zone V.

49. **P. concìnna** Koehne. Shrub to 2 m.; young brts. sparingly pilose, soon glabrous: lvs. purplish when unfolding, narrow-elliptic to oblong-ovate or oblong-obovate, 3–6 or on shoots to 8 cm. long and lance-oblong, acuminate, rounded or cuneate at base, sharply and rather finely or sometimes doubly serrate, usually sparingly hairy above, grayish green beneath and sparingly hairy chiefly on the veins, at least at first; petioles 3–8 mm. long, sparingly pubescent: fls. 1–4, white, 2–2.5 cm. across; pedicels 8–15 mm. long; calyx-tube tubular, glabrous; sepals ovate to ovate-oblong, entire; petals narrow-obovate, often emarginate: fr. subglobose, 1–1.2 cm. long; stone ovoid, smooth or nearly so. C. China. Intr. 1907. Zone V. Flowering profusely before the lvs.

50. **P. Conradìnae** Koehne. Tree to 8 m.; young brts. glabrous: lvs. obovate to obovate-oblong, rarely broad-ovate, 5–10 cm. long, abruptly acuminate, usually rounded at base, deeply or in the middle doubly serrate, glabrous above, hairy on the veins beneath at first, with 9–12 pairs of veins; petiole 1–1.5 cm. long, glabrous: fls. before the lvs., 1–4, whitish or pinkish, about 2 cm. across; pedicels 5–18 mm. long; bracts caducous; calyx-tube tubular-campanulate; sepals ovate, entire; petals emarginate: fr. oval, about 1 cm. long, red; stone smooth. Gn.87:97. C. China. Intr. 1907. Zone VI? —**P. C. semiplèna** Ingram. Fls. semidouble. G.C.77:217. Orig. before 1925.

Closely related species: **P. Hélenae** Koehne. Lvs. sharply and deeply doubly serrate: petals ovate, acute, white. C. China. Intr. 1907?—**P. Spréngeri** Pamp. Calyx-tube finely pubescent; style pubescent below. C. China. Cult. 1900.

51. **P. yedoénsis** Matsum. Yoshino-zakura. Tree to 16 m., with smooth, pale gray bark; young brts. slightly pubescent: lvs. elliptic-ovate to obovate, 6–12 cm. long, acuminate, strongly doubly serrate with acuminate teeth, glabrous above, pubescent on the veins beneath, light green beneath and green when unfolding; petioles pubescent: fls. white to pink, 3–3.5 cm. across, slightly fragrant, in 5–6-fld. short-peduncled racemes; calyx-tube cylindric, pubescent; sepals serrate; pedicels pubescent; style pubescent or nearly glabrous: fr. globose, black. B.M.9062(c). N.K.5:t.8. Wilson, Cherr. Jap. t.4(h). Cult. in Japan, supposed to be a hybrid between *P. serrulata* and *P. subhirtella*. Intr. 1902. Zone V.—**P. y. perpéndens** Wils., f. Brs. pendulous, very long: pedicels and calyx hairy. Intr. 1910 from Japan.—**P. y. nudiflòra** Koehne, var. Calyx and pedicels glabrous or nearly so.—**P. y. shojo** Wils., f. Fls. double, rosy pink, large.—**P. y. Taizanfukun** Wils., f. Fls. double, pink, of medium size. Icon. Fl. Jap. 1:t.15. J.C.34,1:t.5,f.9(h),t.16, f.70(c). (*P. donarium* f. *T.* Koidz., *P. fruticosa* Miy. f. *ambigua* Miyoshi.)

P. y. × *Sargentii;* see under No. 52.

52. **P. Sargéntii** Rehd. Pyramidal to round-headed tree to 25 m.: bark smooth, chestnut-brown, with large lenticels; brts. glabrous: lvs. purplish when unfolding, elliptic-obovate to oblong-obovate, 7–12 cm. long, long-acuminate, rounded or sometimes subcordate at base, sharply serrate with acuminate teeth, glabrous and glaucescent beneath: petiole 2–3 cm. long: fls. precocious, rose-colored, 3–4 cm. across, in 2–4-fld. sessile umbels; pedicels

1.5–3 cm. long, glabrous like the tubular-campanulate calyx-tube, lobes ovate-oblong, entire; petals obovate, emarginate: fr. globose-ovoid, 1 cm. long, purple-black. Fl.ɪv–v; fr.vɪ–vɪɪ. M.K.t.53(c). B.M.8411(c). G.F.10:463. G.C.III.19:517;55:346. S.L.272(h). B.A.1937:11(h). (*P. serrulata* var. *sachalinensis* Wils., **P**. *sachal.* Koidz.) Japan, Saghal. Intr. 1890. Zone IV. The hardiest and most vigorous of the Japanese cherries and handsome in bloom.

P. S. × *yedoensis* = **P**. Júddii E. Anders. Lvs. brownish when unfolding: fls. flushed pink, 2–4 in short-peduncled racemes; pedicels and style with few hairs at base; sepals slightly glandular-serrate. Orig. 1914. Zone V.

53. **P. serrulàta** Lindl. Tree to 25 m.; bark smooth, dark chestnut-brown; brts. glabrous: lvs. ovate to ovate-lanceolate, rarely obovate, 6–12 cm. long, abruptly long-acuminate, serrate or often doubly serrate with aristate teeth, glabrous, greenish brown when unfolding, glaucescent beneath; petioles 1.5–3 cm. long, usually with 2–4 glands, glabrous: fls. 3–5, white or pink, 3–4 cm. across, racemose with leafy bracts, inodorous; calyx-tube campanulate, glabrous; sepals ovate, acute, slightly serrulate; style glabrous: fr. black. (*Cerasus s.* G. Don, *P. mutabilis* Miyoshi, *P. pseudocerasus* Hort., not Lindl.) Japan, China, Korea. The original *P. serrulata* of Lindl. is a garden form with double white fls. distinguished as **P. s. albo-plena** Schneid., f. Three spontaneous vars. are known: **P. s. spontànea** (Maxim.) Wils., var. Lvs. greenish or reddish brown at first, later glaucescent beneath, teeth scarcely aristate: fls. white or pink, about 2 cm. across, in usually short-stalked, 2–3-fld. racemes. S.I.2:t.27,f.1–14(c). (*P. tenuiflora* Koehne, in part.) Japan, Korea to C. China. Intr. 1900.—**P. s. pubéscens** (Koidz.) Wils., var. Similar to the preceding: lvs. pale green beneath, usually slightly pubescent; petiole hairy, often only above: pedicels usually slightly pubescent. J.C.34,2:269. Japan, Korea, China. Intr. 1907.—**P. s. Lannesiàna** (Carr.) Rehd., var. Bark gray: lvs. slightly reddish or green at first, later pale green beneath, teeth long-aristate: fls. fragrant, pink. B.M.8012(c). T.M.26:117,f.10,11. G.C. III.19:466. (*Cerasus L.* Carr., *P. L.* Wils., *P. s.* f. *L.* Koehne.) Japan. Intr. before 1870. The original *P. L.* Carr. has pink fls., the spontaneous form **P. s. álbida** Mak., f., white fls. J.C.34,2:272,f.7. (*P. speciosa* Ingram.) Cult. 1909.

Almost all the numerous garden forms to which belong most of the Japanese flowering cherries are figured in J.C.34,1:t.1–23(c) and in Miyoshi, Jap. Cherr. t.1–50(c) (1921), many in Russell, Or. Flow. Cherr. (U. S. Dept. Agr. Circ. 313), and some habit pictures in Wilson, Cherr. Jap. (1916). The following are some of the best known; THE FIRST 8 ARE FORMS OF TYPICAL *P. serrulata:* "**Kiku-shidare-zakura.**" Brs. spreading or pendent: fls. very double, pink, with more than 50 petals and sometimes 10 sepals. (*P. s. pendula* Bean, "Cheal's Weeping.")—"**Kiku-zakura.**" Similar to the preceding but brs. upright. (*P. s.* f. *rosea* Wils.)—"**Fugenzo.**" Fls. double, rose pink, with 2 leafy carpels in the centre. One of the most handsome forms. ("James Veitch.")—"**Shirofugen.**" Fls. double, pink in bud, changing to white, with 2 leafy carpels. (*P. s.* f. *albo-rosea* Wils.)—"**Hisakura.**" Fls. double, pale pink.—"**Horinji.**" Fls. in clusters, double or semidouble, pale pink. F.S.21: 2238(c).—"**Sekiyama.**" Fls. rich rose-red, double, large, late.—"**Shogetsu.**" Fls. pale pink, double, very large, long-stalked. (*P. s.* f. *superba* Wils.)— FORMS OF VAR. *Lannesiana:* "**Amanogawa.**" Habit fastigiate: fls. pale pink, semidouble. J.C.34,1:t.5,f.10(h). (*P. L.* f. *erecta* Wils.)—"**Jo-nioi.**" Fls. pure white, single or semidouble. (*P. L.* f. *affinis* Wils.)—"**Sirotae.**" Fls.

pure white, double or semidouble, large; the best of the double white cher-
ries.—**"Yaye-oshima."** Fls. double white. (*P. L.* f. *donarium* Wils.)—
"Ukon." Fls. greenish yellow, double or semidouble, large. Gt.52:t.1513a(c).
(*P. s.* f. *viridiflora* Mak., *P. L.* f. *grandiflora* Wils., *P. pseudocerasus* f. *vires-
cens* Koehne.)—**"Hata-zakura."** Fls. white, tinged pink, semidouble.—
"Fuku-rokuju." Fls. pale pink, fading to white, clustered at end of brts.
(*P. L.* f. *contorta* Wils.)—**"Botan-zakura."** Fls. pale pink, semidouble, very
large. (*P. L.* f. *moutan* Wils.)—**"Ochichima."** Fls. pale pink, double, large.
G.W.6:354.—**"Ojochin."** Fls. semidouble, pink, very large.
    P. s. × *subhirtella;* see No. 51.

    54. P. Siebóldii (Carr.) Wittm. Small tree, to 8 m., with smooth gray
bark; young brts. glabrous; lvs. elliptic to ovate, 6–12 cm. long, abruptly
long-acuminate, rounded at base, sharply and often slightly doubly serrate
with small teeth, densely pubescent on both sides; petioles pubescent, usually with 1 or 2 small glands: fls. about 3 cm. across, double or sometimes
single, pink or sometimes white, 2–4 on a short peduncle; pedicels pubescent; calyx-tube turbinate, or short-campanulate, pubescent, about as long
as the ovate obtuse lobes; style usually hairy at base. R.H.1866:371,t.(c).
Gt.51:t.1494a(c). Gn.33:420. L.I.t.36. G.W.16:355. Wilson, Cherr. Jap. t.8
(h). (*P. pseudocerasus* var. *S.* Maxim., *P. pseudocerasus* f. *Watereri* Koehne.)
Cult. in Japan. Intr. 1864. Zone V.

    Sect. 3. Lobopetalum Koehne. Lvs. with acute or acuminate teeth: fls. in
sessile umbels or 2–6-fld. stalked umbel-like racemes; petals deeply emarginate
or 2-lobed.

    55. P. cantabrigiénsis Stapf. Tree; brts. sparingly pubescent at first,
soon glabrous; lvs. elliptic-ovate or elliptic to elliptic-oblong, to 9 cm. long,
acuminate, rounded at base or broad-cuneate, coarsely doubly serrate with
glandular teeth, pubescent on both sides at first, soon glabrous except on
the veins beneath; petiole 6–7 mm. long, with 2 glands: fls. pink, 2–2.5 cm.
across, 3–6 in subsessile or short-stalked umbels, surrounded by a deciduous
involucre; pedicels to 1.5 cm. long, like the campanulate calyx-tube pilose;
sepals ovate, acutish, entire; petals suborbicular, emarginate: fr. red. B.M.
9129(c). (*P. pseudocerasus* Koidz., not Lindl.) China. Cult. 1826. Zone VI?

    Related species: **P. pseudocérasus** Lindl. Lvs. ovate, rather finely doubly
serrate: fls. in 2–6-fld. racemes; pedicels with small gland-toothed bracts at
base: involucre caducous. B.R.t.800(c). M.D.1917:7. (*P. pauciflora* Bge.)
N. China. Cult. in China and Japan. Intr. 1819. Zone V?

    56. P. Dielsiàna Schneid. Shrub or tree to 10 m.; young brts. glabrous:
lvs. oblong-obovate to oblong, 8–14 cm. long, abruptly acuminate, broad-
cuneate to subcordate at base, simply or doubly serrate with short-acuminate
teeth, glabrous above, thinly villous beneath, more densely on veins, with
10–12 pairs of veins; petioles 8–16 mm. long, villous or nearly glabrous, with
1–3 glands: fls. before the lvs., pink or white, 3–5, umbellate, surrounded by
a large involucre; bracts glandular-fimbriate; pedicels 1–3.5 cm. long, villous;
calyx-tube short-campanulate, villous; sepals oblong to lanceolate, entire;
petals oval, 1–1.4 cm. long; style glabrous: fr. globose, about 8 mm. across,
red; stone smooth. C. China. Intr. 1907. Zone VI?
    P. D. × *canescens?;* see under No. 41.
    Related species: **P. cyclámina** Koehne. Close to No. 56: lvs. glabrous be-
neath or pilose only on the veins; petioles glabrous: fls. coetaneous, pink;
calyx-tube glabrous; petals oblong. C. China. Intr. 1907. Zone (V).—P.
involucràta Koehne. Tree to 5 m.: lvs. pubescent on the veins at first, soon
glabrous, doubly serrate or nearly crenate-serrate with short broad teeth: fls. in
sessile umbels, surrounded by a large involucre persistent during flowering:

pedicels 5–10 mm. long, densely pilose like the calyx. M.D.1917:7. C. China. Intr. ?

Sect. 4. EUCERASUS Koehne. Lvs. dentate with obtuse teeth: fls. in sessile umbels, rarely short-racemose, surrounded at base by the persistent bud-scales.

57. **P. ávium** L. MAZZARD (GEAN). Tree to 24 m., of pyramidal habit; brts. stout: lvs. oblong-ovate, 6–15 cm. long, acuminate, unequally serrate, dull and often slightly rugose above, more or less pubescent beneath, of soft texture; petioles to 4 cm. long: fls. white, in several-fld. umbels, 2.5–3.5 cm. across; scales of fl.-buds rather large, reflexed at anthesis; calyx-tube glabrous, constricted at apex; sepals usually entire: fr. subglobose or ovoid, about 2.5 cm. across. S.E.t.411(c). H.W.3:90,t.55(c). R.I.25:t.93(c). Gn. 78:242(h). M.A.t.25(h). (*Cerasus a.* Moench.) Eu., W. Asia. Cult. since ancient times; intr. to N. Am. about 1625. Zone III. Much cultivated for its fr. in many pomological vars.; some forms planted for ornament.—**P. a. aspleniifòlia** (Kirchn.) Jaeg., var. Lvs. deeply incised.—**P. a. salicifòlia** Dipp. Lvs. narrow.—**P. a. decumàna** (Mord. de Launay) Dipp., var. Lvs. very large, to 25 cm. long. (*P. macrophylla* Poir.)—**P. a. plèna** (West.) Schneid., f. Fls. double. Hedrick, Cherr. N. Y. 30,t(c). G.W.6:329. Gn.78:242;83:94(h). S.L.275(h). (*P. a. fl. pleno* Hort., *Cerasus a.* var. *multiplex* Ser.)—**P. a. péndula** (Ser.) Jaeg., var. Brs. pendulous. Gn.59:267(h).—**P. a. nàna** Bean, var. Dwarf form.—**P. a. Juliàna** (L.) W. Koch, var. HEART-CHERRY (GEAN-CHERRY). Fr. ovoid, heart-shaped, with soft flesh, usually dark-colored. (*P. Cerasus* var. *J.* L.)—**P. a. duràcina** (L.) W. Koch, var. HARD-FLESHED CHERRY (BIGARREAU). Fr. with hard flesh, usually light-colored.—The wild form with small purple-black sweet fr. has been distinguished as **P. a. actiàna** (L.) Schneid., var. (*P. Cerasus* var. *a.* L., *P. avium* var. *sylvestris* Dierb.)

P. a. × *Cerasus* = P. effùsa (Host) Schneid. DUKE CH. Similar to the Heart-Cherry but with sour flesh. R.I.25:t.92,f.34(c). Hedrick, Cherr. N. Y. 31,t(c). (*P. avium* var. *regalis* Bailey, *P. caproniana* Zabel, *Cerasus e.* Host.)—*P. a.* × *Mahaleb* = P. Fontanesiàna Schneid. Similar to *P. avium*, with slightly pubescent brts., smaller and broader lvs. less than 10 cm. long, often rounded or subcordate at base: infl. 4–10-fld. often slightly racemose; fls. 2 cm. across: fr. small, dark red, somewhat bitter. G.W.7:497(h). S.L.276(h). (*P. graeca* Desf., *Cerasus F.* Spach.) Orig. before 1829.—*P. a.* × *canescens;* see under No. 41.

58. **P. Cérasus** L. SOUR CHERRY. Usually round-headed tree to 10 m., with often slender, spreading and pendulous brs., suckering; young brts. glabrous: lvs. elliptic-obovate to ovate, 5–8 cm. long, acute, finely and often doubly serrate, resinous when young, slightly pubescent beneath, of firm texture; petioles 1–2 cm. long: fls. with the lvs., about 2.5 cm. across, in dense clusters; the inner bud-scales often upright and leafy; pedicels 1–3.5 cm. long; calyx-tube obconic, sepals usually serrulate: fr. usually depressed-globose, depressed at apex. R.I.25:t.91(c). S.E.3:t.412(c). Gn.79:236;83: 94(h). W. Asia, S. E. Eu. Cult. since ancient times. Zone III. Often grown for its fr. and some forms for their ornamental fls., particularly the double-fld. forms. It is one of the few fruit-trees suited for shady situations.—**P. C. plèna** L., var. Fls. semidouble. (*P. acida fl. pleno* Kirchn., f. *semiplena* Schneid., *Cerasus caproniana* var. *multiplex* Ser.)—**P. C. Rhéxii** (Kirchn.) Voss, f. With double white fls. F.S.17:t.1805(c). Gn.78:228;81:184;83:94. (*P. C. ranunculiflora* Voss.)—**P. C. persiciflòra** (Ser.) Jaeg., var. Fls. double, light rose or pink. F.S.21:2238(c). (*Cerasus caproniana* var. *p.* Ser., *P. C. fl. roseo pleno* Vanh.)—**P. C. salicifólia** Jaeg., var. Lvs. 8–13 cm. long, 1.5–3 cm. wide, rather coarsely doubly serrate. Cult. 1874.—**P. C. umbraculífera** Jaeg., var. Small-lvd. form of compact roundish habit. Gn.78:209(h). (*P. C.* var. *dumosa* Dipp., *P. C. globosa* Spaeth.)—**P. C. frutéscens** (Neilr.)

Schneid., f. Shrubby small-fruited form. (*P. C.* var. *humilis* Bean.) Occurs wild or escaped.—**P. C. Marásca** (Reichb.) Schneid., f. Lvs. slightly serrate; stipules persistent; pedicels short, to 2.5 cm. long. (*P. M.* Reichb., *P. intermedia M.* Zab.)—**P. C. semperflòrens** (Ehrh.) W. Koch. ALL SAINTS CHERRY. Small tree or shrub: lvs. elliptic to oblong-obovate, irregularly serrate: fls. in 4-fld. racemes at the end of short leafy brts. during the summer. R.H.1877:50,t(c). B.C.5:2837. (*P. s.* Ehrh.)—**P. C. austèra** L., var. MORELLO CHERRY. Frs. dark, with colored juice. Hedrick, Cherr. N. Y. 26,t(c),140,t(c), 178,t(c).—**P. C. caproniàna** L., var. AMARELLE CHERRY. Fr. light-colored with uncolored juice. Hedrick, Cherr. N. Y. 24,t(c),132,t(c),170,t(c). (*P. acida* Ehrh.)

P. C. × *fruticosa* = **P. éminens** Beck. Intermediate between the parents. R.I.25:t.92,f.1–2(c). (*P. intermedia* Host, not Poir.)—Possibly *P. reflexa* Hort., not Walp., belongs here and may be *P. Cerasus semperflorens* × *fruticosa;* it is similar to *P. fruticosa pendula,* but lvs. larger and more serrate than in that form.

59. **P. fruticòsa** Pall. GROUND CHERRY. Spreading shrub, to 1 m.; brts. slender, glabrous: lvs. elliptic-obovate to obovate-oblong, 2–5 cm. long, obtusish to short-acuminate, crenate-serrulate, glabrous and dark glossy green, thickish; petioles 5–12 mm. long: fls. 2–4, in usually sessile umbels, with leafy bracts, white, 1.5 cm. across; pedicels 1.5–2.5 cm. long; sepals broad, obtuse: fr. dark red, globose, about 1 cm. across. R.I.25:t.90(c). H.W.3:92. (*P. chamaecerasus* Jacq., *P. intermedia* Poir.) C. and E. Eu. to Siberia. Cult. 1587. Zone III.—**P. f. pendula** Dipp., f. With slender pendulous brts. G.W. 10:511(h). B.C.5.2836(h). S.L.277(h). (*P. chamaecerasus salicifolia* Zab.)

Sect. 5. MAHALEB Focke. Lvs. crenulate or serrulate: fls. in umbels or few-12-fld. racemes, their basal bud-scales deciduous before anthesis; bracts deciduous.

60. **P. Máhaleb** L. MAHALEB CHERRY. Tree to 10 m., with short stem and spreading brs. forming a loose head; young brts. tomentulose: lvs. orbicular to broad-ovate, 3–6 cm. long, obtusely short-acuminate, rounded or subcordate at base, callously serrulate, pubescent along the midrib beneath, otherwise glabrous; petioles 1–2 cm. long: fls. white, 1.5 cm. across, fragrant, in 6–10-fld. racemes 3–4 cm. long, with small leaf-like bracts at base; sepals ovate, entire, shorter than calyx-tube: fr. about 6 mm. across, black. H.W. 3:t.57(c). R.I.25:t.94(c). S.L.277(h). B.S.2:242(h). (*Cerasus M.* Mill.) Eu., W. Asia. Long cult. Zone V. Used as stock for grafting Cherries and for hedges, also on account of the aromatic bark for the manufacture of pipestems.—**P. M. xanthocárpa** (Roem.) Rehd., f. Fr. yellow. Gn.62:181(h). (*P. M. chrysocarpa* Nichols.)—**P. M. péndula** Dipp., f. Brs. pendulous. G.M.44:210(h).—**P. M. monstròsa** (Kirchn.) Jaeg. Dwarf and compact form with short thick brts. *P. M. globosa* Dieck and *P. M. compacta* Spaeth are probably scarcely different.

P. M. × *avium;* see under No. 57.

61. **P. pensylvànica** L. WILD RED CHERRY (PIN CHERRY). Shrub or small tree to 12 m.; brts. glabrous, slender, reddish and shining: lvs. ovate to oblong-lanceolate, 6–11 cm. long, long-pointed, finely and sharply serrulate, glabrous; petioles 1–2 cm. long: fls. white, 1.2 cm. across, in 2–5-fld. umbels or short racemes often several together; pedicels 1–1.5 cm. long, glabrous; sepals ovate, obtuse, entire, shorter than calyx-tube: fr. globose, 6 mm. across, red. B.M.8486(c). S.S.4:t.156. (*P. persicifolia* Desf., *Cerasus p.* Loisel. *Cerasus borealis* Michx.) Nfd. to B. C., south to N. C. and Colo. Intr. 1773. Zone II. Handsome in bloom and attraotive with its numerous red frs. in

summer.—**P. p. saximontàna** Rehd., var. Usually shrubby: lvs. elliptic-ovate to elliptic-oblong, less acuminate, pale green: umbels with fewer fls. Rocky Mtn. region. Intr. 1882.

62. **P. emarginàta** (Hook.) Walp. Shrub or small tree to 4 m.; young brts. slightly pubescent, soon glabrous: lvs. obovate-oblong to oblanceolate, 3–6 cm. long, usually obtuse or emarginate, cuneate, finely crenulate-serrulate, glabrous above, slightly pubescent or finally glabrous beneath; petioles 6–10 mm. long: fls. dull white, 1 cm. across, in 5–10-fld. clusters or short racemes; pedicels 6–10 mm. long, slightly pubescent; sepals entire, rounded, shorter than calyx-tube, slightly pubescent: fr. globose, about 1 cm. across, red, finally black. Ore. and Cal. to Idaho and Ariz. Intr. 1918. Zone VI.

Closely related species: **P. prunifòlia** (Greene) Shafer. Shrub or tree to 12 m.; young brts. densely pubescent: lvs. obovate or oblong, to 8 cm. long, acute to obtuse, slightly pubescent or nearly glabrous above, pubescent beneath: calyx-tube pubescent. S.S.4:t.157 (as *P. emarginata*). (*Cerasus Pattoniana* Hort., *P. mollis* Walp., not Torr.) B. C. to Calif. Intr. 1865. Zone VI?

Sect. 6. PHYLLOCERASUS Koehne. Lvs. with acuminate or acute teeth: fls. in 1–4-fld. umbels with persistent leafy bracts at base.

63. **P. pilosiúscula** Koehne. Shrub or tree to 12 m.; young brts. glabrous or pilose: lvs. obovate to oblong-obovate, 4–8.5 cm. long, acuminate, usually rounded at base, sharply and doubly serrate, the teeth without or with small glands, sparingly strigillose above, pubescent beneath on the veins; petioles 6–12 mm. long: fls. 1–3, about 2 cm. across, coetaneous; bracts oblong or rotundate, 5–8 mm. long, glandular-serrate; pedicels 1–3 cm. long, glabrous or slightly villous; calyx-tube glabrous or pubescent; petals oval; style villous except at upper third: fr. ellipsoid, 8–9 mm. long, red. B.M.9192(c). (*P. p.* var. *media* Koehne, *P. venusta* Koehne.) C. and W. China. Intr. 1907. Zone V.

Related species: **P. litigiòsa** Schneid. Tree to 10 m.: lvs. ovate to obovate, acuminate, rather finely and sharply serrate, glabrous or sparingly hairy when young: peduncle rarely exceeding 5 mm.; pedicels and calyx glabrous, rarely pedicels slightly pubescent; petals narrow-oblong; involucre persistent during flowering. (*P. pilosiuscula* var. *barbata* Koehne, *P. Rehderiana* Koehne, *P. variabilis* Koehne.) C. China. Intr. 1907. Zone V.—**P. polýtricha** Koehne. Young brts. densely villous: lvs. caudate, the teeth setosely acuminate, pubescent beneath; calyx-tube densely villous; sepals acute; styles pilose at base: fr. oval, about 8 mm. long, red. C. China. Intr. 1907.—**P. tatsienénsis** Batal. Glabrous: lvs. abruptly caudate, the teeth with large terminal conical glands: bracts of infl. glandular-dentate: fr. globose, about 1 cm. across, brownish red. Only var. **stenadènia** Koehne from W. China in cult.: glands of teeth of the bracts narrow-oblong, not disciform as in the type. Intr. 1910. Zone VI.

Sect. 7. PHYLLOMAHALEB Koehne. Lvs. with acuminate to acute teeth: fls. in 4–9-fld. stalked racemes with leafy persistent bracts.

64. **P. Maximowíczii** Rupr. Tree to 16 m., with spreading brs.; young brts. pubescent: lvs. obovate or elliptic-obovate, 4–8 cm. long, abruptly short-acuminate, rounded at base, coarsely doubly serrate, bright green with scattered hairs above, pubescent on the veins beneath; petioles 8–12 mm. long, pubescent: fls. shortly after the lvs., about 1.5 cm. across, yellowish white, in 6–10-fld. stalked racemes, with large leaf-like bracts; pedicels 1.5 cm. long, pubescent; sepals acute, serrate; style glabrous: fr. globose, about 5 mm. across, first red, then black. B.M.8641(c). S.I.2:t.30,f.1–9(c). M.K.t.52(c). N.K.5:t.5. G.F.6:195. Manch., Korea, Japan. Intr. 1892. Zone IV. Planted for its pleasing bright green foliage turning scarlet in autumn.

P. M. × *Maackii* = *P. Meyeri;* see under No. 74.

Related species all differing in the large glands of the teeth of the lvs. and bracts: **P. conadènia** Koehne. Tree to 10 m.; brts. glabrous: lvs. obovate, 4–9 cm. long, caudate-acuminate, subcordate or rounded at base, doubly serrate, the teeth with conical glands, glabrous or nearly so beneath: racemes 5–8-fld., glabrous: pedicels 5–15 mm. long; style villous: fr. ovoid, red; stone sculptured. W. China. Intr. 1908.—P. pleiocérasus Koehne. Tree to 8 m.; brts. glabrous: lvs. obovate-oblong to oblong, 4–9 cm. long, caudate-acuminate, rounded or cuneate at base, unequally serrate with conical glands, glabrous beneath; racemes 5–7-fld., glabrous; pedicels 1–2.2 cm. long; style with few hairs at base: fr. globose, red or nearly black; stone sculptured. W. China. Intr. 1908.—P. macradènia Koehne. Tree to 10 m.; brts. glabrous: lvs. ovate or elliptic-ovate, 4.5–6.5 cm. long, caudate, cuneate or rounded at base, simply or doubly serrate, the teeth with conical glands, pubescent beneath: racemes 3–4-fld., pubescent: fr. globose, dark red, on pedicels 6–20 mm. long; stone slightly ribbed. W. China. Intr. 1911. Zone V.—P. discadènia Koehne. Shrub or tree to 13 m.; brts. glabrous: lvs. obovate to oblong-obovate, 4–10 cm. long, acuminate, cordate or rounded at base, unequally serrate, the teeth with disciform glands, glabrous: racemes 3–9-fld., glabrous; pedicels 8–23 mm. long; sepals glandular-fimbriate, as long as tube: fr. subglobose, red; stone nearly smooth. C. China. Intr. 1907.

Subgen. IV. PADUS (Moench) Koehne. Lvs. usually deciduous, serrate or serrulate: fls. rather small, in many-fld. racemes leafy at base, rarely leafless; calyx-tube short-campanulate; style not furrowed, stigma entire. (*Padus* Moench.)

65. **P. seròtina** Ehrh. BLACK CHERRY. (RUM C.) Tree to 30 m., with dark brown bark, the inner aromatic; young brts. glabrous: lvs. oblong-ovate to lance-oblong, 5–12 cm. long, acuminate, cuneate, serrulate with small incurved callous teeth, lustrous above, light green beneath and often villous along the midrib, thickish and firm at maturity; petioles 6–25 mm. long, glandular: fls. white, 8–10 mm. across, in cylindric glabrous racemes 10–14 cm. long; pedicels 3–8 mm. long; sepals oblong-ovate, often toothed: fr. globose, 8–10 mm. across, finally black. Fls. v–vi; fr.ix–x. M.D.1906:1,t(c). S.S.4:t.159. F.E.32:533(h). (*Cerasus s.* Loisel., *Padus s.* Agardh.) Ont. to N. Dak., Tex. and Fla. Intr. 1629. Zone III. Often planted for its handsome foliage; also valuable timber tree.—P. s. péndula Dipp., f. Brs. pendulous.— P. s. aspleniifòlia (Kirchn.) Jaeg., var. With deeply and irregularly cut lvs. (*Padus s.* f. *a.* Schneid.)—P. s. cartilaginea (Lehm.) Jaeg., var. With long shining lvs.—P. s. phelloìdes Schwerin, f. Lvs. lanceolate. (*P. s.* var. *salicifolia*, Henry, not Koehne.)—P. s. montàna (Small) Britt. Lvs. broader- elliptic, glaucescent beneath: racemes rather few-fld. with pubescent calyx. (*P. s. neomontana* Sudw., *P. s. Smallii* Britt.) Va. to Alo. Intr. ?—P. s. salicifòlia (Kunth) Koehne, var. Lvs. lanceolate, long-acuminate, not pubescent along the midrib beneath, subcoriaceous; racemes stouter, to 18 cm. long: fr. 1.5–2.5 cm. across, usually depressed-globose, edible. Jour. Hered. 13:51–61. L.I.t.34. (*P. capuli* Cav., *P. capollin* Koehne, *P. salicifolia* Kunth.) Mex. to Peru. Intr. 1820. Zone VII?

Closely related species: **P. vírens** (Woot. & Standl.) Shreve. Small tree or shrub: lvs. smaller, usually elliptic, acute, rarely acuminate, more finely serrate; petioles eglandular: fls. smaller, in shorter racemes. N. Mex., Ariz. Intr. 1916. Zone (V).

66. **P. alabaménsis** Mohr. Tree to 10 m.; young brts. tomentose: lvs. ovate or elliptic to oblong-ovate, 6–12 cm. long, short-acuminate, sometimes obtusish, rounded or slightly narrowed at base, serrate with appressed callous teeth, whitish and finely pubescent beneath; petioles 6–12 mm. long, tomentose: fls. about 8 mm. across, in pubescent racemes 8–15 cm. long: fr. subglobose, about 8 mm. across, finally nearly black. S.M.526. (*Padus a.* Small.) Ala. Intr. 1906. Zone (V).

Closely related species: **P. Cuthbertii** Small. Tree to 6 m.: lvs. elliptic to obovate, 4–9 cm. long, glaucescent beneath, tomentose on midrib and pubescent on veins: racemes 5–8 cm. long, pubescent. Ga. Intr. 1912. Zone (V).—P. austràlis Beadle. Tree to 20 m.: lvs. elliptic to obovate, 4–10 cm. long, finely serrate, with rufous or tawny pubescence beneath, not glaucous: racemes pubescent, 7–10 cm. long. S.M.527. Ala. Intr. 1907. Zone VI?

67. **P. serícea** (Batal.) Koehne. Tree to 20 m.; young brts. glabrous: lvs. elliptic to oblong-obovate, 8–12 cm. long, acuminate, rounded or cuneate at base, serrulate, silky-pubescent beneath: fls. about 8 mm. across, in pubescent racemes 10–14 cm. long; calyx glabrous; stamens longer than petals: fr. globose-ovoid, 1.5 cm. long, black. (*P. napaulensis* var. *s.* Batal.) C. and W. China. Intr. 1901 or 1908. Zone VI?

Related species: **P. Wilsònii** (Schneid.) Koehne. Tree to 10 m.: lvs. beneath with white silky glossy tomentum: racemes pubescent; stamens at least 1½ times as long as petals. (*Padus W.* Schneid.) C. China. Intr. 1907. Only var. leióbotrys Koehne with glabrous infl. in cult.—**P. rufomicans** Koehne. Tree to 30 m.: lvs. sharply serrulate, glabrous above, densely covered beneath with rufo-ferrugineous tomentum: fruiting racemes glabrous: fr. subglobose, about 1 cm. across. W. China. Intr. 1908.

68. **P. Pàdus** L. EUROPEAN BIRD CHERRY. Tree to 15 m.; young brts. finely pubescent or glabrous: lvs. elliptic to obovate or oblong-ovate, 6–12 cm. long, abruptly acuminate, rounded or subcordate at base, sharply serrate, dull green above, grayish beneath, glabrous or with axillary tufts; petioles 1–1.5 cm. long, glabrous, glandular: fls. white, 1–1.5 cm. across, fragrant, in drooping loose racemes with the peduncle 10–15 cm. long, glabrous; calyx-tube pubescent inside; fr. globose, 6–8 mm. across, black; stone rugose. H.W. 3:t.56(c). R.I.25:t.95(c). S.E.3:t.413(c). Gn.53:92. (*P. racemosa* Lam., *Padus r.* Schneid., *Cerasus P.* DC.) Eu., N. Asia to Korea and Japan. Long cult. Zone III.—**P. P. aucubaefòlia** (Kirchn.) Jaeg., var. Lvs. spotted yellow.—**P. P. plèna** Schneid., f.. Fls. semidouble. (*P. P. flore pleno* Bean.)—**P. P. parviflòra** (Ser.) K. Koch, var. Fls. smaller, about 1 cm. across in rather dense upright racemes; pedicels 2–5 mm. long. (*Cerasus P.* var. *p.* Ser.)—**P. P. Waterèri** Bean, var. Lvs. with conspicuous axillary tufts of hairs beneath: racemes to 20 cm. long.—**P. P. Spaèthii** Rehd., f. Lvs. like those of the preceding var.: fls. about 2 cm. across; petals obovate.—**P. P. leucocárpos** Reichenb. Fr. yellowish white.—**P. P. chlorocárpos** Reichenb. Fr. yellowish green. (*P. Salzeri* Zdarek.)—**P. P. péndula** Dipp., var. Brs. pendulous.—**P. P. commutata** Dipp., var. Lvs. with coarser, more remote serration, rounded to broad-cuneate, nearly green beneath, unfolding much earlier than the type. M.K.t.55(c). (*P. Regeliana* Zab., *P. Grayana* hort., not Maxim.) E. Asia. Cult. 1890.—**P. P. laxa** Rehd., var. With slender pendulous brts.: lvs. usually oblong-obovate, acuminate, quite glabrous beneath and light green: racemes lax, pendulous: fr. small, with smooth or nearly smooth stone. Korea. Intr. 1906.—**P. P. pubéscens** Reg., var. Young brts. and lvs. beneath more or less pubescent. N. E. Asia. Intr. 1906.

P. P. × virginiana; see under No. 71.

69. **P. pubígera** (Schneid.) Koehne. Tree to 20 m.: lvs. oblong-obovate or obovate, 4–11 cm. long, slightly short-acuminate to acutish, cordate or subcordate at base, minutely serrulate, whitish beneath and glabrous, reticulate: petiole 1–2.5 cm. long, usually puberulous: fls. about 1 cm. across, in puberulous or glabrous racemes, without the stalk 7–14 cm. long; calyx-tube pubescent inside below the middle; stamens about ⅓ shorter than petals: fr. 8 mm. across; stone slightly rugose. (*P. brachypoda* var. *p.* Schneid., *P. p.* var. *Potaninii* Koehne.) W. China.—**P. p. Práttii** Koehne, var. Lvs. of shoots oblong-obovate, broad-cuneate or rounded at base. Intr. 1908.—**P. p. obovàta** Koehne, var. Lvs. of shoots obovate, scarcely subcordate; petioles glabrous. Intr. 1908. Zone V.

70. P. cornùta (Wall.) Steud. HIMALAYAN BIRD CHERRY. Tree to 20 m.; young brts. finely pubescent or glabrous: lvs. oblong-ovate to elliptic or obovate, 8–20 cm. long, acuminate, subcordate to broad-cuneate at base, serrulate, dark green above, paler beneath and pubescent on the nerves when young; petioles 1.5–3 cm. long, usually glandular: fls. 6–8 mm. across, white, in dense glabrous or puberulous racemes 8–16 cm. long; sepals glandular-denticulate: fr. subglobose, about 8 mm. across, red finally dark brownish purple. R.H.1869:275. Gn.6:181. S.H.1:f.351w-w^2,352n. (*P. pachyclada* Zab., *Padus c.* Carr.) Himal. Cult. 1860. Zone VI.

Closely related species: **P. napaulensis** (Ser.) Steud. Lvs. more remotely serrate, cuneate at base; petioles glandless, pubescent: infl. very dense, pubescent: fr. 1.5 cm. across. S.H.1:f.351-o^1-o^2,352k. Himal. Intr. 1881. Zone VII?

71. P. virginiàna L. CHOKE CHERRY. Shrub or tree to 10 m.; brts. glabrous: lvs. broad-elliptic to obovate, 4–12 cm. long, abruptly acuminate, broad-cuneate to rounded at base, closely serrulate, dark green and somewhat lustrous above, glaucescent or grayish green beneath, glabrous except axillary tufts of hairs; petioles 1–2 cm. long, glandular: fls. 8–10 mm. across, white, in dense glabrous racemes, 7–15 cm. long: fr. globose, about 8 mm. across, dark purple; stone smooth. S.S.4:t.158. (*P. nana* Dur., *P. rubra* Ait., *Padus v.* Roem.) Nfd. to Sask., N. Dak. and Neb., south to N. C., Mo. and Kans. Intr. 1724. Zone II.—**P. v. leucocárpa** S. Wats., var. Fr. amber-colored. Intr. 1889.—**P. v. Duerínckii** (Martens) Zab., subsp. Lvs. broad-elliptic (*P. v. rotundifolia* Hort., in part).—**P. v. nana** Bean, var. Dwarf form.—**P. v. melanocárpa** (A. Nels.) Sarg., var. Lvs. usually smaller and thicker: fr. darker, usually nearly black; petioles glandless. (*P. m.* Rydb., *P. demissa* var. *m.* A. Nels.) N. Dak. to B. C., s. to N. Mex., Ariz. and s. Calif. Intr. 1879.—**P. v. xanthocárpa** Sarg., f. A yellow-fruited form of var. *melanocarpa.* Intr. 1912.—**P. v. demíssa** (Torr. & Gr.) Torr. Lvs. usually rounded or subcordate at base, pubescent beneath; petioles glandular: brts. and infl. glabrous or pubescent. S.M.524. (*P. d.* D. Dietr., *Cerasus d.* Torr. & Gr.) Wash. to Calif. Intr. 1892.—**P. v. pachyrrhàchis** (Koehne) Sarg., f. A form of the preceding: lvs. broad-cuneate or rounded at base; brts. and the stout rachis pubescent. (*Padus valida* Woot. & Standl. *Padus calophylla* Woot. & Standl. N. Mex. Intr. 1916. Zone (V).

P. v. × *Padus ?* = P. Laucheàna Bolle. Lvs. broad-obovate, large, glaucescent beneath and with axillary tufts of hair: fls. 1.5 cm. across: stone slightly rugose. (*P. padus* var. *rotundifolia* Hort., *P. virginiana* var. *r.* Hort.) Cult. 1880.

Related species: **P. bícolor** Koehne. Young brts. densely velutinous: lvs. obovate-oblong, short-acuminate, minutely serrate, glabrous and whitish beneath; racemes velutinous: fr. 5–6 mm. across; stone slightly rugose. W. China. Intr. 1908. Zone (V).—**P. velutìna** Batal. Brts. glabrous: lvs. elliptic, acuminate, serrulate, pale and thinly pilose beneath; racemes glabrous or pubescent; petals ⅓ shorter than stamens: stone smooth. S.H.1:f.352p(1). C. China. Intr. 1907.

72. P. Ssiòri F. Schmidt. Tree to 25 m., with pale bark; brts. glabrous: lvs. oblong to oblong-obovate, 8–14 cm. long, long-acuminate, usually cordate, sharply serraté with aristate teeth, glabrous beneath except axillary tufts of hairs; petioles 2–4 cm. long, glandular: fls. small, white in glabrous racemes without peduncle 10–16 cm. long; calyx deciduous; petals as long as stamens: fr. about 1 cm. across, black; stone slightly ribbed. S.I.2:t.28,f. 1–13(c). S.H.1:f.351i-l,352g. (*Padus S.* Schneid.) N. E. Asia, Japan. Intr. 1915. Zone V.

73. P. Grayàna Maxim. Small tree to 10 m.; young brts. glabrous or pubescent: lvs. oblong-ovate, 7–14 cm. long, long-acuminate, usually rounded at base, sharply serrate with aristate teeth, grayish green beneath and slightly pubescent especially on the midrib; petioles short, eglandular: fls. white, about 1 cm. across, in glabrous racemes 7–9 cm. long without peduncle; calyx persistent; petals about as long as stamens and style: fr. 8 mm. across, apiculate, black; stone ovoid, pointed, smooth. M.K.t.56(c). S.H.1:f.351 m-n², 352b. (*P. Padus* var. *japonica* Miq., *Padus G.* Schneid.) Japan. Cult. 1900. Zone V.

74. **P. Maackii** Rupr. Tree to 15 m., with brownish yellow flaky bark; young brts. pubescent: lvs. elliptic to oblong-ovate, 6–10 cm. long, acuminate, rounded at base, finely serrulate, gland-dotted beneath and slightly hairy on the veins; petioles 1–2 cm. long, usually glandular: fls. white, about 1 cm. across, in dense pubescent racemes 5–7 cm. long, leafless at base; calyx-tube tubular-campanulate, longer than the glandular-denticulate sepals; petals oblong-obovate; style about as long as stamens, shorter than petals: fr. 5 mm. across, black; stone rugulose. S.I.2:t.30(c). N.K.5:t.2. S.H.1:f.352 h-i(l). S.L.280(bark). (*Laurocerasus M.* Schneid.) Manch., Korea. Cult. 1878. Zone II. Conspicuous by the brightly colored flaky bark.

A supposed natural hybrid with *P. Maximowiczii* is **P. Meýeri** Rehd. chiefly differing from *P. Maackii* in the darker not flaky bark, the longer and bracted peduncles and shorter style; from *P. Maximowiczii* in the lustrous orange-brown bark of the brs., in the gland-dotted lvs. and in the many-fld. racemes with smaller bracts. Korea. Intr. 1906. Zone V.

75. **P. Buergeriana** Miq. Tree to 10 m.; young brts. pubescent or glabrescent: lvs. elliptic to oblong-elliptic, acuminate, 7–11 cm. long, cuneate, appressed-serrulate, light green beneath and glabrous except axillary tufts of hairs; petioles 8–12 mm. long: fls. about 7 mm. across, in slender puberulous racemes 6–8 cm. long; calyx-tube cup-shaped; sepals short, denticulate; stamens slightly longer than petals; style short: fr. subglobose, black, with persistent calyx. N.K.5:t.1. S.H.1:f.354a-g,355d. (*Laurocerasus B.* Schneid.) Japan, Korea. Intr. 1894 and 1915. Zone V.

Related species: **P. venòsa** Koehne. Lvs. sharply serrate, reticulate beneath and glabrous except axillary tufts of hairs: infl. velutinous. C. China. Intr. 1907.—**P. stellípila** Koehne. Lvs. sharply serrate, reticulate and pubescent beneath: infl. glabrous or puberulous. C. China. Intr. 1907.—**P. perulàta** Koehne. Lvs. serrulate with rather short teeth, slightly hair beneath, more densely along midrib: infl. with persistent involucre at base: rachis velutinous. W. China. Intr. 1908.

Subgen. V. LAUROCERASUS Koehne. Lvs. evergreen, serrate, dentate or entire: racemes leafless at base, otherwise like the preceding subgen. (*Laurocerasus* Roem.)

76. **P. lusitànica** L. PORTUGAL LAUREL. Evergreen shrub or small tree to 20 m : brts. glabrous: lvs. oblong-ovate, 6–12 cm. long, acuminate, rounded at base, shallowly serrate, glabrous, dark lustrous green above, paler beneath; petioles 1.5–2.5 cm. long: fls. white, 8–12 mm. across, in slender glabrous racemes 15–25 cm. long; calyx-tube cup-shaped, with short denticulate lobes: fr. conic-ovoid, about 8 mm. long, dark purple. M.G.27:568(h),569. M.D. 1914:278(h). S.L.281. (*Laurocerasus l.* Roem., *Padus L.* Mill.) Spain, Port. Intr. 1648. Zone VI–VII. Planted for its evergreen bright green and lustrous lvs.—**P. l. variegata** Bean, var. Lvs. margined with white.—**P. l. angusti-fòlia** Dipp., f. Lvs. oblong-lanceolate, 5–8 cm. long. M.D.1907:1,t(c).—**P. l. myrtifòlia** Mouillef. Compact pyramidal shrub: lvs. usually 3–5 cm. long. Bull. Soc. Ort. Tosc. 22:t.2(h).

77. **P. Laurocerasus** L. CHERRY LAUREL. Shrub or small tree to 6 m.; young brts. glabrous or puberulous: lvs. usually oblong or obovate-oblong, 5–15 cm. long, acuminate, cuneate to rounded at base, obscurely serrate to

nearly entire, glabrous, lustrous dark green above; petioles 5–10 mm. long:
fls. about 8 mm. across, in glabrous racemes 5–12 cm. long: fr. conic-ovoid,
about 8 mm. long, black-purple. H!A.4:41(c). Gn.50:313. S.L.2:316(h).
M.D.1911:253(h). (*Padus L.* Mill., *Laurocerasus officinalis* Roem.) S. E. Eu.,
Asia Minor. Intr. 1576. Zone VI–VII. Handsome evergreen shrub with large
lvs.—**P. L. angustifòlia** (Loud.) K. Koch. Lvs. narrow-oblong to lanceolate,
6–12 cm. long.—**P. L. caucásica** (Kirchn.) Jaeg., var. Of upright slender
habit: lvs. to 18 cm. long and 7–8 cm. wide. G.C.III.5:621.—**P. L. cólchica**
Jaeg., var. Of spreading habit, with short brs.: lvs. thinner, to 18 cm. long
and about 5 cm. wide. G.C.III.5:621.—**P. L. magnoliaefòlia** Bean, var. Lvs.
to 25 cm .long and 7–10 cm. wide. G.C.78:249(h).—**P. L. parvifòlia** Bean, var.
Lvs. 3–4 cm. long and 1 cm. wide. G.C.III.5:620 (as var. *angustifolia*).—**P. L.**
schipkaénsis Spaeth. Shrubby: lvs. 5–12 cm. long and 2–3.5 cm. wide, nearly
entire: racemes 6–8 cm. long. R.H.1905:409(h). M.G.17:281(h).—**P. L.**
sérbica Pancic, var. Similar to the last, but of more upright habit and with
obovate rugose lvs.—**P. L. Zabeliana** Spaeth. Similar to the preceding, but
lvs. narrower. G.W.5:177(h). G.C.78:251(h);98:282(h). Cult. 1898. This
and the 2 preceding vars. are the hardiest forms and fairly hardy in Zone V.

47. OSMARÒNIA Greene. Deciduous shrubs: winter-buds stalked, with
few imbricate scales: lvs. alternate, short-petioled, entire, with deciduous
small stipules: fls. polygamo-dioecious, greenish white, in short racemes;
pedicels with 2 bractlets; calyx-tube campanulate, with short triangular
lobes; petals spatulate-oblong; stamens 15, 10 inserted with the petals, 5
below; carpels 5, style not exceeding the calyx-tube: fr. consisting of 1–5
oblong drupes with thin flesh and smooth stone. (Probably from Greek *osme,*
odor, and *aronia,* in reference to its fragrant fls.) Syn.: *Nuttallia* Torr. & Gr.,
not Barton. One or possibly more species in W. N. Am.

O. cerasifórmis (Torr. & Gr.) Greene. Shrub to 5 m. with usually numerous upright stems: brts. glabrous, green: lvs. oblong-lanceolate, 7–10 cm.
long, acute at ends, grayish green and pubescent or glabrous beneath: petioles 5–10 mm. long: fls. fragrant, 8–10 mm. across, in short peduncled 5–10-
fld. glabrous racemes, with the lvs.: fr. 1–1.5 cm. long, bluish black, bloomy.
Fls.iv–v; fr.vii–viii. L.I.t.9. G.C.43:266,267;77:147. Gn.34:78. B.S.2:102(fr).
(*N. c.* Torr. & Gr.) B. C. to Calif. Intr. 1848. Zone (V). Chiefly valued for
its early fragrant fls. and the bright green lvs.

48. PRINSÉPIA Royle. Deciduous shrubs with axillary spines; brs. with
lamellate pith; winter-buds small, with few pubescent scales, enclosed by the
stipules: lvs. alternate, mostly fascicled, petioled, entire or serrulate; stipules small, lanceolate, persistent: fls. 1–4 in the axils of last year's brts., or in
axillary racemes; calyx-tube cup-shaped, with broad and short lobes imbricate in bud; petals 5, spreading, suborbicular, clawed; stamens 10 or many,
with short filaments; ovary 1-celled, style inserted near base; stigma capitate;
ovules 2: fr. a drupe with slightly sculptured stone. (Named for James
Prinsep; 1800–1840.) Syn.: *Plagiospermum* Oliv. Three or four species in
E. Asia to N. W. China and Himal.—Fr. edible and gathered in their native
countries.

Fls. yellow: lvs. obovate-lanceolate to lanceolate..............................1. *P. sinensis*
Fls. white: lvs. linear-oblong to narrow-oblong...............................2. *P. uniflora*

1. P. sinénsis (Oliv.) Oliv. Shrub to 2 m. or taller; brs. light gray-brown;
spines 6–10 mm. long: lvs. slender-petioled, ovate-lanceolate to lanceolate,
5–8 cm. long, long-acuminate, entire or sparingly serrulate, finely ciliate,

Subfam. I. MIMOSOIDEAE Taub. Trees and shrubs rarely herbs, with usually bipinnate lvs.: fls. actinomorphous; petals valvate; stamens 5 to many. (*Mimosaceae* Reichenb.)

1. ALBÍZZIA Durazz. Deciduous trees or shrubs: lvs. bipinnate; lfts. usually small and numerous: fls. in axillary peduncled spikes or globular heads; calyx tubular or campanulate, 5-toothed; corolla small, the segments connate more than ½; stamens numerous, more or less connate at base, exserted: pod large, strap-shaped, without pulp. (After F. degli Albizzi, an Italian nobleman.)—About 25 species in trop. and subtrop. Asia, Afr. and Austr.; one in Mex.

A. Julibríssin Durazz. Tree to 12 m., with broad spreading head; brts. glabrous, angular: lvs. with 10–25 pinnae, each with 40–60 lfts.; lfts. falcate, oblong, very oblique, about 6 mm. long, ciliate and sometimes pubescent on midrib beneath: fls. light pink, in slender-peduncled heads crowded at the upper end of brts.: pod flat, to 15 cm. long. Fl.vi–viii; fr.ix–xi. S.I.1:t.51(c). (*Acacia j.* Willd., *A. nemu* Willd.) Persia to C. China. Intr. 1745. Zone VII. —**A. J. ròsea** (Carr.) Mouillef. Dwarfer and hardier than the type: fls. bright pink. R.H.1870:490,t(c). F.S.t.2199(c). G.C.100:351. N.H.18:70(h). Zone (V).

Closely related species: **A. Kalkora** Prain. Lvs. with 4–12 pinnae, each with 10–28 lfts.; lfts. oblong, 2–3.5 cm. long, very short-stalked, the midrib nearer but not close to the upper margin. (*A. Lebbek* Hemsl., not Benth.) C. and E. China to India. Intr. 1907. Zone VII?

Subfam. II. CAESALPINIOIDEAE Taub. Trees or shrubs, rarely herbs: lvs. simple to bipinnate: fls. nearly regular or imperfectly papilionaceous; calyx with usually free segments; petals 5, rarely fewer, imbricate, the upper petal inside; stamens 10, rarely fewer, usually free. (*Cassiaceae* Link.)

2. CERCIS L. REDBUD. Deciduous shrubs or trees; brts. glabrous; winter-buds several, superposed, small, with several outer scales: lvs. simple, entire, palminerved, petioled, with small caducous stipules: fls. fascicled or racemose, before or with the leaves, papilionaceous; calyx broad-campanulate with short obtuse teeth; petals unequal, the 3 upper smaller; stamens 10, free: ovary stipitate: pod flat, narrow-oblong, thin, narrowly winged on the ventral suture; seeds several, flattened. (*Kerkis*, its ancient Greek name.) Seven species in N. Am. and from S. Eu. to E. Asia.—Planted for their early showy fls.

A. Lvs. rounded or emarginate at apex: fls. fascicled......................1. *C. Siliquastrum*
AA. Lvs. abruptly short-acuminate.
  B. Fls. fascicled.
    c. Lvs. cordate with broad open sinus, without transparent margin, dull beneath when young; fls. less than 1.5 cm. long...................................2. *C. canadensis*
    cc. Lvs. deeply cordate, with transparent cartilaginous margin, lustrous beneath when young: fls. more than 1.5 cm. long...................................3. *C. chinensis*
  BB. Fls. racemose: lvs. truncate or subcordate, pubescent beneath..........4. *C. racemosa*

1. C. Siliquástrum L. JUDAS-TREE. Tree to 10 m.: lvs. suborbicular, 7–12 cm. across, deeply cordate, glabrous: fls. 3–6, rose-purple, 1.8–2 cm. long: pod 7–10 cm. long. Fl.iv–v; fr.x. B.M.1138(c). Gn.44:379;52:5. G.C.52:6 (h). S. Eu., W. Asia. Cult. since ancient times. Zone VI?—**C. S. alba** West., var. Fls. white. (*C. S.* f. *albida* Schneid.) Cult. since the 16th century.

Related species: **C. renifórmis** Engelm. Small tree to 12 m.: lvs. broad-ovate to reniform, 5–8 cm. across, often longer than broad, obtuse to emarginate, glabrous or pubescent below: fls. 1–1.5 cm. long, slender-stalked, occasionally racemose: pod 5–10 cm. long and to 1.5 cm. wide. S.S.3:t.135. (*C. texensis* Sarg.) Tex., N. Mex. Intr. 1901. Zone VII?—**C. occidentàlis** Torr. Shrub: lvs. reniform, 3.5–7 cm. across, broader than long, emarginate, glabrous: fls. 1–1.5 cm. long, usually short-stalked: pod 5–8 cm. long and to 2 cm. wide. U. S. Explor. Exp. 1838–42, 17:t.3. Calif. Cult. 1886. Zone VII?

2. **C. canadénsis** L. Tree to 12 m., with broad round head: lvs. broad-ovate to suborbicular, 7–12 cm. long, usually cordate at base, pubescent to glabrous beneath: fls. 4–8, rosy-pink, 1–1.2 cm. long; pedicels 5–12 mm. long: pod 6–8 cm. long. Fl.iv–v; fr.ix–x. G.O.t.92(c). S.S.3:t.133,134. B.C.2:720. Gg.6:290(h). S.L.121(h). M.G.14:434–5(h). N. J. to n. Fla., w. to Mo. and Tex. and n. Mex. Cult. 1641. Zone IV. Often planted for its early conspicuous fls.—**C. c. pubéscens** Pursh, var. Lvs. more or less pubescent. The type of the species.—**C. c. glabrifòlia** Fern., f. Lvs. glabrous beneath.—**C. c. alba** Rehd., f. Fls. white. Mo. Bot. Gard. Bull. 10:110,t. Orig. before 1903.—**C. c. plena** Sudw. Fls. with some stamens changed to petals. Mo. Bot. Gard. Bull. 23:t.11. Orig. before 1894.

3. **C. chinénsis** Bge. Tree to 15 m.; in cult. usually shrubby: lvs. suborbicular, 7–12 cm. long, deeply cordate, glabrous, lustrous above, subcoriaceous at maturity: fls. 5–8, rosy-purple, 1.5–1.8 cm. long; pedicels 6–15 mm. long: pod 7–12 cm. long, narrow. Fl.v; fr.x. F.S.t.849(c). M.M.2:139. G.F. 6:476(h). B.C.2:721. (*C. japonica* Planch.) C. China. Intr. before 1850. Zone VI. Very handsome in bloom.

4. **C. racemòsa** Oliv. Tree to 10 m.: lvs. broad-ovate, 6–10 cm. long, subcordate or truncate, pubescent beneath: fls. rosy-pink, 1.2 cm. long, slender-stalked, in pendulous racemes 4–10 cm. long: pod 6–10 cm. long. Fl.v; fr.x. H.I.t.1894. C. China. Intr. 1907. Zone VII.

3. **GLEDÍTSIA** L. HONEY-LOCUST. Deciduous trees, usually armed with stout often branched spines; winter-buds usually minute, 3–4 superposed, the upper ones larger and scaly, the lower ones covered by the base of the petiole: lvs. alternate, often fascicled, abruptly pinnate or bipinnate usually on the same tree; lfts. irregularly and slightly crenate; stipules minute: fls. polygamous, in racemes or rarely in panicles; calyx-lobes and petals 3–5; petals nearly equal, not much longer than calyx-lobes; stamens 6–10; style short, with large terminal stigma: pod compressed, usually large, tardily dehiscent or indehiscent, 1–many-seeded; seeds flattened, suborbicular. (After Johann Gottlieb Gleditsch, director of Bot. Garden at Berlin; 1714–1786.) Syn.: *Gleditschia* Scop. About 12 species in N. Am., C. and E. Asia, trop. Afr. and S. Am.—Ornamental trees usually armed with branched spines; the spreading brs. forming a loose head; fls. in May and June; fr. in autumn and remaining on the tree a long time.

A. Pod many-seeded, 8–40 cm. long.
　B. Spines compressed, at least at base: walls of pod papery or leathery; pod flat, usually twisted, not dotted.
　　c. Lfts. usually acute, to 3.5 cm. long, usually more than 20 in pinnate lvs.: ovary pubescent ....1. *G. triacanthos*
　　cc. Lfts. obtuse or emarginate, 2–6 cm. long, usually less than 20: ovary glabrous or pubescent only on margin.
　　　D. Lvs. with 16–20 lfts. 2–4.5 cm. long, often bipinnate: brts. glabrous..2. *G. japonica*
　　　DD. Lvs. with 8–16 lfts. 3–6 cm. long, rarely bipinnate: young brts. pubescent.
　　　　　　　　　　　　　　　　　　　　　　　　　　　　　　3. *G. Delavayi*
　BP. Spines terete; pods straight or falcate, not twisted, convex, with thick woody walls dotted with minute pits: lvs. very rarely bipinnate.
　　c. Lfts. 6–12: pedicels about 1 cm. long............................4. *G. macracantha*
　　cc. Lfts. 8–16: pedicels 2–4 mm. long.......................................5. *G. sinensis*
AA. Pod 1–3-seeded, 2.5–5 cm. long.
　B. Lfts. entire, pubescent beneath: pod 2–3-seeded......................6. *G. heterophylla*
　BB. Lfts. crenulate, glabrous beneath: pod 1–2-seeded........................7. *G. aquatica*

1. **G. triacánthos** L. HONEY-LOCUST (SWEET LOCUST, THREE-THORNED ACACIA). Tree to 45 m., usually with stout simple or branched spines 6–10 cm. long on trunk and brs.: lvs. 14–20 cm. long; rachis pubescent all around, grooved; pinnate lvs. with 20–30 oblong-lanceolate lfts. 2–3.5 cm. long, re-

motely crenate-serrulate, pubescent on the midrib beneath; bipinnate lvs. with 8–14 pinnae, the lfts. 8–20 mm. long: fls. very short-stalked, in narrow racemes 5–7 cm. long: pod 30–45 cm. long, falcate and twisted at length. Fl.vi; fr.x–xii. S.S.3:t.125,126. Gn.32:304. H.H.288,289(b). F.L.6:201,t(h). Am. For. 23:91(h). Pa. to Neb., Tex. and Miss. Intr. about 1700. Zone IV. Often planted; the large branched thorns make the tree conspicuous in winter.—**G. t. inérmis** Willd., var. Unarmed or nearly so and of more slender habit. (*G. t.* var. *laevis* K. Koch.)—**G. t. elegantíssima** (Grosdemange) Rehd., var. Unarmed and of dense bushy habit: lfts. smaller. R.H.1905:513. Orig. about 1880.—**G. t. Bujòti** (Neum.) Rehd., var. Brts. slender, pendulous: lfts. narrower. (*G. B.* Neum., *G. B. pendula* Hort.) Orig. before 1845.—**G. t. nàna** (Loud.) Henry, var. Small compact shrub or tree, with rather short and broad dark green lfts. (*G. sinensis* var. *n.* Loud., *G. ferox* var. *n.* Rehd.) Cult. 1838.

G. t. × *aquatica* = **G. texàna** Sarg. Pod straight, 10–12 cm. long. S.S.13: t.627. Tex. Intr. 1900. Zone VII?

2. **G. japónica** Miq. Tree to 20 or 25 m.; thorns somewhat compressed, 5–10 cm. long, often branched; young brts. purplish: lvs. 25–30 cm. long; pinnate lvs. with 16–20 ovate to oblong or nearly lanceolate lfts. 2–4, rarely to 6 cm. long, entire or remotely crenulate, lustrous above, pubescent on midrib beneath or glabrous; bipinnate lvs. with 2–12 pinnae, lfts. 1–2.5 cm. long; rachis pubescent on edge of groove: fls. short-stalked, in slender racemes: pod 25–30 cm. long, twisted and bullate; seeds near the middle. Fl. vi–vii; fr.x–xi. S.I.1:t.51(c). G.F.6:165. B.C.3:1347. (*G. horrida* Mak., not Willd.) Japan, China. Intr. about 1800? Zone V.

Closely related species: **G. férox** Desf. A tree with very stout compressed spines: lvs. often bipinnate; lfts. 16–30, oblong-ovate to ovate-lanceolate, 1.5–3.5 cm. long. crenate. ?China. Intr. about 1800.—**G. cáspica** Desf. Tree to 12 m.; very spiny; young brts. green: lvs. pinnate with 12–20 ovate to elliptic crenulate lfts. 2–5 cm. long, or bipinnate with 6–8 pinnae; rachis and petiolules pubescent; pod curved, about 20 cm. long, thin. (*G. horrida* var. *c.* Schneid.) S.H. 2:f.6l-o,7d. S.L.185(h). Transcauc., N. Persia. Intr. 1822. Zone VI?

3. **G. Delavàyi** Franch. Tree to 10 m.; young brts. puberulous; spines compressed at base, to 25 cm. long: lvs. pinnate with 8–16 obliquely ovate to ovate-oblong emarginate or obtuse lfts. 3–6 cm. long, the lower ones much smaller than the upper ones, slightly crenate or nearly entire, dark green and lustrous above, the midrib slightly impressed above and pubescent, usually slightly pubescent beneath and scarcely reticulate; on young plants much smaller and often bipinnate: fls. in slender puberulous racemes; ovary glabrous: pod 15–35 or sometimes to 50 cm. long, twisted, with leathery walls. S.H.2:f.6g-h,7b. S. W. China. Intr. 1900. Zone VII.

4. **G. macracántha** Desf. Tree to 15 m., with large spines; brts. glabrous: lvs. simply pinnate; lfts. 6–12, ovate-oblong, rarely obovate, 5–7.5 cm. long, the lower ones smaller and ovate-lanceolate, crenulate, glabrous, except pubescent on the midrib above and less densely so beneath, strongly reticulate; rachis pubescent on edge of groove: fls. in pubescent simple racemes; pedicels slender, about 1 cm. long; ovary pubescent on the margin: pod 15–30 cm. long, 2.5–3.5 cm. broad, slightly convex. C.C.183. C. China. Cult. 1800. Zone VI.

5. **G. sinénsis** Lam. Tree to 15 m., with stout conical often branched spines; brts. glabrous: lvs. pinnate, 12–18 cm. long; lfts. 8–14, rarely to 18, ovate to oblong-ovate, 3–8 cm. long, obtuse or acutish, mucronulate, crenulate, dull yellowish green above, reticulate beneath and slightly pubescent on midrib, more densely above; rachis pubescent on edge of groove and pet-

iolules pubescent: fls. in slender puberulous racemes; pedicels 3–5 mm. long; ovary glabrous, pubescent on the margin: pod nearly straight, 12–25 cm. long and 2–3 cm. broad, convex. S.H.2:f.6b-c,7c-c[1]. U. S. Im. 40,t.4(h). (*G. horrida* Willd.) E. China. Intr. 1774. Zone VI.

6. **G. heterophýlla** Bge. Shrub or small tree; spines slender, simple or trifid, to 3.5 cm. long: young brts. pubescent: lvs. pinnate, with 10–18 oblique-oblong, rarely obovate-oblong lfts. 1–3 cm. long, obtuse, entire, pubescent beneath and grayish green, or bipinnate with 3–4 pairs of pinnae each with 12–20 lfts. 5–10 mm. long: rachis puberulous: fls. subsessile in pubescent spikes sometimes panicled, the fls. in dense clusters: pod long-stipitate, obliquely elliptic to elliptic-oblong, 3.5–5.5 cm. long, thin, glabrous; seeds orbicular-oval, 8–9 mm. long, brown. S.H.2:f.7g(l). N. E. China. Intr. 1907. Zone V.

7. **G. aquática** Marsh. WATER LOCUST. (SWAMP L.) Tree to 20 m.; spiny: pinnate lvs. with 12–18 ovate-oblong lfts. 2–3 cm. long, usually rounded or emarginate, slightly crenulate and often entire below the middle, glabrous except few hairs on the petiolules; bipinnate lvs. with 6–8 pinnae; petioles pubescent on the edges of the groove: fls. in racemes 7–10 cm. long; pedicels short; ovary glabrous; pod 2.5–5 cm. long, long-stipitate, thin. S.S.3:t.127, 128. H.H.290,291(b). (*G. inermis* Mill., not L., *G. monosperma* Walt.) S. C. and Ky. to Fla. and Tex. Intr. 1723. Zone VI?

G. a. × *triacanthos;* see under No. 1.

4. **GYMNÓCLADUS** L. Deciduous trees, unarmed, with stout brs.; winter-buds small, several superposed, indistinctly scaly; terminal bud wanting: lvs. bipinnate; lfts. entire; stipules small, deciduous: fls. in terminal panicles, dioecious or polygamous, regular; calyx tubular, 5-lobed; petals 5, oblong, slightly longer than sepals; stamens 10; ovary with 4–8 ovules; style short: pod broad-oblong, thick, flat, pulpy; seeds large, flattened. (Greek *klados,* branch, and *gymnos,* naked, referring to the stout brs. destitute of twigs.) Two species in N. Am. and China.

G. dioìcus (L.) K. Koch. KENTUCKY COFFEE-TREE. Tree to 30 m.; brts. pubescent at first: lvs. 15–35 cm. long, with 3–7 pairs of pinnae, the lowest usually reduced to simple lfts., the upper with 6–14 lfts.; lfts. ovate or elliptic-ovate, 5–8 cm. long, acute, rounded or cuneate at base, pubescent beneath when young, short-stalked; petioles 4–6 cm. long: pistillate infl. to 25 cm. long, staminate much smaller and denser: fls. about 1.2 cm. long, long-stalked, greenish white, pubescent: pod oblong, 15–25 cm. long, thick, brown; seeds suborbicular, 2–2.5 cm. long. Fl.vi; fr.x(–iv). S.S.3:t.123,124. H.H. 286,287(b). B.C.3:1420. R.H.1897:491. Gn.M.34:138(h). (*G. canadensis* Lam.) N. Y. and Pa. to Minn., Neb., Okl. and Tenn. Intr. before 1748. Zone IV. Lvs. large, pink when unfolding, turning clear yellow in fall; the conspicuous pods persist during the winter.

The related **G. chinénsis** Baill. has oblong obtuse smaller lfts. pubescent on both sides: fr. 7–10 cm. long; thicker: fls. lilac-purple, before the lvs. C.C.181. S.H.2:f.9i-n. C. China. Intr. 1907. Zone VII?

5. **CAESALPÌNIA** L. Trees or shrubs, sometimes climbing, armed or unarmed: lvs. bipinnate, stipulate: fls. in racemes often forming terminal panicles; calyx with short tube and 5 imbricate lobes, the lowest one larger; petals 5, clawed, nearly equal; stamens 10, curved: ovary sessile with few ovules and a slender style: pod ovate to lanceolate, usually compressed, often indehiscent. (After Ándreas Caesalpini, Italian botanist; 1519–1603.) About 40 species in trop. and subtrop. regions.

C. japónica Sieb. & Zucc. Deciduous spreading shrub with long and slender brs. armed with stout recurved prickles: lvs. with 6–16 pinnae, each with 10–20 lfts. oblong, 1.5–2 cm. long, obtuse, pubescent below; rachis prickly: fls. canary-yellow, slender-stalked, in panicles to 30 cm. long; stamens red. Fl.vi; fr.ix. B.M.8207(c). G.C.42:43. R.H.1912:60,t.(c). Gn.40: 588,t.(c) ;76:411. Japan. Cult. 1887. Zone VII?

Subfam. III. PAPILIONATAE Taub. Fls. papilionaceous; the upper petal (standard) enclosing the others in bud; rarely only the standard present. (*Papilionaceae* L., *Fabaceae* Reichenb.)

Tribe 1. SOPHOREAE Taub. Lvs. pinnate; stipules sometimes wanting; stamens free or slightly connate; petals of keel free, rarely connate.

6. MAÀCKIA Rupr. & Maxim. Deciduous tree; winter-buds with several imbricate scales: lvs. odd-pinnate; lfts. opposite or nearly so, entire, short-stalked; fls. white, in dense upright racemes, usually several forming terminal panicles; calyx campanulate, 5-toothed; stamens 10, connate at base; pod linear-oblong, dehiscent, compressed, 1–5-seeded. (For Richard Maack, Russian naturalist; 1825–86.) Six species in E. Asia.

M. amurénsis Rupr. Tree to 15 m.: lfts. 7–11, elliptic to oblong-ovate, 5–8 cm. long, short-acuminate, rounded at base, glabrous: fls. about 8 mm. long, in usually panicled racemes 10–20 cm. long: pod 3.5–5 cm. long. Fl. vii–viii; fr.ix–x. B.M.6551(c). M.K.t.58(c). Gn.33:444. B.S.2:64. (*Cladrastis a.* K. Koch.) Manch. Intr. 1864. Zone IV.—**M. a. Buèrgeri** (Maxim.) Schneid., var. Lfts. pubescent beneath, obtusish. S.I.1:t.50(c). (*Cladrastis a.* var. *floribunda* Shiras.) Japan. Intr. 1892.

Closely related species: **M. chinénsis** Takeda. Tree to 23 m.; lfts. 11–13, ovate to elliptic, 2–6 cm. long, obtuse, pubescent beneath: fls. 1 cm. long. (*M. hupehensis* Takeda.) C. China. Intr. 1908. Zone V.—**M. Faùriei** (Lévl.) Takeda. Tree to 8 m.: lfts. 9–17, elliptic-ovate to oblong, 3–5.5 cm. long, glabrous at maturity: fls. 1 cm. long: pod 3–4.5 cm. long. Not. Bot. Gard. Edinb. 8:t.27,f. 39–43. (*Cladrastis F.* Lév.) Korea. Intr. 1917. Zone V?—**M. Tashiròi** (Yatabe) Mak. Shrub: lfts. 11–15, elliptic-ovate, 2–4 cm. long, slightly pubescent beneath: fls. 7 mm. long: pod 2–3.5 cm. long. Bot. Mag. Tokyo 6:t.10. Japan, Liukiu Isls. Intr. 1919. Zone V?

7. CLADRÁSTIS Raf. Deciduous trees; winter-buds naked, several superposed covered by the base of the petiole: lvs. odd-pinnate; lfts. 7–15, alternate, short-stalked, entire, rather large: fls. white, rarely pinkish, in usually panicled racemes; calyx campanulate, 5-toothed; stamens 10, nearly free: pod narrow-oblong, dehiscent, compressed, 3–6-seeded; valves thin. (Greek *klados*, branch, and *thraustos*, fragile, alluding to the brittle brs.) Four species in N. Am. and E. Asia.

A. Lvs. without stipels: pod not winged.
　B. Panicles drooping: lfts. 7–11 ....1. *C. lùtea*
　BB. Panicles upright: lfts. 9–13..2. *C. sinensis*
AA. Lvs. with stipels: pod winged..3. *C. platycarpa*

1. C. lùtea (Michx.) K. Koch. YELLOW-WOOD. Tree to 15, rarely to 20 m. high, with smooth bark and yellow wood: lfts. 7–11, elliptic or ovate, 7–10 cm. long, abruptly short-acuminate, broad-cuneate, glabrous, bright green: fls. white, 2.5–3 cm. long, fragrant, in panicles 25–40 cm. long: pod 7–8 cm. long. Fl.vi; fr.viii–ix. B.M.7767(c). S.S.3:t.119,120. G.F.1:92(h). G.C.42: 186(h),187. Gg.2:401;5:98(h). (*C. tinctoria* Raf., *Virgilia l.* Michx.) N. C. to Ky. and Tenn. Intr. 1812. Zone III. With fragrant showy white fls. in pendulous panicles; lvs. turning yellow in fall.

2. C. sinénsis Hemsl. Tree to 25 m.: lfts. 9–13, oblong to oblong-lanceolate, 5–10 cm. long, obtuse or acutish, usually rounded at base, grayish green beneath and brownish pubescent chiefly near the midrib; petioles and rachis pubescent: fls. white or pinkish, 1.2 cm. long, in much-branched panicles 12–30 cm. long; ovary finely pubescent: pod 4–6.5 cm. long, glabrous or nearly so. Fl.vii; fr.ix. B.M.9043(c). G.C.74:70. H.B.2:439. K.B.1913:164, t(h). Fls.vi–vii. W. and C. China. Intr. 1901. Zone V.

Related species: **C. Wilsònii** Takeda. Tree to 15 m.: lfts. 7–9, rarely 11, elliptic-ovate to ovate-oblong, 6–12 cm. long, broad-cuneate to rounded at base, nearly glabrous: fls. 1.5–2 cm. long, in panicles 12–18 cm. long; ovary pubescent: pod very shortly stipitate, pubescent. C. China. Intr. 1907. Zone VI?

3. C. platycárpa (Maxim.) Mak. Tree to 20 m.: lfts. 7–15, ovate to elliptic-lanceolate, 5–10 cm. long, acuminate, broad-cuneate to rounded at base, slightly pubescent above chiefly on the veins, green beneath, slightly reticulate and appressed-pilose; petioles 2–2.5 cm. long: fls. 1–1.5 cm. long, in upright panicles about 15 cm. long; standard white with yellow spot at base; pod winged all around, 3–7 cm. long, 1–3-seeded. S.I.2:t.32(c). (*Sophora p.* Maxim., *Platyosprion platycarpum* (Maxim.) Mak.) Japan. Intr. 1919. Zone V.

8. SÓPHORA L. Deciduous or evergreen trees or shrubs, rarely herbaceous; winter-buds small, indistinctly scaly: lvs. odd-pinnate: lfts. opposite, usually small, 7–many; stipules small: fls. in racemes or panicles, calyx with 5 short teeth; standard orbicular to oblong-obovate; stamens 10, free or connate only at base; pod stipitate, terete, rarely compressed, constricted between the seeds, indehiscent or tardily dehiscent, few to many-seeded. (Sophira, Arabian name of a tree with pea-shaped fls.) Including *Styphnolobium* Schott and *Goebelia* Bge. About 20 species in Asia and N. Am.

A. Fls. in large terminal panicles, yellowish white or slightly pinkish; lfts. acute.
        1. *S. japonica*
AA. Fls. in racemes: lfts. obtusish or emarginate.
    B. Lfts. about 3 cm. long: racemes axillary: unarmed small tree..............2. *S. affinis*
    BB. Lfts. about 1 cm. long; racemes terminal: spinescent shrub..............3. *S. viciifolia*

1. S. japónica L. JAPAN PAGODA-TREE. Tree to 25 m., with spreading brs. forming a round head; young brts. glabrous or nearly so, green: lvs. 15–25 cm. long; lfts. 7–17, stalked, ovate to lance-ovate, 2.5–5 cm. long, acute, broad-cuneate to rounded at base, dark green and lustrous above, glaucous beneath and closely appressed-pubescent: fls. 1–1.5 cm. long, in terminal loose panicles 15–30 cm. long; pod stipitate, 5–8 cm. long, terete, glabrous, 1–6-seeded. Fls.viii–ix; fr.x. S.I.1:t.50(c). N.D.3:t.21(c). Gn.24:210,214(h). M.G.13:183(h). F.E.12:1174(h). B.S.2:250(h). (*Styphnolobium japonicum* Schott.) China, Korea. Intr. 1747. Zone IV. Sometimes used as an avenue tree: late-flowering, and lvs. remaining green late into the fall.—**S. j. péndula** Loud., var. A picturesque form with tortuous limbs and pendulous brs. R.H. 1876:194,195(h). Gn.24:202,203(h);89:184(h). G.C.28:479(h). F.E.14:1430, t.43(h). Gn.M.29:167(h).—**S. j. columnàris** Schwer. Of narrow pyramidal habit.—**S. j. violàcea** Carr. Lfts. 15–17, appressed-pubescent beneath: fls. appearing very late, the wings and keel tinged purplish. (*S. violacea* Hort., not Thwait.) Intr. 1858.—**S. j. pubéscens** (Tausch) Bosse, var. Lfts. ovate-oblong to lance-ovate, usually rounded or truncate at base, to 8 cm. long, soft-pubescent beneath: wings and keel of the fl. often tinged purplish. M.D. 1922:t.20(h). (*S. p.* Tausch, *S. Korolkowii* Hort., *S. sinensis* Hort., *S. tomentosa* Hort., not L.) Cult. 1830.

2. S. affìnis Torr. & Gray. Round-headed tree to 6 m.: lvs. 10–20 cm. long; lfts. 13–19, elliptic, 2–4 cm. long, obtusish to emarginate, mucronate, broad-cuneate, glabrous or with scattered hairs beneath and conspicuously

BB. Lvs. simple, alternate.
  c. Brts. spiny.
    D. Infl. racemose.
      E. Brts. pilose or villous: bracts of infl. subulate...............4. *G. germanica*
      EE. Brts. glabrous: bracts of infl. foliaceous..........................5. *G. anglica*
    DD. Infl. capitate ....6. *G. hispanica*
  cc. Brts. unarmed.
    D. Fls. 1–few on axillary short brts.
      E. Lvs. acute: fls. forming racemes to 20 cm. long at end of brs.: upright shrub.
                                                      7. *G. cinerea*
      EE. Lvs. obtuse: racemes short; procumbent shrub...................9. *G. pilosa*
    DD. Fls. in many-fld. terminal racemes: lvs. usually glabrous or nearly so beneath.
                                                    8. *G. tinctoria*
AA. Brts. triangular or 2-winged: procumbent shrubs.
  B. Brts. triangular, glabrous..10. *G. januensis*
  BB. Brts. 2-winged, pubescent...11. *G. sagittalis*

1. G. hórrida DC. Densely branched shrub to 0.3 m., with rigid spiny brts. silky when young: lfts. linear, about 8 mm. long, folded, pubescent: fls. 1–3; keel pubescent; bracts ovate: fr. rhombic-lanceolate, pubescent. Fls. VI–VIII. G.C.53:140(h). Gn.87:620(h). S. W. Eu. Intr. 1821. Zone VII.

2. G. radiàta (L.) Scop. Much-branched shrub to 0.8 m.; brts. pubescent or glabrescent: lfts. linear-lanceolate, 1–1.5 cm. long, glabrous above, pubescent beneath, caducous: fls. in 3–10-fld. heads; calyx campanulate; bracts ovate: pod elliptic, pubescent, 1–2-seeded. Fls.v–vii. B.M.2260(c). R.I.22:t.2083(c). F.D.23:t.2318(c). S.L.183(h). (*Cytisus radiatus* W. Koch, *Enantiosparton radiatum* K. Koch.) S. E. Eu. Intr. before 1758. Zone (V).

3. G. nyssàna Petrovich. Shrub to 0.6 m.; brts. villous: lfts. ellipticlanceolate, 2–3.5 cm. long, villous: fls. in terminal leafy racemes to 20 cm. long; bractlets subulate; teeth of calyx of equal length; keel and standard silky outside: pod rhombic, about 1 cm. long, villous. Fl.vi–vii. I.T.5:t.197. Serbia, Albania. Intr. 1899. Zone VI?

4. G. germànica L. Upright or ascending spiny shrub to 0.6 m.; brts. villous, the flowering ones not spiny: lvs. elliptic-oblong, 1–2 cm. long, deep green, ciliate and villous beneath: fls. rather small, in racemes 3–5 cm. long; bracts subulate, half as long as pedicels; keel and standard silky outside; pod elliptic, 8–10 mm. long, few-seeded, villous. Fls.v–vii. R.I.22:t.2086f.i–ii. D.F.23:t.2302(c). C. and S. Eu. Cult. 1588. Zone V.—**G. g. inérmis** Koch, var. Spineless or nearly so.

Closely related species: **G. silvéstris** Scop. Brts. appressed-pubescent, the flowering ones spiny: lvs. linear to narrow-lanceolate, 1–1.5 cm. long, pubescent beneath: racemes to 10 cm. long; bracts longer than pedicels; calyx with subulate lobes: pod ovoid, usually 1-seeded. R.I.22:t.2084(c). F.D.23:t.2304(c). S. E. Eu. Intr. 1818. Zone VI?—**G. s. pungens** Vis., var. More spiny. B.M. 8075(c). R.I.22:t.2085,f.3. Gn.88:201(h). (*G. dalmatica* Bartl.) Intr. 1893. Zone VII?

5. G. ánglica L. Glabrous spiny shrub to 0.8 m., sometimes procumbent: lvs. elliptic to linear-oblong, 6–8 mm. long, bluish green: racemes few-fld., with leafy bracts longer than the pedicels; pod elliptic-oblong, about 1 cm. long, several-seeded. R.I.22:t.2086,f.3–5(c). D.F.23:t.2303(c). S.E.3:t.326 (c). C. and W. Eu. Cult. 1789. Zone V.—**G. a. subinérmis** Legrand, subvar. Nearly or quite spineless.

6. G. hispànica L. Densely branched shrub to 0.3 m., with numerous thin spines: lvs. ovate-lanceolate, to 1 cm. long, pubescent: fls. in 2–12-fld. heads: calyx pubescent, divided about ½ into lance-ovate teeth: pod rhombic, hirsute. B.M.8528(c). R.H.1888:36,t(c). Gn.87:621(h). M.G.22:388(h). S.L. 183(h). Spain to N. Italy. Intr. 1759. Zone VI.

7. G. cinérea (Vill.) DC. Shrub to 0.9 m.; brts. grooved, pubescent when young; sparingly leafy: lvs. lanceolate, 6–8 mm. long, acute, pubescent on both sides: fls. 1–3, subsessile or very short-stalked, on axillary leafy brts. forming at end of last season's brs.: racemes to 20 cm. long; bractlets lanceolate. caducous; calyx pubescent; keel pubescent: pod to 1.8 cm. long, silky, 2–5-seeded. Fl.IV–VII. B.M.8086(c). R.I.22:t.2092,f.1–2(c). Gn.83:400;86: 564(h). S. Eu., N. Afr. Intr. before 1850. Zone VII?

8. **G. tinctòria** L. DYER'S GREENWEED. Upright or ascending shrub to 1 m., with slender little-branched shoots; brts. striped, glabrous or pubescent. when young: lvs. elliptic-oblong to oblong-lanceolate, 1–2.5 cm. long, nearly glabrous, ciliate, bright green: racemes many-fld., sometimes branched; corolla glabrous: pods narrow-oblong, compressed, glabrous or slightly pubes-. cent, 6–10-seeded. Fls.VI–VIII. R.I.22:t.2088,f.1–2(c). F.D.23:t.2299(c). S.E. 3:t.328(c). B.C.3:1322. (*G. sibirica* Hort., *G. polygalaefolia* Hort., not DC.) Eu., W. Asia; sometimes naturalized in the E. States. Cult. 1789. Zone II. —**G. t. plèna** Rehd., var. With double fls. R.H.1899:573. G.W.16:137(h). (*G. sibirica fl. pleno* Pépin.) Orig. before 1853.—**G. t. hirsùta** DC., var. More branched; brts. and lvs. pubescent; ovary pubescent: pod usually glabrate. (*G. pubescens* Lang.)—**G. t. anxántica** (Ten.) Fiori. Dwarf and quite glabrous: lvs. narrow-elliptic. S.L.55(h). S.B.II.266(c). (*G. a.* Ten.) Italy. Intr. 1818.—**G. t. virgàta** (Willd.) Koch, var. More vigorous and more branched, to 2 m.; quite glabrous; pod 3–6-seeded. R.I.22:t.2088,f.3(c). F.D.23:t.2300(c). (*G. t.* var. *elatior* Schultz, var. *elongata* Rouy, *G. elata* Wender., *G. virgata* Willd., *G. elatior* W. Koch.) Cult. 1790.—**G. t. alpéstris** Bertol., var. Low, with slender procumbent brs.: lvs. narrow: ovary glabrous or pubescent: pod glabrous or glabrate. S. Eu.—**G. t. humílior** (Bertol.) Schneid., var. Similar to the preceding, but pod silky-villous. R.I.22:t.2088,f.4(c). (*G. t.* var. *mantica* Reichenb., *G. mantica* Pollini.) Italy. Intr. 1816.

Closely related species: **G. ovàta** Waldst. & Kit. Ascending or upright shrub, to 0.6 m.; brts. villous: lvs. ovate to lanceolate, villous; pod villous, rarely glabrate. G.O.t.59(c). R.I.22:t.2089,f.3–4(c). L.B.482(c). D.F.23:t.2301(c). (*G. tinctoria* var. *o.* Schultz.) S. France to Rumania. Intr. 1819. Zone V.—**G. lýdia** Boiss. Low prostrate shrub with ascending brs., glabrous: lvs. lanceolate, 5–10 mm. long: fls. in short, usually few-fld. racemes; calyx 2-lipped to the middle, lips with lanceolate lobes. Balk., W. Asia. Intr. 1927. Zone VII?

9. **G. pilòsa** L. Prostrate shrub with rooting knotty stems and short angled ascending brts.: lvs. obovate to oblong, 6–15 mm. long, obtusish, cuneate, appressed-pubescent beneath, dark green and nearly glabrous above: fls. 1–3, axillary, forming short racemes; calyx silky; keel and standard pubescent outside: pod linear, to 2.5 cm. long, silky, 5–8-seeded. Fls.V–VII. S.E.3:t. 327(c). Gn.87:562(h). S.L.184(h). Eu. Cult. 1789. Zone V.

Related species: **G. serícea** Wulf. Prostrate with ascending slender appressed-pilose brts.: lvs. linear- to elliptic-lanceolate, 8–18 mm. long, acute to obtusish, pubescent beneath: fls. in 2–5-fld. racemes; pedicels 3–5 mm. long, villous; standard and keel silky: pod oblong, 3–6-seeded. S.H.2:f.21d-g. Italy to Greece. Intr. 1923. Zone VII?

10. **G. januénsis** Viv. Low, with procumbent stems and ascending triangular slightly winged glabrous brts. 5–20 cm. long: lvs. lance-ovate to lanceolate, to 2 cm. long, with transparent margin; stipules spinescent: fls. in short racemes; bracts longer than pedicels: pod oblong, glabrous, 3–8-seeded. Fl.V–VI. R.I.22:t.2091(c). F.D.23:t.2298(c). L.B.1135(c). (*G. triangularis* Willd., *G. scariosa* Viv., *G. triquetra* Waldst. & Kit.) Italy, S. E. Eu. Cult. 1826. Zone VII?

11. **G. sagittàlis** L. Low Shrub with procumbent stems and ascending or erect broadly 2-winged villous brts. to 0.3 m. high: lvs. ovate to oblong, about 2 cm. long, villous: fls. in short, 6–8-fld. terminal racemes; corolla

glabrous except the pubescent keel; pod linear-oblong, 1–2 cm. long, silky, 3–6-seeded. Fl.vi; fr.viii. R.I.22:t.2081(c). F.D.23:t.2320(c). (*Cytisus s.* Koch.) C. and S. Eu. Cult. 1588. Zone IV.

14. **PETTÈRIA** Presl. Deciduous upright shrub; winter-buds naked, silky: lvs. petioled, 3-foliolate; lfts. entire, subsessile, stipulate: fls. yellow, in terminal upright racemes; calyx tubular, shortly 2-lipped, upper lip split to base, lower lip 3-toothed; claws of wings and keel adnate to staminal tube; ovary sessile, pubescent: pod linear-oblong, flat, dehiscent, with several seeds. (Named for Franz Petter, Dalmatian botanist; died 1853.) One species.

P. **ramentàcea** (Sieber) Presl. Shrub to 2 m.; brts. glabrous, green: lfts. narrow-elliptic to obovate-oblong, 2–6 cm. long, usually obtuse, glabrous, ciliate, dark green above, lighter beneath; petiole 2–4 cm. long: fls. fragrant, short-pediceled, in dense racemes 3–7 cm. long; calyx silky; keel silky: pod to 4.5 cm. long, sparingly silky or glabrate. Fls.v–vi. R.I.22:t.2070(c). F.D. 23:t.2307(c). B.R.29:40(c). (*Cytisus ramentaceus* Sieber, *Laburnum ramentaceum* K. Koch, *Genista r.* Briq.) Istria to Albania. Intr. 1838. Zone (V).

15. **LABÚRNUM** Med. Deciduous trees or shrubs: winter-buds globose-ovoid, with 2–3 outer scales: lvs. alternate, 3-foliolate, petioled, estipulate; lfts. subsessile: fls. yellow, slender-pediceled, in terminal usually pendulous racemes; calyx 2-lipped with obtuse short lips; petals all free; stamens 10, connate; ovary stipitate: pod linear, compressed, tardily dehiscent, with thickened slightly winged margin; seeds several, without appendage. (Ancient Latin name.) Three species in S. Eu. and W. Asia.—Ornamental trees or shrubs; the first two species with very showy pendulous racemes of golden yellow fls.

A. Racemes pendulous: lfts. elliptic to oblong, 2–8 cm. long.
  B. Brts., lvs. beneath and pod appressed-pubescent......................1. *L. anagyroides*
    BB. Brts., lvs. and pod glabrous or nearly so.................................2. *L. alpinum*
AA. Racemes upright: lfts. obovate, 5–15 mm. long...........................3. *L. caramanicum*

1. **L. anagyroìdes** Med. GOLDEN-CHAIN. Large shrub or tree to 7 m.; brts. appressed-pubescent, grayish green: lfts. elliptic to elliptic-oblong or elliptic-obovate, 3–8 cm. long, usually obtuse and mucronulate, broad-cuneate, grayish green and silky-pubescent beneath when young; petioles 2–6 cm. long: fls. about 2 cm. long, in silky-pubescent racemes to 30 cm. long; pedicels usually shorter than fls.: pod about 5 cm. long, with thick keel, appressed-pubescent; seeds black. Fls.v–vi. F.D.23:t.2305(c). G.C.36: 318. Gn.79:246(h);88:15(h). R.H.1912:446a. (*L. vulgare* Bercht. & Prsl., *Cytisus Laburnum* L.—BEAN-TREE.) S. Eu. Cult. 1560. Zone (V).—L. a. **aùreum** (Vanh.) Rehd., f. Lvs. yellow. F.S.21:t.2242–3(c). G.Z.20:129,t(c). (*L. a.* f. *chrysophyllum* (Dipp.) Schneid.) Orig. before 1875.—L. a. **bullàtum** (Jacques) Schneid., f. Lfts. curled and bullate. (*L. vulgare involutum* Hort.) Orig. before 1847.—L. a. **quercifòlium** (Loud.) Schneid., f. Lfts. sinuately lobed. ˙Gn.34:30. S.H.2:f.25c¹. Orig. before 1838.—L. a. **sessilifòlium** (Kirchn.) Schneid., f. Lvs. crowded, subsessile. Orig. before 1847.—L. a. **péndulum** (Bosse) Rehd., var. Brs. pendulous. Gn.25:522(h). G.M.45:317. Orig. before 1840.—L. a. **autumnàle** (Kirchn.) Rehd., var. Blooming a second time in autumn. (*L. vulgare* var. *bifera* Lav., var. *semperflorens* Nichols.)—L. a. **Alschíngeri** (Vis.) Schneid., var. Lfts. more silky and more bluish gray beneath; racemes shorter, often nearly upright; lower lip of calyx longer than upper one. R.I.32:t.2066,f.1,2(c). S.H.2:f.25d-e,26a-b¹. S. Eu. Intr. 1840.—L. a. **Carlièri** (Kirchn.) Schneid., var. Lfts. smaller and

narrower, obovate to narrow-oblanceolate on same br.: fls. in slender racemes; calyx slightly pubescent; ovary glabrous. Orig. before 1864.

L. a. × *alpinum* = **L. Waterèri** Dipp. Lfts. beneath and racemes sparingly pubescent; racemes long and slender: pod with narrow wing, sparingly appressed-pubescent, few-seeded, rarely developed. G.24:355. G.M.45:313. Gs.2: 109(h). (*L. Parksii* Hort., *L. Vossii* Hort.) Orig. before 1864. Zone V.— *L. a.* + *Cytisus purpureus* = *Laburnocytisus Adamii;* see below.

2. **L. alpìnum** Bercht. & Prsl. SCOTCH LABURNUM. Shrub or tree to 10 m.; brts. glabrous or hirsute when young, green: lfts. usually elliptic-oblong, 4–7 cm. long, acute or acutish, ciliate, light green and glabrous or sparingly pilose beneath: fls. less than 2 cm. long, in slender glabrous or sparingly pilose racemes to 40 cm. long; pedicels about as long as fls.: pod thin, with the upper suture winged, glabrous; seed brown. Fl.VI. F.D.23:t.2366(c). B.M.176(c, as *Cystisus Laburnum*). Gn.34:30;88:16(h). R.H.1912:446b. B. S.2:2,t(h). (*Cytisus alpinus* Mill.) Mts. of S. Eu. Cult. 1596. Zone IV. Of more upright stiffer growth than No. 1, with slenderer racemes flowering about two weeks later; hardier.—**L. a. autumnàle** Bean, var. Blooms a second time in fall. (*L. a.* var. *biferum* Arb. Kew.)—**L. a. péndulum** (Loud.) Kirchn., f. Brs. pendulous.

3. **L. caramànicum** (Boiss. & Heldr.) Benth. & Hook. Upright shrub to 2 m.; glabrous; brts. terete: lfts. obovate, 5–15 mm. long, mucronulate, grayish green; petioles 3–10 mm. long: fls. about 1.5 cm. long, in terminal slender racemes 5–15 cm. long; pedicels 5–8 mm. long, with small bractlets in the middle; pod winged on the upper suture, 5–7, glabrous. Fl.VIII. B.M.7898 (c). R.H.1861:410. G.C.48:454. B.S.2:2. (*Podocytisus caramanicus* Boiss. & Heldr., *Cytisus c.* Lav.) Greece, Asia Minor. Cult. 1861. Zone VII?

+ **LABURNOCÝTISUS** Schneid. (*Cytisus* + *Laburnum*). Known only in the following form: **L. Adàmi** (Poit.) Schneid. (*Laburnum anagyroides* + *C. purpureus.*) Habit similar to *L. anagyroides:* lfts. smaller, nearly glabrous; racemes smaller, nodding; fls. usually dull purplish; often developing brs. like true *L. anagyroides,* less often like *C. purpureus.* B.R.1965(c). B.H.21:16–18(c). G.C.36:219;50:162. M.O.t.10. (*Laburnum A.* Kirchn., *Cytisus A.* Poit., *C. Laburnum* var. *purpurascens* Loud.) Orig. about 1826. Zone V. One of the graft-hybrids of the kind termed chimaeras; an interesting plant, but of little ornamental value.

16. **CALYCÓTOME** Lk. Deciduous low spiny shrubs; brts. often opposite: lvs. 3-foliolate, petioled, estipulate; lfts. sessile, small: fls. solitary or fascicled; calyx turbinate, truncate, colored; standard upright; keel obtuse, curved, shorter than standard; filaments connate; ovary sessile; stigma capitate: pod linear-oblong; thickened or 2-winged on upper suture, dehiscent, several-seeded. (Greek *kalyx* and *tome,* cut or section; the upper part of the calyx separates before the flower opens.)—Five species in the Mediterr. region.

C. spinòsa (L.) Lk. Shrub to 1.5 m.; brts. glabrous: lfts. obovate-oblong or obovate, to 1.2 cm. long, obtuse, cuneate, sparingly pubescent beneath; petioles 3–6 mm. long: fls. 1–4, about 1 cm. long; bracts 3-lobed: pod 2–3 cm. long, glabrous. Fl.III–VII. R.I.22:t.2067(c). B.R.32:55(c). S. Eu. Cult. 1846. Zone VII. Excellent for low hedges.

Closely related species: **C. villòsa** (Poir.) Lk. Young brts. and lfts. beneath silky; calyx, pedicels and pod silky-villous: fls. 3–15. R.I.22:t.2067(c). E.N. III.3:f.109a-c. S. Eu., N. Afr. Cult. 1893. Zone VII?

17. ADENOCÁRPUS DC. Deciduous or half-evergreen shrubs or small trees, more or less pubescent: lvs. 3-foliolate, small; stipules caducous: fls. yellow, in terminal racemes; calyx 2-lipped, the 2 upper lobes distinct, the 3 lower ones more or less connate; standard orbicular, spreading; keel strongly incurved, nearly as long as standard; pod sessile, linear or oblong, compressed, viscid-glandular, many-seeded. (Greek *aden,* gland, and *karpos,* fruit; in reference to the glandular pod.) About 10 species in the Mediterr. region and on the high mts. of trop. Afr.

A. decórticans Boiss. Divaricately branched shrub or small tree to 8 m.; bark exfoliating; brts. tomentose: lvs. very crowded; lfts. linear, 8–18 mm. long, with usually involute margin, pubescent; petiole 6–12 mm. long: fls. golden-yellow, in short dense upright racemes 3–6 cm. long; calyx villous, its segments nearly equal; pod 3.5–5 cm. long. Fl.vi. R.H.1883:156,t(c). G.C.II.25:725. Gn.30:498. Spain. Cult. 1879. Zone VII.

The related **A. complicàtus** (DC.) Gren. & Godr. is a dense shrub to 1 m.; brts. glabrescent: lfts. obovate to oblong-lanceolate, pubescent beneath: fls. in elongated racemes; calyx pubescent, usually glandular; middle segment of lower lip longer than the lateral ones, usually much exceeding the upper lip. Fl.vii–viii. R.I.22:t.2055,f.1(c). B.M.1387(c). (*A. divaricatus* Sweet, *A. parvifolius* DC.) S. Eu. Cult. 1780. Zone VII.

18. CYTISUS L. Deciduous or evergreen shrubs, rarely small trees; unarmed, rarely with spinescent brts.: lvs. 3-foliolate, rarely 1-foliolate, sometimes minute or nearly wanting; stipules minute or wanting: fls. yellow or white, rarely purple, axillary or in terminal racemes or heads; calyx 2-lipped with short teeth, the upper 2 connate or free; petals all free; keel obtuse or slightly acuminate; stamens connate; ovary sessile, rarely stipitate; style incurved, with capitate or oblique stigma; pod linear to oblong, flattened, dehiscent, 2–many-seeded; seed with callous appendage. (*Kytisos,* Greek name for a kind of clover.) About 50 species chiefly in the Mediterr. region extending to C. Eu. and Canary Isls. Ornamental shrubs grown for their usually profusely produced fls.

A. Calyx campanulate, as long or slightly longer than wide: brts. grooved or angled.
  B. Fls. axillary along the brs.
    c. Style longer than keel, spirally incurved: fls. 2–2.5 cm. long, usually solitary.
                        Sect. 1. SAROTHAMNUS Benth.
                              1. *C. scoparius*
    cc. Style shorter than keel, slightly curved: fls. smaller.
      D. Habit procumbent: leafy shrubs: fls. yellow.
        E. Lvs. simple ....Sect. 2. COROTHAMNUS Nym.
                              2. *C. decumbens*
        EE. Lvs. 3-foliolate ....Sect. 3. TRIANTHOCYTISUS Griseb.
          F. Lfts. less than 1 cm. long, like the calyx and pod villous. (Lvs. simple in ×
           C. Beanii.) ....3. *C. Ardoinii*
          FF. Lfts. usually more than 1 cm. long, like the brts. and calyx sparingly
           appressed-pubescent ....4. *C. emeriflorus*
      DD. Habit upright; almost leafless shrubs; lvs. often partly 1-foliolate.
                        Sect. 4. SPARTOTHAMNUS Webb & Berth.
        E. Fls. white: brts. slender, arching..............................5. *C. multiflorus*
        EE. Fls. yellow: brts. short, stiff....................................6. *C. purgans*
  BB. Fls. in terminal racemes...................................Sect. 5. PHYLLOCYTISUS Koch.
    c. Lvs. of flowering brts. sessile: glabrous shrub, racemes 4–12-fld......7. *C. sessilifolius*
    cc. Lvs. all petioled: brts., lfts. beneath, calyx and pod appressed-pubescent.
                              8. *C. nigricans*
AA. Calyx tubular, much longer than wide: lvs. always 3-foliolate: brts. terete, not striped.
                        Sect. 6. TUBOCYTISUS DC.
  B. Fls. yellow or white: pubescent shrubs.
    c. Fls. in terminal heads with bracts at base, appearing in summer, only occasionally
      producing axillary fls. in spring; standard silky-pubescent outside.
      D. Fls. yellow.
        E. Brts. and petioles villous....................................9. *C. supinus*
        EE. Brts. and petioles appressed-pubescent........................10. *C. austriacus*
      DD. Fls. white or whitish.....................................11. *C. albus*

cc. Fls. axillary along the brs.; standard glabrous or slightly pubescent outside.
  D. Brts. and calyx with more or less spreading hairs: lvs. pubescent above.
    E. Pubescence of brts. of villous spreading hairs: pod villous........12. *C. hirsutus*
    EE. Pubescence of brts. of partly appressed and partly spreading hairs: pods
      appressed silky-villous ....13. *C. elongatus*
  DD. Brts., calyx and pod appressed-silky: lfts. glabrous above....14. *C. ratisbonensis*
 BB. Fls. purple, rarely white: glabrescent procumbent shrub................15. *C. purpureus*

1. **C. scopàrius** (L.) Lk. Scotch Broom. Upright shrub with slender green
brs. pubescent when young; lfts. obovate to oblanceolate, 8–15 mm. long,
sparingly appressed-pubescent, the upper lvs. often reduced to 1 lft.: fls.
usually 1–2, bright yellow; standard orbicular, 2 cm. across; pedicels and
calyx nearly glabrous: pod narrow-oblong, 3.5–5 cm. long, glabrescent, villous
on the margins. Fl.v–vi. R.I.22:2082(c). F.D.23:2294(c). G.25:169. M.D.
1916:t.64(h);1917:t.7(h). (*Sarothamnus s.* Wimm., *Spartium scoparium*
L.) C. and S. Eu. Long cult. and occasionally naturalized in the E. States,
also on Vancouver. Zone V. Showy with its large yellow fls.—**C. s. albus**
G. Don, var. Fls. yellowish white or nearly white. Orig. before 1830.—**C. s.
sulphùreus** Goldring. "Moonlight Broom." Dwarfer and more compact,
with pale sulphur-yellow fls. Gn.61:299;65:375. G.M.44:580. (*C. s.* f. *ochro-
leucus* Zab., *C. s. pallidus* Hort.)—**C. s. Andreànus** (Puissant) Dipp., var.
Fls. yellow with crimson wings. R.H.1886:373,t.(c). Gn.42:188,t(c). Gt.40:
t.1342(c). R.B.19:129,t(c). Intr. about 1870.—**C. s. plenus** Rehd., f. Fls.
double. (*C. s. var. fl. pleno* Loud.) Cult. 1838.—**C. s. prostràtus** (C. Bailey)
A. B. Jacks., var. With prostrate brs. or pendulous when grafted high. Gn.11:
433(h). G.C.105:387(h). (*Sarothamnus s.* var. *prostratus* C. Bailey, *C. s.* var.
pendulus Nichols. *C. grandiflorus* Hort., *Genista prostrata* Hort., not Lam.)
  C. s. var. *Andreanus* × *multiflorus;* see under No. 5.

2. **C. decúmbens** (Durande) Spach. Prostrate shrub to 0.2 m.; brs. often
rooting; brts. 5-angled, sparingly villous: lvs. sessile, oblong-obovate, 8–20
mm. long, pilose beneath, less so above: fls. 1–3, bright yellow, 1–1.5 cm.
long: calyx sparingly pilose; standard obovate: pod 2–2.5 cm. long, pubescent, 3–4-seeded. Fl.v–vi. B.M.8230(c). L.B.718(c). M.G.50:278(h).
(*Genista d.* Willd.) S. Eu. Intr. 1775. Zone V.
    Closely related species: **C. procúmbens** (Waldst. & Kit.) Spreng. Taller,
to 80 cm.; brts., pedicels and lvs. beneath appressed-pubescent. (*C. Kitaibelii*
Vis., in part.) S. E. Eu. Intr. ?—**C. diffùsus** (Willd.) Vis. Ascending to 25
cm.; brts. soon glabrous: lvs. oblong-lanceolate, glabrous, ciliate when young:
calyx glabrous: pod glabrous or sparingly hairy. R.I.22:2080,f.i,ii(c). (*Genista
humifusa* Jacq., not L.) S. Eu. Intr. ?

3. **C. Ardoìnii** Fournier. Low decumbent shrub, to 0.2 m. high; brts.
slightly grooved, villous; lfts. obovate to oblong, about 8 mm. long, villous;
petioles about 6 mm. long: fls. 1–3, golden-yellow; calyx villous; standard
suborbicular: pod 2–2.5 cm. long, villous, usually 2-seeded. Fl.iv–v. Mog-
gridge, Fl. Mentone, t.58(c). S.H.2:f.28h,30a-e. S. E. France. Intr. 1866.
Zone VII.
    C. A. × *multiflorus* = **C. kewénsis** Bean. Procumbent, to 0.3 m. high; lvs.
sometimes simple; lfts. linear-oblong, pubescent: fls. creamy white or pale
sulphur-yellow. Fl.v. Gn.73:228(h);86:244(h);87:93(h). G.W.16:610. G.M.51:
355. Orig. 1891.—*C. A.* × *purgans* = **C. Beànii** Nichols. Semi-prostrate, to
0.4 m. high; brts. pubescent when young; lvs. simple, linear, about 1 cm. long,
pubescent fls. 1–3, deep golden yellow. B.S.1:457. G.30:207. Orig. 1900. Zone V.

4. **C. emeriflòrus** Reichb. Spreading low shrub, rarely to 1 m.; brs. angular, appressed-pubescent; lfts. elliptic-oblong or obovate, 1–2 cm. long, obtuse, sparingly hairy beneath; petiole 1–2.5 cm. long: fls. 1–4, yellow, about
1.2 cm. long; pedicels about as long, pubescent: pod 2.5–3.5 cm. long, glabrous; seed with very small appendage. Fl.v–vi. B.M.8201(c). B.S.2:588.

(*Cytisus glabrescens* Sart., not Schrank.) Switzerl., N. Italy. Cult. 1890.
Zone V.

5. **C. multiflòrus** (Ait.) Sweet. WHITE SPANISH BROOM. Shrub occasionally to 3 m., with upright slender grooved brts. pubescent when young:
lvs. short-petioled, 3-foliolate on the lower part of the brts., simple above;
lfts. oblong-obovate to linear-oblong, about 1 cm. long or less, sparingly
silky-pubescent: fls. 1–3, white, about 1 cm. long, profusely produced; pedicels about 1 cm. long: pod about 2.5 cm. long, appressed-pubescent, 2–6-
seeded. Fl.v–vi. Gn.64:251(h);89:311(h). G.W.5:111. G.M.49:579(h). (*C.
albus* (Lam.) Link, not Hacq., *C. Linkii* Janka, *Spartium multiflorum* Ait.)
Spain, N. Afr. Intr. 1752. Zone (V).—**C. m. incarnàtus** (Sweet) Aschers. &
Graebn. Fls. slightly blushed. L.B.1052(c).—**C. m. dùrus** (Simon-Louis)
Aschers. & Graebn. A hardier race. (*C. albus durus* Simon-Louis.) Orig.
before 1870.

C. m. × *purgans* = **C. praècox** Bean. Lvs. usually simple, short-stalked,
oblanceolate to linear-spatulate, 8–20 mm. long, silky-pubescent: fls. 1–2, yellowish white or sulphur-yellow, about 1 cm. long, of unpleasant odor. G.C.29:
41(h). Gn.69:318(h). M.G.18:265(h). Orig. about 1867. Zone VI? Very
floriferous and handsome.—**C. p. albus** Th. Smith. Dwarfer and more pendulous: fls. white. Gn.75:192.—**C. p. lùteus** Th. Smith. Dwarf: fls. yellow.—*C. m.*
× *scoparius Andreanus* = **C. Dallimòrei** Rolfe. Shrub similar to *C. scoparius*:
lvs. usually 3-foliolate, pubescent: fls. 1–2, about 1.5 cm. long, yellow suffused
with pink, the wings crimson; calyx brown, slightly pubescent; pedicels about
6 mm. long, pubescent. B.M.8482(c). G.C.51:198. Gn.74:291. (*Cytothamnus
D.* Schneid.) Orig. 1900. Zone VI.—*C. m.* × *Ardoinii;* see under No. 3

6. **C. púrgans** (L.) Spach. Dense shrub to 1 m., with upright stiff grooved
brs. pubescent when young: lvs. usually simple, soon falling, sessile, oblanceolate, 6–12 mm. long, silky-pubescent: fls. 1–2, yellow, about 1 cm. long,
fragrant; pedicels half as long, pubescent: pod 2–2.5 cm. long, pubescent,
3–5-seeded. B.M.7618(c). L.B.1117(c). Gn.86:243(h). (*Genista p.*
L.) Spain, S. France, N. Afr. Cult. 1750. Zone (V).

C. p. × *Ardoinii;* see under No. 3.—*C. p.* × *multiflorus;* see under No. 5.

7. **C. sessilifòlius** L. Upright shrub to 2 m., glabrous; brts. angled: lvs.
nearly sessile on flowering brts., with petioles up to 2 cm. long on leafy
shoots; lfts. obovate or elliptic to oblong-obovate, 8–20 mm. long, usually
rounded at apex, bright green: fls. bright yellow, about 1.2 cm. long, short-
stalked in 4–12-fld. racemes terminal on short brts.: pod about 3 cm. long,
glabrous. Fl.vi. B.M.255(c). R.I.22:2072(c). F.D.23:2309(c). B.S.1:463.
(*Lembotropis s.* K. Koch.) S. Eu., N. Afr. Cult. 1600. Zone VI.—**C. s. leu-
cánthus** Dipp., f. Fls. yellowish white. (*C. Lobelii* Tausch.) Cult. 1864.

8. **C. nígricans** L. Upright shrub to 2 m.; brts. terete, appressed-pubescent; lfts. obovate to oblong-obovate, 1–3 cm. long, acutish, slightly appressed-pubescent beneath; petioles 6–20 mm. long: fls. yellow, about 1 cm.
long, slender-stalked, in terminal racemes 8–30 cm. long; pedicels 4–8 mm.
long, pubescent: pod about 3 cm. long, pubescent. Fl.vi–vii. B.M.8479(c).
R.I.22:2071(c). F.D.23:2308(c). B.S.1:460. C. and S. Eu. Intr. 1730. Zone
V.—**C. n. elongàtus** Willd., var. Blooming again in fall at the end of the
fruiting brs. R.H.1891:149. (*C. n. longespicatus* Hort., *C. n. Carlieri* Hort.)
Cult. 1800.

9. **C. supìnus** L. Shrub to 1 m., upright or sometimes procumbent; brts.
terete, villous: lfts. obovate or elliptic to oblong-obovate, 1.5–2.5 cm. long,
sparingly appressed-pubescent above, villous beneath; petioles about 1 cm.
long, villous: fls. yellow, brownish when fading, 2–2.5 cm. long, in terminal
heads with bracts at base; occasionally developing in spring axillary fls.:

standard silky outside; pod about 3 cm. long, villous. Fl.vi–viii. R.I.22: 2075(c). F.D.23:2313(c). (*C. capitatus* Scop.) C. and S. Eu. Intr. 1755. Zone V.

10. **C. austríacus** L. Shrub to 1 m., similar to the preceding; brts., petioles and·lvs. appressed-silky or sometimes brts. with slightly spreading hairs: lfts. elliptic-oblong to lanceolate, 1.5–3 cm. long, appressed-pubescent on both sides: fls. bright yellow, always capitate; standard silky outside; calyx villous: pod appressed-pubescent. Fl.vii–viii. R.I.22:2078,f.1–2(c). F.D.23:12 var. Slenderer shrub: lfts. smaller, linear-oblong, slightly pubescent above: (c). S. E. Eu., Cauc. Intr. 1741. Zone V.—**C. a. Heuffèlii** (Griseb.) Schneid., pod more silky. R.I.22:2078,f.3(c). (*C. H.* Griseb., *C. supinus* var. *H.* Briq.) Hungary. Cult. 1918.—**C. a. viréscens** Neilr., var. Upright; brts. with appressed hairs above, spreading toward base: lfts. obovate to oblanceolate: pod villous. S. E. Eur. Cult. 1925.

11. **C. albus** Hacq. Spreading shrub to 0.3 m.; brts. with appressed or slightly spreading pubescence: lfts. obovate to oblong, 1–2 cm. long, acutish or obtusish, sparingly pubescent above or nearly glabrous, appressed-pubescent beneath: fls. white or yellowish white, nearly 2 cm. long, 3–10 in a terminal head; calyx appressed-villous; standard silky outside: pod 2–2.5 cm. long, appressed-villous. Fl.vi–vii(–x). B.M.1438(c). R.I.22:2078, f.4(c). (*C. leucanthus* Waldst. & Kit., *C. leucanthus* var. *schipkaensis* Dipp.) S. E. Eu. Intr. 1806. Zone V.—**C. a. pállidus** (DC.) Rehd., var. Fls. pale yellow. (*C. leucanthus* var. *p.* DC.)

Closely related species: **C. Rochèlii** Griseb. & Schenk. Shrub to 1 m.; brts., calyx, and pod villous: lfts. oblong-lanceolate, to 3 cm. long: fls. pale yellow with brownish spots; standard pubescent outside. (*C. leucanthus* var. *obscurus* Roch.) Hungary. Cult. 1878.

12. **C. hirsùtus** L. Shrub to 0.6 m.; brts. villous: lfts. obovate or elliptic to obovate-oblong, 1–2 cm. long, acute to obtuse, villous beneath, slightly so or nearly glabrous above: fls. yellow, about 2.5 cm. long, in axillary clusters of 2–4; standard stained with brown in centre; calyx villous: pod about 3 cm. long, villous. Fl.v–vi. B.M.6819(c, but lfts. not serrate). F.D.23:2315 (c). (*C. falcatus* Waldst. & Kit.) S. E. Eu. Cult. 1739. Zone V.—**C. h. hirsutíssimus** (K. Koch) Boiss., var. More vigorous upright form; brts. more densely villous; lfts. more pubescent above. (*C. h.* K. Koch.) S. E. Eu.

C. h. × *purpureus;* see under No. 15.—*C. h.* × *ratisbonensis;* see under No. 13.

Closely related species: **C. ciliàtus** Wahl. Lfts. nearly glabrous or glabrous above; pods pubescent only at the sutures. S. E. Eu. Intr. 1817.

13. **C. elongàtus** Waldst. & Kit. Shrub to 1.5 m.; brts. with a more appressed tomentum mixed with longer spreading hairs: lfts. obovate to oblong-elliptic, to 2.5 cm. long, more or less appressed-pubescent on both sides: fls. 2–5; standard with reddish brown marks; calyx mostly with spreading and fewer appressed hairs: pod appressed silky-villous. R.I.22:2073(c). B.R.1191(c). (*C. ratisbonensis* var. *e.* K. Koch, *C. hirsutus* subsp. *e.* Briq., *C. multiflorus* Lindl.) C. to S. E. Eu. Intr. 1804. Zone V.—Hybrids between *C. hirsutus* and *C. ratisbonensis* = **C. cètius** Beck, are very difficult to distinguish from this species.

Closely related species: **C. leiocárpus** Kern. Ascending shrub to 0.3 m.; brts. glabrescent: lfts. elliptic or obovate, glabrous above, glabrescent beneath; calyx glabrescent: pod glabrous. Hungary. Cult. 1902.

14. **C. ratisbonénsis** Schaeff. Shrub to 2 m.; brts. appressed silky-pubescent: lfts. oblong-obovate to elliptic-oblong, 1.5–3.5 cm. long, glabrous above, appressed-silky beneath, ciliate: fls. 2–4, bright yellow, 2.5–3 cm. long; calyx

appressed-silky: pod densely appressed-pubescent. Fl.v–vɪ. R.I.22:2074,f. 1–3(c). F.D.23:2314(c). (*C. hirsutus* subsp. *r.* Briq.) C. Eu. to W. Siberia and Caucasus. Intr. about 1800. Zone V.—**C. r. biflòrus** (L'Hérit.) Zab., f. Of more upright habit; lfts. lanceolate-oblong to lanceolate: fls. paler: fr. more silky. B.R.308(c). S. E. Eu. Intr. 1760. Zone V.

C. r. × *hirsutus;* see under No. 13.

15. **C. purpúreus** Scop. Procumbent shrub with ascending brs., to 0.5 m.; glabrous or nearly so: lfts. obovate-elliptic to obovate-oblong, 6–25 mm. long, dark green above, often slightly ciliate; petioles to 2.5 cm. long: fls. 1–3, about 2 cm. long, purple; calyx sparingly pubescent: pod 2.5–3.5 cm. long, glabrous. Fl.v–vɪ. R.I.22:2072(c). F.D.23:2316(c). B.M.1176(c). G.C. 36:217;50:163. Gn.21:421. B.S.1:462,t(h). S. Austria, N. Italy. Intr. 1792. Zone V.—**C. p. albus** Kirchn., f. Fls. white. Gn.21:421. G.6:433. Orig. before 1838.—**C. p. albo-cárneus** Kirchn., f. Fls. pale pink. S.L.145(h). (*C. p. roseus* Hort., *C. p. carneus* Hort.) Orig. before 1840.—**C. p. atropurpúreus** Jaeg., var. Fls. dark purple.—**C. p. eréctus** Kirchn., f. Habit upright. Orig. before 1840.—**C. p. elongàtus** André. With long and slender brts. and violet-purple fls. (*C. p.* f. *pendulus* Dipp.) Sometimes grafted high on Laburnum. Cult. 1872.

C. p. × *hirsutus* = **C. versícolor** Dipp. Upright or spreading shrub to 1 m.; similar to *C. purpureus;* brts. sparingly villous; lfts. glabrous above, sparingly villous beneath; petioles 1–1.5 cm. long, sparingly villous: fls. light purple and yellowish, usually the standard whitish, keel light purple and wings yellowish; calyx villous: pod more or less villous. S.L.146(h). Orig. before 1860. Zone V. —**C. v. Híllieri** (Hillier) Rehd., f. Fls. yellow, flushed pale bronze, changing to buff-pink. (? *C. v.* × *hirsutus hirsutissimus.*)

19. **ÙLEX** L. GORSE (FURZE). Spiny dense shrubs; brts. grooved, ending like all their ramifications in sharp spines: lvs. reduced to a spiny petiole, only on seedlings and occasionally on vigorous shoots developed and 3-foliolate; stipules wanting: fls. 1–2, axillary, often forming terminal racemes, yellow; calyx 2-lipped to base, membranous, colored, persistent; standard ovate, wings and keel obtuse; stigma capitate: pod small, dehiscent, few-seeded; seed with appendage. (Ancient Latin name.) About 20 species in W. Eu.

A. Petals 1½ as long as calyx; calyx villous: fls. in spring..................1. *U. europaeus*
AA. Petals about as long or little longer than calyx; calyx minutely silky; fls. in autumn.
  ʙ. Standard about 1.2 cm. long; wing longer than keel; spines stout............2. *U. Gallii*
  ʙʙ. Standard 8–10 mm. long; wing shorter than keel; spines short and thin....3. *U. nanus*

1. **U. europaèus** L. Dense, much-branched rigid and very spiny shrub, to 1, rarely to 2 m. tall; axillary brts. stout with the spiny tip 2–3 cm. long: young brts. hairy; petioles linear lanceolate, 6–12 mm. long: fls. solitary, golden-yellow; pedicels hairy, about 6 mm. long; bracts ovate; standard 1.5 cm. or more long: pod about 1.5 cm. long, exceeding the calyx. Fl.ɪv–vɪ, sometimes again in autumn. R.I.22:2068(c). S.E.3:t.323(c). G.H.t.123(c). G.W.17:286. S.L.371(h). C. and W. Eu.; naturalized in the middle Atlantic States and on Vancouver. Long cult. Zone VI.—**U. e. plènus** Schneid., f. With double fls. Gn.63:441,89:172(h). G.M.52:393. (*U. e.* var. *fl. pleno* Loud.) Orig. about 1828.—**U. e. stríctus** (Mackay) Webb, var. Of upright columnar habit; fls. but sparingly. (*U. fastigiatus* Hort., *U. hibernicus* Hort.) Intr. about 1815.

2. **U. Gállii** Planch. (? *U. europaeus* × *nanus*). Shrub to 0.5 m., similar to the preceding; spiny tip of axillary brts. not exceeding 1.5 cm.; brts. hairy: fls. bright yellow: calyx minutely silky; wings curved, longer than

keel: pod about 1 cm., scarcely exserted. Fl.viii–ix. F.S.5:441(h). Ann. Sci. Nat. III.11,t.9. W. Eu. Intr. after 1850. Zone VII.

3. **U. nànus** Symons. Dwarf shrub, sometimes procumbent, to 0.6 m. tall; spiny tip of lateral brts. usually not more than 5 mm. long; brts. hairy, with thin and very dense ramifications: fls. golden-yellow; wings straight and shorter than keel; calyx puberulous: pod about 1 cm. long, enclosed in the calyx. Fl.viii–ix. R.I.22:2068(c). S.E.3:t.325. B.S.2:610. W. Eu. Cult. 1789. Zone VII.

Related species: **U. parviflòrus** Pourr. To 1 m.: brts. nearly glabrous, axillary spines often simple, straight: fls. orange-yellow; standard 5–8 mm. long. R.I.22:t.2068(c). S.H.2:f.351. S. W. Eu. Cult. 1904. Zone VII.—**U. p. provinciàlis** (Lois.) Aschers. & Graebn., prol., is a slenderer form (*U. p.* Lois.).

Tribe 4. Trifolieae Taub. Lvs. 3-foliolate; lfts. denticulate: stamens all connate or the upper stamen partly or quite free; petals of keel free or slightly connate on back: pod usually dehiscent.

20. **ONÒNIS** L. Herbs or deciduous shrubs, pubescent and often glandular: lvs. 3-foliolate, rarely pinnate; lfts. denticulate; stipules adnate to petiole, conspicuous: fls. purple to white or yellow, axillary, 1–3, often racemose or paniculate at end of brts.; calyx deeply 5-parted; standard large, suborbicular; keel usually rostrate, incurved; stamens all connate; ovary stipitate, 2–many-ovuled; style incurved with capitate or oblique stigma; pod usually swollen. (Ancient Greek name.) More than 70 species, chiefly Mediterranean, extending to N. Eu. and to the Canary Isls.

O. fruticòsa L. Shrub to 0.6 m.; brts. soon glabrous: lfts. sessile, oblong-ovate to oblanceolate, to 2.5 cm. long, glabrous, grayish green; stipules 2–4-toothed: fls. light rose or whitish with red veins, 1.5–2 cm. long, 2–3 on slender peduncles forming glandular-pubescent terminal panicles; calyx glandular-pubescent, reddish; pod 2–2.5 cm. long, hairy. Fl.vi–viii. R.I.22:t.53(c). B.M. 317(c). G.C.47:420. S.L.241(h). S. Eu., N. Afr. Intr. before 1680. Zone VI.

The following species differ in their orbicular lfts., the middle one distinctly stalked: **O. aragonénsis** Asso. Shrub to 0.3 m.: lfts. about 1 cm. long, glabrous: fls. yellow, about 1 cm. long, short-stalked, 1–2 axillary in terminal racemes 6–14 cm. long: pod about 6 mm. long, glandular-hairy. B.S.2:108. Spain, Algeria. Intr. 1816. Zone VII?—**O. rotundifòlia** L. Subshrub to 0.5 m.; brts. glandular-villous: lfts. 1–3.5 cm. long, slightly glandular-villous: fls. bright rose, about 2 cm. long, 2–4 in axillary peduncled clusters forming terminal leafy panicles: pod to 3 cm. long, very hairy. R.I.22:t.54(c). F.D.23:t.2330(c). B.M. 335(c). S. Eu. Cult. 1600. Zone V.

21. **MEDICÀGO** L. Herbs or rarely deciduous shrubs: lvs. 3-foliolate; lfts. usually denticulate; stipules adnate to petiole: fls. yellow or violet, in axillary heads or racemes; calyx short, with nearly equal teeth; standard obovate or oblong; wings longer than the obtuse keel; ovary sessile or short-stipitate; stigma terminal, oblique: pod spirally twisted or curved, indehiscent, several-, rarely 1-seeded. (From the country Media.) About 50 species in C. and S. Eu., W. Asia and Afr.

M. cretàcea Bieb. Ascending subshrub to 0.25 m.; brts. sparingly appressed-pubescent: lfts. broad-obovate, scarcely more than 8 mm. long, rounded and mucronate at apex, entire or nearly so, pubescent on both sides: fls. about 7 mm. long, yellow, in many-fld. subcapitate racemes on peduncles shorter than the lvs.; calyx villous: pod falcate, compressed, to 1 cm. long, appressed-pubescent or glabrescent. Fl.v–vi. Marschall von Bieberstein, Cent. Pl. Ross. t.76. S.L.236(h). Crimea. Cult. 1908. Zone VI?

Tribe 5. Loteae Taub. Lvs. pinnate or digitate; lfts. entire: filaments all or only 5 dilated at apex; otherwise like the preceding tribe.

22. ANTHÝLLIS L. Herbs or evergreen or deciduous shrubs: lvs. 3-foliolate or odd-pinnate, rarely 1-foliolate; stipules wanting or minute: fls. yellow, white or purple, in axillary heads or clusters; calyx tubular, often inflated after anthesis, with nearly equal teeth, or the 2 upper ones longer and partly connate; standard ovate; wings ovate, longer than the obtuse or apiculate keel, usually adnate to the staminal tube; stamens at first all connate, the upper stamens becoming partly or wholly free; ovary usually stipitate; stigma terminal: pod ovate to linear, enclosed in the calyx or slightly exserted, 1 or few-seeded, indehiscent or tardily 2-valved. (Ancient Greek name.) More than 20 species in the Mediterr. region.

A. Hermánniae L. Deciduous densely branched shrub, to 0.5 m., with tortuous spinescent brs. pubescent when young: lfts. usually 1, oblanceolate, 1–2.5 cm. long, obtuse, silky-pubescent on both sides: fls. orange-yellow, about 8 mm. long, 3–5 in axillary short-stalked clusters; calyx appressed-pubescent: pod oblong, glabrous, 5 mm. long. Fl.vi–vii. B.M.2576(c). S.F. t.683(c). Corsica to Asia Minor. Intr. about 1700. Zone VII. Low shrub suited for sunny rockeries.—**A. H. Aspálathi** Rouy, var. Less pubescent, more spiny; infl. 1–3-fld. (*Aspalathus cretica* L.) Cult. 1910.

23. DORÝCNIUM Adans. Herbs or subshrubs: lvs. 3-foliolate or apparently digitate; the stipules leaf-like and sometimes not different from the lfts.; lfts. entire: fls. white or pink, small, in axillary peduncled umbels or heads, sometimes crowded at end of brts.; calyx with 5 subequal teeth or slightly 2-lipped; standard oblong-ovate; wings oblong-obovate, connate at apex; keel obtusish, incurved; upper stamen free; ovary sessile, 2–many-ovuled; style incurved with capitate stigma: pod oblong to linear, terete, dehiscent. (Ancient Greek name of a poisonous plant.) About 12 species in the Mediterr. region and on the Canary Isls.

D. suffruticòsum Vill. Ascending subshrub, to 0.4 m.; stems slender, appressed pubescent when young: lvs. sessile; lfts. including the similar stipules 5, oblanceolate, those on upper part of the brts. linear, 8–20 mm. long, silky-pubescent, grayish green: fls. pinkish white, about 6 mm. long, sub-sessile, in 10–12-fld. heads on axillary slender stalks 3–6 cm. long at end of stems; calyx silky pubescent: pod subglobose, 1-seeded, about 3 mm. long. Fl.vi–ix. R.I.22:t.137,f.4,5(c). F.D.23:t.2409(c). S. Eu. Intr. before 1650. Zone V.—**D. s. seríceum** (Neilr.) Beck, var. Lower, procumbent at base: lfts. broader, the upper ones not different: pedicels more than ½ as long as calyx; standard 5–7 mm. long. (*D. germanicum* Rouy.) Switzerl. to Balkan Pen.

Related species: **D. réctum** (L.) Ser. Subshrub to 1 m., villous or glabrescent: lfts. obovate, 1.5–2 cm. long; petiole to 1 cm. long; stipules about as long: standard about 4–5 mm. long; pod cylindric, glabrous. Mediterr. reg. Cult. 1800.—**D. hirsùtum** (L.) Ser. Stems hirsute; lfts. obovate to oblong, 2–2.5 cm. long, hirsute beneath; stipules elliptic-ovate, much longer than the very short petiole: fls. white, about 1.5 cm. long, in 6–10-fld. heads; peduncle hirsute: pod about 8 mm. long, usually 4-seeded. R.I.22:t.134,f.1–3(c). S.F.8:t.759(c). S. Eu. Intr. 1680. Zone V.

Tribe 6. GALEGEAE Taub. Lvs. 3-foliolate or pinnate; the upper stamen usually free; filaments not dilated at apex; otherwise like the preceding tribe.

24. INDIGÓFERA L. Deciduous shrubs, subshrubs or herbs, more or less clothed with 2-armed appressed hairs and sometimes also with simple hairs: lvs. usually odd-pinnate, rarely 3-foliolate or 1-foliolate; lfts. usually opposite, short-petioluled, entire, sometimes stipellate; stipules usually small, subulate, adnate at base to petiole: fls. usually pink to purple, in axillary racemes; bracts caducous; calyx small, oblique, with 5 nearly equal teeth or the lowest one longer; standard orbicular to oblong; wings oblong, slightly adhering to keel which has a swelling or spur on either side; ovary sessile or nearly so; anthers with apiculate connective: pod subglobose to linear-oblong, terete or angular, rarely compressed, dehiscent, inside with thin partitions. ("Indigo-bearing"; some species yield indigo.) About 300 species in trop. and subtrop. regions of both hemispheres.—Several species are very ornamental shrubs; even if killed back in colder climates to the ground, young shoots springing from the base flower and fruit the same season.

A. Lfts. 5–13.
  B. Lfts. glabrous above.
    c. Lfts. elliptic-ovate to lance-ovate, acute to obtuse....................1. *I. incarnata*
    cc. Lfts. broad-oval to oblong, rounded or emarginate at apex.........2. *I. hebepetala*
  BB. Lfts. pubescent on both sides.
    c. Fls. 1.5–2 cm. long; peduncle longer than petiole.......................3. *I. Kirilowi*
    cc. Fls. 6–8 mm. long; keel and wings caducous.
      D. Peduncle about as long as petiole.................................4. *I. Potaninii*
      DD. Peduncle much shorter than petiole............................5. *I. amblyantha*
AA. Lfts. 13–27.
  B. Lfts. 13–21, 1–1.5 cm. long: racemes upright...........................6. *I. Gerardiana*
  BB. Lfts. 21–27, 2–3.5 cm. long: racemes pendulous.......................7. *I. pendula*

1. **I. incarnàta** (Willd.) Nakai. Shrub to 0.5 m.; brts. reddish brown, terete, glabrous: lfts. 7–13, elliptic to ovate-lanceolate, 2.5–7 cm. long, acutish or obtuse, mucronate, dark green above, pale beneath and sparingly appressed-pubescent: fls. pink, 1.5–2 cm. long, in slender racemes with the peduncle 10–20 cm. long; peduncle much longer than petiole; pedicels about 6 mm. long; calyx glabrous, with triangular lobes; standard oblong, white, pale crimson toward base, wings pink: pod glabrous. Fl.vii–viii. B.M.5063(c). B.R.32:22(c). P.M.16:290(c). (*I. decora* Lindl.) China, Japan. Intr. 1846. Zone VII?; usually killed back in winter.—I. i. alba (Sarg.) Rehd., f. Fls. white. G.F.7:375. B.C.3:1645. Intr. about 1878. Zone (V).

Related species: I. Fortùnei Craib. Lvs. oval or ovate to broad-oblong, 2–4 cm. long, reticulate beneath and sparingly appressed-pubescent, finally nearly glabrous: fls. to 12 mm. long, white; anthers pilose at apex. (*I. reticulata* Koehne, not Franch., *I. venulosa* Hemsl., not Champ.) China. Intr. before 1890. Zone VI?

2. **I. hebepétala** Benth. Shrub to 1 m. or taller; stems pubescent when young, soon glabrous: lfts. 7–9(5–11), broad-ovate to oblong, 2.5–6 cm. long, rounded or emarginate at apex, sparingly appressed-pubescent beneath: fls. 1–1.5 cm. long, in rather dense racemes 8–20 cm. long, on the upper part of the shoot; peduncle about as long as petiole; standard crimson, pubescent outside, wings and keel rose-colored; calyx with short triangular teeth, pilose: pod 3–5 cm. long, linear-oblong, 8–10-seeded. Fl.viii–ix. B.M.8208(c). I.T. 6:t.219. M.O.t.11. Himal. Cult. 1881. Zone VII.

3. **I. Kirilówii** Maxim. Shrub to 1 m. or taller; brts. slightly angular, slightly pubescent when young, soon glabrous: lfts. 7–11, suborbicular to obovate or elliptic, 1–3 cm. long, mucronate, broad-cuneate or rounded at base, rounded at apex, bright green above, sparingly appressed-pubescent on both sides: fls. rose-colored, about 2 cm. long, in rather dense racemes to 12 cm. long, about as long as leaf; peduncle about twice as long as petiole; calyx 3 mm. long, with unequal lanceolate teeth, slightly pubescent: pod linear-oblong, 3–5.5 cm. long. Fl.vi. B.M.8580(c). B.C.3:1646. M.G.27:271(h). N. China, Korea. Intr. 1899. Zone IV.—I. K. coreàna Craib, var. Racemes nearly twice as long as lvs.; calyx 4 mm. long, with narrower teeth. Korea. Intr. ?

4. I. Potanínii Craib. Upright shrub to 1.5 m. or taller; brts. densely appressed-pubescent at first, soon glabrescent: lfts. 5–9, elliptic-oblong to oblong or obovate-oblong, 1–3 cm. long, rounded and mucronate at apex, cuneate or broadly cuneate at base, grayish green beneath, appressed-pubescent; stipules minute; petiole 1.5–2.5 cm. long: fls. lilac-pink, about 8 mm. long, in racemes 5–12 cm. long; calyx short, the lowest tooth somewhat longer than tube; pedicels 1–2 mm. long: pod up to 3.5 cm. long, glabrate. Fl.vi–vii. N. W. China. Cult. 1925. Zone V?

Related species: **I. Soulièi** Craib. Lfts. oval to elliptic-oblong, 1–2 cm. long: fls. nearly 1 cm. long, in stalked racemes to 15 cm. long; pedicels 3–4 mm. long: pod about 2 cm. long, glabrous. W. China. Intr. 1910. Zone VI?

5. I. amblyántha Craib. Shrub to 2 m.; brts. angled, appressed-pubescent with whitish hairs: lfts. 7–11, elliptic to oblong-elliptic, 1–3.5 cm. long, rounded and mucronate at apex, broad-cuneate, bright green above, glaucescent beneath, appressed-pubescent; petiole 3–4 cm. long: fls. pale lilac-purple, 6–7 mm. long, in dense racemes 6–10 cm. long, shorter than lf.; standard obovate; calyx appressed-pubescent: pod linear-oblong, 3.5–5 cm. long, pubescent. Fl.vii–x. China. Intr. 1908. Zone V.—**I. a. Purdómii** Rehd., var. Fls. larger, lilac-purple, standard 8 mm. long, 6 mm. wide, flat. N. China. Intr. 1911.

Related species: **I. pseudotinctòria** Matsum. Shrub to 2 m.: lfts. 5–11, elliptic-obovate or elliptic to elliptic-oblong, 6–25 mm. long, obtuse and mucronate, glaucescent beneath; petiole 1–2 cm. long: fls. pink or light red, in dense racemes 4–12 cm. long; standard oblong-obovate, 5–6 mm. long: pod 2–3.5 cm. long, slightly appressed-pubescent. Fl.vii–x. Japan, E. and C. China. Intr. 1908. Zone V.

6. I. Gerardiàna Bak. Much-branched shrub to 1 m. or taller; brts. slightly ribbed, appressed-pubescent: lfts. 13–21, oval or obovate to oblong-oblanceolate, 1–1.5 cm. long, rounded or emarginate and mucronulate at apex, appressed-pubescent on both sides: fls. about 1 cm. long, rosy-purple, short-stalked, in rather dense racemes 7–15 cm. long; teeth of calyx equal, lanceolate; standard pubescent outside: pod deflexed at maturity, 3–5 cm. long, 6–10 seeded. Fl.vii–ix. B.R.28:57(c). (*I. dosua* Lindl., not D. Don.) Himal. Cult. 1840. Zone VI?; usually killed back in winter.

7. I. péndula Franch. Shrub to 3 m.; young brts. appressed-puberulous and lenticellate: lvs. to 25 cm. long; lfts. 21–27, elliptic-oblong, 2–3.5 cm. long, rounded at ends, punctulate above, appressed-pubescent beneath, thin: fls. rosy-purple, 1.3 cm. long, in pendulous peduncled racemes to 45 cm. long; calyx appressed-pubescent; standard elliptic-oblong, silky outside: pod 5 cm. long, sparingly strigillose. Fl.viii–ix. B.M.8745(c). W. China. Intr. 1914. Zone VII?; killed back in winter.

Related species: **I. stachyòdes** Lindl. Brts., lf.-rachis and racemes brownish villous: lfts. 25–45, oblong, 1–2 cm. long, mucronate, densely pubescent on both sides: racemes upright, dense, 10–25 cm. long, with long subulate pilose bracts; corolla about 1 cm. long, purple: pod 2.5–3 cm. long, villous. B.R.29:14(c). E. Himal., W. China. Cult. 1840. Zone VII?

25. AMÓRPHA L. Deciduous shrubs or subshrubs, rarely herbs: lvs. odd-pinnate; lfts. small, entire; stipules subulate, caducous: fls. small, bluish violet or whitish or dark purple, in dense terminal often panicled spikes; bracts subulate, caducous; calyx short-campanulate, with 5 equal or unequal teeth, usually gland-dotted; wings and keel wanting; ovary sessile, 2-ovuled: pod short, usually 1-seeded, indehiscent, usually gland-dotted; seed glossy. (Greek *amorphos,* deformed; alluding to the incomplete corolla.) About 15 closely related species in N. Am., s. to Mex.

A. Lowest pair of lfts. close to the stem: low shrubs, usually less than 1 m.
　B. Plant pubescent.
　　c. Calyx-lobes subulate-lanceolate, subequal, nearly as long as tube....1. *A. canescens*
　　cc. Calyx-lobes about half as long as tube, the upper ones triangular....2. *A. herbacea*
　BB. Plant glabrous or nearly so: calyx-lobes subequal, about half as long as tube.3. *A. nana*
AA. Lowest pair of lfts. 1 cm. or more from the stem: taller shrubs, 1–3 m.
　B. Pod nearly straight on back: plant glabrous or nearly so: lfts. 9–19: calyx-lobes very
　　short, rounded ....4. *A. glabra*
　BB. Pod curved on back: plant more or less pubescent: at least the lower calyx-lobes acute.
　　　　　　　　　　　　　　　　　　　　　　　　　　　　　5. *A. fruticosa*

1. **A. canéscens** Nutt. LEAD-PLANT. Subshrub to 1 m.; brts. angled, densely grayish pubescent: lvs. spreading, curved, 5–12 cm. long; lfts. 15–45, elliptic to oblong-lanceolate, 7–20 mm. long, acute or obtuse, rounded at base, densely grayish villous on both sides: fls. blue, in dense, short-peduncled clustered spikes 3–15 cm. long; calyx villous; standard cuneate-obovate, 5 mm. long; pod with straight back, 4 mm. long, villous. Fl.vi–vii. B.M. 6618(c). M.M.5:t.6(c). B.B.2:366. Mich. and Sask. to Ind., Tex. and N. Mex. Intr. 1812. Zone II.—A. c. **glabrata** Gray, var. lvs. sparsely pubescent or glabrate. Mo. to Okl. and Tex. Cult. 1883. Zone V.

2. **A. herbàcea** Walt. Shrub to 1.5 m.; brts. grooved, finely grayish pubescent: lvs. spreading, 4–16 cm. long; lfts. 11–37, elliptic to oblong, 1–2.5 cm. long, rounded at ends, finely grayish pubescent on both sides, black-dotted and reticulate beneath: fls. white to violet-purple, in finely pubescent clustered racemes 10–30 cm. long; calyx villous, the 2 upper lobes triangular, the lower ones subulate; standard cuneate-obovate, 4–5 mm. long: pod with nearly straight back, 4–5 mm. long, puberulous, with conspicuous dark glands. Fl.vi–vii. L.B.689(c). S.H.2:f.42a-b,43b-c. (*A. pubescens* Willd., *A. pumila* Michx.) N. C. to Fla. Cult. 1820. Zone VI?

3. **A. nàna** Nutt. Shrub to 1 m.; brts. glabrous: lvs. 3–10 cm. long, crowded; lfts. 13–19, elliptic to oblong, 5–1.2 cm. long, rounded or emarginate and mucronate at apex, cuneate or rounded at base, glabrous, punctate beneath: fls. purple, in usually solitary racemes, 5–10 cm. long; caiyx glabrous, lobes half as long as tube; standard cuneate-obovate, 4 mm. long: pod straight on back, 5 mm. long, conspicuously glandular. Fl.v–vi. B.B.2:f.2505. Clements, Rocky Mts. Fl.t.29,f.4. S.H.2:f.42h-k,43a. (*A. microphylla* Pursh.) Man. and Sask. to Iowa and N. Mex. Intr. 1811. Zone II.

Related species: **A. brachycárpa** E. J. Palm. Shrub to 1 m.; lfts. 21–45, rounded or subcordate at base: infl. paniculate, 10–25 cm. long; fls. bluish purple; lower calyx-lobes about as long as tube. J.A.12:194–5,f.6,t.36. Mo. Intr. 1920. Zone V.

4. **A. glábra** Poir. Glabrous shrub to 2 m.; brts. purplish, sometimes slightly hairy; lvs. 7–16 cm. long; lfts. 9–19, oval to elliptic-ovate, 2–5 cm. long, rounded or emarginate at apex, rounded or subcordate at base: fls. purple, in usually clustered racemes 6–15 cm. long; calyx with ciliate undulately toothed margin; standard suborbicular, cuneate, 7 mm. long: pod nearly straight on back, 7–8 mm. long, with few small glands. Fl.v–vi. S.H. 2:f.44d,45a-b. (*A. montana* Boynt.) N. C. and Tenn. to Ga. and Ala. Cult. 1800. Zone V.

Related species: **A. cyanostáchya** M. A. Curtis. Shrub to 2 m.: lfts. 11–25, oval, 1–2.5 cm. long, rounded at ends, conspicuously glandular-punctate beneath: fls. blue, in usually solitary racemes 5–15 cm. long; standard obovate: pod conspicuously gland-dotted. S.H.2:f.42s-u,43e-é,44e. (*A. glabra* Boynt., not Poir., *A. caroliniana* Rydb., not Croom.) N. C. to Fla. Cult. 1848. Zone VI?

5. **A. fruticòsa** L. Shrub to 4 m.; brts. sparingly pilose, becoming glabrate: lfts. 11–25, oval or elliptic, 1.5–4 cm. long, rounded at ends, mucronate, finely pubescent or glabrate: fls. purple-blue in clustered spikes 7–15 cm.

long; calyx sparingly pilose or glabrate, its lobes much shorter than tube;
standard orbicular-obovate, about 6 mm. long: pod curved, 7–9 mm. long.
Fl.v–vi. B.R.427(c). B.B.2:f.2504. Conn. to Minn., s. to La. and Fla. Intr.
1724. Zone IV.—**A. f. albiflòra** Sheldon, f. Fls. white.—**A. f. coerùlea** Loud.,
var. Fls. pale blue.—**A. f. péndula** (Carr.) Dipp. Brs. pendulous or recurved.
Cult. 1870.—**A. f. críspa** Kirchn., f. Lfts. with curled margin.—**A. f. hùmilis**
(Tausch) Schneid., var. A low form often dying back to the ground. Cult.
1838.—The following are geographical vars.: **A. f. tennessénsis** (Shuttlew.)
E. J. Palm., var. Lfts. 21–35, narrow-oblong, usually 1–2 cm. long, sparingly
pubescent: standard 4.5 mm. long: pod nearly straight or slightly curved.
J.A.12:194–5,f.20b. (*A. t.* Shuttlew.) N. C. to Fla., w. to Kans. and Tex.
Cult. 1848.—**A. f. angustifòlia** Pursh, var. Brts. appressed-pubescent: lfts.
elliptic or obovate to oblong, narrowed at base, appressed-pubescent: pod
strongly curved. B.M.2112(c, as *A. nana*); S.B.1:t.241(c). (*A. fragrans* Sweet,
A. a. Boynton.) Wisc. to Sask. s. to Kans. and N. Mex. Cult. 1819. Zone II.
—**A. f. emarginata** Pursh, var. Lfts. broader, oval or ovate, obtuse or
emarginate at apex. J.A.12:195,f.20d(l). (*A. e.* Sweet.) Ill. to Ark. and Miss.
Cult. 1827.

Related species: **A. croceo-lanàta** Wats. Shrub to 3 m.; brts. villous: lfts.
13–23, oblong or ovate-oblong, 2.5–6 cm. long, rounded at ends, tawny tomentose
at first, villous beneath at maturity: calyx villous. W.D.2:139(c), J.A.12:194–
5,f.17. (*A. fruticosa* var. *c.* Mouillef.) Ky. to Fla., w. to Mo. and La. Intr.
1812. Zone V.—**A. virgàta** Small. Shrub to 2 m.: lfts. 9–19, oblong-ovate to
oblong, rounded at ends or slightly emarginate at apex, firm and with revolute
margin at maturity, slightly pubescent beneath: calyx glabrous at maturity,
lobes very short, the upper obtuse. J.A.12:194–5,f.16. Ga. to Fla. w. to Okl.
and Miss. Intr. 1923. Zone V.—**A. paniculàta** Torr. & Gr. Brts. tomentose:
lfts. 15–19, oval to oblong, 3–8 cm. long, tomentose beneath: calyx pubescent,
lobes lanceolate, half as long as tube: pod pubescent and glandular. A.J.12:
194–5,f.14. Ark. to Tex. Intr. 1926. Zone V.

26. **WISTÈRIA** Nutt. Wistaria. Deciduous twining shrubs; winter-
buds subglobose or ovoid, with about 3 outer scales: lvs. alternate, odd-pinnate; lfts. petiolulate, alternate, stipellate, 9–19; stipules caducous: fls. blue
to purplish or white, in pendulous racemes; calyx campanulate, shortly 5-
toothed, the lower teeth often longer; standard large, reflexed, usually with 2
callosities at base; wings falcate, auriculate at base; keel obtuse, mucronate;
the upper stamen free; style incurved, with terminal subglobose stigma: pod
stipitate, elongated, flattened, with several seeds, usually slightly constricted
between them, tardily dehiscent. (After Caspar Wistar, Prof. of Anatomy,
University of Pennsylvania; 1761–1818.) Syn.: *Wistaria* Spreng., *Kraunhia*
Raf., *Diplonix* Raf., *Bradleia* Adans. Nine species in N. Am. and E. Asia.—
Ornamental twining shrubs planted for their flowers produced in great profusion in spring.

A. Standard with distinct callosities at base: fls. 1.5–2.5 cm. long, in racemes on short lateral
  brts.
  B. Pod velvety; pedicels 1–3 cm. long.
    c. Lfts. 13–19, nearly glabrous at maturity....................................1. *W. floribunda*
    cc. Lfts. 7–13.
      D. Lfts. nearly glabrous at maturity.....................................2. *W. sinensis*
      DD. Lfts. pubescent on both sides: fls. white............................3. *W. venusta*
  BB. Pods glabrous; pedicels 6–10 mm. long: lfts. 9–13.
    c. Racemes dense, 4–10 cm. long, glandless or slightly glandular; calyx-lobes much
      shorter than the broad tube..4. *W. frutescens*
    cc. Racemes elongated, 20–30 cm. long, glandular; calyx-lobes nearly as long as the
      narrow-campanulate tube ....5. *W. macrostachya*
AA. Standard without callosities at base and not auricled: fls. white, 1–1.3 cm. long, in axillary
  racemes ....6. *W. japonica*

1. **W. floribúnda** (Willd.) DC. JAPANESE W. Tall climber, to 8 m. or more: lfts. 13–19, ovate-elliptic to ovate-oblong, 4–8 cm. long, acuminate, rounded at base, rarely broad-cuneate, appressed-pubescent when young, soon nearly glabrous: fls. violet or violet-blue, 1.5–2 cm. long, in slender racemes, 20–50 cm. long, with the fls. opening gradually from base to apex, fragrant; pedicels 1.2–2.5 cm. long, slightly pubescent; standard broad-oval, auriculate; calyx pubescent, the two upper teeth very short and broad: pod 10–15 cm. long, narrowed toward the base. Fl.v–vi, sometimes later in season with shorter racemes (*W. brachybotrys* S. & Z.). S.I.2:t.32(c). S.Z.1:t.45(c). F.S.9:t.880(c). (*W. polystachya* K. Koch, *Kraunhia fl.* Taub., *K. sinensis* var. *fl.* Mak., *W. grandiflora* Hort.) Japan. Intr. 1830. Zone IV. Very ornamental vine; hardier than the following species.—**W. f. variegàta** (Nichols.) Rehd. & Wils., f. Lvs. variegated.—**W. f. alba** (Carr.) Rehd. & Wils., f. Fls. white; racemes to 60 cm. long. R.H.1891:421. B.S.2:682,t(h).—**W. f. rosea** (Bean) Rehd. & Wils., f. Fls. pale pink, tips of keel and wings purple. M.G. 16:329(h).—**W. f. violaceo-plèna** (Schneid.) Rehd. & Wils., f. With violet double fls. R.H.1887:564,t(c). F.P.1882:t.557(c). Gn.17:105. M.G.16:328.— **W. f. macrobótrys** (Neubert) Rehd. & Wils., f. Lfts. to 10 cm. long: racemes to 1 m., sometimes to 1.5 m. long. F.S.19:t.2002(c). S.Z.1:t.44(c). G.C.69: 149. B.S.2:683. Gn.79:293(h);83:115(h). M.G.18:133(h). (*W. multijuga* Vanh.)

W. f. × *sinensis* = **W. formòsa** Rehd. Lfts. 9–15: racemes about 25 cm. long; fls. about 2 cm. long; pedicels 1–1.5 cm. long; lower calyx-lobes long-acuminate: pod usually 1-seeded. Orig. 1905. All fls. of one raceme open at nearly the same time.

2. **W. sinénsis** (Sims) Sweet. CHINESE W. Lfts. 7–13, ovate-oblong to ovate-lanceolate, 5–8 cm. long, abruptly acuminate, usually broad-cuneate at base, ciliate, densely appressed-pubescent at first, glabrate at maturity: fls. blue-violet, about 2.5 cm. long, slightly fragrant, in rather dense racemes, 15–30 cm. long; pedicels 1–2 cm., rarely to 2.5 cm. long, short-villous; calyx pubescent; all fls. of one raceme opening at nearly the same time: pod 10–15 cm. long, densely velutinous, 1–3-seeded. Fl.v–vi. B.M.2083(c). B.R.650(c). L.B.773(c). B.C.5:t.119(h). (*W. chinensis* DC., *Kraunhia sinensis* Mak., *Glycine s.* Sims.) China. Intr. 1816. Zone (V). Like the preceding species an ornamental vine, but tenderer.—**W. s. alba** Lindl. Fls. white. I.H.5:t. 166(c). Intr. 1846.

3. **W. venústa** Rehd. & Wils. Young brts. pubescent: lfts. 9–13, ovate or elliptic-oblong to oblong-lanceolate, 6–10 cm. long, short-acuminate, rounded to subcordate, silky-pubescent on both sides, more densely beneath: fls. white, 2–2.5 cm. long, in pendulous pubescent racemes 10–15 cm. long; pedicels villous, usually 2.5–3 cm. long; 3 lower calyx-teeth subulate; standard auricled at base; keel truncate at apex: pod 15–20 cm. long, densely velutinous, compressed. Fl.vi–vii. B.M.8811(c). (*W. brachybotrys* var. *alba* Wm. Mill.) Cult. in Japan; introd. before 1900. Zone V.—**W. v. plèna** Rehd. & Wils., f. With double white fls. (*W. chinensis* var. *alba plena* Bean.) Cult. 1914.—**W. v. violàcea** Rehd., f. Fls. violet. Japan. The wild form; not yet introd.

Closely related species: **W. villòsa** Rehd. Brts. villous: lvs. loosely villous finally glabrous above, with persistent grayish white villous hairs beneath: keel emarginate at apex. N. E. China. Intr. 1916. Zone V.

4. **W. frutéscens** (L.) Poir. To 12 m. long: young brts. glabrous or nearly so: lfts. 9–15, elliptic-ovate to oblong or oblong-lanceolate, 2–5 cm. long, acute to obtusish or slightly acuminate, cuneate to rounded at base, glabrous above,

sparingly appressed-pubescent beneath: fls. lilac-purple, 1.5–1.8 cm. long, in dense villous racemes 4–10 cm. long; bracts abruptly pointed; pedicels villous; calyx appressed-pubescent, with very short teeth; standard auricled at base; wings with a slender and a short auricle on either side: pod 5–10 cm. long, compressed. Fl.vi–viii. B.M.2103(c). N.D.3:t.55(c). B.B.2:374. (*W. speciosa* Nutt., *Kraunhia fr.* Greene, *Bradleia fr.* Britt.) Va. to Fla. and Tex. Intr. 1724. Zone V.—**W. f. nivea** Lescuyer. Fls. white (*W. f. alba* Th. Moore.) Cult. 1854.

5. **W. macrostáchya** Nutt. Slender twiner to 8 m.; young brts. sparingly villous, soon glabrous: lfts. usually 9, ovate or elliptic-ovate to lance-elliptic, 3–7 cm. long, acuminate, rounded or subcordate at base, pubescent while young, later only sparingly so beneath: fls. lilac-purple in rather dense racemes 15–35 cm. long; bracts oblong-lanceolate, acuminate; pedicels glandular-pubescent; calyx with the lower teeth at least half as long as tube; standard not prominently auricled; wings with subulate spur about as long as claw: pod 7–12 cm. long, somewhat torulose. Fl.vi–vii. R.H.1862:12,t(c, as *W. fr. Bachousiana*). H.F.1855:t.19(c). F.S.11:t.1151(c). (*W. frutescens* var. *m.* Torr. & Gray, *Kraunhia m.* Small, *Bradleia m.* Small, *W. fr.* var. *magnifica* Herincq.) Mo. to Tenn. and Tex. Cult. 1855, Zone V or VI.—**W. m. albolilácina** (Dipp.) Rehd., f. With lighter colored lilac pinkish fls.

6. **W. japónica** Sieb. & Zucc. Slender twining shrub: brts. glabrous: lfts. 9–13, ovate to ovate-lanceolate, 3–6 cm. long, obtusely acuminate, rounded or subcordate at base, glabrous and lustrous green: fls. white, about 1.2 cm. long, in slender axillary, often branching racemes 15–30 cm. long; calyx glabrous except the ciliate margin, 5 mm. long: pod 8–10 cm. long, glabrous, 6–7-seeded. Fl.vii–viii. S.Z.1:t.43(c). D.L.3:698. S.H.2:f.46a-e,47a. (*Millettia j.* Gray, *Kraunhia j.* Taub.) Japan. Intr. 1878. Zone VII?—Less showy than the preceding species.

27. **ROBÍNIA** L. Deciduous trees or shrubs; winter-buds naked, small, hidden by the base of petiole before leaf-fall, terminal bud wanting; brts. usually with stipular spines: lvs. odd-pinnate; lfts. opposite, petioluled, stipellate: fls. white to pink or pale purple, slender-stalked in pendulous racemes; calyx campanulate, 5-toothed and slightly 2-lipped; standard suborbicular, reflexed; wings curved; keel incurved, its petals united below; upper stamen free or partly free: pod oblong or linear-oblong, flat, 2-valved, with several seeds. (After Jean Robin (1550–1629) and Vespasien R. (1579–1600), herbalists to the king of France.) About 20 species in N. Am. and Mex.—Ornamental trees and shrubs planted chiefly for their showy, often fragrant fls.

A. Brts. glabrous or pubescent.
  B. Pod smooth: brts. glabrate: fls. white (pink in one var.); brts. with stipular spines, glabrous or glabrescent..1. *R. Pseudoacacia*
  BB. Pod hispid or glandular (except in *R. neo-mexicana* under No. 8).
    C. Brts. glabrous or minutely pubescent at first.
      D. Brts. without stipular spines; peduncles glabrous.................2. *R. Boyntonii*
      DD. Brts. with stipular spines; peduncles sparingly glandular-hairy: lfts. glabrous.
                                                                            3. *R. Kelseyi*
    CC. Brts. tomentose when young; peduncles and lfts. beneath grayish pubescent.
                                                                            4. *R. Elliottii*
AA. Peduncles and brts. more or less hispid, glandular or viscid: pod hispid; fls. pink to purple.
  B. Peduncles and brts. hispid or the latter sometimes glabrous: lfts. 7–15.
    C. Brts. and lf.-rachis pubescent and hispid.............................5. *R. longiloba*
    CC. Brts. lf.-rachis and peduncles merely hispid.
      D. Lfts. suborbicular to oval, rounded at apex, glabrous...............6. *R. hispida*
      DD. Lfts. elliptic-ovate to oblong-ovate, acute to obtusish, slightly pubescent beneath.
                                                                            7. *R. fertilis*

BB. Peduncles and brts. glandular-pubescent or viscid: lfts. 13–25.
  c. Rachis of leaf pubescent, glandless, or nearly so: brs. with stipular spines.
                                                   8. *R. luxurians*
  cc. Rachis of lf. glandular or viscid.
    D. Brts., peduncles and petioles puberulous and stipitate-glandular..9. *R. Hartwigii*
    DD. Brts., peduncles and petioles glandular-viscid.......................10. *R. viscosa*

1. **R. Pseudoacàcia** L. Black Locust. Tree to 25 m. with deeply furrowed brown bark; brts. glabrous or slightly pubescent at first: lfts. 7–19, elliptic or ovate, 2.5–4.5 cm. long, rounded or truncate and mucronate at apex, glabrous beneath or slightly pubescent when young: fls. white, very fragrant, 1.5–2 cm. long, in dense racemes 10–20 cm. long; standard with yellow spot at base: pod linear-oblong, 5–10 cm. long, smooth, 3–10-seeded. Fl.VI; fr.IX. H.W.3:104(h),t.58(c). S.S.3:t.112,113. F.E.32:393(h). Gn.61:60(h). R.H. 1919:280,t(h). (False Acacia, Yellow Locust.) Pa. to Ga., w. to Iowa, Mo. and Okla.; naturalized elsewhere in N. Am. and also in Eu. Intr. about 1635. Zone III. Often planted as an ornamental tree chiefly for its fragrant fls., and the many garden forms for their various ornamental qualities; also used for shelter plantations and for afforestation purposes on dry sandy soil.— **R. P. aùrea** Kirchn., f. Lvs. yellow.—**R. P. purpúrea** Schneid., var. Young lvs. purple.—**R. P. coluteoìdes** Neum. Lfts. smaller, oblong-obovate, rounded at apex, cuneate; very floriferous. G.C.64:219. Orig. before 1857.—**R. P. amorphifòlia** Link, var. Lfts. narrow, oblong. Orig. before 1820.—**R. P. microphýlla** Loud., var. Lfts. small and narrow. G.W.2:219. (*R. P. angustifolia* Hort., *R.P. elegantissima* Hort.) Orig. before 1838.—**R. P. myrtifòlia** (K. Koch) Schneid., var. Lfts. 11–19, oval or broadly oval, 1–1.5 cm. long, rounded or slightly emarginate at apex. S.H.2:f.51f(l). Orig. about 1850.— **R. P. crispa** DC., var. Lfts. with undulate and curled margin. Orig. before 1825.—**R. P. lineàris** Kirchn., f. Lfts. linear: of spreading slender habit.— **R. P. dissecta** Mottet. Lfts. linear or broader and dissected: of compact habit with short brs.—**R. P. unifolíola** Talou. Lvs. with one large lft. or occasionally with 2–7. R.H.1860:630,631. (*R. P. monophylla* Carr., *R. P.* var. *heterophylla* Bean.) Orig. 1858.—**R. P. erécta** Rehd., f. Of columnar habit; lvs. with one or few large lfts. (*R. P. monophylla fastigiata* Dieck.) Orig. about 1880.—**R. P. depéndens** Rehd. Of pendulous habit; lvs. with one or few large lfts. (*R. P. monophylla pendula* Dieck.) Orig. about 1880.—**R. P. inérmis** DC. Brs. unarmed. (*R. spectabilis* Dum.-Cours., *R. inermis* Mirbel.) Orig. before 1804.—**R. P. umbraculífera** (DC.) DC., var. Brs. forming a dense subglobose head, unarmed; rarely flowering. M.G.18:630(h). (*R. inermis* Dum.-Cours.) Orig. before 1810. Much used in Europe grafted high for formal plantations and as an avenue tree for narrow streets.—**R. P. Rehdérii** Kirchn., f. A low subglobose form, usually grown on its own roots. G.W. 2:217(h). N.V.12:74,t(h). Orig. 1842.—**R. P. Bessoniàna** Kirchn., f. Similar to *R. P. umbraculifera*, but with slenderer brs. forming a less dense head of more ovoid outline. S.L.314(h). Orig. before 1864.—**R. P. tortuòsa** DC. A slow-growing form with short twisted brs., sometimes pendulous at the tips. G.W.2:218(h). S.L.314(h). Orig. before 1810.—**R. P. Rozynskyàna** Spaeth. Lvs. 25–40 cm. long, pendulous; lfts. 15–21, oblong, 3–6 cm. long: racemes long: fls. large. Gs.7:153(h). Cult. 1920.—**R. P. péndula** Loud., var. With somewhat pendulous brs. Orig. before 1820.—**R. P. Ulriciàna** Hartwig. With slenderer, more decidedly pendulous brs. Orig. before 1890. —**R. P. pyramidàlis** Pepin. A columnar form with unarmed, erect brs. Gt. 6:190(h). I.H.6:20(h). B.H.14:27(h). Gn.83:193(h). G.C.41:151(h). (*R. P. fastigiata* Lem., not Neum.) Orig. before 1850.—**R. P. stricta** Link, var. A pyramidal form with ascending brs. Orig. before 1820.—**R. P. sem-**

offoff*Robinia*   LEGUMINOSAE   *Robinia*

perflòrens Carr. Flowering during the whole summer. R.H.1875:191. Orig. before 1875.—**R. P. Decaisneàna** Carr. Fls. light rose-colored. R.H.1863: 151,t(c). F.S.19:2027(c). Gn.9:36,t(c);34:174. Orig. before 1860.

R. P. × *? hispida* = R. Margarétta Ashe. Shrub; lfts. pubescent beneath: fls. light pink, about 2 cm. long; rachis, pedicels and calyx pubescent and slightly glandular: pod roughened. S. C. Cult. 1920. Zone VI?—*R. P.* × *Kelseyi;* see under No. 3.—*R. P.* × *luxurians;* see under No. 8.—*R. P.* × *viscosa;* see under No. 10.

2. **R. Boyntónii** Ashe. Shrub to 3 m.; brts. unarmed, glabrous or minutely pubescent: lfts. 7–13, elliptic to oblong, 1.5–2.5 cm. long, obtuse, soon glabrous; rachis slightly pubescent: fls. pink or rose-purple with white, about 2 cm. long, in rather loose, 8–10-fld. racemes; calyx-lobes ovate, shorter than tube: pod glandular-hispid. Fl.v–vi. (*R. hispida rosea* Hort.) N. C. and Tenn. to Ga. and Ala. Intr. 1914. Zone V.

Related species: **R. nàna** Ell. Shrub to 30 cm.; brts. minutely pubescent or nearly glabrous, unarmed, rarely with few short spines: lfts. 7–11, elliptic or elliptic-ovate, acutish or obtuse, glabrous: fls. 3–5; calyx-lobes caudate-acuminate, longer than the sparingly pubescent tube; peduncle slightly glandular-hispid. S. C. Cult. 1925. Zone V.

3. **R. Kélseyi** Hutchins. Shrub to 3 m.; brts. glabrous, with slender prickles: lfts. 9–11, oblong-lanceolate, 2–3.5 cm. long, acute, glabrous: fls. rose-colored, 2–2.5 cm. long, in 5–8-fld. racemes; rachis and pedicels sparingly glandular-hairy; calyx finely pubescent, often with glandular hairs, lobes longer than tube: pod oblong, 3.5–5 cm. long; densely covered with purple glandular hairs. Fl.v–vi. B.M.8213(c). Add.1:t.3(c). G.C.44:427(h);47:391; 58:72;61:237(h). M.D.25:101. R.H.1919:339(h). N. C. Intr. 1901. Zone V. Handsome and graceful shrub.

R. K. × *Pseudoacacia* = R. Slavínii Rehd. Lfts. broader, acutish to obtuse: fls. rosy pink; rachis slightly villous, not glandular: pod roughened by minute tubercles. Orig. 1915.

4. **R. Ellióttii** Ashe. Shrub to 1.5 m.; stems virgate with short brs. near summit; brts. with short spines, densely grayish pubescent when young: lfts. 11–15, elliptic, 1.5–2.5 cm. long, grayish pubescent beneath: fls. rose-purple or purple and white, 2–2.3 cm. long, in 5–10-fld. racemes; peduncles, pedicels and calyx grayish pubescent, lobes shorter than tube: pod linear, hispid. Fl.v–vi. (*R. hispida* var. *rosea* Ell.) N. C. to Ga. Intr. about 1901. Zone VI?

5. **R. longíloba** Ashe. Shrub to 60 cm.; brts. loosely villous and more or less hispid, vigorous shoots sometimes with stipular spines: lfts. 7–17, oval, 3.5–5 cm. long, obtuse at ends, mucronate, silky-pubescent beneath, becoming glabrate; rachis slightly pubescent: infl. 7–21-fld., glandular-hispid, corolla rose or purple, about 2 cm. long; calyx puberulous and glandular-hispid; lobes ovate, long-acuminate, longer than tube. N. and S. C. Cult. 1908. Zone V.

Related species: **R. Ashei** Schallert. Shrub to 3 m., similar to the preceding: racemes longer, 18–32-fld.; fls. rose-purple; calyx-lobes 8–10 mm. long. S. C. Cult. 1934.—**R. speciòsa** Ashe. Shrub to 2 m.; brts. densely whitish pubescent and bristly: lf.-rachis densely puberulous, not bristly; lfts. ovate to oval, acute to obtuse; villous beneath, later glabrate: fls. rose, 2–2.5 cm. long, rachis densely puberulous and hispid; calyx-lobes ovate, acuminate, shorter than tube. N. C. Cult. 1925.—**R. pállida** Ashe. Shrub to 20 cm.; brts. densely puberulous, sparingly bristly like the lf.-rachis: lfts. 9–15, ovate to oblong-ovate, usually acute, glabrous or slightly pubescent beneath: fls. pale rose, 5–9; calyx-teeth ovate, shorter than tube. N. C. Cult. 1925.

6. **R. híspida** L. Shrub to 1 m., stoloniferous; stems, brts. and peduncles and often petioles hispid: lfts. 7–13, suborbicular to broad-oblong, 2–3.5 cm. long, obtuse and mucronulate, glabrous or nearly so: fls. rose-colored or pale

510

purple, 2.5 cm. long, in 3–5-fld. hispid racemes: pod 5–8 cm. long, glandular-hispid, rarely developed. Fl.v–vi. Nederl. Fl. & Pom. t.49(c). F.R.2:57. B.C.5:2968. G.4:499. Va. and Ky. to Ga. and Ala. Intr. 1758. Zone V. With large rosy fls.; sometimes grafted high as standard.—R. h. macrophýlla DC., var. Brts. and petioles nearly destitute of bristles; lfts. and fls. somewhat larger. Gn.77:268. G.M.45:512.

Related species: R. pauciflòra Ashe. Shrub to 40 cm.; brts. hispid: lfts. 7–11, ovate or oval, rounded at ends, glabrous: fls. pale bluish purple, 1–4, on slender sparingly hispid peduncles. Tenn. Intr. ?

7. **R. fértilis** Ashe. Shrub to 2 m., stoloniferous; stems, brts., peduncles and petioles hispid; lfts. 9–15, elliptic to oblong-ovate or oblong, 2–5 cm. long, acute to obtusish, mucronate, slightly pubescent beneath when young: fls. rosy-pink, 2–2.5 cm. long; pedicels 5–8 mm. long, like the calyx densely hispid; calyx-lobes lanceolate, about half as long as tube: pod 5–7 cm. long, densely hispid. Fl.vi. (*R. hispida* var. *f.* Clausen.) N. C. to Ga. Cult. 1900. Zone V. Similar to No. 6, but with smaller fls. and freely fruiting.

8. **R. luxùrians** (Dieck) Schneid. Shrub or small tree, to 10 m.; brts. with stipular spines, glandular-pubescent when young: lfts. 15–21, elliptic-oblong or oval, 2–3.5 cm. long, rounded and mucronate or acutish silky-pubescent beneath, at least while young; petioles villous: fls. pale rose-colored or nearly white, about 2 cm. long, in dense, many-fld. racemes; peduncles and pedicels glandular-pubescent; calyx-lobes triangular, upper lip with short acute teeth; pod 6–10 cm. long, glandular-hispid. Fl.vi–viii. B.M.7726(c). S.S.3: t.114. Gt.41:t.1385(c). R.H.1895:112,t(c). S.L.313(h). For. & Irrig. 13:89 (h). (*R. neo-mexicana* var. *l.* Dieck, *R. neo-mexicana* Auth., not Gray.) Colo. to N. Mex., Ariz. and Utah. Intr. 1881. Zone IV.

R. l. × *Pseudoacacia* = R. Holdtii Beiss. Tree: lfts. 3.5–5 cm. long, rather dark and firm: fls. light pink to rose-colored, in less dense racemes: pod with scattered stalked glands. (*R. coloradensis* Dode.) Orig. about 1890.—R. H. britzénsis Spaeth. Fls. whitish. Orig. before 1900.

Related species: R. neo-mexicàna Gray. Shrub to 2 m.; brts. and lf.-rachis grayish puberulous: lfts. 9–15, elliptic to elliptic-lanceolate, 1–4 cm. long, obtuse to acutish, strigulose on both sides: infl. pubescent and glandular-hispid: pod sparingly pilose, not glandular, reticulate. N. Mex. Intr. 1921. Zone V.

9. **R. Hartwígii** Koehne. Shrub to 4 m.; brts., petioles and peduncles densely stipitate-glandular and puberulous: lfts. 13–23, elliptic to lanceolate, 2–3.5 cm. long, mucronate, loosely pubescent above and grayish pubescent beneath: fls. whitish to rosy purple, about 2 cm. long, in rather dense racemes without the peduncle 5–7 cm. long; calyx pubescent and stipitate-glandular; pod oblong, 5–9 cm. long, glandular-bristly and pubescent. Fl.vi. N. C. to Ala. Cult. 1904. Zone V.

10. **R. viscòsa** Vent. Tree to 12 m.; the dark red-brown brts. and usually the petioles and peduncles densely glandular-viscid; stipular spines small or wanting: lfts. 13–25, ovate, 2.5–4 cm. long, obtuse or acute, broad-cuneate at base, pubescent beneath or sometimes glabrous: fls. about 2 cm. long, pink with yellow blotch on standard, in 6–16-fld. racemes 5–8 cm. long; calyx dark red, pubescent: pod narrow-oblong, 5–8 cm. long, sparingly glandular-hispid. Fl.v–vi. B.M.560(c). R.I.22:t.143r–ii(c). S.S.3:t.115. B.S.2:413. (*R. glutinosa* Sims.) N. C. to Ala. Intr. 1791. Zone III.

R. v. × *Pseudoacacia* = R. ambígua Poir. Tree; brts. only slightly viscid, with small spines; lfts. 13–21: fls. light pink. (*R. dubia* Foucault, *R. intermedia* Soul.-Bod.) R.I.22:t.144(c). Add.19:t.624(c). Gn.89:717(h). Orig. before 1812.—R. a. bella-ròsea (Nichols.) Rehd., var. Brts. more viscid: fls. larger and of deeper color. (*R. bella-rosea* Nichols., *R. viscosa* var. *b.* (Nichols.) Voss.) Orig. before 1880.

28. **CARMICHAÈLIA** R. Br. Upright or prostrate shrubs with rush-like or flattened brs.; lvs. of 1–5 lfts., deciduous, often absent: fls. small, in lateral racemes, rarely solitary; calyx campanulate or cup-shaped, 5-toothed; standard orbicular, reflexed, contracted into a short claw; wings curved, auricled at base; keel incurved, obtuse; upper stamen free; style glabrous: pod narrow oblong, rarely nearly orbicular; the face of the valves separating from the thick edges; seeds 1–12, reniform or oblong. (After Dugald Carmichael; 1772–1827.) About 18 species in New Zealand.

C. austràlis R. Br. Upright shrub to 4 m., glabrous, usually leafless; brts. flattened, 3–6 mm. broad, notched: lvs. only on young plants, with 1–5 obcordate lfts. 6–12 mm. long: fls. in short, 3–12-fld. racemes, pale purplish, about 4 mm. long; standard broader than long, emarginate: pod elliptic, flat, about 1 cm. long, beaked; seeds 1–4, red, usually spotted black. Fl.vi–vii. B.R.11:912(c). E.N.III.3:278. N. Zeal. Cult. 1826. Zone VII?

29. **COLÙTEA** L. BLADDER-SENNA. Deciduous unarmed or rarely spiny shrubs; winter-buds small, globose-ovoid, with 2–4 outer scales; brs. with fibrous or flaky bark: lvs. odd-pinnate, with rather small entire lfts.; stipules small: fls. yellow to brownish red, in axillary long-peduncled few-fld. racemes; calyx campanulate, with 5 subequal teeth or the two upper ones shorter; standards suborbicular with two swellings above the claw; petals of keel with partly connate claws; upper stamen free; ovary stipitate; style incurved, bearded near apex, with the stigma below the apex: pod inflated, with papery walls, indehiscent, sometimes open at apex. (*Koloutea*, ancient Greek name of a leguminous tree.) About 10 species from S. Eu. to W. Himal.

A. Pod closed at apex: lfts. 1.5–3 cm. long.
  B. Fls. yellow.
    c. Wings as long or shorter than keel...................................1. *C. arborescens*
    cc. Wings longer than keel...2. *C. cilicica*
  BB. Fls. more or less reddish or brownish...................................3. *C. media*
AA. Pod and ovary open at apex: lfts. usually small, thickish with obscure veins.
  B. Fls. yellow ....4. *C. gracilis*
  BB. Fls. reddish orange to orange-brown...................................5. *C. orientalis*

1. **C. arboréscens** L. Shrub to 4 m.; young brts. pubescent: lfts. 9–13, elliptic to obovate, 1.5–3 cm. long, usually emarginate and mucronate, bright green above, slightly pubescent and paler beneath, membranous, with fairly distinct venation: fls. about 2 cm. long, bright yellow; standard with red markings, in 6–8-fld. racemes; peduncle 2–4 cm. long; pedicels about 1 cm. long; ovary thinly pubescent: fr. glabrescent, greenish or slightly reddish near base, 6–8 cm. long. Fl.v–vii; fr.vii–x. B.M.81(c). S.O.2:t.117(c). R.I. 22:t.141(c). E.N.III.3:282. B.C.2:834. S. Eu., N. Afr. Intr. 1570. Zone V.—
C. a. crispa Kirchn., f. Slow growing form, the lvs. with undulate margin.—
C. a. bullàta Rehd., f. Dwarf and compact: lfts. 5–7, obovate or nearly orbicular and somewhat bullate, 8–15 mm. long.

C. a. × *orientalis;* see No. 3.
Closely related species: **C. brevialàta** Lange. Lower; lfts. usually 11, smaller: fls. 1.2–1.5 cm. long, in 2–6-fld. racemes; wings much shorter than keel and standard. S.H.2:f.53k-m,54a. S. France. Cult. 1860.

2. **C. cilícica** Boiss. Shrub similar to the preceding: lfts. usually 11, oval or obovate, 1–2 cm. long, rounded or truncate and mucronate at apex, slightly hairy beneath, bluish green: fls. yellow, in 3–5-fld. racemes; wings longer than keel. Fl.vi–vii. G.C.III.16:155. S.H.2:f.54h-k,55a-e. (*C. longialata* Koehne, *C. melanocalyx* Hort.) Asia Minor. Cult. 1892. Zone V.

Related species: **C. melanócalyx** Boiss. Lfts. 7–11, broad-elliptic, emarginate, more pubescent beneath: fls. smaller; calyx densely dark brown-pubescent, with broader triangular teeth; wings slightly longer than keel; pod about

5 cm. long. S.H.2:f.54l-m,55f-i. Asia Minor. Cult. 1905. Zone V or VI.—**C. ístria** Mill. Shrub to 2 m.: lfts. 9–13, sometimes to 19, about 1 cm. long: fls. orange-yellow, about 2 cm. long, in 1–4-fld. racemes. S.O.2:t.120(c). S.H.2:f. 53e-i,54p. (*C. halepica* Lam., *C. Pocockii* Ait.) Asia Minor. Intr. 1752. Zon¬ VII?

3. × **C. mèdia** Willd. (*C. arborescens* × *orientalis*). Similar to *C. arborescens:* lfts., 11–13, obovate, 1.5–2.5 cm. long, pubescent beneath, bluish green: fls. brownish red or deep orange, 1.5 cm. long; pod 6–7 cm. long, usually closed at apex, tinged purple. L.D.8:524(c). S.O.2:t.118(c). R.I. 22:t.140(c). Orig. before 1790. Zone V. Often cult. as *C. orientalis.*

4. **C. grácilis** Freyn & Sint. Shrub to 3 m.; young brts. pubescent: lfts. 7–9, obovate, 4–8 mm. long, appressed-pubescent beneath: fls. yellow, 1.2–1.5 cm. long, in 1–4-fld. racemes; wing about as long as keel; keel not rostrate; calyx pubescent with dark hairs; ovary pubescent: pod 3–4 cm. long. S.H.2:f. 56i-k,57a-e. Transcaspia. Cult. 1911. Zone VI?

Related species: **C. pérsica** Boiss. Young brts. glabrous: lfts. 7–13, obovate or broad-obovate, 8–15 mm. long, nearly glabrous beneath, thickish: fls. 2 cm. long; calyx sparingly pubescent; ovary usually glabrous. S.H.2:f.55o-q,56g-h. Kurdistan, Persia. Cult. 1902.—**C. p. Bùhsei** Boiss., var. Lvs. and fls. somewhat larger: pod with scattered appressed hairs. Cult. 1925.—**C. nepalénsis** Sims. Young brts. nearly glabrous: lfts. 9–13, oval, 6–12 mm. long, rounded at apex; pubescent above: fls. about 2 cm. long, in 3–4-fld. drooping racemes: keel rostrate. B.M.2622(c). B.R.1727(c). Afghan. to Nepal. Cult. 1822. Zone VII?

5. **C. orientàlis** Mill. Shrub to 2 m.; young brts. pubescent: lfts. 7–11, broad-obovate, 8–15 mm. long, rounded or emarginate at apex, cuneate, glabrous above, slightly pubescent beneath when young, glaucous, thickish: fls. reddish brown, 1.5 cm. long, in 2–5-fld. racemes; standard with yellow blotch; wings shorter than keel; calyx slightly pubescent: pod 3–3.5 cm. long, usually suffused with violet-purple. Fl.vi–ix. (*C. cruenta* Ait.) S.O.2:t. 119(c). R.I.22:t.142(c). S.L.134(h). Cauc. to Turkest. Intr. 1710. Zone V. Conspicuous by its pale glaucous foliage.

C. o. × *arborescens;* see No. 3.

30. **HALIMODÉNDRON** Fisch. Deciduous shrub; winter-buds ovoid with several outer scales: lvs. abruptly pinnate, with 2 or 4 sessile lfts. and a persistent usually spinescent rachis; stipules subulate, spinescent: fls. pale purple or lilac, in lateral slender-stalked, 2–3-fld, racemes; calyx cup-shaped with 5 short teeth; petals of nearly equal length; standard orbicular, with reflexed sides; keel obtuse, curved; upper stamen free; ovary stipitate, with many ovules; style curved with small terminal stigma: pod obovoid to oblong, inflated, with leathery thick walls, abruptly short-rostrate. (Greek *halimos,* maritime, and *dendron,* tree; referring to its habitat on saline soil.) One species.

H. halodéndron (L.) Voss. SALT-TREE. Shrub to 2 m., with spreading spiny brs. silky pubescent when young: lfts. oblanceolate, 1.5–3.5 cm. long, rounded or mucronate at apex, cuneate, grayish or bluish green, minutely silky or sometimes glabrous: fls. 1.5–1.8 cm. long; calyx pubescent, persistent: fr. 1.5–2.5 cm. long, brownish yellow. Fl.vi–vii. B.M.1016(c). G.O.t.69(c). S.O.1:t.35(c). (*H. argenteum* Fisch.) Transcauc. to Turkest. and Altai. Intr. 1779. Zone II. Handsome and graceful in bloom.—**H. h. purpúreum** Schneid., f. Fls. rosy purple. (*H. speciosum* Carr.) R.H.1876:30,t(c). Orig. before 1876.

31. **CARAGÀNA** Lam. Deciduous shrubs; winter-buds ovoid, with several outer scales; lvs. often fascicled, abruptly pinnate, with 2–18 small entire

lfts.; rachis often persistent and spiny; stipules small, deciduous or persistent and spiny: fls. yellow, rarely whitish or pinkish, solitary or fascicled; calyx tubular or campanulate with nearly equal teeth, the 2 upper usually smaller; standard upright, with recurved sides, like the wings with long claws; keel straight; upper stamen free; ovary subsessile, rarely stipitate; style straight or slightly curved, with small terminal stigma: pod linear, terete or inflated, usually pointed; seed obliquely ellipsoid or subglobose. (Caragan, the Mongolian name of the plant.) More than 50 species from s. Russia to China and Manchuria and Himal. Monograph by Komarov in Act. Hort. Petrop. 29:179–388,16pl.(1908) cited below as A.H.P.—Planted as ornamental shrubs chiefly for their profusely produced bright yellow fls.

A. Lfts. 6–18, or partly 4 on same plant.
  B. Rachis of lf. deciduous.
    c. Lfts. 12–18, 3–8 mm. long...1. *C. microphylla*
    cc. Lfts. 8–14.
      D. Spiny stipules much shorter than petioles; lfts. 1–2.5 cm. long; rachis 3.5–8 cm.
        long ....2. *C. arborescens*
      DD. Spiny stipules usually about half as long as petiole; rachis 1–3 cm. long; lfts. 6–12
        mm. long ....3. *C. decorticans*
  BB. Rachis of lf. persistent, spiny.
    c. Fls. 3–4 on a common peduncle; lfts. 10–14; stipules spinescent......4. *C. brevispina*
    cc. Fls. solitary.
      D. Stipules membranous: fls. whitish or pale yellow; pedicels articulate at base.
        E. Lfts. 8–18 mm. long; auricles of wing as long as claw: brs. very thick, covered
          with crowded lf.-bases and spines...................................5. *C. jubata*
        EE. Lfts. 4–6 mm. long; auricles of wings much shorter than claw; brs. slenderer.
                                     6. *C. Gerardiana*
      DD. Stipules spinescent: fls. bright yellow; wings with short or without auricles;
        pedicels articulate near the middle.
        E. Lvs. pinnate with 4–6 lfts.; spiny rachis short............7. *C. Maximowicziana*
        EE. Lvs. dimorphic, pinnate and nearly digitate on same branch; spiny rachis 2–6
          cm. long ....8. *C. spinosa*
AA. Lfts. always 2 or 4.
  B. Lfts. in 2 remote pairs, obovate; stipules spinescent....................9. *C. Chamlagu*
  BB. Lfts. 2–4, close together, almost digitate.
    c. Lvs. stalked; lfts. 1.5–3 cm. long, usually obovate, obtuse..............10. *C. frutex*
    cc. Lvs. nearly sessile; lfts. 5–10 mm. long, narrow, acute................11. *C. pygmaea*

1. **C. microphýlla** Lam. Shrub to 3 m., with long spreading brs.; young brts. finely silky: lfts. 12–18, oval to obovate, 3–8 mm. long, rounded or emarginate at apex, silky-pubescent at first, grayish green: fls. 1–2, yellow, about 2 cm. long; pedicels 1.5–2.5 cm. long; calyx finely pubescent, tubular with short teeth: pod 2.5–3 cm. long. Fl.v–vi. L.B.1064(c). Gt.10:t.366. B.C. 2:660. (*C. Altagana* Poir.) Siberia, N. China. Intr. 1789. Zone III. Graceful shrub.—**C. m. megalántha** Schneid., var. Lfts. orbicular-obovate, to 1.2 cm. long, or elliptic and to 1.5 cm. long, less pubescent, bright green: fls. about 3 cm. long, pod 3–4 cm. long.

    C. m. × *arborescens;* see under No. 2.

2. **C. arboréscens** Lam. PEA-TREE. Shrub or small tree to 6 m., of upright habit; young brts. pubescent: lfts. 8–12, obovate to elliptic-oblong, 1–2.5 cm. long, rounded at apex and mucronate, pubescent when young, later glabrescent, bright green: fls. 1–4, fascicled, yellow, 1.5–2 cm. long, on pedicels 1.5–2.5 cm. long; calyx with very short teeth: pod 3.5–5 cm. long. Fl.v. G.O.t.67(c). S.O.1:t.33(c). N.D.2:t.19(c). Siberia, Manch. Intr. 1752. Zone II. Much grown for hedges and shelter plantations in the N. W.—**C. a. Lorbérgii** Koehne, f. Lfts. linear, 2–2.5 cm. long; standard and wings narrower. Orig. before 1906. Remarkable and graceful form.—**C. a. péndula** Carr. With stiffly pendent brs.; usually grafted high. M.G.12:425(h). F.E. 91,4:19(h). Orig. 1854.—**C. a. nàna** Jaeg., var. Dwarf stunted shrub with contorted brs. Orig. before 1875.

C. a. × *microphylla* = **C. sophoraefòlia** Tausch. Lfts. usually 12, elliptic to oblong, 8–15 mm. long, cuneate, mucronate: pods about 2 cm. long. (*C. cuneifolia* Dipp., *C. arborescens* var. *c.* Schneid.) Orig. before 1816.

Related species: **C. fruticòsa** (Pall.) Steud. Shrub to 2 m.: lfts. 8–14, oblong to obovate, 1.5–2.5 cm. long, cuneate at base, rounded or acute at apex; stipules herbaceous or slightly spiny: fls. solitary, larger, on longer puberulous peduncles; calyx puberulous, with very short teeth: pod 2–3 cm. long; seeds brown. (*C. arborescens* var. *f.* Dipp., *C. Redowskii* DC.) Amurl., Korea. Cult. 1817.

3. **C. decórticans** Hemsl. Shrub or small tree; bark greenish; stipules spiny, brown, 3–8 mm. long: rachis spiny-pointed; lfts. 6–12, elliptic to obovate, 6–15 mm. long, spiny-mucronate, appressed-puberulous, reticulate: fls. 2.5 cm. long, on slender pedicels to 2 cm. long; calyx campanulate, with triangular spiny-aristate teeth; wings with a spur-like auricle: pod 3–4 cm. long. Fl.vi. H.I.1725. A.H.P.29:t.14A. S.H.2:f.59o-q[1],62a. Afghan. Intr. 1879. Zone V.

Related species: **C. Boìsii** Schneid. Shrub to 2 m.; stipules spiny, to 1 cm. long: lfts. 10–12, obovate to narrow-obovate, 4–18 mm. long, dark green above, light grayish green and slightly pubescent beneath, of firm texture: calyx-teeth not spiny; ovary pubescent. A.H.P.29:t.15B. V.F.57. S.L.2:131(h). (*C. microphylla* var. *crasse-aculeata* Bois.) W. China. Intr. 1895. Zone V.—**C. pekinénsis** Komar. Shrub to 2 m.; stipules spiny, 5–10 mm. long; lfts. 6–12, obovate or elliptic to elliptic-oblong, 8–12 mm. long, mucronulate, grayish pubescent on both sides: calyx tubular, villous, teeth short, not spiny: pod silky-puberulous. N. E. China. A.H.P.29:t.15C. Intr. 1923. Zone V.

4. **C. brevispìna** Royle. Shrub to 2.5 m.; young brts. puberulous: lfts. 10–14, elliptic-oblong to oblong, 8–25 mm. long, rounded at apex, silky when young, nearly glabrous at maturity; rachis 3–7 cm. long, persistent, spiny; stipules spiny, about 6 mm. long: fls. yellow, nearly 2 cm. long, 2–4 on a common peduncle; pedicels with long subulate bractlets; calyx villous, with deltoid, long-acuminate teeth: pod about 5 cm. long, villous inside and slightly so outside. Fl.vi. P.F.2:148. (*C. triflora* Lindl.) N. W. Himal. Intr. before 1850. Zone VII?

Related species: **C. sukiénsis** Schneid. Lfts. 10–14, linear-lanceolate, about 8 mm. long, acute at ends, with prominent lateral nerves and long silky hairs beneath; rachis about 3 cm. long, spiny; stipules membranous: fls. solitary, about 2.5 cm. long; peduncles 3–6 mm. long; pod about 1.5 cm. long, slightly pubescent. N. W. Himal. Intr. 1919. Zone VI?

5. **C. jubàta** (Pall.) Poir. Shrub to 1 or occasionally 5 m. tall, with few upright, sparingly branched stems; brs. thick, densely covered with crowded spines and stipules and shaggy tomentum; stipules scarious with setaceous apex: lfts. 8–14, oblong, 6–18 mm. long, villous, with narrow-triangular teeth; ovary villous: pod about 2 cm. long, hairy. Fl.iv–v. Gt.10:t.331. F.S.19:t. 2013(c). L.B.522(c). S.L.113(h). E. Siberia to W. China and Turkest. Intr. 1796. Zone II. Grown for its odd and curious appearance.

6. **C. Gerardiàna** Royle. Compact, much-branched shrub to 1 m.; brts. densely pubescent when young, close-jointed; stipules scarious; rachis spiny, to 5 cm. long: lfts. 8–12, obovate to oblong-oblanceolate, 5–10 mm. long, mucronate, silky-pubescent: fls. solitary, 2–2.5 cm. long, pale yellow, short-stalked; calyx cylindric, about 1 cm. long, pubescent, with deltoid, cuspidate lobes; wings with short auricle: pod villous, 2–3 cm. long. Fl.iv–v. Jacquemont, Voy. Bot. t.43. A.H.P.29:t.13B. S.L.114(h). (*C. spinosissima* Benth.) N. W. Himal. Intr. before 1870. Zone VI. Remarkable for its long spines and the thick tomentum of its brts.

Related species: **C. Franchetiàna** Komar. Shrub to 3 m.; spiny rachises stout, remote: lfts. 8–10, narrow-obovate to lanceolate, glabrescent above; peduncle with 3 bractlets; calyx with triangular-lanceolate lobes nearly as long as tube; wings with a slender auricle as long as claw and on the upper side with

a slender tooth: pod pubescent, 3–4 cm. long. A.H.P. 29:t.13A. S. W. China.
Intr. 1914. Zone VI?—**C. oreóphila** W. W. Sm. Lfts. usually 16, oblong or oblong-obovate, 5–7 mm. long, silky-villous: corolla nearly 2 cm. long, wings with
a slender auricle: pod about 2 cm. long. W. China. Intr. 1914. Zone VI?—
C. tibética (Maxim.) Komar. Prostrate shrub with ascending brs. to 25 cm.
high: lvs. crowded; rachis 2–3 cm. long; lfts. 6–12, linear-oblong, 5–10 mm. long,
acute, silky-pilose: fls. about 2.5 cm. long, pale yellow, wings with short auricle,
standard emarginate; calyx-teeth short. A.H.P.29:t.10. (*C. tragacanthoides*
var. *t.* Maxim.) W. China. Cult. 1927. Zone V?

7. **C. Maximowicziàna** Komar. Densely branched spreading shrub to
1.5 m. with slender red-brown glabrous or at first slightly pubescent brts.:
stipules deltoid, spinescent; rachis spiny, short; lfts. 4–6, oblong-lanceolate,
5–10 mm. long, spinulose-mucronate, bright green: fls. short-stalked, yellow,
2–2.5 cm. long; calyx cylindric, glabrous, with very short teeth; standard
narrow-obovate; wings without auricle; ovary pilose only on ventral suture.
Fl.v–vi. A.H.P.29:t.11B. W. China. Intr. 1910. Zone II. Shrub with bright
green foliage and fairly large fls.

Related species: **C. tragacanthoìdes** (Pall.) Poir. Low upright or prostrate
shrub, with pubescent spiny brs.; stipules short, spinescent; rachis spiny, to
3 cm. long: lfts. 4–10, obovate to oblanceolate, 8–15 mm. long, cuneate, appressed-
pubescent: fls. 2.5–3 cm. long; calyx broad-cylindric or campanulate, pubescent,
with triangular spinulose teeth; wings auriculate: pod 2.5–3 cm. long, twice as
long as calyx, shaggy pubescent. Pallas, Spec. Astrag. t.86. S.H.2:f.62f,63a-b.
N. W. China to Altai and N. W. Him. Intr. 1816. Zone V.

8. **C. spinòsa** (L.) DC. Shrub to 2 m. or sometimes prostrate, with long
spiny brs. pubescent when young; stipules scarious or sometimes with spinescent apex; rachis silky when young, spiny, 2.5 cm. long, spreading: lfts. 4–8,
oblong-obovate to linear-lanceolate, 8–15 mm. long, rounded or short acuminate, cuneate, slightly silky when young, later glabrate; lvs. of spurs with
4 digitate lfts.: fls. usually solitary, short-stalked, 2–2.5 cm. long; calyx
cylindric, glabrescent, with short deltoid teeth; wings linear-oblong, scarcely
auricled: pod linear-oblong, about 2 cm. long, glabrous. Fl.v–vi. N.D.2:t.
20(c). S.O.1:t.36(c). S.H.2:f.60a,63f-p. (*C. ferox* Lam., *C. spinosissima*
Lam., *C. tragacanthoides* Hort., partly.) Siberia. Intr. 1775. Zone II.—**C. s.
foliòsa** Komar., var. Lfts. crowded, longer; rachis partly persistent.

9. **C. Chamlàgu** Lam. Bushy shrub to 1.5 m., with upright and spreading
brs.: brts. angled, slender, glabrate; stipules usually spinescent, 8 mm. long;
rachis persistent, spiny or caducous: lfts. 4, obovate to cuneate-obovate,
1–3.5 cm. long, rounded or emarginate, dark green and lustrous above, glabrous, chartaceous at maturity and finely reticulate: fls. solitary, 2.5–3 cm.
long, reddish yellow; pedicels about 1 cm. long, articulate about the middle;
calyx campanulate; standard narrow-obovate; pod 3–3.5 cm. long, slightly
compressed, glabrous. Fl.v–vi. N.D.2:t.21(c). G.O.t.30(c). A.H.P.29:t.5B.
S.L.114(h). N. China. Intr. 1773. Zone II.

10. **C. frùtex** (L.) K. Koch. Upright shrub to 3 m., glabrous; brts. slender,
yellowish: lfts. 4, obovate to oblong-obovate, 1.5–2.5 cm. long, rounded or
emarginate, cuneate, membranous, dull green: fls. 1–3, bright yellow, 2–2.5
cm. long, on pedicels nearly as long as fls., articulate about the middle;
calyx campanulate: pod cylindric, 3–3.5 cm. long, glabrous. Fl.v–vi. S.O.
1:t.34(c). S.B.3:t.227(c). B.C.2:660. (*C. frutescens* DC.) S. Russia to
Turkest. and Siber. Intr. 1752. Zone II.—**C. f. macrántha** Rehd., var. Lfts.
larger, to 2.8 cm. long; fls. 2.5–3 cm. long; rachis caducous; calyx broader.
S.H.2:f.64w-y. (*C. frutescens* var. *grandiflora* Rehd., not Reg.)—**C. f. latifòlia** (DC.) Schneid., f. Lfts. to 3.2 cm. long and to 1.4 cm. broad; rachis
caducous. Gt.10:t.348. S.H.2:f.64t-v. (*C. frutescens obtusifolia* Hort.)

11. **C. pygmaèa** DC. Upright or sometimes prostrate shrub, to 1 m., with slender virgate brs., glabrous: stipules spiny, short: rachis deciduous or persistent, 5–8 mm. long: lvs. subsessile; lfts. 4, linear-oblanceolate, 8–15 mm. long, acuminate and spiny pointed: fls. solitary, about 2 cm. long; yellow, on stalks about 1 cm. long and articulate above the middle; calyx narrow-campanulate, with triangular teeth; auricle of wings very short: pod 2–3 cm. long, cylindric, glabrous. Fl.v–vi. B.R.1021(c). S.O.1:t.37(c). S.L.53(h). N. W. China and Siberia. Intr. 1751. Zone III.

Related species: **C. aurantíaca** Koehne. Very similar to the preceding; rachis persistent, about 5 mm. long; fls. 1.5–2 cm. long, orange-yellow; calyx slightly broader than long; auricle of wing at least half as long as claw. B.S. 1:289. (*C. arenaria* Dipp., *C. pygmaea aurantiaca erecta* Hort.) Siberia to Afghan. and Turkest. Cult. 1830, again intr. 1887. Zone V.—**C. grandiflòra** DC. Shrub to 1 m.; rachis persistent, 4–7 mm. long; lfts. obl ng-obovate, rounded or short-acuminate and spiny-pointed, glabrous or puber..ous: fls. 2.5–2.8 cm. long, on pedicels articulate below the middle; calyx tub·ular, saccate at base. S.H.2:t.64e-h. (*C. pygmaea* var. *g.* K. Koch.) S. Ru%ia and Cauc. to Turkest. and Song. Intr. 1823. Zone II.—**C. brevifòlia** Kom·i.. Shrub to 1.5 m.: lf.-rachis and stipules spiny; lfts. narrow-obovate to obovate-lanceolate, 2–6 mm. long, acute: fls. 1.5–1.8 cm. long; pedicels to 5 mm. long; calyx often bloomy, with deltoid spinulose lobes. A.H.P.29:t.17. N. W. China, Kashmir. Intr. 1925. Zone V.—**C. densa** Komar. Shrub to 2.5 m.: lf.-rachis and stipules spiny; lfts. linear-oblanceolate or lanceolate, 8–16 mm. long: fls. about 2 cm. long; pedicel about 5 mm. long, puberulous; calyx tubular, the deltoid teeth much shorter than tube. A.H.P.29:t.7. Intr. 1926. Zone V.

32. **CALÓPHACA** Fisch. Deciduous low shrubs or herbs: lvs. odd-pinnate with small entire lfts.; stipules scarious (in our species) or herbaceous, adnate to the petiole: fls. axillary, racemose (or 1–3 in sect. CHESNEYA Taub.); calyx tubular with 5 nearly equal teeth or the 2 upper somewhat connate; standard upright, with reflexed margin and slightly auriculate base; wings oblong, free, as long as the obtuse or emarginate keel; upper stamen free; ovary sessile, many-ovuled: pod cylindric. (Greek *kalos,* beautiful, and *phaca,* lentil.) About 10 species from S. Russia to India.

C. wolgàrica (L.) Fisch. Shrub to 1 m., often procumbent; young brts. glandular-pubescent: lvs. 5–8 cm long; lfts. 11–17, orbicular to broad-elliptic, 8–15 mm. long, rounded at endy, mucronate, pubescent beneath: fls. bright yellow, 2–2.3 cm. long, in 4–6-fld. axillary peduncled and glandular-pubescent racemes; pedicels about 3 mm. long; calyx-teeth lanceolate: pod 2–3 cm. long, glandular-pubescent, 1-2-seeded. Fl.vi–vii. B.C.2:636. S. Russia to Turkest. Intr. 1756. Zone III. Prefers sunny positions in well drained soil.

Closely related species: **C. grandiflòra** Regel. Lfts. 17–25: fls. 2.5–2.8 cm. long, in 10–16-fld. racemes: pod to 5 cm. long, less pubescent. Gt.35:t.1231(c). Turkest. Intr. about 1880. Zone V.—To sect. CHESNEYA belongs **C. crassicaùlis** (Bak.) Komar. Suffruticose, with thick short upright stems densely clothed with old lf.-rachises; stipules herbaceous; lfts. 21–25, linear-oblong, 4–6 mm. long, pubescent: fls. solitary, yellow to red, about 2 cm. long; pedicel about 1 cm. long; calyx very oblique, densely villous; standard pubescent outside. Himal., W. China. Intr. 1932. Zone VI?

33. **ASTRÁGALUS** L. Herbs or small shrubs: lvs. odd-pinnate or abruptly pinnate, rarely digitate, the shrubby species often with persistent spiny rachis; stipules free, adnate to petiole or connate and opposite to the leaf: fls. whitish, yellowish, purple or violet, in axillary racemes or heads; calyx tubular to campanulate with subequal teeth; standard upright; wings oblong adhering to the obtuse or acutish keel, their claws often adnate to the staminal tube; upper stamen usually free: ovary sessile or stipitate,

Related species: **D. spicàtum** Rehd. Lfts. short-pubescent on both sides; terminal lft. orbicular-obovate, 3–4 cm. long, abruptly mucronate at apex, the lateral ones orbicular-ovate, smaller; petioles 1–3 cm. long; stipules persistent: fls. rosy-lilac to rose-carmine in many-fld. spikes to 10 cm. long, sometimes with smaller ones at base; fr. curved, to 5 cm. long, usually 5-seeded, appressed-pubescent. Fl.ix–x. B.M.8805(c). (*D. cinerascens* Hutchins., not Franch., nor Gray.) S. W. China. Intr. 1896. Zone VII.—**D. floribúndum** G. Don. Shrub to 1.5 m.; lfts. dark green and glabrous above, gray, appressed-pilose and reticulate beneath, the terminal one elliptic or rhombic-elliptic, 5–7.5 cm. long, obtuse and mucronulate, narrowed toward the abruptly rounded base, the lateral ones smaller, rounded at base: petiole 1.5–3.5 cm. long, slightly pilose: fls. rosy-purple, in large terminal panicles; calyx-teeth ovate to lance-ovate: pod 1–2 cm. long, 3–5 seeded, appressed-pilose. Fl.xi. B.M. 2960(c). B.R.967(c). (*D. dubium* Lindl.) Himal., China. Intr. 1823 and again from China 1908. Zone VII.

38. **LESPEDÈZA** Michx. Herbs or deciduous shrubs or subshrubs; winter-buds with several outer scales: lvs. 3-foliolate, rarely 1-foliolate; lfts. entire, without stipels; stipules subulate, deciduous: fls. usually purple to pink or white to yellowish, in axillary racemes or heads, sometimes partly apetalous; pedicels not articulate, usually 2 in the axils of persistent bracts; calyx with short, subequal teeth; petals clawed; standard obovate to oblong; wings oblong, free or slightly adhering to keel; keel obtuse, incurved; upper stamen free, rarely adhering; style incurved, with small terminal stigma: pod short, ovate or elliptic, compressed, rarely subglobose, often reticulate, 1-seeded, not dehiscent. (The name is a misspelling, intended for Cespedez, a Spanish governor of Florida who aided Michaux.) More than 50 species in N. Am., Asia and Australia.

A. Lfts. 2–5 cm. long; petioles 1.5–3.5 cm.: fls. usually in slender racemes.
  B. Racemes slender-stalked: lfts. obtuse.
    c. Suffruticose: calyx-teeth longer than tube: lfts. obtuse.............1. *L. Thunbergii*
    cc. Shrubby: calyx-teeth as long or shorter than tube: lfts. acute to obtuse.2. *L. bicolor*
  BB. Racemes short-stalked or subsessile................................3. *L. Maximowiczii*
AA. Lfts. 1–2 cm. long, linear-oblanceolate: fls. yellowish, in heads..............4. *L. cuneata*

1. **L. Thunbérgii** (DC.) Nakai. Shrub to 2 m.; young brts. grooved, pubescent at first: lfts. 3, elliptic to elliptic-oblong, 3–5 cm. long, acute to obtusish, appressed-pubescent beneath, the middle one long-stalked; petiole appressed-pubescent: fls. rosy-purple, 1.2 cm. long, in racemes 8–20 cm. long, forming terminal panicles 60–80 cm. long; calyx-teeth lanceolate; standard apiculate: pod elliptic, 6–8 mm. long, silky. Fl.ix–x. B.M.6602(c). R.H. 1873:210,t(c). F.S.18:t.1888(c). G.F.5:115. B.C.4:1845. S.L.211(h). (*L. Sieboldii* Miq., *L. racemosa* Dipp., *L. formosa* Koehne in part, *Desmodium penduliflorum* Oudem.) China, Japan. Intr. 1837. Zone (V). Valued for its late profuse fls.

Closely related species: **L. japónica** Bailey. Subshrub with upright stems; lfts. obtuse to emarginate: racemes 3–12 cm. long; fls. white; standard oblong: ovary pilose. (*L. j.* var. *albiflora* Nakai, *L. formosa* var. *albiflora* Schindl.) Jap. Cult. 1900. Zone (V).—**L. j. intermèdia** (Nakai) Nakai, var. Fls. rosy-purple. Probably not in cult.

2. **L. bícolor** Turcz. Shrub to 3 m.; brts. angular, sparingly pubescent at first: lfts. 3, broad-oval to obovate, 2–5 cm. long, rounded at apex and bristle-tipped, dark green above, grayish green beneath and sparingly appressed-pubescent, the middle one long-stalked; petiole glabrous or sparingly hairy: fls. about 1 cm. long, rosy-purple, in axillary racemes with the slender stalk 4–8 cm. long, forming loose and large panicles at the end of the brs.; calyx silky, with ovate to triangular-lanceolate teeth: pod broad-elliptic, rostrate, 6–8 mm. long, slightly appressed-pubescent. Fl.viii–ix. G.F.5:114. B.C.4: 1844. S.H.2:f.70f,71a-d. N. China to Manch. and Japan. Intr. 1856. Zone IV. Handsome shrub, valuable for its late fls.

3. **L. Maximowíczii** Schneid. Shrub to 4 m.; brts. terete, pubescent when young: lfts. elliptic-ovate to ovate, 2.5–5 cm. long, acuminate or acute, rounded or broad-cuneate at base, pale and silky-pubescent beneath; petiole 1–2.5 cm. long, silky-pilose: fls. purple, 8–10 mm. long, in slender racemes 3–8 cm. long, with fls. to the base; calyx-lobes aristate, longer than tube; pedicels 1 mm. long or less: pod elliptic-lanceolate, acuminate, 1–1.5 cm. long. Fl. vii–ix; fr.ix–x. Nakai, Lespedeza, 34. (*L. Buergeri* var. *praecox* Nakai, *L. Friebeana* Schindl.) Korea. Intr. 1917. Zone V.

Related species: **L. Buèrgeri** Miq. Shrub to 6 m.: lvs. elliptic-ovate to ovate-oblong, acute to obtuse: fls. purple-lilac, in axillary racemes 4–10 cm. long, bracted to near base; calyx-lobes lanceolate or ovate, acute, about as long as tube; pedicels 1–3 mm. long. Nakai, Lespedeza, 30. S.H.2:f.70k. Jap. Intr. 1894. Zone V.—**L. cyrtobótrya** Miq. Shrub to 5 m.: lfts. elliptic to obovate, obtuse to emarginate, appressed-pubescent and glaucescent beneath; petioles on flowering brts. short: racemes dense, shorter than lvs.; fls. purple; calyx-lobes acuminate. Nakai, Lespedeza, 43,45.̈ S.H.2:f.70h(l). Jap., Korea. Intr. 1899. Zone V.—**L. Delavayi** Franch. Shrub to 2 m.: lfts. broad-elliptic, rounded at apex, silky white-tomentose beneath: fls. deep violet, changing to dark purple, in large terminal panicles; calyx densely silky. R.H.1890:216. M.O.146. S. W. China. Cult. 1890. Zone VII?

4. **L. cuneàta** G. Don. Subshrub to 1 m. with virgate brs.: lfts. 3, subsessile, linear-oblanceolate, 1–2 cm. long, cuneate, truncate or emarginate, silky-pubescent beneath; petiole 5–15 mm. long: fls. whitish, subsessile, 6 mm. long, in dense clusters shorter than the lvs.; calyx deeply divided into linear-lanceolate teeth, ⅔ as long as corolla; pod broad-oval, 1.5–2 mm. long. Fl.viii–ix. S.H.2:f.70l,71k-m. (*L. sericea* Miq., not Benth., *L. juncea* var. *cuneata* Bean.) China, Korea, Japan, Formosa, Himal. Intr. 1892. Zone V. Of little ornamental value.

39. **CAMPYLÓTROPIS** Bge. Deciduous shrubs: lvs. 3-foliolate; the terminal lfts. slender-stalked: fls. usually purple, in axillary racemes crowded into panicles at the end of the brs.; pedicels slender, solitary in the axils of deciduous or persistent bracts, articulate below the calyx; calyx campanulate, 5-parted, the 2 upper teeth connate; keel curved, rostrate: otherwise much like Lespedeza. (Greek *kampylos*, curved, and *tropis*, keel; referring to the curved keel.) About 40 species in E. and S. Asia.

C. macrocárpa (Bge.) Rehd. Shrub to 1 m.; brts. subterete, silky, pubescent when young: lfts elliptic to oblong, 2–5 cm. long, obtuse to emarginate, glabrous above, silky-pubescent below; petioles 1.5–3.5 cm. long: fls. purple, about 1 cm. long, in rather dense racemes to 8 cm. long; pedicels 5–7 mm. long; bracts deciduous; calyx-teeth acute, shorter than tube; pod elliptic, 1.2–1.5 cm. long. Fl.viii–ix. S.H.2:f.69h-l,70a. (*C. chinensis* Bge., *Lespedeza macrocarpa* Bge.) N. and C. China. Cult. 1871. Zone V. Similar to *Lespedeza Thunbergii.*

Related species: **C. Falcòneri** Schindl. Brts. striate, appressed-pubescent; lfts. obovate, 1–4 cm. long, obtuse or emarginate, pubescent beneath: fls. purple, in dense racemes, 5–20 cm. long; pedicels 2–5 mm. long; bracts persistent: pod 7–9 mm. long, densely silky-pubescent. B.R.32:28(c). (*Oxyrhamphis macrostyla* Lindl., not Wall., *Lespedeza dubia* Schindl., *L. eriocarpa* Bak., partly.) N. W. Himal. Intr. 1837 and 1920. Zone VII?

Tribe 8. PHASEOLEAE Taub. Lfts. 3, with stipels: rachis of infl. usually thickened at the insertion of the fls.: pod 2-valved, dehiscent.

40. **PUERÀRIA** DC. Twining herbs or shrubs: lvs. 3-foliolate, with large stipellate sometimes lobed lfts., stipulate: fls. blue-purple or violet in long and dense axillary racemes; bracts and bractlets small, caducous; calyx campanulate, with unequal lobes, the 2 upper ones more or less connate;

standard orbicular or obovate, auricled, clawed; wings oblong, usually adhering to the keel in the middle; upper stamen free at base, adnate at the middle, rarely free; ovary subsessile, many-ovuled; style incurved, with small terminal stigma: pod elongated, compressed or terete, 2-valved. (M. N. Puerari, botanist of Geneva; 1765–1845.) More than 10 species in trop. Asia, Japan, and Guinea.

P. Thunbergiàna (Sieb. & Zucc.) Benth. KUDZU-VINE. High climbing vine with fleshy tuberous root; brts. striped, appressed-pilose; lfts. entire or slightly lobed, the middle one rhombic-ovate, to 18 cm. long, the lateral ones obliquely ovate, smaller, appressed-pubescent, sometimes glabrescent above, ciliate; petioles 10–20 cm. long, pubescent: fls. violet-purple, 1.5 cm. long, in dense upright pubescent racemes to 25 cm. long; stamens usually all connate: pod oblong-linear, 4–9 cm. long and 6–8 mm. broad, hirsute. Fl.vii–viii. Gt. 45:t.1429(c). G.F.6:505. A.G.13:387;21:505. R.H.1891:31. Gn.61:161. G.W. 5:605. (*P. hirsuta* Schneid., not Kurz, *Pachyrhizus Thunbergianus* S. & Z.) China, Japan. Cult. 1885. Zone VI?; stems usually winter-killed, but grows again from the root. Cult. for ornament as a fast growing large-leafed vine, also as a fibre plant; the root yields starch.

Fam. 41. **ZYGOPHYLLACEAE** Lindl. CALTROP FAMILY

Shrubs, rarely trees, or subshrubs, rarely annual herbs: lvs. opposite, rarely alternate, usually abruptly pinnate, rarely odd-pinnate or simple, stipulate: fls. perfect, regular, usually in terminal circinate infl.; sepals 5, rarely 4, imbricate, rarely valvate, sometimes wanting; stamens 10 or 8, rarely 15, obdiplostemonous, often with stipular appendages; anthers affixed in the middle; ovary superior, 4–5-, rarely 2–12-celled, often with disk at base; ovules 1–several, pendulous; style and stigma 1: fr. a caps., rarely a berry or drupe or splitting into carpels.—About 21 genera with 150 species.

A. Lvs. opposite, pinnate: fr. a capsule..1. *Zygophyllum*
AA. Lvs. alternate, simple: fr. a drupe...2. *Nitraria*

1. **ZYGOPHÝLLUM** L. Low, usually prostrate shrubs or subshrubs, rarely annuals, with fleshy stems and lvs.: lvs. abruptly pinnate, with usually 1 pair of lfts.: fls. solitary or 2, white, yellow or red, 4–5-merous; petals clawed; stamens usually with appendages at base; disk angled and fleshy: fr. a 2–5-angled caps., sometimes winged; cells with 1–several seeds; seeds with thin albumen and oblong cotyledons. (Greek *zygos*, yoke, and *phyllon*, leaf; referring to the paired lfts.) About 60 species, chiefly in the desert regions of the Old World.

Z. xanthóxylum (Bge.) Maxim. Shrub to 1.5 m., often spinescent; brts. glabrous: lfts. 2, linear, about 2 cm. long, fleshy, grayish green: fls. 4-merous; petals cuneate-oblong; stamens longer than petals: fr. 2–3-winged, about 2.5 cm. long and nearly as broad, indehiscent. Linnaea, 17:1,t. D.L.2:358. (*Sarcozygium x.* Bge.) Mongolia. Intr. ? Zone IV? Possibly cult. in some botanical garden; inhabits saline deserts and is difficult to grow.—*Z. Fabago* L., sometimes cult., is herbaceous.

2. **NITRÀRIA** L. Deciduous shrubs with usually spiny brs.: lvs. spatulate, fleshy, entire or crenate, stipulate: fls. small, yellowish green in terminal loose circinate infl.; sepals 5, imbricate, connate at base, persistent; petals valvate, concave; stamens 15–10, without appendages; ovary 3-celled; stigmas 3; each cell with 1 ovule: drupe with thin exocarp and bony endocarp,

1-seeded. (Name referring to the fact that the plant yields soda.) Four species in S. Russia, C. Asia and E. Siberia, N. Afr., Austr.

N. Schòberi L. Low spiny shrub with appressed-silky brts.: lvs. fascicled, oblong-spatulate, 2–3 cm. long, entire, finely silky; stipules deciduous: fls. about 8 mm. across; sepals triangular, short; petals oblong: fr. conic-oblong, 8–10 mm. long. E.N.III.4:91. S.H.2:f.73a-k. S. Russia to E. Siberia and Baluch. Cult. 1819. Zone IV?—Of only botanical interest and rarely cult. in botanical gardens; inhabits saline deserts.

Fam. 42. **RUTACEAE** Juss. RUE FAMILY

Shrubs, trees or herbs; lvs. alternate, rarely opposite, simple or compound, usually with pellucid dots, estipulate: fls. usually perfect and usually regular, 4–5-merous; sepals often cohering, imbricate; petals imbricate or valvate, sometimes wanting; stamens 8–10, rarely 15 or more, inserted at base of a ring-like or cup-like crenate or dentate disk; ovary superior, often raised on a prolongation of the floral axis; carpels 4–5, rarely 1–3, connate or sometimes free at base and united by the styles or stigmas; carpels usually 2-ovuled; styles or stigmas connate: fr. a caps. or berry, or separating into several dehiscent or drupe-like fruitlets, rarely winged.—About 120 genera with about 1000 species, mostly in trop. countries, but extending into the temp. regions of Eurasia and America.

A. Lvs. compound.
  B. Lvs. pinnate.
    c. Lvs. alternate.
      D. Lvs. odd-pinnate; brs. prickly: fr. of dehiscent follicles..........1. *Zanthoxylum*
      DD. Lvs. doubly pinnately dissected; small subshrubs: fr. a dehiscent capsule..5. *Ruta*
    cc. Lvs. opposite, odd-pinnate: trees.
      D. Winter-buds free in the axils of the lvs.: fr. of dehiscent follicles.......2. *Evodia*
      DD. Winter-buds enclosed in base of petiole: fr. a drupe..............7. *Phellodendron*
  BB. Lvs. 3-foliolate.
    c. Lvs. opposite, evergreen: fls. conspicuous, white: fr. dehiscent............4. *Choisya*
    cc. Lvs. alternate: deciduous.
      D. Brs. unarmed: fls. greenish-white in corymbs: fr. a winged samara......6. *Ptelea*
      DD. Brs. spiny, bright green: fls. white, before the lvs.: fr. a large berry...9. *Poncirus*
AA. Lvs. simple.
  B. Lvs. deciduous: fls. small, greenish, in racemes or solitary: fr. a dehiscent capsule.
      3. *Orixa*
  BB. Lvs. evergreen: fls. white, in dense terminal panicles: fr. a small red or black drupe.
      8. *Skimmia*

1. **ZANTHÓXYLUM** L. Deciduous or evergreen aromatic trees or shrubs, sometimes scandent, usually prickly, the prickles mostly in infrastipular pairs; winter-buds small, superposed, with indistinct scales: lvs. alternate, odd-pinnate, rarely 3-foliolate; lfts. opposite, sessile or subsessile, entire or serrate, with pellucid dots: fls. small, dioecious or polygamous, in panicles or rarely fascicled, 3–8-merous; perianth simple or consisting of sepals and petals; filaments subulate; staminate fls. with rudimentary carpels; carpels in pistillate fls. 5–1, usually distinctly stipitate, 2-ovuled; styles distinct or connate, with capitate stigma: mature carpels with a thin exocarp separating from the endocarp, 2-valved, each with 1 shiny black subglobose or ellipsoid albuminous seed. (Greek *xanthos*, yellow, and *xylon*, wood.) Syn.: *Xanthoxylum* Gmel. About 150 species in trop. and subtrop. regions in both hemispheres; few in temp. regions.

A. Fls. before the lvs. in axillary fascicles: lfts. 5–11, pubescent beneath....1. *Z. americanum*
AA. Fls. after the lvs. in corymbs at end of lateral or rarely terminal brts.: lfts. glabrous or nearly glabrous beneath.
  B. Lf.-rachis broadly winged: lfts. 3–5, 3–12 cm. long........................2. *Z. alatum*
  BB. Lf.-rachis not or slightly winged.
    c. Lfts. subsessile; prickles straight: fr. not beaked.
      D. Prickles stout with much flattened broad base: lfts. 7–11, 1.5–5 cm. long.
      3. *Z. cimulans*

DD. Prickles slender: lfts. 11–21, not more than 3 cm. long.
   E. Prickles in pairs: fls. with simple perianth.....................4. *Z. piperitum*
     EE. Prickles solitary: fls. with sepals and petals..................5. *Z. schinifolium*
  CC. Lfts. petioluled, 7–13, 3–7 cm. long; prickles mostly recurved.....6. *Z. stenophyllum*
Subgen I. EUZANTHOXYLUM Endl. Fls. with simple perianth.

1. **Z. americànum** Mill. PRICKLY ASH (Toothache-tree). Shrub or small tree, to 8 m.; young brts. pubescent, with prickles about 1 cm. or less long: lfts. 5–11, ovate or elliptic, 3–6 cm. long, acuminate, entire or crenulate, dark green above, lighter and pubescent beneath, particularly on the midrib: fls. before the lvs., small, yellowish green, in axillary clusters on last year's brts.: pedicels of pistillate fls. 1–6 mm. long, of staminate shorter: fr. blackish, about 5 mm. long; seeds black. Fl.iv–v; fr.viii. M.A.1:33(c). E.N.III.4:f. 65A–G. B.B.2:444. S.H.2:f.74a-i. (*Z. fraxineum* Willd.) Que. to Neb. and Va. Intr. about 1740. Zone III.

2. **Z. alàtum** Roxb. var. **planispìnum** (Sieb. & Zucc.) Rehd. & Wils. Shrub to 4 m.; brts. glabrous; prickles with broad flattened base to 2 cm. long: lfts. 3–5, ovate to ovate-lanceolate, 3–12 cm. long, the terminal one the largest, acuminate, finely serrulate, glabrous; rachis and petioles broadly winged: fls. yellowish, in small panicles 3–4 cm. long; carpels about 5 mm. long, red, warty; seeds lustrous black. Fl.vi; fr.ix. B.M.8754(c). S.I.2:t. 34(c). R.H.1913:17(h). G.35:213. (*Z. pl.* Sieb. & Zucc.) China, Korea, Jap. Cult. 1880. Zone VI. The typical form from the Himal. differs chiefly in its 5–11 lfts.

3. **Z. símulans** Hance. Spreading shrub to 3 m. or small tree to 7 m.: brts. slightly pubescent or glabrous; the stout prickles 6–20 mm. long with a very broad and flattened base to 1.5 cm. wide: lfts. 7–11, ovate to ovate-oblong, 1.5–5 cm. long, the terminal one usually stalked, crenate-serrulate, glabrous; rachis and often the midrib of the lfts. beneath prickly: fls. in sessile corymbs or short panicles 4–6 cm. broad: fr. reddish. Fl.vi–vii; fr. ix–x. D.L.2:348(l). S.H.2:f.74k-m. (*X. Bungei* Hance 1875, not 1866.) N. and C. China. Intr. 1869. Zone V. Handsome shrub with lustrous foliage.

4. **Z. pipéritum** (L.) DC. Shrub or small tree; brts. pubescent when young; prickles rather slender, to 1 cm. long, in infrastipular pairs: lfts. 11–19, ovate to oblong-ovate, 1–3.5 cm. long, the terminal one subsessile, emarginate, cuneate, remotely toothed with a conspicuous gland at the base of each tooth, glabrous; rachis pubescent above, often with a few prickles: fls. greenish, in small corymbs 1.5–3 cm. across; style slender: fr. reddish, gland-dotted; seeds black. Fl.vi; fr.ix. S.I.1:t.52(c). E.N.III.4:f.65J-L. S.H.2:f. 74n-s. N. China, Korea, Japan. Cult. 1877. Zone VI?

Related species: **Z. Piasézkii** Maxim. Shrub to 3 m.: lfts. 7–15, ovate or obovate to oblong, 8–25 mm. long, slightly crenulate or nearly entire; rachis glabrous: fls. in small corymbs; style short: fr. reddish, warty. W. China. Intr. 1897. Zone V or VI.

Subgen. II. FAGARA (L.) G. Don. Fls. with sepals and petals. (*Fagara L.*)

5. **Z. schinifòlium** Sieb. & Zucc. Shrub or small tree; brts. glabrous, with a solitary prickle to 1.2 cm. long at each node: lfts. 13–21, elliptic-lanceolate to lanceolate, 1.5–3.5 cm. long, emarginate at apex, crenate-serrulate, glabrous; rachis prickly: fls. greenish in terminal short-stalked corymbs 5–10 cm. across: fr. greenish or brownish, about 4 mm. long; seeds blue-black. Fl.vi; fr.ix–x. Ad.10:t.326(c). S.I.2:t.33(c). S.H.2:f.75a-c. (*Fagara schinifolia* Engl.) Jap., Korea, E. China. Cult. 1877. Zone V. Graceful shrub with neat foliage and rather conspicuous fruit in fall.

6. **Z. stenophýllum** Hemsl. Scandent shrub to 3 m.; brts. glabrous, with small curved or straight prickles: lfts. 7–13, ovate-oblong to lanceolate, 3.5–7

cm. long, acuminate, cuneate, denticulate, glabrous; rachis usually with
slender hooked prickles: fls. in terminal loose corymbs 5–9 cm. across; stamens exserted: fr. reddish, beaked; seeds black. Fls.vi. (*Fagara stenophylla*
Engl.) W. China. Intr. 1908. Zone VII?

2. **EVÒDIA** Forst. Deciduous or evergreen trees or shrubs; winter-buds
naked: lvs. opposite, petioled, simple or pinnate with entire or nearly entire
punctate lfts.: fls. unisexual, usually 4-merous, sometimes 5-merous, small,
in terminal or axillary panicles or corymbs; sepals imbricate; petals valvate
or slightly imbricate; stamens 4–5, at the base of a cupular disk; carpels
4–5, nearly free or connate, 2-ovuled; style cylindric: fr. of 4–5 2-valved
pods, 1–2-seeded; seeds ellipsoid or subglobose; albumen with straight embryo. (Greek *euodia*, pleasant odor.) About 50 species in E. and S. Asia,
Austr. and Polynesia.—Sometimes planted as ornamental trees.

A. Lfts. 5–11, glabrous beneath or pubescent only along the midrib: fr. beaked at apex.
   B. Lfts. subsessile or short-stalked, with long villous hairs along the midrib and some-
      times along the veins and green beneath: beak of fr. short..............1. *E. Daniellii*
   BB. Lfts. distinctly stalked, glabrous or with short hairs along the base of the midrib and
      glaucescent or pale beneath: beak of fr. long............................2. *E. hupehensis*
AA. Lfts. 7–15, pubescent beneath: fr. rounded at apex.........................3. *E. officinalis*

1. **E. Daniéllii** (Benn.) Hemsl. Small tree: brts. pubescent at first, red-
brown with large pale lenticels the second year: lfts. 7–11, ovate to oblong-
ovate, 5–10 cm. long, acuminate with an obtusish point, rounded at base,
sometimes broad-cuneate or subcordate, finely crenulate, light green beneath;
petiole 3–6 cm. long: fls. 3–4 mm. long, whitish, in puberulous corymbs 10–16
cm. across, stalks of the lower brs. 3–9 cm. long: pods about 8 mm. long,
slightly puberulous or nearly glabrous with a short usually hooked beak;
seeds ellipsoid, 3.5 mm. long, lustrous brownish black or black. Fl.vi; fr.ix.
H.B.1923:61. (*Zanthoxylum D.* Benn.) N. China, Korea. Intr. 1905.
Zone V.

2. **E. hupehénsis** Dode. Tree to 20 m.; brts. glabrous, purple-brown,
lenticellate: lfts. 7–9, rarely 5, ovate to oblong-ovate, 6–12 cm. long, acuminate, oblique and usually rounded at base, rarely cuneate, entire or slightly
crenulate, pale beneath and glabrous, except slightly pilose along the midrib:
fls. whitish, in broad-pyramidal puberulous corymbs 8–16 cm. across; petals
3–4 mm. long: pods reddish brown, without the slender recurved beak 5 mm.
long, glandular, short-pilose or glabrous; seeds ellipsoid, lustrous, black. Fl.
vi–vii; fr.ix–x. R.H.1924:81. G.C.78:429. C. China. Intr. 1907. Zone V.

Closely related species: **E. Hénryi** Dode. Tree to 8 m.; brts. pubescent at
first: lfts. 5–9, oblong-ovate to lance-ovate, rounded or narrowed at base, crenulate: corymbs 5–6 cm. across; pods pubescent, 5–6 mm. long. C. China. Intr.
1907. Zone V.—A species with beaked fr. and pubescent lfts. is **E. velutìna**
Rehd. & Wils. Tree to 12 m.; brts. velutinous: lfts. 7–11, oblong-ovate to lance-
oblong, 6–10 cm. long, nearly rounded at base, soft-pubescent on both sides: infl.
broad-paniculate, to 16 cm. broad: pods 4–5 mm. long, with short beak. W.
China. Intr. 1908. Zone VI?—A species with obtuse fr. and glabrous lfts. is
E. glaùca Miq. Tree to 15 m.: lfts. usually 7, rarely to 11, ovate-lanceolate, long-
acuminate, broad-cuneate at base, obscurely crenulate, glaucescent and glabrous
beneath except pilose along midrib near base: corymbs 15–20 cm. broad: pods
4–5 mm. long, reticulate on back. S.I.2:t.34.f.1–9 (c. as *E. meliaefolia*). Useful
Pl. Jap. 2:t.538. Jap., E. and C. China. Cult. 1915. Zone VII?

3. **E. officinàlis** Dode. Shrub or small tree to 5 m.; brts. pubescent while
young: lfts. 7–15, short-stalked, ovate or elliptic-ovate, rarely oblong, 5–8
cm. long, acuminate or short-acuminate, cuneate to broad-cuneate, rarely
nearly rounded at base, glabrous above except on midrib or sparingly hairy
when young, pubescent beneath: infl. a pubescent corymb 6–11 cm. broad;

pods reddish, warty, rounded at apex, 5–6 mm. long; seeds suborbicular, 4 mm. long, shining steel-blue. Fl.vii; fr.x–xi. C. and W. China. Intr. 1907. Zone VI?
Closely related species: **E. Bodinièri** Dode. Bush to 3 m.: lfts. 5–11, elliptic-ovate to narrow-oblong, 4–10 cm. long, short and obtusely acuminate, cuneate, glabrous above, pubescent at least on the midrib beneath: infl. loose, 6–13 cm. across, pubescent. C. and W. China. Intr. 1910. Zone VI?

3. **ORIXA** Thunb. Deciduous shrub; winter-buds small, with imbricate scales: lvs. alternate, entire, short-petioled, with pellucid dots: fls. dioecious, greenish, small, 4-merous, on last year's brts.; sepals ovate, connate below; petals elliptic, imbricate in bud; staminate fls. in racemes, with a 4-lobed disk and 4 stamens shorter than petals; pistillate fls. solitary with 4 small sterile stamens and 4 carpels united at apex by the short style with 4-lobed stigma: fr. of 4 compressed, 2-valved carpels, cohering only at base, each with a subglobose black albuminous seed; embryo slightly curved with broad cotyledons. (Japanese name.) One species.

O. japónica Thunb. Shrub to 3 m., with spreading brs. pubescent when young: lvs. obovate to oblong, 5–12 cm. long, obtusely pointed, entire or finely crenulate, bright green above, pubescent on the veins at least when young; petiole about 1 cm. long: fls. about 6 mm. across; fr. almost 8 mm. high, 1.8 mm. across, greenish brown. Fl.iv–v. I.T.3:t.101. Gt. 35:t.1232(c). E.N.III.4:f.67t–z. B.C.4:2407. S.L.242(h). (*Celastrus japonica* K. Koch, *Evodia ramiflora* Gray.) Japan. Cult. 1870. Zone V. Shrub with bright green lvs. of pungent odor when bruised.

4. **CHOÌSYA** Kunth. Evergreen shrub, aromatic: lvs. opposite, 3-folio-late; lfts. entire, subsessile, with pellucid dots: fls. white, rather large, per-fect, 5-merous, in terminal and axillary slender-stalked 3–6-fld. cymes clus-tered at the end of the brts.; sepals ovate, thin, deciduous; petals about 4 times as long as sepals, imbricate, finally spreading; stamens 10, much shorter than petals, with flattened, lanceolate filaments, inserted at base of the thick gynophore; carpels 5, connate at base, each with 2 ovules; style with 5-lobed stigma: fr. of 5 2-lobed carpels, with the endocarp separating. (Named for J. D. Choisy, Swiss botanist; 1799–1859.) One species.

C. ternàta Kunth. MEXICAN ORANGE. Shrub to 3 m. forming a round bush; young brts. pubescent: lfts. 3, rarely 2 or 4, obovate-oblong to oblong, 3–7 cm. long, obtuse, cuneate, leathery, glabrous; petiole 1–5 cm. long, pubes-cent: fls. 2.5–3 cm. across, fragrant; petals oblong-obovate. Fl.(iv)v–vi. R.H.1869:332,t(c). Gt.25:t.876(c). Gn.12:232,t(c);86:948(h). G.C.41:382. B.S.1:341. J.L.40:f.3(h). (*C. grandiflora* Reg.) Mexico. Intr. 1866. Zone VI? Ornamental shrub with fragrant white fls. in spring.

5. **RÙTA** L. RUE. Herbs or subshrubs, glandular-punctate and aromatic: lvs. altèrnate, simple, 3-foliolate or pinnately compound: fls. perfect, regular, 4–5-merous, yellow, in terminal cymes or corymbs; sepals connate at base, persistent; petals oblong-obovate, cóncave with denticulate or fringed mar-gin, imbricate in bud; stamens 8–10; disk large, very deeply 4–5-lobed; style with small stigma; fr. a 4–5-lobed capsule with many-seeded cells, dehiscent or indehiscent; seeds angular, albuminous; embryo slightly curved. (Ancient Latin name of the plant.) About 40 species. Mediterr. region and Canary Isls. to E. Siberia.

R. gravéolens L. RUE (HERB OF GRACE). Evergreen subshrub to 1 m., glabrous: lvs. bipinnately dissected, 6–12 cm. long, with obovate-oblong to obovate lobes, bluish green, of strong odor: fls. dull yellow, nearly 2 cm. across, in terminal large and loose cymes; petals very concave, with fringed margin. Fl.vi–ix. F.D.21:t.2088(c). R.I.5:t.157(c). H.A.6:t.8(c). S. Eu. Cult. since ancient times and naturalized elsewhere in Eu. and occasionally in N. Am. Zone V.—**R. g. variegàta** West., var. Lvs. variegated with white. —An old medicinal plant of no ornamental value. There are several closely related species in cult., but these are even less woody.

A closely related genus is **Boenninghausènia** Meissn. differing chiefly in the smaller whitish fls., stipitate ovary and carpels being connate only at base. The only species is **B. albiflòra** (Hook.) Heynhold. Glabrous slender subshrub to 0.5 m.: lvs. up to thrice pinnate; lfts. broad-obovate to oval, 4–15 mm. long, obtuse: fls. in loose leafy panicles, white, 6–8 mm. long; carpels about 4 mm. long. Fl.viii–ix. E.N.III.4:130,f.B-F. Himal. to E. Asia. Cult. 1885. Zone VI? —Rarely cult.

6. PTÉLEA L. Deciduous shrubs or small trees, aromatic; buds superposed, small, pubescent, the terminal one wanting: lvs. alternate, petioled, 3-foliolate, rarely 4–5-foliolate; lfts. subsessile, entire or crenulate, punctate with pellucid dots: fls. small, greenish white, polygamous, 4–5-merous, in corymbs terminal on short lateral brts.; petals oblong, short-pubescent outside, 3–4 times longer than the sepals, both imbricate; stamens 4–5, shorter than petals, in the staminate fls. inserted at the base of a short gynophore bearing a sterile ovary, the filaments villous below; pistillate fls. with 4–5 small staminodes and with a compressed 2-, rarely 3-celled ovary; each cell with 2 ovules; style short: fr. a compressed usually broadly winged and suborbicular, 2-seeded indehiscent samara, rarely 3-celled and 3-winged; seed compressed with thin albumen; embryo straight with oblong cotyledons. (Greek name of the Elm tree; transferred to this plant on account of the similarity of the fruit.) About 7–10 variable species in N. Am. and Mex.

P. trifoliàta L. Hop-tree (Wafer-Ash). Shrub or small round-headed tree to 8 m.; young brts. sparingly pubescent, red-brown the second year: lfts. ovate to elliptic-oblong, 6–12 cm. long, narrowed at ends, sometimes acuminate, the lateral ones oblique at base, smaller, entire or obscurely crenulate, dark green and lustrous above, pale and usually glabrous below: fls. about 1 cm. across, in corymbs 4–8 cm. broad: fr. suborbicular, 1.8–2.5 cm. across, emarginate at apex. Fl.vi: fr.viii–ix. S.O.2:t.76(c). G.O.t.74(c). M.A.1:t.34(c). S.S.1:t.33,34. G.C.III.16:375. Ont. and N. Y. to Fla., w. to Minn.; sometimes escaped from cult. elsewhere. Intr. 1724. Zone IV. Grown for its handsome foliage and the attractive light-colored fr.—**P. t. aùrea** Behnsch ex Hartwig, var. Lvs. yellow. A.F.14:1231(h). Orig. before 1886.— **P. t. pentaphýlla** (Muenchh.) DC., var. Lfts. 3–5, narrower. (*P. t. heterophylla* Kirchn., f.)—**P. t. fastigiàta** Bean, var. Brs. upright, forming a pyramidal bush.—**P. t. pubéscens** Pursh, var. Lfts. pubescent beneath, dull green above: brts. petioles and infl. glabrous or nearly so. Occurs with the type.— **P. t. móllis** Torr. & Gr., var. Young brts., infl. and lfts. beneath densely pubescent or tomentose. (*P. mollis* M. A. Curtis, *P. tomentosa* Raf., *P. t. glauca* Kirchn., *P. t.* var. *Deamiana* Nieuwl.)· Texas to N. C. and Ill.

Related species: **P. Baldwìnii** Torr. Shrubby; brts. brown: lfts. 3–6 cm. long, narrowly elliptic-ovate, or oblong-obovate, pubescent beneath: fls. larger, in smaller corymbs; fr. 1–1.5 cm. across, apiculate. (*P. angustifolia* Benth., *P. trifoliata* var. *angustifolia* Jones.) Calif. Intr. about 1893. Zone VII?— **P. polyadènia** Greene. Brts. dark brown, puberulous or tomentulose; lfts. elliptic-ovate, 3–6 cm. long, obtusish or acutish, crenate, bright green, short-villous beneath, subcoriaceous, strongly gland-dotted. Ariz., N. Mex., Okla. and Tex. Intr. 1916. Zone VI?—**P. nìtens** Greene. Brts. light yellowish brown, glabrate: lfts. rhombic-lanceolate, 3–5 cm. long, acute or acuminate, slightly crenate, glabrous or slightly pubescent along the midrib beneath, light green, strongly gland-dotted, chartaceous: fr. about 1.5 cm. across. Colo., Okla. Cult. 1912. Zone V.—**P. lutéscens** Greene. Brts. white and lustrous, glabrous; lfts. lanceolate, 3–6 cm. long, serrulate, densely and minutely gland-dotted: fr. about 2 cm. across. Ariz. Cult. 1918. Zone VI?

7. PHELLODÉNDRON Rupr. Deciduous trees, aromatic; buds small, naked, pubescent, enclosed by the base of the petiole: lvs. opposite, odd-pinnate, with 5–13 opposite crenulate lfts. punctate with pellucid dots: fls. dioecious, small, yellowish green, in terminal panicles or corymbs; petals 5–8, several times longer than the 5–8 lance-ovate sepals; staminate fls. with 5–6 stamens longer than petals and with a rudimentary pistil; anthers large, ovate, 2-lobed at base; pistillate fls. with 5–6 small staminodes and a 5-celled ovary on a short gynophore; style short and thick with a 5-lobed stigma: fr. a black, subglobose drupe with 5 small, 1-seeded stones; seed with thin albumen; embryo straight, with oblong flat cotyledons. (Greek *phellos*, cork, and *dendron*, tree; referring to the corky bark of the type species.) Eight or 9 species in E. Asia.—Ornamental trees grown for their handsome foliage turning yellow in autumn; the fls. appear in June and the fr. ripens in Sept. and Oct.

A. Lvs. glabrous beneath or with few hairs along the midrib, glaucous or glaucescent.
  B. Bark thick, corky; lfts. ciliate...1. *P. amurænse*
    BB. Bark thin: lfts. not or slightly ciliate.................................2. *P. sachalinense*
AA. Lfts. pubescent beneath, at least on the veins, pale green or grayish green.
  B. Infl. rather loose, about as broad as high: ovary glabrous.
    C. Bark thick, corky: lfts. broadly cuneate at base.....................3. *P. Lavallei*
      CC. Bark thin: lfts. truncate or subcordate at base......................4. *P. japonicum*
    BB. Infl. compact, higher than broad: ovary pubescent: lfts. oblong-lanceolate.
5. *P. chinense*

1. **P. amurénse** Rupr. Amur Cork-tree. Tree to 15 m. with wide-spreading brs.; bark light gray, corky, deeply fissured; mature brts. orange-yellow or yellowish gray: lfts. 5–13, ovate to lance-ovate, 5–10 cm. long, long-acuminate, rounded or narrowed at base, dark green and lustrous above, glabrous beneath or with a few hairs along the base of the midrib: fls. about 6 mm. long in puberulous panicles 6–8 cm. high: fr. about 1 cm. across, of strong turpentine-like odor when bruised. S.I.2:t.33(c). S.T.1:t.93. K.D. 348. Gs.2:37(b). H.B.3:466(h). S.L.252(h). N. China, Manch. Intr. about 1856. Zone III. Conspicuous in winter with its light grày thick and deeply fissured bark.

P. a. × *japonicum*. Raised in 1902 in the Botanic Garden at Lund (see M.D.1912:363).

Closely related species: **P. pirifòrme** E. Wolf. Lfts. more oblique and not rounded at base: sepals scarcely exceeding the base of the ovary; stigma not or little broader than style: fr. pyriform. D.M.1925:216(1). Orig. unknown. Cult. 1891.

2. **P. sachalinénse** (Fr. Schmidt) Sarg. Tree to 15 m.; bark of trunk dark brown, slightly fissured and finally broken into thin plates; mature brts. reddish brown: lfts. 7–11, ovate to ovate-oblong, 6–12 cm. long, acuminate, cuneate or rounded at base, dull green above and glabrous or nearly so beneath: panicle nearly glabrous, 6–8 cm. high: fr. about 1 cm. across. K.M. t.59(c). S.T.1:t.94. G.C.62:186. (*P. amurense* var. *s.* Fr. Schmidt.) Saghal., Korea, N. Japan and W. China. Intr. 1877. Zone III. This species is the hardiest and most satisfactory in cult.

3. **P. Lavállei** Dode. Tree to 10 or occasionally to 15 m.: bark corky; mature brts. purplish brown: lf.-rachis puberulous or pubescent; lfts. 5–13, elliptic-ovate to lance-oblong, 5–10 cm. long, acuminate, cuneate, dull yellowish green above, pubescent beneath when young, at maturity often only

on the veins: infl. puberulous, 6–8 cm. broad: fr. about 8 mm. across. B.M. 8945(c). I.T.5:t.171 (as *P. amurense*). (*P. amurense* var. *L.* Sprague.) C. Japan. Intr. 1862. Zone V.

4. **P. japónicum** Maxim. Tree to 10 m., with dark brown thin and slightly fissured bark; mature brts. reddish brown: lf.-rachis densely villous or tomentose; lfts. 9–13, ovate to ovate-oblong, 6–10 cm. long, acuminate, truncate or subcordate at the very oblique base, dull green above, villous beneath, more densely on the veins: infl. hoary-tomentose, 5–7 cm. across: fr. about 1 cm. across. S.T.1:t.95. C. Japan. Intr. 1863. Zone IV.

5. **P. chinénse** Schneid. Tree to 10 m.: bark dark grayish brown, thin, slightly fissured; mature brts. purplish brown: lfts. 7–13, oblong-ovate to lance-oblong, the margins nearly parallel, 7–14 cm. long, acuminate, rounded or broad-cuneate at base, dark yellowish green above, villous beneath: infl. densely pubescent, compact, paniculate, 5–6 cm. long: fr. about 1 cm. across. Fr.ix–iii. S.H.2:f.79c-d. S.L.253(h). C. China. Intr. 1907. Zone V.—**P. c. glabriúsculum** Schneid., var. Lfts. pubescent only on the veins beneath. (*P. sinense* Dode.) C. and W. China. Intr. 1907. Zone V.

8. **SKÍMMIA** Thunb. Evergreen glabrous shrubs; buds with few outer scales, the terminal one lanceolate: lvs. alternate, short-petioled, entire, dotted with pellucid glands: fls. white, small, 4–5-merous, in terminal panicles, perfect or polygamous; the staminate fls. in larger panicles and fragrant; petals oblong, valvate or slightly imbricate, 3–4 times longer than the imbricate sepals; staminate fls. with 4–5 stamens slightly shorter than petals and with sterile carpels united only at base; filaments filiform; anthers ovate, 2-lobed at base; pistillate fls. with 4–5 staminodes and 2–5 connate carpels, each with 1 pendulous ovule; style short, thick, with 2–5-lobed stigma; fr. an ovoid or obovoid or subglobose drupe with 2–4 1-seeded stones; seed with fleshy albumen; embryo straight with oblong flat cotyledons. (Japanese name Skimmi, meaning a harmful fruit.) Nine species in Himal. and E. Asia. —Ornamental shrubs grown for their handsome evergreen foliage and the bright red berries and also for their fragrant staminate fls.

A. Lvs. generally oblong-obovate, obtusely pointed: fls. usually 4-merous, polygamous: fr. subglobose ....1. *S. japonica*
AA. Lvs. generally oblong-lanceolate, acuminate: fls. usually 5-merous and perfect: fr. obovoid ....2. *S. Reevesiana*

1. **S. japónica** Thunb. Dense shrub to 1.5 m., but usually lower, glabrous except the puberulous infl.: lvs. crowded at end of brts., elliptic-oblong to oblong-obovate, 7–12 cm. long, bright or yellowish green above, yellowish green beneath: fls. usually dioecious, yellowish white, about 8 mm. across in panicles 5–8 cm. long: fr. globose or depressed-globose, 8 mm. across, bright red. Fl.iv–v; fr.x(–v). B.M.8038(c). G.C.III.5:521,524. Gn.87:562(h). R.H. 1869:259;1880:56. G.W.5:261(h). (*S. oblata* T. Moore, *S. fragrans* and *S. fragrantissima* Hort.) The two last synonyms are used for the staminate form. Japan. Cult. 1838. Zone VII?—**S. j. macrophýlla** Mast., var. A staminate form with larger lvs.

S. j. × *Reevesiana* = **S. Foremánii** Knight. Lvs. lanceolate or oblanceolate, yellowish green; petiole reddish: subglobose and obovoid scarlet frs. on the same panicle. G.C.III.5:553. Gn.61:160;67:57. (*S. intermedia* Rehd., not Carr.) Orig. before 1881.—**S. F. Rogérsii** (Mast.) Rehd., var. Lvs. deep green: petiole greenish: fls. perfect; fr. depressed-globose, crimson. Orig. before 1878.

2. **S. Reevesiàna** Fort. Shrub to 0.5 m., similar to the preceding: lvs. lanceolate or oblong-lanceolate, 3–10 cm. long, acuminate, cuneate, dark green above, light green beneath: fls. usually perfect, white, in oblong-ovoid

Closely related species **A. Giráldii** Dode. Young brts. puberulous, brown or brownish: petioles purplish, finely pubescent: lvs. 50–90 cm. long; lfts. 33–41, close-set, lanceolate, 10–15 cm. long, long-acuminate, undulate, with 14–15 pairs of veins, pale green and loosely pubescent beneath: panicle 20–30 cm. long; fr. about 6 cm. long. B.D.1907:191,193A,197B. W. China. Intr. about 1897. Zone V.—**A. G. Duclouxii** Dode, var. Brts. light orange; petiole green; lfts. sparingly pilose beneath, more densely on the veins. Cult. 1914.

2. **A. Vilmoriniàna** Dode. Tree to 16 m.: lvs. 50–90 cm. long: lfts. 17–35, lance-oblong, 10–15 cm. long, acuminate, with 2–4 coarse teeth near base, glabrous or pubescent above, glaucescent and pubescent beneath; petiole often red and sometimes prickly: panicle to 30 cm. long: fr. about 5 cm. long. R.H.1904:445. Gn.75:632(h). B.D.1907:193c. (*A. glandulosa* var. *spinosa* Bois.) W. China. Intr. 1897. Zone VI? Similar to *A. altissima* but not quite as hardy.

Fam. 44. **MELIACEAE** Vent. MAHOGANY FAMILY

Trees or shrubs, rarely subshrubs or herbs: lvs. alternate, very rarely opposite, pinnate, rarely simple, estipulate: fls. perfect, rarely unisexual, regular, in usually axillary panicles; sepals 4–5, usually partly connate, imbricate; petals 4–5, rarely 3–10, valvate, imbricate or convolute, distinct or sometimes connate at base; stamens usually twice as many as petals, usually more or less connate into a tube below, rarely free; ovary superior, surrounded at the base by a disk, 2–5-celled, rarely 1– or 10–20-celled, each cell with 1 or 2, rarely several ovules: fr. a caps., drupe or berry; seeds winged or not winged, albuminous or exalbuminous.—About 40 genera with 600 species in subtrop. and trop. regions, very few in temp. regions.

A. Lvs. odd-pinnate; lfts. 11–23: fls. small, whitish: fr. a caps......................1. *Cedrela*
AA. Lvs. twice-pinnate: fls. pale lilac, nearly 2 cm. across: fr. a drupe................2. *Melia*

1. **CÉDRELA** L. Deciduous or evergreen trees; buds subglobose, with several outer scales: lvs. alternate, usually abruptly pinnate, rarely odd-pinnate; fls. small, whitish or greenish, perfect, in large terminal or axillary panicles; calyx short, 4–5-parted; petals 4–5, keeled inside and adnate with the keel to the gynophore or disk; stamens 4–6, inserted at apex of gynophore, shorter than petals, with subulate filaments; ovary 5-celled, on an elongated or short gynophore; style slightly exceeding the stamens, with capitate stigma; caps. with many winged seeds. (From *Cedrus;* the wood resembles that of the Cedar.) Including *Toona* Roem. About 18 species in trop. Am., S. E. Asia to Australia.

C. sinénsis Juss. Tree to 16 m., with shredding bark; brts. puberulous when young: lvs. long-petioled, 25–50 cm. long; lfts. 10–22, short-stalked, oblong to lance-oblong, 8–15 cm. long, acuminate, remotely and slightly serrate or nearly entire, light green beneath and pubescent on the veins or finally nearly glabrous: fls. white, fragrant, campanulate, about 5 mm. long, in pendulous panicles about 30 cm. long; 5 subulate staminodes alternating with the stamens; ovary glabrous, on a short gynophore: caps. obovoid, woody about 2.5 cm. long; seeds winged above. Fl.vi; fr.ix. R.H.1891:574. S.H.2:f.83b,84l-q. M.O.90. Gng.4:1(h). M.D.1902:495(h). G.C.72:138(h). (*Toona s.* Roem.) China. Intr. 1862. Zone V. Similar to *Ailanthus* but easily distinguished by the absence of the large gland-bearing teeth at the base of the lfts.

2. **MÈLIA** L. Deciduous or half-evergreen trees or shrubs; buds small, roundish with few outer scales, sometimes superposed: lvs. alternate, doubly

pinnate, with entire or serrate lfts.: fls. conspicuous, perfect, in axillary panicles; calyx 5–6-parted, small, imbricate; petals 5–6, free, imbricate in bud; filaments connate into a slender tube, with 10–12 lobes at the apex and bearing 10–12 anthers between the lobes on the inside; ovary on a short disk, 5–8-celled, with a long cylindric style; each cell with 2 ovules: fr. a drupe, with fleshy outer coat. (Ancient Greek name of the Ash.) About 10 species in S. Asia and Austral.

M. Azédarach L. CHINA-TREE (CHINABERRY-TREE). Tree to 15 m. with furrowed bark: lvs. 25–80 cm. long; lfts. ovate to elliptic, 2–5 cm. long, acute, sharply serrate or lobed, light green, glabrous, or puberulous on veins and rachis when young: fls. lilac, nearly 2 cm. across, in loose panicles 10–20 cm. long; petals oblanceolate or narrow-oblong, spreading; ovary 5-celled; fr. subglobose, yellow, about 1.5 cm. across. Fl.ıv–v; fr.ıx–x. B.M.1066(c). S.I. 2:t.35(c). E.N.III.4:f.160a–l. (*M. japonica* Don.) Himal. Cult. since the 16th century; naturalized in all trop. and subtrop. countries. Zone VII.— **M. A. umbraculifórmis** Berckmans. TEXAS UMBRELLA-TREE. Brs. crowded, upright-spreading, forming a flattened head; lfts. narrower. G.F.7:95(h). F.E. 26:187(h). M.M.8:73(h). B.C.4:2024(h). (*M. A. umbraculifera* Hort.) Orig. before 1860.

Fam. 45. **POLYGALACEAE** Reichenb. MILKWORT FAMILY

Herbs, shrubs or small trees: lvs. usually alternate, simple, entire: fls. perfect, irregular; sepals 5, imbricate; the 2 inner ones larger and often petaloid; petals usually 3, rarely 5; stamens usually 8, the filaments connate into a tube or free; ovary superior, 2-celled; cells usually 1-ovuled: fr. a caps. nut or drupe.—About 10 genera with 500 species.

POLÝGALA L. MILKWORT. Herbs, subshrubs or shrubs, rarely trees: lvs. alternate, rarely opposite, without, or with reduced stipules: fls. usually in racemes, variously colored; sepals unequal; the 2 inner ones usually petaloid, wing-like; the lower petal clawed and adnate at base to the staminal tube; the 2 lateral petals usually wanting; stamens 8, very rarely fewer, connate into a tube, slit down to base and open on back; ovary 2-celled; cells 1-ovuled; style straight or curved: fr. a loculicidal caps. with 2 seeds; seeds usually ovoid or subglobose, usually with aril and usually albuminous. (Greek *polys*, much and *gala*, milk; some species were formerly believed to increase the flow of milk.) About 450 species in both hemispheres, mostly herbaceous, the ligneous species chiefly subtrop.

P. Chamaebúxus L. Evergreen dwarf subshrub to 25 cm. high, creeping, with green glabrous or nearly glabrous brts.: lvs. alternate, lanceolate to elliptic or obovate, 1–2.5 cm. long, acutish, cuneate, dull green, coriaceous, glabrous: fls. 1 or 2, axillary or terminal, about 1.2 cm. long; the wings usually creamy white, the keel yellow or reddish near apex, 4-lobed at the dilated apex: caps. flat, suborbicular. Fl.ıv–vı. B.M.3161(c). R.I.18:t.150. F.D.16: t.1524(c). (*Chamaebuxus alpestris* Spach.) C. Eu. Cult. 1658. Zone V.— **P. Ch. grandiflòra** Gaud., var. Fls. with purple or sometimes pink wings and yellowish keel. Gn.13:36,t(c);30:148,t(c). R.I.18:t.150(c). F.D.16:t.1524 (c). (*P. Ch.* var. *purpurea* Neilr., var. *rhodoptera* A. Benn.)

Closely related species: **P. Vayrèdae** Costa. Subshrub to 10 cm.: lvs. narrow-lanceolate to linear, 2–2.5 cm. long: fls. 11–12 mm. long, rosy-purple; keel yellowish at apex. B.M.9009(c). (*Chamaebuxus V.* Willk.) Pyrenees. Cult. 1923. Zone VI.

Fam. 46. **EUPHORBIACEAE** Jaume St. Hil. SPURGE FAMILY

Herbs, shrubs or trees, often with milky juice, very variable in habit: lvs. usually alternate, mostly stipulate: fls. unisexual, usually small, regular, rarely irregular; sepals and petals present, or the latter, rarely both, wanting, usually free; sepals valvate or imbricate; staminate fls. usually with intra-staminal disk and with 1 to many stamens; pistillate fls. with hypogynous disk; ovary usually 3-celled, rarely 1- or 2- or 4–20-celled; ovules 1 or 2 in each cell, pendulous: fr. usually capsular, separating into 3 parts, leaving a central column, rarely indehiscent and berry- or drupe-like; seeds albuminous. Incl. *Dapniphyllaceae* Muell. Arg.—More than 280 genera with about 8000 species mainly in the tropics, few ligneous species in temp. regions.

A. Fr. capsular, dehiscent: lvs. deciduous: fls. solitary or fascicled.
  B. Fls. with petals and epipetalous disk-glands; styles 3, 2-cleft............1. *Andrachne*
  BB. Fls. apetalous.
    C. Stamens 5, filaments free; styles 3, 2-cleft; disk present: caps. 3-celled.2. *Securinega*
    CC. Stamens 3, connate, styles undivided, connate, and caps. 5–8-celled (in our species).
                                                3. *Glochidion*
AA. Fr. a drupe; lvs. evergreen: fls. racemose...............................4. *Daphniphyllum*

1. **ANDRÁCHNE** L. Low shrubs or subshrubs or perennial herbs; buds ovoid, with several outer ciliate scales: lvs. alternate, usually entire, with small stipules: fls. monoecious or incompletely dioecious, small, light yellowish green, 5–6-merous, the staminate in axillary clusters, the pistillate solitary; petals smaller than sepals, with epipetalous disk-glands; stamens not exceeding the sepals; the pistillate sometimes without petals; ovary 3-celled; styles 3, 2-cleft or 2-parted: fr. subglobose or depressed, separating into 3 2-valved carpels, 6-seeded. (Ancient Greek name.) Ten or 12 species in N. Am., Asia and Mal. Archip., Afr.—Occasionally grown in botanical collections.

A. phyllanthoìdes (Nutt.) Muell. Arg. Upright shrub to 1 m., glabrous except the puberulous angled brts.: lvs. elliptic or obovate, 8–20 mm. long, obtuse or emarginate, often mucronulate at apex, rounded or broad-cuneate at base; petioles 1–2 cm. long: fls. 5–6 mm. across, on slender stalks 5–20 mm. long; sepals oblong-obovate; petals of staminate fls. narrow-obovate, little shorter than sepals, 3–4-toothed, of pistillate fls. shorter, obovate, entire: fr. subglobose, about 8 mm. across, with the enlarged persistent sepals at base. Fl.vii–ix; fr.ix–x. (*A. Roemeriana* Muell. Arg.) Mo. to Ark. and Tex. Intr. 1899. Zone V.

Related species: **A. cólchica** Fisch. & Mey. Dense shrub with slender brts. to 1 m., glabrous: lvs. ovate, 6–15 mm. long, obtuse, rounded at base; petals filiform, much shorter than sepals: fr. subglobose, about 5 mm. across. S.L.86 h). Asia Minor. Intr. before 1900. Zone V.—**A. cordifòlia** (Dcne.) Muell. Arg. Shrub to 1 m.: lvs. ovate to oblong, 2–5 cm. long, rounded, rarely cordate at base, soft-pubescent beneath; petals spatulate; caps. depressed-globose, about 6 mm. thick. Klotzsch & Garcke, Bot. Ergeb. Reise Prinz Wald. t.24. Himal. Intr. before 1910. Zone VI?

2. **SECURÍNEGA** Juss. Deciduous shrubs; buds ovoid, with several outer scales: lvs. alternate, short-petioled, entire, stipulate; fls. dioecious or monoecious, small, greenish white, apetalous, axillary, the staminate fascicled, the pistillate 1 or several; sepals 5; stamens usually 5, longer than sepals, inserted at the base of an intrastaminal lobed disk entire in the pistillate fls.; ovary 3-celled; styles 3, 2-lobed; fr. a dehiscent subglobose caps. with persistent calyx at base, 3–6-seeded; embryo straight. (From Latin *securis*, hatchet, and *negare*, to refuse; referring to the hard wood of some

species.) About 10 species in temp. and subtrop. regions of C. and S. Am., Asia, S. Eu. and Afr.—Sometimes planted for their bright green lvs.

S. suffruticòsa (Pall.) Rehd. Shrub to 2 m., with slender spreading greenish brs., glabrous: lvs. short-stalked, elliptic or ovate to lance-ovate, 3–6 cm. long, acute or obtuse, cuneate, bright or yellowish green; petioles 2–4 mm. long; staminate fls. short-pediceled, about 3 mm. across, in 5–10-fld. clusters; pistillate solitary; caps. subglobose, about 5 mm. across, greenish, on slender stalks 1–1.5 cm. long. Fl.vii–viii; fr.ix–x. K.D.352. S.H.2:f.86a-i. J.C.20,3:t.1a. S.L.340(h). (*S. ramiflora* Muell. Arg., *S. flueggeoides* Muell. Arg., *S. japonica* Miq., in part.) N. E. Asia to C. China. Intr. 1783. Zone V.

3. GLOCHÍDION Forst. Deciduous or evergreen trees or shrubs, rarely perennial: lvs. alternate, entire, stipulate: fls. monoecious or dioecious, in axillary clusters; sepals 3–6; disk usually wanting; staminate fls. without rudimentary ovary; stamens 3–8, connate or free; ovary 3–15-celled; styles connate or free, short and thick, rarely 2-fid: fr. a dehiscent caps. (Name from Greek *glochis*, point; referring to the pointed anthers.) About 280 species in trop. and subtrop. Asia and Polynesia.

G. pùberum (L.) Hutchins. Deciduous shrub to 1.5 m.; brts. short-pilose to nearly glabrous: lvs. elliptic-obovate to elliptic- or narrow-oblong, 3–8 cm. long, acute, sometimes obtusish, broad-cuneate, dull green above, glaucescent and short-pilose on veins and veinlets beneath; petiole 1–2 mm. long: fls. monoecious, in axillary clusters, staminate on slender glabrous stalks 3–6 mm. long; sepals 6, 3 mm. long, linear-oblong, longer than the 3 connate anthers; pistillate short-stalked, smaller, the 6 sepals about as long as the tomentose ovary; styles connate into a short annular disk: caps. depressed-globose, furrowed, 12–16 mm. across, 5–8-celled, slightly pubescent, impressed at apex: seeds reddish brown. Fl.vi–ix; fr.viii–x. E. China, n. to Kiangsu and Szechuan. Intr. 1922. Zone VI?

4. DAPHNIPHÝLLUM Bl. Evergreen shrubs or small trees, glabrous; buds with several outer imbricate scales: lvs. alternate, petioled, entire, estipulate; fls. dioecious, small, apetalous, in axillary racemes; calyx small, 3–8-parted; stamens 5–18, with short filaments and large anthers; ovary 2-celled and 4-ovuled; styles 2, short, recurved: fr. a small oblong, usually 1-seeded drupe; seeds with copious albumen and very small straight embryo at apex of seed. (Greek *daphne*, laurel, and *phyllon*, leaf; referring to the shape of the lvs.) About 25 species in E. Asia.

D. macrópodum Miq. Shrub or small tree, occasionally to 15 m. tall, of compact habit; brts. rather stout, green, glaucous and often reddish when young: lvs. oblong, 8–20 cm. long, acuminate, cuneate, dark green above, bluish white or sometimes green below, with 12–17 pairs of veins; petiole 3–4 cm. long, often red like the midrib; fls. pale green, in short racemes, about 2.5 cm. long: fr. oblong, about 1 cm. long, black. Fl.v–vi; fr.x–xi. S.I.1:t.54(c). E.P.IV.147a:10. Gn.48:259(h). S.L.154(h). Gs.2:7(h). (*D. glaucescens* Hort., not Bl.) Japan, Korea, China. Intr. 1879. Zone VII. Grown for its large handsome foliage.—**D. m. variegàtum** Bean., var. Lvs. with broad irregular creamy white margin.

Closely related species: **D. húmile** Maxim. Shrub to 1.5 m.: lvs. elliptic to obovate-oblong, 6–12 cm. long, acute, glaucescent beneath, with 11–14 pairs of veins; petiole 1.5–2 cm. long. S.H.2:87g(1). (*D. macropodum* var. *h.* K. Rosenth., *D. jezoense* Hort.) N. Japan. Intr. 1879. Zone VI?

Fam. 47. **BUXACEAE** Dum. BOX FAMILY

Evergreen shrubs or small trees: lvs. opposite or alternate, estipulate: fls. monoecious, small, apetalous, without hypogynous disk; calyx 4-parted or in the pistillate fls. 4–12-parted or wanting; stamens 4, opposite the sepals or numerous; anthers basifix; ovary superior, 3-celled, rarely 2–4-celled; ovules 2, collateral, rarely 1, pendulous: fr. a dehiscent caps. or fleshy; seeds albuminous.—Six genera with about 40 species in trop. and subtrop. regions, few in temp. countries.

A. Lvs. alternate, usually 3-nerved.
  B. Lvs. entire: infl. subcapitate; styles short.................................1. *Sarcococca*
  BB. Lvs. dentate: infl. a spike; styles elongated: decumbent subshrubs......2. *Pachysandra*
AA. Lvs. opposite, entire, penninerved: fr. capsular..................................3. *Buxus*

1. **SARCOCÓCCA** Lindl. Evergreen glabrous shrubs; buds with several outer imbricate green scales: lvs. alternate, petioled, entire, usually penninerved, coriaceous: fls. whitish, apetalous in short axillary racemes or heads, with the pistillate fls. at base; sepals 4–6; staminate fls. with 4–6 stamens; pistillate fls. with a 2–3-celled ovary and with 2–3 erect or recurved styles; fr. drupe-like, subglobose to ellipsoid, coriaceous or fleshy, 1–2-seeded. (Name from Greek *sarkos,* flesh, and *kokkos,* berry; referring to the fleshy fr.) Five or 6 species from C. and W. China to Mal. Archipelago.—Ornamental shrubs, grown for their handsome evergreen foliage.

A. Lvs. ovate to elliptic-ovate: fr. dark scarlet...............................1. *S. ruscifolia*
AA. Lvs. oblong-lanceolate to lanceolate: fr. black...........................2. *S. Hookeriana*

1. **S. ruscifòlia** Stapf. Shrub to 2 m.; brts. puberulous when young: lvs. ovate or elliptic-ovate, 3–5 cm. long, acuminate, rounded or broad-cuneate at base, dark green and lustrous above, obscurely penninerved; petiole 3–5 mm. long: fls. white, fragrant, in few-, usually 4-fld. racemes: fr. subglobose, about 6 mm. across, dark scarlet. Fl.IX–II; fr.IX–XI. B.M.9045(c). Gn. 83: 73,127. C. and W. China. Intr. 1901. Zone VII?—**S. r. chinénsis** Rehd. & Wils., var. Lvs. elliptic-ovate to lance-elliptic, 3.5–6 cm. long, cuneate. W. China. Intr. ?

2. **S. Hookeriàna** Baill. Shrub to 2 m.; brts. puberulous when young: lvs. lance-oblong to narrow-lanceolate, 3–8 cm. long, acuminate, cuneate; petiole 6–8 mm. long; styles 3: fr. subglobose, 6 mm. across, black. Fl.X–III; fr.IX–XI. Gn.25:359. (*S. pruniformis* var. *Hookeriana* Hook.) W. Himal., Afghan. Cult. 1884. Zone VII?—**S. H. dígyna** Franch., var. Styles 2. W. China. Intr. 1908.—**S. H. húmilis** Rehd. & Wils., var. Shrub 0.3–1.5 m.: lvs. lanceolate to lance-oblong, 3–5 cm. long; midrib more prominent above; stamens less exserted; styles 2–3. B.M.9449(c). Gs. 20:52. (*S. h.* Stapf.) W. China. Intr. about 1907. Zone (V).

Related species: **S. salígna** (Don) Muell. Arg. Brts. glabrous: lvs. lance-oblong or oblong-ovate, 5–12 cm. long, caudate-acuminate, 3-nerved at base: fr. ovoid, about 1 cm. long, purple. B.R.1012(c). I.T.3:t.90. (*S. pruniformis* Lindl.) Himal. Intr. 1820. Zone VII?

2. **PACHYSÁNDRA** Michx. Evergreen or half-evergreen procumbent and ascending subshrubs with fleshy stems: lvs. alternate, dentate, 3-nerved at base: fls. white, in upright spikes, pistillate at base; staminate fls. with 4 sepals and 4 stamens and a rudimentary pistil; filaments thick, much longer than sepals, white; pistillate with 4 or more sepals; ovary 2–3-celled; cells 2-ovuled; styles 2–3, spreading: fr. a 2–3-horned caps. or drupe. (Name from the Greek *pachys,* thick, and *aner, andros,* man; alluding to the thick filaments.) About 5 species in E. Asia and in E. N. Am.

P. terminàlis Sieb. & Zucc. Evergreen; ascending to 25 cm., stoloniferous, glabrous: lvs. obovate to ovate, 5–10 cm. long, cuneate, acutish, coarsely dentate, dark green and lustrous above, petiole 1–3 cm. long, fl.-spike terminal, 3–5 cm. long: fr. whitish, ovoid, about 1 cm. long, '2–3-horned, berry-like. Fl.v. K.D.355. Gs.7:44. H.B.3:92(h). Japan. Intr. 1882. Zone V. Ornamental low evergreen plant; useful as ground cover.—**P. t. variegàta** Manning. Lvs. variegated with white.
Related species: **P. axillàris** Franch. Puberulous or nearly glabrous: lvs. ovate to oblong-ovate, 5–12 cm. long, rounded at base, rarely broad-cuneate, coarsely dentate: fls. white, in short axillary clusters or spikes, 1–2 cm. long: fr. yellowish, 3-horned. Franch., Pl. Delavay. t.26. Cult. 1934. Zone VII?—
P. procúmbens Michx. Half-evergreen; slightly pubescent: lvs. elliptic to obovate; spikes white or pinkish, to 12 cm. long, axillary at the base of the stem. B.M.1964(c). B.R.33(c). G.C.55:335. B.C.5:2426. W. Va. to Fla. Intr. 1800. Zone VI.

3. **BUXUS** L. Box. Evergreen shrubs or trees; buds with several outer scales: lvs. opposite, short-petioled, penninerved, entire, coriaceous, usually glabrous: fls. apetalous, in axillary or terminal clusters consisting usually of a terminal pistillate fl. and several staminate fls., the latter with 4 sepals and 4 stamens much longer than the sepals; pistillate fls. with 6 sepals and a 3-celled ovary with 3 short styles: fr. a subglobose or obovoid, 3-horned caps., separating into 3 2-horned valves, each with 2 lustrous seeds. (Ancient Latin name.) About 30 species in C. Eu., the Mediterr. region, in E. Asia and in the W. Indies and C. Am.

A. Lvs. elliptic to lance-oblong, broadest about or below the middle: brts. usually slightly pubescent ....1. *B. sempervirens*
AA. Lvs. obovate to oblong-obovate, broadest above the middle: brts. usually glabrous.
                                                    2. *B. microphylla*

1. **B. sempérvirens** L. Much-branched, dense shrub or tree to 6 or sometimes to 10 m.; brts. quadrangular, puberulous: lvs. elliptic or ovate to oblong, 1–3 cm. long, obtuse or emarginate at apex, dark green above, light or yellowish green beneath and lustrous on both sides: fls. in axillary clusters; staminate fls. sessile; the rudimentary pistil half as long as calyx; fr. about 8 mm. long. Fl.IV–V. R.I.5:t.153(c). F.D.20:t.2051(c). H.W.3:29. F.E.18: t.81(h). Gn.55:62(h). M.D.1920:t.9,10(h). S. Eu., N. Afr., W. Asia. Cult. since ancient times. Zone (V), VI. Ornamental shrub, much planted for its handsome evergreen foliage.—**B. s. arboréscens** L., var. Tall shrub or small tree: lvs. usually elliptic. The typical form.—**B. s. pyramidàta** (Carr.) Hartw. & Ruempl., var. Of upright pyramidal habit: lvs. generally ovate-oblong, 2–2.5 cm. long, slightly emarginate, dark glossy green. (*B. s.* var. *pyramidalis* Bean.)—**B. s. péndula** Dallimore. Arborescent; brs. slender, pendulous: lvs. oblong-ovate, about 2 cm. long, obtuse.—**B. s. angustifòlia** (Mill.) West., var. Arborescent: lvs. oblong, 2.5–3.5 cm. long. (*B. s.* f. *longifolia* Kirchn., *B. s. salicifolia* Hort.) S.H.2:f.90t.—**B. s. prostràta** Bean, var. Vigorous shrub with horizontally spreading brs.: lvs. mostly ovate-oblong to oblong, 2–3 cm. long, obtuse.—**B. s. handswórthii** (K. Koch) Dallimore. Vigorous shrub with upright brs.: lvs. broad-oval to ovate, usually emarginate, dark green. (*B. s.* var. *handsworthiensis* Henry) G.W.33:152(h).—
B. s. rotundifòlia Baill., var. Lvs. orbicular-obovate to broad-ovate or -oval, to 2.5 cm. long, and 1.5 cm. broad, rounded and emarginate, usually broad-cuneate at base. (*B. s. latifolia* Hort. in part.)—**B. s. bullàta** Kirchn., f. Lvs. broad-oval to obovate, bullate, to 3.5 cm. long and 2 cm. broad, emarginate, dark green. G.W.33:151. (*B. s. latifolia b.* Dallimore, *B. s.* var. *latifolia* Bean, *B. s. latifolia macrophylla* Hort.)—**B. s. glaùca** Kirchn., f. Lvs. oval

to ovate-oblong, 2–2.5 cm. long, obtuse, dull bluish green. G.W.33:151. (*B. s. macrophylla gl.* Hort.)—**B. s. argénteo-variegàta** West., var. Lvs. oval to elliptic-oblong, 1.5–2.5 cm. long, variegated with white. (*B. s.* var. *argentea* Loud.)—**B. s. aùreo-variegàta** West., var. Similar to the preceding, variegated with yellow. (*B. s.* var. *aurea* Loud.)—**B. s. marginàta** Loud., var. Lvs. edged yellow.—**B. s. suffruticòsa** L., var. EDGING Box. Low shrub, rarely exceeding 1 m.: lvs. oval to obovate, 1–2 cm. long, slightly emarginate: infl. usually only terminal. R.I.5:t.153(c). Known for centuries and much used for edgings of flower beds.—**B. s. myrtifòlia** (Lam.) Loud., var. Low shrub: lvs. oval or rhombic-ovate to narrow-oblong, 6–18 mm. long, 4–8 mm. wide, obtuse to acute. D.H.1:t.23f.3(c). S.H.2:f.90u. (?*B. s.* var. *leptophylla* Veillard, *B. s. angustifolia* Kirchn., not West.)—**B. s. rosmarinifòlia** (Madiot) Baill. Low shrub: lvs. linear-oblong, 8–15 mm. long, 3–6 mm. wide, margin revolute, obtuse to acute. (*B. s.* f. *thymifolia* Kirchn.)

Related species: **B. Wallichiàna** Baill. Shrub to 3 m.; brts. pubescent: lvs. linear-lanceolate, 3–6 cm. long, acute or obtusish, less glossy; petiole and midrib beneath puberulous. S.H.2:f.90h-i. Himal. Cult. 1880. Zone VII?—**B. baleàrica** Lam. Shrub or small tree to 20 m.; brts. slightly hairy at first, soon glabrous: lvs. broad-oval to ovate-oblong, 3–4.5 cm. long, emarginate, rarely minutely and abruptly pointed, leathery: staminate fls. stalked, with the rudimentary pistil 4 times shorter than sepals. D.H.1:t.23,f.1(c). Dallimore, Holly, 230,t.(h). Balearic Isls., Spain, Sardinia. Intr. 1780. Zone VII?

2. **B. microphýlla** Sieb. & Zucc. Compact shrub to 1 m. or sometimes prostrate, glabrous; stems sharply quadrangular: lvs. obovate to lance-obovate, 8–25 mm. long, rounded or emarginate, cuneate, fl.-clusters mostly terminal; staminate fls. with a rudimentary pistil about as long as calyx. Fl.v. K.D.355. J.C.20;3:t.6,f.C. S.H.2:f.90m-n(l). Japan. Intr. about 1860. Zone V or VI.—**B. m. japónica** (Muell. Arg.) Rehd. & Wils., var. Shrub to 2 m., with spreading brs.: lvs. obovate or orbicular-obovate, 1–3 cm. long, rounded or emarginate, cuneate, light green; petiole glabrous: fl.-clusters axillary. J.C.20,3:t.6,f.c. S.H.2:f.89v-x,90o-p. (*B. j.* Muell. Arg., *B. sempervirens* var. *j.* Mak., *B. obcordata* Hort.) Japan. Intr. about 1860. Zone V.— **B. m. koreàna** Nakai, var. Upright shrub to 0.6 m.; young brts. and petiole short-pilose: lvs. obovate or elliptic to oblong-elliptic, 6–15 mm. long, emarginate, pubescent on midrib above: fls. axillary and terminal. Korea. Intr. 1919. Zone IV.—**B. m. sínica** Rehd. & Wils., var. Brts. and the lower scales of winter-buds short-pilose: lvs. orbicular or obovate to elliptic-lanceolate, 8–35 mm. long, usually emarginate; petiole and midrib beneath toward the base puberulous. Kanehira, Formos. Trees, 476. China. Intr. about 1900. Zone VI? (?*B. Harlandii* var. *platyphylla* Schneid.)—This species with var. *japonica* and var. *koreana* is the hardiest of the Boxes.

Fam. 48. **EMPETRACEAE** Dum. CROWBERRY FAMILY

Evergreen, small, ericoid shrubs: lvs. alternate, crowded, linear, deeply furrowed beneath, estipulate: fls. polygamous or dioecious, small, regular, apetalous; sepals 2–3, imbricate or sometimes wanting and replaced by bractlets, disk wanting; stamens 2–3: ovary superior, 2–9-celled; cells 2-ovuled; style 2–9-parted with lacinate or toothed stigmas: fr. drupaceous; seeds ascending, with the micropyle turned toward the outside, albuminous. Three genera with about 7 species in arctic and temp. regions of the n. hemisphere; in Am. s. to the Andes.

A. Fls. in terminal heads: fr. dry: small upright shrubs..........................1. *Corema*
AA. Fls. solitary, axillary: fr. berry-like: procumbent shrubs...................2. *Empetrum*

1. **CORÈMA** Don. Evergreen upright shrubs; buds small, globose, with several outer scales: lvs. linear, often whorled: fls. dioecious, 3-merous, in terminal heads, each in the axil of a scale-like bract and with 5 or 6 imbricated bractlets at base, without calyx; stamens 3, rarely 4; style slender, with 3, rarely 4–5 narrow, often toothed stigmas: fr. a small drupe, with usually 3 nutlets. (Name from Greek *korema*, broom; referring to the bushy aspect of the plant.) Syn.: *Oakesia* Tuckerm., *Tuckermannia* Klotzsch. One species in E. N. Am. and one in W. Eu.

    C. Conràdii (Torr.) Loud. Shrub 15–60 cm. tall, nearly glabrous: lvs. linear, 3–6 mm. long, obtuse, often in threes; staminate fls. with long exserted purple filaments and brown anthers: fr. very small, dry. Fls. iv–v. H.I.531. Mem. Am. Acad. II.3:t.1. Nfd. to N. J. Cult. 1885. Zone III. Rarely cult.; attractive in spring with its purple staminate fls.

    Related species: **C. album** (L.) D. Don. Shrub to 60 cm.; brts. pubescent: lvs. linear, 6–10 mm. long, dark green: fls. inconspicuous; fr. white, berry-like, 6 mm. across, in clusters. S.H.2:f.92a-f. Portugal, Spain, Azores. Intr. 1774. Zone VII.

2. **ÉMPETRUM** L. Crowberry. Evergreen procumbent shrubs; buds small, globose, with few outer ciliate scales; lvs. linear-oblong, obtuse, crowded, thick: fls. dioecious or monoecious, axillary, with scale-like bracts at base; sepals 3, somewhat petaloid; stamens 3, with slender filaments; style very short, with 6–9 toothed stigmas: fr. a berry-like drupe with 6–9 nutlets. (Ancient Greek name, meaning "on rocks.") Five species in the arctic zone and extending on the higher mts. to the temp. regions, in Am. to antarctic S. Am.

    E. nígrum L. Procumbent shrub ascending to 25 cm.; brts. glandular when young: lvs. linear to linear-oblong, 4–6 mm. long, glandular on margin when young, spreading and soon reflexed: fls. purplish; anthers pinkish: fr. black, about 5 mm. across. Fl.iv–v; fr.viii–ix. R.I.5:t.158(c). F.D.21:t. 2108(c). S.E.8:t.1251(c). B.B.2:479. S.H.2:f.92g-o. (*E. scoticum* Hook.) N. Eu., N. Asia, in N. Am. s. to N. Y., Mich. and N. Calif. Intr. before 1700. Zone II. Ornamental shrub adapted for rockeries forming dense evergreen patches.—**E. n. purpúreum** (Raf.) DC., var. F. purple. E. Can. Intr. ?— **E. n. leucocárpum** L. M. Neuman, f. Fr. white.

    Closely related species: **E. atropurpúreum** Fern. & Wieg.: lvs. linear-oblong, loosely divergent, on the margin white-tomentose as are the brts.: fr. red to purplish black, 5–7 mm. across. (*E. nigrum* var. *purpureum* auth., not DC., *E. n. tomentosum* Dipp., *E. rubrum* var. *a*. Good.) Gulf St. Lawrence to Me. and N. H. Cult. 1890. Zone II.—**E. Eamèsii** Fern. & Wieg. Lvs. linear-oblong, 3–4 mm. long, ascending, becoming slightly divergent, white-tomentose on the margin as are the brts.: fr. pink or light red, becoming translucent, 4–5 mm. across. (*E. nigrum* var. *purpureum* auth., not DC., *E. rubrum* subsp. *E.* Good.) S. Lab., Nfd. and Que. Intr. 1925. Zone II.

Fam. 49. **CORIARIACEAE** Lem. CORIARIA FAMILY

    Shrubs or herbs with angular glabrous brts.: lvs. opposite or whorled, ovate to lanceolate, entire, estipulate: fls. perfect or polygamous, regular, small, greenish, axillary or in racemes; sepals 5, imbricate; petals 5, smaller, enlarging, becoming fleshy and enclosing the fr.; stamens 10, with short filaments: ovary superior, of 5–10 separate carpels; each with one pendulous ovule; styles free, filiform, papillose throughout: fr. berry-like; the indehiscent 1-seeded dry fruitlets enclosed by the fleshy petals; seed compressed, albuminous. One genus.

CORIÀRIA L. Characters of the family. (Name from Latin *coriarius*, pertaining to leather; referring to the use of the plant for tanning.)

A. Infl. lateral on last year's brts.: lvs. 3-nerved glabrous....................1. *C. japonica*
AA. Infl. terminal, 10-20 cm. long: lvs. 5-9-nerved..............................2. *C. terminalis*

1. **C. japónica** Gray. Shrub usually to 1, rarely to 3 m.: lvs. subsessile, ovate to lance-ovate, 3–10 cm. long, acuminate, 3-nerved, bright green: fls. small, greenish or reddish in racemes 2–3 together and 3–6 cm. long; staminate racemes shorter, drooping: fr: depressed-globose, about 5 mm. across; first bright red, changing to violet-black. Fl.v; fr.viii–ix. B.M.7509(c). G.F. 10:343. B.C.2:846. S.L.135(h).—Japan. Intr. 1892. Zone (V). Shrub with bright green lvs. and conspicuous fr. in fall.

Closely related species: **C. sínica** Maxim. Shrub to 6 m.: lvs. elliptic or broad-elliptic, 3–7 cm. long, abruptly short-pointed: fr. black. S.H.2:f.94e(1). S.L.135(h). C. and W. China. Intr. about 1895. Zone VI? or VII.—**C. myrtifòlia** L. Shrub to 3 m.: lvs. ovate, 2.5–6 cm. long, acute, grayish green: fls. greenish, in racemes about 2.5 cm. long: fr. black, about 6 mm. across. R.I.5:t.160(c). E.N.III.4:f.81. S.H.2:f.93. S. Eu., N. W. Afr. Intr. 1629. Zone VII.

2. **C. terminàlis** Hemsl. Herbaceous or suffruticose to 1 m.; brts. scabrid when young: lvs. subsessile, broad-ovate to lance-ovate, 2.5–7 cm. long, abruptly acuminate: fls. greenish in terminal racemes 12–22 cm. long: fr. black. Fl.vi; fr.viii. H.I.2220. Sikkim to W. China. Intr. 1908. Zone VII?— **C. t. xanthocárpa** Rehd. & Wils., var. Fr. yellow. B.M.8525(c). R.H.1907: 160,t(c). M.D.1897:1,t(c),62(h). G.C.34:282. Sikkim. Cult. 1895. Zone VI. —Particularly the var. is ornamental with its long spikes of yellow translucent berries.

Fam. 50. **ANACARDIACEAE** Lindl. CASHEW FAMILY

Deciduous or evergreen trees or shrubs with resinous bark: lvs. alternate, very rarely opposite, simple or compound, estipulate or very rarely stipulate: fls. perfect or unisexual, regular, small, in panicles, perigynous, epigynous or hypogynous; sepals 3–5; petals 3–5, usually imbricate, or wanting; stamens 5 or 10, rarely more, inserted with the petals at the edge of an annular disk; carpels 1 or 3–5, free or united, 1-ovuled; ovules anatropous; styles 1–5: fr. a drupe or nut, rarely dehiscent; seeds usually exalbuminous or with very thin albumen; embryo curved.—About 60 genera with 400 species chiefly in the trop. and subtrop. zones of both hemispheres.

A. Fls. apetalous: lvs. abruptly pinnate with 10–12 entire lfts....................1. *Pistacia*
AA. Fls. with petals.
  B. Lvs. simple, obtuse: fruiting panicle with long plumose sterile pedicels......2. *Cotinus*
  BB. Lvs. odd-pinnate or ternate; fruiting panicle without plumose pedicels.........3. *Rhus*

1. **PISTÁCIA** L. Evergreen or deciduous trees or shrubs; buds with several outer scales: lvs. alternate, simple, ternate or pinnate: fls. dioecious, apetalous or naked, in lateral panicles; staminate fls. with 2 bractlets at base and 1–2 sepals and with 3–5 stamens with short filaments; pistillate fls. with 2 bractlets, 2–5 sepals and a superior subglobose or ovoid, 1-ovuled ovary; style short, 3-parted: fr. a dry, obliquely ovoid drupe; seed compressed; embryo with plan-convex cotyledons. (Ancient Greek name *pistake,* Latin *pistacia.*) Eight species in the Mediterr. reg., Mex., Tex. and E. Asia.

P. chinénsis Bge. Deciduous tree to 25 m.; brts. puberulous: lvs. abruptly pinnate; lfts. 10–12, short-stalked, lanceolate, 5–9 cm. long, acuminate, oblique, puberulous when young, soon glabrous or nearly so; petiole puberulous: fls. small, the staminate ones in dense panicles 5–8 cm. long, pistillate fls. in longer and looser panicles: fr. globose-obovoid, 5–6 mm. across, compressed, red, finally purple, in much-compound panicles 15–24 cm. long. Fl. IV; fr. X–XI. C.C.218. K.B.1910:393,t(h). M.G.27:25(h). U.S.Im.109:t(h); 117:t(h). China. Intr. about 1890. Zone VII? Lvs. turning crimson in fall; sometimes planted as shade-tree in the S.; also used as stock for the pistachio.

2. **CÓTINUS** Adans. Deciduous shrubs or trees with yellow wood and a strong-smelling juice: lvs. alternate, slender-petioled, entire; buds with several imbricate dark red-brown scales: fls. polygamous or dioecious, yellowish, in large and loose terminal panicles; petals 5, oblong, twice as long as the lance-ovate sepals; stamens shorter than petals; ovary superior with 3 short lateral styles: the fruiting panicles with the pedicels of the numerous sterile fls. lengthened and plumose: fr. a small, dry, obliquely obovoid drupe; embryo with flat cotyledons. (Ancient Greek name of the wild olive.)—One species in N. Am. and one from S. Eu. to C. China.

A. Lvs. abruptly contracted at base, generally oval, glabrous.................1. *C. Coggygria*
AA. Lvs. cuneate, generally obovate, silky-pubescent beneath when young....2. *C. americanus*

1. **C. Coggýgria** Scop. SMOKE-TREE. Shrub of round bushy habit, to 5 m., often broader than high: lvs. oval to obovate, 3–8 cm. long, rounded or slightly emarginate at apex, glabrous; petiole 1–4 cm. long: fls. about 3 mm. across, polygamous: fruiting panicle 15–20 cm. long with numerous sterile pedicels furnished with long spreading purplish or greenish hairs and with few kidney-shaped reticulate frs. 3–4 mm. across. Fl.VI–VII; fr.VIII–IX. F.D.21:t.2174(c). B.C.2:864. G.C.29:92,t(h);72:247(h). Gn.78:606(h). S.L. t.6(hc). (*Rhus Cotinus* L., *C. coccygea* K. Koch.) S. Eur. to C. China and Himal. Cult. 1656. Zone V. Planted for the filmy effect of the plumose fruiting panicles and the yellow and purple autumn tints of the lvs.—**C. C. purpúreus** (Dupuy-Jamin) Rehd., var. Panicle with intensely purple hairs; young lvs. purplish. (*C. C. atropurpurea* Dipp.) Cult. 1870.—**C. C. péndulus** (Burvenich) Dipp. Brs. pendulous. R.B.11:257(h). Cult. before 1885.

2. **C. americànus** Nutt. Upright shrub or small tree to 10 or 12 m.: lvs. obovate to elliptic-obovate, 6–12 cm. long, rounded at apex, silky-pubescent beneath when young; petiole 1.5–3.5 cm. long: fls. dioecious: fruiting panicle 10–15 cm. long, with rather inconspicuous pale purplish or brownish hairs on the sterile pedicels and sparingly produced frs. about 3 mm. across. Fl.VI–VII; fr.VIII–IX. N.S.2:t.81(c). S.S.3:t.98,99. Gn.89:642(h). (*C. cotinoides* (Nutt.) Brit., *Rhus cotinoides* Nutt., *R. americana* Nutt.) Ala. to E. Tenn. and W. Tex. Intr. 1882. Zone V. Chiefly grown for its brilliant scarlet and orange fall coloring; the fruiting panicles are not showy.

3. **RHUS** L. SUMAC. Deciduous or evergreen shrubs, sometimes climbing, or trees; buds small, roundish, naked: lvs. alternate, odd-pinnate, 3-foliolate or simple: fls. small, dioecious or polygamous, in axillary or terminal panicles; petals 5, imbricate, longer than the 5-parted imbricate calyx; stamens 5, inserted below a brownish disk: ovary superior with 1 ovule and 3 terminal styles usually free: fr. a globose or compressed drupe with thin exocarp, resinous mesocarp and bony or crustaceous endocarp; embryo with flat cotyledons. (Ancient Greek name.) Including *Schmaltzia* Desv. and *Toxicodendron* Mill. About 150 species in subtrop. and temp. regions of both hemispheres.

A. Lvs. pinnate.
　B. Infl. terminal: fr. red, hairy.
　　c. Fruiting panicle upright: lfts. serrate (usually entire in No. 4).
　　　D. Rachis terete or winged below the terminal lfts. in No. 3.
　　　　E. Lfts. glabrous beneath or pubescent on the veins, glaucous.

F. Brts. glabrous, glaucous: infl. finely pubescent..................1. *R. glabra*
FF. Brts. and infl. densely pilose.....................................2. *R. typhina*
EE. Lfts. densely brownish pubescent beneath: low shrub to 1 m...3. *R. Michauxii*
DD. Rachis winged (not or slightly so in var. of No. 5).
  E. Lfts. entire or with few teeth toward the apex, 9–21.............4. *R. copallina*
  EE. Lfts. coarsely serrate, usually rounded at base, 7–13..............5. *R. chinensis*
CC. Fruiting panicles pendulous: lfts. entire, only in young plants sometimes serrate;
  rachis not or slightly winged only on the upper part.
  D. Brts. puberulous: lfts. 7–13, subsessile or sessile, pubescent on veins beneath.
                                                            6. *R. punjabensis*
  DD. Brts. glabrous: lfts. 5–9, nearly glabrous, distinctly stalked.........7. *R. Potanini*
BB. Infl. axillary: lfts. entire; lvs. crowded at end of brts.: fr. whitish.
  c. Frs. hispid: lfts. pubescent beneath, 13–17, 4–10 cm. long..........8. *R. trichocarpa*
  cc. Fr. glabrous: lfts. 7–15.
    D. Lfts. pubescent beneath at least on the veins, usually rounded at base: brts.
      pubescent at least when young.
      E. Lfts. to 16 cm. long and to 7 cm. broad, not closely veined, the distance between
        the veins more than 5 mm....................................9. *R. verniciflua*
      EE. Lfts. to 12 cm. long and to 4 cm. broad, closely veined, the veins 5 mm. or less
        distant ....10. *R. sylvestris*
    DD. Lvs. glabrous and glaucous beneath, sometimes pubescent when young, cuneate at
      base; brts. and petioles glabrous....................................11. *R. vernix*
AA. Lvs. ternate.
  B. Fls. in loose axillary panicles: fr. glabrous, white: lfts. 3–16 cm. long, usually glabrous.
                                                           12. *R. radicans*
  BB. Fls. in short and dense panicled spikes, catkin-like before opening: fr. red, pubescent:
    lfts. 1.5–7 cm. long.
    c. Lfts. pubescent, 2.5–7 cm. long, crenate-serrate.....................13. *R. aromatica*
    cc. Lfts. glabrate, 1.5–2.5 cm. long, with few rounded teeth or lobed......14. *R. trilobata*

Sect. 1. SUMAC DC. Fls. in terminal panicles, polygamous: frs. densely
pubescent, red: lvs. pinnate.

1. **R. glábra** L. SMOOTH S. Shrub to 3 or sometimes to 5 m.; brts. glabrous and glaucous: lfts. 11–31, lance-oblong, 5–12 cm. long, acuminate, serrate, glaucous beneath: fls. greenish, in dense panicles 10–25 cm. long,
puberulous: fr. scarlet, viscid-pubescent, in dense panicles. Fl.VII–VIII; fr.
VIII–IX(–IV). Em.572,t(c). M.A.1:36(c). F.E.30:681(h). M.D.1906:t.9(h).
S.L.310(h). (*Schmaltzia g.* Small.) Me. to B. C., s. to Fla. and Ariz. Cult.
1620. Zone II. Chiefly valued for the bright red autumnal foliage and the
scarlet fruiting panicles.—**R. g. laciniàta** Carr. Lfts. pinnately dissected.
F.E.31:875(h). Gn.54:507(h). R.H.1863:7(h). Cult. 1863. Zone VI.

2. **R. týphina** L. STAGHORN S. Shrub or small tree to 10 m.; brts. densely
velvety-hairy: lfts. 11–13, lance-oblong, 5–12 cm. long, acuminate, serrate,
glaucous beneath, pubescent when young: fls. greenish, in dense hairy panicles
10–20 cm. long: fr. crimson, densely hairy. Fl.VI–VII; fr.VIII–IX(–IV). Em.
571,t. S.S.3:102,103. Gn.54:505(h). G.F.2:343(h). M.D.1906:t.8(h). (*R.
hirta* Sudw., *Schmaltzia h.* Small.) Que. to Ont., s. to Ga., Ind. and Iowa.
Cult. 1629. Zone III. Grown for its lvs. turning early in fall to brilliant
scarlet and orange and for the crimson fruit-clusters.—**R. t. laciniàta** Wood.
Lfts. and bracts deeply and lacinately toothed and infl., sometimes partly
transformed into contorted bracts. Cult. ?—**R. t. disséata** Rehd., f. Lfts.
pinnately dissected. M.G.15.211(h). G.M.53:827(h). R.H.1907:10,11(h).
S.L.308(h). (*R. t. laciniata* Manning, not Wood.) Cult. 1898.

R. t. × *glabra* = **R. hýbrida** Rehd. Intermediate between the parents.
Occasionally found wild. Intr. 1923.

3. **R. Michaùxii** Sarg. Low stoloniferous shrub to 1 m.; stems densely
hairy: lfts. 9–15, ovate to oblong-ovate, 5–10 cm. long, acuminate, coarsely
serrate, pubescent above, densely brownish pubescent beneath; rachis winged
below the terminal lfts.: fls. greenish yellow in panicles 10–20 cm. long: fr.
compressed scarlet, densely hairy, in dense panicles. Fl.VI–VII; fr.VIII–IX.
G.F.8:405. (*Schmaltzia M.* Small, *R. pumila* Michx., not Meerb.) N. C. to
Ga. Intr. 1806. Zone V.

4. R. copallìna L. Shining S. Shrub or small tree, occasionally to 10 m.; brts. reddish, puberulous: lfts. 9–21, oblong-ovate to lance-ovate, 4–10 cm. long, usually acute, entire or sometimes with a few teeth near the apex, glabrous and lustrous above, usually pubescent beneath; rachis winged, pubescent: fls. greenish, in dense panicles: fr. hairy, crimson. Fl.vii–viii; fr. ix–x. S.S.3:t.104,105. K.S.81. (*Schmaltzia c.* Small.) Me. and Ont. to Minn., s. to Fla. and Tex. Cult. 1688. Zone IV. Planted for its lustrous lvs. changing to reddish purple in fall and for the crimson fr.-clusters.

Related species: **R. coriària** L. Shrub or small tree; brts. pilose: lfts. 9–15, ovate to elliptic or elliptic-oblong, 2.5–5 cm. long, acute or obtuse, coarsely dentate, pilose beneath, less so or nearly glabrous above; rachis narrowly winged at least near apex: fr. hairy, crimson, in dense narrow panicles. N.D. 2:46(c). F.D.21:t.2174(c). H.W.3:33. S. Eu., W. Asia. Cult. 1648. Zone (V).

5. R. chinénsis Mill. Large shrub or small tree to 8 m., with broad round head: brts. yellowish, glabrous: lfts. 7–13, subsessile, ovate to ovate-oblong, 6–12 cm. long, acute or short-acuminate, coarsely crenate-serrate, brownish pubescent beneath; rachis and often the petiole conspicuously winged, pubescent: fls. creamy-white, in broad panicles 15–25 cm. long: fr. subglobose, orange-red, densely pubescent. Fl.viii–ix; fr.x. S.I.1:t.58(c). M.K.t.62(c). B.C.5:2953. M.G.14:166(h). S.L.310(h). (*R. javanica* Thunb., not L., *R. semialata* Murr., *R. semialata* var. *Osbeckii* DC.) China, Japan. Cult. 1784. Zone V. Valued for its large creamy white fl.-clusters late in summer.—**R. ch. Roxbúrghii** (DC.) Rehd., var. Rachis not or slightly winged. Himal. Intr. ? Zone VII?

6. R. punjabénsis Stew. var. **sínica** (Diels) Rehd. & Wils. Tree to 12 m.; brts. short-pubescent: lfts. 7–11, sessile, ovate-oblong to oblong, 8–12 cm. long, acuminate, rounded to subcordate at the base, entire, pubescent on the veins beneath; upper part of rachis narrowly winged, or on young plants sometimes winged the whole length and lfts. up to 17: fls. whitish in pubescent panicles 12–20 cm. long, with spreading brs.; anthers purple: fr. suborbicular, 4–5 mm. across, red, densely hairy, in drooping panicles. Fls. vi–vii; fr.ix–x. (*R. sinica* Diels, *R. coriarioides* Dipp.) C. and W. China. Cult. 1890. Zone (V). With large pendulous panicles of red fr.

7. R. Potanìni Maxim. Tree to 8 m.; brts. glabrous or minutely pubescent: lfts. 7–9, subsessile or short-stalked, oblong-ovate to oblong-lance-olate, 6–12 cm. long, acuminate, broad-cuneate or rounded at base, entire or on young plants sometimes coarsely toothed, slightly pubescent on the veins beneath or nearly glabrous; rachis terete or sometimes slightly winged between the upper lfts.: fls. whitish, in puberulous panicles 10–20 cm. long; anthers yellowish: fr. dark red, densely hairy, in pendulous panicles. Fl. v–vi; fr.ix. M.D.1910:103. G.M.51:419;52:721. (*R. sinica* Koehne, not Diels, *R. Henryi* Diels.) C. and W. China. Cult. 1902. Zone (V). Similar to the preceding.

Sect. 2. Toxicodendron Gray. Fls. in axillary panicles, polygamous: fr. whitish to brownish, glabrous or hispid: lvs. pinnate or ternate.

8. R. trichocárpa Miq. Tree to 8 m.; young brts. pubescent: lfts. 13–17, short-stalked, ovate to oblong, 4–10 cm. long, acuminate, rounded at base, pubescent beneath and sometimes above, with 10–16 pairs of veins; rachis terete, pubescent: fls. in axillary slender puberulous panicles with the stalk 6–15 cm. long: fr. slightly compressed, hispid, about 6 mm. across, yellowish, the hispid exocarp soon separating and falling off, exposing the white mesocarp. Fls.vi; fr.viii. M.K.t.61(c). G.F.10:384. Japan, China. Intr. 1890.

Zone V. Lvs. changing to orange and scarlet in fall; petioles of young lvs. bright red.

9. **R. verniciflua** Stokes. VARNISH-TREE. Tree to 20 m.; brts. pubescent when young, later glabrous and light yellowish gray or gray, lenticellate: lfts. ovate to oblong-ovate, stalked, 7–20 cm. long and 3–7 cm. broad, acuminate, rounded to broad-cuneate at base, entire, pubescent beneath when young, at maturity at least along the midrib, with 8–16 pairs of veins; rachis terete: fls. yellowish white, in loose drooping panicles 15–25 cm. long: fr. compressed, broader than high, 6–8 mm. across, straw-yellow. Fl.VI; fr.IX. S.I.1:t.57(c). I.T.6:t.201. Gn.34:158;54:507. G.W.1:95(h),97. M.D.21:t.12 (h). S.L.307(h). (*R. vernicifera* DC., *R. vernix* Thunb., not L.—LACQUER-TREE.) Japan, China, Himal. Cult. 1874. Zone V. Planted for its large lvs. and the conspicuous pendulous fruiting panicles; in Japan and China it yields the famous varnish or lacquer of Japan; the oil expressed from the fr. is used for candle-making. The tree is poisonous.

10. **R. sylvéstris** Sieb. & Zucc. Tree to 10 m.; brts. short-pilose: lfts. 7–13, short-stalked, ovate to ovate-oblong, 4–10 cm. long, acuminate, rounded to broad-cuneate at base, pubescent above or nearly glabrous, pubescent beneath, or at least densely rarely slightly on the veins, with 18–25 pairs of conspicuous veins; petiole usually short-pilose: fls. in loose panicles 8–18 cm. long, with spreading brs., usually brownish pubescent: fr. brownish yellow, broader than high and very oblique, about 1 cm. across. Fl.VI; fr.IX–X. S.I. 1:58(c). S.H.2:f.99x-x⁴,100a. China, Japan, Korea. Intr. 1881. Zone VI. Lvs. turning deep red or scarlet in fall.

11. **R. vérnix** L. POISON S. Shrub or small tree to 7 m.; brts. glabrous, glaucous at first, gray at maturity: lfts. 7–13, short-stalked, elliptic to elliptic-oblong, 4–10 cm. long, acuminate, cuneate, entire, slightly pubescent at first, becoming quite glabrous, with 8–12 pairs of veins; petioles glabrous: fls. greenish yellow, in slender panicles 8–20 cm. long: fr. subglobose, compressed, 5–6 mm. across, light yellowish gray. Fl.VI–VII; fr.IX. Em.575,t(c). M.A.1: t.37(c). S.S.3:t.107,108. (*R. venenata* DC.) R. I. and Ont. to Minn., s. to Fla. and La. Cult. 1713. Zone IV. Lvs. orange and scarlet in fall, but highly poisonous to the touch.

Related species: **R. succedànea** L. WAX-TREE. Tree to 10 m.: lfts. 9–15, elliptic-oblong to oblong-lanceolate, 6–12 cm. long, long-acuminate, lustrous above, grayish green or glaucescent beneath, glabrous, with 12–20 pairs of veins: fr. 7–9 mm. across. S.I.1:57(c). S.H.2:f.99y-z²,100b. China, Japan, Himal. Cult. 1863. Zone VII?—**R. Delavayi** Franch. Glabrous shrub: lfts. 5–7, elliptic, 3–5 cm. long, light green beneath: infl. 5–8 cm. long. S.H.2:f.100c(l).—R. D. **quinquéjuga** Rehd. & Wils., var. Lfts. 5–11, slightly pubescent when young. W. China. Intr. 1908. Zone VII?

12. **R. radìcans** L. POISON IVY. Suberect, scrambling over walls and fences or high climbing by aërial rootlets; brts. sparingly pubescent or glabrate: lfts. 3, ovate or rhombic, 3–12 cm. long, acute or short-acuminate, entire or sparingly and coarsely dentate or sinuate, glabrous and lustrous above, more or less pubescent beneath, the lateral ones short-stalked, the terminal one on a stalk 1–3 cm. long; petiole 5–10 cm. long: fls. greenish white, in panicles 3–6 cm. long: fr. subglobose, 5–6 mm. across, whitish or yellowish, glabrous or short-pilose. Fl.VI–VII; fr.X(–III). B.M.1806(c). M.A. 1:t.38(c). Em.577,t(c). F.D.21:t.2175(c). S.L.306(h). (*R. Toxicodendron* auth., not L., *Toxicodendron vulgare* Mill.—POISON OAK.) N. S. to Fla., w. to Minn., Neb. and Ark. Cult. 1640. Zone III. Very showy in autumn with the brilliant scarlet and orange tints of its foliage. Lvs. poisonous to

the touch.—**R. r. Rydbérgii** (Small) Rehd., var. Shrubby, less than 1 m. high: lfts. sinuate-dentate, thickish, nearly glabrous or pubescent on veins beneath. Tex. to Mont. Intr. 1918. Zone V.

Related species, all poisonous, are: **R. Toxicodéndron** L. Upright to 0.5 m.: lfts. broadly rhombic-ovate, 3–7-lobed, pubescent beneath, rather firm: fr. pubescent at first, papillose at maturity. (*R. quercifolia* Robins. & Fern.) N. C. to Fla. and Tex. Cult. 1937. Zone V.—**R. diversíloba** Torr. & Gray. Upright shrub or sometimes climbing: lfts. ovate-elliptic or obovate, 3–7 cm. long, usually obtuse, coarsely crenate-serrate or 3-lobed. B.R.31:38(c). Zoe,1:t.4. S.H. 2:f.98d,99q. B. C. to Calif. Cult. 1845. Zone VI?—**R. orientàlis** (Greene) Schneid. Climbing or shrubby: brts. pubescent when young: lfts. dull green above, always entire, glabrous beneath except axillary tufts of hairs: fr. hispid. (*R. Toxicodendron* var. *hispida* Engl., *Ampelopsis japonica* Hort., ? *R. ambigua* Dipp.) Japan, China. Intr. about 1865. Zone V.

Sect. 3. LOBADIUM DC. Fls. in short, solitary or clustered spikes, catkin-like before opening, polygamo-dioecious, before the lvs.: fr. red, pubescent: lvs. ternate.

13. **R. aromática** Ait. FRAGRANT S. Usually prostrate shrub to 1 m., with ascending or diffuse brs., aromatically fragrant; brts. pubescent: lfts. 3, subsessile, ovate, 2.5–7 cm. long, acute or acuminate, crenate-serrate, pubescent, the terminal one cuneate and often obovate, the lateral ones oblique and rounded at base: fls. yellowish, in solitary or clustered spikes 5–20 mm. long, forming short panicles at the end of the brts.: fr. subglobose, about 6 mm. across, red, hairy. Fls.III–IV; fr.VIII. M.A.1:t.39(c). B.B.2:482. K.S. 89. (*R. canadensis* Marsh., not Mill., *Schmaltzia a.* Desv.) Vt. and Ont. to Minn., s. to Fla. and La. Intr. 1759. Zone III. Conspicuous in early spring with its yellow fls.; lvs. turning orange and scarlet in fall.—**R. a. seròtina** (Greene) Rehd., var. Upright shrub to 2 m.; lfts. acutish or obtuse, with few obtuse teeth or slightly lobed, pubescent beneath: fls. later, with the lvs. Ind. to Okla. Cult. 1929. Zone V.—**R. a. illinoénsis** (Greene) Rehd., var. Upright shrub to 2 m.; lfts. obtuse or rounded at apex, with few rounded teeth, pubescent above, more densely beneath. Mo. to Ill. Intr. 1936. Zone V.

14. **R. trilobàta** Nutt. ILL-SCENTED S. Upright or ascending shrub to 1, rarely 2 m., ill-scented: brts. pubescent: lfts. 3, sessile or subsessile, elliptic or obovate, 1.5–2.5 cm. long, cuneate, with few rounded teeth, the terminal one usually 3-lobed, the lateral ones usually cuneate, slightly pubescent when young, soon glabrate: fls. and frs. similar to those of the preceding species, except fls. greenish and frs. slightly smaller. Fls.III–IV; fr.VIII. B.B.2:483. K.S.91. (*R. canadensis* var. *t.* Gray, *Schmaltzia t.* Small.) Ill. to Wash., Calif. and Tex. Intr. 1877. Zone V. Fls. less conspicuous than those of *R. aromatica* and habit more upright.

Fam. 51. **CYRILLACEAE** Lindl. CYRILLA FAMILY

Shrubs or small trees: lvs. alternate, entire, estipulate: fls. perfect, regular, small, in racemes; sepals 5, imbricate, often enlarged in fr.; petals 5, imbricate; stamens 5 or 10, hypogynous, with dilated filaments; ovary superior, 2–4-celled, each cell with 1–4 pendulous ovules; style short, with 2–4 stigmas: fr. dehiscent or indehiscent and angled or winged; seeds albuminous with small straight embryo. Three genera in N. and S. Am.

A. Racemes axillary; stamens 5: fr. ovoid..1. *Cyrilla*
AA. Racemes terminal; stamens 10: fr. 3–4-winged..2. *Cliftonia*

1. **CYRÍLLA** L. Deciduous to evergreen shrub or small tree; buds small, with several loose pointed scales: lvs. short-petioled, glabrous: fls. white, in narrow slender axillary racemes; petals 5, lance-oblong, about twice

reticulate beneath. Canary Isls., Azores, Madeira, s. Spain. Not hardy within our area.—*I. P.* × *I. Aquifolium;* see under No. 1.

2. **I. cornùta** Lindl. Shrub to 3 m., with spreading brs. forming a broad dense bush: brts. glabrous: lvs. short-stalked, oblong-rectangular, 3.5–10 cm. long, with 3 strong almost equal spines at the broad apex and 1 or 2 strong spines on each side at base, or on older plants rounded at base, dark green and lustrous above: fr. globose, 8–10 mm. across, bright red, on stalks 8–15 mm. long, clustered. Fl.iv–v; fr.ix. B.M.5059(c). G.C.1850:311. F.S.7:216;9:t.895 (c). U. S. Im. 205:t.331,332(c). E. China. Intr. 1846. Zone VII. With lustrous lvs. of unusual shape.—**I. c. Burfórdii** (S. R. Howell) DeFrance, var. Lvs. elliptic or obovate, spiny-pointed, broad-cuneate, entire or with one pair of spiny teeth near apex. N.H.13:193. Cult. 1895.

3. **I. Pérnyi** Franch. Shrub or sometimes tree to 10 m.; young brts. minutely pubescent: lvs. crowded, rhombic or quadrangular-ovate, 1.5–3 cm. long, with 1–3 spines on each side, the upper pair the largest, but shorter than the terminal spine, dark glossy green above, glabrous; petiole 2 mm. long, puberulous; fls. pale yellow, in dense sessile clusters: fr. subsessile, globose-ovoid, 6–8 mm. long, red, clustered. Fl.v; fr.viii. H.I.16:1539. G.C.45:75. R.B.35:24(h). S.L.200(h). C. and W. China. Intr. 1900. Zone VI. Of compact habit with handsome glossy lvs.—**I. P. Veitchii** (Veitch) Bean, var. Lvs. larger and broader, 3.5–5 cm. long, with 4–5 rigid spines on each side. D.H.130,t.,f.4. Intr. 1900.

Closely related species: **I. ciliospinòsa** Loes. Shrub to 4 m.; young brts. densely short-villous: lvs. ovate, 2.5–4 cm. long, spinose-serrate with small aristate teeth pointing forward. M.D.1919:t.2A,B. (*I. bioritsensis* var. *c.* Comber.) C. and W. China. Intr. 1908. Zone VII?

4. **I. dipyrèna** Wall. Tree to 12 m.; young brts. puberulous, angular: lvs. elliptic-ovate to oblong, 5–10 cm. long, acuminate, cuneate, remotely spiny-dentate, or on old trees partly entire, dull green above; petiole 3–6 mm. long: fls. very short-stalked; staminate peduncles usually 1-fld.: fr. subsessile, globose-ovoid, about 8 mm. long, red, with usually 2 stones. Fl.iv–v; fr.x–xii. Wallich, Pl. As. Rar. 3:t.292(c). Brandis, For. Fl.t.15. S.H.2:105r-s²,108c. S.L.199(h). D.H.124,t(h). (*I. Wallichiana* Hort.) Himal. Intr. 1840. Zone VII.—**I. d. paucispinòsa** Loes., var. Lvs. ovate to ovate-oblong, 5–7 cm. long, with only 3–5 teeth on each side. W. China. Intr. 1901?

I. d. × *Aquifolium;* see under No. 1.

5. **I. íntegra** Thunb. Shrub or tree to 12 m.; brts. glabrous, angled: lvs. slender-stalked, elliptic or elliptic-oblong or oblong-obovate, 5–10 cm. long, at the apex contracted into a short obtuse point, cuneate, entire, very rarely with a few teeth, dark green and lustrous above; petiole 8–15 mm. long: fls. fascicled: fr. subglobose, about 1 cm. across, red, on stalks 5–8 mm. long, fascicled or solitary. Fl.iii–iv; fr.viii–ix. S.I.1:t.60(c). G.C.69:15. Japan. Intr. 1864. Zone VII.—**I. i. leucóclada** Maxim., var. Mature brts. pale yellow: lvs. thinner, to 14 cm. long, sometimes slightly serrulate, with acutish point. (*I. l.* Mak.) C. Japan. Intr. 1915. Zone (V).

6. **I. Fargèsii** Franch. Shrub or tree to 6 m.; brts. glabrous: lvs. oblong-lanceolate to oblanceolate or linear-lanceolate, 6–12 cm. long, long-acuminate, cuneate, serrulate above the middle, dull green above; petiole 8–12 mm. long: staminate fls. short-stalked, in dense clusters: frs. globose, 6–8 mm. across, red, usually clustered, on stalks 2–6 mm. long. Fl.v–vi; fr.ix–x. D.H. 130,t,f.1. W. China. Intr. 1900. Zone VI. Easily distinguished from the other species by its long and narrow lvs.

548

Related species: **I. Franchetiàna** Loes. Lvs. elliptic-obovate to lance-oblong or oblanceolate, 4–10 cm. long, abruptly acuminate, usually broad-cuneate, denticulate: frs. short-stalked, in dense clusters. W. China. Intr. 1907. Zone VII?—**I. coràllina** Franch. Tree to 7 m.: lvs. lance-oblong to lanceolate, 6–14 cm. long, sharply serrate or serrulate, acuminate, lustrous above; petiole 4–8 mm. long: frs. 3–4 mm. across, clustered, subsessile. C. and W. China. Intr. about 1900. Zone VII?—**I. latifòlia** Thunb. Tree to 20 m.: lvs. elliptic to oblong-lanceolate, 8–18 cm. long, acuminate, serrate, lustrous: petiole 1–2 cm. long: frs. about 8 mm. across, short-stalked, in dense clusters. B.M.5597(c). P.F.3:f.240. S.I.1:t.62(c). Japan. Intr. 1840. Zone VII.—*I. l.* × *Aquifolium;* see under No. 1.

7. **I. rugòsa** Fr. Schmidt. Low spreading, sometimes prostrate shrub; brts. glabrous, angled: lvs. ovate-oblong to lanceolate, 1.5–5 cm. long, obtusish or acute, rounded to broadly cuneate at base, remotely crenate-serrate, dark green, lustrous and rugose above; petiole 2–3 mm. long; staminate fls. several, short-stalked, pistillate 1 or 2: fr. about 6 mm. across, red, on stalks 2–4 mm. long. Fl.v–vi; fr.viii–ix. Mém. Acad. Sci. St. Pétersb. VII.12,2:t.3. Japan, Saghal. Intr. 1895. Zone III.

Here may be mentioned **I. vomitòria** Ait. YAUPON. Tree to 8 m.; young brts. puberulous: lvs. short-stalked, elliptic to ovate-oblong, 1–3, rarely to 5 cm. long, obtusish, crenate, glabrous: frs. 5–6 mm. across, short-stalked, usually clustered. S.S.1:t.48. B.B.2:487. C.L.13:498(h). (*I. Cassine* Walt., not L., *I. caroliniana* Loes., not Mill.) Va. to Fla., w. to Ark. and Tex. Intr. 1700. Zone VII.

Sect. 2. LIOPRINUS Loes. Fls. or infl. solitary, in the axils of the lvs. on young brts. or at the base of the young brts.

8. **I. opàca** Ait. AMERICAN HOLLY. Tree with spreading brs. forming a narrow pyramidal head, to 15 m.; young brts. finely puberulous: lvs. elliptic to elliptic-lanceolate, 5–10 cm. long, with large remote spiny teeth, rarely nearly entire, dull green above, yellowish green beneath; petiole 6–12 mm. long; staminate fls. in 3–9-fld. stalked cymes: fr. globose, 8–10 mm. across, red, usually solitary. Fl.vi; fr.x(–iv). Em.385,t(c). S.S.1:t.45. Gng.4:276, 277(h). Am. For. 31:726(h);37:725. (*I. querci-folia* Meerb.) Mass. to Fla., w. to Mo. and Tex. Intr. 1744. Zone V. Not as handsome as *I. Aquifolium* but hardier; the berried brs. much used for Christmas decorations.—**I. o. subíntegra** Weatherby, f. Lvs. entire or nearly so.—**I. o. xanthocárpa** Rehd., f. Fr. yellow. Intr. 1901.

I. o. × *Cassine* = **I. attenuàta** Ashe. Lvs. elliptic to oblong-obovate, 4–8 cm. long, spiny-pointed and with 1–4 spreading spiny teeth on each side, pale below and sparingly short-pilose on midrib: infl. pubescent: fr. about 6 mm. across, solitary or in threes on a short stalk. (*I. Topeli* Hort.) Fla., with the parents. Cult. 1931. Zone VII?

9. **I. pedunculòsa** Miq. Shrub or small tree to 10 m., glabrous: lvs. ovate or elliptic, 3–7 cm. long, rounded or broad-cuneate at base, acuminate, entire, lustrous green above; petiole 0.6–1.5 cm. long: fls. in slender-peduncled cymes: fr. subglobose, 6 mm. across, bright red, on slender pedicels 1–2 cm. long, solitary or several on a slender peduncle 2–4 cm. long. Fl.vi; fr.x. S.I. 1:t.61(c). Nat. Nurseryman, 34;127. N.H.18:71. (*I. fujisanensis* Sakato.) Japan. Intr. 1892. Zone (V). One of the hardiest evergreen Hollies.—**I. p. continentàlis** Loes., var. Lvs. 8–12 cm. long, thicker, often remotely appressed-serrulate above the middle: sepals ciliate. C. China. Intr. 1901. Zone VII.

Related species: **I. rotúnda** Thunb. Tree to 12 m., glabrous: lvs. elliptic to oblong, 4–11 cm. long, acute to short-acuminate, broad-cuneate at base, entire; petioles 1–2.5 cm. long: fr. 5–6 mm across, in umbels; pedicels 3–8 mm.; peduncle 6–12 mm. long. S.I.1:t.60(c). F.S.7:216. G.C.1850:311. P.F.1:f.28. Japan, Korea. Intr. about 1850. Zone VII.—**I. venulòsa** Hook. f. Shrub or tree, glabrous: lvs. elliptic-ovate to oblong-ovate, 10–18 cm. long, caudate-acuminate,

broad-cuneate to rounded at base, entire, reticulate beneath; petiole 1.5–2.5 cm.
long: fr. globose, 2.5–3 mm. across, red, in dense stalked umbels. Himal. to W.
China. Cult. 1934. Zone VII.—I. **Cassine** L. DAHOON. Shrub or tree to 12 m.;
brts. usually pubescent: lvs. oblong to oblanceolate, rarely obovate, 4–10 cm.
long, obtuse or acute, entire or with few appressed teeth near apex, finely
pubescent beneath: fls. in peduncled cymes: fr. red, 6–8 mm. across. S.S.1:t.46.
B.B.2:487. S.M.670. (*I. Dahoon* Walt.) Va. to Fla. and La. Intr. 1726. Zone
VII.

10. **I. yunnanénsis** Franch. Shrub to 4 m.; brts. densely short-villous:
lvs. short-stalked, ovate to oblong-ovate, 1.5–3 cm. long, acute, crenate-
serrate or serrulate, lustrous above, pubescent below when young, at least
on the midrib, reddish brown when young: staminate fls. several, on slender
peduncles: pistillate solitary: fr. globose, 6 mm. across, red, on a slender
stalk 4–8 mm. long. M.D.1919:t.1G-L. Fl.VI; fr.IX. W. China. Intr. 1901.
Zone VII? Similar to *I. crenata*, but fr. red.—**I. y. géntilis** Loes., var. Lvs.
and often the brts. glabrous or nearly so. Intr. 1910. Zone (V).

Related species: **I. Sugeròki** Maxim. Dense shrub to 2 m.; brts. finely pubescent: lvs. elliptic, 2–4 cm. long, acute or acutish, cuneate, serrate or crenate-
serrate above the middle, glabrous; petioles short, puberulous: staminate fls.
usually 3 on a peduncle 8–10 mm. long: fr. solitary, about 7 mm. across, on a
stalk 1–2 cm. long (to 4 cm. in *I. S.* f. *longipedunculata* Maxim.). Mém. Acad.
Sci. St. Pétersb. VII,29,3:t.1,f.7. S.I.2:t.38 (as *I. crenata;* frs. should be red).
Japan. Intr. 1914. Zone V?—**I. purpúrea** Hassk. Tree to 13 m., glabrous: lvs.
narrow-elliptic to elliptic-oblong or obovate-oblong, 6–12 cm. long, acuminate,
cuneate at base, rarely rounded, crenate or crenate-serrulate; petiole 5–15 mm.
long: fr. ellipsoid, 6–10 mm. long, red, slender-pedicelled, 1–3, rarely 7, on a
peduncle 5–12 mm. long. N.H.14:330. Japan, China. Cult. 1900. Zone VII.—
I. micrococca Maxim. Shrub or tree to 15 m., glabrous: lvs. elliptic-ovate to
ovate-oblong, 8–16 cm. long, chartaceous, long-acuminate, rounded at base, appressed-serrulate, veins beneath elevated; petiole 1.5–2.5 cm. long: fr. globose,
3 mm. across, red, many in dense cymes 1–2 cm. across. Japan, China. Cult.
1934. Zone VII?

11. **I. glábra** (L.) Gray. INKBERRY. Evergreen or half-evergreen shrub to
2.5 m., with upright brs., puberulous when young: lvs. obovate to oblanceolate,
2–5 cm. long, acute or obtusish, cuneate, with few obtuse teeth near apex or
entire, dark green and lustrous above, glabrous; petiole 3–6 mm. long; staminate fls. several on a slender stalk, pistillate, often solitary, 5–8-merous: fr.
globose, 6 mm. across, short-stalked, black. Fl.VI; fr.IX(-V). L.B.450(c).
B.B.2:487. (*Prinos glaber* L.—WINTERBERRY.) N. S. to Fla., w. to Mo. Intr.
1759. Zone III. With dark green lustrous lvs.

Another black-fruited species is **I. szechwanénsis** Loes. Shrub to 4 m.: lvs.
elliptic-ovate to oblong-lanceolate, 3–6 cm. long, crenately or finely serrulate,
lustrous: fls. 4–6-merous, solitary or the staminate sometimes 2–3-fld., at base
of the young brts. and also on the old brts.: fr. 6–8 mm. across, on a stalk
4–8 mm. long. C. China. Intr. 1907. Zone VII.

12. **I. crenàta** Thunb. Much-branched shrub, rarely small tree to 7 m.;
young brts. minutely puberulous, terete: lvs. crowded, short-stalked, elliptic
or obovate to oblong-lanceolate, 1.5–3 cm. long, acute, cuneate or broad-
cuneate, crenate-serrulate or serrulate, lustrous dark green above, glabrous:
fls. 4-merous, staminate in 3–7-fld. cymes, pistillate solitary: fr. globose, 6
mm. across, black, on a stalk 4–6 mm. long. Fl.V–VI; fr. X. M.D.1919:t.1A-F.
Gg.6:165(h). Gn.M.5:273(h). S.L.201(h). (*I. Fortunei* Hort.) Japan. Intr.
1864. Zone VI. With small dark green lvs. and small black fr.—**I. c. latifòlia** Goldring. Lvs. elliptic or obovate. D.H.118,t.f.6. (*I. c.* var. *typica* Loes.,
I. c. major Hort., *I. c. elliptica* Hort.) The typical form.—**I. c. convéxa** Mak.,
var. Upright slender-branched shrub: lvs. oval or oval-obovate to oblong-
oval, bullate, convex above, concave below. (*I. c.* f. *bullata* Rehd.) Intr.
1919. Zone V.—**I. c. luteo-variegàta** Reg., var. Lvs. spotted yellow. (*I. c.*

aureo-variegata Goldring, *I. c. variegata* Nichols.)—**I. c. longifòlia** Goldring.
Lvs. elliptic-oblong to lanceolate.—**I. c. microphýlla** Maxim., var. Lvs.
elliptic to oblong, 8–14 mm. long. Zone (V).—**I. c. Hélleri** (Craig) Rehd.,
f. Dwarf compact shrub: lvs. oval, 6–12 mm. long, obtusish and mucronulate, with few minute teeth. (*I. H.* Craig.) Cult. 1936. Zone (V).—**I. c.
nummulària** Yatabe, var. Dwarf compact shrub: lvs. very crowded, broad-
ovate to orbicular, 4–15 mm. long, with few small teeth near apex or entire:
fr.-stalk about 2 mm. long. D.H.118,t.f.5. (*I. c. Mariesii* Dallim.) Intr. 1879.
    Subgen. II. PRINOS Gray. Lvs. deciduous: fls. solitary in the axils of the
lvs. or fescicled, together with the lvs.: fr. red. (*Prinos* L.)
    Sect. 1. EUPRINUS Loes. Nutlets smooth on back: frs. 4–8 mm. across: lvs.
and fls. never fascicled.
    13. I. geniculàta Maxim. Slender-branched shrub; brts. glabrous: lvs.
ovate to elliptic-ovate, 3–5 cm. long, acuminate, rounded at base, sharply
serrate, slightly pubescent on midrib beneath: fls. long-stalked; staminate
infl. 3–7-fld.: fr. globose, 5 mm. across, red, on a filiform pendulous stalk 1.5–
3.5 cm. long. Fls. v–vi; fr.viii. Mém. Acad. Sci. St. Pétersb. VII.29,3:t,f.10.
G.C.74:235. H.B.1:77. Japan. Intr. 1894. Zone V. Ornamental shrub, very
attractive and distinct with its red berries on slender pendulous stalks; the
lvs. turn yellow in autumn.
    14. I. serràta Thunb. Shrub to 5 m.; young brts. puberulous: lvs. elliptic
or ovate, 2–5 cm. long, acute or acuminate, serrulate, dull green above,
pubescent beneath: fls. short-stalked, 4–5-merous: fr. globose, red, 4–5 mm.
across. Fl.vi; fr.x. S.I.1:t.61(c). S.T.1:t.15. (*I. Sieboldii* Miq., *I. serrata*
var. *S.* Rehd.) Japan. Intr. 1866. Zone V. Similar to *I. verticillata,* but
smaller in every part; fr. less persistent.—**I. s. xanthocárpa** Rehd., f. Fr.
yellow (*I. s. fr. luteo* Hort.)—**I. s. leucocárpa** Bean, var. Fr. white. (*I. s.
fr. albo* Hort.)—**I. s. argùtidens** (Miq.) Rehd., var. Lvs. glabrous beneath,
the teeth more remote and less fine; petioles shorter: fls. usually 4-merous.
Add. 3:t.106(c). (*I. a.* Miq.) Intr. 1892.
    15. I. verticillàta (L.) Gray. BLACK-ALDER. Shrub to 3 m., with spread-
ing brs.: lvs. elliptic or obovate to oblanceolate or oblong-lanceolate, 3.5–7
cm. long, acute or acuminate, cuneate, serrate or doubly serrate, usually pubescent beneath, at least on the veins: all fls. short-stalked; staminate infl.
2–10-fld.: fr. globose, bright red, about 6 mm. across, often in pairs. Fl.vi–vii;
fr.x(–i). B.M.8832(c). Add.3:t.116(c). Em.388,t(c). G.C.68:201. F.E.24:
779(h). (*Prinos verticillatus* L.) Can. to Fla., w. to Wis. and Mo. Intr.
1736. Zone III. Valued for its bright red berries persisting a long time
on the brs.; the lvs. turn black or brown after frost.—**I. v. chrysocárpa**
Robins., f. Fr. yellow. Intr. 1885.—**I. v. tenuifòlia** (Torr.) S. Wats., var. Lvs.
usually obovate, thinner, larger, pellucid-puncticulate under the lens: fr.
usually solitary. B.B.3:489. (*I. bronxensis* Brit.)—**I. v. padifòlia** (Willd.)
Torr. & Gr., var. Lvs. 5–12 cm. long, tomentulose beneath. Cult. 1920.—**I. v.
fastigiàta** (Bickn.) Fern., var. Dense shrub with ascending brs.; lvs. usually
oblong-lanceolate, 2–4 cm. long, acuminate, cuneate, glabrous or loosely pubescent on veins beneath. E. Can. to Mass. Intr. ?—**I. v. cyclophýlla**
Robins., var. Lvs. suborbicular, small, finely pubescent on veins beneath,
crowded at end of brts. Ill. Cult. 1934.
    16. I. laevigàta (Dum.-Cours.) Gray. WINTERBERRY. Shrub to 2, rarely
3 m., with upright brs. glabrous when young: lvs. lance-ovate to lanceolate,
3–6 cm. long, acuminate, cuneate, appressed-serrulate, lustrous and bright
green above, glabrous or slightly pubescent on the veins beneath; staminate

fls. 1–2 on slender stalks 8–18 mm. long; sepals not ciliate: fr. depressed-globose, 7–8 mm. across, orange-red, solitary, its stalk 2–5 mm. long. Fl.v–vi; fr.ix(–i). Gt.55:t.1551,f.3(c). G.F.4:221. B.C.3:1640. S.L.201(h). Me. to Pa. and Va. Intr. 1812. Zone IV. Planted for its orange-red fr.; the lvs. turn yellow in fall.—I. l. **Herveÿi** Robins., f. Fr. yellow. Intr. ?

Sect. 2. PRINOIDES Gray. Nutlets ribbed or striate on back; fr. 8–12 mm. across: fls. and lvs. often fascicled on short spurs.

17. **I. dùbia** (G. Don) B. S. P. Shrub to 2 m.; young brts. slightly pubescent: lvs. elliptic-oblong to oblong, 3.5–7 cm. long, acutish, rounded to broad-cuneate at base, obscurely serrulate, pubescent and reticulate beneath: fls. slender-stalked, at base of brts. below the lvs.; staminate infl. 6–9-fld.: fr. globose, 8–10 mm. across, scarlet, solitary on a stalk 7–10 mm. long. Fl.vi; fr.x–xi. G.F.2:41. B.C.3:1639. (*I. Amelanchier* M. A. Curt.) Va. to La. Intr. 1880. Zone (V).

Related species: **I. lóngipes** Chapm. Lvs. elliptic to broadly elliptic or elliptic-obovate, 3–5 cm. long, acute or obtusish, remotely crenate-serrulate, glabrous or pubescent when young: staminate fls. solitary: fr. 8–10 mm. long on a stalk 1–2 cm. long. N. C. and Tenn. to Ga. and Ala. Intr. 1906. Zone V.

18. **I. decídua** Walt. Shrub or small tree to 10 m., with light gray spreading brs.; brts. glabrous: lvs. partly fascicled, obovate to obovate-oblong, 3.5–7 cm. long, usually obtusish, cuneate, obtusely serrate, dark green and lustrous above and with impressed veins, pale and pubescent on the midrib beneath, thickish; staminate fls. on slender stalks about 1 cm. long; calyx-lobes obtuse: fr. globose, 7–8 mm. across, orange to scarlet. Fl.v; fr.ix–x(–iv). S.S.1:t.49. G.C.II.14:689. S.H.2:f.105y-z¹;109g-h. (*I. prinoides* Ait., *Prinos deciduus* DC.) Va. to Fla., w. to Tex. Intr. 1760. Zone V.

19. **I. montàna** Gray. Shrub or slender tree to 12 m.; brts. glabrous: lvs. ovate or elliptic-ovate to lanceolate, 6–16 cm. long, acute or acuminate, cuneate, rarely rounded at base, sharply serrate, glabrous or sparingly pubescent on the veins beneath; petiole 1–1.5 cm. long: staminate fls. on stalks 3–8 mm. long; calyx-lobes acute or acutish, ciliate: fr. about 1 cm. across, orange-red, on stalks 2–6 mm. long. Fl.vi; fr.ix(–iv). S.S.1:t.50. B.B.2:488. S.M.674. (*I. monticola* Gray, *I. dubia* var. *monticola* Loes.) N. Y. to S. C., w. to Ala. Cult. 1870. Zone V.—I. m. **mollis** (Gray) Fern., var. Lvs. broad-ovate to ovate-lanceolate, 4–12 cm. long, soft-pubescent beneath. (*I. dubia* var. *m.* Loes.) Mass. to Ga. Cult. ?—I. m. **Beàdlei** (Ashe) Fern., var. Lvs. ovate to elliptic-oblong, scarcely acuminate, 4–9 cm. long, densely pubescent. N. C. and Tenn. to Ga. and Ala. Cult. 1906. Zone VI?—I. m. **macrópoda** (Miq.) Fern., var. Lvs. ovate to elliptic, more coarsely serrate, pubescent beneath, chiefly on the veins; petioles to 2 cm. long. S.I.1:t.59(c). (*I. macropoda* Miq., *I. dubia* var. *macropoda* Loes.) Japan. Intr. 1894.

Related species: **I. macrocárpa** Oliv. Tree to 10 m.; glabrous: lvs. elliptic to lance-oblong, 6–12 cm. long, serrulate: fls. about 1 cm. across, 5–7-merous: fr. about 1.5 cm. across, black. H.I.18:1787. C. China. Intr. 1908. Zone VII?

2. **NEMOPÁNTHUS** Raf. Deciduous slender-branched shrub, glabrous or nearly so; buds ovoid, small, with about 3 outer scales: lvs. alternate, slender-petioled, entire or slightly toothed; stipules small, caducous: fls. polygamo-dioecious, small, whitish, on slender axillary peduncles, the staminate 1–4-fld., the pistillate 1-fld.; sepals 4–5; petals linear, 4–5; stamens free, with slender filaments: fr. a drupe with 4–5 bony nutlets. (Greek *nema*, thread, and *anthos*, flower; referring to the filiform pedicels.) Syn. *Nemopanthes* DC., *Ilicioides* Dum.-Cours. One species.

N. mucronàtus (L.) Trel. MOUNTAIN HOLLY. Shrub to 3 m.; young brts. purplish, older ones ashy-gray: lvs. elliptic to oblong, 2.5–3.5 cm. long, mucronate, entire or sometimes slightly toothed, grayish green beneath; petiole 6–12 mm. long: fls. 4–5 mm. across; pedicels 1–2, in fr. to 3 cm. long: fr. subglobose, 6–8 mm. across, dull red. Fl.v–vi; fr.viii–ix. S.T.3:t.81. B.B.2:490. (*N. canadensis* DC., *N. fascicularis* Raf.) N. S. to Ont., Wis. and Va. Intr. 1802. Zone III. With attractive red frs. in summer; lvs. turning yellow in fall.

Fam. 53. CELASTRACEAE Lindl. STAFF–TREE FAMILY

Shrubs or trees often climbing: lvs. alternate or opposite, simple; stipules small: fls. perfect or unisexual, regular, small, usually greenish, in axillary or terminal cymes or sometimes solitary; sepals and petals 4–5, imbricated; stamens 5, rarely 10; disk present; ovary superior, 2–5-celled, each cell with 1–2 ovules; style short or nearly wanting, with 2–5-lobed stigma: fr. a dehiscent caps., rarely a drupe or samara; seed albuminous, usually arillate; embryo with broad, flat, usually green cotyledons and short radicle.—About 40 genera with 375 species distributed through both hemispheres except the arctic zone.

A. Fr. a dehiscent capsule.
  B. Fr. of 3–5 carpels.
    c. Caps. 4–5-celled, usually lobed: lvs. opposite, rarely alternate and linear; upright or climbing by rootlets..1. *Euonymus*
    cc. Capsule 3-celled, subglobose: lvs. alternate, broad; twining shrubs......2. *Celastrus*
  BB. Fr. usually of 1 carpel: low shrubs with small lvs. 5–40 mm. long.
    c. Lvs. opposite, persistent; unarmed shrubs............................3. *Pachistima*
    cc. Lvs. alternate, deciduous, entire; stamens 10: spiny shrub............ 4. *Forsellesia*
A.A. Fr. indehiscent, 3–winged: fls. in large terminal panicles: lvs. alternate, large.
    5. *Tripterygium*

1. EUÓNYMUS L. SPINDLE–TREE. Deciduous or evergreen shrubs or small trees, sometimes creeping or climbing by rootlets; brts. usually 4-angled; buds usually conspicuous with imbricate scales: lvs. opposite, petioled, rarely alternate or whorled, usually glabrous: fls. 4–5-merous, usually perfect, in axillary cymes; stamens short, inserted on the disk; ovary connate with the disk: fr. a 4–5-celled, or occasionally 2–3-celled caps., usually lobed and sometimes winged; each cell with 1–2 seeds enclosed in a fleshy usually orange aril; seed white to red or black. (*Euonymos*, its ancient Greek name.) Syn.: *Evonymus* L. About 120 species in N. and C. Am., Eu. and Asia, also in Australia.—Ornamental shrubs chiefly planted for their attractive fr.

Lvs. deciduous (half-evergreen in a var. of No. 12 and in No. 4).
  A. Lvs. usually alternate or whorled, linear, entire or nearly entire: fr. 4-lobed....1. *E. nana*
  AA. Lvs. opposite.
    B. Fr. divided nearly to the base into 4 separate pods, sometimes reduced to 1–3; brts. usually with broad corky wings (see also *E. phellomana* under No. 6)........2. *E. alata*
    BB. Fr. at most deeply lobed.
      c. Winter-buds small, conic, scarcely exceeding 5 mm. in length: fr. 4-lobed with obtuse lobes or 5-lobed and warty.
        D. Anthers yellow.
          E. Brts. densely warty; seed black, not wholly covered by the aril..3. *E. verrucosa*
          EE. Brts. smooth.
            F. Caps. tuberculate, depressed-globose: fls. 5-merous.
              G. Lvs. lance-ovate to lance-oblong, half-evergreen: upright shrub.
                4. *E. americana*
              GG. Lvs. obovate, deciduous: procumbent shrub................5. *E. obovata*
            FF. Caps. smooth, 4-lobed.
              G. Fls. greenish.
                H. Fls. 3–5, on a peduncle 2–3.5 cm. long: lvs. 2–8 cm. long..6. *E. europaea*
                HH. Fls. 1–3, subsessile: lvs. 0.8–2 cm. long....................7. *E. nanoides*
              GG. Fls. purple; infl. slender-stalked: lvs. 1.5–2 cm. long.....8. *E. Przewalskii*

7. **E. nanoìdes** Loes. & Rehd. Shrub to 1 m.; brts. sharply 4-angled or narrowly winged, puberulous at first: lvs. short-petioled, narrow- to linear-lanceolate, 0.8–2 cm. long, acutish to obtuse, cuneate, midrib, veins and petioles minutely scabrid: fls. 1–3, subsessile, greenish, about 3 mm. across: filaments very short: frs. 1 or 2, on short stalks, depressed-globose, 1 cm. across, lobed to about the middle, lobes rounded, usually only 2 carpels fertile; seeds dark purple, the orange aril open near apex. W. China. Intr. 1926. Zone V?

Related species: **E. orésbia** W. W. Sm. Shrub to 2 m., glabrous: brts. narrowly winged: lvs. oblanceolate or lanceolate, rarely oblong, 1.5–2 cm. long, obtusish, serrulate: infl. 1–3-fld.: fr. on a stalk 3–10 mm. long, turbinate, with angled lobes; seed as in No. 7. W. China. Cult 1934. Zone VI?

8. **E. Przewálskii** Maxim. Much-branched shrub to 2 m., glabrous; brts. angled, later often slightly corky winged: lvs. lanceolate to oblong-lanceolate, 1.5–3 cm. long, acuminate, crenate-serrulate: fls. dark purple, in slender 3–5-fld. cymes longer than the lf.; pedicels about 1 cm., peduncle 1.5–2.5 cm. long: fr. pinkish or yellowish, slightly lobed; aril orange, half as long as the black seed. N. w. China, E. Tibet. Cult. 1934. Zone V.

Related species: **E. Semenóvii** Reg. & Herd. Small shrub: lvs. lanceolate, 2–4.5 cm. long, thickish, crenate-serrulate; infl. slender-stalked, 3- to several-fld.; aril partly open near apex; seed purplish green. Fedtch., Fl. Aziat. Ross. 5:21. Turkest. Cult. 1910. Zone V.

9. **E. atropurpúrea** Jacq. Burning-bush. Shrub or small tree to 8 m.: lvs. elliptic or ovate-elliptic, 4–12 cm. long, acuminate, serrulate, pubescent beneath; petiole 1–2 cm. long: fls. purple, about 1 cm. across, 7–15 on a slender stalk 2–4.5 cm. long: fr. deeply 4-lobed, 1.5 cm. across, crimson; seed brown, with scarlet aril. Fl.v–vi; fr.x. S.S.2:t.53. M.A.1:t.42(c). B.B.2:491. N. Y. to Fla., w. to Minn., Neb., Okla. and Tex. Intr. 1756. Zone IV. Lvs. turning pale yellow in fall.

Related species: **E. occidentàlis** Nutt. Shrub to 5 m.; winter-buds to 8 mm. long: lvs. ovate to elliptic-lanceolate, glabrous: fls. 5-merous, 1.4 cm. across, purple, 1–4. S.H.2:f.115g-h(1). Ore. to Calif. Cult. 1894. Zone VI?

10. **E. Maàckii** Rupr. Large shrub or small tree, glabrous; brts. subterete: lvs. elliptic-oblong to lance-oblong, 5–8 cm. long, acuminate, gradually narrowed at base, serrulate; petiole 5–8 mm. long: fls. yellowish, about 1 cm. across, in small cymes 1.5–2 cm. across on a stalk 1–1.5 cm. long: fr. pink, 4-lobed, about 8 mm. across; seed red with orange aril sometimes slightly split at apex. Fl.vi; fr.x. M.D.1910:106,f.2,107,f.b. China Jour. 23:178,f.5,6. (*E. Hamiltoniana* Dipp., not Wall.) N. China to Korea. Cult. 1880. Zone IV.

11. **E. híans** Koehne. Large shrub: lvs. ovate-oblong, 6–12 cm. long, short-acuminate, broad-cuneate or nearly rounded at base, serrulate; petiole 6–12 mm. long: fls. yellowish white, about 8 mm. across, usually in 6- or 7-fld. cymes 1.5–3 cm. across on a stalk 1.5–3.5 cm. long; stamens with very short filaments: fr. turbinate, deeply 4-lobed, about 8 mm. across; aril blood-red, split at apex and disclosing the white seed. Fl.v; fr.ix. S.I.2:t.39(c, as *E. europaea*). M.K.t.65(c). M.D.1910:106,f.5,107,f.E. S.H.2:f.115n,116a-e. Japan. Intr. about 1865. Zone V.

Related species: **E. semiexsérta** Koehne. Close to No. 11: lvs. oblong to lance-oblong, usually narrower, crenate-serrulate: fr. whitish pink; aril orange, much split and disclosing nearly ½ of the blood-red seed. M.D.1910:106,f.4;107, f.D. S.H.2:f.604c,605m-p. Japan. Cult. 1895.—**E. nikoénsis** Nakai. Tree: lvs. oblong, 9–12 cm. long, acuminate, serrulate, short-pilose or papillose on midrib and veins beneath: infl. 4–7-fld. on peduncle 1.5–2.5 cm. long: fr. 4-angled, bright red; aril orange, open at apex; seed green. Japan. Cult. 1930. Zone V.

12. **E. lanceifòlia** Loes. Shrub or tree to 10 m.: lvs. elliptic-oblong, to lance-oblong, 8–14 cm. long, acute or acuminate, broad-cuneate, crenate-serrulate, firm at maturity and slightly reticulate beneath and often scabrid-pubescent on the midrib; petioles 4–8 mm. long: fls. 1.2–1.5 cm. across, in usually 7–15-fld. cymes on stalks 5–25 mm. long; filaments longer than anthers, 1–2 mm. long: fr. 4-lobed, pale pink; aril orange, split at apex; seed crimson. Fl.v–vi; fr.x. C. and W. China. Intr. 1900 or 1904. Zone V.

13. **E. yedoénsis** Koehne. Large shrub: lvs. obovate to obovate-oblong, sometimes elliptic, 6–12 cm. long and 3.5–6 cm. broad, abruptly acuminate, broad-cuneate, crenate-serrulate; petiole 6–12 mm. long; cyme many-fld., rather dense, on a stalk 1–2 cm. long; filaments somewhat longer or sometimes shorter than the anthers: fr. deeply 4-lobed, about 1 cm. across, pinkish; aril orange, usually closed or with small opening. Fl.vi; fr.ix. Gt.53: 31. S.T.1:t.62. M.D.1910:106,f.3,107,f.C. F.E.31:125(h). Japan, Korea. Intr. about 1865. Zone IV.—**E. y. calocárpa** Koehne, f. Fr. bright crimson.— **E. y. Koehneàna** Loes., var. Lvs. short-pubescent on the midrib and on the veins below. C. China. Intr. 1907.

14. **E. Bungeàna** Maxim. Shrub or small tree to 6 m., with slender brs.; brts. subterete: lvs. elliptic-ovate to elliptic-lanceolate, 5–10 cm. long, long-acuminate, broad-cuneate at base, serrulate; petiole 8–25 mm. long: fls. yellowish in 3–7-fld. cymes on stalks 1–2 cm. long: fr. deeply 4-lobed, about 1 cm. across, yellowish to pinkish white: filaments about as long as anthers; seeds white or pinkish with orange aril usually open at apex. Fl.vi; fr.x. B.M.8656c). S.T.1:t.63. M.D.1910:106,f.1,107,f.A. M.G.14:569. N. China, Manch. Intr. 1883. Zone IV. Tree of loose habit and with profuse pinkish fr. remaining on the brs. long after the lvs. have fallen; the var. *semipersistens* valued for its half-evergreen foliage.—**E. B. péndula** Rehd., f. With long and slender pendulous brs.: petioles to 3.5 cm. long. Cult. 1902.—**E. B. semipersístens** (Rehd.) Schneid. Lvs. elliptic, half-evergreen and persisting until mid-winter or severe frost: fr. turbinate, pink, sparingly produced. S.H.2:f. 115l(l). (*E. s.* Sprague.)

Related species: **E. Sieboldiàna** Bl. Lvs. slender-petioled, elliptic to elliptic-oblong: fr. obovoid, not lobed, but strongly 4-ribbed. M.D.1906:f.1c;1910: 106,f.6. S.H.2:f.116f-g. Japan. Not in cult., often confused with other species.

15. **E. sanguínea** Loes. Shrub or small tree to 7 m.; terminal winter-bud 6–14 mm. long: brts. nearly terete: lvs. broad-elliptic or ovate to oblong-ovate, 4–10 cm. long, acute or acuminate, broad-cuneate or nearly rounded at base, densely fimbriate-serrulate, dull green above, paler beneath and finely reticulate, reddish when unfolding; petiole 5–10 mm. long: fls. 4- or occasionally 5-merous, purplish, in loose 3–15-fld. cymes 7–10 cm. wide on a slender stalk 3–5 cm. long: fr. slightly lobed, winged, about 2.5 cm. broad, red; wings 6–8 mm. long; aril orange covering the black seed. Fl.v; fr.ix. B.J.29:t.5a-b. C. and W. China. Intr. 1900. Zone V. With handsome foliage and attractive fruit.—**E. s. brevipedunculàta** Loes., var. Peduncles only about 2 cm. long.—**E. s. camptoneùra** Loes., var. Lvs. somewhat narrower, with curved veins (straight in the type.)

Related species: **E. Monbeìgii** W. W. Sm. Close to No. 15: shrub to 8 m.: lvs. ovate to oblong, closely serrate with incurved teeth: fls. green, in large slender-stalked cymes: fr. with triangular wings 3–5 mm. long. Yunnan. Intr. 1926. Zone VII?—**E. fimbriàta** Wall. Lvs. elliptic to oblong-obovate, 4–10 cm. long, abruptly acuminate, finely and doubly fimbriate-serrulate, thickish at maturity: fls. small, in cymes 1.5–2.5 cm. across: fr. with long, pointed wings. Himal. Cult. 1920. Zone VII?—**E. macróptera** Rupr. Lvs. obovate to obovate-oblong, 8–12 cm. long, cuneate: cymes many-fld.: fr. with 4 narrow wings 1–1.8

cm. long. I.T.6:t.233. S.H.2:f.115p,114g. M.I.1:t.38. China Jour. 23:178,f.3,4.
(*E. ussuriensis* Maxim.) N. E. Asia, Japan. Cult. 1906. Zone V.

16. **E. latifòlia** Scop. Shrub or small tree to 7 m.; terminal winter-buds
1–1.5 cm. long: lvs. obovate-oblong or elliptic, 6–12 cm. long, short-acuminate,
broad-cuneate, crenate-serrulate; petiole about 6 mm. long: fls. greenish,
about 1 cm. across, in 7–15-fld. cymes on a stalk 5–6 cm. long: fr. 5-, rarely
4-winged, nearly 2 cm. across, bright red, pendulous; aril orange, seed white.
Fl.v–vɪ; fr.ɪx. R.I.6:t.310,f.5136(c). F.D.21:t.2181(c). B.M.2384(c). Gn.39:
213. Gt.53:30. H.W.3:54. S. Eu., W. Asia. Intr. 1730. Zone V. With handsome lvs. and large bright-colored fr.

17. **E. sachalinénsis** (Fr. Schmidt) Maxim. Shrub to 4 m.: lvs. obovate,
8–12 cm. long, short-acuminate, cuneate, crenate-serrulate; petiole 5–10 mm.
long, flat, not grooved above: fls. in many-fld. loose cymes on slender peduncles 3–7 cm. long: fr. 5-angled, but scarcely winged, broadly conical at apex,
about 18 mm. across. Fl.v; fr.ɪx. M.D.1906:62,f.1a. Gt.53:29. S.L.176. M.G.
33:9(h),10. (*E. planipes* Koehne.) N. E. Asia. Intr. 1892. Zone V. With
large lvs.; fr. handsome, profusely produced.

18. **E. oxyphýlla** Miq. Shrub or small tree; upper winter-buds 5–6 mm.
long: lvs. ovate to ovate-oblong, 4–8 cm. long, acuminate, rounded or broad-
cuneate, serrulate with incurved mucronate teeth, bright green, slightly
reticulate beneath; petiole 3–6 mm. long: fls. greenish, suffused with brown,
8–9 mm. across, in loose many-fld. cymes on a peduncle 4–5.5 cm. long;
anthers subsessile: fr. subglobose, with 5 or sometimes 4 ribs, about 1 cm.
across, dark red, pendulous; aril red. Fl.v; fr.x. S.I.1:t.64(c). M.K.t.64(c).
M.D.1906:63. Japan. Intr. 1892. Zone V.

Related species: **E. nippónica** Maxim. Shrub to 1.5 m.: lvs. elliptic-ovate to
obovate-oblong, 3–5.5 cm. long, up to 2.5 cm. broad, remotely serrulate: infl.
3–5-fld.; peduncle 3–4 cm. long: fr. smaller. S.H.2:f.112z. Japan. Cult. 1903.
Zone V?

19. **E. kiautschòvica** Loes. Half-evergreen or nearly evergreen spreading
shrub to 3 m., lower brs. sometimes prostrate and rooting: lvs. broad-elliptic
or obovate to oblong-obovate or elliptic-oblong, 5–8 cm. long, acute or
obtusish, cuneate, crenate-serrulate, subcoriaceous with obsolete veins beneath; petiole 4–8 mm. long: fls. greenish white, in loose, many-fld. slender-
peduncled cymes 5–7 cm. across: fr. globose, about 1 cm. across, pinkish; seed
pinkish brown, covered by the orange-red aril. Fl.vɪɪɪ–ɪx; fr.x–xɪ. Add.4:t.
158(c). S.T.1:t.64. (*E. patens* Rehd., *E. k.* var. *p.* Loes., *E. Sieboldiana* Hort.,
not Bl.) E. and C. China. Intr. about 1860. Zone VI. Valued for its late
attractive fr.

Related species: **E. pygmaèa** W. W. Sm. Close to No. 19: shrub to 0.7 m.,
glabrous: lvs. chartaceous, elliptic to oblong-elliptic, 4–8 cm. long, obtusely
short-acuminate or obtuse, crenate-serrulate: infl. loose, 3–7-fld.: fr. subglobose;
peduncle 2–4 cm. long; pedicels about 1 cm. W. China. Cult. 1934. Zone VII?
—**E. grandiflòra** Wall. Shrub to 4 m.: lvs. obovate to obovate-oblong, 4–10 cm.
long, acute or obtusish to short-acuminate; crenate-serrulate: fls. about 2 cm.
across, whitish, in loose 5–9-fld. cymes: fr. 4-angled, yellowish; seed black; aril
scarlet. Wallich, Pl. As. Rar. 3:t.254(c). S.H.2:f.112u,114k. Himal., China.
Intr. 1824. Zone VII?—**E. g. salicifòlia** Stapf, f. Lvs. narrow- to oblong-
lanceolate, acute to acuminate. B.M.9183(c). W. China. Cult. 1922.

20. **E. japónica** L. Evergreen upright shrub or small tree to 5 or occasionally 8 m.; brts. slightly quadrangular: lvs. obovate to narrow-elliptic,
3–7 cm. long, acute to obtuse, cuneate, obtusely serrate, lustrous and dark
green above; petiole 6–12 mm. long: fls. greenish white, in 5–12-fld. rather
dense cymes on a peduncle 2–5 cm. long: fr. depressed-globose, about 8 mm.
across, pinkish, aril orange. Fl.vɪ–vɪɪ; fr.x. S.I.2:t.39(c). B.R.30:6(c). S.H.

2:f.111k-p. S. Japan. Intr. 1804. Zone VII. Planted chiefly for its lustrous evergreen lvs. and its compact upright habit.—**E. j. macrophýlla** Reg. Lvs. elliptic, 5–7.5 cm. long. (*E. j. robusta* Hort.)—**E. j. microphýlla** Jaeg. Lvs. narrow-oblong to lance-oblong, 1–2.5 cm. long.—**E. j. argénteo-variegàta** Reg., var. Lvs. edged and marked white.—**S. j. albo-marginàta** T. Moore. Lvs. with a rather narrow white margin.—**E. j. aùreo-variegàta** Reg., var. Lvs. blotched yellow. Lowe, Beautif. Lfd. Pl.t.49(c).—**E. j. aùreo-marginàta** Nichols. Lvs. edged yellow. F.E.16:436;29:815(h).—**E. j. víridi-variegàta** Rehd., var. Lvs. large, bright green, variegated with green and yellow in the middle. ("Duc d'Anjou.")—**E. j. pyramidàta** Carr. Of strictly upright columnar and very compact habit: lvs. crowded, broad-elliptic. (*E. j. columnaris* Carr., *E. j. pyramidalis* Hort.) Another columnar form, but less compact and with narrow-elliptic lvs. is **E. j. fastigiàta** Carr. R.H.1883: 449(h).

21. **E. Fortùnei** (Turcz.) Hand.-Mazz. Shrub climbing with rootlets, or trailing and rooting; brts. subterete, minutely warty: lvs. elliptic or elliptic-ovate, rarely elliptic-obovate, 2.5–6 cm. long, acute or short-acuminate, broad-cuneate, serrulate, veins above slightly raised, distinctly veined beneath: infl., fls. and frs. similar to those of No. 20; secondary axes not exceeding 6 mm. Fl.VI–VII; fr.X. J.A.19:t.218. (*E. jap.* var. *acuta* Rehd., *E. radicans* var. *acuta* Rehd.) China. Intr. 1907. Zone V. The hardiest of the evergreen Euonymus, suitable as ground-cover and for covering walls and tree-trunks; *E. F. Carrierei* and *vegeta* are usually shrubby and bear attractive frs.— **E. F. coloràta** (Rehd.) Rehd., f. Lvs. changing in fall to dark purple above and lighter purple beneath. (*E. rad.* f. *c.* Rehd.) Intr. 1914.—**E. F. radìcans** (Miq.) Rehd., var. Trailing or climbing: Lvs. ovate or broad-elliptic to elliptic, 1–3 cm. long, acute or obtusish, more distinctly serrate, of thicker texture, veins obsolete. G.C.II.20:793. R.H.1885:295. M.D.1906:219. B.C. 2:1188,1187(h). (*E. r.* Miq., *E. jap.* var. *r.* Miq., *E. j.* var. *viridis* Reg.) Japan, s. Korea. Intr. about 1865.—**E. F. reticulàta** (Reg.) Rehd., f. Like the 3 following a form of the preceding var. Lvs. variegated with white along the veins. G.W.1:475. A.G.19:37. (*E. rad.* f. *r.* Schneid., *E. rad.* var. *picta* Rehd.)—**E. F. grácilis** (Reg.) Rehd., f. Lvs. variegated and margined with white or yellow or with pink on the margin. R.H.1876:354;1878:135. (*E. rad.* var. *argenteo-marginata* Rehd., *E. rad. pictus* J. Makoy, *E. rad.* var. *roseo-marginata* Rehd., *E. jap* var. *tricolor* Reg.) A group of variable and inconstant forms.—**E. F. mínima** (Simon-Louis) Rehd., f. Low, usually creeping shrub: lvs. 0.6–1.5 cm. long; sterile. Gs.11:221(h). (*E. rad. minimus* Simon-Louis), *E. rad.* var. *kewensis* Bean.) The form *kewensis* has generally smaller lvs. than *minima*. Intr. 1893.—**E. F. Carrièrei** (Vauvel) Rehd., f. Spreading shrub or somewhat climbing if supported: lvs. elliptic to elliptic-oblong, 3–5 cm. long, acutish, lustrous: fruiting freely. H.B.2:554(h). S.L.176(h). Sometimes producing brs. with the lvs. margined white: "Silver Queen." Cult. 1881.—**E. F. végeta** (Rehd.) Rehd., var. Spreading shrub to 1.5 m. or climbing if supported: lvs. broad-elliptic to nearly suborbicular, 2.5–4 cm. long, acute or obtusish, crenate-serrate, dull green, thickish: fruiting freely. S.T.1:t.65. M.G.23:13. M.D.1927:t.48(h). W.A.96,t(h). (*E. rad.* var. *v.* Rehd.) Japan. Intr. 1876.

22. **E. Wilsònii** Sprague. Shrub to 6 m., climbing: lvs. lanceolate, 6–14 cm. long, acuminate, cuneate, shallowly serrate, conspicuously veined beneath; petiole 6–12 mm. long: fls. yellowish in many-fld. loose cymes 4–8 cm. across on a stalk 3–5 cm. long: fr. 4-lobed clothed with spines about 5 mm.

long, nearly 2 cm. across; aril yellow. Fl.vi; fr.x–xi. G.C.72:49. W. China.
Intr. 1904. Zone VII?
Related species: **E. echinàta** Wall. Prostrate: lvs. elliptic-ovate to lance-
oblong, 4–7 cm. long, acuminate, cuneate, serrate: cymes small, usually 3–7-fld. on
a stalk 1–1.5 cm. long: fr. subglobose, about 8 mm. across. B.M.2767(c). Himal.
Cult. 1827. Zone VII.

23. **E. Sargentiàna** Loes. & Rehd. Shrub to 4 m., with slender brts.: lvs.
obovate to oblong-obovate, 6–9 cm. long, abruptly acuminate, cuneate,
remotely crenate-serrate, dull grayish green above; petiole 8–10 mm. long:
fr. 4-angled, not or scarcely lobed, oblong-obovoid, 1.5 cm. long, attenuate
at base, yellowish, borne in a loose cyme on a stalk about 3 cm. long. Fr.x.
W. China. Intr. 1908. Zone VII?

24. **E. péndula** Wall. Small tree with pendulous brs.: lvs. oblong-lanceolate, 7–14 cm. long, acuminate, broad-cuneate, sharply spinose-serrulate,
lustrous above; petiole 5–10 mm. long: fls. 1.2 cm. across, in many-fld. cymes:
fr. with 4 tapering wings. P.F.2:55. F.S.7:71. (*E. fimbriata* Hort., not Wall.)
Himal. Cult. 1851. Zone VII? With large and lustrous lvs.

25. **E. Aquifòlium** Loes. & Rehd. Shrub to 3 m.; brts. quadrangular: lvs.
subsessile, ovate to ovate-oblong, 4–7 cm. long, spiny sinuate-dentate, dull
green above: fr. usually solitary, depressed-globose, 4-lobed, 1.2–1.5 cm.
across, greenish; seed purple, only partly enclosed by the orange aril. Fr.
x–xi. W. China. Intr. 1908. Zone VII? Remarkable for its holly-like lvs.,
of slow growth in cult.
Related species: **E. ilicifòlia** Franch. Shrub; mature brts. terete; lvs. short-
petioled, elliptic or elliptic-obovate, cuneate, spiny-dentate: frs. subglobose in a
slender-stalked cyme. W. China. Cult. 1934. Zone VII?

2. **CELÁSTRUS** L. STAFF-TREE. Deciduous, rarely evergreen shrubs
usually climbing; brs. with solid or lamellate pith, or hollow; buds with several imbricate scales: lvs. alternate, petioled, serrate or crenate; stipules
small: fls. polygamo-dioecious, small, greenish or whitish, 5-merous, in axillary cymes or terminal panicles; calyx 5-parted; petals oblong-ovate; disk
entire or crenate; stamens short; ovary superior; style short, with 3-lobed
stigma: fr. a caps., usually yellow, dehiscent into 3 valves, each containing 1
or 2 seeds enclosed in a fleshy crimson aril. (*Kelastros*, ancient Greek name
of an evergreen tree, probably *Phillyrea*.) More than 30 species in E. and
S. Asia, Australia and Am.—Ornamental twining shrubs chiefly grown for
their handsome yellow fr. opening at maturity and disclosing the crimson
seeds.

A. Fls. in a terminal panicle.
  B. Brts. terete with solid pith: lvs. 5–10 cm. long.............................1. *C. scandens*
  BB. Brts. angular with lamellate pith: lvs. 10–18 cm. long....................2. *C. angulata*
AA. Fls. in axillary cymes often partly crowded into panicles.
  B. Lvs. glaucous beneath: fls. partly in panicles........................3. *C. hypoleuca*
  BB. Lvs. green beneath.
    C. Stipules deciduous: lvs. 5–12 cm. long.
      D. Cymes partly forming terminal panicles: lvs. rugose, reticulate beneath: pith
        lamellate ....4. *C. rugosa*
      DD. Cymes all axillary, sometimes crowded on short leafless lateral brts.
        E. Brs. with lamellate pith..5. *C. Loeseneri*
        EE. Brs. with solid pith..6. *C. orbiculata*
    CC. Stipules persistent, spinescent, hooked: lvs. 2–6 cm. long, slender-petioled.
                                             7. *C. flagellaris*

1. **C. scandens** L. WAXWORK (AMERICAN BITTERSWEET). Climbing to 7
m.; pith solid, white: lvs. ovate to oblong-ovate, 5–10 cm. long, acuminate,
broad-cuneate at base, serrulate, glabrous; petiole 5–20 mm. long: fls. in
panicles 5–10 cm. long: fr. subglobose, about 8 mm. across, yellow, with crim-

son seeds. Fl.vi; fr.x(–xii). S.O.3:t.140(c). Em.545(c). Gr.G.2:t.170. G.F. 5:569. B.C.2:701. Gg.5:119. Gn.33:393(h). (FALSE BITTERSWEET, CLIMBING B., SHRUBBY B.) Can. to S. Dak. and N. Mex. Intr. 1736. Zone II.

Related species: **C. depéndens** Wall. Brs. with conspicuous lenticels and with brown, partly evanescent pith: lvs. oblong, abruptly acuminate, 8–12 cm. long, crenate-serrulate, lustrous above; petiole 5–10 mm. long: panicle 8–16 cm. long. Himal. to Burma and S. W. China. Cult. 1934. Zone VII?

2. **C. angulàta** Maxim. Climbing to 7 m.; brts. angular, finely lenticellate; pith lamellate: lvs. broad-ovate to nearly orbicular, 10–18 cm. long and 8–14 cm. broad, abruptly short-acuminate, crenate-serrate, glabrous: petiole 1–2.5 cm. long: panicle 10–15 cm. long: fr. subglobose, about 1 cm. across, on thick short pedicels; aril orange-red. Fl.vi; fr.x–xi. H.I.23:2206. S.H. 2:f.117c,118i-k. (*C. latifolius* Hemsl.) Intr. 1900. Zone VII. Remarkable for its large lvs.

3. **C. hypoleùca** Warb. Climbing to 5 m.; brs. with brown evanescent pith; young brts. bloomy: lvs. elliptic to oblong-elliptic, 6–14 cm. long, short-acuminate, remotely serrulate, dark green above, bluish white beneath; petiole 1–1.5 cm. long: terminal panicle 6–12 cm. long, loose, in fr. to 20 cm. long: fr. about 8 mm. across, on slender pedicels 8–15 mm. long. Fl.vi; fr.x. H.I.19:1899. S.H.2:f.117f,118m-q. (*C. hypoglaucus* Hemsl.) C. China. Intr. 1900. Zone VII.

Related species: **C. glaucophýlla** Rehd. & Wils. Brs. dark purplish brown, with lamellate pith: lvs. elliptic to obovate, 5–10 cm. long, acute or abruptly acuminate, remotely crenate-serrate, dull bluish green above, glaucous beneath: fls. axillary and in terminal racemes to 6 cm. long. W. China. Intr. 1908. Zone VII?

4. **C. rugòsa** Rehd. & Wils. Climbing to 6 m.; brts. striate or angular; pith lamellate: lvs. elliptic-ovate or elliptic to elliptic-oblong, 5–13 cm. long, short-acuminate, broad-cuneate or rounded at base, crenate-serrate or crenate-dentate, rugose above, reticulate at maturity beneath, glabrous or puberulous on the veins; petiole 1–1.5 cm. long: fls. partly axillary, partly in a terminal raceme 3–4.5 cm. long, in fr. to 7 cm. long: fr. 8–10 mm. across, orange-yellow, on pedicels 5–8 mm. long. Fl.vi; fr.x. W. China. Intr. 1908. Zone VI?

Related species: **C. Vanièti** (Lévl.) Rehd. Brs. dark red-brown, hollow: lvs. elliptic to elliptic-oblong, 6–10 cm. long, crenate-serrate, scabrid-puberulous on the veins beneath: fls. axillary and in terminal racemes to 12 cm. long: aril dark brown. (*C. spiciformis* Rehd. & Wils.) C. China. Not in cult.—**C. V. laevis** (Rehd. & Wils.) Rehd., var. Lvs. usually narrower, sometimes ovate-lanceolate, glabrous and often slightly glaucescent beneath. W. China. Intr. 1908. Zone VII?

5. **C. Loèseneri** Rehd. & Wils. Climbing to 6 m., glabrous; brts. reddish brown, slightly lenticellate; pith lamellate: lvs. elliptic or elliptic-ovate to elliptic-lanceolate, 5–11 cm. long, acuminate, rounded or broad-cuneate, crenate-serrate, dark green above, pale beneath, thickish; petiole 6–15 mm. long: fls. in short-stalked or subsessile axillary cymes, often forming racemes to 5 cm. long terminating short lateral brts.: fr. yellow; aril red. G.C.90:196, t(c). C. China. Intr. 1907. Zone V.

Related species: **C. Rosthorniàna** Loes. Brs. with lamellate pith: lvs. narrow-elliptic to elliptic-oblong, 4–8 cm. long, acuminate, cuneate, remotely serrate or serrulate, smooth above, with obsolete veinlets beneath, yellowish green, thickish at maturity; petiole 4–8 mm. long: cymes subsessile or short-stalked. C. and W. China. Intr. 1908. Zone VII?—**C. Hoòkeri** Prain. Brs. hollow or sparingly lamellate; young brts. rufous-puberulous, later white-lenticellate: lvs. elliptic or obovate to elliptic-oblong, 7–10 cm. long, on shoots longer, oblong, long-acuminate, crenate-serrulate, scabrid-puberulous on the veins beneath: fls. in short cymes: fr. orange. S. China, Himal. Intr. 1908. Zone VII?

AA. Lfts. 3.
  B. Middle lft. on a slender stalk 1.5–4 cm. long: panicles stalked.
    c. Fls. before the lvs.: fr. not lobed..................................3. *S. holocarpa*
    cc. Fls. after the lvs.: fr. 2–3-lobed.
      D. Lfts. elliptic to ovate, pubescent beneath: stamens not exceeding the petals.
                                        4. *S. trifolia*
      DD. Lfts. broad-elliptic to suborbicular, glabrous: stamens longer than petals.
                                        5. *S. Bolanderi*
  BB. Middle lft. short-stalked: panicle sessile: fr. 2-lobed, compressed........6. *S. Bumalda*

1. **S. pinnàta** L. Upright shrub to 5 m.: lfts. 5–7, ovate-oblong, 5–10 cm. long, acuminate, sharply serrulate, glabrous and glaucescent beneath: fls. about 1 cm. long, in panicles 5–12 cm. long, on peduncles about 5 cm. long; sepals ovate, whitish, greenish at base, reddish at apex, upright; petals oblong: fr. subglobose, much inflated, 2–3-lobed, 2.5–3 cm. long; seeds brownish yellow, about 1 cm. long. Fl.v–vi; fr.ix–x. R.I.5:t.161,f.4823(c). F.D. 21:t.2182(c). G.H.t.36(c). H.W.3:52. Gn.34:280. C. and S. Eu. Cult. 1596. Zone V.

2. **S. cólchica** Stev. Upright shrub to 4 m.: lfts. usually 5, on flowering brts. 3, ovate-oblong, 5–8 cm. long, acuminate, sharply serrate, glabrous and lustrous beneath: fls. 1.2–1.5 cm. long, in panicles 5–10 cm. long and about as broad, upright and peduncled; sepals spreading, narrow-oblong, yellowish white; petals linear-spatulate, white; filaments glabrous: fr. obovoid, 2–3-lobed, much inflated, 4–8 cm. long; seeds about 8 mm. long. Fl.v–vi; fr.ix–x. B.M.7383(c). R.H.1870:257. G.C.III.10:161;59:320(h). Gt.24:837. Gn.76: 171. Cauc. Intr. 1850. Zone VI.—**S. c. Kochiàna** Medwed., var. Filaments pubescent. (*S. c.* var. *lasiandra* Dipp.)—**S. c. laxiflòra** Baas-Beck., var. Lfts. usually 3: infl. longer and slenderer, pendulous; filaments pubescent at base; styles usually 2, spreading at apex. M.D.1921:127.—**S. c. Coulombièri** (André) Zab., var. Of more vigorous growth; lvs. larger; lfts. long-acuminate; stamens glabrous: fr. 6–10 cm. long with spreading lobes. B.S.2:549. Cult. 1872.

S. c. × *pinnata* = S. élegans Zab. Lfts. usually 5: panicles very large and nodding. Cult. 1871.—**S. e. Héssei** Zab., var. Fls. pinkish.

3. **S. holocárpa** Hemsl. Shrub or tree to 10 m.: lfts. 3, elliptic to oblong, 3–10 cm. long, acute to short-acuminate, serrulate, nearly glabrous: fls. white or pinkish, 1 cm. long, in pendulous slender-stalked panicles 3–10 cm. long, axillary on last year's brts.; ovary pubescent: fr. pear-shaped or ellipsoid, 3.5–5 cm. long, abruptly acuminate or sometimes lobed; seeds light grayish brown, lustrous, 6 mm. long. Fl.iv–v; fr.ix. B.M.9074(c). S.H.2:f.120c. C. China. Intr. 1908. Zone V.—**S. h. ròsea** Rehd. & Wils., var. Lfts. whitish-tomentulose beneath when young, later villous along the midrib: fls. pink, slightly larger. Intr. 1908.

4. **S. trifòlia** L. Upright shrub to 5 m.: lfts. elliptic to ovate, 3.5–8 cm. long, acuminate, sharply and unequally serrulate, pubescent beneath, sometimes glabrate at maturity: fls. about 8 mm. long, in nodding panicles or umbel-like racemes; sepals greenish white; petals white, somewhat longer than sepals, style exserted; filaments pubescent below the middle; ovary pubescent: fr. usually 3-lobed, 3–4 cm. long; seeds yellowish, 5 mm. long. Fl.v; fr.ix. N.D.6:t.12(c). Gr.G.2:t.172. Gt.37:529. B.C.6:3227. (*S. trifoliata* West.) Que. to Ont. and Minn., s. to Ga. and Mo. Cult. 1640. Zone III.—**S. t. pauciflòra** Zab., var. Low and suckering: lfts. smaller and broader, becoming glabrous: fls. in short, 3–8-fld. racemes. Cult. 1888.

Related species: **S. emòdi** Wall. Lfts. elliptic to oblong, 5–14 cm. long, finely serrulate, pubescent or nearly glabrous beneath: fls. 12 mm. long in long-peduncled pendulous panicles: fr. 5–8 cm. long. Gt.37:528(l). S.H.2:f.120b(l). Himal. Cult. 1890. Zone VII.

5. **S. Bolánderi** Gray. Shrub: lfts. 3, broad-elliptic or suborbicular, 5–7 cm. long, acute, sharply serrulate, glabrous: fls. in 9–15-fld. nodding panicles, with subverticillate pedicels; stamens and style exserted; filaments glabrous: fr. inflated, 5–6 cm. long, 3-lobed with long-aristate lobes; seed 6 mm. long. Fl.iv–v; fr.viii. G.F.2:545. R.H.1910:305. B.C.6:3228. S.L.354. Calif. Intr. 1879. Zone (V)

6. **S. Bumálda** DC. Shrub to 2 m. with slender spreading brs.: lfts. 3, elliptic or elliptic-ovate, 3.5–6 cm. long, short-acuminate, cuneate, serrulate with mucronate teeth, light green, glabrous except puberulous on veins beneath; middle lft. on a stalk to 1 cm. long: fls. about 8 mm. long, in loose erect panicles 5–7 cm. long; sepals yellowish white, little shorter than the white petals; fr. usually 2-lobed, 1.5–2.5 cm. long, flattened; seed yellowish, lustrous, 5 mm. long. Fl.vi; fr.ix–x. S.Z.1:t.95. I.S.2:t.85. N.F.6:f.97. Japan. Intr. 1812. Zone IV.

2. **EÙSCAPHIS** Sieb. & Zucc. Deciduous shrub or small tree, glabrous; buds with 2 outer scales: lvs. opposite, odd-pinnate, stipulate; lfts. serrulate; petiolulate, stipellate: fls. perfect, in terminal upright panicles: sepals, petals and stamens 5, of nearly equal length; ovary 2–3-celled, with 2 or 3 styles often connate at apex, surrounded at base by an annular disk: fr. consisting of 1–3 spreading leathery dehiscent pods, each with 1–3 seeds covered by a thin fleshy aril. (Greek *eu*, good, and *scaphis*, vessel; referring to the color and shape of the dehiscent pod.) One species.

E. japónica (Thunb.) Kanitz. Shrub to 3 m.: lfts. 7–11, lance-ovate, 4–8 cm. long, acuminate, rounded to broad-cuneate, appressed-serrulate: fls. yellowish green, about 5 mm. across, in broad many-fld. long-peduncled panicles 5–12 cm. across: pods 1–1.3 mm. long, reddish, apiculate; seeds suborbicular, 5–6 mm. across, steel-blue. Fl.v–vi; fr.viii–ix. S.Z.1:t.67(c). S.I.t.70 (c). S.H.2:f.121e–i,122d. (*E. staphyleoides* Sieb. & Zucc.) Japan and C. China. Cult. 1890. Zone VII. Planted chiefly for its handsome foliage and attractive fr.

3. **TAPÍSCIA** Oliv. Deciduous tree; buds with 2 or 3 outer pointed scales: lvs. alternate, odd-pinnate: lfts. short-petioluled, serrate, stipellate; stipules caducous: fls. very small, yellow, andro-dioecious, in axillary panicles; the staminate composed of long slender spikes with densely clustered fls.; the fertile ones much shorter with stouter brs. and with the fls. solitary in the axils of bracts; calyx tubular-campanulate, 5-lobed; stamens 5, exserted; ovary superior with slender style exceeding the stamens; staminate fls. smaller and shorter with rudimentary ovary; fr. a 1-seeded ovoid drupe with thin fleshy epicarp. (Anagram of *Pistacia*.) One species.

T. sinénsis Oliv. Tree to 10 m., rarely to 25 m.; lfts. 5–9, ovate, 6–12 cm. long, acuminate, rounded to cordate at base, sharply serrate, glaucous beneath, glabrous; petiolules 3–10 mm. long: pistillate panicles 5–8, staminate 10–20 cm. long; pistillate fls. 2.5, staminate 1.5 mm. long, fragrant: fr. ovoid, 6–7 mm. long, black. Fl.vii; fr.ix. H.I.20:1928. S.H.2:f.607. K.B.1909:356 (h). C. China. Intr. 1908. Zone VII. With large handsome lvs. turning yellow in fall, and fragrant fls.

Fam. 55. **ACERACEAE** Lindl. MAPLE FAMILY

Trees or shrubs: lvs. opposite, simple or compound, estipulate: fls. bisexual or unisexual, mostly andro-polygamous, or andro-monoecious or dioecious, regular, small, in terminal or lateral racemes or panicles, sepals 4–5, imbricate, rarely connate, petals 4–5, imbricate or wanting; disk usually flat, intrastaminal or extrastaminal, rarely wanting; stamens 4–10, usually 8: ovary superior, 2-celled and 2-lobed, much flattened contrary to the partition; style with 2 stigmas; ovules 2 in each cell: fr. flat, winged, splitting into two 1-seeded samaras; seed exalbuminous, with thin testa; embryo with flat, folded or rolled cotyledons.—Two genera with about 115 species chiefly in the temp. regions of the n. hemisphere.

A. Samara winged all around, with the seed near the middle: lvs. pinnate, 7–15-foliolate.
1. *Dipteronia*
AA. Samara winged only on one side: lvs. simple or 3–7-foliolate........................2. *Acer*

1. **DIPTERÒNIA** Oliv. Deciduous trees; winter-buds small, naked, densely pubescent: lvs. opposite, odd pinnate: lfts. serrate: fls. andro-monoecious, in large upright terminal panicles; sepals 5, longer than the short broad petals; staminate fls. with usually 8 stamens, an extrastaminal disk and a rudimentary ovary; filaments slender; fertile fls. with a 2-celled compressed ovary: fr. consisting of 2 compressed nutlets connate only at base and winged all around. (Greek *dis,* twice, and *pteron,* wing; referring to the winged carpels of the fr.) Two species in China.

D. sinénsis Oliv. Tree to 10 m.: lvs. 20–30 cm. long; lfts. usually 9–13, short-stalked, the upper ones subsessile, oblong-ovate to lance-oblong, the lowest pair sometimes 3-parted or 3-foliolate, 4–10 cm. long, long-acuminate, broad-cuneate, coarsely serrate, glabrous or sparingly pubescent beneath when young; panicle glabrous, 15–30 cm. long: fls. whitish, about 2.5 mm. across, slender-pedicelled: each samara broad-obovate or nearly orbicular, 2–2.5 cm. broad, light brown. Fl.vi; fr.ix. H.I.19:1898. S.I.1:t.36. J.L.28:f.18. G.C.72:139. Gn.89:449. C. China. Intr. 1900. Zone VI. With handsome large lvs. and peculiar fr.

2. **ÁCER** L. MAPLE. Deciduous, rarely evergreen trees, rarely shrubs; winter-buds with imbricate or with 2 outer scales: lvs. opposite, petioled, simple and usually palmately lobed or 3–7-foliolate: fls. usually andro-monoecious or dioecious, 5-merous, rarely 4-merous, in racemes, panicles or corymbs; sepals sometimes connate; petals sometimes wanting; disk usually annular and large, rarely lobed or wanting; stamens 4–10, usually 8; styles or stigmas 2: fr. consisting of 2 long-winged compressed samaras (keys). (The ancient Latin name of the tree.) Including *Negundo* Ludw., *Rulac* Adans. and *Crula* Nieuwl. About 115 species in N. Am., Asia, Eu. and N. Afr.— Ornamental trees chiefly planted for their handsome foliage usually assuming brilliant colors in autumn; some with attractive fls. or frs.

I. **Lvs. simple** (occasionally 3-foliolate in No. 33).
Infl. terminal on short leafy brts. (in Nos. 45–46 the staminate from lateral leafless buds).
  A. Infl. corymbose or paniculate, andro-monoecious; disk extrastaminal.
    B. Lvs. palmately lobed or simple and doubly serrate.
      C. Lobes of lvs. entire or coarsely dentate; winter-buds with imbricate scales.
        D. Infl. corymbose.
          E. Sepals and petals distinct.
            F. Lobes of lvs. acuminate: fr. with flattened nutlets and leathery, scarcely veined walls.
              G. Bark of mature brts. gray or grayish brown, slightly fissured and lenticellate.
                H. Lobes of lvs. coarsely toothed.
                  I. Lvs. glabrous and lustrous beneath; lobes finely pointed.
1. *A. platanoides*
                  II. Lvs. pubescent beneath; lobes bluntly pointed........2. *A. Miyabei*
              HH. Lobes of lvs. entire or rarely with few teeth.
                I. Lvs. truncate at base: wings of fr. about as long as nutlet.
3. *A. truncatum*
                II. Lvs. usually subcordate at base; wings about twice as long as nutlet.
4. *A. Mono*

GG. Bark of brts. smooth and lustrous for several years: lobes of lvs. entire or with few teeth.
  H. Infl. peduncled: lvs. glabrous beneath.
    I. Lvs. usually 3-5-lobed with broad and short lobes: fr. with upright incurved wings ....5. *A. Mayrii*
    II. Lvs. 5-7-lobed, rarely 3-lobed: fr. with spreading wings.
      6. *A. cappadocicum*
  HH. Infl. sessile or subsessile: lvs. pubescent beneath, 3-lobed.7. *A. longipes*
FF. Lobes of lvs. obtusish or acutish: fr. with convex strongly veined nutlets.
  G. Lvs. 2-8 cm. across, usually 3-lobed.
    H. Wings of fr. parallel or spreading at right angles: lvs. chartaceous, glabrous.
      I. Lvs. often without lobes, green beneath...............8. *A. orientale*
      II. Lvs. 3-lobed, glaucous beneath..............9. *A. monspessulanum*
    HH. Wings of fr. horizontally spreading: lvs. 3-5-lobed, pubescent and light green beneath; lobes usually dentate...........10. *A. campestre*
  GG. Lvs. 6-14 cm. across, usually 5-lobed, lobes irregularly dentate: infl. pendulous.
    H. Lvs. shallowly lobed with broad-ovate lobes, pubescent beneath.
      11. *A. Opalus*
    HH. Lvs. deeply lobed, lobes angular with parallel margins, glabrous or nearly so beneath..12. *A. hyrcanum*
EE. Sepals connate; petals wanting: fls. corymbose with slender pendulous pedicels.
  F. Lvs. glaucous or pale beneath or green and glabrous.
    G. Lvs. usually glabrous and sometimes green beneath, rarely villous, lobes entire or with few coarse teeth: corymb subsessile.......13. *A. saccharum*
    GG. Lvs. pubescent beneath, the lobes distinctly lobulate: corymb short-stalked ....14. *A. grandidentatum*
  FF. Lvs. green and pubescent beneath, rarely glabrous.
    G. Lvs. pilose-pubescent beneath, 8-14 cm. across, the basal sinus often closed: bark dark and furrowed............................15. *A. nigrum*
    GG. Lvs. soft-pubescent beneath, rarely glabrous, 5-8 cm. across; the basal sinus open: bark gray...................................16. *A. leucoderme*
DD. Infl. paniculate: fr. with convex strongly veined nutlets.
  E. Panicles pendulous.
    F. Fr. hispid: lvs. 20-30 cm. long, deeply lobed............17. *A. macrophyllum*
    FF. Fr. glabrous: lvs. 10-15 cm. long......................18. *A. Pseudoplatanus*
  EE. Panicles upright.
    F. Lvs. 5-lobed, large.
      G. Middle lobe divided nearly to base........................19. *A. Heldreichii*
      GG. Middle lobe reaching to the middle or little beyond.
        H. Lobes longer than broad; lvs. glaucescent beneath..20. *A. Trautvetteri*
        HH. Lobes about as long as broad; lvs. green beneath......21. *A. velutinum*
    FF. Lvs. 3-lobed, often mixed with undivided ones, 5-8 cm. long.
      22. *A. Buergerianum*
CC. Lobes of lvs. or lvs. serrate or doubly serrate: nutlets of fr. convex and strongly veined.
  D. Winter-buds with imbricate scales: lvs. undivided or 3-lobed, doubly serrate.
    E. Lvs. lustrous dark green, usually with 2 lobes near base.........23. *A. Ginnala*
    EE. Lvs. dull and rather light green, not lobed.....................24. *A. tataricum*
  DD. Winter-buds with only 1 pair of outer valvate scales.
    E. Fls. in panicles.
      F. Panicles narrow, spike-like, upright; lvs. 3-7-lobed, doubly serrate.
        G. Lvs. 3- or rarely 5-lobed, pubescent beneath..............25. *A. spicatum*
        GG. Lvs. 5-7-lobed, glabrous or pubescent beneath............26. *A. caudatum*
      FF. Panicle short, only little longer than broad: lvs. 5-lobed, serrulate.
        G. Lobes irregular and sparingly serrulate......................27. *A. sinense*
        GG. Lobes finely and sharply serrulate......................28. *A. Oliverianum*
    EE. Fls. in few-fld. corymbs.
      F. Lvs. 5-11-lobed, green beneath.
        G. Petioles and peduncles glabrous: ovary glabrous; sepals purplish.
          H. Lvs. divided to about the middle into 7-9 lobes: petals white; sepals purple ....29. *A. circinatum*
          HH. Lvs. divided to beyond the middle into 5-9 lobes; petals purplish.
          30. *A. palmatum*
        GG. Petioles and peduncles pubescent, at least while young: ovary villous.
          H. Fls. yellowish; anthers scabrid: lvs. subcordate or cordate with 7-9 doubly serrate lobes................................31. *A. Sieboldianum*
          HH. Fls. purple; anthers smooth: lvs. deeply cordate with 7-9 incisely serrate lobes ....32. *A. japonicum*
      FF. Lvs. 3-lobed or 3-foliolate, pale and glaucescent beneath, glabrous.
      33. *A. glabrum*
BB. Lvs. undivided, entire or serrulate: infl. paniculate. (See also Nos. 11 and 24 and *A. catalpifolium* under No. 7.)
  C. Lvs. oblong, rounded at base, entire...............................34. *A. oblongum*
  CC. Lvs. ovate, cordate at base, serrulate.............................35. *A. distylum*

AA. Infl. racemose, with fls. of one kind; disk intrastaminal.
  B. Lvs. oblong, doubly serrate with about 20 pairs of veins: fls. apetalous; winter-buds
    with many imbricate scales...*36. A. carpinifolium*
  BB. Lvs. lobed or undivided with about 10 pairs of veins or less: winter-buds with 2 outer
    valvate scales.
    C. Sepals and petals 5; racemes of both sexes on leafy brts.
      D. Lvs. oblong-ovate, undivided or with 2 lobes near base: brts. striped white.
        E. Lvs. not lobed, crenate-serrate...............................*37. A. Davidi*
        EE. Lvs. with 2 lobes near base, the middle lobe elongated..*38. A. crataegifolium*
      DD. Lvs. 5–7-lobed or 3-lobed at apex.
        E. Lvs. 3-lobed above the middle, broad-obovate or ovate: brs. striped.
          F. Lvs. ferrugineous-pubescent beneath when young.
            G. Young brts. not bloomy: young lvs. brownish villous beneath, the pri-
              mary veins glabrescent..............................*39. A. pennsylvanicum*
            GG. Young brts. bloomy: young lvs. densely rufous-pubescent on the veins
              beneath ....*40. A. rufinerve*
          FF. Lvs. glabrous beneath.
            G. Pedicels slender, about 1 cm. long: lvs. reddish when unfolding.
                                                      41. A. capillipes
            GG. Pedicels short: young lvs. bright green.................*42. A. tegmentosum*
        EE. Lvs. 5–7-lobed.
          F. Lvs. rufous-pubescent on the veins beneath at least when young.
                                                 43. A. Tschonoskii
          FF. Lvs. glabrous beneath.....................................*44. A. micranthum*
    CC. Sepals and petals 4; staminate fls. clustered, from leafless lateral buds.
      F. Lvs. 5-lobed, roundish-ovate...............................*45. A. argutum*
      FF. Lvs. undivided or slightly lobed, ovate to oblong-ovate...*46. A. tetramerum*
*Infl. from lateral leafless buds: fls. andro-monoecious or dioecious: winter-buds with imbri-
cate scales.*
  A. Fls. racemose or the staminate corymbose, with the lvs.: disk intrastaminal.
    B. Sepals more or less connate, petals wanting in the staminate fl.: lvs. 5-lobed.
                                                   47. A. diabolicum
    BB. Sepals and petals distinct; fls. of both sexes racemose: lvs. 3-lobed.....*48. A. Francheti*
  AA. Fls. fascicled, before the lvs.: winter-buds with 2 outer scales connate at base.
    B. Lvs. 3–5-lobed with unequally or crenately serrate lobes: fls. slender-stalked; ovary
      glabrous ....*49. A. rubrum*
    BB. Lvs. 5-lobed with deeply serrate or lobulate lobes: fls. short-stalked, apetalous: ovary
      pubescent ....*50. A. saccharinum*

II. Lvs. 3–7-foliolate

  A. Fls. in terminal corymbs, after the lvs.; disk large, extrastaminal: winter-buds with
    many imbricate scales: lfts. 3.
    B. Petioles, lfts. beneath and corymbs pilose.
      C. Lfts. elliptic-oblong, sparingly serrate, 5–12 cm. long; bark close.....*51. A. nikoense*
      CC. Lfts. elliptic, coarsely dentate, 2–5 cm. long; bark flaky..............*52. A. griseum*
    BB. Petioles, lfts. and corymbs glabrous: lfts. lance-oblong..........*53. A. mandshuricum*
  AA. Fls., at least the pistillate ones, in long racemes; disk small or wanting: winter-buds with
    2 outer valvate scales.
    B. Petals present: fls. of both sexes in racemes, sometimes leafy at base: lfts. 3.
      C. Petioles and lfts. beneath pubescent, rarely glabrous: fls. 5-merous; pedicels short.
                                                   54. A. Henryi
      CC. Petioles and lfts. glabrous: fls. 4-merous; pedicels long and slender.*55. A. cissifolium*
    BB. Petals wanting: pistillate fls. in pendulous racemes, staminate ones corymbose, before
      the lvs.: lfts. 3–7...*56. A. Negundo*

    Sect. I. PLATANOIDEA Pax. Fls. andro-polygamous, corymbose (broad-
paniculate in No. 2); staminate fls. perigynous: stamens inserted on the middle
of the disk: fr. with much flattened nutlets and leathery scarcely veined walls:
lvs. 3–5 lobed with coarsely sinuate-dentate or entire lobes, rarely entire; leaf-
stalk with milky juice: winter-buds with imbricate scales.

    1. **A. platanoìdes** L. NORWAY M. Tree to 30 m.; glabrous: lvs. 5-lobed,
10–18 cm. across, lobes acuminate, remotely dentate with pointed teeth,
bright green and lustrous beneath, bearded in the axils of the veins: fls.
greenish yellow, 8 mm. across in erect many-fld. stalked corymbs: fr. pendulous, with nearly horizontally spreading wings, 3.5–5 cm. long, including
the flattened nutlet. Fl.IV–V; fr.IX–X. R.I.5:t.164(c). F.D.16:t.1526(c). H.W.
3:t.45(c). E.N.III.5:264. E.H.3:t.186–188(h). Eu., Cauc. Long cult. Zone
III. Ornamental tree valued for its dense regular habit; the bright green
lvs. appearing early and turn bright yellow in fall; often planted as street
tree.—**A. p. variegàtum** West., var. Lvs. with large white blotches. (*A. p.
albo-variegatum* Hayne.) Cult. 1770.—**A. p. rúbrum** Herd., var. Lvs. green-

ish red when unfolding, turning dark red in late summer. Gt.16:t.545(c). B.H.18:39,t(c). (*A. p.* var. *Reitenbachii* Nichols.) Cult. 1867.—**A. p. Schwédleri** Nichols., var. Lvs. bright red when young, changing to dark green. R.B.32:197,t,f.6(c). Cult. 1870.—**A. p. Stóllii** Spaeth. Lvs. large, usually 3-lobed, with entire lobes, purple when unfolding. Gt.42:585. S.H. 2:f.155f.—**A. p. laciniàtum** Ait., var. EAGLE CLAW M. Of upright columnar habit: lvs. cuneate, irregularly lobed, the lobes curved downward, clawlike. S.O.1:t.5(c). Gt.42:584. Cult. 1789.—**A. p. palmatífidum** Tausch, var. Lvs. palmately divided nearly to the base, the divisions deeply lobed, dark green. Gt.42:584. (*A. p. dissectum* Jacques.)—**A. p. Lorbérgii** Van Houtte. Lvs. palmately divided like the former, but tips ascending from plane of lf., light green. Gt.42:584. (*A. p.* var. *palmatum* Bean.)—**A. p. columnàre** Carr. Of columnar habit with upright brs.: lvs. smaller, less deeply lobed. Orig. about 1855.—**A. p. eréctum** Slavin, f. Narrow-pyramidal tree with short ascending brs.: lvs. larger, dark green.—**A. p. globòsum** Nichols., var. Forming a dense globose head. M.G.18:189(h). G.W.5:14(h). S.L.74(h).

A. p. × *Lobelii* = **A. Diéckii** Pax. Similar to *A. p.*, but lobes entire. S.H.2: f.152a. D.H.2:45(1). (*A. platanoides* var. *integrilobum* Zab.)

2. **A. Miyàbei** Maxim. Tree to 12 m.; brs. with slightly corky bark, pubescent when young: lvs. 5-lobed, 10–15 cm. across, deeply cordate, lobes obtusely acuminate, obtusely lobulate or dentate, pale green and pubescent beneath, pubescent above when young; petioles puberulous; fls. greenish yellow, in slender-stalked 10–15-fld. pyramidal corymbs: wings of fr. horizontally spreading with the flattened velutinous nutlet 4–5 cm. long. Fl.v; fr.ix. S.I. 2:t.45(c). M.K.73(c). G.F.6:143. J.C.32,1:t.31. J.H.29:f.80(h). Japan. Intr. 1892. Zone V. Tree of rather open habit.

3. **A. truncàtum** Bge. Small tree to 8 m., glabrous: lvs. deeply 5-lobed, 6–10 cm. across, truncate at base, lobes acuminate, setosely pointed, entire or the middle lobe sometimes 3-lobed; bright green: fls. greenish yellow, about 1 cm. across, slender-stalked, in erect corymbs 6–8 cm. across: wings of fr. spreading at a right or an obtuse angle, with the compressed nearly smooth nutlet about 3 cm. long, the broad wing about as long as nutlet. Fl.v; fr.ix. S.T.1:t.76. S.H.2:f.150Ad(l). N. China. Intr. 1881. Zone V. Small round-headed tree with graceful foliage purplish when unfolding.

4. **A. Mono** Maxim. Tree to 20 m.; brts. glabrous, becoming yellowish to light gray and slightly fissured the second year: lvs. 5–7-lobed, occasionally 3-lobed, 8–15 cm. across, cordate to subcordate or nearly truncate with ovate-triangular acuminate entire lobes, green and glabrous beneath except axillary tufts of hairs: fls. greenish yellow, in corymbs 4–6 cm. across: wings of fr. spreading about 1½ times as long as the compressed nutlet and with the nutlet 2–3 cm. long. Fl. iv–v; fr.ix. C.C.229. N.K.1:t.12,f.1–4. M.K.t.71(c). (*A. pictum* var. *Mono* Pax, *A. pictum* var. *parviflorum* Schneid.) China, Manch., Korea. Intr. 1880. Zone V. Handsome round-headed tree with bright green lvs.—**A. M. connìvens** (Nichols.) Rehd., f. Fr. with upright, often connivent wings. S.I.1:t.65,f.1–12(c). J.C.32,1:t.32,f.1–5. Japan. Intr. 1865.—**A. M. marmoràtum** (Nichols.) Rehd., f. Lvs. densely dotted and blotched white. (*A. pictum* var. *m.* Nichols., *A. pictum* Thunb. of 1784, not 1783.) Cult. 1881.—**A. M. disséctum** (Pax) Honda, var. Lvs. 5-lobed, divided beyond the middle into oblong, long-acuminate lobes, the middle one usually slightly contracted at base, glabrous. J.C.32,1:62,f.9a. (*A. pictum* var. *d.* Wesm. ex Pax.) Cult. 1907—**A. M. tricúspis** (Rehd.) Rehd., var. Lvs. smaller, 3-lobed, the smallest ones sometimes quite entire and ovate. E.P.

IV,163:53. (*A. pictum* f. *t.* Rehd., *A. tenellum* Pax.) C. China. Intr. 1901.—
A. M. ambíguum (Pax) Rehd., var. Lvs. pilose beneath, fls. unknown.
D.H.2:458. N.K.1:t.12,f.5. (*A. a.* Dipp., not Heer, *A. pictum* var. *a.* Pax,
A. M. var. *Paxii* Honda.) Orig. unknown. Cult. 1892.

Related species: **A. Okamotoànum** Nakai. Close to *A. Mono*: brts. becoming
reddish brown, later grayish brown, not fissured: lvs. 7-lobed: fr. with the wings
connivent or spreading at a right angle; key 3.5–4.5 cm. long. (*A. Okamotoi*
Nakai, in part.) Korea. Intr. 1917. Zone V.—**A. fulvéscens** Rehd. Similar to
A. Mono: lvs. usually 3-lobed, 5–10 cm. across, yellowish or fulvous pubescent
beneath, chiefly on the veins: keys 3 cm. long. C. China. Intr. 1908. Zone V.

5. A. Maÿrii Schwerin. Tree to 25 m.; brts. glabrous and usually bloomy
when young, smooth and lustrous, yellowish or red-brown the second year:
lvs. 3–5-lobed, 8–15 cm. across, truncate or rounded at base, with short, entire
broad-ovate and abruptly acuminate lobes sometimes very short and almost
reduced to a narrow acumen, green and glabrous and reticulate beneath:
fls. greenish white, in corymbs 4–6 cm. across: wings of fr. upright and
incurved or slightly spreading, 1½ or 2 times as long as the compressed
nutlet and with it 2.5–4 cm. long. Fl.ɪv–v; fr.ɪx. M.K.t.72(c). Mayr, Wald-
& Parkb. 440. S.H.2:f.150ᴀ,ɢ. (*A. pictum* var. *M.* Henry.) Japan. Intr
1916. Zone V.

6. A. cappadócicum Gleditsch. Tree to 20 m.; brts. sometimes bloomy
when young, lustrous and green the second year: lvs. 5–7-lobed, usually
cordate at base, 8–14 cm. across, lobes triangular-ovate, long-acuminate,
entire, green and finely reticulate beneath and glabrous except axillary tufts
of hairs; petiole to 10, occasionally to 20 cm. long: fls. pale yellow, small, in
glabrous corymbs: wings of fr. spreading at a wide angle, 2–4 times as long
as the compressed nutlet, with it 3–5 cm. long. Fl.v–vɪ; fr.ɪx. D.H.2:456(l).
Gt.1887:433(l). S.H.2:f.150ᴀʜ,f.151h–k. (*A. laetum* C. A. Mey., *A. pictum
colchicum* Hort.) Cauc. and W. Asia to Him. Intr. 1838. Zone V or VI.—
A. c. rúbrum (Kirchn.) Rehd., f. Lvs. blood-red when unfolding, becoming
green. (*A. laetum rubrum* Kirchn., *A. laetum* f. *horticola* Pax.) Intr. 1838.—
A. c. trícolor (Carr.) Rehd., f. Lvs. blood-red and sprinkled with rosy pink
when young. R.B.12:217,t(c).—**A. c. sínicum** Rehd., var. Lvs. usually 5-
lobed, subcordate to truncate at base, 6–10 cm. across; wings about 2 times
as long as nutlet. S.H.2:f.150ᴀi(l). J.L.29:f.101(l) (as *A. laetum* var. *cul-
tratum*). China. Intr. 1901. Zone V.—**A. c. tricaudàtum** Rehd., f. A form
of the preceding var. with smaller 3-lobed lvs. J.H.29:f.100(h),102(l). S.H.
2:f.150ᴀ,k(l). Intr. 1901.

Related species: **A. Lobèlii** Ten. Tree to 20 m. with ascending brs.; young
brts. bloomy: lvs. usually 5-lobed, 10–16 cm. across, lobes long-acuminate, usually
pointing forward, dark green above, slightly paler beneath: fls. small; calyx
outside and pedicels pilose: wings of fr. spreading at a wide angle, about 1½
times as long as nutlet, with it 2.5–3 cm. long. D.H.2:453. S.H.2:f.152f-g,153g-h.
R.H.1915:524(h). Italy. Cult. 1838. Zone VII?—*A. L.* × *platanoides;* see
under No. 1.—*A. L.* × *campestre;* see under No. 10.

7. A. lóngipes Rehd. Tree to 10 m.; young brts. glabrous green, bark
remaining smooth: lvs. 3-, rarely 5-lobed, 10–16 cm. across, with long-acuminate entire lobes, occasionally mixed with undivided ovate lvs., light green
and soft-pubescent beneath: fls. in glabrous short-peduncled or nearly sessile
loose corymbs about 10 cm. across: wings of fr. spreading at a right angle,
about twice as long as nutlet, with it 2.5–3 cm. long. Fl.v–vɪ; fr.ɪx. S.H.2:
f.152c(l). W. China. Intr. 1900. Zone VI? Lvs. purplish when unfolding.

Related species: **A. amplum** Rehd. Lvs. 5-lobed, occasionally 3-lobed, 10–18
cm. across, with broad-ovate, abruptly acuminate lobes, glabrous: infl. subsessile, loose, 12–15 cm. across; wings spreading at a wide angle. C. China.

Cult. 1937. Zone V?—**A. catalpifòlium** Rehd. Lvs. ovate to ovate-oblong, 10–20 cm. long, undivided or with 2 short rounded lobes near base, abruptly acuminate, light green and glabrous and finely reticulate beneath: corymbs large and loose, sessile: wings of fr. spreading at a very wide angle, about 3 times as long as nutlet, with it 4–5 cm. long. W. China. Intr. 1910. Zone VII?

Sect. II. CAMPESTRIA Pax. Fls. andro-polygamous, on slender often pendulous pedicels, in corymbs; staminate fls. perigynous; stamens inserted near inner margin of disk; nutlet convex with thick strongly veined walls: lvs. 3–5-lobed, with entire or coarsely dentate, rarely crenulate, obtusish lobes, rarely undivided; petiole with milky juice in No. 10: winter-buds with several imbricate scales.

8. **A. orientàle** L. Deciduous or half-evergreen shrub or small tree to 5, rarely 12 m.; brts. glabrous: lvs. ovate or sometimes 3-lobed, 2–5 cm. long, obtuse or acutish, entire or slightly crenulate-denticulate, bright green and glabrous beneath, coriaceous; petiole 3–10 mm. long: fls. in few-fld. upright glabrous corymbs about 2 cm. long: wings of fr. parallel or spreading at a right angle, with the nutlet 1–1.5 cm. long. S.F.4:t.361(c). E.P.IV.163:64. S.H.2:f.159k-o. (*A. creticum* L., *A. sempervirens* L., *A. heterophyllum* Willd.) E. Mediterr. region. Intr. 1756. Zone VII?

Related species: **A. syríacum** Boiss. & Gaillardot. Shrub or small tree, glabrous: lvs. 3-lobed, 4–7 cm. long, sometimes ovate and without lobes, middle lobe triangular, spinulose-denticulate to nearly entire, reticulate and green beneath; infl. few-fld.; keys 2–2.5 cm. long; wings diverging at an acute angle. S.H.2:f. 158e,159g-i. Syria, Cyprus. Cult. 1903. Zone VII?—**A. cineráscens** Boiss. Young brts. pubescent: lvs. 3-lobed, sometimes with 2 additional basal lobes, 2–6 cm. long, with acutish or obtuse, entire or crenulate lobes, pubescent beneath: fr. with upright wings. M.D.1898:47,t. S.H.2:f.158f,159e-f. W. Asia. Cult. 1896. Zone VII?

9. **A. monspessulànum** L. Shrub or round-headed tree to 8 or 12 m.; brts. glabrous: lvs. 3-lobed, 3–8 cm. across, lobes triangular-ovate, entire or sparingly denticulate, lustrous above, glaucescent and reticulate beneath and glabrous except axillary tufts of hairs, subcoriaceous: fls. greenish yellow, slender-pediceled and soon drooping, in several-fld. glabrous corymbs; ovary pubescent: fr. reddish; wings upright and often overlapping or slightly spreading, with the nutlet 2–2.5 cm. long. Fl.v; fr.IX. S.O.1:t.14(c). R.I. 5:t.162(c). F.D.16:t.1528(c). H.W.3:46. E.H.3:t.190(h). G.W.8:195(h). (*A. trilobatum* Lam.) S. Eu., W. Asia. Intr. 1739. Zone V. Lvs. remaining green until late in fall.

A. m. × *campestre;* see under No. 10.—*A. m.* × *opalus;* see under No. 11.— *A. m.* × *Pseudoplatanus;* see under No. 18.—*A. m.* × *tataricum;* see under No. 24.

10. **A. campéstre** L. HEDGE M. Shrub or round-headed tree to 12 or sometimes 25 m.; young brts. pubescent or glabrous, often becoming corky: lvs. 3–5-lobed, 5–10 cm. across, with broad obtuse entire lobes or the middle one 3-lobed, dull green above, pubescent beneath; petiole about as long as blade, with milky juice: fls. greenish, in several-fld. upright pubescent corymbs: fr. usually pubescent; wings spreading horizontally, with the flattened nutlet 2.5–3 cm. long. Fl.v; fr.VIII–IX. S.E.2:t.321(c). R.I.5:t.162(c). F.D.16:t.1527(c). H.W.3:45(h),t.46(c). E.H.3:t.184,185(h). Eu., W. Asia. Cult. Zone IV. Lvs. turning yellow in fall.—**A. c. hebecárpum** DC., var. Fr. pubescent. The typical form.—**A. c. pulveruléntum** Kirchn. Lvs. densely speckled white: fr. glabrous.—**A. c. albovariegàtum** Hayne. Lvs. with large white blotches.—**A. c. postelénse** Lauche. Lvs. golden yellow when young: fr. glabrous.—**A. c. Schwerìnii** Hesse. Lvs. purple when young: fr. glabrous. —**A. c. leiocárpum** Tausch, var. Fr. glabrous.—**A. c. austrìacum** DC., var. Usually a tree: lvs. 5-lobed, with acute, nearly entire lobes, glabrate beneath:

fr. glabrous. F.E.19:t.98(h).—**A. c. taùricum** Kirchn. Lvs. 5-lobed, with lobulate lobes, pubescent beneath: fr. pubescent. S.H.2:f.156c. (*A. c. lobatum* Pax.)

A. c. × *monspessulanum* = **A.** Bornmuèlleri Borb. Lvs. 3–5-lobed, 5–6 cm. across, cordate, glabrous: wings of fr. horizontal, with the convex nutlets 2.5 cm. long. S. E. Eu. Intr. ?—*A. c.* × *Lobelià* = **A. zoeschènse** Pax. Young brts. finely pubescent: lvs. 5-lobed, 8–12 cm. across, cordate, lobes ovate, long-acuminate, lustrous dark green above, paler and pubescent beneath, becoming glabrous: fr. puberulous; wings nearly horizontal, with the nutlet 3 cm. long. Bot. Tidsskr. 19:266. S.H.2:f.152b(1). (*A. neglectum* Lange, not Hoffmanns., *A. aetnense* Hort., *A. c.* × *laetum* Pax.) Cult. 1880. Zone V.—*A. c.* × *?Pseudoplatanus;* see under No. 18.

Related species: **A. divérgens** Pax. Shrub: lvs. 5- or occasionally 3-lobed, 2–6 cm. wide, with broad-ovate, entire, acute or obtusish lobes, truncate or subcordate at base, reticulate beneath, glabrous: wings spreading at a wide angle, 1 cm. wide and 2.5 cm. long with the flat nutlet. Gt.47:123. (*A. quinquelobum* K. Koch, not Gilib.) Transcauc. Intr. 1932. Zone V.

11. **A. Ópalus** Mill. Small tree to 15 m.; brts. glabrous: lvs. shallowly 5-lobed, 6–10 cm. across, cordate or truncate, with short and broad usually acutish obtusely dentate lobes, the middle one often 3-lobed, dark green and glabrous above, glaucescent beneath and pubescent at first, becoming glabrous; petiole 4–9 cm. long: fls. yellow, on slender drooping glabrous pedicels in a many-fld. short-stalked corymb: fr. glabrous; wings spreading at a right angle or connivent, with the thick nutlet 2.5–3.5 cm. long. Fl. IV–V; fr.VIII–IX. R.I.5:t.163(c). L.B.1221(c). E.H.3:t.189(h). (*A. italum* Lauth, *A. opulifolium* Vill.) S. Eu. Intr. 1752. Zone V.—**A. O. obtusàtum** (Kit.) Henry, var. Lvs. usually larger, 8–12 cm. across, cordate, the lobes shorter, obtusish or obtuse, the basal ones very short, often nearly obsolete, softpubescent beneath: pedicels pilose, glabrescent at maturity. R.I.5:t.163,f. 4827(c). D.L.2:443. G.C.75:239. E.H.3:t.206,f.16. (*A. o.* Kit., *A. o.* var. *tomentosum* Schwer.) S. E. Eu. and Italy. Intr. about 1805. Zone VI.— **A. O. tomentòsum** (Tausch) Rehd., var. Lvs. to 16 cm. across, cordate, lobes short and more rounded, tomentose beneath: pedicels pilose until autumn: wings of fr. broader. R.I.5:t.165(c). D.L.2:444. E.H.3:t.206,f.14. (*A. O.* var. *neapolitanum* Henry, *A. opulifolium* var. *t.* Tausch.) Italy. Intr. 1825. Zone VI.—Probably another var. of this species is *A. microphyllum* Kirchn. Dwarf shrub with small glabrous lvs. only about 3 cm. across. M.D. 1894: 47(1). Cult. 1865.

A. O. × *monspessulanum* = **A. Perònai** Schwer. Lvs. 3-lobed, sometimes with small basal lobes, 5–10 cm. across, cordate, lobes triangular, coarsely and sparingly dentate, glaucescent and glabrous beneath. Italy and France. Cult. 1905. Zone V.

12. **A. hyrcànum** Fisch. & Mey. Tree to 10 m.; brts. glabrous: lvs. 5-lobed, 5–10 cm. across, lobes angular, acute, coarsely dentate, the 3 upper ones with nearly straight and parallel margins and often 3-lobed, bright green above, glaucescent beneath and pubescent along the veins; petiole red, slender, 5–10 cm. long: fls. greenish yellow on slender glabrous pendulous pedicels: fr. glabrous; wings nearly upright and 2–2.5 cm. long with the nutlets. Fl.v; fr.IX. Gt.42:361(l). D.H.2:446(l). (*A. italum* var. *h.* Pax, *A. Opalus* var. *h.* Rehd., *A. tauricum* Hort., ?*A. velutinum* Schwer., not Boiss.) S. E. Eu., Crimea, Cauc., Asia Minor. Cult. 1865.

Sect. III. SACCHARINA Pax. Fls. andro-polygamous or sometimes androdioecious, on slender pendulous pedicels, fascicled or corymbose, perigynous; sepals connate; petals wanting; stamens inserted on the inner margin of the disk: fr. with convex veined nutlets spreading horizontally, the wings more or less upright: lvs. 3–5-lobed, the lobes entire or coarsely dentate: winter-buds with many imbricate scales.

13. **A. sáccharum** Marsh. SUGAR M. (ROCK M.) Tree to 40 m., with gray furrowed bark: lvs. 3–5-lobed, 8–14 cm. across, cordate, lobes acuminate, sparingly coarsely dentate with narrow and deep sinuses, light green and glabrous beneath in the typical form: fls. campanulate, about 5 mm. long, greenish yellow on pendulous hairy pedicels 3–7 cm. long in subsessile corymbs; stamens exserted in the staminate fl.: fr. with slightly divergent wings, with the nutlet 2.5–4 cm. long, glabrous. Fl.ɪv; fr.ɪx. M.S.1:t.42(c). S.O.1:t.8(c). Em.2:558,t. S.S.2:t.90. Am. For. 26:87(h);28:12–16. F.L.5:56, t(h). G.F.4:175(h). E.H.3:t.191(h). (*A. barbatum* Michx., *A. saccharinum* Wangh., not L., *A. saccharophorum* K. Koch, *Saccharodendron barbatum* Nieuwl.) E. Can. to Ga., Ala., Miss. and Tex. Intr. 1753. Zone III. Much planted as a street and shade tree in the N. E. States; of dense regular habit and with bright green lvs. turning yellow or orange and scarlet in fall; yields maple sugar.—**A. s. cònicum** Fern., f. Tree with ascending brs. forming a dense conical head. Rh.36:238(h).—**A. s. monumentàle** (Temple) Rehd. Of columnar habit with ascending brs. and short brts. H.B.1:269(h). G.C.A. 38:7(h). Cult. 1900.—**A. s. glaùcum** (Schmidt) Pax, f. Lvs. glaucous beneath. (*A. saccharinum* var. *glaucum* Schmidt.)—**A. s. Schneckii** Rehd., var. Lvs. densely villous on the veins beneath, petioles villous, rarely glabrous. Ind., Ill., Mo. Intr. 1919.—**A. s. Rugélii** (Pax) Rehd., var. Lvs. usually 3-lobed, generally broader than long, with entire lobes, glaucous or sometimes pale green beneath, subcoriaceous. (*A. R.* Pax.) S.S.2:t.91(as var. *nigrum*). Intr. 1903.

14. **A. grandidentàtum** Nutt. Tree to 12 m., with dark brown scaly bark; brts. glabrous: lvs. 3–5-lobed, with broad shallow sinuses, 5–8 cm. across, subcordate, lobes acute or obtuse, lobulate, rarely entire, glaucescent and pubescent beneath especially on the veins; petiole stout, 3–5 cm. long: fls. on slender drooping villous pedicels in several-fld. short-stalked corymbs: calyx often persistent under the fr.: wings spreading, often rose-colored in midsummer, with the nutlet 2.5–3.5 cm. long. Fl.ɪv; fr.ɪx. N.S.2:t.69(c). S.S.2:t.92. D.H.2:440. (*A. saccharum g.* Sudw.) Wyo. to Utah, N. Mex. and n. Mex. Intr. 1882. Zone V.

Related species: **A. floridànum** Pax. Bark of young trees pale and smooth: lvs. 3–5-lobed, truncate or subcordate, with entire or slightly lobulate acute or obtuse lobes, glaucescent and pubescent beneath: fls. in many-fld. nearly sessile corymbs: fr. sparingly villous while young with spreading or sometimes erect wings with the nutlet 2.5–3 cm. long. Va. to Fla. and E. Tex. S.S.2:t.91. G.F. 4:148. (*A. saccharum f.* Sudw.) Intr. ? Zone VII?

15. **A. nígrum** Michx. f. BLACK M. Tree to 40 m., with black deeply furrowed bark; brts. pilose at first, soon glabrous: lvs. 3-lobed, occasionally 5-lobed, 10–14 cm. wide, deeply cordate with usually closed sinus, lobes acute, entire or obtusely toothed, the sides of the blade drooping, dull green above, yellowish green and pilose beneath; petioles usually pubescent, 8–12 cm. long: fls. yellowish green, on pendulous hairy pedicels in nearly sessile many-fld. corymbs: fr. glabrous; wings nearly upright or diverging, with the nutlet 3–4 cm. long. Fl.ɪv; fr.ɪx. M.S.1:t.43(c). S.S.13:t.625. H.H.326,327(b). B.C. 1:203. (*A. saccharum* var. *n.* Brit., *A. saccharinum* var. *n.* Loud.) Que. and N. E. to N. Y., W. Va. and Ky., w. to S. Dak., Iowa and Mo. Intr. 1812. Zone III. Not much planted; with duller lvs. turning yellow in fall.

16. **A. leucodérme** Small. Tree to 8, rarely to 12 m., with light gray or grayish brown bark: lvs. 3–5-lobed, 5–8 cm. across, truncate or subcordate, with acuminate sinuate-dentate lobes, dark yellow green above, lighter and soft-pubescent beneath: fls. yellow, about 4 mm. long, on slender glabrous

pedicels in nearly sessile corymbs: fr. villous, finally glabrous; wings wide-spreading, with the nutlet 1.5–2 cm. long. Fl.ɪᴠ; fr.ɪx. (*A. saccharum* var. *l.* Sarg.) S.S.13:t.624. N. C. to Ga. and La. Cult. 1900. Zone V. Sometimes planted as a street tree in the S.; the lvs. turn scarlet in fall.

Sect. IV. Sᴘɪᴄᴀᴛᴀ Pax. Fls. andro-polygamous, in panicles sometimes broad and nearly corymbiform, hypogynous; stamens inside of the thick disk: fr. with convex, strongly veined nutlets: winter-buds with imbricate scales or with only 2 outer scales: lvs. 3–7-lobed, rarely undivided and serrate, the lobes lobulate to serrate.

17. **A. macrophýllum** Pursh. Oʀᴇɢᴏɴ M. Tree to 30 m.; brts. stout, glabrous: lvs. deeply 3–5-lobed or -cleft, 20–30 cm. across, cordate, the middle lobe mostly 3-lobed, the others lobulate, dark green and lustrous above, pale green and pubescent beneath when young, subcoriaceous; petiole 25–30 cm. long: fls. yellow, fragrant, in narrow pendulous glabrous panicles 10–12 cm. long: nutlets of the fr. with yellow stiff hairs; wings spreading at a right angle or nearly upright, about 3 cm. long. Fl.ᴠ; fr.ɪx. N.S.2:t.67(c). S.S.2: t.86,87. F.E.14:t.44(h). Gn.M.2:107(h). Alaska to Cal. Intr. 1812. Zone VI. —Remarkable for its large lvs. turning bright orange in fall.

18. **A. Pseudoplátanus** L. Sʏᴄᴀᴍᴏʀᴇ M. Tree to 30 m.; brts. glabrous: lvs. 5-lobed, 8–16 cm. across, cordate, lobes ovate, coarsely crenate-serrate, dark green and glabrous above, glaucescent beneath and usually glabrous or pubescent on the veins: fls. yellowish green, in pendulous narrow panicles with the stalk 6–12 cm. long: fr. glabrous; wings spreading at an acute or right angle, with the nutlet 3–5 cm. long. Fl.ᴠ; fr.ᴠɪɪɪ–ɪx. R.I.5:t.164(c). H.W.3:39,40(h),t.44(c). E.H.3:t.179–183(h). F.E.15:t.47(h). Eu., W. Asia. Cult. for centuries. Zone V. Large tree of vigorous growth, with spreading head; thrives in exposed situations and near the seashore.—**A. P. variegàtum** West., var. Lvs. variegated with white, reddish when young. S.O.1:t.2(c). (*A. P. albo-variegatum* Hayne.) Cult. 1730.—**A. P. flavo-variegàtum** Hayne. Lvs. marked with yellow. (*A. P.* var. *aureo-variegatum* Jacques.) Cult. 1822.—**A. P. corstorphinénse** Schwer., f. Lvs. bright yellow when young. G.F.6:205(h). Cult. 1600.—**A. P. Worleèi** Rosenthal. Lvs. deep yellow, orange-yellow when young, petiole reddish.—**A. P. Leopóldii** Lem., var. Lvs. dark rosy pink while young and variegated with yellowish pink. I.H.11:t.411(c).—**A. P. purpúreum** Loud., var. Lvs. purple beneath. (*A. P.* f. *purpurascens* Pax, *A. P. atropurpureum* Spaeth.) Orig. 1828.—**A. P. ery-throcárpum** Carr. Lvs. smaller and more lustrous; fr. bright red. R.H.1864: 171,t(c). M.D.1905:1,t.(c). Gn.76:540.—**A. P. euchlòrum** Spaeth. Lvs. large, dark green above: fr. large, samara to 6 cm. long.—**A. P. tomentòsum** Tausch, var. Lvs. pubescent beneath, more coarsely toothed, subcoriaceous; wings of fr. to 2 cm. broad, rounded at apex. (*A. P.* var. *villosum* Parl.) S. Eu.

A. p. × *monspessulanum* = **A. coriàceum** Tausch. Lvs. 3-lobed, 5–8 cm. across, subcordate, lobes crenate-denticulate, lustrous above, glabrous beneath: fls. in loose corymbs; samaras 2.5 cm. long; wings diverging at an acute angle. S.O.1:t.15(c). D.L.2:433. S.H.2:f.130e. (*A. creticum* Schmidt, not L., *A. poly-morphum* Spach, *A. parvifolium* Tausch.) Orig. unknown, cult. 1790.—The following are probably of the same parentage: **A. hýbridum** Spach. Lvs. 3-lobed, sometimes with 2 small basal lobes, 5–10 cm. across, the lobes pointing forward, acute, denticulate, dull green above, pubescent on the veins beneath: fls. in panicles 8–12 cm. long: samaras 2–2.5 cm. long, wings nearly parallel. D.L.2:422. S.H.2:f.130d. (*A. monspessulanum* × *opalus* Pax.)—**A. Duréttii** Pax. Lvs. 3-lobed, often with 2 small basal lobes, 5–10 cm. across, lobes triangular, irregularly toothed, pubescent on the veins beneath: fls. in corymbs. S.H.2:f.130a(l). (*A. Pseudopl.* × *obtusatum* Pax.)—**A. rotundílobum** Schwer. Lvs. 3-lobed, with rounded obscurely denticulate or nearly entire lobes, glabrous beneath. M.D.

1894:47(1). S.H.2:f.161c(1). (*A. Pseudopl.* × *obtusatum* Pax, *A. barbatum* Booth, not Michx.) Cult. 1889.—Doubtful hybrids of *A. Pseudoplatanus* are: **A. serìceum** Schwer. Lvs. 5-lobed, lobes doubly serrate, pubescent beneath. M.D.1894:47(1). S.H.2:f.130b.—**A. ramòsum** Schwer. Lvs. 3-lobed with doubly serrate lobes, glabrous. M.D.1894:47(1). (?*A. Pseudopl.* × *campestre* Schwer.)

19. **A. Heldreìchii** Orph. Tree of medium height; brts. dark red-brown: lvs. 5-lobed, 8–12 cm. across, lobes oblong, coarsely toothed or lobulate, the middle one divided nearly to the base, the lateral ones halfway, dark green and lustrous above, glaucous beneath and slightly villous along the veins or nearly glabrous at maturity: fls. yellow, in upright ovoid long-stalked panicles: fr. glabrous, wings spreading at an obtuse angle, with the nutlet 3.5–5 cm. long. Fl.v; fr.ix. Gt.34:t.1185. G.C.II.16:141(1). D.H.2:430. S.E. Eu. Intr. 1879. Zone V. Remarkable for its deeply divided lvs.—**A. H. purpuràtum** Schwer. Lvs. red beneath.

20. **A. Trautvétteri** Medwed. Tree to 15 m.; brts. glabrous, dark red-brown at maturity: lvs. deeply 5-lobed, 10–16 cm. across, cordate, lobes ovate-oblong, acuminate, lobulate and irregularly dentate, lustrous dark green above, glaucous beneath, villous along the veins beneath when young, glabrous and finely reticulate at maturity: fls. in upright long-stalked pyramidal panicles: fr. pubescent when young, wings nearly parallel, with the nutlet 4–5 cm. long. Fl.v; fr.ix. B.M.6697(c, as *A. insigne*). Gt.40:264–266. E.H.3:t.206,f.19. G.C.II.16:75. Cauc. Intr. 1866. Zone V.

21. **A. velutìnum** Boiss. Large tree; winter-buds pointed, with 8–10 outer scales; lvs. 5-lobed, 12–18 cm. across, subcordate, lobes ovate, coarsely and irregularly crenate-serrate, bright green above, glaucescent beneath and villous-pubescent; fls. in erect ovoid panicles 8–10 cm. wide: fr. puberulous at maturity; keys 3–4.5 cm. long; wings spreading at a right or obtuse angle. Fl.v; fr.ix–x. G.C.III.10:189. (*A. insigne* var. *velutinum* Boiss.) Cauc., N. Persia. Cult. 1873. Zone VI. Remarkable for its large lvs., particularly var. *VanVolxemii*.—**A. v. VanVolxémii** (Mast.) Rehd., var. Lvs. to 30 cm. broad, cordate at base, with more acutely serrate lobes, glaucous beneath and pubescent in the axils and along the veins: wings of fr. spreading nearly horizontally. G.C.III.10:9,11. D.L.2:432. R.H.1914:225,227,f.68,70(h). (*A. insigne* f. *perckense* Schwer., *A. V.* Mast.)—**A. v. glabréscens** (Boiss. & Buhse) Rehd., var. Lvs. glaucous and glabrous beneath: fr. pubescent only when young. Gt.30:120. R.H.1914:225,226,f.67,69(h). M.D.1932:t.13(h).—**A. v. Wolfii** (Schwer.) Rehd., f. A form of the preceding var. with the lvs. red beneath.

22. **A. Buergeriànum** Miq. Small tree; brts. glabrous; lvs. 3-lobed, 3.5–8 cm. across, 3-nerved at base and rounded or broad-cuneate, lobes triangular, acute and pointing forward, entire or slightly and irregularly serrate, dark green above, pale green or glaucescent beneath and pubescent while young, soon glabrous; petiole about as long as blade: fls. small in a broad-pyramidal pubescent panicle: fr. glabrous; wings parallel and connivent, with the nutlet 2–2.5 cm. long. Fl.v; fr.ix. S.Z.2:t.143. J.C.32,1:t.17. S.H.2:f.126b-c,127a-d. (*A. trifidum* Hook. & Arn., not Thunb.) E. China, Japan. Cult. 1890. Zone VI.—**A. B. trinérve** (Dipp.) Rehd., var. Lvs. deeply 3-lobed with oblong-ovate irregularly and doubly serrate lobes, the lateral ones spreading and shorter. D.L.2:429(1) (*A. t.* Dipp.) Cult. 1890. Probably a juvenile form.

23. **A. Gínnala** Maxim. Shrub or small tree to 7 m.; brts. glabrous, slender: lvs. 3-lobed, 4–8 cm. long, 3–6 cm. wide, rarely undivided and ovate-oblong, subcordate or truncate, the middle lobe usually ovate-oblong, much longer than the lateral ones, doubly serrate, dark green and lustrous above,

light green beneath, glabrous; petiole 1.5–4 cm. long: fls. yellowish white, fragrant, in long-peduncled panicle: fr. glabrous, wings nearly parallel, with the nutlet about 2.5 cm. long. Fl.v; fr.ix. M.K.t.67(c). G.W.12:18,t(c). N.K.1:t.2. Gt.1877:308. B.C.1:201. F.E.17:t.72(h). (A. *tataricum* var. *g.* Maxim., A. *tataricum* var. *aidzuense* Franch.) C. and N. China, Manch., Japan. Intr. about 1860. Zone II. Fr. usually red and conspicuous during the summer; the lvs. turn bright red in fall.—**A. G. Semenòvii** (Reg. & Herd.) Pax, var. Shrubby: lvs. smaller, deeply 3- or nearly 5-lobed, with narrower lobes: fr. with more divergent wings. Bull. Soc. Nat. Mosc. 39:t. 12. (*A. S.* Reg. & Herd.) Turkest. Cult. 1880. Zone IV.

24. A. tatáricum L. TATARIAN M. Shrub or small tree to 10 m.; brts. glabrous: lvs. broad-ovate to ovate-oblong, 5–10 cm. long, rounded to cordate at base, acuminate, irregularly doubly serrate, bright green and glabrous above, pubescent on the veins beneath when young, finally nearly glabrous; petiole 1.5–5 cm. long: fls. greenish white, in upright glabrous long-peduncled panicles: wings of the glabrous fr. nearly parallel, with the nutlet 2–3 cm. long. Fl.v; fr.ix. S.O.1:t.9(c). R.I.5:t.162(c). S.W.3:43. G.O.t.47(c). S. E. Eu., W. Asia. Intr. 1759. Zone IV. With attractive red fr. in late summer and bright green lvs. turning yellow in fall.—**A. t. rubrum** Schwer., f. Lvs. coloring blood-red in fall.

A. t. × *monspessulanum* = **A. pusíllum** Schwer. Shrub: lvs oblong-ovate, 2–4 cm. long, with 2 lobes at base, obtusely doubly serrulate, glabrous. M.D. 1894:47(1). (*A. Boscii* K. Koch, not Spach.) Cult. 1870.—*A. t.* × *pennsylvanicum* = **A. Bóscii** Spach. Lvs. broad-obovate, 8–10 cm. long, 3-lobed near apex, with broad-triangular serrulate lobes, glabrescent. D.L.2:420. S.H.2:f.130c(1). Orig. before 1834.

25. A. spicàtum Lam. MOUNTAIN M. Shrub or small tree, rarely to 10 m.; young brts. grayish pubescent: lvs. 3-lobed or sometimes slightly 5-lobed, 6–12 cm. long, cordate, lobes ovate, acuminate, coarsely and irregularly serrate, yellowish green above, pubescent beneath: fls. small, greenish yellow, in upright pubescent narrow spikes 8–14 cm. long; ovary pubescent: fr. nearly glabrous at maturity, wings divergent at an acute or nearly right angle, with the nutlet about 1.5 cm. long. Fl.vi; fr.ix. M.S.1:t.47(c). Em.567,t. S.S.2:t. 82,83. H.H.328,329(b). Am. For. 28:15,18. (*A. montanum* Ait.) Lab. to Sask., s. to n. Ga. and Iowa. Intr. 1750. Zone II. With light green lvs. turning orange and scarlet in fall; the fr. sometimes bright red in summer.

26. A. caudàtum Wall. Large tree: lvs 5–7-lobed, 8–14 cm. across, cordate, lobes ovate, long-acuminate, incisely serrate, brownish pubescent on the veins beneath: fls. small, in upright cylindric spikes, 12–15 cm. long: fr. small, the wings spreading at a right angle. Wallich, Pl. As. Rar. 2:t.132(c). D.L.2:424. (*A. pictum himalayense* Hort.) Himal. Cult. 1910. Zone VI?—**A. c. ukurunduénse** (Trautv. & Mey.) Rehd., var. Small tree; brts. and petioles pubescent while young: lvs. glabrous above, pubescent beneath, sometimes only along the veins, lobes coarsely serrate; spikes pubescent: fr. with nearly upright wings. S.T.1:t.82. G.C.II.15:172. N.K.1:t.1. M.K.t.66(c). (*A. u.* Trautv. & Mey., A. *spicatum* var. *u.* Maxim., A. *vitifolium* Hort.) Japan, Manch. Cult. 1880. Zone V.—**A. c. multiserràtum** (Maxim.) Rehd., var. Tree to 10 m.; similar to the preceding var., but lvs. glabrous or nearly so beneath. S.H.2:f. 131d(1). (*A. m.* Maxim., A. *erosum* Pax, A. *ukurunduense* var. *m.* Schneid.) C. China. Intr. 1907. Zone V or VI?

Related species: **A. eriánthum** Schwer. Small tree: lvs. 5-lobed, lobes broad, unequally and simply serrate, nearly glabrous beneath except conspicuous axillary tufts of white hairs: fls. with densely villous disk. S.T.1:t.80. China. Intr. 1910? Zone VI?—**A. nippónicum** Hara. Tree: lvs. 3–5-lobed, 10–15 cm.

across, lobes broad-ovate, acute, doubly serrate, pubescent beneath when young, bright green: fls. in narrow puberulous panicles 10–20 cm. long; wings of fr. spreading at an obtuse angle or sometimes ascending. S.I.2:t.42(c). J.C.32, 1:t.1. M.D.1912:359. (*A. parviflorum* Franch. & Sav., not Ehrh., *A. crassipes* Pax, not Heer, *A. brevilobum* Rehd.) Japan. Cult. 1900. Zone (V).

27. **A. sinénse** Pax. Tree to 10 m.; brts. glabrous: lvs. 5-lobed, 8–14 cm. across, cordate and sometimes truncate, lobes ovate, acuminate, sparingly appressed-serrate, dark lustrous green above, glaucescent beneath and glabrous, chartaceous; petiole 3–5 cm. long, usually reddish: fls. greenish white, in pyramidal panicles 5–10 cm. long: wings of fr. spreading at an obtuse angle, with the nutlet about 3 cm. long. Fl.v; fr.ix. S.T.1:t.78. J.H.29:f.88(l), f.99 and f.103(h), probably a juvenile form. C. China. Intr. 1901. Zone VI? Tree with handsome dark green lvs. reddish when unfolding.—**A. s. cóncolor** Pax, var. Lvs. green beneath; fr. with horizontally spreading wings.

Related species: **A. Wílsoni** Rehd. Lvs. 3-lobed, sometimes with small basal lobes, 7–10 cm. across, lobes oblong-ovate to oblong, caudate-acuminate, entire or sparingly serrate, light green beneath and glabrous: wings of fr. spreading at a right angle. S.T.1:t.79. S.H.2:f.126e,133a-d. C. China. Intr. 1907. Zone VI?

28. **A. Oliveriànum** Pax. Tree to 10 m.; brts. glabrous: lvs. 5-lobed, 6–10 cm. across, truncate or subcordate, lobes ovate, caudate-acuminate, finely serrate, the middle lobe with 5–8 pairs of lateral veins, finely reticulate, glabrous and lustrous beneath: fls. whitish, small, in long-stalked glabrous nearly corymbose panicles; keys 2.5–3 cm. long, with nearly horizontally spreading wings. Fls.v; fr.ix. S.T.1:t.77. S.H.2:f.131e,133r-u. C. China. Intr. 1901. Zone VI? Handsome Maple resembling somewhat *A. palmatum*.

Related species: **A. flabellàtum** Rehd. Lvs. 7-, rarely 5-lobed, 8–12 cm. across, deeply cordate, lobes sharply serrate, bearded in the axils of the lateral veins and villous along the primary veins: infl. paniculate. S.T.1:t.81. S.H.2:f.131f, 133v-y. (*A. robustum* Schneid., not Pax.) C. China. Intr. ?—**A. Campbéllii** Hook. f. & Thoms. Lvs. 5–7-lobed, 12–15 cm. wide, rounded or subcordate at base, lobes ovate to ovate-oblong, caudate-acuminate, serrate at least near apex, middle lobe with 10–16 conspicuous pairs of lateral veins, slightly pubescent on veins beneath: infl. paniculate. S.H.2:f.131a,133n-q. E. Himal., S. W. China. Cult. 1934. Zone VII?

Sect. V. PALMATA Pax. Fls. andro-polygamous, in few-fld. corymbs. hypogynous, usually red; stamens inside of the thick disk: fr. with small convex strongly veined nutlets: lvs. 5–11-lobed, with serrate lobes: winter-buds with 2 or 4 outer scales.

29. **A. circinàtum** Pursh. VINE M. Shrub or small tree to 12 m.; brts. glabrous, slender: lvs. 7–9-lobed, 6–12 cm. across, cordate, lobes acute, irregularly and doubly serrate, bright green, puberulous beneath when young, becoming glabrous; petioles 2.5–3.5 cm. long, stout: fls. about 1.2 cm. across in glabrous, 6–20-fld. corymbs; sepals purple; petals smaller, white: wings of fr. spreading almost horizontally, with the nutlet 3.5 cm. long. Fi.iv–v; fr.ix. N.S.2:t.68(c). S.S.2:t.87. B.S.1:138. D.L.2:463. B. C. to Calif. Intr. 1826. Zone V. Usually a wide-spreading shrub with bright green lvs. turning red and orange in fall, attractive in spring with its purple and white fls. and later with the young red frs.

30. **A. palmàtum** Thunb. JAPANESE M. Shrub or small tree to 8 m.; brts. glabrous, slender: lvs. deeply 5–9-lobed or parted, 5–10 cm. across, subcordate, lobes lance-ovate or lance-oblong, acuminate, doubly serrate, glabrous and bright green beneath; petioles glabrous, slender, 1.5–4.5 cm. long: fls. purple, 6–8 mm. across, in small glabrous corymbs; anthers smooth: wings of fr. spreading at an obtuse angle and incurved above, with the glabrous nutlet about 1 cm. long. Fl.vi; fr.ix. S.Z.2:t.145,146(c). S.I.1:t.68(c). J.H.

angle or nearly horizontal, with the oblong nutlet 3–4 cm. long. Wallich, Pl. As. Rar. 2:t.104(c). Himal., China. Intr. 1907. Zone VII.

35. **A. dístylum** Sieb. & Zucc. Deciduous tree to 15 m.; brts. puberulous when young; winter-buds with 2 outer scales: lvs. ovate, 10–16 cm. long, deeply cordate, acuminate, serrulate, green and lustrous beneath, glabrous: petiole 2–6 cm. long, puberulous when young: fls. yellowish, in panicles 5–6 cm. long on stalks of nearly equal length; styles divided to base: fr. in upright panicles; wings spreading at an acute angle, with the nutlet 2.5–3 cm. long. Fl.vi; fr.ix. S.I.2:t.41(c). J.C.32,1:t.2. G.C.II.15:499. J.H.29:f.76(h). Japan. Intr. 1879 to 1881. Zone VII?

Related species: **A. Schwerìnii** Pax. Lvs. ovate, cordate, slightly lobulate and denticulate, 10–16 cm. long, glaucescent beneath. S.H.2:f.141a-b. Orig. unknown. Zone VI?

Sect. VIII. INDIVISA Pax. Fls. andro-monoecious or andro-dioecious, apetalous, 4-merous, hypogynous, racemose; stamens 5–6, inserted outside the disk; styles 2-parted: fr. with compressed elliptic-oblong nutlet: lvs. undivided, oblong, doubly serrate, penninerved: winter-buds with many imbricate scales. (*Carpinifolia* Koidz.)

36. **A. carpinifòlium** Sieb. & Zucc. HORNBEAM M. Tree to 10 m.; brts. glabrous: lvs. ovate-oblong, 8–12 cm. long, subcordate to truncate, long-acuminate, doubly serrate, pubescent on the veins beneath when young, finally glabrous or nearly so; petiole 1–1.5 cm. long: fls. greenish, about 1 cm. across, on slender pedicels in short glabrous racemes: fr. glabrous, on pedicels 2–3 cm. long, wings spreading at a right or obtuse angle, incurved at apex, with the nutlet about 3 cm. long. Fl.v; fr.ix. S.Z.2:142(c). J.C.32,1:t.8. G.C.II.15:564. J.H.29:f.75(h). Japan. Intr. 1881. Zone V. Distinct Maple with bright green lvs. turning bright brownish yellow in fall.

Sect. IX. MACRANTHA Pax. Fls. monoecious or dioecious, hypogynous, racemose; stamens inserted outside of the disk; style deeply 2-lobed: fr. with flattened not strongly veined nutlets: lvs. undivided or 3–5-lobed, serrate or doubly serrate; winter-buds with 2 outer valvate scales, stalked; bark of brts. remaining smooth for several years and striped white.

37. **A. Davìdi** Franch. Tree to 15 m.; brts. glabrous, striate: lvs. ovate to ovate-oblong, 8–16 cm. long, acuminate, subcordate or rounded at base and not prominently 3- or 5-nerved, unequally crenate-serrulate, green beneath and rufous-villous on the veins while young, finally glabrous or nearly so; petiole 1.5–5 cm. long: fls. yellowish in slender glabrous pendulous racemes 6–9 cm. long, the staminate ones shorter: fr. on pedicels 2–8 mm. long; wings spreading nearly horizontally, with the nutlet 2.5–3 cm. long. Fl.v; fr.ix. S.T.1:t.83. I.S.1:t.35. G.C.72:119(b). J.H.29:f.86(h),90. C. China. Intr. 1879 and 1902. Zone V. Distinct Maple with the lvs. turning yellow and purple in fall; the lustrous brs. striped white are conspicuous in winter.

Related species: **A. Hoòkeri** Miq. Lvs. oblong-ovate, 10–14 cm. long, cordate and 5-nerved at base, abruptly caudate-acuminate; sharply serrate, glabrous; petiole 4–7 cm. long: fl. on slender pedicels 4–7 mm. long. D.L.2:408 (juvenile state). E. Himal. Cult. 1892. Zone VII?—**A. sikkiménse** Miq. Lvs. ovate to ovate-oblong, 10–14 cm. long, abruptly acuminate, subcordate and 3-nerved at base, entire or serrulate, glabrous; petiole 2–5 cm. long: racemes in fr. to 15 cm. long; pedicels 1–2 mm. long. E. Himal. and S. W. China. Cult. 1880. Zone VII.

38. **A. crataegifòlium** S. & Z. Small tree to 10 m.; brts. purplish, glabrous: lvs. oblong-ovate, 5–8 cm. long, acuminate, subcordate to truncate, usually with 2 or 4 short lobes near base, unequally serrate, bluish green and glabrous; petiole 1.5–2 cm. long: fls. yellowish white, in erect 5–8-fld. glabrous racemes 3–5 cm. long: fr. glabrous on pedicels about 6 mm. long; wings spreading nearly horizontally, with the nutlet 2–2.5 cm. long. Fl.v; fr.ix.

S.Z.2:147(c). S.I.1:t.67(c). J.C.32,1:t.3. D.L.2:417. Japan. Intr. 1879. Zone (V).—**A. c. Veìtchii** Nichols., var. Lvs. variegated with white or pink. Related species: **A. Veìtchii** Schwer. Brts. greenish: lvs. ovate-oblong, 7–10 cm. long, slightly lobulate greenish beneath; petiole 2–5 cm. long. Orig. unknown. S.H.2:f.144g,145a-b. (?*A. crataegifolium* × *pennsylvanicum* Pax.) Cult. 1890.—**A. laxiflòrum** Pax. Tree to 15 m.: lvs. oblong-ovate, 6–10 cm. long, long-acuminate, cordate, with 2 or 4 short lobes near base, sharply serrate, green and glabrous beneath: racemes slender, pendulous: wings of fr. usually spreading at a right angle. E.P.IV.163:35. W. China. Intr. 1908. Zone VI?

39. **A. pennsylvànicum** L. Moosewood. Small tree, rarely to 12 m.; brts. green, smooth, becoming conspicuously striped with white lines: lvs. roundish-obovate, 3-lobed at apex, 12–18 cm. long, subcordate, the lobes pointing forward, acuminate, serrulate, ferrugineous-pubescent beneath when young; petiole 2–7 cm. long, rufous-pubescent when young: fls. yellow, about 6 mm. across, in pendulous glabrous racemes 10–15 cm. long: fr. on pedicels 1–1.5 cm. long; wings spreading at a wide angle, with the nutlet about 2 cm. long. Fl.v–vi; fr.ix. M.S.2:t.45(c). Em.566,t. S.S.2:t.84,85. H.H.330,331(b). Am. For. 20:505;28:15,17. (*A. striatum* Lam.—Striped M.) Que. to Wis., s. to n. Ga. Intr. 1755. Zone III. The large bright green lvs. turn clear yellow in fall; the striped brs. conspicuous in winter.—**A. p. erythrócladum** Spaeth. Brs. bright red in winter. Cult. 1904.

   A. p. × *tataricum;* see under No. 24.

40. **A. rufinérve** Sieb. & Zucc. Tree to 12 m.; brts. glaucous when young: lvs. 3-lobed, 6–12 cm. long, rounded at base, the lateral lobes somewhat spreading, sometimes with 2 very small basal lobes, unequally doubly serrate, dark green above, veins beneath rufous-pubescent when young like the 2–6 cm. long petiole: fls. in upright ferrugineous-pubescent racemes: fr. pubescent at first, finally glabrous, on pedicels about 5 mm. long; wings spreading at an obtuse angle, with the nutlet about 2 cm. long. Fl.v; fr.ix. S.Z.2:t. 148(c). S.I.1:t.67(c). J.C.32,1:t.9. D.L.2:415. Gs.2:36(b). Japan. Intr. 1879. Zone V. With large dark green lvs. turning crimson in fall.—**A. r. albo-limbàtum** Hook., var. Lvs. with a broad margin of white dots. B.M.5793(c). R.B.4:49,t.(c). Cult. 1869.

   Related species: **A. Grósseri** Pax. Lvs. 3-lobed with triangular-ovate acuminate middle lobe and short acute spreading lateral lobes, at first toward the base beneath and on petiole rufous-pubescent, soon glabrous: fr. in long pendulous racemes; pedicels 3–6 mm. long; keys about 2 cm. long with horizontal, slightly curved wings. C. China.—**A. G. Hérsii** (Rehd.) Rehd., var. Lvs. above the middle with long-acuminate lateral lobes about half as long as middle lobe. I.S.3:t.147. J.A.14:221. (*A. H.* Rehd.) C. China. Intr. 1923. Zone V?

41. **A. capíllipes** Maxim. Tree to 12 m.; brts. smooth, striped: lvs. 3-lobed, 6–12 cm. long, subcordate or rounded at base, lobes acuminate, the lateral ones much shorter, spreading outward, doubly serrate, dark green above, bright green and glabrous beneath, usually with reddish veins; petiole 3–5 cm. long, usually red: fls. greenish white, about 8 mm. across, on slender pedicels 8–15 mm. long, in glabrous drooping racemes 7–10 cm. long: wings spreading at a wide angle or nearly horizontal, with the nutlet 1.5–2 cm. long. Fl.v; fr.ix. S.T.1:t.16. J.C.32,1:t.10. S.H.2:f.163f-g,164a-b. Gn.85:81 (b). Japan. Intr. 1892. Zone V. Lvs. bright green, red when unfolding, turning deep crimson in fall.

42. **A. tegméntosum** Maxim. Tree: brs. striped: lvs. 3-lobed, sometimes with 2 small basal lobes, 7–16 cm. long and nearly as wide, cordate or subcordate, lobes acuminate, the lateral ones much smaller and somewhat spreading, doubly serrulate, glabrous beneath, light green when unfolding;

petiole 3–8 cm. long: fls. in slender pendulous racemes about 8 cm. long: fr. on short pedicels 3–8 mm. long; wings spreading at a wide angle or nearly horizontal, with the nutlets about 3 cm. long. Fl.v; fr.ix. N.K.1:t.13. G.C II.15:75(1). S.H.2:f.163d-e,164f. Manch., Korea. Intr. 1892. Zone IV.

43. **A. Tschonóskii** Maxim. Small tree to 6 m.: lvs. orbicular-ovate, 5-, rarely 7-lobed, 5–10 cm. across, cordate, the lobes ovate, sharply and doubly serrate with acuminate teeth and lobulate, rufous-pubescent along the veins beneath when young; petiole 2–4 cm. long: raceme slender, 6–10-fld., glabrous: fr. on slender pedicels, 1–1.5 cm. long, wings spreading at a right or obtuse angle, incurved, with the nutlet 2.5–3 cm. long. Fl.v; fr.ix. S.I.2:t. 43(c). S.T.1:t.17. N.K.1:t.14. Japan. In*r. 1892. Zone V. Graceful shrubby tree; the lvs. turning bright yellow in fall.—**A. T. rúbripes** Komar., var. Lvs. with longer caudate-acuminate lobes; peticles and young brts. red: wings of fr. more spreading. N.K.1:t.14. N. Korea, Manch. Intr. 1917.

Closely related species: **A. Maximowíczii** Pax. Lvs. 3–5-lobed, 5–8 cm. long, lobes acuminate, the middle lobe elongated and caudate-acuminate, doubly serrate, glaucescent and glabrous beneath: fr. on slender pedicels 5–10 mm. long; wings spreading at a wide angle. S.T.1:t.84. M.I.1:t.10. (*A. urophyllum* Maxim.) C. China. Intr. ?

44. **A. micránthum** Sieb. & Zucc. Shrub or small tree: lvs. 5- or sometimes 7-lobed, 5–8 cm. wide, cordate, the lobes ovate, long-acuminate, incisely and doubly serrate, glabrous beneath; petiole 2–4 cm. long: fls. small, greenish white, in slender racemes 3–7 cm. long; fr. glabrous, on pedicels 2–6 mm. long; wings spreading at a wide angle or nearly horizontal, with the nutlet 1.5–2 cm. long. Fl.v; fr.ix. S.Z.2:t.141(c). S.I.2:t.44(c). J.C.32,1:t.12. Japan. Intr. 1879. Zone V. Graceful shrubby tree.

Sect. X. ARGUTA Rehd. Fls. dioecious, 4-merous, the pistillate ones in racemes terminal on 2-leafed brts., the staminate from leafless lateral buds; stamens 4; disk 4-lobed, intrastaminal: fr. with convex strongly veined nutlets: lvs. serrate or doubly serrate, 3–5-lobed or undivided; winter-buds with 2 outer scales.

45. **A. argùtum** Maxim. Small tree to 8 m.; brts. pubescent: lvs. broad-ovate, 5- or rarely 7-lobed, 5–8 cm. across, lobes ovate, long-acuminate and sharply serrate, pale green beneath and grayish pubescent chiefly on the veins; petiole 2–6 cm. long, pubescent when young: fls. greenish yellow, the pistillate ones in slender many-fld. racemes 4–5 cm. long: fr. on pedicels 1–2 cm. long; wings horizontal, with the nutlets 1.5–2 cm. long. Fl.iv–v; fr.ix. S.I.1t.69(c). S.T.1:t.66. J.C.32,1:t.14. D.L.2:413(1). Japan. Intr. about 1879. Zone V. Graceful small tree.

Related species: **A. barbinérve** Maxim. Lvs. 5-lobed, coarsely doubly serrate, pubescent beneath when young, at maturity only on the veins; petiole 4–9 cm. long: pistillate racemes usually 7-fld.: fr. on pedicels about 2 cm. long; wings spreading at an obtuse angle, with the nutlet about 3.5 cm. long. S.T.1:t.86. N.K.1:t.15. Manch., Korea. Intr. about 1890. Zone IV.—**A. acuminàtum** Wall. Lvs. 3-lobed, 6–11 cm. long, with long-acuminate doubly serrate lobes, glabrous and bright green beneath: wings of fr. spreading at a right angle. G.C.II.15: 364(as *A. laevigatum*). (*A. caudatum* Nichols., not Wall.) Himal. Intr. 1845. Zone VII?

46. **A. tetrámerum** Pax. Slender tree to 10 m.; brs. glabrous: lvs. ovate to oblong-ovate, 5–8 cm. long, acuminate, truncate or rounded and usually 3-nerved at base, unequally incisely serrate or sometimes lobulate, light green and slightly pubescent beneath or nearly glabrous; petiole 1.5–5 cm. long: fls. yellow; stamens sometimes 6; pistillate fls. in elongated racemes: fr. glabrous, on stalks 1–2.5 cm. long; wings spreading at an acute angle, with the nutlet 2.5–3.5 cm. long. Fl.iv; fr.ix. S.T.1:t.85. S.H.2:f.169c-c^1,170h-k.

C. and W. China. Intr. 1901. Zone V.—**A. t. lobulàtum** Rehd., var. Lvs.
distinctly lobulate, nearly glabrous. J.H.29:f.93(h),97. Intr. 1901.—**A. t.
tiliifòlium** Rehd., var. Lvs. ovate, cordate and 5-nerved at base, doubly serrate, not lobulate, pubescent beneath. W. China. Intr. 1910.—**A. t. betulifòlium** (Maxim.) Rehd., var. Lvs. ovate to ovate-oblong, not or very
slightly lobed, glabrous or glabrescent beneath, rounded or sometimes broad-
cuneate at base. N. W. China. Intr. 1927.

Sect. XI. Lithocarpa Pax. Fls. dioecious, 5-merous, perigynous, in corymbs
or racemes from lateral leafless buds; stamens 8; styles divided to the base: fr.
with convex nutlets strongly keeled and veined; embryo with twice conduplicate
and incumbent cotyledons: lvs. 3–5-lobed, coarsely dentate: winter-buds with
many imbricate scales.

47. **A. diabólicum** K. Koch. Tree to 10 m.; young brts. pilose, becoming
glabrous: lvs. 5-lobed, 10–16 cm. across, with broad-ovate short-acuminate
coarsely and remotely dentate lobes, appressed-pilose on both sides when
young, at maturity only sparingly so beneath, more densely on the veins:
petiole 4–10 cm. long, pubescent toward the apex: fls. yellow, the staminate
fascicled, on pendulous pilose pedicels; sepals more or less connate; petals
wanting; stamens exserted, inserted in the middle of the disk; pistillate fls.
in few-fld. racemes; sepals and petals distinct, of equal length: fr. on pedicels
1–2, sometimes to 5 cm. long; wings upright or spreading, with the thick
bristly nutlets 3–4 cm. long. Fl.iv–v; fr.ix–x. S.T.1:t.67. J.C.32,1:t.33. G.C.
II.15:532. Japan. Cult. 1880. Zone V. Round-topped tree with rather large
lvs.; the variety with conspicuous red fls. and red young fr.—**A. d. purpuráscens** (Franch. & Sav.) Rehd., var. Fls. purplish: lvs. reddish when
unfolding: fr. purple when young. S.I.1:t.65(c). (*A. p.* Franch. & Sav.) Japan.
Cult. 1878.

48. **A. Franchèti** Pax. Tree to 6 m.; brts. glabrous: lvs. 3-lobed or sometimes with 2 small basal lobes, 8–12 cm. long and nearly as wide, subcordate,
the lobes pointing forward, triangular-ovate, short-acuminate, irregularly and
remotely toothed, bright green, at maturity pubescent beneath or nearly
glabrous; petiole 5–10 cm. long, pubescent above: fls. yellowish green, in
pubescent racemes; sepals and petals of nearly equal length; disk intrastaminal: fr. on rather stout pedicels, 1–2 cm. long; wings spreading at a right
angle or nearly upright, with the thick sparingly appressed-pilose nutlet
about 5 cm. long. Fl.iv–v; fr.ix. S.T.1:t.87. C. China. Intr. 1901. Zone VI?
Similar to the preceding species.

Related species: **A. villòsum** Wall. Lvs. 3–5-lobed, 14–20 cm. across, coarsely
serrate, tomentose beneath: fr. in long pendulous racemes, often branched at
base; wings nearly upright. Wallich, Pl. As. Rar. 2:t.105(c). P.F.2:148,f.
211(l). D.L.2:412(l). (*A. sterculiaceum* Wall.) Himal. Intr. before 1850.
Zone VII?—**A. pilòsum** Maxim. Lvs. 3-lobed, 4–10 cm. across, with coarsely
toothed or nearly entire acuminate lobes, the middle one much longer and its
margins below the middle nearly parallel, the lateral spreading, glaucescent
beneath and pilose on the veins; petiole slender, red: infl. few-fld., fascicle-like.
Bull. Acad. Sci. St. Pétersb. 27:t.27,f.1–5. S.H.2:f.169e. N. W. China. Intr.
1911. Zone V.

Sect. XII. Rubra Pax. Fls. andro-dioecious or andro-monoecious, in fascicles from lateral leafless buds long before the lvs.: staminate fls. hypogynous,
with 5–8 exserted stamens; petals present or wanting; disk lobed or wanting:
fr. with convex reticulate nutlet: lvs. 3–5-lobed, serrate or coarsely dentate:
winter-buds with few imbricate scales.

49. **A. rúbrum** L. Red M. (Scarlet or Swamp M.). Tree to 40 m.; brts.
glabrous: lvs. 3–5-lobed, 6–10 cm. long, subcordate, with triangular-ovate,
short-acuminate unequally crenate-serrate lobes, dark green and lustrous
above, glaucous beneath and usually pubescent on the veins; petiole 5–10 cm.

long, often red: fls. slender-stalked, red, rarely yellowish, with petals: fr. glabrous, on pendulous stalks, 6–10 cm. long; wings spreading at a narrow angle, with the nutlet 1.5–2 cm. long, usually bright red when young. Fl.III–IV; fr.V–VI. M.S.2:t.41(c). Em.551,t(c). S.S.2:94. H.H.334,335(b). G.C.II.1:173. E.H.3:t.177,191(h). F.L.6:137,t(h). Nfd. to Fla., w. to Minn., Iowa, Okl. and Tex. Cult. 1656. Zone III. Conspicuous in early spring with its red fls. and later with its red fr.: lvs. turning bright scarlet and yellow in fall.—**A. r. columnàre** Rehd., var. Of upright columnar habit. Gn.M.31:382. G.F.7: 65(h, as Sugar M.)—**A. r. globòsum** Rehd., var. Of dwarf compact habit; fls. bright scarlet.—**A. r. pallidiflòrum** Pax, var. Fls. yellowish.—**A. r. trílobum** K. Koch, var. Lvs. smaller, 3-lobed near apex, rounded or sometimes broad-cuneate at base, usually pubescent beneath. S.S.13:t.626. (*A. r.* var. *tridens* Wood, *A. microphyllum* Pax, *A. semiorbiculatum* Pax.)—**A. r. tomentòsum** (Desf.) K. Koch, var. Lvs. 5-lobed, pubescent or nearly tomentose beneath: fls. bright red. (*A. t.* Desf., *A. rubrum* var. *fulgens* Hort.)—**A. r. Drummóndi** (Hook. & Arn.) Sarg., var. Lvs. 5-lobed, 8–14 cm. across, white-tomentose beneath when young, remaining pubescent: fr. bright scarlet; wings with the nutlet 3–3.5 cm. long. N.S.2:t.70(c). S.S.2:t.95. (*A. D.* Hook. & Arn.) Ind. to Tenn., Mo. and La. Intr. 1886. Zone VII?

Closely related species: **A. pycnánthum** K. Koch. Lvs. 3-lobed, 5–9 cm. long, rounded to subcordate, lobes triangular, sometimes very short, obtusely acuminate, doubly obtuse-serrate, glaucous and glabrous beneath: fr. with upright wings. J.C.32,1:t.16. (*A. rubrum* Mak., not L.) Japan. Intr. 1915. Zone V.

50. **A. sacchárinum** L. SILVER-M. Tree to 40 m.: lvs. deeply 5-lobed to 5-cleft, 8–14 cm. across, with deeply and doubly serrate acuminate lobes, the middle one often 3-lobed, bright green above, silvery white beneath and pubescent when young; petiole 8–12 cm. long: fls. short-stalked, greenish, apetalous: fr. pubescent when young, on pendulous pedicels 3–5 cm. long; wings divergent and falcate, with the elliptic-oblong nutlet 3.5–6 cm. long. Fl.II–III; fr.V–VI. M.S.1:t.40(c). Em.556,t(c). S.S.2:t.93. G.C.II.1:37. F.S. 29:983(h);32:443(h). F.L.5:168,t(h). G.W.18:294(h). Gs.3:3(h). (*A. dasycarpum* Ehrh., *A. eriocarpum* Michx.) Que. to Fla., w. to Minn., Neb., Kans., Okla. Intr. 1725. Zone III. Wide-spreading tree with slender often pendulous brs.; the lvs. turning clear yellow in fall.—**A. s. laciniàtum** (Carr.) Pax, var. Lvs. deeply cleft with dissected narrow lobes: brs. pendulous. S.H.2:f. 148e. H.G.35:71. M.G.18:628(h). Here belong "Skinner M." and Wier M." (*A. s.* f. *Wieri* Pax.)—**A. s. tripartìtum** (Schwer.) Pax. f. Lvs. divided nearly to the base into 3 broad lobulate lobes. S.H.2:f.148b(l).—**A. s. lutéscens** (Spaeth) Pax, f. Lvs. yellow, bronze-colored when unfolding. Gart.-Zeit. 2:513,t.f.5(c).—**A. s. péndulum** (Nichols.) Pax, f. Brs. pendulous.—**A. s. pyramidàle** (Spaeth) Pax, f. Brs. upright, forming a narrow-pyramidal head. F.E.67,no.26:19(h).

Sect. XIII. TRIFOLIATA PAX. Fls. andro-dioecious, hypogynous, in terminal few-fld. corymbs on leafy brts.; stamens 8; disk thick, extrastaminal: lvs. 3-foliolate; winter-buds with many imbricate scales.

51. **A. nikoénse** Maxim. NIKKO M. Tree to 15 m.; brts. with pilose pubescence persistent until the 2d year: lfts. ovate to elliptic-oblong, 5–12 cm. long, the middle one short-stalked, the lateral ones subsessile, acute, obtusely dentate or nearly entire, villous-pubescent beneath; petiole densely pilose, 2–4 cm. long: fls. yellow, in usually 3-fld. short-stalked nodding, densely pubescent cymes; stamens exserted: fr. with upright wings curved inward or spreading at a right angle, with the thick densely pubescent nutlet 3–5 cm. long. Fl.V; fr.IX. S.I.1:t.68(c). G.F.6:155. G.C.72:321. Gt.41:149. R.H.

1912:126,127. Gs.3:237,t(c). J.H.29:f.81(h). Japan, C. China. Intr. 1881. Zone V. Lvs. turning brilliant red or purple in fall.

Related species: **A. triflòrum** Komar. Tree to 8 m.; brts. soon glabrous: lfts. oblong-ovate to oblong-lanceolate, 4–8 cm. long, entire or with 1–3 coarse teeth, glaucous beneath and glabrous except pilose along midrib; petiole 3–6 cm. long, sparingly pilose; infl. 3-fld., pubescent: wings nearly straight, spreading at an obtuse angle, with the densely pubescent thick nutlet 3.5–4 cm. long. N.K. 1:t.11. Manch., Korea. Intr. 1923.

52. **A. gríseum** (Franch.) Pax. PAPERBARK M. Tree to 8 m., with cinnamon-brown bark separating in thin papery flakes; young brts. pubescent, becoming glabrous: lfts. elliptic to ovate-oblong, 3–6 cm. long, acute, the middle one short-stalked, coarsely toothed with large bluntish teeth, the lateral ones subsessile, oblique at base, lobulate on the outer margin: fls. in few-fld. short-peduncled pubescent cymes: fr. pendulous, the wings spreading at an acute or nearly right angle, with the thick tomentose nutlet about 3 cm. long. Fl.v; fr.ix. R.H.1912:127. G.C.72:251. Gn.86:543(h);88:816;89:20(h). (*A. nikoense* var. *g.* Franch.) W. China. Intr. 1901. Zone V. Remarkable for its flaky bark resembling that of the River Birch.

53. **A. mandshùricum** Maxim. MANCHURIAN M. Shrub or small tree to 10 m.; brts. glabrous: lfts. oblong to oblong-lanceolate, 5–10 cm. long, acuminate, the middle one slender-stalked, the lateral ones short-stalked, obtusely serrate, dark green above, glaucous beneath and pubescent on the midrib, otherwise glabrous; petiole glabrous, 6–10 cm. long, red: fls. greenish yellow, in 3–5-fld. cymes: fr. glabrous; wings spreading at a right or obtuse angle, with the thick reticulate nutlets 3–3.5 cm. long. Fl.v; fr.ix. N.K.1:t.10. S.H.2:f.139d,140r. Manch., Korea. Cult. 1904. Zone IV. The red petioles forming a pleasing contrast to the dark green lvs.

Sect. XIV. NEGUNDO (Boehmer) K. Koch. Fls. dioecious, in lateral racemes from leafless or occasionally leafy buds, or the staminate ones clustered, 4- or 5-merous, with petals or without; stamens 4–6; disk wanting: lvs. 3–7-foliolate: winter-buds with 2 outer scales. (*Negundo* Ludwig ex Boehmer.)

54. **A. Hénryi** Pax. Small tree to 10 m.; brts. slightly pubescent when young, soon glabrous: lfts. 3, stalked, elliptic, 6–10 cm. long, acuminate, cuneate, remotely dentate, pubescent, rarely nearly glabrous beneath; petiole 5–10 cm. long: fls. nearly sessile, in slender pendulous racemes, sometimes with small lvs. at base: fr. glabrous, in pendulous racemes with the peduncle 10–20 cm. long; wings upright or slightly spreading, with the thick nutlet 2–2.5 cm. long. Fl.iv; fr.ix. H.I.19:1896. I.S.1:t.34. G.C.77:193. J.H.29:f.93 (h),96(as *A. sutchuenense*). C. China. Intr. 1903. Zone V.

55. **A. cissifólium** (Sieb. & Zucc.) K. Koch. Small tree to 10 m.; young brts. pubescent: lfts. 3, stalked, ovate or obovate to elliptic, 5–8 cm. long, acuminate, coarsely and unequally serrate, sparingly ciliate, light green and glabrous or nearly so beneath; petiole 5–8 cm. long, glabrous: fls. small, on pedicels 3–6 mm. long, in slender pubescent racemes 5–10 cm. long: fr. glabrous, in pendulous racemes; wings spreading at an acute angle, with the thick nutlet 2.5 cm. long. Fl.iv; fr.ix. S.I.2:t.41(c). M.K.t.70(c). J.C.32,1: t.15. S.H.2:f:139f,140b-d. (*Negundo c.* Sieb. & Zucc.) Japan. Intr. 1875. Zone (V). Graceful round-headed tree; the lvs. turning red and yellow in fall.

56. **A. Negúndo** L. Box-ELDER. Tree to 20 m.; brts. glabrous: lvs. pinnate; lfts. 3–5, rarely 7 or 9, ovate to lance-oblong, 5–10 cm. long, acuminate, coarsely serrate or the terminal one 3-lobed, bright green, lighter green below and slightly pubescent or nearly glabrous; petiole 5–8 cm. long: fls. yellowish green, before the lvs.; the staminate ones corymbose, on slender

pendulous pubescent stalks 2–3.5 cm. long; the pistillate ones slender-pediceled, in pendulous racemes: fr. glabrous; wings diverging at an acute angle
and usually incurved, with the thick nutlet 2.5–3.5 cm. long. Fl.iii–iv; fr.ix.
S.O.1:t.12(c). M.S.1:t.46(c). F.D.16:1528a(c). S.S.2:t.96. G.G.2:t.175. (*Negundo fraxinifolium* Nutt., *N. aceroides* Moench, *Rulac N.* Hitchc.) The
typical form from N. Eng. and Ont. to Minn., Neb., Kans., Tex. and Fla.
Cult. 1688. Zone II. One of the hardiest Maples and drought resisting, much
planted in the Northwest for shelter-belts. Several of the varieties are
favorite ornamental trees; of rapid growth when young.—**A. N. variegàtum**
Jacques. Lvs. with broad white margin. F.S.17:t.1781(hc). M.D.1896:t.2,f.4
(c). Gn.68:402(h). (*A. N.* var. *argenteo-variegatum* Wesm.) One of the
most conspicuous of all variegated hardy trees.—**A. N. aùreo-variegàtum**
Wesm., var. Lvs. spotted golden yellow.—**A. N. aùreo-marginàtum** Schwer.,
f. Lvs. margined yellow. R.B.32:197,t,f.5(c).—**A. N. auràtum** Spaeth. Lvs.
yellow. R.B.32:197,t,f.3(c). (*A. N. odessanum* H. Rothe, *A. N. californicum
aureum* Hort.)—**A. N. pseudo-califórnicum** Schwer., var. Brts. green,
bloomy; of vigorous growth. (*A. californicum* Hort., not Dietr., *Negundo
californicum* Kirchn., not Torr. & Gr.)—**A. N. violàceum** (Kirchn.) Jaeg.,
var. Brts. purplish or violet with glaucous bloom: lfts. 3–11, usually 5–7, usually pubescent beneath; of vigorous growth. Chiefly in the northwestern part
of the range of the species. (*A. californicum* Hort.)—**A. N. intérius** (Brit.)
Sarg., var. Brts. with short pale pubescence, rarely nearly glabrous: lfts. 3,
slender-stalked, glabrous beneath or villous in the midrib. B.T.655. (*A. in-
terior* Brit.) Alb. and Sask. to Ariz. and N. Mex. Intr. 1914.—**A. N. califórnicum** (Torr. & Gr.) Wesm., subsp. Brts. and winter-buds hoary-tomentose:
lfts. 3, coarsely serrate or nearly entire, pubescent above, tomentose beneath
when young, later densely pubescent: fr. puberulous or glabrous, the nutlet
not constricted at base. N.S.2:t.72(c). S.S.2:t.97. (*A. c.* Dietr., *Negundo c.*
Torr. & Gr.) Calif. Cult. 1865. Zone III?—**A. N. texànum** Pax, var. Brts.
pale-tomentose: lvs. 3-foliolate, tomentose beneath when young, later nearly
glabrous: fr. puberulous, constricted into a short stipe. S. Ohio and w. N. C.,
w. to Kansas and Tex. Intr. 1922. Zone V.

Fam 56. **HIPPOCASTANACEAE** DC. HORSE-CHESTNUT FAMILY

Trees or shrubs: lvs. opposite, digitately 3–9-foliolate or pinnate, estipulate: fls. andro-polygamous, irregular, in terminal panicles; sepals 4–5, distinct or connate, imbricate; petals 4 or 5, unequal, clawed; stamens 5–9,
distinct; disk extrastaminal; ovary superior, 3-celled, with 2 ovules in each
cell; style and stigma 1: fr. usually 1-celled, dehiscent, 3-valved, usually
1-seeded; seeds very large, with a large hilum, exalbuminous. Three genera
with more than 25 species in the temp. regions of the n. hemisphere, in Am.
s. to n. S. Am.—Besides *Aesculus* the Chinese genus *Bretschneidera* may be
hardy in the southern part of our area, but is not yet in cult.

AÈSCULUS L. Horse-chestnut, Buckeye. Deciduous trees or shrubs:
winter-buds large, with several pairs of outer scales: lvs. long-petioled, digitately 5–9-foliolate, serrate: fls. in upright many-fld. panicles; calyx campanulate to tubular, 4–5-toothed; petals 4–5, with long claws. (Ancient Latin
name of an Oak or mast-bearing tree.) About 25 species in N. Am., S. E.
Eu. and E. Asia to India.—Ornamental trees chiefly grown for their showy
fls. and also for their handsome large foliage.

A. Winter-buds resinous; claws of petals not longer than calyx; stamens exserted.
  B. Lfts. sessile (short-stalked in No. 2); petals 5..Sect. I. HIPPOCASTANUM K. Koch.
    c. Lfts. obtusely double-serrate, green beneath: fr. subglobose.
      D. Fls. white, spotted red: fr. echinate...........................1. *A. Hippocastanum*
      DD. Fls. flesh-colored to scarlet: fr. with few small prickles................2. *A. carnea*
    cc. Lfts. nearly equally crenate-serrate, glaucescent beneath: fls. yellowish white: fr.
        broadly pear-shaped, warty...3. *A. turbinata*
  BB. Lfts. stalked: petals 4; calyx 2-lipped: fr. pear-shaped, smooth.
                                                          Sect. II. CALOTHYRSUS K. Koch.
    c. Corolla about 1 cm. long, white...4. *A. Wilsonii*
    cc. Corolla about 2.5 cm. long, white to pink: lvs. glabrous..............5. *A. californica*
AA. Winter-buds not resinous: claws mostly longer than the 5-toothed calyx.
  B. Fls. yellow to scarlet; stamens shorter to slightly longer than the 4 petals: lfts.
     petioled ....Sect. III. PAVIA K. Koch.
    c. Petals villous at the margin (or interspersed with glands in some hybrid forms);
       calyx campanulate ....Ser. I. OCTANDRAE Sarg.
      D. Petals without glands on the margin.
        E. Fr. prickly: fls. yellow; petals of nearly equal length, shorter than stamens.
                                                                          6. *A. glabra*
          EE. Fr. without prickles: fls. yellow or red; petals of unequal length, longer than
              stamens at least the upper ones.
            F. Pedicels and calyx glandular-villous: fls. usually yellow: large tree.
                                                                        7. *A. octandra*
              FF. Pedicels and calyx not glandular: fls. usually red and yellow: small tree or
                  shrub ....8. *A. neglecta*
      DD. Petals with hairs and glands on the margin..........................9. *A. hybrida*
    cc. Petals glandular on the margin; calyx tubular: fls. red or red and yellow: fr.
        without prickles ....Ser. 2. EUPAVIAE Sarg.
      D. Lvs. glabrous or only pubescent on the midrib beneath................10. *A. Pavia*
      DD. Lvs. tomentose or densely pubescent beneath.
        E. Lfts. usually oblong-obovate, tomentose beneath: seed light yellowish brown.
                                                                        11. *A. discolor*
          EE. Lfts. usually lanceolate or oblanceolate, hoary pubescent beneath: seed dark
              chestnut-brown ....12. *A. splendens*
  BB. Fls. white, small; stamens more than twice as long as the 4-5 petals.
                                                      Sect. IV. MACROTHYRSUS K. Koch.
                                                                        13. *A. parviflora*

1. **A. Hippocástanum** L. COMMON H. Tree to 25 m.; brts. usually glabrous: lfts. 5-7, cuneate-obovate, 10-25 cm. long, acuminate, obtusely double-
serrate, rusty floccose-tomentose near base beneath when young: fls. white,
tinged with red, about 2 cm. across, in panicles 20-30 cm. long: fr. echinate,
about 6 cm. across, with 1 or 2 seeds. Fl.v-vi; fr.viii-ix. F.D.21:2117(c).
H.W.3:36,37(h),t.47(c). E.H.2:t.63-65(h). F.E.13:t.13(h). Am. For. 19:145,
t.(h); 21:862(h). Balkan Pen. Intr. 1576. Zone III. One of the most showy
flowering trees and often planted as shade and street tree.—**A. H. Bau-
mánii** Schneid., f. Fl. double, white. I.H.2:50. H.B.7:311. A.G.32:271(h).—
A. H. Memmíngeri (K. Koch) Rehd., var. Lvs. sprinkled with white.—
A. H. lùteo-variegàta West., var. Lvs. variegated with yellow.—**A. H. albo-
variegata** West., var. Lvs. variegated with white.—**A. H. laciniàta** Jacques,
var. Lfts. narrow, deeply and irregularly incised. (*A. H. dissecta* Hort., *A. H.
heterophylla* Hort., *A. H. aspleniifolia* Hort.)—**A. H. pyramidàlis** Henry,
var. Of compact narrow-pyramidal habit.—**A. H. umbraculífera** Jaeg., var.
With a compact round head. M.G.1903;188(h).—**A. H. péndula** Puvilland.
With pendulous brs. E.H.2:t.64(h). R.H.1921:281(h).

2. × **A. cárnea** Hayne (*A. Hippocastanum* × *Pavia*). RED H. Tree to
15 or 25 m.; buds slightly viscid; brts. glabrous: lfts. usually 5, subsessile or
short-stalked, cuneate-obovate, 8-15 cm. long, dark green and somewhat
lustrous above, nearly glabrous beneath: fls. flesh-colored to deep red, in
panicles 12-20 cm. long; petals glandular and villous on the margin: fr.
subglobose, 3-4 cm. across, slightly prickly. Fl.v-vi; fr.ix. G.O.t.22(c).
L.D.6:t.357(c). B.R.1056(c). F.S.t.2229-30(c). M.A.t.64(h). F.E.23:607(h).
(*A. rubicunda* Loisel., *A. intermedia* André.) Orig. before 1818. Zone III.
Round-headed tree, often planted; the lvs. are of darker color and firmer
texture and resist drought better than those of the preceding species.—**A. c.**

péndula Henry, var. With pendulous brs.—**A. c. Briòtii** (Carr.) Nichols. With bright scarlet fls. R.H.1878:370,t(c). (*A. rubicunda Briotii* Carr.) Orig. 1858.—**A. c. plantierénsis** (André) Rehd., var. Lfts. usually 7, to 20 cm. long, bluntly serrate: fls. whitish, suffused with pink and fading to pink: fr. prickly. (*A. p.* André.) Orig. before 1894.

3. **A. turbinàta** Bl. JAPANESE H. Tree to 30 m.: lfts. 5–7, cuneate-obovate, 20–35 cm. long, acuminate, nearly equally crenate-serrate, glaucescent beneath and glabrous except axillary tufts of hairs or pubescent on the veins; petiole glabrous or pubescent: fls. about 1.5 cm. across, yellowish white, with a red spot, in a panicle 15–25 cm. long: fr. broadly pear-shaped, about 5 cm. across, warty; seed brown, about 3 cm. across, with a large hilum covering nearly ½ of the seed. Fl.vi; fr.ix. B.M.8713(c). M.K.t.74(c). G.C.III.5:717;31:187. E.H.2:t.66(h). Japan. Intr. before 1880. Zone V. Fls. less showy than those of *A. Hippocastanum*, but lvs. larger.—**A. t. pubéscens** Rehd., var. Lvs. more or less villous-pubescent beneath. Cult. 1911.

4. **A. Wilsónii** Rehd. Tree to 25 m.; brts. densely pubescent: lfts. 5–7, oblong-obovate or oblong-oblanceolate, 10–22 cm. long, acuminate, rounded or broad-cuneate, closely serrulate, densely grayish pubescent beneath when young, glabrescent at maturity: fls. 1.2–1.5 cm. long, white, the upper petals with a yellow spot, in cylindric panicles 15–30 cm. long: fr. ovoid or obovoid, apiculate, with thin walls; seed 3–3.5 cm. across, the hilum occupying about ⅓ or less of it. Fl.v–vi; fr.ix. C.C.234. S.H.2:f.171f,173b-c. U. S. Inv. 53:t. 3(h). (*A. chinensis* Diels, not Bge.) C. and W. China. Intr. 1908. Zone VI or VII. With long cylindric spikes of white fls.

Closely related species: **A. chinénsis** Bge. Brts. glabrous: lfts. shorter-stalked, cuneate, glabrous beneath, except sparingly hairy on the veins: fls. about 1 cm. long: fr. subglobose, somewhat depressed, with thick walls; seed 2–2.5 cm. across, the hilum occupying about ½ of it. I.S.t.86. G.C.52:346, 347(h). N. China. Cult. 1877, intr. again 1882 and 1912. Zone V.

5. **A. califórnica** Nutt. CALIFORNIAN B. Tree to 12 m.: lfts. 5, sometimes 7, elliptic-oblong to lance-oblong, 8–14 cm. long, acuminate, narrowed or rounded at base, sharply serrate, glabrous; petiolules 1–2.5 cm. long: fls. white to rose-colored, fragrant, about 2.5 cm. long, in dense rather narrow panicles 8–20 cm. long; stamens long-exserted; petals of equal length: fr. obovoid, 5–7 cm. long. Fl.iv–viii; fr.viii–ix. B.M.5077(c). S.S.2:t.71,72. G.C.31:186. Gn.49:490,492(h). G.M.55:577(h). (*Pavia c.* Hartw.) Calif. Intr. 1855. Zone VII?

Related species: **A. índica** Colebr. Tree to 20 m.: lfts. 5–9, short-stalked, obovate-lanceolate, 15–25 cm. long, finely serrate: fls. white, marked red and yellow, the lower part of the unequal petals tinged rose. B.M.5117(c). B.S. 1:171. G.C.33:139,t;36:206,t(h);72:19. R.H.1917:248. Himal. Intr. 1851. Zone VII?

6. **A. glábra** Willd. OHIO B. Small tree to 10 m.: lfts. 5, elliptic to obovate, 8–12 cm. long, acuminate, cuneate, finely serrate, pubescent beneath when young, nearly glabrous at maturity: fls. pale greenish yellow, 2–3 cm. long, in panicles 10–15 cm. long; petals of nearly equal length, their claws as long as calyx; stamens exserted: fr. obovoid, 3–5 cm. long, echinate. Fl.v; fr.ix. B.R.24:51(c). S.S.2:t.67,68. F.E.29:773(h). Am. For. 24:155. (*A. ohioensis* DC., *Pavia g.* Spach.) Pa. to Neb., Kansas and Ala. Cult. 1809. Zone III. Lvs. turning yellow in fall.—**A. g. pallida** (Willd.) Schelle, f. Lfts. with persistent pubescence beneath. (*A. p.* Wilid.) Cult. 1809.—**A. g. leucodérmis** Sarg., var. Tree to 20 m.; bark nearly white: lfts. glabrous and pale green or glaucescent beneath: fls. later. Mo., Ark. Intr. 1901.—**A. g. Sargéntii** Rehd., var. Shrub: lfts. 6–7, obovate-lanceolate, more acuminate,

finely pubescent beneath. (*A. g.* var. *Buckleyi* Sarg., 1905, not 1902; var. *arguta* Robins., in part.) Ohio to Okl. Intr. 1895.—**A. g. montícola** Sarg., var. Lfts. often 6 or 7, glabrous beneath or puberulous on midrib when young: fr. subglobose, 1.5–2 cm. across, usually 1-seeded. Okl. Intr. 1922.

A. glabra × *octandra* = **A. marylándica** Booth. Orig. unknown.—*A. g.* × *hybrida;* see under No. 9.—*A. g.* × *Pavia;* see under No. 9.—*A. g.* × *discolor;* see under No. 9.

Closely related species: **A. argùta** Buckl. Shrub to 2 m.; lfts. 7–9, lanceolate to obovate-lanceolate, 6–12 cm. long, deeply and doubly serrate with obtuse teeth, glabrous or slightly pubescent beneath when young, finally glabrous: fls. light yellowish green. S.T.2:t.198. (*A. glabra* var. *a.* Robins., *A. g.* var. *Buckleyi* Sarg., 1902, partly.) E. Tex. Intr. 1909. Zone V.

7. **A. octándra** Marsh. SWEET B. Tree to 20 or 30 m.: lfts. 5, oblong-obovate or narrow-elliptic, 10–15 cm. long, acuminate, cuneate, finely serrate, dark green above, yellow green and pubescent beneath when young, nearly glabrous at maturity: fls. yellow, 3 cm. long, in panicles 10–15 cm. long; petals very unequal, their claws longer than the calyx; stamens usually 7, shorter than petals: fr. subglobose, 5–6 cm. across, usually 2-seeded. Fl. v–vi; fr.ix. L.B.1280(c). S.S.2:t.69,70. M.A.t.65(h). G.W.7:145(h). (*A. flava* Ait., *A. lutea* Wangh., *Pavia lutea* Poir.) Pa. to Ga. and s. Ill. Intr. 1764. Zone III.—**A. o. virgínica** Sarg. Fls. red, pink or cream-colored. W. Va. Intr. ?—**A. o. vestìta** Sarg., var. Lfts. beneath, petioles and young brts. pubescent or tomentose. N. C. and W. Va. Cult. 1893. Zone V.

A. o. × *glabra;* see under No. 6.—*A. o.* × *Pavia;* see No. 9.

Related species: **A. glaucéscens** Sarg. Shrub to 10 m. Lfts. larger, glabrous and glaucescent beneath: fls. larger; fr. smaller. S.T.2:t.196. Ga. Intr. 1914. Zone V.

8. **A. neglécta** Lindl. Tree to 20 m.: lfts. 5, oblong-obovate, 10–16 cm. long, long-acuminate, simply or sometimes irregularly doubly serrulate, light yellowish green beneath and glabrous except axillary tufts of hairs, rarely without; petiolules 3–8 mm. long, puberulous above; petiole puberulous above, at least near apex: panicles 10–15 cm. long; calyx narrow-campanulate, puberulous: petals very unequal, pale yellow, marked with red veins toward the base; stamens villous below the middle: fr. globose, 2.5–3 cm. across, usually 1-seeded. Fl.v–vi; fr.ix. B.R.1009(c). H.B.1:209. N. C. Cult. 1826. Zone V. Large shrub or tree with large panicles of showy fls., particularly the vars.—**A. n. georgiàna** (Sarg.) Sarg., var. Usually shrubby: panicle broader and denser; calyx often nearly tubular; petals yellow and red, sometimes entirely bright yellow or red. S.T.2:t.197. S.M.706. (*A. g.* Sarg.) N. C. to Fla. and Ala. Intr. 1905.—**A. n. lanceolàta** (Sarg.) Sarg., var. Lfts. lanceolate or nearly oblanceolate: fls. bright red. S.M.707. Ga. Intr. 1917.—**A. n. pubéscens** (Sarg.) Sarg., var. Lfts. pubescent beneath: fls. yellow and red. N. C. to Ga. and Ala. Intr. 1905.—**A. n. tomentòsa** Sarg., var. Lfts. tomentose or densely villous beneath: fls. bright red. (*A. Michauxii* Hort., *A. discolor* Hort., not Pursh.) S. C. Cult. 1880.

A. n. × *Pavia;* see under No. 9.—*A. n.* × *discolor;* see under No. 9.

A related species or hybrid of unknown origin is **A. woerlitzénsis** Koehne. Tree: lfts. oblong-obovate, 10–16 cm. long, yellowish green beneath, sparingly hairy along the midrib and bearded in the axils of the veins, with 17–20 pairs of veins: fls. red, in panicles 10–12 cm. long: calyx tubular; the lateral petals with an oblong-obovate blade cuneate at base. Cult. 1910.—**A. w. Ellwángeri** Rehd., var. Lfts. 12–18 cm. long, slightly pubescent beneath while young, with 20–27 pairs of veins: fls. darker red; calyx narrower, not widened above the middle. (*A. Pavia* var. *Whitleyi* Ellw. & Barry, not Hort. Angl., *A. Pavia atrosanguinea* Hort.) Cult. 1901.

9. × **A. hýbrida** DC. (*A. octandra* × *Pavia.*) HYBRID B. Tree: lfts. 5, oblong-obovate or oblong-elliptic, 10–15 cm. long, acuminate, minutely

crenate-serrate, pubescent beneath along the midrib and veins: fls. yellow
and reddish in panicles 10–16 cm. long; pedicels and calyx stipitate-glandular;
stamens shorter than petals, villous toward the base: fr. subglobose. Fl.
v–vi; fr.ix. W.D.2:164(c, as *A. Pavia*). (*A. versicolor* Wender., *A. Lyoni*
Hort., *A. discolor* Hort., not Pursh, *A. flava* var. *purpurascens* Gray, *Pavia h.*
DC.) Orig. before 1815. Zone V.—Several forms of this hybrid are in cult.
varying in color of the fls. from yellow slightly tinged pink to nearly red.

Other hybrids between species of the Octandrae and Eupaviae with the
petals villous and glandular on the margin are the following of which the first
three have the fr. slightly tuberculate and the lvs. in the first and 2d hybrid
glabrous and in the 3d pubescent beneath, while the 4th has a smooth fr. and glabrous lvs. and the 5th a smooth fr. and the lvs. pubescent beneath.—**A. arnoldiàna** Sarg. (*A. glabra* × *hybrida*.) Lfts. elliptic, finely, often doubly serrate,
pubescent only along the midrib beneath; calyx campanulate, yellow; petals
yellow, the upper marked with red; stamens as long or slightly longer than
petals: fr. with scattered short prickles or tubercles. Orig. about 1900.—**A.
Búshii** Schneid. (*A. glabra* × *discolor*). Tree: brts. and petioles puberulous:
lfts. finely and bluntly serrate, pubescent beneath; calyx red; petals yellow and
pink; stamens longer than petals: fr. slightly tuberculate. Ark., Miss. Intr.
1901.—**A. mississippiénsis** Sarg. (*A. glabra* × *Pavia*). Lfts. elliptic to oblong-
obovate, finely and often doubly serrate, glabrous except axillary tufts of hairs
beneath: fls. dark red and yellow; calyx narrow-campanulate; stamens usually
longer than petals: fr. slightly tuberculate. Miss. Intr. 1913.—**A. Dupóntii**
Sarg. (*A. neglecta* × *Pavia*). Lfts. oblong-obovate to elliptic, acutely serrate,
light green beneath and glabrous except axillary tufts of hairs, with 18–25 pairs
of veins: calyx narrow-campanulate, red; petals yellow or slightly tinged with
red; stamens shorter than petals. Orig. after 1820.—**A. D. Héssei** Sarg., var.
(*A. n. georgiana* × *Pavia*). Lfts. elliptic or elliptic-obovate; panicles compact;
petals yellow, tinged with red. Cult. 1909.—**A. mutàbilis** (Spach) Schelle (*A.
discolor mollis* × *neglecta georgiana*). Lfts. elliptic-oblong, pale and villous
beneath: panicles 12–15 cm. long; calyx narrow-campanulate to tubular, red;
petals red and yellow. (*Pavia m.* Spach.) Cult. 1834.—**A. m. Harbisònii** (Sarg.)
Rehd., var. Lfts. sparingly villous beneath while young and glaucescent: fls.
bright red, in panicles 15–20 cm. long; calyx tubular. (*A. H.* Sarg.) Intr. 1905.
—**A. m. indùta** Sarg., var. (*A. discolor mollis* × *neglecta*). Lvs. densely villous
and glaucescent beneath. (*A. rosea nana* Hesse.) Cult. 1904.—**A. m. pendùli-
flòra** Sarg., var. Lfts. oblong-lanceolate, pale green and soft-pubescent beneath:
panicles loose, slightly pendulous, 14–16 cm. long; calyx tubular, reddish; petals
yellow. (*A. humilis* × *lutea* Spaeth.) Cult. 1902.

10. **A. Pàvia** L. Red B. Shrub or tree to 6, rarely to 12 m.: lfts. 5, short-
stalked, oblong-obovate or narrow-elliptic, 8–14 cm. long, acuminate, irregularly and often doubly serrate, glabrous or slightly pubescent beneath: fls.
bright red, in loose panicles 10–16 cm. long; calyx tubular, dark red; petals
very dissimilar, connivent; stamens usually 8, nearly as long as petals; fr.
subglobose or obovoid. Fl.vi; fr. ix. L.B.1257(c). S.T.2:t.199. G.C.100:2(h).
(*Pavia rubra* Poir., *P. Michauxii* Spach.) Va. to Fla. and La. Intr. 1711. Zone
V. With bright red but comparatively small fls.—**A. P. atrosanguínea** Kirchn.
Fls. dark red.—**A. P. húmilis** (Lindl.) Mouillef., var. Low, sometimes prostrate shrub; lfts. slightly pubescent beneath on veins and veinlets: fls. red,
in small panicles. B.R.1018(c). (*A. h.* Lindl., *A. Pavia* var. *nana* Dipp., *Pavia
rubra* var. *h.* Loud.) Cult. 1826.

A. P. × *Hippocastanum;* see No. 2.—*A. P.* × *octandra;* see No. 9.—*A. P.* ×
glabra; see under No. 9.—*A. P.* × *neglecta;* see under No. 9.

11. **A. díscolor** Pursh. Shrub or small tree to 10 m.; lfts. 5, short-stalked,
elliptic to oblong-obovate, 8–18 cm. long, acuminate, finely crenate-serrate,
dark green and lustrous above, whitish tomentose or tomentulose beneath;
fls. yellow and red, about 3 cm. long, in narrow pubescent panicles 15–20
cm. long; calyx tubular, red, or yellow tinged with red; petals yellow flushed
red, very unequal, connivent, shorter than stamens: fr. usually obovoid, 3.5–6

cm. long; seeds usually 2, light yellow-brown. Fl.v–vi; fr.ix. B.R.310(c). S.S.13:622. (*A. Pavia* var. *d.* Torr. & Gr., *A. octandra* var. *hybrida* Sarg.) Ga. to Mo. and Tex. Intr. about 1812. Zone V. With large panicles of brightly colored fls.—**A. d. móllis** (Raf.) Sarg., var. Fls. bright red. (*A. m.* Raf., *A. austrina* Small.) N. C. to Fla. and Tex. Intr. 1905.—**A. d. Koèhnei** Rehd., var. Low shrub; fls. red and yellow. (*A. humilis* Koehne, not Lindl., *A. Pavia* var. *humilis* Voss, partly.) Cult. 1893.—**A. d. flavéscens** Sarg., var. Fls. yellow. Tex. Intr. ?

A. d. × *neglecta;* see under No. 9.

12. **A. spléndens** Sarg. Shrub to 4 m.: lfts. 5, lanceolate to oblanceolate, 8–14 cm. long, acuminate, finely and often doubly crenate-serrulate, densely hoary-pubescent beneath, rufous-pubescent in autumn: fls. 3.5–4 cm. long, in panicles 10–20 cm. long; calyx tubular, 7–8 mm. in diam., bright red; petals scarlet, very unequal; stamens longer or shorter than petals: fr. subglobose to short-obovoid; seeds dark chestnut-brown. Fl.v; fr.ix. S.T.2:t. 200. Ala. to Miss. and La. Intr. 1911. Zone VI? Apparently the handsomest of all Buckeyes.

13. **A. parviflòra** Walt. Spreading shrub to 4 m.: lfts. 5–7, nearly sessile, elliptic to oblong-obovate, 8–20 cm. long, acuminate, crenate-serrulate, grayish pubescent beneath: fls. white, about 1 cm. long; stamens usually 7, pinkish white, 3–4 cm. long, in long cylindric panicles 20–30 cm. long: fr. obovoid, 2.5–4 cm. long; seed chestnut-brown. Fl.vii–viii; fr.x. B.M.2118(c). Add.2:t.63(c). G.C.31:189;64:33(h). Gn.63:299;79:436(h). Gn.M.9:76(h). B.S.1:173(h). (*A. macrostachya* Michx., *Pavia alba* Poir.) S. C. to Ala. and Fla. Intr. 1785. Zone IV. Valued for its late showy fls.; excellent as a lawn shrub.—**A. p. seròtina** Rehd., var. Lfts. sparsely pubescent or glabrescent and glaucescent beneath: fls. 2 or 3 weeks later. Ala. Intr. 1919.

Fam. 57. **SAPINDACEAE** Juss. SOAPBERRY FAMILY

Trees or shrubs, rarely herbs: lvs. alternate or sometimes opposite, usually abruptly pinnate or odd-pinnate, sometimes bipinnate or 3-foliolate, estipulate: fls. unisexual or apparently polygamous, regular or irregular, small, rarely conspicuous, usually in panicles; sepals 4–5, imbricate, rarely valvate; petals 4–5, sometimes wanting, usually with scales or hairs inside near base; disk well developed, extrastaminal; stamens usually 8 or 10 in 2 whorls, rarely 7 or 6, more or less united at base; ovary superior, mostly 3-celled and deeply 3-lobed; cells usually 1-ovuled; style 1: fr. a caps., berry, drupe, nut or winged fr.; seeds exalbuminous. About 120 genera with more than 1000 species mostly in trop. regions, only few species extending into the temp. zone.

A. Lfts. entire: fls. small, regular, in large panicles: fr. berry-like...............1. *Sapindus*
AA. Lfts. serrate: fls. irregular, conspicuous: fr. capsular.
  B. Lvs. twice pinnate or lfts. incised and lobed: fls. yellow, in large panicles after the lvs.
                                          2. *Koelreuteria*
  BB. Lvs. simply pinnate: lfts. serrate: fls. before the lvs.
    c. Lfts. 9–17: fls. white, in dense racemes..............................3. *Xanthoceras*
    cc. Lfts. 5–7, large: fls. rose-colored, in cymes............................4. *Ungnadia*

1. **SAPÍNDUS** L. SOAPBERRY. Deciduous or evergreen trees or shrubs; winter-buds with few outer pubescent scales: lvs. alternate, abruptly pinnate (simple in one species): lfts. entire, rarely serrate: fls. small, regular, polygamo-dioecious, in ample terminal or axillary panicles; sepals and petals 4–5, the latter with 1 or 2 scales above the claw, or without; disk annular; stamens 8–10; usually only 1 carpel developing into a drupe; seed usually

globose. (Name contracted from *Sapo indicus,* Indian Soap.) About 15 species in the Tropics, few extending into temp. regions.

S. Drummóndii Hook. & Arn. WILD CHINA-TREE. Deciduous tree to 15 m., with scaly red-brown bark; young brts. pubescent: lfts. 8–18, short-stalked, obliquely lanceolate, 4–7 cm. long, acuminate, glabrous above, pubescent beneath; rachis marginless: fls. yellowish white, about 5 mm. across, in loose pubescent panicles 15–25 cm. long; sepals acute, ciliate, shorter than the obovate petals pubescent inside; filaments villous: fr. subglobose, 1–1.5 cm. across, yellow with semitranslucent flesh, finally black. Fl.v–vi; fr.ix–x. S.S.2:t.76,77. B.B.2:500. S. Mo., Kans., N. Mex. and Ariz. to La., Tex. and n. Mex. Cult. 1900. Zone (V). Interesting as the hardiest species of this trop. genus.

Related species: **S. Mukoróssi** Gaertn. Evergreen tree: lfts. 8–13, oblong-ovate to oblong-lanceolate, 8–15 cm. long, glabrous and reticulate beneath; rachis with narrow margin: fr. to 2.5 cm. across, yellow or orange-brown, slightly keeled. S.I.1:t.71(c). C.C.236. E. Asia, Himal. Cult. 1877. Zone VII? —**S. M. carinàtus** Radlk., var. Fr. strongly keeled, fleshier. R.H.1895:304,305. Am. For. 23:686. (*S. utilis* Trabut.)

2. **KOELREUTÈRIA** Laxm. Deciduous trees; winter-buds small, with 2 outer scales: lvs. alternate, odd-pinnate or bipinnate: lfts. serrate: fls. yellow, irregular, in large terminal panicles; calyx deeply and unequally 5-lobed; petals 4, lanceolate, turned upward, clawed, blade cordate at base and with 2 upturned appendages; disk crenate on the upper margin; stamens 8, sometimes less, with long filaments; style 3-fid at apex, shorter than stamens: fr. a bladdery, loculicidal caps. with papery walls and 3 roundish black seeds. (After Joseph G. Koelreuter, professor of natural history at Karlsruhe; 1733–1806.) Four species in E. Asia.

K. paniculàta Laxm. CHINA-TREE. Tree to 10 m.: lvs. pinnate or sometimes partly bipinnate, to 35 cm. long: lfts. 7–15, ovate to ovate-oblong, 3–8 cm. long, coarsely and irregularly crenate-serrate, at base often incisely lobed, glabrous above, pubescent on the veins beneath or nearly glabrous: fls. yellow, about 1 cm. wide, in broad loose panicles to 35 cm. long: fr. oblong-ovoid, gradually narrowed toward the mucronate apex, 4–5 cm. long. Fl.vii–viii; fr.ix–x. S.O.4:t.181(c). B.R.330(c). Add.5:t.191(c). G.C.III.2:561. Gng. 2:353(h). J.L.27:875(h). (*K. japonica* Sieb.—PRIDE OF INDIA, GOLDENRAIN-TREE, VARNISH-TREE.) China, Korea, Japan. Intr. 1763. Zone V. Chiefly valued for its conspicuous panicles of yellow fls. appearing in summer.—**K. p. fastigiàta** Bean, var. A form of narrow columnar habit. Orig. 1888.—**K. p. apiculàta** (Rehd. & Wils.) Rehd., var. Lvs. bipinnate, rarely pinnate with partly pinnatifid lfts., pubescent beneath: sepals orbicular or broad-oval, erose: fr. abruptly mucronate at the rounded apex. G.C.78:307. (*K. a.* Rehd. & Wils.) C. China. Intr. 1900.

Related species: **K. bipinnàta** Franch. Lvs. bipinnate, with ovate to ovate-oblong, equally serrate lfts. 4–10 cm. long. R.H.1888:393. Gn.34:305. D.L.2:392. W. China. Intr. about 1900. Zone VII?

3. **XANTHÓCERAS** Bge. Deciduous shrub or tree; winter-buds ovoid, with several outer scales: lvs. alternate, odd-pinnate; lfts. sessile, narrow, usually opposite, serrate: fls. polygamous, regular, in racemes, the upper fls. of the terminal raceme fertile, the lower ones and those of the lateral racemes sterile, or rarely a few fertile at the apex of the latter; sepals 5, oblong, imbricate; petals obovate, clawed, large; disk thin, 5-lobed, each lobe on its back with an upright horn-like appendage half as long as stamens; stamens 8, half as long as petals; ovary with short thick style: fr. a loculicidally 3-valved

caps. with thick walls; each cell with several globose, dark brown seeds. (Greek *xanthos,* yellow, and *keras,* horn; alluding to the yellow horn-like processes of the disk.) One species in China.

X. sorbifòlium Bge. Shrub or tree to 8 m., with rather stout upright brs., glabrous: lvs. 14–30 cm. long; lfts. 9–17, narrow-elliptic to lanceolate, 3–5 cm. long, sharply serrate, dark green above, lighter beneath: fls. slender-stalked, about 2 cm. across, in racemes 15–25 cm. long; petals thin, white, with a blotch at base changing from yellow to red: fr. green, 4–6 cm. across; seed about 1 cm. thick. Fl.iv–v; fr.viii–ix. B.M.6923(c). Gn.8:524,t(c);71:298(h). G.C.76:77,78(h). G.F.6:285(h). S.L.389(h). Gn.M.32:43(h). N. China. Intr. 1866. Zone V. With showy white fls. in spring and handsome lustrous lvs. remaining green until late in fall.

4. **UNGNÀDIA** Endl. Slender shrub or small tree; winter-buds with many imbricate scales: lvs. alternate, odd-pinnate: lfts. serrate, the lateral ones sessile, the terminal stalked: fls. polygamous, irregular, in lateral fascicles or corymbs, before the lvs.; calyx campanulate, 5-lobed; petals 4 or 5, subequal, clawed, the claws villous and at the apex with a crest of fleshy hairs; disk unilateral, tongue-shaped; stamens 7–10, unequal, exserted; ovary stipitate: fr. a loculicidally 3–4-valved leathery caps.; cells usually 1-seeded. (After Baron Ungnad who introduced the Horse-chestnut to C. Eu.) One species.

U. speciòsa Endl. MEXICAN BUCKEYE. Shrub or tree to 10 m.; brts. pubescent: lfts. 5–9, oblong-ovate to ovate-lanceolate, 8–12 cm. long, acuminate, crenulate-serrate, lustrous dark green above, light green beneath, tomentose when unfolding becoming glabrescent: fls. rose-colored, about 2.5 cm. across, in pubescent fascicles on stalks 3–5 cm. long: fr. broad-pyriform, about 5 cm. across; seeds about 1.5 cm. thick. Fl.iv–v; fr.x. F.S.10:t.1059(c). H.F.1865: 231,t(c). Gr.G.2:t.178,179. S.S.2:t.73. Tex. to n. Mex. Intr. 1848. Zone VII.

Fam. 58. **SABIACEAE** Bl. SABIA FAMILY

Trees or shrubs, sometimes climbing: lvs. alternate, odd-pinnate or simple, estipulate: fls. perfect or polygamous, in axillary or terminal cymes or panicles; sepals 5, rarely 3 or 4, free or connate at base, imbricate, unequal; petals 5, rarely 4, imbricate, the inner 2 often much smaller; stamens 5, opposite the petals, all fertile or the 3 outer sterile and changed to staminodes; ovary superior, usually with disk at base, usually 2-, rarely 3-celled, each cell with 2 or 1 ovule: fr. 1-celled, rarely 2-celled, indehiscent; seed solitary, exalbuminous; embryo with folded cotyledons and large curved hypocotyl.—Four genera with about 70 species in trop. Asia and Am.; few species extending into temp. regions of E. Asia.

A. All stamens fertile; fls. in axillary cymes: lvs. simple: climbing shrubs............1. *Sabia*
AA. Only 2 stamens fertile: fls. in terminal panicles: lvs. simple or pinnate: upright shrubs or trees ....2. *Meliosma*

1. **SÀBIA** Colebr. Deciduous or evergreen climbing shrubs; winter-buds small, with pointed persistent scales: lvs. simple, entire: fls. perfect, rarely polygamous, usually whitish or greenish, in axillary corymbs or solitary; calyx deeply 5- or 4-parted, with imbricate segments; petals 5, rarely 4, nearly opposite the sepals, much longer than sepals; stamens 5 or 4, with subulate filaments and small roundish anthers; ovary with a 5-pointed disk at base; style subulate: fr. 1- or 2-seeded and deeply 2-lobed, with the style at base; exocarp slightly fleshy, mesocarp woody and reticulate. (From its Bengal name, *Sabja-lat.*) About 20 species in E. and S. Asia and Mal.

S. Schumanniàna Diels. Scandent shrub to 3 m.; brts. slender, glabrous, green or yellowish: lvs. oblong-lanceolate or oblong, rarely elliptic, 2–10 cm. long, acuminate, broad-cuneate or nearly rounded at base, scarious and usually crenate-erose at margin, bright green above, lighter green beneath, with 5–8 pairs of ascending veins; petiole 4–10 mm. long: fls. campanulate, greenish, 6 mm. long, in 1–3-fld. cymes on slender peduncles 2.5–4 cm. long; pedicels 3–8 mm. long; petals elliptic-obovate; stamens about as long as petals: fr. reniform, 6–7 mm. across, blue, strongly reticulate. Fl.v; fr.ix. C. and W. China. Intr. 1908. Zone (V)?

Related species: **S. latifòlia** Rehd. & Wils. Brts. pubescent, soon glabrous: lvs. elliptic to elliptic-oblong, 5–12 cm. long, short-acuminate, pubescent at first, at length only on the veins beneath: fls. in usually 3-fld. cymes on peduncles 1–2.5 cm. long, greenish yellow passing into reddish brown. B.M.8859(c). W. China. Intr. 1908. Zone VII?

2. MELIÓSMA Bl. Deciduous or evergreen trees or shrubs; winter-buds naked: lvs. simple and with numerous straight veins or odd-pinnate with opposite lfts., serrate or entire: fls. perfect, rarely polygamous, in terminal and axillary panicles; sepals 5, rarely 4, subequal, imbricate, petals 5, very unequal, the outer 3 rounded, imbricate, the inner 2 much smaller, often bifid or scale-like and often adnate to the fertile stamens; stamens 5, the outer sterile and reduced to cup-shaped staminodes; the inner ones fertile, their anthers surrounded at base by the cup-shaped apex of the short filaments: ovary 2-, rarely 3-celled, at base surrounded by a disk; style subulate, short: fr. a subglobose to oblong, small, usually 1-seeded drupe, black or red. (Name from Greek, *meli,* honey, and *osma,* odor; referring to the fragrant fls.) About 50 species, mostly in trop. E. and S. Asia, also in trop. Amer.

A. Lvs. simple, toothed ....1. *M. cuneifolia*
AA. Lvs. odd-pinnate ....2. *M. Veitchiorum*

1. M. cuneifòlia Franch. Shrub or small tree to 6 m.; young brts. slightly pubescent: lvs. obovate, 8–16 cm. long, acute or abruptly acuminate, narrow-cuneate and decurrent, sinuately toothed, glabrous above, light green and pubescent on the veins beneath and with axillary tufts of hairs, with 20–25 pairs of straight veins; petiole 8–15 mm. long: fls. yellowish white, 6 mm. across, in upright loose panicles with spreading brs., about 15–25 cm. long and nearly as wide; bracts minute, caducous: fr. black, about 6 mm. across. Fl.vii; fr.ix. B.M.8357(c). B.S.2:78. G.C.59:279(h). Gs.8:154(h). W. China. Intr. 1901. Zone VII? With large panicles of fragrant whitish fls.

Related species: **M. myriántha** Sieb. & Zucc. Lvs. elliptic-obovate to oblong-obovate, 10–20 cm. long, short-acuminate, broad-cuneate or sometimes rounded at base, with 24–30 pairs of veins and without axillary tufts of hairs: fls. greenish yellow, smaller, in panicles with ascending brs., 15–20 cm. long; bracts persistent: fr. red. S.I.2:t.46(c). G.C.31:30. Japan. Intr. 1879. Zone VII? —M. ténuis Maxim. Lvs. 5–10 cm. long, glabrous beneath except axillary tufts of hairs and sometimes pubescent on the veins, with 10–15 pairs of veins: infl. without the slender stalk 8–15 cm. long; bracts caducous: fr. black. Japan. Intr. 1915.—M. pendens Rehd. & Wils. Shrub to 5 m.: lvs. elliptic-obovate, 6–15 cm. long, sparingly hairy above, pilose on midrib and veins beneath, without axillary tufts, with 12–20 pairs of veins: panicles pendulous, 12–20 cm. long with the brts. partly reflexed; bracts caducous; fls. fragrant. C. China. Intr. 1907. Zone VII?—M. dilleniifòlia (Wight & Arn.) Walp. Tree to 6 m.; brts. pubescent: lvs. obovate to oblanceolate, 12–30 cm. long, aristate-serrulate, slightly rough above, pubescent beneath: panicle 20–30 cm. long; bracts deciduous. Himal. Cult. 1924. Zone VII?

2. M. Veitchiòrum Hemsl. Tree to 15 m., with stout upright brs.; young brts. hairy, soon glabrous, like the infl. with conspicuous lenticels: lvs. 40–80 cm. long; lfts. 9–11, ovate to ovate-oblong or oblong, 8–16 cm. long, obtuse or short-acuminate, entire, rarely remotely crenate-serrate, glabrous except the pubescent midrib beneath: fls. yellow, 5 mm. across, in drooping panicles 20–40 cm. long: fr. black, subglobose, 6–8 mm. across. Fl.v; fr.ix. K.B.1910: 175(h). B.S.3:230,t(h). C. China. Intr. 1901. Zone VI? With large drooping panicles of fragrant yellowish fls.

Related species: **M. Beaniàna** Rehd. & Wils. Young brts. brownish tomentose: lvs. 15–30 cm. long; lfts. 5–13, ovate to elliptic-lanceolate, 6–15 cm. long, acuminate, usually cuneate, glabrous beneath except axillary tufts of hairs: fls. creamy white, in very numerous fulvous-pubescent lateral panicles before the lvs., 10–16 cm. long. C. China. Intr. 1908. Zone VI.—**M. Oldhami** Miq. Tree to 20 m.: lfts. 7–13, elliptic- or ovate-oblong to lance-oblong, 4–10 cm. long, acuminate, usually cuneate, remotely serrate or serrulate, glabrous or nearly so beneath: infl. terminal, to 20 cm. long and about as broad, glabrous: fr. 5–6 mm. across. G.C.86:345(h). B.S.3:231,t(h). (*M. sinensis* Nakai.) China, Korea. Intr. 1900. Zone VII?

Fam. 59. **RHAMNACEAE** Lindl. BUCKTHORN FAMILY

Trees or shrubs, often spiny, sometimes climbing, rarely herbs: lvs. alternate, rarely opposite, simple, usually stipulate: fls. regular, bisexual or unisexual, small, usually greenish or whitish, in cymes, fascicles or panicles; sepals 5, rarely 4, valvate; petals 5 or 4, sometimes wanting; stamens 5 or 4, opposite the petals; receptacle cup-shaped, lined by the usually well-developed intrastaminal disk; ovary 2–3-celled, rarely 1- or 4-celled, superior or inferior; cells 1-, rarely 2-ovuled; styles 2–4, more or less connate: fr. drupaceous, winged or capsular; seeds usually with scanty albumen, sometimes without; embryo with usually broad, flat cotyledons and small radicle.— About 45 genera and more than 550 species.

A. Stipules changed to spines: lvs. 3-nerved at base.
  B. Fr. dry, winged...1. *Paliurus*
  BB. Fr. fleshy, drupaceous..2. *Zizyphus*
AA. Stipules not spiny.
  B. Lvs. present, usually fairly large: brs. unarmed or with spinescent brts.
    C. Fr. with a single, 1-2-celled stone, drupaceous; brs. not spiny.
      D. Brs. twining: lvs. entire: fls. in terminal panicels or spikes..........3. *Berchemia*
      DD. Brs. not twining: lvs. serrulate: fls. in peduncled terminal and lateral cymes.
                                                4. *Rhamnella*
    CC. Fr. with several, usually 3, stones.
      D. Fls. sessile or subsessile, in clusters forming spikes or panicles: lvs. opposite or nearly opposite: brs. often spiny.....................................5. *Sageretia*
      DD. Fls. pedicelled, usually in axillary clusters or cymes.
        E. Fr. indehiscent, fleshy or leathery.
          F. Infl. not becoming fleshy: lvs. penninerved: fls. greenish.........6. *Rhamnus*
          FF. Infl. a large peduncled cyme, its brs. becoming fleshy: lvs. 3-nerved at base, to 16 cm. long...7. *Hovenia*
        EE. Fr. separating at maturity into 3 dehiscent nutlets: lvs. 3-nerved: fls. white, pink or blue..8. *Ceanothus*
  BB. Lvs. small or wanting: brs. with decussate stout spines: fls. campanulate or tubular. in fascicles or solitary.
    C. Lvs. usually persistent: stipules connected by 2 distinct lines.............9. *Discaria*
    CC. Lvs. usually deciduous; stipules not connected...........................10. *Colletia*

1. **PALIÙRUS** Mill. Deciduous trees or shrubs, sometimes decumbent; stipules usually spiny; winter-buds small, with 2 or 3 outer scales: lvs. alternate, 2-ranked, 3-nerved at base, entire or serrate: fls. perfect, small, 5-merous, in axillary or sometimes terminal cymes; ovary 2–3-celled, united with the receptacle: fr. woody, 2–3-celled, with leathery exocarp, depressed-subglobose and above the middle surrounded by a broad horizontal wing; cells 1-seeded. (Ancient Greek name.) Six species from S. Eu. to E. Asia.

P. spìna-Chrísti Mill. CHRIST-THORN. Spreading spiny shrub or small tree to 6 m.; young brts. pubescent; one of the stipular spines straight, the other hooked or recurved: lvs. ovate, 2–3.5 cm. long, obtuse, rounded and usually oblique at base, minutely serrulate or entire, dark green above, glabrous or slightly pubescent on the veins beneath; petioles 4–12 mm. long: fls. greenish yellow in short-peduncled umbel-like cymes; fr. brownish yellow, 2–2.5 cm. across, glabrous. Fl.vi–viii; fr.x–xii. B.M.1893(c),2535(c). G.C. 50:377. E.N.III.5:402. G.W.4:318. (*P. australis* Gaertn., *P. aculeatus* Lam.) S. Eu. to Himal. and N. China. Cult. 1597. Zone VII. Sometimes grown for its legendary interest, as it is believed to be the tree from which the Crown of Thorns was made; the curious fr. has the aspect of a low-crowned, wide-brimmed hat; the dark green lvs. and the numerous yellow fls. are attractive.

    Related species: **P. Hemsleyànus** Rehd. Tree to 15 m., sometimes unarmed: lvs. 4–10 cm. long, glabrous: fr. 2.5–3.5 cm. broad. (*P. orientalis* Hemsl., in part.) C. China. Intr. 1907. Zone VII?

    2. **ZÌZYPHUS** Mill. Deciduous or evergreen shrubs or trees; winter-buds small, with 2 or few outer scales: lvs. alternate, short-petioled, 3–5-nerved from the base, serrate or entire; stipules usually spiny: fls. usually yellow, small, 5-merous, perfect, in axillary cymes; ovary 2–4-, usually 2-celled; style usually 2-parted; fr. a subglobose to oblong drupe. (*Zizyphon*, ancient Greek name of *Z. Jujuba.*) About 40 species in trop. and subtrop. regions of both hemispheres.

    Z. Jujùba Mill. Common Jujube. Shrub or small tree to 10 m.; glabrous; one spine slender, to 3 cm. long, the other decurved; brts. often fascicled and resembling pinnate lvs.: lvs. oblong-ovate to ovate-lanceolate, rarely ovate, 2–6 cm. long, acutish or obtuse, oblique and 3-nerved at base, crenate-serrulate, glabrous, firm; petiole 1–5 mm. long: fls. yellow, 2–3, axillary, short-stalked: fr. dark red or finally almost black, ovoid to oblong, 1.5–2.5 cm. long, short-stalked. Fl.iv–v; fr.ix–x. N.D.3:t.16(c). E.N.III.5:403g–h. F.E. 19:395,t.96(h). U.S. Im.47:t(h). N.K.9:t.2. (*Z. vulgaris* Lam., *Z. sativa* Gaertn.) S. E. Eu. to S. and E. Asia; nat. in Ala. Intr. about 1640. Zone (V), VII.—The frs. are edible and the tree is cult. in the Mediterr. reg.—**Z. J. inérmis** (Bge.) Rehd., var. Brs. unarmed. N.K.9:t.3. (*Z. vulgaris* var. *i.* Bge.)

    The related **Z. mauritiàna** Lam. (*Z. jujuba* Lam., not Mill.) has the brts. and the under side of the lvs. tomentose and is probably not hardy within our area.

    3. **BERCHÈMIA** Neck. Deciduous twining shrubs; winter-buds small, with 2 or 3 outer scales: lvs. alternate, entire or nearly so, penninerved with conspicuous parallel veins; stipules subulate: fls. perfect, small, 5-merous, in terminal panicles; ovary free, 2-celled; style 2-parted: fr. an oblong or cylindric drupe, with a 2-celled stone. (Named probably after Berthout van Berchem; about 1789.) About 12 species in S. and E. Asia, E. Afr. and N. Am.

A. Fls. in short lateral or terminal panicles with short lateral brs..............1. *B. scandens*
AA. Fls. in large spreading panicles to 15 cm. long with elongated racemose brs..2. *B. racemosa*

    1. **B. scandens** (Hill) K. Koch. Supple-Jack. Shrub to 5 m.: lvs. elliptic-ovate to oblong-ovate, 3–8 cm. long, acute to obtuse, rounded or broad-cuneate at base, often undulate, with 9–12 pairs of veins; petiole to 1 cm. long: fls. greenish white, in terminal panicles 1–4 cm. long: fr. bluish black, oblong, 6–8 mm. long. Fl.vi; fr.vii–viii. S.O.3:t.153(c). Gr.G.2:t.165. B.B. 2:404. E.N.III.5:406d–g. S.H.2:f.183a–e. (*B. volubilis* DC.) Va. to Fla., Mo. and Tex. Intr. 1714. Zone VI.

    Related species: **B. hypochrỳsa** Schneid. Lvs. oblong-ovate or elliptic-oblong, 5–11 cm. long, acuminulate, golden-brown beneath, with 12–14 pairs of veins; petiole 1–2 cm. long: panicle 6–10 cm. long, its lower brs. to 3 cm. long. C. and W. China. Cult. 1920. Zone VII?—**B. polyphýlla** M. A. Laws. Brts. pubescent: lvs. oval or ovate, 1–3 cm. long, obtuse or acute with 5–9 pairs of veins: fls. in terminal or partly axillary racemes 1–6 cm. long: fl.-bud acuminate. Himal., w. China. Not in cult.—**B. p. leióclada** (Hand.-Mazz.) Hand.-Mazz., var. Brts. glabrous, sometimes glaucescent. C. and W. China. Cult. 1911. Zone VII?

2. **B. racemòsa** Sieb. & Zucc. Lvs. ovate, 2.5–6 cm. long, glaucescent beneath, with 7–9 pairs of veins; petiole 1–2 cm. long: fls. greenish, in large terminal panicles 5–15 cm. long; fl.-buds pointed: fr. ovoid or obovoid, 5–6 mm. long, first red, finally black. Fl.vii–ix; fr.vii–viii of the following year. E.N.III.5:406a-c. Japan, Formosa. Intr. 1880. Zone (V).

Related species: **B. Giraldiàna** Schneid. Lvs. ovate to ovate-oblong or oblong, 3.5–7 cm. long, acute to acuminate, sometimes obtuse, with 8–12 pairs of veins; panicle 8–15 cm. long; fl.-bud rounded at apex, abruptly apiculate: fr. oblong, about 7 mm. long. S.H.2:f.182m-n,183k. C. and W. China. Cult. 1911. Zone VII.

4. **RHAMNÉLLA** Miq. Deciduous trees or shrubs; winter-buds small, with several outer scales; terminal bud wanting: lvs. alternate, serrulate, penninerved; stipules subulate: fls. perfect, small, green, in axillary cymes, 5-merous; stamens perigynous; ovary incompletely 2-celled, about ⅓ inferior; style 2-lobed: drupe oblong, black, with a 1-seeded bony nutlet. (Diminutive of Rhamnus.) Six species in E. Asia.

R. frangulòides (Maxim.) Weberb. Small tree to 10 m.: lvs. ovate-oblong, 5–12 cm. long, long-acuminate, rounded at base or broad-cuneate, finely serrulate, glabrous except pubescent on the veins beneath; petioles 3–8 mm. long: fls. in short-peduncled 5–15-fld. clusters; pedicels in fr. 2–4 mm. long; fr. cylindric-oblong, 8 mm. long, black. Fl.v–vi; fr.ix–x. S.I.2:t.48(c). N.K.9:t.5. S.H.2:f.183h-i,186a. (*R. japonica* Miq., *Microrhamnus f.* Maxim.) Japan, Korea, E. China. Cult. 1906. Zone VI? Similar in lf. to *Rhamnus crenata*, but base of stipules persistent and fr. narrow-oblong.

5. **SAGERÈTIA** Brongn. Deciduous or evergreen shrubs, often scandent, usually with spinescent brts.; winter-buds small, with several outer scales; terminal bud wanting: lvs. opposite or subopposite, small, penninerved, entire or serrulate, of firm texture; stipules small, deciduous: fls. perfect, 5-merous, whitish, small, sessile or subsessile, rarely pediceled, forming terminal and axillary spikes often panicled; petals hooded; disk cupshaped, 5-lobed: ovary 2–3-celled, with short 2–3-lobed style: fr. a small subglobose drupe, with fleshy to leathery exocarp and 2–3 indehiscent nutlets with leathery walls. (Named after Auguste Sageret, French botanist; 1763–1851.) About 15 species in E. and S. Asia and in N. Am.

S. pycnophýlla Schneid. Spiny scandent shrub to 2 m.; brts. tomentulose: lvs. elliptic to elliptic-obovate, 5–18 mm. long, or the smaller ones suborbicular, rounded or obtuse at ends, sharply or crenate-serrulate, yellowish green and lustrous beneath and finely reticulate; petioles 1–2 mm. long, pubescent: fls. sessile, glabrous, in spikes 1–3.5 cm. long and usually 1–4 at end of brts. Fl.vi–vii; fr.x. W. China. Intr. 1910. Zone V.

Closely related species: **S. theèzans** Brongn. Lvs. persistent or subpersistent, ovate or broad-elliptic, 8–25 mm. long, obtusish, rounded or subcordate at base: fls. pubescent, in villous usually paniculate spikes: fr. purplish black, subglobose, 5 mm. across. Fl.ix–x; fr.iv–v. N.K.9:t.15. E.N.III.5:409. C. and E. China. Intr. 1908. Zone VII? May be useful as a hedge-plant south; fls very fragrant. —**S. minutiflòra** (Michx.) Trel., a native of the S. E. States (Gr.G.2:t.166) is probably not hardy within our area.

6. **RHAMNUS** L. BUCKTHORN. Deciduous or sometimes evergreen trees or shrubs, often spiny; winter-buds scaly or naked; terminal bud present or wanting: lvs. alternate or opposite, penninerved, serrulate to entire, stipulate: fls. perfect, polygamous or dioecious, small, greenish, yellowish or whit-

ish, 4–5-merous, sometimes apetalous, in axillary clusters, umbels or racemes: ovary 2–4-celled; style usually undivided: fr. a subglobose drupe with 2–4 1-seeded nutlets usually splitting on the inner side. (Ancient Greek name.) About 100 species chiefly native to the temp. regions of the n. hemisphere; few in Brazil and S. Africa.

A. Winter-buds scaly.
  B. Lvs. opposite or subopposite.
    C. Petioles 5–25 mm. long: lvs. with 2–8 pairs of ascending curving veins: brts. usually spinescent.
      D. Lvs. large, 3–10 cm. long.
        E. Lvs. sharply serrulate with acuminate or aristate teeth, rounded or subcordate at base: fr. on pedicels 12–25 mm. long.............................1. *R. arguta*
        EE. Lvs. with short acute or obtuse teeth: fr. on pedicels 3–8 mm. long.
          F. Petioles ¼ to ½ as long as blade.
            G. Lvs. broad-ovate to oblong.
              H. Lvs. brŏad-ovate to elliptic, 4–7 cm. long, thin, light green beneath.
                          2. *R. cathartica*
                HH. Lvs. narrow-elliptic to oblong, 6–10 cm. long, firm, lustrous above, grayish green beneath...................................3. *R. davurica*
            GG. Lvs. obovate to oblong-obovate, narrow-cuneate...........4. *R. japonica*
          FF. Petioles ⅛ to ⅒ as long as blade, 5–12 mm. long: lvs. elliptic-oblong to oblong, with 5–8 pairs of veins....................................5. *R. utilis*
      DD. Lvs. small, 1–3, rarely to 4 or occasionally to 5 cm. long.
        E. Lvs. closely crenate-serrulate, usually elliptic-obovate...........6. *R. saxatilis*
        EE. Lvs. remotely and obscurely crenate-serrulate, those of shoots often rhombic-lanceolate or obovate-lanceolate.
          F. Young brts. and lvs. more or less pubescent.................7. *R. dumetorum*
          FF. Young brts. and lvs. glabrous or nearly so....................8. *R. Rosthornii*
    CC. Petioles 2–4 mm. long: lvs. with numerous parallel straight veins, 6–12 cm. long.
                13. *R. costata*
  BB. Lvs. alternate.
    C. Brs. spinescent; lvs. with 3–6 pairs of veins, 0.6–7 cm. long.
      D. Lvs. lanceolate or elliptic-lanceolate to linear.................9. *R. spathulaefolia*
      DD. Lvs. elliptic or elliptic-ovate to oblong-ovate or obovate.
        E. Lvs. glabrous, obtuse or acutish, not over 4.5 cm. long, chartaceous.
                10. *R. petiolaris*
        EE. Lvs. pubescent, rarely glabrous, acuminate, membranous......11. *R. Schneideri*
    CC. Brts. not spinescent.
      D. Lvs. deciduous.
        E. Stipules persistent: lvs. small: fls. 5-merous...............12. *R. heterophylla*
        EE. Stipules not persistent: lvs. large: fls. 4-merous (except No. 19 and *R. purpurea* under No. 16): lvs. large.
          F. Lvs. with 12–25 pairs of parallel, nearly straight veins.
            G. Lvs. pubescent ....14. *R. imeretina*
            GG. Lvs. glabrous...15. *R. fallax*
          FF. Lvs. with 4–12, rarely to 14 pairs of veins.
            G. Petioles 6–15 mm. long (see also No. 1).
              H. Lvs. subcordate or rounded at base, with 8–12 pairs of veins.
                          16. *R. alpina*
                HH. Lvs. cuneate, with 6–8 pairs of veins....................17. *R. pumila*
            GG. Petioles 3–8 mm. long.
              H. Lvs. elliptic to oblong-lanceolate, serrulate: fls. 4-merous.
                18. *R. lanceolata*
                HH. Lvs. elliptic, crenate-serrate: fls. 5-merous: low shrub..19. *R. alnifolia*
      DD. Lvs. evergreen or half-evergreen, remotely spinulose-denticulate (or crenate-serrate in the hybrid)................................20. *R. Alaternus*
AA. Winter-buds naked.
  B. Lvs. evergreen: infl. peduncled.....................................21. *R. californica*
  BB. Lvs. deciduous.
    C. Fls. in peduncled umbel-like cymes.
      D. Lvs. with 7–15 pairs of veins, 5–15 cm. long.
        E. Lvs. acute to short-acuminate, sometimes obtuse, often nearly entire.
          F. Peduncles usually longer than petiole: lvs. with 8–15 pairs of veins.
                22. *R. Purshiana*
          FF. Peduncles usually shorter than petiole: lvs. with 8–10 pairs of veins.
                25. *R. caroliniana*
        EE. Lvs. distinctly acuminate, closely serrulate......................26. *R. crenata*
      DD. Lvs. with 6–8 pairs of veins, 2–5 cm. long, glabrous: low shrub....23. *R. rupestris*
    CC. Fls. fascicled, sometimes solitary: lvs. with 8 or 9 pairs of veins, usually entire, 3–7 cm. long ....24. *R. Frangula*

Subgen. I. EURHAMNUS Dipp. Winter-buds scaly, terminal bud wanting: lvs. often opposite: fls. polygamo-dioecious, usually 4-merous; style 2–4-parted; seed (not the outer coat of nutlet) with dorsal furrow; cotyledons thin, curved, green.

Sect. I. Cervispina Moench. Brts. usually spinescent and often spur-like with fascicled lvs.

1. **R. argùta** Maxim. Shrub to 3 m., with slender, rarely spinescent brts.: lvs. sometimes alternate, roundish-oval to ovate, 2.5–7 cm. long, obtuse or acutish, rounded or subcordate at base, sharply and finely serrulate, with acuminate or aristate teeth, bright green, lighter beneath, glabrous; petiole 1–2.5 cm. long: pubescent above: fls. slender-pediceled, often in clusters on spurs: fr. subglobose-pyriform, 6–8 mm. long, on pedicels 1.2–2.5 cm. long. Fl.IV–V; fr.IX. S.H.2:f.197l–n,199h-h[1]. N. China. Cult. 1909? Zone V? Distinct on account of the peculiar serration and the long-stalked fr.

2. **R. cathártica** L. Common B. Shrub or small tree to 6 m.: lvs. elliptic or ovate, 4–7 cm. long, acute or obtusish, rounded or subcordate at base, sometimes broad-cuneate, crenate-serrulate, dull green above, light green and usually glabrous beneath, with 3–5 pairs of veins, thin; petiole 6–25 mm. long: fls. yellowish green, in 2–5-fld. clusters: fr. black, subglobose, about 6 mm. across; seed with the furrow open only near base. Fl.V–VI; fr.IX–X. F.D.21:t. 2183(c). S.E.2:t.318(c). M.Am.1:t.41(c). B.B.2:502. M.A.t.68(h). (*R. Willdenowiana* Hort., not Roem. & Schult.—Hart's Thorn, Waythorn, Rhineberry.) Eur., w. and n. Asia; naturalized in the E. States. Cult. for centuries. Zone II. Used as a hedge-plant.—**R. c. pubéscens** Bean. Lvs. pubescent beneath.

See also *R. koraiensis* and *R. rugulosa* under No. 11.

3. **R. davùrica** Pall. Large spreading shrub or small tree to 10 m., with rather stout often spinescent brts., glabrous: lvs. elliptic-obovate to oblong, 4–10 cm. long, acuminate, cuneate, crenate-serrulate, lustrous above, grayish green and glabrous or slightly pubescent beneath, of firm texture: petiole 6–25 mm. long: fls. and fr. like those of preceding sp.; seed usually with narrow furrow. Fl.V–VI; fr.IX–X. G.F.9:425 (as *R. crenata*). N.K.9:t.12. B.C.5:2925. (*R. cathartica* var. *d.* Maxim., *R. mandshurica* Hort.) Dahuria to N. China, Manch. and Korea. Intr. 1817. Zone II. Similar to the preceding, but of more vigorous spreading habit and with larger lustrous lvs.— **R. d. nippónica** Mak., var. Lvs. narrow-oblong, 5–15 cm. long, 2.5–5 cm. broad, light green beneath. N.K.9:t.13. S.H.2:f.197q(l). Japan, Korea. Intr. before 1892. Zone II.

4. **R. japónica** Maxim. Shrub to 3 m.; brts. yellowish or grayish brown, lustrous, often spinescent or spur-like: lvs. obovate to oblong-obovate, 5–8 cm. long, rounded and short-acuminate, cuneate, serrulate, with 3–5 pairs of veins, slightly pubescent beneath or nearly glabrous, bright green; petiole 8–25 mm. long, pubescent: fls. greenish brown, usually in dense clusters on spurs: fr. black, 6–8 mm. across: seeds with usually closed furrow. Fl.V; fr.X. S.I.2:t.48(c). M.K.t.75(c). S.H.2:f.196t–u,197e-k. Japan. Intr. 1888. Zone III. Shrub with bright green lvs. and slightly fragrant fls.

Related species: **R. virgàta** Roxb. Shrub or small tree; young brts. pubescent: lvs. narrow-elliptic to lanceolate, 4–8 cm. long, usually obtusely acuminate, slightly pubescent on both sides, denticulate or erose-denticulate; petiole 4–10 mm. long: fr. bluish black; seed with open furrow. S.H.2:f.192f-h(l). N. W. Himal. Cult. 1919. Zone VII?—**R. leptophýlla** Schneid. Shrub to 2 m.: lvs. elliptic-obovate, 4–7 cm. long, acuminate, remotely denticulate, glabrous beneath, bright green: pedicels and receptacle pubescent outside: seed with an open furrow. S.H.2:f.196v-w,198e-h. C. and W. China. Intr. 1907. Zone V.— **R. l. scabrélla** Rehd., var. Young brts. pubescent: lvs. 2–4 cm. long, scabrid-pilose above, midrib beneath and petiole pilose. Intr. 1926.

5. **R. ùtilis** Dcne. Shrub to 3 m.; brts. usually not spinescent, glabrous: lvs. narrow-elliptic to oblong, 6–12 cm. long, short-acuminate to acuminate,

cuneate, serrulate, yellow-green, glabrous and yellowish green beneath, with
5–8 pairs of yellow veins, sometimes with yellowish pubescence on veins
when young; petiole 5–12 mm. long: fls. yellowish green: fr. black, 6–7 mm.
across, usually 2-seeded; seed furrowed. Fl.ɪv–v; fr.ɪx–x. Rondot, Vert de
Chine,t.1. S.H.2:f.197t-w,1991. (*R. chlorophora* Dipp., not Dcne.) C. and
E. China. Cult. 1870. Zone VI. With rather large bright or yellow-green lvs.

6. **R. saxàtilis** Jacq. Rᴏᴄᴋ B. Low spreading shrub to 60 or 90 cm.; young
brts. minutely pubescent, becoming mostly spiny: lvs. elliptic-ovate to
obovate, 1–2.5 cm. long, often folded, acute or obtusish, cuneate, serrulate,
glabrous, with 2–4 pairs of veins: fls. very small, greenish yellow: fr. turbinate, black; seeds usually 3, with open furrow. Fl.v–vɪ; fr.vɪɪɪ–ɪx. F.D.21:t.
2186(c). S.O.3:t.t.159(c). H.W.3:57. S.H.2:f.193o-o⁴,196a-e. C. and S. Eu.
Intr. 1752. Zone V.

Related species: **R. infectòria** L. Aᴠɪɢɴᴏɴ-ʙᴇʀʀʏ. Spreading shrub to 2 m.,
spiny: lvs. elliptic or sometimes obovate or ovate, 1–4 cm. long, acute, dark
green, usually glabrous above and slightly pubescent beneath; petiole 4–10 mm.
long: seeds usually 2, with only partly open furrow. G.O.t.98(c, as *R. saxatilis*).
F.D.21:t.2185(c). E.N.III.5:f.201B. S.H.2:f.195a-a³,196f-h¹. (*R. saxatilis* ssp.
i. Rouy & Fouc.) S. Eu. Intr. 1683. Zone VI.—**R. tinctòria** Waldst. & Kit.
Shrub to 1.5 m.; young brts. pubescent: lvs. elliptic or narrow-elliptic, 2–5 cm.
long, pubescent beneath and usually above; petiole 4–10 mm. long: seed with
open furrow. F.D.21:t.2184(c). G.O.t.97(c). S.H.2:f.195b-b(1). S. E. Eu.
Intr. 1820. Zone V.—**R. prunifòlia** Sibth. & Sm. Spreading, procumbent or upright shrub: lvs. oval or obovate, 8–18 mm. long, obtuse, cuneate, finely denticulate, glabrous or nearly so; petiole 1–3 mm. long: seed with open furrow. S.H.
2:f.193m-n¹ (not l-l¹). (*R. Simonii* Hort.) S. E. Eu. Intr. before 1858. Zone
VII?

7. **R. dumetòrum** Schneid. Spreading shrub to 2 m., with numerous short
spiny brts. minutely pubescent when young, later usually red-brown: lvs.
elliptic or obovate, 8–20 mm. long, those of shoots elliptic-lanceolate to
obovate-oblong, 1.5–3.5 cm. long, acute or obtuse, cuneate, crenate-denticulate, slightly pubescent above, pubescent on the veins beneath, with 3–4 pairs
of veins; petiole 3–6 mm. long, pubescent: fls. green, sparingly pubescent,
apetalous: fr. globose-obovoid, about 6 mm. across, on very short pedicels:
seed with furrow open only at base. Fl.v–vɪ; fr.x. W. China. Intr. 1910.
Zone V.—**R. d. crenoserràta** Rehd. & Wils., var. Lvs. 4–7 cm. long, crenate-
serrate, usually with 5 pairs of veins: pedicels of fr. about 5 mm. long. W.
China. Intr. 1910. Zone V.

Related species: **R. globòsa** Bge. Spiny shrub; brts. pubescent, rather slender: lvs. usually obovate, sometimes nearly suborbicular, 1.5–4 cm. long, abruptly
and obtusely short-acuminate, crenate-serrulate, pubescent on both sides; petiole
3–10 mm. long: fr. short-stalked, usually 2-seeded; seed with furrow open
only at base. Rondot, Vert de Chine t.2. S.H.2:f.195f-f³,196q-r. (*R. chlorophora*
Dcne., *R. virgata* var. *aprica* Maxim.) N. China Cult. 1890. Zone V.

8. **R. Rosthórnii** Pritzel. Shrub to 2 m.; young brts. glabrous or slightly
pubescent: lvs. obovate to obovate-oblong or lance-oblong, obtusely acuminate or obtusish, gradually narrowed at base, 1.2–4 cm. long, remotely crenate-
denticulate, with usually 3 pairs of veins, glabrous; petiole 2–5 mm. long,
finely pubescent: fr. globose-ovoid, 5 mm. across, on a stalk 2–4 mm. long,
seeds usually 2, with partly open furrow. Fl.v–vɪ; fr.ɪx. S.H.2:f.195g-g²,196i.
W. China. Intr. 1908. Zone VI?

Related species: **R. parvifòlia** Bge. Spiny shrub, to 2 m.: lvs. elliptic-obovate
to elliptic, 1.5–3.5 cm. long, acute, cuneate, dark green and often pilose above,
grayish green and glabrous or with axillary tufts of hairs beneath, with 3–5
pairs of veins; petiole 5–16 mm. long: fr. subglobose, on a stalk 5–10 mm. long;
seed with open or sometimes closed furrow. N.K.9:t.11. S.H.2:f.192i-l,196x-y¹.
(*R. polymorphus* Turcz., *R. virgata* var. *sylvestris* Maxim.) N. E. Asia. Intr.
1910. Zone V.

9. R. spathulaefòlia Fisch. & Mey. Shrub to 2 m.; brts. finely pubescent when young, often becoming spinescent: lvs. elliptic-lanceolate to lanceolate or oblanceolate, 1.5–5 cm. long, acute or obtusish, rarely short-acuminate, gradually narrowed at base, denticulate or remotely crenate-serrulate, pubescent on both sides when young, later glabrescent: petiole 2–10 mm. long: fr. black, on a stalk 4–10 mm. long; nutlet dehiscent; seed with the furrow open only at ends, at apex divided by an inflexed appendix. Fl.v–vi; fr. viii–ix. S.H.2:f.193a-a³,194g. (*R. Pallasii* var. *s.* Maxim.) W. Asia. Cult. 1870. Zone V.

Related species: **R. Pallásii** Fisch. & Mey. Spreading spiny shrub: lvs. linear to linear-lanceolate, 1.5–3.5 cm. long, serrulate, slightly pubescent when young; petiole 3–6 mm. long: fr. usually with 2 splitting nutlets; seed with open furrow, without appendix at apex. Pallas, Fl. Ross. 2:t.14. S.H.2:f.193c-c²,194 b-e¹. S.L.293(h). W. Asia. Cult. 1890. Zone V.—**R. Erythróxylon** Pall. Spreading spiny shrub; young brts. finely pubescent: lvs. linear to linear-lanceolate, 2–5 cm. long, acute, serrulate, slightly pubescent when young; petiole 5–12 mm. long: fr. with 3 indehiscent nutlets; seed with narrow furrow. Pallas, Fl. Ross. 2:t.13(c). L.A.2:535. S.H.2:f.193b,194f. Siberia. Intr. 1823. Zone V.

10. R. petiolàris Boiss. Shrub; brts. dark red-brown: lvs. chartaceous, ovate-oblong to elliptic-ovate, 1.5–4.5 cm. long, obtuse or acute, cuneate or broad-cuneate, crenate-serrulate, glabrous, with 4–5 pairs of veins; petiole 0.8–2.5 cm. long; fr. subglobose, 5–7 mm. across; seeds 3–4, with open furrow. S.H.2:f.195c-d,199f. Asia Minor. Cult. 1906. Zone VII?

Related species: **R. oleoìdes** L. Shrub to 1 m.: lvs. evergreen, obovate, 0.6–2.5 cm. long, obtuse, cuneate, glabrous or pubescent on the veins beneath at first, with 3–4 pairs of veins; petiole 2–5 mm. long: seed with narrow furrow open at base. S.H.2:195c-d. Mediterr. reg. Cult. 1933. Zone VII?

11. R. Schneìderi Lévl. & Vant. Shrub; brs. mostly spiny; brts. glabrous: lvs. sometimes opposite, elliptic to elliptic-obovate, 2.5–6 cm. long, short-acuminate or acute, cuneate, crenate-serrulate, glabrous, with 4–6 pairs of veins; petiole 3–15 mm. long; fls. slender-pedicelled: fr. broad-obovoid; stalk 7–18 mm. long; seeds 2, with furrow open at base only. N.K.9:t.6a. S.H.2:f. 198r-u. Korea.—**R. S. manshùrica** Nakai, var. Young brts. and petioles pubescent; lvs. short-pilose above and on the veins beneath. N.K.9:t.6b. Korea, Manch. Intr. 1917. Zone V.

Related species: **R. koraiénsis** Schneid. Shrub to 1.5 m.; young brts. pubescent: lvs. elliptic or ovate, 2–4 cm. long, obtusely acuminate, cuneate, crenulate, pubescent at first on both sides, later glabrescent: pedicels and calyx pubescent: fr. subglobose; seeds 1–3. N.K.9:t.8. Korea. Cult. 1928. Zone V.—**R. rugulòsa** Hemsl. Shrub to 2 m.; brts. pubescent: lvs. elliptic-ovate to oblong-ovate, 4–7 cm. long, acuminate or sometimes rounded at apex, rounded to broad-cuneate at base, crenulate, densely villous beneath, pubescent or glabrescent above, with 5–6 pairs of veins impressed above, prominent beneath: fls. pubescent: seeds with open furrow. S.H.2:f.196k-m,198a-d. C. and W. China. Cult. 1917. Zone V.

Sect. 2. ESPINOSA K. Koch. Brts. not spinescent: lvs. alternate (except No. 13).

12. R. heterophýlla Oliv. Shrub to 1.5 m., with slender alternate brs.; young brts. densely short-pilose, with persistent, somewhat spinescent stipules: lvs. ovate or sometimes suborbicular to oblong-lanceolate, 5–30 mm. long, acute or acuminate, cuneate to rounded at base, remotely and finely crenate-serrulate, glabrous above, villous on midrib beneath and yellowish green, firm, with 3–4 pairs of veins; petiole 1–2 mm. long: fls. minute, 1 or 2 in the axils, very short-stalked, 5-merous, pubescent outside: fr. subglobose, about 5 mm. across, black, 3-seeded, on stalks about 1 mm. long. Fl.vii; fr. x. H.I.18:1759. W. China. Intr. 1910. Zone VI? Distinct species with small lvs. of different shapes on the same br.

13. R. costàta Maxim. Shrub to 5 m.; brts. stout, glabrous: lvs. opposite, short-petioled, ovate-oblong, 8–14 cm. long, short-acuminate, broadcuneate or narrowed to a subcordate base, crenate-serrulate, rugose above, pubescent beneath chiefly on the veins, with about 20 pairs of veins; petiole 2–4 mm. long: fls. yellowish green, on slender stalks 1.5–3 cm. long: fr. obovoid, about 8 mm. across, 2-seeded; seeds with closed furrow. Fl.vi; fr.x. S.I.2:t.48(c). S.H.2:f.191m(l). M.G.31:29(h),30. S.L.292(h). Japan. Cult. 1908. Zone VI? Distinct and handsome species.

A similar species is **R. Sargentiàna** Schneid. Shrub to 6 m.; lvs. alternate, elliptic-oblong, 4–12 cm. long, sparingly hairy beneath, with 12–18 pairs of veins; petiole 2–5 mm. long: pedicels 2–3 mm. long; fr. about 5 mm. across, 3-seeded. W. China. Intr. 1908. Zone VI?

14. R. imeretìna Kirchn. Shrub to 3 m., with stout brts. slightly pubescent when young: lvs. elliptic-oblong to oblong, 10–25 cm. long, acuminate, rounded or subcordate, serrulate, dark green and glabrescent above, pubescent beneath chiefly on the veins, with 15–25 pairs of veins impressed above; petiole 1–2 cm. long: fls. green, small, in few-fld. clusters: fr. about 6 mm. across. Fl.vi; fr.x. B.M.6721(c). S.H.2:f.190n-n³,191f-g. M.G.21:405(h). (*R. libanotica* Hook. f., not Boiss., *R. colchica* Lipsky, *R. grandifolia* Hort., not Fisch. & Mey., *R. castaneifolia* Hort.) Cauc., W. Asia. Intr. before 1858. Zone V. With large lvs. changing to bronzy purple in autumn.

Related species: **R. libanótica** Boiss. Lvs. smaller, oblong-obovate, 6–12 cm. long, crenate-denticulate, pubescent beneath, with 10–15 pairs of veins; petiole 6–10 mm. long: fr. about 5 mm. across. S.H.2:f.189s,190n-n³. Syria, Cilicia. Cult. 1905. Zone VI?—See also *R. Sargentiana* under No. 13.

15. R. fállax Boiss. CARNIOLAN B. Shrub to 3 m.; brts. rather stout, glabrous, becoming reddish brown: lvs. elliptic-oblong to oblong or oblongobovate, 5–12 cm. long, acuminate, rounded or subcordate at base, crenateserrulate, dark green above, lighter green and glabrous or nearly so beneath, with 12–20 pairs of veins; petiole 6–15 mm. long: fls. yellowish green, in 3–7-fld. clusters; pedicels 3–6 mm. long: fr. subglobose, 5–6 mm. across. Fl.v–vi; fr.vii–ix. S.O.3:t.157(c, as *R. alpinus*). H.W.3:58. H.M.5:341(h). (*R. carniolicus* Kern., *R. alpina* var. *grandifolia* Hort.) Mts. of S. E. Eu. Cult. 1800. Zone V.

16. R. alpìna L. ALPINE B. Shrub to 3 m.; young brts. glabrous or finely pubescent, becoming dull grayish brown: lvs. elliptic, 5–10 cm. long, rounded or abruptly short-acuminate, rounded to subcordate at base, serrulate, glabrous, with 9–12 pairs of veins; petioles 5–15 mm. long: fls. and fr. like the preceding species, but fr. smaller. Fl.v–vi; fr.viii–ix. L.B.1077(c). F.D.21: t.2187(c). S.H.2:f.189i-l,190f-h. S. W. Eu. Intr. 1752. Zone V.

R. a. × *Alaternus;* see under No. 20.

Related species: **R. purpúrea** Edgew. Tall shrub or small tree; brts. glabrous: lvs. elliptic to elliptic-oblong, 7–16 cm. long, acuminate, broad-cuneate, crenate-serrulate, glabrous, with 7–10 pairs of veins; petiole 5–10 mm. long: fls. 5-merous: fr. subglobose, on pedicels of about equal length. M.G.1916:31. Brandis, For. Fl. t.18. Cult. 1916. N. W. Himal. Zone VII?

17. R. pùmila L. DWARF B. Low, often procumbent shrub; young brts. finely pubescent: lvs. suborbicular to elliptic, 2–5 cm. long, acute or acutish, broad-cuneate, crenate-serrulate, glabrous or slightly pubescent on veins beneath, with 5–8 pairs of veins; petiole 3–10 mm. long: fls. yellowish green, on pedicels 4–7 mm. long: fr. bluish black, subglobose. Fl.v–vii; fr.viii–ix. S.H.2:f.189e-h,190o-p. Alps. Intr. 1752. Zone V. Adapted for rockeries.

18. R. lanceolàta Pursh. Upright slender-branched shrub to 2 m.; brts. puberulous, becoming reddish brown: lvs. ovate-lanceolate to oblong-lanceolate, 2.5–8 cm. long, acute or acuminate, often obtuse on flowering brts., cuneate or rounded at base, finely serrulate, glabrous or minutely downy and light green beneath, with 7–9 pairs of veins; petiole 5–10 mm. long: fls. perfect, of 2 forms on distinct plants, one with short clustered pedicels and short style and one with few often solitary pedicels and exserted style: fr. subglobose, about 6 mm. across, 2-seeded. Fl.v; fr.viii–ix. Gr.G.2:t.168. B.B.2: 503. S.H.2:f.190p-s,192a-c. Pa. to Neb., Iowa, Tex. and Ala. Cult. 1870. Zone V. Shrub with bright green lvs.

Closely related species: **R. Smíthii** Greene. Shrub to 5 m.; brts. glabrous, becoming light grayish brown: lvs. oblong-lanceolate to lanceolate, 3–7 cm. long, obtuse or rarely acutish, usually rounded at base, crenate-serrulate, glabrous, yellowish green beneath, firm and thickish. Colo. Intr. 1905. Zone V.

19. **R. alnifòlia** L'Hérit. Low spreading shrub, rarely exceeding 1 m.; young brts. minutely downy: lvs. elliptic to ovate, 4–10 cm. long, acute, cuneate, unequally crenate-serrate, glabrous or slightly pubescent on the veins beneath, with 6–8 pairs of veins; petiole 5–12 mm. long: fls. usually 2–3, apetalous, 5-merous: fr. subglobose, 6 mm. across, black, 3-seeded. Fl. v–vi; fr.ix–x. G.O.t.61(c). B.B.2:503. Hooker, Fl. Bor. Am.1:t.42. S.H.2: f.190t-w,192d-e. S.L.292(h). N. B. and N. J. to B. C. and Calif. Intr. 1778. Zone II. Rather compact shrub with bright green lvs.

20. **R. Alaternus** L. Evergreen shrub to 4 or 6 m.; brts. minutely downy: lvs. elliptic or ovate to ovate-lanceolate, 2–5 cm. long, acute, remotely serrate or nearly entire, dark green and lustrous above, yellowish green and glabrous or nearly so beneath, with 3–5 pairs of veins; petiole 4–6 mm. long: fls. yellowish green, very small, 5-merous, polygamo-dioecious, in short fascicle-like racemes: fr. black, 6 mm. across. Fl.iii–iv; fr.vii–ix. N.D.3:t.14(c). H.W.3:59. S.H.2:f.187a-f,188g-m. Mediterr. region. Intr. about 1700. Zone VII? Evergreen shrub of bushy habit.—**R. A. argénteo-variegàta** (West.) Rehd., i. Lvs. rather narrow, with broad creamy-white margin. S.O.3:t.156, upper fig.(c). (*R. A.* var. *variegata* Bean.)—**R. A. angustifòlia** (Mill.) Dum.-Cours. Lvs. oblong-lanceolate to lanceolate, more deeply toothed. (*R. a.* Mill., *R. Perrieri* Hort.)—**R. A. integrifòlia** Bean, var. Lvs. mostly without teeth, rather conspicuously veined.

R. A. × *alpina* = **R. hýbrida** L'Hérit. Half-evergreen shrub to 4 m.: lvs. elliptic or ovate to elliptic-oblong, 4–10 cm. long, obtuse or acutish, shallowly serrulate, lustrous above, glabrous with about 7 pairs of veins; petiole 4–8 mm. long. S.H.2:f.189a-c. G.W.12:342(h, as *R. latifolia viridis*)? Orig. before 1788. Zone VI?—**R. h.** Billardi Dipp. Lvs. smaller, narrower, more lanceolate and more coarsely denticulate. S.H.2:f.189d.

Related species: **R. cròcea** Nutt. Shrub to 1 m.; brts. glabrous, often spinescent: lvs. elliptic or broad-ovate to suborbicular, 0.6–2 cm. long, rounded and often apiculate at apex, glandular-denticulate, often copper-colored beneath: fls. 4-merous, in short fascicles: fr. red, obovoid. J.H.6:217. S.H.2:f.187g-i,188 a-f. Calif. Intr. 1848. Zone VII?—**R. c. ilicifòlia** (Nutt.) Greene, var. Tree to 6 m.: lvs. 2–4 cm. long, spinulose-dentate. S.M.723. Calif. to Ariz. Intr. ?

Subgen. II. FRANGULA Dipp. Unarmed shrubs; winter-buds naked: lvs. always alternate: fls. perfect, 5-merous, in sessile or peduncled umbel-like cymes, rarely solitary; styles simple with 3-lobed stigma: seed not furrowed; cotyledons flats, thick, hypogeous. (*Frangula* Mill.)

21. **R. califórnica** Eschsch. COFFEE-BERRY. Evergreen shrub to 5 m.; young brts. pubescent: lvs. oblong to oblong-lanceolate, 3–10 cm. long, obtuse or acute, to short-acuminate, usually rounded at base, serrulate or entire, yellowish green and glabrous beneath or pubescent on the veins, with 8–12 pairs of veins; petiole 4–15 mm. long: peduncles longer or shorter than petiole, pubescent: fr. depressed-globose, 8 mm. across, changing from red to purple-black. Fl.v–vii; fr.viii–ix. Hooker, Fl. Bor. Am.1:t.44. R.H.1874:

354. S.H.2:f.186c-f(l). (*R. oleifolia* Hook., *R. Purshiana* var. *c.* Rehd., *Frangula c.* Gray.) Ore. to Calif. Cult. 1871, or possibly 1858? Zone VII?
　Related species: **R. tomentélla** Benth. Brts. and lvs. beneath densely yellowish or grayish tomentose. S.S.2:t.63,f.2. R.H.1858:658;1872:194. (*R. californica* var. *t.* Brew. & Wats., *R. ursina* Greene.) Calif. to Ariz. Cult. 1858.

22. R. Purshiàna DC. CASCARA BUCKTHORN. Tall shrub or tree to 15 m.; young brts. pubescent or tomentose: lvs. elliptic to ovate-oblong, 5–15 cm. long, acute or obtuse, rounded at base, remotely denticulate or sometimes entire, dark green above, lighter and pubescent beneath or nearly glabrous, with 10 to 15 pairs of veins; petiole 1–2 cm. long: infl. pubescent: fr. turbinate, 8 mm. long, purplish black, with 2–3 seeds. Fl.v–vi; fr.ix. S.S.2:t.62,63. Am. For. 29:177(h). K.B.1908:430,t(h). (*Frangula P.* Coop.) B. C. to Mont. and N. Calif. Cult. 1870. Zone VI. The source of the drug "Cascara Sagrada."

23. R. rupéstris Scop. Spreading shrub to 80 cm., sometimes procumbent; young brts. pubescent: lvs. elliptic to elliptic-oblong or sometimes broad-oval to nearly orbicular, 2–5 cm. long, obtuse or acute, rounded at base, denticulate or sometimes entire, pubescent on the veins beneath, with 5–8 pairs of veins; petiole 2–5 mm. long: fls. in pubescent 3–8-fld. umbels: fr. globose-obovoid, 6 mm. across, first red then black. Fl.v–vi; fr.vii–ix. F.D.21:t.2188(c). S.O. 3:t.155(c). S.H.2:f.185e-e³,186m-o. (*Frangula r.* Schur.) S. E. Eu. Cult. 1800. Zone V.

24. R. Frángula L. ALDER B. Shrub or small tree to 6 m.; young brts. pubescent: lvs. oval or obovate to obovate-oblong, 3–7 cm. long, acute, rounded or broad-cuneate at base, entire, dark lustrous green above, lighter green and often slightly pubescent beneath, with 8 or 9 pairs of veins; petiole 6–12 mm. long: fls. in clusters of 2–10, glabrous; pedicels 8–12 mm. long: fr. globose, 6 mm. across, changing from red to dark purple, 2-seeded. Fl.v–vii; fr.vii–ix. S.E.2:t.319(c). F.D.21:t.2189(c). H.W.3:t.48(c). B.B.2:504. Gg. 8:3. (*Frangula Alnus* Mill., *R. Korolkowii* Hort.) Eu., W. Asia, N. Afr.; naturalized in the E. States, also in Ill. Long cult. Zone II. With lustrous lvs. changing to clear yellow in fall and numerous red to purple-black fr. in late summer.—**R. F. latifòlia** (Kirchn.) Dipp. Lvs. larger and broader, to 12 cm. long and to 6 cm. broad: fr. larger. S.H.2:f.186k(l). (*R. l.* Kirchn., not L'Hérit.) Caucas. Cult. 1860.—**R. F. angustifòlia** Loud., var. Lvs. lanceoblong to elliptic-oblong, 1–2 cm. wide.—**R. F. heterophýlla** Mouillef., var. Lvs. lanceolate, with irregular, undulate and often lobed margin.—**R. F. aspleniifòlia** Dipp. Lvs. linear to linear-lanceolate, 4–6 cm. long and 3–5 mm. wide, with wavy margin. Morton Arb. Bull. 4:56. Cult. 1888.
　Related species: **R. latifòlia** L'Hérit. Small tree: lvs. elliptic to ellipticoblong, 10–18 cm. long, entire, with 10–13 pairs of veins, pubescent beneath; receptacle pubescent on both sides. B.M.2663(c). G.O.t.100(c). I.T.3:t.106. Azores. Intr. 1778. Zone VII?

25. R. caroliniàna Walt. INDIAN CHERRY. Shrub or small tree, to 10 m.; young brts. puberulous: lvs. elliptic to oblong or lance-oblong, 5–15 cm. long, acute or acuminate, usually rounded at base, obscurely serrulate or nearly entire, nearly glabrous, with 8–10 pairs of veins; petiole 6–16 mm. long, pubescent: infl. pubescent, 2–8-fld.: fr. globose, 8 mm. across, changing from red to black, sweet; nutlets 3. Fl.v–vi; fr.ix. S.S.2:t.61. B.B.2:503. Gr.G.2: t.167. (*Frangula c.* Gray.) N. Y. to Fla., w. to Neb. and Tex. Intr. 1727. Zone (V). Lvs. changing to yellow in fall.

26. R. crenàta Sieb. & Zucc. Shrub to 3 m.; young brts. and young lvs. rusty-pubescent, soon glabrous: lvs. oblong-ovate to lance-oblong or obovate-oblong, 5–10 cm. long, acuminate, rounded at base, serrulate, bright green above, lighter beneath and pubescent at least on the veins, with 7–12 pairs of veins; petiole 8–15 mm. long: infl. pubescent, on a peduncle to 1 cm. long, sometimes sessile: fr. subglobose, 6–8 mm. across, changing from red to black. Fl.vi; fr.viii–ix. S.I.2:t.47(c). N.K.9:t.14. S.H.2:f.185f-g¹,186p-q. (*Frangula c.* Miq.) Japan and Korea to C. China. Intr. 1905. Zone III.

7. HOVÈNIA Thunb. Deciduous tree; winter-buds with 2 outer caducous scales, pubescent; lvs. alternate, long-petioled, 3-nerved at base, estipulate: fls. perfect, 5-merous, small, greenish, in axillary and terminal cymes; petals convolute, enclosing the stamens; disk pubescent; style 3-parted: fr. 3-celled and 3-seeded, with leathery exocarp, indehiscent; the brs. of the infl. fleshy and twisted at maturity; seed flattened, with lustrous dark brown testa; cotyledons flat, broad. (After David ten Hoven, senator of Amsterdam; 1724–87.) One species.

H. dúlcis Thunb. JAPANESE RAISIN-TREE. Tree to 10 m.: lvs. broad-ovate to elliptic, 10–15 cm. long, acuminate, subcordate or rounded and usually unequal at base, coarsely serrate, glabrous or pubescent on the veins beneath; petiole 3–5 cm. long: fls. 7 mm. across, in many-fld. cymes 4–6 cm. broad on peduncles 1.5–3 cm. long: fr. subglobose, about 8 mm. across, light grayish or brownish; the fleshy brs. of the infl. reddish. Fl.vi–viii; fr.ix–x. B.M.2360(c). B.R.501(c). S.I.2:t.47(c). I.S.1:t.37. S.H.2:291. (*H. acerba* Lindl., *H. inaequalis* DC.) China; cult. in Japan and India. Cult. 1820. Zone (V). Grown for its handsome lvs. and possibly also for the fleshy edible infl.

8. CEANÒTHUS L. Deciduous or evergreen shrubs, rarely small trees, sometimes spiny; winter-buds small, pubescent, with few outer scales: lvs. alternate, sometimes opposite, serrate or entire, usually 3-nerved at base; stipules small, deciduous; fls. perfect, small, 5-merous, in small umbels forming spikes or panicles; sepals often incurved, colored; petals hooded and clawed, spreading or recurved; filaments slender; disk annular; ovary 3-celled, partly or sometimes scarcely adnate to receptacle: fr. usually globose-turbinate, 3-lobed at apex, dry at length and separating into 3 dehiscent parts, the receptacle persisting as a cup; seeds albuminous; embryo with flat cotyledons. (Ancient Greek name.) Nearly 50 species in N. Am. chiefly in the Pacific coast region, s. to Mex.

A. Lvs. alternate, distinctly 3-nerved at base.
  B. Lvs. crenate or serrate.
    c. Lvs. glabrous or pubescent and green beneath.
      D. Lvs. membranous, deciduous.
        E. Fls. white.
          F. Infl. slender-peduncled, at end of the young growth.
            G. Lvs. ovate to oblong-ovate, acute or acuminate..........1. *C. americanus*
            GG. Lvs. elliptic to elliptic-lanceolate, obtuse or acutish..........2. *C. ovatus*
          FF. Infl. short-peduncled, lateral on brts. of the previous season.3. *C. sanguineus*
        EE. Fls. blue or pink.
          F. Lvs. pubescent beneath: fls. blue..............................4. *C. Delilianus*
          FF. Lvs. glabrous or nearly glabrous beneath: fls. pale blue, pink or pinkish.
            5. *C. pallidus*
      DD. Lvs. leathery, persistent, obtuse, glabrous or appressed-pubescent beneath; fls. blue, rarely white..6. *C. thyrsiflorus*
    cc. Lvs. tomentose beneath.
      D. Brts. glabrous: lvs. grayish tomentulose beneath, the veins glabrescent.
        7. *C. velutinus*
      DD. Brts. tomentose: lvs. tawny or whitish tomentose beneath: fls. blue.8. *C. coeruleus*
  BB. Lvs. entire, rarely finely serrulate, 1–2.5 cm. long: fls. white: low spinescent shrub.
    9. *C. Fendleri*
AA. Lvs. opposite, penninerved, thick, small....................................10. *C. cuneatus*

1. **C. americànus** L. NEW JERSEY TEA. Shrub to 1 m., with slender upright brs.; young brts. pubescent: lvs. ovate to ovate-oblong, 3–8 cm. long, acute or acuminate, irregularly serrulate, dull green above, pubescent or nearly glabrous beneath; petiole 6–12 mm. long: fls. in terminal and axillary slender-peduncled panicles forming large corymbose panicles at end of brs.: fr. 5–6 mm. across. Fl.VI–IX; fr.IX–X. B.M.1479(c). Gr.G.2:t.169. B.C.2:696. Gn.56:137(h). Can. to Man., Neb., Tex. and S. C. Intr. 1713. Zone IV. Summer-blooming shrub adapted for borders of shrubberies.—**C. a. inter-mèdius** (Pursh) K. Koch, var. Lvs. ovate to lance-ovate, 1–3 cm. long; fls. in smaller, very slender-peduncled spikes: fr. smaller. S.H.2:f.201e-f(l). (*C. i.* Pursh.) Tenn. to Fla. and Ala. Intr. 1812.

    C. a. × *coeruleus;* see No. 4.

2. **C. ovàtus** Desf. Upright shrub to 60 cm.; brts. slightly pubescent and often slightly glandular: lvs. elliptic to elliptic-lanceolate, 2–6 cm. long, obtuse to acute, crenate-serrulate, lustrous above, nearly glabrous beneath; petiole 4–6 mm. long: infl. like that of the preceding, but smaller and peduncles shorter: fr. 4–5 mm. across. Fl.V–VI; fr.VII–VIII. B.B.2:505. S.H.2:201g-i. (*C. ovalis* Bigel.) N. Eng. to Neb., Colo. and Tex. Cult. 1830. Zone IV.— **C. o. pubéscens** Torr. & Gray. Brts. and lvs. pubescent beneath; lvs. usually smaller and narrower and with more prominent veins. (*C. p.* Rydb.) Mich. to Iowa, Neb. and Tex. Intr. 1904.

    C. o. × *Delilianus;* see No. 5.

3. **C. sanguíneus** Pursh. Shrub to 4 m.; brts. purple or reddish, glabrous: lvs. orbicular or ovate to obovate, 2.5–8 cm. long, obtuse, rounded or sub-cordate at base, serrate, slightly pubescent beneath; petiole 1.5–2.5 cm. long: fls. white, in lateral leafless narrow panicles 4–12 cm. long on stout peduncles: fr. 4 mm. across. Fl.V–VI. B.M.5177(c). S.H.2:f.201k,202a-b. (*C. oreganus* Nutt.) B. C. to Calif. Intr. 1853 (or 1838?). Zone VI?

4. × **C. Deliliànus** Spach. (*C. americanus* × *coeruleus*). Young brts. finely pubescent: lvs. elliptic-ovate or ovate to oblong-ovate, 4–8 cm. long, sometimes 10 cm., acute or short-acuminate, rarely obtuse, rounded at base, dark green and slightly pubescent above, pubescent or sometimes nearly tomentose beneath; petiole 5–10 mm. long: fls. pale to deep blue, in slender-stalked, lateral and terminal narrow panicles; rachis pubescent; pedicels glabrous, 5–8 mm. long. M.G.18:485. Gn.61:223(h);80:76(h). Orig. before 1830. Zone VI–VII.—Here belong: *C. Arnouldii* Carr., *C. versaillensis* Hort., *C. hybridus* Hort., partly, *C. azureus* Hort., not Desf., "Gloire de Versailles," bright blue (Gn.85:595[h]); "Gloire de Plantières," deep blue; "Victor Jouin," dark blue; "Ciel de Provence," deep blue (R.H.1903:322,t[c]); "Léon Simon," pale blue (Nederl. Fl. Pomon.t.72[c]).—The various forms of this and the following hybrid are valued for their showy fls. and their late blooming season.

    C. D. "Indigo" × *floribundus* Hort., not Hook. = **C. Burkwoòdii** Burkwood. Lvs. evergreen: fls. deep blue. Cult. 1929.

5. × **C. pállidus** Lindl. (?*C. Delilianus* × *ovatus*). Brts. terete, slightly pubescent or nearly glabrous, often purplish: lvs. ovate-oblong or elliptic-oblong to oblong, 3–6 cm. long, obtuse, rounded or broad-cuneate at base, serrate, slightly pubescent chiefly on veins beneath or nearly glabrous; petiole 3–6 mm. long: fls. light blue in rather short panicles on long leafy brts.; rachis pubescent. B.R.26:20(c). Orig. before 1830.—**C. p. róseus** (Carr.) Rehd., var. Lvs. larger, to 8 cm. long, usually ovate-oblong, less pubescent or nearly glabrous beneath: fls. pink. R.H.1875:30,t(c). (*C. ovatus*

var. *r*. Carr., *C. r*. Koehne.) Orig. before 1830. Here belongs "Marie Simon," with flesh-colored fls.—**C. p. plènus** Rehd., var. Lvs. similar to those, of the preceding form: fls. white, pink in bud, double. Gn.77:432. Gn.M.28:7(h). (*C. americanus fl. pleno albo* Hort.)

6. **C. thyrsiflòrus** Eschsch. Evergreen shrub or small tree to 10 m.; young brts. glabrous or slightly pubescent, sharply angled: lvs. oblong, 2–5 cm. long, obtuse, crenate-serrulate, lustrous above, light green and glabrous or appressed-pubescent beneath: petiole 6–15 mm. long: fls. blue, rarely white, in lateral narrow panicles 3–7 cm. long. Fl.v–vii. B.R.30:38(c). S.S.2:64. G.C.37:179(h);41:221,t(h). Gn.77:135(h),475(h). Ore. to Calif. Intr. 1837. Zone VII? Fine free-flowering shrub with blue fls.; the hardiest of the taller evergreen species.—**C. t. grìseus** Trel., var. Lvs. broad-ovate, minutely tomentulose beneath: fls. pale lilac. Gn.86:447(h).

C. t. × *dentatus* = **C.** Lobbiànus Hook. Brts. terete: lvs. distinctly 3-nerved: fls. deep blue in oval peduncled heads. B.M.4810 (4811 by error). F.S. 10:t.1016(c). Calif. Intr. 1853.—*C. t.* × *rigidus* = **C.** Veitchiànus Hook. Lvs. obovate, obtuse, glandular-serrate, grayish beneath: fls. deep blue, in dense panicled clusters 3–5 cm. long. B.M.5127(c). G.C.69:211(h);77:431(h). Calif. Intr. 1853.

Related species: **C. foliòsus** Parry. Shrub to 0.3 m.; brts. terete: short-petioled, oval or elliptic, 0.5–2 cm. long, obtuse or obtusish, glandular-serrate, glabrous or nearly so: fls. blue, in panicles to 2.5 cm. long. B.M.9540(c). Calif. Cult. 1933. Zone VII?

7. **C. velutìnus** Dougl. Evergreen tall shrub to 3 or 4 m.; brts. glabrous: lvs. broad-elliptic, 5–7 cm. long, obtuse, rounded or subcordate at base, serrulate, dark green, glabrous and lustrous above, closely tomentose beneath with glabrescent veins; petiole to 12 mm. long: fls. white, in large compound panicles 8–12 cm. long. Fl.vi–vii. B.M.5165(c). G.C.II.22:232. B. C. to Calif. and Colo. Intr. 1853. Zone VI.

8. **C. coerùleus** Lag. Tall shrub; brts. terete, densely tomentose: lvs. ovate to oblong-ovate, 3–8 cm. long, acute or obtuse, rounded at base, serrate, with villous tawny or white tomentum beneath; petiole to 15 mm. long: fls. deep blue, in panicles 8–15 cm. long; pedicels villous, rarely glabrous. Fl.vii–ix. L.B.2:110(c). B.R.4:291(c). P.M.2:74,t(c). Gn.61:223(h);80:76 (h). (*C. azureus* Desf.) Mex. Intr. 1818. Not hardy within our area, but the parent of many beautiful hardier hybrid forms.

9. **C. Féndleri** Gray. Deciduous, usually low, sometimes procumbent, rarely to 2 m. high; brts. terete, tomentulose, spinescent: lvs. elliptic to elliptic-lanceolate, 1–2.5 cm. long, entire or finely serrulate, grayish green and tomentulose beneath; petiole short: fls. white, in clusters 2–3 cm. long, at end of lateral leafy brts. Fl.vi–vii. R.H.1901:423(h). M.G.23:208;27,499(h). S.L. 119(h). S. Dak. to N. Mex. and Ariz. Cult. 1893. Zone V. Adapted for rockeries and sandy banks; the hardiest of the western species.

Related species: **C. parvifòlius** Trel. Evergreen shrub to 1 m., with slender brts., glabrous: lvs. oblong, 1–2.5 cm. long, obtuse, cuneate: fls. blue, in short panicles 1.5–4 cm. long. Calif. Cult. 1933. Zone VII?—**C. cordulàtus** Kellogg. Evergreen spiny rigid shrub, glabrous: lvs. oval or elliptic, 0.8–2.5 cm. long, obtuse, cuneate or sometimes rounded to subcordate at base, sometimes denticulate near apex: fls. white, in dense panicles 1–3 cm. long. Calif. Cult. 1933. Zone VII?

10. **C. cuneàtus** Nutt. Evergreen shrub to 2 m., of spreading habit; brts. pubescent when young: lvs. cuneate-obovate to spatulate, 1–2.5 cm. long, obtuse, entire, dull grayish green, tomentulose beneath: fls. dull white or bluish, in clusters 1–2 cm. across, on short lateral brts. Fl.iv–v. B.H.8:170. S.H.2:f.203g-k(l). Ore. to Calif. Intr. 1848. Zone VII.

Closely related species: **C. prostràtus** Benth. Procumbent: lvs. cuneate-obovate, coarsely spiny-toothed: fls. blue. S.H.2:f.2031-m(1). Wash. to Calif. Cult. 1886. Zone VII?

9. **DISCÀRIA** Hook. Deciduous shrubs with slender opposite spiny brs.: lvs. opposite or clustered, small; stipules connected by narrow ridges or lines: fls. perfect, 4–5-merous, sometimes apetalous, solitary or clustered: disk at base of the campanulate or tubular receptacle with free often undulate margin; stigma 3-lobed, ovary 3-celled: fr. 3-lobed, separating at maturity into 3 dehiscent parts. (Greek *diskos;* referring to the prominent disk.) About 12 species in S. Am., Austr. and N. Zealand.

D. serratifòlia (Vent.) Benth. Shrub to 4 m., with slender pendulous spiny brs.; spines 1.5–2.5 cm. long: lvs. ovate-oblong to oblong-lanceolate, 1–2.5 cm. long, shallowly crenate-serrate, glabrous and lustrous on both sides: fls. greenish white, campanulate, 3–4 mm. across, 5-merous, apetalous, in clusters on last year's brts.; sepals triangular-ovate. Fl.v. G.C.II.6:325. J.H. 8:59. B.S.1:500. (*Colletia s.* Vent.) Chile, Patag. Intr. 1842. Zone VII. Of distinct habit and with fragrant fls. borne in great profusion.

10. **COLLÈTIA** Juss. Deciduous shrubs with opposite spines: lvs. caducous, opposite, small, usually obovate or spatulate, serrate; stipules not connected by lines: fls. small, perfect, 4–6-merous, solitary or fascicled: disk inconspicuous or with rolled-in margin, at base of the campanulate or tubular receptacle; petals minute or wanting, at the mouth of receptacle; ovary 3-celled; stigma 3-lobed: fr. dry, coriaceous, separating into 3 parts. (Named after Philibert Collet, French botanist; 1643–1718.) About 10 species in S. Am.

C. infaùsta N. E. Br. Glabrous shrub to 3 m.; brs. green, rigid, with sharply pointed terete and slightly curved spines 1–2.5 cm. long and about 2 mm. thick: lvs. with the short petiole 4–8 mm. long, elliptic-lanceolate to linear-lanceolate, acute, entire or serrate: fls. greenish white, the tube suffused with red and about 6 mm. long, with recurved ovate acute lobes, apetalous; anthers half-exserted. Fl.II–IV. B.M.3644(c). B.R.1776(c). G.C. 60:132. Gn.75:605(as *C. cruciata*). B.S.3:104. (*C. horrida* Lindl., not Brongn., *C. spinosa* Lindl., not Lam.) Chile. Intr. 1823. Zone VII. Sometimes grown for its striking odd appearance.

Related species: **C. cruciàta** Hook. Brs. stout and rigid, with triangular much compressed spines, 1.5–4 cm. long and sometimes 2 cm. broad at base: lvs. elliptic-ovate, about 6 mm. long, serrate, caducous: fls. yellowish white, urnshaped, about 6 mm. long, with 5 reflexed lobes: fr. 3-lobed. Fl.IX. B.M.5033(c). Add.8:286(c). Gt.16:t.543. G.C.II.8:617. Gn.55:293. S.H.2:299. (*C. bictoniensis* Lindl.) S. Braz., Uruguay. Intr. 1824. Zone VII?—Sometimes slender brs. with nearly terete spines appear on plants of this species and this has given rise to the belief that it is identical with *C. infausta.*—**C. armàta** Miers. Brs. pubescent, spines sometimes glabrous: lvs. elliptic-lanceolate to lanceolate, 5–12 mm. long: fls. 5 mm. long; anthers exserted. Fls.IX–XI. (*C. valdiviensis* Phil.) S. Chile. Intr. about 1880. Zone VII?

Fam. 60. **VITACEAE** Lindl. GRAPE FAMILY

Shrubs, usually climbing by tendrils, rarely upright, or small trees: lvs. alternate, simple or compound, stipulate: fls. bisexual or unisexual, regular, small, in cymes, corymbs or panicles, usually opposite a lf.; sepals 4–5, rarely 3–7, minute or obsolete; petals as many, valvate, rarely connate at base; stamens opposite the petals and as many; disk annular or lobed; ovary superior, 2-, rarely 3–6-celled; each cell with 2, rarely 1 ovule; style 1 or wanting; stigma capitate, peltate or lobed: fr. a berry; seed albuminous;

embryo small; cotyledons flat.—Ten genera with about 450 species, mostly in trop. and subtrop. regions.

A. Petals cohering at apex and cast off as a whole; infl. paniculate; bark without lenticels, finally separating in long strips (except in 2 species); pith brown: lvs. usually simple.
1. *Vitis*
AA. Petals free, expanding at anthesis: infl. usually cymose; bark with lenticels, not shredding; pith white.
  B. Fls. 5-merous (rarely 4-merous and lvs. pinnate); infl. opposite the lf.: lvs. simple, digitate or pinnate to bipinnate.
    C. Tendrils twining without disk-like tips: disk cupular, distinct from the ovary.
2. *Ampelopsis*
    CC. Tendrils with disk-like adhesive tips, rarely without: disk adnate to the ovary, not distinct ....3. *Parthenocissus*
  BB. Fls. 4-merous.
    C. Infl. axillary: fr. 2–4-seeded: lvs. digitate or pedate.
      D. Style nearly wanting; stigma 4-lobed: lfts. 1.5–6 cm. long..........4. *Tetrastigma*
      DD. Style filiform;-stigma small: lfts. 6–15 cm. long, stalked...............5. *Cayratia*
    CC. Infl. opposite the lf.: brts. and lvs. more or less fleshy: fr. 1–2-seeded: lvs. ternate; lfts. sessile ....6. *Cissus*

1. **VĬTIS** L. GRAPE. Deciduous, rarely evergreen shrubs, climbing by tendrils; pith brown, interrupted at the nodes by diaphragms (except in No. 24): lvs. simple, dentate, usually lobed, rarely palmately compound: fls. polygamo-dioecious, 5-merous, in panicles opposite the lf.; sepals minute or obsolete; petals cohering at the apex and falling as a whole at anthesis; disk hypogynous, consisting of 5 nectariferous glands; ovary 2-celled; cells 2-ovuled; style conical, short; fr. a pulpy 2–4-seeded berry; seeds usually pyriform, with a contracted beak-like base, with 2 grooves on the ventral side. (Ancient Latin name of the grape.) About 60 species in the n. hemisphere, chiefly in the temp. regions.—For American species see also L. H. Bailey, Grapes of N. Am. (Bailey, Gent. Herb. 3:151–244. 1934).

Bark without lenticels, on older brs. separating in long strips and fibres; tendrils forked; seeds pyriform.   Subgen. EUVITIS Planch.
A. Brts. glabrous or tomentose: lvs. always simple (3–5-parted in var. of No. 1).
  B. Lvs. green and glabrous or pubescent beneath (occasionally floccose-tomentose when young in No. 1).
    C. Basal sinus of lvs. narrow.
      D. Lvs. suborbicular, usually deeply 3–5-lobed, usually slightly floccose or pubescent beneath ....1. *V. vinifera*
      DD. Lvs. ovate, undivided or slightly 3-lobed, glabrous beneath or pubescent only on veins ....2. *V. vulpina*
    CC. Basal sinus of lvs. wide.
      D. Tendrils well developed; lvs. ovate to orbicular-ovate.
        E. Young brts. and petioles red or reddish: diaphragm thick: lvs. usually distinctly lobed with rounded or obtuse sinuses.
          F. Young brts. and lvs. beneath on veins pubescent: lvs. 12–25 cm. long, short-acuminate ....3. *V. amurensis*
          FF. Young brts. and lvs. glabrous, lvs. 8–12 cm. long, long-acuminate.
4. *V. palmata*
        EE. Young brts. green; diaphragm thin.
          F. Lvs. 8–20 cm. long, coarsely toothed with triangular teeth.
            G. Brts. usually glabrous: lvs. ovate, 3-lobed with acute sinuses.5. *V. riparia*
            GG. Brts. usually pubescent: lvs. suborbicular, scarcely lobed..6. *V. monticola*
          FF. Lvs. 5–10 cm. long, undivided, denticulate or with very short broad teeth, pubescent on the veins beneath...............................7. *V. flexuosa*
      DD. Tendrils usually wanting or small: lvs. usually reniform, broader than high.
8. *V. rupestris*
  BB. Lvs. tomentose beneath at least while young or glaucous.
    C. Lvs. becoming glabrous or nearly so, green beneath.
      D. Lvs. distinctly 3-lobed: brts. angled, pubescent...................9. *V. Baileyana*
      DD. Lvs. indistinctly or slightly 3-lobed.
        E. Lvs. ovate or broad-ovate.
          F. Lvs. with very short, mucronulate teeth broader than high or denticulate.
            G. Lvs. reticulate beneath, remotely denticulate, scarcely toothed: sides of basal sinus at right or wider angle: brts. terete. (See also var. of No. 16.)
10. *V. Wilsonae*
            GG. Lvs. not reticulate, with very broad mucronulate teeth; sides of basal sinus at narrow angle: brts. angled................11. *V. cinerea*
          FF. Lvs. with coarse triangular acute teeth; basal sinus rounded, usually wide: brts. angled ....12. *V. arizonica*

7. **V. flexuòsa** Thunb. Slender vine; young growth rufous-tomentose: lvs. broad- or triangular-ovate, 5–8 cm. broad, acuminate, with broad open sinus or nearly truncate, unequally sinuate-dentate with short small teeth, sometimes angularly 3-lobed, lustrous above, pubescent or floccose on the veins and in the axils beneath, thin and firm: panicle slender, 5–14 cm. long: fr. about 8 mm. across, black, 2–3-seeded. Fl.vi; fr.ix. S.H.2:f.209f-g¹(l). Japan, Korea, China. Cult. 1880. Zone V. Graceful vine.—**V. f. parvifòlia** (Roxb.) Gagnep., var. Lvs. somewhat smaller, lustrous bronzy-green above, purple beneath when young. J.L.28:f.107(l). S.H.2:f.209h-h¹(l). (*V. p.* Roxb., *V. f.* var. *chinensis* Veitch.) Himal. to C. China. Intr. 1900.

8. **V. rupéstris** Scheele. Bush G. Shrub to 2 m., sometimes slightly climbing; tendrils few and small or none; diaphragms thin: lvs. reniform to orbicular-ovate, 7–10 cm. wide, with very wide basal sinus or nearly truncate, coarsely toothed and sometimes slightly 3-lobed, lustrous above, glabrous at maturity or slightly pubescent on the veins beneath, somewhat glaucescent on both sides, thick and firm; panicle slender, 4–10 cm. long: fr. purple-black and somewhat glaucous, 7–14 mm. across, of pleasant taste; seeds small and broad. Fl.vi; fr.viii–ix. S.H.2:f.209i(l) B.B.2:508. S. Pa. to Tenn., Mo., Okla. and S. W. Texas. Intr. about 1860. Zone V.

9. **V. Baileyàna** Muns. High climbing; stems with short internodes and often many short brts.: lvs. ovate to orbicular-ovate, 5–10 cm. long, cordate, toothed with rather small teeth, usually distinctly 3-lobed near apex, with short lobes, bright green above but not lustrous, grayish beneath and pubescent at maturity only on the veins: panicles compact, 8–12 cm. long: fr. 7–10 mm. across, black, not or slightly bloomy; seed small, broadly pear-shaped. Fl.vi; fr.ix. Munson, l.c.,t.24,39. (*V. virginiana* Muns., not Poir.) W. Va. and N. C. to Tenn. and Ga. Intr. about 1890. Zone V.

Related species: **V. Berlandièri** Planch. Spanish G. Lvs. lustrous above, gray-pubescent beneath at first, at maturity only on the veins: panicle 10–20 cm. long; fr. purple, slightly glaucous, pleasant-tasting. Munson,l.c.,t.23,39. B.C. 6:3487. S. W. Tex. and Mex. Intr. before 1883. Zone VI.

10. **V. Wílsonae** Veitch. High climbing: young brts. floccose-tomentose; lvs. reddish when young, broad-ovate, 7–15 cm. wide, cordate to subcordate at the very base with the sides usually diverging at a right or wide angle, short-acuminate, sinuate-dentate or denticulate with short mucronate teeth, floccose-tomentose when young, at maturity glabrous above, cobwebby on the veins beneath and reticulate; panicle slender and narrow, with the stalk 10–20 cm. long: fr. black, bloomy, about 1 cm. across. Fl.vi; fr.ix–x. G.C. 46:236. (*V. reticulata* Pamp., not M. A. Laws.) C. China. Intr. 1907. Zone (V).

Related species: **V. betulifòlia** Diels & Gilg. Lvs. ovate to oblong-ovate, rarely broad-ovate, 5–10 cm. long, cordate to rounded or nearly truncate at base, acuminate, remotely denticulate to dentate with very broad mucronulate teeth, rarely slightly 3-lobed, whitish or tawny floccose-tomentose when young and usually thinly so at maturity; petiole usually 1–4 cm. long: panicle slender, 4–10 cm. long: fr. blue-black. C. and W. China. Intr. 1907. Zone V.

11. **V. cinérea** Engelm. Sweet Winter G. High climbing; young brts. gray-tomentose; diaphragms thick: lvs. broad-ovate, 8–20 cm. across, with wide basal sinus, usually distinctly 3-lobed or 3-angled, unequally toothed with short broad teeth, cobwebby above when young, dull dark green at maturity and with persistent gray cobwebby pubescence beneath: panicle irregular, 15–30 cm. long: fr. 10–14 mm. across, black, scarcely bloomy, becoming sweet after frost. Fl.vi; fr.x. B.C.6:3488. B.B.2:507. Munson, l.c. t.21,39. Ill. to Kans., Tex., Mex. and N. Fla Cult. 1883. Zone V.—**V. c.**

canéscens (Engelm.) Bailey, var. Lvs. almost as broad as long, not lobed. (*V. aestivalis* var. *c.* Engelm.) Mo. and S. Ill. to Tex.

12. **V. arizònica** Engelm. CANYON G. Usually low; brts. angled, with short internodes and thick diaphragms; young growth white-tomentose: lvs. broad-ovate, 4–8 cm. wide, rarely larger, basal sinus wide to nearly truncate, not or indistinctly 3-lobed, with triangular pointed apex, sometimes distinctly lobed on vigorous shoots, dentate with short acute or mucronate teeth, white-cobwebby when young, finally nearly glabrous: panicle short and broad, slender-stalked: fr. 6–8 mm. across, black, pleasant-tasting. Fl.vi; fr.ix. Munson, l.c.t.30. Gn.54:427(h). W. Tex., N. Mex. and Ariz. to s. e. Calif. and n. Mex. Cult. 1890. Zone VI.

13. **V. califórnica** Benth. Usually high climbing; brts. with long internodes and thin diaphragms, white-tomentose when young: lvs. orbicular-ovate to orbicular-reniform, 7–12 cm. wide or more, basal sinus narrow to wide, finely to coarsely crenate-toothed with rounded mucronulate teeth, not or sometimes indistinctly 3-lobed, usually whitish cobwebby until half-grown and remaining pubescent beneath, rarely nearly glabrous: panicle long-stalked and usually forked: fr. about 1 cm. across, glaucous-white, rather dry, but pleasant-tasting; seeds large, pyriform. Fl.vi; fr.ix. B.C.6: 3488. Munson, l.c.t.28. Gn.36:143(h). Ore. to Calif. Cult. 1890. Zone VII? The lvs. turn crimson in autumn.

14. **V. argentifòlia** Muns. BLUE G. Strong high climbing vine, with long internodes and thick diaphragms; young brts. usually glabrous and mostly glaucous: lvs. broad-ovate, 10–30 cm. wide, shallowly 3-lobed on old growth, deeply 3–5-lobed on vigorous shoots, basal sinus deep to shallow, shallowly or sinuately toothed, dull green and glabrous above, glaucous beneath and glabrous or sparingly pubescent on the veins, rather thin; petiole long: panicle 5–10 cm. long, usually long-stalked: fr. about 1 cm. across, purple-black and densely glaucous, sour but pleasant-tasting; seeds rather small and broad. Fl.vi; fr.ix. B.C.6:3489. B.B.2:507. Munson, l.c.t.13. W.A.88,t(h). (*V. bicolor* Leconte, not Raf., *V. Lecontiana* House, *V. aestivalis* var. *bicolor* (Leconte) Deam.—SUMMER G.) N. E. and Ill. to N. C. and W. Tenn. Intr. 1739. Zone V. Easily recognized by the glaucous under side of the large lobed lvs.

V. a. × *riparia:* see under No. 5.

15. **V. aestivàlis** Michx. SUMMER G. Strong high climbing vine, with medium or rather short internodes and thick diaphragms; young brts. floccose: lvs. broad-ovate, 10–30 cm. wide, similar to those of the preceding species, basal lobes often overlapping, more coarsely toothed, dull and glabrescent above, with rusty floccose tomentum beneath, partly persisting at least on the veins; petiole floccose; panicle 10–25 cm. long, slender: fr. about 8 mm. across, black, bloomy, dryish and astringent to juicy and sweet. Fl.vi: fr.ix. Munson, l.c.t.14. B.B.2:506. Am. For. 26:286(trunk). (*V. Labrusca* var. *a.* Reg.) N. Y. to Mo., Fla., and Miss. Intr. 1748. Zone V. Easily recognized by the brown cobwebby tomentum on the under side of the large lobed lvs.; the var. cult. for its fr.—**V. a. Bourquiniàna** (Muns.) Bailey, var. Lvs. only slightly rusty beneath, the pubescence usually grayish or dun-colored, of thinner texture: fr. large and juicy, black to amber-colored. Munson, l.c.t.18. (*V. B.* Muns.) Possibly hybrid. Intr. about 1847.

Related species: **V. Lincecùmii** Buckl. Bushy or high climbing; lvs. as long as broad or little longer, 3-lobed, tomentose beneath; panicle 5–10 cm. long: fr. 12–20 mm. across, black, bloomy, pleasant-tasting: seeds 6–10 mm. long. Munson, l.c.t.11. Mo. to Tenn. and Tex. Intr. about 1860. Zone V.—**V. L. glaùca** Muns., var. Lvs. glaucous below, veins rusty-pubescent. Munson, l.c.t.12. Mo. to Tex.

16. **V. Coignétiae** Planch. Strong growing vine; young brts. floccose-tomentose: lvs. orbicular-ovate, 10–25 cm. broad, deeply cordate with narrow sinus, unequally and shallowly toothed or denticulate, indistinctly lobed, dull and rugose above, nearly glabrous, grayish or rusty-tomentose beneath, reticulate; panicle short, pedunculate: fr. about 8 mm. across, black with purple bloom, not edible. Fl.vi–vii; fr.ix–x. R.H.1892:342;1898:426–8. G.C. III:22:305. B.C.6:3491. Gn.63:124(h),209(h). (*V. Kaempferi* of Rehd., not K. Koch.) Japan. Cult. 1875. Zone V. Handsome vine with large heavy foliage turning crimson in fall.—**V. C. glabréscens** Nakai, var. Lvs. becoming glabrescent beneath at maturity. Cult. 1890.

V. C. × riparia; see under No. 5.

Related species or probably hybrid with *V. amurensis* is **V. pulchra** Rehd. Brts. sparingly floccose, reddish: lvs. 7–12 or 15 cm. wide, coarsely dentate and often slightly 3-lobed, shallowly cordate or nearly truncate at base, crimson when unfolding, becoming lustrous bronzy green above, purplish beneath, later deep green, slightly floccose-tomentose beneath and pilose on the veins: panicle narrow, 6–10 cm. long. (*V. flexuosa major* Hort.) Orig. unknown, intr. about 1880? Zone (V).

17. **V. pentagòna** Diels & Gilg. Brts. gray-tomentose when young, reddish: lvs. ovate, 8–12 cm. long, truncate or nearly so at base, sinuate-denticulate and slightly 5-angled, slightly pubescent on the veins above, grayish or reddish tomentose beneath; petiole 4–9 cm. long: panicle to 16 cm. long, tomentose: fr. 6–7 mm. across; seed pyriform, about 4 mm. long. Fl.vi; fr.ix. S.H.2:f.2071(l). C. and W. China. Cult. 1890. Zone V.—**V. p. béllula** Rehd. & Wils., var. Lvs. 3–5 cm. long, similar to those of *V. flexuosa* var. *parvifolia*, but tomentose beneath. Intr. 1907.

Related species: **V. lanàta** Roxb. Young brts. tomentose: lvs. ovate, 8–15 cm. long, cordate, not lobed, tomentose beneath; panicle short; fls. small, the petals sometimes separating at the top: fr. purple, 5 mm. across. China, Liukiu Isls., Himal. Cult. 1902. Zone VII?

18. **V. Thunbérgii** Sieb. & Zucc. Slender vine; young brts. angled, rusty-tomentose: lvs. deeply 3–5-lobed, 6–10 or to 14 cm. across, cordate, the lobes broad-ovate with rounded sinuses or sometimes with short lobes and acute sinuses, shallowly and irregularly toothed, dark dull green above and glabrous, rusty tomentose beneath: panicle 5–8 cm. long: fr. black with purple bloom, 8–10 mm. across. Fl.vii–viii; fr.ix–x. B.M.8558(c). R.H.1880:210,t (c),279;1882:221. S.H.2:f.207c-d. (*V. Sieboldii* Hort.) Japan, China. Cult. 1879. Zone V. Lvs. turning crimson in fall.—**V. T. sinuàta** (Reg.) Rehd., var. Lvs. smaller, deeply 3–5-lobed with broad rounded sinuses and often lobulate lobes. Gt.22:t.765,f.1. N.K.12:t.5. Japan, China. Cult. 1873.

19. **V. cándicans** Engelm. MUSTANG G. Strong high climbing vine; young growth white-tomentose; diaphragm very thick: lvs. broad-ovate to ovate-reniform, 6–12 cm. broad, basal sinus broad and open or nearly truncate, indistinctly lobed or angled, on vigorous shoots deeply 3–5-lobed, sinuately and shallowly toothed, white-tomentose on both sides when young, later dark green and glabrous above, white tomentose beneath; petiole 3–6 cm. long, white-woolly: panicle 5–12 cm. long: fr. 1.5–2 cm. across, purple or light-colored, with tough skin and of disagreeable taste. Fl.vi; fr.vii–viii. Munson, l.c.t.8,37. S.H.2:f.207h-i(l). (*V. mustangensis* Buckl.) Okla. and Ark. to Tex. Cult. 1860. Zone V?

Related species or hybrid with *V. vulpina* is **V. Doaniàna** Munson. Internodes rather short; diaphragms thin: lvs. orbicular-ovate, 3-lobed at apex, coarsely toothed, bluish green, usually more or less floccose above, tomentose

beneath: panicle small: fr. 12–15 mm. across, black, bloomy, sweet. G.F.9:455.
Munson, l.c.9,37. Okla. to Tex. and N. Mex. Cult. 1890.—*V. c.* × *? rupestris;*
see *V. Champini* under No. 6.

20. **V. Labrúsca** L. Fox G. Strong growing vine; shoots with a tendril
or infl. at every joint, floccose when young: lvs. orbicular-ovate or broad-
ovate, 7–16 cm. wide, basal sinus usually open, undivided or slightly 3-lobed,
rarely deeply lobed with rounded sinuses, shallowly and irregularly toothed,
dark green above, tomentose beneath, at first whitish, later dun-colored or
rusty, thick and strongly veined: panicle little branched, 5–10 cm. long: fr.
globose, 1.5–2 cm. across, purple-black, sometimes red-brown or amber-green,
with thick skin and of sweetish musky taste. Fl.vi; fr.ix. Gr.G.2:t.161. B.B.
2:506. Munson, l.c.t.6,38. N. Eng. to Ga., Tenn. and S. Ind. Intr. 1656.
Zone V. The parent species of the greater part of the cult. American grapes;
also planted for its luxuriant growth and handsome lvs.—**V. L. alba** Prince,
var. Fr. whitish or greenish.

21. **V. Romanéti** Roman. Vigorous vine; young shoots floccose-pubescent
and glandular-bristly, purplish when young: lvs. orbicular-ovate, 10–25 cm.
wide, deeply cordate, obscurely 3-lobed, shallowly toothed, the teeth with
bristle-like tip, dark green above and slightly pubescent on the veins or
nearly glabrous, grayish tomentose beneath, pilose and sparingly glandular-
bristly on the veins, of firm texture; petiole floccose and glandular-bristly;
panicle longer than lvs.: fr. black, 1 cm. across, edible. Fl.v–vi; fr.vii–viii.
R.H.1890:444,t(c). J.L.28:f.98(l). (*V. rutilans* Carr.) China. Intr. 1881.
Zone VII? Young growth purple with bristly pubescence.

22. **V. Davídi** (Roman.) Foëx. Vigorous vine: shoots with straight or
slightly recurved prickles, glabrous: lvs. broad-ovate, 10–20 cm. long, cordate,
acuminate or acute, sinuate-denticulate and obscurely angled, lustrous dark
green and glabrous above, glaucous and nearly glabrous beneath except
glandular-bristly on veins and on the petiole: panicle usually longer than lf.:
fr. black, about 1.5 cm. across. Fl.vi–vii; fr.ix–xi. R.H.1885:55;1890:465.
J.L.28:f.17,83(h),85. (*V. Davidiana* Dipp., *V. armata* Diels & Gilg, *Spinovitis
D.* Roman.) China. Cult. 1885. Zone VI. The lvs. changing to brilliant red
in fall.—**V. D. cyanocárpa** (Gagnep.) Sarg., var. Less prickly: fr. bluish.
J.L.28:389,t(c),f.84(h),89. S.L.385(h). (*V. armata* var. *Veitchii* Veitch.)

23. **V. Piasézkii** Maxim. Young brts. and petioles rufous-pubescent and
glandular-bristly: lvs. variable on same branch, ovate and slightly or deeply
lobed, 4–8 cm. long, cordate with rounded sinus, or 3–5-foliolate, the middle
lft. stalked, rhombic-ovate or ovate, 5–12 cm. long, acute or short-acuminate,
cuneate, the lateral ones sessile and very oblique, smaller, coarsely and angularly toothed, glabrous above, with floccose tomentum beneath, persisting
at least on the veins: panicle to 15 cm. across: fr. about 1 cm. across, black,
bloomy. Fl.v–vi; fr.viii–ix. B.M.9565(c). J.L.28:f.99. S.H.2:f.206a-a¹. (*Par-
thenocissus sinensis* Diels & Gilg.) W. China. Intr. 1807. Zone VI?—**V. P.
Pagnúccii** (Roman.) Rehd., var. Brts. glabrous: lvs. glabrous or nearly glabrous beneath. R.H.1888:f.134;1889:204,t(c). S.H.2:f.206g-g¹. (*V. P.* Roman.,
Ampelovitis Davidii Carr., *Ampelopsis Davidiana* Mottet.) C. China. Cult.
1885. Zone (V).

24. **V. rotundifòlia** Michx. MUSCADINE. Vigorous vine to 30 m., with
close lenticellate bark, sometimes producing aërial roots; pith without diaphragms; tendrils simple; lvs. suborbicular to broad-ovate, 5–12 cm. wide,
acute or acuminate, with shallow basal sinus, coarsely toothed with triangular
teeth, glabrous and lustrous above, yellowish green and glabrous beneath or

slightly pubescent on veins: panicle dense, small: fr. globose, 1.5–2.5 cm. across, dull purple, not bloomy, with very tough skin, of musky flavor. Fl.vi; fr.viii–ix. B.B.2:509. Munson, l.c.t.35,39. (*Muscadinia r.* Small, *V. muscadina* and *V. verrucosa* Hort.) Del. to N. Fla., w. to Mo., Kans., Tex. and Mex. Intr. 1806. Zone V.

2. **AMPELÓPSIS** Michx. Deciduous shrubs, climbing by tendrils: brs. with close lenticellate bark and white pith: winter-buds small, with several outer scales: lvs. alternate, simple or compound, long-petioled: fls. perfect, small, greenish, in long-peduncled dichotomous cymes, opposite the lvs. or terminal, 5-merous, rarely 4-merous; calyx indistinct; petals expanding; stamens short: ovary 2-celled, adnate to a distinct cup-shaped disk, entire or crenulate at the margin; style slender: fr. a 1–4-seeded berry. (Greek *ampelos,* grape, and *opsis,* likeness.) About 20 species in N. Am., C. and E. Asia.

A. Lvs. simple, undivided or lobed.
  B. Lvs. whitish beneath, of firm texture.
    c. Fr. pale yellow or pale bluish or whitish: lvs. bright green and lustrous above.
                                       1. *A. humulifolia*
    cc. Fr. dark blue or violet: lvs. usually not or slightly lobed with shallow rounded mucronulate teeth, with a velvety sheen above when young...........2. *A. Bodinieri*
  BB. Lvs. green beneath, thin.
    c. Lvs. not or slightly lobed: fr. bluish or greenish.......................3. *A. cordata*
    cc. Lvs. 3–5-lobed, rarely scarcely lobed: fr. finally blue..........4. *A. brevipedunculata*
AA. Lvs. compound, sometimes partly simple.
  B. Lvs. 3–5-parted or digitate, sometimes partly simple and 3-lobed.
    c. Segments of lvs. serrate or pinnately lobed, lower lvs. sometimes simple.
      D. Middle lft. short-stalked: fr. dark blue........................5. *A. Delavayana*
      DD. Lfts. sessile, cuneate: fr. orange, sometimes bluish before maturity.
                                   6. *A. aconitifolia*
    cc. Segments of lvs. at least partly pinnate; rachis broadly winged and the pinnae articulate ....7. *A. japonica*
  BB. Lvs. pinnate or bipinnate; lfts. petioled.
    c. Lfts. 1–4 cm. long, coarsely toothed..................................8. *A. arborea*
    cc. Lfts. 5–10 cm. long, crenate-serrate................................9. *A. megalophylla*

1. **A. humulifòlia** Bge. Climbing shrub; brts. glabrous, rarely slightly villous: lvs. broad-ovate, 7–12 cm. long, truncate or cordate with a wide round sinus, 3–5-lobed with rounded sinuses, sometimes slightly lobed, with acute or acuminate coarsely dentate lobes, lustrous bright green and glabrous above, glaucescent and glabrous or pilose on the veins beneath; cymes loose; peduncles slender, longer than petioles: fr. usually few, 6–8 mm. across, usually pale yellow, with bluish cheek, or entirely pale yellow or pale blue, 1–2-seeded. Fl.vii; fr.x. R.H.1868:29. N.I.4:187. Gn.7:199. (*Cissus Davidiana* Carr., *Vitis D.* Nichols.) N. China. Cult. 1868. Zone V. With handsome foliage resembling that of a true Vitis.

2. **A. Bodinièri** (Lévl. & Vant.) Rehd. Climbing to 6 m.; young growth purplish; brts. glabrous: lvs. triangular-ovate and not lobed or broad-ovate and slightly lobed, 5–10 cm. long, subcordate or sometimes truncate at base, short-acuminate, the lateral lobes acute, shallowly and coarsely crenate-serrate, dark green and with a velvety sheen above when young, glaucescent below: cymes long-stalked, rather dense: fr. dark blue. Fl.v–vi; fr.x. ?J.L. 28:f.90. Veitch, Novelties, 1905:5(h,l);1908–9:29(h). (*A. micans* Rehd., *Vitis repens* Veitch, not Wight & Arn., *Vitis flexuosa Wilsonii* Veitch.) C. China. Intr. 1900. Zone V. Similar to the preceding.—**A. B. cinérea** (Gagnep.) Rehd., var. Lvs. grayish pubescent on both sides or only beneath, often deeply 3–5 lobed. Intr. 1907.

Related species: **A. vitifòlia** (Boiss.) Planch. Without tendrils; glabrous: lvs. broad-ovate, 4–7 cm. wide, truncate or subcordate at base, undivided or slightly 3-lobed, coarsely dentate with triangular acuminulate teeth: cymes

slender-stalked. S.H.2:f.213k-l(l). (*A. aegirophylla* Planch., *Vitis persica*
Boiss.) Persia and Turkest. to N. W. Himal. Cult. 1885. Zone VI?

3. **A. cordàta** Michx. High climbing, nearly glabrous: lvs. round-ovate,
5–12 cm. long, acuminate, subcordate or nearly truncate, not or indistinctly
3-lobed, acutely but shallowly serrate, glabrous or sparingly pubescent along
the veins and in the axils beneath; petiole shorter than blade, often pubescent: cymes slender-stalked, loose: fr. 6–8 mm. across, bluish or greenish
blue. Fl.VII; fr.IX–X. M.N.2:t.6(c). B.B.2:509. Ohio Nat. 1:t.1,f.1–2,3–4(h).
(*Vitis indivisa* Willd.) Va. to Ohio and Ill., Fla., Tex. and Mex. Cult. 1796.
Zone V.

4. **A. brevipedunculàta** (Maxim.) Trautv. Vigorous climber; young brts.
hairy: lvs. broad-ovate, 6–12 cm. long, acuminate, cordate, 3-lobed, the lateral
lobes broadly triangular-ovate, spreading, coarsely serrate, dark green above,
lighter beneath and pilose; petioles as long as blade or shorter, hairy: cymes
on pilose stalks 1.5–3.5 cm. long: fr. 6–8 mm. across, changing from pale lilac
to verdigris color and finally to bright blue, rarely whitish. Fl.VII–VIII; fr.
IX–X. B.C.1:277. S.H.2:f.213d²(l). Gn.85:557. (*A. heterophylla* var. *amurensis* Planch., *Vitis b.* Dipp.) N. E. Asia. Cult. 1870. Zone IV. Particularly
handsome in fall with its strikingly colored fr.—**A. b. Maximowíczii** (Reg.)
Rehd., var. Brts. and lvs. glabrous or glabrescent: lvs. more deeply 3–5-lobed,
with rounded sinuses; peduncles longer. B.M.5682(c). Gt.22:t.765,f.2. Gn.
87:541. S.H.2:f.213b-d(l). (*A. heterophylla* Sieb. & Zucc., not Bl., *Vitis h.*
Thunb., *V. h.* var. *humulifolia* Hook.) E. Asia. Cult. 1868.—**A. b. élegans**
(K. Koch) Rehd., f. Lvs. usually smaller, variegated with white and greenish
white and tinged pink while young. H.F.1866:103,t(c). Witte, Flora, t.74(c).
Gn.54:5. (*Vitis e.* K. Koch, *A. heterophylla* f. *e.* Voss, *A. heterophylla tricolor*
Hort.) Cult. 1855.—**A. b. citrulloìdes** (Lebas) Rehd., f. A form with more
deeply 5-lobed lvs., the middle lobe and sometimes the lateral lobes sinuately
lobed or toothed with wide sinuses and much constricted near base and
middle. (*A. c.* Lebas, *A. heterophylla c.* Hort.) Cult. 1875.

5. **A. Delavayàna** Planch. Vigorous vine; young growth hairy and usually
reddish: lvs. broad-ovate, 5–12 cm. long, cordate at base, acuminate, slightly
or deeply 3-lobed and partly 3- or rarely 5-parted, the middle segment elliptic-
oblong, cuneate, the lateral ones very oblique, usually semicordate, coarsely
and shallowly crenate-dentate with rounded mucronulate teeth, usually pubescent beneath; cymes on peduncles 1–3 cm. long, pubescent, rarely nearly
glabrous: fr. dark blue, small. Fl.VII; fr.X. J.L.28:f.102(l). Gn.89:272(l).
S.H.2:f.214g(l). (*Vitis D.* Franch., *A. heterophylla* var. *D.* Gagnep.) C. China.
Intr. 1900. Zone V. Occasionally brs. with all the lvs. simple occur and such
specimens are without frs. almost indistinguishable from *A. brevipedunculata*.

6. **A. aconitifòlia** Bge. Slender luxuriant vine; brts. glabrous: lvs. 5-
foliolate, long-stalked; lfts. lanceolate or rhombic-lanceolate, 4–7 cm. long,
pinnately lobed, often divided nearly to the midrib, with rather narrow
toothed or entire lobes, green beneath and glabrous or pilose on the veins:
cymes glabrous, on peduncles 2–5 cm. long; fr. about 6 mm. across; orange
or yellow when fully ripe, sometimes bluish before maturity. Fl.VIII; fr.IX–X.
R.H.1868:10;1883:318. N.T.1:66. Gn.54:427(h, as *Vitis serjaniaefolia*). J.L.
28:f.87. N.I.1:66. (*Vitis a.* Hance, *A. dissecta* Carr. *A. a.* var. *dissecta*
Koehne.) N. China. Cult. 1868. Zone IV. Very graceful vine.—**A. a. glabra**
Diels, var. Lvs. usually 3-parted; the lower lvs. often only 3-lobed; segments
usually rhombic, coarsely toothed and lobed, rarely pinnatifid. R.H.1867:451.
J.L.28:87(form with narrow segments). (*A. palmiloba* Carr., *A. a.* var. *p.*

obovate, 3–6 cm. long, acuminate, toothed usually only above the middle, velvety green above and variegated with white along the veins at least when young, purplish beneath and glabrous, or pubescent only on the midrib: fls. in narrow panicles 8–15 cm. long: fr. dark blue, usually 3-seeded. Fl.vii; fr.x. G.C.38:309;39:354. Gn.69:341. J.L.28:f.92(l). R.H.1907:211. S.L.249 (h). (*V. H.* Hemsl.) C. China. Intr. about 1895. Zone VII? The handsome coloring of the lvs. is more pronounced in a partly shaded position; it disappears in the full sun.

Closely related species: **P. Thomsòni** (M. A. Laws.) Planch. Young brts. and lvs. purplish when young; tendrils with 3–5 brs.: lfts. long-acuminate, glabrous or slightly pubescent on the midrib beneath: fls. in slender-stalked cymes opposite the lf.: fr. black. Gn.63:203. J.L.28:f.100. (*P. Henryana* var. *glaucescens* Diels & Gilg, *Vitis T.* M. A. Laws., *Ampelopsis T.* Hort.) Himal., C. China. Intr. 1900. Zone VII?

4. **P. tricuspidàta** (Sieb. & Zucc.) Planch. Boston Ivy. High climbing; tendrils short, much-branched: lvs. slender-stalked, broad-ovate, 10–20 cm. wide, 3-lobed with acuminate coarsely serrate lobes, or, chiefly on young plants and basal shoots, smaller and partly 3-foliolate with stalked lfts., the middle one obovate, the lateral ones obliquely broad-ovate, partly simple and broad-ovate, coarsely serrate and not or slightly lobed, glabrous and lustrous above, pubescent on the veins beneath; cymes usually on short 2-lvd. brts., narrow and somewhat elongated: fr. bluish black, bloomy, 6–8 mm. across. Fls.vi–vii; fr.ix–x. B.M.8287(c). G.C.II.14:664. R.H.1877:176. B.C. 5:2479. A.G.15:94(h). S.L.248(h). (*Ampelopsis t.* Sieb. & Zucc., *A. Veitchii robusta* Hort., *A. Hoggii* Hort., *A. japonica* Hort., *Vitis inconstans* Miq.— Japanese Ivy.) Japan, C. China. Intr. 1862. Zone IV. Clinging firmly to walls and forming a dense cover; the lustrous lvs. stand dust and smoke well and turn to a brilliant scarlet and orange in fall.—**P. t. Veìtchii** (Graebn.) Rehd., var. Lvs. smaller, crenate-serrate, purple while young, ovate and simple or 3-foliolate; lfts. with only 1–3 coarse teeth on each side, the lateral ones usually entire inside. B.H.27:224,t(c). R.H.1877:176. M.G.7: 8(h). (*Ampelopsis V.* Hort.) Juvenile form.—**P. t. purpúrea** (Rehd.) Rehd., var. A form of the preceding with dark purple lvs. not changing to green. (*Ampelopsis Veitchii p.* and *atropurpurea* Hort.) Cult. 1889.—**P. t. Lòwii** (Low) Rehd., var. Lvs. small, 2–3 cm. long, simple and often broader than long, incisely dentate and almost palmately lobed with very unequal teeth, or 3-foliolate, apple-green, purplish when young. Gn.71:516. A.F.30:1238. M.G.23:261. R.H.1917:272(h). (*A. L.* Low.) Cult. 1908.

Related species: **P. himalayàna** (Royle) Planch. Lvs. 3-foliolate; lfts. 3, short-stalked, the middle one obovate to ovate or oblong-ovate, the lateral ones obliquely ovate and rounded or semicordate at base, coarsely serrate, glaucous and nearly glabrous beneath; cymes about as long as lf. Collett, Pl. Simla, f.31. S.H.2:f.211k(l). (*Vitis h.* Brandis, *V. semicordata* var. *h.* Hance, *Ampelopsis h.* Royle.) Himal. Cult. 1894. Zone VII?—**P. h. rubrifòlia** (Lévl. & Vant.) Gagnep., var. Lfts. smaller and broader, purplish while young: cymes smaller. (*Vitis r.* Lévl. & Vaniot.) W. China. Intr. 1907. Zone VII?—Closely related to the preceding is **P. semicordàta** (Wall.) Planch. Young shoots and lfts. beneath pilose; lfts. smaller. (*V. s.* Wall.) Himal. Intr. before 1914. Zone VII?

4. **TETRASTÍGMA** Planch. Evergreen or deciduous climbing shrubs: tendrils with adhesive tips or twining: lvs. alternate, digitate or pedate; lfts. 3–5, sometimes reduced to 1: fls. polygamo-dioecious, 4-merous, in axillary cymes or umbels; petals expanding; disk adnate to base of ovary; stigma sessile, 4-lobed or 4-parted: fr. 2–4-seeded; seeds ovoid-globose, sulcate on

the ventral side. (Greek *tetra*, four, and *stigma;* referring to the 4-lobed stigma.) About 40 species in trop. and subtrop. Asia.

T. obtéctum (M. A. Laws.) Planch. Evergreen or half-evergreen climbing shrub with disciferous tendrils; brts. pilose: lfts. long-petioled, digitate; lfts. 5, sessile, cuneate-obovate or elliptic, 1.5–3.5 cm. long, acute, remotely crenate-serrate with mucronate teeth, glabrous or pubescent (var. **pilòsum** Gagnep.) beneath: fls. greenish, small, in slender-stalked umbels; pedicels slender: fr. obovoid, 6 mm. long. Fl.vi–viii; fr.x. (*Vitis obtecta* Wall. ex Laws.) Himal., C. and W. China. Intr. 1904? Zone VII?

Related species: **T. serrulàtum** (Roxb.) Planch. Glabrous: lvs. pedate; lfts. 5 or 3, ovate to elliptic-lanceolate, 1.5–6 cm. long, fls. in compound cymes: fr. globose, black. S.H.2:f.211b,212a-b. (*Vitis capreolata* Don, *Cissus serrulata* Roxb.) Himal. Cult. 1880. Zone VII?

5. CAYRÀTIA Juss. Climbing shrubs, rarely herbaceous; tendrils usually branched: lvs. alternate, 3-foliolate or 5–9-foliolate and pedate, the lfts. stalked: fls. perfect, 4-merous, in axillary, corymbose or umbellate infl.; calyx indistinct; petals valvate, spreading; disk 4-lobed, small, thin, adnate to the ovary; style filiform: fr. 2–4-seeded; seed with 1 or 2 deep ventral grooves. (The latinized Indian name.) Syn. *Columella* Lour., not *Columellia* Ruiz & Pav. About 16 species in e. and trop. Asia.

C. oligocárpa (Lévl. & Vant.) Gagnep. To 3 m. long; young brts., petioles and peduncles finely grayish pubescent; tendrils forked: lvs. long-petioled, pedate; lfts. 5, the middle one on a petiolule 2–4 cm. long, elliptic-ovate, 6–15 cm. long, acuminate, cuneate, the lateral ones smaller and broader and on much shorter stalks, crenate-dentate with short and broad mucronulate teeth, glabrous or nearly so above except on midrib and veins, grayish pubescent on the veins beneath when young, membranous: peduncle 5–8 cm. long; corymb loose, 6–12 cm. across; anthers orbicular: fr. globose, 6–8 mm. across, yellow, finally black: seeds 3–4, with 2 deep ventral grooves. Fl.vi; fr.ix–x. (*Vitis o.* Lévl. & Vant., *Columella o.* (Lévl. & Vant.) Rehd., *Cissus o.* Bailey.) C. and S. China. Intr. 1907. Zone VII.

The related **C. japónica** (Thunb.) Gagnep. (*Cissus j.* Willd.) is herbaceous; it has smaller and broader lfts., a rather dense infl. and elliptic-oblong anthers.

6. CÍSSUS L. Deciduous or evergreen shrubs climbing by tendrils, rarely herbs with usually tuberous roots; stems and lvs. more or less fleshy: lvs. alternate, simple or compound; lfts. sessile: fls. perfect or polygamo-monoecious, 4-merous, in usually umbel-like cymes, opposite the lf. or terminal; petals expanding; disk cupular, 4-lobed or of 4 distinct glands; style filiform, stigma small: fr. 1–2-seeded. (Greek *kissos*, ivy.) About 250 species in trop. and subtrop. countries.

C. incìsa (Torr. & Gr.) Desmoul. MARINE IVY. Stem to 10 m., warty fleshy; glabrous: lvs. 3-parted or 3-foliolate; lfts. or segments ovate or obovate, 1.5–2.5 cm. long, cuneate, coarsely dentate and often lobed: fls. in umbellike peduncled cymes: fr. obovoid, about 8 mm. long, black, on recurved pedicels. Fl.vi–viii; fr.x. B.B.2:210. (*Vitis i.* Nutt. ex Torr. & Gr., not Jacq.) Mo. and Kans. to Ariz., Tex. and Fla. Intr. before 1876. Zone VII?

Fam. 61. TILIACEAE Juss. LINDEN FAMILY

Trees, shrubs or herbs, often with stellate or fascicled pubescence: lvs. alternate, rarely opposite, entire or lobed, stipulate: fls. perfect, regular; sepals 5, rarely 3 or 4, free or connate, usually valvate; petals as many, convolute, valvate or imbricate, rarely wanting; stamens 10 or usually more, hypogynous; filaments distinct or connate only at base; anthers 4-celled, opening by slits or pores; staminodes sometimes present; ovary superior, 2–10-celled; cells with 1 to several ovules; style 1, stigma radiate: fr. a caps. or indehiscent and either nut-like or drupaceous, rarely a berry or separating into drupelets; seed albuminous.—About 35 genera and 300 species in trop., subtrop. and temp. regions.

A. Peduncle with a large adnate, usually oblong bract; ovary sessile; lvs. slender-petioled.
　　　　　　　　　　　　　　　　　　　　　　　　　　　　　　　　　　　　　1. *Tilia*
AA. Peduncle without bract; ovary and stamens borne on an androgynophore: lvs. short-petioled ....2. *Grewia*

1. **TÍLIA** L. LINDEN. Deciduous trees, mostly with fascicled hairs; winter-buds large, obtuse, with few or several scales; terminal bud wanting: lvs. alternate, 2-ranked, slender-petioled, usually cordate or truncate and oblique at base, serrate; stipules caducous: fls. yellowish or whitish, fragrant, in usually drooping cymes; peduncle adnate, usually about ½ to a large ligulate bract; sepals 5, distinct; petals 5, imbricate, often with a staminode opposite each petal; stamens many, distinct or in 5 fascicles opposite the petals; filaments often forked at apex; ovary 5-celled, the carpels opposite the sepals; cells 2-ovuled; style slender, with 5-lobed stigma: fr. globose or ovoid, nutlike, with usually 1–3 seeds; cotyledons palmately 5-lobed. (Ancient Latin name.) LIME-TREE, WHITEWOOD, BASSWOOD. About 30 species in the temp. regions of the n. hemisphere, in N. Am. s. to Mex., but none in W. N. Am.; in Asia s. to C. China and S. Japan.

A. Lvs. glabrous beneath at maturity or pubescent with simple hairs.
　B. Lvs. pubescent beneath and often above, rarely glabrescent: fls. usually 3, without staminodes ....1. *T. platyphyllos*
　BB. Lvs. glabrous beneath except axillary tufts of hairs.
　　C. Fls. without staminodes.
　　　D. Lvs. green or sometimes glaucescent beneath; tertiary veins prominent.
　　　　E. Lvs. lustrous and dark green above, with acuminate teeth.
　　　　　F. Lvs. with aristate teeth: fr. obtuse at ends...................2. *T. dasystyla*
　　　　　FF. Lvs. with acuminate teeth: fr. narrowed at ends...............3. *T. euchlora*
　　　　EE. Lvs. dull green above, sometimes slightly glaucescent beneath, serrate with short acute teeth..4. *T. europaea*
　　　DD. Lvs. glaucous beneath; tertiary veins not prominent.................5. *T. cordata*
　　CC. Fls. with staminodes.
　　　D. Lvs. glaucous or glaucescent beneath, 4–8 cm. long.
　　　　E. Lvs. closely serrate, not lobed.....................................6. *T. japonica*
　　　　EE. Lvs. coarsely serrate and usually 3-lobed........................7. *T. mongolica*
　　　DD. Lvs. green or sometimes glaucescent beneath, 8–15 cm. long........8. *T. americana*
AA. Lvs. with fascicled or stellate, rarely simple pubescence beneath: fls. with staminodes.
　B. Brts. and petioles glabrous.
　　C. Lvs. thinly grayish tomentose or grayish pubescent beneath, ovate or broad-ovate.
　　　D. Lvs. without axillary tufts of hairs beneath, orbicular-ovate........9. *T. Moltkei*
　　　DD. Lvs. with axillary tufts of hairs, ovate............................10. *T. neglecta*
　CC. Lvs. closely and densely tomentose.
　　D. Lvs. oblong-ovate or ovate, sharply serrate, 8–18 cm. long: fr. usually short-ellipsoid, smooth.
　　　E. Petioles to 4 cm. long, tomentum of lf. often brownish; brts. slender.
　　　　　　　　　　　　　　　　　　　　　　　　　　　　　11. *T. heterophylla*
　　　EE. Petiole to 7 cm. long; tomentum of lf. always white; brts. stout.
　　　　　　　　　　　　　　　　　　　　　　　　　　　　　12. *T. monticola*
　　DD. Lvs. orbicular-ovate, 5–10 cm. long, sinuately serrate: fr. globose, tuberculate.
　　　　　　　　　　　　　　　　　　　　　　　　　　　　　13. *T. Oliveri*
　BB. Brts. pubescent or tomentose, at least when young (or glabrate and lvs. denticulate); petioles pubescent.
　　C. Lvs. denticulate or with bristle-like teeth.
　　　D. Lvs. white-tomentose, minutely denticulate, entire below the middle..14. *T. Tuan*
　　　DD. Lvs. brownish-tomentose beneath, with bristle-like teeth........15. *T. Henryana*
　　CC. Lvs. serrate.
　　　D. Lvs. orbicular-ovate.
　　　　E. Tomentum white or grayish white, close: lvs. finely serrate.
　　　　　F. Petiole shorter than half the blade: fr. slightly 5-angled: habit upright.
　　　　　　　　　　　　　　　　　　　　　　　　　　　　　16. *T. tomentosa*
　　　　　FF. Petiole longer than half the blade: fr. 5-furrowed; habit pendulous.
　　　　　　　　　　　　　　　　　　　　　　　　　　　　　17. *T. petiolaris*

EE. Tomentum at least of young brts., petioles and veins beneath brownish: lvs.
    coarsely serrate with long-pointed teeth.
    F. Lvs. without axillary tufts of hairs beneath..............18. *T. mandshurica*
    FF. Lvs. with axillary tufts of hairs beneath..............19. *T. Maximowicziana*
DD. Lvs. triangular-ovate or ovate, coarsely and irregularly serrate with short-pointed
    teeth, often glabrescent with age................................20. *T. Miqueliana*

1. **T. platyphýllos** Scop. LARGE-LEAVED L. Tree to 40 m.; young brts.
pubescent, rarely glabrous: lvs. roundish-ovate, 6–12 cm. long, abruptly
acuminate, obliquely cordate, sharply and regularly serrate, dull and short-
pubescent or glabrous above, light green and pubescent beneath, especially
on the veins, rarely nearly glabrous; petiole pubescent 1.5–5 cm. long: fls.
yellowish white, in pendent 3-, rarely 4–6-fld. cymes; floral bract 5–12 cm.
long, pubescent on midrib below; stamens longer than petals; fr. subglobose
to pyriform, 8–10 mm. long, tomentose, 5-ribbed, hard-shelled. Fl.vi; fr.
IX–X. R.I.6:t.316–18(c)   H.W.3:24,25(h),t.42(c).   G.F.2:256.   M.A.t.74(h).
M.D.1917:t.6(h). (*T. grandifolia* Ehrh., *T. europaea* L., in part, *T. officinarum*
Crantz, in part.) Eu. Zone III. Planted in Eu. for centuries; the earliest
Linden to bloom; very variable, with numerous spontaneous forms; the following are often cult.—**T. p. laciniàta** (Loud.) K. Koch, var. Smaller tree
with deeply and irregularly lobed lvs., often cut to the midrib, with narrow
divisions. S.H.2:f.253h-h¹. M.D.1920:67;1919:t.17(h). G.W.15:662(h). (*T.
p. aspleniifolia* Kirchn., *T. europaea l.* Loud., *T. grandifolia filicifolia* Hort.)
—**T. p. rúbra** (West.) Rehd., var. Brts. red. (*T. p.* var. *corallina* Hartw. &
Ruempl.)—**T. p. aùrea** (Loud.) Kirchn. Brts. bright yellow. (*T. grandifolia*
var. *aurantia* Hort.)—**T. p. fastigiàta** Rehd., f. Of narrow pyramidal habit.
M.G.13:161(h). M.D.14:210(h). (*T. grandifolia pyramidalis* Beiss., not *T. p.
pyramidalis* Schneid.)—**T. p. vitifòlia** (Host) Simonk., var. Lvs. slightly
3-lobed, less pubescent. R.I.6:t.319(c). M.D.1920:67.

    T. p. × *americana* = T. flaccida Host. Lvs. slightly pilose on veins beneath,
serrate with acute or subacuminate teeth, axils of secondary veins bearded;
cymes 3-fld.; stamens as long as petals. S.H.2:f.254a-b,256e-f. (*T. carlsruhensis*
Simonk., *T. praecox* A. Br., not Host.)—*T. p.* × *cordata;* see No. 4.

2. **T. dasýstyla** Stev. Tree to 30 m.; brts. glabrous, red: lvs. firm,
roundish-ovate, 8–14 cm. long, abruptly acuminate, obliquely cordate, sharply
serrate with aristate teeth, glabrous, lustrous dark green above, bright green
and with axillary tufts of whitish hairs beneath: infl. 3–7-fld.; style pubescent
or glabrous: fr. globose-ovoid, about 1 cm. long, slightly 5-ribbed. S.H.2:254
e-f,255e. (*T. rubra* Stev., not DC., *T. begonifolia* Stev., *T. caucasica* Rupr.,
'T. multiflora Ledeb.) S. e. Eu., Cauc. to n. Persia. Cult. 1880. Zone V.

3. × **T. euchlòra** K. Koch (?*T. cordata* × *dasystyla*). Tree to 20 m.;
brts. often slightly pendulous, glabrous when young: lvs. roundish-ovate, 5–10
cm. long, abruptly short-acuminate, obliquely cordate, finely and sharply
serrate with mucronate teeth, lustrous dark green and glabrous above, pale
green and glabrous beneath, except axillary tufts of brown hairs; petiole glabrous, 3–5 cm. long: fls. 3–7, in pendulous cymes; floral bract linear-oblong,
glabrous, 5–8 cm. long; style pubescent near base: fr. short-ellipsoidal, narrowed at ends, slightly 5-ribbed, tomentose. Fl.vii. S.H.2:f.252n-o. M.D.
1920:67. (*T. dasystylu* of Kirchn., not Stev., *T. rubra* var. *e.* Dipp.) Intr.
about 1860. Zone V. One of the handsomest Lindens with smooth glossy lvs.
and of good habit; a valuable avenue tree.

    T. e. × *petiolaris;* see under No. 17.

4. × **T. europaèa** L. (*T. cordata* × *platyphyllos*). COMMON L. Tree to
40 m.; brts. glabrous: lvs. broad-ovate, 6–10 cm. long, short-acuminate, obliquely cordate or nearly truncate, sharply serrate, dark green and glabrous

above, bright green beneath and glabrous except axillary tufts of hairs; petiole 3–5 cm. long; fls. 5–10 in pendulous cymes 7–8 cm. long: fr. subglobose or short-oval, faintly ribbed, tomentose, hard-shelled. Fl.vi–vii. H.A.3:t. 47(c). R.I.6:t.313. G.F.2:256. M.G.19:188(h),189(h). Am. For. 21:782,t(h); 26:214(h). (*T. intermedia* DC., *T. vulgaris* Hayne.) Eu. Zone III. Often planted as street tree.—**T. e. pállida** Reichenb., var. Lvs. larger, yellowish to bluish green beneath. R.I.6:t.315(c). M.G.39:274(h). (*T. vulgaris* var. *p.* Sarg., *T. p.* Simonk.)—**T. e. péndula** Rehd., f. Brs. pendulous. (*T. Beaumontia pendula* Hort.)

5. **T. cordàta** Mill. SMALL-LEAVED EUROPEAN L. Tree to 30 m.; brts. glabrous or slightly pubescent at first: lvs. suborbicular, 3–6 cm. long, sometimes broader than long, abruptly acuminate, cordate, sharply and rather finely serrate, dark green and glabrous and somewhat lustrous above, glaucous or glaucescent and glabrous beneath except axillary tufts of brown hairs; petiole slender, 1.5–3 cm. long: fls. yellowish white, fragrant, 5–7 in pendent or nearly upright cymes; stamens about as long as petals; floral bract 3.5–8 cm. long, glabrous: fr. globose, slightly or not ribbed, thin-shelled. Fl.vii. R.I.6:t.311, 312(c). H.W.3:21,22(h),t.41(c). G.F.2:257. M.G.1904:188(h). G.W.1914:352 (h);494(h). (*T. ulmifolia* Scop., *T. parvifolia* Ehrh., *T. microphylla* Vent., *T. silvestris* Desf., *T. europaea* L. in part.) Eu. Zone III. Planted as shade tree since ancient times.—**T. c. pyramidàlis** Wittm., var. Of narrow pyramidal habit. Gt.45:180(h).

T. c. × *americana* = **T. flavéscens** A. Br. Lvs. 6–8 cm. long, with rather coarse acuminate teeth, glabrous and green beneath; cymes many-fld.; staminodes partly present; stamens shorter than petals. S.H.2:252p-q(l).—Here belongs also *T. floribunda* A. Br. with longer and looser cymes, and *T. Spaethii* Spaeth with larger lvs.—*T. c.* × *dasystyla;* see No. 3.

A related species is **T. amurénsis** Rupr. Bark thin, scaly: lvs. broad-ovate, coarsely serrate with acuminate teeth: fls. 3–20, sometimes with incompletely developed staminodes: fr. subglobose. N.K.12:t.7. I.S.t.177. S.H.2:f.250e-g. (*T. cordata* var. *mandshurica* Maxim., *T. Maximowiczii* Bak.) Manch., Korea. Cult. 1909. Zone V.

6. **T. japónica** (Miq.) Simonk. JAPANESE L. Tree to 20 m., similar to *T. cordata;* young brts. slightly pubescent at first: lvs. suborbicular, 5–8 cm. long, abruptly acuminate, cordate, sharply serrate, light bluish green and pubescent on the veins beneath when young, with axillary tufts of hairs; petiole 2.5–5 cm. long: fls. in 7–40-fld. pendulous cymes; bract stalked: fr. short-ellipsoidal, not ribbed, thin-shelled. Fl.vii. S.I.1:t.72(c). I.S.t.179. M.K. t.76(c). (*T. cordata* var. *j.* Miq.) Japan. Intr. 1875. Zone V.

Related species: **T. insulàris** Nakai. Lvs. broad-ovate, 6–8 cm. long, coarsely serrate, with whitish axillary tufts beneath, thickish: cyme 4.5–7 cm. across; fls. 12–14 mm. across. N.T.12:43(b),t.10. Korea: Dagelet Isl. Intr. 1919. Zone V.—**T. paucicostàta** Maxim. Lvs. ovate, 5–8 cm. long, short-acuminate, obliquely truncate or subcordate at base, rather coarsely toothed, light or slightly bluish green beneath, with axillary tufts of hairs; cymes 7–15-fld.: fr. globose or pyriform, slightly ribbed. S.H.2:f.250n-o. N. and C. China. Intr. 1901. Zone V.—**T. kiusiàna** Mak. & Shiras. Lvs. oblong-ovate, 3–5 cm. long, obliquely rounded or subcordate at base, light green beneath, bearded in the axils; petiole 5–10 mm. long: fls. small, in 20–35-fld. pendulous cymes: fr. globose. S.I.2:t.50(c). Bull. Coll. Agric. Tokyo, 4,2:t.17. S.H.2:f.250a-b. Japan. Intr. 1930. Zone VII?

7. **T. mongòlica** Maxim. MONGOLIAN L. Tree to 10 m.; young brts. glabrous, reddish: lvs. reddish when unfolding, suborbicular to ovate, 4–7 cm. long, coarsely serrate and often 3-lobed, dark green and lustrous above, glaucescent and glabrous beneath without or with small axillary tufts of hairs; petiole reddish, 2–3 cm. long: cyme 6–20-fld.; bract stalked: fr. sub-

globose, thick-walled. Fl.vɪɪ. S.T.1:t.61. I.S.t.180. R.H.1902:476–8. S.H.2:
f.249g-h,250c-d. Mongolia, China. Intr. 1880. Zone IV. Small graceful tree.

8. T. americàna L. AMERICAN L. Tree to 40 m.; brts. glabrous, green:
lvs. broad-ovate, 10–20 cm. long, abruptly acuminate, cordate to truncate at
base, coarsely serrate with long-pointed teeth, light green beneath, with tufts
of hairs in the axils of the lateral veins, wanting at base; petiole 3–5 cm. long:
fls. about 1.5 cm. across, in pendulous 6–15-fld. slender-branched cymes; floral
bract usually stalked, tapering toward the base; stamens shorter than petals:
fr. ellipsoid to subglobose, thick-shelled, without ribs. Fl.vɪɪ. G.O.t.45(c).
S.S.1:t.24. Mn.6:153. F.L.5:136,t(h). M.G.31:357(h). (*T. glabra* Vent., *T.
nigra* Borkh.) Can. to Va. and Ala., w. to N. D., Kans. and Tex. Intr. 1752.
Zone II. Frequently planted as an avenue tree.—**T. a. macrophýlla** (Bayer)
V. Engl., f. Lvs. very large and broad, 12–20 cm. long. (*T. nigra* var. *m.*
Bayer, *T. mississippiensis* Hort., in part, *T. laxiflora* Hort., in part.)—**T. a.
dentàta** (Kirchn.) Rehd., f. Lvs. large, coarsely and irregularly, often nearly
doubly dentate. M.G.39:274(h). (*T. longifolia d.* Kirchn., *T. am.* f. *megalo-
donta* V. Engl.)—**T. a. ampelophýlla** V. Engl., f. Lvs. large, lobed and
coarsely and irregularly toothed with acuminate teeth. (*T. inciso-dentata*
Hort., *T. longifolia dentata* Hort., in part.)—**T. a. fastigiàta** (Slavin) Rehd.,
f. Narrow pyramidal form with ascending brs.

T. a. × *platyphyllos;* see under No. 1.—*T. a.* × *cordata;* see under No. 5.—
T. a. × *petiolaris;* see No. 9.

Closely related species: **T. floridàna** (V. Engl.) Small. Tree to 18 m.: lvs.
tomentose or pubescent beneath when unfolding, soon glabrous, without or with
very small axillary tufts and green or glaucescent beneath: fls. in pubescent few-
fld. rather compact cymes; floral bract subsessile: fr. rusty-tomentose. S.M.738.
S.H.2:f.256i-k. N. C. to Fla., w. to Mo., Okla. and e. Tex. Cult. 1915. Zone V.

9. × T. Móltkei Spaeth (*T. americana* × *petiolaris*). Tree of vigorous
growth with more or less pendent brs.; brts. glabrous or slightly pubescent at
first: winter-buds glabrous or pubescent near apex: lvs. orbicular-ovate, 10–18
cm. long, similar to those of *T. americana* slightly grayish tomentose beneath,
often pilose on veins, without axillary tufts: petiole 5–6 cm. long: cymes
5–8-fld., dense; pedicels tomentulose: fr. subglobose or depressed-globose and
faintly furrowed. Fl.vɪɪ. E.H.7:t.407,f.11. Gt.84:197. S.H.2:f.256g(l). (*T.
spectabilis* Dipp., not Host, *T. Blechiana* Hort., partly, *T. alba spectabilis*
Hort.) Orig. before 1880. Possibly partly *T. americana* × *tomentosa*.

10. T. neglécta Spach. Tree to 30 m.; brts. glabrous, red: lvs. broad-ovate
or ovate, 10–20 cm. long, acuminate, obliquely cordate or truncate, coarsely
serrate with apiculate teeth pointing forward, lustrous and glabrous above,
greenish or grayish and loosely stellate-pubescent beneath, with scattered
mostly simple hairs on the veins, often tinged brownish; petiole glabrous,
3–6 cm. long: cymes rather loose, 5–15-fld.; pedicels pubescent or nearly glabrous; bracts glabrous, usually decurrent nearly to base: fr. subglobose to
ellipsoid, about 8 mm. across, rarely slightly angled. Fl.vɪɪ. S.M.740. (*T.
Michauxii* Sarg., not Nutt., *T. nigra vestita* A. Br., *T. pubescens* Hort., not
Vent.) Can. to N. C., w. to Minn. and Mo. Cult. 1830. Zone IV.

11. T. heterophýlla Vent. Large tree; brts. glabrous, reddish or yellowish
brown: lvs. ovate, 8–13 cm. long, gradually acuminate, obliquely truncate
or rarely subcordate at base, finely serrate with aristate teeth, glabrous above
and lustrous at maturity, beneath with close thick white tomentum or often
brownish on the upper lvs., and with small tufts of reddish brown hairs;
petiole glabrous, 3–4 cm. long: cymes 10–20-fld., 6–8 cm. long, pubescent

except the glabrous peduncle; bract tomentose beneath at first: fr. ellipsoid, 8 mm. long, apiculate, rusty-tomentose. Fl.vii. S.M.745. W. Va. to n. Fla., Ala. and Ind. Cult. 1755. Zone V.—**T. h. Michaùxii** (Nutt.) Sarg., var. Brts. red-brown: lvs. ovate to ovate-oblong, 8–15 cm. long, acute or abruptly acuminate, cordate or rarely obliquely truncate, coarsely serrate, with short white or grayish tomentum beneath; peduncle pubescent at first: fr. subglobose, 6–8 mm. across. (*T. M. Nutt.*) S.M.746. N. Y. to Ohio, Ind., Ark., Ala. and Ga. Cult. 1800. Zone V. With large lvs. white beneath.

12. **T. montícola** Sarg. Tree to 20 m.; brts. glabrous, stout, usually bright red during the first year; winter-buds bloomy: lvs. ovate to ovate-oblong, 10–18 cm. long, gradually acuminate, obliquely truncate or cordate, finely serrate with straight or incurved teeth, dark green and lustrous above, densely white-tomentose beneath, thin: petiole 3–7 cm. long, glabrous: fls. 8–10 mm. long, in usually 7–10-fld. glabrous cymes; pedicels sparingly pubescent: fr. ellipsoid, 6–8 mm. long, rusty-tomentose. Fl.vii. S.M.747. (*T. heterophylla* Sarg., in part, not Vent.) Mts. of Va., Tenn. and N. C. Cult. 1888. Zone V.

13. **T. Olíveri** Szysz. Tree to 15 m.; young brts. glabrous, reddish brown: lvs. broad-ovate or orbicular-ovate, 7–10 cm. long, short-acuminate, obliquely cordate or truncate at base, sinuately denticulate with short gland-tipped teeth, dark green and glabrous above, white-tomentose beneath without axillary tufts; petiole glabrous, 3–5 cm. long: fls. small, in pendulous 7–20-fld. cymes; pedicels short, thickened; floral bract sessile: fr. globose, apiculate, about 8 mm. long, warty, thick-shelled. Fl.vi. I.S.t.184. R.H.1924:188. S.H.2:f.259a-b(l). (*T. pendula* Engl.) C. China. Intr. 1900. Zone V.

14. **T. Tuan** Szysz. Tree to 15 m.; brts. glabrous or pubescent at first: lvs. broad-ovate to ovate, 6–13 cm. long, acuminate, obliquely truncate or subcordate, remotely and minutely denticulate, usually entire below the middle, glabrous above, densely gray-tomentose beneath, with small axillary tufts; petiole pubescent, 3–6 cm. long: fls. in 15–20-fld. cymes; floral bract stellate-pubescent: fr. subglobose, about 8 mm. across, warty, thick-shelled. Fl.vii. H.I.20:1926. C.C.245. I.S.t.191. C. China. Intr. 1901. Zone V.—**T. T. chinénsis** Rehd. & Wils. Brts. tomentose; winter-buds densely pubescent: lvs. ovate to oblong-ovate. Intr. 1907.

15. **T. Henryàna** Szysz. Tree to 15 m.; brts. stellate-pubescent at first, soon glabrous: lvs. broad-ovate to ovate, 5–12 cm. long, short-acuminate, obliquely cordate or truncate, denticulate with bristly teeth, midrib and veins pubescent above, brownish stellate-pubescent beneath with axillary tufts of hairs; petiole 2–4 cm. long, pubescent: fls. whitish, 20 or more in pendulous cymes; floral bract stellate-pubescent: fr. short-ellipsoid, 5-ribbed. Fl.vii–viii. H.I.20:1927. I.S.t.185. C. China. Intr. 1901. Zone V.—**T. H. subglábra** V. Engl., var. Lvs. nearly glabrous beneath.

16. **T. tomentòsa** Moench. Silver L. Tree to 30 m., with upright brs.; young brts. tomentose: lvs. suborbicular, 5–10 cm. long, abruptly acuminate, cordate to nearly truncate at base, sharply and sometimes doubly serrate or even slightly lobulate, dark green and slightly pubescent above at first, white-tomentose beneath; petiole 2–3.5 cm. long, tomentose: fls. 7–10 in pendulous cymes: fr. ovoid, 8–10 mm. long, minutely warty and slightly 5-angled. Fl. vii–viii. R.I.6:t.324(c). H.W.3:26,t.43(c). F.E.14:1154,t(h). M.G.19:189(h). E.H.7:t.373(h). (*T. alba* Ait., *T. argentea* DC., *T. alba pyramidalis* Hort.) S. E. Eu., W. Asia. Intr. 1767. Zone IV. Handsome tree of broad-pyramidal habit.

T. t. × *cordata* = **T. Juranyàna** Simonk. Lvs. lustrous above, with scattered stellate hairs beneath, serrate with mucronate teeth: fr. ovoid, slightly ribbed. Hungary. Cult. ? Zone V.

17. **T. petiolàris** DC. PENDENT SILVER L. Tree to 25 m., with pendent brs.; young brts. tomentose: lvs. orbicular-ovate, 5–11 cm. long, acuminate, obliquely cordate or nearly truncate at base, regularly and sharply serrate, slightly pubescent above, white-tomentose beneath; petiole 3–6 cm. long: fls. whitish, 3–10 in pendulous tomentose cymes: fr. depressed-globose, 8 mm. across, warty and with 5 grooves. Fl.vii. B.M.6737(c). B.S.2:595. G.C. 66:131;100:402(h). E.H.7:t.374(h). Gn.86:579(h). (*T. tomentosa* var. *p.* Kirchn., *T. alba* K. Koch., not Michx., *T. americana pendula* Hort.) Doubtfully native in S. E. Eu. and W. Asia. Intr. before 1840. Zone V. Handsome tree with pendent brs.

    T. p. × *euchlora* = **T. orbiculàris** Jouin. Brs. pendulous: lvs. lustrous and glabrous above, grayish tomentose beneath; petiole shorter. S.H.2:f.2521-m(1). Gn.89:731(h). Orig. about 1870.—*T. p.* × *americana;* see No. 9.

18. **T. mandshùrica** Rupr. & Maxim. MANCHURIAN L. Tree to 20 m.; young brts. and buds with brownish tomentum: lvs. orbicular-ovate, 8–15 cm. long, short-acuminate, usually cordate at base, coarsely serrate with long-pointed teeth, sometimes indistinctly lobed, sparingly pubescent above, grayish or whitish tomentose beneath, without axillary tufts; petiole 3–7 cm. long, tomentose: fls. 7–10 in pendulous brownish tomentose cymes: fr. globose, 5-ribbed toward the base or indistinctly ribbed. Fl.vi–vii. N.K.12:t.12. I.S.t.182. N. E. Asia. Intr. about 1860. Zone IV.

19. **T. Maximowicziàna** Shiras. Tree to 30 m.; young brts. tomentose: lvs. obicular-ovate or broad-ovate, 8–14 cm. long, abruptly acuminate, obliquely cordate, coarsely serrate with broad mucronate teeth, dark green and slightly pubescent above at first, grayish tomentose beneath and with brownish axillary tufts, finally often partly glabrescent; petiole 3–7 cm. long: fls. small, 10–18 in pendulous tomentose cymes; style exserted: fr. subglobose, 5-ribbed, 1 cm. across. Fl.vi. S.I.2:t.50(c). M.K.t.77(c). G.F.6:113 (as *T. Miqueliana*). B.C.6:3348. (*T. Miyabei* Jack.) Japan. Cult. 1880. Zone V.

    Related species: **T. intónsa** Rehd. & Wils. Tree to 20 m.; young brts. pilose: lvs. broad-ovate, 8–14 cm. long, abruptly acuminate, sharply and rather finely serrate, grayish green and stellate-pubescent beneath, usually with axillary tufts: cymes pilose, 1–3-fld.: fr. ovoid, 5-angled. (*T. tonsura* Veitch.) W. China. Intr. 1903.—**T. chinénsis** Maxim. Tree to 15 m.; brts. glabrous: lvs. broad-ovate to ovate, 6–10 cm. long, sharply and closely serrate, glabrous above, thinly tomentose beneath, with fulvous tufts: fr. 5-ribbed. I.S.t.186. (*T. Baroniana* Diels.) Intr. 1925. Zone V.

20. **T. Miqueliàna** Maxim. Tree to 15 m.; young brts. tomentulose: lvs. ovate or triangular-ovate, 6–8, on shoots to 12 cm. long, longer than broad, acute or acuminate, obliquely cordate at base, coarsely serrate with broad mucronate teeth, dark green and glabrous or nearly so above, grayish tomentose beneath, without axillary tufts; petiole 2–4 cm. long, tomentose: fls. 10–20 in pendulous tomentose cymes; stamens 60–75; style shorter than petals: fr. subglobose, 5-ribbed at base. Fl.vi. S.I.1:t.72(c). I.S.t.183. S.H. 2:f.258a-b. E. China; cult in Japan. Intr. before 1900. Zone V.

2. **GRÈWIA** L. Trees or shrubs, more or less stellate-pubescent; winterbuds small, with several pointed narrow scales: lvs. alternate, 2-ranked, short-petioled and usually oblique, entire or serrate, stipulate: fls. 5-merous, rather small, solitary or in terminal or lateral cymes; petals glandular and usually ciliate at base, rarely very small or wanting; stamens many, distinct; an-

thers suborbicular; ovary 5-celled, with 2 to several ovules in each cell: fr. a drupe with 1 or several stones, fleshy or sometimes fibrous; seeds with copious albumen. (After Nehemiah Grew, who wrote on the anatomy of plants; 1628–82.) About 90 species in trop. and subtrop. regions of Asia, Afr. and Austral.

G. bíloba D. Don. Shrub to 2.5 m.; brts. stellate-pubescent: lvs. ovate or rhombic-ovate to rhombic-lanceolate, 5–12 cm. long, acute or acuminate, cuneate or rounded at base, unequally or doubly serrate, nearly glabrous above, sparingly stellate-pubescent or nearly glabrous beneath except on the veins; petiole 3–10 mm. long: fls. creamy yellow, 1–1.5 cm. across, in 5–8-fld. umbels, opposite the lvs., densely pubescent; peduncle 5–20, pedicels 3–6 mm. long; sepals oblong-lanceolate, densely pubescent outside, petals about ⅓ as long: fr. orange or red, usually 2-lobed and 8–12 mm. across, or 3–4-lobed or of only 1 carpel. (*G. parviflora* var. *glabrescens* Rehd. & Wils.) E. China, Formosa. Cult. 1890. Zone VII?—**G. b. parviflòra** (Bge.) Hand.-Mazz., var. Brts. tomentose: lvs. ovate to rhombic-ovate, 4–9 cm. long, broad-cuneate or rounded at base, scabrid above, densely stellate-pubescent beneath. I.T.1:t.12. Gt.38:601. N.K.12:t.16. (*G. p.* Bge.) N. China, Korea. Intr. 1883. Zone (V).

Related species: **G. oppositifòlia** Roxb. Small tree: lvs. ovate, 6–10 cm. long, rounded at base, crenate-serrate, stellate-tomentulose; petiole 4–8 mm. long: fls. about 3 cm. across, on a peduncle 1.5–3 cm. long. Wight, Icon. Pl. 1:t. 32. N. W. Himal. Cult. 1914. Zone VII?

Fam. 62. **MALVACEAE** Neck. MALLOW FAMILY

Herbs, shrubs or trees, usually with stellate pubescence: lvs. alternate, simple, usually palmately veined and more or less lobed, stipulate: fls. perfect, regular, rarely unisexual, solitary or in compound infl.; sepals 5, often united, valvate, often with bractlets at base; petals 5, convolute, often adnate to the stamens; stamens numerous, very rarely 5, the filaments united into a tube; anthers 1-celled; pollen spiny; ovary superior, 2–many-celled; ovules 1–many in each cell; styles and stigmas usually as many as carpels: fr. a caps. or separating into carpels, very rarely fleshy; seed with scant albumen; embryo usually curved, with leafy folded cotyledons.—About 40 genera and 900 species in the temp. and trop. regions over the whole earth.

A. Fr. separating into carpels; calyx without involucel............................1. *Hoheria*
AA. Fr. a dehiscent caps.; calyx with an involucel of bractlets at base.............2. *Hibiscus*

1. HOHERIA Cunningh. Shrubs or small trees with stellate pubescence: lvs. alternate, crenate or serrate, cordate at base: fls. perfect, axillary and solitary or fascicled; calyx 5-toothed, without involucel; staminal column divided at apex into numerous filaments; style divided at apex into as many brs. as carpels; ovary 5–15-celled; ovules one in each cell: mature carpels membranous, separating from the axis, wingless or winged on back. (From the N. Zealand vernacular name *hoheri*). Six species in N. Zeal.

H. glabràta Sprague & Summerh. Tree to 10 m.; brts. sparingly pubescent at first, later glabrous: lvs. ovate to ovate-lanceolate, 5–12 cm. long, acuminate, cordate at base, doubly or simply crenate-serrate, nearly glabrous; petiole 2–7 cm. long: fls. white, 2.5–3.5 cm. across, in 2–5-fld. fascicles; pedicels 1.5–4 cm. long, calyx broad-campanulate with triangular acute lobes; petals obliquely obovate, retuse; ovary 10–15-celled: fr. depressed-globose; carpels wingless on back. Fls.VI. B.M.5935(c). G.C.74:119(h);78:132. Gn.83:421(h);87:443(h). (*H. Lyallii* var. Hook. f., *Plagianthus Lyallii*

Gray, in part, *Gaya Lyallii* E. J. Baker, in part.) Intr. 1871. Zone VII. Handsome in bloom with its numerous white fls.; the hardiest species.

2. **HIBÍSCUS** L. Herbs or deciduous or evergreen shrubs, rarely small trees; winter-buds (of our species) minute, covered by the lf.-basis: lvs. alternate, palmately veined and lobed: fls. usually solitary and axillary, mostly large and conspicuous; calyx 5-toothed or 5-parted, usually with an involucel of bractlets below; corolla usually campanulate, of 5 distinct petals; staminal column with numerous anthers below the 5-toothed apex; style 5-cleft at apex with usually capitate stigmas; ovary 5-celled, with 3–many ovules in each cell: caps. loculicidally dehiscent into 5 valves; the cells sometimes with horizontal walls. (Ancient Latin name.) About 200 species mostly in the Tropics.

H. syríacus L. SHRUBBY ALTHAEA. Shrub to 3 or occasionally small tree to 5 or 6 m.; young brts. villous, later glabrous: lvs. ovate or rhombic-ovate, 5–10 cm. long, more or less 3-lobed and coarsely toothed with rounded or acutish teeth, broad-cuneate or rounded at base and 3-nerved, glabrous except a few hairs on the veins beneath; petiole 5–15 mm. long: fls. solitary, short-stalked, white to red or purple or violet, broad-campanulate, 6–10 cm. across; calyx with unequal ovate-lanceolate lobes and an involucel of linear bractlets shorter than calyx. Fl.viii–ix. B.M.83(c). Gn.52:504,t(c). R.B. 3:25,t(c). F.E.25:459(h);32:127(h). G.W.13:65(h). Gn.75:604(h). (*Althaea frutex* Hort.) China, India. Intr. before 1600. Zone (V). Shrub with showy fls., valued for its late flowering season.—Numerous garden forms of which may be mentioned: "Totus albus." Pure white, single. G.C.II.10:524. Gn. 52:504(c).—"Coelestis." Purplish blue. F.P.1879:t.495(c).—"Speciosus." Fls. double, pinkish, striped and blotched deep rose. R.H.1845:133,t(c).— "Variegatus." Fls. double, purple: lvs. variegated. B.H.18:277,t.(c).—"Puniceus." Red, double.—"Monstrosus." White with dark purple centre.— "Grandiflorus superbus." Rosy, single.—"Pulcherrimus." Pink and white, double.—"Admiral Dewey." Pure white, double.—"Hamabo." Pale blush with large carmine blotch at base of each petal.

Fam. 63. **STERCULIACEAE** Schott. & Endl. STERCULIA FAMILY

Trees, shrubs or herbs, sometimes climbing: lvs. alternate, simple or digitate, stipulate: fls. perfect or unisexual, usually regular; sepals 3–5, valvate, more or less connate; petals convolute or reduced or wanting; stamens in 2 whorls, those opposite the sepals reduced to staminodes or wanting; the anthers united into a tube and variously arranged, 2-celled; ovary superior, sessile or on an androgynophore, 4–5-celled; cells with 2–many ovules; styles 4–5, distinct or connate: fr. usually dry, often separating into carpels; seeds albuminous. About 50 genera and 750 species in the Tropics, few extratropical.

FIRMIÀNA Marsili. Deciduous trees: lvs. alternate, simple, palmately lobed: fls. 5-merous, unisexual, in terminal panicles; sepals colored, petals wanting; androgynophore developed; carpels 5, distinct at base, connate at apex into a single style; rudimentary and free in the staminate fls.: fr. consisting of leathery follicles opening long before maturity and leaf-like, seeds globular, on their edges near the base. (After Karl Joseph von Firmian, governor of Lombardy; 1718–82.) About 10 species in Asia, 1 in Africa.

F. símplex (L.) W. F. Wight. PHOENIX-TREE. Round-headed tree to 15 m., with smooth gray-green bark: lvs. palmately 3–5-lobed, 16–20 cm. long. cordate, lobes acuminate, entire, glabrous or tomentulose beneath; petiole about as long as blade: fls. yellowish green, in terminal panicles 25–50 cm. long; sepals narrow-oblong, about 1 cm. long: carpels 4–5, 3–10 cm. long. Fl.VII; fr.XI. E.N.III.6,f.49(fr). Cavanilles, Diss. 5:t.149. L.A.1:363. (*F. platanifolia* R. Br., *Sterculia p.* L. f.) China, Japan. Intr. 1757. Zone VII. Ornamental tree planted for its large lvs.

Fam. 64. **ACTINIDIACEAE** Tieghem. ACTINIDIA FAMILY

Trees or climbing shrubs: lvs. alternate, serrate to crenate, rarely entire: fls. perfect, polygamous or dioecious, in cymes or panicles or solitary; sepals 5, imbricate; petals 5, imbricate or convolute; stamens many or ten; anthers versatile; ovary superior, 3–5- or many-celled: styles free or connate; ovules several to many, rarely 2, in each cell: fr. a berry or dehiscent caps.; seeds albuminous, with rather large straight embryo. Four genera with about 280 species chiefly tropical and subtrop.

A. Stamens numerous; styles numerous, radiating: fr. a berry....................1. *Actinidia*
AA. Stamens 10; style 1: fr. a caps...2. *Clematoclethra*

1. ACTINÍDIA Lindl. Deciduous twining shrubs; pith solid or lamellate; winter-buds very small, enclosed in the swollen base of the petiole: lvs. alternate, long-stalked, serrate, rarely entire, estipulate: fls. dioecious or polygamous, in axillary cymes or solitary, cup-shaped, white or rarely reddish; sepals 5, rarely less, imbricate; petals 5, rarely 4, convolute, thin; stamens numerous; anthers versatile: ovary superior, many-celled; styles many, radiating: fr. a berry with numerous small albuminous seeds; embryo comparatively large. (Greek *actis*, ray, referring to the radiating styles.) Syn. *Trochostigma* Sieb. & Zucc. About 25 species in Asia from Saghalin to Java and Himal.

A. Brts. glabrous or nearly so: lvs. glabrous or pubescent only on the veins beneath.
  B. Anthers dark purple: lvs. dark green and lustrous above.
    c. Lvs. green beneath, often bristly on the veins.........................1. *A. arguta*
    cc. Lvs. glaucous beneath, glabrous.....................................2. *A. melanandra*
  BB. Anthers yellow.
    c. Lvs. firm, never colored: fr. spotted....................................3. *A. callosa*
    cc. Lvs. thin, often partly colored: fr. not spotted.
      D. Pith of brs. solid, white: lvs. partly white or yellow...............4. *A. polygama*
      DD. Pith of brs. lamellate: lvs. partly pink or white.................5. *A. Kolomikta*
AA. Brts. densely hairy: lvs. tomentose beneath...............................6. *A. chinensis*

1. A. argùta (Sieb. & Zucc.) Miq. High climbing: brs. with brown lamellate pith: lvs. broad-ovate to elliptic, 8–12 cm. long, abruptly acuminate, rounded to subcordate at base, rarely cuneate, setosely and sharply serrate, green beneath and usually setose on midrib; petiole 3.5–8 cm. long, sometimes setose: infl. glabrous, shorter than petiole: fls. 3 or more, about 2 cm. across; sepals elliptic-oblong; petals brownish at base: fr. ellipsoid, about 2.5 cm. long, greenish yellow, edible. Fl.VI–VII; fr.IX–X. B.M.7497(c). L.I.t. 25. R.H.1874:395f.54. M.G.13:378(h). H.B.2:582(h). (*A. volubilis* Carr., not Miq., *A. rufa* Miq., *A. polygama* Hort., not Miq.) Japan, Korea, Manch. Cult. 1874. Zone IV. Vigorous growing vine, forming a dense covering for arbors, etc.—**A. a. cordifòlia** (Miq.) Bean, var. Lvs. broad-ovate, cordate at base, more setose on veins beneath; petiole purple.

A. a. × *chinensis;* see under No. 6.

Related species: **A. purpúrea** Rehd. Lvs. elliptic to elliptic-oblong, 8–12 cm. long, with appressed teeth, dull above, green and glabrous beneath or tomentose at midrib; petiole 3–5 cm. long: pistillate fls. usually solitary, about 1.5 cm.

across; sepals ovate: fr. ovoid to oblong, 2–2.5 cm. long, rostrate, purple, sweet. W. China. Intr. 1908. Zone VI?—**A. Giráldii** Diels. Lvs. broad-elliptic or broad-ovate, 6–12 cm. long, short-acuminate or obtuse, setulose-pilose on the veins and veinlets beneath; petiole strigose: infl. strigulose; sepals concave, 4 mm. long; petals 7 mm. long. C. China. Cult. 1933. Zone VI?

2. **A. melanándra** Franch. High climbing; brts. glabrous, with lamellate pith: lvs. elliptic to oblong, 6–9 cm. long, abruptly acuminate, rounded or cuneate, appressed-serrulate, glaucous beneath and glabrous except axillary tufts of hairs; petiole 2–3.5 cm. long: fls. white, 2–2.5 cm. across, pistillate solitary, staminate several; infl. glabrous, about as long as petiole; ovary bottle-shaped, glabrous: fr. 2.5–3 cm. long, ellipsoid. Fl.vi–vii: fr.ix–x. Japan, C. China. Intr. about 1900. Zone V.

3. **A. callòsa** Lindl. Climbing to 7 m.; brts. with conspicuous lenticels; pith lamellate: lvs. elliptic to oblong, 8–12 cm. long, acuminate, cuneate to rounded, setosely serrulate, glabrous and green beneath; petiole 3–5 cm. long: fls. white or yellow, fragrant, 1.5–2 cm. across, on slender glabrous pedicels; ovary pubescent: fr. oblong-ovoid, greenish or russet, spotted. S.H.2: f.216(l). Himal., S. China. Intr. ?—**A. c. Hénryi** Maxim., var. Lvs. broad-elliptic to elliptic-ovate or oblong-ovate, 5–10 cm. long, sometimes subcordate, bearded in the axils of the veins beneath: infl. usually much shorter than petiole. Fl.vi; fr.x. C. and W. China. Intr. 1907. Zone VI?

Related species: **A. venòsa** Rehd. Climbing to 8 m.; brs. with white lamellate pith: lvs. elliptic to oblong-ovate, 8–15 cm. long, usually rounded at base, tomentulose on the veins beneath at first, later nearly glabrous; the lateral veins connected by conspicuous parallel veinlets: fls. buff-yellow: fr. ovoid or subglobose, spotted. W. China. Intr. 1908. Zone VI?—**A. coriàcea** Dunn. Pith solid, white: lvs. subcoriaceous, oblong to lance-oblong, 6–10 cm. long, remotely serrate, glabrous: fls. small, reddish: fr. ovoid, spotted. G.C.100:245. W. China. Intr. 1908 (distributed as *A. Henryi*).—**A. rubricaùlis** Dunn. Brts. purple, lenticellate; pith solid: lvs. chartaceous, lanceolate to elliptic-oblong, 7–10 cm. long, acuminate, usually rounded at base, serrulate: ovary glabrous. W. China. Cult. 1924. Zone VII?

4. **A. polýgama** (Sieb. & Zucc.) Miq. Silver-Vine. Climbing to 5 m.: lvs. broad-ovate to ovate-oblong, 8–14 cm. long, acuminate, rounded or subcordate at base, appressed-serrate, usually setose on the veins beneath, in part of the lvs. of the staminate plant the upper half or sometimes nearly the whole lf. silvery white or yellowish; petioles bristly: fls. 1–3, white, 1.5 cm. across, fragrant; ovary glabrous, bottle-shaped: fr. yellow, ovoid, beaked, 2–3 cm. long, edible. Fl.vi; fr.ix–x. Ito & Kaku, Fig. Pl. Koishik. Bot. Gard. 2:t. 20(c). S.H.2:f.216f-g,217a-f. (*A. volubilis* Miq.) Manch. to Japan and C. China. Intr. 1861. Zone IV. The staminate plant is very handsome with its partly silvery white lvs. The plant attracts cats.

5. **A. Kolomíkta** (Rupr.) Maxim. Kolomikta-Vine. Climbing usually to 2, rarely to 5 or 7 m.: lvs. ovate-oblong, 10–12 cm. long, acuminate, rounded or cordate at base, unequally setose-serrate, pubescent on the veins beneath when young, part of the lvs., particularly in the staminate plant, with a large white to pink blotch at the apex extending often to the middle or beyond: fls. 1–3, white, 1.5 cm. across, fragrant; ovary cylindric, glabrous: fr. oblong-ovoid, 2–2.5 cm. long, greenish or yellowish, sweet. Fl.v; fr.ix–x. R.H.1898: 36,t.(c). B.M.9093(c). M.G.11:397(h). G.W.3:61(h). N. E. Asia to Japan and C. and W. China. Intr. about 1855. Zone IV. The staminate plant is strikingly handsome with its lvs. blotched pink and white.

• Related species: **A. tetrámera** Maxim. Lvs. narrower and smaller, glabrous except axillary tufts of hairs or rarely setose on the midrib: fls. smaller, tetramerous: fr. yellow, finally brown. C. and W. China. Intr. 1927.

6. **A. chinénsis** Planch. Climbing to 8 m.: brs. with shaggy hairs red when young: pith lamellate: lvs. orbicular or oval, 8–12 cm. long, cordate at base, rounded or emarginate or on shoots acuminate, ciliate-serrulate, finally glabrous above and dark green, whitish tomentose beneath with reddish hairs on the veins: fls. several, 3–4 cm. across, creamy-white, changing to buff-yellow: fr. ovoid to subglobose, 3–5 cm. long, hairy, edible. Fl.vi; fr.viii–ix. B.M.8538(c). G.C.46:77,79,t. H.I.16:1593. U. S. Inv. 50:t. U. S. Im. 111–112:t;164:t. N.H.15:6. S.L.75(h). China. Intr. 1900. Zone VII? With large fls. and large frs. similar in flavor to gooseberries.

A. ch. × *arguta* = **A. Fairchíldii** Rehd. Brts. sparingly villous: lvs. suborbicular or broad-obovate, rounded or short-acuminate at apex, villous on the veins beneath; infl. densely villous; male fls. 2 cm. across; anthers yellowish. Jour. Hered. 18:59. Orig. 1923.

2. **CLEMATOCLÉTHRA** Maxim. Deciduous climbing shrubs; brs. with solid pith; winter-buds conspicuous, with imbricate scales: lvs. alternate, petioled, usually serrate, estipulate: fls. perfect, in axillary cymes, sometimes solitary, white; sepals 5, imbricate, persistent; petals 5, imbricate; stamens 10, short; ovary 5-celled; cells with about 10 ovules; style cylindric, slender: fr. berry-like, with thin flesh, usually 5-seeded. (*Clematis* and *clethra;* referring to the climbing habit and the similarity of the fl. to that of Clethra.) About 10 species in C. and W. Asia.

C. lasióclada Maxim. Climbing to 6 m.; young brts. pubescent: lvs. ovate, 5–10 cm. long, acuminate, rounded or subcordate at base, setosedenticulate, glabrous except pubescent on the midrib above and with axillary tufts of hairs beneath or villous along the midrib and sometimes along the veins, light or pale green beneath; petiole 2–6 cm. long: fls. 1.2–1.5 cm. across, in 2–7-fld. peduncled cymes, shorter than petiole; sepals orbicular-ovate, puberulous like the pedicels and peduncles or nearly glabrous: fr. globose, black, about 8 mm. across. Fl.vii; fr.ix-x. E. N. ed. 2, 21:46. W. China. Intr. 1908. Zone VI?

Related species: **C. scandens** Maxim. Brts. setose: lvs. oblong-ovate to oblong, 5–10 cm. long, rounded or broad-cuneate at base, minutely denticulate, pubescent beneath and hispid on veins; petiole 1–4 cm. long, usually hispid: fl.-clusters usually about as long as petiole. W. China. Intr. 1911.—**C. integrifòlia** Maxim. Brts. glabrous or nearly so: lvs. ovate to ovate-oblong, 3.5–7 cm. long, rounded at base, setose-denticulate, glaucous and glabrous beneath; petiole 2–4.5 cm. long: fls. solitary or in few-fld. clusters much shorter than petioles. N. W. China. Intr. 1908.—**C. actinidioìdes** Maxim. Brts. glabrous: lvs. ovate to ovate-oblong, 4–8 cm. long, rounded to subcordate at base, minutely serrulate, light green and glabrous beneath; petiole 2.5–5 cm. long: fls. long-stalked, often solitary. B.M.9439(c). W. China. Intr. 1908.

Fam. 65. **EUCRYPHIACEAE** Gay. EUCRYPHIA FAMILY

Evergreen trees or shrubs: lvs. opposite, simple or pinnate; stipules connate: fls. perfect, large, white, axillary; sepals 4, imbricate, cohering at apex and separating at base at anthesis; petals 4, large, convolute; stamens very numerous, surrounded at base by tubular excrescences, inserted on the elongated floral axis below the 5–18-celled ovary; cells with several pendulous ovules: fr. a dehiscent caps., separating into 5–18 carpels opening at the inner suture; seeds winged, albuminous.—One genus with 4 species in Chile and Australia.

EUCRÝPHIA Cav. Characters of the family. (Name from Greek *eu*, well, and *kryphios,* covered.)

E. glutinòsa (Poepp. & Endl.) Baill. Evergreen or half-evergreen tree to 5 m., with upright brs. pubescent when young: lvs. pinnate, clustered at the end of the brs.; petiole about 1 cm. long; lfts. 3–5, the lateral ones sessile, elliptic to ovate, 3–6 cm. long, lustrous and dark green above, pubescent when young: fls. 1 or 2, at end of brts., 5–6 cm. across; anthers yellow; fr. pear-shaped, about 1.5 cm. long. Fl.vii–viii. B.M.7067(c). G.C.30:351(h); 81:51,123,t(h). Gn.86:563. B.S.1:536. (*E. pinnatifolia* Gay.) Chile. Intr. 1859. Zone VII? With large white fls.; requires soil free of lime.

E. g. × *cordifolia* = **E. nymansénsis** Bausch. Lvs. partly simple, partly with 3, rarely 5 lfts., serrate, pubescent or puberulous: fls. 6–7 cm. across. G.C.76:167;80:177. Gn.88:621. Orig. 1915. Zone VII? Here belongs "Nymansay."— *E. g.* × *lucida* (Labill.) Baill. = **E. intermèdia** Bausch. Lvs. simple and partly pinnate, entire or with few teeth, glaucescent and glabrous. G.C.100:190. Cult. 1936. Zone VII? Here belongs "Rostrevor."

Fam. 66. **THEACEAE** Mirb. TEA FAMILY

Deciduous or evergreen trees or shrubs: lvs. alternate, simple, entire or serrate, estipulate: fls. usually perfect, regular, axillary or subterminal, usually solitary; sepals 5–7, rarely many, imbricate, usually persistent; petals 5, rarely 4 or more, distinct or connate at base; stamens very many, rarely 5, 10 or 15; free or united at base, often adnate to the petals; ovary superior, 2–10-celled; cells with 1 to many ovules; styles as many as carpels or connate into 1: fr. a loculicidal caps. or indehiscent and dry or drupaceous; seeds 1 to many; albumen wanting or scanty; embryo usually curved. Syn.: *Ternstroemiaceae* R. Br.—About 18 genera and 200 species in trop. and subtrop., few in temp. regions.

A. Fr. a caps.: fls. perfect, upright, 3–10 cm. across.
  B. Lvs. evergreen: fr. subglobose; seeds 1–3, large.............................1. *Camellia*
  BB. Lvs. deciduous: seeds many, small, flattened.
    C. Fr. splitting from above, without persistent central axis: fls. distinctly stalked.
                                               2. *Stewartia*
    CC. Fr. splitting from above and below, with a persistent central axis: fls. subsessile.
                                              3. *Franklinia*
AA. Fr. a berry: fls. dioecious, nodding, about 5 mm. across: lvs. evergreen, 3–6 cm. long.
                                              4. *Eurya*

1. **CAMÉLLIA** L. Evergreen trees or shrubs; winter-buds with many imbricate scales: lvs. alternate, short-petioled, serrulate: fls. perfect, axillary, solitary, rarely 2 or 3, white to red; sepals 5 to many, imbricate; petals 5–7, slightly connate at base; stamens numerous, the outer ones connate and partly adnate to the petals at base, the inner ones free; ovary 3–5-celled; ovules 4–6 in each cell; styles filiform, connate below: fr. a loculicidal woody caps. with a persistent central axis; seeds few, subglobose or angular; embryo straight with thick cotyledons. (After Georg Joseph Kamel, Latinized Camellius, Jesuit priest in the Philippines; 1661–1706.) Syn.: *Thea* L. About 45 species in trop. and subtrop. Asia.

A. Sepals many, deciduous: fls. 7–12 cm. across...............Sect. Eucamellia Cohen Stuart
                                              1. *C. japonica*
AA. Sepals 5, persistent: fls. about 3.5 cm. across, white.........Sect. Theopsis Cohen Stuart
                                               2. *C. cuspidata*

1. **C. japónica** L. CAMELLIA. Shrub or tree to 15 m., glabrous: lvs. ovate to elliptic, 5–10 cm. long, acuminate, lustrous dark green above: fls. subsessile, red in the typical form; petals 5–7, roundish; ovary glabrous; seeds subglobose or angular, 2–2.5 cm. across. Fl.iv–vi; fr.ix–x. B.M.42(c). S.Z.1:t.82(c). F.S.20:t.2121(c). S.I.1:t.73(c). Gn.28:203;36:247. (*Thea j.* (L.) Nois.) China. Japan. Cult. 1742. Zone VII? Ornamental evergreen tree or shrub with large lustrous lvs. and large fls. varying from white to red; many garden

forms with single or double fls. Only precariously hardy within our area like the two following species.

Related species: **C. Sasánqua** Thunb. Shrub of loose habit; young brts. pubescent: lvs. elliptic to oblong-ovate, 4–8 cm. long, bluntly acuminate, crenate-serrate, hairy on the midrib above; fls. 3.5–5 cm. across, white; petals obovate to oblong; ovary pubescent. S.Z.1:t.83(c). S.I.2:t.52(c). Gn.54:142;t(c);82: 33,106. (*Thea Sasanqua* Nois.) China, Japan. Intr. 1811. Zone VII? Several garden forms with white to deep rose, single or double fls.

2. **C. cuspidàta** (Kochs) Veitch. Shrub to 2 m.; young brts. puberulous: lvs. elliptic to ovate-lanceolate, 5–8 cm. long, long-acuminate, rounded or cuneate, indistinctly denticulate, lustrous dark green above or sometimes purplish green, paler and minutely dotted beneath; petiole 3–4 mm. long, slightly pubescent: fls. solitary, white, 3–4 cm. across, on a short pedicel clothed with imbricate green bracts; petals usually 6; ovary glabrous. Fl. v–vi. G.C.51:261. J.L.38:62,f.38. B.S.1:285. (*Thea c.* Kochs.) China. Intr. 1901. Zone VII?

2. **STEWÁRTIA** L. Deciduous shrubs or trees with smooth flaky bark; winter-buds with several imbricate scales, usually silky; lvs. alternate, short-petioled, serrate: fls. perfect, solitary, axillary or subterminal, cup-shaped, with 1 or 2 bracts below the calyx; sepals 5, persistent; petals 5, sometimes 6, rarely to 8, obovate to roundish, crenulate, white, silky outside, connate at base; stamens numerous, adnate at base to the petals; ovary superior, 5-celled; styles 5, free or connate: fr. a woody caps. loculicidally dehiscent into 5 valves; seeds compressed, 1–4 in each cell, usually narrowly winged. (After John Stuart, Earl of Bute, a patron of botany; 1713–92.) Syn.: *Stuartia* L'Hérit. About 8 species in E. N. Am. and E. Asia.

A. Styles united, with 5 stigmas.
  B. Stamens with purple filaments: caps. depressed-globose, apiculate.1. *S. Malacodendron*
  BB. Stamens with whitish filaments (purple in var. of No. 5): caps. ovoid, pointed.
    c. Sepals orbicular, much larger than the orbicular or ovate bracts below; fls. 6–8 cm. across; seeds not or scarcely winged.
      D. Fls. cup-sharped: seeds with acute edge; brts. straight, terete..
                              2. *S. Pseudo-camellia*
      DD. Fls. nearly flat: seeds with rounded edge: brts. mostly zigzag, slightly compressed.
                              3. *S. koreana*
    cc. Sepals and bracts foliaceous, ovate to ovate-oblong, of nearly equal length or bracts longer: seeds narrowly winged.....................4. *S. sinensis*
AA. Styles distinct: lvs. usually rounded at base, 6–12 cm. long....................5. *S. ovata*

1. **S. Malacodéndron** L. Shrub to 6 m.; young brts. pubescent: lvs. short-petioled, elliptic to elliptic-oblong, 6–10 cm. long, acute or short-acuminate, cuneate, serrulate and ciliate, light green and pubescent beneath; petioles 2–5 mm. long, pubescent: fls. 8–10 cm. across; petals obovate, spreading; style shorter than stamens; anthers bluish: fr. about 1.5 cm. across; seeds wingless, lustrous. Fl.vi–vii. B.M.8145(c). Gn.14:136,t(c);34:280. G.C. 77:399,t. B.S.2:553. (*S. virginica* Cav.) Va. and Ark. to Fla. and La. Cult. 1752. Zone VII. With showy white fls.

2. **S. Pseudo-caméllia** Maxim. Shrub or tree to 20 m., with upright brs.; bark red, peeling off in large flakes; brts. glabrous, slender: lvs. elliptic or obovate-elliptic to elliptic-lanceolate, 3–8 cm. long, acuminate, cuneate, remotely crenate-serrulate, bright green, light green and glabrous or with scattered long hairs beneath, thickish; petiole 3–10 mm. long: fls. cup-shaped, 5–6 cm. across, axillary near base of brts. on pedicels 1–3 cm. long; petals suborbicular, concave; stamens white, connate at base; anthers orange: fr. ovoid, 5-angled, about 2 cm. long. Fl.vii–viii; fr.x–xi. B.M.7045(c). S.I.1:t. 73(c). Gn.43:172,t(c). G.F.9:35. G.C.60:217. (*S. grandiflora* Briot, *S. ja-*

ponica var. *grandiflora* Hort.) Japan. Cult. 1874. Zone V. Tree with large white fls.; lvs. changing to dark purple in fall.

3. **S. koreàna** Rehd. Tree to 15 m., with upright brs.; bark flaky, red-brown; brts. glabrous: lvs. elliptic to broad-elliptic, 6–10 cm. long, abruptly acuminate, broad-cuneate or rounded at base, remotely serrate, silky-pubescent at first, finally glabrous above, slightly pubescent beneath: fls. white, 7–7.5 cm. across, in the axils of the lower lvs. on glabrous pedicels 1.5–2 cm. long; bracts 4–7 mm. long; sepals 5, about 1 cm. long, suborbicular, densely pubescent outside; petals 5–6, broadly obovate, spreading, the outer slightly concave, the inner nearly flat: caps. ovoid, rostrate, 2 cm. long; seeds about 5 mm. long, dark brown. Fls. VI–VII; fr.IX–X. N.K.17:t.16. H.B.7:398. Korea. Intr. 1917. Zone V. Tree with showy fls.; lvs. turning orange or orange-red in fall.

4. **S. sinénsis** Rehd. & Wils. Shrub or tree to 10 m.; bark flaky, brown; brts. pilose or glabrous: lvs. elliptic-obovate to oblong-elliptic, 5–10 cm. long, acuminate, cuneate or rarely nearly rounded at base, remotely serrate or crenate-serrulate, sparingly appressed-pubescent beneath or glabrous except the midrib; petiole 5–8 mm. long: fls. about 5 cm. across, cup-shaped; pedicels 4–8 mm. long; bracts ovate to ovate-oblong, 2–2.5 cm. long, acute, serrulate or entire, nearly glabrous outside; sepals similar to bracts, unequal, 1–2.5 cm. long; petals broad-obovate; filaments connate ⅛, pilose below the middle: caps. 5-angled, subglobose, 2 cm. high, 1.5 cm. across, rostrate, pilose or glabrescent; seed oval, 1 cm. long, compressed, narrowly winged, brown. Fls. VII; fr.IX–X. B.M.8778(c). C. China. Intr. 1901. Zone VI? With large white fls.

Related species: **S. monadélpha** Sieb. & Zucc. Tree to 25 m.; brts. pilose: lvs. elliptic to oblong-elliptic, 4–6 cm. long, acute, remotely serrulate, appressed-pubescent beneath: fls. 2.5–3.5 cm. across: pedicels 6–15 mm. long; bracts 1–1.5 cm. long; filaments united below: caps. ovoid, rostrate, 1 cm. long, appressed-pubescent. S.Z.1:t.96(c). Japan. Cult. 1903. Zone VI?—S. serràta Maxim. Young brts. pilose: lvs. elliptic to obovate, 4–7 cm. long, serrate with incurved teeth, pilose on midrib and in the axils of the veins beneath: fls. short-stalked, 5–6 cm. across, with large bracts at base; petals red at base outside; filaments free; ovary glabrous: fr. ovoid, 2 cm. long. B.M.8771(c). Japan. Cult. 1917. Zone VI?

5. **S. ovata** (Cav.) Weatherby. Shrub to 5 m.; brts. glabrous: lvs. ovate or elliptic to ovate-oblong, 6–12 cm. long, acuminate, usually rounded at base, remotely serrulate, sparingly pubescent and grayish green beneath; petiole 3–15 mm. long: fls. cup-shaped, 6–7 cm. across; petals obovate, often 6, concave; filaments white, with orange anthers: fr. ovoid, 1.5–2 cm. long, sharply 5-angled, pointed, pubescent; seeds narrowly winged. Fl.VII–VIII; fr.IX–X. B.M.3918(c). B.R.1104(c). Gr.G.2:t.139. M.G.15:479. Gn.89:468. (*S. pentagyna* L'Hérit., *Malachodendron pentagynum* Dum.-Cours., *M. ovatum* Cav.) N. C. and Tenn. to Fla. Cult. 1800? Zone V. With beautiful large fls. particularly those of the var., and with bright green lvs. changing to orange and scarlet in fall.—**S. o. grandiflòra** (Bean) Weatherby, var. Fls. 8–10 cm. across, stamens purple; petals sometimes up to 8. N.F.8:f.23. Ga. Cult. 1914.

3. **FRANKLÍNIA** Marsh. Deciduous shrub or small tree; winter-buds elongated, naked, pubescent: lvs. alternate, serrate: fls. perfect, axillary, solitary, subsessile: sepals 5, persistent, suborbicular, unequal, silky-pubescent, subtended by 2 minute caducous bracts; petals 5, unequal, concave: stamens inserted on the petals; ovary 5-celled; styles connate, with 5-lobed

stigma: caps. subglobose, woody, 5-valved, dehiscent loculicidally from above and septicidally from below, leaving a persistent central axis; seeds several in each cell, flattened, angular, wingless. (After Benjamin Franklin, American statesman; 1706–1790.) One species in e. N. Am.

F. alatamàha Marsh. FRANKLINIA. Shrub or tree to 10 m., with upright Drs.; bark smooth, thin; young brts. silky: lvs. obovate-oblong, 12–15 cm. long, acute, gradually narrowed into a short petiole, remotely serrate, bright green and shining above, pubescent below: fls. cup-shaped, 7–8 cm. across; petals roundish-obovate, concave, crenulate: fr. globose, 1.5–2 cm. across; seeds wingless. Fl.ix–x; fr.x. S.S.1:t.22. M.M.6:201,t(c). M.G.14:25. Gng. 7:167(h). Gn.M.40:167(h). (*Gordonia a.* Sarg., *G. pubescens* L'Hérit.) Ga. Intr. 1770, but not found wild again since 1790. Zone (V). Lvs. turning crimson in fall; chiefly valued for its large late appearing fls.

4. **EURYA** Thunb. Evergreen shrubs or trees; winter-buds naked: lvs. alternate, serrate to crenate, rarely entire, short-petioled, rarely subsessile: fls. dioecious, axillary, solitary or fascicled: pedicels usually short, with 2 small persistent bracts at apex; sepals 5, persistent: corolla campanulate or urceolate, of 5 petals united at base; staminate fls. with many stamens shorter than petals and with rudimentary ovary or without; pistillate fls. without stamens; ovary 5-celled; styles 3–5, more or less connate or free: fr. a many-seeded berry; seeds albuminous. (Derivation of name uncertain.) More than 50 species in E. Asia, India and Malaysia.

E. japónica Thunb. Shrub or small tree to 7 m.; brts. glabrous; terminal bud glabrous: lvs. elliptic-oblong or elliptic to obovate-oblong, 3–6 cm. long, acute or acuminate with obtuse emarginate apex, cuneate, glabrous, yellowish green beneath, with inconspicuous veins; petiole 2–5 mm. long: fls. 1–3, white, 5–6 mm. across; pedicels nodding, 1–3 mm. long, sepals suborbicular, about half as long as the oval petals; style shorter than petals, 3–4-cleft: fr. globose, 5 mm. across, black. Fl.iii–iv; fr.x–xi. S.I.2:t.53(c). N.K. 17:t.21(as *E. j.* var. *montana*). S.H.2:f.611f-k. Japan, Korea, Formosa. Cult. 1870. Zone VII.

Fam. 67. **GUTTIFERAE** Choisy. GARCINIA FAMILY

Trees or shrubs, rarely herbs, with oil-glands or oil-ducts: lvs. opposite or whorled, rarely alternate; stipules usually wanting: fls. perfect, polygamous or dioecious, solitary or in cymes; sepals 4–5, imbricate; petals as many, imbricate or convolute; stamens usually many and fascicled, rarely few; ovary superior, of 3–5, rarely fewer or more carpels and with as many cells or 1-celled; styles distinct or united; ovules usually many and on parietal placentae: fr. a capsule, drupe or berry-like; seed without albumen. Including *Hypericaceae*.—More than 40 genera and about 650 species chiefly in the Tropics and some in temp. regions.

A. Fls. 4-merous ....1. *Ascyrum*
AA. Fls. 5-merous ....2. *Hypericum*

1. **ASCYRUM** L. ST. PETER'S-WORT. Shrubs or subshrubs with 2-edged brts., glabrous: lvs. opposite, sessile, entire, pellucid-dotted, exstipulate: fls. yellow, 4-merous, in terminal, usually 3-fld. cymes; sepals nearly equal or the 2 outer larger; stamens many, slightly or not united at base; ovary 1-celled, with 2–3, rarely 4 parietal placentae; ovules many; styles distinct or connate at base: fr. a septicidal caps.; seeds not winged. (Ancient Greek

name of a plant, probably Hypericum.) Five species in N. and C. Am. and Himal.

A. hypericoìdes L. St. Andrews Cross. Upright shrub to 80 cm. high: lvs. crowded, linear-oblong to linear-oblancolate, 0.5–2 cm. long, obtuse or acutish, with smaller lvs. in axillary fascicles: fls. about 1.5 cm. across; outer sepals oblong-elliptic to ovate, 5–11 mm. long, inner smaller and narrower; petals narrow-oblong, as long as outer sepals; styles 2, very short: caps. flat. Fls.vi–ix. (*A. Crux-Andreae* L.) Va. and Tenn. to Fla., Tex. and Mex., W. Indies. Intr. 1737. Zone VII.—**A. h. multicaùle** (Michx.) Fern., var. Low and diffuse subshrub with slender ascending brts. 10–30 cm. long: lvs. oblong to oblong-oblanceolate, 1–2 cm. long: outer sepals elliptic, oval or oblong-oblanceolate, rounded at base. M.M.3:65,t(c). G.F.5:257. B.C.1:405. B.B.2: 528. Tex. and Ga. to Mass., Ill. and Kans. Cult. 1870. Zone V. Low short-lived subshrub with bright yellow fls.

Related species: **A. stans** Michx. Upright shrub to 80 cm., with 2-edged or 2-winged brts.: lvs. oblong to obovate, 1–4 cm. long, partially clasping: fls. 2.5–4 cm. broad; outer sepals broad-oval or suborbicular, the inner lanceolate, shorter; petals obovate; styles 3–4. G.G.1:t.91. B.B.2:528. L.I. to Pa., Fla. and Tenn. Intr. 1816. Zone VI.

2. HYPERÌCUM L. St. John's-wort. Herbs or shrubs, sometimes evergreen: lvs. opposite, sometimes whorled, short-petioled or sessile, entire, dotted with pellucid glands, exstipulate: fls. perfect, in terminal or axillary cymes or solitary, yellow, rarely pink or purplish; sepals 5, imbricate or valvate, petals 5, oblique, convolute; stamens usually numerous, distinct or in 3 or 5 bundles, rarely as few as 3: ovary 1–5-celled, with 3–5 parietal placentae; styles 3–5, distinct or connate: fr. a septicidal caps., rarely berry-like; seeds cylindric. (Ancient Greek plant name of obscure meaning.) About 200 species in the temp. and subtrop. regions of the n. hemisphere, few in the s. hemisphere.—Ornamental usually low shrubs or subshrubs chiefly planted for their showy yellow fls.

A. Styles 5.
  B. Lvs. ovate to ovate-lanceolate: fls. 2.5–7 cm. across; stamens in 5 fascicles.
    c. Fls. about 7 cm. across, usually solitary: low suffruticose stoloniferous plant.
                                                              1. *H. calycinum*
    cc. Fls. 3–6 cm. across: plants shrubby.
      D. Styles distinct.
        E. Sepals ovate; petals roundish or obovate.
          F. Brts. 2-edged ....2. *H. patulum*
          FF. Brts. terete ....3. *H. Hookerianum*
        EE. Sepals linear-lanceolate; petals oblong.............................4. *H. Dyeri*
      DD. Styles connate, 1.5–2 cm. long.......................................5. *H. chinense*
  BB. Lvs. linear-oblong to lanceolate: fls. 8–25 mm. across; stamens free.
    c. Cymes many-fld.; fls. about 1 cm. across.........................6. *H. lobocarpum*
    cc. Cymes few-fld.; fls. 1.5–2.5 cm. across............................7. *H. Kalmianum*
AA. Styles 3.
  B. Styles more or less united; stamens distinct, shorter than petals.
    c. Fls. in axillary, few-fld. cymes forming narrow leafy panicles.
      D. Lvs. narrowly linear, 1–4 cm. long: ovary incompletely 3-celled....8. *H. galioides*
      DD. Lvs. narrow-oblong, 2–8 cm. long: ovary completely 3-celled.....9. *H. prolificum*
    cc. Fls. terminal, solitary or in cymes.
      D. Sepals foliaceous: fls. 1–3, 2.5–5 cm. across: ovary incompletely 3-celled.
                                           10. *H. frondosum*
      DD. Sepals not foliaceous: fls. smaller.
        E. Lvs. short-petioled: ovary completely 3-celled.
          F. Fls. many, in large terminal corymbs: upright shrub......13. *H. densiflorum*
          FF. Fls. solitary or few: decumbent shrub........................14. *H. Buckleyi*
        EE. Lvs. sessile: ovary incompletely 3-celled.
          F. Lvs. linear to narrow-oblong; stem 2-edged................12. *H. cistifolium*
          FF. Lvs. ovate to oblong; stem quadrangular..................11. *H. nudiflorum*
  BB. Styles free; stamens in 3 or 5 fascicles.
    c. Lvs. opposite, sessile; stamens about as long as petals
      D. Fr. a caps.; style longer than ovary.

E. Sepals deciduous; style as long as stamens: lvs. of disagreeable goat-like odor
    when bruised ....15. *H. hircinum*
EE. Sepals persistent; styles longer than stamens: lvs. of aromatic odor.
                                      16. *H. elatum*
  DD. Fr. a berry: style shorter than ovary.......................17. *H. Androsaemum*
  CC. Lvs. whorled; stamens shorter than petals............................18. *H. Coris*

1. **H. calýcinum** L. ROSE OF SHARON. Evergreen or half-evergreen sub-shrub, to 30 cm., stoloniferous, with procumbent or ascending 4-angled stems: lvs. short-petioled, ovate-oblong to oblong, 5–10 cm. long, obtuse, dark green above, glaucous beneath, subcoriaceous: fls. solitary, rarely 2 or 3, 7–8 cm. across, bright yellow; sepals large, broad-obovate; stamens in 5 clusters; anthers red; style shorter than stamens, divergent. Fl.vii–ix. B.M.46(c). G.25:333. Gs.8:182. B.C.3:1630. Gn.87:458(h). S. E. Eu., Asia Minor. Intr. 1676. Zone (V). Low plant with large and showy yellow fls., valued as a ground cover, particularly in sandy soil.

H. c. × *patulum;* see under No. 2.

Related species: **H. Ascýron** L. Perennial to 1.5 m. tall, scarcely sub-shrubby; stems 4-angled: lvs. partly clasping, ovate-oblong to ovate-lanceolate, 4–9 cm. long: fls. 3–6 cm. across, in 3–12-fld. cymes; petals narrow-obovate to oblanceolate, persistent until after they wither: caps. 2–3 cm. long. Fl.vii–viii. B.B.2:529. N. E. N. Am., E. and C. Asia. Intr. 1764. Zone III.—**H. A. Vilmorínii** Rehd., var. A form with fls. 7–9 cm. across. B.M.8557(c). Korea. Cult. 1914.

2. **H. pátulum** Thunb. Half-evergreen or evergreen spreading shrub, to 1 m.: brts. arching, 2-edged, usually purplish: lvs. ovate-oblong to ovate-lanceolate, 3–6 cm. long, acutish, glaucous beneath: fls. solitary or in cymes, 4–5 cm. across, golden yellow; sepals orbicular-ovate, about ½ as long as petals; petals roundish, overlapping; styles upright, as long or slightly shorter than stamens. Fl.vii–ix. B.M.5693(c). R.H.1875:170,t(c). Gt.15:513. Gn. W.21:95. Japan. Intr. 1862. Zone VII. Free-flowering shrub with golden-yellow fls.—**H. p. oblongifòlium** (Wall.) Koehne, var. Lvs. 5–10 cm. long, acutish, bluish gray beneath: fls. 3–4 cm. across; sepals less than half as long as petals. (*H. o.* Wall., not Choisy.) Himal.—**H. p. ùralum** (Don) Koehne, var. Lvs. 2–3 cm. long, acute or acutish: fls. 2–2.5 cm. across; sepals less than half as long as petals. G.C.78:329(h). (*H. u.* Don, *H. nepalense* Hort., not Choisy.) Himal.—**H. p. Hénryi** Bean, var. More vigorous: lvs. ovate to ovate-oblong, 5–7 cm. long: infl. larger; fls. 5–6 cm. across; sepals ovate, acute. China. Intr. 1898. Zone (V), VI.—**H. p. Forréstii** Chittenden. Similar to var. *Henryi*, but fls. larger. J.L.48:f.26. S. W. China. Cult. 1922.

H. p. × *calycinum* = **H. Moseriànum** André. Shrub to 40 cm.: stems reddish, arching: lvs. ovate, 4–5 cm. long, obtuse and mucronulate: fls. 1–5, 5–6 cm. across, golden-yellow, with broad petals. R.H.1889:464. Gn.54:409,t(c). R.B.16:97. G.C.III.10:333. Orig. about 1887. Zone VII?—**H. M. trícolor** Mauméné. Lvs. variegated with white and edged red: fls. smaller. J.8:186. Orig. about 1893.

3. **H. Hookeriànum** Wight & Arn. Evergreen or half-evergreen compact shrub, to 2 m.: brts. reddish brown, terete: lvs. subsessile, ovate to ovate-oblong, 3–8 cm. long, obtuse or acutish, dark blue-green above, glaucous beneath: fls. cup-shaped, 5 cm. across, in several-fld. clusters; sepals large, obovate, obtuse; petals broad-obovate; stamens scarcely half as long as petals; styles recurved at apex, slightly longer than stamens: caps. broad-ovoid, furrowed. Fl.viii–ix. B.M.4949(c). Gn.54:490. G.3:463. (*H. oblongi-folium* Hook., not Choisy.) Sikkim, W. China. Intr. before 1853. Zone VII. Very handsome and showy.—**H. H. Leschenaùltii** (Choisy) Dyer. Sepals acute. G.C.74:143. Himal., Java.

4. **H. Dỳeri** Rehd. Half-evergreen shrub to 1 m., with slender spreading brs.; brts. angled: lvs. ovate to ovate-oblong, 2–3.5 cm. long, acute, glaucous

beneath: fls. about 3 cm. across, yellow, in loose leafy cymes; sepals linear-lanceolate; petals oblong; stamens very numerous, about as long as petals; styles upright, shorter than stamens. Fl.viii–ix. V.F.25. R.H.1931:436. (*H. lysimachioides* Wall. ex Dyer, not Boiss. & Noë.) Himal. Intr. 1894. Zone VI.

Related species: H. **kouytchénse** Lévl. Shrub to 0.5 m.: lvs. elliptic-ovate to elliptic-oblong, 2–4.5 cm. long; fls. about 5 cm. across, in 3-fld. cymes; sepals ovate-oblong to ovate-lanceolate; petals oblong-obovate, twice as long as stamens; styles longer than stamens. B.M.9345(c). W. China. Intr. 1907. Zone VI?—H. **cérnuum** Roxb. Brts. terete: lvs. narrow-elliptic to ovate-lanceolate, 3–7 cm. long: fls. pale yellow, 5 cm. across, long-stalked, nodding, solitary or in 3–5-fld. cymes; petals obovate; stamens little shorter than petals; styles slender, nearly as long as stamens. (*H. oblongifolium* Choisy.) Himal. Intr. about 1910. Zone VII.—H. **reptans** Hook. f. & Thoms. Prostrate shrub: lvs. elliptic-oblong, 6–12 mm. long: fls. solitary, about 4 cm. across. Gn.24:267; 30:221. Himal. Cult. 1883. Zone VII?—Sometimes confused with *H. repens* L., a perennial with smaller narrower lvs. and smaller fls. with 3 styles. S.F. 8:t.775(c).

5. H. chinénse L. Half-evergreen shrub to 60 cm.; brts. terete: lvs. sessile, oblong or narrow-oblong, 4–8 cm. long, obtuse: fls. solitary or in 3–7-fld. cymes, bright yellow, 4–6 cm. across; sepals ovate to elliptic-ovate or oblong-ovate, obtuse or acutish; the longer stamens as long as petals; style 1.5–2 cm. long, 5-cleft at apex. Fl.vi–ix. B.M.334(c). G.C.III.1:705; 92:411. S.H.2:f.224a. (*H. monogynum* Willd., *H. salicifolium* Sieb. & Zucc.) China, Japan. Intr. 1753. Zone VII.

6. H. lobocárpum Gattinger. Upright shrub to 2 m.; brts. angled: lvs. sessile or short-petioled, narrow-oblong to oblanceolate, 3–7 cm. long, obtuse or mucronulate, revolute at the margin: fls. 1–1.5 cm. broad, numerous, in dense cymes forming a terminal corymb or panicle; sepals oblong, obtusish; petals cuneate: capsule 5-lobed, 5–7 mm. long. Fl.viii–ix. G.F.10:453. S.H. 2:f.223b-c. N. C. and Tenn. Intr. before 1898. Zone V.

H. l. × *galioides* = H. **arnoldiànum** Rehd. Infl. a cylindric panicle; fr. 3–5-celled. Orig. 1904.—*H. l.* × *prolificum* = H. **Dawsoniànum** Rehd. Similar to *H. prolificum*, but differs in the many-fld. infl. and in the 3–5-celled lobed caps. Orig. 1893.

Closely related species: H. **oklahoménse** E. J. Palmer. Lvs. narrower, firmer, with conspicuous fascicles of smaller lvs.: infl. looser; fls. about 2 cm. across; petals oblong-obovate, about as long as stamens and style: caps. deeply lobed, sharply ridged. Okla. Intr. 1924. Zone V.

7. H. Kalmiànum L. Shrub to 1 m.; stems 4-angled; brts. 2-angled: lvs. linear-oblong to oblanceolate, 2.5–5 cm. long, bluish green above, glaucous beneath: fls. 1.5–2.5 cm. across, bright yellow, in 3-fld. cymes; sepals foliaceous, óblong, acute; stamens about half as long as petals; styles united below, slightly longer than stamens: fr. ovoid, 6–10 mm. across, beaked. Fl.viii. B.M.8491(c). G.F.3:113. M.M.6:t.8(c). Que. and Ont. to Mich. and Ill. Intr. 1760. Zone IV. Handsome hardy species.

H. K. × *densiflorum* = H. **nóthum** Rehd. Fls. more numerous, smaller; sepals narrower; fr. 3–5-celled. Orig. 1903.

8. H. galioìdes Lam. Subshrub to 1 m., with slender stems; brts. nearly terete or 2-edged; lvs. sessile, linear-oblanceolate, 1–5 cm. long, with axillary clusters of smaller lvs., acute, with recurved margin, dark green and conspicuously dotted above: fls. 1–1.5 cm. across, in terminal and axillary few-fld. cymes forming narrow leafy panicles; sepals linear or linear-spatulate, nearly as long as petals; petals cuneate: fr. conic-ovoid, 5–6 mm. long, furrowed. Fl.vii–ix. G.F.10:433. G.C.III.24:301. Del. to Ga., Mo. and Tex. Intr. 1790. Zone V.

H. g. × *lobocarpum;* see under No. 6.

Related species: **H. fasciculàtum** Lam. Shrub to 1.5 m.; brts. sharply 4-angled; lvs. of axillary clusters nearly as long as main pair, subulate, 5–20 mm. long, thick: sepals nearly as long as petals. N. C. to Fla. and Tex. Intr. 1811. Zone VII?

9. **H. prolíficum** L. Shrub with exfoliating light brown bark and rather stout upright brs., to 1.5 m. tall; brts. 2-edged: lvs. short-petioled, narrow-oblong to oblanceolate, 3–8 cm. long, obtuse, dark lustrous green above and pellucid-punctate: fls. about 2 cm. across, bright yellow, in terminal and axillary few- to several-fld. cymes; styles united at base: caps. oblong, 1–1.5 cm. long, not furrowed. Fl.vii–ix. G.F.3:526. W.D.2:t.88(c). (*H. foliosum* Jacq., *Myriandra prolifica* Spach.) N. J. to Iowa and Ga. Intr. about 1750. Zone IV. Often cult.; the most vigorous of the hardier cult. species.

H. p. × *frondosum* = **H. Vanfleètii** Hort. Fls. 2.5–3 cm. across, in terminal cymes, often with a few pairs of axillary solitary fls. below. Cult. 1925.—*H. p.* × *lobocarpum;* see under No. 6.

10. **H. frondòsum** Michx. Upright shrub with rather stout brs., to 1 m. tall, often with a single stem, with thin exfoliating reddish bark; brts. 2-edged: lvs. ovate-oblong to oblong, 2.5–6 cm. long, mucronate, bluish green above, glaucous beneath, pellucid-dotted: fls. terminal, 1 or few, sessile or subsessile, 3–5 cm. across, bright yellow; sepals obovate, unequal, much shorter than the broad-obovate petals; stamens very numerous; fr. ovoid, about 1 cm. long, not furrowed. Fl.vii–viii. B.M.8498(c). G.F.2:185. B.C. 3:1631. Gn.W.20:934. (*H. aureum* Bartr., not Lour., *H. prolificum* var. *a.* Koehne.) S. C. and Tenn. to Ga. and Tex. Intr. 1747. Zone V. Dense shrub with large bright fls.

H. f. × *prolificum;* see under No. 9.

Closely related species: **H. spléndens** Small. Lvs. oblong, 2–4 cm. long: fls. stalked, in several-fld. cymes; stamens orange: caps. with 3 narrow wings. Ga. Intr. 1906. Zone VII.

11. **H. nudiflòrum** Michx. Upright shrub or subshrub, to 1 m.; brts. 4-angled: lvs. elliptic-oblong to oblong-lanceolate, 2–6 cm. long, obtuse, flat, thin: fls. light yellow, 1.5–2 cm. across, in loose dichotomous cymes on a leafless peduncle; sepals elliptic-oblong to elliptic-oblanceolate, 3–4 mm. long: fr. conic-ovoid, 6–7 mm. long. Fl.vii–viii. N. C. to Fla. and Ala. Cult. 1897. Zone (V).

12. **H. cistifòlium** Lam. Stoloniferous subshrub, to 1 m.; stems 4-angled: lvs. narrow-oblong to linear-lanceolate, 2–8 cm. long, obtuse or acutish, often slightly clasping, revolute: fls. 1–1.5 cm. across, nearly sessile, in loose dichotomous cymes; sepals ovate to lanceolate, acute; petals cuneate at base: fr. subglobose to globose-ovoid, 4–6 mm. long, 1-celled. Fl.vii–ix. B.B. 2:532. (*H. sphaerocarpum* Michx.) Ohio to Ill., Ala. and Ark. Intr. 1880. Zone V. May be used as a sand-binding plant.

Related species: **H. túrgidum** Small. Shrub to 60 cm.: lvs. linear to linear-oblanceolate, 1–2.5 cm. long, acute, revolute: fls. about 1 cm. across, in several-fld. cymes; sepals ovate to elliptic: caps. subglobose, broadest above the middle, abruptly pointed, 3.5 mm. across. Ala. Intr. 1907. Zone VI or VII?—**H. glomeràtum** Small. Shrub to 1 m.: lvs. narrow-oblong to linear-oblong, 2–4 cm. long, apiculate: fls. 2–2.5 cm. across, in dense cymes; sepals narrow-oblong: caps. incompletely 3-celled. N. C. Cult. 1905. Zone VI.—**H. adpréssum** Bartr. Subshrub with upright stems or ascending from a creeping base, to 50 cm.: lvs. narrow-oblong to lanceolate, 2–6 cm. long: fls. 1–1.5 cm. across, in terminal cymes; sepals lanceolate or ovate-lanceolate: fr. ovoid, 5–6 mm. long, slender-beaked. B.B.2:531. (*H. fastigiatum* Ell.) Mass. to Ga. and La. Intr. 1888. Zone V.

13. **H. densiflòrum** Pursh. Upright shrub to 2 m.; brts. 2-edged: lvs. linear-oblong to linear, 1–5 cm. long, acute, revolute: fls. 1–1.5 cm. across,

in dense many-fld. corymbs; sepals unequal, oblong to elliptic-oblong: caps. ovoid, 4–6 mm. long, slightly 3-lobed. Fl.vii–ix. G.F.3:527. R.H.1899:517, 518. M.M.4:t.7(c). (*H. prolificum* var. *d.* Gray.) N. J. to Fla., Mo. and Tex. Intr. 1889. Zone V.

14. H. **Buckleyi** M. A. Curtis. Subshrub with decumbent or ascending stems, to 30 cm. high; stems 4-angled: lvs. obovate to elliptic, 5–20 mm. long, rounded at apex: fls. 2–2.5 cm. across, 1–3, terminal; sepals obovate or spatulate, about half as long as the narrow-obovate thin petals; styles connate: caps. conic-ovoid, 6–10 mm. long. Fl.vi–vii. G.F.4:581. N. C. to Ga. Intr. 1889. Zone V. Adapted for rockeries and as ground-cover.

15. H. **hircìnum** L. Half-evergreen subshrub of round compact habit, to 1 m.; brts. 2-edged: lvs. ovate to ovate-lanceolate, 2.5–6 cm. long, acute to obtuse, of goat-like odor when crushed: fls. about 3 cm. across, bright yellow, solitary or in 3-fld. cymes; sepals lanceolate, deciduous, about ⅓ or ¼ the length of the petals; stamens much longer than petals; caps. ovoid, pointed, 5 mm. long. Fl.vii–ix. W.D.2:t.86(c). Mediterr. region. Intr. 1640. Zone VII.—H. h. **pùmilum** Wats., var. Shrub to 30 cm. high, of dwarf compact habit: lvs. smaller. W.D.2:t.87(c). (*H. h.* var. *minus* Bean.)

Related species: H. inodòrum Willd. Slender-branched shrub, to 1.5 m., without goat-like odor: lvs. rather crowded, oblong-ovate, 2.5–5 cm. long, obtuse: fls. 2–2.5 cm. across, one or few; sepals lanceolate, about ½ as long as the narrow petals; stamens little longer than petals. Jaub. & Spach, Ill. 1:t.38. S.H.2:224b. S. E. Eu., Cauc. Cult. 1870.—H. olýmpicum L. Procumbent subshrub, 15–30 cm. high, with little-branched stems; brts. slightly 2-edged or nearly terete: lvs. sessile, elliptic-oblong to oblong, 1–3 cm. long, acutish, grayish green: fls. 1–5, yellow, about 5 cm. across; sepals ovate, acute; stamens in 3 bundles, slightly shorter than the oblong-obovate petals; styles 3, longer than the stamens. B.M. 1867(c). S.F.8:t.772(c). S.E. Eu., Asia Minor. Intr. 1706. Zone VII?—H. polyphýllum Boiss. & Bal. Similar to the preceding, but stems upright or ascending; lvs. narrower, with black dots beneath; sepals sparingly black-dotted. S.St. 123(h). Farrer, Engl. Rock-gard. 1:t.40(h). Asia Minor. Cult. 1910. Zone VII?

16. H. **elàtum** Ait. Half-evergreen shrub, to 1.5 m.; brts. slightly 2-edged: lvs. ovate to ovate-oblong, 3–8 cm. long, obtuse or acutish, often subcordate at base, bluish green beneath, of aromatic odor when bruised: fls. 2–3 cm. across, in several- to many-fld. terminal panicles; sepals ovate to ovate-lanceolate, reflexed in fr.; styles longer than stamens: fr. ovoid, pointed. Fl.vii–viii. R.I.6:t.352(c). S.H.2:f.225d-e. Webb & Berthelot, Fl. Canar.2:t.85(c). (*H. grandifolium* Choisy, *Androsaemum Webbianum* Spach.) Canary Isls., Madeira. Intr. 1762 and sometimes escaped from cult. Zone VII?—The typical Canary Island plant differs in its more reticulate lvs. and in the larger fls. from the cult. form which may be *H. elatum* × *Androsaemum* (*H. multiflorum* Hort., not H.B.K.).

17. H. **Androsaèmum** L. Tutsan. Half-evergreen shrub, to 1 m.; brts. 2-edged: lvs. ovate to ovate-oblong, 5–10 cm. long, obtuse, cordate or subcordate at base, whitish beneath, slightly aromatic: fls. 2–2.5 cm. across, light yellow, in 3–9-fld. cymes or solitary; sepals ovate, about 1 cm. long, little shorter than the petals; styles short, recurved, persistent: fr. berrylike, subglobose, about 8 mm. across, purple-black. Fl.vi–ix. R.I.6:t.352(c). F.D.21:2094(c.) S.H.2:f.225a-c. (*Androsaemum officinale* All.—Sweet-Amber.) W. and S. Eu., W. Asia. Cult. before 1600. Zone VI.

18. H. **Córis** L. Upright or sometimes procumbent subshrub, to 60 cm.; brts. terete: lvs. in whorls of 4–6, linear, 1–2 cm. long, revolute: fls. 2 cm. across, golden-yellow, in terminal panicles; sepals glandular-denticulate,

T. hispida aestivalis Hort., *T. amurensis* Hort.) S. E. Eu. to C. Asia. Cult. 1883. Zone II.—A variable species.

7. **T. odessàna** Stev. Shrub to 2 m., with upright slender brs.: lvs. lanceolate, subulate, decurrent: fls. pink, in slender racemes about 3 cm. long, on short naked peduncles: bracts linear-subulate, longer than the pedicels; pedicels deflexed, about as long as calyx; petals obovate, spreading; disk 5-lobed, with rounded lobes; styles often 4, sublinear, about ½ as long as ovary; anthers apiculate. Fl.vii–ix. Caspian region. Intr. about 1885. Zone IV.

8. **T. chinénsis** Lour. Chinese T. Shrub or small tree to 5 m., with slender spreading, often drooping brs. and very thin brts.: lvs. bluish green, lanceolate, acuminate, keeled: fls. pink, in slender racemes 3–5 cm. long, forming large and loose usually·pendulous panicles; bracts linear-subulate, gibbous at base, longer than pedicels; sepals ovate, much shorter than petals: disk deeply 10-lobed; styles clavate, ⅖–¾ as long as ovary; stamens as long or twice as long as petals; anthers obtuse. Fl.vii–ix. Ito, Fig. Pl. Koishik. 2:t.14(c). China. Intr. 1916 (or earlier?). Zone VII?

The very distinct **T. aphýlla** (L.) Karst. (*T. articulata* Vahl) with jointed brts., minute sheathing lvs. and 5-merous sessile fls. in terminal panicles, from N. E. Afr. and W. Asia is probably not hardy within our area.

2. **MYRICÀRIA** Desv. Deciduous shrubs or subshrubs; lvs. alternate, scale-like: fls. small, pink or white, short-pediceled or subsessile, in terminal or lateral dense racemes; sepals and petals 5; stamens 10, the filaments connate ⅓–½, rarely only at base; anthers introrse; ovary 1-celled, with 3 sessile stigmas; seeds with a stalked tuft of hairs: fr. a 3-valved caps. (Derived from Myrica, probably the ancient name of the Tamarisk.) About 10 species from Eu. to C. Asia, China and Siberia.

M. germànica (L.) Desv. Subshrub to 2 m., with upright wand-like stems, glabrous; lvs. lanceolate, obtuse, glandular-dotted, bluish green: fls. light pink or whitish, in terminal dense racemes, 10–20 cm. long, often with lateral ones at base; bracts ovate-lanceolate, long-acuminate, below with a broad membranous margin, exceeding the fl.-buds; stamens connate about ½. Fl. v–viii. S.O.3:t.131(c). G.H.t.38(c). F.D.13:t.1248(c). (*Tamarix g.* L.) C. and S. Eu., W. Asia. Intr. about 1582. Zone V.

Related species: **M. dahùrica** Ehrenb. Racemes on lateral brts.; bracts oblong-ovate, obtusish, with a membranous margin all around, not exceeding the fl.-buds; stamens connate, often only ⅓. Dahuria, Transbaicalia. Intr. 1816. Zone V.

Fam. 69. **CISTACEAE** Lindl. ROCK–ROSE FAMILY

Shrubs or herbs; lvs. usually opposite, rarely alternate, stipulate or exstipulate: fls. perfect, regular, solitary or in racemes and cymes; sepals 5 or sometimes 3, in ⅖ phyllotaxy; petals 5, rarely 3, caducous, sometimes wanting; convolutions of calyx and corolla in opposite directions; stamens numerous, hypogynous, unequal; ovary superior, 1-celled, with 3–10 parietal placentae; style 1: fr. a caps. dehiscent between the placentae; seeds with copious albumen and crustaceous testa; embryo usually curved.—Seven genera with about 160 species in N. Am. and the Mediterr. region, few in E. Asia and in S. Am.

A. Lvs. usually opposite, longer than 1 cm.: stigma large.
  B. Caps. 5–10-valved: fls. white or red to purple: upright shrubs.................1. *Cistus*
  BB. Caps. 3-valved: fls. often yellow.
    c. Style very short, straight; sepals 3 or 5.............................2. *Halimium*
    cc. Style elongated, curved or bent at base; sepals 5..................3. *Helianthemum*
AA. Lvs. alternate, crowded, 2.5–7 mm. long, scale-like or subulate: fls. small, yellow; stigma
    minute: heath-like shrubs..4. *Hudsonia*

1. **CISTUS** L. Rock-rose. Low upright shrubs, evergreen or half-evergreen, usually villous, more or less glandular and aromatic: lvs. opposite, entire, petioles connate at base, estipulate: fls. large in terminal and axillary cymes at end of brts., rarely solitary, white to purple; sepals 3 or 5; petals 5; stamens numerous; style elongated or short with a large 5–10-lobed stigma; ovary 5–10-celled, with many-ovuled placentae; caps. splitting into 5 or 10 valves. (*Kistos,* the ancient Greek name of the plant.) About 20 species in the Mediterr. region. Low shrubs with showy fls., not hardy north of the middle Atlantic states.

A. Sepals 5.
  B. Fls. red or purple.
    C. Lvs. distinctly 3-nerved, sessile.
      D. Fls. stalked: lvs. with straight revolute margin........................1. *C. albidus*
      DD. Fls. subsessile: lvs. with undulate margin.............................2. *C. crispus*
    CC. Lvs. penninerved, short-petioled...3. *C. villosus*
  BB. Fls. white.
    C. Sepals rounded at base: lvs. sessile, lanceolate, 3–8 mm. broad....4. *C. monspeliensis*
    CC. Sepals cordate at base.
      D. Lvs. sessile, 3-nerved...5. *C. hirsutus*
      DD. Lvs. petioled, penninerved, 3-nerved at base.
        E. Lvs. 1.2–4.5 cm. long...6. *C. salvifolius*
        EE. Lvs. 5–9 cm. long, cordate at base, viscid.....................7. *C. populifolius*
AA. Sepals 3: fls. white: lvs. 3-nerved, viscid.
  B. Lvs. subsessile: fls. usually solitary, long-stalked; sepals lepidote.....8. *C. ladaniferus*
  BB. Lvs. petioled: fls. cymose; sepals hairy................................9. *C. laurifolius*

1. **C. álbidus** L. Shrub to 2 m.; young parts white-tomentose: lvs. sessile, elliptic to ovate-oblong, 2–5 cm. long, obtuse, revolute, 3-nerved at base, reticulate beneath and stellate-tomentose: fls. 3–8, stalked, about 6 cm. across, rosy lilac, the petals blotched yellow at base; sepals broad-ovate, short-acuminate: style longer than stamens. Fl.vi–vii. R.I.3:t.39(c). S.C.31(c). G.C.45:117(h). W. Mediterr. region. Cult. 1640. Zone VII.—**C. a. albus** E. F. Warb., var. Fls. pure white. Cult. 1930.

C. a. × *crispus* = **C. pulveruléntus** Pourr. Low shrub: lvs. undulate, the upper plane or nearly so: fls. short-stalked, subtended by acuminate bracts; sepals ovate-lanceolate. (*C. Delilei* Burnat.) S. W. Eu. Cult. 1929.—*C. a.* × *villosus* = **C. canéscens** Sweet. Lvs. oblong-lanceolate to linear-oblong, stellate-tomentose, 3-nerved, short-petioled. S.C.45(c). Cult. 1827.

2. **C. críspus** L. Compact shrub to 1 m.; young brts. with long white hairs: lvs. sessile, elliptic-ovate to lanceolate, 1–4 cm. long, acute, undulate, rugose above, stellate-tomentose on both sides: fls. subsessile, purplish red, 3.5–4 cm. across, in dense terminal heads; sepals lanceolate, acuminate. Fl. vi–vii. R.I.3:t.38(c). S.C.22(c). B.M.9306(c). Gn.34:252,t(c);79:299(h);83: 176(h). W. Mediterr. region. Intr. 1656. Zone VII.

C. c. × *villosus* var. *creticus* = **C. crispàtus** Bornet. Brts. villous: lvs. sessile, connate, obovate-oblong to oblanceolate, pubescent on both sides: fls. about 5 cm. across, pink; sepals ovate-lanceolate, acuminate, villous. J.L.55:f.11. Cult. 1930.—*C. c.* × *albidus*; see under No. 1.

Related species: **C. várius** Pourr. Lvs. sessile, lanceolate, rugose above, undulate: fls. white, 2–2.5 cm. across; stamens half as long as petals. Willk. Ic. t.87(c). (*C. Pouzolzii* Del., *?C. crispus* × *monspeliensis.*) W. Mediterr. reg. Intr. 1929.

3. **C. villosus** L. Compact shrub to 1 m.; young brts. villous: lvs. elliptic to ovate-oblong, 2.5–6 cm. long, obtuse, abruptly narrowed into a short sheathing petiole, penninerved, rugose and sparingly stellate-pubescent above, more densely so beneath and grayish: fls. purple to rose-colored, 5–6 cm. across, petals yellowish at base, in 3–5-fld. terminal cymes; peduncle grayish tomentose; sepals ovate, acuminate, villous; style about as long as stamens. Fl.vi–vii. B.M.43(c). R.I.3:t.40(c). F.D.13:t.1254(c). S.C.35(c). Gn.27:571. B.S.1 344. Mediterr. region. Intr. about 1650. Zone VI?—**C. v. taùricus**

(Presl) Grosser, var. Lower lvs. roundish, the middle ones obovate-spatulate, the upper lanceolate; pedicels twice as long as sepals. (*C. t.* Presl.) E. Mediterr. region. Cult. 1898. Probably the hardiest variety. Zone (V).— **C. v. crèticus** (L.) Boiss., var. Glandular-pubescent: lvs. rugose, undulate and crisped on the margin, strongly reticulate beneath. H.A.13:t.33(c). Willk. Ic. t.83(c). Cult. 1894.

C. v. × *ladaniferus* = **C. purpúreus** Lam. Young brts. villous and resinous: lvs. nearly sessile, oblong-lanceolate, 3-nerved at base, penninerved above, grayish tomentose beneath: fls. 6–8 cm. across, reddish purple with a dark red blotch at base of each petal. B.R.5:408(c). S.C.17(c). G.C.48:118,119(h). Gn.31:326,t(c);86:305(h). Orig. before 1790.—*C. v.* × *laurifolius.* Here belongs: "Silver Pink" Hillier. Lvs. resembling *C. laurifolius,* but smaller and grayer; fls. pale pink. Orig. before 1933.—*C. v.* × *albidus;* see under No. 1.— *C. v.* × *crispus;* see under No. 2.

Related species: **C. heterophýllus** Desf. Brts. stellate-tomentose and white-pilose: lvs. subsessile, elliptic to ovate-lanceolate, 1.5–2 cm. long, stellate-pubescent and scabrid above, more densely so beneath: fls. long-stalked, 5 cm. across; sepals orbicular, apiculate; petals rose, yellow at base. S.C.t.6(c). Algeria. Intr. 1817.—**C. parviflòrus** Lam. Brts. appressed villous-tomentose: lvs. petioled, 3-nerved, ovate-elliptic or elliptic, 1–2 cm. long, obtuse or acute, whitish-tomentose and reticulate beneath: fls. 2–6, 2.5–3 cm. across, rose; style very short. S.C.t.14(c). Mediterr. reg. Cult. 1825.—*C. p.* × *monspeliensis* = **C. Skanbérgii** Lojac. Brts. densely villous: lvs. petioled, oblong to linear-lanceolate, the lower obtuse, the upper acutish: fls. 2–5; rose; outer sepals broadovate, acuminate. B.M.9514(c). S. Eu. Cult. 1930.

4. C. monspeliénsis L. Shrub to 1.5 m.; brts. pilose, viscid when young: lvs. subsessile, 3-nerved, lanceolate to linear-lanceolate, obtuse or acutish, 2–5 cm. long, revolute at margin, rugose and dark green above, grayish and stellate-pubescent beneath, hairy on the veins: fls. white, about 2.5 cm. across, in 3–10-fld. cymes; sepals ovate, acuminate, long-pilose like the pedicels; stigma subsessile. Fl.vi–vii. R.I.3:t.37(c). F.D.13:t.1252(c). S.C.27(c). W. Mediterr. region. Intr. before 1650. Zone VII.

C. m. × *populifolius* = **C. nígricans** Pourr. Viscid: lvs. ovate-lanceolate, 4–5 cm. long, acute, undulate, attenuate into a short petiole: infl. long-stalked, 3–5-fld.; fls. 5 cm. across; sepals broadly cordate-ovate, apiculate. S.C.12(c). E.N.III.6:302. Cult. 1825.—*C. m.* × *ladaniferus* × *laurifolius* = **C. Hetiéri** Verguin. Viscid: lvs. lanceolate to linear-lanceolate, 3–6 cm. long, sessile and connate at base, whitish tomentose and reticulate beneath: fls. 4 cm. across, on slender villous pedicels; sepals ovate, acuminate, clothed with long white hairs. S. France. Cult. 1930.—*C. m.* × *laurifolius* = **C. glaùcus** Pourr. Lvs. petioled, lanceolate to linear-lanceolate, 3-nerved, gray-tomentose and reticulate beneath: fls. 4–5 cm. across; the 2 outer sepals ovate-lanceolate, half as long as the inner ones. H.A.13:t.36(c). (*C. Ledon* Lam.) Cult. 1900.—*C. m.* × *crispus;* see under No. 2.—*C. m.* × *parviflorus;* see under No. 3.—*C. m.* × *hirsutus;* see under No. 5.—*C. m.* × *salvifolius;* see under No. 6.

5. C. hirsùtus Lam. Shrub to 1 m.; young brts. with long white hairs: lvs. sessile, elliptic-lanceolate, obtuse, 3–6 cm. long, 3-nerved, pilose above, stellate-pubescent beneath: fls. in terminal cymes with alternate bracts, 3–3.5 cm. across, white, the petals yellow at base; bracts alternate; outer sepals cordate, 8–12 mm. long, margin long-pilose, accrescent after anthesis, acuminate, the inner ones smaller, ovate. Fl.vi–vii. S.C.19(c). S. W. Eu. Intr. about 1650. Zone VII.—**C. h. psilocéphalus** (Sweet) Willk., var. Lvs. short-petioled, undulate: outer sepals pilose-ciliate, glabrous on back. S.C. 33(c). Cult. 1826.

C. h. × *monspeliensis* = **C. platysépalus** Sweet. Lvs. sessile, 3-nerved, ovate-lanceolate, nearly glabrous except glandular-pubescent on veins beneath: fls. 3–6; sepals cordate, not revolute on margin, like the pedicels rather sparingly long-pilose. S.C.47(c). J.L.55:f.13. Cult. 1827.—*C. h.* × *salvifolius* = **C. obtusifòlius** Sweet. Lvs. sessile or subsessile, oval to ovate-oblong, rugose and scabrid above, paler and stellate-pubescent beneath: outer sepals smaller, short and sparingly pilose. S.C.42(c). Cult. 1827.—*C. h.* × *populifolius* = **C. laxus** Ait. Lvs. ovate-lanceolate, short-petioled, pubescent on both sides when young and slightly viscid, ciliate; fls. 5 cm. across, on villous stalks; sepals very hairy, acuminate, the outer broader and cordate. S.C.12(c). J.H.55:f.12. (*C. Merinoi* Pau.) Cult. 1656.—*C.? h.* × *ladaniferus* = **C. lusitànicus** Maund, not Mill. Somewhat viscid; lvs. sessile, oblong-lanceolate to lanceolate, 3–6 cm. long, obtuse or acutish, revolute, dull and nearly glabrous above, sparingly stellate-pubescent and reticulate beneath: fls. short-stalked, 6–7 cm. across; petals with purplish blotch; sepals broad-ovate, stellate-pubescent outside. J.H.55:f.9. Gn. 90:447(h). (*C. recognitus* Hort., not Rouy & Fouc.) Cult. 1830.—**C. l. de-cùmbens** Maund. Habit spreading: lvs. oblong-lanceolate, shiny above: petals with conspicuous purple blotch. B.M.8490(c). G.C.66:25(h). Gn.78:428(h), 539;83:304. (*C. Loretii* Hort., not Rouy & Fouc.) Cult. 1830.

6. **C. salvifòlius** L. Shrub to 60 cm.; young brts. thinly stellate-tomentose: lvs. short-petioled, oval to ovate-oblong, 1.5–4 cm. long, grayish green and rugose above, paler beneath, stellate-tomentose on both sides: fls. 1–3, white, the petals yellow at base, 3.5–4.5 cm. across; outer sepals cordate, acuminate, stellate-tomentose. Fl.v–vi. R.I.3:t.36(c). F.D.13:t.1253(c). S.C. 54(c). Gn.83:305(h). G.C.100:25(h). Mediterr. region. Intr. about 1550. Zone VII?

C. s. × *populifolius* = **C. corbariénsis** Pourr. Young brts. minutely pubescent: lvs. petioled, ovate, 2–5 cm. long, cordate or rounded at base, undulate at margin, stellate-pubescent on both sides: fls. 3.5 cm. across. R.I.3:t.36(c). S.C. 8(c). Gn.78:58(h). (*C. populifolius minor* Hort.) Spontaneous hybrid. Zone VII?—*C. s.* × *monspeliensis* = **C. florentinus** Lam. Young brts. tomentose: lvs. short-petioled, elliptic-lanceolate, 2.5–3.5 cm. long, dull green and rugose above, grayish and stellate-pubescent beneath, 3-nerved at base. S.C.t.59(c). Gn.53: 130,134;83:305(h). Spontaneous hybrid.—*C. s.* × *laurifolius* = **C. Cóstei** E.G. Camus. Lvs. petioled, 3-nerved at base, ovate, acuminate, gray-tomentose beneath: fls. 2–3; outer sepals ovate-lanceolate, half as long as the broader inner ones; peduncles and pedicels slender. S. France. Cult. 1930.—*C. s.* × *hirsutus;* see under No. 5.—*C. s.* × *ladaniferus;* see under No. 8.—*C. s.* × *Halimium umbellatum* see *Halimiocistus Sahucii.*—*C. s.* × *Halimium lasianthum* see *Halimiocistus wintonensis,* p. 647.

7. **C. populifòlius** L. Shrub to 2 m.; young brts. slightly pubescent and viscid; lvs. long-petioled, ovate, acuminate, cordate, 5–9 cm. long, glabrous, reticulate beneath; petiole 1–2.5 cm. long, ciliate: fls. 2–5, white, about 5 cm. across; petals yellow at base; outer sepals cordate at base. Fl.vi–vii. S.C. 23 and 70(c). (*C. cordifolius* Mill.) S. W. Eu. Cult. 1656. Zone VII?

C. p. × *monspeliensis;* see under No. 4.—*C. p.* × *hirsutus;* see under No. 5.— *C. p.* × *salvifolius;* see under No. 6.

8. **C. ladaníferus** L. Shrub to 1.5 m.; brts. very viscid: lvs. subsessile, lanceolate or linear-lanceolate, 4–8 cm. long, narrowed at ends, 3-nerved, glabrous and viscid above, gray-tomentose beneath: fls. solitary, 7–10 cm. across, white, each petal with a large purple blotch at base; sepals 3, concave, lepidote, yellow. Fl.vi–vii. H.A.13:t.36(c). L.D.4:t.265(c). S.C.1(c). Gn.30:30,t(c);66:257(h);78:616(h). W. Mediterr. region. Intr. 1629. Zone VII.—**C. l. albiflòrus** Dunal, var. Petals only yellow at base, not blotched purple. S.C.84(c). Gn.89:356. (*C. l. immaculatus* Hort.)

C. l. × *salvifolius* = **C. Verguínii** Coste & Soulié. Slightly viscid: lvs. short-petioled, lanceolate, nearly glabrous or slightly whitish pubescent and reticulate beneath: fls. 4–5 cm. across, solitary or tomentose stalks longer than calyx; petals white with purple blotch; sepals usually 4–5, slightly ciliate. S. France. Cult. 1930.—*C. l.* × *monspeliensis;* see under No. 4.—*C. l.* × *laurifolius* × *monspeliensis;* see under No. 4.—*C. l.* × *hirsutus;* see under No. 5.—*C. l.* × *laurifolius;* see under No. 9.

9. **C. laurifòlius** L. Shrub to 2.5 m.; young brts. hairy and viscid: lvs. petioled, ovate to ovate-lanceolate, 3.5–7 cm. long, acuminate, rounded at base, 3-nerved, undulate at margin, glabrous and dark green above, tomen-

tose beneath, viscid: fls. 3–8, in long-peduncled cymes, 5–7 cm. across, white, petals yellow at base; sepals 3, ovate, concave, pubescent. Fl.vɪ–vɪɪɪ. R.I. 3:t.37(c). S.C.52(c). Gn.53:131;64:234. Gs.2:279(h). M.G.32:297(h). Mediterr. region. Intr. 1731. Zone VII?

C. l. × *ladaniferus* = **C. cýprius** Lam. Shrub to 2.5 m.; young brts. glutinous: lvs. oblong-lanceolate, 4–8 cm. long, narrow at ends, glabrous above, graypubescent beneath, viscid: fls. 3–6, in long-peduncled cymes, about 7 cm. across, white, each petal with a purple blotch; sepals lepidote. S.C.39(c). B.M.112(c, as *C. ladaniferus*). Gn.83:389(h). R.H.1917:327,329(h). J.H.58:306(h). Orig. before 1790.—*C. l.* × *villosus;* see under No. 3.—*C. l.* × *ladaniferus* × *monspeliensis:* see under No. 4.—*C. l.* × *salvifolius;* see under No. 6.

× **HALIMIOCISTUS** Janchen. Hybrids between *Cistus* and *Halimium.*

The following are in cult.: **H. Sahùcii** (Coste & Soulié) Janchen. (*C. salvifolius* × *H. umbellatum*). Lvs. linear-lanceolate or lanceolate: fls. white, 3 cm. across; sepals 4–5, rarely 3, subequal, rounded at base. S. France. Cult. 1933.—**H. wintonénsis** (Hillier) Warb. (*C. salvifolius* × *H. lasianthum*). Lvs. similar to *C. salvifolius:* fls. white, with purple-brown zone at base of petals. (*C. w.* Hillier.) Orig. before 1926.

2. **HALIMIUM** Spach. Evergreen shrubs, subshrubs or herbs: lvs. exstipulate, the lower opposite, the upper alternate or all alternate; fls. in terminal raceme- or umbel-like cymes, yellow or white; sepals 3 or 5; petals 5, fugacious; stamens many; style short, straight, with capitate or 3-lobed stigma: caps. 3-valved with many seeds; embryo strongly curved like a ring or hook. (From Greek *halimos* (*Atriplex Halimus*), in reference to color and shape of lvs.) Seven species in the Mediterr. region and W. Asia.

A. Lvs. linear to linear-lanceolate, sessile......................................1. *H. umbellatum*
AA. Lvs. ovate or obovate to lanceolate, at least partly petioled..............2. *H. lasianthum*

1. **H. umbellàtum** (L.) Spach. Low shrub with upright or ascending brs.: lvs. sessile, clasping, linear to linear-lanceolate, 0.8–2.5 cm. long, revolute, pubescent above, white-tomentose beneath, the upper ones of flowering brts. bract-like, triangular, acuminate: fls. about 2 cm. across, in terminal cymes, white, yellow at base of petals; sepals oval, 5 mm. long, short-pubescent or viscid-puberulous. S.C.5(c). B.S.1:615. (*Helianthemum u.* Mill.) S. Eu., N. Afr. Intr. 1731. Zone VII.

H. u. × *Cistus salvifolius;* see under *Halimiocistus,* above.
Related species: **H. Libanòtis** (L.) Lange. Lvs. linear, 1–3.5 cm. long, glabrous above and grayish tomentulose beneath except midrib: fls. 1–3 at end of lateral brts., on slender pedicels; sepals oval, glabrous. E.P.IV.193:40. (*Helianthemum L.* Willd.) W. Mediterr. reg. Cult. 1894.

2. **H. lasiánthum** (Lam.) K. Koch. Upright shrub to 1 m., with spreading brs.; young brts. grayish stellate-tomentose intermixed with white hairs: lvs. short-petioled, oval to ovate-oblong or lanceolate, 1.5–3.5 cm. long, obtuse or mucronulate, 3-nerved at base, grayish tomentulose and with long white hairs when young; upper and middle lvs. of flowering brts. broad-ovate, sessile, smaller: fls. 1–5 at end of short brts., 3.5 cm. across, yellow, each petal with a brownish purple blotch at base; pedicels silky-villous, 1–2 cm. long: sepals 3, ovate, acuminate, stellate-tomentose. Fl.v–vɪ. B.M.264(c). S.C.50 (c). B.S.1:613. Gn.84:355. (*Helianthemum l.* Pers., *H. formosum* Dun.) Portugal. Intr. 1780. Zone VII?

H. l. × *Cistus salvifolius;* see under *Halimiocistus,* above.
Related species: **H. halimifòlium** (L.) Willk. & Lange. Young brts. lepidote and grayish pubescent: lvs. short-petioled, oblong or oblong-obovate to lanceolate, attenuate at base, white-tomentose and lepidote when young, later grayish

green: fls. 2–7, 3.5 cm. across, yellow, each petal with a small dark blotch; sepals 5, lepidote and pubescent or nearly glabrous, the outer ones smaller. S.C.t.4(c). E.P.IV.193:40. (*Helianthemum h.* Willd.) S. Eu., N. Afr. Cult. 1656.—H. h. multiflórum (Salzm.) Grosser, var. With numerous upright flowering brts.: ivs. stellate-tomentose or lepidote and pilose above: pedicels and sepals lepidote and stellate-pilose. Willk. Ic. t.108(c). N. Afr.—*H. h.* × *alyssoides* = H. cheiranthoïdes (Lam.) K. Koch. Lvs. oblong-lanceolate, stellate-tomentose and lepidote on both sides: fls. 2–3, yellow; outer sepals minute. (*Helianthemum ch.* Pers.) Portugal. Cult. 1894.—H. alyssoïdes (Lam.) K. Koch. Lvs. ovate-lanceolate to oblong-obovate, the lower short-petioled, the upper ones sessile: fls. bright yellow, unblotched, 3.5–4 cm. across; peduncles, pedicels and sepals short-villous. S.C.81(c). (*Helianthemum a.* Vent., *H. scabrosum* Pers.) S. W. Eu. Intr. 1775.—H. ocymoides (Lam.) Willk. & Lange. Lvs. lanceolate to oblong-obovate, the upper ones of the flowering brts. green and sessile, those of the sterile brts. gray and petioled: fls. in loose panicles, bright yellow, each petal purple at base, 2.5–3 cm. across; pedicels slender, sparingly hirsute; sepals ovate-lanceolate, sparingly pilose or nearly glabrous. B.M.627(c). S.C.13,40(c). (*Helianthemum o.* Pers., *H. algarvense* Dunal.) Spain, Portugal. Intr. 1800.

To the closely related genus Crocánthemum Spach, differing from *Halimium* chiefly in the alternate lvs., the presence of small cleistogamous fls. and 5 sepals, belongs C. canadénse (L.) Britt. Perennial: lvs. oblong-lanceolate, 1–3 cm. long, grayish tomentose beneath: normal fls. solitary, yellow, 2–3 cm. across. Gr.G.1:t.87. B.B.2:540. (*Helianthemum c.* Michx.) Me. to N. C. and Miss.

3. HELIÁNTHEMUM Adans. Sun-rose.

Evergreen or half-evergreen, shrubby, suffruticose or herbaceous plants, rarely annual: lvs. mostly oppo-site, or the upper ones alternate, rarely all alternate, entire, with or without stipules: fls. in terminal circinate raceme- or umbel-like or subcapitate cymes, usually yellow; sepals 5, the 2 outer ones smaller; petals 5; stamens many, rarely only 7–20: ovary 1-celled or imperfectly 3-celled; style slender: fr. a 3-valved caps., with several to many seeds; embryo folded. (Greek *helios*, sun, and *anthemon*, flower.) About 70 species in Eu., N. Afr. and W. Asia.— Low, often prostrate, sun-loving plants suited for rockeries, grown for their profuse yellow, rarely white to purple fls.; most species like limestone soil.— For further information see the monograph by Grosser (E.P. IV. 193 [1903]), also Janchen, Die Cistaceen Oesterreich-Ungarns (1909).

A. Style as long or longer than stamens: lvs. stipulate.
   B. Stipules linear-subulate, the lower and middle ones as long as petioles: fls. white.
                                                                    1. *H. apenninum*
   BB. Stipules lanceolate or linear-lanceolate, longer than petiole: fls. usually yellow.
      C. Lvs. stellate-tomentose on both sides (see also *H. sulphureum* under No. 3).
                                                                   2. *H. glaucum*
      CC. Lvs. glabrous or only pilose above, rarely slightly tomentose.
         D. Lvs. grayish tomentose beneath..3. *H. nummularium*
          DD. Lvs. green beneath with scattered stellate hairs................4. *H. grandiflorum*
AA. Style shorter than stamens; fls. yellow: lvs. exstipulate.
   B. Lvs. grayish pubescent beneath: fls. 8–15 mm. across......................5. *H. canum*
   BB. Lvs. green on both sides: fls. 15–20 mm. across............................6. *H. alpestre*

1. H. apennìnum (L.) Mill. Low much-branched subshrub with upright or procumbent stems to 40 cm.; young brts. and lvs. whitish or grayish tomen-tulose: lvs. petioled, oblong-elliptic to linear-oblong, obtusish or acute, 1–3 cm. long, usually revolute, grayish tomentulose on both sides or green above: infl. 3–10-fld., raceme-like; fls. white, 2.5–3 cm. across; sepals 5, the inner elliptic, 5–8 mm. long, white-tomentulose, the outer linear-lanceolate, ⅓–½ as long; petals obovate. Fl.v–viii. S.C.62(c). S.E.19:t.1322(c). R.I.3:f.4554 (c). F.D.13:t.1261(c). (*H. pulverulentum* DC., *H. polifolium* Pers.) W. and S. Eu., Asia Minor. Intr. 1731. Zone VI.—H. a. róseum (Jacq.) Gross., var. Lvs. lanceolate, acutish, 2–3.5 cm. long, with flat margin; greenish above: fls. reddish. S.C.7(c). (*H. a.* var. *rhodanthum* Bean.) S. Eu.—H. a. versícolor (Sweet) Grosser, var. Lvs. about 1.5 cm. long, glabrous and green above: fls. rose, pink or reddish, sometimes variegated. S.C.26(c).

exstipulate: fls. solitary at the end of short brts., yellow; sepals 3, equal, petals 5, obovate-oblong, fugacious; stamens 10–30; ovary 1-celled, with 3 2-ovuled placentae, style filiform; stigma minute; fr. a 3-valved caps. enclosed by the connivent sepals; embryo coiled. (After William Hudson, an English botanist; 1730–93.) Three species in E. N. Am.—Rarely cultivated, difficult to grow and short-lived; they thrive best in sandy soil.

H. tomentòsa Nutt. Tufted shrub to 20 cm. high; hoary-pubescent: lvs. elliptic to oblong, about 2 mm. long, densely imbricated and appressed: fls. bright yellow, 8 mm. across, sessile or nearly so; sepals obtuse: caps. glabrous. Fl.v–vii. G.G.1:t.90. E.P.IV.193:132. S.H.2:f.237. N. B. to Va. and along the Gt. Lakes to Minn.; seashore and lake and river shores. Intr. 1826. Zone IV.

Related species: **H. ericoìdes** L. Soft-pubescent, greenish: lvs. slender, subulate, 6–8 mm. long: fls. on slender pedicels 1–1.5 cm. long; sepals acutish. S.C. 36(c). L.B.2:192(c). N. S. to N. C. Intr. 1805.—**H. montana** Nutt. Slightly villous, green: lvs. subulate, 3–6 mm. long: fls. about 1 cm. across on a pedicel 1 cm. long; sepals acuminate. High mts. of N. C. Intr. ?

Fam. 70. **VIOLACEAE** DC. VIOLET FAMILY

Herbs, shrubs or small trees: lvs. usually alternate, stipulate: fls. perfect, regular or irregular; sepals 5, distinct or nearly so; petals 5, often one spurred; stamens 5, connivent; ovary 1-celled, with 2–5 placentae, ovules usually many, anatropous; style usually club-shaped: fr. a loculicidal caps., rarely a berry.—About 15 genera with 300 species in both hemispheres.

HYMENANTHÈRA R. Br. Evergreen or half-evergreen shrubs or small trees: lvs. alternate, sometimes fascicled, small, entire or toothed; stipules deciduous: fls. small, axillary, solitary or fascicled; sepals and petals 5; anthers nearly sessile, connate into a tube with a membranous appendage at the apex and 5 scale-like appendages on the back; ovary with 2 1-ovuled placentae; style short, with 2-lobed stigma: fr. a berry with 1 or 2 subglobose seeds. (Greek *hymen,* membrane, and anthera; referring to the membranous appendage of the anthers.) Four or 5 species in Australasia.

H. crassifòlia Hook. f. Dense half-evergreen shrub to 2 m., with rigid brs. pubescent when young: lvs. crowded, short-stalked, obovate, 1–2.5 cm. long, rounded or slightly emarginate at apex, entire, glabrous, thickish: fls. solitary or few, short-stalked, yellowish white or brownish, 4 mm. across: fr. subglobose, white, about 6 mm. across. Fl.v; fr.viii. B.M.9426(c). G.C.III. 12:412. Gn.84:122. S.H.2:f.238. New Zeal. Intr. about 1875. Zone VII?

Related species: **H. angustifòlia** R. Br. Half-evergreen, to 3 m.: lvs. linear-spatulate, 0.6–2.5 cm. long, obtuse or emarginate. Tasmania. Cult. 1923. Zone VII?

Fam. 71. **FLACOURTIACEAE** Dum. FLACOURTIA FAMILY

Trees or shrubs, rarely climbing: lvs. usually alternate and often 2-ranked, usually pinnately veined, undivided; stipules usually caducous: fls. usually in cymes, regular, perfect, rarely unisexual; sepals 2–6, usually 4–5, imbricate or valvate, often persistent and accrescent after anthesis; petals as many as sepals, rarely more, sometimes wanting; receptacle often with appendages between the ovary and the petals; stamens numerous, hypogynous or perigynous; ovary superior or nearly so, 1-celled, with usually 3–5 parietal placentae; ovules usually numerous, apotropous or epitropous; styles as many as placentae or 1: fr. a caps. or berry, rarely drupe or achene; seed albuminous; embryo straight. About 85 genera with 500 species, mostly tropical.

A. Fls. dioecious, 0.6–1.5 cm. across.
  B. Fr. a berry: sepals imbricate: lvs. 5–6-nerved at base.........................1. *Idesia*
  BB. Fr. a caps.; sepals valvate; lvs. 3–5-nerved at base.....................2. *Poliothyrsis*
AA. Fls. perfect, 3–3.5 cm. across; sepals valvate: lvs. 3-nerved at base...........3. *Carrierea*

1. **IDÈSIA** Maxim. Deciduous tree; winter-buds glabrous, with several to many imbricate acuminate scales: lvs. alternate, long-petioled, dentate; stipules small, caducous: fls. dioecious or polygamous, apetalous, in large terminal panicles; sepals 3–6, usually 5, imbricate, yellowish, pubescent; staminate fls. with numerous stamens and a small rudimentary pistil; filaments filiform, pubescent; anthers elliptic; pistillate fls. with a subglobose ovary and short staminodes at base; styles usually 5, spreading, with obovate stigmas: fr. a fleshy, many-seeded berry; seeds roundish-ovoid. (After Eberhard Ysbrant Ides, Dutch traveler in China [1691–95].) One species in E. Asia.

I. **polycárpa** Maxim. Tree to 15 m.; bark close, grayish white; brs. spreading, forming a broad round head: lvs. ovate to oblong-ovate, acuminate, cordate or subcordate, 12–25 cm. long, remotely crenate-serrate, deep green above, glaucous beneath, glabrous, except bearded in the axils; petiole 6–15 cm. long, with 1–3 glands about the middle: fls. greenish yellow, fragrant, slender-pediceled, in pendulous panicles 10–25 cm. long; staminate fls. about 1.5 cm., pistillate 8 mm. across; fr. dull orange-red or orange-brown, 7–8 mm. across, in large pendulous panicles. Fl.v–vi; fr.ix–xi. B.M.6794(c). I.S.1:t.38. N.K.17:t.15. G.C.39:13. Gn.13:99. J.L.27:410,t(h). F.E.24:853 (h). (*Polycarpa Maximowiczii* Hort.) S. Japan, C. and W. China. Intr. about 1864. Zone VI?—I. p. **vestìta** Diels., var. Lvs. densely pubescent or tomentose beneath. W. China. Intr. 1908.

2. **POLIOTHÝRSIS** Oliv. Deciduous tree; winter-buds with 2 or 4 outer pubescent scales: lvs. petioled, alternate, dentate; stipules small, caducous: fls. monoecious, apetalous, in terminal panicles; sepals 5, ovate to lanceolate, valvate: staminate fls. with numerous free short stamens and a rudimentary pistil: pistillate fls. with staminodes at base of ovary: styles 3, reflexed, 2-parted at apex: fr. a 3–4-valved caps.; seeds many, oblong, with a broad wing, the seed in the centre. (Greek, *polios*, grayish white, and *thyrsos*, panicle; referring to the color of the infl.) One species in China.

P. **sinénsis** Oliv. Slender tree to 15 m.; young brts. pubescent: lvs. ovate to ovate-oblong, acuminate, usually rounded or truncate at base, 8–16 cm. long, dentate, pubescent beneath or nearly glabrous; petiole 2–4 cm. long: fls. greenish white changing to yellow, 6–8 mm. across, in loose panicles 10–20 cm. long; sepals whitish tomentose outside: caps. oblong-ovoid, nearly 2 cm. long. Fl.vii; fr.x–xi. H.I.19:1885. I.S.2:t,93. Gt.73:180. S.H.2:f.243. C. China. Intr. 1908. Zone VII.

3. **CARRIÈREA** Franch. Deciduous trees; winter-buds small, with 2 outer scales: lvs. alternate, long-petioled, crenate-dentate, exstipulate: fls. perfect, apetalous, in terminal racemes or panicles; sepals 5, free, valvate; stamens numerous, shorter than sepals; ovary obovoid, pubescent, with 3–4 short spreading 3-lobed styles; placentae 3–4: fr. a woody oblong caps. attenuate at ends, tomentulose, dehiscent into 3 or 4 divisions; seeds many, winged. (After Elie Abel Carrière, French horticulturist and botanist; 1816–1896.) Three species in S. E. Asia.

C. **calycìna** Franch. Shrub or tree to 15 m.; bark smooth, lenticellate, grayish brown: lvs. oval to obovate-oblong, 5–15 cm. long, abruptly short-acuminate, rounded to subcordate and 3-nerved at base, lustrous green and glabrous on both sides; petiole 3–5 cm. long: infl. 5–12-fld.; fls. creamy white, cup-shaped, 3–3.5 cm. across; pedicels 2-bracted, 1.5–3 cm. long; sepals ovate, cordate, tomentulose on both sides: fr. 5–6 cm. long; seeds oblong, compressed, 7 mm. long, with terminal wing 1 cm. long. Fl.vi; fr.x–xi. R.H. 1896:498. G.C.88:67;96:294. S.H.2:f.241h,244. W. China. Intr. 1908. Zone VII.

Fam. 72. **STACHYURACEAE** Gilg. STACHYURUS FAMILY

Contains only the following genus.

STACHYÙRUS Sieb. & Zucc. Shrubs or small trees, deciduous to evergreen; brts. with large pith; winter-buds small, with 2–4 outer scales: lvs. alternate, slender-petioled, serrate; stipules small, caducous: fls. regular, perfect or functionally dioecious, subsessile, in pendulous racemes axillary on last year's brs.; sepals and petals 4, imbricate; stamens 8, distinct; ovary superior, incompletely 4-celled by the intrusion of the parietal placentae; style short, with a 4-lobed stigma; ovules many: fr. berry-like, with leathery pericarp; seeds many, with soft arillus, albuminous; embryo straight. (Greek *stachys*, spike, and *urus*, tail; referring to the shape of the infl.) Five or 6 species in E. Asia and the Himal.—Planted for the early appearing racemes of yellow fls.

S. praècox Sieb. & Zucc. Shrub to 4 m., with slender spreading brs.; brts. reddish brown or chestnut-brown, lustrous, glabrous: lvs. elliptic-ovate to ovate-lanceolate, acuminate, rounded at base, 7–14 cm. long, serrate with slightly spreading teeth, glabrous and lustrous beneath or slightly pubescent on the veins; racemes before the lvs., short-stalked, 5–8 cm. long; fls. campanulate, yellow, about 8 mm. long; style shorter than petals: fr. globose, about 8 mm. across; greenish yellow, with reddish cheek. Fl.iii–iv; fr.vii–viii. B.M.6631(c). S.I.1:t.74. R.H.1908:87. Gn.75:204. G.C.III.21:285. B.S. 2:546. M.O.72(h). Japan. Cult. 1865. Zone (V), VI.

Closely related species: **S. chinénsis** Franch. Brts. greenish or dull brown: lvs. ovate to oblong-ovate, 6–12 cm. long, long-acuminate, rounded or subcordate at base, crenate-serrate: fls. more spreading; style as long or slightly longer than petals: fr. about 6 mm. across. G.C.79:229(h). R.H. 1932:95. China. Intr. 1908. Zone VII.

Fam. 73. **CACTACEAE** Lindl. CACTUS FAMILY

Shrubs or trees with fleshy stems branched or unbranched, cylindric, flattened or globular, often constricted or jointed, usually spiny, with watery or milky juice: lvs. alternate, scale-like or wanting, rarely flat and broad, usually with bundles of spines in the axils: fls. perfect, usually regular; sepals and petals usually many, rarely 8–10, similar and gradually passing into each other; stamens many, spirally or in groups, inside of the receptacle; ovary inferior, with 3 or more parietal placentae; style 1 with lobed stigma; ovules many: fr. a berry, sometimes dry; seeds small; embryo straight or curved. Syn.: *Opuntiaceae* H. B. K.—About 25 genera and 1200 species in N., C. and S. Am., few in Africa.—For further information see Britton & Rose, Cactaceae. 4 vols. (1919–23), where 125 genera are recognized.

A. Stems not or not conspicuously jointed: lvs. obsolete: fls. with calyx-tube prolonged beyond the ovary.
  B. Fls. borne on the tubercles or ribs, at or near the areolas; ovary scaly.
    c. Stem ribbed or with vertical rows of tubercles: fls. borne close to the fully developed cluster of spines...1. *Echinocereus*

cc. Stems with tubercles arranged in spiral rows: fls. close to areolas which subsequently develop spines ....2. *Echinocactus*
BB. Fls. arising from the axils of the tubercles or near their base; stem broken into tubercles arranged in spiral rows: ovary naked..........................3. *Mamillaria*
AA. Stems conspicuously jointed, flattened or cylindric: lvs. scale-like: calyx-tube not prolonged beyond the ovary..4. *Opuntia*

1. **ECHINOCÈREUS** Engelm. Stems ovoid to cylindric, ribbed and angled or with tubercles in vertical rows, spiny: fls. from areolas just above the spine-bearing areolas; ovary scaly; style filiform, longer than stamens, shorter than petals: fr. fleshy; seeds tuberculate, almost destitute of albumen; embryo straight. (Greek *echinos*, hedge-hog, and *cereus*.) About 40 species in N. Am. and Mex.

A. Ribs 5–8; fls. scarlet.......................................1. *E. triglochidiatus*
AA. Ribs 12–18.
B. Fls. green: areolas with 12–18 radial spines..........................2. *E. viridiflorus*
BB. Fls. rosy-purple areolas with 20–30 radial spines....................3. *E. Reichenbachii*

1. **E. triglochidiàtus** Engelm. Cespitose, with simple stems erect or spreading, deep green; spines 3–8, usually spreading, 3 cm. or less long, reddish to yellow at first: fls. scarlet, 5–7 cm. long; tube and ovary with few areolas and spines; perianth-segments oblong, obtuse, 3 cm. long: fr. red, 3 cm. across. Fl.v. Britt. & Rose, Cact. 3:10. (*E. gonacanthus* Engelm. & Bigel., *E. paucispinus* Ruempl.) Colo. and N. Mex. to w. Tex. Intr. 1912. Zone V.

2. **E. viridiflòrus** (Engelm.) Engelm. & Gray. Stems solitary or clustered, 8–18 cm. high and 3–5 cm. thick, with 13 ribs; radial spines 12–18, horizontally spreading, straight or slightly curved, the lower lateral ones the longest, to 1.2 cm. long, ruby-red, the others white, central spines usually absent or one, stout, about 2 cm. long and curved upwards, red with brown point: fls. lateral, broad-funnel form, 2.5–3 cm. long; petals green, each with an olivegreen to pink stripe in the middle; ovary and tube spiny: fr. ellipsoid, about 1 cm. long, greenish. Fl.v–vi. B.M.6788(c). B.B.2:569. (*Cereus v.* Engelm.) Wyo. and Kans. to Tex. and N. Mex. Cult. 1844. Zone V.

3. **E. Reichenbáchii** (Walp.) Haage. Stems globose to cylindric-ovoid, to 5 or rarely to 15 cm. high, solitary or in clusters of 6–12; ribs 12–13 with confluent tubercles; spines numerous, white or rarely pink or brown, radial ones 20–30, pectinate, straight or slightly recurved, the lateral ones 4–8 mm. long, the upper and lower ones shorter, central spines wanting or few, short: fls. rotate-funnelform, 6–8 cm. long and nearly as broad; petals rosy-purple: fr. ovoid, 1.8–2 cm. long, greenish. Fl.v. B.M.6669(c). B.B.2: 569. Gt.29:52. (*E. caespitosus* Engelm.) Kans. to Tex. and Mex. Cult. 1844. Zone VI?

Another species is **E. coccineus** Engelm. Stems with 9–11 ribs; spines 1–15, with usually 4 stout central ones, to 3 cm. long: fls. scarlet. B.M.6774(c). (*E. phoeniceus* Ruempl., *E. paucispinus* Hook. f., not Engelm. *E. aggregatus* Rydb.) Colo. to N. Mex., Ariz. and Mex. Cult. 1885. Zone VI?

2. **ECHINOCÁCTUS** Link & Otto. Stems globose to oblong or cylindric, tubercled, the tubercles arranged in spiral or vertical rows, spinebearing: fls. borne on the tubercles, at or near the areolas from which subsequently spines develop; calyx-tube scaly; petals numerous; stamens numerous; style columnar: fr. usually covered with scales and often with tufts of bristles: embryo curved. (Greek *echinos*, hedge-hog, and *cactus*.) About 200 species from N. Am. to S. Am.

E. Simpsònii Engelm. Stems globose, to 15 cm. high and to 10 cm. across; tubercles ovoid, slightly 4-sided at base, 1.2–1.6 cm. long; central spines 5–7, yellowish below, red or red-brown above, 1–3 cm. long, lateral 15–20, slightly shorter, whitish: fls. rosy-pink, about 2 cm. across, borne to one side at end of tubercles; petals oblong, obtuse, crenulate, the inner narrower, acutish; filaments golden-yellow: berry dry, 6–7 mm. across, with a few scales near apex. Fl.iv–v. B.B.2:570. G.C.II.6:242. W.G.2:90. (*Pediocactus S.* Brit. & Rose, *Mamillaria Purpusii* and *M. Spaethii* K. Schum.) Wash. and Mont. to Kans. and N. Mex. Intr. before 1876. Zone V.

3. MAMILLÀRIA Haw.

Stems simple or branched and clustered, usually hemispherical or short-cylindric, often depressed or sometimes elongated; the surface broken up into spirally arranged tubercles (mamillae) spiny at apex: fls. usually short-funnelform, with naked or nearly naked tube and ovary, borne in the woolly axils between the tubercles or at the inner end of a narrow groove on the upper surface: fr. globose to clavate, smooth, berry-like. (Latin *mamilla*, nipple; referring to the shape of the tubercles.) About 600 species in N. and C. Am.

A. Central spines 1 or wanting: fls. yellow.................................1. *M. missouriensis*
AA. Central spines several: fls. purple, 3.5–5 cm. across.........................2. *M. vivipara*

1. M. missouriènsis Sweet. Stems nearly simple, to 6 m. high and 3–5 cm. across or cespitose; tubercles cylindric-conical, spreading, slightly grooved; spines white, weak, puberulent, the radial ones spreading, 12–17, the central one 1–1.2 cm. long, stout, often wanting: fls. tubular, about 2.5 cm. long, yellow to fawn-color with reddish streaks, from the upper surface of the tubercle; sepals fimbriate; petals acute or acuminate; stamens and style shorter than petals: fr. red, subglobose or pyriform, 6–8 mm. long; seeds subglobose, black, pitted. Fl.v. B.B.2:570. (*M. Nuttallii* Engelm., *Cactus m.* Ktze., *Neobesseya m.* Brit. & Rose, *Coryphantha m.* Brit. & Rose.) S. Dak. to Kans., Colo. and Tex. Intr. 1813. Zone V?

2. M. vivípara (Nutt.) Haw. Stems 3–12 cm. high and 3–5 cm. thick; tubercles cylindric-conical, slightly grooved, with 3–8 slender reddish brown central spines 1–2 cm. long, surrounded by 12–25 lateral ones somewhat shorter, whitish or greenish: fls. purple, 3.5–5 cm. across; sepals fringed; petals lanceolate: fr. ovoid, 1.2–1.8 cm. long, green; seeds light brown, obovoid, pitted. Fl.v. B.B.2:571. (*Coryphantha v.* Brit. & Rose.) Man. and Alberta to Minn., Colo. and Kans. Intr. 1913. Zone V.

4. OPÙNTIA Mill.

Stems conspicuously jointed, the joints flattened or terete, procumbent or upright; sometimes tree-like: lvs. scale-like, spirally arranged, caducous, bearing in their axils areolas covered with short wool intermixed with barbed bristles and usually with spines: fls. on the upper part of the joints, on the bristle-bearing part of the areolas; ovary usually with bristle- and spine-bearing areolas; sepals and petals spreading, rotate; style cylindric, with 5–8-lobed stigma: fr. usually pear-shaped, fleshy, frequently edible, rarely dry; seeds flattened or disk-like. (*Opuntia*, ancient Greek name of a plant growing near Opous in Boeotia.) About 130 species in N., C. and S. Am.

A. Joints terete, cylindric: fls. purple..1. *O. imbricata*
AA. Joints flattened or tumid and subglobose to ellipsoid.
  B. Joints flat, 5–14 cm. long.
    C. Spines wanting or few: fls. pale yellow..................................2. *O. humifusa*
    CC. Spines numerous: fls. yellow with darker center or red.
      D. Fls. yellow.
        E. Spines 1–6 in each areola: fr. fleshy..........................3. *O. phaeacantha*
        EE. Spines 5–15 in each areola: fr. dry.............................4. *O. polyacantha*
      DD. Fls. red: spines 2–4 in each areola................................5. *O. rhodantha*
  BB. Joints tumid, 3–5 cm. long, fragile.......................................6 *O. fragilis*

1. O. imbricàta (Haw.) DC. To 3 m. or higher, often tree-like; joints cylindric, the ultimate 2–3 cm. thick; tubercles prominent, 2–2.5 cm. long, laterally flattened; spines 8–30, 2–3 cm. long, brown, with papery sheaths; lvs. terete, 8–24 mm. long: fls. purple, 5–8 cm. across: fr. yellow, 2.5–3 cm. long, tuberculate, spineless. Fl.vii–viii. B.M.8290(c). R.Mo.22:t.6,7. G.C. 34:90(h). (*O. arborescens* Engelm., *O. vexans* D. Griffiths.) Colo. to Tex., N. Mex. and Mex. Intr. 1820. Zone VI.
　　Related species: **O. Davísii** Engelm. & Bigel. Cespitose, with few or many simple stems; joints slender, about 1 cm. thick; spines yellow, 6–12, the longest 4–5 cm. long: fls. olive-green to yellow, 3.5 cm. long; areolas of ovary large, with few spines. B.M.6652(c). N. Mex. and w. Texas. Cult. 1882. Zone V.
2. O. humifùsa Raf. Prostrate; joints usually resting on the ground and rooting on the lower margin, obovate to suborbicular, 5–10 cm. long, thick, pale green; areolas with grayish wool and a few short greenish yellow bristles; spines usually wanting or only 1, stout, less than 2.5 cm. long, yellow or variegated; lvs. thick, 4–5 mm. long: fls. pale yellow, about 5 cm. broad: fr. obovoid or clavate-obovoid, 2–3 cm. long, red. Fl.vii–viii. B.M.2393,7041(c). Add.3:t.105(c). Gn.20:548,t(c). M.A.1:t.61(c). Gs.4:123(h). (*O. vulgaris* Haw., not Mill., *O. mesacantha* Raf., *O. compressa* Macbr., *O. Rafinesquei* Engelm.) Mass. to Ga. and Ala., w. to Mo. and Tenn. Cult. 1596. Zone IV.
3. O. phaeacántha Engelm. Prostrate; joints rooting at the lower margin, broad-obovate to orbicular, 10–15 cm. long, moderately thick; areolas about 2.5 cm. apart, with light brown wool and yellowish brown bristles; spines usually 1–3 (–6), sometimes to 6 cm. long, mostly on marginal areolas reddish brown with lighter tips: fls. 6–8 cm. across, yellow with reddish centre: fr. ovoid to globose, sometimes pyriform, about 3 cm. long, red, sweet. B.B.2:572. Gs.4:123. Ariz. and Tex. Cult. 1885. Zone VII?
4. O. polyacántha Haw. Prostrate, wide-spreading; joints obovate to orbicular, 5–10, rarely to 15 cm. long, often wrinkled and tuberculate, bright green; areolas about 1 cm. apart, all armed, with short grayish wool and reddish brown bristles; spines numerous, lateral ones 5–10, slender, mostly whitish, variegated with red, not exceeding 1.5 cm., central ones 0–5, stout, to 5 cm. long, usually reddish brown with pale tips: fls. yellow or orange-yellow, darker in centre, 5–6 cm. across: fr. obovoid or subglobose, 2–2.5 cm. long, with numerous short spines, dry. Fl.v–vi. B.M.7046(c). G.C.III.28:413;50: 340. B.B.2:573. (*O. missouriensis* Engelm., *O. Schweriniana* K. Schum.) Alb. and N. D. to Okla., Tex. and Utah. Cult. 1814. Zone V.
5. O. rhodántha K. Schum. Prostrate and ascending; joints obovate to obovate-oblong, 7–12 cm. long, slightly tuberculate, deep green; areolas with grayish wool and reddish brown bristles; spines 2–4, to 3 cm. long, grayish, and usually a few smaller ones: fls. 6–7 cm. long and 5.5 cm. broad; petals carmine-red; filaments red, anthers yellow, ovary scaly and bristly. M.M.7: 133. Britton & Rose, Cact. t.35,f.2(c). Colo. Intr. about 1895. Zone VI?—
O. r. xanthostémma (K. Schum.) Rehd., var. Joints tuberculate: fls. carmine-red; filaments yellow below, red above. Gn.58:67. G.W.1:83. (*O. x.* K. Schum.) Colo. Intr. about 1895. Zone VI?
6. O. frágilis Haw. Prostrate, to 10 cm. high; joints tumid, nearly as thick as broad, subglobose to ellipsoidal, 2–5 cm. long, easily detached, bright green; areolas 6–10 mm. apart, with whitish wool and a few white to yellow bristles; spines 1–4 and occasionally a few smaller ones, weak, the upper ones usually longer and stronger, rarely to 2.5 cm. long, dark brown: fls. greenish yellow, 2.5–3 cm. across: fr. ovoid to subglobose, 2–2.5 cm. long, dry, with a few spines. B.B.2:573. Fl.vii–ix. B. C. and Wisc. to Ariz. and Tex. Intr.

1814. Zone V.—**O. f. brachyárthra** (Engelm.) Coult., var. Joints ellipsoid, with more and stronger spines: fls. small: fr. more spiny. Gt.30:413. N.I.2: 502. (*O. b.* Engelm.) Colo. to N. Mex. Cult. 1881.

74. THYMELAEACEAE Reichb. MEZEREUM FAMILY

Shrubs or trees, rarely herbs: lvs. alternate, rarely opposite, simple, entire, exstipulate: fls. perfect or unisexual, regular, usually in terminal spikes, panicles or clusters, sometimes axillary; usually a short or elongated, often colored, calyx-tube bearing at apex 4–5 imbricate, often petaloid, sepals and as many petals or the latter wanting; stamens 4–5 or 8–10, rarely 2; ovary superior, 1-celled, rarely 2-celled; ovule solitary, pendulous; style 1, stigma usually capitate, sometimes sessile: fr. a nut, drupe or berry, rarely a caps.; seed albuminous or exalbuminous; embryo straight with thick cotyledons.— About 40 genera and 450 species widely distributed in both hemispheres.

A. Stamens not exserted; style short or wanting; fls. often in terminal clusters or panicles.
  B. Fls. in terminal or lateral heads or clusters, often with bracts; disk wanting or ring-
    like or of 1 lateral entire scale: lvs. usually alternate.........................1. *Daphne*
  BB. Fls. in terminal spikes, often panicled, without bracts, yellow or whitish; with 1 or
    more usually dentate disk-scales: lvs. usually opposite..................2. *Wikstroemia*
AA. Stamens and style exserted: fls. yellow, with indistinct limb, in a few-fld. lateral clusters
  before the lvs...3. *Dirca*

1. DAPHNE L.

Deciduous or evergreen shrubs; winter-buds small, with several outer scales: lvs. alternate, rarely opposite, short-petioled, entire: fls. perfect, apetalous, in terminal or axillary short racemes or umbels, usually with bracts: calyx-tube (receptacle) campanulate to cylindric, 4- or rarely 5-lobed, corolla-like, usually pubescent outside; stamens 8 or 10 in two rows, included; stigma capitate, sessile or on a short style; ovary without disk at base, or a ring-like disk or 1 entire scale: fr. a leathery or fleshy 1-seeded drupe. (*Daphne*, Greek name of *Laurus nobilis*.) About 50 species in Eu. and Asia.

A. Fls. axillary.
  B. Lvs. deciduous: fls. before the lvs.
    C. Lvs. opposite, silky below: fls. lilac..................Sect. GENKWA Benth. & Hook.
      1. *D. Genkwa*
    CC. Lvs. alternate, glabrous: fls. rosy-purple to white............Sect. MEZEREUM Spach.
      2. *D. Mezereum*
  BB. Lvs. evergreen.
    C. Fls. in sessile racemes: lvs. oblanceolate.............................3. *D. Laureola*
    CC. Fls. in long-peduncled clusters: lvs. obovate to oblong-obovate.......4. *D. pontica*
AA. Fls. in terminal heads....................................Sect. DAPHNANTHES C. A. Mey.
  B. Lvs. deciduous: fls. without bracts, white to yellow.
    C. Lvs. glabrous.
      D. Fls. yellow, glabrous...5. *D. Giraldii*
      DD. Fls. white, pubescent outside...6. *D. altaica*
    CC. Lvs. pubescent: fls. white...7. *D. alpina*
  BB. Lvs. evergreen.
    C. Corolla densely pubescent outside.
      D. Habit upright; shrub to 1 m.: lvs. elliptic to oblong, often pubescent.
        E. Lvs. minutely whitish punctulate, usually acute: fls. without bracts.
          8. *D. oleoides*
        EE. Lvs. not punctulate, usually obtuse: fls. with bracts...............9. *D. collina*
      DD. Habit procumbent or very dwarf: lvs. linear to oblanceolate, glabrous.
        E. Lvs. 8–12 mm. long: dwarf gnarled shrub to 15 cm. tall..........10. *D. petraea*
        EE. Lvs. 1–2.5 cm. long: shrub with slender procumbent stems......11. *D. Cneorum*
    CC. Corolla glabrous or sparingly puberulous outside (see also species under No. 11).
      D. Lvs. obtuse or obtusish: brts. glabrous.
        E. Lvs. less than 5 cm. long: low diffusely branched shrub (see also *D. glomerata*
          under No. 4)...12. *D. Blagayana*
        EE. Lvs. more than 5 cm. long: upright shrub.........................13. *D. odora*
      DD. Lvs. emarginate: young brts. strigose-pubescent....................14. *D. retusa*

1. D. Génkwa Sieb. & Zucc. Shrub to 1 m., with slender upright brs. silky-pubescent when young: lvs. opposite or occasionally alternate, elliptic-oblong, 3–5 cm. long, acute, silky-pubescent on the veins beneath: fls. lilac, 1.2 cm. across, fragrant, 3–7 in short-stalked clusters; tube slender, about 1 cm. long, silky-pubescent outside: fr. white. Fl.IV–V; fr.VI. S.Z.1:t.75(c). Gt.15t.499(c). N.K.17:t.12. F.S.3:t.208(c). Gn.42:94,t(c). (*D. Fortunei* Lindl.) China, Korea; cult. in Japan. Intr. 1843. Zone (V).

2. **D. Mezèreum** L. MEZEREUM. Upright shrub to 1 m., with stout glabrous brs.: lvs. alternate, oblong to oblanceolate, 3–8 cm. long, obtuse to acute, cuneate at base, grayish green beneath, glabrous: fls. long before the lvs., in sessile clusters of usually 3, lilac-purple or rosy-purple, 1.2 cm. across, very fragrant; tube silky-pubescent outside, 6 mm. long: fr. subglobose, 8 mm. across, scarlet. Fl.III–IV; fr.VIII–IX. R.I.11:t.556(c). F.D.10:t. 976(c). Gn.29:602,t(s) ;86:659(h). Eu. to Cauc. and Altai; occasionally naturalized in the N. E. States. Cult. 1561. Zone IV. Planted for its early fragrant fls. and conspicuous scarlet fr.—**D. M. alba** West., var. Fls. white; fr. yellow. Gn.29:602,t(c) ;80:104(h). G.C.III.21:183(h),185. R.H.1905:532.— **D. M. plèna** Schneid., f. Fls. white, double. (*D. M. fl. albo pleno* Hort.) Gn.29:602,t(c).—**D. M. grandiflòra** Dipp., var. Fls. larger, bright purple, from Oct. to Feb . (*D. M. autumnalis* Hort.)

D. M. × *Laureola;* see under No. 3

Related species with yellow fls.: **D. Pseudo-mezèreum** Gray. Low, sometimes procumbent shrub: lvs. oblong to oblong-oblanceolate, acutish: fls. greenish yellow; sepals ovate, obtuse. C. Japan. Cult. 1905. Zone V?—**D. kamtschática** Maxim. Low shrub: lvs. oblong-obovate, obtuse: fls. yellow; sepals ovate to lanceolate, acute. N.K.17:13. N. E. Asia, Korea. Cult. 1912. Zone IV?

3. **D. Lauréola** L. SPURGE LAUREL. Bushy shrub to 1 m.; glabrous: lvs. oblanceolate, 5–8 cm. long, acute, gradually narrowed at base, dark green and lustrous above, light green beneath: fls. in 5–10-fld. nearly sessile racemes, yellowish green, 8 mm. long, scentless or sometimes fragrant: fr. ovoid, bluish black. Fl.III–V. R.I.11:t.555(c). F.D.10:t.977(c). Gn.29:602. G.C.77:218. S.L.27(h). S. Eu., W. Asia. Cult. 1561. Zone VI?—**D. L. Philíppi** (Gren.) Meissn., var. Dwarf; lvs. obovate, 2–5 cm. long: fls. often violet outside, smaller, fragrant. (*D. P.* Gren.) Pyrenees. Cult. 1894.

D. L. × *Mezereum* = **D. Houtteàna** Planch. Upright shrub to 1 m., with stout brs.: lvs. half-evergreen, oblong-lanceolate, purplish: fls. lilac-violet in short-stalked clusters. F.S.6:t.592(c). (*D. Mezereum atropurpurea* Dipp., *D. Laureola purpurea* Hort.) Orig. before 1850.

4. **D. póntica** L. Shrub to 1.5 m.; glabrous, usually with a single stem at base, much branched at the top: lvs. obovate to obovate-oblong, 5–8 cm. long, acute, narrowed toward the base, lustrous above: fls. in long-peduncled 1–3-fld. racemes, greenish yellow, fragrant; tube 8 mm. long; lobes linear-lanceolate. Fl.IV–V. B.M.1282(c). G.C.77:219. B.S.1:473. G.W.5:261(h). Asia Minor. Intr. 1752. Zone VI.

Related species: **D. glomeràta** Lam. Low shrub; glabrous: lvs. obovate-lanceolate, 1.5–3 cm. long: fls. light pink, 1.2 cm. across, in 2–6-fld. racemes, crowded into a terminal head. S.H.2:f.267a-d. Asia Minor. Intr. 1934.

5. **D. Giráldii** Nitsche. Upright shrub to 50 cm. or more; glabrous: lvs. crowded at end of brts., oblanceolate, 3–6 cm. long, acute to obtuse and mucronate, glaucescent below: fls. yellow, glabrous, slightly fragrant, on short glabrous pedicels in 3–8-fld. terminal heads without bracts; tube 6–8 mm. long; lobes acute, about half as long as tube: fr. ovoid, scarlet. Fl.VI; fr.VII. B.M.8732(c). N. W. China. Intr. 1910. Zone V.

6. **D. altáica** Pall. Upright shrub to 1.5 m., much-branched; brts. glabrous: lvs. narrow-oblong to oblanceolate, 3–6 cm. long, acute, cuneate, dull green, glaucescent beneath, glabrous: fls. white, fragrant, in terminal clusters of

6–10; tube slender, 8 mm. long, puberulous outside; lobes ovate-lanceolate, obtuse; ovary glabrous: fr. ovoid, yellowish red. Fl.v–vi. B.M.1875(c). L.B.399(c). G.O.t.13(c). Gt.12:t.409(c). Altai, Songaria. Intr. 1796. Zone V.
  Closely related species: **D. caucásica** Pall. Shrub to 2 m.: lvs. lanceolate or oblanceolate, 3–4 cm. long, obtuse, rarely acuminate, glaucescent beneath: fls. white, silky outside, in 15–20-fld. heads; ovary puberulous at apex. B.M.7388(c). S.L.151(h). Cauc. Cult. 1893. Zone VI?—*D. c.* × *Cneorum* = **D. Burkwoòdii** Burkwood. Habit like *D. caucasica:* fls. creamy white, flushed pink, fragrant. G.C.101:436. Cult. 1935.—**D. Sóphia** Kal. Lvs. oblong-ovate, obtuse or acuminate: fls. white, appressed-puberulous, in 6–15-fld. heads; sepals oblong-ovate, acute. Bull. Soc. Nat. Moscou, 22:t.3. Russia. Cult. 1895. Zone V.
  7. D. alpìna L. Dwarf shrub to 15 cm.; brts. pubescent: lvs. often crowded toward the end of brts., obovate to oblong-obovate, 1–4 cm. long, obtuse or acutish, cuneate, grayish green, pubescent on both sides: fls. white, fragrant, in terminal clusters of 6–10; tube 8 mm. long, silky outside; lobes ovate-lanceolate, acute; ovary pubescent: fr. oblong-ovoid, red, slightly pubescent. Fl.v–vi. R.I.11:t.553(c). F.D.10:t.978(c). L.B.66(c). Gn.29:603. Eu. Alps. Intr. 1759. Zone V.
  8. D. oleoìdes Schreb. Shrub to 1 m.; brts. pubescent: lvs. elliptic-obovate to obovate-lanceolate, 2.5–3.5 cm. long, acute or obtuse and mucronulate, villous-pubescent on both sides or finally glabrous above, minutely whitish dotted beneath, less so above: fls. white to pale lilac, whitish pubescent outside, 1.2–1.5 cm. long, in 3–8-fld. heads, without bracts; lobes ovate to lanceolate, acute: fr. red. Fl.v–vi. R.I.11:t.553(c). S.F.t.357(c). (*D. buxifolia* Vahl.) Mediterr. region. Intr. 1815. Zone VII?
  9. D. collìna Smith. Shrub to 1 m.; brts. villous: lvs. oblong-obovate to oblanceolate, 2.5–4 cm. long, obtuse or obtusish, glabrous and lustrous above, tomentose beneath: fls. rose-purple, about 1 cm. across, in 10–15-fld. heads, with tomentose oval bracts half as long as calyx-tube; lobes oval, obtuse, nearly as long as tube; ovary silky. Fl.v–vi. B.M.428(c). B.R.24:56(c). R.I. 11:t.544(c). F.D.10:t.980(c). Italy, Asia Minor. Intr. 1752. Zone VII?—
D. c. neapolitàna (Lodd.) Lindl., var. Brts. slightly pubescent: lvs. glabrous, glaucous beneath and slightly hairy toward the base: fls. rosy-purple, fragrant. L.B.719(c). B.R.822. (*D. n.* Lodd.)
  D. c. × *odora;* see under No. 13.
  Related species: **D. serícea** Vahl. Shrub to 40 cm.; young brts. pubescent, soon glabrous: lvs. crowded at end of brts., lanceolate, 1–2 cm. long, acuminate, silky beneath, sometimes becoming nearly glabrous: heads 5–8-fld.; fls. pink; lobes broad-ovate, ⅓ as long as the broad-cylindric calyx-tube. Asia Minor. Cult. 1933. Zone VII?
  10. D. petraèa Leyb. Low much-branched shrub to 15 cm. high; brts. slightly puberulous: lvs. crowded, sessile, linear-spatulate, 8–12 mm. long, acutish or obtuse, glabrous, coriaceous: fls. rosy-pink, fragrant, 8 mm. across, puberulous, in 3–5-fld. clusters, tube slender, 1 cm. long; sepals ovate, obtuse. Fl.vi. Gn.87:255;89:227(h). Flora,38:t.13. Gs.3:104,t(hc). (*D. rupestris* Facch.) S. Tyrol. Cult. 1894. Zone V.
  Related species: **D. arbúscula** Čelak. Dwarf shrub; young brts. red: lvs. oblanceolate, 1.5–2.3 cm. long, obtuse, with revolute margin, grooved above, puberulous or glabrous beneath: fls. rosy-pink, tube 1.5 cm. long, appressed-puberulous. G.C.57:268. Gn.79:260. J.L.41:f.93. S.L.150(h). Hungary. Intr. before 1915? Zone V?
  11. D. Cneòrum L. Procumbent shrub with slender trailing and ascending brs.; young brts. pubescent: lvs. crowded, oblanceolate, 1–2 cm. long, usually obtuse and mucronulate, cuneate, dark green and lustrous above, glaucescent beneath, glabrous: fls. bright rosy-pink, 1 cm. across, fragrant, sessile in 6–8-fld. heads; tube 6–7 mm. long, grayish puberulous outside;

sepals ovate, obtuse; bracts spatulate, obtuse, leafy: fr. yellowish brown. Fl.iv–v. B.M.313(c). R.I.11:t.554(c). L.B.1800(c). R.H.1917:252,t(c). G.C. 69:312(h). Gn.88:182(h). M.G.1900:417,418(h). S.L.149(h). Mts. of C. and S. Eu. Intr. 1752. Zone IV. The best of the evergreen Daphnes, forming a dense mat covered with fragrant fls. in spring.—**D. C. major** Dipp. Of more vigorous growth, with larger fls. Gn.51:358;65:457(h).—**D. C. Verlòti** (Gren. & Godr.) Meissn., var. Lvs. linear-lanceolate, 1.5–2.5 cm. long, acute; sepals lanceolate, obtusish; bracts acute. R.H.1901:304,305;1902:552,t(c). C. Eu. Cult. 1894.

D. C. × *caucasica;* see under No. 6.

Related species: **D. striàta** Tratt. Dwarf shrub; brts. glabrous: lvs. oblance-olate, crowded at end of brts.: fls. glabrous, rosy-pink, in 8–12-fld. heads; tube somewhat funnelform, slightly striate. Fl.vi–vii. R.I.11:t.554(c). F.D.10:t. 981(c). Eu. Alps. Cult. 1827. Zone V.—**D. aurantíaca** Diels. Shrub to 1.2 m.; brts. glabrous: lvs. elliptic or obovate to elliptic-oblong, 1–1.5 cm. long, acute, glabrous: fls. terminal and axillary, 2–4, sessile, glabrous, orange-yellow, fragrant; tube 1 cm. long; lobes elliptic-ovate, obtuse; ovary glabrous. S. W. China. Cult. 1924. Zone VII?

12. **D. Blagayàna** Frey. Low diffusely branched shrub, glabrous: lvs. crowded at end of brts., obovate to oblong-obovate, 2.5–4 cm. long, rounded at apex, cuneate; fls. white or yellowish white, 1.2 cm. across, fragrant, in 10–15-fld. heads, with oblong-obovate to lanceolate silky bracts; tube 1.5–1.8 cm. long, sparingly puberulous outside: lobes broad-ovate: fr. globose, pinkish white. Fl.iv–v. B.M.7579(c). Gt.29:t.1020(c). G.C.32:300,301(h). Gn.71:7 (h),247;88:183(h). S.L.31(h). Mts. of S. E. Eu. Intr. 1875. Zone V.

13. **D. odòra** Thunb. Upright shrub to 2 m.; glabrous: lvs. elliptic-oblong, 5–8 cm. long, narrowed at ends, bluntly pointed, dark green above: fls. rosy-purple, fragrant, about 1.5 cm. across, glabrous, in dense terminal peduncled heads; bracts lanceolate, acute, sparingly ciliate, persistent, as long as the calyx-tube; ovary glabrous. Fl.iii–v. B.M.1587(c). Smith, Exot. Bot. t.47 (c). Gn.28:8,t(c). Japan, China. Intr. 1771. Zone VII? Varies with white and spotted fls.

D. o. × *collina* = **D. hýbrida** Lindl. Similar to *D. odora:* lvs. elliptic-oblong, 4–8 cm. long, glabrous or slightly hairy on the veins beneath: fls. reddish purple, pubescent outside, very fragrant. B.R.1177(c). (*D. Delphinii* Hort., *D. Dau-phinii* Hort., *D. Fioniana* Hort.) Orig. about 1820. Zone VII?

14. **D. retùsa** Hemsl. Shrub to 1 m., densely branched; young brts. densely strigose: lvs. oblong to oblong-oblanceolate, 2.5–7 cm. long, obtuse and usually emarginate, cuneate, with revolute margin, glabrous: fls. white inside, rosy-purple outside, 2 cm. across, fragrant, glabrous, on short tomentose pedicels in many-fld. terminal heads; tube 1.5 cm. long; lobes ovate, slightly shorter than tube; bracts obovate or oval, ciliate, deciduous: fr. red. Fl.v. B.M. 8430(c). B.S.1:474. W. China. Intr. 1901. Zone VI?

Related species: **D. tangùtica** Maxim. Brts. densely strigose, later pale yellowish gray, stout: lvs. 3–8 cm. long, oblanceolate to elliptic-oblong: fls. rosy-purple outside, 1.2 cm. across; lobes ovate, obtuse, less than half as long as tube, white inside, stained purple toward the tips; tube 1.5 cm. long. B.M. 8855(c). (*D. Wilsonii* Rehd.) N. W. China. Intr. 1914. Zone VI?—**D. acutíloba** Rehd. Shrub to 1.2 m.; young brts. thinly strigose, later purple-brown, slender: lvs. oblong-lanceolate or oblanceolate, 4–8 cm. long, short-acuminate, with obtuse or slightly emarginate apex: fls. 5–7, white; tube 1 cm. long; lobes ovate-oblong, acute to acuminate. W. China. Cult. 1932. Zone VII.

2. WIKSTROÈMIA Endl.

Deciduous or evergreen shrubs or small trees: lvs. opposite or sometimes alternate: fls. perfect, apetalous, in terminal spikes or racemes, often paniculate; bracts wanting; receptacle cylindric, slender, usually pubescent outside; sepals 4, rarely 5; stamens twice as many as sepals, in two whorls; ovary sessile, pubescent; stigma capitate, subsessile; 1–4 connate or distinct, often toothed disk-scales at base of ovary: fr. a drupe. (After Johan Emanuel Wikstroem, Swedish botanist; 1789–1856.) About 35 species in E. Asia, Malaysia and Australasia.—Of little ornamental merit.

W. Chamaedáphne (Bge.) Meissn. Upright shrub to 50 cm. or more, with slender red-brown glabrous brs.: lvs. opposite or subopposite, oblong-lanceolate to lanceolate, 2–6 cm. long, acute or acutish, narrowed into a very short petiole, pale green beneath, glabrous: fls. small, yellow, subsessile, silky outside, in dense peduncled spikes 0.5–4 cm., rarely to 10 cm. long, usually 3 or more forming terminal panicles; tube slender, 6–8 mm. long; sepals oval, obtuse, ¼ as long as tube. Fl.vii–ix. N. China. Intr. 1910. Zone V.

3. DIRCA L. Deciduous shrubs; winter-buds small, conical, enclosed by the base of the petiole before leaf-fall, terminal bud wanting: lvs. alternate, membranous: fls. perfect, apetalous, in 2–3-fld. clusters axillary on last year's brts., before the lvs.; receptacle narrow-funnelform, indistinctly 4-lobed, deciduous; stamens 8, with filiform filaments exceeding the tube: ovary sessile, glabrous; style slender, as long as stamens, with small stigma: fr. a drupe; seed with bony testa, exalbuminous; embryo with fleshy cotyledons. (*Dirke,* Greek mythological name.) Two species in N. Am.

D. palústris L. LEATHERWOOD. Shrub to 2 m., often with a short single stem; brs. flexible, with very tough bark; brts. glabrous: lvs. short-petioled, elliptic to obovate, 3–7 cm. long, obtuse, cuneate, light green above, glaucescent beneath and pubescent when young: fls. short-stalked, pale yellow, 6–8 mm. long: fr. ellipsoid, 8 mm. long, pale green or reddish. Fl.iii–iv; fr. v–vi. M.A.2:t.146(c). B.R.292(c). G.O.t.49(c). G.C.69:196,197(h). S.L.163 (h). N. B. and Ontario to Fla. and Mo. Intr. 1750. Zone IV. Interesting shrub valued for its early fls.

Fam. 75. **ELAEAGNACEAE** Lindl. OLEASTER FAMILY

Trees or shrubs covered more or less with peltate or stellate silvery or brown scales: lvs. alternate or opposite, entire, exstipulate: fls. perfect or unisexual, regular, apetalous, axillary; calyx-tube (receptacle) with a prominent perigynous disk, developed beyond the ovary, persistent and enclosing the fr., or cup-shaped in the staminate fl.; calyx-lobes 4, rarely 2 or 6, valvate; stamens as many or twice as many as calyx-lobes, inserted in the tube; ovary superior, 1-celled and 1-ovuled; ovule erect, anatropous; style 1, with simple stigma: fr. drupe-like, consisting of the dry fr. proper enclosed by the usually fleshy calyx-tube; seed with bony testa, ex-albuminous or nearly so; embryo straight, with fleshy cotyledons.—Three genera with about 30 species in N. Am., Eu. and Asia s. to Malaysia.

A. Lvs. opposite; stamens 8: fls. dioecious, with 4 sepals......................2. *Shepherdia*
AA. Lvs. alternate: stamens 4.
   B. Fls. dioecious; sepals 2; tube short: lvs. linear to lanceolate............1. *Hippophaë*
   BB. Fls. perfect or polygamous; sepals 4; tube elongated much beyond the ovary: lvs.
      lanceolate to ovate..3. *Elaeagnus*

1. HIPPÓPHAË L. Deciduous shrubs or trees with spiny brs.; the young growth covered with silvery scales or stellate hairs; winter-buds small, round, with few outer scales: lvs. alternate, short-petioled, narrow: fls. dioecious, axillary on last year's brs. in short racemes, the axis of which develops in the pistillate plant usually into brts. or thorns, but usually deciduous in the staminate plant: staminate fls. sessile with reduced tube and 2 valvate sepals; stamens 4, with short filaments; pistillate fls. short-stalked, the calyx-tube with 2 minute lobes; style filiform with cylindric stigma: fr. drupe-like, with a bony ovoid stone. (*Hippophaës* is the ancient Greek name of a spiny plant.) Syn.: *Hippophaës* St.-Lag. Two species in Eu. and Asia.

H. rhamnoìdes L. Sea-Buckthorn. Shrub or tree to 10 m.; brs. gray, usually spiny; winter-buds golden-brown: lvs. linear to linear-lanceolate, 2–6 cm. long, acutish, covered on both sides with silvery-white scales, at maturity often glabrescent above: fls. before the lvs., very small, yellowish: fr. subglobose to ovoid, 6–8 mm. long, orange-yellow. Fl.ɪɪɪ–ɪᴠ; fr.ɪx(–ɪɪɪ). B.M.8016(c). Gn.49:62,t(c) ;65:148(h) ;82:477. G.W.8:115,t(c) ;15:345(h). Eu. to Altai Mts., W. and N. China and N. W. Himal. Long cult. Zone III. Attractive in fr.—**H. r. procèra** Rehd., var. Tree to 18 m.; young brts. villous: lvs. oblong-lanceolate to lanceolate, stellate-pubescent above. W. China. Intr. 1923. Zone VII?

Related species: **H. salicifòlia** D. Don. Tree to 15 m., with pendulous brs., less spiny; young shoots scaly and brownish villous: lvs. lanceolate, to 1 cm. broad, acute, dull green above, stellate-tomentose below, the midrib brown: fr. yellow. S.H.2:f.277k-l,278e-f. M.D.1918:t.27(h). S.L.8(h). Himal. Intr. 1822. Zone VI.

2. SHEPHÉRDIA Nutt. Deciduous or evergreen shrubs; winter-buds with 1 or 2 pairs of outer scales: lvs. opposite, petioled: fls. dioecious, small, nearly sessile, in short axillary spikes or the pistillate often solitary; calyx of staminate fls. 4-parted, with 8 stamens alternating with 8 lobes of the disk; the pistillate with urn-shaped 4-cleft calyx enclosing the ovary, the orifice closed by the lobes of the disk; style slender with 1-sided stigma: fr. drupe-like, ovoid. (After John Shephard, once curator of the Liverpool Botanic Garden; 1764–1836.) Syn.: *Lepargyraea* Raf. Three species in N. Am.; the evergreen *S. rotundifolia* Parry from Utah not in cult.

ᴀ. Lvs. green and nearly glabrous above, silvery and scurfy with brown scales beneath.
                                                                1. *S. canadensis*
ᴀᴀ. Lvs. silvery on both sides...2. *S. argentea*

1. S. canadénsis Nutt. Spreading unarmed shrub to 2.5 m., with brown scurfy brts.: lvs. elliptic to ovate, 2–5 cm. long, obtuse, green and sparingly scurfy above, silvery mixed with brown scales beneath: fls. yellowish about 4 mm. across: fr. ovoid, 4–6 mm. long, yellowish red, insipid. Fl.ɪᴠ–ᴠ; fr. ᴠɪ–ᴠɪɪ. B.B.2:576. S.L.341(h). Nfd. to Alaska, s. to Me., Ohio, N. Mex. and Ore. Intr. 1759. Zone II.—**S. c. xanthocárpa** Rehd., f. Fr. yellow. Intr. 1904.

2. S. argéntea Nutt. Buffalo-berry. Shrub or sometimes nearly tree-like, to 6 m., with often spiny spreading brs. silvery when young: lvs. oblong to oblong-lanceolate, 1.5–6 cm. long, obtuse, cuneate, silvery on both sides: fls. yellowish; fr. ovoid, 4–6 mm. long, scarlet, sour, edible. Fl.ɪᴠ–ᴠ; fr.ᴠɪɪɪ. I.T.2:t.50. Gt.38:625. A.G.1900:827. B.B.2:577. S.L.341(h). Minn. and Man. to Sask., Kans. and Nev. Intr. 1818. Zone II. The fr. is made into jellies and conserves and the shrub used as a hedge plant in the northwest.

S. a. × *canadensis* = **S. gottingénsis** Rehd. The scales of the leaf which are divided to the base in *S. canadensis* and merely dentate in *S. argentea* are divided in the hybrid about ½ to the middle. Orig. about 1892.

3. ELAEÁGNUS L. Oleaster. Deciduous or evergreen shrubs or trees, often spiny: winter-buds small, ovoid, with few outer scales: lvs. alternate, short-petioled, dotted with silvery or brown scales like other parts of the plant: fls. axillary, solitary or clustered, perfect or polygamous, apetalous; calyx-tube (receptacle) campanulate or tubular, 4-lobed; stamens 4, on very short filaments, included: fr. drupe-like, with an ellipsoid striate stone. (Greek *elaia*, olive, and *agnos,* the Greek name of *Vitex agnus-castus*). About 40 species in S. Eu., Asia and N. Am.—Grown for their handsome foliage and decorative frs. and some for their edible frs.

A. Lvs. deciduous: fls. in spring.
  B. Fr. mealy, yellow or silvery: lvs. with silvery scales on both sides.
    c. Brts. silvery: style of perfect fls. enclosed at base by the tubular disk: fr. yellow.
                                                           1. *E. angustifolia*
    cc. Brts. brown: style not enclosed by a tubular disk: fr. silvery, dry..2. *E. commutata*
  BB. Fr. juicy, red-brown to pink, dotted with brown or silvery scales: lvs. often with brown scales beneath.
    c. Calyx-tube much longer than limb, gradually narrowed at base: fr. subglobose to ovoid, on a stalk 8–12 mm. long: brts. sometimes silvery.............3. *E. umbellata*
    cc. Calyx-tube about as long as limb, abruptly contracted at base: fr. ovoid to oblong, on a stalk 1.2–2.5 cm. long: brts. brown............................4. *E. multiflora*
AA. Lvs. persistent: fls. in fall.
  B. Brts. and lvs. beneath silvery white...............................5. *E. macrophylla*
  BB. Brts. brown and lvs. dotted with brown scales beneath.
    c. Lvs. with yellow and brown scales beneath: brts. spineless.............6. *E. glabra*
    cc. Lvs. whitish beneath, dotted with brown scales: brs. usually spiny....7. *E. pungens*

1. E. angustifòlia L. OLEASTER. Shrub or small tree to 7 m., sometimes thorny; young brts. silvery: lvs. oblong-lanceolate to linear-lanceolate, 4–8 cm. long, acute to obtuse, usually broad-cuneate at base, dull green above, silvery beneath; petiole 5–8 mm.: fls. 1–3, short-stalked, on the lower part of the brts., 1 cm. long, yellow inside, silvery outside, fragrant; calyx-tube campanulate, about as long as limb; style of the perfect fls. enclosed at base by a tubular disk: fr. ellipsoid, yellow, about 1 cm. long, yellow and coated with silvery scales, with sweet mealy flesh. Fl.vi; fr.viii–x. R.I.11:t.549(c). F.D. 10:t.972(c). S.O.3:t.134,135(c). S.H.2:f.279a–g. Gs.2:37(b). S.L.9(h). (*E. hortensis* Bieb.—RUSSIAN OLIVE.) S. Eu. to W. and C. Asia, Altai and Himal. Long cult. in Eu.; occasionally escaped. Zone II.—**E. a. spinòsa** (L.) Ktze., var. Brs. usually spiny: lvs. broader, elliptic to elliptic-oblong, 3–7 cm. long, densely scaly: fr. smaller, subglobose to ellipsoid. B.R.1156(c). L.B.1339(c). (*E. hortensis latifolia* Hort., *E. s.* L., *E. hortensis* var. *s.* Boiss.)—**E. a. orientàlis** (L.) Ktze., var. Often spineless: brts. scaly and stellate-pubescent: lvs. elliptic to oblong, 3–7 cm. long, obtuse, usually rounded at base, dull green above, scaly and stellate-pubescent beneath; petiole 4–6 mm. long: fr. to 2 cm. long. A.G.21:405,519,613,645. (*E. o.* L., *E. sativa* Hort.)

2. E. commutàta Bernh. SILVER-BERRY. Upright shrub to 4 m., stoloniferous, unarmed, with reddish brown brts.: lvs. short-petioled, ovate to oblong or ovate-lanceolate, 2–10 cm. long, acute or obtuse, cuneate, silvery on both sides, sometimes with scattered brown scales beneath: fls. 1–3, short-stalked, yellow, silvery outside, 1.2–1.5 cm. long, fragrant: fr. broad-ellipsoid, 1 cm. long, silvery, with dry mealy flesh. Fl.v–vii; fr.ix–x. B.M.8369(c). B.B. 2:576. (*E. argentea* Pursh, not Moench.) E. Can. to N. W. Terr., s. to Minn., S. Dak. and Utah. Intr. 1813. Zone II.

3. E. umbellàta Thunb. Shrub to 4 m., with spreading, often spiny brs.: brts. yellowish brown, often partly silvery: lvs. elliptic to ovate-oblong, 3–7 cm. long, obtuse to short-acuminate, rounded to broad-cuneate at base, often with crisped margin, usually with silvery scales above when young, sometimes glabrous, silvery beneath and usually mixed with brown scales: fls. yellowish white, fragrant, scaly outside, 1.2 cm. long; tube much longer than limb, gradually narrowed toward the base and slightly constricted; style scaly: fr. subglobose to ovoid, 6–8 mm. long, silvery mixed with brown scales at first, finally red, on stalks 8–12 mm. long. Fl.v–vi; fr.ix–x. S.I.2:t.54(c). N.K.17: t.1. R.H.1901:85. M.G.14:569. A.G.12:206. (*E. crispa* Thunb.) China, Korea, Japan. Intr. 1830. Zone III.—**E. u. parvifòlia** (Royle) Servettaz, var. Brts. and winter-buds silvery; lvs. elliptic-ovate to elliptic-lanceolate, usually short-acuminate, usually stellate-pubescent above, finally glabrous. silvery beneath: style stellate-pubescent: fr. short-stalked, subglobose, silvery, finally light red. Fr.vIII. B.R.29:51(c). M.M.5:145. (*E. p.* Royle, *E. japonica* Hort.) Himal. Cult. 1843. Zone (V).

4. **E. multiflòra** Thunb. Shrub to 3 m., with spreading unarmed brs.; brts. reddish brown: lvs. elliptic or ovate to obovate-oblong, 2.5–6 cm. long, short-acuminate to obtusish, broad-cuneate, stellate-pubescent above, becoming glabrous, silvery beneath, with scattered larger brown scales: fls. 1–2, yellowish white, with silvery and brown scales outside; tube campanulate, distinctly constricted above ovary, about as long as limb: fr. oblong, about 1.5 cm. long, red, scaly, of pleasant acid flavor, pendulous on a slender stalk 1.5–2.5 cm. long. Fl.iv–v; fr.vi. B.M.7341(c). Add. 4:t.155(c). G.F.1:499. Gng.1:275, 277. (*E. longipes* Gray, *E. edulis* Carr.) China, Japan. Intr. 1862. Zone IV. —**E. m. ovàta** (Maxim.) Servettaz, var. Lvs. stellate-pubescent above at first, soon glabrous: fls. 1–3: fr. ellipsoid, 8–12 mm. long, red with brown scales, nodding on pedicels 1.2–1.5 cm. long. Fr.vII–vIII. M.G.14:569 and G.C.66:301 (both as *E. multiflora*).

5. **E. macrophýlla** Thunb. Evergreen shrub to 3 m., with spreading unarmed brs.; brts. silvery white: lvs. broad-ovate or broad elliptic, 5–11 cm. long, short-acuminate, rounded at base, scaly above, glabrescent at length, densely silvery-scaly beneath; petiole rather stout, about 1.5 cm. long: fls. 4–6, about 1 cm. long, fragrant, on stalks 6 mm. long, nodding, outside with silvery and brownish scales; tube campanulate, abruptly narrowed above the ovary, as long as limb: fr. ellipsoid, 1.5 cm. long, red, scaly. Fl.ix–xi; fr.v. B.M.7638(c). N.K.17:t.4. G.C.III.25:90. Gn.80:582. S.H.2:f.281a-c,282g-h. Japan, Korea. Intr. 1843. Zone VII.

6. **E. glàbra** Thunb. Evergreen sarmentose or climbing shrub to 6 m., unarmed, very rarely spiny; brts. brown, lustrous: lvs. elliptic-ovate to elliptic-lanceolate, 3–7 cm. long, acutish to acuminate, broad-cuneate at base, lustrous above, with yellow and brown scattered scales beneath, lustrous; petiole 5–10 mm. long, brown: fls. short-stalked, white, brown outside, fragrant, narrowly funnelform; tube slender, gradually narrowed toward the base, twice as long as limb: fr. ellipsoid, 1.2–2 cm. long, gray or ferrugineous, on a stalk 4–10 mm. long. Fl.x–xi; fr.v. S.H.2:f.281i-l,282b-c. C. China, Korea, Japan. Cult. 1888. Zone VII.

7. **E. pungens** Thunb. Spreading shrub, usually spiny, to 4 m.; brts. brown: lvs. elliptic to oblong, 5–10 cm. long, acutish to obtuse, rounded at base, with wavy and often crisped margin, scaly above at first, soon glabrous and lustrous, covered with dull white scales beneath and dotted with brown scales; petiole 6–12 mm. long, brown: fls. 1–3, pendulous, 1.2 cm. long, fragrant, silvery white, tube abruptly contracted above the ovary, longer than the limb: fr. ellipsoid, 1.5 cm. long, brown at first, finally red. Fl.x–xi; fr.v. S.H.2:f.281d-g,282a. Japan. Intr. 1830. Zone VII.—**E. p. aùrea** Servettaz, var. Lvs. margined with deep yellow.—**E. p. variegàta** Rehd., var. Lvs. margined with yellowish white. G.M.54:327.—**E. p. Frederìci** Bean, var. Lvs. rather small and narrow, with pale yellow center and dark green narrow margin. (*E. p. aureo-picta* Hort.)—**E. p. maculàta** Rehd., var. With large deep yellow blotch in the middle. Gs.20:104. A.G.13:122. A.F.23:1015. (*E. p. aureo-maculata* Hort., *E. p.* var. *aureo-variegata* Bean.)—**E. p. Simònii** (Carr.) Nichols., var. Lvs. rather large, elliptic-oblong, without or with few brown scales beneath. Gs.20:53. (*E. S.* Carr.)—**E. p. trícolor** Rehd., var. Lvs. variegated with yellow and pinkish white.—**E. p. refléxa** (Morr. & Dcne.) Servettaz, var. Brs. elongated and less spiny: lvs. ovate-lanceolate, acute

to acuminate, lustrous above, ferrugineous beneath. H.U.4:328,t(c). L.D.II.
4:t.6(c). Gs.20:53. (*E. r.* Morr. & Dcne.) Possibly hybrid between this
species and *E. glabra.*

Fam. 76. **LYTHRACEAE** Lindl.   LOOSE–STRIFE FAMILY

Herbs, shrubs or trees: lvs. opposite or whorled, sometimes alternate,
entire, usually with small stipules: fls. perfect, usually regular, perigynous, in
terminal or axillary racemes, panicles or cymes; calyx-tube (receptacle)
tubular, usually ribbed; sepals 4 or 8, rarely to 16; petals as many, imbricated or wanting; stamens inserted below the petals, usually twice as many,
sometimes fewer or more; ovary superior, with 1 style and an entire or
slightly 2-lobed stigma, usually 2–6-celled, rarely 1-celled; ovules usually
many, on axile placentae: fr. a usually dehiscent caps.; seed exalbuminous;
embryo straight, with flat or rarely folded cotyledons.—Twenty-two genera
with about 450 species, mostly trop., few in temp. regions.

A. Fls. axillary; stamens 8–18: lvs. linear to narrow-oblong.
  B. Fls. yellow, solitary in the axils; stamens 10–18...........................1. *Heimia*
  BB. Fls. rose-purple, in axillary clusters; stamens 8–10.....................2. *Decodon*
AA. Fls. in terminal panicles; stamens 15–200: lvs. elliptic to oblong........3. *Lagerstroemia*

1. **HEIMIA** Link. Deciduous shrubs with virgate brs.: lvs. opposite
or partly alternate or in 3's, subsessile, exstipulate: fls. axillary, solitary,
short-stalked; calyx campanulate, with horn-like spreading processes between the lobes; petals 5–7, yellow; stamens 10–18, about half as long as
petals, equal; style slender, longer than stamens, with capitate stigma; ovary
globose or obovoid, 3–6-celled: caps. loculicidal; seeds small, numerous.
(After Ernst Ludwig Heim, physician in Berlin; 1747–1834.) Two or 3
species from Mex. to Argentine.

H. **salicifòlia** (H. B. K.) Link. Shrub to 3 m., glabrous; brts. slightly
winged: lvs. opposite or partly alternate, linear-lanceolate to narrow-oblong,
1.5–5 cm. long, acute: fls. 1.5–2 cm. across: petals oval. Fl.vii–ix. S.B.3:t.
281(c). L.D.8:567,t(c). (*Nesaea s.* H. B. K.) Mex. to Argentine. Intr. 1821.
Zone VII.—H. **s. grandiflòra** Lindl., var. Fls. larger 2.5–3 cm. across. B.R.
27:t.60(c). H.I.6:t.554,f.A. Intr. 1839.

2. **DÉCODON** J. F. Gmel. Suffruticose plant: lvs. opposite or whorled,
subsessile, entire, exstipulate: fls. in short-peduncled cymes in the axils of the
upper lvs., trimorphous; calyx-tube campanulate, ribbed, sepals 5–7, with as
many horn-like processes at the sinuses; petals lanceolate, crinkled; stamens
10, rarely 8, of 2 lengths, exserted; ovary 3–6-celled; style filiform, of 3
lengths; stigma capitate: caps. subglobose, loculicidal, 3–6-valved; seeds
angled. (Greek *decas,* ten, and *odous* or *odōn,* tooth.) One species in N. Am.

D. **verticillàtus** (L.) Ell. Aquatic subshrub, with slender virgate curved
angled brs., the submerged portion often spongy: lvs. elliptic-lanceolate to
lanceolate, 3–20 cm. long, acuminate, cuneate, with often undulate margin:
fls. in clusters of 2–8; petals rose-purple, 8–10 mm. long; caps. 5 mm. across.
Fl.vii–ix. B.B.2:580. Torrey, Fl. N. Y. 1:t.28(c). House, Wild Fl. N. York,
1:t.143a(c). Mass. to Ont. and Minn., s. to Fla. and La. Intr. 1759. Zone IV.

3. **LAGERSTROÈMIA** L. Evergreen or deciduous shrubs or trees;
winter-buds pointed, with 2 outer scales: lvs. opposite or the upper alternate,
entire, with very small conical and deciduous stipules: fls. in terminal and
axillary panicles, perfect, regular, pink, purple or white; pedicels bracted;
calyx turbinate or hemispheric, often ribbed or winged; sepals 6–9; petals

usually 6, with long and slender claw and crinkled or fringed blade; stamens many, with long filaments: ovary 3–6-celled, with a long style and capitate stigma; caps. loculicidal; seeds winged at the top. (After Magnus von Lager-stroem, a friend of Linnaeus; 1696–1759.) About 30 species in S. and E. Asia, New Guinea, Philipp. Isls., Australia.

L. índica L. CRAPE-MYRTLE. Deciduous shrub or tree to 7 m.; brts. 4–angled, glabrous: lvs. subsessile, elliptic or obovate to oblong, 2.5–7 cm. long, acute or obtuse, broad-cuneate or rounded at base, glabrous or pilose along the midrib beneath: fls. bright pink, 3–4 cm. across, in panicles 6–20 cm. long; calyx smooth outside, not ribbed: fr. a broad-ellipsoid caps., 1–1.2 cm. long. Fl.vii–ix. B.M.405(c). R.H.1874:130,t(c). Gt.6:t.191(c). G.C.66:186(h). Gng.1:151(h);5:281(h). China; much cult. in trop. and subtrop. countries. Intr. 1747. Zone VII. Handsome shrub, much cult. in the South for its pro-fuse summer bloom, hardy as far north as Baltimore; occasionally escaped.— Many color forms from pale pink to cherry red and violet, and one with white fls., **L. i. alba** Nichols.

Fam. 77. **PUNICACEAE** Horan. POMEGRANATE FAMILY

Only one genus which see for characters.

PÙNICA L. Shrubs or small trees; winter-buds small, with 2 pairs of outer scales: lvs. usually opposite and fascicled, entire, exstipulate: fls. perfect, perigynous, 1–5 at end of brts., terminal and axillary; calyx-tube campanu-late or tubular, sepals 5–8, fleshy, valvate; petals 5–7, imbricate; stamens very numerous; ovary inferior or nearly so with the carpels in 1 or 2 superimposed series, 3 with axile placentae in the lower and usually 5–7 with parietal placentae in the upper whorl; style 1 with capitate stigma: fr. a berry, with thick leathery rind, the central pulpy mass formed by the fleshy outer seed-coats; embryo straight, with convolute cotyledons. (The ancient Latin name of the plant.) Two species in the Mediterr. reg. to the Himal. and in Socotra.

P. Granàtum L. POMEGRANATE. Deciduous shrub or small tree to 5, rarely 10 m., with spinescent brs.; brts. angled, glabrous: lvs. short-petioled, obovate to oblong, 2–8 cm. long, acutish, glabrous, lustrous above: fls. short-stalked, scarlet, about 3 cm. across; petals crumpled; calyx purple: fr. sub-globose, 6–8 cm. across, deep yellow, crowned by the persistent calyx. Fl.v̆–vi; fr.ix–x. B.M.1832(c). E.N.III.7:24. S. E. Eu. to Himal. Cult. since time immemorial. Zone VII. Grown for its fls. and fr.—Many forms are known, most of them tenderer than the type.—**P. G. pleniflòra** Hayne. Fls. double, scarlet. Trew, Pl. Ehret. t.71(c). R.B.12,169,t(c).—**P. G. albéscens** DC., var. Fls. white. A.R.t.96(c).—**P. G. múltiplex** Sweet, var. Fls. white, double. R.B.12:169,t(c).—**P. G. flavéscens** Sweet, var. Fls. yellow.—**P. G. Legréllei** Vanh. Fls. double, striped red and yellowish white. F.S.13:t.1385 (c). R.H.1867:232,t(c);1880:130,t(c). I.H.5:t.156(c).—**P. G. nàna** (L.) Pers., var. Low form with smaller linear-lanceolate to linear lvs., smaller fls. and fr. B.M.634(c). L.B.988(c). Zone VI. A double-fld. form is **P. G. plèna** Voss, f.

Fam. 78. **NYSSACEAE** Endl. TUPELO FAMILY

Deciduous trees; winter-buds scaly: lvs. alternate, entire or toothed, ex-stipulate: fls. dioecious or polygamous, in axillary or terminal heads; calyx in the staminate fls. minute, 5-toothed or indistinct, in the pistillate fl. adnate to the ovary; petals 5 or more or wanting; stamens twice as many or fewer than petals, usually in 2 series; ovary 1-celled or 6–10-celled; ovules solitary, anatropous, pendulous; disk epigynous or wanting; style subulate or conic, with simple or divided stigma: fr. drupaceous, crowned with the remnants of the calyx; seed albuminous with thin or membranous testa; cotyledons foliaceous, radicle cylindric. The family is sometimes included in Cornaceae. Three genera in N. Am., W. China, Himal. and Malayan Archipelago.

A. Lvs. cuneate or rounded at base, entire or remotely dentate; infl. without bracts.1. *Nyssa*
AA. Lvs. cordate at base, serrate-dentate: infl. with 2 large bracts....................2. *Davidia*

1. **NYSSA** L. TUPELO. Deciduous trees: winter-buds with imbricate scales: lvs. entire or remotely toothed: fls. minute, greenish white, polygamo-dioecious, in axillary peduncled clusters; the staminate in many-fld. peduncled clusters; calyx disciform or cup-shaped, 5-toothed; petals 5, small, ovate to linear-oblong, inserted on the margin of the conspicuous disk; stamens 5–12, exserted, without rudimentary ovary; pistillate fls. sessile, rarely short-stalked, 1 or 2 to several, with bractlets at base, on slender or sometimes short peduncles; calyx-tube campanulate with 5-toothed limb; petals small; stamens 5–10, short, with often sterile anthers; disk less developed: ovary 1–2-celled, style terete, recurved, stigmatic on the inner face: fr. an oblong drupe, usually 1-seeded, with a bony, ribbed or winged stone; embryo straight. (Greek name of a nymph; alluding to the habitat of the trees, in swampy or moist soil.) Four species in N. Am. and 2 in Asia.

N. sylvática Marsh. TUPELO. Tree to 30 m., with slender spreading usually more or less pendulous brs. forming a flat-topped nearly cylindric or sometimes broad head: lvs. obovate or elliptic, 5–12 cm. long, acute or obtusish, rarely acuminate, cuneate or sometimes rounded at base, entire, rarely coarsely dentate, lustrous above, glaucescent beneath, pubescent on the veins or glabrous at maturity; petiole 6–35 mm. long, terete or wing-margined: fls. on pubescent or tomentose peduncles 1–3.5 cm. long; staminate pediceled, in many-fld. heads; pistillate in 2- or several-fld. clusters: fr. ovoid, 8–12 mm. long, blue-black, with thin acrid flesh; stone slightly 10–12-ribbed. Fl.v–vi; fr.x. S.S.5:t.217. Em.312,t.7(c). G.F.3:491(h);7:275(h). F.L.6:8,t(h). (*N. multiflora* Wangh., *N. villosa* Michx., *N. aquatica* L., partly.—PEPPERIDGE, BLACK GUM, SOUR GUM.) Me., Ont. and Mich. to Fla. and Tex. Intr. before 1750. Zone IV. Tree of distinct habit, with lustrous foliage turning bright scarlet in fall.—**N. s. biflòra** (Walt.) Sarg., var. Lvs. usually narrower and obtuse, subcoriaceous, glabrous at maturity: pistillate fls. in pairs: fr. ellipsoid, about 8 mm. long; stone slightly flattened, prominently ribbed. S.S.5:t. 218. (*N. b.* Walt.) N. C. to Fla. and La. Intr. 1739. Zone VII.

Related species: **N. sinénsis** Oliv. Tree to 15 m.; brts. pubescent: lvs. elliptic, 8–15 cm. long, dull dark green above, light green and pubescent on the veins beneath: pistillate fls. short-pediceled, few, on slender peduncles: fr. oblong, 1.2–1.5 cm. long, bluish. H.I.20:1964. C.C.259. C. China. Intr. 1902. Zone VII?—**N. aquática** L. COTTON GUM. Tree to 30 m.; brts. soon glabrous: lvs. ovate to oblong, 10–16 cm. long, acute or acuminate, entire or remotely toothed, lustrous above, glaucescent and downy-pubescent beneath: pistillate fls. solitary, with 2–4 bractlets at base, on slender hairy peduncles: fr. oblong, 2–2.5 cm. long, purple. S.S.5:t.220. (*N. uniflora* Wangh.) Va. to s. Ill., Fla. and Tex. Intr. before 1735. Zone VII.—**N. Ogèche** Marsh. OGEECHEE LIME. Tree to 20 m.; brts. pubescent: lvs. elliptic to obovate-oblong, 10–14 cm. long, acute to obtuse, entire, at maturity slightly hairy and lustrous above, glaucescent beneath and fulvous-pubescent on the veins or sometimes nearly glabrous: pistillate fls. solitary, on short villous peduncles: fr. oblong, 1.2–1.6 cm. long, red. S.S.5:t.219. S. C. to Fla. Intr. 1806. Zone VII?

2. **DAVÍDIA** Baill. Deciduous tree; winter-buds large, with several imbricate scales: lvs. alternate, slender-petioled, dentate, exstipulate: fls. andromonoecious, apetalous, in dense subglobose heads consisting of numerous staminate fls. and 1 perfect fl., with 2 large bracts at base; sepals and petals wanting; stamens 1–7, with slender filaments; ovary 6–10-celled, with rudimentary perianth and a circle of short stamens on top of the ovary at base of the short thick style; stigmas spreading: fr. a drupe, with 3–5-seeded stone. (After Armand David, French missionary who botanized in China from 1862–74; 1826–1900.) One species in China.

D. involucràta Baill. DOVE-TREE. Tree to 20 m. with ascending brs.: brts. glabrous: lvs. broad-ovate, 8–14 cm. long, acuminate, cordate, dentate-serrate with acuminate teeth, strongly veined, bright green and finally glabrous above, densely silky-pubescent beneath; petiole 3.6–7 cm. long: fl.-heads 2 cm. across on slender peduncles about 7 cm. long and terminal on short lateral spurs; bracts 2, rarely 3, opposite, ovate to oblong-obovate, entire or serrate, creamy-white, the larger one to 16 cm. long, pendulous, the smaller about half as long: fr. pear-shaped, about 3.5 cm. long, green with purple bloom. Fl.v–vi; fr.x. Nouv. Arch. Mus. Paris, II.8:t.10(c). I.S.1:t.40. W. China. Intr. 1904. Zone VI. Pyramidal tree with rather large bright green lvs. and strikingly handsome in bloom with its large creamy-white floral bracts.—D. i. Vilmoriniàna (Dode) Wangerin, var. Lvs. glaucescent or yellowish green and glabrous beneath or only sparingly pubescent on the veins while young. B.M.8432(c). G.C.64:12,13,17(h);78:25(h). R.H.1906:297–9 (h). Gn.82:199. Gn.M.40:131. C. and W. China. Intr. 1897. Zone V. (*D. V.* Dode, *D. laeta* Dode.)

Fam. 79. **ALANGIACEAE** Lindl. ALANGIUM FAMILY

The family contains only the following genus.

ALÀNGIUM Lam. Trees or shrubs, sometimes spiny: lvs. alternate, petioled, entire or lobed, estipulate: fls. perfect, regular, white or yellowish white, in axillary cymes with subulate or linear deciduous bracts; pedicels articulate; calyx-lobes 4–10, petals as many, linear or strap-shaped, valvate, sometimes coherent at base, at first tubular, later recurved; stamens as many as petals or 2 to 4 times as many; filaments free; disk large; ovary inferior, 1-, rarely 2-celled; ovule solitary, pendulous, anatropous; style cylindric, elongated, with entire or 2–3-lobed stigma: fr. an ellipsoid or globose drupe crowned by the calyx, 1-seeded; seed albuminous; embryo straight with foliaceous cotyledons and a long radicula. (Name an anagram of Adanson's name Angolam for this plant.) Syn.: *Marlea* Roxb. About 20 species chiefly in s. Asia extending to Japan, C. China, and Australasia; also in Africa.

A. platanifòlium (Sieb. & Zucc.) Harms. Tree, but usually shrubby in cult.; brs. pubescent when young, soon glabrous: lvs. suborbicular to broadovate, 10–20 cm. long, 3–5-, rarely to 7-lobed, with oblong to triangular acuminate entire lobes, subcordate to broad-cuneate at base, palminerved, dark green above and sparingly pubescent beneath; petiole 2–7 cm. long: fls. 2.5–3 cm. long, fragrant, in 1–4-fld. peduncled cymes; petals linear, usually 6, coherent at base: fr. ovoid, 6–8 mm. long. Fl.vi–vii. I.S.2:t.95. E.P.IV.220b:23. (*Marlea platanifolia* Sieb. & Zucc.) C. China, Japan. Intr. 1867. Zone VII.

Related species: A. chinénse (Lour.) Harms. Lvs. ovate, usually oblique at base, 8–20 cm. long, entire or with few lobes and usually unsymmetrical, acuminate, glabrous above: cymes 3–15-fld.; fls. about 2 cm. long. B.R.24:61(c).

I.S.2:t.94. E.P.IV.220b:20. (*A. begoniifolium* (Roxb.) Baill., *Marlea begonii-folia* Roxb.) C. China to S. Asia, Afr. Intr. 1805. Zone VII?

Fam. 80. **MYRTACEAE** R. Br. MYRTLE FAMILY

Evergreen shrubs or trees, aromatic: lvs. usually opposite, entire, pellucid-dotted, exstipulate: fls. perfect, regular; sepals usually 4–5, imbricate, sometimes lid-like and deciduous; petals as many, imbricate; stamens numerous, often in fascicles opposite the petals; ovary inferior, 1- to many-celled; ovules 1 to many in each cell; style 1: fr. usually a berry or a caps., rarely a drupe or a nut; seeds often angled, exalbuminous.—About 70 genera and 2800 species in trop. and subtrop. regions.

EUCALÝPTUS L'Hérit. GUM-TREE. Evergreen trees, rarely shrubs: lvs. usually alternate and pendulous, petioled, rarely opposite and sessile, but opposite and sessile in the juvenile stage of many species, penninerved, usually glabrous: fls. white to yellow or red, usually in axillary umbels, sometimes corymbose or paniculate; calyx-tube turbinate, campanulate or oblong, adnate to the ovary; calyx-lobes and petals connate into a lid or cap and separating from the calyx-tube at anthesis; stamens numerous; anthers opening by slits or pores: fr. a caps. opening at the top by 3–6 valves; seeds numerous, angled. (Greek *eu*, well, and *calyptein*, to cover; referring to the lid of the fl.) About 300 species in Australia and a few in Malesia.—Much planted in subtrop. countries for timber and ornament; the following species may be precariously hardy at the southern limit of our area.

E. Gúnnii Hook. f. CIDER G. Tree to 25 m., sometimes shrubby: lvs. of young plants opposite or nearly so, orbicular, 2–6 cm. wide, rounded or emarginate at apex, short-petioled or sessile: lvs. of adult plant alternate, lanceolate, 5–10 cm. long, acute at ends; petiole to 2.5 cm. long: umbels 3-fld., short-stalked; fls. about 1.5 cm. across; lid hemispherical, short-pointed, lustrous; stamens yellow, 5–7 mm. long; anthers oval, opening by parallel slits: fr. turbinate, truncate, 6–10 mm. across. Fl.ix–x. G.C.III.2:781;11: 787(h). Maiden, Crit. Rev. Eucal. 3:t.108,f.2–8,t.9,f.1. S. Austral., Tasmania. Intr. about 1850. Zone VII? A variable species; the hardiest form is **E. G. montàna** Hook. f., var. Smaller tree: young lvs. sometimes perfoliate, adult lvs. usually smaller: fr. smaller, more hemispherical, with thinner rim. B.M. 7808(c, excl. f.3,4). B.S.1:534. Maiden, l.c.3:t.83,f.11(as *E. cordata*),t.108,f.1. (*E. Perriniana* F. v. Muell.)

Fam. 81. **ONAGRACEAE** Lindl. EVENING–PRIMROSE FAMILY

Herbs, rarely shrubs or trees: lvs. opposite or alternate or whorled, entire or toothed, rarely lobed; stipules small, deciduous or wanting: fls. perfect, regular, epigynous or perigynous, usually solitary or few, axillary, rarely in racemes or panicles; sepals 4, rarely 2 or 3; petals 4, rarely 2 or wanting, usually clawed, convolute; stamens usually twice as many as petals or as many, rarely fewer; ovary inferior, 2–4-celled; ovules numerous, rarely few, on axile placentae; style 1 with 1–4 stigmas: fr. a caps., rarely a berry or a nut; seeds small, exalbuminous. Syn.: *Epilobiaceae* DC.—About 36 genera with 500 species distributed through both hemispheres but most numerous in Am.—The genus *Zauschneria* sometimes considered woody is scarcely suffruticose and only precariously hardy within our area.

FUCHSIA L. Shrubs or small trees, usually glabrous: lvs. opposite or sometimes whorled or alternate, petioled, dentate, with small caducous stipules: fls. axillary, 1 or several, peduncled and usually pendulous, sometimes forming terminal panicles; calyx-tube prolonged beyond the ovary and campanulate to tubular, with 4 spreading valvate lobes, usually colored, often red; petals 4, sometimes 5, rarely wanting, usually upright; stamens usually 8, often exserted; style exserted, with capitate, simple or 4-lobed stigma: fr. a 4-loculed, soft berry with numerous usually brown seeds. (After Leonard Fuchs, German physician and botanical author; 1501–65.) About 70 species in trop. and subtrop. Am., a few in New Zealand.—Even the hardier species are within our area usually killed to the ground even if protected, but the young shoots springing up from the base flower the same season. One of the hardiest is *F. magellanica* var. *Riccartonii;* it may persist even in Zone V.

F. magellánica Lam. Small shrub: lvs. short-petioled, ovate-oblong, 2.5–5.5 cm. long, acuminate, rounded at base, dentate or denticulate, slightly pubescent on margin and midrib beneath, bright green: fls. usually solitary, pendulous; calyx red, the tube cylindric, less than half as long as the oblong-lanceolate lobes; petals obovate, violet, half as long as calyx-lobes; stamens much exserted. Fl.vi–ix. B.M.97(c). S.H.2:f.285f-g,286c. (*F. coccinea* Curtis, not Ait., *F. macrostemma* Ruiz & Pav.) Peru, Chile. Cult. 1800. Zone VII. A variable species.—**F. m. globòsa** (Lindl.) Bailey, var. Lvs. ovate, glabrous; petiole longer: fl. nearly globose in bud; calyx-tube very short, the lobes often cohering for some time at apex. B.R.1556(c). Gn.55:75. B.C. 3:1299. S.H.2:f.285i,286h. (*F. g.* Lindl., *F. macrostemma* var. *g.* Sweet.) Orig. 1830.—**F. m. riccartònii** (Lebas) Bailey, var. Lvs. oblong-ovate, with purplish tinge; calyx-tube short; lobes shorter and broader. R.H.1896:30; 1926:172,t(c). B.C.3:1300. (*F. R.* Lebas.) Cult. 1835.—**F. m. cònica** (Lindl.) Bean, var. Lvs. broad-ovate or oval, 2–3.5 cm. long: fls. red and purple; calyx-tube 1 cm. long; lobes nearly twice as long; petals obovate. B.R. 1062(c). (*F. c.* Lindl.) Cult. 1827.

The following are of about the same hardiness: **F. exoniénsis** Paxt. Lvs. often in 3's, ovate, 3–8 cm. long, dark green, suffused with red-purple: fls. solitary, slender-stalked; calyx-tube about 1.5 cm. long; lobes oblong-lanceolate, 2.5–3.5 cm. long, scarlet; petals purple, obovate, about half as long as sepals; stamens much exserted. P.M.10:151(c). G.C.II.20:565. (*F. corallina* Porcher.) Probably hybrid of *F. magellanica*. Cult. 1843.—**F. díscolor** Lindl. Dwarf and compact shrub; brts. deep purple, puberulous: lvs. oblong-ovate or narrow-elliptic, 2–4 cm. long, cuneate, remotely denticulate, glabrous or very sparingly hairy beneath; pedicels thin, to 3 cm. long; tube about 1 cm. long, half as long as the narrow lobes; ovary often puberulous. B.R.1805(c). B.C.3:1300. S.H. 2:f.285h;286f-g. (*F. magellanica* var. *d.* Bailey.) Falkland Islands. Intr. before 1835.—**F. grácilis** Lindl. Slender shrub; young brts. and young lvs. puberulous: lvs. oblong-obovate or elliptic-oblong, 3–5.5 cm. long, cuneate, dentate: petioles slender, to 1.5 cm. long: fls. usually solitary; calyx-tube cylindric, about 1.5 cm. long, more than half as long as the lanceolate lobes; pedicels slender, to 4 cm. long, puberulous like the ovary. B.R.847(c),1052(c). B.M.2507(c). Gn. 55:71. B.C.3:1301. (*F. magellanica* var. *g.* Bailey.) Mex. Intr. 1822.—**F. microphýlla** Kunth. Dwarf shrub; brts. puberulous: lvs. broad-elliptic to ovate, 5–15 mm. long, glabrous: fls. polygamous, without the ovary 1–1.3 cm. long; calyx-tube longer than the ovate lobes, deep pink; petals rose-purple; fr. subglobose, 3 mm. across. B.R.1269(c). N.H.13:16. S.H.2:f.285c-d. Mex. Intr. 1825.—**F. ròsea** Ruiz & Pav. Upright shrub: lvs. ovate, 2–3 cm. long, acutish, rounded at base, entire; petiole 5–12 mm. long: fls. slender-stalked, usually several; calyx-tube about 1 cm. long; lobes lanceolate, about as long, reflexed, red, longer than the broad-ovate purple petals: fr. oblong. A.R.2:t.120(c). B.M. 1024(c). (*F. lycioides* Andrews.) Chile. Intr. 1796.—**F. parviflòra** Lindl. Suffruticose, with ascending brs.: lvs. elliptic-ovate or ovate, 2–4 cm. long, acute to obtusish, entire, glabrous or slightly pubescent when young; petiole 0.5–1.5 cm. long: fls. slender-stalked; calyx-tube 5–6 mm. long, pink; lobes triangular-ovate, acuminate, 3–4 mm. long, finally reflexed; petals shorter than sepals, purple: fr. subglobose. B.R.1048(c). Mex. Cult. 1824.—**F. procúmbens**

R. Cunningh. Prostrate shrub: lvs. ovate to orbicular-ovate, 1–1.8 cm. long, cordate, sinuate-dentate; petiole 1–2 cm. long: fls. solitary, erect, 1–1.5 cm. long, apetalous; calyx-tube orange-yellow; lobes ovate-oblong. shorter than tube, finally reflexed; anthers blue; style shorter than tube. B.M.6139(c). Gn.86: 607;88:324(h);90:48(h). Gs.6:171(h). N. Zeal. Intr. about 1855.

Fam. 82. **ARALIACEAE** Vent. GINSENG FAMILY

Shrubs, trees or herbs, often prickly, sometimes climbing; stems usually with large pith: lvs. alternate, entire, lobed or compound; stipules present or wanting: fls. regular, small, perfect or unisexual, epigynous, usually in umbels often forming compound infl.; sepals minute or obsolete; petals 5, rarely more, valvate or imbricate, sometimes cohering at apex and falling off as a cap; stamens usually 5, inserted at the edge of the disk; ovary inferior, 2–15-celled; cells 1-ovuled; styles as many as carpels, often connate: fr. a drupe, rarely splitting into segments; seeds albuminous, with small embryo. Syn. *Hederaceae* Lindl.—About 50 genera and more than 500 species in the trop. and temp. regions of both hemispheres.

A. Lvs. evergreen: stems unarmed.
  B. Stems climbing by rootlets, rarely shrubby: styles connate: lvs. simple, usually 3–5-lobed ....1. *Hedera*
  BB. Stems upright: styles 2–5, distinct or connate at base.
    C. Lvs. palmately lobed; styles 5, distinct.
      D. Lvs. usually 3–5-lobed: styles very short, upright..................1a. *Fatshedera*
      DD. Lvs. palmately 7–9-lobed, large: styles slender, divergent...............2. *Fatsia*
    CC. Lvs. undivided or 3-lobed to 3-foliolate: styles 2–4...................4. *Nothopanax*
AA. Lvs. deciduous: stems prickly, rarely unarmed.
  B. Lvs. palmately lobed: styles 2.
    C. Styles distinct; stems and petioles densely covered with slender prickles; shrubs.
      3. *Oplopanax*
    CC. Styles connate beyond the middle; stems and brs. with stout conical prickles; tree ....5. *Kalopanax*
  BB. Lvs. compound: styles 2–5.
    C. Lvs. digitate: umbels solitary or few..............................6. *Acanthopanax*
    CC. Lvs. pinnate to 3-pinnate; umbels in large panicles.......................7. *Aralia*

1. HÉDERA L. Ivy.

Evergreen shrubs climbing by aërial rootlets; winter-buds ovoid, with several outer scales: lvs. alternate, petioled, entire, coarsely dentate or lobed: fls. perfect, in terminal solitary or racemose umbels; pedicels not articulate; calyx 5-toothed; petals valvate, 5; stamens as many; ovary 5-celled; styles connate into a short column: fr. a 3–5-seeded berry-like drupe. (Ancient Latin name of the Ivy.) Five species in Eu., N. Afr. and Asia.

A. Pubescence of young growth stellate, grayish..................................1. *H. Helix*
AA. Pubescence of young growth scaly.
  B. Lvs. usually lobed, to 15 cm. long; scales with 15–20 rays, gray or yellowish.
    C. Lvs. of sterile brs. with 2–5 lobes on each side: fr. yellow...........2. *H. nepalensis*
    CC. Lvs. of sterile brs. usually 3-, rarely 5-lobed: fr. black...............3. *H. rhombea*
  BB. Lvs. usually entire, to 25 cm. long, thickly coriaceous; scales yellow, with 20–25 rays: fr. black ....4. *H. colchica*

1. H. Hélix L. ENGLISH I. High climbing, to 30 m., or creeping: lvs. of sterile brts. 3–5-lobed, 4–10 cm. long, dark green above, often with whitish veins, pale or yellowish green beneath, those of flowering brts. ovate to rhombic. entire, rounded to truncate at base: umbels globose, usually several forming a raceme; peduncle slender; calyx, pedicels and tips of young brts. with grayish white stellate hairs with usually 5 or 6 rays: fr. black, globose, 6 mm. across. Fl.IX–X; fr.IV–V. R.I.23:t.138b(c). S.E.4:t.633(c). G.H.t.25(c). M.D. 1915.t.31(h);1920:t.15,16(h). Eu. to Caucas. Cult. since ancient times. Zone (V).—Many garden forms and several geographical varieties are known. The following are forms of the typical variety (var. *vulgaris* DC.): **H.H. báltica** Rehd., var. A small-leaved form hardly different from the type, but hardier.

Zone IV.—**H. H. arboréscens** Loud., var. Upright low shrub: lvs. ovate to elliptic, entire. (*H. arborea* Hort.) This form is produced by rooting cuttings from flowering brs.—**H. H. argénteo-variegàta** West., var. Lvs. variegated or irregularly edged with white.—**H. H. aureo-variegàta** West., var. Lvs. variegated with yellow or wholly yellow. Hibberd, Ivy: frontisp., p.62,t.f.6 (c). (*H. H. chrysophylla* Hibb.)—**H. H. marginàta** Hibb. Lvs. broadly triangular-ovate, irregularly edged yellowish white, striped red or pink in autumn. F.E.31:318.—**H. H. trícolor** Hibb. Similar to the preceding, but edges of lvs. becoming red in autumn. (*H. H. marginata rubra* Hibb., *elegantissima* Hort., *Cullisii* Hort.)—**H. H. digitàta** Loud., var. Lvs. rather large and broad, digitately lobed with 5 triangular-oblong lobes, sometimes with 2 small additional lobes at the truncate base. Gn.25:141;34:493.—**H. H. pedàta** Hibb. Lvs. pedately 5-lobed, the middle lobe long and narrow, the lateral lobes much shorter, dark green with whitish veins. Gn.25:141;34:493; 59:154.—**H. H. sagittaefòlia** K. Koch. Lvs. rather small, with triangular, pointed middle lobe and broad obtusish lateral lobes, deeply cordate at base, dull dark green.—**H. H. deltoìdea** Hibb. Lvs. rather small, bluntly deltoid, almost entire, except 2 deep basal lobes. Gn.25:141;34:493. (*H. H. hastata* Hort.)—**H. H. mínima** Hibb. Lvs. small, 1.5–3 cm. long, close-set, 3-lobed or pedately 5-lobed with short and spreading basal lobes, dull purplish brown in winter. Gn.59:154. M.G.1897:229(as var. *digitata*). (*H. H. donerailensis* Hort.)—**H. H. conglomeràta** Nichols. Slow growing; lvs. crowded, small, entire or 3-lobed, undulate. R.H.1890:163.—**H. H. tortuòsa** Hibb. Lvs. ovate or rhombic, entire or obscurely 3-lobed, more or less curled and twisted, more so during cold weather. Gn.55:336. Tobler, Hedera:28.

The following are geographical vars.: **H. H. hibérnica** Kirchn. Lvs. larger and broader, 6–14 cm. across, of light color and thinner texture, with short and broad lobes, often subcordate at base, dark green; stellate hairs mostly with 8, sometimes 12 rays. (*H. H. scotica* Hort., *irlandica* Hort., *H. hibernica* Bean.)—**H. H. maculàta** (Hibb.) Rehd., var. A form of the preceding with the lvs. spotted and striped yellowish white. (*H. hibernica* var. *m.* Bean, *H. grandifolia maculata* Hibb., *H. latimaculata* Hort., *H. latifolia maculata* Hort.)

H. H. poética West., var. Lvs. broad-ovate, shallowly lobed, cordate, often undulate, bright or yellowish green, those of flowering brs. narrower, entire: fr. yellow. Tobler, Hedera: 38–42. (*H. H.* var. *chrysocarpa* Ten., *H. poetarum* Bertol., *H. chrysocarpa* Walsh.) S. E. Eu., Asia Minor.

H. H. taùrica (Tobl.) Rehd., var. Lvs. narrow, usually sagittate with elongated middle lobe and 1 or 2 short spreading lobes, on each side at base, usually undulate; rather more pubescent, the hairs with about 8 rays: fr. yellow. Tobler, Hedera: 43–46. (*H. poetarum* var. *t.* Tobl.) Crimea.

H. H. × *Fatsia japonica* = *Fatshedera Lizei;* see p. 674.

Related species: **H. canariénsis** Willd. High climbing; hairs with 12–20 rays: lvs. roundish-ovate, usually cordate, 5–15 cm. across, entire or with 5–7 short lobes, bright green: fr. larger. Jour. Bot. 3:t.32(c). Mo. Bot. Gard. Rep. 8:t.27. Tobler, Hedera:49. Gn.25:141;34:492,496. (*H. Helix* var. *c.* DC., *H. algeriensis, H. maderensis* and *H. azorica* Hort.) Canary Isls., Madeira, N. Afr. Cult. 1833. Zone VII?

2. **H. nepalénsis** K. Koch. High climbing; hairs scale-like, with 15–20 rays, gray or yellowish: lvs. of sterile brts. triangular-ovate to triangular-oblong, 5–12 cm. long, pinnately lobed, with 2–5 obtusish teeth or lobes on each side, usually truncate at base, those of fertile brts. oblong-ovate to oblong-lanceolate, broad-cuneate at base, entire; petioles scaly: umbels few

to many on rather short stout peduncles: fr. yellow or red. R.H.1884:84,t (c). Tobler, Hedera: 69–74. (*H. himalaica* Tobl., *H. cinerea* Bean, *H. Helix* var. *aurantiaca* André, *H. Helix* var. *cinerea* Hibb.) Himal., Assam to Afghan. and Punjab. Cult. 1880. Zone VII?—**H. n. sinénsis** (Tobl.) Rehd., var. Lvs. of sterile shoots entire or 3-lobed, those of fertile brts. elliptic-ovate to elliptic-lanceolate. Tobler, Hedera: 81–83. (*H. himalaica* var. *s.* Tobl., *H. s.* Hand.-Mazz.) China. Intr. ?

3. **H. rhómbea** (Miq.) Bean. High climbing; hairs scale-like, with 15–20 rays, yellow or yellowish: lvs. of sterile brts. triangular-ovate to broad-ovate, 2–5 cm. long, 3-lobed, rarely 5-lobed, with obtuse lobes, truncate to cordate, those of fertile brts. ovate or rhombic-ovate to oblong-ovate, 5–10 cm. long, rounded to broad-cuneate at base: umbels racemose on slender peduncles; apex of ovary elevated; calyx-limb obsolete: fr. small, black. N.K.16:t.14,15. Tobler, Hedera: 86–88. (*H. Helix* var. *rhombea* Miq., *H. japonica* Tobl., not Jungh., *H. Tobleri* Nakai.) Japan, Korea. Cult. 1867? Zone VI?

4. **H. cólchica** K. Koch. High climbing; hairs scale-like, yellow, with 20–25 rays: lvs. broad-ovate to elliptic or on flowering brts. oblong-ovate, 10–25 cm. long, cordate or rounded at base, entire, rarely slightly lobed, dark green, thick and leathery: calyx-lobes triangular-ovate, conspicuous: fr. black. Gt.11:t.360. Tobler, Hedera: 58–66. Gn.25:141;34:492;86:448(h). (*H. Helix* var. *c.* K. Koch, *H. Roegneriana* Hort., *H. coriacea* Hibb.) Asia Minor, Cauc. to Persia. Cult. 1860. Zone (V.)—**H. c. arboréscens** Paul. Of shrubby habit. Gn.W.20:467.—**H. c. dentàta** Hibb. Lvs. with remote small teeth, of somewhat thinner texture. G.M.30:388;54:318. (*H. Helix* var. *dentata* Reg.)

1a. × **FATSHÉDERA** Guillaum. (*Hedera* × *Fatsia*). Evergreen upright shrub with long-petioled 3–5-lobed lvs.: fls. in large terminal panicles; styles 5, very short.

F. Lìzei (Cochet) Guillaum. (*H. Helix* × *F. japonica*.) Shrub to 2.5 m. or more; stems rusty-pubescent when young: lvs. usually 3–5-lobed, 8–18 cm. long and to 28 cm. across, glabrous, lobes triangular-ovate, entire or sparingly toothed; petiole 4–12 cm. long, usually with 2 stipular subulate appendages at the enlarged base: infl. pubescent; anthers sterile; styles about 1 mm. long, upright. B.M.9402(c). R.H.1912:568;1924:179(h). G.C. 86:423;88:489. (*Aralia L.* Cochet.) Orig. 1911. Zone VII.

2. **FÁTSIA** Dcne. & Planch. Evergreen shrub or small tree, unarmed: lvs. large, deeply palmately 7–9-lobed, exstipulate; petiole enlarged at base: fls. perfect or polygamous, 5-merous, in umbels forming large terminal panicles; pedicels slightly articulate; disk broad-conical; styles 5, diverging, filiform, with small capitate stigma: fr. subglobose, black, fleshy; seeds flattened; albumen solid. (From Fatsi, an incorrect transliteration of its Japanese name.) One species in Japan.

F. japónica (Thunb.) Dcne. & Planch. Shrub or tree to 5 m., glabrous; stems stout: lvs. leathery, 7–9-lobed, usually broader than long, 15–35 cm. across, cordate, divided beyond the middle into oblong-ovate, acuminate, serrate lobes with rounded sinuses, dark lustrous green above, paler beneath; petiole usually 10–30 cm. long: fls. white, in umbels 3–4 cm. across, pedicels 1–1.5 cm. long: fr. about 8 mm. across. Fl.x–xii. S.I.2:57(c). B.M.8638(c). G.C.29:217(h). (*Aralia j.* Thunb.) Japan. Intr. 1838. Zone VII. There are some horticultural varieties probably more tender.

3. **OPLÓPANAX** Miq. Deciduous shrubs, prickly throughout; winter-buds with several outer scales: lvs. alternate, long-petioled, palmately 5–7-lobed, exstipulate: fls. greenish white, in umbels forming terminal panicles; pedicels not articulate; calyx-teeth indistinct; petals 5, valvate; stamens 5; styles, 2, distinct: fr. a compressed drupe; albumen solid. (Greek *hoplon*, weapon, and *panax;* referring to the plant being armed with prickles.) Syn.: *Echinopanax* Dcne. & Planch. Three species in W. N. Am. and E. Asia.

O. hórridus (Sm.) Miq. Devil's Club. Shrub to 4 m. with upright stems densely furnished like the petioles and infl. with slender prickles: lvs. orbicular-ovate, 15–25 cm. across, 5–7-lobed, incisely lobulate and sharply serrate, prickly on both sides, glabrous and bright green above, slightly villous beneath: panicle pubescent, 8–15 cm. long: fr. broad-ellipsoid, 8 mm. long, scarlet. Fl.vii–viii; fr.viii–ix. B.M.8572(c). Gs.2:195(h). (*Panax h.* Sm., *Fatsia horrida* S. Wats., *Echinopanax horridum* Dcne. & Planch.) Alaska to Calif. Intr. about 1829. Zone V. Ornamental shrub with large bright green lvs. and conspicuous scarlet fr.

Closely related species: **O. elàtus** (Nakai) Nakai. Lvs. larger, lobes not lobulate or with 1 small lobe on each side of the middle lobe, closely doubly serrate, setose-pilose on the veins and veinlets beneath. J.C.26,1:t.15. N.K.16: t.11. Korea. Intr. 1917. Zone V.—**O. japónicus** (Nakai) Nakai. Lvs. sometimes peltate, more deeply incised, conspicuously ciliate, with long-acuminate lobes and lobules: pedicels slenderer, in fr. up to 1 cm. long. Japan. Intr. 1915. Zone V.

4. **NOTHÓPANAX** Miq. Evergreen unarmed shrubs or trees, glabrous or nearly so: lvs. digitate or simple and often lobed, slender-petioled, exstipulate or with small appendages at base: fls. 5-merous, in solitary, racemose or paniculate umbels; calyx-limb nearly entire or 5-toothed; petals valvate; ovary 2-, rarely 3–4-celled; styles distinct or connate at base: fr. flattened, rarely subglobose; seeds flattened, with solid albumen. (Greek *nothos*, false, hybrid and *panax;* referring to intermediate character of the genus.) About 15 species chiefly in Australasia, few in China.

N. Dàvidi (Franch.) Harms. Shrub or tree to 6 m., glabrous: lvs. coriaceous, simple, oblong-oval to oblong-lanceolate, 6–15 cm. long, long-acuminate, rounded or broad-cuneate at the 3-nerved base, remotely serrate, sometimes deeply 3-lobed to 3-parted or 3-foliolate, with sessile, narrow-lanceolate lfts.; petiole 5–15 cm. long: umbels about 2.5 cm. across forming panicles to 18 cm. long; calyx minutely 5-toothed; styles 2, connate about ½, diverging above: fr. flattened, 5–6 mm. across, black. Fl.vii–viii; fr.ix–x. R.H. 1919:212. J.L.56:78(h). (*Panax D.* Franch. *Acanthopanax diversifolius* Hemsl.) C. and W. China. Intr. 1907. Zone VII. Handsome evergreen shrub.

5. **KALÓPANAX** Miq. Deciduous tree; brs. stout, armed with short broad-based prickles; winter-buds with 2 or 3 outer scales, glabrous, the terminal broadly conic-ovoid: lvs. palmately lobed, serrulate, long-petioled; infl. terminal, large, consisting of many racemes with 2–8 slender-stalked umbels: fls. slender-stalked, 5-merous, perfect; pedicels not articulate; calyx-limb minutely 5-toothed; petals valvate; disk convex; fr. a 2-seeded drupe; albumen solid. (Greek *kalos*, handsome, and *panax*.) One species in E. Asia.

K. pictus (Thunb.) Nakai. Sparingly branched tree to 30 m.; brs. with numerous stout prickles; lvs. suborbicular, 9–25, sometimes to 35 cm. across, 5–7-lobed with broadly triangular-ovate to oblong-ovate acuminate serrate lobes, dark green above and glabrous or nearly so, light green beneath and usually slightly pubescent when young: petiole 8–50 cm. long: umbels forming a large compound terminal inflorescence 20–30 cm. across; pedicels 5–10 mm. long; fls. white; stamens longer than petals: fr. subglobose, 4 mm. across, bluish black, crowned by the slender style. Fl.vii–viii; fr.ix–x. S.I.2:t.56(c). M.K.t.78(c). N.K.16:t.8–10. M.D.1913:145;1918:t.5,6&8a(h). B.C.1:192. (*K. ricinifolium* Miq., *Acanthopanax r.* Seem., *K. septemlobus* Koidz.) China, Manch., Korea, Japan. Intr. about 1865. Zone IV. Tree of striking subtropical appearance.—**K. p. magníficus** (Zab.) Nakai, var. Brts. nearly unarmed or with few prickles: lvs. with ovate lobes, pubescent beneath. M.D.1918:t.5,j,k,t.8b(h). (*Acanthopanax acerifolius* Schelle.)—**K. p. Maximowíczii** (Vanh.) Hara, var. Lvs. 5–7-lobed beyond the middle, lobes oblong-lanceolate, pubescent beneath. F.S.20:t.2067(h,c). M.G.34:164(h). M.D. 1915:t.8(h);1918:t.5,e,7&8(h). (*Aralia M.* Vanh.) Japan. Cult. 1874. Zone V.

6. **ACANTHÓPANAX** Miq. Deciduous, rarely evergreen trees or shrubs, usually sparingly branched and prickly, rarely unarmed; winter-buds ovoid with several outer scales: lvs. alternate, slender-petioled, digitate, only occasionally entire, exstipulate: fls. perfect or polygamous, in terminal umbels usually few or solitary or forming large terminal panicles; pedicels slightly or not articulate; calyx-teeth minute; petals 5, rarely 4, valvate; stamens as many; ovary 2–5-celled; styles 2–5, connate or free: fr. a 2–5-seeded black drupe; albumen solid. (Greek *acanthos*, spine, and *panax*; referring to the prickly nature of most of the species.) About 20 species in E. Asia and Himal.—Ornamental shrubs with handsome rather large lvs.

A. Styles 5, connate into a column.................Sect. ELEUTHEROCOCCUS (Maxim.) Harms.
  B. Brts. glabrous and smooth, with slender usually reflexed prickles; peduncles glabrous, usually slender.
    c. Lfts. glabrous or pubescent, not setose.
      D. Lvs. 5-foliolate, or only partly ternate.
        E. Brts. usually densely furnished with slender, bristle-like prickles, light yellowish brown ....1. *A. senticosus*
        EE. Brts. with few usually reflexed prickles, greenish.............2. *A. leucorrhizus*
      DD. Lvs. 3-foliolate, rarely a few 4–5-foliolate.....................3. *A. setchuenensis*
    cc. Lfts. on both sides with bristles or setose hairs, usually 5; brts. yellowish or brownish ....4. *A. Simoni*
  BB. Brts. rough-pubescent at first, later glabrous and slightly rough, light yellowish gray, with short conical prickles: peduncles stout, pubescent....................5. *A. Henryi*
AA. Styles 2–5, divided at least at apex.
  B. Brs. prickly.
    c. Fls. subsessile or on short pubescent pedicels 3–10 mm. long: styles 2.
                                Sect. CEPHALOPANAX Baill.
      D. Lfts. usually 5, rough-pubescent beneath.......................6. *A. divaricatus*
      DD. Lfts. usually 3, glabrous or nearly so...........................7. *A. sessiliflorus*
    cc. Fls. slender-pediceled; pedicels glabrous; styles 2–5.
      D. Lfts. usually 5: umbels usually solitary: styles usually 5.
                                Sect. EUACANTHOPANAX Harms.
        E. Umbels at end of elongated leafy brts. on short peduncles: brts. usually with numerous bristly prickles..8. *A. Giraldii*
        EE. Umbels on short lateral spurs, on slender peduncles 4–6 cm. long: brts. with few short stout prickles....................................9. *A. Sieboldianus*
      DD. Lfts. 3, 2–4 cm. long: umbels 4–7 at end of brts., rarely solitary; styles 2.
                            Sect. ZANTHOXYLOPANAX Harms.
                                10. *A. ternatus*
  BB. Brs. unarmed: umbels in large terminal panicles; styles 2, connate.
                            Sect. SCIADOPHYLLOIDES Harms.
                              11. *A. sciadophylloides*

1. **A. senticòsus** (Maxim.) Harms. Shrub to 5 m., with upright sparingly branched stems, usually densely covered with slender bristles or prickles: lfts. 5, sometimes 3, short-stalked, elliptic-obovate to oblong, 6–12 cm. long, short-acuminate, cuneate, sharply and doubly serrate, dark green and with scattered hairs above, light green beneath and brownish pubescent

on the veins when young; petiole slender, 6–12 cm. long; umbels globose, many-fld., 3–4 cm. across, 1 or few on slender peduncles 5–7 cm. long; pedicels –2 cm. long; fls. purplish yellow: fr. subglobose, 8 mm. across. Fl.vii; fr.x. Jt.12:t.393. S.H.2:f.290a(l). S.L.69(h). M.D.1918:t.1(h). (*Eleutherococcus* —. Maxim.) N. China, Manch. Intr. about 1860. Zone II.—**A. s. inérmis** Komar., var. Brts. without or few prickles: lvs. and umbels larger.

2. **A. leucorrhìzus** (Oliv.) Harms. Shrub to 4 m.; brts. yellowish green, with scattered or below the petiole with several reflexed slender prickles or nearly unarmed: lfts. 3–5, short-stalked, oblong-lanceolate, 5–10 cm. long, acuminate, cuneate, sharply and doubly serrate, glabrous; petiole 3–7 cm. long: umbels several or solitary, 4–5 cm. across, on slender stalks 5–10 cm. long; pedicels 1–2 cm. long, glabrous; fls. greenish: fr. globose-ovoid, 6 mm. long. Fl.vii; fr.x. B.M.8607(c). G.C.64:176. B.S.1:130. (*Eleutherococcus l.* Oliv.) C. and W. China. Intr. 1901. Zone V.—**A. l. fulvéscens** Harms & Rehd., var. Lfts. 3–5, scabrous above, fulvous-pubescent on the veins beneath, usually simply serrate. C. and W. China. Intr. 1908.—**A. l. scabérulus** Harms & Rehd., var. Lfts. always 5, smaller and narrower, usually oblong-obovate, doubly serrate, pubescent beneath and setose on the midrib and petiole. C. and W. China. 1907.

3. **A. setchuenénsis** Harms. Upright shrub to 3 m.; brts. yellowish, with few nearly straight prickles: lfts. 3, stalked, oblong-obovate, 5–12 cm. long, long-acuminate, broad-cuneate or nearly rounded at base, remotely serrulate or serrate-dentate to nearly entire, dark green above, glaucescent beneath, glabrous; petiole 4–10 cm. long: umbels 3–7, about 3 cm. across, on peduncles 1–3 cm. long, the middle one sometimes to 10 cm. long; pedicels 6–20 mm. long: fr. black, broad-ellipsoid, 6–8 mm. long, crowned by the short style. Fl.vi; fr.x. M.D.1918:t.2g-k. Gn.85:606. W. China. Intr. 1904. Zone VI.

4. **A. Simòni** (Dcne.) Schneid. Shrub to 3 m.; brts. greenish, smooth, with several stout slightly reflexed prickles below the petioles: lfts. 5, short-talked, oblong to oblanceolate, the middle one 8–12 cm. long, the lateral ones much smaller, acuminate, cuneate, sharply and doubly serrate, bristly on both sides, bright green; petiole 5–7 cm. long; pedicels 4–10 mm. long: fr. 6 mm. across. Fl.vii; fr.x. G.C.38:404(as *A. leucorrhizus*). S.H.2:f.290c(l). M.G.25:25(h). M.D.1913:272;1918:t.1(h). S.L.71(h). (*Eleutherococcus S.* Dcne.) C. China. Cult. 1900. Zone V.

5. **A. Hénryi** (Oliv.) Harms. Shrub to 3 m.; brts. rough-pubescent when young, becoming light yellowish gray, with stout often slightly recurved prickles: lfts. 5, nearly sessile, obovate to oblong, 3–6 cm. long, narrowed toward the ends, serrulate, scabrid above, pubescent beneath; petiole 4–7 m. long, scabrous: umbels usually several, on stout pubescent stalks 1–3 cm. long, rarely longer; pedicels 8–15 mm. long, slightly pubescent or glabrous: fr. black, globose-ellipsoid, 8 mm. long, crowned by the slender style. Fl.viii–x; fr.x. B.M.8316(c). H.I.1718. G.C.38:402. M.D.1913:272;1918:t.7(h). S.L.70(h). (*Eleutherococcus H.* Oliv.) C. China. Intr. 1901. Zone V.

6. **A. divaricàtus** (Sieb. & Zucc.) Seem. Shrub to 3 m., with spreading brs.; brts. glabrous or pubescent, with often paired prickles often recurved at apex: lfts. 5, sessile or short-stalked, oblong-obovate to broad-oblanceolate, 4–12 cm. long, acute or short-acuminate, cuneate, simply or doubly serrate, sparingly pubescent above, villous-pubescent beneath, rarely nearly glabrous; petiole 3–8 cm. long, sometimes prickly: umbels usually 3–7, dense, on rather short pubescent peduncles; pedicels 4–10 mm. long, pubescent: ovary 2-

B.C.1:344(h). (*A. chinensis* var. *mandshurica* (Maxim.) Rehd., *A. chinensis* var. *canescens* Koehne, not Franch. & Sav., *Dimorphanthus elatus* Miq., *D. mandshuricus* Maxim., *A. japonica* Hort.) N. E. Asia. Intr. 1830. Zone III. Like *A. spinosa* of striking appearance with its spiny stems, large bold lvs. surmounted by ample clusters of white fls. in late summer.—**A. e. variegàta** (Rehd.) Nakai, f. Lfts. irregularly bordered with white. G.C.31:231;60:245 (h). (*A. chinensis* var. *albo-marginata* Bean.)—**A. e. aureo-variegàta** (Rehd.) Nakai, f. Lfts. variegated or irregularly margined with yellow. (*Dimorphanthus mandshuricus elegantissimus fol. var.* Hort.)—**A. e. pyramidàlis** (Bean) Rehd., f. Of fastigiate habit with erect brs.: lvs. shorter, less spreading; lfts. smaller, pubescent on the veins beneath when young. (*A. e. f. fastigiata* Rehd.) Cult. 1917.—**A. e. canéscens** (Franch. & Sav.) Nakai, var. Lfts. densely grayish or yellowish pubescent beneath. (*A. spinosa* var. *c.* Franch. & Sav.) Japan. Tenderer.

4. **A. híspida** Vent. BRISTLY SARSAPARILLA. Subshrub to 1 m.; stems woody up to 25 cm.; root-stock creeping: lvs. bipinnate; lfts. ovate or elliptic to oblong, 2–7 cm. long, acute, rounded or broad-cuneate at base, sharply and irregularly serrate, glabrous or pubescent on the veins beneath: umbels on slender peduncles, 3 or more in a terminal loose corymb; fls. white: fr. subglobose, 6–8 mm. across, purple-black. Fl.vi–vii: fr.viii–ix. B.M.1085(c). L.B.1306(c). Nfd. to N. C., w. to Minn. and Ind. Cult. 1788. Zone III.

Related species: **A. nudicaùlis** L. Root-stock creeping; the upright woody stem rarely 10 cm. long, usually with 1 or few lvs. 20–30 cm. high, with three 3–5-foliolate divisions; lfts. elliptic to ovate, 5–12 cm. long, acuminate, serrulate: umbels 2 or 3. Fl.v–vi. B.B.2:506. Nfd. to N. C., w. Man. and Mo. Intr. 1731. Zone III.

Fam. 83. **UMBELLIFERAE** Juss. PARSLEY FAMILY

Herbs, rarely shrubs, containing a volatile oil or balsam; stem usually hollow: lvs. alternate, usually pinnately or ternately compound, rarely simple, exstipulate: fls. small, perfect, regular or the outer fls. irregular, epigynous, in simple or compound umbels; calyx-limb minute; petals 5, valvate; stamens 5, inserted at the margin of the epigynous disk; ovary inferior, 2-celled; cells 1-ovuled; styles 2: fr. consisting of 2 dry winged or ribbed achenes with oil-ducts, separating from each other at maturity but remaining attached at the top to a slender Y-shaped carpophore; seed albuminous; embryo straight. Syn.: *Ammiaceae* Presl.—About 230 genera and 1500 species in boreal, temp. and subtrop. regions.

BUPLEÙRUM L. Herbs or shrubs: lvs. simple, entire, often perfoliate: fls. yellow or yellowish green, in compound umbels; calyx-limb without teeth; petals suborbicular, entire and strongly involute; stylopodium depressed: fr. oblong, compressed; achenes with 5 slender, wing-like ribs. (Ancient Greek name of an umbelliferous plant.) About 75 species in Eu., Asia and Afr., 1 in N. Am.

B. fruticòsum L. Evergreen or half-evergreen upright glabrous shrub to 2.5 m., with slender brs. purplish when young: lvs. subsessile, narrow-elliptic to oblong-obovate, 5–8 cm. long, mucronate, cuneate, entire, bluish green, leathery: fls. yellow, small, in terminal slender-stalked umbels 7–10 cm. across, with a reflexed involucre at base, the umbellets also with reflexed involucres. Fl.vii–viii. E.N.III.8:180. S.F.t.263(c). B.C.1:600. S. Eu. Intr. about 1600. Zone VII. The only shrubby representative of Umbelliferae hardy within our area.

Fam. 84. **CORNACEAE** Lk. DOGWOOD FAMILY

Trees or shrubs, rarely herbs: lvs. opposite, or alternate, entire, rarely toothed or lobed, exstipulate, rarely stipulate: fls. perfect, rarely unisexual, regular, epigynous; sepals 4, rarely 5, minute or wanting; petals 4, rarely 5, usually valvate; stamens as many, inserted on the margin of the usually present epigynous disk; ovary inferior, usually 2-celled, rarely 3–5-celled; ovules solitary, pendulous; style short: fr. a drupe or berry; seeds albuminous, with straight usually small embryo.—Ten genera with about 90 species in the temp. and subtrop. regions of the n. hemisphere, few in the s. hemisphere.

A. Fls. borne on the upper surface of the lvs.: lvs. alternate, deciduous........1. *Helwingia*
AA. Fls. axillary or in a terminal infl.: lvs. usually opposite.
  B. Lvs. evergreen; fls. polygamous, in terminal panicles........................2. *Aucuba*
  BB. Lvs. deciduous; fls. perfect, in corymbs or umbels............................3. *Cornus*

1. **HELWÍNGIA** Willd. Deciduous shrubs; winter-buds small, with few outer scales: lvs. alternate, petioled, serrate; petiole sometimes with stipular appendages: fls. dioecious, small, 3–5-merous, usually 4-merous, in fascicles on the upper surface of the lvs.; calyx-limb obsolete; petals triangular-ovate, valvate; staminate fls. without or with rudimentary styles in the middle of the large disk; pistillate fls. without stamens or staminodes, with a short style with 3–5 thick subulate stigmas; ovary 3–5-celled: fr. a berry-like drupe with 1–4 stones. (After G. A. Helwing, a German clergyman and botanical author; 1666–1748.) Three species in E. Asia and Himal.

H. japónica (Thunb.) F. G. Dietr. Bushy shrub to 1.5 m. with slender green glabrous brts.: lvs. ovate, 3–7 cm. long, acuminate, broad-cuneate, serrulate with bristle-like teeth from near the base, glabrous and bright green on both sides; petiole 1–2.5 cm. long, sometimes with subulate branched small stipules: fls. greenish white, staminate 10–20, short-stalked; pistillate 1–3, subsessile: fr. subglobose, 6 mm. across, black. Fl.vi; fr.viii. S.I.2:t.58(c). S.Z.1:t.68(c). E.P.IV.229:35. A.G.13:8. S.L.192(h). (*H. rusciflora* Willd.) China, Japan. Intr. about 1830. Zone (V). Interesting on account of the position of the fls.

Related species: **H. chinénsis** Batal. Shrub to 2 m.: lvs. ovate-lanceolate to linear-lanceolate, to 12 cm. long, acute, cuneate, with short suberect teeth, entire toward the base: staminate fls. on pedicels 7–25 mm. long. E.P.IV.229:36. W. China. Intr. 1910? Zone VII?

2. **AUCÙBA** Thunb. Evergreen shrubs with stout terete forked brs.: lvs. opposite, petioled, serrate or entire: fls. dioecious, small, purplish, in terminal panicles; pedicels short, with 2 bractlets; calyx minute, 4-toothed; petals 4, ovate to lanceolate, valvate; staminate fls. with 4 stamens and a large 4-angled central disk, without rudimentary ovary; filaments short; pistillate fls. with an inferior, 1-celled and 1-ovuled ovary; style short, thick, with an oblique capitate stigma, without stamens: fr. a 1-seeded berrylike drupe; seed albuminous with the minute embryo at the top. (Name latinized from the Japanese Aokiba.) Three species in E. Asia and Himal.

A. japónica Thunb. JAPANESE AUCUBA. Stout shrub to 5 m.: brts. thick, glabrous, green: lvs. elliptic-ovate to elliptic-lanceolate, 8–20 cm. long, acute to acuminate, with an obtusish apex, broad-cuneate at base, remotely coarsely dentate, lustrous green on both sides; petiole 1–5 cm. long: fls. about 8 mm. across; petals short-acuminate; the staminate fls. in panicles about 5–10 cm. long, rather densely strigillose; the pistillate infl. shorter, rather sparingly strigillose or nearly glabrous: fr. short-ellipsoid, 1.2–1.5 cm. long, scarlet, in dense panicles 5–8 cm. long. Fl.iii–iv; fr.xi(–iii). B.M.5512(c). S.I.2:t.59(c). Gt.25:t.859(c). I.H.11:t.399(c). E.P.IV.229:39. Am. For. 28:103(h). Japan. Intr. first in 1783 in its variegated form and in 1861 in its normal green form distinguished as **A. j. cóncolor** Reg., var. (*A. j. viridis* Hort.). Zone VII.— The best known form is **A. j. variegàta** D'Ombr., not Reg. GOLDDUST-TREE. Lvs. with numerous small yellow spots. B.M.1197(c). F.M.5:t.277(c). R.H.1866:t.292(c). Gs.2:280(h). (*A. j.* var. *maculata* Reg., *A. j. punctata* Hort.)—**A. j. picturàta** T. Moore. Lvs. ovate-oblong with a large irregular blotch in the middle and smaller yellow dots around it. F.M.10:t.527(c). F.W.1876:353. (*A. j. latimaculata* Kirchn., *A. j. picta* Bull, *A. j. aureo-maculata* D'Ombr.)—**A. j. limbàta** Bull. Lvs. large, coarsely dentate, with a greenish yellow margin.—**A. j. dentàta** Carr. Lvs. smaller, elliptic, with few coarse teeth on each side near apex.—**A. j. longifòlia** T. Moore. Lvs. narrow-oblong-lanceolate, 8–12 cm. long, green. (*A. j.* var. *angustifolia* Reg., *A. j.* var. *salicifolia* Bean.)—**A. j. luteo-cárpa** (D'Ombr.) Rehd., var. Lvs. elliptic-oblong, remotely dentate, sparingly dotted: fr. yellow. F.M.1872:t.12(c). (*A. j. fructu luteo* Hort.)

Related species: **A. himaláica** Hook. f. & Thoms. Lvs. ovate-lanceolate to lanceolate, 10–25 cm. long, long and sharply acuminate, serrate to entire: infl. densely fulvous-pubescent; petals long-acuminate; F.S.12:t.1271(c). I.H.6:t. 197(c). (*A. japonica* var. *h.* Dipp.) E. Himal. Cult. 1857. Zone VII.—**A. chinénsis** Benth. Lvs. lanceolate to obovate, 8–20 cm. long, sharply long-acuminate, entire or dentate toward the apex: infl. sparingly strigillose; petals long-acuminate. China. Intr. 1901. Zone VII?

3. **CORNUS** L. DOGWOOD. Deciduous, rarely evergreen trees or shrubs, rarely herbs; winter-buds elongated, with 2 valvate scales, the axillary ones appressed: lvs. opposite, rarely alternate, petioled, entire, usually pubescent with 2-armed appressed hairs: fls. perfect, small, 4-merous, in terminal cymes or heads often surrounded by involucral bracts; calyx with minute teeth; petals ovate to oblong, valvate; style simple, filiform or cylindric; ovary inferior, 2-celled: fr. a drupe with a 2-celled stone. (The ancient Latin name of *C. mas.*) About 40 species in temp. regions of the n. hemisphere; all woody except 2 species.—Ornamental shrubs grown chiefly for their handsome fls. and some for their showy frs. and also for the winter effect of the brightly colored brs.

A. Fls. white in cymes or panicles without an involucre; stone subglobose.

Sect. THELYCRANIA Endl.

  B. Lvs. alternate.
    c. Lvs. beneath with irregularly diverging hairs, usually cuneate at base.
                                                 1. *C. alternifolia*
    cc. Lvs. beneath with straight parallel hairs, usually rounded at base..2. *C. controversa*
  BB. Lvs. opposite.
    c. Fr. white or blue.
      D. Lvs., brts. and infl. with appressed hairs or glabrescent.
        E. Lvs. whitish beneath: fr. white or bluish white.
          F. Mature brts. bright red, or sometimes green or yellow, smooth, rather stout; pith white: cymes flat: stone compressed.
            G. Stone ellipsoid, narrowed at ends: lvs. acute....................3. *C. alba*
            GG. Stone about as broad as high; rounded at base: lvs. acuminate.
                                         4. *C. stolonifera*
          FF. Mature brts. gray, thin; pith white or light brown: cyme convex, paniculate: stone subglobose, not compressed.....................12. *C. racemosa*
        EE. Lvs. green or only slightly paler beneath: pith white.
          F. Fr. pale blue; anthers blue: cyme convex: lvs. acuminate....11. *C. foemina*
          FF. Fr. white; cyme flat: lvs. usually obtusely short acuminate or acutish.
                                         10. *C. glabrata*
      DD. Lvs. with more or less spreading hairs beneath at least on the veins or at least brts. and infl. villous.
        E. Fr. white.
          F. Lvs. smooth above: brts. red-brown or red, smooth, rather stout: pith white, ample ....5. *C. Baileyi*

    FF. Lvs. scabrid above: brts. brownish, slightly rough, thin: pith narrow,
      brown ....9. *C. asperifolia*
  EE. Fr. blue.
    F. Mature brts. greenish, spotted; pith white: lvs. woolly beneath: fr. pale
      blue ....6. *C. rugosa*
    FF. Mature brts. red or purple; pith brown: lvs. pubescent only on the veins:
      fr. usually dark blue, sometimes partly whitish.
      G. Lvs. green beneath, rusty-pubescent on the veins..........7. *C. Amomum*
      GG. Lvs. whitish beneath, grayish or whitish pubescent on the veins.
                                             8. *C. obliqua*
  CC. Fr. black or bluish black (green in a var. of No. 19).
    D. Style cylindric: lvs. with 6–8 pairs of veins, whitish or grayish beneath.
      E. Fls. in broad glabrous panicles: lvs. 10–15 cm. long, closely appressed-pilose
        beneath ....13. *C. macrophylla*
      EE. Fls. in flat more or less villous cymes.
        F. Lvs. with appressed hairs beneath, scabrid............14. *C. Bretschneideri*
        FF. Lvs. more or less villous beneath...........................15. *C. poliophylla*
    DD. Style thickened at apex: lvs. with 2–5 veins, green beneath.
      E. Calyx-teeth longer than disk.
        F. Lvs. with 2–3 pairs of veins, usually oblong, cuneate......16. *C. paucinervis*
        FF. Lvs. with 4–5 pairs of veins, usually ovate, rounded to broad-cuneate.
                                          17. *C. pumila*
      EE. Calyx-teeth shorter than disk.
        F. Petiole 1–3 cm. long; lvs. appressed-pilose beneath............18. *C. Walteri*
        FF. Petiole 0.6–1.2 cm. long; lvs. villous-pubescent beneath......19. *C. sanguinea*
AA. Fls. in dense umbels with an involucre: stone ellipsoid to oblong.
  B. Fls. yellow with a yellowish involucre not exceeding the fls. and deciduous during
    anthesis ....Sect. MACROCARPIUM Spach.
    C. Lvs. without conspicuous tufts of hairs in the axils beneath; pedicels not or slightly
      exceeding the involucre...20. *C. mas*
    CC. Lvs. with conspicuous brown axillary tufts of hairs beneath: pedicels nearly twice as
      long as bracts..21. *C. officinalis*
  BB. Fls. greenish yellow with large white or pink bracts.
    C. Frs. in dense clusters, but individually distinct..........Sect. BENTHAMIDIA K. Koch.
      D. Involucral bracts 4, emarginate......................................22. *C. florida*
      DD. Involucral bracts 4–6, acuminate to obtuse.......................23. *C. Nuttallii*
    CC. Frs. connate into a globose fleshy head............Sect. BENTHAMIA Benth. & Hook.
                                         24. *C. kousa*

    1. C. alternifòlia L. Shrub or small tree to 8 m., with the brs. spreading
in irregular whorls forming horizontal tiers: brts. glabrous, greenish: lvs.
alternate, slender-stalked, usually crowded at end of brts., elliptic-ovate,
6–12 cm. long, acuminate, cuneate, nearly glabrous above, glaucescent beneath and appressed-pubescent, with 5–6 pairs of veins; petiole 2–5 cm.
long: cymes 4–6 cm. across, puberulous, slender-stalked: fr. 6–8 mm. across,
bluish black, bloomy, on red pedicels. Fl.v–vi; fr.viii. Em.463(c). G.O.t.43
(c). S.S.5:t.216. B.C.2:852(h). (*Svida a.* Small.) N. B. to Minn., s. to Ga.
and Ala. Intr. 1760. Zone III.—**C. a. argéntea** Temple. Lvs. variegated with
white. (*C. a. variegata* Hort.)
    2. C. controvérsa Hemsl. Tree to 20 m., similar to the preceding: lvs.
broad-ovate to elliptic-ovate, 7–12 cm. long, abruptly acuminate, usually
rounded at base, glaucous beneath and slightly appressed-pubescent, with
6–9 pairs of veins; cymes 6–12 cm. across: fr. bluish black, 6 mm. across. Fl.
v; fr.viii–ix. B.M.8464(c). M.K.t.81(c). N.K.16:t.25,26. Gn.88:537(h). J.L.
40:f.7(h). (*C. brachypoda* K. Koch, not C. A. Mey., *C. macrophylla* Koehne,
not Wall.) Japan, China. Intr. before 1880. Zone V.—**C. c. variegàta**
(Nichols.) Rehd., var. Lvs. edged white. Gng.3:67;16:291. J.H.III.28:129;
47:147.
    3. C. alba L. Shrub to 3 m. with usually erect stems and blood-red brs.
usually bloomy when young; pith ample, white: lvs. ovate to elliptic, 4–8
cm. long, acute to acuminate usually rounded at base, rugose and often somewhat bullate above and dark green, glaucous beneath, with 5–6 pairs of veins;
petiole 1–2.5 cm. long: fls. yellowish white, in cymes 3.5–5 cm. across: fr.
white or slightly bluish; stone higher than broad, acute at ends, flattened.
Fl.v–vi; fr.viii–ix. S.O.2:t.65(c). N.K.16:t.24. S.H.2:f.294p-r,295m-o. (*C.*

tatarica Mill.) Siberia to Manch. and n. Korea. Intr. 1741. Zone II.—**C. a** **argenteo-marginàta** Rehd., var. Lvs. edged with creamy white. R.H.1906: 421. J.L.40:f.7(h). (*C. alba elegantissima variegata* Hort., *C. alba variegata* Bean.)—**C. a. Gouchaùltii** (Carr.) Rehd., var. Lvs. variegated with yellowish white and pink.—**C. a. Spaèthii** Wittm. Lvs. broadly edged with yellow Spaeth, Cat. 1889–90,t(c). Gn.64:368(h):88:127(h).—**C. a. sibírica** Loud., var. Less vigorous; brts. bright coral-red. C.L.21, No. 4:29. G.M.54:249. (*C. s.* Lodd.)—**C. a. Kesselríngii** (E. Wolf) Rehd., var. Brts. very dark purple, almost purplish black; young unfolding lvs. red. (*C. sibirica* var. *K. E.* Wolf.) Cult. 1906.

Related species: **C. Héssei** Koehne. Dwarf compact shrub, to 0.5 m. high: lvs. crowded, narrow-elliptic to lanceolate, 4–9 cm. long: cymes 2–3 cm. across: fr. bluish white; stone broader than high. S.H.2:f.294k-l,295g-l. ? N. E. Asia. Intr. before 1889. Zone IV.

4. **C. stolonífera** Michx. RED-OSIER DOGWOOD. Shrub to 2.5 m. with prostrate stems and stoloniferous; brts. dark blood-red; pith white, large: lvs. ovate to oblong-lanceolate, 6–12 cm. long, acuminate, rounded at base, dark green above, glaucous beneath, with about 5 pairs of veins; petiole 1–2.5 cm. long: fls. dull white, in cymes 3–5 cm. across; disk usually red: fr. white, globose, 5 mm. across; stone as broad as high or slightly broader, rounded at base. Fl.v-vi; fr.ix-x. B.B.2:662. G.C.II.8:679. B.C.2:852(h). (*C. alba* Wangh., not L.) Nfd. to Man., s. to Va., Ky. and Neb. Cult. 1656. Zone II. —**C. s. flaviràmea** (Spaeth) Rehd., var. Brts. yellow. (*C. alba f.* Spaeth.) Cult. 1899.—**C. s. nítida** (Koehne) Schneid., var. Brts. green in winter: lvs. lustrous above, with 6–8 pairs of veins. (*C. alba* var. *n.* Koehne.)—**C. s. colo-radénsis** (Koehne) Schneid., var. Brts. brownish red: lvs. smaller, less pale beneath: fr. bluish white; stone higher than broad. (*C. alba* var. *c.* Koehne, *C. instolonea* Nels., *C. stolonifera* var. *riparia* Rydb.) Yukon and Man. to N. Mex. and Calif.

C. s. × *rugosa;* see under No. 6.

5. **C. Baìleyi** Coult. & Evans. Upright shrub to 3 m.; brts. dark red in winter, short-villous when young; pith white, large: lvs. ovate to lanceolate, 5–12 cm. long, acute or acuminate, rounded at base, glaucous beneath and with woolly and appressed hairs: cymes 3–5 cm. across, dense, villous: fr. white, 8 mm. across, much broader than high, compressed. Fl.v-vi; fr.vii-viii. G.F.3:465. B.C.2:853. B.B.2:662. S.H.2:295v-x². (*C. stolonifera* var. *B.* Drescher.) Ont. and Minn. to Pa. and Ind. Intr. 1892. Zone IV.

Related species: **C. pubéscens** Nutt. Shrub to 6 m., sometimes nearly tree-like; brts. purple: lvs. elliptic to ovate, 4–10 cm. long, acute to obtusish, slightly pubescent above, glaucous and woolly beneath: fls. yellowish white, in dense cymes 5 cm. across: fr. white; stone much broader than high. (*C. californica* var. *p.* Macbr., *C. Torreyi* S. Wats., *Svida p.* Standl.) S.H.2:f.294s(1). B. C. to Calif. Intr. 1874. Zone VI?

6. **C. rugòsa** Lam. Upright shrub to 3 m., sometimes tree-like; young brts. green, spotted purple, older purplish, sometimes yellowish; pith white: lvs. suborbicular to broad-ovate, 5–12 cm. long, acute or short-acuminate, slightly pubescent above, pale and densely villous beneath, with 6–8 pairs of veins; petiole 1–1.5 cm. long: cymes dense, 5–7 cm. across, slightly villous or nearly glabrous: fr. light blue or greenish white, 5–6 mm. across; stone sub-globose. Fl.v-vi; fr.ix. S.O.2:t.69(c). Em.464(c). E.P.IV.229:61. B.B.2:661. (*C. circinata* L'Hérit.) N. S. to Man., s. to Va., Ill. and Iowa. Intr. 1784. Zone III.

C. r. × *stolonifera* = **C. Slavínii** Rehd. Brts. purple: lvs. intermediate in shape, more or less woolly beneath: fr. bluish, rarely white. Orig. before 1910.

7. C. Amòmum Mill. Shrub to 3 m. with spreading brs.: brts. purple, rarely greenish; pith brown: lvs. elliptic-ovate or elliptic, 5–10 cm. long, short-acuminate, usually rounded at base, dark green and nearly glabrous above, lighter green or slightly paler beneath and with brown hairs on the veins; petiole 8–15 mm. long: fls. yellowish white in flat dense cymes 4–6 cm. across, usually slightly villous: fr. blue or sometimes partly white, 6 mm. across; stone subglobose, furrowed. Fl.vi; fr.ix. S.O.2:t.64(c). Em.466,t (c). B.B.2:661. (*C. sericea* L., *C. cyanocarpa* Moench, *C. coerulea* Lam., *Svida A.* Small.) Mass. to Ga., w. to N. Y. and Tenn. Intr. 1658. Zone V.

C. A. × *macrophylla;* see under No. 13.—*C. A.* × *paucinervis;* see under No. 16.

8. C. oblìqua Raf. Shrub similar to the preceding, but usually more loosely branched: brts. purple to yellowish red: lvs. elliptic-ovate to oblong, 5–8 cm. long, acuminate, cuneate, dark green and glabrous above, glaucous beneath and with grayish white or brownish hairs on the veins: cymes 4–5 cm. across, slightly villous: fr. blue or partly or sometimes nearly white; stone furrowed. Fl.vi; fr.ix. R.H.1888:444,t(c, as *C. stolonifera*). S.T.1:t.39. (*C. Purpusii* Koehne, *C. Amomum* var. *Schuetzeana* Rickett.) Que. to Minn. and Kans., s. Pa., Ill. and Mo. Cult. 1888. Zone III.

C. o. × *racemosa* = **C. arnoldiàna** Rehd. Of more upright habit: brts. slenderer, grayish the second year; cymes less villous: fr. white or light blue; stone less furrowed. S.T.2:t.40. Orig. before 1900.

9. C. asperifòlia Michx. Upright shrub to 5 m., or sometimes small tree to 15 m. with slender spreading brs.; pith brown, narrow; brts. reddish brown, slightly rough, pubescent when young: lvs. elliptic to ovate, 4–10 cm. long, acuminate, rounded or cuneate at base, scabrid above, rarely nearly smooth, woolly pubescent beneath; petiole 5–15 mm. long: fls. yellowish white, in rather loose pubescent corymbs 4–7 cm. across: fr. white, 6 mm. across; stone subglobose, slightly furrowed. Fl.v–vi; fr.ix. G.F.10:105. S.S.14:t.709. B.B. 2:662. (*C. candidissima* Bischoff, not Mill., nor Marsh.) Ont. to Fla., w. to Iowa, Kans. and Tex. Cult. 1836. Zone IV?

C. a. × *macrophylla;* see under No. 13.

10. C. glabràta Benth. Shrub to 4 m., with slender brs., soon glabrous, reddish brown, becoming dark gray-brown; pith white: lvs. narrow-elliptic, 3–8 cm. long, acuminate, cuneate, lustrous and green on both sides and sparingly appressed-pubescent, with 3–4 pairs of veins; petiole 5–10 mm. long: cymes 2.5–3 cm. across, nearly glabrous: fr. white or light blue, 5–6 mm. across; stone subglobose, not ribbed: Fl.v; fr.ix–x. S.H.2:f.296g–h(l). Ore. to Calif. Intr. 1894. Zone VI?

11. C. foèmina Mill. Shrub to 5 m., with purple-brown brs.; pith white, narrow: lvs. elliptic or ovate to ovate-lanceolate, 3–7 cm. long, acuminate, cuneate, sparingly and minutely appressed-pubescent and green on both sides or slightly paler beneath; petiole 5–10 mm. long: cymes 3–6 cm. broad; anthers light blue: drupe subglobose, 5–6 mm. across, pale blue or white; stone usually longer than broad, faintly ribbed. Fl.v–vi; fr.ix. S.O.2:t.67(c). B.B. 2:663,f.3187. L'Héritier, Cornus, t.4. (*C. stricta* Lam., *Svida s.* Small.) Va. to Mo., Fla. and Tex. Intr. 1758. Zone VI?

12. C. racemòsa Lam. Shrub to 5 m., with gray brs.; pith white to light brown: lvs. narrow-elliptic to ovate-lanceolate, 4–10 cm. long, long-acuminate, cuneate, appressed-pubescent or nearly smooth, glaucous beneath; petiole 8–15 mm. long: cymes 3–6 cm. broad, paniculate, rather loose; petals oblong, obtusish: fr. white, 4–5 mm. across, on red pedicels: stone broader than high,

Cornus   CORNACEAE   *Cornus*

slightly ribbed. Fl.vi–vii; fr.ix–x. S.O.2:t.68(c). B.B.2:663,f.3186. Gs.3:270.
(*C. paniculata* L'Hérit., ?*C. candidissima* Marsh., not Mill., ?*C. gracilis*
Koehne, *C. oblongata* Hort.) Me. to Ont. and Minn., s. to Ga. and Neb.
Intr. 1758. Zone IV.

C. r. × *obliqua;* see under No. 8.

13. **C. macrophýlla** Wall. Tree to 15 m.; brts. yellowish or reddish brown:
lvs. elliptic-ovate to elliptic-oblong, 10–16 cm. long, long-acuminate, rounded
or cuneate at base, dark green above and nearly glabrous, glaucous beneath
and appressed-pilose, with 6–8 pairs of veins; petiole 1–3 cm. long: fls. yellowish white in panicle-like cymes 8–14 cm. across; petals oblong; style club-
shaped: fr. bluish black, globose, 6 mm. across. Fl.vii–viii; fr.x. B.M.8261
(c). S.I.1:t.77,f.1–12(c). N.K.16:t.29. I.S.1:t.43. S.T.1:t.41. M.G.28:193(h),
195. (*C. brachypoda* C. A. Mey., *C. corynostylis* Koehne.) Himal., China,
Japan. Intr. 1827. Zone VI. Tree with conspicuous clusters of creamy white
fls. in summer.

C. m. × *Amomum* = **C. Horseÿi** Rehd. Differs chiefly in the smaller and
narrower lvs. pale or grayish green beneath and with scattered fulvous hairs on
the veins and on the petiole, with fewer veins: stone broader than high. Orig.
before 1919. Zone V.—*C. m.* × *asperifolia* = **C. Dunbárii** Rehd. Lvs. smaller
and narrower, scabrid above and with more numerous less closely appressed
hairs beneath: cymes smaller, flattish, more pubescent: fr. blue. Orig. before
1919. Zone V.

14. **C. Bretschneíderi** L. Henry. Shrub to 4 m., with yellowish or reddish
brts. appressed-pubescent when young: lvs. ovate to elliptic-ovate, 5–10 cm.
long, acuminate, usually rounded at base, dull green and slightly scabrid
above, grayish green and loosely appressed-pubescent beneath with scabrid
hairs, with 5–7 pairs of veins; petiole 8–15 mm. long: fls. creamy white in
cymes 6–10 cm. across; calyx-teeth scarcely as long as disk; stamens longer
than petals; style cylindric, shorter than petals: fr. bluish black, 6 mm. across.
Fl.vi; fr.ix. J.13:309. S.H.2:f.298d-d¹(l). (*C. aspera* Wanger.) N. China.
Cult. 1887. Zone V.

Related species: **C. Hemsleÿi** Schneid. & Wanger. Shrub to 6 m.: lvs.
elliptic-ovate, 5–7 cm. long, whitish and slightly scabrid beneath, with 6–7 pairs
of veins; petiole 0.5–1 cm. long, pubescent: infl. 5–7 cm. across; calyx-teeth
longer than disk. S.H.2:f.296m-n. C. China. Intr. 1908. Zone V.

15. **C. poliophýlla** Schneid. & Wanger. Shrub to 4 m.; brts. at first densely
pubescent, later glabrate and brown: lvs. elliptic-ovate or elliptic, 6–12 cm.
long, short-acuminate, rounded at base, deep green above and short-villous,
whitish beneath and densely short-villous, with 7–8 pairs of veins; petiole
1–1.5 cm. long: infl. 8–10 cm. across; peduncle 5 cm. long; calyx-teeth
slightly longer than disk; ovary appressed-pubescent: fr. black. Fl.vi; fr.
ix–x. S.H.2:f.298a. C. China. Intr. 1908. Zone V.

Related species: **C. Monbeígii** Hemsl. Shrub to 3 m.: lvs. elliptic or elliptic-
ovate, 6–8 cm. long, subcordate at base, whitish and densely silky-pubescent
beneath, with 6–7 pairs of veins: infl. about 8 cm. across: ovary with appressed
and spreading hairs. S.H.2:f.296o-p. C. and W. China. Intr. 1917. Zone VII?

16. **C. paucinérvis** Hance. Shrub to 3 m.; brts. quadrangular, appressed-
pubescent when young, usually reddish brown: lvs. elliptic or oblong-obovate
to elliptic-lanceolate, 4–10 cm. long, acute, cuneate, dark green above, lighter
beneath, with appressed hairs on both sides, with 2–4 pairs of ascending veins,
of thickish texture; petiole 3–5 mm. long: cymes dense, long-peduncled, 6–8
cm. across; style club-shaped: fr. sparingly produced, 5–6 mm. across, black.
Fl.vii–viii; fr.ix. G.C.50:95. G.M.54:593. E.P.IV.229:72. Gt.45:285. (*C.
quinquenervis* Franch.) C. China. Intr. 1907. Zone (V) Nearly half-
evergreen.

C. p. × *Amomum* = **C. dúbia** Rehd. Lvs. broader with 3–4 pairs of veins sparingly ferrugineous-pubescent beneath: fr. larger, bluish black; stone ribbed. Orig. before 1920.

17. **C. pùmila** Koehne. Dense shrub to 2 m.; brts. terete, with very short internodes, glabrous: lvs. crowded, broad-ovate, 4–8 cm. long, short-acuminate, abruptly contracted at base, dark green above, paler beneath and appressed-pubescent, with 4–5 pairs of veins; petiole 6–10 mm. long: fls. white, in dense long-peduncled cymes 5–7 cm. broad; style club-shaped: fr. black. Fl.vii; fr.ix. S.H.2:f.298i-k,301e-f. (*C. mas* var. *nana* Dipp.) Orig. unknown. Cult. 1890. Zone V.

18. **C. Wálteri** Wanger. Tree to 12 m.; brts. soon glabrous, greenish yellow to brownish red: lvs. elliptic to oblong-elliptic, 5–12 cm. long, long-acuminate, cuneate, sparingly appressed-pilose above, more densely so beneath and paler green, with 4–5 pairs of veins; petiole 1.5–3 cm. long; cymes corymbose, loose after anthesis, 5–7 cm. across, sparingly appressed-pubescent or nearly glabrous, on a peduncle 1.5–2 cm. long; sepals minute; style club-shaped, shorter than stamens: fr. globose, 6–7 mm. across, black. Fl.vi; fr. ix–x. S.L.137(h, as *C. Wilsoniana*). C. China. Intr. 1907. Zone V.

Related species: **C. coreàna** Wanger. Tree to 20 m.; bark deeply divided into square scaly plates; brts. reddish brown or purple: lvs. elliptic to elliptic-ovate, broad-cuneate to rounded at base; petiole 1–2 cm. long: infl. 7–8 cm. across. N.K.16:t.27,28. Korea. Intr. 1918. Zone V.

19. **C. sanguínea** L. RED DOGWOOD. Shrub to 4 m., with dark red, rarely greenish brs.; lvs. broad-elliptic to ovate, 4–8 cm. long, acuminate, rounded or broad-cuneate at base, villous on both sides, more densely so and lighter green beneath, with 3–5 pairs of veins; petiole 6–15 mm. long: fls. dull white, in pubescent dense cymes 4–5 cm. across; style clavate, as long as stamens, slightly shorter than petals: fr. 6 mm. across, purple-black. Fl.v–vi; fr.ix. R.I.24:t.144(c). F.D.26:t.2704(c). S.O.2:t.66(c). Eu. Long cult. Zone IV. Planted for the dark red brs. in winter and the dark blood-red autumnal color of its lvs.—**C. s. variegàta** West., var. Lvs. variegated with yellowish white. S.O.2:t.66(c, l). G.W.9:247,248(h). Orig. before 1770.—**C. s. atrosanguínea** Gibbs. Brts. of deep red color.—**C. s. viridíssima** Dieck. Brts. and fr. green.

Related species: **C. austràlis** C. A. Mey. Brts. finally glabrous, purplish or greenish: lvs. ovate or elliptic-ovate, to 8 cm. long, densely pilose at first, later sparingly appressed-pilose on both sides, scabrid beneath, with 3–4 pairs of veins; petiole 7–10 mm. long: cymes dense and rather small; style clavate, as long as stamens, shorter than petals: fr. 5–6 mm. across. S.H.2:f.299c(l). (*C. sanguinea* var. *a.* Koehne.) W. Asia. Cult. 1915. Zone V.—**C. a. Koenígii** (Schneid.) Wanger., var. Lvs. larger, on flowering brts. to 13 cm. long; petiole 1–2 cm. long: fr. 8–10 mm. across. S.H.2:f.299d(l). (*C. K.* Schneid.) Transcauc. Intr. 1912. Zone V?

20. **C. mas** L. CORNELIAN CHERRY. Shrub or small tree, to 8 m.; bark close, scaly, dark brown; young brts. minutely appressed-pilose, greenish yellow, later brown: lvs. ovate to elliptic, 4–10 cm. long, acute to acuminate, broad-cuneate at base, appressed-pilose and green on both sides, lustrous above, with 3–5 pairs of veins; petiole 5–10 mm. long: fls. yellow, in short-stalked umbels before the lvs.; bracts yellowish; pedicels about as long as bracts; sepals shorter or as long as disk: fr. ellipsoid, 1.2–1.5 cm. long, scarlet, of pleasant acid taste. Fl.iii–iv; fr.viii. B.M.2675(c). Add. 3:t.101(c). R.I. 24:t.143(c). M.M.5:192. G.C.II.9:399. M.A.t.80(h). (*C. mascula* Hort.) C. and S. Eu., W. Asia. Cult. since ancient times. Zone IV. Chiefly planted for its early yellow fls. and its lvs. remaining green until late in fall; also for its edible fr.—**C. m. aùrea** Schneid., f. Lvs. yellow.—**C. m. elegantíssima**

(T. Moore) Nichols. Lvs. variegated with creamy white and tinged with red. E.P.1877:109,t(c). G.Z.21:169. (*C. m. aureo-elegantissima* Schelle, *C. mascula aurea elegantissima* T. Moore).—**C. m. variegàta** Loud., var. Lvs. bordered white. R.H.1906:420. (*C. m. argenteo-marginata* Schelle.)—**C. m. macrocárpa** Dipp. With larger fr.—**C. m. sphaerocárpa** Cretziou. Fr. globose.—**C. m. flàva** West., var. With yellow fr. (*C. m. f. luteo-carpa* Wanger., var. *xanthocarpa* Bean.)—**C. m. alba** West., var. With white fr. (f. *albocarpa* Schneid.)—**C. m. nàna** Carr. A dwarf form.

21. **C. officinàlis** Sieb. & Zucc. Shrub or small tree, to 10 m. tall, similar to the preceding species; bark flaky, light brown; lvs. ovate to elliptic, rarely ovate-lanceolate, 5–12 cm. long, acuminate, sparingly appressed-pilose above, more densely so beneath and with large fulvous axillary tufts of hairs, with 6–7 pairs of veins; petiole 6–15 mm. long: fls. yellow; pedicels up to twice as long as bracts: fr. oblong, about 1.5 cm. long, scarlet. Fl.III–IV; fr.VIII. S.Z.1:t.50(c). N.K.16:t.23. Add. 3:t.89(c). Japan, Korea. Cult. 1877. Zone V.

To Sect. MACROCARPIUM belongs also: **C. séssilis** Torr. Shrub to 4.5 m.; young brts. silky-pubescent: lvs. ovate to elliptic, 5–9 cm. long, short-acuminate, broad-cuneate, nearly glabrous above, silky-pubescent and whitish beneath; petiole about 1 cm. long: umbels 20–30-fld.; bracts yellow, about as long as fls.: fr. narrow-ellipsoid, 12 mm. long, dark purple. Rep. Expl. Surv. Miss. 4:t.7. Calif. Cult. 1933. Zone VII.

22. **C. flòrida** L. FLOWERING DOGWOOD. Shrub or small tree to 5, rarely to 12 m.; brts. green, soon glabrous: lvs. elliptic or ovate, 8–15 cm. long, abruptly acuminate, broad-cuneate to rounded at base, nearly glabrous above, glaucous beneath and usually only pubescent on the veins, with 6–7 pairs of veins; petiole 5–15 mm. long: fls. greenish white or yellowish; bracts 4, white or pinkish, obovate, emarginate or truncate and mucronate at apex, 4–5 cm. long, during winter enclosing the fl.-buds: fr. ellipsoid, 1 cm. long, crowned by the persistent calyx. Fl.V; fr.IX–X. Em.468(c). B.M.526(c). S.S.5:t.112, 113. Gn.52:177(h);53:222;89:286(h). F.E.23:511(h). S.L.139(h). Am. For. 21:623,786,787(h). (*Cynoxylum floridum* Raf.) Mass. to Fla., w. to Ont., Tex. and to Mex. Cult. 1731. Zone IV. One of the handsomest American flowering trees; the lvs. turn bright scarlet, but remain pale beneath.—**C. f. péndula** Dipp. With pendulous brs. F.E.17:68(h).—**C. f. rúbra** West., var. Bracts of the floral involucre red or pink. B.M.8315(c). R.H.1894:500,t(c). F.E.9:572. A.G.18:441. Cult. in Am. 1731.—**C. f. pluribracteàta** Rehd., f. Infl. with 6–8 larger and several smaller bracts; fls. often aborted. Cult. 1914. —**C. f. xanthocárpa** Rehd., f. With yellow fruit.

23. **C. Nuttállii** Audub. Tree to 25 m.; similar to the preceding: lvs. elliptic ovate to obovate, 8–12 cm. long, short-acuminate, broad-cuneate, appressed-pilose on both sides while young, at maturity only beneath or glabrescent, glaucous beneath, with 5–6 pairs of veins; petiole 6–15 mm. long: involucral bracts usually 6, sometimes 4 or 5, obovate to oblong, usually acute, 5–8 cm. long, white or tinged pink, not enclosing the fl.-buds during the winter: fr. ellipsoid, 1 cm. long, bright red or orange, Fl.V; fr.IX. B.M.8311(c). S.S.5:t.214,215. Gn.79:374,375(h);89:287(h). G.C.63:204(h). K.B.1915:178, t(h). B. C. to S. Calif. Intr. 1835. Zone VII. Beautifuul in bloom, but not doing well in the eastern states.

24. **C. Koùsa** Hance. Tree to 7 m. with spreading brs. and slender green glabrous brts. becoming brown: lvs. elliptic-ovate, 5–9 cm. long, acuminate, cuneate, dark green above, glaucous and appressed-pilose beneath and with large axillary fulvous tufts of hairs; petiole 4–6 mm. long: fls. in a dense

globose head borne on a slender stalk 4–6 cm. long; involucral bracts elliptic-ovate to oblong-ovate, 2.5–5 cm. long, acuminate, cuneate at base: head of frs. globose, pinkish, 1.5–2.5 cm. across; stone ellipsoid, 6 mm. long. Fl.vi; fr.viii. S.Z.1:t.16(c). Add.2:t.43(c). I.S.1:t.42. G.C.68:43(h). Gn.43:152, t(c);60:165. K.B.1915:179,t. (*Benthamia japonica* Sieb. & Zucc., *C. japonica* Koehne, not Thunb.) Japan, Korea. Intr. 1875. Zone V. With showy white fls. in June; lvs. turning scarlet in fall.—**C. K. chinénsis** Osborn, var. Lvs. without or with inconspicuous axillary tufts of hairs beneath, usually larger and more pubescent: bracts 5–6 cm. long. B.M.8833(c). Gn.89:287(h). H.B. 3:258(h). China. Intr. 1907.

Subclass. II. **GAMOPETALAE** Brongn.

Perianth double, the inner whorl more or less connate, rarely distinct or wanting. (*Sympetalae* A. Br., *Metachlamydeae* Engl.)

Fam. 85. **CLETHRACEAE** Klotzsch. WHITE–ALDER FAMILY

Contains only the following genus which see for characters.

CLÉTHRA L. White-Alder. Deciduous or evergreen small shrubs or trees, with stellate pubescence; winter-buds small, pubescent: lvs. alternate, short-petioled, usually serrate, exstipulate: fls. perfect, white or pinkish, in terminal racemes or panicles; sepals 5, distinct, persistent; petals 5, distinct; stamens 10; anthers opening by a pore or a slit; ovary superior, 3-celled, with central placentae; style cylindric, slender, 3-fid at apex: fr. a 3-valved caps., many-seeded; seeds with a loose translucent cellular coat, larger than the body, albuminous. (Ancient Greek name of the Alder, given on account of the resemblance of the lvs.) About 30 species in Am., E. Asia and Madeira. —Ornamental shrubs grown for their handsome spikes of white usually fragrant fls.

> A. Lvs. glabrous or nearly so: racemes panicled; sepals obtuse................1. *C. alnifolia*
> AA. Lvs. pubescent beneath, at maturity at least on the veins.
>   B. Lvs. white-tomentose beneath; pairs of veins 7–10: filaments glabrous..2. *C. tomentosa*
>   BB. Lvs. pubescent beneath, chiefly on the veins; pairs of veins 10–15.
>   c. Racemes usually solitary: sepals acute; filaments pilose.............3. *C. acuminata*
>   cc. Racemes panicled: sepals obtuse; filaments glabrous...............4. *C. barbinervis*

1. **C. alnifòlia** L. Shrub to 3 m.: lvs. obovate to obovate-oblong, 4–10 cm. long, acute to short-acuminate, cuneate, sharply serrate, glabrous or nearly so on both sides, with 7–10 pairs of veins; fls. fragrant, about 8 mm. across, in pubescent upright usually panicled racemes 5–15 cm. long; pedicels 1–6 mm. long; caps. subglobose, 3 mm. across. Fl.vii–ix. Em.426,t. S.O.1:t.47(c). G.O.t.76(c). Gd.W.t.22(c). Gn.19:208,t(c). M.G.18:473,474(h). S.L132(h). (*C. Michauxii* Courtois, *C. paniculata* Ait.) Me. to Fla. Intr. 1731. Zone III. —**C. a. ròsea** Rehd., f. Fls. pinkish. Intr. 1906.

2. **C. tomentòsa** Lam. Shrub to 3 m.: lvs. obovate, 4–10 cm. long, acute or short-acuminate, cuneate, serrate, usually chiefly above the middle, pubescent above, tomentose beneath: fls. fragrant, in pubescent solitary or panicled racemes 6–15 cm. long; pedicels 2–5 mm. long: caps. depressed-globose, 4 mm. across. Fl.viii–ix. B.M.3743(c). G.F.4:65. B.C.2:801. B.S.1: 373. (*C. alnifolia* var. *t.* Michx.) N. C. to Fla. and Ala. Intr. 1731. Zone (V).

3. **C. acuminàta** Michx. Shrub or small tree to 6 m., with upright or spreading brs.: lvs. ovate-elliptic or elliptic to elliptic-oblong, 8–20 cm. long, acuminate, broad-cuneate or rounded at base, serrulate, pubescent beneath at least on the veins: fls. secund, in usually solitary racemes 8–20 cm. long, densely

pubescent; pedicels 3–8 mm. long; sepals oblong-ovate, acutish, ribbed; petals upright; filaments hairy; style glabrous: caps. ovoid, 5 mm. long, nodding Fl.vii–ix. L.D.7:430(c). L.B.1427(c). B.T.f.685. Va. and W. Va. to Ga and Ala., in the mts. Intr. 1806. Zone V.

4. **C. barbinérvis** Sieb. & Zucc. Shrub or tree to 10 m. with spreading brs.; brts. nearly glabrous: lvs. obovate to oblong-obovate, 6–12 cm. long, acuminate, cuneate, sharply serrate, pubescent at first on both sides, at maturity at least on the veins beneath; petiole 6–15 mm. long: fls. fragrant, in panicled pubescent racemes 10–15 cm. long; pedicels 2–8 mm. long; sepals broad-ovate mucronulate; petals 5–6 mm. long, slightly shorter than stamens; filaments and style glabrous: caps. subglobose, 4 mm. across. Fl.vii–ix. S.I.1:t.78(c) B.M.8970(c). Gt.19:654. B.A.1930:58(h). (*C. canescens* auth., not Reinw.) Japan. Intr. 1870. Zone (V).

Related species: **C. Fargèsii** Franch. Shrub to 4 m.; lvs. ovate-oblong or elliptic-oblong, 8–14 cm. long, cuneate or rounded at base, nearly glabrous; petiole 1–2.5 cm. long; racemes panicled 10–20 cm. long; sepals acute: filaments pubescent. C. China. Intr. 1900. Zone VII?—**C. monostáchya** Rehd. & Wils. Closely related to the preceding species: lvs. elliptic-oblong to oblong-lanceolate, nearly glabrous: racemes usually solitary; filaments sparingly pubescent; style appressed-pilose. C. China. Intr. 1908. Zone VII?—**C. Delaváyi** Franch. Shrub or tree to 15 m.; brts. often red: lvs. elliptic-oblong to oblanceolate, pubescent beneath: racemes solitary; calyx red; petals about 1 cm. long, ciliate; stamens half as long as petals; filaments and style appressed-pilose. B.M.8970 (c). G.C.82:83. W. China. Intr. 1913. Zone VII? The handsomest of the Chinese species.

Fam. 86. **PYROLACEAE** Dumort. SHINLEAF FAMILY

Herbs or low suffruticose plants, sometimes parasitic and without chlorophyll: lvs. alternate, estipulate, basal or scattered: fls. perfect, regular, terminal and solitary or in corymbs or racemes; calyx 5-parted, sometimes wanting in the parasitic genera; petals distinct, 5, rarely 4; stamens 10; anthers opening by apical pores or by slits; hypogynous disk present or wanting; ovary superior, 5-celled, many-ovuled; style and stigma 1: fr. a caps. splitting into 5 valves; seed as in the preceding family.—Eleven genera and about 40 species in the boreal and temp. regions of the n. hemisphere.

CHIMÁPHILA Pursh. Evergreen suffruticose plants with creeping stem: lvs. usually crowded into irregular whorls, serrate, thickish: fls. nodding, in terminal stalked umbel-like racemes; sepals persistent, 5; petals 5, orbicular, concave, forming a saucer-shaped corolla; anthers 2-horned, opening with 2 pores; filaments short, dilated about the middle; style very short, with peltate stigma: caps. deeply furrowed, splitting from the apex downward. (Greek, *cheima*, winter, and *philein*, to love; alluding to its popular name Wintergreen.) About 8 species in N. and C. Am., Eu. and N. Asia.

A. Lvs. broadest above the middle, bright green..............................1. *C. umbellata*
AA. Lvs. broadest below the middle, mottled with white.......................2. *C. maculata*

1. **C. umbellàta** (L.) Nutt. WINTERGREEN. Plant 15–25 cm. high: lvs. 3–6 in a whorl, short-petioled, usually oblong-obovate, 2–4.5 cm. long obtuse or acutish, sharply serrate with 4–13 obtusish teeth and with 3–4 slightly elevated pairs of veins beneath, bright green and lustrous above: fls. 3–6, umbellate; about 1.5 cm. across, white or pinkish; pedicels diverging during anthesis; the dilated portion of filament ciliate; caps. globose, 5–6 mm. across. Fl.vii–viii; fr.ix. F.D.20:t.2044(c). K.D.444(a). N. and C. Eu., N. Asia to Japan. Cult. 1796. Zone III?—**C. u. cisatlántica** Blake, var. PIPSISSEWA. Plant to 30 cm.: lvs. oblong-obovate to oblanceolate, 4–7 cm. long, acute and mucronate

with 6–18 acute teeth: fls. 4–8; pedicels ascending during anthesis, more racemose. M.M.7:t.9(c). B.M.778(c). L.B.463(c). (*C. corymbosa* Pursh, in part.—PRINCE'S PINE.) N. S. to Minn., s. to Ga. Intr. 1762.—**C. u. occidentàlis** (Rydb.) Blake, var. Lvs. 3–9 cm. long, acute, with 10–18 acute teeth and with indistinct veins beneath: fls. 4–9; pedicels ascending, more racemose: caps. 6–7.5 mm. across. Brown & Schaeffer, Alp. Fl. Can. 57. (*C. o.* Rydb.) B. C. to Cal., e. Mont. and Colo. Intr. ?

2. **C. maculàta** Pursh. Plant 8–25 cm. high: lvs. usually in threes, ovate-lanceolate to lanceolate, the lower ones ovate, 2.5–7 cm. long, acute or acuminate, rounded or cuneate at base, remotely and sharply serrate, variegated with white along the veins: fls. 2–5, white or pinkish, 1.5–2 cm. across; bracts linear; dilated portion of filaments villous: caps. depressed-globose, 7 mm. across. Fl.vi–vii. B.M.897(c). M.M.9:t.1(c). G.C.74:122. Gn.87:452. Me. to Ont., s. to Mex. Intr. 1747. Zone IV?

Related species: **C. Menzièsii** (R. Br.) Spreng. Plant 8–20 cm.: lvs. alternate or in threes, ovate, to oblong-lanceolate, 2–4 cm. long, acute at ends, sharply serrate, sometimes variegated: fls. 1–3, white, 1.2 cm. across. E.N.IV.1:8. Parsons, Wild Fl. Calif. 105. B. C. to Mex. Intr. ?

Fam. 87. **ERICACEAE** DC. HEATH FAMILY

Shrubs or small trees, often evergreen; lvs. alternate, rarely opposite or whorled, entire or serrate, exstipulate: fls. perfect, regular or slightly irregular, solitary or in racemes, panicles or umbels: calyx 4–5-parted, persistent: corolla gamopetalous, rarely of distinct petals, often urceolate, 4–5-lobed or -parted; stamens as many or twice as many as corolla-lobes, inserted at base of a hypogynous disk; anthers opening by apical pores, rarely by slits, usually with appendages: ovary superior or inferior, 2–5-celled, many-ovuled; style and stigma 1: fr. a caps., rarely a berry or drupe; seeds minute, many in each cell, rarely only 1, albuminous, with small central embryo.—About 70 genera with 1500 species, distributed through both hemispheres, chiefly in the colder and temp. regions, also on high mts. in the tropics.

Ovary superior; calyx free: fr. a caps., rarely berry-like or a berry.
  A. Fr. a caps., with dry calyx.
    B. Corolla of distinct petals.
      c. Fls. in elongated racemes, panicles or solitary; anthers opening by slits: lvs. deciduous.
        D. Petals 3 or 4; fls. in panicles or racemes.
          E. Petals 3; stamens 6..1. *Tripetaleia*
          EE. Petals 4–5; stamens 8–10...2. *Elliottia*
        DD. Fls. solitary; petals 5; stamens 5–10............................3. *Cladothamnus*
      CC. Fls. in terminal umbel-like clusters; anthers opening by pores: lvs. evergreen.
        D. Lvs. tomentose beneath or lepidote, 2–7 cm. long........................4. *Ledum*
        DD. Lvs. glabrous, not exceeding 1.5 cm...............................8. *Leiophyllum*
    BB. Corolla gamopetalous.
      c. Corolla deciduous.
        D. Caps. septicidal.
          E. Corolla without pouches for the anthers; stamens 5–16.
            F. Lvs. alternate or sometimes clustered; anthers opening by pores.
              G. Corolla rotate or broad-campanulate to funnel-form; stamens exserted.
                H. Seed enclosed in a loose elongated testa lacerated at the ends: corolla zygomorphous; stamens 5–20........................5. *Rhododendron*
                HH. Seed with close reticulate testa, obtuse at ends, ovoid: corolla actinomorphous, rotate to rotate-campanulate; stamens 10.
                  I. Lvs. without lepidote glands.
                    J. Lvs. elliptic, ciliate: fls. 1–3...................10. *Rhodothamnus*
                    JJ. Lvs. linear, slightly serrulate: fls. 2–10........10a. *Phyllothamnus*
                  II. Lvs. with lepidote glands beneath, elliptic to elliptic-oblong, entire.
                        11. *Kalmiopsis*
            GG. Corolla globose-campanulate to cylindric; stamens inclosed.
              H. Corolla globose-campanulate or urceolate, 4- or 5-lobed.
                I. Fls. fascicled.
                  J. Lvs. broad: fls. from lateral buds, 4–5-merous.......6. *Menziesia*

ERICACEAE

           JJ. Lvs. linear, heath-like: fls. from terminal buds, 4–6-merous.
                              13. *Phyllodoce*
        II. Fls. in terminal elongated racemes, 4-merous: lvs. linear.
                              14. *Daboecia*
      HH. Corolla cylindric, 8–10 mm. long; ovary 3-celled: fls. 1–2: lvs. 8–12 mm
         long ....7. *Tsusiophyllum*
    FF. Lvs. opposite, small: corolla deeply 5-cleft; stamens 5, included; anthers
        opening by slits...9. *Loiseleuria*
  EE. Corolla broad-campanulate or nearly rotate, with 10 pouches receiving as many
    anthers ....12. *Kalmia*
DD. Caps. loculicidal.
  E. Anther-cells opening by pores or short slits at apex: upright shrubs, or
    prostrate shrubs with minute lvs.
    F. Fls. solitary; corolla campanulate: lvs. scale-like or subulate...16. *Cassiope*
    FF. Fls. in umbels, racemes or panicles.
      G. Calyx 5-lobed or 5-parted, the lobes valvate or separate.
        H. Anthers awned.
          I. Awns of anthers upright or ascending.
            J. Fls. in terminal umbels or racemes.
              K. Lvs. persistent, narrow: fls. in umbels; corolla urceolate: seeds
                numerous, oval ....17. *Andromeda*
              KK. Lvs. deciduous, broad: fls. in racemes or umbels: seeds few in
                each cell, 3–5-angled...........................15. *Enkianthus*
            JJ. Fls. in lateral clusters; corolla campanulate: lvs. half-evergreen.
                      18. *Zenobia*
          II. Awns of anthers reflexed: fls. in terminal panicles; corolla urceolate:
           lvs. evergreen, serrate...........................19. *Pieris*
        HH. Anthers not awned.
          I. Caps. subglobose to ovoid, with thickened sutures, glabrous: fls. in
           racemes or clusters ....20. *Lyonia*
          II. Caps. conical, pubescent, sutures not thickened; flowers in large
           terminal panicles: lvs. deciduous, serrulate, 10–15 cm. long.
                      22. *Oxydendrum*
      GG. Calyx 5-parted, the lobes distinctly imbricate; corolla urceolate.
        H. Lvs. densely scaly beneath, evergreen: fls. in leafy terminal racemes.
                      21. *Chamaedaphne*
        HH. Lvs. not scaly, deciduous or evergreen, serrulate; racemes axillary or
         terminal ....23. *Leucothoe*
    EE. Anther-cells opening through their whole length: evergreen trailing shrub with
      ovate-cordate lvs. ....24. *Epigaea*
  CC. Corolla persistent, 4-merous, enclosing the caps.: lvs. linear, small, persistent.
    D. Calyx longer than the deeply 4-parted corolla, colored.................30. *Calluna*
    DD. Calyx shorter than corolla, not colored; corolla lobes short.
      E. Stamens inserted at base of a high furrowed disk: fls. often axillary or in
        terminal clusters ....31. *Erica*
      EE. Stamens adnate to base of corolla; disk minute; fls. in a dense terminal bract-
        less spike ....32. *Bruckenthalia*
AA. Fr. a berry or surrounded by a fleshy calyx and berry-like: lvs. evergreen (except No. 29).
  B. Calyx accrescent, becoming fleshy and surrounding the caps.............25. *Gaultheria*
  BB. Calyx dry, small, at base of the berry-like fr.
    C. Anthers with short upright appendages at apex: lvs. serrulate: upright shrubs.
                           26. *Pernettya*
    CC. Anthers with 2 long reflexed appendages: habit often prostrate.
      D. Lvs. evergreen, usually entire.
        E. Cells of ovary many-seeded: fr. a berry, granulated or warty: fls. in large
         terminal panicles: lvs. 5–12 cm. long...........................27. *Arbutus*
        EE. Cells of ovary 1-seeded: fr. a drupe, smooth, with several 1-seeded or 1 several-
         seeded stone: fls. in small panicles or racemes: lvs. rarely exceeding 5 cm.
                      28. *Arctostaphylos*
      DD. Lvs. annual, marcescent, serrate: fr. juicy: habit prostrate; clusters few-fld.
                           29. *Arctous*
**Ovary inferior or half-inferior: fr. a berry or berry-like drupe, crowned by the persistent
calyx-lobes.**
  A. Fr. white; ovary free at apex: fls. 4-merous: trailing evergreen with appressed-bristly
    brs. and broad-elliptic lvs. 4–8 mm. long...................................33. *Chiogenes*
  AA. Fr. colored (only exceptionally white): ovary perfectly inferior.
    B. Ovary 10-celled: fr. berry-like with 10 small nutlets: lvs. evergreen, or deciduous and
      resinous-dotted: upright shrubs...................................34. *Gaylussacia*
    BB. Ovary 4–5-celled, rarely incompletely 8–10-celled: fr. a many-seeded berry: lvs. ever-
      green or deciduous, not resinous-dotted; sometimes trailing.............35. *Vaccinium*

    Subfam. I. RHODODENDROIDEAE Drude. Ovary superior, free from
the calyx.

    Tribe 1. RHODODENDREAE Spreng. Fr. a septicidal caps.: corolla deciduous,
sometimes of separate petals.

1. **TRIPETALEÌA** Sieb. & Zucc. Deciduous shrubs; winter-buds with 2 or 3 outer scales: lvs. alternate, short-petioled, entire: fls. white or pinkish. in terminal racemes or panicles; calyx 5-lobed; petals 3, oblong; stamens 6, shorter than petals; anthers opening by a slit; ovary 3-celled, the cells many-ovuled; style slender: caps. septicidal, many-seeded. (Greek *tri-*, three in compound words, and *petalon*.) Two species in Japan.

T. **paniculàta** Sieb. & Zucc. Shrub to 2 m.; brts. red-brown, angled or slightly winged: lvs. rhombic-ovate or rhombic, 2.5–6 cm. long, acute, cuneate, glabrous except pubescent on the midrib beneath: fls. in panicles 5–10 cm. long; bracts subulate; pedicels 2–4 mm. long; calyx small, cupular, with 5 short lobes; petals about 8 mm. long, white tinged with pink; ovary stipitate: caps. subglobose, 3 mm. across. Fl.viii. N.T.1:12. S.H.2:f.311e-f,312c-d. Japan. Intr. 1892. Zone V.

Related species: T. **bracteàta** Maxim. Brts. subterete, light brown: lvs. obovate, obtuse, glabrous: fls. pink, in rarely branched racemes; bracts elliptic to obovate; pedicels 5–15 mm. long, calyx divided to base into 5 foliaceous lobes 5 mm. long: ovary sessile. K.B.1934:192,t. M.I.1:t.71. N.T.1:15. K.B.1934: 192,t. (*Botryostege b.* Stapf.) Japan. Intr. 1915. Zone V?

2. **ELLIÓTTIA** Muhlenb. Deciduous shrub; winter-buds glabrous, with 2 or 3 outer scales: lvs. alternate, petioled, entire: fls. slightly irregular, 4- or occasionally 5-merous, white, in terminal racemes or panicles; calyx small, with 4 rounded apiculate lobes; petals 4, oblong, obtuse; stamens 8, about half as long as petals; anthers opening by a slit; style slender, curved, exserted: ovary 4-, rarely 5-celled: fr. a depressed-globose 4-, rarely 5-valved caps. septicidally dehiscent, many-seeded; seeds suborbicular, compressed, winged all around. (After Stephen Elliott, American botanist who wrote a flora of S. Carolina; 1771–1830.) One species in E. N. Am.

E. **racemòsa** Muhlenb. Shrub to 3 m. or occasionally small tree to 10 m., with slender upright brs. puberulous when young: lvs. oblong or elliptic-oblong, 7–10 cm. long, acute at ends, glandular-mucronate, dull green and glabrous above, paler and sparingly hairy beneath; petiole slender, pubescent, 8–12 mm. long: racemes loose, 10–25 cm. long; pedicels slender, 6–12 mm. long, the lower ones often branched; petals 1–1.5 cm. long; fls. slightly fragrant: caps. 8–10 mm. across; seeds with the wing 3–4 mm. across. Fl.vii. B.M.8413(c). S.S.14:t.712. G.F.7:205. G.C.51:11;78:49. Gn.75:471. A.B. 1938:t.1. S. C. and Ga. Cult. 1813. Zone VII? With fragrant white fls. in summer.

3. **CLADOTHÁMNUS** Bong. Deciduous shrub; winter-buds with 2 or 3 outer scales: lvs. alternate, subsessile, entire: fls. pink, regular, 1–3, terminal, nodding; sepals 5, narrow-oblong, green; petals 5, oblong; stamens 10; anthers opening by a short slit; style slender, shorter than petals: caps. 5–6-celled, many-seeded. (Greek *klados*, branch, and *thamnos*, shrub.) One species in N. W. Am.

C. **pyrolaeflòrus** Bong. Upright much-branched shrub to 3 m.; brts. glabrous, red-brown, angled; lvs. obovate-oblong to oblanceolate, 3–6 cm. long, mucronate, narrowed toward the base, glabrous: fls. usually solitary, 2–2.5 cm. across, pink, yellow toward the end of petals; pedicels 6–12 mm. long: caps. subglobose, 6–7 mm. across, surrounded and exceeded by the leafy sepals. Fl.vi. B.M.8353(c). G.F.10:215. S.H.2:f.312e,313a-d. Alaska to Ore. Cult. 1910. Zone VI?

4. **LEDUM** L. Evergreen shrubs; winter-buds ovoid, with several scales: lvs. alternate, short-petioled, entire, often revolute, tomentose or

glandular beneath: fls. rather small, white, on slender pedicels in umbel-like
terminal clusters; calyx-lobes 5, short and broad; petals 5, spreading; stamens
5–10. with slender filaments; anthers opening by apical pores; ovary 5-celled;
style elongated; caps. opening from the base to the apex into 5 valves.
(Ledon is the Greek name of Cistus.) Probably only 3 species in the colder
regions of the n. hemisphere.

A. Lvs. tomentose beneath, revolute at the margin.
  B. Stamens 7–11: lvs. linear to linear-oblong, sometimes oblong, the midrib more or less
    visible ....1. *L. palustre*
  BB. Stamens 5–8: lvs. elliptic to oblong, densely rusty-tomentose beneath, the midrib not
    visible ....2. *L. groenlandicum*
AA. Lvs. lepidote-glandular and glaucous beneath, not or slightly revolute..3. *L. glandulosum*

1. **L. palústre** L. WILD ROSEMARY. Upright shrub to 1 m.; young brts.
rusty-tomentose: lvs. linear to linear-oblong, 1–4.5 cm. long, strongly revolute,
dark green and somewhat rugose above, rusty-tomentose beneath: fls. 1–1.5
cm. across, in a dense terminal cluster; pedicels glandular-villous; petals
oval; stamens usually 10: caps. ovoid, 4–5 mm. long. Fl.v–vi. S.O.3:163(c).
F.D.20:2033(c). L.B.6:560(c). S.L.210(h). N. Eu. and N. Asia. Intr. 1762.
Zone II.—**L. p. decúmbens** Ait., var. Decumbent, densely branched shrub:
lvs. linear, 1–1.5 cm. long: caps. abruptly bent downward. B.B.2:677. (*L. d.*
Steud.) Arctic Am., N. E. Asia. Intr. 1762.—**L. p. dilatàtum** Wahlbg., var.
Upright shrub: lvs. usually oblong, 2–7 cm. long, less revolute, the rusty
pubescence often restricted to the midrib and veins, exposing a close white
tomentum. N.K.8:t.1,2. (*L. d.* Rupr., *L. hypoleucum* Komar., *L. pacificum*
Small.) N. Eu. to Japan; Sitka. Cult. 1902.

2. **L. groenlándicum** Oed. LABRADOR TEA. Upright shrub to 1 m.; young
brts. rusty-tomentose: lvs. elliptic to oblong or narrow-oblong, 2–5 cm. long,
obtuse, densely rusty-tomentose beneath: fls. 1.5 cm. across; pedicels minutely
puberulous; calyx-lobes acute or acutish; petals oblong: caps. oblong, 5–6.5
mm. long. Fl.v–vi. G.O.t.50(c). S.O.3:t.164(c). L.B.534(c);1049(c). B.S.
2:13. M.G.21:74(h). S.L.46(h). (*L. latifolium* Ait.) Greenl. to Alb. and
Wash., s. to Pa. and Wisc. Intr. 1763. Zone II.—**L. g. compáctum** Bean, var.
Dwarf, with short brs. shorter and broader lvs. and smaller fl.-clusters.

3. **L. glandulòsum** Nutt. Shrub to 2 m.: brts. puberulous: lvs. elliptic or
ovate to oblong, 1.5–5 cm. long, obtuse, not revolute, dark green above,
glaucous and resinous-lepidote beneath; petiole 4–6 mm. long: fls. 1.2 cm.
across; pedicels slender; calyx-lobes obtuse; petals suborbicular to oblong;
stamens 10: caps. subglobose to ovoid, 3–4 mm. long. Fl.v–vi. B.M.7610(c).
Alb. and B. C. to Wyo. and Calif. Intr. 1894. Zone V or VI?

5. **RHODODÉNDRON** L. Evergreen or deciduous shrubs, rarely trees;
buds with several to many imbricate scales: lvs. alternate, petioled, entire,
rarely ciliate-serrulate: fls. pediceled, usually in terminal umbel-like racemes,
sometimes solitary or few, rarely from lateral buds; calyx 5-parted, often
very small, rarely 6–10-parted; corolla rotate to campanulate or funnelform,
sometimes tubular, usually slightly irregular, with 5-, rarely 6–10-lobed limb,
rarely some of the lobes divided to the base; stamens 5–10, rarely more;
anthers opening with apical pores; ovary 5–10-celled; cells many-ovuled;
style slender with capitate stigma; caps. usually ovoid to oblong, septicidal;
seeds minute, numerous, enclosed in a loose elongated testa lacerated at the
ends. (Greek *rhodon*, rose and *dendron*, tree; the ancient Greek name of
Nerium Oleander.) Including *Azalea* L., *Rhodora* L., *Therorhodion* Small,
Azaleastrum Rydb. and *Biltia* Small. More than 600 species distributed
through the colder and temp. regions of the n. hemisphere, also on the high

mts. of s. Asia and Malaysia and extending to N. Guinea and Austr.; 26 species known in N. Am., but none extending into Mex.—Rhododendrons and Azaleas are much planted for their beautiful fls. and the evergreen species also for their foliage; they demand, with few exceptions, soil free from lime. Many hybrids have originated in cult. and make the classification and determination of the garden forms difficult. It is manifestly impossible to give within the scope of this Manual a fairly complete account of the ever increasing number of these hybrids and of the numerous new species introduced chiefly during the last three decades from central and western China and adjoining regions, and only a selection of the hardier and better known species could be included. Descriptions of all species known up to 1930 are given in "Species of Rhododendron" (861 pp., ill. 1930); brief descriptions and much other information will be found in "Bowers, Rhododendrons and Azaleas" (549 pp., ill. 1936), and descriptions of species, varieties and hybrids in "Millais, Rhododendrons" (2 vols., ill. 1917–24).

A. Lvs. evergreen, glabrous, lepidote or tomentose, not ciliate, or ciliate and lepidote, rarely deciduous and lepidote; stamens 5–20; ovary glabrous, lepidote or tomentose, not setose, sometimes more than 5-celled. (See also × Subgen. Azaleodendron with half-evergreen lvs.) ....Subgen. I. EURHODODENDRON
  B. Fls. several or many from a terminal bud, rarely with additional lateral clusters: lvs. persistent.
    c. Lvs. not lepidote, glabrous or tomentose beneath, never less than 5 cm. long; ovary glabrous, glandular or tomentose, never lepidote; stamens 10–20.
                                                        Sect. 1. Leiorhodium
    cc. Lvs. lepidote, sometimes less than 5 cm. long: ovary lepidote.
      D. Corolla rotate or campanulate to funnelform; stamens 10....Sect. 2. Lepipherum
      DD. Corolla salver-shaped, with spreading limb and cylindric tube, villous within; stamens 5–10: lvs. 1–7 cm. long..............................Sect. 3. Pogonanthum
  BB. Fls. solitary or few from lateral buds clustered at end of brts.: lvs. usually deciduous, lepidote: corolla rotate-campanulate; stamens 10................Sect. 4. Rhodorastrum
AA. Lvs. deciduous, pubescent, often strigose and ciliate, never lepidote, sometimes persistent and strigose; stamens 5–10; ovary setose, rarely glabrous, 5-celled (see also × Subgen. Azaleodendron with half-evergreen lvs.)
  B. Fls. from leafless terminal or lateral buds, solitary to many in umbel-like racemes; bracts deciduous; stamens 5–10: upright shrubs.
    c. Fls. solitary or 2 from lateral buds: lvs. deciduous....Subgen. II. AZALEASTRUM
    cc. Fls. in terminal usually many-fld. clusters, rarely solitary.
                                                   Subgen. III. ANTHODENRON
      D. Fls. and leafy brts. from the same terminal bud; fls. 1–3, rarely more.
        E. Brts. with flattened appressed setose hairs: lvs. persistent or sometimes deciduous, scattered: stamens 5–10.................................Sect. 1. Tsutsutsi
        EE. Brts. glabrous or villous: lvs. deciduous, clustered at end of brts., scattered only on vigorous shoots: stamens 8–10.....................Sect. 2. Sciadorhodion
      DD. Fls. from terminal buds, several to many, lvs. from distinct lateral buds below.
        E. Stamens 5–10; corolla rotate-campanulate, sometimes with 1–3 of the lobes divided to or nearly to the base...............................Sect. 3. Rhodora
        EE. Stamens 5; corolla funnelform.............................Sect. 4. Pentanthera
  BB. Fls. on a leafy-bracted peduncle, solitary or in 2–3-fld. racemes with leafy bracts; corolla rotate; stamens 10: procumbent small shrub..Subgen. IV. THERORHODION

Subgen. I. EURHODODENDRON

Sect. 1. Leiorhodium

A. Under side of lvs. glabrous, or pubescent only when young or only on the midrib.
  B. Stamens 10; corolla 5-lobed.
    c. Lvs. glabrous beneath.
      D. Ovary pubescent.
        E. Fls. red, pink or white: bud-scales deciduous.
          F. Pedicels pubescent: ovary glandular-pubescent: lvs. obtuse or obtusish at ends ....1. *R. catawbiense*
          FF. Pedicels glabrous: ovary white-silky: lvs. acute at ends.2. *R. macrophyllum*
        EE. Fls. yellow: bud-scales persistent............................6. *R. chrysanthum*
      DD. Ovary glandular or glabrous.
        E. Fls. red to white.
          F. Lvs. acute at ends..3. *R. ponticum*
          FF. Lvs. rounded to cordate at base: corolla sometimes 6-lobed...15. *R. Souliei*
        EE. Fls. yellow; calyx about as long as ovary.......................16. *R. croceum*
    cc. Lvs. on midrib and brts. with brown shaggy tomentum.....17. *R. longesquamatum*

BB. Stamens more than 10; ovary 6–8-celled; corolla 6–8-lobed, sometimes 5-lobed.
  c. Style glandular to the tip.
    D. Stamens pubescent ....10. *R. decorum*
    DD. Stamens glabrous.
      E. Lvs. rounded or subcordate at base............................11. *R. Fortunei*
      EE. Lvs. cuneate at base..12. *R. discolor*
  cc. Style glabrous, or glandular only at base.
    D. Lvs. rounded at ends or subcordate at base, 5–10(–14) cm. long....13. *R. Fargesi*
    DD. Lvs. cuneate at base, 10–20 cm. long............................14. *R. sutchuenense*
AA. Under side of lvs. tomentose or pubescent.
  B. Sepals about as long as ovary.
    c. Corolla 7-lobed; ovary 6–9-celled (see also *R. Metternichii* under No. 5).
                                             18. *R. auriculatum*
    cc. Corolla 5-lobed.
      D. Lvs. rounded or subcordate at base; ovary glandular (corolla occasionally 6–7-
        lobed in *R. detonsum*, see under No. 21).....................21. *R. adenogynum*
      DD. Lvs. cuneate: ovary glandular-pubescent........................4. *R. maximum*
  BB. Sepals much shorter than ovary.
    c. Ovary tomentose, pubescent or glandular.
      D. Young brts. tomentose.
        E. Infl. rounded; pedicels 2.5–3 cm. long: tomentum of lvs. rufous.
                                     5. *R. Degronianum*
        EE. Infl. elongated; pedicels 3–5 cm. long: tomentum white at first.7. *R. Smirnowi*
      DD. Young brts. glabrous.
        E. Ovary 5-celled.
          F. Tomentum of lvs. close and thin, midrib glabrous or glabrescent.
            G. Lvs. acute at ends: style 3–4 cm. long...................8. *R. caucasicum*
            GG. Lvs. obtuse at ends: style 1.5 cm. long................9. *R. brachycarpum*
          FF. Tomentum of lvs. floccose; midrib woolly-tomentose..........22. *R. rufum*
        EE. Ovary 6–9-celled ....19. *R. Traillianum*
    cc. Ovary glabrous.
      D. Ovary 5–8-celled; corolla slightly spotted....................20. *R. campanulatum*
      DD. Ovary 5-celled; corolla distinctly spotted crimson.............23. *R. Przewalskii*

Sect. 2. LEPIPHERUM

A. Fls. 2.5–5 cm. across: upright shrubs, rarely procumbent.
  B. Fls. yellow.
    c. Brts. pilose: lvs. 2–2.5 cm. long....................................41. *R. megeratum*
    cc. Brts. scaly or glabrous: lvs. 3–8 cm. long.
      D. Calyx small ....24. *R. Keiskei*
      DD. Calyx longer than ovary.......................................25. *R. Hanceanum*
  BB. Fls. pink to purple or white.
    c. Lvs. hirsute on midrib beneath................................26. *R. Augustinii*
    cc. Lvs. quite glabrous beneath.
      D. Style longer than stamens.
        E. Brts. glabrous or scaly.
          F. Fls. partly axillary below the terminal cluster.
            G. Lvs. densely scaly beneath...........................27. *R. Davidsonianum*
            GG. Lvs. beneath with distant scales........................28. *R. yunnanense*
          FF. Fls. all terminal.
            G. Corolla not or slightly scaly outside: lvs. generally lanceolate.
              H. Lvs. with bristly hairs above......................29. *R. hormophorum*
              HH. Lvs. without bristly hairs...............................30. *R. Searsiae*
            GG. Corolla scaly outside: lvs. generally elliptic.
              H. Petioles 4–6 mm. long...............................31. *R. concinnum*
              HH. Petioles 1–1.5 cm. long..............................32. *R. rubiginosum*
        EE. Brts. bristly: calyx 4–8 mm. long.
          F. Corolla scaly and pubescent outside, purple-crimson.......33. *R. saluenense*
          FF. Corolla glabrous outside, white............................34. *R. moupinense*
      DD. Style shorter than stamens.
        E. Tube of corolla shorter or as long as lobes, slightly or not lepidote outside.
                                      35. *R. carolinianum*
        EE. Tube of corolla longer than lobes, lepidote outside.
          F. Corolla about 2.5–3 cm. across: style about 2 cm. long: lvs. 4–10 cm. long.
                                        36. *R. minus*
          FF. Corolla 2–2.5 cm. long; style about 1 cm. long: lvs. 2–6 cm. long.
                                        37. *R. myrtifolium*
AA. Fls. 1–2 cm., rarely 2.5 cm.
  B. Corolla-tube cylindric, longer than limb.
    c. Style at least 3 times as long as ovary: fls. about 2 cm. across....37. *R. myrtifolium*
    cc. Style scarcely twice as long as ovary: fls. about 1.5 cm. across.
      D. Lvs. not ciliate; calyx very short..............................38. *R. ferrugineum*
      DD. Lvs. ciliate; calyx 2.5–3.5 mm. long.........................39. *R. hirsutum*
  BB. Corolla-tube funnelform or campanulate, as long or shorter, rarely longer than lobes;
    fls. white to pink or purple, yellow in No. 41 and in *R. flavidum* under No. 45.
    c. Upright shrubs: lvs. 2.5–8 cm. long: stamens 8–12.

D. Fls. pink, purple or yellow, 1–6; stamens shorter than corolla, pubescent at base.
   E. Calyx-lobes pointed, longer than ovary: lvs. 4–8 cm. long .....40. *R. glaucum*
   EE. Calyx-lobes rounded, shorter than ovary: lvs. 2–3.5 cm. long.
      F. Brts. pilose: fls. yellow....................................41. *R. megeratum*
      FF. Brts. scaly: fls. purple.
         G. Stamens 8; corolla scaly outside........................42. *R. lepidotum*
         GG. Stamens 10–12; corolla glabrous.....................43. *R. campylogynum*
DD. Fls. white, in many-fld. racemes; stamens as long as corolla, glabrous.
                                                    44. *R. micranthum*
CC. Dwarf, usually matted or procumbent shrubs: lvs. 1–3 cm. long: stamens 5–10.
   D. Style pubescent below..45. *R. cantabile*
   DD. Style glabrous.
      E. Corolla not scaly outside.
         F. Style much shorter than stamens..........................46. *R. intricatum*
         FF. Style as long or longer than stamens.
            G. Stamens glabrous ....47. *R. lapponicum*
            GG. Stamens pubescent.
               H. Lvs. about 3 cm. long, narrow-oblanceolate.....48. *R. hippophaeoides*
               HH. Lvs. 1–2 cm. long.
                  I. Calyx ciliate ....49. *R. parvifolium*
                  II. Calyx glabrous ....50. *R. scintillans*
      EE. Corolla scaly outside.......................................51. *R. drumonium*

Sect. 3. POGONANTHUM

A. Stamens 5 ....52. *R. Sargentianum*
AA. Stamens 6–10 ....53. *R. Collettianum*

Sect. 4. RHODORASTRUM

A. Lvs. persistent: fl.-clusters many, racemosely arranged.................54. *R. racemosum*
AA. Lvs. deciduous, rarely evergreen: fl.-clusters few at end of brts.
   B. Lvs. rounded at ends, sometimes evergreen, 2–4 cm. long..............55. *R. dauricum*
   BB. Lvs. acute at ends, 3–7 cm. long, deciduous.....................56. *R. mucronulatum*

Subgen. II. AZALEASTRUM

A. Stamens 10, subequal, pubescent only at base...........................57. *R. albiflorum*
AA. Stamens 5, the 2 upper much shorter and densely pilose............58. *R. semibarbatum*

Subgen. I × III. AZALEODENDRON
Subgen. III. ANTHODENDRON
Sect. 1. TSUTSUTSI

A. Brts. densely clothed with flattened appressed hairs.
   B. Scales of fl.-buds not viscid.
      C. Corolla with cylindric tube and spreading lobes.
         D. Fls. white, about 8 mm. across, tube 3 mm. long; stamens 4–5..59. *R. Tschonoskii*
         DD. Fls. pink to white, dotted carmine, 1.4–2 cm. across, tube 6–8 mm. long: lvs. to
            3.5 cm. long..60. *R. microphytum*
      CC. Corolla funnelform-campanulate, 1.8–5 cm. across.
         D. Stamens 5.
            E. Lvs. crenulate, elliptic-lanceolate to linear-lanceolate...........61. *R. indicum*
            EE. Lvs. elliptic or obovate to lanceolate, entire....................62. *R. obtusum*
         DD. Stamens 10: lvs. elliptic to elliptic-oblong, 2–5 cm. long..............63. *R. Simsii*
   BB. Scales of fl.-buds viscid; stamens 10: lvs. deciduous...................64. *R. yedoense*
AA. Brts. with few appressed hairs and many spreading often glandular hairs: bud-scales
viscid.
   B. Stamens 8–10; fls. white to pale purple..............................65. *R. mucronatum*
   BB. Stamens 5, sometimes 6–10; fls. pink to pale rosy-purple...........66. *R. linearifolium*

Sect. 2. SCIADORHODION

A. Lvs. rhombic, 2–3 at end of brts.
   B. Stamens subequal; corolla red; style villous............................67. *R. Weyrichii*
   BB. Stamens unequal, often declinate; style glabrous or glandular.......68. *R. reticulatum*
AA. Lvs. broad-elliptic to obovate, 4–5 at end of brts.
   B. Corolla white; style glabrous: lvs. 3–5 cm. long..................69. *R. quinquefolium*
   BB. Corolla pink; style glandular: lvs. 5–10 cm. long.................70. *R. Schlippenbachii*

Sect. 3. RHODORA

A. Corolla not divided to base.
   B. Stamens 10; corolla not spotted.
      C. Lvs. obovate to oblong-oblanceolate, pubescent beneath: fls. 3–6, magenta.
                                        71. *R. Albrechti*
      CC. Lvs. elliptic to narrow-elliptic, glabrescent: fls. 1–2, rose-pink..72. *R. pentaphyllum*
                                         73. *R. Vaseyi*
   B. Stamens 5–7: fls. pink or whitish, spotted: lvs. glabrous and green beneath.
AA. Corolla divided to base; stamens 10: lvs. tomentulose beneath...........74. *R. canadense*

Sieb. & Zucc. Shrub to 4 m.: lvs. oblong to lance-oblong: fls. 7-merous; calyx-lobes acute, 2–3 mm. long; corolla 5–6 cm. across, 7-lobed; stamens 14; ovary brown-tomentose. S.Z.1:t.9(c). N.T.1:64. (*R. M.* var. *heptamerum* Maxim.) Japan. Intr. ?

6. **R. chrysánthum** Pallas. Much-branched shrub to 1 m., glabrous; brts. stout, partly covered by the persistent bud-scales: lvs. elliptic to ovate-lanceolate or oblong-obovate, 2.5–8 cm. long, obtuse and mucronulate, cuneate, slightly revolute, rugulose above, light green beneath; petioles stout, 1–1.5 cm. long: fls. 5–8, subtended by persistent bud-scales; corolla funnel-form-campanulate, 2.5–3 cm. across, pale yellow; sepals minute, rounded, pubescent; pedicels floccose-tomentose, 4–6 cm. long, filaments villous at base; ovary rufous-tomentose; style glabrous. Fl.v.–vi. Hooker, Parad. Lond. 2:t.80(c). N.K.8:t.13. N.T.1:68. T.M.41:t.8(h). Altai to Kamchatka, Korea, Japan. Intr. 1796. Zone II.—Difficult to grow.

7. **R. Smirnòwi** Trautv. Shrub or small tree to 6 m.; young brts. white-tomentose: lvs. oblong, 8–15 cm. long, acutish or obtuse, cuneate, dark green and finally glabrous above, with thick woolly tomentum beneath, white at first later pale brown; petioles 8–18 mm. long, tomentose: fls. many; corolla rosy-red, campanulate-funnelform, 6–7 mm. across, lobes longer than tube, with frilled, darker colored margin; stamens pilose below the middle; ovary tomentose; calyx short, tomentose; pedicels 3–5 cm. long, pubescent. Fl.v. B.M.7495(c). Gt.35:t.1226(c). G.C.49:417. W.A.74,t(h). A.B.1927:40 (h). Cauc. Intr. 1886. Zone IV. Distinct and handsome in bloom, but of rather loose habit.—There are crosses with Catawbiense hybrids in cult.; also *R. S.* × *Fortunei* has been raised by J. B. Gable, and crosses with many other species in Eu.

Related species: **R. Ungérni** Trautv. Lvs. oblong, mucronate, with pale brown tomentum beneath: fls. pale rose to white, 5 cm. across, the lobes with flat margin; sepals longer, pointed; pedicels glandular-pubescent. B.M.8332(c). Gt. 35:t.1226(c). Cauc. Intr. 1886. Zone V.

8. **R. caucásicum** Pall. Low dense shrub to 0.5 m. tall, with often pro-cumbent stems; brts. with usually persistent bud-scales, slightly pubescent when young: lvs. narrow-elliptic to obovate-oblong, 5–10 cm. long, acute, cuneate at base, dark green above, with close brown tomentum beneath; petioles 6–8 mm. long: fls. 7–10; corolla funnelform-campanulate, 5 cm. across, with emarginate rounded lobes, pink to yellowish white, spotted greenish; stamens villous near base; ovary rufous-tomentose; calyx minute; pedicels loosely pubescent, about 3 cm. long. Fl.v. B.M.1145(c). Cauc. Intr. 1803. Zone V. Rare in cult.—**R. c. flàvidum** Reg., var. Fl. straw-yellow with greenish spots. Gt.16:t.516(c).—**R. c. stramíneum** Hook., var. Fls. straw-yellow with fulvous spots. B.M.3422(c).

R. c. × *ponticum album* known as "Cunningham's White" is much used in Germany as a stock for hardy Rhododendrons.—*R. c.* × *arboreum* = R. venús-tum Sweet. Fls. rose-colored, paler in the centre, with dark blotch. S.B.II.3: t.285(c). Here also belong *R. Nobleanum* Lindl. Fls. bright rose. B.R.1820(c). Gn.77:30. and *R. pulcherrimum* Lindl. Similar but fls. paler.—The species has also entered into the so-called Catawbiense Hybrids. See No. 1.

9. **R. brachycárpum** D. Don. Shrub to 4 m.; young brts. gray-tomentose: lvs. elliptic to oblong-oblanceolate, 8–20 cm. long, obtuse and apiculate, cuneate to auriculate, dark green and reticulate above, with gray to dun-colored tomentum beneath; petiole stout, 1–3 cm. long, gray-tomentose: corolla broad-funnelform, about 5 cm. across, white or yellowish, striped and flushed pink, spotted greenish or brown; stamens unequal, pubescent near base; style glabrous; ovary brown-tomentose; calyx minute; pedicels slightly

villous. Fl.vi. B.M.7881(c). N.K.8:t.14. G.F.1:292. G.C.77:233. Japan, Korea. Intr. 1861. Zone V.—**R. b. rosaeflòrum** Miyoshi, var. Fls. pink.— **R. b. lutéscens** Koidz., var. Lvs. glabrous beneath: fls. white to yellowish white, slightly or not spotted.

10. **R. decòrum** Franch. Shrub to 6 m.: lvs. oblong to oblong-obovate, 5–15 cm. long, rounded at apex, cuneate or obtuse at base, glaucous beneath with scattered minute hairs, with 12–16 pairs of veins; petiole 2–3 cm. long: fls. 8–10; pedicels glandular; calyx small, glandular; corolla broad-funnel-form, about 5 cm. across, 6–8-lobed, white to pink, usually spotted greenish or pinkish, hairy at base within; stamens 12–16, puberulous at base; ovary and style densely glandular. Fl.v–vi. B.M.8659(c). Millais, Rhod. 2:28(h). (*R. Spooneri* Hemsl. & Wils.) W. China. Intr. 1904. Zone (V).

Related species: **R. seròtinum** Hutch. Lvs. elliptic-oblong, 9–16 cm. long, slightly cordate at base: corolla white, flushed rose outside, blotched red within. B.M.8841(c). W. China. Cult. 1889. Zone (V).

11. **R. Fortùnei** Lindl. Shrub to 4 m.; brts. smooth: lvs. oblong, 10–20 cm. long, abruptly pointed, rounded or subcordate, rarely cuneate, light green above, glaucescent beneath, with minute scattered hairs; petiole 1–2.5 cm. long, purplish: fls. racemose, rosy-lilac or blush, 7-lobed, fragrant, 7–9 cm. across; calyx minute, glandular; stamens 14–16, glabrous; ovary and style sparsely glandular; pedicels slender, stipitate-glandular. Fl.v–vi. B.M.5596 (c). E. China. Intr. 1859. Zone VI.

Related species: **R. vernicòsum** Franch. Brts. glandular when young: lvs. oblong-oval, obtuse to rounded at ends, 6–12 cm. long; petiole 1.5–3.5 cm. long: corolla 7-lobed, white to rose; style covered with dark red glands. B.M.8834(c). G.C.47:120,t. W. China. Intr. 1904. Zone (V).

12. **R. díscolor** Franch. Shrub to 5 m., quite glabrous; young shoots yellowish: lvs. narrow-elliptic to oblong-lanceolate, 10–20 cm. long, acute and mucronulate, cuneate or sometimes subcordate, dark green above, whitish beneath; petiole 1.5–3 cm. long, purplish: fls. about 10; corolla funnelform-campanulate, white to pale pink, 6–10 cm. across, with 6–7 lobes; stamens 12–14; filaments glabrous; ovary and style glandular; calyx 3–5 mm. long, ciliate; caps. 3.5 cm. long. Fl.vi. B.M.8696(c). G.C.72:21. Gn.84:270. Millais, Rhod. 2:128,t(h). C. China. Intr. 1900. Zone VI.—**R. d. cárneum** Wils., f. Fls. bright pink.

R. d. × *catawbiense* hybr. = **R. holmleaénse** Rehd. Lvs. shorter and broader; corolla 5–6-lobed; stamens 10–12; ovary 8-celled, sometimes 6–7-celled. Orig. 1915. Zone (V).

Related species: **R. Houlstónii** Hemsl. Lvs. elliptic- to lance-oblong, 7–15 cm. long, obtuse, cuneate or rounded at base: corolla pink, 7-lobed; pedicels glandular; stamens 14; calyx minute, not ciliate. Gn.91:703(h). C. China. Intr. 1900. Zone VI?

13. **R. Fàrgesi** Franch. Shrub to 6 m.: lvs. elliptic to elliptic-oblong or ovate-oblong, 5–8 cm. long, obtuse, mucronate, truncate to subcordate at base, glaucous beneath and minutely punctulate, with 9–10 pairs of veins fairly distinct beneath: fls. 6–10; pedicels 1.5–2.5 cm. long, glandular; calyx minute, glandular; corolla 7-lobed, about 5 cm. across, white to deep rose, spotted red, glabrous within; stamens 14, glabrous; ovary glandular. Fl.v–vi. B.M.8736(c). G.C.71:42,239. Gn.84:403. C. China. Intr. 1901. Zone (V).

Related species: **R. erubéscens** Hutch. Lvs. elliptic-oblong, rounded at base, with minute scattered hairs beneath: corolla 7-lobed, white, rose-carmine outside, puberulous within; stamens 12–14, pubescent at base; ovary glandular, 6-celled. B.M.8643(c). C. China. Intr. 1902. Zone VII?—**R. oreodóxa** Franch. Young shoots thinly tomentose, soon glabrous: lvs. elliptic to oblong, 5–10 cm. long, obtuse, rounded at base: pedicels short, glandular or nearly glabrous; corolla pale rose, 7–8-lobed; stamens 14, finely puberulous or glabrous at base:

ovary glabrous. B.M.8518(c). S.R.284. G.C.71:239. Gn.84:170;85:225. (*R. haematochilum* Craib.) W. China. Intr. 1904. Zone (V).—**R. orbiculàre** Dcne. Young brts. purplish, glandular: lvs. suborbicular to broad-ovate, 5–10 cm. long, rounded and mucronate at apex, cordate, glaucous beneath, glabrous: fls. broad-campanulate, 5 cm. across, rosy-red, 7-lobed; pedicels 4–6 cm. long, nearly glabrous; stamens 14; ovary glandular; style and pedicels glabrous. B.M.8775(c). G.C.71:274;101:1,t(c). M.D.1937:t.30a(c). (*R. rotundifolium* Franch.) W. China. Intr. 1904. Zone VII.

14. R. sutchuenénse Franch. Shrub to 5 m.; brts. thinly tomentose at first: lvs. oblong-oblanceolate to oval-oblong, 10–25 cm. long, acutish or obtuse, cuneate, glabrous beneath except the floccose-tomentose midrib; petioles 1.5–3 cm. long, tomentose at first: fls. 8–10, on stout pedicels 1.5–2.5 cm. long; calyx small; corolla 5-, rarely 6-lobed, rose-pink, spotted darker rose within, 6–8 cm. across: stamens 12–15, pubescent at base; anthers blackish purple; ovary 12-celled, glabrous. Fl.iv–v. B.M.8362(c). R.H.1922: 150(h),t(c). G.C.73:171. Gn.87:159. C. and W. China. Intr. 1911. Zone (V). —**R. s. Geráldii** Hutchins., var. Fls. with a dark red-purple blotch.

Related species: **R. praevérnum** Hutchins. Lvs. elliptic-oblanceolate, midrib beneath glabrous: corolla 5-lobed, white or flushed rose, with dark wine-red blotch at base; stamens 15; ovary glabrous. G.C.73:159. Gn.84:115;87:521. C. China. Intr. 1907.—**R. calóphytum** Franch. Tree to 12 m.; brts. gray-pubescent: lvs. oblong-obovate to oblanceolate, 20–30 cm. long, acuminulate, cuneate, slightly pubescent on midrib beneath at first: corolla 7–8-lobed, white to rose-color with dark blotch; stamens 16–20, glabrous; ovary glabrous. Gn.86:215. G.C.77:431. W. China. Intr. 1904. Zone VII.—**R. Dàvidi** Franch. Lvs. oblong to oblong-oblanceolate, acute or abruptly short-acuminate; petiole 2 cm. long: fls. 8–12, racemose; rachis 5–10 cm. long; pedicels about 1 cm. long, glandular; corolla broad-campanulate, 7–8-lobed, 4–5 cm. across, rosy-red or lilac-purple spotted; stamens 14–16; glabrous; ovary glandular. S.R.263. W. China. Intr. 1904. Zone VII.

15. R. Soulièi Franch. Shrub to 3 m.; young brts. purplish, glandular: lvs broad-ovate, 5–8 cm. long, rounded and mucronate at apex, bluish green, glabrous: fls. about 6; pedicels 2–3.5 cm. long, glandular; corolla pale rose or white, cup-shaped, 5–7 cm. across, with 5 or sometimes 6 broad short lobes; stamens 8–10; style and ovary glandular; calyx-lobes unequal, oblong, obtuse, glandular; pedicels 3–5 cm. long. Fl.v–vi. B.M.8622(c). G.C.45:380. Gn.73: 278. S.R.731. W. China. Intr. 1905. Zone VII?

Related species: **R. Williamsiànum** Rehd. & Wils. Shrub to 1.5 m. high, usually low and spreading: lvs. broad-oval to suborbicular, 1.5–4 cm. long, cordate: fls. 2–4; pedicels 2 cm. long; calyx minute; corolla campanulate, 5–6 cm. across, pale rose. B.M.8935(c). G.C.93:2,t;106,43(h). B.S.3:430,t. M.D. 1937:t.30(h). M.G.52:325(h). W. China. Intr. 1908. Zone (V).—**R. Thomsónii** Hook f. Lvs. broad-oval to suborbicular, 4–8 cm. long, rounded and mucronate at apex, rounded or subcordate at base; infl. racemose; pedicels 1–2 cm. long, glabrous; corolla cup-shaped, 5–6 cm. across, blood-red, greenish toward the base; style and the 6–10 celled ovary glabrous. B.M.4997(c). S.R. 744. Himal. Intr. 1849. Zone VII.

16. R. cròceum Balf. f. & W. W. Sm. Shrub to 6 m. high; brts. glandular when young: lvs. oblong to oval-oblong, rarely oval, 5–12 cm. long, rounded and apiculate at apex, usually subcordate at base, pale green beneath; petiole 2–2.5 cm. long, glandular at first: fls. 7–8; pedicels 4–5 cm. long, glandular; calyx 1 cm. long, with oval to oblong glandular-ciliate lobes; corolla cup-shaped, 5–7 cm. across, yellow, sometimes with a crimson blotch: stamens 10, glabrous; ovary and style to the tip glandular. Fl.v–vi. G.C.79:335. Intr. 1913. Zone (V)?

Related species: **R. litiénse** Balf. f. Close to the preceding: lvs. oblong to oval, 4–8 cm. long, glaucous beneath; pedicels 1.5–2.5 cm. long; corolla about 5 cm. across, without markings. W. China. Intr. 1913.—**R. Wàrdii** W. W. Sm. Lvs. oblong-oval to suborbicular, 5–10 cm. long, glaucous beneath and reticulate:

ds. 7–14; pedicels 2.5–4 cm. long, slightly glandular; corolla 5–7 cm. across, without markings. B.S.3:428.t. G.C.89:416. N.F.4:7. W. China. Intr. 1913. Zone VII?

17. **R. longesquamàtum** Schneid. Shrub to 3 m.; young brts. covered with brown shaggy hairs; scales of buds persistent: lvs. obovate-oblong, 6–12 cm. long, acute, rounded or subcordate at base, dark green above, on midrib beneath densely rufous-villous like the petioles: fls. 6–15 cm.; corolla broad-campanulate, 5–6 cm. across, pink with dark red blotch; stamens shorter than corolla, pubescent at base; sepals densely rufous-villous and glandular like the pedicels; ovary stipitate-glandular; style glandular at base. Fl.vii. B.M. 9430(c). (*R. Brettii* Hemsl.) W. China. Intr. 1904. Zone VII?

Related species: **R. pachýtrichum** Franch. Brts. with brown bristly hairs; bud-scales deciduous: lvs. narrow-oblong to oblong-ovate, 8–15 cm. long, acuminate or apiculate, rufous-pubescent on midrib beneath and on petioles; corolla 3–4 cm. across, campanulate, pale pink to white; sepals small, triangular; pedicels shaggy. W. China. Intr. 1903. Zone VII?—**R. strigillósum** Franch. Shrub to 6 m.; young brts. with white bristly hairs, often glandular: lvs. oblong-lanceolate, 7–14 cm. long, acuminate, cordate, with brown bristly hairs beneath chiefly on midrib: fls. campanulate, red, sometimes white, 3.5 cm. across; filaments glabrous; pedicels and calyx bristly. B.M.8864(c). G.C.73: 135. W. China. Intr. 1904. Zone VII?

18. **R. auriculàtum** Hemsl. Shrub to 7 m.; winter-buds with acuminate or aristate scales; brts. stipitate-glandular: lvs. oblong, 12–30 cm. long, obtuse and apiculate, auriculate at base, dark green above, rusty-tomentose beneath; petiole glandular-pubescent: fls. 8–15, fragrant; pedicels 2.5–3.5 cm. long, glandular-villous; calyx with short glandular-pubescent lobes; corolla white to pinkish, spotted with green or rose-color, campanulate-funnelform, 7-lobed, 6–9 cm. wide; stamens 14, glabrous; style longer than stamens, shorter than corolla, glandular; ovary glandular. Fl.viii. B.M.8786(c). Gn.86:455;87:539. Millais, Rhod. 2:48,t(h). C. China. Intr. 1900. Zone VII?

19. **R. Traillanum** Forrest & W. W. Sm. Shrub or small tree to 10 m.; young brts. floccose: lvs. elliptic or lanceolate to oblong-lanceolate, 6–11 cm. long, rounded or short-acuminate, rounded to subcordate at base, minutely rugulose above, with a close tawny or grayish green tomentum beneath; petiole 1.5–2.5 cm. long: fls. 10–15; pedicels about 2 cm. long, floccose; calyx small, fimbriate; corolla funnel-campanulate, 3.5–4 cm. across, white or flushed rose, with crimson spots, lobes rounded, emarginate; filaments hairy at base; ovary 8–9-celled, sparingly pilose; style glabrous. Fl.v–vi. W. China. Cult. 1933. Zone VII.

Related species: **R. dictyòtum** Tagg. Lvs. oblong-elliptic to oblanceolate, with a loose detachable tomentum beneath, midrib glabrescent; corolla 4–5 cm. across, flushed pink, spotted crimson; ovary densely floccose, 6-celled. S. E. Tibet. Intr. 1923. Zone VII.

20. **R. campanulàtum** D. Don. Shrub to 5 m.; young brts. glabrous: lvs. elliptic to elliptic-oblong, 8–14 cm. long, usually obtuse and mucronate, broad-cuneate to subcordate, dark green and glossy above, ferrugineous-tomentose beneath: fls. many; corolla broad-campanulate, 5 cm. across, rosy-purple, spotted purple; stamens pubescent at base; ovary 6–7-celled, glabrous; calyx small, pubescent. Fl.v. B.M.3759(c). L.B.1944(c). H.U.1:255. Gn.59:294. Sikkim, Nepal. Intr. 1825. Zone VII?

Related species: **R. Wallíchii** Hook. f. Lvs. elliptic, cordate at base, beneath with a loose tomentum of separate tufts: ovary 5–6 celled. B.M.4928(c). (*R. campanulatum* var. W. Hook. f.) Sikkim. Cult. 1856. Zone VII?—**R. aeruginòsum** Hook. f. Lvs. elliptic or oval, apiculate at apex, obtuse or subcordate at base, glaucous with a verdigris bloom above, particularly when young, with a rusty woolly tomentum beneath: fls. lilac-rose to reddish purple; ovary 5–8-celled. Hook. f. Rhodod. Sikkim t.22. Sikkim. Intr. about 1850. Zone VII.

21. R. adenógynum Diels. Shrub to 3 m.: lvs. oblong-ovate to lance-oblong, 5–12 cm. long, acute to acuminate, rounded or subcordate at base with a thick woolly tawny tomentum beneath; petiole 2 cm. long: fls. about 12; pedicels 1.5–3 cm. long, glandular and tomentose; calyx 1.5 cm. long, with unequal stipitate-glandular and gland-ciliate lobes: corolla funnel-campanulate, 5 cm. across, white, flushed rose and spotted crimson, with broad rounded lobes; filaments pubescent at base: ovary glandular, 5–6-celled; style glandular near base. Fl.v–vi. B.M.9253(c). G.C.79:339;89:33. S.R.632. W. China. Cult. 1917. Zone VII.

Related species: **R. Balfouriànum** Diels. Lvs. lance-ovate, 5–8 cm. long, acute to acuminate, with a crustaceous pale cinnamon tomentum beneath: calyx 1 cm. long; corolla pale rose with crimson markings. W. China. Intr. 1906. Zone VII.—**R. detónsum** Balf. f. & Forrest. Lvs. oblong to oblong-elliptic, abruptly short-acuminate or obtusish, with a floccose brownish detachable tomentum beneath: calyx 3–5 mm. long; corolla 5–7-lobed, rose-pink with a few crimson spots; stamens 10–14; style glandular except near apex. W. China. Cult. 1933. Zone VII.

22. R. rùfum Batal. Shrub to 5 m.; brts. whitish floccose at first, soon glabrous: lvs. elliptic to oblong or oblong-obovate, 7–11 cm. long, obtuse or acutish, obtuse or rounded at base, tawny or rust-brown woolly-tomentose beneath including midrib; petiole 1.5–2 cm. long: fls. 6–12: pedicels 1.5 cm. long, floccose; calyx minute; corolla funnel-campanulate, 3–4 cm. across, white to pinkish purple, spotted crimson, puberulous within at base; filaments puberulous at base; ovary woolly. Fl.v–vi. J.A.9:t.13(h). N. W. China. Intr. 1925. Zone V or IV? Of slow growth.

Related species: **R. cucullàtum** Hand.-Mazz. Lvs. narrow-obovate to oblanceolate, acute to obtuse and mucronate, cuneate, beneath with a woolly rusty-red tomentum including the midrib; petiole short: infl. compact; calyx minute; corolla funnelform, about 4 cm. across, white, spotted crimson; ovary glandular. W. China. Cult. 1933. Zone VII.—**R. Wàsoni** Hemsl. & Wils. Lvs. elliptic or ovate to oblong-ovate, 4–8 cm. long, acute to short-acuminate, rounded to subcordate at base, rarely broad-cuneate, beneath with soft bright brown tomentum: pedicels floccose-tomentose; corolla funnel-campanulate, 3.5–4.5 cm. across, pink to creamy-white, spotted; anthers nearly black; ovary tomentose. B.M.9190(c). W. China. Intr. 1904. Zone VII?

23. R. Przewálskii Maxim. Compact shrub to 2.5 m.; young brts. yellow, glabrous: lvs. oval or obovate to ovate, 5–10 cm. long, 2–4 cm. broad, acute or abruptly apiculate, rounded to subcordate at base, rarely broad-cuneate, dark green above, with close scurfy brown tomentum beneath; petiole yellow: flowers 12–15; corolla campanulate-funnelform, 3–4 cm. across, white to deep pink, spotted purple, lobes short and broad, emarginate; stamens glabrous or slightly pubescent at base; ovary and style glabrous; calyx short, with rounded lobes, glabrous; pedicels glabrous, about 1 cm. long. Fl.vi–vii. (*R. kialense* Franch.) N. W. China. Intr. 1880. Zone V.

Related species: **R. sphaeroblástum** Balf. f. & Forrest. Lvs. oval to oval-oblong, 7.5–15 cm. long, 4–6.5 cm. broad, abruptly mucronate, rounded at base, rusty woolly-tomentose beneath: calyx ciliate; corolla white, spotted crimson; filaments puberulous at base. W. China. Cult. 1933. Zone VII.—**R. agglutinàtum** Balf. f. & Forrest. Lvs. oblong-oval or broad-obovate, 4–7.5 cm. long, abruptly apiculate, rounded at base, with a tawny thin tomentum beneath: corolla white, tinged rose, spotted crimson; filaments hairy below the middle. W. China. Cult. 1925. Zone VII.—**R. schizopéplum** Balf. f. & Forrest. Lvs. elliptic to oblong, 6–8 cm. long, abruptly apiculate, rounded at base, beneath with a rather thin light brown tomentum splitting irregularly: pedicels 1 cm. long; corolla campanulate, 4–5 cm. across, rose, spotted crimson; filaments hairy below the middle. W. China. Intr. ? Zone VII.—**R. flavorùfum** Balf. f. & Forrest. Lvs. oval to oval-oblong, 4.5–12 cm. long, abruptly apiculate, rounded or subcordate at base, beneath with a thin yellow tomentum later reddish and splitting: corolla funnel-campanulate, 4–5 cm. across, white or rose, with a few crimson spots; filaments hairy below the middle. W. China, S. E. Tibet. Cult. 1925. Zone VII.—**R. aganníphum** Balf. f. & Ward. Lvs. oblong to elliptic-oblong, 6–9 cm. long, acute or abruptly apiculate, rounded or subcordate at base, beneath with a white or light yellowish lustrous tomentum: corolla funnel-campanulate, 4.5–5 cm. across, white or flushed rose, spotted crimson; filaments sparingly puberulous at base. W. China, S. E. Tibet. Cult. 1933. Zone VII.

Sect. 2. LEPIPHERUM Don.

(Series: Triflorum, 24–31; Heliolepis, 32; Saluense, 33; Moupinense, 34; Carolinianum, 35–37; Ferrugineum, 38–39; Glaucum, 40; Boothii, 41; Lepidotum, 42; Campylogynum, 43; Micranthum, 44; Lapponicum, 45–51.)

24. R. Keìskei Miq. Shrub to 3 m. or sometimes procumbent; brts. slightly scaly: lvs. elliptic-oblong to lanceolate, 3–6 cm. long, acute to rounded at ends, mucronate, sometimes subauriculate at base, sparingly scaly above, densely so and pale beneath; petiole 4–6 mm. long, bristly and pubescent like base of midrib: fls. 3–6; corolla broad-campanulate, with short tube, sparingly scaly without, 4 cm. across, pale yellow; stamens exserted, slightly pilose near base; style glabrous, longer than stamens; calyx minute; pedicels densely scaly. Fl.v. B.M.8300(c). Millais, Rhodod. 198. R.H.1917:348,t(c). N.T.1:71. Japan. Intr. 1905. Zone (V).

Related species: **R. ambíguum** Hemsl. Lvs. elliptic to lanceolate, 4–7 cm. long, acute, subcordate or rounded at base, slightly scaly above, more densely so beneath: fls. pale yellow, spotted yellow-green, 5 cm. across, slightly scaly outside. B.M.8400(c). Gs.7:125(h). W. China. Intr. 1904. Zone VII?—**R. lutéscens** Franch. Shrub to 2 m.; brts. scaly: lvs. lanceolate or ovate-lanceolate, 3–8 cm. long, long-acuminate, cuneate, sparingly scaly above, more densely so and light green beneath: fls. pale yellow, rotate-funnelform, 3–4 cm. across; calyx minute, scaly. Millais, Rhod. 2:244,t(c). R.H.1914:324,t(c). B.M.8851 (c). S.R.789. J.L.49:t.14. W. China. Intr. 1904. Zone VII?

25. R. Hanceànum Hemsl. Shrub to 1 m.; brts. slightly scaly: lvs. elliptic-lanceolate to elliptic-obovate, 4–8 cm. long, acute to acuminate, rounded to broad-cuneate at base, minutely scaly beneath; petiole 3–8 mm. long: fls. 5–many, racemose, with persistent acuminate bud-scales; calyx-lobes oblong, 6 mm. long, glabrous or slightly scaly and ciliate; corolla funnel-campanulate, 2.5 cm. across, pale yellow, glabrous; stamens exserted, pilose below. Fl.v. B.M.8669(c). K.B.1914:202,t. W. China. Intr. 1909. Zone VII?

26. R. Augustìni Hemsl. Shrub to 6 m.; brts. scaly and pubescent: lvs. oblong-lanceolate to elliptic-oblong, 3–8 cm. long, acuminate or acute, broad-cuneate, dark green and minutely rugulose and puberulous above, scaly beneath and setose on midrib like petiole: fls. 3–4; corolla broad-campanulate, 3.5–5 cm. across, pale to purple pink, rarely nearly white, spotted yellow, tube much shorter than lobes; stamens as long or slightly shorter than corolla, pubescent toward the base; style longer, sepals short, ciliate; pedicels 1–2 cm. long. Fl.iv–v. B.M.8477(c). G.C.97:217,t. Gn.91:123(h). F.R.3:162. R.H.1909:18. Millais, Rhodod. 24,t(c);2:88,t(h). C. and W. China. Intr. 1899. Zone VII.—**R. A. album** Wils., f. Fls. white.

Related species: **R. villòsum** Hemsl. & Wils. Brts. scaly and setose: lvs. ovate-oblong, 5–8 cm. long, sparingly scaly and bristly above, more scaly but less bristly beneath and pubescent on midrib: fls. light to dark purple, 3.5–4 cm. across; corolla funnelform; stamens with tuft of hairs near base. W. China. Intr. 1904.

27. R. Davidsoniànum Rehd. & Wils. Brts. sparingly scaly: lvs. elliptic to oblong, rarely lanceolate, 2.5–6 cm. long, acute or short-acuminate, cuneate, sparingly scaly above, densely so and glaucous beneath, thinly coriaceous: fls. in few- to several-fld. terminal and axillary clusters; corolla funnelform-campanulate, 2.5–3 cm. across, pink, glabrous, lobes ovate, as long as tube; stamens slightly exserted, villous at base; style glabrous, longer than stamens; calyx minute. Fl.v. B.M.8605(c). R.H.1914:323,324. Gn.78:316. W. China. Intr. 1908. Zone VII?

28. **R. yunnanénse** Franch. Half-evergreen shrub to 2 m.; brts. slightly scaly: lvs. thin, narrow-elliptic or oblong-obovate to elliptic-lanceolate, 4–7.5 cm. long, acute at ends, ciliate, sparingly bristly above or sometimes glabrous, slightly scaly on both sides, thin: fl.-clusters terminal and often also axillary, 4–5-fld.; corolla broad-funnelform, 4–5 cm. across, white or slightly pinkish, with crimson spots; stamens exserted, hairy near base; style glabrous, longer than stamens; calyx minute. Fl.v. B.M.7614(c). G.C.54:396(h),397. Gn.88: 168(h). M.G.1903:173. F.R.2:360. W. China. Intr. 1889. Zone VI.

Related species: **R. siderophýllum** Franch. Lvs. elliptic to elliptic-oblong, 3–6 cm. long, acute or acuminulate, broad-cuneate, slightly scaly and not bristly above, paler and with yellow scales beneath, coriaceous: fls. 6–8, pale blush, spotted dark brown, 3–3.5 cm. across, lower lobes longer than upper ones; style as long, stamens shorter than corolla. W. China. Intr. 1904. Zone VII.

29. **R. hormóphorum** Balf. f. & Forrest. Shrub to 1 m.; young brts. scaly: lvs. short-petioled, lanceolate to narrow-elliptic, 3–5 cm. long, acute at ends, ciliate and with bristly hairs above, pale green beneath and sparingly scaly: fls. 2–4; pedicels sparingly scaly, 6–8 mm. long; calyx minute; corolla funnel-campanulate, about 3 cm. across, lavender or rose, spotted; stamens pubescent below. Fl.v. Gn.89:659. W. China. Intr. 1918. Zone VII?

30. **R. Seàrsiae** Rehd. & Wils. Shrub to 5 m.; brts. densely scaly: lvs. oblanceolate, 5–8 cm. long, acuminate, cuneate, glaucescent and densely scaly beneath; petioles 5–8 mm. long: fls. 3–8; pedicels 1 cm. long, densely scaly; calyx lobes unequal, the longer 4–5 mm. long, glandular and ciliate; corolla funnel-campanulate, white or pale purple; stamens pubescent at base. Fl.vi. B.M.8993(c). S.R.808. W. China. Intr. 1908. Zone VII.

Related species: **R. Bodinièri** Franch. Lvs. lance-oblong to obovate, long-acuminate, rounded to broad-cuneate at base, laxly scaly beneath: fls. 6–7, rose, spotted purple; calyx minute. W. China. Cult. 1933. Zone VII.—**R. longístylum** Rehd. & Wils. Lvs. oblanceolate to elliptic-oblong, 2.5–5 cm. long, acute, attenuate at base, laxly and minutely scaly beneath; fls. 8–20, pink, 2–2.5 cm. across; calyx-lobes unequal, to 5 mm. long, slightly ciliate. R.H.1914:232,233 (h). M.O.303(h). W. China. Intr. 1908. Zone VII.

31. **R. concínnum** Hemsl. Shrub to 3 m.; brts. densely scaly: lvs. elliptic-obovate or elliptic-ovate to lance-oblong, 3–5 cm. long, acute, broad-cuneate or rounded at base, scaly on both sides, densely so and glaucescent beneath; petiole 4–5 mm. long: fls. 3–6; calyx very short; corolla funnel-campanulate, pale or rosy purple, rarely white, spotted brown, scaly, sometimes slightly so; stamens densely villous at base; style glabrous. Fl.vi. B.M.8280,8620(c). R.H.1917:348,t(c). Gs.7:124(h). (*R. yanthinum* Bur. & Franch., *R. Benthamianum* Hemsl., *R. coombense* Hemsl.) W. China. Intr. 1901. Zone VII. —**R. c. laetévirens** Cowan, f. Lvs. green beneath between the scales, larger: corolla deep crimson-purple, scaly.—**R. c. lepidánthum** (Rehd. & Wils.) Rehd., var. Lvs. larger and broader, to 7.5 by 3 cm.: corolla larger, dark purple, rather densely villous and scaly outside. (*R. pseudoyanthinum* Balf. f.) Cult. 1908.

Related species: **R. polýlepis** Franch. Lvs. oblanceolate to oblong-oblanceolate, acute at ends, 5–10 cm. long, with overlapping scales beneath: corolla dark purple; style minutely pubescent at base or glabrous. R.H.1914:324. W. China. Intr. 1904. Zone VII.—**R. bracteàtum** Rehd. & Wils. Lvs. elliptic-ovate to oblong, 3.5–5 cm. long, obtusely mucronate, rounded at base, rather densely scaly beneath, passing toward base of brts. into linear or spatulate bracts: pedicels slender, 2 cm. long; corolla white, spotted red, laxly scaly outside, pubescent within at base; style with a few hairs near base. B.M.9031(c). W. China. Intr. 1908. Zone VII?

32. **R. rubiginòsum** Franch. Shrub or tree to 10 m.; brts. scaly, purplish: lvs. elliptic to lance-elliptic, 3.5–8 cm. long, acute to acuminate, cuneate, densely red-brown scaly beneath; petiole 6–10 mm. long: fls. 4–8; pedicels 1 cm. long, densely scaly; calyx very short; corolla funnelform, 3.5–5 cm. across, rosy-lilac, spotted brown; stamens pubescent at base; style glabrous. Fl.ɪv–v. B.M.7621(c). S.R.329. G.C.78:227,t. Gn.89:376(h). W. China. Intr. 1889. Zone VII.

Related species: **R. heliólepis** Franch. Lvs. elliptic-oblong, 7–10 cm. long, acute to acuminate, distinctly mucronate, rounded or broad-cuneate at base, fairly densely scaly beneath, aromatic: corolla 3–3.5 cm. across, rosy-red, spotted crimson; style pubescent at base. W. China. Intr. 1912. Zone VII.

33. **R. saluenénse** Franch. Shrub to 0.70 m.; brts. scaly and bristly: lvs. ovate-elliptic or oval-obovate to elliptic-oblong, 2–3 cm. long, rounded or obtuse and mucronate, rounded or broad-cuneate at base, laxly scaly above, densely so beneath; petiole short, bristly: fls. 2–3; calyx-lobes oval, 6–8 mm. long, scaly along the middle and puberulous, ciliate; corolla broad-campanulate, 3.5–4.5 cm. across, purple-crimson with darker markings, scaly and pubescent outside; filaments villous near base. Fl.ɪv–v. B.M.9095(c). S.R. 599. W. China. Intr. 1914. Zone VII.

34. **R. moupinénse** Franch. Shrub to 1 m.; brts. bristly: lvs. oval or ovate-elliptic to oblong-elliptic, 3–5 cm. long, obtuse or sometimes acute, mucronate, rounded or broad-cuneate at base, glaucescent and rather densely scaly beneath; petiole bristly and scaly: fls. 1–3; pedicels very short; calyx 4 mm. long, scaly, lobes rounded; corolla broad-funnelform, 4–5 cm. across, white, spotted, glabrous outside; stamens pubescent below; anthers dark purple; style glabrous. Fl.ɪv. B.M.8598(c). S.R.504. J.L.62:f.104(h). G.C. 75:161(h) ;94:373,t. W. China. Intr. 1909. Zone VII.

35. **R. caroliniànum** Rehd. Upright shrub to 2 m., usually lower and compact: lvs. elliptic to narrow-elliptic, 5–8 cm. long, acutish or abruptly short-acuminate, broad-cuneate, glabrous above, ferrugineous scaly, often very densely so beneath, sometimes glaucescent; petiole 5–10 mm. long: fls. 5–10, before or with the young lvs.; corolla broad-funnelform, 3–4 cm. across, pale rosy purple, not or slightly spotted, tube gradually widened from the base, as long or shorter than lobes, glabrous or sparingly scaly outside; stamens shorter than corolla, villous at base; style glabrous, about 1.5 cm. long. Fl.v–vi. B.R.37(c). Add.1:t.1(c). M.G.32:58(h). (*R. punctatum* Small, not Andr.) N. C. Cult. 1815. Zone V.—**R. c. album** Rehd., var. Fls. white or nearly white. (*R. c.* var. *Margarettae* Ashe.) N. C. Intr. 1895.—**R. c. foliàtum** Rehd., var. Shrub to 5 m., of looser habit: lvs. usually longer and narrower:· fls. slightly smaller, spotted, more lepidote outside, appearing after the lvs. N. C. Intr. before 1880.

R. c. × *ferrugineum;* see under No. 37.

36. **R. mínus** Michx. Straggling shrub to 3 m.: lvs. narrow-elliptic to lanceolate, 4–10 cm. long, acute at ends, sometimes acuminate, quite entire, glabrous above, scaly and often glaucous beneath: fls. 6–10; corolla funnelform, 2.5–3 cm. across, rosy-pink, spotted greenish, scaly outside, tube cylindric or nearly so, longer than the ovate lobes crinkled at margin; stamens about as long as corolla; style shorter, glabrous, 2–2.5 cm. long; sepals short. Fl.vi–vii. A.R.36(c). B.M.2285(c). (*R. punctatum* Andr., *R. Cuthberti* Small.) S. C. to Ga. and Ala. Intr. 1786. Zone V.

R. m. × *hirsutum;* see No. 37.—*R. m.* × *ferrugineum;* see under No. 37.

Related species: **R. Chapmánii** Gray. Brs. upright, rigid: lvs. oblong to oval, 2–5 cm. long, obtuse, revolute; petiole 3–6 mm. long: fls. rose-colored; corolla-tube 1.5–2 cm. long. N.H.18:49. W. Fla. Intr. 1936. Zone VII?

37. ✕ **R. myrtifòlium** Lodd. (*R. hirsutum* ✕ *minus*). Compact shrub to 1.5 m.: lvs. elliptic, 2.5–6 cm. long, slightly crenulate, densely scaly beneath with brown scales, occasionally ciliate near base when young: corolla funnel-form, about 2.5 cm. across, light rosy pink, with cylindric tube, longer than the spreading lobes; stamens little longer than tube; style shorter than stamens, about 3 times as long as ovary, sepals ovate, about half as long as ovary. Fl.vi. L.B.908(c). S.L.294(h). (*R. ovalifolium* Hort., *R. ovatum* Hort., not Hook.) Orig. before 1824. Zone V.

Similar hybrids: **R. arbutifòlium** Rehd. (*R. ferrugineum* ✕ *minus*). Lvs. elliptic to narrow-elliptic, 3–6 cm. long, acute at ends, dark dull green above, scaly beneath with pale scales interspersed with darker ones: fls. rose-colored; calyx minute. (*R. daphnoides* Hort., *R. Hammondii* Hort.) Origin unknown.—**R. laetévirens** Rehd. (*R. carolinianum* ✕ *ferrugineum*). Similar to the preceding: low wide-spreading shrub: lvs. somewhat narrower and longer, brighter green: fls. somewhat larger, about 3 cm. across. (*R. Wilsoni* Hort., not Nutt., *R. punctatum* Hort., not Andr., *R. oleaefolium* Hort.)

38. **R. ferrugíneum** L. Dense shrub to 1 m.; young brts. covered with rusty scales: lvs. elliptic-oblong to oblong-lanceolate, 2–4 cm. long, acute at ends, lustrous dark green and sparingly scaly above, densely rusty-scaly beneath: fls. 6–12, pink to carmine; corolla funnelform, scaly outside, the tube about twice as long as the oblong spreading lobes, about 1.5 cm. across; style nearly twice as long as ovary; sepals very short; pedicels scaly, about 8 mm. long. Fl.vii–viii. L.B.65(c). R.I.17:t.106,f.1,2(c). F.D.20:t.2029(c). Mts. of C. Eu. Intr. 1752. Zone IV.—**R. f. album** D. Don, var. Fls. white. S.B.II.3:t.258(c).—**R. f. atrococcíneum** Bean, var. Fls. nearly scarlet.

R. f. ✕ *hirsutum* = **R. halénse** Gremblich. Intermediate between the parents. (*R. intermedium* Tausch, not Wender., *R. hirsutiforme* Gremblich.) R.I.17:t.1157(c). F.D.20:t.2030(c). Occurs occasionally with the parents. Cult. 1870.—*R. f.* ✕ *carolinianum;* see under No. 37.

A related species is **R. Kótschyi** Simonk. Smaller and lower: lvs. elliptic-oblong, 1–2 cm. long, obtusish, glabrous above: fls. rosy-pink; style as long or shorter than ovary. R.I.17:t.1157,f.2,3(c). Gn.56:159. (*R. myrtifolium* Schott & Kotschy, not Lodd., *R. ferrugineum* var. *m.* Schroet.) Carpathian Mts. Intr. 1846. Zone V.

39. **R. hirsùtum** L. Shrub to 1 m.; young brts. scaly and hirsute: lvs. elliptic-oblong to obovate, 1–3 cm. long, obtuse to acutish, bright green and glabrous above, bright green and with scattered scales beneath, crenulate and ciliate with long hairs: fls. similar to those of the preceding species; corolla slightly scaly outside; pedicels 1–2.5 cm. long, hirsute and scaly; sepals lance-olate, as long as ovary, hirsute. Fl.vi. L.B.479(c). B.M.1853(c). R.I.17:t.107, f.3–5(c). F.D.20:t.2031(c). Mts. of Eu. Intr. 1685. Zone IV. Thriving in limestone soil.—**R. h. albiflòrum** Schroet., var. Fls. white. (*R. h.* var. *album* Schinz & Kell.)—**R. h. laciniàtum** Schroet., f. Lvs. deeply toothed or incised, at least near base: fls. white. Schroeter, Pflanzenleben Alp. 113.

40. **R. glaùcum** Hook. f. Shrub to 2 m.; brs. scaly: lvs. oval to elliptic-oblong or lance-oblong, 3–8 cm. long, acute or obtuse, mucronate, rounded to broad-cuneate at base, dull green above, glaucous beneath, with scattered brown and smaller yellow scales; petiole 3–8 mm. long: fls. 5–6; pedicels scaly, 1–2 cm. long; calyx-lobes lance-ovate, 8 mm. long, acute, scaly; corolla campanulate, with spreading rounded lobes, pink, 2.5 cm. across; stamens 10, pubescent near base. Fl.iv–v. S.R.299. G.C.67:275;101:215,t. Himal. Intr. about 1850. Zone VII.

41. **R. megèratum** Balf. f. & Forrest. Dwarf shrub to 0.5 m., sometimes prostrate; brts. pilose: lvs. elliptic or elliptic-obovate, 2–3 cm. long, obtuse and mucronate, broad-cuneate to rounded at base, bright green above,

glaucous and rather densely scaly beneath, sometimes sparingly ciliate; petiole bristly: fls. 1–3; pedicels densely bristly; calyx 8 mm. long, with oval rounded lobes; corolla campanulate, 2–2.5 cm. across, yellow, slightly scaly; stamens villous near base. Fl.v–vi. B.M.9120(c). G.C.89:431;100: 337(h). W. China. Cult. 1926. Zone VII?

42. **R. lepidòtum** Wall. ex G. Don. Shrub to 1 m.; brts. slightly scaly: lvs. elliptic to oblanceolate, 2–3.5 cm. long, obtuse or acute at apex, cuneate, densely scaly beneath with contiguous scales; petiole short: fls. 1–4; pedicels slender, 1.5–2 cm. long, densely glandular; calyx-lobes 4 mm. long, broad-oval, scaly; corolla campanulate, about 2.5 cm. across, with short and broad tube, purple or rosy-crimson, spotted, densely scaly outside; stamens 8, pubescent below; style 3 mm. long, thick, decurved. Fl.v–vi. B.M.4657(c). S.R.441. Himal. to W. China. Cult. 1852. Zone VII.

43. **R. campylógynum** Franch. Shrub to 2 m.; brts. glandular: lvs. obovate to oblong-obovate, 1–2.5 cm. long, obtuse and mucronate, cuneate, margin recurved and crenulate, pale green or glaucescent beneath and sparingly scaly at first; petiole short: fls. 1–4; pedicels 2–3 cm. long, slightly scaly; calyx 3–5 mm. long, glabrous, lobes rounded; corolla campanulate, 1.5–2 cm. long and as wide, with 5–6 short rounded lobes, rosy-purple to black-purple, glabrous outside; stamens 10–12, pubescent near base; ovary glandular-scaly; style thick, 1 cm. long, decurved. Fl.v–vi. B.M.9407A(c). J.L. 59:f.127(h). W. China. Intr. 1912. Zone VII?

44. **R. micránthum** Turcz. Shrub to 2.5 m.; brts. scaly and slightly pubescent at first: lvs. elliptic-oblong to oblanceolate, 2–3.5 cm. long, acute at ends, glabrous above, densely ferrugineous-scaly beneath; petiole 1–3 mm. long: fls. in many-fld. dense racemes 3–3.5 cm. across; corolla campanulate, white, with oval spreading lobes, as long or shorter than the tube, 1 cm. across, scaly outside; style longer than corolla, shorter than stamens; filaments glabrous; sepals ovate to lanceolate, often ciliate; pedicels scaly, 1–2 cm. long: fr. oblong, 5–8 mm. long. Fl.v–vi. B.M.8198(c). Gn.84:270. M.O.t.29. N.K. 8:t.7. N. Korea to Manch. and N. China. Intr. 1900. Zone IV. Very distinct species, in habit and fls. resembling Ledum.

45. **R. cantàbile** Hutch. Shrub to 1 m.; brts. scaly: lvs. ovate- to oblong-elliptic, 2–3 cm. long, obtuse at ends, densely scaly on both sides, rusty beneath; petiole short: infl. dense, 5–10-fld.; calyx-lobes oval, 4–5 mm. long, ciliate, scaly only at base; corolla funnelform, purple-blue or violet, 2–2.5 cm. across, glabrous outside; stamens villous toward the base; style villous below the middle. Fl.v. B.M.8963(c). W. China. Cult. 1922. Zone VII? One of the best of this group.

Related species: **R. Websteriànum** Rehd. & Wils. Densely branched upright shrub; brts. densely grayish scaly: lvs. oval or elliptic-oblong, 6–15 mm. long, obtuse, usually cuneate, densely scaly on both sides, light yellowish gray or grayish white beneath: fls. 1–3, rosy-purple, 2.5–3 cm. across; stamens 10; sepals ovate, rounded, 2–5 mm. long. W. China. Intr. 1908. Zone VI?—**R. flàvidum** Franch. Shrub to 1 m.: lvs. oblong-ovate, 1–1.5 cm. long, dark green above, paler beneath, scaly on both sides: fls. 3–6, yellow, 2 cm. across; corolla with very short tube and spreading wavy lobes; stamens and style scarcely as long as corolla; sepals oblong, 5–6 mm. long, scaly; pedicels short. B.M.8326(c). G.C. 47:229. J.L.36:55. B.S.359. (*R. primulìnum* Hemsl.) W. China. Intr. 1905. Zone VI.

46. **R. intricàtum** Franch. Shrub to 0.5 m.; young brts. scaly: lvs. broad-ovate to elliptic, 6–12 mm. long, dark green above, paler beneath, densely scaly on both sides: fls. 5–6: corolla broad-funnelform, with short rounded lobes, 1.5 cm. across, violet-purple; stamens pubescent at base, included in

the tube; style shorter than stamens; sepals short, triangular, scaly. Fl.vɪ
B.M.8163(c). G.C.41:262(h);63:143(h). Gn.78:29,t(c,h),190(h);87:512(h)
S.L.293(h). (*R. nigro-punctatum* Hort., not Franch.) W. China. Intr. 1904
Zone VI?

47. **R. lappònicum** Wahlenb. Prostrate shrub, rarely to 0.5 cm. tall
young brts. very scaly: lvs. oblong, 6–20 mm. long, obtuse or abruptly pointed
dark green and rugose above, densely covered with brownish scales beneath
petiole 2–3 mm. long: fls. 3–6; corolla broad-campanulate, 1.5 cm. across
bright purple; stamens 5–8, as long as corolla, glabrous; sepals triangular
ciliate; pedicels 6–10 mm. long. Fl.vɪ–vɪɪ. B.M.3106(c). M.G.25:136(h)
Mts. of N. Am., N. Eu., N. Asia. Intr. 1825. Zone II.

48. **R. hippophaeoìdes** Balf. f. & W. W. Sm. Upright shrub to 1 m.: lvs
oval-oblong to oblong, 2–3 cm. long, obtuse and mucronate, cuneate, densely
scaly on both sides, beneath pale gray with often overlapping scales: fls
4–8; pedicels 3–4 mm. long; calyx 2 mm. long, usually ciliate; corolla blue
purple to bluish rose, broad-campanulate, 2–2.5 cm. across, tube hairy within
stamens pubescent at base, alternately longer and shorter; anthers dark red
brown; style as long as stamens. Fl.ɪv. B.M.9156(c). G.C.77:94,t. N.F.ɪ
93(h). Gt.79:161(h). W. China. Intr. 1913. Zone VII.

49. **R. parvifòlium** Adams. Shrub to 1 m., with erect and spreading brs.
scaly when young: lvs. narrow-elliptic to oblong or lance-oblong, 5–20 mm
long, acute or obtuse and mucronate, cuneate, dark green and scaly above
densely covered beneath with pale or rusty scales: fls. 2–5, with persistent
bud-scales, corolla broad-campanulate, deeply 5-lobed, 1.5–2 cm. across, rosy
purple; stamens 10, slightly shorter than corolla, villous near base; style
longer than stamens; sepals ovate to oblong-ovate, 1–2 mm. long, scaly
ciliate, sometimes only slightly so. Fl.ɪv–v. Gt.26:t.904(c). B.M.9229(c)
G.C.63:76;87:123(h). N.K.8:t.6,8. Gn.89:113(h). (*R. confertissimum* Nakai.)
Siberia, Korea. Cult. 1877. Zone IV.

Related species: **R. impéditum** Balf. f. & W. W. Sm. Lvs. elliptic to oblong,
8–12 mm. long, obtuse, densely scaly, red-brown beneath: fls. 1–2; calyx-lobes
oblong, 3 mm. long, slightly scaly; corolla mauve or purple-blue, 1.5 cm. across,
tube villous within; stamens long-exserted, villous at base. G.C.78:41,t. J.L.
50:f.65(h). W. China. Cult. 1918. Zone VII.—R. **fastigiàtum** Franch. Lvs
elliptic to elliptic-oblanceolate, 6–8 mm. long, obtuse, densely scaly: fls. 4–5;
calyx-lobes oval, 3–4 mm. long, slightly scaly; corolla 2 mm. across, light purple.
G.C.39:263(h). J.L.50:f.64(h). W. China. Intr. 1911. Zone VII.

50. **R. scintíllans** Balf. f. & W. W. Sm. Small upright shrub; brts. densely
scaly; lvs. elliptic-oblanceolate to oblong, 1–1.5 cm. long, obtuse and mucronate, densely scaly on both sides, pale brown beneath: fls. 2–3; pedicels
very short, densely scaly; calyx very short, scaly; corolla, 1.5 cm. across
lavender-blue; stamens villous near base. Fl.ɪv–v. G.C.75:78. Gn.88:70. W
China. Cult. 1924. Zone VI.

Related species: **R. nitídulum** Rehd. & Wils. Brts. densely fuscous-scaly:
lvs. oval to ovate, 7–12 mm. long, obtuse, densely scaly on both sides: fls. 1–2,
violet-purple, rotate-funnelform, 2.5 cm. across; stamens 8–10, as long as corolla;
sepals ovate to oblong-ovate, 2 mm. long. W. China. Intr. 1904. Zone VI?—
R. n. nubígenum Rehd. & Wils., var. Lvs. 4–8 mm. long: fls. lilac-purple, about
2 cm. broad; sepals oblong, nearly as long as ovary, usually colored. W. China.
Intr. 1903.

51. **R. drumònium** Balf. f. & Ward. Shrub to 0.5 m.; brts. short, crowded
scaly: lvs. elliptic to narrow-elliptic, 4–8 mm. long, obtuse to acutish, mucronate, densely scaly on both sides, red-brown beneath, often with scattered
darker scales: fls. solitary; calyx 2 mm. long, scaly, ciliate; corolla broad-

funnelform, 1–1.5 cm. across, mauve, villous within the tube; style slightly shorter than stamens. Fl.v–vi. W. China. Cult. 1933. Zone VI.

Related species: **R. achroánthum** Balf. f. & W. W. Sm. Lvs. oval to oval-oblong, 8–15 mm. long, rounded at ends or broad-cuneate at base; fls. 2–3, magenta-red, stamens 5–6; style longer than stamens. W. China. Cult. 1933. Zone VII.

Sect. 3. POGONANTHUM G. Don.
(Series: Cephalanthum, 52; Anthopogon, 53.)

52. R. Sargentiànum Rehd. & Wils. Low shrub to 0.6 m., with upright or ascending brs.; brts. fuscous-tomentose: lvs. oval, 8–15 mm. long, obtuse and mucronulate, broad-cuneate, revolute, scaly above at first, soon glabrous and slightly rugulose, densely rusty-scaly beneath, aromatic: petiole 2–4 mm. long, scaly: fls. 6–12; corolla about 1 cm. across, white or pale yellow, scaly and sparingly pubescent outside; tube 6–7 mm. long; lobes suborbicular; stamens 5, glabrous, inclosed; style glabrous, shorter than stamens; sepals obovate, 3–4 mm. long, ciliate near apex. Fl.vi. B.M.8871(c). W. China. Intr. 1904. Zone VI?

Related species: **R. cephalánthum** Franch. Shrub to 1 m.: lvs. oval to oblong, 1.5–3 cm. long, obtuse, pale brown beneath: fls. in dense clusters, white, about 1 cm. across; stamens slightly pubescent at base; sepals ovate-oblong. Millais, Rhod. 2:40,t(h). W. China. Intr. 1908. Zone VI?—**R. Adámsii** Rehd. Shrub to 0.5 m.: lvs. elliptic or elliptic-ovate, 1.5–2 cm. long, acute, rounded at base: fls. pink or white, glabrous outside; stamens puberulous at base; sepals ovate, 1–2.5 mm. long. Mém. Acad. Sci. St. Pétersb. 2:t.14. (*R. fragrans* Maxim., not Paxt.) E. Siberia. Apparently not yet intr., but probably the hardiest species of this group.

53. R. Collettiànum Aitch. Low shrub, occasionally to 3 m.; brts. fuscous-scaly: lvs. elliptic to elliptic-lanceolate, 4–7 cm. long, acute at ends, dull green above, fulvous-scaly beneath, aromatic: fls. white, in clusters 5–6 cm. across; corolla 2.5 cm. across; lobes oblong, upright-spreading; stamens 10; sepals oblong, ciliate. Fl.v–vi. B.M.7019(c). G.C.III.4:297. J.L.36:331. Afghan. Intr. 1879. Zone VI.

Related species: **R. anthopògon** D. Don. Lvs. oval or obovate, 2–3.5 cm. long, rusty-scaly beneath; fls. sulphur-yellow, about 1.5 cm. across; stamens 6–8; sepals oblong, ciliate. B.M.3947(c). S.R.5. E. Himal. Intr. 1820. Zone VI?

Sect. 4. RHODORASTRUM Maxim.
(Series: Virgatum, 54; Dauricum, 55–56.)

54. R. racemòsum Franch. Upright shrub to 2 m.; brts. scaly: lvs. elliptic to oval or obovate, 1.5–3.5 cm. long, obtuse or acutish, rounded or broad-cuneate at base, glabrous above, glaucous and scaly beneath: fls. in numerous few-fld. clusters along the brts.; corolla pink, wide-campanulate, tube shorter than the oblong lobes; stamens 10, pubescent at base, longer than lobes. Fl.iv–v. B.M.7301(c). Gn.42:t.320(c);87:565(h). Gt.57:t.1577(c). G.C.47: 343. N.H.7:109. W. China. Intr. 1889. Zone (V).

55. R. daùricum L. DAHURIAN R. Upright much-branched shrub to 2 m.; brts. scaly: lvs. deciduous or partly persistent till spring, elliptic to elliptic-ovate to oblong-ovate, 1–5 cm. long, obtuse, rounded or broad-cuneate at base, dark green and slightly scaly above, paler and densely scaly beneath, aromatic: fls. solitary, from axillary buds at end of brts.; corolla rotate-campanulate, 2.5–3.5 cm. across, rosy-purple, puberulous outside, lobes longer than tube; stamens about as long as lobes, villous below the middle; style longer than stamens; calyx minute. Fl.iii–iv. A.R.1:t.4(c). B.M.636(c). L.B. 605(c). G.C.III.12:701;53:51. N.K.8:t.9. N.T.1:73. (*R. dahuricum* DC., *Azalea dahurica* K. Koch.) Altai Mts. to Korea, Manch. and N. Japan. Cult.

1780. Zone IV.—**R. d. sempérvirens** Sims, var. Lvs. dark green, persistent or partly persistent: fls. darker, purple. B.M.1883(c). B.R.194(c). L.B.1584 (c). R.H.1908:198. Gt.53:267. (*R. d.* var. *atrovirens* Ker.)

R. d. × *ciliatum* Hook f. = **R. praecox** Carr. Evergreen or half-evergreen shrub: lvs. elliptic, 2.5–5 cm. long, obtusish to acute, sparingly ciliate, lustrous dark green above, rusty-scaly beneath, sparingly ciliate: fls. few, bright rosy purple, broad-funnelform, about 4 cm. across; sepals ovate, ciliate. Fl.III–IV. R.H.1868:210,t(c). Gn.61:428(h). Gt.56:t.1567(c). G.C.III.12:771. Orig. about 1855.—**R. p. rubrum** Wats. Fls. deeper colored. Gn.38:32,t(c).—**R. p.** "Early gem." Lvs. more ciliate; fls. larger, pale lilac. G.C.II.11:335. Zone (V).

56. **R. mucronulàtum** Turcz. Upright shrub to 2 m.; brts. sparingly scaly: lvs. deciduous, thin, elliptic-lanceolate to lanceolate, 3–7 cm. long, acute or acuminate, cuneate, laxly scaly on both sides, pale green beneath; petiole 3–5 mm. long: fls. before the lvs., 3–6 at end of brts.; pedicels short, scaly; calyx small, scaly; corolla funnel-campanulate, 3–4 cm. across, pale rosy-purple, puberulous outside; stamens villous below the middle; style glabrous, longer than stamens. Fl.III–IV. B.M.8304(c). M.D.1898:1,t(c). G.F. 9:65. G.C.74:41(h). W.A.54,t(h, as *Azalea mucronulata*). (*R. dauricum* var. *m.* Maxim.) N. China, Manch., Korea, Japan. Intr. 1882. Zone IV. Valued for its early profuse fls.; lvs. changing to yellow and bronzy crimson in fall.— **R. m. ciliàtum** Nakai, var. Lvs. and petioles ciliate, lvs. with a few appressed hairs above. N.K.8:t.11. N.T.1:75. (*R. dauricum* var. *c.* Wils.) Korea, Jap. Intr. 1917.—**R. m. acuminàtum** Hutchins., var. Blooms several weeks later.

× Subgen. AZALEODENDRON Rodig. (*Eurhododendron* × *Anthodendron, Rhodazalea* Croux.).

R. azaleoìdes Dum.-Cours. (*R.* ?*nudiflorum* × *ponticum*). Lvs. rather large, acuminate, green beneath: fls. pale purple, not spotted, with wavy lobes. A.R.6:t. 379(c). (*R. ponticum* var. *deciduum* Andr.) Orig. before 1800.—Here belongs also: *R. gemmiferum* Bean. Lvs. broader, obtusish or acutish, pubescent beneath: fls. rose-purple, 3 cm. across. Orig. unknown. Zone (V).

R. hýbridum Ker (*R. viscosum* × *maximum*). Lvs. oblong, 5–10 cm. long, acute at ends, glaucous beneath: fls. whitish, tinged with pink or purple, upper lobe spotted yellow, fragrant, 3 cm. across. B.R.t.195(c). (*R. azaleoides* Bean, not Dum.-Cours.) Orig. before 1850.

R. fragrans Paxt. (*R. catawbiense* × *viscosum*). Lvs. shorter and broader: fls. pale pinkish, fragrant. P.M.10:147,t(c). Orig. about 1820.

R. norbitonénse W. Smith (*R. molle* × [*maximum* × *ponticum*]). A hybrid with yellow fls., originated about 1830, of which the two following vars. are occasionally cult.: **R. n. broughtoniànum** Rehd., var. Young brts. pubescent: lvs. persistent, oblong to oblong-obovate, 5–12 cm. long, pale green beneath, finely pubescent on both sides: fls. 8–16 in dense clusters, primrose-yellow, spotted reddish brown, about 6 cm. across; sepals oblong. G.C.51:53. B.S.2:345. Millais, Rhodod. 184,t(h). (*R. broughtonii aureum* W. Wats.)—**R. n. aùreum** (Paxt.) Rehd., var. Similar to the preceding, but lvs. glaucous beneath: fls. paler; pedicels longer; sepals narrower. P.M.9:79,t(c). F.R.2:152,t(c). F.S. 1:45.t(c). (*R. Smithii aureum* Paxt.)

R. azaleodéndron Vilm. & Bois. (*R. japonicum* × *Eurhododendron hybrids*). Evergreen: fls. white to rosy-red or rose-lilac, conspicuously spotted. G.C.III.13: 663. R.B.19:177,t(c). R.H.1893:369.

Subgen. AZALEASTRUM Planch.
(Series: Albiflorum, 57; Semibarbatum, 58.)

57. **R. albiflòrum** Hook. Deciduous shrub to 2 m.; young brts. hairy and glandular: lvs. elliptic-oblong to oblong, 2.5–6 cm. long, acute at ends, appressed-pilose above and on the midrib beneath, slightly ciliate, pale green; petiole strigose: fls. nodding on short glandular-pubescent pedicels, white; corolla rotate-campanulate, 2 cm. across, with ovate lobes; stamens 10, pubescent at base; sepals oval to obovate-oblong, 7–12 mm. long, glandular-ciliate. Fl.VI–VII. B.M.3670(c). (*Azalea albiflora* Ktze.) B. C. and Alb. to

Ore. and Colo. Intr. before 1837, but rare in cult. and not thriving well in the East. Zone V.

58. **R. semibarbàtum** Maxim. Shrub to 2 m.; brts. pubescent and glandular-pilose: lvs. deciduous, thin, elliptic or elliptic-ovate to elliptic-oblong, 2–4 cm. long, acute or obtusish and mucronate, broad-cuneate, minutely crenulate and ciliate, light green beneath and glabrous except the short-villous and sparingly setose midrib; petiole 4–10 mm. long, pubescent and glandular-setose: fls. few at end of brts. beneath the young leafy shoot; calyx-lobes ovate, 2–3 mm. long, glandular-setose, ciliate; corolla rotate-funnelform, 2–2.5 cm. across, with wide ovoid tube 5–6 mm. long and spreading broad-oval lobes, white, flushed pink, spotted red at throat: stamens 5, very unequal, the 3 lower ones as long as limb, puberulous only at base, the upper ones half as long, densely pilose; ovary glandular-setose; style glabrous. Fl.vi. B.M.9147(c). Gt.19:t.666(c). N.T.1:77. S.R.608. Japan. Intr. about 1860. Zone V. A very distinct species, but fls. insignificant.

Subgen. III. ANTHODENDRON Endl.

Sect. 1. Tsutsutsi G. Don.

(Series Azalea, subser. Obtusum, 59–66.)

59. **R. Tschonóskii** Maxim. Deciduous densely branched shrub, to 1.5, rarely 2.5 m. tall, sometimes low and depressed: lvs. crowded at ends of brts., elliptic or oblong to ovate-lanceolate or lanceolate-oblong, 8–35 mm. long, acute at ends, pale green beneath, appressed-pilose on both side, with 1–3 prominent veins: fls. 2–6, short-stalked; corolla funnelform, about 1 cm. across, with cylindric tube, villous inside, sometimes with 4 lobes (*f. tetramerum* Makino); stamens exserted, pilose below the middle; calyx setose: fr. ovoid. Fl.vi. N.T.1:112. N.K.8:t.17. S.H.2:f.332l-o. (*Azalea T.* Ktze.) Japan, Korea. Intr. 1878. Zone V. Fls. insignificant; lvs. changing to orange-red and crimson in fall.

60. **R. microphỳtum** Franch. Shrub to 2 m.; lvs. persistent, elliptic to lance-oblong or lanceolate, 1–4 cm. long, acute or obtusish and mucronulate, cuneate or rounded at base, dark green above, pale green beneath, with scattered hairs on both sides or glabrescent above: fls. 3–6; pedicels short; calyx-lobes lanceolate, 1–3 mm. long, strigose; corolla funnelform, 1.5–2.5 cm. across, rose to nearly white, spotted carmine or crimson, tube cylindric, 5–8 mm. long, with oval or oblong spreading lobes; stamens longer than corolla, puberulous below the middle. S.R.90. H.B.6:244(h). W. China. Intr. 1913. Zone (V).

61. **R. índicum** (L.) Sweet. Evergreen or half-evergreen, dense and low shrub, rarely to 2 m. tall: lvs. short-petioled, elliptic-lanceolate to lanceolate or oblanceolate, 2–3.5 cm. long, acute at ends, dark green and somewhat lustrous above, glaucescent beneath, remotely crenulate-serrulate, ciliolate, sparingly strigose on both sides: fls. 1–2; corolla broad-funnelform, bright red to scarlet, 5–7 cm. across; stamens 5, about as long as corolla; style longer. Fl.vi. B.R.1700(c). S.B.II.3:t.261(c). N.T.1:125. (*R. macranthum* G. Don, *R. lateritium* Planch., *R. i.* var. *macranthum* Maxim., *Azalea indica* L.) Japan. Cult. 1680. Zone (V).—**R. i. laciniàtum** Mak., f. Corolla deeply 5-parted, with lanceolate obtuse lobes.—**R. i. balsaminaeflòrum** (Carr.) Nichols., var. Dwarf form: lvs. 1–2.5 cm. long: fls. double, salmon-red. R.H.1882:432,t(c). Gn.18:254,t(c). F.M.19:t.418(c). (*R. i.* var. *rosaeflorum* Rehd., *Azalea Rollisonii* Moore.) Intr. about 1877. Zone (V).—**R. i. crispiflòrum** (Hook.) Schneid., var. Lvs. thicker: lobes of corolla with wavy margin. B.M.4726(c). F.S.9:79,t(c). Intr. about 1850. Zone VI?

divided into linear-lanceolate segments. B.M.5769(c). S.H.2:f.330g-k,331f
(*R. Burmanii* f. *l.* Nakai, *Azalea linearifolia* Hook. f.) Cult. in Japan. Intr.
before 1867. Zone VII.—**R. l. macrosépalum** (Maxim.) Mak., var. Deciduous or nearly deciduous shrub to 1 m., rarely taller; brts. villous and sparingly strigose: lvs. elliptic-ovate to ovate-lanceolate, 2–5 cm. long, short-
acuminate to acute, sparingly glandular-hairy above, more densely so beneath, summer-lvs. oblanceolate and obtuse: fls. 2–10, fragrant: corolla rose-
lilac to rose-purple, spotted, 3–5 cm. across; stamens 5, sometimes 6–10 (f.
decandrum Wils.) shorter than corolla; style longer; sepals lanceolate, 1–3
cm. long, glandular-pubescent. Gt.19:t.662(c). D.L.1:420. N.T.1:156. (*R. m.*
Maxim., *R. Burmanii* var. *m.* Nakai.) Japan. Intr. 1863. Zone VII.—**R. l.
dianthiflòrum** (Carr.) Wils., f. A form of the preceding var. with double fls.
R.H.1891:60,t(c). (*R. d.* Millais.) Intr. 1889.

Sect. 2. SCIADORHODION Rehd. & Wils.

(Series: Azalea, Subser. Schlippenbachii, 67–70.)

67. R. Weyríchii Maxim. Deciduous shrub to 5 m.; young brts. ferrugineous-pubescent, becoming glabrous and purple: lvs. 2–3 at end of brts.,
broad-ovate or rounded-ovate to rhombic, 3.5–8 cm. long, acutish or obtuse
and mucronulate, broad-cuneate or rounded at base, at first rufous-pubescent
on both sides, soon glabrous, lustrous dark green above; petioles 5–10 mm.
long, rufous-pubescent and setose: fls. 2–4, with the lvs.; corolla red, funnelform, 3.5–6 cm. across, stamens 6–10, shorter than corolla; sepals minute;
pedicels, calyx and ovary densely rufous-pubescent: fr. cylindric to oblong-
ovoid, 1.5–2 cm. long, pubescent. Fl.v. B.M.9475(c). G.C.87:359,t. N.K.8:
t.16. N.T.1:96. (*Azalea W.* Ktze.) Japan, Korea. Intr. 1914. Zone VI. Fls.
red; lvs. turning vinous-purple in fall.

68. R. reticulàtum D. Don. Deciduous much-branched shrub to 8 m.;
young brts. pubescent, soon glabrous, yellow-brown; winter-buds acute, pubescent: lvs. 2 or 3 at end of brts., broad-ovate or ovate to rhombic, 3–6 cm.
long, acute and mucronate, usually broad-cuneate, fulvous pubescent and
strigose at first, at maturity dark green and sparingly strigose or glabrous
above, pubescent on the veins beneath and sparingly strigose or nearly glabrous, pale or glaucescent, reticulate; petioles 4–8 mm. long, pubescent and
strigose: fls. 1–2, rarely to 4, before the lvs.; corolla rotate-campanulate,
slightly 2-lipped, rose-purple to magenta, not or slightly spotted; stamens
usually 10, declinate, the longer ones as long, the shorter ones half as long
as the corolla; anthers purple; style glabrous, or pubescent or glandular or
both; ovary villous; pedicels and the minute calyx pubescent: fr. cylindric,
curved, 1–1.5 cm. long. Fl.iv-v. Gt.17:225,t(c). B.M.6972(c). G.C.III.20:38.
N.T.1:91,93. Gn.72:267(h). A.B.1930:20(h). (*R. rhombicum* Miq., *R. dilatatum* Miq., *Azalea reticulata* K. Koch.) Japan. Intr. 1865. Zone V. With
rose-purple fls. before the lvs.—**R. r. pentándrum** Wils., f. Lvs. usually
quite glabrous at maturity: stamens 5. B.M.7681(c). S.I.2:t.61(c). N.T.1:
100. (*R. dilatatum* Maxim., not Miq.) Japan. Cult. 1880.—The generally
cult. form with 10 stamens, glandular style and villous ovary has been distinguished as *R. wadanum* Mak. N.T.1:95.

69. R. quinquefòlium Biss. & Moore. Deciduous shrub or small tree to
8 m.; young brts. glabrous, lustrous brown, old stems gray-brown, scaly;
winter-buds acute, glabrous: lvs. 4–5 at end of brts., broad-elliptic to obovate,
3–5 cm. long, obtuse or acutish, mucronate, cuneate, ciliate and often red on
margin, villous beneath at least on midrib; petiole very short, villous: fls.

716

1–3, with the lvs.; corolla white, spotted green, rotate-campanulate, about 4 cm. across; stamens 10, unequal; filaments greenish, villous at base; ovary glabrous; sepals deltoid to lanceolate, glandular-ciliate; pedicels slender, glandular-pubescent: fr. cylindric, 1–1.5 cm. long. Fl.v. Millais, Rhod. 2:218,t. N.T.108. M.I.1:t.30. Wilson, Pl. Hunt. 2:t.117(h). (*Azalea quinquefolia* Stand. Pl. Names.) Japan. Intr. 1896. Zone VI.

70. **R. Schlippenbáchii** Maxim. Deciduous shrub to 5 m.; young brts. glandular-pubescent, glabrous the 2d year: lvs. usually 5 at ends of brts., short-petioled, obovate or broad-obovate, 5–10 cm. long, truncate or rounded to emarginate at apex, mucronate, cuneate, slightly undulate, sparingly pubescent when young, later glabrous except on veins beneath, dark green above, pale beneath: fls. 3–6, fragrant, with the lvs.; corolla pale to rosy pink, rotate-funnelform, 6–8 cm. across, spotted red-brown; stamens 10, unequal, the longest as long as corolla; sepals ovate, 5 mm. long; pedicels glandular-pubescent: fr. oblong-ovoid, 1.5 cm. long, glandular. Fl.v. B.M. 7373(c). Gn.46:80,t(c). G.C.55:9,t. N.T.1:107. W.A.58,t(h). (*Azalea S.* Ktze.) Korea, Manch., Japan. Intr. 1893. Zone IV. With large pink fls. in spring; the lvs. changing to yellow, orange and crimson in fall.

Sect. 3. RHODORA G. Don.
(Series Azalea, Subser. Canadense, 71–74; Subser. Nipponicum, under 72.)

71. **R. Albréchti** Maxim. Shrub to 1.5 m.; young brts. glandular-pubescent, becoming glabrous and purple-brown: lvs. about 5 at end of brts., obovate to oblanceolate, 4–12 cm. long, acute or acutish, mucronulate, ciliate-serrulate, sparingly appressed-pilose above, gray-pubescent beneath, membranous; petiole short, winged: fls. with the lvs., 3–5; corolla rotate-campanulate, about 5 cm. across, red-purple; stamens 10, unequal, the longest as long as the corolla, style longer; sepals small, ciliate, purple; pedicels 1–2 cm. long, glandular-pubescent: fr. conic-ovoid, 1–1.2 cm. long, glandular-pubescent. Fl.v–vi. B.M.9207. N.T.1:83. S.H.2:f.325m-n,327e. (*Azalea A.* Ktze.) Japan. Intr. 1892. Zone V. Similar to *R. Schlippenbachii*, but less showy; the lvs. turn yellow in fall.

72. **R. pentaphýllum** Maxim. Shrub to 8 m.; young brts. sparingly pilose, soon glabrous; winter-buds acute, glabrous, purple-brown: lvs. usually 5 at end of brts., elliptic to elliptic-lanceolate, 3–6 cm. long, acute and mucronulate, cuneate, ciliolate-serrulate, villous on midrib above and beneath, otherwise glabrous, chartaceous, reticulate; petiole 3–8 mm. long, usually pilose and glandular: fls. 1–2, before or with the lvs.; corolla rotate-campanulate, 4–5 cm. across, rose-pink, unspotted; stamens 10; unequal, villous at base, shorter than corolla, style longer, glabrous; sepals triangular to deltoid, 1–5 mm. long, glabrous; pedicels 1–1.5 cm. long, glandular-pubescent to glabrous: fr. spindle-shaped, about 1.5 cm. long, verruculose. Fl.iv–v. N.T.1:86. M.I.3:t.168(c). (*R. quinquefolium* var. *roseum* Rehd.) Japan. Intr. 1914. Zone (V). Handsome shrub with soft-pink fls. in spring and orange to crimson lvs. in autumn.

Another species of this section is **R. nippónicum** Matsum. Shrub to 2 m.; brts. glandular-pubescent: lvs. scattered, subsessile, obovate-oblong, 6–18 cm. long, rounded or truncate at apex, appressed-pilose on both sides: fls. 6–15, with or after the lvs.; corolla tubular-campanulate, 1.5–2 cm. long, white, with short slightly spreading lobes; stamens and style included: the slender pedicels and small calyx glandular-pubescent. N.T.1:78. M.I.1:t.5. S.R.74. Japan. Intr. 1914. Zone VI? Fls. hidden by the lvs. which turn orange to crimson in fall.

73. **R. Vaseỳi** Gray. Shrub to 5 m.; brts. puberulous and sparingly pilose at first, soon glabrous, light red-brown, older brs. with grayish brown flaky

bark; winter-buds broad-ovoid, obtuse, with 7–10 ciliolate scales: lvs. scattered, elliptic to elliptic-oblong, 5–12 cm. long, acuminate, cuneate, with ciliate and usually slightly undulate margin, glabrous above except the midrib, green and glabrous beneath or sparingly pilose on midrib; petiole slender, 3–7 mm. long, glabrous or sparingly pilose: fls. 5–8, before the lvs.; corolla rotate-campanulate, 2-lipped, 2.5–3 cm. long, tube about 5 mm. long, the upper lip less deeply divided, light rose, spotted orange; stamens 5–7, usually 7, the longer exceeding the corolla, glabrous; style longer than stamens, glabrous or with few glands near base; sepals short, rounded, glandular-ciliate; pedicels 5–15 mm. long, stipitate-glandular. Fl.iv–v. B.M.8081(c). M.M.7: 121,t(c). Gn.54:282,t(c);56:119(h). G.F.1:377. M.G.14:332,333(h). S.L.302 (h). (*Azalea V.* Rehd., *Biltia V.* Small.) N. C. Intr. about 1880. Zone IV. Handsome shrub with profuse light rose fls. before the lvs.—**R. V. album** Bean, var. Fls. white. Intr. 1891.

74. **R. canadénse** (L.) Torr. Rhodora. Much-branched shrub to 1 m.; brts. puberulous when young, yellowish red or pinkish, often bloomy; winterbuds with acute to acuminate puberulous and ciliolate scales: lvs. petioled, elliptic to oblong, 2–4.5, rarely to 6 cm. long, obtuse or acutish, cuneate, with ciliate and revolute margin, dull bluish green above, thinly grayish tomentulose beneath, usually sparingly glandular and pilose on midrib: fls. 3–7, before the lvs.; corolla 2-lipped, 1.5–2 cm. long, the lower lip divided to or nearly to the base into 2 narrow-oblong lobes, the upper lip with 3 short ovate lobes, rose-purple; stamens 10, about as long as corolla, pubescent near base; style slightly longer, glabrous or nearly so; sepals very short, unequal, setose-ciliate; pedicels 3–7 mm. long, puberulous, usually sparingly glandular: fr. ovoid-oblong, 1–1.5 cm. long, puberulous and setose. Fl.iv–v. B.M.474(c). Em.2:441,t(c). G.O.t.14(c). C.L.11:496. M.G.17:287(h). S.L.301(h). (*R. Rhodora* Gmel., *Rhodora canadensis* L.) Nfd. and Lab. to c. N. Y. and Pa. Intr. before 1756. Zone II. Valued for its early fls.—**R. c. albiflòrum** (Rand & Redf.) Rehd., f. Fls. white. (*R. c. f. album* Voss.) Cult. 1894.

R. c. × *japonicum;* see under No. 75.

Sect. 4. Pentanthera G. Don.
(Series Azalea, Subser. Luteum, 75–85.)

75. **R. japónicum** (Gray) Suringar. Shrub with stout erect brs. to 2 m.; winter-buds ovoid, acute or acutish, slightly puberulous; brts. glabrous, sometimes setose: lvs. obovate to obovate-oblong, 4–10 cm. long, obtuse and mucronulate, cuneate, ciliate, appressed-setose above and on the veins beneath: fls. 6–12, before the lvs.; corolla campanulate-funnelform, 5–6 cm. across, orange-red or salmon-red to brick-red; stamens shorter than corolla, pilose below the middle, anthers brown; sepals small, ovate, setose; pedicels usually setose. Fl.iv–v. B.M.5905(c). Gt.57:516,t(c). F.S.19:t.2034–5(c). S.I. 2:t.62. Gn.59:503. C.L.11:495. N.T.1:81. Gng.4:279. (*R. molle* Sieb. & Zucc., not G. Don, *R. molle* var. *glabrior* Miq., *Azalea japonica* Gray, *R. glabrius* Nakai.) Japan. Intr. 1861. Zone V: Vigorous shrub with conspicuous fls. in spring.—**R. j. aùreum** Wils., f. Fls. yellow.

R. j. × *molle* = **R. Kosteriànum** Schneid. Many garden forms ranging in color from white to red: lvs. only slightly pubescent beneath. Here belongs "Anthony Koster" and "Miss Louisa Hunnewell." R.B.17:121,t(c); 20:277,t(c). G.C.III.13:513.—*R. j.* × *canadense* = **R. Fràseri** W. Wats. Young brts. and winter-buds finely pubescent: lvs. elliptic-oblong to oblong, 4–6 cm. long, acute at ends, pubescent on both sides: fls. rosy-lilac, spotted, 2-lipped, with very short tube and deeply divided lower lip, 3.5–4 cm. across. Orig. 1912.—*R. j.* × *roseum* Gable. N.H.18:257.—*R. j.* × *atlanticum* Gable. N.H.18:259.

76. R. mólle (Bl.) G. Don. Shrub to 1.5 m.; young brts. pubescent and often setose; winter-buds grayish pubescent: lvs. oblong to oblong-lanceolate or oblanceolate, 6–15 cm. long, obtuse and mucronulate, cuneate, ciliate and often revolute, pubescent above at least when young, grayish soft-pubescent beneath: fls. many; corolla campanulate-funnelform, about 5–6 cm. across, finely pubescent outside, golden-yellow, spotted greenish: stamens as long or longer than corolla; sepals short, ciliate; pedicels puberulous, not or slightly setose. Fl.ɪv–v. S.B.3:290(c). L.B.885(c). B.R.1253(c). S.H.2:f.328 g–h;329a–b. (*R. sinense* Sweet, *Azalea mollis* Bl.) China. Intr. 1823. Zone (V). Shrub with conspicuous yellow fls.

R. m. × *occidentale* = R. álbicans Waterer. Lvs. pubescent beneath: fls. large, usually light-colored, white to light pink or rose, with an orange blotch divided by lighter veins; stamens not or slightly exserted. F.P.1883:177,t(c). Gn.29:550,t(c), partly. Orig. before 1880. Here belongs "Graciosa" and "Exquisite."—*R. m.* × *japonicum;* see under No. 75—*R. m.* × *gandavense;* see under No. 77.—*R. m.* × *viscosum;* see under No. 84.—*R. m.* × (*maximum* × *ponticum*) = *R. norbitonense:* see p. 712.

77. R. lùteum Sweet. Shrub to 4 m.; brts. glandular-pubescent when young; winter-buds minutely pubescent, viscid: lvs. oblong to oblong-lanceolate or oblong-oblanceolate, acute or obtuse and mucronate, ciliate-serrulate, hairy on both sides; villous and glandular when young: fls. many, very fragrant; corolla yellow, funnelform, about 5 cm. across, with narrow-cylindrical tube, 1.5–2 cm. long; stamens much exserted, shorter than style; ovary glandular; sepals ovate to oblong, glandular-ciliate; pedicels, calyx and corolla outside glandular: fr. cylindric-oblong, 2–2.5 cm. long, glabrescent. Fl.v. B.M.433(c). S.O.3:t.169(c). R.I.17:t.108(c). Millais, Rhodod. 12:t(h);165, t(c). Gn.29:550. (*R. flavum* G. Don, *Azalea pontica* L.) Asia Minor, Cauc., E. Eu. Intr. 1792. Zone (V). Handsome shrub with very fragrant yellow fls. —**R. l. macránthum** (Bean) Wils., var. Fls. to 6.5 cm. across.

R. l. × *Mortieri* = R. gandavénse (K. Koch) Rehd. Here belong the so-called Ghent Azaleas representing hybrids of the preceding species with *R. calendulaceum* and *R. nudiflorum* and possibly other hybrids. Ann. Soc. Agric. Bot. Gand, 2:t.81,83,106(c). Witte, Flora, t.73(c). Orig. about 1840.—R. g. plènum Rehd., var. Forms with double fls. F.S.13t.1298(c); 19:t.2021–24(c). F.P. 1880:t.516(c).—*R. gandavense* × *molle* = R. mixtum Wils. Mostly double-fld. forms, pink, red or yellow. R.B.19:232,t(c). G.W.15:493(h). Millais, Rhodod. 220(h). Orig. before 1890.

78. R. occidentàle Gray. Shrub to 3 m.; young brts. soft-pubescent or glabrous; winter-buds puberulous or sometimes nearly glabrous: lvs. elliptic to oblong-lanceolate, 3–9 cm. long, acute or obtusish and mucronulate, cuneate, ciliate, thinly pubescent on both sides when young or nearly glabrous, at maturity usually pubescent only on midrib above and strigose on midrib beneath: fls. 6–12, usually after or with the lvs., rarely before; corolla funnelform, white or pinkish, with yellow blotch, villous and glandular-pilose outside, 3.5–5 cm. across; tube about 2 cm. long, gradually dilated upward, as long as lobes; stamens exserted, style as long or longer; ovary glandular-pilose; sepals broad-ovate to oblong-ovate, 1.5–4 mm. long, ciliate; pedicels usually glandular-pubescent: fr. ovate-oblong, 1–2 cm. long, setose-pilose. Fl. vɪ–vɪɪ(v–vɪɪɪ). B.M.5005(c). F.S.14:t.1422(c).. Gn.34:416,t(c). G.C.II.26:105. G.W.11:8(h). (*Azalea Californica* Torr. & Gr.) Ore., Calif. Intr. 1850. Zone VI or VII. Handsome shrub with showy fls.; lvs. turning scarlet and yellow in autumn.

R. o. × *molle;* see under No. 76.—*R. o.* × *arborescens* Gable. N.H.16:255.— There are also hybrids with *R. calendulaceum* and with × *R. gandavense.*

79. R. calendulàceum (Michx.) Torr. Shrub to 3 m., rarely to 5 m.; young brts. pubescent and strigillose; winter-buds glabrous, with ciliolate scales: lvs. broad-elliptic to elliptic-oblong or obovate-oblong, 4–8 cm. long, acute and gland-tipped, broad-cuneate, finely pubescent above and more densely so beneath when young: fls. usually 5–7, shortly after the lvs.; corolla yellow or orange to scarlet, nearly scentless, about 5 cm. across, glandular and pubescent outside, tube gradually dilated above the middle, 1.5–2 cm. long, as long or shorter than the ovate lobes; stamens much exserted, style as long or longer; ovary setose, glandless; sepals oblong, 3–4 mm. long or ovate and shorter; pedicels setulose and usually glandular: fr. ovoid-oblong, 1.5–2 cm. long, setose and pubescent. Fl.v–vi. S.H.2:f.329q-r,330a. K.S.351. C.L. 11:496. (*R. luteum* Schneid., not Sweet, *Azalea calendulacea* Michx., *A. lutea* L., partly.) Pa. to Ga. w. to Ohio and Ky. Cult. 1800. Zone V. The most showy American species. The chief color forms are the following: **R. c. croceum** Sweet, var. Fls. yellow to orange-yellow. B.M.1721(c). L.B.132(c).— **R. c. aurántium** (Lodd.) Rehd., f. Fls. deep orange-red to scarlet. B.R.145(c). L.B.1255(c).

R. c. × *nudiflorum* = **R. Mortièri** Sweet (possibly including *R. speciosum* × *nudiflorum*). Fls. more or less pinkish, with orange blotch: lvs. glabrescent. S.B.II.1:t.10(c). L.B.1382(c). B.R.1366,1402,1407,1559(c). Orig. before 1830. —*R. c.* × *arborescens* = **R. Annelièsae** Rehd. Lvs. glabrous and usually glaucous beneath, with strigose midrib: fls. fragrant, usually pinkish with yellow blotch, tube longer than lobes. Orig. about 1896; also spontaneous in N. C.

Another yellow-fld. species related to *R. canescens* is **R. austrìnum** (Small) Rehd. Brts. pubescent and glandular; winter-buds pubescent: lvs. elliptic to oblong-obovate, finely pubescent on both sides: fls. many, before or with the lvs., yellow to orange, usually with purplish stripes outside, tube cylindric, longer than lobes; ovary setose and glandular; pedicels and calyx glandular. (*Azalea austrina* Small.) Fla. Intr. 1914. Zone VII.

80. **R. speciòsum** (Willd.) Sweet. Shrub to 2 m.; young brts. finely pubescent and strigillose; winter-buds glabrous: lvs. elliptic or obovate to oblong, 3–6 cm. long, acute or obtusish and mucronate, broad-cuneate, strigillose above, finely pubescent beneath or sometimes nearly glabrous except on midrib: fls. 6–15, with the lvs.; corolla scarlet or bright red with yellow blotch, 4–5 cm. across, pubescent and pilose outside, tube slender, 2–2.5 cm. long, longer than lobes; stamens much exserted, slightly shorter than style; ovary setose, not glandular; sepals broad-ovate to oblong, ciliate; pedicels strigillose: fr. ovoid to narrow-oblong, 2–3 cm. long, strigose. Fl.v. B.M.180(c). G.O.t.31(c). W.D.116(c). L.B.624(c). (*R. calendulaceum* f. *s.* Voss, *A. speciosa* Willd., *A. nudiflora* var. *coccinea* Ait.) Ga. to S. C. Cult. 1789. Zone VI. Handsome shrub with bright red fls.

R. s. × *nudiflorum*. Probably some forms of *R. Mortieri* (see under No. 79) represent this cross.

81. **R. nudiflòrum** (L.) Torr. Shrub to 2, rarely to 3 m.; young brts. slightly pubescent and strigillose or nearly glabrous; winter-buds glabrous or slightly pubescent: lvs. elliptic or obovate to oblong or oblong-obovate, 3–8 cm. long, acute or acuminate, cuneate, ciliate, glabrous and green beneath, except strigillose or sometimes slightly pubescent on midrib: fls. 6–12, before the lvs., scentless; corolla usually light pink or white with pink tube, 3–4 cm. across; tube cylindric, 1.5–2 cm. long, gradually dilated above, strigose-pilose and puberulous outside, longer than the rather narrow and acuminate lobes; stamens much exserted, nearly 3 times as long as tube; style slightly longer; ovary setose, glandless; sepals roundish to ovate, rarely oblong, 1.5–2 mm. long; pedicels strigillose and sometimes puberulous, rarely glandular: fr. oblong to narrow-oblong, 1–2 cm. long. Fl.iv–v. S.O.3:t.170(c). B.R.120(c). Em.440,t(c). K.S.347. Gn.M.5:218(h). W.A.52,t(h). (*Azalea nudiflora* L., *A. lutea* L., partly, *A. periclymenoides* M:chx.) Mass. to N. C.

w. to Ohio. Intr. about 1730. Zone III. Shrub with white to pink fls. before the lvs.—**R. n. album** Sweet, var. Fls. white.—**R. n. glandíferum** (Porter) Rehd., var. Corolla puberulous and glandular-pilose outside, usually pink to carmine. (*Azalea nudiflora* var. *glandifera* Porter.) L.B.51(c).

 R. n. × *luteum;* see under No. 77.—*R. n.* × *calendulaceum;* see under No. 79.—*R. n.* × *atlanticum;* see under No. 83.—*R. n.* × *ponticum* = *R. azaleoides;* see p. 712.

 82. R. ròseum (Loisel.) Rehd. Shrub to 3, rarely to 5 m.; young brts. finely pubescent and usually sparingly strigillose; buds grayish pubescent: lvs. elliptic or obovate to obovate-oblong, 3–7 cm. long, acute or short-acuminate, dull bluish green and sparingly pubescent above, grayish pubescent beneath: fls. 5–9, with the lvs., fragrant; corolla bright pink, rarely whitish, about 4 cm. across, tube rather gradually dilated, 1.5–2 cm. long, about as long as the ovate lobes; stamens about twice as long as tube, style longer, purple above; ovary setose and glandular; sepals roundish to ovate, pubescent, glandular-ciliate; pedicels villous and glandular: fr. oblong, 1.5–2 cm. long, slightly puberulous and glandular-setose. Fl.v. N.D.5:t.64(c). M.M.2: t.2(c). K.S.349. A.B.1927:26(h). (*R. canescens* Porter, not Sweet, *R. prinophyllum* Millais, *Azalea rosea* Loisel., *A. prinophylla* Small.) N. H. and s. Quebec to Va. (not on the coastal plain), w. to Ill. and Mo. Intr. 1812 or possibly about 1790. Zone III. Shrub with fragrant pink fls. appearing with the bluish green lvs.

 R. r. × *japonicum;* see under No. 75.

 Related species: **R. canéscens** (Michx.) Sweet. Sparingly branched shrub to 5 m.; young brts. villous-pubescent: lvs. oblong-obovate or oblong to oblanceolate, 4–9 cm. long, grayish pubescent or tomentose beneath: fls. before or with the lvs., slightly fragrant, about 3.5 cm. across, tube slender, 1.5–2.3 cm. long, villous and sometimes glandular outside, longer than lobes, tube usually pink, lobes white; stamens much exserted; ovary villous, sparingly setulose; glandless. Abbot, Nat. Hist. Lepidopt. Georgia,1:t.27(c). (*Azalea c.* Michx., *A. bicolor* Pursh.) N. C. and Fl. to e. Tex. Intr. 1750? Zone VII?—**R. c. candidum** (Small) Rehd., var. Lvs. glaucous beneath and pubescent. (*Azalea candida* Small.) Ga. to n. Fla.—**R. c. subglábrum** Rehd., f. Lvs. glabrous or glabrescent. Ga. and Ala. to e. Tex. Intr. 1916. Zone VII?—**R. alabaménse** Rehd. Low shrub; young brts. strigose-pilose; buds glabrous: lvs. elliptic or obovate to obovate-oblong, 3–6 cm. long, slightly puberulous above when young, pale or glaucescent and short-villous beneath: fls. with the lvs., fragrant, white, 4–5 cm. across, tube gradually dilated, 2–2.8 cm. long: stamens twice as long as tube. Ala. Intr. 1922. Zone VII?

 83. R. atlánticum (Ashe) Rehd. Stoloniferous shrub, to 0.5 m., sometimes taller; young brts. sparingly strigillose, sometimes glandular; buds glabrous or slightly pubescent: lvs. obovate to oblong-obovate, rarely elliptic, 3–6 cm. long, roundish or acutish at apex, glabrous above, bright green or glaucous and glabrous beneath except the strigillose and sometimes pubescent midrib, fls. 4–10, before or with the lvs., very fragrant; corolla white, usually flushed pink or purplish, glandular-pilose outside, not or slightly villous; tube cylindric, 2–2.5 cm. long, glabrous inside; stamens twice as long as tube, style longer; ovary setose, with or without glands; sepals glandular-ciliate, rarely eglandular; pedicels hirsute or glandular-hirsute: fr. ovoid-oblong, 1.5–2 cm. long. Fl.ɪv–v. Jour. Elisha Mitchell Soc. 36:t.1(c). N.H.11:54(h). (*Azalea atlantica* Ashe.) Del. to S. C. Intr. about 1916. Zone VI? Low shrub with very fragrant white to purplish fls.—**R. a. negléctum** Rehd. Fls. purplish pink, tube slightly shorter, wider and more villous outside. N. and S. C.— **R. a. lùteo-álbum** (Coker) Rehd., var. Brts. stipitate-glandular: lvs. bluish green, finely pubescent: fls. white, often yellowish in bud. S. C. Cult. 1928.

 R. a. × *nudiflorum* = **R. pennsylvànicum** (Gable) Rehd. Lvs. elliptic, glaucous beneath and strigose on the midrib, ciliate; corolla white, flushed pink, densely setose-pilose, scarcely glandular, not or scarcely villous. (*Azalea penn-sylvanica* Gable.) Pa. Intr. about 1926.—*R. a.* × *japonicum;* see under No. 75.

84. **R. viscòsum** (L.) Torr. Shrub to 3, rarely to 5 m.; young brts. strigil-lose or hirsute; buds glabrous or sometimes pubescent, with 8–12 ovate obtusish and usually mucronulate scales: lvs. ovate or elliptic-obovate to oblong-oblanceolate, 2–6 cm. long, acute or obtuse, glabrous except the slightly villous and strigillose midrib beneath, sometimes strigillose above, bright green or glaucescent beneath: fls. 4–9, after the lvs.; corolla white or suffused with pink, finely villous and glandular-hirsute outside; tube cylindric, some-what dilated near apex, 1.5–2.5 cm. long, about 1½ times as long as the ovate-oblong lobes, slightly pubescent inside above the middle; stamens some-what longer than lobes, style longer, pale or purplish near apex; ovary glandular-setose, sometimes glandless; sepals roundish to ovate, about 1 mm. long, setose-ciliate; pedicels pubescent and glandular: fr. oblong-ovoid, 1.3–2 cm. long. Fl.vi–vii. Em.438,t(c). S.O.3:t.171(c). M.M.10:81,t.6(c). (*Azalea viscosa* L.) Me. to S. C., in swamps. Cult. 1731. Zone III. Grown chiefly for its late and fragrant fls.—**R. v. rhodánthum** Rehd., f. Fls. bright pink.—**R. v. glaùcum** (Ait.) Torr., var. Lvs. glaucous beneath and sometimes bluish green above. S.O.3:t.172(c). W.D.t.5(c). (*Azalea v.* var. *glauca* Ait.) With the type; a form with intensely pink fls. is **R. v. rubéscens** (Lodd.) Sweet, var. (*R. v.* var. *roseum* Hollick, *Azalea v.* var. *rub.* Sweet.)—**R. v. nítidum** (Pursh) Gray, var. Lvs. obovate-oblong to oblanceolate, acute or abruptly acuminate, green on both sides, sometimes strigillose above: fls. usually pinkish.—**R. v. montànum** Rehd., var. Low shrub to 1.2 m.; brts. puberulous and hirsute like the pedicels and midrib beneath; winter-buds silky-pubescent, with 5–7 rounded scales: lvs. obovate to obovate-oblong, bright green: fls. suffused with pink and with numerous stipitate red glands. N. C. Intr. 1919. —**R. v. coeruléscens** Rehd., f. A form of the preceding var. with the lvs. glaucous beneath and bluish green above and the fls. more highly colored. Intr. 1913.—**R. v. tomentòsum** (Dum.-Cours.) Rehd., var. Lvs. densely pubescent beneath and slightly above. (*Azalea tomentosa* Dum.-Cours.)

R. v. × *molle* = R. viscosépalum (Gard. Chron.) Rehd. Lvs. larger, thinly pubescent and glaucescent beneath: fls. larger, white with yellow blotch, yellow-ish in bud; tube shorter, more dilated, more puberulous outside; stamens not or slightly exceeding the lobes. (*Azalea viscosepala* Gard. Chron., *A. viscocephala* Arb. Kew.) Orig. about 1840.—**R. v. Davièsii** (Gard. Chron.) Rehd., var. Fls. larger, with more conspicuous yellow blotch and with shorter wider tube. Gt. 42:65,t(c). B.R.28:27. Gs. 20:183. (*Azalea D.* Gard. Chron.)—*R. c.* × *maxi-mum* = R. hybridum; see p. 712.—*R. v.* × *catawbiense* = R. fragrans; see p. 712.

Related species: **R. serrulàtum** (Small) Millais. Shrub to 7 m.; young brts. usually densely strigose; buds glabrous or sometimes grayish pubescent, with 15–20 mucronate to aristate scales: lvs. elliptic to obovate or obovate-oblong, 4–8 cm. long, usually acute, serrulate-ciliate, glabrous except the midrib or some-times pubescent: fls. white, very fragrant; tube slender, 2.5–3.3 cm. long, about twice as long as the ovate-lanceolate lobes; style much longer than stamens. N.H.18:252. Ga. to Fla. and La. Intr. 1919. Zone VII?—**R. oblongifòlium** (Small) Millais. Shrub to 2 m.; brts. finely villous and sparingly strigose or nearly glabrous; buds grayish pubescent: lvs. obovate to oblong-lanceolate, 4–10 cm. long, acute or acutish, pubescent beneath to nearly glabrous and sometimes glaucescent: fls. before the terminal buds are formed, white, tube abruptly dilated at apex, 2.5–3 cm. long, villous outside and often sparingly glandular-hirsute; sepals ovate to lanceolate, 1–3 mm. long. (*Azalea oblongifolia* Small.) Ark., Okl. and Tex. Intr. 1917. Zone VII?

85. **R. arboréscens** (Pursh) Torr. Shrub to 3, rarely to 6 m.; brts. gla-brous, rarely with few scattered hairs, often slightly bloomy; buds glabrous: lvs. obovate to elliptic or oblong-oblanceolate, 3–8 cm. long, acute or obtuse,

ciliate, glabrous and bright green above, glaucous or sometimes green beneath and glabrous or sparingly strigose or pubescent on midrib, fragrant when dry; petioles slender, glabrous or nearly so: fls. 3–6, after the lvs., very fragrant; corolla white or pinkish, glandular-hirsute outside and sometimes slightly villous; tube 2.5–3 cm. long, slightly dilated at apex, pubescent inside, longer than the ovate-oblong acuminate lobes; stamens about twice as long as tube, purple above; style as long or longer than stamens, usually glabrous, purple above; ovary glandular-setose; sepals ovate to narrow-oblong, 3–6 mm. long, glandular-ciliate; pedicels glandular-hirsute or glandless, sometimes nearly glabrous: fr. oblong-ovoid, 1–1.7 cm. long. Fl.vi–vii. L.B.1632 (c, as *Azalea verticillata*.) L.S.t.75(c). G.F.1:401. C.L.11:496. (*Azalea a.* Pursh.) S. Pa. to Ga. and Ala., chiefly in the mts. Intr. before 1814. Zone IV. Handsome shrub with large white deliciously fragrant fls.—**R. a. Richardsònii** Rehd., var. Lower, to 1.5, rarely to 2.5 m.: lvs. somewhat smaller; fls. more villous and more glandular; sepals shorter, villous outside; style pubescent near base. High mts. of N. C. Intr. 1917. Zone V.

R. a. × *occidentale;* see under No. 78.—*R. a.* × *calendulaceum;* see under No. 79.

Related species: **R. prunifòlium** (Small) Millais. Glabrous shrub to 3 m.; lvs. elliptic to oblong, 3–12 cm. long, light green beneath, acute to acuminate: fls. 4–5, crimson, glabrous or sparingly hirsute outside; stamens much exserted, style longer, to 8 cm. long. glabrous; ovary glandless. (*Azalea prunifolia* Small.) Ga. to Ala. Intr. 1918. Zone VII.

Subgen. IV. THERORHODION Maxim.
(Series Camtschaticum, 86.)

86. **R. camtscháticum** Pall. Shrub to 30 cm. high; young brts. sparingly glandular-pilose: lvs. short-petioled or nearly sessile, obovate to oblong-obovate, rounded and mucronate at apex, cuneate, ciliate, sparingly pilose beneath, thin and reticulate: fls. 1–3 on glandular-pilose pedicels 1.5–3.5 cm. long; corolla rose-purple, 2.5–3.5 cm. across, with short tube; stamens villous near base; style longer than stamens. Fl.vii–viii. B.M.8210(c). Gt. 36:t.1200. P.F.1:t.22(c). N.T.1:41. G.W.13:554(h). (*R. kamtschaticum* Pall., *Therorhodion c.* Small.) N. E. Asia, N. Japan, Alaska to B. C. Intr. about 1800. Zone II? Difficult to grow; best in rockery in moist and cool situation.

6. **MENZIÈSIA** J. E. Sm. Small deciduous shrubs; buds small, with several outer scales: lvs. alternate, petioled, entire: fls. in terminal clusters, 4–5-merous; sepals short; corolla campanulate or urceolate, with 4–5 short rounded lobes; stamens 5–10, included, rarely the anthers exserted; anthers opening by apical pores; disk 8–10-lobed; ovary 4–5-celled; ovules many: caps. 4–5-valved, leathery; seeds linear, pointed or caudate at ends. (After Archibald Menzies, English surgeon and naturalist; 1754–1842.) Seven species in N. Am. and E. Asia.—Interesting shrubs for the rockery.

M. pilòsa (Michx.) Juss. Shrub to 2 m.; brts. slightly pubescent: lvs. elliptic to oblong-obovate, 1.5–5 cm. long, abruptly mucronate, cuneate, ciliate, sparingly appressed-pilose above, less so and glaucous beneath, short-petioled: fls. few, drooping, 4-merous; pedicels 1–2.5 cm. long, glandular-pubescent; sepals ciliate; corolla campanulate, 6–7 mm. long, yellowish white or pinkish; stamens included, 8, glabrous; style as long as corolla: caps. ovoid, 3–4 mm. long, glandular-setose. Fl.v–vi. B.M.1571(c). G.O.t.27(c). I.T.3:t.104. B.B.2:682. B.S.2:80. (*M. globularis* Salisb.) Pa. to Ga. and Ala. on the mts. Intr. 1806. Zone V.

Related species: **M. ferrugínea** Sm. Lvs. glandular-ciliate; petiole pilose: pedicels glandular-hirsute; calyx long-ciliate; corolla 4-merous, cylindric, 9–13 mm. long; filaments pubescent. Smith, Pl. Icon. Ined. 565. Brown & Schäffer, Alp. Fl. Can.t.61. Alaska to Ore. Intr. 1811.—**M. glabella** Gray. Lvs. obovate, usually obtuse, crenate-serrulate and minutely ciliate; glabrous or nearly so and glaucous beneath: corolla 4-merous, ovoid-campanulate, 7–9 mm. long; filaments pubescent below. B.B.2:682, Henshaw, Mtn. Fl. Am.t.98. B. C. and Alb. to Wyo., Minn. and Idaho. Intr. about 1885.—**M. ciliicalyx** (Miq.) Maxim. Brts. glabrous: lvs. elliptic, ciliate, otherwise glabrous; pedicels glandular-hispid; calyx ciliate; corolla 4–5-merous, yellowish green with purplish limb, oblong-ovoid, 1.5 cm. long; stamens 8–10, pubescent. N.T.1:46. G.C.103:55. S.H.2:f.334h-i. Japan. Intr. 1915.—**M. c. multiflòra** (Maxim.) Mak., var. Fls. 6–10; pedicels glabrous. J.C.27,11:t.3,f.5–8(c). G.C.104:457. (*M. m.* Maxim.) Japan. Intr. 1915.—**M. purpúrea** Maxim. Lvs. elliptic to elliptic-obovate, 2.5–4 cm. long, obtuse and mucronulate, sparingly strigose above and on the midrib beneath: fls. 4–5-merous, campanulate, 12–15 mm. long, bright red, the lobes ciliolate; filaments pubescent; sepals ciliate. S.H.2:f.334. N.T.1:44. Japan. Intr. 1915. Zone V? Very handsome with its bright fls.—**M. pentándra** Maxim. Lvs. elliptic to elliptic-oblong, 1.5–4 cm. long, acute, ciliate: corolla ·5-merous, whitish, globose-urceolate, 5–7 mm. long, 5-lobed; stamens 5, glabrous. N.T.1:51. S.H.2:f.334a-b. Saghal., Japan. Intr. 1905 or 1892?

7. **TSUSIOPHYLLUM** Maxim. Half-evergreen low shrub, with strigose pubescence; winter-buds with few scales: lvs. alternate, small, entire: fls. 1–2, terminal, 5-merous; sepals oblong, small; corolla tubular, with short spreading limb; stamens 5, included; style shorter than stamens; anthers opening by slits; ovary 3-celled. (*Tsusia,* a subgenus of Rhododendron, and Greek *phyllon,* leaf.) One species in Japan.

T. Tánakae Maxim. Shrub to 0.5 m.; brts. strigose: lvs. elliptic-ovate, 8–12 mm. long, acute, strigose above, glaucous and glabrous beneath except the strigose midrib: fls. short-stalked, white or pinkish; corolla about 1 cm. long, pubescent outside and inside; ovary strigose. Fl.vi. N.T.1:38. S.H.2:f.334o-q. Japan. Intr. 1915. Zone (V). Interesting low shrub for the rockery.

8. **LEIOPHÝLLUM** Hedwig f. Evergreen low shrubs; buds minute, pointed, with indistinct scales: lvs. alternate or opposite, short-petioled, crowded, small, entire, coriaceous: fls. slender-pediceled, in terminal umbel-like corymbs; sepals 5, narrow-oblong to lanceolate, about half as long as petals; petals 5, broad-ovate to ovate-oblong, white or pink; stamens 10, longer than petals, glabrous; anthers opening lengthwise, disk 10-lobed; ovary 2–3-, rarely 5-celled; style slender, not exceeding the stamens: caps. ovoid, surrounded by the persistent calyx, 2–5-valved, many-seeded. (Greek *leios,* smooth, and *phyllon,* leaf.) Syn.: *Ammyrsine* Pursh, *Dendrium* Desv. One species in E. N. Am.

L. buxifòlium (Berg.) Ell. Upright shrub to 0.5 m., glabrous: lvs. usually alternate, oblong or obovate-oblong, 3–8 mm. long, lustrous above, paler beneath: pedicels glabrous; petals ovate-oblong to oblong, 2–2.5 mm. long; disk minute; stamens about twice as long as petals; style twice or thrice as long as ovary; caps. ovoid, 3 mm. long, smooth. Fl.v–vi. B.R.531(c). Gd.W.t. 49(c). L.B.52(c). Gn.87:243(h). (*Dendrium b.* Desv., *Ledum b.* Berg.) N. J. Intr. 1736. Zone V. Attractive low shrubs with small white fls. in spring.— **L. b. Hùgeri** (Small) Schneid., var. Upright shrub to 0.4 m.: lvs. alternate, oblong to oblong-ovate, 9–15 mm. long: pedicels finely pubescent and glandular; petals broad-ovate to rhombic-ovate; stamens slightly longer than petals; style less than twice as long as ovary: caps. scabrous on back. B.M. 6752(c, as *L. buxifolium*). (*L. H.* K. Schum., *Dendrium H.* Small.) N. J. to N. and S. C. Cult. 1880.—**L. b. prostràtum** (Loud.) Gray, var. Prostrate or diffuse shrub: lvs. mostly opposite, oval to elliptic-oblong, 4–7 mm. long; otherwise similar to the preceding var., caps. tuberculate on back. Lounsberry, S. Wild Fl. t.122. (*L. Lyoni* Sweet, *Ammyrsine Lyoni* Sweet, *Dendrium L.* Small.) Mts. of N. C. and Tenn. Intr. 1870.

9. **LOISELEÙRIA** Desv. Evergreen prostrate shrub, glabrous; buds minute with indistinct scales: lvs. mostly opposite, small, usually crowded, entire, coriaceous, short-petioled: fls. few, in terminal clusters, short-pediceled; calyx-lobes 5, about half as long as corolla; corolla broad-campanulate, with spreading ovate lobes about as long as tube; stamens 5, shorter than corolla, glabrous; anthers opening lengthwise; ovary 2–3-celled seated on a disk; style cylindric, shorter than stamens: caps. surrounded by the persistent calyx, 2–3-valved; seeds many. (After J. C. A. Loiseleur-Deslongchamps, prominent French botanist and physician; 1774–1849.) Syn.: *Azalea L., Chamaecistus* S. F. Gray. One circumpolar species.

L. procúmbens (L.) Desv. Depressed shrub, rarely to 20 cm. high: lvs. oval to oblong, 3–8 mm. long, obtuse, revolute, often glaucous beneath, with prominent midrib: fls. 1–5, on pedicels 3–10 mm. long; calyx-lobes oblong to oblong-lanceolate, corolla pink or whitish, 4–5 mm. long: caps. ovoid, 3–4 mm. long. Fl.vii–viii. L.B.762(c). R.I.17:t.108,f.2(c). F.D.20:t.2028(c). N.T.1: 28. G.C.53:343. S.L.47(h). (*Azalea p.* L., *Chamaecistus p.* Ktze.) Eu., N. Asia, in N. Am. from Alaska to Nfdl., s. to N. H. Cult. 1800. Zone II. Attractive low shrub for the alpine rockery.

10. **RHODOTHÁMNUS** Reichenb. Evergreen dwarf shrub: lvs. alternate, short-petioled, small, entire: fls. terminal, 1–3, on slender pedicels; sepals 5, half as long as corolla; anthers opening by apical pores, dark brown; style about as long as stamens; ovary 5-celled: caps. 5-valved, many-seeded. (Greek *rhodon*, rose, and *thamnos*, shrub; alluding to the rose-colored fls.) Syn.: *Adodendrum* Neck. One species.

R. Chamaecístus (L.) Reichenb. Diffusely branched shrub to 0.3 m.; brts. slender, glandular-pubescent when young: lvs. narrow-elliptic to cuneate-oblong, 8–12 mm. long, acute, ciliate, dark green and sparingly setose above, paler and glabrous beneath: fls. 2–2.5 cm. across, bright purple; pedicels and calyx glandular-hirsute. Fl.v–vi. B.M.488(c). L.B.1491(c). F.S.19:t.1962(c). R.I.17:t.106,f.4,5(c). G.C.33:293. Gn.89:264(h). (*Rhododendron C.* L., *Adodendron C.* Ktze.) Eu. Alps, E. Siberia. Intr. about 1790. Zone V? Low shrub with handsome fls. for the alpine rockery.

R. e. × *Phyllodoce empetriformis;* see 10a. *Phyllothamnus.*

10a. × **PHYLLOTHÁMNUS** Schneid. (*Phyllodoce* × *Rhodothamnus*). Small shrub with the fls. resembling *Rhodothamnus,* the lvs. *Phyllodoce;* from the former it differs chiefly in the broad-campanulate corolla longer than the stamens and in the linear, slightly ciliate-serrulate lvs. with revolute margin, from the latter in the shape of the corolla and in the narrowly revolute lvs. with the midrib beneath glabrous and elevated.

P. eréctus (Lindl.) Schneid. (*Phyllodoce empetriformis* × *Rhodothamnus Chamaecistus*). Evergreen shrub to 0.3 m.; lvs. linear, about 1.2 cm. long, slightly serrulate, glabrous: fls. 2–10, rotate-campanulate, about 1.2 cm. across, rosy pink, on pubescent pedicels; sepals about ⅓ as long as corolla. Fl.vi–viii. F.S.7:t.659(c). E.P.IV.1:39. J.F.1:58. P.F.1:t.19(c). S.H.2:f.337o. (*Phyllodoce e.* Drude, *Bryanthus e.* Lindl.) Orig. about 1845. Zone V.

11. KALMIÓPSIS Rehd. Evergreen shrub; winter-buds with few foliaceous scales: lvs. alternate, petioled, entire, glandular-lepidote beneath: fls. solitary in the axils of bracts forming short racemes at end of brts.; calyx 5-parted, persistent; corolla broad-campanulate, 5-lobed, stamens 10, about as long as corolla; anthers oblong, opening by apical pores; disk small; style straight, with capitate, slightly lobed stigma; ovary 5-celled: caps. septicidally 5-valved, valves bifid at apex, separating from the central axis; seeds numerous, ovoid, with reticulate testa. (*Kalmia* and Greek *opsis*, likeness.) One species in N. W. N. Am.

K. Leachiàna (Henderson) Rehd. Upright shrub to 25 cm.; young brts. puberulous and sparingly glandular: lvs. coriaceous, short-petioled, elliptic or elliptic-obovate to elliptic-oblong, 1–2 cm. long, acute or obtusish, mucronulate, cuneate, minutely ciliolate or glabrous on the margin, lustrous dark green above, paler green beneath and with scattered immersed glandular scales, midrib and lateral veins slightly impressed above: fls. 3–10 at end of brts.; pedicels 1–1.5 cm. long, minutely glandular-puberulous; calyx gibbous at base, lobes ovate to oblong, 4–5 mm. long, glandular-ciliate; corolla 12–15 mm. across, rosy-purple, with broad-ovate spreading lobes about as long as tube; filaments ciliate only at the very base; anthers 2 mm. long, lilac; style slightly longer or half as long as corolla; ovary glandular-lepidote: caps. subglobose, 4–5 mm. across, enclosed by the persistent calyx. Fl.vi. J.A.13:t.40. N.H.12:172(h). N.F.9:f.77(h). (*Rhododendron Leachianum* Henderson.) Ore. Intr. 1933. Zone VI. Handsome shrub for the rock garden.

12. KÁLMIA L. Evergreen, rarely deciduous shrubs; buds with about 2 outer scales: lvs. alternate, opposite or whorled, entire, petioled, rarely sessile: fls. in terminal or lateral corymbs or solitary; pedicels in the axils of small thick bracts; calyx 5-parted, small, persistent; corolla saucer-shaped or broad-campanulate; stamens 10, with slender filaments; anthers opening by apical pores, held back in little pouches and springing up suddenly by the straightening of the slender filaments when the corolla expands or if touched; style slender; ovary 5-celled; caps. subglobose to globose-ovoid, 5-valved; seeds numerous, minute. (After Peter Kalm, Swedish botanist; traveled from 1748–1751 in N. Am.) About 8 species in E. N. Am. and W. Ind.

A. Fls. terminal
  B. Infl. compound: lvs. alternate, 5–10 cm. long, acute, petioled..............1. *K. latifolia*
    BB. Infl. simple: lvs. opposite or ternate, 0.5–3 cm. long, obtuse, subsessile...2. *K. polifolia*
AA. Fls. lateral; corolla 5–10 mm. across: lvs. usually opposite, obtuse or acutish, 2–6 cm.
  long ....3. *K. angustifolia*

1. K. latifòlia L. MOUNTAIN-LAUREL. Shrub or small tree, occasionally to 10 or 12 m.; glabrous except infl.: lvs. alternate or irregularly whorled, elliptic to elliptic-lanceolate, 5–10 cm. long, acute or short-acuminate, cuneate, dark green above, yellowish green beneath; petiole 1–2 cm. long: fls. in large terminal glandular-pubescent corymbs; pedicels slender, 1–3.5 cm. long; corolla saucer-shaped, 2–2.5 cm. across, viscid outside, usually rose-colored, with purple markings within; ovary glandular: caps. 5–7 mm. across. Fl. v–vi. B.M.175(c). Em.443,t(c). M.M.8:183,t(c). S.S.5:t.236. Gng.7:289(h). G.C.66:203(h). M.G.18:576–9(h). A.B.1927:45(h). Quebec and N. B. to Fla. w. to Ohio and Tenn. Intr. 1734. Zone IV or (III). One of the most beautiful American flowering shrubs.—**K. l. alba** Bosse, var. Fls. white or nearly white. Cult. 1840.—**K. l. rúbra** K. Koch, f. Fls. deep pink. R.H.1888: 540,t(c). (*K. l. Pavartii* André.) Cult. 1870.—**K. l. fuscàta** Rehd., var.

Corolla inside with a broad dark purplish brown band. Cult. 1903.—**K. l. poly-pétala** Nichols., var. Corolla divided into 5 narrow petals which give the infl. a feathery appearance. G.F.3:453. B.C.3:1734. (*K. l.* var. *monstrosa* Mouillef.) Intr. about 1885.—**K. l. myrtifòlia** Jaeg., var. Low slow-growing shrub with darker green smaller lvs. only 2–5 cm. long. G.F.8:317. R.H.1883:11. Gn.29:379.33:603. B.C.3:1734. (*K. l. nana* Hort., *K. l. minor* Hort.) Cult. 1840.—**K. l. obtusàta** Rehd., var. Of compact habit and slow growth; lvs. elliptic, obtuse at ends, 5–7 cm. long. Intr. 1886.—**K. l. laevipes** Fern., var. Pedicels glabrous or nearly so. Va. to Ga. and Ala. Intr. 1939.

2. **K. polifòlia** Wangenh. Low straggling shrub to 0.7 m.; brts. 2-edged, glabrous or puberulous; lvs. sessile or nearly so, usually oblong, 2–3.5 cm. long, obtuse, revolute, glaucous-white beneath, glabrous: fls. in several-fld. terminal umbels; pedicels slender, 2–3 cm. long, glabrous; calyx-lobes ovate-oblong, obtuse: corolla 1–1.5 cm. across, rose-purple; caps. glabrous. Fl.v–vi. B.M.177(c). L.B.1508(c). Em.441,t(c). Gd.W.t.18(c). (*K. glauca* Ait., *K. occidentalis* Small.) Lab. and Hudson Bay to Pa. and Minn. and from Alaska to Wash. Intr. 1767. Zone II. With attractive rosy-purple fls.—**K. p. rosmarinifòlia** (Pursh) Rehd., var. Lvs. linear-oblong, strongly revolute. (*K. glauca* var. *r.* Pursh.)—**K. p. microphýlla** (Hook.) Rehd., var. Low diffusely branched shrub to 20 cm. high: lvs. ovate or obovate to elliptic-oblong, 5–20 mm. long, scarcely revolute; pedicels longer; corolla 8–12 mm. long. Brown & Schäffer, Alp. Fl. Can. t.61(c). N.F.31:f.57(h). G.C.89:180(h). (*K. glauca* var. *m.* Hook, *K. m.* Heller.) Yukon to Mont., Colo. and Calif. Intr. 1904.

3. **K. angustifòlia** L. Sheep-Laurel (Lamb-kill). Shrub to 1 m., rarely to 1.5 m.; brts. glabrous or nearly so: lvs. short-petioled, oblong to lanceolate, 2–6 cm. long, obtuse or acutish, bright green above, paler beneath, glabrous at least at maturity: fls. in many-fld. axillary clusters; pedicels puberulous; calyx-lobes ovate, slightly glandular; corolla about 1 cm. across, usually purple: caps. sparingly puberulous and glandular. Fl.vi–vii. B.M.331(c). M.N.II.2:t.45(c). Em.445,t(c). Nfd. and Hudson Bay to Mich. and Ga. Intr. 1736. Zone II.—**K. a. rúbra** Lodd. Fls. dark purple; lvs. usually broader. L.B.502(c).—**K. a. cándida** Fern., f. Fls. white.—**K. a. ovàta** Pursh, var. Lvs. ovate or elliptic.

Related species: **K. carolìna** Small. Young growth pubescent: lvs. gray-tomentulose beneath: corolla 5–7 mm. across, pink or purple. B.B.2:684. Va. to S. C. Intr. 1906. Zone V.—**K. cuneàta** Michx. Deciduous or half-evergreen shrub to 1 m.: lvs. alternate, obovate-oblong, 1.5–5 cm. long, obtusish, cuneate, pubescent beneath when young: fls. few, slender-pediceled, about 1.5 cm. across, whitish. B.M.8319(c). G.F.8:435. B.C.3:1735. B.S.1:680. N. and S. C. Intr. 1820. Zone VI?—**K. hirsùta** Walt. Evergreen shrub to 0.6 m.: lvs. alternate, subsessile, elliptic to lanceolate, 5–10 mm. long, hirsute: fls. solitary, 1–1.5 cm. across, on slender hirsute pedicels; sepals deciduous, oblong-lanceolate, hirsute. B.M.138(c). L.B.1058(c). L.S.t.126(c). (*Kalmiella h.* Small.) Va. to Fla. and Ala. Intr. 1790. Zone VII?

13. **PHYLLÓDOCE** Salisb. Evergreen prostrate or ascending shrubs: lvs. alternate, crowded, linear, revolute, usually serrulate: fls. in terminal umbels, nodding, on slender pedicels; calyx 4–6-parted, small, persistent: corolla urceolate or campanulate, 4–6-lobed; stamens 8–12; anthers oblong, opening by a large pore; style slender; caps. globose to ovoid, 4–6-valved, many-seeded. (After Phyllodoce, a sea-nymph.) Six or 7 species in N. Am., N. Eu. and N. Asia.—Low evergreen shrubs with heath-like foliage and attractive fls. for the alpine rock garden.

A. Corolla urceolate, slightly lobed; calyx pubescent..........................1. *P. coerulea*
AA. Corolla campanulate; calyx glabrous or glandular.....................2. *P. empetriformis*

1. **P. coerulea** (L.) Bab. Depressed shrub to 15 cm. tall: lvs. linear 4–9 mm. long, obtuse, serrulate, slightly glandular at first: fls. 2–6, ovoid to urceolate, 7–8 mm. long, glabrous, purple, turning bluish in drying; sepals linear to lanceolate; stamens included, glabrous. Fl.vi–viii. L.B.164(c). S.E.6:t.886 (c). N.K.8:t.5. N.T.1:35. G.W.17:261. S.L.34(h). (*P. taxifolia* Salisb., *Andromeda c.* L., *Bryanthus taxifolius* Gray.) Greenland to Que., s. to N. H.; N. Eu., N. Asia. Cult. 1800. Zone I.
Related species: **P. glanduliflòra** (Hook.) Cov. To 30 cm. tall: lvs. linear to linear-oblong, 4–14 mm. long: fls. 3–8; calyx glandular; corolla sulphur-yellow, pubescent outside; filaments pubescent; sepals lanceolate to oblong-lanceolate. Brown & Schäffer, Alp. Fl. Can. t.59b. Henshaw, Mtn. Fl. Am. t.26. Alaska to Mont. and Ore. Intr. about 1885.—**P. aleùtica** (Spreng.) A. Heller. To 20 cm. tall: lvs. linear: fls. 6–14, white or whitish, globose-urceolate; sepals linear to linear-lanceolate; filaments glabrous. N.T.1:30. Alaska, N. E. Asia. Intr. 1915.

2. **P. empetrifórmis** (Sm.) D. Don. Ascending shrub to 15 cm.: lvs. linear to linear-oblong, 6–15 mm. long, obtuse or acutish, serrulate, glabrous: fls. several to many; corolla urceolate, 7–9 mm. long, rosy-purple, its lobes much shorter than tube; stamens included, filaments as long as anthers; sepals ovate to ovate-oblong, obtuse, glabrous. Fl.v–vii. B.M.3176(c). C.L.21:41. B.S.2: 148. S.L.258(h). (*Bryanthus e.* Gray.) B. C. to Calif., e. to Mont. Cult. 1830. Zone V.
P. e. × *glanduliflora* = **P. intermèdia** Rydb. Differs from the preceding chiefly in the more elongated paler corolla and the narrower acute sepals. Montana. Cult. 1933. Zone V.—*P. e.* × *Rhodothamnus Chamaecistus;* see 10a. *Phyllothamnus.*
Related species: **P. nippónica** Mak. To 15 cm. tall: lvs. linear, 5–10 mm. long, serrulate: fls. 3–10; corolla open campanulate, white, 7–8 mm. long; stamens and style included, filaments twice as long as anthers; sepals ovate, acute, purple, glabrous; pedicels glandular, 1–1.5 cm. long. Japan. G.C.78:29. N.T.1: 31. J.L.60:f.153(h);64:f.69(h). Intr. 1915. Zone V.—**P. n. amàbilis** (Stapf) Stoker, var. Lvs. smaller: sepals red; corolla smaller, with pinkish lobes; anthers crimson. B.M.8405(c). J.L.63:570. (*P. a.* Stapf.) Cult. 1910.—**P. Brèweri** (Gray) Heller. To 30 cm. high: lvs. linear, 6–20 mm. long: fls. axillary, forming terminal racemes; corolla divided to the middle; stamens exserted, filaments much longer than anthers. B.M.8146(c). G.C.78:27. Calif. Intr. about 1896. Zone VI?
A related genus is **Bryánthus** S. G. Gmelin; it differs chiefly in its 4-merous fls. borne in peduncled 3–10-fld. racemes, rotate corolla and 8 stamens. Its only species **B. muscifórmis** (Poir.) Nakai (*B. Gmelini* Don) is a prostrate shrub with evergreen linear remotely denticulate lvs. 2–3 mm. long: fls. rosy pink, 3–4 mm. across. Trans. Linn. Soc. 10:t.30B. N.T.1:25. Kamch. to Japan. Intr. ?

14. **DABOÈCIA** D. Don. Low evergreen shrub: lvs. alternate, entire, subsessile: fls. in terminal racemes; calyx small, 4-parted; corolla campanulate-urceolate, with 4 short recurved lobes; stamens 8, included; anthers with apical pores: caps. 4-valved; seeds small, globose-ovoid, verruculose. (St. Dabeoc's Heath, its Irish name.) Syn. *Boretta* Neck. One species in W. Eu.
D. cantábrica (L.) K. Koch. IRISH HEATH. Upright shrub to 0.5 m.; brts. glandular-pubescent: lvs. elliptic, 6–12 mm. long, the uppermost narrower, narrowed at ends, mucronate, revolute, dark green and lustrous above, whitish tomentose beneath; racemes elongated, glandular-pubescent: fls. short-pediceled, nodding; corolla 8–12 mm. long, purple. Fl.vi–xi. Gt.47:257,t(c). R.B.3:121,t(c). Gn.52:344,t(c);71:442(h). M.G.32:179(h). (*D. polifolia* Don, *Menziesia polifolia* Juss., *Boretta c.* Ktze.) Irel. to N. Spain and Azores. Cult. 1800. Zone (V). Handsome summer-flowering shrub; prefers peaty soil. —**D. c. alba** (D. Don) Dipp., f. Fls. white. S.B.II.3:t.276(c). Gt.47:257,t(c). Gn.22:302;76:491(h). (*D. polifolia* var. *a.* Don.) Intr. about 1820.—**D. c.**

bícolor (Koopmann) Dipp., f. Fls. striped white and purple. Gt.47:257,t(c). (*D. polifolia striata* Hort., *D. p. versicolor* Hort.)—**D. c. pallida** (Bosse) Rehd., f. Fls. pink. (*Boretta c.* var. *rosea* Koopm.)—**D. c. atropurpúrea** Dipp., f. Fls. rich purple.—**D. c. nàna** (Lodd.) Rehd., var. Dwarf form with smaller and narrower lvs. L.B.20:1907(c). (*Menziesia polifolia n.* Lodd., *D. p.* var. *pygmaea* Nichols.)

Tribe 2. ANDROMEDEAE Drude. Fr. a loculicidal caps.: calyx dry, small: corolla deciduous.

15. ENKIÁNTHUS Lour. Deciduous, rarely evergreen shrubs with whorled brs.; winter-buds ovoid, with several outer scales: lvs. alternate, mostly crowded at end of brts., petioled, usually serrulate; fls. in terminal umbels or racemes, usually nodding; sepals 5, small; corolla campanulate or urceolate, 5-merous, white to red; stamens 10, included; anthers 2-awned at apex, opening by short slits; style slender, longer than stamens: caps. 5-valved; cells with 1–few, 3–5-angled or winged seeds. (Greek *egkyein*, to be pregnant, and *anthos*, flower: the large colored involucre of *E. quinqueflorus* resembles a flower enclosing smaller fls.) Syn.: *Enkyanthus* DC.; including *Meisteria* Sieb. & Zucc. About 10 species in E. Asia and Himal.

A. Corolla gibbous or saccate at base, urceolate, with reflexed lobes: fr. on straight pedicels.
  B. Fls. in umbels, before the lvs.: corolla about 8 mm. long....Sect. EUENKIANTHUS Palib.
                                                                                1. *E. perulatus*
  BB. Fls. in pendulous racemes after the lvs.; corolla 5 mm. long..Sect. ANDROMEDINA Palib.
                                                                                2. *E. subsessilis*
AA. Corolla not gibbous at base, campanulate; fls. after the lvs.: fruiting pedicels recurved at
  apex.
  B. Corolla with 5 short lobes....................................Sect. ENKIANTELLA Palib.
    c. Ovary and style glabrous...3. *E. campanulatus*
    cc. Ovary and style pubescent..4. *E. deflexus*
  BB. Corolla with irregularly laciniate limb............Sect. MEISTERIA (Sieb. & Zucc.) Palib.
                                                                                5. *E. cernuus*

1. E. perulàtus (Miq.) Schneid. Shrub to 2 m.: lvs. elliptic-ovate to obovate, 2–5 cm. long, acute, sharply appressed-serrulate, glabrous and bright green above, pubescent on the veins beneath; petiole 8–13 mm. long: fls. in 3–10-fld. umbels, slender-pediceled, nodding; corolla white, urceolate, 8 mm. long; filaments pubescent below the middle; caps. oblong-ovoid, 8 mm. long. Fl.v. B.M.5822(c). S.I.2:t.62(c). G.C.III.21:357. N.T.1:199. Gt.80:359(h). (*E. japonicus* Hook. f., *Andromeda perulata* Miq.) Japan. Intr. about 1870. Zone V. Attractive shrub with small white fls. before the lvs.; the foliage turning partly scarlet in fall.

Related species: **E. serrulàtus** (Wils.) Schneid. Shrub to 6 m.: lvs. elliptic-oblong, 4–9 cm. long, acuminate, serrulate, glabrous, reticulate: fls. 3–5, white, campanulate with reflexed lobes, 10–12 mm. long. S.H.2:f.340h(1). (*E. quinqueflorus* var. *s.* Wils.) C. and W. China. Intr. 1900. Zone VI?—The closely related *E. quinqueflorus* Lour. with evergreen entire lvs. and pink fls. is probably not hardy within our area.

2. E. subséssilis (Miq.) Mak. Dense shrub to 3 m.: lvs. elliptic to rhombic-obovate, 2–4.5 cm. long, acute, serrulate, pale green beneath and pubescent along the midrib; petiole 2–5 mm. long: fls. in pendulous racemes 4–6 cm. long; rachis pubescent; pedicels glabrous, about 1 cm. long; corolla globose-urceolate, 5 mm. long, white: fr. ovoid, 4 mm. long, on straight pedicels. Fl.v. S.I.2:t.62(c). S.T.1:t.25. N.T.1:185. (*E. nikoensis* Mak., *Andromeda s.* Miq.) Japan. Intr. 1892. Zone V. Lvs. brilliant red in fall.

3. E. campanulàtus (Miq.) Nichols. Shrub or tree to 10 m.: lvs. elliptic to rhombic-elliptic, 3–7 cm. long, acute or acuminate, appressed-serrulate with aristate teeth, with scattered bristly hairs above and on the veins beneath; petiole 8–15 mm. long: fls. in pendulous umbel-like racemes; pedicels to 2 cm.

thickened suture, loculicidal; seeds numerous, small, angled. (Zenobia, quee of Palmyra.) One species in E. N. Am.

Z. pulverulénta (Bartr.) Pollard. Shrub to 28 m., glabrous, with uprigl or arching terete brs.: lvs. oval to oblong, 2–7 cm. long, obtuse or acutish, gle brous and covered more or less with glaucous bloom: fls. on slender noddin pedicels 1–2 cm. long; corolla white, 6–8 mm. long; sepals ovate or triangulai ovate; caps. 6–7 mm. across. Fl.v–vi. B.M.667(c). L.B.551(c). Gn.24:572,t(c) 81:19;86:656. G.C.III.7:612;23:328,f.119(h). (*Z. speciosa* D. Don, *Andromed. p.* Bartr., *A. dealbata* Lindl., *A. glauca* and *A. candida* Hort.) N. C. to Fla Intr. 1801. Zone V. With white fls. and conspicuous bluish white lvs.—**Z. p nùda** (Vent.) Rehd., var. Lvs. green, without bloom; fls. and caps. some what smaller. Gn.86:656. B.M.970(c). S.B.II.t.330(c). (*Z. cassinefolic* (Vent.) Pollard, *Andromeda cassinefolia* Vent., *A. wilmingtonia* Michx., *A speciosa* var. *nitida* Michx., *A. speciosa* var. *viridis* Hort.) Occurs with the type.

19. PÍERIS D. Don. Evergreen shrubs or small trees; winter-buds ovoic with several outer scales: lvs. alternate, rarely opposite, petioled, serrate to cremulate, rarely entire: fls. in terminal panicles, rarely reduced to small racemes; calyx-lobes separate; corolla ovoid-urceolate, with 5 short lobes; stamens 10, included; anthers with a pair of reflexed awns on back: caps. subglobose, usually depressed, 5-valved, the sutures not thickened, loculicidal; seeds small, scobiform. (Pieris, Greek mythological name.) Syn. *Portuna* Nutt. About 8 species in N. Am., E. Asia and Himal.

A. Brts. strigose: panicles upright..1. *P. floribunda*
AA. Brts. glabrous; panicles drooping..2. *P. japonica*

1. **P. floribúnda** (Pursh) Benth. & Hook. Shrub with erect stems to 2 m.; lvs. elliptic-ovate to oblong-lanceolate, 3–8 cm. long, acute or short-acuminate, obtuse at base, crenate-serrulate and ciliate, otherwise glabrous; fls. nodding, white, in dense panicles 5–10 cm. long; calyx-lobes ovate; corolla angled, 5–6 mm. long; caps. globose-ovoid, 5–6 mm. long, slightly angled. Fl.iv–v. B.M. 1566(c). Add. 5:t.l63(c). Gn.31:612;86:222(h). G.C.45:408(h). S.L.47(h). (*Andromeda f.* Pursh, *Portuna f.* Nutt.) Va. to Ga. Intr. 1800. Zone IV. Dense shrub valued for its early profuse white fls.

2. **P. japónica** (Thunb.) D. Don. Shrub to 3 m., with spreading brs.; lvs. obovate-oblong to oblanceolate, 3–8 cm. long, crenate-serrate, lustrous dark green above, lighter green beneath, glabrous: fls. white, in pendulous panicles, 6–12 cm. long, calyx-lobes oblong-lanceolate; corolla ovoid, 6–8 mm. long; caps. depressed-globose, 5–6 mm. across. Fl. iv–v. S.I.1:t.78(c). R.B.11:109 (c). B.H.21:272,t(c). N.T.1:201. Gn.12:98,t(c);57:399(h). B.S.2:167. G.W. 9:354(h). (*Andromeda j.* Thunb.) Japan. Cult. 1870. Zone (V). With lustrous lvs., beautiful and graceful in bloom.—**P. j. variegàta** (Carr.) Bean, var. Lvs. smaller, with whitish margin. Yatabe, Icon. Fl. Jap. I:t.30a(c). (*P. j.* var. *albo-marginata* Rehd., *Andromeda j. variegata* Carr.) Cult. 1880.—**P. j. pygmaèa** (Maxim.) Rehd., var. Dwarf form with smaller narrow-oblance-olate lvs. Yatabe, Icon. Fl. Jap. 1:t.30b(c). (*Andromeda j.* var. *p.* Maxim.)

Related species: **P. formòsa** (Wall.) D. Don. Shrub or small tree to 6 m.: lvs. elliptic-oblong to lanceolate, 6–15 cm. long, acuminate, broad-cuneate, serrulate: fls. white or tinged with pink, in drooping panicles to 15 cm. long. B.M. 8283(c). I.H.5:t.162(c). G.C.II.15:569. Gn.54:77;81:408(h). (*Lyonia f.* Hand.-Mazz.) E. Himal. Cult. 1858. Zone VII?—**P. Forréstii** Harrow. Upright shrub with pendent brs.; young growth red: lvs. oblong-lanceolate or oblanceolate, 6–12 cm. long, serrulate: pedicels 5 mm. long; sepals whitish; corolla urceolate, 9 mm. long, with narrow 5-angled mouth and upright lobes; filaments sparingly pilose; style as long as corolla. G.35:266. G.C.75:339. S. W.

China. Intr. about 1910.—**P. taiwanénsis** Hayata. Shrub to 2 m.: lvs. oblanceolate or lanceolate to elliptic, 4–7.5 cm. long: panicles upright, 8–15 cm. long, lateral brs. often drooping; calyx-lobes ovate, 3–3.5 mm. long; corolla 7–8 mm. long. B.M.9016c). G.C.71:139;73:63. Formosa. Intr. 1918. Zone VII.

A distinct species is **P. nàna** (Maxim.) Mak. Prostrate shrub; brts. puberulous: lvs. usually in whorls of 3, elliptic to elliptic-oblong, 5–10 mm. long, mucronulate, entire, very coriaceous: fls. terminal, in 3's or in short racemes; corolla globose-urceolate, 4 mm. long, white. N.T.1:168. G.C.75:217(h). (*Arcterica n.* Mak., *A. oxycoccoides* Cov., *Andromeda n.* Maxim.) N. E. Asia. Intr. 1915. Zone I.

20. **LYONIA** Nutt. Evergreen or deciduous shrubs, rarely small trees; brs. angled or terete; winter-buds ovoid, with 2 or several outer scales: lvs. alternate, short-petioled, entire or shallowly toothed or serrulate, sometimes lepidote: fls. in axillary clusters or racemes or collected into terminal panicles; calyx 5-, rarely 4–8-lobed, with separated lobes; corolla urceolate or cylindric-campanulate, with short lobes; stamens 10, rarely 8–16; filaments with a pair of appendages near apex or without; anthers obtuse, without appendages, opening by apical pores; caps. subglobose or ovoid with thickened sutures separating from the valves; seeds small, scobiform. (Named for John Lyon, American botanist, d. about 1818.) Syn.: *Xolisma* Raf. About 30 species in N. Am., W. Ind. and E. Asia and Himal.

A. Fls. in terminal panicles: lvs. deciduous, entire or serrulate.................1. *L. ligustrina*
AA. Fls. in axillary clusters or racemes: lvs. entire.
  B. Brts. angled: lvs. persistent; corolla conic-ovoid...........................2. *L. lucida*
  BB. Brts. terete: lvs. deciduous or half-evergreen; corolla cylindric-ovoid.
    C. Fls. in axillary fascicles: lvs. obtuse or acute, cuneate.................3. *L. mariana*
    CC. Fls. in axillary racemes: lvs. acuminate or acute, rounded at base....4. *L. ovalifolia*

1. **L. ligustrìna** (L.) DC. MALE-BERRY. Deciduous much-branched shrub to 4 m., glabrous or somewhat pubescent: lvs. short-petioled, elliptic or obovate to oblong-lanceolate, 3–7 cm. long, usually acute, or abruptly acuminate, entire or obscurely serrulate, pubescent on the veins beneath or glabrous: fls. whitish, in leafless racemes forming dense panicles 6–15 cm. long; calyx-lobes triangular-ovate; corolla globose- or ovoid-urceolate, puberulous, 3–4 mm. long; filaments flat, without appendages: caps. subglobose 3 mm. across. Fl.v–vii. L.B.1110(c). W.D.t.37,38,127,128(c). B.B.2:691. (*Andromeda l.* Muhlb., *A. paniculata* Ait., *Xolisma l.* Britt., *Arsenococcus ligustrìnus* Small.) Canada to Fla., w. to Tenn. and Tex. Intr. 1748. Zone III.—**L. l. pubéscens** Gray. Lvs. appressed-pubescent above, villous on the veins beneath and loosely pubescent on the surface, thickish, reticulate, entire or nearly so: infl. slightly leafy; corolla short-villous. (*Andromeda tomentosa* Dum.-Cours.) Cult. 1810.—**L. l. foliosiflòra** (Michx.) Fern., var. Racemes less crowded, often elongated, conspicuously leafy-bracted: lvs. leathery, serrulate, usually lustrous above. (*Xolisma frondosa* Small, *A. paniculata* var. *foliosiflora* Michx.) Va. to Fla. and La. Intr. ?

2. **L. lùcida** (Lam.) K. Koch. FETTER-BUSH. Evergreen shrub to 2 m. with sharply angled brs.; glabrous: lvs. broad-elliptic or obovate to oblong, 3–8 cm. long, abruptly acuminate, cuneate, entire, revolute, with a vein close to the margin, bright green and lustrous above: fls. in axillary clusters forming terminal leafy racemes; calyx-lobes lanceolate; corolla conic-ovoid, 6–8 mm. long, white to pink; filaments glabrous, with a pair of appendages near apex: caps. globose-ovoid, 4 mm. long. Fl.iv–v. B.M.1095(c). B.B.2:690. (*Andromeda l.* Lam., *A. nitida* Marsh., *Lyonia n.* Fern., *Xolisma lucida* Rehd., *Desmothamnus lucidus* Small.) Va. to Fla. and La. Intr. 1765. Zone VII.—**L. l. rúbra** (Lodd.) Rehd., f. Fls. deep pink. L.B.672(c). (*Andromeda coriacea rubra* Lodd.)

3. **L. mariàna** (L.) D. Don. STAGGER-BUSH. Deciduous shrub to 2 m., glabrous or nearly so: lvs. elliptic to oblong, 3–6 cm. long, acute or obtuse, cuneate, entire, subcoriaceous and somewhat reticulate: fls. nodding, in axillary clusters forming terminal leafless racemes; calyx-lobes lanceolate; corolla cylindric-ovoid, about 1 cm. long, white or pinkish; filaments pubescent, with a pair of appendages near apex: caps. ovoid-pyramidal, 7–9 mm. long, about as long as sepals. Fl.v–vi. B.M.1579(c). M.N.2:t.47(c). G.O.t.113(c). A.G. 10:281. B.C.5:2623. (*Andromeda m.* L., *Pieris m.* Benth. & Hook., *Neopieris m.* Britt., *Xolisma m.* Rehd.) R. I. to Fla., w. to Tenn. and Ark. Intr. 1736. Zone V. With profuse white or pinkish fls.

4. **L. ovalifòlia** (Wall.) Drude. Half-evergreen or deciduous shrub or tree to 12 m.; brts. glabrous: lvs. ovate or elliptic to ovate-oblong, 5–14 cm. long, short-acuminate, or acute, usually rounded at base, entire, glabrous or hairy on the veins beneath, subcoriaceous: fls. in lateral racemes, 5–14 cm. long, with a few lvs. or leafy bracts near base; sepals ovate or triangular-lanceolate; corolla oblong-urceolate, 8 mm. long, slightly pubescent; caps. 4–5 mm. across. Fl.v–vi. Wight, Icon. 1199. G.C.106:247. (*Andromeda o.* Wall., *Pieris o.* D. Don., *Xolisma o.* Rehd.) Himal., S. W. China. Intr. 1825. Zone VII? Similar in bloom to *Leucothoe racemosa*. Doubtful if at present in cult. —**L. o. lanceolàta** (Wall.) Hand.-Mazz., var. Lvs. elliptic-oblong to oblong-lanceolate, cuneate or broad-cuneate, rarely rounded at base; sepals narrower, greenish. Wight, Icon. t.1198. (*Pieris o.* var. *l.* Clarke.) Himal., W. China. Intr. 1908.—**L. o. ellíptica** (Sieb. & Zucc.) Hand.-Mazz., var. Lvs. deciduous, thinner; caps. 3–4 mm. across; racemes generally shorter. S.I.2: t.60(c). N.T.1:205. S.H.2:f.346p-r,347e-g. (*Andromeda e.* Sieb. & Zucc., *Pieris o.* var. *e.* Rehd. & Wils., *P. e.* Nakai.) China, Japan. Intr. 1892. Zone VI?

21. **CHAMAEDÁPHNE** Moench. Low evergreen shrub, buds small, with several outer scales: lvs. alternate, short-petioled, scurfy, especially beneath, obscurely toothed or nearly entire, more or less appressed to the stem: fls. nodding, short-pediceled, in terminal leafy racemes; calyx small, 5-lobed, subtended by two bractlets: corolla oblong-urceolate, with 5 short lobes; stamens 10, included; anther-sacs terminating into an elongated tube opening by a terminal pore: caps. depressed-globose, with thickened sutures; the wall splitting into 2 layers, the inner one 10-valved; seeds small wingless. (Greek *chamai*, on the ground, and *daphne*, laurel; alluding to the low habit and evergreen lvs.) Syn.: *Cassandra* D. Don. One circumpolar species.

C. calyculàta (L.) Moench. Upright shrub with spreading or horizontal brs., to 1.5 m.: lvs. elliptic or obovate to oblong or lanceolate, 1–5 cm. long, obtuse or acute, revolute, dull green and slightly scaly above, densely so beneath: racemes 4–12 cm. long; corolla 6–7 mm. long, white; caps. 4 mm. across. Fl.iv–vi. B.M.1286(c). L.B.530,1464,1582(c). M.N.1:125,t(c). R.I.17:t.110, f.2(c). (*Andromeda c.* L. *Cassandra c.* D. Don, *Lyonia c.* Reichenb.) N. Eu., N. Asia; in N. Am. s. to Ga., Ill. and B. C. Cult. 1748. Zone II.—**C. c. angustifòlia** (Ait.) Rehd., var. Lvs. linear-lanceolate, wavy on the margin. (*Andromeda c.* var. *a.* Ait.)—**C. c. nàna** (Lodd.) Rehd., var. Low, not exceeding 30 cm., with horizontal brs. and smaller lvs. L.B.862(c). Gs.13:90(h). (*Andromeda c.* var. *n.* Lodd., *A. vaccinioides* Hort.) Cult. 1820.

22. **OXYDÉNDRUM** DC. Deciduous tree; winter-buds small, with about 3 outer scales: lvs. alternate, petioled, serrulate: fls. whitish, in terminal panicles of 6 or more slender one-sided racemes; calyx deeply divided into

5 separated lobes; corolla cylindric-ovoid, puberulous, with 5 short lobes; stamens 10; anthers linear-oblong, awnless, opening from the apex to the middle; style slightly exserted; caps. ovoid-pyramidal, slightly angled, 5-valved, loculicidal; seeds numerous, the loose reticulate seed-coat slender-pointed at ends. (Greek *oxys,* sour, and *dendron,* tree, referring to the acid taste of the lvs.) One species in N. Am.

O. arbóreum (L.) DC. Sorrel-tree. Tree, sometimes to 25 m. tall; bark deeply fissured; brts. glabrous or sparingly puberulous: lvs. slender-petioled, elliptic-oblong to oblong-lanceolate, 8–20 cm. long, acuminate, broad-cuneate, serrulate, lustrous above, glabrous, sparingly pubescent on veins beneath; petiole 8–15 mm. long, slender: panicles 10–25 cm. long, drooping; corolla 6–8 mm. long: caps. 5 mm. long, grayish pubescent. Fl.vii–viii; fr.ix–x. Add. 4:t.139(c). B.M.905(c). L.B.1210(c). S.S.5:t.235. F.E.24:131(h). M.G.19:253(h). (*Andromeda arborea* L.—Sour-wood.) Pa. to Fla., w. to Ind. and La. Intr. 1747. Zone IV. Lvs. turning scarlet in fall, but remaining pale beneath; also valued for its late fls.

23. **LEUCÓTHOË** D. Don. Evergreen or deciduous shrubs; winter-buds small, roundish, with several outer scales: lvs. alternate, short-petioled, serrulate: fls. in axillary or terminal racemes or panicles; corolla ovoid or cylindric; anthers obtuse or 2- or 4-awned; caps. subglobose, 5-lobed, loculi-cidal, the sutures not thickened; seeds pendulous, scobiform. (Leucothoe, daughter of the mythological king Orchamus.) (Including *Eubotrys* Nutt. and *Agarista* D. Don.) About 35 species in N. and S. Am., Madag., Himal. and Japan.

A. Anthers awnless; lvs. evergreen or half-evergreen; calyx without bractlets at base.
                                            Subgen. EU-LEUCOTHOE Drude.
  B. Fls. in axillary dense racemes; filaments pubescent.
    c. Lvs. long-acuminate, closely serrulate; petiole 1–1.5 cm. long........1. *L. Catesbaei*
    cc. Lvs. abruptly acuminate, remotely serrulate; petiole 5–10 mm. long...2. *L. axillaris*
  BB. Fls. in terminal upright panicles or racemes.
    c. Lvs. glabrous, distinctly petioled, serrulate toward the apex, evergreen: racemes
       usually panicled ....3. *L. Davisiae*
    cc. Lvs. ciliate and more or less pilose, subsessile, entire, usually half-evergreen:
       racemes usually solitary...4. *L. Grayana*
AA. Anthers awned; racemes or panicles terminal on short brts.; calyx with 2 bractlets at
    base: lvs. deciduous..................................Subgen. EUBOTRYS (Nutt.) Gray.
  B. Panicles nearly straight; anthers with 4 awns...........................5. *L. racemosa*
  BB. Panicles recurved; anthers with 2 awns...................................6. *L. recurva*

1. **L. Catesbaèi** (Walt.) Gray. Evergreen shrub to 2 m., with spreading and arching brs. reddish and puberulous when young: lvs. ovate-lanceolate to lanceolate, 6–15 cm. long, long-acuminate, rounded or broad-cuneate at base, appressed ciliate-serrulate, lustrous dark green above, lighter beneath, glabrous: racemes 4–7 cm. long; sepals oblong-ovate, scarcely imbricate: corolla cylindric-ovoid, about 6 mm. long, white, usually reddish in bud; caps. depressed-globose, 4–5 mm. across. Fl.iv–v. Add. 4:t.151(c). B.M.1955(c). L.B.1320(c). Gn.M.2:18. G.W.6:279(h). N.F.9:f.72(h). (*Andromeda C.* Walt.) Va. to Ga. and Tenn. Intr. 1793. Zone IV. With rather large lustrous lvs.—**L. C. Rollisòni** Bean, var. Lvs̓. smaller and narrower, 5–10 cm. long and 1–1.8 cm. wide.

2. **L. axillàris** (Lam.) D. Don. Evergreen shrub to 2 m., with arching brs. puberulous when young: lvs. elliptic to oblong-lanceolate, 5–10 cm. long, abruptly short-acuminate or acute, remotely serrulate, often entire toward the base, lustrous above, sparingly pubescent beneath when young; racemes 2–7 cm. long; pedicels very short; sepals ovate, imbricate; corolla cylindric-ovoid, 6–7 mm. long, white, greenish in bud. Fl.iv–v. G.O.114(c). B.B.2:687.

(*Andromeda a.* Lam.) Va. to Fla. and Miss. Intr. 1765. Zone VI? Similar to the preceding, but less hardy.

Related species: **L. populifòlia** (Lam.) Dipp. Shrub to 4 m.; brts. with lamellate pith: lvs. ovate-lanceolate, 3–10 cm. long, acuminate, entire or obscurely serrulate: racemes peduncled, few-fld.; pedicels slender; corolla 8–10 mm. long. Smith, Exot. Bot. t.89(c). S.H.2:f.345h-k,346k. (*Andromeda p.* Lam., *A. lùcida* Jacq., not Lam., *A. acuminata* Ait., *L. acuminata* G. Don.) S. C. to Fla. Intr. 1765. Zone VII?

3. L. Davísiae Torr. Evergreen upright shrub to 1 m.; brts. glabrous: lvs. short-petioled, ovate-oblong to oval, 2–7 cm. long, obtuse to acute, entire or slightly toothed, lustrous dark green, glabrous: fls. nodding, in terminal upright panicles 6–10 cm. long; sepals ovate; corolla urceolate, 6–8 mm. long; pedicels short: caps. 5–6 mm. across. Fl.vi. B.M.6247(c). B.S.2:20. Gn.86:222. (*Andromeda D.* Schneid., *Oreocallis D.* Small.) Ore. to Calif. Intr. 1853. Zone (V). With conspicuous panicles of white fls.

Related species: **L. Keiskei** Miq. Slender shrub; lvs. ovate to ovate-oblong, 3.5–8 cm. long, long-acuminate, broad-cuneate or rounded, remotely and indistinctly crenate-serrate, glabrous; petiole 2–4 mm. long: racemes terminal and axillary at end of brs., short, to 4 cm. long; pedicels slender about 1 cm. long, nodding; corolla cylindric, 1.5 cm. long, white. N.T.1:175. M.I.1:t.34. Japan. Intr. 1915. Zone V. Graceful shrub with rather large white pendulous fls.

4. L. Grayàna Maxim. Half-evergreen shrub to 1 m., with stout upright glabrous brs.: lvs. subsessile, broad-elliptic or obovate to oblong-ovate or -obovate, 5–8 cm. long, acute or short-acuminate, rounded at base, ciliate, otherwise nearly glabrous or slightly pilose, often rugose above: fls. in terminal racemes 5–10 cm. long, leafy at base; upper bracts linear-lanceolate or subulate, longer than the short pedicels; sepals ovate to ovate-lanceolate, glandular-ciliate: corolla urceolate-campanulate, 4–5 mm. long, greenish white to pinkish: ovary glabrous or pubescent: caps. depressed-globose, 4–5 mm. across. Fl.vii–ix. N.T.1:179. N. and C. Japan. Intr. 1890. Zone V.

5. L. racemòsa (L.) Gray. Deciduous upright shrub to 4 m.: lvs. short-petioled, oblong to elliptic or lance-oblong, 2–7 cm. long, acute, serrulate, pubescent beneath, at least on the veins: fls. in upright or spreading racemes, 3–8 cm. long; sepals triangular-ovate to triangular-lanceolate; corolla cylindric, 8–9 mm. long, white or pinkish; caps. subglobose, 4 mm. broad; seeds wingless. Fl.v–vi. G.O.t.57(c). Em.423,t. B.S.2:21. B.B.2:689. (*Andromeda r.* Lam., *Lyonia r.* Don, *Eubotrys r.* Nutt.) Mass. to Fla. and La. Intr. 1736. Zone V. With bright green lvs. turning scarlet in fall and with slender racemes of white fls. in spring.—**L. r. projécta** Fern., var. Racemes 6–20 cm. long, glabrous. Rh.31:t.578,f.1,2. Va. to Ga. and Tenn.

6. L. recúrva (Buckl.) Gray. Deciduous spreading shrub, to 4 m.: lvs. short-petioled, elliptic-ovate or obovate to elliptic-lanceolate, 4–10 cm. long, acute or short-acuminate, serrulate, pubescent on the veins beneath or nearly glabrous: racemes spreading and curved, 2–10 cm. long; sepals ovate to oblong-ovate; corolla cylindric, 6–8 mm. long; anthers with 2 awns: caps. subglobose, 5–6 mm. broad; seeds winged. Fl.iv–vi. G.F.9:225. B.C.4:1850. I.T.1:t.40. B.B.2:688. (*Andromeda r.* Buckl., *Eubotrys r.* Britt.) Va. to Ga. and Ala. Cult. 1880. Zone V. Similar to the preceding species .

24. EPIGAÈA L. Prostrate evergreen shrub with creeping stems: lvs. alternate, petioled: fls. perfect or dioecious, in short terminal and axillary bracted spikes; pedicels with 2 bractlets; sepals 5, imbricate, large, green: corolla salverform, with 5 spreading lobes; stamens 10, included; filaments adnate to base of corolla; anthers opening by slits; stigma 5-lobed; ovary hairy: caps. depressed-globose, fleshy, hirsute, 5-valved, loculicidal; seeds minute on a white succulent placenta. (Greek *epi*, on, and *gaea*, earth; in allusion to the creeping habit.) Two species in N. Am. and Japan.

E. rèpens L. MAYFLOWER (TRAILING ARBUTUS). Stems hirsute, to 30 cm. long: lvs. ovate or suborbicular to oblong-ovate, 2–8 cm. long, rounded and mucronulate, rarely acute at apex, subcordate or rounded at base, ciliate, scabrous on both sides with persistent stiff hairs; petiole 5–30 mm. long: fls. white to pink, very fragrant; sepals ovate to lanceolate, acuminate, 5–8 mm. long; corolla-tube about 1.5 cm. long; staminate fls. larger: caps. berry-like after dehiscence, 8–9 mm. across, whitish. Fl.ιv–v. L.B.160(c). B.R.201(c). B.B.2:692. Gd.W.t.37(c). M.M.3:t.2(c). G.C.42:343(h). Mass. to Ga., w. to Ohio and Tenn. Intr. 1736. Zone II. With white to pink sweetly fragrant fls. Rarely seen in cult.—**E. r. glabrifòlia** Fern., var. Mature lvs. glabrous or glabrate, lustrous. Em.431,t(c). Lab. to Sask., s. to N. C., Tenn. and Wisc.— A form of this var. is **E. r. plena** Rehd., f. Fls. double.

Closely related species: **E. asiática** Maxim. Lvs. ovate-oblong or oval-oblong, lightly scabrid above, usually acute: petiole 0.5–1.5 cm. long: pedicels 1–1.5, rarely 3 cm. long; corolla broad-campanulate, tube 9 mm. wide, glabrous inside, except minutely pubescent near base, lobes broad-ovate, short. B.M.9222(c). N.T.1:172. M.I.1:t.28. J.L.64:f.115. Japan. Cult. 1930. Zone V.

Related genus: **Orphanidèsia** Boiss. Evergreen shrub with large hirsute ovate-oblong lvs.: fls. 1–2, axillary, salver-shaped; anthers with apical pores: caps. subglobose. One species **O. gaultherioides** Boiss. in Asia Minor (Lazistan). Jt.40:469. Intr. about 1885. Zone VI. Apparently not now in cult.

Tribe 3. GAULTHERIEAE Niedenz. Fr. a loculicidal caps. surrounded by the accrescent fleshy calyx and berry-like: corolla deciduous.

25. GAULTHÈRIA L. Evergreen, upright or prostrate shrubs, rarely small trees: winter-buds ovoid, with several outer scales: lvs. alternate, rarely opposite, short-petioled, usually serrate: fls. 5-, rarely 4-merous, in terminal panicles or axillary, racemose, clustered or solitary; pedicels bracteolate; calyx 5-parted, accrescent and usually becoming fleshy: corolla urceolate, or campanulate; stamens 10; anthers with 2 or 4 awns or obtuse; disk 10-lobed; ovary glabrous: fr. a 5-valved caps. enclosed by the fleshy calyx and often highly colored, berry-like; seeds numerous, minute. (After Dr. Gaultier, a physician in Quebec, about 1750.) More than 100 species in N. Am. to Chile, e. and s. Asia, Malaysia and Austral. Evergreen shrubs more conspicuous in fr. than in bloom.

A. Fls. in few- to many-fld. racemes.
  B. Racemes many-fld.: lvs. 4–10 cm. long.
    c. Lvs. subcordate to rounded at base, usually ovate; pedicels about as long as corolla.
                                                              1. *G. Shallon*
    cc. Lvs. broad-cuneate to round at base, usually oblong: pedicels much shorter than
        corolla ....2. *G. Veitchiana*
  BB. Racemes 2–5-fld.: lvs. 1.5–3.5 cm. long.........................3. *G. Miqueliana*
AA. Fls. solitary and axillary, rarely terminal.
  B. Corolla urceolate, short-lobed; anthers awned.......................4. *G. procumbens*
  BB. Corolla campanulate, deeply lobed; anthers awnless...................5. *G. humifusa*

1. G. Shállon Pursh. SHALLON. Diffuse shrub with upright and ascending stems, to 0.5 m.; brts. glandular-hirsute: lvs. ovate to orbicular-ovate, 5–12 cm. long, acute or short-acuminate, rounded to cordate at base, serrulate, glabrous at maturity; petiole 3–6 mm. long: racemes slender, 5–12 cm. long, in terminal panicles, glandular-pubescent; bracts ovate or ovate-oblong; calyx-lobes triangular, whitish, pubescent; corolla ovoid, about 1 cm. long, white to pink, pubescent: fr. purple, becoming black, about 1 cm. across, hairy. Fl.v–vi; fr.ιx–x. B.M.2843(c). B.R.1411(c). L.B.1372(c). Gn.31:379.

to the Falkland Islands; 1716–1801. Spelled *Pernettia* in a preliminary report
About 25 species in Am. from Mex. to the Magellan reg.

P. mucronàta (L.) Gaud. Much-branched shrub to 0.5 m.; brts. puberulous and often sparingly strigose: lvs. nearly 2-ranked, ovate to ovate-
lanceolate, 1–2 cm. long, spiny-pointed, serrate, lustrous, lateral veins obsolete beneath: fls. solitary, nodding; pedicels shorter than lvs., with 2–4 bractlets; corolla 5 mm. long, white, tinged pink: fr. white to dark purple, red in
the typical form, 8–12 mm. across. Fl.v–vi;ix–iii. B.M.3093(c);8023(c). B.R.
1695(c). Gn.23:470,t(c);59:41;79:609. M.G.13:397(h). Chile to Magellan
region. Cult. 1828. Zone VI–VII.—Chiefly grown for the profusely produced variously colored frs. which stay on the plant all winter.—Numerous
forms have been raised in gardens; some of the more important color forms
are: **P. m. alba** Davis. Fr. white. B.M.8023,f.(c). R.B.12:253,t,f.1(c). Gn.23:
470,t,f.(c).—**P. m. ròsea** Davis. Fr. pink. Gn.23:470,t.f.(c).—**P. m. coccínea**
Davis. Fr. bright red. F.M.1879:339,t(c). Gn.23:470,t(c).—**P. m. lilácina**
Davis. Fr. lilac. F.M.1879:339,t(c). R.B.12:253,t(c).—**P. m. purpúrea** Davis.
Fr. violet-purple. F.M.1879:339,t(c). Gn.23:470,t(c).—Spontaneous vars.:
P. m. angustifòlia (Lindl.) Nichols. Lvs. lanceolate to narrow-lanceolate,
acute at ends, usually recurved, of thinner texture: fls. smaller; anthers twice
as long as filaments. B.M.3889(c). B.R.26:63(c). E.N.IV.1:146,f.30a-e. (*P.
a.* Lindl.) Chile, Argentine. Cult. 1840.—**P. m. rupícola** (Phil.) Reiche. Lvs
elliptic or narrow-elliptic, 6–12 mm. long, acute at ends, of thinner texture
lateral veins visible beneath: calyx more than half as long as corolla; stamens
shorter than ovary. K.D.470. S.H.2:f.253c(1). (*Pr.* Phil.) Chile, Argentine
P. m. × *Gaultheria Shallon;* see *Gaulthettya,* p. 739.
    Related species: **P. pùmila** (L. f.) Hook. Usually prostrate: lvs. dense,
ovate- to oblong-elliptic, 3–6 mm. long, acutish, minutely serrulate, lustrous: fls.
on slender stalks 1–2 cm. long, campanulate, 5–6 mm. across; calyx dry in fr.;
fr. white to pink, 6 mm. across. H.I.1:t.9. (*P. empetrifolia* Gaudich.) Magellan Straits, Falkland Isls. Cult. 1933. Zone VII.—**P. tasmánica** Hook. f. Prostrate shrub; brts. slightly pubescent: lvs. elliptic-oblong, 4–8 mm. long, acutish,
obscurely serrulate or nearly entire: fls. short-stalked, campanulate, 4 mm.
long; anthers obtusish; calyx becoming fleshy, nearly half as long as the red to
pink fr. Hook. f., Fl. Tasman, 1:t.73b. Tasmania. Intr. 1930? Zone VII.—
P. prostràta (Cav.) Sleumer. Usually prostrate: lvs. elliptic to oblong-elliptic,
5–10 mm. long, acute, serrulate: fls. short-pedicelled, urceolate, 6–8 mm. long,
white: fr. pink or purple. Venez. to Chile.—**P. p. Pentlándii** (DC.) Sleumer,
var. Shrub to 0.5 m.; brts. pubescent and sparingly bristly: lvs. elliptic-oblong,
1.2–2 cm. long, glabrous beneath or bristly on midrib; corolla globose-ovoid,
8 mm. long: fr. 6–9 mm. across, blue-purple with the ovate acute calyx-lobes
swollen and colored. B.M.6204(c). (*P. P.* DC.) Venez. to Chile. Cult. 1874.
Zone VII.—**P. p. purpúrea** (Don) Sleumer, var. Lvs. elliptic-ovate to broad-
elliptic, 1–1.5 cm. long: brts. often setose. Costa Rica to Chile. Cult. 1937.
Zone VII?

    Tribe 4. Arbuteae Drude. Fr. an indehiscent drupe or berry; calyx dry,
small: corolla deciduous.

27. ÁRBUTUS L. Evergreen trees or shrubs; bark of brs. and young
stems smooth and exfoliating, usually reddish: lvs. alternate, petioled, serrate
or entire: fls. in terminal panicles; calyx deeply 5-lobed, persistent; corolla
urceolate; stamens 10, included; anthers with 2 slender awns, opening by
terminal pores; disk usually 10-lobed; ovary 5-, rarely 4-celled, ovules numerous: fr. a subglobose, berry-like drupe with mealy flesh, usually granular
outside. (Ancient Latin name.) About 12 species in W. N. and C. Am. and
in the Mediterr. region.

A. Panicle broad, drooping, not exceeding 10 cm..1. *A. Uned.*
AA. Panicle upright, pyramidal, larger..2. *A. Menziesii*

1. **A. Ùnedo** L. STRAWBERRY-TREE. Tree to 10 or rarely 12 m.; young brts. glandular-pubescent: lvs. elliptic-oblong or elliptic-obovate, 5–10 cm. long, acute, cuneate, serrate, lustrous dark green above, glabrous; petiole 6 mm. long, glandular: panicles about 5 cm. long; calyx-lobes triangular, ciliolate; corolla 6 mm. long, white or pinkish: fr. strawberry-like, 1.5–2 cm. across, orange-red, warty. Fl. and fr. IX–XII. F.D.20:t.2040(c). L.B.123(c). G.C. III.14:329. S.L.87. Gn.82:437(h);89:608(h). S. W. Ireland and S. Eu. Cult. for centuries. Zone (VII). Conspicuous in late fall with its bright red frs. and white fls.—**A. U. rubra** Ait., var. Fls. deep pink. Gn.26:506;33:320. F.R. 2:375. (*A. U. Croomii* Hort.)—**A. U. integérrima** Sims, var. Lvs. entire. B.M.2319(c).

Related species: **A. Andráchne** L. Tree to 12 m.; young brts. glabrous: lvs. ovate to elliptic-oblong, 5–10 cm. long, obtuse, usually entire; petiole 1–2.5 cm. long; panicles to 10 cm. long and broad; fls. dull white; fr. 1–1.5 cm. across, minutely warty. B.M.2024(c). B.R.113(c). G.C.III.4:724. R.H.1911:307(h). M.A.t.96(h). E. Mediterr. region. Intr. 1724. Zone VII.—*A. A.* × *Unedo* = **A. andrachnoïdes** Lk. Intermediate between the parents. B.R.619(c). L.B.580 (c). G.C.II.9:211. (*A. hybrida* Ker, *A. serratifolia* Lodd.) Orig. about 1800; also wild in Greece.

2. **A. Menziésii** Pursh. MADRONA. Tree to 15 or occasionally 30 m.; bark reddish brown: lvs. oval or obovate to oblong, 5–12 cm. long, obtuse or acutish, subcordate to broad-cuneate, entire, glabrous or slightly pubescent when young, glaucous beneath; petiole 1–3 cm. long; panicle 6–15 cm. long; corolla 7–8 mm. long, white: fr. broad-ellipsoid or obovoid, 10–13 mm. long, orange-red. Fl.V–VI; fr.X–XII. B.M.8249(c). S.S.5:t.231. G.F.3:515(h);5:151 (h). Gn.83:324(h);87:471(h). (*A. procera* Dougl.) B. C. to Calif. Intr. 1827. Zone VII. With conspicuous fls. and frs.

28. ARCTOSTÁPHYLOS Adans.

Evergreen shrubs. sometimes prostrate, rarely small trees, with flaky bark; winter-buds ovoia, small, with few outer scales: lvs. alternate, petioled or sessile, entire, rarely toothed, often vertical and similar on both surfaces: fls. small, nodding, in terminal racemes or panicles; calyx 4–5-parted, persistent; corolla urceolate, or oblong-campanulate, 4–5-lobed; stamens 8–10, included; anthers short, with 2 recurved dorsal awns, opening by apical pores; disk 10-lobed: ovary 4–10-celled; cells 1-ovuled; style slender; fr. a smooth or warty, red or yellowish to brownish drupe, with granular, mealy or fleshy pulp or dry and with 4–10 nutlets. (Greek *arctos*, bear, and *staphyle*, bunch of grapes; a translation of bearberry.) Syn. *Uva-ursi* Moench.; including: *Comarostaphylis* Zucc., *Xylococcus* Nutt. and *Schizococcus* Eastw. About 50 species in N. and C. Am., and one circumpolar.

A. Lvs. entire and flat or slightly revolute.
  B. Ovary glabrous: lvs. glabrous: brts. glabrous or tomentulose.
    c. Prostrate shrubs; lvs. 1–2 cm. long.....................................1. *A. Uva-ursi*
    cc. Upright shrubs: lvs. 1.5–5 cm. long.................................2. *A. Manzanita*
  BB. Ovary pubescent: lvs. tomentose to glabrous beneath: brts. puberulous or tomentulose and usually pilose.
    c. Lvs. 2.5–4 cm. long, tomentose or villous beneath: fr. 8–10 mm. across.
                                            3. *A. tomentosa*
    cc. Lvs. 1–2 cm. long, glabrous or nearly so: fr. about 4 mm. across.
                                            4. *A. nummularia*
AA. Lvs. strongly revolute and entire or serrulate.
  B. Infl. short and dense: lvs. entire..... ....5. *A. bicolor*
  BB. Infl. a long and slender raceme: lvs. serrulate.......................6. *A. diversifolia*

1. **A. Uva-ursi** (L.) Spreng. BEARBERRY. Prostrate; rooting brs. to 50 cm. long; young brts. glabrous or slightly tomentulose: lvs. obovate or obovate-oblong, 1.5–2 cm. long, cuneate, revolute, glabrous, bright green, lighter be-

neath: fls. few; pedicels 3–4 mm. long; corolla urceolate, 4–6 mm. long, white, tinged pinkish: fr. globose, 6–8 mm. across, bright red, lustrous. Fl.iv; fr.vii–ix. R.I.17:t.116,f.3(c). Em.431,t(c). Add.13:t.418(c). Gn.14:68(h). G.W. 14:69(h). (*A. officinalis* Wimm. & Grab., *Uva-ursi procumbens* Moench.) Eu. and N. Asia; in N. Am. s. to Va., N. Mex. and N. Calif. Cult. 1800. Zone II. Trailing evergreen shrub forming large mats, valuable for covering rocky slopes and sandy banks.

Related species: **A. nevadénsis** Gray. Procumbent shrub, brs. sometimes rooting: lvs. oblong-obovate to oblanceolate, mucronate or acute: fls. in short racemes or panicles: fr. depressed-globose, brown. S.H.2:f.357e-g(1). Calif. to Ore. Cult. 1933. Zone VII?—**A. pùmila**. Prostrate shrub with ascending brs.; brts. and lvs. beneath white-puberulous: lvs. obovate to oblong-obovate: fls. in dense clusters; corolla 3 mm. long: fr. globose. Calif. Cult. 1933. Zone VII?

2. **A. Manzanìta** Parry. MANZANITA. Shrub to 4 m.; brts. and infl. white-tomentulose, older brs. dark red-purple: lvs. broad-ovate to obovate, 2.5–5 cm. long, obtuse and mucronate, usually rounded at base, dull green, puberulous when young; petiole 5–10 mm. long: fls. in dense panicles about 3 cm. long; corolla 7–8 mm. long, white or light pink: fr. depressed-globose, 8–12 mm. across, brownish red. Fl.iv–v; fr.viii–x. B.M.8128(c). G.F.4:571. G.C.44: 163. Gn.83:68(h),69;88:756. S.L.88(h). Ore. to C. Calif. Intr. 1897. Zone VII? Shrub with dense panicles of white or pink fls. in spring.

Related species: **A. pátula** Greene. Shrub to 2 m.; young brts. and infl. glandular-puberulous: lvs. orbicular to broad-elliptic, obtuse or acutish, rounded at base, 2.5–4.5 cm. long: infl. short, dense; corolla 6–7 mm. long, pink; fr. globose, 8–10 mm. across, dark brown or black, glossy. Calif. Cult. 1933. Zone VII?—**A. púngens** H.B.K. Shrub to 1 m.; young brts. and infl. white-tomentulose: lvs. elliptic to oblong, 1.5–2.5 cm. long, acute: infl. small, dense; corolla white or pinkish, 5 mm. long: fr. 6–8 mm. across, dark brown. B.M.3927(c). Ariz. and Calif. to Mex. Cult. 1840. Zone VII.—**A. víscida** Parry. Shrub to 3 m.; brts. glabrous and glaucous: lvs. orbicular to elliptic, 2–4.5 cm. long, obtuse to abruptly acute, rounded at base, glaucous: fls. in panicles or racemes 2–4 cm. long; pedicels glandular; corolla light pink, 6 mm. long: fr. deep red, 6–8 mm. across, viscid, rarely glabrous. Calif. Cult. 1933. Zone VII?

3. **A. tomentòsa** (Pursh) Lindl. Shrub to 1.5 m.; young brts. white-tomentose and often hirsute: lvs. oval or ovate to oblong, 2.5–4 cm. long, usually acute, truncate or rounded at base, tomentose or villous beneath; petiole 2–8 mm. long: panicles to 3 cm. long, densely villous; bracts foliaceous lanceolate, longer than pedicels; corolla 6–7 mm. long, white: fr. depressed-globose, 8–10 mm. long, across, brownish red. Fl.iii–v; fr.vii–ix. B.M.3320(c) B.R.1791(c). B. C. to Calif. Cult. 1835. Zone VII?

4. **A. nummulària** Gray. Shrub to 25 cm., with spreading or ascending brs.; young brts. pubescent and pilose: lvs. crowded, orbicular-ovate to elliptic, rarely oblong, 1–2 cm. long, obtuse and mucronate, rounded at base, glossy and glabrous or nearly so, usually ciliate: racemes 1–1.5 cm. long; corolla 4-lobed, 4–5 mm. long, white; stamens 8: fr. ovoid, 4–5 mm. long, greenish, separating into 2–4 thin-shelled nutlets. Fl.iii–v. (*Schizococcus nummularius* Eastw.) Calif. Cult. 1933. Zone VII.

Closely related species: **A. myrtifòlia** Parry. Diffuse shrub to 40 cm.: lvs. elliptic or ovate, 8–15 mm. long, acute, usually broad-cuneate: corolla 5-lobed: fr. separating into 5 nutlets. (*Schizococcus myrtifolius* Eastw.) Calif. Cult. 1933. Zone VII.

5. **A. bícolor** (Nutt.) Gray. Shrub to 3 m.; young brts. and infl. finely pubescent: lvs. oblong to elliptic, 2–5 cm. long, acute, broad-cuneate at base with strongly revolute margin, glabrous above, white-tomentose beneath: infl. short and dense; corolla about 8 mm. long, pink: fr. globose, 6–7 mm.

across, dark red; stone solid. Fl.ɪɪɪ–ɪv; fr.vɪɪ–vɪɪɪ. Apgar, Orn. Shrubs, f.415. (*Xylococcus b.* Nutt.) Calif. Cult. 1933. Zone VII.

6. **A. diversifòlia** Parry. Shrub or small tree to 6 m.; young brts. and infl. white-pubescent: lvs. elliptic to oblong-ovate or narrow-oblong, 3–7 cm. long, acute or obtuse, broad-cuneate, closely serrulate, white-pubescent beneath; petiole 4–6 mm. long: racemes 5–12 cm. long; pedicels 4–8 mm. long; bracts deciduous; corolla 6 mm. long, white: fr. subglobose, 5–6 mm. across, granulate, red; stone solid, 3–5-celled. Fl.v–vɪ; fr.vɪɪɪ–ɪx. G.C.97:336. (*Comarostaphylis d.* Greene.) Calif. Cult. 1926. Zone VII.

29. **ARCTÒUS** Niedenz. Deciduous depressed glabrous shrubs; winter-buds with several outer scales: lvs. alternate, petioled, serrulate: fls. few, in terminal clusters; calyx persistent, 4–5-lobed; corolla urceolate, with 4–5 small lobes; stamens included, 8 or 10; anthers awned; ovary 4–5-celled: fr. a berry-like juicy drupe with 4–5 separate nutlets. (Greek *arctōus*, boreal; referring to its distribution.) Three circumpolar species.

A. alpìnus (L.) Niedenz. Low depressed shrub: lvs. obovate to oblanceolate, obtuse or acutish, narrowed into a short petiole, often ciliate, bright green, reticulate: fls. 2–4, 4 mm. long, white, tinged pinkish, with ciliate lobes: fr. black or purplish black, 6–10 mm. across. Fl.ɪv–vɪ; fr.vɪɪɪ–x. R.I.17:t.116,f. 4(c). F.D.20:t.2041(c). S.E.6:t.880(c).. M.G.25:138(h). (*Arctostaphylos alpina* Spreng., *Mairania alpina* Desv.) N. Eu., N. Asia; in N. Am. from Greenl. and Nfd. to Que. and N. H. Cult. 1789. Zone II. Lvs. turning bright red in fall; suited for a cool place in the alpine garden.

Closely related species: **A. rúber** (Rehd. & Wils.) Nakai. Lvs. usually obovate, brighter green: corolla narrower, with entire or obscurely erose lobes: fr. bright red, 9–13 mm. across. N.T.1:217. (*A. alpinus* var. *r.* Rehd. & Wils., *A. erythrocarpa* Small, *Arctostaphylos r.* Fern.) Man. to Alaska and B. C.; W. China, Korea. Intr. ? Zone V?

Tribe 5. Erɪceae Drude. Corolla persistent: fr. a septicidal, rarely loculicidal caps.: evergreen shrubs with opposite or whorled, small needle-shaped or scale-like lvs.

30. **CALLÙNA** Salisb. Heather. Evergreen small shrub; winter-buds minute, with few scales: lvs. scale-like, opposite, 4-ranked, sessile, keeled: fls. in terminal spikes; calyx 4-parted, colored, with 4 small bractlets at base, longer than the 4-parted campanulate corolla, both becoming scarious and persistent; stamens 8, shorter than corolla, with 2 reflexed appendages on back; style slender, about as long as calyx: caps. 4-valved, septicidal, included in the persistent perianth, few-seeded. (Greek, *kallunein*, to sweep; referring to the use of the branches for brooms.) One species in Eu. and Asia Minor.

C. vulgàris (L.) Hull. Heather. Upright shrub to 0.4, rarely to 0.8 m.; lvs. oblong-ovate, 1–3 mm. long, sagittate at base, puberulous or nearly glabrous: fls. nodding or spreading, usually rosy-pink, in dense racemes 3–15 cm. or sometimes to 25 cm. long; calyx about 6 mm. long, the lobes ovate-oblong: caps. 2–2.5 mm. broad. Fl.vɪɪ–ɪx. R.I.17t.111,f.2(c). F.D.20:t.2022(c). M.M.9:t.5(c). B.C.2:631. Gn.85:208(h);86:27(h). (*Erica v.* L.) Eu., Asia Minor; naturalized in n.e. N. Am. Cult. for centuries. Zone IV. Low evergreen shrub valued for its late fls.; effective when planted in masses, and adapted for planting on sandy banks and slopes.—Numerous forms are in cult. of which the following may be mentioned: **C. v. alba** (West.) Don, var. Fls. white.—**C. v. Hammóndii** Bean, var. Tall; lvs. bright green; fls. white, rather large.—**C. v. Seárlei** H. Fraser. Tall, pinnately branched: fls. white late, Sept. to Nov. (*C. v.* var. *Serlei* Bean.)—**C. v. purpúrea** Don, var. Fls. dark purple. (*C. v. rubra* Kirchn.)—**C. v. plèna** (Waitz) Reg. Fls. double, pink. (*C. v.* f. *polypetala* Beijerinck, ? *C. v.* var. *multiplex* Sweet.)— **C. v. variegàta** Reg. Lvs. variegated with white.—**C. v. aùrea** Don, var. Lvs. golden yellow.—**C. v. cúprea** Bean, var. Lvs. golden yellow in summer, bronzy-red in winter.—**C. v. decúmbens** Don, var. With spreading, partly prostrate brs.; fls. pink, in short racemes. (*C. v. prostrata* Kirchn.)—**C. v. nàna** Kirchn. Low, only 10–20 cm. high.: fls. purple. (*C. v. pygmaea* and *C. v. minima* Hort.)—**C. v. Fóxii** Bean, var. Dwarf and dense, forming close cushion-like tufts. (*C. v.* f. *compacta* Beijerinck.)—**C. v. hirsùta** (Waitz) S. F. Gray, var. Brts. and lvs. pubescent or grayish tomentose. (*C. v.* var. *tomentosa* Don, *C. v.* var. *pubescens* Koch, *C. v.* var. *incana* Reichb.)—Forms of this var. are: **C. v. átrorúbens** Loud., var. Grayish pilose: fls. crimson. (*C. v. Alportii* Kirchn.)—**C. v. seròtina** Loud., var. Pubescent: fls. white, late, Sept. to Nov.

31. ERÌCA L. HEATH. Evergreen shrubs or rarely small trees: winter-buds minute: lvs. usually whorled, short-petioled, small, usually strongly revolute and linear: fls. terminal or axillary and often forming terminal spikes or panicles; calyx free, 4-parted; corolla campanulate, tubular or ventricose; lobes usually 4, very short, white, pink or rarely yellow; stamens 8; filaments slender; anthers with or without appendages; style slender: caps subglobose, 4-valved, loculicidal, enclosed in the persistent corolla; seeds many, minute. (*Ereike,* the ancient Greek name of the Heath.) About 500 species, mostly in S. Africa, also in the Mediterr. region and C. and N. Eu.

A. Lvs. and calyx-lobes conspicuously ciliate.
  B. Fls. in terminal umbel-like clusters; anthers appendaged.................1. *E. Tetralix*
  BB. Fls. in terminal spikes; anthers without appendages......................2. *E. ciliaris*
AA. Lvs. and sepals glabrous.
  B. Anthers included in the corolla-tube.
    c. Brts. finely pubescent: fls. in terminal racemes or panicles; corolla about 6 mm. long.
                                                             3. *E. cinerea*
    cc. Brts. glabrous: fls. axillary, forming cylindric spikes; corolla 2–3 mm. long.
                                                            4. *E. scoparia*
  BB. Anthers exserted, without appendages; fls. lateral.
    c. Sepals less than ½ as long as corolla, usually ovate: corolla broad-campanulate.
                                                               5. *E. vagans*
    cc. Sepals more than ½ as long as corolla, lanceolate; corolla ovoid-oblong..6. *E. carnea*

1. E. Tétralix L. CROSS-LEAFED H. Shrub to 0.6 m.; brts. minutely villous and glandular-hirsute: lvs. in whorls of 4, linear, 3–4 mm. long, puberulous and glandular-ciliate: fls. 4–12, in dense umbel-like clusters; sepals ovate-lanceolate, pubescent, ciliate; corolla oblong-ovoid, contracted at the mouth, 6–7 mm. long, rosy; anthers with appendages: caps. pubescent. Fl. vi–ix. R.I. 17:t.112,f.1(c). F.D.20:t.2023(c). S.E.6:t.889(c). N. and W. Eu.; naturalized in Mass. Cult. 1789. Zone III.—**E. T. alba** Ait., var. Fls. white. —**E. T. Martinèsii** DC., var. Brts. and lvs. white-tomentose. (*E. T.* var. *canescens* Reg.)—**E. T. móllis** Bean, var. A form of the preceding var. with white fls.

E. T. × *ciliaris* = E. **Mackaìi** Hook. Lvs. in whorls of 4, ovate-oblong, glabrous above; fls. in umbels; corolla shorter and broader: caps. nearly glabrous. S.E.6:t.890(c). (*E. Mackaiana* Bab.) Spontaneous with the parents. Intr. 1833.—E. M. **plèna** Rehd., var. Fls. double. (*E. m.* var. *fl. pleno* Bean, *E. Crawfurdii* Hort.)—**E. M. Watsònii** (Benth.) Rehd., var. Fls. in short racemes; corolla longer, obliquely urceolate. S.E.6:t.888(c). (*E. ciliaris* subsp. *W.* Benth., *E. W.* Bean.)—*E. T.* × *vagans* = E. **Williámsii** Druce. Brts. puberulous: lvs. sparingly ciliate, minutely puberulous in the middle above or nearly glabrous; corolla rose, urceolate; stamens included. Spontaneous with the parents. Intr. about 1911.

2. **E. ciliàris** L. FRINGED H. Shrub with prostrate stems and ascending brs., to 0.7 m.; young brts. densely pubescent: lvs. ternate, ovate, 2–3 mm. long, glabrous but glandular-ciliate: fls. in whorls of 3, forming terminal racemes 5–12 cm. long; sepals lanceolate, ciliate; corolla obliquely urceolate, 8–10 mm. long; rosy-purple; anthers without appendages: caps. glabrous. Fl.vi–x. B.M.484(c). L.B.1805(c). S.E.6:t.887(c). Gn.53:364,t(c). W. Eu. from the Brit. Isles to Spain. Intr. 1773. Zone VII?—**E. c. Maweàna** (Backh.) Bean, var. Of more vigorous and more upright habit: lvs. darker green; corolla 1.2 mm. long. B.M.8443(c). Gn.26:259. (*E. M.* Backh.) Portugal. Intr. 1872.

E. c. × *Tetralix;* see under No. 1.

3. **E. cinérea** L. TWISTED H. Shrub with ascending brs. to 0.6 m.; young brts. minutely pubescent: lvs. usually ternate, linear, 5–7 mm. long, glabrous except minutely ciliolate, lustrous above: fls. in umbels or terminal racemes to 7 cm. long; sepals narrow-lanceolate; corolla ovoid, 6 mm. long, rosy-purple; anthers with dentate appendages: caps. glabrous. Fl.vi–ix. R.I.17: t.112,f.3(c). F.D.20:t.2024(c). S.E.6:t.891(c). W. Eu.; nat. in Mass. Cult. 1750. Zone V.—**E. c. atropurpúrea** Lodd. Fl. deep purple. L.B.1409(c).— **E. c. pállida** Lodd. Fls. light rose. L.B.1505(c).—**E. c. alba** Sinclair. Fls. white. Gn.61:430(h).—**E. c. fúlgida** Reg., var. Fls. red, not purple. (*E. c.* var. *coccinea* Bean.)

Related species: **E. terminàlis** Salisb. Upright shrub to 1 m.: lvs. minutely pubescent, 4–5 mm. long, usually in whorls of 4: fls. 4–8, in umbels; sepals lanceolate: corolla oblong-ovoid, 6 mm. long, rosy; anthers with entire appendages: caps. silky. B.M.8063(c). (*E. stricta* Andr., not Willd., *E. multicaulis* Salisb., *E. corsica* DC.) S. Eu. Intr. 1765. Zone VII?—**E. arbórea** L. Shrub or tree to 6 m.; young brts. pubescent, with branched hairs: lvs. usually ternate, 3–6 mm. long, glabrous: fls. in large pyramidal panicles, fragrant; sepals ovate; corolla subglobose, 3–4 mm. long, nearly white; anthers with short appendages. R.I.17:t.113,f.1(c). F.D.20:t.2025(c). Gn.79:288(h). K.V.12:t12,16(h). Mediterr. reg. Intr. 1658. Zone VII.—**E. a. alpìna** Bean, var. A lower and stiffer plant: lvs. bright green. Gn.75:384. G.C.65:283(h). (*E. alpina* Osborn.) Spain. Cult. 1899. Zone VI.—*E. a.* × *lusitanica* = **E. Veitchii** Bean. Similar to *E. arborea*, but hairs of brts. partly simple: stigma pink. G.C.37:138. Gn.71:101 (h). Orig. before 1905. The other parent, *E. lusitanica* Rudolphi, is not hardy within our area.

4. **E. scopària** L. BESOM H. Shrub to 3 m., with upright brs.; brts. glabrous: lvs. in whorls of 3 or sometimes 4, linear, 4–6 mm. long, acute, lustrous dark green, glabrous: fls. 1–4, axillary, short-stalked, forming long cylindric spikes: corolla greenish, 2 mm. long; stamens without appendages: caps. glabrous. Fl.v–vi. R.I.17:t.113,f.3(c). D.H.1:379. W. Mediterr. region, n. to C. France. Intr. 1770. Zone VII? With profuse, but insignificant fls. in spring.—**E. s. mínima** Sinclair. Dwarf, rarely exceeding 0.5 m.: lvs. smaller. (*E. s.* var. *pumila* Bean.)

5. **E. vágans** L. CORNISH H. Low spreading and decumbent shrub, to 0.5 m.: brts. glabrous; yellowish gray: lvs. in whorls of 4–5, spreading, linear, 4–10 mm. long, dark green, glabrous: fls. usually in axillary pairs on slender pedicels about 8 mm. long, forming cylindric racemes 8–16 cm. long; corolla broad-campanulate with obtuse, nearly upright, lobes, about 3 mm. long, pinkish purple; anther-cells separated nearly to the base, without appendages. Fl.vii–x. R.I.17:t.113,f.2(c). F.D.20:t.2027(c). S.E.6:t.893(c). Gn.84:420(h). S.L.50(h). W. Eu., from Ireland to Portugal. Cult. 1811. Zone V. Forming large patches and flowering in late summer and fall.—**E. v. grandiflòra** Bean, var. Fls. larger than in the type.—**E. v. rúbra** Dipp. Fls. more deeply colored. —**E. v. alba** Sinclair. Fls. white.

E. v. × *Tetralix;* see under No. 1.
Related species: **E. verticillàta** Forsk. Brts. whitish gray: lvs. usually 3,
more upright, 4–6 mm. long: fls. on shorter pedicels in less dense spikes. R.I.17:
t.115,f.3(c). S. E. Eu. Intr. 1774. Zone V.—**E. multiflòra** L. Upright shrub
to 1 m.: lvs. 5–6: fls. in dense spikes; corolla pink, about 5 mm. long; sepals
lanceolate, slightly less than half as long; anther-cells only slightly separated at
top. R.I.17:t.114,f.2(c). L.B.1572(c). Gt.50:t.1483,f.9(c). S. Eu. Intr. 1731.
Zone VII.

6. **E. cárnea** L. SPRING H. Spreading shrub with decumbent stems, to
0.3 m., rarely taller; brts. glabrous: lvs. usually in whorls of 4, linear, 4–8
mm. long, bright green: fls. 2–4, axillary, forming terminal one-sided racemes
2–5 cm. long; pedicels about as long as calyx; corolla ovoid, 5–6 mm. long,
rosy-red, like the sepals; anthers dark red; exserted. Fl.III–v. B.M.11(c).
R.I.17:t.114,f.1(c). F.D.20:t.2026(c). Gn.72:176(h);78:101(h);80:605(h);86:
27(h). S.L.170(h). (*E. herbacea* auth., not L.) C. and S. Eu. Intr. 1763.
Zone V. Handsome low shrub chiefly valued for its early bright fls.—**E. c.
purpuráscens** Reg., var. Fls. purple.—**E. c. alba** Bean, var. Fls. white.

E. c. × *mediterranea* = **E. darleyénsis** Bean. Taller than *E. carnea,* and
without the single upright stem of *E. mediterranea:* anthers less exserted. Gn.
78:6(h);88:79(h). (*E. mediterranea hybrida* Bean, *E. hybrida* Hort.) Orig.
before 1894.
Related species: **E. mediterrànea** L. Upright shrub to 3 m.: fls. smaller,
with broader corolla-lobes; anthers half-exserted. R.I.17:t.115,f.1(c). B.S.1:
523. G.W.17:369(h). (*E. carnea* var. *occidentalis* Benth.) W. Eu., Ireland to
Portugal and Spain. Intr. 1765. Zone VI?—**E. m. alba** Bean, var. Fls. white.—
E. m. hibérnica Hook. & Arn., var. Shrub to 1 m.: lvs. glaucous. S.E.6:t.893(c).
(*E. m. glauca* Hort., *E. h.* Syme.) Ireland.

32. **BRUCKENTHÀLIA** Reichenb. Evergreen low shrub: lvs. alternate
or in whorls of 4, linear: fls. 4-merous, in short terminal dense spikes; calyx
4-lobed to about the middle, lobes denticulate, colored; corolla campanulate,
deeply 4-lobed; stamens 8, included; filaments connate at base and adnate
to corolla; anthers ellipsoid, attached at base to filament, opening by oblong
terminal pores; disk rudimentary; style exserted: caps. subglobose, 4-valved,
loculicidal, enclosed in the persistent calyx. (After Samuel von Bruckenthal,
1721–1803, and Michael v. B., Austrian noblemen.) One species.
B. spiculifòlia (Salisb.) Reichenb. SPIKE-HEATH. Dwarf shrub to 25 cm.,
with upright slender brs.; young brts. downy: lvs. crowded, spreading, linear,
3–5 mm. long, bristle-pointed, slightly glandular and pubescent; racemes
about 2 cm. long; corolla pink, 3 mm. long; calyx half as long. Fl.VI–VIII. B.M.
8148(c). R.I.17:t.111,f.1(c). B.S.1:268. S.L.50(h). (*Erica s.* Salisb., *B. spiculi-
flora* Reichenb. f.) S. E. Eu. and Asia Minor. Cult. 1880. Zone V. Interesting small shrub adapted for the rock garden.

Subfam. II. VACCINIOIDEAE Drude. Ovary inferior, rarely only half-
inferior; fr. a berry crowned by the persistent calyx-lobes.

33. **CHIÓGENES** Salisb. Evergreen trailing and creeping plant with
slender slightly woody stems: lvs. alternate, small, short-petioled, ovate: fls.
axillary, solitary; pedicels short, nodding, with 2 large bractlets under the
4-parted calyx; corolla campanulate, deeply 4-cleft; stamens 8, included;
filaments short, inserted on the 8-toothed disk; anther-cells separate, each
minutely 2-pointed at apex and opening by a large chink down to the middle;
ovary 4-celled, adnate below the middle to the calyx-tube and growing into
an almost wholly inferior, white, many-seeded berry crowned by the 4 calyx-
teeth. (Greek *chion,* snow, and *genos,* offspring; in allusion to the snow-
white berries.) Two species in N. Am. and E. Asia.

C. hispídula Torr. & Gr. Brts. appressed-setose: lvs. orbicular-ovate to ovate, 4–10 mm. long, narrowed at ends, revolute, lustrous and glabrous above, paler beneath and rusty-strigose on midrib: fls. 4 mm. long, white: fr. subglobose, about 6 mm. across, usually minutely bristly, aromatic. Fl.v–vi; fr. viii–ix. Torrey, Fl. N. Y. 1:t.68(c). B.B.2:704. (*C. serpyllifolia* Salisb.) Nfd. to B. C., s. to N. C. and Mich. Intr. about 1880. Zone III.—Forming a dense bright green carpet studded with white berries in summer; adapted for a cool half-shady place in the rock garden.

34. GAYLUSSÀCIA H. B. K. HUCKLEBERRY.

Deciduous or evergreen shrubs; winted-buds ovoid, with about 3 outer scales: lvs. alternate, short-petioled, usually entire: fls. in axillary, usually few-fld., racemes; calyx 5-lobed; corolla tubular-campanulate or urceolate, 5-lobed; stamens 10; filaments short; anthers narrowed upward and opening by terminal pores or chinks: ovary 10-celled: fr. a berry-like drupe with 10 1-seeded nutlets, crowned by the persistent calyx-lobes. (After J. L. Gay-Lussac, eminent French chemist; 1778–1850.) Incl.: *Lasiococcus* Small, *Buxella* Small, *Decachaena* Torr. & Gr. About 50 species in N. and S. Am.

A. Lvs. evergreen, obtusely serrate, not resinous.............................1. *G. brachycera*
AA. Lvs. deciduous, entire, resinous-dotted beneath.
  B. Resin glands on the lower surface of the lf. only: fls. in loose racemes.
    c. Pubescence glandular; bracts as long as pedicels, persistent............2. *G. dumosa*
    cc. Pubescence not glandular or absent; bracts shorter than the pedicels, deciduous.
      D. Lvs. acuminate or acute: fr. black.................................3. *G. ursina*
      DD. Lvs. obtuse: fr. blue, bloomy.....................................4. *G. frondosa*
  BB. Resin glands on both surfaces of the lf.: fls. in dense short racemes.......5. *G. baccata*

1. **G. brachýcera** (Michx.) Gray. Box-H. Shrub to 0.5 m., with creeping and ascending stem and spreading glabrous angled brs.: lvs. elliptic, 1.5–2.5 cm. long, slightly revolute, glabrous: fls. few, in short racemes with caducous bracts and bractlets: corolla cylindric-ovoid, 4 mm. long, white or pink. Fl.v–vi; fr.vii–viii. B.M.928(c). Add.6:t.201(c). L.B.648(c). B.B.2:696. Pa. to Va., Tenn. and Ky. Intr. 1796. Zone V.

2. **G. dumòsa** (Andrews) Torr. & Gr. DWARF H. Shrub with creeping stem and erect somewhat glandular-hairy brs., to 0.5 m.: lvs. subsessile, obovate-oblong to oblanceolate, 2.5–4 cm. long, mucronate, lustrous above, lighter green and glandular-pubescent beneath: racemes loose, with foliaceous persistent bracts; corolla 5–7 mm. long, white, pink or red: fr. black, 6–8 mm. across, insipid. Fl.v–vi; fr.vii–ix. B.M.1106(c). B.S.1:584. B.B.2: 696. Nfd. to Fla. and La.; in sandy swamps. Intr. 1774. Zone II?—**G. d. Bigeloviàna** Fern., var. Lvs. elliptic-obovate to oblong-obovate, glandular on both sides as are the bracts; corolla 8–9 mm. long. Nfd. to R. I. and Conn.

3. **G. ursìna** (M. A. Curtis) Torr. & Gr. BUCKBERRY. Shrub to 2 m., with spreading brs.; young brts. slightly pubescent: lvs. obovate to oblong, 4–10 cm. long, acute or short-acuminate, cuneate or rounded, slightly pubescent on both sides, green beneath, thin; fls. in 6–10-fld. racemes 2–5 cm. long; pedicels slender, about 1 cm. long; calyx glandular; corolla short-campanulate, 4–5 mm. long, with recurved lobes, whitish or reddish: fr. shining black, 8–12 mm. across, sweet. Fl.v–vi; fr.vii–viii. Mem. Am. Acad. II.3:t.10. N. and S. C. Intr. 1891. Zone V.

4. **G. frondòsa** (L.) Torr. & Gr. DANGLEBERRY (TANGLEBERRY, BLUE H.). Shrub to 2 m., with spreading brs.; brts. glabrous: lvs. elliptic-obovate to oblong, 2.5–6 cm. long, obtuse or emarginate, pale green above, glaucescent, puberulous and resin-dotted beneath, rather firm: fls. in slender racemes 3.5–7

cm. long; pedicels 1–2.5 cm. long; corolla broad-campanulate, 5 mm. long, greenish purple: fr. 8–12 mm. across, edible. Fl.v–vi; fr.vii–viii. A.R.2:t.140 (c). Em.451,t(c). G.C.III.7:580. B.B.2:695. N. H. to Fla. Intr. 1761. Zone IV.

5. **G. baccàta** (Wangh.) K. Koch. Black H. Shrub to 1 m., upright; young growth densely resinous and sticky: lvs. elliptic to oblong-lanceolate or elliptic-obovate, 2.5–5 cm. long, obtuse or mucronulate, yellowish green above, paler and resin-dotted beneath: fls. in dense drooping racemes 1–2.5 cm. long; pedicels 2–8 mm. long; corolla conic-ovoid 5 mm. long, dull red: fr. 6–8 mm. across, lustrous black, edible. Fl.v–vi; fr.vii–viii. B.M.1288(c). Em.451,t(c). I.T.4:t.152. (*G. resinosa* Torr. & Gr.) Nfd. to Man., s. to Iowa, Ill. and Ga. Intr. 1772. Zone II.—**G. b. glaucocárpa** (Robins.) Mackenzie, f. Fr. larger, blue, bloomy.—**G. b. leucocárpa** (Porter) Fern., f. Fr. white to pinkish, somewhat translucent.

35. **VACCÌNIUM** L. Deciduous or evergreen shrubs, rarely trees; winter-buds small, ovoid, with 2 or several outer scales: lvs. alternate, short-petioled, entire or serrate: fls. axillary or terminal, solitary or in racemes; calyx-lobes 4–5, rarely obsolete; corolla cylindric, urceolate or campanulate, 4–5-lobed or sometimes 4-parted; stamens 8 or 10; anthers awned or awnless, prolonged into terminal tubes, with an opening at the apex; ovary inferior, 4–10-celled: fr. a many-seeded berry crowned by the persistent calyx-lobes. (Ancient Latin name of obscure derivation.) About 130 species in the n. hemisphere, from the arctic circle to high mts. in the Tropics.

A. Corolla campanulate or urceolate to cylindric, 4–5-lobed.
  B. Disk of fl. not or indistinctly lobed: fr. fleshy, many-seeded: lvs. deciduous, except Nos. 1 and 18–22.
    C. Ovary incompletely, but distinctly 10-celled (5-celled in No. 12).
      D. Corolla broad-campanulate; anthers awned: fr. insipid.
        E. Anthers included; corolla closed before anthesis; lvs. half-evergreen.
                1. *V. arboreum*
        EE. Anthers exserted; corolla open before anthesis..............2. *V. stamineum*
      DD. Corolla urceolate to cylindric; anthers awnless: fr. edible, usually blue or black.
        E. Fls. in elongated bracted racemes: lvs. serrulate................3. *V. Oldhami*
        EE. Fls. in short cluster-like racemes or 1–3.
          F. Pedicels short: fls. in dense clusters or short racemes.
            G. Ovary and fr. glandular-hirsute............................4. *V. hirsutum*
            GG. Ovary and fr. glabrous.
              H. Shrubs to 4 m. tall.
                I. Corolla cylindric: lvs. pubescent beneath, 2–5 cm. long.
                          5. *V. virgatum*
                II. Corolla urceolate to ovoid-cylindric: lvs. 3–8 cm. long.
                  J. Lvs. densely pubescent beneath...................6. *V. atrococcum*
                  JJ. Lvs. glabrous or slightly pubescent beneath....7. *V. corymbosum*
              HH. Shrubs to 0.5 m. or only slightly taller: lvs. 1.5–4 cm. long.
                I. Lvs. entire.
                  J. Brts. and lvs. glabrous or the latter pubescent beneath.
                          8. *V. vacillans*
                  JJ. Brts. and lvs. on both sides pubescent............9. *V. canadense*
                II. Lvs. serrulate ....10. *V. angustifolium*
          FF. Pedicels longer than calyx-tube; fls. 1–3: lvs. serrulate.
            G. Lvs. acute to acuminate, pilose at least on midrib: shrub to 1.5 m. tall.
                        11. *V. Smallii*
            GG. Lvs. obtuse to acutish, glabrous: subshrub to 15 cm., with creeping root-
                stock ....12. *V. praestans*
    CC. Ovary 5- or 4-celled (10-celled in No. 19).
      D. Lvs. deciduous.
        E. Fls. axillary, 1–4: anthers awned.
          F. Brts. terete.
            G. Fls. 4-merous, 1–4...13. *V. uliginosum*
            GG. Fls. 5-merous, solitary...................................14. *V. cespitosum*
         FF. Brts. angled.
            G. Lvs. serrate.
              H. Lvs. 1–2 cm. long: shrub to 0.5 m. tall.................15. *V. Myrtillus*
              HH. Lvs. 2–5 cm. long: shrub to 1.5 m. tall..........16. *V. membranaceum*
            GG. Lvs. entire or nearly so.................................17. *V. ovalifolium*

      EE. Fls. in bracted axillary racemes; anthers not or indistinctly awned: lvs. 3–10 cm. long ....18. *V. Arctostaphylos*
    DD. Lvs. evergreen.
      E. Fls. in axillary or terminal clusters.
        F. Corolla 5-lobed: fr. black.
          G. Corolla cylindric-ovoid: lvs. broadest above the middle.19. *V. Myrsinites*
          GG. Corolla campanulate: lvs. broadest below the middle.......20. *V. ovatum*
        FF. Corolla 4-lobed, campanulate: fr. dark red,.................21. *V. Vitis-idaea*
      EE. Fls. in terminal racemes 2–5 cm. long: brts. hirsute or bristly.
                                            22. *V. Nummularia*
  BB. Disk of fls. distinctly 5-lobed; racemes 3–10 cm. long: fr. leathery, few-seeded: lvs. evergreen.
    c. Racemes with persistent foliaceous bracts; anthers awnless........23. *V. bracteatum*
    cc. Racemes with small caducous bracts; anthers awned...............24. *V. Sprengelii*
AA. Corolla deeply 4-cleft or 4-parted with revolute lobes.
  B. Lvs. deciduous: upright shrubs.
    c. Lvs. pubescent on the veins above and beneath................25. *V. erythrocarpum*
    cc. Lvs. quite glabrous or pubescent only near the base beneath.......26. *V. japonicum*
  BB. Lvs. evergreen: trailing shrubs.
    c. Lvs. ovate, acute...27. *V. Oxycoccus*
    cc. Lvs. oblong, obtuse..28. *V. macrocarpum*

Subgen. I. BATODENDRON (Nutt.) A. Gray. Corolla campanulate, 5-lobed; stamens included; style exserted; fls. in racemes, jointed with the pedicle; ovary incompletely 10-celled; fr. black. (*B.* Nutt.)

1. V. arbóreum Marsh. FARKLEBERRY. Spreading shrub or small tree, to 9 m., evergreen in the S.; young brts. glabrous or slightly pubescent: lvs. obovate to oblong, 2–5 cm. long, acute or obtuse, entire or obscurely denticulate, glabrous and lustrous above, sometimes pubescent beneath, subcoriaceous: fls. axillary or in terminal bracted racemes 2–6 cm. long; pedicels 6–15 mm. long; corolla white, 6 mm. long: fr. globose, 6 mm. across, black, inedible. Fl.vii–viii; fr.x–xi. B.M.1607(c). L.B.1885(c). S.S.5:t.230. B.B.2: 698. (*Batodendron a.* Nutt., *B. andrachneforme* Small.) Va. and N. C. to Fla., S. Ill. and Tex. Intr. 1765. Zone VII.—**V. a. glaucéscens** (Greene) Sarg., var. Lvs. glaucescent, glabrous or pubescent: bracts of inflorescence larger. S.M.804. S. Ill. and S. Mo. to La. and Tex.

Subgen. II. POLYCODIUM (Raf.) Sleumer. Corolla campanulate, 5-lobed; stamens exserted: fls. not jointed, in bracted racemes; ovary incompletely 10-celled: fr. greenish or yellowish or nearly black. (*P.* Raf.)

2. V. stamíneum L. DEERBERRY. Diffusely branched shrub to 0.8 m.; brts. pubescent: lvs. elliptic or ovate to ovate-oblong, 3–10 cm. long, acute, entire, glaucous and pubescent beneath: fls. in many-fld. leafy-bracted downy racemes 3–6 cm. long; pedicels 4–8 mm. long; calyx glabrous; corolla greenish white or purplish, 6–8 mm. long, open in bud: fr. globular or pear-shaped, greenish, bloomy, inedible. Fl.v–vi; fr.ix. A.R.t.263(c). N.F.11:f.100. M.O. t.28. B.B.2697. (*Polycodium s.* Greene, *P. candicans* Small.) Mass. to Minn. s. to Fla. and La. Intr. 1772. Zone V. With pale lvs. and conspicuous fls. in spring.

    Closely related species: **V. negléctum** (Small) Fern. Glabrous: lvs. oblong lanceolate to narrow-obovate, short-acuminate, green or slightly glaucous beneath: fls. white or pink. (*Polycodium n.* Small.) Va. to Kans., Fla. and La. Intr. ? Zone VII.—**V. melanocárpum** C. Mohr. Young growth white-pubescent: calyx white-tomentose: fr. dark purple, lustrous, edible. N. C. to Ga. and Ala. Intr. 1909. Zone V.

Subgen. III. CYANOCOCCUS Gray. Corolla urceolate to cylindric or ovoid-campanulate, with 5 short lobes; anthers awnless; filaments pubescent: fls. in racemes or clusters from separate buds: ovary usually incompletely 10-celled. (*C.* Rydb.)

3. V. Oldhami Miq. Upright much-branched shrub, to 4 m.; young brts. pubescent: lvs. short-petioled, ovate to elliptic, 3–8 cm. long, acute to acuminate, sometimes obtusish and mucronulate, ciliate-serrulate, setose on the

sweet. Fl.vi; fr.viii–ix. N.T.1:266. Trans. Linn. Soc. 10:t.9. Kamch., Saghal., N. Japan. Intr. 1914. Zone III. In habit similar to *Gaultheria procumbens;* the large frs. of strawberry-like fragrance.

Subgen. IV. EUVACCINIUM Gray. Ovary 4–5-celled.

Sect. 1. MYRTILLUS Koch. Lvs. deciduous: corolla urceolate; anthers awned; filaments glabrous; fls. axillary, 1–4. (*M.* Gilib.)

13. **V. uliginòsum** L. Bog Bilberry. Low shrub to 0.5 m.; brts. terete, glabrous or puberulous: lvs. subsessile, oval or obovate, 1–2.5 cm. long, obtuse or retuse, entire, pale and glaucous on both sides, slightly pubescent and reticulate beneath: fls. 1–4, subsessile; corolla 4 mm. long, pink or white: fr. blue-black, bloomy, 6 mm. across, sweet. Fl.v–vi; fr.viii–ix. R.I.17:t.117, f.3,4(c) F.D.20:t.2037(c). G.H.t.42(c). N.K.8:t.25. N. Eu., N. Asia, and N. Am., s. to the mts. of N. H. and N. Y. Cult. 1789. Zone II.

Related species: **V. occidentàle** Gray. Shrub to 1 m.: lvs. oblong-obovate to oblanceolate, slightly reticulate and slightly paler beneath: fr. 4–5 mm. across. B. C. to Mont., Utah and Calif. Intr. 1918. Zone V?

14. **V. cespitòsum** Michx. Dwarf Bilberry. Dwarf tufted shrub to 0.3 m.; brts. terete, glabrous: lvs. obovate to oblanceolate or spatulate, 1–4 cm. long, obtuse or acutish, cuneate, serrulate, bright green on both sides, lustrous above: fls. solitary, short-pediceled; corolla ellipsoid, 5-, rarely 4-toothed, 5 mm. long, white or pink: fr. black, bloomy, 6 mm. across, sweet. Fl.v; fr.viii. B.M.3429(c). Hooker. Fl. Bor. Am. t.126. D.H.1:333. B.B.2:699. Lab. to Alaska, s. to N. H., n. N. Y., Mich., Colo. and Calif. Intr. 1823. Zone II.

Closely related species: **V. deliciòsum** Piper. Shrub to 0.3 m.; lvs. obovate or oval, remotely serrulate, thickish, glaucescent beneath; corolla subglobose. Wash. Intr. 1920. Zone V.

15. **V. Myrtíllus** L. Whortleberry. Shrub to 0.5 m.; brts. sharply angled, glabrous: lvs. very short-stalked, ovate or elliptic, 1–3 cm. long, acute, sometimes rounded or subcordate at base, serrate, conspicuously veined beneath: fls. solitary, short-pediceled; calyx-limb nearly entire; corolla globose-ovoid, 6 mm. long, usually pinkish: fr. black, bloomy, 8 mm. across, sweet. Fl.v; fr.viii–ix. R.I.17:t.118,f.1,2(c). F.D.20:t.2036(c). G.H.t.41(c). N.D.2:t.29(c). Eu., N. Asia, N. W. Am. Cult. 1789. Zone IV.—**V. M. leucocárpum** Dumort., var. Fr. white.

V. M. × *Vitis-idaea;* see under No. 21.

16. **V. membranàceum** Torr. Upright shrub to 1.5 m.; brts. slightly angled: lvs. ovate to oblong-ovate, 2–7 cm. long, acute or obtusish, serrulate, bright green and glabrous or nearly so, reticulate beneath, thin: fls. solitary, nodding; pedicel 5–15 mm. long, upright in fr.; calyx-limb nearly entire: corolla depressed-globose to globose-ovoid, 6 mm. across, greenish or purplish: fr. black, 6–8 mm. across, acid. Fl.vi; fr.vii–ix. B.M.3447(c). D.H.1:331. B.B.2:699. (*V. myrtilloides* Hook., not Michx., *V. macrophyllum* Piper.) Mich. to Mont., Ore. and B. C. Intr. 1828. Zone V.

Related species: **V. scopàrium** Leib. Grouseberry. Low shrub to 20 cm.: lvs. ovate to elliptic-ovate, 4–10 mm. long, serrulate, light green: corolla 3 mm. long, globose-urceolate, white: fr. red, 5 mm. across. (*V. erythrococcum* Rydb., *V. microphyllum* Rydb.) B. C. and Alb. to Calif. and Colo. Intr. 1904. Zone V.

17. **V. ovalifòlium** Sm. Slender shrub to 4 m.; brts. sharply angled, glabrous: lvs. oval to oblong, 2.5–5 cm. long, obtuse, sometimes mucronulate, broad-cuneate or rounded, entire, pale green above, glaucous beneath, glabrous: fls. solitary, nodding; pedicels 5–12 mm. long, calyx-limb 10-toothed; corolla ovoid-urceolate, about 8 mm. long: fr. bluish purple, bloomy, about

1 cm. across, rather acid. Fl.vi; fr.vii–ix. Hooker, Fl. Bor. Am. t.127. B.B. 2:700. D.H.1:330. Que. to Mich., Alaska and Ore. Intr. 1880. Zone IV.

Related species: **V. parvifòlium** Sm. Shrub to 3 m.: lvs. broad-oval to obovate, 6–12 mm. long, obtuse, dull green; calyx-limb 5-toothed; corolla subglobose, pinkish white: fr. red, 6 mm. across, acid. Hooker, Fl. Bor. Am. t.128. D.H.1:332. Proc. Iowa Acad. Sci. 23:t.28. Alaska to N. Calif. Intr. 1881. Zone V.

Sect. 2. HEMIMYRTILLUS Sleumer. Lvs. deciduous: corolla campanulate; anthers not or slightly awned; fls. in long racemes.

18. **V. Arctostáphylos** L. Shrub to 3 m.; young brts. terete, glabrous or pubescent: lvs. ovate-oblong, 3–10 cm. long, acute or acuminate, broadcuneate or rounded, serrulate, dark green above and pubescent on veins, paler and pubescent beneath, more densely on veins, sometimes nearly glabrous: racemes 3–5 cm. long; pedicels 5–8 mm. long, as long or shorter than the leafy elliptic bracts; corolla campanulate, 6–8 mm. long, greenish white, tinged purple; sepals triangular: fr. globose, 6–8 mm. across, purple. Fl.v–vi; fr.viii–ix. B.M.974(c). L.D.1:t.38(c). B.S.2:623. Cauc. Intr. 1800. Zone V.

Sect. 3. VITIS-IDAEA (Moench) Koch. Lvs. evergreen: corolla campanulate; filaments pubescent; fls. in short racemes. (*Vitis-idaea* Moench.)

19. **V. Myrsinìtes** Lam. EVERGREEN BLUEBERRY. Evergreen shrub decumbent or upright, to 0.6 m., glabrous or nearly so: lvs. obovate to oblonglanceolate or spatulate, 1–3 cm. long, entire or denticulate, lustrous above, veiny beneath and glabrous or puberulent: fls. in short racemes; bracts and calyx-lobes acute: corolla cylindric, 6–8 mm. long, white; fr. 5–8 mm. across, blue-black. Fl.iv–v; fr.v. B.M.1550(c). Va. to Fla. Cult. 1813. Zone VII.

Related species: **V. crassifòlium** Ait. Procumbent shrub: brts. finely pubescent: lvs. oval or elliptic to obovate or suborbicular, 8–15 mm. long, acutish to obtuse, entire or slightly toothed: corolla campanulate, 4 mm. long, rose-red: fr. black. B.M.1152(c). A.R.2:t.105(c). (*Herpothamnus crassifolius* Small.) N. C. to Ga. Intr. 1787. Zone VII?

20. **V. ovàtum** Pursh. Evergreen shrub to 4 m.; brts. pubescent: lvs. numerous, ovate to oblong-ovate or lance-oblong, 1–5 cm. long, acute, rounded to subcordate at base, serrulate, bright green above, paler beneath, glabrous: fls. in short racemes; calyx-lobes acute; corolla campanulate, 6 mm. long, white or pink, with 5 short lobes: fr. black, 8 mm. across, with or without bloom, acid. Fl.iv–v; fr.vii–viii. B.M.4732(c). B.R.1354(c). L.B.1605(c). B. C. to C. Calif. Intr. 1826. Zone VII. The cut brs. are used extensively by florists for decoration.

21. **V. Vitis-idaèa** L. COWBERRY. Low evergreen shrub, with creeping rootstock and upright stems to 0.3 m. high: lvs. oval to obovate, 1–3 cm. long, obtuse or emarginate, dark green and lustrous above, pale and blackdotted beneath, coriaceous: fls. in short subterminal racemes, nodding; corolla campanulate, 4-lobed, 6 mm. long, white or pinkish: fr. dark red, acid and bitter, 8–10 mm. across. Fl.v–vi; fr.viii–x. R.I.17:t.117,f.1(c). F.D.20:t.2038 (c). B.C.6:3424. N.K.8:t.24. (*Vitis-idaea punctata* Moench, *Vitis-idaea V.* Brit.) Eu., N. Asia. Cult. 1789. Zone V.—**V. V. màjus** Lodd. Lvs. and frs. larger. L.B.616(c).—**V. V. minus** Lodd. MOUNTAIN CRANBERRY. Dwarf, forming dense mats to 10, rarely 20 cm. high; lvs. 5–18 mm. long: corolla pink or red. L.B.1023(c). B.B.2:697. Lab. and Mass. to Alaska and B. C. Cult. 1825. Zone II. Fr. used for jellies and preserves.

V. V. × *Myrtillus* = **V. intermèdium** Ruthe. Evergreen or nearly evergreen; brts. slightly angled: lvs. serrate, without black dots beneath: fr. dark violet. R.I.17:t.118,f.4,5(c). D.H.1:338. Jour. Linn. Soc. Bot. 24:125,t. Occasionally with the parents. Intr. 1870.

Related species: **V. floribúndum** H.B.K. Shrub; brts. and petioles pubescent: lvs. elliptic to ovate-elliptic, 8–15 mm. long, acute at ends, serrulate-crenate: fls. in short dense racemes 4-merous; corolla urceolate, 5–8 mm. long; anthers awnless. B.M.6872(c, as *V. Mortinia*). Colombia to Peru. Cult. 1884. Zone VII?—V. f. ramosíssimum (Dun.) Sleumer, var. Lvs. elliptic or ovate, 7–10 mm. long. Costa Rica to Peru. Cult. 1936.

22. **V. Nummulària** Clarke. Upright small shrub; brts. densely hirsute or bristly: lvs. subsessile, ovate or oval, 1–1.5 cm. long, obtuse, nearly entire, revolute at margin, rugose above, glabrous: racemes terminal, 2–5 cm. long; pedicels 6 mm. long, glabrous; bracts elliptic, caducous; calyx ciliate; corolla tubular, 5 mm. long, rose-red to pinkish; filaments pilose; anthers with long awns: fr. globose, 6 mm. across, black. Fl.v–vi. J.L.60:f.155(h). Himal. Intr. 1850. Zone VII.

Related species: **V. Delavaỳi** Franch. Brts. short-hispid: lvs. obovate, 10–13 mm. long, usually emarginate, cuneate, entire, glabrous: racemes 1.5–2.5 cm. long; pedicels hispid; calyx ciliate; corolla globose-urceolate, 4 mm. long, creamy white: fr. globose, 4–5 mm. across, dark crimson. W. China. Cult. 1933. Zone VII.—V. moupinénse Franch. Brts. pubescent: lvs. obovate to oblong-obovate, obtuse or rounded at apex: racemes 2–2.5 cm. long; pedicels and calyx glabrous; corolla urceolate, 5 mm. long, brownish red: fr. 6 mm across, purple-black. W. China. Intr. 1909. Zone VII.

Subgen. V. EPIGYNIUM (Klotzsch) Benth. & Hook. Lvs. evergreen: corolla urceolate or conic: filaments pubescent; anthers awned; disk distinctly 5-lobed; ovary 5- or 10-celled: fr. leathery, few-seeded. (*Epigynium Klotzsch*.)

23. **V. bracteàtum** Thunb. Evergreen shrub to 1.5 m.: lvs. elliptic to elliptic-oblong, 2.5–6 cm. long, acute, broad-cuneate, remotely serrulate, glabrous or nearly so: racemes 2–5 cm. long, with persistent, lanceolate, leafy bracts; the short pedicels and calyx puberulous; corolla cylindric-ovoid, 6–7 mm. long, puberulous: fr. red. S.I.2:t.61(c). L.B.1648(c, as *Andromeda chinensis*). N.T.1:242. J.L.64:f.55. Japan, China. Cult. 1830. Zone VII.

24. **V. Sprengélii** (Don) Sleumer. Evergreen upright shrub, glabrous or slightly pubescent: lvs. subsessile, oblong-ovate to lanceolate, about 6 cm. long, acuminate, crenate-serrulate, glabrous: racemes 3–10 cm. long, several at end of brts.; bracts small, caducous; calyx glabrous; corolla tubular, 6 mm. long, white, glabrous within; anthers with 3 mm. long awns: fr. globose, 5 mm. across. (*V. mandarinorum* Diels, *V. Donnianum* Wight.) China, Himal. Intr. about 1908. Zone VII.

To this subgen. belong also: **V. frágile** Franch. Shrub to 1 m.: lvs. broad-ovate to oval, acutish or obtuse and mucronulate, serrulate, glabrous or setulose on midrib beneath: racemes 2.5–5 cm. long, pubescent; bracts red; calyx ciliate; corolla urceolate, 4–6 mm. long, rosy-red to white: fr. 5 mm. across, black. W. China. Intr. about 1920. Zone VII.—V. Merrilliànum Hayata. Low shrub; brts. hispid: lvs. obovate, about 8 mm. long, rounded and emarginate, cuneate, entire, rugulose above, glabrous; petiole 1–2 mm. long: racemes terminal, short: calyx glabrous; corolla urceolate, 4 mm. long; anthers with short awns: fr. about 1 cm. across, 10-celled. J.C.25,19:t.24. Hayata, Ic. Formos. 2:117. Formosa. Cult. 1933. Zone VII.—V. urceolàtum Hemsl. Shrub to 2 m.: lvs. elliptic-ovate to oblong-ovate, 6–9 cm. long, subsessile, long-acuminate, glabrous: fls. broad-urceolate, about 5 mm. long, pink, in axillary racemes; anthers partly exserted; bracts large, ovate, caducous: fr. globose, 6–7 mm. across, black. W. China. Intr. 1910. Zone VII?

Subgen. VI. OXYCOCCOIDES (Benth. & Hook.) Sleumer. Corolla deeply 4-cleft with revolute linear-oblong lobes; ovary 4-celled: fls. solitary, axillary, nodding, jointed with the pedicel: lvs. deciduous. (*Hugeria* Small.)

25. **V. erythrocárpum** Michx. Shrub to 2 m., with spreading brs.; brts. pubescent: lvs. short-petioled, ovate to oblong-lanceolate, 3–7 cm. long, acuminate, rounded at base or broad-cuneate, setose-serrulate, green on both sides; slightly pubescent on the veins above and beneath: pedicels about 1

cm. long; corolla about 1 cm. long, pale red: fr. about 6 mm. across, bright red at first, later purplish red, acid. Fl.v; fr.ix. B.M.7413(c). Ad.21:674(c). B.B.2:705. (*Oxycoccus erythrocarpus* Pers., *Hugeria erythrocarpa* Small.) Va. to Ga. Intr. 1806. Zone V.

26. **V. japónicum** Miq. Shrub to 1 m.; brts. angular, glabrous: lvs. very short-petioled, ovate to ovate-oblong, 2–6 cm. long, acute to acuminate, rounded or subcordate at base, serrulate with bristly teeth, bright green and somewhat rugulose above, glaucescent beneath, quite glabrous: pedicels 1–1.5 cm. long; corolla 8 mm. long, pinkish: fr. sometimes pyriform, 5–7 mm. across, scarlet, pendulous. Fl.vii; fr.ix. N.K.8:t.20. N.T.1:228. (*Oxyccoides japonicus* Nakai, *Hugeria japonica* Nakai.) Japan, Korea. Intr. 1892. Zone V.—**V. j. sínicum** (Nakai) Rehd., var. Lvs. ovate-oblong to ovate-lanceolate, smaller, pubescent on and along the midrib beneath near base. China. Intr. 1907. Zone VI.

Subgen. VII. OXYCOCCUS (Hill) Gray. Corolla 4-parted to the base or nearly to the base, with revolute linear-oblong lobes; ovary 4-celled: fls. on slender pedicels, axillary or in racemes: trailing evergreen shrubs. (*Oxycoccus* Adans., *Schollera* Roth.)

27. **V. Oxycóccus** L. SMALL CRANBERRY. Creeping, with filiform stems to 0.5 m. long: lvs. ovate to oblong-ovate, 4–10 mm. long, acute, strongly revolute, dark green above, glaucous beneath: fls. 1–4 in a terminal raceme, on slender pedicels, 1.5–2.5 cm. long, with 2 small colored bracts near the middle: petals 5–6 mm. long, recurved; filaments half as long as anthers: fr. globose to pyriform, 6–8 mm. across, red. Fl.v–vii; fr.ix–xi. R.I.17:t.118,f.6(c). F.D.20:t.2039(c). B.B.2:704. (*Oxycoccus palustris* Pers.) N. Eu., N. Asia and N. Am., s. to Pa., Mich. and Wisc. Cult. 1789. Zone II. Fr. used for jellies and preserves.—**V. O. intermèdium** Gray, var. Coarser: lvs. 6–15 mm. long, acute or obtuse, slightly revolute: fls. 2–10 on a longer rachis; petals 6–8 mm. long: fr. 8–10 mm. across. Nfd. to B. C., s. to Mich. and to N. C. in the mts.; also N. Asia.

28. **V. macrocárpum** Ait. LARGE CRANBERRY. Creeping, with slender stems to 1 m. long, ascending at ends: lvs. elliptic-oblong to oblong, 6–18 mm. long, flat or slightly revolute, slightly whitened beneath: pedicels 1–10, from an elongated rachis terminated by a leafy shoot; pedicels with 2 leaf-like bracts near apex; petals 6–10 mm. long; filaments scarcely ⅓ the length of the anthers: fr. 1–2 cm. across. Fl.vi–viii; fr.ix–xi. B.M.2586(c). Em. 456,t(c). Gt.21:1,t(c). M.N.2:t.28(c). (*Oxycoccus macrocarpus* Pers.—AMERICAN C.) Nfd. to Sask., s. to N. C., Mich. and Minn. Intr. 1760. Zone II. Cult. for its fr., which is extensively used for jellies and preserves.

Fam. 88. **DIAPENSIACEAE** Lindl. DIAPENSIA FAMILY

Suffruticose plants or perennial herbs, evergreen: lvs. alternate or opposite, simple, estipulate: fls. perfect, 5-merous, gamopetalous or petals separate, solitary or racemose; stamens 5, adnate to corolla or sometimes monadelphous; anthers opening by longitudinal slits; staminodes sometimes present; disk absent; fr. a loculicidal caps. with several or numerous seeds; ovary 3-celled; style 1, with 3-lobed stigma.—Six genera with about 10 circumpolar species, s. to Ga. and to Himal. in Asia.

A. Fls. on 1-fld. peduncle: densely tufted plant..................................1. *Diapensia*
AA. Fls. sessile: creeping plant..2. *Pyxidanthera*

1. **DIAPÉNSIA** L. Evergreen suffruticose plants forming dense convex tufts: lvs. crowded, narrow-spatulate, mostly opposite, entire: fls. solitary on

a terminal peduncle, 3-bracted under the calyx; sepals coriaceous, broad; corolla campanulate, 5-lobed with rounded lobes: filaments broad, adnate to the corolla up to the sinus; anther-cells ovoid, divergent below, obtuse: caps. inclosed in the calyx, cartilaginous; cells few-seeded. (Ancient Greek name of uncertain meaning.) Four species in N. Am., N. Eu. and Asia.

D. lappònica L. Tufts, up to 10 cm. high: lvs. obtuse, 5–15 mm. long, obtuse: fls. white, 1.5–2 cm. across, on a peduncle finally 1.5–3 cm. long: fr. ovoid, 4–6 mm. long. Fl.vi–vii. B.M.1108(c). E.P.IV.1:82. S.H.2:f.370a-e. Circumpolar, in N. Am. s. to alpine summits of N. H. and N. Y. Intr. 1801. Zone I. Interesting plant adapted for the alpine rock garden.

2. **PYXIDANTHÈRA** Michx. Evergreen prostrate and creeping plant: lvs. mostly alternate, narrow-oblanceolate: fls. solitary, sessile; sepals thin, obtuse; corolla campanulate, 5-lobed with broad lobes; stamens short, inserted at base of sinus; anthers short, opening transversely, pointed at base; ovary 3-celled: caps. globose. (Greek *pyxis*, small box, and *anthera*; the anthers opening as if by a lid.) One species.

P. barbulàta Michx. FLOWERING MOSS. Lvs. awl-pointed, 3–8 mm. long, slightly hairy near base: fls. 4–6 mm. broad, white or pink. Fl.iv–v. B.M. 4592(c). M.M.8:t.33(c). Gn.27:209. B.B.2:583. N. J. to N. C.; in sandy pine barrens. Intr. 1806. Zone VI. Dotted with white or pink fls. in early spring; adapted for the rock garden.

Fam. 89. **MYRSINACEAE** Lindl. MYRSINE FAMILY

Trees or shrubs: lvs. usually alternate, coriaceous, glandular-dotted, estipulate: fls. perfect or unisexual, regular; calyx 4–5-parted, persistent; corolla gamopetalous, 4–5-lobed, rarely petals distinct; stamens 5, mostly epipetalous, separate or monadelphous; staminodes often present; ovary superior or inferior, 1-celled, with basal or central placenta; ovules few or numerous; style and stigma 1; fr. usually a drupe, 1- or few-seeded, rarely many-seeded; seeds albuminous. More than 30 genera with about 550 species, chiefly trop.

ARDÍSIA Swartz. Evergreen trees or shrubs; lvs. entire or dentate: fls. usually in cymes or panicles; corolla rotate, 5-, rarely 4- or 6-parted, the divisions dextrorsely convolute in bud; calyx 4–6-parted, small, persistent; stamens inserted on throat of corolla, with very short filaments and large sagittate anthers opening by longitudinal slits: fr. a 1-seeded drupe, with thin flesh. (Greek *ardis*, point; referring to the pointed anthers.) About 200 species, chiefly in trop. and subtrop. regions.

A. japónica (Thunb.) Bl. Upright shrub to 0.4 m.; lvs. crowded at end of stems, elliptic, 4–10 cm. long, acute at ends, lustrous bright green, glabrous except the puberulous midrib; petiole 5–10 mm. long, puberulous: racemes 2–6-, rarely many-fld. and paniculate; corolla about 1.2 cm. across, with spreading ovate acute lobes, white: fr. globose, 6 mm. across, red. Fl.viii–ix; fr.ix–xi. B.R.1892(c). N.T.1:278. S.H.2:f.371a-e. (*Bladhia j.* Thunb.) Japan, China. Intr. about 1830. Zone (V) or VI.

The related family of **PRIMULACEAE** which differs chiefly in its dehiscent many-seeded capsular fr. contains mostly herbs and only few suffruticose plants of which none seem to be in cult. A suffruticose genus worth trying within our area is **Dionýsia** Fenzl with about 15 species from the high mts. of Persia and Afghanistan; the species are plants of the habit of Diapensia with salver-shaped usually yellow fls.; they would find their proper place in the alpine rock garden.

Fam. 90. **PLUMBAGINACEAE** Lindl. LEADWORT FAMILY

Herbs or shrubs: lvs. alternate, linear to elliptic, usually entire: fls. perfect, regular, in panicles, spikes or heads, 5-merous; calyx scarious, persistent, plicate, angled or winged, often colored, bracted at base: corolla gamopetalous or petals nearly separate, convolute in bud; stamens 5, epipetalous; ovary superior, 1-celled, with 1 basal ovule; styles or stigmas 5: fr. a caps. or utricle surrounded by the calyx.—About 10 genera with 250 species chiefly in the Mediterr. region and C. Asia.

CERATOSTÍGMA Bge. Shrubs or perennial herbs: lvs. alternate, lanceolate to obovate, ciliate: fls. usually in terminal and axillary bracted heads; calyx tubular, 5-parted, with narrow lobes, 10-nerved at base, eglandular: corolla salver-shaped with long tube and spreading obovate lobes, rose or violet; stamens inserted at the middle of the corolla-tube; style slender, with 5 stigmas: caps. 5-valved, inclosed in the calyx. (Greek, *keras, keratos,* horn, and *stigma;* referring to the shape of the stigmas.) Syn. *Valoradia* Hochst. About 8 species in C. Africa, Himal. and W. China.

C. **Willmottiànum** Stapf. Much-branched shrub to 1.5 m.; brts. grooved, strigillose; young brts. scaly at base: lvs. subsessile, rhombic or rhombic-obovate to rhombic-lanceolate, 3–5 cm. long, acute, gradually narrowed at base, ciliate, strigose above, more densely beneath and glandular-scurfy: fl.-heads surrounded by stiff lanceolate acuminate bracts rigidly ciliate, 8–14 mm. long; corolla salver-shaped, tube rosy-red, limb bright blue, 1.5–2 cm. across, the lobes truncate-obovate; anthers purple; style exserted. Fl.vii–xi. B.M.8591. W. China. Intr. 1908. Zone VII? Loosely branched rather sparingly leafy shrub with handsome bright blue fls.

Closely related species: C. **mínus** Prain. Smaller plant, with generally obovate obtuse and mucronulate lvs. and smaller terminal and axillary heads forming spikes at end of the brts. (*C. Polhilli* Bulley.) W. China. Intr. about 1900.—The best known species, C. **plumbaginoìdes** Bge. (*Plumbago Larpentae* Lindl.), is an herbaceous perennial to 0.3 m. tall with deep blue fls. in dense heads or clusters. B.M.4487(c). Add.5:t.183(c).

Related genus: **Acantholìmon** Boiss. Low tufted subshrubs or herbs with linear rigid lvs.: calyx funnelform; corolla white or rose; stamens inserted at base. More than 80 species from the e. Mediterr. region to C. Asia.—A. **venústum** Boiss. Subshrub to 25 cm.: lvs. crowded, subulate, about 3 cm. long, nearly pungent, concave above, rounded at back; peduncles 7–10 cm. long; spikes 5–8 cm. long, curved; fls. about 1.5 cm. across, rose; calyx yellow-brown. Fl.vii–viii. Asia Minor. Cult. 1866. Zone VII?

Fam. 91. **SAPOTACEAE** Dumort. SAPODILLA FAMILY

Trees or shrubs with milky juice: lvs. alternate, entire, more or less coriaceous, exstipulate: fls. usually perfect, regular, axillary; sepals 5, or in 2 whorls of 2, 3 or 4; corolla gamopetalous, lobes as many as sepals or twice as many, imbricate, sometimes with appendages; stamens as many as corolla-lobes and opposite them; staminodes often present; ovary superior, 4- to many-celled; 1 basal ovule in each cell; style and stigma 1: fr. a drupe.—More than 30 genera with about 400 species chiefly in trop. and subtrop. regions.

BUMÈLIA Swartz. Deciduous or evergreen trees and shrubs with milky or gummy sap and very hard wood; brs. often thorny; winter-buds ovoid, small, with several outer scales: fls. minute, usually perfect, in axillary clusters, slender-pediceled; calyx 5-lobed, persistent, with obtuse lobes; corolla campanulate, 5-lobed, lobes longer than tube, with a small appendage on

757

each side; stamens 5, adnate to corolla, with short filaments, alternating with petaloid staminodes; ovary 5-celled, pubescent: fr. 1-seeded, berry-like (Ancient Greek name of an ash tree.) About 25 species in Am. from the S States to the W. Indies and Brazil.

A. Lvs. beneath, pedicels and calyx pubescent...................................1. *B. lanuginosa*
AA. Lvs., pedicels and calyx glabrous...2. *B. lycioides*

1. **B. lanuginòsa** Pers. CHITTIMWOOD. Shrub or small tree to 8 m., with rigid spreading brs. usually spiny; young brts. tomentose: lvs. oblong-obovate to cuneate-obovate, 3–8 cm. long, rounded and often apiculate at apex, cuneate, lustrous dark green above, with rusty or pale woolly tomentum beneath, subcoriaceous, falling late in autumn or during the winter in the S.; petiole 4–16 mm. long: fls. white, 3 mm. across; in many-fld. clusters; pedicels 2–8 mm. long: fr. ellipsoid or obovoid, about 1 cm. long, black. Fl.vi–vii; fr.x. S.S.5:t.247. H.H.376. B.B.2:720. (SHITTIMWOOD, GUM ELASTIC, WOOLLY BUCKTHORN.) Va. to Ill., Mo., Tex. and Fla. Intr. 1747. Zone (V). Lvs remaining green until very late in fall.

2. **B. lycioìdes** Gaertn. f. SOUTHERN BUCKTHORN. Shrub or small tree to 8 m., with spreading unarmed or spiny brs.: lvs. elliptic or narrow-obovate to lanceolate, 5–13 cm. long, acute or obtusish, sometimes acuminate, cuneate, bright green above, lighter green beneath and silky-villous at first, usually soon glabrous, reticulate, firm, falling late in autumn: petiole 1–2 cm. long, slender: fls. in many-fld. clusters; pedicels 4–10 mm. long, glabrous: fr. subglobose or ellipsoid, about 1 cm. long, black. Fl.vi–viii; fr.x. S.M.816. N.S. 3:t.91(c). N. C. to s. Ind. and Mo., s. to Fla. and Tex. Intr. 1720. Zone (V). —**B. l. virginiàna** Fern., var. Lvs. oblanceolate, rounded at apex. S.S.5:t.248. Va. Intr. ?

Fam. 92. **EBENACEAE** Juss. EBONY FAMILY

Trees or shrubs with watery juice and hard wood: lvs. alternate, entire, exstipulate: fls. dioecious or polygamous, regular, axillary, articulate with the 2-bracteolate pedicel; calyx 3–7-lobed, persistent; corolla gamopetalous, 3–7-lobed, lobes involute in bud; disk wanting; stamens 2 to 3 times as many as corolla-lobes, inserted on the tube, usually some imperfect ones in the pistillate fl.; anthers introrse; ovary several-celled, with usually 2 suspended ovules in each cell; styles 2–8, distinct or united at base: fr. a several-seeded berry; seeds with copious albumen; embryo small, with large foliaceous cotyledons.—About 6 genera with nearly 300 species, chiefly trop.

DIOSPỲROS L. PERSIMMON. Deciduous or evergreen trees and shrubs; winter-buds ovoid, with about 3 outer scales, the terminal bud wanting: fls. dioecious, white or whitish, the pistillate usually solitary; the staminate ones cymose; calyx and corolla usually 4-lobed, rarely 3–7-lobed; stamens usually 8–16, ovary 4–12-celled; styles 2–6: fr. a large juicy berry, 1- to 10-seeded, usually with the enlarged calyx at base; seeds large, flattened. (Greek *Dios*, Jove's, and *pyros*, grain; in allusion to the edible fr.) About 200 species chiefly in trop. and subtrop. regions.

A. Lvs. acuminate, large.
  B. Young brts. glabrous or grayish pubescent: fr. pale orange or yellowish, rarely nearly black, 1–3.5, rarely to 7 cm. across.
    c. Petioles 1.5–2 cm. long: fls. 1–1.5 cm. long...........................1. *D. virginiana*
    cc. Petioles 1–1.5 cm. long: fls. 5–10 mm. long.........................2. *D. Lotus*
  BB. Young brts. brownish pubescent: fr. orange-red to golden-yellow, 4–7 cm. across.
                                                     3. *D. Kaki*
AA. Lvs. obtuse, 2–6 cm. long...4. *D. armata*

1. **D. virginiàna** L. COMMON P. Tree to 15, rarely to 30 m., with round-topped head and spreading, often pendulous brs.; brts. pubescent at least when young; bark dark, deeply divided into square scaly thick plates: lvs. ovate to elliptic, 6–14 cm. long, usually rounded at base, lustrous dark green above, paler beneath and usually glabrous at maturity: corolla campanulate, with 4 reflexed lobes; staminate fls. usually in 3's, about 1 cm. long, with 16 stamens; the pistillate short-stalked, solitary, 1.5 cm. long, with 4 2-lobed styles: fr. globose or obovoid, 2–3.5 cm. across, yellowish to pale orange, often with red cheek, edible; seeds oblong, about 1 cm. long. Fl.v–vi; fr.ix–xi. Add.3:t.85(c). S.S.6:t.252,253. G.F.8:265. Gn.57:146. M.M.4:21(b). G.W. 16:230(h). Conn. to Fla., w. to Kans. and Tex. Intr. 1629. Zone IV. Sometimes planted for its edible fr.—**D. v. pubéscens** (Pursh) Dipp., var. Brts. densely pubescent: lvs. pubescent beneath. Cult. 1889.—**D. v. platycárpa** Sarg., var. Lvs. broader, rounded or cordate at base, pubescent beneath: fr. depressed-globose, 4–7 cm. across. Mo. and Ark. Intr. 1904. Zone V.

2. **D. Lotus** L. DATE-PLUM. Round-headed tree to 14 m.; bark furrowed; brts. pubescent, later gray-brown; winter-buds glabrous, acute: lvs. elliptic to oblong, 6–12 cm. long, rounded to broad-cuneate at base, pubescent above at first, later usually glabrous, grayish or glaucescent and pubescent beneath at least on the veins: fls. reddish or greenish white; staminate fls. 2–3, about 5 mm. long, with 16 stamens; pistillate subsessile, 8–10 mm. long: fr. globose, about 1.5 cm. across, yellow, often bloomy and sometimes becoming blue-black. Fl.vi; fr.x–xi. S.I.1:t.79(c). R.I.17:t.38(c). N.D.6:t.27(c). Gn.32:68. U. S. Im. 113:t.(fr.) W. Asia to N. W. Himal., China and Japan. Cult. 1597. Zone (V). Similar to the preceding species; fr. of inferior quality.

3. **D. Kàki** L. f. KAKI P. Round-headed tree to 14 m.; bark scaly; winter-buds pubescent, obtuse: lvs. elliptic-ovate to oblong-ovate or obovate, 6–18 cm. long, usually broad-cuneate, soon glabrous and lustrous, dark green above, lighter green and pubescent beneath; petiole 1–1.5 cm. long, pubescent: fls. yellowish white; staminate fls. in 3's, about 1 cm. long, with 16–24 stamens; pistillate 1.5–1.8 cm. long; styles divided to base, pubescent: fr. ovoid to depressed-globose, 3.5–7 cm. across, orange to bright yellow, edible. Fl.vi; fr.viii–xi. B.M.8127(c). N.K.13:t.7. G.C.41:22. Gn.49:171. Gn.M.34:102(h). U. S. Inv. 38:t.10(h). (*D. chinensis* Bl., *D. Schitse* Bge., *D. Roxburghii* Carr.) Cult. in China and Japan for its fr.; intr. to Eu. in 1796, but little known before 1870. Zone VII.—**D. K. costàta** (Carr.) Mouillef., var. Fr. large, depressed-globose, with 4 furrows, orange-red. R.H.1870:410,t(c). G.C.III.9: 171;13:51. Gn.49:171.—**D. K. Mazèlii** (Carr.) Mouillef., var. Fr. depressed-globose, with 8 furrows, orange-yellow. R.H.1874:70,t(c).—**D. K. silvéstris** Mak., var. Brts. and petioles more densely fulvous-pubescent, lvs. usually smaller, broad-ovate to lanceolate, pubescent beneath: fls. smaller; ovary pubescent: fr. 1.5–5 cm. across, golden-yellow. China, Korea. Intr. 1907. Zone VII? The wild type of the cult. kaki.

4. **D. armàta** Hemsl. Half-evergreen or deciduous tree, to 8 m., with wide-spreading spiny brs.; young brts. tomentose: lvs. short-petioled, elliptic or obovate to oblong, 1.5–6 cm. long, obtuse, cuneate, dark lustrous green above, minutely pubescent beneath; staminate fls. in small corymbs, creamy white, fragrant, tomentose, 4–5 mm. long: fr. subglobose about 2 cm. across, yellow, setose, on a pedicel about 1 cm. long. Fl.v. C. China. Intr. 1904. Zone VII.

Related species: **D. sinénsis** Hemsl. Shrub or small tree; brts. pubescent: lvs. oblong-lanceolate, 4–6, rarely 10 cm. long, obtuse or obtusish, narrowed at ends, glabrous: pistillate fls. solitary; pedicels 3–6 cm. long; sepals ovate, 1.5 cm.: fr. globose, 1.5 cm. across, yellow. H.I.29:2804. C., W. and S. China. Intr. 1907. Zone VII?

Fam. 93. **SYMPLOCACEAE** Miers. SWEETLEAF FAMILY

Contains only the following genus.

SÝMPLOCOS Jacq. Sweetleaf. Deciduous or evergreen trees or shrubs; winter-buds usually several, superposed, small, with several outer scales: lvs. alternate, simple, estipulate: fls. perfect or sometimes unisexual, regular, in axillary clusters or in racemes or panicles; calyx with 5, rarely 4 imbricate lobes; corolla 5- or 10-, rarely 4-lobed, sometimes divided nearly to the base, lobes imbricate; stamens 15 to many, rarely 4–10, often in several series, distinct or united in fascicles, usually adnate to the corolla; ovary inferior or half-inferior, 2–5-celled, with usually 2 ovules in each cell; style 1, with 1–5 stigmas: fr. a drupe with a 1–5-seeded stone. (Greek *symplokos*, connected, in reference to the often united stamens.) Includ. *Hopea* L., *Bobua* DC., *Palura* D. Don. About 290 species widely distributed in trop. and subtrop. regions except Africa, in Am. n. to Del.

A. Lvs. sharply serrulate: fls. in panicles......................................1. *S. paniculata*
AA. Lvs. obscurely toothed, half-evergreen: fls. in axillary clusters..............2. *S. tinctoria*

1. **S. paniculàta** (Thunb.) Miq. Asiatic S. Shrub or tree to 12 m., with slender spreading brs.; young brts. pubescent: lvs. short-petioled, elliptic or obovate to oblong-obovate, 3–7 cm. long, acute or acuminate, usually broad-cuneate, bright green and glabrous or nearly so above, conspicuously veined beneath and usually pubescent, rarely glabrous: fls. white, fragrant, 8–10 mm across, with spreading elliptic-oblong, nearly distinct petals, in panicles 4–8 cm. long, terminal and axillary on short lateral brts.; stamens distinct, numerous; fr. ellipsoid, about 8 mm. long, bright blue; stone 1-seeded. Fl.v–vi; fr.ix. S.I.2:t.68(c). G.F.5:89. G.C.74:263;75:38,t(h). M.G.16:100(h),101. S. L.361(h). (*S. crataegoides* D. Don, *Palura p.* Nakai.) Himal. to China and Japan. Intr. 1875. Zone V. With conspicuous white fls. in spring and attractive bright blue frs. in fall.

Related species: **S. chinénsis** (Lour.) Merr. Lvs. elliptic, acute, pubescent on both sides: fls. in short panicles; calyx-teeth acute. B.R.710(c). (*S. sinica* Ker.) E. China. Intr. 1823, apparently not now in cult. Zone VII?

2. **S. tinctòria** L'Hérit. Sweetleaf (Horse-sugar). Half-evergreen shrub or small tree to 10 m.; young brts. rufous-pubescent or nearly glabrous: lvs. elliptic to oblong-oblanceolate, 7–15 cm. long, acute or acuminate, cuneate, obscurely serrate or nearly entire, lustrous above at maturity, paler and pubescent beneath, thickish, turning yellow-green in drying: fls. yellowish, 1 cm. across, fragrant, short-stalked, in sessile, dense axillary clusters; petals oblong, obtuse, nearly distinct; stamens numerous in 5 clusters; ovary glabrous, 3-celled: fr. ellipsoid, 6 mm. long, orange or brown. Fl.v; fr.viii–ix. S.S.6:t.255,256. Del. to Fla. and La. Cult. 1780. Zone VII.

Fam. 94. **STYRACACEAE** A. DC. STORAX FAMILY

Shrubs or trees usually with stellate pubescence: lvs. alternate, simple, exstipulate: fls. perfect, regular, solitary or in racemes or panicles; calyx 4–5-lobed or -cleft, free or adnate to ovary; petals 4–8, usually united only at base, imbricate or valvate; stamens twice as many or as many as petals: ovary superior or inferior; 3–5-celled below, with 1 or rarely several ovules in each cell; style with 1–5 stigmas: fr. dry or drupaceous; seeds albuminous.

—Six genera and about 100 species from N. to S. Am., in E. Asia and the Mediterr. reg.

A. Ovary superior: fr. neither ribbed nor winged: fls. racemose or solitary.........1. *Styrax*
AA. Ovary inferior.
  B. Corolla 4-lobed; fls. fascicled: fr. 2–4-winged.................................2. *Halesia*
  BB. Corolla 5–7-parted, divided nearly to base.
    c. Fls. in lateral leafless racemes or panicles: fr. 4–8 cm. long.......3. *Rehderodendron*
    cc. Fls. in racemes or panicles terminating lateral leafy brts.: fr. 1–2.5 cm. long.
      D. Fls. slender-stalked, in 3–5-fld. racemes: fr. not ribbed..............4. *Sinojackia*
      DD. Fls. short-stalked, in large many-fld. panicles......................5. *Pterostyrax*

1. STÝRAX L. SNOWBELL (STORAX).

Deciduous or evergreen shrubs or trees; winter-buds usually several superposed, with 1 outer scale: lvs. short-stalked, entire or serrate: fls. white, in racemes or clusters terminal on short lateral brts., sometimes axillary and solitary; calyx campanulate, obscurely 5-toothed or truncate, persistent; corolla deeply 5-, rarely 8-lobed; stamens 10, rarely to 16, inserted at base of corolla; ovary superior, but adnate at base to calyx, 3-celled below, 1-celled above; style slender: fr. a usually subglobose dry or fleshy drupe with irregularly dehiscent pericarp; seeds 1–2, large, subglobose. (Ancient Greek name of *Styrax officinalis*.) About 100 species in trop. to warm-temp. regions of Am., Asia and Eu.—Ornamental shrubs or trees with showy white fls.

A. Tube of corolla shorter than lobes.
  B. Fls. in few-fld. clusters or racemes.
    c. Pedicels about as long as calyx, puberulous.
      D. Lvs. 3–9 cm. long...1. *S. americana*
      DD. Lvs. 1–2.5 cm. long...2. *S. Wilsonii*
    cc. Pedicels 1.5–2.5 cm. long, glabrous....................................3. *S. japonica*
  BB. Fls. in many-fld. racemes.
    c. Lvs. tomentose or densely pubescent beneath, 6–20 cm. long.
      D. Base of petiole not enlarged: infl. 6–10 cm. long...................4. *S. grandiflora*
      DD. Base of petiole sheath-like and enclosing the bud: infl. 9–20 cm. long..5. *S. Obassia*
    cc. Lvs. glabrous or sparingly pubescent beneath, 5–14 cm. long.
      D. Petiole 5–15 mm. long: corolla-lobes imbricate in bud...........6. *S. Hemsleyana*
      DD. Petiole 1–3 mm. long: corolla-lobes valvate in bud.................7. *S. dasyantha*
AA. Tube of corolla longer than lobes: lvs. broad-elliptic to suborbicular, coarsely dentate.
                                        8. *S. Shiraiana*

1. S. americàna Lam. Shrub to 3 m.; brts. nearly glabrous: lvs. elliptic to oblong, 2–7 cm. long, acute or acuminate, cuneate, entire or serrulate, bright green and sparingly stellate-pubescent; petiole 2–4 mm. long: fls. 1–4, nodding, at end of short brts.; pedicels 6–12 mm. long, puberulous; calyx with minute triangular lobes; corolla about 1.5 cm. long, with spreading or reflexed oblong-lanceolate lobes: fr. obovoid, 8 mm. long. Fl.IV–VI. B.M.921(c). L.B. 906(c). (*S. laevigata* Ait.) Va. to Fla., w. to Mo., Ark. and La. Intr. 1765. Zone (V).—**S. a. pulverulénta** (Michx.) Perk., var. Lvs. sparingly stellate-pubescent above, more densely beneath: calyx and pedicels tomentose. B.B. 2:723. (*S. p.* Michx.) Va. to Fla. and Tex. Intr. 1794. Zone VI?

2. S. Wilsónii Rehd. Much-branched shrub to 3 m.; young brts. stellate-tomentose: lvs. rhombic-ovate to elliptic, 1–2.5 cm. long, obtuse or acutish, sparingly toothed or denticulate, usually entire below the middle, sparingly pubescent above, more densely so or tomentose beneath, or the first lvs. glabrate: fls. 3–5, short-stalked, 1.5–1.8 cm. across; calyx stellate-pubescent; corolla-lobes oblong: fr. globose-ovoid, 8 mm. long. Fl.V–VI. B.M.8444(c). R.H.1914:33. G.M.56:369. W. China. Intr. 1908. Zone VII. Shrub of dense habit, blooming when only a few inches high.

3. S. japónica Sieb. & Zucc. Shrub or small tree to 10 m., with slender spreading brs.; young brts. and lvs. with quickly disappearing stellate pubescence: lvs. broad-elliptic to elliptic-oblong, 2–8 cm. long, acute to acuminate, cuneate, remotely denticulate, glabrous except axillary tufts beneath:

beneath at least on the veins; fls. 3–6 in clusters or short racemes; pedicels 1.5–3 cm. long, tomentose like the calyx; corolla 2–2.5 cm. long, with very short tube and oval to obovate lobes; stamens usually 8, filaments villous; ovary 2-celled, rarely 4-celled: fr. oblong or oblong-obovate, 3.5–5 cm. long, with 2 broad wings, often with 1 or rarely 2 very narrow wings between them. Fl.v. L.B.1172(c). S.S.6:t.259. E.P.IV.241:98. M.G.32:281(h),282. S. C. and Tenn. to Fla. and Tex. Intr. 1758. Zone VI. Similar to the first species, but usually not as free-flowering.

3. REHDERODÉNDRON Hu. Deciduous trees; winter-buds with 2–3 outer scales: lvs. petioled, serrulate, exstipulate: fls white, in axillary leafless panicles or racemes; calyx-lobes 5, short; petals 5, connate only at base, imbricate in bud; stamens 10, unequal, about as long as petals; filaments connate only at base and adnate to corolla; ovary inferior except the conical apex, 3–4-celled; cells 4-ovuled; style slender, slightly longer than stamens; fr. oblong or ellipsoid, large, with the calyx-limb at apex, 5–10-ribbed, woody, indehiscent, with thin corky exocarp and fibrous-spongy endocarp; seeds 1–3, cylindric. (After Alfred Rehder of the Arnold Arboretum, and Greek *dendron,* tree.) Eight species in S. and W. China.

R. macrocárpum Hu. Tree to 9 m.; brts. glabrous: lvs. elliptic or elliptic-ovate to oblong-ovate, 8–11 cm. long, acute or acuminate, broad-cuneate, minutely serrulate, stellate-pilose on veins beneath; petiole 1–1.5 cm. long: racemes 6–7-fld., before the lvs., tomentulose, 4–5 cm. long; pedicels 3–10 mm. long, articulate below calyx; calyx-lobes triangular; petals elliptic-oblong, 12 mm. long, pubescent on both sides; filaments glabrous: fr. oblong, 6–7 cm. long, 8–10-ribbed, glabrous. Fl.iv–v; fr.ix–xi. I.S.t.245. W. China. Intr. 1934. Zone VII?

4. SINOJÁCKIA Hu. Deciduous trees; winter-buds with 2 outer pubescent scales: lvs. short-petioled, serrulate, exstipulate: fls. white, in lateral leafy racemes; pedicels slender; calyx turbinate, with 5–7 short lobes; petals 5–7, cohering at base, imbricate in bud; stamens 10–14, stellate-pilose; filaments distinct, adnate to base of corolla; ovary 3–4-celled, cells 8-ovuled; style slender, exceeding the stamens; fr. ovoid to cylindric-oblong, woody, usually 1-seeded, with the calyx-limb about ⅓ below the conical apex; seed cylindric. (After J. G. Jack of the Arnold Arboretum; the prefix in reference to his connection with Chinese botany.) Three species in China.

S. xylocárpa Hu. Small tree to 6 m.; brts. and pedicels sparsely stellate-pilose: lvs. elliptic to elliptic-obovate, 3–7 cm. long, short-acuminate, rounded at base, ovate and cordate on flowering brts., denticulate, glabrous except slightly stellate at first on midrib beneath; petiole 3–5 mm. long; fls. 3–5, about 2.5 cm. across; pedicels to 3 cm. long; calyx-tube turbinate, stellate-pubescent; lobes triangular-lanceolate; petals usually 6–7, elliptic-oblong, 12 mm. long: fr. ovoid, 1.5–2 cm. long, 1–1.3 cm. across, with broad-conical, obtuse apex. Fl.iv–v; fr.ix–x. I.S.t.98. E. China. Intr. 1934. Zone VII?

Related species: **S. Rehderiàna** Hu. Tree to 5 m.: lvs. elliptic to elliptic-obovate, 2–9 cm. long, acuminate, cuneate to rounded or subcordate at base, minutely serrulate, sparsely pubescent on the veins: pedicels 2 cm. long; petals 5–6: fr. cylindric-oblong, 2.5 cm. long including the 1 cm. long beaked apex. I.S.t.199. E. China. Intr. 1930. Zone VII.

5. PTERÓSTYRAX Sieb. & Zucc. Deciduous trees or shrubs; winter-buds with 2 outer scales: lvs. petioled, serrate: fls. in large panicles terminating short lateral brts.; calyx 5-toothed; petals 5, distinct or sometimes slightly cohering at base, imbricate in bud; stamens 10, exserted, connate below into a tube or nearly free; ovary 3-, rarely 4–5-celled, nearly inferior or not more than ⅓ superior; each cell 4-ovuled; style slender, slightly longer than stamens: fr. an oblong dry drupe, ribbed or winged, 1–2-seeded. (Greek *pteron*, wing, and *styrax*; referring to the winged fr. of one species.) Four species in E. Asia.

P. híspida Sieb. & Zucc. Epaulette-tree. Tree to 15 m., with slender spreading brs. forming an open head; brts. sparingly pubescent: lvs. oblong to obovate-oblong, 7–17 cm. long, acute or short-acuminate, rounded or cuneate at base, minutely denticulate, glabrous and bright green above, sparingly pubescent beneath at least on the veins and grayish green; petiole 1–2 cm. long: panicle 12–25 cm. long, pendulous, stellate-pubescent; fls. creamy-white, fragrant, subsessile or short-stalked; petals 8–10 mm. long, narrow-oblong; stamens subequal, nearly free: fr. cylindric, about 1 cm. long, 10-ribbed, densely bristly. Fl.vi. B.M.8329(c). Ad.5:t.290(c). G.C.58:6. G.F. 5:389. F.E.14:t.21(h). (*Halesia h.* Mast.) Japan. Intr. 1875. Zone V. With large pendulous panicles of creamy-white fragrant fls.

Related species: **P. corymbòsa** Sieb. & Zucc. Shrub or tree: lvs. elliptic or ovate, 6–12 cm. long, serrulate with bristly teeth, sparingly stellate-pubescent: panicle corymbose, 8–12 cm. long; stamens unequal, connate below: fr. obovoid, 1–1.5 cm. long, 5-winged, stellate-tomentose. S.Z.1:t.47(c). S.I.2:t.65(c). N.T. 1:331. E.P.IV.241:101. (*Halesia c.* Nichols.) Japan. Intr. 1850. Zone VI?

Fam. 95. **OLEACEAE** Lindl. OLIVE FAMILY

Trees or shrubs: lvs. opposite, rarely alternate, simple or pinnate, exstipulate: fls. perfect or unisexual, regular; calyx 4-lobed or 4-parted, rarely 5–16-lobed; corolla gamopetalous, 4-lobed or rarely 6–12-lobed, sometimes of distinct petals or wanting; stamens 2, rarely 3–5, adnate to corolla and alternate with the lobes; ovary superior, 2-celled, with usually 2 ovules in each cell; style 1 or wanting with simple or 2-lobed stigma: fr. a drupe or berry, caps. or samara; seeds anatropous, with large straight embryo, with or without albumen.—More than 20 genera with over 400 species in temp. and trop. regions.—Many ornamental species; a few are of economic importance and some are valuable timber-trees.

A. Fr. a winged samara.
  B. Lvs. simple, entire: fr. suborbicular, winged all around; fls. perfect.
    c. Corolla of 4 distinct small petals..1. *Fontanesia*
    cc. Corolla gamopetalous, 4-lobed.......................................2. *Abeliophyllum*
  BB. Lvs. pinnate, rarely simple and serrate: fr. elliptic to linear, with elongated apical wing: fls. apetalous or with 2 or 4 narrow petals...........................3. *Fraxinus*
AA. Fr. a caps. or drupe.
  B. Fr. a caps.: lvs. simple, rarely 3-foliolate or pinnate, deciduous.
    c. Fls. yellow, with imbricate lobes: brs. hollow or with lamellate pith: lvs. usually serrate ....4. *Forsythia*
    cc. Fls. never yellow, with valvate lobes: brs. with solid pith: lvs. entire or pinnate.
          5. *Syringa*
  BB. Fr. a drupe or berry.
    c. Lvs. simple, opposite: fls. white; fr. never 2-lobed.
      D. Corolla-lobes short or corolla wanting.
        E. Fls. in terminal panicles or spikes: corolla-lobes valvate: lvs. entire, deciduous or evergreen ....6. *Ligustrum*
        EE. Fls. axillary; corolla with imbricate lobes or wanting.
          F. Corolla present: lvs. evergreen, entire or serrate.
            G. Fr. with crustaceous fragile endocarp; fls. fascicled.
              H. Stamens exserted; corolla-tube short, shorter than lobes..7. *Phillyrea*
              HH. Stamens included; anthers slightly exceeding the tube.
                I. Corolla-tube about as long as lobes; fls. slender-stalked.
                    7a. *Osmarea*
                II. Corolla-tube cylindric, much longer than the short spreading lobes; fls. very short-stalked...........................8. *Siphonosmanthus*
            GG. Fr. with bony endocarp: fls. fascicled or paniculate.........9. *Osmanthus*
        FF. Corolla wanting: lvs. deciduous: fls. minute, before the lvs....10. *Forestiera*

DD. Corolla-lobes linear, many times longer than tube, valvate: fls. in pendulous
    panicles: lvs. deciduous..11. *Chionanthus*
CC. Lvs. pinnate, opposite or alternate, rarely simple and entire: fls. yellow, rarely
    white or pink: fr. often 2-lobed...12. *Jasminum*

1. **FONTANÈSIA** Labill. Deciduous shrubs; winter-buds globose-ovoid,
with 2 or 3 pairs of outer scales: brts. quadrangular: lvs. opposite, short-
petioled, entire or minutely serrulate: fls. perfect, small, in short axillary
racemes and terminal panicles forming leafy panicles on lateral brts.; calyx
minute, 4-parted; petals 4, narrow, small; stamens exceeding the petals;
ovary superior, 2-celled; stigma 2-lobed: fr. a flat nutlet winged all around;
seeds albuminous. (After Réné Louiche Desfontaines, French botanist; 1752–
1833.) Two species in W. Asia and China.

    F. Fortùnei Carr. Shrub to 5 m., with slender upright brs., glabrous: lvs.
lanceolate or ovate-lanceolate, 3–11 cm. long, acuminate, cuneate, entire, lustrous bright green; petiole 1–3 mm. long: fls. greenish white, 3 mm. long,
short-pediceled; terminal panicle 3–5 cm. long, the axillary much shorter:
fr. oval, 8 mm. long. Fl.v–vi. R.H.1859:43. S.H.2:f.511a-d. (*F. philly-
reoides* var. *sinensis* Debeaux, *F. californica* Hort.) China. Intr. 1845. Zone
IV. Upright graceful shrub with bright green foliage.
    Closely related species: **F. phillyreoïdes** Labill. Shrub to 3 m., densely
branched and more spreading: lvs. ovate-lanceolate or elliptic-oblong, 2–7 cm.
long, minutely serrulate or scabrid on the margin, grayish green; petiole 2–5
mm. long; fr. suborbicular to oval, 6–8 mm. long. L.B.1308(c). G.O.t.91(c).
D.H.f:104. (*F. angustifolia* Dipp.) Asia Minor. Intr. 1787. Zone VII?

2. **ABELIOPHÝLLUM** Nakai. Deciduous shrub; winter-buds usually
2, superposed, with 2 or 4 outer scales: pith lamellate: lvs. opposite, simple,
entire: fls. perfect, in short racemes from axillary buds on last year's brs.;
calyx 4-lobed, with imbricate lobes; corolla with broad spreading imbricate
lobes about as long as tube; stamens 2, filaments short; ovary 2-celled;
ovules solitary, pendulous; style short: fr. compressed, suborbicular, winged
all around. (Abelia and Greek *phyllon*, leaf; referring to the Abelia-like lvs.)
One species in Korea.

    A. dístichum Nakai. Shrub to 1 m.; brts. quadrangular, glabrous: lvs.
spreading in 2 ranks, ovate to elliptic-ovate, 2–5 cm. long, acuminate, broad-
cuneate or rounded at base, appressed-pilose on both sides; petiole 2–5 mm.
long: racemes 5–10 mm. long; corolla 1.5 cm. across, white: fr. 2–2.5 cm.
broad. Fl.v; fr.viii. N.K.10:t.26. C. Korea. Intr. 1924. Zone V.

3. **FRÁXINUS** L. Ash. Deciduous trees, rarely shrubs: winter-buds
often superposed, with 1 or 2 pairs of outer scales, usually brown or black
and scurfy, the outer pair sometimes foliar, i.e., obscurely pinnate at apex
(cf. J.A.15:t.87–89): lvs. opposite, pinnate, rarely reduced to 1 lft.: fls. perfect
or unisexual, small, in panicles; calyx small, 4-parted or 4-lobed or wanting:
corolla of 2–6, usually 4 distinct petals, rarely connate at base, or wanting;
stamens usually 2; ovary 2-celled; stigmas 2: fr. a 1-seeded nutlet with a
usually elongated wing at the apex; seed oblong, albuminous. (Ancient Latin
name of the ash.) About 65 species in the n. hemisphere, in Am. s. to Mex.,
in Asia s. to Java.—Ornamental trees with handsome foliage, some with
conspicuous fls.; several species are important timber-trees.

A. Fls. in terminal panicles on leafy shoots, perfect or polygamous, with or after the lvs.
                                                         Sect. ORNUS
  B. Corolla present.
     c. Corolla divided to the base or nearly to the base; stamens with long filaments.
      D. Lowest pair of lfts. not or only slightly smaller than others.
        E. Lfts. pubescent along the midrib beneath at least near base.

F. Lfts. stalked, usually 7, 5–8 cm. long..............................1. *F. Ornus*
FF. Lfts. sessile, 7–9, 12–18 cm. long..................................5. *F. Paxiana*
EE. Lfts. quite glabrous, generally 5, 2–4 cm. long.................2. *F. Bungeana*
DD. Lowest pair of lfts. much smaller than others, only occasionally nearly as long.
E. Petiole not conspicuously enlarged at base; lfts. usually more or less stalked.
F. Lfts. quite glabrous beneath, 5–7, 5–8 cm. long.................3. *F. Mariesii*
FF. Lfts. pubescent beneath along the midrib, at least near base.
G. Petiole and rachis grooved above; lfts. pubescent along the midrib and
on the lateral veins.......................................4. *F. pubinervis*
GG. Petiole and rachis not or slightly grooved: lfts. pubescent only along mid-
rib or nearly glabrous.....................................7. *F. longicuspis*
EE. Petioles conspicuously enlarged at base: lfts. sessile............6. *F. Spaethiana*
CC. Corolla connate into a tube exceeding the sepals; anthers subsessile: lfts. 3–6 cm.
long, lanceolate ....8. *F. cuspidata*
BB. Corolla wanting: lfts. 5–7, stalked, pubescent along the midrib beneath ..9. *F. chinensis*
AA. Fls. from leafless axillary buds, unisexual, before the lvs.; corolla wanting or with 2 petals
in *F. dipetala* (see under No. 10)..Sect. FRAXINASTER
B. Fls. with a calyx persistent on the fr.; anthers linear or linear-oblong: lfts. usually
5–7: buds brown.
c. Lvs. with winged rachis; lfts. 5–9, 1–4 cm. long: fls. perfect....Subsect. SCIADANTHUS
10. *F. xanthoxyloides*
cc. Lf.-rachis not winged; lfts. 5–15 cm. long: fls. dioecious........Subsect. MELIOIDES
D. Fr. lanceolate or oblanceolate, its body terete or nearly so: lvs. pinnate: brts.
terete.
E. Wing of fr. terminal, not or slightly decurrent: lfts. slender-stalked, papillose
beneath.
F. Lvs. and brts. glabrous......................................11. *F. americana*
FF. Lvs. and brts. pubescent...................................12. *F. biltmoreana*
EE. Wing of fr. decurrent to or below the middle, hence body margined (scarcely to
the middle in No. 15).
F. Fr. 2–7 cm. long; wing much longer than body: lfts. 5–9.
G. Lfts. stalked, 7–9, usually 9.
H. Fr. 5–7 cm. long; brts. and petioles tomentose........13. *F. tomentosa*
HH. Fr. 2.5–6 cm. long; brts. and petioles pubescent or glabrous.
14. *F. pennsylvanica*
GG. Lfts. sessile or nearly sessile.
H. Petioles not dilated at base: lfts. 5–7, rarely 9; brts. and lvs. pilose.
16. *F. oregona*
HH. Petioles dilated at the tomentose base: lfts. 7–11: brts. glabrous.
17. *F. platypoda*
FF. Fr. 1–2 cm. long; wing as long or shorter than body: lfts. 3–7, short-stalked
or nearly sessile; lvs. and brts. pubescent or glabrous.........15. *F. velutina*
DD. Fr. obovate or elliptic to oblong-elliptic, compressed, winged to the base.
E. Brts. terete: lfts. 5–7.......................................18. *F. caroliniana*
EE. Brts. quadrangular.
F. Lfts. usually 5, ovate, acute....................................19. *F. Lowellii*
FF. Lfts. reduced to 1, ovate to suborbicular......................20. *F. anomala*
BB. Fls. without calyx (or a deciduous minute calyx in No. 21); anthers cordate, rarely
broad-oblong: lfts. usually 7 or more...........................Subsect. BUMELIOIDES
c. Brts. 4-angled and usually winged: lfts. 7–11: fls. perfect, with minute deciduous
calyx ....21. *F. quadrangulata*
cc. Brts. terete or nearly so: fls. without calyx.
D. Rachis at base of lfts. with thick rufous tomentum: fls. dioecious.
E. Lfts. sessile, nearly rounded at base.............................22. *F. nigra*
EE. Lfts. narrowed into a very short stalk.........................23. *F. mandshurica*
DD. Lfts. without conspicuous tomentum at base of lfts.: fls. perfect or polygamous,
rarely dioecious.
E. Lfts. sessile or subsessile.
F. Lfts. glabrous or pubescent only along the midrib beneath: ovary glabrous.
G. Lfts. 7–13.
H. Winter-buds black or nearly black: lfts. appressed-serrate or serrate,
usually villous along the midrib beneath.............24. *F. excelsior*
HH. Winter-buds brown: lfts. sinuate-dentate or serrate, usually remotely
so.
I. Lfts. elliptic to broad-elliptic or obovate, obtuse to acute, 9–13.
25. *F. rotundifolia*
II. Lfts. lanceolate or narrow-oblong.
J. Lfts. 9–13, rarely 7, glabrous beneath: fr. rounded at base.
26. *F. angustifolia*
JJ. Lfts. 7–9, rarely 5, pubescent along the midrib beneath: fr. nar-
rowed at base. ....27. *F. oxycarpa*
GG. Lfts. 3–5, rarely 7, lanceolate, glabrous.....................28. *F. syriaca*
FF. Lfts. pubescent on both sides or at maturity only beneath..29. *F. holotricha*
EE. Lfts. distinctly stalked: brts. and lvs. glabrous.................30. *F. potamophila*

Sect. ORNUS DC. Fls. in terminal and lateral panicles on leafy brs., with
or after the lvs., perfect or polygamous. (*Ornus* Pers.)

767

Subsect. EUORNUS Koehne & Lingelsh. Corolla present: scales of termina.
bud entire.

1. **F. Ornus** L. FLOWERING A. Round-headed tree to 20 m.; bark smooth
gray; winter-buds grayish or brownish: lfts. usually 7, stalked, oblong t
ovate, the terminal one obovate, 3–7 cm. long, abruptly pointed, usually
broad-cuneate, irregularly serrate, glabrous except pubescent along the base
of the midrib beneath: fls. white, fragrant, in dense terminal panicles 7–1
cm. long; petals linear, 6 mm. long: fr. narrow-oblong, 2–2.5 cm. long, trun
cate or emarginate at apex. Fl.v–vi. R.I.17:t.31,f.1–2(c). H.W.3:120(h),t.6
(c). Gn.48:286;79:362(h). F.E.22:61(h). B.S.1:572,t(h). (*Ornus europaec*
Pers., *F. floribunda* Hort., not Wall.) S. Eu., W. Asia. Intr. before 1700
Zone V. Round-headed tree attractive when in bloom.—**F. O. juglandifòlia**
Ten., var. Lfts. ovate-oblong, 5–10 cm. long and 2.5–5 cm. broad. D.H.1:70(l)
—**F. O. rotundifòlia** Ten., var. Lfts. broad-elliptic to orbicular-obovate
S.H.2:513c(l). (*F. r.* Lam., not Mill.)

2. **F. Bungeàna** DC. Small tree to 5 m. or shrub; winter-buds nearly
black: brts. puberulous: lfts. usually 5, rarely 3 or 7, slender-stalked, ovate
or orbicular-ovate, 2–4 cm. long, obtusish to short-acuminate, broad-cuneate
serrate, glabrous: panicles 5–7 cm. long, puberulous, filaments longer than
the linear petals: fr. narrow-oblong, 2.5–3 cm. long, obtuse or emarginate
Fl.v. G.F.7:5. B.C.3:1274. (*F. B.* var. *parvifolia* Wenz., *F. Dippeliana*
Lingelsh., *F. parvifolia* Lingelsh.) N. China. Intr. 1881. Zone III. Distinct
species handsome in bloom.

Related species: **F. raibocárpa** Reg. Small tree: lfts. 3–5, elliptic to obovate
or oblong-obovate, 2–6 cm. long, obtuse or acute; petiole wing-margined: fr.
curved, 2.5 cm. long, with rhombic wing. E.P.IV.243,1:20. D.H.1:93. Turkest.
Cult. 1884. Zone V?

3. **F. Marièsii** Hook. f. Shrub or small tree to 8 m.; winter-buds grayish;
young brts. puberulous: lfts. 3–5, rarely 7, usually closely set, subsessile
elliptic to ovate-lanceolate, 3–8 cm. long, acute or acuminate, crenate-serrulate or nearly entire, pale beneath, subcoriaceous; petiole and petiolules
purple near base; panicle 8–14 cm. long; calyx minute; petals sometimes 5–6:
fr. 1.5–3 cm. long, oblanceolate. Fl.vi. B.M.6678(c). B.S.1:570. I.T.4:t.158
N.F.9:f.13(h). C. China. Intr. 1878. Zone VII? Free-flowering; frs. attractive in summer by their purple color.

Related species: **F. retùsa** Champ. Lfts. 3–7, slender-stalked, ovate to oblong,
5–15 cm. long, acuminate, dentate or entire, quite glabrous, subcoriaceous and
reticulate beneath: calyx large. E. China. Not in cult.—**F. r. Henryàna** Oliv.,
var. Tree to 12 m.: lfts. on stalks 4–15 mm. long, oblong to lanceolate, serrulate;
panicle dense, 10–15 cm. long: fr. 2–2.5 cm. long, emarginate. H.I.1930. C.
China. Intr. 1900. Zone VII?—**F. Griffíthii** C. B. Clarke. Trees to 15 m.: lfts.
5–11, ovate to elliptic-oblong, 5–14 cm. long, acuminate, entire: fls. in large loose
bracted puberulous panicles. (*F. bracteata* Hemsl.) China to Philipp. and Mal.
Intr. 1900 from China. Zone VII?

4. **F. pubinérvis** Bl. Tree; lfts. 5–11, stalked, elliptic to ovate-oblong,
5–10 cm. long, acuminate, broad-cuneate, crenate-serrate, dark green and
glabrous or nearly so above, hairy along the midrib and on the primary
veins beneath: fr. oblanceolate, 3–3.5 cm. long. N.T.1:401. (*F. Bungeana*
var. *p.* Wenzig.) Japan. Intr. before 1900. Zone V.

Related species: **F. floribúnda** Wall. Tree to 40 m.; brts. glabrous: lfts.
7–9, short-stalked, ovate-oblong to oblong, 10–15 cm. long, long-acuminate,
sharply serrate, with prominent pubescent veins beneath; rachis slightly winged:
panicles 20–30 cm. long: fr. linear-spatulate, 3 cm. long, obtuse or emarginate.
E.P.IV.243,1:21. Himal. Intr. 1822 and 1876. Zone VII?

5. **F. Paxiàna** Lingelsh. Tree to 20 m.; winter-buds rusty-tomentose:
lfts. 7–9, short-stalked, ovate to oblong-lanceolate, 8–18 cm. long, acuminate

rounded or broad-cuneate at base, crenulate, glabrous: panicle large; calyx large; petals linear-spatulate, as long as stamens: fr. linear-spatulate, 2.5–3 cm. long. Fl.vi. B.M.9024(c). M.G.51:381. S.H.2:f.515d(l). China, Himal. Intr. about 1904. Zone V. Handsome tree with large lvs.

6. **F. Spaethiàna** Lingelsh. Tree: lfts. 5–9, sessile, oblong to oblong-obovate, 8–16 cm. long, the lowest pair much smaller, short-acuminate, irregularly and rather coarsely crenate-serrate, dark green above, lighter beneath and glabrous except along the midrib near base; petiole grooved, much enlarged near base and reddish brown: fr. oblanceolate, 3–3.5 cm. long, obtuse. S.H.2:f.516g(l). N.T.1:400. (*F. stenocarpa* Koidz.) Japan. Cult. 1873. Zone V. Handsome tree with large lvs.

7. **F. longicúspis** Sieb. & Zucc. Small tree to 15 m.; winter-buds rufous-pubescent; brts. glabrous, slightly quadrangular, slender: lfts. usually 5, rarely 7, stalked, elliptic to ovate-lanceolate, 5–10 cm. long, long-acuminate, cuneate, serrate or crenate-serrate, glabrous or nearly glabrous; petiole grooved above: fls. in panicles 6–12 cm. long; calyx minute; petals linear-oblong, as long as stamens: fr. linear-oblong or oblanceolate, 2–3.5 cm. long, obtuse. Fl.vi. S.I.1:t.81(c). N.T.1:404. Japan. Intr. about 1870. Zone V. Graceful tree with white fls. and lvs. turning purple in fall.—**F. l. Sieboldiàna** (Bl.) Lingelsh., var. Lfts. acuminate, sometimes short-acuminate, 3.5–8 cm. long, the lowest pair sometimes ovate, crenate-serrulate, sometimes nearly entire, pubescent along the midrib beneath. M.K.t.84(c). N.T.1:392. N.K. 10:t.7. (*F. S.* Bl.) Japan, Korea.

8. **F. cuspidàta** Torr. Shrub or rarely small tree, with slender brs.; winter-buds dark reddish brown, glutinous: lfts. usually 7, slender-stalked, lanceolate or oblong-lanceolate, 3–6 cm. long, acuminate, cuneate, coarsely serrate, glabrous with obscure veins; petiole slender, sometimes wing-margined: fls. fragrant, in panicles 6–10 cm. long; corolla about 1.5 cm. long, divided to below the middle into linear-oblong lobes; anthers subsessile, not exceeding the tube: fr. spatulate-oblong, 2–2.5 cm. long. Fl.iv–v. S.S.6:t.260. E.P.IV. 243,1:27. (*Ornus c.* Nieuwl.) Ariz. and N. Mex. to Tex. and Mex. Intr. 1914. Zone VII.—**F. c. macropétala** (Eastw.) Rehd., var. Lfts. usually 3–5, often ovate and usually entire. (*F. m.* Eastw.) N. Ariz. Intr. ?

Subsect. 2. ORNASTER Koehne & Lingelsh. Corolla wanting: outer scales of terminal bud foliar.

9. **F. chinénsis** Roxb. Tree to 15 m.; winter-buds brownish black: lfts. 5–9, short-stalked to subsessile, elliptic to elliptic-ovate, 3–10 cm. long, acuminate, serrate to crenate-serrate, pubescent along the midrib beneath and on the primary veins; petiole enlarged at base: panicle large and loose, 8–15 cm. long; calyx campanulate, irregularly lobed; anthers ovoid to oblong-ovoid, about as long as filaments: fr. oblanceolate, 3–4.5 cm. long and 4–6 mm. broad. Fl.v. C.C.280. E.P.IV.243,1:29. China. Intr. 1891. Zone V. One of the trees on which the wax insect lives.—**F. c. acuminàta** Lingelsh., var. Lfts. usually 3–5, stalked, ovate-lanceolate to lanceolate, to 12 cm. long, long-acuminate, more sharply serrate. E.P.IV.243,1:f.8d(l). (*F. Koehneana* Lingelsh.) China. Intr. 1910.—**F. c. rhynchophýlla** (Hance) Hemsl., var. Lfts. usually 5, broad-ovate or obovate, rarely oblong-obovate, 6–15 cm. long, acuminate, rarely obtusish, coarsely crenate-serrate, rarely subentire, usually pubescent on the veins beneath, rarely glabrous; rachis usually rufous-pubescent at the nodes: panicle shorter. G.F.6:485. S.H.2:f.516c,518a-e. N.K. 10:t.4. (*F. r.* Hance, *F. obovata* Schneid., not Bl., *F. Bungeana* Hance, not D.C.) N. E. Asia. Intr. 1892.

Sect. II. **FRAXINASTER** DC. Panicles from leafless lateral buds; fls. usually apetalous, appearing before the lvs.

Subsect. 1. SCIADANTHUS Coss. & Dur. Fls. with calyx, polygamous, in dense panicles; lvs. with winged rachis; lfts. 3–13, small, not exceeding 4 cm., obtuse: outer scales of terminal bud foliar.

10. **F. xanthoxyloìdes** (Don) DC. Shrub or small tree with spreading brs.; brts. minutely puberulous at first: lf.-rachis narrowly winged, slightly pubescent; lfts. 5–9, subsessile, the lower short-stalked, oval to oblong or oblong-ovate, 2–4 cm. long, acute to obtusish, crenate-serrate, slightly pilose on midrib beneath: fls. in short dense panicles; anthers large, subsessile: fr. narrow-oblong to spatulate, 3–4 cm. long, 6–7 mm. broad, obtuse or emarginate; body with a furrow in the middle. D.L.1:f.34. S.H.2:f.518k. (*Ornus x.* Don.) Himal. to Afghan. Cult. 1870. Zone VII?—**F. x. dimórpha** (Coss. & Durieu) Wenz., var. Brts. and lvs. glabrous or nearly so; lfts. subsessile, oval or ovate, 1–2.5 cm. long, obtuse or obtusish, on sterile brts. 7–11, shorter and broader: fr. 4–5 cm. long, obtuse or acutish. M.A.t.18B(c). D.L.1:f.35. S.H.2:f.518g. E.P.IV.243:f.9E. (*F. d.* Coss. & Durieu.) N. Afr. Intr. 1855? Zone (V) or VI.—**F. x. dumòsa** (Carr.) Lingelsh., var. A shrubby dense form of the preceding with suborbicular to ovate lfts. 5–15 mm. long. Cult. 1865.

A species of the subsect. DIPETALAE with axillary fls. and with petals is **F. dipétala** Hook. & Arn. Shrub or small tree; brts. quadrangular: lfts. usually 5, stalked, broad-elliptic to ovate, 1.5–4 cm. long, usually obtuse, serrate, glabrous: fls. with the lvs., in panicles 5–10 cm. long; petals 2, oval, 4–5 mm. long: fr. oblanceolate, 2.5 cm. long. S.S.6:t.261. (*Petlomelia d.* Nieuwl.) Calif. Intr. 1878. Zone VII?

Subsect. MELIOIDES Endl. Fls. with calyx, usually dioecious: lfts. large; rachis not winged: terminal bud-scales entire. (Sect. *Leptaliæ* Koehne, sect. *Ornus* subs. *L.* Wesmael, *Calycomelia* Kostel.)

11. **F. americàna** L. WHITE A. Tall tree to 40 m.; young brts. dark green or brownish, glabrous and lustrous: lfts. 5–9, usually 7, stalked, ovate to ovate-lanceolate, 6–15 cm. long, acuminate, cuneate or rounded at base, usually entire, or slightly dentate toward the apex, dark green above, glaucous beneath and usually glabrous; petiolules 5–15 mm. long; anthers oblong, apiculate: fr. 3–5 cm. long, with terete body, the wing narrow-oblong to spatulate, not decurrent, emarginate or obtuse. S.S.6:t.268,269. E.H.4:t. 246(h). G.F.7:405(h). F.E.23:427(h). (*F. acuminata* Lam., *F. Novae-Angliae* Mill., *F. alba* Marsh.) N. S. to Minn., s. to Fla. and Tex. Intr. 1724. Zone III. Vigorous tree with the lvs. turning deep purple or yellow in fall.—**F. a. ascidiàta** Meunissier, var. Lfts. pitcher-shaped at base. G.C.76:335. Intr. about 1910.—**F. a. iodocárpa** Fern., f. Fr. red-purple, conspicuous in summer —**F. a. subcoriàcea** Sarg., var. Lfts. oblong-ovate, thicker, 7.5–13 cm. long, entire or slightly serrate, silvery white beneath. (*F. a.* var. *crassifolia* Sarg.) Intr. 1874.—**F. a. juglandifòlia** (Lam.) Rehd., var. Lfts. more or less serrate or crenate-serrate, less lustrous above, more or less pubescent beneath and less glaucous. (*F. j.* Lam.) More common north. Cult. 1800.

Related species: **F. texénsis** Sarg. Tree to 15 m.; lfts. usually 5, elliptic to nearly obovate, 3–8 cm. long or larger on young trees, acute or obtuse, crenulate-serrate chiefly above the middle, reticulate beneath: fr. 1.5–3 cm. long. S.S.6:t 270. Tex. Intr. 1901. Zone VII?

12. **F. biltmoreàna** Beadle. Tree to 15 m.; brts. and petioles densely short-pubescent: lfts. 7–9, rarely 11, stalked, ovate-oblong to lanceolate and often falcate, 8–15 cm. long, acuminate, broad-cuneate or rounded at base entire or obscurely toothed, dark green and glabrous above, glaucous and pu-

bescent beneath, more densely on the veins; petiolules 3–5 mm. long: panicles
pubescent;. anthers oblong, acute: fr. 3–4 cm. long; body terete; wing not
decurrent, linear-oblong, emarginate. S.S.14:t.716. E.H.4:t.247(h). N. J. to
Ga., Ala. and Mo. Cult. about 1800. Zone V. Handsome Ash similar to the
preceding species.

13. **F. tomentòsa** Michx. f. PUMPKIN A. Tree to 40 m.; brts. and petioles
tomentose: lfts. usually 7–9, stalked, elliptic or lanceolate, 10–25 cm. long,
acuminate, broad-cuneate or rounded at base, entire or slightly serrate, nearly
glabrous above at maturity, soft-pubescent beneath; petiolules 5–10 mm.
long; anthers oblong, apiculate, on slender filaments: fr. 5–7 cm. long; wing
oblong, rounded or emarginate, decurrent to below the middle or nearly to
the base of the thick terete body. S.S.14:t.714–5. (*F. profunda* (Bush) Britt.,
F. Michauxii Britt.) W. N. Y. to Ill., La. and n. w. Fla. Intr. 1913. Zone V.
Handsome large-leaved Ash.

14. **F. pennsylvànica** Marsh. RED A. Tree to 20 m.; brts. and petioles
densely pubescent: lfts. 5–9, stalked, ovate to oblong-lanceolate, 8–14 cm.
long, acuminate, broad-cuneate, crenate-serrate or entire, pubescent beneath;
petiolules 3–6 mm. long: panicle rather compact, tomentose; anthers linear-
oblong, on short filaments: fr. 3–6 cm. long; wing lanceolate to oblong-
obovate, rounded to acuminate, rarely emarginate, decurrent to below the
middle or nearly to base. S.S.6:t.271. (*F. pubescens* Lam.) N. S. to Man.,
s. to Ga., Ala. and Miss. Intr. 1783. Zone III. A variable species, the type
gradually passing into the var. *lanceolata.*—**F. p. aucubaefòlia** (K. Koch)
Rehd., var. Lfts. mottled with yellow.—**F. p. lanceolàta** (Borkh.) Sarg., var.
GREEN A. Brts. and petioles glabrous; lfts. elliptic-oblong to lanceolate, 5–12
cm. long, irregularly serrate, bright green above, glabrous on both sides or
pubescent along the midrib beneath; panicles glabrous. S.S.6:t.272. (*F. l.*
Borkh., *F. viridis* Michx.) Me. to Fla., w. to Sask., Mont. and Tex. Intr. 1824.
Zone II.

Related species: **F. Berlandieriàna** DC. Tree to 10 m., rarely more: lfts.
3–5, slender-stalked, lanceolate or elliptic to obovate, 7–10 cm. long, acuminate,
broad-cuneate, remotely serrate or nearly entire, hairy in the axils of the veins
beneath or glabrous: fr. oblong-obovate to spatulate, 2.5–3.5 cm. long; wing
decurrent to near the base. S.S.6:t.273. Tex. to n.e. Mex. Intr. 1879. Zone
VII?

15. **F. velutìna** Torr. Tree to 15 m.; brts. velvety-pubescent: lfts. 3–5,
short-stalked or subsessile, elliptic to ovate, 2–4 cm. long, acute, rarely obtusish, broad-cuneate, crenate-serrulate above the middle, pubescent beneath
and somewhat reticulate: panicles pubescent; anthers oblong, apiculate: fr.
1–1.8 cm. long, wing oblong-obovate to elliptic, shorter than the terete body
and decurrent scarcely to the middle. S.M.848. Ariz. and N. Mex. to Mex.
Intr. ? Zone VII? Recommended as a street tree for a dry climate, particu-
arly the var. *Toumeyi.*—**F. v. coriàcea** (S. Wats.) Rehd., var. Lfts. more
coriaceous and more reticulate, less pubescent or glabrescent. Rep. N. S.
Geog. Surv. West 100th Mer. 6:t.22. (*F. c.* S. Wats.) Utah, Calif. Cult. 1900.
Zone VII?—**F. v. glabra** Rehd., var. Lfts. 3–7, glabrous like brts. (*F. v.* var.
glabrata Lingelsh.—MODESTO ASH.) Intr. 1916. Ariz. to Mex. Zone VII?—
F. v. Toumeỳi (Britt.) Rehd., var. Young brts. pubescent or glabrescent:
lfts. 5–7, elliptic to lanceolate, 3–7 cm. long, acuminate, cuneate, serrulate
above the middle, finely pubescent beneath; petiolules 3–10 mm. long: fr.
1.5–2.5 cm. long; wing spatulate or oblong, about as long or rarely slightly
onger than the terete body. S.S.6:t.267. S.M.849. B.T.803. M.G.28:556(h).
(*F. T.* Britt.) Ariz., N. Mex. and Mex. Intr. 1891. Zone VI?

16. **F. orégona** Nutt. Tree to 25 m.; brts. usually pilose: lfts. 5–9, usually 7, sessile, rarely stalked, elliptic or obovate to oblong, 8–16 cm. long, acute broad-cuneate, entire or remotely and slightly serrate, pubescent above at first, becoming glabrous, pubescent beneath, light green: panicles glabrous anthers oblong, on short filaments: fr. 3–5 cm. long; wing elliptic-oblong to oblanceolate, decurrent nearly to the base of the slightly compressed body S.S.6:t.276. (*F. californica* Hort.) Wash. to s. Calif. Cult. 1870. Zone VI

17. **F. platýpoda** Oliv. Tree to 22 m.: petiole enlarged and tomentose at base: lfts. 7–11, sessile, elliptic-oblong or ovate-lanceolate, 5–10 cm. long short-acuminate, serrulate, gray-green and quite glabrous above, pale and papillose and pilose on the veins beneath: panicle 12–15 cm. long; fr. oblong 4–5 cm. long, narrowed at ends, compressed, winged to the base. H.I.1229 C.C.282. China. Intr. 1909. Zone V.

18. **F. caroliniàna** Mill. WATER A. Tree to 15 m.; winter-buds chestnut brown; brts. glabrous or pubescent: lfts. 5–7, stalked, elliptic or ovate to oblong, 5–12 cm. long, acuminate, broad-cuneate or sometimes rounded at base, serrate, rarely entire, glabrous or sparingly pilose on the veins, rarely pubescent (var. *pubescens* [M. A. Curtis] Fern.) beneath: anthers linear apiculate, on slender filaments: fr. elliptic to oblong-obovate, 3–5 cm. long acute to emarginate; body compressed and surrounded by the wing, sometimes 3-winged. S.S.6:t.274,275. (*F. platycarpa* Michx.) Va. to Fla., w. to Ark. and Tex. usually in swamps. Intr. 1724. Zone VII?

19. **F. Lowéllii** Sarg. Tree to 8 m.: brts. quadrangular and winged: lfts 5, rarely 3 or 7, short-stalked, ovate or elliptic-ovate, 5–8 cm. long, acute or acuminate, broad-cuneate, remotely and slightly toothed, yellow-green, glabrous or slightly pubescent: fr. oblong-obovate or elliptic-oblong, 2.5–3.5 cm long, usually rounded at apex; body compressed, winged to the base. S.M.836 Ariz. Intr. 1914. Zone VII.

20. **F. anómala** S. Wats. SINGLE-LEAF A. Shrub or tree to 7 m.; brts quadrangular, slightly winged, glabrous: lvs. simple or occasionally with 2–3 lfts. broad-ovate or suborbicular, 3–6 cm. long, rounded or acutish at apex entire or sparingly crenate-serrate, glabrous and dark green above, pale beneath and pubescent when young; petiole 1–3 cm. long, rusty-pubescent when young: fls. in short panicles, with the lvs., perfect or unisexual; anthers linear-oblong, on slender filaments: fr. obovate-oblong, 2 cm. long, rounded or emarginate. S.S.6:t.266. E.P.IV.243,1:39. Colo. to Utah, S. Calif. Cult 1890. Zone VI. Distinct and interesting Ash.

Subsect. 3. BUMELIOIDES Endl. Fls. without calyx and corolla; only in No 21 a minute deciduous calyx: fls. dioecious or polygamous; anthers broad-oblong to cordate: lfts. usually more than 7: outer scales of terminal bud foliar.

21. **F. quadrangulàta** Michx. BLUE A. Tree to 25, rarely to 40 m.; brts 4-angled and usually slightly winged, glabrous: lfts. 7–11, short-stalked, ovate to lanceolate, 6–12 cm. long, acuminate, broad-cuneate or rounded at base sharply serrate, yellow-green, glabrous except along midrib near base beneath: fls. perfect, in short panicles: anthers short-oblong, obtuse, nearly sessile: fr. oblong, 3–5 cm. long, emarginate, winged to the base. S.S.6:t.263 Mich. to Ark. and Tenn. Intr. 1823. Zone III. Lvs. turning pale yellow in autumn; a valuable timber tree.

22. **F. nígra** Marsh. BLACK A. Tree to 25 m.; winter-buds dark brown brts. terete, glabrous: lfts. 7–11, sessile, oblong to oblong-lanceolate, 7–12 cm long, long-acuminate, obliquely cuneate or rounded at base, serrate with small incurved teeth, dark green above, lighter green beneath, glabrous

except the rusty tomentum at base and along the midrib beneath: fls. dioecious; anthers oblong, apiculate, on short filaments: fr. narrow-oblong to oblong-obovate, 2.5–3.5 cm. long, rounded or emarginate; body flat; wing decurrent to base. S.S.6:t.264–5. Em.382. Am. For. 21:728(h). (*F. sambucifolia* Lam.) Nfd. to Lake Winnipeg, s. to W. Va., Iowa and Ark.; in moist places. Intr. 1800. Zone II.

23. **F. mandshùrica** Rupr. MANCHURIAN A. Tree to 30 m.; brts. obtusely quadrangular, glabrous; winter-buds dark brown: lfts. 9–11, sessile, oblong-ovate to oblong-lanceolate, 7–12 cm. long, long-acuminate, cuneate, sharply serrate, dull green above and often sparingly hispid, usually pilose or hispid on the veins beneath, rufous-tomentose at base; rachis slightly winged: fls. dioecious: fr. oblong-lanceolate, 2.5–3.5 cm. long. M.K.t.85(c). N.K.10:t.8. N.T.1:406. (*F. m.* var. *japonica* Maxim.) N. E. Asia. Intr. 1882. Zone III. Like the preceding species usually not satisfactory under cult.

24. **F. excélsior** L. EUROPEAN A. Tree to 30 or 40 m.; winter-buds black or nearly so: brts. glabrous: lfts. 7–11, sessile, ovate-oblong to ovate-lanceolate, 5–11 cm. long, acuminate, cuneate, serrate, dark green above, lighter green beneath, glabrous except villous along the midrib beneath: fls. polygamous; anthers ovoid, apiculate, shorter than filaments: fr. lanceolate to narrow-oblong, 2.5–4 cm. long, obtuse or emarginate to acute. H.W.3:115(h), 116,t.59(c). R.I.17:t.31,f.3–6(c). S.E.6:t.902(c). F.E.24:395(h). E.H.4:t.239–244(h). Eu., Asia Minor. Cult. for centuries. Zone III.—**F. e. argénteo-variegàta** West., var. Lfts. variegated or margined white. (*F. e. albovariegata* Hayne, *F. e.* f. *argentea* Lingelsh.)—**F. e. aùreo-variegàta** West., var. Lvs. variegated or margined yellow. (*F. e.* var. *lutea* Loud.)—**F. e. aùrea** Willd., var. With yellow brts.—**F. e. diversifòlia** Ait., var. Lvs. simple or sometimes 3-parted and usually incised-dentate. S.E.6:t.903(c). Gn.22:273. S.H.2:f.523h-l. M.D.1915:294,t(h). (*F. simplicifolia* Willd., *F. monophylla* Desf., *F. heterophylla* Vahl, *F. e. simplicifolia laciniata* Kirchn.)—**F. e. eròsa** (Willd.) Loud., var. Lfts. very narrow, incisely serrate or erose-dentate.—**F. e. aspleniifòlia** Kirchn. Lfts. linear, slightly serrulate. S.H.f.523g(l).—**F. e. críspa** Willd., var. With small very dark green, curled and twisted lfts.; of slow growth. S.H.2:f.523f(l). (*F. e. atrovirens* Hort., *F. e. cucullata* Hort.)—**F. e. nàna** (Pers.) Hayne, var. A dwarf compact slow-growing form with very small lfts. S.H.2:f.523k(l). M.G.19:380(h). (*F. nana* Pers., *F. polemoniifolia* Poir., *F. e. globosa* Hort.)—**F. e. péndula** Ait., var. With pendulous brs. Gn. 38:400(h). E.H.4:t.238(h). L.A.6:t.158(h). (*F. e. Wentworthii* Hort.)—**F. e. "aurea péndula"** Loud., var. With yellow pendulous brs.—**F. e. horizontàlis** (Desf.) Poir., var. With horizontally spreading limbs and pendulous brs. forming a broad flat head. Gn.39:451(h). G.W.20:53(h).

Related species: **F. Hoòkeri** Wenzig. Tree; buds nearly black, with conspicuous margin of pale fulvous tomentum: lfts. 5, elliptic to oblong, 6–12 cm. long, acuminate, denticulate or nearly entire, usually villous along the midrib beneath: fls. dioecious: fr. lanceolate, 4–4.5 cm. long, sulcate in the middle. N. W. Himal. Intr. 1920. Zone V?

25. **F. rotundifòlia** Mill. Shrub or small tree to 5 m., with slender often purplish brs.: lfts. 7–13, sessile, orbicular-ovate to elliptic or obovate, rarely elliptic-oblong, 1–3 cm. long, acute or rounded at apex, serrate, glabrous or pubescent along the midrib beneath near base: fr. oblong, about 3 cm. long. S.H.2:f.524h-i(l). D.H.1:95(l). (*F. parvifolia* Lam., *F. p.* var. *minor* Dipp., *F. oxycarpa* var. *parvifolia* Wenz.) S. Eu., W. Asia. Cult. 1750. Zone VI.— **F. r. péndula** (Loud.) Rehd., var. Brs. pendulous. (*F. parvifolia* f. *p.* Dipp., *F. lentiscifolia* var. *p.* Loud.)

Related species: **F. numídica** Dipp. Lfts. 7–9, elliptic, 2–3 cm. long, acute cuneate, serrate, sparingly hairy above and on the veins beneath; rachis an petiole narrowly winged, sparingly short-pilose. D.H.1:96(1). Mediterr. re Cult. 1890.

26. **F. angustifòlia** Vahl. Tree to 25 m.; winter-buds dark brown; brt glabrous: lfts. 7–13, sessile, oblong-lanceolate to narrow-lanceolate, 3–7 cn long, acuminate, cuneate, sharply and remotely serrate, dark green abov lighter beneath, glabrous; rachis with closed groove open only at nodes panicles short, few-fld.; anthers ovoid, cordate, about as long as filaments fr. elliptic-oblong to oblanceolate, 3–4 cm. long, acute or obtuse, rounded a base. D.H.1:91. E.H.4:t.245(h), 262,f.6(l). (*F. oxycarpa* var. *a.* Lingelsb *F. tamariscifolia* Vahl.) S. Eu., N. Afr., W. Asia. Cult. 1800. Zone VI?- **F. a. lentiscifòlia** (Desf.) Henry, var. Lfts. more spreading and more remot lf. sometimes to 25 cm. long. (*F. l.* Desf.)—**F. a. monophýlla** Henry, va Lvs. simple or with 2–3 lfts., lanceolate, 5–12 cm. long, glabrous. (*F. Vel heimii* Dieck.) E.H.4:t.262,f.3(l). Cult. 1885.—**F. a. austràlis** (Gay) Schneid var. Lfts. beneath near midrib and rachis hairy. (*F. a.* Gay, ? *F. tamarisc folia* Dipp., not Vahl.) S. Eu., N. Afr. Cult. 1890. Zone VI.

Related species: **F. Elónza** Kirchn. Small tree; brts. gray-green or yellowis with whitish warts: lfts. 9–13, elliptic-ovate to ovate-lanceolate, 2.5–6 cm. lon acute, broad-cuneate, villous beneath along the midrib: fr. narrow-oblong. D.F 1:87. Origin unknown; cult. 1864. Zone V.—**F. oblìqua** Tausch. Small tree lfts. 9–11, subsessile, elliptic-ovate to ovate-lanceolate, 4–8 cm. long, the termina to 12 cm. long, acuminate, broad-cuneate, glabrous; rachis with continued ope groove: fr. oblong-obovate, 2.5–3 cm. long, acute. S.H.2:f.424c(1). (*F. Wil denowiana* Koehne, *F. rotundifolia* Hort., not Mill.) W. Asia. Cult. 1834.

27. **F. oxycárpa** Willd. Tree; winter-buds dark brown: lfts. 7–9, rarely or 11, sessile, ovate-oblong to lanceolate, 4–7 cm. long, acuminate, cuneate o broad-cuneate, sharply serrate, light green on both sides and glabrous excep villous along the midrib beneath: fr. obovate-oblong to lanceolate, 3–4 cn long, acute or obtusish, narrowed at base of the compressed body. S.H.2 f.522f-g,525n-p. D.H.1:89. (*F. oxyphylla* Bieb.) S. Eu. to Persia and Turkes Intr. 1815. Zone V.

28. **F. syríaca** Boiss. Syrian A. Small tree, brs. often with shortened inter nodes and crowded whorled lvs.: lfts. 3–5, rarely 7, lanceolate, 3–10 cm. lon acuminate, cuneate, sharply serrate, bright green, quite glabrous, stomati erous on both sides: fls. in short panicles: fr. obovate-oblong, 3–4 cm. lon obtuse or acute. D.H.1:92. S.H.2:f.524e,525a-d. (*F. sogdiana* Dipp., no Bge., *F. turkestanica* Carr.) W. and C. Asia. Cult. 1880. Zone V.

29. **F. holótricha** Koehne. Small tree; brts. and petioles pubescent: lfts 9–13, short-stalked or subsessile, ovate or oblong-lanceolate, 3–8 cm. lon acuminate, sharply serrate, pubescent on both sides when young: ovar pubescent; anthers oval, subsessile. M.D.1910:114;1925:281,f.1,4. S.H.2: 524b(l). E. Balkan Pen. Cult. 1870. Zone V.

Related species: **F. Pallisae** Wilmott. Lfts. 5–9, rarely 11, sessile, ovate lanceolate, rounded to broad-cuneate at base, remotely crenate-serrate: anthe on short filaments: fr. oblong, obtuse, 4–5 cm. long. M.D.1925:281,f.2,3,£ Balkan Pen. Intr. about 1840? Zone V?

30. **F. potamóphila** Herd. Tree to 10 m.; brts. green, glabrous: lfts. 9–11 sometimes 7 or 13, stalked, broad-elliptic or elliptic-ovate, 2–5 cm. long, acut narrowed into a stalk 5–10 mm. long, serrate, glabrous or pubescent alon midrib beneath, stomatiferous on both sides: fr. elliptic-oblong, 3–5 cm. lon acute or obtuse. D.H.1:97,98. S.H.2:f.522b,523c(l). E.H.4:t.262,f.8. U. £ Inv. 50:t.4(h). (*F. Regelii* Dipp.) Turkest. Cult. 1890. Zone V.

Related species: **F. sogdiàna** Bge. Small tree: lfts. 7–11, ovate-lanceolate, 3–6 cm. long, spinulose-dentate, quite glabrous: fr. oblong-obovate, 3 cm. long, obtuse or emarginate. S.H.2:f.524d(1). Turkest. Cult. 1890. Zone V.

4. FORSȲTHIA Vahl. Golden-bell.

Deciduous shrubs, glabrous, rarely lvs. pubescent; winter-buds with several outer scales, superposed and often laterally branching; brs. hollow or with lamellate pith: lvs. opposite, petioled, serrate or entire, occasionally 3-parted or 3-foliolate, thickish: fls. 1–6, axillary, heterostylous, before the lvs.; calyx deeply 4-lobed, persistent; corolla yellow, with 4 oblong lobes, longer than the campanulate tube usually striped orange within; stamens 2, inserted at the base of corolla, not or slightly exserted; style slender, with 2-lobed stigma, in the macrostyle form longer, in the microstyle form shorter than the stamens: fr. a 2-celled dehiscent caps. with many winged seeds. Six or 7 species in E. Asia, one in S. E. Eu. (After Wm. Forsyth, prominent English horticulturist; 1737–1800.)—Ornamental shrubs very showy in early spring with profuse yellow fls.; the lvs. remaining green until late in fall and are not attacked by insects.

A. Brs. hollow, with solid pith at the nodes: lvs. often 3-foliolate or 3-parted: fr. ovate, narrowed at base, warty..1. *F. suspensa*
  AA. Brts. with lamellate pith (often only partly so in No. 2).
    B. Pith solid at the nodes, lamellate or partly so between, rarely hollow: lvs. often 3-parted on shoots...2. *F. intermedia*
    BB. Pith lamellate throughout, only at base of vigorous shoots sometimes wanting: lvs. never 3-parted or exceptionally so in No. 4).
      C. Lvs. usually entire or with few shallow teeth, ovate to ovate-lanceolate: fr. smooth, narrowed at base...3. *F. europaea*
      CC. Lvs. serrate, only occasionally nearly entire: fr. smooth, rounded at base.
        D. Lvs. elliptic-oblong to lanceolate, cuneate at base, serrate usually only above the middle; brts. quadrangular, green...............................4. *F. viridissima*
        DD. Lvs. ovate, usually rounded at base and serrate nearly to base: brts. terete or nearly so, yellowish..5. *F. ovata*

1. F. suspénsa (Thunb.) Vahl. Shrub to 3 m., with upright stems and spreading or pendulous brs.; brts. slightly 4-angled: lvs. ovate to oblong-ovate, serrate, 6–10 cm. long, acute, broad-cuneate or rounded at base: fls. 1–3, sometimes to 6, golden yellow, about 2.5 cm. long; calyx-lobes oblong, about as long as corolla-tube: fr. narrow-ovoid, slightly compressed, 1.5 cm. long. Fl.iv–v. S.Z.1:t.3(c). (*Syringa s.* Thunb.) China, cult. in Japan. Zone V. Very showy in spring; the var. *Sieboldii* may be used like a climbing shrub for covering arbors, trellises, etc., and is very effective hanging down over rocks and walls.—**F. s. Siebóldii** Zabel, var. Shrub with very slender pendulous brs., often trailing on the ground and rooting at the tips: lvs. usually simple, ovate or broad-ovate: fls. usually solitary; corolla-lobes rather broad, flat, slightly spreading. B.M.4995(c). F.S.12:t.1253(c). G.F.4:79. Gt.55:205. Gn.86:370(h). Gn.M.29:115(h). (*F. Sieboldii* Dipp.) Intr. from Japan in 1833. Zone V. The type of the species.—**F. s. Fortùnei** (Lindl.) Rehd., var. Vigorous upright shrub with arching or spreading brs.: lvs. ovate to oblong-ovate, on long shoots often 3-foliolate or 3-parted: corolla with narrow, spreading usually twisted lobes. Ad.4:t.129(c). R.H.1861:291. F.E.31:421. Gn.73:243(h);78:182(h). (*F. Fortunei* Lindl.) China. Intr. about 1860.—Forms of this var. are: **F. s. variegàta** Butz. Lvs. variegated with yellow: fls. deep yellow. (*F. s.* f. *aureo-variegata* Koehne.)—**F. s. decípiens** Koehne, f. Fls. solitary, deep yellow, macrostyle; pedicels 1–2 cm. long. Gt.55:203.—**F. s. pállida** Koehne, f. Fls. solitary, pale yellow.—**F. s. atrocaùlis** Rehd., f. Young growth purplish and brts. dark purple: corolla-lobes 13–15 mm. broad. R.H.1930:206,t.f.2(c). G.C.71:167. Intr. 1908. Zone VI?—**F. s. pubéscens** Rehd., f. Young brts. and lvs. on both sides or only beneath short-pubescent, purplish when young. Intr. 1908. Zone VI.

2. × **F. intermèdia** Zab. (*F. suspensa* × *viridissima*). Shrub to 3 m.;
similar in habit to *F. s.* var. *Fortunei*: lvs. usually ovate-oblong to oblong-
lanceolate, sometimes 3-parted on vigorous shoots, 8–12 cm. long: fls. usually
several; calyx shorter than corolla-tube. Fl.ɪv–v. Gt.34:t.1182;40:397. Gn.
W.22:181. Gn.86:No.2622(h). (*F. i. divaricata* Koehne.) Orig. before 1880.
Zone IV.—**F. i. vitellìna** Koehne. Corolla about 2.5 cm. long, deep yellow,
macrostyle. R.H.1930:206,t.f.1(c). Gt.55:227,228. (*F. v.* Koehne.)—**F. i.**
primulìna Rehd., var. Fls. crowded at base of brts., pale yellow, with revolute lobes, microstyle.—**F. i. densiflòra** Koehne. With spreading and pendulous brs.: fls. much crowded, rather pale, with rather flat, slightly recurved
lobes, macrostyle. Gt.55:230,231. (*F. d.* Koehne.)—**F. i. spectàbilis** (Koehne)
Spaeth. Corolla more than 3 cm. long, bright yellow, sometimes 5- or 6-
merous; fls. crowded, microstyle. Gt.55:229. G.C.71:167. Gn.79:176. B.H.
37:85(h). (*F. s.* Koehne.) This is perhaps the most showy of all Forsythias.
3. **F. europaèa** Deg. & Bald. Upright shrub to 2 m., with upright brts.,
green: lvs. ovate to ovate-lanceolate, 5–8 cm. long, acute, rounded or broad-
cuneate at base, usually entire or at end of brts. with shallow teeth, rather
thick, glabrous or slightly pubescent beneath; petiole 4–6 mm. long: fls.
usually solitary, short-stalked; calyx shorter than corolla-tube; corolla yellow,
about 2 cm. long, with narrow-oblong lobes 5–6 mm. wide: fr. ovoid, about 1.2
cm. long. Fl.v. B.M.8039(c). Gt.54:291. G.C.36:123. F.E.18:348. Albania.
Intr. 1899. Zone V. Less ornamental than other species
   F. europaea × *ovata* has been raised at the Arnold Arboretum in 1935.
   Related species: **F. Giraldiàna** Lingelsh. Lvs. elliptic-oblong to lanceolate-
oblong, 6–10 cm. long, long-acuminate, usually sparingly pilose at veins beneath:
fls. short-stalked: fr. ovoid, broad at base, rostrate. E.P.IV.243:111. N. China.
Cult. 1938. Zone V.
4. **F. viridíssima** Lindl. Shrub with upright stems and brs., to 3 m.; brts.
green: lvs. elliptic-oblong to lanceolate, rarely obovate-oblong, broadest about
or above the middle, 8–14 cm. long, acute, cuneate, usually serrate only above
the middle, sometimes nearly entire, dark green; petiole 6–12 mm. long: fls.
1–3, calyx-lobes oval, about half as long as corolla-tube; corolla 2–2.5 cm.
long, bright yellow with a slight greenish tinge, the lobes narrow-oblong,
revolute: fr. ovoid, rostrate, 1.5 cm. long. Fl.v. B.M.4587(c). F.S.3:t.261.
B.R.33:39(c). Gn.33:563. B.S.1:560. China. Intr. 1844. Zone (V), VI. Less
handsome than *F. suspensa*, but var. *koreana* is about as showy.—**F. v.**
koreàna Rehd., var. Upright shrub with more or less spreading brs.: lvs.
elliptic-ovate to ovate-oblong or oblong-lanceolate, broadest below the
middle, 5–12 cm. long, usually serrate from about the middle, sometimes
nearly entire, broad-cuneate; fls. bright yellow; calyx more than half as long
as corolla-tube, corolla about 2.5 cm. long. N.K.10:t.2. (*F. k.* Nakai.) Korea.
Intr. 1917. Zone V.
5. **F. ovàta** Nakai. Shrub to 1.5 m., with spreading brs.; brts. grayish
yellow or yellowish, gray when older: lvs. ovate or broad-ovate, 5–7 cm. long,
abruptly acuminate, truncate or sometimes subcordate or broad-cuneate, serrate or sometimes nearly entire; petiole 8–12 mm. long: fls. solitary, short-
stalked; sepals broad-ovate, half as long as corolla-tube; corolla amber-
yellow, 1.5–2 cm. long, with broad-oblong lobes. Fl.ɪv–v. B.M.9437(c). N.K.
10:t.3. Gn.88:273. G.C.95:225. Korea. Intr. 1917. Zone IV. Distinct species,
the earliest to bloom.
   Related species: **F. japónica** Mak. Shrub with spreading brs.: lvs. ovate to
broad-ovate, 5–12 cm. long, rounded at base, short-acuminate, rather closely
serrate from near base, pubescent beneath; petiole pubescent: fls. solitary,

about 1.5 cm. long. N.T.1:360. C. Japan. Intr. ?—F. j. saxátilis Nakai, var. Brts. brownish or yellowish gray: lvs. ovate to oblong-ovate, 3–6 cm. long, pilose on veins below when young; petiole 5–10 mm. long, pubescent: calyx-lobes ovate, acutish, 3 mm. long, scarious, brown, whitish at apex; corolla pale yellow, lobes narrow-oblong. Korea. Intr. 1924. Zone V.

5. SYRÍNGA L. LILAC.

Deciduous shrubs or small trees; winter-buds ovoid, with several outer scales, the terminal bud often wanting: lvs. opposite, petioled, entire or sometimes lobed or pinnate: fls. perfect, in terminal or lateral panicles on the brs. of the previous season; calyx small, campanulate, 4-toothed, irregularly dentate or nearly truncate, small, persistent; corolla salver-shaped, with cylindric tube and 4 spreading valvate lobes; stamens 2, included or exserted; style with 2-lobed stigma, not exceeding the stamens; ovary 2-celled: fr. an oblong, leathery loculicidal caps. with 2 winged seeds in each cell. (Probably from Greek *syrinx*, pipe, in reference to the stems of Philadelphus to which the name originally had been applied, until Lobel transferred it to this genus.) Including *Ligustrina* Rupr. Monograph by S. D. McKelvey, The Lilacs, with 171 pl. (1928). About 28 species in Asia and S. E. Eu.—Ornamental shrubs with large and showy panicles of often fragrant fls. in spring and early summer.

A. Corolla-tube much longer than calyx; anthers subsessile.
                                  Subgen. I. EUSYRINGA K. Koch.
  B. Panicles from terminal buds, leafy at base (sometimes lateral in No. 9).
                              Ser. 1. VILLOSAE Schneid.
    C. Lvs. papillose, glaucous and glabrous beneath.
      D. Anthers exserted ½; corolla-lobes finally reflexed.......................1. *S. emodi*
      DD. Anthers not or slightly exserted; corolla-lobes upright-spreading.
                                   2. *S. yunnanensis*
    CC. Lvs. not papillose, green to glaucescent and usually pilose at least along the midrib.
      D. Corolla-tube funnelform, gradually widened above the middle, lobes more or less upright; anthers below the mouth.
        E. Panicles upright; anthers not reaching the mouth.
          F. Lvs. 6–12 cm. long, glaucescent beneath.......................3. *S. Josikaea*
          FF. Lvs. 10–16 cm. long, grayish green beneath.......................4. *S. Wolfi*
        EE. Panicles pendulous or nodding, dense; anthers reaching the mouth.
          F. Fls. whitish inside, pink outside, carmine in bud; panicles slender, 12–25 cm. long ....5. *S. reflexa*
          FF. Fls. purple-pink, lighter outside; panicles compact, cylindric, 5–15 cm. long.
                                  6. *S. Komarowi*
      DD. Corolla-tube cylindric or nearly so, lobes spreading.
        E. Anthers reaching the mouth; infl. with 2 pairs of lvs.: lvs. cuneate at base.
          F. Lvs. pilose along the veins beneath or nearly glabrous, glaucescent: infl. compact ....7. *S. villosa*
          FF. Lvs. soft-pubescent beneath: infl. loose.......................8. *S. tomentella*
        EE. Anthers below the mouth: infl. with 1 pair of small lvs. or none, often with lateral panicles below: lvs. rounded or broad-cuneate at base.9. *S. Sweginzowii*
  BB. Panicles from lateral buds; terminal bud usually wanting...Ser. 2. VULGARES Schneid.
    C. Lvs. pubescent at least on midrib beneath: anthers usually violet or bluish gray; corolla about 6 mm. across.
      D. Anthers inserted slightly below the mouth, equaling ½–⅓ of the tube: brts. usually short-pubescent.
        E. Infl. and pedicels short-pilose: lvs. short-pubescent above, villous beneath.
                                 10. *S. Julianae*
        EE. Infl. puberulous; pedicels glabrescent: lvs. slightly pubescent or glabrous above, pubescent at least on veins beneath.......................11. *S. velutina*
      DD. Anthers inserted above the middle of the tube, much below the mouth, equalling ¼ or ⅕ of the tube.
        E. Corolla-tube 1 cm. or less long; lvs. usually pubescent beneath.
                                12. *S. microphylla*
        EE. Corolla-tube slender, over 1 cm. long.
          F. Lvs. with 3–5 pairs of veins, abruptly contracted at base, pubescent at least on veins near base: fls. pale lilac.............................13. *S. pubescens*
          FF. Lvs. with 2–3 pairs of veins, cuneate, glabrous beneath or only pubescent near base: fls. purple-lilac.............................14. *S. Meyeri*
    CC. Lvs. glabrous, or if pubescent broad-ovate and truncate or subcordate at base.
      D. Lvs. entire, or 3–7-lobed in No. 18: corolla about 1 cm. across: flowering brs. without terminal bud.
        E. Lvs. broad-ovate or ovate, subcordate to abruptly broad-cuneate at base: infl. large.

F. Lvs. broad-ovate, subcordate at base, changing orange to purple in fall anthers slightly above middle of tube..........................15. *S. oblat*
FF. Lvs. ovate, subcordate to broad-cuneate at base, remaining green: anthe; just below throat...16. *S. vulgar*
EE. Lvs. oblong-ovate to oblong-lanceolate, cuneate.
  F. Lvs. always entire, 4–7 cm. long: infl. large and loose.........17. *S. chinens*
    FF. Lvs. often 3–7-lobed, 2–4 cm. long: infl. 5–8 cm. long...........18. *S. persic*
DD. Lvs. pinnate, with 7–9 lfts.: infl. 3–7 cm. long: flowering brs. usually with ter minal bud developing into a leafy shoot..............Ser. 3. PINNATIFOLIAE Reh¢
                                            19. *S. pinnatifol*
AA. Corolla-tube not or little longer than calyx; anthers exserted on slender filaments; fl white ....Subgen. II. LIGUSTRINA (Rupr.) K. Koch
  B. Lvs. narrowed at base, ovate to ovate-lanceolate, glabrous; veins not or slightly ele vated; petiole 1.5–2.5 cm. long, slender..................................20. *S. pekinensi*
  BB. Lvs. rounded or subcordate at base, veins elevated; petiole 1–2 cm. long.
                                            21. *S. amurensi*

1. **S. emòdi** G. Don. HIMALAYAN L. Shrub to 5 m., with upright rathe stout brs.; brts. brownish or dark olive-green, dotted with pale lenticels: lv; elliptic to oblong, 8–15, rarely to 20 cm. long, dark green above, glaucous be neath, glabrous; petiole 1–1.5 cm. long: fls. pale lilac or whitish, not pleasantl; scented, in puberulous or glabrescent rather broad and dense panicles 8–1. cm. long; calyx puberulous; corolla with narrow tube 8 mm. long and lance olate acute lobes: fr. cylindric-oblong, about 1.5 cm. long, acuminate, smootl or nearly so. Fl.VI. B.R.31:6(c). R.H.1876:368. Gn.39:106. B.S.2:567. E.F IV.243,1:82,f.3a-b. (*S. villosa* var. *emodi* Rehd.) Afghan., W. Himal. t¢ Kumaon. Intr. about 1840. Zone VI.—**E. e. aùreo-variegàta** Lav. ex Rehd var. Lvs. variegated with yellow. (*S. e. variegata* Nichols., not Van Kleef.)— **S. e. aùrea** Carr. Lvs. yellow.

2. **S. yunnanénsis** Franch. YUNNAN L. Upright shrub to 3 m., with rathe; slender brs.; young brts. glabrous, red-brown, with conspicuous lenticels: lv; elliptic-oblong to elliptic-lanceolate, 3–8 cm. long, short-acuminate, cuneate minutely ciliolate, glaucous beneath; petiole 5–10 mm. long, glabrous, purple fls. pink, in puberulous slender panicles 8–15 cm. long: calyx glabrous witl short teeth; corolla with slender tube about 5 mm. long and acute upright spreading lobes; anthers reaching the mouth: fr. about 1.5 cm. long, pointed smooth. Fl.VI. S.H.2:f.488p-r,489g. Yunnan. Intr. 1906. Zone V. Loosely branched shrub, one of the less showy species.

3. **S. Josikaèa** Jacq. HUNGARIAN L. Shrub to 4 m., with rather stout brs slightly pubescent at first, sparingly lenticellate: lvs. broad-elliptic to elliptic oblong, 6–12 cm. long, acute to acuminate, broad-cuneate to rounded at base ciliolate, dark green and lustrous above, glaucescent beneath, and sparingly hairy on the veins or nearly glabrous; petiole about 1 cm. long: fls. lilac violet, slightly fragrant, subsessile or short-stalked, in rather narrow panicles 10–18 cm. long; calyx pubescent; corolla 1–1.5 cm. long, with ovate upright spreading lobes; anthers inserted much below the mouth: fr. acute, smooth about 1 cm. long. Fl.VI. B.M.3278(c). B.R.1733(c). Hungary, Galicia. Intr about 1830. Zone V. Similar to *S. villosa* but less handsome.—**S. J. exímia** Froebel. Fls. reddish rose, changing to light pink, in large compact panicles G.C.42:280. M.G.16:561. M.D.1907:262.—**S. J.** "H. Zabel" is similar but fls. purplish lilac.

S. J. × villosa; see under No. 7.—*S. J. × reflexa;* see under No. 5.

4. **S. Wólfi** Schneid. Upright shrub to 6 m.; brts. glabrous, sparingly lenticellate: lvs. elliptic-oblong, 10–16 cm. long, acute, or short-acuminate, cuneate or broad-cuneate, grayish green beneath, glabrous except slightly villous along the veins beneath and on margin; petiole 1–1.5 cm. long: fls. lilac, fragrant, stalked, in large slightly pubescent panicles 20–30 cm. long; their lower brs. often recurved; calyx glabrous or short-pilose; corolla 1.5–1.8

cm. long; lobes ovate-oblong, with a conspicuous incurved point; anthers inserted much below the mouth: fr. obtuse, 1.4 cm. long, smooth. Fl.vi. N.K. 10:t.24. S.H.2:f.489i-k,490o-r. (*S. formosissima* Nakai, *S. robusta* Nakai.) Manch., Korea. Cult. 1910. Zone IV.—**S. W. hirsùta** (Schneid.) Rehd., var. Brts., infl. and calyx densely pilose; lvs. pilose beneath. N.K.10:t.25. N. Korea, Manch. Cult. 1938.

5. S. refléxa Schneid. NODDING L. Shrub to 4 m., with rather stout brs.; bark smooth, lenticellate; brts. gray or purple-gray, lenticellate; older brs. pale gray, not fissured: lvs. ovate-oblong to oblong-lanceolate, sometimes elliptic-obovate, 8–15 cm. long, acuminate, cuneate, glabrous above, villous beneath, chiefly along the veins; petioles 1–2 cm. long: infl. narrow, often nearly cylindric, nodding or pendulous, 10–25 cm. long, and 4–5 cm. through, sparingly villous; corolla pinkish outside, white inside, usually carmine in bud, about 1 cm. long; lobes slightly spreading, with incurved tips; anthers reaching the mouth or slightly exserted: fr. oblong, 1.2 cm. long, obtusish and mucronate, smooth or slightly warty, reflexed on the pendulous infl. Fl.vi. B.M.8869(c). G.W.28:409(h). M.G.40:398(h). C. China. Intr. 1901. Zone V. Distinct and handsome species with the fls. in long pendulous panicles.

S. r. × *villosa* = **S. Préstonae** McKelvey. Lvs. pubescent beneath: infl. rather loose with spreading brs.; fls. purple-lilac; corolla-tube funnel-form, slender. McKelvey, Lilacs, t.45–47. G.C.97:193(h). Orig. before 1925.—*S. r.* × *Josikaea* = **S. josifléxa** Preston. Similar to the preceding, but infl. slenderer and slightly nodding. Cult. 1938.—*S. r.* × *Sweginzowii* = **S. swegifléxa** Hesse. Infl. large, dense: fls. deep red in bud, changing to pink. M.G.51:393. Cult. 1935.

6. S. Komarówi Schneid. Shrub to 5 m.; young brts. pubescent, older brs. with gray-brown fissured bark becoming scaly: lvs. ovate-oblong to oblong-lanceolate, 10–16 cm. long, acuminate, cuneate, nearly glabrous above, pubescent beneath, at least on the veins; petiole 1–2 cm. long: panicles nodding, compact, cylindric to oblong-ovoid, 8–14 cm. long; calyx and pedicels slightly pubescent to glabrous; corolla purple-pink, lighter outside, lobes upright, not incurved; anthers usually slightly exserted: fr. usually smooth. Fl.vi. S.H. 2:f.489b-c,490s-u. McKelvey, Lilacs, t.29–33. (*S. Sargentiana* Schneid.) W. China. Intr. 1911. Zone V.

7. S. villòsa Vahl. Bushy shrub of dense habit, to 3 m.; brts. stout, lenticellate, glabrous or slightly pubescent when young: lvs. broad-elliptic to oblong, 5–18 cm. long, acute at ends, dull dark green above, glaucescent beneath and usually pubescent near the midrib, rarely glabrous; petiole 1–2 cm. long: fls. rosy-lilac to whitish, short-stalked, in pyramidal rather dense usually pubescent panicles 8–18 cm. long; calyx slightly pubescent or glabrous; corolla-tube about 1.2 cm. long, with spreading obtuse lobes; anthers inserted near mouth; fr. 1–1.5 cm. long, obtùse or acutish, smooth or nearly so. Fl.v–vi. R.H.1888:492,t(c);1914:332(h). G.F.1:521. Gn.39:91. Gt.44:500. H.B.3:279(h). (*S. Bretschneideri* Lemoine, *S. Emodi* var. *rosea* Cornu.) N. China. Cult. 1882. Zone II. Valued for its dense habit and late and profuse fls.

S. v. × *Josikaea* = **S. Hénryi** Schneid. Similar to *S. villosa,* but panicle larger and looser; corolla pale violet-purple; tube gradually widened above the middle. B.M.8292(c, as *S. villosa*). R.H.1902:40,t(c). J.L.27:800. Orig. 1890. "Lutèce" is the type of this hybrid.—*S. Henryi* × *Sweginzowii* = **S. nanceiàna** McKelvey. In the form of fl. and infl. it resembles the second parent, in the color *S. Henryi.* Orig. before 1925. "Floréal" is the type of this hybrid.—*S. v.* × *reflexa;* see under No. 5.

8. S. tomentélla Bur. & Franch. Slender shrub to 3 m.; brts. brownish, thinly pubescent, later brown, lenticellate: lvs. elliptic to oblong-lanceolate,

3–10 cm. long, acute or acuminate, cuneate, dark green and slightly pubescent above chiefly on the veins, paler beneath and soft-pubescent, rarely only on the veins, ciliolate; petiole about 1 cm. long, pubescent: fls. lilac or whitish, subsessile or short-stalked in a loose pubescent panicle, 10–16 cm. long, its lateral brs. forming dense spikes of subsessile fls. in crowded whorls; calyx pilose; corolla-tube about 1 cm. long, with oblong-lanceolate acute lobes; anthers slightly exserted; fr. 1–1.2 cm. long, acuminulate, smooth. Fl.vi. B.M. 8739(c). Gn.84:35;87:51. (*S. albo-rosea* N. E. Br., *S. Adamiana* Balf. f. & W. W. Sm., *S. Wilsonii* Schneid.) W. China. Intr. 1904. Zone V.

9. **S. Sweginzòwii** Koehne & Lingelsh. Shrub to 3 m.; young brts. purple-brown, glabrous: lvs. oblong or ovate, 5–10 cm. long, usually abruptly acuminate, broad-cuneate to nearly rounded at base, deep green above, light green beneath and pilose on the veins near base or nearly glabrous, thin; petiole 7–10 mm. long: fls. reddish lilac or pale lilac, fragrant, in glabrous or finely puberulous panicles 15–20 cm. long; corolla-tube 8 mm. long, with acutish ovate-oblong lobes; anthers near the mouth; fr. about 1 cm. long, acute, smooth. Fl.vi. G.C.57:344;64:27. M.D.1910:112. G.W.28:411. M.G.40:399. N. W. China. Intr. 1894. Zone V.—**S. S. supérba** Lemoine is scarcely different.

S. S. × *reflexa;* see under No. 5.

10. **S. Juliànae** Schneid. Spreading shrub to 2 m.; brts. densely short-pilose: lvs. elliptic-ovate, 3–6 cm. long, acute or acuminate, broad-cuneate, dark green and short-pubescent above, paler and villous-pubescent beneath, more densely on the veins; petiole 4–8 mm. long, pubescent: fls. lilac-purple, pale inside, fragrant, in slightly pubescent panicles 5–10 cm. long, purplish-violet like the glabrous calyx; corolla-tube 6–8 mm long, with ovate-oblong spreading lobes; anthers light brown, not reaching the mouth: fr. about 1 cm. long, acuminate, verrucose. Fl.v–vi. B.M.8423(c). B.S.2:568. Gn.79:194. (*S. verrucosa* Schneid.) W. China. Intr. 1900. Zone V. Graceful species with fragrant fls.

Related species: **S. Potaníni** Schneid. Shrub to 3 m.: lvs. ovate or elliptic-ovate, 3–6 cm. long, rather densely pubescent above, densely villous-pubescent beneath, usually short-acuminate; petiole 2–5 mm. long: infl. 6–10 cm. long; calyx often pilose; anthers yellow: fr. 10–15 mm. long, short-acuminate, smooth. B.M.9060(c). W. China. Intr. 1905.—**S. pinetòrum** W. W. Sm. Young brts. densely pilose; lvs. ovate to ovate-lanceolate, 2–3.5 cm. long, sparingly pilose or glabrous above, pilose on the veins beneath, petiole 2–5 mm. long; panicle 10–18 cm. long; calyx glabrous, with ciliolate teeth; anthers yellow. S. W. China. Intr. about 1923? Zone VI?

11. **S. velutìna** Komar. Shrub to 3 m.; brts. slightly pubescent or puberulous to nearly glabrous, often glandular: lvs. elliptic to ovate-oblong, acuminate, broad-cuneate or rounded at base, slightly pubescent to glabrous above, densely pubescent beneath or pilose only on midrib or veins; petiole 5–10 mm. long: fls. lilac, in pubescent panicles 6–20 cm. long; calyx pubescent or nearly glabrous; corolla-tube slender, 8–10 mm. long, with short, obtuse or acute, usually cucullate lobes; anthers violet, not reaching the mouth: fr. oblong, 1 cm. long, warty, acute. Fl.v. N.K.10:t.20. McKelvey, Lilacs, t.67–73. (*S. Koehneana* Schneid., *S. Palibiniana* Nakai, *S. Kamibayashii* Nakai.) N. China, Korea. Cult. 1902. Zone III.

12. **S. microphýlla** Diels. Small shrub; young brts. more or less pilose; lvs. orbicular-ovate to elliptic-ovate, 1–4 cm. long, obtuse or abruptly acuminate, broad-cuneate to rounded at base, slightly pilose above, grayish green and pubescent beneath, at maturity only on the veins, ciliolate, or nearly glabrous; petiole 5–10 mm. long: fls. pale lilac, in loose pubescent panicles 3–7

cm. long; calyx pubescent or glabrescent; corolla-tube slender, 1 cm. long, with ovate-lanceolate acute lobes: fr. slender, 1–1.5 cm. long, acuminate, often curved, warty. Fl.vi. S.H.2:f.486z-z^2,487n-p. E.P.IV.243,1:87. N. China. Intr. 1910. Zone V.

13. **S. pubéscens** Turcz. Shrub to 2 m.; brts. slender, slightly quadrangular, glabrous: lvs. orbicular-ovate to rhombic-ovate or ovate, 3–7 cm. long, short-acuminate, broad-cuneate, ciliolate, dark green and glabrous above, pubescent beneath chiefly on the veins; petiole 6–12 mm. long: fls. pale lilac, fragrant, in rather dense glabrous panicles 7–12 cm. long; corolla-tube slender, 1.2–1.5 cm. long, with spreading narrow lobes; anthers inserted much below the mouth: fr. about 1 cm. long, obtusish, warty. Fl.iv–v. B.M.7064(c). G.F.1:415;6:266. G.C.38:123. Gn.M.34:43(h). H.B.3:233(h). (*S. villosa* Dcne., not Turcz.) N. China. Intr. 1880. Zone V. Handsome lilac valued for its early fragrant fls.

14. **S. Meỳeri** Schneid. Small dense shrub; young brts. slightly quadrangular, glabrous or puberulous: lvs. elliptic-ovate to sometimes elliptic-obovate, 2–4 cm. long, acute or obtusish, broad-cuneate, glabrous above, scarcely paler beneath and pubescent on the veins near base, with 2–3 pairs of veins from base nearly to apex; petiole 5–10 mm. long: fls. violet, in dense puberulous panicles 3–8 cm. long, usually several pairs at end of brs.; calyx dark violet, glabrous; corolla-tube very slender, about 1.5 cm. long, scarcely dilated at apex, with spreading acute lobes 3–4 mm. long; anthers inserted below the mouth: fr. verrucose. Fl.v–vi. N. China. Intr. 1908. Zone V. Compact low shrub, flowering when not more than 25 cm. tall, distinct with its dense panicles of violet fls.

15. **S. oblàta** Lindl. Shrub or small tree to 4 m.; brts. rather stout, glabrous: lvs. orbicular-ovate or reniform, often broader than long, 4–10 cm. broad, abruptly acuminate, cordate to subcordate, glabrous; petiole 1–2 cm. long: fls. pale to purple-lilac, in dense rather broad panicles 6–12 cm. long; calyx slightly glandular; corolla-tube 10–12 mm. long, with spreading obtuse lobes: fr. compressed, 1–2 cm. long, acuminate, smooth. Fl.iv–v. B.M.7806(c). G.F.1:221. G.W.5:549. (*S. vulgaris* var. *o.* Franch.) N. China. Intr. 1856. Zone III. The type is a compact early blooming shrub with handsome foliage turning vinous-red in autumn; the vars. are taller and more loosely branched. —**S. o. alba** Rehd., var. Lvs. smaller, minutely pubescent beneath, on flowering brts. often glabrous, ciliolate: fls. white. R.H.1908:301. (*S. affinis* L. Henry, *S. o.* var. *affinis* Lingelsh.) Intr. 1880.—**S. o. Giráldii** (Lemoine) Rehd., var. Lvs. more gradually acuminate, minutely puberulous or sometimes pubescent beneath, ciliolate, or glabrous on flowering brs.: fls. purplelilac, in slender panicles 10–15 cm. long; rachis and calyx purple-violet. R.H. 1909:335. (*S. G.* Lemoine.) N. China. Intr. about 1895.—**S. o. dilatàta** (Nakai) Rehd., var. Lvs. ovate, to 12 cm. long, long-acuminate, usually truncate at base, quite glabrous: infl. loose; corolla-tube slenderer, 12–15 mm. long. N.K.10:t.18. (*S. d.* Nakai.) Korea. Intr. 1917.

S. o. × *vulgaris* = S. hyacinthiflòra Lemoine. Intermediate between the parents, with broad-ovate lvs. turning purplish in autumn; only known in the double form, var. **S. h. plèna** Lemoine. There are also hybrids of var. *Giraldi* and *S. vulgaris,* as "Lamartine" and "Mirabeau" of taller, slenderer habit and with single fls.—*S. o.* × *pinnatifolia;* see under No. 19.

16. **S. vulgàris** L. Upright shrub or small tree to 7 m.; brts. glabrous: lvs. ovate or broad-ovate, 5–12 cm. long, acuminate, truncate or subcordate to broad-cuneate, glabrous; petiole 1.5–3 cm. long: fls. very fragrant, usually lilac, in panicles 10–20 cm. long; corolla-tube slender, about 1 cm long,

with spreading ovate obtuse lobes: fr. 1–1.5 cm. long, acute, smooth. Fl.iv–v. B.M.183(c). R.I.17:t.32(c). F.E.22:5(h). M.G.14:205(h). S. E. Eu. Cult. 1563. Often escaped from cult. Zone III. One of the most popular ornamental shrubs with numerous horticultural forms mostly of French origin.—**S. v. alba** West., var. Fls. white: brts. yellowish gray; winter-buds yellowish green. Blooms a week earlier than other vars.—**S. v. coerùlea** West., var. Fls. blue, in rather loose panicles. This is the typical form.—**S. v. purpúrea** West., var. Fls. purplish red, in rather dense panicles.—**S. v. violàcea** Ait., var. Fls. violet-lilac, in rather loose panicles.—**S. v. plèna** Oudin. Fls. blue, double. *S. v.* × *oblata;* see under No. 15.—*S. v.* × *persica;* see No. 17.

Related species: **S. rhodópea** Velenovsky. Lvs. broad-ovate, subcordate: panicle to 20 cm. long, spreading: corolla-tube about 8 mm. long, lobes mostly 5: fr. acuminate. Bulgaria. Cult. 1922. Zone V. Intermediate between the two preceding species.

17. **S. chinénsis** Willd. (*S. persica* × *vulgaris*.) Shrub to 5 m., with slender spreading and often arching brs., glabrous: lvs. ovate-lanceolate, 4–8 cm. long, acuminate, cuneate; petiole about 1.5 cm. long: fls. purple-lilac, in large and rather loose glabrous panicles; corolla-tube 7–8 mm. long, with 4 ovate obtuse or acutish lobes. Fl.v. R.H.1883:8. (*S. rothomagensis* Mord. de Laun., *S. dubia* Pers., *Lilac media* and *L. varina* Dum.-Cours.) Orig. about 1777. Zone V.—**S. c. alba** (Kirchn.) Rehd., var. Fls. white. (*S. rothomagensis alba* Kirchn., *S. correlata* A. Br.)—**S. c. meténsis** (Simon-Louis) Dieck. Fls. rosy-lilac.—**S. c. Saugeàna** (Loud.) Rehd., var. Fls. lilac-red. (*S. dubia rubra* Lodd., *S. rothomagensis* var. *S.* Loud.)—**S. c. dúplex** (Lemoine) Rehd., var. Fls. purplish lilac, double.

18. **S. pérsica** L. PERSIAN L. Shrub to 2 m., with upright or arching brs., glabrous: lvs. lanceolate, 3–6 cm. long, acuminate, cuneate, sometimes 3-lobed or pinnatifid; petiole 5–12 mm. long: fls. pale lilac, fragrant, in loose broad glabrous panicles 5–8 cm. long; pedicels as long or longer than calyx; corolla-tube slender, about 1 cm. long, with ovate acutish lobes: fr. 4-angled, 8–10 mm. long, obtusish, smooth. Fl.v. B.M.486(c). S.H.2:f.485k-s,486n-q. W.A.50,t(h). Persia to N. W. China. Intr. about 1614. Zone V.—**S. p. integrifòlia** Vahl., var. Lvs. all or almost all undivided. The typical form. —**S. p. alba** West., var. Fls. white or whitish. (*S. Steencruysii* Hort.)—**S. p. laciniàta** (Mill.) West., var. Lvs. all or partly 3–9-lobed; of dwarfer habit and usually with smaller panicles. R.H.1901:40,41. L.B.1107(c). B.S.2:570. (*S. pteridifolia* Hort., *S. filicifolia* Hort., *S. p.* var. *pinnata* Jacques.) Spontaneous in N. W. China.

19. **S. pinnatifòlia** Hemsl. PINNATE L. Upright shrub to 3 m.: lvs. pinnate, 4–8 cm. long; lfts. 7–11, ovate to ovate-lanceolate, 1–3 cm. long, only the upper pairs decurrent, the lower ones contracted at base, acute, ciliolate; petiole 1–2 cm. long: fls. white, tinged pale lilac, in panicles 3–7 cm. long; corolla-tube slender, about 1 cm. long, with recurved obtusish lobes. Fl.v–vi. G.C.55:369. E.P.IV.243,1:91. W. China. Intr. 1904. Zone IV. Interesting for its pinnate lvs., but fls. not conspicuous.

S. p. × *oblata* = **S. diversifòlia** Rehd. Brts. with or without terminal bud: lvs. partly entire and ovate-oblong, rounded at base, or pinnatifid with 3–5 acuminate lobes: infl. to 11 cm. long, usually 1 pair at end of brts.; anthers just reaching the mouth. Orig. 1929.

20. **S. pekinénsis** Rupr. Large shrub to 5 m., with slender spreading brs. brownish red when young: lvs. ovate to ovate-lanceolate, 5–10 cm. long and 2–3.5 cm. broad, acuminate, cuneate, dark green above, grayish green beneath and scarcely veined, quite glabrous; petiole 1.5–2.5 cm. long: fls. yellowish

white, in large glabrous panicles 8–15 cm. long: corolla 6 mm. across; stamens about as long as limb: fr. oblong, acute, 1.5–2 cm. long, warty or smooth. Fl.vi. G.F.3:165;7:385. M.G.14:425. S.L.366(h). (*S. amurensis* var. *p.* Maxim., *Ligustrina p.* Reg.) N. China. Intr. 1881. Zone IV. Handsome large shrub with profuse yellowish white fls.—**S. p. péndula** (Temple) Dipp., f. With slender pendulous brs. W. Am. Sci. 4:39(h).

21. **S. amurénsis** (Rupr.) Rupr. Amur L. Shrub or small tree to 6 m., with upright or spreading brs.: lvs. broad-ovate to ovate, 5–12 cm. long and 3.5–6.5 cm. broad, abruptly to gradually acuminate, usually rounded or truncate at base, bright green above, grayish green and reticulate beneath and glabrous or slightly pubescent; petiole 1–2 cm. long: panicles rather loose, large, 10–15 cm. long; stamens almost twice as long as limb: fr. oblong, 1.5 cm. long, obtusish, smooth or slightly verrucose. Fl.vi. Gt.12:t.396;45:64. G.F.2:271. Gn.12:623,624. R.H.1877:453–5. (*S. rotundifolia* Dcne., *S. ligustrina* Leroy, *S. sibirica* Hort. partly, *Ligustrina a.* var. *mandshurica* Maxim., *L. a.* Reg.) Manch., N. China. Intr. about 1855. Zone IV. Similar to the preceding, but of more upright and stouter habit.—**S. a. japónica** (Maxim.) Fr. & Sav., var. Tree to 10 m.: lvs. to 14 cm. long, often broad-ovate and subcordate, pubescent beneath at least when young: fr. to 2 cm. long, warty. Fl.vi–vii. B.M.7534(c). M.K.t.86(c, as *S. amurensis*). G.F.2: 293(h). Gn.76:356(h). M.G.14:424(h);40:398(h). (*S. japonica* Dcne., *Ligustrina amurensis* var. *j.* Maxim.) Japan. Intr. 1876. Zone IV. Valuable for its late blooming season.

6. **LIGÚSTRUM** L. Privet. Deciduous or evergreen shrubs or rarely trees; winter-buds ovoid, with about 2 outer scales: lvs. opposite, shortpetioled, entire: fls. perfect, white, small, in terminal panicles, rarely from lateral leafless buds; calyx campanulate, 4-toothed: corolla salver-shaped, with usually short or sometimes elongated tube and with 4 spreading lobes; stamens 2, enclosed or exserted; style cylindric, not exceeding the stamens; ovary 2-celled; cells 2-ovuled: fr. a 1–4-seeded berry-like drupe, normally black or bluish black; endocarp in one species dehiscent. (The ancient Latin name of the privet.) About 50 species, chiefly in E. Asia and Malaysia to Australia, one in Eu. and N. Afr.—Ornamental shrubs or small trees mostly grown for their handsome foliage or for their often profusely produced white fls.

A. Corolla-tube shorter than limb or only slightly longer.
  B. Lvs. deciduous or only half-evergreen.
    c. Fls. pediceled.
      D. Brts. minutely puberulous or glabrous: lvs. glabrous: anthers not exceeding the corolla-lobes.
        E. Lvs. with 4–5 pairs of indistinct veins, 3–6 cm. long, obtuse or acute.
                                  1. *L. vulgare*
        EE. Lvs. with about 10 pairs of veins, 5–12 cm. long, acuminate....2. *L. compactum*
      DD. Brts. densely pubescent; lvs. pubescent on midrib beneath: anthers exceeding the corolla-lobes ....3. *L. sinense*
    cc. Fls. sessile in long narrow spikes forming panicles; anthers exceeding the corolla-lobes ....4. *L. Quihoui*
  BB. Lvs. persistent, coriaceous: brts. and infl. glabrous (except in *L. indicum* under No. 3).
    c. Corolla-lobes about as long as tube: lvs. 6–12 cm. long, acuminate.....5. *L. lucidum*
    cc. Corolla-lobes slightly shorter than tube: lvs. 4–8 cm. long, short-acuminate or obtusish ....6. *L. japonicum*
AA. Corolla-tube 2 or 3 times as long as lobes.
  B. Lvs. persistent; corolla-tube about 2 times as long as lobes.
    c. Infl. cylindric, short, leafy at base: lvs. broad-cuneate to rounded at base, 1–3 cm. long ....7. *L. Delavayanum*
    cc. Infl. pyramidal: lvs. usually rounded at base, 2–5.5 cm. long..............8. *L. Henryi*
  BB. Lvs. deciduous or half-evergreen: corolla-tube about 3 times as long as lobes.
    c. Brts. and lvs. glabrous; lvs. half-evergreen........................9. *L. ovalifolium*

cc. Brts. pubescent and lvs. usually on midrib beneath.
  D. Calyx and pedicels glabrous, or pedicels slightly pubescent.
    E. Anthers exserted, equaling the lobes or slightly longer........10. *L. acuminatum*
    EE. Anthers exserted about ½, not exceeding the middle of the corolla-lobes.
      F. Infl. few-fld., to 1.5 cm. long; anthers nearly included...........11. *L. Ibota*
      FF. Infl. many-fld., to 3 cm. long.
        G. Lvs. acuminate to acute, pubescent on midrib beneath: shrub with
           spreading brs. ....12. *L. acutissimum*
        GG. Lvs. obtusish to acute, finally glabrous or glabrate: shrub with upright
            brs. ....13. *L. amurense*
  DD. Calyx and pedicels pubescent; anthers nearly as long as lobes: shrub with spread-
      ing brs. ....14. *L. obtusifolium*

1. **L. vulgàre** L. COMMON P. Deciduous or half-evergreen shrub to 5 m.,
with slender spreading brs.; young brts. and panicles minutely puberulous:
lvs. oblong-ovate to lanceolate, 3–6 cm. long, obtuse to acute, glabrous;
petiole 3–10 mm. long: fls. pediceled, in rather dense panicles, 3–6 cm. long;
anthers exceeding the tube, shorter than limb: fr. subglobose or ovoid, 6–8
mm. long, black, lustrous. Fl.vi–vii; fr.ix–x(–iii). S.O.3:t.147(c). R.I.17:
t.33(c). H.W.3:122(c). F.E.33:1273(h). Eu., N. Afr.; naturalized in E. N.
Am. Cult. since ancient times. Zone IV. Much used as a hedge plant.—
Many garden forms; the most important are:—**L. v. aùreum** Jaeg., var. Lvs.
yellow—**L. v. aureo-variegàtum** West., var. Lvs. blotched yellow. S.O.3:t.
147,f.(c).—**L. v. argenteo-variegàtum** West., var. Lvs. variegated with white.
S.O.3:t.147,f.(c).—**L. v. glaùcum** Mouillef., var. Lvs. bluish green with narrow
white margin. G.W.2:495. (*L. v. glaucum albo-variegatum* Spaeth.)—**L. v.
buxifòlium** Nichols. Lvs. ovate to oblong-ovate, obtuse, 1.5–2.5 cm. long,
half-evergreen.—**L. v. sempérvirens** Ait., var. Lvs. lanceolate to narrow-
lanceolate, nearly evergreen. (*L. v.* var. *italicum* Hayne, *L. italicum* Mill.,
L. foliosum Hort.)—**L. v. chlorocárpum** Loud., var. Fr. greenish.—**L. v.
leucocárpum** Sweet, var. Fr. white.—**L. v. xanthocárpum** G. Don, var. Fr.
yellow.—**L. v. péndulum** Carr. With pendulous brs. Orig. 1854.—**L. v.
pyramidàle** Spaeth. Of pyramidal habit, with upright brs.—The form distributed as "Polish Privet" is apparently not different from the typical form;
"Lodense" is a dwarf compact form.

Closely related species: **L. insulàre** Dcne. Brts. more velvety-pubescent:
lvs. narrow-oblong or lanceolate, 5–10 cm. long, acuminate, often pendulous,
yellow-green: infl. larger; fr. larger. D.H.1:122. Cult. 1878. Orig. uncertain.

2. **L. compáctum** Hook. f. & Thoms. Half-evergreen shrub or small tree
to 10 m.; brts. and petioles glabrous or minutely puberulous: lvs. elliptic-
lanceolate to lanceolate, 8–15 cm. long, acuminate, occasionally coarsely
toothed, bright green and lustrous above, light green beneath, with 8–15 pairs
of veins; petiole 6–15 mm. long: fls. small, in large panicles 10–16 cm. long;
anthers about as long as corolla-lobes: fr. ellipsoid, 7–10 mm. long, bluish
black. Fl.vi–vii; fr.x. R.H.1902:498–500. M.D.1915:t.3(l). (*L. yunnanense*
L. Henry, *L. longifolium* Hort, *L. salicifolium* Carr.) Himal., S. W. China.
Cult. 1877. Zone VII.

Closely related species: **L. Chenaùltii** Hickel. Deciduous; brts. with conspicuous white lenticels; winter-buds acute: lvs. lanceolate, rounded at base, to
25 cm. long. B.D.1925:51(1). S. W. China. Intr. 1908.

3. **L. sinénse** Lour. CHINESE P. Shrub to 4 m., with spreading brs., or
small tree to 7 m.; brts. densely pubescent: lvs. elliptic to elliptic-oblong, 3–7
cm. long, acute to obtuse, usually broad-cuneate, dull green above, pubescent
on the midrib beneath; petiole 3–6 mm. long: fls. distinctly stalked, in loose
pubescent panicles 6–10 cm. long; calyx pubescent; corolla-tube shorter than
lobes; stamens exceeding the lobes: fr. subglobose, about 4 mm. across. Fl.
vii; fr.ix–x(–i). M.D.1915:t.1,2. G.C.66:142(h). B.S.2:28,t(h). (*L. villosum*

May, *L. sinense* var. *villosum* Rehd., *L. Fortunei* Hort.) China. Intr. 1852. Zone VII. One of the most graceful and handsomest Privets when covered with its numerous large panicles.—**L. s. multiflòrum** (Bowles) Bean, var. Anthers reddish brown. G.C.50:237(h). (*L. ovalifolium multiflorum* Bowles.)— **L. s. Stauntònii** (DC.) Rehd., var. Less high and more spreading; brts. less pubescent: lvs. elliptic to ovate, usually obtuse: panicles broader and looser. G.C.II.10:365. G.F.3:213. S.L.212. (*L. S.* DC., *L. chinense nanum* Carr.)

　　Related species: **L. índicum** (Lour.) Merr. Half-evergreen tree: brts. short-villous: lvs. ovate-elliptic to ovate-lanceolate, 4–8 cm. long, acuminate, cuneate, pubescent beneath or only on midrib: infl. loose, pyramidal, to 12 cm. long, pubescent; calyx glabrous: fr. subglobose, 5 mm. across. Wall. Pl. As. Rar. 3:t.270(c). (*L. nepalense* Wall.) Himal., Indochina. Cult. 1933. Zone VII.

　　4. **L. Quihoùi** Carr. Shrub to 2 m., with spreading, rather rigid brs.; brts. and panicles finely pubescent: lvs. elliptic to elliptic-oblong or obovate to obovate-oblong, 2–5 cm. long, obtuse, sometimes slightly emarginate, glabrous, subcoriaceous; petiole 1–3 mm. long, puberulous: fls. sessile, in small clusters forming long cylindric spikes collected into panicles 10–20 cm. long: corolla-tube as long as lobes; anthers exceeding the lobes. Fl.VIII–IX; fr.X–XI. G.C. II.18:277;70:157(h). Gn.66:292(h);89:669(h). (*L. brachystachyum* Dcne.) China. Intr. 1862. Zone VI. Distinct Privet valuable on account of its late fls.

　　Closely related species: **L. Purpùsii** Hoefker. Lvs. broader, usually elliptic, thinner; panicle shorter and broader, more pyramidal; corolla-lobes less spreading. M.D.1915:t.5. China. Cult. 1904.

　　5. **L. lùcidum** Ait. Glossy P. Large shrub or tree to 10 m., with spreading glabrous lenticellate brs.: lvs. ovate to ovate-lanceolate, 8–12 cm. long, acuminate or acute, usually broad-cuneate, with 6–8 pairs of veins usually distinct above and beneath, veinlets beneath often impressed; petiole 1–2 cm. long: panicles 12–20 cm. long and nearly as wide; fls. subsessile; corolla-tube about as long as calyx; stamens about as long as corolla-lobes: fr. oblong, about 1 cm. long, blue-black. Fl.VIII–IX; fr.IX–X(–II). B.M.2565(c),2921(c). G.C.II.10:753. M.D.1915:t.1,4. N.T.1:388. (*L. japonicum macrophyllum* Hort., *L. magnoliaefolium* Hort., *L. sinense latifolium robustum* Hort., *L. spicatum* Hort.) China, Korea, Japan. Intr. 1794. Zone VII. Planted as street tree in warmer regions; one of the white-wax trees in China.

　　6. **L. japónicum** Thunb. Japanese P. Shrub to 3, rarely to 6 m.; glabrous except young brts. and infl. minutely puberulous at first, lenticellate: lvs. broad-ovate to ovate-oblong, 4–10 cm. long, obtusely short-acuminate or acute to obtusish, usually rounded at base, with reddish margin and midrib, with 4–5 pairs of indistinct veins; petiole 6–12 mm. long: panicles 6–15 cm. long, pyramidal; fls. short-stalked, corolla-tube exceeding the calyx; stamens slightly longer than lobes. Fl.VII–IX; fr.X–XI. R.B.25:84(c). S.I.1:t.82(c). B.S.2:26. N.T.1:386. G.W.2:567. Japan, Korea. Intr. 1845. Zone VII? Handsome evergreen shrub.—**L. j. variegàtum** Nichols. Lvs. margined and blotched with creamy-white.—**L. j. rotundifòlium** Bl., var. Compact shrub to 2 m., with stiff short brs.: lvs. crowded, broad-ovate or suborbicular, 3–6 cm. long, obtuse or emarginate, dark lustrous green, thick, often curved; panicle compact, 5–10 cm. long; fls. sessile: fr. subglobose, about 5 mm. across. B.M.7519(c). G.C.53:265. R.H.1874:418;1888:440. (*L. coriaceum* Carr., *L jap. coriaceum* Lav.) Intr. 1860.

　　Another evergreen species is **L. sempérvirens** (Franch.) Lingelsh. Glabrous shrub to 2 m.: lvs. suborbicular or broad-elliptic to ovate, 1.5–4 cm. long, obtuse or short-acuminate, lustrous, thick: infl. dense, 4–7 cm. long; fls. sessile or sub sessile; tube of corolla scarcely twice as long as lobes; filaments much shorter than lobes: fr. ellipsoid, 8 mm. long; endocarp finally dehiscent with 2 valves. (*Syringa s.* Franch., *Parasyringa s.* W. W. Sm.) W. China. Intr. 1922. Zone VII? It forms the sect. SARCOCARPION Mansfeld characterized by the dehiscent endocarp.

7. **L. Delavayànum** Hariot. Evergreen shrub to 2 m., with slender spreading brs.; brts. pubescent: lvs. ovate or elliptic, rarely oblong-obovate, 1–3 cm. long, acute, broad-cuneate to rounded at base, dark lustrous green above, glabrous except downy on midrib above; petiole 1–2 mm. long; panicle pubescent, narrow, 2–5 cm. long, leafy at base; pedicels 1–4 mm. long, glabrous or nearly so; calyx glabrous; corolla-tube 5 mm. long; anthers nearly as long as lobes, violet. Fl.VI; fr.X. R.H.1901:496. S.H.2:f.509k-l,510b. G.C.71:179 (h). J.L.49:t.5(h). (*L. Prattii* Koehne, *L. ionandrum* Diels.) W. China. Intr. 1890. Zone VII? Low shrub with small lvs.

8. **L. Hénryi** Hemsl. Shrub to 4 m.; brts. pubescent: lvs. orbicular-ovate or ovate to ovate-lanceolate, 1.5–5 cm. long, obtusely short-acuminate, usually rounded at base, dark green and lustrous above; petiole 1–2 mm. long: panicle pubescent, pyramidal, short-stalked, 4–12 cm. long; calyx glabrous; corolla 6–7 mm. long; anthers nearly as long as corolla-lobes: fr. ovoid-oblong, 8 mm. long. Fl.VIII. B.S.2:25. S.H.2:f.509f-i,510a. C. China. Intr. 1901. Zone VII. Similar to the preceding species but lvs. and infl. larger.

Related species: **L. strongylophýllum** Hemsl. Shrub or small tree: brts. minutely pubescent: lvs. suborbicular to broad-ovate, 1–2.5 cm. long, dark green, glabrous: panicle pyramidal, rather loose, 5–10 cm. long; corolla about 7 mm. long; tube about 1½ as long as lobes; anthers shorter than lobes. B.M.8069(c). C. China. Intr. 1879. Zone VII.—**L. Massalóngianum** Vis. Shrub to 1 m.; brts. pilose: lvs. linear-lanceolate, 3–8 cm. long, gradually narrowed at ends, glabrous: panicle 6–8 cm. long, pilose: fls. pediceled; anthers about ½ as long as corolla-lobes. G.C.II.16:149. Rep. Sp. Nov. 1:10. Himal. Intr. 1877. Zone VII?

9. **L. ovalifòlium** Hassk. CALIFORNIA P. Deciduous or half-evergreen upright shrub to 5 m.; brts. glabrous: lvs. elliptic-ovate to elliptic-oblong, 3–6 cm. long, acute, broad-cuneate, dark lustrous green above, yellowish green beneath, glabrous; petiole 3–4 mm. long: fls. creamy-white, rather unpleasantly scented, subsessile, in compact glabrous panicles 5–10 cm. long; corolla 8 mm. long; anthers as long as lobes: fr. subglobose, 5–7 mm. across, black. Fl.VII; fr.X–XI. S.I.1:t.84(c). F.E.33:1223(h). (*L. medium* Fr. & Sav., *L. californicum* Hort., *L. japonicum* Hort., not Thunb.) Japan. Cult. 1847. Zone (V). Upright shrub of rather stiff habit with lustrous lvs.; much used for hedges.—**L. o. variegàtum** T. Moore. Lvs. variegated with pale yellow. (*L. o. robustum variegatum* Hort., *L. o. aureum* Carr.)—**L. o. aùreo-marginàtum** Rehd., var. Lvs. with broad yellow margin or almost entirely yellow. (*L. o.* var. *aureum* Bean.)

L. o. × *obtusifolium* = **L. ibòlium** Coe. Upright shrub; brts. puberulous: lvs. pubescent on midrib beneath: infl. puberulous; calyx glabrous; anthers about as long as corolla-lobes. Orig. about 1910. Zone V.—Useful as a hedge plant, hardier than the preceding species.

10. **L. acuminàtum** Koehne. Shrub to 2 m., with upright and spreading brs.: lvs. rhombic-ovate to ovate-lanceolate, 3–8 cm. long, acute to acuminate, cuneate, appressed-pubescent near margin above and ciliolate, pubescent on midrib beneath; petiole 2–5 mm. long, pubescent: panicle 3–6 cm. long, pubescent: fls. subsessile; corolla 9–10 cm. long; anthers exserted: fr. ovoid, 8 mm. long, lustrous black. Fl.VI; fr.IX–X. S.T.1:t.71. M.D.1904:74. N.T.1:383. (*L. ciliatum* Rehd., not Bl., *L. medium* Hort., not Franch. & Sav.) Japan. Intr. 1888. Zone IV. Lvs. turn yellow in fall and drop rather

early.—**L. a. macrocárpum** (Koehne) Schneid., var. More strictly upright: lvs. larger: fr. to 12 mm. long. N.T.1:281. M.D.1904:75. (*L. m.* Koehne.) Japan. Intr. before 1900.

11. **L. Ibòta** Sieb. & Zucc. Shrub to 2 m., with spreading brs.; brts. slightly pubescent, the shoots usually glabrous: lvs. rhombic-ovate to elliptic-oblong, 1.5–5 cm. long, acute, cuneate, ciliolate, light green beneath and pubescent on midrib: infl. nearly capitate, 1–1.5 cm. long, 4–8-fld., slender-peduncled; corolla 8 mm. long; anthers slightly exceeding the tube: fr. globose-ovoid, 7–8 mm. long. Fl.vi; fr.ix–x. N.T.1:368. M.D.1904:73. S.H. 2:f.507n-q,508f. (*L. ciliatum* Sieb., *L. ibota* var. *ciliatum* Dipp.) Japan. Cult. 1870. Zone V. One of the least ornamental species.

12. **L. acutíssimum** Koehne. Shrub to 3 m., with spreading brs.; brts. pubescent: lvs. elliptic- or ovate-oblong to lanceolate, 1–7 cm. long, acute or acuminate, cuneate or broad-cuneate, dark green above, light green beneath and pubescent on midrib and often sparingly on the face; petiole 1–2 mm. long: panicles narrow, nearly cylindric, 2–5 cm. long; anthers reaching the middle of the lobes: fr. globose-ovoid or ovoid, 8–9 mm. long, bluish black. Fl.vi; fr.ix–x. S.H.2:f.505m-n²,506a-d. Rep. Sp. Nov. 1:8. C. China. Intr. about 1900. Zone V. Similar to *L. obtusifolium,* but less graceful.

13. **L. amurénse** Carr. Amur P. Shrub to 5 m., with upright brs., nearly pyramidal; brts. pubescent: lvs. elliptic to oblong, 2.5–6 cm. long, obtuse to acute, rounded or broad-cuneate at base, ciliolate, sometimes lustrous above, glabrous except pubescent on midrib beneath; petiole 2–4 mm. long, usually pubescent: panicle 3–5 cm. long, pubescent; calyx glabrous or slightly pubescent near base; corolla 7–9 mm. long; anthers slightly exserted, not reaching the middle of the lobes: fr. globose-ovoid, 6–8 mm. long, black, slightly bloomy. Fl.vi–vii; fr.ix–x. S.T.1:t.72. M.D.1904:72. R.H.1861:352. (*L. ibota* var. *a.* Hort.) N. China. Cult. 1860. Zone III. Somewhat similar to *L. ovalifolium;* hardier.

14. **L. obtusifòlium** Sieb. & Zucc. Shrub to 3 m., with spreading or arching brs.; brts. pubescent: lvs. elliptic to oblong or oblong-obovate, 2–6 cm. long, acute or obtuse, cuneate or broad-cuneate, glabrous above, pubescent beneath or only on midrib: petiole 1–4 mm. long, pubescent; panicles nodding, 2–3.5 cm. long, usually numerous on short brts. along the brs.; calyx pubescent; corolla 8–10 mm. long; anthers nearly as long as lobes: fr. subglobose, about 6 mm. long, black, slightly bloomy. Fl.vii; fr.ix–x. S.I.1:t.83(c). G.F.6:425. B.C.4:1861. Gn.M.29:225(h). S.L.213(h). (*L. ibota* Sieb.) Japan. Intr. about 1860. Zone III. Graceful floriferous shrub.—**L. o. Regeliànum** (Koehne) Rehd., var. Low shrub with almost horizontally spreading brs.: lvs. usually more pubescent, oblong to obovate: panicle shorter; anthers broader. M.D.1904:70. R.H.1904:434(h),435. N.T.1:365. S.L.214(h). (*L. R.* Koehne.) Japan. Cult. 1885. Zone V.

7. **PHILLÝREA** L. Evergreen shrubs or small trees: lvs. opposite, short-petioled, serrate or entire: fls. small, whitish, dioecious, in axillary short, usually clustered, racemes; calyx 4-toothed; corolla 4-lobed, the lobes imbricate in bud, longer than tube; stamens 2, exserted, on short filaments; style shorter than stamens; ovary 2-celled, with 2 pendulous ovules in each cell: fr. a 1-seeded black drupe. (The ancient Greek name of the plant.) Four species in the Mediterr. region.

A. Lvs. 1–6 cm. long: fr. subglobose to ovoid....................................1. *P. latifolia*
AA. Lvs. 7–12 cm. long: fr. oblong, about 1 cm. long............................2. *P. decora*

1. **P. latifòlia** L. Spreading shrub or small tree to 10 m.; young brts. puberulous: lvs. ovate or elliptic-ovate, rarely ovate-oblong, 2–6 cm. long, acute, subcordate or rounded to broad-cuneate, usually sharply or sometimes indistinctly serrate, dark green and lustrous above, light green beneath and usually pubescent on midrib, with 5–12 pairs of veins; petiole very short, puberulous: fls. greenish white, about 5 mm. across, in small clusters; pedicels 2–5 mm. long; corolla-lobes ovate: fr. subglobose, about 6 mm. across, blue-black. Fl.v–vi. R.I.17:t.34.f.i–iii(c). H.W.3:123. S.H.2:f.4931-s. S. Eu., Asia Minor. Cult. 1597. Zone VII. Densely branched shrub or tree; very variable in the shape of its lvs.—**P. l. spinòsa** West., var. Lvs. spinulose-serrate. (*P. ilicifolia* Willd.)—**P. l. mèdia** (L.) Schneid., var. Usually shrubby or tree to 6 m.; lvs. elliptic-ovate to oblong-ovate or ovate-lanceolate, 1.5–5 cm. long, crenate-serrulate or entire: fr. often ovoid and pointed. R.I.17:t.34,f.3(c). G.O.t.116(c). N.D.2:t.27(c). (*P. m.* L.) S. Eu., Asia Minor. Intr. before 1597. —**P. l. rotundifòlia** Rehd., var. Lvs. broad-obovate to elliptic, 3–5.5 long, to 3.5 cm. broad, obtuse or obtusish, slightly serrulate. Cult. 1896.

Closely related species: **P. angustifòlia** L. Shrub to 3 m.; brts. glabrous; lvs. oblong-lanceolate to linear-lanceolate, 2–6 cm. long, acute, cuneate, usually entire, yellowish green and glabrous beneath, with 5–6 pairs of veins: fr. globose or globose-ovoid, pointed. R.I.17:t.35,f.3,4(c). G.O.t.115(c). (*P. vulgaris* var. *a.* Caruel.) S. Eu., N. Afr. Cult. 1597. Zone VII?

2. **P. decòra** Boiss. & Bal. Shrub to 3 m., with upright-spreading brs.; brts. glabrous: lvs. oblong to oblong-lanceolate, acuminate, broad-cuneate, entire, rarely remotely serrate, dark green and lustrous above, yellowish green beneath, glabrous: petiole 1–1.5 cm. long: fls. white, in dense clusters; pedicels 3–15 mm. long; corolla 6–7 mm. across, with narrow-oblong lobes: fr. oblong-ovoid, purplish black, about 1.5 cm. long. Fl.iv–v; fr.viii–ix. B.M. 6800(c). G.C.III.4:673;16:369. M.G.13:349(h). Gs.2:7(h),80. (*P. Vilmoriniana* Boiss. & Bal., *P. laurifolia* Hort.) W. Asia. Intr. 1867. Zone VI or (V). The handsomest and hardiest species of the genus.

P. d. × *Siphonosmanthus Delavayi;* see 7a. *Osmarea.*

7a. × **OSMÀREA** Burkwood (*Phillyrea* × *Siphonosmanthus*). Differs from the former in the corolla-tube about as long as lobes and in the only slightly exserted anthers, from the latter in the slender pedicels and the corolla-tube about as long as lobes. (Name an abbreviated compound of *Osmanthus* and *Phillyrea*).

O. Burkwoòdii Burkwood (*P. decora* × *S. Delavayi*). Evergreen shrub; brts. puberulous: lvs. short-petioled, elliptic or elliptic-ovate to oblong-ovate, 2–4 cm. long, acute, broad-cuneate or nearly rounded at base, serrulate, sometimes very slightly so, glabrous: fls. white, fragrant, in terminal and axillary 5–7-fld. fascicles; pedicels 5–8 mm. long; calyx-lobes 2 mm. long, acute and dentate at apex, greenish white; corolla-tube 4–5 mm. long, lobes oblong, as long or slightly shorter; anthers slightly exceeding the mouth; style as long as calyx. Fl.iv–v. Orig. before 1928. Zone VI.

8. **SIPHONOSMÁNTHUS** Stapf. Evergreen shrubs; winter-buds with 2 outer pubescent scales: lvs. opposite, short-petioled, serrate: fls. polygamous, in terminal and lateral fascicles, short-stalked; calyx 4-lobed, whitish; corolla-tube cylindric, with 4 short, spreading lobes; stamens 2, inserted just below the mouth; anthers slightly exserted, introrse; ovary 2-celled: fr. a small 1-seeded drupe with crustaceous endocarp. (Greek *siphōn*, tube, and *Osmanthus*.) Syn.: *Osmanthus* sect. *Siphosmanthus* Franch. Two species in S. W. China and India.

S. Delavàyi (Franch.) Stapf. Shrub to 2 m.; young brts. puberulous: lvs. ovate to elliptic-ovate, 1–2.5 cm. long, acute or acutish, broad-cuneate at base, sharply or indistinctly toothed, gland-dotted beneath, glabrous: fls. short-stalked or subsessile, white, fragrant, in 4–8-fld. fascicles; calyx-lobes ciliate; corolla-tube about 1 cm. long, lobes oval, about 4 mm. long: fr. ovoid, mucronulate, about 1.2 cm. long, bluish black. Fl.ɪv. B.M.8459(c). Gn.79:232 (h);83:185;88:757(h). B.S.2:112. (*Osmanthus D.* Franch.) W. China. Intr. 1890. Zone VII.

Closely related species: **S. suàvis** (Clarke) Stapf. Lvs. lance-oblong to lanceolate, 3–7 cm. long, acuminate, crenate-dentate: petiole 5–7 mm. long: corolla-tube 6–9 mm. long. B.M.9176(c). N. E. India. Cult. 1929. Zone VII?

9. OSMÁNTHUS Lour.

Evergreen shrubs or small trees; winter-buds with 2 outer scales, sometimes superposed: lvs. opposite, short-petioled, entire or serrate: fls. perfect, polygamous or dioecious, in axillary or terminal cymes or panicles; calyx short, 4-toothed; corolla with short, rarely long tube and 4 imbricate lobes; stamens 2, rarely 4, included; style cylindric, with capitate stigma, usually about as long as tube; ovary 2-celled, each cell with 2 ovules: fr. an ovoid drupe with a one-seeded stone. (Greek *osme*, fragrance, and *anthos*, flower; in reference to the fls. of *O. fragrans*.) About 15 species in E. and S. Asia, Polynesia and 2 in N. Am.

A. Fls. slender-stalked, fascicled: lvs. often serrate.............................1. *O. ilicifolius*
AA. Fls. subsessile, paniculate; corolla-tube about as long as lobes: lvs. entire.
2. *O. americanus*

1. **O. ilicifòlius** (Hassk.) Mouillef. Shrub or small tree to 6 m.: lvs. elliptic or ovate to elliptic-oblong, 2–6 cm. long, spiny-pointed, cuneate or broad-cuneate, with 1–4 pairs of strong spiny teeth, rarely entire, lustrous and dark green above, yellowish green and veined beneath; petiole 8–12 mm. long: fls. fragrant, in axillary clusters; pedicels 3–8 mm. long; sepals triangular, entire; corolla divided nearly to base, with reflexed lobes: fr. ovoid, about 1.5 cm. long, bluish black. Fl.vɪ–vɪɪ. S.I.1:t.82(c). G.C.II.7:239,f.38. K.B. 1911:177,t. S.L.242(h). (*O. Aquifolium* Benth. & Hook., *Olea Aquifolium* Sieb. & Zucc., *Olea ilicifolia* Hassk.) Japan. Intr. 1856. Zone VI. Evergreen shrubs with handsome lustrous lvs.—**O. i. variegàtus** (Standish) Rehd., f. Lvs. variegated with white. (*O. i. argenteo-marginatus* Bean.)—**O. i. aùreo-marginàtus** Bean. Lvs. variegated with yellow. (*O. i. aureus* Rehd.)—**O. i. purpuráscens** Bean. Lvs. purple at first, later green with purple tinge. (*O. i. f. purpureus* Rehd., *O. A.* var. *atropurpureus* Schneid.)—**O. i. myrtifòlius** (Dipp.) Mouillef., var. Lvs. elliptic to elliptic-oblong, 2.5–4.5 cm. long, entire, acute or acuminate. Gn.50:86. (*O. Aquifolium* var. *m.* Dipp.)—**O. i. rotundi-fòlius** (Jaeg.) Rehd., f. Lvs. broad-elliptic, often obovate, about 2.5 cm. long, entire or with short obtusish teeth; like the preceding a dwarf slow-growing form. S.H.2:f.496k-l. (*O. Aquifolium* var. *r.* Dipp.)

O. i. × *fragrans* = **O. Fortùnei** Carr. Shrub to 2, rarely to 6 m.; lvs. elliptic-ovate to oblong-ovate, 6–10 cm. long, with usually 6–10 pairs of spiny teeth, rarely entire: fls. very fragrant; sepals denticulate. R.H.1864:70. K.B. 1911:177,t. (*O. japonicus* Mak.) Intr. from Japan in 1856.—*O. fragrans* Lour. is not hardy within our area.

Related species: **O. armàtus** Diels. Shrub to 5 m.; young brts. densely puberulous: lvs. lance-oblong to lanceolate, 8–14 cm. long, broad-cuneate to sub-cordate, remotely spiny-toothed, reticulate; petiole 3–6 mm. long, puberulous, reddish: fls. fragrant, slender-stalked; corolla 4–5 mm. long, divided to the middle. Fl.ɪx–x. B.M.9232(c). Gs.20:53. G.C.68:117(h). W. China. Intr. 1902. Zone VII?—**O. Forréstii** Rehd. Shrub to 8 m.; brts. glabrous: lvs. lance-ovate to oblong-lanceolate, 6–20 cm. long, acuminate, broad-cuneate to rounded at base, entire or spiny-toothed, reticulate beneath and with 10 to 16 conspicuous veins: fls. creamy-white, fragrant; pedicels to 1 cm. long, slender; corolla 5 mm. long, divided nearly to base, about 8–10 mm. across: fr. ovoid, 1–1.5 cm. long. W. China. Intr. 1923. Zone VII.—**O. serrulàtus** Rehd. Shrub to 4 m.; young brts. puberulous: lvs. elliptic-oblong to obovate- or lance-oblong, 6–12 cm. long, slender-acuminate, cuneate, sharply serrulate or serrate to entire: fls. fragrant; pedicels 8–18 mm. long; corolla divided nearly to base, 10–12 mm. across: fr. oblong, about 1 cm. long. W. China. Intr. 1910. Zone VII.

2. **O. americànus** (L.) Gray. Shrub or tree to 15 m., glabrous: lvs. lance-oblong to obovate, 5–15 cm. long, acute to obtuse, rarely emarginate, cuneate, entire and somewhat revolute at the margin; petiole 1–2 cm. long; fls. white, fragrant, short-stalked or sessile, in short panicles; calyx-lobes acute; corolla-tube 3–4 mm. long, lobes ovate, spreading; anthers slightly exserted or included: fr. ovoid, 10–14 mm. long, dark blue. Fl.iv; fr.ix–iii. S.S.6:t.279. S.M.857. N. C. to Fla. and Miss. Cult. 1758. Zone VI.

10. **FORESTIÈRA** Poir. Deciduous, rarely evergreen trees or shrubs: lvs. opposite, short-petioled, entire or serrate: fls. polygamo-dioecious, apetalous, small, in lateral clusters or racemes on brts. of the previous season; sepals 4–6, unequal, fugacious, sometimes wanting; stamens 2–4; ovary 2-celled, with 2 pendulous ovules in each cell; style slender, with capitate, sometimes 2-lobed stigma: fr. a small, usually black, 1-, rarely 2-seeded drupe. (After Charles Le-Forestier, French physician and naturalist; about 1800.) Syn. *Adelia* Michx., not L., *Borya* Willd., not Lab. About 20 species from N. Am. and the W. Indies to Brazil.—Shrubs of little ornamental value.

ᴀ. Lvs. acuminate, 3–10 cm. long...1. *F. acuminata*
ᴀᴀ. Lvs. obtusish or acute, 1–4 cm. long....................................2. *F. neo-mexicana*

1. **F. acuminàta** (Michx.) Poir. Deciduous shrub to 3 m. or small tree sometimes to 10 m.; glabrous: lvs. ovate-oblong to ovate-lanceolate, acuminate, cuneate, slightly serrate, principally above the middle, light green; petiole 5–15 mm. long: fls. greenish, minute; the staminate in dense bracted clusters, the pistillate in short panicles: fr. narrow-oblong, 1.2–1.5 cm. long, dark purple. Fl.iv–v; fr.vi–vii. S.M.854. B.B.2:728. (*Adelia a.* Michx.) Ill. and Mo. to Ga. and Tex. Intr. 1812. Zone V.

2. **F. neo-mexicàna** Gray. Deciduous shrub to 3 m.; with spreading brs. sometimes spinescent: lvs. oblong-obovate to oblanceolate, 1.5–4 cm. long, narrowed into a short petiole, slightly crenulate-serrate, grayish green, glabrous: pistillate and staminate fls. in clusters; the pistillate with 2–4 usually sterile stamens; pedicels 3–4 mm. long: fr. short-ellipsoid, 4–5 mm. long. Fl. iv–v; fr.viii. M.D.1919:72. (*F. acuminata* var. *parvifolia* Gray, *Adelia parvifolia* Cov.) Tex. to N. Mex. and Colo. Cult. 1913. Zone V.

Closely related species: **F. pubéscens** Nutt. Brts. pubescent: lvs. elliptic to oblong-obovate, slightly serrate, pubescent; pistillate fls. stalked: fr. oblong, 6–7 mm. long; stone ribbed. (*Adelia p.* Ktze.) Ark. to Fla. and Tex. Cult. 1900. Zone V.—**F. ligustrìna** (Michx.) Poir. Shrub to 3 m.; brts. pubescent or glabrescent: lvs. petioled, elliptic to oblong or oblong-obovate, obtuse, cuneate, appressed-serrulate, pubescent beneath: fls. sessile or subsessile: fr. ellipsoid, 7–8 mm. long. Fl.viii. S.H.2:f.407f-h,408d-e. (*Adelia l.* Michx.) Tenn. to Ga. and Fla. Cult. 1810. Zone VI?

11. **CHIONÁNTHUS** L. Fʀɪɴɢᴇ-ᴛʀᴇᴇ. Deciduous trees or shrubs; winter-buds with several outer acute scales: lvs. opposite, petioled, entire: fls. dioecious or functionally dioecious, white, in loose panicles from lateral buds near the end of year-old brs.; calyx 4-cleft; corolla divided nearly to the base into 4 narrow petals; anthers 2, subsessile, or on very short filaments; style very short, with 2-lobed stigma; ovary 2-celled; cells 2-ovuled: fr. a

1-seeded oval dark blue drupe. (Greek *chion,* snow, and *anthos* flower; in reference to the abundant white fls.) Two species in N. Am. and China.

A. Lvs. generally oblong, 8–20 cm. long...1. *C. virginicus*
AA. Lvs. elliptic or ovate 4–10 cm. long..2. *C. retusus*

1. **C. virgínicus** L. Large shrub or tree to 10 m.; brts. stout, pubescent when young: lvs. narrow-elliptic to oblong or obovate-oblong, 8–20 cm. long, acute or acuminate, cuneate, dark green and lustrous above, paler and pubescent at least on the veins beneath, usually becoming glabrate; petiole 1–2.5 cm. long, pubescent; panicles 10–20 cm. long, usually with leafy bracts at base; calyx-lobes triangular; petals 1.5–3 cm. long, about 2 mm. broad, sometimes 5 or 6 in the staminate fl.; staminate fl. with sterile pistil: fr. ellipsoid, 1.5–2 cm. long, dark blue. Fl.v–vi; fr.ix. S.S.6:t.267. S.M.855. G.F.7: 325(h). M.G.14:412,413(h);15:413(h). Am. For. 24:157(h). N. J. to Fla. and Tex. Intr. 1736. Zone IV. Striking shrub when covered with feathery white fls.; the staminate plant has larger panicles and large fls., but lacks the ornamental fr.; the lvs. turn bright yellow in fall.—**C. v. marítimus** Pursh, var. Lvs. beneath and panicles pubescent. Gt.16:t.564. (*C. v.* var. *pubescens* Dipp.)

2. **C. retùsus** Lindl. & Paxt. Shrub with spreading brs. or small tree to 6 m.; young brts. pubescent: lvs. elliptic or ovate to elliptic-oblong or sometimes obovate, 3–10 cm. long, acute to obtuse or sometimes emarginate, broad-cuneate to rounded, entire, serrulate on young plants, pubescent on the veins beneath at least when young, reticulate: fls. in broad panicles 6–10 cm. long, at end of lateral leafy shoots; calyx-lobes lanceolate; petals 1.2–2 cm. long, about 3 mm. broad; staminate fl. without pistil: fr. ellipsoid, 1.2–1.5 cm. long, dark blue. Fl.vi–vii; fr.ix–x. N.K.10:t. N.T.1:346. G.C.47:328(h),329. G.F. 7:327. B.S.1:339,t(h),340. A.G.22:363(h). China, Korea, Japan. Intr. 1845, reintr. 1879. Zone V. Almost as handsome as the preceding species, blooming later.

12. **JASMÌNUM** L. JASMINE. Deciduous or evergreen, twining or upright shrubs, with usually green angled brs.; pith lamellate or solid: lvs. opposite or alternate, odd-pinnate or simple; lfts. entire: fls. usually in terminal cymes or lateral on year-old brts., perfect, regular, yellow or white, rarely pink, salver-shaped, with slender tube and 4–9 lobes convolute in bud; calyx campanulate, with 4–9 minute or subulate lobes; stamens 2, included; ovary 2-celled, each cell with 1–4 usually upright ovules: fr. a 2-lobed, usually black berry, each carpel 1–2-seeded; seed with little albumen. (The latinized Arabic name.) About 200 species chiefly in trop. and subtrop. regions; in Am. only 1 species.

A. Lvs. opposite.
  B. Fls. lateral, solitary, yellow: lfts. 3......................................1. *J. nudiflorum*
  BB. Fls. terminal, usually several.
    C. Lvs. simple: fls. pink..2. *J. Beesianum*
    CC. Lvs. pinnate: fls. white...3. *J. officinale*
AA. Lvs. alternate, pinnate or pinnatifid.
  B. Lfts. and brts. glabrous.
    C. Calyx-teeth subulate, as long or longer than calyx-tube.
      D. Infl. many-fld.; lfts. 3–5...4. *J. floridum*
      DD. Infl. 2–5-fld.: lfts. 3..5. *J. fruticans*
    CC. Calyx-teeth shorter than calyx-tube (except in var.)....................6. *J. humile*
  BB. Lfts. and brts. pubescent: calyx-teeth pilose, subulate...................7. *J. Giraldii*

1. **J. nudiflòrum** Lindl. WINTER J. Deciduous shrub with slender upright and arching brs., to 5 m.; brts. angled, glabrous: lfts. 3, ovate to oblong-ovate, 1–3 cm. long, narrowed at ends, mucronulate, ciliolate; petiole 5–10 mm. long: fls. bright yellow, solitary and axillary along last year's brs., on

stalks about 6 mm. long and covered with narrow green bracts; calyx-lobes linear, green, as long or longer than calyx-tube; corolla 2–2.5 cm. across, with usually 6 often wavy obovate lobes about half as long as tube. Fl.ɪɪ–ɪᴠ. B.M. 4649(c). B.R.32:48(c). G.C.III.11:181. Gs.2:248(hc). Gn.89:537(h). (*J. Sieboldianum* Bl.) China. Intr. 1844. Zone (V). Valued for its early fls.— **J. n. aùreum** Dipp., f. Lvs. variegated with yellow.

Closely related species: **J. Mésnyi** Hance. Pʀɪᴍʀᴏsᴇ J. Evergreen shrub to 3 m.: lfts. elliptic-oblong to lanceolate, 2–7 cm. long: fls. sometimes on elongated leafy brts.; corolla about 4 cm. across with 6–10 lobes, sometimes double; calyx-lobes lanceolate, much longer than calyx-tube. B.M.7981(c). R.H.1906: 472,t(c). Gn.71:270,t(c);87:195. G.C.33:197. (*J. primulinum* Hemsl.) W. China. Intr. 1900. Zone VII?

2. **J. Beesiànum** Forrest & Diels. Rosʏ J. Slender shrub to 1 m. or climbing to 2 m.; brts. grooved, slightly pubescent, chiefly near the nodes: lfts. solitary, ovate-lanceolate to lanceolate, 3–5 cm. long, acuminate, slightly pubescent on both sides; petiole 1–3 mm. long: fls. 1–3, pink or deep rose, fragrant; calyx-teeth subulate, 6 mm. long; corolla about 1.5 cm. across, with broad-elliptic to suborbicular lobes about half as long as tube. Fl.ᴠ. G.C.77: 131. W. China. Intr. about 1910. Zone VI.—Remarkable for its pink fls. though less showy than those of most other species.

J. B. × *officinale* f. *grandiflorum* = **J. stephanénse** Lemoine. Lvs. simple or with 3–5 lfts., the terminal usually ovate-lanceolate, 2–4 cm. long, acuminate, slightly pubescent beneath: fls. pale pink, fragrant, in 3–5-fld. corymbs; corolla-tube 1 cm. long, limb about as wide. Orig. about 1918, also found in W. China. Zone VII.

3. **J. officinàle** L. Cᴏᴍᴍᴏɴ Wʜɪᴛᴇ J. Deciduous or half-evergreen climbing or sarmentose shrub, sometimes to 10 m.; brts. slender, angled, glabrous or nearly so: lfts. 5–7, rarely 9, elliptic-ovate to oblong-ovate, 1–6 cm. long, acute or acuminate, sessile, the terminal larger and stalked, glabrous: fls. white, fragrant, slender-pediceled in 2–10-fld. terminal cymes; calyx-teeth linear, 6–10 mm. long, corolla about 2.5 cm. across with 4–5 oblong lobes about as long as tube. Fl.ᴠɪ–x. S.O.3:t.150(c). B.M.31(c). B.C.3:1718. Persia to Kashmir and China. Cult. since ancient times. Zone VII. With fragrant white fls.—**J. o. aùreo-variegàtum** West., var. Lvs. blotched yellow. (*J. o.* var. *aureum* Bean.)—**J. o. affìne** (Lindl.) Nichols. Corolla pink outside B.R.31:26(c). R.H.1878:428. (*J. a.* Carr.)—**J. o. grandiflòrum** (L.) Kobuski. Fls. about 4 cm. across; tube 1.5–2 cm. long. B.R.91(c). (*J. g.* L.)

Related species: **J. polyánthum** Franch. Lfts. 5–7, oblong-ovate to lance-ovate, 3–7 cm. long, acuminate or long-acuminate, usually rounded or subcordate and 3-nerved at base: infl. many-fld., paniculate; calyx-teeth subulate, as long or shorter than calyx-tube: corolla pink outside, white inside, fragrant; tube about 2 cm. long, lobes half as long. R.H.1891:270. W. China. Intr. 1906? Zone VII.

4. **J. flòridum** Bge. Half-evergreen shrub, with upright or spreading flexuose brs.; brts. angled, glabrous: lfts. usually 3, sometimes 5, elliptic-ovate to ovate-oblong, 1–3.5 cm. long, acute: fls. yellow in terminal many-fld cymes; calyx-teeth subulate, as long as tube. Fl.ᴠɪɪ–ɪx. B.M.6719(c). S.H. 2:f.527h-i,528a-c. China. Intr. 1850. Zone VII.

5. **J. frúticans** L. Evergreen or half-evergreen shrub with slender upright or spreading weak brs., to 3 m.; brts. angled, glabrous: lfts. 3, rarely 1, obovate-oblong or oblong to spatulate, 8–20 mm. long, obtuse, cuneate, ciliolate: fls. yellow, in 2–5-fld. cymes on short lateral brts.; calyx campanulate, with subulate teeth; corolla about 1.5 cm. across, with 5 ovate obtuse lobes. Fl. ᴠɪ–ᴠɪɪ. B.M.461(c). S.O.3:t.148(c). S.H.2:f.527f-g,528k-n. S. Eu., N. Afr., W. Asia. Intr. about 1570. Zone VII.

6. **J. hùmile** L. Evergreen or nearly evergreen shrub, to 1.5 m. high, glabrous; brts. slightly angled: lfts. 3, sometimes 5, rarely 7, ovate or elliptic to oblong, obtuse or acute, dark green above, pale beneath: infl. 2–6-fld.; calyx-teeth minute, triangular to subulate; corolla yellow; tube about 1 cm. long, limb about 1 cm. across. Fl.vi–vii. B.R.350(c). S.O.3:t.149(c). W. China; naturalized in Persia and elsewhere. Cult. 1650. Zone VII.—**J. h. kansuénse** Kobuski, var. Lfts. usually 3, rarely 5, sometimes 1, ovate to oval or elliptic or obovate, 8–15 mm. long: infl. 3–7-fld; calyx-teeth subulate, about as long as tube. N. W. China. Intr. 1926. Zone VI?—**J. h. siderophýllum** (Lévl.) Kobuski, var. Brts. strongly angled: lfts. 5, often 3, ovate to ovate-lanceolate, acute to acuminate, the terminal subcaudate, short-setose above along the revolute margin: infl. 3–7-fld.: corolla-tube 1 cm. long, limb. 1–1.5 cm. across. W. China. Intr. 1923.—**J. h. revolùtum** (Sims) Kobuski, var. Lfts. 5–7, ovate to ovate-lanceolate, rarely oval, 2–6 cm. long, acute to acuminate: infl. many-fld.; corolla-tube 1.5 cm. long, limb 2–2.5 cm. across. B.M.1731(c). L.B.966(c). (*J. r.* Sims.) W. Himal. to Kashmir. Cult. 1814.— **J. h. glabrum** (DC.) Kobuski, var. Brts. strongly angled: lfts. 7–13, ovate to lanceolate, 2–5 cm. long, acute to acuminate, the terminal usually caudate-acuminate: infl. 1–3-fld.; corolla-tube 1–1.5 cm. long, limb about 1.5 cm. across. B.R.1409(c). (*J. pubigerum* var. *g.* DC., *J. Wallichianum* Lindl.) Nepal. Intr. 1912.

Related species: **J. diversifòlium** Kobuski. Brts. subterete, glabrous: lvs. subcoriaceous, simple or 3-foliolate; lfts. ovate-lanceolate, 8–14 cm. long, lustrous above, glabrous: fls. yellow, in many-fld. corymbs 10 cm. across, puberulous; calyx-teeth minute; corolla-tube 8–10 mm. long, lobes about 6 mm. long. Wall. Pl. As. Rar. 3:t.275(c). (*J. heterophyllum* Roxb., not Moench.) E. Himal. Intr. 1820. Zone VII?—**J. d. glabricymòsum** (W. W. Sm.) Kobuski, var. Lfts. 4–9 cm. long: corymbs smaller, glabrous. Cult. 1933. W. China. Cult. 1915. Zone VII.

7. **J. Giráldii** Diels. Deciduous shrub to 2 m., with spreading brs.; brts. angled, pilose: lfts. 3, rarely 5, elliptic or ovate or oblong-ovate, 1–4 cm. long, obtuse and mucronate to acute, sparingly hairy above, glaucescent and pilose beneath, densely so on the veins; petiole 5–10 mm. long, hairy: fls. yellow, in 3–9-fld. cymes; calyx-teeth subulate, pilose, slightly shorter, rarely longer than tube; corolla 1.2–1.5 cm. across, with slightly spreading ovate lobes. Fl. v–vi. C. China. Intr. 1907. Zone VII.

Related species: **J. Párkeri** Dunn. Low shrub to 30 cm.; brts. angled, like lvs. and calyx puberulous: lfts. 3–5, ovate, 3–6 mm. long, obtuse: fls. solitary, terminal and axillary; calyx-teeth subulate, half as long as tube: corolla yellow, about 1.5 cm. across with 6 lobes half as long as tube. N. W. Himal. Intr. 1923. Zone VII?—Close to *J. humile* is **J. Fárreri** Gilmour. Brts. pubescent when young; lfts. usually 3, narrow-lanceolate to lanceolate or sometimes broad-lanceolate, the terminal 2–8 cm. long, the lateral 1–4 cm., acuminate, pubescent on both sides: calyx-teeth triangular, apiculate. B.M.9351(c). Burma. Intr. 1919. Zone VII.

Fam. 96. **LOGANIACEAE** Lindl. LOGANIA FAMILY

Herbs, shrubs or trees: lvs. usually opposite, simple, stipulate: fls. usually perfect and regular, usually in cymes or panicles; calyx 4- or 5-lobed or -parted; corolla 4- or 5-lobed, rarely with 8–16 lobes; lobes imbricate or convolute in bud; stamens as many as corolla-lobes and usually alternate with them, rarely reduced to 1; ovary superior, 2-celled; ovules usually many; style with 2 or rarely 4 stigmas: fr. a caps., rarely a berry or drupe; seed albuminous, sometimes winged.—More than 30 genera and about 400 species, mostly trop. or subtrop., few in N. Am.

1893.—**B. D. magnífica** (Wils.) Rehd. & Wils., var. Similar to the preceding
var., with larger deep rose-purple fls. in very dense spikes, with deep orange
eye and the margins of the corolla-lobes reflexed. Gn.69:288,t(c). R.B.33:
281,t(c). S.L.109(h). Intr. 1900.—**B. D. supérba** (De Corte) Rehd. & Wils.,
var. Similar to the preceding, but corolla-lobes not reflexed and panicles
larger. R.B.35:12,t(c). Intr. 1900.—**B. D. Wilsònii** (Wils.) Rehd. & Wils.,
var. Tall and arching, with longer and narrower lvs. and looser drooping
spikes, sometimes to 70 cm. long; corolla smaller, rose-lilac, the lobes with
reflexed margin. Intr. 1900.—**B. D. nanhoénsis** (Chittenden) Rehd., var.
Shrub to 1.5 m., with slender spreading brs.: lvs. lanceolate, up to 12 cm. long
and 2–4.5 cm. broad. Kansu. Intr. 1914. (*B. variabilis* var. *n.* Chittenden.)
　　B. D. × *asiatica* = B. hýbrida Farquhar. Lvs. densely white-tomentose beneath, serrulate: spikes slender: corolla pubescent outside; in the form "Eva
Dudley" pale lavender-pink with orange throat. Orig. before 1918. Zone VII.
B. asiatica Lour. is not hardy in our area.—*B. D.* × *globosa;* see under No. 8.
　　6. **B. stenostáchya** Rehd. & Wils. Shrub to 3 m.; brts. terete, like infl.
and lvs. beneath densely white-tomentose; lvs. lance-oblong to oblong-ovate,
12–20 cm. long, acuminate, cuneate, crenate-serrate or nearly entire, dull green
and glabrescent above; petiole 4–8 mm. long; spikes usually 3 at end of brs.,
narrow-cylindric, 15–45 cm. long; corolla lilac, tube 8 mm. long, pubescent
without and within; stamens inserted above the middle of tube: caps.
cylindric-oblong, 8–12 mm. long. Fl.viii–ix. W. China. Intr. 1908. Zone VII.
　　Related species: **B. cándida** Dunn. Young brts. terete, tomentose: lvs.
lanceolate or lance-oblong, 12–17 cm. long, rugulose and pubescent above, densely
woolly beneath; petiole 1 cm. long: spikes 10–12 cm. long, slender; corolla-tube
6 cm. long, tomentose outside, lobes small, violet. E. Himal. Intr. 1928. Zone
VII?—**B. Fallowiàna** Balf. f. & W. W. Sm. Brts. terete, tomentose: lvs. ovate-
lanceolate, 6–14 cm. long, crenate-denticulate, dull above, densely white- or
fulvous-tomentose beneath; petiole 5–10 cm. long, sometimes with auriculate
stipules at base: infl. dense, spike-like, 8–14 cm. long; corolla about 8 mm. long,
lavender, tomentose outside. B.M.9564(c). N.F.1:f.30(h). G.C.80:489 (as *B.
Forrestii*). Gs.14:154(h). W. China. Cult. 1921. Zone VII?—**B. myriántha**
Diels. Brts. quadrangular, slender, thinly tomentose, glabrescent: lvs. lanceolate, 8–15 cm. long, acuminate, auriculate, serrate, closely white or yellowish
tomentose beneath; petiole short: spikes 10–20 cm. long, slender; corolla purple,
tomentose outside. W. China, Burma. Cult. 1933. Zone VII?
　　7. **B. crispa** Benth. Shrub to 5 m.; brts. white or tawny villous-tomentose: lvs. oblong-lanceolate to lanceolate, 5–12 cm. long, acuminate, truncate
to subcordate or subhastate at base, coarsely toothed, pubescent above and
white- or tawny-tomentose beneath; petiole 8–20 mm. long: fls. fragrant,
in narrow-pyramidal dense panicles 5–10 cm. long, with leaf-like bracts at
base, and usually also with short and dense lateral panicles below; corolla
lilac, with white throat; tube about 8 mm. long, pubescent outside, glabrous
inside above the middle. Fl.vi–ix. B.M.4793(c). F.S.9:958(c). (*B. paniculata* Clarke, not Wall., *B. tibetica* W. W. Sm.) N. W. Himal. and Afghan.
Cult. 1854. Zone VII.—**B. c. Fárreri** (Balf. f. & W. W. Sm.) Hand.-Mazz.,
var. Lvs. to 30 cm. long; petiole to 5 cm. long: terminal panicles to 20 cm.
long; the lateral ones to 5 cm. long; corolla-tube glabrous outside, 7–8 mm.
long, pale rose-lilac with yellow throat. B.M.9027(c). (*B. F.* Balf. f. & W. W.
Sm.) N. W. China. Intr. about 1918. Zone VI?
　　Related species: **B. helióphila** W. W. Sm. Lvs. short-petioled, elliptic-ovate
to ovate-oblong, 5–8 cm. long, acuminate, broad-cuneate to rounded at base, yellowish tomentulose beneath, slightly pubescent above: fls. fragrant, in panicles
6–15 cm. long, mostly from short lateral brts., rather loose, puberulous or nearly
glabrous; calyx tomentulose; corolla rose-lavender, tube about 12 mm. long,
tomentulose outside. W. China. Intr. 1913. Zone VII.—Very distinct is **B.
salvifòlia** Lam. Half-evergreen shrub to 5 m.; young brts. tomentose, quad-

rangular: lvs. very short-stalked, stipulate, lanceolate, 2.5–10 cm. long, acuminate, cordate to hastate at base, crenulate, rugose above, reticulate and brown-tomentose beneath: panicles terminal, pyramidal, 6–15 cm. long, 3.5–8 cm. wide, tomentose: fls. pale lilac with orange throat, brown-tomentose outside. Sim, For. Fl. Cape Col. t.114. S. Afr. Cult. 1873. Zone VII?

8. **B. globòsa** Hope. Half-evergreen shrub to 5 m. or more; brts. and lvs. beneath yellowish-tomentose: lvs. elliptic-ovate to lanceolate, 8–20 cm. long, acuminate, cuneate, crenate, rugose and glabrous above: fls. small, fragrant, bright yellow, in dense long-peduncled axillary heads 2 cm. across forming terminal panicles 10–20 cm. long. Fl.VI. B.M.171(c). Gn.33:369. F.R.3:335(h). (*B. capitata* Jacq.) Peru. Intr. 1774. Zone VII? Very distinct.

B. g. × *Davidii* = B. **Weyeriana** Weyer. Fls. grayish yellowish, grayish to violet in subglobose heads crowded into dense terminal panicles; in "Golden Glow" buff-colored; G.C.68:181;74:208. Gn.87:526,679; in "Moonlight" creamy buff; Gn.87:526. Orig. about 1915.

Fam. 97. **APOCYNACEAE** Lindl. DOGBANE FAMILY

Herbs, shrubs or trees, often climbing, with milky juice: lvs. opposite or verticillate, rarely alternate, entire, exstipulate, rarely with minute interpetiolar stipules or lines: fls. perfect, regular, in cymes, panicles or solitary; calyx 4–5-parted, with imbricate lobes, persistent: corolla usually with appendages in the throat, 4–5-lobed, lobes convolute in bud, rarely valvate; stamens 5, rarely 4, adnate to the tube; anthers usually sagittate and acute; pollen granular; carpels usually 2, mostly superior, distinct, rarely more or less united, usually many-ovuled, with an entire or lobed disk at base; style 1, simple or divided: fr. usually of 2 dehiscent follicles, sometimes berry-like or drupe-like; seeds usually compressed and often with a tuft of hairs; albumen usually scanty, sometimes wanting.—About 130 genera and 1100 species chiefly in trop. and subtrop. regions.

A. Fls. solitary, axillary; trailing plant...1. *Vinca*
AA. Fls. in cymes: climbing shrub...2. *Trachelospermum*

1. **VINCA** L. PERIWINKLE. Evergreen or deciduous subshrubs or herbs, trailing, the flowering shoots upright: lvs. decussate: fls. rather large, usually blue; calyx small, 5-parted, with narrow acuminate teeth; corolla salverform, the lobes twisted to the left; stamens adnate to the middle of the tube; anthers free; filaments curved and thick; connective dilated, large; disk of 2 glands; carpels with 6–8 ovules; stigma large, with 5 tufts of hairs: follicles cylindric; seeds cylindric. (The ancient Latin name of the plant.) About 5 species in Eu. and W. Asia.—Evergreen trailing subshrubs, chiefly used as ground-cover and for window-boxes.

A. Lvs. and calyx-lobes glabrous; lvs. narrowed at base........................1. *V. minor*
AA. Lvs. at base and calyx-lobes ciliate; lvs. truncate or subcordate at base......2. *V. major*

1. **V. mínor** L. SMALL P. Flowering stems to 15 cm.: lvs. elliptic-ovate to elliptic-lanceolate, 2–4 cm. long, acutish or obtuse, lustrous dark green above; petiole 2–5 mm. long: fls. lilac-blue, about 2.5 cm. across; pedicels 1–3 cm. long; calyx-lobes lanceolate, 3 mm. long: follicles 7–8 cm. long. Fl.IV–IX. R.I.17:t.21(c). F.D.16:t.1577(c). S.E.6:t.906(c). Eu. and W. Asia. Often escaped from cult. Cult. since ancient times. Zone V.—**V. m. argenteo-variegàta** West., var. Lvs. blotched with white.—**V. m. aùreo-variegàta** West., var. Lvs. blotched with yellow.—**V. m. alba** West., var. Fls. white.—**V. m. atropurpúrea** Sweet, var. Fls. purple.—**V. m. múltiplex** Sweet, var. Fls. purple, double. (*V. m.* var. *purpurea plena* West.)—**V. m. azùrea** Bean, var. Fls. sky-blue.

2. **V. màjor** L. Flowering stems to 30 cm.: lvs. ovate, 2–7 cm. long, acute or obtusish, dark lustrous green, ciliate, at least near base; petiole 8–1.2 mm long, ciliate: fls. bright blue, 3–3.5 cm. across; pedicels 3–5 cm. long; calyx-lobes linear, about 1 cm. long: fr. 4–5 cm. long. Fl.v–ix. R.I.17:t.22,f.3(c) F.D.16:t.1576(c). S.E.6:t.905(c). S. Eu., W. Asia. Cult. 1789. Zone VII.— **V. m. variegàta** Loud., var. Lvs. blotched and margined yellowish white (*V. m. elegantissima* Nichols.)

Related species: **V. diffórmis** Pourr. Quite glabrous: lvs. ovate, 2–7 cm. long broad-cuneate to truncate: fls. 3–3.5 cm. across, pale lilac-blue, with rhombic acute lobes. Fl.ix–xii. B.M.8506(c). Gn.84:569(h). (*V. media* Hoffmanns. & Link, *V. acutiflora* Bertol.) S. W. Eu., N. Afr. Cult. 1880. Zone VII?

2. TRACHELOSPÉRMUM Lem.

Evergreen twining shrubs; winter-buds minute, densely pubescent: lvs. opposite, short-petioled, distinctly veined, usually with minute interpetiolar stipules: fls. white in terminal or axillary cymes; calyx small, 5-parted, with 5–10 glands or scales inside at base; corolla salverform, tube cylindric, lobes ovate to oblong, twisted to the left and overlapping to the right; disk annular, truncate or 5-lobed; stamens inserted above the middle of the tube; filaments short, anthers united and adhering to the large stigma; style filiform; carpels 2, many-ovuled: fr. of 2 terete follicles; seeds linear with long tuft of hairs. (Greek *trachelos*, neck and *sperma*, seed; though seed without neck.) About 16 species in trop. and subtrop. E. Asia.

T. asiáticum (Sieb. & Zucc.) Nakai. Climbing to 5 m. or more; brts densely pubescent, red-brown: lvs. elliptic or ovate to elliptic-oblong, 2–5 cm. long, usually obtuse, lustrous dark green above; petiole about 5 mm. long: fls. yellowish white, fragrant, in peduncled terminal several-fld. cymes; pedicels 5–10 mm. long; buds long-acuminate; corolla 2 cm. across, tube about 8 mm. long; calyx-lobes narrow, pointed; anthers slightly exserted: follicles 12–22 cm. long, nearly parallel or spreading at acute angle. Fl.iv–vi. N.T.1: 420. N.K.14:t.2. (*T. divaricatum* Kanitz, *T. crocostemon* Stapf, *Malouetia asiatica* Sieb. & Zucc.) Japan, Korea. Cult. 1880. Zone VII.

The closely related **T. jasminoìdes** Lem. has narrower lvs., pure white fls., acute in bud, included anthers, sepals reflexed at apex and spreading follicles. B.M.4737(c). China. Tender, often grown as a greenhouse plant.

Fam. 98. ASCLEPIADACEAE Lindl. MILKWEED FAMILY

Herbs or shrubs, often twining, rarely trees, with milky juice: lvs. opposite, sometimes verticillate or alternate, usually entire, exstipulate: fls. perfect, regular, in terminal or axillary umbels, cymes or racemes; calyx 5-parted, imbricate; corolla 5-lobed, with usually reflexed lobes; corona usually present, either an outgrowth of the corolla or of the stamens or of both; stamens 5, the filaments more or less united and the anthers adhering to the stigma; pollen in groups of 4 (tetrades) and granular, or cohering into waxy masses (pollinia) attached to glandular appendages of the stigma: carpels 2, many-ovuled; styles 2, united into a discoid stigma; disk absent: fr. of 2 follicles; seeds usually with a long tuft of hairs.—About 220 genera and 2000 species in trop. and subtrop. regions of both hemispheres.

A. Fls. brown-purple inside; lvs. rounded to cuneate at base: twining shrub: pollen granular ....1. *Periploca*
AA. Fls. white: lvs. cordate to rounded at base: pollen cohering into pollinia.
　　B. Corolla-lobes narrow-oblong, more or less upright, white: upright or slightly climbing shrub ....2. *Marsdenia*
　　BB. Corolla-lobes ovate or elliptic-ovate, dotted red inside, spreading: twining shrub.
　　　　　　　　　　　　　　　　　　　　　　　　　　　　　　　　　　　3. *Wattakaka*

1. PERÍPLOCA L. Deciduous or evergreen twining shrubs, glabrous; winter-buds small, hairy, with few outer scales: lvs. opposite, entire: fls. in axillary or terminal cymes; calyx 5-lobed, glandular within; corolla rotate, 5-parted, with a 5 or 10-lobed crown at base of corolla; lobes overlapping to the right, often hairy above; stamens with very short free filaments and the anthers connected at apex and villous on back; pollen granular; style short, with a broad stigma: fr. of 2 follicles with numerous small winged seeds. (Greek *peri*, around, and *plokein*, to twine.) About 12 species from S. Eu. to trop. Afr., E. Asia and India.

A. Lvs. generally elliptic, up to 5 cm. broad.....................................1. *P. graeca*
AA. Lvs. generally lanceolate, up to 2.5 cm. broad.................................2. *P. sepium*

1. P. graèca L. SILK-VINE. Deciduous twining shrub to 15 m.: lvs. ovate or elliptic to oblong-lanceolate, 4–10 cm. long, acuminate, dark green and glossy above; petiole 6–12 mm. long: fls. about 2.5 cm. across, greenish yellow at the margin and outside, brown-purple inside, in loose long-peduncled 8–12-fld. cymes; corolla-lobes spreading, oblong, villous above; crown of 5 slender thread-like corona-lobes recurved at apex: follicles cylindric, 10–12 cm. long, usually cohering at apex. Fl.vii–viii; fr.ix–x. B.M.2289(c) B.R.803(c). L.B. 1389(c). Gn.84:78. S. Eu., W. Asia. Cult. 1597. Zone VI. Climber with dark green lustrous lvs. remaining green until late in fall.

2. P. sèpium Bge. Similar to the preceding species; less high: lvs. lance-olate to oblong-lanceolate, 4–10 cm. long, long-acuminate; petiole 10–15 mm. long: fls. about 2 cm. across, in few-fld. cymes; corolla-lobes revolute: follicle 10–15 cm. long. Fl.vi–vii; fr.ix–x. Yabe, Icon. Fl. Manch.1:t.9(c). B.C.5: 2553. N. China. Intr. 1905. Zone IV. Slenderer than the preceding species and foliage less dense, turning yellow in fall; hardier.

2. MARSDÈNIA R. Br. Twining or upright shrubs: lvs. opposite, usually broad: fls. usually small, in panicles or umbels; sepals small, usually ovate and obtuse, glandular or glandless; corolla campanulate or urceolate to rotate or salverform, the lobes overlapping to the right; corona-lobes 5, scaly, adnate to the stamens and to the gynostegium; pollen cohering into pollinia one in each anther-cell; stigma flat to rostrate: follicle thick, smooth or winged, often fleshy. (After William Marsden, author of a history of Sumatra; 1754–1836.) About 80 species in subtrop. and trop. regions.

M. erécta (L.) R. Br. Deciduous twining shrub to 8 m., or low with pros-trate brs.; young brts. slightly pubescent, green, becoming light gray-brown: lvs. ovate, 3.5–8 cm. long, acuminate, cordate, bright green and glabrous above, minutely pubescent on the veins at first, later glabrous, petiole 1–4 cm. long: fls. white, fragrant, 8 mm. across, in terminal and axillary peduncled cymes 3–7 cm. across; corolla-lobes narrow-oblong, obtuse; stamens with small petaloid appendages on the back: fr. conic-oblong or spindle-shaped, 7–8 cm. long; each seed with a tuft of hairs about 2.5 cm. long. Fl.v–vii; fr. viii–ix. D.H.1:161. S.H.2:f.535e-k,536c-d. (*Cynanchum erectum* L.) S. E. Eu., W. Asia. Cult. 1597. Zone (V). Of little ornamental merit.

3. WATTAKAKA (Dcne.) Hassk. Twining shrubs: lvs. cordate or rounded at base: fls. in axillary peduncled umbels; calyx 5-parted with small ovate to oblong lobes and 5 small glands between; corolla rotate, with very shallow cup-like tube, the lobes overlapping to the right; corona-lobes fleshy, knob-shaped, star-like, spreading; anthers with membranous tips appressed to the style-head; pollinia erect, narrowly club-shaped, with clavate translators: follicles horizontally spreading, slightly longitudinally ribbed to nearly smooth or with transverse corrugations. (Wattakaka-Rodi is the native Malabar name of *W. volubilis* (L. f.) Stapf.) Three species in S. Asia and Malaysia.

W. sinénsis (Hemsl.) Stapf. Twining shrub to 3 m.; brts., pedicels and infl. pubescent: lvs. ovate or broad-ovate, 4–9 cm. long, acuminate or acute, cordate or rounded at base, bright green above, densely grayish pubescent beneath, usually 5-nerved at base; petiole 1–4.5 cm. long, pubescent: fls. 8–25 in umbels on a stalk 3–6 cm. long; corolla star-shaped, 1.5 cm. across, lobes ovate to elliptic, ciliolate, white with red dots; corona-lobes white: follicles attenuated upwards, 5.5–7 cm. long, finely pubescent, with faint ribs or rough with transverse corrugations. Fl.vi–vii; fr.x–xi. B.M.8976(c) (*Dregea s.* Hemsl.) C. and W. China. Intr. 1908. Zone VII?

Fam. 99. **POLEMONIACEAE** Juss. PHLOX FAMILY

Herbs, rarely shrubby: lvs. alternate or opposite, simple, pinnate or digitate, exstipulate: fls. perfect, regular or nearly so; calyx 5-cleft: corolla 5-lobed, the lobes convolute; stamens 5, inserted on the corolla-tube; ovary superior, 2–5-celled, with a disk at base; cells with many, rarely 1 ovule; style 1, 3-fid, rarely 5-fid at apex: fr. a loculicidal, rarely septicidal caps.; seed with copious albumen and a straight embryo.—About 12 genera and 270 species in Eu., Asia and Am.

GÍLIA Ruiz & Pav. Herbs or subshrubs: lvs. divided or entire, alternate or opposite: fls. solitary or in panicles; calyx tubular or campanulate, teeth of equal length: corolla salver- to funnelform or campanulate; stamens inserted in tube or at the mouth; filaments naked; style glabrous, with 3 filiform stigmas: caps. ovoid or oblong, 3-celled and 3-valved, few- to many-seeded; seeds small, not winged. (After Felipe Luis Gil, Spanish botanist; wrote on exotic plants about 1790.) Including *Leptodactylon* Hook. & Arn. More than 100 species in W. N. Am., few in S. Am.

G. califórnica (Hook. & Arn.) Benth. Subshrub with decumbent or upright much-branched villous stems to 80 cm.: lvs. alternate, crowded, palmately pinnatifid into 3–7 subulate pungent pilose segments 3–8 mm. long: fls. rose-pink, 1 or several on short brts. along the stems; calyx pilose, tubular with subulate teeth; corolla salver-shaped, tube 1.5 cm. long, limb 3 cm. across. Fl.vii. B.M.4872(c). G.C.80:11. N.F.1:102. (*Leptodactylon californicum* Hook. & Arn.) Calif. Cult. 1855. Zone VII.

Fam. 100. **BORAGINACEAE** Lindl. BORAGE FAMILY

Herbs, rarely shrubs or trees: lvs. usually alternate, usually rough-hairy, simple, usually entire, exstipulate: infl. cymose or usually scorpioid and spike-like, simple or forked: fls. perfect, usually regular: calyx 5-parted; corolla 5-lobed, with imbricate, rarely convolute lobes, rarely 4-lobed, often appendaged in the throat; stamens 5, inserted on the corolla-tube; ovary superior, of two 2-ovuled carpels, often deeply 4-lobed as if consisting of 4 1-ovuled carpels, with the style basal between the lobes: fr. usually of 4 nutlets, rarely berry-like; seed with straight or curved embryo and scant albumen.—About 85 genera and 1500 species in temp. and trop. regions.

A. Fr. a drupe: style terminal; fls. in panicles: trees or tall shrubs...............1. *Ehretia*
AA. Fr. of nutlets; style basal: fls. in scorpioid spikes or solitary: low shrubs or subshrubs.
  B. Stamens exserted ....2. *Moltkia*
  BB. Stamens included ....3. *Lithospermum*

1. **EHRÈTIA** L. Deciduous or evergreen trees or shrubs; winter-buds ubglobose, with imbricate scales: lvs. alternate, entire or serrate: fls. small, usually white, in terminal, rarely axillary panicles or corymbs; calyx small, 5-parted; corolla short-funnelform to rotate, with 5 spreading obtuse lobes imbricate in bud; stamens 5, usually exserted, with oblong or ovate anthers; filaments slender: ovary 2- or 4-celled: fr. a usually globose drupe with 4 1-celled or two 2-celled nutlets. (After G. D. Ehret, botanical painter, born in Germany about 1710; died in England 1770.) About 50 species in trop. and subtrop., few extending into temperate regions.

A. Lvs. glabrous or nearly so..1. *E. thyrsiflora*
A. Lvs. pubescent beneath, rough-hairy above..........................2. *E. Dicksoni*

1. **E. thyrsiflòra** (Sieb. & Zucc.) Nakai. Deciduous tree, to 15 m.; brts. glabrous: lvs. obovate to oblong-obovate, 5–18 cm. long, acute or short-acuminate, broad-cuneate or sometimes rounded at base, serrate, glabrous except axillary tufts of hairs beneath; petiole 1–2.5 cm. long: fls. white, subsessile, in panicles 8–20 cm. long; sepals rounded, ciliolate; corolla rotate, about 6 mm. across, with oblong lobes longer than tube; stamens about as long as corolla-lobes: fr. globose, 4 mm. across, first orange, later brownish black. Fl.vi–vii; fr.viii. N.K.14:t.4. N.T.1:443. I.S.2:t.99. (*E. acuminata* of Hemsl., not R. Br., *E. serrata* Fr. & Sav., not Roxb.) China, Japan, Korea. Formosa. Intr. 1900. Zone V. Small tree with upright brs. and large panicles of white fls., interesting as the only arborescent representative of the family, hardy as far north as Mass.

2. **E. Dícksoni** Hance. Deciduous tree to 10 m.; brts. slightly pubescent at first: lvs. broad-elliptic to elliptic, 8–20 cm. long, short-acuminate, rounded at base to subcordate or broad-cuneate, serrate, rough-pubescent above, more or less densely pubescent beneath, rarely glabrescent; petiole 1–3 cm. long: fls. white, fragrant, subsessile, in corymbose panicles 5–10 cm. long and nearly as broad; calyx pubescent, with ovate to ovate-oblong ciliate lobes; corolla about 1 cm. across, with short-funnelform tube as long or longer than lobes: fr. subglobose, beaked, 1–1.5 cm. across, yellowish. Fl.v–vi; fr.ix. R.H.1914: 174(h),175. M.O.362. (*E. macrophylla* Hemsl., not Wall.) China, Formosa, Liukiu Isls. Intr. 1897. Zone VII?

2. **MÓLTKIA** Lehm. Herbs or half-evergreen subshrubs: lvs. alternate, narrow, entire: fls. purple, blue or yellow in dense scorpioid terminal infl.; calyx 5-cleft, with linear lobes; corolla tubular-funnelform, sometimes pubescent in the throat, with 5 upright lobes; stamens with slender filaments, exserted; anthers linear-oblong, often curved; style filiform, with small stigma: nutlets often only 1 or 2, oblique or curved, smooth or rugose. (After Count Joachim Gadske Moltke, of Denmark; died 1818.) Six species in Mediterr. region to Himal.

M. petraèa (Tratt.) Griseb. Upright subshrub, to 30 cm. tall, stems densely grayish strigose: lvs. sessile, linear to oblanceolate, 1–3 cm. long, recurved at margin, appressed-pubescent on both sides: fls. pinkish purple at first, becoming violet-blue, in forked scorpioid cymes 2–3 cm. long and about as wide: corolla tubular, 8 mm. long, with 5 short rounded lobes; stamens exceeding the corolla-lobes: nutlets smooth. Fl.vi. B.M.5492(c). B.R.29:26 (c). Gn.89:140(h). (*Lithospermum petraeum* A. DC.) S. E. Eu. Intr. 1840. Zone VI? Attractive subshrub; suited for a sunny place in the rockery.

Closely related species: **M. coerùlea** (Pers.) Lehm. Stems erect, rigid: lvs. oblong-spatulate, obtuse, those of the stem linear-lanceolate, acutish, canescent: fls. blue; calyx-lobes linear-lanceolate; stamens exserted: nutlets rugose. Leh-

mann, Icon. Asperifol. t.43. Asia Minor. Intr. 1829.—**M. suffruticòsa** (L.)
Brand. Subshrub with ascending stems, to 50 cm. high: lvs. linear, 5–12, or
flowering brs. 2–6 cm. long, revolute, appressed-pubescent above, white-tomen
tose beneath, setulose on midrib: fls. purple-blue, pink in bud; stamens not ex
ceeding the corolla-lobes: nutlets rugose. R.I.18:t.114.f.2(c). G.C.47:213(h)
Gn.65:147(h). (*Lithospermum suffruticosum* Kern., *L. graminifolium* Viv.)
Italy. Cult. 1895.

3. LITHOSPÉRMUM L.

Herbs or subshrubs, hairy: lvs. alternate, en
tire: fls. white, yellow or violet, in scorpioid leafy infl. or the lower one
axillary: calyx 5-parted; corolla funnelform or salver-shaped, with 5 spread
ing lobes, tube cylindric, appendaged in throat; stamens included, on usually
short filaments; style with 2 stigmas; nutlets upright, straight, smooth o
rugose. (Greek *lithos,* stone, and *sperma,* seed; referring to the shape of the
nutlets.) About 50 species in the temp. regions of both hemispheres.

L. diffùsum Lag. Evergreen prostrate subshrub 15 to 30 cm. high; stem
strigose and hirsute: lvs. sessile, linear-oblong to lanceolate, 1–2 cm. long
obtuse, appressed-setose on both sides, slightly revolute: fls. deep blue, faintly
striped reddish violet, purple in bud; sessile in the axils of leafy bracts
corolla 1.5 cm. long, with broad rounded lobes and cylindric tube about
times as long as calyx, pubescent outside, villous in throat; stamens inserted
above the middle. Fl.v–vi. M.B.G.1:t.13,f.2(c). G.C.30:238(h). Gn.88:4
(h). (*L. prostratum* Lois., *L. fruticosum* Brot., not L.) S. Eu. Intr. 1825
Zone VII. Forming large mats; calciphobe, while *L. fruticosum* is calciphile

Closely related species: **L. oleifòlium** Lapeyr. Prostrate shrub: lvs. elliptic
oblong, 1–1.8 cm. long, on shoots to 4 cm. long: fls. dimorphous; calyx-lobes a
long or half as long as corolla-tube; whitish tomentose beneath: corolla 1.5–1.8
cm. long, glabrous inside, limb campanulate; stamens inserted on throat. B.M
8994,9559(c). Pyrenees. Intr. about 1900. Zone VII?—**L. fruticòsum** L. Up
right, to 50 cm.: lvs. narrow, strongly revolute, white-tomentose beneath excep
strigose midrib, pubescent above: corolla glabrous outside and glabrous i
throat, tube about twice as long as calyx; stamens inserted near middle of tube
R.I.18:t.114,f.1(c). S. Eu. Intr. 1683. Zone VII?

Fam. 101. VERBENACEAE Juss. VERVAIN FAMILY

Herbs, shrubs or trees: lvs. opposite, rarely whorled and very rarely alter
nate, simple or compound, exstipulate: fls. perfect, usually oblique or 2
lipped, rarely regular, usually in cymes or panicles; calyx 4–5-, rarely 6–8
toothed; corolla 4–5-lobed, with imbricate lobes; stamens 4, didynamous
sometimes equal, rarely 5 or 2, adnate to the corolla; disk usually small
ovary superior, of 2, 4 or 5 carpels, entire or 2–4-lobed, 2–5-celled, with
ovules in each cell or 5–10-celled by false partitions and cells 1-ovuled; styl
slender: fr. a drupe or berry, often separating into drupelets; seed with
straight embryo and with or usually without albumen.—About 70 genera an
750 species chiefly in trop. and subtrop. regions of both hemispheres.

A. Stamens included; corolla 5-lobed; fls. in racemes: lvs. 4–20 mm. long.
  B. Fr. 4-seeded ....1. *Verben*
  BB. Fr. 2-seeded ....2. *Dioste*
AA. Stamens exserted: fls. in cymes: lvs. larger.
  B. Corolla regular, 4-lobed, with short tube; stamens equal.................3. *Callicarp*
  BB. Corolla oblique; tube usually long; stamens didynamous.
    c. Lvs. compound ....4. *Vite*
    cc. Lvs. simple.
      D. Fr. drupe-like: fls. white to red: lvs. 8–20 cm. long...............5. *Clerodendro*
      DD. Fr. a caps.: fls. blue: lvs. 2–8 cm. long............................6. *Caryopter*

1. VERBÈNA L.

Herbs or shrubs: lvs. usually opposite, toothed o
lobed, rarely entire: fls. in racemes, sometimes in panicles or umbels; caly
tubular, 5-toothed, 5-ribbed; corolla slightly 2-lipped with straight or curve

tube and 5 spreading lobes; stamens 4, didynamous, included, inserted above the middle; ovary 4-celled, 4-ovuled; style short, 2-lobed at apex: fr. enclosed by the calyx, dry, separating into 4 stones. (Ancient Latin name for sacred herbs; as *Verbenaca* the name for *Verbena officinalis*.) About 80 species chiefly in trop. and extratrop. Am., few in the Old World.

V. trídens Lag. MATE NEGRA. Evergreen shrub to 2 m.; brs. erect, virgate: lvs. dimorphous; lvs. of shoots opposite, crowded, puberulous, sessile, 3-lobed, 2–4 mm. long, lobes stout, pointed, grooved beneath; lvs. of axillary brts. decussate and closely packed, short, thick, blunt: fls. sessile, white to rosy-lilac, very fragrant, in short terminal, 6–12-fld. spikes; corolla pubescent outside and in throat, tube 6–8 mm. long and about as wide. Fl.vii. Princeton Univ. Exp. Patag.t.23(c). G.C.90:378(h). (*V. Carroo* Spegazz.) Patag. Intr. 1928. Zone VII.

2. DIÓSTEA Miers. Deciduous shrubs: lvs. opposite or whorled, sessile, entire or sparingly toothed; fls. in terminal or axillary short racemes: calyx campanulate or short-tubular, with 4–5 short teeth; corolla slightly 2-lipped, with cylindric straight or curved tube, 5-lobed; stamens 4, didynamous, included or slightly exserted, with a small staminode; ovary 2-celled, 2-ovuled; style included or slightly exserted: fr. a drupe inclosed in the persistent calyx, with 2 1-seeded stones; seeds without albumen. (Greek *di-*, double, *osteon*, pl. *ostea*, bone, here nutlet.) Two species in S. Am.

D. júncea (Schau.) Miers. Shrub or small tree to 6 m., with slender rush-like brs.: lvs. distant, 8–20 mm. long, ovate-oblong, with few coarse teeth, slightly downy: fls. pale lilac, in dense spikes 2–3 cm. long, terminal on short lateral brts.; calyx cylindric, puberulous; corolla about 8 mm. long, with 5 short rounded lobes. Fl.vi. B.M.7695(c). B.S.1:495. (*Baillonia j.* Briq.) Andes of Chile and Peru. Intr. 1890. Zone VII? Distinct shrub, resembling *Spartium junceum* in habit.

3. CALLICÁRPA L. Deciduous or evergreen shrubs or trees, often with stellate or scurfy pubescence; winter-buds naked, superposed: lvs. opposite, usually serrate: fls. small, in axillary cymes; calyx short-campanulate, truncate or slightly 4-toothed, rarely 4-parted; corolla with short tube, 4-lobed; stamens 4, of equal length, exserted: ovary 4-celled, 4-ovuled; style slender, with simple small stigma: fr. a subglobose, small berry-like drupe, with 2–4 stones. (Greek *kallos*, beauty, and *karpos*, fruit.) About 40 species, chiefly in the trop. and subtrop. regions of E. Asia, Mal., Australia and N. and C. Am. —Ornamental shrubs chiefly grown for the attractive fls. and handsome frs. late in autumn; rather tender, but even if killed back, the young shoots usually flower and fruit the same season.

A. Peduncles longer than petioles: lvs. glabrous or sparingly pubescent beneath.
  B. Lvs. crenate-serrate above the middle: anthers opening by a slit........1. *C. dichotoma*
  BB. Lvs. serrulate from near base: anthers opening by a terminal pore........2. *C. japonica*
AA. Peduncles as long or shorter than petioles.
  B. Lvs. fasciculate-pubescent or glabrescent beneath; peduncles about half as long or
    as long as petioles ....3. *C. Bodinieri*
  BB. Lvs. tomentose beneath: infl. subsessile................................4. *C. americana*

1. C. dichótoma (Lour.) K. Koch. Upright shrub to 1.5 m.; brts. scurfy-pubescent: lvs. elliptic or obovate, 3–8 cm. long, acuminate, cuneate, coarsely serrate except toward the base and at the apex, glandular beneath and light green; petiole 2–4 mm. long: cymes few- to many-fld., 1.2–2 cm. broad, on slender peduncles 5–12 mm. long; fls. pink, with the stamens 5 mm. long: fr. lilac-violet, 3–4 mm. across. Fl.viii; fr.x–xi. Gn.23:540,t(c). N.K.14:t.5.

N.T.1:451. S.H.2.f.382k-l,385m. (*C. purpurea* Juss., *C. gracilis* Sieb. & Zucc
C. koreana Hort. Vilm.) E. and C. China, Korea, cult. in Japan; rare
escaped in the E. States. Intr. 1857. Zone (V).

2. **C. japónica** Thunb. Shrub to 1.5 m.; brts. tomentulose at first, soo
glabrous: lvs. elliptic to ovate-lanceolate, 6–12 cm. long, long-acuminat
cuneate, serrulate, glandular beneath; petiole 2–5 mm. long: cymes many-fld
1.5–3 cm. across, on peduncles 5–10 mm. long; calyx shallowly lobed; fls. pin
or whitish, with the stamens about 6 mm. long; style nearly glabrous; anthe
opening by a pore at apex: fr. violet, 4 mm. across. Fl.VIII; fr.X–XI. Ad.3:
103(c). S.I.1:t.70(c). N.T.1:453. H.F.1861:12,t(c). B.C.2:628. Japan. Int
about 1845. Zone (V).—**C. j. leucocárpa** Sieb., var. Fr. white. Intr. 1845.–
C. j. angustàta Rehd., var. Lvs. oblong-lanceolate to oblanceolate, 5–12 cn
long and 1.2–3.5 cm. broad. N.T.1:456. C. China. Intr. 1907.

C. j. × *mollis* = C. Shirasawàna Mak. Lvs. elliptic to ovate-lanceolate o
obovate-oblong, serrate, sparingly fasciculate-pubescent and glandular beneath
calyx distinctly lobed; fls. lilac. N.T.1:462. Orig. before 1895 in Japan.

3. **C. Bodinièri** Lévl. Shrub to 3 m.; brts. scurfy-pubescent: lvs. broac
elliptic or elliptic-ovate to lance-oblong, 5–12 cm. long, acuminate, cuneat
or broad-cuneate, denticulate or dentate, slightly pubescent above, fasciculate
late-pilose beneath, particularly on the veins; petiole 5–15 mm. long; cyme
dense, 2–3 cm. across, densely fasciculate-pilose; peduncles 3–15 mm. long; fl
lilac, with the exserted stamens about 7 mm. long; lobes rounded, shorte
than stamens: fr. lilac-violet, 3–4 mm. across (*C. Giraldiana* var. *subcanescen*
Rehd.) C. and W. China.—**C. B. Giráldii** (Rehd.) Rehd., var. Lvs. glabrou
above; sparingly fasciculate-pubescent and glandular beneath: cymes le
pubescent. Fl.VII–IX; fr.IX–X. B.M.8682(c). M.D.1912:366. R.H.1923:391,
(c). G.W.29:51. (*C. G.* and *C. Giraldiana* Hesse ex Rehd.) E. to W. Chin
Cult. 1900. Zone (V).

Related species: **C. mollis** Sieb. & Zucc. Lvs. elliptic to oblong-lanceolat
tomentose beneath; petiole 5–8 mm. long, peduncle about as long; calyx deepl
lobed; corolla glandular outside; stamens not exceeding the lobes: fr. du
purple. N.T.1:457. N.K.14:t.9. Japan, Korea. Cult. 1870. Zone VII?—*C. n*
× *japonica;* see under No. 2.

4. **C. americàna** L. Shrub to 2 m.; brts. tomentose: lvs. elliptic-ovate
ovate-oblong, 7–14 cm. long, acuminate, cuneate, crenate-serrate, pubescen
above, tomentose and glandular beneath; petiole 1–3 cm. long: cymes short
stalked or nearly sessile, shorter than petiole, dense; calyx obscurely toothed
corolla bluish, glabrous outside; filaments exceeding the corolla-lobes: f
violet, 4 mm. across. Fl.V–VII; fr.X. B.B.3:99. Gr.M.690. Va. to Tex. an
W. Ind. Intr. 1724. Zone VII.—**C. a. láctea** F. J. Muller, var. Fr. white
(*C. a.* var. *alba* Rehd.)

4. **VÌTEX** L. Deciduous or evergreen shrubs or trees; winter-buds wit
indistinct scales, superposed: lvs. opposite, digitate, rarely reduced to 1 lft.
fls. small, white, blue or yellowish in often panicled cymes; calyx campanu
late, often 5-toothed; corolla tubular-funnelform, with 5-lobed oblique c
slightly 2-lipped limb; stamens 4, didynamous, usually exserted; ovary 4
celled, 4-ovuled; style bifid at apex: fr. a small drupe with a 4-celled ston
surrounded by the persistent calyx; seed without albumen. (Ancient Lati
name of *V. Agnus-castus.*) About 60 species in trop. and subtrop. regions c
both hemispheres, few in temp. regions.

A. Infl. a dense spike: lfts. 5–7, entire or serrate..........................1. *V. Agnus-castu*
AA. Infl. a loose wide panicle: lfts. 3–5, usually incised-serrate to pinnatifid....2. *V. Negund*

1. **V. Agnus-castus** L. CHASTE-TREE. Shrub to 3 m.; grayish tomentose and of aromatic pungent odor; brts. 4-angled: lfts. 5–7, short-stalked, lanceolate or narrow-lanceolate, 5–10 cm. long, entire or with few coarse teeth, grayish tomentose beneath; petiole 1.5–5 cm. long: fls. lilac or pale violet, fragrant, in dense usually sessile clusters forming dense, often panicled spikes 10–18 cm. long; calyx-teeth triangular, very short; corolla about 8 mm. long, pubescent outside and in throat; stamens and style about as long as lobes: fr. globose 3–4 mm. across, of pungent flavor. Fl.vi–ix. Ad.1:t.18(c). G.C.51:52(h). Gn.83:587. M.M.2:44. (*Agnus-castus vulgaris* Carr.—HEMP-TREE, MONKS' PEPPER-TREE.) S. Eu., W. Asia. Intr. 1570. Zone (VI) or VII. Valued for its late fls.; if killed back the young shoots flower the same season.—**V. A. alba** West., var. Fls. white. (*V. albiflora* Hort.)—**V. A. rosea** Rehd., f. Fls. pink.—**V. A. latifòlia** (Mill.) Loud., var. Lfts. mostly oblong-lanceolate, up to 2.5 cm. broad: plant more vigorous and hardier. H.B.11:290. (*V. macrophylla* Hort.)

2. **V. Negúndo** L. Shrub or small tree to 5 m.; brts. 4-angled: lfts. usually 5, sometimes 3, stalked, elliptic-ovate to lanceolate, 3–10 cm. long, entire or serrate, grayish tomentulose beneath; petiole 1.5–5 cm. long: fls. lilac or lavender, in rather loose clusters, at least the lower ones stalked, forming slender spikes collected into terminal panicles 12–20 cm. long; corolla 5–6 mm. long; style and stamens shorter than lobes: fr. about 2 mm. across. H.T.5: t.199. China, India. Intr. about 1697. Probably not hardy within our area.—**V. N. incìsa** (Bge.) Clarke, var. Lfts. incisely serrate or nearly pinnatifid, 2–8 cm. long, in extreme forms deeply pinnatifid with narrow remote segments (f. *multifida* Rehd.) Fl.vii–viii. B.M.364(c). B.C.6:3481. N.K.14:t. 12. N. China, Mong., Korea. (*V. i.* Bge., *V. chinensis* Mill.) Intr. about 1750. Zone (V). Shrub of loose open habit, with small fls.

5. **CLERODÉNDRON** L. Deciduous or evergreen trees or shrubs, often climbing; winter-buds conical, superposed: lvs. opposite or verticillate, entire or toothed, sometimes lobed: fls. in usual terminal cymes or panicles; calyx campanulate, rarely tubular, 5-toothed or 5-lobed, persistent; corolla-tube usually slender, cylindric, the limb spreading, with 5 nearly equal or unequal lobes; stamens 4, inserted on the corolla-tube, long-exserted and curved; style exserted, 2-cleft at apex: ovary incompletely 4-celled, 4-ovuled: fr. a globose or obovoid drupe often enclosed in the calyx, with juicy exocarp, the stone splitting into 4 or 2 parts. (Greek *kleros*, chance, fortune, and *dendron* tree; in reference to 2 species in Ceylon called by early botanists *arbor fortunata* and *arbor infortunata*.) About 100 species in trop. and subtrop. regions.

C. trichótomum Thunb. Upright shrub or small tree to 8 m.; young brts. puberulous: lvs. ovate to elliptic, 10–20 cm. long, acuminate, broad-cuneate to truncate, entire or sometimes remotely toothed, pubescent beneath; petiole 3–10 cm. long, pubescent: fls. fragrant, white, in long-stalked cymes in the axils of the upper lvs., forming a loose terminal infl. 12–24 cm. across; calyx reddish, deeply 5-parted with ovate to ovate-oblong acute lobes; corolla about 3 cm. across, with 5 oblong lobes; stamens and style much exserted: fr. blue, 5–8 mm. across, subtended by the spreading crimson calyx. Fl.viii–ix; fr.ix–x. B.M.6561(c). Ad.1:t.15(c). N.T.1:468. Gn.75:67(h),447. F.E.29:653(h). Gs.4:27(h). (*C. serotinum* Carr., *Volkameria japonica* Hort., not Thunb.) E. China, Japan. Cult. 1880. Zone VI? Large-leaved, rather coarse shrub valued for its late fls. and conspicuously colored frs.—**C. t. Fargèsii** (Dode)

or rose, usually in whorls of 4 forming a loose terminal secund spike; calyx and bracts usually red-brown; corolla nearly 1.5 cm. long, the tube exceeding the calyx. Fl.vii–ix. R.I.18:t.38,f.4(c). F.D.18:t.1875(c). C. and S. Eu., W. Asia. Cult. 1750. Zone V.

Related species: **T. Pólium** L. Subshrub to 0.5 m.; brts. and lvs. closely white-tomentose: lvs. subsessile, narrow-oblong to oblong, 1–2.5 cm. long, obtuse, crenate, revolute: fls. in usually several terminal heads; calyx densely white-tomentose; corolla white to yellowish, about 6 mm. long, tube enclosed in the calyx. F.D.18:t.1877(c). Mediterr. reg. Cult. 1562. Zone VII.—**T. flàvum** L. To 50 cm. high, with ascending brs.: lvs. ovate, crenate-serrate, velutinous: fls. yellow, 1.8 cm. long in whorls of 4–6 forming spikes. S. Eu. Intr. 1640. Zone VII?

2. ROSMARÌNUS L. Rosemary.

Evergreen aromatic shrub: lvs. opposite, sessile, narrow, entire: fls. subsessile, in short axillary racemes; calyx campanulate, 2-lipped, the upper lip minutely 3-toothed, the lower 2-toothed: corolla with the upper lip emarginate or 2-lobed, the lower lip 3-lobed with the middle lobe large, concave, declined; stamens 2 and 2 minute staminodes; style not basal: nutlets smooth, globose-ovoid, with an oblique base. (*Rosmarinus*, sea dew, the ancient Latin name of the plant.) One Mediterranean species.

R. officinális L. Upright shrub to 2 m.; young brts. pubescent: lvs. linear, 1.5–2.5 cm. long, revolute, lustrous dark green above, white-tomentose beneath, thick: fls. violet-blue, rarely white, about 1 cm. long. Fl.iv–v. R.I 18:t.43(c). F.D.18:t.1784(c). B.S.2:449. Gn.74:620(h);89:458(h). S. Eu., Asia Minor.. Cult. for centuries. Zone (VI).

3. LAVÁNDULA L. Lavender.

Perennial herbs, subshrubs or shrubs: lvs. opposite, entire, toothed or dissected: fls. blue, violet or lilac, in 2–10-fld. whorls forming stalked cylindric spikes with often imbricate bracts, sometimes branched at base; calyx tubular, 13–15-nerved, 5-toothed; corolla tubular, with short, 2-lipped limb, upper lip 2-, lower 3-lobed; stamens 4, included, declined; style basal, nutlets smooth. (Latin *lavare*, to wash; referring to its use by the Romans in the bath.) About 20 species chiefly Mediterranean, from the Canary Isls. to India.

L. officinàlis Chaix. Subshrub to 1 m.; brts. tomentulose: lvs. linear to lanceolate, 2–4 cm. long, obtuse, revolute, white-tomentose, finally usually glabrate: fls. lavender, 8–10 mm. long, in spikes 3–6 cm. long borne on peduncles 5–15 cm. long; floral bracts triangular-ovate, acuminate, shorter than calyx, scarious. Fl.vii–viii. R.I.18:t.26,f.1(c). F.D.18:t.1772(c). (*L. Spica* L. in part, *L. vera* DC., *L. angustifolia* Moench.) S. Eu., N. Afr. Cult. since ancient times. Zone V.—**L. o. alba** (Sweet) Rehd., f. Fls. white.

Closely related species: **L. latifòlia** L. Lvs. broader, oblanceolate to oblong, to 5 cm. long, flat; floral bracts linear, longer, herbaceous. R.I.18:t.26,f.2(c). (*L. Spica* DC., *L. Spica* var. *l.* L. f.) H.A.t.38(c). S. Eu. Cult. 1568. Zone V?

4. PHLÓMIS L.

Herbs, subshrubs or shrubs, mostly pubescent or tomentose: lvs. opposite, rather large, rugose: fls. sessile, in dense many-fld. axillary bracted whorls; calyx tubular or campanulate, truncate or 5-toothed, 5–10-nerved; corolla-tube slightly exserted or enclosed, upper lip large, hooded, lower lip 3-lobed with the middle lobe much larger; stamens 4, with diverging anther-cells; style 2-lobed at apex, the posterior lobe shorter; nutlets triangular-ovoid, glabrous, rarely slightly pubescent. (Greek *phlómis* a woolly plant, probably Verbascum.) About 70 species in the Mediterranean reg. to China.—Coarse plants with yellow, purple or white fls. in dense whorls.

P. fruticòsa L. JERUSALEM SAGE. Evergreen shrub tc 1.5 m.; brts. stout, calyx densely villous; corolla 8–10 mm. long. Fl.vɪɪɪ–ɪx. B.M.8441(c). R.H. 4-angled, tomentose: lvs. thickish, oblong-ovate to oblong-lanceolate, 5–12 cm. long, obtuse, rounded to broad-cuneate, rugose and pubescent above, reticulate and densely whitish tomentose beneath; petiole 6–25 mm. long: fls. in dense terminal woolly heads, sometimes with axillary whorls below, with numerous ovate bracts; calyx funnelform, 1.5 cm. long, woolly, with 5 spreading subulate tips; corolla 2.5–3 cm. long, yellow, densely pubescent outside, middle lobe of lower lip emarginate. Fl.vɪ–vɪɪ. B.M.1843(c). Gn.79:114 (h);87:428(h). S. Eu. Cult. 1597. Zone VII. Demands a sheltered and dry position.

5. SÁLVIA L. SAGE. Herbs, subshrubs or shrubs: lvs. opposite, entire, toothed or pinnatisect: fls. variously colored, in 2-many-fld. whorls forming racemes, spikes or panicles, rarely solitary; calyx usually 2-lipped, the upper lip entire or 3-toothed, the lower 2-toothed; corolla usually 2-lipped, upper lip entire or emarginate, concave; stamens 2, inserted on the throat of the corolla; anther-cells widely separated on a long and slender connective articulate with the filament, the upper end of the connective bearing a perfect anther-cell, the lower end an imperfect one or none; nutlets triangular-ovoid, smooth. (Ancient Latin name of *S. officinalis*, from *salvere*, to be well; referring to the medicinal properties of the plant.) About 500 species in the temp. and warmer regions of both hemisphere. Many of them highly ornamental plants with showy fls., but the following chiefly grown as a pot-herb.

S. officinàlis L. GARDEN S. Upright aromatic subshrub, to 50 cm.; young brts. grayish tomentulose, 4-angled: lvs. oblong, 3–5 cm. long, obtuse to acute, crenulate, rugose above, grayish tomentulose beneath; petiole 1–4 cm. long: fls. bluish purple in many-fld. whorls forming an interrupted spike: calyx campanulate, the lower lip longer than the upper one: corolla about 1.5 cm. long, pubescent outside; tube with a hairy ring inside. Fl.vɪ–vɪɪ. R.I.18:t. 44(c). F.D.18:t.1785(c). S. Eu. Cult. since ancient times, chiefly for its medicinal properties. Zone V.—**S. o. albiflòra** Alef. Fls. white: lvs. larger.— **S. o. rubriflòra** Alef. Fls. red. (*S. o.* var. *purpurea* Bean.)—**S. o. variegàta** Sweet, var. Lvs. variegated.

An ornamental species is: **S. Greggii** Gray. Shrub to 1 m., glabrescent; brts. slender, puberulous: lvs. oblong to oblong-obovate or oblanceolate, 1.5–3 cm. long, obtuse, cuneate, dull pale green, gland-dotted: racemes 6–12-fld., slender, glandular and puberulous; calyx narrow-campanulate, glandular outside, purplish, lobes about equal; corolla carmine, 2.5–3 cm. long, lower lip about 2 cm. broad, upper lip smaller, paler. Fl.vɪɪ–x. B.M.6812(c). R.H.1927:496,t(c). Tex., Mex. Cult. 1882. Zone VII.

6. PERÓVSKIA Karel. Herbs or subshrubs: lvs. opposite, serrate or pinnatifid: fls. in distant whorls forming terminal spikes; calyx 2-lipped, tubular-campanulate, upper lip 3-toothed or entire, lower lip 2-toothed; corolla with short funnelform tube, upper lip 4-lobed, lower lip undivided, deflexed: fertile stamens 2, exserted, with 2 pendulous, distinct, but contiguous anther-cells; staminodes 2, small: nutlets oblong-ovoid, smooth. (After Vasili Aleksievich Perovski, governer of the Russian prov. Orenburg; 1794–?1857.) Four species from W. Asia to the Himal. and W. Tibet.

P. atriplicifòlia Benth. Upright subshrub to 1.5 m., of aromatic sage-like odor when bruised; stems hoary-tomentulose: lvs. ovate-lanceolate to lanceolate, 3–6 cm. long, acutish, unequally and coarsely serrate, pubescent at first, finally glabrescent, glandular; petiole 3–8 mm. long: fls. blue, in 2–6-fld. remote whorls in slender spikes forming terminal panicles 30–45 cm. long; 1905:344,t.(c). Gn.80:562(h);88:725. S.L.252(h). Afghan. to W. Himal. and Tibet. Cult. 1904. Zone (V). Valued chiefly for its late blue fls.

Related species: **P. scrophulariaefòlia** Bge. Brts. 4-angled, grayish tomentulose; lvs. ovate-oblong to elliptic-oblong, to 4 cm. long, obtuse, cuneate, doubly crenate-dentate, rugose above, puberulous on the veins beneath when young, glandular: fls. pink. Turkest. Cult. 1935. Zone VI.—**P. abrotanoìdes** Karel. Lvs. pinnatifid to bipinnatifid, 3–6 cm. long, segments linear, puberulous; fls. pink. Bull. Soc. Nat. Mosc. 14:t.1(c). Transcaspia to W. Himal. Cult. 1935. Zone VI.

7. SATURÈJA L. SAVORY. Herbs or subshrubs of aromatic odor: lvs. opposite, narrow and entire or broader and toothed: fls. in few- to many-fld. whorls in the axils of foliage lvs. or forming terminal panicles or racemes, calyx tubular-campanulate, 5-toothed or sometimes 2-lipped; corolla 2-lipped, the upper lip flat, emarginate or entire, the lower lip 3-parted with flat lobes, the middle one usually larger and emarginate; stamens 4; nutlets ovoid, smooth. (Ancient Latin name of the plant.) About 130 species in the warmer regions of both hemispheres.

S. montàna L. WINTER S. Half-evergreen upright subshrub, to 35 cm. of pleasant aromatic odor; stems minutely pubescent: lvs. sessile, narrow-oblong to oblanceolate, 1–2.5 cm. long, acute, the lower obtuse, entire, glandular, hispid-ciliate: floral whorls few- to many-fld., forming terminal leafy panicles; calyx setulose and glandular, campanulate, 10- or 13-nerved, with unequal subulate lobes, slightly 2-lipped; corolla white or purplish, about 1 cm. long; tube little or not exserted. Fl.vii–viii. R.I.18:t.72(c). F.D.18:t. 1800(c). S.L.338(h). Gs.6:191(h). (*Calamintha m.* Lam., *Micromeria m.* Reichenb.) S. Eu. and N. Afr. to Cauc. Cult. since ancient times. Zone VI? Chiefly grown as a pot-herb.

An American species is **S. caroliniàna** (Michx.) Briq. Subshrub to 0.6 m., fragrant; brts. puberulous: lvs. ovate or elliptic to oblong-ovate, 1–3 cm. long, obtusish, broad-cuneate, shallowly serrate: fls. axillary, 3–6; calyx 2-lipped, glabrous and glandular outside, villous inside; lower lip 2-parted with 2 subulate lobes, the upper shorter, 3-toothed; corolla white to purple, 10–12 mm. long, lobes of lower lip subequal. Fl.vii–x. B.M.997(c. as *Thymus grandiflorus*). (*Calamintha c.* Nutt., *Clinopodium carolinianum* Heller, not Mill., *C. georgianum* Harper.) N. C. to Fla. and Miss. Cult. 1807. Zone VII.

8. CONRADÌNA Gray. Shrubs: lvs. opposite, entire, revolute, crowded, often with axillary fascicles of smaller lvs.: fls. axillary in 2–6-fld. cymes; calyx 2-lipped, 13-nerved; corolla 2-lipped, tube longer than calyx, upper lip upright, entire or retuse, lower lip 3-parted, with emarginate middle lobe; stamens 4, ascending; anther-cells parallel, with a tuft of hairs at base: nutlets globose, smooth. (After Solomon W. Conrad of Philadelphia, professor of botany; 1779–1831.) Three species in s. e. U. S.

C. verticillàta Jennison. Shrub to 0.5 m.; brts. 4-angled, puberulous: lvs. linear, 1–2 cm. long, obtuse, green and glandular above, white-tomentose beneath with prominent pubescent midrib: fls. lavender; pedicels short; calyx hirsute; corolla 1.5 cm. long, pilose outside, lower lip 3-lobed, 8–10 mm. long. Fl.v. (*C. montana* Small.) Tenn. Cult. 1935. Zone VII.

9. HYSSOPUS L. HYSSOP. Subshrub of aromatic odor: lvs. opposite, narrow, entire: fls. in many-fld. whorls forming leafy spikes; calyx tubular, 15-nerved, equally 5-toothed; corolla 2-lipped, with flat lobes, upper lip 2-lobed, lower 3-lobed; stamens 4, exserted, divergent: nutlets ovoid and

slightly 3-sided, smooth. (Ancient Greek name of uncertain application.)
One Mediterranean species.

H. officinàlis L. Slender upright subshrub to 45 cm., nearly glabrous;
brts. quadrangular: lvs. subsessile, linear to oblong, 2–4 cm. long, acute or
the lower obtuse, minutely ciliate, glandular-dotted on both sides: floral
whorls in terminal secund spikes 6–12 cm. long; corolla usually blue, about
1 cm. long. Fl.vi–ix. B.M.2299(c). R.I.18:t.58(c). F.D.18:t.1812(c). Mediterr. region to C. Asia. Cult. since ancient times. Zone V. Grown chiefly as
a pot-herb.—**H. o. albus** West., var. Fls. white.—**H. o. ruber** West., var. Fls.
red. F.D.18:t.1812,f.B(c).

10. **THYMUS** L. Thyme. Small evergreen or half-evergreen shrubs and
subshrubs, of aromatic odor: lvs. opposite, small, entire: floral whorls usually
few-fld., axillary and distant or forming terminal clusters or short spikes;
calyx ovoid to cylindric, hairy in throat, 10–13-nerved, 2-lipped, upper lip
3-toothed, the lower lip cut into 2 ciliate teeth; corolla somewhat 2-lipped,
upper lip nearly flat, emarginate, the lower 3-lobed; tube exserted or included: nutlet ovoid or oblong, smooth. (Ancient Greek name.) About 35
species in Eu., W. Asia and Afr.

    A. Stems upright: lvs. tomentulose beneath....................................1. *T. vulgaris*
    AA. Stems prostrate: lvs. glabrous or slightly pubescent beneath..............2. *T. Serpyllum*

1. **T. vulgàris** L. Common T. Upright subshrub, to 20 cm. high; brs.
usually whitish pubescent: lvs. subsessile, ovate-oblong to linear, 4–15 mm.
long, tomentulose beneath, revolute: floral whorls in head-like clusters or in
interrupted spikes; pedicels slender, as long as calyx-tube; corolla lilac or
purplish, about 6 mm. long; tube little or not exserted; stamens scarcely
exserted. Fl.v–vi. R.I.18:t.63,f.1(c). F.D.18:t.1796(c). S. Eu. Cult. since
ancient times. Zone V. Grown as a pot-herb.

2. **T. Serpýllum** L. Mother-of-Thyme. Prostrate subshrub or nearly
herbaceous, cespitose or trailing, with rooting stems: ascending at the ends,
pubescent all around or on opposite sides: lvs. short-petioled, ovate or elliptic
to oblong, 5–12 mm. long, obtuse, broad-cuneate, glabrous beneath or pubescent and ciliate, floral lvs. similar: floral whorls in dense terminal heads or
the lower ones distant; calyx pubescent; corolla purplish, about 6 mm. long;
tube scarcely exserted; stamens exserted. Fl.vi–ix. R.I.18:t.63,f.2,64–67(c).
F.D.18:t.1797(c). S.St.245(h). H.B.4:7(h). Eu., W. Asia, N. Afr. Cult. for
centuries. Zone IV. Adapted for the rock garden and rocky slopes; also used
as an edging plant.—An exceedingly variable species divided into many spontaneous subspecies and varieties often considered distinct species; there are
also a number of garden forms; one of the most distinct vars. sometimes cult.
is **T. S. lanuginòsus** (Mill.) Sweet, var. Stems pubescent all around: lvs. on
both sides and infl. pubescent with long white hairs. F.D.18:t.1997,ii,f.B(c).
Gn.87:264(h). (*T. l.* Mill.)

Closely related species: **T. glàber** Mill. Stems ascending to 20 cm., without
trailing and rooting stems: lvs. oval to elliptic-oblong, 6–15 mm. long, glabrous
except sparingly ciliate at base: fls. in terminal spikes, usually 2–3 cm. long;
calyx hirsute, upper lip much shorter than lower. S.E.7;t.1044(c). H.M.5:2324.
(*T. Chamaedrys* Fries, *T. Serpyllum* subsp. *Ch.* Vollmann.) Eu. Cult. for
centuries. Zone V.

11. **ELSHOLTZIA** Willd. Herbs or subshrubs, usually aromatic: lvs.
opposite, short-petioled, serrate, often glandular-punctate: fls. small, in many-
fld. whorls forming one-sided spikes; calyx tubular or campanulate, 5-
toothed; corolla 2-lipped or slightly so, upper lip emarginate, concave, lower

3-lobed; stamens 4, usually exserted; anther-cells diverging; anterior part of disk developing into a nectary often longer than ovary: nutlets ovoid to ovoid-oblong, smooth or rugose. (After Johann Sigismund Elsholtz, Prussian physician and botanical writer; 1623–1688.) About 20 species in E. and C. Asia, south to Java; 1 in Eu. and 1 in Abyssinia.

E. Stauntòni Benth. Subshrub to 1.5 m., with terete pubescent brts.: lvs. ovate-oblong to oblong-lanceolate, 6–12 cm. long, acuminate, serrate, bright green and glabrous above, lighter green and densely glandular beneath: fls. lilac-purple, in dense one-sided spikes 10–20 cm. long, usually panicled at end of brs.; stamens and style long exserted; nutlets smooth. Fl.ix–x. B.M.8460(c). R.H.1914:60,t(c). G.C.51:21. Gn.75:533. M.G.25: 541(h),542. S.L.169(h). N. China. Intr. 1905. Zone IV. Chiefly valued for its late-appearing profusely produced spikes of lilac-purple fls.

Related species: **E. fruticòsa** (D. Don) Rehd. Subshrub to 2 m.: lvs. ellipticoblong to lanceolate, pubescent on the veins beneath and glandular: fls. white, in slender spikes 5–14 cm. long. L.B.487(c). Wallich, Pl. As. Rar. 1:t.33(c). (*E. polystachya* Benth.) Himal., W. China. Intr. about 1903? Zone VII?

12. **PLECTRÁNTHUS** L'Hérit. Herbs, subshrubs or shrubs: lvs. opposite, usually toothed: fls. mostly small, in axillary loose cymes, spikes or panicles, rarely in dense whorls; calyx campanulate, equally 5-toothed or 2-lipped, enlarged in fr.; corolla-tube exserted, often gibbous or spurred, curved or straight, upper lip 3–4-lobed, lower lip elongated, entire; stamens 4, free, spreading along the lower lip; disk on the anterior side elongated, longer than ovaries: nutlets ovoid or oblong, smooth or punctulate. (Greek *plēktron*, spur, and *anthos*, flower.) About 100 species in trop. and subtrop regions of Afr., Asia and Austral.

P. díscolor Dunn. Shrub to 1 m.; brts. slender, 4-angled, puberulous at first: lvs. ovate, 6–15 mm. long, obtuse, rounded or broad-cuneate at base, crenulate or dentate to entire, minutely puberulous above, white-tomentose beneath; petiole 1–4 mm. long: cymes few-fld.; peduncle longer than petiole; pedicels 2–3 mm. long; calyx campanulate, 10-nerved, tomentulose; corolla 6–8 mm. long, pale lavender, tube gibbous at base, longer than limb, upper lip upright, 3-lobed, lower spreading; stamens slightly exserted. Fl.vii–x. (*P. parvifolius* (Batal.) P'ei, not Talbot.) W. China. Intr. 1911. Zone VI?

Fam. 103. **SOLANACEAE** Pers. NIGHTSHADE FAMILY

Herbs or shrubs, sometimes climbing, or small trees: lvs. usually alternate, entire or toothed to pinnate, exstipulate: fls. mostly perfect and regular, solitary or cymose, often seemingly extra-axillary; calyx 5-lobed; corolla rotate or campanulate to tubular, sometimes irregular, the 5 lobes valvate or plicate in bud; stamens usually as many as corolla-lobes, often connivent by their anthers, sometimes 1 or more sterile; ovary superior, usually with a disk at base, mostly 2-celled, with usually many ovules on axile placentae; style 1; stigma simple or lobed: fr. a berry or caps.; seeds albuminous, rarely without albumen; embryo straight or curved.—About 75 genera and more than 2000 species in trop. and temp. regions of both hemispheres.

A. Corolla rotate; anthers connivent around the stigma: climbing plant..........1. *Solanum*
AA. Corolla salverform; anthers distinct: upright or sarmentose shrubs.
   B. Stamens exceeding the tube: brs. often spiny...............................2. *Lycium*
   BB. Stamens included: brs. unarmed..3. *Cestrum*

1. **SOLÀNUM** L. NIGHTSHADE. Herbs or shrubs, many climbing, sometimes trees: brs. sometimes spiny: lvs. alternate, simple or compound: infl.

mostly supra-axillary or opposite the lvs., cymose, rarely fls. solitary; calyx
5-10-toothed or -parted, persistent; corolla rotate or shallow-campanulate,
the lobes plicate in bud, variously colored, often showy; stamens 5, with
short filaments, inserted on the throat of the corolla; anthers connivent,
opening at apex by a pore or short slit; ovary usually 2-celled, many-ovuled:
fr. a berry. (Ancient Latin name, probably from *solari*, to quiet; referring
to its medicinal properties.) More than 1200 species chiefly in trop. and
subtrop. regions of both hemispheres.

S. Dulcamàra L. BITTER-SWEET (CLIMBING NIGHTSHADE) Suffruticose
climber, to 2.5 m.; brts. glabrous or pubescent: lvs. entire, ovate to ovate-
oblong, or with 1–3 pairs of lobes at base, 4–10 cm. long, acuminate, usually
cordate, bright green and usually sparingly pubescent; petiole 1–3 cm. long:
fls. violet in long-peduncled cymes; corolla-lobes oblong-lanceolate, reflexed,
with 2 green spots near base: fr. ovoid, about 1 cm. long, scarlet. Fl.vi–viii;
fr.viii–x. S.O.3:t.146(c). R.I.20:t.12,f.1,2(c). F.D.16:t.1600(c). Eu., N. Afr.
to E. Asia; often naturalized in N. Am. Cult. 1561. Zone IV. The scarlet
frs. are conspicuous and ornamental, but poisonous.—**S. D. album** West., var.
Fls. white.—**S. D. variegàtum** West., var. Lvs. variegated with white.—**S. D.
villosíssimum** Desv., var. Brts. and lvs. densely pubescent. (*S. D.* var. *lito-
rale* (Raab) Brand, var. *tomentosum* Koch.)—**S. D. indivìsum** Boiss., var.
All lvs. undivided, ovate-oblong: fr. larger. (*S. persicum* Roem. & Schult.,
S. D. var. *p.* Dipp.)

2. LÝCIUM L. BOX-THORN.

Deciduous or evergreen shrubs, thorny or
unarmed; winter-buds small, superposed, with few outer scales: lvs. alternate, often fascicled, short-petioled, entire: fls. axillary, solitary or clustered,
usually slender-stalked; calyx campanulate, 5-toothed or irregularly 3–5-
toothed; corolla funnelform or salver-shaped, with usually 5-lobed limb;
stamens usually 5, usually exserted; ovary 2-celled: fr. a berry with few to
many seeds, usually red. (*Lykion*, ancient Greek name for a thorny shrub.)
About 100 species in temp. and subtrop. regions of both hemispheres.—Ornamental shrubs chiefly valued for their showy scarlet berries.

  A. Fls. violet or purplish; limb not less than ½ as long as tube; filaments pubescent at base.
    B. Lvs. and brts. glabrous; calyx-teeth short and irregular.
      c. Corolla-tube shorter than limb, rather wide: lvs. rhombic-ovate to ovate-lanceolate.
                                   1. *L. chinense*
      cc. Corolla-tube longer than limb, narrowed below the middle: lvs. usually lanceolate.
                                2. *L. halimifolium*
    B. Lvs. and brts. puberulous: corolla-tube shorter than limb; calyx-lobes 5, lanceolate.
                                3. *L. Grevilleanum*
  AA. Fls. greenish white; limb about ⅓ as long as tube; filaments glabrous.....4. *L. pallidum*

1. L. chinénse Mill. CHINESE MATRIMONY-VINE. Rambling shrub with
arching and often prostrate brs. to 4 m. long, usually unarmed; brts. light
yellowish gray: lvs. rhombic-ovate to ovate-lanceolate, 3–8 cm. long, acute
or obtusish, broad- to narrow-cuneate, bright green; petioles rarely exceeding
1 cm.: fls. 1–4; pedicels 3–8, rarely 12 mm. long; calyx 3–5-toothed, usually
divided less than ½, with acute lobes; corolla purple, about 1 cm. long: fr.
ovoid to oblong, 1.5–2.5 cm. long, scarlet to orange-red. Fl.vi–ix; fr.viii–x.
R.I.20:t.14,f.2,3(c). G.F.4:102. N.D.1:t.30(c). F.E.28:641(h). G.W.15:346
(h). (*L. barbarum* Lour., not L.) E. Asia. Intr. before 1709. Zone IV.
Handsome with its long brs. laden with scarlet fr.: lvs. remaining green until
very late in fall.—**L. ch. ovàtum** (Poir.) Schneid., var. Lvs. rhombic-ovate,
to 10 cm. long; fr. very obtuse and impressed at apex, large. (*L. rhombifolium*
Dipp., *L. ch.* var. *rh.* Bean.)

2. **L. halimifòlium** Mill. COMMON MATRIMONY-VINE. Upright or spreading shrub with arching or recurving brs., to 3 m., usually spiny; brts. light gray: lvs. oblong-lanceolate to lanceolate, rarely elliptic-lanceolate, 2–6 cm. long, acute or obtusish, narrowed into a slender petiole 5–20 mm. long, grayish green, thickish: fls. 1–4; pedicels 8–20 mm. long; calyx usually 1–3-lobed, divided about ½, with obtuse lobes: corolla dull lilac-purple: fr. ovoid or short-oblong, 1–2 cm. long, scarlet to orange-red. Fl.vi–ix; fr.viii–x. R.I.20: t.14,f.1,2(c). F.D.16:t.1595(c). B.B.3:168. (*L. barbarum* Ait., not L., *L. vulgare* Dun., *L. flaccidum* K. Koch.) S. E. Eu. to W. Asia; sometimes escaped from cult. Long cult. Zone IV. Sometimes used for hedges.—**L. h. lanceolàtum** (Poir.) Schneid., var. Lvs. lanceolate: fr. ellipsoid. N.D.1:t. 32(c)—**L. h. subglobòsum** (Dun.) Schneid., var. Dwarfer: lvs. lanceolate: fr. subglobose.

Related species: **L. turcománicum** Turcz. Slender spiny shrub: lvs. lanceolate, 2–7 cm. long, thickish, with obsolete veins: fls. short-stalked, pink, small, with slender tube nearly twice as long as limb; calyx irregularly 5-toothed: fr. small, globose, red. Miers, Ill. S. Am. Pl. 2:t.69E. Turkest. Intr. before 1890. Zone V?—**L. ruthènicum** Murr. Upright spiny shrub: lvs. linear or linear-lanceolate, 1–3 cm. long, thickish: fls. about 1.2 cm. long; calyx usually 3-toothed with broad obtuse teeth: fr. black. Intr. 1804. Miers. Ill. S. Am. Pl. 2:t.70A. D.H.1:27. S. Russia to Persia and W. Siberia. Intr. 1804. Zone VI?—*L. barbarum* L. and *L. europaeum* L. which are not hardy within our area are sometimes confused with *L. halimifolium*, but are easily distinguished by the glabrous filaments and the narrower and smaller lvs. and the second also by the slenderer corolla-tube.

3. **L. Grevilleànum** Miers. Much-branched shrub to 2 m., with unarmed spreading or decumbent brs.; brts. puberulous when young: lvs. obovate to oblanceolate, 1–2 cm. long, on vigorous shoots to 5 cm. long, narrow-cuneate, ciliate and puberulous, rather fleshy: fls. solitary or 2, about 1 cm. across; calyx-teeth lanceolate, ciliate; corolla funnelform, yellowish white, with purplish limb, lobes longer than tube; filaments hairy at base: fr. globose, about 8 mm. across, orange-red. Fl.vi–viii. Miers, Ill. S. Am. Pl. 2:t.73F. S.H. 2:f.396h-k. Argentine. Cult. 1890. Zone VII?

The similar **L. chilénse** Bert. differs chiefly in its glandular pubescence and the broader more obtuse lvs. and is still tenderer. Chile.

4. **L. pállidum** Miers. Much branched upright shrub to 2 m., with spreading, often tortuous, spiny brs.: lvs. partly fascicled, lanceolate to oblanceolate, 1.5–5 cm. long, narrow-cuneate, glaucous, somewhat fleshy: fls. 1 or 2, nodding; calyx-lobes 5, triangular-ovate, acute: corolla funnelform, about 2 cm. long, greenish yellow, tinged purplish, tube about 3 times as long as the short rounded lobes: fr. subglobose, 1.2 cm. across, scarlet, usually sparingly produced. Fl.v–vi; fr.vii–viii. B.M.8440(c). G.C.46:232. G.F.1:341. B.S.2:63. M.G.23:209. S. Utah to N. Mex. and Mex. Cult. 1878. Zone (V). Distinct shrub, attractive in bloom.

3. **CESTRUM** L. Deciduous or evergreen shrubs or small trees: lvs. simple and entire: fls. in axillary or terminal cymes; calyx 5-toothed, short; corolla salver-shaped, variously colored, with long slender tube, enlarged or contracted at the mouth, with short spreading limb; stamens inserted about the middle of the tube, included; ovary 2-celled, with 3–6 ovules in each cell; style slender: fr. a few- or 1-seeded small berry; seed albuminous. (*Kestron*, Greek plant name of uncertain application.) About 150 species in trop. and subtrop. Am.

C. Parqui L'Hérit. WILLOW-LEAVED JESSAMINE. Upright shrub to 2 m., glabrous: lvs. lanceolate, 5–14 cm. long, acuminate, cuneate, bright green,

slightly paler beneath; petiole 5–10 mm. long: fls. in axillary and terminal
cymes forming panicles at end of brs.; corolla yellowish green, fragrant at
night; tube slender, dilated at mouth, about 2 cm. long, with spreading acute
lobes: fr. violet-brown, 3–4-seeded. Fl.vii–ix. B.M.1770(c). S.O.3:t.133(c).
Chile. Intr. 1787. Zone VII. Grown chiefly for its fragrant fls.; when killed
to the ground the young shoots will bloom the same season.

Fam. 104. **SCROPHULARIACEAE** Lindl. FIGWORT FAMILY

Herbs, shrubs or trees: lvs. alternate, opposite or verticillate, exstipulate:
fls. perfect, usually irregular, in cymes, racemes or panicles, or solitary and
axillary: calyx 4–5-toothed or -parted: corolla rotate to campanulate, or with
cylindric tube, 4–5-lobed with subequal lobes or 2-lipped; stamens usually
4, didynamous, inserted on the corolla-tube, sometimes 2 or 5; ovary superior,
perfectly or imperfectly 2-celled, with central placentae and usually many
ovules: fr. a caps. or berry; seeds albuminous.—About 180 genera and 3000
species widely distributed in both hemispheres.

A. Stamens 4.
  B. Lvs. not exceeding 6 cm., usually narrow: low shrubs or subshrubs: caps. septicidal.
                                                                   1. *Penstemon*
  BB. Lvs. large and broad: trees: caps. loculicidal..............................2. *Paulownia*
AA. Stamens 2.
  B. Caps. loculicidal, laterally compressed: subshrubs or herbs.................3. *Veronica*
  BB. Caps. septicidal, dorsally compressed or turgid: evergreen shrubs or trees......4. *Hebe*

1. **PENSTEMON** Schmidel. Perennial herbs or small shrubs: lvs. opposite or whorled, the lower ones petioled, upper sessile, entire or serrate: fls. in
terminal racemes or panicles; calyx 5-parted, with imbricated segments;
corolla tubular, usually dilated at throat, 2-lipped, upper lip 2-lobed, lower
3-lobed; fertile stamens 4, the 5th sterile and sometimes bearded; style filiform, with capitate stigma: fr. a septicidally dehiscent caps., with numerous
wingless seeds. (Greek *pente*, five, and *stemon*, stamen; the 5th stamen being
present, though sterile.) Syn.: *Pentstemon* Ait., *Pentastemon* Batsch. About
150 species in N. Am. and Mex., one in E. Asia.—Handsome low shrubs or
subshrubs best suited for well-drained positions in the rock garden.

A. Anther-cells opening their whole length or nearly their whole length, diverging: lvs.
   usually serrate.
  B. Corolla blue, purple or yellowish, shallowly 2-lipped, with funnelform tube.
    c. Anthers bearded: infl. racemose............................Sect. ERIANTHERA Benth.
      D. Lvs. lanceolate to oblong, acute, rarely obtuse: stems upright or ascending.
                                                                   1. *P. Scouleri*
        DD. Lvs. oval, to suborbicular or spatulate, obtuse: stems procumbent.2. *P. Menziesii*
      cc. Anthers glabrous or ciliate: infl. paniculate..............Sect. EUPENTSTEMON Benth.
                                                                   2. *P. Lemmoni*
  BB. Corolla scarlet, tubular and strongly 2-lipped....................Sect. ELMIGERA Benth.
                                                                   3. *P. cordifolius*
AA. Anther-cells opening only on the upper part by short confluent slits, horseshoe-shaped:
   lvs. entire ....Sect. SACCANTHERA Benth.
                                                                   4. *P. heterophyllus*

1. **P. Scouleri** Dougl. Shrub with upright or ascending stems, 20–50 cm.
tall; young brts. puberulous: lvs. lanceolate to spatulate or linear-lanceolate,
2–4 cm. long, acute, narrowed into a short petiole, sharply serrulate except at
base: racemes 5–11-fld., sparingly and minutely glandular-pubescent; sepals
subulate-lanceolate, 1–1.5 cm. long, glandular-hairy; corolla tubular-funnelform, lilac-purple, 3.5–4 cm. long; sterile filament long and glabrous. Fl.v–vii.
B.M.6834(c). B.R.1277(c). D.H.1:41. G.C.III.7:204;65:39(h). (*P. Men-
ziessii* var. *Scouleri* Gray.) B. C. to Idaho and n. Calif. Intr. 1828. Zone V.
  Related species: **P. fruticosus** (Pursh) Greene. Upright shrub to 1 m.: lvs.
obovate or elliptic-oblong to lanceolate, obtuse or acute, serrulate: corolla

purple, about 3 cm. long; sepals lanceolate, 5–10 mm. long. Wash. and Ore. to Wyo. and Mont. Cult. 1924. Zone V?—**P. f. crassifòlius** (Lindl.) Krautter, var. Lvs. narrower, entire or nearly so. B.R.24:16(c). (*P. c.* Lindl.) Wash. to Wyo. and Mont. Cult. 1838. Zone V?

2. **P. Menzièsii** Hook. Suffruticose, with procumbent stem and ascending brs. to 20 cm. high: lvs. obovate to broad-spatulate or suborbicular, 5–15 mm. long, obtuse or rounded at apex, dentate, thickish: racemes 3–7-fld.; calyx 8 mm. long, slightly viscid, lobes lanceolate; sterile filament short, sometimes hairy. Henshaw, Mtn. Wild Fl. Am. t.70. B. C. to Alb. and Wash. Cult. 1902. Zone V.

Related species: **P. Davidsónii** Greene. Lvs. obovate or elliptic, 6–10 mm. long, entire: racemes 1–5-fld.: corolla 2.5 cm. long, lilac-purple. (*P. Menziesii* D. Piper.) N. Calif. Cult. 1898. Zone VII?—**P. Cardwéllii** Howell. Subshrub to 30 cm.: lvs. elliptic-ovate to lanceolate, 1–2.5 cm. long, serrate, petioled, the upper sessile and oval to obovate: sepals narrow-lanceolate; corolla purple, 2.5–3.5 cm. long. (*P. fruticosus* C. Piper.) Ore. Cult. 1930. Zone VI.—**P. Newbérryi** Gray. Subshrub to 40 cm.; lvs. ovate-elliptic to elliptic or ovate-oblong, 1–3 cm. long, acute or acutish, serrulate: sepals lanceolate, long-acuminate; corolla rosy-purple or carmine, 2–3 cm. long. G.C.1872:969. B.C.5:2539. (*P. Menziesii* var. *N.* Gray.) Wash. to Calif. Cult. 1872. Zone VI?

3. **P. Lémmoni** Gray. Upright shrub to 1 m.: lvs. subsessile, the pairs distant, ovate to oblong-lanceolate, 1–3 cm. long, acute, subcordate or truncate, serrulate: infl. paniculate; axis and peduncles glabrous; sepals ovate-lanceolate, like pedicels glandular-hairy; corolla 1.2 cm. long, pinkish yellow, upper lip red-violet inside, lower lip striped red-violet. Calif. Cult. 1898. Zone VII?

4. **P. cordifòlius** Benth. Sarmentose shrub; brts. obscurely quadrangular: lvs. short-petioled, ovate, 2–5 cm. long, acute, cordate to truncate, serrate or denticulate: fls. in glandular-hairy terminal panicles; sepals ovate-lanceolate, glandular-hairy; corolla scarlet; tube straight, 2–2.5 cm. long; limb 1.2 cm. long, upper lip erect, lower deflexed. Fl.vi–viii. B.M.4497(c). G.C.70:102. Calif. Intr. 1848. Zone VII?

Related species: **P. corymbòsus** Benth. Upright shrub to 50 cm.: lvs. elliptic to oblong, 1.2–2.5 cm. long, obtusish, cuneate or broad-cuneate, dentate, often obscurely so: fls. in corymbiform racemes. Calif. Cult. 1898. Zone VII?

5. **P. heterophýllus** Lindl. Upright shrub to 1.5 m., with slender brs.; glabrous: lvs. sessile or subsessile, lanceolate to linear, 2–6 cm. long, acute, narrow-cuneate: racemes elongated, sometimes paniculate at base, usually many-fld.; pedicels 3–10 mm. long; sepals ovate, acuminate, 3–4 mm. long, glabrous; corolla purple to lilac, 2.5–3 cm. long, both lips slightly recurving, tube much narrowed below the middle. Fl.vi–vii. B.M.3853(c). B.R.1899(c). Calif. Intr. 1828. Zone VII?

Related species: **P. Bridgèsii** Gray. Subshrub to 60 cm.: lvs. spatulate to linear, obtuse or acutish, petioled, the upper sessile: fls. in panicles; sepals glandular-pubescent; corolla scarlet, tube 2.5 cm. long, slightly narrowed below the middle, upper lip erect. Calif. to Ariz. and Utah. Cult. 1898. Zone VII?

2. **PAULÒWNIA** Sieb. & Zucc. Deciduous trees; winter-buds with several outer scales, superposed: lvs. opposite, petioled, entire or shallowly lobed, toothed on young plants: fls. in terminal panicles; calyx deeply 5-lobed; corolla tubular-funnelform, with spreading oblique 5-lobed limb; stamens 4, with distinct spreading anther-cells, sterile stamen wanting: caps. loculicidally dehiscent by 2 valves; seeds very numerous, small, winged. (After Anna Paulowna, princess of the Netherlands; 1795–1865.) About 10 species in China.

P. tomentòsa (Thunb.) Steud. Paulownia. Round-headed tree to 15 m.,
with stout spreading brs.; brts. densely soft-pubescent when young, becoming glabrous: lvs. broad-ovate to ovate, 12–25 cm. long, or on vigorous shoots
to 50 cm. long, acuminate, cordate, entire or sometimes shallowly 3-lobed,
pubescent above, densely so or tomentose beneath; petiole 8–20 cm. long:
panicle pyramidal, 20–30 cm. long; calyx broad-campanulate, with 5 ovate
obtuse lobes, rusty-tomentose like the pedicels; corolla funnelform-campanulate, 5–6 cm. long, pale violet, with darker spots and yellow stripes inside,
glandular-pubescent outside; caps. ovoid, beaked, 3–4 cm. long, woody. Fl.
iv–v; fr.ix–xi. S.Z.1:t.10(c). B.M.4666(c). G.C.51:430(h),431;56:150. Gn.60:
130;80:406(h). (*P. imperialis* Sieb. & Zucc.) China, cult. in Japan; escaped
in the E. States from s. N. Y. to Ga. Intr. 1834. Zone (V). Strikingly handsome in spring with its large violet slightly fragrant fls. appearing just before
the lvs.; the fl.-buds which are formed the previous season often winter-killed
in the N. The large lvs. are also a prominent feature of the tree.—**P. t.
pállida** (Dode) Schneid., var. Fls. pale, whitish violet: lvs. dull green above.
(*P. t. flore albo* Hort.)—**P. t. lanàta** (Dode) Schneid., var. Lvs. more densely
yellowish tomentose beneath; calyx more tomentose, with longer acutish
lobes. G.C.72:167(h). Intr. 1908.

Related species: **P. coreàna** Uyeki. Similar to *P. tomentosa:* lvs. remotely
serrate or entire, fulvous-tomentose beneath: corolla violet, without darker
spots, yellow in throat. Bull. Agr. For. Coll. Suigen, 1:t.16(c). M.D.1932:t.53(h).
Korea. Intr. 1928. Zone VI?—**P. lilacina** Sprague. Lvs. never lobed, less pubescent beneath: upper calyx-lobe obtuse, the others apiculate or acute; corolla
pale violet, striped pale yellow in throat, with wide-spreading, strongly 2-lipped
limb. B.M.8927(c). G.C.86:51 (as *P. Fargesii*). ? W. China. Cult. 1908. Zone
VI?—**P. Fargèsi** Franch. Tree to 20 m.; bark smooth; young brts. usually pilose
or villous, soon glabrous: lvs. smaller, sparingly pubescent and glandular above,
slightly pubescent beneath, entire or with few coarse teeth; panicle smaller;
calyx tomentose with triangular acutish lobes; corolla whitish or lavender,
slightly pubescent or glabrescent outside, 6 cm. long. W. China. Intr. about
1896. Zone VII?

3. **VERÒNICA** L. Speedwell. Herbs or subshrubs: lvs. opposite, rarely
alternate or whorled, the floral lvs. often alternate: fls. in terminal or axillary
racemes, sometimes solitary and axillary; calyx 4–5-parted; corolla with
usually short tube and spreading 4–5-lobed limb, the lateral lobes or the lower
usually narrower; stamens 2, exserted: caps. compressed, usually obtuse or
emarginate, 2-grooved, loculicidally dehiscent; seeds few to many. (Probably named in honor of St. Veronica, or possibly misprint for Betonica.)
About 150 species in the colder and temperate regions of both hemispheres.

V. frúticans Jacq. Procumbent, with ascending pubescent stems, to 20
cm. high, woody only at base: lvs. elliptic to oblong, 6–12 mm. long, crenulate or entire, glabrous: racemes 2–6-fld.; corolla blue, 1.2 cm. across; sepals
elliptic, pubescent, eglandular: caps. ovoid, scarcely emarginate. Fls.vii–viii.
R.I.20:t.96,f.1,2(c). F.D.17:t.1649(c). E.P.IV:3b84. (*V. saxatilis* Scop.) Eu.
Intr. 1768. Zone V.

Closely related species: **V. fruticulòsa** L. Stems finely strigillose: lvs. oblong,
1–2 cm. long, obtuse, crenulate, sparingly hairy, finally glabrous, ciliolate: fls.
pink, in loose racemes: sepals glandular-pubescent. R.I.20:t.96:f.3(c). F.D.17:
t.1648(c). (*V. frutescens* Scop.) S. Eu. Cult. 1796.

4. **HÈBE** Commers. ex Juss. Evergreen shrubs or trees; brts. with conspicuous lf.-scars: lvs. opposite, coriaceous, entire, rarely serrate: fls. in axillary racemes; calyx 4-, rarely 3- or 5-parted; corolla-tube longer or shorter
than calyx, spreading limb, 4-, rarely 3- or 5-6-lobed; stamens 2, exserted;

1. BIGNÒNIA L. Evergreen high climbing vine: lvs. opposite, 2-foliolate, the rachis ending in a branched tendril clinging by small disks: fls. in axillary cymes; calyx campanulate, shallowly 5-lobed or truncate; corolla funnelform-campanulate, with spreading, slightly 2-lipped limb; stamens 4, included, inserted near base of corolla: disk annular; ovary linear, many-ovuled: caps. linear, flattened parallel to the partition, septifragally dehiscent, with leathery valves; seeds elliptic, winged. (After Abbé Jean Paul Bignon, court librarian to Louis XIV; 1662–1743.) Syn.: *Anisostichus* Bur., *Doxantha* Schum., Miers in part. One species in N. Am.

B. capreolàta L. CROSS-VINE. Climbing to 20 m.; glabrous: petiole 1–2 cm. long: lfts. 2, stalked, oblong-ovate to oblong-lanceolate, 5–15 cm. long, obtusely acuminate, cordate, entire: cymes short-stalked, 2–5-fld., pedicels 2–4 cm. long: corolla red-orange, lighter within, 4–5 cm. long, lobes rounded, about ¼ as long as tube: caps. 10–17 cm. long, compressed. Fl.v–vi. B.M. 864(c). Gng.1:370–1. (*Doxantha c.* Miers, *Anisostichus c.* Bur., *B. crucigera* L., partly.—TRUMPET-FLOWER, QUARTER-VINE.) Va. and S. Ill. to Fla. and La. Cult. 1653. Zone (V). With showy large fls.—**B. c. atrosanguinea** Hook. f., var. Lfts. longer and narrower; fls. dark red-purple. B.M.6501(c).

2. ECCREMOCÁRPUS Ruiz & Pav. Vines climbing by tendrils or twining: lvs. opposite, pinnate or bipinnate: fls. yellow, orange or scarlet, in terminal racemes; calyx campanulate, with 5 valvate lobes; corolla with elongated tube and small, 5-lobed or 2-lipped limb; stamens 4, included; disk annular: caps. ovoid or ellipsoid, 1-celled, loculicidal; seeds orbicular, with broad wing. (Greek *ekkrĕmes*, pendulous, and *karpos*, fruit.) Three or 4 species in Peru and Chile.

E. scáber Ruiz & Pav. Climbing to 4 m.; glabrous; stems grooved: lvs. bipinnate, the primary pinnae with 3–7 lfts.; lfts. ovate to oblong-ovate, 8–30 mm. long, acute or obtuse, often cordate, entire or serrate: racemes 10–15 cm. long; corolla orange-red, 2–2.5 cm. long, tubular, ventricose above the middle, constricted at mouth, with small rounded lobes: caps. 3–3.5 cm. long. Fl.vi–ix. B.M.6408(c). B.R.939(c). S.H.2:f.405a–g. (*Calampelis scabra* Don.) Chile. Intr. 1824. Zone VII. With showy fls. in summer; where it is not hardy, it may be treated as an annual or perennial.

3. CAMPSIS Lour. TRUMPET-CREEPER. Deciduous shrubs usually climbing by aërial rootlets: lvs. opposite, odd-pinnate; lfts. serrate: fls. orange to scarlet, in terminal cymes or panicles; calyx tubular-campanulate, 5-lobed; corolla funnelform, enlarged above the calyx, with large, spreading, 5-lobed, oblique limb, lobes rounded; stamens 4, didynamous, included: ovary 2-celled, with large disk at base: caps. elongated, stipitate, loculicidally dehiscent, with leathery valves separating from the septum; seeds numerous, compressed, with 2 large wings. (Greek *kampsis*, curvature; referring to the curved stamens.) One species in N. Am. and 1 in E. Asia.

A. Lfts. pubescent beneath at least along the midrib: calyx-teeth short, triangular-ovate.
1. *C. radicans*
AA. Lfts. glabrous beneath: calyx 5-lobed to the middle.....................2. *C. grandiflora*

1. C. radìcans (L.) Seem. TRUMPET-VINE. Climbing to 10 m. or more, with aërial rootlets: lfts. 9–11, short-stalked, elliptic to ovate-oblong, 3–6 cm. long, acuminate, cuneate, serrate: fls. usually orange outside, with scarlet limb; calyx-lobes triangular, much shorter than the tube; corolla tubular-funnelform, 6–9 cm. long, the tube almost 3 times as long as the calyx, limb 4–5 cm. broad: caps. cylindric-oblong, 8–12 cm. long, beaked, keeled along the sutures. Fl.vii–ix. B.M.485(c). M.N.II.2:t.1(c). B.C.2:651. (*Bignonia r.* L., *Tecoma r.* Juss.—TRUMPET-HONEYSUCKLE.) Pa. to Mo., Fla. and Tex. Intr. 1640. Zone IV. Firmly clinging to walls and tree-trunks; with large brilliantly colored fls. in summer.—**C. r. praècox** (Jaeg.) Schneid., f. Fls. scarlet, appearing in June.—**C. r. flàva** (Bosse) Rehd., f. Fls. orange-yellow. (*C. r.* var. *aurea* Rehd., *T. r.* var. *lutea* Kirchn.) Cult. 1842.—**C. r. speciòsa** (Parsons) Rehd., var. Scarcely climbing, usually a bush with long slender stems: lfts. smaller, elliptic, abruptly long-acuminate: fls. orange-red, with rather straight tube, limb about 3 cm. across.

2. **C. grandiflòra** (Thunb.) Loisel. CHINESE T. Climbing, with few or no aërial rootlets: lfts. 7–9, ovate to ovate-lanceolate, 3–6 cm. long, acuminate, serrate, glabrous: fls. in larger and looser terminal cymes or panicles; corolla scarlet, funnelform-campanulate, shorter and broader; tube little or not exceeding the lanceolate calyx-lobes, limb 7–8 cm. across: caps. obtuse at apex. Fl.viii–ix. B.M.1398(c). N.T.1:496. Gn.47:373. G.F.3:393. B.C.2: 652. (*Bignonia chinensis* Lam., *Tecoma c.* K. Koch, *C. ch.* Voss.) China, cult. in Japan. Intr. 1800. Zone VII? Less high climbing and showier than the preceding species; blooms when quite small.—**C. g. Thunbérgii** (Carr.) Rehd., f. Fls. orange, with very short tube and reflexed lobes. (*Tecoma T.* Sieb.)

C. g. × *radicans* = **C. Tagliabuàna** (Vis.) Rehd. Intermediate: lfts. 7–11, usually pubescent on the veins beneath: fls. in loose panicles; calyx divided about ⅓ into acuminate lobes much shorter than the corolla-tube; corolla about 8 cm. long and 5–6 cm. across. S.T.1:t.47. M.G.19:123. (*C. hybrida* Zab., *T. intermedia* Schelle, *Bignonia Princei grandiflora* Hort., *B. radicans grandiflora atropurpurea* Hort.) Orig. before 1858. Zone (V). Almost as showy as No. 2, harlier.

4. **CATÁLPA** Scop. Deciduous, rarely evergreen trees; winter-buds with several outer scales, terminal bud wanting: lvs. opposite, sometimes whorled, long-petioled, entire or coarsely lobed, 3–5-veined at base, usually with purple glandular spot in the axils of the veins beneath: fls. in terminal panicles or racemes; calyx irregularly splitting or 2-lipped; corolla campanulate, 2-lipped, with 2 small upper and 3 larger lower lobes; fertile stamens 2, included; style slightly longer than stamens: caps. cylindric, very long and narrow, separating into 2 valves, with numerous oblong seeds bearing a tuft of long white hairs on each end. (The Indian name of the tree.) About 10 species in N. Am., the West Indies and in E. Asia.

A. Fls. yellowish, 1.5–2 cm. long: lvs. usually lobed and usually nearly glabrous beneath.
                                                                        1. *C. ovata*
AA. Fls. white or rosy pink, 3–5 cm. long: lvs. not or rarely lobed.
  B. Infl. glabrous: lvs. glabrous beneath or pubescent with simple hairs.
    c. Lvs. pubescent beneath, to 30 cm. long: fls. in a large panicle.
      D. Lvs. abruptly acuminate: fls. 4–5 cm. across; panicle many-fld..2. *C. bignonioides*
      DD. Lvs. long-acuminate; fls. about 6 cm. across: panicle several-fld....3. *C. speciosa*
    cc. Lvs. quite glabrous beneath, to 15 cm. long: fls. in a 3–12-fld. raceme..4. *C. Bungei*
  BB. Infl. pubescent: lvs. tomentose or densely pubescent beneath, with branched hairs.
                                                                        5. *C. Fargesi*

1. **C. ovàta** Don. Tree to 10, or sometimes to 15 m., with spreading brs.; brts. glabrous, rarely sparingly hirsute: lvs. broad-ovate, 10–25 cm. long, abruptly acuminate, often shallowly 3–5-lobed, with broad abruptly acuminate lobes, dull green above, light green beneath and pubescent on the veins and veinlets or nearly glabrous; petiole 6–14 cm. long: panicle pyramidal, 10–25 cm. long: fls. yellowish white, striped orange inside and spotted dark violet: pod 20–30 cm. long, about 8 mm. wide. Fl.v. B.M.6611(c). S.I.2: t.71(c). L.I.t.10. (*C. Kaempferi* Sieb., *C. Henryi* Dode.) China, cult. in

Japan. Intr. 1849. Zone IV.—**C. o. flavéscens** Bean, var. Fls. yellow. Cult. 1879.

2. **C. bignonioìdes** Walt. Common C. Tree to 15, rarely 20 m. tall, with widespreading brs. forming a broad roundish head; bark light brown, separating into thin scales: lvs. often whorled, ovate, 10–20 cm. long, abruptly acuminate, truncate to subcordate at base, sometimes with a pair of small lobes, light green and nearly glabrous above, pubescent beneath, especially on the veins, of unpleasant odor when crushed; petiole 8–16 cm. long; panicle broad-pyramidal 15–20 cm. high; fls. 4–5 cm. across, white, with 2 yellow stripes inside and thickly spotted purple-brown, with oblique limb and entire lower lobes: fr. 20–40 cm. long, 6–8 mm. thick, with thin walls. Fl.vi-vii. B.M. 1094(c). L.B.1285(c). S.S.6:t.288–9. G.C.44:10,t(h),312,t(h). B.S.1:312,t(h). G.F.3:537,539. (*C. Catalpa* Karst., *C. syringaefolia* Sims, *C. cordifolia* Moench.) Ga. to Fla. and Miss.; naturalized n. to N. Y. Intr. 1726. Zone IV. Handsome tree, very showy when in bloom.—**C. b. aùrea** Bur., var. Lvs. yellow. G.M.53:709.—**C. b. Koèhnei** Dode, var. Lvs. yellow with a dark green blotch below the middle and green veins. G.W.19:445.—**C. b. nàna** Bur., var. Dwarf; usually grafted high and forming a standard with dense broad head. Gng.3:195(h). M.G.18:616. (*C. Bungei* Hort., not C. A. Mey.)

C. b. × *ovata* = **C. hýbrida** Spaeth. Hybrid C. Intermediate; lvs. resembling more those of *C. ovata* and purplish when unfolding, larger and usually more pubescent beneath, the fls. more like those of *C. bignonioides*, but smaller. Gt.47:t.1454(c). G.F.2:305. G.W.3:569(h). Jour. Hered. 11:16–24. (*C. Teasii* Penh., *C. Teasiana* Dode.) Orig. about 1874. Handsome floriferous tree of rapid growth.—**C. h. japónica** (Dode) Rehd., var. Lvs. broader and more abruptly acuminate, nearly glabrous beneath. (*C. j.* Dode.) B.D.1907:198.—**C. h. purpúrea** (Rehd.) Rehd., var. Young lvs. and shoots dark purple, nearly black when quite young, becoming finally green. (*C. h. atropurpurea* Spaeth, *C. ovata* var. *purpurea* Bean.)

3. **C. speciòsa** Warder. Western C. Tree to 30 m., of pyramidal habit; bark red-brown, broken into thick scales: lvs. ovate to ovate-oblong, 15–30 cm. long, long-acuminate, truncate to cordate, bright green and glabrous above, densely pubescent beneath, scentless: petiole 10–15 cm. long: panicle comparatively few-fld., about 15 cm. high: fls. about 6 cm. across, with slightly oblique limb, the lower lobe emarginate, inside with 2 yellow stripes and inconspicuously spotted purple-brown: caps. 20–45 cm. long, and about 1.5 cm. thick, with a thick wall. Fl.vi. R.H.1895:136,t(c). S.S.6:t.290–1. G.C. 66:34(h). M.G.18:229–30(h). (*C. cordifolia* Jaume St.-Hil., not Moench.) S. Ill. and Ind. to W. Tenn. and N. Ark.; naturalized elsewhere. Cult. 1754. Zone IV. Handsome pyramidal tree more vigorous and hardier than the preceding species; the wood very durable in soil and in water.

4. **C. Búngei** C. A. Mey. Small tree: lvs. triangular-ovate to ovate-oblong, 6–15 cm. long, long-acuminate, truncate to broad-cuneate, sometimes with 1 or few pointed teeth near base; dark green above, lighter beneath; petiole 2–8 cm. long: raceme corymbose, 3–12-fld.; corolla white, with purple spots inside, 3–3.5 cm. long; caps. 25–35 cm. long. S.H.2:403g-h,404e-g. N. China. Cult. 1877. Zone V. Pyramidal tree, apparently not as floriferous as the other species.—**C. B. heterophýlla** C. A. Mey., var. Lvs. with several pointed teeth near base; raceme 3–5-fld. Nouv. Arch. Mus. Paris, II.6:t.4. B.D.1907: 198b(l). (*C. h.* Dode.)

5. **C. Fárgesi** Bur. Tree to 20 m.; young shoots stellate-pubescent: lvs. ovate, 8–14 cm. long, long-acuminate, rounded or subcordate, 3-lobed on young plants, slightly pubescent above, densely so beneath; petiole 4–10 cm. long: raceme corymbose, 7–15-fld.; fl. about 3.5 cm. long, rosy pink or rosy

purple, with purple-brown dots on throat. Nouv. Arch. Mus. Paris, II.6:t.3.
(*C. vestita* Diels.) W. China. Cult. 1900. Zone V.—**C. F. Ducloùxii** (Dode)
Gilmour, f. Glabrous. B.M.9458(c). B.D.1907:198. (*C. D.* Dode.) Intr.
about 1900.

5. **CHILÓPSIS** Don. Deciduous shrub or small tree; brts. without terminal bud; winter-buds with several imbricate scales, rusty-pubescent: lvs.
opposite or alternate, narrow, entire: fls. in terminal racemes or panicles;
calyx 2-lipped, upper lip with 3, the lower with 2 teeth; corolla funnelform-
campanulate, slightly 2-lipped, the upper lip 2-lobed, the lower 3-lobed; stamens 4, included, and 1 staminode: caps. elongated, 2-valved; seeds numerous, winged, with a fringe of hair at the ends. (Greek *cheilos,* lip, and *opsis,*
likeness, referring to the distinct corolla-lip.) One species in N. Am.

C. lineàris (Cav.) Sweet. DESERT-WILLOW. Shrub or tree to 10 m.: lvs.
short-petioled or sessile, linear to linear-lanceolate, 15–30 cm. long, gradually narrowed at ends, glabrous, often viscid: infl. 7–10 cm. long; calyx pubescent; corolla white, tinged pale purple, 2–3.5 cm. long and nearly as wide:
fr. slender, 16–30 cm. long, 6 mm. thick. Fl.vi–viii. S.S.6:t.292. S.M.870. (*C.
saligna* Don.) S. Calif. to Tex., s. to Mex. Cult. before 1800. Zone VII.

Fam. 106. **GLOBULARIACEAE** DC. GLOBULARIA FAMILY

Herbs or shrubs: lvs. alternate, simple, entire or toothed, exstipulate: fls.
perfect, on a chaffy receptacle in involucrate heads; calyx usually 5-parted,
regular or 2-lipped; corolla 2-lipped, with imbricate lobes; stamens 4, didynamous, exserted; the hypogynous disk reduced to a lateral gland; ovary superior, 1-celled, 1-ovuled; style filiform, with 1 or 2 stigmas: fr. a nutlet enclosed by the persistent calyx; seeds albuminous, with straight embryo.—
Three genera and about 20 species in the Mediterr. reg.

GLOBULÀRIA L. Herbs, subshrubs or shrubs: fls. in globose heads terminal on the main axis; corolla exceeding the calyx. (Name referring to the
globular fl.-heads.) About 18 species in S. Eu. and W. Asia.

G. cordifòlia L. Procumbent subshrub to 10 cm. high; glabrous: lvs. obovate, 2–3 cm. long, emarginate and mucronate to 3-toothed at apex, gradually narrowed at base: fls. blue, in peduncled heads about 1 cm. across; corolla
2-lipped, upper lip 2-, lower lip 3-lobed with linear to linear-oblong lobes.
Fl.v–viii. R.I.20:t.195,f.1,2(c) F.D.18:t.1770(c). S.H.2:f.405h-i. Mts. of S.
Eu. Intr. before 1759. Zone V. Suited for the rock garden.

Fam. 107. **PLANTAGINACEAE** Juss. PLANTAIN FAMILY

Herbs, rarely shrubby: lvs. alternate or opposite, exstipulate: fls. perfect,
rarely unisexual, usually in heads or spikes; calyx 4-cleft; corolla 4-lobed,
with scarious imbricate lobes; stamens 4, exserted: ovary superior, 1–2-,
rarely 4-celled; cells with 1 to many ovules: style and stigma 1: fr. a circum-
cissile caps. or nutlet inclosed by the persistent calyx; seeds often peltate,
albuminous.—Three genera and about 200 species distributed over the world.

PLANTÀGO L. PLANTAIN. Herbs, subshrubs or shrubs: lvs. alternate,
rarely decussate: fls. perfect or polygamous, in dense head-like or cylindric
spikes; corolla small, with 4 scarious reflexed lobes; stamens 4, rarely 2, with
long filaments and cordate anthers; ovary 2-, rarely 3-4-celled; each cell with
1 to many ovules; style filiform: caps. 2-many-seeded, opening transversely

with the top falling off like a lid; seeds peltate, with straight embryo. (Anci
Latin name of the plant.) About 200 species mostly in the temp. regions.

P. Cýnops L. Ascending subshrub to 40 cm. high, slightly pubescent: 1
opposite, linear, 3–7 cm. long, thickish and slightly triangular, with scab
margins: fls. whitish, in small ovoid heads about 1 cm. long, on slender axilla
peduncles 3–10 cm. long; bracts broad-ovate, acuminulate, with broad hya
margin. Fl.vi–vii. F.D.20t.2021(c). S.H.2:f.628k. S. Eu. Cult. 1596. Zone
Of interest as a woody representative of the genus.

Fam. 108. **RUBIACEAE** Juss. MADDER FAMILY

Trees, shrubs or herbs: lvs. opposite or whorled, usually entire, stipulate
the stipules of the opposite lvs. usually connate, sometimes reduced to
stipular line: fls. perfect, rarely unisexual, regular, sometimes slightly irregu
lar, usually 4- or 5-merous; calyx with open, rarely imbricate lobes; coroll
with cylindric to campanulate tube, rarely rotate, lobes usually valvate
stamens 4–6, inserted on the tube; ovary inferior, usually 2-celled, rarely 1
to many-celled; ovules 1 to many in each cell; style filiform, with capitate o
branched stigma: fr. a caps., berry or drupe; seeds usually albuminous.—
About 350 genera and 4500 species distributed over the whole world, mostly
in the tropics.

A. Fls. in dense globose peduncled heads: fr. a dry achene: lvs. 6–15 cm. long.
                                            1. *Cephalanthus*
AA. Fls. not in globose heads: lvs. usually smaller.
  B. Plant twining: lvs. 5–12 cm. long: fls. in panicles; style deeply 2-parted: fr. berry-
     like, dry ....2. *Paederia*
  BB. Plants upright or prostrate shrubs.
    c. Fr. a caps.
      D. Style 2-lobed at apex; infl. a terminal large panicle; fls. white, some with one
        calyx-lobe large and lf.-like: tree................................3. *Emmenopterys*
      DD. Style 4-parted at apex; fls. in dense bracted clusters; calyx equally 5-toothed:
        shrubs ....4. *Leptodermis*
    cc. Fr. berry-like.
      D. Style 2-parted to base: fls. 1–4: prostrate shrub......................5. *Coprosma*
      DD. Style 4-parted at apex; fls. in peduncled pairs; trailing subshrub....6. *Mitchella*

1. **CEPHALÁNTHUS** L. BUTTONBUSH. Deciduous or evergreen shrubs
or small trees; winter-buds small, often superposed, terminal bud wanting:
lvs. opposite or whorled, entire, with triangular interpetiolar stipules: fls.
small, 4-merous, sessile, in axillary globose heads; calyx-lobes short, ovate
obtuse; corolla with long slender tube and 4-lobed limb; stamens included;
style long-exserted, with capitate stigma: fr. separating into 2 1-seeded nutlets. (Greek *kephalē*, head, and *anthos*, flower.) About 6 species in Asia, Afr.
and Am.

C. occidentàlis L. Deciduous shrub or rarely small tree to 5 m.: lvs. ovate
to elliptic-lanceolate, 6–15 cm. long, acuminate, lustrous bright green above,
lighter and glabrous or somewhat pubescent beneath; petiole 6–20 mm. long:
fls. creamy-white, in globose heads without the projecting styles 2.5–3 cm.
across, on peduncles 3–6 cm. long. Fl.vii–ix. Ad.5:t.169(c). Em.394,t. S.S.
14:t.711. B.C.2:714. R.H.1889:280. N. B. and Ont. to Fla., Tex. and Calif.;
also E. Asia. Intr. 1735. Zone IV. Attractive in late summer with its slender-
stalked fl.-heads.—**C. o. angustifòlius** André. Lvs. oblong-lanceolate, usually
in 3's. R.H.1889:281.—**C. o. pubéscens** Raf., var. Brts. and lvs. soft-pubescent beneath. Ill. to Ga., La. and Tex. Tenderer.

2. **PAEDÈRIA** L. Twining shrubs: lvs. opposite, rarely whorled, petioled,
entire; stipules small, deciduous: fls. perfect or polygamo-dioecious, small,
in axillary cymes forming usually terminal panicles; calyx 4–5-toothed,

corolla tubular or funnelform, with 4–5 small valvate crisped lobes; stamens included; style deeply 2-parted, twisted; ovary 2-celled; cells 1-ovuled: fr. dry, the exocarp fragile, breaking away and freeing the 2 compressed nutlets. (Latin *paedor*, bad smell; referring to the foliage when bruised.) About 20 species in trop. and subtrop. Asia and Am.

P. scandens (Lour.) Merr. Deciduous shrub climbing to 5 m., emitting a disagreeable odor when bruised: lvs. ovate to ovate-lanceolate, 5–12 cm. long, acuminate, rounded or truncate, rarely subcordate or cuneate, dark green above, lighter green beneath and pubescent or nearly glabrous; petiole 1–5 cm. long: fls. in axillary cymes forming long terminal panicles; corolla 1–1.5 cm. long, 4–6 mm. across, scurfy-pubescent and whitish outside, with purple eye: fr. globose, 5–6 mm. across, orange. Fl.vii–viii; fr.ix–x. N.K.14: t.21. N.T.1:531. R.H.1919:298. M.O.281. (*P. chinensis* Hance, *P. tomentosa* Maxim., not Bl., *P. foetida* Thunb., not L., *P. Wilsonii* Hesse.) China, Japan, Korea. Intr. 1907. Zone VI. Of little ornamental merit.

3. EMMENÓPTERYS Oliv. Deciduous tree, glabrous; terminal winter-bud with one outer convolute scale, conical, pointed: lvs. opposite, petioled, entire; stipules deciduous: fls. in many-fld. terminal glabrous panicles; calyx with 5 rounded, short, ciliate lobes, some fls. with 1 lobe lf.-like, petioled, large, ovate to oblong, whitish, persistent in fr.; corolla funnelform-campanulate, tomentulose outside, tube narrow at base, pubescent within, lobes 5, ovate, spreading tomentulose within; stamens 5, included; style not exceeding the stamens, 2-lobed at apex; ovary 2-celled: fr. an oblong caps. with numerous irregularly winged seeds. (Greek *emmeno*, persist, and *pteryx*, wing; referring to the persistent wing-like calyx-lobe.) Two species in China, Siam and Burma.

E. Hénryi Oliv. Tree to 30 m.: lvs. chartaceous, elliptic, 10–15 cm. long, acute, cuneate, slightly pubescent beneath, at least on veins and midrib; petiole 2–5 cm. long; panicle 10–18 cm. long; the enlarged calyx-lobe 3–5 cm. long, on a stalk about as long; corolla about 2.5 cm. long: caps. 3–6 cm. long. Fl.vii. H.I.19:1823. I.S.1:t.47. G.C.86:267(h). China. Intr. 1907. Zone VII. Showy in bloom.

Related genus: **PINCKNEYA** Michx. Infl. corymbose: calyx-lobes lanceolate, in some fls. 1 or 2 lobes leaf-like, petioled, rose-colored; corolla light yellow, salver-form with narrow tube, lobes 5, oblong, reflexed, marked with red lines and pilose inside; stamens 5, exserted: caps. subglobose, 2-valved. (After Charles C. Pinckney, revolutionary patriot; 1746–1825.) Two species in S. E. N. Am. and Colombia.—**P. pùbens** Michx. GEORGIA-BARK. Shrub or tree to 10 m.: lvs. elliptic to oblong-ovate, 5–20 cm. long, acute or short-acuminate, tomentulose at first, later puberulous: infl. 15–20 cm. across; corolla-tube 1.5–2 cm. long, lobes shorter: caps. about 2 cm. across. F.S.19:t.1937(c). S.S.5:t.227,228. S.M.876. S. C. to Fla. Intr. 1786. Zone VII.

4. LEPTODÉRMIS Wall. Deciduous shrubs: lvs. opposite, entire, with triangular interpetiolar stipules: fls. heterostylous, in axillary head-like bracted clusters; calyx 5-toothed, persistent; corolla tubular-funnelform, with spreading 5-lobed limb; stamens 5; style 5-parted at apex; either style or stamens exserted; ovary 5-celled, cells 1-ovuled: fr. a caps., the outer wall splitting into 5 valves, the inner wall net-like, closed, enveloping the seeds. (Greek *leptos*, thin, and *derma* skin; referring to the inner wall of the fr.) About 30 species in E. Asia and the Himal.

L. oblónga Bge. Shrub to 1 m.; brts. finely pubescent: lvs. elliptic-ovate to oblong, 1–2 cm. long, acute, narrowed into a short petiole, usually scabrid

1. **S. nígra** L. EUROPEAN E. Large shrub or tree to 10 m., with deeply furrowed bark; brts. gray, strongly lenticellate: lfts. 3–7, usually 5, short-stalked, elliptic to elliptic-ovate, 4–12 cm. long, acute, sharply serrate, dark green above, lighter and sparingly hairy on the vein beneath, of disagreeable odor when bruised: fls. yellowish white, of heavy odor, in 5-rayed flat cymes, 12–20 cm. across; ovary usually 3-celled: fr. lustrous black, 6–8 mm. across, Fl.v–vi; fr.viii–ix. R.I.12:t.730(c). S.E.4:t.637(c). M.D.1920:213(h). G.W. 19:345(h). Eu., N. Afr., W. Asia. Cult. since ancient times. Zone V.—**S. n. albo-variegàta** West., var. Lvs. variegated with white. S.O.3:t.144a(c). J.L. 33:f.47(h).—**S. n. aùreo-variegàta** West., var. Lvs. variegated with yellow.— **S. n. aùrea** Sweet, var. Lvs. golden yellow. G.W.2:565.—**S. n. laciniàta** L., var. Lfts. regularly and deeply dissected. S.O.3:t.144b(c). R.I.13:730,f.1436 (c). S.H.2:f.408a.—**S. n. heterophýlla** Endl., var. Lfts. irregularly cut and erose, partly reduced almost to the midrib.—**S. n. rotundifòlia** Endl., var. Lfts. broad-ovate to suborbicular, usually 3. S.H.2:f.408b.—**S. n. víridis** West., var. Fr. greenish. S.O.3:t.143a(c). M.D.1909:8,t,f.2(c). (*S. n.* var. *chlorocarpa* Hayne.)—**S. n. alba** West., var. Fr. whitish. (*S. n.* var. *leucocarpa* Hayne.)—**S. n. pyramidàlis** Jaeg., var. Of upright columnar habit.— **S. n. péndula** Dipp., f. Brs. prostrate or pendulous.

S. n. × *corulea;* see under No. 3.

2. **S. canadénsis** L. AMERICAN E. Stoloniferous shrub to 4 m.; brts. pale yellowish gray, slightly lenticellate: lfts. usually 7, short-stalked, elliptic to lanceolate, 5–15 cm. long, acuminate, sharply serrate, bright green, slightly puberulous on the veins beneath or nearly glabrous: fls. white, in 5-rayed, slightly convex cymes, to 25 cm. across; ovary usually 4-celled: fr. purple-black, 4–5 cm. across. Fl.vi–vii; fr.ix. M. Am. 1:t.75(c). B.C.6:3068,t. Gg.6: 88(h). M.G.14:169(h). M.D.1909:36a(h). N. S. and Man. to Fla. and Tex. Intr. 1761. Zone III.—**S. c. rubra** Palmer & Steyerm., f. Fr. bright red. Intr. 1932.—**S. c. aùrea** Cowell, var. Lvs. golden-yellow: fr. cherry-red. F.E.22: 433. (*S. c.* f. *delicatissima* Schwer.)—**S c. máxima** (Hesse) Schwer., f. Lvs. larger; cymes to 35 cm. across; a very vigorous form. G.M.51:451. G.W.11: 397(h). S.L.335(h).—**S. c. acutíloba** Ellw. & Barry. Lfts. much dissected, the lower ones pinnatifid, the upper ones incisely serrate and narrow. F.S.R.1:151. (*S. c.* var. *laciniata* Cowell, not Gray.)—**S. c. chlorocàrpa** Rehd., f. Fr. greenish; lvs. pale green.—**S. c. submóllis** Rehd., var. Lfts. beneath grayish green and soft-pubescent. Ill. to Ark. and Tex.

3. **S. coerùlea** Raf. Large shrub or small tree occasionally to 15 m.; brts. rather slender, bloomy when young: lfts. 5–7, oblong to oblong-lanceolate, 6–15 cm. long, coarsely serrate, bright green, glabrous: fls. yellowish white, in convex 5-rayed cymes, 10–15 cm. across: fr. blue-black, whitened by a heavy bloom. Fl.vi–vii; fr.viii–ix. S.S.5:t.222. Gs.5:181,t(c). (*S. glauca* Nutt.) B. C. to Calif., e. to Mont. and Utah. Cult. 1850. Zone V. Conspicuous when covered with its bluish white frs.—**S. c. neo-mexicàna** (Wooton) Rehd., var. Lfts. 3–5, narrow-lanceolate, grayish green, slightly pubescent beneath. (*S. intermedia* Carr., *S. n.* Wooton.) Ariz. and N. Mex. Cult. 1875. Zone V.— **S. c. velutìna** (Durand) Schwer., var. Young brts. and lvs. densely short-pubescent. (*S. v.* Durand, *S. californica* K. Koch.) Calif. Intr. before 1870. Zone VII?

S. c. × *nigra* = **S. fontenaỳsii** Carr. Intermediate between the parents: lvs. bluish green: fr. black, bloomy. Orig. before 1870.

4. **S. melanocárpa** Gray. Shrub to 4 m.; brs. red-brown; pith white or light brown at first, darker the 2d year: lfts. 5–7, short-stalked, oblong-

lanceolate, 8–15 cm. long, long-acuminate, coarsely serrate, dark green, pubescent beneath when young, later glabrate: fls. yellowish white, in a broad-ovoid to hemispherical cyme 5–7 cm. across and about as high, its brs. often alternate: fr. 6 mm. across; nutlets rugulose. Fl.vii–viii; fr.viii–ix. I.T.5: t.173. G.F.10:135. M.D.1909:8,t.f.4(c),45. B. C. to Idaho and Calif. Intr. 1894. Zone V.—**S. m. Fuerstenbérgii** Schwer., f. Fr. reddish brown. Intr. 1903.

5. **S. micróbotrys** Rydb. Low shrub, rarely to 2 m.; bark light brown; pith white, at least at first: lfts. 5–7, subsessile or short-petioled, ovate-lanceolate, 5–10 cm. long, long-acuminate, sharply and rather coarsely serrate, light green, glabrous: fls. whitish, in short, nearly hemispherical cymes about 5 cm. high and as broad: fr. scarlet or orange-red, 4 mm. across, nutlets finely rugulose. Fl.vi–vii; fr.viii–ix. M.D.1909:44. Calif. to Nev. and Colo. Cult. 1900. Zone V.

Related species: **S. callicárpa** Greene. Taller and larger: lfts. pubescent along the midrib: cymes larger. M.D.1909:8,t,f.5(c).45. (*S. racemosa* var. *c.* Jeps.) Calif., Ore. Intr. about 1900.

6. **S. racemòsa** L. European Red E. Shrub to 4 m.; brs. light brown; young brts. and lvs. glabrous: lfts. 5–7, subsessile, ovate or elliptic to ovate-lanceolate, 4–8 cm. long, acuminate, sharply and rather coarsely serrate: fls. yellowish white in a dense ovoid or oblong-ovoid panicle 3–6 cm. long, its lower brs. usually reflexed with stalks 5 mm. or less long: fr. scarlet, about 5 mm. across; nutlets finely rugulose. Fl.iv–v; fr.vi–vii. R.I.12:t.731(c). F.D.28:t.2909(c). S.O.3:t.141(c). Eu., W. Asia. Cult. 1596. Zone IV. Attractive in fr. and some of the forms with handsome foliage.—**S. r. plumòsa** Carr. Lfts. incisely serrate to about the middle, with long and narrow teeth, purplish when unfolding. S.H.2:f.410b(l).—**S. r. plumòso-aùrea** Schwer. Lfts. like in the preceding, but golden yellow.—**S. r. laciniàta** Koch, var. Lfts. regularly and deeply dissected, green when unfolding. R.I.12:t.731,f.1438. (*S. r. serratifolia* Carr.)—**S. r. tenuifòlia** (Carr.) Schwer., f. Lfts. finely and deeply dissected, with very narrow segments, purplish when unfolding.— **S. r. ornàta** (Carr.) Schwer., f. The first lvs. like those of *S. r. plumosa*, the later ones like those of the preceding form. (*S. plumosa pteridifolia* Carr.)— **S. r. purpúrea** Sweet, var. Fls. purplish or pinkish outside, purple in bud.— **S. r. flavéscens** Schwer. Fr. yellow or sometimes with red cheek. M.D. 1909:8,t.f.6(c). (*S. r. xanthocarpa* Hort.)

Closely related species: **S. kamtschática** E. Wolf. Lower: lfts. elliptic, rounded and usually acuminulate at apex, finely serrate: infl. pubescent, usually broader than high: petals much longer than calyx-tube, dentate. M.D.1923:32, f.1–3,33,f.1. Kamchatka. Cult. 1923. Zone II.

7. **S. pùbens** Michx. Red-berried E. Shrub to 4 or sometimes to 8 m.; brts. pale yellow-brown; brts. and lvs. finely pubescent when young: lfts. 5–7, stalked, ovate-oblong to oblong-lanceolate, 5–10 cm. long, serrate, pubescent beneath or sometimes finally glabrous: infl. ovoid or pyramidal, to 10 cm. long, loose, stalks of lower brs. 5–15 mm. long; fls. yellowish white: fr. scarlet, about 5 mm. across; nutlets rugulose. Fl.v; fr.vi–vii. M.N.II.2:t. 21(c). B.B.3:268. M.D.1909:44. (*S. racemosa* of Gray, not L., *S. rac.* var. *p. S.* Wats.) N. B. to Minn., s. to Ga. and Colo. Intr. 1812. Zone IV. Shrub with attractive scarlet fr.—**S. p. dissécta** Britt. Lfts. deeply and regularly dissected. (*S. rac.* var. *laciniata* Gray, not Koch.)—**S. p. leucocárpa** (Bernh.) Torr. & Gr., var. Fr. white. (*S. p. albicocca* Britt.)—**S. p. xanthocárpa** (Cock.) Nieuwl., var. Fr. and amber-yellow. (*S. rac.* f. *xanthocarpa* Cock., *S. r.* var. *chrysocarpa* Eames & Godfr.)

The western form has been separated as **S. leiospérma** Leib. Brts., lvs. and infl. glabrous or nearly glabrous: nutlets faintly rugulose or nearly smooth G.F.10:174. S.M.886. (*S. callicarpa* Sarg., not Greene, *S. pubens* var. *dimidiata* Schwer.) Alaska to Wash. and Wyo. Intr. 1904.

8. **S. Sieboldiàna** Graebn. Shrub or small tree to 6 m.: brts. yellowish glabrous when young, with 2 blue rings at the nodes; winter-buds acute: lfts usually 7, on shoots sometimes 11, oblong to oblong-lanceolate, 6–20 cm. long long-acuminate or caudate, sharply and closely serrate, light green, glabrous: fls. yellowish white, small, in ovoid panicles about 7 cm. long and 5 cm across, its brts. often slightly reflexed; fr. scarlet, 3–4 mm. across, nutlets rugulose. Fl.iv–v; fr.vi–vii. S.I.2:t.74(c). H.N.3:t.1. N.T.1:571. M.D.1920:20 (1). (*S. racemosa* of Shiras., not L., *S. rac.* var. *S.* Miq.) Japan, China. Intr. 1907. Zone V?

Closely related species: **S. Williámsii** Hance. Winter-buds obtuse: lvs. sometimes whorled, dark green; lfts. oblong-ovate to elliptic-oblong, rather coarsely serrate: infl. looser; fr. 5–5.5 mm. across, purple-black. H.N.3:t.2. N. China Intr. 1938. Zone V.

2. **VIBÚRNUM** L. Deciduous or sometimes evergreen shrubs or small trees; winter-buds naked or scaly: lvs. opposite, rarely whorled, entire, dentate or lobed, exstipulate or sometimes with small stipules adnate to the petiole: fls. small, white or pinkish, in umbel-like or paniculate compound cymes; calyx minutely 5-toothed; corolla rotate to campanulate or tubular 5-lobed; stamens 5; ovary 1-celled: fr. a drupe with a 1-seeded usually compressed stone. (The ancient Latin name of *V. Lantana.*) About 120 species in N. and C. Am., in Eu., N. Afr. and in Asia s. to Java.—Many species are highly ornamental with showy fls. and attractive frs.

Lvs. not lobed, penninerved, sometimes 3-nerved at base.
A. Cyme paniculate, pyramidal to subglobose, its brs. opposite.
  B. Corolla tubular.
    c. Fls. before the lvs.; panicle 3–5 cm. long....................1. *V. fragrans*
    cc. Fls. after the lvs.: panicles 6–12 cm. long..................2. *V. erubescens*
  BB. Corolla rotate.
    c. Lvs. acuminate, with 5–7 pairs of veins.................................3. *V. Henryi*
    cc. Lvs. rounded or acute, with 7–10 pairs of veins.......................4. *V. Sieboldi*
AA. Cyme umbel-like, usually flat (globose in the snowball forms of Nos. 15, 17 and 43).
  B. Winter-buds naked; shrubs with stellate tomentum.
    c. Infl. without enlarged and sterile marginal fls.: seed with solid albumen.
      D. Lvs. dentate or denticulate, deciduous.
        E. Veins of lvs. straight, ending in the teeth.
          F. Corolla salver-shaped, with a tube nearly 1 cm. long...........5. *V. Carlesi*
          FF. Corolla rotate or wide-funnelform.
            G. Corolla-lobes shorter than tube; cymes usually with 5 rays.
                      6. *V. cotinifolium*
            GG. Corolla-lobes longer than tube; cymes usually 7-rayed.
              H. Calyx stellate-tomentose: lvs. remotely toothed..........7. *V. Veitchi*
              HH. Calyx glabrous or slightly stellate-pubescent: lvs. closely denticulate.
                      8. *V. Lantana*
        EE. Veins of lvs. anastomosing before reaching the margin, rarely partly ending in the teeth.
          F. Corolla rotate or rotate-campanulate.
            G. Lvs. usually obtuse: fls. mostly on rays of the 3d order; ovary glabrous.
                      9. *V. schensianum*
            GG. Lvs. usually acute: fls. mostly on rays of the 2d order; ovary pubescent.
                      10. *V. burejaeticum*
          FF. Corolla with cylindric tube, much longer than limb.
            G. Lvs. obtuse to acute, pubescent.........................11. *V. mongolicum*
            GG. Lvs. acuminate, nearly glabrous.........................12. *V. urceolatum*
      DD. Lvs. entire or sometimes obscurely and remotely denticulate, evergreen: corolla rotate.
        E. Lvs. smooth above, 3–6 cm. long................................13. *V. utile*
        EE. Lvs. rugose above, 10–18 cm. long......................14. *V. rhytidophyllum*
    cc. Infl. with sterile and enlarged marginal fls. (except in *V. cordifolium* under No. 16).
      D. Lvs. rounded at base; veins anastomosing before reaching the margin: albumen solid ....15. *V. macrocephalum*
      DD. Lvs. cordate at base; veins straight, ending in the teeth: albumen ruminate.
                      16. *V. alnifolium*

BB. Winter-buds scaly with 1 or 2 pairs of scales.
  c. Cymes with enlarged sterile margina! fls.: veins of lvs. straight, ending in the teeth: tomentum stellate ....17. *V. tomentosum*
  cc. Cymes without sterile fls.: tomentum not stellate.
    D. Veins of lvs. curving and anastomosing before reaching the margin.
      E. Lvs. deciduous: stone compressed, with solid albumen.
        F. Cyme peduncled.
          G. Lvs. usually entire: peduncle as long or longer than cyme...18. *V. nudum*
          GG. Lvs. usually denticulate: peduncle shorter than cyme....19. *V. cassinoides*
        FF. Cyme sessile: lvs. finely and sharply serrate.
          G. Petiole with broad wavy margin: brs. slender..............20. *V. Lentago*
          GG. Petiole with narrow, not wavy margin: brs. rather rigid.
            H. Winter-buds and petioles rusty-tomentose............21. *V. rufidulum*
            HH. Winter-buds and petioles not rusty-tomentose.......22. *V. prunifolium*
      EE. Lvs. evergreen: stone not compressed, ruminate.
        F. Corolla rotate: lvs. 3-nerved at base........................23. *V. Davidi*
        FF. Corolla cylindric-campanulate: lvs. not 3-nerved..........24. *V. cylindricum*
    DD. Veins of lvs. straight, ending in the teeth.
      E. Fr. red; stone flattened.
        F. Petiole without stipules.
          G. Lvs. evergreen, glabrous..................................25. *V. japonicum*
          GG. Lvs. deciduous.
            H. Lvs. 3-nerved at base, 2–8 cm. long....................26. *V. foetidum*
            HH. Lvs. not 3-nerved, usually larger.
              I. Infl. and brts. glabrous.
                J. Lvs. generally ovate-oblong, broadest below the middle: stamens as long or shorter than corolla....................27. *V. setigerum*
                JJ. Lvs. broader, at least partly broadest above the middle: stamens longer than corolla................................28. *V. Wrightii*
              II. Infl. and brts. pubescent.
                J. Lvs. at least those below the infl. broadest above the middle.
                  29. *V. dilatatum*
                JJ. Lvs. broadest below the middle...................30. *V. Wilsonii*
        FF. Petiole with subulate stipules.
          G. Petiole 1–3 cm. long.
            H. Corolla glabrous.
              I. Cyme short-stalked: fr. globose-ellipsoid, 6 mm. long: lvs. usually rhombic-ovate to elliptic-oblong...............31. *V. betulifolium*
              II. Cyme long-stalked: fr. subglobose, 8 mm. long: lvs. broad-ovate or obovate ....32. *V. lobophyllum*
            HH. Corolla pubescent outside...........................33. *V. dasyanthum*
          GG. Petiole 3–6 mm. long..34. *V. erosum*
      EE. Fr. blue-black; stone scarcely flattened or flattened in Nos. 37–38.
        F. Fr. globose-ovoid, stone with a deep groove on one side, round on back: petioles usually without stipules.
          G. Brts. glabrous: lvs. glabrous except bearded in the axils of the veins beneath ....35. *V. dentatum*
          GG. Brts. slightly pubescent and lvs. pubescent, sometimes slightly so beneath.
            36. *V. pubescens*
        FF. Fr. ellipsoid; stone flattened, with grooves on both sides; petioles with stipules.
          G. Petiole 2–12 mm. long: lvs. rounded to subcordate at base: bark close.
            37. *V. Rafinesquianum*
          GG. Petiole 1.5–3 cm. long: lvs. deeply cordate: bark exfoliating..38. *V. molle*
Lvs. palmately 3–5-nerved at base, lobed, rarely not lobed: petioles stipulate.
A. Fr. purple-black; stone grooved; cymes with all the fls. perfect, on elongated upright brs. ....39. *V. acerifolium*
AA. Fr. scarlet or orange-red; stone not or scarcely grooved; cymes on short lateral brts.
  B. Cyme without sterile marginal fls.: petiole not glandular.
    c. Lvs. shallowly 3-lobed or undivided, 5–8 cm. long..................40. *V. pauciflorum*
    cc. Lvs. deeply 3–5-lobed, 2–5 cm. long.........................41. *V. kansuense*
  BB. Cymes with enlarged sterile marginal fls.; petiole with glands near apex.
    c. Anthers yellow; bark of stems thin.
      D. Petiole with a shallow groove and small glands: lvs. usually glabrous.
        42. *V. trilobum*
      DD. Petiole with a narrow groove and large disk-like glands: lvs. pubescent beneath.
        43. *V. Opulus*
    cc. Anthers purple, rarely yellow: bark of stems thick and slightly corky: upper lvs. usually with elongated entire middle lobe............................44. *V. Sargenti*

Sect. 1. THYRSOSMA (Raf.) Rehd. Petiole without stipules; cymes panicu-late, with opposite brs.: drupe ovoid to ellipsoid, blue-black or purple; stone slightly compressed, with a deep ventral furrow; albumen solid or ruminate.

1. **V. fràgrans** Bge. Shrub to 3 m.; brts. slightly pubescent; brs. brown: vs. elliptic, 4–7 cm. long, acute, broad-cuneate or cuneate, serrate with

triangular teeth, sparingly pubescent above and pubescent on veins beneath finally glabrous or nearly so, with 5–6 pairs of veins and the veinlets impresse above and below, thickish; petiole 1–1.5 cm. long, purplish: panicle 3–5 cm long, glabrous or nearly so; corolla salver-shaped, white, pinkish in bu tube about 8 mm. long, limb spreading about 1 cm. across; stamens inserte above the middle, unequally high. Fl.iv–v. B.M.8887(c). H.N.3:t.26. Gn.35 118;88:221. G.C.69:109;88:267,t(c),340(h). B.A.1931:3. N. China. Int 1910. Zone V. The fragrant and attractive fls. appear before the lvs.

Closely related species: **V. grandiflòrum** Wall. Shrub to 2 m.: lvs. elliptic oblong, 6–9 cm. long, acuminate, pubescent beneath on the veins and in thei axils, pairs of veins 7–8: panicle short and dense, pubescent: corolla-tube ove 1 cm. long; stamens inserted at and below the middle. B.M.9063(c). (*V. foeten* Dcne., *V. nervosum* Hook. f. & Thoms., not D. Don.) Himal. Intr. 1914. Zon VII?

2. **V. erubéscens** Wall. Deciduous shrub or small tree: lvs. elliptic o ovate to oblong, 5–10 cm. long, acuminate, cuneate or rounded at base, pubes cent on the veins beneath or glabrous, with 5–7 pairs of veins; petiole 1–2. cm. long: panicle loose, pendulous, 4–8 cm. long, slightly pubescent or gla brate, on a peduncle 2–6 cm. long; corolla white, tinged with pink, about cm. long, with spreading round lobes: fr. broad-ellipsoid, 6 mm. long, firs red, then black. Wallich, Pl. As. Rar. 2:t.134(c). Himal., W. China. Intr. —**V. e. gracílipes** Rehd., var. Lvs. usually elliptic, rounded at base, glabrou or nearly so: infl. loose, 7–12 cm. long: fls. partly slender-pediceled. Fl.vi; fr ix. C. China. Intr. 1910. Zone (V). Distinct with its pendulous panicles.

3. **V. Hénryi** Hemsl. Evergreen or half-evergreen shrub or small tree t 3 m.; brts. stiff, glabrous: lvs. elliptic-oblong to oblong-obovate, 5–12 cm long, acuminate, cuneate to rounded at base, shallowly toothed, lustrou dark green above, glabrous except sparingly stellate-pubescent on midril beneath; petiole 1–2 cm. long: panicle broad-pyramidal, 5–10 cm. long: fls about 6 mm. across: fr. ovoid, 6 mm. long, first red, then black. Fl.viii. B.M 8393(c). S.T.2:t.116. B.S.2:649. G.C.48:264,265,t(h);60:193(h). S.L.384(h) C. China. Intr. 1907. Zone VII. Handsome in fruit.

4. **V. Sieboldii** Miq. Shrub or tree to 10 m.; brts. stout, pubescent wher young: lvs. elliptic or obovate to oblong-obovate, 6–12 cm. long, acute t rounded, broad-cuneate, coarsely crenate-serrate, dark lustrous green above stellate-pubescent chiefly on the veins beneath, with 7–10 pairs of prominen veins; petiole 8–15 mm. long: panicle 7–10 cm. long and as broad; coroll rotate-campanulate, 8 mm. across, creamy white: fr. oblong-ovoid, 1 cm long, changing from pink to blue-black. Fl.v–vi; fr.vii–ix. Ad.5:t.178(c) S.I.1:t.86(c). G.F.2:559. F.E.23:345. Japan. Cult. 1880. Zone IV. Witl lustrous large lvs. of disagreeable odor when bruised; attractive in fl. and fr —**V. S. reticulàtum** (Hort.) Rehd., var. Smaller in every part; lvs. glab rescent.

Sect. 2. Lantana Spach. Shrubs with stellate tomentum and naked winter buds: lvs. deciduous, rarely persistent, usually denticulate: stone much flattened with 3 ventral and 2 dorsal grooves sometimes obsolete; albumen solid.

5. **V. Carlésii** Hemsl. Shrub to 1.5 m., with spreading brs.; young brts. petioles and infl. stellate-tomentose: lvs. broad-ovate to elliptic, 3–10 cm long, acute, usually rounded at base, irregularly toothed, dull green and stellate-pubescent above, densely so and paler beneath; petiole 5–10 mm long: fls. with the lvs., very fragrant, in dense hemispherical cymes 5–7 cm across; corolla 1–1.4 cm. across, with a cylindric tube 6–10 mm. long, white, pink outside; stamens included, inserted above the middle, filaments shorter

than anthers: fr. ellipsoid, 10 mm. long, blue-black. Fl.ɪv–v; fr.ɪx–x. B.M.
8114(c). G.C.43:346;45:340(h). B.S.2:644. Gn.84:154;88:222. J.L.35:f.85(h).
S.L.375(h). Korea. Intr. 1902. Zone IV. Broad round bush, valued for its
very fragrant handsome early fls.

V. C. × *bitchiuense* = **V.** Juddii Rehd. Lvs. ovate to ovate-oblong; petiole
4–9 mm. long: infl. 6–8 cm. across, rather loose; rays 1.5 cm. long; filaments
about 1½ as long as anthers, inserted about or slightly below the middle of the
tube. Orig. in 1920. Zone V.—*V. C.* × *utile* = **V.** Burkwoòdii Burkwood. Lvs.
glabrous above, tomentose beneath, with brown veins: infl. about 6 cm. across;
corolla 1 cm. across, tube as long as lobes; stamens inserted at base, as long as
tube. G.C.85:291. Orig. 1924. Zone V.

Closely related species: **V.** oitchiuénse Mak. Slenderer, more straggling
shrub: lvs. smaller, usually obtuse, often subcordate: fls. in smaller cymes;
anthers inserted below the middle; filaments about twice as long as anthers.
G.C.69:247. N.T.1:588. B.S.3:497,t. (*V. Carlesii* var. *b.* Nakai, *V. C.* var.
syringiflorum Hutch.) Japan. Cult. 1909. Zone V.—*V. b.* × *Carlesii;* see
under No. 5.

6. V. cotinifòlium D. Don. Shrub to 4 m., with spreading brs. stellate-
tomentose when young: lvs. orbicular-ovate to ovate, 5–12 cm. long, obtuse
or abruptly acuminulate, rounded or cordate, crenulate-dentate or nearly entire, grayish stellate-tomentose beneath, slightly so above and finally often
glabrescent: cymes 5–8 cm. across; corolla funnelform-campanulate, about 6
mm. long, white, tinged pink: fr. ovoid, 8–10 mm. long, red, finally black.
Fl.v; fr.ɪx. B.R.1650(c). G.F.5:245. G.W.13:141(h). (*V. multratum* K.
Koch.) Himal. Intr. 1830. Zone (V).

7. V. Veìtchii C. H. Wright. Shrub to 2 m.; young brts. and petioles
stellate-tomentose: lvs. ovate, 7–12 cm. long, acuminate, cordate or rounded
at base, remotely dentate, sparingly stellate-pubescent above, densely so
beneath: petiole 1–2.5 cm. long: fls. white, 6 mm. across, in dense short-
stalked stellate-tomentose cymes 5–12 cm. across, on a peduncle 6–50 mm.
long: fr. short-ellipsoid, 8 mm. long, red, finally black. Fl.v–vɪ; fr.ɪx. C.
China. Intr. 1901. Zone V. Handsome shrub.

Closely related species: **V.** buddleifòlium C. H. Wright. Shrub to 2 m.; lvs.
oblong-lanceolate, 8–15 cm. long, rounded or subcordate at base, shallowly
toothed, grayish stellate-tomentose beneath: cyme about 8 cm. across; corolla
8 mm. across. C. China. S.H.2:f.419i(1). Intr. 1900. Zone (V).—*V. b.* ×
rhytidophyllum; see under No. 14.

8. V. Lantàna L. WAYFARING-TREE. Upright shrub sometimes to 5 m.
tall and tree-like; brts. scurfy-pubescent: lvs. ovate to oblong-ovate, 5–12
cm. long, acute or obtuse, cordate to rounded at base, rather closely denticulate, sparingly stellate-pubescent and wrinkled above, stellate-tomentose beneath; petiole 1–3 cm. long: cyme 6–10 cm. across, stellate-pubescent: fr.
ovoid-oblong, 8 mm. long, changing from red to black. Fl.v–vɪ; fr.vɪɪ–ɪx.
Ad.4:t.148(c). R.I.17:t.120,f.1–2(c). A.G.18:453(as *V. lantanoides*). Gn.61:
324(h). Eu., W. Asia. Long cult. and occasionally escaped in the E. States.
Zone III. With attractive fls. and frs.; the lvs. turning red in fall.—**V. L.
variegàtum** Bull. Lvs. variegated with yellow.—**V. L. rugósum** Lange, var.
With larger, more wrinkled lvs. and larger cymes.—**V. L. díscolor** Huter,
var. Lvs. smaller and of firmer texture, white-tomentose beneath. S.H.2:
f.419n–o(l). (*V. maculatum* Pantocsek.)

V. L. × *rhytidophyllum;* see under No. 14.

9. V. schensiànum Maxim. Slender-branched shrub; young brts. stellate-
pubescent: lvs. ovate-elliptic, 2–5 cm. long, obtuse or acutish, rounded at
base, sometimes broad-cuneate, denticulate, sparingly pubescent or glabrous
above, stellate-pubescent beneath, with 5–6 pairs of veins usually anastomos-

ing, or partly ending in the teeth; petiole 5–10 mm. long; cyme 5-rayed, 5–
cm. across, stellate-pubescent, on a stalk 5–25 mm. long, sometimes sessile
corolla rotate-campanulate, 6 mm. long; ovary glabrous; drupe short
ellipsoid, 8 mm. long, blue-black; stone with convex back. Fl.v–vi; fr.ix. S.T
2:t.140. H.N.3:t.28. N. W. China. Intr. 1910. Zone V.

10. **V. burejaèticum** Reg. & Herd. Shrub to 5 m.; young brts. stellate
pubescent, glabrous and light gray the 2d year: lvs. ovate or elliptic to elliptic
obovate, 4–10 cm. long, acute to obtuse, rounded or subcordate, sinuately
denticulate, sparingly hairy above, sparingly stellate-pubescent beneath
chiefly on the veins, becoming glabrous; petiole 3–8 mm. long, scurfy-pubes
cent: fls. white, in dense 5-rayed usually pubescent cymes 4–5 cm. across: fr
ellipsoid to ellipsoid-oblong, 1 cm. long, bluish black; stone grooved on both
sides. Fl.v; fr.ix. Gt.11:47,t. H.N.3:t.30. D.H.1:186. Manch., N. China
Cult. 1900. Zone V or IV.

11. **V. mongòlicum** (Pall.) Rehd. Shrub to 2 m., with spreading brs.
young brts. stellate-pubescent, glabrous and yellowish gray the 2d year: lvs
broad-ovate to elliptic, 3–6 cm. long, acute to obtuse, rounded at base, shal
lowly dentate, sparingly pubescent above, sparingly stellate-pubescent be
neath; petiole 3–8 mm. long; cymes stalked, with rather few fls., 2–4 cm
across; fls. mostly on rays of the 1st order; corolla tubular-campanulate, 6–
mm. long, with short, slightly spreading lobes; ovary glabrous: fr. ellipsoid
black. Fl.v; fr.ix. D.H.1:198. H.N.3:t.29. (*V. davuricum* Pall.) E. Siberia
N. China. Intr. 1785. Zone V.

12. **V. urceolàtum** Sieb. & Zucc. Straggling shrub to 1 m., with procum
bent rooting stems; brts. glabrous or sparingly scurfy, becoming reddish o
yellowish brown: lvs. ovate to ovate-lanceolate, 6–12 cm. long, acuminate
rounded at base, rarely broad-cuneate, crenate-serrate, glabrous above, scurf
on the veins beneath; petiole 1–2 cm. long: cymes usually 5-rayed, glabrou
or nearly so, 3–6 cm. across, on long slender peduncles; corolla pinkish white
cylindric-campanulate, 3–4 mm. long, with short erect lobes; anthers ex
serted: fr. ovoid, 6 mm. long, black; stone much compressed, grooved or
both sides. Fl.v; fr.ix. S.T.2:t.141. N.T.1:583. Japan. Intr. 1916. Zone V
Distinct species, but scarcely ornamental.

13. **V. ùtile** Hemsl. Evergreen shrub to 2 m., of open habit, with slende
brs. stellate-pubescent when young: lvs. elliptic-ovate to ovate-oblong, 2–
cm. long, obtuse, rarely acutish, broad-cuneate or rounded, entire, lustrou
dark green above, whitish stellate-tomentose beneath with 5–6 pairs of vein
elevated beneath; petiole 4–8 mm. long: fls. white, in dense stellate-pubescen
5-rayed cymes 5–8 cm. across: fr. broad-ellipsoid, 6–8 mm. long, bluish black
Fl.v. B.M.8174(c). S.T.2:t.143. R.H.1919:264,t(c). S.L.382(h). C. China
Intr. 1901. Zone VI.

V. u. × *Carlesii;* see under No. 5.

14. **V. rhytidophýllum** Hemsl. Evergreen shrub to 3 m., with stout up
right brs. stellate-tomentose when young: lvs. ovate-oblong to ovate-lance
olate, 7–18 cm. long, acute or obtuse, rounded or subcordate at base, entire
or obscurely denticulate, lustrous dark green, glabrous and strongly wrinkled
above, prominently reticulate beneath and gray or yellowish tomentose
petiole 1–3 cm. long: fls. yellowish white, 6 mm. across, in stellate-tomentos
cymes formed in autumn and remaining naked through the winter, 10–2
cm. across, 7–11-rayed, on a stout peduncle 2–4 cm. long; ovary pubescent
fr. short-ellipsoid, 8 mm. long, first red, then lustrous black. Fl.v–vi; fr.ix–x
B M.8382(c). G.C.42:220;68:277(h). Gn.78:283(h). C. and W. China. Intr

1900. Zone (V). Very distinct species with bold lustrous lvs.—**V. r. roseum** Gard. Chron. Fls. bright pink in bud. G.C.104:171,t(c).

V. r. × *Lantana* = **V. rhytidophylloìdes** Suring. Lvs. elliptic-ovate or oblong-ovate, 8–20 cm. long, similar to *V. rhytidophyllum*, but broader and less rugose: infl. stout; stamens about as long as corolla. (*V. lantanophyllum* Lemoine.) Cult. 1927. Zone V.—*V. r.* × *buddleifolium* = **V. rhytidocárpum** Lemoine. Lvs. intermediate between the parents: fr. rugose. Cult. 1936. Zone VI.

15. **V. macrocéphalum** Fort. CHINESE SNOWBALL. Deciduous or half-evergreen shrub to 4 m., with spreading brs. scurfy-pubescent at first: lvs. ovate or elliptic to ovate-oblong, 5–10 cm. long, acute or obtusish, rounded at base, denticulate, dark green and nearly glabrous above, stellate-pubescent beneath; petiole 8–20 mm. long: fls. white, about 3 cm. wide, in large globose heads 8–15 cm. across. Fl.v–vi. B.R.33:43(c). F.S.3:t.263(c). Gn.79:336(h); 38:205(h). A.F.16:1547(h). Gn.M.30:8(h). China. Intr. 1844. Zone VI. Very showy, with larger heads than the European and Japanese Snowballs, distinguished as **V. m. stérile** Dipp., f. (*V. Fortunei* Hort.) from the wild form with only the marginal fls. sterile and enlarged: **V. m. Keteleèri** (Carr.) Nichols. R.H.1863:270. Gn.45:423.

Sect. 3. PSEUDOTINUS Clarke. Deciduous shrubs with denticulate lvs. and stellate tomentum; winter-buds naked: cymes terminal, usually with radial fls.: fr. purple-black; stone compressed, with a deep ventral furrow; albumen ruminate.

16. **V. alnifòlium** Marsh. HOBBLE-BUSH. Shrub to 3 m., with forked brs., sometimes procumbent and rooting; brts. scurfy-pubescent: lvs. in distant pairs, broad-ovate or suborbicular, 10–20 cm. long, short-acuminate, cordate, irregularly denticulate, stellate-pubescent above at first, later glabrous, more densely pubescent beneath, chiefly on the veins; petiole 3–6 cm. long, scurfy: fls. white, in sessile stellate-pubescent cymes 8–12 cm. across; sterile fls. 2–2.5 cm. wide; stamens as long as corolla-lobes: fr. broad-ellipsoid, 8 mm long, first red, then purple-black. Fl.v–vi; fr.ix. L.B.1570(c). G.F.2:535. B.B.3: 269. (*V. lantanoides* Michx.—AMERICAN WAYFARING-TREE.) N. B. and Mich. to N. C.; in the mts. Intr. 1820. Zone III. With large foliage turning deep claret-red in autumn; prefers half-shady and moist situations.—**V. a. praècox** Hesse. Fls. 3 weeks earlier. M.D.1912:370. G.W.16:495(h).

Related species: **V. furcàtum** Bl. Of more upright habit; stamens about half as long as corolla; stone with the ventral furrow broader and more open. S.I.2:t. 4(c). S.T.2:119. Japan. Intr. 1892. Zone V.—**V. sympodiàle** Graebn. Lvs. narrow-ovate to elliptic-ovate, rounded or subcordate at base and more finely serrulate; petiole stipulate: cymes 6–9 cm. across. S.T.2:t.139. China. Intr. 1900? Zone V?—**V. cordifòlium** Wall. ex DC. Lvs. ovate, cordate or rounded at base: infl. without sterile fls.; stamens about half as long as corolla. S.T.2:t. 38. W. China, E. Himal. Intr. 1932. Zone VII?

Sect. 4. PSEUDOPULUS Dipp. Deciduous shrubs with dentate lvs. and stellate tomentum; winter-buds with 2 scales; cymes with radiant fls., on short lateral brts.: fr. blue-black; stone compressed, with broad ventral furrow; albumen solid.

17. **V. tomentòsum** Thunb. Shrub to 3 m., with almost horizontally spreading brs. stellate-tomentose when young: lvs. broad-ovate to oblong-ovate, sometimes elliptic-obovate, 4–10 cm. long, acute or abruptly acuminate, rounded to broad-cuneate, dentate-serrate, dark green and nearly glabrous above, stellate-pubescent beneath, with 8–12 pairs of nearly straight veins; petiole 1–2 cm. long: cymes long-peduncled, stellate-pubescent, usually 8-rayed, 6–10 cm. across, with sterile marginal fls. about 3 cm. wide: fr. ellipsoid, red, then blue-black. Fl.v–vi; fr.viii–ix. S.Z.1:t.38(c). S.I.1:t.86(c). J.C.36:234. G.F.4:594. Gg.5:311(h). S.L.377(h). B.C.6:3458,t(h). (*V. plica-*

835

tum Miq., not Thunb.) Japan, China. Intr. about 1865. Zone IV. Distinc shrub, with showy fls. and attractive frs. red before maturity; lvs. changin to vinous red in fall. The snowball form is one of the showiest shrubs.—**V. t Marièsii** Veitch. Cymes and sterile fls. larger, otherwise not different from the type. Gn.88:222(h). S.L.376(h). J.L.27:863(h).—**V. t. stérile** K. Koch var. JAPANESE SNOWBALL. All fls. sterile, pure white, forming globose cyme 6–8 cm. across: lvs. less pubescent. G.C.29:72(h). Gn.78:427(h),472(h) ;88 125(h). Gg.1:263(h). (*V. t.* var. *plicatum* Maxim., *V. t.* f. *plenum* Rehd., *V plicatum* Thunb.) Cult. in China and Japan. Intr. 1814.—**V. t. rotundifòliun** Rehd., var. Much like the preceding form, but blooming about 2 weeks earl ier and lvs. broader.—**V. t. parvifòlium** (Miq.) Rehd., var. Lvs. elliptic t oblong, 3–5 cm. long, long-acuminate: dwarfer and of slower growth. (*V. t* var. *cuspidatum* Maxim.)—**V. t. lanceàtum** Rehd., var. Similar to the preced ing, but lvs. narrower, lanceolate on the shoots, more gradually acuminate more pubescent beneath: infl. smaller, with fewer sterile fls. Intr. 1892.

Sect. 5. LENTAGO DC. Deciduous shrubs: lvs. entire or serrulate, with curv ing and anastomosing veins: winter-buds with 1 pair of scales: cymes without sterile marginal fls.: fr. blue-black or black; stone convex on back and with 3 shallow ventral grooves; albumen solid.

18. **V. nudum** L. SMOOTH WITHE-ROD. Upright shrub, sometimes to 5 m. ; brts. slightly scurfy: lvs. elliptic or ovate to obovate-elliptic or elliptic- lanceolate, 5–12 cm. long, acute or obtuse, broad-cuneate, entire or obscurely crenulate, slightly revolute, scurfy on both sides when young, glabrous above at length: fls. white or yellowish white, in cymes 6–12 cm. across, on slender stalks as long or longer than the cyme: fr. subglobose, about 8 mm. long blue-black. Fl.VI–VII; fr.IX–X(–XII). B.M.2281(c). B.B.3:273. L. I. to Fla. w. to Ky. and La. Intr. 1752. Zone VI.—**V. n. angustifòlium** Torr. & Gr., var Lvs. smaller and narrower, more lustrous above and of firmer texture. (*V. n* var. *nitidum* Zab., *V. anglicum* Hort.)

V. n. × *Lentago;* see under No. 20.

19. **V. cassinoìdes** L. WITHE-ROD. Upright shrub to 2 m., occasionally t 4 m., similar to the preceding species: lvs. elliptic or ovate to oblong, 3–10 cm. long, acute or bluntly acuminate, obscurely dentate or denticulate, dull green above, nearly glabrous: peduncle usually shorter than the cyme. Fl VI–VII; fr.IX. Ad.7:t.233(c). Em.2:411,t(c). G.F.9:305. S.L.383(h). N.F.9: f.71. Gn.M.29:223(h). (*V. nudum* var. c. Torr. & Gr.—APPALACHIAN TEA.) Nfd. to Man. and Minn., s. to N. C. Intr. 1761. Zone III.

20. **V. Lentàgo** L. SHEEP-BERRY (NANNY-BERRY). Shrub or small tree to 10 m., with slender brs.; brts. slightly scurfy: winter-buds gray, the terminal long-pointed: lvs. ovate to elliptic-obovate, 5–10 cm. long, acuminate, broad- cuneate to rounded at base, finely toothed, glabrous or scurfy on the veins be- neath; petiole 1–2.5 cm. long, mostly winged with wavy margin: cymes 6–12 cm. broad, sessile: fr. ellipsoid, 1.2–1.5 cm. long, blue-black, bloomy. Fl.V–VI; fr.IX–X. S.O.3:t.176(c). G.O.t.102(c). S.S.5:t.223,224. Hudson Bay to Man., s. to Ga. and Miss. Intr. 1761. Zone II. Handsome often arborescent shrub —**V. L. sphaerocárpum** Gray, var. Fr. subglobose.

V. L. × *nudum* = **V. Vétteri** Zabel. Similar to No. 19, but lvs. more closely and distinctly denticulate and more distinctly acuminate, petioles below infl. narrowly winged. Orig. before 1879.—*V. L.* × *prunifolium* = **V. Jáckii** Rehd. Differing chiefly in the broader, less acuminate lvs., more finely serrate, less pale beneath, in the less broadly winged petiole, the shorter winter-buds and denser habit. Orig. before 1900. Similar to *V. prunifolium* var. *Bushii* Palm. & Steyerm. which has narrower lvs. and the petioles not winged.

21. V. rufídulum Raf. SOUTHERN BLACK-HAW. Large shrub or small tree
10 m., with rather stout rigid brs.; winter-buds scarcely pointed, obtuse,
ke the young brts. and petioles rusty-pubescent: lvs. elliptic to elliptic-obo-
ate, 5–10 cm. long, usually obtuse, serrulate, lustrous and glabrous above,
usty-pubescent beneath, chiefly toward the base: petiole usually narrowly
inged, 6–12 mm. long: fls. pure white, in cymes 8–12 cm. across: fr. ellipsoid,
ark blue, bloomy, 1.2–1.5 cm. long. Fl.v–vi; fr.ix–x. S.S.5:t.225(partly).
.M.890. (*V. rufotomentosum* Small, *V. ferrugineum* Small, *V. prunifolium*
ar. *ferrugineum* Torr. & Gr.) Va. to Fla., w. to Ill. and Tex. Intr. 1883. Zone
. Handsome arborescent shrub with lustrous dark green lvs. and attractive
s. and frs.

22. V. prunifòlium L. BLACK-HAW. Large shrub or small tree to 5 m.,
ith rigid spreading brs.; winter-buds short-pointed, reddish pubescent; brts.
labrous: lvs. broad-elliptic to ovate, 3–8 cm. long, acute or obtuse, rounded
t base or broad-cuneate, serrulate, glabrous or nearly so; petiole not or
arrowly winged, 8–16 mm. long: fls. pure white, in sessile cymes 5–10 cm.
cross: fr. short-ellipsoid to subglobose, 8–12 mm. long, blue-black and
loomy. Fl.iv–v; fr.ix–x. Ad.3:t.110(c). D.H.1:195. Gng.5:310(h). A.F.
2:1100(h). (*V. pyrifolium* Poir.—STAG-BUSH.) Conn. to Fla., w. to Mich.
nd Tex. Intr. 1727. Zone III. Similar to the preceding.

V. p. × *Lentago;* see under No. 20.

Sect. 6. TINUS Maxim. Evergreen usually glabrous shrubs: lvs. entire or
bscurely toothed, often 3-nerved at base with curving and anastomosing veins;
etiole exstipulate; winter-buds with 1 pair of scales: corolla rotate: drupe sub-
lobose to ellipsoid, blue or blue-black; stone without grooves; albumen rumi-
ate.

23. V. Davìdi Franch. Evergreen compact shrub to 1 m.; brts. warty:
vs. elliptic to elliptic-obovate, 5–14 cm. long, short-acuminate, broad-cuneate
o nearly rounded at base, distinctly 3-nerved, sometimes obscurely toothed,
hiefly above the middle, dark green above, paler below, glabrous except
xillary tufts of hairs beneath; petiole 6–25 mm. long: fls. dull white, in dense
ymes 5–8 cm. across, on a stalk 1.5–3 cm. long; fr. ovoid or globose-ovoid, 6
m. long, blue. Fl.vi; fr.ix–x. J.L.38:f.44. R.H.1926:69(h). Gn.86:633. G.C.
2:225. W. China. Intr. 1904. Zone VII. Shrub with attractive fr.

Related species: **V. cinnamomifòlium** Rehd. Taller, sometimes tree to 6 m.:
vs. elliptic-oblong, 8–13 cm. long, 3-nerved, nearly entire, glabrous; cymes loose,
2–17 cm. across: fr. ovoid, 4 mm. long, blue-black, lustrous. S.T.2:t.114. W.
'hina. Intr. 1904. Zone VII?—**V. propínquum** Hemsl. Shrub with red-brown
ustrous brts.: lvs. elliptic or ovate to elliptic-oblong or ovate-lanceolate, 4–9
m. long, acuminate, broad-cuneate, 3-nerved, remotely denticulate, lustrous
bove: fls. greenish white, in slender-stalked cymes 4–7 cm. across: fr. globose-
void, 5–6 mm. long. S.T.2:t.115. C. and W. China. Intr. 1901. Zone VII.—
. **Harryànum** Rehd. Shrub to 3 m.; young brts. minutely stellate-tomentose:
vs. orbicular-ovate to obovate, 8–25 mm. long, obtuse, broad-cuneate, entire or
bscurely toothed, dark dull green above, glabrous; cymes 3–3.5 cm. across: fr.
void, 4 mm. long, black. W. China. Intr. 1904. Zone VII.—**V. calvum** Rehd.
hrub to 3 m.: lvs. narrow-ovate or rhombic-elliptic, 3–8 cm. long, acute or
btusish, cuneate, entire or serrulate, with 5–8 pairs of veins: infl.3–5 cm. across;
tamens shorter than corolla: fr. globose-ovoid, 5–6 mm. long, lustrous blue-
lack. (*V. Schneiderianum* Hand.-Mazz.) W. China. Cult. 1933. Zone VII?

Sect. 7. MEGALOTINUS Maxim. Lvs. usually evergreen, entire or denticulate,
enninerved with anastomosing veins; petiole exstipulate: corolla rotate or
ylindric-campanulate; drupe blue-black or purple; stone compressed, with dor-
al and ventral grooves; albumen usually solid; winter-buds with 1 pair of scales.

24. V. cylíndricum D. Don. Evergreen shrub or tree to 13 m.; brts.
varty: lvs. elliptic to oblong, 8–18 cm. long, acuminate, cuneate, entire or
emotely and obscurely toothed above the middle, dark dull green above and

covered with a thin waxy layer, with 3–4 pairs of veins; petiole 1–3 cm. long
cyme usually 7-rayed, 8–12 cm. across, on a stalk 2–6 cm. long: corolla white
tubular-campanulate, 4–5 mm. long, with short erect lobes; anthers exserte
lilac: fr. ovoid, 4–5 mm. long; stone slightly compressed, with shallow groove
1 ventral and 2 dorsal. Fl.vii–ix; fr.x–xii. S.T.2:t.143. G.C.52:371. M.C
254(h). (*V. coriaceum* Bl.) W. China, Himal. Intr. 1881. Zone VII. Distinc
on account of its small cylindric fls.

Sect. 8. ODONTOTINUS Rehd. Lvs. deciduous, rarely evergreen, dentate, wit
straight veins ending in the teeth, very rarely anastomosing, sometimes 3-nerve
and lobed; petioles with or without stipules; corolla rotate: stone with 3 or
ventral and 2 often obsolete dorsal grooves: shrubs with fascicled pubescence o
glabrous; winter-buds with 2 pairs of outer scales.

25. **V. japónicum** Spreng. Evergreen shrub to 2 m.; brts. glabrous: lv
broad- or rhombic-ovate, 8–14 cm. long, acute or short-acuminate, broad
cuneate or rounded at base, remotely and shallowly dentate above th
middle, dark lustrous green above, glabrous; petiole 1–3 cm. long: fls. fragran
in short-peduncled cymes 6–10 cm. across: fr. globose-ovoid, 8 mm. long, re
Fl.vi; fr.x. Ann. Hort. Bot. Pays-Bas, 2:97,t(c). N.T.1:600. D.H.1:193. (*V
macrophyllum* Bl., *V. Buergeri* Miq.) Japan. Intr. 1859. Zone VII. Hanc
some shrub with large lustrous lvs. and fragrant fls.

26. **V. foètidum** Wall. Half-evergreen shrub to 3 m.; young brts. stellate
pubescent: lvs. elliptic to oblong, 4–10 cm. long, acute to acuminate, cuneate
3-nerved at base and with 1–2 pairs of lateral veins, toothed above the middl
or nearly entire, glabrous above, pubescent on the veins beneath; petiole 5–
mm. long, pubescent: fls. small, in pubescent cymes 5–8 cm. across, on later
spreading brs.: fr. broad-ellipsoid, 6–8 mm. long, scarlet. Fl.vi; fr.ix. Wa
Pl. As. Rar. 1:t.61(c). Himal., Burma. Intr. ?—**V. f. rectangulàtu**
(Graebn.) Rehd., var. Slender shrub with long lateral brts. spreading at
right angle: lvs. lanceolate or lance-obovate: infl. usually subsessile. B.M
9509(c). W. China. Cult. 1927. Zone VII?—**V. f. ceanothoìdes** (C. I
Wright) Hand.-Mazz., var. Upright shrub to 2 m., with usually short later
brts.: lvs. obovate to elliptic-oblong, 2–5 cm. long, acute to rounded at ape
cuneate; petiole 2–6 mm. long: peduncle 5–15 mm. long. G.C.96:313. (*V.
C. H. Wright.) W. China. Intr. 1901. Zone VII?

27. **V. setígerum** Hance. Upright shrub to 4 m.; brts. glabrous: lv
ovate-oblong, 7–12 cm. long, acuminate, rounded at base, remotely denticu
late, dark green above, glabrous except silky hairs on the veins beneath, wit
6–9 pairs of veins; petiole 1–2 cm. long, glabrous: cymes 5-rayed, 3–5 cn
across, on a peduncle 1–2.5 cm. long; calyx purple, glabrous; stamens abou
half as long or as long as corolla: fr. ovoid, 8 mm. long, red. Fl.v–vi; fr.x. S.7
2:t.121. (*V. theiferum* Rehd.) C. and W. China. Intr. 1901. Zone (V). Wit
large lvs. and bright red fr. in autumn.—**V. s. aurantíacum** Rehd., f. F
orange-yellow. Intr. 1907.

Related species: **V. phlebótrichum** Sieb. & Zucc. Shrub to 2 m.: lvs. ovat
to elliptic-ovate, 3–6 cm. long; petiole 2–5 mm. long; cymes slender-stalked, no
ding, 2–4 cm. across; stamens very short, the filaments shorter than anther
S.I.2:t.73(c). S.T.2:t.120. N.T.1:607. Japan. Cult. 1890. Zone VII?

28. **V. Wrìghtii** Miq. Upright shrub to 3 m.: brts. nearly glabrous: lv
usually suborbicular to broad-obovate on flowering brts., ovate or broa
ovate on sterile shoots, 8–14 cm. long, abruptly acuminate, rounded or broa
cuneate at base, coarsely dentate, nearly glabrous except slightly pubescer
on the veins beneath and with axillary tufts of hairs; petiole 6–20 mm. long
cymes 5-rayed, 5–10 cm. across, glabrous or slightly pubescent, on a sta

$-20 mm. long; stamens longer than corolla: fr. globose-ovoid, 8 mm. long, ed. Fl.v–vi; fr.ix–x. S.I.1:t.19. N.T.1:604. Japan. Intr. 1892. Zone V. With showy fr.; the lvs. turning crimson in autumn.—**V. W. Héssei** (Koehne) Rehd., var. Of dwarfer habit, lvs. ovate with fewer and shallower teeth: ymes smaller; stamens about as long as corolla. (*V. H.* Koehne.) Gt.58: •1(l). Japan. Intr. before 1809.

29. **V. dilatàtum** Thunb. Upright bushy shrub to 3 m.; young brts. pilose: vs. suborbicular to broad-ovate or obovate, 6–12 cm. long, abruptly short-,cuminate, rounded or subcordate at base, coarsely toothed, hairy on both ides, with 5–8 pairs of veins; petiole 6–16 mm. long: cymes very numerous, $-12 cm. across, pilose, on a peduncle 1–3 cm. long; stamens longer than the ›ubescent corolla: fr. broad-ovoid, 8 mm. long, scarlet. Fl.v–vi; fr.ix–x. Ad.5:t.161(c). B.M.6215(c). G.F.4:150. A.F.15:123(h). S.L.379(h). E. Asia. ntr. before 1845. Zone V. Free-flowering shrub, with showy fls. and decora-ive fr. in fall remaining a long time on the brs.—**V. d. xanthocárpum** Rehd., . Fr. yellow. Gn.90:8(h). Cult. 1919.

Related species: **V. corylifòlium** Hook. f. & Thoms. Similar to *V. dilatatum*, ›ut brts., petioles and peduncles with long spreading fulvous hairs. E. Himal., 2. and W. China. Intr. 1907. Zone VI.

30. **V. Wilsónii** Rehd. Shrub to 3 m.; brts. and petioles fasciculate-•ilose: lvs. ovate to oblong-ovate, 4–8 cm. long, long-acuminate, rounded to ›road-cuneate at base, serrate from near base, loosely pilose above and below ›r nearly glabrous below, with 6 or 7 pairs of veins; petiole 1–1.5 cm. long; ymes about 5 cm. across, yellowish velvety-pubescent; peduncle about 2 cm. ong; rays usually 6: stamens about as long as the pubescent corolla; ovary •ubescent: fr. ovoid, 8 mm. long, bright red, with scattered hairs. Fl.vi; fr.x. V. China. Intr. 1908. Zone VII?

31. **V. betulifòlium** Batal. Shrub to 4 m.; brts. glabrous, becoming red-•rown: lvs. ovate or rhombic-ovate, sometimes elliptic-oblong, 3–8 cm. long, ,cute or short-acuminate, broad-cuneate, coarsely dentate except near base, ·labrous above, lighter beneath and sparingly hairy on the veins and bearded n the axils, often glandular, with 4 or 5 pairs of veins; petioles slender, 1–1.5 m. long: cymes 6–10 cm. across, short-stalked, rather loose, usually 7-rayed, ›paringly hairy or nearly glabrous; ovary glandular and sparingly hairy or ₁early glabrous; stamens longer than corolla: fr. globose-ellipsoid, about 6 ₁m. long, red. Fl.vi–vii; fr.ix–x. B.M.8672(c). S.T.2:t.147. G.C.106:301. 2. and W. China. Intr. 1901. Zone V. Shrub with attractive fr.

32. **V. lobophýllum** Graebn. Shrub to 5 m.; brts. glabrous or sparingly ₁airy at first, becoming dark red-brown: lvs. ovate to orbicular-ovate or broad-•bovate, 5–11 cm. long, acuminate, often abruptly so, truncate or broad-uneate at base, dentate with shallow mucronate teeth, glabrous except pu-•escent on the midrib above and slightly hairy on the veins beneath, with 5 ›r 6 pairs of veins; petiole 1–3 cm. long: cyme 7-rayed, 5–10 cm. across, on a talk 1–2.5 cm. long, minutely pubescent and glandular, rarely glabrescent; •vary glandular and sparingly hairy; stamens longer than the corolla: fr. ubglobose, 8 mm. long, bright red. Fl.vi–vii; fr.ix–x. S.T.2:t.148. G.C.60: •97. Gn.89:614. C. and W. China. Intr. 1901. Zone V.

Related species: **V. ovatifòlium** Rehd. Lvs. ovate to oblong-ovate, acuminate, ›ounded at base, 5–7 cm. long, with 7–8 pairs of veins slightly hairy beneath: ymes 4–6 cm. across, 5–7 rayed; ovary stellate-pubescent; stamens shorter than ›orolla. W. China. Intr. 1904 or 1908? Zone V.

33. **V. dasyánthum** Rehd. Shrub to 2.5 m.; brts. glabrous, becoming red-•rown or dark purple: lvs. ovate or elliptic to ohlong, 6–12 cm. long, acu-

minate, rounded at base, rarely broad-cuneate, remotely denticulate, dark green and glabrous above, bearded in the axils beneath, with 6–7 pairs of veins; petiole 1.5–2 cm. long, glabrous, usually purplish, stipulate: cyme 7- rarely 5-rayed, 8–10 cm. across; peduncle 1–3 cm. long, purplish, like the rays of the 1st order glabrous, those of the 2d order villous; ovary densely villous; corolla villous outside; stamens longer than corolla: fr. short ellipsoid, 8 mm. long, bright red. Fl.vi–vii; fr.ix–x. S.T.2:t.149. C. China Intr. 1907. Zone VI?

Related species: **V. hupehénse** Rehd. Brts. stellate-pubescent, later glabres cent: lvs. broad-ovate or ovate, 5–7 cm. long, truncate or subcordate at base coarsely dentate, pubescent on both sides; petiole 8–15 mm. long: cyme 4–5 cm across, villous, usually 5-rayed; corolla pubescent outside. C. China. Intr. 1907 Zone V.

34. **V. eròsum** Thunb. Upright shrub to 2 m.; brts. pubescent when young, slender: lvs. elliptic-ovate or oblong-ovate to oblong-obovate, 4– cm. long, acuminate, rounded or broad-cuneate at base, sharply dentate, with 7–10 pairs of veins, glabrous except on the veins and in their axils beneath or slightly pubescent above and beneath; petiole 2–6 mm. long, stipulate cymes 6–8 cm. across, usually 5-rayed, rather loose, on a slightly pubescent stalk 1–2.5 cm. long; stamens slightly longer than corolla; ovary glabrous: fr globose-ovoid, 6 mm. long, red. Fl.v–vi; fr.ix. G.F.9:85. N.T.609. Japan China. Intr. 1844. Zone V.—**V. e. Taquétii** (Lévl.) Rehd., var. Lvs. oblong lanceolate, coarsely dentate or incisely dentate, often with 2 lobes near base Korea. Intr. ?

Closely related species: **V. ichangénse** Rehd. Lvs. ovate to ovate-lanceolate 3–6 cm. long, scabrid above, pubescent beneath, rarely glabrescent: cymes 2.5– cm. across; ovary densely villous; stamens shorter than corolla. S.T.2:t.150 C. and W. China. Intr. 1901. Zone VI?

35. **V. dentàtum** L. Arrow-wood. Upright bushy shrub to 5 m.; brts glabrous, becoming gray: lvs. suborbicular to ovate, 3–8 cm. long, short acuminate, rounded or subcordate, coarsely dentate, glabrous and lustrou above, glabrous beneath or bearded in the axils of the veins, with 6–10 pair of veins; petiole 1–2.5 cm. long: cymes slender-stalked, 5–8 cm. across, gla brous; stamens longer than corolla: fr. globose-ovoid, 6 mm. long, blue-black Fl.v–vi; fr.x. G.O.t.103(c). W.D.1:25(c). G.F.10:332. Em.2:414,t. N. B. to Minn., s. to Ga. Intr. 1736. Zone II. With conspicuous fls.

36. **V. pubéscens** Pursh. Shrub to 3 m.; young brts. stellate-pubescent becoming grayish brown: lvs. ovate to suborbicular, 5–10 cm. long, acute or short-acuminate, rounded or subcordate, coarsely dentate, glabrous or spar ingly hairy above, stellate-pilose beneath chiefly on the veins, with 7–9 pair of veins; petiole 1–2 cm. long, pubescent, exstipulate: cymes slender-stalked 6–10 cm. across, slightly pubescent: fr. globose-ovoid, 6 mm. long, blue-black Fl.vi–vii; fr.ix–x. S.T.1:t.43. G.F.4:29. B.C.6:3462. S.O.3:t.179(c, as *V dentatum*). (*V. venosum* Brit., *V. dentatum* var. *p.* Ait., *V. molle* of auth. not Michx., *V. nepalense* Hort.) Mass. to Va. Intr. 1739. Zone V. Simila to the preceding, blooming later.—**V. p. Cánbyi** (Rehd.) Blake. Lvs. thinner larger and broader, those below the infl. often 5–8 cm. broad, less pubescen beneath: cymes larger. W.A.20,t(h). S.L.380(h). (*V. venosum* var. *C.* Rehd *V. C.* Sarg.) Del. to Pa. Cult. 1884.—**V. p. indianénse** Rehd. Similar to the preceding, but brts. glabrous, lvs. more coarsely dentate, and petioles usually with subulate stipules. Ind. Intr. 1923. Zone V.—**V. p. Deàmii** Rehd. Lvs usually orbicular-ovate, sparingly pubescent above, rather soft-pubescen beneath, with 9–11 pairs of veins; petioles often with subulate stipules

V. *Deamii* Bush.) Ind. Intr. 1923. Zone V.—**V. p. longifòlium** (Dipp.)
Blake, var. Lvs. narrower and longer, usually ovate-oblong, pubescent on
both sides, more densely beneath; petiole exstipulate: infl. glabrous or pubes-
ent. S.H.2:f.415k(l). (*V. dentatum* var. *l.* Dipp., *V. venosum* var. *l.* Rehd.)
Cult. 1830?

Related species: **V. scabréllum** Chapm. Brts. scabrid: lvs. ovate to oblong-
vate, rarely broad-ovate, remotely dentate, with shallow, often rounded teeth,
with 5–7 pairs of veins; petiole 5–15 mm. long: cyme densely stellate-pubescent
on a stalk 2–4 cm. long: fr. short-ellipsoid, 6–8 mm. long. B.B.3:271. (*V. molle*
of auth., not Michx., *V. semitomentosum* Rehd.) Pa. to Fla. and Tex. Cult.
830. Zone VI.

37. V. Rafinesquiànum Schult. Shrub to 2 m.; brts. glabrous, later gray-
brown: lvs. ovate to nearly elliptic, 3–5 cm. long, acute or acuminate, rounded
or subcordate at base, coarsely dentate, glabrous or slightly pubescent above,
densely soft-pubescent beneath, with 4–6 pairs of veins; petiole 2–6 mm.
ong: cymes 3–6 cm. across, dense, on a glabrous stalk 1–3 cm. long; rays 5–7:
r. ellipsoid, 7–9 mm. long, bluish black. Fl.v–vi; fr.ix. G.F.3:125. B.C.6:
463. Gng.5:311(h). (*V. pubescens* auth., not Pursh, *V. affine* var. *hypomala-
zum* Blake.) Que. to Ga., w. to Man. and Ill. Cult. 1830. Zone II. Dense
hrub, very floriferous.—**V. R. affìne** (Schneid.) House, var. Lvs. glabrous or
lightly pubescent on the veins beneath, 3–8 cm. long; petiole 2–10 mm. long.
S.L.381(h). (*V. a.* Bush ex Schneid., *V. pubescens* var. *a.* Rehd.) Va. to
Minn., Mo. and Ark.

Related species: **V. bracteàtum** Rehd. Shrub to 3 m.: lvs. orbicular-ovate,
4–12 cm. long, cordate or subcordate, obtusely sinuate-dentate, pubescent on the
veins beneath; petiole 1.5–2 cm. long; cyme 4–8 cm. across, with conspicuous
bractlets: fr. 1 cm. long. S.T.1:t.68. Ga. Cult. 1904. Zone V.

38. V. mólle Michx. Shrub to 4 m.; bark exfoliating in thin flakes; brts.
glabrous, becoming light gray: lvs. suborbicular to broad-ovate, 6–12 cm.
ong, short-acuminate, deeply cordate, coarsely dentate, glabrous and dark
green above, paler and pubescent beneath; petiole 1.5–3 cm. long, stipulate:
cymes long-stalked, puberulous, 5–8 cm. across: fr. ellipsoid, 1 cm. long,
flattened, blue-black. Fl.vi; fr.viii–ix. B.B.3:272. Bot. Gaz. 22:t.8. (*V.
Demetrionis* Deane & Robins.) Ind. to Ky. and Mo. Intr. 1923. Zone V.
Distinct shrub easily recognized by the flaky bark and the light gray young
brts.—**V. m. leiophýllum** Rehd., f. Lvs. glabrous or nearly so beneath. Intr.
1900.

39. V. acerifòlium L. DOCKMACKIE. Upright shrub to 2 m.; young brts.
pubescent: lvs. suborbicular to ovate, 3-lobed, sometimes slightly so, 6–10
cm. long, rounded to cordate at base, the lobes acute to acuminate, coarsely
dentate, slightly pubescent above, more densely so and with black dots beneath; petiole 1–2.5 cm. long: fls. yellowish white, in long-stalked cymes 3–8
cm. broad: fr. ellipsoid, 6–8 mm. long, nearly black. Fl.v–vi; fr.ix. G.O.t.
104(c). W.D.t.118(c). Em.2:414,t. N. B. to Minn., s. to N. C. Intr. 1736.
Zone III. The lvs. turn bright crimson in fall.—**V. a. glabréscens** Rehd., var.
Lvs. glabrous or nearly so. N. C. Intr. 1912.—**V. a. ovàtum** Rehd., f. Lvs.
ovate, remotely dentate, subcordate. Cult. 1920.

Related species: **V. orientàle** Pall. Lvs. suborbicular, 3-lobed, 6–15 cm. long,
cordate to subcordate, glabrescent except bearded in the axils beneath and
without black dots. Gt.17:8,t. S.L.374. W. Asia, Cauc. Intr. 1827. Zone V.—
V. ellípticum Hook. Shrub to 2.5 m.: lvs. broad-elliptic, sometimes suborbicular,
to elliptic-oblong, 3–7 cm. long, obtuse or acute, subcordate, 3-nerved at base,
coarsely dentate above the middle, pubescent beneath at least on the veins;
petiole 6–20 mm. long: cymes 4–5 cm. across, long-stalked, pubescent: fr. ellipsoid, about 12 mm. long. D.H.1:182. S.H.2:f.415p-r(l). Wash. to Calif. Intr.
1908. Zone (V).

Sect. 9. OPULUS DC. Lvs. deciduous, 3–5-nerved at base, lobed, rarely witl out lobes, stipulate: drupe red; stone flattened, not or scarcely grooved: winte> buds with 2 connate outer scales: glabrous shrubs, or pubescent with simpl hairs.

40. **V. pauciflòrum** Raf. MOOSEBERRY. Straggling shrub, to 1.5 m.; brt glabrous: lvs. suborbicular to broad-elliptic, 5–8 cm. long, with 3 short acut lobes at apex, rounded or truncate at base, unequally serrate, glabrous c slightly pubescent beneath; petiole 1–2.5 cm. long: cyme 1.5–2.5 cm. across stamens shorter than corolla: fr. globose-ellipsoid, about 8 mm. long, re⟨ Fl.v; fr.vIII–IX. G.F.3:5. (*V. eradiatum* House.) Nfd. and Lab. to Alask₂ s. to N. H., Vt., Colo. and Wash ; N. E. Asia. Intr. 1880 Zone. II. Rarel cultivated; succeeds best in a half-shady, moist and cool situation.

41. **V. kansuénse** Batal. Shrub to 3 m., with gray brs.; brts. glabrous lvs. broad-ovate to oblong-ovate in outline, deeply 3–5-lobed, 2.5 cm. lons acuminate, broad-cuneate to subcordate, the lobes acuminate to acut⟨ coarsely toothed with mucronulate teeth, sparingly pubescent above, ₂ least on veins, bearded in the axils beneath: petiole slender, 1–2.5 cm. long: fl pinkish white, in 5–7-rayed cymes about 3 cm. wide; stamens longer tha' corolla: fr. ellipsoid, 8–10 mm. long, red. Fl.vi–vII; fr.IX. W. China. Int> 1908. Zone V?

42. **V. trílobum** Marsh. CRANBERRY-BUSH. Shrub to 4 m., with gray brs. brts. glabrous: lvs. broad-ovate, 5–12 cm. long, rounded or truncate at bas⟨ lobes acuminate, coarsely dentate, sometimes the middle lobe elongated an⟨ entire, pilose on the veins beneath or nearly glabrous: petiole 1–3 cm. lonş with shallow groove and small, usually stalked glands: cyme 7–10 cm. acros⟨ on a stalk 1.5–3 cm. long; stamens about twice as long as corolla: fr. sub globose or short-ellipsoid, 8–10 mm. long, scarlet. Fl.v–vII; fr.vIII–II. G.O.⟨ 20(c). B.B.3:270. (*V. americanum* auth., not Mill., *V. Opulus* var. *a.* Ait., *V. C* var. *pimina* Michx., *V. edule* Pursh, *V. Oxycoccus* Pursh, *V. Opulus* Am. auth not L.—HIGH CRANBERRY.) N. B. to B. C., s. to N. Y., Mich., S. D. and Or⟨ Intr. 1812. Zone II. With ornamental fr. beginning to color end of July an⟨ remaining on the brs. all winter.

43. **V. Opulus** L. EUROPEAN CRANBERRY-BUSH. Shrub to 4 m., with rath⟨ smooth light gray brs. and stems; brts. smooth and glabrous: lvs. simila to those of No. 42, with rather shorter, more-toothed lobes, pubescent beneatl or sometimes glabrous; petiole 1–2 cm. long, with narrow groove and a fe⟨ large disk-like glands: cyme on a stalk 1–3.5 cm. long: fr. subglobose, 8 mm across, red. Fl.v–vi; fr.vIII–IX. S.E.4:t.639. F.D.28:t.2912(c). Eu., N. Afr N. Asia. Cult. for centuries. Zone III.—**V. O. variegàtum** West., var. Witl variegated lvs.—**V. O. xanthocárpum** Endl., var. Fr. yellow. Gn.88:204.– **V. O. nànum** David. Dwarf compact form with small lvs., rarely flowering.– **V. O. ròseum** L., var. COMMON SNOWBALL. All fls. sterile, forming a globos⟨ head 5–6 cm. across. Gng.1:9(h). Gn.M.39:146(h). Gn.76:35(h);88:204. (*V O. var. sterile* DC., *V. roseum* Hort.—GUELDER-ROSE.) The Snowball-tree i often planted for its large globose fl.-heads; the lvs. turn deep red in autumn

44. **V. Sargénti** Koehne. Similar to the preceding, but bark darker, fissure⟨ and somewhat corky: brts. with prominent lenticels, pilose or glabrous whe⟨ young: lvs. of thicker texture, often larger, the upper ones usually with mucl elongated entire middle lobe and short spreading lateral lobes, sometime⟨ oblong-lanceolate and without lobes; petiole 2–3.5 cm. long, with larg⟨ disk-like glands: cymes on a stalk 2–6 cm. long; stamens with purple anthers sterile fls. larger, to 3 cm. across: fr. subglobose, 8–10 mm. long, scarlet. Fl

v–vi; fr.viii–x. S.I.2:t.73(c). S.T.1:t.42. H.N.3:t.27. N.T.1:611. Gn.M.33:39 (h). (*V. Opulus* var. *S.* Takeda.) N.E. Asia. Intr. 1892. Zone V or IV.—**V. S. calvéscens** Rehd., var. Lvs. glabrous or nearly so beneath. Intr. 1892.— **V. S. flávum** Rehd., f. With yellow fr.; fls. with yellow anthers: lvs. pubescent on the veins beneath. Intr. 1904.

3. SYMPHORICÁRPOS Duham. Deciduous upright or sometimes prostrate shrubs; winter-buds with about 2 pairs of outer scales: lvs. opposite, short-petioled, entire or occasionally on vigorous shoots, lobed, exstipulate: fls. perfect, axillary, usually forming axillary or terminal clusters or terminal spikes; calyx 4–5-toothed: corolla campanulate to tubular, 4–5-lobed; stamens 4–5, inserted on the tube, included or slightly exserted; style slender, with capitate stigma: ovary with 2 fertile 1-ovuled and 2 sterile several-ovuled cells: fr. a berry-like drupe with 2 nutlets. (Greek *symphorein*, to bear together, and *karpos*, fruit; referring to the clustered fr.) Syn.: *Symphoria* Pers. About 15 species in N. Am., s. to Mex. and 1 in China.—Ornamental shrubs chiefly cultivated for their showy frs.

A. Fr. white or pinkish; corolla usually pubescent inside.
  B. Fls. campanulate, often slightly ventricose at base.
    c. Style and stamens exserted...1. *S. occidentalis*
    cc. Style and stamens included.
      d. Corolla 6–8 mm. long: upright shrub...................................2. *S. albus*
      dd. Corolla 4–5 mm. long: prostrate shrub............................3. *S. hesperius*
  BB. Fls. tubular to funnelform; style and stamens included.
    c. Anthers reaching to about the middle of the corolla-lobes.
      d. Corolla 6–8 mm. long, tube pubescent within: lvs. pubescent...4. *S. rotundifolius*
      dd. Corolla 8–12 mm. long, glabrous or nearly so within: lvs. often glabrous.
                                        5. *S. oreophilus*
    cc. Anthers as long as corolla-lobes..................................6. *S. microphyllus*
AA. Fr. red or bluish black; corolla campanulate.
  B. Fls. in leafy spikes or axillary dense clusters: fr. red: pubescent shrub.7. *S. orbiculatus*
  BB. Fls. in peduncled terminal spikes: fr. bluish black: glabrous shrub........8. *S. sinensis*

1. S. occidentàlis Hook. WOLFBERRY. Shrub to 1 or 1.5 m., with upright rather stiff brs.: lvs. oval or ovate, 2–7 cm. long, obtuse, cuneate to rounded at base, entire or undulate-crenate, grayish green and pubescent beneath or glabrate: fls. in clusters or spikes 1–3 cm. long; corolla pinkish, 6 mm. long, densely hairy within; stamens and style slightly longer than corolla-lobes: fr. subglobose, white, about 1 cm. across. Fl.vi–vii; fr.ix. G.F.3:297. G.C.49: 104,t. B.B.3:277. Mich. to B. C., s. to Ill., Colo. and Kans. Cult. 1880. Zone II.—**S. o. Heỳeri** Dieck, var. Lvs. thinner, less distinctly veined beneath; style and stamens somewhat shorter. D.L.1:281(l). (*S. Heyeri* Dipp.) Colo. Cult. 1888. Zone II.

2. S. albus Blake. SNOWBERRY. Shrub to 1 m., with upright slender brs.; brts. usually slightly puberulous: lvs. oval to elliptic-oblong, 2–5 cm. long, obtuse, on shoots often sinuately lobed, pubescent beneath: fls. in terminal spikes or clusters; corolla pinkish, about 6 mm. long, pubescent inside: fr. globose or ovoid, 8–12 mm. long. Fl.vi–ix; fr.ix–xi. (*S. racemosus* Michx.—WAXBERRY.) N. S. to Alb., s. to Minn. and Va. Intr. 1879? Zone III. The shrub chiefly planted for its white fr. conspicuous in fall and early winter is *S. a. laevigatus*; typical *S. albus* is sometimes grown as *S. rac.* var. *pauciflorus*; the true *S. a.* var. *pauciflorus* (Gray) Blake has smaller lvs. and 1–3 fls. at end of brts.; it is apparently not in cult.—**S. a. laevigàtus** (Fern.) Blake, var. Taller, to 2 m.; brts. glabrous: lvs. usually larger and broader, 3–7 cm. long, glabrous: fr. larger, in terminal spikes. Ad.3:t.94(c). B.M.2211(c). Gn.77:527;84:17(h); 86:477. (*S. rivularis* Suksd.) Alaska to Calif., e. to Mont. and Colo.; often escaped from cult. Intr. 1806.—**S. a. ovàtus** (Spaeth) Rehd., var. A form of

5. ABÈLIA R. Br. Deciduous, rarely evergreen shrubs; winter-buds small, ovoid, with several pairs of outer scales: lvs. opposite, short-petioled, small or medium-sized, entire or dentate: fls. on 1 or 2-fld. peduncles axillary or terminal, sometimes forming terminal panicles or clusters; sepals 2–5, conspicuous, accrescent, persistent; corolla tubular or salver-shaped to campanulate, 5-lobed; stamens 4, didynamous, inserted at base of corolla-tube; ovary 3-celled, only 1 cell fertile and 1-ovuled; style elongated: fr. a 1-seeded leathery achene, crowned by the persistent sepals. (After Dr. Clarke Abel, physician and author on China; 1780–1826.) About 25 species in E. Asia, 1 in the Himal., and 2 in Mex.—Ornamental shrubs planted chiefly for their handsome fls.

A. Corolla campanulate-funnelform; brts. pilose, villous or glabrous, slender; sepals 2 or 5.
    Sect. 1. EUABELIA Rehd.
  B. Sepals 2.
    c. Corolla 1.5–2 cm. long..1. *A. Engleriana*
    cc. Corolla 2.5–3 cm. long...2. *A. Schumannii*
  BB. Sepals 5 or 2–5.
    c. Sepals 2–5 on the same plant.......................................3. *A. grandiflora*
    cc. Sepals 5 ....4. *A. chinensis*
AA. Corolla salver-shaped with cylindric tube; brts. with reflexed setose hairs, rarely glabrate, thickened at the nodes; sepals 4 or 5: bark of stem thick, fluted with 6 grooves.
    Sect. 2. ZABELIA Rehd.
  B. Sepals 5: infl. subcapitate...5. *A. triflora*
  BB. Sepals 4: fls. usually 2 at end of short brts.......................6. *A. Zanderi*

1. A. Engleriàna (Graebn.) Rehd. Bushy shrub to 2 m., with spreading slender brs.; young brts. puberulous: lvs. ovate to elliptic-ovate or elliptic-lanceolate, 2–3.5 cm. long, acute to acuminate, cuneate, sparingly serrulate, lustrous green, sparingly hairy on the veins beneath: fls. several on short lateral brts.; sepals oblong-elliptic, 8 mm. long; corolla rosy pink, tubular below the middle, campanulate above, gibbous at base. Fl.VI–VII. (*Linnaea E.* Graebn.) C. and W. China. Intr. 1908. Zone V.

Related species: **A. serràta** Sieb. & Zucc. Lvs. rhombic-ovate, 1.5–2.5 cm. long, entire or with few shallow teeth; peduncles 2-fld.; corolla funnelform, gradually widened toward the apex. S.Z.1:t.34(c). N.T.1:453. Japan. Intr. before 1900? VII.

2. A. Schumánnii (Graebn.) Rehd. Slender shrub; young brts. dark purple and puberulous: lvs. ovate or elliptic-ovate, 1.5–2.5 cm. long, obtusish and mucronulate, cuneate, entire or slightly serrulate, ciliate, villous along the midrib beneath: fls. several on 1-fld. axillary stalks near end of short brts.; sepals elliptic, 6–10 mm. long; corolla rosy pink, campanulate, tubular at the lower third, gibbous at base, minutely glandular-puberulous outside; filaments hirsute. Fl.VI–VIII. (*Linnaea S.* Graebn.) B.M.8810(c, as *A. longituba*). W. China. Cult. 1915. Zone VII.

Related species: **A. Graebneriàna** Rehd. Shrub to 3 m.: lvs. ovate to oblong-ovate, 3–5 cm. long, acuminate, remotely serrate, pubescent on the midrib beneath: fls. on 1-fld. peduncles, few at end of short lateral brts.; corolla campanulate, 2.5 cm. long, pink, yellow in throat. C. China. Intr. 1910. Zone VI or VII.—**A. uniflòra** R. Br. Evergreen shrub to 2 m.; lvs. ovate, 2–5 cm. long, acuminate, sparingly serrulate, lustrous dark green above, paler beneath and pubescent on the midrib: fls. on 1–3-fld. peduncles, several at end of brts.; corolla campanulate, 2.5 cm. long, white, tinged pink, orange in throat. B.M. 4694(c). G.C.37:323. F.S.8:t.824(c). Gn.27:425. E. China. Intr. 1845. Zone VII?

3. × A. grandiflòra (André) Rehd. (*A. chinensis* × *uniflora*). Half-ever-green shrub to 2 m.; brts. puberulous: lvs. ovate, 1.5–3.5 cm. long, acute, rounded or cuneate at base, lustrous dark green above, paler beneath and glabrous except bearded near base of midrib: fls. in leafy panicles at end of lateral brts.; sepals varying from 2–5, often partly connate, purplish; corolla campanulate, about 2 cm. long, white, flushed pink. Fl.vi–xi. Ad.2:t.49(c). Gt.41:113,t(c). Gn.76:528(h). (*A. rupestris* var. *g.* André, *A. rupestris* Hort., not Lindl., *Linnaea Spaethiana* and *L. Perringiana* Graebn.) Orig. before 1880. Zone (V). Handsome shrub planted for its long flowering season and its lustrous half-evergreen lvs.

4. **A. chinénsis** R. Br. Deciduous spreading shrub, to 1.5 m.; young brts. puberulous, reddish: lvs. ovate, 2–3.5 cm. long, acute or short-acuminate, rounded at base, serrate or serrulate, villous beneath near base of midrib and lateral veins, sometimes with scattered hairs above: fls. fragrant, in dense axillary and terminal cymes forming terminal dense and short panicles; sepals oblong-obovate, 6 mm. long, puberulous; corolla funnelform, about 1 cm. long, white; stamens exserted. Fl.vii–viii. B.R.32:8(c). P.F.2:t.201(c). Gn. 27:424. C. and E. China. Intr. 1844. Zone VII?

Related species: **A. spathulàta** Sieb. Shrub to 1 m.: lvs. elliptic-lanceolate to ovate, 2–5 cm. long, unequally serrate, sparingly hairy above, downy on veins beneath: fls. in pairs at end of short brts.: corolla funnelform-campanulate, 2–2.5 cm. long, white with yellow throat; stamens shorter than corolla. B.M. 6601(c). S.Z.1:t.34(c). N.T.1:618. Japan. Intr. 1880. Zone VII?

5. **A. triflòra** R. Br. Shrub of upright habit, to 4 m.; bark of stems corrugated; young brts. reflexed-setose: lvs. lanceolate to ovate-lanceolate, 3–7 cm. long, long-acuminate, entire or with few coarse teeth, ciliate and sparingly hairy on both sides or nearly glabrous: fls. fragrant, in terminal clusters about 5 cm. across; sepals linear, 1–1.5 cm. long, hairy; corolla rosy-white, with pubescent tube about 1.5 cm. long and with spreading rounded lobes, limb about 1.2 cm. across. Fl.vi. B.M.9131(c). R.H.1870:511,t(c). G.C.II. 16:34. (*Linnaea t.* A. Br. & Vatke.) N. W. Himal. Intr. 1847. Zone VII.

6. **A. Zánderi** (Graebn.) Rehd. Upright shrub to 3 m.; brts. glabrous, except scattered reflexed bristles near base: lvs. ovate-oblong to ovate-lanceolate, 3–7 cm. long, acuminate, broad-cuneate, rarely rounded at base, sparingly dentate or entire, sparingly hairy above, sparingly pilose beneath, more densely so on veins; petiole 2–4 mm. long: peduncles 2-fld., 2–6 mm. long, terminal on short lateral brts.; pedicels short; ovary glabrous; sepals oblanceolate to oblong, 7–10 mm. long, glabrous or minutely ciliolate: corolla salvershaped, glabrous outside, tube 8–10 mm. long, with rounded spreading lobes; style as long as tube; stamens slightly shorter. Fl.vi. H.N.3:t.35. (*Linnaea Z.* Graebn.) C. and N. W. China. Intr. 1910. Zone V. Very variable.

Related species: **A. biflòra** Turcz. Lvs. usually narrower and usually incisely serrate: fls. in terminal pairs; peduncle wanting; pedicels short; ovary setose, usually curved. H.N.3:t.32. N. China, Manch. Intr. 1923. Zone V.—**A. umbellàta** (Graebn. & Buchw.) Rehd. Lvs. elliptic or elliptic-lanceolate, 3–8 cm. long, acute or acuminate, coarsely dentate to entire, pubescent on the veins beneath or glabrous: fls. 4–7 on a slender peduncle 1–1.5 cm. long; corolla-tube 10–12 mm. long. C. and W. China. Intr. 1907. Zone VII?

6. **LINNAÈA** Gronov. ex L. TWINFLOWER. Evergreen trailing subshrub: lvs. opposite, small, petioled, crenate, exstipulate: fls. in pairs on slender upright peduncles terminal on short brts.; calyx 5-parted; corolla campanulate, 5-lobed; stamens 4, ovary 3-celled, stipitate-glandular: 1 cell fertile and 1-ovuled: fr. ovoid, dry, indehiscent, 1-seeded. (Named by Gronovius for Linnaeus at his own request.) One circumpolar very variable species.

L. boreàlis L. Stems slender, sparingly pubescent: lvs. roundish or obovate, 6–25 mm. long, acute or obtuse, with few crenate teeth, usually ciliate and with scattered hairs above: fls. fragrant, pediceled, on slender peduncles 4–7 cm. long; sepals lanceolate, 1.5–3 mm. long: corolla campanulate, 6–9 mm. long, white, tinged and striped rose-purple: fr. yellow, about 3 mm.

long. Fl.vi–viii. R.I.17:t.119,f.1(c). S.E.4:t.644(c). Gn.24:177. M.G.25:138
(h). Act. Hort. Berg. 4,7:t.1–13. (*L. serpyllifolia* Rydb.) N. Eu., N. Asia,
N. Am. (Alaska). Cult. 1762. Zone II. Handsome trailing plant; suited for a
moist and half-shady position in the rock garden.—**L. b. americàna** (Forbes)
Rehd., var. Lvs. usually glabrous, ciliate near base: corolla 8–15 mm. long,
the tubular portion exceeding the calyx; sepals 1.5–3 mm. long. B.B.3:276.
(*L. a.* Forb.) Lab. to Alaska, s. to W. Va., Ind., Colo., Utah and N. Calif. Intr.
1800.—**L. b. longiflòra** Torr., var. Lvs. slightly larger; corolla more funnelform, 10–16 mm. long, the tubular portion exceeding the calyx; sepals 3–5 mm.
long. Act. Hort. Berg. 4,7:t.13,f.12. B. C. to Calif.

7. **KOLKWÍTZIA** Graebn. Deciduous upright shrub; winter-buds with
several pairs of pointed pubescent scales: lvs. opposite, short-petioled, exstipulate: fls. in pairs forming terminal corymbs on short lateral brts.; sepals
5, narrow, pilose, spreading; corolla campanulate, 5-lobed; stamens 4, about
as long as tube; the two ovaries inserted one above the other, sometimes
partly connate, ellipsoid, narrowed into a long beak, hispid, with adnate
bractlets, 3-celled, 1 cell fertile and 1-ovuled, the other sterile, several-ovuled:
fr. dry, hispid like the pedicels and sepals. (After Richard Kolkwitz, professor
of botany, Berlin; b. 1873.) One species in China.

K. amàbilis Graebn. BEAUTY-BUSH. Shrub to 2 m.; young brts. pilose,
older with brown flaky bark: lvs. broad-ovate, 3–7 cm. long, acuminate,
rounded at base, remotely and shallowly toothed or nearly entire, ciliate,
dull green above and sparingly hairy, pilose on the veins beneath; petiole
pilose, 2–3 mm. long: fls. in corymbs 5–7 cm. across; peduncles 6–10 mm.
long, pilose; corolla about 1.5 cm. long, pink, yellow in throat, puberulous: fr.
ovoid, 6 mm. long, bristly. Fl.v–vi. B.M.8563(c). H.I.2937. H.N.3:t.37. G.C.
74:4,5,7;106:55t(h). H.B.2:487(h). C. China. Intr. 1901. Zone V.—Graceful
shrub, very handsome in spring with its profuse pink fls.

8. **DIERVÍLLA** Adans. Deciduous low stoloniferous shrubs; winter-
buds with several pairs of pointed scales: lvs. opposite, serrate, exstipulate:
fls. in 3- to many in terminal or subterminal cymes, yellow or greenish yellow;
calyx-lobes 5, subulate, distinct; corolla 2-lipped, with funnelform tube; the
5 stamens and the style exserted; stigma capitate; ovary elongated, 2-celled:
caps. thin-walled, beaked, crowned by the shriveled calyx, indehiscent or
imperfectly splitting, valves not separating; core hollow; seeds many, minute,
reticulate, not winged. (After Diereville or Dierville, French surgeon; traveled in Canada 1699–1700 and intr. *D. Lonicera* to France.) Three species in
N. Am.—Fls. not conspicuous and therefore not much planted.

A. Brts. and lvs. glabrous or nearly so.
  B. Lvs. petioled ....1. *D. Lonicera*
  BB. Lvs. subsessile ....2. *D. sessilifolia*
AA. Brts. and lvs. pubescent; lvs. subsessile...,................................3. *D. rivularis*

1. **D. Lonícera** Mill. Shrub to 1 m.; brts. nearly terete: lvs. ovate to
ovate-oblong, 4–10 cm. long, acuminate, subcordate to broad-cuneate, serrate
and ciliolate; petiole 3–6 mm. long: fls. yellow, in usually 3-fld. peduncled
cymes; limb of corolla nearly as long as tube: caps. about 8 mm. long. Fl.vi–
vii. B.M.1796(c). (*D. Diervilla* Macm., *D. canadensis* Willd., *D. trifida*
Moench.) Nfd. to Sask., s. to N. C. and Mich. Intr. 1720. Zone III.

2. **D. sessilifòlia** Buckl. Shrub to 1.5 m.; brts. 4-angled: lvs. subsessile,
ovate-lanceolate, 6–15 cm. long, acuminate, cordate or rounded at base,
sharply serrate: fls. sulphur-yellow, in 3–7-fld. cymes often crowded into a

dense terminal panicle; limb of corolla shorter than tube: caps. 9–12 mm. long. Fl.vi–viii. G.C.42:427. L.I.t.8. N. C. to Ga. and Ala. Intr. 1844. Zone IV.

   D. s. × *Lonicera* = **D. spléndens** (Carr.) Kirchn. Similar to No. 2, but lvs. short-petioled. (*Weigela s.* Carr.) Orig. about 1850.

   3. D. rivulàris Gatt. Shrub to 2 m.; brts. terete, densely short-pilose: lvs. subsessile, ovate to oblong-lanceolate, 4–8 cm. long, acuminate, cordate to truncate, doubly serrate, pubescent on both sides: cymes few- to many-fld., crowded into terminal panicles; corolla lemon-yellow; limb about as long as tube: fr. 6 mm. long. Fl.vii–viii. G.C.38:339. N. C. to Ga. and Ala. Cult. 1898. Zone V.

   9. WEÌGELA Thunb. Deciduous shrubs; winter-buds with several pointed scales: lvs. opposite, petioled, rarely subsessile, serrate, exstipulate: fls. rather large, 1 to several in axillary cymes on short brts. lateral on last year's brs., white to pink, purple or crimson; calyx-lobes 5, connate below or distinct; corolla tubular-campanulate or funnelform, zygomorphous, tube much longer than the 5 broad lobes; stamens 5, shorter than corolla; style sometimes exserted; stigma capitate; ovary 2-celled, elongated: caps. generally oblong, beaked, opening with 2 valves, leaving a central column; seeds many, angular, minute, often winged. (After C. E. von Weigel, professor in Greifswald, Germany; botanical author; 1748–1831.) Including *Macrodier-villa* Nakai (*Calyptrostigma* Trautv. & Mey., not Klotzsch) and *Weigel-astrum* Nakai. About 12 species in E. Asia.—Ornamental shrubs with showy fls.; many garden forms and hybrids.

<small>A. Anthers not cohering nor connivent; calyx not 2-lobed: central column of fr. exserted.
  B. Calyx divided to base into linear, usually pilose lobes: seeds with narrow wing.
                                  Sect. 1. Utsugia (A. DC.) Bailey
    c. Lvs. and brts. pubescent.
      D. Fls. peduncled, pink, carmine or white; style not or slightly exceeding the corolla.
        E. Lvs. pubescent beneath chiefly on the veins: corolla funnelform-campanulate, gradually widening ....1. *W. japonica*
        EE. Lvs. gray-tomentose or densely soft-pubescent beneath: corolla cylindric below, campanulate above.....................................2. *W. hortensis*
      DD. Fls. sessile, dark crimson (except in var.); style much exserted; ovary pubescent.
                                     3. *W. floribunda*
    cc. Fls. sessile: lvs. and brts. glabrous....................................4. *W. coraeensis*
  BB. Calyx divided to about the middle; lobes lanceolate: seeds not winged.
                             Sect. 2. Calysphyrum (Bge.) Bailey
    c. Lvs. glabrous above, pubescent on veins beneath or only on midrib.....5. *W. florida*
    cc. Lvs. pubescent above, soft-pubescent beneath........................6. *W. praecox*
AA. Anthers pilose, connected in a ring about the style or only connivent and partly free; stigma calyptrate; calyx 2-lipped; central column of fr. not exceeding the valves.
  B. Valves separating at apex from the persisting central column; seeds with narrow lateral wing ....Sect. 3. Weigelastrum (Nakai) Rehd.
                                   7. *W. Maximowiczii*
  BB. Valves cohering at apex; seeds winged at ends.Sect. 4. Calyptrostigma (Koehne) Rehd.
                                   8. *W. Middendorffiana*</small>

   1. W. japónica Thunb. Shrub to 3 m.; young brts. glabrous or with 2 rows of hairs: lvs. elliptic to oblong-obovate, 5–10 cm. long, acuminate, rounded or cuneate at base, serrate, slightly pubescent above, pilose-pubescent on veins beneath; petiole 2–5 mm. long: peduncles 3-fld., several on short lateral brts.; corolla campanulate-funnelform, 2.5–3 cm. long, whitish at first, changing to carmine, slightly pubescent or nearly glabrous outside; style slightly exserted; ovary glabrous or sparingly pilose: caps. glabrous. Fl.v–vi. S.I.2:t.74(c). G.F.9:405. B.C.2:1008. (*Diervilla j.* DC.) Japan. Intr. 1892. Zone V.— **W. j. sínica** (Rehd.) Bailey, var. Shrub to 6 m.: lvs. soft-pubescent beneath; petiole 8–10, rarely 5–7 mm. long: corolla abruptly contracted below the middle into a narrow tube, pale pink; ovary densely pubescent. (*D. j.* var. *s.* Rehd.) C. China. Intr. 1908. Zone VI.

Related species: **W. decòra** (Nakai) Nakai. Lvs. villous beneath on th veins: fls. short-peduncled; ovary nearly glabrous; corolla changing from greenish to white and finally pink; style somewhat exserted. Japan. Cult 1933. Zone V?

2. **W. horténsis** (Sieb. & Zucc.) C. A. Mey. Shrub to 3 m.; young brts pilose: lvs. ovate or obovate to oblong, 5–10 cm. long, acuminate, serrulate slightly pubescent above at first, later glabrate, densely grayish pubescent o tomentose beneath; petiole 2–5 mm. long: fls. on elongated 3-fld. pubescen peduncles: corolla tubular-campanulate, carmine; style exserted, as long o slightly longer than lobes; ovary pilose: caps. glabrous. Fl.v–vi. S.Z.1:t.29,3 (c). N.T.1:701. (*Diervilla h.* Sieb. & Zucc., *D. japonica* var. *h.* Rehd.) Japan Cult. 1870. Zone VI.—**W. h. nívea** Bonard. Fls. white. G.C.II.10:80. Gn.22 185;34:352. (*W. h.* var. *albiflora* Nakai, *D. japonica* var. *nivea* Rehd., *D japonica* var. *alba* Mak.) Intr. about 1864.

3. **W. floribúnda** (Sieb. & Zucc.) C. A. Mey. Shrub to 3 m., with slende brs.; young brts. pubescent or at least with 2 rows of hairs: lvs. elliptic t oblong-ovate or oblong-obovate, 7–10 cm. long, acuminate, broad-cuneate serrate, sparingly pubescent above, villous-pubescent beneath chiefly on th veins; petiole 2–5 mm. long: fls. sessile, crowded on short lateral brts.; corolla tubular-funnelform, 2.5–3 cm. long, pubescent outside, dark crimson, brown ish crimson in bud, the lobes about 5 times shorter than tube; stamens a long as corolla; style exserted, often exceeding the lobes by 1 cm.: caps. pu bescent. Fl.v–vi. S.Z.1:t.32(c). I.H.10:t.383(c). N.T.1:696. (*Diervilla f* Sieb. & Zucc., *D. multiflora* Lem.) Japan. Intr. 1860. Zone V.—**W. f. grandi flòra** (Dipp.) Rehd., f. Fls. larger, brownish crimson. (*W. arborescens* Hort.) —**W. f. versícolor** (Sieb. & Zucc.) Rehd., var. Fls. greenish white at first changing to red or crimson: lvs. pilose on the veins beneath. S.Z.1:t.33(c) (*D. v.* Sieb. & Zucc.)

Related species: **W. subséssilis** (Nakai) Bailey. Lvs. subsessile, broad-ovate to obovate-oblong, subcordate to rounded at base, pilose on the veins beneath: fls. sessile; corolla greenish yellow or yellowish pink; style about as long as corolla: caps. sparingly pilose. N.K.11:t.41. Korea. Intr. ?

4. **W. coraeénsis** Thunb. Shrub to 5 m.; brts. stout, glabrous: lvs. broad-elliptic or elliptic to obovate, 8–12 cm. long, abruptly acuminate, broad-cuneate, crenate-serrate, lustrous above and glabrous except on the veins, sparingly hairy on the veins beneath or quite glabrous, petiole 5–10 mm. long: fls. in peduncled cymes, several on short lateral brts.; corolla campanulate-funnelform, abruptly narrowed below the middle, 2.5–3 cm. long, glabrous pale rose or whitish at first, changing to carmine; sepals linear-lanceolate, glabrous or ciliate; ovary glabrous. Fl.v–vi. S.Z.1:t.31(c). S.I.2:t.74(c). F.S 8:t.855(c). (*Diervilla c.* DC., *D. grandiflora* Sieb. & Zucc., *D. amabilis* Carr.) Japan. Cult. 1850. Zone V.—**W. c. alba** (Voss) Rehd., f. Fls. yellowish white, changing to pale rose. (*D. c.* var. *arborea* Rehd., *Weigela grandiflora alba* and *W. arborea grandiflora* Hort.)

Related species: **W. suàvis** (Komar.) Bailey. Shrub to 2 m.; young brts. with 2 rows of curly hairs: lvs. subsessile, ovate- to oblong-lanceolate, 2–5 cm. long, acute or acuminate, obtusely serrate, sparingly ciliate and sometimes with a few hairs on midrib beneath, membranous: corolla purple-pink, 2–2.5 cm. long, puberulous outside. Manch. Intr. about 1910?

5. **W. flòrida** (Sieb. & Zucc.) A. DC. Shrub to 3 m.; brts. with 2 rows of hairs: lvs. short-petioled to subsessile, elliptic to ovate-oblong, or obovate, 5–10 cm. long, acuminate, rounded to cuneate at base, serrate, glabrous above except on midrib, pubescent or tomentose on veins beneath; sepals nearly

glabrous, connate about ½; ovary slightly pubescent; corolla funnelform-campanulate, about 3 cm. long, abruptly narrowed below the middle, rosy pink outside, pale within, with rounded spreading lobes; stigma 2-lobed: caps. glabrous. Fl.v–vi. B.M.4396(c). F.S.3:t.211(c). R.H.1849:381,t(c). (*Diervilla f.* Sieb. & Zucc., *W. rosea* Lindl., *W. amabilis* Hort., *D. pauciflora* Carr.) N. China, Korea. Intr. 1845. Zone V. One of the handsomest species and particularly the var. *venusta* is one of the most graceful and hardiest of the Weigelas.—**W. f. alba** (Moore) Rehd., f. Fls. white, changing to light pink. R.H.1861:331,t(c). (*D. f. f. candida* Voss, *Weigela rosea alba* Moore.)—**W. f. variegàta** (Bean) Bailey, var. Lvs. edged with pale yellow; fls. deep rose. B.S.1:490.—**W. f. venústa** (Rehd.) Nakai, var. Lvs. smaller, usually obovate, 3–6 cm. long, usually nearly glabrous; fls. in dense clusters with small lvs. at base; corolla rosy-pink, about 3.5 cm. long, rather gradually narrowed toward the base, lobes oval. Fl.v. B.M.9080(c). N.K.11:t.39. (*W. v.* Bailey, *D. f. var. v.* Rehd., *D. v.* Stapf.) Korea. Intr. 1905. Zone IV.

6. **W. praècox** (Lemoine) Bailey. Shrub to 2 m.; brts. glabrous or pilose: lvs. short-petioled or subsessile, elliptic or elliptic-ovate to obovate, 5–8 or on vigorous shoots to 12 cm. long, acuminate, serrate, hairy above, soft pubescent beneath: fls. nodding, 3–5 on short lateral brts.; calyx and ovary pilose or the latter glabrate toward the base; corolla funnelform-campanulate, abruptly narrowed below the middle, rosy pink or purplish pink, yellow in throat, pubescent outside: caps. glabrous. Fl.v. Gt.46:t.1441(c). R.H.1905: 314,315. H.B.3:73(h). N.K.11:t.38. (*Diervilla praecox* Lemoine, ?*D. Wolfiana* Schneid.) Korea. Cult. 1894. Zone V. The earliest of all species to bloom.

7. **W. Maximowíczii** (S. Moore) Rehd. Shrub to 1.5 m.; brts. with 2 rows of hairs: lvs. subsessile, elliptic-ovate or obovate to ovate-oblong, 4–8 cm. long, acuminate, broad-cuneate, with scattered hairs above, pilose on the veins beneath: fls. usually 2, sessile; calyx 2-lipped, the upper lip 3-lobed, the 2 lower lobes distinct, sparingly pilose; corolla funnelform-campanulate, the tubular portion exceeding the calyx, greenish yellow, about 3.5 cm. long; stamens and style shorter than corolla; anthers connivent; ovary nearly glabrous: caps. about 2 cm. long. N.T.1:692. (*Diervilla Middendorffiana* var. *M.* S. Moore, *D. Maximowiczii* Mak., *Weigelastrum M.* Nakai.) Japan. Intr. 1915. Zone V.

8. **W. Middendorffiàna** (Carr.) Lem. Shrub to 1.5 m.; young brts. with 2 rows of hairs: lvs. subsessile or sessile, ovate-oblong to ovate-lanceolate, 5–8 cm. long, acuminate or acute, cuneate or rounded at base, serrulate, bright green, pilose on veins above and below, rarely nearly glabrous: peduncles 1–3-fld. in terminal cyme; corolla campanulate-funnelform, 3–3.5 cm. long, glabrous, sulphur-yellow, dotted orange on lower lobes; calyx 2-lipped, longer than the narrow portion of corolla, its upper lip with spreading lobes; anthers coherent; caps. glabrous. Fl.v–vi. B.M.7876(c). Gt.6:t.183(c). F.S.11:t.1137 (c). N.T.1:690. G.C.III.7:581. (*Diervilla M.* Carr., *Macrodiervilla M.* Nakai, *Calyptrostigma M.* Trautv. & Mey.) Manch., N. China, Japan. Intr. 1850. Zone IV. Shrub with handsome fls.; like the preceding it demands a sheltered, cool and moist situation.

W. M. × (*florida* × *coraeensis*) = **W. Wàgneri** (Kusnetz.) Bailey. Lvs. ovate-oblong, glabrous except on veins beneath; sepals lanceolate, distinct or partly connate; corolla pink, tinged yellow. Gt.48:t.1461(c). Orig. about 1890.

A large number of garden forms, mostly of hybrid origin, are in cult. for which the untenable name *W. hybrida* Jaeg. (*D. h.* Dipp.) has been used. They are hybrids between the species Nos. 2–5 and the best known are enumerated below under their probable parents, though some are probably ternary or ever quaternary hyrids.

2 × 3. *W. hortensis* × *floribunda:* Desboisii.

2 × 4. *W. hortensis* × *coraeensis:* Dame Blanche.

2 × 5. *W. hortensis* × *florida:* Abel Carrière, Dr. Bulliard, Gratissima, Intermedia, Montblanc, Pavillon Blanc, Stelzneri, Vanhouttei.

3 × 4. *W. floribunda* × *coraeensis:* Congo, E. André, Eva Rathke, Lavallei, Othello, Styriaca.

3 × 5. *W. floribunda* × *florida:* Hendersonii, Lowei, P. Duchartre.

4 × 5. *W. coraeensis* × *florida:* André Thouin, Candida, Gustave Mallet, Mme. Couturier, Mme. Lemoine, Marc Tellier, Venosa.

5 × ?. *W. florida* × *?:* Isoline, Groenewegenii.

6 × ?. *W. praecox* × *?:* Avalanche, Conquérant, Espérance, Fleur de Mai, Floréal, Gracieux, Séduction, Vestale.

10. **LONÍCERA** L. HONEYSUCKLE. Deciduous, rarely half-evergreen or evergreen shrubs, rarely tree-like, upright or climbing; winter-buds with several or 2 outer scales: lvs. opposite, usually short-petioled, sometimes sessile, entire, rarely lobed, exstipulate, rarely with intrapetiolar stipules: fls in axillary peduncled pairs, each pair with 2 bracts and 4 bractlets, the latter often connate, rarely wanting, or fls. in sessile whorls; calyx 5-toothed, corolla with slender or short, often gibbous tube, 2-lipped or nearly equally 5-lobed; stamens 5; ovary inferior, 2–3- rarely 5-celled; the pairs sometimes partly or wholly connate; style slender with capitate stigma: fr. few- to many-seeded. (After Adam Lonicer or Lonitzer, a German physician and botanist; 1528–1586.) Including *Caprifolium* Adans., *Periclymenum* Mill., *Xylosteum* Mill., *Chamaecerasus* Med., *Distegia* Raf., *Nintooa* Sweet. About 180 species throughout the n. hemisphere; in Am. s. to Mex., in the Old World to N. Afr. Java and the Philippines.—Ornamental shrubs, grown for their attractive fls and frs.; about 100 species have been intr. into cult.

Fls. in pairs, rarely solitary: lvs. always distinct.
  A. Brs. with solid white pith.
    B. Corolla with regular or nearly regular 5-lobed limb, lobes shorter than tube.
      C. Corolla equal at base, not ventricose; bractlets connate, at least half as long as ovary: lvs. not or slightly exceeding 3 cm. in length, conduplicate or flat in bud.
        D. Stamens and style included.
          E. Style half as long as corolla-tube: fr. red.
            F. Ovaries connate, 2-celled...1. *L. Myrtillus*
            FF. Ovaries distinct, 3-celled.
              G. Corolla outside and lvs. beneath glabrous................2. *L. syringantha*
              GG. Corolla pubescent outside: lvs. pubescent or tomentose beneath, rarely glabrous on sterile shoots...................................3. *L. thibetica*
          EE. Style as long as corolla-tube: fr. black..........................4. *L. tomentella*
        DD. Stamens and style exserted: fr. whitish or pale purple, bloomy: lvs. linear.
                                      5. *L. spinosa*
      CC. Corolla ventricose or saccate at base: lvs. convolute.
        D. Bracts narrow, usually subulate.
          E. Ovaries not inclosed by a cupula.
            F. Bractlets connate or wanting: ovary usually 2-celled.
              G. Ovaries connate or partly connate.
                H. Bractlets present: fr. bluish black.
                  I. Corolla purple, 1.5 cm. long: lvs. pubescent beneath.
                                      6. *L. purpurascens*
                  II. Corolla whitish, 1 cm. long: lvs. glabrous.............7. *L. obovata*
              HH. Bractlets wanting (except in *L. trichopoda* under No. 8): fr. red.
                I. Corolla ventricose at base; lvs. to 3 cm. long, glabrous beneath.
                                      8. *L. tangutica*
                II. Lvs. saccate at base: lvs. to 5 cm. long, pubescent beneath.
                                        9. *L. saccata*
              GG. Ovaries distinct or nearly so: corolla gibbous at base.
                H. Style exceeding the limb: fls. whitish, in pairs........11. *L. canadensis*
                HH. Style shorter than limb; fls. red, solitary.
                  I. Lvs. and fls. glabrous.............................12. *L. gracilipes*
                  II. Lvs. and fls. glandular-pubescent......................13. *L. tenuipes*
             FF. Bractlets distinct, acute, half as long as ovaries..............25. *L. pyrenaica*
          EE. Ovaries and fr. distinct, enclosed by a persistent cupula.
            F. Fr. blue, bloomy, consisting of a fleshy cupula, tightly enclosing the ovaries, these therefore seemingly connate: lvs. deciduous..............14. *L. coerulea*

852

FF. Fr. pale purple, splitting at maturity the dry cupula: lvs. half-evergreen, lustrous ....15. *L. pileata*
DD. Bracts large, more or less enveloping the ovaries.
E. Bractlets wanting: fls. white: fr. red: terminal winter-bud wanting.
F. Winter-buds with 2 outer scales, acute.
G. Ovaries glabrous or glandular: corolla with slender tube.....22. *L. hispida*
GG. Ovaries setose and glandular-pilose; corolla-tube stout, saccate: lvs. pubescent beneath ....23. *L. chaetocarpa*
FF. Winter-buds with several outer scales, small, obtuse....24. *L. strophiophora*
EE. Bractlets large: fls. yellow to scarlet: fr. purple-black.
F. Stamens as long as limb: lvs. glabrous or slightly pubescent.
26. *L. involucrata*
FF. Stamens not exceeding the mouth of the tube: lvs. pubescent beneath.
27. *L. Ledebourii*

BB. Corolla 2-lipped.
C. Winter-buds with 2 outer scales: fls. white or yellowish.
D. Ovaries enclosed by a cupula: terminal winter-bud present.
E. Lvs. acuminate, to 10 cm. long..................................17. *L. Ferdinandi*
EE. Lvs. obtuse, to 4 cm. long.......................:...............18. *L. iberica*
DD. Ovaries not inclosed by a cupula: terminal bud wanting.
E. Ovaries more or less connate.
F. Lvs. acuminate: brts. setose...............................19. *L. Standishii*
FF. Lvs. obtusish or acute: brts. glabrous..................20. *L. fragrantissima*
EE. Ovaries distinct ....21. *L. Altmannii*
CC. Winter-buds with several outer scales.
D. Tube of corolla about as long as limb: lvs. 1-2.5 cm. long.......10. *L. microphylla*
DD. Tube much shorter than limb: lvs. larger.
E. Winter-buds ovoid, terete, with ovate obtuse rarely lanceolate scales: peduncles long (except in No. 16); calyx with obtuse or obsolete teeth: fr. red, rarely whitish.
F. Bractlets connate into a cupula as high as ovaries......16. *L. gynochlamydea*
FF. Bractlets distinct or wanting.
G. Ovaries partly or wholly connate.
H. Corolla finely pubescent outside, yellowish: lvs. obtusish.
28. *L. oblongifolia*
HH. Corolla glabrous or pilose outside, usually tinged purple: lvs. acuminate ....29. *L. alpigena*
GG. Ovaries distinct.
H. Corolla yellowish, tinged purplish: lvs. more or less glandular, to 12 cm. long ....30. *L. Webbiana*
HH. Corolla dark purple: lvs. pilose, not glandular, 3-6 cm. long.
31. *L. tatsienensis*
EE. Winter-buds oblong-ovoid, acute, 4-angled, with acute lanceolate scales, persistent at base of brts.: fls. yellowish to lilac.
F. Fr. red.
G. Peduncles much longer than petioles.
H. Bracts caducous, bractlets minute or indistinct......32. *L. conjugialis*
HH. Bracts persistent; bractlets at least ¼ as long as ovaries.
I. Lvs. distinctly petioled, acute to acuminate.
J. Lvs. green and glabrescent or pubescent beneath.
33. *L. Maximowiczii*
JJ. Lvs. grayish tomentulose beneath..............34. *L. Tatarinovii*
II. Lvs. subsessile, rounded at base, obtuse, rarely acute.
35. *L. Chamissoi*
GG. Peduncles shorter than petioles: fls. 4-merous, whitish...36. *L. subsessilis*
FF. Fr. black or bluish black.
G. Ovaries connate; bractlets connate into distinct pairs; peduncles often shorter than petioles.....................................37. *L. orientalis*
GG. Ovaries distinct, rarely connate ½; bractlets connate into a short cupula; peduncles longer than petioles.
H. Peduncles not exceeding 1.5 cm.: lvs. glabrous............38. *L. nervosa*
HH. Peduncles 1.5-4 cm. long: lvs. pubescent beneath at least along midrib.
39. *L. nigra*

AA. Brts. hollow: ovaries distinct.
B. Habit upright.
C. Peduncles much longer than petioles.
D. Corolla light pink to rosy red, sometimes white, but not changing to yellow.
E. Bractlets distinct or nearly so; the 2 outer lobes of upper lip of corolla divided to base of limb...40. *L. tatarica*
EE. Bractlets of each fl. connate at base; lateral lobes of upper lip divided to the middle or slightly beyond: lvs. 1-4 cm. long..................41. *L. Korolkowii*
DD. Corolla white, sometimes slightly tinged pinkish, changing to yellow or yellowish.
E. Winter-buds elongated, pointed, with long-ciliate pubescent scales.
F. Lvs. broad-ovate to obovate or elliptic, acute, soft-pubescent to glabrescent: fls. often tinged pink....................................42. *L. Xylosteum*
FF. Lvs. rhombic-ovate to ovate-lanceolate, acuminate, pilose or glabrescent: fls. yellowish white...43. *L. chrysantha*

EE. Winter-buds small, obtusish, glabrescent.
  F. Ovary sparingly glandular and pilose; lvs. 1.5–3 cm. long, acute to obtusish.
                                                                    44. *L. demissa*

  FF. Ovary glabrous: lvs. 3–10 cm. long.
    G. Bractlets about as long as ovary, pubescent; upper lip of corolla divided
        to base, with spreading lobes: lvs. acute to obtusish.......45. *L. Morrowii*
    GG. Bractlets small, glabrous or glandular-ciliate; upper lip divided about ½,
        upright: lvs. acuminate................................46. *L. Ruprechtiana*
CC. Peduncles shorter or slightly longer than petioles: bractlets connate into pairs; calyx
    cup-shaped or campanulate, often splitting.
  D. Fr. red.
    E. Calyx divided to about the middle into ovate to lanceolate lobes; upper lip of
        corolla divided to about the middle into oblong lobes............47. *L. Maackii*
    EE. Calyx campanulate, with short, often indistinct teeth, becoming scarious,
        splitting; upper lip with short ovate lobes.
      F. Lvs. acuminate, pubescent, 4–8 cm. long.....................48. *L. deflexicalyx*
      FF. Lvs. obovate to ovate, obtuse to acutish, glabrate, 3–5 cm. long.
                                                                    49. *L. trichosantha*
  DD. Fr. white, translucent, with blackish seeds; calyx cup-shaped, not splitting.
                                                                    50. *L. quinquelocularis*
BB. Habit twining: fr. black: corolla-tube slender, not or only slightly ventricose.
  C. Bracts. subulate.
    D. Tube of corolla as long or slightly longer than limb: corolla 1.5–3 cm. long, yellow-
        ish red to purple red.
      E. Corolla glabrous outside; lvs. glabrate...........................51. *L. Henryi*
      EE. Corolla densely pilose outside: lvs. pilose.......................52. *L. Giraldii*
    DD. Tube of corolla much longer than limb, not ventricose; corolla 4–8 cm. long,
        deeply 2-lipped, white, changing to yellow.
      E. Ovary glabrous: lvs. white-tomentose beneath, 4–9 cm. long......53. *L. similis*
      EE. Ovary pubescent: lvs. grayish pubescent beneath, 3–6 cm. long....54. *L. confusa*
  CC. Bracts leafy ovate: corolla white, changing to yellowish, often purplish outside.
                                                                    55. *L. japonica*

Fls. in usually 6-fld. sessile whorls at end of brts.; the pairs of lvs. below the whorls
usually connate: fr. red; habit twining, rarely sarmentose or suberect.
  A. Corolla with short, nearly regular or short-lipped limb, tube ventricose below the middle;
      stamens inserted below the mouth.
    B. Floral whorls remote, forming a peduncled spike: lvs. not ciliate....56. *L. sempervirens*
    BB. Floral whorls 1–3, close, forming a peduncled head: lvs. ciliate............57. *L. ciliosa*
  AA. Corolla deeply 2-lipped; stamens inserted at mouth.
    B. Corolla 1.5–2.5, rarely to 3.5 cm. long, ventricose or gibbous below the middle, pubescent
        inside (glabrous in No. 63); style usually glabrous.
      C. Bractlets half as long as ovaries; corolla 1.2–1.8 cm. long, gibbous....58. *L. hispidula*
      CC. Bractlets not more than ⅓ as long as ovaries.
        D. Lvs. ciliate and pubescent beneath; brts. pubescent; corolla glandular outside.
                                                                    59. *L. hirsuta*
        DD. Lvs. not ciliate; brts. glabrous; corolla glabrous outside or sparingly pilose.
          E. Disk of connate lvs. elliptic to oblong, pointed at ends, concave.
            F. Corolla gibbous, 1.5–2 cm. long.................................60. *L. dioeca*
            FF. Corolla with slender tube, 2–3 cm. long.....................61. *L. yunnanensis*
          EE. Disk of connate lvs. suborbicular to oval, rounded at ends, nearly flat: corolla
              2.5–3 cm. long.
            F. Corolla inside and style pubescent: disk of lvs. glaucous above.
                                                                    62. *L. prolifera*
            FF. Corolla inside and style glabrous; disk bright green or slightly glaucous
                above ....63. *L. flava*
    BB. Corolla 3.5–8 cm. long; tube slender; glabrous inside and style glabrous (except No.
        64).
      C. Floral whorls all or the lower ones in the axils of connate lvs., more or less remote.
        D. Corolla-tube 3 to 4 times as long as limb; stamens much shorter than limb.
                                                                    64. *L. implexa*
        DD. Corolla-tube not more than 1½ as long as limb; stamens at least as long as limb.
                                                                    65. *L. Caprifolium*
      CC. Floral whorls in the axils of small bract-like lvs.
        D. Lvs. below the infl. connate into a disk, rarely distinct and subsessile.
          E. Infl. an elongated spike with remote whorls....................66. *L. Heckrottii*
          EE. Infl. a dense head or short spike, or only of 1 or 2 whorls.
            F. Bractlets rarely more than ⅓ as long as ovaries.
              G. Floral whorls 1 or 2, glabrous, short-peduncled; corolla 7–8 cm. long.
                                                                    67. *L. tragophylla*
              GG. Floral whorls 3–5, sessile, glandular; corolla 4–5 cm. long..68. *L. splendida*
            FF. Bractlets about as long as ovaries; floral heads long-peduncled, often in 3's.
                                                                    69. *L. etrusca*
        DD. Lvs. below the inflorescence distinct, petioled; whorls forming a dense head.
                                                                    70. *L. Periclymenum*

  Subgen. I. CHAMAECERASUS L. Upright or twining shrubs: lvs. always
distinct: fls. in axillary pairs, sometimes reduced to 1 fl.

Sect. 1. Isoxylosteum Rehd. Upright, rarely prostrate shrubs; axillary buds solitary: lvs. usually small, conduplicate or nearly flat in bud: corolla regular, tubular or campanulate, 5-lobed, with 5, rarely 3 nectaries at base inside; bracts usually leafy; bractlets always present, usually connate into a cupula.

1. L. Myrtíllus Hook. f. & Thoms. Small shrub with slender brs. glabrous or slightly pubescent when young: lvs. very short-petioled, oval or ovate to oblong, 6–25 mm. long, dark green above, grayish green beneath, glabrous: peduncle upright, short; bracts narrow-oblong, longer than calyx; corolla tubular-campanulate, 6–8 mm. long, yellowish white, glabrous; tube about twice as long as limb; cupula half as long as ovary: fr. orange-red, 6 mm. across. Fl.v–vi; fr.vii–viii. S.T.1:t.44. (*L. parvifolia* var. *M.* Clarke.) Afghan. to Sikkim. Cult. 1879. Zone (V).—**L. M. depréssa** (Royle) Rehd., var. Peduncle longer, sometimes as long as lf.; bractlets larger and broader, usually elliptic. S.L.219(h). (*L. d.* Royle, *L. parvifolia* Hook. f. & Thoms., not Hayne, nor Edgew.) Himal. Cult. 1910.

Related species: **L. myrtilloídes** Purpus. Young brts. glandular-pubescent: lvs. elliptic to ovate-oblong or narrow-oblong, 1–3 cm. long, sparingly pubescent at least on midrib: peduncles 1 cm. long, nodding; bracts narrow-oblong; cupula about as long as ovaries; corolla pubescent outside, fragrant. M.D.1907:255,t. S.H.2:f.436a-c,437b-c. Himal. Cult. 1907. Zone (V). Possibly a hybrid between *L. Myrtillus* and *L. angustifolia.*—**L. angustifòlia** Wall. ex DC. Shrub to 3 m.; brts. pubescent: lvs. oblong to oblong-lanceolate, 2–5 cm. long, acuminate, pubescent beneath; peduncles 1–2 cm. long, nodding; bracts linear to lanceolate; corolla pinkish white, fragrant, glabrous or pubescent outside, often 4-merous; tube 3 times longer than limb. F.S.4:407,408b. S.H.2:f.436f-g,437d. Kashmir to Sikkim. Intr. about 1849. Zone VII?

2. L. syringántha Maxim. Upright slender-branched shrub, to 2 or 3 m., glabrous: lvs. short-petioled, often in whorls of 3's, elliptic to oblong, 1–2.5 cm. long, obtusish or acutish: peduncle to 5 mm. long; bracts linear oblong, exceeding the calyx; cupula shorter than ovaries; calyx-teeth lanceolate, often longer than ovary; corolla tubular-campanulate, 1.2–1.5 cm. long, pinkish white to rosy lilac, fragrant, tube 3–4 times as long as limb: fr. red. Fl.v–vi; fr.viii. B.M.7989. R.H.1907:281. H.N.3:t.8. Gn.89:126(h). N. W. China. Intr. about 1890. Zone IV. With profusely produced fragrant fls.—**L. s. Wólfii** Rehd., var. Much branched shrub with partly prostrate brs.: lvs. narrower and more acute, to 3.5 cm. long; calyx-teeth more connate at base, ciliate; corolla carmine. S.H.2:f.436n-o,437h. (*L. W.* Hao.) Cult. 1900.

3. L. thibética Bur. & Franch. Spreading shrub to 1.5 m., with slender partly prostrate brs. loosely tomentose when young: lvs. often in 3's, oblong-lanceolate, 1–3 cm. long, acute, rarely obtusish, dark green and lustrous above, white-tomentose beneath: peduncle to 1 cm. long; bracts linear-lanceolate, about as long as calyx, bractlets about half as long as ovaries, glandular-ciliate; corolla tubular-campanulate, 1–1.5 cm. long, pale purple, pubescent outside, tube 2 or 3 times as long as limb; style half as long as corolla-tube: fr. red, ellipsoid, about 6 mm. long. Fl.v–vi; fr.viii–ix. S.T.1:t.45. H.N.3:t.7. R.H.1902:449. B.S.2:57. (*L. rupicola* var. *t.* Zab.) W. China. Intr. 1897. Zone IV. Suited for planting on rocky slopes.

Closely related species: **L. rupícola** Hook. f. & Thoms. Young brts. slightly villous or glabrous: lvs. ovate-oblong to oblong, 1.2–2.5 cm. long, obtuse or acutish, bluish green above, grayish green and pubescent beneath or nearly glabrous: fls. pale purple, pubescent outside. S.H.2:f.436k-l,437f. Himal. Cult. 1888. Zone VI.

4. L. tomentélla Hook. f. & Thoms. Upright shrub to 2 m.; brts. pubescent: lvs. elliptic to ovate-oblong, 1–3.5 cm. long, obtusish or acute, dull green above, pubescent beneath: fls. short-stalked, nodding; bracts linear-oblong; bractlets about half as long as the partly or wholly connate ovaries; calyx-lobes triangular-ovate, short; corolla tubular-funnelform, about 1.5 cm. long, pinkish white, pubescent outside; style as long as corolla-tube: fr. blue-black. Fl.vi. B.M.6486(c). Sikkim. Intr. 1849. Zone VII?

5. **L. spinòsa** Walp. Low shrub with rigid spinescent brs.; glabrous lvs. linear-oblong, 1.5–2.5 cm. long, often with 2 teeth at base: peduncles upright to 1 cm. long; bracts linear; ovaries usually connate only at base; cupula about half as long; corolla tubular-funnelform, glabrous outside, with slender tube, lobes ovate; filaments about as long as anthers. Jacquemont, Voy. Inde, 4:t.86. N. W. Himal. Not in cult.—**L. s. Albérti** (Reg.) Rehd., var. Low shrub with slender arching or often prostrate brs.: lvs. to 3 cm. long, often with 2–4 teeth at base, glaucous or bluish green: corolla rosy-pink, fragrant, tube slender, about 1 cm. long; stamens nearly as long as lobes; filaments much longer than anthers: fr. pale bluish red or whitish, bloomy, about 8 mm. across. Fl.vi; fr.viii. B.M.7594(c). Gt.30:t.1065(c). (*L. A.* Reg.) Turkest. Intr. about 1880. Zone III. Graceful shrub with narrow bluish green lvs. and rosy pink fls.

Sect. 2. Isika DC. Upright or nearly prostrate shrubs; accessory superposed buds often present; pith solid or evanescent: lvs. involute or convolute in bud: corolla more or less irregular, usually 2-lipped, sometimes with regular limb, but tube ventricose or gibbous with 1–3 nectaries: bractlets either distinct or connate, sometimes wanting: ovary 2–3-, rarely 5-celled.

6. **L. purpuráscens** Walp. Shrub to 3 m.; brts. pubescent: lvs. ovate to oblong or obovate-oblong, 2–4 cm. long, obtuse or acute, sparingly pubescent or nearly glabrous above, pubescent beneath: fls. nodding, on slender stalks; bracts linear-lanceolate, longer than ovaries; bractlets glandular-ciliate, ⅓ as long as ovaries; corollâ tubular-funnelform, 1.5 cm. long, dull purple, pubescent outside, gibbous at base: ovaries ⅓ connate; stamens as long, style longer than limb: fr. blue-black. Fl.v. Jacquemont, Voy. Inde, 4:t.87. Sikkim to Afghan. Cult. 1894. Zone VI?

7. **L. obovàta** Royle. Shrub to 2 m., glabrous: lvs. obovate, 5–12 mm. long, obtuse or acutish, cuneate, whitish beneath: fls. nodding on short stalks; bracts about as long as ovaries; bractlets ⅓ as long as the connate ovaries; corolla 1 cm. long, glabrous outside, whitish; stamens as long, style longer than limb: fr. blue-black, short-ellipsoid. Fl.v. S.H.2:f.439a-d,440e. (*L. parvifolia* Edgew., not Hayne.) Sikkim to Kashmir and Afghan. Cult. 1894. Zone V.

8. **L. tangùtica** Maxim. Low shrub, with slender spreading brs.; brts. glabrous: lvs. obovate to elliptic- or obovate-oblong, 1.5–3 cm. long, acute or obtusish, cuneate, ciliate, usually sparingly hairy above, whitish beneath and glabrous: fls. pendulous on slender stalks 1.5–3 cm. long; bracts subulate, about as long as ovaries; corolla tubular-funnelform, 1–1.4 cm. long, slightly ventricose at base, glabrous outside, yellowish white, tinged pink; stamens shorter than limb, style longer, usually glabrous; ovaries usually connate ½: fr. scarlet. Fl.v–vi; fr.vii. Gt.40:581. H.N.3:t.21. S.H.2:f.439m-o,440i. W. China. Cult. 1890. Zone IV? The pendulous scarlet frs. are attractive.

Related species: **L. szechuànica** Batal. Lvs. obovate, 8–25 mm. long, obtuse, quite glabrous: peduncles 5 mm., rarely 2 cm. long; bracts subulate, slightly longer than the connate ovaries; style glabrous. S.H.2:f.439h-i,440g. W. China. Intr. 1908. Zone V.—**L. Schneideriàna** Rehd. Lvs. obovate to oblong-obovate 1–2.5 cm. long, obtuse, quite glabrous: peduncles about 2.5 cm. long; bracts subulate, scarcely half as long as ovaries; corolla slightly gibbous; stamens slightly exceeding the limb; style pubescent. S.H.2:f.439k-l,440h. W. China. Intr. 1911. Zone V.—**L. trichópoda** Franch. Brts. pubescent: lvs. pubescent on both sides: peduncle 1–1.5 cm. long; bracts as long as the wholly connate ovaries;

ractlets present, ¼–½ as long as ovaries; corolla-tube slender, scarcely gibbous. V. China. Cult. 1925. Zone VI?

9. **L. saccàta** Rehd. Upright shrub to 1.5 m.; brts. glabrous: lvs. oblong-lliptic to oblong, 1.5–5 cm. long, obtuse, cuneate, glabrous above or sparingly ubescent at first, pubescent beneath, becoming glabrous except on the veins: s. nodding on slender stalks 1–2.5 cm. long; bracts narrow-oblong, exceeding he calyx; corolla tubular-funnelform, 1.2–1.5 cm. long, whitish tinged pink, accate at base; stamens about as long as limb, style longer, pubescent below he middle: fr. scarlet. Fl.v; fr.vi. S.T.1:t.20. C. and W. China. Intr. 1910. Zone V.

10. **L. microphýlla** Willd. Much-branched shrub, to 1 m.; brts. glabrous r puberulous: lvs. obovate to elliptic or oblong, 1–2.5 cm. long, obtuse or cutish, puberulous on both sides, sometimes glabrate: fls. upright or nodding, n stalks 5–15 mm. long; bractlets subulate, usually slightly longer than alyx; bractlets wanting; calyx indistinctly 5-toothed; corolla 2-lipped, about cm. long, yellowish white, glabrous or puberulous; limb about as long as he gibbous tube; upper lip divided to the middle; stamens and style scarcely s long as limb: berries usually wholly connate, orange-red. Fl.v; fr.vi–vii. Ledebour, Ic. Pl. Ross. t.213. H.N.3:t.17. S.H.2:f.441a-c,440l. (*L. Sieveriana* Bge.) C. Asia. Intr. 1818. Zone V.

11. **L. canadénsis** Marsh. FLY-H. Shrub with spreading brs., to 1.5 m.; rts. glabrous: lvs. ovate to ovate-oblong, 4–8 cm. long, acute, rounded to cordate at base, ciliate, slightly pubescent beneath at first or glabrous; petiole 6–8 mm. long: fls. nodding on slender stalks 2–2.5 cm. long; bracts subulate, not exceeding the calyx; bractlets ciliate, small, sometimes obsolete; corolla ubular-funnelform, 1.5–2 cm. long, yellowish white, often tinged reddish, glabrous outside, strongly gibbous at base; stamens slightly, style much exceeding the limb: berries red, connate only at base. Fl.iv–v; fr.vi. Torrey, Fl. N. Y. t.42(c). Ad.21:677(c). B.B.2:381. (*L. ciliata* Muhlenb.) Que. to Sask., s. to Pa., Mich., Wisc. and Minn. Intr. 1641. Zone III.

Closely related species: **L. utahénsis** S. Wats. Lvs. broad-ovate to oblong. obtuse, usually rounded at base, not or only slightly ciliate near base: corolla shorter, slightly gibbous. S.H.2:f.440n(1). B. C. to Ore., Utah and Wyo. Intr. 1904. Zone V.

12. **L. gracílipes** Miq. Upright shrub to 2 m., with spreading brs.; young rts. glabrous or slightly pubescent: lvs. short-petioled, broad-ovate or rhombic-ovate to elliptic, 3–7 cm. long, acute or acutish, rounded at base, bright green above and usually with reddish margin, slightly ciliate when young, light bluish green and slightly pubescent beneath at first; vigorous brs. often with interpetiolar roundish stipules: fls. usually solitary, pendulous on slender stalks 2–3 cm. long; bracts subulate, unequal; bractlets minute; corolla funnelform, enlarged above the middle, 1.5 cm. long, pink to carmine, glabrous outside; stamens about half as long as the ovate-oblong lobes; style slightly shorter than lobes: berries ellipsoid, scarlet. Fl.iv–v; fr.vi. S.I.2:t. 73(c). G.F.10:265. N.T.1:654,f.D. B.C.3:1907. (*L. uniflora* Bl., *L. Philomelae* Carr.) Japan. Intr. about 1870. Zone V. The form described is var. *glabra* Miq.; the typical form has ciliate lvs. pubescent beneath, particularly on the midrib and is apparently not in cult. N.T.1:654,f.a. Handsome and distinct species, one of the earliest to bloom; very attractive in fr.—**L. g. albiflòra** Maxim., var. Fls. white.

13. **L. tenúipes** Nakai. Shrub to 2 m.; brts. pilose or nearly glabrous, changing to red- or yellow-brown: lvs. elliptic or elliptic-ovate to ovate- or obovate-oblong, 3–6 cm. long, pilose above, densely pilose beneath with brown

hairs; petiole pilose and glandular: fls. usually solitary on slender pedicel 1–2 cm. long and pilose and stipitate-glandular; bracts pilose and sparingly glandular, usually only one developed; calyx glandular-ciliate; corolla 1.2–1.8 cm. long, red, pilose outside, gibbous at base; ovary glandular; stamen shorter, the pilose style nearly as long as lobes: fr. ellipsoid, red. Fl.IV–V fr.VI. N.T.1:657. (*L. gracilipes* var. *glandulosa* Maxim.) Japan. Intr. 1915 Zone V.

14. **L. coerùlea** L. Much-branched upright or spreading shrub, to 1.5 m. brts. glabrous or pubescent, later yellowish or red-brown, with flaky bark winter-buds spreading, with 2 outer scales; vigorous brs. often with inter petiolar stipules: lvs. roundish ovate or oval to ovate-oblong or oblong, 2–8 cm. long, acute to obtusish, usually rounded at base, at least slightly pubescen when young, rarely quite glabrous, bright green: fls. on short nodding stalks bracts subulate, exceeding the short-ciliate calyx; corolla tubular-funnelform 1.2–1.5 cm. long, yellowish white, usually pubescent outside, with gibbous tub usually longer than the oblong upright-spreading lobes; stamens longer than limb; style longer than stamens, glabrous: fr. subglobose to ellipsoid, 6–12 mm. long, dark blue, bloomy. Fl.IV–V; fr.VI. B.M.1965(c). R.I.17:t.124,f.1(c) F.D.28:t.2819(c). N. and C. Eu., N. Asia to Japan. Long cult. Zone II. Very variable.—**L. c. glabréscens** Rupr., var. Brts. glabrous or puberulous, yel lowish brown: lvs. usually oblong, 3–6 cm. long, pubescent when young or a least ciliate; corolla with rather short thick tube glabrous outside. (*L. c var. praecox* Dipp.) Eu. to N. E. Asia. This is the typical var.—A form o it is **L. c. salicifòlia** Dipp., var. Lvs. oblong to lanceolate. D.H.1:266. N.T 1:664.—**L. c. depéndens** Reg. ex Dipp., var. Brts. red-brown, glabrous o nearly so: lvs. elliptic, 1.5–3 cm. long, ciliate, pubescent when young; coroll with slender pubescent tube. Turkest.—A form of this is **L. c. graciliflòr** Dipp., var. Upright shrub with red-brown brs.: lvs. ovate to ovate-oblong 2–4 cm. long, bluish green, finely pubescent on both sides; corolla with slende tube: fr. oblong. Turkest. (*L. Karelini* Hort., not Bge.)—**L. c. viridifòli** Dipp., var. Similar, but lvs. ovate to obovate, 1.5–3 cm. long, bright green corolla with rather short tube. (*L. Kirilowii* Hort.)—**L. c. angustifòlia** Reg. var. Brts. finely velutinous: lvs. oblong to oblong-lanceolate, 2–4 cm. long finely pubescent when young: corolla small, slightly pubescent; cupula some times divided at apex and not closely appressed. S.H.2:f.442c(l). Turkest —**L. c. altáica** (Pall.) Sweet, var. Upright shrub with hirsute brts.: lvs elliptic to oblong, 4–7 cm. long, pilose on both sides; stamens slightly or no exceeding the limb; corolla pubescent outside: fr. subglobose. Ledebou Icon. Pl. Ross. 2:t.131. (*L. Pallasii* Ledeb.) N. Eu. to Japan.—**L. c. edüli** Reg., var. Brts. pubescent: lvs. oblong to lanceolate, pubescent; stamen longer than limb: fr. oblong. Bull. Soc. Nat. Mosc. 53,1:t.3,f.1–2. E. Siberia Tibet.

Related species: **L. villòsa** (Michx.) Roem. & Schult. Low shrub, with up right or ascending brs. and winter-buds; accessory buds and stipules wanting brts. tomentose or densely short-pilose: lvs. densely villous on both sides: coroll tubular-campanulate, villous or pilose outside; tube as long or shorter tha limb: fr. blue, edible. (*L. coerulea* var. *v.* Torr. & Gr., *L. coerulea* Am. auth. not L.) Lab. to Pa., Minn. and Man. Intr. ? Zone II.—The type occurs from Lab. and Que. to N. H. and is probably not in cult.; the following vars. are les pubescent and have a glabrous or rarely pilose corolla: **L. v. Solònis** (Eat.) Fern., var. Young brts. pilose and puberulous: lvs. pilose beneath, Cult. 1871.— **L. v. calvescens** (Eat.) Fern., var. Brts. puberulent: lvs. pilose to glabrate be neath.—**L. v. tónsa** (Fern. & Wieg.) Fern., var. Brts. glabrous: lvs. sparingl pilose to glabrous beneath. Cult. 1889.—**L. cauriàna** Fern. Shrub to 1.5 m., wit upright or ascending brs.: lvs. narrow-obovate to oblong, 2–9 cm. long, villous ciliate on margin and veins beneath: corolla slightly 2-lipped, pilose: fr. red. Wyo. to Wash. and Calif. Intr. ?

15. L. pileàta Oliv. Evergreen or half-evergreen low shrub, with spreading sometimes prostrate brs.; brts. pubescent: lvs. ovate to oblong-lanceolate, 5–40 mm. long, obtusish, cuneate, dark green and lustrous above, pale green and sparingly pubescent on midrib beneath or glabrous, sparingly ciliate: fls. short-stalked, upright, fragrant; bracts subulate, as long as ovaries or longer and oblong; calyx with a cap-like downward production at base covering the rim of the cupula; corolla funnelform, 8 mm. long, whitish, glandular-pubescent or glabrous outside, gibbous at base; stamens and style exceeding the limb: fr. violet-purple or amethyst color. Fl.ɪv–v; fr.x. B.M.8060(c). G.C. 47:236;68:195(fr.). H.I.16:1585. C. and W. China. Intr. 1900. Zone (V). Low shrub with handsome evergreen foliage.—**L. p. yunnanénsis** (Franch.) Rehd., f. Spreading shrub: lvs. suborbicular to ovate, usually rounded at base. Gs.19:16,t.,f.3(c).

Closely related species: **L. nítida** Wils. Upright shrub to 2 m.: lvs. broad-ovate to ovate-oblong, 6–12 mm. long, subcordate to broad-cuneate: fls. slightly larger. B.M.9352(c). G.C.71:137(h). Gn.89:163(h). H.B.2:517(h). W. China. Intr. 1908. Zone VII .

16. L. gynochlamýdea Hemsl. Deciduous upright shrub; brts. glabrous, usually purplish: lvs. oblong-lanceolate to narrow-lanceolate, 5–10 cm. long, acuminate, cuneate or rounded at base, pubescent on the midrib on both sides or sometimes villous beneath along the midrib: fls. upright, short-stalked; bracts subulate, about as long as ovaries; calyx and cupula as in No. 15; corolla 2-lipped, 8–12 mm. long, white, tinged pink, pubescent outside; tube stout, gibbous at base, shorter than limb; stamens longer than limb, style shorter, pilose: berries pale purple to white, distinct; seeds nearly black. Fl.v; fr.ɪx–x. S.H.2:f.441p-r,442g. W. China. Intr. 1907. Zone V.

17. L. Ferdinándi Franch. Upright shrub, to 3 m., with spreading brs.; brts. usually setose; interpetiolar stipules often present on vigorous brs.: lvs. ovate to lanceolate, 3–5.5 cm. long, acuminate, rounded to broad-cuneate at base, ciliate, dark green and sparingly strigose or nearly glabrous above, lighter green beneath and hirsute along the veins: fls. on short stalks; bracts ovate, short-petioled, about 1 cm. long, ciliate; cupula urceolate, villous, adhering by matted hairs to the base of the calyx; corolla 2-lipped, 1.5–2 cm. long, glandular-pubescent and usually reflexed-setose outside; tube gibbous at base, about as long as limb: berries distinct, bright red, surrounded by the split cupula. Fl.v–vɪ; fr.ɪx. H.N.3:t.12. N. China. Intr. 1910. Zone V.—**L. F. leycesterioìdes** (Graebn.) Zabel, var. Brts. nearly glabrous: lvs. oblong-ovate to lanceolate, 4–7 cm. long: corolla not or slightly setose. S.H.2:f.443c-e. (*L. l.* Graebn.) Cult. 1900. Zone V.—**L. F. indùta** Rehd., var. Brts. densely villous and pilose: lvs. 3–7 cm. long, rounded to cordate at base, soft-pubescent beneath: corolla not setose, with rather slender, scarcely gibbous tube. N. China. Intr. 1923.

Closely related species: **L. vesicària** Komar. Brts. stout, setose, otherwise glabrous: lvs. subcoriaceous, ovate to ovate-oblong, 5–10 cm. long, truncate or rounded at base, glabrous except sparingly setose above, setose on midrib and veins beneath and ciliate; petiole 3–10 mm. long: bracts ovate to oblong, acuminate, 1.5 cm. long; corolla reflexed-setose; cupula split finally by the red berries. R.Mo.14:t.10. Korea. Cult. 1924. Zone V?

18. L. ibèrica Bieb. Densely branched shrub to 2 m.; brts. pubescent: lvs. orbicular-ovate to ovate, 2–3.5 cm. long, acute or acutish, rounded to cordate at base, ciliate, hairy on both sides: fls. short-stalked, at end of short brts.· bracts elliptic to ovate-oblong, about twice as long as ovary; cupula

very short petiole, bluish green above, pale beneath: fls. nodding, on slende stalks 2.5–4 cm. long; bracts oblong-lanceolate, usually twice as long, bract lets ovate to oblong-ovate, acute, ½ as long as ovaries; corolla funnelform campanulate, 1.5–2 cm. long, white, often flushed pink, gibbous at base, gla brous outside, with oval spreading lobes; stamens shorter, style slightly longe than limb: berries distinct, subglobose, red. Fl.v; fr.vii. B.M.7774(c). L.B 1361(c). B.S.2:53. Pyrenees and Balear. Isls. Intr. 1739. Zone (V). Attrac tive in bloom.

26. **L. involucràta** (Richards.) Banks ex Spreng. Upright shrub to 3 m. brts. glabrous, slightly angled: lvs. elliptic-ovate to oblong-lanceolate, 5–1 cm. long, acuminate, cuneate, bright green, glabrous or slightly pubescent be neath when young; petiole 3–12 mm. long: fls. on upright glabrous stalks 1.5– cm. long; bracts ovate or broad-ovate, acute, glandular-pubescent, reaching t the middle of the corolla; bractlets large, exceeding the ovaries; corolla tubu lar 1–1.5 cm. long, with upright ovate lobes, yellow or slightly tinged red glandular-pubescent outside; stamens as long as limb; style glabrous, slightl longer: berries globose, lustrous purple-black, surrounded by the enlarge bractlets and bracts, the latter finally reflexed. Fl.v–vi; fr.vi–vii. B.R.1179(c) B.B.3:282. (*Distegia i.* Cock.) Que. to Alaska and in the Rockies s. to Mex Cult. 1828. Zone III. Chiefly valued for its conspicuous fr.; var. *serotina* i distinct in bloom.—**L. i. seròtina** Rehd., f. Lvs. nearly glabrous; corolla to ? cm. long, orange-yellow flushed scarlet; bracts not reflexed in fr. Fl.vi–viii Colo. Intr. 1903.—**L. i. húmilis** Rehd., f. Dwarf, not exceeding ½ m.; brts sparingly pubescent: lvs. ovate-oblong, 4–6 cm. long, sparingly pubescent be neath; bracts green; stamens slightly longer than limb. Colo. Cult. 1903.— **L. i. flavéscens** (Dipp.) Rehd., var. Lvs. oblong- or ovate-lanceolate, 7–1? cm. long, light green, glabrous or nearly so: corolla gibbous, not saccate a base. Gt.37:7. D.H.1:260. (*L. f.* Dipp., *L. Webbiana* Hort., not Wall.) B. C to Ore., Wyo. and Utah. Cult. 1880.

27. **L. Ledebòurii** Eschsch. Upright shrub, sometimes with sarmentos brs. to 5 m. long, closely related to the preceding species; brts. glabrous o sparingly pubescent: lvs. oblong or ovate-oblong to ovate-lanceolate, 6–1? cm. long, acuminate, broad-cuneate to rounded at base, dark green an slightly lustrous above, paler and pubescent beneath, thickish; petiole 3– mm. long: fls. on upright glabrous or pubescent stalks 2–4 cm. long; bract broad-ovate, yellow or reddish, covering the base of the corolla; corolla 1.5–? cm. long, orange and scarlet outside, with slightly spreading short lobes stamens not exceeding the tube; style longer than limb. Fl.vi–vii; fr.vii–ix B.M.8555(c). Gt.2:289,t(c). (*Distegia L.* Greene.) Calif. Intr. 1838. Zon (V).—Handsomer than No. 26, with dark green lvs. and showier fls.

L. L. × *alpigena* = **L. propínqua** Zabel. Known in two forms; one more like the first, the other like the second parent: corolla yellowish brown, 2-lipped strongly gibbous; bracts slightly longer, bractlets half as long as the partly con nate ovaries, glandular-pubescent. Orig. 1884.

28. **L. oblongifòlia** (Goldie) Hook. Swamp Fly-H. Upright shrub to 1.? m.; brts. minutely pubescent: lvs. subsessile, elliptic-oblong to oblong lanceolate, 3–8 cm. long, obtusish, abruptly narrowed at base, short-pubescen on both sides or glabrate above, bluish green above, grayish green beneath fls. upright on slender stalks about 2.5 cm. long; bracts small and caducous bractlets obsolete; ovaries wholly or ½ connate; corolla deeply 2-lipped, 1–1.? cm. long, yellowish white, upper lip with short lobes, longer than the gibbou tube; stamens shorter, style about as long as limb: fr. red. Fl.v; fr.vii

ooker, Fl. Bor. Am. 1:t.100. B.B.3:281. N. B. to Man., s. to Pa., Mich. and
Iinn. Intr. 1823. Zone II.—**L. o. altíssima** (Jennings) Rehd., var. Glabrous
r nearly so. Ann. Carnegie Mus. 4:t.20. (*L. a.* Jennings.) Pa.

29. **L. alpígena** L. Upright shrub to 3 m., with gray brs.; young brts.
ightly pubescent and glandular or glabrous: lvs. elliptic to oblong-obovate
r oblong, 5–10 cm. long, acuminate, rounded to cuneate at base, dark green
nd glabrous above, lighter beneath and often slightly pubescent when young;
etiole 1–1.5 cm. long: fls. upright on slender stalks 2–4.5 cm. long; bracts
near, about twice, and bractlets about ¼ as long as ovaries, glandular-ciliate;
rolla 2-lipped, 1–1.5 cm. long, yellowish or greenish yellow, tinged dull red
r brown-red, glabrous outside; tube strongly gibbous, much shorter than
mb; stamens about as long as limb, style slightly longer; anthers red; ovaries
ore or less connate: fr. globose-ovoid, scarlet. Fl.v; fr.vIII–Ix. G.H.1:t.10
). R.I.17:t.1175,f.3,4(c). Mts. of C. and S. Eu. Cult. 1600. Zone V. Attrac-
ve in summer with its drooping scarlet frs.—**L. a. nàna** (Carr.) Nichols.
warf form: lvs. beneath and peduncles pubescent.

L. a. × *Ledebourii;* see under No. 27.
Related species: **L. Glèhnii** Fr. Schmidt. Brts. peduncles and petioles glan-
ular-pubescent: lvs. usually rounded or subcordate at base, pubescent beneath:
rolla yellowish; anthers yellow. N.T.1:675. (*L. alpigena* var. *G.* Nakai.)
apan, Saghal. Intr. ?

30. **L. Wébbiana** Wall. Shrub to 3 m., with stout brs.; brts. glandular-
ubescent or nearly glabrous: lvs. elliptic to ovate-oblong or oblong-lance-
ate, 5–12 cm. long, acuminate, usually cuneate, pilose and glandular on both
des, sometimes nearly glabrous above; petiole 5–10 mm. long, glandular-
ubescent: peduncles glandular-pubescent, 2.5–3 cm. long; bracts slightly or
ot longer than ovaries, glandular-ciliate like the ovate bractlets; corolla 1.5
n. long, yellowish, tinged with red, sparingly pilose-glandular outside; tube
ick, strongly gibbous, much shorter than limb; stamens about as long as
mb, style shorter, pubescent: berries distinct, short-ellipsoid, scarlet. Fl.Iv–v;
.vIII–Ix. S.T.1:t.69. (*L. alpigena W.* Nichols.) S. E. Eu., Afghan., Himal.
ult. 1885. Zone (V).
Related species: **L. heterophýlla** Dcne. Brts. glabrous: lvs. glabrous, some-
mes irregularly lobed: corolla yellowish, tinged reddish, usually glandular and
lose outside. Himal.—In cult. only **L. h. Karelini** (Bge.) Rehd., var. Lvs.
sually not lobed, glandular on midrib on both sides. (*L. K.* Bge.) C. Asia.
ult. 1906. Zone V.

31. **L. tatsienénsis** Franch. Shrub to 2.5 m.; brts. glabrous; scales of
inter-buds becoming reflexed: lvs. ovate or elliptic-ovate to oblong-lance-
ate, 4–7 cm. long, acuminate, rounded to cuneate at base, on sterile vigorous
oots often deeply lobed, pilose on both sides or nearly glabrous; petiole
-10 mm. long: peduncles glabrous, 2.5–4 cm. long; bracts and the small bract-
ts glandular-ciliate; corolla dark purple, about 1.2 cm. long, glabrous outside
r sparingly hairy, with very short, scarcely gibbous but abruptly widened
be; stamens about as long as limb, filaments pubescent at base, longer than
athers: fr. red. Fl.v–vI; fr.vIII. W. China. Intr. 1910. Zone V.—Distinct on
ccount of its often lobed lvs. and dark fls.
Related species: **L. heteróloba** Batal. Similar to No. 31, but lvs. smaller,
ore pilose, densely so on midrib: stamens shorter than limb; filaments gla-
ous, shorter than anthers. N. W. China. Intr. 1911. Zone V.—**L. mupinénsis**
ehd. Shrub to 3 m.; brts. glandular or glabrous; winter-buds with lanceolate,
uminate upright scales persisting at base of brts.: lvs. oblong-obovate to
long-lanceolate, 6–12 cm. long, abruptly acuminate, pilose on veins beneath or
metimes nearly glabrous; petiole glandular: peduncles to 6 cm. long; corolla
ark purple, glabrous. W. China. Intr. 1908. Zone V.—**L. adenóphora** Franch.

Shrub to 6 m.: lvs. elliptic-obovate, 4–12 cm. long, short-acuminate, ciliat
glandular beneath, otherwise glabrous: corolla glandular outside, dark purple
bractlets ovate-lanceolate, half as long as the glandular ovaries. W. Chin
Cult. 1933. Zone VI?

32. **L. conjugiàlis** Kell. Upright much-branched shrub to 1.5 m.; br
glabrous or sparingly pubescent: lvs. short-petioled, elliptic or ovate
obovate, 2.5–5 cm. long, acute or short-acuminate, cuneate, ciliate, pubesce
or nearly glabrous beneath; peduncles 1.5–2.5 cm. long; bracts small, decid
ous; bractlets minute or obsolete; corolla dark red, about 1 cm. long, glabro
outside; tube gibbous, shorter than limb; stamens about as long as lim
pubescent below the middle; style pubescent to apex; ovaries connate:
subglobose, 8 mm. across, red. Fl.vi; fr.viii. S.H.2:f.450g,451k-m. Wash.
Calif. and Nev. Intr. 1896. Zone (V).

33. **L. Maximowíczii** Reg. Shrub to 3 m.; brts. glabrous, purplish: lv
elliptic or ovate to ovate-oblong, 3–7 cm. long, acute to acuminate, usuall
rounded at base, dark green and glabrous above, lighter green and pubesce
beneath: peduncles 1.5–2.5 cm. long, glabrous; bracts subulate, about ⅓ as lon
as ovaries; bractlets shorter, roundish, ciliate; corolla about 1 cm. long, gl
brous outside, violet-red; limb longer than the gibbous tube; stamens slight
longer than limb; style as long as limb; ovaries connate: fr. ovoid, red. F
v–vi; fr.viii. Gt.17:t.597. H.N.3:t.20. Manch., Korea. Intr. about 1855. Zor
IV. Attractive in fruit; flowers of the var. more conspicuous.—**L. M. sach
linénsis** Fr. Schmidt, var. Lvs. broader, less acuminate, glabrous or nearly
and glaucescent beneath, red when unfolding; fls. dark purple. N.K.11:t.3
N.T.1:686. (*L. s.* Nakai.) Saghal., Korea. Intr. 1917.

34. **L. Tatarinòvii** Maxim. Upright shrub to 1.5 m.; brts. glabrous: lv
oblong-lanceolate, 3–7 cm. long, acuminate, glabrous above, grayish or whi
ish tomentulose beneath; petiole 2–5 mm. long: peduncle 1–2 cm. lon
bracts and bractlets ⅓ to ½ as long as the connate ovaries; corolla about
mm. long, dark purple, glabrous outside; tube gibbous, shorter than limb
stamens and the pubescent style shorter than limb: fr. subglobose, red. Fl.
vi; fr.vii–ix. N.K.11:t.35. H.N.3:t.19. N. China, Korea. Intr. 1913. Zone
—**L. T. leptántha** Nakai, var., is scarcely different.

35. **L. Chamissoi** Bge. Upright shrub to 1 m.; brts. glabrous: lvs. su
sessile, ovate to elliptic, 2.5–5 cm. long, obtuse, rarely acute, rounded at bas
glabrous, conspicuously veined: peduncles slender, subterminal, 6–14 mr
long; bracts and bractlets about ¼ as long as ovaries, glabrous; calyx-teet
triangular; corolla 1.2 cm. long, dark violet, glabrous outside, with sho
gibbous tube; stamens and style shorter than limb, glabrous; berries connat
red. Fl.v–vi; fr.viii. N.T.1:680. S.H.2:f.450m,452c-e. N. E. Asia, Japan. Cul
1909. Zone IV.

36. **L. subséssilis** Rehd. Shrub to 2 m., glabrous; brts. purplish; lvs. ova
or elliptic-ovate, 3–5.5 cm. long, acute or short-acuminate, broad-cuneat
the lower ones sometimes obtusish and rounded at base, bright green abov
pale beneath, distinctly veined; petiole 2–5 mm. long; fls. slightly fragran
subsessile or on stalks shorter than the petioles, bracts shorter than bractlet
the latter connate into a cupula ⅓ as long as the wholly or partly conna
ovaries; corolla white to yellowish, 1.2 cm. long, upper lip 3-lobed, muc
longer than the gibbous tube; stamens 4, as long as limb; style slightly longe
fr. bright red, 6–8 mm. long. Fl.vi; fr.viii–ix. N.K.11:t.34. (*L. diamantiac*
Nakai.) Korea. Intr. 1917. Zone V. Differing from all related species in i
4-merous fls.

37. L. orientàlis Lam. Shrub to 3 m.; brts. glabrous: lvs. ovate to ovate-
anceolate, rarely elliptic, 4–10 cm. long, usually acuminate, rounded to broad-
uneate, pubescent and light green beneath; petiole 6–10 mm. long: peduncles
horter or as long as petioles (in some vars. longer); bracts subulate, not exceeding the ovaries; bractlets connate into small distinct pairs; calyx-teeth
anceolate; corolla about 1.2 cm. long, dull pink to violet, glabrous outside,
ube gibbous, much shorter than limb; stamens and style shorter than limb;
varies connate: fr. black. Jaubert & Spach, Ill. Pl. Or. 1:t.71. Asia Minor.
Not intr.—**L. o. caucásica** (Pall.) Zab., var. Lvs. elliptic to elliptic-oblong,
–7 cm. long, 1.5–5 cm. broad, broad-cuneate at base, glaucescent and gla-
rous beneath: corolla-tube less gibbous. Fl.v–vi; fr.viii–ix. Gt.11:t.359.
Transcauc., Armenia. Intr. about 1825. Zone III.—**L. o. longifòlia** Dipp., var.
Lvs. oblong to lanceolate, 2.5–6 cm. long, about 1–2 cm. broad: fls. smaller,
eddish, with slightly or scarcely gibbous tube. Gt.40:124. (*L. Kesselringii*
Reg., *L. kamtchatica* and *L. savranica* Hort.) Intr. 1888, supposedly from
Kamchatka.

Closely related species: **L. díscolor** Lindl. Shrub to 2 m., glabrous: lvs.
lliptic to elliptic-oblong, glaucous beneath: fls. yellowish white, often tinged
ed, on slender stalks 1.5–3 cm. long. B.R.33:t.44(c). (*L. orientalis* var. *d.*
larke.) Kashmir to Afghan. Cult. 1847. Zone (V).

38. L. nervòsa Maxim. Shrub to 3 m., with upright and spreading slender
rs., glabrous: lvs. red when unfolding, elliptic to ovate-oblong, 2.5–6 cm.
ong, acute at ends, bright green, usually with red midrib and reddish veins,
luish green beneath; petiole 3–5 mm. long; peduncles about 1 cm. long;
racts subulate, scarcely as long as ovaries: bractlets connate into a lobed
upula half as long as ovaries, sometimes in distinct pairs, ovate-lanceolate,
landular-ciliate or glabrous: corolla about 1 cm. long, light pink; limb some-
vhat longer than the gibbous tube; stamens about as long as limb; style
horter, pubescent to near the apex: berries distinct, black. Fl.v–vi; fr.viii–ix.
I.N.3:t.14. S.H.2:f.452m-o,453l. N. W. China. Intr. about 1890. Zone V.

Related species: **L. lanceolàta** Wall. Shrub to 4 m.; brts. glandular-puberu-
us: lvs. ovate to ovate-lanceolate, 4–10 cm. long, acuminate, pubescent beneath
n the veins and sparingly glandular on both sides: peduncles 1–1.5 cm. long;
upula as long or somewhat shorter than ovaries, glandular-ciliate; corolla pale
iolet, strongly gibbous at base. S.H.2:f.452p-r,453c-d. (*L. decipiens* Hook. f. &
Thoms.) Himal. and W. China. Intr. about 1904 from China. Zone (V).

39. L. nígra L. Shrub to 1.5 m.; brts. glabrous: lvs. elliptic to ovate-
anceolate, 4–6 cm. long, acute or obtusish, broad-cuneate or rounded at base,
right green and glabrous above, light bluish green beneath and villous along
he midrib, finally often glabrous; petiole 2–5 mm. long: peduncles 3–4 cm.
ong, glabrous; bractlets connate into a glandular-ciliate cupula, like the
racts about ½ as long as ovaries: berries nearly distinct, bluish black. Fl.
–vi; fr.viii–ix. R.I.17:t.123,f.3(c). F.D.28:2918(c). Eu., Korea. Cult. 1683.
one V.

The supposed hybrid with *L. orientalis* is probably a form of × *L. xyloste-*
ides and that with *L. Xylosteum* a form of the latter species.

Sect. 3. COELOXYLOSTEUM Rehd. Brs. with quickly evanescent pith, fistulose:
varies always distinct, 3-celled; bractlets distinct or connate into pairs above
he bracts; corolla always 2-lipped; fr. red, yellow or white.

40. L. tatarica L. TATARIAN H. Upright shrub to 3 m., glabrous; older
rs. gray: lvs. ovate to ovate-lanceolate, 3–6 cm. long, acute to acuminate,
arely obtusish, rounded or subcordate at base, dark green above, light to
luish green beneath; petiole 2–6 mm. long: peduncles slender, 1.5–2 cm.

long; bracts usually linear-lanceolate, not or slightly longer than calyx; bract
lets distinct, roundish to broad-oblong, ⅓–½ as long as ovaries; corolla pinl
to white, 1.5–2 cm. long; tube slightly gibbous at base, shorter than limb
lateral lobes of upper lip divided to the base, spreading; stamens and styl
shorter than limb: berries globose, red. Fl.v–vi; fr.vii–viii. B.M.8677(c). B.R
31(c). G.O.t.87(c). S. Russia to Altai and Turkest.; occasionally escaped
from cult. Cult. 1752. Zone IV. Popular ornamental shrub, much plante
for the profusely produced fls. and the attractive red frs. Very variable an
many forms are cult. in gardens.—**L. t. latifòlia** Loud., var. Lvs. large, to 1
cm. long and to 5 cm. broad: fls. large, pink. Gt.18:t.627,f.1(c). (*L. t.* var
splendens Reg.)—**L. t. sibìrica** Pers., var. Lvs. smaller: fls. deep pink. B.M
2469(c). F.D.17:t.123,f.4–5(c).—**L. t. rósea** Reg., var. Fls. rosy pink out
side, light pink inside. Gt.18:t.627,f.4(c).—**L. t. alba** Loisel., var. Fls. pur
white. (*L. t.* var. *albiflora* DC.)—**L. t. angustifòlia** (Wender.) Kirchn. Lvs
narrow, ovate-lanceolate, 4–6 cm. long and 1–2 cm. wide: fls. light pink.—
L. t. lùtea Loud., var. Fr. yellow. (*L. t.* var. *xanthocarpa* Endl.)—**L. 1**
Leroyàna (Zab.) Rehd., f. Low compact shrub: lvs. oblong-lanceolate, to
cm. long, rounded at base, ciliolate: fls. sparingly produced, pink. G.W.19:20.
(h).—**L. t. nàna** Alphand, var. Dwarf shrub: lvs. oblong-ovate, 2–5 cm. long
broad-cuneate: fls. small, pinkish, numerous; bracts usually leafy.—**L. 1**
parvifòlia (Hayne) Jaeg., var. Lvs. ovate-elliptic to ovate-oblong, 2–5 cm
long, obtusish, often bluish green: fls. small, white, upper lip with broad an
short lobes: fr. orange-red. (*L. p.* Hayne.) Turkest.—**L. t. pállens** Rehd
var. Lvs. small and narrow, pale bluish green: fls. pinkish, finally nearly white
Turkest.

L. t. × *Korolkowii* = L. amoèna Zab. Very floriferous shrub with smal
ovate lvs. and slender-stalked fls.; bractlets connate into pairs. Orig. befor
1895.—**L. a. ròsea** Zab., f. with rose-colored fls.—**L. a. alba** Zab., f. with white fls
—**L. a. arnoldiàna** Rehd., var. Lvs. oblong-lanceolate, 2–3.5 cm. long: fls. white
flushed pink; very floriferous and graceful. A.B.1931:35. Orig. 1899.—*L. t.* ×
Xylosteum = L. xylosteoìdes Tausch. Lvs. usually rhombic-ovate, broad-cuneat
at base, bluish green, slightly pubescent: fls. small, pinkish. D.H.1:233. (*L*
nepalensis Kirchn., *L. coerulescens* Dipp., *L. micrantha* Zab., not Reg.) Orig
before 1838.—*L. micranthoides* Zab. supposed to be a hybrid of *L. tatarica* an
L. nigra probably belongs here: lvs. glabrate, elliptic to elliptic-obovate: fl
small and usually malformed.—*L. x.* × *Ruprechtiana;* see under No. 46.—*L. t*
× *Morrowii;* see under No. 45.—*L. t.* × *Ruprechtiana;* see under No. 46.

41. L. Korolkòwii Stapf. Shrub to 4 m., with spreading brs.; young brts
finely pubescent: lvs. ovate to elliptic, 1–2.5 cm. long, usually acute, cuneat
to rounded at base, slightly pubescent above, more densely so beneath, rarel
glabrate, bluish green; petiole 3–6 mm. long; peduncles 1–2.5 cm. long, pu
berulous; bracts about as long and bractlets about ⅓ as long as ovaries, con
nate into pairs, ciliate or glabrous; corolla rose-colored, rarely white, abou
1.5 cm. long; lateral lobes of upper lip divided to the middle or slightl
beyond, tube slightly gibbous; stamens and style shorter than limb: fr. brigh
red. Fl.v–vi; fr.viii. G.F.7:35. H.B.1929:377(h). (*L. floribunda* var. *K.* Zab.
Turkest. Cult. 1880. Zone IV.—**L. K. auròra** Koehne, var. Lvs. ovate t
elliptic: corolla to 1.8 cm. long, with slender tube, rosy pink; bractlets ½ a
long as ovaries. M.D.1910:117,f.c.—**L. K. floribúnda** Nichols. Lvs. broad
ovate, usually rounded or sometimes subcordate at base. Gt.42:103,f.4–6. (*L*
f. Zab., not Boiss. & Buhse.)—**L. K. Zabèlii** (Rehd.) Rehd., var. Lvs. usuall
broad-ovate, rounded to subcordate at base, glabrous. Gt.42:103,f.1–3. (*L. Z*
Rehd.)

L. K. × *tatarica;* see under No. 40.

42. L. Xylósteum L. EUROPEAN FLY-H. Shrub to 3 m.; brts. glabrous or pubescent: lvs. broad-ovate or elliptic-ovate to obovate, 3–6 cm. long, acute, broad-cuneate to rounded at base, dark or grayish green and sparingly pubescent or glabrous above, paler and pubescent, rarely glabrate beneath; petiole 3–8 mm. long: peduncles 1–2 cm. long, pubescent; bracts subulate, not exceeding the ovaries; bractlets broad, about half as long as ovaries, pubescent and glandular; ovaries glandular; corolla about 1 cm. long, whitish or yellowish white, often tinged reddish, pubescent outside; tube short, gibbous; stamens nearly as long as limb, style shorter; filaments pubescent at base: fr. dark red. Fl.v–vi; fr.viii–ix. R.I.17:t.123,f.1–2(c). F.D.28:t.2917(c). B.B.3:282. Eu. to Altai; sometimes escaped. Long cult. Zone IV. The fls. are rather insignificant, but the frs. are attractive.—**L. X. móllis** Reg., var. Lvs. densely pubescent on both. sides.—**L. X. glabréscens** Zab., f. Lvs. elliptic-oblong, glabrous or nearly so above; peduncles about as long as the yellowish white corolla.—**L. X. lùtea** Loisel., var. Fr. yellow: lvs. pubescent. (*L. X.* var. *xanthocarpa* DC.)—*L. segreziensis* Lav. supposed to be a hybrid with *L. quinquelocularis* is probably only a form of *L. Xylosteum*.

L. X. × *chrysantha* = L. pseudochrysántha A. Br. Similar to *L. chrysantha*, but bractlets broad and about half as long as ovaries and ciliate. (*L. Regeliana* Dipp., in part, not Kirchn.)—*L. X.* × *tatarica;* see under No. 40.

43. L. chrysántha Turcz. Upright shrub to 4 m.; young brts. pilose, rarely nearly glabrous: lvs. rhombic-ovate to rhombic-lanceolate or ovate-lanceolate, 6–12 cm. long, acuminate, rounded to broad-cuneate at base, dark green and nearly glabrous above, lighter green and pilose at least on the veins beneath; petiole 3–5 mm. long: peduncles pilose, 1.5–2.5 cm. long; bracts as long or longer than ovaries; bractlets ovate-oblong to suborbicular, ⅓–½ as long as ovaries, glandular and sparingly long-cilate; corolla yellowish white, changing to yellow, 1.5–2 cm. long, sparingly pubescent outside, upper lip divided about ½; tube strongly gibbous, short; stamens about as long as limb, pubescent below the middle; ovaries usually oblong-ovoid, glandular; berries coral-red. Fl.v–vi; fr.viii–ix. Gt.12:t.404(c). N.T.1:642. H.N.3:t.16. N. E. Asia to C. Japan. Intr. about 1854. Zone III.—**L. c. Regeliàna** (Kirchn.) Zab. Differs in the smaller more yellowish fls.—**L. c. latifòlia** Korsh., var. Lvs. broad-elliptic to ovate-elliptic, usually rounded at base, only sparingly pilose beneath, somewhat thickish. (*L. c.* f. *turkestanica* Rehd.) —**L. c. villòsa** Rehd., f. Lvs. elliptic to elliptic-ovate, sparingly pubescent above, villous beneath, chiefly on the veins.—**L. c. lóngipes** Maxim., var. Lvs. more sparsely pubescent with longer hairs: peduncles 2–3 cm. long. N. V. China, Japan. Intr. 1926.

L. c. × *Xylosteum;* see under No. 42.

Related species: **L. Koehneàna** Rehd. Lvs. densely soft-pubescent beneath and grayish green; bractlets connate into pairs, about half as long as ovaries, upper lip of corolla divided about ⅓; ovaries subglobose, glandular and pilose; anthers with pilose connective: fr. dark red. S.T.1:t.21. H.N.3:t.15. W. China. Intr. about 1904. Zone V.

44. L. demíssa Rehd. Much-branched shrub to 4 m., with spreading brs.; brts. short-villous; winter-buds small, ovoid: lvs. obovate or elliptic-obovate, on vigorous shoots elliptic, 1.5–3 cm. long, acute or obtusish and mucronulate, broad-cuneate, dull-green and appressed-pilose above, more densely so and pale green beneath; petiole 1–2 mm. long; peduncle 6–12 mm. long, ose; bracts twice as long, bractlets half or nearly as long as ovaries, ciliate and sparingly pilose; corolla whitish changing to yellowish, about 1 cm. long; per lip with short oval lobes; stamens slightly longer than limb: berries nose, 6–9 mm. across, scarlet. Fl.v–vi; fr.ix. N.T.1:646. (*L. ibotaeformis*

Nakai.) Japan. Intr. 1914. Zone V. Dense small-leaved shrub, handsome in fr.

45. **L. Morròwii** A. Gray. Shrub to 2 m., with wide-spreading brs.; young brts. soft-pubescent: lvs. elliptic to ovate-oblong or obovate-oblong, 3–5 cm. long, acute or obtusish and mucronulate, rounded at base, sparingly pubescent above at least when young, soft-pubescent beneath; petiole 2–3 mm. long: peduncles 5–15 mm. long, pubescent; bracts pubescent, usually exceeding the calyx; bractlets about as long as ovaries, pubescent; corolla white, changing to yellow, 1.5 cm. long, pubescent outside; upper lip divided to base into spreading oblong lobes; tube rather slender, gibbous; stamens shorter than limb, glabrous: fr. dark red, rarely yellow. Fl.v–vi; fr.vii–viii. S.I.2:t.73(c) N.T.1:644. Gs.10:215(h). J.L.35:362(h). Japan; naturalized occasionally in the E. States. Intr. about 1875. Zone III. Distinct shrub of widespreading habit, handsome in bloom and in fr.—**L. M. xanthocárpa** Teuscher. Fr yellow. Ad.17:t.563(c).

L. M. × *Ruprechtiana* = L. muscaviénsis Rehd. Differs from No. 45 in the acuminate lvs. and from No. 46 in the longer pubescent bracts and bractlets Gt.42:101,f.1–3. Orig. before 1888.—*L. M.* × *tatarica* = L. bélla Zab. Lvs glabrescent, more acute: fls. pink or pinkish, fading to yellowish. A.B.1929:54 Orig. before 1878.—L. b. cándida Zab., f. Fls. pure white.—L. b. rósea Zab., f Fls. rose-pink.—L. b. atrorosea Zab., f. Fls. dark pink.—*L. bella* × *Ruprech tiana* = L. muendeniénsis Rehd. Similar to *L. bella*, but lvs. more acuminate and darker green. Gt.42:101,f.4–6. Orig. before 1883.—*L. M.* × *xylosteoide* = L. minutiflòra Zab. Lvs. oblong, rather small, nearly glabrous: fls. small Orig. 1878.

46. **L. Ruprechtiàna** Reg. Shrub to 3 m., with upright and spreading brs. young brts. slightly pubescent: lvs. oblong-obovate to lanceolate, 6–10 cm long, acuminate, cuneate, dark green above and glabrous or nearly so, pale beneath and pubescent; petiole about 5 mm. long, pubescent; peduncle 1–2 cm. long, slightly pubescent; bracts subulate, pubescent, usually exceeding the calyx; bractlets usually ovate, ¼–⅓ as long as the glabrous ovaries, glabrou or glandular-ciliate; corolla 1.5–1.8 cm. long, white, changing to yellow, gla brous outside; tube thick, strongly gibbous; upper lip divided about ½ stamens about ⅔ as long as limb: fr. coral- or orange-red. Fl.v–vi; fr.viii–ix Gt.19:t.645. H.N.3:t.18. Manch. to N. China. Intr. about 1860. Zone II —**L. R. xanthocárpa** Rehd., var. Fls. smaller, yellowish: fr. yellow.—**L. R calvéscens** Rehd., var. Lvs. almost glabrous, only sparingly hairy on the veins beneath: fr. dark dull red. Cult. 1910.

L. R. × *tatarica* = L. notha Zab. Lvs. usually ovate-oblong, acuminate glabrate: fls. more or less pinkish, fading to yellowish. Orig. 1878. A few un important color forms have been described.—*L. R.* × *xylosteoides* = L. salici fòlia Zab. Lvs. narrow, acuminate: fls. small, similar to a small-flowered forn of *L. xylosteoides*. (*L. Ruprechtiana* var. *s.* Dieck, *L. R.* × *micranthoides* Zab. Orig. before 1880.—*L. R.* × *Morrowii;* see under No. 45.—*L. R.* × *bella;* se under No. 45.

47. **L. Maàckii** Maxim. Shrub to 5 m.; brts. short-pubescent; winter-bud small, ovoid: lvs. ovate-elliptic to ovate-lanceolate, 5–8 cm. long, acuminate broad-cuneate, rarely rounded at base, dark green above, lighter beneath usually pubescent only on the veins on both sides; petiole 3–5 mm., glandular pubescent; peduncles shorter than petiole, glandular-pubescent; bracts linear longer than ovaries; bractlets connate into pairs, ½ or as long as ovaries calyx-limb campanulate, divided to the middle into ovate to lanceolate teeth corolla to 2 cm. long, white, changing to yellowish, usually glabrous outside fragrant; tube thin, not gibbous, ⅓–½ as long as limb; stamens and styl ½–⅔ as long as limb: fr. dark red. Fl.vi; fr.ix–x. Gt.33:t.1162(c). N.T.1:64**

G.C.62:252;96:312. R.H.1920:122. U. S. Im. 74:t(h). Manch., Korea. Intr. 1855 or 1860. Zone II. Valued for its conspicuous fragrant white fls. and the attractive late fr.; the var. retains its dark green lvs. until November.—**L. M. podocárpa** Rehd., f. Habit more spreading: lvs. usually elliptic-ovate or elliptic, abruptly acuminate, more pubescent and darker green: fls. slightly smaller, pubescent outside; ovaries raised above the bracts on a very short, but distinct stalk; stamens sometimes as long as limb. H.N.3:t.13. Gn.81: 549(fr.) Gn.M.33:40(h). China. Intr. 1900. Zone IV.—**L. M. erubéscens** Rehd., f. A form of the preceding var. with larger fls. flushed pink.

48. **L. deflexícalyx** Batal. Upright shrub to 3 m., with spreading or arching brs.; brts. finely pubescent: lvs. oblong-lanceolate to lanceolate, 4–8 cm. long, acuminate, broad-cuneate or rounded at base, bright green and sparingly pubescent above, light grayish green and pubescent on the veins beneath; petiole 3–5 mm. long: peduncles usually slightly longer than petioles, pubescent or nearly glabrous; bracts subulate, scarcely longer than calyx; bractlets about ¾ as long as ovaries, glabrous; calyx campanulate, 2–3 mm. long, shallowly or indistinctly toothed, scarious and usually splitting to the base in 1 or 2 places; corolla yellowish, later yellow, 1.5 cm. long, appressed-pubescent outside; tube short, strongly gibbous; lobes of upper lip short: fr. brick-red. Fl.vi; fr.vii–viii. B.M.8536(c). B.S.2:42. W. China, Tibet. Intr. 1904. Zone V. Floriferous shrub of distinct appearance.—**L. d. xerócalyx** (Diels) Rehd., var. Lvs. lanceolate to narrow-lanceolate, 6–10 cm. long, rounded or truncate at base, glaucescent beneath; bractlets connate into a truncate or 2-lobed cupula, longer than ovaries; calyx about 4 mm. long. (*L. x.* Diels). S. W. China. Cult. 1915. Zone (V).

L. d. × *quinquelocularis;* see under No. 50.

49. **L. trichosántha** Bur. & Franch. Spreading shrub to 1.5 m., with slender sometimes sarmentose brs.; brts. glabrous or slightly pubescent: lvs. ovate to obovate, 2.5–5 cm. long, obtuse and usually mucronulate, rounded or truncate at base, bright green, glabrous above, pilose beneath at least on the veins and reticulate: peduncles shorter than petioles: fls. like those of No. 48: fr. bright red. Fl.vi; fr.viii. S.H.2:f.456r-s,457a-b. (*L. ovalis* Batal.) W. China, Tibet. Intr. 1904.—**L. t. glabràta** Rehd., f. Lvs. generally broadoval or -ovate, rounded and usually without mucro at apex, sometimes subcordate at base, glabrous beneath and not reticulate.—**L. t. acutiuscula** Rehd., . Lvs. usually elliptic or elliptic-ovate, acute or acutish, rounded to broad-cuneate at base, usually 2–2.5 cm. long on flowering brts., slightly pilose at least on veins beenath. Zone V.

Related species: **L. prostràta** Rehd. Prostrate shrub forming dense mats, or sometimes a low depressed shrub with sarmentose brs.: lvs. ovate or elliptic, –2 cm. long, acute or acutish: fls. smaller. W. China. Intr. 1904. Zone V.

50. **L. quinqueloculàris** Hardw. Upright shrub with spreading brs.; brts. short-pubescent: lvs. broad-ovate to elliptic or oblong-ovate, 3–7 cm. long, acute or short-acuminate, broad-cuneate to rounded at base; slightly pubescent above, more densely and grayish green beneath; petiole 3–5 mm. long; peduncles very short; bracts subulate, not exceeding the calyx; bractlets ⅔ to nearly as long as ovaries; calyx-limb cup-shaped with broad short teeth; corolla 1.5–2 cm. long, yellowish, densely appressed-pubescent outside; tube slender, slightly or scarcely gibbous, usually only slightly shorter than limb; stamens and style about as long as limb: berries whitish, translucent, with blackish violet seeds. Fl.vi; fr.ix–x. B.R.30:33(c). H.I.9:807. Gt.55:t.1551, 1(c, fr.) (*L. diversifolia* Wall., *L. Royleana* Wall.) Himal. to Afghan. and

Baluch. Cult. 1840. Zone (V).—**L. q. translùcens** (Carr.) Zab., f. Lvs. ovate to ovate-oblong, usually subcordate to rounded at base; corolla smaller; tube rather short, stouter and distinctly gibbous. Gs.9:376. G.C.89:7. (*L. t.* Carr.) Cult. 1870.

L. q. × *deflexicalyx* = **L.** **Vilmorìnii** Rehd. Similar to No. 48: lvs. smaller, broader and less acuminate; calyx distinctly 5-toothed; peduncles shorter: fr. yellowish pink, minutely dotted red. Orig. about 1900. Zone (V).

Related species: **L. arbórea** Boiss. Shrub to 3 m.: lvs. broad-ovate to ovate-oblong, 2–4 cm. long, obtuse or acutish, pubescent beneath; peduncles short; bractlets about ⅓ as long as ovaries; calyx with ovate to ovate-lanceolate teeth: corolla reddish white; tube gibbous, half as long as limb. S.H.2:f.453o-p,458d-f. Spain, N. Afr. Cult. 1900. Zone VI?—**L. a. pérsica** (Jaub. & Spach) Rehd., var. Lvs. smaller, often acute, less pubescent to nearly glabrous: corolla-tube not gibbous, longer than half the limb. S.F.3:t.223(c). Jaubert & Spach, Ill. Pl. Or. t.69,70. (*L. p.* and *L. nummulariifolia* Jaub. & Spach, *L. turcomanica* Fisch. & Mey.) S. E. Eu. to Afghan. and Turkest. Cult. 1880. Zone V.

Sect. 3. NINTOOA DC. Twining shrubs with usually hollow brs. and with usually evergreen or half-evergreen lvs.: fls. in axillary pairs often forming terminal spikes or panicles: bracts usually subulate; bractlets and ovaries distinct (except in *L. calcarata*); calyx distinctly toothed; corolla 2-lipped, with slender tube: fr. black, rarely white or yellow.

51. **L. Hénryi** Hemsl. Half-evergreen twining or prostrate shrub; brts. densely strigose: lvs. oblong-lanceolate to lanceolate, 4–8 cm. long, acute to acuminate, rounded to subcordate at base, ciliate, usually pubescent on midrib beneath: fls. on pubescent or glabrous stalks 2–10 mm. long, often forming short spikes at the end of brts.; calyx-teeth triangular-ovate, ciliate or glabrous; corolla 1.5–2 cm. long, yellowish red to purple-red; tube slightly ventricose, usually slightly longer than limb: fr. black. Fl.vi–viii; fr.ix–x. B.M. 8375(c). W. China. Intr. 1908. Zone V.—**L. H. subcoriàcea** Rehd., var. Lvs. ovate-oblong, 5–10 cm. long, not ciliate, subcoriaceous; corolla slightly longer with longer tube. Intr. 1910.

Related species: **L. alseuosmoìdes** Graebn. Brts. glabrous: lvs. lanceolate to narrow-lanceolate, 3–6 cm. long, 8–15 mm. broad: corolla 1.5 cm. long; tube longer than limb. S.H.2:f.457h,458m-o. W. China. Intr. 1908.

52. **L. Giráldii** Rehd. Twining shrub; brts. like petioles and peduncles densely clothed with spreading yellowish hairs: lvs. oblong-lanceolate to lanceolate. 3.5–8 cm. long, acuminate, truncate or subcordate at base, pilose on both sides; petiole 2–4 mm. long: fls. on short stalks crowded at end o brts.; bracts longer than calyx, like bractlets and calyx-teeth pilose; coroll: purplish red, about 2 cm. long, yellowish hairy outside; tube slightly ventri cose, longer than limb; stamens and style slightly exceeding the limb: fr purple-black. Fl.vi–viii. B.M.8236(c). N. W. China. Intr. 1899. Zone V Distinct in the yellowish pubescence of the red fls.

53. **L. símilis** Hemsl. Half-evergreen climbing shrub; brts., petioles an peduncles hirsute: lvs. oblong-lanceolate to lanceolate, 4–9 cm. long, acumi nate, truncate to subcordate at base, ciliate, bright green and glabrous abov whitish tomentose and hirsute beneath; petiole about 5 mm. long: fls. race mose at end of brts.; lower peduncles to 4 cm. long, decrescent toward th apex; corolla white, changing to pale yellow, 4–6 cm. long, hirsute and glar dular outside; tube slender, longer than limb; stamens and style exceedin the limb: fr. black. Fl.viii. H.N.3:t.5. S.H.2:f.457o-p,458i-k. C. and W China. Only the following var. in cult.—**L. s. Delavaỳi** (Franch.) Rehd var. Glabrous or nearly so in all parts except the white-tomentose under sic of the slightly ciliate lvs.: corolla to 8 cm. long. B.M.8800(c). M.O.267. (*l D.* Franch.) W. China. Intr. 1901. Zone VII?

Related species: **L. affìnis** Hook. & Arn. Brts. usually glabrous: lvs. ovate
o ovate-lanceolate, acuminate, glabrous: lower peduncles to 1.5 cm. long;
orolla 3.5–4.5 cm. long, white, glabrous. N.T.1:637. S.H.2:f.457u-v,461a.
'hina, Japan. Intr. ?—**L. a. pubéscens** Maxim., var. Brts. usually pubescent
r pilose: lvs. pubescent and usually glandular beneath: corolla pilose and
landular. S.H.2:461b-c. (*L. hypoglauca* Miq.) Cult. 1930. Zone (V).

54. L. confùsa DC. Half-evergreen twining shrub; brts. pubescent: lvs.
▸vate to ovate-oblong, 3–6 cm. long, acute, usually rounded at base, dark
;reen above and finally glabrous, short-pubescent and grayish green beneath;
▸etiole about 5 mm. long: fls. short-stalked in short and dense panicles at end
▸f brts.; bracts, bractlets and ovaries pubescent; corolla about 4 cm. long,
▸hite, changing to yellow, very fragrant, pubescent and glandular outside;
▸ube slender, slightly longer than limb; stamens and style longer than limb:
▸. black. Fl.vi–ix. B.R.70(c). L.D.t.132(c). (*L. japonica* Andr., not Thunb.)
▸. China. Intr. 1805. Zone VII?

Closely related species: **L. biflòra** Desf., readily distinguished by the gla-
▸rous ovaries. Desfontaines, Fl. Atl. t.52. S. W. Eu., N. Afr. Cult. 1889-
▸one VII?

55. L. japónica Thunb. Half-evergreen twining shrub; brts. pubescent:
▸vs. ovate to oblong-ovate, 3–8 cm. long, acute to short-acuminate, rounded
▸o subcordate at base, pubescent on both sides when young, later glabrate
▸bove; petiole about 5 mm. long: peduncle usually solitary, axillary, longer,
▸arely shorter than petioles; bracts leafy, broad-ovate to elliptic; bractlets
▸3–½ as long as ovaries; corolla 3–4 cm. long, pubescent and glandular out-
▸ide, white, tinged purple, very fragrant; tube about as long as limb; style
▸nd stamens longer than limb: fr. black. Fl.vi–ix; fr.ix–x. N.T.1:635. H.N.
▸:t.6. E. Asia, often naturalized in the E. States. Intr. 1806. Zone IV. Valued
▸or its handsome fragrant fls. appearing during the summer; also used as
▸round-cover.—**L. j. Halliàna** (Dipp.) Nichols., var. Similar to the type,
▸ut fls. pure white at first, changing to yellow; upper lip divided nearly to the
▸niddle into oblong lobes. Gng.3:293. M.G.16:609(h).—**L. j. chinénsis**
▸Wats.) Baker, var. Lvs. nearly glabrous, but usually ciliate and often slightly
▸ubescent on the veins beneath, usually tinged more or less red purple when
▸oung; corolla carmine outside, upper lip divided more than ½. B.R.712(c).
▸.M.3316(c). (*L. c.* Wats., *L. flexuosa* Ker, not Thunb.) Cult. 1825.—**L. j.
▸èpens** (Sieb.) Rehd., var. Lvs. oval or ovate to oblong-ovate or elliptic-
▸blong, acute or obtusish, rounded to broad-cuneate at base, nearly glabrous,
▸eins often purplish; the basal lvs. sometimes lobed: corolla white or tinged
▸ale purple; limb longer than tube; upper lip divided about ⅓; bractlet
▸ounded or truncate, often as long as ovaries. Jaarb. Maatsch. Anmoed.
▸uinb.1845:t.7(c). Baker, Ref. Bot.4:t.224(c, as var. *chinensis*). (*L. j.* var.
exuosa Nichols., *L. fl.* Thunb., *L. brachypoda* DC.) Intr. 1843.—A form with
▸sually smaller lvs. netted with yellow is **L. j. aùreo-reticulàta** (T. Moore)
▸lichols., var. I.H.9:t.337(c). B.H.21:59,t(c). (*L. brachypoda reticulata*
▸Vitte.) Intr. about 1860.

Subgen. II. **PERICLYMENUM** L. Twining, rarely dumose shrubs; brs.
▸ollow: lvs. deciduous or persistent, usually one or several pairs below the infl.
▸onnate into a disk: fls. at end of brts. in 3-fld. sessile cymes, rarely reduced to
▸or 2 fls., forming whorls in the axils of bracts or connate lvs.; bractlets dis-
▸inct or sometimes wanting (connate in *L. Griffithii*), calyx-lobes short, some-
▸imes inconspicuous; corolla 2-lipped or sometimes nearly regular: fr. red.

56. L. sempérvirens L. TRUMPET H. High-climbing glabrous shrub: lvs.
▸ery short-petioled or subsessile, elliptic or ovate to oblong, 3–8 cm. long,
▸btuse or acutish, usually cuneate, dark green above, glaucous beneath and

sometimes pubescent, 1 or 2 pairs below the infl. connate into a suborbicula to oblong disk, rounded and mucronate at ends: infl. a slender peduncled spike with remote whorls; corolla about 5 cm. long; tube slender, slightly ventricos below the middle, 5 to 6 times as long as the ovate nearly equal upright lobes orange yellow and scarlet; stamens and style slightly exceeding the limb Fl.v–viii; fr.ix–x. B.M.781(c). R.H.1856:351,t(c). Gn.45:307. Conn. to Fla w. to Neb. and Tex.; sometimes escaped from cult. Intr. 1686. Zone III Handsome summer-blooming vine, valued for its brightly colored fls.—**L. s superba** Reg., var. Fls. of bright scarlet color. F.S.11:t.1128(c). (*L. s speciosa* Carr.)—**L. s. sulphùrea** Jaques. Fls. yellow. Gt.2:t.38(c). (*L. s* var. *flava* Reg.)—**L. s. mínor** Ait., var. Lvs. elliptic to oblong-lanceolate often half-evergreen; corolla usually 4 cm. long. B.M.1753(c). B.R.556(c) Gn.34:300,t(c).

 L. s. × *hirsuta* = **L. Brównii** (Reg.) Carr. Similar to No. 56, but coroll more or less 2-lipped and tube slightly gibbous at base: lvs. sometimes sparingl ciliate and slightly pubescent beneath and petiole sparingly glandular. Gt.2:t 38(c). F.S.11:t.1133(c). (*L. sempervirens Brownii* André.) Orig. before 1850 Zone V.—Cult. in several forms: **L. B. punícea** (Kirchn.) Rehd., var. Fls orange-red.—**L. B. Yoùngii** (K. Koch) Rehd., var. More vigorous: fls. deepe orange-red.—**L. B. fuchsioídes** (Nichols.) Rehd., var. Fls. scarlet outside, dis tinctly 2-lipped. G.F.9:496.—**L. B. plantierénsis** (André) Rehd., var. Fls. coral red, lobes orange. I.H.18:t.86(c). (*L. p.* André.)—Also *L. Hendersonii* Hort belongs here.—*L. s.* × *americana;* see No. 66.—*L. s.* × *tragophylla;* se under No. 67.

 57. L. ciliòsa Poir. Twining or procumbent: lvs. short-petioled or sub sessile, ovate or elliptic to oblong-elliptic, 5–10 cm. long, obtuse or acutish broad-cuneate, rarely rounded at base, ciliate, bluish green beneath, sometime pubescent when young; the upper pair connate into an elliptic disk usuall; acute at ends; petioles to 6 mm. long; fls. in short-stalked heads of one o few whorls; corolla 3–4 cm. long, usually sparingly hairy outside, yellow sometimes tinged purple, tube ventricose at base, 3–4 times as long as the 2-lipped limb; style pubescent and like the stamens longer than limb. Fl.vi fr.viii–ix. S.H.2:f.460h,462d-e. B. C. to Calif., Mont. and Utah. Intr. 1825 Zone V.—**L. c. occidentàlis** (Hook.) Nichols. More vigorous, with large more brightly colored fls. glabrous outside. B.R.1457(c). D.H.1:214. (*L. c* Hook., *L. ciliosa volubilis* Zab.) Intr. 1824.

 Closely related species: **L. arizònica** Rehd. Lvs. ovate to oval, 2–4, rarel to 7 cm. long, ciliate; petiole 6–12 mm. long: corolla with nearly regular limb 3.5–4.5 cm. long, tinged scarlet outside, glabrous. S.T.1:t.23. Ariz., N. Mex Cult. 1900.—Another species with subregular limb is **L. subaequàlis** Rehd Lvs. elliptic to obovate-oblong, 6–10 cm. long, obtuse, the upper pair connate elliptic, pointed at ends, bearing the sessile fl.-whorl; corolla funnelform, 2.5– cm. long, sparingly glandular outside; stamens about as long as limb, style longer glabrous. R.Mo.14:t.4,f.5–9. W. China. Intr. 1908. Zone VI?

 58. L. hispídula (Lindl.) Torr. & Gr. Bushy shrub with sarmentose brs rarely twining; brts. usually hirsute and glandular: lvs. ovate to ovate-oblong 3–6 cm. long, acute or abruptly acuminate, rarely obtuse, rounded to subcor date at base, ciliate, glabrous to sparingly pilose above, pubescent beneath the upper pair usually connate into a usually acute disk; the pair below often with foliaceous stipules; petiole to 8 mm. long: fl.-whorls usually sev eral, approximate, forming long-peduncled spikes; bractlets ½ as long a ovaries; corolla 2-lipped, about 1.5 cm. long, pilose or glabrous outside, whit ish, tinged purple; tube about as long as limb; stamens and style as long a limb. Fl.vi–vii; fr.viii–ix. B.R.1761(c). D.H.1:211. (*L. h.* var. *Douglas* Gray.) B. C. to n. Calif. Intr. about 1830. Zone VI.—**L. h. vacíllans** Gray ar. More vigorous; lvs. ovate-oblong, 3–8 cm. long, usually acute, usually glabrous above, glabrous or pubescent beneath: infl. longer, sometimes paniculate; corolla to 1.8 cm. long. (*L. h. californica* Rehd.) B.C. to s. Calif. Intr. about 1880.

59. **L. hirsùta** Eaton. High climbing shrub; brts. usually hirsute: lvs. short-petioled, elliptic, 5–11 cm. long, dark green and often pilose above, gray-sh green and pubescent beneath, 1 or 2 pairs connate into an elliptic acute disk: fls. in short usually peduncled glandular-pubescent spikes; corolla 2–2.5 m. long, orange-yellow, glandular-pubescent outside; tube longer than limb, entricose below the middle; style and stamens exceeding the limb. Fl.vi–vii; r.ix–x. B.M.3103(c). G.F.9:344. S.L.223(h). (*L. pubescens* Sweet.) Que. o Sask., s. Pa., Ohio, Mich., Neb. Intr. about 1825. Zone III. Attractive vine.

L. h. × *sempervirens;* see under No. 56.—*L. h.* × *prolifera;* see under No. 62.—Hybrids of *L. h.* with *L. dioica* and *L. flava* have been recorded.

60. **L. dioìca** L. Slightly twining or bushy shrub with sarmentose brs.; glabrous: lvs. very short-petioled or subsessile, elliptic to oblong, 4–8 cm. ong, obtuse or acutish, cuneate, with cartilaginous, transparent, often wavy nargin, glaucous beneath, the upper pair connate: fls. in sessile or short-stalked spikes of usually several whorls; corolla about 1.5 cm. long, greenish or whitish yellow, often tinged purplish, glabrous outside; stamens as long as imb, style longer, usually glabrous. Fl.v–vi; fr.vii–ix. B.R.138(c). S.O.2:t. 109(c). Gs.13:193. (*L. glauca* Hill, *L. media* Murr., *L. parviflora* Lam.) Que. to Sask., s. to N. C., Ohio and Iowa. Intr. 1636? Zone II.

Hybrids of *L. d.* with *L. hirsuta, L. prolifera* and *L. flava* have been recorded.
Closely related species: **L. glaucéscens** Rydb. Lvs. pubescent beneath; corolla about 2 cm. long, often pubescent outside; tube slightly longer than imb; style usually pubescent; ovary sometimes glandular. (*L. hirsuta glaucescens* Rydb., *L. Douglasii* Koehne, not DC.) B.B.3:279. S.H.2:f.460n-o,463 a–c. Que. to Alb., s. to Va., Ohio and Neb. Cult. 1890? Zone III.—**L. g. dasýgyna** Rehd., var. Ovaries densely glandular and hirsute. Cult. 1928.

61. **L. yunnanénsis** Franch. Twining shrub; brts. glabrous: lvs. very short-stalked, oblong to oblong-obovate or oblong-lanceolate, 4–8 cm. long, acutish, glabrous above, glaucous and glabrous or slightly pubescent beneath, the upper pair or 2 pairs connate: fls. in a short-peduncled head of one to several whorls; corolla 2–2.5 cm. long, yellow, glabrous; tube slightly ventricose, longer than limb, pubescent inside. S. W. China. Intr. ?—**L. y. ténuis** Rehd., var. Smaller and slenderer: lvs. oblong, about 3 cm. long, sparingly pilose beneath on veins: infl. of 1 whorl; corolla scarcely 2 cm. long, white, changing to yellow. M.O.270. S. W. China. Intr. about 1900. Zone VII?

Related species: **L. albiflòra** Torr. & Gray. Bushy or somewhat climbing shrub: lvs. elliptic or ovate, 2–3.5 cm. long, obtuse, glabrous: infl. of 1 or 2 sessile whorls; corolla 2–3 cm. long, with slender tube, yellowish white. Ark. and Tex. Intr. about 1850. Zone V.

62. **L. prolífera** (Kirchn.) Rehd. Twining or almost bushy shrub; brts. glabrous: lvs. sessile or very short-petioled, elliptic to oblong-obovate, 5–9 cm. long, obtuse rarely acute, bright green and often bloomy above, glaucous beneath and usually short-pubescent, usually more than 2 pairs connate into suborbicular or oval flat disks obtuse or emarginate at the ends, thickish and densely bloomy above: fls. in peduncled spikes of 2–4 whorls, often with 2 smaller spikes at base; corolla 2.5–3 cm. long, pale yellow, glabrous outside, with slender tube pubescent inside and slightly ventricose below the middle; style pubescent. Fl.vi–vii; fr.ix–x. R.H.1856:222,t(c). G.F.3:191. Gn.60:

285. (*L. Sullivantii* Gray, *Caprifolium proliferum* Kirchn.) Ohio to Tenn Mo., Iowa and Wis. Cult. 1840. Zone IV.

L. p. × *hirsuta* = **L. Sargéntii** Rehd. Lvs. more pubescent beneath an〈 sparingly ciliate; disk slightly or not bloomy above: fls. orange-yellow, usuall〉 slightly pubescent outside. G.F.9:345. Orig. 1880.—Also hybrids of *L. p.* wit〉 *L. dioica* and *L. flava* have been recorded.

63. L. flàva Sims. Slightly twining, glabrous: lvs. short-petioled, broad〉 elliptic to elliptic, 4–8 cm. long, obtuse or acutish, bright green above, bluis〉 green beneath, the upper or 2 upper pairs connate into a suborbicular or ova〉 disk rounded and usually mucronulate or acuminulate at ends, green o〉 slightly bloomy above, rather thin: fl.-whorls 1–3 on a short, sometimes t〉 1.5 cm. long peduncle; corolla about 3 cm. long, orange-yellow, fragrant, wit〉 slender not ventricose tube, glabrous or nearly so inside; style glabrous. F〉 v–vi; fr.viii–ix. B.M.1318(c). L.D.3:162(c). G.F.3:190. N. C. to Mo., Ark〉 and Okl. Cult. 1810. Zone V.—One of the handsomest of the America〉 species, with fragrant fls.

64. L. impléxa Ait. Evergreen, much-branched twining or sometime〉 bushy shrub, glabrous: lvs. usually sessile, elliptic or ovate to narrow-oblong 2.5–8 cm. long, acute to rounded and mucronulate, cuneate to subcordate a〉 base, glaucous beneath, glabrous or pubescent, the upper pairs connate int〉 concave, usually pointed disks; fl.-whorls several, all or the lower ones in th〉 axils of connate lvs.; bractlets wanting; corolla 3.5–4.5 cm. long, yellowis〉 white, often tinged red, glabrous or pubescent outside; tube much longe〉 than the short limb, pubescent inside; stamens and the pubescent style slightl〉 exceeding the tube. Fl.vi–viii. B.M.640(c). R.I.17:t.122,f.4(c). F.D.28:〉 2914(c). Mediterr. reg. Intr. 1772. Zone (VII). Very variable.

Hybrids with *L. Caprifolium* and *L. etrusca* are known.

65. L. Caprifòlium L. Twining shrub, glabrous: lvs. short-petioled, broad〉 elliptic to elliptic, 4–10 cm. long, obtuse, dark green above, bluish gree〉 beneath, sometimes slightly pubescent when young, the 2 or 3 upper pair〉 connate into elliptic acutish disks: usually 1 or 2 fl.-whorls in the axils o〉 connate lvs.; bractlets minute or wanting; corolla 4–5 cm. long, white c〉 yellowish white, sometimes slightly purplish, very fragrant, glabrous or spar〉 ingly pilose; tube slightly longer than limb; stamens and the glabrous sty〉 as long as limb: fr. orange-red. Fl.v–vi; fr.viii–ix. R.I.17:t.122,f.3(c). F.D.28〉 2913(c). Gs.9:241(h);15:109(h). (*L. pallida* Host.) Eu. and W. Asia. Cul〉 for centuries; occasionally naturalized in the E. States. Zone V.—**L. C. pauc〉 flòra** Carr. Corolla tinged purple outside. R.I.17:t.122,f.1–2(c). (*L. C.* va〉 *rubra* Tausch, not West.)

L. C. × *etrusca* = **L. americàna** K. Koch. Lvs. broad-elliptic to obovat〉 glabrous: several fl.-whorls at end of brts.; the lower in the axils of connate lvs〉 the upper in the axils of bracts, close; bractlets about half as long as ovarie〉 those of upper fls. smaller; corolla 4–5 cm. long, yellowish, usually purple ou〉 side and glandular-pubescent or glandular, fragrant. Fl.vi–vii. S.O.2:t.106(c〉 F.S.11:t.1120(c, as *L. Caprifolium major*). G.C.102:441,t(c). Gn.45:307(a〉 *L. etrusca* and *L. Caprifolium*); 54:26. (*L. italica* Schmidt, *L. grata* Ait〉 Orig. before 1750. Zone V.—**L. a. rubélla** (Tausch) Rehd., var. Fls. pale purpl〉 —**L. a. atrosanguínea** (Carr.) Rehd., var. Fls. dark purple.

66. L. Heckróttii Rehd. (? *L. americana* × *sempervirens*). Shrub wit〉 sarmentose or upright brs., glabrous: lvs. subsessile, elliptic to elliptic-oblong 3–6 cm. long, acute or acutish, glaucous beneath: fls. in elongated peduncle〉 spikes, with several remote whorls; bractlets about half as long as ovaries〉 corolla 3.5–5 cm. long, sparingly glandular and purple outside, yellowish an〉 sparingly hairy within. Fl.vi–ix. Gn.85:502;89:638. B.H.3:89(h). Origi〉 unknown, before 1895. Zone V. Floriferous handsome plant.

67. **L. tragophýlla** Hemsl. High climbing; brts. glabrous: lvs. short-
petioled, oblong, rarely elliptic, 5–12 cm. long, acute to obtuse, cuneate, gla-
rous and bright green above, glaucous beneath and pubescent at least along
he midrib, the upper pair connate: fls. in terminal short-peduncled glabrous
eads of usually 2 whorls; corolla 7–8 cm. long, bright yellow, glabrous out-
ide, sparingly pubescent within; tube nearly 3 times as long as limb. Fl.vi.
B.M.8064(c). S.T.1:t.46. H.N.3:t.4. G.C.71:271(h);78:7,t(h). W. China.
ntr. about 1900. Zone (V). Remarkable for its large yellow fls.

L. t. × *sempervirens* = **L. Tellmanniàna** Spaeth. Lvs. oblong, obtuse: fls. in
peduncled heads of usually 2 whorls; corolla deep yellow, 2-lipped, tube about
cm. long, limb about half as long. G.C.90:421,t(c). Orig. about 1920. Zone V.

68. **L. spléndida** Boiss. Evergreen twining shrub: lvs. of flowering brts.
essile or connate at base, obovate-oblong to oblong, 2–5 cm. long, obtuse,
grayish green, glaucous beneath, glabrous, usually more than 2 pairs connate;
terile brs. with smaller, petioled, oval or ovate, usually pilose lvs.: fls. fra-
rant in dense sessile glandular-pubescent spikes of 3–5 whorls; bractlets ¼–
⅓ as long as ovaries; corolla 4–5 cm. long, yellowish white, purple and glan-
lular outside; tube about 1½ times as long as limb. Fl.vii. F.S.11:t.1130(c).
B.M.9517(c). Gt.39:65. Spain. Cult. 1880. Zone VII. Handsome species,
ut tender.

69. **L. etrúsca** Santi. Evergreen or half-evergreen, high-climbing; young
rts. glabrous, usually tinged purple: lvs. short-petioled, obovate to broad-
val or elliptic, 3–8 cm. long, obtuse or acutish, usually glabrous above, pubes-
ent beneath and glaucous, rarely glabrous, the upper ones connate: fls.
ragrant, in dense spikes of several whorls on stalks to 4 cm. long, often in
's at end of brs., glabrous or glandular; bractlets nearly as long as ovary,
uborbicular; corolla 4–5 cm. long, yellowish white, often tinged purple,
glabrous or glandular-pubescent outside; tube very slender, about 1½ times
s long as limb. Fl.vi–vii. R.I.17:t.121,f.5(c). F.D.28:t.2915(c). Mediterr.
eg. Cult. 1750. Zone VII.—**L. e. supérba** W. Wats. Vigorous form: fl.-
eads forming large terminal panicles. B.M.7977(c). (*L. gigantea* Carr.)—
L. e. pubéscens Dipp., var. Lvs. soft-pubescent on both sides, large. Garten-
eit. 1886:557. (*L. gigantea* Zab., not Carr.)—**L. e. viscídula** Boiss., var. Lvs.
–4 cm. long, densely glandular above like the brts., glaucous and less glan-
lular beneath. Asia Minor.

L. e. × *Caprifolium;* see under No. 65.—There is also a hybrid with *L.
mplexa.*

70. **L. Periclýmenum** L. Woodbine. Climbing or scrambling over
ushes; young brts. pubescent or glabrous: lvs. all distinct, petioled or the
upper pair sessile, ovate or elliptic to ovate-oblong, 4–6 cm. long, acute, some-
imes obtuse, dark green above, bluish green beneath, glabrous or slightly
ubescent when young: fls. fragrant, in peduncled spikes of 3–5 whorls; bract-
ets at least half as long as ovary, glandular; corolla 4–5 cm. long, yellowish
white, often slightly tinged purple, glandular outside; tube slender, longer
han limb; stamens and style as long as limb. Fl.vi–viii; fr.viii–ix. R.I.17:t.
121,f.3,4(c). F.D.28:t.2916(c). Eu., N. Afr., Asia Minor. Long cult. Zone
[V. The two last named vars. most frequently cult.—**L. P. aùrea** Lind. &
André. Lvs. variegated with yellow. I.H.18:t.59(c).—**L. P. quercìna** West.,
var. Lvs. sinuately lobed and often with narrow white margin.—**L. P. bélgica**
Ait., var. Dutch W. Of more shrubby habit: lvs. glabrous, somewhat thick-
sh: fls. purple outside, usually fading to yellowish.—**L. P. seròtina** Ait.,
var. Fls. dark purple outside, fading to pale purple, yellow within. Fl.vii–ix.
Gn.45:307,t(c). (*L. semperflorens* Goldring.)

Another species with distinct lvs. is **L. Griffithii** Hook. f. & Thoms. Climb
ing: lvs. broad-ovate to ovate-oblong, glabrous, the pair below the infl. sub
orbicular, petioled: fls. in a dense peduncled sparingly pilose and glandula
head; bractlets of each whorl connate into a cupula as high as ovaries; coroll
about 2.5 cm. long, glandular and pilose outside, glabrous inside; tube about a
long as limb. S.T.1:t.24. G.C.60:43. Afghan. Intr. about 1900. Zone VII?

11. LEYCESTÈRIA Wall. Deciduous shrubs: lvs. opposite, petiolec
with or without stipules: fls. in whorls in the axils of leafy bracts, formin,
terminal spikes; calyx unequally 5-lobed, persistent; corolla funnelform
nearly equally 5-lobed, ventricose above the base; stamens 5; style slende
with capitate stigma; ovary 5–8-celled: fr. a many-seeded berry. (After Wm
Leycester, judge in Bengal.) Incl. *Pentapyxis* Hook. f. Three species in th
Himal. and S. China.

L. formòsa Wall. Shrub to 2 m., with hollow stems, glabrous and bloom;
when young: lvs. broad-ovate to ovate-lanceolate, 5–18 cm. long, acuminate
cordate, entire or toothed, finely pubescent when young; petiole 5–15 mm
long: spikes drooping, 3–10 cm. long, terminal and axillary: fls. sessile i
the axils of purplish bracts 1.5–3.5 cm. long; corolla 1.5–2 cm. long, purplish
calyx with subulate hairy lobes about ⅓ as long as corolla: fr. subglobose
about 1 cm. across, glandular-pubescent, red-purple. Fl.VIII–IX. B.M.369
(c). Gt.28:181. M.G.23:330(h). Himal., S. W. China. Intr. 1824. Zone VII
Conspicuous in bloom on account of its colored bracts.

Fam. 110. **DIPSACACEAE** Lindl. TEASEL FAMILY

Herbs or dwarf shrubs: lvs. opposite, rarely whorled, usually lobed, exstip
ulate: fls. perfect, small, sessile, mostly irregular, surrounded by a cup-shape
scarious involucel and crowded into involucrate heads; calyx various; coroll
4–5-lobed with imbricate lobes; stamens 4, rarely 2–3, adnate to the corolla
ovary inferior, 1-celled and 1-ovuled; style with 2 stigmas: fr. an achene
seed albuminous with straight embryo.—Ten genera and about 150 specie
in the warm-temp. regions of the Old World.

PTEROCÉPHALUS Adans. Annual or perennial herbs, rarely shrubs
lvs. opposite: scales of the receptacle small or wanting; involucels with :
grooves extending to the base and with spreading limb; calyx-limb of 12–2
bristles; corolla 5-fid.; stigma simple or divided. (Greek *pteron*, wing, an
kephale, head; referring to the feathery appearance of the heads after flower
ing.) About 20 species chiefly in the Mediterr. reg.

P. parnàssi Spreng. Tufted subshrub, densely gray-pubescent: lvs. ovate
1–2 cm. long, obtuse, broad-cuneate to truncate at base, incisely crenate
dentate and often pinnatifid at base; petiole often nearly as long as blade
fls. lilac-pink, in depressed-hemispherical heads, 2–3 cm. across; disk-fls. nearly
regular; ray-fls. 2-lipped, upper lip with 2 rounded lobes, the lower with :
ovate obtuse lobes. Fl.VII. B.M.6526(c). G.C.104:142(h). (*Scabiosa ptero
cephala* L.) S. E. Eu. Cult. 1880. Zone VI. Suited for the rock garden; th
fl.-heads conspicuous on account of the long plumose bristles of the calyx.

Fam. 111. **COMPÓSITAE** Adans. COMPOSITE FAMILY

Herbs, shrubs or rarely trees, sometimes twining, often with milky juice
lvs. alternate, rarely opposite or whorled, exstipulate: fls. bisexual or uni
sexual, regular or irregular, sessile on a flat or conical axis (receptacle) an
forming small or large involucrate heads, sometimes reduced to 1 fl.; caly:

reduced to scales, awns or hairs (pappus) or wanting; corolla gamopetalous, 4–5-lobed, regular or ligulate (with an elongated limb on one side), rarely 2-lipped; stamens 4–5; anthers connate into a tube around the style; style 1, with 2, rarely 1 stigma; ovary inferior, 1-celled and 1-ovuled: fr. an achene, often crowned by the persistent pappus; seed exalbuminous. Includ. *Carduaceae* Neck. and *Cichoriaceae* Reichb.—About 800 genera with about 20,000 species in all parts of the world, the woody species chiefly confined to trop. and subtrop. regions.

A. Heads with ray-fls.
  B. Involucre of several series of imbricate bracts.
    c. Lvs. linear: heads small, yellow, with 3–4 rays...........................1. *Gutierrezia*
    cc. Lvs. lanceolate to elliptic: rays many.
      D. Lvs. entire or slightly serrulate, tomentose beneath: heads about 8 mm. across.
        E. Lvs. evergreen, 0.5–2.5 cm. long..3. *Olearia*
        EE. Lvs. deciduous, lanceolate, 5–12 cm. long..........................4. *Microglossa*
      DD. Lvs. toothed or lobed, glabrous or pubescent beneath: heads larger.
                                                10. *Chrysanthemum*
  BB. Involucre of one series of bracts, often with small linear bracts at base: ray-fls.
    yellow ....13. *Senecio*
AA. Heads without ray-fls.
  B. Lvs. pinnate.
    c. Heads solitary, slender-peduncled: lvs. pectinately pinnate, evergreen..9. *Santolina*
    cc. Heads in panicles, small: lvs. usually twice pinnate, deciduous.........11. *Artemisia*
  BB. Lvs. entire or dentate.
    c. Infl. corymbose.
      D. Fls. white: lvs. evergreen.
        E. Lvs. glabrous: receptacle not scaly.............................6. *Ozothamnus*
        EE. Lvs. tomentose beneath; receptacle usually scaly....................7. *Cassinia*
      DD. Fls. yellow: lvs. deciduous.
        E. Involucral bracts in several series: lvs. 3–7 cm. long..........2. *Chrysothamnus*
        EE. Involucral bracts 4–6, in one series: lvs. 1–2 cm. long............12. *Tetradymia*
    cc. Infl. not corymbose.
      D. Heads paniculate or spicate: lvs. toothed, rarely entire.
        E. Pappus present: lvs. glabrous, entire or toothed, penninerved.
          F. Involucral bracts in several series, imbricate; fls. white: lvs. deciduous.
                                              5. *Baccharis*
          FF. Involucral bracts in one series; fls. yellow: lvs. evergreen.........13. *Senecio*
        EE. Pappus wanting.
          F. Lvs. at least partly opposite, serrate, 3-nerved: involucre with about 5
            bracts ....8. *Iva*
          FF. Lvs. alternate, entire or toothed at apex: involucre with many imbricate
            bracts ....11. *Artemisia*
      DD. Heads solitary: lvs. entire...14. *Pertya*

Tribe 1. ASTEREAE. Lvs. usually alternate, entire or toothed, rarely pinnate; heads radiate or discoid; involucral bracts usually unequal and in many series; receptacle usually naked; disk-fls. usually yellow; anthers without tail at base; style-brs. of pistillate fls. flattened, with marginal stigmatic lines and a hairy triangular to lanceolate appendage; pappus various or none.

1. **GUTIERRÈZIA** Lag. Shrubs or subshrubs, much-branched, usually glabrous, often glutinous: lvs. alternate, linear, entire: heads small, yellow, forming paniculate or fastigiate cymes, of few to several fls.; ray-fls. 1–6, pistillate; disk-fls. usually perfect or a few staminate; involucre oblong to narrow-campanulate, with several imbricated coriaceous bracts; receptacle naked; achenes short, terete, ribbed or angled; pappus of chaffy scales. (After Piedro Gutierrez, correspondent of the botanical garden of Madrid.) About 20 species in W. N. Am., Mex. and S. Am.

G. Saróthrae (Pursh) Brit. & Rusby. BROOM-WEED. Much-branched subshrub to 60 cm., with upright or ascending brs., glabrous or minutely pubescent; heads few-fld., forming rather loose corymbose panicles usually 4–8 cm. across; rays usually 3–4, 1.5–2 mm. long; involucre oblong, about 5 mm. long; scales of pappus linear-oblong; achenes pubescent. Fl.VIII–IX. B.B.3:370. S.H.2:f.472g-k. S.L.186(h). (*G. Euthamiae* Torr. & Gr.) Minn. and Man. to Nev., Calif. and Tex. and n. Mex. Cult. 1900. Zone IV.

2. CHRYSOTHÁMNUS Nutt. Shrubs: lvs. alternate, rarely opposite, linear to oblanceolate, entire, 1–3-nerved: fls. yellow, tubular, perfect, in small, 3(–20)-fld. heads; involucre oblong to narrow-campanulate, with narrow appressed and densely imbricated bracts, often forming vertical rows; corolla with upright lobes; style-brs. exserted; achenes narrow, angled, pubescent; pappus a single row of capillary roughened bristles. (Greek *chrysos*, gold, and *thamnos*, shrub; referring to the color of the fls.) About 25 species in western N. Am.

C. graveòlens (Nutt.) Greene. Much-branched shrub to 1.5 m., of aromatic odor when bruised, with very leafy upright brs. white-tomentulose when young: lvs. narrow-linear, 3–7 cm. long, glabrous at maturity: heads 1–1.5 cm. high, very numerous, in terminal corymbs 3–10 cm. across; involucre narrow-campanulate, of oblong or linear-oblong acute glabrous or nearly glabrous bracts in about 4 series; achenes appressed-pubescent; pappus with copious soft bristles. Fl.viii–x. B.M.8155(c). B.B.3:376. (*C. nauseosus* var. *graveolens* Piper, *Bigelowia g.* Gray.) Mont. and Neb. to Utah and N. Mex. Cult. 1886. Zone III. With large corymbs of golden-yellow fls.; suited for well drained sunny positions. It contains rubber, though not in sufficient quantity for commercial exploitation.

Related species: **C. nauseòsus** (Pursh) Brit. Shrub to 1 m.; brts. permanently white-tomentose: lvs. 3–6 cm. long, tomentose; bracts of involucre strongly carinate on back, tomentose: achenes hirsute-strigose. (*Bigelowia graveolens* var. *albicaulis* Gray.) B. C. and Ore. to Mont., Wyo. and Utah. Intr. ?—**C. viscidiflòrus** (Hook.) Nutt. Shrub to 1 m.; brts. glabrous or nearly so: lvs. linear-lanceolate, 2–4 cm. long, 2–3 mm. wide, glabrous: involucre glabrous. (*Bigelowia Douglasii* Gray.) Wyo. to Colo., Ariz. and Utah. Cult. 1886. Zone V?—**C. v. tortifolius** (Gray) Greene, var. Lvs. linear, serrulate, ciliate, twisted. Cult. 1933.

3. OLEÀRIA DC. Evergreen shrubs or subshrubs, sometimes small trees: lvs. alternate, rarely opposite, usually tomentose beneath: heads heterogamous, small, with several to many usually white to purple short ray-fls., rarely without; involucre of several rows of bracts with scarious margin; anthers often pointed or minutely caudate at base; achenes terete or slightly compressed, usually 5-ribbed; pappus with several rows of bristles, the outer row often short. (Name referring to the similarity of some species to those of Olea.) Syn.: *Shawia* Forst. About 100 species in Australia and N. Zeal.

O. Haàstii Hook. f. Bushy shrub to 3 m.; young brts. whitish tomentose: lvs. alternate, short-stalked, crowded, elliptic or ovate, 1–2.5 cm. long, obtuse, entire, lustrous dark green above, white-tomentose beneath, leathery: heads about 8 mm. across, in axillary peduncled cymes at end of brs. and forming a flattened corymb 5–8 cm. across; ray-fls. 3–5, white; disk yellow: achenes ribbed, pubescent. Fl.vii. B.M.6592(c). G.C.49:52(h). Gn.78:473(h). S.L. 241(h). N. Zeal. Intr. 1858. Zone VII? One of the most ornamental of the hardier shrubby Composites.

Related species probably hardy in Zone VII: **O. nummulariifòlia** Hook. f. Lvs. orbicular to oblong, 5–12 mm. long, thick, with recurved margins: heads about 1 cm. long, solitary or few on peduncles longer than the lvs. Laing & Blackwell Pl. N. Zeal. ed. 2:411. N. Zeal. Intr. 1889.—**O. álbida** Hook. f. Shrub or small tree to 6 m.: lvs. oblong or ovate-oblong, 4–10 mm. long, obtuse, rounded or narrowed at base: heads many, in corymbs about 5 cm. across; fls. 3–6; ray-fls. 1–3. J.L.60:f.168(h). N. Zeal. Cult. 1928.—**O. odoràta** Petrie. Shrub to 4 m.: lvs. opposite or fascicled, linear-spatulate to linear-obovate, 0.6–2.5 cm. long: heads in axillary fascicles, fragrant; bracts and corolla of disk-fls. viscid; disk-fls. 20–35; ray-fls. 8–18. N. Zeal. Intr. 1908.—**O. lineàta** (Kirk) Cockayne. Shrub to 3 m., with slender often pendulous brs.: lvs. opposite with fascicles of lvs. in the axils, narrow-linear, 1–2.5 cm. long, strongly revolute: heads fascicled; bracts villous; disk–fls. 6–12; ray-fls. 8–14. N. Zeal. Cult. 1933.

4. **MICROGLÓSSA** DC. Climbing or upright shrubs: lvs. alternate, usually entire: heads rather small, in panicles or corymbs; ray-fls. pistillate, with short rays, white or bluish; disk-fl. perfect; receptacle flat, naked or nearly so; involucre of narrow bracts in many rows, membranous, the outer shorter: achenes not compressed, with slender pappus-hairs in 1 or 2 rows. (Greek *micros*, small, and *glosse*, tongue; referring to the short rays.) About 10 species in trop. Asia and Himal., also in Afr.

M. albéscens (DC.) C. B. Clarke. Shrub or subshrub to 1 m.; brs. slightly grooved, grayish pubescent, with ample white pith: lvs. lanceolate, 5–12 cm. long, acute at ends, entire or slightly serrulate, grayish tomentulose beneath: heads about 8 mm. across, in terminal compound corymbs 7–15 cm. across; ray-fls. about 14, narrow, pale lilac-blue or nearly white; disk yellow. Fl.vii–viii. B.M.6672(c). R.H.1907:523. S.L.237(h). (*Amphirhaphis a.* DC., *Aster a.* Koehne, *A. cabulicus* Lindl.) Temp. Himal. and China. Intr. about 1840. Zone VII.

Related genus: **Aster** L. Heads rather large, with conspicuous rays and yellow disk; anthers obtuse at base: fr. usually compressed, without or with 1 or few ribs on the faces. More than 200 species mostly herbaceous.—**A. statici-fólius** Franch. Much-branched shrub to 50 cm. tall: lvs. spatulate, 1.5–8 cm. long, obtuse or slightly emarginate, glabrous or puberulous, ciliolate, minutely glandular-punctate: heads solitary on slender stalks to 10 cm. high; involucre with 15–18 linear glabrous bracts; disk to 1 cm. across; ray-fls. 15–18, with purple-blue linear limb 1–1.5 cm. long: fr. silky, smooth on one side, obscurely ribbed on the other. B.M.9081(c). G.C.60:116. J.L.48:f.25. W. China. Intr. 1906. Zone VII?

5. **BÁCCHARIS** L. Deciduous or evergreen shrubs or herbs; glabrous, sometimes viscid or lepidote: lvs. alternate, usually toothed: heads small, many-fld., in terminal panicles or corymbs or axillary, dioecious, white or yellowish, without ray-fls.; involucre of many imbricate bracts; receptacle flat, naked; pistillate fls. with filiform corolla; achenes compressed, usually 10-ribbed; pappus of pistillate fls. of long bristly hairs. (*Bakkharis*, ancient Greek name for different shrubs.) More than 250 species in N. to S. Am.

A. Lvs. petioled, deciduous...1. *B. halimifolia*
AA. Lvs. sessile, evergreen...2. *B. patagonica*

1. **B. halimifòlia** L. GROUNDSEL-BUSH. Shrub to 4 m., much-branched: lvs. short-stalked, obovate to oblong, 2–7 cm. long, acute, cuneate, coarsely toothed, the upper ones entire, resinous; heads 4–6 mm. long, in peduncled clusters of 3–5 forming large panicles: achenes about 1 mm. long; pappus about 8 mm. long. Fl.viii–ix; fr. x–xi. Ad.2:t.55(c). Gg.7:113(h). Mass. to Fla. and Tex. Intr. 1683. Zone IV. Conspicuous in fr. with its white pappus.

Related species: **B. salicìna** Torr. & Gray. Shrub to 1 m.: lvs. subsessile, narrow-oblong to linear-lanceolate, 2–4 cm. long, obtuse or obtusish, slightly toothed or nearly entire. Fl.v–vii; fr.viii. B.B.3:445. Kansas and Colo. to W. Tex. Cult. 1894. Zone V.—**B. pilulàris** DC. Ascending shrub to 1 m.: lvs. subsessile, elliptic to obovate, 1–2.5 cm. long, toothed. Ore. to Calif. Intr. before 1910. Zone VII?

2. **B. patagònica** Hook. & Arn. Much-branched evergreen shrub to 3 m; brts. angled, viscid when young: lvs. sessile, obovate to oblong, 8–20 mm. long, obtuse, cuneate, with few coarse teeth, deep green above, scurfy on both sides: heads axillary, sessile, usually solitary, yellowish white: pappus about 1 cm. long. Fl.v–vi; fr.viii. Dumont d'Urville, Voy. Pole Sud, Bot. 2:t.26. Patag. Cult. 1880. Zone VII.

Tribe 2. INULEAE. Lvs. usually alternate, entire or nearly so: heads usually discoid; involucral bracts usually dry and scarious, in several series, sometimes foliaceous or petaloid; receptacle naked or scaly; anthers tailed at base; style various, pappus usually capillary.

6. **OZOTHÁMNUS** R. Br. Evergreen shrubs: lvs. alternate, entire: heads few- to many-fld., in terminal or lateral corymbs, without ray-fls.; involucre with several rows of imbricate bracts; receptacle without scales; fls. tubular, usually all perfect; pappus of numerous slender bristles, thickened or barbellate at apex. (Greek *ozo*, to be scented, and *thamnos*, shrub.) More than 20 species in Tasmania, N. Zeal. and Australia.

O. Antennària (DC.) Hook. f. Shrub to 1 m.; young brts. puberulous, soon glabrous: lvs. petioled, narrow-obovate, 1–2.5 cm. long, rounded or slightly emarginate at apex, cuneate, whitish pubescent at first, soon glabrous, pale gray beneath: corymbs about 3 cm. across, pubescent; heads cylindric-campanulate, 4–5 mm. long; bracts up to 20, the inner with hyaline white tips; fls. 16–18, the 3 or 4 outer pistillate; pappus of about 24 scaberulous white bristles. Fl.vi. B.M.9152(c). (*Helichrysum antennarium* F. v. Muell.) Tasmania. Cult. 1885. Zone VII?

6. **CASSÍNIA** R. Br. Evergreen shrubs: lvs. alternate, entire: heads small, in panicles or corymbs, with perfect or a few pistillate fls., without ray-fls.; involucre with scarious colored bracts, the inner often with spreading appendage; receptacle usually with long deciduous scales: achenes with setose pappus. (After Count A. H. G. Cassini, French botanist; 1781–1832.) About 18 species in Australia, N. Zeal., and S. Afr.

C. fúlvida Hook. f. Shrub to 2 m., with upright brs. viscid when young, yellowish pubescent: lvs. crowded, oblong-obovate to linear-spatulate, 4–8 mm. long, with revolute margin, dark green and slightly viscid above, yellowish tomentulose beneath: heads 5 mm. long, with 5–8 fls., white, in terminal dense corymbs 2–5 cm. across; outer bracts glabrous; receptacle with few or no scales; achenes puberulous. Fl.vi–vii. Gt.39:241. S.L.115(h). (*Diplopappus chrysophyllus* Koehne.) N. Zeal. Cult. 1880. Zone VI? Shrub of heath-like habit.

Related species, all with scaly receptacle and glabrous achenes: **C. leptophýlla** R. Br. Brts. grayish pubescent: lvs. linear or linear-spatulate, 3–5 mm. long, dark green above, yellowish or whitish tomentose beneath: heads in terminal corymbs 3–5 cm. across; outer bracts glabrous. P.F.3:16. N.H.14:12. N. Zeal. Intr. 1824. Zone VII?—**C. Vauvilliérsii** (Dcne.) Hook. f. Shrub to 2 m.; brts. yellowish or whitish tomentose: lvs. linear-obovate to linear-oblong, 6–10 mm. long, usually glutinous above, fulvous or whitish beneath: heads in terminal rounded corymbs; outer bracts tomentose or glabrate. Laing & Blackwell, Pl. N. Zeal. ed. 2:431. New Zeal. Cult. 1902. Zone VII?—**C. retórta** DC. Shrub to 5 m.: lvs. spreading and recurved, linear-obovate to linear-oblong, 3–5 mm. long, white-tomentose beneath: heads numerous, in small corymbs; outer bracts tomentose. N. Zeal. Cult. 1933. Zone VII?

Tribe 3. HELIANTHEAE. Lvs. usually opposite, at least the lower ones: heads mostly radiate; involucral bracts usually herbaceous, in 1 to many series; receptacle usually scaly; anthers not tailed; style-brs. truncate or appendaged, usually with a ring of hairs below the brs.: pappus never capillary.

8. **ÍVA** L. Herbs or shrubs: lower lvs. opposite, upper alternate, serrate or entire, thickish; heads small, of staminate and a few marginal pistillate fls., not radiate, axillary; involucre with few roundish bracts; receptacle chaffy; anthers scarcely coherent: achenes glabrous or slightly pubescent, compressed, without pappus. (Medieval name of a medicinal plant [Ajuga Iva].) About 12 species in N. and C. Am. and in the W. Indies.

I. frutéscens L. MARSH-ELDER. Shrub to 3.5 m.; brts. strigose: lvs. short-petioled, lanceolate, 10–15 cm. long, acute, serrate, cuneate, slightly strigose, 3-nerved, the upper ones smaller, nearly linear; heads greenish, hemispheric, 4 mm. across, with 5, rarely 4, orbicular-ovate bracts; pistillate fls. about 5. Fl.vii–ix. Va. to Fla. and Tex. Cult. 1711. Zone VII?—**I. f. orària** (Bartlett) Fern. & Griscom, var. Subshrub to 1 m.: lvs. elliptic-ovate or elliptic, acute or obtuse, on the flowering brts. nearly linear: heads 5–6 mm. across, with 5, rarely 6 bracts. B.B.3:339. K.D.564. (*I. o.* Bartlett.) Mass. to Md. Intr. 1880. Zone V.

Tribe 4. ANTHEMIDEAE. Usually aromatic or strong-scented: lvs. usually alternate and usually dissected: heads radiate or discoid; involucral bracts imbricate, in 2 to many series, wholly or in part dry and scarious; receptacle scaly, pubescent or naked; anthers not tailed at base: style-brs. of the perfect fls. usually truncate: pappus a short crown or none.

9. SANTOLÌNA L.
Evergreen subshrubs or herbs, aromatic: lvs. alternate, pinnate: heads many-fld., discoid, yellow or rarely white, solitary on long peduncles; fls. all perfect; involucre campanulate, with appressed imbricate bracts; receptacle chaffy; stigmas truncate: achenes 3–5-angled, without pappus. (Derivation of name doubtful.) About 8 species in the Mediterr. reg.

S. Chamaecyparíssus L. LAVENDER-COTTON. Much-branched subshrub, with procumbent stem and ascending brs., to 50 cm., whitish tomentose: lvs. pinnate, 1–4 cm. long, with short-oblong obtuse segments, 1–2 mm. long, often in 3 or 4 rows; heads yellow, hemispheric, 1–2 cm. across, long-peduncled. R.I. 16:t.121,f.2(c). F.D.29:t.3030(c). B.S.2:498. Fl.vii–viii. (*S. incana* Lam.) S. Eu. Cult. 1596. Zone VII.

Related species: **S. neapolitàna** Jord. Whitish tomentose: lvs. 2–5 cm. long, segments 2–6 mm. long, obtusish to acute: heads yellow, 6–12 from each stem. Italy. Cult. 1930. Zone VII.—**S. vírens** Mill. Green, glabrate: lvs. 2–5 cm. long, with acute teeth, 1–2 mm. long: fls. yellow. (*S. viridis* Willd.) S. Eu. Cult. 1727. Zone VII.—**S. pinnàta** Viv. Glabrous or nearly so: lvs. 2–3.5 cm. long, segments 3–5 mm. long: fls. dull white; heads 1–1.5 cm. across, Gs.7:211. Italy. Cult. 1791. Zone VII.

10. CHRYSÁNTHEMUM L.
CHRYSANTHEMUM. Herbs or subshrubs: lvs. alternate, entire, dentate or lobed: heads rather large and long-peduncled or small and corymbose; radiate disk-fls. perfect; ray-fls. pistillate; involucre of several series of imbricate appressed bracts with usually scarious margin: receptacle flat or convex, naked; achenes angled or ribbed; pappus wanting or reduced to a scale-like border. (Greek *chrysos*, golden, *anthemos*, flower.) About 150 species in Eu., Asia and Afr.

A. Lvs. lobed, deciduous.
  B. Lvs. more or less pubescent..1. *C. morifolium*
  BB. Lvs. glabrate ....2. *C. sibiricum*
AA. Lvs. obtusely serrate, evergreen...3. *C. nipponicum*

1. C. morifòlium Ram. FLORISTS' C. Suffruticose or nearly herbaceous: lvs. usually ovate in outline, 4–12 cm. long, pinnately lobed, with broad obtuse lobes dentate or lobulate, pubescent or tomentose; heads usually several in terminal corymbs, about 5 cm. across, or smaller or much larger, of various colors; involucre of oblong bracts; the wild form has white ray-fls. and yellow disk-fls.; in the garden forms the fls. are usually all changed into ray-fls. or sometimes into tubular fls. Fl.ix–xii. B.M.327(c). G.C.31:302. B.C. 2:755. (*C. sinense* Sabine, *C. hortorum* Bailey.) Intr. from China 1790.— The hardier forms with smaller fl.-heads are hardy in zone V, the highly developed greenhouse forms with much larger fl.-heads are tender.

2. **C. sibíricum** Fisch. KOREAN C. Suffruticose, to 30 cm., with uprigł stems from a procumbent woody base, glabrous or puberulous toward the en of the brs.: lvs. pinnatifid, 3–5 cm. long, with ovate or elliptic, incised-serrat to lobulate acutish lobes, truncate or broad-cuneate at base and decurrer into the margined petiole 3–5 cm. long in the lower lvs., upper lvs. smalle short-petioled, with undivided lobes: heads 4–5 cm. across, with white c pinkish rays on solitary slender peduncles forming loose racemes or panicle at end of stems; bracts of involucre oblong, obtuse, scarious, with gree midrib and fuscous margin. Fl.IX–X. (*C. coreanum* Hort.) N. E. Asia. Int 1905. Zone V. Valuable for its late blooming season.

Hybrids between this and garden forms of the preceding species with var ously colored fls., the heads mostly with all ray-fls., are in cult. as HYBRI KOREAN C.

3. **C. nippónicum** (Franch.) Sprenger. Evergreen subshrub, to 50 cm glabrous: lvs. subsessile, oblanceolate to oblong-obovate, 6–10 cm. long, ob tuse, cuneate, irregularly dentate with small obtusish teeth, dark green abov(paler beneath, thickish: heads solitary, 5–7 cm. across, on stalks 4–10 cm long; involucre hemispherical, the oval, obtuse bracts with scarious margin ray-fls. white, linear, minutely 5-toothed; disk pale greenish yellow. Fl.IX–x B.M.7660(c). R.H.1905:47. G.C.III.24:349. (*Leucanthemum n.* Franch. Japan. Cult. 1895. Zone VI. Chiefly valued for its late blooming season.

11. **ARTEMÌSIA** L. Herbs, subshrubs or shrubs, aromatic: lvs. alter nate, entire, dentate, lobed or pinnatisect: heads small and inconspicuous yellowish or whitish, without ray-fls., in terminal leafy spikes or panicles involucre with imbricate bracts in few series, the outer shorter; receptacle no chaffy: fls. all or only the marginal ones fertile; stigmas truncate; achene without pappus. (Mythological name, wife of Mausolus.) About 200 specie chiefly in the n. hemisphere.

A. Lvs. lobed or dissected.
  B. Lvs. finely dissected; receptacle usually glabrous.
    C. Lvs. glabrous or slightly pubescent, with long filiform segments.....1. *A. Abrotanun*
    CC. Lvs. pubescent, at least beneath; pinnae pectinately pinnatifid.......2. *A. sacrorur*
  BB. Lvs. coarsely lobed; marginal fls. pistillate.
    C. Lvs. 5–12 cm. long, with oblong lobes................................3. *A. Absinthiur*
    CC. Lvs. 1–4 cm. long, with short linear lobes................................4. *A. frigid*
AA. Lvs. 3-toothed at apex or entire, cuneate: fls. all perfect and fertile.......5. *A. tridentat*

1. **A. Abrótanum** L. SOUTHERNWOOD. Subshrub to 1.5 m., with uprigł brs. glabrous or puberulous when young: lvs. 2–6 cm. long, simply to thric(pinnate, with linear obtuse lobes usually exceeding 1 cm., glabrous or slightl] pubescent: heads very numerous, several-fld., 4–5 mm. across, yellow, witł perfect fls. and marginal pistillate fls., all fertile: involucre nearly hemi spherical, pubescent; outer bracts lanceolate, acute, inner obovate. Fl.VIII–x R.I.16:t.150,f.2(c). F.D.29:t.3006(c). B.B.3:526. S.L.2:104(h). S. Eu. Lon] cult. and often escaped. Zone V.—Grown for its aromatic odor.

Related species: **A. procèra** Willd. Subshrub to 2.5 m., more spreading lvs. 5–8 cm. long, thrice pinnate, dark green: fls. yellowish green, smaller; in volucre glabrous. S. E. Eu. and Asia Minor. Cult. 1800; sometimes escaped Zone V.—**A. camphoràta** Vill. Subshrub to 70 cm.: lvs. green and glabrous o] nearly so, dotted, lower ones thrice pinnate, with rather few pinnae, the uppe] entire; petioles auriculate; heads nodding, in narrow panicles; involucral bract: linear, obtuse. R.I.16:t.142,f.2. S. Eu., N. Afr. Intr. 1820. Zone V.—Th closely related **A. suàvis** Jord. differs chiefly in its naked receptacle: lvs. witł few long linear segments: heads nodding, peduncled, 5 mm. across. Rouy, Ill Pl. Eu. Rar. 8:t.186. S. France. Cult. 1904. Zone VII.—**A. Cina** K. Berg. Sub shrub to 0.5 m., puberulous: lvs. slender-petioled, bipinnatifid, 1.5–2 cm. long segments linear: heads 3–6-fld., about 3 mm. long, upright, sessile, in raceme orming narrow panicles; bracts glabrous, grayish or yellowish brown. Koehler, Ied.-Pfl. 1:t.48(c). C. Asia. Cult. 1927. Zone VI.

2. **A. sacròrum** Ledeb. Subshrub to 1.5 m., gray-pubescent: lvs. slender-etioled, ovate in outline, 4–7 cm. long, twice pinnate, pinnae pectinately ivided, with linear or linear-oblong acute segments, pubescent beneath; achis and petiole winged: heads 15–20-fld., about 3 mm. across, with pistil-ate marginal fls., in slender racemes forming large terminal panicles 15–40 m. long; involucre villous, outer bracts lanceolate, the inner elliptic with arious margin. Fl.VIII–IX. S. Russia, Siberia to N. E. Asia. Cult. 1828. one IV.—**A. s. víridis** Taylor, var. SUMMER-FIR. Green. Usually grown as n annual; of pyramidal habit with much dissected bright green foliage.— **A. s. latíloba** Ledeb., var. Pinnae of lvs. narrow-oblong and incisely serrate to innatisect with mostly incisely serrate narrow segments. N. E. Asia. Cult. 927.

Related species: **A. póntica** L. ROMAN WORMWOOD. Shrub to 1.5 m.: lvs. wice pinnatisect, 1.5–5 cm. long, pinnae pinnatifid with linear lobes, gray-ubescent; heads whitish yellow, small, in large and narrow panicles. R.I.16:t. 50,f.3(c). F.D.29:t.3007(c). B.B.3:527(c). Eu.; escaped in the N. E. States. Cult. 1810. Zone V.—**A. austríaca** Jacq. Subshrub, grayish tomentulose; lvs. uborbicular in outline, 6–15 mm. long, twice pinnatisect, upper lvs. subsessile, lmost digitately divided, the uppermost entire: heads small, in narrow dense anicles. R.I.16:t.143,f.2(c). S. E. Eu. to Altai Mts. Cult. 1810. Zone V.— **A. salìna** Willd. Subshrub 0.3–1 m., whitish or grayish tomentose: lower lvs. talked, twice or thrice pinnatifid, 1–2.5 cm. long, the upper sessile, smaller, innatifid; segments linear: heads ovoid, few-fld., 2–3 mm. long; the lower hort-stalked, in racemes usually nodding at apex, forming panicles; bracts blong, the outer pubescent, the inner with scarious margins. R.I.16:1039(c). *A. maritima* var. *salina* Koch.) C. Eu. Cult. 1935. Zone V.

3. **A. Absínthium** L. WORMWOOD. Subshrub to 1.5 m., whitish silky; lvs. –12 cm. long, the lower long-petioled, twice or thrice pinnate, with lanceolate, btuse lobes: heads short-stalked, hemispherical, 4–5 mm. broad, yellow, umerous in large leafy panicles; outer bracts of involucre linear; receptacle ubescent. Fl.VII–X. R.I.16:t.138,f.1(c). F.D.29:t.3001(c). B.B.3:525. Eu. .ong cult. and often escaped. Zone V. Grown for medicinal use as a vermi-uge; in Eu. it is also used for a liquor "absinth."

Related species: **A. arboréscens** L. Shrub to 1 m., with erect and angled rs., silvery white: lower lvs. to 10 cm. long and petioled, twice to thrice pinnate ith linear lobes; heads about 7 mm. across, in 1-sided racemes. Fl.v–VI. R.I.16: .138,f.2(c). S.H.2:f.478m-r,479c. S. Eu. Intr. 1640. Zone VII?—**A. Stelleriàna** ess. BEACH WORMWOOD (DUSTY MILLER). Subshrub, white-tomentose, with reeping stem and ascending brs. to 0.5 m.: lvs. obovate, 3–10 cm. long, pinnat-fid with oblong, obtuse lobes: heads rather large, with oblong obtuse lobes blong-campanulate, in a narrow panicle; receptacle glabrous. Gt.15:t.498. B.B. :527. B.C.1:399. Que. to N. J., N. E. Asia. Cult. 1870. Zone II.

4. **A. frígida** Willd. Subshrub with procumbent stems and ascending brs., o 50 cm., silky-canescent: lvs. 1–4 cm. long, ternately or quinately divided nto linear entire lobes, the lower ones petioled and often auricled, the upper essile: heads about 4 mm. across, numerous, in racemes or raceme-like pan-cles; involucre hemispherical, with oblong canescent bracts; receptacle pubes-ent. Fl.VIII–IX. B.B.2:525. Yukon and Minn. to Idaho and w. Tex.; also in Siberia. Intr. 1597. Zone II.—Handsome plant for the rock garden.

5. **A. tridentàta** Nutt. SAGE-BRUSH. Much-branched shrub to 3 m.; ilvery-canescent: lvs. sessile, narrowly cuneate, 1–4 cm. long, 3–7-toothed at he truncate apex: heads 5–8-fld., 2–3 mm. broad, very numerous, sessile or early so, in large dense panicles 30–50 cm. long; involucre oblong, the inner racts oblong, obtuse, the outer shorter, ovate, tomentose; fls. all perfect and

fertile. Fl.vɪɪɪ-ɪx. B.B.3:530. S.L.52(h). B. C., Mont. and Neb. to Calif
Utah and Colo. Cult. 1894. Zone V.

Related species: **A. càna** Pursh. Shrub to 60 cm.; lvs. linear to narrow
lanceolate, 3–5 cm. long, acute and usually entire, rarely with 2 or 3 acut
teeth; heads forming a narrow almost spike-like panicle; involucre campan
late, 3–5 mm. broad. B.B.3:530. Neb. to Colo., N. Dak. and Sask. Intr. befor
1903. Zone V.—**A. arbúscula** Nutt. To 30 cm. tall: lvs. 3-lobed, with obovat
often 2-lobed lobes: heads upright, in spike-like panicles. Colo. and Wyo. t
Sask. Intr. ? Zone V ?

Tribe 5. SENECIONEAE. Lvs. usually alternate; heads commonly radiate
involucral bracts mostly equal, not scarious, in 1 or 2 series, with or withou
accessory bracts at base; receptacle naked; anthers usually tail-less at base
style-brs. truncate or obtuse, with or without appendages, usually more or les
hairy; pappus capillary.

12. TETRADÝMIA DC. Low rigid shrubs, gray- or white-tomentose
lvs. alternate, entire: heads with few fls. usually all perfect and fertile, with
out ray-fls., in terminal corymbs; involucre oblong or cylindric, of one serie
of 4–6 concave overlapping bracts; receptacle flat; corolla with lanceolat
spreading lobes; anthers with triangular tips, sagittate at base; style-brs. fla
obtuse: achenes terete, 5-nerved; pappus of numerous white, minutely sca
brid bristles. (Greek *tetradymos*, fourfold; referring to the number of fl
and involucral bracts.) About 6 species in western N. Am.

T. canéscens DC. Shrub to 1 m., densely white-tomentose: lvs. linear t
narrow-lanceolate, 1.5–3 cm. long, acute and spinulose, silky-villous: head
4–5-fld., 1.5 cm. high, yellow, peduncled, in terminal clusters of 3–5, usuall
forming broad corymbs at end of brs.; involucre cylindric, with 4 linear
oblong bracts; achenes densely silky-hirsute. Fl.vɪɪ–vɪɪɪ. S.H.2:f.480g-m,48
e-f. B. C. to Calif., Idaho and Utah. Intr. ? Zone V?

13. SENÉCIO L. Herbs, shrubs or trees: lvs. alternate, entire, serrat
or pinnatifid: heads in terminal or axillary corymbs or panicles; involucre c
many bracts in one series, usually with small bracts at base: fls. many; ray
fls. usually present, usually yellow; disk-fls. tubular; receptacle usuall
naked; achenes usually terete and ribbed; pappus of soft whitish bristle
(From Latin *senex, senecis*, old man, in reference to the white pappus.) Abou
1200 species in all parts of the world.

A. Lvs. pinnatifid, white-tomentose: subshrub..............................1. *S. Cinerari*
AA. Lvs. undivided, entire or dentate, rarely with a few lobes at base.
  B. Climbing subshrub: lvs. membranous..................................2. *S. scander*
  BB. Upright shrubs: lvs. coriaceous.....................................3. *S. rotundifoliu*

1. S. Cineràra DC. Subshrub to 0.5 m., white-tomentose: lvs. thickis
pinnatifid, with 4–6 obtuse 3–5-lobed segments, densely tomentose beneat
less so above: heads 8–12 mm. high, in large flat or convex corymbs; ray-fl
10–12, oblong-elliptic, bright yellow: achenes nearly glabrous. Fl.vɪ–vɪɪ
R.I.16:t.968(c). H.M.6:728,729. B.C.3157. (*Cineraria maritima* L.) S. Eu
Algeria. Cult. 1633. Zone V.

2. S. scandens Don. Climbing subshrub to 5 m.; brts. slender, striate
slightly pubescent: lvs. ovate- or triangular-lanceolate, 4–9 cm. long, acumi
nate, hastate to broad-cuneate, dentate or denticulate, rarely with a fe
lobes at base, puberulous or nearly glabrous; petiole 4–15 mm. long: inf
terminal and axillary, paniculate or racemose; heads hemispheric, 4–8 mm
long, slender-stalked; bracts linear, acute, nearly glabrous; ray-fls. about 1
rays to 8 mm. long, 4-nerved, bright yellow: achenes cylindric, 5-ribbed, sca
brous. Fl.ɪx–x. R.H.1909:407. S. Asia, S. China, Japan. Intr. 1895. Zone VI

3. **S. rotundifòlius** Hook. f. Shrub or tree to 10 m.; brts., petioles, lvs. beneath and infl. densely tomentose: lvs. coriaceous, orbicular to ovate-oblong, 5–12 cm. long, obtuse, rounded or subcordate at base, dark green and lustrous above, margin entire, revolute; petiole 2–7 cm. long: heads without ray-fls., campanulate, 8 mm. across, in large terminal panicles; bracts 9–12, linear-oblong; pistillate fls. 1–4: achenes grooved, hispid. Fl.vi–vii. Kirk, For. Fl. N. Zeal. t.116. N. Zeal. Cult. 1904. Zone VII.

Related species: **S. laxifòlius** Buchan. Shrub to 1.5 m.; white-tomentose: lvs. lanceolate to elliptic-lanceolate, 2.5–6 cm. long, acute at ends; petiole 1–3.5 cm. long: heads with 12–15 narrow yellow ray-fls., 2–2.5 cm. across, in pyramidal panicles 10–20 cm. long; bracts 12–15: achenes glabrous. B.M.7378(c). G.C.68: 49;85:622. J.L.55:f.36. N. Zeal. Cult. 1894. Zone VII? More ornamental than the two preceding species, but tenderer.

Tribe 6. **Mutisieae.** Lvs. usually alternate and entire; heads with or without rays; involucral bracts imbricate, usually in many series: corolla bilabiate, deeply 5-cleft, or ligulate; receptacle usually naked; anthers long-tailed at base; style-brs. usually short, not appendaged: pappus usually capillary.

14. **PÉRTYA** Schultz Bip. Deciduous shrubs: lvs. alternate, often crowded under the fl.-heads, entire or serrulate: heads solitary, terminal on short brts., of 4–15 perfect fls.; involucre campanulate, with few large imbricate bracts; corolla tubular, deeply 5-lobed; style hairy on upper part, shortly 2-lobed: achenes pubescent, with conspicuous whitish or purplish pappus. (After J. A. Maximilian Perty, professor of natural history at Berne, Switzerland; 1804–1884.) Four species in E. and C. Asia.

P. sinénsis Oliv. Slender upright shrub to 2 m.: lvs. ovate to oblong-lanceolate, 5–8 cm. long, acutish, entire, often with 1–3 sharp teeth, on year-old brs. fascicled, smaller and entire; heads pinkish, 10–12-fld., about 1 cm. across, on slender pedicels 1–2.5 cm. long; involucre nearly glabrous; achenes sericeous; pappus whitish. Fl.vi–vii. H.I.23:t.2214. C. China. Intr. 1901. Zone V. Botanically interesting, but of little ornamental merit.

Class II. MONOCOTYLEDONEAE Juss.
MONOCOTYLEDONS

Stems without central pith or annular layers: embryo with a single cotyledon, the first lvs. always alternate; lvs. mostly parallel-veined: parts of the fl. usually in threes or sixes, never in fives.

112. GRAMINEAE Juss. GRASS FAMILY

Herbaceous, sometimes shrubby or tree-like plants, with usually hollow stem (culm): lvs. alternate, 2-ranked, consisting of a sheath enveloping the stem and usually open on one side, and a parallel-veined usually linear blade, at the junction of blade and sheath inside a membranous appendage (ligula): fls. perfect, rarely unisexual, naked or with a perianth of 1–2 minute scales, borne in spikelets forming panicles, spikes or racemes; each spikelet consisting of 3 or more 2-ranked scales, the first 1–6, usually 2, are empty and are called glumes (or empty glumes), the others are called lemmas (lower paleas) or fertile glumes each bearing a fl. in its axil; the fl. is subtended and usually enveloped by a bract (palea or upper palea) with its back to the axis and bears usually 2 small scales or lodicules at the base; stamens usually 3, rarely 1, 2 or 6, exserted; pistil with a 1-celled, 1-ovuled ovary and usually 2 styles with mostly plumose stigmas: fr. a nutlet (caryopsis) with a starchy endosperm and a small embryo. Syn.: *Poaceae* R. Br.—About 400 genera with more than 5000 species distributed all over the earth. Divided into many subfamilies of which only the following is of interest to us:

Subfam. **Bambuseae** Lindl. (*Bambusaceae* Link). Stems woody, at least at the base: leaf-blade often constricted into a distinct petiole, finally separating from the sheath: spikelets usually many-fld., rarely 1-fld.; glumes many-nerved, usually not aristate. About 250 species chiefly in the Tropics and Subtropics.—Most species bloom but rarely and many die after flowering, only some of the smaller kinds flower every year; of many species the flowers are yet unknown. Therefore in the following specific descriptions the floral characters have been omitted, as of little practical value for the determinations of the cultivated species.—Sometimes *Arundo* and *Phragmites* of the Subfam. Festuceae are included among the woody Gramineae, but their stems are annual, though stout and nearly ligneous at maturity.

A. Culms terete: style short with 3 stigmas or styles 2.
  B. Brs. solitary, rarely 2 at the nodes: stem-sheaths persistent.
    C. Lf.-sheaths with rigid scabrous bristles; nodes more or less elevated: stamens 6.
                                                            1. *Sasa*
    CC. Lf.-sheaths with smooth and flexuose bristles or without; nodes scarcely elevated: stamens 3, rarely 4–5...2. *Pseudosasa*
  BB. Brs. several at each node.
    C. Infl. without conspicuous bracts enveloping the spikelets.
      D. Stem-sheaths persistent.
        E. Each node with 1 bud; br. branching from the very base; bristles of lf.-sheath rigid, scabrous ....3. *Arundinaria*
        EE. Each node with 2 or more buds; bristles of lf.-sheaths smooth..4. *Pleioblastus*
      DD. Stem-sheaths caducous.
        E. Style 1 with 3 stigmas: stems to 4–15 m. tall.
          F. Lvs. 1.5–2.5 cm. broad, with 5–6 pairs of veins; lf.-sheaths with rigid bristles ....5. *Semiarundinaria*
          FF. Lvs. 0.6–1.5 cm. broad, with 2–4 pairs of veins; lf.-sheaths with flexuose bristles ....6. *Sinarundinaria*
        EE. Styles 2: stems to 2 m. tall; lvs. 0.6–1.5 cm. broad.........7. *Chimonobambusa*
    CC. Infl. with large bracts enclosing the spikelets; stems 10–15 m. tall; lvs. 7–15 cm. long, with 12–15 pairs of veins....................................8. *Thamnocalamus*
AA. Stems more or less flattened on one side of the node; each node with several brs.; style long, with 3 stigmas.
  B. Lvs. lanceolate to linear-lanceolate; stems straight, 3–8 m. tall.......9. *Phyllostachys*
  BB. Lvs. ovate-oblong to ovate-lanceolate, distinctly stalked; stems zigzag, 1–2 m. tall.
                                                      10. *Shibataea*

1. SASA Mak. & Shibata. Shrubs or subshrubs with creeping rootstock to 2 m.; stems terete, fistulose, not spotted, with 1, rarely 2 brs. at each node; sheaths persistent, appendiculate; lvs. crowded at end of brts.; sheaths with rigid scabrid bristles or without: infl. a lax panicle; spikelets 2–9-fld.; glumes 2, small; palea 2-keeled and 2-fid, shorter than the acuminate lemma; stamens 6; style short, with 3 stigmas; ovary glabrous; caryopsis oblong, often grooved at base, slightly exceeding the lemma. (Japanese name for the small bamboos.) About 70 species in E. Asia.

A. Lvs. with 5–18 pairs of veins, 2–10 cm. wide.
  B. Pairs of veins 15–18; stem-sheaths with involute margin, loosely appressed.
                                                      1. *S. tessellata*
  BB. Pairs of veins 5–13; stem-sheaths convolute, firmly appressed.
    C. Lf.-sheaths at apex without bristles; lvs. 7–8 cm. broad.............2. *S. senanensis*
    CC. Lf.-sheaths at apex with brown bristles; lvs. 3–6 cm. broad, discoloring in fall along margin ....3. *S. Veitchii*
AA. Lvs. with 2–6 pairs of veins, 0.5–2, rarely 3 cm. broad....................4. *S. chrysantha*

1. Sasa tessellàta (Munro) Mak. & Shib. Stems to 1.5 m. tall, slightly fistulose, soon arching; nodes 3–8 cm. distant; stem-sheaths persisting, each clasping also parts of the 2 or 3 sheaths above it, ciliate: lvs. to 60 cm. long and to 10 cm. broad, long-pointed, abruptly contracted at the base, sharply serrate, light green above, glaucous beneath and minutely pubescent, hairy on one side of the yellow midrib toward the base, with 15–18 pairs of veins, tessellate. G.C.III.18:189(h). C.Ba.t.3,f.B,t.7,f.B. B.S.1:78,t(h). (*Bambusa t.* Munro,

Arundinaria t. Bean, not Munro, *A. Ragamowskii* Pfitzer.) Japan. Intr. before 1845. Zone VI. Striking on account of its large lvs., forming broad rounded masses.

2. **S. senanénsis** (Franch. & Sav.) Rehd. Stems to 2 m., waxy, particularly below the nodes, hollow; nodes 12–15 cm. distant; stem-sheaths terminated by a deciduous lanceolate, strongly tessellated, ciliate tongue; lvs. 15–32 cm. long, 7–8 cm. broad, long-pointed, abruptly contracted at base, serrulate, bright green and lustrous above, glaucous beneath and minutely puberulous, with 7–13 pairs of veins, minutely tessellate. C.Ba.t.2,c,D. I.B.t. 11,f.7–15. (*Arundinaria kurilensis* var. *paniculata* F. Schmidt, *Bambusa s.* Franch. & Sav., *S. paniculata* Mak. & Shib.) Japan. Cult. 1913. Zone VI. Handsome bamboo spreading by suckers.—**S. s. nebulòsa** (Mak.) Rehd., var. Stems tinged with purple; sheaths of the brts. with small round spots. G.C. 35:280,t.(h). Gn.49:59(h). B.S.1:218,t(h). (*Arundinaria paniculata* var. *n.* Mak., *A. palmata* Bean, *Bambusa metallica* Mitf.) Intr. about 1889.

3. **S. Veìtchii** (Carr.) Rehd. Stems 0.5, rarely to 1.2 m. tall, green, narrow-fistulose; nodes 8–12 cm. distant; stem-sheaths persistent, pubescent at first; leaf-sheaths with tufts of bristle at apex; lvs. 10–20 cm. long, 3–6 cm. broad, rather abruptly long-pointed, abruptly contracted at the base, dark green above, glaucous and minutely pubescent beneath, turning yellow along the margin in fall, midrib yellow beneath, with 6–9 pairs of veins. I.B.t.11,f.21–27(c). (*S. albo-marginata* Mak. & Shib., *Bambusa V.* Carr., *Arundinaria V.* N. E. Br.) Japan. Intr. 1880. Zone VI. Forms dense patches and spreads rapidly; the discolored edges of the lvs. give it an injured appearance in fall.

4. **S. chrysántha** (Mitf.) E. G. Camus. Stems 0.5–2 m. tall, hollow; nodes 5–12 cm. distant; brs. several at one node; stem-sheaths ciliate on one margin: lvs. 8–12 cm. long, 1.2–2 cm. broad, rather abruptly long-pointed, rounded at base, bright green above or often more or less variegated with yellow, glabrous, with 4–6 pairs of veins. (*Arundinaria c.* Mitf.) Japan. Intr. 1892. Zone VI. Spreading rapidly; of little ornamental value.

2. **PSEUDOSASA** Mak. Shrubs with creeping rootstock; stems terete, fistulose, to 5 m. tall; stem-sheaths persistent, hispid outside; each node with one br.; lf.-sheaths with flexuose smooth bristles or without: spikelets 2–8-fld.; lemma subaristate, curving, enveloping the palea; palea bifid at apex; stamens 3, rarely 4; style short, with 3 stigmas. (Greek *pseudos,* false, and Japanese *sasa.*) Three species in Eastern Asia.

P. japónica (Sieb. & Zucc.) Mak. Stems to 2 or 3, rarely to 5 m. tall, stout; stem-sheaths covered at first with compressed bristles, soon turning pale brown, very persistent, terminated by a persistent awl-shaped tongue to 7 cm. long; lvs. 8–24 cm. long and 2–4 cm. wide, long-pointed, narrowed at base, serrulate on one margin, lustrous dark green above, glaucescent beneath except a green strip on one margin, with 6–10 pairs of veins, minutely tessellated. G.C.III.18:185(h). Gs.3:38(h). I.B.t.4,f.1–3,t.13,f.4(c). C.Ba.t.5,f.A, t.13,f.A. (*Arundinaria j.* Sieb. & Zucc., *Sasa j.* Mak., *Bambusa metake* Sieb.) Japan. Intr. 1850. Zone VI.

3. **ARUNDINÀRIA** Michx. Shrubs to 10 or 15 m. tall, with cespitose or creeping rootstock; stems upright or arching; each node with 1 bud, the br. branching from the base: lf.-sheaths with scabrid rigid bristles: infl. lateral; spikelets 5–15-fld.; glumes small; lemma subaristate; stamens 3; style 1, with 3 stigmas. (Derived from Latin *arundo,* cane.) Six species in N. Am. and E. and S. Asia.

A. gigantèa (Walt.) Chapm. CANE REED. Stems upright, to 9 m., wit. numerous short divergent branches: lvs. 10–30 cm. long, 2–3 cm. broad rounded at base, denticulate, glabrous or pubescent, with 6–14 pairs of veins fls. on old stems on leafy brs.; spikelets 3.5–7 cm. long, many-fld. B.B.1:29 C.Ba.t.14,f.c. (*A. macrosperma* Michx., *Arundo gigantea* Walt.) Va. to Fla west to Ohio and La., along river banks. Intr. ? Zone VI.

The closely related **A. tecta** (Walt.) Muhlb. (*A. macrosperma* var. *t.* Nees) from Md. and Ind. to Texas is smaller, only 1–4 m. tall and the fls. appear o leafless shoots of the year. In *A. tecta* var. *decidua* Beadle the lvs. turn yellow in autumn and drop.

4. PLEIOBLÁSTUS Nakai. Low, or tall shrubs to 10 m.; with cespi tose or creeping rootstock; stems upright or arching; each node with 3– brts.; stem-sheaths persistent; lf.-sheaths with smooth flexuose bristles a apex: spikelets with articulate rachis; lemma falcate-convolute, tessellate palea 2-keeled; lodicules 3, one twice as large as the others; stamens 3; styl with 3 stigmas. (Greek *pleios*, more, and *blastos*, bud; referring to the sev eral buds at each node.) About 30 species in E. Asia.

```
A. Lvs. glabrous or slightly hairy.
   B. Stems to 6 or 8 m. tall; lvs. quite glabrous.
      c. Lvs. rounded or broadly cuneate at base...............................1. P. Simon
      cc. Lvs. gradually narrowed at base.........................................2. P. Hinds
   BB. Stems to 1.5 m. tall; lvs. usually slightly hairy.
      c. Lvs. distichous, 2–6 cm. long........................................3. P. distichu
      cc. Lvs. not distichous, larger.
         D. Stems with waxy bloom; stem-sheaths with a ring of hairs at base..4. P. pumilu
         DD. Stems without waxy bloom; stem-sheaths without ring of hairs at base.
                                                                              5. P. humili
AA. Lvs. soft-pubescent beneath.
   B. Lvs. green or striped with yellow, sparingly puberulous or nearly glabrous above.
                                                                          6. P. viridi-striatu
   BB. Lvs. striped with white, pubescent on both sides...................7. P. variegatu
```

1. P. Simòni (Riv.) Nakai. Stems to 8 m. tall, very hollow, 2–3 cm. thic at the base, the outer stems arching outward; rootstock creeping; stem sheaths to 25 cm. long, purplish when young, rather persistent: lvs. 8–30 cm long, 0.8–3 cm. broad, long-pointed, broadly cuneate at the base, bright gree above, often striped white or whitish, glaucescent beneath on one side o the midrib, nearly green on the other, with 4–7 pairs of veins. G.C.III.15 301;18:181. N.K.20:t.6. I.B.t.7,f.1–5,t.13,f.2(c). (*Arundinaria S.* Riv.) Japan Intr. 1862. Zone VI.—**P. S. variegàtus** (Hook. f.) Nakai, var. Lvs. stripe white. B.M.7156(c). (*Arundinaria S.* var. *v.* Hook. f., *A. S.* var. *striata* Mitf *A. S.* var. *albo-striata* Bean.)

Related species: **P. Chino** (Franch. & Sav.) Mak. Stems 1–1.5 m. tall; lvs 3.5–25 cm. long, 0.5–2 cm. broad, green beneath, with 3–7 pairs of veins. I.B.t.5 f.7–14(c). (*Arundinaria Simoni* var. *C.* Mak., *A. Maximowiczii* Riv.) Japan Cult. 1876. Zone VI.—**P. C. Laydékeri** (Bean) Nakai, var. Lvs. with dark yel low stripes. (*Arundinaria L.* Bean.) Cult. 1894.—**P. angustifòlius** (Mitf.) Nakai Stems to 1, rarely 2 m. tall, narrow-fistulose; lvs. 2.5–15 cm. long, 3–6 mm. broad green with white stripes, margin spinulose. Japan. Cult. 1895. Zone VI.

2. P. Híndsii (Munro) Nakai. Stems to 4 m. tall, quite erect, to 2.5 cm thick, hollow, dark olive-green, bloomy at first, internodes to 20 cm. long brs. erect, in dense clusters; lvs. mostly erect, 16–20 cm. long, 1–2 cm. broad long-pointed, tapering at the base, denticulate on one side, dark green above glaucescent beneath, with 3–6 pairs of veins, tessellated. I.B.t.5,f.4–6,t.14 fig. 2. R.H.1921:367(h). (*Thamnocalamus H.* E. G. Camus, *Arundinaria H* Munro, *A. erecta* Hort., *Bambusa gracilis* Hort.) China, Japan. Intr. 1875 Zone VII.

Related species: **P. gramíneus** (Bean) Nakai. Slenderer: lvs. much nar rower, scarcely exceeding 1 cm. in width, with 2–4 pairs of veins. I.B.t.5,f.1–3 t.14,f.5. (*Arundinaria Hindsii* var. *g.* Bean.) Japan. Intr. 1877. Zone VI. Hardier and handsomer than *P. Hindsii.* Cult. 1894.

3. **P. dístichus** (Mitf.) Nakai. Stems slender, 25–75 cm. tall, green, hollow; nodes 3–8 cm. distant; stem-sheaths pubescent at first, ciliate; lvs. distichous, 2–6 cm. long, 5–8 mm. broad, slender-pointed, narrowed into a short petiole, setosely serrulate, bright green on both sides, with 2–3 pairs of veins. I.Ba.t.6,f.5–6. (*Bambusa disticha* Mitf., *B. nana* Hort., not Roxb., *Sasa disticha* E. G. Camus, *P. pygmaeus* var. *distichus* Nakai.) Japan. Cult. 1870. Zone V.

4. **P. pùmilus** (Mitf.) Nakai. Stems slender, 30–60 cm. tall, fistulose, stemsheaths tessellate, the upper ones tinged with purple; lvs. 7–15 cm. long, 0.8–2 cm. broad, usually abruptly long-pointed, rounded at base, serrulate, bright green, slightly hairy on both sides, with 4–5 pairs of veins. C.Ba.t.7,f.a. (*Arundinaria pumila* Mitf., *A. variabilis* var. *p.* Houzeau de Lehaie.) Japan. Cult. 1896. Zone VI.

5. **P. húmilis** (Mitf.) Nakai. Stems 0.5–1 m. tall, very slender, narrowly fistulose, green, with usually 2 or 3 branches at one node, long in proportion to the stem; stem-sheaths purplish at first; leaf-sheaths with 2 clusters of bristles at the apex: lvs. 10–15 cm. long, 0.8–2 cm. broad, long-pointed, rounded at the base, scarcely hairy, pale green, with 3–5 pairs of veins. C.Ba.t.5,f.D. (*Arundinaria h.* Mitf., *A. Fortunei viridis* Hort., *A. gracilis* Hort.) Japan. Cult. 1896. Zone VII?

6. **P. viridi-striàtus** (André) Mak. Root-stock somewhat creeping; stems to 1.25 m. tall, slender, dark purplish green, fistulose: lf.-sheaths minutely and irregularly ciliate, sparsely fimbriate or naked at apex; lvs. 8–20 cm. long, 1–3 cm. broad, abruptly long-pointed, rounded at base, serrulate, striped green and golden yellow, at first sparingly puberulous above, soft pubescent beneath, with 5–6 pairs of veins. I.H.19:t.108(c). H.I.27:2613. (*Bambusa viridistriata* Sieb. ex André, *B. Fortunei aurea* Hort., *Arundinaria auricoma* Mitf., *Sasa a.* E. G. Camus.) Japan. Cult. 1870. Zone VI.—**P. v. vagans** (Gamble) Nakai, var. Root-stock creeping and spreading: lvs. green. I.Ba.t.6,f.7–8(c). (*Arundinaria v.* Gamble, *Bambusa pygmaea* Mitf., not Miq., *Sasa p.* E. G. Camus.) Japan. Cult. 1896. Zone VI. Spreading rapidly and forming dense thickets.

7. **P. variegàtus** (Miq.) Mak. Stems 0.3–1 m. tall, very slender, narrowly fistulose, somewhat zigzag: lvs. 8–15 cm. long, 0.8–2 cm. broad, abruptly long-pointed, rounded at base, serrulate, green, striped with white, hairy on both sides; with 3–5 pairs of veins. F.S.15,t.1535(c). (*Arundinaria variegata* Mak., *A. Fortunei* Riv., *Sasa v.* E. G. Camus, *Bambusa v.* Miq.) Japan. Intr. before 1863. Zone VI? Spreading rapidly, forming large tufts.

5. **SEMIARUNDINÀRIA** Mak. Upright shrubs; stems terete; upper internodes flattened; stem-sheaths with appendages, deciduous; brs. several at each node; lf.-sheaths with rigid smooth bristles: lemma tessellate; stamens 3; style short, with 3 stigmas. (Latin *semi-,* half, and *Arundinaria:* referring to the close relation to that genus.) Three species in Japan and S. Asia.

S. fastuòsa (Mitf.) Mak. Stems erect, to 7, rarely to 15 m. tall, very hollow, to 3.5 or to 8 cm. diam., terete, but the upper internodes flattened, dark green, marked with purplish brown; brs. erect; stem-sheaths to 22 cm. long, purplish and pubescent at first, early deciduous: lvs. 10–18 cm. long, 1.5–2.5 cm. broad, long-pointed, gradually narrowed into a rather long petiole, lustrous dark green above, glaucous on one side beneath, puberulous, with 5–6 pairs of veins, tessellated. B.S.1:215,t(h). C.Ba.t.7.f.c.t.9,f.c,t.13,f.a. (*Bambusa f.* Mitf., *Phyllostachys f.* Nichols., *Arundinaria f.* Mak., *A. narihira* Mak.) Japan. Intr. 1892. Zone VI.

6. **SINARUNDINÀRIA** Nakai. Shrubs to 6 m. tall, with creeping rootstock, cespitose; stem-sheaths with appendages, deciduous; each node with several brs.; lvs. glabrous; lf.-sheaths with flexuose smooth bristles; infl. paniculate on leafy brts.; stamens 3; style short, with 3 stigmas. (Latin *Sina*, China, and *Arundinaria;* referring to the habitat of the genus.) Three species in China and Himal.

S. nítida (Mitf.) Nakai. Stems to 6 m., hollow, erect and leafless the first year, branching and arching the second year; stem-sheaths purplish, pubescent; lvs. 5–8 cm. long, 0.6–1.2 cm. broad, slender-pointed, rounded at the base, denticulate on one side, bright green above, glaucescent beneath, with 3–4 pairs of rather faint veins. G.C.III.18:179(h);24:211(h). M.O.t.40. C.Ba t.9,f.a.t.12,f.a. S.L.110(h). (*Arundinaria n.* Mitf.) C. & W. China. Intr. 1889. Zone V. Demands partial shade and abundant moisture.

Related species: **S. Murièlae** (Gamble) Nakai. Stems yellow, with waxy bloom when young; stem-sheaths glabrous, ciliate; lvs. petioled, 7–12 cm. long, 1–1.5 cm. broad, long-acuminate into a setaceous point. (*Arundinaria M* Gamble.) C. China. Intr. 1907. Zone VII?

7. **CHIMONOBAMBÙSA** Mak. Shrubs with creeping rootstock; stems nearly solid, terete; stem-sheaths with conspicuous appendages, deciduous; each node with several brs.; lf.-sheaths with smooth bristles at apex: spikelets racemose; lemma not tessellate, with prominent nerves; stamens three; styles 2. (Greek *cheimon*, winter, and *Bambusa;* referring to the season of the innovation of the shoots.) 12 species in E. and S. Asia.

C. marmórea (Mitf.) Mak. Stems to 2 m. tall, slender, purplish, branching the second year; stem-sheaths at first purplish, mottled with pinkish gray; brs. usually 3 at each node; lvs. 6–12 cm. long, 6–15 mm. wide, constricted about 1 cm. below apex into a slender point, narrowed into a short petiole minutely serrulate on both sides, with 4–5 pairs of veins. I.B.t.4,f.4–8,t.14,f.3 (c). C.Ba.t.10,f.b. (*Arundinaria m.* Mak.) Japan. Cult. 1893. Zone VII?

8. **THAMNOCÁLAMUS** Munro. Shrubs with creeping rootstock; stems terete, fistulose; stem-sheaths caducous; lvs. small, usually inconspicuously tessellate: infl. large, paniculate; brts. with conspicuous bracts enveloping the 1–4 spikelets in their axils; palea long-acuminate, as long or longer than lemma; lodicules 3, ciliate; stamens 3; stigmas 3, sessile. (Greek *thamnos*, thicket, and *calamus*, cane; referring to its habit.) About 5 species in India.

T. spathiflòrus (Trin.) Munro. Stems to 12 m. tall; internodes 15–35 cm long; stem-sheaths glabrous, 15–20 cm. long, with a caducous blade 5–10 cm long; lvs. 7–12 cm. long, 8–12 mm. broad, narrowed into a short petiole, with 12–15 pairs of veins; lf.-sheaths coriaceous, fimbriate at apex. C.Ba.t.30,f.a (c). (*Arundinaria spathiflora* Trin.) Himal. Cult. 1913. Zone VII?

9. **PHYLLOSTACHYS** Sieb. & Zucc. Usually tall shrubs with creeping rootstock, rarely cespitose; stems with rather short hollow internodes flattened or grooved on one side or sometimes on two sides; nodes prominent brs. usually 2–3 at each node, rebranched; stem-sheaths caducous; lvs. petioled, small or moderately large, articulated, tessellate; lf.-sheaths with sca

rous bristles: fls. in terminal leafy panicles; spikelets 2–3, 1–4 fld., subtended
by imbricated bracts: glumes usually unequal, many-nerved, glabrous; lemma
ovate-lanceolate, acuminate; palea 2-keeled, often with 2 mucros; stamens 3,
long-exserted; ovary glabrous; style long, with 3 long stigmas. (Greek
phyllos, leaf, and *stachys*, spike; referring to the leafy inflorescence.) About
30 species in E. Asia and Himal.

A. Stem-sheaths glabrous at the margin, as long or longer than the internodes; scales at
    base of brts. not divided or only to the middle, persistent.
    B. Stems dark-colored at maturity: lf.-sheaths without bristles............1. *P. flexuosus*
    BB. Stems green or yellow; lf.-sheaths with bristles.
      C. Stems spaced; stem-sheaths striped with purple............2. *P. viridi-glaucescens*
      CC. Stems tufted.
        D. Stem-sheaths without or with few small spots; stems yellow; lvs. 1–2 cm. broad.
                                  3. *P. aureus*
        DD. Stem-sheaths with large spots.
          E. Nodes at base of stem congested; sheaths spotted brownish........4. *P. edulis*
          EE. Nodes not congested; sheaths mottled with purple..........5. *P. bambusoides*
AA. Stem-sheaths with ciliate margin, at maturity shorter than internodes; scales at base
    of brts. deeply divided, soon shriveling...6. *P. niger*

1. **P. flexuòsus** (Carr.) Riv. Stems to 6 m. tall, usually lower, bright
green at first, becoming darker with age, sometimes nearly black; brs. rather
long, flexuose; lf.-sheaths without bristles: lvs. 5–10 cm. long, 0.8–1.5 cm.
broad, slender-pointed, abruptly narrowed at base, serrulate on one margin,
dark green above, glaucous beneath, with 4–6 pairs of veins. C.Ba.31,f.a.
(*Bambusa f.* Carr., not Munro.) China. Intr. 1864. Zone VI.

2. **P. víridi-glaucéscens** (Carr.) Riv. Stems to 6 m. or more, yellowish
green, purplish at the nodes, very hollow; the outer stems arching; stem-
sheaths scabrous, striped with purple, deciduous; lf.-sheaths purplish with
tufts of bristles at apex: lvs. 5–10 cm. long, 0.8–2 cm. wide, long-pointed,
abruptly narrowed at the base, denticulate on one margin, bright green above,
glaucous beneath and pubescent near the base, with 4–7 pairs of rather indistinct veins. G.C.III.15:433(h). Gn.7:279(h). C.Ba.t.29,f.a. China. Intr.
1846. Zone VI.

3. **P. aùreus** (Carr.) Riv. Stems 3–6 m. tall, erect, 2–2.5 cm. thick, yellow
or yellowish, with slightly creeping rootstock; nodes often crowded at the
base of stem, the upper internodes to 15 cm. long, with a swollen band beneath
each node: stem-sheaths deciduous; lf.-sheaths with 2 tufts of bristles at
apex: lvs. linear, 5–12 cm. long, 1–2 cm. broad, long-pointed, cuneate at the
base, denticulate on one side, dark green above, glaucous beneath, glabrous,
with 4–5 pairs of veins. B.F.69:233(fl.). Gn.8:206. A.F.5:41(h). I.B.t.3,f.
1–6(c). (*Bambusa a.* Carr.) China, Japan. Intr. before 1870. Zone VI.

4. **P. edùlis** (Carr.) Houzeau de Lehaie. Stems to 20 m. or more, yellowish; stem-sheaths pubescent, spotted brownish; lf.-sheaths with tufts of
bristles at apex; lvs. 6–12 cm. long, 0.8–2 cm. broad, slender pointed, round
or cuneate at base, denticulate on one side, dark green above, glaucous beneath, with 3–6 pairs of rather indistinct veins. C.Ba.t.26,f.A. B.D.1909;t.257,
259. (*Bambusa mitis* Bean, not Riv., *P. pubescens* Houzeau de Lehaie.)
China, Japan. Intr. 1877. Zone VI.

5. **P. bambusoìdes** Sieb. & Zucc. Stems to 6, or sometimes to 22 m., 2–3
cm. thick, bright green, bloomy below the nodes: brs. long; stem-sheaths
mottled with purple; lf.-sheaths with tufts of bristles at apex; lvs. 8–15 cm.
long, 1.2–3 cm. broad, rather abruptly long-pointed, narrowed into a short
petiole, serrulate on one side, bright green above, glaucous beneath and
pubescent near base, with 5–7 pairs of veins. Gamble, Ind. Bamb. t.27. I.B.
t.1,f.5–8. Gs.3:37(h). (*P. reticulata* K. Koch in part, *P. Quilioi* Riv., *P.*

Mazelii Hort.) China. Intr. 1866. Zone VI.—**P. b. Castillòni** (Marliac) Mak., var. Smaller and slenderer; stems yellow, striped with green, and green on the flattened portion: lvs. shorter and narrower, usually striped more or less with pale yellow. I.B.t.2,f.1–4. (*P. C.* Mitf.) Japan. Intr. about 1890.—**P. b. marliàceus** (Mitf.) Mak., var. Stem wrinkled, particularly near the base; stem-sheaths dark green. (*P. m.* Mitf., *P. Quilioi* var. *m.* Bean.) I.B.t.2,f.11–13,t.15,f.4(c). Tenderer.

Related species: **P. sulphùreus** Riv. Stems yellow, often with 2 narrow green stripes; stem-sheaths glabrous, spotted; lvs. scabrous and puberulent toward the base beneath, sometimes with few whitish stripes. C.Ba.t.32,f.A. China Intr. 1865. Zone VII?—**P. s. víridis** Young, var. Stems green: lvs. not striped (*P. mitis* Riv.) Cult. 1878.

6. **P. níger** (Lodd.) Munro. Stems to 7 m., green at first, changing to purple-black, very hollow, very leafy; nodes conspicuously edged with white below; the brs. usually spotted; lvs. 5–10 cm. long, 0.6–1.5 cm. broad, very thin, denticulate, glabrous, glaucous beneath, with 3–6 pairs of veins. Zone VI. B.M.7994(c). G.C.III.15:369;18:185. Gs.3:36(h). (*P. puberula* v. *nigra* Houzeau de Lehaie.) China, Japan. Intr. 1827.—**P. n. punctàtus** Bean, var. A more robust and hardier form with yellow stems dotted with black. I.B.t. 15,f.1.(c). N.K.20:t.13. (*P. puberula* var. *nigro-punctata* Houzeau de Lehaie) —**P. n. Henònis** (Mitf.) Rendle, var. Stems green or greenish, finally yellowish, to 17 m. tall; stem-sheaths greenish or reddish brown, unspotted. H.I 2614. B.D.1909:237,t. (*P. H.* Mitf., *P. puberula* Mak.) China. Intr. 1890 Zone VI.—**P. n. Boryànus** (Mitf.) Mak. Form of the preceding var.; stems green at first, changing to pale yellow with purplish brown blotches. I.B.t.2 f.5–19,t.15, f.3(c).

10. **SHIBATAÈA** Mak. Shrubs to 1.5 m. tall; stems zigzag, much flattened, nearly solid; brs. very short, 3–5 at each node: lvs. terminal on short brs., short-petioled; sheaths without bristles: infl. on leafless brs.; spikelets 1–2-fld.; lodicules 3; stamens 3; style long, with 3 stigmas. (After Keita Shibata, Japanese botanist.) Two species in E. Asia.

S. Kumasasa (Steud.) Mak. Stems 1, sometimes 2 m. tall, upright, very zigzag, much flattened, narrow fistulose, green; internodes 3–8 cm. long; brs. 2–5 at each node: lvs. distinctly stalked, ovate-oblong to ovate-lanceolate, 6–12 cm. long, 1.5–2.5 cm. broad, long-pointed, broadly cuneate at the base, lustrous dark green above, slightly glaucescent, and at first puberulous beneath, with 6–7 pairs of veins. G.C.III.15:369;18:189. I.B.t.11,f.1–6(c). (*S. kumasaca* Nakai, *Phyllostachys ruscifolia* Nichols.) Japan. Cult. 1870. Zone VI. Very distinct on account of its comparatively broad leaves; of low tufted habit.

113. **LILIACEAE** Adans. LILY FAMILY

Herbs, shrubs or trees, sometimes climbing: lvs. alternate, parallel-veined: fls. perfect, rarely unisexual, regular, solitary or in racemes, panicles or umbels; perianth of 6 similar parts in 2 series; stamens 6, rarely less; anthers 2-celled; ovary superior, usually 3-celled, rarely 3 free carpels; ovules 1 to many in each cell; style and stigma 1–3: fr. a usually dehiscent capsule or a berry; seeds with a small embryo and copious albumen. Incl. *Ruscaceae* Spreng., *Asparagaceae* Walp., *Philesiaceae* Lindl., *Smilacaceae* Vent., *Dracaenaceae* Link, and *Agavaceae* Hutchins., in part.—About 200 genera with 2000 species widely distributed through both hemispheres; mostly herbaceous.

.. Fr. a berry; slender-branched climbing or upright shrubs.
  B. Plants with scale-like lvs. and lf.-like brts. (cladodes): fls. small white.
    c. Fls. in clusters in the middle of broad cladodes, dioecious; stamens 3......1. *Ruscus*
    cc. Fls. axillary or terminal.
      D. Cladodes linear or filiform...2. *Asparagus*
      DD. Cladodes ovate-lanceolate or lanceolate...................................3. *Danaë*
  BB. Plants with normal lvs.
    c. Fls. large, rosy-red, solitary or few; upright shrub........................4. *Philesia*
    cc. Fls. small, white or greenish, in umbels: climbing shrubs, rarely low and upright,
      usually prickly ....5. *Smilax*
.. Fr. a caps., sometimes indehiscent or fleshy: plants with thick cylindric stem, not or
  sparsely branched, or acaulescent, with a dense head of narrow evergreen lvs.
  B. Fls. 3–6 cm. long; stamens shorter than perianth: lvs. with fibrous or serrulate margin.
                                        6. *Yucca*
  BB. Fls. small; stamens longer than perianth: lvs. with spiny margin.........7. *Dasylirion*

1. RUSCUS L.

Low evergreen shrubs or subshrubs with green stems, spreading by suckers: brs. bearing alternate leaf-like cladodes in the axils of minute, scale-like lvs.: fls. dioecious, small, borne in bracted clusters in the middle of the upper surface of the cladodes; perianth-segments 6, distinct; stamens 3 with the filaments connate into a tube: ovary 1-celled, 2-vuled; style short: fr. a 1–2-seeded red berry. (The old Latin name of the plant.) Four or 5 species in the Medit. reg.—Valuable for planting in shady places.

.. Cladodes spiny-pointed, stiff...1. *R. aculeatus*
.. Cladodes not spiny ....2. *R. Hypoglossum*

1. R. aculeàtus L. BUTCHERS-BROOM. Rigid evergreen shrub, 0.5–1.2 m. tall, with grooved branched stems: cladodes sessile, ovate, 2–3.5 cm. long, .6–2 cm. broad, dark green: fls. 1 or 2 in the axils of a bract in the middle of the spiny-pointed cladode, short-stalked, white, 6 mm. across: fr. globose or ovoid, red, 1–1.5 cm. thick. Fl.III–IV; fr.x–III. R.I.10:t.437(c). P.B.1: .20(c). Gn.34:231. R.H.1894:545. S. and W. Eu. north to S. Engl. Cult. before 1750. Zone VII?—**R. a. angustifòlius** Boiss., var. with narrower cladodes.—**R. a. latifòlius** Bean, var. Cladodes up to 5 cm. long and 2–2.5 cm. broad.

Related species: **R. hyrcanus** Woronow. Brs. in whorls of 3–5 at the end of the stems: fls. 2–5. Transcauc., N. Persia. Intr. 1911. Zone VI?

2. R. Hypoglóssum L. Subshrub 25–40 cm. tall; stems unbranched: cladodes narrowly oval to oblanceolate, tapering at the ends, 7–11 cm. long, .5–3.5 cm. broad: fls. small, yellowish, borne in the axils of a leaf-like bract .5–3.5 cm. long, 6–8 mm. broad, on the upper surface of the cladodes: fr. globose, red, about 1 cm. thick. Fl.III–IV; fr.x–III. R.I.10,t.437(c). F.D.4,t. 9(c). S. Eu. Intr. before 1600. Zone VII.

Related species: **R. Hypophýllum** L. Cladodes oval or ovate, 3.5–7 cm. long; fls. slender-stalked, in the axil of a small bract. B.M.2049(c). Canary Ils. to auc. Cult. 1625. Zone VII?

2. ASPÁRAGUS L.

Shrubs, subshrubs or herbs, often climbing: lvs. scale-like, alternate, often spiny, subtending lf.-like, linear or sometimes broad cladodes: fls. polygamous or dioecious, small, greenish to white, axillary or in umbels or racemes; perianth-segments 6, connivent; stamens 6; ovary 3-celled: fr. a 1- or few-seeded berry. (*Asparagos,* the ancient Greek name of the plant.) About 150 species in Asia, Mediterr. reg. and Afr.

A. cochinchinensis (Lour.) Merr. Climbing subshrub to 3 m., rarely taller, with tuberous edible roots; stems and brs. terete or nearly so, with spiny lf.-scales; brts. angled; cladodes linear, 2–4, flat, 1–4 cm. long: fls. axillary, 1–3, campanulate, white; pedicels articulate about the middle: fr. globose, 4–7 mm. across, white to pinkish. A.G.13:78. (*A. lucidus* Lindl.) E. Asia: Korea to Indochina. Cult. 1844. Zone VI?

Related species: **A. verticillàtus** L. Climbing subshrub; cladodes 3–8, fi‑
form, angled, 2–5 cm. long: fls. subglobose: fr. about 6 mm. across, red. R.B.2‑
154. G.W.14:648. W. Mediterr. reg. Cult. 1894. Zone VI?—**A. aphýllus** ‑
Densely branched subshrub to 1 m.; brts. angled, scabrous; cladodes fascicle
rigid, pungent, 7–30 mm. long: fls. axillary, few; fr. bluish black. S.F.4:t.3‑
(c). S. Eu. Cult. 1640. Zone VII.

3. **DÁNAÉ** Medic. Evergreen much-branched shrub with alternate lea‑
like cladodes borne in the axils of small scale-like lvs.: fls. in short termin
racemes, perfect; perianth gamopetalous, subglobose, 6-lobed; stamens
inserted below the limb of the perianth; filaments connate; style short, wit
capitate stigma; ovary 3-celled, cells 2-ovuled: fr. a globose red berry, I
rarely 2-seeded. (Danae, daughter of King Acrisius of Argos.) One specie

D. racemòsa (L.) Moench. ALEXANDRIAN LAUREL. Upright shrub to 1 m
cladodes ovate-lanceolate or lanceolate, acuminate, gradually narrowed int
a short stalk, many-nerved, 6–10 cm. long, 1–2.3 cm. broad: fls. white, smal
fr. red. W.D.t.145(c). S.H.2:860. G.W.2:99(h). (*Ruscus racemosus* L
Fl.vi–vii. Syria, Transcauc., Persia. Intr. 1739. Zone VII.

4. **PHILÈSIA** Juss. Evergreen glabrous shrub, with erect stem an
angled brts.: lvs. alternate: fls. terminal, solitary or few, perfect; periantl
segments 6, connivent, the inner whorl 2–3 times longer than the outer; st‑
mens 6, with the filaments connate below the middle: ovary 1-celled, wit
numerous ovules; style elongated, stigma capitate: fr. a berry. (Greek prop‑
name, from *philein*, to love.) One species from Chile to Strait of Magellan.

P. magellànica Gmel. Shrub to 1 m.: lvs. short-stalked, narrow-oblon
stiff, 2.5–3.5 cm. long, dark green above, glaucous beneath, with reflexed ma
gins: fls. short-stalked, nodding, tubular-campanulate, 5 cm. long, rosy-red
sepals oblong, petals oblanceolate. Fl.ix–x. B.M.4738(c). G.C.55:398,t(c
Gn.87:86(h). (*P. buxifolia* Lam.) Intr. 1847. Zone VII?—Strikingly hand
some; demands peaty soil and half-shady sheltered position.

5. **SMILAX** L. GREEN-BRIER. Deciduous or evergreen, woody or herb‑
ceous climbers, rarely upright; stems often prickly, little branched at base
the lower lvs. reduced to scales, the upper entire or slightly lobed, 3–9-nerve
often blotched with white or gray; stipules usually ending in long tendril‑
fls. dioecious, rather small, greenish, yellowish or whitish, in axillary usuall
peduncled umbels, with the pedicels nearly uniform in length; periantl
segments 6, deciduous; stamens 6, rarely to 15; pistillate fl. with 6 or 3‑
staminodes: ovary 3-celled, cells 1–2-ovuled; stigmas nearly sessile: fr.
small berry, 1–several-seeded. (Ancient Greek name.) About 200 species i
the temp. and trop. regions of both hemispheres.

A. Umbels in the axils of lvs.
  B. Stipules distinct, with tendrils.
    C. Stipules narrow.
      D. Peduncles much longer than petioles.
        E. Berries black.
          F. Lvs. green or slightly glaucescent beneath.
            G. Lvs. ovate to ovate-oblong, quite entire.
              H. Pedicels 5–10 mm. long.
                I. Tendrils near base of petiole: fr. black.
                  J. Lvs. usually truncate or cuneate....................2. *S. hispia*
                  JJ. Leaves cordate to truncate.........................3. *S. Siebold*
                II. Tendrils near apex of petiole: lvs. ovate to ovate-oblong, 5–7 cr
                  long; fr. blue-black...........................9. *S. menispermoid*
              HH. Pedicels 1.5–2 cm. long: lvs. elliptic to ovate-oblong, rounded ‑
                broadly cuneate at base.........................10. *S. longip‑*
            GG. Lvs. at least those of vegetative brs. hastate or 3-lobed, more or less spin‑
            toothed: fr. black...7. *S. bona-n‑*
        FF. Lvs. very glaucous beneath: fr. blue-black, bloomy..............8. *S. glauc*

EE. Berries red.
　F. Lvs. broadly cuneate at base or rounded, ovate to oblong, sometimes reni-
　　form: prickles small, reflexed.
　　G. Lvs. glaucous beneath, generally oblong..................11. *S. megalantha*
　　GG. Lvs. green beneath, generally ovate to suborbicular...........12. *S. China*
　FF. Lvs. subcordate or truncate at base, triangular-ovate: prickles stout,
　　straight ....13. *S. excelsa*
DD. Peduncles of the pistillate plant shorter than petioles (sometimes longer in
　No. 15).
　E. Fruit red.
　　F. Lvs. deciduous: fr. coral-red....................................6. *S. Walteri*
　　FF. Lvs. persistent: fr. dark red..............................14. *S. lanceolata*
　EE. Fr. black.
　　F. Lvs. oblong to oblong-lanceolate.
　　　G. Lvs. coriaceous, 2-3.5 cm. broad: peduncle distinct........15. *S. laurifolia*
　　　GG. Lvs. deciduous, 1-1.5 cm. broad: fls. in nearly sessile clusters.
　　　　　　　　　　　　　　　　　　　　　　　　　　　1. *S. microphylla*
　　FF. Lvs. broad-ovate to ovate-oblong.
　　　G. Prickles small, bristle-like: lvs. oblong-ovate............4. *S. scobinicaulis*
　　　GG. Prickles stout: lvs. broad-ovate.........................5. *S. rotundifolia*
　CC. Stipules enlarged into a semicircular auricle as long as the very short petiole: lvs.
　　usually cordate ....18. *S. discotis*
BB. Stipules not distinct from the petiole, without tendrils: plant unarmed.
　C. Petiole glabrous, striate..16. *S. vaginata*
　CC. Petiole scabrous, papillose-pubescent..............................17. *S. trachypoda*
, Umbels borne on special leafless brs.: lvs. evergreen, often blotched white...19. *S. aspera*

Sect. 1. COILANTHUS A. DC. Perianth-segments of staminate fls. incurved,
ually less than 3 mm. long.

1. S. microphýlla C. H. Wright. Stems to 4 m. long: brs. angled, with
ort stout prickles: lvs. short-stalked, oblong to oblong-lanceolate, acute or
oruptly acuminulate, 2-6 cm. long, 5-18 mm. broad, glaucous beneath, 3-5-
erved: fls. yellowish, in very short-stalked or nearly sessile umbels; pedicels
ender: fr. black, 5 mm. thick, 1-seeded. Fl.VI; fr.X-XI. C. and W. China.
utr. 1908. Zone VII?

Sect. 2. EUSMILAX A. DC. Perianth-segments spreading or reflexed, longer
an 3 mm.

2. S. híspida Muhlb. Deciduous: root-stock woody, not much spreading:
ems to 15 m. long, densely prickly below; prickles straight, slender, blackish:
's. ovate or broad-ovate, the larger cordate, pointed, slightly rough-margined,
-12 cm. long, green beneath, 5-9-nerved: peduncle 2-5 cm. long: fr. black,
mm. across, usually many in one umbel. Fl.VI; fr.IX-X. G.F.5:53. B.B.1:
29. (*S. pseudo-china* auth., not L.) Conn. to Ont. and Minn., s. to N. C.
d Tex. Cult. 1688. Zone IV. Does not spread by stolons.

3. S. Siebóldii Miq. Deciduous, similar to the preceding species: stem
rmed with slender prickles; brs. angular: lvs. membranous, triangular-ovate,
cuminate, cordate, rough-margined, 4-8 cm. long, green on both sides, 5-7-
erved: peduncle about 1.5 cm. long; fr. black, 8 mm. thick, usually few in
ne umbel. Fl.VI; fr.IX-X. Japan, Korea. Intr. 1905. Zone V.

4. S. scobinicaùlis C. H. Wright. Deciduous: climbing to 3 m.: brs.
rooved, often densely beset with small dark bristly prickles, sometimes
narmed: petioles 5-10 mm. long, with the tendrils above the middle: lvs.
vate to oblong-ovate, acute or acuminate, rounded or subcordate at base,
-10 cm. long and 2.5-4.5 cm. broad, green beneath, 7-nerved: peduncles 4-10
m. long: pedicels 2-5 mm. long: fr. black, 5-8 mm. thick, 1-3-seeded. Fl.VI;
.X-XI. China. Intr. 1907. Zone V.

5. S. rotundifòlia L. HORSE-BRIER (COMMON GREEN-BRIER). Deciduous:
oot-stock scarcely tuberous, long-creeping; stems and brs. terete, with few
out prickles never present on the nodes; brts. angled: lvs. ovate to sub-
rbicular, acute or cuspidate, rounded or cordate at base, 3-15 cm. long:
etioles 6-12 mm. long: peduncles 6-12 mm. long; pedicels 2-8 mm. long:

fr. bluish black, 6 mm. diam., 1–3-seeded. Fl.vi; fr.ix–x. B.B.1:528. N. S. t
Ga., w. to Minn., Ill. and Tex. Intr. about 1760. Zone IV.—**S. r. quadrangu**
làta Wood, var. Brs. and brts. quadrangular.
    Related species: **S. Cantab** Lynch. Evergreen; lvs. triangular, to 12 cm. long
cordate: peduncles as long or slightly longer than petioles. Origin unknown
probably hybrid. Cult. 1890.
    6. **S. Wálteri** Pursh. Deciduous: stems slightly angled, prickly below
unarmed above; brts. angled: lvs. ovate to ovate-lanceolate or oblong, acum
nate, cordate to broadly cuneate at base, 5–11 cm. long, 2–6 cm. broad, gree
beneath, 5–7-nerved: peduncles 4–10 mm. long; pedicels 4–6 mm. long: f
coral-red, 6–8 mm. thick, 2–3-seeded. Fl.vi; fr.ix–x. B.B.1:530. N. J. an
Tenn. to Fla. and La. Intr. before 1820. Zone VI.
    7. **S. bòna-nox** L. SAW-BRIER. Partially evergreen: underground stem
spiny: stems green, densely prickly below: lower part of larger stems with
peculiar stiff stellate pubescence: lvs. at least of vegetative brs. hastate o
3-lobed, spiny on the margins and on the midrib below, the upper lvs. tr
angular-ovate, 4–12 cm. long, green and lustrous on both sides: peduncle
1.5–3 cm. long: fr. black, about 5 mm. thick, 1-seeded. Fl.vi; fr.ix–x. B.I
1:529. N. J. to Fla. west to Kans. and N. Mex. Intr. 1720. Zone VI.
    8. **S. glaùca** Walt. CAT-BRIER. Partially evergreen: underground stem
spiny, tuberous, with long rhizomes: stems and brs. terete, slender, with sca
tered stout prickles or unarmed; brts. slightly angular: lvs. ovate or broad
ovate, abruptly acuminulate, rounded or subcordate at base, 5–7 cm. long
glaucous beneath (sometimes the whole plant glaucous): peduncle 1–2.5 cm
long; fr. blue-black, bloomy, 6–8 mm. thick. Fl.vi; fr.ix–x. G.F.5:425. B.M
1846(c). W.D.2:t.111. Mass. to Fla. and Tex. Cult. 1664. Zone V.
    9. **S. menispermoìdes** A. DC. Deciduous: climbing to 3 m., unarmed
brs. nearly terete, brts. slightly angled: petioles 7–10 mm. long, with th
tendrils near the apex: lvs. ovate, rounded at base, 3–7 cm. long, 1.5–4 cm
broad, glaucescent beneath, 5–7-nerved; peduncle 2–3, in fr. to 4 cm. long
pedicels slender, 5–8 mm. long: fr. blue-black, 5–8 mm. thick. Fl.vi; fr.x
Himal., W. China. Intr. 1908. Zone VI?
    10. **S. lóngipes** Warb. Deciduous: climbing to 5 m.; brs. nearly terete
with scattered short, slightly reflexed prickles: lvs. elliptic to ovate-oblong
abruptly pointed, rounded or broad-cuneate at base, 6–12 cm. long, 3.5–7 cm
broad, with cartilaginous margin, glaucescent beneath, 5–7-nerved; peduncl
2.5–8 cm. long; pedicels 1.5–2 cm. long: fr. blue-black, 6–7 mm. thick, usuall
3-seeded. Fl.v; fr.x. C. China. Intr. 1907. Zone VII.
    11. **S. megalántha** C. H. Wright. Evergreen: climbing to 6 m.; brs. wit
stout spines; brts. angled: lvs. ovate to narrow-oblong, acuminate or abruptl
pointed, broadly cuneate or obtuse at base, 6–12 cm. long, 3–5 cm. wide
glaucescent beneath, 3–5-nerved; peduncles 1–3 cm. long; pedicels 0.5–2 cm
long: fr. red, 1.2 cm. across, often 1-seeded. G.C.68:251. Fl.v; fr.x. Chin
Intr. 1907. Zone VII? Handsome with its large coral-red frs. and evergree
lustrous lvs.
    12. **S. Chìna** L. Deciduous: climbing to 5 m.; brs. and brts. more or le
angled, with few small spines or unarmed: lvs. usually elliptic, abruptl
pointed, broad-cuneate or rounded, 5–7 cm. long, 2.5–3.5 cm. broad, some
times roundish and subcordate and as broad as long, green beneath, 5-nerved
peduncle 1.5–3 cm. long; pedicels about 1 cm. long: fr. red, 8–10 mm. thick
seeds several. Fl.vi; fr.ix–x. C. and E. China. China, Japan, Korea. Int
before 1759 and again 1907. Zone VI?

Related species: **S. biflòra** Miq. Dwarf shrub to 30 cm.; stems zigzag, spiny ⲅ unarmed: lvs. broad-oval to elliptic-oblong, 2.5–5 cm. long; petiole short; tipules with abortive tendrils: peduncles 3–10 mm. long, usually 2-fld.; pedicels –5 mm. long: fr. 6–8 mm. across, red. Japan. Intr. 1864. Zone VII?

13. **S. excélsa** L. Deciduous: tall climber: brs. angled, with stout straight ⲣrickles to 7 mm. long: lvs. triangular-ovate to orbicular-ovate, acute or bruptly pointed, truncate or subcordate at base, 4–8 cm. long, 3.5–7.5 cm. ⲅide, green beneath, 5–7-nerved: peduncle about 1.5 cm. long; pedicels 5–7 ⲙm. long: fr. red, about 1 cm. thick; seeds 3–1. Fl.v–vi; fr.x–xi. N.D.1:t.54. ⵙ. E. Eu., W. Asia to Persia, Azores. Intr. 1739. Zone VI.

14. **S. lanceolàta** L. Evergreen: climbing to 10 m.; with fleshy tubers; ⲧems stout, glaucous when young, with stout recurved prickles below; brts. ⲗightly angled: lvs. rather thin, ovate-lanceolate to lanceolate, acute or ⲥuminate, cuneate-at base, 5–8 cm. long, dull green or glaucescent beneath, –7-nerved; peduncle 6–15 mm. long; pedicels 5–14 mm. long: fr. dark red, –7 mm. thick, usually 2-seeded. Fl.vi; fr.x. B.B.1:530. Va. to Fla., w. to ⲁrk. and Tex. Intr. 1737. Zone VII. Of vigorous growth with dense bright ⲅreen foliage.

15. **S. laurifòlia** L. FALSE CHINA-BRIER. Evergreen: high climbing; stem ⲅmed with stout straight prickles; brs. angled, unarmed: lvs. coriaceous, ⲗliptic to oblong-lanceolate, acute or acuminate, cuneate at base, 6–12 cm. ⲟng, dark green above, glaucescent below, 3-nerved; peduncle 4–20 mm. ⲟng; pedicels 4–6 mm. long: fr. globose-ovoid, 4–6 mm. long, usually 1-seeded. ⲗl.vii–viii; fr. the following year. B.B.1:530. N. J. to Fla., w. to Ark. and ⲧex. Intr. 1739. Zone VII.

16. **S. vaginàta** Dcne. Deciduous: climbing to 3 m. or shrubby: stem ⲛd branches terete, unarmed; petioles 5–15 mm. long, vaginate below the ⲙiddle and gradually narrowed into the slender upper part, without tendrils: ⲅs. thin, ovate, acute or short-acuminate, rounded or subcordate at base, –6.5 cm. long, 1.5–3 cm. wide, pale or glaucescent beneath, 3–5-nerved: ⲣeduncle slender, 1–3 cm. long; pedicels slender, to 1 cm. long: fr. black, –10 mm. thick, 1–2-seeded. Fl.vi; fr.x–xii. Himal., W. China. Intr. 1908. ⲟne VI?

17. **S. trachýpoda** Norton. Deciduous: 1–4 m. tall, upright or climbing; ⲧems terete, unarmed: petioles 1.5–3 cm. long, papillose-pubescent, gradually ⲁrrowed from a vaginate base, without tendrils: lvs. ovate, acuminate, cor- ⲁte at base, 7–10 cm. long, 4–6 cm. wide, entire or slightly erose at the margin, ⲅeins 5–7, papillose-pubescent below toward the base: peduncles 3–5 cm. ⲟng; pedicels 3–10 mm. long, those of the staminate fls. 10–15 mm. long: fr. ⲗue-black, bloomy, 6–8 mm. thick, 1–2-seeded. Fl.vi; fr.x. C. and W. China. ⲛtr. 1908. Zone VII?

18. **S. discòtis** Warb. Deciduous: climbing to 5 m.; stems nearly terete, ⲓke the angled or grooved brs. with scattered hooked prickles or unarmed; ⲣetioles usually 2–4 mm. long; stipules as long or longer, dilated into a broad ⲁuricle, rarely petiole about 5 mm. long and exceeding the auricle, without ⲅr with short tendrils: lvs. ovate to ovate-lanceolate, acute or acuminate, ⲥordate or rarely rounded at base, 3–9 cm. long, 1.5–4 cm. broad, glaucous ⲛd coarsely reticulate beneath, 3–5-nerved; peduncle 1–4 cm. long; pedicels –10 mm. long: fr. blue-black, 6–8 mm. thick. Fl.vi; fr.x. C. & W. China. ⲛtr. 1908?—**S. d. cóncolor** Norton, var. Lvs. larger, to 9 cm. long and to 5 ⲙm. wide, green beneath; petioles 5–10 mm. long, stipules somewhat shorter, ⲙore often with tendrils. C. China. Intr. 1907. Zone VII?

19. S. áspera L. Evergreen: climbing: stems and the zigzag brs. angled with short stout prickles or unarmed: lvs. deltoid-ovate to lanceolate, usually cordate at base, or broad-cuneate, 4–12 cm. long, often prickly on the margin and on the midrib below, often blotched with white, green below, 5–9-nerved: fls. greenish white, sweet-scented, in 5–7-fld. clusters forming axillary and terminal racemes 3–10 cm. long: fr. red, 6 mm. thick, usually 3-seeded. F VIII–IX; fr.I–III. L.B.18:1799(c). Gt.46:t.1443(c). G.C.II:22:784. Gn.62:397 S. Eu. to India. Intr. about 1650. Zone VII.—**S. a. maculàta** (Roxb.) A. DC var. Lvs. blotched with white. Gt.20:t.683(c). (*S. a.* var. *punctata* Reg.)– **S. a. mauritànica** (Desf.) Gren. & Godr., var. A robust form with larger lvs and fewer spines. F.S.10:t.1049. (*S. m.* Desf.) Medit. reg.

6. YUCCA L. YUCCA. Evergreen plants with thick, simple or branched stem, or acaulescent; the longe sword-shaped lvs. crowded into dense ter minal clusters; fls. perfect, cup- or saucer-shaped, large, usually pendent white, sometimes tinged with violet, in large usually erect, terminal panicle or racemes; petals distinct or nearly so, thickish; stamens much shorter tha the petals, with fleshy filaments and small sagittate anthers; style short, wit 3 stigmas: fr. ovoid to oblong, more or less 6-angled, incompletely 6-celled capsular and usually dehiscent, or fleshy and indehiscent; seeds compressed subglobose to obovoid, black. (Yuca, the Carib name for the manihot, errone ously applied by Gerarde to this plant.) About 30 species in N. and C. Am.— Besides the species described below many hybrids are cult. in Europea gardens, but they are little known in this country. For monographs se Trelease in Rep. Mo. Bot. Gard. 13:42–116,99 pl. (1902); Molon, Le Yucch (1914); and McKelvey, Yuccas of the S. W. U. S. 150 pp., 80 pl. (1938).

A. Lvs. entire, with marginal threads.
  B. Lvs. nearly flat: fr. dehiscent, capsular.
    C. Lvs. 2–4 cm. wide.
      D. Lvs. upright ....1. *Y. filamentos*
      DD. Lvs. flaccid, recurving...2. *Y. flaccia*
    CC. Lvs. 8–12 mm. wide..3. *Y. glauc*
  BB. Lvs. concave, thick and rigid, about 5 cm. wide: fr. fleshy, indehiscent...6. *Y. baccai*
AA. Lvs. denticulate at first, finally slightly filiferous, nearly flat: fr. dry, indehiscent.
  B. Lvs. stiff ....4. *Y. glorios*
  BB. Lvs. flaccid, recurving...5. *Y. recurvifol*

1. Y. filamentòsa L. ADAMS NEEDLE. Acaulescent, spreading by sho stolons: lvs. erect and spreading, linear-lanceolate, acute, 25–75 cm. long slightly or scarcely glaucous, with numerous curly threads at the margin panicle 1–3 m. tall, rather broad, usually glabrous; fls. pendulous, yellowis white, 5–7 cm. across: fr. 5 cm. long; carpels rounded on back. Fl.VII–VII B.M.900(c). G.C.37:187. R. Mo. 13:t.8–12(h). S. C. to Miss. and Fla. Cul 1675. Zone IV.—**Y. f. variegàta** Carr. Lvs. striped with yellow or white L.H.t.50(c).—**Y. f. concàva** (Haw.) Bak., var. Lvs. stiff, concave, to 10 cn broad. R. Mo. 13:t.10.

Y. f. × *glauca;* see under No. 3.

2. Y. fláccida Haw. Similar to the preceding species but lvs. gradual attenuate, recurving, with thinner straighter threads: panicle usually pubes cent, shorter: carpels with angular back. Gn.58:447;78:433. R. Mo. 13:t.1 17(h). N. C. to Ala. Intr. 1816. Zone IV.—**Y. f. màjor** (Bak.) Rehd., va Lvs. glaucous, broader: panicle pubescent; petals narrower. B.M.6316(c (Var. *glaucescens* Trel., *Y. orchioides major* Bak.)—**Y. f. íntegra** Trel., f. Lv smaller, without fibres on the margin. B.M.2662(c, as *Y. glauca*).—**Y. orchioìdes** Trel., f. Lvs. stiffer, more erect, without fibres on the margin: in racemose. R.H.1861:370.

3. **Y. glaùca** Nutt. Acaulescent or with prostrate short stem: Lvs. narrow-near, 30–70 cm. long, 6–12 mm. broad, grayish or glaucous green, with a arrow white margin, with few threads: fls. pendulous, greenish white, 6–7 m. long, in a narrow, rarely branched infl. 1–2 m. tall; style swollen, green. l.vii–viii. B.M.2236(c). Gn.76:402. F.E.14:34(h). R. Mo. 13:t.25(h). (*Y. ngustifolia* Pursh.) S. D. to N. Mex. Intr. about 1656. Zone IV.—**Y. g. rícta** (Sims) Trel. With a distinct erect stem and a larger branched infl. .M.2222(c). Gn.8:130. R. Mo. 13:t.26(h). (*Y. stricta* Sims.)—**Y. g. rósea** . M. Andrews. Fls. tinted rose-pink outside.

Y. g. × *filamentosa* = **Y. karlsruhénsis** Graebener. Lvs. about 2 cm. wide: ifl. branched below the middle. G.W.10:83(h). M.G.50:296(h). Orig. 1899. one IV.

Related species: **Y. angustíssima** Trel. Acaulescent; lvs. narrow-linear, 20–) cm. long, 2–5 mm. broad, white-bordered, filiferous: infl. 1–1.5 m. tall, race-ose with few short brs. at base; style oblong, white; fr. smaller. R.Mo.13:t.23, l,t.24,f.1. Utah, Nev. to Ariz. Cult. 1933. Zone VII?—**Y. rupícola** Scheele. caulescent; lvs. 30–60 cm. long, 2.5–3.5 cm. broad, finely denticulate, not liferous on margin: infl. paniculate, 1.5–2 m. tall; fls. 5–6 cm. long. B.M.7172). R.Mo.3:t.51. Tex. Intr. about 1850. Zone VII?—**Y. Harrimániae** Trel. caulescent: lvs. linear to spatulate-lanceolate, 20–40 cm. long, 6–15, rarely to mm. broad, glaucous, with brown fibrous margin: infl. 25–50 cm. high, race-ose; fls. greenish; style slender, oblong. R.Mo.13:t.28,29. Utah to Colo. Cult.)36. Zone VI?—**Y. neomexicàna** Woot. & Standl. Acaulescent, cespitose; lvs. near-lanceolate, 25–30 cm. long, 8–10 mm. broad, with white filiferous margin: ifl. 60–90 cm. high, racemose; fls. white, about 4 cm. long; style short, swollen. *Y. Coloma* D. M. Andrews.) N. Mex. Cult. 1933. Zone VII?

4. **Y. gloriòsa** L. With a short trunk and cespitose, or sometimes to 5 m. ill and branched: lvs. stiff, straight, 40–60 cm. long, 5–6 cm. broad, spine-pped, nearly flat, smooth, glaucous green, usually with a few teeth while oung and a few threads when old: panicle narrow, 1–1.5 m. tall; fls. pendu-us, creamy white, often tinged with purple: fr. oblong-ovoid, 5–6 cm. long. l.vii–ix. S.S.10:503. G.C.28:262. R. Mo. 13;t.43,44(h). (*Y. acuminata* weet.) S. C. to Fla. Intr. about 1550. Zone VII.—**Y. g. robústa** Carr. iter lvs. usually somewhat recurving. B.M.1260(c).—**Y. g. nòbilis** Carr. imilar, but lvs. glaucous. Ref. Bot. 5;t.317. (*Y. gloriosa* var. *Ellacombei* ak.)—**Y. g. plicàta** Carr. With glaucous lvs. plicate toward the end. Gn.49: 32. G.C.III.8:692;15:304.—**Y. g. supérba** Bak., var. is similar, but taller nd green.

5. **Y. recurvifòlia** Salisb. To 2 m. tall and more or less branched: lvs. 5–1 m. long, 3.5–5.5 cm. broad, nearly plane, flexible, recurved, at first glau-ous, narrowly yellow- or brown-margined: fls. 5–7 cm. across, creamy white, a narrow panicles to 1 m. tall: fr. 5–6 cm. long, erect. Gt.17:t.580(c). Gn.47: 37(h). R. Mo. 13:t.46,47(h). B.S.1:58,t(h). (*Y. gloriosa r.* Engelm., *Y. ecurva* Haw., *Y. obliqua* Reg., *Y. pendula* Groenl.) Coast of Ga. and Miss. ntr. 1794. Zone VI.—**Y. r. marginàta** (Carr.) Trel., f. Lvs. bordered with ellow.—**Y. r. variegàta** (Carr.) Trel., f. Lvs. striped with yellow.

6. **Y. baccàta** Torr. Nearly acaulescent or with short prostrate trunk: lvs. gid, spreading, about 60 cm. long, concave, rough, narrowly brown-bordered, parsely filiferous: fls. pendulous, 7–8 cm. long, in an upright dense panicle bout 1 m. tall: fr. conic-ovoid, very large, to 20 cm. long, fleshy. G.C.28:103. H.20:115. R.H.1887:368. McKelvey, t.8–12. Colo. to N. Mex. and Nev. ntr. about 1887. Zone VII.

7. **DASYLÌRION** Zucc. Evergreen plants with thick simple stem or caulescent; lvs. crowded, rigid, narrow, with spiny margin: fls. dioecious, nall, white, rarely purplish, in crowded spikes forming long narrow panicles;

perianth campanulate, of 6 distinct segments, usually the outer whorl toothed the inner entire; stamens 6, exserted; ovary 1-celled, stigmas 3: fr. 1-seeded dry, indehiscent, 3-winged. (Greek *dasys*, dense, crowded, and *leirion*, lily referring to the crowded lvs. and crowded fls.) About 15 species in Mexico Texas and Ariz.

D. texànum Scheele. Stem to 40 cm. tall; lvs. linear, 50–90 cm. long, 1– cm. broad, margin with hooked prickles, splitting into fibres near apex: scap 3–5 m. tall, with conspicuous ovate to ovate-lanceolate bracts, often longe than the fl.-spikes; perianth 2–3 mm. long: fr. 6–7 mm. long. Tex. Cult. 1936 Zone VII.

ADDITIONS AND EMENDATIONS

Page 240, between No. 43 and No. 44 insert:
Related species: **B. reticulàta** Bijhouwer. Brs. purple-brown the second
ear: lvs. obovate to oblong-obovate, 2–4 cm. long, spinulose-serrulate, grayish
nd reticulate beneath: racemes subumbellate, 3–8-fld., with the short peduncle
5–2 cm. long: fr. oval, 7–10 mm. long, red, slightly pruinose. N. China. Intro-
uced 1910. Zone V.

Page 260, at end of **Lindera cercidifolia** insert:
Related genus: **Laurus** L. LAUREL. Evergreen, very aromatic: lvs. entire,
enninerved: fls. dioecious, in axillary peduncled 4-bracted umbels; staminate
ith 8–14, usually 12, stamens; pistillate with 4 staminodes; sepals 4. Two
ecies in the Mediterr. reg.—**L. nòbilis** L. SWEET BAY. Shrub or tree to 10 m.,
abrous, lvs. short-stalked, elliptic to elliptic-lanceolate, 5–10 cm. long, cuneate,
ute to short acuminate, often with crisp margin, reticulate beneath: fls.
reenish-white, about 1 cm. across: fr. ovoid 1.5–2 cm. long, dark green, finally
ack. R.I.12:t.673(c). F.D.10:t.938(c). H.M.4,1:t.122(c). Cult. since ancient
mes. Zone (VI). The laurel of history and poetry; often grown in tubs for
ecoration; easily trimmed into formal shapes. Lvs. used as condiment, the
il of the fr. in perfumery.

Page 441, under No. 34, after **Rosa Macounii** insert:
—**R. ultramontàna** (S. Wats.) Heller. Prickles slender, straight: lvs. oval
oval-oblong, puberulent and dull green beneath; stipules narrow, except the
pper ones: fls. several. B. C. to N. Calif., Utah and Wyo. Cult. 1888. Zone V.

Page 452, at end of **Maddenia hypoleuca**, add:
Closely related species: **M. hypoxántha** Koehne: Lvs. yellowish green and
ppressed-pubescent beneath, at least on the veins. W. China. Intr. ?

Page 535, insert before 4. **Daphniphyllum:**
Gen. 1–3 belong to the tribe PHYLLANTHOIDEAE Pax, Gen. 4 to DAPHNI-
HYLLOIDEAE, the following to CROTONOIDEAE: **Sàpium** P.Br. Shrubs or trees,
eciduous or evergreen, glabrous: lvs. alternate, entire; petioles usually bi-
andular at apex: fls. monoecious, in terminal racemes or panicles; calyx 3-
bed or 3-fid.; male fls. several in the axils of bracts, with 2–3 stamens;
istillate fls. at base of infl.; ovary 2–3-celled, cells 1-ovuled; styles free or con-
ate at base: fr. a crustaceous or fleshy caps. More than 100 species trop. or
btrop.—**S. sebíferum** Roxb. CHINESE TALLOW-TREE. Tree to 10 m.: lvs. broadly
ombic-ovate or suborbicular, 3.5–7 cm. long and about as broad, abruptly
uminate, broad-cuneate: petioles 2–5 cm. long, slender: racemes slender, 5–10
n. long: caps. subglobose, 1–1.5 cm. across, seeds subglobose with waxy coat.
.N.R.19c:201. B.T.601 (*Excoecaria sebifera* Muell.-Arg.) China; nat. in s.e.
.Am. Cult. 1850. Zone VII. The waxy seed coat used for candles in China.
vs. turning red in fall.

Page 542, add at end of No. 1. **Rhus glabra:**
—**R. g. cismontàna** (Greene) Daniels. Low: lfts. 11–13, 4–8 cm. long: infl.
 fr. pyramidal, compact. Mont. and Neb. to Ariz. Cult. 1916.—**R. g. flavéscens**
D. M. Andr.) Rehd., f. A form of the preceding var. with yellow fr.; lvs. turn-
g yellow in fall. Cult. 1925.

Page 611, under No. 5 after Related species, before **Vitis Longii** insert:
V. nòvae-ángliae Fern. Lvs. suborbicular or reniform-ovate, indistinctly
lobed, with broad deltoid teeth, pilose beneath at least on the veins and with

901

ADDITIONS AND EMENDATIONS

cobwebby pubescence when young, usually rufescent at first: fr. 1.2–1.6 cm across. Me. to Conn. Intr. 1918. Zone III.—

Page 634, after **Camellia cuspidata** add:

To the Sect. THEA (L.) Cohen Stuart, differing in its long-stalked fls., persistent calyx and pubescent ovary belongs **C. sinénsis** (L.) Ktze. TEA. Shrub o tree to 15 m.: lvs. short-petioled, elliptic-lanceolate to elliptic, 4–12 cm. long obtusish or obtusely short-acuminate, cuneate, crenate-serrate, glabrous: fl 2.5–3.5 cm. across, white, nodding, 1–3 in the axils on stalks about 1 cm. long ovary pubescent: seeds subglobose, 1.5 cm. across. B.M.988,3148(c). H.A.7: 28(c). E.P.R.21:130. (*C. Thea* Lk., *C. theifera* Griff., *Thea s.* L., *Th. chinensi* Sims, *Th. Bohea* L., *Th. viridis* L.) Assam, much cult. in China. Intr. abou 1770. Zone VII.

Page 751, after No. 8. **V. corymbosum** insert:

V. c. × *angustifolium* = **V. atlánticum** Bickn. Shrub to 1 m.: lvs. ellipti oblong to elliptic-lanceolate, 3–5 cm. long, ciliolate-serrulate, usually pubescen only on the midrib beneath, rarely glabrous: corolla usually urceolate: fr. blue glaueous. U. S. to N. Y. w. to Wisc. Cult. 1905. Zone III.

Page 805, at end of 2. **Vitex Negundo** add:

Related species: **V. rotundifólia** L. f. Prostrate or ascending to 1 m: lv simple, obovate to oval, 2–6 cm. long, rounded to obtusish at apex, broac cuneate, entire, white tomentulose beneath: panicles 4–12 cm. long, 1.5–4 cm wide at base, rather loosely branched; fls. blue, 1–1.5 cm. long, upper lip muc longer than lower. N.K.14:t.11 (*V. ovata* Thunb., *V. trifolia* var. *simplicifoli* Cham., *V. t.* var. *unifoliolata* Schau.) Mal. to E. Asia, n. to Shantung an Korea. Cult. 1930. Zone VII.

GLOSSARY

Abortive. Imperfectly or not developed; barren.

Achene. A dry indehiscent, 1-celled and 1-seeded fruit or carpel.

Acicular. Needle-shaped.

Actinomorphous or *actinomorphic.* Capable of division by two or more planes into equal halves.

Aculeate. Prickly; beset with prickles.

Acuminate. Tapering at the end; long-pointed.

Acuminulate. Abruptly ending in a short point.

Acute. Sharp-pointed; ending in a point.

Adnate. United with another part, as the filament with the corolla-tube or an anther attached for its whole length to the filament.

Aestivation. The arrangement of the parts of the perianth in the bud.

Albumen. The nutritive material surrounding the embryo in the seed.

Albuminous. Having albumen.

Alternate. Not opposite to each other on the axis.

Ament. A catkin.

Amphitropous (ovule). Half-inverted and straight with the hilum lateral.

Anastomosing (veins). Connecting by cross-veins and forming a network.

Anatropous (ovule). Inverted and straight with the micropyle next to the hilum.

Andro-dioecious. Staminate and bisexual flowers on different plants.

Androgynophore (or *Androphore*). Stipe-like elongation of the floral axis between peri-anth and stamens.

Androgynous. With both staminate and pistillate flowers in the same inflorescence.

Andro-monoecious. Staminate and bisexual flowers on the same plant.

Angiospermous. Having the seeds borne within a pericarp.

Annular. In the form of a ring.

Anterior. On the front side of the flower toward the subtending bracts.

Anther. The pollen-bearing part of the stamen.

Apetalous. Having no petals.

Apical. At the apex or summit of an organ.

Apiculate. Contracted into a minute point.

Apophysis (in Pinus). The exposed, mostly swollen part of the cone-scales.

Appressed. Lying close and flat against.

Aril. An appendage growing out from the hilum and covering the seed partly or wholly.

Aristate. Awned; tipped by a bristle.

Articulate. Jointed; having a node or joint.

Ascending. Rising somewhat obliquely and curving upward.

Attenuate. Slenderly tapering.

Auriculate. Furnished with ear-shaped appendages (auricles), as the base of a petal or leaf.

Awl-shaped. Tapering from the base to a slender and stiff point.

Axil. The upper angle formed by a leaf or branch with the stem.

Axile. Belonging to the axis, chiefly used in reference to the position of the placentae.

Axillary. Situated in an axil.

Axis. The central line of an organ or the support of a group of organs.

Baccate. Berry-like; pulpy or fleshy.

Basifixed. Attached or fixed by the base.

Beaked. Ending in a beak or prolonged tip.

Bearded. Ending in a long awn or furnished with long or stiff hairs.

Berry. A fruit with the whole pericarp fleshy or pulpy.

Bi- or *bis-.* A Latin prefix signifying two or twice.

Bifid. Two-cleft.

Bilabiate. Two-lipped.

Bipinnate. Twice pinnate.

Bisexual. Having both stamens and pistils; hermaphrodite.

Blade. The expanded portion of the leaf.

Bract. A modified reduced leaf subtending a pedicel or peduncle or belonging to an inflorescence or occurring at the base of shoots.

Bractlet. A secondary bract, particularly as borne on the pedicel.

Bracteate. Having bracts.

Branchlet. A small branch, referring to the branches of the currant and usually also to those of the preceding year.

Bullate. Blistered or puckered.

Caducous. Falling off very early.

Calyx. The outer perianth of the flower.

Campanulate. Bell-shaped.

Canaliculate. Longitudinally channeled.

Canescent. Gray-pubescent and hoary.

Capitate. Head-like; collected into a dense cluster.

Capsular. Belonging to or of the nature of a capsule.

Capsule. A dry dehiscent fruit of more than one carpel.

Carinate. Keeled.

Carpel. A simple pistil or a member of a compound pistil.

Catkin. A scaly-bracted spike of usually unisexual flowers.

Cell. One of the minute vesicles of which plant tissues are formed; also a cavity of an anther or ovary.

Chaff. A small thin scale or bract; particularly on the receptacle of the Compositae.

Channeled. Deeply grooved longitudinally.

Chartaceous. Having the texture of stiff writing paper.

Ciliate. Fringed with hairs.

Ciliolate. Minutely ciliate.

Circinate. Involute from the top into a coil.

Circumscissile. Dehiscing by a transverse circular line; the upper part usually coming off as a lid.

Clasping. Said of the base of a leaf partly or wholly surrounding the stem.

Clavate. Club-shaped; gradually thickened upward.

Cleistogamous. Closed, self-fertilized flowers.

Coalescent. Two or more similar parts united.

Coetaneous. Appearing or existing at the same time, as leaves and flowers in some trees and shrubs.

Coherent. Two or more similar parts or organs joined.

Columnar. Having the shape of a column.

Compound. Composed of two or more similar parts as a compound leaf, or an inflorescence with the flowers on axes of the second or a higher order.

Conduplicate. Folded together lengthwise.

Conelet. The young cone in Pinus during the first season after fertilization.

Connate. United; joined into one organ.

Connective. The portion of the stamen which connects the cells of an anther.

Connivent. Converging; coming together, but not connate.

Convolute. Rolled up longitudinally.

Cordate. Heart-shaped; usually referring to the base of a leaf with two rounded lobes and a sinus.

Coriaceous. Of leathery texture.

Corolla. The inner series of floral envelopes, consisting of either connate or distinct petals.

Corona. An appendage on the inside of the corolla, usually near the throat.

Corymb. A flat-topped or convex flower-cluster with the outer flowers opening first.

Cotyledon. The primary leaf or leaves in the embryo.

Crenate. Toothed with rounded, shallow teeth.

Crenulate. Finely crenate.

Crested. With an irregular or toothed ridge.

Crown. Same as corona or an annular outgrowth at the top of an organ.

Cucullate. Hooded or hood-shaped.

Culm. The stem of grasses and sedges.

Cuneate. Wedge-shaped; triangular, with the narrow end at point of attachment.

Cuspidate. Sharp-pointed; ending in a sharp pointed cusp.

Cyme. A convex or flat flower-cluster of the determinate type; the central flowers opening first.

Cymose. Arranged in cymes; cyme-like.

Deciduous. Falling, not persistent.

Decompound. More than once compound.

Decumbent. Reclining, but with the ends ascending.

Decurrent (leaf). Extending down the stem below the insertion.

Decussate. Alternating in pairs at right angles; opposite leaves forming four longitudinal rows.

Dehiscent. Opening to emit the contents, as a capsule or anther.

Deliquescent. Said of a trunk of a tree dividing into several stems or limbs, without main axis.

Deltoid. Triangular; delta-like.

Dentate. Toothed with the teeth directed outward.

Denticulate. Minutely dentate.

Depressed. Flattened from above.

Di, dis. Greek prefix, signifying two or twice.

Diaphragm. A cross-partition at the node of hollow or pithy stems or branches.

Dichotomous. Forked regularly in pairs.

Didynamous. With four stamens in pairs of unequal length.

Diffuse. Loosely or widely spreading.

Digitate. With the members arising from one point.

Dimorphous or *dimorphic.* Occurring in two forms.

Dioecious. Staminate and pistillate flowers on different plants.

Diplostemonous. Flowers with twice as many stamens as petals, the outer opposite to the sepals.

Discoid. Resembling a disk; discoid head (in Compositae), one without ray-flowers.

Disk. A development of the receptacle at or around the base of the pistil.

Dissected. Divided into many narrow segments.

Dissepiment. A partition in an ovary or fruit.

Distichous. Arranged in two vertical ranks; two-ranked.

Distinct. Separate; not united with parts of the same series; not connate; also evident.

Divaricate. Spreading; widely divergent.

Divided. Separated to the base.

Dorsal. Relating to the back or outer surface of an organ.

Double. Said of flowers with more than the normal number of floral envelopes, particularly of petals.

Drupe. A fleshy indehiscent fruit with bony, usually one-seeded endocarp.

Drupelet. A drupe in a fruit consisting of an aggregate of small drupes as in Rubus.

E, ex. A Latin prefix usually denoting that parts are missing, as exstipulate, without stipules.

Ellipsoid. A solid body elliptic in the longitudinal section.

Elliptic. With an outline of an ellipse and about two times as long as wide.

Emarginate. With a shallow notch at the apex.

Embryo. The rudimentary plant within the seed.

Endocarp. The inner layer of the pericarp.

Entire. Without toothing or division.

Epigynous. Borne on the top of the ovary.

Epiphytic. Growing on other plants, but not parasitic.

Erose. With jagged margin, as if gnawed.

Estipulate. See exstipulate.

Exalbuminous. Without albumen.

Excurrent. With a projecting tip, as the nerve of a leaf projecting beyond the margin.

Exfoliating. Peeling off in thin layers.

Exocarp. The outer layer of the pericarp.

Exserted. Prolonged beyond the surrounding organs, as stamens from the corolla.

Exstipulate. Without stipules.

Extrastaminal. Like intrastaminal, chiefly used in reference to the disk, whether it inside (intrastaminal) or outside (extrastaminal) of the stamens.

Extrorse. Facing outward.

Eye. The differently colored centre of flower.

Falcate. Sickle- or scythe-shaped.

Fascicle. A dense cluster.

GLOSSARY

ascicled. Borne in dense clusters; said of several or many long hairs arising from a common base.

astigiate. With stems or branches erect and near together.

errugineous. Rust-colored.

ertile. Capable of producing fruit or seeds; also said of pollen-bearing anthers.

ibro-vascular. Composed of woody fibres and ducts.

ilament. The stalk of an anther.

iliform. Thread-like; very slender and terete.

imbriate. Fringed.

laccid. Not rigid; lax and weak.

loccose. Clothed with flocks of soft hair or wool.

loriferous. Flower-bearing.

oliaceous. Leaf-like in texture or appearance.

ollicle. A dry dehiscent fruit or carpel opening only along one suture.

oveolate. Pitted.

ree. Not joined to other organs; not adnate.

ruit. The seed-bearing product of a plant.

ruticose. Shrubby; with woody persistent stems and branches.

rutescent. Nearly shrubby.

ugacious. Falling or withering away very early.

unicle. The stalk of an ovule or seed.

unnelform. Said of a corolla with the tube gradually widening upward into the spreading limb.

urrowed. With longitudinal channels or grooves.

uscous. Grayish brown.

usiform. Spindle-shaped, narrowed toward the ends from a swollen middle.

Jamopetalous. Having the petals more or less united.

Jeniculate. Bend abruptly like a knee.

Jibbous. Swollen on one side.

Jlabrate. Nearly glabrous or becoming glabrous with age.

Jlabrescent. Becoming nearly glabrous with age.

Jlabrous. Not hairy.

Jland. A secreting part or appendage, but often used for gland-like organs.

Jlandular. Bearing glands or gland-like appendages.

Jlaucous. Covered with a bloom; bluish white or bluish gray.

Jlomerate. In compact clusters.

Jlomerulate. In small compact clusters.

Jlume. A chaff-like bract; particularly one of the two empty bracts at the base of the spikelet in grasses.

Jranular, granulose. Composed of or appearing as if covered by minute grains.

Jymnospermous. Bearing naked seeds, without an ovary.

Jynophore. The stipe of an ovary.

Jynostegium. The structure resulting from the union of stamens and pistil in Asclepiadaceae.

Jastate. Halberd-shaped; like an arrowhead, but with the basal lobes pointing outward nearly at right angles.

Jead. A dense cluster or short dense spike of sessile or nearly sessile flowers.

Heart-shaped; see cordate.

Heteromorphous. Parts of different shape.

Hilum. The scar or point of attachment of the seed.

Hirsute. With rather coarse or stiff hairs.

Hirtellous. Minutely hirsute.

Hispid. Beset with rigid hairs or bristles.

Hispidulous. Minutely hispid.

Hoary. Covered with a close whitish or grayish white pubescence.

Homogamous. Bearing only one kind of flowers.

Homomorphous. Parts of like shape.

Hybrid. A plant resulting from a cross between two or more parents that are more or less unlike.

Hypanthium. The cup-shaped or tubular receptacle on which the perianth and the stamens are inserted.

Hypogeous. Said of cotyledons remaining below ground.

Hypogynous. Borne on the receptacle beneath the ovary; said of stamens and petals.

Hypostyle. The free portion on the ventral side of the stone in Crataegus and Cotoneaster, differing conspicuously in texture from the rest of the stone.

Imbricate. Overlapping, as shingles on a roof.

Incised. Sharply and more or less deeply and irregularly cut.

Included. Not protruding or exserted.

Indehiscent. Not opening.

Inferior. Beneath or below, as an inferior ovary, one that is below the perianth.

Inflated. Blown up; bladdery.

Inflorescence. The flowering part of the plant; mode of flower-bearing.

Infra-. In composition, below; as infrastipular, below the stipules.

Inserted. Attached.

Inter- or *intra-.* In composition, between, as interpetiolar, between the petioles of opposite leaves like the stipules of many Rubiaceae.

Internode. The portion of the stem between two nodes.

Intrastaminal. See under extrastaminal.

Introrse. Facing inward toward the axis.

Involucel. A secondary involucre.

Involucre. A whorl of bracts surrounding a flower-cluster or a single flower.

Involute. Rolled inward.

Irregular flower. Some parts different from other parts of the same whorl; usually applied to zygomorphous flowers.

Keel. A central ridge; the two anterior united petals of a papilionaceous flower.

Laciniate. Cut into narrow pointed lobes.

Lamellate. Having thin flat plates or a laterally flattened ridge, as lamellate pith, one consisting of thin transverse plates, also called chambered.

Lanceolate. Lance-shaped, about 4 times as long as wide and broadest below or about the middle.

Leaf-cushion. In Conifers the basal part of the leaf decurrent on the stem.

Leaflet. Part of a compound leaf.

Legume. The fruit of Leguminosae, consisting of a single carpel and dehiscent at maturity by one or two sutures.

905

GLOSSARY

Lemma. The lower of the two bracts enclosing the flower in the Grasses.
Lepidote. Beset with small scurfy scales.
Ligneous. Woody.
Ligulate. Provided with or resembling a ligule.
Ligule. A strap-shaped organ; a usually scarious projection from the summit of the sheath in the Grasses.
Limb. The expanded part of a petal, sepal or of the corolla.
Linear. Long and narrow with nearly parallel margins.
Lip. The divisions of a two-lipped corolla.
Lobe. A segment of an organ, particularly if rounded.
Lobed. Divided into or bearing lobes.
Lobulate. Divided into small shallow lobes.
-locular. In composition, having locules or cells, as bilocular, two-celled.
Loculicidal. Dehiscent on the back of the cells of a capsule.
Lodicules. Two or rarely 3 small hyaline scales at the base of the flower in Gramineae.
Lyrate. Pinnatifid with a large terminal lobe and small basal lobes.

Macrostylous. In dimorphus flowers the form with the longer style.
Marcescent. Withering but persistent.
Medullary. Pertaining to the pith or medulla.
Membranous. Thin and rather soft.
-merous. As 3-merous or 4-merous, with a
Mesocarp. The middle layer of a pericarp.
Micropyle. The orifice of the ovule and the whorl or whorls of 3 or 4 parts. corresponding place in the seed.
Microstylous. In dimorphous flowers the form with the shorter style.
Midrib. The central vein or rib of a leaf.
Monadelphous. Stamens united in one group by their filaments.
Moniliform. Resembling a string of beads, as the legume of Sophora.
Monoecious. With unisexual flowers of both sexes on the same plant.
Mucronate. Tipped with a short abrupt point or mucro.
Mucronulate. With a minute mucro.
Multinodal; see p. 35.
Muricate. Roughened with short hard points.
Mutic. Said of the unarmed and obtuse umbo of the cone-scales in Pinus.

Naked flower. A flower without perianth.
Nectary. A place or organ where sugar or nectar is secreted.
Nerve. A slender unbranched rib or vein.
Nodal. On or close to a node, relating to a node.
Node. The place upon the stem which normally bears a leaf or leaves.
Nut. An indehiscent one-seeded hard and bony fruit.
Nutlet. A small nut or a small stone or stones of a drupaceous fruit.

Ob-. Latin prefix usually signifying inversion.
Obcordate. Inversely heart-shaped.

Obdiplostemonous (flowers). With twice as many stamens as petals and the outer one opposite to the petals.
Oblanceolate. Lanceolate but broadest near the apex.
Oblique. Unequal-sided.
Oblong. About 3 times as long as wide and with nearly parallel sides.
Obovate. Inversely ovate.
Obovoid. Inversely egg-shaped.
Obsolete. Not evident; rudimentary.
Ocrea. A tubular stipule or a pair of stipules united into a sheath.
Odd-pinnate (leaf). Pinnate with a terminal leaflet.
Orbicular. Circular; round in outline.
Orthotropous (ovule or seed). Erect with the micropyle at the apex.
Oval. Broad-elliptic, about 1½ times as long as broad and round at the ends.
Ovary. The ovule-bearing part of the pistil.
Ovate. Having an outline like a hen's egg.
Ovoid. An oval or ovate body.
Ovule. The body which after fertilization becomes the seed.

Palea. The upper bract which with the lemma encloses the flower in Grasses.
Paleaceous. Chaffy.
Palmate (leaf). Radiately lobed or divided with 3 or more veins arising from one point.
Pandurate. Fiddle-shaped; constricted about the middle.
Panicle. A compound inflorescence of the racemose type with pediceled flowers.
Panicled, paniculate. Borne in a panicle or resembling a panicle.
Papilionaceous (corolla). Having a standard, wings and keel.
Papillose. Bearing minute nipple-shaped projections.
Pappus. The modified calyx-limb in Compositae, forming a crown of bristles, awns or scales.
Parietal. Borne on or pertaining to the wall of a fruit.
Parted. Cleft nearly but not quite to the base.
Pectinate. Comb-like; pinnatifid with narrow, closely set segments.
Pedate. Palmately divided with the lateral segments 2-cleft.
Pedicel. The stalk of a flower.
Pediceled or *pedicellate.* Borne on a pedicel.
Peduncle. The stalk of a flower-cluster; also used for the stalk of a solitary flower.
Peduncled or *pedunculate.* Borne on a peduncle.
Peltate. Shield-shaped; attached to its stalk inside the margin.
Pendulous. Hanging.
Penninerved. Nerves arising along a central midrib.
Perfect (flower). Having both stamens and pistil; bisexual.
Perianth. The floral envelope; commonly used when there is no clear distinction between calyx and corolla.
Pericarp. The wall of the ripened ovary.
Perigynous. Borne around the ovary and not at its base, as in flowers in which perianth and stamens are borne on a cup-shaped hypanthium.
Persistent. Remaining attached; not falling off.

GLOSSARY

Petal. One of the separate leaves of the corolla.
Petaloid. Petal-like; resembling a petal in color and shape.
Petiole. Leaf-stalk.
Petioled. Having a petiole.
Petiolule. Stalk of a leaflet.
Pilose. With soft long straight hairs.
Pinna. A primary division of a pinnate leaf.
Pinnate (leaf). Compound, with the leaflets placed on each side of the rachis.
Pinnatifid. Cleft or divided in a pinnate way.
Pinnatisect. Cleft to the midrib in a pinnate way.
Pinnule. A secondary pinna.
Pistil. The seed-bearing organ of the flower consisting of ovary, style and stigma.
Pistillate. Having a pistil and no stamens.
Pitted. Marked with pits or small depressions.
Placenta. Part of the ovary which bears the ovules.
Plicate. Folded into plaits.
Plumose. Feathery; furnished with long hairs, as the tail of the achene in some Clematis.
Pod. A dry dehiscent fruit.
Pollen. Spores or grains borne by the anther, usually granular.
Polygamous. Bearing unisexual and bisexual flowers on the same plant.
Pome. A fleshy fruit like the apple and the pear.
Posterior. In an axillary flower the side nearest the axis.
Prickle. A spine-like outgrowth from the bark or epidermis.
Procumbent. Lying on the ground or trailing.
Prostrate. Lying flat on the ground.
Pruinose. Bloomy.
Puberulent or *puberulous.* Minutely pubescent.
Pubescent. Covered with hairs, particularly if short and soft.
Punctate. With translucent or colored dots or depressions.
Pungent. Termination in a rigid sharp point; acrid.
Pyriform. Pear-shaped.

Raceme. A simple inflorescence of stalked flowers on a more or less elongated rachis.
Racemose. In racemes or resembling a raceme.
Rachis. An axis bearing flowers or leaflets.
Radiate. Spreading from a common centre; with ray-flowers.
Radicle. The portion of the embryo below the cotyledons.
Ray. The branch of an umbel; the marginal flowers (ray-flowers) of an inflorescence if distinct; the strap-like part of the corolla of the ray-flowers in Compositae.
Receptacle. The more or less expanded portion of an axis which bears the organs of a flower or the collected flowers of a head.
Recurved. Curved downward or backward.
Reflexed. Abruptly turned downward.
Regular (flower). With the parts of each whorl alike.
Reniform. Kidney-shaped.
Repand. With a slightly sinuate margin.
Resin-ducts or *resin-canals.* Canals in the plant-tissue containing resin.

Retuse. Slightly notched at the rounded apex.
Revolute. Rolled backward; margin rolled toward the lower side.
Rib. A primary or prominent vein in a leaf.
Rostrate. Having a beak.
Rotate (corolla). Wheel-shaped; with a flat and circular limb and without or with a very short tube.
Rufous. Reddish brown.
Rugose. Wrinkled.
Ruminate. Appearing as if chewed. Said of albumen with deeply indented furrows.

Saccate. Sac-shaped.
Sagittate. Shaped like an arrow-head, with the basal lobes directed downward.
Salver-shaped (flower). With a slender tube abruptly expanded in a flat limb.
Samara. An indehiscent flattened fruit.
Scabrid. Slightly rought to the touch.
Scabrous. Rough to the touch.
Scale. A minute leaf or bract, usually appressed or dry; minute gland-like flat appendages of the epidermis.
Scarious. Thin and dry, not green.
Scobiform. Having the appearance of sawdust.
Seed. The ripened ovule consisting of the embryo and its integuments.
Segment. One of the parts of a leaf or other organ that is divided but not compound.
Sepal. A division of the calyx.
Septicidal. Dehiscing along or in the partitions.
Septifragal. Dehiscing with the valves breaking away from the dissepiment.
Septum. A partition.
Sessile. Not stalked.
Setose. Beset with bristles.
Sheath. A tubular envelope.
Sheathing. Enclosing as by a sheath.
Shrub. A woody plant branched from the base.
Silky. Covered with appressed fine and straight hairs.
Sinuate. With a strongly wavy margin.
Sinus. The recess between the lobes.
Smooth. Without roughness; also used in the sense of glabrous.
Spatulate. Gradually narrowed from a rounded summit.
Spicate. Arranged in or resembling a spike.
Spadix. A spike with fleshy axis.
Spike. A simple inflorescence with the flowers sessile or nearly so on a common axis.
Spine. A sharp-pointed woody outgrowth from the stem.
Spinescent. Becoming spiny; with short spine-like branchlets.
Spur. A sac-like or tubular extension of some part or parts of the perianth, usually nectariferous; a short branchlet with much shortened internodes, usually bearing a cluster of leaves.
Stamen. The pollen-bearing male organ of the flower.
Staminode. A sterile stamen or similar structure inserted between the corolla and the pistil.
Standard. The upper broad petal of a papilionaceous flower.
Stellate. Star-shaped; said of hairs with radiating branches or of a cluster of radiating hairs.

GLOSSARY

Stem. The main axis of a plant.

Sterigmata. The peg-like projections of the leaf-cushions in some Conifers, as in the Spruces.

Sterile. Not fertile; a flower without or with rudimentary pistil, or stamens without fertile pollen.

Stigma. The part of the pistil that receives the pollen.

Stipe. The stalk of a pistil or similar organ.

Stipel. Stipule of a leaflet.

Stipellate. Furnished with stipels (stipellae).

Stipitate. Having a stipe.

Stipular. Belonging to the stipules.

Stipule. An appendage of the base of the petiole, usually one on each side.

Stolon. A subterranean stem; sucker.

Stoloniferous. Bearing stolons or suckers.

Stoma (pl. *stomata*). An orifice in the epidermis of a leaf.

Stomatic or *stomatiferous.* Bearing stomata.

Stone. The hard usually 1-seeded endocarp of a drupe.

Striate. Marked with fine longitudinal lines.

Strict. Very straight and upright.

Strigose. Beset with appressed straight and stiff hairs.

Strobile. A small cone.

Style. The usually attenuate part of the pistil between the ovary and the stigma.

Stylopodium. The disk-like expansion at the base of the style.

Subshrub. An undershrub, a suffruticose plant; also applied to a small low shrub.

Subulate. Awl-shaped.

Suffrutescent. Slightly woody; woody at the base.

Suffruticose. A perennial plant with only the lower part of the stem and of the branches woody and persistent.

Sulcate. Grooved or furrowed.

Superior (ovary). Borne above the insertion of the perianth and free from it.

Suture. A line of splitting.

Symmetrical (flower). Having the same number of parts in each whorl.

Syncarp. A fleshy aggregate fruit.

Tapering. Gradually becoming smaller in diameter or width toward one end.

Tendril. A coiling thread-like organ by which a plant grasps an object for support.

Terete. Circular in transverse section.

Ternate. In threes.

Tessellate. Checkered; divided into little squares as the reticulation in certain bamboo leaves.

Testa. The outer seed-coat.

Thyrse. A compact narrow panicle.

Thyrsoid. Like a thyrse.

Tomentose. With dense woolly pubescence.

Tomentulose. Closely and finely tomentose.

Tomentum. A dense covering of matted hairs.

Torus. The receptacle of a flower bearing the ovaries.

Tortuous. Twisted or bent.

Tree. A woody plant with one main stem and at least 4 or 5 m. tall.

Tri-. A Latin prefix signifying three or thrice, as trifoliolate, with 3 leaflets.

Truncate. Ending abruptly, as if cut off.

Tumid. Swollen.

Turbinate. Top-shaped; inversely conical.

Turgid. Swollen.

Umbel. An inflorescence with pedicels or branches arising from the same point.

Umbellate. Borne in umbels.

Umbelliform. Umbel-like; resembling an umbel.

Umbo. The parts of the apophysis of the cone-scales of Pinus, usually differing in color, which represents the exposed part of the conelet.

Umbonate. Bearing an umbo or boss.

Undulate. With wavy surface or margin.

Uninodal; see p. 35.

Unisexual. Of one sex, either staminate or pistillate.

Urceolate. Ovoid or cylindric and contracted at the mouth; urn-shaped.

Valvate. Opening by valves; in aestivation, meeting by the edges without overlapping.

Vascular. Furnished with vessels or ducts.

Veins. Threads of fibro-vascular tissue in a leaf or similar organ; nerves, but especially the smaller branched nerves.

Velutinous. Velvety.

Venation. Arrangement of veins.

Ventral. Relating to the inner face or part of an organ; the part nearer to the axis.

Vernation. The arrangement of leaves in bud.

Versatile. Relating to an anther attached near the middle and moving freely on its support.

Verticillate. Disposed in a whorl.

Villous. Bearing long and soft, usually curved or curly, hairs.

Virgate. Wand-like.

Whorl. An arrangement of three or more organs in a circle around the axis.

Wing. A membranous or thin and dry expansion or appendage of an organ; one of the lateral petals of a papilionaceous flower.

Woolly. Clothed with long and soft and curled or matted hairs.

Zygomorphous or *zygomorphic.* Capable of division into equal halves by only one plane.

EXPLANATIONS OF AUTHORS' NAMES [1]

ABEL—Clarke A...; 1780–1826. Gt. Br.
ADAMS—Johannes Michael Friedrich A...; 1780–1838. Russ.
ADAMS, J. W.—J. W. A...; contemp. Nurs. U. S. A.
ADANS.—Michel Adanson; 1727–1806. Fr.
AGARDH—Jacob Georg A...; 1813–1901. Swed.
AHRENDT—Leslie Walter Allan A...; 1903–. Gt. Br.
AIRY-SHAW — Herbert Kenneth A...-S...; 1902–. Gt. Br.
AIT.—William Aiton; 1731–1793. Gt. Br.
AIT. F.—William Townsend Aiton, the son; 1766–1849. Gt. Br.
AITCH.—James Edward Tiery Aitchison; 1836–1898. Gt. Br.
ALEF.—Friedrich Alefeld; 1820–1872. Germ.
ALL.—Carlo Allioni; 1725–1804. Ital.
ALLAN—Henry Howard A...; 1882–. N. Zeal.
ALPHAND—Jean Charles Adolphe A... (1875). Hort. Fr.
ALSTROEM—Clas A...; 1736–1794. Swed.
AMES, L. M.—Lawrence M. A...; 1900–. U. S. A.
ANDERS.—Nils Johan Andersson; 1821–1880. Swed.
ANDERS., E. — Edgar Anderson; 1897–. U. S. A.
ANDERS., G.—George Anderson; 17..–1817. Gt. Br.
ANDERS., T.—Thomas Anderson; 1832–1870. India.
ANDR.—Henry C. Andrews; 17..–1830. Gt. Br.
ANDR., D. M.—D. M. Andrews (1897–1938). Nurs. U. S. A.
ANDRÉ—Édouard A...; 1840–1911. Fr.
ANT.—Franz Antoine; 1815–1886. Austria.
ARCANG.—Giovanni Arcangeli; 1840–1921. Ital.
ARENDS—H. A...; contemp. Nurs. Germ.
ARMSTR.—John B. Armstrong (1880–1885). N. Zeal.
ARN.—George Arnold Walker Arnott; 1799–1868. Gt. Br.
ARNOLD—Arnold (1785). Austria.
ARRHEN.—Johan Pehr Arrhenius; 1811–1889. Swed.
ASAMI—Yoshichi A... (1925–1927). Jap.
ASCHERS.—Paul Friedrich August Ascherson; 1834–1913. Germ.
ASHE — William Willard A...; 1872–1932. U. S. A.
ASSO—Ignacio Jordan de A... y del Rio; 1742–1814. Spain.
AUBL.—J. B. C. F. Aublet; 1720–1778. Fr.
AUDIB.—Audibert frères (1810–1830). Nurs. Fr.
AUDUB.—John James Audubon; 1785–1851. U. S. A.
AUTH.—authors; referring to usage by various authors.

BAAS-BECK.—Miss Baas-Becking (1918–1921). Holl.

BAB.—Charles Cardale Babington; 1808–1895. Gt. Br.
BABCOCK—Ernest Brown B...; 1877–. U. S. A.
BACKH.—James Backhouse; 1825–1890. Nurs. Gt. Br.
BAENITZ—Carl Gabriel B...; 1837–1913. Germ.
BAILEY—Liberty Hyde B...; 1858–. U. S. A.
BAILEY, C.—Charles B....; 1838–1924. Gt. Br.
BAILL.—Henri Ernest Baillon; 1827–1895. Fr.
BAKER—John Gilbert B...; 1834–1920. Gt. Br.
BAKER F.—Edmund Gilbert B..., the son; 1864–. Gt. Br.
BALDACCI—Antonio B...; 1867–. Ital.
BALF.—John Hutton B...; 1808–1884. Gt. Br.
BALF. F.—Isaac Baily B..., the son; 1853–1922. Gt. Br.
BALF. F. & WARD—I. B. Balfour. — Francis Kingdon Ward; 1885–. Gt. Br.
BALL—Carlton Roy B...; 1873–. U. S. A.
BALL, J.—John B...; 1818–1889. Gt. Br.
BANKS—Sir Joseph B...; 1743–1820. Gt. Br.
BARBIER—B... & fils (1900). Nurs. Fr.
BARRAT—Josef B...; 1797–1882. U. S. A.
BARRON—William B... (1852–1880). Nurs. Gt. Br.
BARTLETT—Harley Harris B...; 1886–. U. S. A.
BARTL.—Friedrich Gottlieb Bartling; 1798–1875. Germ.
BARTR.—William Bartram; 1739–1823. U. S. A.
BAST.—Toussaint Bastard; 1784–1846. Fr.
BATAL.—Alexander Batalin; 1847–1898. Russ.
BATSCH—August Johann Georg Karl B...; 1761–1802. Germ.
BATT. — Jules Aimé Battandier; 1848–1922. Algiers.
BAUMANN—Charles (1830) & Constantin Auguste Napoléon B...; 1804–1884. Nurs. Fr.
BAUSCH—J. B. B... (1938). Holl.
BAYER—Johann Nepomuk B...; 1802–1870. Austria.
BEADLE—Chauncey Delos B...; 1866–. U. S. A.
BEAN—William Jackson B...; 1863–. Gt. Br.
BEAUV.—A. M. F. J. Palisot de Beauvois; 1755–1820. Fr.
BEBB — Michael Schuck B...; 1833–1895. U. S. A.
BECHST. — Johann Matthaeus Bechstein; 1757–1822. Germ.
BECK—Guenther B... von Mannagetta; 1856–1931. Austria.
BEIJERINCK—Willem B...; 1881–. Holl.
BEISS.—Ludwig Beissner; 1853–1927. Germ.
BENN. — John Joseph Bennett; 1801–1876. Gt. Br.
BENN., A.—Alfred William Bennett; 1833–1902. Gt. Br.
BENTH.—George Bentham; 1800–1884. Gt. Br.
BENTH. & HOOK.—George Bentham.—J. D. Hooker (Hook. f.).
BERCHT. & PRESL — Friedrich, Graf von Berchtold; 1781–1876; Austria.—Presl.

[1] The names are followed by the dates of birth and death; if these could not be ascertained, the period of their literary activity appears in parenthesis, or "contemp." (contemporary) is used if the author is living and the date of birth unknown. Following the dates, the country (mostly abbreviated) is given where the author resided during his active botanical career, rather than that of his birth, if different. In some cases "Nurs." or "Hort." is inserted after the dates to indicate that the authors are nurserymen (or seedsmen) or horicultural writers.

EXPLANATIONS OF AUTHORS' NAMES

CAREY, J.—John C...; 1797–1880. Gt. Br.

CARR.—Elie Abel Carrière; 1816–1896. Hort. Fr.

CARRUTH. — William Carruthers; 1830–1922. Gt. Br.

CARUEL—Teodoro C...; 1830–1898. Ital.

CASP.—Johann Xavier Robert Caspary; 1818–1887. Germ.

CASS. — Alexandre Henri Gabriel Cassini; 1781–1832. Fr.

CASTIGL.—Luigi Castiglioni; 1757–1832. Ital.

CAV. — Antonio José Cavanilles; 1745–1804. Spain.

CELAK.—Ladislav Josef Čelakovski; 1834–1902. Czekosl.

CHAIX—Dominique C...; 1731–1800. Fr.

CHAM.—Adalbert von Chamisso; 1781–1838. Germ.

CHAMBRAY—Georges de C...; 1783–1849. Fr.

CHAPM.—Alvin Wentworth Chapman; 1809–1899. U. S. A.

CHEESEM.—Thomas Frederick Cheeseman; 1846–1923. N. Zeal.

CHENAULT—Léon C...; 1833–1930. Nurs. Fr.

CHENG—Wan Chun C...; contemp. China.

CHEVAL.—Auguste Chevalier; 1873–. Fr.

CHITTENDEN—Frederick James C...; 1873–. Hort. Gt. Br.

CHOIS.—Jacques Denis Choisy; 1799–1859. Switz.

CHRIST—Hermann C...; 1833–1933. Switz.

CHUN—Woon Young C...; 1894–. China.

CLARKE—Charles Baron C...; 1832–1906. Gt. Br.

CLAUSEN—Robert Theodore C...; 1911–. U. S. A.

CLEMENCEAU—C... (1866–1872). Hort. Fr.

CLEMENTI—Giuseppe C...; 1812–1873. Ital.

COCHET — Pierre Charles Marie Cochet-Cochet; 1866–1936. Nurs. Fr.

COCKAYNE—Leonard C...; 1855–1934. N. Zeal.

COCKAYNE & ALLAN—L. C...—H. H. A...

COCKERELL — Theodore Dru Alison C...; 1866–. U. S. A.

COE — Ernest F. C...; contemp. Hort. U. S. A.

COHEN STUART—Combert Pieter C... S...; 1889–. Holl.

COKER — William Chambers C...; 1872–. U. S. A.

COLE—Cole Nursery Co.; contemp. U. S. A.

COLLETT—Sir Henry C...; 1836–1901. Gt. Br.

COMBER—Harold Frederick C... (1933). Gt. Br.

COOP.—James Graham Cooper; 1830–1902. U. S. A.

CORNU—Maxine C...; 1843–1901. Fr.

CORR.—J. Henry Correvon; 1855–1939. Hort. Switz.

CORREA—José Francisco Corréa [Correia] da Serra; 1751–1823. Port.

COSS.—Ernest St.-Charles Cosson; 1819–1889. Fr.

COSS. & DUR.—E. St.-Ch. Cosson.—Michel Charles Durieu de Maisonneuve; 1796–1878. Fr.

COSTA—Antonio Cipriano C... y Cuxart; 1817–1886. Spain.

COSTE & SOULIÉ—Hippolyte Jacques C...; 1858–1924.—Jean André S...; 1858–1905. Fr.

COULT. — John Merle Coulter; 1851–1928. U. S. A.

COURTIN—Albert C... (1850–1858) Germ.

COURTOIS—Richard Joseph C...; 1806–1835. Belg.

COV.—Frederick Vernon Coville; 1867–1937. U. S. A.

COWAN—John Marqueen C... (1928–1935). Gt. Br.

COWELL—John F. C...; 1852–1915. U. S. A.

CRAIB—William Grant C...; 1882–1933. Gt. Br.

CRAIG—William N. C...; contemp. Nurs. U. S. A.

CRANTZ — Heinrich Johann Nepomuk von C...; 1722–1797. Austria.

CRÉP.—François Crépin; 1830–1903. Belg.

CRETZOIU—Paul C...; contemp. Rumania.

CRIPPS—Cripps (1876–1880). Nurs. Gt. Br.

CRIVELLI—Giuseppe Gabriel Balsamo-C...; 1800–1874. Ital.

CROOM—Hardy Bryan C...; 1797–1837. U.S.A.

CROUX—Croux & fils; Gabriel C...; 1817–1883; Gustave C..., the son; 1848–1921. Nurs. Fr.

CUNNINGH.—Allan Cunningham; 1791–1839. Gt. Br.

CUNNINGH., R. — Richard Cunningham; 1793–1835. Gt. Br.

CURT.—William Curtis; 1746–1799. Gt. Br.

CURT., M. A.—Moses Ashley Curtis; 1808–1872. U. S. A.

DALLIM.—William Dallimore; 1871–. Gt. Br.

DAMMER—Udo D...; 1860–1920. Germ.

DANIEL—Lucien D...; 1856–. Fr.

DANIELS—Francis P. D...; 1869–. U. S. A.

DAUVESSE—D... (1880). Nurs. Fr.

DAVID—Armand D...; 1826–1900. Fr.

DAVID—Irenée D...; 1791–1862. Hort. Fr.

DAVIES—Hugh D...; 1739–1821. Gt. Br.

DAVIS—L. D. D... (1878). Nurs. Gt. Br.

DAVIS, K. C.—Kay Cadmus D...; 1867–1936. U. S. A.

DAVIS, W. T.—William Thompson D...; 1862–. U. S. A.

DC.—Augustin Pyramus de Candolle; 1778–1841. Switz.

DC., A.—Alphonse de Candolle; the son; 1806–1893. Switz.

DCNE.—Joseph Decaisne; 1809–1892. Fr.

DEANE—Walter D...; 1842–1930. U. S. A.

DEBEAUX—J. Odon D...; 1826–1910. Fr.

DE CORTE—C. deCorte (1909). Belg.

DE-FRANCE—Jesse Allison De-F...; 1899–. U. S. A.

DEGEN—Árpad von D...; 1866–1934. Hung.

DEG. & BALD.—Degen.—Baldacci.

DEL.—Alire Raffeneau Delisle; 1778–1850. Fr.

DÉSÉGL.—Pierre Alfred Déséglise; 1823–1883. Fr.

DESF. — Réné Louiche Desfontaines; 1750–1833. Fr.

DESMOUL. — Charles Desmoulins; 1797–1875. Fr.

DESPORTES—Narcisse Henri François D...; 1776–1856. Fr.

DESROUSS.—Louis Auguste Joseph Desrousseaux; 1753–1838. Fr.

DESV.—Augustin Nicaise Desvaux; 1784–1856. Fr.

DIECK—Georg D...; 1847–1926. Nurs. Germ.

DIELS—Ludwig D...; 1874–. Germ.

DIERB. — Johann Heinrich Dierbach; 1788–1845. Germ.

DIETR.—Friedrich Gottlieb Dietrich; 1768–1850. Germ.

DIETR., A.—Albert Dietrich; 1795–1856. Germ.

DIETR., D.—David Nathanael Friedrich Dietrich; 1799–1888. Germ.

DIPP.—Ludwig Dippel; 1827–1914. Germ.

DODE—Louis Albert D...; 1875–. Fr.

DOELL — Johann Christoph D...; 1808–1885. Germ.

DOERFL.—Ignaz Doerfler; 1866–. Austria.

EXPLANATIONS OF AUTHORS' NAMES

Dole—Eleazar Johnson D...; 1888-. U.S.A.

D'Ombr. — Henry Honywood D'Ombrain (1862–1866). Hort. Gt. Br.

Don—George D...; 1798–1856. Gt. Br.

Don, D.—David D...; 1799–1841. Gt. Br.

Donn—James D...; 1758–1813. Gt. Br.

Dop—Paul D...; 1876-. Fr.

Dougl.—David Douglas; 1799–1834. Gt. Br.

Drescher—A. A. D... (1933). U.S.A.

Duby—Jean Etienne D...; 1798–1885. Switz.

Duchartre — Pierre Etienne Simon D...; 1811–1894. Fr.

Dudley—Margaret Gertrude D...; contemp. Can.

Duham.—Henri Louis Duhamel du Monceau; 1700–1781. Fr.

Dum.-Cours.—Georges Louis Marie Dumont de Courset; 1746–1824. Fr.

Dumort. — Barthélemy Charles Dumortier; 1797–1887. Belg.

Dun.—Michael Felix Dunal; 1789–1856. Fr.

Dunn—Stephen Troyte D...; 1868–1938. Gt. Br.

Dupuy-Jamin—D...-J... (1857–1870). Hort. Fr.

Dur.—See Du Roi.

Durand — Elias Magloire D...; 1794–1873. U.S.A.

Durante—Jean François D...; 1730–1794. Fr.

Durazz.—Antonio Durazzini (1772). Ital.

Du Roi—Johann Philipp D...; 1741–1785. Germ.

Duthie—John Ferminger D...; 1845–1922. Gt. Br.

Dyer—Sir William Turner Thiselton-D...; 1843–1929. Gt. Br.

Eames & Godfr.—Arthur Johnson E...; 1881- U.S.A. — C. Castlidge Godfrey; 1855–1927. U.S.A.

Eastw.—Alice Eastwood; 1859-. U.S.A.

Eat.—Amos Eaton; 1776–1842. U.S.A.

Edgew. — Michael Packenham Edgeworth; 1812–1881. Gt. Br.

Eggl. — Willard Webster Eggleston; 1863–1935. U.S.A.

Ehrh.—Friedrich Ehrhart; 1742–1795. Germ.

Ehrh., B.—Balthasar Ehrhart; 1700–1756. Germ.

Eichl.—August Wilhelm Eichler; 1839–1887. Germ.

Ell.—Stephen Elliott; 1771–1830. U.S.A.

Ellis—John E...; 1710–1776. Gt. Br.

Ellw. & Barry—George Ellwanger; 1816–1906. —Patrick Barry; 1816–1890. Nurs. U.S.A.

Endl.—Stephan Ladislaus Endlicher; 1804–1849. Austria.

Engelm. — George Engelmann; 1809–1884. U.S.A.

Engl. — Heinrich Gustav Adolph Engler; 1844–1930. Germ.

Engl., V.—Victor Engler; 1885–1917. Germ.

Esch.—Johann Friedrich Eschscholtz; 1793–1831. Russ.

Exell—Arthur Wallis E...; contemp. Gt. Br.

Fabric. — Philipp Konrad Fabricius; 1714–1774. Germ.

Facch.—Francesco Facchini; 1788–1852. Ital.

Farquhar—John K. M. L. F...; 1858–1921. Nurs. U.S.A.

Farr—Edith May F...; 1864-. U.S.A.

Farwell—Oliver Atkins F...; 1867-. U.S.A.

Fedde—Friedrich Karl Georg F...; 1873-. Germ.

Fedtch. — Boris Aleksyevitch Fedtchenko; 1873-. Russ.

Fenzl—Eduard F...; 1808–1879. Austria.

Fern. — Merritt Lyndon Fernald; 1873- U.S.A.

Fern. & Griscom—M. L. Fernald.—Ludlow Griscom; 1890-. U.S.A.

Fiek—Emil F...; 1840–1897. Germ.

Finet & Gagnep.—Achille Finet; 1862–1913.— F. Gagnepain. Fr.

Fiori & Paol.—Adriano Fiori; 1865-.—Giulio Paoletti; 1865-. Ital.

Fisch. — Friedrich Ernst Ludwig von Fischer; 1782–1854. Russ.

Fisch. & Mey.—F. E. L. von Fischer.—C. A. Meyer.

Fitschen—Jost F...; 1869-. Germ.

Fletcher—Fletcher & Sons (1913). Nurs. Gt. Br.

Fluegge—Johann Fluegge; 1775–1816. Germ.

Focke — Wilhelm Olbers F...; 1834–1922. Germ.

Foëx—Gustave F...; 1844–1906. Hort. Fr.

Forb.—James Forbes; 1773–1861. Gt. Br.

Forrest—George F...; 1873–1932. Gt. Br.

Forsk.—Pehr Forskål; 1738–1768. Swed.

Forst.—Georg Forster; 1754–1794. Germ.

Forst., E.—Edward Forster; 1765–1849. Gt. Br.

Fortune—Robert F...; 1812–1880. Gt. Br.

Foucault—Emmanuel de F... (1813). Fr.

Foug.—Auguste Denis Fougeroux; 1732–1789. Fr.

Fournier—Eugène F...; 1834–1884. Fr.

Frahm—G. F... (1898). Nurs. Germ.

Franch.—Adrien R. Franchet; 1834–1900. Fr.

Franch. & Rochebr.—Franchet.—Alphonse F. de Rochebrune; 1834–1912. Fr.

Franch. & Sav.—Franchet.—Ludovic Savatier; 1830–1891. Fr.

Fraser, H.—Hugh F...; 1834–1904. Gt. Br.

Freeman—Oliver M. F...; 1891-. U.S.A.

Freyer—C. F. F...; 1802–1866. Austria.

Freyn—Joseph F...; 1845–1903. Austria.

Freyn & Sint.—J. F...—Paul Ernst Emil Sintenis; 1847–1907. Germ.

Fries—Elias Magnus F...; 1794–1878. Swed.

Fries, Th.—Theodor Magnus F...; 1832–1913. Swed.

Fritsch—Karl F... (of Prague); 1812–1878. Austria.

Fritsch, K.—Karl F... (of Graz); 1864–1934. Austria.

Froebel—Karl Otto F...; 1844–1906. Nurs. Switz.

Gable — Joseph B. G...; contemp. Nurs. U.S.A.

Gaertn.—Joseph Gaertner; 1732–1791. Germ.

Gagnep.—François Gagnepain; 1866-. Fr.

Gand.—Michel Gandoger; 1850–1926. Fr.

Gatt.—August Gattinger; 1825–1903. U.S.A.

Gaud. — Jean François Gottlieb Philippe Gaudin; 1766–1833. Switz.

Gaudich. — Charles Gaudichaud - Beaupré; 1789–1854. Fr.

Gay, C.—Claude G...; 1800–1873. Fr.

Gay, J.—Jacques E. G...; 1786–1864. Fr.

Germain—Jacques Nicolas Ernest Germain de St. Pierre; 1815–1882. Fr.

Gibbs—Vicary G...; 1853–1932. Gt. Br.

Gilg—Ernst G...; 1867–1933. Germ.

Gilib.—Jean Emmanuel Gilibert; 1741–1814. Fr.

Gillek.—L. Guillaume Gillekens; 1833–1905. Belg.

Gilmour—J. S. L. G... (1934). Gt. Br.

Gleditsch — Johann Gottlieb G...; 1714–1786. Germ.

EXPLANATIONS OF AUTHORS' NAMES

GMEL.—Johann Friedrich Gmelin; 1748–1804. Germ.

GMEL., K. C.—Karl Christian Gmelin; 1762–1837. Germ.

GMEL., S. G. — Samuel Gottlich Gmelin; 1743–1774. Russia.

GOD.—Charles Henry Godet; 1797–1879. Switz.

GOEPP.—Heinrich Robert Goeppert; 1800–1884. Germ.

GOLDIE—John G...; 1793–1886. Gt. Br.

GOLDRING—W. G...; 1854–1919. Hort. Gt. Br.

GOMBOCZ—Endre G...; 1882–. Hung.

GOOD—R. D'O. G... (1927). Gt. Br.

GORD.—George Gordon; 1806–1879. Gt. Br.

GOUAN—Antoine G...; 1733–1821. Fr.

GRAB.—Heinrich Emanuel Grabowsky; 1792–1842. Germ.

GRAEBENER—G... (1893–1925). Hort. Germ.

GRAEBN. — Karl Otto Robert Peter Paul Graebner; 1871–1933. Germ.

GRAEBN. & BUCHW. — Graebner. — Johannes Buchwald (1892–1921). Germ.

GRAHAM—Robert G...; 1786–1845. Gt. Br.

GRAY—Asa G...; 1810–1888. U. S. A.

GRAY, S. F.—Samuel Frederick G...; 1780–1836. Gt. Br.

GREEN — Mary Letitia G... (Mrs. T. A. Sprague); 1886–. Gt. Br.

GREENE—Edward Lee G...; 1842–1915. U.S.A.

GREENM. — Jesse More Greenman; 1867–. U. S. A.

GREMBLICH—P. Julius G...; 1851–1905. Austria.

GREN.—Jean Charles Marie Grenier; 1808–1875. Fr.

GREN. & GODR.—J. C. M. Grenier.—Dominique Alexandre Godron; 1807–1880. Fr.

GRIFF.—William Griffith; 1810–1845. Gt. Br.

GRIFFITHS, D. — David G...; 1867–1935. U.S.A.

GRIGGS—Robert Fiske G...; 1881–. U. S. A.

GRIGNAN—G. T. G... (1898–1900). Hort. Fr.

GRISEB.—Heinrich Rudolph August Grisebach; 1814–1879. Germ.

GRISEB. & SCHENK—Grisebach—Joseph August von S...; 1815–1891. Germ.

GROENLAND—Johannes G...; 1824–1891. Nurs. Holl.

GROSDEMANGE—Charles G... (1893–1897). Hort. Fr.

GROSSER—Wilhelm G...; 1869–. Germ.

GUILLAUM.—André Guillaumin; 1885–. Fr.

GUMBLETON—W. E. G...; 1830–1911. Gt. Br.

GUNNARSSON—Johann Gottfried G...; 1866–. Swed.

GUSS—Giovanni Gussone; 1787–1866. Ital.

HAAGE—Ferdinand H...; 1859–1930. Germ.

HACQUET—Balthasar H...; 1740–1815. Austria.

HALL, W.—William H...; 17. .–1800. Gt. Br.

HANCE — Henry Fletcher H...; 1827–1886. Gt. Br.

HAND.-MAZZ. — Heinrich von Handel-Mazzetti; 1862–1940. Austria.

HANSEN—Carl H...; 1848–1903. Denm.

HANSEN—Niels Ebbesen H...; 1866–. U.S.A.

HAO—Kin Shen H... (1931–1936). China.

HARA—Hiroshi H...; 1911–. Jap.

HARBISON—T. G. H...; 1862–1936. U. S. A.

HARDW. — Thomas Hardwicke; 1757–1835. Gt. Br.

HARIOT—Paul Auguste H...; 1854–1917. Hort. Fr.

HARMS — Hermann August Theodor H...; 1870–. Germ.

HARPER — Roland Macmillan H...; 1878–. U. S. A.

HARROW—Robert Lewis H...; 1867–. Gt. Br.

HARTM. — Carl Johan Hartman; 1790–1849. Swed.

HARTW.—Karl Theodor Hartweg; 1812–1871. Germ.

HARTW. & RUEMPL.—A. K. J. Hartwig.—T. Ruempler.

HARTWIG — August Karl Julius H...; 1823–1913. Hort. Germ.

HASSK. — Justus Carl Hasskarl; 1811–1894. Java.

HAUSSKN.—Heinrich Carl Haussknecht; 1838–1903. Germ.

HAW. — Adrian Hardy Haworth; 1768–1833. Gt. Br.

HAYATA—Bunzo H...; 1874–1934. Jap.

HAYEK—August H...; 1871–1928. Austria.

H. B. K.—F. W. H. A. von Humboldt; 1769–1859. Germ.—A. J. A. Bonpland.—C. S. Kunth.

HEDL. — Johan Theodor Hedlund; 1861–. Swed.

HEDW. F.—Romanus Adolf Hedwig (son of Johann H.; 1730–1799); 1772–1806. Germ.

HEER—Oswald H...; 1809–1883. Switz.

HEGETSCHW.—Johann Jacob Hegetschweiler; 1789–1839. Switz.

HEGI—Gustav H...; 1876–1932. Switz.

HELDR.—Theodor von Heldreich; 1822–1902. Greece.

HELLER—Amos Arthur H...; 1867–. U. S. A.

HEMSL. — W. Botting Hemsley; 1843–1924. Gt. Br.

HENDERSON—Louis Fourniquet H...; 1853–. U. S. A.

HENK. & HOCHST.—Johann Baptist Henkel; 1815–1871. — Wilhelm Hochstetter; 1825–1881. Germ.

HENKEL—Heinrich H... (1897–1914). Nurs. Germ.

HENRY—Augustine H...; 1857–1930. Gt. Br.

HENRY, J. K.—Joseph Kaye H...; 1866–1913. Can.

HENRY, L.—Louis H...; 1853–1903. Hort. Fr.

HÉRINQ—François H...; 1820–1891. Hort. Fr.

HERRM.—Johann Herrmann; 1738–1800. Fr.

HEYNH. — Gustav Heynhold (1838–1850). Germ.

HESSE—Hermann Albrecht H...; 1852–1937. Nurs. Germ.

HIBB.—James Shirley Hibberd; 1825–1890. Hort. Gt. Br.

HICKEL—Robert H...; 1861–1935. Fr.

HILL—John H...; 1716–1775. Gt. Br.

HILL, E. J.—Ellsworth Jerome H...; 1833–1917. U. S. A.

HILLIER — Hillier & Sons; contemp. Nurs. Gt. Br.

HITCHC.—Albert Spear Hitchcock; 1865–1935. U. S. A.

HOCHST.—Christian Friedrich Hochstetter; 1787–1860. Germ.

HOEFKER—Hinrich H...; 1859–. Germ.

HOESS—Franz H...; 1756–1840. Austria.

HOFFM.—Georg Franz Hoffmann; 1761–1826. Germ.

HOFFMANNS.—Johann Centurius von Hoffmannsegg; 1766–1849. Germ.

HOLZ.—John M. Holzinger; 1858–1929. U.S.A.

HONDA—Masaji H...; 1897–. Jap.

HOOIBRENK—Daniel H... (1848–1861). Austria.

HOOK.—William Jackson Hooker; 1785–1865. Gt. Br.

HOOK. & THOMS.—J. D. Hooker.—Thomas Thomson; 1817–1878. Gt. Br.

HOOK. F.—Joseph Dalton Hooker, the son; 1817–1911. Gt. Br.

EXPLANATIONS OF AUTHORS' NAMES

HOOPES — Josiah H...; 1832–1904. Hort. U. S. A.

HORAN.—Pavel Fedorovich Horaninow; 1796–1866. Russ.

HORNIBR. — Murray Hornibrook; contemp. Gt. Br.

HORSEY—R. E. H...; contemp. U. S. A

HORT.—Hortorum or hortulanorum; of gardens or gardeners. Hort. Angl.— English gardens; Hort. Gall.— French gardens.

HOST — Nicolaus Thomas H...; 1761–1834. Austria.

HOUSE—Homer Doliver H...; 1878–. U. S. A.

HOUTT. — Martinus Houttuyn; 1720–1798. Holl.

HOUZEAU DE LEHAIE—Jean H...; 1820–1888. Belg.

HOWELL—Thomas H...; 1842–1912. U. S. A.

HOWELL, J.—John Thomas H...; 1903–. U. S. A.

HOWELL, S. R.—S. R. H... (1934). Nurs. U. S. A.

HRYNIEWIECKI & KOBENDZA—Boleslaw H...; 1875–.—Roman K...; 1886–. Pol.

HU—Hsen Hsu Hu; 1894–. China.

HUBENY—Joseph H... (1830–1843). Hung.

HUDS.—William Hudson; 1730–1793. Gt. Br.

HUGHES—Dorothy K. H... (Mrs. Wilson Popenoe); 1899 – 1932. Gt. Br. & U. S. A.

HULL—John H. H...; 1761–1843. Gt. Br.

HURST — Charles Chamberlain H...; 1870–. Gt. Br.

HUTCHINS.—J. Hutchinson; 1884–. Gt. Br.

HUTER—Rupert H...; 1859–1934. Austria.

ITO—Tokutaro I...; 1868–. Jap.

INGRAM—Collingwood I... (1929–1939). Gt. Br.

JACK—John George J...; 1861–. U. S. A.

JACKS., A. B.—Albert Bruce Jackson; 1876–. Gt. Br.

JACQ.—Nicolaus Joseph Jacquin; 1727–1817. Austria.

JACQUES — Henri Antoine J...; 1782–1866. Hort. Fr.

JAEG. — Hermann Jaeger; 1815–1890. Hort. Germ.

JAENNICKE—Friedrich J...; 1831–1907. Germ.

JAMES—Edwin J...; 1797–1861. U. S. A.

JANCHEN—Erwin J...; 1882–. Austria.

JANCZ. — Edward Janczewski von Glinka; 1846–1920. Pol.

JANKO—Johan Jankó (1890). Hung.

JAUB.—Hippolyte François de Jaubert; 1798–1874. Fr.

JAUME ST.-HIL.—Jean Henri Jaume Saint-Hilaire; 1772–1845. Fr.

JENNISON—Harry Milliken J...; 1885–1940. U. S. A.

JEPS.—Willis Linn Jepson; 1867–. U. S. A.

JESSON—Miss E. M. J... (1915). Gt. Br.

JOHNST. — Ivan Murray Johnston; 1898–. U. S. A.

JONES — Marcus Eugene J...; 1852–1934. U. S. A.

JONES, G. N.—George Neville J...; 1904– U. S. A.

JORD. & FOUR.—Alexis Jordan; 1814–1897.— Jules Fourneau (1866–1868). Fr.

JOUIN—Victor J...; 1839–1909.—Victor Emile J...; contemp. Nurs. Fr.

JUEHLKE—Ferdinand J...; 1815–1893. Hort. Germ.

JUSS.—Antoine Laurent de Jussieu, nephew of B. de J...; 1748–1836. Fr.

JUSS., A.—Adrien de Jussieu, son of A. L. J...; 1797–1843. Fr.

JUSS., B.—Bernard de Jussieu; 1699–1777. F

KACHE—Paul K...; contemp. Hort. Germ.

KAL.—Ivan Osipovich Kaleniczenko; 180 1876. Russ.

KALM—Pehr K...; 1717–1779. Swed.

KANITZ—Agost K...; 1843–1896. Hung.

KAREL. & KIRIL.—Grigorij Silych Karelir 1801–1872. — Ivan Petrovitch Kiril (1821–1842). Russ.

KARST. — Gustav Karl Wilhelm Hermar Karsten; 1817–1908. Germ.

KEARN. — Thomas Henry Kearney; 1874 U. S. A.

KELLER—Robert K...; 1854–. Switz.

KELLOGG—Albert K...; 1813–1887. U. S. A.

KER—John Bellenden K..., or more correct John Ker Bellenden; before 18(John Gawler; 1765–1842. Gt. Br.

KERN.—Anton Josef Kerner von Marilaun 1831–1898. Austria.

KERN., J.—Josef Kerner; 1829–1906. Austria

KIKUCHI—Akio K...; 1883–. Jap.

KIRCHN.—Georg Kirchner; 1837–1885. Hor Germ.

KIRK, T.—Thomas K...; 1828–1898. N. Zea

KIT.—Paul Kitaibel; 1757–1817. Hung.

KLOTZSCH—Johann Friedrich K...; 1805–186 Germ.

KMET—Andreas K...; 1841–1908. Austria.

KNIGHT — Josef K...; 1781–1855. Nur Gt. Br.

KNIGHT & PERRY—J. Knight—Thomas A P... Nurs. Gt. Br. Holl.

KNOOP—Johann Hermann K... (1757–1763) Holl.

KOBUSKI — Clarence Emmeren K...; 1900– U. S. A.

KOCH—Wilhelm Daniel Joseph K...; 1771 1849. Germ.

KOCH, K.—Karl Heinrich Emil K...; 1809 1879. Germ.

KOCHS—Julius K... (1900). Germ.

KOEHNE—Emil K...; 1848–1918. Germ.

KOERN. — Friedrich Koernicke; 1828–1908 Russ.

KOMAR.—Vlademir Leontyevitch Komarov 1869–. Russ.

KOMATSU—Shunzö K... (1918). Jap.

KOOPM.—Karl Koopmann (1879–1900). Hort Germ.

KORSH. — Sergyei Ivanovitch Korshinsky 1861–1900. Russ.

KORT—Antoine K... (1905). Belg.

KOSTEL.—Vincenz Franz Kosteletzky; 1801– 1887. Czekosl.

KOSTER—M. Koster & Sons; contemp. Nurs Holl.

KOTSCHY—Theodor Kotschy; 1813–1866. Austria.

KRAETZL—Franz K...; 1852–. Austria.

KRASSN.—Andrei Nikolayevitch Krassnov; 1862–1915. Russ.

KRAUTTER—Louis K...; 1880–1909. U. S. A.

KTZE.—Carl Ernst Otto Kuntze; 1843–1907 Germ.

KUNTH — Carl Sigismund K...; 1788–1850 Germ.

KUNZE—Gustav K...; 1793–1851. Germ.

KUSNEZ. — Nikolai Ivanovitch Kusnezov; 1864–1932. Russ.

L.—Carl von Linné (Linnaeus); 1707–1778. Swed.

L. F.—Carl von Linné, the son; 1741–1783. Swed.

914

EXPLANATIONS OF AUTHORS' NAMES

ABILL.—Jacques Julien Houtton de Labillardière; 1755-1834. Fr.

AG.—Mariano Lagasca y Segura; 1776-1839. Spain.

AM.—Jean Baptiste Antoine Pierre Monnet Lamarck; 1744-1829. Fr.

AMB.—Aylmer Bourke Lambert; 1761-1842. Gt. Br.

ANG—Adolph Franz Láng; 1759-1863. Hung.

ANG, T.—Thomas L... (1853). Gt. Br.

ANGE—Johan Martin Christian L...; 1818-1898. Denm.

AUCHE — Wilhelm L...; 1827-1882. Hort. Germ.

AUTH—Thomas L...; 1758-1826. Fr.

AV.—Alphonse Lavallée; 1835-1884. Fr.

AWS., M. A.—Marmaduke Alexander Lawson; 1840-1896. Gt. Br.

AWSON—Lawson & Son; Peter L... (17..-1820); Charles L... (1794-1873), author of Agric. Man. Gt. Br.

AXM.—Erich Laxmann; 1737-1796. Russ.

EBAS—E. L... (1866-1888). Nurs. Fr.

E CONTE—John Eaton Le C...; 1784-1860. U.S.A.

EDEB—Carl Friedrich von Ledebour; 1785-1851. Russ.

EES—Edwin L...; 1800-1887. Gt. Br.

EGRAND—O. Le Grand (1895). Fr.

EHM.—Johann Georg Christian Lehmann; 1792-1860. Germ.

EIB.—John B. Leiberg; 1853-1913. U.S.A.

EM.—Charles Lemaire; 1800-1871. Belg.

EMOINE — Victor L...; 1823-1911; Emile L...; 1862-. Nurs. Fr.

EMM.—John Gill Lemmon; 1832-1908. U.S.A.

EROY—André L...; 1801-1875; Louis L...; 1808-1887. Nurs. Fr.

ESCUYER.—O. L... (1855-1872). Hort. Fr.

ESKE — Nathanael Gottfried L...; 1751-1786. Germ.

ETOURN.—Aristide Horace Letourneux; 1820-1890. Fr.

ÉVL.—Auguste Abel Hector Léveillé; 1863-1918. Fr.

ÉVL. & BLIN—Léveillé.—Blin. Fr.

ÉVL. & VANT.—Léveillé.—Eugène Vaniot. Fr.

EY—Augustin L...; 1842-1911. Gt. Br.

EYB.—Friedrich Ernst Leybold; 1804-1864. Austria.

L'HÉR.—Charles Louis L'Héritier de Brutelle; 1746-1800. Fr.

IEBLEIN — Franz Kaspar L..; 1744-1810. Germ.

IND.—J. J. Linden; 1817-1898. Nurs. Belg.

INDL.—John Lindley; 1799-1865. Gt. Br.

INGELSH. — Alexander Lingelsheim; 1874-1937. Germ.

INK — Heinrich Friedrich L...; 1767-1851. Germ.

IPSKY—Vladimir Ippolitovich L...; 1863-1937. Russ.

ITVIN.—Dmitri Ivanovitch Litvinov; 1854-1929. Russ.

ODD.—Conrad Loddiges; 1732-1826; George Loddiges, the son; 1784-1846. Nurs. Gt. Br.

OES.—Ludwig Eduard Theodor Loesener; 1865-. Germ.

OISEL.—Jean Louis Auguste Loiseleur-Deslongchamps; 1774-1849. Fr.

OJAC. — Michele Lojacono Pojero; 1853-. Ital.

OUD. — John Claudius Loudon; 1783-1843. Hort. Gt. Br.

OUR.—Juan Loureiro; 1715-1796. Portug.

OW—Hugh L... & Co. (1908). Nurs. Gt. Br.

LUDWIG—Christian Gottlieb L...; 1709-1773. Germ.

LUTZ—Karl L... (1920-1927). Nurs. Germ.

LYNCH — Richard Irwin L...; 1850-1924. Hort. Gt. Br.

MAACK—Richard M...; 1825-1886. Russ.

MACBR.—J. Francis Macbride; 1892-. U.S.A.

MACBR. & NELS.—Macbride.—A. Nelson.

McCLATCHIE—Alfred James M...; 18..-1906. U.S.A.

MACFARL. — John Muirhead Macfarlane; 1855-. U.S.A.

MACK.—Kenneth Kent Mackenzie; 1877-1934. U.S.A.

MACK. & BUSH—K. K. Mackenzie.—B. F. Bush.

MACM. — Conway MacMillan; 1867-1929. U.S.A.

McCLELLAND—John M...; 1805-1883. Gt. Br.

McKELVEY — Susan Delano M...; 1883-. U.S.A.

MADIOT—M...; 1780-1832. Fr.

MAK.—Tomitaro Makino; 1863-. Jap.

MAK. & SHIB.—T. Makino.—Shibata.

MANNING—Jacob W. M...; 1826-1904. Nurs. U.S.A.

MANSF.—Rudolph Mansfeld; 1901-. Germ.

MARCHANT—M...; contemp. Nurs. Gt. Br.

MARQUAND—Cecil Victor Boley M...; 1897-. Gt. Br.

MARQUAND & SHAW—Marquand.—Airy-Shaw.

MARSH. — Humphrey Marshall; 1722-1801. U.S.A.

MARSILI—Giovanni M...; 1727-1795. Ital.

MARTENS—Martin M...; 1797-1863. Belg.

MAST.—Maxwell Tylden Masters; 1833-1907. Gt. Br.

MAST., W.—W. Masters; 1796-1874. Gt. Br.

MATSUM.—Jinzo Matsumura; 1855-1928. Jap.

MATTEI—Giovanni Ettore M...; 1865-. Ital.

MATTF.—Johannes Mattfeld; 1895-. Germ.

MATTUSCHKA—Heinrich Gottfried von M...; 1734-1779. Germ.

MAUMENÉ—Albert M... (1894-1902). Hort. Fr.

MAUND—Benjamin M...; 1790-1863. Hort. Gt. Br.

MAXIM. — Carl Johann Maximowicz; 1827-1891. Russ.

MAY—M... (1870-1885). Hort. Fr.

MAYR—Heinrich M...; 1856-1911. Germ.

MED. — Friedrich Casimir Medicus; 1736-1808. Germ.

MEDWED. — Yakov Sergyeevich Medwedew (Medvyedev); 1847-1923. Russ.

MEEH.—Thomas Meehan; 1826-1901. Nurs. U.S.A.

MEERB. — Nicolaus Meerburg (1775-1798). Holl.

MEISN.—Carl Friedrich Meisner (or Meissner); 1800-1874. Germ.

MÉRAT—François Victor M...; 1780-1851. Fr.

MERC.—E. Mercier; 1802-1863. Switz.

MERR.—Elmer Drew Merrill; 1876-. U.S.A.

METHVEN—John M... (1890). Nurs. Gt. Br.

MEUNISSIER—A. M...; contemp. Fr.

MEY. — Ernst Heinrich Friedrich Meyer; 1791-1858. Germ.

MEY., C. A.—Carl (Karl) Anton Meyer; 1795-1855. Russ.

MEY., F.—F. Meyer (1934). Hort. Germ.

MEY., G. F. W.—Georg Friedrich Wilhelm Meyer; 1782-1856. Germ.

MEZ—Karl Christian M...; 1864-. Germ.

MICHX.—André Michaux; 1746-1802. Fr.

MICHX. F.—François André Michaux, the son; 1770-1855. Fr.

EXPLANATIONS OF AUTHORS' NAMES

MIERS—John M...; 1789–1879. Gt. Br.
MILL.—Philip Miller; 1691–1771. Gt. Br.
MILL., W. — William Tyler Miller; 1869–. U. S. A.
MIQ. — Friedrich Anton Wilhelm Miquel; 1811–1871. Holl.
MITF.—Algernon Bertram Freeman-Mitford, Lord Redesdale; 1837–1916. Gt. Br.
MIYABE—Kingo M...; 1860–. Jap.
MIYABE & KUDÔ—Miyabe.—Yûshun K...; 1887–1932. Jap.
MIYOSHI—Manabu M...; 1861–1939. Jap.
MOEHL—Heinrich M... (1861–1890). Germ.
MOENCH—Konrad M...; 1744–1805. Germ.
MOHR — Charles Theodor M...; 1824–1901. U. S. A.
MOLINA — Juan Ignacio M...; 1737–1829. Spain.
MOORE—Albert Hanford M...; 1883–. U. S. A.
MOORE, S.—Spencer Le Marchant M...; 1851–1931. Gt. Br.
MOORE, T.—Thomas M...; 1821–1887. Gt. Br.
MORD. DE LAUN.—Jean Claude Michel Mordant de Launay; 1750–1816. Fr.
MORIC.—Moise Etienne Moricand; 1779–1854. Switz.
MORITZI—Alexander M...; 1806–1850. Switz.
MORR.—Charles Jacques Edouard Morren; 1833–1886. Belg.
MOSER—Jean Jacques M... (1889–1925). Nurs. Fr.
MOSS — Charles Edward M...; 1872–1930. Gt. Br.
MOTT. — Seraphin Mottet; 1861–1930. Hort. Fr.
MOUILLEF. — Pierre Mouillefert; 1845–1903. Hort. Fr.
MUELL.-ARG.—Jean Mueller (Argoviensis, i.e., of Aargau); 1828–1896. Switz.
MUELL., F. v.—Ferdinand von Mueller; 1825–1896. Austral.
MUELL., P. J.—Philipp Jakob Mueller; 1832–1889. Fr.
MUENCHH.—Otto von Muenchhausen; 1716–1774. Germ.
MUHL.—Henry Ludwig Muhlenberg; 1756–1817. U. S. A.
MULLER, F. G.—F. G. M... (1889). U. S. A.
MULLIGAN—Brian O. M...; 1907–. Gt. Br.
MUNRO—William M...; 1816–1880. Gt. Br.
MUNS.—Thomas Volney Munson; 1823–1913. Nurs. U. S. A.
MURR.—Johann Andreas Murray; 1740–1791. Germ.
MURR., A.—Andrew Murray; 1812–1878. Gt. Br.
MUTIS—José Celestino M...; 1732–1808. Colombia.

NAKAI—Takenoshi N...; 1882–. Jap.
NASH — George Valentine N...; 1864–1919. U. S. A.
NAUD.—Charles Naudin; 1815–1899. Fr.
NECK.—Noel Joseph de Necker; 1729–1793. Fr.
NEES—Christian Gottlieb Nees von Esenbeck; 1776–1858. Germ.
NEES & EBERM.—C. G. Nees.—Carl Heinrich Ebermaier; 1802–1870. Germ.
NEILL—Patrick N...; 1776–1851. Gt. Br.
NEILR.—August Neilreich; 1803–1871. Austria.
NELS., A.—Aven Nelson; 1859–. U. S. A.
NELS., E. — Elias Emanuel Nelson; 1876–. U. S. A.
NELSON—John N... (Senilis) (1866). Gt. Br.
NESTL.—Christian Gottfried Nestler; 1778–1832. Fr.

NEUBERT—Wilhelm N...; 1808–1905. Hor Germ.
NEUMAN, L. M.—Leopold Martin N...; 1852 1922. Swed.
NEUMANN — Joseph Henri François N... 1800–1858. Hort. Fr.
NEUMANN, L.—Louis N...; 1827–1903. Hort Fr.
NICHOLS. — George Nicholson; 1847–1908 Hort. Gt. Br.
NIEDENZ.—Franz Niedenzu; 1857–1937. Germ
NIEMETZ — W. F. N... (1898–1922). Nurs Hung.
NIEUWL.—Julius Aloysius Nieuwland; 1878 U. S. A.
NITSCHE—Walter N...; 1883–. Germ.
NOERDL. — Hermann Noerdlinger; 1818–1897 Germ.
NOIS.—Louis Claude Noisette; 1772–1849. Fr
NORTON—Jesse Baker N...; 1877–1938. U. S. A
NUTT.—Thomas Nuttall; 1786–1859. U. S. A
NYM.—Carl Fredrik Nyman; 1820–1893. Swed

OED. — Georg Christian Oeder; 1728–1791 Germ.
OERST. — Anders Sande Oersted; 1816–1872 Swed.
OHLENDORFF—J. H. O... (1832–1834). Nurs Germ.
OLIV.—Daniel Oliver; 1830–1917. Gt. Br.
OLIVIER—Guillaume Antoine O...; 1756–1814 Fr.
OPIZ—Philipp Maximilian O...; 1787–1858 Czekosl.
ORPH. — Theodoros Georgios Orphanides 1817–1886. Greece.
ORR—Matthew Young O...; contemp. Gt. Br
OSBECK—Pehr O...; 1723–1805. Swed.
OSBORN—Arthur O...; contemp. Gt. Br.
OSTENF.—Carl Emil Hansen Ostenfeld; 1873 1931. Swed.
OSTEN. & SYRACH—Ostenfeld.—Lassen Car S...; 1898–. Swed.
OTTO—Friedrich O...; 1782–1856. Germ.
OTTO & DIETR.—Otto.—A. Dietrich.
OTTOLANDER — Cornelius Johannes Wilhelm O...; 1822–1887. Nurs. Holl.
OUDEM.—Cornelius Antoon Jan Abraham Ou demans; 1825–1906. Holl.
OUDIN—Oudin (1841). Nurs. Fr.

PALL.—Peter Simon Pallas; 1741–1811. Russ
PALM. & STEYERM.—Palmer.—Steyermark.
PALMER, E. J.—Ernest Jesse Palmer; 1875– U. S. A.
PAMPAN.—Renato Pampanini; 1875–. Ital.
PANTOCSEK—Josef P...; 1846–1916. Austria.
PARDÉ—Léon Gabriel Charles P...; 1865–. Fr
PARL.—Filippo Parlatore; 1816–1877. Ital.
PARRY—Charles Christopher P...; 1823–1890 U. S. A.
PARSONS—Samuel B. P...; 1819–1906. Nurs U. S. A.
PATSCHKE—Wilhelm P...; 1888–. Germ.
PAU — Carlos P... y Español; 1857–1937 Spain.
PAX—Ferdinand P...; 1858–. Germ.
PAXT.—Joseph Paxton; 1802–1865. Gt. Br.
PENH.—David Pearce Penhallow; 1854–1910 Can.
PENNELL — Francis Whittier P...; 1886– U. S. A.
PÉPIN—Pierre Denis P... (1836–1869). Hort Fr.
PERKINS — Janet Russell P...; 1853–1933 U. S. A.
PERS.—Christian Hendrik Persoon; 1755–1837 Germ.

EXPLANATIONS OF AUTHORS' NAMES

Peterm.—Wilhelm Ludwig Petermann; 1806–1855. Germ.

Petrie—D. P... (1891). N. Zeal.

Petrovich—Sava Petrovič; 1839–1889. Serbia.

Phil.—Rudolph Amandus Philippi; 1808–1904. Chile.

Pierce — Newton Barris P...; 1856–1916. U. S. A.

Pilger—Robert P...; 1876–. Germ.

Piper—Charles Vancouver P...; 1867–1926. U. S. A.

Planch.—Jules Emile Planchon; 1833–1900. Fr.

Poech—Joseph P...; 1816–1846. Austria.

Poederlé — Eugène Joseph Charles Gilain Hubert d'Olmen, Baron de P...; 1742–1813. Belg.

Poepp. & Endl.—Eduard Friedrich Poeppig; 1798–1868. Germ.—Endlicher.

Pohl—Johann Baptist Emanuel P...; 1782–1834. Austria.

Poir.—Jean Louis Marie Poiret; 1755–1834. Fr.

Poit. — Antoine Poiteau; 1766–1854. Hort. Fr.

Poll. — Johann Adam Pollich; 1740–1780. Germ.

Pollard—Charles Louis P...; 1872–. U. S. A.

Pollini—Ciro P...; 1782–1833. Ital.

Pomel—August P...; 1821–1898. Fr.

Popov — Michail Grigorievich P...; 1893–. Russ.

Porcher—Felix P... (1848–1870). Hort. Fr.

Porter — Thomas Conrad P...; 1822–1901. U. S. A.

Pott — Johann Friedrich P...; 1738–1805. Germ.

Pourr.—Pierre André Pourret; 1754–1818. Fr.

Prain—David P...; 1857–. Gt. Br.

Presl — Karel Bořiwog P...; 1794–1852. Czekosl.

Preston—Isabelle P...; contemp. Can.

Prévost — Honoré Albert P...; 1822–1883. Hort. Fr.

Prévost—P... jr. (1825–1831). Hort. Fr.

Prince — William Robert P...; 1795–1869. Nurs. U. S. A.

Pritz.—Ernst Pritzel; 1875–. Germ.

Puissant—A. P... (1886). Fr.

Purkyně—Emanuel P...; 1831–1882. Austria.

Purp. — Joseph Anton Purpus; 1860–1933. Germ.

Pursh—Frederick P... (Friedrich Traugott Pursch); 1774–1820. U. S. A.

Puvilland—P... (1879). Nurs. Fr.

Pynaert — Edouard Christophe P...-van Geert; 1835–1900. Nurs. Belg.

Raab—Raab; 17..–1835. Germ.

Racib.—Maryjan Raciborski; 1863–1917. Pol.

Raeuschel — Ernest Adolph R... (1772). Germ.

Raf. — Constantino Samuel Rafinesque-Schmaltz; 1784–1842. U. S. A.

Rafn—Johannes Hendrik R...; 1854–. Nurs. Denm.

Ram.—Louis François Elisabeth Ramond de Carbonnières; 1753–1827. Fr.

Rand & Redf.—Edward Lothrop R...; 1859–1924.—John Howard Redfield; 1815–1895. U. S. A.

Raoul—Edouard Fiacre Louis R...; 1815–1852. Fr.

Rau—Ambrosius R...; 18..–1870. Germ.

Raup—Hugh Miller R...; 1901–. U. S. A.

Réaubourg—G. R... (1906). Fr.

Reg.—Eduard August von Regel; 1815–1892. Russ.

Reg. & Schmalh.—Regel.—Johannes Theodor Schmalhausen; 1849–1894. Russ.

Reg. & Tiling — Regel. — Heinrich Sylvester Theodor T...; 1818–1871. Russ.

Reg. & Winkl.—Regel.—Constantin [Alexander] W...; 1848–1900. Russ.

Rehd.—Alfred Rehder; 1863–. U. S. A.

Reichb.—Heinrich Gottlieb Ludwig Reichenbach; 1793–1879. Germ.

Reichb. f.—Heinrich Gustav Reichenbach, the son; 1823–1889. Germ.

Reiche—Karl R...; 1860–1929. Chile.

Rendle—Alfred Barton R...; 1865–1938. Gt. Br.

Req.—Esprit Requien; 1788–1851. Fr.

Retz. — Andres Johan Retzius; 1742–1821. Swed.

Rich.—Louis Claude Marie Richard; 1754–1821. Fr.

Richards.—Sir John Richardson; 1787–1865. Gt. Br.

Ricker—Percy Leroy R...; 1878–. U. S. A.

Rickett — Harold William R...; 1896–. U. S. A.

Riv. — Marie Auguste Rivière; 1821–1877; Charles Marie R...; 1845–. Nurs. Fr.

Rivers—Thomas R... (1837–1869). Nurs. Gt. Br.

Robins.—Benjamin Lincoln Robinson; 1864–1935. U. S. A.

Robins., W.—William Robinson; 1839–1935. Hort. Gt. Br.

Robs.—Edward Robson; 1763–1813. Gt. Br.

Roch.—Anton Rochel; 1770–1847. Austria.

Rod.—Emile Rodigas; 1831–1902. Belg.

Roem.—Johann Jacob Roemer; 1763–1819. Switz.

Roem., M. J.—Max J. Roemer (1835–1846). Germ.

Roess. — Karl Gottlob Roessig; 1752–1806. Germ.

Rolfe—Robert Allen R...; 1855–1921. Gt. Br.

Roman. — Frédéric Romanet du Caillaud (1881–1888). Fr.

Rose—Joseph Nelson R...; 1862–1928. U. S. A.

Rosenth. — R. C. Rosenthal (1882–1888). Nurs. Austria.

Rosenth., K.—Käthe Rosenthal (1919). Austria.

Rostk.—Friedrich Wilhelm Gottlieb Rostkovius; 1770–1848. Germ.

Roth — Albrecht Wilhelm R...; 1757–1834. Germ.

Rothe—H. R... (1890). Nurs. Germ.

Rothr. — Joseph Trimble Rothrock; 1839–1922. U. S. A.

Rouy—Georges R...; 1851–1924. Fr.

Rouy & Fouc. — Rouy. — Julien Foucaud; 1847–1904. Fr.

Rovelli — Renato R...; 1806–1880; Carlo R...; 18..–1902; Achille R... (1880). Nurs. Ital.

Rowlee—Willard Winfield R...; 1861–1923. U. S. A.

Roxb.—William Roxburgh; 1759–1815. Gt. Br.

Royle—John Forbes R...; 1800–1858. Gt. Br.

Rudolphi — Karl Asmund R...; 1771–1832. Germ.

Ruempl. — Theodor Ruempler; 1817–1891. Hort. Germ.

Ruiz & Pav.—Hippolito R... [-Lopez]; 1764–1815.—José Antonio Pavon; 17..–1844. Spain.

Rupr. — Franz Josef Ruprecht; 1814–1870. Russ.

Rusby—Henry Hurd R...; 1855-. U.S.A.
Russell—Paul George R...; 1889-. U.S.A.
Ruthe—Johann Friedrich R...; 1788-1859. Germ.
Rydb.—Per Axel Rydberg; 1860-1931. U.S.A.

Sabine—Joseph S...; 1770-1837. Gt. Br.
Sakata—T. S...; Sakata & Co. (1938). Nurs. Jap.
Salisb.—Richard Anthony Salisbury; 1761-1829. Gt. Br.
Salm-Dyck—Joseph, Prince Salm-Reifferscheidt-Dyck; 1773-1861. Germ.
Salzm.—Philipp Salzmann; 1781-1853. Fr.
Sander—Henry F. C. S...; 1847-1920 (Sander & Sons). Nurs. Gt. Br.
Sandw.—Noel Y. Sandwith; 1901-. Gt. Br.
Santi—Giorgio S...; 1746-1822. Ital.
Sarg.—Charles Sprague Sargent; 1841-1927. U.S.A.
Sarg., H. W. — Henry Winthrop Sargent; 1810-1822. U.S.A.
Sart. — Giovanni Battista Sartorelli; 1780-1853. Ital.
Sauter—Anton Eleutherius S...; 1800-1881. Austria.
Sav.—Ludovic Savatier; 1830-1891. Fr.
Savi—Gaetano Savi; 1769-1844. Ital.
Schaeffer—Jakob Christian S...; 1718-1790. Germ.
Schallert—Paul Otto S...; 1879-. U.S.A.
Schau.—Johan Konrad Schauer; 1813-1848. Germ.
Scheele—Georg Heinrich Adolph S...; 1808-1864. Germ.
Schelle—Ernst S... (1893-1929). Germ.
Schindl. — Anton Karl Schindler; 1879-. Germ.
Schinz & Kell.—Hans S...; 1858-.—Robert Keller.
Schinz & Thell.—Schinz.—Albert Thellung; 1881-1928. Switz.
Schk.—Christian Schkuhr; 1741-1811. Germ.
Schlecht. — Diedrich Franz Leonhard von Schlechtendal; 1794-1866. Germ.
Schleich. — Johann Christoph Schleicher; 1768-1834. Switz.
Schleid.—Matthias Jacob Schleiden; 1804-1881. Germ.
Schmidel — Casimir Christoph S...; 1718-1792. Germ.
Schmidt—Franz S...; 1751-1834. Austria.
Schmidt, Fr. — Friedrich S...; 1832-1908. Russ.
Schneid.—Camillo (Karl) Schneider; 1876-. Germ.
Schoch — Gottlieb S...; 1853-1905. Hort. Germ.
Schott — Heinrich Wilhelm Schott; 1794-1865. Austria.
Schrad.—Heinrich Adolph Schrader; 1767-1836. Germ.
Schreb.—Johann Christian Daniel von Schreber; 1739-1810. Germ.
Schreiner & Stout—Ernst Jefferson Sch...; 1902-.—Arlow Burdett St...; 1876-. U.S.A.
Schrenk—Alexander Gustav Schrenk; 1816-1876. Russ.
Schroet.—Carl Schroeter; 1855-1939. Switz.
Schuebl. & Mart.—Gustav Schuebler; 1787-1834.—Georg Matthias von Martens; 1788-1872. Germ.
Schult.—Joseph August Schultes; 1773-1831. Austria.
Schultz Bip.—Karl Heinrich S...; (Bipontinus, i.e., of Zweibrücken); 1805-1867. Germ.

Schultz, K. F.—Karl Friedrich S...; 1765-1837. Germ.
Schum.—Heinrich Christian Friedrich Schumacher; 1757-1830. Denm.
Schum., K.—Karl Moritz Schumann; 1851-1904. Germ.
Schur — Philipp Johann Ferdinand S... 1799-1878. Austria.
Schwarz—Otto S...; contemp. Germ.
Schwein.—Lewis David de Schweinitz; 1780-1834. U.S.A.
Schwer.—Graf Fritz von Schwerin; 1856-1934. Germ.
Scop.—Giovanni Antonio Scopoli; 1723-1788. Ital.
Sealy—J. R. S... (1938). Gt. Br.
Seem.—Berthold Carl Seemann; 1825-1871. Germ.
Seemen—Otto von S...; 1838-1910. Germ.
Selys-Longch.—Michel Edmond de Selys Longchamps; 1813-1900. Belg.
Sénécl.—Adrien Sénéclauze (1840-1867). Hort. Fr.
Ser. — Nicolas Charles Seringe; 1776-1858. Fr.
Servett.—Camille Servettaz (1909). Switz.
Shafer—John Adolph S...; 1863-1918. U.S.A.
Sheldon—John Lewis S...; 1865-. U.S.A.
Shibata—Keita S...; 1878-. Jap.
Shirai—Mitsutarô S...; 1863-1932. Jap.
Shiras.—Homi Shirasawa; 1868-. Jap.
Shiras. & Koyama—Shirasawa.—M. K... (1914). Jap.
Shreve—Forrest S...; 1878-. U.S.A.
Shull—Charles Albert S...; 1879-. U.S.A.
Sibth.—John Sibthorp; 1758-1796. Gt. Br.
Sieb.—Philipp Franz von Siebold; 1796-1866. Holl.
Sieb. & Zucc.—Siebold.—Zuccarini.
Sieber—Franz Wilhelm S...; 1785-1844. Austria.
Siehe—Walter S...; 1859-1928. Germ.
Simmonds—A. Simmonds (1933). Gt. Br.
Simonkai—Lajos tól Simonkai (né Simkovics); 1851-1910. Hung.
Simon-Louis — Simon-Louis; Léon Louis 1834-1913. Nurs. Fr.
Sims—John S...; 1792-1838. Gt. Br.
Sinclair—George Sinclair; 1786-1834. Gt. Br.
Skan—Sydney Alfred S...; 1870-1940. Gt. Br.
Skeels—Homer C. S...; 1873-1934. U.S.A.
Slavin — Arthur Daniel S...; 1903-. Hort. U.S.A.
Sm.—Sir James Edward Smith; 1759-1828. Gt. Br.
Sm., J.—John Smith; 1798-1888. Gt. Br.
Sm., James—James Smith; 1760-1840. Nurs. Gt. Br.
Sm., R.—Richard Smith & Co. (1875). Nurs. Gt. Br.
Sm., Th.—Thomas Smith (1911). Nurs. Gt. Br.
Sm., W.—William Smith (1835). Nurs. (of Norbiton) Gt. Br.
Sm., W. W.—Sir William Wright Smith 1875-. Gt. Br.
Small—John Kunkel S...; 1869-1938. U.S.A.
Soland.—Daniel Solander; 1736-1782. Gt. Br.
Solemacher — von S... - Antweiler (1936). Germ.
Somm.—Stefano Sommier; 1848-1922. Ital.
Soul.-Bod.—Etienne Soulange-Bodin (1827-1842). Nurs. Fr.
Soy.-Willem.—Hubert Félix Soyer-Willemet 1791-1861. Fr.
Spach—Edouard S...; 1801-1879. Fr.

EXPLANATIONS OF AUTHORS' NAMES

ꜱᴘᴀᴇ — Dieudonné S...; 1819-1858. Nurs. Belg.

ꜱᴘᴀᴇᴛʜ — Franz Ludwig S...; 1839-1913; Hellmut Ludwig S...; 1885-. Nurs. Germ.

ꜱᴘᴇɢᴀᴢᴢ.—Carlos Spegazzini; 1858-1926. Arg.

ꜱᴘɪɴɢᴀʀɴ—Joel Elias S...; 1875-1939. U. S. A.

ꜱᴘʀᴀɢᴜᴇ — Thomas Archibald S...; 1877-. Gt. Br.

ꜱᴘʀᴇɴɢ.—Kurt Sprengel; 1766-1833. Germ.

ꜱᴘʀᴇɴɢᴇʀ—Karl S...; 1847-1918. Nurs. Ital.

ꜱᴛᴀɴᴅɪsʜ—John S... (1850-1871). Nurs. Gt. Br.

ꜱᴛᴀɴᴅʟ. — Paul Carpenter Standley; 1884-. U. S. A.

ꜱᴛᴀᴘꜰ—Otto S...; 1857-1933. Gt. Br.

ꜱᴛᴀʀᴋᴇʀ — Thurman James S...; 1890-. U. S. A.

ꜱᴛᴇᴘʜ.—Friedrich Stephan; 1757-1814. Russ.

ꜱᴛᴇᴜᴅ.—Ernst Gottlieb Steudel; 1783-1856. Germ.

ꜱᴛᴇᴠ.—Christian von Steven; 1781-1863. Russ.

ꜱᴛᴇᴡ.—John Lindsay Stewart; 1832?-1873. Gt. Br.

ꜱᴛᴇʏᴇʀᴍ.—Julian Alfred Steyermark; 1909-. U. S. A.

ꜱᴛ.-Hɪʟ.—August de Saint-Hilaire; 1779-1853. Fr.

ꜱᴛ. Jᴏʜɴ—Harold St. J...; 1892-. U. S. A.

ꜱᴛ.-Lᴀɢ.—Jean Baptiste Saint-Lager; 1825-1912. Fr.

ꜱᴛᴏᴋᴇʀ—Fred S... (1938). Gt. Br.

ꜱᴛᴏᴋᴇꜱ—Jonathan S...; 1755-1831. Gt. Br.

ꜱᴜᴅᴡ. — George Bishop Sudworth; 1864-1927. U. S. A.

ꜱÜɴᴅᴇʀᴍ. — F. Sündermann (1923). Nurs. Germ.

ꜱᴜᴋꜱᴅ. — William N. Suksdorf; 18..-1932. U. S. A.

ꜱᴜᴍᴍᴇʀʜ. — Victor Samuel Summerhayes; 1897-. Gt. Br.

ꜱᴜʀɪɴɢ.—Jan Valckenier Suringar; 1865-1932. Holl.

ꜱᴡ.—Olof Swartz; 1760-1818. Swed.

ꜱᴡᴇᴇᴛ—Robert S...; 1783-1835. Gt. Br.

ꜱᴡɪɴɢʟᴇ — Walter Tennyson S...; 1871-. U. S. A.

ꜱʏᴍᴏɴꜱ—Jelinger S...; 1778-1851. Gt. Br.

ꜱʏᴍᴏɴꜱ-Jᴇᴜɴᴇ—Bertram Hanmer Bunbury S...-J.... Nurs. Gt. Br.

ꜱᴢʏꜱᴢ.—Ignaz Szyszylowicz; 1857-1910. Pol.

ᴛᴀɢɢ—H. F. T...; 1874-1933. Gt. Br.

ᴛᴀᴋᴇᴅᴀ—Hisayoshi T... (1913-1927). Jap.

ᴛᴀʟᴏᴜ—A. de T... (1858-1866). Hort. Fr.

ᴛᴀᴛᴀʀ—Mathias T... (1878). Austria.

ᴛᴀᴛᴇᴡᴀᴋɪ—Misao T...; 1899-. Jap.

ᴛᴀᴜʙ. — Paul Hermann Wilhelm Taubert; 1862-1897. Germ.

ᴛᴀᴜꜱᴄʜ — Ignaz Friedrich T...; 1793-1848. Austria.

ᴛᴀʏʟᴏʀ—Norman T...; 1883-. U. S. A.

ᴛᴇᴍᴘʟᴇ—F. L. Temple & Beard (1887-1893); Nurs. U. S. A.

ᴛᴇɴ.—Michele Tenore; 1780-1861. Ital.

ᴛᴇᴜꜱᴄʜᴇʀ—Henry T...; 1891-. Can.

ᴛʜᴏᴍᴀꜱ—David T...; 1776-1859. U. S. A.

ᴛʜᴏᴍᴀꜱ, F.—Friedrich August Wilhelm T...; 1840-1918. Germ.

ᴛʜᴏʀɴʙᴇʀ—John James T...; 1872-. U. S. A.

ᴛʜᴏʀʏ—Claude Antoine T...; 1759-1827. Fr.

ᴛʜᴏᴜɪɴ—André T...; 1747-1824. Fr.

ᴛʜᴜɴʙ. — Carl Peter Thunberg; 1743-1822. Swed.

ᴛɪᴅᴇꜱᴛ.—Ivar Tidestrom; 1865-. U. S. A.

ᴛɪɴᴇᴏ—Vincenzo T...; 1791-1856. Ital.

ᴛᴏʙʟᴇʀ—Friedrich T...; 1879-. Germ.

ᴛᴏᴇᴘꜰ.—Adolph Toepffer; 1853-1931. Austria.

ᴛᴏᴘꜰ—Alfred T... (1851-1857). Hort. **Germ.**

ᴛᴏʀʀ.—John Torrey; 1796-1873. U. S. A.

ᴛᴏʀʀ. & Gʀ.—J. Torrey.—A. Gray.

ᴛᴏʀʀᴇʏ, G. S.—George Safford T...; 1891-. U. S. A.

ᴛᴏᴜʀɴ. — Joseph Pitton Tournefort; 1656-1708. Fr.

ᴛʀᴀʙᴜᴛ—Louis T...; 1853-1929. Fr.

ᴛʀᴀᴛᴛ.—Leopold Trattinick; 1764-1849. Austria.

ᴛʀᴀᴜᴛᴠ.—Ernst Rudolph von Trautvetter; 1809-1889. Russ.

ᴛʀᴇʟ.—William Trelease; 1857-. U. S. A.

ᴛʀᴇᴡ — Christoph Jacob T...; 1695-1769. Germ.

ᴛᴜᴄᴋᴇʀᴍ.—Edward Tuckerman; 1817-1886. U. S. A.

Tᴜʀᴄᴢ. — Nikolai Stepanovich Turczaninow; 1796-1864. Russ.

ᴛᴜʀʀᴀ—Antonio T...; 1730-1796. Ital.

Uꜱᴛᴇʀɪ—Alfred U...; 1869-. Switz., S. Am.

Uʏᴇᴋɪ—Homiku U... (1921-1938). Jap.

Vᴀʜʟ—Martin V...; 1749-1804. Denm.

Vᴀɴʜ.—Louis van Houtte; 1810-1876; son, 1845-1938. Belg.

Vᴀɴɪᴏᴛ—Eugène V... (1904-1910). Fr.

Vᴀɴ Kʟᴇᴇꜰ—C. van K... (1877). Hort. Holl.

Vᴀɴ Tɪᴇɢʜ. — Philippe van Tieghem; 1839-1914. Fr.

Vᴀᴛᴋᴇ—Georg Karl Wilhelm V...; 1849-1889. Germ.

Vᴀᴜᴠᴇʟ—L. V... (1869-1870). Hort. Fr.

Vᴇɪʟʟᴀʀᴅ—V... (1810?). Fr.

Vᴇɪᴛᴄʜ—John Gould V...; 1839-1867; Harry James V...; 1840-1924; Nurs. Gt. Br.

Vᴇʟᴇɴ—Joseph Velenovsky; 1858-. Czekosl.

Vᴇɴᴛ.—Etienne Pierre Ventenat; 1757-1808. Fr.

Vᴇʀɢᴜɪɴ—Louis V...; 1866-1936. Fr.

Vᴇʀʟᴏᴛ—Bernard V...; 1837-1897. Fr.

Vᴇʀꜱᴄʜ. — Ambroise Verschaffelt; 1825-1886. Nurs. Belg.

Vɪᴄᴛᴏʀɪɴ—Fr. Marie-V...; 1885-. Can.

Vɪɢɴᴇᴛ—A. von V... (1795). Austria?.

Vɪʟʟ.—Dominique Villars; 1745-1814. Fr.

Vɪʟᴍ.—Maurice Levêque de Vilmorin; 1849-1919; Philippe de V...; 1872-1917. Nurs. Fr.

Vɪꜱ.—Roberto de Visiani; 1800-1878. Ital.

Vɪᴛᴍ.—Fulgenzio Vitman; 1728-1806. Ital.

Vɪᴠ.—Domenico Viviani; 1772-1840. Ital.

Vᴏʟʟᴍᴀɴɴ—Franz V...; 1858-1917. Germ.

Vᴏꜱ—C. deV... (1876-1886). Hort. Holl.

Vᴏꜱꜱ—Andreas V...; 1857-1924. Hort. Germ.

Wᴀʜʟ.—Goran Wahlenberg; 1780-1851. Swed.

Wᴀʜʟʙ.—Pehr Fredrick Wahlberg; 1800-1877. Swed.

Wᴀɪᴛᴢ — Karl Friedrich W...; 1774-1848. Germ.

Wᴀʟᴅꜱᴛ.—Franz de Paula Adam, Graf von Waldstein; 1759-1823. Austria.

Wᴀʟʟ—A. W.... (19..). N. Zeal.

Wᴀʟʟ.—Nathaniel Wallich; 1786-1854. India.

Wᴀʟʟʀ.—Carl Friedrich Wilhelm Wallroth; 1792-1857. Germ.

Wᴀʟᴘ. — Wilhelm Gerhard Walpers; 1816-1853. Germ.

Wᴀʟꜱʜ—Rev. Robert W...; 1772-1852. Gt. Br.

Wᴀʟᴛ.—Thomas Walter; 1740-1788. U. S. A.

Wᴀɴɢʜ.—Friedrich Adam Julius von Wangenheim; 1747-1800. Germ.

Wᴀɴɢᴇʀ.—Walter Wangerin; 1884-1938. Germ.

EXPLANATIONS OF AUTHORS' NAMES

WARB.—Otto H. Warburg; 1859–1938. Germ.
WARB., O. E.—Sir Oscar E. Warburg (1930). Gt. Br.
WARSCZ. — Joseph Warsczewicz; 1812–1866. Pol.
WATERER—Anthony W...; 1822–1896. Nurs. Gt. Br.
WATERER, J.—J. Waterer & Crisp; contemp. Nurs. Gt. Br.
WATS. — Peter William Watson; 1761–1830. Gt. Br.
WATS., S.—Sereno Watson; 1826–1892. U.S.A.
WATS., W. — William Watson; 1858–1925. Hort. Gt. Br.
WAUGH—Frank Albert W...; 1869–. U.S.A.
WEATHERBY — Charles Alfred W...; 1875–. U.S.A.
WEBB—Philip Barker W...; 1793–1854. Gt. Br.
WEBER — Georg Heinrich W...; 1752–1828. Germ.
WEBERB.—August Weberbauer; 1871–. Peru.
WEBSTER—Angus Duncan W... (1893–1920). Hort. Gt. Br.
WEIHE—Carl Ernst August W...; 1779–1834. Germ.
WENDER.—Georg Wilhelm Franz Wenderoth; 1774–1861. Germ.
WENDL.—Johann Christoph Wendland; 1755–1828. Germ.
WENDL., H.—Hermann Wendland, grandson of J. C. W...; 1823–1903. Germ.
WENDL., H. L.—Heinrich Ludolph Wendland, son of J. C. W...; 1792–1869. Germ.
WENZ.—Theodor Wenzig; 1824–1892. Germ.
WEST.—Richard Weston; 1733–1806. Gt. Br.
WETTST.—Richard von Wettstein; 1862–1931. Austria.
WEYER—W. van de W... (1920). Gt. Br.
WHERRY — Edgar Theodore W...; 1904–. U.S.A.
WHITE—Francis Buchanan W...; 1842–1894. Gt. Br.
WIEG.—Karl McKay Wiegand; 1873–. U.S.A.
WIGHT—Robert W...; 1796–1872. Gt. Br.
WIGHT & HEDR.—W. F. W....—Ulysses Prentiss Hedrick; 1870–. U.S.A.
WIGHT, W. F. — William Franklin W...; 1874–. U.S.A.
WILLD.—Karl Ludwig Willdenow; 1765–1812. Germ.

WILLK. & LGE.—Heinrich Moritz Willkomm; 1821–1895. Germ.—J. M. C. Lange.
WILLM.—Ellen Ann Willmott; 1860–1934. Gt. Br.
WILMOTT—Alfred James W...; 1888–. Gt. Br.
WILS. — Ernest Henry Wilson; 1876–1930. U.S.A.
WIMM.—Christian Friedrich Heinrich Wimmer; 1803–1868. Germ.
WINKLER—Hubert J. P. W...; 1875–. Germ.
WINKLER, HANS—Hans Karl Albert W...; 1877–. Germ.
WITH.—William Withering; 1741–1799. Gt. Br.
WITTE — Heinrich W...; 1825–1917. Hort. Holl.
WITTM.—Max Carl Ludwig Wittmack; 1839–1929. Germ.
WITTR.—Veit Brecher Wittrock; 1839–1914. Swed.
WOHLF.—Rudolf Wohlfahrt; 1830–1888. Germ.
WOLF, E.—Egbert W...; 1860–1931. Russ.
WOLF, TH.—Theodor W... (1901–1903). Germ.
WOOD—Alphonso W...; 1810–1881. U.S.A.
WOODALL—Edward H. W. W...; 1843–1937. Gt. Br.
WOOT.—Elmer Otis Wooton; 1865–. U.S.A.
WORONOW — Jurij Nicolaievich W...; 1874–1931. Russ.
WRIGHT, C. H.—Charles Henry W...; 1864–. Gt. Br.
WULF.—Franz Xaver von Wulfen; 1728–1805. Austria.
WYMAN — A. Phelps W... (1916). Nurs. U.S.A.

YATABE—Ryokichi Y...; 1851–1899. Jap.
YOUNG—Maurice Y... (1872). Nurs. Gt. Br.
YOUNG, R. A. — Robert Armstrong Y...; 1876–. U.S.A.

ZAB.—Hermann Zabel; 1832–1912. Germ.
ZAMELIS—Aleksandrs Z... (1939). Latvia.
ZDÁREK—Robert Z... (1881–1900). Austria.
ZEDERB.—Emerich Zederbaur; 1877–. Austria.
ZEMAN—Franz Z...; contemp. Hort. Czekosl.
ZENGERL.—Zengerling (1889). Austria.
ZENARI—Silvia Z...; 1896–. Ital.
ZUCC.—Joseph Gerhard Zuccarini; 1797–1848. Germ.
ZUCCAGNI—Attilio Z...; 1754–1807. Ital.

INDEX

INDEX

INDEX

INDEX

INDEX

INDEX

INDEX

INDEX

INDEX

INDEX

INDEX

INDEX

INDEX

INDEX

INDEX

INDEX

INDEX

INDEX

941

INDEX

INDEX

943

INDEX

INDEX

INDEX

INDEX

INDEX

INDEX

INDEX

INDEX

INDEX

INDEX

INDEX

INDEX

957

INDEX

INDEX

INDEX

961

INDEX

INDEX

INDEX

INDEX

INDEX

INDEX

969

INDEX

INDEX

INDEX

972

INDEX

INDEX

974

INDEX

INDEX

976

INDEX

INDEX

INDEX

INDEX

INDEX

983

INDEX

INDEX

INDEX

INDEX

987

INDEX

INDEX

990

INDEX

992

INDEX

INDEX

INDEX

INDEX